W9-ADE-619

THE
DICTIONARY
OF
CANADIAN
LAW

Third Edition

by

DATE DUE	RETURNED
MAR 1 4 2012	MAR 0 5 2012
MAY 08 2012	MAY 1 1 2012
	APR 2 7 2012
NOV 1 1 2013	NOV 1 7 2013
FEB 1 1 2014	FEB 0 4 2014

DISCARD
HUMBER COLLEGE
LAKESHORE CAMPUS
LEARNING RESOURCE CENTRE
3199 LAKESHORE BLVD. WEST
TORONTO, ONTARIO M8V 1K8

©2004 Thomson Canada Limited

All rights reserved. No part of this publication may be reproduced, stored in a retrieval system, or transmitted, in any form or by any means, electronic, mechanical, photocopying, recording, or otherwise, without the prior written permission of the publisher.

The publisher is not engaged in rendering legal, accounting or other professional advice. If legal advice or other expert assistance is required, the services of a competent professional should be sought. The analysis contained herein represents the opinions of the authors and should in no way be construed as being official or unofficial policy of any government body.

Canadian Cataloguing in Publication Data

Dukelow, Daphne A., 1948-
        The dictionary of Canadian law / by Daphne A. Dukelow. — 3rd ed.
Includes bibliographical references
ISBN 0-459-24129-X (bound). — ISBN 0-459-24151-6 (pbk.)

1. Law — Canada — Dictionaries.   I. Title

KE183.D83   2004   349.71'03   C2004-903822-2
KF156.D85   2004

∞   The paper used in this publication meets the minimum requirements of American National Standard for Information Sciences – Permanence of Paper for Printed Library Materials, ANSI Z39.48-1984.

Composition: Computer Composition of Canada Inc.

THOMSON

CARSWELL

One Corporate Plaza, 2075 Kennedy Road, Scarborough, Ontario M1T 3V4
Customer Service:
Toronto 1-416-609-3800
Elsewhere in Canada/U.S. 1-800-387-5164
Fax 1-416-298-5094

Preface to the Third Edition

I am honoured to have the opportunity to prepare this third edition of the dictionary. New statutory and regulatory material from all jurisdictions has been provided. As well, more material from judicial decisions, particularly of the appellate courts, is added. Some historic material is maintained. Of course, it is impossible to enter all the new material available.

As before, the text of any source cited should be consulted for complete accuracy. I have edited material from sources to suit more general needs. Definitions from multiple sources do not have a reference cited. This is the reason for the deletion of references in some definitions.

In preparing the first edition I was impressed by the "Fs", fur, farm, fish and forestry (and mining), the most universally Canadian industries. Now, digital, electronic, terrorism, cloning, genetics indicate the wider range of interests we have in this decade. It is a privilege to take time to obtain this overview of the activity of the work of the legislatures and the courts of the country. Two other "F" words, food and family, have evolving meanings.

Political correctness manifests itself in statutory language. A dumb show becomes a mime. Feeble-minded person, retarded, handicap, illegitimacy, and mental defective disappear. Also, the language of the courts and the legislatures adapts to the plain language movement.

Thank you to Steven Iseman, Ken Mathies, and the other people at Carswell who have brought this edition together quickly and efficiently. Also thank you to Sarah Payne, editor, for her diligent work.

Thank you to my friends who have supported me through the work on this edition and who have been willing to adapt their schedules to my obsession. Much of the work Betsy did on the first two editions remains.

Vancouver, B.C.   Daphne A. Dukelow
March 2004.

Preface to the Second Edition

We are grateful to Gary Rodrigues, Vice-president – Publishing, and Catherine Campbell, Publisher, for the opportunity to revise *The Dictionary of Canadian Law* in such a timely fashion. Our thanks to Sherry MacIsaac, our new editor in Ottawa, for her support and understanding and to Sharon Rodrigues, Lorie Acton, Pamela Juneau and Norma Rodrigues who collected and collated new statutory material for us.

We have updated material from statutes and legal texts cited in the first edition. But most importantly, we have included for the first time in this work a substantial number of definitions from case law. Our aim has been to increase both the depth and currency of this dictionary by identifying new and important terms and by providing more useful definitions of many others. There are consequently over 3,300 new entries in this edition.

Humber College Library

Tracking and defining the terminology of this lively profession is a never-ending task, but we are grateful both to Carswell and to those users whose purchase of the first edition and helpful comments on it enabled this edition to be done.

Vancouver and Cobble Hill, B.C.
September, 1994

Daphne Dukelow
Betsy Nuse

Preface to the First Edition

This first edition of The Dictionary of Canadian Law realizes the wish of publishing vice-president Gary Rodrigues, that Carswell undertake the monumental task of publishing a truly comprehensive, Canadian common law dictionary. We are grateful to Gary for the opportunity to work on this project, to Sharon Rodrigues, Lorie Acton, Diann Devins and Anne Walasek who collected statutory material over the years and to publisher Catherine McKeown for her understanding and support.

In compiling this work, we have attempted, as much as the constraints of time allowed, to honour the best current lexicographical principles. Thus this dictionary — both word list and definitions — was created largely from primary, Canadian sources: a term bank of definitions from federal and provincial statutes and regulations and a library of basic Canadian legal textbooks. The unique character of Canada is strongly reflected in the large number of terms which relate to the regulation of our country's natural resources, to agriculture and related industries. Where we needed to rely on another dictionary, our source has been the second edition Jowitt's Dictionary of English Law, published by Sweet and Maxwell of England. We are grateful to that company for the use of its material.

We wish to thank our good friends in Ontario and British Columbia who patiently listened to reports of our several trips through the alphabet and to bulletins regarding the most fascinating term of the day or week. To paraphrase Dr. Johnson, our work is ended, but not complete.

We know that this first effort will be improved upon. We believe that The Dictionary of Canadian Law underlines the importance of indigenus work to Canadian lexicography and will be useful to all people in the common law jurisdictions of Canada.

Galiano, B.C.
December, 1990

Daphne Dukelow
Betsy Nuse

How to Use This Dictionary

HEADWORD

ABBUTTALS. *n.* Limits or boundaries of land.

ABC. *abbr.* Advance booking charter. — abbreviation

ABDICATE. *v.* To refuse or renounce a thing.

FUNCTIONAL LABEL

ABSOLUTA SENTENTIA EXPOSITORE NON INDIGET. [L.] A clean statement requires no exposition. — ETYMOLOGY

DEFINITIONS

ABSOLUTE LIABILITY. 1. Liability regardless of intention or negligence. 2. An offence for which an accused is criminally liable even though the accused acted under a reasonable mistake of fact. *R. v. Metro News Ltd.* (1986), 23 C.R.R. 77 at 89, 16 O.A.C. 319, 56 O.R. (2d) 321, 53 C.R. (3d) 289, 29 C.C.C. (3d) 35, 32 D.L.R. (4th) 321 (C.A.), the court per Martin J.A.

ABUSE OF PROCESS. 1. ". . . [I]n *R. v. D. (T.C.)* (1987), 38 C.C.C. (3d) 434 at 447 . . . (Ont. C.A.), [it was] held that the onus of establishing that an abuse of process has occurred is on the respondent who must establish, on a balance of probabilitites, that the Crown has acted in an oppressive or vexatious manner or that the prosecution is offensive to the principles of fundamental justice and fair play." *R. v. Miles of Music Ltd.* (1989), 24 C.P.R. (3d) 301 at 309, 31 O.A.C. 380, 69 C.R. (3d) 361, 48 C.C.C. (3d) 96 (C.A.), Krever J.A. 2. ". . . [T]he unreasonable multiplication of proceedings . . ." *General Foods Ltd. v. Struthers Scientific & International Corp.* (1971), 4 C.P.R. (2d) 97 at 105, [1974] S.C.R. 98, 23 D.L.R. (3d) 313, the court per Pigeon J. 3. ". . . [F]rivolous and vexatious, or if the process . . . is in fact being used for an ulterior or improper purpose, or if the process is being used in such a way as to be in itself an abuse . . ." *Canada Metal Co. v. Heap* (1975), 7 O.R. (2d) 185 at 192 (C.A.). 4. "The essence of the tort of abuse of process is the misuse or perversion of the court's process for an extraneous or ulterior purpose. There must be a purpose other than that which the process was designed to serve . . ." *D.K. Investments Ltd. v. S.W.S. Investments Ltd.*

CITATION OF AUTHORITY –

— case law

(1984), 59 B.C.L.R. 333 (S.C.), Finch J., affirmed (1986), 6 B.C.L.R. (2d) 291 (C.A.).

ACCEPTANCE. *n.* 1. Signification by an offeree of willingness to enter into a contract with an offeror on the offeror's terms. G.H.L. Fridman, *The Law of Contract in Canada*, 2d ed. (Toronto: Carswell, 1986) at 41. 2. Of a bill, the signification by the drawee of assent to the drawer's order to pay the bill. F.L.G. Tyler & N.E. Palmer, eds., *Grossley Vaines' Personal Property*, 5th ed. (London: Butterworths, 1973) at 235. 3. An acceptance completed by delivery or notification. *Bills of Exchange Act*, R.S.C. 1985, c. B-4, s. 2. 4. In sale of goods, involves taking possession of the goods by the buyer. See BLANK ~; CONDITIONAL ~; LOCAL ~; NON- ~; PARTIAL ~; QUALIFIED ~.

— text

— statute

— none

ACCIDENT. *n.* A wilful and intentional act, not being the act of the employee, and a fortuitous event occasioned by a physical or natural cause. *Workers Compensation acts.* See AIRCRAFT ~; ENVIRONMENTAL ~; FATAL ~; INDUSTRIAL ~; INEVITABLE ~; NON-INDUSTRIAL ~.

CROSS REFERENCES

ACCIDENTAL DEATH INSURANCE. Insurance undertaken by an insurer as part of a contract of life insurance whereby the insurer undertakes to pay an additional amount of insurance money in the event of the death by accident of the person whose life is insured. *Insurance acts.*

CITATION OF AUTHORITY – general topical

ACCOMMODATION FACILITIES. See TRANSIENT ~.

HEADWORD USED FOR CROSS-REFERENCE ONLY

A4. Facsimile by amplitude modulation of the main carrier either directly or by frequency modulated sub-carrier. *General Radio Regulations, Part II*, C.R.C., c. 1372, s. 42.

TERM WITH A
NUMERAL

AIR TIME. *var.* **AIR-TIME.** In respect of any aircraft, means the period of time commencing when the aircraft leaves the surface of the earth and terminating when the aircraft touches the surface of the earth at the next point of landing. See PRICE OF ~.

VARIANT
SPELLING

ASSUMPSIT. [L. one promised] A form of action to recover damages for breach of a simple contract.

TRANSLATION
INSIDE
ETYMOLOGY
BRACKET

BAIT. *v.* To set one animal against another which is tied or contained.

BAIT. *n.* Corn, wheat, oats or other cultivated grain or any product thereof or any manufactured product or material that may attract migratory game birds and includes plastic corn and any other imitation grain. *Migratory Birds Regulation*, C.R.C., c. 1035, s. 2.

HOMOGRAPH

BARGAINING COLLECTIVELY. 1. Negotiating in good faith with a view to the conclusion of a collective bargaining agreement, or a renewal or revision of a bargaining agreement, the embodiment in writing or writings of the terms of agreement arrived at in negotiations or required to be inserted in a collective bargaining agreement by this Act, the execution by or on behalf of the parties of such agreement, and the negotiating from time to time for the settlement of disputes and grievances of employees covered by the agreement or represented by a trade union representing the majority of employees in an appropriate unit. *The Trade Union Act*, R.S.S. 1978, c. T-17, s. 2. 2. Negotiating in good faith with a view to the conclusion of a collective bargaining agreement or a renewal or revision or a collective bargaining agreement and the embodiment in writing of the terms of agreement arrived at in negotiations or required to be inserted in a collective bargaining agreement by statute. Saskatchewan statutes.

CITATION OF
AUTHORITY
general
geographical

How to Use This Dictionary

Definitions in this dictionary are based largely on primary, Canadian sources: case law, a term bank of definitions from the statutes of Canada, all provinces and the Northwest Territories and Ontario and federal regulations and a library of basic Canadian legal textbooks.

In general, material is presented not historically but by frequency of use in the sources considered. Some historical terms hvae been included, e.g. "capital number", "non-capital murder" and any term which appeared in an earlier statute revision if this was the only definition available to us at the time.

Where definitions have been rewritten, we have attempted to remove sexual and racial bias, but material quoted verbatim has not been edited in this way.

Alphabetization

1. This dictionary is alphabetized absolutely by letter. Thus, the term "residential property" will be found after the term "resident" but before the term "resident owner".
2. Terms which include numerals are entered as though the numerals were spelled out. Thus, the term "A2" (= A- two) will be found after the term "attrition" and before the term "au besoin".
3. Abbreviations are integrated into the main work in the alphabetical order described above, rather than listed separately.
4. Homographs are ordered by function: first verbs, then nouns, abjectives, adverbs, abbreviations. Thus, the entry for "charge" used as a verb precedes the entry for "charge" used as a noun.

Elements of Each Entry

1. HEADWORD/HEADWORDS
(a) The words or phrase is presently in boldface, upper case letters.
(b) Variant spellings follow the most common spelling, in order of the frequency of their use.

2. FUNCTIONAL LABEL
(a) This identifies the grammatical part of speech or function (e.g. use as an abbreviation) of the headword/headwords. See the Table of Abbreviations Used in This Dictionary (on the inside front cover) for the abbreviations used here.
(b) A headword entered for cross-reference purposes only is assigned a functional label only to distinguish it from any homograph.

3. ETYMOLOGY
(a) Presented in square brackets, these characters show the language of origin of a word or phrase which is or was originally in a language other than English. See the Table of Abbreviations Used in This Dictionary (on the inside front cover) for the abbreviations used here.
(b) Where the word or phrase has adopted a more general meaning over time, a literal translation from the original language may be offered inside the brackets.
(c) A headword entered for cross-reference purposes only is assigned no etymological label.

4. DEFINITIONS

Multiple definitions are numbered. The most common or general definition is given first, less general or common definitions follow, ranked by frequency of use. In entries where case law is used, definitions are ranked from general to specific and also, where necessary, by the currency and weight of the authority.

5. CITATON OF AUTHORITY

(a) Where no authority is cited, the definition is derived from multiple sources.

(b) Specific citations of case law are complete and include pinpoint page reference from one law report. Most frequently, decisions have been quoted verbatim; such definitions are enclosed by quotation marks. Those definitions from case law which have been paraphrased or summarized do not contain quotation marks.

(c) Specific citations of legislation provide the chapter and section numbers. In most cases, legislation has been quoted verbatim, but occasionally minor editing has been done in the interest of clarity. Since this editing has been done and in some cases only the latest statute law revision has been used, those wishing to cite exactly are urged to refer to the original statutes.

(d) Specific citations of textual material provide exact page references. Since all textual material has been paraphrased or rewritten, those wishing to cite exactly are urged to refer to the original text.

(e) A general topical citation (italicized) limits a definition to a particular area of law.

(f) A general geographical citation (in ordinary type) limits a definition to a particular region or jurisdiction.

6. CROSS-REFERENCES

These refer the reader to more narrow or specific applications of the word or phrase or occasionally to related terms.

In the interest of saving space, the character "~" has been used to represent the headword/headwords in the cross-references which follow it.

A. *abbr* 1. Anonymous. 2. Ampere. 3. Atto.

AB. *abbr*. Abridgment.

AB ABUSU AD USUM NON VALET CONSEQUENTIA. [L.] One can draw no conclusion as to the legitimate use of a thing from its abuse.

ABANDON. *v.* 1. Includes (a) a wilful omission to take charge of a child by a person who is under a legal duty to do so, and (b) dealing with a child in a manner that is likely to leave that child exposed to risk without protection. *Criminal Code*, R.S.C. 1985 c. C-46 s. 214. 2. ". . .[A]bandon [as used in the *Adoption Act*, R.S.B.C. 1979, c. 4, s. 8] means: ~To desert surrender, forsake, or cede. To relinquish or give up with intent of never again resuming one's right or interest . . . to relinquish all connection with or concern in . . . ' This definition illustrates that both physical and mental components are involved in the definition of abandonment." *B. C. Birth Registration No. 77-09-010612, Re* (1989), 64 D.L.R. (4th) 432 at 436 (B.C. S.C.), Melnick L.J.S.C. 3. [To abandon property requires] an intention to desert or relinquish a right permanently. There must be a sense of finality to the action. *Arndt Estate v. First Galesburg National Bank & Trust Co.*, 2001 CarswellSask 329, 2001 SKQB 234, 206 Sask. R. 261, 42 R.P.R. (3d) 66 Saskatchewan Court of Queen's Bench, Hunter J.

ABANDONED MINE. A mine for which all permit obligations under this Act have been satisfied and in respect of which the mineral claims have reverted to the government. *Mines Act*, R.S.B.C. 1996, c. 293, s. 1.

ABANDONED MOTOR VEHICLE. A vehicle that has been left unattended without lawful authority and that appears to an officer, by reason of its age, appearance, mechanical condition or lack of number plates, to be abandoned. *Environmental Protection Act* R.S.O. 1990 c. E.19, s. 60.

ABANDONED MOTOR VEHICLE SITE. (a) A waste disposal site, (i) that is classified by the regulations as a derelict motor vehicle site, (ii) that is not exempt under the regulations relating to Part V or this Part, and (iii) for which a certificate of approval or a provisional certificate of approval has been issued pursuant to Part V, or (b) any place that is approved in writing by the Director for the purpose of receiving and storing abandoned motor vehicles. *Environmental Protection Act*, R.S.O. 1990, c. E.19, s. 60.

ABANDONED VEHICLE. A vehicle, other than a derelict vehicle, that has been abandoned at an airport or otherwise remains unclaimed at an airport for a period of not less than 30 days. *Airport Personal Property Disposal Regulations*, C.R.C., c. 1563 s. 2.

ABANDONEE. *n.* A person to whom rights to property are left.

ABANDONMENT. *n.* A. Relinquishing, surrender, giving up property or rights. 2. "Abandonment of an acquired domicile to be effective must be complete; there must be an animus relinquendi . . ." *Lauritson v. Lauritson* (1932), 41 O.W.N. 274 at 274 (H.C.), Kelly J. 3." . . . In order to find that a trade mark has indeed been abandoned, the non-use of the trade mark in question must be accompanied with an intention to abandon said trade mark. . ." *Labatt Brewing Co. v. Formosa Spring Brewery Ltd (1992), (sub nom. Labatt Brewing Co. v Molson Breweries, A Partnership)* 42 C.P.R. (3d) 481 at 490, 55 F.T.R. 266, Dubé J. 4. To constitute abandonment, we find the test in *Simpson v. Gowers* (1981), 121 D.L.R. (3d) 709 (Ont. C.A.) to be apt. In that case, a case involving property, specifically chattels, McKinnon, A.C.J.O., said at p. 711 quoting from R. A. Brown, in his text *The*

Law of Personal Property, 2nd ed. (1955), at p. 9: "Abandonment occurs when there is a giving up, a total desertion, and absolute relinquishment of private goods by the former owner. It may arise when the owner with the specific intent of desertion and relinquishment casts away or leaves behind his property . . . " *Ericsson Inc. v. Novatel Inc.* 2001 ABCA 199, 286 A.R. 190, 253 W.A.C. 190, 12 C.P.C. (5th) 212. 5. A defence to a charge of conspiracy in which the accused alleges that she abandoned the conspiracy, the agreement.

ABANDONMENT OF BARGAINING RIGHTS. The Ontario *Labour Relations Act*, 1995, S.O. 1995, c. 1 ("the Act") does not speak of abandonment of bargaining rights. The concept was developed in the Board's jurisprudence to allow termination of the bargaining rights of a union that fails to "actively promote those rights". *I.B.E.W., Local 894 v. Ellis-Don Ltd.*, 2001 CarswellOnt 99, 2001 SCC 4, 265 N.R. 2, 194 D.L.R. (4th) 385, 52 O.R. (3d) 160 (note), 2001 C.L.L.C. 220-028, 26 Admin. L.R. (3d) 171, 140 O.A.C. 201, [2001] 1 S.C.R. 221, Per Binnie J. (dissenting) (Major J. concurring).

AB ANTIQUO. [L.] From ancient times.

AB ASSUETIS NON FIT INJURIA. [L.] From things to which one has become accustomed, no wrong can arise.

ABATE. *v.* To break down, destroy or remove; to lower the price.

ABATEMENT. *n.* Termination, reduction, destruction. See PLEA IN ~; TAX ~.

ABATEMENT OF NUISANCE. Removing or putting an end to nuisance.

ABATEMENT PROJECT. A project for the abatement of an undesirable environmental condition affecting premises by (a) the removal and relocation of the development causing the condition; or (b) the removal and relocation of the premises affected by the condition. The Environment Act, S.M. 1987-88, c. 26, s. 1.

ABATER. *n.* One who puts an end to a nuisance.

ABATOR. *n.* One who puts an end to a nuisance.

ABBATOIR. *n.* Premises where animals are slaughtered; premises where animals are slaughtered and meat is cut, wrapped, frozen, cured, smoked or aged.

ABBROACHMENT. *n.* Forestalling a market by buying up goods intended to be sold there.

ABBROCHEMENT. *n.* Forestalling a market by buying up goods intended to be sold there.

ABBUTTALS. *n.* Limits or boundaries of land.

ABC. *abbr.* Advance booking charter.

ABC (DOMESTIC). *abbr.* Advance booking charter (domestic).

ABCA. The neutral citation for the Alberta Court of Appeal.

ABPC. The neutral citation for the Alberta Provincial Court.

ABQB. The neutral citation for the Alberta Court of Queen's Bench.

AB EXTRA. [L.] From without.

AB INCONVENIENTE. [L.] Because of inconvenience.

ABDICATE. *v* To refuse or renounce a thing.

ABDICATION. *n.* Where a person in office voluntarily renounces it or gives it up.

ABDUCTION. *n.* 1. Take, or cause to be taken away, a person under 16 years of age from the possession of and against the will of the parent or guardian who has lawful charge of that person. *Criminal Code*, R.S.C. 1985, c. C-46, s. 280. 2. Unlawfully taking, enticing away, concealing, detaining, receiving or harbouring a person under 14 years of age with intent to deprive a parent or guardian of the possession of that person. *Criminal Code*, R.S.C. 1985 c. C-46, ss. 281283. 3. Forcible stealing or carrying away any person. See CHILD~.

ABERRANCE. *n.* Behaviour.

ABERRATIO ICTUS. [L.] " . . . '[A] mistake of the bullet' that has led to the controversy surrounding the doctrine of transferred intent. In this . . . situation the perpetrator aims at X but by chance or lack of skill hits Y." *R. v Droste* (1984), 10 C.C.C. (3d) 404 at 410 1984 1 S.C.R. 208, 39 C.R. (3d) 26, 6 D.L.R. (4th) 607, 52 N.R. 176, 3 O.A.C. 179, Dickson J. See TRANSFERRED INTENT.

ABET. *v.* " . . . [T]o instigate, promote, procure or encourage the commission of an offence." *R. v. Stevenson* (1984), 11 C.C.C. (3d) 442 at 449, 62 N.S.R. (2d) 193, 136 A.P.R. 193 (C.A.), the court per Macdonald J.A. See AID AND ABET.

ABETTOR. *n.* One who promotes, procures, encourages.

AB EXTRA. [L.] From without.

ABEYANCE. *n.* 1. Lapse of an inheritance because it has no present owner. 2. In expectation.

ABIDE. *v.* " . . . [T]o accept without dispute or appeal any such order, and to fulfil or carry out such order if made." *Paulson v. Murray* (1922), 68 D.L.R. 643 at 644, 32 Man. R. 327, [1922] 2 W.W.R. 654 (K.B.), Dysart J.

ABILITY. *n.* Capacity to perform an act; skill. See NON~.

AB INCONVENIENTE. [L.] Because of inconvenience.

AB INITIO. [L.] From the beginning.

AB INTESTATO. [L.] From an intestate.

AB IRATO. [L.] By a person in anger.

ABJURATION. *n.* Renunciation of an oath.

ABJURE. *v.* To renounce or abandon an oath.

ABLE SEAMAN CONVENTION. In respect of an able seaman or an efficient deckhand, means the Certification of Able Seamen Convention, 1946. *Crewing Regulations*, SOR/97-390, s.(1).

ABODE. *n.* Residence. *R. v. Braithwaite*, [1918] 2 K.B. 319 at 330, [1918-19] All E.R. Rep. 1145 (U.K. C.A.), Scrutton L.J. See PLACE OF ~; USUAL PLACE OF~.

ABOLISH. *v.* To do away with.

ABOLITION. *n.* Doing away with something; destruction of thing.

ABORIGINAL. *adj.* Relating to the Indian, Inuit or Métis peoples of Canada.

ABORIGINAL COMMUNITY. A traditional collectivity of Aboriginal people that has a distinctive culture that includes engaging in traditional hunting practices.

ABORIGINAL FISHING RIGHTS. The spectrum of fishing rights consists of the right to fish for food, the right to exchange fish for money or other goods and the right to fish commercially.

ABORIGINAL GOVERNMENT. 1. A governing body that is established by or under or operating under an agreement between Her Majesty in right of Canada and aboriginal people and that is empowered to enact laws respecting (a) the protection of the environment; or (b) for the purposes of Division 5 of Part 7, the registration of vehicles or engines. *Canadian Environmental Protection Act, 1999*, S.C. 1999, c. 33, s. 3(1). 2. An Indian, an Inuit or a Métis government or the "council of the band", as defined in subsection 2(1) of the Indian Act. *Federal-Provincial Fiscal Arrangements Act*, R.S.C. 1985, c. F-8, s. 2(1)

ABORIGINALITY-RESIDENCE. An analogous ground of discrimination under section 15 of the *Charter of Rights and Freedoms*. Refers to different treatment of those living off a reserve. Recognized as an analogous ground because the decision to live on or off-reserve is a "personal characteristic essential to a band member's personal identity" which can be changed "only at great cost, if at all". *Corbiere v. Canada (Minister of Indian and Northern Affairs)*, [1999] 2 S.C.R. 203.

ABORIGINAL LANGUAGE. An aboriginal language as defined in the Official Languages Act. *Elections Act*, S.N.W.T. 1986 (2d Sess.), c. 2, s. 204.

ABORIGINAL LAND. Reserves, surrendered lands and any other lands that are set apart for the use and benefit of a band and that are subject to the Indian Act; land, including any water, that is subject to a comprehensive or specific claim agreement, or a self-government agreement, between the Government of Canada and aboriginal people where title remains with Her Majesty in right of Canada; and air and all layers of the atmosphere above and the subsurface below land. *Canadian Environmental Protection Act, 1999*, S.C. 1999, c. 33, s. 3(1), part.

ABORIGINAL LAW. The law relating to aboriginal people and their rights and claims.

ABORIGINAL MIDWIFERY. Traditional aboriginal midwifery practices such as the use and administration of traditional herbs and medicines and other cultural and spiritual practices, contemporary aboriginal midwifery practices which are based on, or originate in, traditional aboriginal midwifery practices, or a combination of traditional and contemporary aboriginal midwifery practices. *Midwives Regulation Act*, B.C. Reg.103 95, s.1.

ABORIGINAL ORGANIZATION. Includes an Indian band, an Indian band council, a tribal council and an organization that represents a territorially based aboriginal community. *Aboriginal Communal Fishing Licences Regulations*, SOR/93-332, s. 2.

ABORIGINAL PEOPLES. Persons who are Indians, Inuit or Métis.

ABORIGINAL PERSON. A person of Indian or Inuit ancestry, including a Métis person, or a person recognized as being a member of an Indian, Inuit or Métis group by the other members of that group, who at any time ordinarily resided in the territory that is now Canada. *Canadian Cultural Property Export Control List*, C.R.C., c. 448, s. 1.

ABORIGINAL RIGHT LANDS. Those lands on which only specific aboriginal rights exist (e.g., the right to hunt for food, social and ceremonial purposes) because the occupation and use by the particular group of aboriginal people is too limited and, as a result, does not meet the criteria for the recognition, at common law, of aboriginal title. In these cases, the aboriginal rights on the land are restricted to residual portions of the aboriginal title—such as the rights to hunt, fish or trap—or to other matters not connected to land; they do not, therefore, entail the full *sui generis* proprietary right to occupy and use the land. Both the Canadian Parliament and provincial legislatures can enact legislation, pursuant to their respective general legislative competence, that affect native activities on aboriginal right lands. *R. v. Van der Peet*, [1996] 2 S.C.R. 507 (per L'Heureux-Dube, dissenting).

ABORIGINAL RIGHTS. 1. The test for identifying the aboriginal rights recognized and affirmed by s. 35(1) must be directed at identifying the crucial elements of those pre-existing distinctive societies. Identifying those traditions, customs and practices that are integral to distinctive aboriginal cultures will serve to identify the crucial elements of the distinctive aboriginal societies that occupied North America prior to the arrival of Europeans. The person or community claiming the existence of an aboriginal right protected by s. 35(1) need only show that the particular practice, custom or tradition which it is claiming to be an aboriginal right is distinctive, not that it is distinct. *R. v. Van der Peet* [1996] 2 S.C.R. 507, per Lamer, J. 2. Three factors that should guide a court's characterization of a claimed aboriginal right: (1) the nature of the action which the applicant is claiming was done pursuant to an aboriginal right; (2) the nature of the governmental legislation or action alleged to infringe the right, i.e. the conflict between the claim and the limitation; and (3) the ancestral traditions and practices relied upon to establish the right. *Mitchell v. Minister of National Revenue* [2001] 1 S.C.R. 911. See EXISTING ~.

ABORIGINAL TITLE. 1." . :. [A] legal right derived from the Indians' historic occupation and possession of their tribal lands." *Calder v. Attorney General of British Columbia*, [1973] S.C.R. 313, cited in *Guerin v R.*, [1985] 1 C.N.L.R. 120 at 132 (S.C.C.), Dickson J. 2. Aboriginal title is a right in land and, as such, is more than the right to engage in specific activities which may be themselves aboriginal rights. Rather, it confers the right to use land for a variety of activities, not all of which need be aspects of practices, customs and traditions which are integral to the distinctive cultures of aboriginal societies. Those activities do not constitute the right *per se*; rather, they are parasitic on the underlying title. However, that range of uses is subject to the limitation that they must not be irreconcilable with the nature of the attachment to the land which forms the basis of the particular group's aboriginal title. This inherent limit [. . .] flows from the definition of aboriginal title as a *sui generis* interest in land, and is one way in which aboriginal title is distinct from a fee simple. [. . .] Aboriginal title at common law is protected in its full form by s. 35(1) [of the *Constitution Act, 1982*]. This conclusion flows from the express language of s. 35(1) itself. . .[Section] 35(1) did not create aboriginal rights; rather, it accorded constitutional status to those rights which were "existing" in 1982. . . In order to make out a claim for aboriginal title, the aboriginal group asserting title must satisfy the following criteria: (i) the land must have been occupied prior to sovereignty, (ii) if present occupation is relied on as proof of occupation pre-sovereignty, there must be a continuity between present and pre-sovereignty occupation, and (iii) at sovereignty, that occupation must have been exclusive. *Delgamuukw v. British Columbia* [1997] 3 S.C.R. 1010, Per Lamer C.J.C. (Cory and Major JJ. concurring) 3. [T]he aboriginal right of possession is derived from the historic occupation and use of ancestral lands by aboriginal peoples. Put another way, "aboriginal title" is based on the continued occupation and use of the land as part of the aboriginal peoples' traditional way of life. This *sui generis* interest is not equated with fee simple ownership; nor can it be described with reference to traditional property law concepts. . . [T]he aboriginal right of occupancy is further characterized by two principal features. First, this *sui generis* interest in the land is personal in that it is generally inalienable except to the Crown. Second, in dealing with this interest, the Crown is subject to a fiduciary obligation to treat aboriginal peoples fairly. *Del-*

gamuukw v. British Columbia [1997] 3 S.C.R. 1010, Per La Forest J. (L'Heureux-Dubé J. concurring).

ABORIGINAL TITLE LANDS. Aboriginal title lands are lands which the natives possess for occupation and use at their own discretion, subject to the Crown's ultimate title; federal and provincial legislation applies to aboriginal title lands, pursuant to the governments' respective general legislative authority. Aboriginal title of this kind is founded on the common law and strict conditions must be fulfilled for such title to be recognized. Aboriginal title can also be founded on treaties concluded between the natives and the competent government. *R. v. Van der Peet*, [1996] 9 W.W.R. 1 (per L'Heureux-Dube, dissenting).

ABORIGINE. *n*. The first, original or indigenous inhabitants of a country.

ABORTIFACIENT. *n*. Any instrument or substance used to cause an abortion.

ABORTION. *n*. 1. Miscarriage or the premature expulsion of the fetus. 2. The interruption of a speedypregnancy. See THERAPEUTIC~COMMITTEE.

ABORTIONIST. *n*. One who carries out abortions.

ABOUT. *adv*. Approximately; nearly; around.

ABOUT TO. On the point of.

ABOVE. In the context of disability insurance, above a finger joint means toward the wrist, not toward the tip of the finger. *Labelle v. Great-West Life Assurance Co.* (1996), 17 C.C.L.I. 173 (B.C.S.C.).

ABOVE PAR. At a premium, at a price above face or nominal value.

ABPC. The neutral citation for the Alberta Provincial Court.

ABQB. The neutral citation for the Alberta Court of Queen's Bench.

ABRADED MARGIN. An area of abrasion surrounding the wound where a bullet entered. F.A. Jaffe, *A Guide to Pathological Evidence*, 3d ed. (Toronto: C arswell, 1991) at 211.

ABR. *abbr*. Abridgment.

ABRASION. *n*. 1. Rubbing off; wearing. 2. Injury to the skin's surface.

ABRIDGE. *v*. To shorten.

ABRIDGMENT. *n*. 1. Of law, a digest. 2. Of time, shortening. 3. *The Canadian Abridgment*.

ABROACHMENT. *n*. Forestalling a market by buying up goods intended to be sold there.

ABROAD. *adv*. 1. Outside the country. 2. At large, out of doors.

ABROGATE. *v*. To annul or cancel.

ABROGATION. *n*. Annulment; repeal of a law.

ABS. *abbr*. Automatic Block Signal System.

ABSCESS. *n*. A zone of tissue containing pus.

ABSCOND. *v*. 1. To abscond from a trial means voluntarily absenting oneself from the trial for the purpose of impeding or frustrating it or with the intention of aborting its consequences. *R. v. Garofoli* [1990] 2 S.C.R. 1421. 2." . . . One who absconds from a particular place not only leaves but leaves it with the purpose of frustrating or rendering more difficult, by his absence, the effective application of the laws current in the jurisdiction whence he absconds.*Carolus v. Minister of National Revenue*, [1976] C.T.C. 608 at 610 (Fed. T.D.), Mahoney J.

ABSCONDING DEBTOR. A debtor who hides to avoid arrest or service, or simply is not in the province. C.R.B. Dunlop, *Creditor-Debtor Law in Canada* (Toronto: Carswell, 1981 at 206.

ABSENCE. *n*. 1. Non-existence; want; lack. 2. Not being present. *R. v. Brunet* (1918), 57 S.C.R. 83 at 91, 92, 95, 30 C.C.C. 16 42 D.L.R. 405, Anglin J. See LEAVE OF ~.

ABSENCE CUM DOLO ET CULPA. [L.] Wilful non-appearance to a writ or subpoena in order to avoid arrest or defeat or delay creditors.

ABSENCE WITHOUT LEAVE. A person absents himself without leave who (a) without authority leaves his place of duty; (b) without authority is absent from his place of duty; or (c) having been authorized to be absent from his place of duty, fails to return to his place of duty at the expiration of the period for which the absence of that person was authorized. *National Defence Act*, R.S.C. 1985, c. N-5, s. 90(2).

ABSENT. *v*. To be away; to not be present. *R. v. Brunet* (1918), 57 S.C.R. 83 at 91, 92, 95, 30 C.C.C. 16, 42 D.L.R. 405, Anglin J.

ABSENT. *adj*. Away; not present.

ABSENTEE. *n*. Within the meaning of this Act means a person who, having had his or her usual place of residence or domicile in Ontario, has disappeared, whose whereabouts is unknown and as to whom there is no knowledge as to whether he or she is alive or dead. *Absentees Act*, R.S.O. 1990, c. A.3, s. 1.

ABSENTEEISM. *n*. 1. Absence from work. 2. When employees absent themselves from work for insufficient reasons.

ABSENTE REO. [L.] The defendant being absent.

ABSOLUTA SENTENTIA EXPOSITORE NON INDIGET. [L.] A clear statement requires no exposition.

ABSOLUTE. *adj*. 1. Unconditional. *R. v. Helliwell* (1914), 18 D.L.R. 550 at 552, 5 O.W.N. 936, 23 C.C.C. 146, 30 O.L.R. 594 (C.A.), the court per Meredith C. J.O. 2. Unqualified. *Bank of Montreal v. Brett* (1984), 53 B.C.L.R. 346 at 348-49 (S.C.), McLachlin J. 3. Complete. See DECREE ~; ORDER ~; RULE~.

ABSOLUTE ALCOHOL. Alcohol of a strength of 100 per cent. *Food and Drug Regulations*, C.R.C., c. 870, s. B.02.002.

ABSOLUTE ASSIGNMENT. An instrument cannot be both a security interest and an absolute assignment since an absolute assignment is complete and perfect in itself. There cannot be a residual right remaining with the debtor to recover the assets. It is simply the sale of the book debts of the company. *Alberta Treasury Branches v. Minister of National Revenue* [1996] 1 S.C.R. 963, per Cory, J.

ABSOLUTE CERTIFICATE OF TITLE. A certificate of title issued on the registration of an absolute fee and includes such a certificate issued before October 31, 1979. *Land Title Act*, R.S.B.C. 1996, c. 250, s. 1.

ABSOLUTE DISCHARGE. A sentence by which accused is discharged although the charge is proven or a plea of guilty entered. The effect of an absolute discharge is that the person is deemed to not be convicted of the offence.

ABSOLUTE INTEREST. Complete and full ownership.

ABSOLUTE LIABILITY. 1. Describes an offence for which proof of a guilty mind is not necessary. *R. v. Heywood* (1992), 18 C.R. (4th) 63, (B.C. C.A.). 2. An offence for which an accused is criminally liable even though the accused acted under a reasonable mistake of fact. *R. v. Metro News Ltd.* (1986), 23 C.R.R. 77 at

89, 16 O.A.C. 319, 56 O.R. (2d) 321, 53 C.R. (3d) 289, 29 C.C.C. (3d) 35, 32 D.L.R. (4th) 321 (C.A.), the court per Martin J.A.

ABSOLUTE LIABILITY OFFENCE. Guilt follows proof of the proscribed act in such an offence.

ABSOLUTELY. *adv*. Unconditionally.

ABSOLUTE PRIVILEGE. Exemption from censure granted to (a) a defamatory statement made by an executive officer acting in the course of duty, (b) matters relating to the affairs of state, (c) statements by members of Parliament during the course of its proceedings by it or any of its constituent bodies, or (d) any communication made in the course of, or incidental to, judicial and quasi-judicial proceedings. R.E. Brown, *The Law of Defamation in Canada* (Toronto: Carswell, 1987) at 11.

ABSOLUTE RESPONSIBILITY. Criminal liability regardless of fault. D. Stuart, *Canadian Criminal Law: a treatise*, 2d ed. (Toronto: Carswell, 1987) at 157.

ABSOLUTION. *n*. Acquittal; dispensation.

ABSOLVE. *v*. To pardon; to acquit of a crime.

ABSORBED DOSE. The quotient, in gray, obtained by dividing the energy absorbed through exposure to radiation by the mass of the body or part of the body that absorbs the radiation. *Radiation Protection Regulations*, SOR/2000-203, s. 1(1).

ABSORPTION PLANT. Any plant for treating or processing gas by absorption or otherwise for the extraction from it of natural gasoline or other hydrocarbons. *Gas Utilities Act*, R.S.A. 2000, c. G-5, s. 1.

ABSQUE HOC. [L.] Without this.

ABSQUE IMPETITIONE VASTI. [L.] Without liability for waste.

ABSQUE TALI CAUSA. [L.] Without such cause.

ABSTENTION. *n*. Refusal to vote or debate.

ABSTRACT. *v*. To abridge; to remove.

ABSTRACT. *n*. Abridgment.

ABSTRACT. *adj*. Having no basis in fact.; conceptual.

ABSTRACT BOOK. Record in which each parcel of land is assigned a separate page on which details describing the document affecting title are inscribed. B.J. Reiter, B.N. McLellan & P.M. Perell, *Real Estate Law*, 4th ed. (Toronto: Emond Montgomery, 1992) at 389.

ABSTRACT INDEX. See REGISTER OF TITLE AND ~.

ABSTRACT OF TITLE. History of the title to land which shows any conveyance of the land or any interest in the land in chronological order.

ABSURD. *adj*. An "absurd" interpretation of a statute is one which leads to a ridiculous or frivolous consequences or is "extremely unreasonable". *Pointe Claire v. Quebec (Labour Court)* (1997), 146 D.L.R. (4th) 1, S.C.C., per L'Heureux-Dube, dissenting.

ABSURDITY. *n*. " . . . [I]n relation to the construction of statutes refers to disharmony between the parts of a statute or between a part and the whole, or inconsistency between the statute taken as a whole and a particular result of its application . . ." *Carfrae Estates Ltd v. Gamble* (1979), 97 D.L.R. (3d) 162 at 164, 24 O.R. (2d) 113 (Div. Ct.), Reid J.

ABUNDANS CAUTELA NON NOCET. [L.] Great caution causes no harm.

ABUSE. *v*. 1. To make improper or excessive use of. 2. " . : . [T]o cause unnecessarily substantial suffering to any animal." *R. v. Linder*, [1950] 1 W.W.R. 1035 at 1037, 10 C.R. 44, 97 C.C.C. 174 (B.C. C.A.), Bird, J.A. 3. To mistreat.

ABUSE. *n*. 1. Misuse; maltreatment. 2. Condition of (a) physical harm wherein a child suffers physical injury but does not include reasonable punishment administered by a parent or guardian; (b) malnutrition or mental ill-health of a degree that if not immediately remedied could seriously impair growth and developmment or result in permanent injury or death or (c) sexual molestation. 3. A state or condition of being physically harmed, sexually molested or sexually exploited. *Child and Family Services Act*, R.S.O. 1990, c. C.11, s. 79(1). 4. Of a child by the person means that the child (a) has suffered physical harm, inflicted by the person or caused by the person's failure to supervise and protect the child adequately; (b) has been sexually abused by the person or by another person where the person, having the care of the child, knows or should know of the possibility of sexual abuse and fails to protect the child; or (c) has suffered serious emotional harm demonstrated by severe anxiety, depression, withdrawal, or self-destructive or aggressive behaviour, caused by the in-

tentional conduct of the person. *Children and Family Services Act*, S.N.S.1990 c. 5 s. 62. 5. Mistreatment of an adult that causes the adult physical, mental or emotional harm, or damage to or loss of assets, and includes intimidation, humiliation, physical assault, sexual assault, overmedication, withholding needed medication, censoring mail, invasion or denial of privacy or denial of access to visitors, failing to provide adequate nutrition, medical attention, misappropriating or improperly converting money or possessions. *Adult Guardianship statutes*. See ALCOHOL~; ALCOHOL AND DRUG CHILD ~; DRUG ~; SUBSTANCE ~.

ABUSE OF DISTRESS. Use of chattels lawfully seized.

ABUSE OF PROCESS. 1. Conduct on the part of government authorities that undermines the fundamental principles that underlie the community's sense of decency and fair play. *R. v. La* [1997] 8 W.W.R. 1 (S.C.C.), per Sopinka, J. at pp. 11-12. 2. The tort of abuse of process exists where the abuser has used the legal process for a purpose other than that which it was designed to serve, a collateral, extraneous, ulterior, improper or illicit purpose. There is no abuse where the litigant employs regular legal process to its proper conclusion even if with bad intentions. *Levi Strauss & Co. v. Roadrunner Apparel Inc.* (1997), 221 N.R. 93 (Fed. C.A.), per Letourneau, J.A. 3. The doctrine of abuse of process is intended to prevent the re-litigation of an issue which was determined in an earlier proceeding and which would be determinative of the later case. *Glenko Enterprises Ltd. v. Keller* 2000 MBCA 7, [2001] 1 W.W.R. 229, 5 C.L.R. (3d) 1, 150 Man. R. (2d) 1. 4. " . . . [I]n *R. v. D. (T.C.)* (1987), 38 C.C.C. (3d) 434 at 447 . . .(Ont. C.A.), [it was] held that the onus of establishing that an abuse of process has occurred is on the respondent who must establish, on a balance of probabilities, that the Crown has acted in an oppressive or vexatious manner or that the prosecution is offensive to the principles of fundamental justice and fair play." *R. v. Miles of Music Ltd* (1989), 24 C.P.R. (3d) 301 at 309, 31 O.A.C. 380, 69 C.R. (3d) 361, 48 C.C.C. (3d) 96 (C.A.), Krever J.A. 5. " . . . [T]he unreasonable multiplication of proceedings. . ." *General Foods Ltd v. Struthers Scientific & International* Co . (1971), 4 C.P.R. (2d) 97 at 105, [1974] S.C ~ 989 23 D.L.R. (3d) 313 the court per Pigeon J. 6. " . . . ' [F]rivolous and vexatious, or if the process . . . is in fact being used for an ulterior or improper purpose, or if the process is being used in such a way as to be in itself an abuse . . ." *Canada Metal Co. v. Heap* (1975), 7 O.R. (2d) 185 at 192 (C.A.). 7. "The essence of the tort of abuse of process is the misuse or perversion of the court's process for an extraneous or ulterior purpose. There must be a purpose other than that which the process was designed to serve . . ." *D.K. Investments Ltd. v S. W. S Investments Ltd*. 1984 5 B.C.L.R. 333 (S.C.), Finch J., affirmed (1986), 6 B.C.L.R. (2d) 291 (C.A.).

ABUSE OF STATUTORY POWERS. Abuse of process or abuse of office. Malicious prosecution is a specific tort of this category. *Starline Entertainment Centre v. Ciccarelli* (1995), 41 C.P.C. (3d) 99 (Ont. Gen. Div.).

ABUT. *v.* 1. To border upon. 2. Includes having access thereto directly. *Community Planning Act*, R. S.N.B. 1973, c. C-12, s. 1.

ABUTTALS. *n.* Limits or boundaries of land.

ABUTTING DIRECTLY. In relation to works of constructing, enlarging or extending a sewer or water main, applies to mains through private lands as well tmains under streets. *Local Government Act*, R.S.B.C. 1996, c. 323, s. 620.

ABUTTING PARCEL. A lot or parcel of land abutting on that portion of the street wherein or whereon a work is or is to be made. *Municipalities Act*, R.S.N.B. 1973, c. M-22, s. 118.

A.C. *abbr.* Law Reports, Appeal Cases, 1891-.

A/C. *abbr.* Account.

ACADEMIC STAFF. Includes professors, associate professors, assistant professors, lecturers, instructors.

ACADEMIC YEAR. The portion of the calendar year between the opening and closing dates of a school.

ACCEDAS AD CURIAM. [L.] That you go to the court.

ACCEDE. *v.* To consent; to agree.

ACCELERATED TRUST. A trust for a spouse created when it is an advantage for the taxpayer who created the estate that tax be levied when the trust comes into effect. D.M.W. Waters, *The Law of Trusts in Canada*, 2d ed. (Toronto: Carswell, 1984) at 30.

ACCELERATE-STOP DISTANCE AVAILABLE. In respect of a runway, the length of the take-off run available plus the length of the stopway, where a stopway is provided. *Canadian Aviation Regulations*, SOR/96-433, s. 101.01(1).

ACCELERATING PREMIUM. Bonus or incentive paid to employees and which increases as production increases.

ACCELERATION. *n.* "The doctrine of acceleration is that all interests which fail or are undisposed of are captured by a residuary gift or go on an intestacy, but that a testator is presumed to have intended an acceleration of subsequent interests where a life interest fails in consequence of the donee being prevented by law from taking." *Kebty-Fletcher's Will Trusts Re* (1967), (*sub nom. Public Trustee v. Swan*) [1967] 3 All E.R. 1076 at 1080 (U.K. Ch.), Stamp J.

ACCELERATION CLAUSE. A clause in a contract which makes several periodic payments become due immediately upon default of the payor or permits a lender to call for payment of money due.

ACCELERATOR. See PARTICLE~.

ACCELERATOR CONTROL SYSTEM. See DRIVER-OPERATED~.

ACCEPTABLE QUALITY. The characteristics and the quality of a consumer product that consumers can reasonably expect the product to have, having regard to all the relevant circumstances of the sale of the product, including the description of the product, its purchase price and the express warranties of the retail seller or manufacturer of the product.

ACCEPTANCE. *n.* 1. Signification by an offeree of willingness to enter into a contract with an offeror on the offeror's terms. G.H.L. Fridman, *The Law of Contract in Canada*, 2d ed. (Toronto: Carswell, 1986) at 41. 2. The acceptance of a bill is the signification by the drawee of his assent to the order of the drawer. *Bills of Exchange Act*, R.S.C. 1985, c. B-4, s. 34(1). 3. An acceptance completed by delivery or notification. *Bills of Exchange Act* R.S.C. 1985 c. B-4, s. 2. 4. In sale of goods, involves taking possession of the goods by the buyer. See BANKER'S ~; BLANK ~; CONDITIONAL ~; GENERAL ~; LOCAL ~; NON- ~; PARTIAL ~; QUALIFIED ~.

ACCEPTANCE LIMITS OF ERROR. The limits of error that apply to a device when the performance of the device is tested (a) at the time the class, type or design of that device is examined for approval, (b) at the time the device is inspected prior to its first use in trade, (c) at the time the measuring elements of the device are overhauled or repaired following the failure of the device on inspection to measure within the applicable limits of error, or (d) at any time within 30 days after the time referred to in paragraph (b) or (c). *Weights and Measures Regulations* C.R.C., c. 1605 s. 2.

ACCEPTANCE OF BILL. The signification by the drawee of assent to the drawer's order to pay the bill. E.L.G. Tyler & N.E. Palmer, eds., Crossley Vaines' Personal Property, 5th ed. (London: Butterworths 1973) at 235.

ACCEPTANCE OF SERVICE. To endorse on the back of a document or a copy of it acknowledgement that the document was duly served.

ACCEPTED VALUE. The value that would be attributed by a municipal taxing authority to federal property, without regard to any ornamental, decorative or non-functional features thereof, as the base for computing the amount of real estate tax applicable to that property if it were taxable property.

ACCEPTOR. *n.* One who accepts a bill of exchange. The person to whom a depository bill is addressed and who signs it. *Depository Bills and Notes Act, 1998*, S. C. 1998, c. 13, s. 2.

ACCESS. *n.* 1. Either the opportunity to examine an original record or the provision of a copy, at the option of the Government. *Freedom of Information Act*, R.S.N.S. 1989, c. 180, s. 2. 2. "... [I]mplies that the custody of a child has been awarded to another person. Kay J., in *Evershed v. Evershed* (1882) 46 L.T. 690 at 691 (Ch.), stated at p. 691: 'The meaning of access is clear; it is that someone is to have leave to see children in custody of someone else ...'" *Glasgow v. Glasgow* (1982), 51 N.S.R. (2d) 13 at 24, 67 A.P.R. 473, 102 A.P.R. 13 (Fam. Ct.), Niedermayer Fam. Ct. J. 3. "... '[R]ights to visit'..." *W. (E C.) . H. (P.J.J.)* 26 R.F.L. (2d) 164 at 177, [1982] 2 W.W.R. 313, 13 Man. R. (2d) 259, 131 D.L.R. (3d) 630 (C.A.), Matas J.A. (dissenting). 4. Includes visitation. *Family Relations Act*, R.S.B.C. 1996, c. 128, s. 21. 5. An exit from or an entrance to a highway. *The Highways Protection Act*, R.S.M. 1987, c. H50, s. 1. See LEVEL ~; NON- ~; RIGHT OF ~.

ACCESSIBLE. *adj.* Approachable by person or tools as required , without undue hindrance or impediment.

ACCESSIBLE LOCATION. Any point that can be reached by any part of the human body.

Radiation Emitting Devices Regulations, C.R.C. c. 1370, s. 1.

ACCESSIO CEDIT PRINCIPALI. [L.] Any accessory thing, when incorporated in a principal thing, becomes part of that principal thing.

ACCESSION. *n.* Something belonging to one person which becomes the property of a second person because it was added to or incorporated with the second person's thing.

ACCESSION OF THE SOVEREIGN. The heir at once becomes the sovereign when a sovereign dies.

ACCESSIONS. *n.* Goods that are installed in or affixed to other goods.

ACCESS ORDER. A custody order under the Divorce Act includes an access order. An order relating to access to children by one or both of the parents.

ACCESSORIUM NON DUCIT, SED SEQUITUR SUUM PRINCIPALE. [L.] The incident passes with the grant of the principal, but the principal does not pass by the grant of the incident.

ACCESSORIUM NON TRAHIT PRINCIPALE. [L.] An accessory thing does not carry its principal with it.

ACCESSORIUM SEQUITUR PRINCIPALE. [L.] An accessory thing goes with its principal.

ACCESSORIUS SEQUITUR NATURAM SUI PRINCIPALIS. [L.] An accessory and the principal offender are of the same nature.

ACCESSORY. *n.* 1. Anything joined to another; thing incident to another. 2. One who is not the chief actor in an offence but who is in some way concerned in it either before the act was committed, or at its commission, or soon after the initial and main act has been committed. *R. v. Smith* (1876), 38 U.C.Q.B. 218 at 227 (C.A.), Harrison C.J. See PRINCIPAL AND ~.

ACCESSORY AFTER THE FACT. One who, knowing that a person has been a party to the offence, receives comforts or assists that person for the purposes of enabling that person to escape. *Criminal Code*, R.S.C. 1985, c. C-46 s. 23.

ACCESSORY BEFORE THE FACT. At common law, one who counsels or procures another to commit an offence but who is not present or active when it is committed. *R. v. Berryman*

(1990), 78 C.R. (3d) 376 at 383, 48 B.C.L.R. (2d) 105, 57 C.C.C. (3d) 375 (C.A.), the court per Wood J.A.

ACCESSORY BUILDING. A subordinate building or portion of a main building that is not used for human habitation.

ACCESSORY USE. Use naturally and normally incidental to the principal use.

ACCESS RIGHT. A right, granted in an order or agreement, of access to or visitation of a child. Family Orders acts.

ACCESS ROAD. 1. A road located on land not owned by a municipality and not dedicated and accepted as or otherwise deemed at law to be, a Public highway, that serves as a motor vehicle access route to one or more parcels of land. *Road Access Act*, R.S.O. 1990, c. R.34, s. 1. 2. A road of a temporary nature used to reach sources of material or parts of a construction project, or for fire protection in timbered areas and access to mining claims. See FOREST ~; TEMPORARY ~.

ACCESS TO COMPANY PREMISES. A clause permitting union representatives entry to an employer's premises even if they are not employees.

ACCESS-TO-PLANT CLAUSE. A clause which permits union representatives entry to an employer's premises even if they are not employees.

ACCIDENT. *n.* 1. " . . . [T]he expression 'accident' is used in the popular and ordinary sense of the word as denoting an unlooked-for mishap or an untoward event which is not expected or designed." *Fenton v. Thorley & Co. Ltd*, [1903] A.C. 443 at 448, Macnaghten L.J. 2. A wilful and an intentional act, not being the act of the employee, a fortuitous event occasioned by a physical or natural cause, or disablement arising out of and in the course of employment. *Workers Compensation acts*. See ENVIRONMENTAL ~; FATAL ~; INDUSTRIAL ~; INEVITABLE ~; NONINDUSTRIAL ~.

ACCIDENTAL. *adj.* 1. " . . . [I]ndicating an unlooked for mishap or an untoward event which is not expected or designed; or as an event which takes place out of the usual course of events without the foresight of expectation of the person injured; or as an injury happening by chance unexpectedly, not as expected. . ." *Voison v. Royal Insurance Co. of Canada* (1988), 33 C.C.L.I. 1 at 6, 66 O.R. (2d) 45, 53 D.L.R. (4th)

299, [1988] I.L.R. 1-2358, 29 O.A.C. 227 (C.A.), the court per Robins J.A. 2. employed in contradistinction to wilful . . . produced by mere chance, or incapable of being traced to any cause. *Filliter v. Phipard* (1848),11 Q.B. 347, 17 L.J.Q.B. *89*, 116 E.R. 506 (U.K.), Lord Denman.

ACCIDENTAL DEATH INSURANCE. Insurance undertaken by an insurer as part of a contract of life insurance whereby the insurer undertakes to pay an additional amount of insurance money in the event of the death by accident of the person whose life is insured. *Insurance acts*.

ACCIDENTAL MEANS. 1. In my view, the phrase "accidental means" conveys the idea that the consequences of the actions and events that produced death were unexpected. Reference to a set of consequences is therefore implicit in the word "means". "Means" refers to one or more actions or events, seen under the aspect of their causal relation to the events they bring about. *Martin v. American International Assurance Life Co.* 2003 SCC 16. 2. ". . . [A]n effect which is not the natural or probable consequence of the means which produced it, an effect which does not ordinarily follow and cannot be reasonably anticipated from the use of those means, an effect which the actor did not intend to produce and which he cannot be charged with the design of producing, . . . Such an effect is not the result of design, cannot be reasonably anticipated, is unexpected, and is produced by an unusual combination of fortuitous circumstances; . . ." *Western Commercial Travellers' Assn. v Smith* (1898), 40 L.R.A. 653.

ACCIDENT FUND. The fund provided for the payment of compensation, medical aid outlays and expenses. *Workers Compensation acts*.

ACCIDENT INSURANCE. 1. Insurance by which the insurer undertakes, otherwise than incidentally to some other class of insurance defined by or under the Insurance Act, to pay insurance money in the event of accident to the person or persons insured, but does not include insurance in which the insurer undertakes to pay insurance money both in the event of death by accident and in the event of death from any other cause. *Insurance acts*. 2. Includes personal accident insurance, public liability insurance and employers' liability insurance. 3. The obligation of the insurer under this Act to benefits if loss from bodily injuries is sustained by an insured as the result of one of the perils mentioned in section 22. *The Automobile Accident Insurance Act*, R.S.S. 1978, c. A-35, s. 2. See GROUP ~.

ACCIDENT PREVENTION ASSOCIATION. A group formed by employers to provide education in accident prevention. D. Robertson, *Ontario Health and Safety Guide* Toronto: Richard De Boo Ltd., 1988) at 5.13.

ACCIDENT PRONENESS. The tendency of a person to have accidents.

ACCLAMATION. *n*. Occurs when only the number of candidates required to fill an office is nominated. The candidate(s) is (are) elected..

ACCOMMODATION. *n*. 1. Refers to what is required in the circumstances of employment or service provision to avoid discrimination under human rights legislation. Employers and others governed by human rights legislation are now required in all cases to accommodate the characteristics of affected groups within their standards, rather than maintaining discriminatory standards supplemented by accommodation for those who cannot meet them. Incorporating accommodation into the standard itself ensures that each person is assessed according to her or his own personal abilities, instead of being judged against presumed group characteristics. *British Columbia (Superintendent of Motor Vehicles) v. British Columbia (Council of Human Rights)*, [1999] 3 S.C.R. 868, 131 B.C.A.C. 280, 214 W.A.C. 280, McLachlin, J. for the court. 2. Sleeping facilities provided on a commercial basis to the general public. *Air Carrier Regulations*, C.R.C. c . 3 s. 23. 3. The provision of lodging in hotels and motels. See HOSTEL ~; HOUSING ~; SANITARY ~; SEMI-PRIVATE ~; SERVICED HOUSING ~; SLEEPING ~ SLEEPING ~S; TOURIST ~; TRANSIENT~

ACCOMMODATION BILL. A bill accepted or endorsed without value to accommodate a party to the bill. The party who accommodates thus is in fact a surety for a principal debtor who may or may not be a party to the bill. I.F.G. Baxter, *The Law of Banking*, 3d ed. (Toronto: Carswell, 1981) at 116.

ACCOMMODATION CHARGE. The charge in respect of nursing home care payable by a resident for accommodation and meals in a nursing home or an approved hospital. *Nursing Homes Act*, S.A. 1985, c. N-14.1, s. 1.

ACCOMMODATION FACILITIES. See TRANSIENT ~.

ACCOMMODATION PARTY. An accommodation party to a bill is a person who has signed a bill as drawer, acceptor or endorser, without receiving value therefor, and for the purpose of lending his name to some other person. *Bills of Exchange Act*, R.S.C. 1985, c. B-4, s. 54(1).

ACCOMMODATION SPACE. (a) Passenger spaces, (b) crew space, (c) offices, (d) pantries, and (e) space similar to any of the foregoing not being service spaces or open spaces on deck. *Hull Construction Regulations*, C.R.C, c. 1431, s. 2.

ACCOMMODATION SURETY. A party who enters into a guarantee in the expectation of little or no remuneration and for the purpose of accommodating others or of assisting others in the accomplishment of their plans. *Johns-Manville Canada Inc. v. John Carlo Ltd.*, [1983] 1 S.C.R. 513, at 521.

ACCOMMODATION UNIT. A room for the accommodation of the public that contains at least one bed.

ACCOMPLICE. *n*. " . . . What is necessary to become an accomplice is a participation in the crime involved, and not necessarily the actual commission of it . . ." *R. v Morris* (1979 10 C.R. (3d) 259 at 281, [1979] 2 S.C.R. 1041, 26 N.B.R. (2d) 273, 55 A.P.R. 273, 27 N.R. 313, 47 C.C.C. (2d) 257, 99 D.L.R. (3d) 420, Spence J. (dissenting) (Laskin C.J.C., Dickson and Estey JJ. concurring).

ACCORD. *v*. To agree.

ACCORD. *n*. Agreement by which an obligation in contract or tort is discharged. *Coulter Electronics of Canada Ltd v. Motorways (1985) Ltd* (1990), 42 C.P.C. (2d) 90 at 93, 65 Man. R. (2d) 45 (C.A.), O'Sullivan, Philp and Helper JJ.A.

ACCORD AND SATISFACTION. "Accord and satisfaction is the purchase of a release from an obligation whether arising under contract or tort by means of an valuable consideration not being the actual performance of the obligation itself. The accord is the agreement by which the obligation is discharged. The satisfaction is the consideration which makes the agreement operative." *Coulter Electronics of Canada Ltd. v. Motorways (1985) Ltd* (1990), 42 C.P.C. (2d) 90 at 93, 65 Man. R. (2d) 45 (C.A.), O'Sullivan, Philp and Helper JJ.A.

ACCOST. *v*. To solicit.

ACCOUNT. *n.* 1. Settlement of debits and credits between parties. 2. Any monetary obligation not evidenced by any chattel paper, instrument or securities, whether or not it has been earned by performance. 3. An account with a bank. See ~S; BANK ~; CAPITAL ~; CASH ~; CHARGE ~; DUTY TO ~; EXPENSE ~; HOLD BACK ~ MARGIN ~; MONEY OF ~; OMNIBUS ~; OPEN ~; PASS AN ~; STATEMENT OF ~; UNSETTLED ~.

ACCOUNTABLE. *adj.* Liable; responsible.

ACCOUNTABLE ADVANCE. (*a*) a sum of money advanced to a person from an appropriation, and (*b*) a sum of money advanced to a person from the sum of money described in paragraph (*a*) for which the person is accountable and includes imprest funds and working capital advances administered under an imprest system. *Accountable Advances Regulations,* SOR/86-438 s 2.

ACCOUNTABLE RECEIPT. A written acknowledgement of receipt of a chattel or money, for which the person receiving it must account.

ACCOUNTANCY. See PUBLIC~.

ACCOUNTANT. *n.* 1. A chartered accountant, a certified general accountant or a registered industrial accountant. 2. An accountant of the court. See FIRM OF ~S; PUBLIC ~.

ACCOUNTING. *n.* "... [T]he art of recording, classifying, and summarizing in a significant manner and in terms of money, transactions and events which are, in part at least, of a financial character and interpreting the results thereof." *Toromont Industrial Holdings Ltd. v. Thorne Gunn, Helliwell & Christenson* (1975), 23 C.P.R. (2d) 59 at 74, 10 O.R. (2d) 65, 62 D.L.R. (3d) 225 (H.C.), Holland J. See ACCRUAL METHOD OF ~; ACTION FOR ~; PRICE LEVEL ADJUSTED ~; PUBLIC ~ AND AUDITING.

ACCOUNTING PERIOD. Usually a year; fiscal year; period in respect of which financial statements are prepared.

ACCOUNTING PRACTICE. See EXCLUSIVE ~.

ACCOUNTING PRINCIPLES. See GENERALLY ACCEPTED ~.

ACCOUNT IS TO BE TAKEN. The account in credit and debit form, verified by affidavit, is brought into court.

ACCOUNT PAYABLE. An amount that is owed to a regular trade creditor.

ACCOUNT RECEIVABLE. An amount that a regular trade debtor owes. See ACCOUNTS RECEIVABLE.

ACCOUNTS. *n.* 1. The statement of profit and loss and the balance sheet. 2. Deposits in a bank are known as accounts of the depositors. See ACCOUNT; BOOK ~; PUBLIC ~.

ACCOUNTS OF CANADA. The accounts that show the expenditures made under appropriations, the revenues of Canada and other payments into and out of the Consolidated Revenue Fund.

ACCOUNTS RECEIVABLE. 1. The amounts that are owing by customers to a business for goods shipped to them or for services rendered. 2. Existing or future book debts, accounts, claims, moneys and choses in action or any class or part thereof and all contracts, securities, bills, notes, books, instruments and other documents securing, evidencing or in any way relating to the same or any of them, but shall not include uncalled share capital of the company or calls made but not paid. *Canada Corporations Act,* R.S.C. 1970, c. C-32, s. 3.

ACCOUNT STATED. " ... I agree with the observation of Patterson, J.A., in Watson v. Severn, 6 A.R. 559, at p. 565 ... 'An account stated is a settlement of accounts, in which both parties or their agents agree upon the amount due from the one to the other:' Bates v. Townley, 2 Exch. 152 ... " *Robb v. Murray* (1889), 16 O.A.R. 503 at 506 (C.A.), the court per Osler J.A.

ACCREDIT. *v.* To furnish a diplomat with sufficient credentials and authority to be duly received.

ACCREDITED EMPLOYERS' ORGANIZATION. An organization of employers that is accredited under this Act as the bargaining agent for a unit of employers. *Labour Relations Act,* 1995, S.O. 1995, c. 1, Sched. A, s. 1.

ACCREDITED HOSPITAL. A hospital accredited by the Canadian Council on Hospital Accreditation in which diagnostic services and medical, surgical and obstetrical treatment are provided. *Criminal Code,* R.S.C. 1985, c. C-46, s. 287(6).

ACCRETION. *n.* 1. " ... [T]he increase which land bordering on a river or on the sea undergoes through the silting up of soil, sand or other substance, or the permanent retiral of the waters. This increase must be formed by a process so slow and gradual as to be . . . imperceptible, by which is meant that the addition cannot be observed in its actual progress from moment to moment or from hour to hour, although, after a certain period, it can be observed that there has been a fresh addition to the shore line. The increase must also result from the action of the water and not from some unusual or unnatural action by which a considerable quantity of soil is suddenly swept from the land of one man and deposited on, or annexed to, the land of another." *Clarke v Edmonton (City)*, [1930] S.C.R. 137 at 144, [1949] 4 D.L.R. 1010, the court per Lamont J. 2. Something which the mortgagor adds to property to improve its value for the mortgagee's benefit. W.B. Ra ner R .H. & .H. McLaren *Falconbridge on Mortgages*, 4th ed. (Toronto: Canada Law Book, 1977) at 19. 3. " . . . [D]esignate[s] an enlargement or widening of an existing bargaining unit by the addition of a number of employees, for whatever reason, when said employees, as compared to the actual members of the bargaining unit involved, shall occupy classifications the incumbents of which will perform similar work . . ." *C. O. T. U. v. Teleglobe Canada* (1979), 3 Can. L.R.B.R. 86 at 135, 32 di 270 (Can.), Lapointe (Chair), Archambault and Bernstein (Members).

ACCRUAL. *n.* Gradual vesting of a right in a person, without active intervention.

ACCRUAL METHOD OF ACCOUNTING. A method in which income is reported as it is earned and costs are recorded as they are incurred.

ACCRUE. *v.* 1. A right can only be said to accrue to a person at the point when the person can actually exercise the right. To say that a right accrues to a person is a passive way of saying that the person "acquires" that right. *R. v. Puskas (sub nom. R. v. Chatwell)*, (1998), 227 N.R. 1 (S.C.C.). 2. " . . . [T]o fall (to any one) as a natural growth, to arise as a natural growth." *Hockin v. Bank of British Columbia* (1989), 36 B.C.L.R. (2d) 22 at 226 (S.C.), Spencer J.

ACCRUED. *adj.* 1. Earned or accumulated but not yet received or receivable. 2. Vested.

ACCRUED BENEFIT COST METHOD. A method of determining the annual cost of benefits under a pension plan whereby the cost of such benefits applicable to a particular plan year is taken as the actuarial value of the benefits that accrued in respect of service for that year. *Pension Benefits Standards Regulations*, C.R.C., c. 1252, s. 2.

ACCRUED DIVIDEND. A dividend declared but not yet paid.

ACCRUED LIABILITY. The amount owing on a given day in respect of salaries, periodic payments, interest and similar items. S.M. Beck *et al, Cases and Materials on Partnerships and Canadian Business Corporations* (Toronto: The Carswell Company Limited, 1983) at 779.

ACCRUED RIGHT. " . . . [A] right which has come into existence . . . one that may be enjoyed at a period of time that is current or past, . . ." *Chafe v. Power* (1980), 117 D.L.R. (3d) 117 at 122, 125 (Nfld. T.D.), Goodridge J.

ACCRUED TAX. Tax that has not yet become due and payable but that can be charged.

ACCRUING. *adj.* " . . . [N]ecessarily, or inevitably, not possibly or even probably, arising in due course . . . the events giving rise to it or the condition upon which it depends for its existence, must have been so set in train or engaged as inevitably to give rise in due course to the right and its corresponding duty." *Scott v College of Physicians and Surgeons (Saskatchewan)* (1992), 95 D.L.R. (4th) 706 at 719, [1993] 1 W.W.R. 533, 100 Sask. R. 291, 18 W.A.C. 291 (C.A.), the court per Cameron J.A. See OWING OR ~.

ACCRUING DEBT. "An accruing debt, therefore, is a debt not yet actually payable, but a debt which is represented by an existing obligation." *Webb v. Stenton* (1883), 11 Q.B.D. 518 at 527 (C.A.), Lindley L.J.

ACCRUING RIGHT. " . . . [A] vested (or possibly contingent) one that may only be enjoyed at a future time." *Chafe v. Power*, (1980), 117 D.L.R. (3d) 117 at 125 (Nfld. T.D.), Goodridge J.

ACCT. *abbr.* account.

ACCUMULATED DIVIDEND. A dividend due but not yet paid.

ACCUMULATED PROFITS. Profits which have not been distributed.

ACCUMULATED WEALTH. See LOSS OF ~.

ACCUMULATION. *n.* 1. Adding of dividends, rents, and other incomes to capital. 2. Income from property is separated from the ownership of the property either to be an accretion to or to form the capital of any fund, or to be a restriction on and postponement of beneficial enjoyment of that property. In most jurisdictions there is a statutory provision which limits provisions directing accumulation of income T. Sheard, R. Hull & M.M.K. Fitzpatrick, *Canadian Forms of Wills* 4th ed. (Toronto, Carswell 1982) at 227-28.

ACCUMULATIONS ACT. The Act of Great Britain being chapter 98 of 39 and 40 George III, known as The Accumulations Act, 1800 or The Thellusson Act. *The Perpetuities and Accumulations Act*, R.S.M. 1987, c. P33, s. 1.

ACCUMULATION TRUST. A trust requiring the trustee to accumulate specified income. D.M.W. Waters, *The Law of Trusts in Canada* 2d ed. (Toronto: Carswell, 1984) at 491.

ACCUMULATIVE DIVIDEND. A dividend which accumulates from year to year if not paid.

ACCUSARE NEMO SE DEBET. [L.] One must not accuse oneself

ACCUSARE NEMO SE DEBET NISI CORAM DEO. [L.] One is not bound to accuse oneself, except to God.

ACCUSATION. *n.* A charge that a person has committed a crime.

ACCUSATOR POST RATIONABILE TEMPUS NON EST AUDIENDUS, NISI SE BENE DE OMISSIONE EXCUSAVERIT. [L.] An accuser should not be heard after a reasonable time, unless the delay can be satisfactorily accounted for.

ACCUSE. *v.* To charge with a crime or fault. *R. v Kempel* (1900), 31 O.R. 631 at 633 (C.A.).

ACCUSED. *n.* 1. One charged with a crime. *R. v Kempel* (1900), 31 O.R. 631 at 633 (C.A.). 2. Includes (a) a person to whom a peace officer has issued an appearance notice under s. 496, and (b) a person arrested for a criminal offence. *Criminal Code*, R.S.C. 1985, c. C-46, s. 493. 3. Includes a defendant in summary conviction proceedings and an accused in respect of whom a verdict of not criminally responsible on account of mental disorder has been rendered. *Criminal Code*, R.S.C. 1985, c. C–46, s. 672.1.

ACCUSTOMED. *adj* Habitual; usual.

A.C.D.I. *abbr.* Annuaire canadien de droit international (Canadian Yearbook of International Law).

A.C.D.P. *abbr.* Annuaire canadien des droits de la personne (Canadian Human Rights Yearbook).

AC ETIAM. [L.] And also.

ACID. See MINERAL ~; ORGANIC ~; PHOSPHORIC ~.

ACID PHOSPHATASE. Enzymes found in significant concentration only in the secretion of the prostate gland. F.A. Jaffe *A Guide to Pathological Evidence*, 3d ed. (Toronto: Carswell 1991) at 211.

ACID TEST. To analyze balance sheets by calculating the ratio of liquid assets to current liabilities.

ACKNOWLEDGE. *v.* 1. To admit; to accept responsibility. 2. [T]he ordinary meaning of "acknowledge" is to admit or affirm that a person is the biological father of a child. If the legislature had intended otherwise, it could have said so. *Herrington v. Green*, 1999 CarswellBC 2060, 178 D.L.R. (4th) 568 S.C.

ACKNOWLEDGEMENT. *n.* An admission that some claim or liability exists or that one owes a debt.

ACKNOWLEDGEMENT OF INSTRUMENT. A person certifies before someone in authority that the instrument is a free act.

A COELO USQUE AD CENTRUM. [L.] From the heavens down to the centre of the earth.

A COMMUNI OBSERVANTIA NON EST RECEDENDUM. [L.] There should not be a departure from common usage.

ACOUSTIC. *adj.* 1. Relating to sound. 2. Natural as opposed to amplified, in relation to a musical instrument. See ELECTRO-MAGNETIC ~ MECHANICAL OR OTHER DEVICE.

ACOUSTIC REPRESENTATION. A broadcast of music over a cable television network even though the sound is communicated by electro-magnetic rather than acoustic waves. *Canadian Cable Television Assn. v. Canada* [1993] 2 F.C. 138 (C.A.).

ACQUIESCE. *v.* To agree tacitly, silently, or passively to something such as the children remaining in a jurisdiction that is not their habitual residence. Thus, acquiescence implies unstated consent. *Katsigiannis v. Kottick-Katsigiannis* (2001), 55 O.R. (3d) 456 (C.A.).

ACQUIESCED.*v.* Within the context [of the Canada Agricultural Products Act] means impliedly consented or tacitly agreed to, raised no objection to, accepted, permitted to be done. *R. v. A & A Foods Ltd.* 1997 CarswellBC 2541, 120 C.C.C. (3d) 513.

ACQUIESCENCE. Acquiescence has three different senses depending on the context. The first is as a synonym for estoppel where the plaintiff stands by and watches the deprivation of her rights and does nothing. The second meaning is as an aspect of laches. After the deprivation of rights and in full knowledge of their existence, the plaintiff delays. The third usage is a confusing one related to the second branch of the laches rule in the context of an alteration of the defendant's position in reliance on the plaintiff's inaction. *M. (K.) v. M. (H).* [1992] 3 S.C.R. 6, per La Forest, J. 2. See ACTIVE~; PASSIVE~.

ACQUIRE. *v.* 1. To obtain by any method and includes accept, receive, purchase, be vested with, lease, take possession, control or occupation of, and agree to do any of those things, but does not include expropriate. *Interpretation Act*, R.S.B.C. 1996, c. 238, s. 29. 2. Includes take expropriate, and purchase, irrespective of whether the acquisition by the Corporation be of its own volition, or pursuant to an obligation created or imposed upon it by, or under a statutory, enactment or any contract. *Electric Power* R.S.N.B. 1973 c. E-S, s.1.3. . . [O]btaining or getting by paying or compensating therefor." *Felker v McGuigan Construction Co.* (1909), 1 O.W.N. 946 at 948 16 O.W.R. 417 (C.A.), Moss C.J.O. (Garrow and Meredith JJ.A. concurring). 4. " . . . [C]apable of being read as meaning, to get without payment or other consideration as by way of gift' . . ." *Felker v McGuigan Construction Co.* (1909) 1 O.W.N. 946 at 948, 16 O.W.R. 417 (C.A.), Moss C.J.O. (Garrow and Meredith JJ.A. concurring). See OFFER TO ~.

ACQUISITION. *n.* Includes every action or method bar which land or a right, interest or estate in it may be obtained.

ACQUISITION COST AMOUNT. 1. For each eligible share of an eligible corporation that has been contributed to any stock savings plan, (i) if the share is contributed to a stock savings plan of an eligible investor immediately on its being withdrawn from another stock savings plan of the same eligible investor, an amount equal to the disposition cost amount of that share, and (ii) in any other case, an amount equal to the product obtained when the cost amount of the eligible share is multiplied by the eligible percentage applicable to the eligible share on the date it was acquired by the eligible investor. *Stock Savings Plan acts.* 2. With respect to each eligible security that has been contributed to any stock savings an: (i) if the security is contributed to a stock savings plan of an eligible investor immediately on its being withdrawn from another stock savings plan of the same eligible investor, an amount equal to the disposition cost amount of that security; and (ii) in any other case, an amount equal to 30% of the cost amount of the eligible security. *The Stock Savings Tax Credit Act*, S.S. 1986, c. S-59.1, s. 2.

ACQUISITION COSTS. The consideration or compensation paid for acquisition of land, or on the expropriation of land, or the value thereof other than the value of any service or benefit that accrues to, passes to, or is provided to the persons from whom the land is acquired at the expense of the authority for which the land is required, or as a result of the use or development of the land by the authority, and includes the cost of any surveys or appraisals made in respect of the acquisition for or in respect of which a fee is paid, and the legal costs of the authority in respect of the acquisition or the expropriation. *The Land Acquisition Act*, R.S.M. 1987, c. L40, s. 1.

ACQUISITIVE PRESCRIPTION. Prescription by which one acquires a right.

ACQUIT. *v.* 1. To find not guilty. 2. Originally, to free from pecuniary liability.

ACQUITTAL. *n.* A finding of "not guilty".

ACQUITTANCE. *n.* A written acknowledgement that a debt was paid.

ACQUITTED. *adj.* Absolved; found free from guilt. See FINALLY

ACRE. *n.* 1. A measure of land. 2. 4840 square yards. *Weights and Measures Act*, S.C. 1970-7172 c. 36 schedule II. See QUOTA~S.

ACREAGE. See ACCEPTED ~; INSURABLE~.

ACROSS. *prep.* " . . . [F]rom side to side of and over or above." *Bell Telephone Co. v. Middlesex (County)*, [1947] S.C.R. 1 at 10-11, [1947] 1 D.L.R. 248, 60 C.R.T.C. 1, Rinfret C.J. (Kerwin and Taschereau JJ.).

ACROSS-THE-BOARD ADJUSTMENT. A change in pay rates for all employees of an employer or in one plant of the employer.

ACRYLONITRILE. *n.* A substance designated under the Ontario Occupational Health and Safety Act. D. Robertson, *Ontario Health and Safety Guide* (Toronto: Richard De Boo Ltd., 1988) at 5-17.

ACT. *v.* 1. To perform; to carry out functions. 2. To carry out a function or fill an office on a temporary basis.

ACT. *n.* 1. A statute. *R. v Thompson*, [1931] 2 D.L.R. 282 at 285, [1931] 1 W.W.R. 26, 39 Man. R. 277, 55 C.C.C. 33 (Man. C.A.), Dennistoun J.A. (Trueman and Robson JJ.A. concurring). 2. An act (a) of commission, or, (b) in certain particular cases, of omission, (c) by a human being, (d) that is voluntary, and, (e) has caused consequences, if consequences are included in the definition of the offence. D. Stuart, *Canadian Criminal Law: a treatise*, 2d ed. (Toronto: Carswell, 1987) at 66. 3. Includes (a) an Act of Parliament, (b) an Act of the legislature of the former Province of Canada, (c) an Act of the legislature of a province, and (d) an Act or ordinance of the legislature of a province, territory or place in force at the time that province, territory or place became a province of Canada. *Criminal Code*, R.S.C. 1985, c. C46, s. 2. 4. An Act of Parliament. *Interpretation Act*, R.S.C. 1985, c. 1-21, s. 2. 5. As meaning an Act of a legislature, includes an ordinance of the Northwest Territories and a law of the Legislature of Yukon or of the Legislature for Nunavut. *Interpretation Act*, R.S.C. 1985, c. I-21, s. 35(1). 6. An Act of the Legislature. 7. Includes enactment. *Interpretation Act* R.S.O. 1990, c.I-11, s. 29. See ACCUMULATIONS ~; ADMINISTRATIVE ~; ADOPTIVE ~; ANTICOMPETITIVE ~; ANTI-INFLATION (CANADA) ~; APPRENTICESHIP ~; ASSESSING ~; AUTHENTIC ~; BRITISH NORTH AMERICA ~, 1867; BULK SALES ~; CAMPBELL'S (LORD) ~; CANADA ~, 1982; CARRIAGE BY AIR ~; COLONIAL LAWS VALIDITY ~,1865; CONSOLIDATION ~; CONSTITUTION ~, 1867; CORPORATE ~; DECEPTIVE ~ OR PRACTICE; DELIBERATE ~; DOWER ~S; DUTY TO ~ FAIRLY; EXTRA-PROVINCIAL ~; FEDERAL ~; FINAL ~; FRAUDULENT ~; GOLD CLAUSES ~; HOUSING ~S; IMPERIAL ~S; INCOME TAX ~; JUDICIAL ~; LEGISLATIVE ~ ; LOCAL ~; LOCKE KING'S ~; LORDS DAY ~; MARRIED WOMEN'S PROPERTY ~; MERCHANT SHIPPING ~S; MORTMAIN ~; NOTARIAL ~; OVERT ~; PERSONAL PROPERTY SECURITY ~; PIRATICAL ~ ; ~S; PROHIBITED ~; PROVINCIAL ~; QUEBEC ~, 1774; REGISTRY ~ REVENUE ~; SALE OF GOODS ~; SPECIAL ~; UNLAWFUL ~; WRONGFUL ~.

ACT. *abbr.* Acton, Privy Council.

ACTA GRIM. *abbr.* Acta Criminologica.

ACTA EXTERIORA INDICANT INTERIORA SECRETA. [L.] Exterior actions show interior secrets.

ACTA GESTIONIS. [L.] Private—commercial acts. J.G. McLeod, *The Conflict of Laws* (Calgary: Carswell, 1983) at 72.

ACTA IMPERIL [L.] Public acts. J.G. McLeod, *The Conflict of Laws* (Calgary: Carswell, 1983) at 72.

ACT FAIRLY. "In general it means a duty to observe the rudiments of natural justice for a limited purpose in the exercise of functions that are not analytical judicial but administrative. " *Nicholson v. Haldimand-Norfolk (Regional Municipality) Commissioners of Police* (1978), 88 D.L.R. (3d) 671 at 680, [1979] 1 S.C.R. 311, 78 C.L.L.C. 14,181, 23 N.R. 410, Laskin C.J.C. See DUTY TO ~; FAIRNESS.

ACTING ATTORNEY-GENERAL. " . . . [I]s in a very different position to that of a deputy or agent of the Attorney-General. He is the Attorney-General for the time being and clothed by statute with all the powers and authority of the office." *R. v. Faulkner* (1911) 16 B.C.R. 229 at 235, 18 W.L.R. 634,19 C.C.C. 47 (C.A.), MacDonald C.J.A.

ACTING JOINTLY OR IN CONCERT. For the purposes of this Part, it is a question of fact as to whether a person or company is acting jointly or in concert with an offeror and, without limiting the generality of the foregoing, the following are presumed to be acting jointly or in concert with an offeror: (a) every person who or company that, as a result of any agreement, commitment or understanding, whether formal or informal, with the offeror or with any other person or company acting or in concert with the offeror: (i) acquires or acquire; or (ii) intends to exercise jointly or in concert with the offeror or with any other person or company acting jointly or in concert with the offeror any voting rights attaching to any securities of the offeree issuer; or (b) every associate and affiliate of the offeror. *The Securities Act*, 1988 S.S. 1988-89, C. S–42.2, s. 100.

ACT IN PAIS. An act not contained in a deed or record.

ACT IN THE LAW. Any expression of the intention or will of the person concerned to create, transfer, or make extinct of a right, which is effective in law for that purpose.

ACTIO CONTRA DEFUNCTUM CAEPTA CONTINUITUR IN HAEREDES. [L.] Any action begun against a person who dies continues against that person's heirs.

ACTIO IN PERSONAM. [L.] " . . . [W]here the subject matter of the proceeding is the personal rights of the litigants and where the judgment affects only the immediate parties to the action . . ." Works v Holt (1976), 22 R.F.L. 1 at 5 (Ont. Prov. Ct.), Beaulieu Prov. J.

ACTIO IN REM. [L.] " . . . [W]here the subject matter touches questions of status of the person or some thing and where the judgment binds all the world . . ." *Works v. Holt* (1976), 22 R.F.L. 1 at 5 (Ont. Prov. Ct.), Beaulieu Prov. J.

ACTION. *n*. 1. One party (the plaintiff) brings suit against another party (the defendant) for the protection or enforcement of a right, the prevention or redress of a wrong, or the punishment of an offence. 2. A civil proceeding in the court, commenced in such a manner as is prescribed in the rules, and without limiting the generality of the foregoing, includes set-off, counter-claim and garnishment, interpleader, and third party proceedings. 3. "The word 'action' [in the Railway Act, R.S.C. 1970, c. R-2, s. 262(7)] connotes a proceeding in the Courts. It is to be contrasted with the use of the words 'application' and 'complaint' with reference to proceedings before the Commission under the Railways Act . . ." *Kiist v. Canadian Pacific Railway* (1981) 123 D.L.R. (3d) 434 at 444, [1982] 1 F.C. 361, 37 N.R. 91 (C.A.), the court per Le Dain J.A. 4. Includes counter-claim and set-off. *Bills of Exchange Act*, R.S.C. 1985, c. B-4, s. 2. 5. A civil and includes a civil proceeding, by or against the Crown. 6. A civil proceeding that is not an application and includes a proceeding commenced by claim, statement of claim, notice of action, counterclaim, crossclaim, third or subsequent party claim, or divorce petition or counterpetition. *Courts of Justice Act*, R.S.O. 1990, c. C.43, s. 1. 7. Includes any civil proceeding, inquiry, issue, matter, reference, investigation, arbitration, and prosecution for an offence committed against a statute of the province or against a by-law or regulation made under the authority of any such statute, and any other prosecution or proceeding authorized or permitted to be tried, heard had or taken, by or before a court under the law of the province. 8. A civil proceeding that is not an application and includes a proceeding commenced by, (a) claim, (b) statement of claim, (c) notice of action, (d) counterclaim, (e) crossclaim, (f) third or subsequent party claim, or (g) divorce petition or counterpetition. Courts of Justice Act, R.S.O. 1990, c. 43, s. 1. See AFFIRMATIVE ~; BRING AN~; CAUSE OF ~; CHOSE IN ~; CIRCUITY OF ~; CIVIL ~; CLASS ~; CONSOLIDATION OF ~S; CONTRACTUAL RIGHT OF ~; CROSS ~; DERIVATIVE ~; DISCIPLINARY ~; DISCRIMINATORY ~; DOUBLE ~; ENEMY ~ OR COUNTERACTION AGAINST THE ENEMY; FAINT ~; FORMS OF ~; FROST ~; INDUSTRIAL ~; JOB ~; LIMITATION OF ~; MORAL ~; NOTICE OF ~; PERSONAL ~; REAL ~; RELATOR ~; REPRESENTATIVE ~; RIGHT OF ~; SCIENTER ~; SYSTEMS ~; VEXATIOUS ~.

ACTIONABILITY. See DOUBLE ~.

ACTIONABLE. *adj*. Capable of sustaining or giving rise to an action.

ACTION AREA PLAN. The statement of the city's policies and proposals for the comprehensive treatment during a period prescribed in it of an action area as a whole, by development, redevelopment or improvement of the whole or part of the area, or by the establishment and implementation of a social development program, or partly by one and partly by another method, and the identification of the types of treatments selected, and may be expressed in texts, maps or illustrations. *The City of Winnipeg Act*, S.M. 1971, c. 105, s. 569.

ACTIONEM NON. [L.] A statement by a defendant in pleadings that a plaintiff should not have brought the action against the defendant.

ACTION EX DELICTO. An action to remedy a tort.

ACTION FOR ACCOUNTING. A cause of action which a debtor may have against a security holder who has seized and sold assets or a beneficiary may have against a trustee or other person acting in a fiduciary capacity to make known what has been done with property and to adjust and settle accounts between them.

ACTION FOR COLLISION. An action for damage caused by one or more ships to another ship or ships or to property or persons on board another ship or ships as a result of carrying out or omitting to carry out a manoeuvre, or as a result of non-compliance with law, even though there has been no actual collision. *Federal Courts Act*, R.S.C. 1985, c. F-7, s. 2.

ACTION FOR DETINUE. A claim for damages caused by the improper withholding from the plaintiff of a chattel. D.M.W. Waters, *The Law of Trusts in Canada*, 2d ed. (Toronto: Carswell, 1984) at 1035.

ACTION FOR MONEY HAD AND RECEIVED. An action to recover money a defendant has received and which for reasons of equity the defendant should not retain.

ACTION FOR NEGLIGENCE. The fundamental principle is that the plaintiff in an action for negligence is entitled to a sum of damages which will return the plaintiff to the position the plaintiff would have been in had the accident not occurred, insofar as money is capable of doing this. This goal was expressed in the early cases by the maxim restitutio in integrum. The plaintiff is entitled to full compensation and is not to be denied recovery of losses which he has sustained. *Cunningham v. Wheeler*, [1994] 1 S.C.R. 359, McLachlin, J. dissenting.

ACTION FOR RECOVERY OF LAND. An action brought by an owner against one unlawfully in possession of land. See EJECTMENT.

ACTION FOR REPLEVIN. An action in which a plaintiff seeks to recover possession of a chattel. D.M.W. Waters, *The Law of Trusts in Canada*, 2d ed. (Toronto: Carswell, 1984) at 1035-36.

ACTION FOR SALE. A mortgagee's action to obtain an order to require the sale of property on which he holds a mortgage when the mortgagor is in default.

ACTION FOR TORT. It may be well to state once again the principle of recovery in an action for tort. Simply, it is to compensate the injured party as completely as possible for the loss suffered as a result of the negligent action or inaction of the defendant. However, the plaintiff is not entitled to a double recovery for any loss arising from the injury. *Cunningham v. Wheeler*, [1994] 1 S.C.R. 359, Cory, J.

ACTION IN PERSONAM. An action brought against a person for recovery of damages or other relief.

ACTION IN REM. " . . . [A] proceeding to determine the status or condition of the thing itself, and a judgment is a decision as to the disposition of the thing." *Fry v. Botsworth* (1902), 9 B.C.R. 234 at 239 (C.A.), Irving J.A.

ACTION LEVEL. The level of a substance identified in a worker's body. D. Robertson, *Ontario Health and Safety Guide* (Toronto: Richard De Boo Ltd., 1988) at 5-18.

ACTION OF ACCOUNT. An action to settle an account between a debtor and creditor.

ACTION OF CONTRACT. An action arising on a breach of contract.

ACTION OF EJECTMENT. An action to recover possession of land. W.B. Rayner & R.H. McLaren, *Falconbridge on Mortgages*, 4th ed. (Toronto: Canada Law Book, 1977) at 411-412. See EJECTMENT.

ACTIO. NON. *abbr*. Actionem non.

ACTIO NON ACCREVIT INFRA SEX ANNOS. [L.] A plea in which the defendant alleges that the plaintiff's cause of action has not arisen within six years.

ACTIO NON DATUR NON DAMNIFICATO. [L.] No cause of action exists without the plaintiff having suffered damages.

ACTION ON THE CASE. 1. In the context of the Ontario Limitations Act has something of a residual character. Is a catch-all or short-hand expression to embrace personal actions for damages based upon breach of a legal duty not otherwise caught by the Act. *Perry, Farley & Onyschuk v. Outerbridge Management Ltd.* (2001), 54 O.R. (3d) 131 (C.A.). One of the common law forms of action. It is not confined to torts but includes claims such as assumpsit. 2. An action brought to recover damages for injury or loss resulting indirectly or consequentially from the act corn lained of. *Burd v. Macau* (1924) 20 Alta. E .R. 352 at 356 358 [1924] 2 W.W.R. 393, [1924] 2 D.L.R. 815 (C.A.), the court per Stuart J.A.

ACTION TO REDEEM. An action brought by anyone who has an interest in the equity of redemption in mortgaged property or by a person who is liable for the mortgage debt. The purpose is to recover the property.

ACTIONUM GENERA MAXIME SUNT SERVANDA. [L.] The forms of action are to be preserved.

ACTION UPON THE CASE. See ACTION ON THE CASE.

ACTIO PER QUOD CONSORTIUM AMISIT. [L.] The right of action of a husband against a defendant who has imprisoned, taken away or done physical harm to his wife so that he is deprived of her services or society. K.D. Cooper-Stephenson & I.B. Saunders, *Personal Inquiry Damages in Canada* (Toronto: Carswell, 1981) at 485.

ACTIO PER QUOD SERVITIUM AMISIT. [L.] "The action per quod [servitium amisit] is born of the relationship of master and servant, and though of very early origin in my opinion still persists in the common law provinces of Canada in one form or another. The action recognizes the right in the master to recover damages as against a wrongdoer who has injured his servant and thus deprived the master of his services." *R. v. Buchansky* (1983), 24 C.C.L.T. 266 at 271, [1983] 1 S.C.R. 481, [1983] 5 W.W.R. 577, 145 D.L.R. (3d) 1, 47 N.R. 208, 22 Man. R. (2d) 121, Ritchie J. (Estey, Lamer and Wilson JJ. concurring).

ACTIO PERSONALIS MORITUR CUM PERSONA. [L.] A personal action and the person die together.

ACTIO QUAELIBET IN SUA VIA. [L.] Each action follows its own course.

ACTIVE. *adj.* Opposite of passive; engaged in activity.

ACTIVE ACQUIESCENCE. Involves some step by the aggrieved parent that is demonstrably inconsistent with insistence on the summary return of the child to the place of the child's habitual residence. *Katsigiannis v. Kottick-Katsigiannis* (2001), 55 O.R. (3d) 456 (C.A.).

ACTIVE ASSET. Money and the market value of assets readily convertible into money.

ACTIVE DEBT. A debt upon which one pays interest.

ACTIVE DEVICE. A medical device that depends for its operation on a source of energy other than energy generated by the human body or gravity. A medical device that transmits or withdraws energy or a substance to or from a patient without substantially altering the energy or the substance is not an active device. *Medical Devices Regulations*, SOR/98-282, s. 1.

ACTIVE DIAGNOSTIC DEVICE. An active device that, whether used alone or in combination with another medical device, is intended to supply information for the purpose of detecting, monitoring or treating a physiological condition, state of health, illness or congenital deformity. *Medical Devices Regulations* SOR/98-282, s. 1.

ACTIVE DOCUMENT. A document in current use for administrative or legal purposes. Archives Act, R.S.Q. c.A-21.1, s. 2.

ACTIVE DUTY. Something that requires a trustee to carry out an activity such as making a maintenance payment, ensuring that an investment policy balances between income return and capital growth in the interest of both the one holding the remainder and the life tenant keeping accurate accounts and retaining and instructing solicitors to the trust. DVW. Waters *The Law of Trusts in Canada 2d* ed. (Toronto: Carswell, 1984) at 28. See ACTIVE TRUST.

ACTIVE INGREDIENT. A component of a pest control product to which the intended effects of the product are attributed and includes a synergist but does not include a solvent, diluent, emulsifier or other component that is not primarily responsible for those effects. *Pest Control Products Act*, S.C. 2002, c. 28, s. 2(1).

ACTIVE MILITARY SERVICE. Full-time service in the armed forces of Canada or an ally at any time during World War II between September 10, 1939 and September 30, 1947, and at any time during the Korean Campaign between June 30 1950 and January 1 1954. *Members Superannuation Act*, R.C.S.N.B. 1973,c. M-8, s. 3.1(1).

ACTIVE SERVICE. 1. Any service of a kind specified in the regulations to be active service, which service is deemed for the purposes of this Part to have terminated on discharge or, in the case of a person who underwent treatment in a veterans hospital, as defined in the regulations, immediately following his discharge, on his release from that hospital. *Royal Canadian Mounted Police Superannuation Act*, R.S.C. 1985 c. R-11 s. 3. 2. Full-time service as a member of (a) a component of the naval, army or air forces of Canada while that component was on active service having been placed on active service by the Governor in Council pursuant to the Militia Act, or (b) a component of the naval, army or air forces of Her majesty other than the forces specified in paragraph (a) while members of that component were subject to service in a theatre of war. *Royal Canadian Mounted Police Superannuation Regulations*, C.R.C., c. 1393, s. 3.

ACTIVE SERVICE IN THE FORCES. 1. Any service in the forces of a kind designated in the regulations to be active service, which service is deemed for the purposes of this Part to have terminated on discharge or, in the case of a person who underwent treatment in a veterans' hospital, as defined in the regulations, immediately following his discharge, on that person's release from hospital. *Public Service Superannuation Act*, R.S.C. 1985 c. P-36 s. 3. 2. Full-time service as a member of (a) a component of the naval, army or air forces of Canada while that component was on active service having been placed on active service by the Governor in Council pursuant to the Militia Act, or (b) a component of the naval, army or air forces of Her Majesty other than the forces specified in paragraph (a), or any of the Allies of Her Majesty, while members of that component were subject to service in a theatre of war. *Public Service Superannuation Regulations*, C.R.C., c. 1358, s. 3.

ACTIVE THERAPEUTIC DEVICE. An active device that, whether used alone or in combination with another medical device, is intended to support, modify, replace or restore a biological function or structure for the purpose of treating or mitigating an illness or injury or a symptom of an illness or injury. *Medical Devices Regulations* SOR/98-282, s. 1.

ACTIVE TRUST. A trust which requires a trustee to carry out duties connected with it. See ACTIVE DUTY.

ACTIVE TUBERCULOSIS. Includes (i) pulmonary tuberculosis that produces sputum containing tubercle bacilli; and (ii) tuberculosis other than the pulmonary form in which tubercle bacilli are found in the discharges from the diseased tissue; and (iii) a condition in which evidence by means of X-ray or other examination discloses that tuberculosis disease is active even though the affected person cannot or will not submit a specimen for examination. *Health Act*, R.S.N.S. 1989, c. 195 s. 74.

ACTIVITIES OF DAILY LIVING. Include personal hygiene, dressing, grooming, meal preparation and the taking of medication. *Homes for Special Care Act*, R.S.N.S. 1989, c. 203, s. 2(1).

ACTIVITY. *n.* Business; actions which occupy one. See BUSINESS; COMMERCIAL ~; CONCERTED ACTIVITIES ~; CONTINUOUS ~; FILM ~; MANUFACTURING OR PROCESSING ~, RECREATIONAL ACTIVITIES.

ACTIVITY DUTY. In occupiers' liability, a duty base on the risk entailed in an activity carried on by the occupier or someone else.

ACT OF ATTAINDER. An act attainting a person.

ACT OF BANKRUPTCY. An act which entitles another person to have a receiving order made against a debtor.

ACT OF GOD. " . . . [A]mounts to an interference in the course of nature so unexpected that any consequence arising from it is to be regarded as too remote to be foundation for successful legal action." *Tomchak v. Ste-Anne (Rural Municipality)* (1962), 39 W.W.R. 186 at 188, 33 D.L.R. (2d) 481 (Man. C.A.), Monnin J.A. (Miller C.J.M., Schultz and Guy JJ.A. concurring; Freedman J.A. concurring in the result).

ACT OF GOD CLAUSE. " . . . [G]enerally operates to discharge a contracting party when a supervening, sometimes supernatural, event, beyond the control of either party, makes performance impossible. The common thread is that of the unexpected, something beyond reasonable human foresight and skill." *Atlantic Paper Stock Ltd. v St. Anne-Nackawic Pulp & Paper Co.* (1975), 10 N.B.R. (2d) 513 at 516, [1976] 1 S.C.R. 580 4 N.R. 539, 56 D.L.R. (3d) 409, the court per Dickson J. See FORCE MAJEURE CLAUSE.

ACT OF PARLIAMENT. A statute.

ACT OF STATE. 1. "In the broad sense of the term, many lawful acts of the executive government, and many instances of the exercise of the prerogative of the Crown, might be designated acts of state; ' . . ." *Baird v. Walker* (1891) 11 C.L.T. 223 at 226 (Nfld. S.C.), the court per Pinsent J., appeal dismissed (sub nom. *Walker v. Baird*) [1892] A.C. 491 C.R. [10] A.C. 262. 2. " . . . [T]here is a narrower sense, and that in which the term is more technically if not exclusively employed, which related to acts done or adopted by the ruling powers of independent states, in their political and sovereign capacity, particularly an act injurious to the person or to the property of some person who is not at the time of that act a subject of Her Majesty; which act is done by any representative of Her Majesty's authority, civil or military, and is either previously sanctioned or subsequently ratified by Her Majesty:' Stephen's History of the Criminal Law, p. 61." *Baird v. Walker* 1891 11 C.L.T. 223 at 226 (Nfld. S.C.), the court per Pinsent J., anneal dismissed (sub nom. *Walker v. Baird*) [1892] A.C. 491 C.R. [10] A.C. 262.

ACT OF THE LAW. The creation, transfer or extinction of a right by the operation of the law itself, in no way dependent on the consent of any concerned party.

ACT OF THE PARTY. Any expression of the intention or will of the person concerned to create, transfer, or make extinct a right, which is effective in law for that purpose.

ACTOR. *n*. A doer, a person who acts. See JOINT ~.

ACTORE NON PROBANTE ABSOLVITUR REUS. [L.] When a plaintiff does not prove his or her case, judgment is for the defendant; when the prosecution fails to prove its case, the accused is acquitted.

ACTORI INCUMBIT ONUS PROBANDI. [L.] The plaintiff or prosecution carries the burden of proof.

ACTOR SEQUITUR FORUM REI. [L.] A plaintiff must take the case to the defendant's jurisdiction.

ACT OR STATUTE. An Act of the Legislature and includes an Ordinance of the Northwest Territories in force in Saskatchewan. *The Interpretation Act*, S.S. 1995, c. I-11.2, s. 27(1).

ACTUAL. *adj*. Real, in opposition to constructive, as in actual possession or actual occupation.

ACTUAL AUTHORITY. " . . . [A] legal relationship between principal and agent created by a consensual agreement to which they alone are parties. . ." *Freeman & Lockyer v. Bockhurst Park Properties*, [1964] 2 Q.B. 480 at 502-3 (C.A.), Diplock L.J.

ACTUAL BODILY HARM. Includes any injury or hurt.

ACTUAL CAUSATION. Causation in fact.

ACTUAL EXPRESS AUTHORITY. See EXPRESS AUTHORITY.

ACTUAL FRONTAGE. The distance which a parcel of land actually abuts on the highway.

ACTUAL IMPLIED AUTHORITY. See IMPLIED AUTHORITY.

ACTUALITÉS. *n*. The periodical, Actualités.

ACTUALITÉS-JUSTICE *n*. The periodical, Actualités-Justice.

ACTUALLY. *adv*. " . . . [A] word of emphasis: Robinson v. Marsh, [1921] 2 K.B. 640 (C.A.); Canadian National Fire Insurance Co. v. Colonsay Hotel Co. [1923] S.C.R. 688." *King, Re* (1925), 57 O.L.R. 144 at 154 (C.A.), Hodgins J.A. (Mulock C.J.O., Magee and Smith W.A. concurring).

ACTUALLY RECEIVED. The sum of money or benefit received by the borrower from the lender.

ACTUAL NOTICE. " : .. [A]ctual knowledge of the very fact required to be established, whereas constructive notice means knowledge of other facts which put a person on inquiry to discover the fact required to be established. The classic distinction, . . .is that of Strong J. in Rose v. Peterkin (885), 13 S.C.R. 677 a 694: 'What such actual and direct notice is may well be ascertained very shortly by defining constructive notice, and then taken actual notice to be knowledge, not resume as in the case of constructive notice, but shown to be actually brought home to the party to be charged with it, either by proof of his own admission or by the evidence of witnesses who are able to establish that the very fact, of which notice is to be established, not something which would have led to the discovery of the fact if an inquiry had been pursued, was brought to his knowledge.'" *Stoimenov v. Stoimenov* (19 8 5), 35 R.P.R. 150 at 158 44 R.F.L. 2d 14 7 O.A.C. 220 (C.A.), the court per Tarnopolsky J.A. See CONSTRUCTIVE NOTICE.

ACTUAL POSSESSION. Physical possession of goods or land.

ACTUAL PREJUDICE. The fact that a piece of evidence is missing that might or might not affect the defence will not be sufficient to establish that irreparable harm has occurred to the right to make full answer and defence. Actual prejudice occurs when the accused is unable to put forward his or her defence due to the lost evidence and not simply that the loss of the evidence makes putting forward the position more difficult. To determine whether actual prejudice has occurred, consideration of the other evidence that does exist and whether that evidence contains essentially the same information as the lost evidence is an essential consideration. *R. v. Bradford* (2001) 52 O.R. (3d) 257 (C.A.).

ACTUAL PRODUCER. Producer actually engaged in the production of grain. *Canadian Wheat Board Act* R.S.C. 1985 c. C-24 s. 2.

ACTUAL RESIDENCE. Physical presence. *Giradin v Giradin* (1974), 15 R.F.L. 16 at 22, [1974] 2 W.W.R. 180, 42 D.L.R. (3d) 294 (Sask. Q.B.), Disbery J.

ACTUAL TOTAL LOSS. Either the insured item is destroyed or so damaged that it ceases to be what it was, or the assured is permanently deprived of the item.

ACTUAL VALUE. 1. " . . . [C]ash market value . . ." *Canadian National Fire Insurance Co. v. Colonsay Hotel Co.*, [1923] 3 D.L.R. 1001 at 1004, [1923] S.C.R. 688, [1923] 2 W.W.R. 1170, Idington J. 2. " . . . [E]xchangeable value the price which the subject will bring when exposed to the test of competition." *Lord Advocate v. Earl of Home*, (1881) 28 Sc. L.R. 289 at 293, Lord MacLaren, cited with approval in *Montreal Island Power Co. v. Laval-des-Rapides (Ville)*, [1935] S.C.R. 304 at 305, [1936] 1 D.L.R. 621, Duff C.J.

ACTUARIAL ASSUMPTIONS. The assumptions made in calculating the present value of benefits expected to be provides and the present value of contributions and special payments expected to be made under a pension plan concerning (a) the rates of investment income, and (b) the occurrence of events and existence of circumstances that govern the amount of benefits and contributions that are payable or may become payable and the time when they will be paid. *Pension Benefits Standards Regulations* C.R.C., c. 1252 s. 2(1).

ACTUARIAL BASIS. The assumptions and methods generally accepted and used by fellows of the Canadian Institute of Actuaries to establish, in relation to the contingencies of human life such as death, accident, sickness and disease, the costs of pension benefits, life insurance, disability insurance, health insurance and other similar benefits, including their actuarial equivalents. *Benefit Plans Act*, O. Reg. 286/01, s. 1.

ACTUARIAL GAIN. In respect of a plan, the aggregate of (a) the experience gain of the plan, (b) the amount by which the going concern liabilities of the plan decrease as a result of an amendment to the plan, and (c) the amount by which the going concern liabilities of the plan decrease or the going concern assets of the plan increase as a result of a change in the methods or bases of valuation of the plan. *Pension Ben-*

efits Standards Regulations, 1985, SOR/87-19, s. 2(1), as am.

ACTUARIALLY EQUIVALENT. Equivalent in accordance with the appropriate actuarial tables.

ACTUARIALLY SOUND. That on the basis of statistical data sufficient premiums will be credited to pay the anticipated indemnities that will have to be met and provide a reasonable reserve against unforeseen losses.

ACTUARIAL METHOD. See ARITHMETICAL OR ~.

ACTUARIAL TABLE. Statistical data organized to show average life expectancies of persons.

ACTUARY. *n.* A Fellow of the Canadian Institute of Actuaries.

ACTUS CURIAE NEMINEM GRAVABIT. [L.] The act of a court harms no one.

ACTUS DEI NEMINEM GRAVABIT. [L.] No one should be prejudiced by an act of God.

ACTUS DEI NEMINI FACIT INJURIAM. [L.] No person is responsible for the act of God.

ACTUS DEI NEMINI NOCET. [L.] No one should be prejudiced by an act of God.

ACTUS INCEPTUS CUJUS PERFECTIO PENDET EX VOLUNTATE PARTIUM REVOCARI POTEST; SI AUTEM PENDET EX VOLUNTATE TERTIAE PERSONAE VEL EX CONTINGENTI, REVOCARI NON POTEST; SI AUTEM PENDET EX VOLUNTATE TERTIAE PERSONAE VEL EX CONTINGENTI, REVOCARI NON POTEST. [L.] A transaction begun but not completed may be rescinded if its completion requires the parties' mutual consent; but it cannot be rescinded if its completion depends on a third party's consent or on a contingency.

ACTUS JUDICIARIUS CORAM NON JUDICE IRRITUS HABETUR; DE MINISTERIALI AUTEM A QUOCUNQUE PROVENIT RATUM ESTO. [L.] A judicial act done outside of or exceeding jurisdiction is invalid but a ministerial act done outside of jurisdiction can be approved.

ACTUS LEGIS NEMINI EST DAMNOSUS. [L.] An act in the law should prejudice no one.

ACTUS LEGIS NEMINI FACIT INJURIAM. [L.] An act of the law can wrong no one.

ACTUS LEGITIMI NON RECIPIUNT MODUM. [L.] When the law sanctions doing something only in a particular manner, then it cannot be done differently.

ACTUS ME INVITO (FACTUS) NON EST MEUS ACTUS. [L.] When my will does not concur, what I do is not my act at all.

ACTUS NON FACIT REUM NISI MENS SIT REA. [L.] Both intent and act must concur to constitute a crime.

ACTUS REUS. [L.] 1. " . . . [T]he use of the expression 'actus reus' . . . is liable to mislead, since it suggests that some positive act on the part of the accused is needed to make him guilty of a crime and that a failure or omission to act is insufficient to give rise to criminal liability unless some express provision in the statute that creates the offence so provides." *R. v. Miller*, [1983] 1 All E.R. 978 a 979 (H.L.) Di lock L.J. 2. A voluntary act of commission or of omission which caused results that constitute a criminal offence or form part of the criminal offence.

ACT WITHIN SCOPE OF EMPLOYMENT. To carry out assigned duties, functions or activities contemplated.

ACUPUNCTURE. *n*. An act of stimulation, by means of needles, of specific sites on the skin, mucous membranes or subcutaneous tissues of the human body to promote, maintain, restore or improve health, to prevent a disorder, imbalance or disease or to alleviate pain and includes the administration of manual, mechanical, thermal and electrical stimulation of acupuncture needles, the use of laser acupuncture, magnetic therapy or acupressure, and moxibustion (Jiu) and suction cup (Ba Guan).

A.C.W.S. *abbr* All Canada Weekly Summaries.

A.D. *abbr*. Anno Domini.

ADAPTED. *adj*. Section 369(*b*) and s. 342.01(1)(*d*) [of *Criminal Code*] . . . are related provisions. They must be read together. The French version of s. 342.01(1)(d) uses the word "*modifié*" for the English word "adapted". In contrast, in s. 369(*b*), the word "*adapté*" is used together with the English expression "adapted". This makes clear that, in the first case, "adapted" means altered or modified, while in the second case it does not. Thus the common meaning of "adapted/*adapté*" in s. 369(*b*) is "suitable for". *R. v. Mac* [2002] 1 S.C.R. 856.

ADAPTER. *n*. Any means by which the coupling of one section or portion of standard hose of one thread may be connected to a hydrant, nozzle or another adapter or to the coupling of another section or portion of standard hose of a different thread. *Standard Hose Coupling Act*, R.S.N.S. 1989, c. 439, s. 2.

AD ARBITRIUM. [L.] At will.

AD AVIZANDUM. [L.] To be deliberated on.

AD DAMNUM. [L.] To the damage.

ADDENDUM. *n*. Something added.

ADDICT. *n*. 1. Any person addicted to the improper use of cocaine, opium, or their derivatives, or any other narcotic drug. 2. A person who is addicted to a substance other than alcohol. *Alcoholism and Drug Addiction Research Foundation Act*, R.S.O. 1990, c. A.16, s. 1.

ADDICTION. *n*. Addiction to a substance other than alcohol. *Alcoholism and Drug Addiction Research Foundation Act*, R.S.O. 1990 c. A.16 s. 1.

AD DIEM. [L.] On the day appointed.

ADDITIONAL VOLUNTARY CONTRIBUTION. Under a pension plan means an optional contribution by a member that does not give rise to an obligation on the employer to make additional contributions.

ADDITIONAL WRITTEN WARRANTY. Any undertaking in writing by a warrantor that he will repair, replace, make a refund or take other remedial action with respect to a consumer product that breaks down, malfunctions or fails to meet the specifications set forth in the undertaking, and includes a service contract. *The Consumer Products Warranties Act*, R.S.S. 1978, c. C-30, s. 2.

ADDITIVE. See FOOD ~.

ADDRESS. *n*. 1. A petition. 2. A place of residence or business. 3. (i) Of the merchant means the place of that merchant's establishment or office indicated in the contract or of a new establishment or office . See CLOSING ~; JOINT ~; RECORDED ~.

ADDRESS MAIL. Mail bearing the return address of the sender but not bearing a specific request that the mail be returned. *Undeliverable and Redirected Mail Regulations*, C.R.C., c. 1298, s. 2.

ADDUCE. *v*. To present; to lead, in connection with evidence, to bring forward.

AD EA QUAE FREQUENTIUS ACCIDUNT JURA ADAPTANTUR. [L.] The laws are fitted to more frequently occurring cases.

ADEMPTION. *n.* 1. " . . . [T]he taking away of the benefit by the act of the testator . . . ' *Tracy, Re* (1913), 5 O.W.N. 530 at 531, 25 O.W.R. 413 (H.C.), Boyd C. 2. What occurs when a testator dies and the subject matter of a gift was converted into something else or destroyed by the testator's act or by duly appointed authority. T. Sheard, R. Hull & M.M.K. Fitzpatrick, *Canadian Forms of Wills* 4th ed. (Toronto: Carswell, 1982) at 168.

ADEMPTION BY ADVANCEMENT. When a testator provides in a will for a child or another person to whom that testator stands *in loco parentis* and after that advances to that child or person a sum of money, it is presumed that the testator did not intend to provide a double portion to that child or person at the expense of other children. T. Sheard, R. Hull & M.M.K. Fitzpatrick, *Canadian Forms of Wills*, 4th ed. (Toronto: Carswell, 1982) at 170.

ADEQUATE. *adj.* Sufficient; suitable.

ADEQUATE CONSIDERATION. Sufficient consideration; reasonable value for what is received.

ADEQUATE NOTICE. Reasonably sufficient notice.

ADEQUATE VALUABLE CONSIDERATION. A consideration of fair and reasonable money value with relation to that of the property conveyed, assigned or transferred or a consideration of fair and reasonable money value with relation to the known or reasonably to be anticipated benefits of the contract, dealing or transaction. *Bankruptcy and Insolvency Act*, R.S.C. 1985, c. B3, s. 97(2).

AD FILUM AQUAE. [L.] To the centre line of a stream.

AD FILUM VIAE. [L.] To the centre of a road.

AD FINEM. [L.] Near or at the end.

ADFREEZING. *n.* The adhesion of soil to a foundation unit resulting from the freezing of soil water. *Building Code*, O. Reg. 403/97, s. 1.1.3.2(1).

AD HOC. [L.] l. For a particular purpose. 2. Appointed specially for a specified short period of time or until the occurrence of a stated event. *Formal Documents Regulations*, C.R.C., c. 1331, s. 2.

AD HOC ARBITRATION. Arbitration of a particular dispute or group of related disputes.

AD IDEM. [L. at the same point] Said when parties agree.

AD INFINITUM. [L.] With no limit.

AD INQUIRENDUM. [L.] To make inquiry.

AD INTERIM. [L.] In the meantime.

ADIPOCERE. *n.* An easily crumbled, waxy substance derived from fatty tissues. F.A. Jaffe, *A Guide to Pathological Evidence*, 3d ed. (Toronto: Carswell, 1991) at 9.

ADIPOCIRE. *n.* An easily crumbled, waxy substance derived from fatty tissues. F.A. Jaffe, *A Guide to Pathological Evidence*, 3d ed. (Toronto: Carswell, 1991) at 211.

ADJACENT. *adj.* "'Adjacent' is not a word to which a precise and uniform meaning is attached by ordinary usage. It is not confined to places adjoining, and it includes places close to or near. What degree of proximity would justify the application of the word is entirely a question of circumstances." *Mayor of Wellington v. Mayor of Lower Hutt*, [1904] A.C. 773 at 775-6 (P.C.).

ADJACENT CLAIMS. Claims that are contiguous or are intended by the locator to be contiguous. *Canada Mining Regulations*, C.R.C., c. 1516, s. 2(1).

ADJACENT LAND. Land that is contiguous to the parcel that is the subject of the application for subdivision approval and includes land or a portion of land that would be contiguous if not for a public roadway, river or stream. *Planning Act*, R.S.A. 1980 c P-9 s. 106.

ADJACENT SEAT. A designated seating position so located that a portion of its occupant space is not more than 25.4 cm from an emergency exit for a distance of at least 38.1 cm measured horizontally and parallel to the emergency exit. *Motor Vehicle Safety Regulations*, C.R.C., c. 1038, s. 2(1).

ADJECTIVE LAW. Law which relates to practice and procedure.

ADJOINING. *adj.* 1. Touching; coterminous. 2. "The word 'adjoining' is different from the word 'adjacent'. 'Adjoining' as its derivation implies signifies being joint together 'adjacent' is simply lying near." *Bowker & Richards, Re* 1905 1 W.L.R. 194 at 1 *96* (B.C. S.C.), Irving J. 3. The word 'adjoining' as applied to parcels of land, does not necessarily imply that the parcels are to be in physical contact with each other; . . ." *McKenzie v Miniota School District*, [1931] 2 W.W.R. 105 at 106, [1931] 2 D.L.R. 695 (Man. K.B.), Dysart J.

ADJOINING CLAIMS. Those mineral claims that come into contact one with the other at some point on the boundary lines or that share a common boundary.

ADJOINING LAND. 1. (i) Parcels of land that adjoin or corner, (ii) parcels of land, separated by a road allowance or a surveyed highway or road that would adjoin or corner if they were not so separated. 2. Land immediately adjacent to the subject land.

ADJOURN. *v*. To postpone; to recess.

ADJOURNAMENTUM EST AD DIEM DICERE SEU DIEM DARE. [L.] Adjournment is appointing a day or giving a day.

ADJOURNMENT. *n*. 1. Postponement or putting off business to another time or place. 2. Of Parliament, an interruption during the course of one and the same session. A. Fraser, W.A. Dawson, & J. Holtby, eds., *Beauchesne's Rules and Forms of the House of Commons of Canada*, 6th ed. (Toronto: Carswell, 1989) at 6.

ADJUD. *abbr*. Adjudicator.

ADJUDGE. *v*. " . . . [T]o pronounce judicially . . ." *R. v. Morris*, 91 D.L.R. (3d) 161 at 182, [1979] 1 S.C.R. 405, 23 N.R. 109, 6 C.R. (3d) 36, 43 C.C.C. (2d) 129, Pratte J.

ADJUDICATE. *v*. To determine; to decide after a hearing.

ADJUDICATION. *n*. 1. The decision or judgment of a court. 2. Any decision, determination, refusal or award made under this Act pertaining to an allowance. *War Veterans Allowance Act*, R.S.C. 1985, c. W-3, s. 2. 3. A procedure to determine a rights dispute. *Civil Service Collective Bargaining Act*, R.S.N.S. 1989 c. 71 s. 2.

ADJUDICATION DIVISION. A division of the Immigration and Refugee Board.

ADJUDICATIVE FACTS. 1. " .. ; [T]wo categories of facts in constitutional litigation: 'adjudicative facts' and 'legislative facts' . . . Adjudicative facts are those that concern the immediate parties: . . ." *Danson v. Ontario (Attorney General)*, 50 C.R.R. 59 at 69, 43 C.P.C. (2d) 165, 73 D.L.R. (4th) 686, [1990] 2 S.C.R. 1086, 41 O.A.C. 250, 74 O.R. (2d) 763n, 112 N.R. 362, the court per Sopinka J. 2. Adjudicative facts are those that concern the immediate parties and disclose who did what, where, when, how and with what motive or intent. *Public School Boards' Assn. (Alberta) v. Alberta (Attorney General)*, 2000 CarswellAlta 678, 2000 SCC 2, [2000] 1 S.C.R. 44, 182 D.L.R. (4th) 561, 251 N.R. 1, 250 A.R. 314, 213 W.A.C. 314, [2000] 10 W.W.R. 187, 82 Alta. L.R. (3d) 211, 9 C.P.C. (5th) 36. Binnie, J.

ADJUDICATOR. *n*. A person who hears and determines a reference to adjudication.

ADJUNCT. *n*. Thing necessarily and actually employed in use of other thing. *McQueen v. R.* (1887), 16 S.C.R. 1.

ADJUNCT. *adj*. Additional.

ADJUNCTUM ACCESSORIUM. [L.] An appurtenance; an accessory.

ADJURATION. *n*. Binding upon oath; swearing.

ADJUST. *v*. To determine amount to be paid by insurer to insured when loss occurs.

ADJUSTED EQUITY. An amount determined by correcting to their realizable value the book value of liabilities and assets on a balance sheet. A. Bissett-Johnson & W.M. Holland, eds., *Matrimonial Property Law in Canada* (Toronto: Carswell, 1980) at V.3.

ADJUSTER. *n*. A person who, (a) on behalf of an insurer or an insured, for compensation, directly or indirectly solicits the right to negotiate the settlement of or investigate a loss or claim under a contract or a fidelity, surety or guaranty bond issued by an insurer, or investigates, adjusts or settles any such loss or claim, (b) holds himself, herself or itself out as an adjuster, investigator, consultant or adviser with respect to the settlement of such losses or claims, but does not include, (c) a barrister or solicitor acting in the usual course of the practice of law, (d) a trustee or agent of the property insured, (e) a salaried employee of a licensed insurer while acting on behalf of such insurer in the adjustment of losses, (f) a person who is employed as an appraiser, engineer or other expert solely for the purpose of giving expert advice or evidence, or (g) a person who acts as an adjuster of marine losses only. See CLAIMS~.

ADJUSTMENT. *n*. 1. Settlement and ascertainment of the amount of indemnity which an insured may receive under a policy. 2. A change, usually an increase, in a salary, rate or benefit.

3. A calculated procedure, force or thrust designed to move one structure in relation to another, of the spinal column, to remove subluxations or fixations and to mobilize the affected structures for the purpose of restoring or maintaining health. *Chiropractic Profession* Act, R.S.A. 1980, c. C-9, s. 1. See ACROSS-THE-BOARD ~; CHIROPRACTIC ~; COST-OF-LIVING ~; GENERAL ~; STATEMENT OF ~S.

ADJUSTMENT HARDWARE. Hardware designed for adjusting the size of a seat belt assembly to fit the user, including such hardware as may be integral with a buckle, a retractor or attachment hardware. *Motor Vehicle Safety Regulations*, C.R.C., c. 1038, s. 209(1).

ADJUSTMENT LEVY. In the context of product marketing schemes, a pooling of proceeds, so that producers' returns are equalized even if the product was actually sold at different prices in different markets. P.W. Hogg, *Constitutional Law of Canada*, 2d ed. (Toronto: Carswell, 1985) at 614.

AD LARGUM. [L.] At large.

AD LIB. *abbr*. Ad libitum.

AD LIBITUM. [L.] At pleasure.

AD LITEM. [L.] For a suit; for the purposes of a suit. See GUARDIAN ~.

AD LONGUM. [L.] At length.

ADM. CT. *abbr*. Admiralty Court.

ADMEASUREMENT. *n*. Ascertainment.

AD MEDIUM FILUM AQUAE. [L.] .Up to the imaginary line down the centre of a river.

AD MEDIUM FILUM VIAE. [L.] Up to the imaginary line down the centre of a road.

ADMIN. *abbr*. Administrator.

ADMINISTER. *v*. 1. To manage; to control. 2. Includes prescribe, give, sell, furnish, distribute or deliver. *Food and Drug Regulations*, C.R.C., c. 870, c. 6.04.001.

ADMINISTERED. *adj*. " . . . [A] narcotic is not 'administered' until it enters the intended recipient's system parenterally or otherwise." *R. v. Tan* (1984) 35 Sask. R. 74 at 78 [1985] 1 W.W.R. 377, 42 C.R. (3d) 252, 15 C.C.C. (3d) 303 (C.A.), Tallis J.A. (Vancise J.A. concurring).

ADMINISTERING. *adj*. Acting as guardian or custodian or trustee or executor or administrator of the estate of a person or a deceased person. *Public Trustee Act*, R.S.N.S. 1989, c. 379, s. 2.

ADMINISTRATION. *n*. 1. "There is nothing in the words 'administration' and 'administrative' which excludes the proprietary or business decisions of governmental organizations. On the contrary, the words are full broad enough to encompass all conduct engaged in by a governmental authority in furtherance of governmental policy business or otherwise. ' *B. C. Development Corp. v Friedmann*, [1984] 2 S.C.R. 447.2. " . . . [T]he winding-up and distribution of the estate of a deceased person, . . ." *Flynn v. Capital Trust Corp.* (1921), 51 O.L.R. 424 at 425, 62 D.L.R. 427 (H.C.), Middleton J. 3. Letters of administration of the property of deceased persons, whether with or without the will annexed and whether granted for general, special or limited purposes. 4. In respect of a ship, the government of the country in which the ship is registered. See ANCILLARY ~; GRANT OF ~; GRANT OF ~ WITH WILL ANNEXED; LETTERS OF ~; LETTERS OF ~ WITH WILL ANNEXED; LIMITED ~.

ADMINISTRATION AGREEMENT. An agreement between the Government of Canada and the government of a province or an aboriginal government under which (a) the Government of Canada will administer and enforce an Act of the legislature of the province, or legislation made by an aboriginal government, that imposes a tax and will make payments to the province or the aboriginal government in respect of the taxes collected, in accordance with the terms and conditions of the agreement, or (b) the government of the province will administer and enforce an Act of Parliament that imposes a tax and will make payments to the Government of Canada in respect of the taxes collected, in accordance with the terms and conditions of the agreement. *Federal-Provincial Fiscal Arrangements Act*, R.S.C. 1985, c. F-8, s. 2(1).

ADMINISTRATION COSTS. Salaries and travelling expenses of members and employees of an authority, office rent, maintenance and purchase of office equipment, expenses connected with exhibits, visual equipment and printed matter for educational purposes, and all expenditures necessary for carrying out the objects of an authority other than capital expenses and maintenance costs of projects. *Conservation Authorities Act*, R.S.O. 1990, c. 27, s. 1.

ADMINISTRATION OF JUSTICE. 1. (a) "[Di Iorio v. Montreal Jail (1976), 33 C.C.C.

(2d) 2891 establishes that the police, criminal investigations, prosecutions, corrections, and the court system, all comprise part of the 'administration of justice' [as found in the *Constitution Act*, 1867 (30 & 31 Vict.), c. 3]." *MacKeigan v. Hickman* (1989), 61 D.L.R. (4th) 688 at 724, 99 N.R. 227n, 50 C.C.C. (3d) 449 (S.C.C.), McLachlin J. (L'Heureux-Dube and Gonthier JJ. concurring). (b) "Since Keable No. 1 [Quebec (Attorney General) v. Canada (Attorney General) (1978), [1979] 1 S.C.R. 218 . . . and [Putnam v. Alberta (Attorney General) (1981), 37 N.R. 1 J., then it is clear that the boundaries of the 'administration of justice' do not include the discipline, organization and management of the R.C.M.P. In my dissent in Putnam J. sought to make clear, however, that the 'administration of justice' does include the organization and management of police forces created by provincial legislation.' *Robinson v. British Columbia* (1987) (sub nom. *O'Hara v. British Columbia*) 38 C.C.C. (3d) 233 at 243-44, [1988] 1 W.W.R. 216, 80 N.R. 127, 45 D.L.R. (4th) 527, 189 B.C.L.R. (2d) 273, [1987] 2 S.C.R. 591, Dickson C.J.C. (Beetz, McIntyre, Lamer, Wilson, Le Dain, La Forest and L'Heureux-Dube JJ. concurring). (c) " . . . [I]nclude but are not limited to, the constitution, maintenance and organization of provincial Courts of civil and criminal jurisdiction and they include procedure in civil matters . . ." *Di Iorio v. Montreal Jail* (1977), 73 D.L.R. (3d) 491 at 527, [1978] 1 S.C.R. 152, 35 C.R.N.S. 57, 8 N.R. 361, Dickson J. (Marsand, Judson, Ritchie and Spence JJ. concurring). 2. The provision, maintenance and operation of, (a) the courts of justice of the Province of Ontario, (b) land registry offices, (c) jails, and (d) the offices of coroners and Crown Attorneys, for the performance of their functions, including any functions delegated to such courts, institutions or offices or any official thereof by or under any Act. *Administration of Justice Act*, R.S.O. 1990, c. A.6, s. 1. 3. (a) Provision maintenance and operation of (i) courts of justice in British Columbia, (ii) court registry and land title offices, (iii) correctional centres as defined in the Correction Act, and prisons and lockups operated by police forces; (iv) the offices of coroner, Crown counsel, probation officers, court workers and sheriffs, and their officers; and (v) the police forces, for the purpose of their functions, including functions given to the courts or offices, or to any official of them under an Act or rule or regulation made under an Act; (b) prosecution of offences; and (c) provision of adequate legal services, including the operation of legal aid offices. *Justice Administration Act*, R.S.B.C. 1996, c. 243, s. 1.

ADMINISTRATIVE. *adj.* 1. " . . . [I]t is reasonable to interpret 'administrative' as describing those functions of Government which are not performed by the Legislative Assembly and the Courts. Broadly speaking, it describes that part of Government which administers the law and governmental policy." *Ontario (Ombudsman) v. Ontario (Health Disciplines Board)* (1979), 26 O.R. (2d) 105 at 148 (C.A.). 2. That which concerns ministerial or executive action, used in contradistinction to judicial, quasi-judicial or legislative.

ADMINISTRATIVE ACT. To adopt a policy, to make and issue a specific direction, and to apply a general rule to a particular case. To be contrasted with legislative and judicial acts.

ADMINISTRATIVE AND TECHNICAL STAFF. People with communication, secretarial or clerical duties. J.G. McLeod, *The Conflict of Laws* (Calgary: Carswell, 1983) at 76.

ADMINISTRATIVE DISCRETION. In the work of an administrative agency, consideration not entirely susceptible of proof or disproof in relation to which the agency must make decisions.

ADMINISTRATIVE LAW. 1. Law relating to public administration. 2. The law which relates to the organization, duties and quasi–judicial and judicial powers of the executive, to proceedings before tribunals and to the making of subordinate legislation.

ADMINISTRATIVE NOTICE. The equivalent of judicial notice for an administrative tribunal. Those matters which a tribunal may accept as generally known without evidence being lead to prove the matters.

ADMINISTRATIVE PURPOSE. In relation to the use of personal information about an individual, means the use of that information in a decisionmaking process that directly affects that individual. Privacy Act, R.S.C. 1985, c. P-21, s. 3.

ADMINISTRATIVE TORT. Exists once it is shown that the invalid decision by a public officer is tainted by either malice or knowledge of lack of authority. *Comeau Sea Foods v. Canada (Fisheries & Oceans)* (1995), 123 D.L.R. (4th) 180, Fed. C.A.

ADMINISTRATIVE TRIBUNAL. A person or body before whom a matter is heard, contrasted with a court.

ADMINISTRATOR. *n.* 1. The Governor in Council may appoint an Administrator to act as Commissioner during the Commissioner's absence or illness or other inability or when that office is vacant. *Yukon Act, 2002*, S.C. 2002, c. 7, s. 5. The administrator of the federal government is the Chief Justice of Canada who acts when the Governor General is absent. The Chief Justice of each province performs the same function in the absence of the Lieutenant Governor. 2. " . . . [T]he person to whom the property of a person dying intestate is committed for administration and whose duties with respect thereto correspond with those of an executor." *Minister of National Revenue v. Parsons* (1983), 4 Admin L.R. 64 at 79, [1983] C.T.C. 321, 83 D.T.C. 5329 (Fed. T.D.), Cattanach J. See LITIGATION~; URBAN MUNICIPAL ~.

ADMINISTRATOR AD LITEM. An administrator of an estate appointed for the purpose of conducting litigation. May now be referred to as a litigation administrator.

ADMINISTRATOR DE SON TORT. A person who is neither an executor nor an administrator but is either involved with the deceased's personal property or does other things characteristic of an executor.

ADMINISTRATOR WITH WILL ANNEXED. An administrator appointed to administer a testator's estate where the executors named in the will refuse or are unable to act.

ADMINISTRATRIX. *n.* A woman appointed to administer the estate of a person who died without appointing an executor in a will or without leaving a will.

ADMIN. L.J. *abbr.* Administrative Law Journal.

ADMIN. L.R. *abbr.* Administrative Law Reports, 1983-.

ADMIRALTY COURT. The Federal Court.

ADMIRALTY LAW. Maritime law.

ADMIRALTY PROCEEDING. The Federal Court Act sets out the maritime or Admiralty jurisdiction of the Federal Court. See CANADIAN MARITIME LAW.

ADMISSIBLE EVIDENCE. Relevant evidence not otherwise excluded.

ADMISSION. *n.* 1. A confession, concession or voluntary acknowledgement made by a party, or someone identified with him in legal interest, of the existence of a fact which is relevant to the cause of an adversarial party. *Vector Energy v. Canadian Pioneer Energy Inc.* (1996) 50 C.P.C. (3d) 148 (Alta. Q.B.). 2. Excludes confession. *R. v. Rothman* (1981), 20 C.R. (3d) 97 at 122, [1981] 1 S.C.R. 640, 59 C.C.C. (2d) 30, 121 D.L.R. (3d) 578, 35 N.R. 485, Este J. (dissenting) (Laskin C.J.C. concurring). 3. Facts admitted by the opposite party in civil proceeding or allegations made by the plaintiff and not disputed the defendant. 4. Silence may be taken as an admission where a denial would be the only reasonable course of action expected if that person were not responsible. *R. v. Warner* (1994), 94 C.C.C. (3d) 540 (Ont. C.A.). 5. Entry to any place of entertainment. 6. Entry or landing. Immigration Act, R.S.C. 1985, c. I-2, s. 2. 7. Call to the bar. 8. Official acceptance of a patient or resident into the hospital or facility. See FIRST ~; FORMAL ~; PRICE OF ~; SOLEMN ~; UNSOLEMN ~.

ADMISSION AGAINST INTEREST. A statement made by one of the parties to an action which amounts to a prior acknowledgement by him that one of the material facts relevant to the issues is not as he now claims it is. *Vector Energy v. Canadian Pioneer Energy Inc.* (1996) 50 C.P.C. (3d) 148 (Alta. Q.B.).

ADMISSION DIAGNOSIS. The diagnosis given to explain admission to a hospital or facility.

ADMISSION IN JUDICIUM. A solemn admission. P.K. McWilliams, *Canadian Criminal Evidence*, 3d ed. (Aurora: Canada Law Book, 1988) at 14-1.

ADMISSION OF SERVICE. Acknowledgement that a true copy of the document was received.

ADMISSION PRICE. (a) The greater of the face value of the ticket and the amount paid for entrance or admission to a place of amusement, (b) the amount paid for (i) a ride or the use of a thing, or (ii) participation in an amusement, and (c) the amount paid for the right to sit in or use any seat, box or stand in a place of amusement. *The Municipal Act*, C.C.S.M., c. M225, s. 329. See PRICE OF ADMISSION.

AD OFFICUM JUSTICIARIORUM SPECTAT, UNICUIQUE CORAM EIS PLACITANTI JUSTITIAM EXHIBERE. [L.] It is the duty of judicial officers to administer justice to everyone who pleads before them.

ADOLESCENT. *n.* An individual who is 16 or 17 years of age. *The Employment Standards Code*, C.C.S.M., c. E110, s. 84(1).

ADOPT. *v.* 1. To accept a contract as binding; to select; to choose. 2. A witness may adopt a videotaped statement if he or she, whether or not presently recalling the events discussed, believes them to be true because he or she recalls giving the videotaped statement and attempting at that time to be honest and truthful. *R. v. Meddoui* [1991] 2 W.W.R. 289 (Alta. C.A.). 3. To take on responsibility for a child as if the child were one's own biological child. 4. A local government adopts a bylaw where it approves or accepts the bylaw.

ADOPTED CHILD. A person who was adopted in Ontario. For all purposes of law, as of the date of the making of an adoption order, (a) the adopted child becomes the child of the adoptive parent and the adoptive parent becomes the parent of the adopted child; and (b) the adopted child ceases to be the child of the person who was his or her parent before the adoption order was made and that person ceases to be the parent of the adopted child, except where the person is the spouse of the adoptive parent, as if the adopted child had been born to the adoptive parent. *Child and Family Services Act*, R.S.O. 1990, c. C.11, s. 158(1), (2).

ADOPTION. *n.* 1. " . . . [I]n its popular sense it means the act by which a person adopts as his own the child of another or, in other terms, the acceptance by a person of a child of other parents to be the same as his own child." *Anderson v. Minister of National Revenue*, [1947] 4 D.L.R. 262 at 2 80, [1947] Ex C.R. 3 89, [1947] C.T.C. 223, Angers J. 2. " . . . '[A]doption' bears the meaning 'putting into operation' or 'passing' when used in s. 240 [of the Municipal Act, R.S.B.C. 1960, c. 255] with reference to a resolution . . ." *Winter v. Surrey (District)* (1976), 72 D.L.R. (3d) 273 at 274 (B.C. S.C.), Legg J. 3. Adoption is not another form of custody. It is the total extinguishment of the birth parents' rights and the establishment of legally, retroactively and permanently, of a parent-child relationship between a child and a person who is not the biological parent of the child. *K. v. B.* (1995), 125 D.L.R. (4th) 653 (Ont. Prov. Ct.). 4. Adoption of a cheque by signing a written acknowledgement of responsibility for its face value is similar to a ratification of the cheque. *Newell v. Royal Bank of Canada* (1997), 147 D.L.R. (4th) 268 (N.S.C.A.). 5. A trade-mark is deemed to have been adopted by a person when that person or his predecessor in title commenced to use it in Canada or to make it known in Canada or, if that person or his predecessor had not previously so used it or made it known, when that person or his predecessor filed an application for its registration in Canada. See INDEPENDENT ~; INTERCOUNTRY~.

ADOPTION BY REFERENCE. Incorporation of a separate statement, statute, by-law, etc. into the original statement, statute, by-law, etc. by referring to it.

ADOPTION OF CONTRACT. Acceptance of a contract as binding.

ADOPTIVE ACT. An act must be adopted either by the vote of a public body or the vote of a particular number of persons.

AD PROXIMUM ANTECEDENS FIAT RELATIO, NISI IMPEDIATUR SENTENTIA. [L.] Unless the context requires otherwise, relative words refer to the last antecedent] " . . . [I]t is a rule both of grammar and of law that relative words must ordinarily be referred to the last antecedent, the last antecedent being the last word which can be made an antecedent so as to give a meaning." *Hinton Avenue, Ottawa, Re* (1920), 47 O.L.R. 556 at 563, 54 D.L.R. 115 (C.A.), Riddell J.A.

AD QUAESTIONEM (OR QUESTIONES) FACTI NON RESPONDENT JUDICES; AD QUAESTIONEM (OR QUESTIONES) JURIS NON RESPONDENT JURATORES. [L.] In cases tried by a judge and jury, the judge should not decide questions of fact and the jury should not decide questions of law.

AD QUAESTIONEM LEGIS RESPONDENT JUDICES. [L.] Judges decide points of law.

AD QUEM. [L.] To whom; to which.

AD QUOD DAMNUM. [L.] To what damage.

ADR. Alternative dispute resolution.

ADS. *abbr* [L. ad sectam] At the suit of. Used when the defendant's name is put first in the title of a proceeding.

AD SECTAM. ·[L. at the suit of] Used in its abbreviated form ads. or ats. when the defendant's name is put first in the title of a proceeding.

A.D.T. *abbr* Anti-Dumping Tribunal.

AD TUNC ET IBIDEM. [L.] Then and there.

ADULT. *n*. One who is neither a young person nor a child. See DEPENDENT ~; NEGLECTED ~.

ADULT BASIC EDUCATION. Programs and courses that are designed to develop and improve the basic literacy and numeracy skills of adults. *Education* Act, R.S.O. 1990, c. E.2, s. 189(1).

ADULTERATED. *adj* Deteriorated by the addition of any substance to a maple product or the substitution for any maple product or for any part thereof of any colourable imitation.

ADULTERATION. *n*. Mixing into any substance intended for sale an ingredient which is either dangerous to health or which turns the substance into something other than what it is represented to be.

ADULTERINE. *n*. The child of an adulterous relationship.

ADULTERY. *n*. Voluntary sexual intercourse between a spouse and any person other than his wife or her husband while the marriage exists.

ADULT FILM. A film that produces or reproduces an adult motion picture. *Motion Picture Act*, R.S.B.C. 1996, c. 314, s. 1.

ADULT FILM DISTRIBUTOR. A person who distributes adult films to an adult film retailer or to another adult film distributor. *Motion Picture Act*, R.S.B.C. 1996, c. 314, s. 1.

ADULT FILM RETAILER. A person who distributes adult films to the public, but does not include an adult film distributor. *Motion Picture Act*, R.S.B.C. 1996, c. 314, s. 1.

ADULT IN NEED OF PROTECTION. An adult who, in the premises where he resides, (i) is a victim of physical abuse, sexual abuse, mental cruelty or a combination thereof, is incapable of protecting himself therefrom by reason of physical disability or mental infirmity, and refuses, delays or is unable to make provision for his protection therefrom, or (ii) is not receiving adequate care and attention, is incapable of caring adequately for himself by reason of physical disability or mental infirmity, and refuses, delays or is unable to make provision for his adequate to care and attention. *Adult Protection Act* R.S.N.S. 1989 c. 2 s. 3.

ADULT INTERDEPENDENT PARTNER. A person is the adult interdependent partner of another person if (a) the person has lived with the other person in a relationship of interdependence (i) for a continuous period of not less than 3 years, or (ii) of some permanence, if there is a child of the relationship by birth or adoption, or (b) the person has entered into an adult interdependent partner agreement with the other person under section 7. *Adult Interdependent Relationships Act*, S.A. 2002, c. A-4.5, s. 3(1).

ADULT INTERDEPENDENT RELATIONSHIP. The relationship between 2 persons who are adult interdependent partners of each other; *Adult Interdependent Relationships Act*, S.A. 2002, c. A-4.5, s. 1(1).

ADULT PERSON. A person eighteen years of age or more. *The Devolution of Real Property Act*, R.S.S. 1978, c. D-27, s. 2.

ADULT SENTENCE. In the case of a young person who is found guilty of an offence, means any sentence that could be imposed on an adult who has been convicted of the same offence. *Youth Criminal Justice Act*, S.C. 2002, c. 1, s. 2(1).

A. DU N. *abbr*. Annales du notariat et de l'enregistrement.

ADV. *abbr*. [L.] Adversus.

AD VALOREM. [L.] According to their value, used in reference to customs or duties.

AD VALOREM DUTY. Duty is imposed in the form of a percentage on the value of the dutiable property.

ADVANCE. *v*. 1. To pay. *Foster v. Minister of National Revenue*, [1971] C.T.C. 335 at 339, 71 D.T.C. 5207 (Ex. Ct.), Jackett P. 2. Pay before due. *Bronester Ltd. v. Priddle*, [1961] 3 All E.R. 471 at 475 (C.A.), Holroyd Pearce L.J. 3. Includes lend and give.

ADVANCE. *n*. 1. Payment made before due. 2. " . . . [A]dvances of money either by way of loan or payment at the request of the legatee . . ." *Hauck v Schmaltz*, [1935] S.C.R. 478 at 482, [1935] 3 D.L.R. 691, the court per Lamont J. 3. Although the word could refer to something other than money the primary meaning is in relation to money. *Klaue v. Bennett* (1989), 62 D.L.R. (4th) 367 (B.C. C.A.). 4. The word "advance" is typically used in connection with payments made by a lender to a borrower. *Air Canada, Re* 66 O.R. (3d) 257 (C.A.). See ACCOUNTABLE ~; FUTURE ~; HARVESTING ~S; PROGRESS ~S; STANDING ~; TEMPORARY ~.

ADVANCE BOOKING CHARTER. A round-trip passenger flight originating in Canada that is operated according to the conditions of a contract entered into between one or two air carriers and one or more charterers that requires the charterer or charterers to charter the entire passenger seating capacity of an aircraft for resale by them to the public, at a price per seat, not later than a specified number of days prior to the date of departure of the flight from its origin in Canada. *Air Transportation Regulations*, SOR/88-58, s. 2.

ADVANCED EXPLORATION. The excavation of an exploratory shaft, adit, or decline, the extraction of material in excess of the prescribed quantity, the installation of a mill for test purposes or any other prescribed work. *Mining Act*, R.S.O. 1990, c. M.14 s. 139(1).

ADVANCED ULTRA-LIGHT AEROPLANE. An aeroplane that has a type design that is in compliance with the standards specified in the manual entitled *Design Standards for Advanced Ultra-light Aeroplanes. Canadian Aviation Regulations*, SOR/96-433, s. 101.01(1).

ADVANCEMENT. *n*. 1. Promotion. 2. A single outlay for a defined purpose. 3. Paying to a beneficiary part of the capital of a gift before the actual time when the capital falls into the beneficiary's hands. D.M.W. Waters, *The Law of Trusts in Canada*, 2d ed. (Toronto: Carswell, 1984) at 930. 4. The doctrine of advancement creates a presumption that where property is purchased in the name of another, or transferred to another without consideration, a resulting trust arises in favour of the person who paid the purchase price. *Chartier v. Chartier* (1999), 235 N.R. 1 (S.C.C.). See ADEMPTION BY ~; PRESUMPTION OF ~.

ADVANCEMENT OF EDUCATION. One of the four heads of charity in the classic definition of that term by Lord MacNaghten. It includes the training of the mind and the improvement of a useful branch of human knowledge and its public dissemination. See CHARITY.

ADVANCE PAYMENT. 1. A payment made by or on behalf of Her Majesty under the terms of a contract before the performance of that art of the contract in reset of which the payment is made. *Government Contracts Regulations*, SOR/402, s. 2. 2. A payment for grain made to a producer under the authority of this Act. *Prairie Grain Advance Payments Act*, R.S.C. 1985, c. P-18, s. 2.

ADVANCE POLL. A poll taken in advance of polling day. *Election Act*, R.S.A. 2000, c. E-1, s. 1(1).

ADVANCE POLLING DAY. The day preceding ordinary polling day.

ADVANCE VOTE. A vote taken in advance of election day. Local *Authorities Election Act*, R.S.A. 2000, c. L 21, s. 1.

ADVANTAGE. See COLLATERAL ~; NO MAN CAN TAKE ~ OF HIS OWN WRONG.

ADVENTITIOUS. *adj*. Incidental; unexpected.

AD VENTREM INSPICIENDUM. [L.] To inspect the womb.

ADVENTURE. *n*. A hazardous enterprise. See JOINT ~; MARINE ~; MIS~.

ADVENTURE IN THE NATURE OF TRADE. 1. A transaction of the same kind carried on in the same way as a transaction of an ordinary trader or dealer in property of the same kind as the subject matter of the transaction. *Loewen v. Minister of National Revenue* (1994), 166 N.R. 266 (Fed. C.A.). 2. An adventure is in the nature of trade when it has none of the essential characteristics of an investment, but is a mere speculation if the purpose is not to earn income, but to turn to profit on prompt realization. *M.N.R. v. Sissons* 1969 S.C.R. 507 1969 C.T.C. 184 69 5152.

ADVERSARIAL SYSTEM. A system by which disputes between opposing parties are resolved be an impartial arbiter after hearing evidence and argument presented by both parties.

ADVERSARY. *n*. A party opposed to another in interest; a litigant.

ADVERSARY SYSTEM. "Procedure in our Courts is based on the adversary system, that is to say each party must present the evidence on which it seeks to rely and attempt to refute the other party's evidence by cross-examination of its witnesses or rebuttal proof . . ."*Canadians for the Abolition of the Seal Hunt v. Canada (Minister of Fisheries & the Environment)* (1980), 20 C.P.C. 151 at 162, [1981] 1 F.C. 733, 10 C.E.L.R. 1, 111 D.L.R. (3d) 222 (T.D.), Walsh J. See ADVERSARIAL SYSTEM.

ADVERSE. *adj*. Opposed in interest; unfavourable; hostile.

ADVERSE CLAIM. Includes a claim that a transfer was or would be unauthorized or wrongful or that a particular adverse person is the owner of or has an interest in the security. *Corporations acts.*

ADVERSE DRUG REACTION. A noxious and unintended response to a drug that occurs at doses normally used or tested for the diagnosis, treatment or prevention of a medical condition or the modification of an organic function. *Marihuana Medical Access Regulations*, SOR/2001-227, s. 1(1).

ADVERSE EFFECT. 1. An unwanted effect brought about by the normal dose of a drug. F.A. Jaffe, *A Guide to Pathological Evidence*, 3d ed. (Toronto: Carswell, 1991) at 81. 2. One or more of, (a) impairment of the quality of the natural environment for any use that can be made of it, (b) injury or damage to property or to plant or animal life, (c) harm or material discomfort to any person, (d) an adverse effect on the health of any person, (e) impairment of the safety of any person, (f) rendering any property or plant or animal life unfit for human use, (g) loss of enjoyment of normal use of property, and (h) interference with the normal conduct of business. *Environmental Protection Act*, R.S.O. 1990, c. E.19, s. 1. *Environment Enforcement Statute Law Amendment Act*, S.O. 1986, c. 68, s. 1.

ADVERSE EFFECT DISCRIMINATION. 1." . . . [A]rises where an employer for genuine business reasons adopts a rule or standard which is on its face neutral, and which will apply equally to all employees, but which has a discriminatory effect upon a prohibited ground on one employee or group of employees in that it imposes because of some special characteristic of the employee or group obligations, penalties, or restrictive conditions not imposed on other members of the workforce . . ." *Ontario (Human Rights Commission) v. Simpsons-Sears Ltd.* (1985), 9 C.C.E.L. 185 at 199, [1985] 2 S.C.R. 536, 52 O.R. (2d) 799, 17 Admin L.R. 89, 86 C.L.L.C. 17,002, 64 N.R. 161, 7 C.H.R.R. D/3102, 23 D.L.R. (4th) 321, 12 O.A.C. 241, the court per McIntyre J. 2. Adverse effect discrimination occurs when a law, rule or practice is facially neutral but has a disproportionate impact on a group because of a particular characteristic of that group. *Egan v. Canada*, 1995 CarswellNat 6, 12 R.F.L. (4th) 201, 95 C.L.L.C. 210-025, C.E.B. & P.G.R. 8216, 124 D.L.R. (4th) 609, 182 N.R. 161, 29 C.R.R. (2d) 79, [1995] 2 S.C.R. 513, 96 F.T.R. 80 (note), [1995] 2 S.C.R. 513. Per Cory and Iacobucci JJ. (dissenting). See MEIORIN TEST.

ADVERSE INFERENCE. 1. The "adverse inference" principle is derived from ordinary logic and experience, and is not intended to punish a party *who exercises its right not to call the witness* by imposing an "adverse inference" which a trial judge in possession of the explanation for the decision considers to be wholly unjustified. *R. c. Jolivet*, 2000 CarswellQue 805, 2000 SCC 29, 144 C.C.C. (3d) 97, 33 C.R. (5th) 1, 185 D.L.R. (4th) 626, [2000] 1 S.C.R. 751, 254 N.R. 1. Binnie, J. for the court. 2. The adverse interest doctrine is more a matter of logic than of law. The law permits an adverse inference to be drawn against a party in certain circumstances. It does not require it. Generally, the drawing of such an inference is a matter exclusively for the trial judge. One of the circumstances in which it may be drawn occurs when a party with knowledge of a relevant fact fails to testify. The judge may infer that if the party had testified the testimony would have been against the party's interest. *L.(F.A.) v. B. (A.B.)* [1995] 6 W.W.R. 570 (Man. C.A.).

ADVERSE IN INTEREST. A party is adverse in interest to another if he has a direct pecuniary or other substantial legal interest adverse to the legal interest of the other party even though they are on the same side of the record and there is no issue on the record that the court will be called upon to adjudicate between them.

ADVERSE PARTY. The opposite party.

ADVERSE POSSESSION. 1. "The essentials to be established in a case of adverse possession are that the claimant be in possession and that the true owner be out of possession . . ." *Lutz v. Kawa* (1980), 15 R.P.R. 40 at 54, 112 D.L.R. (3d) 271, 23 A.R. 9 (C.A.), the court per Laycraft J.A. 2. " In order for possession to extinguish true title the adverse claimant must prove that the possession was open, notorious and continuous, to the exclusion of the owner for the full statutory period. Acts of possession which are simply equivocal, or occasional will not be enough to displace paper title." *Burke Estate v. Nova Scotia Attorney General* 1991 107 N.S.R. (2d) 91 at 103, 290 A.P.R. 91 (T.D.), Saunders J.

ADVERSE REACTION. A noxious and unintended response to a natural health product that occurs at any dose used or tested for the diagnosis, treatment or prevention of a disease or for modifying an organic function. *Natural Health Products Regulations*, SOR/2003-196, s. 1(1).

ADVERSE WITNESS. A hostile witness, one hostile in mind to the party calling him, or a witness who gives evidence that is contrary to the prior statement of the party who calls him and who shows intention not to tell the truth. *Skender v. Barker* (1987), 18 B.C.L.R. (2d) 57 (S.C.).

ADVERSUS. [L.] Against, abbreviated v.

ADVERSUS EXTRANEOS VITIOSA POSSESSIO PRODESSE SOLET. [L.] Prior possession is good title unless anyone can show better.

ADVERTENT NEGLIGENCE. Imports an element of intentionally driving in a manner one knows or recognizes to be dangerous or negligent. *R. v. Mason* (1990), 60 C.C.C. (3d) 338, at 340 (B.C. C.A.).

ADVERTISE. *v.* To make any representation to the public by any means whatever for the purpose of promoting directly or indirectly the sale of a product.

ADVERTISEMENT. *n.* 1. Any representation by any means whatever for the purpose of promoting directly or indirectly the sale or disposal of any product. 2. Includes (i) an advertisement in a newspaper, magazine or other publication or circular; (ii) an advertisement shown on a billboard sign, handbill or similar item that is located elsewhere than on the business premises of the credit grantor on whose behalf the advertisement is being made; (iii) a message broadcast by television or radio. See POLITICAL ~; PUBLIC ~.

ADVERTISER. *n.* A person who prepares, publishes or broadcasts an advertisement or who causes an advertisement to be prepared, published or broadcast. *Consumer Protection Act*, R. S.Q. c. P-40.1, s. 1.

ADVERTISING. *n.* Includes television and radio commercials, newspaper and magazine advertisments and all other sales material generally disseminated through the communications media. *Securities Act*, R.S.O. 1990 c. S-5, s. 50(2). See POLITICAL ~.

ADVERTISING EXPENSES. Election expenses, including production expenses, incurred for advertising (a) in newspapers, magazines or other periodical publications, and (b) on radio or television, and (c) on billboards, buses, or other property normally used for purposes of commercial advertising. *The Elections Finances Act* R.S.M. 1987 c. E32 s. 1.

ADVERTISING MATERIAL. Any commercial message and programming that promotes a station, network or program, but does not include (*a*) a station or network identification, (*b*) the announcement of an upcoming program that is voiced over credits, (*c*) a program that consists exclusively of classified announcements, if the program is broadcast not more than once during a broadcast day and has a duration of not more than one hour, or (*d*) a promotion for a Canadian program or a Canadian feature film, notwithstanding that a sponsor is identified in the title of the program or the film or is identified as a sponsor of that program or that film, where the identification is limited to the name of the sponsor only and does not include a description, representation or attribute of the sponsor's products or services. Federal regulations.

ADVICE. *n.* " . . . [I]n ordinary parlance means primarily the expression of counsel or opinion, favourable or unfavourable as to action, but it may, chiefly in commercial usage, signify information or intelligence . . ." *J.R. Moodie Co. v. Minister of National Revenue*, [1950] 2 D.L.R. 145 at 148, [1950] C.T.C. 61 (S.C.C.), Rand J. (Rinfret C.J.C. concurring). See APPROPRIATE ~; INDEPENDENT ~.

ADVISE. *v.* To notify.

ADVISEMENT. *n.* Deliberation.

ADVISER. *var.* **ADVISOR**. *n.* A person or company engaging in or claiming to engage in the business of advising others as to the investing in or the buying or selling of securities. See LEGAL -~

ADVISORY COMMITTEE. A committee established under a statute to provide advice, usually to the government of the day.

ADVISORY COUNCIL. See ADVISORY COMMITTEE; CANADIAN ~ ON THE STATUS OF WOMEN.

ADVISORY OPINION. An answer to a hypothetical question put to a court.

ADVISORY SERVICES. The provision of one aeronautical radio station to another such station of flight safety information, including aeronautical weather information and serviceability reports in respect of aerodromes, air navigation aids and approach aids, but does not include the provision of IFR air traffic control clearances, instructions or procedures. Aeronautical *Communications Standards and Procedures Order*, C.R.C., c. 20, s. 2.

ADVOCACY. *n.* 1. The act of pleading for, supporting a position or viewpoint. 2. Skillful advocacy involves taking information acquired as a result of the trial, the evidence, the other party's theory of the case, and various other, intangible factors, and weaving this information together with law, logic and rhetoric into a persuasive argument. *R. v. Rose* (1998), 20 C.R. (5th) 246, at 289, (S.C.C.) per Cory, Iacobucci and Bastarache, JJ.

ADVOCATE. *n.* 1. The supporter of a cause who assists a client with advice and pleads for the client. 2. A barrister and solicitor.

ADVOCATE. *n.* The periodical, Advocate.

ADVOCATES' Q. *abbr.* The Advocates' Quarterly.

ADVOCATES' SOC. J. *abbr.* The Advocates' Society Journal.

ADVOCATE (TOR.) *abbr.* The Advocate, published by the Student Law Society, Faculty of Law, University of Toronto.

ADVOCATE (VAN.) *abbr.* The Advocate, published by the Vancouver Bar Association.

ADVOW. *v.* To maintain or justify an act.

ADWARE. *n.* Advertising placed in other software with the intent of generating revenue.

AECB. *abbr.* Atomic Energy Control Board.

AECL. *abbr.* Atomic Energy of Canada Limited.

AEDIFICARE IN TUO PROPRIO SOLO NON LICET QUOD ALTERI NOCEAT. [L.] One is permitted to build on one's own land any structure as long as it does not interfere with the rights of another.

AEDIFICATIO (OR AEDIFICATUM) SOLO, SOLO CEDIT. [L.] Whatever is built on land becomes part of the land.

AEQUITAS EST CORRECTIO JUSTAE LEGIS QUA PARTE DEFICIT QUOD GENERATIM LATA EST. [L.] Equity corrects a just law which is defective because of its universality.

AEQUITAS EST PERFECTA QUAEDAM RATIO QUAE JUS SCRIPTUM INTERPRETATUR ET EMENDAT; NULLA SCRIPTURA COMPREHENSA, SED SOLUM IN VERA RATIONE CONSISTENS. [L.] Equity is a complete system, which though unwritten and based on right reason alone, interprets and amends the law.

AEQUITAS EST QUASI EQUALITAS. [L.] Equity is, in a manner of speaking, equality.

AEQUITAS FACTUM HABET QUOD FIERI OPORTUIT. [L.] Equity regards that what ought to have been done was done.

AEQUITAS NUNQUAM CONTRAVENIT LEGIS. [L.] Equity never contravenes the commonlaw.

AEQUITAS SEQUITUR LEGEM. [L.] Equity follows the law.

AEQUUM ET BONUM EST LEX LEGUM. [L.] What is equitable and good is the law of laws.

AERIAL TRAMWAY. Any type of overhead transportation effected by the use of a cable or cables .

AERIAL WORK. A commercial air service other than an air transport service or a flight training service. *Canadian Aviation Regulations*, SOR/96-433, s. 101.01(1).

AERIAL WORK ZONE. An area, delineated in an aerial work zone plan, in which aerial work is being conducted and that is over a built-up area of a city or town or over or adjacent to an area where persons may assemble. *Canadian Aviation Regulations* SOR?96-433, s. 101.01(1).

AERIAL WORK ZONE PLAN. A risk management plan for proposed aerial work. *Canadian Aviation Regulations*, SOR?96-433, s. 101.01(1).

AEROBATIC MANOEUVRE. A manoeuvre where a change in the attitude of an aircraft results in a bank angle greater than 60 degrees, an abnormal attitude or an abnormal acceleration not incidental to normal flying. *Canadian Aviation Regulations* SOR/96-433, s. 101.01(1).

AERODROME. n. Any area of land, water (including the frozen surface thereof) or other supporting surface used, designed, prepared, equipped or set apart for use either in whole or in part for the arrival, departure, movement or servicing of aircraft and includes any buildings, installations and equipment situated thereon or associated therewith. *Aeronautics Act*, R.S.C. 1985 (1 st Supp.), c. 33, s. 3. See ALTERNATE~.

AERODROME TRAFFIC. All traffic on the movement area of an aerodrome and all aircraft operating at or in the vicinity of the aerodrome. *Canadian Aviation Regulations* SOR 96-433, s. 101.01A(1).

AERONAUTICAL PRODUCT. Any aircraft, aircraft engine, aircraft propeller or aircraft appliance or part or the component parts of any of those things, including any computer system and software. *Aeronautics Act*, R.S.C. 1985, c. A-2, s. 3

AERONAUTICAL SERVICE. A radiocommunication service that provides for the safety and navigation and other operations of aircraft, and that may also include the exchange of air-to-ground messages on behalf of the public. *Radiocommunications Regulations*, SOR/96-484 s. 2.

AERONAUTICS. *n*. 1. " . . . [A]ir transportation as a whole." *Bensol Customs Brokers v Air Canada* (1979), 99 D.L.R. (3d) 623 at 630, [1979] 2 F.C. 575 (T.D.), Le Dain J. 2. " . . . [A]s used in this section [Federal Court Act; R.S.C. 1970, c. 10, s. 23], certainly includes the control and regulation of air navigation over Canada, and regulation and control of aerodromes and air stations as well as the investigation of air accidents, such as one in the Aeronautics Act, R.S.C. 1970, c. A-3." *Canadian Fur Co. v KLM Royal Dutch Airlines* (1974), 52 D.L.R. (3d)128 at 133, [1974] 2 F.C. 944 (T.D.), Addy J. 3. Parachuting involves aeronautics since the parachutist navigates his or her fall and controls the motion and direction of the fall. *Mercier v. Alberta (Attorney General)* (1997), 145 D.L.R. (4th) 692 (Alta. C.A.).

AEROPLANE. *n*. A power-driven heavier-than-air aircraft, that derives its lift in flight from aerodynamic reactions on surfaces that remain fixed during of flight. *Canadian Aviation Regulations*, SOR 96-433, s. 101.01 See LARGE~.

AFFAIRS. *n*. 1. That which concerns a person in trade or property. 2. The relationships among a body corporate, its affiliates and the shareholders, directors and officers of those bodies corporate but does not include the business carried on by those bodies corporate. 3. Professional or public business. *Law Society of Upper Canada v. Ontario (Attorney General)*, 1995 CarswellOnt 800, 31 Admin. L.R. (2d) 134, 21 O.R. (3d) 666, 121 D.L.R. (4th) 369. 4. To be distinguished from the business of a company. A time limit for sending of proxies relates to the affairs of a company, not to its business. *Beatty v. First Exploration Fund 1987 & Co.* (1988),

25 B.C.L.R. (2d) 377 (S.C.). See CONSUMER AND CORPORATE CANADA ~ EXTERNAL ~ CANADA~; INDIAN AND NORTHERN ~ INTERGOVERNMENTAL ~; VETERANS ~.

AFFECT. *v*. " . . . '[T]o act upon or have an effect upon' . . ." *Desjarlais v. Piapot Bang No. 75* (1989), [1990] 1 C.N.L.R. 39 at 41, [1989] 3 F.C. 605, 12 C.H.R.R. C/466 (C.A.), Desjardins J.A.

AFFECTED LIVESTOCK. Livestock having a communicable disease. *Livestock Diseases Act*, R.S.A. 2000, c. L-15, s. 1.

AFFECTED SECURITY. A participating security of a corporation in which the interest of the holder would be terminated by reason of a going private transaction. *Business Corporations Act*, R.S.O. 1990, c. B.16, s. 190.

AFFECTION. See NATURAL ~.

AFFECTUS PUNITUR LICET NON SEQUATUR EFFECTUS. [L.] A person is punished for an attempt, even though the person fails.

AFFIANCE. *n*. The promise between a man and woman to marry.

AFFIANT. *n*. A person who makes an affidavit.

AFFIDAVIT. *n*. 1. A written statement supported by the oath of the deponent or by a solemn affirmation, administered and attested by any person authorized by law to administer oaths. Includes a statutory declaration. Various statutes. 3. An affirmation when made by a person entitled to affirm. Various statutes. Includes a solemn declaration, or statutory declaration, and an agreed statement of facts. *Judicature Act*, R.S.Nfld. 1990, c. J-4, s. 2. See COMMISSIONER FOR TAKING ~S; CROSS-EXAMINATION ON ~; OATH OR ~.

AFFIDAVIT OF DOCUMENTS. A descriptive listing of the documents which a party to an action possesses, controls or has in their power.

AFFIDAVIT OF MANUFACTURER. An attestation submitted by a manufacturer on a form acceptable to the chief inspector that the boiler or pressure vessel described in it has been fabricated in accordance with an approved design which has been registered. *Public Safety Act*, S.N. 1996, c. P.-41.01, s. 9.

AFFIDAVIT OF MERITS. An affidavit which a defendant files and which responds to a specially endorsed writ.

AFFIDAVIT OF SERVICE. An affidavit certifying that a document has been served on a party to a proceeding.

AFFILIATE. *n*. Where used to indicate a relationship between corporations, means any corporation where one is the subsidiary of the other, or both are subsidiaries of the same corporation, or (a) each of them is controlled by the same person or the same group of persons, or (b) one of them is controlled by one person and the other is controlled by an associate. See FOREIGN ~.

AFFILIATED BARGAINING AGENT. A bargaining agent that, according to established trade union practice in the construction industry, represents employees who commonly bargain separately and apart from other employees and is subordinate or directly related to, or is, a provincial, national or international trade union and includes an employee bargaining agency. *Labour Relations Act*, S.O. 1995, c. 1, Sched. A, s. 151.

AFFILIATED COMPANY. One company is affiliated with another company if one of them is the subsidiary of the other or both are subsidiaries of the same company or each of them is controlled by the same person. Manitoba Statutes.

AFFILIATED POLITICAL ORGANIZATION. Any political organization that is affiliated with and endorsed by a political party or one or more constituency associations registered under this Act. *Election Finances Act*, R.S.O. 1990, c. E.7, s. 26(4).

AFFILIATION. *n*. 1. The establishment of a bond between two or more organizations. 2. A process through which a child's parentage is determined. *Kirkpatrick v. Maroughan* 1927 3 D.L.R. 546 at 548, 60 O.L.R. 495 (C.A.), Middleton J.A. See POLITICAL ~.

AFFILIATION AGREEMENT. An agreement between any person and a station that includes a provision for reserved time. *Broadcasting regulations*.

AFFILIATION ORDER. " . . . There are two parts to the order; in some jurisdictions, such as Nova Scotia, there are two distinct orders. The first part of the one order or the first of two orders establishes the respondent's paternity while the second directs the payment of maintenance for the child. Maintenance can be directed if, and only if, paternity is established." *Works v. Holt* (1976), 22 R.F.L. 1 at 11 (Ont. Prov. Ct.), Beaulieu Prov. J.

AFFILIATION PROCEEDING. An application or action to determine paternity of a child.

AFFINITAS AFFINITATIS. [L.] A relationship which is not based on affinity or consanguinity, i.e. the relationship between one's brother and one's spouse's sister.

AFFINITY. *n*. Relationship through marriage.

AFFIRM. *v*. 1. To promise in solemn form to tell the truth while giving evidence or when making an affidavit. 2. To confirm a lower court's decision. 3. When a party who is entitled to void a contract but chooses not to avoid the contract, to carry it out or act as though bound by it, the party is said to affirm the contract.

AFFIRMANCE. *n*. Confirmation of something which could be voided.

AFFIRMANT. *n*. One who solemnly affirms.

AFFIRMANTI NON NEGANTI INCUMBIT PROBATIO. [L.] The burden of proof lies on the party who is affirming a fact not on the party trying to disprove it.

AFFIRMATION. *n*. A solemn declaration with no oath. A person who objects to taking an oath may affirm, and the affirmation has the same effect as an oath. See OATH OR ~ OF CITIZENSHIP.

AFFIRMATIVE. *adj*. Asserting positively.

AFFIRMATIVE ACTION. "Affirmative action has been defined by Laycraft J.A. (as he then was) and adopted by the Supreme Court of Canada [in] Athabasca Tribal Council v. Amoco Can. Petroleum Co., [1981] 1 S.C.R. 699 . . . :'Terms and conditions imposed for the benefit of groups suffering from economic and social disadvantages, usually as a result of past discrimination, and designed to assist them to achieve equality with other segments of the population are referred to as "affirmative action" programs.'" *Shewchuk v. Ricard* (1986), 24 C.R.R. 45 at 52 2 B.C.L.R. (2d) 324 1, [1986] 4 W.W.R. 289, 1 R.F.L. (3d) 337, 28 D.L.R. (4th) 429 (C.A.), Nemetz C.J.B.C.

AFFIRMATIVE DEFENCE. Also called confession and avoidance. The defendant confesses or admits the facts alleged but then states fresh facts or grounds which afford an answer to them. *Ryan v. Kirby* (1993), 25 C.P.C. (3d) 34 (P.E.I. T.D.).

AFFIRMATIVE EASEMENT. Confers a right on its holder to commit an act or acts upon the servient easement.

AFFIRMATIVE PREGNANT. An assertion implying a negation in favour of the adverse party.

AFFIXED. *adj*. As applied to goods means erected upon or affixed or annexed to land in such manner and under such circumstances as to constitute them fixtures. *Conditional Sales* acts.

AFFOREST. *v*. To change land into forest.

AFFORESTATION. *n*. Changing land to forest.

AFFRANCHISE. *v*. To make free.

AFFRAY. *n*. The act of fighting in any public street or highway, or fighting to the alarm of the public in any other place to which the public have access. *Criminal Code*, R.S.C. 1927, c. 36, s. 100.

AFFREIGHTMENT. *n*. A contract in which a shipowner agrees to carry goods in exchange for a reward.

AFL. *abbr*. American Federation of Labour.

AFORESAID. *adj* Mentioned previously.

AFORETHOUGHT. *adj*. Considered or thought of previously. See MALICE ~.

A FORTIORI. [L.] 1. By so much stronger reason. 2. Much more.

AFFRONT. *v*. To insult; to offend especially by showing disrespect.

AFFRONT. *n*. A word or act showing intentional disrespect.

AFTER-ACQUIRED CLAUSE. In a security instrument, a charge on the debtor's future or after-acquired property as well as any additions to the property which the debtor may acquire. F. Bennett, *Receiverships* (Toronto: Carswell, 1985) at 28.

AFTER-ACQUIRED PROPERTY. Property acquired after marriage. See AFTERACQUIRED CLAUSE.

AFTERBIRTH. *n*. Placenta.

AFTERCARE. *n*. The assistance made available to persons discharged from imprisonment, parole or probation. *Corrections Act*, R.S.N.W.T. 1988, c. C-22, s.1.

AFTER DATE. In a bill of exchange, a phrase fixing the date of payment, e.g., two months after date, pay . . .".

AFTERGLOW. *n*. The glow remaining on the splint of a match after the flame has been extinguished. *Hazardous Products (Matches) Regulations* C.R.C., c. 929 s. 2.

AFTER-MARKET. *n*. The market in a security once it has been sold initially by the issuer.

AFTER PERPENDICULAR. A perpendicular that coincides with the after end of the length (L) of a ship. *Load Line Regulations (Inland)*, C.R.C., c. 1440, s. 1.

AFTER SIGHT. To specify time for payment of a bill of exchange the time must be specified and begins with the date of acceptance by the drawee.

AFT PERPENDICULAR. A perpendicular that coincides with the after side of the rudder post, or where no rudder post is fitted, with the centreline of the rudder stock. *Arctic Shipping Pollution Prevention Regulations*, C.R.C., c. 353, schedule VI, s. 1.

A(F) ULTIMATE AND A(F) AND A(M) ULTIMATE TABLES. The tables so entitled appearing in the "Mortality of Annuitants 1900-1920" published on behalf of the Institute of Actuaries and The Faculty of Actuaries in Scotland, 1924. *Public Service Superannuation Regulations*, C.R.C., c. 1358, s. 2.

A(F) ULTIMATE TABLE. The table so entitled appearing in the "Mortality of Annuitants 1900-1920" published on behalf of the Institute of Actuaries and the Faculty of Actuaries in Scotland, 1924.

A.G. *abbr*. Attorney General.

AGAINST INTEREST. Used to describe a statement or admission which is adverse to the position or interest of the person making the statement or admission.

AGE. *n*. 1. " . . . [I]ndicia of maturity, reflecting a length of time which a being or thing has been in existence . . ." *R. v. Panarctic Oils Ltd.* (1982), 12 C.E.L.R. 78 at 92 (N.W.T. Terr. Ct.), Bourassa Terr. Ct. J. 2. 18 years of age or older. *Human Rights, Citizenship and Multiculturalism Act*, R.S.A. 2000, c. H-14, s. 44(1). 3. Any age of 18 years or more but less than 65 years. *Saskatchewan Human Rights Code*, S.S. 1979, c. S-24.1, s. 2. 4. An age that is 18 years or more, except in subsection 5(1) where "age" means an age that is 18 years or more and less than 65 Years. *Human Rights Code* R.S.O. 1990, c. H.19, s.10(1)/5. The period during which an alcoholic beverage is kept under such conditions of storage as may be necessary to render it potable or to develop its characteristic flavour or bouquet. *Food and Drug Regulations*, C.R.C., c. 870, s. B.02.002. See CERTIFICATE OF ~; FULL ~; LEGAL ~; NON ~; PENSIONABLE ~ RETIREMENT ~.

AGE CERTIFICATE. Document issued in connection with statutory restrictions on child labour and authorizing employment of a minor.

AGED. *adj.* An individual who has reached 65 years of age or in some cases 55. *Alcoholism Foundation of Manitoba v. Winnipeg (City)* [1990] 6 W.W.R. 232 (Man.C.A.).

AGENCY. *n.* 1. A relationship existing between two persons. One, called the agent, is legally considered to represent the other, called the principal, in a way which affects the principal's legal position in relation to third parties. G.H.L. Fridman, *The Law of Agency*, 6th ed. (London: Butterworths, 1990) at 9. 2. " . . . [A] local place of business from which an agent acts for his principal, ..." Minister *of National Revenue v. Panther Oil & Grease Manufacturin Co.*, [1961] C.T.C. 363 at 378 61 D.T.C. 1212 (Ex. Ct.), Thorson P. See APPROPRIATE ~; BURGLAR ALARM ~; CANADIAN INTERNATIONAL DEVELOPMENT~; CHIEF ~; CHIEF EXECUTIVE OFFICER OF AN ~; CLEARING ~; COLLECTION ~; CROWN ~; DESIGNATED ~; DETECTIVE ~; DOUBLE ~; EMERGENCY SERVICE AGENCIES; EMPLOYMENT ~; EXPRESS~; EXTRA-PROVINCIAL ~; GOVERNMENT~; GOVERNMENT RELATED ~; HEALTH~; INDIAN ~; INNOCENT ~; INSURANCE ~; LAW OF ~; MARKETING ~; NONPROFIT ~; PAY ~; PERSONAL REPORTING ~; PLACEMENT PROMOTIONAL~; PUBLIC ~; PUBLIC HOUSING ~; REPORTING ~; SECURITY GUARD ~; SELLING ~; SETTLEMENT ~.

AGENCY BY ESTOPPEL. A relationship legally treated as one of principal and agent, in which the parties conduct seems to express consent that they are principal and agent. G.H.L. Fridman, *The Law of Agency*, 6th ed. (London: Butterworths, 1990) at 98-9.

AGENCY FROM COHABITATION. A rebuttable presumption of fact that one spouse actually still cohabiting with the other is the other's agent. G.H.L. Fridman, *The Law of Agency*, 6th ed. (London: Butterworths, 1990) at 130.

AGENCY OF A FOREIGN STATE. Any legal entity that is an organ of the foreign state but that is separate from the foreign state. *State Immunity Act*, R.S.C. 1985, c. S-18, s. 2.

AGENCY OF GOVERNMENT. Any board, commission, association, or other body, whether incorporated or unincorporated, that is established under an Act of the Legislature and all the members of which, or all the members of the board of management or board of directors of which, (i) are appointed by an Act of the Legislature or the Lieutenant Governor in Council, and (ii) in the discharge of their duties are public officers or servants of the Crown, or for the proper discharge of their duties are, directly or indirectly, responsible to the Crown.

AGENCY OF NECESSITY. A form of agency which arises when a person, in an emergency, acts on behalf of another despite the lack of a formal agreement between the persons to this effect.

AGENCY OF THE CROWN. (i) Any board, commission, association, or other body, whether incorporated or unincorporated, all the members of which, or all the members of the board of management or board of directors of which, (A) are appointed by an Act of the Legislature or by order of the Lieutenant Governor in Council; or (B) if not so appointed, in the discharge of their duties are public officers or servants of the Crown, or for the proper discharge of their duties are, directly or indirectly, responsible to the Crown; or (ii) any corporation the election of the board of directors of which is controlled by the Crown, directly or indirectly, through ownership of shares of the capital stock thereof by the Crown or by a boar commission, association, or other body to which sub-cause applies. See CROWN AGENT.

AGENCY OF THE GOVERNMENT. Any board, commission, association, or other body, whether incorporated or unincorporated, all the members of which, or all the members of board of management or board of directors of which, (a) are appointed by an Act of the Legislature or by the Lieutenant Governor in Council; or (b) if not so appointed, are, in the discharge of their duties, public officers or servants of the Crown, or, for the proper discharge of their duties are, directly or indirectly responsible to the Crown. Manitoba statutes.

AGENCY STORE. A liquor store operated by an agent.

AGENDA. *n*. A schedule or list of the business items to be considered at a meeting.

AGENT. *n*. 1. One who acts for another whether for any form of remuneration or not. 2. [A]nyone who does something for another is for that very limited purpose an "agent" *Penderville Apartments Development Partnership v. Cressey Development Corp.* (1990), 43 B.C.L.R. (2d) 57 (B.C. C.A.), Southin, J.A. 3. A person who, for another or others, for compensation, gain or reward, or hope or promise thereof, either alone or through one or more officials or salesmen, trades in real estate. 4. Used to describe the position of a person who is employed by another to perform duties often of a technical or a professional nature which he discharges as that other's alter ego and not merely as a conduit pipe between the principal and the third party. *MacDonald v. Roth*, 2000 CarswellBC 2416, 2000 BCSC 1670, 83 B.C.L.R. (3d) 171.5. A person who has a mandate to represent a candidate in a polling-station. *Elections acts*. 6. In relation to the government of a foreign state or any political subdivision thereof, a person empowered to perform a function or duty on behalf of the government of the foreign state or political subdivision, other than a function or duty in connection with the administration or management of the estate or property of an individual. 7. A person appointed by the owner of a mine site, mine or coal processing plant to act as a representative of the owner. 8. Includes an employee. Criminal Code, R.S.C. 1985, c. C-46, s. 426(4). See AUTHORIZED ~; BARGAINING ~; BIOLOGICAL ~; BUSINESS~; CANDIDATE'S ~; CHIEF ~; COLLECTING ~; COLLECTION~; COMMISSION ~; CROWN ~; DEL CREDERE ~; DIRECT ~; EMPLOYER'S ~; EXCLUSIVE~; FISCAL ~; FORWARDING ~; GELLING~; GENERAL ~; IMMUNIZING ~; INFECTIOUS ~; INSURANCE ~; JELLING ~; LAND ~; LITERARY~; MANAGING ~; MERCANTILE ~; NEWS~; OFFICIAL ~; PARLIAMENTARY ~; PARTICULAR ~; PATENT ~; PRINCIPAL AND ~; RECORDED ~; RECORDING ~; REGISTERING ~; REVISING ~; SOLICITING ~; SPECIAL ~; TRADE MARK ~; TRANSFER ~; TRAVEL ~.

AGENT CORPORATION. A Crown corporation that is expressly declared by or pursuant to any other Act of Parliament to be an agent of the Crown. *Financial Administration Act*, R.S.C. 1985, c. F-11, s. 83.

AGENTES ET CONSENTIENTES PARI POENA PLECTENTUR. [L.] Those who do something and those who consent to its being done are punished equally.

AGENT-GENERAL. *n*. The representative of a province in another country.

AGENT OF A CANDIDATE. A person authorized in writing by a candidate to represent that candidate at an election or at any proceeding of an election.

AGENT OF A PARTICIPANT. A person who by a record admitted in evidence under this section appears to be or is otherwise proven to be an officer, agent, servant, employee or representative of a participant. *Competition Act*, R.S.C. 1985, c. 34, s. 69(1).

AGENT OF NECESSITY. See AGENCY OF NECESSITY.

AGENT OF THE CROWN. See CROWN AGENCY.

AGENT OF THE STATE. A peace officer and a person acting under the authority of, or in cooperation with, a peace officer. *Criminal Code*, R.S.C. 1985, c. C-46, s. 184.1(4).

AGENT PROVOCATEUR. ". . . [O]ne who . . . provides the opportunity for a person to commit a crime that of his own volition and intent and without encouragement he intended to commit when opportunity presented itself, . . ." *R. v. Shipley*, [1970] 2 presented 411 at 414 (Co. Ct.), McAndrew Co. Ct. J.

AGENT'S LIEN. The right of an agent to retain goods in her possession until the principal pays the amount owing to the agent in respect of the goods.

AGE OF CONSENT. The age at which a person may marry without parental approval.

AGE OF CRIMINAL RESPONSIBILITY. The age at which a child may be held responsible for a criminal act.

AGE OF MAJORITY. 18 or 19 years of age; traditionally was 21 years of age; the age at which a person has full rights and responsibilities in legal matters.

AGE OF RETIREMENT. Of a judge, means the age, fixed by law, at which the judge ceases to hold office. *Judges Act*, R.S.C. 1985, c. J-1, s. 2. See RETIREMENT AGE.

AGGRAVATED ASSAULT. Wounding, maiming, disfiguring or endangering the life of the complainant. *Criminal Code* R.S.C. 1985 c. C46, s 268.

AGGRAVATED DAMAGES. 1. " . . . [A]warded to compensate for aggravated damage . . . take account of intangible injuries and by definition will generally augment damages assessed under the general rules relating to the assessment of damages . . ." *Vorvis v. Insurance Corp. of B.C.*, [1989] 1 S.C.R. 1085 at 1099, McIntyre J. 2. Aggravated damages may be awarded in circumstances where the defendant's conduct has been particularly high-handed or oppressive, thereby increasing the plaintiff's humiliation and anxiety arising from the libellous statement. If aggravated damages are to be awarded, there must be a finding that the defendant was motivated by actual malice, which increased the injury to the plaintiff, either by spreading further afield the damage to the reputation of the plaintiff, or by increasing the mental distress and humiliation of the plaintiff. *Hill v. Church of Scientology* [1995] 2 S.C.R. 1130.

AGGRAVATED SEXUAL ASSAULT. Wounding, maiming, disfiguring or endangering the life of the complainant in committing a sexual assault. *Criminal Code*, R.S.C. 1985, c. C-46, s. 273.

AGGRAVATING CIRCUMSTANCE. In sentencing an individual convicted of an offence, the following are deemed to be aggravating circumstances: (i) evidence that the offence was motivated by bias, prejudice or hate based on race, national or ethnic origin, language, colour, religion, sex, age, mental or physical disability, sexual orientation, or any other similar factor, (ii) evidence that the offender, in committing the offence, abused the offender's spouse or common-law partner or child, (iii) evidence that the offender, in committing the offence, abused a position of trust or authority in relation to the victim, or (iv) evidence that the offence was committed for the benefit of, at the direction of or in association with a criminal organization. *Criminal Code*, R.S.C. 1985, c. C-46, s. 718.2,(part).

AGGRAVATION. *n*. Increasing the enormity of a wrong.

AGGREGATE. *n*. 1. Collection of people, parts or things in order to form a whole. 2. " . . . [I]mplies a plurality of units whose total amount it represents." *Minister of National Revenue v. Imperial Oil Ltd.*, [1960] C.T.C. 275 at 297, [1960] S.C.R. 735, 60 D.T.C. 1219, 25 D.L.R.

(2d) 321, Ritchie J. (Kerwin C.J.C., Judson and Martland JJ. concurring). 3. Gravel, sand, clay, earth, shale, stone, limestone, dolostone, sandstone, marble, granite, rock other than metallic ores, or other prescribed material. Aggregate Resources Act, R.S.O. 1990, c. A.8, c. 1. See CORPORATION ~; INDUSTRIAL ~.

AGGREGATE LAND HOLDING. Of a person, includes all land holdings of that person and all land holdings of that person's spouse and dependent children.

AGGREGATION. *n*. Adding together all property passing at death in a single estate to ascertain succession.

AGGRESSOR. *n*. One who begins a quarrel or dispute.

AGGRIEVED. *adj*. 1. " . . . [A] party is aggrieved or may be aggrieved [under the Ombudsman Act, R.S.B.C. 1979, c. 306, s. 10] whenever he genuinely suffers, or is seriously threatened with, any form of harm prejudicial to his interests, whether or not a legal right is called into question." *British Columbia Development Corp. v. British Columbia (Ombudsman)* (1984), 11 Admin L.R. 113 at 136, [1984] 2 S.C.R. 447, [1985] 1 W.W.R. 193, 55 N.R. 298, 14 D.L.R. (4th) 129, the court per Dickson J. 2. " . . . [W]ronged . . ." *Friends of Toronto Parkland v. Toronto (City)* (1991), 6 O.R. (3d) 196 at 205, 86 D.L.R. (4th) 669, 8 M.P.L.R. (2d) 127 (Div. Ct.), O'Driscoil, Hartt and O'Brien JJ. See PERSON ~.

AGISTER. *n*. A person other than a livery, boarding or sales stable keeper who, for a money consideration or its equivalent, feeds, grazes, stables, boards or cares for animals. *Agisters and Livery Stable Keepers Act*, R.S.N.W.T. 1974, c. A-2, s. 2.

AGISTMENT. *n*. . . . [A] contract of bailment for the benefit of both bailor and bailee. The contract implies, in the absence of special agreement, that the agister will use due care and diligence in keeping the animals taken in by him in return for compensation to be paid by their owner . . ." *McCauley v. Huber* (1920), 54 D.L.R. 150 at 153, [1920] 3 W.W.R. 123, 13 Sask. L.R. 401 (C.A.), Lamont J.A. (Elwood J.A. concurring).

AGL. Above ground level. *Canadian Aviation Regulations*, SOR/96-433, s. 101.01(1).

AGNATE. *n*. A relative by the father's side.

AGNATION. *n.* Relatedness by the father's side.

AGNOMEN. *n.* Nickname; a name which originates in a personal condition or attribute.

AGNOMINATION. *n.* A surname.

AGONAL. *adj.* Relating to the last moments of life. F. A. Jaffe, *A Guide to Pathological Evidence*, 3d ed. (Toronto: Carswell, 1991) at 211.

AGONY OF COLLISION. The doctrine of agony of collision arises in circumstances where a party, often a motorist, is suddenly confronted by an emergency situation of someone else's making, which the party is then unable to avoid. The doctrine comes to the assistance of such a party who may happen to make a wrong decision in attempting to avoid the hazard *provided that* the party confronted by the emergency has not been negligent. *Leddicote v. Nova Scotia (Attorney General)* 2002 NSCA 47, 203 N.S.R. (2d) 271, 635 A.P.R. 271, 28 M.V.R. (4th) 189.

AGONY OF THE MOMENT. This doctrine relieves a driver from having to exercise extraordinary skill, presence of mind, poise or self control when an emergency situation arises through no fault of her own. If the driver's instantaneous reaction was not inherently unreasonable her contract will not attract liability even though it might otherwise be considered to be negligent in other circumstances.

AGREE. *v.* To concur; to make an agreement.

AGREED. *adj.* Settled.

AGREED CHARGE. A charge agreed on between a carrier and a shipper as provided in this Act and includes the conditions attached thereto. *Transport Act*, R.S.C. 1985, c. T-17, s. 2.

AGREED STATEMENT OF FACTS. A statement of facts relating to evidence to which the parties agree and on which the case will be decided. P.K. McWilliams, *Canadian Criminal Evidence*, 3d ed. (Aurora: Canada Law Book, 1988) at 1-13.

AGREEING PROVINCE. A province that has entered into an agreement with the government of Canada under which the government of Canada will collect taxes payable under that province's income tax statute and will make payments to that province in respect of the taxes so collected. *Provincial Income Tax acts.*

AGREEMENT. *n.* 1. Two or more persons together express a common intention in order to alter their duties and rights. 2. A contract. 3. A collective agreement. 4. ". . . [I]n its more proper and correct sense, as signifying a mutual contract on consideration between two or more parties . . ." *Wain v. Walters* (1804), 5 East 10 at 16-17, Lord Ellenborough C.J. 5. " . . . used, as synonymous to promise or undertaking,. . ." *Wain v. Walters* (1804), 5 East 10 at 16-17, Lord Ellenborough C.J. 6. Conspiracy is a form of agreement which may be actual or tacit. An agreement requires the meeting of minds. Discussion, negotiation and talking alone do not constitute an agreement. See AFFILIATION ~; ALLUNION ~; APPRENTICESHIP ~; ARBITRATION~; AREA~; ASSOCIATION ~; ASSUMPTION ~; BACK-TO-WORK ~; BOUNDARY BY~; COHABITATION ~; COLLECTIVE ~; COLLECTIVE BARGAINING ~; COMMERCIAL ~; COMPANY-WIDE~; CREDIT ~; CULTURAL PROPERTY ~; CUSTODY ~; GUARDIANSHIP ~; HIRE-PURCHASE ~; INDUSTRY-WIDE ~; INTERGOVERNMENTAL ~; INTERIM ~; LISTING ~; LOAN ~; MARY CARTER ~; MASTER ~; MEDICAL-SURGICAL SERVICES ~; MEMORANDUM OF ~; NATURAL RESOURCES ~; PAROL ~; PATERNITY ~; POOLING ~; PRICE MAINTENANCE ~; PRODUCTIVITY ~; PURCHASE ~; RECIPROCAL TAXATION ~; RECIPROCAL TRANSFER ~; RECOGNITION ~; RECREATIONAL ~; REINSURANCE ~; RESIDENTIAL TENANCY ~; SECURITY ~; SEPARATION ~; SOLUS ~; SPECIALIZATION ~; SPOUSAL ~; SUBDIVISION ~; TAX RENTAL ~; TENANCY ~; TIMBER ~; TIME SALE ~; TRADE ~; UNANIMOUS SHAREHOLDER ~; UNDERWRITING ~; UNIT ~; VARIABLE RATE ~.

AGREEMENT FOR SALE. A contract for the sale of an interest in land under which the purchaser agrees to pay the purchase price over a period of time, in the manner stated in the contract, and on payment of which the vendor is obliged to convey the interest in land to the purchaser, but does not include a contract under which (a) the purchase price is payable in less than 6 months from the time the contract was entered into, and (b) the purchaser is not, during the 6 month period, entitled to possession of the land that is the subject-matter of the contract. British Columbia statutes.

AGREEMENT OF TRANSFER. The agreement made on the twentieth day of March, 1930, between the Government of Canada and the Government of Saskatchewan for the transfer of the natural resources of the province, and set forth in the schedule to chapter 87 of the statutes of 1930, and includes all amendments pursuant thereto. *The Provincial Lands Act*, R.S.S. 1978, c. P-31, s. 2.

AGREEMENT TO SELL. 1. A contract of sale in writing under which (i) an interest in goods may be transferred to a purchaser (A) at a time in the future, or (B) subject to some condition to be fulfilled. 2. A written agreement, made between a grain elevator operator and an owner of grain, for the sale of grain that is stored or to be stored. *Grains Act*, R.S.O. 1990, c. G.10, s. 1.

AGRICULTURAL. *adj*. Pertaining to agriculture, farming.

AGRICULTURAL AND VOCATIONAL COLLEGE. A college established pursuant to this Act for the purpose of teaching practical and scientific farming, household economy, domestic science and such other subjects as the Board prescribes. *Agricultural and Vocational Colleges Act*, R.S.A. 1970, c. 9, s. 2.

AGRICULTURAL CHEMICAL. Any substance or mixture of substances intended or represented for use, or sold, as a fertilizer, pesticide, plant growth regulator or soil supplement, or any other substance or mixture of substances used to control plant or animal pests or to promote or control plant growth, except drugs and medicines intended for human or veterinary use.

AGRICULTURAL COMMODITY. Any natural or processed product of agriculture.

AGRICULTURAL CORPORATION. A corporation: (i) that is engaged in the business of farming; and (ii) the majority of issued voting shares of which are legally or beneficially owned by producers who are resident persons. *The Saskatchewan Farm Security Act*, S.S. 1988-89, c. S-17.1, s. 2(1).

AGRICULTURAL CREDIT. Financial assistance given to a farm operator. *Agricultural Credit Act*, R.S.B.C. 1996, c. 9, s. 1.

AGRICULTURAL EQUIPMENT. Implements, apparatus, appliances and machinery, of any kind usually affixed to real property for use on a farm but does not include property, farm electric system.

AGRICULTURAL EXPLOITATION. A farm, developed by the farmer personally or through employees. Quebec statutes.

AGRICULTURAL FAIR ASSOCIATION. An organization of district, county or provincial scope whose purpose is to hold exhibitions of livestock, poultry, agricultural produce and the products of kindred agricultural and homemaking arts. *Agricultural Associations Act*, R.S.N.B. 1973, s. A-5, s. 1.

AGRICULTURAL FEEDS. Includes all feed for livestock, all hay and straw and any drug or medicine fed to or injected into livestock or poultry. *Retail Sales Tax Act*, R.R.O. 1990, Reg. 1012, s. 1(1).

AGRICULTURAL IMPLEMENT. A vehicle designed and adapted exclusively for agricultural, horticultural or livestock raising operations. *Highway Traffic Act*, S.S. 1986, c. H-3.1, s. 2.

AGRICULTURAL IMPLEMENTS. Tools, implements, apparatus, appliances and machines, of any kind not usually affixed to real property, for use on or in connection with a farm, and vehicles for use in the business of farming and, without restricting the generality of the foregoing, includes plows, harrows, drills, seeders, cultivators, mowing machines, reapers, binders, threshing machines, combines, leaf tobacco tying machines, tractors, movable granaries, trucks for carrying products of agriculture, equipment for bee-keeping, cream separators, churns, washing machines, spraying apparatus, portable irrigation apparatus, incubators, milking machines, refrigerators and heating and cooking appliances for farming operations or use in the farm home of a kind not usually affixed to real property. *Bank Act*, R.S.C. 1991, c. 46, s. 425(1).

AGRICULTURAL INDUSTRY. Includes all aspects of the production, processing and distribution of agricultural products and related services. *Farm Product Industry Act*, R.S.B.C. 1979, c. 124, s. 1.

AGRICULTURAL LAND. Land that is zoned for agricultural use, or is assessed or is actually used as farm or agricultural land or as an orchard.

AGRICULTURAL LIMESTONE. Includes pulverized limestone and marl for use on lands. *Agriculture and Marketing Act*, R.S.N.S. 1989, c. 6, s. 72.

AGRICULTURAL OPERATION. 1. The production or any step in the production of livestock, grain, forage crops, poultry, furs, honey or any other agricultural product. 2. An agricultural, aquacultural, horticultural or silvicultural operation that is carried on in the expectation of gain or reward. *Farming and Food Production Protection Act, 1998*, S.O. 1998, c. 1, s. 1(1). *Farm Practices Protection Act*, R.S.O. 1990 c. F.6 s. 1.

AGRICULTURAL OPERATIONS COOP-ERATIVE. A cooperative whose main object and principal activity is the operation of an economic farm of which it is the owner or lessee, provided that all of its members are natural persons, that at least sixty per cent of the common shares are owned by farm operators and that the majority of its members are farm operators among whom the principal occupation of the majority is the operation of such farm. Quebec statutes.

AGRICULTURAL OPERATIONS COR-PORATION. A corporation whose principal object and principal activity is the operation of an economic farm of which it is the owner or lessee, provided that all of its shareholders are physical persons and that not less than sixty per cent of the issued shares of each class are owned by farm operators among whom the principal occupation of the majority is the operation of such farm. Quebec statutes.

AGRICULTURAL OPERATIONS PART-NERSHIP. (1) A partnership whose principal object is the joint operation of an economic farm of which it is the owner or lessee, composed of natural persons and in which at least sixty per cent of the interests are owned by one or several farm operators the principal occupation of whom or of the majority of whom is the operation of such farm; or (2) several natural persons who are the undivided owners of an economic farm when at least sixty per cent of the property rights in such farm are held by one or several farm operators the principal occupation of whom or the majority of whom is the operation of such farm. Quebec statutes.

AGRICULTURAL PRODUCT. 1. Livestock (including fur-bearing animals raised in captivity), eggs, poultry, milk, vegetables, fruit, honey and maple syrup and products thereof, leaf tobacco, grass seed, legume seed, feed grains and oil seed, fleeces and skins of animals. (i) Any product of agriculture or of a forest, lake or river; (ii) any edible or inedible article that is wholly or partly manufactured or derived from a product described in subclause (i); or (iii) any product that may be of benefit to the agriculture or food industry that the Lieutenant Governor in Council

may designate by regulation as an agricultural product. *The Agri-Food Act*, S.S. 1990-91, c. A-15.2, s. 2.

AGRICULTURAL PROPERTY. Includes dwelling-houses, stables, barns, sheds and out buildings and their contents, wagons, carriages, and other vehicles, saddles and harnesses, agricultural engines, implements, tools, instruments, appliances and machinery, household goods, wearing apparel, provisions, musical instruments, libraries, livestock, growing crops, and crops severed from the land, fruit and ornamental trees, shrubs and plants, and live or standing timber, being upon farms as farm property, and owned by members of the insurer in which the property is insured. *Insurance Act*, R.S.O. 1990, c. 1.8, s. 142.

AGRICULTURAL SOCIETY. A community group of farmers organized for the general promotion of agriculture within that community. *Agricultural Associations Act*, R.S.N.B. 1973, c. A-5, s. 1.

AGRICULTURAL WASTE. Waste, other than sewage, resulting from farm operations, including animal husbandry and where a farm operation is carried on in respect of food packing, food preserving, animal slaughtering or meat packing, includes the waste from such operations. *General —Waste Management Act*, R.R.O. 1990, Reg. 347, s. 1(1).

AGRICULTURE. *n.* 1. The cultivation of the soil or the raising of livestock. 2. Includes tillage of the soil, livestock raising, beekeeping, poultry raising, dairying, fruit growing, woodlot management and fur farming. See PRODUCTS OF ~.

AGRICULTURE CANADA. The federal government department responsible for programmes, policies and regulations which relate to agriculture and food.

AGRICULTURIST. *n.* A person who uses farm land for agricultural or forestry production. *Pesticides Act*, R.R.O. 1990, Reg. 914, s. 1.

AGROLOGIST. *n.* A person who is qualified to teach or to practise the science and art of agriculture or to conduct scientific experiments and research in relation thereto.

AGROLOGIST IN TRAINING. A person registered as an agrologist in training under an act.

AGROLOGY. *n.* 1. The acquisition or application of scientific knowledge relating to agriculture. 2. Engaging in a professional capacity in advising on, investigating, experimenting in, teaching or demonstrating scientific principles and practices relating to any of the following: (a) the cultivation, production, improvement, use or protection of agricultural plants; (b) the raising, feeding, improving, protecting or using of farm animals or poultry; (c) the production or protection of milk; (d) the classification, cultivation, use, fertilization, conservation or improvement for agricultural purposes of arable, forest and range land; (e) the making of economic surveys of any aspect of the agricultural industry; (f) the agricultural use of machinery or equipment; (g) the identification or control of pests of agricultural plants and animals; *Agrologists Act*, R.S.B.C. 1996, c. 12, s. 1. See PRACTISE ~.

A.I.C. *abbr*. Affaires d'immigration en appel.

AID. *v*. " . . . [T]o assist or help." *R. v. Stevenson* (1984), 11 C.C.C. (3d) 443 at 449, 62 N.S.R. (2d) 193, 136 A.P.R. 193 (C.A.), the court per Macdonald J.A.

AID. *n*. 1. Assistance. 2. A useful device. 3. A person who provides assistance. See FIRST- ~; HEARING ~; LEGAL ~; MEDICAL ~; VETERINARY ~.

AID AND ABET. 1. Aiding and abetting in the commission of an offence requires two components, a physical, (act, gesture, words done, made or spoken during the commission of the offence), and a mental component, (intention). 2. "Mere presence at the scene of a crime is not sufficient to ground culpability. Something more is needed: encouragement of the principal offender; an act which facilitates the commission of the offence, such as keeping watch or enticing the victim away, or an act which tends to prevent or hinder interference with accomplishment of the criminal act, such as preventing the intended victim from escaping or being ready to assist the prime culprit . . . Presence at the commission of an offence can be evidence of aiding and abetting [Criminal Code, R.S.C. 1970, c. C-34, s. 21(1)(b)] if accompanied by other factors, such as prior knowledge of the principal offender's intention to commit the offence or attendance for the purpose of encouragement." *R. v. Dunlop* (1979) 99 D.L.R. 3d 301 at 301 at 313, 317, [1979] 2 S.C.R. 881, [1979] 4 W.W.R. 599, 47 C.C.C. (2d) 93, 8 C.R. (3d) 349, 12 C.R. (3d) 330, 27 N.R. 153, Dickson J. (Laskin C.J.C., Spence and Estey JJ. concurring). 3. "An accused who is present at the scene of an offence and who carries out no overt acts to aid or encourage the commission of the offence may none the less be convicted as a party if his purpose in failing to act was to aid in the commission of the offence . . . The authorities to which I have referred support the conclusion that where the accused had a duty to prevent the commission of an offence, or where he was in a position to have control over the acts of the offender and failed to prevent the commission of the offence, he will be guilty as an aider and abettor." *R. v. Nixon* (1990), 57 C.C.C. (3d) 97 at 109, 114, 47 B.C.L.R. (2d) 222, 78 C.R. (3d) 349, [1990] 6 W.W.R. 253 (C.A.), the court per Legg J.A.

AIDE. See NURSING ~; TEACHER ~.

AIDS. *abbr*. The acquired immune deficiency syndrome.

AID TO NAVIGATION. A buoy, beacon, lighthouse, landmark, radio aid to marine navigation or any other structure or device installed, built or maintained in or on water or on land for the purpose of assisting with marine navigation. *Canada Shipping Act, 2001*, S.C. 2001, c. 26, s. 125.

AIR. *n*. 1. The atmosphere, but does not include the atmosphere in a mine or human-made enclosure that is not open to the weather. 2. Open air not enclosed in a building, structure, machine, chimney, stack, tank, building, or flue. 3. Includes enclosed air. *Environmental Assessment Act*, R.S.O. 1990, c. E.18, s. 1. See AMBIENT ~; CARRIAGE BY ~ ACT; COMPRESSED ~; OPEN ~.

AIR AMBULANCE. Ambulance service using aircraft.

AIR BRAKE SYSTEM. A system that uses air as a medium for transmitting pressure or force from the driver control to the service brake, but does not include a system that uses compressed air or vacuum only to assist the driver in applying muscular force to hydraulic or mechanical components. *Motor Vehicle Safety Regulations*, C.R.C., c. 1038, s. 2.

AIR BREAK. The unobstructed vertical distance between the lowest point of an indirectly connected waste pipe and the flood level rim of the fixture into which it discharges. *Building Code*, O. Reg., 403/97, s. 1.1.3.2(1).

AIR CARRIER. Any person who operates a commercial air service. See CANADIAN ~; CERTIFIED ~; FOREIGN ~; .

AIR CONDITIONING. The process of treating air to control simultaneously its temperature, humidity, cleanliness, and distribution to meet the comfort requirements of the occupants of the conditioned space. *Building Code*, O. Reg., 403/97, s. 1.1.3.2(1). See REFRIGERATION AND ~ MECHANIC.

AIR CONTAMINANT. Any solid, liquid, gas or odour or a combination of any of them that, if emitted into the ambient air, would create or contribute to the creation of air pollution.

AIRCRAFT. *n.* 1. Any machine capable of deriving support in the atmosphere from reactions of the air. 2. Flying machines and guided missiles that derive their lift in flight chiefly from aerodynamic forces, and flying devices that are supported chiefly by their buoyancy in air, and includes any aeroplane, balloon, kite balloon, airship, glider or kite; *National Defence Act*, R.S.C. 1985, c. N-5, s. 2(1). See CANADIAN ~; COMMERCIAL ~; DANGEROUS OPERATION OF ~; FALLING ~ INSURANCE; HEAVIER-THAN-AIR ~; INTERNATIONAL ~; JET-POWERED ~; LIGHTER THAN-AIR ~; MULTI-ENGINE ~; PRESSURIZED ~; PRIVATE STATE ~; TRANSPORT CATEGORY ~.

AIRCRAFT GASOLINE. Any fuel used for the operation of an aircraft or in the testing of the engine of an aircraft on the round. *Gasoline Tax Act*, R.S.M. 1987, c. G40, s. 1.

AIRCRAFT FLIGHT MANUAL. A manual, requirements for which may be established by the Minister in Part V, that contains information in respect of an aircraft. *Canadian Aviation Regulations*, SOR 96/433, s. 101.01(1).

AIRCRAFT INSURANCE. Insurance against loss of or damage to an aircraft and against liability for loss or damage to persons or property caused by an aircraft or by the operation thereof. *Insurance acts.*

AIRCRAFT MATERIAL. Engines, fittings, armament, ammunition, bombs, missiles, gear, instruments and apparatus, used or intended for use in connection with aircraft or the operation thereof, and components and accessories of aircraft and substances used to provide motive power or lubrication for or in connection with aircraft or the operation thereof. *National Defence Act*, R.S.C. 1985, c. N-5, s. 2.

AIR CUSHION VEHICLE. 1. A machine designed to derive support in the atmosphere primarily from reactions against the earth's surface of air expelled from the machine. 2. Hovercraft.

AIR EMBOLISM. Blockage of blood vessels by air bubbles. F.A. Jaffe, A *Guide to Pathological Evidence*, 3d ed. (Toronto: Carswell, 1991) at 218.

AIR GAP. The unobstructed vertical distance through air between the lowest point of a water supply outlet and the flood level rim of the fixture or device into which the outlet discharges. *Building Code Act*, O. Reg, 403/97, s. 1.1.3.2.

AIR HANDLING SYSTEM. An assembly of connected ducts, plenums or other air passages with associated fittings through which air is conducted, but does not include a cooking exhaust system. *Hotel Fire Safety Act*, R.R.O. 1980, Reg. 505, s. 2.

AIRLINE. See COMMERCIAL~.

AIR LOCK. A chamber designed for the passage of persons or material or both persons and material from one place to another place having a different air pressure. *Occupational Health and Safety Act*, O. Reg. 213/91, s. 332.

AIRPLANE. See AEROPLANE.

AIR OF REALITY. A judge in a criminal case must instruct a jury on any defence which has an "air of reality". The threshold test for air of reality is met when there is an evidentiary basis for the defence which, if believed, would allow a reasonable jury properly instructed to acquit. *R. v. Lemky* [1996] 1 S.C.R. 757.

AIR OPERATOR. The holder of an air operator certificate. *Canadian Aviation Regulations*, SOR/96-433, s. 101.01(1).

AIR OPERATOR CERTIFICATE. A certificate issued that authorizes the holder of the certificate to operate a commercial air service. *Canadian Aviation Regulations*, SOR/96-433, s. 101.01(1).

AIRPLANE. See AEROPLANE

AIR POLLUTION. A condition of the air, arising wholly or partly from the presence in the air of any substance, that directly or indirectly (a) endangers the health, safety or welfare of humans; (b) interferes with the normal enjoyment of life or property; (c) endangers the health of animal life; (d) causes damage to plant life or to property; or (e) degrades or alters, or forms part of a process of degradation or alteration of, an ecosystem to an extent that is detrimental to its use by humans, animals or plants. *Canadian Environmental Protection Act, 1999*, S.C. 1999, c. 33, s. 3(1).

AIR POLLUTION EPISODE. An occasion when air contamination is at such a level and for such a period of time that the air contamination may become the cause of increased human sickness and mortality. *General—Air Pollution Act*, R.R.O. 1990, Reg. 346, s. 1.

AIR POLLUTION INDEX. A series of numbers expressing the relative levels of air pollution and taking into consideration one or more air contaminants. *General—Air Pollution Act*, R.R.O. 1990, Reg. 346, s. 1.

AIRPORT. *n*. 1. An aerodrome in respect of which a Canadian aviation document is in force. *Aeronautics Act*, R.S.C. 1985, c. A-2, s. 3. See ALTERNATE ~; CONTROLLED ~; FEDERAL ~; OPEN ~.

AIRPORT LOUNGE. A room in an airport restricted to passengers waiting to board a departing aircraft. *Liquor Licence Act*, R.R.O. 1980, Reg. 581, s. 1.

AIRPORT MANAGER. The Department of Transport official in charge of the airport or that person's duly authorized representative.

AIRPORT SITE. Any land, not being a part of an existing airport, (a) the title to which is vested in or that otherwise belongs to Her Majesty in right of Canada, or (b) in respect of which a notice of intention to expropriate under section 5 of the Expropriation Act has been registered and that is declared by order of the Governor in Council to be required for use as an airport. *Aeronautics Act*, R.S.C. 1985 c. A-2, s. 5.4(1).

AIRPORT TRAFFIC. All traffic on the manoeuvring area of an airport or aerodrome and all aircraft flying in the vicinity of an airport or aerodrome.

AIR RACE. See LOW-LEVEL ~.

AIR RAID PRECAUTIONS WORKER. A person registered as a volunteer worker in a designated area by an official body organized for air raid precautions purposes, a duly registered voluntary evacuation worker or a person designated as such by the Commission. *Civilian War-related Benefits Act* R.S.C. 1985 c. C31, s. 30.

AIR ROUTE. The airspace within the boundaries or along the tracks specified in the *Designated Airspace Handbook*. *Canadian Aviation Regulations*, SOR/96-433, s. 101.01(1).

AIR SAMPLING. See ENVIRONMENTAL MONITORING.

AIR SERVICE. A service, provided by means of an aircraft, that is publicly available for the transportation of passengers or goods, or both. *Canada Transportation Act,*, S.C. 1996, c. 10, s. 55(1). See COMMERCIAL ~.

AIRSHIP. *n*. A power-driven lighter-than-air aircraft. *Canadian Aviation Regulations*, SOR 96-433, s. 101.01.

AIR SHOW. An aerial display or demonstration before an assembly of persons by one or more aircraft. *Canadian Aviation Regulations*, SOR 96-433, s. 101.01.

AIRSPACE. *var*. **AIR SPACE**. See CONTROLLED ~; HIGH LEVEL ~; LOW LEVEL.

AIR SPACE PARCEL. A volumetric parcel, whether or not occupied in whole or in part by a building or other structure, shown as such in an air space plan. *Land Title Act*, R.S.B.C. 1996, c. 250, s. 138.

AIR SPACE PLAN. A plan that (a) is described in the title to it as an air space plan, (b) shows on it one or more air space parcels consisting of or including air space, and (c) complies with the requirements. *Land Title Act*, R.S.B.C. 1996, c. 250, s. 138.

AIR-SUPPORTED STRUCTURE. A structure consisting of a pliable membrane which achieves and maintains its shape and support by internal air pressure. *Building Code*, R.R.O. 1980, Reg. 87, s. 1.

AIR-TERMINAL. *n*. A pointed tube or rod extending upwards from a conductor. *Lightning Rods Act*, R. R.O. 1980, Reg. 577 s. 1.

AIR-TERMINAL SUPPORT. A device used for the purpose of holding an air-terminal firmly in position. *Lightning Rods Act*, R.R.O. 1980, Reg. 577, s. 1.

AIR TIME. *var*. **AIR-TIME**. With respect to keeping technical records, the time from the moment an aircraft leaves the surface until it comes into contact with the surface at the next point of landing. *Canadian Aviation Regulations*, SOR/96-433, s. 101.01(1). See PRICE OF ~.

AIR TRAFFIC ADVISORY SERVICES. The provision by an air traffic control unit or flight service station of aeronautical safety information, including aviation weather information and serviceability reports in respect of aerodromes and radio navigation aids, but does not include the provision of IFR air traffic control messages; *Canadian Aviation Regulations*, SOR 96-433, s. 101.01.

AIR TRAFFIC CONTROL CLEARANCE. An authorization issued by an air traffic control unit that authorizes an aircraft to proceed within controlled airspace in accordance with the conditions specified by that unit; *Canadian Aviation Regulations*, SOR/96-433, s. 101.01(1).

AIR TRAFFIC CONTROL INSTRUCTION. A directive issued by an apron traffic control unit for airport apron traffic and gate control purposes. *Airport Traffic Regulations*, C.R.C., c. 886, s. 64.

AIR TRAFFIC CONTROL RECORDING. The whole or any part of any recording, transcript or substantial summary of voice communications respecting matters of air traffic control or related matters that take place between any of the following persons, namely, air traffic controllers, aircraft crew members, vehicle operators, flight service station specialists and persons who relay air traffic control messages. *Canadian Aviation Safety Board Act*,. R.S.C. 1985, c. C-12, s. 36.

AIR TRAFFIC CONTROL UNIT. (*a*) An area control centre established to provide air traffic control service to IFR aircraft, (*b*) a terminal control unit established to provide air traffic control service to IFR aircraft while they are being operated within a terminal control area, or (*c*) an air traffic control tower established to provide air traffic control service at an aerodrome. *Canadian Aviation Regulations*, SOR/96-433, s. 101.01(1).

AIR TRAFFIC SERVICES. Includes air traffic control services and advisory services; *Canadian Aviation Regulations*, SOR/96-433, s. 101.01(1).

AIR TRANSPORT. The carriage by aeroplanes or rotorcraft of persons or property or mail for hire or reward.

AIR TRANSPORT SERVICE. A commercial air service that is operated for the purpose of transporting persons, personal belongings, baggage, goods or cargo in an aircraft between two points. *Canadian Aviation Regulations*, SOR/96-433, s. 101.01(1).

AIR VENT. An outlet at the upper end of the casing that allows for equalization of air pressure between the inside of the well casing and the atmosphere, and for the release of gases from the well. *Wells Act*, R.R.O. 1990, Reg. 903, s. 1.

AIRWAY. The airspace within the boundaries or along the tracks specified in the *Designated Airspace Handbook* and within which air traffic control service is provided; *Canadian Aviation Regulations*, SOR/96-433, s. 101.01(1).

AIRWORTHINESS. See CERTIFICATE OF ~.

AIRWORTHINESS DIRECTIVE. An instruction issued by the Minister or by a civil aviation authority responsible for an aeronautical product type design that mandates a maintenance or operation action to ensure that an aeronautical product conforms to its type design and is in a condition for safe operation; *Canadian Aviation Regulations*, SOR/96-433, s. 101.01(1).

AIRWORTHINESS LIMITATION. A limitation applicable to an aeronautical product, in the form of a life limit or a maintenance task that is mandatory as a condition of the type certificate; *Canadian Aviation Regulations*, SOR/96-433, s. 101.01(1).

AIRWORTHY. *adj.* In respect of an aeronautical product, means in a fit and safe state for flight and in conformity with its type design. *Canadian Aviation Regulations*, SOR/96-433, s. 101.01(1).

AISLE. See POURING~.

ALARM. See FALSE ~ OF FIRE.

ALARM MONITOR. A security employee whose duties are, by his or her security employee licence, restricted to the monitoring of security alarms. *Private Investigators and Security Agencies Act*, R.S.B.C. 1996, c. 374, s. 1.

ALARM SERVICE. A person who (a) sells, supplies, provides, installs or offers to install security alarms, or (b) repairs, maintains, monitors or responds to security alarms that are installed on the property of another, but no person is an alarm service or carries on an alarm service merely because he or she (c) sells, supplies or provides a security alarm, if the person does not, as part of the transaction, visit or inspect premises on which the security alarm is or has been or is to be installed, or (d) monitors a security alarm installed on the property of another, if the person (i) does so for no fee or other consideration, and (ii) is not otherwise required to be licensed under this Act. *Private Investigators and Security Agencies Act*, R.S.B.C. 1996, c. 374, s. 1.

ALARM SIGNAL. An audible signal transmitted throughout a zone or zones or throughout a building to advise occupants that a fire emergency exists. *Building Code*, O. Reg., 403/97, s. 1.1.3.2(1). See RADIOTELEGRAPH ~; RADIOTELEPHONE ~.

ALBERTA. See GOVERNMENT OF ~; LAW OF ~; RESIDENT IN ~; RESIDENT OF ~.

ALBERTA BORDER PRICE. With respect to the term of a federal-provincial agreement or any period during that term, the amount determined as the Alberta border price for the term or that period, as the case may be, under the federal-provincial agreement. *Natural Gas Pricing Agreement Act*, R.S.A. 2000, c. N-4, s.1.

ALBERTA COMPANY. A body corporate incorporated and registered under the Companies Act or any of its predecessors. *Business Corporations Act*, R.S.A. 2000, c. B-9, s. 1.

ALBERTA CONTRACT. A contract of insurance made in Alberta, but does not include a contract of reinsurance. *Insurance Act*, R.S.A. 2000, c. I-3, s. 62.

ALBERTA LAND SURVEYOR. An individual who holds a certificate of registration and an annual certificate to engage in the practice of surveying under this Act. *Land Surveyors Act*, R.S.A. 2000, s. L-3, s. 1.

ALBERTAN. See RESIDENT ~.

ALBERTA RESOURCE PROPERTY. A property that is (i) a right, licence or privilege to explore for, drill for or take petroleum, natural gas or petroleum and natural gas in Alberta, (ii) a petroleum or natural gas well in Alberta, (iii) a rental or royalty computed by reference to the amount or value of production from a petroleum or natural as well in Alberta, or (iv) a right or interest of any nature whatsoever or howsoever described in any property referred to in sub-clauses (i) to (iii) including a right to receive proceeds of disposition in respect of a disposition of that. *Alberta Corporate Income Tax Act*, R.S.A. 2000 c. A-15, s. 26(1).

ALCOHOL. *n.* 1. A product of fermentation or distillation of grains, fruits or other agricultural products rectified once or more than once whatever may be the origin thereof, and includes syn-

thetic ethyl alcohol. 2. Any material or substance whether in liquid or any other form containing any proportion by mass or by volume of absolute ethyl alcohol (C_2H_5OH). *Excise Act*, R.S.C. 1985, c. E-14, s. 3. See ABSOLUTE -~; DENATURED ~; ETHYL ~; GRAIN ~; PURE GRAIN ~; SPECIALLY DENATURED ~; WOOD ~.

ALCOHOL ABUSE. " . . . [P]athological drinking plus interference with an important function of life." *Robson v Ashworth* (1985), 33 C.C.L.T. 229 at 240 (Ont. H.C.), Galligan J.

ALCOHOL AND DRUG ABUSE. The use of any substance by a person in quantities that create a condition in the person that is characterized by physical, psychological or social problems. *Alcoholism and Drug Abuse Act*, R.S.A. 2000 c. 38 s. 1. See ILLICIT DRUG USE.

ALCOHOLIC. *n.* A person who suffers from the illness of alcoholism.

ALCOHOLIC BEVERAGES. The five varieties of beverages defined in this section, namely: alcohol, spirits, wine, cider and beer, and every liquid or solid containing ethyl alcohol, spirits, wine, cider or beer and capable of being consumed by a human being. Any liquid or solid containing more than one of the five varieties above mentioned is considered as belonging to that variety which has the higher percentage of alcohol, in the following order: alcohol, spirits, wine, cider and beer. *An Act respecting the Offences Related to Alcoholic Beverages*, R.S.Q., c. C-I-8.1, s. 2.

ALCOHOLIC LIQUOR. An alcoholic, spirituous, vinous, fermented or malt liquor, or combination of liquors, and all drinks or drinkable liquids and consumable solids, patented or not, containing one per cent and upwards of alcohol by volume. *Liquor Control Act*, R.S. Nfld. 1990, c. L-18, s. 2.

ALCOHOLISM. *n.* 1. Any diseased condition produced by the action of alcohol upon the human system. 2. Any dependent condition produced by the action of alcohol on the human system. 3. A chronic behavioural disorder manifested by the consumption by a person of alcoholic beverages to an extent that substantially interferes with the person's health or ability to function in relation to his or her social and economic responsibilities. *Alcohol and Drug Dependency Commission Act*, R.S. Nfld. 1990, c. A-8, c. 2.

ALDERMAN. *n.* A member of a council of a municipality other than the mayor.

ALDERPERSON. *n.* A member of municipal council other than the mayor.

ALEATORY CONTRACT. A contract which depends on an uncertain event or contingency. Raoul Colinvaux, *The Law of Insurance* 5th ed. (London: Sweet & Maxwell, 1984) at 3.

ALERT SIGNAL. An audible signal to advise designated persons of a fire emergency. *Building Code Act*, O. Reg, 403/97, s. 1.1.3.2.

ALGORITHM. *n.* An algorithm is a formal procedure for any mathematical operation. There can be many algorithmic ways of expressing the same functional requirement. While an algorithm in itself is an idea, the specific expression of algorithms within the context of a computer program can be the subject of copyright. *Teklogix Inc. v. Zaino* (1997), 79 C.P.R. (3d) 1 (Ont. Gen. Div.)

ALGOR MORTIS. [L.] The cold state of the body after death. F.A. Jaffe, A *Guide to Pathological Evidence*, 3d ed. (Toronto: Carswell, 1991) at 212.

ALIA ENORMIA. [L.] Other wrongs.

ALIAS. *n.* A name by which a person is known.

ALIAS DICTUS. [L.] Otherwise called.

ALIAS WRIT. A replacement for an earlier writ which has been lost or has become ineffectual.

ALIBI. *n.* 1. " . . . [P]roof of the absence of the accused at the time a crime is supposed to be committed, satisfactory proof that he is in some place else at the time." *R. v. Haynes* (1914), 22 D.L.R. 227 at 230, 48 N.S.R. 133, 23 C.C.C. 101 (C.A.), Townshend C.J. 2. " . . . [N]ot confined to the situation where the accused claims to have been elsewhere when the actual offence was committed. It may refer to a separate and particular ingredient of an offence, or it may refer to a claim to have been elsewhere when any particular event is alleged to have taken place." *R. v. ONeill* (1973), 6 N.B.R. (2d) 656 at 662, 22 C.R.N.S. 359 (C.A.), the court per Limerick J.A.

ALIEN. *v.* To transfer; to convey.

ALIEN. *n.* 1. At common law, the subject of a foreign government who was not born within the allegiance of the Crown. 2. A person who is not a Canadian citizen, Commonwealth citizen, British subject or citizen of the Republic of Ireland. *Canadian Citizenship Act*, R.S.C. 1970, c. C-19, s. 2. See ENEMY ~; NONRESIDENT ~.

ALIENABILITY. *n.* The quality of being transferable.

ALIENATE. *v.* " ' . . . Has a technical legal meaning, and any transfer of real estate, short of a conveyance of the title, is not an alienation of the estate. No matter in what form the sale may be made, unless the title is conveyed to the purchaser, the estate is not alienated:' Masters v. Madison County Mutual Ins. Co. (1852), 11 Barb 624." *Meek v. Parsons* (1900), 31 O.R. 529 at 533 (Div. Ct.), Armour C.J. (Street J. concurring).

ALIENATIO LICET PROHIBEATUR, CONSENSU TAMEN OMNIUM IN FAVOREM QUORUM PROHIBITA EST POTEST FIERI. [L.] Although alienation is prohibited, those in whose interests it is prohibited may consent to it.

ALIENATION. *n.* " . . . [B]ased on a voluntary transfer of the right of ownership . . ." S*yndicat national des emp és de la comm. scolaire régionale de l'Outaouais v. Union des emp byes de service, Local 298* (1988), 89 C.L.L.C. 14 045 at 12,399, 35 Admin L.R. 153, 95 N.R. 161, 24 Q.A.C. 244, [1988] 2 S.C.R. 1048, Beetz J. See RESTRAINT ON ~.

ALIENATION IN MORTMAIN. The transfer of tenements or lands to any corporation.

ALIENATIO REI PREFERTUR JURI ACCRESCENDI. [L.] The law prefers alienation to the accumulation of property.

ALIENEE. *n.* One to whom property is transferred.

ALIEN FRIEND. The subject of an enemy government who resides in Canada. J.G. McLeod, *The Conflict of Laws* (Calgary: Carswell, 1983) at 64.

ALIENI JURIS. [L.] Under the power of someone else, as opposed to sui juris.

ALIEN NEE. One who is born an alien.

ALIENOR. *n.* A person who transfers property.

ALIGNMENT AND BRAKES MECHANIC. A person engaged in the repair and maintenance of motor vehicles who, (i) tests for and corrects faulty alignment of wheels, axles, frames and steering mechanisms including wheel balancing, and (ii) adjusts, disassembles, repairs and reassembles foundation brake systems, and controls and components pertaining to them. *Apprenticeship and Tradesmen's Qualification Act*, R.R.O. 180 Reg. 21 s. 1.

ALII PER ALIUM NON ACQUIRITUR OBLIGATIO. [L.] One person cannot incur a liability through another.

ALIMENTARY. *adj*. Protective.

ALIMONY. *n*.. " . . . [O]riginally the word 'alimony' was limited to payments made by a husband to his wife up and until their marriage was dissolved and that any payments made or ordered to be paid thereafter were strictly called 'maintenance .*" Rystrom v. Rystrom* (1954), 14 W.W.R. (N.S.) 118 at 119, [1955] 2 D.L.R. 345 (Sask. C.A.), the court per Gordon J.A.

ALIO INTUITU. [L.] With another motive.

ALIQUID CONCEDITUR NE INJURIA REMANEAT IMPUNITA, QUOD ALIAS NON CONCEDITUR. [L.] Something is conceded, which would otherwise not be conceded, so that an injury will be punished.

ALIQUIS NON DEBET ESSE JUDEX IN PROPRIA CAUSA QUIA NON POTEST ESSE JUDEX ET PARS. [L.] No one person should judge their cause, because a person cannot be judge and a party at the same time.

ALITER. [L.] Otherwise.

ALIUD EST CELARE, ALIUD TACERE. [L.] Silence is one thing, concealment another.

ALIUD EST POSSIDERE, ALIUD ESSE IN POSSESSIONE. [L.] To possess is one thing, and to be in possession another.

ALIUNDE. [L.] From some other place or person.

ALKALI METAL AMALGAM. A combination of sodium metal or potassium metal with mercury. *Chlor Alkali Mercury National Emission Standards Regulations*, C.R.C., c. 406, s. 2.

ALL DUE DILIGENCE. A defence to avoid conviction for contravention of a regulatory offence. The defendant must show that he exercised every precaution reasonable in the circumstances. See DUE DILIGENCE.

ALLEGANS CONTRARIA NON EST AUDIENDUS. [L.] One who makes inconsistent statements should not be heard.

ALLEGANS SUAM TURPITUDINEM NON EST AUDIENDA. [L.] A person alleging personal infamy should not be heard.

ALLEGARI NON DEBUIT QUOD PROBATUM NON RELEVAT. [L.] Whatever would be irrelevant if proved should not be heard.

ALLEGATA ET PROBATA. [L.] Things alleged and proved.

ALLEGATIO CONTRA FACTUM NON EST ADMITTENDA. [L.] An allegation contrary to that which a person has made in a deed is not permitted.

ALLEGATION. *n*. Assertion.

ALLEGE. *v*. To state, to assert positively. *R. v. O'Malley*, [1924] 3 D.L.R. 430 at 432, 2 W.W.R. 652 (Alta. C.A.), the court per Stuart J.A. See MIS~.

ALLEGIANCE. *n*. Obedience owed to the sovereign or government. See OATH OF ~.

ALLEGIARE. To justify or defend by due course of law.

ALL-ENGINES-OPERATING TAKE-OFF DISTANCE. The distance from the start of the take-off roll to the point at which the aeroplane reaches the height above the runway elevation specified in the certification basis of the aeroplane. *Canadian Aviation Regulations* SOR/96-433, s. 101.01(1).

ALL-ENGINES-OPERATING TAKE-OFF RUN. The distance from the start of the take-off roll to the point midway between the lift-off point and the point at which the aeroplane reaches the height above the runway elevation specified in the certification basis of the aeroplane. *Canadian Aviation Regulations* SOR 96-433, s. 101.01.

ALL E.R. *abbr*. All England Law Reports.

ALLER SANS JOUR. [Fr.] To go without day.

ALLEVIARE. To pay or levy an accustomed fine.

ALLEY. *n*. 1. A narrow highway intended chiefly to give access to the rear of buildings and parcels of land. *Traffic Safety Act*, R.S.A. 2000, c. T-6, s. 1(1). 2. A highway that is not more than 9 metres wide. *The Highway Traffic Act* C.C.S.M., c. H-60, s. 223(4).

ALL FOURS. A phrase to describe cases which agree in all their circumstances.

ALLIANCE. *n*. 1. A league. 2. Relation by marriage or any form of blood relationship.

ALLIED TRADES FEDERATION. An organization of unions or union locals in the same industry formed to co-ordinate the activities of members.

ALLISION. *n*. One vessel running against another.

ALLOCATED RETAINED EARNINGS. Earnings which have been retained by a credit union in anY form wherein the extent of each member's interest in the retained earnings is or can be identified. *Credit Union Act*, S.S. 1984-85-86, c. C-45-1, s. 2.

ALLOCATION. *n*. Appropriation or assignment of funds to particular purposes or people.

ALLOCATUR. [L.] It is allowed.

ALLOCUTUS. *n*. The unsworn statement of an accused at trial.

ALLODARII. *n*. [L.] Tenants having as great an estate as subjects can enjoy; owners of allodial lands.

ALLODIAL LANDS. var. **ALODIAL LANDS**. Lands held absolutely and not the estate of any lord or superior.

ALLOGRAPH. *n*. A document not written by any of the parties to the document.

ALLONGE. *n*. A slip of paper annexed to a bill of exchange to accommodate endorsements.

ALLOT. *v*. 1. To indicate that something should belong solely to a specific person. 2. To appropriate shares to those who applied for them.

ALL OTHER PERILS. Includes only perils similar in kind to the perils specifically mentioned in the policy. *Marine Insurance Act*, R.S.N.B. 1973, s. M-1, Schedule.

ALLOTMENT. *n*. 1. "As applied to a fixed quantity of anything or a fixed number of shares, the word 'allotment' can mean nothing more than to give, to assign, to set apart, to appropriate . . ." *Nelson Coke & Gas Co. v. Pellatt* (1902), 4 O.L.R. 481 at 489 (C.A.), McLellan J.A. 2. Distribution of land. 3. The portion of land distributed. 4. " . . . [T]he acceptance by the company of the offer to take shares." *Re Florence Land etc. Co., Nicol's Case* (1885), 29 Ch. D. 421 at 426, Chitty J. 5. " . . . [T]here should be some unequivocal act from which acknowledgement of the allottee's right to demand the shares pursuant to the offer can be inferred, and of which he can take advantage to compel the company to give them to him." *Imperial Bank v.*

Dennis, [1926] 3 D.L.R. 168 at 169, 59 O.L.R. 20 (C.A.), Hodgins J.A. (dissenting in part) (Magee J.A. concurring). 6. The total number of dozens of eggs that a producer is entitled to market in intraprovincial, interprovincial and export trade pursuant to the Canadian Egg Marketing Agency Quota Regulations and the order made by the Commodity Board under the Plan. *Ontario Egg Marketing Levies Order*, C.R.C., c. 182, s. 1. 7. An application for shares providing that the applicant takes a specified quantity of shares or a smaller amount if allotted or the board of director's acceptance, by resolution, of such an application of shares. H. Sutherland, D.B. Horsley & J .M. Edmiston, eds., *Fraser's Handbook on Canadian Company Law*, 7th ed. (Toronto: Carswell, 1985) a10.

ALLOW. *v*. 1. To permit; to admit something is valid. 2. Section 167 [of the *Criminal Code*, R.S.C. 1985, c. C-46] requires that the accused "allow" the indecent performance . . . s. 167 is a full *mens rea* offence . . . the requirement that the accused "allow" an indecent performance implies, at the very least, a requirement of concerted acquiescence or wilful blindness on the part of the accused. Indeed, I would equate"allow" in this context with "knowingly" in the context of [*R. v. Jorgensen*, [1995] 4 S.C.R. 55]. *R. v. Mara*: 1997 CarswellOnt 1983, 213 N.R. 41, 115 C.C.C. (3d) 539, 101 O.A.C. 1, 148 D.L.R. (4th) 75, 8 C.R. (5th) 1, 33 O.R. (3d) 384, 44 C.R.R. (2d) 243, [1997] 2 S.C.R. 630. Per Sopinka, J. for the court.

ALLOWABLE. *adj*. When the term is used in connection with a well, means the amount of oil or gas a well is permitted to produce after application of any applicable penalty factor. See BASE ~.

ALLOWABLE ANNUAL CUT. A rate of timber harvesting specified for an area of land. See ANNUAL ALLOWABLE CUT.

ALLOWABLE BEARING PRESSURE. The maximum pressure that may be safely applied to a soil or rock by the foundation unit considered in design under expected loading and subsurface conditions. *Building Code*, O. Reg. 403/97, s. 1.1.3.

ALLOWABLE CUT. See ALLOWABLE ANNUAL CUT; ANNUAL ~.

ALLOWABLE LOAD. The maximum load that may be safely applied to a foundation unit considered in design under expected loading and subsurface conditions. *Building Code*, O. Reg. 403/97, s. 1.1.3.

ALLOWANCE. *n.* 1. A limited predetermined sum of money paid to enable the recipient to provide for certain kinds of expenses; its amount is determined in advance and, once paid, it is at the complete disposition of the recipient who is not required to account for it. *The Queen v. Pascoe*, [1975] C.T.C. 58, 75 D.T.C. 5427 (Fed. C.A.). 2. Any discount, rebate, price concession or other advantage that is or purports to be offered or granted for advertising or display purposes and is collateral to a sale or sales of products but is not applied directly to the selling price. *Competition Act*, R.S.C. 1981, c. C-34, s. 51(3). See CAPITAL COST ~; DEPLETION ~; FLOATING ~; NET ~; RETIRING ROAD ~; SUBSISTENCE ~; TRADE-IN ~; TREATMENT ~.

ALLOWED TIME. The time allowed for faulty material, tool care, rest periods in connection with incentive wage plans.

ALLOY. *n.* When applied to steel, means steel that contains one or more of the following elements in the quantity, by weight, respectively indicated: (a) over 1.65 per cent of manganese; (b) over 0.25 per cent of phosphorus; (c) over 0.35 per cent of sulphur; (d) over 0.60 per cent of silicon (e) over 0.60 per cent of copper; (f) over 0.30 per cent of aluminum; (g) over 0.20 per cent of chromium; (h) over 0.30 per cent of cobalt; (i) over 0.35 per cent of lead; (j) over 0.50 per cent of nickel; (k) over 0.30 per cent of tungsten; or (l) over 0.10 per cent of any other metallic element. *Customs Tariff*, R.S.C. 1985, c. C-54, s. 2. See LEAD ~; LIGHT METAL ~.

ALL PROPER COSTS AND EXPENSES. Costs limited to the tariff scale and to party-and-party costs. M.M. Orkin, *The Law of Costs*, 2d ed. (Aurora: Canada Law Book, 1987) at 113.

ALL RISKS. Coverage under an all risks policy extends to damage caused by fortuitous circumstance or causality not resulting from misconduct or fraud by the insured unless coverage is excluded by a specific provision. It does not extend to ordinary wear and tear or to depreciation.

ALL-ROUND LIGHT. A light showing an unbroken light over an arc of the horizon of 360 degrees. *Collision Regulations*, C.R.C., c. 1416, Rule 3.

ALL TERRAIN VEHICLE. *var.* **ALL-TERRAIN VEHICLE.** 1. Any motor vehicle designed or adapted for off-road use. 2. A wheeled or tracked motor vehicle designed for travel primarily on unprepared surfaces such as open country and marshland. 3. Dirt bikes, dune buggies, motorized snow vehicles and amphibious machines. 4. A self-propelled vehicle designed to be driven, (i) exclusively on snow or ice, or both, or (ii) on land and water.

ALL-UNION AGREEMENT. Collective agreement under which employer agrees to a closed shop.

ALLUREMENT. *n.* An object which is likely to attract persons onto another person's property.

ALLUVION. *n.* An addition to existing land formed when sand and earth wash up from the sea or a river.

ALLY. *n.* 1. A nation which has entered into an alliance. 2. Includes a person who, in the board's opinion, in combination, in concert or in accordance with a common understanding with the employer assists him in a lockout or in resisting a lawful strike. *Labour Code* R.S.B.C. 179 c. 212 s. 85.

ALMS. *n.* Charitable donations.

ALMSHOUSE. *n.* A house where poor people may live free of charge.

ALODY. *n.* Land which may be inherited.

ALTA. *abbr.* Alberta.

ALTA. L.R. *abbr.* Alberta Law Reports, 1908-1932.

ALTA. L.R.B.R. *abbr.* Alberta Labour Relations Board Reports.

ALTA. L. REV. *abbr.* Alberta Law Review.

ALTA. L.R. (2d). *abbr.* Alberta Law Reports, Second Series, 1977-.

ALTA PRODITIO. [L.] High treason.

ALTA TENURA. [L.] Highest or free tenure.

ALTER. *v.* " . . . [Refers to] a change or variation in something, a modification, a change in some elements or ingredients of the thing, but not a change in the whole, a total replacement . . . *R. v. Parkway Chrysler Plymouth Ltd* (1976), 32 C.C.C. (2d) ,116 at 117, 28 C.P.R. (2d) 15 (Ont. C.A.), Wilson J.A.

ALTERATION. *n.* 1. Replacement, removal or addition; change. 2. Addition or erasure. 3. The structural alterations to the exterior or interior of any building or structure that are designed to improve, modernize or increase the usefulness of any building or structure and includes the (a) purchase of material for any such purpose, (b) relocation of any equipment, and (c) alteration of plumbing, heating, ventilating, water supply or air conditioning systems or parts thereof. See MAJOR ~; MATERIAL ~; STRUCTURAL ~; STRUCTURAL ~S OR STRUCTURALLY ALTERED~.

ALTERED. *adj*. Changed.

ALTER EGO. [L.] Second self.

ALTERIUS CIRCUMVENTIO ALII NON PRAEBET ACTIONEM. [L.] A fraud successful on one person does not allow another to bring an action.

ALTERNAT. *n*. A custom among diplomats by which the places and rank of different powers who have similar rights and claims to precedence are varied occasionally, either by lot or in a certain regular order. In some treaties and conventions it is customary for the parties to change place in the preamble and the signatures, so that each power holds, in the copy which will be delivered to it, first place.

ALTERNATE AERODROME. An aerodrome to which a flight may proceed when landing at the intended aerodrome of destination becomes inadvisable. *Canadian Aviation Regulations*. SOR/96-433, s. 101.01(1).

ALTERNATIVA PETITIO NON EST AUDIENDA. [L.] An alternate petition will not be heard.

ALTERNATIVE. *n*. One of several possibilities.

ALTERNATIVE DISPUTE RESOLUTION. 1. A term for processes such as arbitration, conciliation, mediation and settlement, designed to settle disputes without formal trials. 2. This [non-binding arbitration] differs from other forms of ADR [Alternative Dispute Resolution] in which the parties themselves are part of the decision-making mechanism and the neutral third party's involvement is of a facilitative nature: e.g. mediation, conciliation, neutral evaluation, non-binding opinion, non-binding arbitration. Of course, the simplest method—often overlooked—is that of non-involvement by a neutral: a negotiation between the parties. It is not unusual that ADR resolutions are conducted privately; more to the point, I suspect it would be unusual to see a public ADR session especially where the focus is on coming to a consensual arrangement. The parties need to have the opportunity of discussion and natural give and take with brainstorming and conditional concessions giving without the concern of being under a microscope. If the parties were under constant surveillance, one could well imagine that they would be severely inhibited in the frank and open discussions with the result that settlement ratios would tend to dry up. The litigation system depends on a couple of percent of new cases only going to trial. If this were doubled to several percent the system would collapse. Therefore in my view public policy supports the non-trial resolution of disputes . . . *887574 Ontario Inc. v. Pizza Pizza Ltd.*, 1994 CarswellOnt 1069, 35 C.P.C. (3d) 323, 23 B.L.R. (2d) 239, Ontario Court of Justice (General Division), Commercial List, Farley, J.

ALTERNATIVE FORMAT. With respect to personal information, a format that allows a person with a sensory disability to read or listen to the personal information. *Personal Information Protection and Electronic Documents Act*, S.C. 2000, c. 5, s. 2(1).

ALTERNATIVE FUEL. Fuel that is for use in motor vehicles to deliver direct propulsion, less damaging to the environment than conventional fuels, and including ethanol, methanol, propane gas, natural gas, hydrogen or electricity when used as a sole source of direct propulsion energy. *Alternative Fuels Act*, S.C. 1995, c. 20, s. 2(1), part.

ALTERNATIVE LIABILITY. " . . . [I]f an injured party cannot identify which of two or more defendants caused an injury, the burden of proof may shift to the defendants to show that they were not responsible for the harm . . ." *Valleyview Hotel Ltd. v. Montreal Trust Co.* (1985), 33 C.C.L.T. 282 at 286, 39 Sask. R. 229 (C.A.), the court per Tallis J.A.

ALTERNATIVE MEASURES. Measures, other than judicial proceedings, that are used to deal with a person who is alleged to have committed an offence. Refers to consensual measures such as sentencing circles.

ALTIMETER SETTING REGION. The low level airspace so specified, and delineated, in the *Designated Airspace Handbook. Canadian Aviation Regulations*. SOR/96-433, s. 101.01(1).

ALTITUDE. *n*. Height above sea level.

ALTO ET BASSO. [L.] High and low.

ALTUM MARE. [L.] The high sea.

ALUMNI ASSOCIATION. An association of graduates of a university.

ALUMNUS. *n*. [L.] A person educated at a university or college.

A.M. *abbr.* 1. [L. ante meridiem] Before noon. 2. Amplitude modulation. *Radio Broadcasting regulations.*

AMALGAMATED COMPANY. A company that results from an amalgamation.

AMALGAMATION. *n*. 1. The word "amalgamation" does not admit of a single meaning. Used in the corporate law context, an amalgamation may extinguish old entities and create new entities in their place, or it may blend those pre-existing entities and continue them under the auspices of the new amalgamated entity. The effect of a particular amalgamation depends on the purpose the amalgamation is intended to promote, as discerned by an examination of the agreement or statute bringing about the amalgamation. *MacPump Developments Ltd. v. Sarnia (City)* 1994 CarswellOnt 631, 24 M.P.L.R. (2d) 1, 20 O.R. (3d) 755, 75 O.A.C. 378, 120 D.L.R. (4th) 662, 28 Admin. L.R. (2d) 127, 20 O.R. (3d) 755, Doherty, J.A. 2. " . . . [D]erived from mercantile usage and denotes, one might say, a legal means of achieving an economic end. . . The purpose is economc: to build, to consolidate, perhaps to diversify, existing businesses; so that through union there will be enhanced strength. It is a joining of forces and resources in order to perform better in the economic field . . . There are various ways in which companies can be put together . . . in an amalgamation a different result is sought and different legal mechanics are adopted, usually for the express purpose of ensuring the continued existence of the constituent companies . . . the end result is to coalesce to create a homo eneous whole . . ." *R. v Black & Decker Manufacturing Co.* (1974), 13 C.P.R. (2d) 97 at 103, (19751 1 S.C.R. 411, 43 D.L.R. (3d) 393, 1 N.R. 299, the court per Dickson J. See HORIZONTAL ~; STATUTORY~; VERTICAL ~.

AMANUENSIS. *n*. A person who writes or copies on another's behalf.

AMATEUR. *n*. A non-professional. A person who does something for the love of doing it.

AMATEUR. *adj.* Non-professional.

AMATEUR ATHLETIC ASSOCIATION. See REGISTERED CANADIAN ~.

AMATEUR RADIO SERVICE. A radiocommunication service in which radio apparatus are used for the purpose of self-training, intercommunication or technical investigation by individuals who are interested in radio technique solely with a personal aim and without pecuniary interest. *Radiocommunications Regulations*, SOR/96-484, s. 2.

AMATEUR SPORT. 1. Any athletic activity that is engaged in solely for recreation, fitness or pleasure and not as a means of livelihood. 2. Sport in which the participants receive no remuneration for their services as participants. *Competition Act*, R.S.C. 1985 c. C-34, s. 6(2).

AMBASSADOR. *n*. The head of a diplomatic mission.

AMBER. See FOSSIL~.

AMBIDEXTER. *n*. One who takes bribes from both sides.

AMBIENT AIR. The atmosphere surrounding the earth but does not include the atmosphere within a structure or within an underground space.

AMBIGUA RESPONSIO CONTRA PROFERENTEM EST ACCIPIENDA. [L.] An ambiguous response is interpreted against the person who makes it.

AMBIGUIS CASIBUS SEMPER PRAESUPRO REGE. [L.] In doubtful cases, the presumption is always in favour of the Crown.

AMBIGUITAS VERBORUM LATENS VERIFICATIONE SUPPLETUR, NAM QUOD EX FACTO ORITUR AMBIGUUM VERIFICATIONE FACTI TOLLITUR. [L.] A latent ambiguity in wording may be explained by evidence; for whatever ambiguity arises on evidence extrinsic to an instrument may be removed by similar evidence.

AMBIGUITAS VERBORUM PATENS NULLA VERIFICATIONE EXCLUDITUR. [L.] A patent ambiguity in the wording of a written instrument may not be cleared up by extrinsic evidence.

AMBIGUITY. *n*. 1. Doubtfulness. 2. What, then, in law is an ambiguity? To answer, an ambiguity must be "real." The words of the provision must be "reasonably capable of more than one meaning". For this reason, ambiguity cannot reside in the mere fact that several courts—or, for that matter, several doctrinal writers—have come to differing conclusions on the interpretation of a given provision. Just as it would be improper for one to engage in a preliminary tallying of the number of decisions supporting competing interpretations and then apply that which receives the "higher score", it is not appropriate to take as one's starting point the premise that differing interpretations reveal an ambiguity. It is necessary, in every case, for the court charged with interpreting a provision to undertake the contextual and purposive approach set out by Driedger ["Construction of Statutes" (3d ed. 1994)], and *thereafter* to determine if "the words are ambiguous enough to induce two people to spend good money in backing two opposing views as to their meaning" [John Willis, "Statute Interpretation in a Nutshell" (1938), 16 Can. Bar Rev. 1, at pp. 4, 5]. *Bell ExpressVu Ltd. Partnership v. Rex* [2002] 2 S.C.R. 559. 3. Ambiguity in the meaning of criminal statues has always been resolved by choosing the meaning which is most favourable to the accused. The principle that ambiguous penal provisions must be interpreted in favour of an accused does not mean that the most restrictive possible meaning of any word used in the penal statute must always be the preferred meaning. The principle applies only where there is true ambiguity as to the meaning of a word in a penal statute . . . The meaning of words cannot be determined by examining those words in isolation. Meaning is discerned by examining words in their context. True ambiguities in a statute exist only where the meaning remains unclear after a full contextual analysis of the statute. *R. v. Mac* (2001) 140 O.A.C. 270. See LATENT ~; PATENT ~.

AMBIGUOUS. *adj.* "[A word is ambiguous if] no meaning it reasonably has could effect the legislative intent, or if the legislative intent could not be ascertained . . ." *Xerox of Canada Ltd v. Ontario Regional Assessment Commissioner, Region No. 10* (1980), (*sub nom. Ontario Regional Assessment Commissioner, Region No. 10 v. Xerox of Canada Ltd*) 11 O.M.B.R. 23 8 at 244, 30 O.R. (2d) 90, 17 R.P.R. 72, 115 D.L.R. (3d) 428 (C.A.), Jessup J.A.

AMBIGUUM PLACITUM INTERPRETARI DEBET CONTRA PROFERENTEM. [L.] An ambiguous pleading should be interpreted against the party who prepares it.

AMBIT. *n.* Limit; the bounds encompassing any thing.

AMBULANCE. *n.* A conveyance that is used, or intended to be used, for the purpose of transporting persons requiring medical attention or under medical care, and that is designed and constructed, or equipped, for that purpose. See AIR ~.

AMBULANCE ATTENDANT. A person who is employed or engaged, with or without remuneration on a full-time or part-time basis to attend and assist patients while they are receiving ambulance services.

AMBULANCE DRIVER. A person who is employed or engaged, with or without remuneration, on a full-time or part-time basis, to drive or pilot an ambulance vehicle while it is being used to provide ambulance services.

AMBULANCE SERVICE. The service of transporting a patient by means of an ambulance vehicle, and may include the service of carrying the patient into and out of the ambulance vehicle and the service of attending and assisting the patient while being so transported or carried.

AMBULANCE SERVICES PROGRAM. A system for making ambulance services available to a community and includes the ambulance vehicles and other equipment necessary to the provision of the ambulance services. *The Ambulance Services Act* S.M. 1985-86, c. 7, s. 1.

AMBULANCE VEHICLE. Any motor vehicle or aircraft that is used for the transportation of patients.

AMBULATORIA EST VOLUNTAS DEFUNCTI USQUE AD VITAE SUPREMUM EXITUM. [L.] The will of a deceased person is movable until the last moment of life.

AMBULATORY. *adj.* 1. The ability of a person to move about without the assistance of mechanical aids or devices and without assistance from another person. *Homes for Special Care Act*, R.S.N.S. 1989, c. 203 s. 2 (1). 2. Able to be altered or revoked. See SEMI~.

AMBULATORY BUSINESS. A business with no fixed head office.

AMELIORATING WASTE. Acts which improve an inheritance, even though they technically amount to waste. R. Megarry and H.W.R. Wade, *The Law of Real Property*, 5th ed. London: Stevens 1984 at 96.

AMENABLE. *adj.* Capable of being led; tractable; responsible or subject to.

AMEND. *v.* 1. " . . . [T]o change in any way for the better. It includes removing anything that is erroneous or faulty and substituting something else in the place of what is removed. . ." *Kucy v. McCallum*, [1944] 2 D.L.R. 101 at 112, 1 W.W.R. 361, 25 C.B.R. 128 (Alta. C.A.), Ewing J.A. (dissenting). 2. "[In the Judicature Act, R.S.O. 1970, c. 228, s. 114(10)] . . . would include a change in form not involving a change in substance. . ." *Johannes v. Johannes* (1981), 24 R.F.L. (2d) 412 at 419, 34 O.R. (2d) 548, 127 D.L.R. (3d) 88 (Div. Ct.), the court per Morden J.A. 3. " . . . Has several judicial meanings. It has been held to mean 'to annul or remove that which is faulty and substitute that which will improve.' And also, 'to substitute something in place of what is removed.'. . ." *Elizabeth Shoe Co. v. Racine*, [1951] Que. K.B. 624 at 625, Barclay J.A. (Casey J.A. concurring).

AMENDING CLAUSE. Amending procedures for the Constitution absent from the B.N.A. Act but supplied by the *Constitution Act, 1982*.

AMENDING FORMULA. The means by which the Constitution of Canada may be amended. See DOMESTIC~.

AMENDMENT. *n*. 1. The correction of an error. 2. The making of a change to a document. 3. "[As] contemplated by No. 1 of section 92 [Constitution Act, 1867 (30 & 31 Vict.) c. 3] . . . was intended . . . to alter certain details of structure or machinery deemed necessary for the efficient operation of the constitution, the essential design and purpose being preserved." *Reference re Initiative & Referendum Act (Man.)* (1916), [1917] 1 W.W.R. 1012 at 1029, 27 Man. R. 1, 32 D.L.R. 148 (C.A.), Perdue J.A. 4. "Section 32(4) [of the Saskatchewan Human Rights Code, S.S. 1979, c. S-24] only empowers the Court to remit to the board for 'amendment'; . . . rectification of omissions, or the correcting of slips and errors, or attending to incidentals; it does not suggest reconsideration after a failure as fundamental as that which occurred in this case." *Peters v. University Hospital* (1983), 4 C.H.R.R. D/ 1464 at D/ 1478, [1983] 5 W.W.R. 193, 1 Admin L.R. 221, 147 D.L.R. (3d) 385, 23 Sask. R. 123 (C.A.), Cameron J.A. (dissenting). See ARTICLES OF ~.

AMENDS. *n*. Satisfaction.

AMENITY. *n*. A feature adding to enjoyment of property. See LOSS OF AMENITIES.

A MENSA ET THORO. [L.] From board and bed.

AMENTIA. *n*. Insanity.

AMERCIAMENT. var. **AMERCEMENT**. *n*. Pecuniary penalty, at a court's discretion.

AMERICAN FEDERATION OF LABOUR. A federation of labour unions joined to the CIO.

AMERICAN PLAICE. A fish of the species Hippoglossoides platessoides (Fab.). *Northwest Atlantic Fisheries Regulations*, C.R.C., c. 860, s. 2.

AMI. *n*. [Fr.] Friend.

AMICUS CURIAE. [L.] Friend of the court. 1. A barrister who assists the court during the course of a hearing, usually at the court's request. 2. "In England the use of amicus curiae is still substantially restricted to the three traditional situations. The first is where a matter of importance is before the court which could affect many other persons and the court invites the Attorney-General to appear as amicus curiae . . . The second is to address the court to revert injustice. The amicus can call the attention of the court to decisions or points of law that might have been overlooked . . . The third is to represent the unrepresented, for example, . . . I would not call them intervenors because they do not intervene. They are barristers who assist the court, usually at the court's request, and are disinterested." *Canada (Attorney-General) v Aluminum Co. of Canada* (1987), 35 D.L.R. (4th) 495 at 505, 26 Admin L.R. 18, 15 C.P.C. (2d) 289, 10 B.C.L.R. (2d) 371, [1987] 3 W.W.R. 193 (C.A.), Seaton J.A. (Hinkson J.A. concurring).

AMIDSHIPS. *adv*. or *adj*. 1. At the middle of the length. 2. The mid-point of the length of a fishing vessel. *Small Fishing Vessel Inspection Regulations*, C.R.C., c. 1486, s. 2. 3. The middle of the length between the perpendiculars. *Hull Construction Regulations*, C.R.C., c. 1431, Schedule 1 s. 11. 4. The middle of the length of the summer load waterline as defined in subsection (2). *General Load Line Rules*, C.R.C., c. 1425, Schedule 1, s. 1.

AMINO ACIDS. Those L-amino acids commonly found in naturally occurring proteins and such amino acids when they have been modified. *Patent Rules*. SOR/96-423, s. 2.

AMINO ACID SEQUENCE. (*a*) An unbranched sequence of four or more contiguous amino acids, and (*b*) any peptide or protein that includes abnormal linkages, cross links and end caps, non-peptidyl bonds or the like. *Patent Rules*, SOR/96-423, s. 2.

AMITTERE CURIAM. [L. to lose court] To be forbidden to attend court.

AMITTERE LEGEM TERRAE. [L.] To lose the law of the land.

AMITTERE LIBERAM LEGEM. [L.] To lose the liberty of being sworn in court.

AMMONIA. See ANHYDROUS~.

AMMONIA NITROGEN. The nitrogen in ammonia that results from the operation of a plant and that is contained in the effluent from that plant.

AMMONIUM NITRATE. The chemical compound NH_4NO_3 in granular, prilled, flake, crystalline or other solid form. *Ammonium Nitrate Storage Facilities Regulations*, C.R.C., c. 1145, s. 2.

AMMUNITION. *n*. 1. An explosive of any class when enclosed in a case or contrivance or otherwise adapted or prepared so as to form a cartridge or charge for small arms, cannon, any other weapon or blasting, or so as to form any safety or other fuse for blasting or shells or so as to form any tube for firing explosives or so as to form a percussive cap, detonator, shell, torpedo, war rocket or other contrivance other than a firework. 2. A cartridge containing a projectile designed to be discharged from a firearm and, without restricting the generality of the foregoing, includes a caseless cartridge and a shot shell. *Criminal Code*, R.S.C. 1985, c. C-46, s. 84(1). See CENTRE FIRE ~; SHIP'S ~; WADCUTTER ~.

AMNESTY. *n*. A government grant of general pardon for past offences.

AMNIOTIC FLUID. Liquid in which the fetus is suspended in the amniotic sac. F.A. Jaffe, *A Guide to Pathological Evidence*, 3d ed. (Toronto: Carswell, 1991) at 212.

AMNIOTIC FLUID EMBOLISM. An embolism formed from the solid elements of amniotic fluid. F.A. Jaffe, *A Guide to Pathological Evidence*, 3d ed. (Toronto: Carswell, 1991) at 218.

A MORTE TESTATORIS. [L.] From the death of the testator.

AMORTIZATION. *var*. **AMORTISATION**. *n*. 1. Reduction of the amount owing under a mortgage or debt by instalment payments. 2. Of a blended payment mortgage, the period of time needed to pay all the principal and interest, assuming fixed monthly payments. D.J. Donahue & P.D. Quinn, *Real Estate Practice in Ontario*, 4th ed. (Toronto: Butterworths, 1990) at 227.

AMORTIZED VALUE. When used in relation to the value of a redeemable security at any date after purchase, means a value so determined that if the security were purchased at that date and at that value, the yield would be the same as the yield would be with reference to the original purchase price.

AMOTION. *n*. Removal from office.

AMOUNT. *n*. 1. Money expressed in terms of the quantity of money. 2. Rights or things expressed in terms of the money value of the rights or things. 3. In respect of a contract, means the consideration to be given by the contracting authority under the terms of the contract, whether the consideration is fixed or estimated. *Government Contracts Regulations*, C.R.C., c. 701, s. 2. See ACQUISITION COST ~; DEPOSITED ~; LOAN~; MEDIAN ~; PRINCIPAL ~; REASONABLE ~ FOR A RESERVE.

AMOUNT DUE ON THE JUDGMENT. Includes the costs incurred subsequently to those forming part of the judgment, and which may be recovered by an execution issued upon the judgment. *Collection Act* R.S.N.S. 198y c. 76 s. 2.

AMOUNT PAID OUT. That portion of a pool determined by multiplying the pay-out price of each pari-mutuel ticket by the number of such tickets. *Race Track Supervision Regulations*, C.R.C., c. 441; s. 2.

AMOUNT TAXABLE. Taxable paid up capital or taxable paid up capital employed in Canada.

AMOVE. *v*. To remove from a position or place.

AMPACITY. *n*. Current-carrying capacity expressed in amperes.

AMPERE. *n*. 1. The unit of measurement of electric current, being a constant current that, if maintained in two straight parallel conductors of infinite length, of negligible circular cross-section and placed one metre apart in vacuum, would produce between those conductors a force equal to 2×10^{-7} newton per metre of length. *Weights and Measures Act* S.C. 1970-71-72, c. 36 schedule 1. 2. The current that, when constantly maintained in two straight parallel conductors of infinite length, of infinitesimal circular sections and placed one centimetre apart in a vacuum, will produce a force equal to two one-hundredths of a dyne per centimetre of length. *Electric and Photometric Units Act*, R.S.C. 1970, c. E-3, s. 2.

AMPHETAMINE. *n*. A drug which stimulates the central nervous system. F.A. Jaffe, *A Guide* to *Pathological Evidence*, 3d ed. (Toronto: Carswell, 1991 at 91.

AMPHIBIAN. *n*. A vertebrate of the class Amphibia and includes the eggs and other developmental life stages.

AMPHITHEATRE. *n*. An establishment comprising stepped rows of seats and an arena disposed so as to allow the presentation of a match or spectacle.

AMPLIATION. *n*. Deferral of judgment until the matter can be further examined.

AMPLITUDE. See PULSE ~.

AM STATION. A station that broadcasts in the AM frequency band of 525 to 1 705 kHz. It does not include a carrier current undertaking or a transmitter that only rebroadcasts the radiocommunications of another station. *Broadcasting Distribution Regulations*, SOR/97-555, s. 1.

A MULTO FORTIORI. [L.] So much the more.

AMUSEMENT. *n*. Any contest, dance, entertainment, exhibition, game, performance, program, riding device or amusement ride, or show. See PLACE OF ~; TRAVELLING ~.

AMUSEMENT DEVICE. A machine, contrivance, structure or vehicle used in an amusement park to entertain members of the public by moving them or causing them to be moved.

AMUSEMENT MACHINE. A contrivance for providing amusement or a game of skill. *An Act respecting lotteries, racing, publicity contests and amusement machines*, S.Q. 1978, c. 36, s. 1.

AMUSEMENT OWNER. Includes every person who for gain conducts a place of amusement or operates an amusement device, or who for gain permits the public or some of them to participate or indulge in any amusement or recreation whatsoever, but does not include a theatre owner where only a performance is given in the theatre.

AMUSEMENT PARK. 1. A facility, open to the public, used in connection with a carnival, fair, shopping centre, resort, park or place of entertainment where amusement devices are provided. 2. A tract of land used as a temporary or permanent location for amusement devices and includes any place where amusement devices or structures are installed or in operation. *Amusement Devices Safety* Act, R.S.N.S. 1989, c. 12, s. 3.

AMUSEMENT RIDE. A device or combination of devices designed to entertain or amuse people by physically moving them.

AMY. *n*. A friend.

AN. *abbr*. Anonymous.

ANAESTHETIC. *n*. A procedure that causes the loss of sensation of pain in the whole or any part of the body.

ANAGRAPH. *n*. A written record.

ANAL. DE POL. *abbr* Analyse de Politiques.

ANALGESIC. *n*. A drug which relieves pain.

ANALOGY. *n*. Similarity or identity of degree; one may reason by analogy to compare cases governed by the same general principle in a different subject-matter.

ANALOGOUS GROUND. An analogous ground of discrimination refers to any distinction which serves to deny the essential human dignity of a person claiming rights under the *Charter*. It is to be contrasted with one of the enumerated grounds appearing in section 15 of the *Charter*. Spousal status, sexual orientation, and aboriginality-residence have been found to be analogous grounds. Once an analogous ground has been identified, it is a "constant marker of potential legislative discrimination" for all future cases.

ANALOGUE. *n*. A substance that, in relation to a controlled substance, has a substantially similar chemical structure. *Controlled Drugs and Substances Act,* , S.C. 1996, c. 19, s. 2(1).

ANALOGY TO STATUTE. A statutory limitation period applicable to a legal claim may be applied by analogy to an equitable claim if the equitable claim and the legal claim are sufficiently similar. See LIMITATION BY ANALOGY.

ANALYSIS. *n*. 1. Separation into component parts or elements. 2. Physical or bacteriological as well as chemical analysis.

ANALYST. *n*. A person appointed or designated to carry out analysis under a statute. See DEPARTMENTAL ~; PROVINCIAL ~.

ANAPHYLAXIS. *n*. An acute, life-threatening reaction which occurs when an individual is exposed to an allergen to which that person is hypersensitive.

ANARCHY. *n*. Non-existence of government.

ANATOCISM. *n.* Accepting compound interest on a loan.

ANCESTOR. *n.* One from whom a person is descended; progenitor.

ANCESTRAL. *adj.* Relating to ancestors.

ANCESTRY. *n.* " . . . [F]amily descent . . . determined through the lineage of one's parents through their parents, and so on." *Cousens v. Canada (Nurses Assn.)*, [1981] 2 C.H.R.R. D/365 at D/367 (Ont. Bd. of Inquiry), Ratushny.

ANCHORAGE. *n.* 1. A toll to be paid by vessels anchoring in a port. 2. Any area in a harbour where a vessel is permitted to moor by means of its anchor. *National Harbours Board Operating By-law*, C.R.C., c. 1064, s. 2. 3. The provision for transferring seat belt assembly loads to the vehicle structure. *Motor Vehicle Safety Regulations*, C.R.C., c. 1038, s. 210.

ANCIENT. *adj* Old.

ANCIENT DOCUMENT. " . . . [O]ne which meets the requirements for admission as such a document . . ." *Delgamuukw v. British Colum*bia (1989), [1990] 1 C.N.L.R. 20 at 23, 38 B.C.L.R. (2d) 165, [1989] 6 W.W.R. 308 (S.C.), McEachern C.J.B.C.

ANCIENT LEASE. A lease of vacant land within the city that was made before August 2, 1921, on which land the lessee or the lessee's assign has erected a building or has pulled down an old building and erected another and includes an extension of an original lease whether the extension is expressed to be an extension or not of that original lease. *Leaseholds in St. John's Act*, R.S. Nfld. 1990 c. L-10 s. 2(1).

ANCILLARY. *adj.* 1. " . . . [A]uxiliary or subordinate . . ." *Whynot v. Giffin* (1984), 40 C.P.C. 344 at 350, 62 N.S.R. (2d) 112, 136 A.P.R. 112, 7 D.L.R. (4th) 68 (C.A.), the court per Macdonald J.A. 2. " . . . [S]omething grafted on to the primary matter . . ." *Gwyn v. Mellen* (1978), 90 D.L.R. (3d) 195 at 201, 7 R.F.L. (2d) 106 (B.C. S.C.), McKenzie J. 3. " . . . [I]n the constitutional sense. In Re Fisheries Act, 1914; A.-G. Can. v. A.-G. B.C., [1930] 1 D.L.R. 194, [1930] A.C. 111, [1929] 3 W.W.R. 449, it was said that ancillary legislation is that which is necessarily incidental to effective legislation." *Cook v. Cook* (1981), 120 D.L.R. (3d) 216 at 228, 30 Nfld. & P.E.I.R. 42, 84 A.P.R. 42 (Nfld. T.D.), Goodridge J.

ANCILLARY ADMINISTRATION. Administration of a portion of an estate in a second jurisdiction where property of the deceased is located or where the deceased had a cause of action.

ANCILLARY JURISDICTION. Jurisdiction of a federal court in the United States over ancillary proceedings (such as a counterclaim or a third party, issue) which it could not consider if they were independently presented. P.W. Hogg, *Constitutional Law of Canada* 3d ed. (Toronto: Carswell, 1992) at 180.

ANCILLARY RELIEF. Auxiliary relief.

ANCIPITUS USUS. [L.] Of doubtful use.

AND. *conj.* 1. " . . . [N]ormally has a conjunctive meaning, . . ." *Saskatoon (City) . v. Plaxton, Loewen & Wiebe* (1989), 33 C.P.C. (2d) 238 at 258, [1989] 2 W.W.R. 577 (Sask. C.A.), Wakeling J.A. (dissenting). 2. " . . . [A] semantically ambiguous conjunction. The notions which it links may be intended to be regarded jointly or joins and severally." *Bayliner Marine Corp. v. Doral Boats Ltd* (1986) 9 C.I.P.R. 311 at 318, 67 N.R. 139, [1986] 3 F.C. 421, 10 C.P.R. (3d) 289 (C.A.), the court per Mahone J.A. 3. " . . . [R]ead disjunctively to mean 'or' for example] . . ." *R v. Welsh (No. 6)* (1977) 15 O.R. 2d 1 at 9, 32 C.C.C. (2d) 363, 74 D.L.R. (3d) 748 (C.A.), the court per Zuber J.A. 4. " . . . [C]onjunction .. : capable of suggesting a flow of thought from one element to the other . . ." *British Columbia Civil Liberties Assn. v. British Columbia (Attorney General)* (1988), 49 D.L.R . (4th) 493 at 498, 24 B.C.L.R. (2d) 189, [1988] 4 W.W.R. 100 (S.C.), McEachern C.J.S.C.

AND/OR. *conj.* " . . . [U]sed in order to avoid a certain amount of circumlocution. Where things or persons or statements or stipulations are coupled by 'and/or' they are 'to be read either disjunctively or conjunctively' per Cairns, L.C., in Stanton v. Richardson (1875) 45 L.J.C.P. 78 at p. 82." *Export Brewing & Malting Co. v. Dominion Bank*, [1932] 3 D.L.R. 128 at 134, [1932] O.R. 446 (C.A.), Orde J.A.

ANDROLEPSY. *n.* One nation arrests the citizens or subjects of another to compel something of the latter.

A. NELS. *abbr.* Aven Nelson. Weed *Control Act*, R.R.O. 1980, Reg. 944, s. 1.

ANEMIA. *n.* The diminution of the number of red blood corpuscles distinguished by pallour of tissues.

ANENCEPHALY. *n.* The lack of a brain.

ANEURYSM. *n*. A bulge in a blood vessel occurring because of weakness in the wall of the vessel. See ARTERIOR-VENOUS ~; BERRY ~; CONGENITAL ~; MYCOTIC ~; SACCULAR~; TRAUMATIC~.

ANGLE. *v*. To take or attempt to take fish by means of hook and line.

ANGLER. *n*. A person taking or attempting to take fish by means of a hook and line.

ANGLIAE JURA IN OMNI CASU LIBERTATIS DANT FAVOREM. [L.] The laws of England favour liberty in all cases.

ANGLING. *n*. Fishing or attempting to fish with a hook and line, or a hook, line and rod. See ICE~.

ANGLING GUIDE. A person licensed as an angling guide under this Act. *Wildlife Act*, R.S.B.C. 1996, c. 488, s. 1(1).

ANGLO-CANADIAN RULE. " . . . [T]raditionally regarded as that laid down in Phillips v. Eyre [(1870 , L.R. 6 Q.B. 1], subsequently confirmed by the House of Lords in Carr v. Fracis Ties & Co., [1902] A.C. 176, that in order to found an action in England for a wrong committed abroad, two conditions must be fulfilled: the wrong must be of such a character that it would have been actionable if committed in England, and (b) the act must not have been justifiable by the law of the place where it was committed." *Bailey v. Fraser* (1982), (*sub nom. Going v. Reid Brothers Motor Sales Ltd.*) 19 C.C.L.T. 209 at 231, 35 O.R. (2d) 201, 13 M.V.R. 283, 136 D.L.R. (3d) 254 (H.C.), Henry J.

ANHYDROUS AMMONIA. Dry ammonia gas in liquified form and is not to be confused with aqua ammonia which is a solution of ammonia gas in water. *Anhydrous Ammonia Bulk Storage Regulations* C.R.C., c. 114 6, s. 2.

ANIMAL. *n*. 1. Any living being of the animal kingdom other than a human being. *Veterinary acts*. 2. A member of the class Mammalia (mammals), Aves (birds), Reptilia (reptiles) or Amphibia (amphibians), but does not include a human being. *Fish and Wildlife Conservation Act, 1997*, S.O. 1997, c. 41, s. 1(1). 3. All animals except humans and includes vertebrates, invertebrates and micro-organisms whether wild, domestic, living or dead. 4. A mammal, reptile, amphibian or bird. See AQUATIC PLANTS OR ~ S; DANGEROUS ~; DEAD ~; DOMESTIC ~; ENTIRE ~; EXOTIC ~; FALLEN ~; FOOD ~; FUR ~; FUR-BEARING ~; GAME ~; GAME PRODUCTION ~; GUIDE ~; MEAT ~; PREDATORY ~; REGISTERED ~; STRAY ~.

ANIMAL BY-PRODUCT. Includes blood or any of its components, bones, bristles, feathers, flesh, hair, hides, hoofs, horns, offal, skins and wool, and any thing containing any of those things. *Health of Animals Act*, S.C. 1990, c. 21, s. 2(1).

ANIMAL DEADYARD. A place where animal carcasses, animal by-products or disabled or diseased animals are brought when they are not to be prepared for human consumption. *Health of Animals Act*, S.C. 1990, c. 21, s. 2(1).

ANIMAL EMBRYO. The fertilized ovum of an animal.

ANIMAL FOOD. Any thing that is capable of being a nutriment for animals and includes any of the constituent elements of an animal ration. *Health of Animals Act*, S.C. 1990, c. 21, s. 2(1).

ANIMAL FOOD STORAGE PLANT. A business that provides facilities to store frozen food for animal consumption.

ANIMAL HEALTH TECHNICIAN. A person: (i) who holds a certificate or document indicating completion of a course of formal study or training approved by the association; (ii) whose name has been entered by the registrar on the current register of animal health technicians; and (iii) who, under the direction or supervision of a member named by the association, is permitted to perform the technical procedures set out in the bylaws of the association. *Veterinarians acts*.

ANIMAL PRODUCT. 1. Includes cream, eggs, milk, non-fertilized ova and semen. *Health of Animals Act*, S.C. 1990, c. 21, s. 2(1). 2. Any product produced by or from an animal and includes any part of an animal, whether edible or non-edible, and any by-product of an animal or imitation animal product.

ANIMAL RUNNING AT LARGE. (i) An animal that is off the premises of its owner, and is not under the immediate, continuous and effective control of its owner, or (ii) an animal, whether under the control of its owner or not, grazing upon lands other than lands in respect of which the owner of the animal has the right of occupation, or upon a highway or road allowance.

ANIMALS DOMITAE NATURAE. [L.] " . . . [A]nimals which are generally , tame, living in association with man, . . . subject of absolute ownership with all the rights duties privileges and obligations that legal relationship entails. *Diversified Holdings Ltd. v. R.* 1982 33 D.L.R. (3d) 712 at 716, [1982] 3 W.W.R. 516, 35 B.C.L.R. 349, 20 C.C.L.T. 202 (S.C.), Wallace J.

ANIMALS FERAE NATURAE. [L.] " . . . [A]nimals which under normal circumstances are usually found at liberty,. . . are not the subject of absolute ownership, although a qualified property in such animals might be acquired by taking taming them or while they are on one's estate . . ." *Diversified Holdings Ltd v. R.* (1982), 133 D.L.R. (3d) 712 at 716-17, [1982] 3 W.W.R. 516, 35 B.C.L.R. 349, 20 C.C.L.T. 202 (S.C.), Wallace J.

ANIMAL UNIT MONTH. The amount of forage required for one month by an average animal of the genus bos, aged 6 months or older. *Range Act*, R.S.B.C. 1979, c. 355 s. 1.

ANIMO. *adv.* [L.] With intention.

ANIMUS. *n.* [L.] Intent; intention.

ANIMUS AD SE OMNE DUCIT. [L.] Intention draws all law to itself.

ANIMUS CANCELLANDI. [L.] Intention to cancel or destroy.

ANIMUS CONTRAHENDI. [L.] Having an intention to enter into a contract.

ANIMUS DOMINI. [L.] Intention to hold as owner.

ANIMUS ET FACTUM. [L.] Combination of an intention with an act.

ANIMUS FURANDI. [L.] The intention to steal.

ANIMUS HOMINIS EST ANIMA SCRIPTI. [L.] A person's intention is the soul of whatever is written.

ANIMUS MANENDI. [L.] Intention to remain.

ANIMUS NON REVERTENDI. [L.] Intention not to return.

ANIMUS POSSIDENDI. [L.] Intention to possess.

ANIMUS QUO. [L.] Intention with which.

ANIMUS RECIPIENDI. [L.] Intention to receive.

ANIMUS REVERTENDI. [L.] Intention to return.

ANIMUS REVOCANDI. [L.] Intention to revoke.

ANIMUS TESTANDI. [L.] Intention to make a will.

ANN. AIR & SPACE L. *abbr.* Annals of Air and Space Law (Annales de droit aérien et spatial).

ANN. AIR & SP. L. *abbr.* Annals of Air and Space Law.

ANN. CAN. D. DE LA PERSONNE *abbr.* Annuaire canadien des droits de la personne (Canadian Human Rights Yearbook).

ANN. CAN. D. INT. *abbr.* Annuaire canadien de droit international (Canadian Yearbook of International Law).

ANN. D. AÉRIEN & SPATIAL *abbr.* Annales de droit aérien et spatial (Annals of Air and Space Law).

ANNEX. *v.* To add to.

ANNEXATION. *n.* 1. Adding land to a municipality or nation. 2. Incorporation of a municipality into another municipality. 3. " . . . [I]f the object of setting up the articles is to enhance the value of the premises or improve its usefulness for the purposes for which it is used, and if they are affixed to the freehold even in a slight way, but such as is appropriate to the use of the articles, and showing an intention not of occasional but of permanent affixing, then both as to the degree of annexation and as to the object of it, it may very well be concluded that the articles are become part of the realty, at least in questions as between mortgagor and mortgagee." *Haggart v. Brampton (Town)* (1897) 28 S.C.R. 174 at 182 the court per King J. 4. " . . . [W]here a plan is clearly identifiable . . . and is referred to in the .. Crown grant as going to determine the extent of the Crown grant, then there is a form of constructive annexation and it is not necessary that the plan be physically annexed." *British Columbia v. Hilyn Holdings Ltd* (1989) 4 D.L.R. (4th) 95 at 104 (B.C. &C. MacDonald L.J " [U]niting of the affidavit and the exhibits in one parcel . . . constituted sufficient annexation of them to the affidavit." *James v. Yarimi Enterprises Ltd.* (1984), 57 B.C.L.R. 131 at 133 (Co. Ct.), Cowan J.

ANNI NUBILES. [L.] When one is old enough to marry.

ANNIVERSARY. *n.* " . . . [A]ssociated precisely with a period of one year, usually in the sense of a recurring one-year interval." *Peking Palace v. Trizec Costruction Ltd.* (1987), 20 B.C.L.R. (2d) 161 at 164, 48 R.P.R. 4 (C.A.), Lambert J.A.

ANNIVERSARY DATE. In relation to a timber licence means the first day of April in each year regardless of the day and month when that licence is issued. *Crown Lands Act*, R.S.N.B. 1973, c. C-38, s. 1.

ANNIVERSARY MONTH. The month in each year that is the same as the month in which the original event occurred.

ANNO DOMINI. [L.] In the year of the Lord.

ANNO REGNI. [L.] In the year of the reign.

ANNOTATION. *n.* Description; explanation; comment.

ANNOUNCEMENT. See CLASSIFIED ~.

ANNOYANCE. *n.* " . . . [C]onduct of a sort which a reasonably minded person would regard as disturbing or as a source of anxiety or irritation to himself or to a substantial degree . . ." *Sniderman v. Sniderman* (1981), 25 R.F.L. (2d) 319 at 323 (Ont. H.C.), Pennell J.

ANNUAL. *adj.* 1. " . . . [T]he word 'annual' [in s. 3 of the Income War Tax Act, R.S.C. 1927, c. 97] as applied to profit or gain or gratuity does not mean that the profit or gain or gratuity must necessarily be of a recurring nature from year to year, but rather that it is the profit or gain or gratuity of or in or during the year in respect of which the assessment is made." *Consolidated Textiles Ltd v. Minister of National Revenue*, [1947] 2 D.L.R. 172 at 175, [1947] C.T.C. 63, [1947] Ex. C.R. 77, 3 D.T.C. 958, Thorson P. 2." . . . [I]nfers the quality of being recurrent or being capable of recurrence." *Lucas v. Minister of National Revenue* (1987), [1988] 13 F.T.R. 77 at 79, 87 D.T.C. 5277, [1987] 2 C.T.C. 23, Cullen J.

ANNUAL ALLOWABLE CUT. The total volume of timber that may be harvested in one year or the total amount of forested land on which the timber may be harvested in one year. *Forests Act*, R.S.A. 2000, c. F-22, s. 1.

ANNUAL CUT. See ALLOWABLE ~; ANNUAL ALLOWABLE CUT.

ANNUAL DEBT CHARGES. The amount required in each year to meet the payments of principal and interest due on money borrowed.

ANNUAL EMPLOYMENT PLAN. A system under which an employer provides a specified number of hours of work in a year.

ANNUAL GENERAL MEETING. Includes the general meeting of shareholders at which the directors of a company are elected.

ANNUAL HOLIDAY PAY. In respect of any period of employment of an employee: (i) subject to subclause (ii), means, during each year of his employment or portion thereof with any one employer, three fifty-seconds of the employee's total wage for that year of employment or portion thereof during which the employee worked; (ii) means during the year of his employment or portion thereof with any one employer in which he first becomes entitled or would have become entitled to four weeks' annual holiday under section 30 and during each year thereafter, four fifty-seconds of the employee's total wage for the year of employment or portion thereof during which the employee worked. *The Labour Standards Act*, R.S.S. 1978 c. L-1 s. 2.

ANNUAL INCOME. See NET ~.

ANNUALLY. *adv.* Yearly.

ANNUAL OUTLAY. All yearly maintenance, operation and depreciation costs, and necessary amortization costs other than instalments of the capital cost, incurred in respect of regulating or storage works together with interest on the capital cost. *Dominion Water Power Regulations*, C.R.C., c. 1603, s. 55.

ANNUAL PERCENTAGE RATE. In relation to a credit transaction, the percentage rate for each period of time that, when multiplied by the principal amount owing under the credit transaction that is outstanding at the end of each period, will produce an amount or amounts the total of which is equal to the credit charges in relation to the credit transaction, expressed as a rate per annum. *Consumer Credit Transactions Act*, S.A. 1985, c. 22.5, s. 1.

ANNUAL REGISTER. The register of names of members of a profession who have paid their annual fees for the current year.

ANNUAL RETURN. A yearly statement which companies are required to file under. governing legislation.

ANNUAL SALARY RATE. An employee's basic hourly or daily or bi-weekly rate of pay, as the case may be, multiplied by the number of basic hours or days or multiplied periods in one year of continuous employment.

ANNUAL STATEMENT. A yearly statement which companies are required to file under governing legislation.

ANNUAL SUMMARY. A yearly statement which companies are required to file under governing legislation.

ANNUAL VALUE. The rental value of a property for a year.

ANNUAL WEALTH TAX. This form of tax on wealth is a tax of a person's total assets minus the person's liabilities. W. Grover & F. Iacobucci, *Materials on Canadian Income Tax*, 4th ed. (Toronto: Richard De Boo Ltd., 1980) at 36.

ANNUITANT. *n*. 1. A person in receipt of, or entitled to the receipt of, an annuity. 2. (i) Until such time after maturity of the plan as his spouse becomes entitled, as a consequence of his death, to receive benefits to be paid out of or under the plan, the individual referred to in subparagraph (j) (i) or (ii) for whom under a retirement savings plan, a retirement income is to be provided, and (ii) thereafter, his spouse. *Income Tax Act*, R.S.C. 1952 c. 148 (as am. S.C. 1979 c. 5, s. 46), c. 146(1)(a). 3. Under a retirement income fund at any particular time means the individual to whom the carrier has undertaken to make the payments described in paragraph (f) out of or under the fund. *Income Tax Act*, R.S.C. 1952, c. 148 (as am. S.C. 1977-78, c. 32, s. 35), c. 146.3(1)(a).

ANNUITIES. *n*. Includes salaries and pensions. *Apportionment acts*.

ANNUITY. *n*. 1. An annuity consists of an alienation of capital, a sum of money or capital asset, which is then turned into a flow of income so that the capital is used up and replaced by the flow of capital. 2. "... [U]sual purpose is simply to provide, by the deposit either of a lump sum or of payments over a period of years, a sum of money sufficient, with accumulated years, to provide interest to provide an annuity to commence in one's later years, either for the life of the annuitant or for a fixed term of years. The sum repayable on death if the annuitant dies before he has reached the age when the annuity has commenced or before the stipulated number of annual payments have been made is nothing more than a refunding of moneys deposited for a defined purpose, when that purpose has wholly or partially failed owing to the death of the annuitant." *Gray v. Kerslake* (1957),11 D.L.R. (2d) 225 at 234, [1958] S.C.R. 3, Locke J. 3. "... [S]tated sums of money payable at regular inter-

vals ... derived from a fund or source in which the annuitant has no further property beyond the right to claim payment. Under the annuity contract, the issuer obligates himself to make those payments in return for the premium which he has extracted." *Rektor, Re* (1983), 3 P.P.S.A.C. 32 at 34, 47 C.B.R. (ICS.) 267 (Ont. S.C.), Smith J. 4. "... [T]he annuity income—the annual amount to be paid under the annuity contract ..." *Minister of National Revenue v E.*, [1950] Ex. C.R. 509 at 514, [1950] C.T.C. 345, Cameron J. See DEFERRED ~; IMMEDIATE ~; LIFE ~.

ANNUITY CONTRACT. A contract that provides for payment of an income for a specified period or for life and under which the sole benefit stated to be payable by reason of death does not exceed the sum of the amounts paid as consideration for the contract together with interest.

ANNUITY METHOD. Manner of calculating the cost of an annuity to provide income and to cover medical expenses for a successful plaintiff .

ANNUL. *v*. To deprive of effectiveness or operation.

ANNULAR SPACE. Open space between the casing and the sides of a well.

ANNULMENT. *n*. Making void; depriving of effectiveness or operation.

ANON. *abbr*. Anonymous.

A NON POSSE AD NON ESSE SEQUITUR ARGUMENTUM NECESSARIE NEGATIVE, LICET NON AFFIRMATIVE. [L.] Because a thing cannot be done, you draw the conclusion that it was not done but just because a thing has not been done, you should not conclude it is impossible.

ANONYMOUS. *n*. A nameless person.

ANONYMOUS. *adj*. Nameless.

ANOXIA. *n*. Lack of oxygen..

ANSI. *Abbr*. American National Standards Institute.

ANSWER. *n*. The respondent's pleading provided in response to a petition filed to commence an action or proceeding. See FULL ~AND DEFENCE.

ANSWERING POINT. See PUBLIC SAFETY~; SECONDARY PUBLIC SAFETY ~.

ANTE. [L.] Before.

ANTECEDENT. *n.* Some time prior.

ANTECEDENT. *adj.* Prior in time.

ANTEDATE. *v.* To date a document before the day it is executed.

ANTE LITEM MOTAM. [L. before litigation was begun] Declarations as to pedigree or family history are reliable only if the declarations were made ante litem motam. Once a disagreement which may create bias among members of a family exists, any subsequent statement as to pedigree is inadmissible whether the person making the statement knew of the dispute or not when making the statement. J. Sopinka and S.N. Lederman, *The Law of Evidence in Civil Cases* (Toronto: Butterworths, 1974) at 100.

ANTE-NUPTIAL. *var* **ANTENUPTIAL**. *adj.* Before marriage.

ANTERIOR. *adj.* Before, facing towards the front, in front of.

ANTHEM. see NATIONAL ~.

ANTHROPOMETRY. *n.* Measurement of the human body.

ANTHROPOMORPHIC TEST DEVICE. A representation of a human being used in the measurement of the conditions that a human being would experience.

ANTHROPOPHAGY. *n.* The act of animals eating a human body.

ANTIBIOTIC. *n.* A drug or a veterinary biologic prepared from micro-organisms or made synthetically that inhibits the growth of microorganisms.

ANTICIPATED. *adj.* "To be anticipated, an invention described in a patent must already have been fully described in a previous document . . ." *Brushtech Inc. v. Liberty Home Products Corp.* (1988) 23 C.P.R. 3d 370 at 376, 21 C.I.P.R. 27, 23 F.T.R. 300, Dubé J.

ANTICIPATION. *n.* 1. Taking or doing something before the chosen time. 2. In patent law, occurs when there is an invention but it has been disclosed to the public prior to the application for the patent. 3. Prior knowledge, prior use, prior publication and prior sale, which are together referred to as "anticipation". The legal question is whether the prior publication, "contains sufficient information to enable a person of ordinary skill and knowledge in the field to understand 'the nature of the invention and carry it into practical use without the aid of inventive genius but purely by mechanical skill'" The touchstone test [is] set out by Hugessen J.A. in *Beloit Canada Ltée/Ltd. v. Valmet Oy* (1986), 8 C.P.R. (3d) 289 (Fed. C.A.), at 297, which requires that One must, in effect, be able to look at a prior single publication and find in it all the information which, for practical purposes, is needed to produce the claimed invention without the exercise of any inventive skill. The prior publication must contain so clear a direction that a skilled person reading and following it would in every case and without the possibility of error be led to the claimed invention. Anticipation alleges that "your invention, though clever, was already known." *SmithKline Beecham Pharma Inc. v. Apotex Inc.* 2002 FCA 216, 21 C.P.R. (4th) 129, 219 D.L.R. (4th) 124, [2003] 1 F.C. 118, 226 F.T.R. 144 (note).

ANTICIPATORY BREACH. 1. Anticipatory breach occurs when a party, by express language or conduct, or as a matter of implication from what he has said or done, repudiates his contractual obligations before they fall due. The conduct of the repudiating party must be such that the other party to the contract is entitled to conclude that the repudiating party no longer intends to be bound by the provisions of the contract. For this type of breach to occur, there must be conduct amounting to a total rejection of the obligations under the contract and lack of justification for such conduct." *Armada Lines Ltd. v. Chaleur Fertilizer Ltd.* [1995] 1 F.C. 3, (Fed. C.A., per Pratte, J.A.). 2. " . . . [A] party is in breach from the moment that his actual breach becomes inevitable. Since the reason for the rule is that a party is allowed to anticipate an inevitable event and is not obliged to wait til it happens, it must follow that the breach which he anticipates is of just the same character as the breach which would actually have occurred if he had waited." *Universal Cargo Carriers Corporation v. Citati*, [1957] 2 Q.B. 401 at 436 (C.A.), Lord Devlin.

ANTICIPATORY CREDIT. Permitting an exporter to draw on credit prior to shipment by tender of particular documents. I.F.G. Baxter, *The Law of Banking*, 3d ed. (Toronto: Carswell, 1981) at 156.

ANTI-COMPETITIVE ACT. Without restricting the generality of the term, includes any of the following acts: (*a*) squeezing, by a vertically integrated supplier, of the margin available to an unintegrated customer who competes with the supplier, for the purpose of impeding or preventing the customer's entry into, or expansion in, a market; (*b*) acquisition by a supplier of a customer who would otherwise be available to a competitor of the supplier, or acquisition by a customer of a supplier who would otherwise be available to a competitor of the customer, for the purpose of impeding or preventing the competitor's entry into, or eliminating the competitor from, a market; (*c*) freight equalization on the plant of a competitor for the purpose of impeding or preventing the competitor's entry into, or eliminating the competitor from, a market; (*d*) use of fighting brands introduced selectively on a temporary basis to discipline or eliminate a competitor; (*e*) pre-emption of scarce facilities or resources required by a competitor for the operation of a business, with the object of withholding the facilities or resources from a market; (*f*) buying up of products to prevent the erosion of existing price levels; (*g*) adoption of product specifications that are incompatible with products produced by any other person and are designed to prevent his entry into, or to eliminate him from, a market; (*h*) requiring or inducing a supplier to sell only or primarily to certain customers, or to refrain from selling to a competitor, with the object of preventing a competitor's entry into, or expansion in, a market; (*i*) selling articles at a price lower than the acquisition cost for the purpose of disciplining or eliminating a competitor; (*j*) acts or conduct of a person operating a domestic service, as defined in subsection 55(1) of the *Canada Transportation Act*, that are specified under paragraph (2)(*a*); and (*k*) the denial by a person operating a domestic service, as defined in subsection 55(1) of the *Canada Transportation Act*, of access on reasonable commercial terms to facilities or services that are essential to the operation in a market of an air service, as defined in that subsection, or refusal by such a person to supply such facilities or services on such terms. *Competition Act*, R.S.C. 1985, c. C-34, s. 78(1).

ANTIGRAPHY. *n.* The counterpart or copy of a deed.

ANTI-HANDLING DEVICE. A device intended to protect a mine and that is part of, linked to, attached to or placed under the mine and that activates when an attempt is made to tamper with or otherwise intentionally disturb the mine. *Anti-Personnel Mines Convention Implementation Act*, S.C. 1997, c. 33, s. 2.

ANTI-INFLATION ACT (CANADA). An Act to provide for the restraint of profit margins, prices, dividends and compensation in Canada passed by the Parliament of Canada at the First Session of the Thirtieth Parliament. *Anti-Inflation (Nova Scotia) Act*, S.N.S. 1975, c. 54, s. 2.

ANTI-MANIFESTO. *var.* **ANTI MANIFESTO**. The reply to another belligerent's manifesto.

ANTIMONY. *n.* 1. A poisonous metallic element used in making the core of jacketed bullets and soft bullets. F.A. Jaffe, *A Guide to Pathological Evidence*, 3d ed. (Toronto: Carswell, 1991) at 212. 2. A contradiction between two legal propositions; opposition to a particular law.

ANTI-PERSONNEL MINE. A mine that is designed, altered or intended to be exploded by the presence, proximity or contact of a person and that is capable of incapacitating, injuring or killing one or more persons. Mines that are designed, altered or intended to be detonated by the presence, proximity or contact of a vehicle as opposed to a person, and that are equipped with anti-handling devices, are not considered to be anti-personnel mines as a result of being so equipped. *Anti-Personnel Mines Convention Implementation Act*, S.C. 1997, c. 33, s. 2.

ANTIQUE. *n.* Curios, objects of art or of historical interest and home furnishing that through passage of time have increased in interest and value. *Salvage Dealers Licensing acts.*

ANTIQUE FIREARM. Any firearm manufactured before 1898 that was not designed to discharge rim-fire or centre-fire ammunition and that has not been redesigned to discharge such ammunition, or any firearm that is prescribed to be an antique firearm. *Criminal Code*, R.S.C. 1985, c. C-46, s. 84(1).

ANTIQUE MOTOR VEHICLE. A motor vehicle that is 25 years of age or older, is owned as a collector's item and is operated solely for use in exhibitions, club activities, parades and other similar functions and is not used for general transportation. *Highway Traffic Act*, R.S.A. 1980 c. H-7, s. 1.

ANTIQUE REPRODUCTION VEHICLE. A vehicle that is designed to be a scaled reproduction of an antique vehicle and (a) may contain contemporary design components; (b) has a motor that produces 8 kW (10.7 3 bhp) or less; (c) is intended for use exclusively in parades, exhibitions and demonstrations; and (d) bears a label, permanently affixed in a conspicuous position, stating that the vehicle is not to be used for public transportation, but is intended for use in parades, exhibitions and demonstrations.

ANTIQUE VEHICLE. A vehicle more than 30 years old that, when restored to a condition comparable to that on the date of its manufacture, retains the original components or incorporates replacement components with original design characteristics. Canada regulations.

ANTITRUST LAW. A law of a foreign jurisdiction having directly or indirectly as a purpose the preservation or enhancement of competition between business enterprises or the prevention or repression of monopolies or restrictive practices in trade or commerce.

ANTON PILLER ORDER. An ex parte order for seizure, inspection or preservation of property. The defendant or defendants (or at least of the main defendant or defendants) is known at the time the order is granted. There is evidence before the Court of the particular acts of copyright, trademark, or sometimes patent infringement, that it is alleged the defendants are committing. *Nike Canada Ltd. v. Jane Doe* (1999), 174 F.T.R. 131.

A., N.W.T. & Y. TAX R. *abbr.* Alberta, N.W.T. & Yukon Tax Reports.

ANY. *adj.* 1. All, each and every, whichever. *Aerlinte Eireann Teoranta v. Canada (Minister of Transport)* (1990), 68 D.L.R. (4th) 220 at 225, 107 N.R. 129 (Fed. C.A.), the court per Heald J.A. 2. Several. *Nolan v. Nolan* (1977), 1 R.F.L. (2d) 280 at 282, 15 O.R. (2d) 358, 75 D.L.R. (3d) 662 (H.C.), Morden J.

ANYONE. *n.* "[In s. 24 of the Charter] . . . includes a corporation and is not to be restricted to a human person." *R v. B. (G.)*, 4 C.C.C. (3d) 59 at 61 [1983]23 W.W.R. 141, 24 Alta. L.R. (2d) 226, 42 A.R. 383,146 D.L.R. (3d) 673, 4 C.R.R. 296 (Q.B.), Dea J.

ANYTHING. *n.* 1. " . . . [T]he wording of s. 283 [of the Criminal Code, R.S.C. 1985, c. C-46] restricts the meaning of 'anything' in two ways. First, whether tangible or intangible, anything must be of a nature such that it can be the subject of a proprietary right. Second, the property must be capable of right taken or converted in a manner that results in the deprivation of the victim . . . to be the object of theft, 'anything' must be property in the sense that to be stolen, it has to belong in some way to someone. For instance,

no conviction for theft would arise out of a taking or converting of the air that we breathe, because air is not property. . . 'anything' is not restricted to tangibles, but includes intangibles. To be the subject of theft it must, however: 1. be property of some sort; 2. be property capable of being: a) taken—therefore intangibles are excluded, or (b) converted—and may be an intangible; (c) taken or converted in a way that deprives the owner of his proprietary interest in some way . . . confidential information does not come within the meaning of the word 'anything' of s. 283 of the Criminal Code." *R. v. Stewart* (1988), 19 C.I.P.R. 161 at 188, 194, 85 N.R. 171, [1988] 1 S.C.R. 963, 28 O.A.C. 219, 63 C.R. (3d) 305, 41 C.C.C. (3d) 481, 50 D.L.R. (4th) 1, 39 B.L.R. 198, 65 O.R. (2d) 637n, 21 C.P.R. (3d) 289, the court per Lamer J. 2. " . . . [P]assive or trivial acts are not encompassed by the word 'anything' as used in [section 172 of the Criminal Code, R.S.C. 1970, c. C-34]. . . must be read down so as to extend only to things in the nature of profane discourse, rude or indecent behaviour or making a noise . . ." *R. v. Hafey* (1985), (*sub nom. Skoke-Graham v. R.*) 44 C.R. (3d) 289 at 308, 311, [19851 1 S.C.R. 106, 17 C.C.C. (3d) 289, 67 N.S.R. (2d) 181, 155 A.P.R. 181, 16 D.L.R. (4th) 321, 57 N.R. 321, Wilson J.

AORTA. *n.* The main artery which emerges from the heart.

APARTHEID. *n.* The crime of apartheid means inhumane acts of a character similar to those referred to elsewhere in the Statue, committed in the context of an institutionalized regime of systematic oppression and domination by one racial group over any other racial group or groups and committed with the intention of maintaining that regime; Rome Statute, Article 7.

APARTMENT. *n.* A self-contained residential accommodation unit that has cooking, sleeping, bathroom and living room facilities.

APARTMENT BLOCK. A house or building, portions of which are rented or leased as residents to five [or three] or more tenants or families living independently of each other but having common rights in the halls, stairways, yards or other conveniences. Saskatchewan statutes.

APARTMENT BUILDING. A building that is divided into multiple dwelling units or suites.

APARTMENT COMPLEX. A group of physically related apartment buildings.

APARTMENT-TYPE BUILDING. A building intended for residential purposes in whole or in part that contains more than four residential units.

APATISATIO. *n.* Compact; agreement.

APIARY. *n.* A place where bees are kept.

APICES JURIS NON SUNT JURA. [L.] Extremes in law make bad law.

APOLOGY. *n.* [In the context of a defamation suit], "any apology so offered or made must amount to a full and frank withdrawal of the charges conveyed and should be worded so that "an impartial person would consider it reasonably satisfactory in all the circumstances". [You must make and publish an apology] expressing sorrow, withdrawing the imputation, rehabilitating the plaintiff's character as well as you can; not stipulating that the plaintiff is to accept it; not making any terms but publishing it in the interest of truth, and because you are anxious to undo whatever harm which may have accrued from a wrong which you find you have been the unconscious instrument of inflicting. Quoted with approval in *Carter v. Gair* (1999) 64 B.C.L.R. (3d) 272 (C.A.).

APNOEA. *n.* Lack of breath.

A POSTERIORI. [L.] From what comes after.

APP. *abbr.* Appeal.

APPARATUS. *n.* 1. Includes any machine, instrument or device. *Electricity and Gas Inspection Act*, R.S.C. 1985, c. E-4, s. 2. 2. Any device, mechanism or instrument using gas to produce heat, light or power, including its connecting piping and its vent for carrying off the products of as combustion. *Gas Distibution Act* R.S.Q. 1977, c. D-10, s. 1. 3. System electrical equipment of which system conductors form part or are connected thereto and includes all electrical transmission circuits, electrical machines, switch-gear, fittings and accessories. *Coal Mines Regulation Act*, R.S.N.S. 1989 c. 73 s 85(1). See BREATHING ~; BROADCASTING RECEIVING ~; RADIO ~; SCIENTIFIC ~.

APPARENT. *adj.* Readily perceived.

APPARENT AUTHORITY. " . . . [A] legal relationship between the principal and the contractor created by a representation, made by the principal to the contractor, intended to be and in fact acted upon by the contractor, that the agent has authority to enter on behalf of the principal into a contract of a kind within the scope of the 'apparent' authority, so as to render the principal liable to perform any obligations imposed upon him by such contract. To the relationship so created the agent is a stranger. He need not be (although he generally is) aware of the existence of the representation but he must not purport to make the agreement as principal himself . . ." *Freeman & Lockyer v. Buckhurst Park Properties (Mangal) Ltd.*, [1964] 2 Q. B. 480 at 502 (C.A.), Diplock L.J.

APPARENT EASEMENT. An easement which is shown by some sign, audible or visible or otherwise perceptible upon reasonable inspection.

APP. CAS. *abbr.* Law Reports, Appeal Cases, 1875-1890.

APPEAL. *n.* 1. A review of a decision of an inferior body by a superior court for the purpose of testing the soundness of the decision. 2. A reconsideration by a higher court of a decision of a lower court. 3. Proceeding to set aside or vary any judgment of the court appealed from *Supreme Court Act*, R.S.C. 1985, c. S-26, s. 2. 4. The distinction between "an appeal by holding a trial de novo and an appeal to the provincial Court of Appeal is that although the object of both is to determine whether the decision appealed from was right or wrong, in the latter case the question is whether it was right or wrong having regard to the evidence upon which it was based, whereas in the former the issue is to be determined without any reference, except for purposes of cross-examination, to the evidence called in the court appealed from and upon a fresh determination based upon evidence called anew and perhaps accompanied by entirely new evidence. A trial de novo envisages a new trial before a different tribunal than the one which originally decided the issue. *McKenzie v. Mason*, 1992 CarswellBC 282, 72 B.C.L.R. (2d) 53, 9 C.P.C. (3d) 1, 96 D.L.R. (4th) 558, 18 B.C.A.C. 286, 31 W.A.C. 286, Toy, J.A. 5. [I]n s. 18.5 of the *Federal Court Act*, has as its essential nature the review of the decision of an inferior body by a superior court for the purpose of testing the soundness of the decision. An 'appeal' may include a trial de novo, an appeal to the Governor-in-Council, a stated case appeal and traditional appeals upon the record created in the tribunal or court below. *Canada Post Corp. v. Canada (Minister of Public Works)*, 1993 CarswellNat 826, 21 Admin. L.R (2d) 152, 68 F.T.R. 235, McKeown J. See COURT OF~; CROSS ~;

FEDERAL COURT-DIVISION; FEDERAL COURT OF ~; NOTICE OF ~; RIGHT OF ~; TRIBUNAL ~.

APPEAL BOARD. A board established under a statute to hear appeals from administrative decisions or from decisions of first level tribunals. See IMMIGRATION ~; PENSION APPEALS BOARD.

APPEAL COURT. The Court of Appeal in a province or territory or the Appeal Division of the Supreme Court in a province. Also refers to the Supreme Court of Canada and Federal Court of Appeal. May refer to the Supreme Court of a province or the provincial court of a province if that court is fulfilling an appellate function under a statute. Also may refer to the Court Martial Appeal Court of Canada. See COURT MARTIAL ~.

APPEAL DIVISION. A division of the Immigration and Refugee Board called the Immigration Appeal Division.

APPEALS TRIBUNAL. See APPEAL BOARD.

APPEAL TRIBUNAL. See APPEAL BOARD.

APPEAR. *v.* To enter into court and submit to the court's jurisdiction. In some situations, an appearance may be entered by filing a document. See PROMISE TO ~.

APPEARANCE. *n.* A document filed in court which indicates that a person will participate in proceedings or will defend. See CONDITIONAL ~; NON~.

APPEARANCE FORFEIT. The amount of money that a boxer, under a written contract to appear in a professional boxing contest or exhibition agrees to pay in accordance with this Regulation upon his failure to so appear. *Athletics Control Act* R.R.O. 1980 Reg. 76 s. 2.

APPEARANCE NOTICE. 1. A document which requires people to appear in court to answer charges against them. 2. A notice in Form 9 issued by a peace officer. *Criminal Code*, R.S.C. 1985, c. C-46, s. 493.

APPEARANCE OF THE INJURY OR DISEASE. Includes the recurrence of an injury or disease that has been so improved as to have removed the resultant disability. *Pension Act*, R.S.C. 1985, c. P-6, s. 2.

APPEARING CONSPICUOUSLY. Written in such a way that the person against whom

words so noted or appearing are to operate ought reasonably to notice them. *Business Corporations Act*, R.S.O. 1990, c. B.16, s. 53.

APPELLANT. *n.* The party bringing an appeal.

APPELLATE. *adj.* Appealed to.

APPELLATE COURT. 1. In respect of an appeal from a court, means the court exercising appellate jurisdiction with respect to that appeal. 2. " . . . [W]hen the [Divorce Act, R.S.C. 1985 c. 3 (2d Supp.), s. 21(1), (4) and (6)] refers to an appellate court it means something different than a single judge of the appellate court." *Khera v. Khera* (1990), 25 R.F.L. (3d) 82 at 84 (B.C. C.A.), Proudfoot J.A.

APPELLATE JURISDICTION. 1. A superior court's power to review the decision of a lower court. 2. May refer to the jurisdiction of any court or tribunal to review the decision of another person or body.

APPELLEE. *n.* One against whom the appeal is made.

APPELLOR. *n.* A criminal who accuses an accomplice; a person who challenges a jury.

APPENDANT. *adj.* That which the operation of law attaches to land. R. Megarry and H.W.R. Wade, *The Law of Real Property*, 5th ed. (London: Stevens, 1984) at cxxiii. See APPURTENANT.

APPENDIX. *n.* In connection with an appeal, a volume referred to which contains the material documents or other evidence used in the lower court.

APPERTAIN. *v.* To belong to.

APPERTIZE. *v.* To heat food immediately after it is hermetically sealed in a container at a temperature and for a time (a) sufficient to destroy pathogenic and spoilage organisms; and (b) so that it will remain stable and safe under non-refrigerated conditions of storage and distribution. *Meat Inspection Regulations*, C.R.C., c. 1032, s. 2.

APPLE JUICE FROM CONCENTRATE. The product that is obtained by the addition of water to concentrated apple juice. *Processed Fruit and Vegetable Regulations*, C.R.C., c. 291, Schedule I, c. 5.

APPLIANCE. *n.* 1. Any device which utilizes gas to produce light, heat or power or any combination of them. 2. A device that uses a hydrocarbon and includes all valves, fittings, controls and components attached or to be attached thereto. *Energy Act* R.S.O. 1990 c. E.16, s. 1. 3. See DENTAL ~S; HOUSEHOLD ~; OPHTHALMIC ~; OPTICAL ~; ORTHOPAEDIC ~S; PROSTHETIC ~; SPACE-HEATING ~.

APPLICABLE. *adj.* " . . . [W]hen courts have considered what laws of England are applicable to a province under the above-quoted section [Saskatchewan Act, 4 & 5 Edw. VII, c. 42, s. 16], applicable . . . has been interpreted to mean 'suitable' or 'properly adapted to the condition of the country' and not 'intended to apply to.'" *Miller-Morse Hardware Co. v. Smart* (1917 28 D.L.R. 171 at 174, [1917] 3 W.L.R. 1113, 10 Sask. L.R. 409 (C.A.), the court per McKay J.A.

APPLICANT. *n.* 1. A person who applies or on whose behalf an application is made for assistance, a benefit, a loan or grant. 2. A person applying for a licence, registration, permit or passport. 3. One who brings an application or petition.

APPLICATIO EST VITA REGULAE. [L.] The application is the life of a rule.

APPLICATION. *n.* 1. A request. 2. A motion to a judge or court. 3. The commencement of proceedings before a court of tribunal. 4. " . . .The expression application in this context [s. 24(1) of the Charter] is intended to refer simply to the fact that the substantive right to relief which the section gives may be invoked by proceedings taken in court of competent jurisdiction for that purpose . . . a compendious term which denotes the types of procedings which by law are available to secure the form of relief sought . . ." *R.L. Crain Inc. v. Couture* (1983), 6 D.L.R. (4th) 478 at 487, 30 Sask. R. 191, 10 C.C.C. (3d) 119, 9 C.R.R. 287 (Q.B.), Scheibel J. 5. A civil proceeding that is commenced by notice of application or by application. *Courts of Justice Act*, R.S.O.1990 c. C.43 s.1. See DUE ~; EXTERNAL ~; INTERLOCUTORY ~; NOTICE OF ~; SUMMARY ~.

APPLICATION FOR CERTIFICATION. A request by a trade union to a labour relations board for designation as bargaining agent for a unit of employees.

APPLICATION PROGRAM. A program designed for a specific task, ordinarily chosen by the user, such as to maintain records, perform certain calculations or display graphic charts. "Application programs" are normally written in high level languages that are designed to be eas-

ily used by the unsophisticated. *Apple Computer Inc. v. Macintosh Computers Ltd.* 3 C.I.P.R 133, 3 C.P.R. (3d) 34, F.C.T.D. Cullen J.

APPLIED BIOLOGICAL SCIENCE. A biological science, including botany, zoology, ecology, biochemistry and microbiology, if the biological science is applied to the management, use, conservation, protection, restoration, or enhancement of (a) aquatic or terrestrial ecosystems, or (b) biological resources within these ecosystems. *College of Applied Biology Act*, S.B.C. 2002, c. 68, s. 1.

APPLIED BIOLOGY. The application of the applied biological sciences, including collecting or analyzing inventories or other data or carrying out of research or assessments, to design, evaluate, advise on, direct or otherwise provide professional or technical support to projects, works, undertakings or field practices on public or private lands, but does not include (a) pure scientific research, or (b) teaching. *College of Applied Biology Act*, S.B.C. 2002, c. 68, s. 1.

APPLIED BIOLOGY TECHNICIAN. A person admitted or reinstated to the college of applied biology as an applied biology technician, whose name appears in the register of the college. *College of Applied Biology Act*, S.B.C. 2002, c. 68, s. 1.

APPLIED SCIENCE. See SCHOOL OF ~.

APPLY. *v.* 1. To request; to make application; to bring a motion to a court. 2. In respect of a label, to attach to, imprint on, include in or cause to accompany in any other way a product. 3. In relation to a mark, includes any application or attachment thereof to, or any use thereof on in connection with or in relation to (a) an article, (b) anything attached to an article, (c) anything to which an article is attached, (d) anything in or on which an article is, or (e) anything so used or placed as to lead to a reasonable belief that the mark thereon is meant to be taken as a mark on an article. See LIBERTY TO ~.

APPOINT. *v.* To select; to designate; to assign an office or duty.

APPOINTED DAY. A day designated for a particular purpose.

APPOINTEE. *n.* A person chosen for some purpose.

APPOINTMENT. *n.* 1. Designation of a person to fill an office. 2. An appointment made in the exercise of a power to appoint property among several objects. 3. As used in the Public Service Employment Act, R.S.C. 1970, c. P-32, s. 2, means assignment. *Lucas v. Public Service Commission Appeal Board* (1987), 40 D.L.R. (4th) 365 at 372 (Fed. C.A.), the court per Heald J.A. 4. A scheduled meeting or consultation. See POWER OF ~.

APPOINTOR. *n.* One given a power; a person who names someone else for an office.

APPORTIONMENT. *n.* A division of a whole into proportional parts according to the claimants' rights.

APPRAISAL. *n.* Valuation. See COLLECTIVE ~.

APPRAISAL REMEDY. " . . . [T]he statutory right granted to minority shareholders [Canada Business Corporations Act, S.C. 1974-75-76, c. 33, s. 184], even where 'oppression' as such is not in issue, to oblige either the majority or the corporation to purchase the shares of those minority shareholders who dissent from some basic change imposed by the majority. That purchase is at an appraised value effected by an independent outside instrumentality; . . ." *Domglas Inc. v. Jarislowsky Fraser & Co.* (1980) 13 B.L.R. 135 at 161, [1980] C.S. 925 (Que.), Greenberg J.

APPRAISAL RIGHT. See APPRAISAL REMEDY.

APPRAISE. *v.* To estimate or set the value of a thing.

APPRAISEMENT. *n.* The act of valuing property. Appraisement of a ship may be ordered by Federal Court.

APPRAISER. *n.* 1. "In determining whether the proceeding . . . is a valuation or an arbitration, . . . Generally speaking, if the person to whom a reference is made is intended to use his skill and knowledge of the particular subject without taking any evidence or hearing the parties, he is not prima facie an arbitrator, he is a valuer or appraiser." *Pfeil v. Simcoe & Erie General Insurance Co.*, [1986] 2 W.W.R. 710 at 715, 45 Sask. R. 241, 24 D.L.R. (4th) 752, [1986] I.L.R. 1-2055 (C.A.), the court per Vancise J.A. 2. A person appointed to engage in valuations. 3. A property valuator. See DAMAGE ~; QUALIFIED ~.

APPRECIATE. *v.* 1. "The verb 'know' has a positive connotation re a bare awareness, the act of receiving information without more. The act

of appreciating, on the other hand, is a second stage in a mental process, requiring the analysis of knowledge or experience in one manner or another. It is therefore clear on the plain meaning of the section [Criminal Code, R.S.C. 1970, c. C-34, s. 16] that Parliament intended that for a person to be insane within the statutory definition, he must be incapable, firstly, of appreciating in the analytical sense the nature and quality of the act or of knowing in the positive sense that his act was wrong." *R. v. Kjeldsen* (1981), 24 C.R. (3d) 289 at 295, [1981] 2 S.C.R. 617, [1982] 1 W. W. R. 577, 17 Alta. L.R. (2d) 97, 28 C.R. (3d) 81, 39 N.R. 376, 64 C.C.C. (2d) 161, 131 D.L.R. (3d) 121, 34 A.R. 576, the court per McIntyre J. 2. "To 'know' the nature and quality of an act may mean merely to be aware of the physical act, while to appreciate may involve estimation and understanding of the consequences of that act." *R. v. Cooper* (1980), 13 C.R. (3d) 97 at 119 (Eng.), [1980] 1 S.C.R. 1149, 18 C.R. (3d) 138 (Fr.), 51 C.C.C. (2d)129, 31 N.R. 234, 4 L. Med. Q. 227, 110 D.L.R. (3d) 46, Dickson J. (Laskin C.J.C., Beetz, Estey and McIntyre JJ. concurring). 3. " . . . [I]mports an additional requirement to mere knowledge of the physical quality of the act. The requirement, unique to Canada is that of preception an ability to perceive the consequences, impact and results of a physical act. An accused may be aware of the physical character of his action (i.e., in choking) without necessarily having the capacity to appreciate that, in nature and quality, that act will result in the death of a human being." *R. v Cooper* (1980), 13 C.R. (3d) 97 at 120 En . 19 1 S.C.R. 1149, 18 C.R. (3d) 138 (Fr.), 51 C.C.C. (2d) 129, 31 N.R. 234, 4 L. Med. Q. 227, 110 D.L.R. (3d) 46, Dickson J. (Laskin C.J.C., Beetz, Estey and McIntyre JJ. concurring). 4. To increase in value.

APPRECIATION. *n.* 1. Growth in value. *Waters v. Waters* (1986), 4 R.F.L. (3d) 283 at 293, 44 Man. R. (2d) 109 (C.A.), Twaddle J.A. (Huband J.A. concurring). 2. An accused's appreciation of the nature and quality of an act or omission refers to an accused's ability to perceive the consequences, impact and results of a physical act and *not* to an accused's ability to appreciate that the *legal* consequences of an act are applicable to him or her. *R. v. Abbey*, [1982] 2 S.C.R. 24, per Dickson, J. as he then was.

APPREHEND. *v.* " . . . [A]s used in s. 12 of the Act [Child Welfare Act, 1954 (Ont.), c. 8] contemplates a physical possession and custody of the child and taking him to place of safety and detaining him there until he can be brought before a Judge." *Blackmore, Re* (195 8), 120 C.C.C13 19 at 23 (Ont. C.A.), Laidlaw J.A.

APPREHENSION. *n.* 1. Capturing a person on a criminal charge. 2. The act of taking a child into custody. 3. Apprehension is an interim child protection measure. Where it involves the physical removal of a child from his or her parents' care, it is also one of the most disruptive forms of intervention undertaken to protect children. *Winnipeg Child & Family Services (Central Area) v. W. (K.L.)* 2000 CarswellMan 469, 2000 SCC 48, [2001] 1 W.W.R. 1, 260 N.R. 203, 10 R.F.L. (5th) 122, 78 C.R.R. (2d) 1, [2000] 2 S.C.R. 519, 150 Man. R. (2d) 161, 230 W.A.C. 161, 191 D.L.R. (4th) 1 Per L'Heureux-Dubé J. (Gonthier, Major, Bastarache, Binnie JJ. concurring). See REASONABLE ~ OF BIAS.

APPREHENSION OF BIAS. The test for finding a reasonable apprehension of bias has challenged courts in the past. It is interchangeably expressed as a "real danger of bias," a" real likelihood of bias," a "reasonable suspicion of bias" and in several other ways. The test for reasonable apprehension of bias is that set out by de Grandpré J. in *Committee for Justice & Liberty v. Canada (National Energy Board)*(1976), [1978] 1 S.C.R. 369. The apprehension of bias must be a reasonable one, held by reasonable and right-minded persons, applying themselves to the question and obtaining thereon the required information... [T]hat test is "what would an informed person, viewing the matter realistically and practically—and having thought the matter through—conclude. Would he think that it is more likely than not that [the decision-maker], whether consciously or unconsciously, would not decide fairly." The grounds for this apprehension must, however, be substantial and I . . . [refuse] to accept the suggestion that the test be related to the "very sensitive or scrupulous conscience". See REASONABLE ~; REASONABLENESS.

APPREHENSION OF IMPROPRIETY. "[In the context of disqualifying a lawyer] . . . the inquiry should be whether a reasonable and right-minded former client who knew the facts and was prepared to understand them, would have an apprehension of impropriety." *Bank of Nova Scotia v. Imperial Developments (Canada) Ltd.* (1989), 72 C.B.R. (ICS.) 285 at 294, [1989] 3 W. W.R. 21, 5 8 Man. R. (2d) 100 (Q.B.), Simonsen J.

APPREHENSIVE. *adj.* " . . . [S]uspicious, or fearful of something. *Golding v. Waterhouse* (1876), 16 N.B.R. 313 at 319 (U.) Allen C.J. (Duff and Fisher JJ.A. concurring).

APPRENDRE. *n.* [Fr.] A profit or fee to be received or taken.

APPRENTICE. *n.* 1. A person who is at least sixteen years of age and who has entered into a contract under which he or she is to receive, from or through an employer, training and instruction in a trade. 2. A person who works as assistant to a journeyman with a view to qualify as a journeyman. 3. A person who has been duly registered with the association for training in pharmacy pursuant to the provisions of this Act and the bylaws, rules and regulations. *The Pharmacy Act*, R.S.S. 1978, c. P-9, s. 2. See PRE-~.

APPRENTICE PILOT. A person who is training to become a licensed pilot. *Pilotage Act*, R.S.C. 1985, c. P-14, s. 2.

APPRENTICESHIP. *n.* A method of vocational training including a period of practical training with an employer and, generally, courses in relevant technical and vocational subjects. See CONTRACT OF ~; INDENTURED ~; TERM OF ~.

APPRENTICESHIP ACT. Statute governing the terms of apprenticeships.

APPRENTICESHIP AGREEMENT. A written agreement under which an employee is to receive job training, on-the-job instruction, practical work and experience provided by an employer and related technical instruction in a designated trade.

APPRENTICESHIP PROGRAM. A program of training in a designated trade under which an apprentice receives formal instruction and on the job training.

APPRO. *abbr.* Approval.

APPROACH. See COST ~; FUNCTIONAL ~.

APPROACH ANGLE. The smallest angle, in a plan side view of a vehicle, formed by the level surface on which the vehicle is standing and a line tangent to the front tire static loaded radius arc and touching the underside of the vehicle forward of the front tire. *On-Road Vehicle and Engine Emission Regulations*, SOR/2003-2, s. 1(1).

APPROACH SURFACE. 1. An imaginary inclined plane extending upward and outward from the end of each strip along and at right angles to the projected centre line thereof. *Airport Zoning Regulations*, Canada regulations. 2. An imaginary inclined plane the lower end of which is a horizontal line at right angles to the centre line of a strip and passing through a point at the strip end on the centre fine of the strip. *Airport Zoning Regulations*, Canada regulations.

APPROACH WHARF. That section of a wharf or wall as defined by appropriate signs immediately above and below a lock. *Canal Regulations*, C.R.C., c. 1564, s. 2.

APPROPRIATE. *v.* 1. " . . . [T]o take it with a view to using it as one's own, to become indeed the owner in fact whatever the legality of the relationship is." *R. v. Dalzell* (1982), 3 C.C.C. (3d) 232 at 243, 54 N.S.R. (2d) 239, 111 A.P.R. 239 (Co. Ct.), O'Hearn Co. Ct. J. 2. To earmark for a purpose.

APPROPRIATE. *adj.* " . . . [E]mbraces a concept of suitableness, proper, and fitting to a particular situation . . . Appropriate is the equivalent of 'convenable' in the sense of being the correct or suitable remedy or reparation; . . ." *Kodellas v. Saskatchewan (Human Rights Commission)* (1989), 89 C.L.L.C. 17,027 at 16,303, [1989] 5 W.W.R. 1, 10 C.H.R.R. D/6305, 60 D.L.R. (4th) 143, 77 Sask. R. 94 (C.A.), Vancise J.A.

APPROPRIATE ADVICE. 1. In relation to any fact or circumstance means the advice of competent persons qualified, in their respective spheres, to advise on the professional or technical aspects of that fact or that circumstance, as the case may be. *Limitation of Actions Act*, S.M. 1980, c. 28, s. 3. 2. " . . . [S]uitable in the circumstances of those facts . . ." *Levitt v. Carr* (1992),12 C.C.L.T. (2d)195 at 209, 66 B.C.L.R. (2d) 58, [1992] 4 W.W.R. 160, 8 C.P.C. (3d) 101, 12 B.C.A.C. 27, 23 W.A.C. 27, Hutcheon, Toy, Cumming, Gibbs and Goldie JJ.A.

APPROPRIATE AGENCY. The agency for the province or territory in which the person by whom or on whose behalf a notice of intention is signed has his place of business or if that person has more than one place of business in Canada and the places of business are not in the same province or territory, the agency for the province or territory in which that person has his principal place of business or if that person has no place of business, then agency for the province or territory in which the person resides; and, in respect of a notice of intention registered be-

fore December 1,1980 means the office in which registration was required to be made by the law in force at the time of such registration. *Bank Act*, R.S.C. 1985 c. B-1 s. 178(5).

APPROPRIATE AND JUST REMEDY. In the circumstances of a *Charter* claim is one that meaningfully vindicates the rights and freedoms of the claimants. It must employ means that are legitimate within the framework of our constitutional democracy. Is a judicial one which vindicates the right while invoking the function and powers of a court. It will not be appropriate for a court to leap into the kinds of decisions and functions for which its design and expertise are manifestly unsuited. One that, after ensuring that the right of the claimant is fully vindicated, is also fair to the party against whom the order is made. The remedy should not impose substantial hardships that are unrelated to securing the right. The judicial approach to remedies must remain flexible and responsive to the needs of a given case. *Doucet-Boudreau v. Nova Scotia (Department of Education)* 2003 SCC 62, per Iacobucci and Arbour, JJ.

APPROPRIATE AUTHORITY. The public body or agency designated as responsible for a particular subject matter.

APPROPRIATE BARGAINING AGENT. The recognized bargaining agent authorized to negotiate terms and conditions of employment on behalf of employees.

APPROPRIATE CHIEF JUSTICE. (a) In relation to the Province of Ontario, the Chief Justice of the Ontario Court; (b) in relation to the Province of Quebec, the Chief Justice of the Superior Court; (c) in relation to the Provinces of Prince Edward Island and Newfoundland, the Chief Justice of the Supreme Court, Trial Division; (d) in relation to the Provinces of New Brunswick, Manitoba, Saskatchewan and Alberta, the Chief Justice of the Court of Queen's Bench; (e) in relation to the Provinces of Nova Scotia and British Columbia, the Chief Justice of the Supreme Court; and (f) in relation to Yukon, the Northwest Territories and Nunavut, the Chief Justice of the Court of Appeal. *Criminal Code*, R.S.C. 1985, c. C-46, s. 745.6(3).

APPROPRIATE FOR COLLECTIVE BARGAINING. With reference to a unit, means a unit that is appropriate for such purposes whether it is an employer unit, craft unit, technical unit, plant unit, or any other unit and whether or not the employees therein are employed by one or more employer.

APPROPRIATE PERSON. (a) The person specified by the security or by special endorsement to be entitled to the security; (b) if a person described in paragraph (a) is described as a fiduciary but is no longer serving in the described capacity, either that person or his successor; (c) if the security or endorsement mentioned in paragraph (a) specifies more than one person as fiduciaries and one or more are no longer serving in the described capacity, the remaining fiduciary or fiduciaries, whether or not a successor has been appointed or qualified; (d) if a person described in paragraph (a) is an individual and is without capacity to act by reason of death, incompetence, infancy, minority or otherwise, his fiduciary; (e) if the security or endorsement mentioned in paragraph (a) specifies more than one person with right of survivorship and by reason of death all cannot sign, the survivor or survivors; (f) a person having power to sign under applicable law or a power of attorney; (g) or to the extent that a person described in paragraphs (a) to (f) may act through an agent, his authorized agent. *Business Corporations acts.*

APPROPRIATE UNIT. A unit of employees appropriate for the purpose of bargaining collectively.

APPROPRIATION. *n.* 1. Means by which Parliament or a legislature regulates the expenditure of public money voted to be applied to particular purposes. 2. Any authority of Parliament to pay money out of the Consolidated Revenue Fund. *Financial Administration Act*, R.S.C. 1985, c. F-11, s. 2. 3 . Any authority of a legislature to pay money out of the Consolidated Fund. See MIS~; STATUTORY ~.

APPROPRIATION BILL. A bill ordered to be brought in by the House when it concurs with the Estimates. A. Fraser, W.A. Dawson, & J. Holtby, eds., *Beauchesne's Rules and Forms of the House of Commons of Canada*, 6th ed. (Toronto: Carswell, 1989) at 263.

APPROVAL. *n.* Confirmation; acceptance; ratification. See SALE ON ~.

APPROVE. *v.* To confirm, accept, ratify.

APPROVED. *adj.* Authorized, directed or ratified.

APPROVED CONTAINER. (a) In respect of breath samples a container of a kind that is designed to receive a sample of the breath of a person for analysis and is a roved as suitable for the purposes of section 358 by order of the At-torney General of Canada; and (b) in respect of blood samples, a container of a kind that is designed to receive a sample of the blood of a person for analysis and is approved as suitable for the purposes of section 258 by order of the Attorney General of Canada. *Criminal Code,* R.S.C. 1985 c. C-46 s. 254(1).

APPROVED CREDIT AGENCY. A lending agency that may be approved by the Lieutenant Governor in Council for the purpose of making loans to the society or the company for the purposes of this Act. The Co-operative Guarantee Act, R.S.S. 1978, c. C-35, s. 2.

APPROVED HOME. A home certified in accordance with legislation in which patients may be placed from a psychiatric facility.

APPROVED HOSPITAL. A hospital in a province approved for the purposes of this section by the Minister of Heal of that province-*Criminal Code* R.S.C. 1985 c. C 46, s. 287(6).

APPROVED INSTRUMENT. An instrument of a kind that is designed to receive and make an analysis of a sample of the breath of a person in order to measure the concentration of alcohol in the blood of that person and is approved as suitable for the purposes of section 258 by order of the Attorney General of Canada. *Criminal Law Amendment Act* R.S.C. 1985 (1 st Supp.), c. 27 s. 254.

APPROVED LENDER. A lender or lending institution approved for purposes of making loans under governing legislation.

APPROVED PROGRAM OF STUDY. Courses leading to a certificate, diploma or degree.

APPROVED SCREENING DEVICE. *A* device of a kind that is designed to ascertain the presence of alcohol in the blood of a person and that is approved for the purposes of this section by order of the Attorney General of Canada. *Criminal Law Amendment Act*, R.S.C. 1985 (1st Supp.), c. 27, s. 254.

APPROVED SHARE. A share of the capital stock of a prescribed labour-sponsored venture capital corporation, but does not include (a) a share issued by a registered labour-sponsored venture capital corporation the venture capital business of which was discontinued before the time of the issue, and (b) a share issued by a prescribed labour-sponsored venture capital corporation (other than a registered labour-sponsored venture capital corporation) if, at the time of the issue, every province under the laws of which the corporation is a prescribed labour-sponsored venture capital corporation has suspended or terminated its assistance in respect of the acquisition of shares of the capital stock of the corporation. *Income Tax Act*, R.S.C. 1985, c. 1 (5th Supp.), s. 127.4(1).

APPROVEMENT. *n*. Improvement.

APPROXIMATELY. *adv*. 1. "...'[A]bout'..." *British Whig Publishing Co. v. E.B. Eddy Co.* (1921), 62 S.C.R. 576 at 583, 59 D.L.R. 77, Anglin J. 2. :... '[M]ore or less.'" *British Whig Publishing Co. v. E.B. Eddy Co.* (1921), 62 S.C.R. 576 at 589, 59 D.L.R. 77, Mignault J. 3. "...[I]s given a primary meaning of 'very near or nearly resembling'. [In the case of a taxation of solicitor's bill] a margin of 10 per cent is the maximum that can be considered within the word 'approximately'." *Paolini v. Evans, Keenan* (1976), 2 C.P.C. 113 at 116, 13 O.R. (2d) 767 (H.C.), Osler J.

APPROXIMATE ODDS. The odds that are calculated by an association before the close of betting on a race. *Pari-Mutuel Betting Supervision Regulations*, SOR/91-365, s. 2.

APPURTENANCE. *n*. One thing which belongs to another thing.

APPURTENANT. *adj*. 1. Belonging or pertaining to. 2. "...[A]nnexed'...." *Moreau Estate v. Regnier*, [1986] 4 W.W.R. 548 at 551 (Man. Q.B.), Hansen J. 3. That which an act of parties attaches to land. R. Megarry and H.W.R. Wade, *The Law of Real Property*, 5th ed. (London: Stevens, 1984) at cxxiii. See APPENDANT.

A.P.R. *abbr*. Atlantic Provinces Reports, 1975-.

A PRIORI. [L.] From cause to effect.

APRON. A part of an aerodrome, other than the manoeuvring area, that is intended to be used for the loading and unloading of passengers and cargo, the refuelling, servicing, maintenance and parking of aircraft and the movement of aircraft, vehicles and persons engaged in services necessary for those purposes. *Canadian Aviation Regulations*, SOR/96-433, s. 101.01(1).

APRON TRAFFIC. All aircraft, vehicles, pedestrians and equipment utilizing the apron area of the airport. *Airport Traffic Regulations*, C.R.C., c. 886, s. 2.

APRON TRAFFIC CONTROL CLEARANCE. Authorization by an apron traffic control unit for an aircraft to proceed on a controlled apron. *Airport Traffic Regulations*, C.R.C., c. 886, s. 64.

APRON TRAFFIC CONTROL UNIT. Staff of an airport that provides apron traffic control service at the airport and includes the staff of a mobile control vehicle. *Airport Traffic Regulations*, C.R.C., c. 886, s. 64.

APT. *abbr*. Apartment.

APT DESCRIPTIVE WORDS. Metes and bounds description and includes an abbreviated description.

APTITUDE. *n*. "...'[N]atural or acquired abilities for performing a task'..." *Brossard (Town) v. Quebec (Commission des droits de la personne)* (1989), 10 C.H.R.R. D/5515 at D/5530, 88 C.L.L.C. 17,031, [1988] 2 S.C.R. 297, 88 N.R. 321, 18 Q.A.C. 164, 53 D.L.R. (4th) 609, Beetz J. (McIntyre, Lamer and La Forest JJ. concurring.)

APTITUDE TEST. A test designed to measure abilities such as mechanical or clerical, or to determine ability to learn a second or subsequent language.

APT WORDS. Words which produce the intended legal effect. *Holloway v. Miner* (1916), 10 W.W.R. 995 at 999 (Man. K.B.), Curran J.

AQUA CEDIT SOLO. [L.] The water goes with the soil.

AQUACULTURAL ELECTRIC SYSTEM. All machinery, apparatus and appliances for the generation or distribution of electricity in an aquaculture operation, whether or not affixed to real property. *Bank Act*, S.C. 1991, c. 46, s. 425(1).

AQUACULTURAL EQUIPMENT. Implements, apparatus, appliances and machinery of any kind usually affixed to real property for use in an aquaculture operation, but does not include an aquacultural electric system. *Bank Act*, S.C. 1991, c. 46, s. 425(1).

AQUACULTURAL IMPLEMENTS. Tools, implements, apparatus, appliances and machines of any kind not usually affixed to real property, for use in an aquaculture operation, and includes net pen systems, vehicles and boats for use in aquaculture. *Bank Act*, S.C. 1991, c. 46, s. 425(1).

AQUACULTURAL PRODUCE. Aquatic flora and fauna raised or being raised as part of an aquacultural operation. *Aquaculture Act*, R.S.N.S. 1989, c. 18, s. 2.

AQUACULTURE. *n*. The cultivation of aquatic plants and animals. *Bank Act*, S.C. 1991, c. 46, s. 425(1).

AQUACULTURE FACILITY. (i) A site where aquaculture is being carried on, or (ii) a parcel of land with respect to which an application has been made to carry on aquaculture and includes all structures, machinery, equipment and tools on the site or parcel of land. *Aquaculture Act*, R.S. Nfld. 1990, c. A-13, s. 2.

AQUACULTURE OPERATION. Any premises or site where aquaculture is carried out.

AQUACULTURIST. Includes the owner, occupier, landlord and tenant of an aquaculture operation.

AQUA CURRIT ET DEBET CURRERE. [L.] Water flows and should flow.

AQUAGE. *n*. Watercourse.

AQUAGIUM. *n*. Watercourse.

AQUATIC. *adj*. Refers to fresh, brackish or marine water. *Aquaculture Act*, R.S.N.S. 1989, c. 18, s. 2.

AQUATIC BROODSTOCK. Any aquatic plants and animals used to produce aquatic seedstock. *Bank Act*, S.C. 1991, c. 46, s. 425(1).

AQUATIC PLANT. Includes benthic and detached algae, marine flowering plants, brown algae, red algae, green algae and phytoplankton. *Fisheries Act*, R.S.B.C. 1979, c. 137, s. 12.

AQUATIC PLANTS OR ANIMALS. Plants and animals that, at most stages of their development or life cycles, live in an aquatic environment. *Bank Act*, S.C. 1991, c. 46, s. 425(1).

AQUATIC RESERVE. An area, consisting mainly of fresh water, salt water or brackish water, established to protect all or part of a body of water or watercourse, including associated wetlands, because of the exceptional value it holds from a scientific, biodiversity-based viewpoint, or to conserve the diversity of its biocenoses or biotopes; *Natural Heritage Conservation Act*, R.S.Q., c.C-61.01, s. 2.

AQUATIC RIGHTS. Rights which persons have to running or still water.

AQUATIC SEEDSTOCK. Aquatic plants and animals that at any stage of their development are purchased or collected by an aquaculturist

for cultivation. *Bank Act*, S.C. 1991, c. 46, s. 425(1).

AQUATIC SPECIES. A wildlife species that is a fish, as defined in section 2 of the *Fisheries Act*, or a marine plant, as defined in section 47 of that Act. *Species at Risk Act*, S.C. 2002, c. 29, s. 2(1).

AQUICULTURAL PLANT. See ECONOMIC ~.

AQUIFER. *n*. A water-bearing formation that is capable of transmitting water in sufficient quantities to serve as a source of water supply. *Wells Act*, R.R.O. 1990, Reg. 903, s. 1.

A QUO. [L.] From which.

A.R. *abbr* 1. Anno Regni. 2. Alberta Reports, 1977-.

ARABLE. *adj*. Suitable for purposes of cultivation.

ARABLE LAND. 1. Land which is suitable for cultivation. 2. "The test of arable land, in my opinion, is: Can it reasonably be cultivated, and, if so, is the soil of such a quality that it will, when cultivated, produce a reasonable crop of grain—not necessarily wheat—in an ordinary season? . . ." *Mutual Life Assurance Co. v. Armstrong*, [1924] 3 W.W.R. 659 at 664, 19 Sask. L.R. 90, [1924] 4 D.L.R. 1144 (C.A.), Lamont J.A. (Haultain C.J.S. concurring).

ARACHNOID MATER. The middle membrane which covers the brain and spinal cord. F.A. Jaffe, *A Guide to Pathological Evidence*, 3d ed. (Toronto: Carswell, 1991) at 212.

ARB. *abbr* Arbitrator.

ARB. BD. *abbr*. Arbitration Board.

ARBITER. *n*. Referee; arbitrator.

ARBITRABILITY. *n*. The capability of matter to be determined by an arbitrator or referee.

ARBITRABLE. *adj*. The term "arbitrable" is generally used by labour lawyers as a synonym for "within jurisdiction", but this begs the question. Arbitrable [as used in s. 44(1) of the *Labour Relations Act*, R.S.O. 1980, c. 228] encompasses, in a restricted sense, a determination of whether the collective agreement under arbitration is in force. If the issue is arbitrable, then the arbitrator has jurisdiction, at least in the limited sense of being empowered to decide that question." *Dayco (Can.) Ltd. v. C.A.W.* 1993 CarswellOnt 883, 14 Admin. L.R. (2d) 1, 13

O.R. (3d) 164 (note), 152 N.R. 1, 63 O.A.C. 1, (*sub nom. Dayco v. N.A.W.*) C.E.B. & P.G.R. 8141, (*sub nom. Dayco v. C.A.W.*) 93 C.L.L.C. 14,032, [1993] 2 S.C.R. 230, 102 D.L.R. (4th) 609. Per La Forest, J.

ARBITRAGE. *n*. The act of purchasing in one place, where a thing is cheaper, and selling somewhere else simultaneously.

ARBITRAL AWARD. An award made by a board or an arbitrator appointed in respect of a dispute.

ARBITRAL ERROR. An error made by an arbitrator in the course of an arbitration that constitutes misconduct and includes (a) corrupt or fraudulent conduct, (b) bias, (c) exceeding his powers, or (d) failure to observe the rules of natural justice.

ARBITRAL TRIBUNAL. A sole arbitrator or a panel of arbitrators.

ARBITRAMENT. *n*. The award or decision of arbitrators upon a matter of dispute.

ARBITRAMENT AND AWARD. When parties had submitted a question to an arbitrator and received an award, they could successfully plead this in an action for damages as a good defence to the action.

ARBITRAMENTUM AEQUUM TRIBUIT CUIQUE SUUM. [L.] A just arbitrament awards right to each person.

ARBITRARILY. *adv*. Capriciously; without limits of power.

ARBITRARILY DETAINED. Detained without proper procedures having been followed.

ARBITRARILY IMPRISONED. Imprisoned without proper procedures having been followed.

ARBITRARY. *adj*. 1. " . . . A discretion if arbitrary is there are no criteria express or implied, which govern its exercise." *R. v. Hufsky* (1988), 84 N.R. 365 at 377 (S.C.C.), Le Dain J. 2. . . . [C]apricious, despotic or unjustifiable." *R. v. Cayer* 11988 28 O.A.C. 105 at 114 6 M.V.R. (2d) 1 (C.A.), Howland C.J.O., Martin and Griffiths JJ.A.

ARBITRARY PUNISHMENT. Punishment ordered at a judge's discretion.

ARBITRATION. *n*. 1. "The common law has . . . developed two concepts which it regards as characteristic of arbitration: the existence of a dispute and the duty or intent of the parties, as the case may be, to submit that dispute to arbitration." *Zittrer c. Sport Masks Inc*. (1988), 38 B.L.R. 221 at 284, 83 N.R. 322, [1988] 1 S.C.R. 564, 13 Q.A.C. 241, L'Heureux-Dube J. (Lamer, Wilson and Le Dain JJ. concurring). 2. The determination of a dispute by an arbitrator. 3. A procedure to determine an interest dispute. See AD HOC ~; COMMERCIAL ~; COMPULSORY ~; GRIEVANCE ~; INTEREST ~; LABOUR ~; RIGHTS ~; STAY OF ~.

ARBITRATION AGREEMENT. An agreement by the parties to submit to arbitration all or certain disputes which have arisen or which may arise between them in respect of a defined legal relationship, whether contractual or not. An arbitration agreement may be in the form of an arbitration clause in a contract or in the form of a separate agreement. See INTERNATIONAL ~.

ARBITRATION BOARD. A board constituted by or pursuant to a collective agreement or by agreement between the parties of a collective agreement.

ARBITRATION CLAUSE. The clause in a contract providing for submission of disputes under contract to arbitration for resolution.

ARBITRATOR. *n*. 1. A person who decides disputes on the basis of evidence which the parties adduce. Generally disputes are referred to an arbitrator on consent by the parties to the dispute or under the terms of an agreement between the parties. 2. " . . . [A] person appointed under an agreement which contemplates such an appointment for the purpose of resolving a dispute between the parties to the agreement, . . .' *Concord Pacific Developments Ltd v. British Columbia Pavilion Corp*. (1991), 60 B.C.L.R. (2d) 121 at 132, 85 D.L.R. (4th) 402 (C.A.), Lambert J.A. 3. Includes umpire and referee in the nature of an arbitrator. See BROADCASTING ~; PERMANENT ~; PROFESSIONAL ~.

ARBITRIUM EST JUDICIUM. [L.] The award of an arbitrator is the same as a judgment.

ARBOR DUM CRESCIT; LIGNUM CUM CRESCERE NESCIT. [L.] While growing a tree is called a tree, but it is called timber when it has reached its fullest growth.

ARCHAEOLOGICAL ARTIFACT. Any tangible evidence of human activity that is more than 50 years old and in respect of which an unbroken chain of possession or regular pattern of usage cannot be demonstrated, and includes a Denesuline archaeological specimen referred to in section 40.4.9 of the Nunavut Land Claims Agreement. *Nunavut Archaeological and Palaeontological Sites Regulations*, SOR/2001-220, s. 1.

ARCHAEOLOGICAL INVESTIGATION. Investigation by any person in or on lands in or of the province for the purpose of discovering in or forming part of the soil (including, without limitation of the generality of the word "soil", soil under any water, fresh or salt) within or of the province remains of ancient civilization or historic objects but does not include studies, surveys or examinations which do not involve interference with or removal of, (i) the soil (ii) any historic objects in, or partly in, the soil.

ARCHAEOLOGICAL OBJECT. An object that is the product of human art, workmanship or use, including plant and animal remains that have been modified by or, deposited due to human activities, and that is of value for its historic or archaeological significance.

ARCHAEOLOGICAL PROPERTY. Property indicating prehistoric or historic human occupation. *Cultural Property Act*, R.S.Q., c.B-4, s. 1.

ARCHAEOLOGICAL RESOURCE. A work of humans that (i) is primarily of value for its prehistoric, historic, cultural or scientific significance, and (ii) is or was buried or partially buried in land in Alberta or submerged beneath the surface of any watercourse or permanent body of water in Alberta, and includes those works of man or classes of works of humans designated by the regulations as archaeological resources. *Historical Resources Act* R.S.A. 2000, c. H-9, s. 1.

ARCHAEOLOGICAL SITE. 1. A place where archaeological property is found. 2. A site or work of archaeological, ethnological or historical importance, interest or significance or where an archaeological specimen is found, and includes explorers' cairns.

ARCHAEOLOGICAL SPECIMEN. An object or specimen of archaeological, ethnological or historical importance, interest or significance and includes explorers' documents.

ARCHETYPE. *n.* The original from which copies are made.

ARCHITECT. *n.* 1. A person who is engaged for hire, gain or hope of reward in (i) the planning, designing or supervision of, or (ii) the supplying of plans, drawings or specifications for, the erection, construction, enlargement or alteration of buildings for other persons, but does not include a person employed by a registered architect as a draftsman, student clerk of works, superintendent or in any other similar capacity, nor a superintendent of buildings paid by the owner thereof and acting under directions and control of a registered architect. 2. A person who is registered or licensed or who holds a certificate of practice or a temporary licence under the Architects Act or is registered as a member of the provincial association of architects.

ARCHITECT'S CERTIFICATE. A certificate of completion required by a building contract.

ARCHITECTS FIRM. A partnership or corporation (i) that (a) confines its practice to providing architectural consulting services, or (b) if it does not confine its practice to providing architectural consulting services, engages in a practice satisfactory to the Joint Board, and (ii) in which registered architects (a) hold a majority interest, and (b) control the partnership or corporation, and that is otherwise entitled to engage in the practice of architecture. Alberta statutes.

ARCHITECTURAL SERVICES. Services that are part of or are related to the practice of architecture. *Architects Act*, S.O. 1984, c. 12, s. 1.

ARCHITECTURAL WORK. Any building or structure or any model of a building or structure. *Copyright Act*, R.S.C. 1985, c. C-42, s. 2

ARCHITECTURE. See PRACTICE OF ~.

ARCHIVES. *n.* 1. A place where old records are kept. 2. The body of documents of all kinds, regardless of date, created or received by a person or body in meeting requirements or carrying on activities, preserved for their general information value by a government. Archives Act, S.Q. 1983, c. 38, s. 2. See PRIVATE ~; PUBLIC ~; PUBLIC ~ CANADA.

ARCHIVIST. *n.* One who collects, catalogues and maintains archives.

ARCTIC WATERS. The waters adjacent to the mainland and islands of the Canadian arctic within the area enclosed by the sixtieth parallel of north latitude, the one hundred and forty-first meridian of west longitude and a line measured seaward from the nearest Canadian land a distance of one hundred nautical miles, except that in the area between the islands of the Canadian arctic and Greenland, where the line of equidistance between the islands of the Canadian arctic and Greenland is less than one hundred nautical miles from the nearest Canadian land, that line shall be substituted for the line measured seaward one hundred nautical miles from the nearest Canadian land. *Arctic Waters Pollution Prevention Act*, R.S.C. 1985, c. A-12, s. 2.

AREA. *n.* 1. A district designated for a particular purpose. 2. A city, town, village, county, municipal district or improvement district. 3. A polling district or districts, or a part of a polling district or districts. See BUILDING ~; BUILT-UP ~; BUSINESS IMPROVEMENT ~; CLAIM ~; COMMON ~S; COMMUNITY IMPROVEMENT PROJECT ~; COMPULSORY PILOTAGE ~; CONTROL ~; CONTROLLED ~; CONVENTION ~; COURT ~; DESIGNATED SMOKING ~; DRAINAGE ~; EMERGENCY ~; FELLING ~; FIRE HAZARD~; FLOOR ~; FOREST ~; GREATER TORONTO~; GREENSPOND ~; GROSS ~; GULF ~; HEAD IMPACT ~; LABOUR MARKET ~; LAKE SHORE ~; LANDING ~; LEASE ~; LICENCE ~; LOCAL OPTION ~; LOT ~; LURE CROP ~; MANOEUVRING~; MARINE ~; METROPOLITAN ~; MINING ~; MOVEMENT ~; NATURAL ~; NATURE CONSERVANCY ~; NEIGHBOURHOOD IMPROVEMENT ~; NO SHOOTING ~; OCEAN SHORE ~; OFF-SHORE ~; PELVIC IMPACT ~; PERMIT ~; PROTECTED~; PUBLIC PARKING ~; PURE WATER ~S; QUARANTINE ~; RAMP ~; RESTRICTED ~; RESTRICTED SPEED ~; RETENTION ~; RURAL ~; SERVICE ~; SHORE ~; SPACING ~; TAILINGS IMPOUNDMENT ~; TARGET ~; TAXATION ~; UNIT ~; URBAN ~; WORKING ~.

AREA AGREEMENT. A collective agreement covering a geographical area.

AREA AUTHORITY. The governing body of an area. *Conservation and Development Amendment Act*, 1979, S.S. 1979, c. 11, s. 3.

AREA DRAIN. A drain installed to collect surface water from an open area.

AREA MUNICIPALITY. (a) A town, other than a separated town, township or village in a county, and (b) a city, town, village or township in a regional, metropolitan or district municipality. *Development Charges Act*, R.S.O. 1990, c. D.9, s. 1.

AREA PRACTICE. The custom prevailing in a geographical area concerning employees' rights and benefits.

AREA TAX. Any tax levied on the owners of real property or immovables that is computed by applying a rate to all or part of the assessed dimension of the property and includes any tax levied on the owners of real property or immovables that is in the nature of a local improvement tax, a development tax or a redevelopment tax, but does not include a tax in respect of mineral rights. *Payments in Lieu of Taxes Act*, S.C. 2000, c. 8, s. 3.

AREA-WIDE BARGAINING. Negotiation of a collective agreement between a union and the employers in a geographical area.

AREA YIELD. The average yield of an insurable crop in an area greater than an insurance unit. *The Saskatchewan Crop Insurance Act*, R.S.S. 1978, c. S-12, s. 2.

ARENDRE. *var.* **A RENDRE.** *v.* [Fr.] To yield; to render.

ARENTARE. *v.* To rent.

A RESCRIPTIS VALET ARGUMENTUM. [L.] An argument based on ancient writs is sound.

ARGENTINE. *n.* A fish of the species Argentiva silvus. *Northwest Atlantic Fisheries Regulations*, C.R.C., c.. 860, s. 2.

ARGUABLE ISSUE. On appeal, an arguable issue is one which if raised by a ground of appeal would result in the appeal being allowed if the ground of appeal were successfully demonstrated by the appellant.

ARGUENDO. [L.] While arguing.

ARGUMENT. *n.* 1. A method of establishing belief by using a course of reasoning. 2. The closing comments of counsel or the parties or their representatives in a hearing or trial. There may also be argument made by these persons on jurisdictional, procedural or evidentiary issues during the hearing or trial. See CLOSING ~; ORAL ~.

ARGUMENT A CONTRARIO. A reason advanced to treat two compared propositions in contrary fashion.

ARGUMENTATIVE. *adj.* 1. In describing a pleading, containing not only allegations of fact but arguments as to how those facts bear on the disputed matter. 2. In the old common law pleading, described a pleading in which a material fact was stated by inference only.

ARGUMENTUM AB AUCTORITATE EST FORTISSIMUM IN LEGS. [L.] An argument based on authority is the most effective known to the law.

ARGUMENTUM AB AUCTORITATE PLURIMUM VALET IN LEGE. [L.] An argument based on authority has the greatest weight in the law.

ARGUMENTUM AB IMPOSSIBILI PLURIMUM VALET IN LEGE. [L.] An argument deduced from the fact that something is impossible has much weight in the law.

ARGUMENTUM AB INCONVENIENTI PLURIMUM VALET IN LEGE. [L.] An argument based on inconvenience has great weight in the law.

ARGUMENTUM A COMMUNITER ACCIDENTIBUS IN JURE FREQUENS EST. [L.] The argument that an event or thing commonly happens is often made in the law.

ARGUMENTUM A DIVISIONE EST FORTISSIMUM IN JURE. [L.] Argument by division is the most effective known to the law.

ARGUMENTUM A FORTIORI. [L.] Argument from the stronger to the weaker.

ARGUMENTUM A MAJORI AD MINUS NEGATIVE NON VALET; VALET E CONVERSO. [L.] Argument in the negative from the greater to the less is not useful; but argument in the negative from the less to the greater is.

ARGUMENTUM A SIMILI VALET IN LEGE. [L.] An argument from a similar case prevails in law.

ARITHMETICAL OR ACTUARIAL METHOD. The court first determines the appropriate discount rate to deal with projected interest and inflation rates when calculating a lump sum to produce an annual income of a certain amount which will exhaust itself after a certain period. K.D. Cooper-Stephenson & I.B. Saunders, *Personal Injury Damages in Canada* (Toronto: Carswell, 1981) at 74.

ARMA IN ARMATOS SUMERE JURA SINUNT. [L.] To use arms against persons who are armed is justifiable.

ARMED. *adj.* "Being 'armed' with an offensive weapon and 'using an offensive weapon' are not synonymous. A person is 'armed' with an offen-

sive weapon if he is equipped with it; see *R. v. Sloan* (1974) 19 C.C.C. (2d) 190 at 192 (B.C. C.A.)." *R v. Langevin* (No. I) (1979), 10 C.R. (3d) 193 at 200, 47 C.C.C. (2d) 138 (Ont. C.A.), the court per Martin J.A.

ARMED FORCES. 1. Includes army, naval and air forces or services, combatant or non-combatant, but does not include surgical, medical, nursing and other services that are engaged solely in humanitarian work and under the control or supervision of the Canadian Red Cross or other recognized Canadian humanitarian society. *Foreign Enlistment Act*, R.S.C. 1985, c. F-28, s. 2. 2. The Merchant Marine, Naval, Army and Air Forces of Canada or an ally. *Members Superannuation Act*, S.N.B. c. M-8, s. 3.1.

ARMISTICE. *n.* Cessation of hostilities.

ARM OF THE SEA. A river, bay, port, cove, or creek where water, salt or fresh; ebbs and flows.

ARMORED CABLE. A cable provided with a wrapping of steel wires forming an integral part of the assembly, primarily for the purpose of mechanical protection but which may also be used to provide continuity to round. *Coal Mines Regulation Act* R.S.N.S. 1989, c. 73, s. 85(1).

ARMOURED CAR SERVICE. A person who provides the service of transporting property in an armoured vehicle and who employs for that purpose a person who is in possession of a firearm for use in connection with his employment. *Private Investigators and Security Agencies Act*, S.B.C. 1980, c. 45, s. 1.

ARM'S LENGTH. *var.* **ARM'S-LENGTH.** 1. Arm's-length negotiation suggests negotiation between parties with opposing interests, each having an economic stake in the outcome. 2. A transaction "not at arm's length" is one in respect of which unrelated persons are, in the eyes of the law, in the same position as persons related by blood or marriage. In other words, if a transaction between unrelated persons has the same essential characteristics as one between related persons, i.e., the parties are influenced in their bargaining by something other than individual self-interest, those unrelated persons are said not to deal at arm's length. *Skalbania (Trustee of) v. Wedgewood Village Estates Ltd.* 37 B.C.L.R. (2d) 88 (C.A.), per Esson, J.A. 3. Where the "mind" directing the bargaining of one party to a contract is the same "mind" directing the bargaining of the other party, the parties cannot be said to be dealing at "arm's length". This principle applies whether the same person dictates the terms of the bargain on behalf of both parties, or whether several parties (either natural persons or corporations or a combination of the two) concertedly act in the same interest, and thereby direct or dictate the conduct of another person or persons. Cattanach, J. in *Minister of National Revenue v. T.R. Merritt Estate*, [1969] 2 Ex. C.R. 51, [1969] C.T.C. 207. See AT ~; NOT AT ~.

ARMY. *n*. The military force of a country intended to operate on land.

AROSE. *v*. " . . . [A] cause of action arises for purposes of a limitation period when the material facts on which it is based have been discovered or ought to have been discovered by the plaintiff by the exercise of reasonable diligence, . . ." *Central & Eastern Trust Co. v. Rafuse* (1986), 37 C.C.L.T. 117 at 180, 42 R.P.R. 161, 34 B.L.R. 187, [1986] 2 S.C.R. 147, 31 D.L.R. (4th) 481, 75 N.S.R. (2d)109,186 A.P.R. 109, 69 N.R. 321, the court per Le Dain J.

ARPENT. *n*. 1. As a measure of area 32 400 square feet (French measure), a unit of measurement to describe certain land in Quebec. *Weights and Measures Act*, S.C. 1970-71-72, c. 26, Schedule III. 2. As a measure of length 180 feet (French measure), a unit of measurement to describe certain land in Quebec. *Weights and Measures Act*, S.C. 1970-71-72, c.26, Schedule III.

ARRAIGN. *v*. To bring a prisoner to the bar of a court to answer a charge.

ARRAIGNMENT. *n*. Calling a prisoner by name, reading the indictment, demanding of the prisoner whether he or she is guilty or not guilty, and entering the prisoner's plea.

ARRANGEMENT. *n*. 1. A structure or combination of things designed to accomplish a purpose. *Pozniak Estate v. Pozniak* [1993] 7 W.W.R. 500 (Man. C.A.). 2. With respect to a corporation, includes, (a) a reorganization of the shares of any class or series of the corporation or of the stated capital of any such class or series; (b) the addition to or removal from the articles of the corporation of any provision or the change of any such provision; (c) an amalgamation of the corporation with another corporation; (d) an amalgamation of a body corporate with a corporation that results in an amalgamated corporation; (e) a transfer of all or substantially all the property of the corporation to another body corporate in exchange for securities, money or other property of the body corporate; (f) an exchange of securities of the corporation held by security holders for other securities, money or other property of the corporation or securities, money or other property of another body corporate that is not a take-over bid as defined in the Securities Act; (g) a liquidation or dissolution of the corporation; (h) any other reorganization or scheme involving the business or affairs of the corporation or of any or all of the holders of its securities or of any options or rights to acquire any of its securities that is, at law, an arrangement; and (i) any combination of the foregoing. See EXTRA-DITION ~; FAMILY ~; PREVENIENT ~; TRADE-IN ~.

ARREARAGE. *n*. An amount overdue and unpaid.

ARREARS. *n*. " . . . [S]omething which is behind in payment, or which remains unpaid, . . ." *Corbett c.. Taylor*(1864), 23 U.C.Q.B. 454 at 455 (C.A.), the court per Draper C.J. See IN ~; TAX~.

ARREARS OF TAX. Tax unpaid and outstanding after the expiry of the year in which they were imposed, and includes penalties for default in payment.

ARRENDARE. *v*. To lease land by the year.

ARREST. *n*. 1. " . . . [I]n general an arrest is effected by the compulsory restraint of a person either by actual seizure or by the touching of his body with a view to his detention. The person being arrested must be informed that he is being arrested and the reasons therefor. Until it has been made clear to the person that he is under arrest, the arrest is not complete in law: . . ." *R. v. Delong* (1989), 47 C.C.C. (3d) 402 at 417 (Ont. C.A.), the court per Griffiths J.A. 2. "To constitute an arrest it is not necessary to touch the person arrested if he acquiesces in the situation by acknowledging that he is deprived of his liberty: . . ." *Kozak v. Beatty* (1957) 7 D.L.R. (2d) 88 at 93 20 W.W.R. 497, 118 C.C.C. 72 (Sask. C.A.), Martin J.A. 3. "The best expressed view of the matter that I have found is a note to *Nicholl v. Darley* (1828), 2 Y. & J. 399 [(U.K.)], at p. 405, (Philad. ed.,1869) viz.: 'The distinction seems to be, that if the party does not acquiesce, there must be an actual touching of his person by the officer, to constitute an arrest; and any touching of the person by the officer, in the execution of a writ, will be an arrest. But if the party submits and comes within the power of the officer, who thereupon abstains from interference with his person, this is such a conclusive confession of arrest as is equivalent in law to an arrest.'" *Higgins v. MacDonald*, [1928] 4 D.L.R. 241 at 243, [1928] 3 W.W.R. 115, 50 C.C.C. 353, 50 B.C.R. 150 (C.A.), Martin J.A. 4. An admiralty action brought against a ship. See CARDIAC ~; FALSE ~.

ARRESTOR. See FLAME ~.

ARRESTS, ETC., OF KINGS, PRINCES, AND PEOPLE. Refers to political or executive acts, and does not include a loss caused by riot or by ordinary judicial process. *Marine Insurance acts.*

ARREST WARRANT. A document issued by a judge or justice commanding peace officers to arrest the person named in the document.

ARROW. See FISH ~.

ARSENAL. *n.* Storage place for arms.

ARSENIC. *n.* A common, poisonous constituent of insecticides, weed killers, and rat killers which is a designated substance under the Ontario Occupational Health and Safety Act. D. Robertson, *Ontario Health and Safety Guide* Toronto: Richard De Boo Ltd., 1988) at 5-26.

ARSON. *n.* (1) Wilfully setting fire to (a) a building or structure, whether completed or not; (b) a stack of vegetable produce or of mineral or vegetable fuel; (c) a mine; (d) a well of combustible substance; (e) a vessel or aircraft, whether completed or not; (f) timber or materials placed in a shipyard for building, repairing or fitting out a ship; (g) military or public stores or munitions of war; (h) a crop, whether standing or cut down; or (i) any wood, forest, or natural growth, or any lumber, timber, log, float, boom, dam or slide. (2) Wilfully and for a fraudulent purpose setting fire to property not mentioned in subsection (1). *Criminal Code* R.S.C. 1985 c. C-46, s. 433.

ART. *n.* 1. " . . . [C]onnotation of 'learning' or 'knowledge' as commonly used in expressions such as 'the state of the art' or 'the prior art'.. : ." *Shell Oil Co. v. Canada (Patent Commissioner)* (1982), 142 D.L.R. (3d) 117 at 127, [1982] 2 S.C.R. 536, 44 N.R. 541, 67 C.P.R. (2d) 1, the court per Wilson J. 2. " . . . [As found in s. 2(d) of the Patent Act, R.S.C. 1952, c. 203] or operation is an act or series of acts performed by some physical agent upon some physical object and producing in such object some change either of character or of condition. It is abstract in that, it is capable of contemplation of the mind. It is concrete in that it consists in the application of physical agents to physical objects

and is then apparent to the senses in connection with some tangible object or instrument . . . 'method' is synonymous with 'art' . . ." *Lawson v. Canada (Commissioner of Patents)* (1970), 62 C.P.R. 101 at 109, 110 (Ex. Ct.), Cattanach J. See TERM OF ~; WORDS OF ~; WORK OF ~.

ARTEFACT. *n.* An artificially produced, not a natural, change. F.A. Jaffe, *A Guide to Pathological Evidence*, 3d ed. (Toronto: Carswell, 1991) at 212. See IATROGENIC ~; POST MORTEM ~.

ARTERIOR-VENOUS ANEURYSM. An aneurysm including a direct connection between an artery and a vein. F.A. Jaffe, *A Guide to Pathological Evidence*, 3d ed. (Toronto: Carswell, 1991) at 212.

ARTERIOSCLEROSIS. *n.* Hardening, thickening and loss of elasticity of the walls of arteries, often accompanied by narrowing of their lumens. F.A. Jaffe, *A Guide to Pathological Evidence*, 3d ed. (Toronto: Carswell, 1991) at 212.

ARTERY. *n.* A vessel which carries blood from the heart to the body's tissues. F.A. Jaffe, *A Guide to Pathological Evidence*, 3d ed. (Toronto: Carswell, 1991 at 212. See CORONARY ~.

ARTICLE. v. To serve a period of training with an established member of a profession.

ARTICLE. *n.* 1. Real and personal property of every description including (a) money, (b) deeds and instruments relating to or evidencing the title or right to property or an interest immediate, contingent or otherwise, in a corporation or in any assets of a corporation (c) deeds and instruments giving a right to recover or receive property, (d) tickets or like evidence of right to be in attendance at a particular place at a particular time or times or of a right to transportation, and (e) energy, however generated. *Competition Act*, R.S.C. 1985 c. C-34, s. 2(1). 2. Includes each separate type, size, weight and quality in which an article, within the meaning assigned by section 2, is produced. *Competition Act* R.S.C. 1985, c. C-34 s. 85. 3. Any thing that is made by hand, tool or machine. *Industrial Design Act*, R.S.C. 1985, c. I-9, s. 2. See DANGEROUS ~; MANUFACTURED ~; MULTI-SERVICE ~; PATENTED ~; PLATED ~; PRECIOUS METAL ~; SECOND-HAND ~; SINGLE-SERVICE ~.

ARTICLED CLERK. A student-at-law bound by contract in writing to service with a member of the Law Society, who has filed articles of clerkship in accordance with the governing legislation.

ARTICLED STUDENT. 1. Any person validly holding a certificate of admission to the training period prescribed by by-law of the General Council. *Barreau du Quebec Act*, R.S.Q. 1977, c. B-1, s. 1. 2. A person enrolled in the Bar Admission Course during the time he is not in attendance at the teaching period thereof. *Legal Aid Act*, R.R.O. 1980, Reg. 575 s. 1. 3. A person over eighteen years of age who has been duly registered by the council as a student. *The Saskatchewan Embalmers Act* R.S.S. 1978 c. S-15, s. 2.

ARTICLES. *n*. 1. Clauses contained in a document. 2. The document itself. 3. The agreement between a member of a profession, the principal, and a student, the articled student, regarding the student's training from and work for the member. 4. An agreement repecting training and service between a member of the Association and a student. *Surveyors acts*. 5. The original or restated articles of incorporation, articles of amendment, articles of amalgamation, articles of continuance, articles of reorganization, articles of arrangement, articles of dissolution articles of revival, a statute letters patent, a memorandum of association, certificate of incorporation, a special act and any other instrument by which a corporation is incorporated or which evidences the corporate existence of a body corporate continued as a corporation under this Act and includes any amendments thereto. *Corporation acts*.

ARTICLES OF AMENDMENT. A document which changes the capital structure or the constitution of a company and is ordinarily authorized by a special resolution of the shareholders.

ARTICLES OF ASSOCIATION. Contain the internal regulations of a corporation. One of the incorporating documents in some jurisdictions.

ARTICLES OF CONTINUANCE. A document which permits a body corporate incorporated in one jurisdiction to be reconstituted in another.

ARTICLES OF INCORPORATION. 1. Incorporation takes place when these articles are delivered to the appropriate Director and a certificate of incorporation is issued. 2. The original or restated articles of incorporation, articles of amalgamation, letters patent, supplementary letters patent, a special Act and any other instrument by which a corporation is incorporated, and includes any amendments thereto. 3. Correspond to memorandum of association in those jurisdictions using that method of incorporation.

ARTICLES OF WAR. A code of laws which regulates armed forces.

ARTICULABLE CAUSE. 1. Term used to contrast arbitrary detention. Where an officer has articulable cause to detain a person there is no arbitrary detention. "Where an individual is detained by the police in the course of efforts to determine whether that individual is involved in criminal activity being investigated by the police, that detention can only be justified if the detaining officer has some "articulable cause" for the detention. What is required is a number of objectively discernible facts which give the detaining officer reasonable cause to suspect that the detainee is criminally implicated in the activity under investigation. A "hunch" based entirely on intuition gained by experience cannot suffice, no matter how accurate that "hunch" might prove to be. Such subjectively based assessments can too easily mask discriminatory conduct based on such irrelevant factors as the detainee's sex, colour, age, ethnic origin or sexual orientation. The inquiry into the existence of an articulable cause is, however, only the first step in the determination of whether the detention was justified in the totality of the circumstances and consequently a lawful exercise of the officer's common law powers. *R. v. Simpson* (1993), 20 C.R. (4th) 1, Ont. C.A. per Doherty, J.A. 2. Exists where the grounds for stopping the motorist are reasonable and can be clearly expressed. *R. v. Brown* (2003) 173 C.C.C. (3d) 23 (Ont. C.A.).

ARTICULATED VEHICLE. A vehicle which can be divided into more than one part.

ARTIFACT. *n*. 1. An object that is the product of human art or workmanship or both and that is of value primarily for its historic or archaeological importance or interest.

ARTIFICE. *n*. Contrivance or device; used to refer to fraud or deceit.

ARTIFICER. *n*. A person who is employed largely in manual labour.

ARTIFICIAL BREEDING ASSOCIATION. Any organization or person carrying on the business of the artificial insemination of domestic animals.

ARTIFICIAL BREEDING SERVICE CENTRE. An establishment where semen is collected, processed or stored and supplied to an artificial breeding association.

ARTIFICIAL FLY. 1. A single or double hook dressed with silk, tinsel, wool, fur, feathers or any combination of these or other materials commonly used in making artificial flies, but does not include a fly that has a spinning device or a weight to cause the fly to sink. 2. A wet or dry fishing fly (a) the body of which is made of plastic, cork or rubber, (b) that has not more than two hooks on a common shank, and (c) to which is attached no biological material, paste, eggs or worms other than feathers, fur, hair or fibre.

ARTIFICIAL INDUCEMENT OF RAIN. A person artificially induces rain if he causes it to fall artificially or attempts to cause it to fall artificially. *An Act respecting the artificial inducement of rain*, R.S.Q., c. P-43, s. 3.

ARTIFICIAL INSEMINATION. Depositing semen in the genital tract of a female domestic animal by other than the natural method.

ARTIFICIAL INSEMINATION BUSINESS. The business of collecting, acquiring, processing, storing, distributing or inseminating semen, as the case may be.

ARTIFICIAL INSEMINATION CENTRE. An establishment where semen is collected, stored or distributed for purposes of artificial insemination.

ARTIFICIAL ISLAND. Any man-made extension of the seabed or a seabed feature, whether or not the extension breaks the surface of the superjacent waters. *Oceans Act*, S.C. 1996, c. 31, s. 2.

ARTIFICIAL PERSON. A body corporate or other body given the status of a person by law.

ARTIFICIALLY PROPAGATED. Grown from seeds, spores, pollens, tissue culture or other propagules under controlled conditions. *Wild Animal and Plant Trade Regulations*, SOR/96-263, s. 2.

ARTIST. *n*. Any natural person who practises an art on his own account and who offers his services for remuneration, as a creator or performer in any field of artistic endeavour referred to in section 1. *An Act respecting the professional status and conditions of engagement of performing, recording and film artists*, R.S.Q., c. S-32.1, s. 2.

ARTISTIC CHARACTERISTICS. See TRADITIONAL OR ~.

ARTISTIC DEFENCE. To a charge of obscenity, test which assesses whether the exploitation of sex has a justifiable role in advancing the plot or the theme, and in considering the work as a whole, does not merely represent "dirt for dirt's sake" but has a legitimate role when measured by the internal necessities of the work itself. *R. v. Butler* [1992] 1 S.C.R. 452

ARTISTIC ENDEAVOURS. The stage, including the theatre, the opera, music, dance and variety entertainment, the making of films, the recording of discs and other modes of sound recording, dubbing, and the recording of commercial advertisements. *An Act respecting the professional status and conditions of engagement of performing, recording and film artists*, R.S.Q., c. S-32.1, s. 1.

ARTISTIC MERIT. Defence to criminal charge of possession of child pornography. "the defence must be established objectively, since Parliament cannot have intended a bare assertion of artistic merit to provide a defence. . . The second meaning that can be ascribed to "artistic merit" is " possessing the quality of art", or "artistic character". On this meaning, a person who produces art of any kind is protected, however crude or immature the result of the effort in the eyes of the objective beholder. This interpretation seems more consistent with what Parliament intended. It is hard to conceive of Parliament wishing to make criminality depend on the worth of the accused's art. It would be discriminatory and irrational to permit a good artist to escape criminality, while criminalizing less fashionable, less able or less conventional artists. Such an interpretation would run counter to the need to give the defence a broad and generous meaning. I conclude that "artistic merit" should be interpreted as including any expression that may reasonably be viewed as art. *R. v. Sharpe*; 2001 CarswellBC 82; 2001 SCC 2, per McLachlin, C.J.C. for majority.

ARTISTIC WORK. Includes paintings, drawings, maps, charts, plans, photographs, engravings, sculptures, works of artistic craftsmanship, architectural works, and compilations of artistic works. *Copyright Act*, R.S.C. 1985, c. C-42, s. 2. See EVERY ORIGINAL LITERARY, DRAMATIC, MUSICAL AND ~.

ARTS. *n*. The arts of the theatre, literature, music, painting, sculpture, architecture or the graphic arts, and includes any other similar creative or interpretive activity. See NATIONAL ~ CENTRE; PERFORMING ~.

ARTS AND CRAFTS. The production of original works which are unique or in multiple copies, intended for a utilitarian, decorative or expressive purpose and conveyed by the practice of a craft related to the working of wood, leather, textiles, metals, silicates or any other material. *An Act respecting the professional status of artists in the visual arts, arts and crafts and literature, and their contracts with promoters*, R.S.Q., c. S-32.01, s. 2.

A RUBRO AD NIGRUM. [L. from the red to the black] To deduce the meaning of a statute (formerly printed in black) from its title (formerly printed in red).

AS AGAINST. To contrast the positions of two people by referring to a different relationship between one of them and a third person.

ASBESTOS. *n*. Naturally occurring, highly fibrous, heat insulating, and chemically inert silicate minerals belonging to either serpentine or amphibole groups and include chrysolite, crocidolite, amosite, anthophyllite, tremolite and actinolite and any other mineral commonly known as asbestos.

ASBESTOS FIBRE. A fibre of asbestos with a length of more than five microns and a ratio of length to breadth of three to one or more. *Asbestos Mines and Mills Release Regulation*, SOR/90-341, s. 2.

ASBESTOSIS. *n*. An industrial disease of the lungs.

AS BETWEEN. To contrast the positions of two people by referring to a different relationship between one of them and a third person.

ASCAP. *abbr*. American Society of Composers, Authors and Publishers.

ASCENDANT. *n*. The ancestor of a family.

ASCENDING REGISTER. A mechanical device in a postage meter that records the total value of impressions made by an impression die or the total dollar value of postage used.

ASCERTAIN. *v*. To decide upon. *Stinson v. College of Physicians & Surgeons (Ontario)* (1913), 27 O.L.R. 565 at 581, 10 D.L.R. 699 (C.A.), Riddell J.A.

ASCERTAINABLE. *adj*. Capable of being made certain or of being determined.

ASCERTAINABLE POINT. A point found or re-established in its original position on a line or boundary established during the original survey or on a line or boundary established during the survey of a plan of subdivision registered under the *Land Titles Act* or the *Registry Act*. *Surveys Act*, R.S.O. 1990, c. S.30, s. 1.

ASCERTAINED GOODS. " . . . [D]efined by Atkin L.J. *In re Waite*, [1927] 1 Ch. 606 in these words: 'Ascertained' probably means identified in accordance with the agreement after the time a contract of sale is made . . .'" *George Eddy Co. v. Noble Corey & Son* (1951), 28 M.P.R. 140 at 154, [1951] 4 D.L.R. 90 (N.B. C.A.), Michaud C.J.K.B.D.

ASDA. Accelerate-stop distance available. *Canadian Aviation Regulations*, SOR/96-433, s. 101.01(1).

ASH. See INCINERATOR~.

ASL. Above sea level. *Canadian Aviation Regulations*, SOR/96-433, s. 101.01(1).

ASPECT. See DOUBLE ~ DOCTRINE.

ASPHALT PAVING PLANT. Equipment designed to dry aggregate material and to mix the aggregate material with bituminous asphalt. *Environmental Protection Act*, R.R.O. 1980, Reg. 297, s. 1.

ASPHYXIA. *n*. Describes the state of lack of oxygen which is terminal, not the means of bringing about that state. F.A. Jaffe, *A Guide to Pathological Evidence*, 3d ed. (Toronto: Carswell, 1991) at 139. See TRAUMATIC ~.

ASPIRATION. The entry of a liquid or solid chemical product directly through the oral or nasal cavity, or indirectly from vomiting, into the trachea or lower respiratory system.

ASPORTATION. *n*. Carrying away.

ASPORTAVIT. [L.] One carried away.

ASSASSINATION. *n*. Murder of a public figure for political motives.

ASSAULT. *n*. 1. Applying force intentionally to another person, directly or indirectly, without their consent; attempting or threatening, by an act or gesture, to apply force to another person if he has or causes the other person to believe upon reasonable grounds that he has, present ability to effect his purpose; or accosting or impeding another person or begging while openly wearing or carrying a weapon or imitation thereof. *Criminal Code* R.S.C. 1985, c. C-46, s. 265(1). 2. In tort law, intentionally causing another person to fear imminent contact of a harmful or offensive nature. John G. Fleming,

The Law of Torts, 8th ed. (Sydney: The Law Book Company Limited, 1992) at 25. See AGGRAVATED ~; COMMON ~; INDECENT ~.

ASSAULT AND BATTERY. The actual carrying out of the threatened harmful or offensive contact. John G. Fleming, *The Law of Torts*, 8th ed. (Sydney: The Law Book Company Limited, 1992) at 25.

ASSAY. *n*. The quantitative determination by a recognized method for a metal or other constituent of a mine sample.

ASSAYER. *n*. A person who performs an assay.

ASSEMBLE NATIONALE. See PRESIDENT OF THE ~.

ASSEMBLY. *n*. 1. A meeting of persons. 2. The Legislative Assembly of a province. 3. The House of Assembly of a province. 4. " . . . [P]utting things together to make a whole . . ." *Engineering Industry Training Board v. Foster Wheeler John Brown Boilers Ltd.*, [1970] 1 All E.R. 490 at 498 (U.K. Q.B.), Bridge J. See AXLE~; FIFTH WHEEL ~; GENERAL ~; LAND ~; LEGISLATIVE ~; MULTI-OUTLET ~; OCCUPANT RESTRAINT ~; PLACE OF ~; PRODUCT RESTRAINT ~; UNLAWFUL ~.

ASSEMBLY BUILDING. A building or portions of buildings used for the congregating of persons for civic, political, social, travel, educational, recreational, or like purposes or for the consumption of food or drink. *Fire Prevention Act*, R.S.N.S. 1989, c. 171, s. 2.

ASSEMBLY LANGUAGE. "A second level of [computer] language, which can be referred to as an intermediate level, consists of mnemonics which correspond more explicitly to the operations the computer must perform . . . This intermediate level is referred to as assembly language." *Apple Computer Inc. v. Mackintosh Computers Ltd.* 1986), 10 C.P.R. (3d) 1 at 7, 8 C.I.P.R. 153, 3 F.T.R. 118, [1987] 1 F.C. 173, 28 D.L.R. (4th) 178 (T.D.), Reed J.

ASSEMBLY-LINE WORK. The item being manufactured is moved along a conveyor system in order that employees may perform specific tasks on the item.

ASSEMBLY OCCUPANCY. Occupancy for gatherings of persons for civic, educational political, recreational, religious, social, travel or other similar purpose, or for the consumption of food or drink.

ASSEMBLY YARD. Premises to which producers may deliver their hogs. Canada regulations.

ASSEMBLY YARD OPERATOR. The owner or operator of an assembly yard. Canada regulations.

ASSENSIO MENTIUM. [L.] Mutual consent needed to validate a contract.

ASSENT. *v*. 1. To agree to, concur in or recognize a matter. 2. " . . . [T]o be valid, must be given by a majority of eligible band members in attendance at a meeting called for the purpose of giving or withholding assent." *Cardinal v. R*, [1982] 3 C.N.L.R. 3 at, [1982] 3 W.W.R. 7, 41 N.R. 300, 133 D.L.R. (3d) 513, [1982] 1 S.C.R. 508, the court per Estey J.

ASSENT. *n*. n. Acceptance. Concurrence. See MUTUALITY OF ~; ROYAL ~.

ASSENTED. *v*. Within the context [of the Canada Agricultural Products Act] means concurred in, agreed or consented to, approved or permitted. *R. v. A & A Foods Ltd,.* 1997 CarswellBC 2541, 120 C.C.C. (3d) 513.

ASSERTION. *n*. " . . . [S]tatement, tale or news is an expression which, taken as a whole and understood in context, conveys an assertion of fact or facts and not merely the expression of opinion . . . Expression which makes a statement susceptible of proof and disproof is an assertion of fact; . . .' *R. v. Zundel* (1992) 75 C.C.C. (3d) 449 at 492, 95 D.L.R. (4th) 202, [1992] 2 S.C.R. 731, 140 N.R. 1, 56 O.A.C. 161, 16 C.R. (4th) 1, 10 C.R.R. (2d) 193, Cory and Iacobucci JJ. (dissenting) (Gonthier J. concurring). See OPINION.

ASSESS. *v*. 1. " . . . '[I]mpose a liability to be taxed' . . ." *Ottawa (City) v. Nantel* (1921), 51 O.L.R. 269 at 274, 69 D.L.R. 727 (C.A.), Latchford J.A. 2. "As used in Section 46(1) [of the *Income Tax Act*, R.S.C. 1952, c. 148] . . . roughly equivalent to 'ascertain and fix' and it seems to have two possible senses in one of which the mere acts of ascertaining and calculating only are included, and the other that of computing and stating the tax in the manner prescribed by the statute." *Scott v. Minister of National Revenue*, 1960 C.T.C. 402 at 415, [1961] Ex. C.R. 120, 60 D.T.C. 1273, Thurlow J. 3. " . . . [T]o consider and determine the whole amount necessary to be raised by rate . . ." *Nova Scotia Car Works Ltd v. Halifax (City)* (1913), 47 S.C.R. 406 at 414, 12 E.L.R. 282, 11 D.L.R.

55, Fitspatrick C.J. 4. To value property for tax purposes.

ASSESS. *abbr.* Assessment.

ASSESSABLE PROPERTY. The property shown on the assessment roll of a municipality and in respect of which (i) taxes for school purposes are required to be paid, or (ii) grants in lieu of taxes for school purposes are paid under an Act of the Legislature or an Act of Parliament.

ASSESSED. See SPECIALLY ~.

ASSESSED COSTS. Costs which have been assessed by an assessment officer; taxed costs.

ASSESSED DIMENSION. The frontage, area, other dimension or other attribute of real property established by an assessment authority for the purpose of computing a frontage or area tax. *Payments in Lieu of Taxes Act*, R.S.C. 1985, c. M-13, s. 2.

ASSESSED VALUE. The value established for any real property by an assessment authority for the purpose of computing a real property tax. *Payments in Lieu of Taxes Act*, R.S.C. 1985, c. M-13, s. 2.

ASSESSING ACT. Any Act pursuant to which an assessing authority is empowered to assess and levy rates, charges or taxes on land or in respect of the ownership of land, and includes any bylaws or regulations made under the authority of any such Act.

ASSESSING AUTHORITY. A local authority, school board or other authority having power to assess and levy rates, charges or taxes on land or in respect of the ownership of land.

ASSESSMENT. *n.* 1. Valuation of property for taxation purposes. 2. The determination of an amount payable. 3. The work to be done or the payment to be made each year to entitle the owner of a mineral claim to a certificate of work. *Yukon Quartz Mining Act*, R.S.C. 1985, c. Y-4, s. 2. 4. "In *Income Tax Comm'rs for London v. Gibbs*, [1942] A.C. 402 at p. 406, Viscount Simon L.C, in reference to the word 'assessment' said: 'The word "assessment" is used in our income tax code in more than one sense. Sometimes, by "assessment" is meant the fixing of the sum taken to represent the actual profit for the purpose of charging tax on it, but in another context the "assessment" may mean the actual sum in tax which the taxpayer is liable to on his profits.' That the latter meaning attached to the word 'assessment' under the [*Income War Tax Act*, R.S.C. 1927, c. 97] as it stood before the enactment of Part VIII . . . is clear. . ." *Okalta Oils Ltd v. Minister of National Revenue*, [1955] 5 D.L.R. 614 at 615, [1955] S.C.R. 824, [1955] C.T.C. 271, 55 D.T.C. 1176, Fauteux J. See CERTIFICATE OF ~; COMMERCIAL ~; CORPORATION ~; ENVIRONMENTAL ~; ENVIRONMENTAL IMPACT ~; EQUALIZED ~; LEVEL OF ~; MUNICIPAL ~ PER CAPITA; RISK~; OF~; SCHOOL~; SECURITY~; SPECIAL ~; UNIT OF ~.

ASSESSMENT AUTHORITY. An authority that has power by or under an Act of Parliament or the legislature of a province to establish an assessed dimension or assessed value of real property or immovables. *Payments in Lieu of Taxes Act*, R.S.C. 1985, c. M-13, s. 2.

ASSESSMENT LIST. A copy of the assessment and tax roll for a municipality or other taxing authority. *An Act to Amend the Assessment Act*, S.N.B. 1983, c. 12, s. 1.

ASSESSMENT OF COSTS. Calculation of the procedural costs to which a party is entitled, formerly taxation of costs.

ASSESSMENT OFFICER. Taxing officer; officer of the court who carries out assessments of costs.

ASSESSMENT ROLL. An assessment roll prepared in accordance with a municipal act. See REVISED ~.

ASSESSMENT WORK. The prescribed work required to be carried out under a licence. *Mineral Act*, S. Nfld. 1975-76, c. 44, s. 2.

ASSESS O. *abbr.* Assessment Officer.

ASSESSOR. *n.* 1. The official who evaluates property for tax purposes. 2. A specialist who assists the court in determining a matter. D. Sgayias *et al., Federal Court Practice 1988* (Toronto: Carswell 1987) at 494.

ASSET. *n.* 1. Any real or personal property or legal or equitable interest therein including money, accounts receivable or inventory. 2. ' . . . [I]nclude[s] only such properties of the debtor as are available for the payment of this debt . . . *Sandberg v. Meurer* (1948), [1949] 1 D.L.R. 422 at 427, [1949] C.T.C. 35, [1949] 1 W.W.R. 117, 56 Man. R. 391 (C.A.), Adamson J.A. (MacPherson C.J.M., Richards and Coyne JJ.A. concurring). See ACTIVE ~; BUSINESS ~; BUSINESS ~S; CAPITAL ~S; COMMERCIAL ~; CONTINGENT ~S; CURRENT ~S;

FAMILY~; FARMING ~S; FISHING ~S; FIXED ~; GOING CONCERN ~S; LIQUID ~S; MATRIMONIAL ~S; MINING ~S; PROCESSING ~S; QUALIFIED ~S; REDUNDANT ~; SURPLUS ~S; TOTAL ~S; WASTING ~.

ASSEVERATION. *n.* Positive assertion, affirmation.

ASSIGN. *v.* 1. To transfer property. 2. For a person to execute and perform every necessary or suitable deed or act for assigning, surrendering or otherwise transferring land of which that person is possessed, either for the whole estate or for any less estate. *Trustee acts.* 3. For a tenant to transfer the tenant's remaining interest in a lease or tenancy agreement.

ASSIGN. *n.* 1. A person to whom something is transferred or given. *Quaal Estate, Re*; [1920] 2 W.W.R. 271 at 272, 51 D.L.R. 720 (Sask. K.B.), Embury J. 2. . .. [A]nyone to whom an assignment is made . . . *National Trust Co. v. Mead* (1990) 12 R.P.R. (2d) 165 at 177, [1990] 2 S.C.R. 410, [1990] 5 W.W.R. 459, 71 D.L.R. (4th) 488, 112 N.R. 1, 87 Sask. R. 161, Wilson J. (Lamer C.J.C., La Forest, L'Heureax-Dubé Gonthier and Cory JJ. concurring).

ASSIGNATUS UTITUR JURE AUCTORIS. [L:] An assignee enjoys the authority of the principal.

ASSIGNED RISK PLAN. A plan operated by insurers licensed to issue motor vehicle liability policies.

ASSIGNEE. *n.* 1. The person to whom property is transferred. *Minister of National Revenue v. Parsons* (1983), 4 Admin L.R. 64 at 79, [1983] C.T.C. 321, 83 D.T.C. 5329 (Fed. T.D.), Cattanach J. 2. Includes any person in whom the right or benefit concerned has become vested, as a result of any assignment or series of assignments. *Consumer Protection acts.* 3. Any person to whom an assignment of book debts is made. *Assignment of Book Debts acts.*

ASSIGNMENT. *n.* 1. " . . . [P]roperty is transferred to another . . ." *Minister of National Revenue v. Parsons* (1983), 4 Admin L.R. 64 at 79, [1983] C.T.C. 321, 83 D.T.C. 5329 (Fed. T.D.), Cattanach J. 2. "[In s. 205(1)(b) of the Canada Shipping Act, R.S.C. 1970, c. S-9] . . . a transfer of a right from one person to another. . ." *Makar v. "Rivtow Lion" (The) (1982)*, (*sub nom. Makar v. Rivtow Straits Ltd.*) 82 C.L.L.C . 14, 209 at 364, 43 N.R. 245, 140 D.L.R. (3d) 6 (Fed. C.A.),

Thurlow C.J.A. (Verchere D.J.A. concurring). 3. Act of assigning, or the document by which a thing is assigned. 4. A transfer by a tenant of the full term remaining under the tenant's lease. W.B. Rayner & R.H. McLaren *Falconbridge on Mortgages*, 4th ed. (Toronto: Canada Law Book, 1977) at 100. 5. Includes every legal and equitable assignment, whether absolute or by way of security, and every mortgage or other charge upon book debts. *Assignment of Book Debts acts.* 6. In bankruptcy, a voluntary act by a debtor or his legal representative for the benefit of the debtor's creditors. It transfers control over the debtor's property so that it can be distributed among his creditors. The debtor cannot continue to carry on business. 7. " . . . As between mortgagors, an assignment would be an agreement between the original mortgagor and his purchaser by which the latter would assume the mortgage debt in exchange for valuable consideration . . ." *National Trust Co. v. Mead* (1990), 12 R.P.R. (2d) 165 at 177, [1990] 2 S.C.R. 410, [1990] 5 W.W.R. 459, 71 D.L.R. (4th) 488, 112 N.R. 1, 87 Sask. R. 161, Wilson J. (Lamer C.J.C., La Forest, L'Heureux-Dubé, Gonthier and Cory JJ. concurring). See ABSOLUTE ~.

ASSIGNMENT OF BOOK DEBTS. Includes every legal or equitable assignment by way of security of book debts and every mortgage or other charge upon book debts. *Corporation Securities Registration acts.*

ASSIGNMENT OF SECURITY INTEREST. A notice of the assignment of a security interest or any part thereof in respect of which a security notice has been registered under this Part. *Canada Petroleum Resources*, R.S.C. 1985 (2d Supp.), c. 36, s. 84.

ASSIGNOR. *n.* 1. One who makes a transfer. 2. A corporation making an assignment of book debts. *Corporation Securities Registration acts.* 3. Any person making an assignment of book debts. *Assignment of Book Debts acts.*

ASSISE. *var.* **ASSIZE**. *n.* The trial of a civil action before a travelling judge.

ASSISTANCE. *n.* 1. Aid in any form to or in respect of persons in need for the purpose of providing or providing for all or any of the following: (a) food, shelter, clothing, fuel, utilities, household supplies and personal requirements (hereinafter referred to as "basic requirements"); (b) prescribed items incidental to carrying on a trade or other employment and other prescribed special needs of any kind; (c) care in a home for special care, (d) travel and transportation; (e) funerals and burials; (f) health care services; (g) prescribed welfare services purchased by or at the request of a provincially approved agency; and (h) comfort allowances and other prescribed needs of residents or patients in hospitals or other prescribed institutions. *Canada Assistance Plan*, R.S.C. 1985, c. C-1, s. 2. 2. Old age assistance provided under provincial law to the persons and under the conditions specified in this Act and the regulations. *Old Age Assistance Act*, R.S.C. 1970, c. O-5, s. 2. See CANADA ~ PLAN; FINANCIAL ~; GOVERNMENT ~; MUNICIPAL ~; SOCIAL ~; STUDENT FINANCIAL ~; WRIT OF ~.

ASSISTANT. *n.* 1. A person who takes part in an action, a helper or an aide. 2. Any person employed in or about a shop and wholly or mainly employed in serving customers receiving orders or despatching goods or in any office connected with a shop. See CLERK ~; ELECTION ~; LAY ~; NURSING ~.

ASSISTANT ENGINEER. A person, other than a rating, who is in training to become an engineer. *Shipping Regulations*.

ASSISTANT RETURNING OFFICER. A person appointed by the clerk to assist in the conduct of the election. *Municipal Elections Act*, R.S.O. 1990, c. M.5 3, s. 1.

ASSISTANT REVISING OFFICER. A person appointed by the clerk to assist in the revision of the list of electors. *Municipal Elections Act* R.S.O. 1990, c. M.5 3, s. 1.

ASSIZE. *n.* " . . . [A] sitting of a Judge of the Supreme Court with a jury." *Imperial Bank v. Alley*, [1926] 3 D.L.R. 86, 59 O.L.R. 1 (C.A.), the court per Orde J.A. See ASSISE.

ASSN. *abbr*. Association.

ASSN. CAN. REL. IND. *abbr*. Association canadienne des relations industrielles. Congrès. Travaux. (Canadian Industrial Relations Association. Annual Meeting. Proceedings).

ASSOCIATE. *n.* 1. " . . . [M]ay include the [partner] . . . may also signify a mere companion or companionship." *Derby Development Development Corp. v. Minister of National Revenue*, [1963] C.T.C. 269 at 279 (Ex. Ct.), Kearney J. 2. Where used to indicate a relationship with any person or company means, (i) any company of which such person or company beneficially owns directly or indirectly, voting securities carrying more than 10 per cent of the voting rights attached to all voting securities of the company for the time being outstanding, (ii) any partner of that person or company, (iii) any trust or estate in which such person or company has a substantial beneficial interest or as to which such person or company serves as trustee or in a similar capacity, (iv) the spouse or any parent, son or daughter, brother or sister of that person, or (v) any relative of such person or of that person's spouse who has the same home as such person.

ASSOCIATED GOVERNMENT. Her Majesty's Government in the United Kingdom, any other government of the Commonwealth, the government of a country that is a member of the North Atlantic Treaty Organization or the government of any other country designated by the Governor in Council as being a country the defence of which is vital to the defence of Canada. *Defence Production Act*, R.S.C. 1985, c. D-1, s. 2.

ASSOCIATED TRADE MARKS. Confusing trade marks which the applicant owns. H.G. Fox, *The Canadian Law of Trade Marks and Unfair Competition*, 3d ed. (Toronto: Carswell, 1972) at 210.

ASSOCIATED WORDS RULE. Rule of statutory interpretation which states that when terms are connected by "and" or "or", the terms' common feature may be "relied on to resolve ambiguity or limit the scope of the terms". Thus, when a specific term such as "medical evidence" is followed by a general term such as "other evidence", the general term is interpreted in such a way as to limit its scope in light of the preceding specific term. *R. v. Soosay* 2001 ABCA 287, 18 M.V.R. (4th) 11, 160 C.C.C. (3d) 437, 293 A.R. 292, 257 W.A.C. 292.

ASSOCIATION. *n.* 1. An employers' organization, a trade union, a professional association or a business or trade association. 2. Any association of persons formed in any foreign country on the plan known as Lloyd's, whereby each member of the association that participates in a policy becomes liable for a stated, limited or proportionate part of the whole amount payable under the policy. *Foreign Insurance Companies Act*, R.S.C. 1985 c. I-13 s. 2. 3. " . . . [I]n its ordinary meaning is wide enough to include an incorporated company. . ." *Minister of National Revenue v. St. Catherines Flying & Training School Ltd.*, [1953] C.T.C. 362 at 369, [1953] Ex. C.R. 259, 53 D.T.C. 1232, Thorson P. 4. An association incorporated by or pursuant to an Act of Parliament or of the legislature of a province that owns or leases a race-course and conducts horse-races in the ordinary course of its business and, to the extent that the applicable legislation requires that the purposes of the association be expressly stated in its constituting instrument, having as one of its purposes the conduct of horse-races. *Criminal Code* R.S.C. 1985 (1st Supp.), c. 47, s. 1(12). See ACCIDENT PREVENTION ~; AGRICULTURAL FAIR ~; ALUMNI ~; ARTICLES OF ~; ARTIFICIAL BREEDING ~; BOND OF ~; BUSINESS OR TRADE ~; CANADIAN PAYMENTS ~; CANADIAN STANDARDS ~; CERTIFIED ~; COMPENSATION ~; CONSTITUENCY ~; CONSUMERS' OF CANADA ~; COOPERATIVE ~; DISTRICT ~; ELECTORAL DISTRICT~; EMPLOYERS' ~; FACILITY ~; FEEDER ~; FREEDOM OF ~; GRAZING AND FODDER ~; HOUSING ~; INSTRUCTORS ~; LABOUR ~; LAKE, FOREST AND FUR ~; LAND IMPROVEMENT ~; LIVESTOCK ~; LLOYD'S ~; MACHINERY ~; MANUFACTURING ~; MEMORANDUM OF ~; MUTUAL ~; NATIONAL FIRE PREVENTION ~; OCCUPATIONAL ~; POLICE ~; PRODUCTION SERVICE ~; PROFESSIONAL ~; RIGHT OF ~; TRAVEL ~; UNINCORPORATED ~; UNION ~.

ASSOCIATION AGREEMENT. Collective bargaining agreement made with an employers' association.

ASSOCIATION OF EMPLOYEES. 1. A group of employees constituted as a professional syndicate, union, brotherhood or otherwise, having as its objects the study, safeguarding and development of the economic, social and educational interests of its members and particularly the negotiation and application of collective agreements. *Labour Code*, R.S.Q. 1977, c. C-27, s. 1. 2. A group of employees (i) organized for the purpose of improving their economic conditions, and (ii) free from undue influence, domination, restraint or interference by employers or associations of employers. *Alberta Labour Act*, R.S.A. 1970, c. 196, s. 43.

ASSOCIATION OF PRODUCERS. A farmers' cooperative syndicate, a farmers' cooperative association, a cooperative agricultural association, a farmers' association or professional syndicate, a union, a federation or confederation of such bodies or a professional or cooperative group of producers. Quebec statutes.

ASSOCIATION STEWARD. A person appointed by an association to act as its representative. *Race Track Supervision Regulations*, C.R.C., c. 441, s. 2.

ASSUETUDE. *n.* Custom.

ASSUME. *v.* 1. To take on a debt or obligation. *Thompson v. Warwick* (1894), 21 O.A.R. 637 at 644 (C.A.), MacLennan J.A. 2. To take for granted. *Gillespie v. R.*, [1983] 1 W.W.R. 641 at 647, 82 D.T.C. 6334, [1982] C.T.C. 378, 45 N.R. 77, 141 D.L.R. (3d) 725 (Fed. C.A.), the court per Thurlow C.J.F.C.

ASSUMED JURISDICTION. There are two sources from which the Court of Queen's Bench in Saskatchewan acquires jurisdiction over an *in personam* action. The first is the common law which provides that this Court has jurisdiction where there is service of the process within the province. The second is what is frequently called "assumed jurisdiction", which is a creation of legislation. It empowers a court to assume jurisdiction over a cause of action which arose in this province despite the fact that the defendant's residence is elsewhere and the process must be served *ex juris*. This new jurisdiction was introduced in England by *The Common Law Procedure Act*, 1852, 15 & 16 Vict., c. 76. That same jurisdiction was incorporated into the law of Saskatchewan by the enactment of s. 12 of *The Queen's Bench Act*, R.S.S. 1978, c. Q-1. *Gray v. Dow Corning Corp.* (1996), 48 C.P.C. (3d) 50 (Sask. Q.B.), appeal to C.A. dismissed.

ASSUMPSIT. [L. one promised] A form of action to recover damages for breach of a simple contract.

ASSUMPTION AGREEMENT. An arrangement by which a purchaser in a new subdivision contracts directly with a mortgagee to make mortgage payments so that the developer is released from the covenant with the mortgage lender. D.J. Donahue & P.D. Quinn, *Real Estate Practice in Ontario*, 4th ed. (Toronto: Butterworths, 1990) at 231.

ASSUMPTION OF RISK. See VOLUNTARY ~.

ASSUMPTIONS. See ACTUARIAL ~.

ASSURANCE. *n.* A transfer, deed or instrument, other than a will, by which land may be conveyed or transferred. *Limitation of Actions acts*. 2. Insurance. See FINANCIAL~; RE ~.

ASSURANCE FUND. A fund established under a statute to indemnify certain persons against loss. See LAND TITLES ~.

ASSURANCES. *n*. The periodical, Assurances.

ASSURE. *v*. To make certain; to insure.

ASSURED. *n*. One who is indemnified against particular events.

ASSURER. *n*. Indemnifier, insurer.

ASTIPULATION. *n*. Mutual agreement.

ASTM. *abbr*. The American Society for Testing and Materials.

ASYLUM. *n*. 1. A sanctuary. 2. A place for the treatment of the mentally ill.

AT AN ELECTION. 1. In respect of an election in any electoral district, means the period commencing with the issue of the writ for that election and terminating on polling day or, where the writ is withdrawn or deemed to be withdrawn, terminating on the day that the writ is withdrawn or deemed to be withdrawn. 2. Includes the period between the dissolution of the House of Assembly, or the occurrence of a vacancy in consequence of which a writ for an election is eventually issued, and when a candidate is declared elected. *Elections acts.*

AT ARM'S LENGTH. Parties are said to be at arm's length when they are not under the control or influence of each other.

ATAXIA. *n*. A condition in which it is difficult to perform voluntary movements. F.A. Jaffe, *A Guide to Pathological Evidence*, 2d ed. (Toronto: Carswell, 1983) at 78.

ATC. *abbr*. An air traffic control unit. *Flight Plans and Flight Notifications Order*, C.R.C., c. 45, s. 2.

A TEMPORE CUJUS CONTRARII MEMORIA NON EXISTET. [L.] From a time of which no memory to the contrary exists.

ATHEROMA. *n*. A form of arteriosclerosis in which fibrous tissue locally proliferates and fat deposits narrow the lumen. F.A. Jaffe, *A Guide to Pathological Evidence*, 3d ed. (Toronto: Carswell, 1991) at 213.

ATLANTIC ACCORD. The memorandum of agreement between the Government of Canada and the government of the province on offshore oil and gas resource management and revenue sharing dated February 11, 1985, and includes any amendments to the memoradum of agreement. *Canada-Newfoundland Atlantic Accord Implementation (Newfoundland) Act*, R.S. Nfld. 1990, c. C-2, s. 2.

ATLANTIC FISHERIES. All the activities relating to the harvesting, processing and marketing of fish in the Provinces of Quebec, Nova Scotia, New Brunswick, Prince Edward Island and Newfoundland and in the fishing zones of Canada, as defined pursuant to subsection 4(1) of the *Territorial Sea and Fishing Zones Act*, on the Atlantic coast of Canada. *Atlantic Fisheries Restructuring Act*, R.S.C. 1985, c. A-14, s. 2.

ATLANTIC PROVINCES. The Provinces of Nova Scotia, New Brunswick, Prince Edward Island and Newfoundland.

ATLANTIC REGION. The region comprising the Provinces of New Brunswick, Nova Scotia, Prince Edward Island and Newfoundland.

ATLANTIC SALMON. Includes "ouananiche". *Ontario Fishery Regulations*, C.R.C., c. 849, s. 2.

AT LARGE. 1. Off the premises of the owner and not muzzled or under the control of any person. *The Sheep Protection and Dog Licensing Act*, R.S.S. 1978, c. S-49, s. 2. 2. Not under control. *Dog Act*, R.S.P.E.I. 1988, c. D-13, s. 1(a). 3. ". . . [L]eft unattended." *Thompson v. Grand Trunk Railway* (1895), 22 O.A.R. 453 at 461 (C.A.), the court per Osler J.A. 4. "[Refers to animals] . . . which are away from home." *Hupp v. Canadian Pacific Railway* (1914), 16 D.L.R. 343 at 347, 6 W.W.R. 385, 27 W.L.R. 398, 17 C.R.C. 66, 20 B.C.R. 49 (C.A.), Galliher J.A. 5. "Damages in libel actions are 'at large' and rest upon a consideration of the injury to the plantiff, the conduct of the defendant and the plaintiff and, in some cases, the deterrent effect sought to be accomplished. Except to the extent that they are intended to be a deterrent, they are compensatory and not punitive." *Munro v. Toronto Sun Publishing Corp.* (1982), 21 C.C.L.T. 261 at 294, 39 O.R. (2d) 100 (H.C.), J. Holland J. 6. "[In Criminal Code, R.S.C. 1970, c. C-34, s. 133(1)(b)] . . . has been defined, sensibly I think, in *Joliffe v. Dean* (1954), 54 S.R. 1V.S.W. 157 . . . as free or at liberty . . . *R. v. MacCaud* (1975), 22 C.C.C. (2d) 445 at 446 (Ont. C.A.), Donohue J. See DAMAGES ~; RUN ~; RUNNING ~.

ATLAS. See PRINTED ~ OR CARTOGRAPHIC BOOK.

AT LEAST. 1. ". . . '[N]ot less than' . . ." *R. v. Robinson* (1951), 12 C.R. 101 at 108, [1951] S.C.R. 522, 100 C.C.C. 1, Locke J. (Rand and Kellock JJ. concurring). 2. ". . . '[A]s much as'." *R. v. Robinson* (1951),12 C.R. 101 at 108, [1951]

S.C.R. 522, 100 C.C.C. 1, Locke J. (Rand and Kellock JJ. concurring). 3. ". . . [W]hen the term 'at least' is used in reference to the days between two events, that means 'clear days.' . . . when the term 'at least' is used in reference to the period between two events, whether that period is expressed in years, months, weeks, hours or minutes . . . the same effect must be given to those words as is given to them when the period is expressed in days. There can be no basis for anything but a consistent interpretation of such words." *R. v. Davis*, [1978] 1 W.W.R. 381 at 384, 35 C.C.C. (2d) 224 (Sask. C.A.), the court per Culliton C.J.S.

ATMOSPHERE. *n*. The ambient air surrounding the earth, excluding the air within any structure or underground space.

ATOMIC ENERGY CONTROL BOARD. The federal body which enforces and administers the *Atomic Energy Control Act* and its regulations.

ATOMIC ENERGY OF CANADA LIMITED. A federal corporation with mandate to research and develop peaceful uses for atomic energy, including developing nuclear power systems and applications for radioisotopes and radiation in industry and medicine.

AT PAR. Of stocks or bonds, sold or issued at face value.

AT PLEASURE. Refers to employment, generally by the Crown, that can be terminated by the employer without notice and without cause.

ATS. *abbr*. 1. At the suit of. Used when the defendant's name is put first in the title of a proceeding. 2. Air traffic services. *Canadian Aviation Regulations*, SOR/96-433, s. 101.01(1).

AT SIGHT. In reference to bills of exchange, payable on demand.

ATTACH. *v*. To take or apprehend; to take goods as well as persons. See ATTACHMENT.

ATTACHE. *n*. [Fr.] A person associated with an embassy.

ATTACHED. *adj*. 1. " . . . [P]laced . . . with 'some kind of permanency' . . ." *Boomars Plumbing & Heating Ltd v. Marogna Brothers Enterprises Ltd.* (1988), 51 D.L.R. (4th) 13 at 24, 50 R.P.R. 81, 27 B.C.L.R. (2d) 305, [1988] 6 W.W.R. 289 (C.A.), the court per Esson J.A. 2. " . . . '[T]o lay hold of person or property by virtue of some process of law.' . . ." *Barnard v.*

Walkem (1880), 1 B.C.R. (Pt. 1) 120 at 127 (C.A.), Begbie C.J.

ATTACHMENT. *n*. 1. Arresting a person under an order of committal. 2. "Garnishee proceedings . . . stop orders and a writ of attachment against the goods of an absconding debtor . . . appointment of a receiver under judicial process, that is by order of the Court . . ." *W. C. Fast Enterprises Ltd v. All-Power Sports (1973) Ltd* (1981), 123 D.L.R. 3d 27 at 38, 16 Alta. L.R. (2d) 47 (C.A.), the court per McGillivray C.J.A. 3. The security interest is said to have attached [as found in s. 12(1) of the *Personal Property Security Act*, R.S.O. 1980, c. 375] when all events necessary for the creation of that interest have taken place. At that time, the rights of the debtor in the collateral assets are restricted and effected by the rights of the secured party . . . Attachment defines the commencement of the relationship betweeen the debtor and the secured party . . ." *Royal Trust Corporation of Canada v. No. 7 Honda Sales Ltd* (1987) 7 P.P.S.A.C. 51 at 55-6 (Ont. Dist. Ct.), Kane Dist. Ct. J. See GARNISHMENT ~; RE-~; WRIT OF ~.

ATTACHMENT HARDWARE. Hardware designed for securing a seat belt assembly to a vehicle. *Motor Vehicle Safety Regulations*, C.R.C., c. 1038, s. 209.

ATTACHMENT OF DEBTS. Where judgment for the payment of money is obtained against a person to whom another person owes money, an order is made that all debts owing or accruing from that person (called the garnishee) to the judgment debtor be applied to the judgment debt.

ATTACHMENT OF WAGES. " . . . [A] continuous deduction or diversion of wages at source by an employer . . . [which] originates by court order, . . ." *Ruthven v. Ruthven* (1984), 38 R.F.L. (2d) 102 at 106 (Ont. Co. Ct.), Dandie Co. Ct. J. See GARNISHMENT.

ATTACK DIRECTED AGAINST ANY CIVILIAN POPULATION. A course of conduct involving the multiple commission of acts referred to in paragraph 1 against any civilian population, pursuant to or in furtherance of a State or organizational policy to commit such attack. Rome Statute, Article 7.

ATTAINDER. *n*. Formerly, when judgment of outlawry or death was made against a person convicted of felony or treason, the principal consequences were the forfeiture and escheat of the convict's lands and the corruption of the convict's blood so that the convict was not able to hold or inherit land or transmit a title by descent to any other person. See ACT OF ~.

ATTAINT. *adj*. Describing a person under attainder.

ATTAINTURE. *n*. Censure under law.

ATTEMPT. *n*. 1. Having an intent to commit an offence, and doing or omitting to do anything for the purpose of carrying out the intention whether or not it was possible under the circumstances to commit the offence. *Criminal Code*, R.S.C. 1985, c. C-46, s. 24(1). 2. The crime of attempt consists of an intent to commit the completed offence together with some act more than merely preparatory taken in furtherance of the attempt. Section 24(1) draws no distinction between attempts to do the possible but by inadequate means, attempts to do the physically impossible, and attempts to do something that turns out to be impossible "following *completion*". All are varieties of attempts to do the "factually impossible"and all are crimes. Only attempts to commit imaginary crimes fall outside the scope of the provision. *United States of America v. Dynar*, [1997] 2 S.C.R. 462, per Cory and Iacobucci, JJ. for the majority.

ATTEND. *v*. " . . . '[T]o be present' or 'go regularly to'. . ." *Howell v. Ontario (Minister of Community and Social Services)* (1987), 17 O.A.C. 349 at 353 (Div. Ct.), the court per Griffiths J. See ATTENDANCE.

ATTENDANCE. *n*. " . . . [A]ttendance in court necessarily involves making one's presence known to the presiding judge. One does not comply merely by being physically present .. " *R. v. Anderson* (1983) 37 C.R. (3d) 67 at 73, 29 Alta. L.R. (2d) 66, 49 A.R. 122, 9 C.C.C. (3d) 539 (C.A.), Kerans J.A. (Moir J.A. concurring).

ATTENDANCE BONUS. A bonus paid to an employee for an especially good attendance record.

ATTENDANCE FEE. " . . . [I]ncludes the cost of going to, staying at and returning from the place of examination to the extent that these amounts may be reasonably calculated in advance together with at least one day's per diem fee . . ." *M. Hodge & Sons Ltd v. Monaghan* (1984), 39 C.P.C.112 at 116 46 Nfld. & P.E.I.R. 279, 135 A.P.R. 279 (Nfld. T.D.), Goodridge J.

ATTENDANCE MONEY. 1. Conduct money. 2. Reimbursement paid to a witness for reasonable expenses incurred while going to, staying at and returning from the place where a discovery or trial is held.

ATTENDANT. *n*. 1. A person who operates an elevating device. 2. A person who owes duty or service to another person. See AMBULANCE ~; CABIN ~; FIRST AID ~; SERVICE STATION ~.

ATTENDANT. *adj*. Accompanying.

ATTENDING DENTIST. A member of the dental staff who attends a patient in the hospital.

ATTENDING PHYSICIAN. The physician to whom responsibility for the observation, care and treatment of a patient has been assigned.

ATTENDING PSYCHIATRIST. The psychiatrist to whom responsibility for the observation, care and treatment of a patient has been assigned.

ATTENUATION. *n*. The decrease in radiation intensity caused by absorption and scattering in a medium.

ATTEST. *v*. To witness an event or act.

ATTESTATION. *n*. 1. Witnessing a written instrument and signing it as a witness. 2. " . . . [C]onsists, at the very least, of witnessing the execution of an instrument . . ." *Cameron, Re* (1984), 63 N.S.R. (2d) 103 at 107, 141 A.P.R. 103 (S.C.), Hallett J.

ATTESTATION CLAUSE. The witness to the execution of a written instrument signs this sentence, stating that he or she has witnessed it.

ATTESTING WITNESS. A person who has seen someone else sign a written document or execute a deed.

ATTIC. *n*. The space between the roof and the ceiling of the top storey or between a dwarf wall and a sloping roof. *Building Code Act*, R.R.O., 1980, Reg. 87, s. 1.

ATTINCTUS. *adj*. [L.] Under attaint.

ATTITUDINAL BIAS. Arises where a decision-maker has prejudged an issue and has not brought an open mind to the decision-making process. The rule against bias disqualifies decision-makers with attitudinal biases. *Halfway River First Nation v. British Columbia*, 1997 CarswellBC 1745 (S.C.).

ATTO. *pref*. 10^{-18}, prefix for multiples and submultiples of Basic, Supplementary and Derived Units of Measurement. *Weights and Measures Act*, S.C. 1970-71-72, c. 36, schedule 1, part V.

ATTORN. *v.* 1. To turn over. 2.To agree to recognize a new owner as landlord. 3. To attorn to a foreign court is to voluntarily submit to its jurisdiction. "It is a well-accepted principle of private international law that where a defendant, although he does not reside within the jurisdiction of that court, appears in a foreign court solely to preserve assets that have been seized by that court, he does not attorn to the jurisdiction of the foreign court." *Amopharm Inc. v. Harris Computer Corp*, 10 O.R. (3d) 27 (C.A.).

ATTORNARE REM. [L.] To appropriate or assign goods or money to a particular service or use.

ATTORNEY. *n.* 1. A person appointed to act in place of or to represent another. 2. Lawyer. 3. Patent agent. 4. The donee of a power of attorney or where a power of attorney is given to two or more persons, whether jointly or severally or both, means any one or more of such persons. *Powers of Attorney Act*, R.S.O. 1990, c. P.20, s. 1. 5. A person who is, by virtue of section 11 of the Act, an officer of the Court. *Federal Court Rules*, C.R.C., c. 663, s. 2. See CROWN~; POWER OF ~.

ATTORNEY GENERAL. *var.* **ATTORNE-YGENERAL**. 1. The principal law officer of the Crown, a Minister of the Crown. 2. The office of Attorney General started in England as early as the thirteenth century as the King's Attorney. In essence, the Attorney General exercised on the King's behalf the prerogative to bring and terminate prosecutions. Although there are great differences between the constitution of the Canadian and English offices of Attorney General, the power to manage prosecutions of individuals for criminal acts has changed little since these early times and between these countries. In Canada, the office of the Attorney General is one with constitutional dimensions recognized in the *Constitution Act, 1867*. Although the specific duties conventionally exercised by the Attorney General are not enumerated, s. 135 of that Act provides for the extension of the authority and duties of that office as existing prior to Confederation. A similar provision applicable to the Attorney General of Alberta is found in the *Alberta Act*, S.C. 1905, c. 3 (reprinted in R.S.C. 1985, App. II, No. 20), at s. 16(1). Furthermore, s. 63 of the *Constitution Act, 1867* requires that the cabinets of Quebec and Ontario include in their membership the Attorneys General. Attorneys General in this country are, of course, charged with duties beyond the management of prosecutions. As in England, they serve as Law Officers to their respective legislatures, and are responsible for providing legal advice to the various government departments. Unlike England, the Attorney General is also the Minister of Justice and is generally responsible for drafting the legislation tabled by the government of the day. The numerous other duties of the provincial and federal Attorneys General are broadly outlined in the various Acts establishing the Departments of Justice in each jurisdiction. The gravity of the power to bring, manage and terminate prosecutions, which lies at the heart of the Attorney General's role, has given rise to an expectation that he or she will be in this respect fully independent from the political pressures of the government. It is a constitutional principle in this country that the Attorney General must act independently of partisan concerns when supervising prosecutorial decisions. This side of the Attorney General's independence finds further form in the principle that courts will not interfere with his exercise of executive authority, as reflected in the prosecutorial decision-making process. *Krieger v. Law Society (Alberta)* [2002] 3 S.C.R. 372. 3. See ACTING ~.

ATTORNEY GENERAL OF THE PROVINCE. The minister of the Crown of the province who is responsible for judicial affairs. *Judges Act*, R.S.C. 1985 c. J-1 s. 2.

ATTORNMENT. *n.* Agreement to become a new owner's tenant or a mortgagee's tenant. See BAILMENT BY ~.

ATTRIBUTABLE. *adj.* That which is a natural and reasonable consequence; causally connected.

ATTRIBUTE. *n.* With reference to a person, means the race, creed, colour, nationality, ancestry, place of origin, sex or geographical location of the person and includes the race, creed, colour, nationality, ancestry, place of origin, sex or geographical location of a person connected with the person or of nationals of a country with the government of which the person conducts, has conducted or may conduct business. *Discriminatory Business Practices Act*, R.S.O. 1990, c. D.12, s. 4(2). See OTHER ~.

ATTRIBUTION. *n.* To assign income or property to another person for certain purposes.

ATTRITION. *n.* Reduction of number of members of the work force by death, retirement or resignation.

AU BESOIN. [Fr.] In the event of need.

AUCTION. *n.* Public sale of property to the highest bidder. See DUTCH ~.

AUCTIONEER. *n.* 1. ". . . [A] person who sells property of any kind by public auction . . ." *Merritt v. Toronto (City)* (1895) 22 O.A.R. 205 at 213 (C.A.), MacLennan J.A. (Hagarty C.J.O. and Burton J.A. concurring). 2. An individual who conducts the bidding at a sale by auction of any property.

AUCTION MARKET. See LIVESTOCK ~.

AUCTOR. *n.* [L.] Vendor; seller.

AUCTOR IN REM SUAM. [L.] Agent for personal advantage.

AUCTOR REGIT ACTUM. [L.] It is the law of the country that bestows on someone the power to perform an act which determines the validity of any act committed in that capacity. J.G. McLeod, *The Conflict of Laws* (Calgary: Carswell, 1983) at 779.

AUCUPIA VERBORUM SUNT JUDICE INDIGNA. [L.] Quibbles are beneath a judge's dignity.

AUDI ALTERAM PARTEM. [L. hear the other side] 1. The Latin expression and best known name for one of the main principles of natural justice. 2. " . . . [P]arties must be made aware of the case being made against them and [be] given an opportunity to answer it. . ." *Canadian Cable Television Ass. v. American College Sorts Collective of Canada Inc.* (1991), 4 Admin L.R. (2d) 61 at 72, 81 D.L.R. (4th) 376, 36 C.P.R. (3d) 455, 129 N.R. 296, [1991] 3 F.C. 626 (C.A.), the court per MacGuigan J.A. 3. The broad scope of the rule in Canada is demonstrated in L'Alliance des Professeurs case . . . [[1953] 2 S.C.R. 140] where Rand J. said at p. 161: 'Audi alteram partem is a pervading principle of our law, and is peculiarly applicable to the interpretation of statutes which delegate judicial action in any form to inferior tribunals: in making decisions of a judicial nature they must hear both sides, and there is nothing in the statute here qualifying the application of that principl.'" *Downing v. Graydon* (1978), 9 C.C.E.L. 260 at 264 21 O.R. 2d 292 78 C.L.L.C. 14, 183, 92 D.L.R. (3d) 355 (C.A.), Blair J.A. 4. "... [T]he audi alteram partem rule . . . is one of the basic requirements of procedural fairness. According to that rule, a party to a decision must have an opportunity to be heard and, in particular, the decision-maker cannot hear evidence in the absence of a party whose conduct is under scrutiny.

(See *Kane v. University of British Columbia*, [1980] 1 S.C.R. 1105 . . .). . ." *Ontario (Attorney General) v. Grady* (1988), 34 C.R.R. 289 at 317 (Ont. H.C.), Callaghan A.C.J.H.C.

AUDIENCE. *n.* Interview; hearing. See PRE ~.

AUDIENCE ROOM. Any room or apartment that, in any public building, is intended to accommodate or to be used for any public meeting or assemblage of persons. *Public Buildings Act*, R.S.M. 1970 c. P200 s. 2.

AUDIOLOGIST. *n.* A person whose name is entered in the register as an audiologist. *Speech-Language Pathology and Audiology Act* S.N.B. 1987, c. 71, s. 2.

AUDIOLOGY. *n.* The assessment of auditory function and the treatment and prevention of auditory dysfunction to develop, maintain, rehabilitate or augment auditory and communicative functions. Audiology is the assessment of auditory function and the treatment and prevention of auditory dysfunction to develop, maintain, rehabilitate or augment auditory and communicative functions. *Audiology and Speech-Language Pathology Act, 1991*, S.O. 1991, c. 19, s. 3, as am.

AUDIO RECORDING MEDIUM. A recording medium, regardless of its material form, onto which a sound recording may be reproduced and that is of a kind ordinarily used by individual consumers for that purpose, excluding any prescribed kind of recording medium. *Copyright Act*, R.S.C. 1985, c. C-42, s. 79.

AUDIT. *n.* 1. " . . . [A]n examination of books of account and supporting evidence to determine the reliability of the information recorded." *Toromont Industrial Holdings Ltd v. Thorne Gunn Helfwell & Christenson* (1975) 23 C.P.R. (2d) 59 at 74, 10 O.R. (2d) 65, 62 D.L.R. (3d) 225 (H.C.), Holland J. 2. (i) An independent examination of records for the purpose of expressing an opinion or (ii) the preparation of a report or certificate or the preparation or expression of an opinion as to whether financial information is presented fairly. See INSPECTION ~.

AUDITA QUERELA. [L.] After the dispute has been heard a writ which could be delivered to call into question a judgment or execution.

AUDIT COMMITTEE. A committee of the board of directors of a corporation who nominate auditors and work with them.

AUDITING. See PUBLIC ACCOUNTING AND ~.

AUDITING STANDARDS. See GENERALLY ACCEPTED ~.

AUDITOR. *n.* 1. One who reviews and verifies accounts. 2. A person who is a member in good standing of any corporation, association or institute of professional accountants, and includes a firm, every partner of which is such a person. 3. " . . . [A] person whose position is an independent one, whose duty it is to discover and point out the errors or mistakes of the directors, if any, the gains and losses of the company, to show in fact, exactly the true state of the accounts; so that he stands, as it were, between the directors and the shareholders as an independent investigator of all business transactions, in which the directors, as the managers of the affairs of the company, have been engaged . . ." *Ontario Forge & Bolt Co. Re* (1896) 27 O.R. 230 at 232 H.C. Robertson J. See PROVINCIAL ~; QUALIFIED ~.

AUDITOR GENERAL. 1. The Auditor General of Canada appointed pursuant to subsection 3(1). *Auditor General Act*, R.S.C. 1985 c. A-17 s. 2. 2. Some provinces use the same title to describe the person who carries out similar functions for the provincial government.

AUDITOR GENERAL OF CANADA. 1. The officer appointed pursuant to subsection 3(1) of the *Auditor General Act. Financial Administration Act*, R.S.C. 1985, c. F-11, s. 2. 2. The federal official who examines Canada's public accounts, including those relating to public property, Crown corporations and the Consolidated Revenue Fund.

AUGUSTA LEGIBUS SOLUTA NON EST. [L.] The spouse of a ruler is not above the law.

AUNT. *n.* In relation to any person, means a sister of the mother or father of that person. *Immigration Regulations*, C.R.C., c. 940, s. 2.

AUTHENTIC. *adj.* Original; genuine.

AUTHENTIC ACT. Something executed before a notary or another duly authorized public official.

AUTHENTICATION. *n.* 1. An attestation made by an officer certifying that a record is in proper form and that the officer is the proper person to so certify. 2. A municipal corporation's signing and sealing of a by-law.

AUTHENTICITY. *n.* 1. Proven of an original when it was written, printed, executed or signed as it claims to have been. 2. Proven of a copy when it is a true copy of the original. 3. Proven of the copy of a letter, telecommunication or telegram when the original was sent as claimed and received by the addressee.

AUTHOR. *n.* 1. One should always keep in mind that one of the purposes of the copyright legislation, historically, has been "to protect and reward the *intellectual* effort of the *author* (for a limited period of time) in the work" (my emphasis). The use of the word "copyright" in the English version of the Act has obscured the fact that what the Act fundamentally seeks to protect is "le droit d'auteur". While not defined in the Act, the word "author" conveys a sense of creativity and ingenuity. *Tele-Direct (Publications) Inc. v. American Business Information Inc.* 1997 CarswellNat 2111, 221 N.R. 113, 154 D.L.R. (4th) 328, 76 C.P.R. (3d) 296, 134 F.T.R. 80 (note), [1998] 2 F.C. 22, 37 B.L.R (2d) 101, Federal Court of Appeal, Decary, J.A. for the court. 2. " . . . [T]he person who expressed the ideas in an original or novel form: . . ." *New Brunswick Telephone Co. v. John Maryon International Ltd* (1982), 24 C.C.L.T. 146 at 199, 43 N.B.R. (2d) 469, 113 A.P.R. 469,141 D.L.R. (3d) 193 (C.A.), the court per La Forest J.A. 3. Includes the legal representatives of a deceased author. *Copyright Act*, R.S.C. 1985, c. C-42, s. 60(3). See CANADIAN ~; WORK OF JOINT ~SHIP.

AUTHORITY. *n.* 1. Power or right to enforce obedience or to influence the conduct and actions of others. 2. A statute, case or text cited in support of a legal opinion or argument. 3. A legal power given by one person to another to do some act. 4. Body given powers by statute to oversee or carry out a government function. 5. " . . . '[J]urisdiction'. . ." *Toronto (City) v. Morson* (1916), 37 O.L.R. 369 at 376, 28 D.L.R. 188 (C.A.), Masten J.A. See ACTUAL ~; APPARENT ~; APPROPRIATE ~; AREA ~; ASSESSING ~; ASSESSMENT ~; BINDING ~; CITATION OF AUTHORITIES; COMPETENT ~; CONFIRMING ~; CUSTOMARY ~; EDUCATION ~; ELECTED ~; EXPROPRIATING ~; EXPROPRIATION ~; HIGHWAY ~; IMPLIED ~; LICENSING~; LOCAL ~; MUNICIPAL ~; OPERATING ~; OSTENSIBLE ~; PARTY ~; PERSUASIVE PUBLIC ~; REGULATION-MAKING ~; ROAD ~; ST. LAWRENCE SEAWAY ~; STATUTORY ~; DEFENCE; SUPPLY ~; USUAL OR CUSTOMARY ~.

AUTHORIZATION. *n.* 1. Licence; certificate; registration. 2. An authorization to intercept a private communication given under section 186 or subsection 188(2). *Criminal Code*, R.S.C. 1985, c. C-46, s. 183. See SPECIAL ~.

AUTHORIZE. *v.* To empower.

AUTHORIZED. *adj.* 1. Properly empowered to perform any specified duty or to do any specified act. 2. "A work is authorized by statute whether the statute is mandatory or permissive, if the work is carried out in accordance with the statute." *Tock v. St. John's (City) Metropolitan Area Board* (1989), 1 C.C.L.T. (2d) 113 at 154, 47 M.P.L.R. 113, [1989] 2 S.C.R. 1181, 64 D.L.R. (4th) 620, 104 N.R. 241, 82 Nfld. & P.E.I.R. 181, 257 A.P.R. 181, Sopinka J. 3. Within the context [of the *Canada Agricultural Products Act*] means empowered, enabled, sanctioned, approved or permitted. *R. v. A & A Foods Ltd,.* 1997 CarswellBC 2541, 120 C.C.C. (3d) 513.

AUTHORIZED AGENT. Any person authorized by the Minister to accept subscriptions for or make sales of securities. *Financial Administration Act*, R.S.C. 1985, c. F-11, s. 2.

AUTHORIZED CAPITAL. The total amount of capital which, by its incorporating documents, a company is authorized to issue.

AUTHORIZED CHARGE. A charge made directly to a patient for insured services. *Hospitals or Health Insurance acts*.

AUTHORIZED EMERGENCY VEHICLE. (a) A motor vehicle operated by a peace officer in the course of duty or employment, (b) a fire department or fire fighting vehicle, and (c) an ambulance. *Motor Vehicle Act*, R.S.N.B. 1973, c. M-17, s. 1.

AUTHORIZED EXPLOSIVE. Any explosive that is declared to be an authorized explosive in accordance with the regulations. *Explosives Act*, R.S.C. 1985, c. E-17, s. 2.

AUTHORIZED INSURER. An insurance company lawfully authorized or permitted to carry on business in a province.

AUTHORIZED INVESTMENT. A security in which a trust permits its trustee to invest funds.

AUTHORIZED OFFICIAL. A person who is authorized to act as the representative of a collection agent or broker and is named in the licence of the collection agent or broker.

AUTHORIZED PARTY. See CANDIDATE OF AN ~.

AUTHORIZED PERSON. A person authorized by legislation to perform a specified function under it.

AUTHORSHIP. See JOINT~.

AUTO. *abbr.* Automobile.

AUTO BODY REPAIRER. A person engaged in the repair of motor vehicles who, (i) hammers out dents in body panels, fenders and skirting, (ii) files, grinds, sands, fills and finishes ready for any dented, welded or pierced area, (iii) by heat treatment, shrinks or stretches metal panels, (iv) welds breaks in body areas, (v) tests for and corrects faulty alignment, alignment of frames, (vi) paints and glazes, and (vii) removes and installs body parts. *Apprenticeship and Tradesmen's Qualification Act*, R.R.O. 1980, Reg. 22, s. 1.

AUTOBUS. *n.* A vehicle equipped for the transportation of persons, at least eight at a time, and effects such transportation for a pecuniary consideration. *Highway Code*, R.S.Q. 1977, c. C-24, s. 1.

AUTOCRACY. *n.* Unlimited monarchy.

AUTOGRAPH. *n.* 1. The handwriting of a person. 2. The signature of a person.

AUTOLYSIS. *n.* Enzymes normally present in cells and tissues dissolving them. F.A. Jaffe, *A Guide to Pathological Evidence*, 3d ed. (Toronto: Carswell, 1991) at 213.

AUTOMATED TELLER. A machine normally unattended by an employee of a credit union or bank; that (a) receives cash from; (b) disburses cash to; or (c) provides services of the credit union to a member on receiving an instruction from the member or customer.

AUTOMATED WEATHER OBSERVATION SYSTEM. A set of meteorological sensors, and associated systems designed to electronically collect and disseminate meteorological data. *Canadian Aviation Regulations*, SOR/96-433, s. 101.01(1).

AUTOMATIC. *adj.* 1. Involuntary. 2. Refers to machinery not requiring the assistance of a human operator to complete its function or functions. See SEMI- ~.

AUTOMATIC CHECK-OFF. The deduction of union dues from wages by an employer.

AUTOMATIC ENFORCEMENT. After someone assigns the order for payment of maintenance to an enforcement office, all of the debtor's payments are made to the office instead of to the creditor so that the office may monitor compliance with the order. C.R.B. Dunlop, Cred*itor-Debtor Law in Canada*, Second Cumulative Supplement (Toronto: Carswell, 1986) at 222.

AUTOMATIC FIREARM. A firearm that is capable of, or assembled or designed and manufactured with the capability of, discharging projectiles in rapid succession during one pressure of the trigger. *Criminal Code*, R.S.C. 1985, c. C-46, s. 84(1).

AUTOMATIC-LOCKING RETRACTOR. A retractor incorporating adjustment hardware that has a positive self-locking mechanism that is capable when locked of withstanding restraint forces. *Motor Vehicle Safety Regulations*, C.R.C., c. 103 8, s. 209.

AUTOMATIC RENEWAL. Extension of an agreement from year to year or period of time to period of time when no notice of termination is given by either party.

AUTOMATIC TABULATING EQUIP-MENT. Apparatus that automatically examines and totals votes recorded on ballot cards and tabulates the results.

AUTOMATIC WAGE ADJUSTMENT. A wage increase which occurs upon the happening of a specified event.

AUTOMATIC WAGE PROGRESSION. A system of wage increases based upon length of service.

AUTOMATIC WEAPON. Any firearm that is capable of firing bullets in rapid succession during one pressure of the trigger.

AUTOMATISM. *n.* 1. Two forms of automatism are recognized at law: insane automatism and non-insane automatism. Involuntary action which does not stem from a disease of the mind gives rise to a claim of non-insane automatism. If successful, a claim of non-insane automatism entitles the accused to an acquittal. . . On the other hand, involuntary action which is found, at law, to result from a disease of the mind gives rise to a claim of insane automatism. It has long been recognized that insane automatism is subsumed by the defence of mental disorder, formerly referred to as the defence of insanity. *R. v. Stone*, 1999 CarswellBC 1064, [1999] 2

S.C.R. 290, [1999] 2 S.C.R. 290, 24 C.R. (5th) 1, 239 N.R. 201, 63 C.R.R. (2d) 43, 173 D.L.R. (4th) 66, 134 C.C.C. (3d) 353, 123 B.C.A.C. 1, 201 W.A.C. 1 Bastarache, J. for the majority. 2. The two concepts [of automatism and provocation] are quite distinct and their application depends on the nature of the impact on an accused of the triggering event. The key distinction between the two concepts is that automatism relates to a lack of voluntariness in the accused, an essential element of the offence, while provocation is a recognition that an accused who "voluntarily" committed all the elements of murder may nevertheless have been provoked by a wrongful act or insult that would have been sufficient, on an objective basis, to deprive an ordinary person of the power of self-control. *R. v. Stone*, 1999 CarswellBC 1064, [1999] 2 S.C.R. 290, [1999] 2 S.C.R. 290, 24 C.R. (5th) 1, 239 N.R. 201, 63 C.R.R. (2d) 43, 173 D.L.R. (4th) 66, 134 C.C.C. (3d) 353, 123 B.C.A.C. 1, 201 W.A.C. 1. 3." . . . [A]s it is employed in the defence of non-insane automatism, has in my opinion been satisfactorily defined by Mr. Justice Lacourciere of the Court of Appeal of Ontario in the case of *R. v. K.* (1970), 3 C.C.C. (2d) 84 . . . : 'Automatism is a term used to describe unconscious, involuntary behavior, the state of the person who, though capable of action, is not conscious of what he is doing. It means an unconscious, involuntary act, where the mind does not go with what is being done.'" *Rabey v. R.* (1980), 54 C.C.C. (2d) 1 at 6 (S.C.C.), Ritchie J.

AUTOMOBILE. *n.* 1. Any vehicle propelled by any power other than muscular force and adapted for transportation on the public highways but not on rails. Quebec statutes. 2. Includes all self-propelled vehicles, their trailers, accessories and equipment, but not railway rolling stock, watercraft or aircraft of any kind. *Insurance acts*. 3. Includes a trolley bus and a self-propelled vehicle, and the trailers, accessories and equipment of automobiles, but does not include railway rolling stock that runs on rails, watercraft or aircraft. *Insurance acts*. 4. A motor vehicle. See DAMAGE CAUSED BY AN ~; SCRAP ~; UNIDENTIFIED ~; UNINSURED ~; USED ~.

AUTOMOBILE DEALER. A person who carries on the business of buying or selling new or used automobiles.

AUTOMOBILE INSURANCE. Insurance (a) against liability arising out of, (i) bodily injury to or the death of a person, or (ii) loss of or damage to property, caused by an automobile or the use or operation thereof; or (b) against loss of or damage to an automobile and the loss of use thereof, and includes insurance otherwise coming within the class of accident insurance where the accident is caused by an automobile or the use or operation thereof, whether liability exists or not, if the contract also includes insurance described in clause (a). *Insurance acts.*

AUTOMOBILE JUNK YARD. Premises where three or more unserviceable, discarded or junked motor vehicles, bodies, engines or other component parts thereof are gathered, located or placed.

AUTOMOBILE MASTER KEY. Includes a key, pick, rocker key or other instrument designed or adapted to operate the ignition or other switches or locks of a series of motor vehicles. *Criminal Code*, R.S.C. 1985, c. C-46, s. 353(5).

AUTOMOBILE SERVICE STATION. A place for supplying fuel, oil and minor accessories for motor vehicles at retail prices directly to the user and for making minor servicing or running repairs essential to the operation of motor vehicles. Canada regulations.

AUTOMOTIVE MACHINIST. A person who reconditions and rebuilds internal combustion engines and associated components, power trains, brake system components and suspension system components. *Apprenticeship and Tradesmen's Qualification Act*, R.R.O. 1980, Reg. 23, s. 1.

AUTOMOTIVE PAINTER. A person engaged in the refinishing of motor vehicle bodies who, (i) sands, spot fills, primes and paints, (ii) dries or bakes newly painted surfaces, (iii) masks and tapes for multi-tone paint work and protective requirements, (iv) applies decals, transfers, stencils and other types of identification to finished paint work, (v) mixes paint and components and matches colours, and (vi) refinishes galvanized outer panels and anodized aluminum moulding. *Apprenticeship and Tradesmen's Qualification Act*, R.R.O. 180 Reg. 24 s. 1.

AUTONOMY. *n.* National political independence. See LOCAL ~.

AUTOPSY. *n.* 1. Necropsy; postmortem. F.A. Jaffe, *A Guide to Pathological Evidence*, 3d ed. (Toronto: Carswell, 1991) at 1. 2. The dissection of a body for the purpose of examining organs and tissues to determine the cause of death or manner of death or the identity of the deceased and may include chemical, histological, microbiological or serological tests and other laboratory investigations.

AUTOROUTE. *n.* 1. A toll-charge, limited access, rapid-transit highway. *Autoroutes Act*, R.S.Q. 1977, c. A-34, s. 1. 2. A public highway defined as an autoroute by the Minister and specially identified as such by an official traffic sign. Such word does not include an autoroute within the meaning of the *Autoroutes Act* (chapter A-34). *Highway Code*, R.S.Q. 1977, c. C-24, s. 56.

AUTO TRANSPORTER. A truck and a trailer designed for use in combination to transport motor vehicles where the truck is designed to carry cargo other than at the fifth wheel and that cargo is to be loaded only be means of the trailer. *Motor Vehicle Safety Regulations*, C.R.C., c. 1038, s. 2.

AUTRE. *adj.* [Fr.] Another.

AUTRE DROIT. [Fr.] In another's right.

AUTREFOIS ACQUIT. [Fr. formerly acquitted] 1. A plea which an accused may make in her own defence. 2. To make out the defence of autrefois acquit, the accused must show that the two charges laid against him are the same. In particular, he must prove that the following two conditions have been met: (1) the matter must be the same, in whole or in part; and (2) the new count must be the same as at the first trial, or be implicitly included in that of the first trial, either in law or on account of the evidence presented if it had been legally possible at that time to make the necessary amendments. *R. v. Van Rassel* (1990), 53 C.C.C. (3d) 353 (S.C.C.), McLachlin, J. for the court. 3. An accused may not be prosecuted when he or she has been tried for and acquitted of the same offence. *R. v Wright.* (1965), 45 C.R. 38 at 39, [1965] 2 O.R. 337, [1965] 3 C.C.C. 160, 50 D.L.R. (2d) 498 (C.A.), Porter C.J.O.

AUTREFOIS CONVICT. [Fr. formerly convicted] " . . . [A]n absolutely effective plea in bar to the second information, if the accused has been . . . convicted and it was attempted again to prosecute them for the same offence." *A. v. Esker*, [1929] 3 D.L.R. 760 at 761, 64 O.L.R. 1, 51 C.C.C. 409 (C.A.), Latchford C.J.

AUTRE VIE. [Fr.] The life of another (period of time).

AUXILIARY. *n*. See DENTAL ~; RELIGIOUS ~.

AUXILIARY. *adj*. Assisting.

AUXILIARY EMISSION CONTROL DEVICE. Any element of design that senses temperature, vehicle speed, engine RPM, transmission gear, manifold vacuum, or any other parameter for the purpose of activating, modulating, delaying, or deactivating the operation of any part of an emission control system. *On-Road Vehicle and Engine Emission Regulations*, SOR/2003-2, s. 1(1).

AUXILIUM. *n*. [L.] Aid.

AUXILIUM CURIAE. [L.] The suit or request of one party that a court cite and convene another party to warrant something.

AUXILIUM FACERE ALICUI IN CURIA REGIS. [L.] To become the friend and solicitor of another in the sovereign's courts.

AUXILIUM REGIS. [L. the king's aid] Money levied for royal and public service use such as taxes which Parliament grants.

AVAIL. *n*. Profit from land.

AVAILABLE. *adj*. " . . . [D]oes not mean 'existing.' It means 'in such condition as that it can be taken advantage of.'" *Devitt v. Mutual Life Insurance Co.* (1915), 33 O.L.R. 473 at 478, 2 D.L.R. 183 (C.A.), Riddell J.A. (Falconbridge C.J.K.B. concurring).

AVAILABLE CHANNEL. Any unrestricted channel of a distribution undertaking in a licensed area, other than a channel on which is distributed (a) the programming service of a licensed programming undertaking other than a video-on-demand programming undertaking; (b) community programming; (c) the House of Commons programming service; or (d) a programming service consisting of the proceedings of the legislature of the province in which the licensed area is located. *Broadcasting Distribution Regulations*, SOR/97-555, s. 1.

AVAILABLE MARKET. A particular situation of trade, area and goods in which there is enough demand that, if a purchaser defaults, the goods in question can readily be sold. G.H.L. Fridman, *Sale of Goods in Canada*, 3d ed. (Toronto: Carswell, 1986) at 359.

AVAILS. *n*. Proceeds; profits.

AVAL. *n*. [Fr.] Surety.

AVER. *v*. To allege.

AVERAGE. *n*. 1. A medium. 2. Loss or damage to goods on board a ship. See RACE ~.

AVERAGE DAILY WAGE. The daily wage of an employee averaged over the employee's employment with an employer.

AVERAGE NATIONAL RATE OF UNEMPLOYMENT. The monthly national rates of unemployment in a year averaged for the year.

AVERAGE YIELD. The average total orchard production of the insured person over the preceding six years allowing for, (i) age of trees, (ii) biennial bearing, (iii) tree removal, and (iv) change in acreage. Ontario regulations. See LONG TERM ~.

A VERBIS LEGIS NON EST RECEDENDUM. [L.] The words of a statute must not be departed from.

AVERMENT. *n*. 1. Allegation. *R. v. Bellman*, [1938] 3 D.L.R. 548 at 551, 70 C.C.C. 171, 13 M.P.R. 37 (N.B. C.A.), Baxter C.J. 2. In a pleading, affirmation of any matter. See IMMATERIAL ~; PREFATORY ~.

AVIATION. See CANADIAN ~ SAFETY BOARD; SPECIAL ~ EVENT.

AVIATION FUEL. Any gas, hydrocarbon substance or liquid that is sold to be used or is used to create power to propel an aircraft.

AVIATION FUEL IN BULK. Aviation fuel stored, transported or transferred by any means other than in a fuel tank of an aircraft or a motor vehicle in which aviation fuel for generating power in an aircraft or the motor vehicle is kept. *Gasoline Tax Act*, R.S.O. 1990, c. G.5, s. 1.

AVIATION OCCURRENCE. (a) Any accident or incident associated with the operation of aircraft; and (b) any situation or condition that the Board has reasonable grounds to believe could, if left unattended, induce an accident or incident described in paragraph (a). *Canadian Transportation Accident Investigation and Safety Board Act*, S.C. 1989, c. 3, s. 2.

A VINCULO MATRIMONII. [L.] From the ties of wedlock.

AVOCAT. *n*. [Fr.] Barrister, advocate.

AVOID. *v*. To make a transaction void.

AVOIDABLE HAZARD. A threat of injury to the health of the user of a cosmetic that can be (a) predicted from the composition of the cosmetic, the toxicology of the ingredients and the site of application thereof; (b) reasonably anticipated Burin normal use; and (c) eliminated specified limitations on the usage of the cosmetic. *Cosmetic Regulations*, C.R.C., c. 869, s. 24.

AVOIDANCE. *n*. Avoiding, setting aside or vacating. See CONFESSION AND ~; TAX ~.

AVOIDANCE TRANSACTION. Any transaction, (a) that, but for this section, would result directly or indirectly in a tax benefit, unless the transaction may reasonably be considered to have been undertaken or arranged in good faith primarily for purposes other than to obtain the tax benefit, or (b) that is part of a series of transactions which would result directly or indirectly in a tax benefit but for this section, unless the transaction may reasonably be considered to have been undertaken or arranged in good faith primarily for purposes other than to obtain the tax benefit. *Corporations Tax Act*, R.S.O. 1990, c. C.40, s. 5(1).

AVOIRDUPOIS. *n*. [Fr.] The method of measuring and weighing in which 16 ounces equals a pound.

AVOUCH. *v*. To maintain or justify an act.

AVOUCHER. *n*. Requesting that an undertaking be fulfilled by the warrantor.

AVOW. *v*. To maintain or justify an act.

AVULSION. *n*. 1. Land which current or flood tears off from property to which it originally belonged and adds to the property of another or land joined to another's property when a river changes its course. 2. Tearing away a tissue or part.

AWARD. *n*. 1. Judgment. 2. Instrument which embodies an arbitrator's decision. 3. A pension, allowance, bonus or grant payable under this Act. *Pension Act*, R.S.C. 1985, c. P-6, s. 2. 4. Includes umpirage and a certificate in the nature of an award. *Arbitration acts*. See ARBITRAL ~; ARBITRAMENT AND ~.

AWG. The American (or Brown and Sharpe) wire gauge as applied to non-ferrous conductors and nonferrous sheet metal. *Power Corporation Act*, R.R.O. 1980, Reg. 794.

A.W.L.D. *abbr.* Alberta Weekly Law Digest.

AWNING. *n*. A roof-like covering of canvas or similar fabric material or metal that projects outwards above a window or doorway of any building.

AWOS. Automated weather observation system. *Canadian Aviation Regulations*, SOR/96-433, s. 101.01(1).

AXIOM. *n*. A truth which is indisputable.

AXLE. *n*. 1. A straight line, real or imaginary, extending the width of the vehicle at right angles to the centre line thereof, on which the wheels revolve and which transfers the load carried by it approximately equally to the wheel or wheels attached to each end of the axle. See DUAL ~; PONY ~; SINGLE ~; TANDEM ~; TRIPLE ~.

AXLE ASSEMBLY. All the wheels of a vehicle, the centres of which may be included between two vertical parallel transverse planes one metre apart, extending across the full width of the vehicle. *The Highway Traffic Act*, S.M. 1985-86, c. 3, s. 1.

AXLE GROUP. Two or more axle assemblies the centres of which are not less than one metre and not more than 1.8 metres apart and which are either articulated from a common attachment to the vehicle or are separately attached to the vehicle and have a common connecting mechanism that equalizes the load carried by each axle assembly. *The Highway Traffic Act*, S.M. 1985-86, c. 3, s. 1. See FOUR ~; THREE ~; TWO ~.

AXLE LOAD. The mass measured under the wheels of an axle or of the axles included in one category established by regulation, resulting from the distribution on such wheels of the mass of a road vehicle or combination of road vehicles, including accessories, equipment and load. *Highway Safety Code*, S.Q. 1986, c. 91, s. 462.

AXLE MASS. The mass indicated when the vehicle is weighed with the rear wheels or with the front wheels on the scales or weighing device or with other wheels on the scales or weighing device where those wheels are mounted on the same axle. *Highway Traffic Act*, R.S. Nfld. 1990, c. H-3, s. 2.

AXLE WEIGHT. The combined weight which all the wheels on any one axle impose on the road. See TANDEM ~.

AZOOSPERMIA. *n*. Total absence of sperm cells in semen. F.A. Jaffe, *A Guide to Pathological Evidence*, 3d ed. (Toronto: Carswell, 1991) at 213.

B. *abbr*. 1. Baron. 2. Of a ship, breadth.

BACHELOR. *n*. 1. The first degree in a university. 2. A never married man.

BACK. *v*. To countersign; to endorse.

BACKADATION. *n*. The percentage which a seller of shares, deliverable on a certain date, pays for the privilege of delaying delivery until another date.

BACK A WARRANT. For one justice to endorse a warrant issued by the justice of another district or jurisdiction permitting it be executed in the first justice's jurisdiction. *R. v. Solloway Malls & Co.* (1930), 65 O.L.R. 677 at 679, 54 C.C.C. 214 (C.A.), the court per Hodgins J.A.

BACK-BENCHER. *n*. A Member of Parliament or of a legislature who is a member of the government party but is not a member of Cabinet and does not hold an office in the party caucus. The name refers to where the member is likely to sit in the legislature.

BACK-BOND. *var*. **BACKBOND**. *n*. A bond of indemnity which one gives to a surety.

BACK FLOW. A flowing back or reversal of the normal direction of the flow.

BACKFLOW PREVENTER. A device or a method that prevents backflow in a water distribution system.

BACKING. *n*. The structural base to which the pile, face or outer surface is woven, tufted, hooked, knitted or otherwise attached in a pile fabric or floor covering. *Textile Labelling and Advertising Regulations*, C.R.C., c. 1551, s. 25.

BACK LANE. A highway situated wholly within the limits of any city, town or village or restricted speed area or reduced restricted speed area which has been designed, constructed and intended to provide access to and service at the rear of places of residence or business and includes alleys having a width of not more than 9 metres. *The Highway Traffic Act*, C.C.S.M. c. H60, s. 1.

BACK PAY. Wages due for services performed in the past.

BACKSHEET. *n*. A page attached to the back and facing in the opposite direction to other pages of a document filed in a court proceeding; gives the title of the proceeding and other information.

BACK-SIPHONAGE. Backflow caused by a negative pressure in the supply system.

BACK-SIPHONAGE PREVENTER. A device or a method that prevents back-siphonage in a water distribution system.

BACK-TO-BACK CREDIT. Secondary credit which an exporter requests the confirming bank to extend to a supplier of goods. It covers the same goods which are the subject of the confirmed credit to the exporter. I.F.G. Baxter *The Law of Banking*, 3d ed. (Toronto: Carswell 1981) at 156.

BACK-TO-WORK AGREEMENT. Terms under which employees will return to work following settlement of a strike.

BACK-TO-WORK MOVEMENT. An effort to persuade employees to end a strike.

BACKTRACK. *v*. To displace junior employees when the seniority rights of other workers are exercised.

BACK VENT. A pipe that is installed to vent a trap off the horizontal section of a fixture drain or the vertical leg of a water closet or other fixture that has an integral siphonic flushing action.

BACKWARDATION. *n*. The percentage which a seller of shares, deliverable on a certain date, pays for the privilege of delaying delivery until another date.

BACKWATER VALVE. A check valve designed for use in a gravity drainage system.

BACTERIAL CULTURE. The coagulum made by growth of harmless acid-producing bacteria in milk, reconstituted milk powder or reconstituted skim milk powder.

BAD. *adj*. In pleadings, unsound.

BAD DEBT. A debt which is irrecoverable.

BAD FAITH. 1. Bad faith has been found in situations where there has been a blatant disregard for the *Charter* rights of an accused or where more than one *Charter* right has been violated. *R. v. Wise* [1992] 1 S.C.R. 527. 2. Used in municipal and administrative case law to cover a wide range of conduct in the exercise of legislatively delegated authority. Bad faith has been held to include dishonesty, fraud, bias, conflict of interest, discrimination, abuse of power, corruption, oppression, unfairness, and conduct that is unreasonable. The words have also been held to include conduct based on an improper mo tive, or undertaken for an improper, indirect or ulterior purpose. In all these senses, bad faith describes the exercise of delegated authority that is illegal and renders the consequential act void. And in all these senses bad faith must be proven by evidence of illegal conduct, adequate to support the finding of fact. Bad faith, however, is also used to describe the exercise of power by an administrative body that is beyond the scope or the ambit of the powers delegated to that body by the legislature. In those cases the exercise of powers is sometimes described as unauthorized, or beyond the scope, or outside the limit of the delegated power. It is an act that is ultra vires. Frequently, allegations of bad faith include both the aspect of illegality in the first sense and in the sense of ultra vires. To the extent that the allegation focuses on the way the delegated power was exercised, or on the conduct of the administrative body, there is an issue of fact. In those cases where powers are said to have been exceeded, however, there is another issue. That is the scope, or the amplitude, of the powers delegated by the legislature. That issue invariably requires an interpretation of the empowering statutes, and that raises an issue of law. *Mac-Millan Bloedel Ltd. v. Galiano Island Trust Committee* (1995), 10 B.C.L.R. (3d) 121 (C.A.) per Finch, J.A. (leave to appeal to S.C.C. refused).

BADGE. *n*. " . . . [H]ad its origin in heraldry as meaning a distinctive device worn by the adherents of the lord. The badge is not comprised of the arms of the lord, which are exclusive to him, but usually it utilizes the crest. In Scotland the badge worn by a clansman is the crest of the chief within a belt and buckle with the chief's motto inscribed on the belt." *Insurance Corp. of British Columbia c. Canada (Registrar of Trade Marks)* (1978), 44 C.P.R. (2d) 1 at 7, [1980] 1 F.C. 669 (T.D.), Cattanach J.

BADGES OF FRAUD. 1. "(1) [S]ecrecy[,] (2) generality of conveyance[,] (3) continuance in possession by debtor[, and] (4) some benefit retained under the settlement to the settlor." *Re Dougmor Realty Mg. Ltd.; Fisher v. Wilgorn Invt. Ltd.*, [1967] 1 O.R. 66 (Ont. H.C.). 2. These include: the precarious financial situation of the grantor; secrecy; showing the property after the transfer as an asset of the grantor; the preservation by the grantor of an interest in the property; substantially reducing the property of the grantor that would, but for the transfer, be available to his creditors; the effect of the transfer being to delay and defeat creditors; knowledge by the grantee that the asset is worth substantially more than what he is paying for it; inadequacy of the consideration; no immediate or early change of possession following the conveyance. *Phaneuf Fertilizer Sales Ltd. v. LeBlanc* [1999] 1 W.W.R. 659 (Sask. Q.B.).

BAD TITLE. 1. Unmarketable title. 2. One which conveys no or a very limited interest to the purchaser and a purchaser cannot be forced to accept.

BAFFLE. *n*. A non-liquid-tight transverse partition in a cargo tank.

BAG. *n*. 1. Something containing drugs. F.A. Jaffe, *A Guide to Pathological Evidence*, 3d ed. (Toronto: Carswell, 1991) at 213. 2. 50 pounds. *Crop Insurance Act (Ontario)*, R.R.O. 1980, Reg. 213, s. 3. See MAIL ~.

BAGGAGE. *n*. Such articles, effects and other personal property of a passenger as are necessary or appropriate for wear, use, comfort or convenience in connection with his trip.

BAG LIMIT. The total number of a species that may be taken by a hunter, trapper or fisherman per day per season or for any time period specified.

BAG NET. A net (a) that is attached to stakes, (b) the bag of which floats with the tide or current, and (c) that is capable of catching fish without enmeshing them. *Canada Regulations*.

BAIL. *v*. To free a person arrested or imprisoned after a particular day and place to appear are set and security is taken.

BAIL. *n*. 1. Security given by the persons into whose hands an accused is delivered. They bind themselves or become bail for the person's due appearance when required and, if they fear the person's escape, they have the legal power to deliver that person to prison. 2. In common parlance, "bail" sometimes refers to the money or other valuable security which the accused is required to deposit with the court as a condition of release. Restricting "bail" to this meaning would render s. 11(*e*) nugatory because most accused are released on less onerous terms. In order to be an effective guarantee, the meaning of "bail" in s. 11(*e*) must include all forms of judicial interim release. *R. v. Pearson* [1992] 3 S.C.R. 665, per Lamer, C.J.C. 3. "...[P]roperly the contract whereby the man is bailed (i.e. delivered) to his sureties but it is also applied to the sureties themselves ..." *R. v, Sandhu* (1984), 38 C.R. (3d) 56 at 63 (Qué. S.C.), Boilard J. 4. In an admiralty proceeding, security given in order to obtain release of property under arrest. See JUSTIFY ~.

BAILABLE. *adj*. Possible to give bail.

BAIL-BOND. *n*. An instrument executed by sureties.

BAILEE. *n*. 1. A person to whom goods are entrusted for a specific purpose with no intention of transferring the ownership. 2. A person who receives possession of a thing from another or consents to receive or hold possession of a thing for another under an agreement with the other person that she will keep and return the thing or that she will deliver the thing to him or that she will do what she is directed to do with the specific thing.

BAILER. *n*. A container that can be held in the hand and used for clearing a boat of water.

BAILIFF. *n*. 1. A sheriff's officer or person employed by a sheriff to make arrests, carry out executions, and serve writs. 2. A person who, for remuneration, acts or assists a person to act, or represents to a person that she or he is acting or is available to act, on behalf of another person in repossessing, seizing or distraining any chattel, or in evicting a person from property. 3 As used today, the word "bailiff" has two meanings. In the first meaning, it refers to a person employed in an official capacity to serve a Crown-appointed officer (such as a sheriff) or a court. In the second meaning, it refers to an agent of a private person who collects rents or manages real estate. *R. v. Burns* 2002 MBCA 161, [2003] 2 W.W.R. 638, 170 C.C.C. (3d) 288, 170 Man. R. (2d) 55, 285 W.A.C. 55.

BAILING. See PACKING AND ~.

BAILIWICK. *n*. Geographic jurisdiction of a sheriff or bailiff.

BAILMENT. *n*. "... [T]he delivery of personal chattels on trust, usually on a contract, express or implied, that the trust shall be executed and the chattels delivered in either their original or an altered form as soon as the time for which they were bailed has elapsed ... the legal relationship of bailor and bailee can exist independently of a contract. It is created by the voluntary taking into custody of good[s] which are the property of another ..." *Punch v. Savoy's Jewellers Ltd.* (1986), 33 B.L.R. 147 at 154, 54 O.R. (2d) 383, 35 C.C.L.T. 217, 14 O.A.C. 4, 26 D.L.R. (4th) 546 (C.A.), the court per Cory J.A. See GRATUITOUS ~.

BAILMENT BY ATTORNMENT. Occurs when, with the bailor's consent, a bailee delivers the goods to another person to hold, making that person bailee of the bailor. E.L.G. Tyler & N.E. Palmer eds. *Crossley Vaines' Personal Property*, 5th ed. (London: Butterworths, 1973) at 84.

BAILOR. *n*. A person who entrusts something to another person for a specific purpose.

BAIT. *v*. To set one animal against another which is tied or contained.

BAIT. *n*. Corn, wheat, oats or other grain, pulse or any other feed, and includes any imitation thereof that may attract migratory game birds; *Migratory Birds Regulations*, SOR/98-282, s. 2.

BAIT AND SWITCH. To advertise at a bargain price a product that the person does not supply in reasonable quantities having regard to the nature of the market in which the person carries on business, the nature and size of the person's business and the nature of the advertisement. A selling practice reviewable under the Competition Act. *Competition Act*, R.S.C. 1985, c. C-34, s. 74.04.

BAIT CROP AREA. An area of cropland, harvested or unharvested, that is intended to attract migratory birds and that is designated as such an area by poster, notice or sign. *Migratory Birds Regulations*, SOR/98-282, s. 2.

BAIT STATION AREA. An area established pursuant to an agreement between the Government of Canada and the government of a province where bait is deposited for the purpose of luring migratory birds from unharvested crops, and designated as such an area by poster, notice or sign. *Migratory Birds Regulations*, SOR/98-282, s. 2.

BAIT TRAP. A fishing device that (a) has no wings or leaders, (b) is made of netting or plastic or wire mesh, (c) is fastened to hoops or frames, (d) has a maximum length of 60 cm and a maximum width of 25 cm, and (e) is equipped with funnel-shaped openings, the smallest diameter of which does not exceed 2.5 cm. *Quebec Fishery Regulations, 1990* SOR/90-214, s. 2.

BAKESHOP. *n.* A building, premises, workshop, room or place in which bread and other food items are made for sale or sold.

BALANCE. *n.* The difference between the total debit entries and total credit entries in an account; the remainder. See OPERATING ~.

BALANCE OF CONVENIENCE. A determination of which of the two parties will suffer the greater harm from the granting or refusal of an interlocutory injunction, pending a decision on the merits. *Metropolitan Stores (MTS) Ltd. v. Manitoba Food & Commercial Workers, Local 832* [1987] 1 S.C.R. 110, Beetz, J. for the court.

BALANCE OF PROBABILITIES. Where one thing is more probable than another; greater likelihood of one thing than another.

BALANCE OF TRADE. The difference between the value of the imports into and exports from a country.

BALANCE-SHEET: *n.* A statement showing the assets and liabilities of a business.

BALE. *n.* Goods wrapped in cloth and bound with cord.

BALEEN WHALE. Any whale other than a toothed whale. *Whaling Convention Act*, R.S.C. 1970, c. W-8, Schedule, s. 18.

BALLAST. *n.* Anything within a vessel which keeps it in proper trim and prevents capsizing.

BALLASTAGE. *n.* A toll paid when ballast is taken from the bottom of a harbour or port.

BALLAST WATER. Water, carried in a vessel for stability and seaworthiness, that is discharged from the vessel to a refinery prior to loading the vessel and includes water used for cargo or ballast tank cleaning. *Petroleum Refinery Liquid Effluent Regulations*, C.R.C., c. 828, s. 2.

BALLISTICS. *n.* The study of the behaviour of projectiles, particularly in the firing of weapons. See EXTERNAL ~; INTERNAL ~; TERMINAL ~; WOUND ~.

BALLOON. *n.* A non-power-driven lighter-than-air aircraft. *Canadian Aviation Regulations* SOR 96-433, s. 101.01.

BALLOON PAYMENT. A large payment at the end of the term of a mortgage when the mortgage amount is not amortized over the term.

BALLOT. *n.* 1. The paper by which a voter casts his vote at an election. Contains the names of candidates in the election, arranged alphabetically, taken from their nomination papers. 2. The portion of a ballot paper which has been marked by an elector detached from the counterfoil, and deposited in the ballot box. See SPOILED ~.

BALLOT PAPER. As soon as possible after the issue of the writ, the Chief Electoral Officer shall provide the returning officer with the paper on which the ballots are to be printed. The weight and opacity of the paper shall be determined by the Chief Electoral Officer. *Canada Elections Act*, S.C. 2000, c. 9, s. 115. See REJECTED ~; SPOILED ~.

BAN. *v.* 1. To exclude. 2. To expel. 3. To prevent.

BAN. *n.* A proclamation or public notice which publicizes an intended marriage.

BANC. *n.* A bench or seat of justice.

BANCO. *n.* A bench or seat of justice.

BAND. *n.* 1. A body of Indians (a) for whose use and benefit in common, lands, the legal title of which is vested in Her Majesty, have been set apart before, on or after September 4, 1951, (b) or whose use and benefit in common, moneys are held by Her Majesty, or (c) declared by the Governor in Council to be a band for the purposes of this Act. *Indian Act*, R.S.C. 1985, c. I-5, s. 2. 2. With reference to a reserve or surrendered lands, means the band for whose use and benefit the reserve or the surrendered lands were set apart. *Indian Act*, R.S.C. 1985, c. I-5, s. 2. 3. The definition of "band" does not constitute an Indian Band as a legal entity. Rather, I take it from the definition of "band", and other provisions of the *Indian Act*, that in relation to rights to an Indian reserve, a band is a distinct population of Indians for whose use and benefit, in common, a reserve has been set aside by the Crown. It does not follow that because an Indian band is not a legal entity, rights accruing to the band are the rights of its members or their descendants in their individual capacities. The definition of "band" uses the term "in common" in relation to the interest that the members of the band have in the reserve. The term "in common" connotes a communal, as opposed to a private, interest in the reserve, by the members of the band. In other words, an individual member of a band has an interest in association with, but not independent of, the interest of the other members of the band. *Blueberry River Indian Band v. Canada (Department of Indian Affairs & Northern Development)*, 2001 CarswellNat 963, 2001 FCA 67, 6 C.P.C. (5th) 1, 201 D.L.R. (4th) 35, 274 N.R. 304, Rothstein, J.A. for the court. See COUNCIL OF THE ~; CUSTOM ~; INDIAN ~; MEMBER OF A ~.

BAND COUNCIL. The council of the band as defined in the *Indian Act* (Canada). See INDIAN ~.

BAND COUNCILLOR. A councillor of a band within the meaning of the *Indian Act* (Canada).

BANDIT. *n.* An outlaw; a person who is put under the ban by law.

BAND LIST. A list of persons that is maintained under section 8 by a band or in the Department. *Indian Act*, R.S.C. 1985 (1st Supp.), c. 32, s. 1.

BAND'S CUSTOM. Include practices for the choice of a council which are generally acceptable to members of the band, upon which there is a broad consensus. *Bigstone v. Big Eagle*, (1992), 52 F.T.R. 109 (F.C.T.D.), Strayer, J.

BANG'S DISEASE. Brucellosis in cattle. *Animal Husbandry Act*, R.S.M. 1970, c. A90, s. 109.

BANISHMENT. *n.* 1. Expulsion from a nation; loss of nationality. 2. One of the possible outcomes of a sentencing circle.

BANK. *n.* 1. A bank listed in Schedule I or II to the *Bank Act, Interpretation Act*, R.S.C. 1985, c. I-21, s. 35. 2. An incorporated bank or savings bank carrying on business in Canada. 3. A bank to which the Bank Act or the Quebec Savings Banks Act applies. 4. Includes every member of the Canadian Payments Association established under the Canadian Payments Association Act and every local cooperative credit society, as defined in that Act, that is a member of a central,

as defined in that Act, that is a member of the Canadian Payments Association. *Bills of Exchange Act*, R.S.C. 1985, c. B-4, s. 164. 5. The Bank of Canada. *Bank of Canada Act*, R.S.C. 1985, c. B-2, s. 2. 6. An organization or corporation that is set up to accept deposits of money from persons and to pay out the money according to their instructions on demand. 7. "... [E]dge' ... the margin of the lake; ..." *Burke v. Niles* (1870) 13 N.B.R. 166 at 170 (C.A.), the court per Ritchie C.J. 8. ... Banks are fast land on which vegetation appropriate to such land in the particular locality grows wherever the bank is not too steep to permit such growth,. . ." *Robo Management Co. v Byrne* (1989), 8 R.P.R. (2d) 245 at 25 3, 76 Sask. R. 40 (Q.B.), Walker . J. See BED; CHARTERED ~; CONFIRMING ~; DATA ~; DISTRIBUTING ~; FEDERAL BUSINESS DEVELOPMENT ~; FOREIGN; OFFICER OF A ~; ORGAN AND TISSUE ~; PERSONAL INFORMATION ~; RESPONSIBLE OFFICER OF THE ~; SAVINGS ~; SEMEN ~.

BANK ACCOUNT. 1. "[Both a] ... debt, ... [and] property , . . ." *Ontario (Securities Commission) v. Greymac Credit Corp.* (1986) 34 B.L.R. 29 at 45, 23 E.T.R. 81, 30 D.L.R. (4th) 1, 55 O.R. (2d) 673, 17 O.A.C. 88 (C.A.), the court per Morden J.A. 2. A chequing account, savings accounts, certificate of deposit or transfer account and includes any other type of account authorized to be established by bank. *Financial Administration Act*, R.S.N.W. 1974, c. F-4, s. 2. See DEPARTMENTAL ~; JOINT ~.

BANK-BOOK. *n.* 1. A record of deposits and withdrawals from a bank account. 2. " ... [E]vidence of a debt . . ." *Cusack v Day*, [1925] 2 W.W.R. 715 at 722, 3 D.L.R. 1028, 36 B.C.R. 106 (C.A.), MacDonald J.A. See BANK PASS BOOK.

BANK DEBENTURES. Instruments evidencing unsecured indebtedness of a bank.

BANK DEPOSIT. The money left with a bank by a customer. It is loaned to the bank and is to be repaid on demand by the customer. The bank pays interest while the money remains on deposit with it.

BANKER. *n.* 1. " ... [A] person or corporation who carries on the business of banking, and to whom members of the public have access for the purpose of depositing money, opening accounts, drawing cheques borrowing money, and a variety of other services such as are offered by banks." *655 Developments Ltd. v. Chester Dawe Ltd.* (1992) 42 C.P.R. 3d 500 at 515 97 Nfld. & P.E.I.R. 247, 308 A.P.R. 246 (Nfld. T.D.), Wells J. 2. " . . . '[A] dealer in credit.'" *Reference re Alberta Legislation*, [1938] S.C.R. 100 at 116, [1938] 2 D.L.R. 81, Duff C.J. (Davis J. concurring).

BANKER'S ACCEPTANCE. A draft drawn on and accepted by a bank used to pay for goods sold in import-export transactions and as a source of financing in trade.

BANKING. *n.* 1. From an institutional point of view, the point of view adopted by the court, involves a set of interrelated financial activities carried out by an institution that operates under the nomenclature and terms of incorporation which clearly identify it as having the distinctive institutional character of a bank. Other approaches were considered. According to the functional approach, the relation between a banker and a customer who pays money into the bank is not a fiduciary one. It is the ordinary relation of debtor and creditor, with a superadded obligation arising out of the custom of bankers to honour the customer's cheques. Possession of or property in the deposit remains with the bank, the obligation of which is a debt under a contract of mutuum, not commodatum. From the economic point of view, a view widely held in the nineteenth century, banks were considered as the main channel for the transfer of savings; the function of banking was one of financial intermediation in which the public had an interest with respect to solvency and allocation of financial resources. But under this particular economic view the list of financial intermediaries would include, as well as chartered banks, some other very different types of institutions such as life insurance companies, finance companies, mortgage companies, trust companies, etc. From a legal point of view, includes the following: (1) Receiving money on deposit from its customers, (2) Paying a customer's cheques or drafts on it to the amount on deposit by such customers, and holding Dominion Government and bank notes and coin for such purpose; (3) Paying interest by agreement on deposits; (4) Discounting commercial paper for its customers; (5) Dealing in exchange and in gold and silver coin and bullion; (6) Collecting notes and drafts deposited; (7) Arranging credits for itself with banks in other towns, cities and countries; (8) Selling its drafts or cheques on other banks and banking correspondents; (9) Issuing letters of credit; (10) Lending money to its customers (*a*) on the customers' notes; (*b*) by way of overdraft; (*c*) on bonds, shares and other securities. The business of a Canadian chartered bank is wider still because of the statutory rights and powers given to a bank under the provisions of *The Bank Act*. The business carried on by most banks includes the totality of these functions enumerated, but, of course, a banking business can be carried on without performing all of them and most corporations and individuals engaged in a financial business of any kind are required to carry on or perform some of them and it does not follow from the fact that banks perform them that every exercise of one or more of the functions is a form of banking. *Canadian Pioneer Management Ltd. v. Saskatchewan (Labour Relations Board)* [1980] 1 S.C.R. 433, per Beetz, J. for the majority. 2. "The legislative authority conferred by these words [s. 91.15 of the Constitution Act, 1867 (30 & 31 Vict.), s. 3] is not confined to the mere constitution of corporate bodies with the privilege of carrying on the business of bankers. It extends to the issue of paper currency . . ." *Tennant v. Union Bank of Canada*, [1894] A.C. 31 at 46 (P.C.), Lord Watson.

BANKING BUSINESS. " . . . [I]ssuing letters of credit . . . lending money; and . . . accepting term deposits . . . are within what, in common knowledge, would be considered the hard core of banking." *R. v. Milelli* (1989), 45 B.L.R. 209 at 215, 51 C.C.C. (3d) 165, 35 O.A.C. 241 (C.A.), the court per Finlayson J.A.

BANKING INSTRUMENT. A cheque, draft, telegraphic or electronic transfer or other similar instrument.

BANKING PRACTICES. See GENERALLY ACCEPTED ~.

BANK MORTGAGE SUBSIDIARY. A wholly-owned subsidiary of a bank that receives deposits that are guaranteed by the bank and whose investments in mortgages equal at least 85 per cent of its deposits. *Loan and Trust Corporations acts.*

BANK-NOTE. *n.* 1. Includes any negotiable instrument (a) issued by or on behalf of a person carrying on the business of banking in or out of Canada and (b) issued under the authority of Parliament or under the lawful authority of the government of a state other than Canada, intended to be used as money or as the equivalent of money, immediately on issue or at some time subsequent thereto, and includes bank bills and bank post bills. *Criminal Code*, R.S.C. 1985, c. C-46, s. 2. 2. " . . . [A]n instrument which is a promissory note payable to bearer on demand." *R. v. Brown* (1854), 8 N.B.R. 13 at 15 (C.A.), the court per Carter C.J.

BANK OF CANADA. The federal body which devises and carries out monetary policy and is the fiscal agent of the government of Canada. By the Bank of Canada Act, this is the only body authorized to issue notes for circulation in Canada.

BANK OF CANADA RATE. The rate of interest set by the Bank of Canada for loans by the Bank of Canada to the chartered banks, as published by the Bank of Canada.

BANK PASS BOOK. A record of the credits and debits in a customer's account.

BANK RATE. The bank rate established by the Bank of Canada as the minimum rate at which the Bank of Canada makes short-term advances to banks listed in Schedule I to the Bank Act. *Courts of Justice Act*, R.S.O. 1990, c. C.43, s. 127(1).

BANKRUPT. *n*. A person who has made an assignment or against whom a receiving order has been made. *Bankruptcy and Insolvency Act*, R.S.C. 1985, c. B-3, s. 2.

BANKRUPT. *adj*. The legal status of a person who has made an assignment or against whom a receiving order has been made. *Bankruptcy and Insolvency Act*, R.S.C. 1985, c. B-3, s. 2.

BANKRUPTCY. *n*. 1. The state of being bankrupt or the fact of becoming bankrupt. *Bankruptcy and Insolvency Act*, R.S.C. 1985, c. B-3, s. 2. 2. The debtor's property is vested in a trustee who is required to realize on the debtor's property and distribute the receipts to the debtor's creditors according to the scheme set out in the Bankruptcy and Insolvency Act. When the bankruptcy is ended, the debtor is free of his debts except for certain debts for which he remains liable. See ACT OF ~; CLAIM PROVABLE IN ~; TRUSTEE IN ~.

BANKRUPTCY AND INSOLVENCY. 1. A federal head of power. *Constitution Act, 1867* (U.K.), 30 & 31 Vict., c. 3, s. 91(21). 2. " . . . [I]t is a feature common to all the systems of bankruptcy and insolvency to which reference has been made, that the enactments are designed to secure that in the case of an insolvent person his assets shall be rateably distributed amongst his creditors whether he is willing that they shall be so distributed or not . . ." Reference *re Assignments & Preferences Act (Ont.)*, s. 9, [1894] A.C. 189 at 201, 70 L.T. 538, 63 L.J.P.C. 59 (Ont. P.C.), the board per Lord Chancellor.

BANNS. *n*. (pl.) A proclamation or public notice which publicizes an intended marriage.

BANNER. *v*. To carry picket signs on the picket line.

BANNS OF MARRIAGE. The proclamation of an intended marriage in a church.

BANQUIER. *n*. The periodical, Le Banquier.

BAR. *v*. To stop; to prohibit.

BAR. *n*. 1. A barrier which separates the judge's bench and the front row of counsel's seats from the rest of the court; Queen's counsel are the only counsel allowed within the bar. 2. Obstacle; barrier. 3. Used to refer to the legal profession as a whole, usually in a geographical area. See CALL TO THE ~; IRON ~; OUTER ROCK ~.

BAR ADMISSION EXAMINATION. An examination in general subjects related to the practice of law including practice and procedure, ethics and the general law of a province and of Canada. The examination or set of examinations a person must take to qualify as a lawyer in a province.

BAR AND BENCH. Refers to members of the legal profession and the judiciary.

BARBER. *n*. Any person who, for hire, gain, or hope of reward, performs any one, or any combination, of the following services for other persons: (a) cuts or trims hair, (b) tints, bleaches or dyes hair, (c) shampoos hair and scalp, (d) gives hair or scalp treatments or facial massages, (e) curls or waves hair by any means, (f) performs any other operation with respect to dressing hair to obtain an intended effect or according to a particular style. *Barbers Act*, R.S.M. 1487, c. B-10, s. 1.

BARBERING. *n*. Engaging in the shaving of the face or cutting or trimming or singeing of the hair or beard for hire, gain or hope of reward or in connection with any of the foregoing the shampooing or massaging or the treating of the head or face.

BARBER SHOP. *var*. **BARBERSHOP**. *n*. A place, room, premises, building or part of them where the occupation of barbering is carried on.

BARBITURATE. *n*. A general term for synthetic compound derivatives of barbituric acid which are hypnotics or sedatives. F.A. Jaffe, *A Guide to Pathological Evidence* 3d ed. (Toronto: Carswell, 1991) at 88.

BAR CODE. A unique bar code in the symbology of the Universal Product Code (UPC) or the European Article Number (EAN).

BARE-BOAT CHARTER. (*var.* **BARE-BOAT CHARTER**) 1. A vessel charter agreement under which the charterer has complete possession and control of the vessel, including the right to appoint its master and crew. *Canada Shipping Act, 2001*, S.C. 2001, c. 26, s. 2. 2. A charter of a ship without master or crew is commonly known as a "bareboat" charter. *North Ridge Fishing Ltd. v. "Prosperity" (The)* 2000 CarswellBC 982, 2000 BCCA 283, 74 B.C.L.R.(3d) 383, 186 D.L.R. (4th) 374 Per Cumming J.A. (Prowse and Saunders JJ.A. concurring).

BARE LAND STRATA PLAN. (a) A strata plan on which the boundaries of the strata lots are defined on a horizontal plane by reference to survey markers and not by reference to the floors, walls or ceilings of a building, or (b) any other strata plan defined by regulation to be a bare land strata plan. *Strata Property Act*, S.B.C. 1998, c. 43, s. 1.

BARE LAND UNIT. A unit defined by delineation of its horizontal boundaries without reference to any buildings on a plan referred to in subsection 6(5). *Condominium Act*, C.C.S.M., c. C-170, s. 1.

BARE LICENSEE. " . . . [A] person merely permitted by the owner to enter without there being any obligation so to permit and with the right in the owner to revoke the permission at any time." *Musselman v. Zimmerman*, [1922] 66 D.L.R. 350 at 351 1922 2 W.W.R. 640 18 Alta. L.R. 104 (C.A.), Stuart J.A. (Scott C.J., Beck and Clarke JJ.A. concurring).

BARE TRUST. "[A trust under the terms of which] . . . a trustee's only duty is to hold the legal estate until called upon by the beneficiary to convey . . ." *Creasor v. Wall* (1982), 25 R.P.R. 1 at 16, 38 O.R. (2d 35 (H.C.), White J.

BARGAIN. *v.* To contract; to enter into an agreement; to negotiate an agreement.

BARGAIN. *n.* Contract; agreement. See CATCHING ~; PLEA ~.

BARGAIN AND SALE. A contract for the sale of chattels, of an estate or of any interest in land followed by payment of the price agreed.

BARGAIN AND SELL. Convey for a consideration. *Conveyancing Act*, R.S.N.S. 1967, c. 56, s. 6.

BARGAIN COLLECTIVELY. To negotiate in good faith with a view to entering into, renewing or revising a collective agreement.

BARGAINEE. *n.* The person to whom the subject matter of a bargain and sale passes.

BARGAINER. *n.* The person who transfers the subject matter of a bargain and sale.

BARGAINING. *n.* " . . . '[N]egotiating.'" *Bloedel, Stewart & Welch Ltd v. Stuart* (1942), 58 B.C.R. 351 at 356, [1943] 1 W.W.R. 128, [1943] 1 D.L.R. 183 (C.A.), Sloan J.A. See AREA WIDE ~; BLUE-SKY ~; COLLECTIVE ~; COMPANY-WIDE ~; HARD ~; INDIVIDUAL ~; INDUSTRY WIDE ~; MULTI-EMPLOYER ~; MULTI-PLANT ~; MULTI-UNION ~; PACKAGE ~; PATTERN ~; SINGLE-PLANT ~; SURFACE ~.

BARGAINING AGENCY. See EMPLOYEE ~; EMPLOYER ~.

BARGAINING AGENT. 1. A trade union employee organization or other organization that acts on behalf of employees or other groups of workers or has exclusive bargaining rights in collective bargaining or acts as party to a collective agreement or to a recognition agreement with their employer or an employers' organization. 2. An employee organization. See AFFILIATED ~; APPROPRIATE ~; CERTIFIED ~.

BARGAINING COLLECTIVELY. Negotiating in good faith with a view to the conclusion of a collective bargaining agreement or a renewal or revision or a collective bargaining agreement and the embodiment in writing of the terms of agreement arrived at in negotiations or required to be inserted in a collective bargaining agreement by statute.

BARGAINING COUNCIL. A council of trade unions.

BARGAINING HISTORY. The relationships which have existed between the parties.

BARGAINING RIGHT. " . . . [O]nly entitle[s] a union to be recognized as the exclusive bargaining agent for a particular group of employees . . ." " *Metropolitan Toronto Apartment Builders Association* [1978] O.L.R.B. Rep. Nov. 1022 at 1034. See EXCLUSIVE ~.

BARGAINING UNIT. 1. A unit of employees appropriate for collective bargaining. 2. A group of employees usually designated by class of employee, geographical location, work performed, or by a combination of these concepts. D.J.M. Brown and D.M. Beatty, *Canadian Labour Arbitration*, 3d ed. (Aurora: Canada Law Book, 1988-) at 5-4. 3. " . . . [F]or the purpose of s. 57 [Labour Relations Act, R.S.O. 1980, c. 228], is a unit consisting only of those of the employer's employees whom the trade union is entitled to represent." *Snow v. S.M.W., Loc. 285*, [1984] O.L.R.B. Rep. 1004 at 1010, Gray (ViceChair), Bell and Kobryn (Members).

BARGAINING UNIT WORK. Tasks which form part of the job description of a bargaining unit member.

BARGAINOR. *n*. The person who transfers the subject matter of a bargain and sale.

BARGAIN PRICE. (a) A price that is represented in an advertisement to be a bargain price by reference to an ordinary price or otherwise; or (b) a price that a person who reads, hears or sees the advertisement would reasonably understand to be a bargain price by reason of the prices at which the product advertised or like products are ordinarily supplied. *Competition Act*, R.S.C. 1985, c. C-34, s. 74.04(1).

BARGE. *n*. A non-self-propelled barge, scow, dredge, pile-driver, hopper, pontoon or houseboat. *Collision Regulations*, C.R.C., c. 1416, s. 2.

BARKING. *n*. The process of removing bark from the trunk of a tree prior to processing it.

BARLEYCORN. *n*. A nominal rent.

BAR OF DOWER. Giving up of dower.

BARON. *n*. The former title of judges of certain courts. See COVERT ~.

BARR. *abbr*. The Barrister (Can.).

BARRATOR. *n*. A person who routinely brings, stirs up or maintains quarrels or suits.

BARRATRY. *n*. 1. Includes every wrongful act wilfully committed by the master or crew to the prejudice of the owner, or, as the case may be, the charterer. *Insurance acts*. 2. The difference between champerty and barratry appears to be that while champerty is purely self-interested, barratry requires the additional intent to harm the third person: " . . . if the design was not to recover his own right, but only to ruin and op-

press his neighbour, that is barratry." Maintenance is further distinguished from barratry and champerty on the basis that it appears to be motivated by altruism. That is, it requires a person to "lay out money on behalf of another in suits at law to recover a just right, and this may be done in respect of the poverty of the party; but if he lends money to promote and stir up suits, then he is a barrator". In Canada, the common law criminal offences of champerty, maintenance and barratry (as well as refusing to serve in office and being a "common scold") were abolished after the 1950 *Report of the Royal Commission on the Revision of the Criminal Code*. There is no reference to a tort of barratry in torts texts. Nonetheless, for the purpose of this motion I will assume, but not decide, that there is such a thing as the tort of barratry. *McIntyre Estate v. Ontario (Attorney General)* 26 C.P.C. (5th) 312, (Ont. C.A.)

BARRED. Not permitted. Ended. See STATUTE ~.

BARREL. *n*. 1. 34.9722 standard gallons within the meaning of subsection 13(1) of the Weights and Measures Act, being chapter W-7 of the Revised Statutes of Canada, 1970. *Petroleum Administration Act*, S.C. 1974-75-76, c. 47, s. 4. 2. 35 standard Canadian gallons as defined by the Weights and Measures Act (Canada). *Environmental Protection Act*, R.R.O. 1980, Reg. 303, s.1. 3. The portion of a firearm in the shape of a tube through which a projectile passes. F.A. Jaffe *A Guide to Pathological Evidence* 3d ed. (Toronto: Carswell, 1991) at 213.

BARREN BOTTOM. Includes those parts of the beds and bottoms of any bays, rivers, harbors or creeks where no natural or live oyster beds are found to exist.

BARRETOR. *n*. A person who routinely brings, stirs up or maintains quarrels or suits.

BARRIER. See FIXED COLLISION

BARRIER-FREE. That a building and its facilities can be approached, entered, and used by persons with physical or sensory disabilities.

BARRING. *conj*. or *prep*. " . . . '[I]n the absence of'." *Price v. Williams* (1990) 46 C.C.L.I. 161 at 164, [1990] I.L.R. 1-2681 (B.C. C.A.), the court per Hinds J.A.

BARRISTER. *n*. When used alone, usually refers to a lawyer who appears as an advocate in court.

BARRISTER. *abbr*. Barrister (1894-1897).

BARRISTER AND SOLICITOR. 1. The title given to a lawyer who is a member of a provincial law society in the common law provinces and territories of Canada. The legal profession is not divided into barristers and solicitors but the two words are still used, usually together to describe lawyers. When the words are used alone they tend to be used according to their original meanings. 2. He is entitled to vote at an election of benchers . . . 3. He is eligible to become a bencher . . . 4. He is eligible to become an officer of the society . . ." *Maurice v. Priel* (1987), 60 Sask. R. 241 at 245-6, [1988] 1 W.W.R. 491, 46 D.L.R. (4th) 416 (C.A.), Bayda C.J.S. (Brownridge J.A. concurring).

BAR SEINE. Netting that is floated at the top, weighted at the bottom and used to impound fish along the shore.

BAR SINK. A receptacle for the disposal of liquid wastes only.

BARTER. *v*. To exchange goods for goods.

BASE. *n*. Bottom; foundation. See CAPITAL ~; OPERATING ~; RATE ~; REVENUE ~.

BASE. *adj*. Inferior; impure.

BASE ALLOWABLE. The amount of production that according to a Board order could be taken if no penalty factor, whether its purpose be for proration, for avoidance of waste or for protection of the rights of others, were to be applied. *Oil and Gas Conservation Act* R.S.A. 2000, c. O-6, s. 1.

BASE BID. A bid in which an amount of money is stated as the sum for which the bidder offers to perform the work described in the bidding document, exclusive of adjustments.

BASE CALENDAR YEAR. The calendar year ending immediately before the current fiscal year.

BASE LENGTH. The distance measured between the centres of the first axle of the front axle of a vehicle or combination of vehicles and the last axle of a vehicle or combination of vehicles.

BASEMENT. *n*. A storey or storeys of a building located below the first storey.

BASE PURPOSE. " . . . [D]efined as meaning to vilify sex and to treat it as something 'less than beautiful' or to write in a manner calculated to serve aphrodisiac purposes:. . ." *R. v. Ariadne Developments Ltd*. (1974), 19 C.C.C. (2d) 49 at 54 (N.S. C.A.), the court per MacDonald J.A.

BASE RATE. The rate of pay for work excluding bonuses and overtime.

BASIC BAND. The 12 analog cable channels that are commonly identified by the numbers 2 to 13 and that are used in the frequency bands 54 to 72 MHz, 76 to 88 MHz and 174 to 216 MHz. *Broadcasting Distribution Regulations*, SOR/97-555, s. 1.

BASIC EARNINGS PER SHARE. The amount of income attributable to each outstanding share that carries as an incident of ownership the right to participate in earnings to an unlimited degree.

BASIC EDUCATION. See ADULT ~.

BASIC EQUIPMENT. All equipment approved by the Minister as necessary and reasonable to enable a facility to commence its function as determined at the time of its completion or renovation, provided that such equipment is installed and ready for use not later than twelve months after the date of completion of the construction project or renovation program. Ontario regulations.

BASIC FACT. See PRESUMPTION WITH A ~; PRESUMPTION WITHOUT A ~.

BASIC MONTHLY FEE. The total amount that a licensee is authorized to charge to a subscriber on a monthly basis for provision of the basic service to an outlet to which a television receiver, FM receiver, channel converter or other terminal device may be connected in the subscriber's residence or premises. It does not include federal or provincial taxes. *Broadcasting Distribution Regulations*, SOR/97-555, s. 1.

BASIC NECESSITIES. Things, goods and services essential to a person's health and well-being, including food, clothing, shelter, household and personal requirements, medical, hospital, optical, dental and other remedial treatment, care and attention, and an adequate funeral on death.

BASIC PREMIUM. That portion of the premium that is based upon criteria established but does not include any additional premium or any surcharge.

BASIC RATE OF WAGES. The basic hourly wage rate of an employee excluding any premium or bonus rates paid under any specific conditions of his employment.

BASIC SERVICE. The services distributed in a licensed area by a licensee as a package consisting of the programming services the distribution of which is required under sections 17, 22, 32 or 37, or a condition of its licence, and any other services that are included in the package for a single fee. *Broadcasting Distribution Regulations*, SOR/97-555, s. 1.

BASIC UNIT RENT. The amount of rent charged for a rental unit exclusive of any separate charges.

BASIC VEHICLE FRONTAL AREA. The area enclosed by the geometric projection of the basic vehicle, which includes tires but does not include mirrors or air deflectors, along the longitudinal axis of the vehicle onto a plane perpendicular to that axis. *On-Road Vehicle and Engine Emission Regulations*, SOR/2003-2, s. 1.

BASIC WAGE. Minimum wage.

BASIC WELL-HEAD PRICE. The price at the well-head of a barrel of oil.

BASIN. *n.* Any navigable area, whether or not it includes a part of the normal canal prism provided for the loading, unloading, turning or passing of vessels. *Canal Regulations*, C.R.C. c. 1564, s. 2. See LOWER CHURCHILL ~.

BASIS. *n.* Foundation, main principle, starting point. See ACTUARIAL ~; CASH ~; COOPERATIVE ~; FULL-TIME ~; PART-TIME ~.

BASIS POINT. One one-hundredth of a cent or of a percentage point.

BASKET CLAUSE. 1. Clause intended to ensure that the document covers a larger number of persons or instances than are actually specified in the document. 2. In pleadings, a request for such other relief as to this court may seem just. 3. In a wiretap authorization, a clause which would permit interception of any persons unknown to the police at the time of the application for the authorization and which would permit the police to intercept such communications at any place provided that there are reasonable and probable grounds to believe that the interception may assist. *R. v. Thompson* [1990] 2 S.C.R. 1111.

BASKET DRAG RAKE. A drag rake with a device attached to the rear and forward portions so as to form an enclosure.

BASTARD. *n.* A person born to unmarried parents.

BASTARDIZE. *v.* To declare someone a bastard; to give evidence to prove that someone is a bastard.

BASTARDY ORDER. Affiliation order.

BASTARDY PROCEEDING. Affiliation proceeding.

BASTART. *n.* Bastard.

BATHROOM. A room containing a bathtub or a shower.

BATTERED WOMAN. A woman who has experienced a cycle of tension-building, acute battering and loving contrition more than once. A feature of the cyclical nature of the abuse is that it begets a degree of predictability to the violence that is absent in an isolated violent encounter between two strangers. *R. v. Lavallee* [1990] 1 S.C.R. 852, per Wilson, J.

BATTERED WOMAN SYNDROME. Not a legal defence in itself such that an accused woman need only establish that she is suffering from the syndrome in order to gain an acquittal. It is a psychiatric explanation of the mental state of women who have been subjected to continuous battering by their male intimate partners, which can be relevant to the legal inquiry into a battered woman's state of mind. *R. v. M. (M.A.)* [1998] 1 S.C.R. 123. L'Heureux-Dubé J. (McLachlin J. concurring).

BATTERY. *n.* 1. " . . . [T]he intentional infliction of unlawful force on another person." *Norberg v. Wynrib* (1992), 12 C.C.L.T. (2d) 1 at 16, [1992] 4 W.W.R. 577, 68 B.C.L.R. (2d) 29, 138 N.R. 81, 9 B.C.A.C. 1, 19 W.A.C. 1, 92 D.L.R. (4th) 449, [1992] 2 S.C.R. 226, La Forest J. (Gonthier and Cory JJ. concurring). 2. A system or arrangement of tanks or other surface equipment receiving the effluents of one or more wells prior to delivery to market or other disposition, and may include equipment or devices for separating the effluents into oil, gas, crude bitumen or water and for measurement. *Oil and Gas acts*. See ASSAULT AND ~; STORAGE ~.

BATTERY SITE. That portion of the surface of land, other than a well site or roadway, required for access to and to accommodate separators, treaters, dehydrators, storage tanks, surface reservoirs, pumps and other equipment, including above ground pressure maintenance facilities, that are necessary to measure, separate or store prior to shipping to market or disposal, or necessary to produce the fluids minerals, and water, or any of them from wells. *Surface Rights acts.*

BAWDY HOUSE. *var.* **BAWDY-HOUSE.** *n.* A brothel. *Singleton v. Ellison* [1895] 1 Q.B. 607, Wills J. See COMMON ~.

B.C. *abbr.* British Columbia.

B.C.A.A. *abbr.* B.C. Assessment Authority.

B.C.B.C. *abbr.* B.C. Buildings Corporation.

B.C. BR. LECT. *abbr.* Canadian Bar Association, British Columbia Branch Lectures.

BCCA. *abbr.* The neutral citation for the British Columbia Court of Appeal.

BCCAT. *abbr.* British Columbia Council of Administrative Tribunals.

BCCLS. *abbr.* B.C. Courthouse Library Society.

B.C. CORPS. L.G. *abbr.* British Columbia Corporations Law Guide.

B.C.E.C. *abbr.* B.C. Enterprise Corporation.

B.C.F.C. *abbr.* B.C. Ferry Corporation.

B.C.F.R. *abbr.* B.C. Forest Resources Commission.

B.C.H.P. *abbr.* B.C. Hydro and Power Authority.

BCHRT. *abbr.* The neutral citation for the British Columbia Human Rights Tribunal.

B.C.L.C. *abbr.* B.C. Lottery Corporation.

B.C.L.N. *abbr.* British Columbia Law Notes.

B.C.L.R. *abbr.* British Columbia Law Reports, 1977-1988.

B.C.L.R.B. DEC. *abbr.* British Columbia Labour Relations Board Decisions.

B.C.L.R. (2D). *abbr.* British Columbia Law Reports (Second Series) 1988-.

BCPC. *abbr.* The neutral citation for the British Columbia Provincial Court.

B.C.P.C. *abbr.* B.C. Pavilion Corporation.

B.C.P.E. *abbr.* B.C. Petroleum Corporation.

B.C.R. *abbr.* 1. British Columbia Reports, 18671947. 2. B.C. Rail Ltd.

BCSC. *abbr.* The neutral citation for the British Columbia Supreme Court.

B.C.S.C. *abbr.* B.C. Systems Corporation.

BCSECCOM. *abbr.* The neutral citation for the British Columbia Securities Commission.

B.C.S.T. *abbr.* B.C. Stena Lines Ltd.

B.C.T. *abbr.* B.C. Transit.

B.C.T.C. *abbr.* B.C. Trade Development Corporation.

B.C.T.R. *abbr.* British Columbia Tax Reports.

B.C.U.C. *abbr.* B.C. Utilities Commission.

B.C.W.L.D. *abbr.* British Columbia Weekly Law Digest.

BD. *abbr.* Board.

BEACH. *n.* " . . . [S]hore . . . the land lying between high water and low water over which the tide ebbs and flows . . ." *Lee v. Arthurs* (1918), 46 N.B.R. 185 at 194 (S.C.), Grimmer J.

BEACH SEINE. Netting that is floated at the top, weighted at the bottom and used to impound fish along the shore.

BEACON. *n.* Lighthouse.

BEAD. *n.* That part of the tire made of steel wires wrapped or reinforced by ply cords, that is shaped to fit the rim.

BEAD SEPARATION. A breakdown of bond between components in the bead area of a tire.

BEAM. *n.* 1. The light projected from a pair of lighted headlamps. 2. A collection of rays that may be parallel, convergent or divergent. See USEFUL ~.

BEAR. *n.* One who expects a fall in the price of shares.

BEARER. *n.* 1. The person in possession of a bill or note that is payable to bearer. *Bills of Exchange Act*, R.S.C. 1985, c. B-4, s. 2. 2. The person in possession of a security payable to bearer or endorsed in blank. See FUR-~.

BEARER FORM. A security is in bearer form if it is payable to bearer according to its terms and not by reason of any endorsement.

BEARING SUPPORT. A structural member or system of structural members supporting masonry and resisting all applied loads.

BEARING SURFACE. The contact surface between a foundation unit and the soil or rock upon which it bears. *Building Code Act*, 1992, O.Reg 403/97, s.1.1.3.

BEAR MARKET. Name for a market when it is going down in value.

BECOME. *v.* " . . . [T]o come into being, . . ." *R. v. Guaranty Properties Ltd* (1990), 48 B.L.R. 197 at 209, 109 N.R. 284, 90 D.T.C. 6363, [1990] 2 C.T.C. 94, [1990] 3 F.C. 337, 37 F.T.R. 239n (C.A.), the court per MacGuigan J.A.

BED. *n.* 1. " . . . [S]oil of a different character [than that of the bank], and having no vegetation, or only such as exists, when commonly submerged in water." *Robo Management Co. v. Byrne* (1989) 8 R.P.R. (2d) 245 at 253 76 Sask. R. 40 (Q.B.), Walker J. 2. " . . . [T]he whole bed of the river and all the river occupies, even if high water up to the high water mark; without overflowing or flooding the surrounding country. All that it covers up, to high water mark, without speaking of floods . . ." *Chauret v. Pilon* (1908), 17 Que. K.B. 283 at 285, 5 E.L.R. 234, the court per Trenholme J.A. See BANK; RIVER ~.

BEDDING. *n.* Any mattress, mattress type pad, boxspring, quilt, comforter, sleeping bag, mattress protector pad, pillow or quilted bedspread that contains stuffing concealed by fabric or other flexible material or any such article that can be used for sleeping or reclining purposes.

BEDROCK. *n.* The solid rock underlying unconsolidated material such as sand, gravel and clay. *Ontario Water Resources Act* R.R.O. 1980 Reg. 739 s. 1.

BEE. *n.* The insect (i) Apis mellifera, or (ii) Megachile rotundata. See PACKAGE ~S.

BEEF. *n.* Live cattle for slaughter or the whole or any part of a cattle carcass of any variety, grade or class.

BEEHIVE EQUIPMENT. Hives, supers, hive covers, hive floors, queen excluders, frames, comb, and includes the honey, brood and pollen in the combs.

BEEKEEPER. *var.* **BEE-KEEPER**. *n.* 1. A person who owns, or partnership that owns or possesses any bees or any honeycombs or brood combs suited to the maintenance and keeping of bees. 2. A person who owns or controls bees or beehives or beekeeping equipment.

BEEKEEPING EQUIPMENT. Hives, parts of hives, and utensils used in the maintenance and keeping of bees and includes, when kept in conjunction with hives, parts of hives and utensils used in the maintenance and keeping of bees, honey, wax, pollen and royal jelly.

BEER. *n.* 1. Liquor made in whole or in part from grain, malt or other saccharine matter, whether or not the liquor is fermented or unfermented. *Excise Act*, R.S.C. 1985, c. E-14, s. 33. Any beverage containing alcohol in excess of the prescribed amount obtained by the fermentation of an infusion or decoction of barley, malt and hops or of any similar products in drinkable water. *Liquor Licence Act*, R.S.O. 1990, c. L-19, s. 1. See LIGHT ~.

BEER LICENCE. A beer parlour licence, a beer vendor's licence, a brewer's retail licence, or a club beer licence. *Liquor Control Act*, R.S.M. 1970, c. L 160, s. 2.

BEES-WAX REFUSE. Damaged honeycombs, honeycomb cappings or the material remaining after the first rendering of used honeycombs or honeycomb cappings.

BEGGAR. *n.* A person who begs or gathers alms.

BEGIN. *v.* To start, to commence. See RIGHT TO ~.

BEHAVIOUR. *n.* Conduct; comportment. See MIS ~.

BEING. *adj.* Living; existing. See IN ~.

BELGIUM. *n.* Used in a geographical sense means the territory of the Kingdom of Belgium, including any area beyond the territorial waters of Belgium which is an area within which Belgium may exercise rights with respect to the seabed and sub-soil and their natural resources. *Canada-Belgium Income Tax Convention Act*, S.C. 1974-75-76, c. 104, Schedule II, Article III, s. 1.

BELIEF. *n.* " . . . [M]ore than acceptance, and involves knowledge, probably knowledge of consequences . . . *R. v. Budin* (1981), 20 C.R. (3d) 86 at 96, 32 O.R. (2d) 1, 58 C.C.C. (2d) 352, 120 D.L.R. (3d) 536 (C.A.), Brooke J.A. (concurring).

BELLIGERENT. *n.* A country or group of people waging war as determined by the law of nations.

BELITTLE. *v.* To make one appear inferior to another.

BELLO PARTA CEDUNT RESPUBLICAE. [L.] The spoils of war belong to the Crown.

BELL TRAP. A trap where the pipe conveying water from the trap is covered by a bell so that the water flowing through the trap passes under the rim of the bell and over the end of the pipe. *Ontario Water Resources Act* R.R.O. 1980 Reg. 736, s. 85.

BELLUM JUSTUM. [L.] Just war.

BELONG. *v.* 1. To be the property of, to be owned. 2. ". . . [B]roader than legal ownership." *Agnew v. Ontario Regional Assessment Commissioner, Region No. 7* (1990), 1 M.P.L.R. (2d) 13 8 at 140, 74 D.L.R. (4th) 154 (Ont. Gen. Div.), Philp J.

BELOW PAR. At a price lower than face or nominal value; at a discount.

BELT. See SAFETY ~; SEAT ~.

BELT ASSEMBLY. See SEAT ~.

BELT INJURY. See SEAT ~.

BELUGA. *n.* A cetacean (Delphinapterus leucas) of the dolphin family, also known as the white whale.

BELUGA CALF. A beluga that is dark in colour and less than 2 m in length, measured from the point of the upper jaw to the notch between the tail flukes. *Marine Mammals Regulation*, SOR/93-56, s. 2.

BENCH. *n.* 1. The judge's seat in a court. 2. A single judge. 3. Judges collectively. See QUEEN'S ~.

BENCHER. *n.* A member of the governing body of a provincial law society. May be elected by lawyers in a region of the province, in the province as a whole or may be appointed by the government to be a member of the governing body.

BENCH WARRANT. 1. A court-issued warrant to arrest a person. 2. Where an indictment has been preferred against a person who is at large, and that person does not appear or remain in attendance for his trial, the court before which the accused should have appeared or remained in attendance may issue a warrant for his arrest. *Criminal Code*, R.S.C. 1985, c. C-46, c. 597.

BENDS. See DECOMPRESSION SICKNESS.

BENEDICTA EST EXPOSITIO QUANDO RES REDIMITUR A DESTRUCTIONE. [L.] Well-spoken is the statement which saves anything from destruction.

BENEFICIAL INTEREST. 1. " . . . [E]quitable and not a legal interest . . ." *Vancouver A & W Drive-Ins Ltd v. United Food Services Ltd*. (1980), 13 B.L.R. 89 at 102, 10 E.T.R. 34, 38 B.C.L.R. 30 (S.C.), Fulton J. 2. The interest of a beneficiary or beneficial owner. 3. An interest arising out of the beneficial ownership of securities. 4. Includes ownership through a trustee, legal representative, agent or other intermediary.

BENEFICIAL OWNER. " . . . [T]he real owner of property even though it is in someone else's name. *Csak v Aumon* (1990), 69 D.L.R. (4th) 567 at 570 (Ont. H.C.), Lane J.

BENEFICIAL OWNERSHIP. Includes ownership through a trustee, legal representative, agent or other intermediary.

BENEFICIAL USE. A use of water, including the method of diversion, storage, transportation, and application, that is reasonable and consistent with the public interest in the proper utilization of water resources, including but not being limited to domestic, agricultural, industrial, power, municipal, navigational, fish and wildlife and recreational uses.

BENEFICIARY. *n.* 1. A person designated or appointed as one to whom or for whose benefit insurance money is to be payable. 2. A person entitled to benefit from a trust or will. 3. A person entitled to receive benefits under a statutory scheme. See CONTRACT ~; IRREVOCABLE ~; PREFERRED ~.

BENEFICIARY COUNTRY. A country that is a beneficiary of the General Preferential Tariff. *General Preferential Tariff and Least Developed Country Tariff Rules of Origin Regulations*, SOR/98-34, s. 1.

BENEFIT. *n.* 1. A pension; a monetary amount paid under a pension or other plan. 2. A drug or other good or service that is supplied to an eligible person. 3. Compensation or an indemnity paid in money, financial assistance or services. 4. A material acquisition which confers an economic benefit on the taxpayer and does not constitute an exemption, e.g. loan or gift. (adopted by Dickson, J. in *R. v. Savage* [1983] 2 S.C.R. 428nb). 5. The positive effect of one thing on another, the advantage one thing confers on another. 6. Must mean that the individual receiving it ultimately receives a net transfer of resources without expectation for repayment. *Maynard v. Maynard* 1999 CarswellBC 333, 45 R.F.L. (4th) 395 S.C. See BRIDGING ~; COLLAT-

ERAL ~; CONDITIONAL ~; CONTRIBU-TORY ~; DEATH ~; DEFINED ~; DE-FINED ~ PENSION PLAN; DEFINED CONTRIBUTION ~; FEDERAL ~S; FRINGE ~; LABOUR ADJUSTMENT ~S; MUTUAL ~S; PENSION ~; SICK AND FU-NERAL ~S; STRIKE ~; TAX ~.

BENEFIT COST STATEMENT. A statement relating the anticipated benefits expressed in dollars to the total estimated cost of a project.

BENEFIT PERIOD. 1. " . . . [T]he period during which a claimant receives unemployment insurance benefits." *Canada (Canada Employment & Immigration Commission) v. Gagnon* (1988), 33 Admin. L.R. 1 at 11, 22 C.C.E.L. 17, [1988] 2 S.C.R. 29, 86 N.R. 268, 88 C.L.L.C. 14,034, 52 D.L.R. (4th) 42, L'Heureux-Dubé J. (Wilson J. concurring). 2. The period of time during which an insured person is entitled to insured services.

BENEFIT PLAN. See DEFINED ~; EM-PLOYEE ~; HEALTH INSURANCE OR ~.

BENEFIT PROVISION. See DEFINED ~.

BENEFITS. The term "benefits" has been broadly interpreted to include anything to which the employee would have been entitled during a period of reasonable notice. To limit entitlement to benefits where there has been "payment in lieu", would be tantamount to giving the company the power to circumscribe benefits during the notice period where notice is provided. In the absence of such a power having been expressly reserved in the termination policy itself, it follows that the phrase "or similar employment benefits" should be construed broadly so as to equate "payment in lieu" as closely as possible with the "notice" alternative. *Gilchrist v. Western Star Trucks Inc.* 2000 CarswellBC 2136, 2000 BCSC 1523, 82 B.C.L.R. (3d) 99, 25 C.C.P.B. 22.

BENEFIT SOCIETY. See FRATERNAL ~; TRADE UNION ~.

BENEVOLENCE. See CONTRACT OF ~.

BENEVOLENT. *adj.* Charitable; conferring benefits; philanthropic.

BENEVOLENTIA REGIS HABENDA. [L.] Having the sovereign's good will; having the sovereign's pardon.

BENEVOLENT PURPOSE. A charitable, educational, religious, or welfare purpose or other purpose to the public advantage or benefit.

BENIGNAE FACIENDAE SUNT INTER-PRETATIONES ET VERBA INTENTIONI DEBENT INSERVIRE. [L.] Liberal interpretation ought to be the rule, and words ought to serve intention.

BENIGNAE SUNT FACIENDAE INTER-PRETATIONES CARTARUM PROPTER SIMPLICITATEM LAICORUM UT RES MAGIS VALEAT QUAM PEREAT. [L.] Because of the simplicity of laypeople, charters should be interpreted liberally so that the intention prevails rather than goes to waste.

BENIGNIOR SENTENTIA IN VERBIS GE-NERALIBUS SEU DUBIIS, EST PRAEFER-ENDA. [L.] A more favourable construction should be placed on general or doubtful terms.

BENTONITE. *n.* Also known as Fuller's earth, a soft, plastic rock that is a type of clay.

BENZENE. *n.* A cyclic hydrocarbon.

BEQUEATH. *v.* To leave through a will.

BEQUEST. *n.* Personal property given by will. See RESIDUARY ~; SPECIFIC ~.

BEREAVEMENT. *n.* Being deprived of, or losing, a relative.

BEREAVEMENT LEAVE. "Time off without loss of pay to gather together with relatives at a time of personal tragedy for mutual comfort, to assist in making arrangements for the funeral of the deceased and for the immediate and after care of the deceased's survivors, and to enable the employee to bear his grief privately without immediate exposure to the comparative harshness of his working environment." *Re Dominion Glass Co. Ltd.* (1973), 4 L.A.C. (2d) 345 at 353.

BERM. *n.* Dyke constructed of earth or tailings.

BERNE CONVENTION. The international convention drawn up at Berne in 1886 which created an international union for the protection of artistic and literary copyright.

BERRY ANEURYSM. The rupture of this aneurysm involving an artery at the base of the brain commonly causes sudden death in young or middle aged adults. F.A. Jaffe, *A Guide to Pathological Evidence*, 3d ed. (Toronto: Carswell, 1991) at 212.

BERTH. *n.* 1. A location at any wharf, pier, quay or similar facility at which a vessel may be secured. 2. Includes a wharf, pier, anchorage or mooring buoy. See FOREST MANAGE-

MENT ~; PULPWOOD ~; SLEEPER ~; TIMBER ~.

BERTHAGE. *n.* 1. A charge on a vessel (a) while occupying a berth or while fast to or tied up alongside any other vessel occupying a berth at any wharf, pier, jetty, bulkhead or other similar facility under the administration management and control of or under lease from the Commissioners within the harbour, and (b) while not moored at but loading or unloading by lighter from or to any facilities referred to in paragraph (a). 2. A charge levied on a vessel in respect of the period of time that the vessel is (a) moored to a wharf, (b) occupying a berth or any space at or near a wharf, or (c) secured in any manner whatever to a vessel that is subject to berthage.

BESET. *v.* To approach, importune, assail another person.

BESTES KE GAIGNENT SA TERRE. [Fr.] Beasts of the plough.

BEST EFFORTS. 1. " . . . [T]aking, in good faith, all reasonable steps to achieve the objective, carrying the process to its logical conclusion, and 'leaving no stone unturned' . . ." *Bruce v. Waterloo Swim Club* (1990), 31 C.C.E.L. 321 at 336, 73 O.R. (2d) 709 (H.C.), Lane J. 2. In summary, the principles extracted from the cases on the issue of "best efforts" are: 1. "Best efforts" imposes a higher obligation than a "reasonable effort". 2. "Best efforts" means taking, in good faith, all reasonable steps to achieve the objective, carrying the process to its logical conclusion and leaving no stone unturned. 3. "Best efforts" includes doing everything known to be usual, necessary and proper for ensuring the success of the endeavour. 4. The meaning of "best efforts" is, however, not boundless. It must be approached in the light of the particular contract, the parties to it and the contract's overall purpose as reflected in its language. 5. While "best efforts" of the defendant must be subject to such overriding obligations as honesty and fair dealing, it is not necessary for the plaintiff to prove that the defendant acted in bad faith. 6. Evidence of "inevitable failure" is relevant to the issue of causation of damage but not to the issue of liability. The onus to show that failure was inevitable regardless of whether the defendant made "best efforts" rests on the defendant. 7. Evidence that the defendant, had it acted diligently, could have satisfied the "best efforts" test is relevant evidence that the defendant did not use its best efforts. The "no stone unturned" test has been applied to contracts relating to a wide variety of subject matter. Further, courts routinely imply a term in contracts that the parties will make reasonable efforts to fulfil their respective contractual obligations. Where the parties include a "best efforts" clause in a contract, as they did in the case at bar, they must surely intend that something more than "reasonable efforts" be used. *Atmospheric Diving Systems Inc. v. International Hard Suits Inc.* 1994 CarswellBC 158, 89 B.C.L.R. (2d) 356, [1994] 5 W.W.R. 719, 53 C.P.R. (3d) 459, 13 B.L.R. (2d) 243 British Columbia Supreme Court, Dorgan J.

BEST EVIDENCE RULE. Wherever possible, the original of a document must be produced. P.K. McWilliams, *Canadian Criminal Evidence* 3d ed. (Aurora: Cnada Law Book, 1988) at 6-1.

BESTIALITY. *n.* The act of a human being having sexual intercourse with an animal.

BEST INTERESTS OF THE CHILD. 1. ". . . [T]he physical comfort and material advantages that may be available in the home of one contender or the other. The welfare of the child must be decided on a consideration of these and all other relevant factors, including the general psychological, spiritual and emotional welfare of the child . . ." *King v. Low* (1985), 16 D.L.R. (4th) 576 at 587, [1985] 1 S.C.R. 87, the court per McIntyre J. 2. The ultimate test in all cases is the best interest of the child. This is a positive test, encompassing a wide variety of factors. One of the factors which the judge seeking to determine what is in the best interests of child must have regard to is the desirability of maximizing contact between the child and each parent. But in the final analysis, decisions on access must reflect what is in the best interests of the child. *Young v. Young,* 1993 CarswellBC 264, 84 B.C.L.R. (2d) 1, [1993] 8 W.W.R. 513, 49 R.F.L. (3d) 117, 160 N.R. 1, 34 B.C.A.C. 161, 56 W.A.C. 161, 108 D.L.R. (4th) 193, [1993] 4 S.C.R. 3, 18 C.R.R. (2d) 41, [1993] R.D.F. 703, Per McLachlin, J. 3. The "best interests of the child" principle is best understood as an important underlying social value that informs many legislative and policy initiatives, rather than as a principle of fundamental justice under s. 7 of the [Canadian Charter of Rights and Freedoms]. *Canadian Foundation for Children, Youth & the Law v. Canada (Attorney General)* 2000 CarswellOnt 2409, 146 C.C.C. (3d) 362, 188 D.L.R. (4th) 718, 49 O.R. (3d) 662, 36 C.R. (5th) 334, 76 C.R.R. (2d) 251 SC.

BET. *n.* 1. A bet that is placed on any contingency or event that is to take place in or out of

Canada, and without restricting the generality of the foregoing, includes a bet that is placed on any contingency relating to a horse-race, fight, match or sporting event that is to take in or out of Canada. *Criminal Code*, R.S.C. 1985, c. C-46, s. 197. 2. A bet placed under the system known as pari-mutuel wagering. See TRIAC-TOR ~.

BETTER BUSINESS BUREAU. An organization which provides information to consumers regarding local businesses.

BETTER EQUITY. When one claimant should have priority over the others because of notice, priority in time or some other reason.

BETTERMENT. *n*. Increasing property value.

BETTING. *n*. A wagering contract under which financial consideration is made payable as the result of a contingency.

BETTING HOUSE. See COMMON~.

BETTOR. *n*. A person who bets.

BEVERAGE. *n*. Beer, carbonated soft drinks and any other liquor intended for human consumption by drinking. See ALCOHOLIC ~S.

BEYOND A REASONABLE DOUBT. The standard of proof required in criminal cases. " . . . The burden cast upon the Crown is to prove all essential ingredients of the crime charged beyond a reasonable doubt, viz. 'outside the limit or sphere of ' or 'past' a reasonable doubt. . ." *R. v. Lachance* (1962), 39 C.R. 127 at 130, [1963] 2 C.C.C. 14 (Ont. C.A.), Porter C.J.O., Roach, Aylesworth, Schroeder and Kelly JJ.A.

BEYOND SEAS. 1. ". . . [O]utside the jurisdiction." *Schacht v. Schacht* (1982), 30 C.P.C. 52 at 54, [1982] 5 W.W.R. 189 (B.C. C.A.), the court per Hutcheon J.A. 2. Does not include any part of Canada, or of the British dominions in North America, or of the United States of America in North America. *Limitation of Actions Act*, R.S.N.B. 1973, c. L-8, s. 1.

BEYOND THE SEAS. In this Act, shall be meant any place beyond the limits of the Government of Newfoundland. *Limitation of Actions (Personal) and Guarantees Act*, R.S. Nfld. 1970, c. 206, s. 7.

B.F.L.R. *abbr*. Banking & Finance Law Review.

BFR. Bona fide requirement.

BIAS. *n*. 1. Prejudice. 2. [B]ias denotes a state of mind that is in some way predisposed to a particular result, or that is closed with regard to particular issues. *R. v. S. (R.D.)* 1997 CarswellNS 301, 151 D.L.R. (4th) 193, 118 C.C.C. (3d) 353, 10 C.R. (5th) 1, 218 N.R. 1, 161 N.S.R. (2d) 241, 477 A.P.R. 241, [1997] 3 S.C.R. 484, 1 Admin. L.R (3d) 74, Cory, J. 3. An allegation of bias is a serious charge against those who have accepted the obligations of independence and impartiality which go with judicial or quasi-judicial office, as have the members of this commission. To charge such persons with bias is not merely to say that they would be likely to decide a particular matter in a particular way, but to say that they would do so improperly. The charge implies that the quasi-judicial decision-maker would not decide the case independently, and on the basis of the evidence, but would do so under improper influence, and with a view to achieving an extraneous or otherwise improper purpose. *Bennett v. British Columbia (Superintendent of Brokers)*, 1994 CarswellBC 762, 36 C.P.C. (3d) 96, 7 C.C.L.S. 165, 30 Admin. L.R. (2d) 283, 48 B.C.A.C. 56, 78 W.A.C. 56 Taylor, J.A. 4. " . . . [C]overs a spectrum of disqualification ranging from partiality on one hand, to the extreme of corruption on the other . . ." *Calgary General Hospital c. U. N. A., Local 1* (1983), 6 Admin. L.R. 80 at 85, 29 Alta. L.R. (2d) 3, 84 C.L.L.C. 14,032, 50 A.R. 250, 5 D.L.R. (4th) 54 (C.A.), the court per Stevenson J.A. 5. "Bias may be of two kinds. It may arise from an interest in the proceedings. . . Sometimes it is a direct pecuniary or proprietary interest in the subject-matter of the proceedings. A person possessing such an interest is disqualified from sitting as a judge thereon. Sometimes the interest is not financial but arises from a connection with the case or with the parties of such a character as to indicate a real likelihood of bias. . . the second kind of bias—namely actual bias in fact." *Gooliah v. R.* (1967), (*sub nom. Gooliah, Re*) 63 D.L.R. (2d) 224 at 227-8, 59 W.W.R. 705 (Man. C.A.), Freedman J.A. 6. In the context of challenges for cause, refers to an attitude that could lead jurors to discharge their function in the case at hand in a prejudicial and unfair manner. It is evident from the definition of bias that not every emotional or stereotypical attitude constitutes bias. Prejudice capable of unfairly affecting the outcome of the case is required. Bias is not determined at large, but in the context of the specific case. What must be shown is a bias that could, as a matter of logic and experience, incline a juror to a certain party or conclusion in a manner that is unfair. *R. v. Find*, 2001 CarswellOnt 1702, 2001 SCC 32, 42 C.R.

(5th) 1, 154 C.C.C. (3d) 97, 199 D.L.R. (4th) 193, 269 N.R. 149, 146 O.A.C. 236 McLachlin C.J.C., for the court. See ATTITUDINAL ~; INSTITUTIONAL ~; REASONABLE APPREHENSION OF ~.

BIAS PLY TIRE. A pneumatic tire in which the ply cords that extend to the beads are laid at alternate angles substantially less than 90 degrees to the centreline of the tread. Canada Regulations.

BI-CAMERAL. *adj.* Having two chambers: in Canada, refers to the two houses of Parliament, the House of Commons and the Senate.

BICAMERAL COUNCIL. Describes the council of any Ontario city which has a board of control as well as aldermen.

BICYCLE. *n.* Every device propelled by human power upon which a person may ride, having two tandem wheels. See MOTOR ASSISTED ~; MOTOR ASSISTED PEDAL ~; POWER ~.

BID. *v.* 1. To make an offer at an auction. 2. To submit a response to a call for tenders.

BID. *n.* 1. " . . . [T]he submission, of a tender, . . ." *Ron Engineering & Construction (Eastern) Ltd v. Ontario* (1981), 13 B.L.R. 72 at 122-23, 119 D.L.R. (3d) 267, 35 N.R. 40, [1981] 1 S.C.R. 111, Estey J. 2. "[In the Combines Investigation Act, R.S.C. 1970, c. C-23 s. 32.2(1)(b)] . . . must be interpreted to be an offer which may be accepted by the offeree binding the offeror . . ." *R. v. Coastal Glass & Aluminum Ltd.* (1984), 8 C.P.R. (3d) 46 at 59, 17 C.C.C. (3d) 313 (B.C. S.C.), Lander J. 3. A take over bid or an issuer bid. 4. Documentation submitted by a contractor in response to a tender for a construction contract. 5. A "Tender" is that which a General Contractor submits to an Owner. It is not to a "Bid" which is what a Subcontractor submits to a General Contractor. *Ken Toby Ltd. v. British Columbia Buildings Corp.* 1997 CarswellBC 1087, 34 B.C.L.R. (3d) 263, [1997] 8 W.W.R. 721, 34 C.L.R. (2d) 81, 31 B.L.R. (2d) 224, British Columbia Supreme Court, Burnyeat J. *Securities acts.* See BASE ~; EXPIRATION OF ~; ISSUER ~; QUALIFIED ~; REFERENTIAL ~; TAKE OVER ~.

BID BOND. 1. A bond given to guarantee entry into a contract. 2. A bond that is conditioned upon the bidder on a contract entering into the contract, if the contract is awarded to him, and furnishing any required payment bond and performance bond.

BID CIRCULAR. A take over bid circular or an issuer bid circular, as the case may be.

BIDDER. *n.* At an auction, a person who makes an offer.

BIDDING. *n.* Quoting cost or price for a contract in response to a request or call for bids or tenders.

BID-RIGGING. *n.* (a) An agreement or arrangement between or among two or more persons whereby one or more of those persons agrees or undertakes not to submit a bid in response to a call or request for bids or tenders, or (b) the submission, in response to a call or request for bids or tenders, of bids or tenders that are arrived at by agreement or arrangement between or among two or more bidders or tenderers, where the agreement or arrangement is not made known to the person calling for or requesting the bids or tenders at or before the time when any bid or tender is made by any person who is a party to the agreement or arrangement. *Competition Act*, R.S.C. 1985, c. C-34, s. 47.

BIENS. *n.* [Fr.] Property.

BIGAMOUS. *adj.* Said of marriage entered into by a party already married.

BIGAMUS. *n.* A bigamous person.

BIGAMY. *n.* Every one commits bigamy who (a) in Canada, (i) being married, goes through a form of marriage with another person, (ii) knowing that another person is married, goes through a form of marriage with that person, or (iii) on the same day or simultaneous goes through a form of marriage with more than one person; or (b) being a Canadian citizen resident in Canada leaves Canada with intent to do anything mentioned in subparagraphs (a)(i) to (iii) and, pursuant thereto, does outside Canada anything mentioned in those subparagraphs in circumstances mentioned therein. *Criminal Code*, R.S.C. 1985, c. C-46, s. 290(1).

BIG GAME. Bison, pronghorn antelope, mountain sheep or mountain goat, any of the deer family whether known as elk wapiti, caribou, moose, deer or otherwise, bear, cougar and musk-ox.

BIG GAME FARM. A place on which big game animals are kept for the purposes of propagation or for sale, gain, profit or pleasure.

BILAGINE. *n.* By-law.

BILATERAL. *adj.* Involving two agreeing parties.

BILATERAL CONTRACT. A contract in which each of the two parties is bound to fulfil obligations towards the other.

BILGE BOUNDARY LINE. A line that in elevation is parallel to the line of the keel and coincident amidships with the boundary between the side of the hull and the upper turn of bilge. *Arctic Shipping Pollution Prevention Regulations*, C.R.C., c. 353, Schedule VI, s. 1.

BILINGUAL. *adj.* Having the ability to speak two languages. Usually refers to the ability to speak both of Canada's official languages. See RECEPTIVE ~S.

BILINGUAL POSITION. A position identified as having duties that require a knowledge and use of both official languages.

BILL. *n.* 1. Writing; a letter. 2. An account. 3. In parliamentary practice, the first star in the enactment of a statute. 4. An order. 5. A bill of exchange. *Bills of Exchange Act*, R.S.C. 1985, c. B-4, s. 2. See ACCEPTANCE OF ~; ACCOMMODATION ~; APPROPRIATION ~; EXCHEQUER ~; FOREIGN ~; GOVERNMENT ~; INLAND ~; INTERNATIONAL ~ OF HUMAN RIGHTS; MONEY ~; PRIVATE ~; PRIVATE MEMBER'S ~; PUBLIC ~; SHIPPING ~; SKELETON ~; TREASURY ~; TRUE ~; WAY- ~.

BILLA VERA. [L.] True bill.

BILLBOARD. *n.* 1. An announcement at the commencement or end of any program naming the sponsor, if any. 2. A large outdoor sign for advertising.

BILLET. *v.* To offer accommodation to soldiers and their horses.

BILLET. *n.* A dwelling in which soldiers stay.

BILLFISH. *n.* A fish of the species Scomberesox saurus.

BILLIARD-RICOCHET EFFECT. Deflection of succeeding shot gun pellets by the pellets which had already penetrated the tissue and been slowed. F.A. Jaffe *A Guide to Pathological Evidence*, 3d ed. (Toronto: Carswell 1991) at 213.

BILLIARDS. *n.* Includes pool, bagatelle or any other similar game.

BILLIARD TABLE. In addition to its proper meaning, also means boards used for the games of pigeon-hole, Mississippi, pool, bagatelle or other like games.

BILLING. See EXTRA ~.

BILLING PERIOD. The time between two consecutive meter readings taken at approximately the same date each month.

BILL OF COSTS. A document setting out the claim for legal fees and disbursements in a proceeding.

BILL OF EXCHANGE. An unconditional order in writing, addressed by one person to, another, signed by the person giving it, requiring the person to whom it is addressed to pay, on demand or at a fixed or determinable future time, a sum certain in money to or to the order of a specified person or to bearer. *Bills of Exchange Act*, R.S.C. 1985, c. B-4, s. 16(1). See CONSUMER BILL.

BILL OF INDICTMENT. The printed or written accusation of crime made against one or more people.

BILL OF LADING. Includes all receipts for goods, wares and merchandise accompanied by an undertaking (a) to move the goods, wares and merchandise from the place where they were received to some other place, by any means whatever, or (b) to deliver to a place other than the place where the goods, wares and merchandise were received a like quantity of goods, wares and merchandise of the same or a similar grade or kind. *Bank Act*, S.C. 1991, c. 46, s. 425.

BILL OF RIGHTS. 1. The Canadian Bill of Rights. S.C. 1960, c. 44, Pt. 1. 2. The English Statute 1688, 1 Will. & Mary, sess. 2, c. 2. 3. The first 10 amendments to the U.S. Constitution. See CANADIAN ~.

BILL OF SALE. A document in writing in conformity with this Act evidencing a sale or mortgage of chattels but does not include a bill of lading, a warehouse receipt, a warrant or order for the delivery of goods, or any other document used in the ordinary course of business as proof of the possession or control of goods or authorizing or purporting to authorize the possessor of the document to transfer either by endorsement or delivery or to receive goods thereby represented. *Bills of Sale acts*.

BIN. *abbr.* The Business Identification Number (BIN) is a 9-digit number used by the Ontario government to identify provincial business accounts. It also appears on the Ontario Master Business Licence.

BIND. *v.* To obligate; to secure payment.

BINDER. *n.* A written memorandum providing temporary insurance coverage until a policy is issued. *Kline Brothers & Co. v. Dominion Fire Insurance Co.* (1913), 47 S.C.R. 252 at 255, 9 D.L.R. 231, Fitzpatrick C.J. (Davies, Idington, Duff and Brodeur JJ. concurring). See MEAT ~.

BINDING ARBITRATION. A binding arbitration is a non-court equivalent to a court trial. In either case a neutral third party hears the case and makes his decision which (subject to appeal) is binding upon the parties. This differs from other forms of ADR [Alternative Dispute Resolution] in which the parties themselves are part of the decision-making mechanism and the neutral third party's involvement is of a facilitative nature: e.g. mediation, conciliation, neutral evaluation, non-binding opinion, non-binding arbitration. Of course, the simplest method—often overlooked—is that of non-involvement by a neutral: a negotiation between the parties. *887574 Ontario Inc. v. Pizza Pizza Ltd.* 1994 CarswellOnt 1069, 35 C.P.C. (3d) 323, 23 B.L.R. (2d) 239 Ontario Court of Justice (General Division), Commercial List, Farley J.

BINDING AUTHORITY. Compelling authority; a decision of a higher court which a lower court must follow.

BIND OVER. To enter into a bond before the court to keep the peace and be of good behaviour.

BINNING. See SPECIAL ~.

BIOACCUMULATION FACTOR. The ratio of the concentration of a substance in an organism to the concentration in water, based on uptake from the surrounding medium and food. *Persistence and Bioaccumulation Regulations*, SOR/2000-107, s. 1.

BIOCHEMICAL OXYGEN DEMAND. The quantity of oxygen utilized in the biochemical oxidation of organic matter during a 5-day period.

BIOCHEMICAL OXYGEN DEMANDING MATTER. The substance contained in the effluent from a plant that results from the operation of a plant and that will exert a biochemical oxygen demand.

BIOCONCENTRATION FACTOR. The ratio of the concentration of a substance in an organism to the concentration in water, based only on uptake from the surrounding medium.

Persistence and Bioaccumulation Regulations, SOR/2000-107, s. 1.

BIOLOGICAL AGENT. Includes sera, immune globulins, vaccines and toxoids.

BIODIVERSITY. *n.* The variability among living organisms from all sources including terrestrial, marine, estuarial and freshwater ecosystems and the ecological complexes of which they are a part; those terms include diversity within species, between species and of ecosystems.

BIODIVERSITY RESERVE. An area established in order to maintain biodiversity and in particular an area established to preserve a natural monument — a physical formation or group of formations — and an area established as a representative sample of the biological diversity of the various natural regions of Québec. *Natural Heritage Conservation Act*, R.S.Q., chapter C-61.01, s. 2.

BIOLOGIC. See VETERINARY ~.

BIOLOGICAL DIVERSITY. The variability among living organisms from all sources, including terrestrial and marine and other aquatic ecosystems and the ecological complexes of which they form a part and includes the diversity within and between species and of ecosystems.

BIOLOGICAL FATHER. The man (i) who is married to the biological mother at the time of the birth of the child, (ii) acknowledged by the biological mother as the biological father of the child, (iii) declared by a court to be the biological father of the child, or (iv) who satisfies a Director that he is the biological father of the child. *Child Welfare Act*, S.A. 2000, c. C-12, s. 1. See BIRTH PARENT.

BIOLOGICAL MOTHER. The woman who gave birth to the child. *Child Welfare Act*, S.A. 2000, c. C-12, s. 1. See BIRTH PARENT.

BIOLOGY. *n.* The study of life forms. See APPLIED ~.

BIOMETRIC INFORMATION. 1. Information derived from an individual's unique characteristics but does not include a photographic or signature image. 2. Information derived from an individual's personal characteristics other than a representation of the individual's signature.

BIOMETRICS. The use of measurable human characteristics, such as fingerprints or iris images, to identify individuals.

BIOTECHNOLOGY. The application of science and engineering in the direct or indirect use of living organisms or parts or products of living organisms in their natural or modified forms. *Canadian Environmental Protection Act*, 1999, S.C. 1999, c. 33, s. 3.

BIOTECHNOLOGY PRODUCTS MANUFACTURING PLANT. A plant that produces products using the application of science and engineering in the direct or indirect use of living organisms or parts or products of living organisms in their natural or modified form.

BIPARTITE. *adj*. Having two parts.

BIRD. *n*. An animal of the class Aves, and its eggs. See GALLINACEOUS ~; GAME ~; MIGRATORY ~S; SONG ~.

BIRD OF PREY. Any hawk, falcon, eagle, owl, osprey, vulture or any other species of the families Falconidae, Cathartidae, Accipitridae, Pandionidae, or Strigidae, the eggs of those birds and any part of those birds or eggs.

BIRD OF THE PARROT FAMILY. Parrot, Amazon, Mexican double head, African grey, cockatoo, macaw, love-bird, lorie, lorikeet, and any other member of the species psittacidae. *Health of Animals Regulations*, C.R.C., c. 296, s. 2.

BIRRETUM. *n*. [L.] A thin cap fitted close to the shape of the head; cap worn by judges; black cap.

BIRRETUS. *n*. [L.] A thin cap fitted close to the shape of the head; cap worn by judges; black cap.

BIRTH. *n*. The complete expulsion or extraction from its mother, irrespective of the duration of pregnancy, of a product of conception in which, after such expulsion or extraction, there is breathing, beating of the heart, pulsation of the umbilical cord or unmistakable movement of voluntary muscle, whether or not the umbilical cord has been cut or the placenta is attached. *Vital Statistics acts*.

BIRTH FATHER. (a) In the case of a child who has not been previously adopted, the biological father of the child, who: (i) at the time of the child's birth or conception, was living with the birth mother, whether or not they were married to each other; (ii) together with the child's birth mother, has registered the child's birth pursuant to *The Vital Statistics Act, 1995*; (iii) has access to or custody of the child by order of a court having jurisdiction over the matter or by agreement; (iv) acknowledges that he is the birth father and has supported or maintained the child or the birth mother; (v) is not registered as the father of the child pursuant to *The Vital Statistics Act, 1995* but has been named as the birth father by the birth mother and acknowledges that he is the birth father; or (vi) has been declared by the court to be the father of the child pursuant to Part VI of *The Children's Law Act, 1997*; or (b) in the case of a child who has been previously adopted, a person who is the father of the child by virtue of an order of adoption. *Adoption Act, 1998*, S.S. 1998, c. A-5.2, s. 2.

BIRTH INJURY. An injury like brain damage or a fracture to the skull sustained during the birth of an infant. F.A. Jaffe, *A Guide to Pathological Evidence*, 3d ed. (Toronto: Carswell, 1991) at 213.

BIRTH MOTHER. (i) In the case of a child who has not been previously adopted, the mother of the child; or (ii) in the case of a child who has been previously adopted, a person who is the mother of the child by virtue of an order of adoption. *The Adoption Act*, S.S. 1998, c.A-5.2, s. 2.

BIRTH PARENT. 1. The biological mother or father of a child. 2. When used in reference to a child, means a person who is the child's parent at the time of the child's birth. See BIOLOGICAL FATHER; BIOLOGICAL MOTHER.

BIRTH RELATIVE. An adult person who is a birth parent, birth sibling, birth grandparent, birth aunt or birth uncle of the adult adoptee.

BIRTH SIBLING. A brother or sister.

BISHOP. *n*. The cleric appointed to administer a diocese.

BISSEXTILE. *n*. The extra day added in leap years.

BITUMEN. *n*. A mixture of hydrocarbons that results naturally from the degradation of oil and that can be transformed into crude oil. *Gulf Canada Resources Ltd. v. R.* [1996] 2 C.T.C. 55, Pratte, J.A. for majority. See CRUDE ~.

BITUMINOUS SHALE. Bituminous shale, oil shale, albertite, kerogen and includes all other such substances intimately associated therewith.

BITUMINOUS SHALE BY-PRODUCTS. All minerals intimately associated with bituminous shale and which because of this intimate association are produced with or recovered from bituminous shale and bituminous shale products during bituminous shale production operations. *Bituminous Shale Act*, S.N.B., c. B-4.1, s. 1.

BITUMINOUS SHALE EVALUATION WELL. A hole made or being made by drilling, boring, or in any other manner, for the purpose of ascertaining the existence of bituminous shale in the subsurface, or from which bituminous shale products are to be obtained. *Bituminous Shale Act*, S.N.B., c. B-4.1, s. 1.

BITUMINOUS SHALE PRODUCTION OPERATIONS. Any operation or process for the recovery of bituminous shale products, including open pit mining, underground mining or, any in situ process which reduces organic matter, or hydrocarbons not otherwise recoverable by conventional oil and natural gas production techniques, contained in the bituminous shale, to bituminous shale products. *Bituminous Shale Act*, S.N.B., c. B-4.1, s. 1.

BLACK CAP. The cap worn by judges when pronouncing sentence of death.

BLACKCOD POT. A metal framed enclosure that is covered with netting or expanded metal and has one or more openings through which the fish enter the enclosure.

BLACKCOD TRAP. See BLACKCOD POT.

BLACK LIST. 1. A list of persons with whom those compiling the list advise that no one should have dealings of a certain type. 2. " . . . [H]istorical described the practice utilized by employers to identify and boycott unwanted employees, particularly trade-union activists and supporters." *Pacific Gillnetters Assn. v. U.F.A.W., British Columbia Provincial Council*, [1979] 1 Can. L.R.B.R. 506 at 518 (B.C.), Germaine (Vice-Chair), Fritz and Smith (Members).

BLACKMAIL. *n*. Menacing and making unwarranted demands. See EXTORTION.

BLACK MARKETING. Unauthorized dealing in or offering rationed, prohibited or restricted goods or services.

BLACK ROT. A condition in which the interior of an egg appears partially or wholly black in colour.

BLACK STEEL. Steel that is not coated with any metallic substance.

BLACK WROUGHT IRON. Wrought iron that is not coated with any metallic substance.

BLANK ACCEPTANCE. An acceptance written across a bill before it is filled out.

BLANK AUDIO RECORDING MEDIUM. An audio recording medium onto which no sounds have ever been fixed, and any other prescribed audio recording medium. *Copyright Act*, R.S.C. 1985, c. C-42, s. 79.

BLANK ENDORSEMENT. An endorsement written on the back of a bill of exchange before the bill is filled out.

BLANKET INSURANCE. That class of group insurance which covers loss arising from specific hazards incident to or defined by reference to a particular activity or activities. *Insurance acts*.

BLANKET MORTGAGE. A second mortgage which is granted and which includes in its principal sum the amount of the smaller first mortgage, although this amount is not advanced initially. The mortgagee continues to make payments on the first mortgage. Once the first mortgage matures, the mortgagee must pay it off and obtain a discharge of it so that the second mortgage becomes the first.

BLASPHEMY. *n*. " . . . [T]he profane speaking of God or sacred things . . . It may also bear the meaning of evil speaking or defamation, . . ." *Ralston v. Fomich* (1992), 66 B.C.L.R. (2d) 166 at 168, [1992] 4 W.W.R. 284 (S.C.), Spencer J.

BLASTER. *n*. A person who has charge of explosives and their use in a surface mine.

BLDG. *abbr*. Building.

BLEND. *v*. Of payment of principal and interest, to mix so that they are indistinguishable and inseparable. W.B. Rayner & R.H. McLaren, *Falconbridge on Mortgages*, 4th ed. (Toronto: Canada Law Book, 1977) at 665.

BLENDED. *adj*. 1. Describes a combined payment of principal money with interest. W.B. Rayner & R.H. McLaren *Falconbridge on Mortgages*, 4th ed. (Toronto: Canada Law Book 1977) at 662. 2. " . . . '[M]ixed so as to be inseparable and indistinguishable.'" *Kilgoran Hotels Ltd. v. Samek*, [1968] S.C.R. 3 at 5, 65 D.L.R. (2d) 534, the court per Hall J. 3. As applied to any fur, means that the surface of the fur has been treated by brushing with reagents to change its colour.

BLENDED FUND. A mixed fund obtained from different sources.

BLENDED PAYMENT. A periodic payment on a loan, a definite amount of which is applied first towards interest and the rest of which is applied to reducing the principal.

BLIND. *adj*. 1. If the visual acuity in both eyes with proper refractive lenses is 20/200 (6/60) or less with Snellen Chart or equivalent, or if the greatest diameter of the field of vision in both eyes is less than 20 degrees. *Blind Persons Regulations*, C.R.C., c. 371, s. 2. 2. A person is deemed to be blind if his vision renders him incapable of doing work for which sight is necessary. *Workmen's Compensation Act*, R.S.Q 1977, c. A-3, s. 121.

BLIND PERSON. 1. A person who is registered as blind with the Canadian National Institute for the Blind, or who, on account of blindness, receives a pension, or who is certified by a qualified eye specialist as not having more than 6/60 vision according to Snellen's Chart after correction with glasses. 2. A person who is apparently blind and dependent on a guide dog or white cane.

BLIND TRUST. A trust in which an office holder transfers all personal wealth to a trustee to invest, reinvest and manage in a normal way according to the powers given to the trustee by an instrument. At no time may the trustee give any account to the settlor or office holder of the actual assets held. D.M.W. Waters, *The Law of Trusts in Canada*, 2d ed. (Toronto: Carswell, 1984) at 438.

BLINKING REFLEX TEST. A test administered to a seal to confirm that it has a glassy-eyed, staring appearance and exhibits no blinking reflex when its eye is touched while the eye is in a relaxed condition. *Marine Mammal Regulations*, SOR/93-56, s. 2.

BLISTER. *n*. Fluid which collects underneath the surface layer of the skin. F.A. Jaffe, *A Guide to Pathological Evidence*, 3d ed. (Toronto: Carswell, 1991) at 13.

BLOATER FILLETS. Fillets of salted, smoked, round herring.

BLOATERS. *n*. Salted, smoked, round herring.

BLOCK. *n*. 1. A piece of land in a registered subdivision that is not itself subdivided. 2. An area or part of a pool consisting of production spacing units grouped for the purpose of obtaining a common, aggregate production allowable. See APARTMENT ~; QUARTER HOUR ~; STEREOTYPE ~.

BLOCKADE. *n*. Cutting off all of an enemy's external communication. See PACIFIC ~; PAPER ~.

BLOCK OUTLINE SURVEY. A survey in which special survey monuments are established at suitable points at or near certain or all street intersections or angles in street lines, or in cases where no streets exist, then at other suitable points.

BLOOD. *n*. Cells suspended in fluid plasma. F.A. Jaffe, *A Guide to Pathological Evidence*, 3d ed. (Toronto: Carswell, 1991) at 195. See CORRUPTION OF ~; PULLORUM TEST OR ~ TEST.

BLOOD GROUPS. Classification of blood types based on the two red cell antigens, A and B. F.A. Jaffe, A *Guide to Pathological Evidence*, 3d ed. (Toronto: Carswell, 1991) at 213-14.

BLOOD MEAL. Dried blood of an animal.

BLOOD RELATIONSHIP. " . . . [D]escribed the relationship existing between two or more persons who stand in lawful descent from a common ancestor. . ." *Army & Navy Department Store Ltd. v. Minister of National Revenues*, [1953] C.T.C. 293 at 300, [1953] 25 S.C.R. 496, [1954] 1 D.L.R. 177, 53 D.T.C. 1185, Locke J. (Taschereau and Fauteux JJ. concurring).

BLOOD SPOT. A small particle of blood on the yolk or in the albumen of an egg.

BLOWGUN. See YAQUA ~.

BLOWOUT. *n*. The unintentional and uncontrolled escape of oil or gas, as from a drilling well when high formation pressure is encountered. *Canada Oil and Gas Drilling and Production Regulations*, C.R.C., c. 1517, s. 2.

BLOWOUT PREVENTER. A casing-head control fitted with special gates or rams that can be closed around the drilling pipe and completely close the top of the casing if the pipe is withdrawn. *Canada Oil and Gas Drilling and Production Regulations*, C.R.C., c. 1517, s. 2.

B.L.R. *abbr*. Business Law Reports, 1977-.

BLUEBACK. A hooded seal that has not moulted its blue coat. *Marine Mammal Regulations*, SOR/93-56, s. 2.

BLUE CHIP. Highest quality securities.

BLUE COLLAR WORKER. An employee engaged in maintenance or production as opposed to one employed in an office or professionally.

BLUEFIN. *n.* Any fish of the species Thunnus thynnus.

BLUENOSE. *n.* The schooner which was featured on the Canadian dime.

BLUE-SKY BARGAINING. Proposals by negotiators which are so unreasonable that there is no chance of their acceptance.

BLUE-SKY LAW. A law to protect investors from fraud in connection with sales of securities.

BLUE WHALE. Any whale known by the name of blue whale, Sibbald's rorqual, or sulphur bottom.

BN. *abbr.* Business number. A 9-digit federal client identification number to which businesses can register program accounts.

B.N.A. ACT(S). *abbr.* British North America Act(s).

BOARD. *n.* 1. A body of persons to which certain powers are delegated or assigned or who are elected for certain purposes. 2. The governing body of an institution purposes. 3. The board of directors of a corporation. 4. The board of governors, management or directors, or the trustees, commission or other person or group of persons having the control and management of an accredited or approved hospital. *Criminal Code*, R.S.C. 1985, c. C-46, s. 287(6). 5. "... [A] succession of meals obtained from day to day, or from week to week, or from month to month, &c..." *R. v. McQuarrie* (1862), 22 U.C.Q.B. 600 at 601, the court per Draper C.J. See APPEAL ~; ARBITRATION ~; ATOMIC ENERGY CONTROL ~; CANADA LABOUR RELATIONS ~; CANADIAN AVIATION SAFETY ~; CANADIAN WHEAT ~; CHECK IN ~; CONCILIATION ~; DIVING ~; EXAMINING ~; EXPROPRIATION ~; FEDERAL ~ COMMISSION OR OTHER TRIBUNAL; HOSPITAL ~; JOINT PRACTICE ~; LIBRARY~; LOCAL ~; NATIONAL ENERGY ~; NATIONAL FILM ~; PANEL ~; PENSION APPEALS ~; PRODUCERS' ~; PUBLIC SERVICE STAFF RELATIONS ~; REVIEW ~; SELECTION ~; TARIFF ~; TREASURY ~ OF CANADA; TRIPARTITE ~.

BOARD FOOT. A unit of measurement used to measure sawn lumber or to estimate the lumber volume that can be sawn from a log.

BOARDING. Suggests that the owner of the animal makes an arrangement to leave it in the care of the boarding facility. *Woodman v. Capital (Regional District)*, 1999 CarswellBC 2193, 6 M.P.L.R. (3d) 128. See PET ~.

BOARDING CHARGE. A charge for placing cargo on customer pallets.

BOARDING HOME. A building, part of a building, group of buildings or other place in which, for a fee, gain or reward, food and lodging together with care or attention are furnished.

BOARDING HOUSE. A building or structure or part of a building or structure kept, used or advertised as or held out to be a place where sleeping accommodation is furnished to the public as regular roomers.

BOARDING STABLE KEEPER. A person who, for a money consideration or its equivalent, stables, boards or cares for animals.

BOARDING STATION. See PILOT ~.

BOARD LOT. A unit in which shares are traded on a stock exchange.

BOARD OF CONTROL. In cities over 100,000 in population a body required by the Ontario Municipal Act unless dispensed with by approval of the Ontario Municipal Board. Other large municipalities may have a board of control. I.M. *Rogers, The Law of Canadian Municipal Corporations*, 2d ed. (Toronto: Carswell, 1971-) at 280.11.

BOARD OF GOVERNORS. 1. The board of directors, board of management or other head of a hospital legally authorized to manage the affairs of the hospital. *The Hospital Standards Act*, R.S.S. 1978, c. H-10, s. 23. 2. The board of governors of a university.

BOARD OF HEALTH. The board of health of a city, town, village or rural municipality.

BOARD OF POLICE COMMISSIONERS. See POLICE COMMISSIONER.

BOARD OF REFEREES. Consists of a chairperson and one or more members chosen from employers or representatives of employers and an equal number of members chosen from insured persons or representatives of insured persons. The first level of appeal from decisions of the employment commission.

BOARD OF TRADE. An association of persons who are directly or indirectly engaged or interested in trade, commerce or the economic and social welfare of any district, whether residents of the district or not, may associate themselves together as a board of trade for the purpose of promoting and improving trade and commerce and the economic, civic and social welfare of the district.

BOARDS. *v*. Includes lives, abides, dwells and lodges.

BOAT. *n*. Includes any vessel used or designed to be used in navigation of water. [A]ny craft afloat, which carries goods or passengers . . ." *R. v. Conrad*, [1938] 2 D.L.R. 541 at 543, 12 M.P.R. 588, 70 C.C.C. 100 (N.S. T.D.), the court per Chisholm C.J. See EXCURSION ~; HOUSE- ~;   MOTOR ~;   PLEASURE; POWER ~.

BOAT-HOUSE. *n*. A structure in which one or more boats is stored.

BOAT-OWNER.   See   INDEPENDENT ~ FISHERMAN.

BOAT TRAILER. A trailer that is designed to transport a boat and has cradle-type mountings that permit the launching of the boat from the rear of the trailer. *Motor Vehicle Safety Regulations*, C.R.C., c. 1038, s. 100.

B.O.D. *abbr*. Biochemical oxygen demand.

BODILY HARM. Any hurt or injury to a person that interferes with the health or comfort of the person and that is more than merely transient or trifling in nature. *Criminal Code*, R.S.C. 1985, c. C-46, s. 2. See ACTUAL ~; GRIEVOUS ~; SERIOUS ~.

BODILY INJURY. Physical, psychological or mental injury including death as well as damage to the clothing worn by the victim at the time of the accident.

BODILY INJURY LIABILITY INSURANCE. The obligation of the insurer to pay insurance money in the event of the death of or bodily injury to any person as the result of one of the perils mentioned.

BODY. *n*. 1. The main section of any document or instrument. 2. In writs, a person. 3. A human body. See CAROTID ~; COOPERATIVE ~; DEAD ~;   GOVERNMENT ~;   PAROCHIAL ~; PERSON LAWFULLY IN POSSESSION OF THE ~; PUBLIC ~; RELIGIOUS ~;   SELF   REGULATING ~; WATER ~.

BODY CAVITY SEARCH. Involve a physical inspection of the detainee's genital or anal regions. While the mouth is a body cavity, it is not encompassed by the term "body cavity search". Searches of the mouth do not involve the same privacy concerns. *R. v. Golden* 2001 SCC 83.

BODY CORPORATE. 1. A company or other body corporate with or without share capital wherever or however incorporated. 2. Any incorporated corporation, incorporated association, incorporated syndicate or other incorporated organization wheresoever incorporated. See EXTRA-PROVINCIAL ~.

BODY-GRIPPING TRAP. A device designed to capture or kill an animal by seizing and holding it by a part of its body, and includes a spring trap, steel trap, gin, deadfall, snare or leghold trap but does not include a device designed to capture or kill a mouse or rat. *Fish and Wildlife Conservation Act, 1997*, S.O. 1997, c. 41, s. 1.

BODY OF WATER. 1. Includes any body of flowing or standing water whether naturally or artificially created. 2. ". . .That which lies within defined limits (such as a lake or a pond) and although it might form part of a watercourse it is distinguished from it in that the water in it is not subject to the same degree of continuous flow which is usually observed within the banks of a river or stream . . ." *Murphy Oil Co. v. Continental Insurance Co.*, [1981] I.L.R. 1-1409 at 381, 33 O.R. (2d) 853 (Co. Ct.), Fogarty Co. Ct. J. See OPEN ~; STANDING ~.

BODY ORIFICE. A natural opening or a permanent artificial opening in the body, such as a stoma. *Medical Devices Regulations* SOR/98-282, s. 1.

BODY POLITIC. A nation; a corporation.

BODY-RUB. *n*. Includes the kneading, manipulating, rubbing, massaging, touching, or stimulating, by any means, of a person's body or art thereof but does not include medical or therapeutic treatment given by a person otherwise duly qualified, licensed or registered so to do under the laws of the Province of Ontario. *Municipal Act*, R.S.O. 1990, c. M.45, s. 224(9).

BODY-RUB PARLOUR. Includes any premises or part thereof where a body-rub is performed, offered or solicited in pursuance of a trade, calling, business or occupation, but does not include any premises or part thereof where the body-rubs performed are for the purpose of medical or therapeutic treatment and are performed or offered by persons otherwise duly qualified, licensed or registered so to do under the laws of the Province of Ontario. *Municipal Act*, R.S.O. 1990, c. M.45, s. 224(9).

BOILER. *n.* 1. A vessel in which steam or other vapour can be generated under pressure or in which a liquid can be put under pressure by the direct application of a heat source. 2. An appliance intended to supply hot water or steam for space heating, processing or power purposes.See CHEMICAL RECOVERY ~; COILED TUBE ~; DUAL CONTROL ~; ELECTRIC ~; FIRED STEAM HEATING ~; HIGH PRESSURE ~; HOT WATER ~; LOCOMOTIVE ~; LOW PRESSURE ~; MINIATURE ~; POWER ~; STEAM ~; THERMAL LIQUID ~.

BOILER AND MACHINERY INSURANCE. Insurance against loss or damage to property and against liability for loss or damage to persons or property through the explosion, collapse, rupture or breakdown of, or accident to, boilers or machinery of any kind. *Insurance acts*.

BOILER INSURANCE. Insurance against (a) liability arising out of (i) bodily injury to, or the death of, a person, or (ii) the loss of, or damage to, property, or (b) the loss of, or damage to, property, caused by the explosion or rupture of, or accident to, pressure vessels of any kind and pipes, engines and machinery connected therewith or operated thereby. See STEAM ~.

BOILER PLANT. Any plant which consists of one or more vessels or structures in which, by the application of heat, steam may be generated or water put under pressure.

BOILERPLATE. *n.* Standard clauses used in legal documents of a particular kind.

BOILER PLATE PROVISION. A standard clause which is inserted, by the drafter, usually *verbatim*, in instruments of the same type. *BC Tel v. Seabird Island Indian Band (Assessor of)* 2002 FCA 288, [2002] 4 C.N.L.R. 1, 216 D.L.R. (4th) 70, 292 N.R. 120, [2003] 1 F.C. 475, 231 F.T.R. 159 (note). Per Noël J.A., dissenting.

BOILER RATING. The rating for measuring the capacity of a boiler in kilowatts as determined in the regulations. *Boilers and Pressure Vessels acts*.

BOIL-OVER. *n.* A term used to describe the action that occurs when a hot layer of crude petroleum or similar liquid comes into contact with an underlying layer of a more volatile liquid

and causes that liquid to flash into vapour; the expansion produced by the conversion of the entrapped liquid vapour results in a violent surface action. *Flammable Liquids Bulk Storage Regulations*, C.R.C., c. 1148, s. 2.

BOLUS. *n.* A round, moist mass of food for swallowing. F.A. Jaffe, *A Guide to Pathological Evidence*, 2d ed. (Toronto: Carswell, 1983) at 170.

BOLUS DRINKING. A pattern of consuming large quantities of alcohol immediately before driving.

BOMB. See TEAR ~S.

BONA. *n.* [L.] Goods; property.

BONA. *adj.* [L.] Good.

BONA FIDE. [L. in good faith] " ... '[H]onestly', 'genuinely' or 'in good faith': ..." *Extendicare Health Services Inc. v. Canada (Minister of National Health & Welfare)* (1987), 14 C.E.R. 282 at 286, 87 D.T.C. 5404, 15 F.T.R. 187, [1987] 3 F.C. 622, [1987] 2 C.T.C. 179, Can S.T.R. 80-127, Jerome A.C.J.

BONA FIDE DEALER. A person who deals generally with the sale of supplies of the type being purchased and who trades generally through normal trade channels.

BONAE FIDEI POSSESSOR IN ID TANTUM QUOD AD SE PERVENERIT, TENETUR. [L.] One who possesses in good faith is liable only for what has come to her or him.

BONA FIDE OCCUPATIONAL QUALIFICATION. " ... [M]ust be imposed honestly, in good faith, and in the sincerely held belief that such limitation is imposed in the interests of the adequate performance of the work involved with all reasonable dispatch, safety and economy, and not for ulterior or extraneous reasons . . . it must be related in an objective sense to the performance of the employment concerned, in that it is reasonably necessary to assure the efficient and economical performance of the job without endangering the employee, his fellow employees and the general public." *Ontario (Human Rights Commission) v. Etobicoke (Borough)*, [1982] 1 S.C.R. 202 at 208, 40 N.R. 159, 82 C.L.L.C. 17,005, 132 D.L.R. (3d) 14, 3 C.H.R.R. D/781, McIntyre J.

BONA FIDE OCCUPATIONAL REQUIREMENT. 1. The Supreme court has established a new test, the unified approach or Meiorin test: Having considered the various alternatives, I propose the following three-step test for determining whether a prima facie discriminatory standard is a BFOR. An employer may justify the impugned standard by establishing on the balance of probabilities: (1) that the employer adopted the standard for a purpose rationally connected to the performance of the job; (2) that the employer adopted the particular standard in an honest and good faith belief that it was necessary to the fulfilment of that legitimate work-related purpose; and (3) that the standard is reasonably necessary to the accomplishment of that legitimate work-related purpose. To show that the standard is reasonably necessary, it must be demonstrated that it is impossible to accommodate individual employees sharing the characteristics of the claimant without imposing undue hardship upon the employer. *British Columbia (Public Service Employee Relations Commission) v. B.C.G.E.U.* 1999 CarswellBC 1907, 99 C.L.L.C. 230-028, [1999] 10 W.W.R. 1, 176 D.L.R. (4th) 1, 244 N.R. 145, 66 B.C.L.R. (3d) 253, 127 B.C.A.C. 161, 207 W.A.C. 161, 46 C.C.E.L. (2d) 206, 35 C.H.R.R. D/257, 68 C.R.R. (2d) 1, [1999] 3 S.C.R. 3, Supreme Court of Canada, McLachlin, J. for the court. 2. Equivalent to bona fide occupational qualification. *Central Alberta Dairy Pool v. Alberta (Human Rights Commission)* (1990), 33 C.C.E.L. 1 at 14-15, 21, [1990] 2 S.C.R. 489, [1990] 6 W.W.R. 193, 72 D.L.R. (4th) 417, 76 Alta. L.R. (2d) 97, 90 C.L.L.C. 17,025, 113 N.R. 161, 12 C.H.R.R. D/417, 111 A.R. 241, Wilson J. (Dickson C.J.C., L'Heureux-Dubé and Cory JJ. concurring).

BONA FIDE PURCHASER. 1. A purchaser for value in good faith and without notice of any adverse claim who takes delivery of a security in bearer form or of a security in registered form issued to her or him, endorsed to her or him or endorsed in blank. 2. A purchaser for value, in good faith and without notice of any adverse claim, (i) who takes delivery of a security certificate in bearer form or order form or of a security certificate in registered form issued to him or endorsed to him or endorsed in blank, (ii) in whose name an uncertificated security is registered or recorded in records maintained by or on behalf of the issuer as a result of the issue or transfer of the security to him, or (iii) who is a transferee or pledgee as provided in section 85. *Business Corporations Amendment Act*, S.O. 1986, c. 57, s. 7.

BONA FIDE REQUIREMENT. Once the plaintiff establishes that the standard is prima facie discriminatory, the onus shifts to the defendant to prove on a balance of probabilities that the discriminatory standard is a BFOR or has a bona fide and reasonable justification. In order to establish this justification, the defendant must prove that: (1) it adopted the standard for a purpose or goal that is rationally connected to the function being performed; (2) it adopted the standard in good faith, in the belief that it is necessary for the fulfillment of the purpose or goal; and (3) the standard is reasonably necessary to accomplish its purpose or goal, in the sense that the defendant cannot accommodate persons with the characteristics of the claimant without incurring undue hardship. *British Columbia (Superintendent of Motor Vehicles) v. British Columbia (Council of Human Rights)* 1999 CarswellBC 2730, [2000] 1 W.W.R. 565, 47 M.V.R. (3d) 167, 249 N.R. 45, 70 B.C.L.R. (3d) 215, 181 D.L.R. (4th) 385, 36 C.H.R.R. D/129, [1999] 3 S.C.R. 868, 131 B.C.A.C. 280, 214 W.A.C. 280, McLachlin for the court.

BONA FIDE RESIDENT OF NEWFOUNDLAND. A person with Canadian citizenship who has resided in the province for a continuous period of not less than one year. *Fishing Ships (Bounties) Act*, R.S. Nfld. 1970, c. 137, s. 2.

BONA FIDES. [L.] Good faith.

BONA FIDES NON PATITUR UT BIS IDEM EXIGATUR. [L.] Good faith does not permit the same thing to be demanded twice.

BONA FIDE SUPPLIER. A person who deals generally with the sale of supplies of the type being purchased and who trades generally through normal trade channels.

BONA FORISFACTA. [L.] Forfeited goods.

BONA GESTURA. [L.] Good behaviour.

BONA MOBILIA. [L.] Movable goods and effects.

BONA VACANTIA. [L.] 1. Personal property without an owner, including the property of an intestate who dies without heirs, becomes the property of the Crown. 2. ". . . [T]he ultimate surplus of assets of the defunct company remaining after all obligations of the company are satisfied . . . the residue after all obligations were discharged . . . the residue only . . . being the bona vacantia." *Embree v. Millar* (1917), 33 D.L.R. 331 at 334, [1917] 1 W.W.R. 1200, 11 Alta. L.R. 127 (C.A.), the court per Beck J.A.

BONA WAVIATA. [L.] Goods thrown away or waived.

BOND. *n*. 1. ". . . [A] written instrument under seal whereby the person executing it makes a promise or incurs a personal liability to another." *Grimmer v. Gloucester (County)* (1902), 32 S.C.R. 305 at 310, the court per Sedgewick J. 2. A government debt obligation which is unsecured or a debt obligation of a large public corporation. 3. An agreement in writing signed by the guarantor under which the guarantor undertakes, upon the default of another person named in the agreement in paying a debt or a debt of a class of debts specified in the agreement (i) to pay a sum of money; or (ii) to pay the debt. See BACK~; BAIL~; BID ~; BONDS; BOTTOMRY ~; CONTRACT ~; COUPON ~; DOUBLE ~; FIDELITY ~; GOVERNMENT GUARANTEED ~; GUARANTEE ~; IN ~; JOINT INSURED ~; LABOUR AND MATERIAL ~; MORTGAGE PAYMENT ~; PEACE ~; PERFORMANCE ~; SINGLE INSURED ~; SURETY ~.

BONDAGE. *n*. Enslavement.

BONDED CARRIER. Any person who has been authorized to transport goods in bond.

BONDED GOODS. Dutiable goods for which a bond was given for payment of the duty.

BONDED MANUFACTURER. A person who carries on under bond and subject to ministerial regulations the manufacture of articles in the production of which goods subject to excise are used in combination with other materials. *Excise Act*, R.S.C. 1985, c. E-14, s. 5.

BONDED MANUFACTORY. Any place or premises licensed to use spirits or other goods subject to excise in the manufacture of articles under formula approved by the Minister, and every place or premises where any of those articles are warehoused stored or kept shall be held to form a part of the bonded manufactory to which it is attached or appurtenant. *Excise Act*, R.S.C. 1985, c. E-14, s. 5.

BONDED WAREHOUSE. A place licensed as a bonded warehouse by the Minister.

BONDEE. *n*. A person named in a bond upon whose default in paying a debt or a debt of a class of debts specified in the bond the guarantor undertakes to pay a sum of money or to pay the debt.

BONDHOLDERS' TRUST. Assets pledged by a company which is borrowing from bondholders and held in trust.

BONDING WAREHOUSE. Any warehouse in which goods subject to excise may be stored or deposited without payment of the duty imposed by this Act. *Excise Act*, R.S.C. 1985, c. E-14, s. 2.

BOND OF ASSOCIATION. Includes groups having a common bond of occupation or association, the residents within a well defined neighbourhood, community or rural or urban district, including a rural trading area, employees of a common employer or members of a bona fide fraternal, religious, co-operative, labour, rural, educational and similar organizations, and members of the immediate family of such persons. *Credit Unions and Caisses Populaires Act*, S.M. 1986-87, c. 5, s. 1.

BONDS. *n*. 1. Includes debentures. 2. All securities issued or guaranteed by any government, including treasury bonds, short-term notes and deposit certificates, whether negotiable or not, shall be regarded as bonds. *Caisse de Dépôt et Placement du Québec Act*, R.S.Q. 1977, c. C-2, s. 24. See BOND; LONG-TERM ~ OF CANADA.

BONDSMAN. *n*. A surety.

BONE MARROW EMBOLISM. An embolism in a blood vessel caused by bone marrow fragments. F.A. Jaffe, *A Guide to Pathological Evidence*, 3d ed. (Toronto: Carswell, 1991) at 218.

BONE MEAL. Ground animal bones, hoofs or horns.

BONI JUDICIS EST AMPLIARE JURISDICTIONEM. [L.] 1. "Boni judicis est ampliare jurisdictionem is a maxim that is open, when literally rendered . . . of being a 'foolish saying', but, in modern paraphrase, it enjoins no more than to amplify remedies for the attainment of substantial justice without usurping jurisdiction." *Brereton v. Canadian Pacific Railway* (1898), 29 O.R. 57 at 63, 18 C.L.T. 63 (H.C.), Boyd C. 2. "The supposed legal maxim, Boni judicis est ampliare jurisdictionem, derives from times when Judges were paid largely by fees and the more cases the more pay; it has been long discredited and the more reasonable dictum substituted, Boni judicis est ampliare justiciam: *Rex v. Philips* (1757), 1 Burr. 292, at p. 304, per Lord Mansfield . . ." *Sereda v. Consolidated Fire & Casual Insurance Co.*, [1934] O.R. 502 at 505, [1934] 3 D.L.R. 504 (C.A.), the court per Riddell J.A. See BONI JUDICIS EST AMPLIARE JUSTITIAM.

BONI JUDICIS EST AMPLIARE JUSTI-TIAM. [L.] It is the duty of a good judge to amplify the remedies.

BONI JUDICIS EST JUDICIUM SINE DI-LATIONE MANDARE EXECUTIONI. [L.] It is the duty of a good judge to order that judgment be executed without delay.

BONI JUDICIS EST LITES DIRIMERE, NE LIS EX LITE ORITUR, ET INTEREST REI-PUBLICAE UT SINT FINES LITIUM. [L.] A good judge disposes of cases so that one lawsuit does not lead to another; and it is in the public interest that there should be limits on litigation.

BONUS. *n.* 1. Gratuity; premium. 2. " . . . [M]ay be a mere gift or gratuity as a gesture of goodwill, and not enforceable. Or it may be something which an employee is entitled to on the happening of a condition precedent and is enforceable when the condition is fulfilled. But in both cases it is something in addition to or in excess of that which is ordinarily received." *Minister of National Revenue v. Great Western Garment Co.* (1947), [1948] 1 D.L.R. 225 at 233, [1947] C.T.C. 343, [1947] Ex. C.R. 458, O'Connor J. 3. Discount, premium, dues, commission, brokerage fee, finders fee or other payment made by a borrower to a mortgage lender or mortgage broker. ATTENDANCE ~; GROUP ~.

BONUSING. The practice of conferring benefits upon businesses in order to attract them to a municipality. *Telus Communications Inc. v. Opportunity (Municipal District) No. 17*, (1998), 235 A.R. 258.

BONUS JUDEX SECUNDUM AEQUUM ET BONUS JUDICAT, ET AEQUITATEM STRICTO JURI PRAEFERT. [L.] A good judge decides using fairness and good, and prefers equity to legal strictness.

BOOK. *n.* 1. A volume or a part or division of a volume, in printed form, but does not include (a) a pamphlet, (b) a newspaper, review, magazine or other periodical, (c) a map, chart, plan or sheet music where the map, chart, plan or sheet music is separately published, and (d) an instruction or repair manual that accompanies a product or that is supplied as an accessory to a service. *Copyright Act*, R.S.C. 1985, c. C-42, s. 2. 2. Library matter of every kind, nature and description and includes any document, paper, record, tape or other thing published by a publisher, on or in which information is written, recorded, stored or reproduced. *National Library Act*, R.S.C. 1985, c. N- 2, s. 2. 3. The National Library Act requires the publisher of a book published in Canada shall, at the publisher's own expense and within one week after the date of publication, send two copies of the book to the National Librarian, who shall give to the publisher a written receipt therefor. See ABSTRACT ~; BOOKS; CASH ~; DAY- ~; HORN~; INCLUDIBLE ~; PERMIT ~; POLL ~; PRINTED ~ OF PHOTOGRAPHS; PRINTED ~ OF PICTURES OR DESIGNS; PRINTED ~ OR PAMPHLET.

BOOK ACCOUNTS. All the accounts and debts current and future as in the ordinary course of business would be entered in the books whether entered or not, and includes all books, documents and papers relating to the accounts and debts. *Book Accounts Assignment Act*, R.S.B.C. 1979, c. 32, s. 1. See ASSIGNMENT OF ~.

BOOK DEBTS. All existing or future debts that in the ordinary course of business would be entered in books, whether actually entered or not. See ASSIGNMENT OF ~.

BOOK DEPOSIT. Two copies of a book published in Canada which its publisher must deliver to the National Librarian.

BOOKMAKER. *n.* " . . . [A] person who engages in the occupation of taking bets (or even in negotiating bets) and the keeping of accounts, . . ." *R. v. Decome* (1991), 63 C.C.C. (3d) 460 at 472, [1991] R.J.Q. 618, 40 Q.A.C. 92, Proulx J.A. (Gendreau J.A. concurring).

BOOKS AND PAPERS. Includes accounts, deeds, writings and documents.

BOOKSELLER. *n.* An individual, firm or corporation that is directly engaged in the sale of books in Canada for at least 30 consecutive days in a year and (a) whose floor space is open to the public and is located on premises consisting of floor space, including book shelves and customer aisles, of an area of at least 183 m² (600 sq. ft.); or (b) whose floor space is not open to the public and that derives 50% of his or her or its gross revenues from the sale of books. *Book Importation Regulations*, SOR/99-324, s. 1.

BOOKS OR PAPERS. Includes accounts, deeds, writings and documents.

BOOK VALUE. 1. " . . . [V]alue at which property is recorded in the financial accounts of its owner. Usually, property is recorded at historical cost less, in the case of depreciable property, the amount of accumulated depreciation . . . *Domglas Inc. v. Jarislowsky, Fraser & Co.* (1980), 13 B.L.R. 135 at 199, [1980] C.S. 925 (Que.), Greenberg J. 2. In respect of an asset, means the cost of acquisition to the person acquiring the asset, including all direct costs associated with the acquisition. See NET ~.

BOOM. *n*. The projecting part of a back-hoe, shovel, crane or similar lifting device from which a load is likely to be supported. Ontario regulations.

BOOM CHAIN. A chain with toggles attached for use in the booming of logs.

BOOTH. See POLLING ~.

BOOZE CAN. A colloquial expression which means a place where liquor is served illegally after closing time, usually at a higher price than at a regular bar or tavern.

BORDER TREE. One category of "boundary trees". Trees whose trunks are solely on one property at ground level, but whose roots encroach into an adjoining property, or whose canopy of branches invades the air space above an adjoining property. *Koenig v. Goebel*, (1998), 162 Sask. R. 81.

BORE. *v*. To bore, drill or dig into the ground.

BORE. *n*. The interior of a firearm barrel. F.A. Jaffe, *A Guide to Pathological Evidence*, 3d ed. (Toronto: Carswell, 1991) at 214.

BORE DIAMETER. Caliber. F.A. Jaffe, *A Guide to Pathological Evidence*, 3d ed. (Toronto: Carswell, 1991) at 214.

BOROUGH. *n*. A town.

BORROWER. *n*. 1. A person to whom a loan has been made. 2. A person who receives credit. See JOINT ~S.

BORROWING. *n*. A loan obtained including a line of credit. See COST OF ~.

BOSS. *n*. 1. Employer, supervisor. 2. A protuberance or knob that is on the outside of a pipe and that causes the pipe wall to be thicker at that point than the rest of the pipe wall. *Ontario Water Resources Act*, R.R.O. 1980, Reg. 736, s. 1.

BOTTLE TRAP. A trap that retains liquids in a closed chamber and the water seal of which is made by submerging the inlet or outlet pipe in the liquids or by a partition submerged in the liquids.

BOTTLE-YOUR-OWN PREMISES. Premises in which, in accordance with the laws of the province in which they are located, alcohol is supplied from a marked special container of alcohol for the purpose of being packaged by a purchaser. *Excise Act, 2001*, S.C. 2002, c. 22.

BOTTOM. See BARREN ~.

BOTTOMRY BOND. 1. The hypothecation or mortgage of a ship in which her bottom or keel is pledged. 2. An agreement entered into by a ship's owner in which the borrower undertakes to repay money advanced for the use of the ship with interest if the ship ends her voyage successfully.

BOULEVARD. *n*. 1. In an urban area, that part of a highway that (i) is not roadway, and (ii) is that part of the sidewalk that is not especially adapted to the use of or ordinarily used by pedestrians. 2. The area between the curb lines, the lateral lines or the shoulder of a roadway and the adjacent property line.

BOUNDARY. *n*. 1. Limit of territory; an imaginary line which divides two pieces of land. 2. The international boundary between Canada and the United States as determined and marked by the Commission. *International Boundary Commission Act*, R.S.C. 1985, c. I-16, s. 2. 3. Patent claims are frequently analogized to "fences" and "boundaries", giving the "fields" of the monopoly a comfortable pretence of bright line demarcation. Thus, in *Minerals Separation North American Corp. v. Noranda Mines Ltd.*, [1947] Ex. C.R. 306 (Can. Ex. Ct.), Thorson P. put the matter as follows, at p. 352: By his claims the inventor puts fences around the fields of his monopoly and warns the public against trespassing on his property. His fences must be clearly placed in order to give the necessary warning and he must not fence in any property that is not his own. The terms of a claim must be free from avoidable ambiguity or obscurity and must not be flexible; they must be clear and precise so that the public will be able to know not only where it must not trespass but also where it may safely go. In reality, the "fences" often consist of complex layers of definitions of different elements (or "components" or "features" or "integers") of differing complexity, substitutability and ingenuity. A matrix of descriptive words and phrases defines the monopoly, warns the public and ensnares the infringer. In some instances, the precise elements of the "fence" may be crucial or "essential" to the working of the invention as claimed; in others the inventor may contemplate, and the reader skilled in the art appreciate, that variants could easily be used or substituted without making any material difference to the working of the invention. The interpretative task of the court in claims construction is to separate the one from the other, to distinguish the essential from the inessential, and to give to the "field" framed by the former the legal protection to which the holder of a valid patent is entitled. *Free World Trust c. Électro Santé Inc.* 2000 CarswellQue 2728, 2000 SCC 66, 194 D.L.R. (4th) 232, 263 N.R. 150, [2000] 2 S.C.R. 1024, 9 C.P.R. (4th) 168, Binnie, J. See CONVENTIONAL ~; NATURAL ~; OBLITERATED ~; SEAWARD ~.

BOUNDARY BY AGREEMENT. A conventional boundary located by agreement between the government and the adjoining owner. *Land Act*, R.S.B.C. 1996, c. 245, s. 1.

BOUNDARY MONUMENT. A buoy, post, tablet, cairn or other object or structure placed, erected or maintained by the Commission to mark the boundary and includes a reference monument, triangulation station or other marker or structure erected or maintained by the Commission to assist in determining the boundary. *International Boundary Commission Act*, R.S.C. 1985, c. I-16, s. 2.

BOUNDARY SURVEY. A survey to determine the boundaries of land.

BOUNDARY TREE. One whose trunk, roots or branches encroach on the property or air space of an adjoining property. Includes border trees and straddle trees. *Koenig v. Goebel*, (1998), 162 Sask. R. 81.

BOUNDARY WATERS. The waters from main shore to main shore of the lakes and rivers and connecting waterways, or the portions thereof, along which the international boundary between the United States and Canada passes, including all bays, arms, and inlets thereof, but not including tributary waters which in their natural channels would flow into such lakes, rivers and waterways, or waters flowing from such lakes, rivers, and waterways, or waters flowing across such lakes, rivers, and waterways, or the waters of rivers flowing across the boundary. *Canada Water Act*, R.S.C. 1985, c. C-11, s. 2.

BOUND OVER. See BIND OVER.

BOUNDS. See METES AND ~.

BOUNTY. *n.* 1. Money or premium paid for the fulfilment of a particular service. 2. A bounty payable for killing a predator or a nuisance animal.

BOUT. *n.* A contest or exhibition between two contestants.

BOW. *n.* 1. A tool for projecting arrows which consists of a handle and one or more flexible limbs which are held bent by a string or cable which is drawn, pulled or released or held in a drawn position by hand or hand-held release and not by any mechanical device attached to any portion of the bow other than the bowstring. Nova Scotia statutes. 2. A longbow or crossbow. See CROSS ~; LONG ~.

BOW FISHING. Fishing with a bow and arrow.

BOWHEAD CALF. A bowhead whale that is mottled in appearance and less than 7.5 m in length, measured from the point of the upper jaw to the notch between the tail flukes. *Marine Mammal Regulations*, SOR/93-56, s. 2.

BOW SECTION. The foremost (a) one-third length of a ship, in the case of a ship 50 feet in length or under, (b) 17 feet of a ship, in the case of a ship over 50 feet but under 70 feet in length, and (c) one-quarter length of a ship, in the case of a ship 70 feet in length or over. *Hull Construction Regulations*, C.R.C., c. 1431, s. 100.

BOX. *n.* Any crate, carton, or other outer covering or wrapper in which containers are packed. See END ~; LOCK ~; MAIL ~; SERVICE ~.

BOXER. *n.* A person who engages in boxing for monetary reward.

BOX NET. A net that (a) is made and set in the form of a box, (b) has a trap into which fish are guided by a leader, and (c) is capable of catching fish without enmeshing them.

BOY. *n.* Any male person under the age of 18 years.

BOYCOTT. *v.* To take part in a boycott.

BOYCOTT. *n.* An organized refusal to deal with a particular person or business. See CONSUMER ~; PRODUCTION ~; SECONDARY ~.

B.R. *abbr.* 1. Cour du Banc de la Reine/du Roi. 2. Recueils de jurisprudence de la Cour de banc de la Reine (du Roi) de Québec. 3. Rapports judiciaires du Québec, Cour du Banc de la Reine (ou du Roi) (Quebec Official Reports, Queen's (or King's) Bench, 1892-1941).

[]B.R. *abbr.* 1. Rapports judiciaires du Québec, Cour du Banc de la Reine (ou du Roi) 1942-

1966. 2. Recueils de jurisprudence du Québec, Cour du Banc de la Reine, 1967-1969.

BRACING CHARGE. A charge for furnishing labour or materials for bracing or securing goods on railway cars or other vehicles, but does not include the cost of covering goods. *Pacific Terminal Tariff By-law*, C.R.C., c. 1083, s. 41.

BRACKISH WATER. Water situated in tidal areas where fresh water mixes with marine water. *Aquaculture Act*, R.S.N.S. 1989, c. 18, s. 2.

BRAIN INFARCT. Blockage of an artery in the brain. F.A. Jaffe, *A Guide to Pathological Evidence*, 2d ed. (Toronto: Carswell, 1983) at 46.

BRAKE. See AIR ~ SYSTEM; EMERGENCY ~; PARKING ~; SERVICE ~.

BRAKE FLUID. Brake fluid for use in hydraulic brake systems, except hydraulic system mineral oil. *Motor Vehicle Safety Regulations*, C.R.C., c. 103 8, s. 2.

BRAKE HORSE POWER. *var.* **BRAKE HORSEPOWER**. 1. The aggregate horse power on a shaft from all elements driving it. *Steam and Pressure Plants Act*, R.S.M. 1987, c. S210, s. 1. 2. The effective or useful horsepower developed by a prime mover as measured by a weigh scale and a brake applied to its driving shaft or by other means approved by the chief officer, and one brake horsepower is equivalent to 2,544 British thermal units per hour or to 0.02544 Therm-hours. *Operating Engineers Act*, R.S.O. 1990, c. O.42, s. 1. 3. As applied to motor-driven ships, means the continuous brake horsepower as rated by the manufacturer of the engine. *Marine Engineers Examination Regulations*, C.R.C., c. 1443, s. 2.

BRANCH. *n.* 1. (a) in respect of a bank, means an agency, the head office or any other office of the bank, and (b) in respect of an authorized foreign bank, means an agency, the principal office or any other office of the authorized foreign bank in Canada at which is carried on the business in Canada of the authorized foreign bank. *Bank Act*, S.C. 1991, c. 46, s. 2. 2. " . . . [I]ncludes a local and subordinate office . . . it also includes a component portion of an organization or system or a section, division, subdivision or department of a business." *Minister of National Revenue v. Panther Oil & Grease Manufacturing Co.*, [1961] C.T.C. 363 at 377, 61 D.T.C. 1272 (Ex. Ct.), Thorson P. See HORIZONTAL ~.

BRANCH CIRCUIT. That part of a circuit extending beyond the final overcurrent devices in the circuit. See MULTI-WIRE ~.

BRANCH LINE. A line of railway in Canada of a railway company within the legislative authority of Parliament that, relative to a main line within the company's railway system in Canada of which it forms a part, is a subsidiary, secondary, local or feeder line of railway, and includes a segment of any such subsidiary, secondary, local or feeder line of railway. *National Transportation Act, 1987*, S.C. 1987, c. 34, s. 157(1).

BRANCH OFFICE. Any location, other than the head office, at which business is carried on.

BRANCH VENT. A vent pipe that is connected at its lower end to the junction of 2 or more vent pipes and is connected at its upper end either to a stack vent, vent stack or header, or is terminated in open air.

BRAND. *n.* 1. A character or combination of characters impressed or intended to be impressed on the skin or hide of stock to show ownership of the stock. 2. Any mark, stencil, stamp, label or writing placed on any milk product or package. See IDENTIFICATION ~; SINGLE CHARACTER ~.

BRANDEIS BRIEF. A social science brief in which empirical data is appended to or included in a factum.

BRANDHEMATOM. *n.* Blood clots collected extradurally in a body which has been exposed to intense heat. F.A. Jaffe, *A Guide to Pathological Evidence*, 3d ed. (Toronto: Carswell, 1991) at 214.

BRAND NAME. A name in English or French, whether or not it includes the name of a manufacturer, corporation, partnership or individual (a) that is used to distinguish the natural health product; and (b) under which a natural health product is sold or advertised. *Natural Health Products Regulations*, SOR/2003-196, s. 1.

BRAND-NAME DRUG. A prescription drug product, usually one sold by a corporation with patent rights in the product. Contrasted with generic drug. *Apotex Inc. v. Canada (Attorney General)*, (1997), 123 F.T.R. 161.

BRAND READER. A person appointed by a municipality to give an accurate description of an estray. *Domestic Animals (Municipalities) Act*, R.S.A. 1970, c. 112, s. 2.

BRANDY. See CANADIAN ~.

BRAWL. *v.* To create a disturbance.

BREACH. *n.* 1. Encroachment of a right. 2. Disregard of a duty. 3. Non-execution of a contract. See ANTICIPATORY ~; FUNDAMENTAL ~; POUND ~; PRISON ~; SUBSTANTIAL ~.

BREACH OF CLOSE. Unjustified entry on another person's land.

BREACH OF CONFIDENCE. " ... [C]onsists in establishing three elements: that the information conveyed was confidential, that it was communicated in confidence, and that it was misused by the party to whom it was communicated." *International Corona Resources Ltd. v. Lac Minerals Ltd.* (1989), 44 B.L.R. 1 at 16, [1989] 2 S.C.R. 574, 26 C.P.R. (3d) 97, 69 O.R. (2d) 287, 61 D.L.R. (4th) 14, 6 R.P.R. (2d) 1, 35 E.T.R. 1, 101 N.R. 239, 36 O.A.C. 57, La Forest J. (Wilson and Lamer JJ. concurring).

BREACH OF CONTRACT. The failure to complete a contract according to its terms. See CRIMINAL ~; INTENTIONAL INDUCEMENT OF ~.

BREACH OF CONTRACT, INDUCING. A concise statement of the tort of inducing breach of contract was provided by Lord Morris in *D.C. Thomson & Co. Ltd. v. Deakin*, [1952] Ch. 646 (Eng. C.A.), at page 702: The breach of contract must be brought about or procured or induced by some act which a man is not entitled to do, which may take the form of direct persuasion to break the contract or the intentional bringing about of a breach by indirect methods involving wrongdoing. *923087 N.W.T. Ltd. v. Anderson Mills Ltd.* 1997 CarswellNWT 36, 35 B.L.R. (2d) 1, 13 C.P.C. (4th) 357, [1997] N.W.T.R. 212, 40 C.C.L.T. (2d) 15, Northwest Territories Supreme Court, Vertes J.

BREACH OF PRISON. Escape from a prison.

BREACH OF PRIVILEGE. Contempt of Parliament.

BREACH OF PROMISE TO MARRY. Conduct which permitted a common law action for damages.

BREACH OF STATUTORY DUTY. A tort involving the elements that a statutory duty is owed to the plaintiff, the injury is of the kind the statute was designed to prevent, defendant must be in breach and the breach of the duty must have caused the loss.

BREACH OF THE PEACE. 1. An act or acts which result in actual or threatened harm to someone. The act or acts may not be unlawful standing alone. *Brown v. Durham Regional Police Force* (1998), 21 C.R. (5th) 1 (Ont. C.A.) 2. Has a narrower meaning than the breach of the Queen's peace which is supposed to underlie every crime. The most flagrant instance of a breach of the peace is a riot. An unlawful assembly which has not yet become a riot is a breach of the Queen's peace. A fight between two or more persons is a breach of the peace.

BREACH OF TRUST. 1. The exercise of authority which is vested in a public official by virtue of his or her office, other than for the public benefit. Any breach of the appropriate standard of responsibility and conduct demanded of the holder of an office as a senior civil servant. *R. v. Power* (1993), 82 C.C.C. (3d) 73 (N.S.C.A.) 2. There are three ways in which a stranger to a trust can be held liable as a constructive trustee for breach of trust. First, a stranger to the trust can be liable as a trustee *de son tort*. Secondly, a stranger to the trust can be liable for breach of trust by knowingly assisting in a fraudulent and dishonest design on the part of the trustees ("knowing assistance"). Thirdly, liability may be imposed on a stranger to the trust who is in receipt and chargeable with trust property ("knowing receipt") *Citadel General Assurance Co. v. Lloyds Bank Canada* 1997 CarswellAlta 823, 152 D.L.R. (4th) 411, (*sub nom.* Citadel General Life Assurance Co. v. Lloyds Bank Canada) 206 A.R. 321, (*sub nom.* Citadel General Life Assurance Co. v. Lloyds Bank Canada) 156 W.A.C. 321, 19 E.T.R. (2d) 93, 35 B.L.R. (2d) 153, 47 C.C.L.I. (2d) 153, [1997] 3 S.C.R. 805, 219 N.R. 323, [1999] 4 W.W.R. 135. See CRIMINAL ~.

BREACH OF WARRANTY OF AUTHORITY. Breach of warranty of authority is a contractual cause of action. It focuses primarily on whether the plaintiff was induced by the specific misrepresentation (warranty) of the defendant that it had the authority of a third party. The misrepresentation in question must have induced the plaintiff to act to his or her detriment. In a breach of warranty of authority cause of action the agent's belief in the existence of his authority is immaterial so it matters not whether the warranty was given deliberately, negligently, innocently, or mistakenly. *Alvin's Auto Service Ltd. v. Clew Holdings Ltd.* 1997 CarswellSask 433, 33 B.L.R. (2d) 11, 157 Sask. R. 278, 37 C.C.L.T. (2d) 135, [1997] 9 W.W.R. 5, 13 R.P.R. (3d) 107 Saskatchewan Court of Queen's Bench, Baynton J.

BREAD. *n*. All products of flour or meal in which yeast, or any other ingredient for raising flour is used, irrespective of variety, colour, form or name.

BREADED FISH. Fish or fish flesh that is coated with batter and breading.

BREADTH. *n*. The maximum breadth of a ship, measured amidships, (a) in the case of a ship with a metal shell, to the moulded line of the frame, and (b) in the case of a ship with a shell of a material other than metal, to the outer surface of the hull. Canada regulations.

BREAK. *v*. (a) To break any part, internal or external, or (b) to open any thing that is used or intended to be used to close or to cover an internal or external opening. *Criminal Code*, R.S.C. 1985, c. C-46, s. 321.

BREAK. *n*. See AIR ~; PAID ~.

BREAK AND ENTER. Obtain entrance by a threat or artifice or by collusion with a person within, or enter without lawful justification or excuse by a permanent or temporary opening. *Criminal Code*, R.S.C. 1985, c. C-46, s. 350(b). See ENTER.

BREAKDOWN. *n*. An event, a point in time, at which an object stops functioning correctly. *Triple Five Corp. v. Simcoe & Erie Group* (1994), 29 C.C.L.I. (2d) 219 (Alta. Q.B.). 2. Some collapse in function, mechanical, electrical or electronic malfunction. *Clark v. Waterloo Insurance Co.* (1992), 98 D.L.R. (4th) 689 (Ont. Gen. Div.).

BREAKER. See CIRCUIT~; VACUUM ~.

BREAK FEE. In a hostile takeover of a corporation, a payment employed by the target corporation for the purpose of enticing another competitive bidder to enter the fray. It is paid to the competitive bidder when its bid fails or is superseded by a better offer. *CW Shareholders v. WIC Western International* (1998), 160 D.L.R. (4th) 131 (Ont. Gen. Div.).

BREAKING AND ENTERING. See BREAK AND ENTER.

BREAK-OVER ANGLE. The supplement of the largest angle, in the plan side view of a vehicle, that can be formed by two lines tangent to the front and rear static loaded radii arcs and intersecting at a point on the underside of the vehicle. *On-Road Vehicle and Engine Emission Regulations*, SOR/2003-2, s. 1.

BREATHALYZER. *n*. An instrument to measure alcohol content in the blood by analysis of a breath sample. See APPROVED INSTRUMENT.

BREATHING APPARATUS. An approved apparatus that, in an oxygen deficient atmosphere or an atmosphere contaminated by a toxic or dangerous substance, will provide oxygen or an adequate supply of air that is safe to breathe to a person engulfed in that atmosphere.

BRED IN CAPTIVITY. (a) in the case of sexual reproduction, born or otherwise produced in a controlled environment of parents that mated or whose gametes were otherwise transmitted under controlled conditions, and (b) in the case of asexual reproduction, produced or developed under controlled conditions *Wild Animal and Plant Trade Regulations*, SOR/96-263, s. 2.

BREECHING. *n*. A flue pipe or chamber for receiving flue gases from one or more flue connections and for discharging these gases through a single flue connection. *Building Code Act*, 1992, O. Reg. 403/07, s.1.1.3.

BREEDING POND. A body of water used for breeding fish for non-commercial purposes with a view to restocking.

B.R.E.F. *abbr*. 1. Bureau de revision de l'évaluation foncière. 2. Decisions du Bureau de revision de l'évaluation foncière du Québec.

BREVE. *n*. [L.] A writ to summon a person or which commands something to be done.

BREVE ITA DICITUR, QUIA REM DE QUA AGITUR, ET INTENTIONEM PETENTIS, PAUCIS VERBIS BREVITER ENARRAT. [L.] A writ is so named because it states briefly in few words the matter in dispute, and the intention of the party who seeks relief.

BREVE JUDICALE NON CADIT PRO DEFECTU FORMAE. [L.] A judicial writ does not fail through a formal defect.

BREVET RANK. The authority of the rank immediately above that held by an officer.

BREVIATE. *n*. Explanatory memorandum accompanying a bill in the legislature.

BREVI MANU. [L.] By direct action.

BREW. *v*. To make beer or other alcoholic beverage.

BREW. *n*. 1. A beverage made by brewing. 2. Colloquially, a beer.

BREWER. *n*. A manufacturer of beer for commercial purposes.

BREWERY. *n*. Any place or premises where any beer is manufactured, and all offices, granaries, mash-rooms, cooling-rooms, vaults, yards, cellars and store-rooms connected therewith or in which any material to be used in the manufacture of beer is kept or stored.

BREW ON PREMISE FACILITY. Premises where equipment for the making of beer or wine on the premises is provided to individuals. *Liquor Licence Act*, R.S.O. 1990, c. L-19, s. 1.

BRIBE. *v*. 1. To offer a person a payment or thing in circumstances which amount to a bribe. 2. It is an offence to offer a bribe to influence an elector to vote or refrain from voting or to vote or refrain from voting for a particular candidate. It is also an offence to accept or agree to accept a bribe, during an election period, offered to vote or refrain from voting for a particular candidate. *Canada Elections Act, 2000*, S.C. 2000, c. 9, s. 481.

BRIBE. *n*. 1. A gift to any person holding a position of trust or in public or judicial office intended to induce that person to betray trust or disregard official duty for the giver's benefit. 2. " . . . For the purposes of the civil law a bribe means the payment of a secret commission which only means (i) that the person making the payment makes it to the agent of the other person with whom he is dealing; (ii) that he makes it to that person knowing that that person is acting as the agent of the other person with whom he is dealing; and (iii) that he fails to disclose to the other person with whom he is dealing that he made that payment to the person whom he knows to be the other person's agent. Those three are the only elements necessary to constitute the payment of a secret commission or bribe for civil purposes." *Indust. & Gen. Mtge. Co. v. Lewis*, [1949] 2 All E.R. 573 at 575 Slade J. 3. A secret payment by one contracting party to the agent of another when it puts the agent in a position where the agent's interest is in conflict with the agent's duty to the principal. This course of dealing constitutes a "fraud" on the principal. *Ruiter Engineering & Construction Ltd. v. 430216 Ontario Ltd.* (1989), 41 B.L.R. 213 (Ont. C.A.).

BRIBERY OF JUDICIAL OFFICER. Occurs when the holder of a judicial office, or a member of Parliament or a legislature corruptly accepts or obtains, agrees to accept or attempts to obtain any money, valuable consideration, office, place or employment for himself or another person in respect of anything done or omitted or to be done or omitted by him in his official capacity or, when another person gives or offers corruptly to a person who holds a judicial office or is a member of Parliament or a legislature any money, valuable consideration, office place or employment in respect of anything done or omitted or to be done or omitted by him in his official capacity for himself or another person. *Criminal Code*, R.S.C. 1985, c. C-46, s. 119.

BRIBERY OF OFFICERS. Occurs when (a) a justice, police commissioner, peace officer, public officer, or officer of a juvenile court, or being employed in the administration of criminal law, corruptly (i) accepts or obtains, (ii) agrees to accept, or (iii) attempts to obtain, for himself or any other person any money, valuable consideration, office, place or employment with intent (iv) to interfere with the administration of justice, (v) to procure or facilitate the commission of an offence, or (vi) to protect from detection or punishment a person who has committed or who intends to commit an offence, or (b) anyone gives or offers, corruptly, to a person mentioned in paragraph (a) any money, valuable consideration, office, place or employment with intent that the person should do anything mentioned in subparagraph (a)(iv), (v) or (vi). *Criminal Code*, R.S.C. 1985, c. C-46, s. 120.

BRICK AND STONE MASON. A person who (i) constructs, erects, installs and repairs with brick, concrete block, insulation and other masonry units, walls, arches, paving, floors, fireplaces, chimneys, smoke-stacks and other structures, (ii) cuts and trims all brick, concrete block and other masonry units by hand tools and power activated equipment, (iii) lays firebrick and other refractory materials to walls, arches and floors in the construction of furnaces or to lining furnaces and retorts or to enclosing boilers, tanks and heat treating furnaces, (iv) has a comprehensive knowledge of tools to perform in the trade, (v) reads and understands blueprints, sketches, specifications, codes and manufacturers' literature used in the layout and erection of a structure. *Apprenticeship and Tradesmen's Qualification Act*, R.R.O. 1980, Reg. 26, s. 1.

BRIDE'S TROUSSEAU. Goods acquired for use in the household of a newly married couple.

BRIDGE. *n*. 1. Any structure used or intended to be used for the purpose of carrying traffic on a highway over or across a river, stream, ravine, railway or other highway. 2. Includes a viaduct, culvert, subway and embankment, and a pavement on a bridge. See COUNTY ~; INTERNATIONAL ~; OVERHEAD ~; TOLL- ~.

BRIDGE FINANCING. Financing arranged for a short period of time, for example when one has purchased or is building a new home and is waiting to sell an existing home.

BRIDGEMASTER. *n.* A person actually on duty in charge of a bridge. *Canal Regulations*, C.R.C., c. 1564, s. 2.

BRIDGE POLICE. Any National Harbours Board constable in charge of traffic on the bridge. Canada regulations.

BRIDGE TOLL. A charge on every vehicle, including the driver and passengers, entering upon or using a bridge.

BRIDGING BENEFIT. A periodical payment provided under a pension plan to a member of the pension plan for a temporary period of time after retirement for the purpose of supplementing the members pension benefit until the member is eligible to receive benefits under the Old Age Security Act or commences to receive retirement benefits under the Canada Pension Plan or the Quebec Pension Plan. *Pension Benefits acts*.

BRIEF. *v.* To brief a case means to summarize it and its salient points.

BRIEF. *n.* A file of all pleadings, documents and memoranda which serves as the basis for argument by the lawyer in the matter in court. See BRANDEIS ~; CHAMBERS ~; SOCIAL SCIENCE ~.

BRINE. *n.* An aqueous solution of mineral salts. See EXPLORATION LICENCE FOR ~; OIL FIELD ~.

BRINE CURING PLANT. See SALMON ~.

BRINE PACK. A pack in which a water and salt solution is used as the packing media.

BRINE WELL. A hole or opening in the ground for use in brining. *Mining Act*, R.S.O. 1990, c. M.4, s. 154(1).

BRING AN ACTION. The issuance of the writ to commence an action. Does not include serving the writ. *Kemp v. Metzner* 2000 CarswellBC 1616, 2000 BCCA 462, 78 B.C.L.R. (3d) 187, 190 D.L.R. (4th) 388.

BRINING. *n.* The extraction of salt in solution by any method. *Mining Act*, R.S.O. 1990, c. M.14, s. 154(1) .

BRISTLES. See RAW WOOL, HAIR OR ~.

BRITISH COLUMBIA. The Province of British Columbia other than (a) the art known as the Peace River District, and (b) except for the purpose of making payments related to the cost of feed grain transported into the Creston-Wynndel Areas, the part known as the Creston-Wynndel Areas. *Livestock Feed Assistance Act*, R.S.C. 1985, c. L-10, s. 2.

BRITISH COMMONWEALTH. Has the same meaning as Commonwealth. *Interpretation Act*, R.S.C. 1985, c. I-21, s. 35.

BRITISH COMMONWEALTH OF NATIONS. Has the same meaning as Commonwealth. *Interpretation Act*, R.S.C. 1985, c. I-21, s. 35.

BRITISH COMPANY. Any corporation incorporated under the laws of the United Kingdom or of any other Commonwealth country, or any political subdivision or dependent territory thereof other than Canada or a province, for the purpose of carrying on the business of insurance, and includes any association of persons formed in any such country, political subdivision or dependent territory on the plan known as Lloyd's, whereby each member of the association that participates in a policy becomes liable for a stated, limited or proportionate part of the whole amount payable under the policy. *Canadian and British Insurance Companies Act*, R.S.C. 1985, c. I-12, s. 2.

BRITISH NORTH AMERICA ACT, 1867. The Statute of the Parliament of the United Kingdom which formed the federation of Canada in 1867 from the four provinces, Lower Canada, Upper Canada, Nova Scotia and New Brunswick. Since the patriation of the constitution in 1982, it is known as the Constitution Act, 1982. Renamed the Constitution Act, 1867 in 1982, this Act gave effect to the confederation scheme by uniting the provinces of Canada, Nova Scotia and New Brunswick.

BRITISH POSSESSION. Any dominion of Her Majesty exclusive of the United Kingdom of Great Britain and Northern Ireland, and Canada. *Evidence acts*.

BRITISH THERMAL UNIT. The amount of heat required to raise the temperature of one pound of water by one degree Fahrenheit.

BROADCASTER. *n.* A body that, in the course of operating a broadcasting undertaking, broadcasts a communication signal in accordance with the law of the country in which the broadcasting undertaking is carried on, but excludes a body whose primary activity in relation to communication signals is their retransmission. *Copyright Act*, R.S.C. 1985, c. C-42, s. 2.

BROADCASTING. *n*. 1. Any radiocommunication in which the transmissions are intended for direct reception by the general public. 2. Any transmission of programmes, whether or not encrypted, by radio waves or other means of telecommunication for reception by the public by means of broadcasting receiving apparatus, but does not include any such transmission of programs that is made solely for performance or display in a public place. *Broadcasting Act*, S.C. 1991, c. 11, s. 2(1). 3. The dissemination of writing, signs, signals, pictures and sounds of all kinds, intended to be received by the public either directly or through the medium of relay stations, by means of (i) any form of wireless radioelectric communication utilizing Hertzian waves, including radiotelegraph and radiotelephone, or (ii) cables, wires, fibre-optic linkages or laser beams. See CANADIAN ~ CORPORATION; DIRECT TO HOME ~.

BROADCASTING ARBITRATOR. The person appointed Broadcasting Arbitrator by the Chief Electoral Officer pursuant to this Act. *Canada Sections Act*, R.S.C. 1985, c. E-2, s. 2.

BROADCASTING LICENCE. A licence to carry on a broadcasting undertaking issued under this Act. *Broadcasting Act*, R.S.C. 1985, c. B-9, s. 2.

BROADCASTING RECEIVING APPARATUS. A device, or combination of devices, intended for or capable of being used for the reception of broadcasting. *Broadcasting Act*, S.C. 1991, c. 22, s. 2(1).

BROADCASTING RECEIVING UNDERTAKING. " . . . [A] cable distribution system, at least one which receives signals from a broadcaster and sends them through the system, . . ." *Capital Cities Communications Inc. v. Canada (Canadian Radio-Television & Telecommunications Commission)* (1977), 36 C.P.R. (2d) 1 at 19, [1978] 2 S.C.R. 141, 81 D.L.R. (3d) 609, 18 N.R. 181, Laskin C.J. (Martland, Judson, Ritchie, Spence and Dickson JJ. concurring).

BROADCASTING UNDERTAKING. 1. Includes a distribution undertaking, a programming undertaking and a network. *Broadcasting Act*, S.C. 1991, c. 11, s. 2(1). 2. Includes a broadcasting transmitting undertaking, a broadcasting receiving undertaking and a network operation located in whole or in part within Canada or on a ship or aircraft registered in Canada. See FOREIGN ~.

BROADCAST WEEK. A period of seven consecutive days beginning on a Sunday. *Broadcasting Distribution Regulations*, SOR/97-555, s. 1.

BROADCAST YEAR. The period beginning on September 1 in a calendar year and ending on August 31 of the following calendar year. *Broadcasting Distribution Regulations*, SOR/97-555, s. 1.

BROCAGE. *n*. The commission which one pays to a broker.

BROKEN CONCESSION. A concession any boundary of which is broken in whole or in part by a lake or river. *Surveys Act*, R.S.O. 1990, c. S.30, s. 1.

BROKEN FRONTS. In Ontario surveys, the base line followed the inner ends of inlets and consequently an irregularly shaped area, known as broken fronts, frequently appeared in front of the line. B.J. Reiter, B.N. McLellan & P.M. Perell, *Real Estate Law*, 4th ed. (Toronto: Emond-Montgomery, 1992) at 535.

BROKEN LOT. An irregular lot or a regular lot whose area is diminished or increased by a natural or artificial feature shown on the original plan. *Surveys Act*, R.S.O. 1990, c. S.30, s. 1

BROKEN STOWAGE. In a ship, space which is not occupied by cargo.

BROKER. *n*. 1. One who negotiates or makes contracts for the sale of property. 2. A person who is engaged for full or part time in the business of buying and selling securities and who, in the transaction concerned, acts for, or buys a security from, or sells a security to a customer. 3. A person who, for another or others, for compensation, gain or reward or hope or promise thereof, either alone or through one or more officials or salespersons, trades in real estate, or a person who claims to be such a person. 4. A person who, for compensation, acts or aids in any manner in negotiating contracts of insurance or placing risks or effecting insurance, or in negotiating the continuance or renewal of insurance contracts for another person. *Insurance acts*. See CUSTOMS ~; INSURANCE MINERAL INTEREST ~; MINERAL LEASE ~; MONEY ~; SPECIAL ~; SUBMORTGAGE ~; TAXI-CAB ~; VESSEL ~.

BROKERAGE. *n*. The commission which one pays to a broker.

BROKERAGE FEE. The payment that a borrower makes or agrees to make to a loan broker who assists or attempts to assist the borrower in arranging a credit agreement, and includes an amount that the lender deducts from an advance and pays to the broker. *Consumer Protection Act, 2002*, S.O. 2002, c. 30, Sched. A, s. 66.

BROKER-DEALER. *var*. **BROKER DEALER**. Any person or company that is recognized as a broker-dealer that engaged either for full or part time in the business of trading in securities in the capacity of an agent or principal.

BROMOFLUOROCARBON. *n*. A fully halogenated bromofluorocarbon each molecule of which contains one, two or three carbon atoms and at least one atom each of bromine and fluorine. *Ozone-depleting Substances Regulations, 1998*, SOR/99-7, s. 1.

BROOD COMB. A structure of cells in which bees lay their eggs or in which immature bees are being reared or have been reared.

BROS. *abbr*. Brothers.

BROTHEL. *n*. " . . . [T]he same thing as a 'bawdy-house', . . . applies to a place resorted to by persons of both sexes for the purpose of prostitution . . ." *Singleton v. Win*, [1895] 1 Q.B. 607 at 608, Wills J.

BROTHER. *n*. 1. Includes half-brother. *Criminal Code*, R.S.C. 1985, c. C-46, s. 155(4). 2. Includes brother-in-law. See HALF ~.

BROUGHT. *v*. 1. (Said of an action or charge or proceeding) " . . . '[I]nitiate[d]' . . ." *R. v. Henderson*, [1929] 2 W.W.R. 209 at 214, [1929] 4 D.L.R. 984, 52 C.C.C. 82, 41 B.C.R. 242 (C.A.), Macdonald J.A. 2. " . . . '[C]ommenced' . . ." *Krueger v. Raccah* (1981), 24 C.P.C. 14 at 16, 12 Sask. R. 130, 128 D.L.R. (3d) 177 (Q.B.), Cameron J. See BRING AN ACTION.

BRUCELLOSIS. *n*. An infectious disease of cattle caused by the organism brucella abortus.

BRUISE. *n*. A hemorrhage into the tissue under the skin. F.A. Jaffe, A *Guide to Pathological Evidence*, 3d ed. (Toronto: Carswell, 1991) at 13.

BRUTUM FULMEN. [L. an empty noise] An empty threat.

B-S GAUGE. The Brown and Sharp wire gauge which applies to nonferrous conductors.

B.T.U. *abbr*. British Thermal Unit.

BUCKET SHOP. " ... [A] place where bets are made against the rise or fall of stocks or commodities, and where the pretended transactions of purchase or sale are fictitious . . ." *Richardson v. Beamish* (1913), 21 C.C.C. 487 at 503, 4 W.W.R. 815, 13 D.L.R. 400, 23 Man. R. 306 (C.A.), Perdue J.A.

BUCKING. *n*. The act of sawing a log or a tree that has been felled into smaller pieces.

BUCKLE. *n*. A quick release connector that secures a person in a seat belt assembly. *Motor Vehicle Safety Regulations*, C.R.C., c. 1038, s. 209.

BUCK SHOT. Shotgun pellets. F.A. Jaffe, A *Guide to Pathological Evidence*, 3d ed. (Toronto: Carswell, 1991) at 214.

BUDGET. *n*. A statement of the amounts of estimated revenues and expenditures. See CASH ~.

BUDGETARY REQUIREMENTS. The basic requirements of a person and his dependants, if any, and any other of the items and services described in paragraphs (b) to (h) of the definition assistance in section 2 of the Act that, in the opinion of the provincial authority, are essential to the health or well-being of that person and his dependants, if any. *Canada Assistance Plan Regulations*, C.R.C., c. 382, s. 2.

BUGGERY. *n*. Sodomy, anal intercourse.

BUILD. See RE~.

BUILDER. *n*. A person who builds houses for sale or for rent. See OWNER-~.

BUILDER AND CONTRACTOR. A person, company or corporation contracting with, or employed directly by, the proprietor for the doing of work or the placing or furnishing of machinery or materials on, in, or about, any building or erection, or in connection with any building or erection.

BUILDER'S CERTIFICATE. A certificate which the builder of a ship signs which contains (a) an accurate account of the tonnage and denomination of the ship, as the builder estimates, (b) the place where and the time when it was built (c) the name of any people on whose account the ship was built, and (d) if there was any sale of the ship or a share of it, the bill of sale under which the ship was vested in the applicant for registry. R.M. Fernandes & C. Burke., *The*

Annotated Canada Shipping Act (Toronto: Butterworths, 1988) at 42.

BUILDERS' LIEN. Provides a security or charge against real property to secure a claim for goods, services and work carried out on the property by a contractor.

BUILDER'S MORTGAGE. A mortgage of a recorded vessel. *Canada Shipping Act*, R.S.C. 1985, c. S-9, s. 2.

BUILDING. *n*. 1. A structure consisting of foundations, walls or roof, with or without other parts. 2. A structure that is used or intended to be used for the purpose of supporting or sheltering persons or animals or storing property. 3. Includes a structure, erection, well, pipe line, mine or work built, erected or constructed on or in land. 4. Includes a trailer, mobile home or portable shack. 5. A structure, erection, excavation, alteration or improvement placed on, over or under land, or attached, anchored or moored to land, and includes mobile structures, vehicles and marine vessels adapted or constructed for residential, commercial, industrial and other similar uses, and part of a building as so defined and fixtures that form part of a building. *Urban and Rural Planning Act*, R.S. Nfld. 1990, c. U-7, s. 2. 6. (i) A public building, (ii) an apartment-type building, (iii) a hotel, and (iv) a building link. *Buildings Accessibility Act*, R.S. Nfld. 1990 c. B-10 s. 2. 7. Includes any structure or enclosure occupied by employees. Canada regulations. 8. In respect of a ship, includes the conversion of a ship. *Shipbuilding Industry Assistance Regulations*, C.R.C., c. 348 s. 2. See ACCESSORY ~; APARTMENT ~; APARTMENT-TYPE ~; ASSEMBLY ~; BUILDINGS; CHURCH ~; DILAPIDATED ~; FARM ~; INSTITUTIONAL ~; MERCANTILE ~; MULTI-UNIT RESIDENTIAL ~; NONCOMBUSTIBLE ~; NON-CONFORMING ~; OFFICE ~; POST-DISASTER ~; PRECINCTS OF THE ~; PUBLIC ~; RESIDENTIAL ~; ROAD ; SUBORDINATE ~.

BUILDING AREA. The greatest horizontal area of a building within the outside surface of exterior walls or, where a firewall is to be constructed, within the outside surface of exterior walls and the centre line of firewalls.

BUILDING CODE. Detailed specifications for the design and construction of buildings which ensure structural safety, fire safety and the occupants' health. See NATIONAL ~ OF CANADA.

BUILDING CONSTRUCTION CODE. A code of building construction standards.

BUILDING CONSTRUCTION STANDARD. A standard for (a) construction materials, or plumbing or electrical materials or installations, or equipment or appliances, or any combination thereof, to be used or installed in any building or part of a building, or (b) the method to be used in the construction or demolition of any building or part of a building.

BUILDING CONTRACT. A contract to build anything.

BUILDING CONTROL VALVE. The valve on a water system that controls the flow of potable water from the water service pipe to the water distribution system.

BUILDING DRAIN. Sanitary building drain or storm building drain.

BUILDING FACING. See EXPOSING ~.

BUILDING HEIGHT. The number of storeys contained between the roof and the floor of the first storey.

BUILDING INSPECTOR. An inspector appointed by a municipality to administer and enforce the building code.

BUILDING LEASE. 1. A lease of a vacant piece of land on which the lessee covenants to erect a building or to pull down an old building and erect a new one on the site. 2. The lease of land for a rent called ground rent.

BUILDING LINE. The line to which the front of all buildings shall be set back from the road improvement line or road line.

BUILDING LINK. A structure which connects a building to another building.

BUILDING MATERIALS. Includes goods that become so incorporated or built into a building, that their removal therefrom would necessarily involve the removal or destruction of some other part of the building and thereby cause substantial damage to the building apart from the value of the goods removed; but does not include goods that are severable from the land merely by unscrewing, unbolting, unclamping, uncoupling, or by some other method of disconnection; and does not include machinery installed in a building for use in the carrying on of an industry, where the only substantial damage, apart from the value of the machinery removed, that would necessarily be caused to the building in removing the machinery therefrom, is that arising from the removal or destruction of the bed or casing on or in which the machinery is set and the main or enlargement of an opening in the walls of the building sufficient for the removal of the machinery. *Conditional Sales acts.*

BUILDING PERMIT. A permit, issued under a building bylaw of a municipality, authorizing the construction of all or part of any structure.

BUILDING PROJECT. A project composed of one or more of the following elements: (i) the purchase or other acquisition of all or any part of an existing building or buildings including the land contiguous thereto, (ii) any renovations or alterations to an existing building or buildings, (iii) additions to an existing building or buildings, (iv) the purchase or other acquisition of vacant land for the purpose of constructing a building or buildings thereon, (v) the erection of a new building, or any part thereof, (vi) the demolition of a building, and (vii) the installation of public utilities, sewers and items or services necessary for access to the land or building or buildings.

BUILDINGS. *n*. Any structure that is assessable as part of assessable property but does not include the earth or soil upon which it rests. Manitoba statutes. See BUILDING; FACTORY BUILT ~; FARM ~; PARLIAMENT ~.

BUILDING SCHEME. 1. " . . . [U]sed to define a scheme whereby the owner of a large block of land has endeavoured to protect those who acquire parts of it from himself as the common vendor, and sometimes to protect himself as well as to lands he wishes to retain, by imposing restrictions as to the use of the land or the character or location or number of the buildings to be erected thereon . . ." *Rowan v. Eaton* (1926), 59 O.L.R. 379 at 382, [1926] 4 D.L.R. 582 (H.C.), Orde J.A. 2. A scheme of development which comes into existence where defined land is laid out in parcels and intended to be sold to different purchasers or leased or subleased to different lessees, each of whom enters into a restrictive covenant with the common vendor or lessor agreeing that his particular parcel shall be subject to certain restrictions as to use; the restrictive covenants constituting a special local law applicable to the defined land and the benefit and burden of the covenants passing to, as the case may be, the purchaser, lessee or sublessee of the parcel and his parcel and his successors in title. *Land Title Act*, R.S.B.C. 1979, c. 219, s. 1.

BUILDING SEWER. Sanitary building sewer or storm building sewer.

BUILDING SITE. The location on which construction of a structure is about to commence or is in progress, and may be all or part of a subdivided parcel of land.

BUILDING TRADES COUNCIL. Association of craft unions in the construction and building industry.

BUILDING TRAP. A trap that is installed in a sanitary building drain or sanitary building sewer to prevent circulation of air between a sanitary drainage system and a public sewer.

BUILDING UNIT. See MODULAR ~.

BUILDING USED FOR SLEEPING ACCOMMODATIONS. Includes, (a) a hotel, (b) a building in which lodgings are let, (c) a building in which an educational institution lodges its students, (d) a hospital, sanatorium or infirmary, (e) a convent, and (f) a building in which inmates of an orphanage, children's home, home for aged persons or almshouse are lodged.

BUILT-UP AREA. An area of land where (i) not less than 50 per cent of the frontage upon one side of a road for a distance of not less than 200 metres is occupied by dwellings, buildings used for business purposes, schools or churches, or (ii) not less than 50 per cent of the frontage upon both sides of a road for a distance of not less than 100 metres is occupied by dwellings, buildings used for business purposes, schools or churches, or (iii) not more than 200 metres of a road separates any land described in subparagragh (i) or (ii) from any other land described in subparagraph (i) or (ii), or (iv) a plan of subdivision has been registered.

BULK. See FUEL IN ~; GASOLINE IN ~; GOODS IN ~; IN ~; PROPANE IN ~; STOCK IN ~.

BULK CARGO. Such goods as are loose or in mass and generally must be shovelled, pumped, blown, scooped or forked in the handling.

BULK GASOLINE. Gasoline stored in tanks or other containers that are not part of the regular fuel storage system of a motor vehicle, engine, machine or equipment.

BULK GOODS. Carloads of coal, coal products, wood, sand, gravel, brick, scrap metal, and of such other goods as may be approved by the Commission. *Railway Act*, R.S.C. 1985, c. R-3, s. 311(3).

BULKHEAD. *n.* A structure built for impounding water or confining air under pressure in a crosscut, drift or other mine opening and constructed in a manner to close off completely the crosscut, drift or other mine opening.

BULKHEAD DECK. The uppermost deck up to which transverse watertight bulkheads are carried. *Hull Construction Regulations*, C.R.C., c. 1431, s. 2.

BULK MILK COOLER. A stationary farm storage tank maintained in a milkhouse and used for cooling and storing milk for sale.

BULK MILK TRANSFER STATION. Any location where bulk milk or cream is transferred from one tank-truck to another.

BULK PLANT. One or more storage tanks, including the appurtenances thereof, where gasoline or an associated product is received by pipe line, tank vessel, tank car or tank vehicle and is stored in bulk for subsequent transmission by pipe line or transportation or distribution by tank vessel, tank car or tank vehicle. See PROPANE ~.

BULK SALE. The sale of all or a large portion of the stock in trade of a business when that sale takes place other than in the normal course of business. See SALE IN BULK.

BULK SALES ACT. A provincial statute which is intended to protect the creditors of a business when a business enters into a bulk sale. See BULK SALE; SALE IN BULK.

BULK STORAGE CONTAINER. A bin; a hopper; a silo.

BULK STORAGE TANK. Includes any static storage tank in which gasoline or an associated product is contained, but does not include a supply tank that is connected to the heating appliance that it serves.

BULK TANK. See FARM ~.

BULK TRANSPORT FACILITIES. Includes any property, real or personal, designed or suited, or capable of being used, for the transportation of goods in bulk either by means of ships or by a company to which the Railway Act applies including facilities for loading, unloading and storing goods in bulk and any facilities owned or controlled by or in possession of any person operating transport facilities.

BULL. *n.* One who buys shares expecting prices on the stock exchange to rise. See SCRUB ~.

BULL. ACBD. *abbr.* Bulletin ACBD (CALL Newsletter).

BULL. AVOCATS. *abbr.* Le Bulletin des avocats (Solicitor's Journal).

BULL. CCDJ. *abbr.* Bulletin d'information juridique du CCDJ (CLIC's Legal Materials Letter).

BULLET. *n.* A projectile which a rifled weapon fires. F.A. Jaffe, *A Guide to Pathological Evidence*, 3d ed. (Toronto: Carswell, 1991) at 214. See TANDEM ~.

BULLET EMBOLISM. An embolism caused by a bullet or bullet fragments. F.A. Jaffe, *A Guide to Pathological Evidence*, 3d ed. (Toronto: Carswell, 1991) at 218.

BULLETIN. See INFORMATION ~. *Tax Act*, R.R.O. 1980, Reg. 639, s. 1.

BULLION. *n.* 1. Uncoined silver and gold. 2. A precious metal alloy product of processing in the form of bars, plates, lumps or other masses and includes crude bullion and refined bullion. *Mining Tax Act*, R.R.O. 1980, Reg. 639, s. 1.

BULL MARKET. Name for a market which is going up in value.

"BULLOCK" ORDER. 1. Named after the case of Bullock *v.* London General Omnibus Co., [1907] 1 K.B. 264 (C.A.). " . . . [O]rder under which the plaintiff paid the costs of the successful defendant and recovered them together with his own from the unsuccessful defendant . . ." *Rowe v. Investors Syndicate Ltd.* (1984), 46 C.P.C. 209 at 215 (Ont. H.C.), Henry J. 2. A Bullock order directs an unsuccessful defendant to reimburse the plaintiff for the recovered costs of a successful defendant. A Sanderson order directs that the payment go directly to the successful defendant. The rational behind both orders is the same. Where the allocation of responsibility is uncertain, usually because of interwoven facts, it is often reasonable to proceed through trial against more than one defendant. In these cases, a Bullock or Sanderson order provides a plaintiff with an appropriate form of relief. *Rooney (Litigation Guardian of) v. Graham* (2001) 53 O.R. (3d) 685 (C.A.).

BULL SPREAD. In the commodities market buying one contract and selling another in anticipation of a profit on the difference in prices at two different points in time. In a bull spread, the client is long in the nearby month and short in the later month.

BUMPER. *n.* A device designed to be affixed to the front and rear of a motor vehicle of the passenger car type and capable of preventing or minimizing the damage to other parts of the motor vehicle.

BUMPER FRACTURE. A below-the-knee leg fracture caused by the bumper of a motor vehicle. F.A. Jaffe, *A Guide to Pathological Evidence*, 2d ed. (Toronto: Carswell, 1983) at 176 and 177.

BUMPING. *n.* As a result of a layoff, an employee with more seniority can displace, bump, an employee with less seniority. Various rules concerning bumping may appear in the collective bargaining agreement governing the jobs in question. See CLOCK ~.

BUMP UP. To receive a promotion, in effect, as a result of the bumping process.

BUNCHING. *n.* When gains which have accrued over several years are, for tax purposes, realized and recognized in a single year. W. Grover & F. Iacobucci *Materials on Canadian Income Tax*, 4th ed. (Toronto: Richard De Boo Ltd., 1980) at 157.

BUNKER FUEL. A residual fuel oil which when used for heating requires or would ordinarily require preheating. See MARINE ~.

BUNKING. See DOUBLE ~.

BUOY. *n.* 1. A navigation marker. 2. Any type of buoy or float anchored in position either permanently or temporarily and maintained as a signal or aid to navigation. See FAIRWAY ~; GOVERNMENT ~; PORT HAND ~; PRIVATE ~; STARBOARD HAND ~.

BUOYAGE. *n.* A charge on a vessel for the use of a buoy, dolphin or similar facility.

BURDEN. *n.* The duty to perform an obligation. See EVIDENTIAL ~; EVIDENTIARY ~; LEGAL ~ OF PROOF; MAJOR ~; PERSUASIVE ~; PRIMARY ~.

BURDEN OF PERSUASION. The burden of convincing the court of the existence or non-existence, or probable existence or non-existence, of any fact. *Military Rules of Evidence*, C.R.C., c. 1049, s. 2.

BURDEN OF PROOF. " . . . [M]ay be applied to cases like this in two distinct senses: . . . The first is in the sense of establishing a case. This is a matter of substantive law, . . . The other sense

in which the term may be applied is that of introducing evidence. This is a matter of procedure, . . ." *R. v. Primak* (1930), 24 Sask. L.R. 417 at 419, [1930] 1 W.W.R. 755, [1930] 3 D.L.R. 345, 53 C.C.C. 203 (C.A.), the court per Mackenzie J.A.

BUREAU. *n.* 1. An office. 2. A name applied to certain public bodies. See BETTER BUSINESS ~; CREDIT ~; RATING ~.

BUREAUCRACY. *n.* An organization with a hierarchical structure, inflexible rules and procedures.

BURGESS. *n.* 1. A person who is entitled to vote as a burgess in a municipality. *The Major Urban Centres Integrated Hospitals Act*, R.S.S. 1978, c. M-2, s. 2. 2. A person who: (i) is at least eighteen years of age; and (ii) is a Canadian citizen or other British subject; and (A) is the registered owner of taxable real property in the municipality; provided that where property is owned under bona fide agreement for sale burgess shall mean the purchaser; or (B) is assessed as an occupant in the municipality; or (C) is assessed for a business in the municipality; or (D) is a shareholder of a duly incorporated co-operative association located in the municipality and established to provide housing for its members residing therein; or (E) where such person is not in his own right qualified under paragraph (A), (B), (C) or (D), he is the spouse of a person mentioned in paragraph (A), (B), (C) or (D) and resides with that person in the municipality; except where the municipality is a summer resort village, in which case the spouse resides with that person in the province. *The Urban Municipal Elections Act*, R.S.S. 1978, c. U-9, s. 2. See RESIDENT ~.

BURGLAR ALARM AGENCY. The business of selling, providing, installing or servicing burglar alarm systems or of monitoring a signal from premises protected by a burglar alarm system or of providing the services of a burglar alarm agent. *Private Investigators and Security Guards acts*.

BURGLAR ALARM SYSTEM. A system consisting of a device or devices to provide warnings against intrusion including burglary, robbery, theft or vandalism. *Private Investigators and Security Guards acts*.

BURGLARY. *n.* The common law offence of breaking and entering a dwelling-house at night with intent to commit a crime there.

BURGLARY INSURANCE. Insurance against loss or damage by burglary, housebreaking, robbery or theft.

BURIAL. *n.* The burial of human remains and includes the permanent placement of human remains in a building or structure.

BURIAL PERMIT. A permit to bury, cremate, remove or otherwise dispose of a dead body. *Vital Statistics acts.*

BURIAL SITE. Land containing human remains.

BURIED FACILITIES. Telecommunication facilities buried below ground surface and which are not encased in cement, wood or some other enclosure.

BURIED VALLEY. A valley containing coarse-grained fluvial or glacial fluvial deposits covered by glacial fill. *Activities Designation Regulation* Alta. Reg. 276/2003, s. 2.

BURKING. *n.* An assailant sits on the victim's chest causing traumatic asphyxia. F.A. Jaffe, *A Guide to Pathological Evidence*, 3d ed. (Toronto: Carswell, 1991) at 214.

BURKISM. *n.* The practice of killing persons for the purpose of selling their bodies for dissection.

BURN. *n.* An injury effected by dry heat. F.A. Jaffe, *A Guide to Pathological Evidence*, 3d ed. (Toronto: Carswell, 1991) at 214.

BURSAR. *n.* 1. The business administrator of a School. 2. A college treasurer.

BURSARY. *n.* 1. A sum of money granted without having special regard to the quality of the academic work of the person to whom it is granted.

BUS. *n.* 1. Any vehicle adapted to carry more than six to twelve adult passengers in addition to the driver. 2. A conductor which serves as a common connection for the corresponding conductors of two or more circuits. *Power Corporation Act*, R.R.O. 1980, Reg. 794, s. 0. See AUTO~; EXTRA-PROVINCIAL ~ TRANSPORTATION PUBLIC MOTOR ~; SCHOOL ~; TROLLEY~.

BUS. & L. *abbr.* Business & the Law.

BUSHEL. *n.* 1. 8 gallons. *Weights and Measures Act*, S.C. 1970-71-72, c. 36, Schedule II. 2. 56 pounds of shelled corn or seed corn the kernal moisture content of which does not exceed 15.5 per cent. *Crop Insurance Act (Ontario)*, R.R.O. 1980, Reg. 205, s. 3. 3. In this Act, unless a bushel by measure is expressly referred to, and in any contract respecting grain, unless the parties otherwise expressly agree, the word "bushel", when used with respect to oats, means a quantity weighing 34 pounds, when used with respect to barley or buckwheat, means a quantity weighing 48 pounds, when used with respect to Indian corn, flaxseed or rye, means a quantity weighing 56 pounds, or when used with respect to peas or wheat, means a quantity weighing 60 pounds. *Canada Grain Act*, R.S.C. 1970, c. G-16, s. 165.

BUSINESS. *n.* 1. Includes a profession, calling, trade, manufacture or undertaking of any kind whatsoever and includes an adventure or concern in the nature of trade but does not include an office or employment. 2. An undertaking carried on for the purpose of gain or profit, and includes an interest in any such undertaking. *Real Estate and Business Brokers acts.* 3. Those lawful objects and purposes for which a company is established. 4. The land and buildings used for a commercial enterprise. 5. A line must be drawn under the *Act* [i.e. the *Income Tax Act*, R.S.C. 1985, c. 1 (5th Supp.)] between a mere investment in property and an activity or activities that constitute a business. The expansive definition of the term "business" in section 248 is not exhaustive. It extends to any endeavour that occupies time, labour and attention with a view to profit. To the extent that income is derived from human activity rather than from the passive ownership of property, its source can be properly described as business. *Dansereau v. R.* 2001 CarswellNat 2275, 2001 FCA 305, 2001 D.T.C. 5642, Noel, J.A. for the court. 6. An individual who, for the purpose of gain or profit, is carrying on a commercial or industrial undertaking of any kind or providing professional, personal or other services, and a corporation, whether or not operating for the purpose of gain or profit. See AMBULATORY ~; ARTIFICIAL INSEMINATION ~; BANKING ~; CANADIAN ~; CARRYING ON ~; CARRY ON ~; COMMON FORM ~; CONTENTIOUS ~; COURSE OF ~; DEPOSIT ~; DEPOSIT TAKING ~; DOING ~; EMBRYO TRANSFER ~; ENGAGING IN ~; FAMILY ~; CORPORATION; FEDERAL ~ DEVELOPMENT BANK; FEDERAL WORK, UNDERTAKING OR ~; INCOME FROM A ~ (OR PROPERTY); INSEMINATING ~; INSURANCE ~; MANUFACTURING ~;

NON-CONTENTIOUS ~; OPERATING ~; PRINCIPAL PLACE OF ~; RESIDENT ~; RETAIL ~; SECURITY ~; TRUST ~.

BUSINESS ACTIVITY. Includes any profession, activity or enterprise which may lawfully be carried on.

BUSINESS AGENT. Executive officer of a local union who administers the union's affairs.

BUSINESS ASSET. 1. " . . . [A]ssets which have as their purpose the generation of income in an entrepreneurial sense . . ." *Clarke v. Clarke* (1990), 28 R.F.L. (3d) 113 at 134, 73 D.L.R. (4th) 1, 113 N.R. 321, [1990] 2 S.C.R. 795, the court per Wilson J. 2. Property owned by one spouse and used principally in the course of a business carried on by that spouse, either alone or jointly with others, and includes shares that the spouse owns in a corporation through which he or she carries on a business.

BUSINESS ASSETS. Real or personal property primarily used or held for or in connection with a commercial, business, investment or other income-producing or profit-producing purpose.

BUSINESS COMBINATION. An acquisition of all or substantially all of the property of one body corporate by another or an amalgamation of two or more bodies corporate.

BUSINESS CONTACT INFORMATION. An individual's name, position name or title, business telephone number, business address, business e-mail, business fax number and other similar business information; *Personal Information Protection Act 2003*, S.A. 2003, c. P-6.5, s. 1.

BUSINESS DAY. 1. A day other than Saturday or a holiday. 2. In respect of any investments of a company listed or dealt in on a stock exchange, a day on which the principal stock exchange is open for trading in stocks and securities.

BUSINESS DISTRICT. The territory contiguous to a portion of a highway along which there are buildings used for business, industrial or public purposes.

BUSINESS ENTERPRISE. An industry, trade, service or tourist business or commercial business undertaking.

BUSINESS IDENTIFICATION NUMBER. A 9-digit number used by the Ontario government to identify provincial business accounts. It also appears on the Ontario Master Business Licence.

BUSINESS IMPROVEMENT AREA. A commercial area of a municipality which, in the opinion of a council and in the interest of that council requires improvement, beautification or maintenance and which has been designated as such.

BUSINESS IMPROVEMENT LOAN. A loan made by a lender to a proprietor of a small business enterprise for the purpose of financing (a) the purchase installation renovation, improvement or modernization of equipment of a kind usually affixed to real property, (b) the purchase, renovation, improvement or modernization of equipment of a kind not usually affixed to real property, (c) the renovation, improvement or modernization of premises or the purchase, construction, alteration or extension of premises, or (d) the purchase of land necessary for the operation of a business enterprise. *Small Business Loans Act*, R.S.C. 1985, c. S-11 s. 2.

BUSINESS JUDGMENT RULE. In assessing whether directors have met their fiduciary and statutory obligations, this rule shields from court intervention decisions which have been made honestly, prudently, in good faith and on reasonable ground.. *CW Shareholders v. WIC Western International* (1998), 160 D.L.R. (4th) 131 (Ont. Gen. Div.).

BUSINESS NAME. The name under which a business is carried on or is to be carried on and includes a firm name.

BUSINESS NUMBER. 1. The number (other than a Social Insurance Number) used by the Minister to identify a corporation or partnership, or any other association or taxpayer that carries on a business or is required by the Income Tax Act to deduct or withhold an amount from an amount paid or credited or deemed to be paid or credited under the Act and of which the Minister has notified the corporation, partnership, association or taxpayer. *Income Tax Act*, R.S.C. 1985, c. 1 (5th Supp.), s. 248. A 9-digit federal client identification number to which businesses can register program accounts. 2. A number used by provincial officials to identify a business entity for purposes of the province.

BUSINESS OCCUPANCY. Occupancy for the transaction of business.

BUSINESS OCCUPANCY TAX. A tax levied on occupants in respect of their use or occupation of real property or immovables for the purpose of or in connection with a business. *Payments in Lieu of Taxes Act, 2000*, S.C. 2000, c. 8, s. 3.

BUSINESS OF INSURANCE. The making of any contract of insurance, and includes any act or acts of inducement to enter into a contract of insurance, and any act or acts relating to the performance thereof or the rendering of any service in connection therewith.

BUSINESS OF INVESTMENT. With respect to a corporation, means the borrowing of money by the corporation on the security of its bonds, debentures, notes or other evidences of indebtedness and the use of some or all of the proceeds of such borrowing for (a) the making of loans, whether secured or unsecured, (b) the purchase of (i) bonds, debentures, notes or other evidences of indebtedness of individuals or corporations, (ii) shares of corporations, (iii) bonds, debentures, notes or other evidences of indebtedness of or guaranteed by a government or a municipality, or (iv) conditional sales contracts, accounts receivable, bills of sale, chattel mortgages, bills of exchange or other obligations representing part or all of the sale price of merchandise or services, (c) the purchase or improvement of real property other than real property reasonably required for occupation or anticipated occupation by the corporation, or any corporation referred to in subsection (4), in the transaction of its business, or (d) the replacement or retiring of earlier borrowings some or all of the proceeds of which have been used for the purposes set out in a paragraphs (a) to (c). *Investment Companies Act*, R.S.C. 1985, c. I-22, s. 2.

BUSINESS OF SUPPLY. Considering estimates for interim supply, passing all stages of any bill based on them, and considering opposition motions. A. Fraser, W.A. Dawson, J. Holtby, eds., *Beauchesne's Rules and Forms of the House of Commons of Canada*, 6th ed. (Toronto: Carswell, 1989) at 255.

BUSINESS ORGANIZATION. A corporation, a partnership or a sole proprietorship.

BUSINESS OR TRADE ASSOCIATION. An organization of persons that by an enactment, agreement or custom has power to admit, suspend, expel or direct persons in relation to any business or trade. *Human Rights codes*.

BUSINESS PREMISES. 1. A site where a person carries on business. 2. Does not include a dwelling.

BUSINESS PROPERTY. Real property used for or occupied by any industry, trade, business, profession or vocation.

BUSINESS PURPOSES. See COMMERCIAL OR ~.

BUSINESS RECORDS. 1. A category of records for purposes of the evidence acts and questions of admissibility. They are defined in the following terms. 2. " . . . [T]hree prerequisites to their reception as admissible evidence of what they record—(1) if they are made in the usual and ordinary course of such business; (2) if it was in the usual and ordinary course of such business to make such a writing or record; (3) the record or writing was made at the time of the act, transaction occurrence or event or a reasonable time thereafter." *Tobias v. Nolan* (1985), 71 N.S.R. (2d) 92 at 102, 171 A.P.R. 92 (T.D.), MacIntosh J.

BUSINESS TAX. " . . . [O]ne imposed upon, and proportioned to, either the volume of business done in or the volume of profits derived from, some business—though the latter would perhaps be rather in the nature of an income tax . . ." *Dominion- Express Co. v. Brandon (City)* (1910), 20 Man. R. 304 at 306, 17 W.L.R. 71 (C.A.), Richards J.A.

BUSINESS TRANSACTED IN THE PROVINCE. (a) In the case of property insurance, all contracts on which premiums are receivable from, or in respect of, persons whose property was situated in the province at the time their premiums became payable; and (b) in the case of other insurance, all contracts on which premiums are receivable from, or in respect of persons who were resident in the province at the time their premiums became payable.

BUS. Q. *abbr*. Business Quarterly.

BUS SERVICE. A service for the transportation of passengers by bus for reward between points. See CHARTERED ~.

BUS TRAILER. A vehicle having a designated seating capacity of more than 10 and designed primarily to be drawn behind another vehicle. *Motor Vehicle Safety Regulations*, C.R.C., c.103 8, s. 2 .

BUSWAY. *n*. A raceway consisting of a system of metal troughing, including its elbows, tees, crosses and straight runs, containing conductors supported on insulators.

BUTCHER. *n*. A person who is engaged in the business of dealing in and selling to the public by retail the flesh of meat animals.

BUT FOR TEST. Causation in negligence is established when the plaintiff proves on a balance of probabilities, that the defendant caused or contributed to the injury. The generally applicable test is the "but for" test. This test "requires the plaintiff to show that the injury would not have occurred but for the negligence of the defendant" ([*Athey v. Leonati*, [1996] 3 S.C.R. 458], at para.14). *Cottrelle v. Gerrard* (2003), 178 O.A.C. 142.

BUTTER. *n.* The food prepared by gathering the milk-fat of milk or cream into a mass. See DAIRY ~; PROCESS ~; WHEY ~.

BUTTERFAT DIFFERENTIAL. The value in cents of each 1/10th of a kilogram of butterfat above or below 3.6 kilograms per hectolitre of milk. *Milk Prices Review Act*, R.S.M. 1987, c. M130, s. 1.

BUTTERFLY. *n.* 1. Used to describe a corporate reorganization under which the assets are distributed to some or all of the shareholders in proportion to their respective shareholdings without triggering at that time such things as the realization in taxation of any approved gain and recapture of capital cost allowance for income tax purposes in those assets. *Public Trustee v. Brown* (1993), 2 E.T.R. (2d) 181 (B.C.C.A.). 2. " . . . [A] distribution of assets of a corporation in a proportional manner to shareholders of the corporation without tax being payable." *Canadian Pacific Ltd., Re* (1990), 47 B.L.R. 1 at 24, 72 O.R. (2d) 545, 68 D.L.R. (4th) 9 (H.C.), Austin J.

BUTTERMILK. *n.* Grade A milk from which a portion of the milk-fat is removed and that (i) is prepared by adding a bacterial culture to milk, partly-skimmed milk or skim-milk, (ii) exhibits a developed acidity in excess of that found in the milk product to which the bacterial culture has been added, and (iii) may contain added salt and stabilizers.

BUTTERMILK POWDER. Dried buttermilk that contains not more than 5 per cent by weight of water and no fat or oil other than milk fat.

BUY. *v.* To purchase; to acquire by payment of money or equivalent.

BUY AND BUST. An undercover police operation in which police try to buy illicit drugs from individuals who appear to be inclined to sell drugs. If the officer if successful, the individuals are arrested.

BUY-DOWN. See INTEREST ~.

BUYER. *n.* 1. A purchaser. 2. A person who buys or agrees to buy goods. 3. A person who buys or hires goods by a conditional sale. 4. A person who acquires stock in bulk. *Bulk Sales acts.* 5. A person who purchases goods or services on credit and includes that person's agent. 6. An individual who leases or purchases goods or services under an executory contract, and includes his agent. *Consumer Protection acts.* 7. Someone who has bought something. 8. A hirer on a retail hire-purchase. *Consumer Protection Act*, R.S.M. 1987, c. C200, s. 1. See FUR ~; GRAIN ~, HOME ~; PROSPECTIVE ~; SECOND ~.

BUY IN. For the original owner or person with interest in a property to purchase it at a mortgage, tax or other forced sale.

BUY ON MARGIN. To purchase securities partly on credit extended by a broker.

BY. *adv.* At the side of, near, close.

BY. *prep.* As a result of; because of; through the agency of; no later than.

BY. *prefix.* Subordinate; secondary; incidental.

BY-ELECTION. *n.* 1. An election other than a general election. Usually required to fill a vacancy in an elected position. 2. An election held in a constituency on a date on which there is no general election. 3. An election held to fill a vacancy in the office of mayor, councillor or trustee at a time other than a general election.

BY-LAW. *var.* **BYLAW**. *n.* 1. " . . . [N]ot an agreement, but a law binding on all persons to whom it applies, whether they agree to be bound by it or not. All regulations made by a corporate body, and intended to bind not only themselves and their officers and servants, but members of the public who come within the sphere of their operation, may be properly called 'by-laws'." *London Association of Shipowners and Brokers v. London and Index Docks Joint Committee* (1892), 3 Ch. 242 at 252, Lindley L.J. 2. A law which a municipality makes. 3. " . . . [A] local law, . . ." *White v. Morely* (1899), 2 Q.B. 34 at 39, Channell J. 4. Includes a resolution on which the opinion of the electors is to be obtained. Includes an order or resolution. 5. When used in relation to a cemetery, means the rules under which a cemetery or crematorium is operated. See LOCAL OPTION ~; MONEY ~; ORDINARY ~; PROPOSED ~; REFERRED ~; SPECIAL ~; ZONING ~.

BY-PRODUCT. See ANIMAL ~; MEAT ~.

C. *abbr*. 1. Court. 2. Chapter. 3. Chancellor. 4. Centi. 5. Coulomb.

C.A. *abbr*. 1. Court of Appeal. 2. Cour d'appel. 3. Recueils de jurisprudence de la Cour d'appel de Québec (Quebec Court of Appeals Reports).

[] C.A. *abbr*. Recueils de jurisprudence du Québec, Cour d'appel, 1970-.

CAB. " . . . [A] vehicle of a sedan type for hire for the transportation of passengers from place to place and ordinarily having a seating capacity for one to five or six passengers . . ." *Emslie v. R.* (1959), 22 D.L.R. (2d) 650 at 653, [1959] O.W.N. 279, 124 C.C.C. 253 (C.A.), Laidlaw J.A. (Aylesworth J.A. concurring). See TAXI ~.

CABAL. *n*. 1. A small association formed for the purpose of intrigue. 2. An intrigue.

CABARET. *n*. A room in which musical entertainment occurs in association with a restaurant.

CAB CARD. See CAVR ~.

CABIN. *n*. A one-room structure equipped for sleeping. *Tourism Act*, R.R.O. 1980, Reg. 936, s. 1.

CABIN ATTENDANT. A crew member, other than a flight crew member, assigned to duty in a passenger-carrying aeroplane or rotorcraft during flight time. Canada regulations.

CABIN ESTABLISHMENT. A tourist establishment comprised of cabins arranged singly or in pairs.

CABINET. *n*. 1. A body composed of the Prime Minister or Premier and Ministers of the Crown or a committee of Privy Council (federal) or Executive Council (provincial) which determines the direction of and makes policy decisions for the government. It is usually composed of members of the Prime Minister's or Premier's political party who have been elected as members of the House of Commons or the Legislature and is often referred to as "the government". 2. Enclosure hung on a wall or a self-supporting enclosure.

CABINET DOCUMENTS. 1. Minutes, records of Cabinet and committee meetings and recommendations made by Ministers and policy advisors to Cabinet to assist in deliberations. 2. " . . . [A] term which encompasses generally not only documents comprising minutes and other records of what is reported to have transpired at Cabinet or Cabinet committee meetings, but also documents which are prepared by ministers or their policy advisers and which set out policy options, advice or recommendations for the assistance of Cabinet and its committees in formulating policies and reaching decisions . . . also includes copies of documents used in Cabinet which are kept in the custody of the Secretary of the Cabinet because, although the texts of the documents may be public, the copies have been annotated or have had comments noted on them which impart to them a special quality . . ." *R. v. Carey* (1983), 38 C.P.C. 237 at 248, 43 O.R. (2d) 161, 3 Admin. L.R. 158, 7 C.C.C. (3d) 193, 1 D.L.R. (4th) 498 (C.A.) the court per Thorson J.A.

CABINET GOVERNMENT. Government in which Prime Minister or Premier selects members of her or his own party elected to Parliament and perhaps others to be Ministers of the Crown. This group collectively forms the Cabinet, the policy-making arm of government. The Ministers and Cabinet are responsible to Parliament for the conduct of the government. The government remains in power so long as it has the confidence of a majority of the House of Commons or the Legislature. In theory, the Privy Council or Executive Council advises the formal head of state (the Governor General or Lieutenant Governor) though, in fact, the Committee of Council, known as the Cabinet, carries out this function in most situations.

CABINET MINISTER. A member of Cabinet who is responsible for a portfolio, usually a ministry or department of government. This person acts as political head of the ministry or department and is responsible to Parliament for the affairs of that ministry or department or the conduct of that portfolio.

CABIN PRESSURE ALTITUDE. The pressure altitude in the cabin of an aircraft.

CABLE. *n*. 1. The rope to which the anchor of a ship is fastened. 2. A number of wires twisted or braided to form a conductor. 3. One or more stranded conductors insulated from one another and further insulated from the mass of the earth. See ARMORED ~; FERRY ~; RAISED ~.

CABLECASTER. See COMMERCIAL~; COMMUNITY~.

CABLECASTING FIRM. A person who operates a cable or wire network or system that distributes one or more audio or audio and video programmings intended to entertain, inform or instruct the audience linked with it. *An Act respecting educational programming*, R.S.Q. c. P-30.1, s. 1.

CABLECAST PROGRAMMING. The orderly presentation of messages by a cablecaster.

CABLE DISTRIBUTION UNDERTAKING. An undertaking that distributes broadcasting to subscribers predominantly over closed transmission paths. *Broadcasting Distribution Regulations*, SOR/97-555, s. 1.

CABLE REEL TRAILER. A vehicle designed to be drawn behind another vehicle for the exclusive purpose of carrying a drum or reel of cable. *Motor Vehicle Safety Regulations*, C.R.C., c. 1038, s. 2.

CABLETROUGH. *n*. A raceway consisting of metal troughing and fittings constructed that insulated conductors and cables may be readily installed or removed without injury either to conductors or their covering.

CAB SIGNAL. A signal located in engineman's compartment or cab, indicating a condition affecting the movement of a train or engine and used in conjunction with interlocking or block signals, or in lieu of block signals. *Regulations No. 0-8, Uniform Code of Operating Rules*, C.R.C., Part III, s. 2.

C.A.C.F.P. *abbr*. Comité d'appel de la commission de la Fonction publique.

CACHEXIA. *n*. The advanced state of constitutional disorders, wasting, anemia, hydremia or weakness.

CABLE DISTRIBUTION UNDERTAKING. An undertaking that distributes broadcasting to subscribers predominantly over closed transmission paths. *Broadcasting Distribution Regulations*, SOR/97-555, s. 1.

CADASTRAL MAPPING.The portion of the mapping system that deals with the land survey system. *Land Titles Act*, R.S.A. 2000, c. S-26, s. 1.

CADASTRAL OPERATION. A division, a subdivision, a new subdivision, a redivision, a cancellation, a correction, an addition or a replacement of lot numbers effected under the Cadastre Act. *An Act to Amend Various Legislative Provisions Respecting Municipalities*, S.Q. 1982, c. 2, s. 53.

CADASTRAL SURVEYING. Surveying in relation to (a) the identification, establishment, documentation or description of a boundary or the position of anything relative to a boundary; or (b) the generation, manipulation, adjustment, custody, storage, retrieval or display of spatial information that defines a boundary. *Canada Lands Surveyors Act, 1998*, S.C. 1998, c. 14, s. 2. See PRACTICE OF ~.

CADASTRAL SURVEYING, PRACTICE OF. Advising on, reporting on, conducting or supervising the conducting of surveys to establish, locate, define or describe lines, boundaries or corners of parcels of land or land covered with water. *Surveyors Act*, R.S.O. 1990, c. S. 29, s.1.

CADAVER. *n*. A dead body, a corpse.

CADAVERIC. *adj*. Related to a dead body. F.A. Jaffe, *A Guide to Pathological Evidence*, 3d ed. (Toronto: Carswell, 1991) at 214.

CADAVERIC RIGIDITY. See RIGOR MORTIS.

CADAVERIC SPASM. See RIGOR MORTIS.

CADIT QUAESTIO. [L.] The matter allows no further argument.

CAESAREAN OPERATION. Delivery of a fetus through an abdominal incision.

CAETERIS PARIBUS. [L.] Other things being equal.

CAF. The French neutral citation for the Federal Court of Appeal.

CAFÉ CORONARY. Asphyxia caused by a bolus of food impacting the windpipe or larynx.

CAGETENDER. *n.* A person designated to give mine shaft signals, to supervise a shaft conveyance, to maintain discipline, to enforce load limits and to notify the hoist operator of heavy or irregular loads. D. Robertson *Ontario Health and Safety Guide* (Toronto: Richard De Boo Ltd., 1988) at 5-41.

CAHIERS PROP. INTEL. *abbr.* Les Cahiers de propriété intellectuelle.

C.A.I. *abbr.* 1. Commission d'appel de l'immigration 2. Décisions de la Commission d'accès à l'information.

CAISSON. *n.* 1. A casing sunk or constructed below ground or water level whether or not it is designed to contain air above atmospheric pressure and includes an excavation drilled by an auger into which a worker enters or is required to enter to work. 2. A deep foundation unit, made of materials such as wood, steel or concrete or combination thereof, which is either premanufactured and placed by driving, jacking, jetting or screwing, or cast-in-place in a hole formed by driving, excavating or boring. *Building Code Act*, R.R.O. 1980, Reg. 87, s. 1.

CALCULATE. *v.* " . . . [P]lan deliberately . . ." *Belmont v. Millhaven Institution* (1984), 41 C.R. (3d) 91 at 95, 9 Admin. L.R. 181 (Fed. T.C.), Dubé J.

CALCULATED. *adj.* 1. " . . . [F]itted, suited, apt . . ." *R. v. Hill* (1976), 33 C.C.C. (2d) 60 at 68 (B.C.C.A.), McIntyre J.A. 2. In the context of the phrase "calculated to mislead" means 'likely' to mislead". *Bond v. Dupras* (1995), 1995 CarswellBC 1044, 32 Admin. L.R. (2d) 161 (S.C. [In Chambers]) Spencer J. 3. Planned, intended.

CALCULATED TO DECEIVE. Of a trademark, meant to so nearly resemble another that it is likely to cause confusion about the origin of the goods or services with which it is associated or to suggest that the goods or services are from the same source as the trademark with which there is confusion.

CALCULATING POOL. The portion of the net pool that remains after deduction of the total value or the net value as determined pursuant to paragraph 119(4)(*a*), as the case may be, of all

bets on the winning horses in that pool. *Pari-Mutuel Betting Supervision Regulations*, SOR/91-365, s. 2.

CALCULATOR. *n.* A person who calculates the pay-out prices in any pool. *Race Track Supervision Regulations*, C.R.C., c. 441, s. 2.

CALDERBANK LETTER. " . . . [A letter written] on a 'without prejudice' basis not only setting out an offer of settlement but expressly reserving the right, if the settlement offer was not accepted, to bring this letter to the attention of the trial Judge, after judgment, on the issue of costs . . ." *Goodman v. Goodman* (1992), 2 C.P.C. (3d) 316 at 319 (B.C. S.C.), Sinclair Prowse J.

CALENDAR. *n.* The order of the division of time into years, months, weeks, days.

CALENDAR MONTH. May refer to an actual month or to a period from a day in one month to the same day in the next month. See MONTH.

CALENDAR QUARTER. Three consecutive months. May refer to three complete months or to the period from the day in the first month until the same day in the fourth month.

CALENDAR YEAR. The year from January 1 to December 31. May refer to a period of one year commencing on any day of a year and running until the same day of the next year. See BASE ~; YEAR.

CALF. *n.* 1. A head of cattle under the age of one year. 2. An immature marine mammal.

CALIBER. *n.* Of a firearm's barrel, the inside diameter. In a rifled barrel, the distance from land to land. F.A. Jaffe, *A Guide to Pathological Evidence*, 3d ed. (Toronto: Carswell, 1991) at 214.

CALL. *v.* 1. To make a request or demand. 2. To demand shareholders pay amount remaining on unpaid shares.

CALL. *n.* 1. Includes instalment, assessment and any other amount paid, payable or agreed to be paid in respect of a share. H. Sutherland, D.B. Horsley & J.M. Edmiston, eds., *Fraser's Handbook on Canadian Company Law*, 7th ed. (Toronto: Carswell, 1985) at 136. 2. " . . . [A] contract purchased for an agreed premium entitling holder, at his option, to buy from the vendor on or before a fixed date a specified number of shares at a pre-determined price. . ." *Posluns v. Toronto Stock Exchange*, [1964] 2 O.R. 547 at 553, 46 D.L.R. (2d) 210 (H.C.), Gale J. 3. A request or command to come or assemble. 4. A demand for payment. 5. An option transferable by delivery to demand delivery of a specified number or amount of securities at a fixed price within a specified time. 6. The summons of a person to the bar of the court to be admitted to the Bar of the province.

CALL. *abbr*. Canadian Association Of Law Librarians.

CALLABLE. *adj*. Describes an option to pay on call before maturity.

CALL-BACK CLAUSE. A provision in a collective agreement concerning the calling back of an employee to the workplace after he has left after his regular shift.

CALL-BACK PAY. A minimum number of hours' pay guaranteed to an employee who is called back to work at a time outside the employee's scheduled hours of work.

CALLING. *n*. A business; occupation; profession; trade; vocation.

CALL-IN CLAUSE. A provision in a collective agreement concerning the calling in of an employee to the workplace from his home.

CALL-IN PAY OR PREMIUM. A minimum number of hours' pay paid to an employee required to report to work outside the employee's scheduled work time.

CALLIPHORA VOMITORIA. The larvae of this common fly hatch in recently dead bodies and help the tissues disintegrate. F.A. Jaffe, *A Guide to Pathological Evidence*, 3d ed. (Toronto: Carswell, 1991) at 214.

CALL NEWSL. *abbr*. CALL Newsletter (Bulletin ACBD).

CALL TO THE BAR. 1. Admission to the Law Society of a province or to membership in the legal profession of a province. 2. The conferral on students of the degree of barrister-at-law.

CALLUS. *n*. Tissue which grows to connect fragments of a broken bone. F.A. Jaffe, *A Guide to Pathological Evidence*, 3d ed. (Toronto: Carswell, 1991) at 214.

CALUMNIATOR. *n*. One who accuses falsely.

CAM. *abbr*. Cameron's Privy Council Decisions, 1832-1929.

CA MAG. *abbr*. CA Magazine.

CAMBIST. *n*. One who deals in bills of exchange and promissory notes.

CAM. DIG. *abbr*. Cameron's Digest.

CAMERA. *n*. 1. A judge's chambers. 2. A room. See IN ~.

CAMERALISTICS. *n*. The study of public finance.

CAMP. *n*. A person's temporary place to live while away from the usual place of residence. See DAY ~; LOGGING ~; OUTPOST ~; RECREATIONAL ~; TOURIST ~; TRAILER ~; VACATION ~.

CAMPAIGN EXPENSE. Any expense incurred in relation to an election by or on behalf of a political party, constituency association or candidate during the period commencing with the issue of a writ for an election and terminating on polling day.

CAMPAIGN PERIOD. The period commencing with the issue of the writ for an election and terminating on polling day or at a later date specified by statute.

CAMPBELL'S (LORD) ACT. The name by which the Fatal Accidents Act, 1846, U.K. is known.

CAMPER. *n*. A person in attendance at a camp.

CAMPGROUND *var*. **CAMP GROUND**. See PUBLIC ~.

CAMPING ESTABLISHMENT. Premises operated for the accommodation of the travelling or vacationing public comprising land used or maintained as grounds for camping or for parking recreational vehicles.

CAM. S.C. *abbr*. Reports Hitherto Unpublished, Supreme Court of Canada, Cameron, 1880-1900.

CAN. *n*. Includes any hermetically sealed glass bottle, package or container.

CAN. *abbr*. Canada.

CANADA. *n*. 1. The geographic unit. 2. The juristic federal unit. *Reference re Legislative Authority of Parliament of Canada* (1979), (*sub nom. Reference re Legislative Authority of Parliament to Alter or Replace Senate*) 102 D.L.R. (3d) 1 at 12, [1980] 1 S.C.R. 56, 30 N.R. 271, Laskin C.J.C., Martland, Ritchie, Pigeon, Dickson, Estey, Pratte and McIntyre JJ. 3. For greater certainty, includes the internal waters of Canada and the territorial sea of Canada. *Interpretation Act*, R.S.C. 1985, c. I-21, s. 35. See AUDITOR GENERAL OF ~; BANK OF ~; COASTAL

WATERS OF ~; COAST OF~; CONSTITU-TION OF ~; CONSUMERS' ASSOCIATION OF ~; CORPORATION INCORPORATED IN ~; COURT OF ~; DEFENCE OF ~; EASTERN ~; ECONOMIC COUNCIL OF~; GOVERNMENT OF ~; GOVERNOR OF ~; INFORMATION COMMISSIONER OF ~; INLAND WATERS OF ~; LAW OF ~; LAW REFORM COMMISSION OF ~; LAWS OF ~; LONG-TERM BONDS OF ~; LOWER ~; MEDICAL RESEARCH COUN-CIL OF~; MINOR WATERS OF ~; NA-TIONAL BUILDING CODE OF ~; NA-TIONAL LIBRARY OF ~; NATIONAL MUSEUMS OF ~; NATIONAL RESEARCH COUNCIL OF ~; NATURAL' SCIENCES AND ENGINEERING RESEARCH COUN-CIL OF~; PAID-UP CAPITAL EMPLOYED IN ~; PARLIAMENT OF ~; POLICYHOL-DER IN ~; POLICY IN ~; PRIVACY COM-MISSIONER OF ~; PUBLISHED IN ~; QUEEN'S PRIVY COUNCIL FOR ~; RESI-DENT OF ~; SCIENCE COUNCIL OF ~; SO-CIAL SCIENCES AND HUMANITIES RE-SEARCH COUNCIL OF ~; STANDARDS COUNCIL OF ~; SUPREME COURT OF ~; TREASURY BOARD OF ~; WESTERN ~; WITHIN ~; WORKS FOR THE GENERAL ADVANTAGE OF ~.

CANADA ACT, 1982. The statute of the Parliament of the United Kingdom, which gave effect to the Constitution Act, 1982, proclaimed in force April 17, 1982. This statute patriated the Constitution and terminated the power of the U.K. Parliament to legislate for Canada.

CANADA AIR PILOT. An aeronautical information publication that contains information on instrument procedures and that is published under the authority of the Minister. *Canadian Aviation Regulations* SOR 96-433, s. 101.01.

CANADA ASSISTANCE PLAN. A group of income-support programmes and social services which began in the 1940s and 1950s. P.W. Hogg, *Constitutional Law of Canada*, 3d ed. (Toronto: Carswell, 1992) at 145.

CANADA CORPORATION. A body corporate incorporated by or under an Act of the Parliament of Canada.

CANADA COUNCIL. A federal body which offers services and grants to arts organizations and professional artists in music, dance, theatre, visual and media arts, writing and publishing.

CANADA CUSTOMS AND REVENUE AGENCY. The Agency is responsible for (a) supporting the administration and enforcement of the program legislation; (b) implementing agreements between the Government of Canada or the Agency and the government of a province or other public body performing a function of government in Canada to carry out an activity or administer a tax or program; (c) implementing agreements or arrangements between the Agency and departments or agencies of the Government of Canada to carry out an activity or administer a program; and (d) implementing agreements between the Government of Canada and an aboriginal government to administer a tax. *Canada Customs and Revenue Agency Act, 1999*, S. C. 1999, c. 17, s. 5.

CANADA DAY. July 1, not being a Sunday, is a legal holiday and shall be kept and observed as such throughout Canada under the name of "Canada Day". When July 1 is a Sunday, July 2 is a legal holiday and shall be kept and observed as such throughout Canada under the name of "Canada Day". July 1 is the anniversary of confederation in 1867.

CANADA DEPOSIT INSURANCE COR-PORATION. A federal body with power to insure qualified Canadian currency deposits which member institutions hold and which makes loans to those institutions and to co-operative credit societies, finance corporations and other related organizations.

CANADA FLIGHT SUPPLEMENT. An aeronautical information publication published under the authority of the Minister of Transport and the Minister of National Defence that is intended to be used to supplement enroute charts and the *Canada Air Pilot*. *Canadian Aviation Regulations* SOR 96-433, s. 101.01.

CANADA LABOUR RELATIONS BOARD. An administrative tribunal whose functions and powers are established by the Canada Labour Code.

CANADA LANDS. 1. (*a*) Any lands belonging to Her Majesty in right of Canada or of which the Government of Canada has power to dispose that are situated in Yukon, the Northwest Territories, Nunavut or in any National Park of Canada and any lands that are (i) surrendered lands or a reserve, as defined in the *Indian Act*, (ii) Category IA land or Category IA-N land, as defined in the *Cree-Naskapi (of Quebec) Act*, chapter 18 of the Statutes of Canada, 1984, (iii) Sechelt lands, as defined in the *Sechelt Indian Band Self-Government Act*, chapter 27 of the Statutes of Canada, 1986, (iv) settlement land, as defined in the *Yukon First Nations Self-Government Act*, and lands in which an interest is transferred or recognized under section 21 of that Act, or (v) lands in the Kanesatake Mohawk interim land base, as defined in the *Kanesatake Interim Land Base Governance Act*, other than the lands known as Doncaster Reserve No. 17; and (*b*) any lands under water belonging to Her Majesty in right of Canada or in respect of any rights in which the Government of Canada has power to dispose. *Oil and Gas Act*, R.S.C. 1985, c. O-6, s. 1.

CANADA LANDS SURVEYOR. A person who holds a commission. *Canada Lands Surveyors Act, 1998*, S.C. 1998, c. 14, s. 2.

CANADA MORTGAGE AND HOUSING CORPORATION. The federal corporation which administers the National Housing Act, insures the mortgage loans which approved lenders make for new and existing homeowner and rental housing or for dwellings which non-profit and co-operative associations build.

CANADA PENSION PLAN. A contributory federal social insurance plan which provides benefits upon retirement from employment, on disability and for survivors of beneficiaries of the plan.

CANADA POST CORPORATION. The body which gathers, sorts and delivers mail in Canada.

CANADA POST OFFICE. The activities [formerly] conducted under the direction and control of the Postmaster General. *Post Office Act*, R.S.C. 1970, c. P-14, s. 2.

CANADA REVENUE AGENCY. See CANADA CUSTOMS AND REVENUE.

CANADA TWIST. The unstemmed, unflavoured and unpressed leaf of tobacco grown in Canada, twisted and made into coils by a manufacturer of tobacco. *Excise Act*, R.S.C. 1985, c. E-14, s. 6.

CANADIAN. *n.* 1. A Canadian citizen. 2. A permanent resident of Canada. 3. A Canadian government, whether federal, provincial or local, or an agency thereof. 4. An entity that is Canadian-controlled. See NON~; NON-RESIDENT ~; RESIDENT ~.

CANADIAN ADVISORY COUNCIL ON THE STATUS OF WOMEN. A body estab-lished to offer the federal government advice concerning issues which affect women and to increase public awareness of those issues.

CANADIAN AIR CARRIER. Any air carrier that carries on business principally in Canada and (a) is incorporated or registered in Canada, or (b) has its head office in Canada. *Air Carrier Regulations*, C.R.C., c. 3, s. 2.

CANADIAN AIRCRAFT. An aircraft regis-tered in Canada.

CANADIAN ARMED FORCES. The Cana-dian Forces are the armed forces of Her Majesty raised by Canada and consist of one Service called the Canadian Armed Forces.

CANADIAN AUTHOR. A writer or translator who is a Canadian citizen or who has been law-fully admitted to Canada for permanent resi-dence.

CANADIAN AVIATION SAFETY BOARD. An independent body with mandate to advance aviation safety. It investigates aviation occur-rences, makes public reports of its findings and recommends measures to reduce or eliminate safety problems. See CANADIAN TRANS-PORTATION ACCIDENT INVESTIGATION AND SAFETY BOARD.

CANADIAN BILL OF RIGHTS. This bill, en-acted by 8-9 Elizabeth II, c. 44 S.C. 1960, c. 44 (R.S.C. 1985, Appendix III), was the first at-tempt in Canada to give statutory recognition and protection to certain human rights, funda-mental freedoms of religion, speech, assembly and association and the press and procedural rights. See BILL OF RIGHTS.

CANADIAN BLOOD COMMITTEE. An or-ganization comprised of representatives of the federal government and of each of the provinces. It is responsible for developing and implement-ing policies for collecting, processing, distrib-uting, and utilizing whole blood and blood prod-ucts in Canada, and for supervising and directing programs instituted under policies formulated in that regard by the federal and provincial govern-ments. It is responsible for providing funding annually to the Canadian Red Cross. *Endean v. Canadian Red Cross Society* (1997), 148 D.L.R. (4th) 158 (B.C. S.C.).

CANADIAN BRANDY. Spirits distilled exclu-sively from the juices of native fruits, without the addition of sugar or other saccharine matter. *Excise Act*, R.S.C. 1985, c. E-14, s. 3.

CANADIAN BROADCASTING CORPO-RATION. The publicly owned corporation with mandate to provide Canada's national broadcasting service.

CANADIAN BUSINESS. Business carried on in Canada that has (a) a place of business in Canada, (b) an individual or individuals in Canada who are employed or self-employed in connection with the business, and (c) assets in Canada used in carrying on the business. *Investment Canada Act*, R.S.C. 1985 (1st Supp.), c. 28, s. 3.

CANADIAN CHARTER OF RIGHTS AND FREEDOMS. Part I of the Constitution Act, 1982 which guarantees rights and freedoms. See CHARTER.

CANADIAN CITIZEN. A citizen within the meaning of the Citizenship Act.

CANADIAN COAST GUARD SHIP. A government ship entrusted for management or operation to the Marine Operations Branch of the Department of Transport. *Registration of Government Ships Regulations*, C.R.C., c. 1463, s. 2.

CANADIAN COMMODITY FUTURES EXAMINATION. An examination relating to the Canadian commodity futures industry that has been prepared and is administered by the Canadian Securities Institute.

CANADIAN COMPANY. A company formed or incorporated by or under any Act of Parliament of Canada or of the Legislature of any province.

CANADIAN-CONTROLLED PRIVATE CORPORATION. A private corporation that is a Canadian corporation other than (a) a corporation controlled, directly or indirectly in any manner whatever, by one or more non-resident persons, by one or more public corporations (other than a prescribed venture capital corporation), by one or more corporations described in paragraph (c), or by any combination of them, (b) a corporation that would, if each share of the capital stock of a corporation that is owned by a non-resident person, by a public corporation (other than a prescribed venture capital corporation), or by a corporation described in paragraph (c) were owned by a particular person, be controlled by the particular person, or (c) a corporation a class of the shares of the capital stock of which is listed on a prescribed stock exchange. *Income Tax Act*, R.S.C. 1985, c.1 (5th Supp.), s. 125(7).

CANADIAN CORPORATION. 1. At any time means a corporation that is resident in Canada at that time and was (a) incorporated in Canada, or (b) resident in Canada throughout the period that began on June 18, 1971 and that ends at that time, and for greater certainty, a corporation formed at any particular time by the amalgamation or merger of, or by a plan of arrangement or other corporate reorganization in respect of, 2 or more corporations (otherwise than as a result of the acquisition of property of one corporation by another corporation, pursuant to the purchase of the property by the other corporation or as a result of the distribution of the property to the other corporation on the winding-up of the corporation) is a Canadian corporation because of paragraph 89(1) "Canadian corporation: (a) only if (c) that reorganization took place under the laws of Canada or a province, and (d) each of those corporations was, immediately before the particular time, a Canadian corporation. 2. A corporation incorporated by or under a law of Canada or a province. *Income Tax Act*, R.S.C. 1985, c.1 (5th Supp.), s. 89(1).

CANADIAN CUSTOMS WATERS. The waters forming that part of the sea that is adjacent to and extends nine marine miles beyond Canadian waters.

CANADIAN DOMESTIC AIRSPACE. The airspace specified, and delineated as such, in the *Designated Airspace Handbook*. *Canadian Aviation Regulations* SOR 96-433, s. 101.01.

CANADIAN EDITION. An edition of a book that is published under an agreement conferring a separate right of reproduction for the Canadian market, and that is made available in Canada by a publisher in Canada. *Book Importation Regulations*, SOR/99-324, s. 1.

CANADIAN ELECTRICAL CODE. The code of electrical facility standards published by the Canadian Standards Association.

CANADIAN ENTITY. An entity that is incorporated or formed by or under an Act of Parliament or of the legislature of a province and that carries on business, directly or indirectly, in Canada.

CANADIAN EQUIVALENT RATE. The interest rate that the issuer of the foreign debt would have been required to undertake to pay if the debt had been issued in Canada.

CANADIAN FABRIC. A fabric that has been woven in Canada, whether or not it contains imported materials. *Customs Drawback Shirting Fabrics Regulations* C.R.C., c. 478, s. 2.

CANADIAN FEATURE FILM. A feature film or feature film production in respect of which the Corporation has determined (a) that the completed film will in the judgment of the Corporation have a significant Canadian creative, artistic and technical content, and that arrangements have been made to ensure that the copyright in the completed film will be beneficially owned by an individual resident in Canada, by a corporation incorporated under the laws of Canada or a province or by any combination of such persons; or (b) that provision has been made for the production of the film under a co-production agreement entered into between Canada and another country. *Canadian Film Development Corporation Act*, R.S.C. 1970, c. C-8, s. 10.

CANADIAN FILM. Film manufactured in Canada or entered for consumption into Canada in accordance with the Customs Act. *Exposed and Processed Film and Recorded Video Tape Remission Order*, C.R.C., c. 763, s. 2.

CANADIAN FINANCIAL INSTITUTION. 1. A financial institution that is incorporated or formed by or under an Act of Parliament or of the legislature of a province. 2. Any of the following that is authorized to carry on business under the laws of Canada or a province, namely, (i) a bank, (ii) an authorized foreign bank, (iii) a loan company, (iv) a trust company, (v) an insurance company to which the *Insurance Companies Act* applies, (vi) an insurance corporation incorporated by or under an Act of the legislature of a province, (vii) a central cooperative credit society, (viii) a cooperative credit association, or (ix) a local cooperative credit society; (b) Alberta Treasury Branches, established under the *Alberta Treasury Branches Act* of the Province of Alberta; or (c) the Fédération des caisses Desjardins du Québec. *Canada Regulations.*

CANADIAN FIREARMS REGISTRY. The registry established by the Registrar under section 83 of the *Firearms Act*. Records shall be kept in the Canadian Firearms Registry of the following matters: (*a*) every application for a licence, registration certificate or authorization that is issued or revoked by the Registrar, as well as all information accompanying the application; (*b*) any information provided to the Registrar concerning firearms that are taken as samples or seized under the Act or any other Act of Parliament; (*c*) the names of the individuals who

are designated as chief firearms officers or firearms officers within the meaning of subsection 2(1) of the Act; (*d*) information concerning prohibition orders made under section 147.1 of the *National Defence Act*; (*e*) the names of the individuals who are approved verifiers within the meaning of the *Conditions of Transferring Firearms and other Weapons Regulations*; and (*f*) information concerning any other matter relevant to the Registrar's responsibilities under the Act, that is required to be collected under the Act or any other Act of Parliament.

CANADIAN FISHERIES WATERS. All waters in the fishing zones of Canada, all waters in the territorial sea of Canada and all internal waters of Canada.

CANADIAN FISHING VESSEL. A fishing vessel that is registered or licensed in Canada under the Canada Shipping Act and is owned by one or more persons each of whom is a Canadian citizen, a person resident and domiciled in Canada or a corporation incorporated under the laws of Canada or of a province, having its principal place of business in Canada, or that is not required to be registered or licensed in Canada but is owned as described.

CANADIAN FORCES. The armed forces of Her Majesty raised by Canada.

CANADIAN FORCES ELECTOR. A person is a Canadian Forces elector if he or she is qualified as an elector under section 3 and is not disentitled from voting at an election under section 4: (*a*) a member of the regular force of the Canadian Forces; (*b*) a member of the reserve force of the Canadian Forces on full-time training or service or on active service; (*c*) a member of the special force of the Canadian Forces; and (*d*) a person who is employed outside Canada by the Canadian Forces as a teacher in, or as a member of the administrative support staff for, a Canadian Forces school. *Canada Elections Act*, S.C. 2000, c. 9, s. 191.

CANADIAN FORCES POST OFFICE. A military post office operated outside Canada by the Canadian Forces Postal Services to provide postal facilities.

CANADIAN GOODS. Goods that are the growth, produce or manufacture of Canada.

CANADIAN GOVERNMENT RAILWAYS. (a) The lines of railway or parts thereof, (b) the property, works or interests, and (c) the powers, rights or privileges the management and operation of which are entrusted to the National Company by any order in council.

CANADIAN HUMAN RIGHTS COMMISSION. The federal commission which administers the Canadian Human Rights Act.

CANADIAN IMPORT TRIBUNAL. The federal tribunal which determines if subsidized, dumped or low-cost imports threaten or cause material injury to production of like goods in Canada.

CANADIAN INTERNATIONAL DEVELOPMENT AGENCY. The federal body which controls and supervises the official international development assistance program of Canada.

CANADIAN INVESTMENT FINANCE COURSE. A course prepared and conducted by the Canadian Securities Institute.

CANADIAN INVESTMENT FUNDS COURSE. A course prepared and conducted by the Educational Division of the Investment Funds Institute of Canada.

CANADIAN JUDICIAL COUNCIL. The objects of the Council are to promote efficiency and uniformity, and to improve the quality of judicial service, in superior courts and in the Tax Court of Canada.

CANADIAN LABOUR CONGRESS. See CENTRAL LABOUR CONGRESS.

CANADIAN LEGAL INFORMATION INSTITUTE. CanLII is an initiative of the Federation of Law Societies of Canada, funded by law societies and by law foundations. It is designed as a free Canadian virtual law library to serve both the profession and the public. Accessible at: www.canlii.org.

CANADIAN MARITIME LAW. 1. " . . . [I]ncludes all that body of law which was administered in England by the High Court on its Admiralty side in 1934 as such law may, from time to time, have been amended by the federal Parliament, and as it has developed through judicial precedent to date . . . a body of federal law dealing with all claims in respect of maritime and admiralty matters . . . the words 'maritime' and 'admiralty' should be interpreted within the modern context of commerce and shipping. In reality, the ambit of Canadian maritime law is limited only by the constitutional division of powers in the Constitution Act, 1867 (30 & 31 Vict.), c. 3. . . a body of federal law encompassing the common law principles of tort, contract

and bailment." *Miida Electronics Inc. v. Mitsui O.S.K. Lines Ltd.* (1986), (*sub nom. ITO—International Terminal Operators Ltd. v. Miida Electronics Inc.*) 28 D.L.R. (4th) 641 at 654, 656, 660, [1986] 1 S.C.R. 752, 68 N.R. 241, 34 B.L.R. 251, McIntyre J. (Dickson C.J.C., Estey and Wilson JJ. concurring). 2. Administered by the Exchequer Court of Canada on its Admiralty side by virtue of the Admiralty Act, chapter A-1 of the Revised Statutes of Canada, 1970, or any other statute or that would have been so administered if that Court had had, on its Admiralty side, unlimited jurisdiction in relation to maritime and admiralty matters, as that law has been altered by this Act or any other Act of Parliament. *Federal Court Act*, R.S.C. 1985, c. F-7, s. 2.

CANADIAN NATIONAL. Canadian national as defined in the Canadian Nationals Act, chapter 21 of the Revised Statutes of Canada, 1927. *Civilian War Pensions and Allowances Act*, R.S.C. 1985, c. C-31, s. 6.

CANADIAN OFFENDER. A Canadian citizen, within the meaning of the Citizenship Act, irrespective of age, who has been found guilty of an offence and is subject to supervision either in confinement or at large by reason of parole, probation or any other form of supervision without confinement, in a foreign state. *Transfer of Offenders Act*, R.S.C. 1985, c. T-15, s. 2.

CANADIAN-OWNED. *adj*. Wholly owned by any of the following individuals, corporations or groups carrying on business in Canada: (a) an individual who is a resident of Canada within the meaning of section 250 of the Income Tax Act, (b) a corporation incorporated in Canada under federal or provincial law, or (c) a group comprised of individuals or corporations or both at least one of the members of which is a person referred to in paragraph (a) or (b). *Customs and Excise Offshore Application Act*, R.S.C. 1985, c. C-53, s. 2.

CANADIAN PAYMENTS ASSOCIATION. A corporation established by the federal government to facilitate transactions among financial institutions. The Association shall consist of the following members: (*a*) the Bank of Canada; (*b*) every bank; (*c*) every authorized foreign bank; and (*d*) any other person who is entitled under this Part to be a member and who, on application to the Association for membership in the Association, establishes entitlement to be a member. Each of the following persons is entitled to be a member of the Association if they meet the requirements set out in the regulations and the by-laws: (*a*) a central, a trust company, a loan company and any other person, other than a local that is a member of a central or a cooperative credit association, that accepts deposits transferable by order to a third party; (*c*) Her Majesty in right of a province or an agent thereof, if Her Majesty in right of the province or the agent thereof accepts deposits transferable by order to a third party; (*d*) a life insurance company; (*e*) a securities dealer; (*f*) a cooperative credit association; (*g*) the trustee of a qualified trust; and (*h*) a qualified corporation, on behalf of its money market mutual fund. *Canadian Payments Act*, R.S.C. 1985, c. C-21, s. 4.

CANADIAN PRODUCTION FUND. The Canada Television and Cable Production Fund, or its successor. *Broadcasting Distribution Regulations*, SOR/97-555, s. 1.

CANADIAN PROGRAMMING SERVICE. (a) A programming service that originates entirely within Canada or is transmitted by a licensed station; (b) a programming service consisting of community programming; (c)a specialty service; (d) a pay television service; (e) a television pay-per-view service; (f) a DTH pay-per-view service; (g) a video-on-demand service; or (h) a pay audio service. *Broadcasting Distribution Regulations*, SOR/97-555, s. 1.

CANADIAN RADIO-TELEVISION AND TELECOMMUNICATIONS COMMISSION. The federal body which supervises and regulates every aspect of Canadian broadcasting (television, radio, cable and pay television and specialty services) and regulates federal telecommunications carriers.

CANADIAN SECURITIES COURSE. A course prepared and conducted by the Canadian Securities institute and so designated.

CANADIAN SECURITIES DEALER. A person who holds, under a law of a province relating to trading in securities, a subsisting and unsuspended licence or registration that entitles him to trade in the shares of companies.

CANADIAN SHIP. A ship registered in Canada either under this Act or under the Merchant Shipping Acts before August 1, 1936. *Canada Shipping Act*, R.S.C. 1985, c. S-9, s. 2. See HER MAJESTY'S ~.

CANADIAN STANDARDS ASSOCIATION. A national standard-setting organization

which certifies products covered by its standards. D. Robertson, *Ontario Health and Safety Guide* (Toronto: Richard De Boo Ltd., 1988) at 5-42.

CANADIAN TRANSPORTATION ACCIDENT INVESTIGATION AND SAFETY BOARD. The body charged with the investigation of accidents involving modes of transportation within the federal sphere, particularly aviation and railways.

CANADIAN TRANSPORT COMMISSION. The federal body which regulates transportation which is under federal jurisdiction in Canada (i.e. by air, water, rail and commodity pipeline) and certain kinds of interprovincial commercial motor transport.

CNAADIAN VESSEL. A vessel registered or listed under Part 2 of the Canada Shipping Act. *Canada Shipping Act, 2001*, S.C. 2001, c. 26, s. 2.

CANADIAN WARSHIP. A ship of war, a military transport or a military supply ship owned by, or operated by or on behalf of, the Government of Canada.

CANADIAN WATERS. The territorial sea of Canada and all internal waters of Canada.

CANADIAN WHEAT BOARD. The federal body, established under the Canadian Wheat Board Act, which supervises export sales of barley, oats and wheat produced in Western Canada and domestic sales of these grains intended for human consumption. It controls the delivery of all major grains, coordinating grain movement to terminal elevators. The object of the board is to market in an orderly manner, in interprovincial and export trade, grain grown in Canada.

CANADIAN WORKFORCE. All persons in Canada of working age who are willing and able to work.

CANAL. *n*. A canal, lock or navigable channel and all works and property appertaining or incidental to the canal, lock or channel. See OWNERS OF A DOCK OR ~.

CAN-AM L.J. *abbr*. Canadian-American Law Journal.

CAN. BANKER. *abbr*. Canadian Banker.

CAN. BAR. J. *abbr*. Canadian Bar Journal.

CAN. BAR REV. *abbr*. The Canadian Bar Review (La Revue du Barreau canadien).

CAN. BUS. L.J. *abbr*. Canadian Business Law Journal (Revue canadienne du droit de commerce).

CANCEL. *v*. 1. To revoke a will. *Bishop Estate v. Reesor* (1990), 39 E.T.R. 36 at 38 (Ont. H.C.), Kurisko L.J.S.C. 2. In the case of an instrument, to draw lines across it intending to indicate it is no longer in force.

CANCELLATION. *n*. " . . . [U]sed in relation to an insurance policy implies the bringing to an end of the policy during its term, i.e. for some reason rendering invalid what would otherwise be valid." *Bank of Nova Scotia v. Commercial Union Assurance of Canada* (1991), 104 N.S.R. (2d) 313 at 319, 283 A.P.R. 313, 6 C.C.L.I. (2d) 178 (T.D.), Tidman J. See PURCHASE FOR ~.

CANCELLATION CLAUSE. A clause in an agreement that permits the parties to cancel and terminate their agreement.

CANCELLED CHEQUE. A cheque which bears the indication that it has been honoured by the bank upon which it was drawn.

CANCELLI. *n*. [L. lattice] 1. The rails enclosing the bar of a court. 2. The lines drawn on the face of a document indicating the document is revoked or annulled.

CANCER. *n*. Includes all forms and types of malignant growth and precancerous conditions.

CAN. C.L.G. *abbr*. Canadian Commercial Law Guide.

CAN. COMMUNIC. L. REV. *abbr*. Canadian Communications Law Review.

CAN. COMMUNITY L.J. *abbr*. Canadian Community Law Journal (Revue canadienne de droit communautaire).

CAN. COMPET. POLICY REC. *abbr*. Canadian Competition Policy Record.

CAN. COMP. POL. REC. *abbr*. Canadian Competition Policy Record.

CAN. COMPUTER L.R. *abbr*. Canadian Computer Law Reporter

CAN. COM. R. *abbr*. Canadian Commercial Reports, 1901-1905.

CAN. COUNCIL INT. L. *abbr*. Canadian Council on International Law. Conference. Proceedings. (Conseil canadien de droit international. Congrès. Travaux).

CAN. COUNCIL INT'L L. PROC. *abbr*. Canadian Council on International Law, Proceedings.

CAN. CRIM. FORUM. *abbr*. Canadian Criminology Forum (Le Forum canadien de criminologie).

CAN. CURR. TAX. *abbr*. Canadian Current Tax.

CAN. CURRENT TAX. *abbr*. Canadian Current Tax.

CANDELA. *n*. The unit for the measurement of luminous intensity, being the luminous intensity, in the perpendicular direction, of a surface of 1/600 000 square metre of a full radiator at the temperature of freezing platinum under a pressure 101 325 newtons per square metre.

C. & F. *abbr*. Cost and freight. In a sales contract, means that the price includes cost and freight and the buyer must arrange insurance.

CANDIDATE. *n*. 1. Any person elected to serve as a member, any person who has been nominated as a candidate at an election or any person who declares himself or herself to be an independent candidate at the election in the electoral district. 2. Includes a person who, after the dissolution of the House of Assembly or the occurrence of a vacancy in its membership, and until the return of the writ for the next election is publicly represented personally or by others as standing or intending to stand, and who intends to stand, or has stood, for election as a member of the House of Assembly for a seat then vacant. *Newspapers and Books Act*, R.S. Nfld. 1990, c. N-4, s. 2. 3. " . . . [A]ny person having applied for the job." *Landriault v. Canada (Attorney General)* (1982), 143 D.L.R. (3d) 163 at 166, [1983] 1 F.C. 636, 45 N.R. 570 (Fed C.A.), Pratte J. 4. An applicant for a commission. *Canada Lands Surveys Act*, R.S.C. 1985, c. L-6, s. 2. See AGENT OF A ~; ELECTION EXPENSES OF A ~; INDEPENDENT ~; OFFICIAL ~; REGISTERED ~.

CANDIDATE AT AN ELECTION. A person elected to serve in a legislature and a person who is nominated as a candidate at an election or who declares or is declared by others to be a candidate on or after the date of the issue of the writ or after the dissolution or vacancy in consequence of which the writ has been issued.

CANDIDATE OF AN AUTHORIZED PARTY. A person designated by an authorized party to be the candidate of this party for office.

CANDIDATE'S AGENT. A person authorized in writing by a candidate to represent that candidate at an election or at any proceeding of an election.

CANDLING. *n*. Examination of the internal condition of an egg by rotating it in front of or over a source of light that illuminates the contents.

C & S. *abbr*. Clarke & Scully's Drainage Cases (Ont.), 1898-1903.

CANDY. *n*. Cocaine.

CANDY MAN. A seller of cocaine.

CANE. See WHITE ~.

CAN. ENV. L.N. *abbr*. Canadian Environmental Law News.

CAN. F.L.G. *abbr*. Canadian Family Law Guide.

CAN. H.R. ADVOC. *abbr*. Canadian Human Rights Advocate.

CAN. HUM. RTS. Y.B. *abbr*. Canadian Human Rights Yearbook (Annuaire canadien des droits de le personne).

CAN. IND. REL. ASSOC. *abbr*. Canadian Industrial Relations Association. Annual Meeting. Proceedings (Association canadienne des relations industrielles. Congrès. Travaux).

CAN. INTELL. PROP. REV. *abbr*. Canadian Intellectual Property Review.

CAN. I.T.G.R. *abbr*. Canada Income Tax Guide Report.

CAN. J. CRIM. *abbr*. Canadian Journal of Criminology (Revue canadienne de criminologie).

CAN. J. GRIM. & CORR. *abbr*. Canadian Journal of Criminology and Corrections.

CAN. J. FAM. L. *abbr*. Canadian Journal of Family Law (Revue canadienne de droit familial).

CAN. J. INS. L. *abbr*. Canadian Journal of Insurance Law.

CAN. J.L. & JURIS. *abbr*. The Canadian Journal of Law and Jurisprudence.

CAN. J.L. & SOCIETY. *abbr*. Canadian Journal of Law and Society (Revue canadienne de droit et société).

CAN. J. WOMEN & LAW. *abbr*. Canadian Journal of Women and the Law (Revue juridique "La femme et le droit").

CAN. LAW. *abbr*. Canadian Lawyer.

CAN. LAWYER. *abbr*. Canadian Lawyer.

CAN. LEGAL STUD. *abbr*. Canadian Legal Studies.

CANLII. Canadian Legal Information Institute. CanLII is an initiative of the Federation of Law Societies of Canada, funded by law societies and by law foundations. It is designed as a free Canadian virtual law library to serve both the profession and the public. Accessible at: www.canlii.org. See LEGAL INFORMATION INSTITUTE; PUBLIC ACCESS TO LAW.

CAN. L.J. *abbr*. Canada Law Journal.

CAN. L.R.B.R. *abbr*. Canadian Labour Relations Board Reports, 1974-.

[] CAN. L.R.B.R. *abbr*. Canadian Labour Relations Board Reports.

CAN. L. REV. *abbr*. Canadian Law Review (1901-1907).

CAN. L.T. (1881-1922). *abbr*. Canadian Law Times.

CAN. MUN. J. *abbr*. Canadian Municipal Journal.

CANNABIS. *n*. Derived from the plant Cannabis sativa, known commonly as hemp. F.A. Jaffe, *A Guide to Pathological Evidence*, 3d ed. (Toronto: Carswell, 1991) at 93.

CANNED FISH. Includes any fish packed in a hermetically sealed container and treated with heat to prevent spoilage and to destroy pathogenic organisms.

CANNERY. *n*. The buildings, structures, machinery, appurtenances, appliances, apparatus and chemicals occupied or used in the business of canning or bottling fish or shellfish. See HERRING ~; SALMON ~; SHELL FISH ~; TUNA FISH ~.

CANON. *n*. 1. A rule of law. 2. A church dignitary.

CANONIST. *n*. A professor of church law.

CANON LAW. A body of Roman church law, compiled from the opinions of the fathers of the church, the decrees of general councils and the Vatican.

CANOPY. *n*. Any roof-like structure projecting more than twelve inches from the wall of a building.

CAN. PETRO. TAX J. *abbr*. Canadian Petroleum Tax Journal.

CAN. PUB. POL. *abbr*. Canadian Public Policy.

CAN. S.L.R. *abbr*. Canadian Securities Law Reports.

CAN. S.T.R. *abbr*. Canadian Sales Tax Reports.

CAN. TAX FOUND. *abbr*. Canadian Tax Foundation (Conference Report).

CAN. TAX J. *abbr*. Canadian Tax Journal (Revue fiscale canadienne).

CAN. TAX N. *abbr*. Canadian Tax News.

CAN. TAX'N: J. TAX POL'Y. *abbr*. Canadian Taxation: A Journal of Tax Policy.

CANTEEN. *n*. A wardroom, mess, cafeteria, dining area, common room, or other room to which the public is not ordinarily admitted situated in or on a base, station, camp, campus, institution or other facility. See FORCES ~; MILITARY ~.

CAN.-U.S. L.J. *abbr*. Canada-United States Law Journal.

CANVASS. *v*. To go door to door in sequence down a street soliciting customers or providing information and soliciting votes for a candidate at an election.

CANVASSER. *n*. 1. Any person who approaches electors to obtain their votes in favour of a candidate. 2. To solicit donations by going door to door.

CAN. Y.B. INT. L. *abbr*. Canadian Year Book of International Law (Annuaire canadien de droit international).

CAN. Y.B. INT'L. L. *abbr*. Canadian Year Book of International Law.

CAP. *n*. A capsule; a quantity of a drug like cocaine. F.A. Jaffe, *A Guide to Pathological Evidence*, 2d ed. (Toronto: Carswell 1983) at 171. See BLACK ~.

CAP. *abbr*. Chapter.

CAPABLE. *adj*. Having potential to do or be; having the qualities or nature required.

C.A.P.A.C. *abbr*. Composers, Authors and Publishers Association of Canada Limited.

CAPACITY. *n*. The capacity to understand and appreciate the nature of a consent or agreement and the consequences of giving, withholding, or revoking the consent or making, not making or terminating the agreement. See CARRYING ~; CONFIDENTIAL ~; CONTRACTUAL ~; DESIGN ~; FISCAL ~; MAXIMUM ~; RATED BED ~; RATED ~; RATED GENERATOR ~; REPRESENTATIVE ~; TESTAMENTARY ~; TRUST ~.

CAPAX DOLL [L.] Capable of committing crime.

CAPELIN. *n*. A fish of the species Mallotus villosus.

CAPIAS. [L. that you take] The name of writs which direct the sheriff to arrest the person named in the writs.

CAPIAS AD AUDIENDUM JUDICIUM. [L. that you take to hear judgment] A writ of capias issued in order to bring a criminal to receive judgment.

CAPIAS AD RESPONDENDUM. [L. that you take to answer] A writ issued for the arrest of a person.

CAPIAS AD SATISFACIENDUM. [L. that you take to satisfy] A writ for the arrest of the judgment debtor in a civil action when the judgment had not been satisfied.

CAPIAS EXTENDI FACIAS. [L. that you take and cause to be extended] A writ of execution issued against a debtor of the Crown, commanding the sheriff to arrest the debtor and "cause to be extended" the debtor's lands and goods.

CAPIAS IN WITHERNAM. [L. and AS. that you take by way of reprisals] A writ directing the sheriff to take other goods of the defendant when the goods ordered to be replevied were concealed so that the sheriff could not replevy them.

CAPIAS PRO FINE. [L. that you take for the fine] A writ issued for the arrest of a person who was fined for an offence.

CAPITAL. *n*. 1. The means with which a business is carried on. 2. In estates, used in contradistinction to income. " . . . [W]hen applied to estate problems would clearly mean the value of the assets of the estate as of the date of the testator's death." *Thomson v. Morrison* (1980), 6 E.T.R. 257 at 266, 28 O.R. (2d) 403, 111 D.L.R. (3d) 390 (H.C.), Holland J. 3. Money raised through issuing shares, certificates, bonds, debentures, long-term notes or any other long-term obligation, contributed or earned surplus and reserves. See AUTHORIZED ~; CIRCULAT-

ING ~; EQUITY ~; FIXED ~; FLOAT-ING ~; ISSUED ~; LIQUID ~; LOAN ~; NATIONAL ~ COMMISSION; NATIONAL ~ REGION; NOMINAL ~; SHARE ~; STATED ~; SUBSCRIBED ~; UNCALLED ~; WORKING ~.

CAPITAL ACCOUNT. The amount by which the assets of a person employed in the business exceed the liabilities arising from the business and all money advanced or loaned to the person for capital account.

CAPITAL ASSETS. Things used in a business to earn the income—land, buildings, plant, machinery, motor vehicles, ships. *Canada Steamship Lines Ltd. v. M.N.R.*, [1966] C.T.C. 255, 66 D.T.C. 5305 (Exch. Ct.).

CAPITAL BASE. The shareholders' equity of a company.

CAPITAL COST. The cost involved in acquiring, constructing, designing, equipping, adding to, replacing or altering a capital work. See NET EDUCATION ~.

CAPITAL COST ALLOWANCE. " . . . [A] tax term signifying the writing-off of the capital cost of an asset in an amount allowed by income tax regulations." *Canning v. C.F.M. Fuels (Ontario) Ltd.*, [1977] 2 S.C.R. 207 at 214, 12 N.R. 541, 71 D.L.R. (3d) 321, the court per Dickson J.

CAPITAL EXPENDITURE. An outlay or the incurrence of a liability for the construction or acquisition or, for the addition to, a tangible asset.

CAPITAL GAIN. The profit earned when property is sold for more than was paid for it. See TAXABLE ~.

CAPITAL GAIN OR LOSS. On the sale of an item of capital property, the difference between the proceeds of the disposition and the total of the adjusted cost base and the value of expenses incurred in making the disposition. A positive figure is a gain and a negative is a loss.

CAPITAL IMPROVEMENT. An addition to or an extension, enlargement, alteration, replacement or other improvement of a work of such nature or character that it is usually and properly accounted for as a capital asset.

CAPITAL INTEREST. Of a taxpayer in a trust means all rights of the taxpayer as a beneficiary under the trust, and after 1999 includes a right (other than a right acquired before 2000 and disposed of before March 2000) to enforce payment of an amount by the trust that arises as a consequence of any such right, but does not include an income interest in the trust. *Income Tax Act*, R.S.C. 1985, c. 1 (5ᵗʰ Supp.), s. 108(1).

CAPITALISATION. *var.* **CAPITALIZATION**. *n.* 1. The total amount of shares and other securities issued by a corporation. 2. " . . . [U]nless the earnings as such actually or constructively pass from the company to the shareholder there is, for all purposes, capitalization. . . . When earnings are 'capitalized', they cease at that moment to be 'earnings'; they become part of the capital assets; . . ." *Waters, Re (sub nom. Waters v. Toronto General Trusts Corp.)* [1956] C.T.C. 217 at 222, [1956] S.C.R. 889, 56 D.T.C. 1113, 4 D.L.R. (2d) 673, Rand J. 3. An estimate of yearly revenue in terms of the amount of capital which it is necessary to invest at a given rate of interest in order to receive that revenue.

CAPITAL LOSS. See CAPITAL GAIN OR LOSS; CARRY-OVER OF ~ES.

CAPITAL MAINTENANCE. Replacement of the capital resources of a firm before profit is calculated. W. Grover & F. Iacobucci, *Materials on Canadian Income Tax*, 4th ed. (Toronto: Richard De Boo Ltd., 1980) at 601.

CAPITAL MURDER. A classification formerly used under the Criminal Code where a person personally caused or assisted in causing the death of (a) a police officer, police constable, constable, sheriff, deputy sheriff, sheriff's officer or other person employed for the preservation and maintenance of the public peace, acting in the course of that officer's duties, or (b) the warden, deputy warden, instructor, keeper, gaoler, guard or other officer or permanent employee of a prison, acting in the course of that officer's duties, or counselled or procured another person to do any act causing or assisting in causing the death.

CAPITAL PROPERTY. (i) Any depreciable property of the taxpayer, and (ii) any property (other than depreciable property), any gain or loss from the disposition of which would if the property were disposed of, be a capital gain or a capital loss, as the case may be, of the taxpayer. *Income Tax Act*, R.S.C. 1985, c. 1 (5ᵗʰ Supp.), s. 54(1).

CAPITAL PUNISHMENT. Punishment by death.

CAPITAL RECEIPTS. All principal money received by a province from the sale of Crown lands, or other assets of a province and all principal repayments of capital advances and principal money received through the sale, pledge or other disposition of securities of a province for capital purposes.

CAPITAL SECURITY. Any share of any class of shares of a company or any bond, debenture, note or other obligation of a company, whether secured or unsecured.

CAPITAL STOCK. See PAID IN ~.

CAPITAL TRANSACTION. The general concept is that a transaction whereby an enduring asset or advantage is acquired for the business is a capital transaction. *Associated Investors v. M.N.R.*, [1967] C.T.C. 138, 67 D.T.C. 5096.

CAPITAL WORKS. Any building or other structure built on or into the land and machinery, equipment, and apparatus that are affixed to or incorporated into such building or structure for the purpose of improving the serviceability or utility of the building.

CAPITATION. *n*. A person-by-person tax.

CAPITULARY. *n*. A legal code.

CAPITULATION. *n*. The act of surrendering upon negotiated terms.

CAPON. See CHICKEN ~.

CAPPED FUSE. A safety fuse to which a detonator has been attached by crimping.

CAPPINGS. *n*. The covering and adhering honey over comb cells, pollen or brood, that is removed before the honey extracting process.

CAPRICIOUS. *adj*. Arbitrary.

CAPTATOR. *n*. A person who receives a gift or legacy by means of artifice.

CAPTION. *n*. The formal heading of an affidavit, deposition, indictment, information or recognisance which states before whom it was taken, found or made.

CAPTIVE INSURANCE COMPANY. An insurance company that is a pure captive insurance company, an association captive insurance company or a sophisticated insured captive insurance company. *Insurance (Captive Company)* Act, R.S.B.C., 1996, c. 227, s. 1.

CAPTIVE UNION. A union formed or controlled by the employer.

CAPTURE. *v*. To take; arrest; seize.

CAPTURE. *n*. See FREE OF ~ AND SEIZURE.

CAPUT ANNI. [L.] New Year's Day.

CAPUT MORTUUM. [L.] Obsolete; dead.

CAR. See COMPETITION ~; DELIVERY ~; PASSENGER ~; RAILWAY ~; STREET ~; TANK ~; TOW ~.

CARAT. *n*. 200 milligrams. *Weights and Measures Act*, S.C. 1970-71-72, c. 36, Schedule II.

CARCASS. *n*. 1. The body of a dead animal. Canada regulations. 2. The tire structure except tread and sidewall rubber. Canada regulations. See DRESSED ~; LAMB ~; MUTTON ~.

CARCER AD HOMINES CUSTODIENDOS, NON AD PUNIENDOS, DARI DEBET. [L.] A prison should be used for the custody not the punishment of persons.

CARCINOGEN. *n*. An agent or substance which can induce cancer.

CARD. See CREDIT ~; INSURANCE ~; RACING ~; SHOP ~.

CARDIAC ARREST. The state in which no effective heart beat occurs when the heart stops totally or the heart muscle quivers ineffectually. F.A. Jaffe, *A Guide to Pathological Evidence*, 3d ed. (Toronto: Carswell, 1991) at 214.

CARDIAC PACEMAKER. An implantable device that consists of a pulse generator and one or more leads and is designed to deliver electrical impulses to stimulate the heart.

CARDIAC TAMPONADE. Compression of the heart when fluid accumulates rapidly in the pericardial sac, caused by bleeding into the pericardial cavity when the heart is ruptured or is wounded by penetration. F.A. Jaffe, *A Guide to Pathological Evidence*, 3d ed. (Toronto: Carswell, 1991) at 214.

CARE. *n*. 1. Safekeeping. 2. " . . . [I]ncludes such things as feeding, clothing, cleaning, transporting, helping and protecting another person." *Thornborrow v. MacKinnon* (1981) (*sub nom. Schmidt, Re*) 16 C.C.L.T. 198 at 207, 32 O.R. (2d) 740, 123 D.L.R. (3d) 124 (H.C.), Linden J. 3. " . . . [I]mplies at least physical possession of the motor vehicle with an element of 'control' and carries the sense of responsibility and includes a sense of charge, possession and management." *R. v. Young* (1979), 4 M.V.R. 38 at 43, 21 Nfld. & P.E.I.R. 77, 56 A.P.R. 77 (P.E.I. C.A.), M.J. McQuaid J.A. (Peake J.A. concurring). 4. Includes such nursing, personal or supervisory care as is normally provided by or under the supervision of skilled nursing personnel. *Nursing Home Care Benefits Regulations*, C.R.C., c. 334, s. 2. 5. The physical care and control of a child. *Children and Family Services Act*, S.N.S. 1990, c. 5, s. 2. See AFTER~; CHILD IN ~; COMMUNITY ~ FACILITY; CONTINUING ~; CUSTODIAL ~; CUSTOMARY ~; DAY ~; ENDOWMENT ~; EXTENDED ~; FOSTER ~; HABILITATION AND ~; HEALTH ~; MEDICAL ~; NURSING ~; NURSING HOME ~; PARENTAL ~; PERPETUAL ~; PERSONAL ~; PROTECTIVE~; RESIDENTIAL ~; SUPERVISORY ~; SURGICAL ~.

CARE AND CUSTODY. All parental rights, duties and responsibilities toward a child.

CARE FACILITY. A hospital or a similar institution that provides care and treatment for chronic diseases.

CARE FUND. An irrevocable trust fund required to be established by an operator for the specified care and maintenance of graves in a cemetery.

CARELESS. *adj.* 1. " . . . [I]nfers an element of negligence or recklessness. It describes a state of conscious in difference [sic] or oblivion to the potential consequences of an act or a course of action." *R. v. Pawlivsky* (1981), 8 Sask. R. 356 at 359 (Div. Ct.), affirmed (1981), 10 Sask L.R. 179 (C.A.). 2. " . . . [N]ot caring . . ." *R v. King* (1984), 37 Sask. R. 29 at 32 (Q.B.), Hrabinsky J.

CARELESSLY. See DRIVE ~.

CARE OR CONTROL. In reference to a motor vehicle, may be exercised without an intent to set the vehicle in motion when a person performs an act or series of acts involving the use of the car, its fittings or equipment and unintentionally sets the vehicle in motion. *R. v. Ford*, [1982] 1 S.C.R. 231, per Ritchie, J. for the majority.

CARE SERVICES. Services consisting of provision of continual residential accommodations with meals and housekeeping, supervisory services, personal services.

CARETAKER'S PREMISES. Residential premises used for residential purposes by a person employed as a caretaker, janitor, manager, watchman, security guard, or superintendent in respect of the building in which the residential premises are situated.

CARETAKER'S UNIT. A rental unit used by a person employed as a caretaker, janitor, manager, watchman, security guard or superintendent in respect of the residential complex in which the rental unit is situated.

CAREY. *abbr.* Manitoba Reports, temp. Wood, 1875.

CARGO. *n.* The load of a ship or other carrier. See BULK ~; FIXED ~GEAR; GENERAL ~; GRAIN ~; HOT ~; TIMBER DECK ~.

CARGO CONTAINER. A container or chassis that is rigid, reusable, capable of being mounted or dismounted and handled by standard container lifting equipment and that is used by ocean carriers for transportation of goods on board vessels and includes any container that is insulated, refrigerated or dry cargo or described as flat rack, vehicle rack, liquid tank or open top.

CARGO SHIP. A ship that is not a fishing vessel, a passenger ship or a pleasure craft. *Canada Shipping Act*, R.S.C. 1985, c. S-9, s. 2, as am.

CARGO TANK UNIT. A mobile unit consisting of a tank mounted on a truck, trailer or semi-trailer chassis and of a type that is commonly employed for the road transportation of liquids and gases.

CARNAL KNOWLEDGE. Coitus, copulation, sexual intercourse.

CARNET. *n.* An A.T.A. (Admission Temporaire-Temporary Admission) Carnet referred to in the Custom Convention on the A.T.A. Carnet for the Temporary Admission of Goods. Canada regulations.

CAROTID BODY. An organ located in the side of the neck and concerned with blood pressure regulation. F.A. Jaffe, *A Guide to Pathological Evidence*, 3d ed. (Toronto: Carswell 1991) at 214-15.

CAR POOL VEHICLE. A motor vehicle as defined in the Highway Traffic Act, (a) with a seating capacity of not more than twelve persons, (b) while it is operated transporting no more than twelve commuters including the driver, none of whom pay for the transportation more frequently than on a weekly basis, (c) that is not used by any one driver to transport commuters for more than one round trip per day, and (d) the owner, or if the vehicle is subject to a lease, the lessee, of which does not own or lease another car pool vehicle unless the owner or lessee is the employer of a majority of the commuters transported in the vehicles, but does not include a motor vehicle while being operated by or under contract with a school board or other authority in charge of a school for the transportation of children to or from school. *Public Vehicles Act*, R.S.O. 1990, c. P.54, s. 1.

CARPORT. *n.* An open-sided roofed automobile shelter. *Jasper Townsite Zoning Regulations*, C.R.C., c. 1111, s. 2.

CARRIAGE. *n.* 1. A contract of carriage generally begins when the goods are loaded aboard the carrying vessel or vehicle and continues until the goods are delivered to the final destination. May include salvage. *Bombardier Inc. v. Canadian Pacific Ltd.* (1991), 6 B.L.R. (2d) 166 (Ont. C.A.). 2. " . . . [C]an be used to cover an incidental carriage of goods as well as a whole cargo of goods . . . anything so long as it is carried on the vehicle." *Customs & Excise Commissioners v. Jack Bradley (Accrington) Ltd.*, [1958] 3 All E.R. 487 at 489, [1959] 1 Q.B. 219 (U.K.), Lord Parker C.J.

CARRIAGE BY AIR ACT. This act gives binding force in Canada to the Warsaw convention. J.G. McLeod, *The Conflict of Laws* (Calgary: Carswell, 1983) at 106.

CARRIER. *n.* 1. Any person engaged for hire or reward in transport of persons or commodities by railway, water, aircraft, motor vehicle undertaking or commodity pipeline. 2. An insurer. 3. A person who, without apparent symptoms of a communicable disease, harbours and may disseminate an infectious agent. 4. A person with whom a shipper of goods enters into a contract of carriage of the goods by water. *Canada Shipping Act, 2001*, S.C. 2001, c. 26, s. 247. See AIR ~; CHEMICAL ~; COMBINATION ~; COMMON ~; CONNECTING ~; CRANE ~; INTERJURISDICTIONAL ~; LOCAL ~; MOTOR ~; OCEAN ~; PAPER ~; PRIVATE ~; PUBLIC ~; SEA ~.

CARRY. *v.* 1. Includes to store or have in possession. 2. In connection with insurance, to possess or hold.

CARRY COSTS. A verdict carries costs when the party for whom the verdict is given becomes entitled to costs as an incident of the verdict.

CARRYING CAPACITY. In respect of a vehicle, means the gross vehicle weight rating (manufacturer's rating) of the vehicle less the aggregate of the weight of the unloaded vehicle and the weight of all necessary equipment fuel and tires. *Explosives Regulations*, C.R.C., c. 599, s. 48.

CARRYING CHARGE. A charge made by creditor in addition to interest.

CARRYING COSTS. A verdict carries costs when the party for whom the verdict is given becomes entitled to costs as an incident of the verdict.

CARRYING ON BUSINESS. Involves continuity of time or operations as is involved in the ordinary sense of a 'business'. *Friesen v. R.* (1995), 127 D.L.R. (4th) 193 (S.C.C.). See DOING BUSINESS.

CARRY ON. To carry on, perform, operate, keep, hold, occupy, deal in or use, for gain, whether as principal or as agent.

CARRY ON BUSINESS. 1. Any action for the promotion or execution of any purpose of business. 2. Transaction of business. See DOING BUSINESS.

CARRY ON BUSINESS AS A MORTGAGE BROKER. (i) Solicit a person to borrow or lend money to be secured by a mortgage, (ii) negotiate a mortgage transaction, (iii) collect mortgage payments and otherwise administer mortgages, or (iv) buy, sell or exchange mortgages or offer to do so, on behalf of another person and for money or other consideration.

CARRY-OVER OF CAPITAL LOSSES. If a taxpayer does not have sufficient capital gains against which to deduct capital losses experienced in one taxation year, the taxpayer may carry the losses forward to another year. This is known as carry-over.

CARSWELLALTA. Citation of case originating in Alberta in Carswell's eCarswell system.

CARSWELLB. Citation of case originating in British Columbia in Carswell's eCarswell system.

CARSWELLMAN. Citation of case originating in Manitoba in Carswell's eCarswell system.

CARSWELLNAT. Citation of case originating in the Federal court or before a federal tribunal in Carswell's eCarswell system.

CARSWELLNB. Citation of case originating in the New Brunswick courts in Carswell's eCarswell system.

CARSWELLNFLD. Citation of case originating in Newfoundland in Carswell's eCarswell system.

CARSWELLNS. Citation of case originating in Nova Scotia in Carswell's eCarswell system.

CARSWELLNUN. Citation of case originating in Nunavut in Carswell's eCarswell system.

CARSWELLNWT. Citation of case originating in the Northwest Territories in Carswell's eCarswell system.

CARSWELLONT. Citation of case originating in Ontario in Carswell's eCarswell system.

CARSWELLPEI. Citation of case originating in Prince Edward Island in Carswell's eCarswell system.

CARSWELLQUE. Citation of case originating in the province of Quebec in Carswell's e-Carswell system.

CARSWELLSASK. Citation of case originating in Saskatchewan in Carswell's eCarswell system.

CARSWELLYUKON. Citation of case originating Yukon in Carswell's eCarswell system.

CARTA DE NON ENTE NON VALET. [L.] A charter concerning something which does not exist is of no worth.

CARTA DE UNA PARTE. A one-sided charter; a deed poll.

CARTAE LIBERTATUM. [L.] The British charters of liberties, the Carta de Foresta and Magna Carta.

CARTA NON EST NISI VERTIGIUM DONATIONIS. [L.] The deed is nothing but the covering of the grant; the grant is what is really important.

CARTARUM SUPER FIDEM, MORTUIS TESTIBUS, AD PATRIAM, DE NECESSITUDINE, RECURRENDUM EST. [L.] When the witnesses are dead the validity of charters must be decided by a jury.

CART. B.N.A. *abbr.* Cartwright's Constitutional Cases (Can.), 1868-1896.

CARTE BLANCHE. [Fr. white card] 1. Unlimited authority. 2. A blank card signed at the bottom which gives another person power to write anything above the signature.

CARTEL. *n.* 1. An agreement between producers of raw materials or goods. 2. A wartime agreement regarding the treatment or liberation of prisoners, the treatment of messengers between the conflicting sides or maintenance of postal and telegraphic communication.

CARTEL-SHIP. *n.* A vessel commissioned in wartime which sails under safe conduct to exchange prisoners or to carry a particular proposal from one side to another.

CARTER. See MARY ~ AGREEMENT.

CARTILAGE. See THYROID ~.

CARTOGRAPHIC BOOK. See PRINTED ATLAS OR ~.

CARTOGRAPHIC RECORD OR DOCUMENT. (a) A collection of cartographic representations composed of manuscript or printed material that is bound, stitched or fastened together to form a unit that has no established dates of printing for the unit as a whole, (b) a single sheet containing thereon cartographic representations irrespective of folding, or (c) cartographic material (i) unattached and issued in a combination other than a printed book, such as boxed maps, irrespective of their dates of printing, or (ii) in a loose format that clearly forms a single unit of visual information. *Canadian Cultural Property Export Control List*, C.R.C., c. 448, s. 1.

CARTRIDGE. *n.* 1. A unit of ammunition composed of projectile, cartridge case, primer and propellant, or, in the case of shotgun ammunition, shell, pellets and wads. F.A. Jaffe, *A Guide to Pathological Evidence*, 3d ed. (Toronto: Carswell, 1991) at 215. 2. A stick of explosives enclosed in a wrapping of waterproof paper. See LARGE-CAPACITY ~ MAGAZINE; PRIMER ~; RIM-FIRE SHELL OR ~; SAFETY ~.

CARTRIDGE CASE. A metal or plastic cylinder of firearm ammunition containing propellant; primer and projectile are inserted into it. F.A. Jaffe, *A Guide to Pathological Evidence*, 3d ed. (Toronto: Carswell, 1991) at 215 .

CARTRIDGE MAGAZINE. A device or container from which ammunition may be fed into the firing chamber of a firearm. *Criminal Code*, R.S.C. 1985, c. C-46, s. 84(1).

CARVING STONE. Serpentinite, argillite or soapstone that is suitable for carving. *Nunavut Waters and Nunavut Surface Rights Tribunal Act, 2002*, S.C. 2002, c. 10, s. 2.

CAR WASH. A building or place where motor vehicles are washed, cleaned or polished for a fee or charge.

C.A.S. *abbr.* 1. Children's Aid Societ(y)(ies). 2. Décisions de la Commission des affaires sociales.

CA. SA. *abbr.* Capias ad satisfaciendum.

CASE. *v.* 1. For a potential thief or burglar to inspect a premises. 2. The operation of adding to raw leaf tobacco any flavouring materials. *Excise Act*, R.S.C. 1985, c. E-14, s. 6.

CASE. *n.* 1. " . . . '[S]uit' or 'appeal' and that . . . it also included 'decision, question or matter'." *lantsis (Papatheodorou) v. Paparheodorou* (1971), 3 R.F.L. 158 at 164, [1971] 1 O.R. 245, 15 D.L.R. (3d) 53 (C.A.), the court per Schroeder J.A. 2. Instance. *Lovibond v. Grand Trunk Railway*, [1934] O.R. 729 at 743, 43 C.R.C. 38, [1935] 1 D.L.R. 179 (C.A.), Macdonnell J.A. (Fisher J.A. concurring). 3. A sealed package, carton or container. See ACTION ON THE ~; CARTRIDGE ~; HALLMARK ~; LEADING ~; MCNAGHTEN'S ~; PRIMA FACIE ~; SPECIAL ~; STATED ~; TEST ~.

CASE-BY-CASE PRIVILEGE. The communications are not privileged unless the party opposing disclosure can show they should be privileged according to the fourfold utilitarian test elaborated by Wigmore: (1)The communications must originate in a confidence that they will not be disclosed. (2)This element of *confidentiality must be essential* to the full and satisfactory maintenance of the relation between the parties. (3)The *relation* must be one which in the opinion of the community ought to be sedulously. (4)The *injury* that would inure to the relation by the disclosure of the communications must be *greater than the benefit* thereby gained for the correct disposal of litigation. *A. (L.L.) v. B. (A.)*, [1995] 4 S.C.R. 536, per L'Heureux-Dube, J.

CASE-CONTROL STUDY. A medical or scientific study which compares the differences between two populations of persons who are matched except for the feature being studied. A moderately reliable source of clinical evidence.

CASE LAW. The decisions of judges relating to particular matters in contrast to statute law; case law is a source of law and forms legal precedents.

CASE READY FOR JUDGMENT. A case in which the trial has been completed and which has been taken under advisement.

CASE REPORT. A medical or scientific study which reports on an individual or small number of cases of a particular condition. Provides the weakest clinical evidence of causation.

CASE SERIES. A medical or scientific study of a number of cases of a particular condition. More reliable than individual case reports.

CASE STATED. A written statement requesting an opinion on a question of law.

CASE TO MEET. The Crown establishes a case to meet only when it adduces evidence which, if believed, would establish proof beyond a reasonable doubt. In short, "the Crown must prove its case before there can be any expectation that [the accused] will respond." *R. v. Noble*, 1997 CarswellBC 710, 210 N.R. 321, 6 C.R. (5th) 1, 89 B.C.A.C. 1, 145 W.A.C. 1, 114 C.C.C. (3d) 385, 146 D.L.R. (4th) 385, [1997] 1 S.C.R. 874, [1997] 6 W.W.R. 1, 43 C.R.R. (2d) 233, McLachlin J. (dissenting).

CASH. *v.* To convert a negotiable instrument to money.

CASH. *n.* 1. Currency. *Irving Oil Co. Assessment, Re* (1948), 22 M.P.R. 63 at 72, [1948] 2 D.L.R. 774 (N.S. C.A.), Doull J.A. (Chrisholm C.J., Graham and MacQuarrie JJ.A. concurring). 2. Bank notes and coins. 3. May refer to cheques and bills of exchange as well as to bank notes and coins. See PETTY ~ EXPENDITURE.

CASH ACCOUNT. 1. In bookkeeping, a record of cash transactions. 2. A brokerage firm account which is settled on a cash basis. See MARGIN ACCOUNT.

CASH AGAINST DOCUMENTS. An invoiced amount due when a bill of lading is presented.

CASH BASIS. An accounting method which recognizes income when actually received and expenses when actually paid out. See ACCRUAL METHOD OF ACCOUNTING.

CASH BOOK. An accounting record that combines cash receipts and disbursements.

CASH BUDGET. The estimated cash receipts and disbursements for a future period.

CASH DIVIDEND. The portion of profits and surplus paid to shareholders by a corporation in cash, in contrast with a stock dividend.

CASHIER. *v*. To dismiss from command or a position of authority.

CASHIER. *n*. 1. A person who collects and records payments at a business. 2. A person who cashes winning pari-mutuel tickets.

CASH LAPPING. An illegal practice whereby employees of an armoured car company remove cash from customers' bags, use it for company operations, then replace it on the next day with cash taken from other customers' bags. *Moss v. National Armoured Ltd.* (1996), 44 C.C.L.I. (2d) 268 (Ont. Gen. Div. [Commercial List]).

CASH METHOD. An accounting method which recognizes income when actually received and expenses when actually paid out. See ACCRUAL METHOD OF ACCOUNTING.

CASH-MUTUAL CORPORATION. A corporation without share capital that is empowered to undertake insurance on both the cash plan and the mutual plan.

CASH-MUTUAL INSURANCE COMPANY. A company without share capital or with guarantee capital stock subject to repayment by the company, in respect of which the dividend rate is limited by its act or instrument of incorporation, which is empowered to undertake insurance on both the cash plan and the mutual plan.

CASH ON DELIVERY. A sale of goods on condition that cash be paid on delivery.

CASH PRICE. The price that would be charged by the seller for the goods or services to a buyer who paid cash for them at the time of purchase or hiring.

CASH SURRENDER VALUE. The amount an insurer will return to a policyholder upon cancellation of the policy.

CASING. *n*. 1. Pipe or tubing installed in a well to support the sides of the well. 2. A skinlike case for processed meat. 3. The operation of adding to raw leaf tobacco any flavouring materials. *Excise Act*, R.S.C. 1985, c. E-14, s. 6.

CASKET. A container intended to hold a dead human body for funeral, cremation or interment purposes.

CASPAR'S RULE. At roughly similar temperature a body after lying in the open air putrifies in one week the same amount as a body lying in water putrifies in two weeks or a body lying in earth in the usual manner putrifies in eight weeks. F.A. Jaffe, *A Guide to Pathological Evidence*, 3d ed. (Toronto: Carswell, 1991) at 215.

CASSETUR BILLA. [L.] Let the bill be quashed.

CASSETUR BREVE. [L.] Let the writ be quashed.

CASS. PRAC. CAS. *abbr*. Cassels' Practice Cases (Can.).

CASS. S.C. *abbr*. Cassels' Supreme Court Decisions.

CAST. *v*. To deposit formally, as to cast a ballot.

CASTING VOTE. The deciding vote to break equality of votes, cast by the chair or presiding officer. Whether the chair has a casting vote depends on provisions of the relevant statute, by-laws, standing orders, regulations or articles.

CASUAL. adj " . . . [T]he antonym of 'regular' and means occasional or coming at uncertain times without regularity in distinction from stated or regular. . ." *R. v. C.U.P.E.* (1981), 125 D.L.R. (3d) 220 at 224 (N.B. C.A.), the court per Stratton J.A.

CASUAL EMPLOYEE. A person engaged to perform work of a casual nature or in an emergency.

CASUAL EMPLOYMENT. 1. " . . . [E]mployment at uncertain times or irregular intervals or employment lacking continuity and has reference to the nature of the employment and not its duration." *R. v. C.U.P.E.* (1981) 125 D.L.R. (3d) 220 at 224 (N.B. C.A.), the court per Stratton J.A. 2. " . . . [T]he product of a given employer's unforeseen need to have work performed and the chance, random and voluntary availability of a given employee." *Bank of Montreal v. U.S.W.A.* (1987), 87 C.L.L.C. 16,044 (Can.).

CASUAL IMPORTER. A person who is not normally engaged in the importation of goods into Canada. *Casual Importer Regulations*, C.R.C., c. 453, s. 2.

CASUALTY. See SHIPPING ~.

CASUAL WORKER. A person who works occasionally.

CASUS BELLI. [L.] An incident which causes or justifies war.

CASUS FOEDERIS. [L.] An event which, through the terms of a treaty, entitles one allied nation to help from another or others.

CASUS FORTUITUS NON EST SPERAN- DUS; ET NEMO TENETUR DIVINARE. [L.] No reliance should be placed on an event which may or may not happen; and, if it does happen, no one can foresee that it will happen.

CASUS NON PRAESTATUR. [L.] An accident for which one did not take responsibility.

CASUS OMISSUS. [L.] Something which should have been, but was not, provided for.

CASUS OMISSUS ET OBLIVIONI DATUS DISPOSITIONI COMMUNIS JURIS RE- LINQUITUR. [L.] A point not treated by statute law must be decided according to common law.

CATALOGUE. *n.* 1. A bound, stitched, sewed or stapled book or pamphlet containing a list and description of goods, wares, merchandise or services, with specific information, with or without price. 2. A publication in printed, electronic or microfiche form that (*a*) is updated at least once a year; (*b*) lists all book titles currently in print that are available from at least one exclusive distributor; and (*c*) identifies the title, the International Standard Book Number, the exclusive distributor, the author and the list price in Canada for each book listed. *Book Importation Regulations*, SOR/99-324, s. 1.

CATALYST. *n.* A substance that produces or modifies a chemical reaction and that, at the end of the reaction, is unchanged.

CATALYTIC CONVERTER. A device through which exhaust from a motor is passed in order to prevent or lessen the emission of a contaminant and which device would be impaired in its functioning by the use of leaded gasoline as a fuel for operation of the motor.

CATCH. *n.* Any unprocessed product or natural by-product of the sea or of any other body of water caught or taken by a crew and includes Irish moss, kelp and whales. See FRESH ~; IN- CIDENTAL ~.

CATCHING BARGAIN. An agreement to loan or pay money made on unfavourable terms to a person having property in reversion or expectancy.

CATCHPOLE. *n.* A bailiff or sheriff's officer.

CATCH-WEIGHT. *n.* A product that because of its nature cannot ordinarily be portioned to a predetermined quantity and is, as a result, usually sold in packages of varying quantity.

CATCHWEIGHT PACKAGE. Any transparent package sold on a weight basis in which the produce is readily visible.

CATCH WEIGHT PRODUCT. A product that because of its nature cannot normally be portioned to a predetermined quantity and is, as a result, usually sold in packages of varying quantity.

CATCH-WEIGHTS. *n.* When used in a professional boxing contract means the actual weights of the contestants where no mention of specific weights is made in the contract.

CATEGORY. See OCCUPATIONAL ~.

CATEGORY 1 SERVICE. A Canadian programming service designated as such by the Commission. *Broadcasting Distribution Regulations*, SOR/97-555, s. 1.

CATEGORY 2 SERVICE. A Canadian programming service designated as such by the Commission. *Broadcasting Distribution Regulations*, SOR/97-555, s. 1.

C.A.T. (QUÉ.). *abbr.* Commission des accidents du travail (Québec).

CAT ROAD. An unsurfaced road of a temporary nature over which logs or materials are dragged by any means.

CATTLE. *n.* 1. Neat cattle or an animal of the bovine species by whatever technical or familiar name it is known, and includes any horse, mule, ass, pig, sheep or goat. *Criminal Code*, R.S.C. 1985, c. C-46, s. 2. 2. A bull, cow, ox heifer, steer or calf. 3. Animals of the species *Bos taurus* or *Bos indicus. Health of Animals Regulations*, C.R.C. 296, s. 2. See PURE-BRED ~.

CATTLE PEST. The insect known as Hypoderma bovis or Hypoderma lineatum and commonly known as the warble fly. *Cattle Pest Control Act*, R.S.N.S. 1989, c. 61, s. 2.

CATTLE WITH HORNS. Cattle that are not polled or have not been dehorned.

CATV. *abbr.* 1. Community Antenna Television. 2. ". . . [I]t provides a well-located antenna with an efficient connection to the viewer's television set . . ." *Fortnightly Corp. v. United Artists Television Inc.* (1968), 392 U.S. 390 at 399 Stewart J., cited with approval in *Capital Cities Communications Inc. v. Canada (Canadian Radio-Television & Telecommunications Commission)* (1977), 36 C.P.R. (2d) 1 at 13, [1978] 2

S.C.R. 141, 81 D.L.R. (3d) 609, 18 N.R. 181, Laskin C.J. (Martland, Judson, Ritchie, Spence and Dickson JJ. concurring).

CAUCUS. *n.* The members of Parliament or a legislature who belong to the same party. See OPPOSITION ~; THIRD PARTY ~.

CAUSA CAUSANS. [L.] The immediate cause; the last of a chain of causes.

CAUSAE DOTIS, VITAE, LIBERTATIS, FISCI, SUNT INTER FAVORABILIA, IN LEGE. [L.] Causes of dower, life, liberty, revenue are among the things favoured in law.

CAUSA MORTIS. [L.] Because of death; in case of death.

CAUSA PROXIMA. [L.] The immediate cause.

CAUSA PROXIMA NON REMOTA SPECTATUR. [L.] The immediate, not the remote, cause should be considered.

CAUSA SINE QUA NON. [L.] The cause without which the event would not have occurred.

CAUSATION. *n.*1. " . . . [A]n expression of the relationship that must be found to exist between the tortious act of the wrongdoer and the injury to the victim in order to justify compensation of the latter out of the pocket of the former." *Snell v. Farrell* (1990), 4 C.C.L.T. (2d) 229 at 243, 110 N.R. 200, [1990] 2 S.C.R. 311, the court per Sopinka J. 2. Is established, in negligence, when the plaintiff proves on a balance of probabilities, that the defendant caused or contributed to the injury. The generally applicable test is the "but for" test. This test "requires the plaintiff to show that the injury would not have occurred but for the negligence of the defendant" (*[Athey v. Leonati*, [1996] 3 S.C.R. 458], at para.14). *Cottrelle v. Gerrard* (2003), 178 O.A.C. 142 (C.A.). See ACTUAL ~; FACTUAL ~; LEGAL ~.

CAUSE. *v.* " . . . [A] transitive verb which in its ordinary usage contemplates that someone or something brings about an effect." *Astro Tire & Rubber Co. v. Western Assurance Co.*, [1979] I.L.R. 1-1098 at 188, 24 O.R. (2d) 268, 97 D.L.R. (3d) 515 (C. A.), Blair J.A.

CAUSE. *n.* 1. A suit or action. *Hampton Lumber Mills v. Joy Logging Ltd* (1977), 2 C.P.C. 312 at 317, [1977] 2 W.W.R. 289 (B.C. S.C.), Ruttan J. 2. That which produces an effect and includes any action, suit or other original proceeding between a plaintiff and a defendant and any criminal proceeding by the Crown. 3. In negligence

cases, the defendant's fault is a cause of the damage if the damage would not have occurred but for the defendant's fault and the fault is not a cause if the damage would have happened with or without the defendant's fault. John G. Fleming, *The Law of Torts*, 8th ed. (Sydney: The Law Book Company Limited, 1992) at 194. 4. "[In the context of dismissal for cause] . . . relates to the acts or the omissions of the employee, not the acts or the omissions of the employer." *Alberta v. A. E.P.E.* (1987), 53 Alta. L.R. (2d) 275 at 278, 82 A.R. 19 (Q.B.), Dea J. 5. In the context of a landlord's having cause, means reason. See CHALLENGE FOR ~; COSTS IN THE ~; DISMISSAL FOR ~; GOOD ~; MATRIMONIAL ~; NECESSARY ~; NO MAN SHALL BE JUDGE IN HIS OWN ~; PROBABLE ~; REASONABLE AND PROBABLE ~; SHOW ~ ORDER; TESTAMENTARY MATTERS AND ~S.

CAUSE CÉLÈBRE. [Fr.] A matter of great interest or importance.

CAUSED. *v.* "[In s. 231(5) of the Criminal Code, R.S.C. 1985, c. C-46] . . . where the combined effect of assaults by two or more persons upon a victim is the death of the victim and death was the very purpose of the assaults, then those persons who jointly assaulted the victim caused the death." *R. v. Harbottle* (1992), 14 C.R. (4th) 363 at 374, 72 C.C.C. (3d) 257, 54 O.A.C. 32, 8 O.R. (3d) 385 (C.A.), Galligan J.A. (Tarnopolsky J.A. concurring).

CAUSE OF ACTION. "The classic definition of a cause of action as stated by Diplock L.J. in Letang *v.* Cooper, [1965] 1 Q.B. 232 . . . (H.L.) is as follows: 'A cause of action is simply a factual situation the existence of which entitles one person to obtain from the court a remedy against another person.' . . ." *Consumers Glass Co. v. Foundation Co. of Canada/Cie fondation du Canada* (1985), 1 C.P.R. (2d) 208 at 215, 51 O.R. (2d) 385, 33 C.C.L.T. 104, 30 B.L.R. 87, 13 C.L.R. 149, 9 O.A.C. 193, 20 D.L.R. (4th) 126 (C.A.), the court per Dubin J.A. See REASONABLE ~.

CAUSE OF ACTION ESTOPPEL. " . . . [P]recludes a person from bringing an action against another when the same cause of action has been determined in earlier proceedings by a court of competent jurisdiction . . ." *Angle v. M.N.R.*, [1975] 2 S.C.R. 248 at 253-55, Dickson J.

CAUSE OF DEATH. 1. Whatever violence or disease disrupts the vital processes and brings about death. P.A. Jaffe, *A Guide to Pathological Evidence*, 3d ed. (Toronto: Carswell, 1991) at 12. 2. The medical cause of death according to the International Statistical Classification of Diseases, Injuries and Causes of Death as last revised by the International Conference assembled for that purpose and published by the World Health Organization. *Fatality Inquiries acts.*

CAUTION. *n.* 1. A warning. 2. A warning given to an accused concerning possibly incriminating statements. 3. " . . . [N]otice of adverse claim equivalent to a lis pendens and expires by lapse of time or otherwise as may be directed by the Court in an action: . . ." *Ontario (Attorney General) v. Hargrave*, [1906] 11 O.L.R. 530 at 536 (H.C.), Master.

CAUTIO PRO EXPENSIS. [L.] Security for costs.

CAUTIOUS. *adj.* Careful.

C.A.V. *abbr.* Curia advisari vult.

CAVEAT. *n.* [L. let one take heed] 1. "A caveat [under the Land Titles Act, R.S.A. 1980, c. L5] is a warning, a notice and a prohibition. It creates no new rights, but prevents new ones arising other than subject to the claim of which it gives notice after registration. It is intended strictly to preserve the status quo . . ." *Royal Bank v. Donsdale Developments Ltd.* (1986), 43 R.P.R. 59 at 75, 48 Alta. L.R. (2d) 289, [1987] 2 W.W.R. 14, 74 A.R. 161 (Q.B.), Andrekson J. 2. A document filed by an inventor before filing an application. 3. "[In the context of estates]. . . 'a formal notice or caution given by a person interested, to a Court, Judge, or public officer, against the performance of certain judicial or ministerial acts.' A caution, or caveat, while in force, may stop probate or administration from being granted without notice to or knowledge of the person who enters it . . ." *McDevitt, Re* (1913), O.W.N. 333 at 335, 25 O.W.R. 309 (H.C.), Britton J.

CAVEAT ACTOR. [L.] Let the doer beware.

CAVEAT EMPTOR. [L. let the buyer beware] "The rule . . . [means] that a buyer gets only what he bargains for." *Moretta v. Western Computer Investment Corp.* (1983), 26 B.L.R. 68 at 84, [1984] 2 W.W.R. 409, 29 Alta. L.R. (2d) 193 (C.A.), Kerans J.A.

CAVEAT EMPTOR; QUI IGNORARE NON DEBUIT QUOD JUS ALIENUM EMIT. [L.] A purchaser must be on guard; for the purchaser has no right to ignore the fact that what was bought belongs to someone else besides the vendor.

CAVEATOR. *n.* The person who gives, files or registers a caveat.

CAVEAT PAYMENT. A person who wants to prevent paying money out of court may file a notice and the Registry must enter a caveat in its caveat payment book. D. Sgayias *et al., Federal Court Practice 1988* (Toronto: Carswell, 1987) at 546.

CAVEAT RELEASE. A person who wants to prevent releasing property under arrest may file a notice, and the Registry must enter a caveat in its caveat release book. D. Sgayias *et al., Federal Court Practice 1988* (Toronto: Carswell, 1987) at 546.

CAVEAT VENDITOR. [L.] Let the seller beware.

CAVEAT VIATOR. [L.] Let the traveller beware.

CAVEAT WARRANT. To give bail to an action or counter-claim that may be or may have been brought against property so that the Registry enters a caveat in its caveat warrant book. D. Sgayias *et al., Federal Court Practice 1988* (Toronto: Carswell, 1987) at 545.

CAVITY. *n.* A structure that encloses and confines a microwave field. See PERMANENT ~; TEMPORARY ~.

CAVITY WALL. A construction of masonry laid up with a cavity between the wythes tied together with metal ties or bonding units, the cavity of which may or may not contain insulation.

CAVR CAB CARD. A permit issued pursuant to the Canadian Agreement on Vehicle Registration.

C.B.A. PAPERS. *abbr.* Canadian Bar Association Papers.

C.B.A. Y.B. *abbr.* Canadian Bar Year Book.

CBC. *abbr.* Canadian Broadcasting Corporation.

C.B.E.S. *abbr.* Cour du Bien-être social.

C.B.R. *abbr.* Canadian Bankruptcy Reports, 1920-1960.

C.B.R. (N.S.). *abbr.* Canadian Bankruptcy Reports, New Series, 1960-.

CC. *abbr.* Cubic centimetre.

C.C.A.S. *abbr*. Catholic Children's Aid Societ(y)(ies).

CCAT. *abbr*. Council of Canadian Administrative Tribunals.

C.C.C. *abbr*. Canadian Criminal Cases, 1893-1962.

[] **C.C.C**. *abbr*. Canadian Criminal Cases, 1963-1970.

C.C.C. (2D). *abbr*. Canadian Criminal Cases (Second Series), 1971-1983.

C.C.C. (3D). *abbr*. Canadian Criminal Cases (Third Series), 1983-.

C.C.D.P. *abbr*. Commission canadienne des droits de la personne.

C.C.E.A. *abbr*. Commission de contrôle de l'énergie atomique.

C.C.E.L. *abbr*. Canadian Cases on Employment Law, 1983-.

CCFTA. The Canada-Chile Free Trade Agreement.

C. CIRC. *abbr*. Cour de circuit.

CCL. *abbr*. Canadian Congress of Labour, which is now part of the Canadian Labour Congress.

[] **C.C.L**. *abbr*. Canadian Current Law.

C.C.L.I. *abbr*. Canadian Cases on the Law of Insurance, 1983-.

C.C.L.R. *abbr*. Canada Corporations Law Reports.

C.C.L.T. *abbr*. Canadian Cases of the Law of Torts, 1976-.

C.C.P. *abbr*. Commission canadienne des pensions.

CCRA. Canada Customs and Revenue Agency.

C.C.R.T. *abbr*. Conseil canadien des relations de travail.

CD. *abbr*. Candela.

C. DE D. *abbr*. Les Cahiers de droit.

C. DE L'É. *abbr*. Cour de l'Échiquier.

C. DE L'I.Q.A.J. *abbr*. Cahiers de l'institut québécois d'administration judiciaire.

CDIC. *abbr*. Canada Deposit Insurance Corporation.

C. DIST. *abbr*. Cour de district.

C. DIV. *abbr*. Cour divisionnaire.

CDN. *abbr*. Canadian.

CDRP. Canadian internet registration authority domain name dispute resolution policy.

CEASE. *v*. To stop; to suspend activity.

C.E.B. & P.G.R. *abbr*. Canadian Employment Benefits and Pension Guide Reports.

C.E.C.M. *abbr*. Commission des écoles catholiques de Montreal.

CEDE. *v*. 1. To give up or yield. 2. To transfer. 3. To surrender.

C.E.G.S.B. *abbr*. Crown Employees Grievance Settlement Board.

CEILING. *n*. 1. An upper limit on wages or hours. 2. The lowest height at which a broken or overcast condition exists, or the vertical visibility when an obscured condition such as snow, smoke or fog exists, whichever is the lower.

CELEBRATION OF MARRIAGE. The formal act by which two persons become husband and wife.

CELIBACY. *n*. The state or condition of remaining single or unmarried, usually used in connection with one who has vowed to remain single or unmarried.

CELL. *n*. In respect of a landfilling site, means a deposit of waste that has been sealed by cover material so that no waste deposited in the cell is exposed to the atmosphere. See MERCURY ~.

CELLAR. *n*. 1. An underground room; a basement. 2. A basement that is more than 50 per cent below grade.

CELL ROOM. In respect of (a) a structure housing one or more mercury cells, means the structure, and (b) mercury cells not housed in a structure, means the mercury cells. *Chlor-Alkali Mercury National Emission Standards Regulations*, C.R.C., c. 406, s. 2.

CELLULAR DEATH. The death of cells or even whole organs which follows death by several hours. F.A. Jaffe, *A Guide to Pathological Evidence*, 3d ed. (Toronto: Carswell, 1991) at 3 and 4.

CELLULAR FLOOR. An assembly of metal or concrete floor members containing cells. *Power Corporation Act*, R.R.O. 1980, Reg. 794, s. 0.

C.E.L.R. *abbr*. Canadian Environmental Law Reports.

C.E.L.R. (N.S.). *abbr*. Canadian Environmental Law Reports (New Series).

CEMENTED SAND AND GRAVEL. A mixture of sand and gravel or boulders thoroughly cemented together as a hard layer which will not soften in its natural bed when wet.

CEMENT MASON. A person who does concrete finishing by hand or with mechanical equipment, does all phases of waterproofing and restoration of concrete, does rubbing-up and repairing of hardened concrete surfaces, places and finishes epoxy, plastic and other composition materials, and finishes and exposes aggregate in pre-cast and architectural concrete.

CEMETERY. *n*. Land set aside to be used for the interment of human remains and includes a mausoleum, columbarium or other structure intended for the interment of human remains. See COMMERCIAL ~; FAMILY ~; PREARRANGED ~ CONTRACT; PRENEED ~ PLAN.

CEMETERY COMPANY. A corporation that is the owner of a cemetery.

CEMETERY GOODS OR SERVICES. The goods supplied by the cemetery or crematorium in conjunction with the burial or cremation of human remains or the services performed by the cemetery or crematorium relative to the installation or provision of any of the goods.

CEMETERY OR PERPETUAL CARE TRUST. A trust, usually created by will, to keep up and maintain one or more designated graves or other burial places within a burial site or cemetery. D.M.W. Waters, *The Law of Trusts in Canada*, 2d ed. (Toronto: Carswell, 1984) at 436.

CEMETERY SERVICES. 1. The opening and closing of graves, compartments, crypts or other spaces and services related thereto. 2. In respect of a lot, (i) opening and closing of a grave, (ii) interring or disinterring human remains, (iii) providing temporary storage in a receiving vault, (iv) construction of a foundation for a marker, (v) setting of corner posts, (vi) providing, a tent or canopy, carrying and lowering devices, and ground cover, for an interment service, and (vii) preparing flower beds and planting flowers and shrubs, (b) in respect of a crypt or compartment in a mausoleum, (i) opening, closing and sealing of the crypt or compartment, (ii) providing tem-porary storage in a vault or crypt, (iii) providing a tent or canopy for an interment service, and (iv) providing elevating devices, (c) in respect of a niche or compartment in a columbarium, (i) opening, closing and sealing of the niche or compartment, and (ii) providing a tent or canopy for an interment service, (d) in respect of a crematorium, all services provided by the owner of the crematorium at the crematorium, and (e) in respect of a cemetery, such other services as are provided by the owner of the cemetery at the cemetery. *Cemeteries Act (Revised)* R.S.O. 1990, c. C.4, s. 1, as am. See PRENEED ~ PLAN.

CEMETERY SUPPLIES. Burial vaults, grave stones, grave markers, flowers, shrubs and artificial wreaths and other articles intended to be placed in a cemetery, monuments or bases for use in a cemetery.

CENSOR. *n*. A person who regulates or prohibits distribution, production or exhibition of films or publication of books, plays, etc.

CENSORSHIP. *n*. The prohibition or regulation of publication, distribution or production of books, plays, films.

CENSURE. *n*. An official reprimand; condemnation.

CENSUS. *n*. A count or enumeration of the people. See GENERAL ~; PENULTIMATE DECENNIAL ~.

CENSUS REGALIS. [L.] The annual income or revenue of the Crown.

CENT. *n*. 1. A coin. 2. One hundredth part of a dollar.

CENTAL. *n*. 100 pounds. *Weights and Measures Act*, S.C. 1970-71-72, c. 36, schedule II.

CENTI. *pref*. 10^{-2}. A prefix for multiples and submultiples of basic, supplementary and derived units of measurement. *Weights and Measures Act*, S.C. 1970-71-72, c. 36, Schedule 1.

CENTIMETRE. See CUBIC ~.

CENTIN. *n*. Used in the French version of the laws of Quebec, means the coin called "cent" in the laws of Canada and in the English version of the laws of Quebec. *Interpretation Act*, R.S.Q. 1977, c. I-16, s. 61.

CENTRAL CARDIOVASCULAR SYSTEM. The heart, pericardium, pulmonary veins, pulmonary arteries, cardiac veins, coronary arteries, common carotid arteries, cerebral arteries, brachiocephalic artery, aorta, inferior and superior vena cava, renal arteries, iliac arteries and femoral arteries. *Medical Devices Regulations* SOR/98-282, s. 1.

CENTRAL CLAIMS DRAFTING PRINCIPLE. The *Patent Act* [R.S.C. 1985, c. P-4] requires the letters patent granting a patent monopoly to include a specification which sets out a correct and full "disclosure" of the invention, i.e., "correctly and fully describes the invention and its operation or use as contemplated by the inventor" (s. 34(1)(*a*)). The disclosure is followed by "a claim or claims stating distinctly and in explicit terms the things or combinations that the applicant regards as new and in which he claims an exclusive property or privilege" (s. 34(2)). It is the invention thus claimed to which the patentee receives the "exclusive right, privilege and liberty" of exploitation (s. 44). These provisions, and similar provisions in other jurisdictions, have given rise to two schools of thought. One school holds that the claim embodies a technical idea and claims construction ought to look to substance rather than form to protect the inventive idea underlying the claim language. This is sometimes called the "central claims drafting principle" and is associated with the German and Japanese patent systems. The other school of thought supporting what is sometimes called the "peripheral claiming principle" emphasizes the language of the claims as defining not the underlying technical idea but the legal boundary of the state-conferred monopoly. Traditionally, for reasons of fairness and predictability, Canadian courts have preferred the latter approach. *Free World Trust c. Électro Santé Inc.*, 2000 CarswellQue 2728, 2000 SCC 66, 194 D.L.R. (4th) 232, 263 N.R. 150, [2000] 2 S.C.R. 1024, 9 C.P.R. (4th) 168, Binnie, J.

CENTRAL COOPERATIVE CREDIT SOCIETY. A body corporate organized on cooperative principles by or under an Act of the legislature of a province, one of whose principal purposes is to receive deposits from and provide liquidity support to local cooperative credit societies, and (a) whose membership consists solely or primarily of local cooperative credit societies, or (b) whose directors are wholly or primarily persons elected or appointed by local cooperative credit societies. *Federal acts.*

CENTRAL COUNTER-PARTY. A corporation, association, partnership, agency or other entity in a clearing and settlement system with whom all participant's payment rights and obligations are netted to produce a single amount owing as between each participant and the central counter-party. *Payment Clearing and Settlement Act*, S.C. 1996, c. 6, Sch., s. 2.

CENTRAL CREDIT UNION. An organization of credit unions.

CENTRAL HIRING HALL. A central location where unionized workers are referred to seasonal or casual jobs.

CENTRALIST. *adj*. Describes a form of federal government in which greater power is given to the central or federal government.

CENTRAL LABOUR CONGRESS. An affiliation of unions, directly chartered locals, provincial labour federations and local labour councils organized to co-ordinate activities at the national level.

CENTRAL NERVOUS SYSTEM. The brain, meninges, spinal cord and cerebrospinal fluid. *Medical Devices Regulations* SOR/98-282, s. 1.

CENTRAL POLITICAL PARTY ORGANIZATION. The permanent and continuing office and staff of a recognized political party. *Election Act*, R.S.M. 1970, c. E30, s. 2.

CENTRAL STANDARD TIME. The mean time of the ninetieth degree of longitude west from Greenwich which is six hours behind Greenwich time.

CENTRE. *n*. A building or facility. See CLASSIFICATION ~; COMMUNITY ~; CORRECTIONAL ~; DAY CARE ~; DISPATCH ~; DRYING ~; GERIATRIC ~; HOSPITAL ~; INFORMATION ~; JUDICIAL ~; MENTAL HEALTH ~; NATIONAL ARTS ~; RECREATION ~; REMAND ~; SHOPPING ~; TREATMENT ~.

CENTRE FIRE AMMUNITION. Firearm ammunition in which the primer is located in the centre of the base of the cartridge case in a well. F.A. Jaffe, *A Guide to Pathological Evidence*, 3d ed. (Toronto: Carswell, 1991) at 215.

CENTRE LINE. 1. Either (a) the centre of a roadway measured from the curbs or, in the absence of curbs, from the edges of the roadway, or (b) where on a laned roadway there are more lanes available for traffic in one direction than the other direction the line dividing the lanes for traffic in different directions except, in both cases, on a one-way roadway. 2. (a) In the case of a highway on which traffic is permitted to move in opposing directions, the marked line or median that divides traffic moving in opposing directions on the highway or, where there is no marked line or median, the centre of the roadway; and (b) in the case of a highway designated for the use of one-way traffic the left curb or edge of the roadway. *Highway Traffic Act*, R.S.O. 1990, c. H.8, s. 141(1).

CENTRE OF OSSIFICATION. A point where bone forms. F.A. Jaffe, *A Guide to Pathological Evidence*, 3d ed. (Toronto: Carswell 1991) at 223.

CENTRE POINT OF AN INTERSECTION. The point where the centre line of the through part of a highway meets the centre line of, or the centre line of the prolongation of, another highway that intersects or meets the highway.

CENTURY. *n.* 1. One hundred. 2. One hundred years.

C.E.P.A.R. *abbr*. Canadian Estate Planning and Administration Reporter.

CEPI CORPUS ET PARATUM HABEO. [L. I have taken the body and have it ready] The return to a writ of capias or attachment by a sheriff to indicate that the defendant is in custody.

CEPIT. [L.] Did carry away.

CEPIT IN ALIO LOCO. [L.] A plea in replevin, stating that the defendant has taken the goods in a different place than the one mentioned in the declaration.

C.E.P.R. *abbr*. Canadian Estate Planning and Administration Reporter.

C.E.R. *abbr*. Canadian Customs and Excise reports, 1980-.

CEREBRAL EDEMA. A swelling of brain tissue. F.A. Jaffe, *A Guide to Pathological Evidence*, 3d ed. (Toronto: Carswell, 1991) at 157.

CEREBROSPINAL FLUID. A clear fluid which circulates in the cavities of the brain and the space surrounding the spinal cord and brain. F.A. Jaffe, *A Guide to Pathological Evidence*, 3d ed. (Toronto: Carswell, 1991) at 215.

CEREMONY. A formal event to mark an occasion. See CIVIL ~.

CERTA DEBET ESSE INTENTIO, ET NARRATIO, ET CERTUM FUNDAMENTUM, ET CERTA RES QUAE DEDUCITUR IN JUDICIUM. [L.] In a pleading, the intention, the declaration and the cause of action

should be clear, and so should the point which the court is asked to decide.

CERTAIN. *adj.* 1. Definitive. 2. Free from doubt.

CERTAINTY. *n.* 1. Accuracy; absence of doubt. 2. Precision. See THREE CERTAINTIES.

CERTAINTY OF INTENTION. One of the "three certainties" required of a trust. The transferor of the property to the trust must be found to have intended to create a trust.

CERTAINTY OF OBJECTS. One of the "three certainties" required of a trust. The intended beneficiaries of the trust must be ascertainable.

CERTAINTY OF SUBJECT MATTER. One of the "three certainties" required of a trust. The property which is subject to the trust must be identifiable.

CERTIFICATE. *n.* 1. An official assurance or representation concerning a matter within the knowledge or authority of the person making the certificate. 2. A document issued to show that a person has completed a course of study or training. See AGE ~; ARCHITECT'S BUILDER'S ~; DUPLICATE ~; EMPLOYMENT ~; FIRST AID ~; GUARANTEED INVESTMENT ~; HEALTH ~; HUNTER'S ~; LOAD LINE CONVENTION ~; MEDICAL ~; NOTARIAL ~; OPERATOR'S ~; OWNER'S ~; QUOTA ~; SECURITY ~; SECURITY OR SECURITY ~; SHARE STREET ~; TONNAGE MEASUREMENT ~.

CERTIFICATE OF AGE. A document issued in connection with statutory restrictions on child labour and authorizing employment of a minor. See AGE CERTIFICATE.

CERTIFICATE OF AIRWORTHINESS. A conditional certificate of fitness for flight issued in respect of a particular aircraft under Part II of these Regulations or under the laws of the state in which the aircraft is registered. *Air Regulations*, C.R.C., c. 2, s. 101.

CERTIFICATE OF ASSESSMENT. A document given to prove that a review of the costs awarded in an action or billed by a solicitor has been completed by an assessment officer of the court.

CERTIFICATE OF CITIZENSHIP. A certificate of citizenship issued or granted under an act.

CERTIFICATE OF COMPLETION. A certificate given by an architect under whose supervision a building contract has been carried out; contractor is generally not entitled to payment until the certificate is given.

CERTIFICATE OF CONTINUANCE. An indication that a corporation originally incorporated in one jurisdiction has transferred its governance to another jurisdiction and that the corporation's existence continues. This change must be authorized by the original jurisdiction as well as the new one.

CERTIFICATE OF CONVICTION. A certificate stating that an accused was convicted of an indictable offence, drawn up by a judge or magistrate when requested to do so by the prosecutor, the accused or a peace officer.

CERTIFICATE OF INCORPORATION. Documentary evidence, including letters patent, a special act or any other instrument, by which a corporation is incorporated stating that a corporation exists and was duly incorporated under the appropriate statute.

CERTIFICATE OF LIS PENDENS. A document registered against land to warn that there is litigation pending concerning an interest in the land. See CERTIFICATE OF PENDING LITIGATION.

CERTIFICATE OF NATURALIZATION. A certificate of naturalization granted under any act that was in force in Canada at any time before January 1, 1947.

CERTIFICATE OF PENDING LITIGATION. A document registered against land to warn that there is litigation pending concerning an interest in the land. See CERTIFICATE OF LIS PENDENS.

CERTIFICATE OF READINESS. A former term for the document which a party in an action filed to indicate that the party is ready for trial. See now NOTICE OF READINESS FOR TRIAL.

CERTIFICATE OF REGISTRATION. A certificate of registration issued under the authority of this Act for an animal of a distinct breed. *Animal Pedigree Act*, R.S.C. 1985, c. 8 (4th Supp.), s. 2.

CERTIFICATE OF RENUNCIATION. A certificate of renunciation issued under section 9. *Citizenship Act*, R.S.C. 1985, c. C-29, s. 2.

CERTIFICATE OF TAXATION. A document given to prove that a review of the costs awarded in an action or billed by a solicitor has been completed by a taxation officer of the court. See also CERTIFICATE OF ASSESSMENT.

CERTIFICATE OF TITLE. A certificate of title granted pursuant to a Land Titles Act. See ABSOLUTE ~; DUPLICATE ~.

CERTIFICATION. *n.* 1. " . . . [A] mechanism whereby an association which counts among its members an absolute majority of all an employer's employees, or of a separate group of an employer's employees, is recognized as the sole representative of those employees to this employer for collective bargaining purposes . . . " *Union des employés de service, local 298 v. Bibeault* (1988), 35 Admin L.R. 153 at 204, 95 N.R. 161, [1988] 2 S.C.R. 1048, the court per Beetz J. 2. " . . . [T]he name given to the marking of a cheque by the drawee bank to show that it is drawn by the person purporting to draw it, that it is drawn upon an existing account with the drawee, and that there are funds sufficient to meet it. Certification is demonstrated by some physical marking on the cheque, normally stamping on its face 'certified' . . ." *A.E. LePage Real Estate Services Ltd. v. Rattray Publications* (1991), 84 D.L.R. (4th) 766 at 767, 5 O.R. (3d) 216 (Div. Ct.), Montgomery J. 3. A written attestation of a training organization as to the level of achievement attained by a student in an occupational training program. 4. The entry of the name of a person in the register. See APPLICATION FOR ~.

CERTIFICATION MARK. A mark that is used for the purpose of distinguishing or so as to distinguish wares or services that are of a defined standard with respect to (a) the character or quality of the wares or services, (b) the working conditions under which the wares have been produced or the services performed, (c) the class of persons by whom the wares have been produced or the services performed, or (d) the area within which the wares have been produced or the services performed, from wares or services that are not of that defined standard. *Trademarks Act*, R.S.C. 1985, c. T-13, s. 2.

CERTIFICATION OF LABOUR UNION. Official recognition by a labour relations board of a union as bargaining representative for employees in a particular bargaining unit.

CERTIFIED AIR CARRIER. (*a*) An air carrier who is authorized by the Canadian Transportation Agency under Part II of the *Canada Transportation Act* to operate a domestic service or an international service, and (*b*) an air carrier, other than an air carrier described in paragraph (*a*), who, personally or by agent, sells in Canada transportation of a person by air that is to be provided in whole or in part by an air carrier described in paragraph (*a*). *Excise Tax Act*, R.C.S. 1985, E-15, s. 8.

CERTIFIED ASSOCIATION. The association recognized by decision of the Commission as the representative of all or some of the employees of an employer. *Labour Code*, R.S.Q., c. C-27, s. 1.

CERTIFIED BARGAINING AGENT. A bargaining agent that has been certified under this Act and the certification of which has not been revoked.

CERTIFIED CHEQUE. A cheque which the drawer has taken to his bank and the funds are withdrawn from his account pending the cashing of the cheque. If the cheque is certified by the holder the same action occurs and the payment of the obligation is complete.

CERTIFIED COPY. 1. A copy certified to be a true copy. 2. (a) In relation to a document of a corporation, a copy of the document certified to be a true copy by an officer thereof, (b) in relation to a document issued by a court, a copy of the document certified to be a true copy the seal of the court and signed by the registrar or clerk thereof, (c) in relation to a document in the custody of the Director, a copy of the document certified to be a true copy by the Director and signed by the Director or by such officer of the Ministry as is designated by the regulations. *Business Corporations Act*, R.S.O. 1990, c. B.16, s. 1.

CERTIFIED INSTITUTION. A non-profit organization or charity that holds a valid and subsisting certificate issued under subsection (2); (2) On application in the prescribed form and manner and containing the prescribed information, the Minister may issue a certificate to the applicant for the purposes of this section, if the Minister is satisfied that the applicant is a non-profit organization or charity (*a*) whose principal purpose is to provide care, of such type as the Governor in Council may prescribe by regulation on the recommendation of the Minister and the Minister of Finance, (i) to children, or to aged, infirm or incapacitated persons, who are in need of care on a continuous or regular basis, and (ii) on its own premises by means of qualified persons in sufficient numbers in relation to

the type of care provided; or (*b*) whose only purpose is to provide administrative services solely to one or more non-profit organizations or charities having the principal purpose described in paragraph (*a*) and holding a certificate under this subsection. *Excise Tax Act*, R.S.C. 1985 (2d Supp.), c. 7, s. 68.24.

CERTIFIED MAIL. Mail for which (a) a signature is obtained on delivery, (b) proof of delivery is returned to the sender, and (c) a record of delivery is retained.

CERTIFIED RECORD. A plan or field notes prepared in a manner satisfactory to the registrar-general, and certified to as accurate by a surveyor, showing the particulars of a survey made by the surveyor. *Surveys Act*, C.C.S.M., c. S240, s. 2.

CERTIFIED STATUS. With respect to seed, means that (*a*) where the crop from which the seed is derived was grown in Canada, (i) a crop certificate designated "Certified" has been issued for that crop by the Association, and (ii) the seed meets the standards for varietal purity established by the Association for seed of that kind or species, or (*b*) where the crop from which the seed is derived was not grown in Canada, (i) the crop meets the standards established by an official certifying agency and approved by the Association, and (ii) the seed meets the standards for varietal purity established by the official certifying agency for seed of that kind or species and approved by the Association. *Seeds Regulations*, C.R.C., c. 1400 s. 2.

CERTIFIED UNION. A union recognized by a labour relations board as bargaining agent of a group of workers.

CERTIFIER. See PAYMENT ∼.

CERTIFY. *v*. 1. "... [H]as the connotation that the person so doing formally vouches for the statement or guarantees its certainty ..." *First Investors Corp., Re*, Doc. No. Edmonton Appeal 8803-0942-AC (Alta. C.A.), the court per Laycraft J.A. 2. ... [A] word of wide import which may also refer merely to a formal or legal certificate." *R. v. Lines* (1986), 27 C.C.C. (3d) 377 at 380 (N.W.T. C.A.), the court per Laycraft C.J.N.W.T.

CERTIORARI. *n*. "... [T]he prerogative writ adopted to quash a decision based upon an error of law which is apparent from the record ..." *Minister of National Revenue v. Parsons* (1983), 4 Admin. L.R. 64 at 72, [1983] C.T.C. 321, 83 D.T.C. 5329 (Fed. T.D.), Cattanach J.

CERTIORARI IN AID. Certiorari ordered in connection with habeas corpus. *Perepolkin v. Superintendent of Child Welfare for British Columbia (No. 2)* (1958), 27 C.R. 95 at 97, 23 W.W.R. 592, 120 C.C.C. 67, 11 D.L.R. (2d) 417 (B.C. C.A.), Smith J.A.

CERTUM EST QUOD CERTUM REDDI POTEST. [L.] What is capable of being made certain is to be treated as certain.

CERVIX. *n*. The neck of the uterus which connects the vagina with the uterine cavity. F.A. Jaffe, *A Guide to Pathological Evidence*, 3d ed. (Toronto: Carswell, 1991) at 215.

C.E.S.H.G. *abbr*. Canadian Employment, Safety and Health Guide.

CESSANTE CAUSA, CESSAT EFFECTUS. [L.] When the cause ceases, the effect ceases.

CESSANTE RATIONE LEGIS, CESSAT IPSA LEX. [L.] When the reason of the law ceases, the law itself ceases.

CESSANTE STATU PRIMITIVO, CESSAT DERIVATIVUS. [L.] When the original estate determines, the derivative estate ceases.

CESSAT EXECUTIO. [L.] Suspension or stopping of execution.

CESSATION OF CHARGE. An instrument which acknowledges that the claim against real property contained in a charge has been discharged.

CESSER. *n*. Occurs when a term annuity determines or comes to an end.

CESSET PROCESSUS. [L.] A stay of proceedings which is entered on a record.

CESSION. *n*. Ceding, yielding, giving up.

CESSURE. *n*. Ceding, giving over; departing from.

CESTUI QUE TRUST. *pl*. **CESTUIS QUE TRUST**. A beneficiary; beneficial owner of trust property.

CESTUI QUE USE. A grantee to whom property was conveyed to use.

CESTUI QUE VIE. One for whose life someone else holds an estate or interest in property. See TENANT PUR AUTRE VIE.

CETERIS PARIBUS. [L.] Other things being equal.

CF. *abbr*. Compare.

C.F. *abbr*. 1. Cour fédérale 2. In sales contract, means price included cost and freight. 3. Recueils de jurisprudence de la Cour fédérale du Canada.

C.F. & I. See C.I.F.

C.F. (APPEL). *abbr*. Cour fédérale du Canada-Cour d'appel.

CFC. A fully halogenated chlorofluorocarbon each molecule of which contains one, two or three carbon atoms and at least one atom each of chlorine and fluorine. *Ozone-depleting Substances Regulations, 1998*, SOR/99-7, s. 1.

C.F.I. See C.I.F.

C.F.L.Q. *abbr*. Canadian Family Law Quarterly.

CFPI. The French neutral citation for the Federal Court, Trial Division.

CFPO. *abbr*. Canadian Forces Post Office.

C.F. (1RE INST.). *abbr*. Cour fédérale du Canada-Division de premiere instance.

C.F.S. COMM. *abbr*. Corporate and Financial Services Commission.

CGSB. *abbr*. The Canadian Government Specifications Board. Canada regulations.

CH. *abbr*. 1. Chapter. 2. Chancery.

[] CH. *abbr*. Law Reports, Chancery, 1891-.

CHAIN. *n*. 1. 22 yards. *Weights and Measures Act*, S.C. 1970-71-72, c. 36, Schedule II. 2. An old surveyors' measure equal to 100 links or 66 feet. See BOOM ~.

CHAIN. *adj*. One of a number of stores or outlets under the same ownership.

CHAIN OF TITLE. Tracking successive transfers or other conveyances of a particular parcel of land.

CHAIN PICKETING. Patrolling a place of business by a single file of closely ranked persons to form a human chain barring the entrance.

CHAIRMAN. *n*. 1. A person who presides at meetings of the board of directors of a corporation. 2. A person occupying the position of chairman, by whatever name called, of the board of directors of a corporation.

CHALLENGE. *v*. 1. To object. 2. To take exception against a juror. See PEREMPTORY ~.

CHALLENGE FOR CAUSE. The suitability of a juror is objected to on basis of knowledge of the case or lack of qualifications or impartiality.

CHAMBER. *n.* The place where legislative assemblies are held; the assemblies themselves. See FIRING ~; WORKING ~.

CHAMBERLAIN. *n.* The keeper, manager or director of a chamber or chambers.

CHAMBER OF COMMERCE. An organization organized to promote business in a community.

CHAMBERS. *n.* Judge's office; a room in which motions or applications or other business not required to be carried out in court is transacted.

CHAMBERS BRIEF. " . . . [A]ssist[s] in clarifying the issues and so reduce[s] the length of time for hearing a motion or trial . . . it should contain the following: (a) Description of the motion. (b) Authority for the motion. (c) Statement of facts. (d) Authorities. (e) Relief asked. (f) Form of Order." *Eileen's Quality Catering Ltd. v. Depaoli* (1985), 1 C.P.C. (2d) 152 at 154, 158 (B.C. S.C.), Bouck J.

CHAMOIS. *n.* Leather produced from (a) the skin of the mountain antelope or chamois, or (b) sheep or lamb skin from which the grain has been removed prior to tanning, where the tanning process is restricted to the oxidation of fish or marine animal oils and where a suede finish has been applied to one or both sides of the leather.

CHAMPAGNE. *n.* Wine produced in the district of France called Champagne.

CHAMPERTOR. *n.* A person who brings suits in order to have part of the gain or proceeds.

CHAMPERTY. *n.* 1. " . . . [A] bargain by which A, a stranger to B, having no interest recognized by law in a given property, agrees to help B to recover such in a Court of Justice in consideration of getting a portion of the fruits of the suit, . . ." *Hopper v. Dunsmuir* (1906), 3 W.L.R. 18 at 33 (C.A.), Martin J.A. 2. [T]o bargain with a plaintiff to pay the expenses of a suit wholly or in art on condition that the plaintiff will divide with the party who so shares plaintiff expenses the land or other matter sued for, if successful in such suit, is undeniably champerty." *Meloche v. Deguire* (1903), 34 S.C.R. 24 at 37, Taschereau C.J. (Sedgewick, Nesbitt and Killam JJ. concur-

ring). 3. A form of maintenance. *Pioneer Machinery (Rentals) Ltd. v. Aggregate Machine Ltd.* (1978), 8 C.P.C. 168 at 170 15 A.R. 588 [1978] 6 W.W.R. 484, 93 D.L.R. (3d) 726 (T.D.), Laycraft J.

CHANCE. *n.* An accident; absence of explainable causation; risk. See GAME OF ~; LOSS OF ~; MIXED GAME OF ~ AND SKILL; SALE OF A ~.

CHANCELLOR. *n.* 1. The highest official of a university. 2. The presiding judge of a court of chancery. 3. The cleric entrusted with the keeping of the archives of a diocese. *An Act Respecting Fabriques*, R.S.Q., c. F-1, s. 1. See VICE-~.

CHANCE-MEDLEY. *n.* A sudden or casual affray.

CHANCERY. *n.* 1. A court which administered equity before the Judicature Acts combined this court with the common law court. 2. Originally an office where writs were issued. See COURT OF ~.

CHANGE. *v.* To alter; substitute; modify; exchange.

CHANGE. *n.* 1. Alteration, replacement, modification. *Simplex Floor Finishing Appliance Co. v. Duranceau*, [1941] 4 D.L.R. 260 at 264 (S.C.C.), Taschereau J. 2. Any change by way of alteration, substitution, modification, addition or abandonment. *Change of Name acts.* 3. Exchange of money for money of another denomination. See MATERIAL ~; POST MORTEM ~; SIGNIFICANT ~; STRUCTURAL ~; TECHNOLOGICAL ~.

CHANGE OF NAME. 1. Refers to alteration of an individual's name by court order or by assumption of a different name. 2. Any change in the name of a physical person by alteration, substitution, addition or abandonment. *Change of Name Act*, R.S.Q. 1977, c. C-10, s. 1.

CHANGE OF PARTIES. Occurs where parties to litigation are added or substituted.

CHANGE OF POSSESSION. Such change of possession as is open and reasonably sufficient to afford public notice thereof. *Bills of Sale Acts.*

CHANGE OF SOLICITOR. The change of lawyer representing a client in an action effected by filing notice in court.

CHANGE ROOM. A room that is used by employees as a room within which to change from their street clothes to their work clothes before starting work, and from their work clothes to their street clothes after finishing work, and includes a locker room.

CHANNEL. *n*. 1. The bed in which a river flows; watercourse; the course followed in navigating a river or other body of water. 2. Includes a space between a transmitter and receiver of telecommunications and any other channel of transmission of telecommunications. See AUGMENTED ~ SERVICE; COMMUNITY ~; RESTRICTED ~.

CHAPEL. *n*. A place of worship.

CHAPELRY. *n*. A territory canonically erected as a chapelry for the purposes of the Roman Catholic religion and the benefit of the faithful of such religion. *An Act Respecting Fabriques*, R.S.Q., c. F-1, s. 1.

CHAPLAIN. *n*. The member of the clergy attached to a unit of the armed forces or an institution such as a hospital, university or prison.

CHAR. *n*. Arctic char Salvelinus alpinus and includes sea-run speckled trout Salvelinus Fontinalis.

CHARACTER. *n*. 1. A device, name, signature, word, letter or numeral. 2. The inclination of a person to act in a particular way relating to integrity, peaceableness, lawfulness, honesty and ultimately veracity. P.K. McWilliams, *Canadian Criminal Evidence*, 3d ed. (Aurora: Canada Law Book, 1988) at 39-1. 3. "[As found in the Trade Marks Act, R.S.C. 1970, c. T-10, s. 12(1)(b)] . . . refers to the characteristic or special feature of the product . . ." *Bagagerie SA v. Bagagerie Willy Ltée* (1987), 17 C.P.R. (3d) 209 at 217, 12 F.T.R. 245, 17 C.I.P.R. 95, Rouleau J. 4. " . . . [O]f a job does not just mean the individual acts which make up the particular job. 'Character' means feature, trait, essential peculiarity, nature, sort . . ." *Kennedy v. William C. Cavell Enteprises Ltd.* (1987), 88 C.L.L.C. 14,004 at 12,015, 18 C.C.E.L. 52, 23 O.A.C. 349 (Div. Ct.), Campbell J. See HERITAGE ~; UNCHASTE ~.

CHARACTERISTICS. See TRADITIONAL OR ARTISTIC ~.

CHARACTERIZATION. *n*. A matter of classifying, categorizing or assimilating elements of a concept into the overall concept. J.G. McLeod, *The Conflict of Laws* (Calgary: Carswell 1983) at 26.

CHARGE. *v*. 1. To give instructions to a jury. 2. " . . . [E]xists only when a formal written complaint has been made against the accused and a prosecution initiated. . ." *R. v. Chabot* [1980] 2 S.C.R. 985 at 1005 Dickson J. 3. To lay a duty upon a person. 4. To impose a tax. 5. To purchase on credit. 6. " . . . [I]n Section 8(2)(d) [of the Human Rights Code, R.S.B.C. 1979, c. 186] means 'the things specified in the information and the circumstances surrounding them' rather than simply 'the nature of the offence charged.' " *Woodward Stores (British Columbia Ltd. v. McCartney* (1983), 4 C.H.R.R. D/1325 at D/1327, 43 B.C.L.R. 314, 83 C.L.L.C. 17,015, 145 D.L.R. (3d) 193 (S.C.), MacDonald J.

CHARGE. *n*. 1. An instrument creating security against property for payment of a debt or obligation. 2. The amount required, as the price of a thing or service sold or supplied. 3. A judge's instruction to a jury. 4. A price or rate. 5. A registered interest less than fee simple and a registered encumbrance on land. 6. As related to taxation or other financial encumbrance or burden imposed on or in respect of land, personal property, or persons, (A) the imposition of that taxation encumbrance, or burden; or (B) that tax, encumbrance, or burden itself. 7. A charge on land given for the purpose of securing the payment of a debt or the performance of an obligation. 8. Includes every encumbrance on land. 9. An explosive and a detonator, or an explosive, a detonator and primer that is exploded as a single unit. See ACCOMMODATION ~; AGREED ~; AUTHORIZED ~; BOARDING ~; BRACING ~; CARRYING ~; CESSATION OF ~; CHARGES; CONTAINER HANDLING ~; CONTAINER REHANDLING ~; CRANE HIRE ~; CRANE MOVING ~; DEBT ~; DELIVERY ~; DEVELOPMENT ~; DIRECT ~ CO-OPERATIVE; EQUITABLE ~; FIXED ~; FLOATING ~; HANDLING ~; HAVE ~ OF; HEAVY-LIFT ~; INSURANCE ~; LIGHTER ~; LOADING ~; OFFICER IN ~; OVER-TIME ~; PASSENGER ~; PREFER A ~; PROPRIETARY ~; RECEIVING ~; REDOCUMENTATION ~; REGULATORY ~; RENT ~; SALVAGE ~; SPECIFIC ~; STORAGE ~; SUB-ORDER DELIVERY ~; SWITCHING ~; TERMINAL ~; THROUGHPUT ~; TIME ~; UNLOADING ~; USER ~; WINTERING ~.

CHARGEABLE. *adj*. Capable of or subject to being charged with a duty or obligation.

CHARGE ACCOUNT. An arrangement with a store or financial institution permitting purchase of goods and services on credit under which purchaser agrees to pay within specified time or periodically.

CHARGED. *adj*. 1. "The word 'charged' or 'charge' is not one of fixed or unvarying meaning at law. It may be and is used in a variety of ways to describe a variety of events. A person is clearly charged with an offence when a charge is read out to him in court and he is called upon to plead. . ." *R. v. Kalanj* (1989), 48 C.C.C. (3d) 459 at 465, 70 C.R. (3d) 260, [1989] 6 W.W.R. 577, [1989] 1 S.C.R. 1594, 96 N.R. 191, McIntyre J. (La Forest and L'Heureux-Dubé JJ. concurring). 2. " . . . [A] person is 'charged with an offence' within the meaning of s. 11 of the Charter when an information is sworn alleging an offence against him, or where a direct indictment is laid against him when an information is sworn. . ." *R. v. Kalanj* (1989), 48 C.C.C. (3d) 459 at 469, 70 C.R. (3d) 260, [1989] 6 W.W.R. 577, [1989] 1 S.C.R. 1594, 96 N.R. 191, McIntyre J. (La Forest and L'Heureux-Dubé JJ. concurring).

CHARGE D'AFFAIRES. [Fr.] A diplomatic agent.

CHARGEE. *n*. A person in whose favour a charge is given.

CHARGES. *n*. Expenses; costs. See BORROWER'S ~; CHARGE; CREDIT ~; CROWN ~, DEBT ~; SEPARATE ~.

CHARGE-SHEET. *n*. A paper kept at a police station to record the names of the persons brought into custody, the accusation, and the accuser's name in each case.

CHARGE THE JURY. A judge gives instructions to a jury before it deliberates with regard to the law as it applies to the case heard by them.

CHARGE TO THE JURY. The instructions which a judge gives a jury before the jury begins its deliberations at the end of a trial. See CHARGE THE JURY.

CHARGING ORDER. 1. A creditor can apply to a judge to order that shares of or in any public company stand charged with the payment of the judgment debt. 2. An order made for the benefit of a solicitor against funds in court or property realized through the endeavours of the solicitor.

CHARGOR. *n*. A person who gives a charge against property.

CHARITABLE. *adj*. Having purposes of a charity.

CHARITABLE CORPORATION. A body constituted exclusively for charitable purposes no part of the income of which is payable to, or is otherwise available for the personal benefit of, any proprietor, member or shareholder thereof.

CHARITABLE FOUNDATION. A corporation or trust, other than a charitable organization, constituted and operated exclusively for charitable purposes.

CHARITABLE INSTITUTION. All or any part of a building or buildings maintained and operated by an approved corporation for persons requiring residential, sheltered, specialized or group care.

CHARITABLE PURPOSE. 1. "The starting point for a discussion of what may or may not constitute a good charitable purpose is the decision of the House of Lords in the case of Commrs. for Special Purposes of Income Tax v. Pemsel, [1891] A.C. 531 [(U.K.)] and in particular, the legal meaning of the word 'charity' given by Lord Macnaghten at p. 583 of the report: 'How far then, it may be asked does the popular meaning of the word "charity" correspond with its legal meaning?. "Charity" in its legal sense comprises four principal divisions: trusts for the relief of poverty; trusts for the advancement of education; trusts for the advancement of religion; and trusts for other purposes beneficial to the community, not falling under any of the preceding heads.' That definition has been applied time after time in this country and has been approved by the Supreme Court of Canada (see Guaranty Trust Co. (Towle Estate) v. M.N.R., [1967] S.C.R. 133 at p. 141) . . ." *Native Communications Society of British Columbia v. Minister of National Revenue* (1986), 23 E.T.R. 210 at 218, 86 D.T.C. 6353, 67 N.R. 146, [1986] 2 C.T.C. 170, [1986] 4 C.N.L.R. 79, [1986] 3 F.C. 471 (C.A.), Stone J.A. (Heald and Mahoney JJ.A. concurring). 2. Any charitable, benevolent, philanthropic, patriotic, athletic, artistic, or civic purpose and any purpose that has as its object the promotion of a civic improvement or the provision of a public service. *Charities Endorsement Act*, C.C.S.M., c. C60, s. 1.

CHARITABLE TRUST. A trust for purposes which the law treats as charitable.

CHARITY. *n*. 1. An organization with a charitable purpose. 2. (a) Trusts for the relief of poverty, (b) trusts for the advancement of education,

(c) trusts for the advancement of religion, (d) trusts for other purposes beneficial to the community not falling under any of the preceding heads. *Commrs. of Income Tax v. Pemsel*, [1891] A.C. 531 at 583, Lord Macnaghten. 3. Any person, association, institute or organization under whose auspices funds for benevolent, educational, cultural, charitable or religious purposes are to be raised. See EMPLOYEES' ~ TRUST; REGISTERED ~.

CHARTER. *v.* " . . . [I]s not synonymous with 'hire'. It has such a meaning only when it is used in relation to a means of transportation." *Seaway Forwarding Ltd. v. Western Assurance Co.*, [1981] I.L.R. 1-1400 at 351 (Ont. H.C.), Galligan J.

CHARTER. *n.* 1. The Canadian Charter of Rights and Freedoms, Part I of the Constitution Act, 1982. 2. Includes any act, statute, or ordinance by or under which a corporation has been incorporated and any letters patent, supplementary letters certificate of incorporation, memorandum patent, of association, and other document evidencing corporate existence. 3. The corporation's articles, notice of articles or memorandum, regulations, bylaws or agreement or deed of settlement, and every alteration to them. 4. If the corporation was incorporated, continued or converted by or under, or if the corporation resulted from an amalgamation under, an Act, statute, ordinance, letters patent, certificate, declaration or other equivalent instrument or provision of law, that record and every alteration to it applying to the corporation. 5. An agreement to supply a vessel or aircraft for a voyage for a period of time. See ADVANCE BOOKING ~; INCLUSIVE TOUR ~; TERM ~; TIME ~.

CHARTER AND REGULATIONS. The charter of a corporation and its articles, bylaws, rules and regulations.

CHARTER BY DEMISE. A charter by demise operates as a lease of the ship itself for a period of time which puts the ship altogether out of the power and control of the owner and vests that power and control in the charterers. *North Ridge Fishing Ltd. v. "Prosperity" (The)*, 2000 CarswellBC 982, 2000 BCCA 283, 74 B.C.L.R. (3d) 383, 186 D.L.R. (4th) 374 (C.A.). Cumming J.A. for the court.

CHARTERED BANK. A bank to which the *Bank Act* (Canada) applies, and includes a branch agency, and office of a bank.

CHARTERED BUS SERVICE. Service by means of a bus that is engaged solely to transport the persons engaging it on one occasion or for one trip to a stated destination and if so required, return therefrom to the point of origin.

CHARTERED COMPANY. A company incorporated by Royal Charter such as the Hudson's Bay Company.

CHARTERED SHIP. A ship hired; a ship subject to charter party.

CHARTERED TRIP. One specific trip for which a public vehicle is engaged, hired or chartered for the transportation exclusively of a group of persons and for which one fare or charge only is collected.

CHARTERER. *n.* One who hires a ship or aircraft for a certain period or for a voyage.

CHARTER PARTY. *vars.* **CHARTER-PARTY, CHARTER-PARTY**. An agreement to use or hire a ship or to convey goods for a specified period or on a specified voyage.

CHASE. *v.* To pursue rapidly with intent to overtake or send away.

CHASE. *n.* A pursuit with a view to catching, not a test between rivals as in a "race". *McGill v. Insurance Corp. of British Columbia* (1992), 10 C.C.L.I. (2d) 65 (B.C. S.C.).

CHASSIS-CAB. *n.* A vehicle consisting of a chassis that is capable of being driven, drawn or self-propelled, upon which may be mounted a cab, and that is designed to receive (a) a passenger-carrying body including a body that incorporates a prime mover, or (b) a work performing structure other than a fifth-wheel coupling.

CHASTE. *adj.* " . . . [T]he principle is well established that virginity and chastity are not necessarily synonymous terms. . ." *R. v. Trecarain* (1980), 32 N.B.R. (2d) 621 at 623, 78 A.P.R. 621 (Q.B.), Dickson J. See UNCHASTE CHARACTER.

CHASTITY. *n.* The state of being chaste.

CHATTEL. *n.* 1. Colloquially used to refer to chattel mortgage. 2. An item of personal property. See CHATTELS; INCORPOREAL ~.

CHATTEL MORTGAGE. "To constitute a chattel mortgage, the contract between the parties must import a transfer of the property in the chattels from the mortgagor to the mortgagee, as security for a debt, defeasible on payment of the debt; . . ." *Dealers Finance Corp. v. Masterson*

Motors Ltd., [1931] 4 D.L.R. 730 at 735, [1931] 2 W.W.R. 214 (C.A.), Martin J.A.

CHATTEL PAPER. One or more than one writing that expresses both a monetary obligation and a security interest in or lease of specific goods and accessions.

CHATTELS. *n*. 1. "...[I]nclude[s] all personal property..." *Ontario (Attorney General v. Royal Bank*, [1970] 2 O.R. 467 at 472, 11 D.L.R. (3d) 257 (C.A.), the court per Brooke J.A. 2. "...[T]he principles as summarized in [Stack v. Eaton Co. (1902), 4 O.L.R. 335 (C.A.) by Meredith C.J.] ... at p. 338, [are] as follows: 'I take it to be settled law: (1) That articles not otherwise attached to the land than by their own weight are not to be considered as part of the land, unless the circumstances are such as shew that they were intended to be part of the land. (2) That articles affixed to the land even slightly are to be considered part of the land unless the circumstances are such as to shew that they were intended to continue chattels. (3) That the circumstances necessary to be shewn to alter the prima facie character of the articles are circumstances which shew the degree of annexation and object of such annexation, which are present to all to see. (4) That the intention of the person affixing the article to the soil is material only so far as it can be presumed from the degree and object of the annexation.' " *Dolan v. Bank of Montreal* (1985), 5 P.P.S.A.C. 196 at 201-2, 42 Sask. R. 202 (C.A.), Matheson J.A. 3. "...[I]n the context of a chattel mortgage the word 'chattels' is confined to those which by their nature are susceptible of assignment." *209991 Ontario Ltd. v. Canadian Imperial Bank of Commerce* (1988), 39 B.L.R. 44 at 53, 24 C.P.C. (2d) 248, 8 P.P.S.A.C. 135 (Ont. H.C.), Anderson J. 4. 4. May refer to goods and other items capable of transfer by delivery but not chattel interests in land. See GOODS AND PERSONAL ~.

CHATTELS PERSONAL. "Pure personalty", either in action or in possession. E.L.G. Tyler & N.E. Palmer, eds., *Crossley Vaines' Personal Property*, 5th ed. (London: Butterworths, 1973) at 11.

CHATTELS REAL. Leaseholds.

CHAUD-MEDLEY. See CHANCE-MEDLEY.

CHAUFFEUR. *n*. A person who drives motor vehicles as a means of livelihood.

CH. D. *abbr*. Law Reports, Chancery Division, 1875-1890.

CHEAP. *adj*. With low price.

CHEAT. *v*. "... [T]o defraud ..." *Hackworth v. Baker*, [1936] 1 W.W.R. 321 at 348 (Sask. C.A.), Turgeon J.A.

CHECKERBOARD. *v*. To divide land in the manner of a checkerboard so that one person owns the "red squares" and another owns the "black squares". The owners on title may be nominees or trustees for the actual landowner, or the actual landowner might retain "one set of squares" and transfer the "other set" to a nominee. B.J. Reiter, B.N. McLellan & P.M. Perell, *Real Estate Law*, 4th ed. (Toronto: Emond Montgomery, 1992) at 340.

CHECK-IN BOARD. A board on which employees hang brass checks to show attendance.

CHECKLIST. *n*. List of items to be covered in an agreement or in a transaction.

CHECK-OFF. *n*. A system which requires the employer to deduct from wages and remit to the union the dues stipulated, with respect to the persons covered by the collective agreement. See AUTOMATIC ~.

CHEDDAR CHEESE. Cheese made (i) from the matted and milled curd of milk by the cheddar process, or (ii) from milk by another procedure that produces a finished cheese having the same physical and chemical properties as the cheese produced by the cheddar process, and (b) may contain (i) a colouring matter approved under the Food and Drug Regulations, or (ii) bacterial culture.

CHEESE. *n*. Cheese made by coagulating the casein of milk, skim milk, evaporated milk, evaporated skim milk, cream, milk powder or skim milk powder, or a mixture thereof, with or without the addition of cream, milk powder, skim milk powder or small amounts of other ingredients such as ripening ferments, harmless acid-producing bacterial cultures, special mould cultures, salt, seasoning, special flavouring materials, food colour or permitted preservatives. See CHEDDAR ~; PACKAGE ~; PROCESS ~; WHOLE ~.

CHEESE FACTORY. A place where milk from cows or goats is manufactured into cheese.

CHEMICAL. See AGRICULTURAL ~; CORROSIVE ~; HAZARDOUS ~; NEW ~.

CHEMICAL CARRIER. A ship that is specially constructed or adapted for the carriage of dangerous chemicals and is engaged in the carriage of such chemicals. *Navigating Appliances Regulations*, C.R.C., c. 1449, s. 2.

CHEMICAL INTERMEDIARY. A substance which is not in and of itself suitable for therapeutic or clinical use as a medicine but is within the category of substances "intended or capable of being used for medicine or for the preparation or production of medicine". *ICN Pharmaceuticals Inc. v. Canada (Patented Medicine Prices Review Board)* (1996), [1997] 1 F.C. 32 (C.A.).

CHEMICAL RECOVERY BOILER. A boiler that is capable of being fuelled by the black liquor that results from the Kraft sulphate pulp manufacturing process. *Power Engineers and Boiler and Pressure Vessel Safety Act*, R.S.B.C. 1996, c. 368, s. 1.

CHEMICAL STILL. Any distilling apparatus that is kept and used by any person for the sole purpose of distilling water or claiming alcohol previously used in or for the preparation or manufacture of chemical, medicinal or pharmaceutical preparations, or that is used for scientific or industrial purposes, and not used for the manufacture or distillation of spirits. *Excise Act*, R.S.C. 1985, c. E-14, s. 3.

CHEMICAL TANKER. A ship constructed and used for the carriage in bulk of any chemical listed in Chapter 17 of the *International Code for the Construction and Equipment of Ships Carrying Dangerous Chemicals in Bulk*, published by the International Maritime Organization, as amended from time to time. *Shipping Regulations*.

CHEMIST. See MARINE ~; PHARMACEUTICAL ~.

CHEMISTRY. See PRACTICE OF PROFESSIONAL ~.

CHEQUE. *n.* 1. A bill drawn on a bank, payable on demand. 2. Includes a bill of exchange drawn on any institution that makes it a business practice to honour bills of exchange or any particular kind thereof drawn on it by depositors. *Criminal Code*, R.S.C. 1985, c. C-46, s. 362(5) and 364(3). 3. " . . . [A] direction to some one, who may or may not have in his possession funds of the drawer, authorising him to pay to the payee a certain sum of money. . ." *Re Bernard* (1911), 2 O.W.N. 716 at 717 Chief Justice of Exchequer Division. See CROSSED ~; STALE ~.

CHEQUE REQUISITION. A requisition issued for a payment to be made by means of a cheque.

CHEST. See FLOATING ~.

CHEVISANCE. *n.* An unlawful contract or bargain.

C.H.F.L.G. *abbr.* Canadian Health Facilities Law Guide.

CHICANE. *v.* To use trickery.

CHICK. *n.* A chick hatched from a broiler hatching egg from the time of hatch until it is placed in the facilities of a chicken producer for raising and not for resale.

CHICKEN. *n.* A bird of the species *Gallus domesticus* having flexible cartilage at the posterior end of the breast or keel bone, tender meat and soft skin of smooth texture.

CHICKEN CAPON. A male bird of the species *Gallus domesticus* whose testes are surgically removed before it is six weeks old and who has flexible cartilage at the posterior end of the breast or keel bone, tender meat and soft skin of smooth texture.

CHICKEN FAT CLOT. Mainly of white blood cells, bright yellow in colour, forming the top layer of a clot. It is used to determine the position of a body after death. F.A. Jaffe, *A Guide to Pathological Evidence*, 3d ed. (Toronto: Carswell, 1991) at 215.

CHICKEN HADDIE. Canned haddock, cod, cusk or hake, or any combination thereof, that has not been ground.

CHICKS. *n.* Poultry under one month old.

CHICKS-FOR-PLACEMENT. Female chickens twenty weeks of age or less.

CHICOT. *n.* A dead tree or a dead limb of a tree. *Occupational Health and Safety Act*, R.R.O. 1980, Reg. 692, s. 107.

CHIEF. *adj.* Head, principal. See DEPUTY ~; FIRE ~; IN ~.

CHIEF ADMINISTRATOR. Has all the powers necessary for the overall effective and efficient management and administration of all court services, including court facilities and libraries and corporate services and staffing. The Chief Administrator, in consultation with the Chief Justices of the Federal Court of Appeal, the Federal Court, the Court Martial Appeal Court and the Tax Court of Canada, shall establish and maintain the registry or registries for those courts in any organizational form or forms and prepare budgetary submissions for the requirements of those courts and for the related needs of the Service. *Courts Administration Service Act, 2002*, S.C. 2002, c. 8, s. 7.

CHIEF AGENCY. The principal office or place of business.

CHIEF AGENT. 1. In respect of a registered party, means the chief agent named in the application for registration as required by paragraph 366(2)(*h*). *Canada Elections Act*, S.C. 2000, c. 9, s. 2. 2. The chief agent of a company in Canada, named as such in a power of attorney.

CHIEF ELECTORAL OFFICER. The Chief Electoral Officer appointed under The Elections Act.

CHIEF ENGINEER. The person who is responsible for the operation of a boiler or steam plant.

CHIEF EXECUTIVE OFFICER. 1. The person appointed by the board of governors of a hospital to be responsible to the board for the day by day administration of the hospital. 2. (i) The Deputy Minister in any Department of the Government of the province, (ii) the Auditor General, (iii) the Clerk of the Executive Council and (iv) any other official head of any agency designated by the Lieutenant Governor in council to function as a Deputy Minister.

CHIEF EXECUTIVE OFFICER OF AN AGENCY. The person entrusted by law, with regard to his staff or the staff of an agency, with the powers of the chief executive officer of an agency, or, if such is not the case, the person exercising the highest authority in the agency.

CHIEF FINANCIAL OFFICER. (a) Where used to refer to the chief financial officer of a registered political party, means the person shown in the registers or records of the Chief Electoral Officer as the chief financial officer of the registered political party, and (b) where used to refer to the chief financial officer of a candidate, means the person appointed in the nomination papers of the candidate as the official agent of the candidate or subsequently appointed by the candidate as his official agent.

CHIEF GOVERNMENT WHIP. See CHIEF WHIP.

CHIEF INSPECTOR. The officer employed as chief inspector for the purpose of an act.

CHIEF JUDGE. 1. The person having authority to assign duties to the judges of a court. 2. The chief justice, chief judge or other person recog-

nized by law as having rank or status senior to all other members of, or having the supervision of, that court, but where that court is a superior court constituted with divisions, then the person having such rank or status in relation to all other members of the division of which the particular judge is a member.

CHIEF JUSTICE. Of any court of which a particular judge is a member means the chief justice or other person recognized by law as having rank or status senior to all other members of, or having the supervision of, that court, but if that court is constituted with divisions, then it means the person having that rank or status in relation to all other members of the division of which the particular judge is a member. *Judges Act*, R.S.C. 1985, c. J-1, s. 41(4). See APPROPRIATE ~; ASSOCIATE ~.

CHIEF OPERATING ENGINEER. An operating engineer who at all times has charge of and the responsibility for the safe operation of a plant.

CHIEF OPERATOR. An operator or an operating engineer who at all times has charge of and the responsibility for the safe operation of a compressor plant or a refrigeration plant.

CHIEF OPPOSITION WHIP. See CHIEF WHIP.

CHIEF STATISTICIAN. Chief Statistician of Canada appointed under subsection 4(1) of the Statistics Act. *Statistics Act*, R.S.C. 1985, c. S-19, s. 2.

CHIEF WHIP. Each party in Parliament has a 'person who keeps members of that party informed about the business of the House, ensures these members attend, determines pairing arrangements so that the votes of members who cannot attend divisions will be neutralized and not lost, and supplies lists of members to serve on the various House committees. A. Fraser, W.A. Dawson, & J. Holtby, eds., *Beauchesne's Rules and Forms of the House of Commons of Canada*, 6th ed. (Toronto: Carswell, 1989) at 57.

CHILD. *n*. 1. " . . . [H]as two primary meanings. One refers to chronological age and is the converse of the term 'adult'; the other refers to lineage and is the reciprocal of the term 'parent'. A child in the first sense was defined at common law as a person under the age of 14. This definition may be modified by statutory provision . . . No statutory modification however, fixed an age higher than the age of majority which in

Ontario, pursuant to the Age of Majority and Accountability Act, R.S.O. 1980, c. 7, s. 1(1) is 18 years. A child in the second sense was defined at common law as the legitimate offspring of a parent, but in most jurisdictions this definition has been amended by statute to constitute all offspring, whether legitimate or not, as the children of their natural or adoptive parents . . ." *R. v. Ogg-Moss* (1984), [1985] 11 D.L.R. (4th) 549 at 558, [1984] 2 S.C.R. 173, 54 N.R. 81, 14 C.C.C. (3d) 116, 5 O.A.C. 81, 6 C.H.R.R. D/ 2498, 41 C.R. (3d) 297, the court per Dickson J. 2. Includes a person toward whom another person has demonstrated a settled intention to treat as a child of his or her family, except under an arrangement where the child is placed for valuable consideration in a foster home by a person having lawful custody. 3. A person who has not attained the age of majority. 4. A person who (i) has not reached the age of majority, (ii) has not been married, and (iii) is not a parent with legal custody of his or her child. 5. An unmarried person under the age of majority. 6. Includes, where the context requires, a child en ventre sa mere. 7. Includes son, daughter, grand-son, grand-daughter, step-son, and step-daughter. 8. Includes a child lawfully adopted. 9. Any other child to whom another person stood in loco parentis. 10. An individual of compulsory school age. 11. Includes an adopted child and an illegitimate child. *Criminal Code*, R.S.C. 1985, c. C-46, s. 214. 12. A Person who is or, in the absence of evidence to the contrary, appears to be under the age of twelve years. *Youth Criminal Justice Act*, S.C. 2002, c. 1, s. 2. 13. A person under the age of 13, 14, 15, 16, 17, 18, 19, or 21 years of age. 14. A person who is between the ages of 6-12, or 5-13 years inclusive. See ADORED ~; BEST INTERESTS OF THE~; DEPENDANT ~; DEPENDENT DESERTED ~; DISABLED CONTRIBUTOR'S ~; DOMICILE OF THE ~; FATHER OF A ~; FOSTER ~; HANDICAPPED ~REN; ILLEGITIMATE ~; IMMIGRANT ~; INFANT ~; INVALID ~; MINOR ~; MODERATELY RETARDED NATURAL ~; NEGLECTED ~; NEWLY-BORN ~; PARENT; POSTHUMOUS ~.

CHILD ABDUCTION. The kidnapping of a child by the parent not awarded custody.

CHILD ABUSE. 1. Physical, mental, sexual, emotional mistreatment of a child. 2. Corporal punishment which causes injury is child abuse. Spanking [which does not cause physical harm] is not child abuse. *Canadian Foundation for Children, Youth & the Law v. Canada (Attorney General)* (2000), 2000 CarswellOnt 2409, 146 C.C.C. (3d) 362, 188 D.L.R. (4th) 718, 49 O.R. (3d) 662, 36 C.R. (5th) 334, 76 C.R.R. (2d) 251 (S.C.J.).

CHILD CARE RESOURCE. A child's own home, a foster home, group living home, community sponsored home, diagnostic centre, attendance centre, any other facility established for the care, treatment, training and rehabilitation of children.

CHILD CARE SERVICES. Assessment, counselling, referral, child protection and child placement services, voluntary care, homemaker, day care, consulting services, research and evaluation services with respect to child care services and similar services.

CHILD DEVELOPMENT SERVICE. A service for a child with a developmental or physical handicap, for the family of a child with a developmental or physical handicap, or for the child and the family.

CHILD IN CARE. 1. Except in Sections 67 to 87, a child who is in the care and custody of an agency (i) pursuant to an agreement made pursuant to this Act, (ii) as a result of being taken into care or (iii) pursuant to a court order made pursuant to this Act. *Children and Family Services Act*, S.N.S. 1990, c. 5, s. 2. 2. A child who is receiving residential services from a service provider and includes (a) a child who is in the care of a foster parent; and (b) a child who is detained in a place of temporary detention, committed to secure or open custody under the Young Offenders Act (Canada), or held in a place of open custody under section 95 of Part IV (Young Offenders). *Child and Family Services Act*, R.S.O. 1990, c. C.11, s. 99.

CHILD IN NEED OF PROTECTION. A child (a) who is not receiving proper care, education, supervision, guidance or control; (b) whose parent is unable or unwilling to care for the child, or whose behaviour or way of life creates a danger for the child; (c) who has been abused, neglected or sexually exploited or is in danger of consistently threatening behaviour; (d) who is forced or induced to do work disproportionate to his strength or to perform for the public in a manner that is unacceptable for his age; (e) whose behaviour, condition, environment or associations is injurious or threatens to be injurious to himself or others; (f) for whom the parent or person is whose custody he is neglects or refuses to provide or obtain proper medical or surgical care or treatment necessary for his health and well-being where it is recommended by a duly qualified medical practitioner; (g) whose emotional or mental health and development is endangered or is likely to be endangered by the lack of affection, guidance and discipline or continuity of care in the child's life; (h) for whom the parent or person is whose custody he is neglects, refuses or is unable to provide the services and assistance needed by the child because of the child's physical, mental, or emotional handicap or disability; (i) who is living in a situation where there is severe domestic violence; (j) who is beyond the control of the person caring for him; (k) who is living apart from his parents without their consent; or (l) who is pregnant and refuses or is unable to provide properly and adequately for the health and welfare needs of herself and her child both before and after the birth of her child.

CHILD LABOUR. Work prohibited by statute by minors when minor is under age specified by statute.

CHILD OF THE MARRIAGE. A child of two spouses or former spouses who, at the material time, (a) is under the age of majority and who has not withdrawn from their charge, or (b) is the age of majority or over and under their charge but unable, by reason of illness, disability or other cause, to withdraw from their charge or to obtain the necessaries of life. *Divorce Act*, R.S.C, 1985, c. 3 (2nd Supp.), s. 2, as am.

CHILD PORNOGRAPHY. A photographic, film, video or other visual representation, whether or not it was made by electronic or mechanical means, (i) that shows a person who is or is depicted as being under the age of eighteen years and is engaged in or is depicted as engaged in explicit sexual activity, or (ii) the dominant characteristic of which is the depiction, for a sexual purpose, of a sexual organ or the anal region of a person under the age of eighteen years; or any written material or visual representation that advocates or counsels sexual activity with a person under the age of eighteen years that would be an offence under this Act. *Criminal Code*, R.S.C. 1985, c. C-46, s. 163.1.

CHILDREN. *n*. " . . . Prima facie, the word 'children', in such context [using the words 'to her children in equal shares per stirpes'], denotes persons of the first degree of descent, and therefore is a word of designation." *Simpson, Re,*

[1928] S.C.R. 329 at 331, [1928] 3 D.L.R. 773, the court per Duff J. See CHILD.

CHILDREN'S AID SOCIETY. An organized or incorporated society having among its objects the promotion of family and child welfare.

CHILDREN'S INSTITUTION. All or any part of a building or buildings maintained and operated for children and other persons requiring sheltered, specialized or group care.

CHILDREN'S RESIDENCE. A parent model residence where five or more children not of common parentage, or a staff model residence where three or more children not of common parentage, live and receive residential care, and includes a foster home or other home or institution that is supervised or operated by a children's aid society.

CHILD-RESISTANT CONTAINER. Must (*a*) be constructed so that it can be opened only by operating, puncturing or removing one of its functional and necessary parts using a tool that is not supplied with the container; or (*b*) meet the child test protocol requirements of one of CSA-Z76.1, ISO 8317 or 16 CFR 1700.20 or a standard that is at least equivalent. *Consumer Chemicals and Containers Regulations, 2001,* SOR/2001-269, s. 9.

CHILD RESTRAINT SYSTEM. Any device, other than a safety-belt, that is designed to restrain, seat or position a person and that complies with the applicable standards of airworthiness set out in Chapter 537 of the *Airworthiness Manual*. *Canadian Aviation Regulations* SOR 96-433, s. 101.01.

CHILD SUPPORT GUIDELINES. 1. The Governor in Council may establish guidelines respecting the making of orders for child support, based on the principle that spouses have a joint financial obligation to maintain the children of the marriage in accordance with their relative abilities to contribute to the performance of that obligation. *Divorce Act*, R.S.C., 1985, c. 3 (2nd Supp.), s. 26.1. 2. Where both spouses or former spouses are ordinarily resident in the same province at the time an application for a child support order or a variation order in respect of a child support order is made, or the amount of a child support order is to be recalculated pursuant to section 25.1, and that province has been designated by an order made under subsection (5), the laws of the province specified in the order are for that purpose the child support guidelines, and (b) in any other case, the Federal

Child Support Guidelines. *Divorce Act*, R.S.C, 1985, c. 3 (2nd Supp.), s. 2.

CHILD SUPPORT ORDER. A court of competent jurisdiction may, on application by either or both spouses, make an order requiring a spouse to pay for the support of any or all children of the marriage. *Divorce Act*, R.S.C, 1985, c. 3 (2nd Supp.), s. 15.1.

CHILD TREATMENT SERVICE. A service for a child with a mental or psychiatric disorder, for the family of a child with a mental or psychiatric disorder, or for the child and the family. *Child and Family Services Act*, R.S.O. 1990, c. C.11, s. 3.

CHILD WELFARE SERVICE. A residential or non-residential service, child protection service, adoption service, individual or family counselling.

CHILLED SHOT. Shot pellets which are especially hardened. F.A. Jaffe, *A Guide to Pathological Evidence*, 3d ed. (Toronto: Carswell, 1991) at 226.

CHILLERS. *n*. Those heat recovery units or heat recovery chillers that are installed in a central air-conditioning system specifically designed to incorporate such units or chillers for the purpose of recovery of heat from the system and its subsequent utilization.

CHILLING EFFECT. " . . . [P]resent in respect of any law or practice which has the effect of seriously discouraging the exercise of a constitutional right . . ." *R. v. Smith* (1987), 31 C.R.R. 193 at 226, [1987] 5 W.W.R. 1, 75 N.R. 321, 15 B.C.L.R. (2d) 273, 58 C.R. (3d) 193, [1987] 1 S.C.R. 1045, 34 C.C.C. (3d) 97, 40 D.L.R. (4th) 435, McIntyre J. (dissenting).

CHIMERA. *n*. An embryo into which a cell of any non-human life form has been introduced; or an embryo that consists of cells of more than one embryo, foetus or human being.

CHIMERIC PLANT GENE. One that has been molecularly engineered using multiple sources that may include plant, viral and bacterial DNA. *Monsanto Canada Inc. v. Schmeiser* (2002), 218 D.L.R. (4th) 31, 293 N.R. 340, [2003] 2 F.C. 165, 231 F.T.R. 160 (note), 21 C.P.R. (4th) 1 (C.A.).

CHIMNEY. *n*. A primarily vertical shaft enclosing at least one flue for conducting flue gases to the outdoors. See FACTORY-BUILT ~; METAL ~.

CHIMNEY LINER. A conduit containing a chimney flue used as a lining of a masonry, or concrete chimney.

CHINESE WALL. 1. A method in which a law firm may represent more than one client in the same transaction by having the lawyer who presents one side keep everything confidential from the lawyer who represents the other. 2. " . . . If the attorney practices in a firm, there is a presumption that lawyers who work together share each other's confidences. Knowledge of confidential matters is therefore imputed to other members of the firm. This latter presumption can, however, in some circumstances be rebutted. The usual methods used to rebut the presumption are the setting up of a 'Chinese Wall' . . . at the time that the possibility of the unauthorized communication of confidential information arises. A 'Chinese Wall' involves effective 'screening' to prevent communication between the tainted lawyer and other members of the firm." *MacDonald Estate v. Martin* (1990), 48 C.P.C. (2d) 113 at 126, [1991] 1 W.W.R. 705, 121 N.R. 1, 77 D.L.R. (4th) 249, 70 Man. R. (2d) 241, [1990] 3 S.C.R. 1235, Sopinka J. (Dickson C.J., La Forest and Gonthier JJ. concurring). 3. "These two subsections [of the Securities Act, R.S.O. 1980, c. 466, s. 75(1) and (3)] provide for what is commonly referred to as a 'Chinese Wall' defence. That means the establishment within an organization of informational barriers to prevent the improper transmission of information within the organization concerning a material fact or material change that has not been generally disclosed. Chinese Walls are designed to insulate and to keep to a minimum persons in an organization who make investment decisions from persons in that organization who have confidential information which could affect those decisions." *R. v. Saliga* (1991), 14 O.S.C.B. 4777 at 4783 (Prov. Div.), Masse J. See CONE OF SILENCE.

CHIROGRAPH. *n*. A deed or other public instrument in writing, which was attested by the subscription of witnesses.

CHIROGRAPHUM APUD DEBITOREM REPERTUM PRAESUMITUR SOLUTUM. [L.] When a person possesses a document requiring payment of money, this gives rise to a presumption that the money was paid.

CHIROPODIST. *n*. A person, other than a legally qualified medical practitioner, who practises the treatment of any ailment, disease, defect or disability of the human foot.

CHIROPODY. *n.* The assessment of the foot and the treatment and prevention of diseases, disorders or dysfunctions of the foot by therapeutic, orthotic or palliative means. See PRACTICE OF THE PROFESSION OF ~.

CHIROPRACTIC. *n.* That system of therapeutics based on the science and art of adjusting the articulations or segments of the body, especially those of the spinal column, without the use of drugs or surgery.

CHIROPRACTIC ADJUSTMENT. A form of treatment that entails the application of force to a joint in the human body toward the immediate end of bringing about movement of the parts of the joint, which is to say sufficient, though not excessive, movement toward the ultimate end of producing the desired remedial effect, namely, the correction of a structural dysfunction and the resulting relief of the associated ailment. *Simpson v. Chiropractors' Assn. (Saskatchewan)*, 2001 SKCA 22, 31 Admin. L.R. (3d) 87, 203 Sask. R. 231, 240 W.A.C. 231 (C.A.).

CHIROPRACTOR. *n.* A person whose method of treatment of the human body for disease and the causes of disease is confined solely to chiropractic.

CHIRURGEON. *n.* A surgeon.

CHITTY'S L.J. *abbr.* Chitty's Law Journal, 1953-.

CHLORATE MIXTURE. Any explosive containing a chlorate.

CHLORINE. *n.* The chemical element Cl_2 in liquid or gaseous form. See RESIDUAL ~ CONTENT.

CHLOROBIPHENYLS. *n.* Those chlorobiphenyls that have the molecular formula $C^{12}H^{10-n}Cl^n$ in which "n" is greater than 2.

CHLOROFLUOROCARBON. *n.* A fully halogenated chlorofluorocarbon each molecule of which contains one, two or three carbon atoms and at least one atom each of chlorine and fluorine. *Ozone-depleting Substances Regulations, 1998*, SOR/99-7, s. 1.

CHOICE OF LAW. " . . . [R]efers to the conflicts rules which have developed, through legislation or jurisprudence, in order to determine which system of substantive law the forum court will apply in respect of a legal matter having connection with other jurisdictions. There are difference [*sic??*] choice of law rules for differ-

ent areas of law." *Tolofson v. Jensen* (1992), 4 C.P.C. (3d) 113 at 118, 65 B.C.L.R. (2d) 114, 9 C.C.L.T. (2d) 289, [1992] 3 W.W.R. 743, 89 D.L.R. (4th) 129, 11 B.C.A.L. 94, 22 W.A.C. 94, the court per Cumming J.A.

CHOKE. *n.* Narrowing of the muzzle end of a shotgun barrel so that the area of scatter of shotgun pellets is smaller. F.A. Jaffe, *A Guide to Pathological Evidence*, 3d ed. (Toronto: Carswell, 1991) at 215.

CHOKE HOLD. A sudden seizure of a suspect's throat by police personnel in an attempt to prevent the swallowing of illicit drugs which might be evidence.

CHOKING. *n.* Suffocation caused by obstructing the upper air passages. F.A. Jaffe, *A Guide to Pathological Evidence*, 3d ed. (Toronto: Carswell, 1991) at 215.

CHOREOGRAPHIC WORK. Includes any work of choreography, whether or not it has any story line. *Copyright Act*, R.S.C. 1985, c. C-42, s. 2.

CHOSE. *n.* [Fr.] A chattel personal, either in action or in possession. See CHATTEL.

CHOSE IN ACTION. 1. "In Torkington v. Magee, [1902] 2 K.B. 427 at p. 430, Channel J. said: "'Chose in action" is a known legal expression used to describe all personal rights of property which can only be claimed or enforced by action, and not by taking physical possession. The term covers multifarious rights, many diverse in their essential nature, such as debts, company shares, negotiable instruments and rights of action founded on tort or breach of contract." *Di Guilo v. Boland* (1958), 13 D.L.R. (2d) 510 at 513, [1958] O.R. 384 (C.A.), the court per Morden J.A. 2. " . . . [A]n incorporeal right to something not in one's possession and, accordingly, it is not possible for the debtor to have possession of it. . ." *Ontario (Attorney General) v. Royal Bank*, [1970] 2 O.R. 467 at 472, 11 D.L.R. (3d) 257 (C.A.), the court per Brooke J.A.

CHOSE IN POSSESSION. A tangible thing which is in someone's possession.

CH. R. *abbr.* Upper Canada Chambers Reports, 1857-1872.

C.H.R.C. *abbr.* Canadian Human Rights Commission.

CHRISTIAN NAME. The name given at baptism; first name. See SURNAME AND ~S.

CHRISTMAS DAY. December 25.

CHRISTMAS TREE. A tree, whether sheared or unsheared, that is, (i) sold, offered for sale or intended to be sold severed from its root system and with its bark, branches and foliage mainly intact, and (ii) of the coniferous species, including but not limited to, (A) Douglas fir (Pseudotsuga Menziesii), (B) Balsam fir (Abies balsomea), (C) Black spruce (Picea mariana), (D) White spruce (Picea glauca), (E) Scotch pine (Pinus sylvestis), (F) Norway spruce (Picea excelsa), (G) Red Pine (Pinus resinosa), and (H) Red spruce (Picea rubens).

CHRISTMAS TREE PLANTATION. A group of coniferous trees that are planted or growing on land for the production of Christmas trees.

CHROMATIN. *n*. The carrier of genetic information in the nuclei of cells which can be stained with basic dyes. F.A. Jaffe, *A Guide to Pathological Evidence*, 3d ed. (Toronto: Carswell, 1991) at 215. See SEX ~.

CHRONIC. *adj*. Used in connection with diseases, of long duration or with slowly progressive symptoms; distinguished from acute.

CHRONICALLY ILL PERSON. A person afflicted with or suffering from any chronic illness, sickness, injury or other condition of a long-term nature requiring treatment.

C.H.R.R. *abbr*. Canadian Human Rights Reporter, 1980-.

C.H.S. CHART. *abbr*. Canadian Hydrographic Service Chart.

CHUNKING. *n*. The breaking away of pieces of the tread or sidewall of a tire.

CHURCH. *n*. 1. Any church, chapel, meetinghouse or other building or place used for public worship. 2. A group of persons who form a religious body.

CHURCH BUILDING. A church, chapel or meeting house or a residence for the minister.

CHURCHILL. See LOWER ~ BASIN.

CHURCHWARDEN. *n*. 1. The guardian or keeper of the church. 2. The representative of the parish. 3. An officer of a church or congregation.

CHURNING. *n*. Excessive trading of a client's account by a stockbroker.

CHUTE. See LETTER ~.

CHY. CHRS. *abbr*. Upper Canada Chancery Chambers Reports.

C.I.B.C. *abbr*. Canadian Imperial Bank of Commerce.

CICA. The Canadian Institute of Chartered Accountants.

CICA HANDBOOK. The handbook prepared and published by the Canadian Institute of Chartered Accountants, as amended from time to time.

CIDA. *abbr*. Canadian International Development Agency.

CIDER. *n*. The beverage obtained by the alcoholic fermentation of fruit juice. See STRONG ~; WEAK ~.

CIE. *abbr*. [Fr. compagnie] Company.

C.I.F. *abbr*. Cost insurance and freight.

C.I.F. CONTRACT. A contract in which price includes cost of the goods, insurance while in transit and freight charges incurred. G.H.L. Fridman, *Sale of Goods in Canada*, 3d ed. (Toronto: Carswell, 1986) at 480.

CIFTA. The Canada-Israel Free Trade Agreement Implementation Act.

CIGAR. *n*. Includes (*a*) a cigarillo or cheroot; and (*b*) any roll or tubular construction intended for smoking that consists of a filler composed of pieces of natural or reconstituted leaf tobacco, a binder of natural or reconstituted leaf tobacco in which the filler is wrapped and a wrapper of natural or reconstituted leaf tobacco. *Excise Act, 2001*, S.C. 2002, c. 22, s. 2.

CIGARETTE. *n*. Includes any roll or tubular construction intended for smoking, other than a cigar or a tobacco stick. If a cigarette exceeds 102 mm in length, each portion of 76 mm or less is considered to be a separate cigarette. *Excise Act, 2001*, S.C. 2002, c. 22, s. 2.

CIGAR MANUFACTORY. Any place or premises where raw leaf tobacco is worked up into a cigar, and every workshop, office, storeroom, shed, yard or other place where any of the raw material is or is to be stored, where any process connected with the manufacture or preparation of cigars is or is intended to be carried on or where any of the products of the manufacture are or are intended to be stored. *Excise Act*, R.S.C. 1985, c. E-14, s. 6.

CIGAR MANUFACTURER. Any person who either personally or by an agent, carries on the manufacture of cigars, and the casing, packing, cutting, pressing, grinding, rolling, drying, crushing or stemming of any raw leaf tobacco for manufacture into cigars. *Excise Act*, R.S.C. 1985, c. E-14, s. 6.

CIGAR STAMP. Any stamp affixed to any package of cigars. *Excise Act*, R.S.C. 1985, c. E-14, s. 6.

C.I.L.R. *abbr*. 1. Canadian Insurance Law Reports. 2. Canadian Insurance Law Review.

CINEMATOGRAPH. *n*. 1. A moving picture machine or other similar apparatus. 2. Includes any work produced by any process analogous to cinematography. *Copyright Act*, R.S.C. 1985, c. C-42, s. 2.

CINEMATOGRAPHIC FILM. Positive or negative film containing continuous images designed to create the illusion of motion and includes film issued in any form in a set under a single title.

CINEMATOGRAPHIC WORK. Includes any work expressed by any process analogous to cinematography, whether or not accompanied by a soundtrack. *Copyright Act*, R.S.C. 1985, c.C-42, s. 2.

CIO. *abbr*. Congress of Industrial Organizations, a federation of national and international industrial unions.

CIPO. *abbr*. Canadian Intellectual Property Office.

C.I.P.R. *abbr*. Canadian Intellectual Property Reports, 1984-.

CIRCA. [L.] About; around.

CIRC. CT. *abbr*. Circuit Court.

CIRCUIT. *n*. 1. Any complete conductor, loop, path or unit current-carrying part of the system conductors and that portion of a system controlled by a switch or protected by a cut-out. 2. A single telecommunication channel of intelligence by signals, sounds, pictures or writings of all kinds. 3. One or more race courses on which successive days of racing or race meetings are held. See BRANCH ~; CONTROL ~; NON-INCENDIVE ~; REMOTE CONTROL~; SIGNAL ~; VOLTAGE OF A ~.

CIRCUIT-BREAKER. *n*. An electromechanical device designed to automatically open a current-carrying circuit on a pre-determined over-current, under both overload and short-circuit conditions without injury to the device.

CIRCUIT INTERRUPTER. See GROUND FAULT ~.

CIRCUITUS EST EVITANDUS. [L.] Circuity should be avoided.

CIRCUIT VENT. A vent that functions for two or more traps and extends to a vent stack from a point on a horizontal branch in front of the last connected fixture.

CIRCUITY OF ACTION. A more complex course of proceeding than is necessary; a multiplicity of actions.

CIRCULAR. *n*. A take-over bid circular; an issuer bid circular; an amendment to a take-over bid circular or issuer bid circular; a notice of change; and a notice of variation. See BID ~; INFORMATION ~.

CIRCULAR NOTE. A bank's request in writing that one of its correspondents abroad pay a certain sum to a certain person.

CIRCULATING CAPITAL. A part of the subscribed capital of a company intended to be temporarily circulated in business in the form of goods, money or other assets, which capital, or its proceeds, is intended to return to the company increased so that it can be used repeatedly, always to return with some increase. W. Grover & F. Iacobucci, *Materials on Canadian Income Tax*, 4th ed. (Toronto: Richard De Boo Ltd., 1980) at 298.

CIRCULATION. *n*. 1. Transmission from person to person or place to place. 2. Of a newspaper or periodical, the number of readers or number of copies printed.

CIRCULATION COIN. A coin composed of base metal that is put into circulation in Canada for use in day-to-day transactions.

CIRCUMSTANCE. *n*. 1. An attendant or auxiliary fact. 2. Includes any communication made to or information received by the assured. *Insurance acts*. See DANGEROUS ~S.

CIRCUMSTANTIAL EVIDENCE. 1. Evidence which creates an inference that a particular fact exists. 2. Evidence tending to establish the existence or non-existence of a fact that is not one of the elements of the offence charged, where the existence or non-existence of that fact reasonably leads to an inference concerning the existence or non-existence of a fact that is one of the elements of the offence charged. *Military Rules of Evidence*, C.R.C., c. 1049, s. 2.

CIT. *abbr.* 1. Citizen. 2. Citizenship.

C.I.T. *abbr.* Canadian Import Tribunal.

CITATIO AD REASSUMENDAM CAUSAM. [L.] A citation to revive a cause which issues against the heir of the party who died pending the original suit.

CITATION. *n.* 1. Calling on a person who is not a party to a proceeding or an action to appear in court. 2. In probate matters, notice of proceedings given to anyone whose interests are or may be affected. 3. A precise reference to a case or enactment. 4. The act of referring to a case or an enactment. See CORE OF ~; NEUTRAL ~ STANDARD.

CITATION OF AUTHORITIES. 1. A reference to case or statute law to establish or support propositions of law advanced. 2. The act of referring to a case or an enactment.

CITATOR. *n.* A set of books which provides historical information regarding statutes, cumulates amendments to statutes since the last revision or consolidation of the statutes and traces judicial consideration of sections of statutes.

CITE. *v.* 1. To refer to legal authorities. 2. To name in citation. 3. To put a defendant on notice that he or she must show cause why he or she should not be found in contempt of court. See CITING IN CONTEMPT.

CITE. *n.* Citation of a case or enactment.

CITING IN CONTEMPT. The expression "citing in contempt", should be used not as an expression of a finding of contempt but instead, as a method of providing the accused with notice that he or she has been contemptuous and will be required to show cause why they should not be held in contempt. *R. c. Arradi*, 2003 SCC 23.

CITIZEN. *n.* 1. A Canadian citizen. *Citizenship Act*, R.S.C. 1985, c. C-29, s. 2. 2. In the Charter, refers to a natural person, not a corporation. See CANADIAN ~; SENIOR ~.

CITIZENSHIP. *n.* Canadian citizenship. Citizenship *Act*, R.S.C. 1985, c. C-29, s. 2. 2. Refers to a political status conferred by a state. See CERTIFICATE OF ~; OATH OR AFFIRMATION OF ~.

CITIZENSHIP COURT. A place where a citizenship judge or citizenship officer performs duties under the Act. *Citizenship Regulations, 1993*, SOR/93-246, s. 2.

CITIZENSHIP JUDGE. A citizenship judge appointed under the Citizenship Act. *Citizenship Act*, R.S.C. 1985, c. C-29, s. 2.

CITIZENSHIP OFFICER. A person who is authorized by the Minister in writing to perform the duties of a citizenship officer prescribed by these Regulations. *Citizenship Regulations, 1993*, SOR/93-246, s. 2.

CITY. *n.* A municipal corporation incorporated as a city.

CITY CENTRAL. A council created to correlate activities of union locals within a community.

CITY INDUSTRIAL UNION COUNCIL. A body composed of CIO locals from a city.

CITY MOTOR VEHICLE OPERATOR. A motor vehicle operator who operates exclusively within a 10-mile radius of his home terminal and is not a bus operator and includes any motor vehicle operator who is classified as a city motor vehicle operator in a collective agreement entered into between his employer and a trade union acting on his behalf or who is not classified in any such agreement but is considered to be a city motor vehicle operator according to the prevailing industry practice in the geographical area where he is employed. *Motor Vehicle Operators Hours of Work Regulations*, C.R.C., c. 990, s. 2.

CIVIC HOLIDAY. The first Monday in August.

CIVIL. *adj.* 1. Of legal matters, private as opposed to criminal. 2. Used to distinguish the criminal courts and proceedings in them from military courts and proceedings. 3. Used to distinguish secular from religious.

CIVIL ACTION. Any type of action except criminal proceedings.

CIVIL AIRCRAFT. 1. Any aircraft other than a military aircraft. 2. All aircraft other than aircraft operated by the Canadian Forces, a police force in Canada or persons engaged in the administration or enforcement of the Customs Act, the Excise Act or the Excise Act, 2001. *Criminal Code*, R.S.C. 1985, c. C-46, s. 78(2).

CIVIL AVIATION INSPECTOR. (a) An employee who is required to conduct flight tests to determine the competency of flight crew personnel and to inspect commercial air operations, or (b) an employee who is required to monitor in-flight cabin procedures in use in commercial air operations. *Flying Accidents Compensation Regulations*, C.R.C., c. 10, s. 2.

CIVIL CEREMONY. A marriage performed by a judge or justice of the peace, distinguished from a religious ceremony.

CIVIL CODE. The *Civil Code of Québec*, S.Q., 1991, c. 64.

CIVIL COMMOTION INSURANCE. Insurance against loss of or damage to the property insured caused by bombardment, invasion, insurrection, mutiny, civil war or commotion, riot, act of foreign enemy, hostilities or warlike operations, whether war is declared or not, revolution, rebellion, conspiracy, usurped power or military, naval or air force operations, vandalism or malicious mischief.

CIVIL CONSPIRACY. 1. " . . . [W]hereas the law of tort does not permit an action against an individual defendant who has caused injury to the plaintiff, the law of torts does recognize a claim against them in combination as the tort of conspiracy if: (1) whether the means used by the defendants are lawful or unlawful, the predominant purpose of the defendants' conduct is to cause injury to the plaintiff; or, (2) where the conduct is directed towards the plaintiff (alone or together with others), and the defendants should know in the circumstances that injury to the plaintiff is likely to and does result." *Canada Cement LaFarge Ltd. v. British Columbia Lightweight Aggregate Ltd.*, [1983] 1 S.C.R. 452 at 471-2, Estey J. 2. A summary of the law relating to claims of civil conspiracy was provided by McLachlin J. (as she then was) in *Nicholls v. Richmond (City)* (1984), 52 B.C.L.R. 302 (S.C.), at pages 311-312: There are two categories of civil conspiracy: (1) where the predominant purpose of the defendants' conduct is to injure the plaintiff; and (2) where the defendants effect their agreed end by unlawful means knowing that the plaintiff may be injured. While only the first category is available in the United Kingdom since the decision of the House of Lords in *Lonrho Ltd. v. Shell Petroleum Co.* (1981), [1982] A.C. 173, [1981] 3 W.L.R. 33, [1981] 2 All E.R. 456 (H.L.), both categories are recognized in Canada: *Canada Cement LaFarge Ltd. v. British Columbia Lightweight Aggregate Ltd.*, [1983] 6 W.W.R. 385, 21 B.L.R. 254, 24 C.C.L.T. 111, 72 C.P.R. (2d) 1, 145 D.L.R. (3d) 385, 47 N.R. 191 (S.C.C.). The requirements of conspiracy to injure the plaintiff are an agreement between two or more persons whose predominant purpose is to injure the plaintiff and which when acted upon results in damage to the plaintiff. It is not a requirement that the conduct of the defendants in effecting their agreement be unlawful. The requirements of the second type of conspiracy, conspiracy by unlawful means, are an agreement between two or more persons which is effected by unlawful conduct where the defendants should know in the circumstances that damage to the plaintiff is likely to ensue and such damage does in fact ensue. Unlike the first category of conspiracy, it is not a requirement of conspiracy by unlawful means that the predominant purpose of the defendants be to cause injury to the plaintiff. Rather, a constructive intent is derived from the fact that the defendants should have known that damage to the plaintiff would result from their conduct. *923087 N.W.T. Ltd. v. Anderson Mills Ltd.*, 1997 CarswellNWT 36, 35 B.L.R. (2d) 1, 13 C.P.C. (4th) 357, [1997] N.W.T.R. 212, 40 C.C.L.T. (2d) 15 (S.C.), Vertes J.

CIVIL CONTEMPT. 1. Breach of the rules of a court, a court order or other misconduct in a private matter causing a private injury or wrong. 2. " . . . [T]he purpose . . . is to secure compliance with the process of a tribunal including, but not limited to, the process of a court . . . initiated by a party or person affected by the order sought to be enforced. In order to secure compliance in a proceeding for civil contempt, a court may impose a fine or other penalty which will be exacted in the absence of compliance. However, the object is always compliance and not punishment." *U.N.A. v. Alberta (Attorney General)* (1992), 13 C.R. (4th) 1 at 22, [1992] 3 W.W.R. 481, 89 D.L.R. (4th) 609, 71 C.C.C. (3d) 225, 135 N.R. 321, 92 C.L.L.C. 14,023, 1 Alta. L.R. (3d) 129, 125 A.R. 241, 14 W.A.C. 241, [1992] 1 S.C.R. 901, 9 C.R.R. (2d) 29, Sopinka J. (dissenting). 3. " . . . [A] private wrong. The intervention of the court is called upon primarily to assist the position of one of the litigants to enforce an order favourable to that party. . ." *R. v. Clement* (1980), 17 R.F.L. (2d) 349 at 362, [1980] 6 W.W.R. 695, 4 Man. R. (2d) 18, 54 C.C.C. (2d) 252, 114 D.L.R. (3d) 656 (C.A.), Matas J.A. (Freedman C.J.M. concurring).

CIVIL COURT. A court of ordinary criminal jurisdiction in Canada and includes a court of summary jurisdiction. *National Defence Act*, R.S.C. 1985, c. N-5, s. 2.

CIVIL CUSTODY. The holding under arrest or in confinement of a person by the police or other competent civil authority, and includes confinement in a penitentiary or civil prison. *National Defence Act*, R.S.C. 1985, c. N-5, s. 2.

CIVIL DEFENCE. Planning, organization, establishing and operating salvage, precautionary safety measures controls, facilities and services of all kinds vital and necessary for the public welfare for meeting, preventing, reducing and overcoming the effects of enemy action or civil disaster.

CIVIL DISASTER. A disaster occurring within the province from fire, flood, earthquake, tempest, or other cause, not attributable to enemy attack, sabotage, or other hostile action, whereby injury or loss is or may be caused to some or all of the citizens of the province or to their property, or both.

CIVIL EMERGENCY PLAN. A plan, measure, procedure or arrangement (a) for dealing with an emergency by the civil population, or (b) for dealing with a civil emergency by the Canadian Forces. *Emergency Preparedness Act*, R.S.C., 1985, c. 6 (4th Supp.), s. 2.

CIVILIAN. *n.* 1. A private citizen, not a member of the armed forces. 2. A person knowledgeable in civil law.

CIVILISATION. *n.* A law, act of judgment or justice which makes a criminal matter civil.

CIVILITER MORTUUS. [L. civilly defunct] Dead in law.

CIVIL LAW. 1. The legal system of Quebec based on the Civil Code and ultimately Roman law. 2. " . . . [A] body of private law, consists largely, although not exclusively, of the law enunciated in the Civil Code of Lower Canada and the Civil Code of Quebec, L.R.Q. 1977, c. C-25." *Laurentide Motels Ltd. c. Beauport (Vine)* (1989), 45 M.P.L.R. 1 at 11, 94 N.R. 1, [1989] 1 S.C.R. 705, 23 Q.A.C. 1, Beetz J. (McIntyre, Lamer, Wilson and La Forest JJ. concurring).

CIVIL LIABILITY CONVENTION. The International Convention on Civil Liability for Oil Pollution Damage, concluded in Brussels on November 29,1969, as amended by any protocol that is in force for Canada.

CIVIL LIBERTIES. Essentially that which is not a prohibited act. Include the rights protected by the Charter of Rights and Freedoms: freedom of association, assembly, religion, expression, mobility rights, voting rights, procedural and legal rights, right to equal treatment under the law, and language rights. See EGALITARIAN ~; LEGAL ~; POLITICAL ~.

CIVIL LITIGATION. Litigation involving private parties as opposed to criminal proceedings.

CIVIL MARRIAGE CEREMONY. A marriage performed by a judge or justice of the peace, distinguished from a religious ceremony.

CIVIL MATTER. A cause, issue or matter, other than a criminal matter.

CIVIL ONUS. The standard of proof for the party bearing the onus is on a balance of probabilities.

CIVIL PRISON. Any prison, jail or other place in Canada in which offenders sentenced by a civil court in Canada to imprisonment for less than two years can be confined, and, if sentenced outside Canada, any prison, jail or other place in which a person sentenced to that term of imprisonment by a civil court having jurisdiction in the place where the sentence was passed, can for the time being be confined. *National Defence Act*, R.S.C. 1985, c. N-5, s. 2.

CIVIL PROCEDURE. The law governing the process and practice of civil litigation. See RULES OF ~.

CIVIL RIGHTS. 1. Those rights referred to in the list of provincial powers in the Constitution Act, 1867 are primarily proprietary, contractual or tortious rights. 2. Procedural rights of an individual. See CIVIL LIBERTIES; PROPERTY AND ~.

CIVIL RIGHTS IN THE PROVINCE. Proprietary, contractual or tortious rights referred to in the Constitution Act, 1867.

CIVIL SERVANT. 1. A person appointed to the service of the Crown. 2. A member of the civil service. 3. A member of the staff of a department or Ministry of Government.

CIVIL SERVICE. The employees of the government.

CIVIL STATUS. " . . . [U]nder s. 10 [of the Quebec Charter of Rights and Freedoms, R.S.Q. 1977, c. C-12] includes a range of facts (and not necessarily recorded facts) relating to the three classical elements of civil status—birth, marriage, and death—to which arts. 39 et seq. C.C.L.C. refer. These facts are sometimes recorded in a person's own acts of civil status, sometimes recorded in the acts of another person, and sometimes not recorded in any act at all . . . Other facts, such as interdiction or emancipation, which do not relate to birth, marriage or death but instead to legal capacity may also be included in civil status under s. 10 . . . family relationships [are included in] 'civil status'. Like filiation, fraternity and sorority fall within the parameters which have ascribed to civil status under s. 10 in this respect as well . . ." *Brossard (Ville) v. Québec (Commission des droits de la personne)* (1989), 10 C.H.R.R. D/ 5515 at D/ 5520, D/5522, 88 C.L.L.C. 17,031, [1989] 2 S.C.R. 279, 88 N.R. 321, 18 Q.A.C. 164, 53 D.L.R. (4th) 609, Beetz J. (McIntyre, Lamer and La Forest JJ. concurring). See ACTS OF ~; OFFICERS OF ~.

CIVIL SUIT. A proceeding involving private parties or a private party and the government as opposed to a criminal matter. Usually refers to a claim for damages by one party against the other. See CIVIL ACTION; SUIT.

C.J. *abbr*. Chief Justice.

C.J.A.L.P. *abbr*. Canadian Journal of Administrative Law & Practice.

C.J.C. The Chief Justice of Canada. The Chief Justice of the Supreme Court of Canada.

C.J.W.L. *abbr*. Canadian Journal of Women and the Law (Revue juridique "La femme et le droit").

CLADDING. See EXTERIOR ~.

CLAIM. *n*. 1. The demand or the subject matter for which any action, suit, or proceeding is brought. 2. A right, title, interest, encumbrance or demand of any kind affecting land. 3. A parcel of land marked out on the ground under a prospector's licence in conformity with the Mining Act. *Mining Act*, R.S.Q. 1977, c. M-13, s. 1. 4. An assertion. 5. An area granted or used for mining purposes. 6. A means of defining boundaries within which an inventor asserts his patent rights. 7. "[A] means of defining in precise terms the boundaries of that which (within what, has in general terms, been described as his invention in the 'specification') the inventor asserts as his claim [under the Patent Act, R.S.C. 1970, c. P-4] to an exclusive privilege. . ." *Leithiser v. Pengo Hydra-Pull of Canada Ltd.* (1974), 17 C.P.R. (2d) 110 at 114, [1974] 2 F.C. 954, 6 N.R. 301 (C.A.), Jackett C.J. (MacKay D.J. concurring). See ADJACENT ~S; ADJOINING ~S; ADVERSE ~; BORING ~; COUNTER~; CROSS~; DORMANT ~; FULL ~; MINERAL ~; MINING ~; NOTICE OF ~; PROFESSIONAL LIABILITY ~; PROVABLE ~; QUARRYING ~; QUIT ~; STATEMENT OF ~; THIRD PARTY ~; TWO POST ~; UNPATENTED MINING ~.

CLAIMANT. *n*. 1. One who makes a claim. 2. A person who has or is alleged to have a right to maintenance or support. Any person who claims or asserts or seeks to realize a lien. 4. A person who applies or has applied for benefit or compensation. 5. A person other than an insured to whom monies may be payable under a contract. *Insurance Adjusters, Agents and Brokers Act*, R.S. Nfld. 1990, c. I-9, s. 2. See LIEN ~; MAJOR ATTACHMENT ~; MINOR ATTACHMENT ~; ORIGINAL ~; PREFERRED ~.

CLAIM AREA. The land covered by a mineral claim.

CLAIM CONSTRUCTION. Claim construction is a question of law, based on the patent alone without resort to extrinsic evidence. This issue precedes other issues.

CLAIM PROVABLE. Any claim or liability provable in proceedings under this Act by a creditor. *Bankruptcy Act*, R.S.C. 1985, c. B-1, s. 2.

CLAIM PROVABLE IN BANKRUPTCY. Any claim or liability provable in proceedings under this Act by a creditor. *Bankruptcy Act*, R.S.C. 1985, c. B-3, s. 2.

CLAIMS ADJUSTER. Every person who, in insurance matters, on behalf of another and for remuneration or on behalf of an employer, investigates a loss, assesses damage arising from it or negotiates settlement of the claim.

CLAIMS MADE AND REPORTED POLICY. Coverage under such policies applies only to claims which are both made of the insured *and reported to the insurer* during the policy period. *Reid Crowther & Partners Ltd. v. Simcoe & Erie General Insurance Co.*, 1993 CarswellMan 96, [1993] 2 W.W.R. 433, 6 C.L.R. (2d) 161, 147 N.R. 44, 13 C.C.L.I. (2d) 161, [1993] 1 S.C.R. 252, 99 D.L.R. (4th) 741, 83 Man. R. (2d) 81, 36 W.A.C. 81, (sub nom. *Simcoe & Erie General Insurance Co. v. Reid Crowther & Partners Ltd.*) [1993] I.L.R. 1-2914 McLachlin, J. for the court.

CLAIMS MADE POLICY. [T]he policy may focus on the time the claim is made by the third party on the insured. Under a "claims-made" policy, the insurer is liable to indemnify the insured for claims made during the currency of the policy, regardless of when the negligence giving rise to those claims may have occurred. Liability for negligent acts predating the policy is covered provided a claim arising from any such negligent act is made during the policy period. On the other hand, liability for negligent acts which occur within the policy period is covered only if a claim is made against the insured on their account within the policy period. *Reid Crowther & Partners Ltd. v. Simcoe & Erie General Insurance Co.*, 1993 CarswellMan 96, [1993] 2 W.W.R. 433, 6 C.L.R. (2d) 161, 147 N.R. 44, 13 C.C.L.I. (2d) 161, [1993] 1 S.C.R. 252, 99 D.L.R. (4th) 741, 83 Man. R. (2d) 81, 36 W.A.C. 81, (sub nom. *Simcoe & Erie General Insurance Co. v. Reid Crowther & Partners Ltd.*) [1993] I.L.R. 1-2914 McLachlin, J. for the court.

CLAIMS RATIO. With respect to any particular period for policies issued by a company with respect to a particular class of insurance, the ratio of the claims incurred during that period under those policies, including applicable adjustment expenses, to the premiums earned during that period in respect of those policies. See EXPECTED ~.

CLAM. *n.* Includes a soft shell, long neck or squirt clam, bar clam and quahaug. Canada regulations.

CLAM DELINQUENTES MAGIS PUNIUNTUR QUAM PALAM. [L.] Those who sin secretly are punished more severely than those who sin openly.

CLAM, VI, AUT PRECARIO. [L.] Secretly, violently or suppliantly.

CLARITY ACT. *An Act to give effect to the requirement for clarity as set out in the opinion of the Supreme Court of Canada in the Quebec Secession Reference*, received Royal Assent on June 29, 2000. Its purpose was stated as: The Government of Quebec can ask Quebec voters the question of its choice. But the Government of Canada and the House of Commons, as political actors, have a duty to make their own assessment of whether the question and the majority indicate a clear support for secession before concluding that the Government of Canada is bound to enter into negotiations on the break-up of Canada.

CLASS. *n.* 1. A group of persons or things having common attributes. 2. A group of securities with defined rights attached to it which distinguish it from another class of securities issued by the same issuer. 3. Includes any series of the class. 4. A group of positions involving duties and responsibilities so similar that the same or like qualifications may reasonably be required

for, and the same schedule or range of pay can be reasonably applied to all positions in the group. See ~ A SHARE; ~ B SHARE; COMMERCIAL ~; CONSTRAINED-~; FEMALE-DOMINATED ~; GOODS OF THE SAME ~ OR KIND; INADMISSIBLE ~; JOB MALE-DOMINATED ~; SHARE~; TRAIN OF SUPERIOR ~.

CLASS ACTION. 1. A representative proceeding. 2. "It is necessary to consider the difference between a class action which is derivative in nature, and a representative action by persons having the same interest in the subject of the litigation. Derivative type class actions are those in which a wrong is done to the entity to which the members belong. Such an action may be brought by a member or members, but it is brought on behalf of the entity. A representative action can be brought by persons asserting a common right, and even where persons may have been wronged in their individual capacity." *Pasco v. Canadian National Railway* (1989), (*sub nom. Oregon Jack Creek Indian Hand v. Canadian National Railway*) [1990] 2 C.N.L.R. 85 at 87, 34 B.C.L.R. (2d) 344, 56 D.L.R. (4th) 404 (C.A.), MacFarlane J.A.

CLASS A SHARE. In respect of a corporation, means a share of a class of shares that entitle the holders thereof to, (a) receive notice of and, subject to the legislation under which the corporation is organized, to attend and vote at all meetings of the shareholders of the corporation, (b) receive dividends at the discretion of the board of directors of the corporation, and (c) receive, on dissolution of the corporation, all the assets of the corporation that remain after payment of all amounts payable to the holders of all other classes of shares of the corporation. *Community Small Business Investment Funds Act*, S.O. 1992, c. 18, s. 1 as am.

CLASS B SHARE. In respect of a corporation, means a share of a class of shares that do not entitle the holders thereof to receive dividends but do entitle the holders thereof to, (a) receive notice of and, subject to the legislation under which the corporation is organized, to attend and vote at all meetings of the shareholders of the corporation, (b) receive, on dissolution of the corporation, an amount equal to the amount of the equity capital received by the corporation on the issue of the Class B shares, and (c) in the case of a corporation registered under Part II or III, vote as a class to elect a majority of the board of directors of the corporation. *Community Small*

Business Investment Funds Act, S.O. 1992, c. 18, s. 1 as am.

CLASS COMPLAINT. A complaint in which each member of the class is said to be suffering essentially the same type of injury and is entitled, if the complaint succeeds, to the same type of remedy. *Canada Safeway Ltd. v. Saskatchewan (Human Rights Commission)* (1997), [1998] 1 W.W.R. 155 (Sask. C.A.).

CLASS COMPOSITION. Deals with the type of student a teacher will teach. *Flin Flon Teachers' Assn. v. Flin Flon School Division No. 46*, 2000 MBCA 78, [2000] 9 W.W.R. 575, 150 Man. R. (2d) 94, 230 W.A.C. 94 (C.A.).

CLASSED SHIP. A ship that is classed with a classification society.

CLASS GIFT. A gift to a number of persons who are united or connected by some common tie . . . the testator was looking to the body as a whole rather than to the members constituting the body as individuals . . . if one or more of that body died in his lifetime the survivors should take the gift between them. *Kingsbury v. Walter*, [1901] A.C. 187 at 191, per Lord Macnaghten.

CLASSIFICATION. See COLOUR ~; FIRE HAZARD ~; JOB ~; OCCUPATIONAL ~.

CLASSIFICATION CENTRE. An institution for the study and diagnosis of persons under sentence to determine the type of institution and type of treatment most suitable to effect the rehabilitation of those persons.

CLASSIFICATION OFFICER. A person responsible for classifying a prisoner as maximum, medium or minimum for security purposes.

CLASSIFICATION OF MURDER. Murder is first degree murder or second degree murder. *Criminal Code*, R.S.C. 1985, c. C-46, s. 231(1).

CLASSIFICATION SOCIETY. 1. A society or association for the classification and registry of shipping approved by the Minister of Transport under the Canada Shipping Act. Canada regulations. 2. Lloyd's Register of Shipping, Bureau Veritas American Bureau of Shipping Det norske Veritas, Germanischer Lloyd, and Registro Italiano Navale. *Steamship Machinery Construction Regulations*, C.R.C., c. 1491, Schedule 1, s. 2.

CLASSIFIED ANNOUNCEMENT. An announcement respecting goods or services offered or sought by persons not normally engaged in the business of dealing in those goods or services. *Television Broadcasting Regulations*, C.R.C., c. 381, s. 2.

CLASSIFY. *v.* In relation to a position means to assign a class and grade to a position.

CLASS MEETING. A meeting of members who hold shares of a particular class.

CLASS OF OCCUPANCY. The use or intended use of a building.

CLASS OF POSITIONS. A group of positions involving duties and responsibilities so similar that the same or like qualifications may reasonably be required for, and the same schedule or grade of pay can be reasonably applied to, all positions in the group.

CLASS OF SECURITIES. A group of securities to which certain rights, privileges or limitations are attached. Classes of securities are used in incorporating documents to provide preferential treatment of some securities.

CLASS OF SHARES. A group of shares to which certain rights, privileges or limitations are attached. Classes of shares are used in incorporating documents to provide preferential treatment of some shares.

CLASS OF SUBSTANCES. 1. Any two or more substances that (i) contain the same chemical moiety, or (ii) have similar chemical properties and the same type of chemical structure. 2. Class of substances whose members have similar physio-chemical or toxicological properties.

CLASS PRIVILEGE. " . . . [A] privilege which was recognized at common law and one for which there is a prima facie presumption of inadmissibility (once it has been established that the relationship fits within the class) unless the party urging admission can show why the communications should not be privileged (i.e., why they should be admitted into evidence as an exception to the general rule). Such communications are excluded not because the evidence is not relevant, but rather because, there are overriding policy reasons to exclude this relevant evidence. Solicitor-client communications appear to fall within this first category . . ." *R. v. Fosty* (1991), 7 C.R.R. (2d) 108 at 123, [1991] 6 W.W.R. 673, 8 C.R. (4th) 368, 130 N.R. 161, 75 Man. R. (2d) 112, 6 W.A.C. 112, 67 C.C.C. (3d) 289, [1991] 3 S.C.R. 263, Lamer C.J.C. (La Forest, Sopinka, Cory, McLachlin, Stevenson and Iacobucci JJ. concurring).

CLASS SIZE. Deals with the number of students the teacher will teach. *Flin Flon Teachers'*

Assn. v. Flin Flon School Division No. 46, 2000 MBCA 78, [2000] 9 W.W.R. 575, 150 Man. R. (2d) 94, 230 W.A.C. 94 (C.A.).

CLAUSE. *n.* 1. A paragraph or division of a contract. 2. A sentence or part of a sentence. 3. A numbered portion of a bill called a section once the bill becomes law. A. Fraser, W.A. Dawson, & J. Holtby, eds., *Beauchesne's Rules and Forms of the House of Commons of Canada*, 6th ed. (Toronto: Carswell, 1989) at 193-4. See ACCELERATION ~; ACCESS-TO-PLANT ~; ACT OF GOD ~; AFTER-ACQUIRED ~; AMENDING ~; ARBITRATION ~; ATTESTATION ~; BASKET ~; CALL-BACK ~; CALL-IN ~; CANCELLATION ~; COLA ~; DEEMING ~; DEFEASANCE ~; DEROGATORY ~; DISCIPLINE ~; DISCLAIMER ~; ENACTING ~; ENTRENCHMENT ~; ESCALATION ~; EXCEPTIONS ~; EXCLUSION ~; EXCLUSIVE JURISDICTION ~; EXEMPTION ~; FINALITY ~; FORCE MAJEURE ~; "GENERAL WELFARE" ~; GRANDFATHER ~; GREEN ~; HIMALAYA ~; INCHMAREE ~; INTERPRETATION ~; MOST FAVOURED NATION ~; NO-CERTIORARI ~; PRIVATIVE RECOGNITION ~; RED ~; REMEDY ~; REOPENING ~; RESCISSION ~; RESOLUTORY ~; REVERSE ONUS ~.

CLAUSULAE INCONSUETAE SEMPER INDUCUNT SUSPICIONEM. [L.] Unusual clauses in a document always create suspicion.

CLAUSULA GENERALIS DE RESIDUO NON EA COMPLECTITUR, QUAE NON EJUSDEM SINT GENERIS CUM US QUAE SPEC DICTA FUERINT. [L.] A general remainder clause does not include things which are not of the same kind with those which have been named specially.

CLAUSULA GENERALIS NON REFERTUR AD EXPRESSA. [L.] A general clause does not refer to matters expressly provided.

CLAUSULA REBUS SIC STANTIBUS. [L.] Agreement is intended by the parties to be binding only until there is a vital change in the circumstances.

CLAUSULA VEL DISPOSITIO INUTILIS PER PRESUMPTIONEM VEL CAUSAM REMOTAM EX POST FACTO NON FULCITUR. [L.] An unnecessary clause or disposition is not supported by a remote presumption or a cause arising after the event.

CLAY. *n.* A soil (i) the particles of which are not visible to the naked eye, (ii) dry lumps of which are not easily powdered by the fingers, (iii) that, after shaking a small saturated pat vigorously in the hand, does not exhibit a wet shiny surface, and (iv) that shines when moist and stroked with a knife.

CLAY-SHALE. *n.* Fine-grained, finely laminated, will swell on wetting, and will disintegrate on its first drying and wetting cycle.

CLC. *abbr.* Canadian Labour Congress.

CLEAN. *adj.* Of fruit, the appearance is not affected by dirt, dust, spray residue or other foreign material.

CLEANER. See DRY ~.

CLEAN HANDS DOCTRINE. 1. " . . . [E]quity will refuse relief to any party who, in the matter of his claim, is himself tainted with fraud, misrepresentation, illegality or impropriety by reason of which his opponent has suffered a detriment of a kind rendering it unjust that the order sought should be made." *Miller v. F. Mendel Holdings Ltd.* (1984), 26 B.L.R. 85 at 100, [1984] 2 W.W.R. 683, 30 Sask. R. 298 (Q.B.), Wimmer J. 2. " . . . [T]he theory of the doctrine is that a shareholder cannot invoke an equitable remedy when he himself is a principal source of the conflict and controversy which threaten the future of the corporation. . ." *Journet v. Superchef Food Industries Ltd.* (1984), 29 B.L.R. 206 at 224, [1984] C.S. 916 (Que.), Gomery J. See HE WHO COMES INTO EQUITY MUST COME WITH CLEAN HANDS; NO MAN CAN TAKE ADVANTAGE OF HIS OWN WRONG; NO ONE CAN BE ALLOWED TO DEROGATE FROM HIS OWN GRANT.

CLEAN SHELL COMPANY. A company which has neither assets nor liabilities.

CLEAR. *adj.* 1. Free from doubt. 2. Free from encumbrance, lien or charge. 3. Free from deductions.

CLEARANCE. *n.* 1. A certificate issued to indicate compliance with law or regulations. 2. The distance from an object to the nearest point of roof, sides or floor. 3. An authorization by a marine traffic regulator for a vessel, a seaplane or an air cushion vehicle to proceed or manoeuvre as authorized.

CLEAR DAYS. Complete days in counting time for items such as notice; both first and last days are omitted.

CLEARED. *adj.* An offence is cleared when an information has been laid or when there is enough evidence to lay an information against an identified offender although such information is not in fact laid. *R. v. Slavens* (1991), 64 C.C.C. (3d) 29 (B.C. C.A.).

CLEAR FUEL. Fuel which contains no dye or less dye than the minimum quantity of dye prescribed. *Fuel Tax Act*, R.S.O 1990, c. F.35, s. 1.

CLEARING. *n.* 1. In banking, making exchanges and settling balances among banks. 2. In transport, departing having complied with customs regulations.

CLEARING AGENCY. (a) A person that (i) in connection with trades in securities, acts as an intermediary in paying funds, in delivering securities or in doing both of those things, and (ii) provides centralized facilities for the clearing of trades in securities, or (b) a person that provides centralized facilities as a depository in connection with trades in securities. *Securities acts*. See SECURITY WITH A ~.

CLEARING AND SETTLEMENT SYSTEM. A system or arrangement for the clearing or settlement of payment obligations or payment messages in which (*a*) there are at least three participants, at least one of which is a bank, (*b*) clearing or settlement is all or partly in Canadian dollars, and (*c*) the payment obligations that arise from clearing within the system or arrangement are ultimately settled through adjustments to the account or accounts of one or more of the participants at the Bank and, for greater certainty, includes a system or arrangement for the clearing or settlement of securities transactions, foreign exchange transactions or other transactions where the system or arrangement also clears or settles payment obligations arising from those transactions. *Payment Clearing and Settlement Act, 1996*, S.C. 1996, c. 6, Sch., s. 2.

CLEARING HOUSE. 1. A corporation, association, partnership, agency or other entity that provides clearing or settlement services for a clearing and settlement system, but does not include a stock exchange or the Bank. *Payment Clearing and Settlement Act*, S.C. 1996, c. 6, Sch., s. 2. A corporation, association, partnership, agency or other entity that carries on in Canada the business of providing its participants with the clearing and settlement of transactions in securities that are deposited with it. *Depository Bills and Notes Act*, S.C. 1998, c. 13, s. 2. 3. A body that acts as an intermediary for its

clearing members in effecting securities transactions. *Bankruptcy and Insolvency Act*, R.S.C. 1985, c. B-3, s. 95. 4.

CLEARING MEMBER. A person engaged in the business of effecting securities transactions who uses a clearing house as intermediary. *Bankruptcy and Insolvency Act*, R.S.C. 1985, c. B-3, s. 95.

CLEARING SYSTEM. A means by which transactions in securities and commodity contracts are settled between members of the system.

CLEARLY DESCRIPTIVE. In the context of trade marks, material to the composition of the goods or products and referring to an intrinsic quality or characteristic of the product.

CLEAR TITLE. 1. Good title; title free from encumbrances. 2. Title is "clear" of an encumbrance once the registrar has endorsed a note of cancellation on the registry. It may be clear when the encumbrancer has been paid off but has not delivered the discharge or when application is made to register the discharge. *Norfolk v. Aikens* (1989), 64 D.L.R. (4th) 1 (B.C. C.A.).

CLEAT. *n.* A member of shoring and timbering that directly resists the downward movement of a wale or strut.

CLERGY. *n.* 1. A minister of a religious denomination. 2. Collectively: ministers, priests, rabbis.

CLERGYMAN. *n.* 1. A minister, priest, commissioner and staff officer of the Salvation Army and rabbi. 2. A person duly ordained, appointed or commissioned by a religious body. 3. Includes any priest, rabbi, elder, evangelist, missionary or commissioned officer ordained or appointed by the religious body to which he belongs. See REGISTERED ~.

CLERIC. *n.* A person who is charged with the solemnization of the ceremony of marriage by a religious denomination. See MINISTERING ~.

CLERICAL. *adj.* 1. Pertaining to clergy. 2. Relating to the office of clerk.

CLERICAL ERROR. 1. " . . . In Re Robert Sist Dev. Corpn. Ltd. (1977), 17 O.R. (2d) 305 . . . (S.C.), Henry J. dealt with the meaning of 'clerical error' and adopted the definition given in [John Burke, ed.] Jowitt's Dictionary of English Law, 2nd ed. ([London: Sweet and Maxwell,] 1977), that a 'clerical error' is 'an error in a document which can only be explained by considering it to be a slip or mistake of the party preparing or copying it'. We believe that this furnishes an adequate definition of 'clerical error'. . ." *Ovens, Re* (1979), 32 C.B.R. (N.S.) 42 at 47, 26 O.R. (2d) 468, 1 P.P.S.A.C. 131, 8 B.L.R. 186, 103 D.L.R. (3d) 352 (C.A.), the court per Houlden J.A. 2. "[In the Patent Act, R.S.C. 1970, c. P-4, s. 8] . . . errors caused by a clerk or stenographer." *Novopharm Ltd. v. Upjohn Co.* (1983), *(sub nom. Upjohn Co. v. Pat. Commr.)* 74 C.P.R. (2d) 228 at 232 (Fed. T.D.), Muldoon J.

CLERK. *n.* 1. The officer of a court who accepts filings, issues process, keeps records. 2. An officer of a municipality. 3. An officer of the Legislative Assembly or House of Commons. 4. A research assistant to a judge or judges. See ARTICLED ~; COURT ~; ELECTION ~; LAW ~ AND PARLIAMENTARY COUNSEL; MUNICIPAL ~; POLL ~.

CLERK ASSISTANT. A person appointed by Letters Patent under the Great Seal to assist the Clerk of the House. A. Fraser, W.A. Dawson & J. Holtby, eds., *Beauchesne's Rules and Forms of the House of Commons of Canada*, 6th ed. (Toronto: Carswell, 1989) at 60.

CLERK OF THE COURT. The officer of a court who accepts filings, issues process, keeps records.

CLERK OF THE HOUSE OF COMMONS. The chief procedural advisor to the House, its members and the Speaker, who provides procedural services, directs and controls all officers and clerks employed by the House. A. Fraser, W.A. Dawson, & J. Holtby, eds., *Beauchesne's Rules and Forms of the House of Commons of Canada*, 6th ed. (Toronto: Carswell, 1989) at 59-60.

CLERK OF THE PEACE. The person who assists justices of the peace to draw indictments, enter judgments, issue process and administer the courts.

CLERK OF THE QUEEN'S PRIVY COUNCIL. Clerk of the Privy Council and Secretary to the Cabinet. *Interpretation Act*, R.S.C. 1987, c. I-21, s. 35.

CLERKSHIP. *n.* The training given in a pharmacy by a pharmacist to a student or graduate.

CLIC LETTER. *abbr.* CLIC's Legal Materials Letter (Bulletin d'information juridique du CCDJ).

CLIENT. *n.* 1. A person who receives services. 2. A person or body of persons on whose behalf a lawyer receives money for services. 3. A person or body of persons on whose behalf an agent receives money in connection with his business. See SOLICITOR AND HIS OWN ~ COSTS.

CLIMATOLOGIST. *n.* A person who specializes in dealing with climates and their phenomena.

CLINIC. *n.* 1. A student organization offering free legal assistance. 2. An independent community organization structured as a corporation without share capital that provides legal aid services to the community it serves on a basis other than fee for service. *Legal Aid Services Act, 1998*, S.O. 1998, c. 26, s. 2. 3. A medical facility. See FORENSIC ~; MENTAL HEALTH ~; SEXUALLY TRANSMITTED DISEASES ~.

CLINIC LAW. The areas of law which particularly affect low-income individuals or disadvantaged communities, including legal matters related to, (a) housing and shelter, income maintenance, social assistance and other similar government programs, and (b) human rights, health, employment and education. *Legal Aid Services Act, 1998*, S.O. 1998, c. 26, s. 2

CLIP. *n.* The removable magazine of a firearm which contains unfired cartridges. F.A. Jaffe, *A Guide to Pathological Evidence*, 3d ed. (Toronto: Carswell, 1991) at 215.

CLIPPING. *n.* Impairing, diminishing or lightening a current gold or silver coin with intent that it should pass for a current gold or silver coin. *Criminal Code*, R.S.C. 1985, c. C-46, s. 413.

C.L.L.C. *abbr.* Canadian Labour Law Cases.

C.L.L.R. *abbr.* Canadian Labour Law Reports, 1973-.

CLOCK-BUMPING. *n.* Receiving credit on a time card, as a worker, for more hours than were actually worked.

CLOCK HOUR. A period of 60 minutes beginning on each hour and ending immediately before the next hour. *Broadcasting Distribution Regulations*, SOR/97-555, s. 1.

CLOCK OVERTIME. A premium for work after specified regular working hours.

CLOG ON EQUITY OF REDEMPTION. 1. A provision, repugnant to either a contractual or an equitable right to redeem which is void. 2. A device which prevents a mortgagor from getting property back after the obligations under the mortgage are discharged.

CLOSE. *n.* 1. Conclusion. 2. An area of land enclosed by a fence or other boundary markings; 3. An interest in land. See BREACH OF ∼.

CLOSE COMPANY. A company in which shares are held by one shareholder or a very small number of shareholders.

CLOSE CORPORATION. A corporation in which shares are held by one shareholder or a very small number of shareholders.

CLOSED. *adj.* Not open for the serving of customers or the receiving of orders from customers. See EFFECTIVELY ∼.

CLOSED CIRCUIT TELEVISED. Shown through the means of closed circuit television, film projection or any other electronic projection device.

CLOSED-CIRCUIT TELEVISION COMPANY. Includes a person operating for a fee or charge a television-signal receiving antenna or similar device, or equipment for the transmission of television signals to television receivers or subscribers.

CLOSED CIRCUIT TELEVISION CORPORATION. Includes a person operating for a fee or charge a television signal receiving antenna or similar device or equipment for the transmission of television signals to television receivers of subscribers.

CLOSED COMPANY. A company whose constituting documents provide for restrictions on the free transfer of shares, prohibit any distribution of securities to the public and limit the number of its shareholders to 50, exclusive of present or former employees of the company or of a subsidiary.

CLOSED COMPETITION. A competition that is open only to employees.

CLOSED-LOOP SYSTEM. In respect of a medical device, means a system that enables the device to sense, interpret and treat a medical condition without human intervention. *Medical Devices Regulations* SOR/98-282, s. 1.

CLOSED MIND TEST. Because the Commission must make policy decisions and its members are expected to have experience and views on the matters to which the policies relate, the Commission is not an adjudicative body and the

appropriate test for a reasonable apprehension of bias is the "closed mind" test. The question is whether it can be shown that a member of the Commission had prejudged the matter to the extent that representations to the contrary would be futile. *Doctors Hospital v. Ontario (Health Services Restructuring Commission)* (1997), 1997 CarswellOnt 3405, 103 O.A.C. 183, 3 Admin. L.R. (3d) 116 (Div. Ct.).

CLOSED PACKAGE. Any package the contents of which cannot be satisfactorily inspected without removing the cover, lid or other closing device.

CLOSED SEASON. A specified period during which a species of wildlife or fish shall not be hunted, taken or fished.

CLOSED SHOP. " . . . [O]ne in which membership in a particular union is a condition of employment. Its effect is not only to exclude non-union labour from jobs but also prevents the employer from hiring or retaining in his employment any one but members of a particular union." *B.S.O.I.W., Local No. 97 v. Canadian Ironworkers Union No. 1* (1970), 5 C.L.L.C. 236 at 252, 73 W.W.R. 172, 13 D.L.R. (3d) 559 (B.C. C.A.), Nemetz J.A. (dissenting).

CLOSED SHOP CONTRACT. " . . . [T]he effect of a 'closed shop' provision is to preclude a person from obtaining employment unless he is a member of the union certified as the bargaining agent for the bargaining unit." *Bhindi v. British Columbia Projectionists, Local 340 International Alliance of Picture Machine Operators of United States & Canada* (1986), 24 C.R.R. 302 at 321, 4 B.C.L.R. (2d) 145, [1986] 5 W.W.R. 303, 86 C.L.L.C. 14,052, 29 D.L.R. (4th) 47 (C.A.), Anderson J.A. (dissenting).

CLOSED SPIRIT-RECEIVER. The vessel or vessels into which the spirit is conveyed for measurement. *Excise Act*, R.S.C. 1985, c. E-14, s. 3.

CLOSED TIME. A specified period during which fish, to which the expression applies, may not be fished. *Fishery regulations*.

CLOSED-TYPE HOT-WATER HEATING SYSTEM. A system in which water is heated and circulated and which is not vented to the atmosphere. *Boiler and Pressure Vessel Act*, R.S. Nfld. 1970, c. 24, s. 2.

CLOSED TYPE HOT WATER SYSTEM. A system in which water is heated and circulated and which is not vented to atmosphere.

CLOSED UNION. A union in which membership is restricted.

CLOSELY HELD CORPORATION. A private corporation the shares of which are not listed on a stock exchange.

CLOSE OF PLEADINGS. Pleadings end in a proceeding when the last permitted pleading is delivered and filed or the time for doing so has expired.

CLOSE SEASON. A period during which the hunting or fishing for migratory birds, fur animals, game or fish is prohibited.

CLOSE SUBSTITUTE. Within the meaning of the Competition Act, said of products if buyers are willing to switch from one product to another in response to a relative change in price. *Canada (Director of Investigation & Research) v. Southam Inc.* (1995), 127 D.L.R. (4th) 263 (Fed. C.A.).

CLOSE THE DEAL. To complete a transaction by exchanging documents and funds.

CLOSE TIME. A specified period during which fish to which it applies may not be fished.

CLOSING ADDRESS. A statement made by counsel at conclusion of a trial before a jury.

CLOSING ARGUMENT. A statement made by counsel at conclusion of a trial before a judge.

CLOSING A TRANSACTION. A meeting between the lawyers or agents representing the parties to complete the transaction by exchanging documents and funds.

CLOSING DAY. See UNIFORM ~.

CLOSING-OUT SALE. Any sale or intended sale at retail of goods, wares or merchandise: (i) that is in any way represented, held out, advertised or described by any of the terms "bankrupt", "insolvent", "assignee's", "adjuster's", "trustee's", "executor's", "administrator's", "receiver's", "liquidation", wholesaler's", "jobber's", "manufacturer's", "moving out", "selling out", "closing-out", "closing stock", "fire", "smoke", "water damage", "landlord's", "lease expired", "creditor's" or "forced", or by any similar words or expressions; or (ii) wherein it is in any way represented, held out or advertised that the goods, wares or merchandise are the property of or have been acquired or purchased from or are being sold by or on behalf of any bankrupt, insolvent person, assignee, adjuster, trustee, executor, administrator, receiver, wholesaler, jobber, or manufacturer, or are the property of or have been acquired or purchased from or are being sold by or on behalf of any other retailer, or (iii) wherein it is in any way represented, held out or advertised that the goods, wares or merchandise have been damaged by fire, smoke, water or any other injurious agent, or are offered or will be offered for sale by reason of any action on the part of a landlord or creditor, or because of the expiry of a lease, or because the vendor thereof or any agent or principal of the vendor is either discontinuing business or changing his place of business, or has done so, or intends to do so, or because the vendor or any agent or principal of the vendor is in any way forced to offer the goods, wares or merchandise for sale. *The Closing-out Sales Act*, R.S.S. 1978, c. C-13, s. 2.

CLOSURE. *n.* 1. A procedure to conclude debate to force the House of Commons to decide a subject. A. Fraser, G.A. Birch & W.A. Dawson, eds., *Beauchesne's Rules and Forms of the House of Commons of Canada*, 5th ed. (Toronto: Carswell, 1978) at 117. 2. The temporary suspension, inactivity or close out of advanced exploration mining or mine production. 3. A device for shutting off an opening through a construction assembly, such as a door or a shutter, and includes all components such as hardware, frames and anchors.

CLOT. *n.* A semi-solid, soft coagulated mass formed in stagnant blood. F.A. Jaffe, *A Guide to Pathological Evidence*, 3d ed. (Toronto: Carswell, 1991) at 215. See BLOOD ~; CHICKEN FAT ~; CURRANT JELLY ~; POST MORTEM ~.

CLOTHING. See TEXTILE AND ~ GOODS.

CLOTTING. See COAGULATION.

CLOVER. *n.* Red clover, alsike clover or white clover or a mixture thereof.

C.L.R. *abbr.* Construction Law Reports, 1983-.

C.L.R.B. *abbr.* Canada Labour Relations Board.

C.L.R.B.R. (N.S.). *abbr.* Canadian Labour Relations Board Reports (New Series).

C.L.S. *abbr.* Canada Labour Service.

C.L.T. *abbr.* Canadian Law Times, 1881-1922.

C.L.T. (OCC. N.). *abbr.* Canadian Law Times, Occasional Notes.

CLUB. *n.* 1. "Clubs are associations of a peculiar nature. They are societies the members of which are perpetually changing. They are not partnerships; they are not associations for gain; and the feature which distinguishes them from other societies is that no member as such becomes liable to pay to the funds of the society or to any one else any money beyond the subscriptions required by the rules of the club to be paid so long as he remains a member. . ." *Taylor v. Peoples' Loan & Savings Corp.* (1928), 62 O.L.R. 564 at 568-69 [1928] 4 D.L.R. 598 (H.C.), Raney J. 2. An association of individuals for purposes of mutual entertainment and convenience. 3. A social, sporting, community, benevolent or fraternal order or society or any branch thereof. See FLYING ~; FRATERNAL ~; LABOUR ~; MEMBER OF A ~; VETERANS' ~.

CLUB MEMBER. A person who, whether as a charter member or admitted in accordance with the by-laws or rules of a club, has become a member thereof, who maintains membership by the payment of regular periodic dues in the manner provided by the rules or by-laws, and whose name and address are entered on the list of members.

CLUE FACT. A fact which increases the probability that a subordinate fact will be discovered and thus that an ultimate fact, and the crime, will be proved. *R. v. S. (R.J.)* (1995), 121 D.L.R. (4th) 589 (S.C.C.).

C. MAG. *abbr.* Cour de magistrat.

C.M.A.R. *abbr.* Canadian Court Martial Appeal Reports, 1957-.

CMHC. *abbr.* 1. Canada Mortgage and Housing Corporation. 2. Central Mortgage and Housing Corporation.

C.M.M. *abbr.* Cour municipale de Montréal.

CMND. *abbr.* Command papers.

C.M.P.R. *abbr.* Canadian Mortgage Practice Reports.

C.M.Q. *abbr.* Cour municipale de Québec.

CMRRA. The Canadian Musical Reproduction Rights Agency.

C. MUN. *abbr.* Cour municipale.

CMVSS. abbr. Canada Motor Vehicle Safety Standard.

CN. *abbr.* 1. Canadian National. 2. Canadian National Railway Company.

C.N.L.C. *abbr.* Commission nationale de libérations conditionnelles.

C.N.L.R. *abbr.* Canadian Native Law Reporter.

C.N.R. *abbr.* Canadian National Railway Company.

CO. *abbr.* Company.

C/O. symbol In care of. *McLennan, Re* [1940] 1 W.W.R. 465 at 472 (Sask. Surr. Ct.), Bryant Surr. Ct. J.

COACH. See HIGHWAY ~; TRAILER TROLLEY ~.

COADJUTOR. *n.* A helper, assistant or ally.

CO-ADVENTURE. A person is engaged in a co-adventure if despite the legal character of the person's association with the business, he retains a form of interest in the business along with other persons. *Canada (Attorney General) v. Tremblay* (1986), 91 N.R. 102 (Fed. C.A.).

COAGULATION. *n.* 1. Transformation of a liquid to a semi-solid or solid mass. 2. In blood, formation of fibrin which creates a thrombus or clot. F.A. Jaffe, *A Guide to Pathological Evidence*, 3d ed. (Toronto: Carswell, 1991) at 215-16.

COAL. *n.* 1. A combustible sedimentary rock, other than peat, composed of altered and hardened carbonized vegetable matter. 2. Anthracite coal and bituminous coal.

COALBED GAS. All substances (a) that can be recovered to the surface through a wellbore from subsurface coal deposits and any reservoirs in communication with the coal deposits, and (b) the volume of which, if measured at the surface immediately following that recovery, would be measured as a gas. *Coalbed Gas Act* , S.B.C. 2003, c. 18, s. 1.

COAL GAS. Methane occurring naturally in coal seams and associated strata and includes methane obtainable by methane extraction.

COAL MINE. Any opening or excavation in or working of ground for the purpose of prospecting, exploring, mining, opening up, developing or proving any coal or coal bearing deposit.

COAL MINER. A person employed underground in any coal mine to cut, shear, break or loosen coal from the solid, whether by hand or machinery.

COAL PROCESSING PLANT. An installation for upgrading the quality of coal or for producing a marketable solid fuel.

COARSE FISH. 1. (a) Any member of the gar family Lepisosteidae, (b) bowfin or dogfish, Amia calva Linnaeus, (c) bullhead, catfish or any member of the family Ictaluridae, (d) burbot or ling, Lota Iota (Linnaeus), (e) carp , Cyprinus carpio Linnaeus or any member of the family Cyprinidae (f) eel, Anguilla rostrata (LeSueur), (g) freshwater drum or sheepshead, Aplodinotus grunniens Rafinesque, (h) smelt, Osmerus mordax (Mitchill), and (i) sucker, mullet, red horse or any member of the family Catostomidae. 2. Any fish other than sport fish but does not include Atlantic salmon.

COARSE GRAIN. Oats, barley, and any oat product or barley product.

COAST. *n*. The edge of land bordered by a sea.

COASTAL CADIZ. *abbr*. Coastal Canadian Air Defence Identification Zone.

COASTAL TRADE. The regular employment and operation of ships in the waters of the region, the waters of Puget Sound, the Strait of Juan de Fuca and the coastal waters of the State of Alaska not west of Cook Inlet. *Pacific Pilotage Regulations*, C.R.C., c. 1270, s. 2.

COASTAL WATERS. Includes waters in the fishing zones of Canada adjacent to British Columbia, all waters in the territorial sea of Canada adjacent to British Columbia, and all internal waters of British Columbia. *Fisheries Act*, R.S.B.C. 1996, c. 149, s. 12.

COASTAL WATERS OF CANADA. 1. Includes all of Queen Charlotte Sound, all the Strait of Georgia and the Canadian waters of the Strait of Juan de Fuca. *Criminal Code*, R.S.C. 1985, c. C-46, s. 339(6). 2. All Canadian fisheries waters not within the geographical limits of any province. *Fisheries Act*, R.S.C. 1985, c. F-14, s. 47.

COAST GUARD. Provides services for the safe, economical and efficient movement of ships in Canadian waters through the provision of (i) aids to navigation systems and services, (ii) marine communications and traffic management services, (iii) ice breaking and ice management services, and (iv) channel maintenance; provides the marine component of the federal search and rescue program; provides for pleasure craft safety, including the regulation of the construction, inspection, equipment and operation of pleasure craft; provides for marine pollution prevention and response; and provides support of departments, boards and agencies of the Government of Canada through the provision of ships, aircraft and other marine services.

COAST GUARD SHIP. See CANADIAN ∼.

COASTING. *n*. The carrying by water transportation of goods and materials of every description to or from its in the province of Newfoundland.

COASTING TRADE. Is defined as (a) the carriage of goods by ship, or by ship and any other mode of transport, from one place in Canada or above the continental shelf of Canada to any other place in Canada or above the continental shelf of Canada, either directly or by way of a place outside Canada, but, with respect to waters above the continental shelf of Canada, includes the carriage of goods only in relation to the exploration, exploitation or transportation of the mineral or non-living natural resources of the continental shelf of Canada, (b) subject to paragraph (c), the carriage of passengers by ship from any place in Canada situated on a lake or river to the same place, or to any other place in Canada, either directly or by way of a place outside Canada, (c) the carriage of passengers by ship from any place situated on the St. Lawrence River northeast of the Saint Lambert lock or on the Fraser River west of the Mission Bridge (i) to the same place, without any call at any port outside Canada, other than one or more technical or emergency calls, or (ii) to any other place in Canada, other than as an in-transit call, either directly or by way of a place outside Canada, (d) the carriage of passengers by ship from any place in Canada other than from a place to which paragraph (b) or (c) applies (i) to the same place, without any call at any port outside Canada, other than one or more technical or emergency calls, or (ii) to any other place in Canada, other than as an in-transit call, either directly or by way of a place outside Canada, (e) the carriage of passengers by ship (i) from any place in Canada to any place above the continental shelf of Canada, (ii) from any place above the continental shelf of Canada to any place in Canada, or (iii) from any place above the continental shelf of Canada to the same place or to any other place above the continental shelf of Canada where the carriage of the passengers is in relation to the exploration, exploitation or transportation of the mineral or non-living natural resources of the continental shelf of Canada, and (f) the engaging, by ship, in any other marine activity of a commercial nature in Canadian waters and, with respect to waters above the continental shelf of

Canada, in such other marine activities of a commercial nature that are in relation to the exploration, exploitation or transportation of the mineral or non-living natural resources of the continental shelf of Canada. *Coasting Trade Act, 1992*, S. C. 1992, c. 31, s. 2.

COAST OF CANADA. The sea-coast of Canada and the salt water bays, gulfs and harbours on the sea-coast of Canada. *Canada Shipping Act*, R.S.C. 1985, c. S-9, s. 2.

COAT. See STATION WAGON OR CAR ~.

COAT-TAIL RIDER. 1. A unionized employee who has not paid dues. 2. An employee who is not a union member but benefits from the advantages won by a union.

COCAINE. *n*. An alkaloid made from the leaves of the bush Erythroxylon coca, a nervous system stimulant, local anaesthetic, appetite repressant, euphoriant, and blood vessel constrictor. F.A. Jaffe, *A Guide to Pathological Evidence*, 3d ed. (Toronto: Carswell, 1991) at 89.

COCK PIT. Keeping a cock pit is illegal. *Criminal Code*, R.S.C. 1985, c. C-46, s. 447.

COCKTAIL MIXING UNIT. A combination food holding tray and sink forming part of the bar facilities were alcoholic beverages are dispensed.

CO. CT. *abbr*. County Court.

COD. *n*. A fish of the species Gadus morhua. See LING ~.

C.O.D. *abbr*. See CASH ON DELIVERY.

CODE. *n*. 1. A collection or system of laws, i.e. Code Napoléon or Civil Code. 2. A consolidation of existing statute and common law, i.e. Criminal Code. 3. Guidelines for a process or use of equipment to ensure safety, efficiency or a level of quality established and published by a competent authority, i.e. building code, safety code. 4. A group of letters or symbols identifying pari-mutuel tickets with a particular race or racing card. 5. A set of letters, numbers or symbols used to identify something or someone. See BUILDING ~; BUILDING CONSTRUCTION ~; CIVIL ~; CRIMINAL ~; CSA ELEVATOR ~; FIRE ~; FORWARD SORTATION AREA ~; I.M.C.O. ~; OBJECT ~; POSTAL ~; RECOGNIZED ~; UNIFORM ~.

CODE CIVIL. The civil law of Quebec.

CODE MARK. A combination of letters, symbols and numbers that identifies an inspector.

CODE NAPOLÉON. A collection of civil law prepared by Napoléon Bonaparte.

COD-END. *n*. A bag-like extension attached to the after end of the belly of a trawl net and used to retain the catch. Canada regulations.

CODE OF CONDUCT. The regulations made pursuant to section 38. *Royal Canadian Mounted Police Act*, R.S.C. 1985 (2d Supp.), c. 8, s. 2.

CODE OF SERVICE DISCIPLINE. 1. The provisions of Part of the *National Defence Act* which sets out offences which may be committed by a member of the forces and the procedures involved in charging and prosecuting a member charged with an offence under the code. 2. The provisions of Part III. *National Defence Act*, R.S.C. 1985, c. N-5, s. 2.

CODE OF SIGNALS. See STANDARD ~.

CODICIL. *n*. An addition or change made to a will by a testator.

CODIFICATION. *n*. The collection of all the principles of any system or subject of law into one body of statutes or single statute.

CODIFYING STATUTE. A single statute which aims to state all the law on a particular subject by combining pre-existing statutory provisions with common law rules relating to the subject.

CO-EMPT. *v*. To purchase all of any commodity.

COERCION. *n*. 1. " . . . [I]ncludes not only such blatant forms of compulsion as direct commands to act or refrain from acting on pain of sanction, coercion includes indirect forms of control which determine or limit alternative courses of conduct available to others." *R. v. Big M Drug Mart Ltd*. (1985), 13 C.R.R. 64 at 97-8 (S.C.C.), Dickson C.J.C. 2. Compelling by force or threats. 3. A threat of serious consequences should a contract not be executed. Does not arise out of an existing state of affairs. *Permaform Plastics Ltd. v. London & Midland General Insurance Co*., [1996] 7 W.W.R. 457 (Man. C.A.).

COFFERDAM. *n*. A structure constructed all or in part below water level or below the level of the water table in the ground and intended to provide a place in which to work that is free of water.

COGENT. *adj*. [T]he word "cogent" is not synonymous with "admissible" or "relevant." . . .

"Cogency" . . . relates to "force," "power" and "incisiveness." "Cogent" evidence is desirable, but is not essential to proof. *Terracon Development Ltd. v. Winnipeg (City) Assessor*, 2002 MBCA 117, 218 D.L.R. (4th) 515, 166 Man. R. (2d) 245, 39 M.P.L.R. (3d) 67 (C.A.).

COGITATIONIS POENAM NEMO MERETUR. [L.] No one deserves punishment for a thought.

COGNISANCE. *n.* 1. Knowledge. 2. To take cognisance means to take judicial notice.

COGNIZOR. *n.* Shall include any number of cognizors in the same recognizance, whether as principals or sureties, unless such interpretation be inconsistent with the context. *Criminal Cases Recognizance Act*, R.S.Q. 1977, c. C-7, s. 1.

COGNOVIT. [L.] He or she has confessed.

COGNOVIT ACTIONEM. [L.] He has admitted the action. An instrument signed by a defendant in an action admitting that the plaintiff's demand is just and authorizing the signing of judgment against the defendant.

COHABIT. *v.* 1. To live together in a conjugal relationship, whether within or outside marriage. 2. To live together in a family relationship. *Child and Family Services and Family Relations* Act, S.N.B. 1980, c. C-2.1, s. 1.

COHABITATION. *n.* Dwelling or living together as spouses. See AGENCY FROM ~; PERIOD OF ~.

COHABITATION AGREEMENT. Two persons of the opposite sex or the same sex who are cohabiting or intend to cohabit and who are not married to each other may enter into an agreement in which they agree on their respective rights and obligations during cohabitation, or on ceasing to cohabit or on death, including, (a) ownership in or division of property; (b) support obligations; (c) the right to direct the education and moral training of their children, but not the right to custody of or access to their children; and (d) any other matter in the settlement of their affairs. *Family Law Act*, R.S.O. 1990, c. F-3, s. 53, as am.

COHAEREDES SUNT QUASI UNUM CORPUS, PROPTER UNITATEM JURIS QUOD HABENT. [L.] Co-heirs are considered one person because of the unity of title which they possess.

CO-HEIR. *n.* One of several people among whom an inheritance is divided.

CO-HEIRESS. *n.* A woman who shared an inheritance equally with another woman.

COHERENCE, PRESUMPTION OF. In determining the legislator's intention there is a presumption of coherence between related statutes. Provisions are only deemed inconsistent where they cannot stand together. The co-existence of a short limitation period and a rule for its postponement is not an absurd result. *Murphy v. Welsh*, 1993 CarswellOnt 428, 18 C.P.C. (3d) 137, 47 M.V.R. (2d) 1, 156 N.R. 263, 65 O.A.C. 103, [1993] 2 S.C.R. 1069, 106 D.L.R. (4th) 404, 18 C.C.L.T. (2d) 101. Major, J. for the court.

COHORT STUDY. A medical or scientific study of a large population over time to track the appearance of and progress of a disease or condition. The most reliable form of individual study.

COILED TUBE BOILER. A boiler with one or more coiled tubes having attached thereto a forced circulation water pump, a pressure limiting and a prepurge flame failure device.

COIN. *v.* To stamp pieces of metal into a set shape and size and place marks on them under the aegis of a government. See PRECIOUS METAL ~.

COIN. *n.* A piece of metal stamped with certain marks and put into circulation as money of a certain value by a government. See SUBSIDIARY ~.

CO-INSURANCE. *n.* The insured bears a portion of any loss in excess of the insurance on it. The insurer is liable only for the portion of the insured property or risk which represents the portion of the property or risk insured.

COITUS INTERRUPTUS. [L.] Interrupted sexual intercourse.

COKE OVEN EMISSIONS. Condensed vapours and benzene soluble particulates emitted into the atmosphere from a metallurgical coke oven.

COLA. *abbr.* Cost-of-living adjustment.

COLA CLAUSE. An agreement to provide employees with an increase in wages tied to an index such as the Consumer Price Index prepared by Statistics Canada.

COLD-ROLLED. See HOT-ROLLED OR ~.

COLD STORAGE. The storage of articles of food at or below a temperature of 7 degrees Celsius.

COLD STORAGE PLANT. Buildings, structures, machinery, appurtenances, appliances and apparatus occupied or used in the business of freezing and storing any article for human consumption. See FISH ~.

COLD TURKEY. To stop taking drugs suddenly. F.A. Jaffe, *A Guide to Pathological Evidence*, 2d ed. (Toronto: Carswell, 1983) at 172.

COLLABORATIVE LAW. The use of non-adversarial methods, mediation techniques, legal advocacy and advice, governed by the notion that cases settle. Practice of law in a manner which avoids litigation if at all possible.

COLLATERAL. *n*. 1. Property used to secure the payment of a debt or performance of an obligation. 2. A blood relation who is neither a descendant nor an ancestor.

COLLATERAL. *adj*. "... '[P]arallel' or 'additional' or 'side by side with'." *Manitoba Development Corp. v. Berkowits* (1979), 9 R.P.R. 310 at 313, [1979] 5 W.W.R. 138, 101 D.L.R. (3d) 421 (Man. C.A.), the court per O'Sullivan J.A.

COLLATERAL ADVANTAGE. Something which makes a lender's remuneration for a loan exceed the proper interest rate.

COLLATERAL ATTACK. An attack made in proceedings other than those whose specific object is the reversal, variation, or nullification of the order or judgment.

COLLATERAL ATTACK, RULE AGAINST. A court order, made by a court having jurisdiction to make it, stands and is binding and conclusive unless it is set aside on appeal or lawfully quashed. It is also well settled in the authorities that such an order may not be attacked collaterally. *R. v. Wilson*, [1983] 2 S.C.R. 594, at p. 599.

COLLATERAL BENEFIT. The provision of money to the defendant in a tort claim by an insurer.

COLLATERAL BENEFITS, DOCTRINE OF. Precludes a tortfeasor from setting off monies paid to the plaintiff under an insurance contract against the damages payable to the plaintiff.

COLLATERAL, CONTRACT. 1. "... [A]n oral agreement ancillary to a written agreement..." *Ahone v. Holloway* (1988), 30 B.C.L.R. (2d) 368 at 373 (C.A.), the court per McLachlin J.A. 2. A statement, on the strength of which a person enters into a contract, may give rise to an entirely separate contract "collateral" to the main contract made between the maker of the statement and the person to whom the statement was made.

COLLATERAL ESTOPPEL. Is a subcategory of "res judicata" that has been accepted in the United States courts but not, so far, in Canada. It differs from "issue estoppel" in that the condition of identity of parties applies only to the party who is attempting to relitigate a question of fact, not to the party who is asserting the plea. *Connaught Laboratories Ltd. v. Medeva Pharma Ltd.* (1999), 1999 CarswellNat 2809, 4 C.P.R. (4th) 508, 179 F.T.R. 200 (T.D.).

COLLATERAL FACT RULE. Subject to certain exceptions, a party is not entitled to introduce extrinsic evidence to contradict the testimony of an adversary's witness unless that extrinsic evidence is relevant to some issue in the case other than merely to contradict the case. *R. v. P. (G.)* (1996), 31 O.R. (3d) 504 (C.A.).

COLLATERAL QUESTION. A question connected to the merits or the heart of an inquiry but which is not the major question to be decided.

COLLATERAL RELATIVE. A person whose relationship to a second person is not in the direct line of descent from the second person, i.e. a brother's child.

COLLATERAL SECURITY. "... [A]ny property which is assigned or pledged to secure the performance of an obligation and as additional thereto, and which upon the performance of the obligation is to be surrendered or discharged: ..." *Royal Bank of Canada v. Slack* (1958), 11 D.L.R. (2d) 737 at 746 (Ont. C.A.), Schroeder J.A., cited in *MacLaren, Re* (1978), 88 D.L.R. (3d) 222 at 231, 30 N.S.R. (2d) 694, 49 A.P.R. 694, 4 B.L.R. 191, 28 C.B.R. (N.S.) 56 (S.C.), Cowan C.J.T.D.

COLLATERAL TERM. Outside or distinct from the terms of the main contract.

COLLATIO BONORUM. [L.] A contribution of goods.

COLLATION. *n*. Comparing a copy with its original to ensure its accuracy and completeness.

COLLECT. *v*. To enforce a money judgment by execution.

COLLECTING AGENT. A person whose business is the collecting, either by himself or through a representative, of debts owing to other persons.

COLLECTION. *n*. 1. A bank's handling of commercial and financial documents according to instructions received. 2. The process of obtaining payment of debts owing. See PARTIC-ULATE ~ EFFICIENCY.

COLLECTION AGENCY. A person other than a collector who obtains or arranges for payment of money owing to another person, or who holds out to the public as providing such a service or any person who sells or offers to sell forms or letters represented to be a collection system or scheme.

COLLECTION AGENT. A person other than a collector who: (i) collects debts for others; (ii) offers or undertakes to collect debts for others; (iii) solicits accounts for collection; (iv) collects debts owed to him under a name which differs from that under which he is the creditor; (v) mails to debtors or offers or undertakes to mail to debtors, on behalf of a creditor collection letters; (vi) for a fee or other consideration or hope or promise thereof, enters into an arrangement under the terms of which he agrees or undertakes to pay to a vendor any amount is respect of goods or services sold or supplied by the vendor to a person other than the collection agent; (vii) offers or undertakes to act for a debtor in arrangements or negotiations with his creditors; or (viii) receives money periodically from a debtor for distribution to his creditors and includes a person who takes an assignment of a debt or debts due at the date of assignment from a specified debtor or debtors. *The Collection Agents Act*, R.S.S. 1978, c. C-15, s. 2.

COLLECTION AGREEMENT. See TAX ~.

COLLECTION FACILITY. See RE-GIONAL ~.

COLLECTION SYSTEM. See INDIVID-UAL ~.

COLLECTIVE AGREEMENT. An agreement in writing between an employer or an employer's organization acting on behalf of employers, and a bargaining agent of employees acting on behalf of a unit of employees containing respecting terms and conditions of employment and related matters. More than a private arrangement, it provides the foundation for labour relations and exists to provide and maintain peace in labour relations.

COLLECTIVE APPRAISAL. A sampling taken on various cultivated farms in the same zone to determine the actual yield of the insured crops in the zone. *Crop Insurance Act*, R.S.Q., c. A-30, s. 1.

COLLECTIVE BARGAINING. Negotiating with a view to the conclusion of a collective agreement or the renewal or revision thereof. The implementation of freedom of association in the workplace. See APPROPRIATE FOR ~.

COLLECTIVE BARGAINING AGREE-MENT. An agreement in writing between an employer or an employer's organization acting on behalf of an employer, on the one hand, and a bargaining agent of employees acting on behalf of the employees, on the other hand, containing terms or conditions of employment of employees.

COLLECTIVE INDEPENDENCE. "Judicial control over . . . assignment of judges, sittings of the court, and court lists . . . as well as the related matters of allocation of court-rooms and direction of the administrative staff engaged in carrying out these functions, has generally been considered the essential and minimum requirement . . ." *R. v. Valente (No. 2)* (1985), 19 C.R.R. 354 at 368, 372, 376, 379-80, [1985] 2 S.C.R. 673, 52 O.R. (2d) 779, 37 M.V.R. 9, 49 C.R. (3d) 97, 23 C.C.C. (3d) 193, 24 D.L.R. (4th) 161, 64 N.R. 1, 14 O.A.C. 79, [1985] D.L.Q. 85n, the court per Le Dain J.

COLLECTIVE SOCIETY. A society, association or corporation that carries on the business of collective administration of copyright or of the remuneration right conferred by section 19 or 81 for the benefit of those who, by assignment, grant of licence, appointment of it as their agent or otherwise, authorize it to act on behalf in relation to that collective administration, and (a) operates a licensing scheme, applicable in relation to a repertoire of works, performer's performances, sound recordings or communication signals of more than one author, performer, sound recording maker or broadcaster, pursuant to which the society, association or corporation sets out classes of uses that it agrees to authorize under this Act, and the royalties and terms and conditions on which it agrees to authorize those classes of uses, or (b) carries on the business of collecting and distributing royalties or levies payable pursuant to this Act. *Copyright Act*, R.S.C. 1985, c. C-42, s. 2.

COLLECTIVE WORK. (a) An encyclopedia, dictionary, year book or similar work, (b) a newspaper, review, magazine or similar periodical, and (c) any work written in distinct parts of works of different authors are incorporated. *Copyright Act*, R.S.C. 1985, c. C-42, s. 2.

COLLECTOR. *n*. 1. A person authorized or required by or pursuant to a revenue act or by agreement to collect a tax. 2. Every officer of customs and excise who is appointed to collect the duties imposed by this Act in any defined district or excise division. *Excise Act*, R.S.C. 1985, c. E-14, s. 2. 3. A person employed, appointed or authorized by a collection agency to solicit business or collect debts for the agency or to deal with or trace debtors for the agency. 4. A person engaged in the business of collecting dead animals. *Dead Animal Disposal Act*, R.S.O. 1990, c. D.3, s. 1. See DISTRICT ~; GENUINE GUN ~.

COLLEGATARY. *n*. One of a group of people who shares a common legacy.

COLLEGE. *n*. 1. A corporation, company, or society having certain privileges, i.e., College of Physicians and Surgeons. 2. A community college. 3. A regional college. 4. A college of applied arts and technology. See AGRICULTURAL AND VOCATIONAL ~; HERALDS' ~; PRIVATE ~.

COLLEGE OF PHYSICIANS AND SURGEONS. The licensing, and governing body of the medical profession in a province.

COLLIERY. *n*. A mine.

COLLIMATOR. *n*. A device or mechanism that limits the shape and size of the useful beam. *Radiation Emitting Devices Regulations*, C.R.C., c. 1370, s. 1.

COLLISION. *n*. 1. " . . . [I]mplies an impact, the sudden contact of a moving body with an obstruction in its line of motion. Both bodies may be in motion, or one in motion and the other stationary." *Aberdeen Paving Ltd. v. Guildhall Insurance Co.* (1966), 52 M.P.R. 349 at 362, 60 D.L.R. (2d) 45 (N.S. C.A.), Cowan J.A. 2. The striking by a vessel of another vessel or a ship. 3. An action for collision includes an action for damage caused by one or more ships to another ship or ships or to property or persons on board another ship or ships as a result of carrying out or omitting to carry out a manoeuvre, or as a result of non-compliance with law, even though there has been no actual collision. *Federal Court Act*, R.S.C. 1985, c. F-7, s. 2. See ACTION FOR ~; FIXED ~ BARRIER.

COLLISION REGULATIONS. The regulations made under section 562.11. *Canada Shipping Act*, R.S.C. 1985, c. S-9, s. 2.

COLLOQUIUM. *n*. In pleading in a libel or slander action, the plaintiff must show that the statement complained of was "published of and concerning the plaintiff." R.E. Brown, *The Law of Defamation in Canada* (Toronto: Carswell, 1987) at 218.

COLLUSION. *n*. 1. Agreement to deceive. *Edison General Electric Co. v. Vancouver & New Westminster Tramway Co.* (1896), 4 B.C.R. 460 at 483 (C.A.), Drake J.A. 2. An agreement or conspiracy to which an applicant for a divorce is either directly or indirectly a party for the purpose of subverting the administration of justice, and includes any agreement, understanding or arrangement to fabricate or suppress evidence or to deceive the court, but does not include an agreement to the extent that it provides for separation between the parties, financial support, division of property or the custody of any child of the marriage. *Divorce Act*, R.S.C. 1985, (2d Supp.), c. 3, s. 11(4).

COLONIAL LAW. In a colony discovered and occupied, the laws of England; in a conquered colony or one ceded to England, its own laws until England changed them.

COLONIAL LAWS VALIDITY ACT, 1865. The British Act confirming the capacity of legislatures in the colonies to enact laws inconsistent with English laws.

COLONY. *n*. 1. A place settled by people from an older city or country. 2. A number of persons who hold land or any interest therein a communal property, whether as owners, lessees or otherwise, and whether in the name of trustees or as a corporation or otherwise, and includes a number of persons who propose to acquire land to be held in such manner. 3. Queen, brood and accompanying bees.

COLORE OFFICI. [L.] Colour of office. See DURESS ~.

COLOUR. *v*. In respect of fuel means the addition to fuel of dye in the proportion prescribed.

COLOUR. *n*. Appearance, pretext or pretence, apparent or prima facie. See FOOD ~; SYNTHETIC ~.

COLOURABILITY. *n*. A doctrine invoked when a statute is addressed to a matter outside jurisdiction though it bears the formal trappings of a matter within the jurisdiction of the enacting legislature.

COLOURABLE. *adj*. In appearance but not in substance what it claims to be.

COLOURABLE IMITATION. A trademark with such similar appearance as a registered trade mark that confusion is likely, though there is not a deliberate imitation intended to deceive.

COLOURED FUEL. Fuel which contains dye.

COLOURED FUEL OIL. Any fuel oil that has been coloured.

COLOURING. *n.* The adding to fuel oil of any quantity of natural or chemical products furnished for the purpose of identifying fuel oil.

COLOURING PERMIT. A permit issued by the Minister that authorizes a person to colour tax-exempt gasoline.

COLOUR OF OFFICE. Pretense of authority to carry out an act for which the actor has no authority.

COLOUR OF RIGHT. 1. The essence of the defence is that the accused genuinely believes that he or she has a lawful claim to property. A belief in a moral right to property is not sufficient to ground the defence of colour of right. *R. v. Gamey* (1993), 80 C.C.C. (3d) 117 (Man. C.A.) 2. " . . . [G]enerally, although not exclusively, refers to a situation where there is an assertion of a proprietary or possessory right to the thing which is the subject-matter of the alleged theft. . . The term . . . is also used to denote an honest belief in a state of facts which, if it actually existed would at law justify or excuse the act done; . . ." R. *v. DeMarco* (1973), 13 C.C.C. (2d) 369 at 372, 22 C.R.N.S. 258 (Ont. C.A.), Martin J.A.

COLUMBARIUM. *n.* A structure designed to store the ashes of cremated human remains.

COLUMN. See STEERING ~.

COMA. *n.* A profoundly unconscious state. F.A. Jaffe, *A Guide to Pathological Evidence* 3d ed. (Toronto: Carswell, 1991) at 216.

COMB. *n.* A structure of cells composed of beeswax. *Bee Act*, R.S.B.C. 1979, s. 27, s. 1. See BROOD ~.

COMB HONEY. Honey that is in the honey comb.

COMBINATION. *n.* Used in reference to trade unions. An association of persons for a particular purpose. See BUSINESS ~; TRACTOR-FLOAT ~; TRACTOR-TRAILER ~; TRADE ~.

COMBINATION CARRIER. A tanker designed to carry, in bulk, oil or solid cargoes.

COMBINATION OF ROAD VEHICLES. A combination of vehicles consisting of a motor vehicle drawing a trailer, a semi-trailer or a detachable axle.

COMBINATION OF VEHICLES. Every combination of truck, truck trailer, semi-trailer and trailer.

COMBINED PIPELINE. A commodity pipeline through which oil or gas, or both, can be moved.

COMBUSTIBLE CONSTRUCTION. As applied to a building means that type of construction in which the structural elements are constructed wholly or partly of wood members which do not meet the requirements for heavy timber (mill type) construction and may include noncombustible as well as combustible elements.

COMBUSTIBLE DUST. Any dust that will burn or explode in the air when exposed to a flame or any other ignition source.

COMBUSTIBLE MATERIAL. Material other than incombustible material.

COMFORT STATION. A building containing flush water closets, electrical lighting and running water.

COMIC. See CRIME ~.

COMITATU COMMISSO. [L.] A commission or writ to act as sheriff.

COMITATUS. *n.* [L.] A county.

COMITY. *n.* 1. " . . . [T]he informing principle of private international law, which has been stated to be the defence [sic] and respect due by other states to the actions of a state legitimately taken within its territory. . . For my part, I much prefer the more complete formulation of the idea of comity adopted by the Supreme Court of the United States in Hilton v. Guyot, 159 U.S. 113 . . . (1895) at p. 1634 in a passage cited by Estey J. in Spencer v. R., [1985] 2 S.C.R. 278 at p. 283 . . . as follows: "Comity" in the legal sense, is neither a matter of absolute obligation, on the one hand, nor of mere courtesy and good will, upon the other. But it is the recognition which one nation allows within its territory to the legislative, executive or judicial acts of another nation, having due regard both to international duty and convenience, and to the rights of its own citizens or of other persons who are under the protection of its laws.' " *Morguard Investments Ltd. v. De Savoye* (1990), 46 C.P.C. (2d) 1 at 17,

19, 15 R.P.R. (2d) 1, 16, 52 B.C.L.R. (2d) 160, [1991] 2 W.W.R. 217, 76 D.L.R. (4th) 256, 122 N.R. 81, [1990] 3 S.C.R. 1077, the court per La Forest J. 2. The name given to the general principle that encourages the recognition in one country of the judicial acts of another. Its basis is not simply respect for other nations, but convenience and necessity, recognizing the need to facilitate interjurisdictional transactions. The Supreme Court of Canada has said, in the context of a case involving the recognition of one province of Canada of a decision of the Courts of another province, that the content of comity must be adjusted in light of a changing world order. Connaught Laboratories Ltd. v. Medeva Pharma Ltd. 1999 CarswellNat 2809, 4 C.P.R. (4th) 508, 179 F.T.R. 200. 3. " . . . [T]he Courts of one jurisdiction will give effect to the laws and judicial decision of another jurisdiction, not as a matter of obligation but out of mutual deference and respect. A foreign request is given full force and effect unless it be contrary to the public policy of the jurisdiction to which the request is directed . . . or otherwise prejudicial to the sovereignty or the citizens of the latter jurisdiction." *R. v. Zingre* (1981), 23 C.P.C. 259 at 266-7, [1981] 2 S.C.R. 392, 10 Man. R. (2d) 62, 38 N.R. 272, 61 C.C.C. (2d) 465, 127 D.L.R. (3d) 223, the court per Dickson J. See INTERNATIONAL ~.

COMITY OF NATIONS. A code of behaviour towards one another which nations observe from mutual convenience or courtesy.

COMM. *abbr*. Commission.

COMMAND. See SECOND-IN- ~; VESSEL NOT UNDER ~.

COMMANDEER. *v*. To seize a thing or require a thing to be used for military purposes.

COMMAND PAPERS. In Britain, papers presented to Parliament at the Crown's command. Include the reports of Royal Commissions.

COMMENCEMENT. *n*. When used with reference to an enactment, means the time at which the enactment comes into force.

COMMERCE. *n*. Trade; exchange of goods or property. See CHAMBER OF ~; TRADE AND ~.

COMMERCIA BELLI. [L.] Agreements between warring states, such as a capitulation or truce.

COMMERCIAL. *adj*. 1. Connected with trade and commerce in general. 2. Of real property, principally used for the sale of goods or services.

COMMERCIAL AGREEMENT. An agreement arising out of a commercial relationship and includes, but is not limited to, agreements respecting the following kinds of transactions: (a) a trade transaction for the supply or exchange of goods; (b) a distribution agreement; (c) a commercial representation or agency; (d) factoring; (e) leasing; (f) construction of works; (g) consulting; (h) engineering; (i) licensing; (j) financing; (k) banking; (l) insurance; (m) an exploitation agreement or concession; (n) joint venture and other related forms of industrial or business cooperation; (o) carriage of goods or passengers by air, sea, rail or road; (p) investing. *Commercial Arbitration Act*, R.S.B.C. 1996, c. 55, s. 1.

COMMERCIAL AIRCRAFT. An aircraft operated or available for operation for hire or reward. Canada regulations.

COMMERCIAL AIRLINE. A person who operates a commercial air service.

COMMERCIAL AIR SERVICE. Any use of aircraft for hire or reward. *Aeronautics Act*, R.S.C. 1985 , c. A-5, s. 3.

COMMERCIAL AIR SERVICE STANDARDS. The standards published under the authority of the Minister that apply in respect of commercial air services operated by air operators. *Canadian Aviation Regulations* SOR 96-433, s. 101.01.

COMMERCIAL ARBITRATION. An adjudicative process, either voluntary or ad hoc, involving the application and interpretation of agreements concerning business or trade matters. See COMMERCIAL AGREEMENT.

COMMERCIAL ASSESSMENT. (a) The assessment of real property that is used as the basis for computing business assessment including the assessment for real property that is rented and occupied or used by the Crown in right of Canada or any province or any board, commission, corporation or other agency thereof, or by any municipal corporation or local board thereof, and (b) business assessment, and (c) the assessment for mineral lands, pipelines, railway lands, other than railway lands actually in use for residential and farming purposes. *Municipal Act*, R.S.O. 1990, c. M.45, s. 366(1). See EQUALIZED ~.

COMMERCIAL ASSET. An asset that is not a family asset. *Marital Property Act*, C.C.S.M., c. 24, s. 1.

COMMERCIAL CABLECASTER. Any cablecaster other than a community cablecaster.

COMMERCIAL CEMETERY. A cemetery operated for the purpose of making a profit for the owner.

COMMERCIAL CONSIGNMENT. A transaction under which goods are delivered for sale, lease or other disposition to a consignee who, in the ordinary course of the consignees business, deals in goods of that description, by a consignor who, (i) in the ordinary course of the consignor's business, deals in goods of that description, and (ii) reserves an interest in the goods after they have been delivered, but does not include an agreement under which goods are delivered to an auctioneer for sale or to a consignee for sale, lease or other disposition if it is generally known to the creditors of the consignee that the consignee is in the business of selling or leasing goods of others. *Personal Property Security Act*, R.S.A., 2000, c. P-7, s. 1(1).

COMMERCIAL CROP. Plants grown on a cultivated farm and intended mainly for sale, including grain-corn and alfalfa grown for commercial purposes. *Crop Insurance Act*, R.S.Q., c. A-30, s. 1.

COMMERCIAL DISCOVERY. A discovery of oil, gas or petroleum that has been demonstrated to contain reserves that justify the investment of capital and effort to bring the discovery to production.

COMMERCIAL ENTERPRISE. A sole proprietorship, partnership, co-operative or corporation having for its object the acquisition of gain.

COMMERCIAL ESTABLISHMENT. Any establishment or other place where commodities are, or merchandise is, sold or offered for sale at retail.

COMMERCIAL FISH. Fish other than game fish.

COMMERCIAL FISHER. The master and crew of a fishing vessel, the master and crew of a fish packing vessel and any other person who contributes in any manner to the catching or landing of fish for sale or commercial use. *Workers' Compensation Act*, R.S.B.C. 1996, c. 492, s. 4.

COMMERCIAL FISHING. Fishing for sale or barter. See FIXED ~ UNIT.

COMMERCIAL FISHING VESSEL. 1. Any fishing vessel (a) the catch or any portion of the catch of which is sold, offered for sale, traded or bartered, (b) that is used in processing fish, or (c) that is used in transporting unprocessed fish.

COMMERCIAL FISH POND. An artificially constructed pond that is used by the owner to sell angling rights to the general public.

COMMERCIAL FOREST OPERATION. An operation involving the cutting or felling of trees for sale.

COMMERCIAL LAW. The law of contracts, bankruptcy, intellectual property, corporations and partnerships and any other subjects dealing with rights and relations of persons engaged in commerce or trade.

COMMERCIAL LETTER OF CREDIT. 1. An irrevocable document issued by a buyer's bank in favour of a seller. The issuing bank will accept drafts drawn upon it for the price of the goods when the seller tenders shipping documents. G.H.L. Fridman, *Sale of Goods in Canada*, 3d ed. (Toronto: Carswell, 1986) at 260. 2. A document issued by a bank on an importer's application in which the bank undertakes to pay an exporter when the exporter complies with certain terms. I.F.G. Baxter, *The Law of Banking*, 3d ed. (Toronto: Carswell, 1981) at 141.

COMMERCIAL LICENCE. See ZONE ~.

COMMERCIAL LIST. A special list of cases to be heard, established to provide a forum in which commercial disputes can be resolved economically and efficiently and heard by judges with accumulated expertise in commercial law.

COMMERCIALLY AVAILABLE. In relation to a work or other subject-matter, (a) available on the Canadian market within a reasonable time and for a reasonable price and may be located with reasonable effort, or (b) for which a licence to reproduce, perform in public or communicate to the public by telecommunication is available from a collective society within a reasonable time and for a reasonable price and may be located with reasonable effort. *Copyright Act*, R.S.C. 1985, c. C-42, s. 2.

COMMERCIAL MARINA. A place located on or adjacent to a body of water or a watercourse where overnight moorings, moorings for a fee, storage, repairs, or marine fuel are ordinarily provided for or supplied to pleasure boats in which toilets are installed and includes a place operated by a boat or yacht club. *Environmental Protection Act*, R.R.O. 1990, Reg. 351, s. 1.

COMMERCIAL MESSAGE. An advertisement that is intended to sell or promote goods, a service or an activity, directly or indirectly, or an announcement that mentions or displays in a list of prizes the name of the person selling or promoting those goods or that service or activity. *Broadcasting Distribution Regulations*, SOR/ 97-555, s. 1.

COMMERCIAL MOTOR VEHICLE. A motor vehicle having attached thereto a truck or delivery body and includes an ambulance, hearse, casket wagon, fire apparatus, police patrol, motor bus, and other motor vehicles used for the transportation of goods.

COMMERCIAL OPERATION. See INDUSTRIAL OR ~.

COMMERCIAL PAPER. A bill of exchange, cheque, promissory note, negotiable instrument, conditional sale agreement, lien note, hire purchase agreement, chattel mortgage, bill of lading, bill of sale, warehouse receipt, guarantee, instrument of assignment things in action and, in addition, any document of title that passes ownership or possession and on which credit can be raised. *Interpretation Act*, R.S.B.C. 1996, c. 238, s. 29.

COMMERCIAL PARKING LOT. Land used for the parking of vehicles that is accessible to the public and for which a fee is charged.

COMMERCIAL PART. In respect of an aircraft, means a part (*a*) that is not specifically designed or produced for use as an aeronautical product, (*b*) that is made to a specification or catalogue description and marked under an identification scheme of the maker, and (*c*) whose failure does not adversely affect the continued safe flight and take-off and landing of the aircraft. *Canadian Aviation Regulations* SOR 96-433, s. 101.01.

COMMERCIAL PASSENGER VEHICLE. Any taxi, bus or other vehicle used or intended for use in the transportation of persons for compensation. *Airport Traffic Regulations*, C.R.C., c. 886, s. 2.

COMMERCIAL PRODUCTION. Output from a well of such quantity of crude oil, liquid hydrocarbons, natural gas and natural gas liquids as, having regard to the cost of drilling and pro-

duction and the price, kind and quality of such production, would justify from a commercial and economic standpoint the drilling of a similar well in the immediate surroundings.

COMMERCIAL PROPERTY. 1. All property except residential property and resource property. 2. Land that is a service station, garage, store, shopping centre, office, office building, restaurant, transient accommodation, theatre, cinema, arena, assembly hall.

COMMERCIAL QUANTITY. Applied to a discovery of petroleum or natural gas, means a quantity obtained or anticipated which justifies the drilling of new wells in the vicinity of the discovery, taking into account the quality of the product, possible markets and other economic factors.

COMMERCIAL REALTY. Real property owned by the Crown or any person, used for or occupied by any industry, trade, business, profession, vocation or government business,

COMMERCIAL RIVER RAFTING. The carrying on of a business in which an outfitter supplies equipment and personnel to transport a person down a river on a raft. *Commercial River Rafting Safety Act*, R.S.B.C.,1996, c. 56, s. 1.

COMMERCIAL SAMPLE. (a) Any goods that are representative of a particular category of goods produced outside Canada and that are imported solely for the purpose of being exhibited or demonstrated to solicit orders for similar goods to be supplied from outside Canada, and (b) any films, charts, projectors and scale models, and similar items, imported solely for the purpose of illustrating a particular category of goods produced outside Canada to solicit orders for similar goods to be supplied from outside Canada. *Commercial Samples Remission Order*, C.R.C., c. 751, s. 2.

COMMERCIAL SCALE. See WORK ON A ~.

COMMERCIAL SPEECH. "[In considering s. 2(b) of the Charter] . . . whatever else may be subsumed within the rubric 'commercial speech', (a) speech which does no more than propose a commercial transaction; (b) expression related solely to the economic interests of the speaker and audience, and (c) speech which advertises a product or service for profit or a business purpose may fairly be regarded as included. . ." *R. v. Smith* (1988) 44 C.C.C. (3d) 385 at 424 (Ont. H.C.), Watt J. See FREEDOM OF EXPRESSION; HATRED.

COMMERCIAL STRUCTURE. See MOBILE INDUSTRIAL OR ~.

COMMERCIAL TENANT. A tenant of a commercial property.

COMMERCIAL TIME. Any period of two minutes or less during which a broadcaster normally presents commercial messages, public service announcements or station or network identification. *Canada Elections Act, 2000*, S.C. 2000, c. 9, s. 344.

COMMERCIAL TREATY. An international treaty concerning financial or economic relations.

COMMERCIAL UNIT. In human rights legislation, any building or other structure or part thereof that is used or occupied or is intended, arranged or designed to be used or occupied for the manufacture, sale, resale, processing, reprocessing, displaying, storing, handling, garaging or distribution of personal property, or any space that is used or occupied or is intended, arranged or designed to be used or occupied as a separate business or professional unit or office in any building or other structure or a part thereof.

COMMERCIAL USE. 1. A use in connection with a trade, business, profession, manufacture or other venture for profit. 2. Any use other than for residential or agricultural purposes.

COMMERCIAL VEHICLE. 1. A motor vehicle designed or adapted for the carrying of freight, wares or merchandise. 2. A motor vehicle goods, trailer operated on a highway for the transportation of livestock or livestock products for gain or compensation, or by or on behalf of a person dealing livestock or livestock products. See PUBLIC ~.

COMMERCIUM JURE GENTIUM COMMUNE ESSE DEBET, ET NON IN MONOPOLIUM ET PRIVATUM PAUCORUM QUAESTUM CONVERTENDUM. [L.] Trade, by law, ought to be free to all, and not monopolized into private gain for a few.

COMMINGLE. *v.* 1. To mass together. 2. Of funds, to mix into one larger fund.

COMMINUTED FISH. Fish flesh that has been ground to a fine, uniform consistency.

COMMINUTED FRACTURE. A fracture with several fragments because the bone splintered. F.A. Jaffe, *A Guide to Pathological Evidence*, 3d ed. (Toronto: Carswell, 1991) at 219.

COMMISSARY. *n.* 1. A person who is sent or delegated to execute some function as the representative of a superior. 2. In the military, an officer who is responsible for furnishing provisions, clothing, etc.

COMMISSION. *n.* 1. The authority or order to act. 2. Remuneration paid to an agent or employee based on price. 3. . . . [I]n the section s. 207(3) of the Criminal Code R.S.C. 1927, c. 36] is not restricted to the actual instantaneous act constituting the crime but includes the preparations for same and all factors which naturally arise in connection with such crime." *R. v. Roher* (1953), 10 W.W.R. (N.S.) 309 at 312, 17 C.R. 307, 61 Man. R. 311, 107 C.C.C. 103 (C.A.), McPherson C.J.M. (Coyne J.A. concurring). 4. An authority given to a person or persons to administer a program or statute, manage a fund or a public utility, investigate a matter or perform some other public function. 5. The name of a body which carries out the functions listed in definition #4. 6. The Governor in Council may, whenever the Governor in Council deems it expedient, cause inquiry to be made into and concerning any matter connected with the good government of Canada or the conduct of any part of the public business thereof. Where an inquiry is not regulated by any special law, the Governor in Council may, by a commission, appoint persons as commissioners by whom the inquiry shall be conducted. Provincial governments have similar powers. See CANADIAN HUMAN RIGHTS ~; CANADIAN RADIO-TELEVISION AND TELECOMMUNICATIONS ~; CANADIAN TRANSPORT ~; DEL CREDERE ~; EUROPEAN ~ OF HUMAN RIGHTS; EXTRA-PROVINCIAL ~; FEDERAL BOARD, ~ OR OTHER TRIBUNAL; INTERNATIONAL JOINT ~; LAW REFORM ~ OF CANADA; MUNICIPAL ~; NATIONAL CAPITAL ~; ONTARIO SECURITIES ~; PROPRIETOR ~; PUBLIC SERVICE ~; PUBLIC UTILITIES ~; RESTRICTIVE TRADE PRACTICES ~; ROYAL ~; SERVICE ~.

COMMISSION AGENT. 1. A person who receives goods for a principal and is employed to sell them for remuneration or commission. 2. Any person who receives and handles produce on commission. *Fruit, Vegetables and Honey Act*, R.S.C. 1970, c. F-31, s. 2.

COMMISSION COUNSEL. A counsel employed by the Minister to assist the court holding an investigation. *Shipping Inquiries and Investigations Rules*, C.R.C., c. 1479, s. 2.

COMMISSIONER. *n*. 1. A person authorised by letters patent, statute or other lawful warrant to examine any matters or execute a public office. 2. A member of a commission. 3. A person authorized to take the evidence of another person. 4. The Commissioner of the Royal Canadian Mounted Police. *Criminal Code*, R.S.C. 1985, c. C-46, s. 84. 5. The Commissioner of the Northwest Territories. *Northwest Territories Act*, R.S.C. 1985, c. N-27, s. 2. 6. A Commissioner of Yukon shall be appointed by order of the Governor in Council. *Yukon Act, 2002*, S.C. 2002, c. 7, s. 4. 7. The Commissioner of Nunavut. 8. The Commissioner of one of the territories is the chief executive officer of the territory. The Commissioner administers the territory under the instructions of the Governor in Council or the Minister. See CITY ~S; CONCILIATION ~; DOMINION FIRE ~; FAMILY LAW ~; FIRE ~; HYDROELECTRIC ~; INFORMATION ~; INFORMATION ~ OF CANADA; MARRIAGE ~; POLICE ~; PRIVACY ~; PRIVACY ~ OF CANADA.

COMMISSIONER FOR TAKING AFFIDAVITS. One authorized to administer affirmations or oaths. A lawyer may be a commissioner for taking affidavits because of his status as a member of the provincial law society. The same may be true of certain officers of public bodies. Others have to apply to the provincial government for the appointment as a commissioner.

COMMISSIONER IN COUNCIL. The Commissioner of the Northwest Territories or Yukon acting by and with the advice and consent of the Council. The Commissioner acting by and with the advice and consent of the Council. The council consists of elected members representing the electoral districts in the territory. The Commissioner is chief executive officer of the Territory. The Commissioner administers the territory under the instructions of the Governor in Council or the Minister. The members of council are elected to represent electoral districts in the territory. In the Yukon, continued as the Legislature of Yukon, consisting of the Commissioner and the Legislative Assembly by the *Yukon Act*, 2002, S.C. 2002, c. 7.

COMMISSIONER OF COMPETITION. Appointed under the Competition Act and responsible for the administration and enforcement of the Competition Act, the administration of the *Consumer Packaging and Labelling Act*, the enforcement of the *Consumer Packaging and Labelling Act* except as it relates to food, as that term is defined in section 2 of the *Food and Drugs Act*; and the administration and enforcement of the *Precious Metals Marking Act* and the *Textile Labelling Act*.

COMMISSIONER OF OFFICIAL LANGUAGES. The federal official empowered to see that both Canada's official languages, French and English, have equal status, rights and privileges in federal institutions.

COMMISSION EVIDENCE. A way to preserve or secure evidence when a witness is, because of (i) physical disability caused by illness, or (ii) any other good and sufficient reason, not able to attend a trial at the time it is held. The evidence is given and recorded before a commissioner appointed or recognized by the court. See COMMISSION ROGATORY; LETTERS ROGATORY; PERPETUATE TESTIMONY; ROGATORY; ROGATORY LETTERS.

COMMISSION FIRM. A person who buys or sells cattle for another on commission.

COMMISSION OF INQUIRY. An investigation into an issue or series of events. The findings of the commissioner are findings of fact and statements of opinion by the commissioner at the end of the inquiry. Neither a criminal trial nor a civil action for determination of liability. *Canada (Attorney General) v. Canada (Commissioner of the Inquiry on the Blood System)*, (sub nom. *Canada (Attorney General) v. Canada (Commission of Inquiry on the Blood System)*) [1997] 3 S.C.R. 440, per Cory, J.

COMMISSION OF THE PEACE. A commission by which a number of persons are appointed as justices of the peace.

COMMISSION ROGATORY. A means of collecting evidence for courts of one country through the courts of another country. See COMMISSION EVIDENCE; LETTERS ROGATORY; PERPETUATE TESTIMONY; ROGATORY; ROGATORY LETTERS.

COMMISSION STEWARD. A person appointed by a Commission to represent that commission at races.

COMMIT. *v*. 1. To complete or carry out an act or acts which constitute an offence. 2. To send to prison by reason of lawful authority. 3. To send to trial, i.e. a provincial court judge commits a person to trial before another court. 4. To refer a bill to a committee in which the bill is considered and reported. A. Fraser, W.A. Dawson, & J. Holtby, eds., *Beauchesne's Rules and Forms of the House of Commons of Canada*, 6th ed. (Toronto: Carswell, 1989) at 203. 5. To direct that a person be confined in a psychiatric facility. See RE ~.

COMMITMENT. *n.* 1. An agreement or promise to do something. 2. Sending a person to prison. 3. Directing that a person be confined in a psychiatric facility. See GOVERNMENT ~; LOAN ~; MORTGAGE ~.

COMMITMENT LETTER. A letter prepared by a lender, setting out the conditions and terms upon which the lender is willing to advance money to a borrower.

COMMITTAL ORDER. A court order for the committal of a person to a correctional facility or a federal penitentiary.

COMMITTED. *adj.* ". . . [An] offence is committed when the offender has completed the unlawful act or acts. . ." *R. v. MacDonald* (1989), 51 C.C.C. (3d) 191 at 192, 18 M.V.R. (2d) 276, 98 A.R. 308 (C.A.), Stevenson, Foisy and Irving JJ.A.

COMMITTEE. *n.* 1. A group of persons elected or appointed to whom any matter is referred by a legislative body, corporation or other institution. 2. A person appointed by the court to look after a person or the affairs of a person incapable of managing their own affairs because of a mental disorder. See ADVISORY ~; AUDIT ~; DISCIPLINE ~; FINANCE GRAIN STANDARDS ~; HOSPITAL MEDICAL STAFF REVIEW ~; JOINT ~; JOINT PRACTICE ~; JOINT TRAINING ~; JUDICIAL ~; LEGISLATIVE ~; MEDICAL STAFF ~; PARLIAMENTARY ~; PROVINCIAL REVIEW ~; SAFETY AND HEALTH SELECT ~; SPECIAL ~; STANDING STEERING ~; STRIKING ~; TERRITORIAL ~.

COMMITTEE OF THE WHOLE HOUSE. The membership of the House when a chairman instead of the Speaker presides. This committee may, deliberate any questions which, in the opinion of the House, it may more fitly discuss, including provisions of public bills. After second reading bills founded on a supply motion are referred to this committee. A. Fraser, W.A. Dawson & J. Holtby, eds., *Beauchesne's Rules and Forms of the House of Commons of Canada*, 6th ed. (Toronto: Carswell, 1989) at 249.

COMMODATUM. *n.* [L.] An agreement to loan useful goods or chattels free of charge, to be used and later restored in specie. E.L.G. Tyler & N.E. Palmer, eds., *Crossley Vaines' Personal Property*, 5th ed. (London: Butterworths, 1973) at 85. See CONTRACT OF ~.

COMMODITY. *n.* 1. ". . . [A]nything that is usable for a purpose."' *R. v. Robert Simpson Co.* (1964), 43 C.R. 366 at 371, [1964] O.R. 227, [1964] 3 C.C.C. 318 (H.C.), Landreville J. 2. Tangible personal property of every kind. 3. The various kinds of freight, merchandise and goods carried on a public motor truck. 4. Any agricultural product, forest product, product of the sea, mineral, metal, hydrocarbon fuel, currency or precious stone or other gem in the original or a processed state. incapable of managing their own affairs because of a mental disorder. See AGRICULTURAL ~; DANGEROUS ~; ENERGY~; INDIVIDUALLY MEASURED~; NAMED ~.

COMMODITY BOARD. A local board under the *Farm Products Marketing Act* or a marketing board under the Milk Act. *Commodity Boards and Marketing Agencies Act*, R.S.O. 1990, c. C-19, s. 1.

COMMODITY CONTRACT. A commodity futures contract or commodity futures option. See OPEN ~.

COMMODITY EXCHANGE. An association or organization, whether incorporated or unincorporated, operated to provide the facilities necessary for the trading of commodity contracts by open auction.

COMMODITY FUTURES CONTRACT. A contract to make or take delivery of a specified quantity and quality, grade or size of a commodity during a designated future month at a price agreed upon when the contract is entered into on a commodity futures exchange pursuant to standardized terms and conditions set forth in such exchange's by-laws, rules or regulations. See OPEN ~.

COMMODITY FUTURES EXAMINATION. See CANADIAN ~; NATIONAL ~.

COMMODITY FUTURES EXCHANGE. An association or organization, whether incorporated or unincorporated, operated for the purpose of providing the physical facilities necessary for the trading of contracts by open auction.

COMMODITY FUTURES OPTION. A right, acquired for a consideration, to assume a long or short position in relation to a commodity futures contract at a specified price and within a specified period of time and any other option of which the subject is a commodity futures contract.

COMMODITY GROUP. An organized body of producers of specific agricultural product or products.

COMMODITY OPTION. A right, acquired for a consideration, to assume a long or short position in relation to a commodity at a specified price and within a specified period of time and any other option of which the subject is a commodity.

COMMODITY PIPELINE. A pipeline that is used or is proposed to be used for the transportation of commodities and that connects a province with any other or others of the provinces or extends beyond the limits of a province.

COMMODITY PIPELINE COMPANY. A person named in an Act of Parliament and having authority under that Act to construct or operate a commodity pipeline, or a person authorized by an Act of Parliament to construct or operate a commodity pipeline with respect to which that Act has special reference.

COMMODITY RATE. A toll applicable to specifically named commodities.

COMMODITY SUPERVISORS' EXAMINATION. An examination relating to the supervision of a dealer's business that has been prepared by and is administered by the Canadian Securities Institute and is so designated by that Institute.

COMMODUM EX INJURIA NON ORITUR. [L.] No legal advantage can arise out of a wrong.

COMMON. *n.* An interest one person can enjoy in the land of another, i.e. common of pasture is the right to pasture cattle on another person's land. See TENANCY IN ~.

COMMON. *adj.* Usual, ordinary; shared.

COMMONABLE. *adj.* Used of something by, over or in respect of which one may exercise a right of common.

COMMONALTY. *n.* The people.

COMMON AREAS. 1. Areas controlled by a landlord and used for access to residential premises or for the service or enjoyment of a tenant. 2. In a condominium or strata property, the areas owned by the strata corporation for the benefit of all owners of the property.

COMMON ASSAULT. "[At common law]... any act in which one person intentionally caused another to apprehend immediate and unlawful violence... The traditional common law definition always assumed that the absence of consent was a required element of that offence." *R. v. Jobidon* (1991), 7 C.R. (4th) 233 at 245, 66 C.C.C. (3d) 454, 128 N.R. 321, 49 O.A.C. 83, [1991] 2 S.C.R. 714, Gonthier J. (La Forest, L Heureux-Dubé, Cory and Iacobucci JJ. concurring).

COMMON ASSET. (a) personal property held by or on behalf of a strata corporation, and (b) land held in the name of or on behalf of a strata corporation, that is (i) not shown on the strata plan, or (ii) shown as a strata lot on the strata plan. *Strata Property Act*, S.B.C. 1998, c. 43, s. 1.

COMMON BAWDY-HOUSE. A place that is (a) kept or occupied, or (b) resorted to by one or more persons for the purpose of prostitution or the practice of acts of indecency. *Criminal Code*, R.S.C. 1985, c. C-46, c. 197.

COMMON BETTING HOUSE. A place that is opened, kept or used for the purpose of (a) enabling, encouraging or assisting persons who resort thereto to bet between themselves or with the keeper, or (b) enabling any person to receive, record, register, transmit or pay bets or to announce the results of betting. *Criminal Code*, R.S.C. 1985, c. C-46, s. 197.

COMMON CARRIER. "... [O]ne who holds himself out to the public to carry the goods of such persons as may choose to employ him." *Engel Canada Inc. v. Bingo's Transport* Drivers (1990), 23 M.V.R. (2d) 193 at 197 (Ont. H.C.), Austin J.

COMMON ELEMENTS. All property, except the condominium units, owned in common by all of the owners of units.

COMMON EMPLOYMENT DOCTRINE. "... [C]ommon law doctrine... operated to prevent an employee from suing his employer for damages suffered as a result of the negligence of a fellow employee. It did not in the past and it does not now prevent an employee from suing a negligent co-worker unless such an action is otherwise barred by statute: ..." *Berger v. Willowdale A.M.C.* (1983), 23 B.L.R. 19 at 33, 41 O.R. (2d) 89, C.E.S.H.G. 95,063, 145 D.L.R. (3d) 247 (C.A.), Cory J.A. (Brooke J.A. concurring).

COMMON EXPENSES. The expenses of the performance of the objects and duties of a condominium corporation and any expenses specified as common expenses in a declaration.

COMMON FACILITY. An improvement in the common property that is available for the use of all the owners of a condominium.

COMMON FORM BUSINESS. The business of obtaining probate or administration where there is no contention as to the right thereto, including the passing of probate and administration through court when the contest is terminated, and all business of a non-contentious nature to be taken in a surrogate court in matters of testacy and intestacy not being proceedings in a suit and also the business of lodging caveats against the grant of probate or administration.

COMMON GAMING HOUSE. A place that is (a) kept for gain to which persons resort for the purpose of playing games, or (b) kept or used for the purpose of playing games (i) in which a bank is kept by one or more but not all of the players, (ii) in which all or any portion of the bets on or proceeds from a game is paid directly or indirectly, to the keeper of the place, (iii) in which, directly or indirectly, a fee is charged to or paid by the players for the privilege of playing or participating in a game or using gaming equipment, or (iv) in which the chances of winning are not equally favourable to all persons who play the game, including the person, if any, who conducts the game. *Criminal Code*, R.S.C. 1985, c. C-46, s. 197.

COMMON INTEREST. 1. "[In the context of a representative action refers to the fact that] . . . the plaintiff and all those whom he claims to represent will gain some relief by his success, though possibly in different proportions and perhaps in different degrees." *A.E Osler and Co. v. Solman* (1926), 59 O.L.R. 368 at 372 (H.C.), Orde J.A. 2. In condominium law, the interest in the common elements appurtenant to a unit. 3. In occupier's liability, a mutuality of interest or advantage to invitor and invitee.

COMMON INTEREST PRIVILEGE. 1. ". . . [A] privilege in aid of anticipated litigation in which several persons have a common interest. . ." *Buttes Gas & Oil Co. v. Hammer (No. 3)*, [1980] 3 All E.R. 475 at 483-84 (C.A.), Lord Denning M.R. 2. Arises in a situation where solicitor-client privilege exists with the added element that a communication of privileged material is made in confidence to a party with a common interest in the matter. *Anderson Exploration Ltd. v. Pan-Alberta Gas Ltd.*, [1998] 10 W.W.R. 633 (Alta. Q.B.).

COMMON ISSUES. 1. Common but not necessarily identical issues of fact, or common but not necessarily identical issues of law that arise from common but not necessarily identical facts. *Class Proceedings acts*. 2. In the context of the [*Class Proceedings Act*, R.S.B.C. 1996, c. 50], "common" means that the resolution of the point in question must be applicable to all who are bound by it. *Harrington v. Dow Corning Corp.*, 2000 CarswellBC 2183, 2000 BCCA 605, 82 B.C.L.R. (3d) 1, [2000] 11 W.W.R. 201, 47 C.P.C. (4th) 191, 193 D.L.R. (4th) 67 (C.A.).

COMMON JAIL. Any place other than a penitentiary in which persons charged with offences are usually kept and detained in custody.

COMMON KNOWLEDGE. 1. " . . . [K]nowledge of a general nature which has been acquired in common with other members of the general public. . ." *Maslej v. Canada (Minister of Manpower & Immigration)*, [1977] 1 F.C. 194 at 198 (C.A.), the court per Urie J. 2. " . . . [T]he common knowledge possessed by every man on the street, of which courts of justice cannot divest themselves . . ." *In re Price Bros. Etc.* (1920), 60 S.C.R. 265 at 279, Anglin J.

COMMON LAW. 1. In contrast to statute law, law which relies for its authority on the decisions of the courts and is recorded in the law reports as decisions of judges along with the reasons for their decisions. Judge-made law. Includes the interpretation of statutes and subordinate legislation by judges. 2. In contrast to canon (or ecclesiastical) and the civil (or Roman) law, the system of law in provinces other than Quebec.

COMMON LAW LIEN. A right at common law in one person to retain the property belonging to another and continuously and rightfully in his possession until the property owner satisfies the possessor's claims against the property, example a mechanic's lien, a repairperson's lien.

COMMON LAW MARRIAGE. *var.* **COMMON-LAW MARRIAGE**. " . . . [A] voluntary union of a man and woman during their joint lives to the exclusion of all others which, for historical reasons, was treated as being just as valid as a regular marriage." *Louis v. Esslinger* (1981), 15 C.C.L.T. 137 at 161 1981 3 W.W.R. 350, 22 C.P.C. 68, 29 B.C.L.R. 41, 121 D.L.R. (3d) 17 (S.C.), McEachern C.J.S.C.

COMMON-LAW PARTNER. In relation to an individual, means a person who is cohabiting with the individual in a conjugal relationship.

COMMON-LAW PARTNERSHIP. The relationship between two persons who are common-law partners of each other.

COMMON-LAW RELATIONSHIP. " . . . [S]ome sort of a stable relationship which involves not only sexual activity but a commitment between the parties. It would normally necessitate living together under the same roof with shared household duties and responsibilities as well as financial support . . . such a couple would present themselves to society as a couple who were living together as man and wife. All or none of these elements may be necessary depending upon the intent of the parties." *Soper v. Soper* (1985), 44 R.F.L. (2d) 308 at 314, 67 N.S.R. (2d) 49, 155 A.P.R. 49 (C.A.), the court per Morrison J.A.

COMMON LAW SPOUSE. *var.* **COMMON-LAW SPOUSE**. Includes any man or woman who although not legally married to a person lives and cohabits with that person as the spouse of that person and is known as such in the community in which they have lived.

COMMON LAW UNION. 1. A union of two persons who live together on a daily basis over an extended period of time and who share privileges and obligations. 2. Cohabitation by a man and a woman who publicly present themselves as spouses.

COMMON-LAW WIFE. A woman who, although not legally married to a man, cohabits with him and is recognized as his wife in the community in which they live.

COMMON MARKET. The popular name for the European Economic Community.

COMMON MISTAKE. See MISTAKE.

COMMON NUISANCE. The offence of committing a common nuisance consists of doing an unlawful act or failing to discharge a legal duty and thereby (a) endangering the lives, safety, health, property or comfort or the public or (b) obstructing the public in the exercise or enjoyment or any right that is common to all the subjects of Her Majesty in Canada. *Criminal Code*, R.S.C. 1985, c. C-46, s. 10.

COMMON OF FISHERY. The right enjoyed by several persons but not the whole public. *R. v. Robertson* (1882), 6 S.C.R. 52.

COMMON OF PASTURE. A type of profit a prendre, the right to feed animals upon another's land.

COMMON OF PISCARY. The liberty or right, held in common with others, of fishing in water covering the soil of another's land or in a river running through another's land. The right enjoyed by all the public on the sea or to the ebb and flow of the tide. *R. v. Robertson* (1882), 6 S.C.R. 52.

COMMON PARENTAGE. Having one common parent.

COMMON PLEAS. The British court which was a superior court of record.

COMMON PROPERTY. 1. The part of the land included in a condominium plan that is not included in any unit shown in the condominium plan. This property is available for the benefit of all members of the condominium corporation. 2. (a) that part of the land and buildings shown on a strata plan that is not part of a strata lot, and (b) pipes, wires, cables, chutes, ducts and other facilities for the passage or provision of water, sewage, drainage, gas, oil, electricity, telephone, radio, television, garbage, heating and cooling systems, or other similar services, if they are located (i) within a floor, wall or ceiling that forms a boundary (A) between a strata lot and another strata lot, (B) between a strata lot and the common property, or (C) between a strata lot or common property and another parcel of land, or (ii) wholly or partially within a strata lot, if they are capable of being and intended to be used in connection with the enjoyment of another strata lot or the common property; *Strata Property Act*, S.B.C. 1998, c. 43, s. 1.

COMMON ROAD. An access road on which public money has been expended for its repair or maintenance. *Road Access Act*, R.S.O. 1990, c. R.34, s. 1.

COMMONS. *n*. The House of Commons is referred to colloquially as the commons. See HOUSE OF ~.

COMMON SHARE. 1. A share to which no special rights or privileges attach. 2. A share of a corporation (i) the older of which is not precluded upon the reduction or redemption of the capital stock from participating in the assets of the corporation beyond the amount paid up on the share plus a fixed premium and a defined rate of divided, and (ii) that carries a number of voting rights in the issuing corporation, in all circumstances and regardless of the number of shares held, that is not less than the number attached to any other share of the capital stock of that corporation. 3. A share in a body corporate, the rights of the holders of which are equal in all respects, including equal rights to (a) receive dividends declared by the body corporate on the shares; and (b) receive the remaining property of the body corporate on dissolution. *Canada Cooperatives Act*, S.C. 1998, c. 1, s. 284.

COMMON SURPLUS. The excess of all receipts of the corporation over the expenses of the corporation. *Condominium Act, 1998*, S.O. 1998, c. 19, s. 1.

COMMON TRUST FUND. A fund maintained by a trust company in which money belonging to various estates and trusts in its care are combined to facilitate investment.

COMMON USE. Used by more than one person.

COMMONWEALTH. *n.* 1. The association of countries named in the schedule. *Interpretation Act*, R.S.C. 1985, c. I-21, s. 35. 2. The social state of a country. 3. A republic. 4. The Australian federation called the Commonwealth of Australia. 5. The British government from 1649 to 1660. See BRITISH ~.

COMMONWEALTH AND DEPENDENT TERRITORIES. The several Commonwealth countries and their colonies, possessions, dependencies, protectorates, protected states, condominiums and trust territories. *Interpretation Act*, R.S.C. 1985, c. I-21, s. 35.

COMMONWEALTH COUNTRY. 1. A country (a) whose government was a party to the British Commonwealth Merchant Shipping Agreement signed at London on December 10, 1931, or (b) that was included within the ambit of that Agreement in 1931 and the government of which as a government of a separate entity within the association of the Commonwealth of Nations, continues to participate in that Agreement, and includes the colonies possessions, dependencies, protectorates, protected states, condominiums and trust territories of any such country. *Canada Shipping Act*, R.S.C. 1985, c. S-9, s. 2. 2. A country that is a member of the association of such countries.

COMMONWEALTH OF NATIONS. The association of countries named in the schedule to the Act. *Interpretation Act*, R.S.C. 1985, c. I-21, s. 35. The countries are former colonies or pos-

sessions of the United Kingdom and the United Kingdom itself. See BRITISH ~.

COMMORIENTES. *n.* [L.] People who die in the same accident or on the same occasion.

COMMR. *abbr.* Commissioner.

COMMUNAL PROPERTY. (i) Land held by a colony in such a manner that no member of the colony has any individual or personal ownership or right of ownership in the land, and each member shares in the distribution of profits or benefits according to his needs or in equal measure with his fellow members and (ii) land held by a member of the colony by personal ownership or right of ownership or under a lease, if the land is used in conjunction with and as part of other land held in the manner described in subclause (i). *Communal Property Act*, R.S.A. 1970, c. 59, s. 2.

COMMUNE. *n.* A small community of people who share common interests and who own property together.

COMMUNE CONCILIUM REGNI. [L.] The common council of the monarch and parliament.

COMMUNICABLE DISEASE. 1. An illness due to an infectious agent or its toxic products which is transmitted directly or indirectly to a well person from an infected person or animal or through the agency of an intermediate animal host, of vector, or of the inanimate environment. 2. An infectious or contagious disease. 3. Includes measles, influenza, rubella (rotheln), scarlet fever, smallpox, varicella (chicken pox), typhus fever, relapsing fever, diptheria, typhoid fever, paratyphoid fever lethargic encephalitis, Asiatic cholera, tuberculosis (of any organ) bubonic plague, tetanus, anthrax, glanders, cerebrospinal meningitis, leprosy, infectious diseases of the eye (trachoma, suppurative conjunctivitis, ophthalmia neonatorum), erysipelas, puerperal septicaemia, whooping cough, yellow fever, malaria, syphilis or other venereal disease, and communicable diseases of the skin, mumps, actinomycosis, anterior poliomyelitis, pneumonia, rabies and pediculosis. *Health Act*, R.S.N.S. 1989, c. 195, s. 2.

COMMUNICATE THE EVIDENCE. The phrase "communicate the evidence" indicates more than mere verbal ability. The reference to "the evidence" indicates the ability to testify about the matters before the court. It is necessary to explore in a general way whether the witness is capable of perceiving events, remembering events and communicating events to the court.

If satisfied that this is the case, the judge may then receive the child's evidence, upon the child's promising to tell the truth under s. 16(3). It is not necessary to determine in advance that the child perceived and recollects the very events at issue in the trial as a condition of ruling that her evidence be received. That is not required of adult witnesses, and should not be required for children. *R. v. Marquard*, 1993 CarswellOnt 127, 25 C.R. (4th) 1, 159 N.R. 81, 66 O.A.C. 161, 85 C.C.C. (3d) 193, 108 D.L.R. (4th) 47, [1993] 4 S.C.R. 223. Per McLachlin, J. for the majority.

COMMUNICATING. *n.* Includes communicating by telephone, broadcasting or other audible or visible means. *Criminal Code*, R.S.C. 1985, c. C-46, s. 319(7).

COMMUNICATION. *n.* 1. [I]nvolves the passing of thoughts, ideas, words or information from one person to another. . ." *R. v. Goldman*, 108 D.L.R. (3d) 17 at 32, [1980] 1 S.C.R. 976, 30 N.R. 453, 51 C.C.C. (2d) 1, 13 C.R. (3d) 228 (Eng.), 16 C.R. (3d) 330 (Fr.), McIntyre J. (Martland, Ritchie, Pigeon, Dickson, Beetz, Estey and Pratte JJ. concurring). 2. Making available. 3. Connotes an intention to impart, convey or exchange ideas or knowledge or at least the awareness that this may be the result. *Chmara v. Nguyen*, [1993] 6 W.W.R. 286 (Man. C.A.). 4. Any form of contact, and includes oral, written or electronic communication. *Unclaimed Intangible Property Act*, R.S.O. 1990, c. U.1, s. 1. See CONFIDENTIAL ~; DISTRESS ~; PENITENTIAL ~; PRIVATE ~; PRIVILEGED ~; RADIO-~.

COMMUNICATION LINE. A line for telegraphic, telephonic, signalling or other intelligence purposes. *Wire Crossings and Proximities Regulations*, C.R.C., c. 1195, s. 2.

COMMUNICATIONS. *n.* 1. A method, manner or means by which information is transmitted, imparted or exchanged and includes the transmission and reception of sound, pictures, signs, signals, data or messages by means of wire, cable, waves or an electrical, electronic, magnetic, electromagnetic or optical means. 2. The business of radio and television broadcasting and the furnishing of community antenna services, telephone services and other electrical or electronic communication services. *Small Business Loans Regulations*, C.R.C., c. 1501, s. 3. See DEPARTMENT OF ~; PUBLIC ~.

COMMUNICATION SIGNAL. Radio waves transmitted through space without any artificial guide, for reception by the public.

COMMUNICATIONS SECURITY ESTABLISHMENT. A body within the federal public service that is charged with the following duties. (*a*) to acquire and use information from the global information infrastructure for the purpose of providing foreign intelligence, in accordance with Government of Canada intelligence priorities; (*b*) to provide advice, guidance and services to help ensure the protection of electronic information and of information infrastructures of importance to the Government of Canada; and (*c*) to provide technical and operational assistance to federal law enforcement and security agencies in the performance of their lawful duties.

COMMUNICATION SYSTEM. An electrical system whereby intelligence or signals may be transmitted to or through a central station, including telephone, telegraph, district messenger, fire and burglar alarm, watchman or sprinkler supervisory system, and other central station systems of similar nature which commonly receive the power supply necessary for their operation from central office or local power sources.

COMMUNIS ERROR FACIT JUS. [L.] A common error may make law.

COMMUNITY. *n.* 1. "[In s. 24 of the Taxation Act, R.S.B.C. 1960, c. 376] . . . must be interpreted in the sense that it means the public in general and not a community in the sense of an isolated or identifiable area or group." *Piers Island Assn. v. Saanich & Islands Area Assessor* (1976), 71 D.L.R. (3d) 270 at 275, 1 B.C.L.R. 279 (S.C.), Fulton J. 2. A city, town or village. *The Community Planning Profession Act*, R.S.S. 1978, c. C-21, c. 2. 3. A geographic unit or group of persons sharing common interests within a geographic unit who provide or receive services on a collective basis. 4. A group of persons living together and observing common rules under the direction of a superior. 5. The Communauté urbaine de Montréal, the Communauté urbaine de Québec or the Communauté régionale de l'Outaouais. 6. Any area which is not a municipality. 7. "[In the context of selecting a jury] . . . a reasonably distinct, distinguishable group by language and culture. It should occupy, as well, a unique geographic area. If those conditions are met, then, it seems that those people living in that area should qualify as a community . . ." *R. v. Fatt* (1986), 54 C.R. (3d) 281 at 291, [1986] N.W.T.R. 388, 30 C.C.C. (3d) 69, 24 C.R.R. 259, [1987] 1 C.N.L.R. 74 (S.C.), Marshall J. See CREE ~; FULL ~; NATIVE ~; REMOTE ~; SEPARATED ~; VACATED ~.

COMMUNITY ANTENNA TELEVISION. A system by which television signals are received from distant stations on large antennae and transmitted by cable to individual consumers.

COMMUNITY-BASED RESIDENTIAL FACILITY. A place that provides accommodation to offenders who are on parole, statutory release or temporary absence. *Corrections and Conditional Release Act*, S.C. 1992, c. 20, s. 66(3).

COMMUNITY CABLECASTER. A provider of cablecast service and cablecast programming.

COMMUNITY CARE FACILITY. A facility that provides personal care, supervision, social or educational training, physical or mental rehabilitative therapy, with or without charge to persons not related by blood or marriage to an operator of the facility.

COMMUNITY CENTRE. Any public land improved, or buildings erected and equipped to provide recreational, sporting, cultural, or adult educational facilities for the public use of the community.

COMMUNITY CHANNEL. The channel of a distribution undertaking that is used for the distribution of community programming in a licensed area. *Broadcasting Distribution Regulations*, SOR/97-555, s. 1.

COMMUNITY CREDIT UNION. A credit union whose membership is open to all persons residing or working within a defined geographical area.

COMMUNITY DEVELOPMENT SERVICES. Services designed to encourage and assist residents of a community to participate in or continue to participate in improving the social and economic conditions of the community for the purpose of preventing, lessening or removing the causes and effects of poverty, child neglect or dependence on public assistance in the community.

COMMUNITY HALL. Includes the building, lands or other property used or intended to be used or capable of being used for social, educa-

tional, recreational or community purposes, public meetings, public library or for entertainment or amusement, and includes all lands and buildings used or intended to be used or capable of being used for athletic purposes. *Community Act*, R.S.N.S. 1989, c. 80, s. 2.

COMMUNITY IMPROVEMENT. The planning or replanning, design or redesign, resubdivision, clearance, development or redevelopment, reconstruction and rehabilitation, or any of them, of a community improvement project area, and the provision of such residential, commercial industrial, public, recreational, institutional, religious, charitable or other uses, buildings, works, improvements or facilities, or spaces therefor, as may be appropriate or necessary. *Planning Act*, R.S.O. 1990, c. P.13, s. 28.

COMMUNITY IMPROVEMENT PLAN. A plan for the community improvement of a communiy improvement project area. *Planning Act*, R.S.O. 1990, c. P.13, s. 28.

COMMUNITY IMPROVEMENT PROJECT AREA. A municipality or an area within a municipality, the community improvement of which in the opinion of the council is desirable because of age, dilapidation, overcrowding, faulty arrangement, unsuitability of buildings or for any other environmental, social or community economic development reason. *Planning Act*, R.S.O. 1990, c. 213, s. 28.

COMMUNITY OF INTEREST DOCTRINE. An exception to the general rule against covenants in restraint of trade. Covenants restricting tenants' business in shopping centre leases may be upheld as mutually and reciprocally enforceable as between landlord and tenant and between tenants if it is clear from the respective leases that a community of interest is created.

COMMUNITY OF PROPERTY. See COMMUNITY PROPERTY REGIME; DEFERRED ~.

COMMUNITY ORGANIZATION. See LOCAL ~.

COMMUNITY PASTURE. (i) A community grazing reserve, or (ii) public land subject to a grazing lease or permit between the Government and a grazing association or a group of individuals. *Livestock Identification and Brand Inspection Act*, R.S.A. 2000, c. L-16, s. 1.

COMMUNITY PLAN. See OFFICIAL ~.

COMMUNITY PLANNING. See PRACTICE OF PROFESSIONAL ~.

COMMUNITY PLANNING OFFICE. An office, whether of a department or agency of a government or of a person or persons engaged in private business, in which the principal work is the preparation of comprehensive plans of development and in which is employed on a full-time basis, in a senior position, a person who has a degree or diploma in community planning from a recognized university or an institution of learning of equivalent status. *The Community Planning Profession Act*, R.S.S. 1978, c. C-21, s. 2.

COMMUNITY PLANNING SCHEME. See MASTER PLAN.

COMMUNITY PROGRAMMING. In relation to a licensed area, programming that is produced (*a*) by the licensee in the licensed area or by members of the community served in the licensed area; (*b*) by the licensee in another licensed area or by the members of the community served in that other licensed area and that is relevant to the community referred to in paragraph (*a*); (*c*) by another licensee in a licensed area or by the members of the community served in that licensed area and that is relevant to the community referred to in paragraph (*a*); or (*d*) by a person licensed to operate a network for the purpose of producing community programming for distribution by the licensee on a community channel. *Broadcasting Distribution Regulations*, SOR/97-555, s. 1.

COMMUNITY PROPERTY. Real and personal property held for or owned by the community. *Community Act*, R.S.N.S. 1989, c. 80, s. 2.

COMMUNITY PROPERTY REGIME. An arrangement whereby spouses share all property which one or both may own.

COMMUNITY RECREATION CENTRE. Land or all or any part of a building or buildings or structure established in accordance with this Act that is maintained and operated for community recreation activity. *Community Recreation Centres Act*, R.S.O. 1990, c. C.22, s. 1(1).

COMMUNITY SALE. A sale or offering for sale of livestock at an established and recognized place of business where livestock is assembled for that purpose, or, at a railway depot, siding or car or at dock side or from a vessel thereat.

COMMUNITY SANCTIONS. " . . . [R]efers to sanctions other than custody. It includes com-munity programs or resources (e.g. supervised probation) or compensation to the community (e.g. fines or service). The sanctions are to be served or performed in the community with the community taking an active role in the rehabilitation, responsibility for, and treatment of the offender. . ." *R. v. P. (J.A.)* (1991), 6 C.R. (4th) 126 at 135, [1991] N.W.T.R. 301 (Y.T. Terr. Ct.), Lilles C.J.T.C.

COMMUNITY SERVICE. " . . . [A]n alternative to a custodial sentence in those cases where the public interest does not demand that the offender should be imprisoned. It allows the offender to continue to live in the community with his wife and family, supporting them by his normal work. It demonstrates to the offender that society is involved in his delinquency and that he has incurred a debt which can de repaid in some measure by work or service in the community. . ." *R. v. Jones* (1975), 25 C.C.C. (2d) 256 at 259 (Ont. G.S.P.), Stortini Co. Ct. J.

COMMUNITY SERVICE CENTRE. See LOCAL ~.

COMMUNITY SERVICE ORDER. An order requiring an offender to perform unpaid work in the community under supervision.

COMMUNITY SOCIAL SERVICES. Services that are protective, preventive, developmental or rehabilitative in nature and which (a) facilitate access to the necessities of life; (b) assist disabled or disadvantaged persons to live as normally and independently as possible or support them in doing so; (c) prevent the need for institutional care as well as provide alternatives to it; (d) support or assist the aged, children or families; (e) facilitate or support the involvement and participation of people in their communities; (f) enhance or maintain employment skills and capabilities of persons; (g) provide protection to children and adults; (h) provide information and refer people to available services.

COMMUNITY STANDARD. 1. [In the context of a publisher on trial for publishing an obscenity,] " . . . [C]oncerned not with what Canadians would not tolerate being exposed to themselves, but what they would not tolerate other Canadians being exposed to." *R. v. Butler* (1992), 70 C.C.C. (3d) 129 at 145, [1992] 2 W.W.R. 577, [1992] 1 S.C.R. 452, 11 C.R. (4th) 137, 134 N.R. 81, 8 C.R.R. (2d) 1, 89 D.L.R. (4th) 449, 78 Man. R. (2d) 1, 16 W.A.C. 1, Sopinka J. (Lamer C.J.C., La Forest, Cory, Mc-

Lachlin, Stevenson and Iacobucci JJ. concurring). 2. " . . . [A]re not set by those of lowest taste or interest. Nor are they set exclusively by those of rigid, austere, conservative, or puritan taste and habit of mind. Something approaching a general average of community thinking and feeling has to be discovered. . .Community standards must be contemporary . . ." *R. v. Dominion News & Gifts Ltd.* (1963), 40 C.R. 109 at 126, 42 W.W.R. 65, [1963] 2 C.C.C. (Man. C.A.), Freedman J.A. (dissenting).

COMMUNITY SUPPORT SERVICE. A support service or prevention service provided in the community for children and their families. *Child and Family Services Act*, R.S.O. 1990, c. C.11, s. 3.

COMMUNITY WELFARE. Includes the establishment, maintenance and operation of any one or more of the following: a public or community hall, a club room, a rest room, a library, a recreational ground, a theatre, an ice rink, or any other facilities operated solely for social welfare, health, civic improvement, public entertainment or recreation, no part of the income of which is payable to or otherwise available for the personal benefit of any member or patron. *The Co-operative Associations Act*, R.S.S. 1978, c. C-34, s. 82.

COMMUTATION. *n.* 1. Conversion. 2. Reduction of a punishment or penalty. 3. Change to the right to receive a gross or fixed payment from the right to receive a periodic or variable payment.

COMMUTED. *adj.* 1. Of a sentence or penalty, changed from greater to lesser. 2. Refers to a periodic payment which has been converted into a fixed sum payable presently. 3. Refers to the exercise of an aspect of the Crown's pardoning power with respect to a sentence imposed for the commission of a criminal offence.

COMMUTED PENSION. A final payment in lieu of annual pension.

COMMUTED VALUE. In relation to benefits that a person has a present or future entitlement to receive, the actuarial present value of those benefits determined, as of the time in question, on the basis of actuarial assumptions and methods that are adequate and appropriate and in accordance with generally accepted actuarial principles.

COMPANION. *n.* The title granted certain members of honorary orders. See CONSTANT ~.

COMPANY. *n.* 1. An association of people formed to carry on some business or undertaking in the association's name. 2. Any body corporate. 3. A body corporate with share capital. 4. May include unincorporated association, co-operative association, partnership, single proprietor or person. 5. An entity distinct and separate in law from its individual shareholders or members. H. Sutherland, D.B. Horsle & J.M. Edmiston, eds., *Fraser's Handbook on Canadian Company Law*, 7th ed. (Toronto: Carswell, 1985) at 1. See AFFILIATED ~; ALBERTA ~; AMALGAMATED ~; BRITISH ~; CANADIAN ~; CANADIAN NATIONAL RAILWAY ~; CASH-MUTUAL ~; CEMETERY ~; CHARTERED ~; CLEAN SHELL ~; CLOSE ~; CLOSED ~; COMMODITY PIPELINE ~; CONSTRAINED-SHARE ~; CONTROLLED ~; DEBTOR ~; DEFUNCT ~; DISTRIBUTION ~; DOMESTIC ~; DOMICILED ~; DOMINION ~; ELEVATOR ~; EXTRA-PROVINCIAL ~; EXTRA-TERRITORIAL ~; FEDERAL ~; FINANCE ~; FOREIGN ~; GAS ~; GAS EXPORT ~; GUARANTEE ~; HOLDING ~; HOUSING ~; HUDSON'S BAY ~; INCORPORATED ~; INDUSTRIAL ~; INSURANCE ~; INVESTMENT ~; JOINT STOCK ~; LIFE ~; LIMITED ~; LIMITED LIABILITY ~; LOAN ~; MANAGEMENT ~; MINING ~; MUTUAL ~; MUTUAL INSURANCE ~; NATIONAL ~; NON-RESIDENT ~; NOT-FOR-PROFIT ~; OFFEREE ~; PARENT ~; PIPE LINE ~; PRIVATE ~; PROSPECTING ~; PROVINCIAL ~; PUBLIC ~; RAILWAY ~; RELATED COMPANIES; RELATED PERSON OR ~; REPORTING ~; REVIVED ~; SHIPPING ~; SMALL LOANS ~; SPECIALLY LIMITED ~; STORAGE SUBSIDIARY ~; SURETY ~; TELEGRAPH ~; TELEPHONE ~; TRADING ~; TRANSPORTATION ~; UTILITY ~.

COMPANY DOMINATED ORGANIZATION. A labour organization, the formation or administration of which an employer or employer's agent has dominated or interfered with or to which an employer or employer's agent has contributed financial or other support. *Trade Union Act*, R.S.S. 1978, c. T-17, s. 2.

COMPANY-DOMINATED UNION. A union created with employer support or controlled by the employer.

COMPANY LIMITED BY GUARANTEE. A company having the liability of its members limited by the memorandum to the amount that the members may respectively thereby undertake to contribute to the assets of the company in the event of its being wound up. *Companies Act*, R.S.A. 2000, c. C-21, s. 1.

COMPANY LIMITED BY SHARES. A company having the liability of its members limited to the amount, if any, unpaid on the shares respectively held by them. *Companies Act*, R.S.A. 2000, c. C-21, s. 1.

COMPANY MAN. An employee who is extremely loyal to the employer.

COMPANY PIPELINE. A pipeline to transport oil, gas, solids or water that a company under this Act is authorized to construct or operate, and includes all branches, extensions, tanks, reservoirs, pumps, racks and loading facilities; interstation systems of communication by telephone, telegraph or radio; property and works connected with it. *Pipeline Act*, R.S.B.C. 1996, c. 364, s. 1.

COMPANY STORE. A store maintained by an employer.

COMPANY TOWN. A community owned by an employer.

COMPANY UNION. 1. A union the membership of which is limited to one company. 2. A union dominated by an employer.

COMPANY-WIDE AGREEMENT. An agreement between an employer and a union affecting all plants belonging to the employer.

COMPANY-WIDE BARGAINING. Negotiation of an agreement between an employer operating more than one plant and the union representing workers in all the plants.

COMPARABLE. *adj*. In respect of two or more programming services, means that not less than 95% of the video and audio components of those programming services, exclusive of commercial messages and of any part of the services carried on a subsidiary signal, are the same. *Broadcasting Distribution Regulations*, SOR/97-555, s. 1.

COMPARABLE UNCONTROLLED PRICE METHOD. According to the OECD Guidelines, there are a number of methods for determining an arm's length price in the context of international transactions. The method that is said to be in principle the most appropriate and in theory the easiest is the comparable uncontrolled price method, or "CUP" method. In general, the CUP method requires a direct reference to prices in comparable transactions between enterprises that are independent of each other. *SmithKline Beecham Animal Health Inc. v. R.*, 2002 FCA 229, [2002] 4 C.T.C. 93 (C.A.).

COMPARTMENT. *n*. A lower hold, or a cargo space bounded by permanent bulkheads at each end and having decks with closed hatchways above and below. See FILLED ~; FIRE ~; PARCEL ~ ASSEMBLY; PARCEL ~ UNIT; WATERTIGHT ~.

COMPARTMENT DOOR. See INTERIOR ~.

COMPASSING. *n*. Contriving; imagining.

COMPELLABILITY. *n*. The state of being subject to legal compulsion to testify in proceedings.

COMPELLABLE. *adj*. Required by law to give evidence.

COMPELLATIVUS. *n*. [L.] An accuser; an adversary.

COMPELLED. *adj*. 1. "[In s. 11(c) of the Charter] . . . indicates to me that the section is referring to a legal compulsion forcing an accused to give evidence in proceedings brought against him or her. The tactical obligation felt by the accused will no doubt increase with the strength of the Crown's case, but it remains a tactical and not a legal compulsion. The decision whether or not to testify remains with the accused free of any legal compulsion." *R. v. Boss* (1988), 42 C.R.R. 166 at 182, 30 O.A.C. 184, 68 C.R. (3d) 123, 46 C.C.C. (3d) 523 (C.A.), the court per Cory J.A. 2. [In interpreting the words "compelled statement"] the test for compulsion under s. 61(1) of the *Motor Vehicle Act*, R.S.B.C. 1979, c. 288 is whether, at the time that the accident was reported by the driver, the driver gave the report on the basis of an honest and reasonably held belief that he or she was required by law to report the accident to the person to whom the report was given. *R. v. White*, 1999 CarswellBC 1224, 63 C.R.R. (2d) 1, 240 N.R. 1, 24 C.R. (5th) 201, 135 C.C.C. (3d) 257, 174 D.L.R. (4th) 111, 42 M.V.R. (3d) 161, 123 B.C.A.C. 161, 201 W.A.C. 161, [1999] 2 S.C.R. 417.

COMPELLING PRESUMPTION. Facts sufficient to require that a given conclusion be drawn from them.

COMPENDIA SUNT DISPENDIA. [L.] Summaries are not reliable.

COMPENDIUM. *n*. 1. The CPS [Compendium of Pharmaceutical Specialities] is a reference book which lists the dosages, ingredients and directions for certain drugs, and is widely used by pharmacists and physicians. *AB Hassle v. Canada (Minister of National Health & Welfare)*, 2002 FCA 421, 22 C.P.R. (4th) 1, 298 N.R. 323 (C.A.). 2. The *Compendium of Monographs* published by the Department of Health and as amended from time to time. *Natural Health Products Regulations*, SOR/2003-196, s. 1.

COMPENSABLE INJURY. A personal injury to a worker for which the worker is entitled to receive benefits under the workers' compensation system. A personal injury arising out of and in the course of employment.

COMPENSATION. *n.* 1. " . . . [A]n equitable monetary remedy which is available when the equitable remedies of restitution and account are not appropriate. By analogy with restitution, it attempts to restore to the plaintiff what has been lost as a result of the breach, . . ." *Canson Enterprises Ltd. v. Boughton & Co.* (1991), 9 C.C.L.T. (2d) 1 at 41, [1991] 1 W.W.R. 245, 61 B.C.L.R. (2d) 1, 85 D.L.R. (4th) 129, 131 N.R. 321, 43 E.T.R. 201, 39 C.P.R. (3d) 449, [1991] 3 S.C.R. 534, 6 B.C.A.C. 1, 3 W.A.C. 1, McLachlin J. (Lamer C.J.C. and L'Heureux-Dubé J. concurring). 2. A rate, remuneration, reimbursement or consideration of any kind paid, payable, promised, demanded or received, directly or indirectly. 3. The total amount of money or value that is required to be paid in respect of land expropriated. 4. In expropriation proceedings, when a public body acts to acquire the property of a person, ". . . [T]he owner [of land taken] is made 'economicially whole'. . . ." *British Columbia (Minister of Highways) v. Richland Estates Ltd.* (1973), 4 L.C.R. 85 at 86 (B.C. C.A.), Farris C.J.B.C. 5. " . . . [T]he indemnity which the statute [Exchequer Court Act, R.S.C. 1906, c. 140] provides to the owners of lands which are compulsorily taken in, or injuriously affected by, the exercise of statutory powers." *John Pigott & Son v. R.* (1916), 53 S.C.R. 626 at 627, 32 D.L.R. 461, Fitzpatrick C.J. 6. " . . . [T]he term 'compensation' [in Criminal Code, R.S.C. 1970, c. C-34, ss. 653 and 654] covers the making of a financial payment as a replacement for property so taken, or as payment for damage to property as a result of the offence." *R. v. Groves* (1977), 39 C.R.N.S. 366 at 380, 17 O.R. (2d) 65, 37 C.C.C. (2d) 429, 79 D.L.R. (3d) 561 (H.C.), O'Driscoll J. 7. All payments and benefits paid or provided to or for the benefit of a person who performs functions that entitle the person to be paid a fixed or ascertainable

amount. *Pay Equity Act*, R.S.O. 1990, c. P.7, s. 1(1). 8. Gain or reward. 9. Indemnification, that which is necessary to restore an injured party to his former position, is the meaning in which [compensation] is used in these mortgage contracts. It is used in the sense of indemnification or recompense for such loss that the Credit Union may sustain by reason of the plaintiff exercising her right to prepay. I do find that the term "compensation", when used in regards to the first prepayment provision, that of three months interest on the amount prepaid, is used to reflect a penalty charged by the defendant. *Pfeiffer v. Pacific Coast Savings Credit Union*, 2000 CarswellBC 2541, 2000 BCSC 1472, 83 B.C.L.R. (3d) 147 (S.C.). See CRIMINAL INJURIES ~; IMPORT ~; TOLL, GAIN OR ~; WORKERS' ~.

COMPENSATION ASSOCIATION. A body corporate or unincorporated association the purpose of which is to provide compensation to claimants and policyholders of insolvent insurers.

COMPENSATION OF VICTIMS OF CRIME. Benefits provided by the government to victims of crime in the form of ex gratia payments.

COMPENSATION ORDER. A court by which a person is convicted or discharged may make an order requiring that person to pay compensation for any loss or damage to property resulting from the offence.

COMPENSATION PLAN. The provisions, however established, for the determination and administration and implementation of compensation, and includes such provisions contained in a collective agreement or established bilaterally between an employer and an employee, unilaterally by an employer of an employee, established by an arbitrator or an arbitration board or by or pursuant to an enactment. See DEFERRED ~; GROUP ~.

COMPENSATION RATES. Single rates of remuneration or ranges of rates of remuneration, including cost-of-living adjustments, or, where no such rates or ranges exist, any fixed or ascertainable amounts of remuneration.

COMPENSATORY DAMAGES. 1. Compensatory damages may include special damages for pecuniary loss. Compensatory damages embrace general damages and, if aggravating circumstances exist, aggravated damages. *Grassi v. WIC Radio Ltd.*, 2000 CarswellBC 209, 49

C.C.L.T. (2d) 65, [2000] 5 W.W.R. 119 (S.C.). 2. In a libel case, are intended to compensate the plaintiff for the injury which he or she sustained as a result of the lessening of his or her esteem in the eyes of the community, as well as for the injury caused to the plaintiff's feelings by the defendant's defamatory statements. *Hill v. Church of Scientology of Toronto* (1994), 18 O.R. (3d) 385 (C.A.). 3. "In assessing compensatory damages, the element of aggravation resulting from the defendant's conduct must be taken into account: ... not confined in their scope to pecuniary losses: ..." *Vogel v. Canadian Broadcasting Corp.* (1982), 1 C.C.L.T. 105 at 205, [1982] 3 W.W.R. 97, 35 B.C.L.R. 7 (S.C.), Esson J.

COMPENSATORY TIME OFF. 1. Time off in lieu of overtime pay. 2. Extra time off allowed when an employee's regular day off falls on a holiday.

COMPETENCE. *n.* 1. Jurisdiction. 2. Suitability and fitness. See SUBJECT MATTER ~; TERRITORIAL ~.

COMPETENCY. *n.* Testimonial competence comprehends: (1) the capacity to observe (including interpretation); (2) the capacity to recollect; and (3) the capacity to communicate. . .The judge must satisfy him- or herself that the witness possesses these capacities. Is the witness capable of observing what was happening? Is he or she capable of remembering what he or she observes? Can he or she communicate what he or she remembers? The goal is not to ensure that the evidence is credible, but only to assure that it meets the minimum threshold of being receivable. The enquiry is into *capacity* to perceive, recollect and communicate, not whether the witness *actually* perceived, recollects and can communicate about the events in question. *R. v. Marquard*, 1993 CarswellOnt 127, 25 C.R. (4th) 1, 159 N.R. 81, 66 O.A.C. 161, 85 C.C.C. (3d) 193, 108 D.L.R. (4th) 47, [1993] 4 S.C.R. 223 Per McLachlin, J. for the majority.

COMPETENT. *adj.* 1. Legally allowed to give evidence during a trial. 2. Having adequate skill and knowledge. 3. " ... '[Of sound mind, memory and understanding' ..." *McHugh v. Dooley* (1903), 10 B.C.R. 537 at 546 (S.C.), Martin J. See MENTALLY ~.

COMPETENT AUTHORITY. A person or body authorized by statute to perform the act or carry out the function in question.

COMPETENT COURT. 1. The Federal Court or any superior, county or district court, except where the context otherwise requires. *Commercial Arbitration Act*, R.S.C. 1985 (2d Supp.), c. 17, s. 6. 2. For the purposes of the International Law, a reference to "court" or "competent court", where in the context it means a court in New Brunswick, means The Court of Queen's Bench of New Brunswick except where the context otherwise requires. *International Commercial Arbitration Act*, C.S.N.B., c. I-12.2, s. 9.

COMPETENT JURISDICTION. See COURT OF ~.

COMPETENT PERSON. A person who, (a) is qualified because of knowledge, training and experience to organize the work and its performance, (b) is familiar with the provisions of this Act and the regulations that apply to the work, and (c) has knowledge of any potential or actual danger to health or safety in workplace. *Occupational Health and Safety Act*, R.S.O. 1990, c. O.1, s. 1(1).

COMPETITION. *n.* 1. A situation when two or more businesses seek customers in the same marketplace. 2. An event in which participants take part to demonstrate their skills or abilities in comparison to each other. See CLOSED ~; FREE ~; OPEN ~.

COMPETITION CAR. A four-wheeled vehicle designed for use exclusively on racing circuits. Canada regulations.

COMPETITION LAW. The law governing competition in the market place, corporate mergers, anti-trust legislation, franchising, pricing.

COMPETITION VEHICLE. A vehicle that is designed for use exclusively in closed-course competition and (*a*) bears a label affixed by the manufacturer stating, in both official languages, that the vehicle is a competition vehicle and is for use exclusively in closed-course competition, or (*b*) is accompanied by a signed declaration clearly indicating that the vehicle is a competition vehicle and is for use exclusively in closed-course competition. *Motor Vehicle Safety Regulations*, C.R.C. 1038, s. 2.

COMPILATION. *n.* 1. A work resulting from the selection or arrangement of literary, dramatic, musical or artistic works or of parts thereof, or a work resulting from the selection or arrangement of data. *Copyright Act*, R.S.C. 1985, c. C-42, s. 2. 2. Essentially, for a compilation of data to be original, it must be a work that was independently created by the author and which displays at least a minimal degree of skill, judgment and labour in its overall selection or arrangement. The threshold is low, but it does exist. *Tele-Direct (Publications) Inc. v. American Business Information Inc.* (1997), 1997 CarswellNat 2111, 221 N.R. 113, 154 D.L.R. (4th) 328, 76 C.P.R. (3d) 296, 134 F.T.R. 80 (note), [1998] 2 F.C. 22, 37 B.L.R. (2d) 101 (C.A.), Decary, J.A. for the court.

COMPLAINANT. *n*. 1. The victim of an alleged offence. *Criminal Code*, R.S.C. 1985, c. C-46, s. 2. 2. A person who lodges or files a formal complaint.

COMPLAINT. *n*. 1. "In a rape case, . . . any statement made by the alleged victim which, given circumstances of the case, will, if believed, be of some probative value in negating the adverse conclusions the trier of fact could draw as regards her credibility had she been silent." *R. v. Timm* (1981), 21 C.R. (3d) 209 at 229, [1981] 2 S.C.R. 315, 28 C.R. (3d) 133, [1981] 5 W.W.R. 577, 37 N.R. 204, 29 A.R. 509, 59 C.C.C. (2d) 396,124 D.L.R. (3d) 582, the court per Lamer J. 2. An allegation or allegations, made orally or in writing by a member of the public, concerning misconduct of a public officer or of a contravention or violation of a statute. 3. An extra-judicial statement concerning an offence made after the alleged commission of that offence to a person other than the accused by the person in respect of whom it is alleged to have been committed. *Military Rules of Evidence*, C.R.C., c. 1049, s. 31. 4. An extra-judicial statement concerning an offence or violation of a statute made after the alleged commission of that offence or violation of a statute to a person other than the accused or violator by the person in respect of whom the offence or violation is alleged to have been committed. 5. Includes identification of the complainant, the victim, the time during which the alleged violation took place, the location and nature of the alleged violation, the relevant section of the statute and an affirmation that the violation took place. 6. An expression of concern about the care provided or other aspects of the professional relationship which identifies a registrant of the governing body of a profession. See CLASS ~.

COMPLEMENT. *n*. The persons, including the master, who comprise the crew of a ship. See APPROVED ~.

COMPLETE. *v*. To finish.

COMPLETE. *adj*. Finished; entire.

COMPLETED. *adj*. Whenever used with reference to a contract for an improvement, means substantial performance, not necessarily total performance.

COMPLETED CONTRACT METHOD. "The completed contract or substantially completed contract method [of accounting recognizes profit only when the contract has been completed or substantially completed. The completed or substantially completed contract method has the advantage that costs are known or virtually known at the time the profit is taken." *Toromont Industrial Holdings Ltd.* v. *Thorne, Gunn, Helliwell & Christenson* (1975), 23 C.P.R. (2d) 59 at 77, 10 O.R. (2d) 65, 62 D.L.R. (3d) 225 (H.C.), Holland J.

COMPLETE DENTURE. A dental prosthesis supported by soft tissue which replaces the natural teeth and associated structures in an edentulous arch and is not attached to or supported by natural teeth or implants and which is removable by the patient. *Health Professions Act*, B.C. Reg.

COMPLETE HEAVY-DUTY VEHICLE. A heavy-duty vehicle having a GVWR of 6350 kg (14,000 pounds) or less that is powered by an Otto-cycle engine and that has a primary load carrying device or container attached at the time the vehicle leaves the control of the manufacturer of the engine. *On-Road Vehicle and Engine Emission Regulations*, SOR/2003-2, s. 1.

COMPLETE SURVEY. A survey which, in addition to the requirements for a block outline survey, defines on the ground every angle of every parcel.

COMPLETION. *n*. Full performance of a contract. *Lambton (County) v. Canadian Comstock Co.* (1959), 21 D.L.R. (2d) 689 at 695, [1960] S.C.R. 86, the court per Judson J. See CERTIFICATE OF ~; DATE OF ~.

COMPLETION BOND. A guarantee to the owner of property that the contractor will finish the job contracted. See PERFORMANCE BOND.

COMPLETION DATE. The date on which the total depth of a well is reached.

COMPLETION LOAN. The advance of the whole amount, minus costs, of a mortgage loan by a lender to a borrower when construction of the borrower's new building is completed, the lender has inspected the building and is satisfied..

COMPLETION OF THE CONTRACT. Substantial performance, not necessarily total performance, of the contract. *Mechanics' Lien acts.*

COMPLEX. *n*. Several related buildings in a setting. See APARTMENT ~; HOUSING OFFICE ~; RESIDENTIAL ~.

COMPLEX. *adj*. Having many interrelated parts, patterns or elements, difficult to understand fully.

COMPLIANCE. The distinction between the meaning of "compliance" and the meaning of "consent" is real. To consent means to actually agree and cooperate. Compliance has a more subtle meaning involving the failure to object. *R. c. Knox*, 1996 CarswellQue 1041, 202 N.R. 228, 109 C.C.C. (3d) 481, 23 M.V.R. (3d) 93, [1996] 3 S.C.R. 199, 38 C.R.R. (2d) 222, 139 D.L.R. (4th) 1, 1 C.R. (5th) 254 per Lamer, C.J.C. See SUBSTANTIAL ~.

COMPLIANCE ORDER. Either an order, like a quia timet order or order for specific performance, that someone take positive action, or an order, like an injunction, that certain conduct be stopped.

COMPLICE. *n*. An accomplice, an associate.

COMPLICITY. *n*. 1. Being an accomplice; being involved in crime or conspiracy. 2. The distinction between the meaning of "compliance" and the meaning of "consent" is real. To consent means to actually agree and cooperate. Compliance has a more subtle meaning involving the failure to object. *R. c. Knox*, 1996 CarswellQue 1041, 202 N.R. 228, 109 C.C.C. (3d) 481, 23 M.V.R. (3d) 93, [1996] 3 S.C.R. 199, 38 C.R.R. (2d) 222, 139 D.L.R. (4th) 1, 1 C.R. (5th) 254 per Lamer, C.J.C.

COMPLY. *v*. To conform; yield; accept.

COMPONENT. *n*. An individual unit of food that is combined as an individual unit of food with one or more other individual units of food to form an ingredient. Canada regulations. See PRESSURE ~; PRICE ~; VEHICLE ~.

COMPOSITE. See INDUSTRIAL ~.

COMPOSITE SAMPLE. (*a*) A quantity of effluent consisting of not less than three equal volumes or three volumes proportionate to flow that have been collected at approximately equal time intervals over a sampling period of not less than seven hours and not more than 24 hours; or (*b*) a quantity of effluent collected continuously at a constant rate or at a rate proportionate to the rate of flow of the effluent over a sampling period of not less than seven hours and not more than 24 hours. *Metal Mining Effluent Regulations,* SOR/2002-222, s. 1.

COMPOSITE UNIT. A pushing vessel and an associated pushed vessel that are rigidly connected and that are designed as a dedicated and integrated tug and barge combination. *Collision Regulations*, C.R.C., c. 1416, s. 2.

COMPOSITION. *n*. 1. An arrangement for the payment of debts. 2. Refers to the total number of judges of a court and number of judges who must be drawn from each different region. See FIREWORKS ~.

COMPOSITION OF MATTER. 1. If the words "composition of matter" [*Patent Act*, R.S.C. 1985, c. P-4, s. 2] are understood this broadly, then the other listed categories of invention, including "machine" and "manufacture", become redundant. This implies that "composition of matter" must be limited in some way. This phrase does not include higher forms of life. As a result a mouse was not patentable. *Harvard College v. Canada (Commissioner of Patents)*, 2002 SCC 76, Bastarache, J. for the majority. 2. An open-ended expression. Statutory subject matter must be framed broadly because by definition the *Patent Act* [R.S.C. 1985, c. P-4] must contemplate the unforeseeable. The definition is not expressly confined to inanimate matter, and the appellant Commissioner agrees that composition of organic and certain living matter can be patented. In the case of the oncomouse, the modified genetic material is a physical substance and therefore "matter". The fertilized mouse egg is a form of biological "matter". The combination of these two forms of matter by the process described in the disclosure is thus, as pointed out by Rothstein J.A. ([2000] 4 F.C. 528 (C.A.), at para. 120), a "composition of matter". *Harvard College v. Canada (Commissioner of Patents)*, [2002] 4 S.C.R. 45, Per Binnie J. (dissenting), (McLachlin C.J.C., Major and Arbour JJ. concurring).

COMPOS MENTIS. [L.] Sound mind.

COMPOST FACILITY. A waste management facility where waste, not including hazardous waste, is decomposed through a controlled bio-oxidation process that results in a stable humus-like material.

COMPOSTING. *n*. The treatment of waste by aerobic decomposition of organic matter by bacterial action for the production of stabilized humus.

COMPOUND. *v*. 1. To compromise; to effect a composition with a creditor. 2. To combine; to unite. 3. To charge interest on interest on a loan or debt. 4. To pay interest on the interest payable on a deposit or investment.

COMPOUND. *n*. See IGNITION ~.

COMPOUND. *adj*. Combined; added to.

COMPOUND FRACTURE. A fracture which communicates through a wound to the outside.

COMPOUND INTEREST. 1. Interest charged on interest. 2. "... [A]t periodic intervals unpaid interest is added to unpaid principal, and interest then begins to accrue on the aggregate sum ... To compound, the first overdue instalment is added to the principal, and the new amount ... commences to bear interest." *Elman v. Conto* (1978), 82 D.L.R. (3d) 742 at 747, 18 O.R. (2d) 449 (C.A.), the court per Arnup J.A.

COMPREHENSIVE COVERAGE. "... [A] form of automobile insurance that pays for loss or damage to the insured vehicle caused otherwise than by collision ..." *Turner v. Cooperative Fire & Casualty Co.* (1983), 1 C.C.L.I. 1 at 7, [1983] I.L.R. 1-1678, 147 D.L.R. (3d) 342, 58 N.S.R. (2d) 1, 123 A.P.R. 1 (C.A.), Macdonald J.A. (Morrison J.A. concurring).

COMPREHENSIVE INSURANCE. The obligation of the insurer pursuant to Part III to pay insurance money to an insured in the event of loss of or damage to a vehicle. *Automobile Accident Insurance Act*, R.S.S. 1978, c. A-35, s. 2.

COMPREHENSIVE PLAN OF DEVELOPMENT. A study of the development characteristics of a community or region, made for the purpose of formulating plans, reports or legal instruments to guide, control or otherwise influence the physical development of the community or region or any part thereof, where such plans, reports or legal instruments are an integral part of and are contained in and expressed by the study and include an examination of at least the population, land use, economic base and transportation characteristics of the community or region in terms of their existing conditions, trends and probable future conditions, together with a formulation of development proposals relating to those aspects of the community or region or any part thereof provided that the information contained in the study is in sufficient detail to permit the evaluation of the implications that the characteristics examined may have for any plans, reports or legal instruments designed to influence the physical development of the community or region or any part thereof.

COMPREHENSIVE ZONE SYSTEM. Regulations containing text and zoning maps designed to regulate the development or redevelopment of land.

COMPRESSED AIR. Air mechanically raised to a pressure higher than atmospheric pressure.

COMPRESSED-AIR PLANT. A plant in which pressure vessels contain, distribute or otherwise handle air under pressure of more than fifteen pounds.

COMPRESSED GAS. A gas or a combination of gases that is contained under pressure whether or not the gases are liquefied, vapourized, dissolved or in any combination of these states.

COMPRESSED GAS PLANT. *var*. **COMPRESSED-GAS PLANT**. A plant used for producing, manufacturing, transferring, storing, distributing or otherwise handling compressed gas.

COMPRESSED GAS SYSTEM. The complete installation of pressure vessels, piping, fittings, compressors, machinery and other equipment used for producing, manufacturing, transferring, storing, distributing or otherwise handling compressed gas.

COMPRESSED INFLAMMABLE GAS. Any product, material or mixture that (*a*) has a critical temperature less than 50°C, an absolute vapour pressure greater than 295 kPa at 50°C or an absolute pressure in a pressure vessel greater than 275 kPa at 21.1°C or 716 kPa at 54.4°C, and (*b*) is flammable when in a mixture of 13 per cent or less by volume with air at normal atmospheric temperature and pressure or has a flammable range with air wider than 12 per cent regardless of the lower limit. *Railway Prevention of Electric Sparks Regulations*, SOR/82-1015, s. 2.

COMPRESSED WORK WEEK. Longer hours worked each of a smaller number of days than is usual.

COMPRESSION INJURY. An injury caused when a force acts perpendicularly to the surface of a tissue or organ. F.A. Jaffe, *A Guide to Pathological Evidence*, 3d ed. (Toronto: Carswell, 1991) at 221.

COMPRESSOR PLANT. Includes the machinery and equipment used for compressing or storing air or other gas under pressure.

COMPRISING. *v.* In a deed, made up of, consisting of, namely.

COMPROMISE. *v.* To settle differences, claims and to reach an agreement as to those differences or claims.

COMPROMISE. *n.* 1.The settlement of an action by agreement under which the plaintiff agrees not to take action and the intended defendant makes a promise in return. 2. An arrangement between a company and its shareholders and creditors. 3. An arrangement for the taxpayer to pay a lesser amount than the full amount of taxes owed and for the taxing authority to accept that lesser amount in order to settle the matter with the taxing authority.

COMPROMISSARII SUNT JUDICES. [L.] Those who arbitrate are judges.

COMP. TRIB. *abbr.* Competition Tribunal.

COMPTROLLER. *n.* 1. One who examines the accounts of collectors of public money. 2. The senior financial officer of a company or organization. See CONTROLLER.

COMPULSION. *n.* 1. Duress; force. 2. The overbearing nature of statements or conduct such that the person speaking or acting is able to control the conduct of the person to whom the statements or conduct are directed. See PRACTICAL ~.

COMPULSORY. *adj.* Forced; coerced; mandatory, required.

COMPULSORY ARBITRATION. Arbitration that is required by law.

COMPULSORY LICENCE. A licence of a patent which is mandated for production of medicine or food in certain circumstances and one which is mandated if there has been an abuse of exclusive rights.

COMPULSORY PILOTAGE. In respect of a ship, the requirement that the ship be under the conduct of a licensed pilot or the holder of a pilotage certificate.

COMPULSORY PILOTAGE AREA. An area of water in which ships are subject to compulsory pilotage.

COMPULSORY PURCHASE. To acquire land for public purposes.

COMPULSORY RETIREMENT AGE. 65 years of age.

COMPULSORY SCHOOL AGE. Over the age of 7 years and under the age of 16 years.

COMPULSORY SCHOOL ATTENDANCE. The attendance of a child at school that is required by statute.

COMPULSORY SCHOOL LAW. A statute requiring children to attend school.

COMPULSORY TRUCE. A cooling-off period imposed by statute during which a labour dispute is investigated by an official agency, and strikes and lock-outs are prohibited.

COMPULSORY UNIONISM. Employment conditional on union membership.

COMPURGATION. *n.* "Oath-helping . . . a method used to prove one's case in pre-Norman England. The accused in a criminal case or the defendant in a civil case could prove his innocence by providing a certain number of compurgators who would swear the truth of his oath. The compurgators swore a set oath. If they departed from it in the slightest, the 'oath burst' and the opposing party won. The practice fell into desuetude in the 13th century." *R. c. Béland* (1987), 60 C.R. (3d) 1 at 44, 79 N.R. 263 9 Q.A.C. 293, [1987] 2 S.C.R. 398, 36 C.C.C. (3d) 481, 43 D.L.R. (4th) 641, Wilson J. (dissenting) (Lamer J. concurring).

COMPURGATOR. *n.* A person who swore that she or he believed the accused in a criminal matter or the defendant in a civil matter.

COMPUTER. *n.* 1. " . . . [F]unction . . . is to permit the making of complex calculations, to process and correlate information and to store it, and to enable it to be retrieved." *R. v McLaughlin* (1980),113 D.L.R. (3d) 386 at 390, [1980] 2 S.C.R. 331, 32 N.R. 350, [1981] 1 W.W.R. 298, 53 C.C.C. (2d) 417, Laskin C.J.C. 2. " . . . [A] complex system of interconnected, integrated electrical circuits. It consists of a circuit board ('mother board') into which have been pinned or soldered a number of electronic components. The components communicate with one another by means of the traces (sometimes called buses, sometimes called wires) etched into the board. The main electronic components of the system are the input-output devices, the microprocessor (CPU) and the memory." *Apple Computer Inc. v. Mackintosh Computers Ltd.* (1986), 10 C.P.R. (3d) 1 at 12, 8 C.I.P.R. 153, 3 F.T.R. 118, [1987]

1 F.C. 173, 28 D.L.R. (4th) 178 (T.D.), Reed J. See DUAL ~.

COMPUTER L. *abbr*. Computer Law.

COMPUTER LANGUAGE. ". . . [A] code for writing a program. A language is said to be 'higher' or lower' depending upon the ease with which it can be read . . ." *Apple Computer Inc. v. Mackintosh Computers Ltd.* (1986), 10 C.P.R. (3d) 1 at 7, 8 C.I.P.R. 153, 3 F.T.R. 118, [1987] 1 F.C. 173, 28 D.L.R. (4th) 178 (T.D.), Reed J.

COMPUTER PASSWORD. Any data by which a computer service or computer system is capable of being obtained or used.

COMPUTER PROGRAM. 1. Data representing instructions or statements that, when executed in a computer system, causes the computer system to perform a function. *Criminal Code*, R.S.C. 1985, c. C-46, s. 342.1(2), as added by *Criminal Law Amendment Act*, R.S.C. 1985 (1st Supp.), c. 27, s. 45. 2. A set of instructions or statements, expressed, fixed, embodied or stored in any manner, that is to be used directly or indirectly in a computer in order to bring about a specific result. *Copyright Act*, S.C. 1989, c. 15, s. 1(3).

COMPUTER SERVICE. Includes data processing and the storage or retrieval of data. *Criminal Code*, R.S.C. 1985, c. C-46, s. 342.1(2) as added by *Criminal Law Amendment Act*, R.S.C. 1985 (1st Supp.), c. 27, s. 45.

COMPUTER SOFTWARE. Packaged or prewritten computer software programs that are designed for general application, or the right to use those programs, and includes modifications to those programs.

COMPUTER SYSTEM. A device that, or a group of interconnected or related devices one or more of which, (a) contains computer programs or other data, and (b) pursuant to computer programs, (i) performs logic and control, and (ii) may perform any other function. *Criminal Code*, R.S.C. 1985, c. C-46, s. 342.1(2) as added by *Criminal Law Amendment Act*, R.S.C. 1985 (1st Supp.), c. 27, s. 45.

CON. *v*. To deceive, to trick.

CON. *adj*. Short form for confidence, as a "con game".

CON. *prep*. [L.] 1. With. 2. Against

CON. *pref*. 1. Together. 2. Against

CONCEAL. *v*. To hide, cover, keep from view; to prevent discovery.

CONCEALED. *adj*. 1. "[In R. v. Lemire (1980), 18 C.R. (3d) 166 at 170 (B.C. Co. Ct.)] Melvin Co. Ct. J. (as he was then) . . . reviewed the authorities and dictionary definitions of the word 'concealed' [as used in s. 87 of the Criminal Code, R.S.C. 1970, c. C-34]: 'In my view, the definition of the word "conceal" clearly demonstrates that some purpose is required in addition to the object being merely not capable of being seen. To conceal, in a sense of keeping from the knowledge or observation of others or hide, imports into this offence regarding the act of concealment a mental element on the part of the accused . . . ' . . . The mens rea articulated by Mr. Justice Cavanaugh [in R. v. Coughlan (1974), 27 C.R.N.S. 195 at 195 (Alta. Q.B.)] for a interpretation of the word 'concealed' was[:] 'In : 'In m view, these definitions clearly impart the idea of an intentional putting out of sight for the purpose of being out of sight.'" *R. v. Felawka* (1991), 9 C.R. (4th) 291 at 297, 303, 68 C.C.C. (3d) 481, 3 B.C.A.C. 241, 7 W.A.C. 241, Toy J.A. (McEachern C.J.B.C., Wallace and Proudfoot JJ.A. concurring). 2. Rendered permanently inaccessible by the structure or finish of a building.

CONCEALED DANGER. A deceptively safe appearance which hides a potential cause of injury.

CONCEALING BODY OF CHILD. It is an offence to dispose of the dead body of a child with intent to conceal the fact that its mother has been delivered of it whether it died before, during or after birth. *Criminal Code*, R.S.C. 1985, c. C-46, s. 243.

CONCEALMENT. *n*. In insurance law describes the situation when an applicant for insurance fails to inform the insurer of a material fact which is known to the applicant. See HEADLAMP ~ DEVICE.

CONCEALMENT OF BIRTH. See CONCEALING BODY OF CHILD.

CONCEALS. *v*. " . . . [A]s used in s. 350(a)(ii) [of the Criminal Code, R.S.C. 1970, c. C-34] contemplates some positive conduct on the part of the debtor [to conceal assets] as opposed to a mere failure to disclose the existence of the property, even though under a duty to do so under the Bankruptcy Act, R.S.C. 1970, c. B-3, ss. 129 and 132]." *R. v Goulis* (1981), 125 D.L.R. (3d)137 at 142, 33 O.R. (2d) 55, 20 C.R. (3d) 360, 37 C.B.R. (N.S.) 290, 60 C.C.C. (2d) 347 (C.A.), the court per Martin J.A. See CONCEAL.

CONCENTRATE. *v*. To separate and accumulate valuable minerals from gangue in one or more stages by removing the valuable minerals from it to form a concentrate without changing the chemical identity of these minerals.

CONCENTRATE. *n*. See APPLE JUICE FROM ~.

CONCENTRATION. *n*. Any treatment of ore, reject or tailing to separate a mineral substance from its gangue and obtain a concentrate.

CONCEPTION. *n*. The beginning of pregnancy; fertilization of the ovum by spermatozoon.

CONCERN. *v*. To relate, be of interest or importance to. See PERSON ~ ED.

CONCERNING. *adj*. Relating to; affecting.

CONCERT. *n*. 1. Agreement. 2. To act in concert is to act together to bring about a planned result.

CONCERTED ACTIVITIES. Employees acting together to achieve improvements in conditions of work.

CONCESSI. [L.] I granted.

CONCESSIMUS. [L.] We granted.

CONCESSION. *n*. 1. A tier of township lots. *Surveys Act*, R.S.O. 1990, c. S.30, s.1. 2. A public authority grants land to a private person to establish something, i.e. an industry, a railway. 3. A grant by an owner of a place of amusement or business to a person permitting them to perform a service or sell articles on the premises. See BROKEN ~; FOREST ~; MINING ~; TAX ~; UNDERGROUND MINING ~.

CONCESSION OPERATOR. A person holding a concession, right or privilege to perform any service or sell any articles at a particular location.

CONCESSIO VERSUS CONCEDENTEM LATAM INTERPRETATIONEM HABERE DEBET. [L.] A grant should be given a wide interpretation, that is to be strictly construed against the grantor.

CONCESSIT SOLVERE. [L.] One granted and one agreed to pay.

CONCESSOR. *n*. One who grants.

CONCILIATION. *n*. The process by which a third party attempts to assist an employer and a trade union to achieve a collective agreement.

CONCILIATION BOARD. A board established under labour legislation for the investigation and conciliation of a dispute.

CONCILIATION COMMISSIONER. A person appointed by the Minister of Labour under the Labour Code. *Labour Code*, R.S.C. 1985, c. L-2, s. 3.

CONCILIATION OFFICER. A person whose duties include the conciliation of disputes and who is under the control and direction of the Minister of Labour or other Minister.

CONCILIATOR. *n*. A person appointed to assist the parties to collective bargaining in reaching agreement.

CONCILIUM. *n*. [L.] A court; the time and place set for a meeting.

CONCLUDE. *v*. To finish; to bar or estop.

CONCLUDED CONTRACT. " . . . [O]ne which settles everything that is necessary to be settled, and leaves nothing still to be settled by agreement between the parties. Of course, it may leave something which still has to be determined, but then that determination must be a determination which does not depend on the agreement between the parties." *May & Butcher Ltd. v. R.*, [1929] All E.R. Rep. 679 at 683-84 (U.K. H.L.), Viscount Dunedin.

CONCLUSION. *n*. 1. The finish, end, summation. 2. A rule of law or an irrefutable presumption.

CONCLUSION OF FACT. An inference or result drawn from evidence.

CONCLUSION OF LAW. A finding of law; a statement of law applicable to a matter.

CONCLUSIVE. *adj*. Final, decisive, clear.

CONCLUSIVE PRESUMPTION. A presumption where when one fact is proven, another fact must be taken as true and beyond dispute by a party opposing the presumption or its effect.

CONCORD. *n*. An agreement to settle or refrain from bringing an action.

CONCORDAT. *n*. 1. An agreement between two or more governments. 2. A treaty or agreement between the Pope and a head of state.

CONCUBINAGE. *n*. " . . . [I]mplies a cohabitation extending over an appreciable period of time . . ." *Wilson, Re*, [1938] 1 W.W.R. 856 at 856 (B.C. S.C.), Fisher J.

CONCUBINE. *n.* A woman who cohabits with a man. *Wilson, Re*, [1938] 1 W.W.R. 856 at 856 (B.C. S.C.), Fisher J.

CONCUR. *v.* 1. To agree, consent. 2. "... [A]s used in [s. 4 of the Trade-unions Act, R.S.B.C. 1960, c. 384] means 'to combine in action' or to 'co-operate with' ..." *Perini Pacific Ltd. v. I.U.O.E, Local 115* (1961), 36 W.W.R. 49 at 66, 28 D.L.R. (2d) 727 (B.C. S.C.), Monroe J.

CONCURRENCE. *n.* Agreement, consent.

CONCURRENT. *adj.* Contemporaneous.

CONCURRENT CAUSE. A cause acting contemporaneously with another cause and together causing injury which would not have occurred in the absence of either cause.

CONCURRENT JURISDICTION. Two or more courts or tribunals having authority to try or hear the same subject matter.

CONCURRENTLY. *adv.* At the same time, contemporaneously.

CONCURRENT NEGLIGENCE. The failure of two or more persons to fulfil their duty of care to a third person. Generally requires contribution between the tortfeasors.

CONCURRENT SENTENCE. Two or more terms of imprisonment served simultaneously.

CONCURRENT WRIT. A duplicate of an original writ. See ALIAS WRIT.

CONCURRING OPINION. The decision of a judge agreeing in the decision though not necessarily the reasons of another judge or judges.

CONCUSSION. *n.* A violent impact causing diffuse injury to an organ.

CONDEMN. *v.* 1. To find guilty. 2. To sentence. 3. In admiralty law, to find that a vessel is a prize or that the vessel is unfit. 4. To expropriate. 5. To declare a building unfit for use or occupation. 6. In relation to a food animal or a meat product, means to determine that the food animal or meat product is unfit for human or animal food.

CONDEMNATION. *n.* 1. An order that a building is unfit for use or occupation. 2. Expropriation. 3 . A judgment that a prize or captured vessel has been lawfully captured or that the vessel is unfit.

CONDENSATE. *n.* A mixture consisting mainly of pentanes and heavier hydrocarbons that is recovered or recoverable through a well from a reservoir and that might be gaseous in its virgin reservoir state but is liquid at the conditions under which its volume is measured or estimated.

CONDENSED MILK. Milk from which water has been evaporated and to which sugar or dextrose, or both, with or without added vitamin D, have been added.

CONDENSERY. See MILK ~.

CONDITIO BENEFICIALIS QUAESTATUM CONSTRUIT, BENIGNE, SECUNDUM VERBORUM INTENTIONEM, EST INTERPRETANDA; ODIOSA, AUTEM, QUAE STATUM DESTRUIT, STRICTE, SECUNDUM VERBORUM PROPRIETATEM, ACCIPIENDA. [L.] A beneficial condition which creates an estate should be interpreted generously, according to the intention behind the words; but a condition which destroys an estate is undesirable and should be interpreted strictly.

CONDITIO DICITUR CUM QUID IN CASUM INCERTUM QUI POTEST TENDERE AD ESSE AUT NON ESSE CONFERTUR. [L.] When something is given on an uncertain event which may or may not come into existence, it is called a condition.

CONDITION. *n.* 1. A provision in an agreement or declaration that contains an event which must occur or an action that must be taken before other provisions of the same agreement or declaration come into force or occur or are required. 2. "... [A] contractual term which the parties intended to be fundamental to its performance." *Jorian Properties Ltd. v. Zellenrath* (1984), 26 B.L.R. 276 at 285, 4 O.A.C. 107, 46 O.R. (2d) 775, 26 B.C.L.R. 276, 10 D.L.R. (4th) 458 (C.A.), Blair J.A. (dissenting). 3. "... [O]f the parties [in s. 11(1) of the Divorce Act, R.S.C. 1970, c. D-8] includes their ages; their states of health, both physical and mental; their backgrounds; their education; their attitude toward family; their motives for seeking custody; their comparative abilities to provide psycological [sic], spiritual and emotional needs of the children; their respective modes of living; and so on." *Burgmaier v. Burgmaier* (1986), 50 R.F.L. (2d) 1 at 11, 46 Sask. R. 1 (C.A.), the court per Cameron J.A. 4. Includes a warranty, representation or proviso. 5. An observable medical symptom, sign or condition, or combination of related medical symptoms, signs or conditions. See DEPENDENT ~; EXPRESS ~; IMPLIED ~; INSANITARY ~; LOADED ~;

PERMISSIBLE ~; PRECEDENT ~; PREEXISTING OR UNDERLYING ~; RESOLUTIVE ~; RESOLUTORY ~; SANITARY ~; TURNING-OUT ~; WORKING ~S.

CONDITIONAL. *adj*. Dependent upon, subject to.

CONDITIONAL ACCEPTANCE. The acceptor pays only when a condition stated in the bill is fulfilled.

CONDITIONAL ADMISSIBILITY. Evidence is admitted until it is examined further.

CONDITIONAL APPEARANCE. 1. "Middleton J. in Wolsely Tool & Motor Car v. Jackson Potts & Co. (1914), 6 O.W.N. 109 (H.C.), described the conditional appearance as follows: 'A conditional appearance is not intended to be a provisional appearance, as in England, but a form of appearance to be used where for some reason it is not convenient to determine the question whether the case can be brought within Rule 25 until the hearing of the action.' " *Sea Electronics Aids Inc. v. Kaytronics Ltd*. (1979), 11 C.P.C. 275 at 277, 24 O.R. (2d) 38 (H.C.), Grange J. 2. A motion filed by a defendant, with leave of the Court, to object to an irregularity in the commencement of the proceeding or the court's jurisdiction.

CONDITIONAL BENEFIT. A benefit which may be received only if the potential recipient is not awarded damages in a tort action for the same loss which the benefit is supposed to compensate.

CONDITIONAL DEBT. A debt the payment of which is dependent upon a fact which may never happen.

CONDITIONAL DISCHARGE. 1. Disposition of a criminal matter by which a person is deemed not to be convicted after serving a period of probation. Sentence which may be imposed upon conviction for a criminal offence. 2. " . . . [P]uts the accused conditionally, at liberty, . . ." *Ahluwalia, Re* (1989), 25 F.T.R. 208 at 217, [1989] 3 F.C. 209, Muldoon J.

CONDITIONAL LICENCE. A licence authorizing an activity prior to the issue of a final licence.

CONDITIONAL OFFER. 1. An offer which is not final until a condition is fulfilled. 2. A proposal to settle a strike with reservations.

CONDITIONAL SALE. 1. A contract for the sale of goods under which possession is to be delivered to a buyer and the property in the goods is to vest in her or him at a subsequent time on payment of the whole or part of the price or on the performance of an other condition. 2. A contact for the hiring on goods under which it is agreed that the hirer will become or have the option of becoming the owner of the goods on compliance with the terms of the contract.

CONDITIONAL SENTENCE. 1. Where a person is convicted of an offence, except an offence that is punishable by a minimum term of imprisonment, and the court (a) imposes a sentence of imprisonment of less than two years, and (b) is satisfied that serving the sentence in the community would not endanger the safety of the community and would be consistent with the fundamental purpose and principles of sentencing set out in the Code, the court may, for the purpose of supervising the offender's behaviour in the community, order that the offender serve the sentence in the community, subject to the offender's complying with the conditions of a conditional sentence order. *Criminal Code*, R.S.C. 1985, c. C-46, s. 742.1. 2. Incorporates some elements of a non- custodial sentence and some of a custodial sentence. It will generally be more effective in achieving restorative goals of sentencing than a carceral sentence because it is served in the community. It is however a punitive sanction and therefore capable of satisfying the objectives of denunciation and deterrence. It is this punitive aspect that distinguishes the conditional sentence from probation. A sentence under s. 742.1 is not just a choice between imprisonment or not. It is a community-based sentence that permits a great deal of creativity for fulfilling the objectives outlined in ss. 718 to 718.2 as well as establishing consequences for a breach of the sentence. . . Parliament, in a typically Canadian way, has tried to blend traditional retributive goals of sentencing with concepts of restorative justice. *R. v. Laliberte*, 2000 SKCA 27, 31 C.R. (5th) 1, [2000] 4 W.W.R. 491, 143 C.C.C. (3d) 503, 189 Sask. R. 190 (C.A.).

CONDITIONAL WILL. A will which takes effect only in the event of the testator's death in a certain way, such as by accident, or during a certain period, such as on a trip; the will does not take effect unless the specified condition is met.

CONDITION DEFECT. Any defect that may develop in an agricultural product during storage or transit.

CONDITIONER. *n*. See WATER ~.

CONDITIONES QUAELIBET ODIOSAE; MAXIME AUTEM CONTRA MATRIMONIUM ET COMMERCIUM. [L.] All conditions are objectionable, but especially those which are in restraint of marriage and trade.

CONDITION OF EMPLOYMENT. 1. A qualification or circumstance required for employment. 2. All matters and circumstances in any way affecting employers and employees it respect of the employment relationship.

CONDITION OF SALE. A term upon which an interest is to be sold by auction or tender.

CONDITION PRECEDENT. " . . . [A]n external condition upon which the existence of the obligation depends . . . a future uncertain event the happening of which depends entirely upon the will of a third party . . ." *Turney v. Zhilka*, [1959] S.C.R. 578 at 583, Judson J. See TRUE ~.

CONDITION SUBSEQUENT. 1. A term of an agreement requiring that the agreement be valid and binding unless and until a specified event or occurrence happens. 2. After a gift is made, a condition subsequent may operate to defeat the gift.

CONDITIO PRAECEDENS ADIMPLERI DEBET PRIUSQUAM SEQUATUR EFFECTUS. [L.] The condition precedent must be fulfilled before any effect can follow.

CONDO. *abbr.* Condominium.

CONDOM. *n.* A sheath or covering intended to be worn on the penis during coitus for the purpose of preventing conception or reducing the risk of transmission of disease.

CONDOMINIUM. *n.* 1. A system of property ownership of multi-unit housing or commercial projects in which each unit owner is a tenant-in-common of the common elements and each unit is owned separately in fee simple. 2. Two or more subjects of international law jointly exercise sovereignty over one territory. See TIME-SHARING ~.

CONDOMINIUM PLAN. A plan that (i) is described in the heading thereto as a condominium plan; (ii) shows the whole or any part of the building included therein as being divided into two or more units; and (iii) complies with the requirements of the legislation.

CONDOMINIUM PROJECT. The lands and interests appurtenant thereto that are described or proposed to be described in any description required by the Condominium Act and which include or are proposed to include units to be used as homes.

CONDOMINIUM UNIT. A bounded space in a building designated or described as a unit on a registered condominium or strata lot plan or description, or a similar plan or description registered pursuant to the laws of a province, and intended for human habitation and includes any interest in land appertaining to ownership of the unit. *National Housing Act*, R.S.C. 1985, c. N-11, s. 2.

CONDONATION. *n.* 1. Acquiescence, forgiveness. 2. " . . . [T]he reinstatement in his or her former marital position of a spouse who has committed a matrimonial wrong of which all material facts are known to the other spouse, with the intention of forgiving and remitting the wrong, on condition that the spouse whose wrong is so condoned does not thenceforward commit any further matrimonial offence." *MacDougall v. MacDougall*, [1970] 3 R.F.L. 175 at 176 (Ont. C.A.). 3. "In *McIntyre v. Hockin* (1889),16 O.A.R. 498 [(C.A.)], Maclennan J.A., speaking for the Court, said at pp. 501-502: 'If [the employer] retains the servant in his employment for any considerable time after discovering his fault that is condonation, and he cannot afterwards dismiss for that fault without anything new. No doubt the employer ought to have a reasonable time to determine what to do, to consider whether he will dismiss or not, or to look for another servant. So, also, he must have knowledge of the nature and extent of the fault, for he cannot forgive or condone matters of which he is not full informed. Further, condonation is subject to an implied condition of future good conduct, and whenever any new misconduct occurs, the old offences may be invoked and may be put on the scale against the offender as cause for dismissal.' " *Nossal v. Better Business Bureau of Metropolitan Toronto* (1985), 12 C.C.E.L. 85 at 89, 51 O.R. (2d) 279, 19 D.L.R. (4th) 547, 9 O.A.C. 184 (C.A.), the court per Zuber J.A.

CONDUCIVE. *v.* Tending to a specific end, bringing about, leading to a particular result.

CONDUCT. *v.* 1. To manage or operate. *Saskatchewan Telecommunications v. Central Asphalt Ltd.* (1988), 70 Sask. R. 235 at 239, [1988] 6 W.W.R. 459 (Q.B.), Wright J. 2. To lead or guide. *R. v. Mackenzie* (1982),135 D.L.R. (3d) 374 at 379, 36 O.R. (2d) 562, 66 C.C.C. (2d) 528 (C.A.), the court per Cory J.A.

CONDUCT. *n.* 1. Any act or omission. 2. Personal behaviour. 3. ' . . . [I]ncludes the role of the parties in the break-up of the home; their behaviour in relation to one another, the children, and the family, both before and after the break-up; such agreements, if any, as they may have arrived at; and such other conduct tending to demonstrate their characters, personalities and temperaments, and other matters bearing upon their abilities to rear the children." *Burgmaier v. Burgmaier* (1986), 50 R.F.L. (2d) 1 at 10, 46 Sask. R. 1 (C.A.), the court per Cameron J.A. See CODE OF ~; CORRUPT ~; EXCUSABLE ~; IMPROPER ~; MIS~; SAFE~; UNPROFESSIONAL ~.

CONDUCT CRIME. The conduct, the behaviour, of the accused is itself a crime. No particular result is required to constitute a conduct crime.

CONDUCTIO. See CONTRACT OF LOCATIO ET ~.

CONDUCT MONEY. 1. Fees payable to witnesses to defray expenses of coming to testify. 2. Attendance money.

CONDUCTOR. *n.* 1. A wire, cable or other form of metal installed for the purpose of conveying electric current from one piece of electrical equipment to another or to ground. 2: A person in charge or having the chief direction of any railway train. See BRANCH-~; DEAD-END ~; DOWN-~; GROUNDING ~; NEUTRAL ~.

CONDUCT UNBECOMING. Any act or conduct, whether or not disgraceful or dishonourable, which (i) is inimical to the best interests of the public or the members of the society; or (ii) tends to harm the standing of the legal profession generally. *Legal Profession Amendment Act 1981*, S.S. 1980-81, c. 64, s. 3.

CONDUCT UNBECOMING A LAWYER. Includes a matter, conduct or thing that is considered, in the judgment of the benchers or a panel, (a) to be contrary to the best interest of the public or of the legal profession, or (b) to harm the standing of the legal profession. *Legal Profession Act*, S.B.C. 1998, c. 9, s. 1.

CONDUIT. *n.* 1. i. A sewer, ii. a water main, iii. a duct or cable for a telegraphic, telephonic, television or electrical service, iv. a pipe or duct for the transportation of any solid, liquid or gas. 2. A raceway of circular cross-section into which it is intended that conductors be drawn.

CONE OF SILENCE. " . . . Knowledge of confidential matters is therefore imputed to other members of the firm. This latter presumption can, however, in some circumstances, be rebutted. The usual methods used to rebut the presumptions are the setting up of a . . . 'cone of silence' . . . at the time that the possibility of the unauthorized communication of confidential information arises . . . A 'cone of silence' is achieved by means of a solemn undertaking not to disclose by the tainted solicitor." *MacDonald Estate v. Martin* (1990), 48 C.P.C. (2d) 113 at 126, [1991] 1 W.W.R. 705, 121 N.R. 1, 77 D.L.R. (4th) 249, 70 Man. R. (2d) 241, [1990] 3 S.C.R. 1235, Sopinka J. (Dickson C.J.C., La Forest and Gonthier JJ. concurring). See CHINESE WALL.

CONFABULATE. *v.* To fabricate facts or events which the person cannot recall.

CONF. COMMEM. MEREDITH. *abbr.* Conférences commémoratives Meredith (Meredith Memorial Lectures).

CONFECTIONER. *n.* A person, firm, or corporation, who sells by retail only all or any of the following: biscuits, plain or fancy, bon-bons, cakes, candied gums, candies, chewing gum, chocolate bars, chocolates, ice cream, ice cream cones, pastries, popcorn, confectionery, bread, milk, butter, or soft drinks. *Shops Regulation Act*, C.S.S.M., c. S110, s. 3.

CONFECTIONS. *n.* Includes chocolate coated nuts and preparations of fruits, nuts or popcorn in combination with chocolate, sugar or honey. *Retail Sales Tax Act*, R.R.O. 1990, Reg. 1013, s. 1.

CONFEDERACY. *n.* In international law, two or more states joined for their mutual welfare.

CONFEDERATION. *n.* 1. The joining together of the original four provinces into the Dominion of Canada on July 1, 1867. 2. A loose association of states in which the state governments take precedence over the central government. 3. A league of nations or states. 4. A compact for mutual support.

CONFER. *v.* Grant or bestow. *Minister of National Revenue v. Pillsbury Holdings Ltd*, [1964] C.T.C. 294 at 300, [1965] 1 Ex. C.R. 676, 64 D.T.C. 5184, Cattanach J.

CONFERENCE. *n.* 1. A meeting of persons for consideration of matters, exchange of opinions. 2. An association of organizations or businesses for a particular purpose. 3. A group of persons who are convened to give advice in accordance with section 19. A youth justice court judge, the provincial director, a police officer, a justice of the peace, a prosecutor or a youth worker may convene or cause to be convened a conference for the purpose of making a decision required to be made. The mandate of a conference may be, among other things, to give advice on appropriate extrajudicial measures, conditions for judicial interim release, sentences, including the review of sentences, and reintegration plans. *Youth Criminal Justice Act*, S.C. 2002, c. 1, ss. 2, 19. The representative assembly of a church. 4. An association of athletic teams. 5. An association of ocean carriers that has the purpose or effect of regulating rates and conditions for the transportation by those ocean carriers of goods by water. *Shipping Conferences Exemption Act, 1987*, S.C. 1987, c. 22, s. 2(1). See FIRST MINISTERS' ~; PRE-TRIAL ~; SHIPPING ~.

CONFESS. *v.* To admit; to concede.

CONFESSIO FACTA IN JUDICIO OMNI PROBATIONE MAJOR EST. [L.] An admission made during judicial proceedings has greater weight than any proof.

CONFESSION. *n.* 1. An admission of guilt. 2. In civil procedure, a formal admission. 3. Formerly, a plea of guilty. F. Kaufman, *The Admissibility of Confessions*, 3d ed. (Toronto: Carswell, 1980) at 1. 4. " . . . [S]tatements made by an accused to a person in authority; . . ." *R. v. Rothman* (1981), 20 C.R. (3d) 97 at 122, [1981] 1 S.C.R. 640, 59 C.C.C. (2d) 30, 121 D.L.R. (3d) 578, 35 N.R. 485, Estey J. (dissenting) (Laskin C.J.C. concurring). 5. A statement made by an accused person, whether before or after he is accused of an offence, that is completely or partially self-incriminating with respect to the offence of which he is accused. *Military Rules of Evidence*, C.R.C., c. 1049, s. 2. See EXCULPATORY ~; INCULPATORY ~; VOLUNTARY STATEMENT ~.

CONFESSION AND AVOIDANCE. 1. A pleading in which, though the defendant admits the plaintiff's allegation, the defendant then sets out other facts which deprive the allegation of the legal consequences for which the plaintiff argued. 2. " . . . [A] submission [by the defendant] that if the plaintiff's allegations are true there are facts which provide a legal justification for the defendant's conduct . . ." *Royal Bank v. Rizkalla* (1984), 50 C.P.C. 292 at 295, 59 B.C.L.R. 324 (S.C.), McLachlin J.

CONFESSIONS RULE. In its modern formulation the confessions rule postulates that any statement by an accused to a person in authority will be disallowed as evidence on the basis of an inducement negating voluntariness if there is a reasonable doubt about whether the quid pro quo offer that it conveys caused the will of the accused to be overborne. *R v. Tessier*, 2001 NBCA 34, 153 C.C.C. (3d) 361, 41 C.R. (5th) 242, 245 N.B.R. (2d) 1, 636 A.P.R. 1 (C.A.).

CONFESSES IN JUDICIO PRO JUDICATO HABETUR, ET QUODAMMODO SUA SENTENTIA DAMNATUR. [L.] Those who make confessions are held to have decided their own cases against themselves.

CONFIDENCE. *n.* 1. Trust, reliance. 2. A communication made in reliance on another's discretion. See BREACH OF ~.

CONFIDENCE GAME. Obtaining money or property by a trick or device.

CONFIDENCE OF THE QUEEN'S PRIVY COUNCIL FOR CANADA. Includes, without restricting the generality thereof, information contained in (a) a memorandum the purpose of which is to present proposals or recommendations to Council; (b) a discussion the purpose of which is to present background paper explanations analyses of problems or policy options to Council for consideration by Council in making decisions; (c) an agendum of Council or a record recording deliberations or decisions of Council; (d) a record used for or reflecting communications or discussion between ministers of the Crown on matters relating to the making of government decisions or the formulation of government policy; (e) a record the purpose of which is to brief Ministers of the Crown in relation to matters that are brought before, or are proposed to be brought before, Council or that are the subject of communications or discussion referred to in paragraph (d); and (f) draft legislation. *Canada Evidence Act*, R.S.C. 1985, c. C-5, c. 39(2).

CONFIDENTIAL. *adj.* Intended to be kept secret.

CONFIDENTIAL CAPACITY. 1. The question under the statute is not to be determined by the test whether the employee has incidental access to this information; it is rather whether between the particular employee and the employer there exists a relation of a character that stands out from the generality of relations, and bears a special quality of confidence. Between the management and the confidential employee there is an element of personal trust which permits some degree of "thinking aloud" on special matters: it may be on matters in relation to employees, competitors or the public or on proposed action of any sort or description; but that information is of a nature out of the ordinary and is kept within a strictly limited group. In many instances it is of the essence of the confidence that the information be not disclosed to any member of any group or body of the generality of employees. *Canada Safeway Ltd. v. British Columbia (Labour Relations Board)*, [1953] 2 S.C.R. 46, per Rand, J. 2. " . . . [A] regular material involvement in matters relating to labour relations which are confidential because their disclosure would adversely affect the interest of the employer . . ." *United Steelworkers of America v. Falconbridge Nickel Mines Ltd*, [1966] O.L.R.B.R. Rep. 379 at 388. See PERSON EMPLOYED IN A MANAGERIAL OR ~.

CONFIDENTIAL COMMUNICATION. Privileged communication; a statement made in circumstances which indicate an intention that it be kept in confidence.

CONFIDENTIAL INFORMATION. 1. " . . . [T]he statement of Lord Greene in Saltman Engineering Co. v. Campbell Engineering Coy. (1948), 65 R.P.C. 203 . . . at 215 . . . (C.A.) is apposite: 'The information, to be confidential, must, I apprehend, apart from contract, have the necessary quality of confidence about it, namely, it must not be something which is public property and public knowledge. On the other hand, it is perfectly possible to have a confidential document, be it a formula, a plan, a sketch, or something of that kind, which is the result of work done by the maker upon materials which may be available for the use of anybody; but what makes it confidential is the fact that the maker of the document has used his brain and thus produced a result which can only be produced by somebody who goes through the same process.' " *International Corona Resources Ltd. v. Lac Minerals Ltd.* (1989), 44 B.L.R. 1 at 77, [1989] 2 S.C.R. 574, 26 C.P.R. (3d) 97, 69 O.R. (2d) 287, 61 D.L.R. (4th) 14, 6 R.P.R. (2d) 1, 35 E.T.R. 12, 101 N.R. 239, 36 O.A.C. 57, Sopinka J. (dissenting) (McIntyre and Wilson JJ. concurring in part). 2. Information obtained in the solicitor-client relationship concerning the affairs of a client.

CONFIDENTIALITY. *n.* " . . . There are four fundamental conditions: (1) The communica-

tions must originate in a confidence that they will not be disclosed. (2) The element of confidentiality must be essential to the full and satisfactory maintenance of the relation between the parties. (3) The relation must be one which in the opinion of the community ought to be sedulously fostered. (4) The injury 'that would inure to the relation by the disclosure of the communications must be greater than the benefit thereby gained for the correct disposal of the litigation.' *Slavutych v. Baker* (1975), [1976] 1 S.C.R. 254.

CONFIDENTIAL RELATION. A relation of trust which gives rise to an expectation that communications will be held in confidence; fiduciary relation.

CONFIGURATION. See FORWARD CONTROL ~.

CONFINED. *adj.* Imprisoned, shut in.

CONFINED SPACE. A space in which, because of its construction, location, contents or work activity therein, the accumulation of a hazardous gas, vapour, dust or fume or the creation of an oxygen-deficient atmosphere may occur. See HAZARDOUS ~.

CONFINEMENT. *n.* "The essential ingredients of the offence may then be taken to be: (a) physical restraint; (b) contrary to the wishes of the person restrained; (c) to which the victim submits unwillingly; (d) depriving him of his liberty to move from one place to another." *R. v. Moore* (1989), 51 C.C.C. (3d) 566 at 572, 73 C.R. (3d) 120, 78 Nfld. & P.E.I.R. 284, 244 A.P.R. 284 (P.E.I. T.D.), McQuaid J. See SOLITARY ~.

CONFIRM. *v.* 1. To ratify; to make firm or certain; to give approval. 2. Approve. *R. v. Briardale Investments Ltd.* (1964), 50 W.W.R. 517 at 530, 45 C.R. 358, [1965] 2 C.C.C. 273, 48 D.L.R. (2d) 315 (Man. Q.B.), Smith J. 3. " . . . '[R]evive' . . . By confirming the will of 1909, the testator revived it and made it a new will of the date of the codicil-the last will of the testator." *Findlay v. Pae* (1916), 37 O.L.R. 318 at 325, 31 D.L.R. 281 (H.C.), Latchford J.

CONFIRMARE EST ID QUOD PRIUS INFIRMUM FUIT FIRMARE. [L.] To confirm is to strengthen that which was weak before.

CONFIRMARE NEMO POTEST PRIUSQUAM JUS EI ACCIDERIT. [L.] No one can confirm a right before the right accrues.

CONFIRMATIO EST NULLA UBI DONUM PRAECEDENS EST INVALI-

DUM. [L.] Confirmation is void where the preceding gift was void.

CONFIRMATION. *n.* 1. Formal approval. 2. Ratification; a document which validates an agreement. 3. "The Civil Code appears to treat the words 'confirmation' and 'ratification' as synonyms . . . The legislator follows current usage on this point, though the writers distinguish ratification from confirmation. They define confirmation as the waiver of an action to rescind and ratification as the approval of an act done without authority." *Denis-Cossette v. Bermain*, [1982] 1 S.C.R. 751 at 796-7, 48 N.R. 1, 24 R.P.R. 56, the court per Beetz J. 4. An order of the court confirming the order of another court.

CONFIRMATION ORDER. 1. A confirmation order made under the Reciprocal Enforcement of Maintenance Orders Act or under the corresponding enactment of a reciprocating state. The second state confirms the original order requiring that maintenance be paid. The order is then enforced as an order of the second court in the second jurisdiction. 2. An order of a court confirming the order of another court.

CONFIRMATIO OMNES SUPPLET DEFECTUS, LICET ID QUOD ACTUM EST AB INITIO NON VALUIT. [L.] Confirmation makes up for any defects, even though what had been done was not valid at the beginning.

CONFIRMED CREDIT. A credit in which another bank adds its confirmation.

CONFIRMED LETTER OF CREDIT. " . . . [W]hen a letter of credit is issued and confirmed by a bank, the bank must pay it if the documents are in order and the terms of the credit are satisfied. Any dispute between buyer and seller must be settled between themselves. The bank must honour the credit . . ." *Edward Owen Enrg. Ltd. v. Barclays Bank Internat. Ltd.*, [1978] 1 All E.R. 976 at 981 (U.K. C.A.), Lord Denning M.R.

CONFIRMING AUTHORITY. (a) Where the authority is a municipality, the council therof; (b) where the authority is a school division, school area or school district, the board of trustees thereof; (c) where the authority is the Crown, notwithstanding The Land Acquisition Act, the member of the Executive Council who signed or authorized the signing of the declaration, or the member of the Executive Council who is charged with the administration of the program or project for which the land is required; (d) where the authority is a Crown agency, the member of the Executive Council through whom the agency reports to the assembly; and (e) in every other case, the Lieutenant Governor in Council. *Expropriation Act*, C.C.S.M., c. E190, s. 1.

CONFIRMING BANK. A bank that agrees to honour the credit issued by another bank.

CONFISCATE. *v.* To seize property; to forfeit property.

CONFISCATION. *n.* 1. Seizure or forfeiture of property. 2. " . . . [T]he bringing of something into the treasury of a Government, . . ." *R. v. Lane*, [1937] 1 D.L.R. 212 at 214, 67 C.C.C. 273, 11 M.P.R. 232 (N.B. C.A.), Baxter C.J. (Grimmer C.J. concurring).

CONFITENS REUS. [L.] An accused who admits guilt.

CONFLICT. See FALSE ~.

CONFLICT OF INTEREST. 1. " . . . [T]he test must be such that the public represented by the reasonably informed person would be satisfied that no use of confidential information would occur. . . Typically, these cases require two questions to be answered: (1) Did the lawyer receive confidential information attributable to a solicitor-and-client relationship relevant to the matter at hand? (2) Is there a risk that it will be used to the prejudice of the client?" *MacDonald Estate v. Martin* (1990), 48 C.P.C. (2d) 113 at 137, [1991] 1 W.W.R. 705, 121 N.R. 1, 77 D.L.R. (4th) 249, 70 Man. R. (2d) 241, [1990] 3 S.C.R. 1235, Sopinka J. (Dickson C.J.C., La Forest and Gonthier JJ. concurring). 2. "It is not part of the job description that municipal councillors be personally interested in matters that come before them beyond the interest that they have in common with the other citizens in the municipality. Where such an interest is found, both at common law and bar statute, a member of council is disqualified if the interest is so related to the exercise of public duty that a reasonably well-informed person would conclude that the interest might influence the exercise of that duty. This is commonly referred to as a conflict of interest . . ." *Old St. Boniface Residents Assn. v. Winnipeg (City)* (1990), 75 D.L.R. (4th) 385 at 408, 46 Admin. L.R. 161, 2 M.P.L.R. (2d) 217, [1991] 2 W.W.R. 145, 116 N.R. 46, 69 Man. R. (2d) 134, [1990] 3 S.C.R. 1170, Sopinka J. (Wilson, Gonthier and McLachlin JJ. concurring). 3. " . . . [A] situation in which an employee engages in activities which are external and parallel to those he performs as part of his job, and which conflict or compete with the latter." *Canadian Imperial Bank of Commerce v. Boisvert* (1986), 13 C.C.E.L. 264 at 292, [1986] 2 F.C. 431, 68 N.R. 355 (C.A.), Marceau J.A. (Lacombe and MacGuigan JJ.A. concurring). 4. " ... [P]ersonal interest sufficiently connected with his professional duties that there is a reasonable apprehension that the personal interest may influence the actual exercise of the professional responsibilities." *Cox v. College of Optometrists (Ontario)* (1988), 33 Admin. L.R. at 298, 28 O.A.C. 337, 65 O.R. (2d) 461, 52 D.L.R. (4th) 298 (Div. Ct.), the court per Campbell J.

CONFLICT OF LAWS. 1. Private international law, the branch of law concerned with private relations which contain a foreign element. 2. The body of laws which each province has in common law and in statute to govern issues concerning extraterritoriality. These issues are: (a) the provincial court's jurisdiction in cases in which facts or parties are outside the province, (b) the provincial court's recognition of judgments obtained in other jurisdictions, and (c) the choice of law in any case involving extraterritorial elements and over which the court has jurisdiction.

CONFORM. *v.* Comply. *Bourk v. Temple* (1990), 50 M.P.L.R. 125 at 132, 73 Alta. L.R. (2d) 302, 105 A.R. 61, [1990] 5 W.W.R. 87 (Q.B.), Conrad J.

CONFORMATION. *n.* The general outline of the muscle formation of a carcass.

CONFORMING USE. In zoning or planning, use of property which complies with restrictions of use in effect in respect of the property.

CONFORMITY. *n.* Correspondence in some respect; agreement.

CONFORMITY PREJUDICE. A form of juror prejudice which arises when the case is of significant interest to the community causing the juror to perceive a strong feeling in the community and an expectation in the community concerning the outcome of the case.

CONFUSING. *adj.* 1. When applied as an adjective to a trade-mark or trade-name, means a trade-mark or trade-name the use of which would cause confusion in the manner and circumstances described in the Trade-Marks Act. *Trade-Marks Act*, R.S.C. 1985, c. T-13, s. 2. 2. In relation to a corporate name, means a corporate name the use of which causes confusion with a trade mark or trade name in the manner de-

scribed in section 13. *Canada Business Corporations Regulations*, C.R.C., c. 426, s. 12.

CONFUSION. *n.* To decide whether the use of a trade-mark or of a trade-name causes confusion with another trade-mark or another trade-name, the Court must ask itself whether, as a matter of first impression on the minds of an ordinary person having a vague recollection of that other mark or name, the use of both marks or names in the same area in the same manner is likely to lead to the inference that the services associated with those marks or names are performed by the same person, whether or not the services are of the same general class. *Miss Universe Inc. v. Bohna* (1994), [1995] 1 F.C. 614 (C.A.).

CON GAME. Obtaining money or property by a deceiving or tricking the owner. See CONFIDENCE GAME.

CONGENITAL. *adj.* Present at birth.

CONGENITAL ANEURYSM. The rupture of this aneurysm involving an artery at the base of the brain commonly causes sudden death in young or middle aged adults. F.A. Jaffe, *A Guide to Pathological Evidence*, 3d ed. (Toronto: Carswell, 1991) at 212.

CONGESTION LIVIDITY. Lividity caused when the blood distends the skin capillaries. F.A. Jaffe, *A Guide to Pathological Evidence*, 3d ed. (Toronto: Carswell, 1991) at 222. See HYPOSTATIC OR ~.

CONGREGATION. *n.* A body of individuals, whether or not incorporated, that adheres to the practices and beliefs of the religious organization of which it is a constituent part. See MEMBER OF A ~.

CONGRESS. *n.* An assembly of persons who meet to consider measures related to their common concerns.

CONGRESS OF INDUSTRIAL ORGANIZATIONS. A federation of national and international industrial unions.

CONJECTURE. *n.* "The dividing line between conjecture and inference is often a very difficult one to draw. A conjecture may be plausible but of no legal value, for its essence is that it is a mere guess. An inference in the legal sense, on the other hand, is a deduction from the evidence, and if it is a reasonable deduction it may have the validity of legal proof. The attribution of an occurrence to a cause is, I take it, always a matter of inference . . ." *Jones v. Great Western Rwy. Co.* (1930), 47 T.L.R. 39 at 45 (U.K. H.L.), Lord Macmillan.

CONJOINTS. *n.* People married to one another.

CONJUGAL. *adj.* Related to the married or marriage-like state.

CONJUGAL RIGHTS. Each spouse's right to the society, comfort and affection of the other spouse.

CONJUNCTIVE. *adj.* Joining two concepts.

CONJURATIO. *n.* [L.] An oath.

CONMINGLE. *v.* With reference to gas, means the mixing together or blending of gases for transmission through pipelines and other facilities.

CONNECTED. See PERSON ~.

CONNECTING CARRIER. A railway company, other than a local carrier, that moves traffic to or from an interchange over a portion of a continuous route in respect of which the railway company and the shipper agree on the movement of the traffic, including the applicable rate. *Canada Transportation Act*, S.C. 1996, c. 10, s. 111.

CONNECTING FACTOR. Part of the choice of law rule: an element which connects a system of law with the facts of a particular case.

CONNECTOR. *n.* A device used to make a connection between two conductors or between a conductor and another part of a system or between a conductor and a metallic object. See VENT ~.

CONNIVANCE. *n.* Culpable agreement to do wrong.

CONQUEST. *n.* In international law, the occupation of enemy territory by force.

CONSANGUINITY. *n.* Relationship by descent: either collaterally, i.e. from a common ancestor or lineally, i.e. mother and daughter. See LINEAL ~.

CONSCIENCE. *n.* " . . . [S]elf-judgement [sic] on the moral quality of one's conduct or the lack of it. . ." *MacKay v. Manitoba* (1985), 23 C.R.R. 8 at 11, [1986] 2 W.W.R. 367, 24 D.L.R. (4th) 587, 39 Man. R. (2d) 274 (C.A.), Twaddle J.A. (Philp J.A. concurring). See FREEDOM OF AND RELIGION.

CONSCIENTIOUS OBJECTOR. A person who, on moral or religious grounds, thinks it wrong to resist force with force and to kill.

CONSCIOUSNESS OF GUILT EVIDENCE. Evidence of after-the-fact conduct is commonly admitted to show that an accused person has acted in a manner which, based on human experience and logic, is consistent with the conduct of a guilty person and inconsistent with the conduct of an innocent person. It is introduced to show that the accused was aware of having committed the crime in question and acted for the purpose of evading detection and prosecution. That label is somewhat misleading and its use should be discouraged. "Consciousness of guilt" is simply one inference that may be drawn from the evidence of the accused's conduct; it is not a special category of evidence in itself. *R. v. White*, [1998] 2 S.C.R. 72.

CONSCIOUS PARALLELISM. " . . . [C]onformity is the result of price leadership by the industry leader and a conscious effort by other members of the industry to follow the leader to parallel its prices . . . 'without agreement or arrangement, direct or tacit. *R. v. Atlantic Sugar Refineries Co.* (1975), 26 C.P.R. (2d) 14 at 97, [1976] C.S. 421, Mackay J.

CONSCRIPTION. *n.* Compulsory enrolment in the military service.

CONSCRIPTIVE EVIDENCE. 1. Concerning unreasonable search and seizure " . . . [R]efers to evidence which emanates from the accused following a violation of s. 10(b) of the [Charter] . . ." *R. v. Wise* (1992), 11 C.R. (4th) 253 at 265, [1992] 1 S.C.R. 527, 70 C.C.C. (3d) 193, 133 N.R. 161, 8 C.R.R. (2d) 53, 51 O.A.C. 351, Cory J. (Lamer C.J.C., Gonthier, Stevenson JJ. concurring). 2. Evidence is conscriptive when an accused is compelled to incriminate himself in violation of his Charter rights means of a statement, use of the body, or production of bodily samples.

CONSECUTIVE. *adj.* One after the other; following.

CONSECUTIVE INTERPRETATION. It may be useful to keep in mind the distinction between "consecutive" (after the words are spoken) and "simultaneous" (at the same time as words are spoken). Although consecutive interpretation effectively doubles the time necessary to complete the proceedings, it offers a number of advantages over simultaneous interpretation. Consecutive interpretation, on the other hand, has the advantage of allowing the accused to react at the appropriate time, such as when making objections. It also makes it easier to assess on the spot the accuracy of the interpretation, something rendered more difficult when one has to listen to the original language *and* its translation at the same time, as would be the case with simultaneous interpretation. *R. v. Tran*, [1994] 2 S.C.R. 951.

CONSECUTIVELY. *adv.* Following immediately upon. *R. v. Cadeddu* (1980),19 C.R. (3d) 93 at 90, 57 C.C.C. (2d) 264 (Ont. C.A.), the court per Morden J.A.

CONSECUTIVE SENTENCES. One sentence follows another in time.

CONSEIL CAN. D. INT. *abbr*. Conseil canadien de droit international. Congrès. Travaux (Canadian Council of International Law. Conference. Proceedings).

CONSENSUAL TREE. Tree planted along a common boundary with the consent of the adjoining owners, or their predecessors in title. *Koenig v. Goebel* (1998), 162 Sask. R. 81 (Q.B.).

CONSENSUS AD IDEM. [L. agreement to the same thing] The consent required for a contract to be binding.

CONSENSUS FACIT LEGEM. [L.] Consent makes the law.

CONSENSUS NON CONCUBITUS FACIT MATRIMONIUM; ET CONSENTIRE NON POSSUNT ANTE ANNOS NUBILES. [L.] Consent, not coitus, constitutes marriage; and the parties cannot consent before reaching marriageable years.

CONSENSUS TOLLIT ERROREM. [L.] Consent removes error.

CONSENT. *v.* To agree to something, such as the removal of children from their habitual residence. *Katsigiannis v. Kottick-Katsigiannis* (2001), 55 O.R. (3d) 456 (C.A.).

CONSENT. *n.* 1. Freely given agreement. 2. There is a difference in the concept of "consent" as it relates to the state of mind of the complainant *vis-à-vis* the *actus reus* of the offence and the state of mind of the accused in respect of the *mens rea*. For the purposes of the *actus reus*, "consent" means that the complainant in her mind wanted the sexual touching to take place. In the context of *mens rea*—specifically for the purposes of the honest but mistaken belief in consent—"consent" means that the complainant had affirmatively communicated by words or conduct her agreement to engage in sexual activity with the accused. This distinction should always be borne in mind and the two parts of the analysis kept separate. *R. v. Ewanchuk*, 1999 CarswellAlta 99, 131 C.C.C. (3d) 481, 169 D.L.R. (4th) 193, 235 N.R. 323, 22 C.R. (5th) 1, 232 A.R. 1, 195 W.A.C. 1, 68 Alta. L.R. (3d) 1, [1999] 6 W.W.R. 333, [1999] 1 S.C.R. 330 Per Major, J. for majority. 3. The distinction between the meaning of "compliance" and the meaning of "consent" is real. To consent means to actually agree and cooperate. Compliance has a more subtle meaning involving the failure to object. *R. c. Knox*, 1996 CarswellQue 1041, 202 N.R. 228, 109 C.C.C. (3d) 481, 23 M.V.R. (3d) 93, [1996] 3 S.C.R. 199, 38 C.R.R. (2d) 222, 139 D.L.R. (4th) 1, 1 C.R. (5th) 254 per Lamer, C.J.C. See AGE OF ~; INFORMED ~; ROYAL ~.

CONSENTIENTIS ET AGENTIS PARI POENA PLECTANTUR. [L.] Those consenting to and those perpetrating a crime are punished equally.

CONSENT JUDGMENT. A judgment the terms of which are agreed to by the parties.

CONSENT ORDER. An order which constitutes a bargain between the parties. *Kitchen v. Crown Coal Co.*, [1932] 1 W.W.R. 696 (Alta. C.A.).

CONSENT SURVEILLANCE. " . . . [T]erm to describe a practice where only one party to a conversation has agreed to have it recorded . . . I shall therefore use the term 'participant surveillance.' *R. v. Sanelli* (1990), 74 C.R. (3d) 281 at 286, 103 N.R. 86, 37 O.A.C. 322, [1990] 1 S.C.R. 30, 53 C.C.C. (3d) 1, 65 D.L.R. (4th) 240, 71 O.R. (2d) 575, 45 C.R.R. 278, La Forest J.

CONSEQUENCE. *n.* 1. "[Within the meaning of s. 16 of the Criminal Code, R.S.C. 1985, c. C-46] . . . refers to the physical consequences of the act: . . ." *R. v. Charest* (1990), 76 C.R. (3d) 63 at 88, 28 Q.A.C. 258, 57 C.C.C. (3d) 312 (C.A.), the court per Fish J.A. 2. "[In the Family Law Act, 1986, S.O. 1986, c. 4, s. 56(4)(b)] . . . would seem to reach the effect or impact of the [domestic contract] document upon the spouses' affairs." *Grant-Hose v. Grant-Hose* (1991), 32 R.F.L. (3d) 26 at 46 (Ont. U.F.C.), Mendes da Costa U.F.C.J. See TRUE PENAL ~.

CONSEQUENTIAL DAMAGES. The loss which occurs indirectly from the act complained of.

CONSEQUENTLY. *adv.* " . . . [C]an, in the one instance, import an inevitable sequence of events, one necessarily flowing from, and as a direct result of, the other . . . On the other hand, it may also import something which follows by logical inference." *Campbell v. Blackett* (1978), 80 D.L.R. (3d) 252 at 257, 13 Nfld. & P.E.I.R. 64, 29 A.P.R. 64 (P.E.I. C.A.), the court per McQuaid J.A.

CONSERVATION. *n*. 1. Includes the prevention of waste, improvident or uneconomic production or disposition of natural resources. In relation to heritage, any activity undertaken to protect, preserve or enhance the heritage value or heritage character of heritage property or an area. See MANAGEMENT AND ~ ZONE.

CONSERVATION AUTHORITY LAND. Land owned by a conservation authority. *Conservation Land Act*, R.S.O. 1990, c. C.28, s. 1.

CONSERVATION LAND. Includes wetland, areas of natural and scientific interest, land within the Niagara Escarpment Planning Area, conservation authority land and such other land owned by non-profit organizations that through their management contribute to provincial conservation and heritage program objectives. Conservation Land Act, R.S.O. 1990, c. C.28, s. 1.

CONSERVATION PURPOSE. The use and storage of water or the construction of works in and about streams for the purpose of conserving fish or wildlife. *Water Act*, R.S.B.C. 1996, c. 483, s. 1.

CONSERVATOR. *n*. One who protects, preserves, or maintains.

CONSERVE. *v*. To keep; to save.

CONSIDER. *v*. 1. To examine, inspect; to turn one's mind to. 2. To go about deciding a case. 3.County Council was required by s. 25.4 of the *Municipal Act* [R.S.O. 1990, c. M.45] to do no more than "consider" the Minister's principles. In my opinion, that imposes no greater requirement on County Council than to take the principles into account when developing a restructuring proposal to be submitted to the Minister. Section 25.4 does not state how or when the principles are to be considered. Moreover, to "consider" is a somewhat conditional requirement in the sense that it does not imply that the principles must be followed in the development of a restructuring proposal. *Bruce (Township) v. Ontario (Minister of Municipal Affairs & Housing)* (1998), 1998 CarswellOnt 3382, 112 O.A.C. 68, 164 D.L.R. (4th) 443, 48 M.P.L.R. (2d) 201, 41 O.R. (3d) 309, 8 Admin. L.R. (3d)

21 (C.A.) Court: Ontario Court of Appeal, Osborne for the court.

CONSIDERATIO CURIAE. [L.] The judgment of the court.

CONSIDERATION. *n*. 1. In a contract, an interest, right, profit or benefit accrues to the one party while some detriment, forebearance, loss or responsibility is suffered or undertaken by the other party. G.H.L. Fridman, *The Law of Contract in Canada*, 2d ed. (Toronto: Carswell, 1986) at 75. 2. In a contract for the sale of goods, it is called the price and must be in money. G.H.L. Fridman, *Sale of Goods in Canada*, 3d ed. (Toronto: Carswell, 1986) at 42. 3. " . . . [U]sed to describe that which is given or promised in order to bring a binding contract into existence. It is also used, however, to describe the performance of the promise . . ." *Kiss v. Palachik* (1983), 146 D.L.R. (3d) 385 at 393, [1983] 1 S.C.R. 623, 47 N.R. 148, 22 R.F.L. (2d) 225, 15 E.T.R. 129, the court per Wilson J. See ADEQUATE ~; EXECUTED ~; EXECUTORY ~; FUTURE~; GOOD~; MERITORIOUS ~; PAST ~; PRESENT ~; VALUABLE ~.

CONSIDERATUM EST PER CURIAM. [L.] The court has considered.

CONSIDERED. *adj*. Determined; regarded.

CONSIGN. *v*. To send goods to another to be sold to third parties.

CONSIGNED. *adj*. Shipped, consigned or entrusted to a mercantile agent for sale, reconsignment or other disposition. *The Sales on Consignment Act*, R.S.S. 1978, c. S-4, s. 2.

CONSIGNEE. *n*. A person to whom the goods are sent.

CONSIGNMENT. *n*. 1. "In its simplest terms, . . . the sending of goods to another. An arrangement whereby an owner sends goods to another on the understanding that such other will sell the goods to a third party and remit the proceeds to the owner after deducting his compensation for effecting the sale is an example of a consignment agreement." *Stephanian's Persian Carpets Ltd., Re* (1980), 34 C.B.R. (N.S.) 35 at 37, 1 P.P.S.A.C. 119 (Ont. S.C.), Saunders J. 2. The goods themselves. See COMMERCIAL ~.

CONSIGNOR. *n*. 1. A person who consigns goods. 2. A person who sends goods to another to be sold to third parties.

CONSIST. *v*. To be made up of.

CONSISTENT. *adj*. Harmonious; in agreement with.

CONSOL. *abbr*. Consolidated.

CONSOLATION DOUBLE. The pay-out price of a daily double ticket that combines a horse, entry or mutuel field that is declared the winner in the official result of the first race of the daily double with a horse, entry or mutuel field in the second race of the daily double where, after the official result of the first race is posted, (*a*) the second race of the daily double is cancelled, or (*b*) the horse, entry or mutuel field in the second race of the daily double is scratched from that race. *Pari-Mutuel Betting Supervision Regulations*, SOR/91-365, s. 2.

CONSOLIDATE. *v*. 1. To combine, unite. 2. In relation to statutes, to bring together several pieces of legislation into one dealing with the topic more generally. 3. In relation to statutes or regulations, to pull together all amendments to the original statute so that only provisions currently in force are contained in the consolidation made.

CONSOLIDATED FUND. The aggregate of all public money that is on hand and on deposit to the credit of a province.

CONSOLIDATED LOAN. 1. A loan acquired for the purpose of consolidating liabilities. 2. In relation to statutes, to bring together several pieces of legislation into one dealing with the topic more generally. 3. In relation to statutes or regulations, to pull together all amendments to the original statute so that only provisions currently in force are contained in the consolidation made.

CONSOLIDATED REVENUE FUND. 1. Aggregate of all public moneys that are on deposit at the credit of the Receiver General. *Financial Administration Act*, R.S.C. 1985, c. F-11, s. 2. 2. The aggregate of all public moneys that are on deposit at the credit of the Treasurer or in the name of any agency of the Crown approved by the Lieutenant Governor in Council. *Ministry of Treasury and Economics Act*, R.S.O. 1990, c. M.37, s. 1.

CONSOLIDATED STATUTE. A version of a statute prepared by drawing all amendments to the original statute together and creating a document which provides all the currently in force provisions of the statute.

CONSOLIDATING STATUTE. A statute which draws together, with only minor amend-

ments and improvements, all statutory provisions related to a particular topic into a single act.

CONSOLIDATION. *n*. 1. In statute law, the uniting of many acts of Parliament into one. 2. The healing or stabilization of an employment injury following which no improvement of the state of health of the injured worker is foreseeable. *An Act Respecting Industrial Accidents and Occupational Diseases*, S.Q. 1985, c. 6, s. 2. See POSTAL ~ POINT.

CONSOLIDATION ACT. An act, usually with amendments, which repeals a number of earlier acts and includes, sometimes, some rules of the common law.

CONSOLIDATION OF ACTIONS. The combination of proceedings involving the same parties or issues.

CONSORT. *n*. A man and a woman who are married and cohabit, or who live together as husband and wife. See QUEEN ~.

CONSORTIUM. *n*. "The term 'consortium' is not susceptible of precise or complete definition but broadly speaking, companionship, love, affection, comfort, mutual services, sexual intercourse—all belonging to the marriage state—taken together make up what we refer to as consortium" *Kungl v. Schiefer*, [1961] O.R. 1 at 7 (C.A.), Schroeder J.A.

CONSPICUOUSLY. *adv*. "... '[S]triking', 'manifest', 'notable' or 'flagrant' ..." *Henfrey Samson Belair Ltd. v. Wedgewood Village Estate Ltd.* (1986), 59 C.B.R. (N.S.) 38 at 58 (B.C. S.C.), Taylor J. See APPEARING ~; NOTED ~.

CONSPIRACY. *n*. 1. "A conspiracy consists not merely in the intention of two or more, but in the agreement of two or more to do an unlawful act, or to do a lawful act by unlawful means. So long as such a decision rests in intention only, it is not indictable. When two agree to carry it into effect, the very plot is an act in itself, and the act of each of the parties, promise against promise, actus contra actum, capable of being enforced if lawful, punishable if for a criminal object or for the use of criminal means." *Mulcahy v. R.* (1868), L.R. 3 H.L. 306 at 317, Willes J. 2. There must be an intention to agree, the completion of an agreement, and a common design. Conspiracy is in fact a more "preliminary" crime than attempt, since the offence is considered to be complete before any acts are taken that go beyond mere preparation to put the common design into effect. The Crown is simply required to prove a meeting of the minds with regard to a common design to do something unlawful, specifically the commission of an indictable offence. See s. 465(1)(c) of the *Criminal Code*. A conspiracy must involve more than one person, even though all the conspirators may not either be identified, or be capable of being convicted. *United States v. Dynar*, 1997 CarswellOnt 1981, (sub nom. *United States of America v. Dynar*) 115 C.C.C. (3d) 481, (sub nom. *United States of America v. Dynar*) 213 N.R. 321, (sub nom. *United States of America v. Dynar*) 147 D.L.R. (4th) 399, (sub nom. *United States of America v. Dynar*) 101 O.A.C. 321, 8 C.R. (5th) 79, (sub nom. *United States of America v. Dynar*) 33 O.R. (3d) 478 (headnote only), (sub nom. *United States of America v. Dynar*) 44 C.R.R. (2d) 189, (sub nom. *United States of America v. Dynar*) [1997] 2 S.C.R. 462, Cory and Iacobucci for the majority. 3. A pleading of civil conspiracy must describe who the parties are and the relationship with each other. It should allege the agreement between the defendants to conspire, and state precisely what the purpose or what were the objects of the alleged conspiracy. The pleading must set forth with clarity and precision the overt acts which are alleged to have been done by each of the alleged conspirators in furtherance of the conspiracy. Finally, the pleading must allege the injury and damage occasioned to the plaintiff. Once these formal requirements are met, the plaintiff must show that the allegations are supported by the available evidence. To establish the tort of conspiracy, the plaintiff must show that there was an agreement to injure between the defendants, that the defendants intended to injure the plaintiff and that damages resulted and that there was no justification for the act. *Belsat Video Marketing Inc. v. Astral Communications Inc.* (1998), 81 C.P.R. (3d) 1 (Ont. Gen. Div.). 4. " . . . [W]hereas the law of tort does not permit an action against an individual defendant who has caused injury to the plaintiff, the law of torts does recognize a claim against them in combination as the tort of conspiracy if (1) whether the means used by the defendants are lawful or unlawful, the predominant purpose of the defendants' conduct is to cause injury to the plaintiff; or (2) where the conduct of the defendants is unlawful, the conduct is directed toward the plaintiff . . . and the defendants should know in the circumstances that injury to the plaintiff is likely to and does result. In situation (2) it is not necessary that the predominant purpose of the defendants' conduct be to cause injury to the plaintiff but, in the prevailing circumstances, it must be a constructive intent derived from the fact that the defendants should have known that injury to the plaintiff would ensue. In both situations, however, there must be actual damage suffered by the plaintiff." *Canada Cement LaFarge Ltd. v. British Columbia Lightweight Aggregate Ltd.* (1983), 21 B.L.R. 254 at 274, [1983] 1 S.C.R. 452, [1983] 6 W.W.R. 385, 24 C.C.L.T. 111, 72 C.P.R. (2d) 1, 145 D.L.R. (3d) 385, 47 N.R. 191, the court per Estey J. See CIVIL ~; CRIMINAL ~; SEDITIOUS ~.

CONSPIRACY DOCTRINE. An early labour law theory which considered self-organization of employees as equivalent to a conspiracy at common law.

CONSPIRATOR. *n.* A person who takes part in a conspiracy.

CONSPIRE. *v.* "The word 'conspire' derives from two Latin words, 'con' and 'spirare', meaning 'to breathe together'. To conspire is to agree. . ." *Cotroni v. R.*, [1979] 2 S.C.R. 256 at 276-77, Dickson J.

CONSTABLE. *n.* 1. " . . . '[T]he holder of a police office' . . . exercising, so far as his police duties are concerned, an original authority . . . a member of a civilian force, and I take his assimilation to a soldier . . . to be an assimilation related only to whether an action per quod lies against a tortfeasor at common law for the loss of his services and not to assimilation for other purposes, such as liability to peremptory discharge, if that be the case with a soldier." *Nicholson v. Haldimand-Norfolk (Regional Municipality) Commissioners of Police* (1978), 9 C.L.L.C. 249 at 253, [1979] 1 S.C.R. 311, 88 D.L.R. (3d) 671, 78 C.L.L.C. 14, 181, 23 N.R. 410, Laskin C.J.C. 2. Any member of a police force other than an officer. 3. Any member of the Royal Canadian Mounted Police other than a commissioned officer. 4. Includes any sheriff, deputy sheriff, police officer, constable bailiff keeper of a jail or prison, or other person employed or deputized for the preservation of the public peace. 5. A constable, police or other officer, and any person acting to aid such an officer. See PRIVATE ~; SPECIAL ~.

CONSTANT COMPANION. Being a belt containing a concealed stainless steel knife.

CONSTANT WAGE PLAN. A method of paying steady amount of wages during fluctuating work weeks without incurring charges for overtime.

CONSTAT. [L.] It appears.

CONSTATING INSTRUMENT. Includes a statute other than the Companies Act, letters patent, memorandum of association, articles of association, certificate of incorporation, certificate of continuance, by-laws, regulations or other instrument by which a body corporate is incorporated or continued or that governs or regulates the affairs of a body corporate. *Corporations Act*, R.S. Nfld. 1990, c. C-36, s. 2.

CONSTITUENCY. *n.* 1. A place or territorial area entitled to return a member to serve in a legislative assembly or in Parliament. 2. The voters, or more generally, the people who live in the area described in definition 1. 3. The supporters of a particular person or group or the persons who share the interest of a particular person or group. See URBAN ~.

CONSTITUENCY ASSOCIATION. In an electoral district, means the association or organization endorsed by a registered party as the official association of that party in the electoral district.

CONSTITUENCY WORK. Any work directly connected with a member's responsibilities as a member. *Legislative Assembly and Executive Council Act*, S.N.W.T. 1985 (2d Sess.), c. 4, s. 2.

CONSTITUENT. *n.* 1. One entitled to vote in a constituency. 2. Includes sulphur extracted from natural gas. *Natural Gas Price Act*, S.B.C. 1985, c. 53, s. 1.

CONSTITUENT PART. (a) Any of the following parts of a consumer textile article: (i) a section or backing described in section 34 or 35, or (ii) a lining, interlining, padding or filling described in section 37 or 38 or any trimming or findings, or (b) a consumer textile article exclusive of any part that (i) is described in subparagraph (a)(ii), and (ii) the article contains. *Textile Labelling and Advertising Regulations*, C.R.C., c. 1551, s. 25.

CONSTITUTION. *n.* 1. The body of law which establishes the framework of government for a nation or an organization. 2. The supreme law of Canada. *Constitution Act, 1982*, s. 52(1) being Schedule B of the *Canada Act, 1982*, (U.K.), 1982, c. 11. 3. " ... [I]s drafted with an eye to the future. Its function is to provide continuing framework for the legitimate exercise of governmental power and, when joined by a Bill or a

Charter of Rights for the unremitting protection of individual rights and liberties. Once enacted its provisions cannot easily be repealed or amended. It must, therefore, be capable of growth and development over time to meet new social, political and historical realities often unimagined by its framers. *Canada (Director of Investigation & Research) v. Southam Inc.* (1984), 27 B.L.R. 297 at 307, [1984] 2 S.C.R. 145, 33 Alta. L.R. (2d) 193, 41 C.R. (3d) 97, [1984] 6 W.W.R. 577, 14 C.C.C. (3d) 97, 55 A.R. 291, 55 N.R. 241, 2 C.P.R. (3d) 1, 9 C.R.R. 355, 11 D.L.R. (4th) 641, 84 D.T.C. 6467, the court per Dickson J. 4. The memorandum of association and articles of association of a corporation. *Share Ownership Plan Act*, S.N.S. 1992, c. 10, s. 2.

CONSTITUTION ACT, 1867. The act originally called the British North America Act (BNA Act). It became known as the Constitution Act when the constitution was patriated in 1982.

CONSTITUTIONAL CONVENTION. "We respectfully adopt the definition given by the learned Chief Justice of Manitoba, Freedman C.J.M. in the Manitoba Reference [Reference re Amendment of the Constitution of Canada (No. 3) (1981), 120 D.L.R. (3d) 385] ... : ' ... a convention occupies a position somewhere in between a usage or custom on one hand and constitutional law on the other. There is a general agreement that if one sought to fix that position with greater precision he would place convention nearer to law than to usage or custom. There is also a general agreement that "a convention is a rule which is regarded as obligatory by the officials to whom it applies": Hogg, Constitutional Law of Canada (1977), p. 9.' ... The existence of a definite convention is always unclear and a matter of debate. Furthermore conventions are flexible, somewhat imprecise and unsuitable for judicial determination." *Reference re Questions Concerning Amendment of the Constitution of Canada as set out in O.C. 1020/80 (1981), (sub nom. Resolution to Amend the Constitution of Canada; Re)* 1 C.R.R. 59 at 137-38, [1981] 1 S.C.R. 753, [1981] 6 W.W.R. 1, 11 Man. R. (2d) 1, 39 N.R. 1, 34 Nfld. & P.E.I.R. 1, 95 A.P.R. 1, Martland, Ritchie, Dickson, Beetz, Chouinard and Lamer JJ. See CONVENTION.

CONSTITUTIONAL EXEMPTION. A device which enables the court to uphold a law that is valid in most of its applications. The court does this by creating an exemption, declaring the law unconstitutional and invalid, in their application to specific individuals or groups.

CONSTITUTIONALISM. The constitutionalism principle bears considerable similarity to the rule of law, although they are not identical. The essence of constitutionalism in Canada is embodied in s. 52(1) of the *Constitution Act, 1982* [*Constitution Act, 1982*, being Schedule B of the *Canada Act 1982* (U.K.), 1982, c. 11], which provides that "[t]he Constitution of Canada is the supreme law of Canada, and any law that is inconsistent with the provisions of the Constitution is, to the extent of the inconsistency, of no force or effect." Simply put, the constitutionalism principle requires that all government action comply with the Constitution. The rule of law principle requires that all government action must comply with the law, including the Constitution. *Reference re Secession of Quebec*, 1998 CarswellNat 1299, 161 D.L.R. (4th) 385, 228 N.R. 203, 55 C.R.R. (2d) 1, [1998] 2 S.C.R. 217 Per curiam.

CONSTITUTIONAL LAW. The body of law which deals with the distribution or exercise of the powers of government.

CONSTITUTIONAL REMEDY. A remedy under section 24(1) of the Canadian Charter of Rights and Freedoms other than a remedy consisting of the exclusion of evidence or consequential on such exclusion. *Constitutional Question Act*, R.S.B.C. 1996, c. 68, s. 8.

CONSTITUTIONES TEMPORE POSTERIORES POTIORES SUNT HIS QUAE IPSAS PRAECESSERUNT. [L.] More recent laws prevail over those which preceded them.

CONSTITUTION OF CANADA. 1. Includes (a) The Canada Act 1982, including this Act; (b) the Acts and orders referred to in the schedule; and (c) any amendment to any Act or order referred to in paragraph (a) or (b). *Constitution Act, 1982*, s. 52(2), being Schedule B of the *Canada Act, 1982* (U.K.), 1982, c. 11. 2. Section 52(1) of Constitution provides that the Constitution of Canada is the supreme law of Canada and any law that is inconsistent with the provisions of the Constitution is, to the extent of the inconsistency, of no force or effect. 3. " . . . [T]he phrases 'Constitution of Canada' and 'Canadian Constitution' do not refer to matters of interest only to the federal government or federal juristic unit. They are clearly meant in a broader sense and embrace the global system of rules and principles which govern the exercise of constitu-

tional authority in the whole and in every part of the Canadian state." *Reference re Questions Concerning Amendment of the Constitution of Canada as set out in O.C. 1020/80 (1981), (sub nom. Resolution to Amend the Constitution of Canada, Re)* 1 C.R.R. 59 at 131, [1981] 1 S.C.R. 753, [1981] 6 W.W.R. 1, 11 Man. R. (2d) 1, 39 N.R. 1, 34 Nfld. & P.E.I.R. 1, 95 A.P.R. 1, Martland, Ritchie, Dickson Beetz, Chouinard and Lamer JJ. 4. " . . . [M]eans the constitution of the federal Government, as distinct from the provincial Governments . . ." Reference re Legislative Authority of Parliament of Canada (1979), (sub nom. Reference re Legislative Authority of Parliament to Alter or Replace Senate) 102 D.L.R. (3d) 1 at 12, [1980] 1 S.C.R. 56, 30 N.R. 271, Laskin C.J.C., Martland, Ritchie, Pigeon, Dickson, Estey, Pratte and McIntyre JJ. 5. The "Constitution of Canada" certainly includes the constitutional texts enumerated in s. 52(2) of the Constitution Act, 1982. Although these texts have a primary place in determining constitutional rules, they are not exhaustive. The Constitution also "embraces unwritten, as well as written rules". Finally, the Constitution of Canada includes the global system of rules and principles which govern the exercise of constitutional authority in the whole and in every part of the Canadian state. These supporting principles and rules, which include constitutional conventions and the workings of Parliament, are a necessary part of our Constitution because problems or situations may arise which are not expressly dealt with by the text of the Constitution. In order to endure over time, a constitution must contain a comprehensive set of rules and principles which are capable of providing an exhaustive legal framework for our system of government. Such principles and rules emerge from an understanding of the constitutional text itself, the historical context, and previous judicial interpretations of constitutional meaning. *Reference re Secession of Quebec*, 1998 CarswellNat 1299, 161 D.L.R. (4th) 385, 228 N.R. 203, 55 C.R.R. (2d) 1, [1998] 2 S.C.R. 217 Per curiam.

CONSTRAINED-CLASS. *n*. The class of persons specified in the articles of a constrained share corporation as being ineligible to hold, as a class, more than the maximum aggregate holdings. *Canada Business Corporations Regulations, 2001*, SOR/2001-512, s. 73.

CONSTRAINED SHARE CORPORATION. A corporation that has provisions in its articles imposing a constraint. *Canada Business Cor-*

porations Regulations, 2001, SOR/2001-512, s. 73.

CONSTRAINT. A restriction on (*a*) the issue or transfer of shares of any class or series to persons who are not resident Canadians; (*b*) the issue or transfer of shares of any class or series to enable a corporation or any of its affiliates or associates to qualify under a law referred to in paragraph 87(1)(*a*) (i) to obtain a licence to carry on any business, (ii) to become a publisher of a Canadian newspaper or periodical, or (iii) to acquire shares of a financial intermediary as defined in paragraph 87(1)(*b*); or (*c*) the issue, transfer or ownership of shares of any class or series in order to assist a corporation or any of its affiliates or associates to qualify under a law referred to in subsection 87(2) to receive licences, permits, grants, payments or other benefits by reason of attaining or maintaining a specified level of Canadian ownership or control. *Canada Business Corporations Regulations, 2001*, SOR/2001-512, s. 73.

CONSTRUCT. *v.* 1. To do anything in the erection, installation, extension, material alteration or repair of a building. 2. When used with respect to a well, means bore, dig, drill or otherwise make, extend or alter. *Ontario Water Resources Act*, R.S.O. 1990, c. 0.40, s. 35(1). 3. Includes to reconstruct, wholly or in part, when the lifetime of the work has expired.

CONSTRUCTIO LEGIS NON FACIT INJURIAM. [L.] The law is construed so as not to create injury.

CONSTRUCTION. *n.* 1. "[In Chatenay v. Brazilian Submarine Telegraph Co., [1891] 1 Q.B. 79] . . . Lindley L.J. at p. 85 said the following: 'The expression "construction" as applied to a document, at all events as used by English lawyers, includes two things: first the meaning of the words; and second their legal effect, or the effect which is to be given to them. The meaning of the words I take to be a question of fact in all cases whether we are dealing with a poem or a legal document. The effect of the words is a question of law."' *Wald v. Greater York Developments Ltd.* (1978), 8 C.P.C. 12 at 15 (Ont. H.C.), Sandler (Master). 2. The activity of building or erecting. 3. May include demolition, alteration, repairing. 4. Refers to the creation of something new, the execution of a design. See CLOSED ~; COMBUSTIBLE ~; COST OF ~; DENTURE ~; FIRE RESISTIVE ~; HEAVY TIMBER ~; LANDSCAPE ~; MILL ~; NON-COMBUSTIBLE ~; OPEN ~.

CONSTRUCTION CONTRACT. 1. A contract for erecting, remodelling or repairing a building or other structure on land and includes lump-sum, cost-plus and time and material contracts. 2. A contract entered into for the construction, repair, renovation or restoration of any work except a vessel and includes (*a*) a contract for the supply and erection of a prefabricated structure, (*b*) a contract for dredging, (*c*) a contract for demolition, or (*d*) a contract for the hire of equipment to be used in or incidentally to the execution of any contract referred to in this definition. *Government Contracts Regulations*, SOR/87-402 s. 2.

CONSTRUCTION CONTRACTOR. A person who undertakes a construction project, whether for his own benefit or for the benefit of another, or who enters into a contract, agreement or other arrangement whereby he agrees to undertake a construction project. *Construction Projects Labour-Management Relations Act*, R.S.N.S. 1989, c. 90, s. 2(1).

CONSTRUCTION HOIST. A mechanism used in connection with the construction, alteration, maintenance or demolition of a building, structure or other work, including its hoistway enclosure, affixed to a building or structure and equipped with a car, bucket or platform that (a) moves in guides, or is otherwise guided, at an angle exceeding 70 degrees from the horizontal, and (b) is used for raising or lowering workers materials or both, in connection with the construction, alteration, maintenance or demolition of a building, structure or other work.

CONSTRUCTION INDUSTRY. The businesses that are engaged in constructing, altering, decorating, repairing or demolishing buildings, structures, roads, sewers, water or gas mains, pipe lines, tunnels, bridges, canals or other works at the site thereof.

CONSTRUCTION LIEN. A claim secured against real property made to ensure payment for materials furnished or work performed during construction.

CONSTRUCTION LOAN. A loan to finance construction. The loan permits the borrower to take draws or advances from time to time during the course of construction.

CONSTRUCTION PROJECT. Construction work that is carried out as a separate and distinct undertaking. See NEW ~.

CONSTRUCTION SITE. A place where foundation, erection, maintenance, renovation, repair, alteration or demolition work is carried out in respect of a building or of civil engineering works, on and at the site itself, including the preparatory work of land clearing or earth moving and the lodging, eating or recreational facilities put at the disposal of the construction workers by the employer.

CONSTRUCTION SUBCONTRACTOR. A person who enters a contract, agreement or other arrangement with a construction contractor or with a person who has a contract, agreement or other arrangement with a construction contractor for the performance of any construction work on a construction project. *Construction Projects Labour-Management Relations Act*, R.S.N.S. 1989, c. 90, s. 2(1).

CONSTRUCTION TRADE NEWSPAPER. A newspaper having circulation generally throughout Ontario, that is published no less frequently than on all days except Saturdays and holidays, and in which calls for tender on construction contracts are customarily published, and that is primarily devoted to the publication of matters of concern to the construction industry. *Construction Lien Act*, R.S.O. 1990, c. C.30, s. 1(1).

CONSTRUCTION WORK. Foundation, erection, maintenance, renovation, repair, alteration and demolition work on buildings and on civil engineering works carried out on the job site itself and in the vicinity thereof, including the preparatory work on the site.

CONSTRUCTIVE. *adj.* 1. Implied or inferred. 2. Arising out of law without reference to any party's intention.

CONSTRUCTIVE DESERTION. One spouse by misconduct forces the other spouse to leave the home.

CONSTRUCTIVE DISCHARGE. Actions by the employer which cause an employee to resign.

CONSTRUCTIVE DISCRIMINATION. Occurs where an employer unilaterally makes a fundamental or substantial change to an employee's contract of employment — a change that violates the contract's terms — the employer is committing a fundamental breach of the contract that results in its termination and entitles the employee to consider himself or herself constructively dismissed. The employee can then claim damages from the employer in lieu of reasonable notice. *Farber c. Royal Trust Co.* [1977] 1 S.C.R. 846.

CONSTRUCTIVE DISMISSAL. A neutral "requirement, qualification or consideration" which gives rise to constructive discrimination is only allowed to operate as an exception where it is reasonable and *bona fide* in the circumstances. And it is only reasonable in the circumstances if accommodation cannot be accomplished without undue hardship. *Central Alberta Dairy Pool v. Alberta (Human Rights Commission)*, [1990] 2 S.C.R. 489. See ADVERSE EFFECT DISCRIMINATION.

CONSTRUCTIVE EVICTION. Acts by the landlord which deprive a tenant of enjoyment of the property so that it is untenantable.

CONSTRUCTIVE FRAUD. 1. "... [E]quivalent of breach of fiduciary duty..." *Proprietary Mines Ltd v. MacKay*, [1939] 3 D.L.R. 215 at 246, [1939] O.R. 461 (C.A.), Masten J.A. (Middleton J.A. concurring). 2. An equitable principle which permits the court to set aside transactions where conduct falling below the standards demanded of equity; classified under four headings: undue influence, abuse of confidence, unconscionable bargains, and frauds on powers. *Ogilvie v. Ogilvie Estate* (1998), 106 B.C.A.C. 55 (C.A.).

CONSTRUCTIVE KNOWLEDGE. Knowledge of circumstances which would indicate the facts to an honest person or knowledge of facts which would put an honest person on inquiry. *Air Canada v. M & L Travel Ltd.*, [1993] 3 S.C.R. 787.

CONSTRUCTIVE LAYOFF. A significant reduction in hours in circumstances where a particular employee is singled out may amount to constructive layoff.

CONSTRUCTIVE NOTICE. 1. "... [K]nowledge of other facts [other than the very fact required to be established] which put a person on inquiry to discover the fact required to be established. The classic distinction, . . . , is that of Strong J. in *Rose v. Peterkin* (1885),13 S.C.R. 677 at 94: 'What such actual and direct notice is may well be ascertained very shortly by defining constructive notice, and then taking actual notice to be knowledge, not presumed as in the case of constructive notice, but shown to be actually brought home to the party to be charged with it, either by proof of his own admission or by the evidence of witnesses who are able to establish that the very fact, of which notice is to be established, not something which would have led to the discovery of the fact if an inquiry had been pursued, was brought to his knowledge.' " *Stoimenov v. Stoimenov* (1985), 35 R.P.R. 150 at 158, 44 R.F.L. (2d) 14, 7 O.A.C. 220 (C.A.), the court per Tarnopolsky J.A. 2. Knowledge attributed to someone who fails to make proper inquiries into the title of property purchased, who fails to investigate a fact, brought to notice, which suggests that a claim exists, or who deliberately does not inquire in order to avoid notice. See EQUITABLE DOCTRINE OF ~.

CONSTRUCTIVE POSSESSION. " . . . The doctrine [of constructive possession] is described in Harris v. Mudie (1882), 7 O.A.R. 414 (C.A.) at p. 427, as follows: ' . . . when a party having colour of title enters in good faith upon the land professed to be conveyed, he is resumed to enter according to his title, and thereby gains a constructive possession of the whole land embraced in his deed.' . . . The party must establish visible and exclusive possession of part of the property described in the deed, but occupation of a portion of the property will be extended by construction to all of the land within the boundary of the deed: *Wood v. LeBlanc* (1903), 36 N.B.R. 47 affirmed 34 S.C.R. 627." *Port Franks Properties Ltd. v. R.* (1979), [1981] 3 C.N.L.R. 86 at 99, 99 D.L.R. (3d) 28 (Fed. R.C.), Lieff D.J.

CONSTRUCTIVE TOTAL LOSS. 1. "In Sailing Ship 'Blairmore' Company v. Macredie (1898), A.C. 593 the second paragraph of the headnote succinctly sets forth the law: ' . . . In considering whether a constructive total loss has occurred, the question is whether a shipowner of ordinary prudence and uninsured would have gone to the expense of raising a sunken ship and repairing her.' " *Captain J.A. Cates Tug & Wharfage Co. v. Franklin Fire Insurance Co.* (1926), 37 B.C.R. 539 at 542, [1926] 3 W.W.R. 362, [1926] 4 D.L.R. 638 (B.C. C.A.), McPhillips J.A. 2. A loss where (a) an insured property is abandoned because it appears to the Minister, on reasonable grounds, that the total loss of the property is unavoidable, or (b) the expenditure necessary to avoid the total loss of the insured property and to repair such property would exceed the insured value for total loss thereof. *Fishing Vessel Insurance Regulations*, C.R.C., c. 325, s. 2.

CONSTRUCTIVE TRUST. 1. Imposed as a " . . . [A] remedy against unjust enrichment and that before unjust enrichment may . . . exist, three elements must be shown—an enrichment, a corresponding deprivation and the absence of any 'juristic reason' for the enrichment (per Dickson J. in Becker v. Pettkus, [1980] 2 S.C.R. 834 . . .")." *Hyette v. Pfenniger* (1991), 39 R.F.L. (3d) 30 at 41 (B.C. S.C.), Newbury J. 2. Unjust enrichment" in equity permitted a number of remedies, depending on the circumstances. One was a payment for services rendered on the basis of quantum meruit or quantum valebat. Another equitable remedy, available traditionally where one person was possessed of legal title to property in which another had an interest, was the constructive trust. The remedy of constructive trust arises, where monetary damages are inadequate and where there is a link between the contribution that founds the action and the property in which the constructive trust is claimed. In order for a constructive trust to be found, in a family case as in other cases, monetary compensation must be inadequate and there must be a link between the services rendered and the property in which the trust is claimed. *Peter v. Beblow*, 1993 CarswellBC 44, 77 B.C.L.R. (2d) 1, [1993] 3 W.W.R. 337, 44 R.F.L. (3d) 329, 48 E.T.R. 1, 150 N.R. 1, 23 B.C.A.C. 81, 39 W.A.C. 81, 101 D.L.R. (4th) 621, [1993] 1 S.C.R. 980, [1993] R.D.F. 369 McLachlin, J. for the majority. See REMEDIAL ~; SUBSTANTIVE ~; VALUE RECEIVED; VALUE SURVIVED.

CONSTRUCTIVE TRUSTEE. There are three ways in which a stranger to a trust can be held liable as a constructive trustee for breach of trust. First, a stranger to the trust can be liable as a trustee *de son tort*. Secondly, a stranger to the trust can be liable for breach of trust by knowingly assisting in a fraudulent and dishonest design on the part of the trustees ("knowing assistance"). Thirdly, liability may be imposed on a stranger to the trust who is in receipt and chargeable with trust property ("knowing receipt").. *Citadel General Assurance Co. v. Lloyds Bank Canada*, 1997 CarswellAlta 823, 152 D.L.R. (4th) 411, (sub nom. *Citadel General Life Assurance Co. v. Lloyds Bank Canada*) 206 A.R. 321, (sub nom. *Citadel General Life Assurance Co. v. Lloyds Bank Canada*) 156 W.A.C. 321, 19 E.T.R. (2d) 93, 35 B.L.R. (2d) 153, 47 C.C.L.I. (2d) 153, [1997] 3 S.C.R. 805.

CONSTRUCTOR. *n.* 1. A person who contracts with any person to undertake all or part of the work on a construction site. 2. An owner who contracts with more than one person for the work or part of the work at a construction site, or undertakes all or part of the work at a construction site.

CONSTRUE. *v.* To interpret; to ascertain the meaning of.

CONSUETUDINARY LAW. Customary law.

CONSUETUDO. *n.* [L.] Custom.

CONSUETUDO DEBET ESSE CERTA; NAM INCERTA PRO NULLIS HABEN-TUR. [L.] A custom ought to be certain because uncertain things are considered worthless.

CONSUETUDO EST ALTERA LEX. [L.] Custom is another law.

CONSUETUDO EST OPTIMUS INTER-PRES LEGUM. [L.] The best interpreter of law is custom.

CONSUETUDO ET COMMUNIS ASSUE-TUDO VINCIT LEGEM NON SCRIPTAM, SI SIT SPECIALIS; ET INTERPRETATUR LEGEM SCRIPTAM, SI LEX SIT GENER-ALIS. [L.] Custom and common sense override unwritten law, if it is special; and interpret the written law if it is general.

CONSUETUDO EX CERTA CAUSA RA-TIONABILI USITATA PRIVAT COMMU-NEM LEGEM. [L.] The common law is superceded by a custom grounded in a particular cause and reasonably applied.

CONSUETUDO, LICET SIT MAGNAE AUCTORITATISM NUNQUAM TAMEN PRAEJUDICAT MANIFESTAE VERI-TATI. [L.] A custom, though it be of great authority, should never prejudice manifest truth.

CONSUETUDO LOCI OBSERVANDA EST. [L.] One should observe the custom of a place.

CONSUETUDO NEQUE INJURIA ORIRI NEQUE TOLLI POTEST. [L.] An unlawful act can neither establish nor abrogate a custom.

CONSUETUDO REGNI ANGLIAE EST LEX ANGLIAE. [L.] England's custom is England's law.

CONSUETUDO SEMEL REPROBATA NON POTEST AMPLIUS INDUCI. [L.] Once a custom has been disallowed it cannot be relied upon again.

CONSUETUDO VINCIT COMMUNEM LEGEM. [L.] Custom overrides the common law.

CONSUL. *n.* The agent of a foreign state who assists nationals of the state and protects the state's commercial interests. J.G. McLeod, *The*

Conflict of Laws (Calgary: Carswell, 1983) at 77. See VICE-~.

CONSULAR OFFICER. A consular officer of Canada or any person for the time being discharging the duties of a consular officer of Canada, and, in the absence of a consular officer of Canada or such other person, means a consul general, consul or vice-consul of the United Kingdom or any person ' for the time being discharging the duties of consul-general consul or vice-consul of the United Kingdom, and, when used in relation to a country other than Canada, means the officer recognized by Her Majesty as a consular officer of that count *Canada Shipping Act*, R.S.C. 1985, c. S-9, s. 7. See DIPLOMATIC OR ~.

CONSULATE. *n.* The residence or office of a consul.

CONSULTANT. *n.* A person appointed under a security instrument to review the value of any property which may be realized subject to the security instrument and a debtor's financial viability. F. Bennett, *Receiverships* (Toronto: Carswell, 1985) at 3. See MEDICAL ~; SECU-RITY ~.

CONSULTANT LOBBYIST. 1. An individual who, for payment, undertakes to lobby on behalf of a client. 2. An individual who, for payment, on behalf of any person or organization undertakes to communicate with a public office holder in an attempt to influence the development of any legislative proposal, the introduction of a Bill or resolution or the passage, defeat or amendment of a Bill or resolution before the legislature.

CONSULTARY RESPONSE. The court's opinion in a special case.

CONSULTATION. *n.* 1. Conferring, meeting to discuss with patient or client. 2. Discussion with a view to mutual agreement or understanding, but does not include conciliation, arbitration or any other form of process or authority binding on the parties thereto.

CONSULTATION CIRCLE. Two criteria which are absolutely essential for holding a consultation circle. First, the accused must have the firm intention to rehabilitate himself or herself. Second, the community must desire to become involved for the accused's sake. There are many other factors which should be considered, including the violence of the crime and the difficulty of the case; whether the community is affected by the crime; whether the accused has admitted his or her guilt; and the size of the community in which the accused resides. When a probation period is not applicable, there is no need to hold a circle. Where feasible the victim should participate in the consultation circle. However, the victim should not feel obliged to participate. The court should choose consultation circle members of good character and not impose on the members a duty which exceeds their capacity. *R. v. Alaku* (1993), [1994] N.W.T.R. 193 (C.Q.).

CONSUME. *v.* 1. Includes inhale, inject into the human body, masticate and smoke. *Criminal Code*, R.S.C. 1985, c. C-46, s. 462.1. 2. With respect to liquor, includes putting liquor to any use, by drinking or otherwise.

CONSUMER. *n.* 1. A natural person. 2. An individual. 3. A person who (a) utilizes or intends to utilize within a province goods for personal consumption, or for the consumption of any other person at personal expense, (b) utilize or intends to utilize within province goods on behalf of or as the agent for a who desired or desires to so utilize principal, such goods for consumption by the principal or by any other person at the expense of the principal. 4. An individual acting for personal, family or household purposes and does not include a person who is acting for business purposes. 5. (i) A person who purchases goods or services under a time sale agreement or a continuous deferred payment plan, (ii) a borrower of funds under a loan agreement, or (iii) a person who purchases goods or services or obtains money by the use of a credit card, and includes a person not referred to in subclauses (i) to (iii) who enters into a credit agreement with a credit grantor. See REGISTERED ~.

CONSUMER AGREEMENT. An agreement between a supplier and a consumer in which the supplier agrees to supply goods or services for payment. *Consumer Protection Act, 2002*, S.O. 2002, c. 30, s. 1.

CONSUMER AND CORPORATE AF-FAIRS CANADA. The federal ministry responsible for efficient conduct of the marketplace, satisfactory to both business and consumers, and for promoting confidence in private enterprise.

CONSUMER BILL. A bill of exchange issued in respect of a consumer purchase and on which the purchaser or any person signing to accommodate the purchaser is liable as a party, but does not include (a) a cheque that is dated the date of its issue or prior thereto, or at the time it is issued is post-dated not more than thirty days; or (b) a bill of exchange that (i) would be a cheque within the meaning of section 165 but for the fact that the party on which it is drawn is a financial institution, other than a bank, that as part of its business accepts money on deposit from members of the public and honours any such bill directed to be paid out of any such deposit to the extent of the amount of the deposit, and (ii) is dated the date of its issue or prior thereto, or at the time it is issued is post-dated not more than thirty days. *Bills of Exchange Act*, R.S.C. 1985, c. B-4, s. 189.

CONSUMER BOYCOTT. General refusal to buy an employer's products.

CONSUMER CREDIT. Loans to individuals to facilitate purchase of goods or services.

CONSUMER DEBT. Debt incurred by an individual for personal or household goods and services.

CONSUMER DEBTOR. A natural person who is bankrupt or insolvent and whose aggregate debts, excluding any debts secured by the person's principal residence, do not exceed seventy-five thousand dollars or such other maximum as is prescribed. *Bankruptcy and Insolvency Act*, R.S.C. 1985, c. B-3, s. 66.11.

CONSUMER GOODS. Goods that are used or acquired for use primarily for personal, family or household purposes.

CONSUMER INFORMATION. Credit information or personal information collected and retained by a consumer reporting agency. *Consumer Reporting Agencies Act*, R.S. Nfld. 1990, c. C-32, s. 2.

CONSUMER LEAFLETING. It seeks to persuade members of the public to take a certain course of action by distributing leaflets at the entrance to a business. Seeks to persuade customers to shop elsewhere because of alleged unfair labour practices.

CONSUMER NOTE. A promissory note (a) issued in respect of a consumer purchase; and (b) on which the purchaser or any one signing to accommodate him is liable as a party. *Bills of Exchange Act*, R.S.C. 1985, c. B-4, s. 189.

CONSUMER OF TOBACCO. A person who, within a province, purchases from a vendor tobacco at a retail sale in the province for personal consumption or for the consumption of other persons at personal expense or who, within the purchases from a vendor tobacco at province, retail sale in the province on behalf of or as agent for a principal who desires to acquire such tobacco for consumption by such principal or other persons at the expense of such principal.

CONSUMER ORGANIZATION. A corporation that has as its primary objective the protection or advancement of the interests of consumers and that is not incorporated for the purpose of acquiring financial gain for its members. *Financial Consumers Act*, R.S.A. 2000, c. F-13, s. 28.

CONSUMER PRICE INDEX. 1. The consumer price index for Canada as published by Statistics Canada under the authority of the Statistics Act (Canada). 2. ". . . [T]he phrase, 'cost of living index', is used in Canada commonly and interchangeably for the phrase, 'consumer price index', and especially for the index published by . . . Statistics Canada." *Collins Cartage & Storage Co. v. McDonald* (1980), 30 O.R. (2d) 234 at 236, 16 R.P.R. 71, 116 D.L.R. (3d) 570 (C.A.), the court per Goodman J.A. See COST OF LIVING INDEX; EARLIER ~.

CONSUMER PRODUCT. (i) Any goods ordinarily used for personal, family or household purposes and, without restricting the generality of the foregoing, includes any goods ordinarily used for personal, family or household purposes that are designed to be attached to or installed in any real or personal property, whether or not they are so attached or installed; and (ii) includes any goods bought for agricultural or fishing purposes by an individual or by a family farming corporation.

CONSUMER PROTECTION LEGISLATION. Legislation regulating business practices of those dealing with consumers.

CONSUMER PURCHASE. A purchase, other than a cash purchase, of goods or services or an agreement to purchase goods or services (i) by an individual other than for resale or for use in the course of a business, profession or calling, and (ii) from a person who is engaged in the business of selling or providing those goods or services.

CONSUMER REPORT. A written, oral or other communication by a consumer reporting agency of credit information or personal information, or both, pertaining to a consumer.

CONSUMER REPORTING AGENCY. A person who, for gain or profit, or on a regular cooperative non-profit basis, furnishes consumer reports.

CONSUMER REPRESENTATION. A representation, statement, offer, request or proposal, (i) made respecting or with a view to the supplying of goods or services, or both, to a consumer, or (ii) made for the purpose of or with a view to receiving consideration for goods or services, or both, supplied or purporting to have been supplied to a consumer. *Business Practices acts*.

CONSUMER SALE. A contract of sale of goods or services including an agreement of sale as well as a sale and a conditional sale of goods made in the ordinary course of business to a purchaser for personal consumption or use but does not include a sale, (a) to a purchaser for resale; (b) to a purchaser whose purchase is in the course of carrying on business; (c) to an association of individuals, a partnership or a corporation; or (d) by a trustee in bankruptcy, a receiver, a liquidator or a person acting under the order of a court. *Consumer Protection Act*, R.S.N.S. 1989, c. 92, s. 26(1).

CONSUMERS' ASSOCIATION OF CANADA. A national, non-profit organization that represents and educates consumers.

CONSUMER'S COOPERATIVE. A cooperative which purchases consumer goods for resale to its members.

CONSUMER TEXTILE ARTICLE. (a) Any textile fibre, yarn or fabric, or (b) any product made in whole or in part from a textile fibre yarn or fabric that is in the form in which it is or is to be sold to any person for consumption or use, other than consumption or use in the manufacturing, processing or finishing of any product for sale. *Textile Labelling Act*, R.S.C. 1985, c. T-10, s. 2.

CONSUMER TRANSACTION. 1. (i) A sale or lease of goods or any other disposition of goods for a consideration, whether or not the sale, lease or disposition includes any agreement or arrangement under which services are provided, (ii) an agreement or arrangement under which services are provided for a consideration, or (iii) an award by chance of goods or services or both. 2. Any act or instance of conducting business or other dealings with a consumer, including a consumer agreement. *Consumer Protection Act, 2002*, S.O. 2002, c. 30, s. 1.

CONSUMMATE. *v.* 1. To finish. 2. "A marriage is consummated once sexual intercourse has taken place . . ." *Sau v. Sau* (1970), 1 R.F.L. 250 at 251 (Ont. H.C.), Parker J.

CONSUMMATE. *adj.* Completed; possessing extra skill or ability; excellent.

CONSUMMATION. *n.* Completion; act of sexual intercourse after marriage which completes the marriage.

CONSUMPTION. *n.* 1. Includes (i) use, (ii) the incorporation into any structure, building or fixture, of goods including those manufactured by the consumer or further processed or otherwise improved personally, (iii) the provision of goods by way of promotional distribution. 2. In relation to crude oil, the action of using it as a fuel or energy source or consuming it in the manufacture of products of trade and commerce. *Energy Administration Act*, R.S.C. 1985, c. E-6, s. 20. See FUEL ~.

CONTACT. *n.* 1. "[In s. 16(10) of the Divorce Act, R.S.C. 1985, c. 3] . . . define[s] the quality of the time spent together. It bespeaks a real communication, of the opportunity to know each other well and to appreciate each other as individuals, and of the chance to preserve and to share with each other that special relationship which ought to endure between child and parent." *Young v. Young* (1990), 29 R.F.L (3d) 113 at 204, 50 B.C.L.R. (2d) 1, 75 D.L.R. (4th) 46 (C.A.), Wood J.A. 2. Any person or animal suspected to have been in association with an infected person or animal or a contaminated environment to a sufficient degree to have had the opportunity to become infected with a disease. See PERSONAL ~.

CONTACT FLATTENING. The shaping of muscles caused by contact with any hard surface during rigor mortis. F.A. Jaffe, *A Guide to Pathological Evidence*, 3d ed. (Toronto: Carswell, 1991) at 216.

CONTACT INFORMATION. Information to enable an individual at a place of business to be contacted and includes the name, position name or title, business telephone number, business address, business email or business fax number of the individual.

CONTACT RING. See GREY RING.

CONTAGIOUS. *adj.* Communicable by close contact or inoculation.

CONTAGIOUS DISEASE. A disease which may be transmitted by one animal or person to another by direct contact or otherwise. See INFECTIOUS DISEASE.

CONTAINER. *n.* 1. The articles and devices used to package tangible personal property for shipment or delivery, such as bags, cans, barrels, boxes, bottles, drums, carboys, cartons, sacks, pallets and cores. 2. A receptacle, package, wrapper or confining band in which a product is offered for sale but does not include package liners or shipping containers or any outer wrapping or box that is not customarily displayed to consumer. *Consumer Packaging and Labelling Act*, R.S.C. 1985, c. C-38, s. 2. 3. An article of transport equipment, including one that is carried on a chassis, that is strong enough to be suitable for repeated use and is designed to facilitate the transportation of goods by one or more means of transport without intermediate reloading, but does not include a vehicle. *Transportation of Dangerous Goods acts*. See APPROVED ~; BULK ~; BULK STORAGE ~; CARGO ~; CHILD-RESISTANT ~; CONSUMER ~; DISPOSABLE ~; MASTER ~; NON-REFILLABLE ~; NON-RETURNABLE ~; ORNAMENTAL ~; PORTABLE ~; REFILLABLE ~; RETURNABLE ~; SHIPPING ~.

CONTAINERIZED GOODS. Goods that are received in a container for movement intact between vessels and inland carriers.

CONTAMINANT. *n.* 1. Any solid, liquid, gas, waste, odour, heat, sound, vibration, radiation, or a combination of any of them that (i) is foreign to or in excess of the natural constituents of the environment; or (ii) affects the natural, physical, chemical, or biological quality of the environment; or (iii) is or is likely to be injurious to the health or safety of a person; or (iv) is or is likely to be injurious or damaging to property; or (v) is or is likely to be injurious or damaging to plant or animal life; or (vi) interferes likely to interfere with visibility; or (vii) interferes or is likely to interfere with the normal conduct of business, or (viii) interferes or is likely to interfere with the comfort, well-being or enjoyment of a person. 2. Any solid, liquid, gas, odour, heat, sound, vibration, radiation or combination of any of them resulting directly or indirectly from human activities that may cause an adverse effect. *Environmental Protection Act*, R.S.O. 1990, c. E.19, s. 1(1). See AIR ~; EFFLUENT; SOURCE OF ~; WATER ~.

CONTAMINATED. *adj.* In respect of grain, containing any substance in sufficient quantity that the grain is unfit for consumption by persons and animals. *Canada Grain Act*, R.S C. 1985, c. G-10, s. 2.

CONTAMINATION. *n.* The presence of an infectious agent on a body surface, or on or in an inanimate article or substance including food. *Public Health, Act*, R.S.A. 2000, c. P-37, s. 1. See SOURCE OF ~.

CONTANGO. *n.* A charge paid by a buyer of stock for being allowed to delay taking delivery until a date later than that originally agreed.

CONTEMNOR. *n.* One who commits contempt of court.

CONTEMPLATE. *v.* To view, consider, study, ponder.

CONTEMPLATION. *n.* 1. Consideration of a matter. 2. Contemplation of marriage refers to a time when the parties have committed themselves to marry each other.

CONTEMPLATION OF MARRIAGE. " . . . [I]nfers a situation where the parties have agreed on, or committed themselves to, a marriage and where the transfer or gift can be said to have been made in that context. . ." *Fediuk v. Gluck* (1990), 26 R.F.L. (3d) 454 at 459 (Man. Q.B.), Wright J.

CONTEMPORANEA EXPOSITIO EST FORTISSIMA IN LEGE. [L.] The meaning openly given by current or long professional use should be taken as the true one.

CONTEMPORANEA EXPOSITIO EST OPTIMA ET FORTISSIMA IN LEGE. [L.] The current meaning is the best and most compelling in law.

CONTEMPORANEOUS INTERPRETATION. It may be useful to keep in mind the distinction between "consecutive" (after the words are spoken) and "simultaneous" (at the same time as words are spoken). While it is generally preferable that interpretation be consecutive rather than simultaneous, the overriding consideration is that the interpretation be contemporaneous. *R. v. Tran*, [1994] 2 S.C.R. 951.

CONTEMPT. *n.* 1. Contempt of court is the mechanism which the law provides for the protection of the authority of the court from improper interference. It is part of the court's inherent jurisdiction and is not enacted or prescribed. 2. " . . . [I]nterfering with the administration of the law and . . . impeding and perverting the course of justice." *R. v Kopyto* (1987), 61 C.R. (3d) 209 at 222, 24 O.A.C. 8, 62 O.R. 449, 39 C.C.C. (3d) 1, 47 D.L.R. (4th) 213 (C.A.), Dubin J.A. 3. Disobeying an order of the court. 4. "Acts which interfere with persons having duties to discharge in a Court of Justice, including parties, witnesses, jurors and officers of the Court, . . ." *B.C.G.E.U., Re* (1988), 30 C.P.C. (2d) 221 at 242, [1988] 6 W.W.R. 577, 71 Nfld. & P.E.I.R. 93, 220 A.P.R. 93, 87 N.R. 241, [1988] 2 S.C.R. 214, 88 C.L.L.C. 14,047, 53 D.L.R. (4th) 1, 31 B.C.L.R. (2d) 273, 44 C.C.C. (3d) 289, the court per Dickson C.J.C. 5. A person who was required by law to attend or remain in attendance for the purpose of giving evidence, who fails, without lawful excuse, to attend or remain in attendance, is guilty of contempt of court. *Criminal Code*, R.S.C. 1985, c. C-46, s. 708 1. 6. An act before a court or tribunal which shows disrespect for a court's authority or tends to hinder the course of justice. See CIVIL ~; CRIMINAL ~; SCANDALIZE THE COURT.

CONTEMPT EX FACIE. Contempt committed outside the court.

CONTEMPT IN FACIE. Contempt committed in the face of the court.

CONTEMPT IN PROCEDURE. Disobedience of the judgments, orders or other process of a court in circumstances which involve an injury to a private litigant.

CONTEMPT IN THE FACE OF THE COURT. " . . . [A]ny word spoken or act done in or in the precinct of the court which obstructs or interferes with the due administration of justice or is calculated to do so." *R. v. Kopyto* (1987), 39 C.C.C. (3d) 1 at 9, 24 O.A.C. 8, 61 C.R. (3d) 209, 62 O.R. (2d) 449, 47 D.L.R. (4th) 213 (C.A.), Cory J.A.

CONTEMPT NOT IN THE FACE OF THE COURT. " . . . [I]ncludes words spoken or published or acts done which are intended to interfere or are likely to interfere with the fair administration of justice." *R. v. Kopyto* (1987), 39 C.C.C. (3d) 1 at 9, 24 O.A.C. 8, 61 C.R. (3d) 209, 62 O.R. (2d) 449, 47 D.L.R. (4th) 213 (C.A.), Cory J.A.

CONTEMPT OF COURT. 1. Contempt may be dealt with by one of two procedures: the ordinary procedure, which provides the accused with the usual procedural guarantees of a criminal trial, or the summary procedure, which allows the judge to avoid the formalities of a criminal trial to convict a person of contempt of court, even *instanter* in some cases. Using the summary contempt of court procedure can be justified only in cases where it is *urgent* and *imperative* to act immediately. The summary procedure consists of citing, convicting and sentencing. *R. c. Arradi*, 2003 SCC 23. 2. Contempt of court, both civil and criminal, has existed for centuries. It is the tool used by the courts to ensure compliance with its orders and to protect its process. Is clearly aimed at punishing public acts which tend to bring the administration of justice into disrepute and interfere with the due administration of justice. *R. v. Edmonton Sun*, 2003 ABCA 3, 320 A.R. 217 (C.A.).

CONTEMPT OF PARLIAMENT. To obstruct the due course of proceedings in either House of Parliament.

CONTEMPT OUTSIDE THE COURT. " . . . [W]ords spoken or otherwise published, or acts done, outside court which are intended or likely to interfere with or obstruct the fair administration of justice . . ." *R. v. Cohn* (1984), 42 C.R. (2d) 1 at 10, 48 O.R. (2d) 65, 70 C.R.R. 142, 15 C.C.C. (3d) 150, 13 D.L.R. (4th) 680, 4 O.A.C. 293 (C.A.), the court per Goodman J.A.

CONTEMPTUOUS DAMAGES. Small damages awarded to a plaintiff who sustained no loss, but whose legal rights were technically infringed.

CONTENT. See CANADIAN ~; JOB ~; PROVINCIAL ~; RESIDUAL CHLORINE ~.

CONTENTIOUS. *adj*. Contested.

CONTENTIOUS BUSINESS. (i) The proving of a will in solemn form, (ii) proceedings in which the right to obtain or retain a grant is in dispute, and (iii) proceedings to discharge a caveat. *Administration of Estates Act*, R.S.A. 1980, c. A-1, s. 1.

CONTENTIOUS JURISDICTION. Authority to hear and determine matters which parties dispute.

CONTEST. *v*. To oppose, resist, dispute.

CONTEST. *n*. A boxing match in which the contestants compete for monetary reward and includes a closed circuit televised contest. *Boxing Authority Act*, R.S.N.S. 1989, c. 43, s. 2. See LEADERSHIP ~ PERIOD; PHYSICAL ~; PROFESSIONAL ~ OR EXHIBITION; PUBLICITY ~.

CONTESTANT. See LEADERSHIP ~.

CONTESTATIO LITIS EGET TERMINOS CONTRADICTARIOS. [L.] The joinder of issue requires contradictory terms.

CONTESTATION. *n*. 1. A controversy; a disputed issue. 2. Any elector who was eligible to vote in an electoral district, and any candidate in an electoral district, may, by application to a competent court, contest the election in that electoral district on the grounds that the elected candidate was not eligible to be a candidate; or there were irregularities, fraud or corrupt or illegal practices that affected the result of the election. *Canada Elections Act*, S.C. 2000, c. 9, s. 524.

CONTESTED DIVORCE. A divorce action in which a respondent delivers an answer. That is, the respondent disputes the grounds alleged by the petitioner or the remedies sought by the petitioner.

CONTEXT. *n*. 1. Parts of text surrounding the portion under consideration. 2. For purposes of constitutional analysis includes the circumstances which led to the enactment and the mischief at which it was directed. 3. Of words in a statute, refers to the whole of the statute and other indicators of legislative meaning.

CONTEXTUAL APPROACH. 1. Refers to the method of interpretation of the Charter in which a particular right or freedom is considered in its particular context to determine the aspect of the right or freedom which is at issue. 2. Looking at the broader context of a statutory provision, such as other provisions of the same statute and parliamentary intent as an aid to interpretation of a provision.

CONTIGUITY. *n*. In international law, proximity to neighbouring territory.

CONTIGUOUS. *adj*. "One area is contiguous to another where both have a common boundary or even a common point of contact." *R. v. Alegria* (1992), 96 Nfld. & P.E.I.R. 128 at 140, 305 A.P.R. 128 (Nfld. C.A.), the court per Goodridge C.J.N.

CONTIGUOUS LAND. One or more parcels or lots of lands the aggregate area of which is continuous and unbroken, so that, in the case of there being more than one parcel or lot, each parcel or lot thereof touches or adjoins one or more of the other parcels or lots.

CONTIGUOUS ZONE. 1. In relation to Canada, means the contiguous zone of Canada as determined under the *Oceans Act*, and in relation to any other state, means the contiguous zone of the other state as determined in accordance with international law and the domestic laws of that other state. *Interpretation Act*, R.S.C. 1985, c. I-21, s. 35. 2. The contiguous zone of Canada consists of an area of the sea that has as its inner limit the outer limit of the territorial sea of Canada and as its outer limit the line every point of which is at a distance of 24 nautical miles from the nearest point of the baselines of the territorial sea of Canada, but does not include an area of the sea that forms part of the territorial sea of another state or in which another state has sovereign rights. *Oceans Act*, S.C. 1996, c. 31, s. 10.

CONTINENTAL SHELF. 1. The shallow area of the ocean which adjoins each continent. 2. In relation to Canada, means the continental shelf of Canada as determined under the *Oceans Act*, and in relation to any other state, means the continental shelf of the other state as determined in accordance with international law and the domestic laws of that other state. *Interpretation Act*, R.S.C. 1985, c. I-21, s. 35. 3. The continental shelf of Canada is the seabed and subsoil of the submarine areas, including those of the exclusive economic zone of Canada, that extend beyond the territorial sea of Canada throughout the natural prolongation of the land territory of Canada (*a*) subject to paragraphs (*b*) and (*c*), to the outer edge of the continental margin, determined in the manner under international law that results in the maximum extent of the continental shelf of Canada, the outer edge of the continental margin being the submerged prolongation of the land mass of Canada consisting of the seabed and subsoil of the shelf, the slope and the rise, but not including the deep ocean floor with its oceanic ridges or its subsoil; (*b*) to a distance of 200 nautical miles from the baselines of the territorial sea of Canada where the outer edge of the continental margin does not extend up to that distance; or (*c*) in respect of a portion of the continental shelf of Canada for which geographical coordinates of points have been prescribed pursuant to subparagraph 25(*a*)(iii), to lines determined from the geographical coordinates of points so prescribed. *Oceans Act, 1996*, S.C. 1996, c. 31, s. 17.

CONTINGENCY. *n.* 1. Accident, sickness, strikes and unemployment. K.D. Cooper-Stephenson & I.B. Saunders, *Personal Injury Damages in Canada Supplement to June 30, 1987* (Toronto: Carswell, 1987) at 244. 2. An uncertain event on which an estate, interest, liability, right or obligation depends for its existence. See MITIGATION ∼.

CONTINGENCY AGREEMENT. An agreement which provides that the remuneration paid to a solicitor for legal services provided to or on behalf of the client is contingent, in whole or in part, on the successful disposition or completion of the matter in respect of which services are provided.

CONTINGENCY CONTRACT. A contract between a member and a person (referred to in this section as "the client") under which the member is to receive or retain, as remuneration for services rendered or to be rendered to the client, in lieu of or in addition to other remuneration for those services, (a) a portion of the proceeds of the subject matter of the action or proceedings in which the member is or will be acting for the client; (b) a portion of the money or property in respect of which the member is or may be retained or employed; or (c) a commission or a percentage of (i) the amount recovered or defended, or (ii) the value of the property that is the subject of a transaction, action, or proceeding. *The Legal Profession Act*, S.M. 2002, c. 44, s. 55.

CONTINGENCY FEE. The fee paid under an agreement which provides that the remuneration paid to a solicitor for legal services provided to or on behalf of the client is contingent, in whole or in part, on the successful disposition or completion of the matter in respect of which services are provided.

CONTINGENCY INSURANCE. An agreement by an insurer to pay when an event occurs regardless of the loss suffered. Examples are life or accident insurance.

CONTINGENCY LEVY. An assessment or levy made on members of a society, order, association, or corporation on the occasion of the happening to any member thereof of any one or more of certain contingencies upon the happening of which that member or the member's beneficiaries become entitled to receive the proceeds of that assessment or levy.

CONTINGENCY RESERVE FUND. A fund for common expenses that usually occur less often than once a year or that do not usually occur, *Strata Property Act*, S.B.C. 1998, c. 43, s. 1.

CONTINGENCY WITH A DOUBLE ASPECT. An interest that will vest only if the next preceding interest never vests in any way.

CONTINGENT. *adj.* Conditional upon the occurrence of some future uncertain event.

CONTINGENT ASSETS. Assets without known value to the company until fulfilment of conditions regarded as uncertain.

CONTINGENT INTEREST. A possibility conditioned on the happening of a future uncertain event.

CONTINGENT LEGACY. A legacy bequeathed payable on happening of a contingency.

CONTINGENT LIABILITIES. Liabilities that may, under certain conditions, become obligations of the company but are not direct or assumed obligations on the date of the balance sheet. Canada regulations.

CONTINGENT LIABILITY. " . . . [A] liability to make a payment is contigent if the terms of its creation include uncertainty in respect of any of these three things: (1) whether the payment will be made; (2) the amount payable; or (3) the time by which payment shall be made . . ." *Samuel F. Investments Limited v. M.N.R.* (1988), 88 D.T.C. 1106 at 1108 (T.C.C.).

CONTINGENT REMAINDER. A remainder which depends on an uncertain condition or event that may never be performed or happen, or which may not be performed or happen until after a preceding estate is determined.

CONTINGENT RIGHT. Includes a contingent or executory interest, a possibility coupled with an interest, whether the object of the gift or limitation of the interest or possibility is or is not ascertained, also a right of entry, whether immediate or future, and whether vested or contingent.

CONTINUANCE. 1. Keeping up, going on with, maintaining. 2. The ongoing existence of a company which is transferred from regulation by the jurisdiction where it was incorporated to be regulated under the control of another jurisdiction. See CERTIFICATE OF ~;

CONTINUATION. *n*. Statutes governing corporations may permit a corporation to continue its corporate existence under the law of another jurisdiction.

CONTINUE. See ORDER TO ~.

CONTINUED. *adj*. A company incorporated under one act may in certain circumstances be "continued" under the laws of some other jurisdiction so that its existence is maintained subject to the laws of the second jurisdiction.

CONTINUING. *adj*. Ongoing; enduring.

CONTINUING CARE. Health care services to persons with a frailty or with an acute or chronic illness or disability that do not require admission to a hospital.

CONTINUING CAUSE OF ACTION. A cause of action which arises from a repetition of the act or omission giving rise to the cause.

CONTINUING EDUCATION. Includes education or training offered by an institution to adult persons on a part time or short term basis. *College and Institute Act*, R.S.B.C. 1996, c. 52, s. 1.

CONTINUING GARNISHMENT. Refers to the taking of money coming due at intervals by garnishment proceedings.

CONTINUING GRIEVANCE. A grievance which recurs or in which the circumstances upon which the grievance are based are repeated.

CONTINUING OFFENCE. " . . . [N]ot simply an offence which takes or may take a long time to commit. It may be described as an offence where the conjunction of the actus reus and the mens rea, which makes the offence complete, does not, as well, terminate the offence. The conjunction of the two essential elements for the commission of the offence continues and the accused remains in what might be described as a state of criminality while the offence continues. . . Conspiracy to commit murder could be a continuing offence. The actus reus and the mens rea are present when the unlawful agreement is made and continue until the killing occurs or the conspiracy is abandoned. Whatever the length of time involved, the conspirators remain in the act of commission of a truly continuing offence. . ." *R. v. Bell* (1983), 8 C.C.C. (3d) 97 at 110, 36 C.R. (3d) 289, 3 D.L.R. (4th) 385, 50 N.R. 172, [1983] 2 S.C.R. 471, McIntyre J. (Beetz, Estey and Chouinard JJ. concurring).

CONTINUING TORT. One involving the continuance of the act which caused the damage.

CONTINUOUS. *adj*. 1. Uninterrupted. *New Brunswick v. C.U.P.E.* (1981), 125 D.L.R. (3d) 220 at 224 (N.B. C.A.), the court per Stratton J.A. 2. In relation to membership in a pension plan or to employment, means without regard to periods of temporary interruption of the membership or employment. *Pension Benefits Standards Act*, R.S.C. 1985 (2d Supp.), c. 32, s. 2.

CONTINUOUS ACTIVITY. Work requiring an employee be constantly available.

CONTINUOUS DEFERRED PAYMENT PLAN. A sale or an agreement to sell under which (i) purchases on credit can be made from time to time by a purchaser, and (ii) the credit charges, if any, are computed from time to time in relation to the unpaid balance on all the purchases.

CONTINUOUS DISCLOSURE. An ongoing obligation imposed on a company with publicly traded securities to make public statements concerning any material changes in its affairs in order that there is a continuous flow of information to the securities market.

CONTINUOUS INDUSTRY. A manufacturing process carried on without interruption.

CONTINUOUSLY. *adv.* Without ceasing; without break.

CONTINUOUSLY EMPLOYED. Includes the employment of seasonal workers who are engaged under a contract of service for 2 or more consecutive seasons of at least 5 months in each season during which the employee is occupationally engaged. *Labour Standards Act*, R.S. Nfld. 1990, c. L-2, s. 55.

CONTINUOUSLY-OPERATING PLANT. *var.* **CONTINUOUSLY OPERATING PLANT**. (i) An industrial plant; or (ii) an establishment factory, works, or undertaking, in or about any industry, in which, in each seven-day period, operations once commenced normally continue day and night without cessation until the completion of the regularly scheduled operations for that period.

CONTINUOUS MINER. Machine used in coal mining operations. It has a rotating head with picks that are in physical contact with the working face of a mine. The head loosens the rock and the fragments are then directed along a conveyor system. *Sandvik Tamrock Canada Ltd. v. Deputy Minister of National Revenue (Customs & Excise)*, 2001 FCA 340, 284 N.R. 183, 6 T.T.R. (2d) 302 (C.A.).

CONTINUOUS OPERATION. An operation or that part of an operation that normally continues 24 hours a day without cessation in each seven-day period until it is concluded for that period. *Employment Standards Act, 2000*, S.O. 2000, c. 41, s. 1. See EMPLOYED IN A ~.

CONTINUOUS PERIOD. See SERVICE FOR A ~.

CONTINUOUS RATING. The brake horsepower speed stated by the manufacturer to be the highest at which an engine will give satisfactory service when operating continuously for not less than 24 hours. *Large Fishing Vessel Inspection Regulations*, C.R.C., c. 1435, s. 2.

CONTINUOUS SERVICE. Uninterrupted service of a person as an employee. May include time spent on certain types of leave.

CONTINUOUS TRIGGER THEORY. Under this theory, the property damage is effectively deemed to have occurred from the initial exposure to the time when the damage became manifest or ought to have become manifest to the plaintiffs, and if alerted, to the insured. In that case, all policies in effect over that period are called upon to respond to the loss. *Alie v. Bertrand & Frère Construction Co.* (2002), 62 O.R. (3d) 345 (C.A.).

CONTINUOUS WASTE AND VENT. A vent pipe that is a vertical extension of a vertical waste pipe and includes the vertical waste pipe. *Building Code Act, 1992* O. Reg. 403/97, s. 1.1.3.

CONTOUR. See OFFICIAL ~.

CONTRA. [L.] Against.

CONTRABAND. *n.* 1. Goods not permitted to be exported or imported, bought or sold. 2. Anything that is in a prisoner's possession in circumstances in which possession thereof is forbidden by any act or regulation, or by an order of general or specific application within the prison or penitentiary in which the prisoner is confined. 3. An intoxicant; a weapon or a component thereof, ammunition for a weapon, and anything that is designed to kill, injure or disable a person or that is altered so as to be capable of killing, injuring or disabling a person, when possessed without prior authorization; an explosive or a bomb or a component thereof; currency over any applicable prescribed limit, when possessed without prior authorization; and, any item not described that could jeopardize the security of a penitentiary or the safety of persons, when that item is possessed without prior authorization. *Corrections and Conditional Release Act*, S.C. 1992, c. 20, s. 2.

CONTRA BONOS MORES. [L.] Contrary to good morals.

CONTRACAUSATOR. *n.* A criminal; a person prosecuted for a crime.

CONTRACEPTIVE. *n.* A device for preventing conception.

CONTRACEPTIVE. *adj.* Preventing conception.

CONTRACEPTIVE DEVICE. Any instrument, apparatus, contrivance or substance other than a drug, that is manufactured, sold or represented for use in the prevention of conception. *Food and Drugs Act*, R.S.C. 1985, c. F-27, s. 2.

CONTRACT. *n.* 1. An agreement between two or more persons, recognized by law, which gives rise to obligations that the courts may enforce. 2. A promise, or set of promises, which one person gives in exchange for the promise, or set of promises, of another person. See ACTION OF ~; ADOPTION OF ~; ALBERTA ~; ALEATORY ~; ANNUITY ~; BILATERAL~; BRITISH COLUMBIA ~; BUILDING ~; C.I.F. ~; CLOSED SHOP ~; COLLATERAL ~; COMMODITY ~; COMMODITY FUTURES ~; COMPLETED ~ METHOD; COMPLETION OF THE ~; CONCLUDED ~; CONSTRUCTION ~; CONTINGENCY ~; COST PLUS ~; DEFENCE ~; DEPOSIT ADMINISTRATION DIRECT SALES ~; DISTRIBUTION ~; DOMESTIC ~; EMPLOYMENT ~; ESSENCE OF THE ~; EXCHANGE ~; EXECUTED ~; EXECUTORY ~; FIRM PRICE ~; FIXED PRICE ~; FOOD PLAN ~; F.O.R. ~; FORMAL ~; FREEDOM OF ~; FUTURES ~; GAS ~; GAS PURCHASE ~; GOODS ~; GOVERNMENT ~; GROUP ~; HONEYMOON ILLEGAL ~; IMMORAL ~; IMPLIED INDUSTRIAL ~; INFORMAL ~; INSULATION ~; INVESTMENT ~; LAW OF ~; LOYALTY ~; MANAGEMENT ~; MANITOBA ~; MARRIAGE ~; MATERIAL ~; MEDICAL ~; MULTI-YEAR ~; NAKED~; NEWFOUNDLAND ~; ONTARIO ~; ORAL ~; PAROL ~; PATRONAGE ~; PREARRANGED CEMETERY ~; PRE-EXISTING ~; PRE-INCORPORATION ~; PREPAID ~; PROBATIONARY ~; PRODUCER-SHIPPER ~; QUASI-~; REGULAR PAYMENT ~; RELATIONAL ~; SALES ~; SASKATCHEWAN ~; SERVICE ~; SIMPLE ~; SPECIALTY ~; STIPULATED PRICE ~; TERM ~; TRAINING ~; UNILATERAL ~; UNION ~; UNIT PRICE ~; VALUE OF THE ~; WAGERING ~.

CONTRACT BENEFICIARY. The individual: (i) who is named in a prepaid contract; and (ii) on whose death funeral services or cremation services or both are to be provided pursuant to that prepaid contract. *The Funeral and Cremation Services Act*, S.S. 1999, c. F. 23.3, s. 2.

CONTRACT BOND. " . . . [C]ontract of suretyship and guarantee. . ." *Johns-Manville Canada Inc. v. John Carlo Ltd.* (1980), (*sub nom. Canadian Johns-Manville Co. v. John Carlo Ltd.*) 12 B.L.R. 80 *at* 87, 29 O.R. (2d) 592, 113 D.L.R. (3d) 686 (H.C.), R.E. Holland J. See LABOUR AND MATERIAL BOND; PERFORMANCE BOND.

CONTRACT DATE. The date on which a contract is signed by both parties.

CONTRACT DELIVERY POINT. (i) With reference to a gas sales contract, the point at which delivery is taken by the original buyer under the gas sales contract, or (ii) with reference to a resale contract, the point at which delivery is taken by the second buyer under the resale contract.

CONTRACTED. *adj.* Agreed upon; effected.

CONTRACT EMPLOYEE. An employee engaged by means of a contract for temporary employment for a fixed term.

CONTRACT FIELD PRICE. With reference to a gas sales contract or a resale contract, the price of gas under the contract, whether the price is specified in the contract or is redetermined pursuant to the contract by agreement or by arbitration. *Natural Gas Pricing Agreement Act*, R.S.A. 1980, c. N-4, s. 1.

CONTRACT FOR FUTURE SERVICES. An executory contract that includes a provision for services of a prescribed type or class to be rendered in the future on a continuing basis.

CONTRACT FOR SALE. A sale in which the thing sold is exchanged for a consideration in money or money's worth.

CONTRACT FOR SERVICES. The engagement of a person as an independent contractor.

CONTRACT HOLDER. An individual who has entered into an income-averaging annuity contract with a trustee. *Queen's Bench Act, 1998*, S.S. 1998, c. Q-1.01, s. 74.

CONTRACTING ELECTRICIAN. A person who, for another, carries out, or causes to be carried out, electrical installation work, or renovation, alteration or repair work on electrical installations for purposes of electric lighting, heating or power.

CONTRACTING IN. Refers to an employer's bringing persons into a workplace to perform the same work as bargaining unit employees.

CONTRACTING OUT. The action of an employer who arranges with a second employer to have the second employer perform work on behalf of the first employer.

CONTRACTING STATE. Any state that has ratified or adhered to a convention and whose denunciation thereof has not become effective. See COURT OF A ~.

CONTRACT IN RESTRAINT OF TRADE. " . . . Lord Hodson, [in Esso Petroleum Co. v. Harper's Garage (Stourport) Ltd., [1968] A.C. 269] at p. 317, adopted the dicta of Diplock, L.J., in Petrofina (Great Britain) Ltd. v. Martin [1966] Ch. 146 at p. 180: 'A contract in restraint of trade is one in which a party (the covenantor) agrees with any other party (the convenantee) to restrict his liberty in the future to carry on trade with other persons not parties to the contract in such manner as he chooses.' " *Stephens v. Gulf Oil Canada Ltd.* (1975), 25 C.P.R. (2d) 64 at 77, 11 O.R. (2d) 129, 65 D.L.R. (3d) 193 (C.A.), the court per Howland J.A.

CONTRACT LAW. The branch of private law dealing with drafting, interpretation and enforcement of contracts between persons.

CONTRACT OF APPRENTICESHIP. A written agreement entered into in accordance with this Act and the regulations between a person who is sixteen years of age or older and an employer, under which the person agrees with the employer to learn a trade requiring a minimum of four thousand hours of reasonably continuous employment and which provides for a course of related technical instruction for the person. *Apprenticeship Act*, R.S. Nfld. 1990, c. A-12, s. 2.

CONTRACT OF BENEVOLENCE. A contract made which benefits only one contracting party, as a mandate or deposit.

CONTRACT OF COMMODATUM. A contract concerning a loan of useful goods. D.M.W. Waters, *The Law of Trusts in Canada* 2d ed. (Toronto: C arswell, 1984) at 63.

CONTRACT OF DEPOSITUM. A contract of deposit. D.M.W. Waters, *The Law of Trusts in Canada*, 2d ed. (Toronto: Carswell, 1984) at 63.

CONTRACT OF EMPLOYMENT. A contract by which an employee agrees to provide services to an employer.

CONTRACT OF GUARANTEE. In the contract of guarantee, the guarantor agrees to repay the lender if the debtor defaults. The exact nature of the obligation owed by the guarantor to the lender depends on the construction of the contract of guarantee, but the liability of the guarantor is usually made coterminous with that of the principal debtor. Generally speaking, if the principal debt is void or unenforceable, the contract of guarantee will likewise be void or unenforceable. *Communities Economic Development Fund v. Canadian Pickles Corp.*, [1991] 3 S.C.R. 388.

CONTRACT OF INDEMNITY. 1. In a contract of indemnity, the indemnifier assumes a primary obligation to repay the debt, and is liable regardless of the liability of the principal debtor. An indemnifier will accordingly be liable even if the principal debt is void or otherwise unenforceable. *Communities Economic Development Fund v. Canadian Pickles Corp.*, [1991] 3 S.C.R. 388. 2. " . . . [A] contract by which one party agrees to make good a loss suffered by the other and includes most contracts of insurance. . ." *Callaghan Contracting Ltd. v. Royal Insurance Co. of Canada* (1989), [1990] 39 C.C.L.I. 65 at 70, 97 N.B.R. (2d) 381, 245 A.P.R. 381 (C.A.), the court per Stratton C.J.N.B.

CONTRACT OF INSURANCE. 1. "In . . . Re Bendix Automotive of Can. Ltd. and U.A.W., [1971] 3 O.R. 263 . . . (Ont. H.C.), [the court considered] the . . . definition of contract of insurance at p. 269: 'The basic elements which are common to all of these definitions may be stated as follows; i) an undertaking of one person; ii) to indemnify another person; iii) for an agreed consideration; iv) from loss or liability in respect of an event; v) the happening of which is uncertain.' " *Arkhe v. Haskell* (1986) 25 C.C.L.I. 277 at 282, 284, 33 D.L.R. (4th) 458, [1987] I.L.R. 1-2176 (B.C.C.A.), McLachlin J.A. (Hutcheon and MacFarlane JJ.A. concurring). 3. An agreement by which an insurer, for a premium, agrees to indemnify the insured against loss. 2. A policy, certificate, interim receipt, renewal receipt, or writing evidencing the contract, whether sealed or not, and a binding oral agreement.

CONTRACT OF LIFE INSURANCE. See REPLACEMENT OF A ~.

CONTRACT OF LOCATIO ET CONDUCTIO. A contract about hiring. D.M.W. Waters, *The Law of Trusts in Canada*, 2d ed. (Toronto: Carswell, 1984) at 63.

CONTRACT OF MARINE INSURANCE. A contract under which an insurer agrees to indemnify the insured, in the way and to the extent agreed, against marine losses.

CONTRACT OF PIGNUS. A contract relating to a pledge. D.M.W. Waters, *The Law of Trusts in Canada*, 2d ed. (Toronto: Carswell, 1984) at 63.

CONTRACT OF SALE. Includes an agreement to sell as well as sale. *Sale of Goods acts*.

CONTRACT OF SERVICE. 1. "In Short v. J. and W. Henderson, Ltd. (1946), 174 L.T. 416, an appeal to the House of Lords from a decision of the Court of Session, Lord Thankerton . . . referred to four indicia of a contract of service which had been derived from the Lord Justice Clerk from the authorities referred to by him. They were, (a) the master's power of selection of his servant; (b) the payment of wages or other remuneration; (c) the master's right to control the method of doing work, and (d) the master's right of suspension or dismissal." *Marine Pipeline Dredging Ltd. v. Canadian Fina Oil Ltd.* (1964) 46 D.L.R. (2d) 495 at 502 (Alta. C.A.). 2. There is a relationship of subordination between the parties. The worker, in other words, is a true employee of the employer, and not merely a contractor working for the employer pursuant to a contract of enterprise. 3. Contractor is defined variously as a person who undertakes a contract, esp. to provide materials, conduct building operations; one who contracts on predetermined terms to provide labour and materials and to be responsible for the performance of a construction job in accordance with established specifications or plans; one who contracts to provide work or labour, but not a vendor of a chattel. *Daishowa-Marubeni International Ltd. v. Toshiba International Corp.* (2000), 2000 CarswellAlta 1518, [2001] I.L.R. I-3915, 86 Alta. L.R. (3d) 76, [2001] 5 W.W.R. 357, 12 B.L.R. (3d) 297, 278 A.R. 388, 28 C.C.L.I. (3d) 309 (Q.B.), Kent J.

CONTRACTOR. *n.* 1. Any person who, for another, carries out construction work or causes it to be carried out or makes or submits tenders, personally or through another person, to carry out such work for personal profit. 2. One who agrees to supply work or labour. 3. A person who enters into a pre-incorporation contract in the name of or on behalf of a corporation before its incorporation. 4. Any person or body that has undertaken to supply electricity or gas to any purchaser. See BUILDER AND ~; BUILDING CONSTRUCTION ~; DEPENDENT ~; ELECTRICAL ~; FARM LABOUR ~; GEN-ERAL ~; INDEPENDENT ~; MAIL ~; NON-RESIDENT ~; PERSONAL SERVICE ~; PLUMBING ~; PRIME ~; PRINCIPAL SERVICE ~.

CONTRACT OUT. 1. To make a contract or agreement in accordance with which a significant part of the work regularly done by the employees of an employer is to be done by some other person or persons. *Trade Union Act*, R.S.N.S. 1989, c. 460, s. 2. 2. To agree with others for whose benefit a statute has been passed to deprive oneself of the benefit of the statute.

CONTRACT PRICE. The price to be paid under a contract or sub-contract for performance of the contract or sub-contract. *The Builders' Liens Act*, C.C.S.M., c. B91, s. 1. See TOTAL ~.

CONTRACT RATE. The rate to be charged for the transportation of goods shipped by a shipper pursuant to a loyalty contract. *Shipping Conferences Exemption Act, 1987*, S.C. 1987, c. 22, s. 2(1).

CONTRACTUAL CAPACITY. Ability in law to enter into a contract.

CONTRACTUAL EMPLOYEE. A person employed for a certain term for the purpose of performing certain specified work and whose terms and conditions of employment are specifically stated in a written contract. *Public Service Commission Act*, R.S. Nfld. 1990, c. P-43, s. 2.

CONTRACTUAL ENTRANT. One who has contracted and paid for the right to enter onto premises.

CONTRACTUAL PLAN. Any contract or other arrangement for the purchase of shares or units of a mutual fund by payments over a specified period or by a specified number of payments where the amount deducted from any one of the payments as sales charges is larger than the amount that would have been deducted from such payment for sales charges if deductions had been made from each payment at a constant rate for the duration of the plan. *Securities Act*, R.S.O. 1990, c. S.5, c. 1(1).

CONTRACTUAL PROMISE. An undertaking or an assurance given for consideration.

CONTRACTUAL RELATIONS. See UNLAWFUL INTERFERENCE WITH ~.

CONTRACTUAL RIGHT OF ACTION. A right of action against an issuer for rescission or damages, which right, (i) is available to an investor to whom an offering memorandum prospectus has been delivered by or on behalf of the seller of securities referred to in the offering memorandum prospectus if the offering memorandum prospectus contains a misrepresentation, (ii) is exercisable on notice given to the issuer not later than 90 days after the date on which payment was made for the securities or after the initial payment, where payments after the initial payment are made a under a contractual commitment assumed before, or concurrently with, the initial payment, (iii) reasonably corresponds to the rights provided in section 130 applicable to a prospectus, and may be subject to defences equivalent to a defence available under subsection (2) of that section, and (iv) includes a provision stating that the right is in addition to another right or remedy available at law to the investor. *Securities Act*, R.S. Nfld. 1990, c. S-13, s. 2(1).

CONTRACT UNDER SEAL. A contract in writing which is signed and sealed by the parties; a specialty contract.

CONTRACTUS EX TURPI CAUSA VEL CONTRA BONOS MORES, NULLUS EST. [L.] A contract based on a base consideration or against morality is null.

CONTRADICT. *v*. To disprove; to prove a fact conflicting with other evidence.

CONTRADICTION IN TERMS. A group of words the parts of which are expressly inconsistent.

CONTRADICTORY EVIDENCE. Evidence disproving earlier evidence.

CONTRAFACTION. *n*. Counterfeiting.

CONTRA FORMAM STATUTI. [L.] Against the form of the statute: the concluding words of an indictment.

CONTRAINDICATION. *n*. A potential concern to a consumer of a drug or pharmaceutical.

CONTRA NEGANTEM PRINCIPIA NON EST DISPUTANDUM. [L.] There is no arguing with a person who refuses to admit first principles.

CONTRA NON VALENTEM AGERE NULLA CURRIT PRAESCRIPTIO. [L.] No time limitation runs against a person unable to bring an action.

CONTRA PACEM. [L.] Against the peace.

CONTRA PROFERENTEM. [L. against the party putting forward] 1. "Estey J. . . wrote in McClelland & Stewart Ltd. v. Mutual Life Assurance Co. of Canada, [1981] 2 S.C.R. 6[:] 'That principle of interpretation [the contra proferentem rule] applies to contracts and other documents on the simple theory that any ambiguity in a term of a contract must be resolved against the author if the choice is between him and the other party to the contract who did not participate in the drafting.'" *McKinlay Motors Ltd. v Honda Canada Inc.* (1989), 46 B.L.R. 62 at 77 (Nfld. T.D.), Wells J. 2. *Contra proferentem* operates to protect one party to a contract from deviously ambiguous or confusing drafting on the part of the other party, by interpreting any ambiguity against the drafting party. When both parties are in agreement as to the proper interpretation of the contract, however, it is not open to a third party to assert that *contra proferentem* should be applied to interpret the contract against *both* contracting parties. Indeed, a third party has no basis at all upon which to rely upon *contra proferentem*. *Eli Lilly & Co. v. Novopharm Ltd.*, 1998 CarswellNat 1061, 227 N.R. 201, 161 D.L.R. (4th) 1, [1998] 2 S.C.R. 129, 152 F.T.R. 160 (note), 80 C.P.R. (3d) 321 Iacobucci, J. for the court.

CONTRARY. *adj*. Against; opposed to.

CONTRA SPOLIATOREM OMNIA PRAESUMUNTUR. [L.] All is presumed against a despoiler.

CONTRATENERE. [L.] To withhold.

CONTRAVENE. *v*. 1. To violate, to not comply. 2. " . . . [T]o prevent, to obstruct the operation of and to defeat or nullify." *Collins v. Ontario (Attorney General)* (1969), 6 C.R.N.S. 82 at 88-9, [1970] 1 O.R. 207, [1970] 1 C.C.C. 305 (H.C.), Addy J.

CONTRAVENTION. *n*. 1. Failure to comply. 2. Non-compliance. 3. " . . . [S]omething done in violation of a provision of the [Highway Traffic] Act [R.S.M. 1940, c. 93, s. 82] and it does not include a non-compliance with a provision which results from pure accident . . . or non-compliance resulting from vis major or the act of a third party. " *Currie v. Nikon* (1954), 13 W. W.R. (N.S.) 497 at 501, 62 Man. R. 325 (Q.B.), Tritschler J. 4. An offence that is created by an enactment and is designated as a contravention by regulation of the Governor in Council. *Contraventions Act*, S.C. 1992, c. 47, s. 2.

CONTRAVENTIONS COURT. In respect of a contravention alleged to have been committed in, or otherwise within the territorial jurisdiction of the courts of, a province, a court designated by order of the Governor in Council in respect of that province. *Contraventions Act*, S.C. 1992, c. 47, s. 2.

CONTRE COUP FRACTURE. Stress at a point of impact causes this fracture, usually of bones in the skull. F.A. Jaffe, *A Guide to Pathological Evidence*, 3d ed. (Toronto: Carswell, 1991) at 219.

CONTRECOUP INJURY. *var.* **CONTRE COUP INJURY** *var.* **CONTRE-COUP INJURY**. Injury to an organ which occurs on the side opposite to the one which suffered impact. F.A. Jaffe, *A Guide to Pathological Evidence*, 3d ed. (Toronto: Carswell, 1991) at 216.

CONTRECTATIO REI ALIENAE, ANIMO FURANDI, EST FURTUM. [L.] To appropriate property not one's own, with the intention of stealing, is theft.

CONTRIBUTION. *n.* 1. Indemnity may arise by contract, by statute, or by the nature of the relationship itself. An obligation to indemnify means an obligation to protect against or keep free from loss, to repay for what has been lost or damaged, to compensate for a loss. Contribution, on the other hand, is *only* available when a co-debtor has paid more than his equal share of the debt. Contribution among co-debtors is an equitable concept, and a co-debtor, while liable to the creditor for the full amount, is only liable as among the co-debtors for his or her share. *Lafrentz v. M & L Leasing Ltd. Partnership* (2000), 2000 CarswellAlta 1121, 2000 ABQB 714, 8 B.L.R. (3d) 219, [2001] 1 W.W.R. 629, 85 Alta. L.R. (3d) 233, 275 A.R. 334 (Q.B.), Perras J. 2. Indemnity. 3. ". . . [D]escribes a situation where the wrongdoer who has paid the plaintiff's damages, or more than his share of them, is entitled to receive a portion of this amount from the other wrongdoer . . ." *Peter v. Anchor Transit Ltd.*, [1979] 4 W.W.R. 150 at 153, 100 D.L.R. (3d) 37 (B.C. C.A.), the court per Craig J.A. 4. The performance by all parties jointly liable, by contract or otherwise, of their shares of the liability. 5. An amount payable or sum paid under an agreement, usually a pension plan or agreement between governments. 6. Any money or real or personal property that is provided (i) to a political party, constituency association or candidate, or (ii) for the benefit of a political party, constituency association or candidate with its or the candidate's consent, without compensation from that political party, constituency association or candidate. See ADDITIONAL VOLUNTARY ~; DEFINED ~ BENEFIT; EMPLOYEE ~S; EMPLOYER'S ~; MERITORIOUS ~; RATES OF ~; RETURN OF ~S; VOLUNTARY ADDITIONAL ~; VOLUNTARY ~S.

CONTRIBUTOR. *n.* 1. An employee required to make contributions to a pension plan. 2. A person who ships stock to a livestock auction sale area, slaughterhouse, feed lot or stockdealer. See DISABLED ~'S CHILD.

CONTRIBUTORY. *n.* A person liable to contribute to the assets of a company that is being wound up.

CONTRIBUTORY. *adj.* Joining in the promotion of a purpose.

CONTRIBUTORY BENEFIT. A pension benefit or part of a pension benefit to which a member is required to make contributions under the terms of the pension plan. *Pension Benefits Act*, R.S.O. 1990, c. P.8, s. 1.

CONTRIBUTORY MONTHS. See BASIC NUMBER OF ~.

CONTRIBUTORY NEGLIGENCE. ". . . [A] failure to take reasonable care for one's own safety in circumstances where one knows or reasonably ought to foresee danger to oneself. . ." *Reekie v. Messervey* (1989), 48 C.C.L.T. 217 at 277, 36 B.C.L.R. (2d) 316, 59 D.L.R. (4th) 481, 17 M.V.R. (2d) 94 (C.A.), Southin J.A. (dissenting in part).

CONTRIBUTORY PENSION BENEFIT. A pension benefit or part of a pension benefit to which a member is required to make contributions under the terms of a pension plan. *Pension Benefits Act*, S.N.B. 1987, c. P-5.1, s. 1.

CONTRIBUTORY PENSION PLAN. A plan for pension of employees to which employees themselves contribute as well as employer.

CONTRIBUTORY SERVICE. Service for which an employee makes the contributions required by this Act, and includes: (i) periods of absence: (A) for which the employee makes the required contributions; or (B) with respect to which the requirement to make contributions has been waived pursuant to subsection 16(1.31); (ii) one-half of any period of actual service with an employer that the member was required to complete pursuant to section 14, as it existed at the relevant time, before becoming a member; and (iii) periods that the employee is entitled to count as contributory service pursuant to section 2.1. *The Municipal Employees Superannuation Act*, R.S.S. 1978, c. M-26, s. 2.

CONTROL. *v*. With reference to a noxious or nuisance weed, to (i) carry out measures designed to inhibit propagation of the weed, (ii) destroy the weed, or (iii) carry out measures prescribed by an inspector for the control of the weed. *Weed Control Act*, R.S.A. 2000, c. W-5, s. 1.

CONTROL. *n*. 1. Power to direct. 2. In respect of a body corporate, means (a) control in any manner that results in control in fact, whether directly through the ownership of shares, stocks, equities or securities or indirectly through a trust, a contract, the ownership of shares stocks, equities or securities of another body corporate or otherwise or (b) the ability to appoint, elect or cause the appointment or election of a majority of the directors of the body corporate, whether or not that ability is exercised. See BOARD OF ~; DEVELOPMENT ~; EFFECTIVE ~; EXPORT ~ LIST; FIRE ~ AUTHORITY; GAS HAZARD ~ STANDARDS; MEDICAL ~; OPERATIONAL ~; SERVICE SURVEY ~; UNDER ~; USER ~.

CONTROL AREA. The controlled airspace that is specified as the Northern Control Area or the Southern Control Area in the *Designated Airspace Handbook* and that extends upwards vertically from a specified altitude or a specified pressure-altitude. *Canadian Aviation Regulations* SOR 96-433, s. 101.01.

CONTROLLED. *adj*. "It has long been decided that for the purposes of this section [s. 39(4)(a) of the Income Tax Act, R.S.C. 1952, c. 148] ' . . . the word "controlled" contemplates the right of control that rests in ownership of such a number of shares as carries with it the right to a majority of the votes in the election of the Board of Directors' . . ." *Imperial General Properties Ltd. v. R.* (1985), 85 D.T.C. 5500 at 5502, [1985] 2 S.C.R. 288, [1985] 2 C.T.C. 299, 31 B.L.R. 77, 62 N.R. 137, 21 D.L.R. (4th) 741, Estey J.. (Beetz, Chouinard and La Forest JJ. concurring).

CONTROLLED-ACCESS HIGHWAY. *var*. **CONTROLLED ACCESS HIGHWAY**. 1. A highway (a) on to which persons have a right to enter from abutting land, and (b) from which persons have a right to enter on to abutting land, only at fixed locations. 2. The highway or por-

tions designated or designed for through traffic. *Highway Act*, R.S.B.C. 1979, c. 167, s. 55. 3. A provincial highway.

CONTROLLED AERODROME. An aerodrome at which an air traffic control unit is in operation. *Canadian Aviation Regulations* SOR 96-433, s. 101.01.

CONTROLLED AIRSPACE. An airspace of fixed dimensions that is so specified in the *Designated Airspace Handbook* and within which air traffic control service is provided. *Canadian Aviation Regulations* SOR 96-433, s. 101.01.

CONTROLLED AREA. The area between the limited access highway or freeway and the control line in relation thereto. *Highways Protection Act*, C.C.S.M., c. H50, s. 1.

CONTROLLED COMPANY. A company is controlled by another person or company or by two or more companies if (a) voting securities of the first-mentioned company carrying more than 50% of the votes for the election of directors are held, otherwise than by way of security only, by or for the benefit of the other person, company or companies; and (b) the votes carried by the securities are entitled, if exercised, to elect a majority of the board of directors of the first-mentioned company. *The Commodity Futures Act*, S.M. 1996, c. 73, s. 1.

CONTROLLED CORPORATION. See SUBSIDIARY ~.

CONTROLLED DRUG. See CONTROLLED SUBSTANCE.

CONTROLLED FINANCIAL CORPORATION. See SUBSIDIARY ~.

CONTROLLED OPERATION. See SUBSIDIARY ~.

CONTROLLED PRODUCT. 1. Any product, material or substance specified by the regulations made pursuant to paragraph 15(1)(*a*) to be included in any of the classes listed in Schedule II. *Hazardous Products Act*, R.S.C. 1985, c. H3, s. 2. 2. Products which pose a hazard in the workplace and are regulated under WHMIS (workplace hazardous materials information system).

CONTROLLED SUBSIDIARY. " . . . [C]ompany so described is subordinate to a dominant company which is able, through share ownership, to exert influence or control over its affairs." *Cominco Ltd. v. Canadian Pacific Ltd.* (1988), 39 B.L.R. 172 at 182, 24 B.C.L.R. (2d) 124 (S.C.), Gibbs J.

CONTROLLED SUBSTANCE. A substance included in Schedule I, II, III, IV or V. Includes narcotics. *Controlled Drugs and Substances Act, 1996*, S.C. 1996, c. 19, s. 2.

CONTROLLER. *n*. 1. An official who examines and verifies the accounts of other officials. 2. The chief financial officer of a corporation or organization. See COMPTROLLER.

CONTROL LINE. (a) In the case of a limited access highway or a part thereof, or a freeway or a part thereof, in respect of which the traffic board has not specifically established control lines, a line that is parallel to the centre line of the limited access highway or freeway 125 feet distant from the edge of the right-of-way thereof; (b) in the case of a limited access highway or a part thereof or a freeway or a part thereof in respect of which the traffic board has specifically established control lines a line that is parallel to the centre line thereof and such distance from the edge of the right-of-way thereof as the traffic board may have designated or a line that forms the circumference, or part of the circumference of a circle with the centre at the point of intersection of the centre line of a limited access highway or freeway and another highway and a radius of such length as the traffic board may have designated. *Highways Protection Act*, R.S.M. 1987, c. H50 s. 1.

CONTROLLING INTEREST. The interest that a person has in a corporation when that person beneficially owns, directly or indirectly, or exercises control or direction over, equity shares of the corporation carrying more than 10 per cent (or in some statutes, 25 per cent) of the voting rights attached to all equity shares of the corporation for the time being outstanding.

CONTROL LIST. The Canadian Cultural Property Export Control List established under the Act. *Cultural Property Export and Import Act*, R.S.C. 1985, c. C-51, s. 2. See AREA ~; IMPORT ~.

CONTROL NUMBER. A unique series of letters, numbers or symbols, or any combination of these, that is assigned to a medical device by the manufacturer and from which a history of the manufacture, packaging, labelling and distribution of a unit, lot or batch of the device can be determined. *Medical Devices Regulations* SOR/ 98-282, s. 1.

CONTROL ORDER. An order issued under the Environmental Protection Act to regulate discharge of contaminants into the environment.

CONTROL PERSON. Any person or company or any combination of persons and companies holding (i) a sufficient number of any of the securities of an issuer so as to affect materially the control of that issuer; or (ii) more than 20% of the voting rights attached to all voting securities of the issuer for the time being outstanding, except where there is evidence showing that the holding of those voting rights does not affect materially the control of that issuer. *Securities acts*.

CONTROL PROJECT. See WATER ~.

CONTROL PRODUCT. Any product, device, organism, substance or thing that is manufactured, represented, sold or used as a means for directly or indirectly controlling, preventing, destroying, mitigating, attracting or repelling any pest, and includes (a) any compound or substance that enhances or modifies or is intended to enhance or modify the physical or chemical characteristics of a control product to which it is added, and (b) any active ingredient used for the manufacture of a control product. *Pest Control Products Act*, R.S.C. 1985, c. P-9, s. 2.

CONTROL STATION. Includes (a) a radio room, and (b) any other enclosed space that houses (i) a compass, a direction-finder, radar equipment, a steering wheel or other similar equipment used in navigation, (ii) a central indicator connected with a system for the detection of fire or smoke, or (iii) an emergency generator. *Hull Construction Regulations*, C.R.C., c. 1431, s. 2.

CONTROL STATUS. With respect to a person, whether or not the person is Canadian controlled as determined under this Act and the regulations. *Canadian Ownership and Control Determination* Act, R.S.C. 1985, c. C-20, s. 2.

CONTROL SURVEY MARKER. A marker which is installed in the ground by authority of the minister and the location of which is, or is proposed to be, derived from the Geodetic survey of Canada. *Crown Lands Act*, R.S. Nfld. 1990, c. C-42, s. 2.

CONTROL SYSTEM. See DRIVER-OPERATED ACCELERATOR ~.

CONTROL WORKS. See WATER ~; WATER POLLUTION ~.

CONTROL VALVE. See ELECTRICALLY SUPERVISED ~.

CONTROL ZONE. The controlled airspace that is so specified in the *Designated Airspace*

Handbook and that extends upwards vertically from the surface of the earth up to and including 3,000 feet AGL, unless otherwise specified in that Handbook. *Canadian Aviation Regulations* SOR/96-433, s. 101.01. See TEMPORARY ~.

CONTUMACY. *n.* 1. Failure or refusal to obey an order or to attend court as required. 2. Being in contempt of court.

CONTUSION. *n.* Injury to a tissue with no surface disruption. F.A. Jaffe, *A Guide to Pathological Evidence*, 3d ed. (Toronto: Carswell, 1991) at 13.

CONVALESCENT PERSON. A person whose condition, in the opinion of a medical practitioner, has passed the acute or emergency state and is improving or can be improved by continued medical and skilled nursing care in a convalescent unit or a hospital for convalescent patients.

CONVENIENCE. *n.* 1. " . . . [R]elates to the proper conduct and management of the entire trial including, of course, the decisional process." *Wipfli v. Britten* (1981), 24 C.P.C. 164 at 170, [1982] 1 W.W.R. 709, 32 B.C.L.R. 242 (S.C.), McEachern C.J.S.C. 2. " . . . [A]ccording to McBride J. in MacDonald v. Leduc Utilities Ltd. (1952), 7 W.W.R. (N.S.) 603 at 608 (Alta. T.D.), relates to 'the nature of the issues raised, technical or otherwise, and not to the personal convenience of individual jurymen'." *Przybylski v. Morcos* (1986), 14 C.P.C. (2d) 126 at 130, 49 Alta. L.R. (2d) 164, 75 A.R. 233 (Q.B.), Andrekson J. See FLAG OF ~.

CONVENIENT FORUM. " . . . [T]he applicant must establish that the foreign jurisdiction is the more appropriate or natural forum to try the actions in the sense that the foreign jurisdiction has the most real and substantial connection with the lawsuit." *Bonaventure Systems Inc. v. Royal Bank* (1986), 16 C.P.C. (2d) 32 at 43, 57 O.R. (2d) 270, 32 D.L.R. (4th) 721, 18 O.A.C. 11 (Div. Ct.), Ewaschuk J.

CONVENTIO. *n.* [L.] A covenant; an agreement.

CONVENTION. *n.* 1. An agreement between states which is intended to be binding in international law. P.W. Hogg, *Constitutional Law of Canada*, 3d ed. (Toronto: Carswell, 1992) at 281. 2. "We respectfully adopt the definition given by the learned Chief Justice of Manitoba, Freedman C.J.M. in the Manitoba Reference [Reference re Amendment of the Constitution of Canada (No. 3) (1981), 120 D.L.R. (3d) 385] . . . : ' . . . a convention occupies a position somewhere in between a usage or custom on one hand and constitutional law on the other. There is a general agreement that if one sought to fix that position with greater precision he would place convention nearer to law than to usage or custom. There is also a general agreement that "a convention is a rule which is regarded as obligatory by the officials to whom it applies": Hogg, Constitutional Law of Canada (1977) . 9. " . . . The existence of a definite convention is always unclear and a matter of debate. Furthermore conventions are flexible somewhat imprecise and unsuitable for judicial determination." *Reference re Questions Concerning Amendment of the Constitution of Canada as set out in O.C 1020/80* (1981), (*sub nom. Resolution to Amend the Constitution of Canada, Re*) 1 C.R.R. 59 at 137-38, [1981] 1 S.C.R. 753, [1981] 6 W.W.R. 1, 11 Man. R. (2d) 1, 39 N.R. 1, 34 Nfld. & P.E.I.R. 1, 95 A.P.R. 1, Martland, Ritchie, Dickson, Beetz, Chouinard and Lamer JJ. 3. A meeting, assembly. See BERNE ~; CIVIL LIABILITY ~; CONSTITUTIONAL ~; EUROPEAN ~ ON HUMAN RIGHTS; GENEVA ~S; HAGUE ~S; LOAD LINE ~; 1968 SAFETY ~; SEAMEN'S ARTICLES ~; SEAMEN'S REPATRIATION ~; SUB-JUDICE ~; UNIVERSAL COPYRIGHT ~; UNIVERSAL POSTAL ~; USAGE.

CONVENTION AGAINST TORTURE. The Convention Against Torture and Other Cruel, Inhuman or Degrading Treatment or Punishment, signed at New York on December 10, 1984. *Immigration and Refugee Protection Act*, S.C. 2001, c. 27, s. 2.

CONVENTIONAL. *adj.* In constitutional law, refers to law which is not found in statute or in decided cases but in the practice of states and governments.

CONVENTIONAL BOUNDARY. A boundary consisting of a straight line or a series of straight lines of fixed direction and length conforming as nearly as possible to the natural boundary, but eliminating minor sinuosities. *Land Act*, R.S.B.C. 1996, s. 245, s. 1.

CONVENTIONAL BOUNDARY-LINE. *var.* **CONVENTIONAL BOUNDARY LINE**. Those portions of the boundary marked on the ground by survey monuments and shown on the map sheets by a series of straight lines connecting the survey monuments.

CONVENTIONAL INTERNATIONAL LAW. Any convention, treaty or other international agreement (*a*) that is in force and to which Canada is a party; or (*b*) that is in force and the provisions of which Canada has agreed to accept and apply in an armed conflict in which it is involved. *Crimes Against Humanity and War Crimes Act, 2000*, S.C. 2000, c. 24, s. 2.

CONVENTIONAL MARRIAGE. " . . . [T]he wife remained at home and was responsible for raising the children and doing the housekeeping while the husband went to work." *Boyd v. Boyd* (1992), 41 R.F.L. (3d) 182 at 183, 68 B.C.L.R. (2d) 201, 13 B.C.A.C. 148, 24 W.A.C. 148 (C.A.), Hinkson J.A. See TRADITIONAL MARRIAGE.

CONVENTIONAL TREATMENT. In respect of a symptom, a medical or surgical treatment that is generally accepted by the Canadian medical community as a treatment for the symptom. *Marihuana Medical Access Regulations* SOR/2001-227, s. 1.

CONVENTION AREA. An area defined in an international convention concerning fishing.

CONVENTION ON THE ELIMINATION OF ALL FORMS OF DISCRIMINATION AGAINST WOMEN. A 1979 enactment of the U.N. General Assembly promoting gender equality, establishing a committee to monitor progress and providing a dispute settlement mechanism for disputes between nations. D. Gibson, *The Law of the Charter: Equality Rights* (Toronto: Carswell, 1990) at 14.

CONVENTION ON THE ELIMINATION OF ALL FORMS OF RACIAL DISCRIMINATION. A 1965 enactment of the U.N. General Assembly requiring that governments themselves not engage in discriminatory practices and that discrimination be prohibited by all levels of public authorities, that discriminatory laws be eliminated, that discrimination by all persons, groups, and organizations be ended, that racial harmony and equality be fostered and that certain affirmative action steps be taken with regard to racial minorities. D. Gibson, *The Law of the Charter: Equality Rights* (Toronto: Carswell, 1990) at 14-15.

CONVENTION REFUGEE. Any person who (a) by reason of a well-founded fear of persecution for reasons of race, religion, nationality, membership in a particular social group or political opinion, (i) is outside the country of the person's nationality and is unable or, by reason of that fear, is unwilling to avail himself of the protection of that country, or (ii) not having a country of nationality, is outside the country of the person's former habitual residence and is unable or, by reason of that fear, is unwilling to return to that country, and (b) has not ceased to be a Convention refugee by virtue of subsection (2), but does not include any person to whom the Convention does not apply pursuant to section E or F of Article 1 thereof, which sections are set out in the schedule to this Act. *Immigration Act*, R.S.C. 1985, c. I-2, s. 2.

CONVENTION SHIP. A sea-going ship, wherever registered, (*a*) carrying, in bulk as cargo, crude oil, fuel oil, heavy diesel oil, lubricating oil or any other persistent hydrocarbon mineral oil, or (*b*) on any voyage following any such carriage of such an oil, unless it is proved that there is no residue of the oil on board. *Canada Shipping Act*, R.S.C. 1985, c. S-9, c. 673.

CONVENTIO PRIVATORUM NON POTEST PUBLICO JURI DEROGARE. [L.] No private agreement can derogate from the rights of the public.

CONVENTIO VINCIT LEGEM. [L.] An express agreement prevails against the law.

CONVERSATION. *n*. 1. " . . . [A]n interchange of a series of separate communications." *R. v. Cremascoli* (1979), (*sub nom. R. v. Goldman*) 108 D.L.R. (3d) 17 at 32, [1980] 1 S.C.R. 976, 30 N.R. 453, 51 C.C.C. (2d) 1, 13 C.R. (3d) 228, McIntyre J. (Martland, Ritchie, Pigeon, Dickson, Beetz, Estey and Pratte JJ. concurring). 2. Behaviour, conduct. See CRIMINAL ∼.

CONVERSE. *n*. The subject and predicate in a proposition are transposed, i.e. the converse of "X is Y" is "Y is X".

CONVERSION. 1. *n*. " . . . [A] taking of chattels with an intent to deprive the Plaintiff of his property in them, or with an intent to destroy them or change their nature." *McLean v. Bradley* (1878), 2 S.C.R. 535 at 550, Strong J. (Taschereau and Fournier JJ. concurring). 2. ". . . [A]ct of wilful interference without justification with property, including money, in a manner inconsistent with the right of the owner whereby the owner is deprived of the use of possession of the property.' *Austin v. Habitat Development Ltd.* (1992), 44 C.P.R. (3d) 215 at 220, 94 D.L.R. (4th) 359, 114 N.S.R. (2d) 379, 313 A.P.R. 379 (C.A.), Hallet J.A. See COST OF ∼; RE∼; SNOWMOBILE ∼ VEHICLE.

CONVERSION UNIT. A mechanical device consisting of a single axle designed to convert a two-axle vehicle into a three-axle vehicle. *Highway Traffic Act*, R.S.O. 1990, c. H.8, s. 1(1).

CONVERT. *v.* To change shares into shares of another class, in the manner specified in the share provisions.

CONVERTER. See CATALYTIC ~.

CONVERTIBLE. *n.* A vehicle that has an A-pillar or windshield peripheral support, the upper portion of which is not joined by a fixed rigid structure to the B-pillar or other rear roof support to the rear of the B-pillar. *Motor Vehicle Safety Regulations*, C.R.C., c. 1038, s. 2.

CONVERTIBLE MORTGAGE. A mortgage in which the lender has the option to purchase the property at a certain price, usually the market value of the property when the term of the mortgage began. D.J. Donahue & P.D. Quinn, *Real Estate Practice in Ontario*, 4th ed. (Toronto: Butterworths, 1990) at 232.

CONVERTIBLE SECURITY. In relation to a security of a particular class: (i) a security convertible into or exchangeable for a security of that class prior to the expiration of the bid; (ii) a security carrying a warrant or right to acquire or to convert into or exchange for a security of that class that is exercisable prior to expiration of the bid; or (iii) an option, warrant, right or subscription privilege or to convert into or exchange for a security of that class or a security mentioned in subclause (i) or (ii) that is exercisable prior to expiration of the bid.

CONVEY. *v.* 1. To create a property right or change it between persons. 2. Applied to any person means the execution by that person of every necessary or suitable assurance for conveying or disposing to another land of or in which the first person is seised or entitled to a contingent right, either for the person's whole estate or for any less estate together with the performance of all formalities required by law to validate the conveyance. *Trustee acts.* 3. Includes the granting, assigning, releasing, surrendering, leasing or disposing of land in Ontario, agreeing to sell land in Ontario, or the giving of an option upon or with respect to any land in Ontario, or the registration of a caution or notice of any kind signifying the existence of an unregistered instrument or writing by which land is conveyed, whether the effect of any of the foregoing is to bring into existence an interest of any kind in land or is only for the purpose of giving effect to or formal recognition to any interest of whatsoever kind that theretofore existed in land, but "convey" does not include any transfer of land for the purpose only of securing a debt or loan, or any transfer by a creditor for the purpose only of returning land that has been used as security for a debt or loan. *Land Transfer Tax Act*, R.S.O. 1990, s. L.6, s. 1(1). 4. To carry. *Nolan v. McAssey*, [1930] 2 D.L.R. 323 at 323 (P.E.I. S.C.), Arsenault J.

CONVEYANCE. *n.* 1. Any instrument by which a freehold or leasehold estate, or other interest in real estate, may be transferred or affected. 2. Includes transfer, assignment, delivery over, appointment, lease, settlement, other assurance and covenant to surrender, payment, gift, grant, alienation, bargain, charge, in cumbrance, limitation of use or uses of in to or out of real property or personal property by writing or otherwise. 3. Includes ships, vessels, aircraft, trains, and motor and other vehicles. See DEED OF ~; DOCUMENT OF ~; FIXED ~; FRAUDULENT ~; MAIL ~; RE~; SHAFT ~; TOWED ~; VOLUNTARY ~.

CONVEYANCE OF LAND. Unless an exception is specially made therein, includes all houses, outhouses, edifices, barns, stables, yards, gardens, orchards, commons, trees, woods, underwoods, mounds, fences, hedges, ditches, ways, waters, watercourses, lights, liberties, privileges, easements, profits, commodities, emoluments, hereditaments and appurtenances whatsoever to such land belonging or in anywise appertaining, or with such land demised, held, used, occupied and enjoyed or taken or known as part or parcel thereof, and, if the conveyance purports to convey an estate in fee simple, also the reversion and reversions, remainder and remainders, yearly and other rents, issues and profits of the same land and of every part and parcel thereof, and all the estate, right, title, interest, inheritance, use, trust, property, profit, possession, claim and demand whatsoever of the grantor into, out of or upon the same land, and every part and parcel thereof, with their and every of their appurtenances. *Conveyancing and Law of Property Act*, R.S.O. 1990, c. 34 s. 15.

CONVEYANCE ORDER. An order for the conveyance of distressed seamen issued to the master of a British ship. *Distressed Seamen Regulations*, C.R.C., c. 1420, s. 2.

CONVEYANCER. *n.* A paralegal or lawyer whose chief practice is conveyancing.

CONVEYANCE SYSTEM. The whole of the pipes used for the conveyance of gas to the point of junction with a distribution network, including the equipment, machines, structures, gasometers, meters and other devices and accessories connected therewith. *Gas Distribution Act*, R.S.Q., c. D-10, s. 1.

CONVEYANCING. *n*. Practice which deals with the creation and transferral of rights in real property.

CONVEYING PURPOSE. The carriage of water for licensees authorized to divert, extract, use or store that water. *Water Act*, R.S.B.C. 1996, c. 483, s. 1.

CONVICT. *v*. To find guilty of offence.

CONVICT. *n*. A person against whom judgment of imprisonment has been pronounced or recorded by a court. See SERVICE ~.

CONVICTED. *adj*. " ... [A]s used in s. 19(1)(c) [of the Immigration Act, R.S.C. 1985, c. I-2] was intended by Parliament to mean 'found guilty', after a plea of guilty or otherwise." *Canada (Minister of Employment & Immigration) v. Burgeon* (1991), 1 Imm. L.R. (2d) 102 at 116, 78 D.L.R. (4th) 103, [1991] 3 F.C. 44, 122 N.R. 228 (C.A.), Mahoney J.A. (concurring in the result).

CONVICTION. *n*. " ... [A] word which has different meanings in different contexts. The different senses in which the word 'conviction' is used include: (i) the verdict or adjudication of guilt; (ii) the sentence; (iii) the verdict or adjudication of guilt plus the judgment of the court, that is, the sentence; (iv) the record of the conviction." *R. v. McInnis* (1973), 23 C.R.N.S. 152 at 156, 1 O.R. (2d) 1, 13 C.C.C. (2d) 471 (C.A.), the court per Martin J.A. See CERTIFICATE OF ~; DATE OF ~; FIRST ~; SECOND ~; SUBSEQUENT ~; THIRD ~.

CONVOCATION. *n*. A regular or special meeting of the benchers convened for the purpose of transacting business of the Society. *Law Society Act*, R.S.O. 1990, c. C.8, s. 1.

CONVOY. *n*. Ships of war sent by a country in wartime to escort and protect merchant ships which belong to that country.

COOK. See SHIP'S ~.

COOK ADM. *abbr*. Cook, Admiralty (Que.), 1873-1884.

COOKING UNIT. See SEPARATE BUILT-IN ~.

COOLER. See BULK MILK ~; WATER ~.

COOLING-OFF PERIOD. *var*. **COOLING OFF PERIOD**. 1. An opportunity to resile from a contract and cancel it within a specified time period. 2. The time before which a strike or lockout may begin.

CO-OP. *abbr*. Cooperative.

COOPERATIVE. *var*. **CO-OPERATIVE**. *n*. 1. A legal person in which persons having economic and social needs in common unite for the prosecution of an enterprise according to the rules of cooperative action to meet those needs. *Cooperatives Act*, R.S.Q. c. 67.2, s. 3. 2. A rental residential property other than a condominium, that is (a) owned or leased or otherwise held by or on behalf of more than one person, where any owner or lessee has the right to present or future exclusive possession of a unit in the rental residential property, or (b) owned or leased or otherwise held by a corporation having more than one shareholder or member where any one of the shareholders or members, by reason of owning shares in or being a member of the corporation, has the right to present or future exclusive possession of a unit in the rental residential. 3. A corporation carrying on an enterprise on a cooperative basis. See AGRICULTURAL OPERATIONS ~; CONSUMER'S ~; DIRECT CHARGE ~; DISTRIBUTING ~; FARM PRODUCTS MARKETING ~; INSIDER OF A ~; INVESTMENT ~; LAND ~.

COOPERATIVE ASSOCIATION. *var*. **CO-OPERATIVE ASSOCIATION**. 1. Any cooperative association or federation incorporated by or pursuant to an Act of Parliament or of the legislature of a province. *Canada Cooperative Associations Act*, R.S.C. 1985, c. C-40, s. 3. 2. A co-operative corporation of producers of farm products to which the Co-operative Corporations Act applies and which was incorporated for the purpose of grading, cleaning, packing, storing, drying, processing or marketing farm products. See FEDERAL ~; PROVINCIAL ~; RURAL GAS ~.

COOPERATIVE BASIS. *var*. **CO-OPERATIVE BASIS**. Organized, operated and administered upon the following principles and methods, (a) each member or delegate has only one vote, (b) no member or delegate may vote by proxy, (c) interest on loan capital and dividends on share capital are limited to a percentage fixed by this Act or the articles of incorporation, and (d) the enterprise of the corporation is operated as nearly as possible at cost after providing for reasonable reserves and the payment or crediting of interest on loan capital or dividends on share capital; and any surplus funds arising from the business of the organization, after providing for such reasonable reserves and interest or dividends, unless used to maintain or improve services of the organization for its members or donated for community welfare or the propagation of co-operative principles, are distributed in whole or in part among the members in proportion to the volume of business they have done with or through the organization. *Co-operative Corporations Act*, R.S.O. 1990, c. C-35, s. 1 as am.

COOPERATIVE CORPORATION. 1. A body corporate organized and operated on co-operative principles. *Cooperative Credit Associations Act, 1991*, S.C. 1991, c. 48, s. 2. 2. Includes a housing cooperative under the *Cooperative Association Act*, any other corporation as defined in the *Company Act* and any partnership or limited partnership that is the owner of land, where a majority of the persons entitled to occupy all or a portion of that land, or the buildings on it, is, or is intended or entitled to become, the shareholders, owners or partners, directly or indirectly, of that housing cooperative, other corporation, partnership or limited partnership. *Real Estate Act*, R.S.B.C. 1996, c. 397, s. 1.

COOPERATIVE CREDIT SOCIETY. A co-operative corporation one of whose principal purposes is to provide financial services to its members. *Cooperative Credit Associations Act, 1991*, S.C. 1991, c. 48, s. 2. See CENTRAL ~; FEDERATION OF COOPERATIVE CREDIT SOCIETIES; LOCAL ~.

COOPERATIVE ENTITY. A body corporate that, by the law under which it is organized and operated, must be organized and operated on—and is organized and operated on—cooperative principles. *Canada Cooperatives Act*, S.C. 1998, c. 1, s. 2.

COOPERATIVE FEDERALISM. The set of relationships which has been developed among the executives of the federal and provincial governments to achieve a redistribution of powers and resources, as required, on a negotiated basis rather than along legalistic lines resolved by the courts.

COOPERATIVE HOUSING ASSOCIATION. A cooperative association incorporated under the laws of Canada or any province, having as its principal aim or object the construction, on a cooperative basis, of single-family dwellings.

CO-OPERATIVE HOUSING CORPORATION. A corporation that was incorporated, by or under a law of Canada or a province providing for the establishment of the corporation or respecting the establishment of cooperative corporations, for the purpose of making supplies by way of lease, licence or similar arrangement of residential units to its members for the purpose of their occupancy as places of residence for individuals where (*a*) the statute by or under which it was incorporated, its charter, articles of association or by-laws or its contracts with its members require that the activities of the corporation be engaged in at or near cost after providing for reasonable reserves and hold forth the prospect that surplus funds arising from those activities will be distributed among its members in proportion to patronage, (*b*) none of its members (except other cooperative corporations) have more than one vote in the conduct of the affairs of the corporation, and (*c*) at least 90% of its members are individuals or other cooperative corporations and at least 90% of its shares are held by such persons. *Excise Tax Act*, R.S.C. 1985, c. E-15, s. 123. See NON-PROFIT ~.

CO-OPERATIVE LISTING. An exclusive listing which permits one agent to use the facilities of sub-agents appointed in one or more was. B.J. Reiter, R.C.B. Risk & B.N. McLellan, *Real Estate Law*, 3d ed. (Toronto: Emond Motgomery, 1986) at 75.

COOPERATIVE MARKETING CONTRACT. A contract entered into by a person with an association to deliver to or sell through the association any thing caught, grown, made or produced by the person, or on the person's behalf, or in which the person has an interest, that person being one of a number of persons with whom the association has entered into contracts of a similar nature. *Cooperatives Association Act*, S.B.C. 1999, c. 28, s. 174.

COOPERATIVE PLAN. An agreement or arrangement for the marketing of agricultural products that provides for (a) equal turns for primary producers for agricultural products of the like grade and quality, (b) the return to primary producers of the proceeds of the sale of all agricultural products delivered under the agreement or arrangement and produced during the year, after deduction of processing, carrying and selling costs and reserves, if any, and (c) an initial payment to primary producers of the agricultural product to which the agreement relates of an amount fixed by regulations made by the Governor in Council on the recommendation of the Minister with respect to a reasonable amount that does not exceed the amount estimated by the Minister to be the amount by which the average wholesale price according to grade and quality of the agricultural product for the year in respect of which the initial payment will be made will exceed the processing, carrying and selling costs thereof for that year. *Agricultural Products Cooperative Marketing Act*, R.S.C. 1985, c. A-5, s. 2.

CO-OPERATIVE PRINCIPLES. (i) Open membership subject to the natural limitations that may be prescribed by the constitution of the society; (ii) one member one vote, with no proxy voting; (iii) low interest on capital; and (iv) the return or credit to members, in proportion to patronage, of the net surplus of the society remaining after provision is made for expenses of operation, bonuses, interest on capital, and reserves, or the collective use of net surplus for the social or economic benefit of members or the disposal of it for those objects. *Co-operative Societies Act*, R.S. Nfld. 1990, c. C-35, s. 2(2).

COOPERATIVE RESIDENCE. A self contained dwelling unit, in a housing project consisting of self-contained dwelling units, and owned by a cooperative association incorporated under the Cooperative Association Act. *Home Purchase Assistance Act*, R.S.B.C. 1996, c. 195, s. 1.

COOPERATIVE UNIT. The interest of a person in a cooperative corporation that includes (a) a right to use or occupy a part of the land that the cooperative corporation owns or has an interest in; or (b) a present or future right of ownership of one or more shares of, or other evidence of ownership of, an interest in the cooperative corporation. *Real Estate Act*, R.S.B.C. 1996, c. 397, s. 1.

COOPERATOR. See SUBSCRIBING ~.

CO-OP SHARE. A share in the capital stock of an association to which no special preferences, rights, conditions, restrictions, limitations or prohibitions are attached either by the articles of association or application for continuation or amalgamation of the association or by the charter by-laws thereof.

CO-ORDINATE. *adj*. Describing clauses in a statute governed equally by another clause.

CO-ORDINATED COVERAGE. The ability of an individual, through the combination of two benefit plans, to obtain reimbursement for his or her insurance claims up to the combined limit of the two plans. *British Columbia Public School Employers' Assn. v. B.C.T.F.*, 2003 BCCA 323, 15 B.C.L.R. (4th) 58 (C.A.).

CO-ORDINATE MONUMENT. A bronze cap suitably inscribed and (a) imbedded in a reinforced concrete post set in a concrete base, or (b) placed as prescribed by regulations under surveys legislation.

CO-ORDINATE SURVEY. A survey made for the purpose of establishing the location of points on the surface of the earth by geographic or grid co-ordinates. *Surveys Act*, R.R.O. 1990, Reg. 1028, s. 1.

CO-ORDINATE SURVEY SYSTEM. A system of plane rectangular co-ordinates for locating points on the earth's surface.

CO-OWNER. *n*. 1. The person who owns property in common or jointly with one or more other persons. 2. Includes co-lessee and co-licensee, and a corporation with share capital and a shareholder thereof shall be deemed to be co-owners. *Mining Act*, R.S.O. 1990, c. M.14, s. 181(1). See JOINT TENANT; TENANCY IN COMMON.

COPARCENER. *n*. A person to whom an estate in common with one or more other persons has descended.

COPIED. *adj*. Includes reproduced by a photographic process.

CO-PILOT. *n*. A licensed pilot assigned to duty as a pilot in an aircraft during flight time, other than as (a) a pilot-in-command, or (b) a pilot receiving flying instruction. See FIRST SECOND ~.

COPULATIO VERBORUM INDICAT ACCEPTATIONEM IN EODEM SENSU. [L.] The joining of words shows that their meaning is to be understood in the same sense.

COPY. *n*. 1. A document written or taken from another document. 2. A reproduction of the original. 3. In relation to any record, includes a print, whether enlarged or not, from a photographic film of the record. *Canada Evidence Act*, R.S.C. 1985, c. C-5, s. 30(12). See CERTIFIED ~; EXAMINED ~; TRUE ~.

COPYRIGHT. *n.* 1. The rights described in (a) section 3, in the case of a work, (b) sections 15 and 26, in the case of a performer's performance, (c) section 18, in the case of a sound recording, or (d) section 21, in the case of a communication signal. *Copyright Act*, R.S.C. 1985, c. C-42, s. 2. 2. In relation to a work, means the sole right to produce or reproduce the work or any substantial part thereof in any material form whatever, to perform the work or any substantial part thereof in public or, if the work is unpublished, to publish the work or any substantial part thereof. *Copyright Act*, R.S.C. 1985, c. C-42, s.3(part). 3. The maker of a sound recording has a copyright in the sound recording, consisting of the sole right to do the following in relation to the sound recording or any substantial part thereof: (*a*) to publish it for the first time, (*b*) to reproduce it in any material form, and (*c*) to rent it out, and to authorize any such acts.. *Copyright Act*, R.S.C. 1985, c. C-42, s. 18(part). 4. A performer has a copyright in the performer's performance, consisting of the sole right to do the following in relation to the performer's performance or any substantial part thereof: (*a*) if it is not fixed, (i) to communicate it to the public by telecommunication, (ii) to perform it in public, where it is communicated to the public by telecommunication otherwise than by communication signal, and (iii) to fix it in any material form, (*b*) if it is fixed, (i) to reproduce any fixation that was made without the performer's authorization, (ii) where the performer authorized a fixation, to reproduce any reproduction of that fixation, if the reproduction being reproduced was made for a purpose other than that for which the performer's authorization was given, and (iii) where a fixation was permitted under Part III or VIII, to reproduce any reproduction of that fixation, if the reproduction being reproduced was made for a purpose other than one permitted under Part III or VIII, and (*c*) to rent out a sound recording of it, and to authorize any such acts. *Copyright Act*, R.S.C. 1985, c. C-42, s. 15. 5. Where a performer's performance takes place on or after January 1, 1996 in a country that is a WTO Member, the performer has, as of the date of the performer's performance, a copyright in the performer's performance, consisting of the sole right to do the following in relation to the performer's performance or any substantial part thereof: (*a*) if it is not fixed, to communicate it to the public by telecommunication and to fix it in a sound recording, and (*b*) if it has been fixed in a sound recording without the performer's authorization, to reproduce the fixation or any

substantial part thereof, and to authorize any such acts. *Copyright Act*, R.S.C. 1985, c. C-42, s. 26. 6. A broadcaster has a copyright in the communication signals that it broadcasts, consisting of the sole right to do the following in relation to the communication signal or any substantial part thereof: (*a*) to fix it, (*b*) to reproduce any fixation of it that was made without the broadcaster's consent, (*c*) to authorize another broadcaster to retransmit it to the public simultaneously with its broadcast, and (*d*) in the case of a television communication signal, to perform it in a place open to the public on payment of an entrance fee, and to authorize any act described in paragraph (*a*), (*b*) or (*d*). *Copyright Act*, R.S.C. 1985, c. C-42, s. 21. 7. " . . . [T]he exclusive right to make copies; and the concomittant right to restrain others from making copies. It is well established that it is a form of property which may be transferred by a will or a deed." *R. v. Stewart* (1983), 24 B.L.R. 53 at 76, 42 O.R. (2d) 225, 5 C.C.C. (3d) 481, 35 C.R. (3d) 105, 149 D.L.R. (3d) 583, 74 C.P.R. (2d) 1 (C.A.), Cory J.A. 8. " . . . [Protects] the expression of ideas. It is, in effect, a right to prevent the appropriation of the expressed result of the labours of an author by other persons. It is the work of the author that is protected but the work must be fixed in some concrete form." *Warner Brothers-Seven Arts Inc. v. CESM-TV Ltd.* (1971), 65 C.P.R. 215 at 225 (Ex. Ct.), Cattanach J. 9. " . . . [T]he exclusive right to make copies; and the concomittant right to restrain others from making copies. It is well established that it is a form of property which may be transferred by a will or a deed." *R. v. Stewart* (1983), 24 B.L.R. 53 at 76, 42 O.R. (2d) 225, 5 C.C.C. (3D) 481, 35 C.R. (3d) 105, 149 D.L.R. (3d) 583, 74 C.P.R. (2d) 1 (C.A.), Cory J.A.

COR. *abbr.* [L. coram] In the presence of.

CORAM JUDICE. [L.] In the presence of a judge; before an appropriate or properly constituted court.

CORAM NON JUDICE. [L.] Without jurisdiction.

CORAM PARIBUS. [L.] Before one's peers.

CORBETT APPLICATION. An application brought by an accused to exclude his or her criminal record from a jury trial because of its likely prejudicial effect on the jury. The decision on a Corbett application involves determining whether the probative value of otherwise admissible evidence (*i.e.* evidence of an accused person's criminal record) outweighs its potential prejudice (*i.e.* the likelihood that the jury will use the evidence for an improper purpose). Named after *R. v. Corbett*, [1988] 1 S.C.R. 670.

CORD. *n.* 1. 128 cubic feet. *Weights and Measures Act*, S.C. 1970-71-72, vol. 1, c. 36, schedule II. 2. The strands forming the plies of a tire. See DETONATING ~; POWER SUPPLY ~; UMBILICAL ~.

CORD SEPARATION. The parting of cords from adjacent rubber compounds. Canada regulations.

CORE OF THE CITATION. The core of the neutral citation consists of three important elements: (i) the year ; (ii) the tribunal identifier ; (iii) the ordinal number of the decision.

CO-RESPONDENT. *n.* A person identified in a divorce pleading as the party involved in a matrimonial offence with a spouse.

COR. JUD. *abbr.* Correspondances Judiciaires (Que.).

CORN. See GRAIN ~; SEED ~.

CORNER. *n.* A point in an intersection of boundaries of land. *Surveys acts.* See LOST ~; UNDISPUTED ~.

CORNER LOT. A lot situated at a junction or intersection of two streets.

CORNER POST. See LEGAL ~.

COROLLARY. *n.* A collateral or secondary consequence.

COROLLARY RELIEF. 1. Relief collateral to or secondary to the main relief granted in an action. 2. In divorce, custody or maintenance.

COROLLARY RELIEF PROCEEDING. A proceeding in a court in which either or both former spouses seek a child support order, a spousal support order or a custody order. *Divorce Act*, R.S.C., 1985, c. 3 (2nd Supp.), s. 2.

CORONARY. See CAFE ~.

CORONARY ARTERY. One of two arteries which arises from the aorta and supplies the heart muscle. F.A. Jaffe, *A Guide to Pathological Evidence*, 3d ed. (Toronto: Carswell, 199 at 212.

CORONARY THROMBOSIS. Obstruction of a coronary artery by a thrombus. F.A. Jaffe, *A Guide to Pathological Evidence*, 3d ed. (Toronto: Carswell, 1991) at 216.

CORONER. *n.* The official who investigates the death of any person who was killed or died in suspicious circumstances.

CORP. *abbr.* Corporation.

CORP. MGMT. TAX CONF. *abbr.* Canadian Tax Foundation. Corporate Management Tax Conference. Proceedings.

CORPORAL. *n.* In the army, a non-commissioned rank.

CORPORAL. *adj.* Bodily; relating to the body.

CORPORAL OATH. Touching the Bible or other holy book with the hand while taking an oath.

CORPORAL PUNISHMENT. Corporal punishment which causes injury is child abuse. Spanking [which does not cause physical harm] is not child abuse. *Canadian Foundation for Children, Youth & the Law v. Canada (Attorney General)* (2000), 2000 CarswellOnt 2409, 146 C.C.C. (3d) 362, 188 D.L.R. (4th) 718, 49 O.R. (3d) 662, 36 C.R. (5th) 334, 76 C.R.R. (2d) 251 (S.C.J.).

CORPORATE ACT. " . . . [T]he 'collective act' of . . . directors as expressed by resolution . . ." *Hill v. Develcon Electronics Ltd.* (1991), 37 C.C.E.L. 19 at 32, 92 Sask. R. 241 (Q.B.), Baynton J.

CORPORATE NAME. A name given to a corporation.

CORPORATE PURPOSES. Any effort to influence the voting of members or debenture holders of a corporation at any meeting, to acquire or sell shares or debentures of the corporation, or to effect an amalgamation or reorganization of the corporation. *Company Act*, R.S.B.C. 1996, c. 62, s. 1.

CORPORATE SEAL. The impression of the company's name which is placed on important documents such as share certificates, bonds and debentures.

CORPORATE VEIL. See PIERCE ~.

CORPORATION. *n.* 1. A legal entity distinct from its shareholders or members with liability separate from its shareholders or members vested with the capacity of continuous succession. 2. A body corporate with or without share capital. See AGENT ~; AGRICULTURAL ~; AGRICULTURAL OPERATIONS ~; ALBERTA ~; ASSOCIATED ~; BANK SERVICE ~; BUILDING DEVELOPMENT CAN-

ADA ~; CANADA DEPOSIT INSURANCE ~; CANADA MORTGAGE AND HOUSING ~; CANADA POST ~; CANADIAN BROADCASTING ~; CANADIAN ~; CASH-MUTUAL ~; CHARITABLE ~; CLOSELY HELD ~; CONSTRAINED SHARE ~; CONTROL OF ~; COOPERATIVE ~; COUNTY ~; CROWN CONTROLLED ~; CROWN ~; CROWN OWNED ~; DEPARTMENTAL ~; DEPOSIT INSURANCE ~; DISTRIBUTING ~; DOMESTIC ~; DOMINION ~; ELEEMOSYNARY ~; EMERGING ~; EXECUTIVE OFFICER OF A ~; EXHIBITION ~; EXPORT DEVELOPMENT ~; EXTRA-PROVINCIAL ~; FACTORING~; FAMILY BUSINESS ~; FAMILY ~; FAMILY FARM ~; FAMILY FARMING ~; FAMILY FISHING ~; FARM ~; FARM CREDIT ~ CANADA; FINANCE ~; FINANCIAL ~; FIRE AND CASUALTY ~; FOREIGN CONTROLLED ~; FOREIGN GOVERNMENT ~; HOLDING ~; INDEPENDENT ~; INVESTMENT ~; LAY ~; LEASING ~; LOAN ~; LOCAL PORT ~; MEMBERSHIP ~; MUNICIPAL ~; MUTUAL ~; MUTUAL FUND ~; MUTUAL INSURANCE ~; NON-PROFIT ~; NON-RESIDENT ~; NORTHERN VILLAGE ~; OFFEREE ~; OFFERING ~; OPERATING ~; PARENT ~; PIPE LINE ~; PRIVATE ~; PROFESSIONAL ~; PROVINCIAL ~; PUBLIC ~; PUBLIC SERVICE ~; REAL ESTATE ~; RESIDENCE OF A ~; SCHOOL ~; SENIOR ~; SERVICE ~; STATUTORY ~; SUBSIDIARY CONTROLLED ~; SUBSIDIARY CONTROLLED FINANCIAL ~; SUBSIDIARY ~; SUBSIDIARY WHOLLY OWNED ~; TERRITORIAL ~; TRUST ~; TRUST OR LOAN ~; VENTURE CAPITAL ~; WATER SUPPLY ~.

CORPORATION AGGREGATE. A corporation with several members, created by the Crown through Royal Prerogative or by statute. G.H.L. Fridman, *The Law* of *Contract in Canada*, 2d ed. (Toronto: Carswell, 1986) at 151.

CORPORATION INCOME TAX. A tax imposed by the Parliament of Canada or by the Legislature of a province or by a municipality in the province that is declared by the regulations to be a tax of general application on the profits of corporations. *Corporations Tax Act*, R.S.O. 1990, c. C.40, s. 16(3).

CORPORATION INCORPORATED IN CANADA. Includes a corporation incorporated

in any part of Canada before or after it became part of Canada.

CORPORATION NUMBER. The number assigned by the Director to a corporation in accordance with the Business Corporations Act. *Business Corporations Act*, R.S.O. 1990, c. B.16, s. 1.

CORPORATION SOLE. 1. The corporate status granted an individual natural person by the law, which is distinct from that individual's natural personality. The main example is the Crown. 2. " ... [O]ne single person being ex officio a corporate body, . . ." *Arnegard v. Barons Consolidated School District* (1917), 33 D.L.R. 735 at 739, [1917] 2 W.W.R. 303, 11 Alta. L.R. 460 (C.A.), the court per Stuart J.A.

CORPORATION TAX. A tax imposed by the Legislature of a province or by a municipality in the province that is declared by the regulations to be a tax on corporations, but does not include, (a) a corporation income tax, or (b) any other tax declared by the regulations not to be corporation tax. *Corporations Tax Act*, R.S.O. 1990, c. C.40, s. 16(3).

CORPORATOR. *n*. A member of a corporation aggregate. The inhabitants and officers of a municipal corporation.

CORPOREAL. *adj*. Describes that which is capable of physical possession.

CORPOREAL HEREDITAMENT. 1. A material object in contrast to a right. It may include land, buildings, minerals, trees or fixtures. 2. Land. *Pegg v. Pegg* (1992), 38 R.F.L. (3d) 179 at 184, 21 R.P.R. 2d 149 1 Alta. L.R. 3d 249, 128 A.R. 132 (Q.B.), Agrios J.

CORPOREAL PROPERTY. Property having a physical existence.

CORPORE ET ANIMO, NEQUE PER SE CORPORE, NEQUE PER SE ANIMO. [L.] Once a domicile is established, it can only be changed by residing in another country together with intending to remain there indefinitely. J.G. McLeod, *The Conflict of Laws* (Calgary: Carswell, 1983) at 779.

CORPS. See MINE RESCUE ~.

CORPS DIPLOMATIQUE. [Fr.] Ambassadors and diplomatic persons at a particular capital.

CORPSE. *n*. The dead body of a person.

CORPUS. *n*. [L.] 1. The capital of a fund in contrast to income. 2. The body, referring to a human body or the aggregation of something, such as laws.

CORPUS DELICTI. [L. body of the offence] The ingredients of an offence: commonly, the dead body.

CORPUS HUMANUM NON RECIPIT AES-TIMATIONEM. [L.] A human body cannot be valued.

CORPUS POSSESSIONIS. [L.] Actual power to direct or retain a thing.

CORRECTION. *n.* For s. 43 [of the *Criminal Code*, R.S.C. 1985, C-46] to apply, the force used on a child must be intended for correction. Punishment motivated by anger, or administered with an intent to injure the child, is not for the purpose of correction. As well, the accused must honestly and reasonably believe that the child is guilty of conduct deserving of punishment. Moreover, the child must be capable of being corrected. Therefore a parent or teacher who applies force on a child who is either too young to appreciate corrective force or mentally handicapped and clearly unable to learn from corrective force is not protected by s. 43. A consideration of what constitutes "correction" should be informed not by the particular notions of the parent or teacher, but by reference to contemporary community standards. *Canadian Foundation for Children, Youth & the Law v. Canada (Attorney General)* (2000), 2000 CarswellOnt 2409, 146 C.C.C. (3d) 362, 188 D.L.R. (4th) 718, 49 O.R. (3d) 662, 36 C.R. (5th) 334, 76 C.R.R. (2d) 251 (S.C.J.).

CORRECTIONAL CENTRE. 1. A lawful place of confinement, jail, prison, lockup, place of imprisonment, camp, correctional institution. 2. " . . . [A] jail where full security is established for the confinement and rehabilitation of persons committed to it . . ." *R. v. Degan* (1985), 20 C.C.C. (3d) 293 at 299, 38 Sask. R. 234 (C.A.), the court per Vancise J.A.

CORRECTIONAL FACILITY. 1. A jail, prison, correctional centre for the custody of offenders. 2. " . . . [I]ncludes a community training residence, is a facility established for the confinement and rehabilitation of a person committed to it . . ." *R. v. Dean* (1985), 20 C.C.C. (3d) 293 at 299, 38 Sask. R. 234 (C.A.), the court per Vancise J.A.

CORRECTIONAL INSTITUTION. Any building, correctional camp, rehabilitation camp, reformatory, forensic clinic, work site, gaol or place for the reception and lawful custody of inmates.

CORRECTIONAL INVESTIGATOR OF CANADA. It is the function of the Correctional Investigator to conduct investigations into the problems of offenders related to decisions, recommendations, acts or omissions of the Commissioner or any person under the control and management of, or performing services for or on behalf of, the Commissioner that affect offenders either individually or as a group. *Corrections and Conditional Release Act*, S.C. 1992, c. 20, s. 167.

CORRECTIONAL SERVICE CANADA. The federal body which supervises federal penal institutions, administers court-imposed sentences of two years and greater, preparing offenders for return to society.

CORRECTIONS EMPLOYEE. A person employed in a correctional facility.

CORRECTIVE DISCIPLINE. Principle that management withholds the ultimate penalty of discharge unless it is clear that the worker is not likely to respond favourably to a lesser penalty.

CORRECTNESS. n. 1.The highest standard of judicial review of tribunals' decisions. Cases in which this standard is applied deal with issues concerning the interpretation of a provision limiting the tribunal's jurisdiction (jurisdictional error) or where there is a statutory right of appeal which allows the reviewing court to substitute its opinion for that of the tribunal and where the tribunal has no greater expertise than the court on the issue in question, for example in the area of human rights. 2. At the correctness end of the spectrum [of standards of review], where deference in terms of legal questions is at its lowest, are those cases where the issues concern the interpretation of a provision limiting the tribunal's jurisdiction (jurisdictional error) or where there is a statutory right of appeal which allows the reviewing court to substitute its opinion for that of the tribunal and where the tribunal has no greater expertise than the court on the issue in question, as for example in the area of human rights. *Pezim v. British Columbia (Superintendent of Brokers)*, 1994 CarswellBC 232, 92 B.C.L.R. (2d) 145, [1994] 7 W.W.R. 1, 14 B.L.R. (2d) 217, 22 Admin. L.R . (2d) 1, 114 D.L.R. (4th) 385, [1994] 2 S.C.R. 557, (sub nom. *Pezim v. British Columbia (Securities Commission)*) 168 N.R. 321, (sub nom. *Pezim v. British Columbia (Securities Commission)*) 46

B.C.A.C. 1, (sub nom. *Pezim v. British Columbia (Securities Commission)*) 75 W.A.C. 1, 4 C.C.L.S. 117 Iacobucci, J. for the court. See PATENTLY UNREASONABLE; REASONABLE.

CORRELATIVE RIGHTS. The rights of an owner to receive the owner's share of oil and gas produced from a pool.

CORRESPONDENCE. See PUBLIC ~.

CORRIDOR. See PEDESTRIAN ~; PUBLIC ~.

CORR. JUD. *abbr*. Correspondances judiciaires (1906).

CORROBORATE. *v*. " . . . As Lord Diplock observed in D.P.P. v. Hester [[1972] 3 All E.R. 1056 at 1071], the ordinary sense in which the verb 'corroborate' is used in the English language is the equivalent of 'confirmed' and (at p. 1073): 'What is looked for under the common law rule is confirmation from some other source that the suspect witness is telling the truth in some part of his story which goes to show that the accused committed the offence with which he is charged.' " *R. v. Vetrovec* (1982),136 D.L.R. (3d) 89 at 104, [1982] 1 S.C.R. 811, 41 N.R. 606, 67 C.C.C. (2d)1, 27 C.R. (3d) 304, [1983] 1 W.W.R. 193, the court per Dickson J.

CORROBORATION. *n*. Confirmation of a witness's evidence by independent testimony.

CORROBORATIVE. *adj*. " . . . [Describes evidence which] enhances the credibility of or at least one material particular of the story which, if true, implicates the accused." *R. v Chayko* (1984), 12 C.C.C. (3d) 157 at 171, 31 Alta. L.R. (2d) 113, 51 A.R. 382 (C.A.), Kerans J.A. (Haddad J.A. concurring).

CORROBORATIVE EVIDENCE. Must be independent of the testimony of the witness whose testimony is sought to be corroborated. It must implicate the accused, that is, connect or tend to connect the accused with the crime. It must be evidence which confirms in some material particular, not only the evidence that the crime has been committed, but also that the accused committed it. *R. v. Whynder* (1996), 149 N.S.R. (2d) 241 (C.A.).

CORROSION-RESISTANT MATERIAL. Any material that maintains its original surface characteristics after, (i) repeated exposure to food, soil, moisture or heat, or (ii) exposure to any substance used in cleansing and disinfecting.

CORROSIVE PRODUCT. A chemical product that (*a*) is capable of inducing necrosis or ulceration of epithelial tissue; (*b*) is capable of causing an erythema or edema of the skin, corneal or iris damage or conjunctival swelling or redness; or (*c*) is identified in Part 2 as a Category 2 corrosive product. *Consumer Chemicals and Containers Regulations, 2001*, SOR/2001-269, s. 1.

CORRUPT. *v*. To alter morals and behaviour from good to bad.

CORRUPT. *adj*. Spoiled; debased; depraved.

CORRUPT CONDUCT. " . . . [I]n the context of s. 18 [of the Commercial Arbitration Act, S.B.C. 1986, c. 3] would be conduct so immoral that the unfairness of the process would be apparent. . . wilfully immoral or dishonest activity or action carried out by an arbitrator which has some bearing on the matter he has been asked to adjudicate. The activity itself might be dishonest or, alternatively, it might be an activity which is undertaken with an evil object in mind." *Zaleschuk Pubs Ltd. v. Barop Construction Ltd.* (1992), 68 B.C.L.R. (2d) 340 at 349 (S.C.), Vickers J.

CORRUPTING MORALS. (1) The offence of (a) making, printing, publishing, distributing, circulating, or having in his possession for the purpose of publication, distribution or circulation any obscene written matter, picture, model, phonograph record or other thing whatever, or (b) making, printing, publishing, distributing, selling or having in his possession for the purpose of publication, distribution or circulation, a crime comic. (2) The offence of knowingly, without lawful justification or excuse, (a) selling, exposing to public view or having in his possession for such a purpose any obscene written matter, picture, model, phonograph record or other thing whatever, (b) publicly exhibiting a disgusting object or an indecent show, (c) offering to sell, advertising, or publishing an advertisement of, or having for sale or disposal, any means, instructions, medicine, drug or article intended or represented as a method of causing abortion or miscarriage, or (d) advertising or publishing an advertisement of an means instructions, medicine drug or article intended or represented as a method for restoring sexual virility or curing venereal diseases or diseases of the generative organs. *Criminal Code*, R.S.C. 1985, C-46, s. 163.

CORRUPTION. *n*. Granting of favours inconsistent with official duties.

CORRUPTION OF BLOOD. An effect of attainder, when a person attainted was considered corrupted by the crime, so that the person could no longer hold land, inherit it or leave it to any heirs.

CORRUPTLY. *adv*. " . . . [In s. 426 of the Criminal Code, R.S.C. 1985, c. C-46] in the context of secret commissions, means without disclosure . . ." *R. v. Kelly* (1992), 14 C.R. (4th) 181 at 196, [1992] 4 W.W.R. 640, 73 C.C.C. (3d) 385, 9 B.C.A.C. 161, 19 W.A.C. 161, 92 D.L.R. (4th) 643, 68 B.C.L.R. (2d) 1, 137 N.R. 161, [1992] 2 S.C.R. 170, Cory J. (L'Heureux-Dubé, Gonthier and Iacobucci JJ. concurring).

CORRUPT PRACTICE. 1. " . . . [A] phrase, a term of art, created by statute for describing or dealing with a series of widely disparate acts and omissions. . . There may be corrupt practices within the meaning of the defined term where there was no debased intent and they may be corrupt practices notwithstanding that there was no element of moral turpitude." *Johansen v. Dickerson* (1980), 117 D.L.R. (3d) 176 at 180, 30 O.R. (2d) 616 (Div. Ct.), the court per Anderson J. 2. " . . . By the 'Common law of Parliament' it included bribery, intimidation of electors and undue influence. Statutes have added treating, which is a form of bribery, hiring vehicles to convey voters to polls, personation and some other acts. . ." *How v. Campbell*, [1939] 1 D.L.R. 431 at 432, 71 C.C.C. 246, 13 M.P.R. 494 (N.S. C.A.), Doull J.A. (concurring in the result). 3. Any act or omission, in connection with an election, in respect of which an offence is provided under the *Criminal Code* (Canada) or which is a corrupt practice under this Act. *Election Act*, R.S.O. 1990, c. E-6, s. 1.

COSEN. *v*. To cheat; to defraud.

COSENAGE. *n*. The condition of being kin, consanguinity.

COSEWIC. The Committee on the Status of Endangered Wildlife in Canada established by section 14. *Species at Risk Act*, S.C. 2002, c. 29, s. 2.

CO-SIGNER. *n*. A person who agrees to sign a promissory note, or other agreement, together with the maker and be responsible if the maker should default.

COSMETIC. *n*. Any substance or mixture of substances manufactured, sold or represented for use in cleansing, improving or altering the complexion, skin, hair or teeth, and includes deodorants and perfumes. *Food and Drugs Act*, R.S.C. 1985, c. F-27, s. 2.

COSMETICS. *n*. Goods, whether possessing therapeutic or prophylactic properties or not, commonly or commercially known as toilet articles, preparations or cosmetics, that are intended for use or application for toilet purposes, of for use in connection with the care of the human body, including the hair, nails, eyes, teeth, or any other part or parts thereof, whether for cleansing, deodorizing, beautifying, preserving or restoring, and includes toilet soaps, shaving soaps and shaving creams, skin creams and lotions, shampoos, mouth washes, oral rinses, toothpastes, tooth powders, denture creams and adhesives, antiseptics, bleaches, depilatories, perfumes, scents and similar preparations. *Excise Tax Act*, R.S.C. 1985, c. E-15, s. 2.

COST. *n*. 1. "[In ss. 40(1)(c) and 54 of the Income Tax Act, S.C. 1970-71-72, c. 63] . . . means the price that the taxpayer gave up in order to get the asset; it does not include any expense he may have incurred in order to put himself in a position to pay that price or to keep the property afterwards." *R. v. Stirling* (1985), 85 D.T.C. 5199, [1985] 1 F.C. 342 , [1985] 1 C.T.C. 275 (C.A.), the court per Pratte J. 2. Of a loan means the whole of the cost of the loan to the borrower whether the cost is called interest or is claimed as discount, deduction from an advance, commission, brokerage, chattel mortgage and recording fees, fines, penalties or charges for inquiries, defaults or renewals or otherwise, and whether paid to or charged by the lender or paid to or charged by any other person, and whether fixed and determined by the loan contract itself, or in whole or in part by any other collateral contract or document by which the charges, if any, imposed under the loan contract or the terms of the repayment of the loan are effectively varied. *Small Loans Act*, R.S.C. 1970, c. S-11 s. 2. See ACTUAL ~; ADMINISTRATION ~; BENEFIT ~ STATEMENT; CAPITAL ~; ~S; DEVELOPMENT ~ METHOD; EDUCATION CAPITAL ~; ELIGIBLE ASSET ~; ELIGIBLE ~ OR EXPENSE; ESTIMATED ~; F.O.B. ~; FUTURE ~ OF INSURED SERVICES; OPPORTUNITY ~; ORIGINAL ~ OF THE LAND; OWNER'S PORTION OF THE ~; OWNER'S SHARE OF THE ~; PAST ~ OF INSURED SERVICES; PUBLICATION ~; PURCHASER'S ~ OF A SHARE; RATE OF ~ CHANGE; REPLACEMENT ~.

COST AMOUNT. With respect to an eligible security issued pursuant to a certificate of eligibility: (i) if the eligible security is issued for consideration consisting only of money, the amount of money paid by the eligible investor for the eligible security, including any applicable underwriters' fees paid by the eligible investor for the eligible security but not including: (A) any brokerage or custody fee or similar charge; or (B) any amount paid to acquire a warrant that evidenced the right to acquire the eligible security; or (ii) if the eligible security is issued for consideration consisting only of property or past service or partly of money and partly of property or past service, an amount not exceeding the amount, if any, by which the aggregate of (A) the amount, if any, of money paid by the eligible investor for the eligible security, as determined in accordance with subclause (i); and (B) the fair market value of the property or past service in consideration for which the eligible security was issued; exceeds the fair market value of any consideration issued or granted by the eligible issuer other than an eligible security or a warrant that evidences the right to acquire an eligible security. *Stock Savings Tax Credit acts.*

COST APPROACH. "[In expropriation] . . . a valuation based upon the current cost of reproducing an improvement less accrued depreciation from all causes plus the value of the land." *A. Merkur & Sons Ltd. v. Ontario Regional Assessment Commissioner, Region 14* (1977), 4 M.P.L.R. 177 at 184, 7 M.P.L.R. 191, 17 O.R. (2d) 339, 7 O.M.B.R. 287 (Div. Ct.), the court per Steele J.

COST OF BENEFIT. See ACCRUED BENEFIT COST METHOD; BASIC ~.

COST OF BORROWING. 1. In respect of a loan made by a bank, (*a*) the interest or discount applicable to the loan; (*b*) any amount charged in connection with the loan that is payable by the borrower to the bank; and (*c*) any charge prescribed to be included in the cost of borrowing. *Bank Act*, S.C. 1991, c. 46, s. 449. 2.All amounts that a borrower is required to pay under or as a condition of entering into a credit agreement other than, (a) a payment or repayment of a portion of the principal under the agreement as prescribed, and (b) prescribed charges. *Consumer Protection Act, 2002*, S.O. 2002, c. 30, s. 66.

COST OF COMPENSATION. See FULL ~.

COST OF CONSTRUCTION. The aggregate of (a) the cost or appraised value of the land, whichever is the lesser, or, in the case of land acquired by gift or devise, the appraised value of the land, (b) actual expenditure for building, (c) the architectural, legal and other expenses and carrying charges necessary to complete the house or housing project, (d) where work is done by the owner, such amount as the Corporation may fix as the value of the work, and (e) land development costs and carrying charges. *National Housing Act*, R.S.C. 1985, c. N-11, s. 2.

COST OF FUTURE CARE. 1. " . . . [A] pecuniary claim for the amount which may reasonably be expected to be expended in putting the injured party in the position he would have been in if he had not sustained the injury. . ." *Andrews v. Grand & Toy Alberta Ltd.* (1978), 3 C.C.L.T. 225 at 235, [1978] 2 S.C.R. 229, [1978] 1 W.W.R. 577, 19 N.R. 50, 8 A.R. 182, 83 D.L.R. (3d) 452, the court per Dickson J. 2. In respect of a loan made by a bank, (*a*) the interest or discount applicable to the loan; (*b*) any amount charged in connection with the loan that is payable by the borrower to the bank; and (*c*) any charge prescribed to be included in the cost of borrowing. *Bank Act, 1991*, S.C. 1991, c. 46, s. 449. 3. Costs which a plaintiff can be expected to expend for care, particularly medical and hospital expenses, as a result of the injuries suffered and for which he is claiming damages.

COST OF LABOUR. (a) The actual wages paid to all workers up to and including the foremen for their time actually spent on the work and in travelling to and from the work, and the cost of food, lodging and transportation for such workers where necessary for the proper carrying out of the work, (b) the cost to the operating corporation of contributions related to such wages in respect of worker's compensation, vacation pay, unemployment insurance, pension or insurance benefits and other similar benefits, (c) the cost of using mechanical labour-saving equipment in the work, (d) necessary transportation charges for equipment used in the work, and (e) the cost of explosives. *Public Service Works on Highways Act*, R.S.O. 1990, c. P.49, s. 1.

COST OF LIVING. The relationship between the cost of goods to the consumer and buying power of wages.

COST-OF-LIVING ADJUSTMENT. A change in wages or pension payments designed to offset changes in cost of living.

COST OF LIVING INDEX. " . . . [U]sed in Canada commonly and interchangeably for the phrase, 'consumer price index,' and especially for the index published by the Dominion Bureau of Statistics. Judicial notice may be taken of the fact that this government department is now known as Statistics Canada." *Collins Cartage & Storage Co. v. McDonald* (1980), 16 R.P.R. 71 at 74, 30 O.R. (2d) 234, 116 D.L.R., (3d) 570 (C.A.), the court per Goodman J.A. See CONSUMER PRICE INDEX.

COST OF THE LOAN. The whole cost to the debtor of money lent and includes interest, discount, subscription, premium, dues, bonus, commission, brokerage fees and charges, but not actual lawful and necessary disbursements made to a registrar of deeds, a prothonotary, a clerk of a county or municipal court, a sheriff or a treasurer of a city, town or municipality. *Unconscionable Transactions Relief acts.*

COST-PLUS CONTRACT. A contract to sell a product or perform work for the selling price or contractor's costs plus a percentage or plus a fixed fee.

COSTS. *n.* 1. An award made in favour of a successful or deserving litigant, payable by another litigant, the award of which is determined at the end of proceedings, payable by way of indemnity for allowable expenses and services relevant to the proceeding and not payable to ensure participation in the proceedings. 2. Modern costs rules accomplish various purposes in addition to the traditional objective of indemnification. An order as to costs may be designed to penalize a party who has refused a reasonable settlement offer; this policy has been codified in the rules of court of many provinces. Costs can also be used to sanction behaviour that increases the duration and expense of litigation, or is otherwise unreasonable or vexatious. In short, it has become a routine matter for courts to employ the power to order costs as a tool in the furtherance of the efficient and orderly administration of justice. *British Columbia (Minister of Forests) v. Okanagan Indian Band*, 2003 SCC 71. 3. Money expended to prosecute or defend a suit which a party is entitled to recover. 4. " . . . [F]or the purpose of indemnification or compensation. *Bell Canada v. Consumers' Assn. of Canada* (1986), 17 Admin L.R. 205 at 228, [1986] 1 S.C.R. 190, 9 C.P.R. (2d) 145, 65 N.R. 1, 26 D.L.R. (4th) 573, the court per Le Dain J. 5. The costs and charges after they have been ascertained, of committing and conveying to prison the person against whom costs have been awarded. *Criminal Code*, R.S.C. 1985, c. C-46,

s. 809(5). 6. Where costs are awarded to a party without any qualification as to their being in the cause, or in any event of the cause, as here, the award must be interpreted as meaning costs in the cause. *Miller v. Miller*, 2000 CarswellBC 350, 2000 BCSC 300 (S.C.). See ACQUISITION ~; ADMINISTRATION ~; ALL PROPER ~ AND EXPENSES; ASSESSED ~; ASSESSMENT OF ~; BILL OF ~; CARRY ~; CARRYING ~; COST; DISTRIBUTIVE ORDER FOR ~; EXTRAJUDICIAL ~; FIXED ~; FULL ~; INCREASED ~; JUDICIAL ~; MAINTENANCE ~; NO ORDER AS TO ~; NORMAL ~; OPERATING ~; PARTY-AND-PARTY ~; SALVAGE ~; SECURITY FOR ~; SOLICITOR-AND-CLIENT ~; SOLICITOR AND HIS OWN CLIENT ~; SPECIAL ~; TANKER FREIGHT ~; TAXABLE ~; TAXATION OF ~; TAXED ~; WITH ~.

COSTS IF DEMANDED. An expression inserted in a judgment when either the successful party is a body like the Crown or the unsuccessful party faces financial ruin. M.M. Orkin, *The Law of Costs*, 2d ed. (Aurora: Canada Law Book, 1987) at 1-12.

COSTS, INSURANCE AND FREIGHT. See C.I.F.; C.I.F. CONTRACT.

COSTS IN THE ACTION. See COSTS IN THE CAUSE.

COSTS IN THE CAUSE. 1. " . . . [T]he costs of this motion are to be taken into account in the final taxation of the costs at the conclusion of the litigation between the parties." *Banke Electronics Ltd. v. Olvan Tool & Die Inc.* (1981), 32 O.R. (2d) 630 at 632-33 (H.C.), Cory J. 2. Where costs are awarded to a party without any qualification as to their being in the cause, or in any event of the cause, as here, the award must be interpreted as meaning costs in the cause. *Miller v. Miller*, 2000 CarswellBC 350, 2000 BCSC 300 (S.C.).

COSTS OF AND INCIDENTAL TO. Party-and-party costs. M.M. Orkin, *The Law of Costs*, 2d ed. (Aurora: Canada Law Book, 1987) at 113.

COSTS OF THE DAY. Costs awarded when adjournment of the trial was caused by one party's default. M.M. Orkin, *The Law of Costs*, 2d ed. (Aurora: Canada Law Book, 1987) at 273.

COSTS OF THE WORK. See VALUE OF THE WORK AND ~.

COSTS OF THIS HEARING. Costs which include both preparation for the hearing and the hearing itself. M.M. Orkin, *The Law of Costs*, 2d ed. (Aurora: Canada Law Book, 1987) at 112.

COSTS OF THIS PROCEEDING. Costs for all interlocutory motions and services, not only costs at trial. M.M. Orkin, *The Law of Costs*, 2d ed. (Aurora: Canada Law Book, 1987) at 112.

COSTS REASONABLY INCURRED. Party-and-party costs. M.M. Orkin, *The Law of Costs*, 2d ed. (Aurora: Canada Law Book, 1987) at 113.

COSTS THROWN AWAY. Refers to expenses incurred in anticipation of a proceeding which did not occur through no fault of the person incurring the expenses.

COSTS TO THE SUCCESSFUL PARTY IN THE CAUSE. See COSTS IN THE CAUSE.

CO-SURETY. *n*. One who shares a surety's obligations.

COT DEATH. See CRIB DEATH.

COTENANCY. *n*. Includes tenancy in common and joint tenancy.

COTTAGE. *n*. 1. A small house. 2. A building to accommodate one or more guests.

COUCHANT. [Fr.] Lying down.

COULOMB. *n*. The quantity of electricity transported in one second by a current of one ampere. *Weights and Measures Act*, S.C. 1970-71-72 c. 36, schedule 1.

COUNCIL. *n*. 1. An assembly of people for governmental or municipal purposes. 2. The governing body of a city, village, summer village, municipal district, county or other municipality. 3. The Queen's Privy Council for Canada committees of the Queen's Privy Council for Canada, Cabinet and committees of Cabinet. *Canada Evidence Act*, R.S.C. 1985, c. C-5, s. 39(3). 4. An advisory body to government. 5. Used to describe the governing body of an association, i.e. professional organizations. 6. Used in the title of administrative agencies. 7. An association of unions within an area. 8. The Council of the Northwest Territories or the Yukon the members of which shall be elected to represent such electoral districts in the Territories as are named and described by the Commissioner in Council. See BAND ~; BARGAINING ~; BICAMERAL ~; BUILDING TRADES ~; CANADA ~; COMMISSIONER IN ~; COUNTY ~; DISTRICT ~; ECO-NOMIC ~ OF CANADA; EXECUTIVE ~; GOVERNOR GENERAL IN ~; GOVERNOR IN ~; HEAD OF ~; HEAD OF THE ~; INDIAN BAND ~; JUDICIAL ~; LEGISLATIVE ~; LIEUTENANT GOVERNOR IN ~; LOCAL ~; MEDICAL RESEARCH ~ OF CANADA; MEMBER OF ~; MEMBER OF THE ~; MUNICIPAL ~; NATIONAL RESEARCH ~; NATIONAL RESEARCH OF CANADA; NATURAL SCIENCES AND ENGINEERING RESEARCH ~ OF CANADA; ONTARIO JUDICIAL ~; ORDER IN ~; PRIVY ~; SCIENCE ~ OF CANADA; SETTLEMENT ~; SOCIAL SCIENCES AND HUMANITIES RESEARCH ~ OF CANADA; STANDARDS ~ OF CANADA; STUDENTS ~.

COUNCILLOR. *n*. A member of or a person serving on a council. See BAND ~.

COUNCIL OF THE BAND. (a) In the case of a band to which section 74 applies, the council established pursuant to that section, (b) in the case of a band to which section 74 does not apply, the council chosen according to the custom of the band, or, where there is no council, the chief of the band chosen according to the custom of the band. *Indian Act*, R.S.C. 1985, c. I-5, s. 2.

COUNCIL OF TRADE UNIONS. 1. Two or more trade unions that have formed a council of trade unions, one of the purposes of which is the regulation of relations between employers and employees. *Canada Labour Relations Band Regulations*, C.R.C., c. 1014, s. 2. 2. A council that is formed for the purpose of representing or that according to established bargaining practice represents trade unions. *Industrial Relations Act*, R.S.N.B. 1973, c. I-4, s. 38. 3. Includes an allied council, a trades council, a joint board or another association of trade unions. See CERTIFIED ~.

COUNSEL. *v*. 1. To procure, solicit or incite. *Criminal Law Amendment Act*, R.S.C. 1985 (1st Supp.), c. 27, s. 7(3). 2. To advise or recommend.

COUNSEL. *n*. 1. A barrister or solicitor, in respect of the matters or things that barristers and solicitors respectively, are authorized by the law of a province to do or perform in relation to legal proceedings. *Criminal Code*, R.S.C. 1985, c. C-46, s. 2. 2. 2. Both singular and plural. 3. " . . . [A]n adviser whether or not he is a lawyer, . . ." *Olavarria v. Canada (Minister of Manpower & Immigra*tion), [1973] F.C. 1035 at 1037, 41

D.L.R. (3d) 472 (C.A.), Jackett, Thurlow and Hyde JJ.A. See COMMISSION ~; CROWN ~; DUTY ~; HOUSE ~; INVEST-MENT ~; QUEEN'S RIGHT TO ~.

COUNSELLING. *n*. " . . . [A]cts or words . . . such as to induce a person to commit the offences that one desires and passive communication does not constitute an offence even if its purpose is to have someone inflict those in *R. v. Dionne* (1987), 38 C.C.C. (3d) 171 at 180 58 C.R. (3d) 351 79 N.B.R. (2d) 297, 201 A.P.R. 297 (C.A.), Ayles J.A. See INVESTMENT ~.

COUNT. *n*. A charge in an information or indictment. *Criminal Code*, R.S.C. 1985, c. C-46, s. 2. See RE~.

COUNTENANCE. *v*. To encourage; to aid and abet.

COUNTERCLAIM. *n*. " . . . [A]n independent action raised by a defendant, which because of the identity of the parties can conveniently be tried with the plaintiff's claim. While a counter-claim frequently (although not necessarily) arises from the same events as the plaintiff's claim, and while it may result in reduction of the plaintiff's claim, its in principle an independent action." *Royal Bank v. Rizkalla* (1984), 50 C.P.C. 292 at 296, 59 B.C.L.R. 324 (S.C.), McLachlin J.

COUNTERFEASANCE. *n*. Forging.

COUNTERFEIT. *n*. An unauthorized imitation intended to be used to defraud by passing off.

COUNTERFEIT COIN. See COUNTERFEIT MONEY.

COUNTERFEIT MONEY. Includes (a) a false coin or false paper money that resembles or is apparently intended to resemble or pass for a current coin or current paper money, (b) a forged bank-note or forged blank bank-note whether complete or incomplete, (c) a genuine coin or genuine paper money that is prepared or altered to resemble or pass for a current coin or current paper money of a higher denomination, (d) a current coin from which the milling is removed by filing or cutting the edges and on which new milling is made to restore its appearance, (e) a coin cased with gold, silver or nickel, as the case may be, that is intended to resemble or pass for a current gold, silver or nickel coin, and (f) a coin or a piece of metal or mixed metals that is washed or coloured by any means with a wash or material capable of producing the appearance of gold, silver or nickel and that is intended to

resemble or pass for a current gold, silver or nickel coin. *Criminal Code*, R.S.C. 1985, c. C-46, s. 448. See UTTERING ~.

COUNTERFEIT TOKEN OF VALUE. A counterfeit excise stamp, postage stamp or other evidence of value, by whatever technical, trivial or deceptive designation it may be described, and includes genuine coin or paper money that has no value as money. *Criminal Code*, R.S.C. 1985, c. C-46, s. 448.

COUNTERFOIL. *n*. The complementary part of a cheque or receipt used to preserve a record of the contents.

COUNTERMAND. *v*. To revoke; to recall.

COUNTER OFFER. *var*. **COUNTER-OF-FER**. A statement by the offeree rejecting the offer and creating a new offer.

COUNTERPART. *n*. A part which corresponds; a duplicate.

COUNTERPETITION. *n*. A claim for relief against the petitioner by respondent in a divorce proceeding.

COUNTER-PROPOSAL. *n*. An opposing offer made in collective bargaining following an offer or proposal by the other party.

COUNTER-SIGN. *var*. **COUNTERSIGN**. *v*. 1. For a second person to sign a document to verify the validity of the original signature of the first person. 2. For a subordinate to sign to vouch for the authenticity of any writing by the superior.

COUNTER-SIGNATURE. *var*. **COUNTER-SIGNATURE**. *n*. The endorsement on a royal instrument or on a document under the sign-manual of the signature of Her Majesty's responsible Canadian minister. *Seals Act*, R.S.C. 1985, c. S-6, s. 2.

COUNTERVAIL. *v*. To compensate; to balance.

COUNTERVAILING DUTIES AGREE-MENT. See SUBSIDIES AND ~.

COUNTRY. *n*. The total territory which is subject under a single sovereign to a single body of law. J.G. McLeod, *The Conflict of Laws* (Calgary: Carswell, 1983) at 5. See BENEFICI-ARY ~; COMMONWEALTH ~; FOR-EIGN ~.

COUNTRY OF EXPORT. 1. In respect of goods, the country from which the goods are shipped directly to Canada. *Customs Act*, R.S.C. 1985, (2d Supp.), c. 1, s. 45. 2. In the case of dumped goods, the country from which the goods were shipped directly to Canada or, if the goods have not been shipped directly to Canada, the country from which the goods would be shipped directly to Canada under normal conditions of trade and, in the case of subsidized goods, the country in which the subsidy originated. *Special Imports Measures Act*, R.S.C. 1985, c. S-15, s. 2.

COUNTRY OF ORIGIN. (a) The country of the Union in which the applicant for registration of a trade-mark had at the date of the application a real and effective industrial or commercial establishment, or (b) if the applicant for registration of a trade-mark did not at the date of the application have in a country of the Union an establishment as described in paragraph (a), the country of the Union where he on that date had his domicile, or (c) if the applicant for registration of a trade-mark did not at the date of the application have in a country of the Union an establishment as described in paragraph (a) or a domicile as described in paragraph (b), the country of the Union of which he was on that date a citizen or national. *Trade-marks Act*, R.S.C. 1985, c. T-13, s. 2.

COUNTRY OF THE UNION. (*a*) Any country that is a member of the Union for the Protection of Industrial Property constituted under the Convention, or (*b*) any WTO Member. *Trade-marks Act*, R.S.C. 1985, c. T-13, s. 2.

COUNTRY SALE. A public sale of livestock at any place other than a market.

COUNTY. *n*. A territorial division for electoral, judicial or local government purposes. See ~ MUNICIPALITY; DISTRICT OR ~; GENERAL ~ LEVY.

COUNTY BRIDGE. A bridge under the exclusive jurisdiction of the council of a county. *Municipal Act*, R.S.O. 1990, c. M.45, s. 258(1).

COUNTY COUNCIL. The municipal council of a county. In Ontario, the members are the reeves and deputy reeves of the unseparated towns, villages and townships in the county. I.M. Rogers, *The Law of Canadian Municipal Corporations*, 2d ed. (Toronto: Carswell, 1971-) at 226.

COUNTY COURT. 1. A court with jurisdiction limited to a county by territory and limited by subject matter or by value of the claim. 2. " . . .

[A]n inferior statutory Court of record and its jurisdiction, namely the County Court Act, R.S.N.S. 1967, c. 64, and its antecedent enactments.'' *Whynot v. Giffin* (1984), 40 C.P.C. 344 at 346, 62 N.S.R. (2d) 112, 136 A.P.R. 112, 7 D.L.R. (4th) 68 (C.A.), the court per Macdonald J.A. 3. In its application to the Province of Ontario includes, and in its application to the Province of Newfoundland means, "district court". *Interpretation* Act, R.S.C. 1985, c. I-21, s. 35.

COUNTY COURT JUDGE. See SENIOR ~.

COUNTY LEVY. See NET ~.

COUNTY MUNICIPALITY. A municipality, other than a city, that forms part of a county or regional municipality that is not in the territorial districts. *Education Act*, R.S.O. 1990, c. E.2, s. 1(1).

COUPLING SLEEVES. Function to allow the attachment of the drill rod to other drill rods or to the rock drill. *Sandvik Tamrock Canada Ltd. v. Deputy Minister of National Revenue (Customs & Excise)* (2001), 2001 FCA 340, 284 N.R. 183, 6 T.T.R. (2d) 302 (C.A.).

COUPON. *n*. Part of a commercial instrument designed to be cut off, which evidences something connected with the contract the instrument represents, usually interest.

COUPON BOND. A bond registrable as to principal only; interest is paid through coupons, payable to bearer, attached to the instrument. H. Sutherland, D.B. Horsley & J.M. Edmiston, eds., *Fraser's Handbook on Canadian Company Law*, 7th ed. (Toronto: Carswell 1985) at 311.

COUPON DEBENTURE. A debenture registrable as to principal only; interest is paid through coupons, pay able to bearer, attached to the instrument. H. Sutherland D.B. Horsley & J.M. Edmiston eds. *Fraser's Handbook on Canadian Company Law*, 7th ed. (Toronto: Carswell, 1985) at 311.

COURIER. *n*. An individual who, on personal account or as an employee of another person, provides to members of the public the service of carrying items of value in personal custody.

COURSE. *n*. 1. "[As used in s. 2(f.1) of the Newfoundland Human Rights Code, R.S. Nfld. 1970, c. 262] . . . imports the need for some series of events." *Aavik v. Ashbourne* (1990), 12 C.H.R.R. D/401 at D/407 (Nfld. Humans Rights Comm.), Gallant (Member). 2. A specific unit of study. *Public Schools Act*, S.M. 1980, c. 33,

s. 1. See CANADIAN SECURITIES ~; DENOMINATIONAL THEOLOGICAL ~; HOME STUDY ~; ORDER OF ~; SECONDARY ~; TRAINING ~; UNIVERSITY ~; UPDATING ~; UPGRADING ~; WATER ~.

COURSE LOAD. See NORMAL FULL-TIME ~.

COURSE OF BUSINESS. The normal activities of business.

COURSE OF CONDUCT. A series of actions similarly motivated, repetitive conduct.

COURSE OF EMPLOYMENT. " . . . [W]ork or job-related . . ." *Robichaud v. Canada (Treasury Board)*, [1987] 2 S.C.R. 84 at 92, La Forest J., cited with approval in *Janzen v. Platy Enterprises* (1989), 47 C.R.R. 274 at 305, [1989] 1 S.C.R. 1252, 25 C.C.E.L. 1, [1989] 4 W.W.R. 39, 59 D.L.R. (4th) 352, 10 C.H.R.R. D/6205, 58 Man. R. (2d) 1, the court per Dickson C.J.C.

COURSE OF JUSTICE. "[In s. 127 (2) of the Criminal Code, R.S.C. 1970, c. C-34] . . . includes judicial proceedings existed [sic] or proposed but is not limited to such proceedings. . . also includes attempts by a person to obstruct, pervert or defeat a prosecution which he contemplates may take place, notwithstanding that no decision to prosecute has been made. *R. v. Spezzano* (1977) 15 O.R. (2d) 489 at 492, 34 C.C.C. (2d) 87, 76 D.L.R. (3d) 160 (C.A.), the court per Martin J.A. Refers to a proceeding in which a decision-making body makes a determination and in which the body's authority is derived from statute.

COURSE OF STUDY. See APPROVED ~.

COURT. *n*. 1. A place where justice is administered; a body or part of the judicial system. 2. A place where a sovereign resides. 3. The court or a judge of the court. 4. A tribunal. 5. " . . . [A]ny judicial or judge whatever its importance or jurisdiction. That is the usual meaning of the word . As well, [it has] a narrow meaning by which . . . 'court' designates more specifically a judicial organism of superior jurisdiction . . ." *Québec (Commission des droites de la personne) c. Canada (Procureur général)* (1978), (*sub nom. Human Rights Commission v. Solicitor-General of Canada*) 93 D.L.R. (3d) 562 at 570 (Que. C.A.), Mayrand J.A. (Bernier J.A. concurring). 6. Includes a judge, arbitrator, umpire, commissioner provincial judge, justice of the peace or other office or person having by law or by the consent of the parties authority to hear,

receive and examine evidence. *Evidence acts*. 7. A court having jurisdiction in an action for the recovery of a debt or money demand to the amount claimed by a creditor in respect of money lent. *Unconscionable Transactions Relief acts*. 8. An authority having jurisdiction to make an order. *Maintenance Orders Enforcement acts*. See ADMIRALTY ~; APPEAL ~; APPELLATE ~; CITIZENSHIP ~; CIVIL CONTEMPT; CIVIL ~; COMPETENT ~; CONTEMPT; CONTEMPT IN THE FACE OF THE ~; CONTEMPT NOT IN THE FACE OF THE ~; CONTEMPT OUTSIDE ~; COUNTY ~; CRIMINAL CONTEMPT; DISTRICT ~; DIVIDED ~; DIVISIONAL ~; ECCLESIASTICAL ~; ELECTION ~; ENCLOSED ~; EUROPEAN ~; EUROPEAN ~ OF HUMAN RIGHTS; EXCHEQUER ~; FEDERAL ~; FOREIGN ~; FRIEND OF THE ~; FULL ~; INFERIOR ~; INTERNATIONAL ~ OF JUSTICE; NAVAL ~; NIGHT ~; OFFICE OF THE ~; OPEN ~; ORDINARY ~; ORIGINAL PAYMENT INTO ~; POLICE ~; PRIZE ~; PROVINCIAL ~; REGISTERING ~; REGISTRATION ~; RULES OF ~; SCANDALIZE THE ~; SERVICE ~; SMALL CLAIMS ~; STATUTORY ~; SUMMARY CONVICTION ~; SUMMARY TRIAL ~; SUPERIOR SUPREME ~; SUPREME ~ OF CANADA; SUPREME ~ OF ONTARIO; TERRITORIAL ~; TRAILER ~; TRIAL ~; YOUTH ~.

COURT APPEALED FROM. The court from which the appeal is brought directly to the Supreme Court, whether that court is one of original jurisdiction or a court of appeal. *Supreme Court Act*, R.S.C. 1985, c. S-26, s. 2.

COURT-APPOINTED RECEIVER. A receiver of property which a court appoints when it judges that it is "just or convenient" to do so.

COURT AREA. An area that is used for the purposes of a court, whether or not the public is normally admitted to the area, and, without restricting the generality of the foregoing, includes an area that is used for conducting court proceedings, for a judge's chambers or judge's office or for an office or workplace used for the purposes of a court and any common areas used in connection with such areas. *Court Security Act*, S.N.S. 1990, c. 7, s. 2.

COURT BELOW. Refers to inferior courts.

COURT CLERK. The chief administrator of a court who issues process, enters orders and performs other duties.

COURTESY VEHICLE. A motor vehicle operated by a commercial enterprise for the purpose of transporting customers of that enterprise between an airport and the place of business of that enterprise. *Government Airport Concession Operations Regulations*, C.R.C., c. 1565, s. 2.

COURT MARTIAL. 1. A court which tries offences against naval, military or air force discipline, or offences committed by a member of the armed forces against the ordinary law. 2. Includes a General Court Martial, a Special General Court Martial, a Disciplinary Court Martial and a Standing Court Martial. *National Defence Act*, R.S.C. 1985, c. N-5, s. 2.

COURT MARTIAL APPEAL COURT. The court established under the National Defence Act which shall hear and determine all appeals referred to it. The judges of the Court Martial Appeal Court are not less than four judges of the Federal Court to be designated by the Governor in Council and such additional judges of a superior court of criminal jurisdiction as are appointed by the Governor in Council.

COURT OF A CONTRACTING STATE. (i) In relation to the United Kingdom, any court of the United Kingdom or of any territory to which this Convention extends pursuant to Article XIII; (ii) in relation to Canada, the Federal Court of Canada or any court of a province or territory to which this Convention extends pursuant to Article XII. *Canada – United Kingdom Civil and Commercial Judgments Convention*, R.S.C. 1985, c. C-30, Sched. 1, s. 1.

COURT OF APPEAL. 1. In the Province of Prince Edward Island, the Appeal Division of the Supreme Court, and in all other provinces, the Court of Appeal. *Criminal Code*, R.S.C. 1985, c. C-46, s. 2, as am. 2. The words "general court of appeal" in s. 101 [of the *Constitution Act, 1867* (U.K.), 30 & 31 Vict., c. 3] denote the status of the Court within the national court structure and should not be taken as a restrictive definition of the Court's functions. In most instances, this Court acts as the exclusive ultimate appellate court in the country, and, as such, is properly constituted as the "general court of appeal" for Canada. Moreover, it is clear that an appellate court can receive, on an exceptional basis, original jurisdiction not incompatible with its appellate jurisdiction. *Reference re Secession of Quebec*, 1998 CarswellNat 1299, 161 D.L.R. (4th) 385, 228 N.R. 203, 55 C.R.R. (2d) 1, [1998] 2 S.C.R. 217, Per curiam.

COURT OF CANADA. The Federal Court of Canada or any court of a province or territory to which this Convention extends pursuant to Article XII. *Canada – United Kingdom Civil and Commercial Judgments Convention*, R.S.C. 1985, c. C-30, Sched. 1, s. 1.

COURT OF CHANCERY. The main English court in which the part of law known as equity was enforced. The Lord Chancellor preside assisted by the Master of the Rolls and judges called Vice-Chancellors.

COURT OF COMPETENT JURISDICTION. 1. One that possesses jurisdiction over the subject matter, jurisdiction over the person, and jurisdiction to grant the remedy. . . whether a court or tribunal possesses the power to grant the remedy sought is first and foremost a matter of discerning legislative intent. The question in all cases is whether Parliament or the legislature intended to empower the court or tribunal to make rulings on *Charter* violations that arise incidentally to their proceedings, and to grant the remedy sought as a remedy for such violations. *R. v. Hynes*, [2001] 3 S.C.R. 623. 2. May include a tribunal which has jurisdiction over the parties and subject matter of the dispute and which is empowered to make the orders sought. 3. " . . . [A] court is competent if it has jurisdiction, conferred by statute, over the person and the subject-matter in question and, in addition, has authority to make the order sought." *R. v. Morgentaler* (1984), 48 O.R. 2d 19 (C.A.), Brooke J.A., cited with approval in *R. v. Mills* (1986), 29 D.L.R. (4th) 161 at 177 (S.C.C.), McIntyre J. and *Cuddy Chicks Ltd. v. Ontario (Labour Relations Board)* (1989), 39 Admin. L.R. 48 at 68, 89 C.L.L.C. 14,051, 79 O.R. (2d) 179, 62 D.L.R. (4th) 125, [1989] O.L.R.B. Rep. 989, 35 O.A.C. 94, 44 C.R.R. 75 (C.A.), Finlayson J.A. (dissenting).

COURT OF CRIMINAL JURISDICTION. (*a*) A court of general or quarter sessions of the peace, when presided over by a superior court judge, (*a*.1) in the Province of Quebec, the Court of Quebec, the municipal court of Montreal and the municipal court of Quebec, (*b*) a provincial court judge or judge acting under Part XIX, and (*c*) in the Province of Ontario, the Ontario Court of Justice. *Criminal Code*, R.S.C. 1985, c. C-46, s. 2.

COURT OF FIRST INSTANCE. A court before which an action is first brought for trial.

COURT OF KING'S BENCH. The superior court of some provinces, known by this name during the reign of a king.

COURT OF LAST RESORT. The court from which there is no further appeal.

COURT OF PROBATE. Any court having jurisdiction in matters of probate.

COURT OF QUEEN'S BENCH. The name given to the superior court of some provinces.

COURT OF RECORD. 1. Any court which keeps a record of its judicial acts and proceedings. 2. " . [A] Court which has power to fine and imprison . . ." *R. v. Fields* (1986), 28 C.C.C. (3d) 353 at 357-58, 16 O.A.C. 286, 53 C.R. (3d) 260, 56 O.R. (2d) 213 (C.A.), Dubin J.A.

COURT OF THE UNITED KINGDOM. Any court of the United Kingdom or of any territory to which this Convention extends pursuant to Article XIII. *Canada – United Kingdom Civil and Commercial Judgments Convention*, R.S.C. 1985, c. C-30, Sched. 1, s. 1.

COURT RECORD. 1. The records of the office of any court and documents filed therein. 2. All documents, records, letters, transcripts, recordings, exhibits and papers of any kind or any thing on which information is recorded or stored by any means including graphic, electronic or mechanical means, deposited or on file with or held by a court.

COURT REPORTER. 1. A person who records proceedings of a court and the evidence given in court. 2. " . . . [A]n officer of the court and enjoys an official status. . ." *R. v. Turner* (1981), 27 C.R. (3d) 73 at 79, [1982] 2 W.W.R. 142, 65 C.C.C. (2d) 335, 14 Sask. R. 321 (C.A.), Bayda C.J.S. (MacDonald J.A. concurring).

COURTS ADMINISTRATION SERVICE. Body established by the federal government. The purposes of this Act are to (*a*) facilitate coordination and cooperation among the Federal Court of Appeal, the Federal Court, the Court Martial Appeal Court and the Tax Court of Canada for the purpose of ensuring the effective and efficient provision of administrative services to those courts; (*b*) enhance judicial independence by placing administrative services at arm's length from the Government of Canada and by affirming the roles of chief justices and judges in the management of the courts; and (*c*) enhance accountability for the use of public money in support of court administration while safeguarding the independence of the judiciary. *Courts*

Administration Service Act, 2002, S.C. 2002, c. 8, s. 2.

COUSIN. *n*. A collateral relation, not including sisters and brothers and their descendants, or the sisters and brothers of an ancestor.

COUSIN-GERMAN. *n*. The child of a brother or sister.

COUT. DIG. *abbr*. Coutlee's Digest.

COUT. S.C. *abbr*. Notes of Unreported Cases, Supreme Court of Canada (Coutlee), 1875-1907.

COVENANT. *n*. 1. An agreement in writing signed and delivered and in the past under seal. 2 " . . . [R]efers to obligations of the landlord not only under any written agreement of lease between landlord and tenant, but also to any obligations imposed upon the landlord by reason of the Landlord and Tenant Act [R.S.O. 1980, c. 232]." *Kingsway v. Pooler* (1988), 4 T.L.L.R. 105 at 108 (Ont. Dist. Ct.), Davidson D.C.J. 3. "No particular form of words beyond such as shew the parties' concurrence in agreeing to abide by some specific course of conduct in future, are needed to constitute a covenant." *Pearson v. Adams* (1914), 50 S.C.R. 204 at 209, 50 C.L.J. 586, Idington J. 4. 4. [As used in s. 248(1)(a)(iii) of the *Income Tax Act*, R.S.C. 1985, c. 1 (5th Supp.)] is a more general word, and can include any contractual promise. However, its scope is limited by the statutory context in which it is used: it must be a promise *similar* to a guarantee, security or indemnity *Citibank Canada v. R.*, 2002 FCA 128, 2002 D.T.C. 6876, [2002] 2 C.T.C. 171 (C.A.). See CONTRACT IN RESTRAINT OF TRADE; DEED OF ~; QUIET ENJOYMENT; RESTRICTIVE ~; SEVERAL ~; USUAL ~.

COVENANT FOR FURTHER ASSURANCE. A standard covenant which a vendor undertakes to protect the purchaser's interest in something purchased; the vendor agrees, at the purchaser's request and cost, to execute a further conveyance or other document to more perfectly assure the subject-matter conveyed.

COVENANT FOR PAYMENT. An agreement that the mortgagor will pay the mortgage money and interest.

COVER. *v*. 1. To insure. 2. To buy back securities sold short.

COVERAGE. *n*. 1. The right conferred upon a person to be indemnified against liability for or to be compensated for, death, injury, loss or damage. *Motor Vehicle Insurace acts*. 2. . . [C]an mean at least two things; a straight naming of the perils insured against, or on a larger view, a bundle of descriptions of the protection offered in the case of each individual peril contained in the one insurance policy. In British Columbia, I prefer the latter, more compendious understanding." *Dressew Supply Ltd. v. Laurentian Pacific Insurance Co.* (1991), [1992] 3 C.C.L.I. (2d) 286 at 310-11, 77 D.L.R. (4th) 317, 57 B.C.L.R. (2d) 198, [1991] 6 W.W.R. 174, [1991] I.L.R. 1-2755 (C.A.), the court per Locke J.A. See COMPREHENSIVE ~; EXCESS ~; EXTENDED ~; INSURANCE ~.

COVERING. See METALLIC ~.

COVER NOTE. A document given to an insured to indicate insurance is in effect.

COVERT. *adj*. 1. Hidden. 2. Of a woman, under the protection of her husband. See FEMME ~.

COVERT-BARON. *adj*. Under the protection of a husband.

COVERTURE. *n*. A woman's condition during marriage; the fact that she is married.

COVIN. *n*. Conspiracy to defraud.

COVINOUS. *adj*. Fraudulent.

COYOTE. *n*. The prairie wolf and includes the immature young of such animal. *The Wolf and Coyote Bounty Act*, R.S.S. 1978, c. W-15, s. 2.

C.P. *abbr*. 1. Canadian Pacific. 2. Common Pleas. 3. Cour provinciale. 4. Recueils de jurisprudence, Cour provinciale.

CP. *abbr*. Compare.

CPIC. Canadian Police Information Centre.

CPC. *abbr*. Common purpose charter.

C.P.C. *abbr*. 1. Carswell's Practice Cases, 1976-1985. 2. Canadian Pension Commission.

CPC EDUCATIONAL PROGRAM. A program for educational purposes organized for the exclusive benefit of full-time elementary or secondary school students, or both. *Air Transportation Regulations*, SOR/88-58, s. 2.

CPC EVENT. A presentation, performance, exhibition, competition, gathering or activity that (*a*) is of apparent significance unrelated to the general interest inherent in travel, and (*b*) is not being created or organized for the primary purpose of generating charter air traffic. *Air Transportation Regulations*, SOR/88-58, s. 2.

C.P.C. (2D). *abbr*. Carswell's Practice Cases (Second Series) 1985-.

C.P.D. *abbr*. Law Reports, Common Pleas Division.

C.P. DIV. CIV. *abbr*. Cour provinciale, Division civile.

C.P. DIV. CRIM. *abbr*. Cour provinciale, Division criminelle.

C.P. DIV. FAM. *abbr*. Cour provinciale, Division de la famille.

C.P. DU N. *abbr*. Cours de perfectionnement du Notariat.

C.P.R. *abbr*. 1. Canadian Patent Reporter, 1942-1971. 2. Canadian Pacific Railway Company.

C.P.R. (N.S.). *abbr*. Canadian Patent Reporter (New [Third] Series).

C. PROV. *abbr*. Cour provinciale.

C.P.R. (2D). *abbr*. Canadian Patent Reporter (Second Series), 1971-1984.

C.P.R. (3D). *abbr*. Canadian Patent Reporter (Third Series), 1985-.

CPS. *abbr*. The CPS [Compendium of Pharmaceutical Specialities] is a reference book which lists the dosages, ingredients and directions for certain drugs, and is widely used by pharmacists and physicians. *AB Hassle v. Canada (Minister of National Health & Welfare)*, 2002 FCA 421, 22 C.P.R. (4th) 1, 298 N.R. 323 (C.A.).

C.P.U. All computers have a Central Processing Unit (C.P.U.) which is a specialized integrated circuit that executes binary programs. The C.P.U. does primary calculations required of all programs and shifts answers to other parts of the system depending upon the requirements of the program controlling it. *Apple Computer Inc. v. Macintosh Computers Ltd.* (1985), 3 C.I.P.R. 133, 3 C.P.R. (3d) 34 (Fed. T.D.) Cullen J.

C.R. *abbr*. Criminal Reports. (Canada), 1946-1967.

CRAB. See SNOW ~; SOFT-SHELLED ~.

CRAB TRAP. (a) A metal or wood framed enclosure covered with netting or wire mesh and having one or more openings, or (b) a similar enclosure constructed from synthetic materials.

C.R.A.C. *abbr.* Canadian Reports, Appeal Cases, 1828-1913.

CRACKING. *n.* Any parting within the tread, sidewall or innerliner of a tire extending to the cord. *Motor Vehicle Tire Safety Regulations*, 1995, SOR/95 -148, s. 2.

CRAFT. *n.* 1. A skilled trade. 2. A small boat. 3. A guild. See PLEASURE ~; WATER-EX-CURSION ~.

CRAFT UNION. A union, membership in which is restricted to workers having a particular skill.

CRAFT UNIT. A collective bargaining unit consisting of employees having a particular skill.

CRANE. *n.* 1. A crane used in handling containers at a container terminal. 2. A cargo crane or a Colby crane. See PRODUCTION ~; SERVICE ~.

CRANE CARRIER. A self-propelled wheeled vehicle that is constructed for the purpose of having a crane unit mounted thereon.

CRANE HIRE CHARGE. A charge for the use of the crane, consisting of a time charge and a lift charge.

CRANE MOVING CHARGE. A charge for moving the crane, whether carrying a lift or not, to or from any job.

CRANE SERVICE. A service provided to a hirer involving the use of the crane in lifting goods without lightering but does not include slinging the goods into or unslinging them from the crane.

CRANIAL SUTURES. Fibrous bands where the bones of the vault of the skull unite. F.A. Jaffe, *A Guide to Pathological Evidence*, 3d ed. (Toronto: Carswell, 1991) at 216.

CRANIUM. *n.* The portion of the skull which surrounds the brain. F.A. Jaffe, *A Guide to Pathological Evidence*, 3d ed. (Toronto: Carswell, 1991) at 216.

CRANKCASE EMISSIONS. Substances that cause air pollution and that are emitted to the atmosphere from any portion of the engine crankcase ventilation or lubrication systems. *On-Road Vehicle and Engine Emission Regulations*, SOR/2003-2, s. 1.

CRAPPIE. *n.* Includes black crappie, calico bass or speckled bass Pomoxis nigromaculatus (LeSueur), and white crappie Promoxis annularis Rafinesque.

CRASSA NEGLIGENTIA. [L.] Gross negligence.

CRAVE. *v.* To ask in a formal manner.

C.R.C. *abbr.* Canadian Railway Cases.

CREAM. *n.* 1. The portion of milk that rises to the surface on standing or is separated by centrifugal force. 2. The fatty liquid obtained by separating the constituents of milk. See MILK AND ~; STERILIZED CANNED ~; WHIPPING~.

CREAMERY. *n.* The premises in which milk or cream is processed into creamery butter.

CREAMERY OPERATOR. A person engaged in the manufacture of creamery butter at a plant.

CREAM RECEIVING STATION. A place where milk or cream is received and purchased for the purpose of being forwarded to a dairy manufacturing plant for processing or manufacturing.

CREAM STATION. Any building operated as a branch of a creamery where cream is received from individual patrons by an agent of the creamery and where that agent weighs, samples, grades, tests or stores the cream before it is transported or forwarded to that creamery in the individual patrons' cans or transferred to shipping cans for the purpose of being transported or forwarded.

CREATE. *v.* To bring into legal existence. *Manco Home Systems Ltd., Re* (1990) 78 C.B.R. (N.S.) 109 at 113 (B.C. C.A.), Southin J.A.

CREATION OF CURRENCY. To create money which forms part of the money supply by printing more currency through the Bank of Canada.

CREATION OF LIEN. Mechanics', construction or builder's liens are created when work or services are performed or materials are placed or furnished at the direction of and on the property of another person.

CREDE EXPERTO. [L.] Trust, believe, an expert.

CREDIBILITY. *n.* 1. Credibility means simply worthiness of belief. *Cooper v. Cooper*, 2001 CarswellNfld 17, 2001 NFCA 4, 13 R.F.L. (5th) 29, 198 Nfld. & P.E.I.R. 1, 595 A.P.R. 1 (C.A.)

Per Green J.A. (Cameron J.A. concurring). 2. " . . . [N]ot merely the appreciation of the witnesses' desire to be truthful but also of their opportunities of knowledge and powers of observation, judgment and memory—in a word, the trustworthiness of their testimony, . . ." *Raymond v. Bosanquet (Township)* (1919), 59 S.C.R. 452 at 460 50 D.L.R. 560 Anglin J. 3. The degree of credit the court should give to the testimony of a witness. *Military Rules of Evidence*, C.R.C., c. 1049, s. 2.

CREDIBLE. *adj*. Believable; worthy of belief.

CREDIT. *n*. 1. Belief in a person's trustworthiness. 2. An arrangement for obtaining loans or advances. *Bank Act*, R.S.C. 1985, c. B-1, s. 202(2). 3. The advancing of money, goods or services to or on behalf of another for repayment at a later time, whether or not there is cost of borrowing, and includes variable credit. *Consumer Protection acts*. 4. Credit for which a borrower is required to pay and that is (i) given under an agreement between a seller and a buyer to purchase goods or services by which all or part of the purchase price is payable after the agreement is entered into; or (ii) given by the advancement of money. 5. Recognition granted to a student as proof that the student has successfully completed a quantity of work. See AGRICULTURAL ~; ANTICIPATORY ~ ; BACK-TO-BACK ~; CONFIRMED ~; CONSUMER ~; CUMULATIVE ~; DOCUMENTARY ~; EXPORT ~S AGENCY; FARM ~ CORPORATION CANADA; INTERNATIONAL DOCUMENTARY ~; IRREVOCABLE ~; IRREVOCABLE LETTER OF ~; LETTER OF ~; PAST SERVICE ~; PENSION BENEFIT ~; PENSION REVOLVING ~; SALE ON ~; SECONDARY ~; SERVICE ~; STANDBY ~; TAX ~; UNIVERSITY ~; VARIABLE ~; WORK ~.

CREDIT ADVANCED. The aggregate of the money and the monetary value of any goods, services or benefits actually advanced or to be advanced under an agreement or arrangement minus the aggregate of any required deposit balance and any fee, fine, penalty, commission and other similar charge or expense directly or indirectly incurred under the original or any collateral agreement or arrangement. *Criminal Code*, R.S.C. 1985, c. C-46, s. 347(2).

CREDIT AGENCY. See APPROVED ~.

CREDIT AGREEMENT. A consumer agreement under which a lender extends credit to a borrower and includes a loan of money, a supplier credit agreement and a consumer agreement under which a loan of money or supplier credit agreement may occur in the future, but does not include an agreement under which a lender extends credit on the security of a mortgage of real property or consumer agreements of a prescribed type. *Consumer Protection Act, 2002*, S.O. 2002, c. 30, s. 66.

CREDIT BALANCES. See FREE ~.

CREDIT BUREAU. An organization which collects information relating to the credit, responsibility and character of individuals and businesses for the purpose of providing the information to its members.

CREDIT CARD. 1. Any card, plate, coupon book or other device issued or otherwise distributed for the purpose of being used (a) on presentation to obtain, on credit, money, goods, services or any other thing of value, or (b) in an automated teller machine, a remote service unit or a similar automated banking device to obtain any of the services offered through the machine, unit or device. *Criminal Code*, R.S.C. 1985, c. C-46, s. 321. 2. A card or device under which a borrower can obtain advances under a credit agreement for open credit. *Consumer Protection Act, 2002*, S.O. 2002, c. 30, s. 1. See UNSOLICITED ~.

CREDIT CHARGES. The amount the consumer must pay under the contract in addition to (a) the net capital in the case of a contract for the loan of money or a contract extending variable credit; (b) the net capital and the down payment in the case of a contract involving credit. *Consumer Protection Act*, R.S.Q. c. P-40.1, s. 69.

CREDITED SERVICE. In connection with pension plans, period of service with an employer or in an office to which holders are entitled to pensions.

CREDIT INFORMATION. 1. Information about a consumer as to name, age, occupation, place of residence, previous places of residence, marital status, spouse's name and age, number of dependants, particulars of education or professional qualifications, places of employment, previous places of employment, estimated income, paying habits, outstanding debt obligations, cost of living obligations and assets. *Consumer Reporting acts*. 2. Information collected or stored for the purpose of assessing the credit rating of consumers. *Consumer Reporting Agencies Act*, R.S. Nfld. 1990, c. C-32, s. 2.

CREDIT INSTITUTION. A bank, treasury branch, credit union or a trust company.

CREDIT INSURANCE. Insurance against loss to the insured through insolvency or default of a person to whom credit is given in respect of goods, wares or merchandise. *Insurance acts.*

CREDIT LINE. The amount of money a lender agrees to supply to a person.

CREDIT NOTE. A note issued by a business indicating that a customer is entitled to be credited by the issuer with a certain amount.

CREDITOR. *n.* 1. A person to whom another person owes a debt. 2. " . . . [A] person entitled to the fulfilment of, an obligation. *Crown Lumber Co. v. Smythe*, [1923] 3 D.L.R. 933 at 952, [1923] 2 W.W.R. 1019, 19 Alta. L.R. 558 (C.A.), Beck J.A. 3. A person having a claim, preferred, secured or unsecured, provable as a claim under this Act. *Bankruptcy Act*, R.S.C. 1985, c. B-3, s. 2. 4. In *G.T. Campbell & Associates Ltd. v. Hugh Carson Co.* (1979), 99 D.L.R. (3d) 529 (Ont. C.A.), for example, the court extended the meaning of the word creditor under the Ontario Act to include any claim against a dissolved corporation whether it be in debt or for unliquidated damages. The definition of "creditor" was stretched to include a claimant who at the time the acts complained of occurred was unable to state the amount of the debt being claimed. *A E Realisations (1985) Ltd. v. Time Air Inc.* (1994), 1994 CarswellSask 287, [1995] 3 W.W.R. 527, 17 B.L.R. (2d) 203, 127 Sask. R. 105 (Q.B.), Noble, J. 5. Includes a surety or guarantor for the debt due to the creditor. *Bankruptcy and Insolvency Act*, R.S.C. 1985, c. B-3, s. 95. 6. (i) In relation to a writ of execution, any person entitled to enforce by execution the payment of any money payable pursuant to any judgment or order that is enforceable by execution, and (ii) in relation to a distress, the person who has the power of distress. 7. The person or corporation entitled to receive the amount due on a judgment. 8. Includes the person advancing money lent and the assignee of any claim arising or security given in respect of money lent. *Unconscionable Transactions acts.* 9. A. person who supplies labour, materials or services used or reasonably required to be used in the performance of contract with the Crown for the construction, alteration, demolition, repair, or maintenance of a public work. *Public Works Creditors' Payment acts.* See EXECUTION ~; JUDGMENT ~; PETITIONING ~; PREFERRED ~; REGISTERED ~; SECURED ~; SECURED TRADE ~; UNSECURED ~; UNSECURED TRADE ~.

CREDITOR'S GROUP ACCIDENT INSURANCE. Accident insurance effected by a creditor whereby the lives or well-being or the lives and well-being of a number of that creditor's debtors are insured severally under a single contract.

CREDITOR'S GROUP INSURANCE. 1. Insurance effected by a creditor in respect of the lives of that creditor's debtors whereby the lives of the debtors are insured severally under a single contract. 2. Insurance effected by a creditor whereby the lives or well-being, or the lives and well-being, of a number of that creditor's debtors are insured severally under a single contract.

CREDITOR'S GROUP SICKNESS INSURANCE. Sickness insurance effected by a creditor whereby the lives or well-being or the lives and well-being of a number of that creditor's debtors are insured severally under a single contract.

CREDITORS' MEETING. The first meeting of creditors of a bankrupt.

CREDITORS' RELIEF STATUTE. A statute which forces a judgment creditor to share pari passu any proceeds of execution with other unsecured creditors who filed writs of execution or certificates with the sheriff.

CREDIT RATE. The actual annual percentage of a credit charge.

CREDIT RATING. Evaluation of the credit worthiness of a business or individual based on ability to pay and past performance in paying debt.

CREDIT RATING ORGANIZATION. Dominion Bond Rating Service Limited; Fitch, Inc.; Moody's Investors Service, Inc.; or, Standard & Poor's Corporation.

CREDIT REPAIR. Services or goods that are intended to improve a consumer report, credit information, file or personal information, including a credit record, credit history or credit rating. *Consumer Protection Act, 2002*, S.O. 2002, c. 30, s. 48.

CREDIT REPAIRER. A supplier of credit repair, or a person who holds themself out as a credit repairer.

CREDIT REPORT. A report of credit information or of a credit rating based on credit information, supplied by a credit reporting agency.

CREDIT REPORTING AGENCY. A person who is engaged in providing credit reports to any other person, whether for remuneration or otherwise.

CREDIT SALE. Analogous to a loan. The vendor of goods or services defers the debt owed by the purchaser. A premium is charged on the deferred amount.

CREDIT SOCIETY. See COOPERATIVE ~.

CREDIT TRANSACTION. (i) A purchase of goods or services under a continuous deferred payment plan or a time sale agreement, (ii) a loan, or (iii) a purchase of goods or services or the obtaining of money by the use of a credit card.

CREDIT UNION. 1. A co-operative society, including caisses populaires, that provides its members with financial and other services. 2. A co-operative, non-profit credit society, incorporated as a limited company under this Act for the purpose of providing a source of credit for provident and productive purposes at fair and reasonable rates of interest, of encouraging and promoting habits of thrift among its members, of affording its members an opportunity to accumulate their savings, and of giving its members the use and control of their money for their mutual benefits. *Credit Unions Act*, R.S.P.E.I. 1988, c. C-29, s. 1(b). See CENTRAL ~; COMMUNITY ~.

CREE COMMUNITY. A collectivity composed of all the Crees enrolled or entitled to be enrolled on a community list in accordance with the Act respecting Cree, Inuit and Naskapi Native persons. *The Cree Villages and the Naskapi Village Act*, R.S.Q., chapter V-5.1, s. 1.

CREED. *n.* " . . . [I]nvolve[s] a declaration of religious belief." *R. v. Ontario (Labour Relations Board)*, [1963] 2 O.R. 376 at 389, 39 D.L.R. (2d) 593, 63 C.L.L.C. 15,459 (H.C.), McRuer C.J.H.C.

CREEK. *n.* All natural watercourses, whether usually containing water or not, and that portion of any stream below the point where it enters the valley of the parent stream, but does not include streams that have an average width of one hundred and fifty feet. *Yukon Placer Mining Act*, R.S.C. 1985, c. Y-3, s. 2.

CREE TALLYMAN. A Cree person recognized by a Cree community as responsible for the supervision of the activities related to the exercising of the right to harvest on a Cree trap-

line. *An Act respecting hunting and fishing rights in the James Bay and New Quebec territories*, R.S.Q , D-13.1, s. 1.

CREE TRAPLINE. An area where the activities related to the exercise of the right to harvest are by tradition carried on under the supervision of a Cree tallyman. *An Act respecting hunting and fishing rights in the James Bay and New Quebec territories*, R.S.Q., D-13.1, s. 1.

CREMATED REMAINS. Human bone fragments that remain after cremation.

CREMATION. *n.* Disposal of a dead body by incineration.

CREMATORIUM. *n.* A building fitted with the proper appliances for the purpose of the incineration and cremation of human remains.

CREMATORY. *n.* A building fitted with proper appliances for the purpose of incinerating or cremating dead human bodies.

CREPUSCULUM. *n.* [L.] Twilight.

CRESCENTE MALITIA CRESCERE DEBET ET POENA. [L.] Where malice increases, punishment should also increase.

CREST. *n.* " . . . [F]orms an integral part of a coat of arms as a whole. It is the figure or device which appears above the wreath on the helmet which surmounts the shield . . ." *Insurance Corp. of British Columbia v. Canada (Registrar of Trade Marks)* (1978), 44 C.P.R. (2d) 1 at 7, [1980] 1 F.C. 669 (T.D.), Cattanach J.

C. REV. *abbr.* Cour de revision.

CREW. *n.* 1. Persons responsible for navigating a ship or aircraft. 2. The officers, seamen and apprentices of a ship. See MEMBER OF A ~.

CREW LIST. A list of members of the crew of a ship or aircraft.

CREW MEMBER. A person assigned to duty in an aircraft during flight time. See FLIGHT ~.

CRIB DEATH. Sudden infant death syndrome: the sudden death of an apparently well infant, who is usually between three and twelve months old. F.A. Jaffe, *A Guide to Pathological Evidence*, 3d ed. (Toronto: Carswell, 1991) at 216.

CRICOID CARTILAGE. The cartilage which is lowermost in the larynx. F.A. Jaffe, *A Guide to Pathological Evidence*, 3d ed. (Toronto: Carswell, 1991) at 216.

CRI DE PAIS. [Fr.] A hue and cry.

CRIER. *n.* An officer of the court who made proclamations.

CRIME. *n.* 1. "... [A]n act which the law, with appropriate penal sanctions, forbids; but as prohibitions are not enacted in a vacuum, we can properly look for some evil or injurious or undesirable effect upon the public against which the law is directed ..." *Margarine Case* (1948), [1949] 1 D.L.R. 433 at 472, [1949] S.C.R. 1, Rand J. 2. Must consist of a physical element of committing a prohibited act, creating a prohibited state of affairs or omitting to do that which is required by law and the conduct must be willed, voluntary. *R. c. Daviault*, [1994] 3 S.C.R. 63. 3. A public wrong involving a violation of public rights and duties owed to the whole community in its social aggregate capacity. *Reference re Alberta Legislation*, [1938] S.C.R. 100. See CONDUCT ~; EXTRADITION ~; GRAVE ~; PROCEEDS OF ~; REAL ~; WAR ~.

CRIME AGAINST HUMANITY. 1. Murder, extermination, enslavement, deportation, persecution or any other inhumane act or omission that is committed against any civilian population or any identifiable group of persons, whether or not it constitutes a contravention of the law in force at the time and in the place of its commission, and that, at that time and in that place, constitutes a contravention of customary international law or conventional international law or is criminal according to the general principles of law recognized by the community of nations. *Criminal Code*, S.C. 1987, c. 36, s. 1(1). 2. Any of the following acts when committed as part of a widespread or systematic attack directed against any civilian population, with knowledge of the attack: (a) murder; (b) extermination; (c) enslavement; (d) deportation or forcible transfer of population; (e) imprisonment or other severe deprivation of physical liberty in violation of fundamental rules of international law; (f) torture; (g) rape, sexual slavery, enforced prostitution, forced pregnancy, enforced sterilization, or any other form of sexual violence of comparable gravity; (h) persecution against any identifiable group or collectivity on political, racial, national, ethnic, cultural, religious, gender as defined in paragraph 3, or other grounds that are universally recognized as impermissible under international law, in connection with any act referred to in this paragraph or any crime within the jurisdiction of the Court; (i) enforced disappearance of persons; (j) the crime of apartheid; (k) other inhumane acts of a similar character intentionally causing great suffering, or serious injury to body or to mental or physical health. *Rome Statute*, Article 7.

CRIME COMIC. A magazine, periodical or book that exclusively or substantially comprises matter depicting pictorially (a) the commission of crimes, real or fictitious; or (b) events connected with the commission of crimes, real or fictitious, whether occurring before or after the commission of the crime. *Criminal Code*, R.S.C. 1985, c. C-46, s. 163(7).

CRIME HAS BEEN COMMITTED IN CANADA. The wording of [s. 18(1)(b) of the Extradition Act, R.S.C. 1985, c. E-23] requires the court to assume that "the crime has been committed in Canada." This has been interpreted to mean that the court should look to the impugned conduct and make its assessment under Canadian law on the basis of that conduct. *D'Agostino, Re* (2000), 2000 CarswellOnt 465, (sub nom. *United States of America v. Commisso*) 47 O.R. (3d) 257, (sub nom. *United States of America v. Commisso*) 143 C.C.C. (3d) 158, (sub nom. *United States of America v. Commisso*) 129 O.A.C. 166, (sub nom. *United States of America v. Commisso*) 72 C.R.R. (2d) 198 (C.A.).

CRIMEN FALSI. [L.] Forgery; perjury; suppression of evidence.

CRIMEN FURTI. [L.] Theft.

CRIMEN INCENDII. [L.] Arson.

CRIMEN LAESAE MAJESTATIS OMNIA ALIA CRIMINA EXCEDIT QUOAD POENAM. [L.] Treason is punished most severely of all crimes.

CRIMEN RAPTUS. [L.] Rape.

CRIMEN ROBERIAE. [L.] Robbery.

CRIME OF SPECIFIC INTENT. One which involves the performance of the actus reus couple with an intent or purpose going beyond the mere performance of the questioned act. *R. v. Bernard*, [1988] 2 S.C.R. 833.

CRIME VICTIM. Any person killed or injured in Quebec: (a) by reason of the act or omission of any other person occurring in or resulting directly from the commission of an offence the description of which corresponds to the criminal offences mentioned in the schedule of this act; (b) while lawfully arresting or attempting to arrest an offender or suspected offender or assisting a peace officer making an arrest; (c) while lawfully preventing or attempting to prevent the commission of an offence or suspected offence, or assisting a peace officer preventing or attempting to prevent the commission of an offence or suspected offence. *Crime Victims Compensation Act*, R.S.Q. 1977, c. I-6, s. 3. See COMPENSATION OF VICTIMS OF CRIME.

CRIMINAL. *n*. A person found guilty of an offence. See FUGITIVE ~; HABITUAL ~.

CRIMINAL. *adj*. Relating to crimes or to the administration of the law in respect of crimes.

CRIMINAL BREACH OF CONTRACT. Wilfully breaking a contract, knowing or having reasonable cause to believe that the probable consequences of doing so, whether alone or in combination with others, will be (a) to endanger human life, (b) to cause serious bodily injury, (c) to expose valuable property, real or personal, to destruction or serious injury, (d) to deprive the inhabitants of a city or place, or part thereof, wholly or to a great extent, of their supply of light, power, gas or water, or (e) to delay or prevent the running of any locomotive engine, tender, freight or passenger train or car, on a railway that is a common carrier, is an offence. *Criminal Code*, R.S.C. 1985, c. C-46, s. 422.

CRIMINAL BREACH OF TRUST. Every one who, being a trustee of anything for the use or benefit, whether in whole or in part, of another person, or for a public or charitable purpose, converts, with intent to defraud and in contravention of his trust, that thing or any part of it to a use that is not authorized by the trust is guilty of an indictable offence. *Criminal Code*, R.S.C. 1985, c. C-46, s. 336.

CRIMINAL CODE. The Criminal Code, R.S.C. 1985, c. C-46 as amended from time to time. The codification of the criminal law and the source of criminal law in Canada. This federal statute is frequently amended to modify the law or to add new offences.

CRIMINAL CONSPIRACY. ". . . [An] agreement of two or more to do an unlawful act, or to do a lawful act by unlawful means." *R. v. O'Brien*, [1954] S.C.R. 666 at 669, 672 and 674.

CRIMINAL CONTEMPT. 1. Private or public conduct which interferes with a court's process or seriously threatens the administration of justice. Dealt with by a summary process. 2. ". . . [W]hen the element of public defiance of the court's process in a way calculated to lessen societal respect for the courts is added to the breach [of a court order], it [the contempt] becomes criminal. . . The gravamen of the offence is rather open, continuous and flagrant violation of a Court order without regard for the effect that [such actions] may have on the respect accorded to edicts of the Court. . . To establish criminal contempt the Crown must prove that the accused defied or disobeyed a court order in a public way (the actus reus), with intent, knowledge or recklessness as to the fact that the public disobedience will tend to depreciate the authority of the court (the mens rea) . . ." *U.N.A. v. Alberta (Attorney General)* (1992), 13 C.R. (4th) 1 at 13-14, [1992] 3 W.W.R. 481, 89 D.L.R. (4th) 609, 71 C.C.C. (3d) 225, 135 N.R. 321, 92 C.L.L.C. 14,023, 1 Alta. L.R. (3d) 129, 125 A.R. 241, 14 W.A.C. 241, [1992] 1 S.C.R. 901, 9 C.R.R. (2d) 29, McLachlin J. (La Forest, Gonthier and Iacobucci JJ. concurring).

CRIMINAL CONVERSATION. A husband's claim for damages for adultery.

CRIMINAL HARASSMENT. Conduct consisting of (a) repeatedly following from place to place the other person or anyone known to them; (b) repeatedly communicating with, either directly or indirectly, the other person or anyone known to them; (c) besetting or watching the dwelling-house, or place where the other person, or anyone known to them, resides, works, carries on business or happens to be; or (d) engaging in threatening conduct directed at the other person or any member of their family. *Criminal Code*, R.S.C. 1985, c. C-46, s. 264(2).

CRIMINAL HISTORY. The convictions which a person has received from the criminal courts during his or her lifetime.

CRIMINAL INJURIES COMPENSATION. A statutory plan to compensate victims of specified crimes, or anyone injured while attempting to arrest a person, assist a peace officer or preserve the peace.

CRIMINALITY. See DOUBLE ~.

CRIMINALIZATION. *n*. Rendering an act criminal and therefore punishable.

CRIMINAL JURISDICTION. See SUPERIOR COURT OF ~.

CRIMINAL JUSTICE SYSTEM. The sum of criminal law processes intended ultimately to control crime. S.A. Cohen, *Due Process of Law* (Toronto: Carswell, 1977) at 1.

CRIMINAL LAW. 1. The prohibition of conduct which interferes with the proper functioning of society or which undermines the safety and security of society as a whole. *RJR-Macdonald c. Canada (Procureur general)* (1995), 127 D.L.R. (4th) 1 (S.C.C.) 2. A law which declares acts to be crimes and prescribes punishment for those crimes. 3. " . . . [L]egislation creating offences which have a national aspect or dimension may properly be characterized as criminal law . . . *R. v. Hoffman-La Roche Ltd.* (1981), 15 B.L.R. 217 at 265, 33 O.R. (2d) 694, 24 C.R. (3d) 193, 58 C.P.R. (2d) 1, 62 C.C.C. (2d) 118,125 D.L.R. (3d) 607 (C.A.), the court per Martin J.A. See CRIME; CRIMINAL CODE.

CRIMINAL MATTER. A prosecution or trial for an offence triable by a judge or jury in accordance with the Criminal Code of Canada.

CRIMINAL NEGLIGENCE. 1. Every one is criminally negligent who (a) in doing anything, or (b) in omitting to do anything that it is his duty to do shows wanton or reckless disregard for the lives or safety of other persons. *Criminal Code*, R.S.C. 1985, c. C-46, s. 219. 2. "In criminal cases, generally, the act coupled with the mental state or intent is punished. In criminal negligence, the act which exhibits the requisite degree of negligence is punished. . ." *R. v. Tutton* (1989), 48 C.C.C. (3d) 129 at 140, 13 M.V.R. (2d) 161, 69 C.R. (3d) 289, 98 N.R. 19, [1989] 1 S.C.R. 1392, 35 O.A.C. 1, McIntyre J. 3. " . . . [T]he well-recognized tort of civil negligence: the sins of omission and commission that cause injury to one's neighbour, elevated to a crime by their magnitude of wanton and reckless disregard for the lives and safety of others." *R. v. Gingrich* (1991), 6 C.R. (4th) 197 at 209, 28 M.V.R. (2d) 161, 44 O.A.C. 290, 65 C.C.C. (3d) 188 (C.A.), Finlayson J.A. (Krever J.A. concurring).

CRIMINAL OFFENCE. 1. An activity which Parliament wishes to suppress through criminal sanction must pose a significant, grave and serious risk of harm to public health, morality, safety or security before it can fall within the purview of the criminal law power. *RJR-Macdonald c. Canada (Procureur general)* (1995), 127 D.L.R. (4th) 1 (S.C.C.). 2. " . . . Where the offence is criminal, the Crown must establish a mental element, namely, that the accused who committed the prohibited act did so intentionally or recklessly, with knowledge of the facts constituting the offence, or with wilful blindness toward them. Mere negligence is excluded from the concept of the mental element required for conviction. Within the context of a criminal prosecution a person who fails to make such inquiries as a reasonable and prudent person would make, or who fails to know facts he should have known, is innocent in the eyes of the law." *R. v. Sault Ste. Marie (City)* (1978), 3 C.R. (3d) 30 at 40, [1978] 2 S.C.R. 1299, 21 N.R. 295, 7 C.E.L.R. 53, 40 C.C.C. (2d) 353, 85 D.L.R. (3d) 161, the court per Dickson J. 2. An offence against an Act of Parliament. *Transfer of Offenders Act*, R.S.C. 1985, c. T-15, s. 2. See QUASI~; SERIOUS ~.

CRIMINAL ONUS. The standard of proof , on the Crown, is that the case or issue must be proved beyond a reasonable doubt.

CRIMINAL ORGANIZATION. Any group, association or other body consisting of five or more persons, whether formally or informally organized, (a) having as one of its primary activities the commission of an indictable offence under this or any other Act of Parliament for which the maximum punishment is imprisonment for five years or more, and (b) any or all of the members of which engage in or have, within the preceding five years, engaged in the commission of a series of such offences. *Criminal Code*, R.S.C. 1985, c. C-46, s. 2.

CRIMINAL ORGANIZATION OFFENCE. An offence under section 467.1 or an indictable offence under this or any other Act of Parliament committed for the benefit of, at the direction of or in association with a criminal organization for which the maximum punishment is imprisonment for five years or more, or a conspiracy or an attempt to commit, being an accessory after the fact in relation to, or any counselling in relation to, an offence referred to. *Criminal Code*, R.S.C. 1985, c. C-46, s. 2.

CRIMINAL PROCEDURE. " . . . In one sense, it is concerned with proceedings in the criminal Courts and such matters as conduct within the courtroom, the competency of witnesses, oaths and affirmations, and the presentation of evidence. Some cases have defined procedure even more narrowly in finding that it embraces the three technical terms—leading evidence and practice. In a broad sense, it encompasses such things as the rules by which, according to the Criminal Code, police powers are exercised, the right to counsel, search warrants, interim release, procuring attendance of witnesses." *Di Iorio v. Montreal Jail* (1977), 73 D.L.R. (3d) 491 at 530, [1978] 1 S.C.R. 152, 35

C.R.N.S. 57, 8 N.R. 361, Dickson J. (Martland, Judson, Ritchie and Spence JJ. concurring).

CRIMINAL PROCEEDING. Includes any prosecution for an offence under any statute of the Province. *Evidence Act*, R.S.N.S. 1989, c. 154, s. 2.

CRIMINAL RATE. An effective annual rate of interest calculated in accordance with generally accepted actuarial practices and principles that exceeds sixty per cent on the credit advanced under an agreement or arrangement. *Criminal Code*, R.S.C. 1985, c. C-46, s. 347(2).

CRIMINAL RECORD. Refers to convictions under the Criminal Code entered in a register or data base, CPIC.

CRIMINAL RESPONSIBILITY. See AGE OF ~; VERDICT OF NOT CRIMINALLY RESPONSIBLE ON ACCOUNT OF MENTAL DISORDER.

CRIMINAL SANCTIONS. Fines, imprisonment and probation.

CRIMINATE. *v.* To implicate.

CRIMINATION. See SELF-INCRIMINATION.

CRIMINOLOGIE. *abbr.* Journal published by Presses de l'Université de Montreal.

CRIMINOLOGY. *n.* The study of the nature, causes, treatment or punishment of criminal behaviour.

CRIM. L.Q. *abbr.* Criminal Law Quarterly.

CRIMOGENIC. *adj.* Contributing to a person's criminality.

CRITERIA. See EXPOSURE ~.

CRITICAL ENGINE. The engine the failure of which would most adversely affect the performance or handling qualities of an aircraft. *Canadian Aviation Regulations*, SOR/96-433, s. 101.01.

CRITICAL HABITAT. The habitat that is necessary for the survival or recovery of a listed wildlife species and that is identified as the species' critical habitat in the recovery strategy or in an action plan for the species. *Species at Risk Act*, S.C. 2002, c. 29, s. 2.

CRITICAL INJURY. A serious injury which results in life being placed in jeopardy, substantial loss of blood, unconsciousness, burns to major part of the body, fracture of a leg or arm, or

loss of sight in an eye. D. Robertson, *Ontario Health and Safety Guide* (Toronto: Richard De Boo Ltd., 1988) at 5-92.

CRITICAL PERIOD. The period concomitant with or consecutive to a natural disaster which creates an emergency situation for a certain number of producers or the period during which an unforeseen and uncontrollable collapse in the selling prices of a designated production seriously affects a large number of producers and that the Gouvernement acknowledges as such for the time that it indicates; the orders in council indicating the beginning and end of a period must be published in the Gazette officielle du Québec. *An Act to Promote Special Credit to Agricultural Producers During Critical Periods*, R.S.Q., c. C-79, s. 1.

CRITICAL WILDLIFE AREA. Land in a wildlife management area which is designated as a critical wildlife area. *Wildlife Act*, R.S.B.C. 1996, c. 488, s. 1.

CRITICISM. *n.* The opinion of any person about a book, play or visual image.

C.R.N.S. *abbr.* Criminal Reports, New Series, 1967-1978.

C.R.O. *abbr.* Commission des relations ouvrieres.

CROOK. *n.* A criminal; swindler.

CROOKED. *adj.* Dishonest, not trustworthy.

CROP. *n.* 1. Field crops, either cultivated or uncultivated. 2. An unharvested agricultural crop, whether standing or cut, but does not include stubble fields or other fields from which the crop has been removed. *Migratory Birds Regulations*, SOR/98-282, s. 2.See COMMERCIAL ~; ~S; FREE GROWING ~; GROWING ~; INDUSTRIAL ~; INSURABLE ~; INSURED ~; MIXED FARMING ~; VINE ~.

CROP INSURANCE. (i) Insurance against loss of an insured crop caused by drought, flood, hail, wind, frost, lightning, excessive rain, snow, hurricane, tornado, wildlife, accidental fire, insect infestation, plant disease or any other peril designated in the regulations; and (ii) insurance against the occurrence or non-occurrence of any climatic event designated in the regulations that has the potential to cause loss to an insurable crop. *Crop Insurance Act*, S.S. 1983-84, c. 47.2, s. 1.

CROP INSURANCE PROGRAM. A program for the insurance of specified agricultural products against loss from natural causes that is established by the laws of a province and administered by the province.

CROPS. *n*. The products of the soil, and without limiting the generality of the foregoing, includes all sorts of grain, grass, hay, hops, fruit, pulse, potatoes, beets, turnips and other products of the soil. See CROP; GRAIN OR ~; HARVESTING OF ~; ROOT ~; STANDING ~.

CROP YEAR. 1. The period commencing on August 1 in any year and terminating on July 31 in the year next following. Canada statutes. 2. The period from the first day of April to the 31st day of March in the next succeeding year.

CROSS. *n*. A mark in the form of an X. See VARIETAL ~.

CROSS-ACTION. *n*. An action brought by a defendant against the plaintiff in the original action.

CROSS-APPEAL. *var*. **CROSS APPEAL**. 1. An appeal by the respondent to an appeal. 2. A cross-appeal is only filed by a respondent to an appeal who seeks to vary the judgment in his own favour. *Morrison v. Hicks* (1991), 82 D.L.R. (4th) 568 (B.C. C.A.).

CROSSBOW. *n*. 1. A device with a bow and a bowstring mounted on a stock that is designed to propel an arrow, a bolt, a quarrel or any similar projectile on a trajectory guided by a barrel or groove and that is capable of causing serious bodily injury or death to a person. *Criminal Code*, R.S.C. 1985, c. C-46, s. 84(1). 2. A bow fixed across a stock with a groove for the arrow or bolt and a mechanism for holding and releasing the string.

CROSSCLAIM. *n*. A claim by one defendant against a co-defendant.

CROSS-COUNTRY RECREATION. A type of recreation characterized by the use of little frequented territory and the use of relatively simple equipment. *Parks Act*, R.S.Q., c. P-9, s. 1.

CROSSED CHEQUE. A cheque which is crossed generally or a cheque which is crossed specially. Two parallel lines drawn across the cheque to indicate it cannot be endorsed.

CROSSED GENERALLY. Where a cheque bears across its face an addition of (a) the word "bank" between two parallel transverse lines, either with or without the words "not negotiable", or (b) two parallel transverse lines simply, either with or without the words "not negotia-

ble", that addition constitutes a crossing, and the cheque is crossed generally. *Bills of Exchange Act*, R.S.C. 1985, c. B-4, s. 168.

CROSSED SPECIALLY. Where a cheque bears across its face an addition of the name of a bank, either with or without the words "not negotiable", that addition constitutes a crossing, and the cheque is crossed specially and to that bank. *Bills of Exchange Act*, R.S.C. 1985, c. B-4, s. 168.

CROSS-EXAMINATION. *n*. The examination of a witness by the party who did not call the witness and who did not examine the witness in chief. The purpose of the cross-examination is to elicit evidence in favour of the party examining the witness, to discredit the witness and to undermine the evidence given by the witness when examined in chief.

CROSS-EXAMINATION ON AFFIDAVIT. The opposite party's examination of an affiant on the contents of the affiant's affidavit.

CROSSING. *n*. 1. A place where pedestrians may cross a street, highway or railway. 2. A railway crossing of a highway or highway crossing of a railway. 3. The addition of (a) the word "bank" between two parallel transverse lines, either with or without the words "not negotiable", or (b) two parallel transverse lines simply, either with or without the words "not negotiable". *Bills of Exchange Act*, R.S.C. 1985, c. B-4, s. 168. See RAILWAY ~; ROAD ~.

CROSSING GUARD. See SCHOOL ~.

CROSSOVER. See PEDESTRIAN ~.

CROSS PICKETING. Picketing by two groups having different objectives.

CROSS WALK. *var*. **CROSSWALK**. (i) A clearly marked pedestrian crossing; or (ii) if there is no clearly marked pedestrian crossing, the prolongation through the intersection of the lateral boundary lines of the adjacent or intersecting sidewalks at the end of a block.

CROWN. *n*. 1. In Canada, the federal government and each of the provincial governments. 2. Depending on the context, Her Majesty the Queen in right of a Province, Canada or both a province and Canada. 3. Used when speaking of the rights, duties or of the sovereign. 4. Any of the prerogatives Commonwealth governments which represent the head, which is Her Majesty. 5. The Sovereign of the United Kingdom Canada and Her other Realms and Territories, and Head of the Commonwealth. 6. "Although at one time it was correct to describe the Crown as one and indivisible, with the development of the Commonwealth this is no longer so. Although there is only one person who is the Sovereign within the British Commonwealth, it is now a truism that in matters of law and government the Queen of the United Kingdom, for example, is entirely independent and distinct from the Queen of Canada. Further, the Crown is a constitutional monarchy, and thus when one speaks today, and as was frequently done in the course of the argument on this application, of the Crown 'in right of Canada', or of some other territory within the Commonwealth, this is only a short way of referring to the Crown acting through, and on the advice of her ministers in Canada or in that other territory within the Commonwealth." *R. v. Foreign & Commonwealth Affairs (Secretary of State)* (1982), 1 C.R.R. 254 at 277, [1982] 2 All E.R. 118 (U.K. C.A.), May L.J. 7. "In Gauthier v. The King (1918), 56 S.C.R. 176 at p. 194 Mr. Justice Anglin said: '. . . a reference to the Crown in a provincial statute shall be taken to be to the Crown in right of the Province only, unless the statute in express terms or by necessary intendment makes it clear that the reference is to the Crown in some other sense. . .' It has been said that the Crown is one and indivisible. That is the ideal conception of the Crown, but in this country we have under our Federal system, a distribution of powers amongst the Dominion Parliament and the Provincial Legislatures, 'the Crown in right of the Dominion,' and the Crown in right of the Province, are expressions which may therefore mean different things. . ." *Montreal Trust Co. v. South Shore Lumber Co.* (1924), 33 B.C.R. 280 at 284, [1924] 1 W.W.R. 657, [1924] 1 D.L.R. 1030 (C.A.), Macdonald C.J.A. See AGENCY OF THE ~; DEMISE OF THE ~; EMPLOYED BY OR UNDER THE ~; FEDERAL ~; LAW OFFICER OF THE ~; MINISTER OF THE ~; PLEA OF THE ~; PREROGATIVE RIGHTS OF THE ~; PROCEEDING AGAINST THE ~.

CROWN AGENCY. 1. Any board, commission, association or other body, whether incorporated or unincorporated, all the members of which, or all the members of the board of management or board of directors of which are appointed by an Act of the Legislature or by the Lieutenant Governor in Council. Manitoba statutes. 2. A board, commission, railway, public utility, university, manufactory, company or agency, owned, controlled or operated by Her Majesty in right of Ontario, or by the Government of Ontario, or under the authority of the Legislature or the Lieutenant Governor in Council. *Crown Agency Act*, R.S.O. 1990, c. C.48, s. 1.

CROWN AGENT. The determination as to whether a particular body is an agent of the Crown depends on the "nature and degree of control" exercised over that body by the Crown. *Westeel-Rosco Ltd. v. Bd. of Gov. of South Sask. Hosp. Centre* (1976), 69 D.L.R. (3d) 334 at 342 (S.C.C.), Ritchie J.

CROWN ASSETS. See SURPLUS ~.

CROWN ATTORNEY. An agent of the Attorney General; prosecutor in criminal matters on behalf of the Crown.

CROWN CHARGES. All charges, fees, assessment levies and dues in respect of Crown timber, costs, expenses and penalties imposed under this Act or the regulations or payable to the Crown by virtue of any contract.

CROWN CONTROLLED CORPORATION. A corporation that is not an agency of the Crown and having 50 per cent or more of its issued and outstanding shares vested in Her Majesty in right of Ontario or having the appointment of a majority of its board of directors made or approved by the Lieutenant Governor in Council. *Audit Act*, R.S.O. 1990, c. A.35, s. 1.

CROWN-CONTROLLED ORGANIZATION. Unless subsection (3) applies, (i) an unincorporated board, commission, council or other body that is not a department or part of a department, 20% or more but fewer than a majority of whose members are appointed or designated, either by their personal names or by their names of office, by an Act of the Legislature or regulations under an Act of the Legislature, by an order of the Lieutenant Governor in Council or of a Minister of the Crown, or by any combination of them, and that is responsible for the administration of public money or assets owned by the Crown, (ii) a corporation, other than a corporation incorporated by or under a local or private Act, 20% or more but fewer than a majority of whose members or directors are appointed or designated, either by their personal names or by their names of office, by an Act of the Legislature or regulations under an Act of the Legislature, by an order of the Lieutenant Governor in Council or of a Minister of the Crown, or by any combination of them, and that is responsible for the administration of public money or assets owned by the Crown, (iii) a corporation, other than a corporation incorporated by or under a local or private Act, 50% or more but less than 100% of whose issued voting shares are owned by the Crown or held in trust for the Crown or are partly owned by the Crown and partly held in trust for the Crown, or (iv) a corporation that is a subsidiary of a corporation described in subclause (ii) or (iii) or that is controlled by a corporation described in subclause (ii) or (iii) directly or indirectly through one or more intermediary corporations, but does not include a regional health authority or subsidiary health corporation under the Regional *Health Authorities Act. Financial Administration Act*, R.S.A. 2000, c. F-12, s. 1.

CROWN CORPORATION. 1. A corporation that is accountable, through a Minister, to the Legislative Assembly or Parliament for the conduct of its affairs. 2. A corporation of which not less than 90 per cent of the shares ordinarily entitled to vote in an election for directors are owned by the government of the Province or of Canada. 3. A corporation of which all the directors or members of the governing body are appointed by the Lieutenant Governor in Council or the Governor General in Council. 4. A corporation which under any Act of the Province or of Canada is designated as such. See PARENT ~.

CROWN COUN. REV. *abbr*. Crown Counsel's Review.

CROWN COUNSEL. A person entitled to practise law in the jurisdiction and who is authorized to represent the Crown before the courts in relation to the prosecution of offences.

CROWN DEBT. Any existing or future debt due or becoming, due by the Crown, and any other chose in action in respect of which there is a right of recovery enforceable by action against the Crown. *Financial Administration Act*, R.S.C. 1985, c. F-11, s. 66.

CROWN DISPOSITION. The rights granted by the Crown under a Crown lease or any other instrument issued under this Act, or under any predecessor statute, by which the Crown has granted to any person any right or privilege to explore or prospect for any Crown mineral or an other right to or interest in any Crown mineral, or any Crown mineral lands. *Crown Minerals Act*, S.S., c. C-50.2, s. 2.

CROWN EMPLOYEE. A person who is, (a) employed in the service of the Crown, or (b) employed in the service of an agency of the Crown that is designated in the regulations. *Public Service Act*, R.S.O. 1990, c. P.47, s. 1.

CROWN ENTITY. For the purposes of this Act, any board, commission, association or other body corporate, all the members of which, or all the members of the board of management or board of directors of which, (a) are appointed by an Act of the Legislature or by the Lieutenant Governor in Council, or (b) are elected, directly or indirectly by the government in its capacity as shareholder, or by a corporation which is owned or controlled by the government, or (c) if not so appointed or elected, are, in the discharge of their duties public officers or servants of the Crown, or, for the purpose of the discharge of their duties are, directly or indirectly, responsible to the Crown, but does not include any board, commission, association or other body, the employees of which are subject to The Civil Service Act. *The Pay Equity Act*, C.C.S.M., c. P-13, s. 1.

CROWN ESTATE. An estate in which the Crown has an interest and which is administered for the use and benefit of Her Majesty. *Ontario (Public Trustee) v. Movesian Estate* (1994), 3 E.T.R. (2d) 149 (Ont. C.A.).

CROWN GRANT. 1. A transfer of Crown lands to a private person. 2. An instrument in writing conveying Crown land in fee simple. *Land Act*, R.S.B.C. 1996, c. 245, s. 1. 3. Letters patent under the Great Seal, an instrument of grant that has the same force and effect as letters patent, a plan that operates as an instrument granting, dedicating, transferring or conveying real property for a road, utility, park or other public purpose, a notification within the meaning of the Territorial Lands Act or any other instrument by which federal real property may be granted. *Federal Real Property and Federal Immovables Act, 1991*, S.C. 1991, c. 50, s. 2.

CROWN IMMUNITY. 1. The common law rule that the Crown is not bound by a statute, unless by express words or necessary implication. *R. v. Eldorado Nuclear Ltd* (1983), 77 C.P.R. (2d) 1 at 8, 50 N.R. 120, 4 D.L.R. (4th) 193, 1 O.A.C. 243, 8 C.C.C. (3d) 449, [1983] 2 S.C.R. 551, 7 Admin L.R. 195, Dickson J. (Laskin C.J.C. and Ritchie J. concurring). 2. Statutory provisions in the various Interpretation Acts to the effect that the Crown is not bound unless by express words.

CROWN LAND. Land, whether or not it is covered by water, or an interest in land, vested in the Crown. See VACANT ~.

CROWN LANDS. 1. Such Crown or public lands or Crown domain as are within the Province and belong to Her Majesty in right of the Province, and whether or not any water flow over or cover the same. 2. (i) All lands within the province except (A) lands that may be in the use or occupation of any department of the government of the province or of an officer or employee of the government of the province in connection with his or her employment (B) lands that may have been lawfully set apart or appropriated for any public purposes, and (C) ands lawfully alienated from the Crown, and (ii) lands deemed to be Crown lands under section 88. *Crown Lands Act*, R.S. Nfld. 1990, c. C-42, s. 2.

CROWN LEASE. A lease issued under this Act, or under any predecessor statute, by which the Crown has granted to any person the right to extract, recover or produce any Crown mineral. *Crown Minerals Act*, S.S., c. C-50.2, s. 2.

CROWN MINERAL. Any mineral that may be found on, in or under any Crown mineral lands. *Crown Minerals Act*, S.S., c. C-50.2, s. 2.

CROWN MINERAL LANDS. The mineral interest of the Crown in any lands in Saskatchewan whether or not the surface rights in any of those lands are also the property of the Crown. Saskatchewan statutes.

CROWN OWNED CORPORATION. Any corporation or entity in which the government owns more than 50 per cent of the issued and outstanding voting shares. *Audit Act*, R.S.P.E.I. 1988, c. A-24, s. 1(1)(d).

CROWN PETROLEUM. Petroleum which is vested in the Crown under this Act. *Petroleum and Natural Gas Act*, R.S. Nfld. 1990, c. P-10, s. 2.

CROWN PRIVILEGE. The rule of evidence which states that relevant evidence which is otherwise admissible must not be admitted if to do so would injure the public interest.

CROWN RANGE. Crown land included within the boundaries of a range district, but does not include Crown land that is subject to a lease issued under the Land Act. *Range Act*, R.S.B.C. 1996, c. 396, s. 1.

CROWN RESERVE. Land which vests in the Crown but which is not dedicated to the public.

CROWN RESERVE LANDS. Lands in respect of which no interest is in force.

CROWN ROYALTY. See INCREMENTAL ~.

CROWN SHARE. The share reserved to Her Majesty.

CROWN SHIP. A ship, as defined in the Canada Shipping Act, that is owned by or is in the exclusive possession of the Crown. *Crown Liability Act*, R.S.C. 1985, c. C-50, s. 2.

CROWN'S NEWSL. *abbr.* Crown's Newsletter.

CROWN TIMBER. 1. Includes any trees, timber and products of the forest in respect whereof the Crown is enabled to demand and receive any stumpage, royalty, revenue or money. 2. Timber on Crown land or timber reserved to the Crown. *Forest acts.*

CROWN VESSEL. A vessel that is owned by or is in the exclusive possession of Her Majesty in right of Canada. *Canada Shipping Act, 2001*, S.C. 2001, c. 26, s.140.

CROWN WARDSHIP ORDER. An order of a court making the Crown the legal guardian of a child in need of protection.

C.R.P. *abbr.* Conseil de revision des pensions.

C.R.R. *abbr.* Canadian Rights Reporter.

C.R.T.C. *abbr.* 1. Canadian Railway and Transport Cases, 1902-1966. 2. Canadian Radio-television and Telecommunications Commission (Conseil de la radio-diffusion et des telecommunications canadiennes).

C.R.T.F.P. *abbr.* Commission des relations de travail dans la Fonction publique.

C.R. (3d). *abbr.* Criminal Reports (Third Series), 1978-.

C.R.T.Q. *abbr.* Commission des relations du travail (Québec).

CRUDE BITUMEN. A naturally occurring viscous mixture, mainly of hydrocarbons heavier than pentane, that may contain sulphur compounds and that, in its naturally occurring viscous state, will not flow to a well.

CRUDE OIL. A mixture mainly of pentanes and heavier hydrocarbons, which may be contaminated with sulphur compounds, that is recovered or is recoverable at a well from an underground reservoir and that is liquid at the conditions under which its volume is measured or estimated, and includes all other hydrocarbon mixtures so recovered or recoverable except raw gas or condensate. See HEAVY ~; SYNTHETIC ~.

CRUDE PETROLEUM. A flammable liquid with a flash point below 150°F and consisting of an unrefined mixture of natural liquid hydrocarbons as obtained from the earth. *Flammable Liquids Bulk Storage Regulations*, C.R.C., c. 1148, s. 2.

CRUEL AND UNUSUAL PUNISHMENT. "The general standard for determining an infringement of s. 12 [of the Charter] was set out by Lamer J. . . in R. v. Smith, [1987] 1 S.C.R. 1045 . . . [at p. 1072]: 'The criterion which must be applied in order to determine whether a punishment is cruel and unusual within the meaning of s. 12 of the Charter is . . . "whether the punishment prescribed is so excessive as to outrage standards of decency". In other words, though the state may impose punishment, the effect of that punishment must not be grossly disproportionate to what would have been appropriate.' " *Chiarelli v. Canada (Minister of Employment & Immigration)* (1992), 16 I.L.R. (2d) 1 at 22, 2 Admin. L.R. (2d) 125, 135 N.R. 161, 90 D.L.R. (4th) 289, 8 C.R.R. (2d) 234, 72 C.C.C. (3d) 214, [1992] 1 S.C.R. 711, the court per Sopinka J.

CRUELTY. *n*. 1. " . . . As used in ordinary parlance 'cruelty' signifies a disposition to inflict suffering; to delight in or exhibit indifference to the pain or misery of others; mercilessness or hard-heartedness as exhibited in action. If in the marriage relationship one spouse by his conduct causes wanton, malicious or unnecessary infliction of pain or suffering upon the body, the feelings or emotions of the other, his conduct may well constitute cruelty which will entitle a petitioner to dissolution of the marriage if, in the court's opinion, it amounts to physical or mental cruelty 'of such a kind as to render intolerable the continued cohabitation of the spouses'. That is the standard which the courts are to apply, and in the context of s. 3(d) of the [Divorce Act, S.C. 1967-68, c. 24] . . . Care must be exercised in applying the standard set forth in s. 3(d) that conduct relied upon to establish cruelty is not a trivial act, but one of a 'grave and weighty' nature, and not merely conduct which can be characterized as little more than a manifestation of incompatability of temperament between the spouses. . ." *Knoll v. Knoll* (1970), 1 R.F.L. 141 at 149, 10 D.L.R. (3d) 199 (Ont. C.A.), the court per Schroeder J.A. 2. Conduct that creates a danger to life, limb or health, and includes any course of conduct that in the opinion of the court is grossly insulting and intolerable, or is of such a character that the person seeking a separation could not reasonably be expected to be willing to live with the other after he or she has been guilty of such conduct. *Domestic Relations acts*. See ACTS OF ~.

CRUISE SHIP. A Canadian ship or any other vessel that has sleeping facilities for over 100 persons who are not crew members but does not include a vessel engaged in passenger or cargo ferry service. *Marine Transportation Security Regulations (Cruise Ships and Cruise Ship Facilities)*, SOR/97-270, s. 1.

CRUMBLING SKULL RULE. A tortfeasor must take his or her victim as the tortfeasor finds the victim even though the plaintiff's losses are greater than they would be for the average person. The victim has a pre-existing condition which is inherent in the victim's condition for purposes of assessing damages.

CRUSH. See INITIAL ~ RESISTANCE; INTERMEDIATE ~ RESISTANCE; PEAK ~ RESISTANCE.

CRUSH SYNDROME. 1. Kidney failure brought about by a serious crushing injury, usually to a limb. 2. Kidney failure following transfusion of incompatible blood. F.A. Jaffe, *A Guide to Pathological Evidence*, 2d ed. (Toronto: Carswell 1983) at 184 and 185.

CRY DE PAIS. See CRI DE PAIS.

CRYER. *n*. A court officer who makes proclamations.

CRYPT. *n*. An underground chamber located under the main floor of a church or other building. *An Act to Amend the Cemetery Companies Act*, S.N.B. 1984, c. 18, s. 1.

CRYSTALLIZATION. *n*. " . . . [O]f a floating charge means that upon the happening of some event or events the charge that had been floating over the assets becomes fixed." *Bayhold Financial Corp. v. Clarkson Co.* (1991), (sub *nom. Barhold Financial Corp. v. Community Hotel Co. (Receiver of)*) 86 D.L.R. (4th) 127 at 149, 10 C.B.R. (3d)159,108 N.S.R. (3d)198, 294 A.P.R. 198 (C.A.), the court per Hallett J.A.

CRYSTALLIZE. *v*. To convert a floating charge into a fixed charge. F. Bennett, *Receiverships* (Toronto: Carswell, 1985) at 33. See DE-~.

C.S. *abbr*. 1. Cour superieure. 2. Cour supreme (provinciale). 3. Recueils de jurisprudence de la Cour supérieure de Québec (Quebec Superior Court Reports). 4. Rapports judiciaires du Québec, Cour supérieure, 1892-1941 (Official Reports, Superior Court).

[] C.S. *abbr*. 1. Rapports judiciaires du Québec, Cour supérieure, 1942-1966. 2. Recueils de jurisprudence du Québec, Cour Supérieure, 1967-.

C.S.A. *abbr*. Canadian Standards Association.

CSA ELEVATOR CODE. The Safety Code for Elevators, Dumbwaiters and Escalators of the Canadian Standards Association, CSA Standard B44-1966, as amended from time to time. Canada regulations.

CSA INDUSTRIAL LIGHTING STANDARD. The Canadian Standards Association Standard C92.1-1967, as amended from time to time. *Canada Safe Illumination Regulations*, C.R.C., c. 1008, s. 2.

CSA STANDARD. A standard published by the Canadian Standards Association. *Occupational Health and Safety Act*, R.R.O. 1980, Reg. 694, s. 1.

CSC. The French neutral citation for the Supreme Court of Canada.

C.S.C. *abbr*. Cour suprême du Canada.

C.S. CAN. *abbr*. Cour Supreme du Canada.

CSE. Communications Security Establishment.

CSIS. The Canadian Security Intelligence Service.

C.S.P. *abbr*. 1. Cour des Sessions de la paix. 2. Recueils de jurisprudence, Cour des Sessions de la Paix.

C.S.P. QUÉ. *abbr*. Cour des sessions de la paix (Québec) (Court of Sessions of the Peace (Quebec)).

C.S. QUÉ. *abbr*. Cour supérieure (Québec).

C.S.R. *abbr*. Commission scolaire régionale.

CT. *abbr*. Court.

C.T. *abbr*. Commission du tarif

C.T.C. *abbr*. 1. Canadian Transport Cases, 1966-. 2. Canadian Transport Commission (Commission canadienne des transports). 3. Centralized Traffic Control.

[] C.T.C *abbr*. Canada Tax Cases, 1917-1971.

CTC(A). The Air Transport Committee of the Canadian Transport Commission. Canada regulations.

[] C.T.C. (N.S.). *abbr*. Canada Tax Cases, 1971-

C.T.C. REGULATIONS. Regulations for the Transportation of Dangerous Commodities by Rail. Canada regulations.

CT. CRIM. APP. *abbr*. Court of Criminal Appeals.

C.T.C.U.M. *abbr*. Commission de transport de la communauté urbaine de Montréal.

CTEE. *abbr*. Committee.

C.T.M. *abbr*. Canada Tax Manual.

CT. MARTIAL APP. CT. *abbr*. Court Martial Appeal Court.

C.T.Q. *abbr*. Commission des transports du Québec.

C. TRANS. C. *abbr*. Canadian Transport Cases.

CT. REV. *abbr*. Court of Review.

CT. SESS. P. *abbr*. Court of Sessions of the Peace.

C.T./T.T. *abbr*. Décisions du Commissaire du travail et du Tribunal du travail.

CUBIC CENTIMETRE. 1. Interchangeable with the term "millilitre". *Food and Drug Regulations*, C.R.C., c. 870, c. A.01.010. 2. In relation to uses, means the quantity of the gases that occupies a volume of 1 cubic centimetre at 25 degrees Celsius and at a pressure of 760 millimetres of mercury (being the equivalent of a pressure of 100.9 kPa). *Asbestos Mining and Milling National Emission Standards Regulations*, C.R.C., c. 405, s. 2.

CUBIC FOOT. 1/27 cubic yard. *Weights and Measures Act*, S.C. 1970-71-72, c. 36, schedule II. See STANDARD ~.

CUBIC INCH. 1/1 728 cubic foot. *Weights and Measures Act*, S.C. 1970-71-72, c. 36, schedule II.

CUBIC METRE. For a volume of (a) natural gas, that volume measured at 101.325 kPa and

15°C; and (b) petroleum, that volume measured at 15°C. *Petroleum or Natural Gas Act*, R.S.B.C. 1979, c. 323, s. 1. See NORMAL ~.

CUBIC METRE (SOLID). A unit of measurement used to measure the solid wood volume of a log. *Forestry Act*, R.S. Nfld. 1990, c. F-23, s. 119.

CUBIC METRE (STACKED). A unit of measurement used to measure the quantity of round timber that can be properly piled within a space of 1 cubic metre without deduction for bark or for normal air space. *Forestry Act*, R.S. Nfld. 1990, c. F-23, s. 119.

CUBIC YARD. A volume equal to that of a cube each side of which measures one yard. *Weights and Measures Act*, S.C. 1970-71-72, c. 36, Schedule II.

CUI BONO. [L.] To whose good.

CUICUNQUE ALIQUID QUID CONCEDIT CONCEDERE VIDETUR ET ID SINE QUO RES IPSA ESSE NON POTUIT. [L.] A grantor must grant that thing without which the first thing granted would be useless.

CUILIBET IN SUA ARTS PERITO EST CREDENDUM. [L.] A person who is skilled in a profession should be believed.

CUILIBET LICET RENUNTIARE JURI PRO SE INTRODUCTO. [L.] Anyone can waive the advantage of a law made solely for the protection and benefit of the individual in a private capacity as long as this does not infringe any public policy or right. P.St.J. Langan, ed., *Maxwell on The Interpretation of Statutes*, 12th ed. (Bombay: N.M. Tripathi, 1976) at 328.

CUI LICET QUOD MAJUS NON DEBET QUOD MINUS EST NON LICERE. [L.] The one who has authority to do a greater thing should not be prevented from doing a lesser thing.

CUJUS EST DARE EJUS EST DISPONERE. [L.] The one who gives something can also control its disposition.

CUJUS EST INSTITUERE EJUS EST ABROGARE. [L.] The one who initiates may also abrogate.

CUJUS EST SOLUM EJUS EST USQUE AD COELUM. [L. one who owns the soil owns up to the sky] " . . . [W]hoever owns the soil owns all that lies above it. . ." *Ramey v. Canada* (1986), 36 L.C.R. 97 at 103, 6 F.T.R. 309, McNair J.

CUL DE SAC. *var*. **CUL-DE-SAC**. A street or road open only at one end.

CULL. *n*. A defective log as defined by the manual of scaling instructions. *Crown Timber Act*, R.S.O. 1990, c. C.51, s. 1.

CULLER. *n*. A person who measures timber cut on lands in the domain of the State including cross cut trees, lopped trees, trees with no crown or trees reduced to chips. *Cullers Act*, R.S.Q., chapter M-12.1, s. 1.

CULMINATING INCIDENT, DOCTRINE OF. Where an employee has engaged in a final act of misconduct or course of conduct for which disciplinary action may be imposed, the employer properly may consider the employment record in determining the sanction that is appropriate for the final incident.

CULPA. *n*. [L.] Fault; neglect, negligence.

CULPABILITY. *n*. Blame, blameworthiness, negligence, guilt, being at fault.

CULPABLE. *adj*. That which is to be blamed, blameworthy, negligent, guilty, criminal, faultful.

CULPABLE HOMICIDE. 1. Murder or manslaughter or infanticide. *Criminal Code*, R.S.C. 1985, c. C-46, s. 222(4). 2. A person commits culpable homicide when he causes the death of a human being, (a) by means of an unlawful act, (b) by criminal negligence, (c) by causing that human being, by threats or fear of violence or by deception, to do anything that causes his death, or (d) by wilfully frightening that human being, in the case of a child or sick person. *Criminal Code*, R.S.C. 1985, c. C-46, s. 222(5).

CULPABLE NEGLIGENCE. Criminal negligence.

CULPA CARET QUI SCIT SED PROHIBERE NON POTEST. [L.] Anyone who knows but cannot prevent is free from blame.

CULPA EST IMMISCERE SE REI AD SE NON PERTINENTI. [L.] It is wrong for someone to interfere in a matter not related to oneself.

CULPA LATA DOLO AEQUIPARATUR. [L.] Gross negligence is equivalent to purposeful wrong.

CULPA LEVISSIMA. [L.] Very slight fault.

CULPRIT. *n*. A person accused of an offence; a person found guilty of an offence.

CULTIVATE. *v.* " ... [C]ommences when seeding takes place and continues until the marijuana plants are harvested or they die. Once a person normally takes on the task of raising a plant or a crop of marijuana to maturity, he is 'cultivating' that crop until such time as he abandons the task or the crop is harvested." *R. v. Arnold* (1990), 74 C.R. (3d) 394 at 398 (B.C.C.A.), Hutcheon, Toy and Taylor JJ.A.

CULTIVATED LAND. 1. (a) Pasture fields seeded with cultivated brass, (b) land on which planted crops are growing, (c) land which is or which is usually prepared for the growing of planted crops, (d) Christmas tree plantations, (e) forest experimental lots, (f) managed sugar bush stands, and (g) orchards. 2. Land that in the year of award was seeded to crop or was in summer-fallow and includes (a) land that was seeded to grass in any year if the productivity thereof was maintained in the year of award, and (b) land of a farmer that in three out of five years immediately preceding the year of award had been seeded or summer-fallowed, but owing to natural causes beyond his control could not be seeded or summer-fallowed in the year of award. *Prairie Farm Assistance Act*, R.S.C. 1970, c. P-16, s. 2. 3. Land tilled for the production of crops other than grass or hay.

CULTIVATION. *n.* The preparation and use of land to raise a crop.

CULTURALLY MODIFIED TREES. For ministry [of Small Business, Tourism & Culture] purposes, CMTs [culturally modified trees] are trees which bear the marks of past aboriginal intervention occurring as part of traditional aboriginal use. Bark may have been stripped from them. Pieces or chunks of wood may have been removed from the trees to make tools or build canoes. Sap or pitch may have been collected from the trees. *Kitkatla Band v. British Columbia (Minister of Small Business, Tourism & Culture)*, [2002] 2 S.C.R. 146.

CULTURAL PROPERTY. A work of art, a historic property, a historic monument or site, an archaeological property or site or a cinematographic, audiovisual, photographic, radio or television work. *Cultural Property Act*, R.S.Q., chapter B-4, s. 1. See FOREIGN ~.

CULTURAL PROPERTY AGREEMENT. In relation to a foreign State, means an agreement between Canada and the foreign State or an international agreement to which Canada and the foreign State are both parties, relating to the prevention of illicit international traffic in cultural property. *Cultural Property Export and Import Act*, R.S.C. 1985, c. C-51, s. 37.

CULTURE. See BACTERIAL ~.

C.U.M. *abbr.* Communauté urbaine de Montreal.

CUM DIV. *abbr.* Cum dividend.

CUM DIVIDEND. With dividend; when a share is sold cum div. the purchaser receives any declared and not yet paid dividend.

CUM DUO INTER SE PUGNANTIA REPERIUNTUR IN TESTAMENTO ULTIMUM RATUM EST. [L.] Where two clauses in a will are inconsistent, the one appearing later in the will should be considered valid.

CUM GRANO SALIS. [L.] With a grain of salt.

CUM IN TESTAMENTO AMBIGUE AUT ETIAM PERPERAM SCRIPTUM EST, BENIGNE INTERPRETARI DEBET ET SECUNDUM ID QUOD CREDIBILE EST COGITATUM CREDENDUM EST. [L.] Where an ambiguous, or even incorrect, expression occurs in a will it should be interpreted liberally and in accordance with what it is thought the testator intended.

CUM ONERE. [L.] With the burden or onus.

CUM PAR DELICTUM EST DUORUM SEMPER ONERATUR PETITOR ET MELIOR HABETUR POSSESSORIS CAUSA. [L.] When both parties are at fault it is the plaintiff who must fail, and the person in possession has the stronger case.

CUM RIGHTS. A purchaser of shares cum rights has the right to claim the rights to new shares or warrants which are about to be issued.

CUM TESTAMENTO ANNEXO. [L. with the will annexed] Administration with the will annexed is granted when a testator has not named an executor or the executor named is not willing to act.

CUMULATIVE. *adj.* Additional, to be added together, to be taken in succession.

CUMULATIVE CREDIT. The amount of credit available for each period is spelled out, and any balance unspent in one period may be carried over into the next. I.F.G. Baxter *The Law of Banking*, 3d ed. (Toronto: Carswell, 1981) at 156.

CUMULATIVE EFFECTS. "Cumulative effects" are not defined in the Act [*Canadian Environmental Assessment Act*, S.C. 1992, c. 37, s. 16(1)(a)]. The Agency has defined cumulative environmental effects as "the effects on the environment, over a certain period of time and distance, resulting from effects of a project when combined with those of other past, existing, and imminent projects and activities." Only likely cumulative environmental effects must be considered. Projects or activities which have been or will be carried out must be considered. However, only approved projects must be taken into account; uncertain or hypothetical projects or activities need not be considered. The Agency's *Reference Guide on Cumulative Effects* suggests, however, that "it would be prudent to consider projects or activities that are in a government approvals process as well." *Bow Valley Naturalists Society v. Canada (Minister of Canadian Heritage)*, 37 C.E.L.R. (N.S.) 1, 266 N.R. 169, 27 Admin. L.R. (3d) 229, [2001] 2 F.C. 461, 2001 CarswellNat 1721, [2001] F.C.J. No. 18 (C.A.).

CUMULATIVE LEGACY. A legacy given in addition to a prior legacy in the same will.

CUMULATIVE PREFERENCE SHARE. A share the dividend of which cumulates from year to year.

CUMULATIVE REMEDY. A mode of procedure available in addition to another possible remedy; opposite to alternative remedy.

CUMULATIVE VOTING. A voting method which permits all votes attached to all a shareholder's shares to be cast for one candidate for board of directors of a corporation.

C.U.Q. *abbr.* Communauté urbaine de Quebec.

CURATIVE. *adj.* Intended to remedy.

CURATIVE SECTION. A provision that if one substantially complies with provisions the transaction will not be invalidated because one failed to comply with the requirements of such a section unless the Court judges that some person was prejudiced thereby (and then the award is only to the extent of that prejudice).

CURATIVE STATUTE. A statute designed to operate on past events, acts or transactions so that irregularities and errors are corrected and acts which would otherwise be ineffective for the intended purpose are rendered valid..

CURATOR. *n.* A protector of property.

CURB. *n.* A raised or guarded place at the edge of a roadway or a safety island, median or boulevard.

CURBING. *n.* Includes a curbing of any material in or along a street, whether constructed in connection with or apart from the laying down of a pavement or sidewalk, or with or without a projection for the purpose of a gutter.

CURB MASS. The actual mass of a motor vehicle when unladen but including the body, battery, loose tools, spare wheels, and other usual equipment and a full supply of water and fuel used for the purpose of propulsion. *Highway Traffc Act*, R.S. Nfld. 1990, c. H-3, s. 2.

CURB WEIGHT. The actual or manufacturer's estimated weight of a vehicle in operational status with all standard equipment and weight of fuel at nominal tank capacity and the weight of optional equipment. *On-Road Vehicle and Engine Emission Regulations*, SOR/2003-2, s. 1.

CURE. *v.* To add a substance to a meat product for the purpose of preventing or delaying undesirable or unwholesome changes as well as to enhance colour, flavour and texture. *Meat Inspection Regulations*, C.R.C., c. 1032, s. 2.

CURED FISH. Fish that has received curing. *Saltfish Act*, R.S.C. 1985, c. S-4, s. 2.

CURE TITLE. To remove encumbrances or claims in order to create good or clear title.

CURFEW. *n.* A law requiring persons to remove themselves from the streets at a certain time of night.

CURIA. *n.* [L.] A court of justice.

CURIA ADVISARI VULT. [L.] The court will consider the matter.

CURIAL DEFERENCE. The degree to which a court will refrain from interfering with a decision of an administrative tribunal or a lower court. Factors such as public interest, expertise of the tribunal, the courts' treatment of a tribunal historically and the existence and type of privative clause in place are important in determining which standard of deference will be applied. See CORRECTNESS; PATENTLY UNREASONABLE; STANDARD OF REVIEW; UNREASONABLE.

CURIA PARLIAMENTI SUIS PROPRIIS LEGIBUS SUBSISTIT. [L.] The court of Parliament functions under its own peculiar laws.

CURIA REGIS. [L.] The monarch's court.

CURING. *n.* Processing with salt or with salt and drying. *Saltfish acts*.

CURING PLANT. See SALMON BRINE ~.

CURRANT JELLY CLOT. Mainly red blood cells, dark red in colour, forming the lower part of a clot. F.A. Jaffe, *A Guide to Pathological Evidence*, 3d ed. (Toronto: Carswell, 1991) at 215.

CURRENCY. *n.* 1. A period during which something is in force. 2. The medium of exchange which circulates in a country. 3. Money. See CREATION OF ~; EURO-MAR-KET.

CURRENT. *n.* See OVER ~ DEVICE.

CURRENT. *adj.* Lawfully current in Canada or elsewhere by virtue of law, proclamation or regulation in force in Canada or elsewhere as the case may be. *Criminal Code*, R.S.C. 1985, c. C-46, s. 448.

CURRENT ASSETS. Cash, accounts receivable, inventory and assets which could be converted to cash in the near future.

CURRENT DEPOSIT. A deposit out of which money may be withdrawn on presentation of a bill of exchange.

CURRENT EXCHANGE RATE. The rate of exchange prevailing on the day on which a transaction takes place, as ascertained from a Canadian bank.

CURRENT EXPENDITURE. An expenditure for operating purposes or a permanent improvement from funds other than those arising from the sale of a debenture, from a capital loan or from a loan pending the sale of a debenture. *Education Act*, R.S. 1990, c. E.2, s. 1(1).

CURRENT LAND VALUE. The actual value of similar land held in fee simple. Thus "current land value" means the price a willing buyer would pay for fee simple title to the land. *Musqueam Indian Band v. Glass* (2000), 2000 CarswellNat 2405, 2000 SCC 52, [2000] 11 W.W.R. 407, 36 R.P.R. (3d) 1, 192 D.L.R. (4th) 385, 82 B.C.L.R. (3d) 199, 261 N.R. 296, 186 F.T.R. 248 (note), [2000] 2 S.C.R. 633, [2001] 1 C.N.L.R. 208, Per McLachlin C.J.C. (dissenting on the appeal) (L'Heureux-Dubé, Iacobucci and Arbour JJ. concurring).

CURRENT LIABILITY. A debt due within a short period of time.

CURRENT REVENUE. All amounts earned and the amounts to which one may become entitled; other than by borrowing, that may be used to meet expenditures.

CURRENT SERVICE COST. An actuarial estimate of the present value of future benefits to members of a pension plan. *Schmidt v. Air Products of Canada Ltd.*, [1994] 2 S.C.R. 611.

CURRENT YEAR TAXES. Unpaid real property taxes levied for the current year.

CURRICULUM. *n.* Studies set out for a particular period.

CURR. LEGAL PROBS. *abbr.* Current Legal Problems.

CURSE. *v.* To swear.

CURSUS CURIAE EST LEX CURIAE. [L.] The practice of the court is the law of the court.

CURTESY. *n.* Formerly, the interest in a wife's fee simple which a husband will have after her death until his own.

CURTILAGE. *n.* The space around a dwelling house necessary, convenient and used for family purposes and carrying out domestic chores. Includes a garden. *R. v. Kelly* (1999), 132 C.C.C. (3d) 122 (N.B. C.A.).

CUSHION TANK. A pressure vessel designed for installation in a closed hot water heating system to provide an air cushion for the expansion of water.

CUSTANTIA. *n.* [L.] Costs.

CUSTODIAL CARE. The personal care, assistance and protection required by a person who has reached the apparent limit of recovery and whose condition is such that such care is necessary or who has such a degree of senile deterioration that such care is necessary but who does not require continued medical and skilled nursing care in a hospital. *Public Hospitals Act*, R.R.O. 1980, Reg. 865, s. 1.

CUSTODIAL PORTION. With respect to a youth sentence imposed on a young person, means the period of time, or the portion of the young person's youth sentence, that must be served in custody before he or she begins to serve the remainder under supervision in the community subject to conditions or under conditional supervision. *Youth Criminal Justice Act*, S.C. 2002, c. 1, s. 2.

CUSTODIA LEGIS. [L.] The custody of the law.

CUSTODIAL EMPLOYEE. A guard; an after hours security guard

CUSTODIAL FACILITY. See YOUTH ~.

CUSTODIAL PERSON. A person who, in the opinion of a medical practitioner, requires custodial care. *Public Hospitals Act*, R.R.O. 1980, Reg. 865, s. 1.

CUSTODIAN. *n*. 1. A person in whose custody a package is placed. 2. A person acting as a custodian for a clearing agency. 3. A person designated by an order to have custody of the property of another person.

CUSTODIAN TRUSTEE. A person in whom title to trust property is vested while management of the trust is left in the hands of other trustees, the managing trustees.

CUSTODY. *n*. 1. "[As used in the Extra-Provincial Enforcement of Custody Orders Act, 1977 (Alta.), c. 20, s. 1(c)] . . . is not a word that has a narrow single meaning. It may mean only the care and control of the child or it may mean all of the rights of guardianship." *Read v. Read*, [1982] 2 W.W.R. 25 at 29, 17 Alta. L.R. (2d) 273 (C.A.), Moir, Laycraft and McClung JJ.A. 2. " . . . Its meaning can range from immediate effective possession and control of the person, as where a jailer has custody of his prisoner, to control by a parent of a child in the widest possible sense, that is, not only physical but also intellectual, educational, spiritual, moral and financial . . . Thus the concept of custody under the Divorce Act [S.C. 1986, c. 4, s. 2] is for all practical purposes, co-extensive with guardianship of the person under the provincial Family Relations Act [R.S.B.C. 1979, c. 121, ss. 1, 25] . . ." *Clarke v. Clarke* (1987), 7 R.F.L. (3d) 176 at 178, 180, 12 B.C.L.R. (2d) 290 (S.C.), Gow L.J.S.C. 3. In the narrow sense of the word, "custody" means physical care and control or day to day care and control of a child. In the broad sense of the word, "custody" means all of the rights and obligations associated with physical, day to day care and control of a child as well as the right and obligation to nurture the child by ensuring, providing for, and making decisions in relation to, a child's physical and emotional health, education, religious or spiritual development, and all other matters that affect the welfare of the child. *Abbott v. Abbott*, 2001 CarswellBC 420, 2001 BCSC 323, 13 R.F.L. (5th) 233, 89 B.C.L.R. (3d) 68 (S.C.), Pitfield J. 4. Physical control. See CARE AND ~; CIVIL ~; DIVIDED ~; JOINT ~; LEGAL ~;

OPEN ~; PLACE OF ~; PLACE OF SECURE ~; PROTECTIVE ~; RIGHT OF ~; SECURE ~; SERVICE ~; SOLE ~.

CUSTODY AGREEMENT. Any agreement with respect to the custody, care or control of a child.

CUSTODY ORDER. 1. The order of any court with respect to the custody, care or control of a child. 2. An order, or that part of an order, of an extra-provincial tribunal that grants custody of a child to any person and includes provisions, if any, granting another person a right of access or visitation to the child. *Extra-provincial Custody Orders Enforcement acts*. 3. A court of competent jurisdiction may, on application by either or both spouses or by any other person, make an order respecting the custody of or the access to, or the custody of and access to, any or all children of the marriage. *Divorce Act*, R.S.C, 1985, c. 3 (2nd Supp.), s. 16.

CUSTODY PROVISION. A provision of an order or agreement awarding custody of a child.

CUSTOM. *n*. 1. An unwritten law or right, established through long use. 2. " . . . [I]n the sense of a rule having the force of law and existing since time immemorial is not in issue in this case. Indeed, Canadian law being largely of imported origin will rarely, if ever, evince that sort of custom. Custom in Canadian law must be given a broader definition. In any event, both courts below were not using the term in such a technical sense, as is clear from the fact that both substituted the term 'practice' as a synonym." *International Corona Resources Ltd. v. Lac Minerals Ltd.* (1989), 26 C.P.R. (3d) 97 at 121, [1989] 2 S.C.R. 574, 69 O.R. (2d) 287, 61 D.L.R. (4th) 14, 6 R.P.R. (2d) 1, 44 B.L.R. 1, 35 E.T.R. 1, 101 N.R. 239, 36 Q.A.C. 57, La Forest J. (Wilson and Lamer JJ. concurring).

CUSTOMARY. *adj*. According to custom; usual.

CUSTOMARY AUTHORITY. An agent who is authorized to act for a principal in a particular business, market or locale has implied authority to act in accordance with the usages and customs of that business, market or locale. G.H.L. Fridman, *The Law of Agency*, 6th ed. (London: Butterworths, 1990) at 66. See USUAL OR ~.

CUSTOMARY CARE. The care and supervision of an Indian or native child by a person who is not the child's parent, according to the custom of the child's band or native community. *Child*

and Family Services Act, R.S.O. 1990, c. C.11, s. 208.

CUSTOMARY INTERNATIONAL LAW. A national practice accepted as international law.

CUSTOM BAND. A First Nations band which devises its own election system for its band council.

CUSTOM DUTY. The fee payable when importing goods.

CUSTOMER. *n.* 1. A client; one who is in a retail establishment to make a purchase. 2. A person who is liable for payment for programming services that are distributed by a licensee and that are received directly or indirectly by one or more subscribers. It does not include the owner or operator of a hotel, hospital, nursing home or other commercial or institutional premises. *Broadcasting Distribution Regulations*, SOR/97-555, s. 1. See CREDIT CARD ~; FOREIGN ~; INDUSTRIAL ~; SEASONAL ~; WHOLESALE ~; YEARLY ~.

CUSTOM-HOUSE. *n.* The office where any duty payable or receivable upon import or export is paid or received.

CUSTOM-MADE DEVICE. A medical device, other than a mass-produced medical device, that (*a*) is manufactured in accordance with a health care professional's written direction giving its design characteristics; (*b*) differs from medical devices generally available for sale or from a dispenser; and (*c*) is (i) for the sole use of a particular patient of that professional, or (ii) for use by that professional to meet special needs arising in the course of his or her practice. *Medical Devices Regulations* SOR/98-282, s. 1.

CUSTOM OF THE TRADE. Any practice usually observed by people dealing in a particular product.

CUSTOM OPERATOR. A person who purchases a new farm implement and uses or permits the use of that farm implement for hire or for service to others for valuable consideration to the extent of at least 50 per cent of the annual use of that farm implement.

CUSTOMS. *n.* Duties charged when goods are imported into, or exported out of, a country. See CANADIAN ~ WATERS; CHIEF OFFICER OF ~; OUTSIDE ~ AREA.

CUSTOMS BONDED WAREHOUSE. A facility operated under licence from the government of Canada where goods on which duty and taxes have not been paid are stored.

CUSTOMS BROKER. A person who acts as agent to clear goods through customs.

CUSTOMS CONTROL. See POST AUDIT ~ SYSTEM.

CUSTOMS DUTY. The tax when goods are imported.

CUSTOMS DUTY STAMPS. Stamps issued by the Deputy Minister indicating the prepayment of customs duty on any goods specified in the tariff item. *Printed Matter Prepayment Regulations*, C.R.C., c. 541, s. 2.

CUSTOMS EXPRESS BRANCH WAREHOUSE. A warehouse for the safekeeping, examination and appraisal by customs of imported goods carried by means of air or rail express. *Customs Warehousing Regulations*, C.R.C., c. 462, s. 2.

CUSTOMS LAWS. See FEDERAL ~.

CUSTOMS OFFICE. A place designated as a customs office by the Minister. *Customs Act*, R.S.C. 1985 (2d Supp.), c. 1, s. 2.

CUSTOMS OFFICER. The collector or chief officer of customs at a port.

CUSTOMS UNION. An agreement between countries for the unification of territories for purposes of customs.

CUSTOMS WAREHOUSE. Includes sufferance warehouse, bonding warehouse and examining warehouse.

CUSTOS ROTULORUM. [L.] A keeper of the records.

CUSTOS STATUM HAEREDIS IN CUSTODIA EXISTENTIS MELIOREM, NON DETERIOREM, FACERE POTEST. [L.] A person can only improve, not worsen, the estate of an heir for whom the person is a guardian.

CUT. *v.* Of drugs, to dilute. F.A. Jaffe, *A Guide to Pathological Evidence*, 3d ed. (Toronto: Carswell, 1991) at 216.

CUT. *n.* The incised wound which a sharp object caused. F.A. Jaffe, *A Guide to Pathological Evidence*, 3d ed. (Toronto: Carswell, 1991) at 216. See PRIMAL ~.

CUTBACK. *n.* A reduction in production of a manufacturer possibly requiring layoffs of employees.

CUTIS ANSERINA. [L.] Goose flesh, goose pimples.

CUT-OFF LANDS. Lands that had before 1916 been appropriated by the government for the use and benefit of Indians but that, under the Indian Affairs Settlement Act, S.B.C. 1919, c. 32, the British Columbia Indian Affairs Settlement Act, S.C. 1920, c. 51, and the report of the Royal Commission on Indian Affairs in the Province of British Columbia of June 30, 1916, as approved by Dominion Privy Council Order 1265 of July 19, 1924 and British Columbia Order in Council 911 of July 26, 1923, ceased to be so appropriated, but "cut-off lands" does not include any lands in the Railway Belt or Peace River Block. *Indian Cut-Off Lands Dispute Act*, R.S.B.C. 1996, c. 218, s. 1.

CUT-OUT. *var.* **CUT OUT**. A device installed to isolate manually a circuit from its source of supply. See THERMAL ~.

CUTTER. See SNOWMOBILE ~.

CWT. *abbr.* 1. One hundred pounds. 2. 112 lb. *Dangerous Goods Shipping Regulations*, C.R.C., c. 1419, s. 2.

CYANIDE. *n.* A poisonous chemical constituent of insecticide. F.A. Jaffe, *A Guide to Pathological Evidence*, 3d ed. (Toronto: Carswell, 1991) at 216.

CYANOSIS. *n.* Blue or grey discolouration of the mucous membranes and skin where insufficiently oxygenated blood has circulated. F.A. Jaffe, *A Guide to Pathological Evidence*, 3d ed. (Toronto: Carswell, 1991) at 216.

CYCLE. *n.* 1. A prescribed amount of time. 2. A bicycle, a motor cycle or a moped. See MOTOR~; MOTOR DRIVEN ~.

CYLINDER. *n.* Of a revolver, the circular magazine. F.A. Jaffe, *A Guide to Pathological Evidence*, 3d ed. (Toronto: Carswell, 1991) at 216. See PORTABLE ~S.

CYLINDRICAL GRADUATED STANDARD. A local standard of volume or capacity that is made of glass or metal, has a cylindrical shape and, if made entirely of glass, shows graduations on the glass and, if made of metal, shows graduations that are adjacent to a glass window in the metal. *Weights and Measures Regulations*, C.R.C., c. 1605, s. 53.

CY-PRES. [Fr. near to it]. 1. Enables a court to apply the property of a charitable trust which would otherwise fail for impracticability or unenforceability to some other charitable purpose which resembles that of the original trust as nearly as possible. *Buchanan Estate, Re* (1997), 44 B.C.L.R. (3d) 283 (C.A.). 2. " . . . [I]f the settlor or testator specifies an object but that object is or afterwards becomes impossible or impracticable of performance, the gift will not fail, but the property will be used for some similar purpose as much resembling the specified object as possible, providing the settlor has expressed, or the Court is able to gather . . . from a trust instrument, the paramount instrument of charity . . ." *Weatherby v. Weatherby* (1927), 53 N.B.R. 403 at 417 (S.C.), Hazen C.J.

D. *abbr*. 1. Day. 2. Deci. 3. Depth for freeboard. 4. Draught.

DA. *abbr*. Deca.

DACTYLOGRAPHY. *n*. The study of fingerprints as means of identifying persons.

DAILY. *adj*. Every day.

DAILY DOUBLE. A type of bet on two races on a racing card to select the winning horse in the official result in each race. *Pari-Mutuel Betting Supervision Regulations*, SOR/91-365, s. 2.

DAILY RATE. Compensation for a day's work.

DAILY WAGE. The wage to which an employee would be entitled if the employee worked on a normal working day of the employer that is not a general holiday. See AVERAGE ~.

DAIRY. *n*. 1. Premises in which milk is processed into fluid milk products. 2. Includes, (a) creamery; and (b) pasteurization plant. 3. A place at which milk or cream is purchased or received for the purpose of being pasteurized, standardized or otherwise processed and resold to the wholesale or retail trade or to the wholesale and retail trade.

DAIRY BUTTER. Butter, other than creamery butter and whey butter.

DAIRY DRINK. Milk to which there has been added chocolate or other flavouring.

DAIRY FARM. 1. A place where cattle are kept for milking. 2. Any place where one or more milking animals are kept, and part or all of the milk produced by those cows or goats is sold, offered for sale or held in possession for sale for human consumption.

DAIRY MANUFACTURING PLANT. 1. An establishment in which dairy product is processed, manufactured, pasteurized, reprocessed, packed or repacked. 2. A dairy, a cheese factory, a creamery, a cream receiving station, a concentrated milk plant, milk receiving station, a milk condensery, an ice cream plant, a process cheese plant, or a skimming station, or a combination of any two or more of them.

DAIRY PLANT. A cheese factory, a creamery, a cream receiving station, a milk condensery, an ice cream plant, a cheese processing plant, a plant where milk or cream is received for the purpose of being pasteurized, homogenized, standardized or otherwise processed for sale to the wholesale or retail trade, or a combination of any two or more of them.

DAIRY PLANT PERSONNEL. Persons engaged in specific duties in relation to dairy products for the performance of which the licences are required.

DAIRY PRODUCT. Milk, cream, butter, cheese, condensed milk, evaporated milk, sterile milk, milk powder, dry milk, ice milk, ice cream, malted milk, sherbet, dried whey, condensed whey, casein, sodium caseinate, yogurt or any other food substance for human consumption manufactured wholly or mainly from milk.

DALHOUSIE L.J. *abbr*. Dalhousie Law Journal.

DAM. *n*. 1. Any structure built for the purpose of impounding water in any drift, crosscut or other mine opening and constructed in such a manner as to permit an unobstructed overflow of the water. 2. Includes a channel, diversion, dock, groyne, light, pier, slide, warning device, wharf or work for the control and regulation of water and any building, road, structure, service or temporary installation necessary or incidental thereto.

DAMAGE. *n*. 1. Harm; loss. 2. " . . . used to refer to [U]sually a particular head of loss for which compensation is awarded. The word 'damages' is generally used to identify the amount of money that is paid by a tortfeasor for inflicting the various items of damage. . . certainly includes injury but it also includes more than that. It includes all of the different heads of damage and various expenses that may be suffered as a result of tortious conduct." *Vile v. Von Wendt* (1979), 14 C.P.C. 121 at 125-6, 26 O.R. (2d) 513, 103 D.L.R. (3d) 356 (Div. Ct.), the court per Linden J. See ACTUAL LOSS OR ~; ~S; NEGATIVE ~; OIL POLLUTION ~; PERSONAL ~; POLLUTION ~; POSITIVE ~; PROPERTY ~; SPECIAL~; STIPULATED SUBSTANTIAL ~.

DAMAGE APPRAISER. A person who, for compensation or for promise or expectation of compensation, engages in the business of establishing the amount of loss resulting from any damage to the real or personal property of another person. *Insurance Act*, R.S.N.B. 1973, c. I-12, s. 1.

DAMAGE CAUSED BY AN AUTOMOBILE. Any damage caused by an automobile, by the use thereof or by the load carried in or on an automobile, including damage caused by a trailer used with an automobile, but excluding damage caused by the autonomous act of an animal that is part of the load and injury or damage caused to a person or property by reason of an action performed by that person in connection with the maintenance, repair, alteration or improvement of an automobile. *Automobile Insurance Act*, R.S.Q., c. A-25, s. 1.

DAMAGE FAISANT. Doing damage.

DAMAGE FEASANT. Doing damage.

DAMAGES. *n.* 1. " . . . [A] monetary payment awarded for the invasion of a right at common law." *Canson Enterprises Ltd. v. Boughton Co.* (1991), 9 C.C.L.T. (2d) 1 at 23, [1991] 1 W.W.R. 245, 61 B.C.L.R. (2d) 1, 85 D.L.R. (4th) 129, 131 N.R. 321, 43 E.T.R. 201, 39 C.P.R. (3d) 449, [1991] 3 S.C.R. 534, 6 B.C.A.C. 1, 3 W.A.C. 1, La Forest J. (Sopinka, Gonthier and Cory JJ. concurring). 2. In an action in contract there is a distinction between debt and damages. In an action on a debt the plaintiff claims money that is owed as money. The law of damages is concerned with the assessment of money compensation for legal wrongs—the translation, so to speak, of a legal wrong into a money sum. *Lafrentz v. M & L Leasing Ltd. Partnership* (2000), 2000 CarswellAlta 1121, 2000 ABQB

714, 8 B.L.R. (3d) 219, [2001] 1 W.W.R. 629, 85 Alta. L.R. (3d) 233, 275 A.R. 334 (Q.B.), Perras J. See AGGRAVATED ~; COMPENSATORY ~; CONSEQUENTIAL ~; CONTEMPTUOUS ~; DAMAGE; DERISORY ~; DISTURBANCE ~; EXEMPLARY ~; FUTURE ~; GENERAL ~; LIQUIDATED ~; MEASURE OF ~; MITIGATION OF ~; NOMINAL ~; PUNITIVE ~; SPECIAL ~; UNLIQUIDATED ~; VINDICTIVE ~.

DAMAGES AT LARGE. "Damages other than for material loss . . . These have been variously defined but appear generally to mean general damages consisting of non-economic loss and exemplary damages in appropriate cases. . . Because they include compensation for loss of reputation, damages at large probably encompasses economic loss that can be foreseen but not readily quantified." *Farrell v. Canadian Broadcasting Corp.* (1987), (*sub nom. Farrell v. Canadian Broadcasting Corp. (No. 1)*) 43 D.L.R. (4th) 667 at 667, 669, 66 Nfld. & P.E.I.R. 145, 204 A.P.R. 145 (Nfld. C.A.), Goodridge C.J.N.

DAMAGES OCCASIONED BY A MOTOR VEHICLE. Section 88(1) of the *Highway Traffic Act* [S.S. 1986, c. H-3.1] bars the bringing of an action for any "damages occasioned by a motor vehicle" after 12 months of the occurrence of the damages. The words, "damages occasioned by a motor vehicle", constitute the standard phraseology used in the limitation periods provided by the various provincial Highway Traffic Acts. The true intent of the statute is that "damages occasioned by a motor vehicle" requires that the presence of a motor vehicle be the dominant feature, or constitute the true nature, of the claim. Conversely, claims, whether framed in contract or in tort, where the presence of a motor vehicle is a fact ancillary to the essence of the action, ought not be regarded as within the scope of that phrase. In my view, it is time for this Court to depart from the sharp distinction that has, in the opinion of some courts, been created by the effect of *Heppel* and *Bruell* between cases framed in contract and cases framed in tort. The legislation aims to have a reasonably wide effect and does not distinguish between these divergent forms of action. It says, simply, "[*n]o action* may be brought against a person for the recovery of damages occasioned by a motor vehicle" (emphasis added) after the expiry of the limitation period. At the same time, I would depart from the view expressed most forcefully in Heppel that, "[i]f a motor vehicle is the occasion for the damage, *i.e.*, if it is the vehicle which brings it about, then the limitation period applies" (p. 710). In so far as this has been taken to be the core of the Heppel decision, that the presence of a motor vehicle in the chain of causation leading to damages for which the action is brought is sufficient to invoke the limitation, I think it must be said that Heppel should no longer be considered the law. In other words, the true intent of the statute is that "damages occasioned by a motor vehicle" requires that the presence of a motor vehicle be the dominant feature, or constitute the true nature, of the claim. Conversely, claims, whether framed in contract or in tort, where the presence of a motor vehicle is a fact ancillary to the essence of the action, ought not be regarded as within the scope of that phrase. *Heredi v. Fensom*, [2002] 2 S.C.R. 741.

DAMKEEPER. *n*. A person actually on duty in charge of a dam. *Canal Regulations*, C.R.C., c. 1564, s. 2.

DAMNA. *n*. [L.] Damages.

DAMNIFICATION. *n*. Whatever causes loss or damage.

DAMNIFY. *v*. To injure; to cause personal loss.

DAMNUM. *n*. [L.] 1. Damage. 2. Harm. 3. Loss.

DAMNUM ABSQUE INJURIA. [L.] Loss without an injury.

DAMNUM SENTIRE NON VIDETUR QUI SIBI DAMNUM DEDIT. [L.] A person is seen not to have suffered damage where that person caused it.

DAMNUM SENTIT DOMINUS. [L.] The owner suffers the damage.

DAMNUM SINE INJURIS ESSE POTEST. [L.] There may be damage inflicted without any thing being done which the law considers an injury.

DAMP GRAIN. Any grain within the meaning of this Act that has a moisture content that classifies it as damp grain in the Canada Grain Regulations made pursuant to the Canada Grain Act. *Prairie Grain Advance Payment Act*, R.S.C. 1985, c. P-18, s. 9(5).

DAMP LOCATION. A location which is normally or periodically subject to condensation of moisture.

DANCE HALL. Any hall, pavilion, place, premises, room, tent or structure of any kind kept or used for public dancing, and includes a cafe, hotel or restaurant where facilities are supplied and used for public dancing.

DANGER. *n*. 1. Any existing or potential hazard or condition or any current or future activity that could reasonably be expected to cause injury or illness to a person exposed to it before the hazard or condition can be corrected, or the activity altered, whether or not the injury or illness occurs immediately after the exposure to the hazard, condition or activity, and includes any exposure to a hazardous substance that is likely to result in a chronic illness, in disease or in damage to the reproductive system. *Canada Labour Code*, R.S.C. 1985, c. L-2, s. 122(1), 2. A present risk. See CONCEALED ~; UNUSUAL ~.

DANGER OF POLLUTION. Any accumulation of material at a particular location, any artificial disturbance of land any material storage or disposal facility, any transfer operation, any transport facility, any pipeline, tank, drum, excavation, depression, pond or impoundment situated in or on the ground or in buildings, whether natural or artificial and whether lined or unlined, for either storage or transport, as the case may be, of useful or waste materials that could through use or misuse, seepage, leaching, accidents, leaks, breaks, negligence, acts of animals or persons or acts of God release contaminants or indirectly into or upon the waters of the Province and any application or disposal of materials or chemicals into or upon the environment unless such material or chemical is a pesticide controlled by or under the Pesticides Control Act. *Clean Environment* Act, R.S.N.B. 1973, c. C-6, s. 1.

DANGEROUS. *adj*. " . . . [L]ikely or probable to cause injury. . ." *Burns v. R.* (1945),19 M.P.R. 178 at 185 (P.E.I. C.A.), Campbell C.J. See GOODS OF A ~ NATURE.

DANGEROUS ANIMAL. Refers to a dangerous individual of the class of animals considered to be animals mansuetae and to all animals ferae.

DANGEROUS ARTICLE. Includes inflammable or corrosive liquids and liquified petroleum gas. *Motor Vehicle Act*, R.S.B.C. 1996, c. 318, s. 1.

DANGEROUS CIRCUMSTANCES. A situation in which, (a) a provision of this Act or the regulations is being contravened; (b) the contravention poses a danger or a hazard to a worker; and (c) the danger or hazard is such that any delay in controlling it may seriously endanger a worker. *Occupational Health and Safety Act*, R.S.O. 1990, c. 0.1, s. 44(1).

DANGEROUS COMMODITY. Any substance subject to the Regulations for the Transportation of Dangerous Commodities by Rail or subject to any other regulation or order issued by the Commission to control its hazard. Canada regulations.

DANGEROUS DISEASE. Any disease, other than a disease included in the schedule, the introduction of which into Canada would, in the opinion of the quarantine officer concerned, constitute a grave danger to public health in Canada. *Quarantine Act*, R.S.C. 1985, c. Q-1, s. 2.

DANGEROUS DRIVING. See DANGEROUS OPERATION OF MOTOR VEHICLES.

DANGEROUS GOODS. 1. Any product, substance or organism included by its nature or by the regulations in any of the classes listed in the schedule. *Transportation of Dangerous Goods acts*. 2. Goods that by reason of their nature, quantity or mode of stowage are either singly or collectively liable to endanger the lives of the passengers or imperil the ship, and includes all substances determined by the Governor in Council, in regulations made by him, to be dangerous goods. *Canada Shipping Act*, R.S.C. 1985 c. S-9, s. 2.

DANGEROUS OPERATION OF AIRCRAFT. Operating an aircraft in a manner that is dangerous to the public, having regard to all the circumstances, including the nature and condition of that aircraft or the place or air space in or through which the aircraft is operated. *Criminal Code*, R.S.C. 1985, c. C-46, s. 249(1)(c).

DANGEROUS OPERATION OF MOTOR VEHICLES. Operating a motor vehicle in a manner that is dangerous to the public, having regard to all the circumstances, including the nature, condition and use of the place at which the motor vehicle is being operated and the amount of traffic that at the time is or might reasonably be expected to be at that place. *Criminal Code*, R.S.C. 1985, c. C-46, s. 249(1)(a).

DANGEROUS OPERATION OF RAILWAY EQUIPMENT. Operating railway equipment in a manner that is dangerous to the public, having regard to all the circumstances, including the nature and condition of the equipment or the place in or through which the equipment is operated. *Criminal Code*, R.S.C. 1985, c. C-46, s. 249(1)(d).

DANGEROUS OPERATION OF VESSELS. Operating a vessel or any water skis, surf board, water sled or other towed object on or over any of the internal waters of Canada or the territorial sea of Canada, in a manner that is dangerous to the public, having regard to all the circumstances, including the nature and condition of such waters or sea and the use that at the time is or might reasonably be expected to be made of such waters or sea. *Criminal Code*, R.S.C. 1985, c. C-46, s. 249(1)(b).

DANGEROUS SEXUAL OFFENDER. A person who, by his conduct in any sexual matter, has shown a failure to control his sexual impulses, and who is likely to cause injury, pain or other evil to any person, through failure in the future to control his sexual impulses. *Criminal Code*, R.S.C. 1970, c. C-34, s. 687.

DANGEROUS SUBSTANCE. Any substance that, because of a property it possesses, is dangerous to the safety or health of any person who is exposed to it.

DANGER TO THE SECURITY OF CANADA. A person constitutes a "danger to the security of Canada" [within the meaning of s. 53(1)(b) of the *Immigration Act*, R.S.C. 1985, c. I-2] if he or she poses a serious threat to the security of Canada, whether direct or indirect ... The threat must be "serious," in the sense that it must be grounded on objectively reasonable suspicion based on evidence and in the sense that the threatened harm must be substantial rather than negligible. *Suresh v. Canada (Minister of Citizenship & Immigration)*, [2002] 1 S.C.R. 3.

DANGER ZONE. An area or space upon a highway which is so marked or indicated under the provisions of this Act by the proper signs plainly visible. *Motor vehicle acts*.

DANS LOCUM CONTRACTUI. [L.] Which gives rise to the contract.

DARE. *v*. [L.] To hand over property.

DARE AD REMANENTIAM. [L.] To give away for ever or in fee.

DARKNESS. *n*. The period from 1/2 hour after sunset to 1/2 hour before sunrise and any other occasion when there is not sufficient light to render clearly discernible a substantial object on the highway at a distance of 60 m. *Motor Vehicle acts*.

DARRAIGN. *v*. 1. To answer an accusation; to settle a controversy. 2. Of a legal account, to clear.

DARREIN. *n*. [Fr.] The last.

DATA. *n*. 1. Facts. 2. Representations of information or of concepts that are being prepared or have been prepared in a form suitable for use in a computer system. *Criminal Code*, R.S.C. 1985, c. C-46, s. 342.1(2).

DATA BANK. A body of information concerning a group of people or a particular topic stored in electronic form.

DATA PROCESSING. A process whereby a computer is used to manipulate information, including the functions of storing, retrieving, sorting, merging, calculating and transforming data according to programmed instructions and those activities required to support this process.

DATA PROCESSING SERVICES. All activities, procedures and methods relating to or facilitating the storing, retrieving, sorting, merging, calculating and transforming of information and data whether manually or with the assistance or by means of the use of machines.

DATE. *n*. 1. " . . . [T]ime 'given' or specified, time in some way ascertained and fixed; . . ." *Bement v. Trenton Locomotive Co.* (1866), 32 N.J.L. 513 at 515-6. 2. The year and the day of the month. See AFTER ~; ANNIVERSARY ~; COMPLETION ~; CONTRACT ~; DECLARATION ~; DUE ~; DURABLE LIFE ~; EFFECTIVE ~; ENUMERATION ~; EXPIRATION~; FIXED ~; INITIAL APPEARANCE~; LAPSE ~; MATURITY ~; PROCLAMATION ~; REDEMPTION VALUATION ~.

DATE OF COMPLETION. The date on which a building or project is certified as substantially complete.

DATE OF CONVICTION. The day on which a conviction for an offence was first entered by a court.

DATE OF DELIVERY. The date when the pregnancy of a woman terminates with the birth of a child or the pregnancy otherwise terminates.

DATE OF DEPOSIT. With respect to any moneys constituting a deposit, the day on which credit for the moneys is given to the account of the depositor or the day on which an instrument is issued for such moneys by the member institution, as the case may be. *Canada Deposit In-surance Corporation Act*, R.S.C. 1985, c. C-3, Sched., s. 1.

DATE OF LEAVING. The day on which a patient leaves.

DATE OF LOADING. The date the product was cleared for export by the host government at the port of loading. Canada regulations.

DATE OF MANUFACTURE. (a) In the case of a product for which a standard of potency exists, the date it satisfactorily passes a potency test, (b) in the case of an animal product for which no standard of potency exists, the date of its removal from the animal, and (c) in the case of a product other than an animal product for which no standard of potency exists, the date of cessation of growth. *Food and Drug Regulations*, C.R.C., c. 870, c. C.04.001.

DATE OF MATURITY. The date, excluding days of grace, on which the debt will be fully paid if every payment is made according to the original terms of the security agreement.

DATE OF POSSESSION. 1. The day upon which the expropriating authority became entitled to take physical possession or make use of the land to which a notice of confirmation relates. 2. The date on which the home is completed for possession by an owner.

DATE OF RETIREMENT. See NORMAL ~.

DATE OF THE OFFER. The day on which an offer was accepted. *Expropriation acts*.

DATE OF THE ORDER. The date the order is made, even if the order is not entered or enforceable on that date, or the order is varied on appeal, and in the case of an order directing a reference the date the report on the reference is confirmed. *Courts of Justice Act*, R.S.O. 1990, c. C.43, s. 127(1).

DATIF. *n*. That which may be disposed of or given at pleasure or will; officially appointed.

DATIVE. *n*. That which may be disposed of or given at pleasure or will; officially appointed.

DATUM. *n*. [L. a thing given] The primary principle.

DAUGHTER. See SON AND ~.

DAUHVAL. *n*. Any unclaimed dead whale found free floating.

DAY. *n*. 1. 86 400 seconds. *Weights and Measures Act*, S.C. 1970-71-72, c. 36, schedule 1. 2. A calendar day. 3. " . . . [C]ommences at midnight and ends the following midnight: . . ." *Thornbury (Town) v. Grey (County)* (1893), 15 P.R. 192 at 194 (Ont. C.A.), the court per Armour C.J. 4. The period between 6 o'clock in the forenoon and 9 o'clock in the afternoon of the same day. *Criminal Code*, R.S.C. 1985, c. C-46, s. 2. 5. Any period of 24 consecutive hours. 6. A clear day and a period of days shall be deemed to commence on the day following the event which began the period and shall be deemed to terminate on midnight of the last day of the period except that if the last day of the period falls on Saturday, Sunday or a holiday the period shall terminate on midnight of the day next following that is a business day. *Securities acts*. 7. The period beginning one half-hour before sunrise and ending one half-hour after sunset and, in respect of any place where the sun does not rise or set daily, the period during which the centre of the sun's disc is less than six degrees below the horizon. *Canadian Aviation Regulations* SOR 96-433, s. 101.01. See APPOINTED ~; BUSINESS ~; CHRISTMAS ~; CLEAR ~S; CONSECUTIVE ~S; COSTS OF THE ~; ELECTION ~; FERIAL ~; FRACTION OF A ~; GALE~; HOURS OF THE ~; INSTRUCTIONAL ~; JURIDICAL ~; LAY ~; LORD'S ~; MAN~; NOMINATION ~; NON-BUSINESS ~S; NON-INSTRUCTIONAL ~; ONE ~; ORDER OF THE ~; PATIENT~; PAY ~; POLLING ~; PRODUCTION ~; REMEMBRANCE ~; RESERVABLE ~; SITTING ~ OF PARLIAMENT; SIR JOHN A. MACDONALD ~; SIR WILFRID LAURIER ~; SPECIFIED ~; TEACHING VALUATION ~; VIMY RIDGE ~; WITHOUT ~; WORK ~; WORKING ~.

DAY-BOOK. *n*. A journal in which the transactions of the day are recorded.

DAY CAMP. A camp or resort that admits persons for temporary custody for a continuous period not exceeding twenty-four hours. *Public Pools Act*, R.R.O. 1990, Reg. 565, s. 1.

DAY CARE. A service that provides daytime care of or services to children outside their own homes by an authorized person, with or without charge. See HOME ~; PRIVATE-HOME ~; SCHOOL ~.

DAY CARE AGENCY. See HOME ~; PRIVATE-HOME ~.

DAY CARE CENTRE. *var.* **DAY CARE CENTER**. Any place in which day care services are offered.

DAY CARE HOME. Premises in which day care either alone or in combination with parental care provided or offered at any time and which is the home of the person providing the daycare. *Community Day Care Standards Act*, R.S.M. 1987, c. C158, s. 1.

DAY LABOURER. An unskilled worker hired by the day.

DAYLIGHT. *n.* 1. One-half hour before sunrise to one-half hour after sunset on the same day. 2. In respect of any place in Canada, the period of time in any day when the centre of the sun's disc is less that 6° below the horizon and in any place where the sun rises and sets daily, may be considered to be the period of time commencing 1/2 hour before sunrise and ending 1/2 hour after sunset.

DAYLIGHT SAVING TIME. The time one hour in advance of (later than) Standard Time.

DAY NURSERY. A building, part of a building or other place, whether known as a day nursery, nursery school, kindergarten, play school or by any other name, which for compensation or otherwise receives, for temporary care or custody or guidance on a daily or hourly basis, children.

DAY OF NOMINATION. The day upon which nominations for an election close.

DAY OF POLLING. The day fixed for holding the poll at an election.

DAY OF REST. See PRESCRIBED ~; WEEKLY ~.

DAY PAROLE. 1. The authority granted to an offender by the Board or a provincial parole board to be at large during the offender's sentence in order to prepare the offender for full parole or statutory release, the conditions of which require the offender to return to a penitentiary, a community-based residential facility or a provincial correctional facility each night, unless otherwise authorized in writing. *Corrections and Conditional Release Act*, S.C. 1992, c. 20, s. 99. 2. Parole the terms and conditions of which require the inmate to whom it is granted to return to prison or correctional centre from time to time during the duration of the parole or to return to prison or correctional centre after a specified period. *Parole acts*.

DAY-PATIENT. *n.* A patient in an in-patient facility who is given sustenance and other services provided to in-patients except that he does not occupy a bed in the facility overnight.

DAY SHIP. A ship on which the crew is not required to sleep on board.

DAYS OF GRACE. Time allowed to make a payment or do some other act when the time originally allowed has expired.

DAYS STAY. The number of days during which a patient is hospitalized.

DAY'S TREATMENT. Necessary medical or surgical treatment in a hospital of a patient for a complete period of 24 hours commencing and ending at midnight, but the hours of necessary treatment in a hospital of a patient during the day of the person's admission and the day of the person's discharge must be counted together as one day's treatment. *Hospital Act*, R.S.B.C. 1996, c. 200, s. 1.

DAY TIME. *var*. **DAYTIME**. One-half hour before sunrise to one-half hour after sunset on the same day.

DAY VFR. In respect of the flight of any aircraft in Canada, a flight conducted in accordance with VFR during the hours of daylight.

DBH. The diameter of the stem of a tree measured at a point that is four and one-half feet above ground. *Trees Act*, R.S.O. 1990, c. T.20, s. 1.

D.C.A. *abbr*. Dorion, Décisions de la Cour d'Appel (Queen's Bench Reports).

D.D.C.P. *abbr*. Décisions disciplinaires concernant les Corporations professionnelles.

DE. *prep*. [L.] Of; from; concerning.

DEACTIVATED FIREARM. A device that, (a) was designed or adapted to discharge, (i) a shot, bullet or other projectile at a muzzle velocity exceeding 152.4 metres per second, or (ii) a shot, bullet or other projectile that is designed or adapted to attain a velocity exceeding 152.4 metres per second, and (b) has been permanently altered so that it is no longer capable of discharging any shot, bullet or other projectile. *Imitation Firearms Regulation Act, 2000*, S.O. 2000, c. 37, s. 1.

DEAD. *adj*. When applied to electrical equipment means that the current-carrying electrical equipment is free from any electrical connection to a source of potential difference and from electrical charge or has not a potential different from that of earth.

DEAD ANIMAL. The carcass, or any part thereof, of a horse, goat, sheep, swine or head of cattle that has died from any cause other than slaughter.

DEAD BODY. A corpse.

DEAD END. A pipe that terminates with a closed fitting. *Building Code Act* O. Reg. 403/97, s. 1.1.3.2(1).

DEAD FREIGHT. " . . . [A] sum agreed to be paid in respect of space not filled according to charter-party or damages provided for by the charter-party, in the event of the freighter not having a full cargo. . .' " *Lord v. Davidson* (1886), 13 S.C.R. 166 at 169 Ritchie C.J.C.

DEADHEAD. *v*. To transport railway equipment or employees, not in service, from one terminal to another.

DEAD HEAT. The official result of a race in which more than one horse finishes in first, second, third or fourth place, as the case may be. *Pari-Mutuel Betting Supervision Regulations*, SOR/91-365, s. 2.

DEAD LOAD. The weight of all permanent structural and nonstructural components of a building. *Building Code Act* O. Reg. 403/97, s. 1.1.3.2(1).

DEAD PLEDGE. A mortgage.

DEAD RENT. A fixed rent payable whether a mine is productive or not.

DEAD SHIP. A ship normally self-propelled that is without the use of its propelling power, but does not include a ship warped from one berth to another solely by means of mooring lines attached to a wharf, to the shore or to a mooring buoy. Canada regulations.

DEAD TIME. 1. Time lost by an employee because of equipment breakdown, lack of materials or other causes beyond the employee's control. 2. "[Time spent in prison which] . . . does not attract any benefit by way of remission for a prisoner. . . " *R. v. Ko* (1979), 11 C.R. (3d) 298 at 309, [1978] 1 W.W.R. 577, 50 C.C.C. (2d) 430 (B.C. C.A.), the court per Aikins J.A.

DEAD USE. Future use.

DEADWEIGHT. *n*. The difference in tonnes between the weight of water of a specific gravity of 1.025 displaced by a ship loaded to the load water line corresponding to the assigned summer freeboard and the weight of such water displaced by the ship without cargo, fuel, lubricating oil, ballast water, fresh water or feedwater in tanks, consumable stores, passengers, crew and their effects. *Fire Detection and Extinguishing Equipment Regulations*, C.R.C., c. 1422, s. 2.

DEADYARD. See ANIMAL ~.

DEAF PERSON. A person whose hearing is impaired to a degree that the person would benefit from a hearing dog and who is certified as a deaf person or the purposes of this Act by the authority nominated for the purpose by the regulations. *Blind Persons' Rights Act*, R.S.A. 2000, c. 7 B-3, s. 1(a.1).

DEALER. *n*. 1. " . . . [O]ne who trades in, buys or sells goods on his own account. It does not necessarily follow he must be the owner of the goods he sells; he may be a broker . . . so long as he is in the business for himself . . ." *Harmon v. Russell* (1927), 21 Sask. L.R. 686 at 699, [1927] 2 W.W.R. 505, [1927] 3 D.L.R. 626 (C.A.), Mackenzie J.A. 2. Person whose business is to buy items and sell them to other persons. 3. A person who trades in securities as principal or agent. *Securities acts*. See AUTO-MOBILE ~; BONA FIDE ~; BROKER-~; CANADIAN SECURITIES ~; COMMODITY CONTRACTS ~; FIRST ~; FISH ~; FUR ~; GRAIN ~; HEARING AID ~; INDEPENDENT INVESTMENT ~; LICENSED ~; LIVE-STOCK ~; MILK ~; MOBILE HOME ~; MONEY MARKET ~S; MORTGAGE ~; MOTOR ~; MOTOR VEHICLE ~; NON-RESIDENT CONTROLLED ~; OIL AND GAS ~; PURPOSES RELATING TO THE BUSINESS OF A ~; QUALIFIED ~; RETAIL ~; SALVAGE ~; SECOND-HAND ~; SEED ~; SUB-BROKER ~; WHOLE-SALE ~.

DEALER-SHIPPER. *n*. Any person who sells or offers to sell, buys, receives, assembles, packs, ships or transports fresh fruit or grapes but does not include (a) a servant employed by and driving a vehicle owned by a producer, shipper or dealer-shipper, (b) a railway company, or (c) a person who transports fresh fruit or grapes by motor vehicle as the agent of the producer. Canada regulations.

DEALER'S PLATE. A plate issued to a dealer to be attached by the plate to a vehicle that is used for demonstration purposes with a view to the sale of the vehicle. *Highway Traffic Act*, R.S. Nfld. 1990, c. H-3, s. 2.

DEALING. See EXCLUSIVE ~.

DEALING IN OR WITH. Includes buying, selling, owning, leasing, hiring, lending, bor-

rowing, exchanging, acquiring, importing, storing, supplying, chartering, operating, delivering, transporting, distributing, dispensing, shipping, conveying, installing or using. *Transport Control Regulations*, C.R.C., c. 1566, s. 2.

DE AMBITU. [L.] Concerning bribery.

DEATH. *n*. 1. The loss of signs of life such as movement, growth, reproduction and metabolism. F.A. Jaffe, *A Guide to Pathological Evidence*, 3d ed. (Toronto: Carswell, 1991) at 3. 2. " . . . [V]ital functions have ceased to operate. . . *R. v. Kitching* (1976), 32 C.C.C. (2d) 159 at 172, [1976] 6 W.W.R. 697 (Man. C.A.), O'Sullivan J.A. 3. The permanent end of all vital functions. F.A. Jaffe, *A Guide to Pathological Evidence*, 3d ed. (Toronto: Carswell, 1991) at 216. 4. The death of a natural person and includes a stillbirth as defined in the Vital Statistics Act. *Coroners Act*, S.N.W.T. 1985 (3d Sess.), c. 2, s. 2. 5. Includes death presumed for official purposes. *Pensioners Act*, R.S.C. 1985, c. P-6, s. 2. See CAUSE OF ~; CELLULAR ~; COT ~; CRIB ~; MANNER OF ~; NEONATAL ~; PROPERTY PASSING ON THE ~; REPORT-ABLE ~; SOMATIC ~; SUDDEN IN-FANT ~ SYNDROME.

DEATH BENEFIT. The amount received by a survivor or the deceased's estate upon or after the death of an employee in recognition of the employee's service in office or employment.

DEATHSMAN. *n*. Hangman; executioner.

DE AUDITU. [L.] Hearsay.

DEBATES. See OFFICIAL REPORT OF ~.

DEBASEMENT. *n*. A reduction of standard of fineness of coinage.

DE BENE ESSE. [L.] 1. To consider something well done for the moment, but when it is examined or tried more fully, it must stand or fall on its own merit. 2. "To do a thing de bene esse signifies allowing or accepting certain evidence for the present until more fully examined, valeat quantum valere otest. It is regarded as an additional examination to be utilized if necessary only in the event that witnesses cannot be examined later in the action in the regular way. This evidence therefore was taken 'for what it was worth.' . . . *C.T. Gogstad & Co. v. "Camosun" (The)* (1941), 56 B.C.R. 156 at 157 (Ex. Ct.), MacDonald D.J.A.

DEBENTURE. *n*. 1. Any corporate obligation unsecured or secured by a floating charge. 2. "

. . . [A] document in which a debt is acknowledged and in which the debtor covenants to repay . . ." *Acmetrack Ltd. v. Bank Canadian National* (1984), 4 P.P.S.A.C. 199 at 206, 48 O.R. (2d) 49, 27 B.L.R. 319, 52 C.B.R. (N.S.) 235, 12 D.L.R. (4th) 428, 5 O.A.C. 321 (C.A.), the court per Zuber J.A. 3. Includes debenture stock, bonds and any other securities of a company constituting a charge on the assets of the company. 4. " . . . [I]n municipal financing [a debenture] is, ordinarily : . . a promise under seal to pay the bearer a principal sum and interest at certain times, and is an instrument transferable on the markets by delivery." *Toronto (City) v. Canada Permanent Mortgage Corp.*, [1954] S.C.R. 576 at 582, [1954] 4 D.L.R. 529, Rand J. See BANK ~S; COUPON ~; MORTGAGE ~.

DEBENTURE STOCK. A fund or stock which represents money borrowed by a company or public body charged on its property. The title of each original holder is entered in a register.

DEBENTURE TRUST DEED. A deed which vests a security in trustees in order to give greater security to the debenture holders.

DEBET ET DETINET. [L.] One owes and detains.

DEBET ET SOLET. [L.] One owes and is accustomed.

DEBILE FUNDAMENTUM FALLIT OPUS. [L.] A weak foundation destroys the work.

DEBIT. *n*. A sum due or owing.

DEBITA SEQUUNTUR PERSONAM DEBITORIS. [L.] Debts follow the debtor's person.

DEBIT NOTE. A note which states that the account of the person to whom it is sent will be debited.

DEBITOR. *n*. A debtor; the person against whom another has a personal right.

DEBITOR NON PRAESUMITUR DONARE. [L.] It is not presumed a debtor will give.

DEBITORUM PACTIONIBUS CREDITORUM PETITIO NEC TOLLI NEC MINUI POTEST. [L.] Creditors' rights can neither be removed nor diminished by agreements among the debtors.

DEBITUM CONNEXIUM. [L.] A debt which gives rise to a lien.

DEBITUM ET CONTRACTUS SUNT NULLIUS LOCI. [L.] Debt and contract have no place.

DEBITUM IN PRAESENTI, SOLVENDUM IN FUTURO. [L.] Owed currently though payable in the future.

DEBITUM RECUPERATUM. [L.] A recovered debt.

DE BONIS ASPORTATIS. [L.] For goods taken away. See TRESPASS ~.

DE BONIS NON. *abbr*. [L.] De bonis non administratis.

DE BONIS NON ADMINISTRATIS. [L.] A grant made when an administrator dies without having fully administered an estate or an executor dies intestate.

DE BONIS PROPRIIS. [L.] Of a person's own goods.

DE BONIS TESTATORIS. [L.] Of a testator's goods.

DEBRIS. *n*. Waste material.

DEBT. *n*. 1. " . . . [I]ncludes any claim, legal or equitable, on contract, express or implied, or under a statute on which a certain sum of money, not being unliquidated damages, is due and payable, though an enquiry be necessary to ascertain the exact amount due." *Boldrick v. Salz*, [1952] O.W.N. 487 at 488 (C.A.), Hope J.A. 2. " . . . [A] sum payable in respect of a liquidated money demand recoverable by action. .." *Walsh v. British Columbia Minister of Finance)* (1979), 5 E.T.R. 179 at 191, [1979] 4 W.W.R. 161, [1979] C.T.C. 251, 13 B.C.L.R. 255 (S.C.), Anderson J. 3. The term 'debt' is a narrower term [narrower than liability] and means a specific kind of obligation for a liquidated or certain sum incurred pursuant to an agreement. The term 'loan' is even narrower and means a specific type of debt. *Royal Trust Co. v. H.A. Roberts Group Ltd.*, 1995 CarswellSask 7, 31 C.B.R. (3d) 207, [1995] 4 W.W.R. 305, 17 B.L.R. (2d) 263, 44 R.P.R. (2d) 255, 129 Sask. R. 161 (Q.B.), Baynton J. 4. In an action in contract there is a distinction between debt and damages. In an action on a debt the plaintiff claims money that is owed as money. The law of damages is concerned with the assessment of money compensation for legal wrongs—the translation, so to speak, of a legal wrong into a money sum. *Lafrentz v. M & L Leasing Ltd. Partnership* (2000), 2000 CarswellAlta 1121, 2000 ABQB 714, 8 B.L.R.

(3d) 219, [2001] 1 W.W.R. 629, 85 Alta. L.R. (3d) 233, 275 A.R. 334 (Q.B.), Perras J. See ACCRUING~; ACTIVE ~; ATTACHMENT OF ~S; BAD ~; BOOK ~S; CONDITIONAL ~; CONSUMER ~; CROWN ~; FAMILY ~; FOREIGN ~; FUNDED ~; INSURANCE OF ~S; JUDGMENT ~; LONG-TERM ~; MARITAL ~S; MUTUAL ~S; NATIONAL ~; PAST ~; PUBLIC ~; SPECIALTY ~; TERRITORIAL ~.

DEBT CHARGE. The amount of money necessary annually, (a) to pay the principal due on long-term debt not payable from a sinking fund, (b) to provide a fund for the redemption of debentures payable from a sinking fund, and (c) to pay the interest due on all debt referred to in clauses a and b.

DEBT CHARGES. The annual debt charges on debentures issued or other borrowings. See ANNUAL~.

DEBTEE. *n.* A creditor.

DEBT OBLIGATION. A mortgage, bond, debenture, note, loan, evidence of indebtedness, guarantee or other similar obligation of a corporation, whether secured or unsecured.

DEBTOR. *n.* 1. One who owes a debt. 2. A person to whom or on whose account money lent is advanced and includes every surety and endorser or other person liable for the repayment of money lent or upon agreement or collateral or other security given in respect thereof. *Unconscionable Transactions Relief acts*. 3. An insolvent person and any person who, at the time an act of bankruptcy was committed by him resided or carried on business in Canada and where the context requires, includes a bankrupt. *Bankruptcy Act*, R.S.C. 1985, c. B-3, s. 2. 4. (i) In relation to a writ of execution, any person liable for the payment of any money under a writ of execution, and (ii) in relation to a distress, the person who is liable for the payment of any money or the delivery up of any goods or chattels, which payment or delivery up is enforceable by distress or by proceedings in the nature of distress. See ABSCONDING ~; ACCOUNT ~; JUDGMENT ~; LOCALITY OF ~; MAINTENANCE ~; PRINCIPAL ~; TAX ~.

DEBTOR COMPANY. Any company that (a) is bankrupt or insolvent, (b) has committed an act of bankruptcy within the meaning of the Bankruptcy and Insolvency Act or is deemed insolvent within the meaning of the Winding-up

and Restructuring Act, whether or not proceedings in respect of the company have been taken under either of those Acts, (c) has made an authorized assignment or against which a receiving order has been made under the Bankruptcy and Insolvency Act, or (d) is in the course of being wound up under the Winding -up and Restructuring Act because the company is insolvent. *Companies' Creditors Arrangement Act*, R.S.C. 1985, c. C-36, s. 2.

DEBT POOLING SYSTEM. An arrangement or procedure whereby a debtor pays to one person money to be distributed or paid, according to a system, by that person to more than 2 creditors of the debtor. *Debt Collection Act*, R.S.B.C. 1996, c. 92, s. 1.

DEBT SECURITY. Any bond, debenture, note or similar instrument representing indebtedness, whether secured or unsecured.

DEBT SERVICE. See GROSS ~ RATIO.

DECA. *pref.* 10^1. Prefix for multiples and submultiples of basic, supplementary and derived units of measurement. *Weights and Measures Act*, S.C. 1970-71-72, c. 36, schedule 1.

DE CAETERO. [L.] From now on.

DEC. B.-C. *abbr.* Décisions des Tribunaux du Bas-Canada (1851-1867).

DECEASED. *n.* 1. A dead person. 2. A testator or a person dying intestate. *Dependants Relief acts*. 3. Includes any deceased person whether or not any tax is payable under this Act in respect of the death of that person. *Estate Tax acts*. See PROPERTY OF THE ~.

DECEASED INMATE. See ESTATE OF A ~.

DECEASED PERSON. The body of a deceased person or of a stillborn child or a foetus.

DECEIT. *n.* " . . . [A] false representation of fact by words or conduct . . . made . . . with the knowledge of its falsity; . . . [and] with the intention that it be acted upon . . . [and that it was in fact acted upon] in reliance upon the representation and that . . . damage [was sustained in so doing]." *Bell v. Source Data Control Ltd.* (1988), 40 B.L.R. 10 at 17, 29 O.A.C. 134, 66 O.R. (2d) 78, 53 D.L.R. (4th) 580 (C.A.), Cory J.A. (dissenting).

DECEIVE. *v.* To induce a person to believe that something which is false is true. See CALCULATED TO ~.

DECEPTIVE ACT OR PRACTICE. False, misleading or deceptive consumer representation. See UNFAIR OR ~S IN THE BUSINESS OF INSURANCE.

DECERTIFICATION. *n.* Removal of a union's right to represent a group of employees for collective bargaining purposes.

DECHARACTERIZE. *v.* To change the natural appearance of a meat product by mixing it with an innocuous substance. *Meat Inspection Regulations*, C.R.C., c. 1032, s. 2.

DECI. *pref.* 10^{-1}. Prefix for multiples and submultiples of basic, supplementary and derived units of measurement. *Weights and Measures Act*, S.C. 1970-71-72, c. 36, schedule 1.

DECIDUOUS TEETH. A child's first teeth. F.A. Jaffe, *A Guide to Pathological Evidence*, 3d ed. (Toronto: Carswell, 1991) at 217.

DECISION. *n.* 1. A judgment, ruling, order, finding, or determination of a court. 2. ". . . [O]f a Court or Judge means the judicial opinion, oral or written, pronounced or delivered, upon which the 'judgment or order' is founded and the 'judgment or order' is the embodiment in legal procedure of the result of such decision . . ." *Fermini v. McGuire* (1984) 42 C.P.C. 189 at 191, 64 N.S.R. (*2d*) 421, 143 A.P.R. 421 (C.A.), Macdonald J.A. 3. An order, a determination and a declaration. *Canada Labour Code*, R.S.C. 1985, c. L-2, s. 20(3). 4. A direction, decision, order, ruling or requirement made under a power or right conferred by this Act or the regulations. *Securities acts*. 5. The reasons given by the court for its judgment or other order. See STATUTORY POWER OF ~.

DECISION HEIGHT. A height specified in the *Canada Air Pilot* or the route and approach inventory at which a missed approach procedure shall be initiated during a precision approach if the required visual reference necessary to continue the approach to land has not been established. *Canadian Aviation Regulations*, SOR/96-433, s. 101.01(1).

DECK. *n.* The area immediately surrounding a pool. *Public Health Act*, R.R.O. 1980, Reg. 849, s. 1. *Public Pools Act*, R.R.O. 1990, Reg. 565, s. 1. See BULKHEAD ~; FREEBOARD ~; MAIN ~; ON ~; PEDESTRIAN ~; SHELTER ~ SPACE; STRENGTH ~; SUPERSTRUCTURE ~; UNDER ~.

DECK COVERING. See PERMANENT ~.

DECK LINE. The line indicating the uppermost complete deck of a ship as defined by the Load Line Rules. *Canada Shipping Act*, R.S.C. 1985, c. S-9, s. 2.

DECK OFFICER. See SENIOR WATCH KEEPING ~.

DECK WATCH. That part of the complement that is required for the purpose of attending to the navigation or security of a ship. Canada regulations. See PERSON IN CHARGE OF THE ~.

DECK WATCH OFFICER. A person who has the immediate charge of the navigation and safety of a ship, but does not include a pilot.

DECLARANDI LEGEM. [L.] Declaring the law.

DECLARANT. *n.* 1. One who makes a declaration. 2. The owner or owners in fee simple of the land described in the description at the time of registration of a declaration and description of the land, and includes any successor or assignee or such owner or owners but does not include a bona fide purchaser of a unit who actually pays fair market value or any successor or assignee of such purchaser. *Condominium acts*. 3. The person who originally makes a hearsay statement. *Military Rules of Evidence*, C.R.C., c. 1049, s. 2.

DECLARATION. *n.* 1. A formal statement of the opinion or decision of a court on the rights of interested parties or the construction of a will, deed or other written instrument. 2. " . . . [D]iffers from other judicial orders in that it declares what the law is without pronouncing any sanction against the defendant, but the issue which is determined by a declaration clearly becomes res judicata between the parties and the judgment a binding precedent." *LeBar v. Canada* (1988) 46 C.C.C. (3d) 103 at 108, 33 Admin. L.R. 107, 22 F.T.R. 160n, 90 N.R. 5 (C.A.), the court per MacGuigan J.A. 3. An instrument signed by the insured. (i) with respect to which an endorsement is made on the policy; or (ii) that identifies the contract or (iii) that describes the insurance or insurance fund or a part thereof, in which the applicant designates, or alters or revokes the designation of, a personal representative or a beneficiary as one to whom or for whose benefit insurance money is to be payable. *Insurance acts*. 4. A solemn declaration in the form and manner from time to time provided by the provincial evidence acts or by the *Canada Evidence Act*. See DYING ~; HOT ~; SOL-

EMN ~; STATUTORY ~; UNIVERSAL ~ OF HUMAN RIGHTS.

DECLARATION DATE. Where used in relation to a commodity futures option, means that date on which the option expires. *Commodity Contract acts.*

DECLARATION OF SYDNEY. A statement made in 1968 by the 22nd World Medical Assembly in Sydney, Australia that determination of death should be the responsibility of a physician and should be based on ordinary clinical criteria supplemented by an electroencephalograph. In a case in which a patient is considered to be a possible organ donor, two physicians should ascertain the point of death and they should have no concern with the subsequent transplant. F.A. Jaffe, *A Guide to Pathological Evidence*, 3d ed. (Toronto. Carswell, 1991) at 227.

DECLARATION OF TRUST. Creation of a trust when the trust property is already held by the intended trustee by execution of a deed declaring that the trustee holds the property in trust for the executor of the deed.

DECLARATION OF WAR. The formal announcement that one nation intends to treat another nation as an enemy.

DECLARATION POLICY. A policy of insurance which covers goods which are declared under the policy.

DECLARATORY JUDGMENT. Declaring the parties' rights or expressing the court's opinion on a question of law, without ordering that anything be done. Can be given without any provision for consequential relief.

DECLARATORY ORDER. A binding declaration of right whether or not any consequential relief is claimed or could be claimed.

DECLARATORY POWER. The power of the federal Parliament under s. 92(10)(C) of the Constitution Act, 1867 to bring a local work into federal jurisdiction by declaring that it is "for the general advantage of Canada". See WORKS FOR THE GENERAL ADVANTAGE OF CANADA.

DECLARATORY RELIEF. " . . . [A] remedy neither constrained by form nor bounded by substantive content, which avails persons sharing a legal relationship, in respect of which a real issue concerning the relative interests of each has been raised and falls to be determined." *Solosky v.*

Canada (1980), 105 D.L.R. (3d) 745 at 753, [1980] 1 S.C.R. 821, 30 N.R. 380, 50 C.C.C. (2d) 495, 16 C.R. (3d) 294, Dickson J. (Laskin C.J.C., Martland, Ritchie and Pigeon JJ. concurring).

DECLARATORY STATUTE. A declaration or formal statement of existing law.

DECLARE. *v.* To assert, proclaim, state formally.

DECOMPOSED. *adj.* Having an offensive or objectionable odour, flavour, colour or textural defect associated with spoilage. *Fish Inspection acts.*

DECOMPRESSION SICKNESS. A condition of bodily malfunction caused by a change from a higher air pressure to a lower air pressure and includes the condition commonly known as the bends.

DECONTAMINATION. See TERMINAL ~.

DE CORPORE COMITATUS. [L.] From the body of the county.

DECOY. *n.* 1. Enticement, lure. 2. An instrument, artificial bird or any equipment used to attract migratory game birds. *Migratory Birds Regulations*, C.R.C., c. 1035, s. 2(1).

DECREE. *n.* Judgment.

DECREE ABSOLUTE. 1. A final decree. 2. The final court order in a divorce action.

DECREE NISI. 1. A provisional decree which will become final or absolute unless there is reason shown not to do so. 2. A provisional court order which terminates marriage.

DECREE OF FORECLOSURE. An order which states that a mortgagor will be finally foreclosed or deprived of the equitable right to redeem, unless, within a specified time, that mortgagor does redeem.

DECRIMINALIZATION. *n.* The removal of a matter from the Criminal Code; changing the law so that an act is no longer a crime.

DE-CRYSTALLIZE. *v.* To discharge the receiver and manager shortly after appointment under a floating charge. F. Bennett, *Receiverships* (Toronto: Carswell, 1985) at 10. See CRYSTALLIZATION.

DEDICATE. *v.* To make public a private road.

DEDICATION. *n.* The express or tacit opening of a road for public use.

DE DIE IN DIEM. [L.] From day to day.

DEDI ET CONCESSI. [L.] I gave and granted.

DEDITION. *n*. Surrender; yielding up.

DE DONIS. [L.] Concerning gifts.

DEDUCT. *v*. Includes withhold. *Canada Pension Plan*, R.S.C. 1985, c. C-8, s. 2.

DEDUCTION. *n*. 1. An amount deducted, taken away. 2. An amount withheld by an employer from an employee's wages for union dues, taxes, pension, insurance. 3. An amount permitted by tax laws to be subtracted from income before computing tax. See ROYALTY ~ ACCOUNT.

DEDUCTION AT SOURCE. A withholding, made by an employer from the remuneration of an employee with respect to the employee's contribution.

DEDUCTIVE VALUE. In respect of goods, the value of the goods determined in accordance with subsection 51(2). *Customs Act*, R.S.C. 1985 (2d Supp.), c. 1, s. 45.

DEED. *n*. 1. A document signed, sealed and delivered, through which an interest, property or right passes. 2. Any instrument whereby real property is conveyed, transferred, assigned to or vested in any person. 3. Every deed or writing of whatsoever nature or kind relating to or affecting any interest in or title to land in the province, except a mortgage. See DISENTAILING ~; EXECUTION OF ~S; PREMISES OF A ~; QUIT-CLAIM ~; REGISTRAR OF ~S; REGISTRY OF ~S; SUPPLEMENTAL ~; TAX ~; TRUST ~.

DEED OF CONVEYANCE. " . . . [A] mere transfer of title, . . ." *Fraser-Reid v. Droumtskeas* (1979), 9 R.P.R. 121 at 139, [1980] 1 S.C.R. 720, 103 D.L.R. (3d) 385, Dickson J.

DEED OF COVENANT. A deed in which one party formally agrees to do certain things with another.

DEED OF GIFT. A deed which transfers property as a gift.

DEED OF GRANT. A deed which grants property.

DEED OF LOAN. A deed of hypothecary loan or of loan on pledged property. *An Act to promote long term farm credit by private institutions*, R.S.Q., c. C-75.1, s. 1.

DEED-POLL. *var*. **DEED POLL**. *n*. 1. A declaration of the act and intention of a grantor of property, so named because it was formerly polled (shaved even) at the top, whereas an indenture was indented (cut in acute angles). 2. A deed with one party only. A sheriff who sells property seized under a writ of execution conveys the property by deed-poll. See INDENTURE.

DEED TO USES. A deed purporting to grant or convey land to such uses as the grantee may appoint, regardless of the method of appointment specified in the deed, and, until appointment appointment or in default of appointment, purporting to grant or convey the land to the use of the grantee absolutely, and includes every such deed containing words of like import, but does not include a mortgage. *Registry Act*, R.S.O. 1990, c. R-20, s. 64(1).

DEEM. *v*. 1. " . . . [W]hen used in a statute . . . to bring in something which would otherwise be excluded . . ." *Hillis v. Minister of National Revenue*, [1983] 6 W.W.R. 577 at 588, 15 E.T.R. 156, [1983] C.T.C. 348, 49 N.R. 1, 83 D.T.C. 5365 (Fed. C.A.), Heald J.A. (dissenting). 2. " . . . [T]o adjudge or decide . . . to decide judicially. . ." *Hunt v. College of Physicians & Surgeons (Saskatchewan)*, [1925] 4 D.L.R. 834 at 839, [1925] 3 W.W.R. 758, 45 C.C.C. 39, 20 Sask. L.R. 305 (K.B.), MacKenzie J.

DEEMED. *adj*. " . . . [M]ay mean 'deemed conclusively or deemed until the contrary is proved'. *Gray v. Kerslake* (1957), 11 D.L.R. (2d) 225 at 239, [1958] S.C.R. 3, [1957] I.L.R. 1279, Cartwright J.

DEEMED TRUST. A trust created by statute and designed to protect some classes of creditors or to insure the recovery of certain prescribed payments.

DEEMING CLAUSE. " . . . [P]urpose of any 'deeming' clause is to impose a meaning, to cause something to be taken to be different from that which it might have been in the absence of the clause." *R. v. Sutherland* (1980), 113 D.L.R. (3d) 374 at 379, [1980] 2 S.C.R. 451, 35 N.R. 161, [1980] 5 W.W.R. 456, 53 C.C.C. (2d) 289, 7 Man. R. (2d) 359, [1980] 3 C.N.L.R. 71, the court per Dickson J.

DEEMING PROVISION. A statutory fiction; as a rule it implicitly admits that a thing is not what it is deemed to be but decrees that for some particular purpose it shall be taken as if it were that thing although it is not or there is doubt as to whether it is. Artificially imports into a word or an expression an additional meaning which it would not otherwise convey besides the normal meaning which it retains where it is used. *R. v. Verrette* (1978), 40 C.C.C. (2d) 273 at 283 (S.C.C.) per Beetz, J.

DEEPENED WELL. An oil or gas well that, after (a) being capable of producing petroleum or gas from an accumulation of petroleum or gas, or (b) being drilled for the purpose of producing petroleum or gas from an accumulation of petroleum or gas and having been abandoned, is deepened by further drilling commenced after March 31, 1985 for the purpose of producing petroleum or as from a different accumulation of petroleum or as. *Petroleum and Gas Revenue Tax Act*, R.S.C. 1985, c. P-12, s. 2.

DEEPEST SUBDIVISION LOADLINE. The water line that corresponds to the greatest draught. *Hull Construction Regulations*, C.R.C., c. 1431, s. 2.

DEEP FOUNDATION. A foundation unit that provides support for a building by transferring loads either by end-bearing to a soil or rock at considerable depth below the building, or by adhesion or friction, or both, in the soil or rock in which it is placed. *Building Code*, O. Reg. 403/97, s. 1.1.3.2(1).

DEEP PRODUCTION. See NEW ~.

DEEP SEA VOYAGE. A voyage, between extreme points called at, of not less than 500 nautical miles to seaward of (*a*) on the east coast, West Point, Anticosti Island, provided that one of the extreme points called at lies outside the Gulf of St. Lawrence and the Strait of Belle Isle; and (*b*) on the west coast, the inside passage of the coast of British Columbia and Alaska. *Marine Certification Regulations*, SOR/97-391, s. 1.

DEEP WELL DISPOSAL. The discharge of liquid waste into a geological formation by means of a well. *Deep Well Disposal Act*, R.R.O. 1990, Reg. 341, s. 1.

DEER FAMILY. 1. The family Cervidae. 2. Moose, caribou and deer. *Wildlife Act*, R.S.N.S. 1989, c. 504, s. 3(1).

DEERJACKING. *v.* Hunting deer by aiming the lights of the hunter's vehicle or other bright lights at an animal and blinding it, giving the hunter an opportunity to shoot the animal.

DE FACTO. [L.] In fact. Characterizes a state of affairs which must be accepted.

DE FACTO ARREST. May occur through the use of words that convey clearly to the accused that he or she is under arrest, in conjunction with certain conduct on the part of the arresting officers and the accused's submission to the officers' authority. A de facto arrest which is lawful cannot constitute an arbitrary detention within the meaning of the Charter. *R. v. Latimer*, [1997] 1 S.C.R. 217.

DE FACTO POSSESSION. Physical control.

DEFALCATION. *n.* 1. " . . . [D]oes not necessarily entail a dishonest or wrongful act. It is sufficient if there is a failure to meet an obligation by a fiduciary. A breach of trust arises whenever a trustee fails to carry out his obligations under the terms of the trust . . ." *Smith v. Henderson* (1992), 64 B.C.L.R. (2d) 144 at 149, 10 C.B.R. (3d) 153, 10 B.C.A.C. 249, 16 W.A.C. 249 (C.A.), the court per Legg J.A. 2. Includes any fraudulent act or omission of a public officer that occasions loss in money or property to (a) Her Majesty, or (b) persons other than Her Majesty, when such money or property was in the custody of the public officer in the course of his official duties, whether such loss is recovered or not. *Public Officers Guarantee Regulations*, C.R.C., c. 723, s. 2.

DEFAMATION. *n.* 1. Libel or slander. *Defamation acts.* 2. The law of defamation is concerned with the protection of reputation against the publication of falsehoods that are defamatory in the sense of tending to lower reputation in the estimation of reasonable persons in the community. *Grassi v. WIC Radio Ltd.*, 2000 CarswellBC 209, 49 C.C.L.T. (2d) 65, [2000] 5 W.W.R. 119 (S.C.). 3. Defamation may flow from the plain and ordinary meaning of published words or from extrinsic facts or circumstances, known to the listener or reader, which give words a defamatory meaning by way of innuendo. *Botiuk v. Toronto Free Press Publications Ltd.* (1995), 126 D.L.R. (4th) 609 (S.C.C.).

DEFAMATORY. *adj.* Tending to lower the reputation of someone in the opinion of right thinking members of society.

DEFAMATORY LIBEL. Matter published without lawful justification or excuse, that is likely to injure the reputation of any person by exposing him to hatred, contempt or ridicule, or that is designed to insult the person of or concerning whom it is published. A defamatory libel may be expressed directly or by insinuation or irony (a) in words legibly marked upon any substance, or (b) bar any object signifying a defamatory libel otherwise than by words. *Criminal Code*, R.S.C. 1985, c. C-46, s. 298.

DEFAULT. *n*. 1. The failure to pay or otherwise perform the obligation secured when due or the occurrence of any event whereupon under the terms of the security agreement the security becomes enforceable. *Personal Property Security acts*. 2. The omission of something one should do; neglect. 3. Non-attendance in court. 4. A tenant's failure to pay rent in a timely fashion is "a default". *SME Holdings Ltd. v. Cappeech Coffee Corp.* (1999), 1999 CarswellBC 1769 (S.C.). See EVENT OF ~.

DEFAULTER. *n*. One who fails, usually in paying.

DEFAULT JUDGMENT. The final judgment awarded to the plaintiff when the defendant fails to file an appearance or statement of defence.

DEFEASANCE. *n*. 1. A condition appended to an estate which defeats the estate when performed or a deed which defeats an estate. 2. A condition on an obligation which defeats it when performed.

DEFEASANCE CLAUSE. A proviso that a mortgage will become void on payment of the mortgage money. Thus, if one pays strictly according to the proviso, the estate without release or reconveyance becomes revested in the mortgagor or becomes vested in any other person entitled to it by subsequent mortgage or assignment from the mortgagor. W.B. Rayner & R.H. McLaren, *Falconbridge on Mortgages*, 4th ed. (Toronto: Canada Law Book 1977) at 366.

DEFEASIBLE. *adj*. 1. Able to be abrogated or annulled. 2. "A gift that is subject to being defeated or terminated on an event such as remarriage. . ." *Dontigny v. R.*, [1974] 1 F.C. 418 at 421, [1974] C.T.C. 532, 74 D.T.C. 6437 (C.A.), Jackett and St.-Germain JJ.A.

DEFEAT. *v*. 1. To frustrate, prevent. 2. To flee from one country to another; to give up one's relation to one country and seek asylum in another country.

DEFECT. *v*. 1. To frustrate, prevent. 2. To flee from one country to another; to give up one's relation to one country and seek asylum in another country.

DEFECT. *n*. Absence of an essential. See CONDITION ~; INHERENT ~; LATENT ~; PATENT ~; PHYSICAL ~.

DEFECT IN A DOCUMENT. Includes any error, omission or want or particularity in a document, any failure of a document to comply with the requirements of this Act, any discrepancy between the contents of a document and the evidence that is given at trial, and every defect that but for this section, might make a document invalid. *Provincial Offences Procedure Act*, S.N.B. 1987, c. P-22.1, s. 105.

DEFECT IN THE PROCEEDINGS. Includes any failure of a judge to exercise jurisdiction or to appear at the time and place to which proceedings are adjourned and every other defect of procedure that, but for this section, might deprive the judge of jurisdiction. *Provincial Offences Procedure Act*, S.N.B. 1987, c. P-22.1, s. 105.

DEFECTUM SANGUINIS. [L.] Failure of bloodline.

DEFECTUS POTESTATIS, NULLITAS NULLITATUM. [L.] A lack of power is a nullity of nullities.

DEFENCE. *n*. 1. " . . . [A] contention that the plaintiff's claim is not established. It adopts one or more of the following positions: (i) an objection on ground of jurisdiction; (ii) a denial of the plaintiff's allegations (traverse); (iii) a submission that if the plaintiff's allegations are true they disclose no cause of action (demurrer); and (iv) a submission that if the plaintiff's allegations are true there are facts which provide a legal justification for the defendant's conduct (confession and avoidance)." *Royal Bank v. Rizkalla* (1984), 50 C.P.C. 292 at 295, 59 B.C.L.R. 324 (S.C.), McLachlin J. 2. In criminal law, an assertion of innocence and denial of guilt. *R. v. Schwartz* (1988), 55 D.L.R. (4th) 1, [1989] 1 W.W.R. 289, 66 C.R. (3d) 251, 88 N.R. 90, [1988] 2 S.C.R. 443, 45 C.C.C. (3d) 97, 56 Man. R. (2d) 92. 3. In criminal law, generally a response to a criminal charge which would defeat the charge or an assertion which if accepted, would require an acquittal. *R. v. Chaulk* (1990), 1 C.R.R. (2d) 1 C.R. (4th) 1, 119 N.R. 161, [1991] 2 W.W.R. 385, 69 Man. R. (2d)161, 62 C.C.C. (3d)193, [1990] 3 S.C.R. 1303. 4. A guard; a justification; a protection. 5. Includes counter-claim. *Bills of Exchange Act*, R.S.C. 1985, c. B-4, s. 2. See CIVIL ~; DEPARTMENT OF NATIONAL ~; EXTRANEOUS ~; FULL ANSWER AND ~; INHERENT ~; MENTAL DISORDER ~; MERITORIOUS ~; SELF-INDUCED INTOXICATION ~; STATEMENT OF ~; STATUTORY AUTHORITY ~.

DEFENCE CONTRACT. (a) A contract with Her Majesty or an agent of Her Majesty, or with an associated government, that in any way relates to defence supplies or to defence projects or to the designing, manufacturing, producing, constructing, finishing, assembling, transporting, repairing, maintaining, servicing or storing of, or dealing in, defence supplies or defence projects, and (b) a defence subcontract. *Defence Production Act*, R.S.C. 1985, c. D-1, s. 2.

DEFENCE ESTABLISHMENT. Any area or structure under the control of the Minister of National Defence, and the material and other things situated in or on any such area or structure.

DEFENCE OF CANADA OR ANY STATE ALLIED OR ASSOCIATED WITH CANADA. The efforts of Canada and of foreign states toward the detection, prevention or suppression of activities of any foreign state directed toward actual or potential attack or other acts of aggression against Canada or any state allied or associated with Canada. *Access to Information Act*, R.S.C. 1985, c. A-1, s. 15(2).

DEFENCE OF DWELLING. Every one who is in peaceable possession of a dwelling-house, and every one lawfully assisting him or acting under his authority, is justified in using as much force as is necessary to prevent any person from forcibly breaking into or forcibly entering the dwelling-house without lawful authority. *Criminal Code*, R.S.C. 1985, c. C-46, s. 40.

DEFENCE OF PROPERTY. Every one who is in peaceable possession of personal property, and every one lawfully assisting him, is justified (a) in preventing a trespasser from taking it, or (b) in taking it from a trespasser who has taken it, if he does not strike or cause bodily harm to the trespasser. *Criminal Code*, R.S.C. 1985, c. C-46, s. 38(1).

DEFENCE PROJECTS. Buildings, aerodromes, airports, dockyards, roads, defence fortifications or other military works, or works required for the protection, maintenance or storage of defence supplies. *Defence Production Act* R.S.C. 1985, c. D-1, s. 2.

DEFENCE PROPERTY. The prescribed lands and premises of defence establishments belonging to Canada. *Municipal and School Board Payments Adjustment Act*, R.S.O. 1990, c. M. 47, s. 1.

DEFENCE SUBCONTRACT. A contract or arrangement between any persons whomever, (a) to perform all or any part of the work or service or make or furnish any article or material for the purpose of any other defence contract, (b) under which any amount payable is contingent on the entry into of any other defence contract or determined with reference to any amount payable under or otherwise by reference to any other defence contract, or (c) under which any part of the services performed or to be performed consists of soliciting, attempting to negotiate or negotiating any other defence contract or soliciting or negotiating for the purchase or sale of an articles, materials or services required to fulfil any other defence contract, and, for greater certainty but not so as to limit the foregoing for the purposes of this definition the expression "other defence contract" includes a defence subcontract. *Defence Production Act*, R.S.C. 1985, c. D-1, s. 2.

DEFENCE SUPPLIES. (a) Arms, ammunition, implements of war, vehicles, mechanical and other equipment, watercraft, amphibious craft, aircraft, animals, articles, materials, substances and things required or used for the purposes of the defence of Canada or for cooperative efforts for defence being carried on by Canada and an associated (b) ships of all kinds, and (c) articles, government, materials, substances and things of all kinds used for the production or supply of anything mentioned in paragraph (a) or (b) or for the construction of defence projects. *Defence Production Act*, R.S.C. 1985, c. D-1, s. 2.

DEFENCE WOUND. A wound, sustained by the victim of an attack, while trying to grab or fend off the attacker's sharp weapon.

DEFEND. *v*. To deny. See NOTICE OF INTENT TO ~.

DEFENDANT. *n*. 1. Includes every person served with any writ of summons or process, or served with notice of, or entitled to attend, any proceedings. 2. A person against whom an action is commenced. 3. A person to whom a summons is issued. 4. Includes a plaintiff against whom a counterclaim is brought.

DEFENDEMUS. [L.] We will defend.

DEFENDERE SE PER CORPUS SUUM. [L.] To defend oneself with one's own body.

DEFENDERE UNICA MANU. [L. to defend oneself with the mere hand] A denial of an accusation under oath.

DEFENERATION. *n*. Lending money on usury.

DEFERENCE. *n.* 1. Respect. 2. The degree to which a court will refrain from interfering with a decision of an administrative tribunal or a lower court. A standard of review is established by the courts in relation to the degree of deference shown to another decision-maker, legislative, administrative or judicial. 3. Considerable deference must be extended to elected representatives undertaking what is essentially a legislative function. In my opinion, courts are not equipped to micro-manage a process such as the restructuring process undertaken in Bruce County. To do so would result in the judicialization of what was intended to be a political process. The courts should only interfere in egregious circumstances where it is manifest that statutorily prescribed pre-conditions have not been met. *Bruce (Township) v. Ontario (Minister of Municipal Affairs & Housing)* (1998), 1998 CarswellOnt 3382, 112 O.A.C. 68, 164 D.L.R. (4th) 443, 48 M.P.L.R. (2d) 201, 41 O.R. (3d) 309, 8 Admin. L.R. (3d) 21 (C.A.) Court: Ontario Court of Appeal, Osborne for the court. See. CURIAL ~; JUDICIAL ~.

DEFERRED. *adj.* 1. Of a debt, time for payment is extended. 2. Delayed.

DEFERRED ANNUITY. An annuity that becomes payable to the contributor at the time he reaches sixty years of age or another age specified by the governing statute.

DEFERRED COMMUNITY OF PROPERTY. Each spouse retains separate property during marriage, but when the marriage dissolves, each spouse is entitled to one-half of all property which forms the community. J.G. McLeod, *The Conflict of Laws* (Calgary: Carswell, 1983) at 372.

DEFERRED COMPENSATION PLAN. The employer pays an amount equal to a percent of the salary into the plan, and the plan pays the employee the accumulated credits thirty days after the employee completes the employment. A. Bissett-Johnson & W.M. Holland, eds, *Matrimonial Property Law in Canada* (Toronto: Carswell, 1980) at BC-18.

DEFERRED LIFE ANNUITY. A life annuity that commences at retirement date.

DEFERRED PAYMENT PLAN. See CONTINUOUS ~.

DEFERRED PENSION. A pension benefit, payment of which is deferred until the person entitled to the pension benefit reaches the normal retirement date under the pension plan.

DEFERRED PENSION BENEFIT. A pension benefit other than an immediate pension benefit. *Pension Benefits Standards Act*, R.S.C. 1985 (2d Supp.), c. 32, s. 2.

DEFERRED PROFIT SHARING PLAN. A plan which allows an employer to share company profits with employees.

DEFERRED SHARING SCHEME. The sharing of matrimonial property is deferred until the happening of an event such as marriage breakdown. A. Bissett-Johnson & W.M. Holland, eds., *Matrimonial Property Law in Canada* (Toronto: Carswell, 1980) at A-5.

DEFERRED STOCK. A stock entitling holders to all the remaining net earnings after dividends have been paid to the preferred stock and ordinary stockholders.

DEFERRED TRUST. Tax is deferred on the spouse's interest under the trust until that spouse's interest ends on his or her death. D.M.W. Waters, *The Law of Trusts in Canada*, 2d ed. (Toronto: Carswell, 1984) at 30.

DEFICIENCY. See EXPERIENCE ~; MARGIN ~; MENTAL ~; OXYGEN ~.

DEFICIENTE UNO (SANGUINE) NON POTEST ESSE HAERES. [L.] A person lacking one bloodline cannot be heir.

DEFICIT. *n.* Loss; an amount by which expenditures exceed revenue. See BASIC ACCOUNT ~.

DE FIDE ET OFFICIO JUDICIS NON RECIPITUR QUAESTIO; SED DE SCIENTIA SIVE SIT ERROR JURIS SIVE FACTI. [L.] No question can be entertained regarding the good faith and integrity of a judge.

DEFILEMENT. *n.* Corruption; debasing.

DEFINE. *v.* To explain the meaning; to limit; to clarify.

DEFINED BENEFIT. A pension benefit other than a defined contribution benefit.

DEFINED BENEFIT PENSION PLAN. A pension plan under which the pension to which a member is entitled upon retirement in accordance with the pension plan is prescribed by the terms of the pension plan on the basis of a period of service under the pension plan or income earned while a member of the pension plan or during a prescribed period of membership in the pension plan or on the basis of both such a period of service and such income earned.

DEFINED BENEFIT PLAN. A pension plan that is not a defined contribution plan. *Pension Benefits Standards Act, 1985*, R.S.C. 1985, c. 32 (2nd Supp.), s. 2(1).

DEFINED BENEFIT PROVISION. A provision of a pension plan under which pension benefits for a member are determined in any way other than that described in the definition "defined contribution provision". *Pension Benefit Standards Act*, R.S.C. 1985 (2d Supp.), c. 32, s. 2.

DEFINED CONTRIBUTION BENEFIT. A pension benefit that is determined with reference to and provided by contributions, and the interest on the contributions, paid by or for the credit of a member of a pension plan and determined on an individual account basis. *Pension Benefits acts*.

DEFINED CONTRIBUTION PLAN. A pension plan that consists of defined contribution provisions and does not contain defined benefit provisions, other than (a) a defined benefit provision relating to pension benefits accrued in respect of employment before the effective date of the pension plan, or (b) a defined benefit provision that provides for a minimum pension benefit whose additional value is not significant in the Superintendent's opinion. *Pension Benefit Standards Act*, R.S.C. 1985 (2d Supp.), c. 32, s. 2.

DEFINED CONTRIBUTION PROVISION. A provision of a pension plan under which pension benefits for a member are determined solely as a function of the amount of pension benefit that can be provided by (a) contributions made by and on behalf of that member, and (b) interest earnings and other gains and losses allocated to that member. *Pension Benefit Standards Act*, R.S.C. 1985 (2d Supp.), c. 32, s. 2.

DEFINITION SECTION. A statutory provision which states that particular words and phrases, when used in the statute, will bear certain meanings.

DEFOG. *v*. To remove moisture from the inside surface of the glass. *Motor Vehicle Safety Regulations*, C.R.C., c. 1038, s. 103.

DEFORCEMENT. *n*. Holding lands to which someone else is entitled.

DEFRAUD. *v*. " . . . [T]wo elements are essential, 'dishonesty' and 'deprivation'. . . . The element of deprivation is satisfied on proof of detriment, prejudice or risk of prejudice to the economic interests of the victim. . ." *R. v. Olan* (1978), 5 C.R. (3d) 1 at 7, [1978] 2 S.C.R. 1175, 86 D.L.R. (3d) 212, 41 C.C.C. (2d) 145, 21 N.R. 504, Dickson J.

DEFROST. *v*. To melt frost or ice.

DEFUNCT. *adj*. No longer in operation; no longer carrying on business.

DEFUNCT COMPANY. A company which is no longer carrying on business.

DEGRADATION. *n*. A loss of dignity.

DEGRADATION TEST. Test for obscenity which considers degrading or dehumanizing materials place women (and sometimes men) in positions of subordination, servile submission or humiliation. They run against the principles of equality and dignity of all human beings; *R. v. Butler*, [1992] 1 S.C.R. 452.

DEGREE. *n*. 1. A difference in relative importance between members of the same species. 2. One step in the line of consanguinity or descent. 3. Any recognition in writing of academic achievement which is called a degree; and includes the degrees of bachelor, master and doctor.

DEGREE OF ARC. π180 radian. *Weights and Measures Act*, S.C. 1970-71-72, c. 36, schedule I.

DE GUSTIBUS NON EST DISPUTANDUM. [L.] One should not argue over tastes.

DEHORS. [Fr.] Outside.

DEHUMANIZATION TEST. Test for obscenity which considers degrading or dehumanizing materials place women (and sometimes men) in positions of subordination, servile submission or humiliation. They run against the principles of equality and dignity of all human beings; *R. v. Butler*, [1992] 1 S.C.R. 452.

DEHYDRATED. *adj*. Dried rapidly by artificial heat.

DEHYDRATOR. *n*. An apparatus designed and used to remove water from raw gas.

DE INCREMENTO. [L.] Of increase.

DE INJURIA SUA PROPRIA ABSQUE TALI CAUSA. [L.] Of a personal wrong and not for the cause alleged.

DEJURATION. *n*. Swearing a solemn oath.

DE JURE. [L.] By right; lawful.

DE JURE JUDICES DE FACTO JURA-TORES RESPONDENT. [L.] Judges answer to the law, a jury to fact.

DELATOR. *n.* [L.] An accuser; an informer.

DELAWARE MERGER. A subsidiary company with minority shareholders is merged with a shell subsidiary in exchange for a cash or share option in the parent company. W. Grover and F. Iacobucci, *Materials on Canadian Income Tax*, 4th ed. (Toronto: Richard De Boo Ltd., 1980) at 1057.

DELAY. *v.* To postpone, to put off.

DELAY. *n.* Postponement. See DISMISSAL FOR ~; INSTITUTIONAL ~; PRE-SCRIBED ~; SYSTEMIC ~.

DELAY DEFEATS EQUITIES. "[A court of equity] . . . has always refused its aid to stale demands, where a party has slept upon his right and acquiesced for a great length of time. Nothing can call forth this court into activity, but conscience, good faith, and reasonable diligence; where these are wanting, the Court is passive, and does nothing." *Smith v. Clay* (1767), 3 Bro.C.C. 639n at 640n, Lord Camden L.C.

DELAYED RETIREMENT. Withdrawal from the workforce after the normal retirement date.

DEL CREDERE. Guarantee; warranty.

DEL CREDERE AGENT. A mercantile agent who will indemnify the principal if the third party fails to pay as contracted in respect of goods. G.H.L. Fridman, *The Law of Agency*, 6th ed. (London: Butterworths, 1990) at 38-9.

DEL CREDERE COMMISSION. An extra commission paid to a del credere agent. G.H.L. Fridman, *The Law of Agency*, 6th ed. (London: Butterworths, 1990) at 38.

DELECTUS PERSONAE. [L.] The selection of a person.

DELEGATA POTESTAS NON POTEST DELEGARI. [L.] A power already delegated cannot be delegated again.

DELEGATE. *v.* The word 'delegate' is properly used to describe the disposition of one's own powers. One cannot delegate what one does not have. *Stenner v. British Columbia (Securities Commission)* (1993), 1993 CarswellBC 1209, 23 Admin. L.R. (2d) 247 (S.C.), Spencer J.

DELEGATE. *n.* 1. A person elected to represent others. 2. The recipient of a power or authority delegated by another.

DELEGATED LEGISLATION. 1. Subordinate legislation made by authorities other than Parliament or a legislature. 2. A statutory instrument.

DELEGATION. *n.* 1. Entrusting someone else to act in one's place. 2. The assignment of a debt to someone else.

DELEGATUS NON POTEST DELEGARE. [L.] 1. One who already is a delegate cannot delegate. 2. " . . . Unless rebutted, it stands for the proposition that there is no authority to re-delegate a delegated power. . ." *Hanson v. Ontario Universities Athletic Assn.* (1975), 25 C.P.R. (2d) 239 at 248, 11 O.R. (2d) 193, 65 D.L.R. (3d) 385 (H.C.), Lieff J.

DELERIUM. *n.* Disorientation of the mind. F.A. Jaffe, *A Guide to Pathological Evidence*, 3d ed. (Toronto: Carswell, 1991) at 217.

DELETERIOUS. *adj.* Harmful.

DELETERIOUS SUBSTANCE. (a) Any substance that, if added to any water, would degrade or alter or form part of a process of degradation or alteration of the quality of that water so that it is rendered or is likely to be rendered deleterious to fish or fish habitat or to the use by man of fish that frequent that water, or (b) any water that contains a substance in such quantity or concentration, or that has been so treated, processed or changed by heat or other means from a natural state that it would, if added to any other water degrade or alter or form part of a process of degradation or alteration of the quality of that water so that it is rendered or is likely to be rendered deleterious to fish or fish habitat or to the use by man of fish that frequent that water, and without limiting the generality of the foregoing includes (c) any substance or class of substances prescribed pursuant to paragraph (2)(a), (d) any water that contains any substance or class of substances in a quantity or concentration that is equal to or in excess of a quantity or concentration prescribed in respect of that substance or class of substances pursuant to paragraph (2)(b), and (e) any water that has been subjected to a treatment, process or change prescribed pursuant to paragraph (2)(c). *Fisheries Act*, R.S.C. 1985, c. F-14, s. 34.

DELIBERANDUM EST DIU QUOD STATUENDUM EST SEMEL. [L.] One should long deliberate on anything which is to be decided once and for all.

DELIBERATE. *v*. To consider.

DELIBERATE. *adj*. " . . . [C]onsidered, not impulsive." *R. v. Nygaard* (1989), 51 C.C.C. (3d) at 432, [1989] 2 S.C.R. 1074, [1990] 1 W.W.R. 1, 70 Alta. L.R. (2d) 1, 72 C.R. (3d) 257, 101 N.R. 108, 102 A.R. 186, Cory. J.

DELIBERATE ACT. " . . . [O]ne proceeding from an intention and an intelligence which knows the nature and quality of the criminal act . . ." *R. v. Pilon* (1965), 46 C.R. 272 at 294, [1968] 2 C.C.C. 53 (Qué. C.A.), Rivard J.A.

DELIBERATION. *n*. " . . . [I]n the case of a tripartite board, . . . an opportunity for a discussion of the issues—or at least some form of communication among the members of the board as to the issues—so that it can be said that each member's reasons, for and against a decision, were considered by the others."' *U.N.A., Local 1 v. Calgary General Hospital* (1989), 39 Admin. L.R. 244 at 246, 99 A.R. 157, 70 Alta. L.R. (2d) 284, 63 D.L.R. (4th) 440 (Q.B.), Virtue J.

DELICATUS DEBITOR EST ODIOSUS IN LEGE. [L.] A luxurious debtor is repugnant in law.

DELICT. *n*. A tort; a crime.

DELICTUM. *n*. [L.] A tort.

DELINEATION WELL. A well that is so located in relation to another well penetrating an accumulation of petroleum, oil or gas that there is a reasonable expectation that another portion of that accumulation will be penetrated by the first-mentioned well and that the drilling is necessary in order to determine the commercial value of the accumulation.

DELINQUENCY. *n*. 1. Failure; omission. 2. " . . . [T]wo categories of acts; the first category includes acts that are in violation of 'any provision of the Criminal Code or of any federal or provincial statute, or of any by-law or ordinance of any municipality' (Juvenile Delinquents Act, R.S.C. 1970, c. J-9, s. 2(1)), or, as Fauteux J. put it in *A.G.B.C. v. Smith (S.)*, [1967] S.C.R. 702 at 710 . . . that are 'punishable breaches of the public law, whether defined by Parliament or the Legislature'; the second category includes sexual immorality or other similar forms of vice which while not illegal in the case of adults, should be repressed in the case of juveniles." *R. v. Morris* (1979), 6 C.R. (3d) 36 at 48, 43 C.C.C.

(2d) 129, [1979] 1 S.C.R. 405, 91 D.L.R. (3d) 161, 23 N.R. 109, Pratte J. (Martland, Ritchie, Pigeon and Beetz JJ. concurring).

DELINQUENT. See JUVENILE ~.

DELERIUM TREMENS. [L.] " . . . [A]n abnormal state of mind which may follow the habitually excessive use of alcohol." *R. v. Malcolm* (1989), 50 C.C.C. (3d) 172 at 179, [1989] 6 W.W.R. 23, 58 Man. R. (2d) 286, 71 C.R. (3d) 238 (C.A.), Twaddle J.A.

DELIST. *v*. To remove a security from its trading on the stock exchange.

DELIVER. *v*. 1. With reference to a notice or other document, includes mail to or leave with a person, or deposit in a person's mail box or receptacle at the person's residence or place of business. 2. " . . . [P]roviding what is wanted (in or for the construction of the building)." *W. & B. Construction Ltd. v. Mahaney* (1978), 4 R.P.R. 5 at 11, 25 N.S.R. (2d) 361, 85 D.L.R. (3d) 425, 36 A.P.R. 361 (C.A.), the court per Coffin J.A. 3. To place by means of a hose or other article capable of transmitting liquids. 4. " . . . [T]urning over the custody of the person . . ." *R. v. Dean* (1991) 5 C.R. (4th) 176 at 183 (Ont. Gen. Div.), Haley J.

DELIVERABLE STATE. Goods in such a state that the buyer would, under contract, be bound to take delivery of them. *Sale of Goods acts*.

DELIVERED. *adj*. ".. [T]he party whose deed the document is expressed to be, having first sealed it, must by words or conduct expressly or impliedly acknowledge his intention to be immediately and unconditionally bound by the expressions obtained therein: . . ." *Metropolitan Theatres Ltd., Re* (1917), 40 O.L.R. 345 at 347 (H.C.), Rose J.

DELIVERED PRICING. The practice of refusing a customer, or person seeking to become a customer, delivery of an article at any place in which the supplier engages in a practice of making delivery of the article to any other of the supplier's customers on the same trade terms that would be available to the first-mentioned customer if his place of business were located in that place. *Competition Act*, R.S.C. 1985, c. C-34.

DELIVERY. *n*. 1. The voluntary transfer of possession from one person to another. *Sale of Goods acts*. 2. Transfer of possession, actual or constructive, from one person to another. 3 " . .

[A] process whereby the addressee of mail is afforded access to that mail. . ." *R. v. Weaver* (1980), 116 D.L.R. (3d) 701 at 702, 30 O.R. (2d) 261, 55 C.C.C. (2d) 564 (C.A.), the court per Jessup J.A. 4. The natural or the lawfully, medically induced end of a pregnancy by child-birth, whether or not the child is viable. 5. Transfer from one premises to another for any purpose. See CASH ON ~; DATE OF ~; GAOL ~; MIS~; NON-~; WRIT OF ~.

DELIVERY CAR. Is equipped for the transportation of merchandise, and effects such transportation for a pecuniary consideration.

DELIVERY CHARGE. See SUB-ORDER ~.

DE LUNATICO INJURENDO. [L.] Concerning an inquiry into lunacy.

DELUSION. *n*. False belief. *Crabbe v. S.*, [1925] 3 D.L.R. 1069 at 1072, [1925] W.W.R. 701, 36 B.C.R. 89 (C.A.), MacDonald J.A.

DEM. *abbr*. On the demise of. In a British action of ejectment before 1852, the plaintiff in the action would be styled "Doe dem. Smith."

DEMAIN. See DEMESNE.

DEMAINE. See DEMESNE.

DEMAND. *n*. 1. A claim that a person offer something due. 2. A request that a person do something which she or he is legally bound to do once the request is made. See BILLING ~; BIOCHEMICAL OXYGEN ~; LIQUIDATED MARKET ~; STALE ~; THIRD PARTY ~.

DEMANDANT. *n*. The plaintiff in a real action.

DEMAND LETTER. A letter requesting immediate payment of debt.

DEMAND NOTE. A promissory note payable on demand.

DEMARCATION POINT. In respect of the wire that is used by a distribution undertaking for the distribution of programming services to a subscriber, means (*a*) if the subscriber resides in a single-unit dwelling, (i) 30 cm outside the exterior wall of the subscriber's premises, or (ii) any point to which the licensee and the customer have agreed; and (*b*) if the subscriber resides in a multiple-unit dwelling, (i) the point inside the dwelling at which the wire is diverted to the exclusive use and benefit of that subscriber, or (ii) any point to which the licensee and the customer have agreed. *Broadcasting Distribution Regulations*, SOR/97-555, s. 1.

DEMEASE. *n*. Death.

DEMENTIA. *n*. Unalterable mental deterioration. F.A. Jaffe, *A Guide to Pathological Evidence*, 3d ed. (Toronto: Carswell, 1991) at 217.

DEMERIT POINT. A point assessed against a driver's licence for an offence committed by a driver under highway traffic legislation.

DEMESNE. *n*. The private property of a lord which was not granted out in tenancy.

DEMESNIAL. *adj*. Relating to a demesne.

DEMIDIETAS. *n*. A half; moiety.

DE MINIMIS NON CURAT LEX. [L.] The law does not bother itself about trifles.

DEMISE. *n*. 1. Includes any and every agreement or transaction whether in writing or by deed or parol whereby one person may become the tenant of another. 2. " . . . [C]reates an implied covenant for quiet enjoyment [pursuant to The Short Form of Leases Act, R.S.O. 1937, s. 159, Schedule B., clause 13] . . ." *Bowra v. Henderson*, [1942] O.R. 734 at 739, [1943] 1 D.L.R. 672 (H.C.), Roach J. 3. " . . . [A]n effective word to convey an estate of freehold, and that it is of like import with and equivalent to the word 'grant.' . . ." *Spears v. Miller* (1882), 32 U.C.C.P. 661 at 663 (Ont.), Armour J. See RE~.

DEMISE OF THE CROWN. The death, deposition or abdication of the sovereign.

DEMOCRACY. *n*. 1. Simply put, "democracy" is a political system by which the citizens of a country govern themselves (in Canada at the federal and provincial levels, not to exclude the territorial, municipal or newly emerging aboriginal levels), where their elected representatives make laws; the executive branch administers those laws and is responsible for the way it does so. *Qu v. Canada (Minister of Citizenship & Immigration)*, 2000 CarswellNat 705, 5 Imm. L.R. (3d) 129, [2000] 4 F.C. 71 (T.D.). 2. Democracy is commonly understood as being a political system of majority rule. Since Confederation, efforts to extend the franchise to those unjustly excluded from participation in our political system—such as women, minorities, and aboriginal peoples—have continued, with some success, to the present day. Democracy is not simply concerned with the process of government. On the contrary democracy is fundamentally connected to substantive goals, most importantly, the promotion of self-government. Democracy accommodates cultural and group identities. The Court must be guided by the values and principles essential to a free and democratic society which embody, to name but a few, respect for the inherent dignity of the human person, commitment to social justice and equality, accommodation of a wide variety of beliefs, respect for cultural and group identity, and faith in social and political institutions which enhance the participation of individuals and groups in society. In institutional terms, democracy means that each of the provincial legislatures and the federal Parliament is elected by popular franchise. In individual terms, the right to vote in elections to the House of Commons and the provincial legislatures, and to be candidates in those elections, is guaranteed to "Every citizen of Canada" by virtue of s. 3 of the *Charter*. Historically, this Court has interpreted democracy to mean the process of representative and responsible government and the right of citizens to participate in the political process as voters and as candidates. In addition, the effect of s. 4 of the *Charter* is to oblige the House of Commons and the provincial legislatures to hold regular elections and to permit citizens to elect representatives to their political institutions. The democratic principle is affirmed with particular clarity in that section 4 is not subject to the notwithstanding power contained in s. 33. *Reference re Secession of Quebec*, 1998 CarswellNat 1299, 161 D.L.R. (4th) 385, 228 N.R. 203, 55 C.R.R. (2d) 1, [1998] 2 S.C.R. 217, Per curiam.

DEMOCRATIC. *adj.* " . . . [R]efer[s] to a system in which the governors are chosen by elections in which all adult citizens have the right to vote . . ." *Griffin v. College of Dental Surgeons (British Columbia)* (1989), 64 D.L.R. (4th) 652 at 677, 40 B.C.L.R. (2d) 188, [1990] 1 W.W.R. 503 (C.A.), Southin J.A. See FREE AND ~; SOCIETY.

DEMOCRATIC INSTITUTION. For the purpose of subpara. 19(1)(f)(i) of the *Immigration Act* consists of a structured group of individuals established in accordance with democratic principles with preset goals and objectives who are engaged in lawful activities in Canada of a political, religious, social or economic nature. *Qu v. Canada (Minister of Citizenship & Immigration)* (2001), 2001 FCA 399, 18 Imm. L.R. (3d) 288, [2001] F.C.J. No. 1945, 284 N.R. 201, [2002] 3 F.C. 3, 217 F.T.R. 198 (note), 2001 CarswellNat 2977 (C.A.).

DEMOLISH. *v.* 1. To destroy. 2. To do anything in the removal of a building or any material

part thereof. *Building Code Act, 1992*, S.O. 1992, c. 23, s. 1(1), as am.

DEMOLITION. *n.* The doing of anything in the removal of a building or any material part thereof.

DEMOLITION ORDER. If a building is unfit for occupation and cannot be repaired at reasonable cost it may be ordered demolished.

DEMONETISATION. *n.* A declaration that certain coins are no longer legal tender.

DEMONSTRABLY JUSTIFIED. Determining whether it has been demonstrated that the impugned distinction is "demonstrably justified in a free and democratic society" involves tow enquiries. First, the goal of the legislation is ascertained and examined to see if it is of pressing and substantial importance. Then the court must carry out a proportionality analysis to balance the interests of society with those of individuals and groups. *Miron v. Trudel*, [1995] 2 S.C.R. 418, per McLachlin, J. See REASONABLE AND ~.

DEMONSTRABLY UNFIT. That then brings us to a consideration of what is meant by the words "demonstrably unfit". "Demonstrably unfit" has been equated with unreasonableness sentences which are clearly or manifestly excessive; "falling outside the acceptable range"; sentences where there is a "substantial and marked departure from the sentences customarily imposed for similar offenders committing similar crimes". The Court again stated that a demonstrably unfit sentence is one that falls outside the acceptable range of sanctions for a similar offence committed by a comparable offender. A wide deviation from the accepted "starting-point" of sentencing for an offence will not, in and of itself, render a sentence demonstrably unfit, but rather is a factor in determining demonstrable unfitness "A demonstrably unfit sentence is one that is clearly outside the range imposed for that type of offence and that type of offender". *R. v. Pankewich*, 2002 SKCA 7, 49 C.R. (5th) 143, 161 C.C.C. (3d) 534, [2002] 4 W.W.R. 648, 217 Sask. R. 111, 265 W.A.C. 111 (C.A.).

DEMONSTRATION. *n.* The act of showing, displaying or exhibiting an object in Canada for the purpose of explaining or proving its qualities and capabilities to prospective customers.

DEMONSTRATION OR RESEARCH PROJECT. (i) A project that is designed to test, in a specified situation, the applicability of new or modified methods of providing welfare services as a means of improving such services, or (ii) a project that is intended to make a contribution to knowledge by systematically collecting, organizing and evaluating data relating to welfare problems or matters by experimentally testing an hypothesis relating to such problems or matters, where the project is to be completed within a specified time and has been approved as a demonstration project or as a research project pursuant to the rules made by the Governor in Council for the purposes of the National Welfare Grants program. *Canada Assistance Plan Regulations*, C.R.C., c. 382, s. 3.

DEMONSTRATIVE EVIDENCE. Real things as opposed to testimony, i.e., weapons, models, maps, photographs.

DEMONSTRATIVE LEGACY. 1. " . . . [T]o be paid not out of the general assets of the testator but out of the segregated bonds." *Lasham, Re* (1924-25), 56 O.L.R. 137 at 139 (Div. Ct.), Middleton J.A. 2. A legacy, general in nature which is supposed to be satisfied out of part of a testator's property or a specified fund. T. Sheard, R. Hull & M.M.K. Fitzpatrick, *Canadian Forms of Wills*, 4th ed. (Toronto: Carswell, 1982) at 158.

DEMONSTRATOR. *n.* " . . . [U]sually indicates a new car that has been used only by the dealer to drive prospective purchasers and exhibit the attributes of the car to those purchasers." *MacHardy v. Alma Motors Ltd.* (1963), 38 D.L.R. (2d) 761 at 763 (N.S. T.D.), Coffin J.

DEMORATUR. [L.] One demurs.

DE MORTE HOMINIS NULLA EST CUNCTATIO LONGA. [L.] There is no long delay concerning a person's death.

DEMOTE. *v.* To reduce the salary of an employee by transferring him to a position with a lower maximum salary or by reducing the salary of his present position.

DEMOTION. *n.* An objective comparison of the two positions must be carried out. A substantial change to the essential terms of an employment contract that warrants a finding that the employee has been constructively dismissed. *Farber c. Royal Trust Co.* (1996), [1997] 1 S.C.R. 846.

DEMOUNTABLE RIM. A supporting member for a tire or tire and tube assembly, that does not have a permanently attached centre component. *Motor Vehicle Safety Regulations*, C.R.C., c. 1038, s. 2.

DEMUR. *v.* To object by demurrer.

DEMURRABLE. *adj.* Said of pleading which does not state facts to support the claim.

DEMURRAGE. *n.* 1. A charge made by railways for the detention of a freight car beyond the free time provided for by the applicable special arrangements tariffs and is intended as an inducement to promptly release the freight car, and alternatively, to compensate partially railways, should the freight car be detained beyond the free time allowance. *Canadian Pacific Railway v. Canada (Transportation Agency)*, 2003 FCA 271, 307 N.R. 378 (C.A.). 2. An allowance made to a shipowner for detaining a ship in port after the agreed-on sailing time.

DEMURRER. *n.* 1. " . . . [A] submission [by the defendant] that if the plaintiff's allegations are true they disclose no cause of action . . ." *Royal Bank v. Rizkalla* (1984), 50 C.P.C. 292 at 295, 59 B.C.L.R. 324 (S.C.), McLachlin J. 2. " . . . [T]o admit all the facts that the plaintiff's pleadings alleged and to assert that these facts were not sufficient in law to sustain the plaintiff's case." *Hunt v. T & N plc.* (1990), (*sub nom. Hunt v. Carey Canada Inc.*), 74 D.L.R. (4th) 321 at 328, 4 C.C.L.T. (2d) 1, 43 C.P.C. (2d) 105, 117 N.R. 321, [1990] 6 W.W.R. 385, 49 B.C.L.R. (2d) 273, [1990] 2 S.C.R. 959, Wilson J.

DENARII. *n.* [L.] Available money.

DENATURE. *v.* To denature spirits into denatured alcohol or specially denatured alcohol using prescribed denaturants in the prescribed manner. *Excise Act, 2001*, S.C. 2002, c. 22, s. 2.

DENATURED ALCOHOL. 1. Alcohol in suitable admixture with such denaturants as to render it in the judgment of the Minister non-potable and to prevent recovery of the ethyl alcohol. *Excise Act*, R.S.C. 1985, c. E-14, s. 243. 2. A mixture of (a) alcohol derived from biomass materials, and (b) soluble by-products of fermentation, containing by volume at least 98% ethanol. *The Gasoline Tax Act*, C.C.S.M., c. G40, s. 1.

DENATURED ETHANOL. A solution that contains ethanol derived from biomass materials.

DENATURED SPIRITS. Spirits in suitable admixture with such denaturants as to render them in the opinion of the Minister non-potable and to prevent recovery of the ethyl alcohol. *Excise Act*, R.S.C. 1985, c. E-14, s. 243.

DENIAL. *n*. 1. Taking issue with and disputing the facts asserted by an opposite party in pleadings in an action. 2. The refusal by a department to provide access to information, to correct a record or to make a notation on a record upon a request being made pursuant to this Act. *Freedom of Information Act*, R.S.N.S. 1989, c. 180, s. 2.

DENIZATION. *n*. Enfranchising, making free.

DENIZEN. *n*. An alien born citizen of a country. *Canepa v. Canada (Minister of Employment and Immigration)* (1992), 10 C.R.R. (2d) 348 at 351, 93 D.L.R. (4th) 589, [1992] 3 F.C. 270 (C.A.), the court per MacGuigan J.A.

DENOMINATION. *n*. 1. A value or size of currency. The denominations of money in the currency of Canada are dollars and cents, the cent being one hundredth of a dollar. 2. A religious organization and members bearing a particular name. 3. The act of naming. See RECOGNIZED ~; RELIGIOUS ~.

DE NON APPARENTIBUS, ET NON EXISTENTIBUS, EADEM EST RATIO. [L.] The rule is the same concerning things which do not appear and things which do not exist.

DE NOVO. [L.] Fresh; new. See HEARING ~; TRIAL ~.

DE NOVO HEARING. 1. A rehearing. 2. The distinction between "an appeal by holding a trial de novo and an appeal to the provincial Court of Appeal is that although the object of both is to determine whether the decision appealed from was right or wrong, in the latter case the question is whether it was right or wrong having regard to the evidence upon which it was based, whereas in the former the issue is to be determined without any reference, except for purposes of cross-examination, to the evidence called in the court appealed from and upon a fresh determination based upon evidence called anew and perhaps accompanied by entirely new evidence. A trial de novo envisages a new trial before a different tribunal than the one which originally decided the issue. *McKenzie v. Mason* (1992), 1992 CarswellBC 282, 72 B.C.L.R. (2d) 53, 9 C.P.C. (3d) 1, 96 D.L.R. (4th) 558, 18 B.C.A.C. 286, 31 W.A.C. 286 (C.A.), Toy, J.A.

DENSITY. *n*. 1. The total number of residential properties in an area municipality divided by the hectares in the area municipality correct to three places of decimals. *Ontario Unconditional Grants Act*, R.S.O. 1990, c. 0.38, s. 1. 2. The

shade of smoke at the point of emission to the outdoor atmosphere. *Air Pollution and Smoke Control Regulations*, C.R.C., c. 1143, s. 2. See FILLING ~.

DENTAL APPLIANCES. (a) Gold, amalgam, porcelain or any other kind of dental filling and cotton used in preparing the patient's teeth for filling and other supplies likewise used materials to be fabricated (b) into, attached to or incorporated processed, into a denture or dental appliance, or (c) impression materials for use in dentistry, if used by a dentist or denture therapist.

DENTAL AUXILIARY. A person other than a dentist who is qualified to perform dental services specified.

DENTAL HEALTH WORKER. A dental nurse, dental hygienist, dental technician, or a dental assistant who is trained and qualified to perform such dental services as are prescribed by the regulations and is duly registered in accordance with this Act. *The Dental Health Workers Act*, C.C.S.M. 1987, c. D31, s. 1.

DENTAL HYGIENE. The practice of dental hygiene is the assessment of teeth and adjacent tissues and treatment by preventive and therapeutic means and the provision of restorative and orthodontic procedures and services.

DENTAL INSTRUMENT. A reusable medical device that is intended for surgical or dental use, including cutting, drilling, sawing, scraping, clamping, hammering, puncturing, dilating, retracting or clipping, without connection to an active device. *Medical Devices Regulations*, SOR/98-282, s. 1.

DENTAL LABORATORY. Any place where the art or business of dental technology is practised or carried on.

DENTAL NURSE. A person who is trained to provide dental nursing services.

DENTAL SERVICES. See SURGICAL-~.

DENTAL INSTRUMENT. A reusable medical device that is intended for surgical or dental use, including cutting, drilling, sawing, scraping, clamping, hammering, puncturing, dilating, retracting or clipping, without connection to an active device. *Medical Devices Regulations*, SOR/98-282, s. 1.

DENTAL STAFF. (a) The oral and maxillofacial surgeons to whom the board has granted the privilege of diagnosing, prescribing for or treating patients in the hospital, and (b) the dentists to whom the board has granted the privilege of attending patients in the hospital in co-operation with a member of the medical staff. *Hospital Management* R.R.O. 1990, Reg. 965, s. 1(1).

DENTAL SURGERY. Any professional service usually performed by a dentist or dental surgeon and includes (a) the diagnosis or treatment of, and the prescribing, treating, and operating for the prevention, alleviation or correction of any injury, disease, pain, deficiency, deformity, defect, lesion, disorder or physical condition of, to, in, or from any human tooth, mandible or maxilla or associated structures or tissues, including the prescribing, treating and administering of x-rays, anaesthetics, drugs and medicines in connection therewith; (b) the making, producing, reproducing, constructing, fitting, furnishing, supplying, altering, or repairing, prescribing or advising the use of any prosthetic denture, bridge, appliance or thing for any of the purposes indicated in paragraph (a) or to replace, improve or supplement any human tooth, or to prevent, alleviate, correct or improve any condition in the human oral cavity, or to be used in, upon or in connection with any human tooth, jaw or associated structure or tissue, or in the treatment of any condition thereof; (c) the taking or making, or the giving of advice or assistance or the providing of facilities for the taking or making of any impression, bite or cast and design preparatory to, or for the purpose of, or with a view to making, producing, reproducing, constructing, fitting, furnishing, supplying, altering or repairing any such prosthetic denture, bridge, appliance or thing; (d) any specialty of dentistry; (e) the dental procedures performed by a dental hygienist or dental assistant.

DENTAL TECHNICIAN. 1. A person who on the prescriptions or orders of dentists or physicians makes, produces, reproduces, constructs, furnishes, supplies, alters or repairs any prosthetic denture, bridge, appliance or thing to be used in, on or in connection with a human tooth or associated structure or tissue, or in the treatment of any condition thereof. 2. A person who practises the art or business of dental technology.

DENTAL TECHNOLOGY. The practice of dental technology is the design, construction, repair or alteration of dental prosthetic, restorative and orthodontic devices.

DENTAL THERAPIST. A person who is trained to provide dental therapy services.

DENTAL THERAPY. The performance of dental services under the direction and control

of a dentist and includes (i) the performance of uncomplicated dental restorations, (ii) the uncomplicated removal of teeth, (iii) the performance of dental prophylaxes, (iv) the application on teeth of topical fluorides or other anticariogenic agents, and (v) the taking and developing of x-rays of teeth.

DENTIST. *n. A* person lawfully entitled to practise dentistry in the place in which the practice is carried on by that person. See ATTENDING ~.

DENTISTRY. *n.* The practice of dentistry is the assessment of the physical condition of the oral-facial complex and the diagnosis, treatment and prevention of any disease, disorder or dysfunction of the oral-facial complex. See PRACTICE OF ~.

DENTURE. See COMPLETE ~; OVER~; PARTIAL ~.

DENTURE CONSTRUCTION. (i) The making and repairing of any complete upper or complete lower denture, or (ii) taking of impressions, bite registrations, try-ins and insertions for the making, producing, constructing and furnishing of any complete upper or lower denture for the intended wearer thereof.

DENTURE TECHNOLOGY. See PRACTICE OF ~.

DENTURE THERAPY. See PRACTICE OF ~; PRACTICE OF SUPERVISED ~.

DENTURISM. The practice of denturism is the assessment of arches missing some or all teeth and the design, construction, repair, alteration, ordering and fitting of removable dentures. *Denturism Act, 1991*, S.O. 1991, c. 25, s. 3.

DENTURIST. *n.* A person who provides a dental prosthetic service.

DENTUROLOGY. See PRACTICE OF ~.

DENUDER. *n.* A horizontal or vertical container that is part of a chlor-alkali mercury cell and in which water and alkali metal amalgam are converted to alkali metal hydroxide, metallic mercury and hydrogen gas in a short-circuited electrolytic reaction. *Chlor-Alkali Mercury National Emission Standards Regulations*, C.R.C., c. 406, s. 2.

DENUNCIATION. *n.* One of the principles of sentencing of those convicted of offences. The principle of denunciation ... is the communication of society's condemnation of an offender's conduct. *R. v. Laliberte*, 2000 SKCA 27, 31 C.R. (5th) 1, [2000] 4 W.W.R. 491, 143 C.C.C. (3d) 503, 189 Sask. R. 190 (C.A.). See SENTENCING.

DENUNCIATORY SENTENCE. Sentence which emphasizes community disapproval of the act and indicates the community finds it reprehensible. The goal is general deterrence.

DEP. *abbr.* Deputy.

DEPARTMENT. *n.* 1. A branch of the civil service over which a minister presides. 2. " . . . [I]nvolves the idea of something which forms part of a larger thing, . . ." *Carlyle v. Oxford (County)* (1914), 18 D.L.R. 759 at 764, 5 O.W.N. 728, 30 O.L.R. 413 (C.A.), the court per Meredith C.J.O. 3. A department, secretariat, ministry, office or other similar agency of the executive government. 4. (a) Any of the departments named in Schedule I, (b) any other division or branch of the public service of Canada, including a commission appointed under the Inquiries Act, designated by the Governor in Council as a department for the purposes of this Act, (c) the staffs of the Senate, the House of Commons and the Library of Parliament, and (d) any department corporations. *Financial Administration Act*, R.S.C. 1985, c. F-11, s. 2. 5. An academic unit administered by a head. See FIRE ~; GOVERNMENT ~; HEAD OF A ~; HEAD OF THE MEDICAL ~; PARI-MUTUEL ~; PUBLIC ~.

DEPARTMENTAL ANALYST. A person employed as a chemical analyst in any department or agency of the government of Canada or of any province. *Excise Act*, R.S.C. 1985, c. E-14, s. 2.

DEPARTMENTAL CORPORATION. A corporation named in Schedule 11. *Financial Administration Act*, R.S.C. 1985, c. F-11, s. 2.

DEPARTMENTAL INVESTIGATION. The minister presiding over any department of the Public Service may appoint, under the authority of the Governor in Council, a commissioner or commissioners to investigate and report on the state and management of the business, or any part of the business, of the department, either in the inside or outside service thereof, and the conduct of any person in that service, so far as the same relates to the official duties of the person. *Inquiries Act*, R.S.C. 1985, c. I-11, s. 6.

DEPARTMENTAL ROAD. (a) A provincial trunk highway; (b) a provincial road; (c) any highway in unorganized territory; (d) an industrial road; but does not include parking lots, or roads or driveways, on grounds appurtenant to a public work as defined in The Public Works Act, any highway the cost of construction or maintenance of which is paid from and out of the Consolidated Fund with moneys authorized to be expended for the purposes of any other Act of the Legislature, any highway built and maintained at the expense of the Government of Canada, or any highway built and maintained on private land by the owner of the land. *The Highways and Transportation Act*, C.C.S.M. 1987, c. H40, s. 1.

DEPARTMENTAL SENIORITY. Seniority which is lost if an employee moves to another department of the employer's business.

DEPARTMENT HEAD. 1. A member of the Executive Council charged with the administration of a department or agency. 2. The non-elected head of a department. See HEAD OF A DEPARTMENT; HEAD OF THE DEPARTMENT.

DEPARTMENT OF JUSTICE CANADA. The federal ministry which oversees every legal matter under federal jurisdiction, advises on legislative acts and provides legal advice to the Governor General.

DEPARTMENT OF NATIONAL DEFENCE. The federal ministry which manages and controls the Armed Forces of Canada and everything related to national defence including civil defence.

DEPARTMENT STORE. " . . . [T]est . . . is whether it deals in so many lines of goods that it has lost its identity as a store dealing in any particular line or lines of goods." *London (City) v. Kingmill's Ltd.*, [1956] O.W.N. 715 at 717 (H.C.), Aylen J.

DEPARTURE ANGLE. The smallest angle, in a plan side view of a vehicle, formed by the level surface on which the vehicle is standing and a line tangent to the rear tire static loaded radius arc and touching the underside of the vehicle rearward of the rear tire. *On-Road Vehicle and Engine Emission Regulations*, SOR/2003-2, s. 1(1).

DEPARTURE TAX. A capital gains tax imposed on taxpayers who cease to be residents of Canada.

DEPENDANT. *n.* 1. A person who depends upon another for maintenance. 2. A person to whom another has an obligation to provide support. 3. The spouse of a person or any child of a person who resides with the person. See DEPENDENT; PRIMARY ~; SECONDARY ~.

DEPENDANT CHILD. A person who (i) is dependent for support upon his or her mother or father, or (ii) is dependent for support upon a person who stands in loco parentis to him or her, and (ii) meets the age requirements and the other particulars as defined in legislation.

DEPENDENCY. *n.* 1. In relation to a narcotic, a state of psychological or physical dependence, or both, on a narcotic following its use on a periodic or continuous basis. 2. A state of psychological or physical reliance, or both, on one or more chemical substances that alter mood, perception, consciousness or behaviour to the apparent detriment of the person or society, or both, as a result of the periodic or continuous use or administration of one or more chemical substances and includes the use of nicotine or alcohol, or both. See DOMICILE OF ~; DRUG ~; LOSS OF ~ ON INCOME.

DEPENDENT. *n.* 1. The father, mother, grandfather, grandmother, brother, sister, uncle, aunt, niece or nephew, or child or grandchild of any age, who at the date of the death of the employee or pensioner is, by reason of mental or physical infirmity, dependent on that person for support. 2. A child or other relative of a deceased victim who was, in whole or in part, dependent upon the income of the victim at the time of the victim's death. 3. A child under the age of eighteen years, an unmarried child under the age of twenty-one years who is attending an approved educational institution on a fulltime basis and the surviving spouse of an employee. See DEPENDENTS.

DEPENDENT ADULT. A person respect of whom (i) a guardianship order is in effect, (ii) a trusteeship order is in effect, or (iii) both a guardianship order and a trusteeship order are in effect. *Dependent Adults Act*, R.S.A. 2000, c. D-11, s. 1.

DEPENDENT CHILD. 1. A dependent child who is under the age of 18 years. "2. Of a contributor means a child of the contributor who is less than eighteen years of age, (b) is eighteen or more years of age but less than twenty-five years of age and is in full-time attendance at a school or university as defined by regulation, or (c) is a child other than a child described in paragraph (b), is eighteen or more years of age

and is disabled, having been disabled without interruption since the time he reached eighteen years of age or the contributor died, whichever occurred later." *Canada Pension Plan*, R.S.C. 1985, c. C-8, s. 42. See SURVIVING SPOUSE WITH DEPENDENT CHILDREN.

DEPENDENT CONDITION. With respect to a person, means the condition of being without sufficient income or assets, other than the premises in which the person resides, to maintain that person. *Pension Act*, R.S.C. 1985, c. P-6, s. 3(1).

DEPENDENT CONTRACTOR. 1. Person, whether or not employed under a contract of employment and whether or not furnishing her or his own tools, vehicles, equipment, machinery, material or any other thing, who performs work or services for another person on such terms and conditions to be in a position of economic dependence upon that person, is under an obligation to perform duties mainly for that person and is in a relationship with that person more closely resembling that of an employee than an independent contractor. 2. (a) The owner, purchaser or lessee of a vehicle used for hauling, other than on rails or tracks, livestock, liquids, goods, merchandise or other materials, who is a party to a contract, oral or in writing, under the terms of which they are (i) required to provide the vehicle by means of which they perform the contract and to operate the vehicle in accordance with the contract, and (ii) is entitled to retain for their own use from time to time any sum of money that remains after the cost of their performance of the contract is deducted from the amount they are paid, in accordance with the contract, for that performance, (b) a fisher who, pursuant to an arrangement to which the fisher is a party, is entitled to a percentage or other part of the proceeds of a joint fishing venture in which the fisher participates with other persons, and (c) any other person who, whether or not employed under a contract of employment, performs work or services for another person on such terms and conditions that they are, in relation to that other person, in a position of economic dependence on, and under an obligation to perform duties for, that other person. *Canada Labour Code*, R.S.C. 1985, c. 2, s. 3(1).

DEPENDENT FATHER. A father who is permanently unemployable by reason of physical or mental disability, and includes a father who is blind or otherwise disabled as defined by the legislation.

DEPENDENT PARENT. A parent who by reason of age, disease or infirmity is unable to maintain himself or herself.

DEPENDENT RELATIVE REVOCATION. Where a will is revoked by a codicil it is a question whether it was the intention of the testator that the provisions of the will are to be effective if those contained in the codicil are declared to be invalid. *Murray v. Murray*, [1956] 1 W.L.R. 605.

DEPENDENT RIGHT. Any right, encumbrance or other consideration in, relating to, dependent on or calculated by reference to the share or production in respect of or imputable to the share of an interest holder, but does not include any debt or other obligation secured by an encumbrance. *Oil and Gas acts*.

DEPENDENTS. *n.* 1. Those members of the victim's family and any stranger who stood in loco parentis to the victim, or to whom the victim stood in loco parentis, and who were wholly or partly dependent upon the victim's income or work for support at the time of death. *Crime Victims Compensation acts*. 2. The members of the family of a worker who were wholly or partly dependent upon that person's earnings at the time of the worker's death. *Workers' Compensation acts*. 3. Such person as a person, against whom a maintenance order is made is liable to maintain according to the law in force in the lace where the maintenance order is made. *Maintenance Orders Enforcement* acts. See DEPENDANT; DEPENDENT.

DEPENDENT TERRITORIES. See COMMONWEALTH AND ~.

DEPLANE. *v.* To disembark from an aircraft for the purpose of terminating a flight.

DE PLANO. [L.] Directly; clearly.

DEPLETION ALLOWANCE. An extra deduction, after the taxpayer amortizes or deducts any actual exploration and development expenses. W. Grover and F. Iacobucci, *Materials on Canadian Income Tax*, 4th ed. (Toronto: Richard De Boo Ltd., 1980) at 1214.

DEP. M.N.R. (CUSTOMS & EXCISE). *abbr.* Deputy Minister of National Revenue for Customs and Excise.

DEPONENT. *n.* 1. A person who testifies that certain facts are true. 2. One who makes an affidavit.

DEPORTATION. *n.* 1. The removal of a person from any place in Canada to the place whence he came to Canada or to the country of his nationality or citizenship or to the country of his birth. 2. Forced displacement of the persons concerned by expulsion or other coercive acts from the area in which they are lawfully present, without grounds permitted under international law. *Rome Statute*, Article 7.

DEPOSE. *v.* 1. To remove from high office or a throne. 2. To affirm by making a deposition.

DEPOSIT. *v.* " . . . [F]iling, handing over, forwarding . . ." *Sacchetti v. Lockheimer*, [1988] 1 S.C.R. 1049 at 1057, 86 N.R. 4, 49 R.P.R. 101, 15 Q.A.C. 89, the court per Lamer J.

DEPOSIT. *n.* 1. " . . . [A] contract by which a customer lends money to a bank. The terms of the loan may vary as agreed upon by the banker and the customer. In the absence of such expressly agreed upon terms, the common law dictates that what is intended is a loan that is payable on demand." *Saskatchewan Co-operative Credit Society Ltd. v. Canada (Minister of Finance)* (1990), 47 B.L.R. 85 at 92, 65 D.L.R. (4th) 437, 32 F.T.R. 91, [1990] 2 F.C. 115, Collier J. 2. Money received that is repayable on demand or after notice or that is repayable upon the expiry of a fixed term. 3. Money paid as an earnest or security for a person to perform a contract. 4. A loan of money at interest or at a discount or repayable at a premium in money or otherwise but does not include a loan of money to a corporation in connection with the issue and sale of its bonds, debentures, notes or other written evidences of indebtedness. *Deposit Regulation acts*. 5. Any discharging, spraying, releasing, spilling, leaking, seeping, pouring, emitting, emptying, throwing, dumping or placing. *Fisheries Act*, R.S.C. 1985, c. F-14, s. 34. See BANK ~; BOOK ~; CURRENT ~; DATE OF ~; NON-CHEQUABLE ~S; OIL SANDS ~; SECURITY ~; SOLICITATION OF ~S.

DEPOSITARY. *n.* A specified government or international organization where instruments of ratification of a multilateral treaty are to be deposited. P.W. Hogg, *Constitutional Law of Canada*, 3d ed. (Toronto: Carswell, 1992) at 284.

DEPOSIT BALANCE. See REQUIRED ~.

DEPOSIT BUSINESS. The business of receiving on deposit money that is repayable (a) on demand, (b) after notice, or (c) on the expiry of a specified term.

DEPOSITED. *adj.* Includes filed, registered, recorded and kept.

DEPOSITED AMOUNT. An amount that, after the coming into force of this section, is put on deposit with the Corporation or left with the Corporation for transmission by post, but does not include an amount paid to the Corporation on account of services or products to be provided at a future date. *Canada Post Corporation Act*, R.S.C. 1985, c. C-10, s. 39.

DEPOSIT INSTITUTION. (a) A bank to which the Bank Act (Canada) applies, (b) a loan corporation or trust company registered under the Loan and Trust Corporations Act, (c) a credit union or credit union league incorporated under the provisions of the Credit Unions and Caisses Populaires Act, and (d) a member commercial bank of the Federal Reserve System of the United States of America. *General Act*, R.R.O. 1990, Reg. 90, s. 7(1).

DEPOSIT INSURANCE. The insurance referred to in paragraph (7)(a). *Canada Deposit Insurance Corporation Act*, R.S.C. 1985, c. C-3, s. 2. See CANADA ~ CORPORATION; POLICY OF ~.

DEPOSIT INSURANCE CORPORATION. (a) A corporation that was incorporated by or under a law of Canada or a province respecting the establishment of a stabilization fund or board if (i) it was incorporated primarily (A) to provide or administer a stabilization, liquidity or mutual aid fund for credit unions, and (B) to assist in the payment of any losses suffered by members of credit unions in liquidation, and (ii) throughout any taxation year in respect of which the expression is being applied, (A) it was a Canadian corporation, and (B) the cost amount to the corporation of its investment property was at least 50% of the cost amount to it of all its property (other than a debt obligation of, or a share of the capital stock of, a member institution issued by the member institution at a time when it was in financial difficulty, or (b) a corporation incorporated by the Canada Deposit Insurance Corporation Act. *Income Tax Act*, R.S.C. 1985, c. 1 (5th Supp.), s. 137.1(5)

DEPOSITION. *n*. Every affidavit, affirmation or statement made under oath.

DEPOSIT OF RECORDS. The handing over of a notary's records to the clerk of the Superior Court of a judicial district for preservation in the archives of such district. *Notarial Act*, R.S.Q., c. N-2, s. 1.

DEPOSITOR. *n*. 1. A person whose account has been or is to be credited in respect of moneys constituting a deposit or part of a deposit or a person to whom a member institution is liable in respect of an instrument issued for moneys constituting a deposit or part of a deposit. *Canada Deposit Insurance Corporation Act*, R.S.C. 1985, c. C-3, Sched. s. 1. 2. A person who has entered into a contract with the minister providing for the making of deposits in a branch. *Treasury Branches acts*. 3. (a) An individual, or (b) an entity that has money on deposit with a trust company, credit union or extraprovincial trust corporation, and includes an individual or entity who holds non-equity shares in a credit union.

DEPOSITORY. *n*. A bank, trust company or person holding by way of deposit or otherwise money, trust funds or assets of any kind relating to the business of a member as a barrister or solicitor.

DEPOSITORY BILL. An unconditional order in writing that is (a) signed by the drawer and addressed to another person, requiring the person to whom it is addressed to pay, at a fixed or determinable future time, a sum certain in money to, or to the order of, a specified person; (b) accepted unconditionally by the signature of the person to whom it is addressed; (c) marked prominently and legibly on its face and within its text, at or before the time of issue, with the words "This is a depository bill subject to the *Depository Bills and Notes Act*" or "Lettre de dépôt assujettie à la *Loi sur les lettres et billets de dépôt*"; (d) not marked with any words prohibiting negotiation, transfer or assignment of it or of an interest in it; (e) made payable, originally or by endorsement, to a clearing house; and (f) deposited with the clearing house to which it is made payable. *Depository Bills and Notes Act*, S.C. 1998, c. 13, s. 4.

DEPOSITORY NOTE. An unconditional promise in writing that is (a) signed by the maker, promising to pay, at a fixed or determinable future time, a sum certain in money to, or to the order of, a specified person; (b) marked prominently and legibly on its face and within its text, at or before the time of issue, with the words "This is a depository note subject to the Depository Bills and Notes Act" or "Billet de dépôt assujetti à la Loi sur les lettres et billets de dépôt"; (c) not marked with any words prohibiting negotiation, transfer or assignment of it or of an interest in it; (d) made payable, originally or by endorsement, to a clearing house; and (e) deposited with the clearing house to which it is made payable. *Depository Bills and Notes Act, 1998*, S.C. 1998, c. 13, s. 5.

DEPOSIT PROTECTION AGENCY. An entity established (a) to provide or administer a stabilization or mutual aid fund for local cooperative credit societies, (b) to assist in the payment of any losses incurred by the members of a local cooperative credit society in the liquidation of the society, or (c) to provide deposit insurance for members of local cooperative credit societies. *Cooperative Credit Associations Act*, S.C. 1991, c. 48, s. 2.

DEPOSIT RECEIPT. When an insured pays all or part of the premium, the combination of a receipt for the premium with a cover note. Raoul Colinvaux, *The Law of Insurance*, 5th ed. (London: Sweet & Maxwell, 1984) at 19.

DEPOSIT-TAKING BUSINESS. Subject to subsection (3), (i) the lending, in the ordinary course of business, of money received by way of deposit, or (ii) any other activity that is financed wholly or to any material extent out of the capital of, or the interest on, money received by way of deposit. *Loan and Trust Corporations Act*, R.S.A. 2000, c. L-20, s. 1(1).

DEPOSITUM. *n*. A simple bailment of goods. E.L.G. Tyler & N.E. Palmer, eds., Crossley *Vaines' Personal Property*, 5th ed. (London: Butterworths, 1973) at 85. See CONTRACT OF ~.

DEPOT. *n*. A place established or operated as a business by any person for the collection and disposal of empty containers. See FILM ~; TRUCKING ~.

DEPRECIATION. *n*. " . . . [A]n accounting term. It signifies . . . the writing-off of the cost of an asset over its useful life." *Canning v. C.F.M. Fuels (Ontario) Ltd.*, [1977] 2 S.C.R. 207 at 214, 12 N.R. 541, 71 D.L.R. (3d) 321, the court per Dickson J. See STRAIGHT-LINE ~.

DEPRECIATION INSURANCE. Any type of coverage under which the insurance company agrees, in effect, to pay the *difference* between actual cash value and full replacement costs." What is insured, simply put, is depreciation. Under replacement coverage, insureds are entitled to receive the amount necessary to rebuild a structure or replace its contents in a new condition, without deducting for depreciation. Recovery is allowed, in the words of many courts, on a new-for-old basis. *Brkich & Brkich Enterprises Ltd. v. American Home Assurance Co.* (1995), 8 B.C.L.R. (3d) 1 (C.A.) appeal to S.C.C. dismissed, reasons of Finch J.A. adopted.

DEPRESSED FRACTURE. A fracture, often in the vault of the skull, in which fragments are depressed towards the brain. F.A. Jaffe, *A Guide to Pathological Evidence*, 3d ed. (Toronto: Carswell, 1991) at 220.

DEPRIVATION. *n*. 1. Removal of an offender's rights in property. S. Mitchell, P.J. Richardson & D.A. Thomas, eds., *Archbold Pleading, Evidence and Practice in Criminal Cases*, 43d ed. (London: Sweet & Maxwell, 1988) at 813. 2. Deprived of the necessities for proper sustenance of life. 3. "[As an element of fraud] . . . detriment, prejudice or risk of prejudice to the economic interests of the victim; it is not essential that there be actual economic loss as the outcome of the fraud: . . ." *R. v. Stewart* (1983), 5 C.C.C. (3d) 481 at 496, 42 O.R. (2d) 225, 35 C.R. (3d) 105, 149 D.L.R. (3d) 583, 74 C.P.R. (2d) 1, 24 B.L.R. 53 (C.A.), Houlden J.A.

DEPRIVE. *v*. To take away from; to deny; to defeat.

DEPRIVED. *adj*. "[Refers to] . . . a loss rather than a change . . ." *Woelk v. Halvorson* (1979), 11 C.C.L.T. 152 at 165, 18 A.R. 580, [1980] 1 W.W.R. 609, 106 D.L.R. (3d) 726 (C.A.), the court per Moir J.A.

DEPT. *abbr*. Department.

DEPTH. *n*. The vertical dimension from the highest point of an excavation to a point level with the lowest point of the excavation. See LOT ~; MOULDED ~; REAR YARD ~; TRENCH ~.

DEPTH FOR FREEBOARD. 1. The distance measured from the same point as moulded depth, and to the upper surface of the freeboard deck or stringer plate, with no allowance for sheathing, and in the case of a ship having a rounded gunwale with a radius greater than four per cent of the breadth (B) or having topsides of unusual form, means the depth for freeboard of a ship having a midship section with vertical topsides and with the same round of beam and area of topside section equal to that provided by the actual midship section. *Load Line Regulations (Inland)*, C.R.C., c. 1440, s. 1. 2. (a) The moulded depth amidships, plus the thickness of the freeboard deck stringer plate, where fitted, plus T (L minus S) if the exposed freeboard deck is sheathed, where T is the mean thickness of the exposed sheathing clear of deck openings, and S of the total length of superstructures as defined in paragraph (9)(d). (b) The depth for freeboard (D) in a ship having a rounded gunwale with a radius greater than four per cent of the breadth (B) or having topsides of unusual form is the depth for freeboard of a ship having a midship section with vertical topsides and with the same round of beam and area of topside section equal to that provided by the actual midship section. *Load Line Regulations (Sea)*, C.R.C., c. 1441, s. 3.

DEPURATION. *n.* The process of removing micro-organisms that may be dangerous to humans from live shellfish in a controlled environment.

DEPUTY. *n.* One who acts instead of another, or who exercises an office in another person's name.

DEPUTY CHIEF. The one person who has been appointed by the council of the municipality to act in the place of the chief of the fire department in his or her absence or in the case of a vacancy in the office. *Fire Departments Act*, R.S.O. 1990, c. F.15, s. 1.

DEPUTY HEAD. *var.* **DEPUTY-HEAD.** 1. The deputy of the member of the Executive Council presiding over a department and all others whom the Governor in Council designates as having the status of deputy. 2. The deputy minister of a department or the chief executive officer of an agency. See APPROPRIATE ~.

DEPUTY MARSHAL. In the Federal Court, each deputy sheriff is ex officio a deputy marshal.

DEPUTY MINISTER. 1. The senior civil servant in a department who advises the minister and is the senior administrator of that department. 2. (a) The deputy of a minister, (b) an officer who, by an Act, is declared to have the status of a deputy minister, or (c) a person designated as a deputy minister.

DEPUTY RETURNING OFFICER. A person appointed to preside over a polling station.

DEPUTY SPEAKER. 1. A member elected by the House of Commons to be a Chairman of Committees of the Whole under Standing Order 7(1). A. Fraser, W.A. Dawson & J. Holtby, eds., *Beauchesne's Rules and Forms of the House of Commons of Canada*, 6th ed. (Toronto: Carswell, 1989) at 52. 2. The Deputy Speaker and Chairman of Committees of a legislative assembly. 3. The Deputy Speaker and chairperson of the Committee of the Whole.

DERAIGN. *v.* To displace; to prove.

DERELICT. *n.* A ship which is voluntarily abandoned by her master and owner without intent of return or recovery.

DERELICT. *adj.* Abandoned.

DERELICTION. *n.* Abandoning something.

DERELICT MOTOR VEHICLE. A motor vehicle that, (a) is inoperable, and (b) has no market value as a means of transportation, or, has a market value as a means of transportation that is less than the cost of repairs required to put it into operable condition. *General — Waste Management Act*, R.R.O. 1990, Reg. 347, s. 1(1).

DERELICT VEHICLE. A vehicle, other than an abandoned vehicle, that (a) has been abandoned at an airport or otherwise remains unclaimed at an airport for a period of not less than 14 days, and (b) has a market value less than $200. *Airport Personal Property Disposal Regulations*, C.R.C., c. 1563, s. 2.

DERISORY DAMAGES. Small damages awarded to a plaintiff who sustained no loss, but whose legal rights were technically infringed.

DERIVATIVA POTESTAS NON POTEST ESSE MAJOR PRIMITIVA. [L.] A derivative power cannot be greater than the power from which it was derived.

DERIVATIVE. *n.* 1. " . . . [S]omething that arises or is produced (is derived) from something else, either directly or indirectly. . ." *Pfizer Co. v. Deputy Minister of National Revenue*, [1973] F.C. 3 at 4, 34 D.L.R. (3d) 537 (C.A.), Jackett J.A. (Thurlow J.A. concurring). 2. " . . . '[A] compound actually obtained from another by chemical reaction.' " *Pfizer Co. v. Deputy Minister of National Revenue*, [1973] F.C. 3 at 21, 34 D.L.R. (3d) 537 (C.A.), Choquette J.A. (dissenting).

DERIVATIVE ACTION. "[Arises when] . . . a wrong is done to the entity to which the members belong. Such an action may be brought by a member or members, but it is brought on behalf of the entity . . ." *Pasco v. Canadian National Railway* (1989), (*sub nom. Oregon Jack Creek Indian Band v. Canadian National Railway*) 34 B.C.L.R. (2d) 344 at 348, 56 D.L.R. (4th) 404, [1990] 2 C.N.L.R. 85 (C.A.), the court per MacFarlane J.A.

DERIVATIVE EVIDENCE. ". . . [I]nclude all facts, events or objects whose existence is discovered as a result of a statement made to the authorities." *Thomson Newspapers Ltd. v. Canada (Director of Investigation & Research, Combines Investigation Branch)* (1990), 54 C.C.C. (3d) 417 at 528, 76 C.R. (3d) 129, 72

O.R. (2d) 415n, 67 D.L.R. (4th) 161, 29 C.P.R. (3d) 97, [1990] 1 S.C.R. 425, 39 O.A.C. 161, 106 N.R. 161, L'Heureux-Dubé J.

DERIVATIVE MORTGAGE. A mortgage of a mortgage or a sub-mortgage.

DERIVED. *adj.* " . . . '[A]rising or accruing'. . ." *Minister of National Revenue v. Hollinger North Shore Exploration Co.*, [1963] C.T.C. 51 at 54, [1963] S.C.R. 131, 63 D.T.C. 1031, 36 D.L.R. (2d) 636, the court per Abbot J.

DERMAL NITRATE TEST. See PARAFFIN TEST.

DEROGATE. *v.* To destroy; to evade; to prejudice. See NO ONE CAN BE ALLOWED TO ~ FROM HIS OWN GRANT.

DEROGATION. *n.* Evading an act passed or a rule made in the interest of the public, not for the actors' benefit.

DEROGATORY CLAUSE. "Constitutional provisions like s. 1 [of the Charter] . . . they permit some derogation from (in the sense of limitation of and not in any pejorative sense) the very human rights which are, in the words of the section, 'guaranteed' . . ." *Black v. Law Society (Alberta)* (1986), 20 C.R.R. 117 at 139, [1986] 3 W.W.R. 590, 44 Alta. L.R. (2d) 1, 20 Admin. L.R. 140, 27 D.L.R. (4th) 527, 68 A.R. 259 (C.A.), Kerans J.A.

DESCENDANT. *n.* Lineal progeny; child; grandchild. See DIRECT ~.

DESCENT. *n.* The title to inherit real property by reason of consanguinity, as well when the heir is an ancestor or collateral relation as where he is a child or other issue. *Probate Act*, R.S.P.E.I. 1988, c. P-21, s. 1. See LINEAL ~; ROOT OF ~.

DESCRIBE. *v.* "[To provide] . . . a detailed description . . ." *R. v. Simpson* (1981), 20 C.R. (3d) 36 at 57, 58 C.C.C. (2d) 122 (Ont. C.A.), the court per Martin J.A.

DESCRIBED MINERAL SPECIMEN. A mineral specimen for which scientific data, illustrations or descriptions appear in a professional publication. *Canadian Cultural Proper Export Control List*, C.R.C., c. 448, s. 1.

DESCRIPTION. *n.* Identification of goods or other attributes which apply to identified, defined goods. G.H.L. Fridman, *Sale of Goods in Canada*, 3d ed. (Toronto: Carswell, 1986) at 175. See LEGAL ~; MIS~; SALE BY ~.

DESCRIPTIVE. *adj.* Words are found to be descriptive of the wares with which they are associated when they describe something which is material to the composition of the goods. It must be material to the composition of the good or product and not in any way be descriptive of the intrinsic character or quality of the product.

DESECRATE. *v.* To profane, violate sanctity.

DESERTED CHILD. A child (A) whose parent, without reasonable excuse, fails to provide reasonable maintenance, or (B) who has left or has been removed from the home of the parent because of neglect by or misconduct or acts of cruelty of the parent.

DESERTION. *n.* 1. " . . . [A] forsaking and an abandonment of the conjugal relationship of husband and wife and requires the intention to desert against the wishes of the other spouse. It is not necessarily a withdrawal from a place, but from a state of things." *Reid v. Reid* (1970), 5 R.F.L. 37 at 42 (Ont. Prov. Ct.), Creighton Prov. Ct. J. 2. A person deserts who, (a) being on or having been warned for active service, duty during an emergency or other important service, is absent without authority with the intention of avoiding that service; (b) having been warned that his vessel is under sailing orders, is absent without authority with the intention of missing that vessel; (c) absents himself without authority from his place of duty with the intention of remaining absent from his place of duty; (d) is absent without authority from his place of duty and at any time during such absence forms the intention of remaining absent from his place of duty; or (e) while absent with authority from his place of duty, with the intention of remaining absent from his place of duty, does any act or omits to do anything the natural and probable consequence of which act or omission is to preclude his being at his place of duty at the time required. *National Defence Act*, R.S.C. 1970, c. N-4, s. 78. See CONSTRUCTIVE ~.

DESIGN. *n.* 1. A plan, sketch, drawing, graphic representation or specification intended to govern the construction, enlargement or alteration of a building or part of a building and related site development. 2. With reference to a boiler, pressure vessel or plant or an elevating device, means its plan or pattern, and includes drawings, specifications, and where required, the calculations and a model. 3. Features of shape, configuration, pattern or ornament and any combination of those features that, in a finished article, appeal to and are judged solely by the eye. *In-*

dustrial Design Act, R.S.C. 1985, c. I-9, s. 2. 4. " . . . [A] pattern or representation which the eye can see and which can be applied to a manufactured article . . ." *Clatworthy & Son Ltd. v. Dale Display Fixtures Ltd.*, [1929] 3 D.L.R. 11 at 12, [1929] S.C.R. 429, the court per Lamont J. See INDUSTRIAL ~; INTERIOR ~; PRINTED BOOK OF PICTURES OR ~S.

DESIGNATE. *n*. A person appointed.

DESIGNATED AGENCY. A person designated by a marketing commission or producer board as the agency by or though which a regulated product is car is not to be marketed.

DESIGNATED AIRSPACE HANDBOOK. The manual that contains information in respect of the designation of airspace and that is published under the authority of the Minister. *Canadian Aviation Regulations*, SOR/96-433, s. 101.01(1).

DESIGNATED EDUCATIONAL INSTITUTION. (a) An educational institution in Canada that is (i) a university, college or other educational institution designated by the Lieutenant Governor in Council of a province as a specified educational institution under the Canada Student Loans Act or recognized by the Minister of Education of the Province of Quebec for the purposes of the Student Loans and Scholarships Act of the Province of Quebec, or (ii) certified by the Minister of Employment and Immigration to be an educational institution providing courses, other than courses designed for university credit, that furnish a person with skills for, or improve a person's skills in, an occupation, (b) a university outside Canada at which the individual referred to in subsection (2) was enrolled in a course, of not less than 13 consecutive weeks duration, leading to a degree, or (c) if the individual referred to in subsection (2) resided, throughout the year referred to therein, in Canada near the boundary between Canada and the United States, an educational institution in the United States to which the individual commuted that is a university, college or other educational institution providing courses at a post-secondary school level. *Income Tax Act*, R.S.C. 1985, c. 1 (5th Supp.), c. 188.6 (1).

DESIGNATED GROUP. Women, aboriginal peoples, persons with disabilities and members of visible minorities. *Employment Equity Act*, R.S.C. 1985 (2d Supp.), c. 23, s. 3.

DESIGNATED INFORMATION. Information as to the race, creed, colour, nationality, ancestry, place of origin, sex or geographical location of a person. *Discriminatory Business Practices Act*, R.S.O. 1990, c. D.12, s. 1.

DESIGNATED MARIHUANA OFFENCE. (*a*) An offence, in respect of marihuana, against section 5 of the Act, or against section 6 of the Act except with respect to importation; or (*b*) a conspiracy or an attempt to commit or being an accessory after the fact in relation to or any counselling in relation to an offence referred to in paragraph (*a*). *Marihuana Medical Access Regulations*, SOR/2001-227, s. 1(1).

DESIGNATED PERILS. Hail, drought, excessive rainfall, excessive moisture, flood, frost, wind including tornado, disease, including rust, and pests. *Crop Insurance Act*, R.S.M. 1970, c. C310, s. 1.

DESIGNATED PROVINCE. A province or territory of Canada that is designated by regulation as a province or territory in which there is in force legislation substantially similar to this Act. *Pension Benefits acts.*

DESIGNATED SEATING CAPACITY. The number of designated seating positions provided in a vehicle or, in the case of a motor home that has a GVWR greater than 4 536 kg, may, at the option of the manufacturer, mean the number of sleeping positions provided in the motor home. *Motor Vehicle Safety Regulations*, C.R.C., c. 1038, s. 2.

DESIGNATED SEATING POSITION. Any plan view position intended by the manufacturer to provide seating accommodation while the vehicle is in motion for a person at least as large as a 5th percentile adult female, as defined in section 100 of Schedule IV, but does not include any plan view position of temporary or folding jump seats or other auxiliary seating accommodation. *Motor Vehicle Safety Regulations*, C.R.C., c. 1038, s. 2. See OUTBOARD ~.

DESIGNATED SMOKING AREA. A separate space set aside for use by smokers and clearly identified as such.

DESIGNATED SMOKING ROOM. An enclosed and independently ventilated space, set aside for use by smokers and clearly identified as such.

DESIGNATED SUBSTANCE. A biological, chemical or physical agent or combination thereof prescribed as a designated substance to which the exposure of a worker is prohibited, regulated, restricted, limited or controlled. *Oc-*

cupational Health and Safety Act, R.S.O. 1990, c. O.1, s. 1(1).

DESIGNATED SUBSTANCE OFFENCE. 1. An offence under Part I of the CDSA [*Controlled Drugs and Substances Act*, S.C. 1996, c. 19], excluding s. 4(1) possession offences, and includes trafficking in cocaine (s. 5(1) CDSA). *R. v. Marriott*, 2001 NSCA 84, 42 C.R. (5th) 339, (sub nom. *Stone Estate, Re*) 155 C.C.C. (3d) 168, 194 N.S.R. (2d) 64 (C.A.). 2. (*a*) An offence against section 39, 44.2, 44.3, 48, 50.2 or 50.3 of the *Food and Drugs Act*, as those provisions read immediately before May 14, 1997; (*b*) an offence against section 4, 5, 6, 19.1 or 19.2 of the *Narcotic Control Act*, as those provisions read immediately before May 14, 1997; (*c*) an offence under Part I of the Act, except subsection 4(1); or (*d*) a conspiracy or an attempt to commit, being an accessory after the fact in relation to or any counselling in relation to an offence referred to in any of paragraphs (*a*) to (*c*). *Marihuana Medical Access Regulations*, SOR/2001-227, s. 1(1).

DESIGNATIO JUSTICIARIORUM EST A REGE; JURISDICTIO VERO ORDINARIA A LEGE. [L.] The sovereign appoints justices, but the law gives them their ordinary jurisdiction.

DESIGNATION. *n*. The instrument designating a person or purpose; specifying which person is to receive a benefit or perform a function or other purpose. See MODEL ~; SIZE ~.

DESIGNATIO PERSONAE. [L.] The description of a party or person to a contract or deed.

DESIGNATIO UNIUS EST EXCLUSIO ALTERIUS, ET EXPRESSUM FACIT CESSARE TACITUM. [L.] Mentioning one thing excludes another; when you mention one thing expressly, anything you did not mention ceases.

DESIGN BEARING PRESSURE. The pressure applied by a foundation unit to soil or rock and which is not greater than the allowable bearing pressure.

DESIGN-BUILD CONTRACT. The client deals with the main contractor who provides the design and the construction under one contract.

DESIGN CAPACITY. The load that a foundation is designed to transfer to the supporting soil or rock.

DESIGNED PRESSURE. The pressure that a boiler, pressure vessel or pressure plant is designed to withstand.

DESIGNER. *n*. The person responsible for the design. *Building Code Act*, R.R.O. 1980, Reg. 87, s. 1.

DESIGN LOAD. The load applied to a foundation unit and which is not greater than the allowable load.

DESIGN PRESSURE. 1. The maximum pressure that a boiler, pressure vessel or plant is designed to withstand safely when operating normally. *Boiler and Pressure Vessels acts*. 2. Synonymous with "maximum allowable working pressure" as used in the A.S.M.E. Boiler and Pressure Vessel Code.

DESIGN PROFESSION. Includes the professional practice of architecture or engineering, landscape architecture, town planning, environment planning, interior design and related professions but does not include the practice of drafting. *Architects Act*, R.S. Nfld. 1990, c. A-15, s. 2.

DESIGN PROPERTY. A property of the soil or rock used in proportioning and determining the design capacity of a foundation.

DE SIMILIBUS IDEM EST JUDICIUM. [L.] In similar cases the judgment is the same.

DESK ORDER DIVORCE. A divorce, permitted by the Rules of Court, obtained by the filing of documents without the necessity of attendance before a Judge.

DE SON TORT. [Fr.] Of his own wrong. See EXECUTOR ~; TRUSTEE ~.

DE SON TORT DEMESNE. Of one's own wrong.

DESPATCH. *v*. To send off quickly.

DESPATCH. *n*. A letter, message or order concerning affairs of state sent with speed.

DESPATCHER. *n*. A person actually on duty operating a marine radiotelephone station for controlling ship traffic entering or within a canal. *Canal Regulations*, C.R.C., c. 1564, s. 2.

DESPITE. *prep*. Even if; notwithstanding.

DESPITUS. *n*. One who is contemptible.

DESPONSATION. *n*. Betrothal of people to each other.

DESPOT. *n*. A person governing with unlimited authority.

DESPOTISM. *n*. Absolute governing power.

DESTINATION. *n*. The point to which the passengers or goods to be transported. See IMMOVEABLE BY ~; PLACE OF ~.

DESTITUTE. *adj*. Without means; not possessing necessaries of life.

DESTROY. *v*. 1. Includes slaughter and other means of disposal of an animal. 2. With reference to a restricted weed, to (i) kill all growing parts of the weed, or (ii) render the reproductive mechanisms of the weed non-viable. *Weed Control acts*.

DESTRUCTIO. *n*. [L.] Waste.

DESTRUCTION SCHEDULES. See RETENTION AND ~.

DESTRUCTIVE TEST. A test on a sample of shaft rope wherein the shaft rope is broken during the test by a tensile testing machine.

DESUETUDE. *n*. Disuse.

DETACHED STORE. (a) A building well and substantially constructed of brick, stone, concrete, or other fire-resistant substance or of wood covered or treated with fire-resistant material, and (b) a bin well and substantially constructed of wood covered or treated with fire-resistant material, which building, or bin is (c) detached from any dwelling house and situated at a safe distance from any highway, street, public thoroughfare, or public place; (d) made and closed so as to prevent unauthorized persons having access thereto, and to secure it from danger from without; and (e) exclusively used for the keeping of explosives. *Explosives Regulations*, C.R.C., c. 599, s. 134.

DETACHIARE. *v*. To seize another's goods or person.

DETAIN. *v*. To restrain; to withhold from. See DETENTION.

DETAINED. *adj*. Within the meaning of section 10 of the Charter the question whether a person has been detained invokes several criteria, including: the language used by the police office; whether the person accompanied the police officer voluntarily; whether the person left after being questioned; the point in the investigation when the person was interviewed; whether there were grounds to believe the person was in fact the guilty party; the nature of the questions asked; the subjective belief of the person. See ARBITRARILY~.

DETAINEE. See SERVICE ~.

DETAINER. *n*. Wrongful retention. See FORCIBLE ~.

DETECTIVE AGENCY. Any person who, for remuneration, acts as a detective, investigates offences, gathers or supplies information on the character or behaviour of others.

DETECTOR. *n*. The image receptor or other device that interacts with the X-rays to produce a signal corresponding to the intensity of the X-rays incident on it. *Radiation Emitting Devices Regulations*, C.R.C. c. 1370, s. 1. See HEAT ~; PRODUCTS OF COMBUSTION ~; SMOKE ~.

DE TEMPORE PRAETERITO. [L.] Concerning time past.

DETENTION. *n*. " . . . [M]ay be effected without the application or threat of application of physical restraint if the person concerned submits or acquiesces in the derivation of liberty and reasonably believes that the choice to do otherwise does not exist. . . Le Dain J.'s extension of 'detention' to instances of 'psychological' restraint or compulsion is predicated on two requirements: (1) a 'demand or direction', in response to which (2) 'the person concerned submits or acquiesces in the deprivation of liberty and reasonably believes that the choice to do otherwise does not exist'." *R. v. Elshaw*, [1991] 3 S.C.R. 24 at 52, 55, 7 C.R. (4th) 333, 59 B.C.L.R. (2d) 143, 67 C.C.C. (3d) 97, 128 N.R. 241, 6 C.R.R. (2d) 1, 3 B.C.A.C. 81, 7 W.A.C. 81, L'Heureux-Dubé J. (dissenting). See HOUSE OF ~; PLACE OF ~; PLACE OF SECURE TEMPORARY ~; PLACE OF TEMPORARY ~; PREVENTIVE ~.

DETENTION HOME. Any place including a reception centre, group foster home, foster home and institution for the reception and temporary detention of a child.

DETENTION ORDER. An order that the accused be denied bail until trial.

DETER. *v*. To discourage; to prevent.

DETERIORATION. *n*. The destructive effect which wear and tear causes to property.

DETERMINABLE. *adj*. Coming to an end.

DETERMINABLE FEE. A type of fee simple which terminates automatically on the happening of a specified event which may not occur.

DETERMINATE SENTENCE. A sentence of imprisonment for a limited period of time.

DETERMINATION. *n.* " . . . [I]mplies an ending or finality, the ending of a controversy. . ." *R. v. Appleby* (1974), 18 C.P.R. (2d) 194 at 200, 10 N.B.R. (2d) 162, 21 C.C.C. (2d) 282 (C.A.), Hughes C.J.N.B. (Ryan J.A. concurring).

DETERMINE. *v.* 1. To decide; to come to a decision. 2. To come to an end.

DETERMINED. *adj.* Decided; fixed; delimited.

DETERMINED LIFE. (i) In the case of wooden ships, up to ten years, (ii) in the case of fibreglass or aluminum ships, up to fifteen years, and (iii) in the case of steel ships, up to twenty years from the date of issue by the director of the certificate referred to in section 12. *Fishing Ships Bounties Act*, R.S. Nfld. 1990, c. F-19, s. 2.

DETERRENCE. *n.* 1. " . . . [T]he achieving of control by fear." *R. v. McGinn* (1989), 49 C.C.C. (3d) 137 at 155, 75 Sask. R. 161 (C.A.), Vancise J.A. (dissenting). 2. One of the principles of sentencing of those convicted of offences.

DETERRENT. *n.* A penalty imposed with view to preventing others from committing same act.

DETERRENT. *adj.* Preventative.

DETINET. [L.] One detains.

DETINUE. *n.* " . . . [W]here there is a wrongful taking [of goods] the victim may have the alternative of claiming in detinue, where the unsuccessful defendant must replace the goods or pay the value at the time of the trial. . ." *Steiman v. Steiman* (1982), 23 C.C.L.T. 182 at 187, 18 Man. R. (2d) 203, 143 D.L.R. (3d) 396 (C.A.), O'Sullivan J.A. (Hall J.A. concurring). See ACTION FOR ~.

DETINUIT. [L.] One detained.

DETONATING CORD. An explosive core contained in a waterproof covering that for detonation requires an ordinary detonator and fuse attached.

DETONATING FUSE. An explosive core contained within a waterproof textile covering which for detonation requires an ordinary detonator and fuse attached thereto.

DETONATOR. *n.* 1. A device used in firing charges of explosives in the form of cartridges and includes a blasting cap, electric blasting cap and delay electric blasting cap. 2. A capsule or case that is of such strength and construction, and contains an explosive of the fulminate class in such quantity that the explosion of one capsule or case will communicate the explosion to other like capsules or cases.

DETROIT RIVER GROUP. The geological formations generally known as the Detroit River Group of formations of Devonian age.

DEUTEROGAMY. *n.* A second marriage.

DEV. *abbr.* Development.

DEVALUATION. *n.* An official reduction in the amount of gold relating to the paper value of currency or the reduction in value of a currency in relation to a standard in use, other than gold.

DEVASTAVIT. [L.] One has wasted.

DEVELOPED LAND. Land that has been subdivided for the uses and purposes specified in an approved plan of subdivision and includes land that has been improved with the provision of sewer or water services.

DEVELOPED LENGTH. When used with reference to a pipe, means its length along the centre line of the pipe.

DEVELOPED UNIT. A drainage unit that has a well completed therein that is capable of producing oil or gas in paying quantities.

DEVELOPED WELL. A well that obtains oil from a producing area and that is not a new well.

DEVELOPER. *n.* 1. The owner of lands on which development is proposed. 2. A person who, on the date that a condominium plan is presented for registration, is the registered owner of the land included in the plan. 3. A person who applies for a building permit in respect of a major retail development. 4. A person who, alone or in conjunction with other persons, sells or offers for sale to the public (i) residential units, or (ii) proposed residential units, that have not previously been sold to the public. See OWNER ~.

DEVELOPMENT. *n.* 1. (a) The carrying out of any construction or excavation or other operations in, on, over or under land, or (b) the making of a change in the use or the intensity of use of land, buildings or premises. 2. Any act or deed which prevents beneficiaries from exercising their hunting, fishing and trapping activities, except for "'pre-development'. *An Act respecting the land regime in the James Bay and New Quebec territories*, S.Q. 1979, c. 25, s. 50. 3. A major retail development. 4. Preparing a deposit of a prescribed mineral resource for production. *Ontario Mineral Exploration Program Act*,

R.S.O. 1990, c. O.27, s. 1. See BUILDING ~; CANADIAN INTERNATIONAL ~ AGENCY; CHILD ~ SERVICE; COMMERCIAL ~; COMMUNITY ~ SERVICES; EXPLORATION AND ~; EXPORT ~ CORPORATION; FEDERAL BUSINESS ~ BANK; HYDRO ~; INITIAL ~; LAND ~ AREA; PLANNED UNIT ~; POWER ~; PRE-~; RE~; RESOURCE PROTECTION AND ~ SERVICE; SPECIAL AGRICULTURAL ~; STORAGE ~; STRIP ~.

DEVELOPMENTAL DISABILITY. A condition of mental impairment present or occurring during a person's formative years, that is associated with limitations in adaptive behaviour. *Ontario acts.*

DEVELOPMENTAL SERVICE. A radiocommunication service that provides for research and development, experimentation or demonstration of radio apparatus, or the assessment of the marketability of radio apparatus, new technology or telecommunication services. *Radiocommunications Regulations*, SOR/96-484, s. 2.

DEVELOPMENT CHARGE. A charge imposed with respect to growth-related net capital costs against land under a by-law passed under section 3. *Development Charges Act*, R.S.O. 1990, c. D.9, s. 1.

DEVELOPMENT CONTROL. A type of land use control carried out by administrative means in contrast with zoning, which is accomplished through legislative means. It is used in Manitoba, Newfoundland and the Niagara Escarpment Region of Ontario. I.M. Rogers, *The Law of Canadian Municipal Corporations*, 2d ed. (Toronto: Carswell, 1971-) at 813. See INTERIM ~; ZONING.

DEVELOPMENT COST METHOD. "The Land, being ready for subdivisional or other such development, is, for example, divided into lots; the gross selling price of each of these lots is estimated, and deducted from this figure is the cost of development to arrive at the contractor's net profit. This then becomes the measure of compensation. . ." *Newfoundland (Minister of Public Works & Services v. Associated Builders Ltd.* (1978), 7 R.P.R. 257 at 265 (Nfld. C.A.), the court per Gushue J.A.

DEVELOPMENT COSTS. See PREPRODUCTION ~; PRODUCTION ~.

DEVELOPMENT EXPENDITURE. See PROVINCIAL ~.

DEVELOPMENT EXPENSE. " . . . [E]xpenses which are incurred in the opening up of an ore body by shafts, drives and subsidiary openings for the various purposes of subsequent mining such as, the valuation of deposits, the estimate of its tonnage and in due course, it extraction." *International Nickel Co. v. Minister of National Revenue*, [1969] C.T.C. 106 at 128, [1969] 1 Ex. C.R. 563, 69 D.T.C. 5092, Gibson J. See ELIGIBLE ~.

DEVELOPMENT LICENCE. *var.* **DEVELOPMENT LICENSE**. A licence by which the holder thereof is granted the right to hold a mineral deposit on a designated area for a period of one year. *Mineral Resources acts.*

DEVELOPMENT PERMIT. A permit, issued by a council of a municipality, that authorizes development.

DEVELOPMENT PLAN. A plan, policy and program, or any part thereof, approved under this act covering a development planning area or a portion thereof, as defined therein, designed to promote the optimum economic, social, environmental and physical condition of the area, and consisting of the texts and maps describing the program and policy. *Planning acts.* See URBAN ~.

DEVELOPMENT WELL. A well that, at the time of application for drilling authority, is so located in relation to another well or wells penetrating an accumulation of oil or gas that it is considered to be a well or art of a well drilled for the purpose of production or observation or for the injection or disposal of fluid into or from the accumulation. *Oil and Gas acts.*

DEVIATION. *n*. A major change in the method of performance which was agreed on in a contract.

DEVICE. *n*. 1. Any article, instrument, apparatus or contrivance, including any component, part or accessory thereof, manufactured, sold or represented for use in (a) the diagnosis, treatment, mitigation or prevention of a disease, disorder or abnormal physical state, or the symptoms thereof, in man or animal, (b) restoring, correcting or modifying a body function or the body structure of man or animal, (c) the diagnosis of pregnancy in humans or animals, or (d) the care of humans or animals during pregnancy and at and after birth of the offspring, including care of the offspring, and includes a contraceptive device but does not include a drug. *Food and Drugs Act*, R.S.C. 1985, c. F-27, s. 2. 2. Any weight, weighing machine, static measure or measuring machine and includes any equipment and accessories attached to or used in conjunction with the device that have or can have an effect on the accuracy of the device. *Weights and Measures Act*, R.S.C. 1985, c. W-6, s. 2. 3. Any article, instrument, apparatus, contrivance or gadget that, by itself or in conjunction with a control product, is used as a means to control pests directly or indirectly. *Pest Control Products Regulations*, C.R. C., c. 125 3, s. 2. 4. A demonstration-type gas discharge device. *Radiation Emitting Devices Regulations*, C.R.C., c. 1370, s. 1. See AMUSEMENT ~; ANTHROPOMORPHIC TEST ~; ANTI-HANDLING ~; APPROVED CONTRACEPTIVE ~; CONTROL ~; ELECTROMAGNETIC, ACOUSTIC, MECHANICAL OR OTHER ~; ELECTROMAGNETIC ~; ELEVATING ~; FIXED ~S; FLUORINATION ~; FUEL METERING ~; HEADLAMP CONCEALMENT ~; HEAT RECOVERY UNIT OR ~; HOLD-OPEN ~; HYDRAULIC ~; LIFTING ~; NEW ~; OVER CURRENT OVERLOAD ~; PACKING ~; PARKING CONTROL ~; RADAR WARNING ~; RADIATION EMITTING ~; REMOVEABLE ~S; SAFETY ~; SUBLIMINAL ~; TRAFFIC CONTROL ~.

DEVISE. *n*. A disposition or gift by will. See EXECUTORY ~; SPECIFIC ~.

DEVISED. *adj*. Left in a will. E.L.G. Tyler & N.E. Palmer, eds., Crossley *Vaines' Personal Property*, 5th ed. (London: Butterworths, 1973) at 7.

DEVISEE. *n*. Includes the heir of a devisee and the devisee of an heir, and any person who claims right by devolution of title of a similar description. *Trustees acts*. See RESIDUARY ~.

DEVISER. *n*. A testator.

DEVISOR. *n*. A testator.

DEVOLUTION. *n*. The transfer of an interest in property from one person to another through the operation of law, e.g., on bankruptcy or death.

DEVOLVE. *v*. To transfer property from one person to another through the operation of law, as on death, property devolves to the administrator of the deceased's estate.

DIAGNOSE. *v*. To identify the disease or condition from which a person or animal is suffering.

DIAGNOSIS. *n*. The process of ascertaining a disease or ailment by its general symptoms. See ADMISSION ~; SECONDARY ~.

DIAGNOSTIC SPECIMEN. Any human or animal material, including excreta, secreta, blood and its components, tissue and tissue fluids, that is to be used for the purposes of diagnoses, but does not include live infected animals. *Human Pathogens Importation Regulations*, SOR/94-558, s. 2.

DIAGNOSTIC X-RAY EQUIPMENT. X-ray equipment used in a medical, dental, chiropractic or other health occupation for the purpose of making a diagnosis.

DIALECTICS. *n*. An area of logic dealing with the modes and rules of reasoning.

DIAMETER. *n*. 1. When applied to pipes and tubes, means the actual inside diameter. *Customs Tariff*, R.S.C. 1985, c. C-54, s. 2. 2. The greatest diameter at right angles to the longitudinal axis. 3. With respect to a laser beam, means the minimum diameter of a circular aperture that, when placed to intercept the beam with the plane of the circular aperture perpendicular to the direction of propagation of the beam, will permit 0.865 of the total beam power to be transmitted. *Radiation Emitting Devices Regulations*, C.R.C., c. 1370, s. 1. See BORE ~.

DIARIUM. *n*. Daily food.

DIATOM. *n*. A single-celled microscopic alga.

DIATOMACEOUS EARTH. A siliceous sedimentary rock consisting of microscopic skeletons of unicellular algae. Its unique properties give it commercial value.

DICTA. *n*. Plural of DICTUM. See JUDICIAL ~; OBITER ~.

DICTUM. *n*. 1. Statement or observation. 2. "Some authorities distinguish between obiter dicta and judicial dicta. The former are mere passing remarks of the judge, whereas the latter consist of considered enunciations of the judge's opinions of the law on some point which does not arise for decision on the facts of the case before him, and so is not part of the ratio decidendi. But there is . . . a third type of dictum, so far innominate. If instead of merely stating his own view of the point in question the judge supports it by stating what has been done in other cases, not reported, then his statement is one which rests not only on his own unsupported view of the law but also on the decisions of those other judges whose authority he has invoked. . . Such a statement of the settled law or accustomed practice carries with it the authority not merely of the judge who makes it but also of an unseen cloud of his judicial brethren. A dictum of this type offers .. the highest authority that any dictum can bear." *Richard West & Partners (Inverness) Ltd v. Dick (1968)*, [1969] 1 All E.R. 289 at 292 (U.K. Ch.), Megarry J. 3. " . . . Sometimes they may be called almost casual expressions of opinion upon a point which has not been raised in the case, and is not really present to the judge's mind . . . Some dicta however are of a different kind; they are, although not necessary for the decision of the case, deliberate expressions of opinion given after consideration upon a point clearly brought and argued before the Court . . . much greater weight attaches to them than to the former class." *Slack v. Leeds Industrial Cooperative Society Ltd.*, [1923] 1 Ch. 431 at 451 (U.K. C.A.), Lord Sterndale M.R.

DIE. See POSTAGE INDICIA IMPRESSION ~; POSTMARK IMPRESSION ~; PRINTING ~; TOOL AND ~ MAKER.

DIES. *n.* Solid or hollow forms used for shaping goods in process by stamping, pressing, extruding, drawing, or threading, and includes taps.

DIES AD QUEM. [L.] A day until which interest is payable.

DIES AMORIS. [L.] A day of favour.

DIES A QUO. [L.] The day from which.

DIES CEDIT. [L.] The day commences.

DIES DATUS. [L.] A given day.

DIES DOMINICUS NON EST JURIDICUS. [L.] The Lord's Day is not a day for legal business.

DIESEL ENGINE. A type of engine that has operating characteristics significantly similar to those of the theoretical Diesel combustion cycle. The non-use of a throttle during normal operation is indicative of a diesel engine. *On-Road Vehicle and Engine Emission Regulations*, SOR/2003-2, s. 1(1).

DIESEL FUEL. 1. Includes any fuel oil that is suitable for use in internal combustion engines of the compression-ignition type, other than any such fuel oil that is intended for use and is actually used as heating oil. *Excise Tax Act*, R.S.C. 1985, c. E-15, s. 2. 2. Any fuel petroleum product other than gasoline. See MARINE ~.

DIESEL HEAVY-DUTY VEHICLE. A heavy-duty vehicle that is powered by a diesel engine. *On-Road Vehicle and Engine Emission Regulations*, SOR/2003-2, s. 1(1).

DIESEL OIL. The products distilled from petroleum which are capable of developing the power required for operating internal combustion engines and which are commonly known as diesel oil, semi-diesel oil or fuel oil and includes any other products determined by the Minister to be diesel oil. *Gasoline and Diesel Oil Tax acts*. See HEAVY ~.

DIES GRATIAE. [L.] A day of grace.

DIES INCEPTUS PRO COMPLETO HABETUR. [L.] A day begun is considered to be complete.

DIES JURIDICUS. [L.] A court-day.

DIES NON. *abbr.* Dies non juridicus.

DIES NON JURIDICUS. [L.] A day on which legal business cannot be transacted.

DIET. *n.* An assembly gathered to consider matters.

DIETETICS. *n.* The practice of dietetics is the assessment of nutrition and nutritional conditions and the treatment and prevention of nutrition related disorders by nutritional means. See PRACTICE OF ~.

DIETITIAN. See REGISTERED ~.

DIE WITHOUT ISSUE. A want or failure of issue in the lifetime or at the time of the death of that person and not an indefinite failure of issue, subject to any contrary intention appearing by the will or to any requirements as to age or otherwise therein contained for obtaining a vested estate. *Wills acts*.

DIE WITHOUT LEAVING ISSUE. A want or failure of issue in the lifetime or at the time of death of that person, and does not mean an indefinite failure of issue unless a contrary intention appears by the will. *Wills acts*.

DIFFACERE. [L.] To destroy.

DIFFERENCE. *n.* A difference arising (i) as to the interpretation, application or operation of a collective agreement, (ii) with respect to a contravention or alleged contravention of a collective agreement, or (iii) as to whether a difference referred to in subclauses (i) and (ii) can be the subject of arbitration under Part 7. *Public Ser-*

vice Employee Relations Act, R.S.A. 2000, c. P-43, s. 1.

DIFFERENTIAL. *n*. Different treatment; different remuneration. See RURAL RATE ~; SEX SHIFT ~; WAGE ~.

DIFFERENTIAL PIECE RATE. A system of wages in which two or more piece rates are used.

DIFFUSION LIVIDITY. Spreading of hemoglobin into the tissues and dependent parts of the skin after approximately 8 hours. F.A. Jaffe, *A Guide to Pathological Evidence*, 3d ed. (Toronto: Carswell 1991) at 6 and 222.

DIGAMIA. *n*. A second marriage entered into after the first marriage ends.

DIGAMY. *n*. A second marriage entered into after the first marriage ends.

DIGEST. *n*. 1. A gathering of rules of law based on particular cases, in contrast to a code. 2. An arrangement of the summarized decisions of courts made either alphabetically or systematically. 3. A private author's collection of abstract rules or principles of law.

DIGITAL RADIO STATION. A station that broadcasts in the frequency band of 1 452 to 1 492 MHz (L-Band) using a digital transmission system. *Broadcasting Distribution Regulations*, SOR/97-555, s. 1.

DIGITAL SERVICE AREA. A service area marked for a licensed digital radio station on the map that pertains to that station and that is most recently published under the *Department of Industry Act* by the Minister of Industry. *Broadcasting Distribution Regulations*, SOR/97-555, s. 1.

DIGITAL SIGNATURE. The result of the transformation of a message by means of a cryptosystem using keys such that a person who has the initial message can determine (a) whether the transformation was created using the key that corresponds to the signer's key; and (b) whether the message has been altered since the transformation was made. *Electronic Payments Regulations*, SOR/98-129, s. 1.

DIGNITY. *n*. 1. Worth. 2. Serious quality. 3. The quality or state of being worthy or honourable. 4. The privilege of bearing a title of honour or nobility. See HUMAN DIGNITY.

DIJUDICATION. *n*. Judicial decision.

DILAPIDATED BUILDING. Includes a building which is structurally sound but by virtue of broken windows, torn roofing or other defects is in a condition of substantial disrepair. *Unsightly Property Act*, R.S.P.E.I. 1988, c. U-5, s. 1.

DILAPIDATION. *n*. Disrepair; decay.

DILATORY. *adj*. 1. Tending to cause delay in decision making. 2. Done for the purpose of causing delay.

DILATORY MOTION. A proposal that the original question be disposed of either permanently or for the time being. A. Fraser, W.A. Dawson & J. Holtby, eds., *Beauchesne's Rules and Forms of the House of Commons of Canada*, 6th ed. (Toronto: Carswell, 1989) at 173.

DILIGENCE. *n*. Care.

DILIGENTIA. [L.] Care, diligence.

DILUENT. *n*. Any substance other than a synthetic colour present in a colour mixture or preparation.

DIMENSION. See ASSESSED ~; PROPERTY ~; SHOULDER ROOM ~.

DIMINUTION. *n*. Decrease.

DINARCHY. *n*. Government by two people.

DINING ROOM. A place established and operated as a business which provides, for a consideration, meals and attendant services for the public.

DIOCESAN. *adj*. Relating to a diocese.

DIOCESE. *n*. 1. A territory under the jurisdiction of a bishop. 2. Area of bishops jurisdiction.

DIPHENYLAMINE TEST. See PARAFFIN TEST.

DIPLOMA. *n*. A certificate, less than a degree, awarded by a college.

DIPLOMACY. *n*. Conduct of negotiations between countries.

DIPLOMATIC OR CONSULAR OFFICER. Includes an ambassador, envoy, minister, charge d'affaires, counsellor, secretary, attaché, consul-general, consul, vice-consul, pro-consul, consular agent, acting consul-general, acting consul, acting vice-consul, acting consular agent, high commissioner, permanent delegate, adviser, acting high commissioner, and acting permanent delegate. *Interpretation Act*, R.S.C. 1985, c. I-21, s. 35.

DIPLOMATIC PRIVILEGE. The privilege from prosecution for offences under domestic law afforded to diplomats residing in a country other than their own while they are on official business.

DIPLOMATIC PROTECTION. Assistance which nations grant to their citizens against other nations.

DIPLOMATICS. *n*. The art of evaluating ancient charters, diplomas or public documents and judging them true and false.

DIP NET. A net the bottom of which is closed to form a bag and that is hung on a ring or frame attached to a pole or handle.

DIPTERA. *n*. The order of insects composed of true flies which includes the species Calliphora vomitoria.

DIR. *abbr*. Director.

DIRECT. *v*. To order; to instruct; to lead.

DIRECT. *adj*. Immediate; by the shortest route.

DIRECT AGENT. A substance that produces or modifies a chemical reaction and that is consumed in the chemical reaction to the point of destruction or dissipation or uselessness for any other purpose.

DIRECT AGREEMENT. A consumer agreement that is negotiated or concluded in person at a place other than, (a) at the supplier's place of business, or (b) at a market place, an auction, trade fair, agricultural fair or exhibition. *Consumer Protection Act, 2002*, S.O. 2002, c. 30, Sched. A, s. 20(1).

DIRECT CHARGE CO-OPERATIVE. A co-operative that deals with its members and prospective members only in products or services on a cost basis and that directly charges its members a fee to cover the operating expenses of the co-operative. *Co-operative Corporations Act*, R.S.O. 1990, c. C.35, s. 1(1).

DIRECT CONTRIBUTION. Financial contributions to property are examples of direct contributions. Homemaking or household management services are an example of indirect contributions. *Sanders v. Tomei*, 2000 CarswellBC 1032, 2000 BCSC 696, 9 R.F.L. (5th) 376 (S.C.).

DIRECT DISCOUNTING OF INCOME METHOD. Method of valuing intellectual property. Estimating the future net economic income associated with the asset and reducing the projected income for corporate income taxes on the income, research and development costs, capital expenditures, working capital, royalties for other technology required to support the income stream; and a capital charge on associated assets.

DIRECT DISCRIMINATION. Direct discrimination involves a law, rule or practice which on its face discriminates on a prohibited ground. *Egan v. Canada*, 1995 CarswellNat 6, 12 R.F.L. (4th) 201, 95 C.L.L.C. 210-025, C.E.B. & P.G.R. 8216, 124 D.L.R. (4th) 609, 182 N.R. 161, 29 C.R.R. (2d) 79, [1995] 2 S.C.R. 513, 96 F.T.R. 80 (note). Per Cory and Iacobucci JJ. (dissenting). See MEIORIN TEST.

DIRECTED. *v*. Advised, guided, ordered or controlled another, or something to be done.

DIRECTED VERDICT. The decision by the trial judge that there is no case to go to the jury for their deliberation. The judge directs that the accused be freed.

DIRECT EQUITY PERCENTAGE. With respect to formal equity owned by a person in any particular person, (a) where the particular person does not have more than one class of formal equity within the meaning of the regulations, the percentage of the formal equity of the particular person that is owned by the person, and (b) where the particular person has more than one class of formal equity within the meaning of the regulations, subject to the regulations, the aggregate fair market value of the formal equity of the particular person that is owned by the person, expressed as a percentage of the aggregate fair market value of all the formal equity of the particular person. *Canadian Ownership and Control Determination Act*, R.S.C. 1985, c. C-20, s. 2.

DIRECT EVIDENCE. 1. A witness' testimony as to what was observed through the senses. P.K. McWilliams, *Canadian Criminal Evidence*, 3d ed. (Aurora: Canada Law Book, 1988) at 1-11. 2. " . . . [A] necessary connection between the facts proven and the principal fact or factum probandum [exists] . . ." *R. v. Mitchell* (1963), 42 C.R. 12 at 26, 45 W.W.R. 199 (B.C. C.A.), Sheppard J.A. 3. Evidence tending directly to establish the existence or non-existence of an element of the offence charged. *Military Rules of Evidence*, C.R.C., c. 1049, s. 2.

DIRECT EXAMINATION. Questioning of a witness by the party which called that witness.

DIRECT EXPANSION COILS. The piping in which liquid refrigerant is vaporized to produce ice in a rink for hockey, skating or curling.

DIRECT INDICTMENT. A procedure available to the Attorney General or Minister of Justice to prefer an indictment without a preliminary inquiry being conducted.

DIRECTION. *n*. 1. " . . . [A]uthoritative command . . ." *R. v. Bazinet* (1986), 25 C.C.C. (3d) 273 at 284, 54 O.R. (2d) 129, 14 O.A.C. 15, 51 C.R. (3d) 139 (C.A.), the court per Tarnopolsky J.A. 2. The judge's instructions to the jury as to what the law is. See FACING ~; MIS~; NON-~; OPPOSING ~; SIDEWARD~; TRAIN OF SUPERIOR ~.

DIRECTIONAL DIVIDING LINE. A line marked or placed on a roadway as provided in section 108, not necessarily at the centre thereof, to indicate to the drivers of vehicles the portions of the roadway that may be used for traffic proceeding in each direction and, in the case of a roadway on which no such line is marked or placed, means the centre line. *The Highway Traffic Act*, C.C.S.M., c. H-60, s. 1(1).

DIRECTION OF TRAFFIC FLOW. The direction for traffic in a route that is indicated by arrows on a reference chart. *Collision Regulations*, C.R.C., c. 1416, s. 2.

DIRECTIONS FOR USE. Full information as to the procedures recommended for achieving optimum performance of a device, and includes cautions, warnings, contra-indications and possible adverse effects. *Medical Devices Regulations*, SOR/98-282, s. 1(1).

DIRECTIVE. *n*. An order, a direction.

DIRECTLY. See YOU CANNOT DO INDIRECTLY WHAT YOU CANNOT DO ~.

DIRECTLY CHARTERED LOCAL. A union local which receives its charter from a central labour congress and is not part of an international or national union.

DIRECTOR. *n*. 1. ". . . [T]hose persons acting collectively to whom the duty of managing the general affairs of the company is delegated by the shareholders. Their duty is to conduct the business of the company for the greatest benefit of the shareholders. . ." *Minister of National Revenue v. Parsons* (1983), 4 Admin. L.R. 64 at 79, [1983] C.T.C. 321, 83 D.T.C. 5329 (Fed. T.D.), Cattanach J. 2. Where used in relation to a person, includes a person acting in a capacity similar to that of a director of a company. *Securities acts*. 3. Includes a trustee, officer, member of an executive committee and any person occupying a similar position. *Societies acts*. 4. Includes commissioners governors and other officials of any body corporate with comparable responsibilities, whether or not they are called directors. 5. The title of the head or administrator of a government program or office. See BOARD OF ~S; FUNERAL ~; INFORMATION BANK ~; LABORATORY ~; MANAGING ~; MEDICAL ~; MEETING OF ~S; OFFICER-~; PARTNERS', ~S' AND SENIOR OFFICERS' QUALIFYING EXAMINATION; PROVINCIAL ~.

DIRECTORY. *n*. A provision from which no invalidating consequence will follow if it is disregarded, unlike a mandatory provision, which must be followed.

DIRECT PLACEMENT. Placement, other than by the superintendent or a licensed adoption agency, of a child with persons intending to adopt the child.

DIRECT SALE. 1. A sale which involves a consumer and takes place at the buyer's dwelling. 2. A sale by a direct seller acting in the course of business as such. *Direct Sellers acts*.

DIRECT SALES CONTRACT. A written or oral agreement for the direct sale of goods or services. *Direct Sellers acts*.

DIRECT SELLER. A person who: (i) goes from house to house selling or offering for sale, or soliciting orders for the future delivery of goods or services; or (ii) by telephone offers for sale or solicits orders for the future delivery of goods or services.

DIRECT SELLING. Selling, offering for sale or soliciting of orders for the sale of goods or services by (i) going from house to house, (ii) telephone communication, or (iii) mail.

DIRECT TAX. 1. ". . . [O]ne that is demanded from the very person who it is intended or desired should pay it." *Reference re Grain Futures Taxation Act (Manitoba)* (1925), (*sub nom. Manitoba (Attorney General) v. Canada (Attorney General)*) [1925] 2 D.L.R. 691 at 694, [1925] 2 W.W.R. 60, [1925] A.C. 561 (Can. P.C.), the board per Viscount Haldane. 2. ". . . [O]ne that is imposed on the consumer. . ." *Chehalis Indian Band v. British Columbia* (1988), [1989] 1 C.N.L.R. 62 at 67, 31 B.C.L.R. (2d) 333, 53 D.L.R. (4th) 761 (C.A.), Marfarlane, Wallace and Locke JJ.A.

DIRECT TAXATION. Direct taxation refers to the method of taxation where taxes are imposed on the person intended to pay them. Income and sales tax are direct taxes.

DIRECT TO HOME BROADCASTING. DTH [direct-to-home] broadcasting makes use of satellite technology to transmit television programming signals to viewers. All DTH broadcasters own or have access to one or more satellites located in geosynchronous orbit, in a fixed position relative to the globe. The satellites are usually separated by a few degrees of Earth longitude, occupying "slots" assigned by international convention to their various countries of affiliation. The DTH broadcasters send their signals from land-based uplink stations to the satellites, which then diffuse the signals over a broad aspect of the Earth's surface, covering an area referred to as a "footprint". The broadcasting range of the satellites is oblivious to international boundaries and often extends over the territory of multiple countries. Any person who is somewhere within the footprint and equipped with the proper reception devices (typically, a small satellite reception dish antenna, amplifier, and receiver) can receive the signal. *Bell ExpressVu Ltd. Partnership v. Rex*, [2002] 2 S.C.R. 559.

DIRECT TRANSFER CHARGE. A charge on goods that are (a) moved directly between a vessel and open railway cars or open motor vehicles, or (b) moved directly between a vessel and barges or scows that are alongside it. *Pacific Terminal Tariff By-law*, C.R.C., c. 1083, s. 41.

DIRECT VISUAL SURVEILLANCE. Direct observation by a person who is physically present at the place that is under observation.

DIRIMENT IMPEDIMENT. A bar to a marriage which invalidates it ipso jure.

DISABILITY. *n*. 1. The absence of legal ability to do certain acts or enjoy certain benefits. 2. The incapacity of a minor or of a person who is mentally incompetent. 3. Any previous or existing mental or physical disability and includes disfigurement and previous or existing dependence on alcohol or a drug. *Canadian Human Rights Act*, R.S.C. 1985, c. H-6, s. 25. 4. The loss or lessening of the power to will and to do any normal mental or physical act. *Pension Act*, R.S.C. 1985, c. P-6, s. 2. 5. "... [P]hysical or mental incapacity, usually arising from injury or disease, although it might arise from other causes..." *Penner v. Danbrook* (1992), 10

C.R.R. (2d) 379 at 382, [1992] 4 W.W.R. 385, 39 R.F.L. (3d) 286, 100 Sask. R. 125, 18 W.A.C. 125 (C.A.), the court per Sherstobitoff J.A. 6. In relation to an injured worker, means the loss of earning capacity of the worker that results from an injury. *Workers' Compensation Act*, R.S.O. 1990, c. W.11, s. 1(1). 7. (a) For the purpose of paragraph 18(2)(b) of the Act, a mental or physical condition that a physician has certified as being likely to shorten considerably the life expectancy of a member; and (b) for the purpose of determining pensionable age, a mental or physical condition that a physician has certified as rendering a member unable to perform the member's duties as an employee. *Pension Benefits Standards Regulations, 1985*, SOR/87-19, s. 2, as am. See MENTAL ~; PARTY UNDER ~; PERSON UNDER ~; PERSON WITH A ~; PERSONS WITH DISABILITIES; PHYSICAL ~; PHYSICAL ~ OR MENTAL ~; SENSORY~; SERIOUS OR PROLONGED ~; TOTAL AND PERMANENT ~; TOTAL ~.

DISABILITY INSURANCE. Insurance undertaken by an insurer as part of a contract of life insurance whereby the insurer undertakes to pay insurance money or to provide other benefits in the event that the person whose life is insured becomes disabled as a result of bodily injury or disease.

DISABILITY PLAN. A long term disability income continuance plan, under which an employee who, as a result of illness or other disability rendering him unable to perform his regular duties, is entitled to be paid a percentage of his salary in accordance with that plan. Alberta states.

DISABLE. *v*. To bring about a disability.

DISABLED. *adj*. Incapable of pursuing regularly any substantially gainful occupation. See PHYSICALLY ~ PERSONS.

DISABLED CONTRIBUTOR'S CHILD. A dependent child of a contributor who is disabled.

DISABLED PERSON. Persons who consider themselves disadvantaged by reason of any persistent physical, mental, psychiatric, learning or sensory impairment or who believe that a potential employer would likely consider them so disadvantaged. *Centennial Flame Research Award Act*, S.C. 1991, c. 17, s. 2. See MENTALLY ~.

DISABLING INJURY. An injury during employment which prevents a worker from earning full wages in the work at which the worker was employed before the injury.

DISAFFECTION. *n.* Disloyalty to established authority.

DISAFFIRM. *v.* To repudiate; to deny.

DISAGREEMENT. *n.* A grantee's or lessee's refusal to accept an estate or lease.

DISALLOWANCE. *n.* 1. The Queen's power to annul any statute enacted by the Parliament of Canada. 2. The federal power vested in the Governor General in Council to annul provincial statutes.

DISAPPEARANCE. *n.* Enforced disappearance of persons means the arrest, detention or abduction of persons by, or with the authorization, support or acquiescence of, a State or a political organization, followed by a refusal to acknowledge that deprivation of freedom or to give information on the fate or whereabouts of those persons, with the intention of removing them from the protection of the law for a prolonged period of time. *Rome Statute*, Article 7.

DISASTER. *n.* 1. A calamity caused by accident, by an act of war or insurrection or by the forces of nature, that has resulted or may result in serious harm to the safety, health or welfare of people, or in widespread damage to property. 2. An emergency in any community caused by fire, flood, tempest or other calamity not resulting from enemy attack, sabotage or other hostile action. See CIVIL ~; NATURAL ~; PEACE-TIME~; POST-~ BUILDING.

DISBAR. *v.* To expel a lawyer from membership in a law society.

DISBARMENT. *n.* Cessation of membership in the law society, and in the case of a barrister means the striking of his name from the barristers' roll, and in the case of a solicitor, means the striking of his name from the solicitors' roll.

DISBURSEMENT. *n.* 1. An expenditure or any other payment or transfer of public money. 2. Money expended or paid out on behalf of the client, such as a fee aid to a court officer or court reporter or witness fees for which a lawyer is entitled to a credit when an account is submitted. 3. " . . . [I]ndicative of an immediate outlay or payment and signifies an expenditure . . . *R. v. McKee*, [1977] C.T.C. 491 at 494, 77 D.T.C. 5345 (Fed. T.D.), Addy J.

DISCARD. *n.* Presently unusable solid or liquid materials removed or rejected during mining or processing operations.

DISCARD SITE. An area within which discard is stored, either temporarily or permanently.

DISCHARGE. *v.* 1. To release a person from an obligation. *R. v. Simmons* (1984), 11 C.C.C. (3d) 193 at 214, 45 O.R. (2d) 609, 39 C.R. (3d) 223, 26 M.V.R. 168, 3 O.A.C. 1, 7 D.L.R. (4th) 719, 8 C.R.R. 333, 7 C.E.R. 159 (C.A.), Howland C.J.O. (Martin, Lacourcière and Houlden JJ.A. concurring). 2. To derive a right or obligation of its binding force. 3. " .. [T]o revoke or to rescind." *Lamontagne v. Lamontagne* (1964), 47 W.W.R. 321 at 33 , 44 D.L.R. (d) 228 (Man. C.A.), Freedman J.A. (Schultz J.A. concurring). 4. Spilling, leaking, pumping, pouring, emitting, emptying, throwing and dumping.

DISCHARGE. *n.* 1. Section 662.1 of the Code gives judges discretion to release an accused after guilt is determined absolutely or on conditions a probation order prescribes. 2. An instrument by which one terminates an obligation under contract. 3. Termination of employment by an employer other than a lay-off. 4. Honourable termination of service in or with the regular forces. 5. Release of a patient. 6. Includes, but not so as to limit its meaning, any spilling, leaking, pumping, pouring, emitting, emptying, throwing or dumping. See ABSOLUTE ~; CONDITIONAL ~; CONSTRUCTIVE ~.

DISCHARGED. *adj.* 1. Relieved from further performance of the contract. *Frustrated Contracts acts.* 2. Of a payment, made or paid. 3. " . . . '[N]ot committed on the charge laid' . . ." *Myers v. R.* (1991), 65 C.C.C. (3d) 135 at 140, 91 Nfld. & P.E.I.R. 37, 286 A.P.R. 37 (Nfld. C.A.), Goodridge C.J.N. (Steele J.A. concurring). 4. " . . . [R]ecognizance is 'discharged' (that is, the debtor is released from his or her obligations), if the conditions of the contract are fulfilled." *Purves v. Canada (Attorney General)* (1990), 54 C.C.C. (3d) 355 at 363 (B.C. C.A.), the court per Legg J.A.

DISCHARGE POINT. See FINAL ~.

DISCHARGE TUBE. See GAS ~.

DISCIPLINARY ACTION. 1. " . . . The reason for disciplinary action is misconduct and the purpose is to punish." *Canada v. Evans* (1983), 49 N.R. 189 at 194 (Fed. C.A.), Le Dain J.A. (Urie J.A. concurring). 2. Action which adversely affects a worker if the employer imposes discipline 3. Action which adversely affects a member of the group which imposes the discipline.

DISCIPLINARY COMMITTEE. See DISCIPLINE COMMITTEE.

DISCIPLINARY COURT MARTIAL. Composed of a military judge and a panel of three members.

DISCIPLINARY MATTER. Any matter involving an allegation of professional misconduct or fitness to practise on the part of a member, student or professional corporation.

DISCIPLINE. *n*. Correction; punishment. See PROGRESSIVE ~.

DISCIPLINE CLAUSE. A clause in a collective agreement permitting an employer to punish employees for disobedience.

DISCIPLINE COMMITTEE. A committee established under a statute regulating one of the self-governing professions. The committee usually has powers to suspend or revoke the professional's authority to practice his profession. Usually, it also has investigatory and hearing powers and duties. It also has the authority, depending on the statute, to impose fines, issue reprimands and to impose other similar types of discipline on members of the profession.

DISCLAIM. *v*. To repudiate; to refuse to recognize.

DISCLAIMER. *n*. 1. The act of renouncing generally substantiated by a deed. 2. Whenever, by any mistake, accident or inadvertence, and without any wilful intent to defraud or mislead the public, a patentee has (*a*) made a specification too broad, claiming more than that of which the patentee or the person through whom the patentee claims was the inventor, or (*b*) in the specification, claimed that the patentee or the person through whom the patentee claims was the inventor of any material or substantial part of the invention patented of which the patentee was not the inventor, and to which the patentee had no lawful right, the patentee may, on payment of a prescribed fee, make a disclaimer of such parts as the patentee does not claim to hold by virtue of the patent or the assignment thereof. *Patent Act*, R.S.C. 1985, c. P-4, s. 48(1). 3. The Registrar may require an applicant for registration of a trade-mark to disclaim the right to the exclusive use apart from the trade-mark of such portion of the trade-mark as is not independently registrable, but the disclaimer does not prejudice or affect the applicant's rights then existing or thereafter arising in the disclaimed matter, nor does the disclaimer prejudice or affect the ap-

plicant's right to registration on a subsequent application if the disclaimed matter has then become distinctive of the applicant's wares or services. *Trade-marks Act*, R.S.C. 1985, c. T-13, s. 35.

DISCLAIMER CLAUSE. A clause in a contract denying that guarantees or other representations have been made.

DISCLAIMER OF REPRESENTATIVE STATUS. A union's statement that it no longer represents certain workers.

DISCLOSED PRINCIPAL. A person whose existence the agent has revealed to the third party, but whose exact identity is still unknown. G.H.L. Fridman, *The Law of Agency*, 6th ed. (London: Butterworths, 1990) at 193.

DISCLOSURE. *n*. 1. A revelation. 2. The provision of documents to a party to a proceeding. May refer to documents held by an opposing party or by an administrative body. 3. "In its simplest form, disclosure will consist of simply displaying what must be disclosed to defence counsel for examination. In its absolute form disclosure will consist of providing copies of the materials to be disclosed where copies are available and copies of notes, copies and 'will says'." *R. v. Vokey* (1992), 10 C.R.R. (2d) 360 at 370, 14 C.R. (4th) 311, 102 Nfld. & P.E.I.R. 275, 323 A.P.R. 275 (Nfld. C.A.), the court per Goodridge C.J.N. 4. The part of the specification other than the claims. *Patent Rules*, C.R.C., c. 1250, s. 2. See CONTINUOUS ~; FULL ~; TIMELY ~.

DISCONTINUANCE. *n*. 1. Breaking off; interruption. 2. "Discontinuance before judgment,. . . amounts to the abandonment of the exercise of a right . . ." *Quebec (Expropriation Tribunal) v. Quebec (Attorney General)* (1983), 29 L.C.R. 6 at 8, [1983] R.D.J. 432 (Qué. C.A.), the court per Jacques J.A.

DISCOUNT. *v*. 1. Lessen, diminish. 2. "To discount a negotiable security is therefore to buy it at a discount; or it may mean, using another sense of the word, to lend money on the security, deducting the interest in advance . . ." *Jones v. Imperial* (1876), 23 Gr. 262 at 270 (Ont. Ch.), Proudfoot V.C.

DISCOUNT. *n*. 1. Lessening, diminishing. 2. The excess of the par or stated value of any security issued or resold over the value of the consideration received for the security. Canada regulations. 3. " . . . [I]n commerce a discount on the sale of an article of trade is an abatement or deduction from the nominal value or price of that article." *Consolboard Inc. v. MacMillan Bloedel (Saskatchewan) Ltd.* (1982), 63 C.P.R. (2d) 1 at 22 (Fed. T.D.), Cattanach J.

DISCOUNTER. *n.* A person who acquires, for a consideration, a right to a refund of tax from the person entitled to it.

DISCOUNT RATE. 1. " . . . [T]he difference between the interest rate that can be earned on the lump sum invested and the rate of inflation . . ." *McDermid v. Ontario* (1985), 5 C.P.C. (2d) 299 at 303, 53 O.R. (2d) 495 (H.C.), Rosenberg J. 2. The rate, expressed as a percentage, used in calculating the resent value of future damages.

DISCOVERABILITY. *n.* " . . . [I]n the case of discovery of pre-existing real evidence as a result of a [Charter] violation, . . . the practical question triggered in such a case is whether the real evidence could have been discovered without the breach. . ." *R. v. Meddoui* (1990), 5 C.R.R. (2d) 294 at 299, 77 Alta. L.R. (2d) 97, 2 C.R. (4th) 316, [1991] 2 W.W.R. 289, 61 C.C.C. (3d) 345, 111 A.R. 295 (C.A.), Kerans J.A. (Harradence J.A. concurring).

DISCOVERABILITY RULE. " . . . [A] cause of action arises for purposes of a limitation period when the material facts on which it is based have been discovered or ought to have been discovered by the plaintiff by the exercise of reasonable diligence, . . ." *Central Trust v. Rafuse*, [1986] 2 S.C.R. 147 at 224, 37 C.C.L.T. 117, 42 R.P.R. 161, 34 B.L.R. 187, 31 D.L.R. (4th) 481, 75 N.S.R. (2d) 109, 186 A.P.R. 109, 69 N.R. 321, Le Dain J.

DISCOVERT. *n.* A spinster; a widow.

DISCOVERY. *n.* 1. Disclosure by the parties before trial of information and documents. 2. " . . . [F]ollows upon the issues having been previously defined by the pleadings and the purpose of such discovery is to prove or disprove the issues so defined, by a cross-examination on the facts relevant to such issues." *Anglo-Cdn. Timber Products Ltd. v. B.C. Electric Co.* (1960), 31 W.W.R. 604 at 605, 23 D.L.R. (2d) 656 (B.C. C.A.), Sheppard J.A. 3. "[In the context of patents] . . . adds to the amount of human knowledge but it does so only by lifting the veil and disclosing something which before had been unseen or dimly seen. . ." *Reynolds v. Herbert Smith & Co. Ltd.* (1903), 20 R.P.C. 123 at 126 (Ch. D.), Buckley J. See COMMERCIAL ~; DIVIDED ~; ELECTRONIC ~; EXAMINATION FOR ~; SIGNIFICANT ~.

DISCREDIT. *v.* To throw doubt on the testimony of a witness.

DISCRETIO EST DISCERNERE PER LEGEM QUID SIT JUSTUM. [L.] Discretion is to distinguish through law what is just.

DISCRETION. *n.* 1. " . . . [W]hen it is said that something is to be done within the discretion of the authorities . . . [it] is to be done according to the rules of reason and justice, not according to private opinion . . . according to law, and no humour. It is to be, not arbitrary vague, and fanciful, but legal and regular." *Sharp v. Wakefield*, [1891] A.C. 173 at 179 Lord Halsbury, cited by Kellock J. in *Wrights Canadian Ropes Ltd. v. Minister of National Revenue*, [1946] S.C.R. 139 at 166. 2. A person's own judgment of what is best in a given situation. See ADMINISTRATIVE ~; JUDICIAL ~; UNFETTERED ~.

DISCRETIONARY. *adj.* At the discretion of someone; not available as of right.

DISCRETIONARY DUTY. Something required of a trustee, such as allocating trust property, choosing how much a beneficiary should have, or choosing who should have a benefit from among a class of beneficiaries, and then how much that particular beneficiary should have. D.M.W. Waters, *The Law of Trusts in Canada*, 2d ed. (Toronto: Carswell, 1984) at 28-29.

DISCRETIONARY REMEDY. Given at a court's discretion, not available as of right.

DISCRETIONARY SERVICE. A programming service that is not included in the basic service and that is distributed to subscribers on a discretionary basis for a fee separate from and in addition to the fee charged for the basic service. *Broadcasting Distribution Regulations*, SOR/97-555, s. 1.

DISCRETIONARY TRUST. A trust in which trustees are given absolute discretion concerning the allocation of the capital and income of the trust fund to beneficiaries.

DISCRIMINATION. *n.* 1. " . . . [A] distinction, whether intentional or not but based on grounds relating to personal characteristics of the individual or group, which has the effect of imposing burdens, obligations, or disadvantages on such individual or group not imposed on others, or which withholds or limits access to opportunities, benefits, and advantages, available to other members of society . . ." *Andrews v. Law Society (British Columbia)* (1989), 56 D.L.R. (4th) 1 at 18, 36 C.R.R. 193, [1989] 2 W.W.R. 289, 25

C.C.E.L. 255, 91 N.R. 255, 34 B.C.L.R. (2d) 273, 10 C.H.R.R. D/5719, [1989] 1 S.C.R. 143, McIntyre J. (Dickson C.J.C., Lamer, Wilson and L'Heureux-Dubé JJ. concurring). 2. Another definition of discrimination is provided by Justice Abella in her Royal Commission Report on *Equality in Employment*, (Ottawa: Minister of Supply & Services, 1984) at p. 2: Discrimination in this context means practices or attitudes that have, whether by design or impact, the effect of limiting an individual's or a group's right to the opportunities generally available because of attributed rather than actual characteristics. What is impeding the full development of the potential is not the individual's capacity but an external barrier that artificially inhibits growth. 3. Discrimination is not only about groups. It is also about individuals who are arbitrarily disadvantaged for reasons having largely to do with attributed stereotypes, regardless of their actual merit. Discrimination on the basis of marital status may be defined as practices or attitudes which have the effect of limiting the conditions of employment of, or the employment opportunities available to, employees on the basis of a characteristic relating to their marriage (or non-marriage) or family. *A. v. B.* (2000), 2000 CarswellOnt 4203, (sub nom. *Ontario (Human Rights Commission) v. Mr. A*) 50 O.R. (3d) 737, 25 Admin. L.R. (3d) 1, 139 O.A.C. 13, (sub nom. *Mr. B. v. Ontario (Human Rights Commission)*) 195 D.L.R. (4th) 405, 7 C.C.E.L. (3d) 177, (sub nom. *Ontario (Human Rights Commission) v. Mr. A*) 2001 C.L.L.C. 230-015 (C.A.). 4. Selection for or the giving of unfavourable treatment. 5. A court that is called upon to determine a discrimination claim under s. 15(1) should make the following three broad inquiries: (A)Does the impugned law (a) draw a formal distinction between the claimant and others on the basis of one or more personal characteristics, or (b) fail to take into account the claimant's already disadvantaged position within Canadian society resulting in substantively differential treatment between the claimant and others on the basis of one or more personal characteristics? (B)Is the claimant subject to differential treatment based on one or more enumerated and analogous grounds? and (C)Does the differential treatment discriminate, by imposing a burden upon or withholding a benefit from the claimant in a manner which reflects the stereotypical application of presumed group or personal characteristics, or which otherwise has the effect of perpetuating or promoting the view that the individual is less capable or worthy of recogni-

tion or value as a human being or as a member of Canadian society, equally deserving of concern, respect, and consideration? *Law v. Canada (Minister of Employment & Immigration)*, [1999] 1 S.C.R. 497. See ADVERSE EFFECT ~; CONSTRUCTIVE ~; CONVENTION ON THE ELIMINATION OF ALL FORMS OF ~ AGAINST WOMEN; CONVENTION ON THE ELIMINATION OF ALL FORMS OF RACIAL ~; DIRECT ~; POISONED ENVIRONMENT SEXUAL HARASSMENT; QUID PRO QUO SEXUAL HARASSMENT; RACIAL ~; REVERSE~; SEX ~; SYSTEMIC ~.

DISCRIMINATORY. *adj.* To be discriminatory within the meaning of section 15 of the Charter, there must be a legislative distinction, the distinction must result in a denial of one of the four equality rights on the basis of the claimant's membership in an identifiable group and the distinction must be capable of either promoting or perpetuating the view that the individual or group adversely affected by this distinction is less capable or less worthy of recognition or value as (a) human being(s) or (a) member(s) of Canadian society.

DISCRIMINATORY ACTION. Any action by an employer which adversely affects a worker with respect to any terms or conditions of employment or opportunity for promotion, and includes the action of dismissal, layoff, suspension, demotion, transfer of job or location, reduction in wages, change in hours of work or reprimand. *Occupational Health and Safety acts.*

DISC WHEEL. A supporting member for a tire or tire and tube assembly, comprising a rim with a dish shaped component that is permanently attached to the inner circumference of the rim. *Motor Vehicle Safety Regulations*, C.R.C., c.1038, s. 2.

DISEASE. *n.* 1. ". . . [A]n ailment that disorders one or more of the vital functions or organs of the body, causing a morbid physical condition." *Tomlinson v. Prudential Insurance Co. of America*, [1954] O.R. 508 at 516, [1954] I.L.R. 1-144 (C.A.), the court per Laidlaw J.A. 2. Any condition that adversely affects the health of an animal. 3. A condition that exists in a plant or seed as the result of the action of virus, fungus, bacterium, or any other similar or allied organism and that inures to or may injure the plant or any part thereof. See APPEARANCE OF THE INJURY OR ~; BANG'S ~; COMMUNICA-

BLE ~; CONTAGIOUS ~; DANGEROUS ~; DUTCH ELM ~; ENDEMIC ~; EPIDEMIC ~; FRUIT TREE~; INDUSTRIAL ~; INFECTIOUS ~; NOTIFIABLE ~; OCCUPATIONAL ~; PLANT ~; REPORTABLE ~; SEXUALLY TRANSMITTED ~; VENEREAL ~; VIRULENT ~.

DISEASED. *adj*. 1. Infected with an infectious or contagious disease. 2. Affected by disease.

DISEASE OF THE MIND. 1. " . . . Any malfunctioning of the mind or mental disorder having its source primarily in some subjective condition or weakness internal to the accused (whether fully understood or not) may be a 'disease of the mind' if it prevents the accused from knowing what he is doing, but transient disturbances of consciousness due to certain specific external factors do not fall within the concept of disease of the mind. . ." *R. v. Rabey* (1977), 40 C.R.N.S. 46 at 62-63, 17 O.R. (2d) 1, 1 L. Med. Q. 280, 37 C.C.C. (2d) 461, 79 D.L.R. (3d) 414 (C.A.), Martin J.A., adopted in *R. v. Rabey* (1980), 15 C.R. (3d) 225 (Eng.), [1980] 2 S.C.R. 513, 54 C.C.C. (2d) 1, 32 N.R. 451, 20 C.R. (3d) 1 (Fr.). 2. " . . . [I]n a legal sense, . . . embraces any illness, disorder or abnormal condition which impairs the human mind and its functioning, excluding, however, self-induced states caused by alcohol or drugs, as well as transitory mental states such as hysteria or concussion. . ." *R. v. Cooper* (1979), 13 C.R. (3d) 97 at 117 (Eng.), [1980] 1 S.C.R. 1149, 18 C.R. (3d) 138 (Fr.), 51 C.C.C. (2d) 129, 31 N.R. 234, 4 Led. Med. Q. 227, 110 D.L.R. (3d) 46, Dickson J. (Laskin C.J.C., Beetz, Estey and McIntyre JJ. concurring). 3. Such a broad definition [as in *R. v. Cooper*] is surely large enough to encompass cases of sleepwalking that create dangers that society must address. *Canada v. Campbell* (2000), 2000 CarswellOnt 2116, 35 C.R. (5th) 314 (S.C.J.) 4. Taken alone, the question of what mental conditions are included in the term disease of the mind is a question of law. However, the trial judge must also determine whether the condition the accused claims to have suffered from satisfies the legal test for disease of the mind. This involves an assessment of the particular evidence in the case rather than a general principle of law and is thus a question of mixed law and fact. *R. v. Stone*, 1999 CarswellBC 1064, [1999] 2 S.C.R. 290. See INSANITY.

DISENTAIL. *v*. To bring an entail to an end.

DISENTAILING DEED. An assurance through which a tenant in tail blocks the entail in order to convert it into a fee simple.

DISENTITLED. *adj*. Not entitled.

DISFIGUREMENT. *n*. An external injury which detracts from personal appearance.

DISFRANCHISEMENT. *n*. Depriving of a franchise, privilege or immunity.

DISGORGEMENT. *n*. The paying over, to the victim, of any secret profit obtained by a fiduciary or trustee at the expense of the person to whom the fiduciary duty is owed.

DISGUISED EXTRADITION. 1. Occurs if the purpose of deportation proceedings is to surrender the subject as a fugitive criminal to a requesting state, and if the proceedings were not undertaken because the Minister genuinely considered the expulsion of the subject to be in the public interest. If the purpose is to surrender the person as a fugitive criminal to a state because it asked for him, that is not a legitimate exercise of the power of deportation. *Shepherd v. Canada (Minister of Employment & Immigration)* (1989), 9 Imm. L.R. (2d) 9 (Ont. H.C.). 2. " . . . [E]stablished when evidence is not strong enough for extradition and the authorities of both countries collude together through deportation to achieve indirectly what they could not achieve through extradition. *Bembenek v. Canada (Minister of Employment & Immigration)* (1991), 15 Imm. L.R. (2d) 229 at 244, 69 C.C.C. (3d) 34 (Ont. Gen. Div.), Campbell J.

DISHONEST. *adj*. " . . . [N]ormally used to describe an act where there has been some intent to deceive or cheat. . ." *Lynch & Co. v. United States Fidelity & Guaranty* Co., [1971] 1 O.R. 28 at 37, 14 D.L.R. (3d) 294 (H.C.), Fraser J.

DISHONESTY. *n*. Conduct which a person knows would be considered dishonest by people generally.

DISHONOUR. *v*. 1. To neglect or refuse to accept or pay a bill of exchange when it is duly presented for payment. 2. A bill is dishonoured by non-payment when (a) it is duly presented for payment and payment is refused or cannot be obtained; or (b) presentment is excused and the bill is overdue and unpaid. When a bill is dishonoured by non-payment, an immediate right of recourse against the drawer, acceptor and endorsers accrues to the holder. *Bills of Exchange*

Act, R.S.C. 1985, c. B-4, s. 94. See NOTICE OF ~.

DISINCARCERATE. *v*. To free from prison; to set at liberty.

DISINFECTION. *n*. 1. The destruction of infectious agents outside the body by any means. *Public Health Act*, S.A. 1984, c. P-27.1, s. 1. 2. The application by inspectors or other persons authorized by the Minister, of chemical materials on infected surfaces, areas or objects for the purpose of killing insects, viruses, fungus, bacteria or other organisms that are designated plant diseases by the regulations. *Plant Disease Eradication Act*, R.S.P.E.I. 1988, c. P-9, s. 1. See TERMINAL ~.

DISINFESTATION. *n*. The destruction or removal, by any physical or chemical process, of animal forms present on domestic animals or humans or in the environment.

DISINTERMENT. *n*. 1. Exhumation. 2. Removal of human remains, along with the casket or container or any of the remaining casket or container holding the human remains, from the lot in which the human remains had been interred.

DISJUNCTIVE TERM. Usually expressed by the word "or" which indicates alternative conditions or matters.

DISMISS. *v*. 1. In employment, to fire, let go, terminate. 2. In proceedings, to refuse the remedy requested.

DISMISSABLE AT PLEASURE. " . . . [W]ithout the requirements of reasons or a hearing." *Hallyburton v. Markham (Town)* (1988), 20 C.C.E.L. 131 at 150, 25 O.A.C. 29, 63 O.R. (2d) 449, 47 D.L.R. (4th) 641 (C.A.), Finlayson J.A. (dissenting).

DISMISSAL. *n*. 1. " . . . [O]f an employee may be effected either by words or conduct. The conduct [must] be such as to amount to a refusal by the employer to continue to be bound by the contract. . ." *Gilson v. Fort Vermilion School Division No. 52* (1985), 12 C.C.E.L. 72 at 74, 61 A.R. 225 (Bd. of Reference), McFayden J. 2. " . . . [I]f made by a court of competent jurisdiction, a final disposition of the case against the accused sufficient to support the plea of autrefois acquit: . . ." *R. v. Dubois* (1986), 25 C.C.C. (3d) 221 at 232, [1986] 1 S.C.R. 366, [1986] 3 W.W.R. 577, 26 D.L.R. (4th) 481, 66 N.R. 289, 18 Admin. L.R. 146, 51 C.R. (3d) 193, 41 Man. R. (2d) 1, the court per Estey J. See CON-STRUCTIVE ~; JUST ~; SUMMARY ~; WRONGFUL ~.

DISMISSAL FOR CAUSE. "[The employer] . . . is entitled to refuse to perform his future obligations because of the prior fundamental breach of the employee. . ." *Carr v. Fama Holdings Ltd.* (1989), 28 C.C.E.L. 30 at 39, 41, 40 B.C.L.R. (2d) 125, 45 B.L.R. 42, [1990] 1 W.W.R. 264, 63 D.L.R. (4th) 25 (C.A.), Wallace J.A. (Hutcheon and Cumming JJ.A. concurring).

DISMISSAL FOR DELAY. Dismissal of the plaintiff's action when that plaintiff has not taken any of certain steps specified within the time permitted.

DISMISSAL FOR WANT OF PROSECUTION. See DISMISSAL FOR DELAY.

DISMISSAL PAY. Severance pay.

DISMISSAL WITHOUT PREJUDICE. One action is dismissed, but another action for the same relief may be commenced.

DISMORTGAGE. *v*. To deliver from mortgage.

DISORDER. See MENTAL ~; PSYCHIATRIC ~; PSYCHOPATHIC ~.

DISORDERLY HOUSE. A common bawdy-house, a common betting house or a common gaming house. *Criminal Code*, R.S.C. 1985, c. C-46, s. 197.

DISPARAGEMENT. *n*. A statement which casts doubt on ownership of property or on quality of goods.

DISPARITY. See WAGE ~.

DISPATCH. *v*. To send off quickly.

DISPATCH. *n*. A letter, message or order concerning affairs of state sent with speed.

DISPATCH CENTRE. A radio station that is equipped to receive calls for ambulance service and to dispatch ambulances by radio or telephone.

DISPATCHER. *n*. A person who operates radio or telephone equipment at a dispatch centre for the purpose of receiving calls for ambulance service and dispatching ambulances.

DISPENSARY. *n*. A place where prescriptions, drugs, chemicals and poisons are (i) sold by retail, or (ii) compounded, or (iii) dispensed, or (iv) supplied or distributed.

DISPENSATION. *n*. Freedom from a legal obligation; liberty to do a forbidden thing.

DISPENSE. *v*. Includes the preparation and release of a drug prescribed in a prescription and the taking of steps to ensure the pharmaceutical and therapeutic suitability of a drug for its intended use.

DISPENSER. *n*. 1. A person who dispenses a drug pursuant to a prescription. 2. A person who is a member of a professional governing body and who is entitled, by virtue of their membership in that body, to manufacture or adapt a medical device in accordance with a health care professional's written directions in order to meet the specific requirements of a patient. *Medical Devices Regulations*, SOR/98-282, s. 1. See LAY ~; OPHTHALMIC ~.

DISPENSING. *n*. Includes the responsibility for taking all reasonable steps to ensure pharmaceutical and therapeutic appropriateness as well as the preparing and releasing of the prescribed medication. *Pharmacy Act*, R.S.N.S. 1989, c. 343, s. 2. See OPHTHALMIC ~; OPTICAL ~.

DISPENSING OPTICIAN. A person who (a) supplies, prepares and dispenses optical appliances, (b) interprets complete prescriptions of duly qualified medical practitioners and Optometrists, and (c) fits, adjusts, and adapts optical appliances to the human face and eyes in accordance with the complete prescriptions of duly qualified medical practitioners and Optometrists.

DISPLAY. See FLYING ~ AREA.

DISPOSAL. *n*. The transfer or sale of the right, title or interest in assets. See DEEP WELL ~; HAZARDOUS WASTE ~ FACILITY; WASTE ~ SITE.

DISPOSE. *v*. 1. "... [O]f property ... to make the property over to another so that no interest therein remains..." *Harman v. Gray-Campbell Ltd.*, [1925] 2 D.L.R. 904 at 908, [1925] 1 W.W.R. 1134,19 Sask. L.R. 526 (C.A.), Lamont. J.A. 2. To transfer by any method and includes assign, give, sell, grant, charge, convey, bequeath, devise, lease, divest, release and agree to do any of those things. *Interpretation Act*, R.S.B.C. 1979, c. 206, s. 29. 3. To destroy. *R. v. Cie Immobilière BCN*, [1979] 1 S.C.R. 865, [1979] C.T.C. 71, 79 D.T.C. 5068, 25 N.R. 361, 97 D.L.R. (3d) 238, the court per Pratte J. 4. "... '[T]o part with', 'to pass over the control of

the thing to someone else' so that the person disposing no longer has the use of the property." *Victory Hotels Ltd. v. Minister of National Revenue*, [1962] C.T.C. 614 at 626, [1963] Ex. C.R. 123, 62 D.T.C. 1378, Noel J.

DISPOSING. *n*. Includes discharging, dumping, throwing, dropping, discarding, abandoning, spilling, leaking, pumping, pouring, emitting or emptying.

DISPOSING MIND. The "disposing mind and memory" essential to testamentary capacity is one able to comprehend, of its own initiative and volition, the essential elements of will-making, such as property, objects, just claims to consideration, revocation of existing dispositions and the like. *Leger v. Poirier*, [1944] S.C.R. 152.

DISPOSITION. *n*. 1. Final settlement or sentencing of a criminal case. 2. "[In the context of the transfer of business from one employer to another] ... something must be relinquished from the first business and obtained by the second." *W.W. Lester (1978) Ltd. v. U.A., Local 740* (1990), 48 Admin. L.R. 1 at 23, 76 D.L.R. (4th) 389, 91 C.L.L.C. 14,002, 123 N.R. 241, 88 Nfld. & P.E.I.R. 15, 274 A.P.R. 15, [1990] 2 S.C.R. 644, McLachlin J. (Lamer C.J.C., La Forest, Sopinka and Gonthier JJ. concurring). 3. The act of disposal or an instrument by which that act is affected or evidenced, and includes a Crown grant, order in council, transfer, assurance, lease, licence, permit, contract or agreement and every other instrument whereby lands or any right, interest or estate in land may be transferred, disposed of or affected or by which the Crown divests itself of or creates any right, interest or estate in land. 4. Disposition hearings in young offender proceedings are equivalent to sentencing hearings in proceedings under the *Criminal Code* [R.S.C. 1985, c. C-46] involving adults. *R. v. H. (J.)* (2002), 161 C.C.C. (3d) 392, 155 O.A.C. 146, [2002] O.J. No. 268, 2002 CarswellOnt 156 (C.A.). A youth court may impose any of the following dispositions on a young offender. Direct that the young person be discharged absolutely, be discharged on such conditions as the court considers appropriate; impose on the young person a fine; order the young person to pay to any other person at such time and on such terms as the court may fix an amount by way of compensation for loss of or damage to property, for loss of income or support or for special damages for personal injury arising from the commission of the offence; order the young person to make restitution to any other person of any property obtained by the young person as a result of the commission of the offence if the property is owned by that other person or was, at the time of the offence, in his lawful possession; order the young person to compensate any person in kind or by way of personal services at such time and on such terms as the court may fix for any loss, damage or injury; order the young person to perform a community service at such time and on such terms as the court may fix; make any order of prohibition, seizure or forfeiture that may be imposed under any Act of Parliament or any regulation made thereunder where an accused is found guilty or convicted of that offence; place the young person on probation; commit the young person to custody, to be served continuously or intermittently, for a specified period; impose on the young person such other reasonable and ancillary conditions as it deems advisable and in the best interest of the young person. *Young Offenders Act*, R.S.C. 1985, c. Y-1, s. 20. 5. In the context of labour relations to accomplish a disposition something must be relinquished by the predecessor business on the one hand and obtained by the successor on the other. A transfer implies a nexus, an agreement or transaction of some sort between the predecessor and successor employers. . . There must be a mutual intent to transfer part of the business. *C.A.W., Local 222 v. Charterways Transportation Ltd.*, 2000 SCC 23, (sub nom. *Ajax (Town) v. CAW, Local 222*) [2000] 1 S.C.R. 538, (sub nom. *Ajax (Town) v. National Automobile, Aerospace & Agricultural Implement Workers Union of Canada (CAW-Canada), Local 222*) 253 N.R. 223, 22 Admin. L.R. (3d) 1, (sub nom. *Ajax (Town) v. National Automobile, Aerospace & Agricultural Implement Workers Union of Canada (CAW-Canada), Local 222*) 133 O.A.C. 43, Per Bastarache J. (dissenting). See CROWN ~; PRE-~ REPORT; TIMBER ~.

DISPOSITIVE. *adj*. Capable of determining an issue.

DISPOSITIVE POWER. 1. The authority to distribute trust property, either capital or income or both, to a beneficiary or among several beneficiaries. 2. The authority of a trustee to draw on capital or income to maintain a beneficiary during infancy, or to give capital to a widow who takes an income interest under a testamentary trust when her husband dies.

DISPOSITIVE POWER OR DISCRETION. Authorization given to a trustee to allocate or distribute trust property to a beneficiary of the trust.

DISPOSSESSION. *n*. Ouster; removal from possession.

DISPROOF. *n*. Proof that not the accused but a third party committed the crime.

DISPROVE. *v*. To refute; to prove to be false.

DISPUTE. *n*. 1. A difference or apprehended difference arising in connection with the entering into, renewing or revision of a collective agreement. 2. Any dispute or difference or apprehended dispute or difference between an employer and one or more employees or a bargaining agent acting on behalf of the employees, as to matters or things affecting or relating to terms or conditions of employment or work done or to be done by the employee or employees or as to privileges, rights and duties of the employer or the employee or employees. See ALTERNATIVE ~ RESOLUTION; INDUSTRIAL ~; INTEREST ~; INTER-UNION ~; JURISDICTIONAL ~; LABOUR ~; LABOUR-MANAGEMENT ~; NOTICE OF ~; PROCESS FOR RESOLUTION OF A ~; WORK ASSIGNMENT ~.

DISQUALIFIED. *adj*. 1. Not eligible. 2. In which some condition precedent was not fulfilled.

DISREGARDS. *v*. Fails to pay attention to. See UNFAIRLY ~.

DISS. *abbr*. Dissentiente.

DISSATISFIED. *adj*. "Dissatisfied" is much broader [than aggrieved]. I take it to mean that the result has failed to meet or fulfil the wish or desire or expectation of the person launching the appeal. *British Columbia (Mushroom Marketing Board) v. British Columbia (Marketing Board)* (1988), 1988 CarswellBC 745, 31 Admin. L.R. 259 (S.C.), Trainor J.

DISSECTION. *n*. Anatomical examination of a corpse.

DISSEISE. *v*. To deprive; to dispossess.

DISSEISIN. *n*. Dispossession. See NOVEL ~; RE~; SEISIN.

DISSEISINAM SATIS FACIT, QUI UTI NON PERMITTIT POSSESSOREM, VEL MINUS COMMODE, LICET OMNINO NON EXPELLAT. [L.] Not permitting the possessor to enjoy or making the enjoyment

less beneficial although not total expulsion, amounts to disseisin.

DISSEISOR. *n*. A person who unlawfully expels another from land.

DISSEISSE. *n*. One turned out of possession.

DISSEMINATION. See INNOCENT ~.

DISSENT. *n*. 1. Disagreement. 2. The decision of a judge who does not agree with the majority of the members of the court. See RIGHT OF ~.

DISSENTIENTE. *adj*. Used in reports of judgments where one or more judges do not agree with the majority of the members of the court.

DISSENTING OFFEREE. 1. An offeree who does not accept a take-over bid or issuer bid. 2. A person who acquires from an offeree a share for which a take-over bid or issuer bid is made.

DISSENTING OPINION. The individual opinion of a judge who does not agree with the majority of the members of the court.

DISSENTING SHAREHOLDER. Includes a shareholder who has not accepted the offer or assented to the plan or arrangement and any shareholder who has failed or refused to transfer his shares to the transferee company in accordance with the contract.

DISSIGNARE. *v*. [L.] To break or open a seal.

DISSIPATE. *v*. To jeopardize the financial security of a household by the squandering of property.

DISSIPATING ASSETS. Jeopardizing the financial security of a household by grossly and irresponsibly squandering assets.

DISSIPATION. *n*. The jeopardizing of the financial security of a household by the gross and irresponsible squandering of an asset. *Marital Property Act*, R.S.M. 1981, c. M45, s. 1.

DISSOCIATION. *n*. In prison, solitary confinement.

DISSOCIATIVE BEHAVIOUR. An impairment of the normally integrative functions of memory, consciousness and identity. The behavioural aspect of a dissociative state is called automatism. *R. v. Sullivan* (1995), 96 C.C.C. (3d) 135 (B.C. C.A.).

DISSOLUTION. *n*. 1. Putting an end to a legal entity or relation. 2. Of marriage, divorce. 3. Of Parliament, dissolution either by the expiration of five years or by proclamation. A. Fraser, W.A.

Dawson & J. Holtby, eds., *Beauchesne's Rules and Forms of the House of Commons of Canada*, 6th ed. (Toronto: Carswell, 1989) at 66. 4. Of a corporation, ending of corporate existence. *Computerized Meetings & Hotel Systems Ltd. v. Moore* (1982), 20 B.L.R. 97, 40 O.R. (2d) 88, 141 D.L.R. (3d) 306 (Div. Ct.), Callaghan J.

DISSOLUTION OF AGE. "[Refers to] . . . the decree absolute." *Pearce, Re* (1974), 18 R.F.L. 302 at 305, [1975] 2 W.W.R. 678, 52 D.L.R. (3d) 544 (B.C. S.C.), MacFarlane J.

DISSOLVE. *v*. To annul; to cancel; to put an end to.

DIST. *abbr*. District.

DISTAL. *adj*. More distant from the origin or from the trunk of the body.

DISTANCE. See LIMITING ~; TRAVEL ~.

DISTANT EARLY WARNING IDENTIFICATION ZONE. The airspace extending upward from the surface of the earth in that area of Canada described in Schedule III. *Security Control of Air Traffic Order*, C.R.C., c. 63, s. 2.

DISTANT TELEVISION STATION. A licensed television station that is not a local television station, regional television station or extra-regional television station. *Broadcasting Distribution Regulations*, SOR/97-555, s. 1.

DIST. CT. *abbr*. District Court.

DISTILLER. *n*. Any person who conducts, works, occupies or carries on any distillery, who rectifies any spirits by any process whatever, either by himself or his agent, or who has in his possession, complete or partially completed, or who imports, makes or manufactures, in whole or in part, any still, worm, rectifying or other apparatus suitable for the manufacture of spirits, and everyone who makes or keeps beer or wash prepared, in preparation or fit for distilling, or low wines or faints, or who has in his possession or use a still or rectifying apparatus, shall be deemed to be a distiller. *Excise Act*, R.S.C. 1985, c. E-14, s. 3.

DISTILLERY. *n*. Any plant or premises where (a) any process of fermentation for the production of wash is carried on, (b) any wash is kept or produced for the purpose of distillation, (c) any mash-tub, fermenting-tub, worm or still for the distillation of spirits is set up or used, (d) any process of distillation whatever of spirits is carried on, (e) any process of rectification of spirits, ether by re-distillation or filtration, or other process is carried on, (f) any spirits are manufactured or produced from any substance whatever, by any process whatever, or (g) any still, rectifier or other apparatus, suitable for the manufacture of spirits, in whole or in part manufactured made or kept, and every office, workshop, warehouse, granary, fermenting-room mash-house, stillroom, rectifying-house, vault, cellar, shed, and or other place owned or occupied by or on behalf of, or for the use of, any distiller, or in which any part of his business as such is transacted where any grain, matter, material or apparatus suitable, for or adapted to the production of spirits, or that is or is to be used in the production or rectification of spirits, is kept or stored, where any other products of the distillery are kept or stored or where any process of manufacture is carried on, shall be held to be included in and to form part of the distillery to which it is attached or appurtenant. *Excise Act*, R.S.C. 1985, c. E-14, s. 3.

DISTINCTION WITHOUT A DIFFERENCE. An expression referring to two expressions which though stated differently mean essentially the same thing. The use of the phrase "damages were sustained" rather than "cause of action arose", in the context of the *HTA*, is a distinction without a difference. *Peixeiro v. Haberman*, [1997] 3 S.C.R. 549.

DISTINCTIVE. *adj.* 1. In relation to a trademark, means a trade-mark that actually distinguishes the wares or services in association with which it is used by its owner from the wares or services of others or is adapted so to distinguish them. *Trade-Marks Act*, R.S.C. 1985, c. T-13, s. 2. 2. In relation to a trade name, means a trade name that actually distinguishes the business in association with which it is used by its owner from the business of others or that is adapted so as to distinguish them. 3. The characteristic of distinctive trade marks in Canada is that they actually distinguish the wares or services of the owner from the wares or services of others or are adapted to distinguish them. *Union Carbide Corp. v. W.R. Grace & Co.* (1987), 1987 CarswellNat 657, 14 C.I.P.R. 59, 14 C.P.R. (3d) 337, 78 N.R. 124 (Fed. C.A.) Urie, J.A. for the court.

DISTINCTIVE CULTURE. The significance of the practice, tradition or custom to the aboriginal community is a factor to be considered in determining whether the practice, tradition or custom is integral to the distinctive culture, but the significance of a practice, tradition or custom cannot, itself, constitute an aboriginal right. To satisfy the integral to a distinctive culture test the aboriginal claimant must do more than demonstrate that a practice, tradition or custom was an aspect of, or took place in, the aboriginal society of which he or she is a part. The claimant must demonstrate that the practice, tradition or custom was a central and significant part of the society's distinctive culture. He or she must demonstrate, in other words, that the practice, tradition or custom was one of the things which made the culture of the society distinctive—that it was one of the things that truly *made the society what it was*. One must ask, to put the question affirmatively, whether or not a practice, tradition or custom is a defining feature of the culture in question. A claim of distinctness is, by its very nature, a claim relative to other cultures or traditions. By contrast, a culture that claims that a practice, custom or tradition is *distinctive*—"distinguishing, characteristic"—makes a claim that is not relative; the claim is rather one about the culture's own practices, customs or traditions considered apart from the practices, customs or traditions of any other culture. It is a claim that this tradition or custom makes the culture *what it is*, not that the practice, custom or tradition is different from the practices, customs or traditions of another culture. *R. v. Vanderpeet*, [1996] 2 S.C.R. 507.

DISTINGUENDA SUNT TEMPORA. [L.] The context of the times must be considered.

DISTINGUISH. *v.* To clarify an essential difference.

DISTINGUISHING GUISE. (a) A shaping of wares or their containers, or (b) a mode of wrapping or packaging wares the appearance of which is used by a person for the purpose of distinguishing or so as to distinguish wares or services manufactured, sold, leased, hired or performed by him from those manufactured, sold, leased, hired or performed by others. *Trade-Marks Act*, R.S.C. 1985, c. T-13, s. 2.

DISTINGUISHING MARK. A distinguishing mark that is appropriated for use on public stores pursuant to Section 416. *Criminal Code*, R.S.C. 1985, c. C-46, s. 417.

DISTRAIN. *v.* To seize goods using distress.

DISTRAINER. *n.* One who seizes a distress.

DISTRAINOR. *n.* One who seizes a distress.

DISTRAINT. *n.* 1. Seizing. 2. Satisfying the wrong committed by taking a personal chattel back from the wrongdoer and delivering to the party injured.

DISTRESS. *n*. 1. Lawfully seizing chattels extrajudicially in order to enforce a right such as payment of rent. 2. Property which was distrained. 3. The state of being in need of proper care, food or shelter or by being injured, sick, abused, in pain or suffering or being subject to undue or unnecessary hardship, privation or neglect. *Animal Protection acts*. See ABUSE OF ~; GRAND ~; POWER OF ~.

DISTRESS COMMUNICATION. A radiocommunication transmitted for the purpose of requesting immediate assistance in a case of grave and imminent danger, preceded, in the case of aeronautical and maritime mobile services, by the signal "SOS" when sent by radiotelegraphy and by the spoken word "MAYDAY" when sent by radiotelephony.

DISTRESS FUND. A public fund established after a disaster.

DISTRIBUTE. *v*. 1. To deliver, handle, keep for sale or sell. 2. Includes rent, lease, sell or supply, or to make an offer to do any of those things. *Motion Picture Act*, S.B.C. 1986, c. 17, s. 1. 3. To calculate a pool in accordance with these Regulations. *Race Track Supervision Regulations*, C.R.C., c. 441, s. 2.

DISTRIBUTING BANK. A bank, any of the issued securities of which are or were part of a distribution to the public and remain outstanding and are held by more than one person. *Bank Act*, R.S.C. 1985, c. B-1, s. 168.

DISTRIBUTING CORPORATION. 1. A corporation, any of the issued securities of which are or were part of a distribution to the public and remain outstanding and are held by more than one person. 2. A corporation (i) any of whose issued shares, or securities which may or might be exchanged for or converted into shares, were part of a distribution to the public, and (ii) which has more than 15 shareholders. *Business Corporations Act*, S.A. 1981, s. B-15 , s. 1.

DISTRIBUTING COOPERATIVE. A cooperative any of whose issued securities, other than membership shares or member loans, are or were part of a distribution to the public and remain outstanding and are held by more than one person. *Canada Cooperatives Act*, S.C. 1998, c. 1, s. 2(1).

DISTRIBUTING PIPE. A pipe to convey water from a service pipe to a fixture or to an outlet and includes the control valves and fittings connected to it.

DISTRIBUTION. *n*. Where used in relation to trading in securities, (a) a trade in a security of an issuer that has not been previously issued, (b) a trade by or on behalf of an issuer in a previously issued security of that issuer that has been redeemed or purchased by or donated to that issuer, (c) a trade in a previously issued security of an issuer from the holdings of a control person, (d) a trade by or on behalf of an underwriter in a security which was acquired by that underwriter, acting as underwriter, before the coming into force of this section, if that security continues, on the day this section comes into force, to be owned by or on behalf of that underwriter so acting, (e) a transaction or series of transactions involving further purchases and sales in the course of or incidental to a distribution. *Securities acts*. See OCCUPANT ~; PRIMARY ~ TO THE PUBLIC; PROMOTIONAL ~; RETAIL ~; WHOLESALE ~.

DISTRIBUTION AND SALE TO THE PUBLIC. Distribution and sale (a) to a person or persons with whom the vendor deals at arm's length, or (b) to a person or persons with whom the vendor does not deal at arm's length for resale directly or indirectly to persons with whom the vendor does deal at arm's length. *Public Utilities Income Tax Transfer Act*, R.S.C. 1985, c. P-37, s. 2.

DISTRIBUTION COMPANY. A person or company distributing securities under a distribution contract. *Securities acts*.

DISTRIBUTION CONTRACT. A contract between a mutual fund or its trustees or other legal representative and a person or company under which that person or company is granted the right to purchase the shares or units of the mutual fund for distribution or to distribute the shares or units of the mutual fund on behalf of the mutual fund. *Securities acts*.

DISTRIBUTION EQUIPMENT. Posts, pipes, wires, transmission mains, distribution mains and other apparatus of a public utility used to supply service to the utility customers.

DISTRIBUTION LINE. 1. A pipe used for transmitting gas for domestic, commercial or industrial purposes and includes the installations in connection with that pipe. 2. A pipe used for transmitting as for domestic, commercial or industrial purposes from a gas line secondary line or a well and includes the installations in connection therewith, but does not include any pipe or installation on, within or under a building.

DISTRIBUTION MAIN. Pipe used for the transmission and distribution of gas at a pressure not exceeding 700 kPa (gauge), for any distance between a city gate and a service pipe.

DISTRIBUTION OF POWERS. The division of legislative powers between regional authorities (provincial legislatures) and a central authority (the federal Parliament) which is the essence of a federal constitution, binds the regional and central authorities, and cannot be altered by the unilateral action of any one of them.

DISTRIBUTION PIPELINE. See LOW PRESSURE ~.

DISTRIBUTION SYSTEM. 1. A system for the supply of electric energy to premises in a city, town, village or hamlet or on a farm, from an electrical generating plant or main substation existing for the purpose of supplying such premises. 2. A system for the supply of gas to consumers' premises from collection or transmission systems. 3. A cable network that carries a signal from the head end into the dwellings of subscribers who pay the cable company fees for the service. See ALLOWABLE ~ PRESSURE; ELECTRIC ~; GAS ~; RURAL ~.

DISTRIBUTION TO THE PUBLIC. Where used in relation to trading in securities, means a distribution that is made for the purpose of distributing to the public securities issued by an issuer, where such trades are made directly or indirectly to the public through an underwriter or otherwise. See GENERATION AND SALE FOR ~.

DISTRIBUTION UNDERTAKING. An undertaking for the reception of broadcasting and the retransmission thereof by radio waves or other means of telecommunication to more than one permanent or temporary residence or dwelling unit or to another such undertaking. *Broadcasting Act*, S.C. 1991, c. 11, s. 2(1).

DISTRIBUTIVE COSTS. Costs ordered on the basis of success on the particular issues in dispute in a matter. See DISTRIBUTIVE ORDER FOR COSTS.

DISTRIBUTIVE ORDER FOR COSTS. ". . . Under this formula the major issues at trial were identified and the party who was successful on each issue was awarded costs for the time and expense attributable to that issue." *Oakville Storage & Forwarders Ltd. v. Canadian National Railway* (1991), 4 C.P.C. (3d) 280 at 287, 84 D.L.R. (4th) 326, 5 O.R. (3d) 1, 52 O.A.C. 188 (C.A.), the court per Carthy J.A.

DISTRIBUTOR. *n.* 1. A person engaged in the business of selling to other persons, for the purpose of resale. 2. A person engaged in selling or distributing a product direct or indirectly to consumer. See AUTOMATIC ~ ELECTRICITY ~; MOTION PICTURE ~; MUTUAL FUND ~; PROMOTIONAL ~; PYRAMID ~; RETAIL ~; VIDEO ~; WHOLESALE ~.

DISTRICT. *n.* 1. A regional administrative unit. 2. A judicial district. 3. A local improvement district. 4. A school district. See BILINGUAL ~; BUILT-UP ~; BUSINESS ~; ELECTORAL ~; GENERAL ~ LEVY; HISTORIC ~; INDIAN ~; JUDICIAL ~; JURY ~; LAND USE ~; LOCAL IMPROVEMENT ~; MULTI-MEMBER ~; NATURAL ~; POLLING ~; RESIDENCE ~; RURAL ~; SINGLE MEMBER ~; TOWN ~; UNORGANIZED ~; URBAN ~; VILLAGE ~.

DISTRICT ASSOCIATION. An association of persons supporting an authorized political party in an electoral district.

DISTRICT COLLECTOR. A collector having jurisdiction over the ports within a customs district. Canada regulations.

DISTRICT COUNCIL. An organization of union locals in a particular geographical area.

DISTRICT COURT. A court limited in territorial jurisdiction by subject matter and by value of property or claim at stake.

DISTRICT COURT OF ONTARIO. Formerly an amalgamation of the county and district courts, the courts of general sessions of the peace and the county and district court judges' criminal courts into a single court of record.

DISTRICTIS. *n.* Distraint; distress.

DISTRINGAS. [L. that you distrain]. A writ directing a sheriff to distrain on a certain person for a particular purpose.

DISTURBANCE. *n.* 1. Infringement of an easement, franchise, profit a prendre or similar right. 2. A disturbance of the peace and quiet of the occupants of an inn by fighting, screaming, shouting, singing or otherwise causing loud noise. 3. Causing a tenant to leave through force, menace, persuasion or otherwise. 4. Odour, dust, flies, light, smoke, noise and vibration. *Farming* *and Food Production Protection Act, 1998*, S.O. 1998, c. 1, s. 1. See GROUND PUBLIC ~; SURFACE ~.

DISTURBANCE DAMAGES. " . . . [A]ll damages, costs and expenses, apart from the market value of lands taken and damages for injurious affection, as are directly attributable to the expropriation of lands or premises on which a business or undertaking was carried on, or proposed to be carried on, . . ." *Dell Holdings Ltd. v. Toronto Area Transit Operating Authority* (1991), 80 D.L.R. (4th) 112 at 121, 3 O.R. (3d) 78, 45 L.C.R. 250, 50 O.A.C. 193 (Div. Ct.), the court per Steele J., adopted from Land Compensation Board decision in *Ridgeport Developments v. Metropolitan Toronto Region Conservation Authority* (1976), 11 L.C.R. 143 at 155.

DITCH. *n.* 1. A drain open or covered wholly or in part whether in the channel or a natural stream, creek or watercourse or not, and includes the work and material necessary for bridges, culverts, catch basins and guards. 2. Includes a flume, pipe, race or other artificial means for conducting water by its own weight, to be used for mining purposes. 3. A ditch open or covered wholly or in part, whether in the channel of a natural stream, creek or watercourse or not, heretofore or hereafter constructed, repaired, maintained or improved, and all the work and materials necessary for any bridge, culvert, catch basin or guards connected therewith. See DRAINAGE ~.

DIV. *abbr.* Divisional.

DIV. & MATR. CAUSES CT. *abbr.* Divorce and Matrimonial Causes Court.

DIV. CT. *abbr.* Divisional Court.

DIVERGENCE. *n.* With respect to a laser beam, means the full angle of spread of the beam. *Radiation Emitting Devices Regulations*, C.R.C., c. 1370, s. 1.

DIVERS. *adj.* [Fr.] Various, sundry.

DIVERSION. *n.* The taking or removing of water from any river, stream, lake or body of water by means of any mechanical contrivance of works and includes the impounding of water.

DIVERSITY. *n.* A prisoner's plea to bar execution, alleging that it was another who was attainted.

DIVERT. *v.* 1. Or a word of similar import, means to take water from a stream, and includes to cause water to leave the channel of a stream

and make a change in or about the channel that permits water to leave it. 2. Includes take, remove, and impound. See TEMPORARILY ~ ED.

DIVEST. *v.* 1. To take away; to deprive. 2. To remove an estate or interest which was already vested in a person.

DIVIDED COURT. Applied to a court consisting of more than one judge when the decision or opinion of the court is not unanimous.

DIVIDED CUSTODY. " . . . [T]he children to divide their time between the two homes, living in each temporarily, on some type of rotating basis. . ." *Colwell v. Colwell* (1992), 38 R.F.L. (3d) 345 at 349, 128 A.R. 4 (Q.B.), Bielby J.

DIVIDED DISCOVERY. Where information may become relevant only after the determination of an issue in the action and the disclosure of the information before the issue is determined would seriously prejudice a party, the court on the party's motion may grant leave to withhold the information until after the issue has been determined (Ontario, Rules of Civil Procedure, r. 31.06(6)). G.D. Watson & C. Perkins, eds., *Holmested & Watson: Ontario Civil Procedure* (Toronto: Carswell, 1984-) at 31-8.

DIVIDED MUNICIPALITY. A local municipality parts of which were annexed to two or more municipalities to constitute an area municipality under a Regional Act. *Regional Municipalities Act*, R.S.O. 1990, c. R.8, s. 1.

DIVIDEND. *n.* 1. The division of profits of a corporation or trust. 2. "A payment from profits, whether in cash specie or the shares of another company, is in essence a dividend." *Canadian Pacific Ltd., Re* (1990) 47 B.L.R. 1 at 30 72 O.R. (2d) 545, 68 D.L.R. (4th) 9 (H.C.), Austin J. 3. Includes bonus or any distribution to shareholders as such. 4. Without restricting the ordinary meaning thereof, includes an amount payable, or subject to be credited, by an insurer to its insured and that is composed in whole or in part of a portion of the amount previously paid by the insured as a premium or as a deposit or payment under a reciprocal contract of indemnity or inter-insurance. *Insurance Companies Tax acts.* See ACCRUED ~; ACCUMULATED ~; ACCUMULATIVE ~; CASH ~; CUM ~; ~S; INTERIM ~; NONCUMULATIVE ~; PATRONAGE ~; SCRIP ~; STOCK ~.

DIVIDENDA. *n.* [L.] One section of an indenture.

DIVIDEND RIGHT. See UNLIMITED ~.

DIVIDENDS. *n*. Includes all payments made by the name of dividend, bonus or otherwise out of revenues of trading or other public companies divisible between all or any of the members, whether such payments are usually made or declared at any fixed times or otherwise, but does not include payments in the nature of a return or reimbursement of capital. *Apportionment acts*. See DIVIDEND.

DIVIDING LINE. See DIRECTIONAL~.

DIVINATIO, NON INTERPRETATIO EST, QUAE OMNINO RECEDIT A LITERA. [L.] An interpretation which departs totally from the original is a guess, not an interpretation.

DIVING BOARD. A flexible board. *Public Pools Act*, R.R.O. 1990, Reg. 565, s. 1.

DIVING PLATFORM. A rigid platform. *Public Pools Act*, R.R.O. 1990, Reg. 565, s. 1.

DIVISA. *n*. [L.] 1. An award, device or decree. 2. A devise. 3. Limits or bounds of a farm or parish. 4. A court held on a boundary in order to settle tenants' disputes.

DIVISIBLE. *adj*. " . . . [T]hat may be taken apart . . . *R. v. Ciesielski* (1958), 26 W.W.R. 695 at 701, 29 C.R. 312, 122 C.C.C. 247 (Alta. C.A.), Porter J.A.

DIVISION. *n*. 1. In the House of Commons, a recorded vote. A. Fraser, W.A. Dawson, & J. Holtby, eds., *Beauchesne's Rules and Forms of the House of Commons of Canada*, 6th ed. (Toronto: Carswell, 1989) at 91. 2. A group of grades taught in a school and into which the school grades are divided. 3. The territory in and for which a small claims court is prescribed. 4. An administrative unit. See EASTERN ~; ELECTORAL ~; ESTATES ~; EXCISE ~; INTERMEDIATE ~; JUNIOR ~; POLLING ~; PRIMARY ~; SENIOR ~; TERRITORIAL ~; TRADE ~; TRIAL ~; WESTERN ~.

DIVISIONAL COURT. *Health Protection and Promotion Act*, R.R.O. 1990, Reg. 565, s. 1.

DIVORCE. *n*. 1. " . . . [D]issolution of marriage . . ." *Hurson v. Hurson* (1970), 73 W.W.R. 765 at 767, 1 R.F.L. 19, 11 D.L.R. (3d) 759 (B.C. C.A.), the court per McFarlane J.A. 2. Dissolution and annulment of marriage and includes nullity of marriage. *Vital Statistics Act*, R.S.O. 1990, c. V.4, s. 1. See CONTESTED ~; NO-FAULT ~; UNCONTESTED ~.

DIVORCE PROCEEDING. A proceeding in a court in which either or both spouses seek a divorce alone or together with a child support order, a spousal support order or a custody order. *Divorce Act*, R.S.C. 1985, c. 3 (2nd Supp.), s. 2(1).

D.L.Q. *abbr*. Droits et libertés au Québec.

D.L.R. *abbr*. Dominion Law Reports, 1912-1922.

[] D.L.R. *abbr*. Dominion Law Reports, 1923-1955.

D.L.R. (4TH). *abbr*. Dominion Law Reports (Fourth Series), 1984-.

D.L.R. (2D). *abbr*. Dominion Law Reports (Second Series), 1956-1968.

D.L.R. (3D). *abbr*. Dominion Law Reports (Third Series), 1969-1984.

DMCA. *abbr*. Digital Millennium Copyright Act, U.S.

DNA. *abbr*. Deoxyribonucleic acid. *DNA Identification Act*, S.C. 1998, c. 37, s. 2. See MITOCHONDRIAL ~.

DNA DATA BANK. The national DNA data bank established by the Solicitor General of Canada under section 5 of the DNA Identification Act. *DNA Identification Regulations*, SOR/2000-300, s. 1.

DNA PROFILE. The results of forensic DNA analysis of a bodily substance. *DNA Identification Act, S.C. 1998, c. 37, s. 2*.

DNA PROFILING. DNA is isolated from the muclei of white blood or tissue cells or sperm. The DNA strands are broken into fragments by enzymes. Some fragments which show individual characteristics are isolated using electrophoresis. Bases are visualized by the use of radioactive probes and the base pattern found is compared with that from other sources. F.A. Jaffe, *A Guide to Pathological Evidence*, 3d ed. (Toronto: Carswell, 1991) at 204.

DND. *abbr*. Department of National Defence.

D.O.A. *abbr*. Dead on arrival.

DOC. *abbr*. Department of Communications.

DOCK. *n*. 1. The physical location in which a prisoner is placed during trial in a criminal court. 2. Includes wet docks and basins, tidal-docks and basins, locks, cuts, entrances, dry docks, graving docks, gridirons, slips, quays, wharfs, piers, stages, landing places and jetties. *Canada Shipping Act*, R.S.C. 1985, c. S-9, s. 578(4). See DRY ~; OWNERS OF A ~ OR CANAL.

DOCKAGE. *n.* 1. Any material intermixed with a parcel of grain, other than kernels of grain of a standard or quality fixed by or under this Act for a grade of that grain, that must and can be separated from the parcel of grain before that grade can be assigned to the grain. *Canada Grain Act*, R.S.C. 1985, c. G-10, s. 2. 2. The charge on a vessel while occupying a berth or while fast to or tied up alongside any other vessel occupying a berth at the wharf. Canada regulations.

DOCKET. *v.* To make a list of entries; to keep track of time spent on matters.

DOCKET. *n.* 1. A record of the time and disbursements a lawyer spent on a particular matter. 2. A list of cases to be heard.

DOCKING. *n.* 1. Deduction from wages as a penalty. 2. The manoeuvring of a ship to a berth. See UN ~.

DOCK WARRANT. A document resembling a bill of lading and issued by a dock owner or dock company authorizing delivery of certain goods to a named person or to that person's assigns by endorsement.

DOCTOR. *n.* Medical practitioner; physician; surgeon.

DOCTOR-PATIENT PRIVILEGE. Recognized by statute provincially. Protects the disclosure of information provided in the doctor-patient relationship.

DOCTRINE. *n.* A rule or principle of law. See CLEAN HANDS ~; COLLATERAL BENEFITS, ~ OF; COMMON EMPLOYMENT ~; COMMUNITY OF INTEREST ~; DOUBLE ASPECT ~; EQUITABLE ~ OF CONSTRUCTIVE NOTICE; IDENTITY ~; INEVITABILITY REGULATED INDUSTRIES ~.

DOCTRINE OF ACQUIESCENCE. "In the first place the plaintiff must have made a mistake as to his legal rights. Secondly, the plaintiff must have expended some money or must have done some act (not necessarily upon the defendant's land) on the faith of his mistaken belief. Thirdly, the defendant, the possessor of the legal right, must know of the existence of his own right which is inconsistent with the right claimed by the plaintiff. If he does not know of it he is in the same position as the plaintiff and the doctrine of acquiescence is founded upon conduct with a knowledge of your legal rights. Fourthly, the defendant, the possessor of the legal right, must know of the plaintiff's mistaken belief of his rights. If he does not, there is nothing which calls upon him to assert his own rights. Lastly, the defendant, the possessor of the legal rights must have encouraged the plaintiff in his expenditure of money or in the other acts which he has done, either directly or by abstaining from asserting his legal right. Where all of these elements exist, there is a fraud of such a nature as will entitle the court to restrain the possessor of the legal right from exercising it, but, in my judgment, nothing short of this will do. *Wilomot v. Barber* (1880), 15 Ch. D. 96 at 105-106, Fry J. See ACQUIESCENCE.

DOCTRINE OF SHELTERING. Anyone who buys with notice from another person who bought without notice can be sheered under the first buyer. W.B. Rayner & R.H. McLaren, *Falconbridge on Mortgages*, 4th ed. Toronto: Canada Law Book, 1977) at 149.

DOCTRINE OF SUBROGATION. If a mortgagee or unpaid vendor insures an interest in property and receives insurance money when a loss occurs and if that mortgagee or vendor afterwards receives the mortgage money or the purchase price with no deduction on account of the insurance, that mortgagee or vendor is liable to the insurer for a sum equal to the insurance money received, because one is not entitled to more than full indemnification. W.B. Rayner & R.H. McLaren, *Falconbridge on Mort*gages, 4th ed. (Toronto: Canada Law Book, 1977) at 792.

DOCTRINE OF THE TABULA IN NAUFRAGIO. An equitable mortgagee who takes with no notice of an earlier equitable mortgage may get in the legal estate and in some cases obtain priority over the earlier mortgagee. W.B. Rayner & R.H McLaren, *Falconbridge on Mortgages*, 4th ed. (Toronto: Canada Law Book, 1977) at 126.

DOCUMENT. *n.* 1. " . . . [S]omething which gives you information . . . something which makes evident what would otherwise not be evident. . . the form which the so-called document takes is perfectly immaterial so long as it is information conveyed by something or other; it may be anything, upon which there is written or inscribed information." *R. v. Hill* [1945] 1 All E.R. 414 at 417 (U.K. K.B.), Humphreys J. 2. Any paper, parchment or other material on which is recorded or marked anything that is capable of being read or understood by a person, computer system or other device, and includes a credit card, but does not include trade-marks on articles of commerce or inscriptions on stone or metal or other like material. 3. Includes an assignment, a renewal statement, an affidavit and a certificate of discharge. *Assignment of Book Debts acts.* See ACTIVE ~; ANCIENT ~; CARTOGRAPHIC RECORD OR ~; DEFECT IN A ~; ~S; ELECTION ~; FALSE ~; IDENTIFICATION ~; INACTIVE ~; MANUSCRIPT, RECORD, OR ~; OFFICIAL ORIGINATING ~; PHOTOGRAPHIC RECORD OR ~; PICTORIAL RECORD OR ~; PRIVILEGED ~; PUBLIC ~; REGISTERED ~; RESPONDING ~; SECURITY ~; SEMI-ACTIVE ~; SHARE OFFERING~; SHIPPING ~; STATE ~.

DOCUMENTARY CREDIT. A conditional letter of credit providing that any draft drawn under it may be negotiated only if bills of lading, invoices and insurance policies valued at least equally to the draft accompany the draft. See INTERNATIONAL ~.

DOCUMENTARY EVIDENCE. A document or paper adduced to prove its contents.

DOCUMENTARY LETTER OF CREDIT. ". . . [T]he obligation of the issuing bank to honour a draft on a credit when it is accompanied by documents which appear on their face to be in accordance with the terms and conditions of the credit is independent of the performance of the underlying contract for which the credit was issued . . ." *Angelica-Whitewear Ltd. v. Bank of Nova Scotia* (1987), 36 B.L.R. 140 at 148, 73 N.R. 158, [1987] 1 S.C.R. 59, the court per Le Dain J.

DOCUMENTED. See PROPERLY ~.

DOCUMENT OF CONVEYANCE. Any instrument by which a land holding is or may be acquired and includes a trust document.

DOCUMENT OF TITLE. 1. Includes any bill of lading, dock warrant, warehousekeeper's certificate and warrant or order for the delivery of goods and any other document used in the ordinary course of business as proof of the possession or control of goods, or authorizing or purporting to authorize, either by endorsement or by delivery, the possessor of the document to transfer or receive goods thereby represented. 2. Any writing that purports to be issued by or addressed to a bailee and purports to cover such goods in the bailee's possession as are identified or fungible portions of an identified mass, and that in the ordinary course of business is treated as establishing that the person in possession of it is entitled to receive, hold and dispose of the document and the goods it covers. *Personal Property Security acts.*

DOCUMENT OF TITLE TO GOODS. 1. Includes a bought and sold note, bill of lading, warrant, certificate or order for the delivery or transfer of goods or any other valuable thing, and any other document used in the ordinary course of business as evidence of the possession or control of goods, authorizing or purporting to authorize, by endorsement or by delivery, the person in possession of the document to transfer or receive any goods thereby represented or therein mentioned or referred to. *Criminal Code*, R.S.C. 1985, c. C-46, s. 2. 2. Any bill of lading, dock warrant, warehouse keeper's certificate, and warrant or order for the delivery of goods, and any other document used in the ordinary course of business as proof of the possession or control of goods, or authorizing or purporting to authorize, either by endorsement or by delivery the possessor of the document to transfer or a goods thereby represented. *Sale of Goods acts.*

DOCUMENT OF TITLE TO LANDS. Includes any writing that is or contains evidence of the title, or any part of the title, to real property, and any notarial or registrar's copy thereof and any duplicate instrument, memorial, certificate or document authorized or required by any law in force in any part of Canada with respect to registration of titles that relates to title to real property or to any interest in real property.

DOCUMENTS. *n.* Includes any of the following, whether computerized or not: books, records, writings, vouchers, invoices, accounts and statements, financial or otherwise. See AFFIDAVIT OF ~; CABINET ~; CASH AGAINST ~; DOCUMENT; ELECTION ~.

DOCUMENT UNDER TIE SIGN-MANUAL. An instrument, in respect of Canada, that, under the present practice, is issued in the name and under the signature of Her Majesty the Queen without any seal. *Seals Act*, R.S.C. 1985, c. S-6, s. 2.

DOG. *n.* 1. A dog, male or female, and includes an animal that is a cross between a dog and a wolf. 2. Any of the species Canis familiaris Linnaeus. See GUARD ~; GUIDE ~; HEARING ~; HUSKY ~; OWNER OF A ~; SLEIGH ~.

DOGFISH. *n*. A fish of the species the family name of which is (Sualidae). *Northwest Atlantic Fisheries Regulations*, C.R.C., c. 860, s. 2.

DOGFISH REDUCTION PLANT. A building, structure, machinery, appurtenances, appliances and apparatus occupied and used in the business of producing oil, fish meal, fish scrap, chicken feed or fertilizer from dogfish. *Fisheries Act*, R.S.B.C. 1996, c. 149, s. 12.

DOG GUIDE. 1. A dog trained to guide a visually handicapped person. 2. A dog trained to assist a person with a disability or a disease which causes the person to require assistance.

DOGWOOD. *n*. The shrub or tree, Cornus nuttallii, commonly known as western flowering dogwood.

DOING BUSINESS. The transaction of any of the ordinary business of a corporation or person, including franchises, whether or not by means of an employee or an agent and whether or not the corporation or person has a resident agent or representative or a warehouse office or place of business in the province. See CARRYING ON BUSINESS; CARRY ON BUSINESS.

DOLE. *n*. 1. The act of distributing. 2. An allotment. 3. Unemployment benefits or welfare assistance.

DOLI CAPAX. [L.] Capable of a criminal act.

DOLI INCAPAX. [L.] Not capable of a criminal act.

DOLLAR. *n*. 1. The monetary unit of Canada is the dollar. It is equivalent to one hundred cents. 2. A money unit equivalent to one hundred cents. See EURO-~.

DOLLY. See TRAILER CONVERTER ~.

DOLO MALO PACTUM SE NON SERVATURUM. [L.] A contract arising through fraudulent deceit will not be upheld.

DOLOSUS VERSATUR IN GENERALIBUS. [L.] A person intending to deceive uses general terms.

DOLUS. *n*. [L.] Fraud; guilt; wilful injury.

DOLUS CIRCUITU NON PURGATUR. [L.] Fraud is not excused by going a roundabout way.

DOLUS DANS LOCUM CONTRACTUI. [L.] Fraud or deceit which gives rise to a contract.

DOM. *abbr*. Dominion.

DOMAIN NAME. An electronic address on the internet.

DOMESTIC. *n*. A natural person engaged by an individual for remuneration, whose main duty is, in the dwelling of the individual, (1) to do housework, or (2) to care for a child or a sick, handicapped or aged person and who lives in the dwelling.

DOMESTIC AIRSPACE. See CANADIAN ~.

DOMESTIC AMENDING FORMULA. A procedure to amend the Constitution in Canada without the need to involve the British Parliament.

DOMESTIC ANIMAL. 1. A horse, a dog or any other animal that is kept under human control or by habit or training lives in association with humans. 2. An animal that is tame or kept, or that has been or is being sufficiently tamed or kept, to serve some purpose for people.

DOMESTIC CONTRACT. 1. A cohabitation agreement, marriage contract, separation agreement or agreement between a deceased spouse's administrator or executor and the surviving spouse. 2. A marriage contract, separation agreement, cohabitation agreement or paternity agreement.

DOMESTIC CORPORATION. A body corporate that is incorporated by or under the authority of an Act of the Legislature and has gain for its purpose or object.

DOMESTIC ESTABLISHMENT. See SELF-CONTAINED ~.

DOMESTIC FISHING. Fishing for personal use but not for sale or barter.

DOMESTIC FISHING LICENCE. A licence authorizing a person to engage in domestic fishing. *Northwest Territories Fishery Regulations*, C.R.C., c. 847, s. 2.

DOMESTIC FLIGHT. A flight between points in Canada.

DOMESTIC HEN. The hen of the domestic chicken of the species Gallus domesticus.

DOMESTIC JURISDICTION. The sphere in which sovereign nations may act freely.

DOMESTIC PETROLEUM. Petroleum from a natural reservoir in Canada and petroleum produced, extracted, recovered or manufactured in Canada otherwise than from a natural reservoir.

Energy Administration Act, R.S.C. 1985, c. E-6, s. 56.

DOMESTIC PURCHASER. A purchaser who uses a taxable product in respect of which he is the purchaser solely to heat or serve a dwelling unit in which he resides.

DOMESTIC PURPOSE. 1. The use of water for household requirements, sanitation and fire prevention, the watering of domestic animals and poultry and the irrigation of a garden. 2. With reference to heating oil, means the use of heating oil in domestic appliances or for heating or lighting premises used as a private dwelling.

DOMESTIC SERVANT. A person who is employed by a householder, (i) as a sitter to attend primarily to the needs of a child who is a member of the household, (ii) as a companion to attend to the needs of an aged, infirm or ill member of the household, or (iii) as a domestic to perform services in the household who works twenty-four hours a week or less. *Employment Standards Act*, R.R.O. 1980, Reg. 285, s. 1.

DOMESTIC SERVICE. An air service between points in Canada, from and to the same point in Canada or between Canada and a point outside Canada that is not in the territory of another country. *Canada Transportation Act*, S.C. 1996, c. 10, s. 55(1).

DOMESTIC TRIBUNAL. " . . . [N]ot created or empowered by statute and is not part of an incorporated entity." *Rees v. U.A., Local 527* (1983), 4 Admin. L. R. 179 at 183, 43 O.R. (2d) 97, 83 C.L.L.C. 14,067, 150 D.L.R. (3d) 493 (Div. Ct.), Henry J.

DOMESTIC USE. The use of waters for household requirements, sanitation and fire prevention, for the watering of domestic animals and poultry and for irrigation of a garden adjoining a dwelling-house.

DOMESTIC VIOLENCE. The following acts or omissions committed against an applicant, an applicant's relative or any child: 1. An assault that consists of the intentional application of force that causes the applicant to fear for his or her safety, but does not include any act committed in self-defence. 2. An intentional or reckless act or omission that causes bodily harm or damage to property. 3. An act or omission or threatened act or omission that causes the applicant to fear for his or her safety. 4. Forced physical confinement, without lawful authority. 5. Sexual assault, sexual exploitation or sexual molesta-tion, or the threat of sexual assault, sexual exploitation or sexual molestation. 6. A series of acts which collectively causes the applicant to fear for his or her safety, including following, contacting, communicating with, observing or recording any person. *Domestic Violence Protection Act, 2000*, S.O. 2000, c. 33, s. 1(2).

DOMESTIC WASTE. Any waste other than industrial waste.

DOMESTIC WASTE WATER. Wastewater being discharged from a residential building and wastewater of a like nature being discharged from other buildings.

DOMESTIC WINE. Wine fermented in Canada.

DOMESTIC WORKSHOP. Every establishment in which only the members of the family are employed.

DOMICILE. *n*. A person's permanent home or principal establishment to which that person intends to return after every absence. See ELECTION OF ~; PLACE OF ~.

DOMICILE BY REVERTER. The domicile of a person who loses a domicile and does not immediately acquire another. J.G. McLeod, *The Conflict of Laws* (Calgary: Carswell, 1983) at 143.

DOMICILE OF CHOICE. " . . . [O]btained if two elements are present: the fact of residing in a legal jurisdiction other than the domicile of origin and doing so with the intention of continuing to reside there indefinitely." *Smallman v. Smallman Estate* (1991), 41 E.T.R. 86 at 95, 35 C.C.E.L. 146 (Ont. Gen. Div.), Haley J.

DOMICILE OF DEPENDENCY. A person's domicile, after domicile of origin, which the law still regards that the person could not select himself or herself. J.G. McLeod, *The Conflict of Laws* (Calgary: Carswell, 1983) at 143.

DOMICILE OF ORIGIN. A person's first domicile, determined by birth. J.G. McLeod, *The Conflict of Laws* (Calgary: Carswell, 1983) at 143.

DOMINA. *n*. [L.] The former title of a woman who was a peeress in her own right; a dame.

DOMINANT PURPOSE TEST. " . . . *Waugh v. British Railways Board*, [1979] 2 All E.R. 1169. Under that authority a party need not produce a document otherwise subject to production if the dominant purpose for which the document was prepared was submission to a legal advisor for advice and use in litigation (whether in progress or as contemplated). Such documents are shielded from production by what is usually described as legal professional privilege. . . the legal professional privilege should only be applied when there is a significant connection between the preparation of the document and the anticipation of litigation. This leads to the introduction of the 'dominant purpose' test." *Nova, An Alberta Corporation v. Guelph Engineering Co.* (1984), 80 C.P.R. (2d) 93 at 95, 97, 1984 3 W.W.R. 314, 42 C.P.C. 194, 30 Alta. L.R. (2d) 183, 5 D.L.R. (4th) 755, 50 A.R. 199 (C.A.), the court per Stevenson J.A. See LEGAL PROFESSIONAL PRIVILEGE; SOLICITOR-CLIENT PRIVILEGE.

DOMINANT TENEMENT. A subject or tenement to the benefit of which an easement or servitude is constituted.

DOMINICAL. *adj.* Belonging to the Lord's Day, or Sunday.

DOMINICUM. *n.* [L.] Demesne.

DOMINION. *n.* 1. Any of the following Dominions, that is to say, the Dominion of Canada, the Commonwealth of Australia, the Dominion of New Zealand, the Union of South Africa, the Irish Free State and Newfoundland. *Statute of Westminster, 1931*, (U.K.), 22 Geo. 5, c. 4, s. 1, reprinted in R.S.C. 1985, App. Doc. No. 27. 2. Dominion of Canada. *Interpretation Act*, R.S.Q. 1977, c. I-16, s. 61. See HER MAJESTY'S ~S.

DOMINION COMPANY. A company incorporated by or under an Act of the Parliament of Canada.

DOMINION CORPORATION. A body corporate that is incorporated by or under the authority of an Act of the Parliament of Canada and has gain for its purpose or object.

DOMINION GEODESIST. The Dominion Geodesist and Director of the Geodetic Survey, in the Department of Energy, Mines and Resources. *Territorial Land Use Regulations*, C.R.C., c. 1524, s. 2.

DOMINION TIMBER BERTH. Any area for which a licence or permit was granted by the Dominion of Canada prior to the fifteenth day of July, 1930, for the cutting of timber. *Forest Act*, R.S.M. 1970, c. F150, s. 2.

DOMINION WATER-POWERS. Any waterpowers on public lands, or any other water-powers that are the property of Canada and have been or may be placed under the control and management of the Minister. *Dominion Water Powers Act*, R.S.C. 1985, c. W-4, s. 2.

DOMINIUM. *n.* [L.] Absolute ownership.

DOMINIUM NON POTEST ESSE IN PENDENTI. [L.] Ownership cannot be held in suspense.

DOMINUS LITIS. [L. master of the suit] One who has control over a judicial proceeding or an action.

DOMINUS NAVIS. [L.] A ship's absolute owner.

DOM. PROC. *abbr.* Domus Procerum.

DOMUS PROCERUM. [L.] The British House of Lords.

DOMUS SUA CUIQUE EST TUTISSIMUM REFUGIUM. [L.] To every person, one's house is one's surest refuge.

DONA CLANDESTINA SUNT SEMPER SUSPICIOSA. [L.] Clandestine gifts are always suspicious.

DONARI VIDETUR, QUOD NULLO JURE COGENTE CONCEDITUR. [L.] A thing is considered to be given when it is transferred any way except by virtue of a right.

DONATIO. *n.* [L.] Gift.

DONATIO INTER VIVOS. [L.] A gift between persons still living.

DONATIO MORTIS CAUSA. [L.] " . . . [T]hree essential conditions,. . . first, the gift must have been made in contemplation, though not necessarily in expectation, of death; second, there must have been delivery to the donee of the subject-matter of the gift; third, the gift must be made under such circumstances as to show that the thing is to revert to the donor in case he should recover." *Szczepkowski v. Eppler*, [1945] 4 D.L.R. 104 at 110, [1945] O.R. 540 (C.A.), the court per Roach J.A. See GIFT MORTIS CAUSA.

DONATION. *n.* 1. Includes any gift, testamentary disposition, deed, trust or other form of contribution. 2. "To constitute a valid donation there must be sufficient words of gift, and an act . . ." *Blain v. Terryberry* (1862), 9 Gr. 286 at 295 (Ont. H.C.), Spragge V.C.

DONATIONES SUNT STRICTI JURIS, NE QUIS PLUS DONASSE PRAESUMATUR,

QUAM IN DONATIONE EXPRESSIT. [L.] Gifts are to be strictly examined to prevent a person being presumed to have given more than is expressed in the grant.

DONATION IN KIND. Any property other than money given or provided to or for the benefit of a recognized party or a candidate without compensation from the recognized party or candidate and includes services of an employee of the taxpayer provided to a recognized party or a candidate without compensation from the recognized party or candidate.

DONATIO NON PRAESUMITUR. [L.] A gift is not enjoyed beforehand.

DONATIO PERFICITUR POSSESSIONE ACCIPIENTIS. [L.] A gift is perfected when the donee possesses the subject-matter.

DONATIO PROPTER NUPTIAM. [L.] A gift on account of marriage.

DONATIVE PROMISE. A promise to confer a benefit by gift.

DONATOR NUNQUAM DESINIT POSSIDERE ANTEQUAM DONATARIUS INCIPIAT POSSIDERE. [L.] The donor never ceases to have possession until the receiver begins to possess.

DONE. See EQUITY LOOKS ON THAT AS ~ WHICH OUGHT TO HAVE BEEN ~.

DONEE. *n.* 1. Any person who receives or has received the benefit of a gift, including a gift deemed, for the purposes of this Act, to have been made. *Gift Tax acts.* 2. One to whom a gift is made. 3. A person to whom a power of appointment is given is sometimes called the donee of the power.

DONOR. *n.* 1. One who gives. 2. Any individual who makes or has made a gift, including a gift deemed, for the purposes of this Act, to have been made. *Gift Tax acts.* 3. A person who, (i) in writing at any time, or (ii) orally in the presence of at least two witnesses during his last illness, has requested that his body or a specified part or parts thereof be used after his death for therapeutic purposes or for the purposes of medical education or research. *Human Tissue acts.*

DOOR. See CARGO-TYPE ~; EXIT ~S; FIRE ~; OUTER ~S.

D.O.R. *abbr.* Desires an opportunity to redeem. A notice filed by a defendant in an action for foreclosure or sale when the defendant wishes to have a chance to redeem the property.

DORMANT CLAIM. A suspended claim.

DORMIT ALIQUANDO LEX, MORITUR NUNQUAM. [L.] A law occasionally sleeps, but it never dies.

DORMIUNT ALIQUANDO LEGES, NUNQUAM MORIUNTUR. [L.] The laws occasionally sleep, but they never die.

DORSAL. *adj.* Posterior.

DOS. *n.* Dower.

DOSAGE FORM. The form in which a prescription drug is manufactured in order to be suitable for administration irrespective of the size or type of container in which it is packaged.

DOSE. *n.* The quantity of energy absorbed per unit of mass by any material from X-rays or from secondary particles generated by X-rays, falling upon or penetrating the material.

DOSEMETER. *n.* Any device that, in the opinion of the Minister, may be reliably used for measuring or estimating dose or dose-rate.

DOSE-RATE. *n.* Dose per unit of time.

DOSIMETER. *n.* A device for measuring a dose of radiation that is worn or carried by an individual. *Radiation Protection Regulations*, SOR/2000-203, s. 1(1).

DOSIMETRY SERVICE. A prescribed facility for the measurement and monitoring of doses of radiation. *Nuclear Safety and Control Act*, S.C. 1997, c. 9, s. 2.

DOTAL. *adj.* Relating to the dos or dower.

DOTATION. *n.* 1. Giving a portion or dowry. 2. In general, endowment.

DOT SPECS. See US ~.

DOUBLE. See CONSOLATION ~; DAILY ~.

DOUBLE ACTION. As applied to handguns, cocking of the hammer when the trigger is pulled. F.A. Jaffe, *A Guide to Pathological Evidence*, 3d ed. (Toronto: Carswell 1991) at 217.

DOUBLE ACTIONABILITY. " . . . [T]he wrongful act alleged must be actionable according to the lex fori (Ontario), and actionable according to the lexi loci delicti (Quebec) . . ." *Bailey v. Fraser* (1982), (*sub nom. Going v. Reid Brothers Motor Sales Ltd.*) 19 C.C.L.T. 209 at 238, 35 O.R. (2d) 201, 13 M.V.R. 283, 136 D.L.R. (3d) 254 (H.C.), Henry J.

DOUBLE AGENCY. A situation occurring when a security holder appoints a receiver/manager to take possession of a debtor's business and realize on it, and at the same time that receiver/manager is considered the debtor's agent in order to manage the business and contract with third parties. F. Bennett, *Receiverships* (Toronto: Carswell, 1985) at 7.

DOUBLE ASPECT DOCTRINE. " ... [S]ubjects which in one aspect and for one purpose fall within sect. 92 [of the Constitution Act 1867 (30 & 31 Vict.), c. 3], may in another aspect and for another purpose fall within sect. 91." *Hodge v. The Queen* (1883), 9 App. Cas. 117 at 130 (P.C.).

DOUBLE BOND. " ... [C]onsists of two parts: first, the obligation and secondly the condition ..." *R. v. London Guarantee & Accident Co.* (1920), 51 D.L.R. 624 at 626, [1920] 2 W.W.R. 83, 19 Ex. C.R. 385, Audette J.

DOUBLE-BREASTING. *n.* " ... [W]here one company, which continues to carry on business subject to a union contract, sets up a second parallel company which operates without a union ..." *W.W. Lester (1978) Ltd. v. U.A., Local 740* (1990), 48 Admin L.R. 1 at 20, 76 D.L.R. (4th) 389, 91 C.L.L.C. 14,002, 123 N.R. 241, 88 Nfld. & P.E.I.R. 15, 274 A.P.R. 15, [1990] 3 S.C.R. 644, McLachlin J. (Lamer C.J.C., La Forest, Sopinka and Gonthier JJ. concurring).

DOUBLE BUNKING. " ... [T]he confinement of two inmates in a prison cell designed and previously utilized for single occupancy." *Ache v. Canada (Solicitor General)* (1989), 36 Admin. L.R. 225 at 227, 47 C.C.C. (3d) 495, 98 N.R. 148 (Fed. C.A.), the court per MacGuigan J.A.

DOUBLE CRIMINALITY. 1. The test under [s. 18(1)(b) of the *Extradition Act*, R.S.C. 1985, c. E-23] embodies the "double criminality" rule. This rule underlies the structure of the extradition process and has its origins in the principle of reciprocity. The rule is designed to protect the fundamental rights of an individual whose extradition is being sought by ensuring that a person is not surrendered to another country for conduct not considered to be a criminal offence in the country from which extradition is sought. *D'Agostino, Re* (2000), 2000 CarswellOnt 465, (sub nom. *United States of America v. Commisso*) 47 O.R. (3d) 257, (sub nom. *United States of America v. Commisso*) 143 C.C.C. (3d) 158, (sub nom. *United States of America v. Commisso*) 129 O.A.C. 166, (sub nom. *United States of America v. Commisso*) 72 C.R.R. (2d) 198 (C.A.). 2. "An extradition crime, as well as being a crime in the demanding country, must also be a crime in the country to which the request for extradition is made. . ." *United States v. Andrews* (1991), 65 C.C.C. (3d) 345 at 348, 73 Man. R. (2d) 131, 3 W.A.C. 131 (C.A.), the court per Philp J.A.

DOUBLE DIPPING. Term that has come to describe the situation where, after an equal division of assets on marriage breakdown, one spouse claims continued support from the previously divided or equalized assets of the other spouse. This usually arises when a pension is involved. Describes the situation where a pension, once equalized as property between spouses, is also treated as income from which the pension-holding spouse must make spousal support payments. *Boston v. Boston*, 2001 CarswellOnt 2432, 2001 SCC 43, 201 D.L.R. (4th) 1, 17 R.F.L. (5th) 4, 271 N.R. 248, 149 O.A.C. 50. Per Major J. (McLachlin C.J.C., Gonthier, Iacobucci, Bastarache, Binnie, Arbour JJ. concurring).

DOUBLE ENTRY. Describing books of account kept by posting each entry as a debit and credit.

DOUBLE FRONT TOWNSHIP. A township where the usual practice in the original survey was to survey the township boundaries, the proof lines and base lines, if any, and the concession lines forming the front boundaries of the half lots and to establish the front corners of the half lots. *Surveys Act*, R.S.O. 1990, c. S.30, s. 24(1).

DOUBLE HEARSAY. Hearsay based upon hearsay.

DOUBLE HOOP NET. A hoop net having two pots joined by one lead.

DOUBLE INDEMNITY INSURANCE. Insurance undertaken by an insurer as part of a life insurance contract whereby the terms of the policy provide for the duration of the insurance for more than one year and for payment only in the event of the death of the insured by accident of an additional amount of insurance money not exceeding the amount payable in the event of death from other causes.

DOUBLE INSURANCE. 1. Two or more insurances on the same interest, the same risk and the same subject. 2. An insured is over-insured by double insurance if two or more marine policies are effected by or on behalf of the insured on the same marine adventure and interest or part thereof and the sums insured exceed the indemnity allowed by this Act. *Marine Insurance Act*, S.C. 1993, c. 22, s. 86.

DOUBLE JEOPARDY. A second prosecution for the same offence. See RULE AGAINST ~.

DOUBLE RECOVERY. 1. Term that has come to describe the situation where, after an equal division of assets on marriage breakdown, one spouse claims continued support from the previously divided or equalized assets of the other spouse. This usually arises, as here, when a pension is involved. Used to describe the situation where a pension, once equalized as property, is also treated as income from which the pension-holding spouse (here the husband) must make spousal support payments. Expressed another way, upon marriage dissolution the payee spouse (here the wife) receives assets and an equalization payment that take into account the capital value of the husband's future pension income. If she later shares in the pension income as spousal support when the pension is in pay after the husband has retired, the wife can be said to be recovering twice from the pension: first at the time of the equalization of assets and again as support from the pension income. *Boston v. Boston*, 2001 CarswellOnt 2432, 2001 SCC 43, 201 D.L.R. (4th) 1, 17 R.F.L. (5th) 4, 271 N.R. 248, 149 O.A.C. 50. Per Major J. (McLachlin C.J.C., Gonthier, Iacobucci, Bastarache, Binnie, Arbour JJ. concurring). 2. n injured plaintiff or dependant in a fatal accident action may both keep a benefit and recover full damages as if no benefit was received. K.D. Cooper-Stephenson & I.B. Saunders, *Personal Injury Damages in Canada* (Toronto: Carswell, 1981) at 469.

DOUBLE RENT. A penalty on a tenant who holds over after notice to quit expires.

DOUBLE TICKETING. The practice of charging the higher of two prices marked on an item.

DOUBLE TIME. Twice the worker's usual rate of pay.

DOUBLE VALUE. A penalty on an overholding tenant of double the yearly value of the land or double rent.

DOUBLE WASTE. Committed by a tenant who allows a house needing repair to be wasted and then illegally fells timber to repair it.

DOUBTFUL LOAN. Any loan in connection with which the board, manager or credit committee of a credit union or an officer of the credit union who has examined the circumstances related to the loan believes there is doubt about the credit union's ability to collect the full amount of the principal and interest owing. See ALLOWANCES FOR ~S.

DO UT DES. [L.] I give so you may give.

DO UT FACIAS. [L.] I give so you may perform.

DOVETAILING. *n*. The practice of merging seniority lists so that employees of both former bargaining units are credited with seniority as of their date of hire with their respective former employers.

DOW. *v*. To endow; to give.

DOWABLE. *adj*. With claim to dower.

DOWAGER. *n*. An endowed widow; the widow of nobility. See QUEEN ~.

DOWER. *n*. A life interest in one-third of any freehold estate of inheritance of which the husband died solely seised in possession either through a tenant or by himself and which he either brought with him into the marriage or acquired afterwards. A. Bissett-Johnson & W.M. Holland, eds., *Matrimonial Property Law in Canada* (Toronto: Carswell 1980) at I-10. See BAR OF ~.

DOWER ACTS. Provincial acts which increased the scope of common law dower by affording the wife right to her husband's equivalent equitable interests in land. A. Bissett-Johnson & W.M. Holland, eds., *Matrimonial Property Law in Canada* (Toronto: Carswell, 1980) at I-10.

DOWER RIGHTS. All rights given by this Act to the spouse of a married person in respect of the homestead and of the married person, and without restricting property the generality of the foregoing, includes (i) the right to prevent disposition of the homestead by withholding consent, (ii) the right of action for damages against the married person if a disposition of the homestead that results in the registration of the title in the name of any other person is made without consent, (iii) the right to obtain payment from the General Revenue Fund of an unsatisfied judgment against the married person in respect of a disposition of the homestead that is made without consent and that results in the registration of the title in the name of any other person, (iv) the right of the surviving spouse to a life estate in the homestead of the deceased married person, and (v) the right of the surviving spouse to a life estate in the personal property of the deceased married person that is exempt from seizure under writ proceedings. *Dower Act*, R.S.A. 2000, D-15, 1.

DOWN GRADING. Demotion to a job with a lower rate of pay.

DOWN PAYMENT. A sum of money, the value of a negotiable instrument payable on demand, or the agreed value of goods, given on account at the time of the contract. *Consumer Protection acts*.

DOWN PERIOD. A period when a plant is closed for repairs to machinery, other maintenance or alterations.

DOWNSTREAM INVESTMENT. Where a person or a group of persons owns beneficially, directly or indirectly, or is deemed to own beneficially, equity shares of a corporation, that person or group of persons shall be deemed to own beneficially a proportion of the equity shares of any other corporation that are owned beneficially, indirectly, by the first mentioned corporation, which proportion shall equal the proportion of the equity shares of the first mentioned corporation that are owned beneficially, directly or indirectly, or that pursuant to this subsection are deemed to be owned beneficially, by that person or group of persons.

DOWNTIME. *n.* A brief period of time during which no work is possible because of machinery breakdown, adjustment or the like.

DOWRESS. *n.* A widow with claim to dower.

DOWRY. *n.* Marriage goods which a wife brings to the marriage.

D.P. *abbr.* Domus Procerum.

D.P.P. *abbr.* Director of Public Prosecutions.

DRACHM. *n.* 1. One eighth of an ounce apothecaries. 2. One eighth of a fluid ounce.

DRAFT. *n.* 1. An order drawn by one person on another for the payment of money, i.e. a bill of exchange or cheque. 2. An order for the payment of money drawn by one banker on another. See RE-~.

DRAFTSMAN. *n.* Any person who drafts a legal document.

DRAGGER. *n.* A vessel (a) of an overall length that does not exceed 100 feet, and (b) that is equipped with an otter trawl or other trawl of a similar type for catching fish. *Otter Trawl Fishing Regulations*, C.R.C., c. 821, s. 2.

DRAG RAKE. Any gear that is towed over the ocean floor bar a vessel for the purpose of collecting marine plants. *Atlantic Coast Marine Plant Regulations*, C.R.C., c. 805, s. 2. See BASKET ~.

DRAG SEINE. A net weighted at the bottom, floated at the top and cast from a boat so as to enclose an area of water between it and the shore, and then drawn ashore. Canada regulations.

DRAIN. *n.* 1. Usually refers to an open channel in contrast to a sewer which is enclosed; includes sewer. 2. Any drain used for the drainage of one building or premises only for the purpose of communicating therefrom with a sewer, septictank, cesspool or other like receptacle, into which the drainage of two or more houses or premises occupied by different persons is conveyed. *City of St. John's Act*, R.S. Nfld. 1970, c. 40, s. 2. 3. A drain open or covered wholly or in part, whether in the channel of a natural stream, creek or watercourse or not, heretofore or hereafter constructed, repaired, maintained or improved, and all the work and materials necessary for any bridge, culvert, catch basin or guards connected therewith. See AREA ~; BUILDING ~; FLOOD ~; FOUNDATION~; HOUSE~; LATERAL ~; SUB-SURFACE ~.

DRAINAGE. *n.* In general refers to artificial interference with the natural flow of water, sewage or waste. May refer to the removal of surface water in order to improve land for agriculture and for flood prevention and to the removal of sewage and other waste for purposes of sanitation. See LAND ~.

DRAINAGE AREA. For a point, the area which contributes runoff to that point.

DRAINAGE DITCH. A man-made water course, added to the natural land drainage system, primarily to collect and convey water and that, for some period each year, does not contain flowing water.

DRAINAGE PIPING. All the connected piping that conveys sewage to a place of disposal, including the building drain, building sewer, soil pipe, soil stack, waste stack and waste pipe but does not include, i. a main sewer, and ii. piping used for sewage in a sewage plant. See STORM ~.

DRAINAGE REFEREE. In Ontario, a judicial officer under the Drainage Act with wide powers over matters relating to drainage. I.M. Rogers, *The Law of Canadian Municipal Corporations*, 2d ed. (Toronto: Carswell, 1971-) at 948.

DRAINAGE SYSTEM. See SANITARY ~.

DRAINAGE UNIT. The area allocated to a well for the purpose of drilling for and producing oil or gas, and includes all subsurface areas bounded by the vertical planes in which the surface boundaries lie. *Oil and Natural Gas acts.*

DRAINAGE WORK. 1. A drainage system constructed of tile, pipe or tubing of any material beneath the surface of agricultural land, including integral inlets and outlets, for the purpose of improving the productivity of the land drained. 2. The construction of a drain and includes the deepening, straightening, widening of, the clearing of obstructions from, or otherwise improving a stream, creek, or watercourse, the lowering of the waters of a lake or pond and the construction of necessary guards in connection therewith.

DRAINAGE WORKS. Includes a drain constructed by any means, including the improving of a natural watercourse, and includes works necessary to regulate the water table or water level within or on any lands or to regulate the level of the waters of a drain, reservoir, lake or pond, and includes a dam, embankment, wall, protective works or any combination thereof *Drainage Act*, R.S.O. 1990, c. D.17, s. 1.

DRAM. *n*. 1/16 ounce. *Weights and Measures Act*, S.C. 1970-71-72, c. 36, schedule II. See FLUID ~.

DRAMATIC WORK. Includes (a) any piece for recitation, choreographic work or mime, the scenic arrangement or acting form of which is fixed in writing or otherwise, (b) any cinematographic work, and (c) any compilation of dramatic works. *Copyright Act*, R.S.C. 1985, c. C-42, s. 2. See EVERY ORIGINAL LITERARY, DRAMATIC, MUSICAL AND ARTISTIC WORK.

DRAPER. *abbr.* Draper (Ont.), 1828-1831.

DRAUGHT. *n*. 1. An order drawn by one person on another for the payment of money, i.e. a bill of exchange or cheque. 2. An order for the payment of money drawn by one banker on another. 3. The vertical distance from the moulded base line amidships to a subdivision load water line (section 2). *Hull Construction Regulations*, C.R.C., c. 1431. 4. The deepest draught of a ship at the time pilotage services are performed. Can-

ada regulations. See SUMMER ~; VESSEL CONSTRAINED BY HER ~.

DRAW. *v*. To write a bill of exchange and sign it.

DRAWBACK. *n*. The remitting or paying back of duties previously paid on a commodity when it is exported.

DRAWEE. *n*. The person to whom a bill of exchange is addressed.

DRAWER. *n*. 1. The person who signs or makes a bill of exchange. 2. The person who addresses a depository bill. *Depository Bills and Notes Act*, S.C. 1998, c. 13, s. 2(1).

DRAWING. *n*. A unique artistic representation or work including calligraphy, usually on paper, parchment or vellum, executed in media such as pen and ink, ink wash, black or colour chalk, pastels, charcoal, graphite, watercolour, gouache or metal-point. *Canadian Cultural Property Export Control List*, C.R.C., c. 448, s. 1.

DREDGE. See MOTOR ~; STEAM ~.

DRESS. *n*. An object that is armour, headdress, pantaloons, a tunic with trappings, accoutrements or such other associated articles that form a part of military apparel. *Canadian Cultural Property Export Control List*, C.R.C., c. 448, s. 1.

DRESSED. *adj.* In relation to softwood lumber, means dressed or surfaced by planing on at least one edge or face. *Softwood Lumber Products Export Charge Act*, S.C. 1987, Sched., Part. 1, s. 1.

DRESSED CARCASS. The edible parts of a carcass but does not include the edible organs.

DRESSED POULTRY. Poultry, other than eviscerated poultry, from which the blood and feathers or blood, feathers and wing tips have been removed. *Dressed and Eviscerated Poultry Regulations*, C.R.C., c. 283, s. 2.

DRESSED STURGEON. A sturgeon from which the head, tail and entrails have been removed. *Ontario Fishery Regulations*, C.R.C., c. 849, s. 2.

DRESSED WEIGHT. The weight of the fish after the gills and entrails have been removed. See HEADLESS ~.

DRIED GRAIN. Damp or tough grain that has been dried by a grain drier.

DRIED MARIHUANA. Harvested marihuana that has been subjected to any drying process. *Marihuana Medical Access Regulations*, SOR/2001-227, s. 1(1).

DRIER. See GRAIN ~.

DRIFT. See TAX ~.

DRIFT NET. 1. A floating gill net that is neither anchored or staked but floats freely with the tide or current. 2. A net that is used to catch fish by enmeshing them and that does not enclose an area of water.

DRILL. *v.* To construct a well by drilling, boring, digging, washing, coring or by any other method by which a well can be constructed.

DRILLED. *adj*. In relation to softwood lumber, softwood flooring or softwood siding, means drilled at intervals for nails, screws or bolts, sanded or otherwise surface processed in lieu of, or in addition to, planing or working, or treated with creosote or other preservatives or with fillers, sealers, waxes, oils, stains, varnishes, paints or enamels but not including anti-stain or other temporary applications that serve only for the purpose of maintaining a product in its rough, dressed or worked condition until installation or further manufacture. *Softwood Lumber Products Export Charge Act*, S.C. 1987, c. 15, Sched., Part 1, s. 1.

DRILLER. *n.* (i) A person who is engaged or authorized by the licensee to undertake, or (ii) a licensee who personally undertakes, a drilling operation at a well or an operation preparatory or incidental to the drilling of a well or the reconditioning or abandonment of a well. See WELL ~.

DRILLING. *n.* The drilling, boring, digging, driving, jetting or reconditioning of a well.

DRILLING MACHINE. A machine, together with attachments, that is designed to be used or is used to drill a well.

DRILLING OR EXPLORATION EXPENSE. Incurred on or in respect of exploring or drilling for petroleum or natural gas includes any expense incurred on or in respect of (a) drilling or converting a well for the disposal of waste liquids from a petroleum or natural gas well, (b) drilling for water or gas for injection into a petroleum or natural gas formation, or (c) drilling or converting a well for the injection of water or gas to assist in the recovery of petroleum or natural as from another well. *Income Tax Act*, R.S.C. 1985, c. 1 (5th Supp.), s. 66(15).

DRILLING RESERVATION. See HOLDER OF A ~.

DRILL RODS. Used in percussive drilling and function to transmit the percussive energy to the host rock, provide rotation to the drill bit, transmit feed pressure to keep the bit constantly on the bottom of the hole and transmit a flushing medium to the bottom of the drill hole. *Sandvik Tamrock Canada Ltd. v. Deputy Minister of National Revenue (Customs & Excise)*, 2001 FCA 340, 284 N.R. 183, 6 T.T.R. (2d) 302 (C.A.).

DRINK. See DAIRY ~; SOFT ~.

DRINKING. See BOLUS ~.

DRIVE CARELESSLY. To drive a vehicle on a highway without due care and attention or without reasonable consideration for other persons using the highway.

DRIVER. *n.* 1. A person who drives or is in actual physical control of a vehicle or who is exercising control over or steering a vehicle being towed or pushed by another vehicle. 2. Includes a person who has the care or control of a motor vehicle whether it is in motion or not. 3. Includes street car operator. 4. Includes the rider of a bicycle. 5. The occupant of a vehicle seated immediately behind the steering control system. *Motor Vehicle Safety Regulations*, C.R.C., c. 1038, s. 2. See AMBULANCE ~; BROKER-~; TAXI ~.

DRIVER IMPROVEMENT PROGRAM. A course of study or instruction for the improvement of the knowledge, attitudes and skills of persons in the operation of motor vehicles.

DRIVER INSTRUCTOR. A person who holds a driver instructor's certificate and who is engaged in the business of giving instruction for hire, fee or tuition in the driving of motor vehicles or the preparation of an applicant for an examination for a licence.

DRIVER-OPERATED ACCELERATOR CONTROL SYSTEM. All components of a vehicle, except the fuel metering device, that regulate engine speed in direct response to movement of the driver-operated control and that return the throttle to the idle position upon release of the driver-operated control. *Motor Vehicle Safety Regulations*, C.R.C., c. 1038, s. 2.

DRIVER OR OPERATOR. A person who drives or is in actual physical control of a vehicle.

DRIVER SALESMAN. Person who works an assigned route, delivering goods and collecting payments as well as selling goods.

DRIVER'S LICENCE. 1. A licence which has been issued authorizing the person to whom it is issued to drive a motor vehicle and which has not expired, been suspended or cancelled. 2. A licence or a permit to drive a motor vehicle on a public highway. 3. Includes a motorized snow vehicle operator's licence.

DRIVER'S LICENSE. A license issued to drive a motor vehicle upon the highway.

DRIVER'S POLICY. A motor vehicle liability policy insuring a person named therein in respect of the operation or use by him of any automobile other than an automobile owned by him or registered in his name. *Insurance acts.*

DRIVER TRAINING SCHOOL. A person, firm or association that is engaged in the business of giving instructions for hire, fee or tuition on the driving of motor vehicles or in the preparation for an examination for a driver's licence.

DRIVEWAY. *n.* A clearly defined private road, way, drive, path or passage or a similar opening or space which is wide enough, but not wider than is necessary, for the passage of a motor vehicle, whereby the owner, occupier or user of property has vehicular access from a roadway to a point within the property. See PRIVATE ~.

DRIVING CARELESSLY. See DRIVE CARELESSLY.

DRIVING INSTRUCTOR. A person who teaches other persons to operate motor vehicles and receives compensation therefor, but does not include a licensed teacher under contract in a recognized educational institution who instructs in the operation of a motor vehicle in a private driver education training course carried on in the institution.

DRIVING PRIVILEGE. (a) The privilege of applying for, obtaining or holding a licence to operate a motor vehicle in the Province, and (b) the privilege of operating a motor vehicle in the province.

DRIVING TIME. The period of time that a motor vehicle operator is at the controls of a motor vehicle and the engine is in operation.

DROIT. *n.* [Fr.] Equity; justice; right.

DROITURAL. *adj.* Relating to right.

DROP DEAD RULE. A rule of court which requires a court to dismiss an action if nothing has been done to materially advance the processing of the action within a certain period of time.

DROP SHIPMENT. Shipment of goods directly from manufacturer to dealer or consumer, not through a wholesaler.

DROVER. *n.* Any person or partnership engaged in the business of selling his livestock at a stockyard on his own account. *Livestock and Livestock Products Act*, R.S.C. 1985, c. L-9, s. 10.

DROWNING. *n.* Death caused by immersing the nose and mouth in fluid. F.A. Jaffe, *A Guide to Pathological Evidence*, 3d ed. (Toronto: Carswell, 1991) at 217. See DRY ~; SECONDARY ~.

D.R.S. *abbr.* Dominion Report Service.

DRUG. *n.* 1. Any substance or mixture of substances manufactured, sold or represented for use in (a) the diagnosis, treatment, mitigation or prevention of a disease, disorder, abnormal physical state, or the symptoms thereof, in man or animal, (b) restoring, correcting or modifying organic functions in man or animal, or (c) disinfection in premises in which food is manufactured, prepared or kept. 2. Any substance that is capable of producing a state of euphoria, depression, hallucination or intoxication in a human being. 3. (i) Any substance that is named in the latest edition from time to time of the British Pharmacopoeia, the British Pharmaceutical Codex, the Pharmacopoeia of the United States of America, the National Formulary, the New and Nonofficial remedies, the Canadian Formulary, the Codex Français or the Pharmacopoea Internationalis, or (ii) any preparation containing any substance mentioned in subclause (i), or (iii) any substance or mixture of substances manufactured, sold or represented for use in (A) the diagnosis, treatment, mitigation or prevention of a disease, disorder, abnormal physical state or the symptoms thereof, in human or animal; (B) restoring, correcting or modifying organic functions in human or animal; or (C) disinfection in premises in which food is manufactured, prepared or kept, or for the control of vermin in such premises. 4. A substance, whether in crude form, refined form, prepared dosage form or any other form whatever, intended or capable of being used for medicine or for the preparation or production of medicine. *Patent Rules*, C.R.C., c. 1250, s. 117. 5. " ... [A]ny substance or chemical agent the consumption of which will bring about impairment as contemplated by s. 234 [of the Criminal Code, R.S.C. 1970, c. C-34]." *R. v. Marionchuk* (1978), 1 M.V.R. 158 at 162, 4 C.R. (3d) 178, [1978] 6 W.W.R. 120, 42

C.C.C. (2d) 573 (Sask. C.A.), the court per Culliton C.J.S. See APPROVED ~ AND PHARMACEUTICAL; BRAND-NAME ~; CONTROLLED ~; DESIGNATED ~; GENERIC ~; HALLUCINOGENIC ~; ILLICIT ~; INTERCHANGEABLE ~; NEW ~; OFFICIAL ~; OPTOMETRIC ~; LICENCE; PRESCRIPTION ~; RESTRICTED ~; SOFT ~; SPECIFIED ~; VETERINARY ~.

DRUG ABUSE. (a) Addiction to a substance other than alcohol; or (b) the use, whether habitual or not, of a substance other than alcohol that is capable of inducing euphoria, hallucinations or intoxication in a person. See ILLICIT DRUG USE.

DRUG ABUSER. A person who abuses or is addicted to a drug.

DRUG DEPENDENCY. A state of psychological or physical reliance, or both, on one or more chemical substances that alter mood, perception, consciousness or behaviour to the apparent detriment of the person or society, or both, as a result of the periodic or continuous use or administration of one or more chemical substances and includes the use of nicotine or alcohol, or both.

DRUGGIST. *n.* A pharmaceutical chemist registered and entitled to practise.

DRUG INTERACTION. Reinforcement or cancellation of each other's effects when two drugs are present in a person's body at the same time.

DRUGLESS PRACTITIONER. A person who practises the treatment of any ailment, disease, defect or disability of the human body by manipulation, adjustment, manual or electrotherapy or by any similar method. *Drugless Practitioners Act*, R.S.O. 1990, c. D.18, s. 1.

DRUGLESS THERAPIST. Any person who practises or advertises or holds himself out in any way as practising the treatment by diagnosis, including all diagnostic methods, direction, advice, written or otherwise, of any ailment, disease, defect or disability of the human body by methods taught in colleges of drugless therapy or naturopathy and approved by the Board. *Drugless Practitioners Act*, R.R.O. 1980, Reg. 250, s. 1.

DRUG PRODUCT. See LISTED ~.

DRUG STORE. A place where prescriptions, medicines, drugs, chemicals and poisons are compounded or prepared or sold by retail.

DRUG USE. See ILLICIT ~; INSTRUMENT FOR ILLICIT ~; LITERATURE FOR ILLICIT ~.

DRUG USER. A person who (i) is addicted to the use of a substance other than alcohol, or (ii) uses, whether habitually or not, a substance other than alcohol for the purpose of inducing euphoria, hallucinations or intoxication.

DRUM HOIST. The type of hoisting engine where the rope is anchored to and spooled on to a drum.

DRUM TRAP. A trap where the inlet and outlet are in the sides of the cylinder of the trap.

DRUNKARD. See HABITUAL ~.

DRUNKENNESS. *n.* Intoxication.

DRY. *adj.* A condition that does not include uncombined water. *National Emission Standards Regulations*, Canada regulations.

DRY CLEANER. A person who understands and is capable of carrying out the process of, (i) cleaning garments in either manual or automatic equipment by immersion and agitation or by immersion only in volatile solvents, including but not being restricted to solvents of the petroleum distillate type, the coal tar distillate type, the chlorinated hydrocarbon type and including any or all of the processes incidental to cleaning garments by immersion in volatile solvents, (ii) wet cleaning of garments by immersion in water or bar the application, manually or by any mechanical device, of water or any detergent and water, or by spraying or brushing the garments with water and any detergent or with water vapour or with chemicals and water or with steam, (iii) pressing or finishing, or both, being the process of restoring garments to their original shape, dimensions or contour or to the condition in which the garments were received from the customer or as directed by the customer, and including the removal of wrinkles, stresses, bulges and impressions, imprint marks and shine from garments by the application, either manually or mechanically and with or without dry or wet cleaning, of pressure, heat, moisture, water vapour or steam, (iv) removing spots or stains or localized areas of soil from garments before or after the garments are dry or wet cleaned or by manual or mechanical means, other than dry or wet cleaning, such as by brushing or spraying with water detergents and volatile or flammable solvents or with chemicals or both, (v) repairing, being the process of making alterations as required the customer to garments, such as by minor repairs and alterations, by reaffixing, replacing or restoring buttons or other fastening devices and decorative materials to the a merits either before or after one of the processes referred to in this clause, (vi) identification of fabrics, fabric construction, designs and finishes, (vii) cleaning shirts by immersion in water, including the use of washing formulae and chemicals, and of special finishes and a knowledge of the control of water and temperature, the operation of necessary equipment and the control of quality in the proper processing and finishing shirt laundry, and (viii) basic management, production, quality control, garment identification pricing, packaging and servicing to the customer. *Apprenticeship and Tradesmen's Qualification Act*, R.R.O. 1980, Reg. 31, s. 1.

DRY DOCK. Includes floating dry docks. *Dry Dock Subsidies Act*, R.S.C. 1985, c. D-4, s. 2.

DRY DROWNING. Suffocation caused by a spasm in the larynx when small quantities of fluid are inhaled. F.A. Jaffe, *A Guide to Pathological Evidence*, 3d ed. (Toronto: Carswell, 1991) at 217.

DRY EXCHANGE. An old term for covering and disguising usury: though something was supposed to pass on both sides, it passed on one side only.

DRYING CENTRE. An establishment, other than a regional centre, where services are offered for the handling, drying, screening and grading of grain in conformity.

DRY LEASE. A lease of an aircraft under the terms of which the lessor does not provide, directly or indirectly, the aircrew to operate the aircraft.

DRY-RENT. *n.* Rent-seck; rent reserved with no distress clause.

DRY SALTERY. See HERRING ~; SALMON ~.

DRY VENT. A vent pipe that is not a wet vent.

D.T.C. *abbr.* Dominion Tax Cases.

DTH DISTRIBUTION UNDERTAKING. A direct-to-home (DTH) satellite distribution undertaking. *Broadcasting Distribution Regulations*, SOR/97-555, s. 1.

DTH ELIGIBLE SATELLITE SERVICE. A programming service included in Appendix C of the Commission's *Revised Lists of Eligible Satellite Services*, as amended from time to time. *Broadcasting Distribution Regulations*, SOR/97-555, s. 1.

DTH PAY-PER-VIEW SERVICE. The pay-per-view service provided by a person licensed to carry on a direct-to-home pay-per-view television programming undertaking. *Broadcasting Distribution Regulations*, SOR/97-555, s. 1.

DUAL AXLE. Any two consecutive axles whose centres are more than forty inches or one metre apart and (i) are articulated from a common attachment to the vehicle, or (ii) designed to equalize the load between the two axles.

DUAL COVERAGE. The ability of an individual, through the combination of two benefit plans, to obtain reimbursement for his or her insurance claims up to the combined limit of the two plans. *British Columbia Public School Employers' Assn. v. B.C.T.F.*, 2003 BCCA 323, 15 B.C.L.R. (4th) 58 (C.A.).

DUAL NATIONALITY. Citizenship in two countries.

DUAL-PURPOSE VEHICLE. A motor vehicle, other than one commonly known as a passenger car, designed by the manufacturer for the transportation of persons and goods. *Truck Transportation Act*, R.S.O. 1990, c. T.22, s. 1(1).

DUAL RATE SYSTEM. An arrangement of the rates to be charged for the transportation of goods into contract rates and non-contract rates, and in which the contract rate for the transportation of specific goods described therein is lower than the non-contract rate for those goods. *Shipping Conference Exemption Act*, R.S.C. 1985, c. S-10, s. 5(2).

DUAL VALUATION. A method of valuation of a fishing vessel for insurance purposes establishing one insured value for total loss and a second insured value for partial loss.

DUAL VENT. A vent pipe connecting at a junction of waste pipes serving two fixtures and serving as a common vent pipe for both fixtures.

DUARCHY. *n.* Government in which two govern jointly.

DUBITANTE. *adj.* [L. doubting] Used in a law report to describe a judge's doubt that a proposition is correct without a decision that it is wrong.

DUCES TECUM. [L.] Bring with you.

DUCT. See EXHAUST ~; RETURN ~; SUP-PLY ~.

DUE. *adj.* 1. Payable; owing. *Mail Printing Co. v. Clarkson* (1895), 25 O.A.R. 1 (C.A.), Moss J.A. 2. " . . . [I]n relation to moneys in respect of which there is a legal obligation to pay them may mean either that the facts making the obligation operative have come into existence with the exception that the day of payment has not yet arrived, or it may mean that the obligation has not only been completely constituted but is also presently exigible. . ." *Ontario Hydro-Electric Power Commission v. Albright* (1922), 64 S.C.R. 306 at 312, [1923] 2 D.L.R. 578, Duff J.

DUE APPLICATION. Includes such information, evidence and material as an official requires to be furnished; and also the payment of the fees prescribed in respect of any application, certificate or document required or issued by virtue of an act.

DUE COURSE. See HOLDER IN ~.

DUE DILIGENCE. 1. A defence that the accused held a reasonable belief in a mistaken set of facts or that the accused took all reasonable steps to avoid the offending event. 2. In the context of an agreement of purchase and sale, refers to the requirement for the purchaser to complete all relevant searches and investigations to satisfy herself that she should complete the transaction.

DUELLING. *n.* Challenging or attempting by any means to provoke another person to fight a duel, attempting to provoke a person to challenge another person to fight a duel, or accepting a challenge to fight a duel is an offence. *Criminal Code*, R.S.C. 1985, c. C-46, s. 71.

DUE PROCESS. " . . . [T]he phrase 'due process of law' as used in s. 1(a) [of the Canadian Bill of Rights, R.S.C. 1970, App. III] is to be construed as meaning 'according to the legal processes recognized by Parliament and the Courts in Canada.' " *Curr v. R.*, [1972] S.C.R. 889 at 916, 18 C.R.N.S. 281, 7 C.C.C. (2d) 181, 26 D.L.R. (3d) 603, Ritchie J.

DUES. *n.* Fees, rates, charges or other moneys payable by any person to the Crown under and by virtue of a lease, licence or permit. See AR-BOUR ~; PILOTAGE ~; UNION ~.

DULOCRACY. *n.* A government in which servants and slaves dominate.

DULY. *adv.* In the proper manner; regularly.

DULY QUALIFIED MEDICAL PRACTI-TIONER. Person registered and holding a current licence from the college authorizing the person to practise medicine.

DUM BENE SE GESSERIT. [L.] During good conduct.

DUMBWAITER. *var.* **DUMB-WAITER**. *n.* A mechanism affixed to a building or structure, equipped with a car or platform that moves in guides in a substantially vertical direction, the total compartment height of which does not exceed four feet that is loaded or unloaded and controlled manually, that is used exclusively for lifting or lowering freight.

DUM CASTA VIXERIT. [L.] As long as she lives chastely.

DUMP. *n.* A place where scrapped objects are deposited, whether or not such objects are intended to be sold or recycled; it includes in particular an old car dump. See RURAL ~.

DUMPED. *adj.* In relation to any goods, means that the normal value of the goods exceeds the export price thereof. *Special Imports Measures Act*, R.S.C. 1985, c. S-15, s. 2.

DUMPING. *n.* 1. " . . . [T]he introduction of dumped goods into the commerce of Canada . . ." *Sacilor Acieries v. Canada (Anti-Dumping Tribunal)* (1985), 9 C.E.R. 210 at 214, 60 N.R. 371 (Fed. C.A.), Hugessen J.A. 2. (a) The deliberate disposal at sea from ships, aircraft, platforms or other anthropogenic structures, including disposal by incineration or other thermal degradation, of any substance, or (b) the disposal of any substance by placing it on the ice in any area of the sea referred to in paragraphs (2)(a) to (e), but does not include (c) any disposal that is incidental to or derived from the normal operations of a ship, aircraft, platform or other anthropogenic structure or of any equipment on a ship, aircraft, platform or other anthropogenic structure, other than the disposal of substances from a ship, aircraft, platform or other anthropogenic structure operated for the purpose of disposing of such substances at sea, and (d) any discharge that is incidental to or derived from the exploration for, exploitation of and associated offshore processing of sea bed mineral resources. *Canadian Environmental Protection Act*, S.C. 1988, c. 22, s. 66(1). See MARGIN OF ~.

DUMP VEHICLE. A commercial motor vehicle used for the transportation and dumping or spreading of sand, gravel, earth, crushed or uncut rock, slag, rubble, salt, calcium chloride, snow, ice or any mixture thereof, asphalt mixes or scrap metal.

DUM SOLA. [L.] As long as she remains single or unmarried.

DUM SOLA ET CASTA. [L.] As long as she remains unmarried and lives chastely.

DUM VIDUA. [L.] As long as she remains a widow.

DUNE. See SAND ~.

DUNGEON. *n*. A secure prison.

DUNNAGE. *n*. Wood or other material laid against the bottom and sides of a vessel's hold.

DUODECIMA MANU. [L.] Twelve witnesses to wipe out a criminal's offence.

DUODENA. *n*. [L.] A jury of 12.

DUODENA MANU. [L.] Twelve witnesses to wipe out a criminal's offence.

DUO NON POSSUNT IN SOLIDO UNAM REM POSSIDERE. [L.] Two people cannot possess one thing in entirety.

DUO SUNT INSTRUMENTA AD OMNES RES AUT CONFIRMANDAS AUT IMPUG-NANDAS, RATIO ET AUCTORITAS. [L.] There are two ways to either confirm or impugn things: reason and authority.

DUPLEX. *n*. 1. " . . . [A] building of two floors in separate occupation, with separate entrances. . ." *Toronto (City) v. William Unser Ltd.*, [1954] 3 D.L.R. 641 at 649 (S.C.C.), Kellock J. (Locke, Cartwright and Taschereau JJ. concurring). 2. A unit within a separate and detached building permanently erected on land within the Province, which building consists of two self-contained units within the confines of the building, each of which provides housing accommodation for a single family within the confines of the unit. *Homeowner's Incentive Act*, R.S.N.S. 1989, c. 202, s. 2. See HOME-OWNER ~; RENTAL ~.

DUPLICATE. *v*. To copy.

DUPLICATE. *n*. 1. A copy. 2. The duplicate, delivered or issued to the person entitled thereto, of the certificate of title in the register. *Land Titles acts*.

DUPLICATE CERTIFICATE. The duplicate, delivered or issued to the person entitled thereto, of the certificate of title in the register. *Land Titles acts*.

DUPLICATE CERTIFICATE OF TITLE. An exact copy of the certificate in the register;

when an entry is made on the certificate in the register, the same entry must be made on the duplicate certificate.

DUPLICATE ORIGINAL. The first copy of a document which was executed as though it were also an original.

DUPLICATE PLAN. A true copy of the plan.

DUPLICATE WILL. One copy of a will kept by the executor, the other deposited with someone else.

DUPLICITY. *n*. 1. " . . . [I]f the information in one count charges more than one offence, it is bad for duplicity . . ." *R. v. Sault Ste. Marie (City)* (1978), 7 C.E.L.R. 53 at 57, [1978] 2 S.C.R. 1299, 3 C.R. (3d) 30, 21 N.R. 295, 40 C.C.C. (2d) 353, 85 D.L.R. (3d) 161, the court per Dickson J. 2. " . . . [T]he practice of including more than one claim in a pleading." *Flexi-Coil Ltd. v. Rite Way Manufacturing Ltd.* (1989), 28 C.P.R. (3d) 256 at 259, 31 F.T.R. 73, [1990] 1 F.C. 108, Giles (Associate Senior Prothonotary).

DURABLE LIFE. The period, commencing on the day on which a prepackaged product is packaged for retail sale, during which the product, when it is stored under conditions appropriate to that product, will retain, without any appreciable deterioration, its normal wholesomeness, palatability, nutritional value and any other qualities claimed for it by the manufacturer.

DURABLE LIFE DATE. 1. A date on packaged goods indicating by when the contents should be consumed; best before date. 2. The date on which the durable life of a prepackaged product ends.

DURA MATER. [L.] A sturdy fibrous membrane attached to the inside of the skull. F.A. Jaffe, *A Guide to Pathological Evidence*, 3d ed. (Toronto: Carswell, 1991) at 153.

DURANTE. [L.] During.

DURANTE ABSENTIA. [L.] During absence.

DURANTE BENE PLACITO. [L.] 1. During pleasure. 2. During the Crown's pleasure.

DURANTE MINORE AETATE. [L.] During the state of minority.

DURANTE VIDUIDATE. [L.] During the widowed state.

DURANTE VITA. [L.] During life.

DURATION. See PULSE ~.

DURESS. *n.* 1. " . . . [A] threat of death or serious physical injury is necessary to constitute duress at common law: . . . Mere fear does not constitute duress in the absence of a threat, either express or implied." *R. v. Mena* (1987), 34 C.C.C. (3d) 304 at 320, 322, 57 C.R. (3d) 172, 20 O.A.C. 50 (C.A.), the court per Martin J.A. 2. ". . . [T]hreats must be made to a person who is a party and with the intention of inducing that person to enter into the agreement sought to be avoided; . . . duress makes a contract voidable at the initiative of the innocent party, but there cannot be duress unless the acts complained of constitute a coercion of the complaining party's will so as to vitiate the consent of that party: . . ." *Byle v. Byle* (1990), 46 B.L.R. 292 at 304, 65 D.L.R. (4th) 641 (B.C. C.A.), the court per Macdonald J.A. 3. "Economic pressure does not amount to duress unless there is a coercion of will to the point that the payment or contract was not a voluntary act." *Century 21 Campbell Munro Ltd. v. S & G Estates Ltd.* (1992), 89 D.L.R. 413 at 417, 54 O.A.C. 315 (Div. Ct.), the court per Campbell J. 4. Can constitute a defence to a criminal charge including one of conspiracy. See ECONOMIC ~.

DURESS COLORE OFFICII. [L.] Abuse of an official or governmental position in which the official requires a person to pay in order to obtain some authority, licence, permission or power to act or proceed in a particular way.

DURESS OF PROPERTY. Wrongful seizure or detention of a plaintiff's goods.

DURESS OF THE PERSON. Actual or threatened physical violence to a person, or violence or threatened violence to the physical safety of others, such as members of a payer's family. The concept now extends to threats of criminal process which might lead to imprisonment.

DURESS PER MINAS. Duress by threat. Codified in section 17 of the Criminal Code as to principals. Parties to offences may seek to have their behaviour excused by duress by threat. *R. v. Hibbert* (1995), 99 C.C.C. (3d) 193 (S.C.C.).

DURHAM REPORT. The 1839 report which recommended that the two Canadas unite.

DURING. *prep.* Throughout; while.

DURING AN ELECTION. 1. In respect of an election in any electoral district, means the period commencing with the issue of the writ for that election and terminating on polling day or, where the writ is withdrawn or deemed to be withdrawn, terminating on the day that the writ is withdrawn or deemed to be withdrawn. 2. The period from issue of a writ of election to the close of the polls on the day on which polling takes place; or, in the case of an election in which no poll is granted, the period from the issue of the writ of election to the close of the nominations on the day of nomination.

DURING THE ELECTION. The period from issue of a writ of election to the close of the polls on the day on which polling takes place; or, in the case of an election in which no poll is granted, the period from the issue of the writ of election to the close of the nominations on the day of nomination. *Election Act*, R.S.M. 1970, c. E-30, s. 2.

DUST. *n.* Solid airborne particles that are mechanically generated. See COMBUSTIBLE ~; SILICEOUS ~.

DUST EXPOSURE OCCUPATION. (i) Any employment underground in a mine; (ii) any employment at the surface of a mine in ore or rock crushing operations in which the ore or rock being crushed is not constantly kept in a moistened or wet condition by the use of water or chemical solutions; (iii) any employment at the surface of a mine that is designated by an inspector as a dust exposure occupation; or (iv) any employment in assay grinding rooms or in wet concentrating plants not isolated from dry crushing plants.

DUTCH AUCTION. Offering property for sale at auction at high value and gradually lowering the price until it is sold.

DUTCH ELM DISEASE. The disease caused by the fungus Ceratocystis Ulmi.

DUTIES. *n.* 1. Any duties or taxes levied on imported goods under the Customs Tariff the Excise Tax Act, the Excise Act, the Special Import Measures Act or any other law relating to customs. 2. In addition to its ordinary meaning, the fees, price or cost of licences or permits, permits, taxes and other imposts and contributions provided for by a fiscal law. See CUSTOM DUTY; CUSTOMS DUTY; PILOTAGE ~.

DUTY. *n.* 1. A requirement which the law recognizes to avoid conduct characterized by unreasonable risk of danger to other persons. 2. A duty imposed by law. *Criminal Code*, R.S.C. 1985, c. C-46, s. 219(2). See ACTIVE ~; CONTINUOUS ~; CUSTOM ~; CUSTOMS ~; DISCRETIONARY ~; ESTATE ~; EX-

CISE ~; INTERMITTENT ~; MINISTE-RIAL ~; PERIODIC ~; PROBATE ~; SHORT TIME ~; STAMP ~; SUCCESSION ~; VALUE FOR ~; VARYING ~.

DUTY COUNSEL. A lawyer appointed to assist any person appearing in court without having retained a lawyer.

DUTY OF CARE. " ... [A] device which the courts have developed to control the extent to which defendants would otherwise be liable in negligence. In its modern manifestation as a basic principle of negligence, it owes its origin to the following words of Lord Atkins in *M'Alister (Donoghue) v. Stevenson*, [1932] A.C. 562 ... at pp. 580-581: 'Who, then, in law is my neighbour? The answer seems to be—persons who are so closely and directly affected by my act that I ought reasonably to have them in contemplation as being so affected when I am directing my mind to the acts or omissions which are called in question.'" *Laden v. Canada Attorney General)* (1991) (*sub nom. Brewer Brothers v. Canada (Attorney General)*) 8 C.C.L.T. (2d) 45 at 68, 129 N.R. 1, [1992] 1 F.C. 25, 45 F.T.R. 325n (C.A.), the court per Stone J.A. See NEIGHBOUR TEST.

DUTY OF FAIRNESS. See DUTY TO ACT FAIRLY.

DUTY PAID VALUE. The value of the article as it would be determined for the purpose of calculating an ad valorem duty on the importation of that article into Canada under the laws relating to the customs and the Customs Tariff whether that article is in fact subject to ad valorem or other duty or not, plus the amount of the customs duties if any, payable thereon. *Excise Tax Act*, R.S.C. 1985, c. E-15.

DUTY TO ACCOMMODATE. Employers and others governed by human rights legislation are now required in all cases to accommodate the characteristics of affected groups within their standards, rather than maintaining discriminatory standards supplemented by accommodation for those who cannot meet them. Incorporating accommodation into the standard itself ensures that each person is assessed according to her or his own personal abilities, instead of being judged against presumed group characteristics. *British Columbia (Superintendent of Motor Vehicles) v. British Columbia (Council of Human Rights)* (1999), 1999 CarswellBC 2730, [2000] 1 W.W.R. 565, 47 M.V.R. (3d) 167, 249 N.R. 45, 70 B.C.L.R. (3d) 215, 181 D.L.R. (4th) 385, 36 C.H.R.R. D/129, [1999] 3 S.C.R. 868, 131 B.C.A.C. 280, 214 W.A.C. 280, McLachlin for the court. See ACCOMODATION.

DUTY TO ACCOUNT. The duty of a trustee to have his accounts always ready, to afford all reasonable facilities for inspection and examination, and to give full information whenever required. *Sandford v. Porter* (1889), 16 O.A.R. 565 at 571.

DUTY TO ACT FAIRLY. 1. "Fairness involves compliance with only some of the principles of natural justice. Professor de Smith, Judicial Review of Administrative Action (1973), 3rd ed. p. 208, expressed lucidly the concept of a duty to act fairly: 'In general it means a duty to observe the rudiments of natural justice for a limited purpose in the exercise of functions that are not analytically judicial but administrative.'" *Martineau v. Matsqui Institution* (1979), 106 D.L.R. (3d) 385 at 411-12, [1980] 1 S.C.R. 602, 12 C.R. (3d) 1, 15 C.R. (3d) 315, 50 C.C.C. (2d) 353, 30 N.R. 119, Dickson J. 2. " ... The basic objective of the duty to act fairly is to ensure that an individual is provided with a sufficient degree of participation necessary to bring to the attention of the decision-maker any fact or argument of which a fair-minded decision-maker would need to be informed in order to reach a rational conclusion." *Kindler v. Canada (Minister of Justice)* (1987), 1 Imm. L.R. (2d) 30 at 37, 8 F.T.R. 222, [1987] 2 F.C. 145, 34 C.C.C. (3d) 78, Rouleau J. See ECONOMIC DURESS; FAIRNESS.

DUTY TO DEFEND. An insurer's duty which arises when the claim against the insured alleges a set of facts which, if proven, would fall within the coverage of the policy issued by the insurer to the insured.

DUTY TO MINIMIZE. The first problem that arises is the question of the existence and effect, in Canadian criminal law, of a duty to minimize impairments of solicitor-client privilege when a search in a lawyer's office is authorized and executed. Under the current law, as set out in the decisions of this Court, there is no doubt that such a duty exists. It rests on the informant who applies for a search warrant, the authorizing judge and those responsible for executing it. There are two aspects to this duty. First, it requires that a search not be authorized unless there is no other reasonable solution. Second, the authorization must be given in terms that, to the extent possible, limit the impairment of solicitor-client privilege. The search must be executed in the same way. *Maranda c. Québec*

(Juge de la Cour du Québec), 2003 SCC 67. per LeBel, J. for the majority.

DUTY TO MITIGATE. The requirement that the plaintiff take all reasonable steps to minimize a loss which follows a breach of contract or injury.

DVFR FLIGHT PLAN. A flight plan that (a) includes the information required in a VFR flight plan as set out in the Flight Plans and Flight Notifications Order, and (b) states the flight level or altitude above sea level to be flown. *Security Control of Air Traffic Order*, C.R.C., c. 63, s. 2.

DWARF SIGNAL. A low signal used as a block or interlocking signal. *Regulations No. O-8, Uniform Code of Operating Rules*, C.R.C., c. 1175, Part III, s. 2.

DWELLING. *n.* 1. ". . . [P]lace of residence, a place in which to live, a habitation." *Read v. Read*, [1950] 2 W.W.R. 812 at 813, [1950] 4 D.L.R. 676 (B.C. C.A.), the court per Sloan C.J.B.C. 2. A premises or any part thereof occupied as living accommodation. See MULTIPLE ~; MULTIPLE-FAMILY ~; MULTIPLE UNIT ~; NEW ~; ONE-FAMILY ~; RAILWAY STATION-~; SEMI-DETACHED ~; SINGLE-FAMILY ~; TWO-FAMILY ~.

DWELLING-HOUSE. *var.* **DWELLING HOUSE.** 1. Dwelling-house does not mean a separate, single-family building. It means any place a person dwells. *R. v. Kutschera*, 1999 CarswellBC 2751, 1999 BCCA 748, 141 C.C.C. (3d) 254, 131 B.C.A.C. 120, 214 W.A.C. 120 (C.A.). Per Southin J. dissenting). 2. The whole or any part of a building or structure that is kept or occupied as a permanent or temporary residence and includes (a) a building within the yard of a dwelling-house that is connected to it by a doorway or by a covered and enclosed passageway, and (b) a unit that is designed to be mobile and to be used as a permanent or temporary residence and that is being used as a residence.

DWELLING UNIT. A room or suite of rooms used or intended to be used as a domicile by one or more persons and usually containing cooking, eating, living, sleeping and sanitary facilities. See BACHEOR ~; RESIDENTIAL ~; SELF-CONTAINED ~.

D.W.I. *abbr.* Died without issue.

DYE. *n.* 1. Chemical substances prescribed for the purpose of blending with fuel to make coloured fuel. *Fuel Tax Act*, R.S.O. 1990, c. F.35, s. 1. 2. The principal dye and associated subsidiary and isomeric dyes contained in a synthetic colour.

DYING DECLARATION. " . . . [S]tatement made under a sense of impending death . . ." *R. v. Davidson* (1898), 30 N.S.R. 349 at 359 (C.A.), Henry J.A.

DYING WITHOUT ISSUE. Dying without any child being born before or after death.

DYKE. *n.* An embankment, wall, fill, piling, pump, gate, floodbox, pipe, sluice, culvert, canal, ditch, drain or any other thing that is constructed, assembled or installed to prevent the flooding of land. *Dyke Maintenance Act*, R.S.B.C. 1979, c. 99, s. 1. See PRIVATE ~.

DYNAMICALLY POSITIONED. In respect of a MODU, means that the MODU is held in position over a well wholly or partly by means of propulsion units. *Crewing Regulations*, SOR/ 97-390, s. 1(1).

DYNE. *n.* That force which, acting on one gramme for one second, generates a velocity of one centimetre per second. *Electric and Photometric Units Act*, R.S.C. 1970, c. E-3, s. 2.

DYSNOMY. *n.* Making unsatisfactory laws.

DYSON DECLARATION. The name refers to *Dyson v. Attorney General* (1910), [1911] 1 K.B. 410 (Eng. C.A.). It is a declaratory judgment in an action in which the Attorney General, as representative of the Crown, is a party. *Cummins v. Canada* (1997), 50 B.C.L.R. (3d) 262 (S.C.).

E

E. *abbr.* Effective length of superstructure or trunk.

EADEM MENS PRAESUMITUR REGIS QUAE EST JURIS, ET QUAE ESSE DEBET, PRAESERTIM IN DUBIIS. [L.] It is presumed that the mind of the sovereign conforms with the law, and what should be, particularly in doubtful cases.

E. & A. *abbr.* Error and Appeal Reports (Grant) (Ont.), 1846-1866.

E. & O.E. *abbr.* Errors and omissions excepted.

EARLY RETIREMENT. Withdrawal of an employee from the workforce before the normal date for retirement.

EARMARK. *n.* A mark of ownership or identity.

EARN. *v.* 1. " . . . [T]o 'earn' income or profit is, . . . to expend the effort or exertion which creates the value to be exchanged . . ." *William Wrigley Jr. Co. v. Manitoba (Provincial Treasurer)*, [1947] C.T.C. 304 at 314, [1947] S.C.R. 431, [1947] 4 D.L.R. 12, Rinfret C.J.C. and Taschereau J. 2. To acquire income on an investment. 3. Of interest, to receive.

EARNED INCOME IN KIND. The expenditure of talent and energy to create goods or services for which goods and services are received.

EARNED REMISSION. Shortening of a sentence in respect of time during which a prisoner applies himself or herself industriously.

EARNEST. *n.* That which is given by a buyer and accepted by a seller to indicate that a contract has been made.

EARNINGS. *n.* 1. The pay received or receivable by an employee for work done for an employer. 2. "[As used in the Unemployment Insurance Act, S.C. 1970-71-72, c. 48, s. 58(q)] . . . in the broad sense are everything the worker derives in the form of pecuniary benefits from his work present or past, and in this sense a pension is still undoubtedly earnings, . . ." *Côté v. Canada (Employment & Immigration Commission)* (1986), 13 C.C.E.L. 255 at 262, 86 C.L.L.C. 14,050, 69 N.R. 126 (Fed. C.A.), Marceau J.A. (Pratte J. concurring). See ALLOCATED RETAINED ~; INSURABLE ~; INTERRUPTION OF ~; MAINTAINABLE~; NET ~; PENSIONABLE ~; PROSPECTIVE LOSS OF ~ OR PROFITS; RECORD OF ~; RETAINED ~.

EARNINGS PER SHARE. See BASIC ~; FULLY DILUTED ~.

EARTHQUAKE INSURANCE. Insurance against loss of or damage to property caused by an earthquake.

EARTH STATION. A station operated in a space service and located on the earth's surface, including a station on board a ship or aircraft. See SATELLITE TELECOMMUNICATION SYSTEM.

EARTHWORK. *n.* 1. Any dump or heap of earth, sand, or gravel or any place from which earth, sand, or gravel has been removed. *Noxious Weeds acts.* 2. Construction composed of clay, shale or heavy loam and containing more than 10 per cent by volume of sand, gravel or stone. *Gasoline Handling Act*, R.R.O. 1980, Reg. 439, s. 1.

EARWITNESS. *n.* One who can bear witness to something heard personally.

EASEMENT. *n.* 1. A landowner's right to use another's land for a particular purpose, for example a right of way or a right to extract a mineral. 2. " . . . [A] right annexed to land which permits the owner of a dominant tenement to require the owner of a servient tenement to suffer something on such land. There are four charac-teristics of an easement: (1) There must be a dominant and a servient tenement. (2) An ease-ment must accommodate the dominant tene-ment. (3) Dominant and servient owners must be different persons. (4) A right over land cannot amount to an easement unless it is capable of forming the subject-matter of a grant." *Vannini v. Sault Ste. Marie Public Utilities Commission* (1972), [1973] 2 O.R. 11 at 16, *32* D.L.R. (3d) 661 (H.C.), Holland J. See AFFIRMATIVE ~; APPARENT ~; NEGATIVE ~; POSI-TIVE ~; PRESCRIPTIVE ~; REGIS-TERED ~.

EASEMENT IN GROSS. An easement created by private grant or statute, e.g. a power line or pipeline. J.V. DiCastri, *Occupiers' Liability* (Vancouver: Burroughs/Carswell 1980) at 212.

EASEMENT OF APPARENT CONVEN-IENCE. An easement which is necessary to the reasonable enjoyment of the property granted and which has been and is at the time of the grant used by the owners of the entirety for the benefit of the part granted. *Wheeldon v. Burrows* (1879), 12 Ch. D. 31 (Eng. C.A.).

EASEMENT OF NECESSITY. A right of way which arises by implication when access to a property is impossible without access over an adjoining property.

EASTERN CANADA. All that part of Canada lying east of the eighty-ninth meridian of west longitude and such other areas in Ontario as the Governor in Council may designate. *Livestock Feed Assistance Act*, R.S. 1985, c. L-10, s. 2.

EASTERN DIVISION. That part of Canada not included in the Western Division. *Canada Grain Act*, R.S.C. 1985, c. G-10, s. 2.

EASTERN GRAIN. Grain grown in the East-ern Division. *Canada Grain Act*, R.S.C. 1985, c. G-10, s. 2.

EASTERNMOST. *adj*. The half compass circle from but not including true north through east to and including true south.

EASTERN ONTARIO. The counties of Has-tings, Prince Edward, Renfrew, Lennox and Ad-dington, Frontenac, Lanark, Leeds, Grenville, Russell Dundas, Stormont, Prescott and Glen-garry and the City of Ottawa. *Development Cor-porations Act*, R.S.O. 1990, c. D.10, s. 1(1).

EAT INDE SINE DIE. [L. that one may go from there without a day] Attendance had been fully satisfied, and the defendant is free to go.

EATING ESTABLISHMENT. See PUB-LIC ~.

EATING PLACE. See PUBLIC ~.

EAVES. *n*. The roof's edge, built to extend be-yond the walls of a building.

EBITDA. *abbr*. Earnings before interest, taxes, depreciation and amortization.

E.C.B. *abbr*. Expropriations Compensation Board.

ECCHYMOSIS. *n*. Bleeding into skin, mucous or serous membrane. F.A. Jaffe, *A Guide to Pathological Evidence*, 3d ed. (Toronto: Car-swell, 1991) at 217.

ECCLESIASTIC. *adj*. Set apart for or belong-ing to the church.

ECCLESIASTICAL. *adj*. Set apart for or be-longing to the church.

ECCLESIASTICAL COURT. A court with jurisdiction in ecclesiastical matters only.

ECCLESIASTICAL LAW. Law which relates to the government, obligations and rights of a church.

ECE. *abbr*. The United Nations Economic Commission for Europe, Inland Transport Com-mittee. *Motor Vehicle Safety Regulations*, C.R.C., c. 1038, s. 2.

ECOLOGICAL INTEGRITY. With respect to a park, a condition that is determined to be characteristic of its natural region and likely to persist, including abiotic components and the composition and abundance of native species and biological communities, rates of change and supporting processes. *Canada National Parks Act, 2000*, S.C. 2000, c. 32, s. 2.

ECOLOGICAL RESERVE. An area estab-lished 1) to conserve the elements constituting biological diversity in their natural state, as in-tegrally as possible and in a permanent manner, in particular by protecting ecosystems and the elements or processes on which their dynamics are based; 2) to set aside land for scientific study or educational purposes; or 3) to safeguard the habitats of threatened or vulnerable species of flora or fauna. *Natural Heritage Conservation Act*, R.S.Q., c. C-61.01, s. 2. See MAN-AGED ~; WHOLLY-PROTECTED ~.

ECOLOGY. *n*. The study of the interrelation-ship of living things, including humans and plants, with their respective environments.

ECONOMIC COUNCIL OF CANADA. An independent federal body which publishes a yearly review of Canada's economic problems and prospects for the medium term and may conduct economic studies at the government's request or on its own.

ECONOMIC DURESS. "[A]s used in recent cases . . . is not more than a recognition that in our modern life the individual is subject to societal pressures which can be every bit as effective, if improperly used, as those flowing from threats of physical abuse. . . It must be a pressure which the law does not regard as legitimate and it must be applied to such a degree as to amount to 'a coercion of the will', . . . or it must place the party to whom the pressure is directed in a position where he has no 'realistic alternative' but to submit to it, . . ." *Stott v. Merit Investment Corp.* (1988), 19 C.C.E.L. 68 at 92, 25 O.A.C. 174, 63 O.R. (2d) 545, 48 D.L.R. (4th) 288 (C.A.), Finlayson J.A. (Krever J.A. concurring).

ECONOMIC EMERGENCY. A dire and exceptional situation precipitated by unusual circumstances such as the outbreak of war of pending bankruptcy. *R. v. Campbell*, (sub nom. *Reference re Remuneration of Judges of the Provincial Court of Prince Edward Island*) [1997] 3 S.C.R. 3.

ECONOMIC ENTERPRISE. An enterprise in which is carried on any industry, trade, business or other undertaking of any kind whatsoever. *The Communities Economic Development Fund Act*, C.C.S.M., c. C-155, s. 1.

ECONOMIC ESPIONAGE. Every person commits an offence who, at the direction of, for the benefit of or in association with a foreign economic entity, fraudulently and without colour of right and to the detriment of Canada's economic interests, international relations or national defence or national security (a) communicates a trade secret to another person, group or organization; or (b) obtains, retains, alters or destroys a trade secret. *Security of Information Act*, R.S.C. 1985, c. O-5, s. 19.

ECONOMIC FARM. Any farm which, taking into account all of its resources, is capable of producing a revenue which enables the operator thereof to pay the operating costs thereof, including maintenance and depreciation, to fulfill his obligations and to support his family adequately. Quebec statutes.

ECONOMIC FARM UNIT. A farm capable of producing income sufficent to support the operator of the farm and the operator's family, if any, and to repay moneys borrowed to establish the unit.

ECONOMIC HARDSHIP. In the context of the Divorce Act and spousal support, is dependent on the circumstances of the parties, is a question of degree, is not to be equated with poverty or extreme privation, can refer to health and career disadvantages arising from the marriage breakdown. It addresses compensatory and non-compensatory factors. *Bracklow v. Brackow*, [1999] 1 S.C.R. 420.

ECONOMIC LOSS. As a cause of action, claims concerning the recovery of economic loss are identical to any other claim in negligence in that the plaintiff must establish a duty, a breach, damage and causation. Nevertheless, as a result of the common law's historical treatment of economic loss, the threshold question of whether or not to recognize a duty of care receives added scrutiny relative to other claims in negligence. In an effort to identify and separate the types of cases that give rise to potentially compensable economic loss, La Forest J., in Norsk Pacific Steamship Co., [*Canadian National Railway v. Norsk Pacific Steamship Co.*, [1992] S.C.R. 1021], endorsed the following categories (at p. 1049): 1. The Independent Liability of Statutory Public Authorities; 2. Negligent Misrepresentation; 3. Negligent Performance of a Service; 4. Negligent Supply of Shoddy Goods or Structures; 5. Relational Economic Loss. The allegation of negligence in the conduct of negotiations does not fall within any of these classifications. As a general proposition, no duty of care arises in conducting negotiations. While there may well be a set of circumstances in which a duty of care may be found, it has not yet arisen. *Martel Building Ltd. v. R.*, 2000 CarswellNat 2678, 2000 SCC 60, 36 R.P.R. (3d) 175, 193 D.L.R. (4th) 1, 262 N.R. 285, 3 C.C.L.T. (3d) 1, 5 C.L.R. (3d) 161, 186 F.T.R. 231 (note), [2000] 2 S.C.R. 860 Per Iacobucci and Major JJ for the court. See PURE ~.

ECONOMIC SANCTION. The enforcement of international duties or responsibilities by asserting financial and economic pressure.

ECONOMIC STRIKE. " . . . [In contrast to an unfair labour practices strike] . . . in the case of a purely 'economic strike', the strikers do not have an absolute right to return to their jobs, . . . *Eastern Provincial Airways Ltd. v. Canada (Canadian Labour Relations Board)* (1983), (sub nom. *Eastern Provincial Airways Ltd. v.*

C.A.L.P.A.) 3 C.L.R.B.R. (N.S.) 75 at 122, 51 di 209 (Can.), Lapointe (Chair), Parent and Shaffer (Members).

ECONOMY. *n*. The acquisition, at the lowest cost and at the appropriate time, of financial, human and physical resources in appropriate quantity and quality.

E CONVERSO. [L.] Conversely.

ECOSYSTEM. *n*. 1. A dynamic complex of plant, animal and micro-organism communities and their non-living environment interacting as a functional unit. *Canadian Environmental Protection Act, 1999*, S.C. 1999, c. 33, s. 3(1). 2. A complete system composed of human beings, other animals and plants in a defined area, and with the soil and climate comprising their habitat in that area. 3. A complete system composed of people, animals, and plants in a defined area, together with the soil, atmosphere and climate comprising their habitat in that area.

ECUMENICAL. *adj*. Universal, general.

EDEMA. *n*. Presence of excess amounts of fluid in tissue. F.A. Jaffe, *A Guide to Pathological Evidence*, 3d ed. (Toronto: Carswell, 1991) at 217. See CEREBRAL ~; PULMONARY ~.

EDENTULOUS ARCH. A dental arch with no remaining natural teeth or roots.

EDIBLE. *adj*. Fit for food. *Meat Inspection Act* (Ontario), R.R.O. 1980, Reg. 607, s. 1.

EDIBLE OIL PRODUCT. A food substance, other than a dairy product, of whatever origin, source or composition that is manufactured for human consumption wholly or in part from a fat or oil other than that of milk. *Edible Oil Products Act*, R.S.O. 1990, c. E.1, s. 1.

EDIBLE SECTION. As applied to a registered establishment, means the part of the establishment in which any meat product is prepared or kept. *Meat Inspection Regulations*, C.R.C., c. 1032, s. 2.

EDICT. *n*. A command, proclamation.

EDITION. *n*. The number of copies of a work printed at one time or from the same typesetting.

EDUCABLE. *adj*. Capable of being educated, having a level of functioning to permit learning skills beyond the most basic ones of personal hygiene and care.

EDUC. & L.J. *abbr*. Education and Law Journal.

EDUCATION. 1. In the context of a charitable purpose, should now be understood to connote information or training provided in a structured manner and for a genuinely educational purpose, that is, to advance the knowledge or abilities of the recipients and not solely to promote a particular point of view or political orientation. Contemplates some legitimate, targeted attempt at educating others, whether through formal or informal instruction, training, plans of self-study or otherwise. *Vancouver Society of Immigrant & Visible Minority Women v. Minister of National Revenue* (1999), 169 D.L.R. (4th) 34 (S.C.C.). 2. " . . . [W]hen . . . used without qualification, it has reference to a fundamental process of learning which is aimed at preparing either for life in general or for a large purpose such as a particular profession or trade, and is in any event without an immediately utilitarian *focus.*" *MacLean Hunter Ltd. v. Deputy Minister of National Revenue (Customs & Excise)* (1987), 15 C.E.R. 340 at 343, 88 D.T.C. *6096*, [1988] 1 C.T.C. 174, Can S.T.R. 80-001, 87 N.R. 195 (Fed. C.A.), the court per MacGuigan J.A. See ADULT BASIC ~; CONTINUING ~; ENGLISH LANGUAGE ~; FRENCH LANGUAGE ~; GENERAL~; OFFICERS OF ~; POST-SECONDARY ~; SECONDARY ~; SELF-IMPROVEMENT ~; VOCATIONAL ~.

EDUCATIONAL AUTHORITY. A body that is (*a*) an independent corporation, within the meaning of section 2 of the *Direction to the CRTC (Ineligibility to Hold Broadcasting Licences)*; or (*b*) a provincial authority, within the meaning of section 2 of the *Direction to the CRTC (Ineligibility to Hold Broadcasting Licences)*. *Broadcasting Distribution Regulations*, SOR/97-555, s. 1.

EDUCATIONAL ESTABLISHMENT. (a) A university established by special charter, the University of Québec, as well as a constituent university or superior school within the meaning of the University of Quebec Act (chapter U-1); (b) a general and vocational college within the meaning of the General and Vocational Colleges Act (chapter C-29); (c) any other establishment designated by the Gouvernement which provides instruction at the college or university level. *An Act to Enable Municipalities to Tax Certain Educational Establishments*, R.S.Q. 1977, c. M-40, s. 1.

EDUCATIONAL INCREMENT. Salary recognition or wage increment provided to employees with certain educational qualifications.

EDUCATIONAL INSTITUTION. 1. An institution of learning that offers courses at a post-secondary level. 2. A technical or vocational school, a university, college or other school of higher education. 3. (a) A non-profit institution licensed or recognized by or under an Act of Parliament or the legislature of a province to provide pre-school, elementary, secondary or post-secondary education; (b) a non-profit institution that is directed or controlled by a board of education regulated by or under an Act of the legislature of a province and that provides continuing, professional or vocational education or training; (c) a department or agency of any order of government, or any non-profit body, that controls or supervises education or training referred to in paragraph (a) or (b), or (d) any other non-profit institution prescribed by regulation. *Copyright Act*, R.S.C. 1985, c. C-42, s. 2. See DESIGNATED ~; SPECIFIED ~.

EDUCATIONAL PROJECT. A procedure by which a school defines its specific objectives drafts and carries out a plan of action and revises the plan periodically with the participation of the plan periodically parents, and the staff of the school and of the school board. *Education Act*, S.Q 1979, c. 80, s. 1.

EDUCATIONAL RADIO PROGRAMMING SERVICE. A radio programming service that provides the programming described in the definition of "independent corporation" in section 2 of the *Direction to the CRTC (Ineligibility to Hold Broadcasting Licences)*. *Broadcasting Distribution Regulations*, SOR/97-555, s. 1.

EDUCATIONAL TELEVISION PROGRAMMING SERVICE. A television programming service that provides the programming described in the definition of "independent corporation" in section 2 of the *Direction to the CRTC (Ineligibility to Hold Broadcasting Licences)*. *Broadcasting Distribution Regulations*, SOR/97-555, s. 1.

EDUCATION AUTHORITY. A corporation that is incorporated by one or more bands or councils of bands for the purpose of providing for the educational needs of the members of the band or bands. *Education Act*, R.S.O. 1990, c. E.2, s. 1(1). See LOCAL ~.

EDUCATION LAW. The law relating to the administration of schools and universities and the students attending them.

EDUCATION SAVINGS PLAN. A contract made at any time between (a) either (i) one individual (other than a trust), or (ii) an individual (other than a trust) and the spouse or common-law partner of the individual, and (b) a person or organization (in this section referred to as a "promoter") under which the promoter agrees to pay or to cause to be paid educational assistance payments to or for one or more beneficiaries. *Income Tax Act*, R.S.C. 1985, c. (5th Supp.), s. 146.1(1).

EDUCATION LAW. The law relating to the administration of schools and universities and the students attending them. See REGISTERED ~.

EDUCATION SERVICES. See SPECIAL ~.

EDUCATOR. See ADULT ~.

EFFECT. *v*. " . . . '[T]o bring about an event or result' . . ." *Gladstone v. Catena*, [1948] 2 D.L.R. 483 at 486-7, [1948] O.R. 182 (C.A.). Laidlaw J.A.

EFFECT. *n*. The actual consequences of legislation. See ADVERSE ~; CHILLING ~; ~S; PARADOXICAL ~; RETROACTIVE ~; RETROSPECTIVE ~; SIDE ~.

EFFECTIVE. *adj*. Suitable for its purpose; accomplishing its purpose.

EFFECTIVE CAUSE RULE. In reference to real estate agency, refers to the situation where a vendor's agent finds a person who does in fact purchase the property even though at a different price and at a later time than following the first introduction of the purchaser to the property. The agent is entitled to commission in such a case as long as there is continuity between the introduction and the purchase. *Robertson v. Ball* (1996), 31 O.R. (3d) 30 (Gen. Div.).

EFFECTIVE DATE. The date upon which a contract, agreement, plan, or legislation comes into operation.

EFFECTIVE DATE OF LAY-OFF. The date of lay-off of an employee that occurs within a layoff period.

EFFECTIVENESS. *n*. The achievement, to the best degree, of the objectives or other intended effects of a program, an organization or an activity.

EFFECTIVE OPENING. The cross-sectional area of a faucet, fitting or pipe at the point of discharge.

EFFECTIVE RATE. The rate of real property tax or of frontage or area tax that, in the opinion of the Minister, would be applicable to any federal property if that property were taxable property. *Payment in Lieu of Taxes Act*, R.S.C. 1985, c. M-13 s. 2.

EFFECTIVE RATE OF INTEREST. The ratio of the amount of interest earned during the year to the amount of principle invested at the beginning of the year.

EFFECTIVITY. *n*. The principle of effectivity proclaims that an illegal act may eventually acquire legal status if, as a matter of empirical fact, it is recognized on the international plane. Our law has long recognized that through a combination of acquiescence and prescription, an illegal act may at some later point be accorded some form of legal status. In the law of property, for example, it is well-known that a squatter on land may ultimately become the owner if the true owner sleeps on his or her right to repossess the land. In this way, a change in the factual circumstances may subsequently be reflected in a change in legal status. It is, however, quite another matter to suggest that a subsequent condonation of an initially illegal act retroactively creates a legal right to engage in the act in the first place. The broader contention is not supported by the international principle of effectivity or otherwise and must be rejected. *Reference re Secession of Quebec*, 1998 CarswellNat 1299, 161 D.L.R. (4th) 385, 228 N.R. 203, 55 C.R.R. (2d) 1, [1998] 2 S.C.R. 217 Per curiam.

EFFECTS. *n*. Chattels, goods and property. See EFFECT.

EFFICIENCY. *n*. The conversion, in the best ratio, of resources into goods and services. See PARTICULATE COLLECTION ~.

EFFICIENT CAUSE RULE. In reference to real estate agency, refers to the situation where a vendor's agent finds a person who does in fact purchase the property even though at a different price and at a later time than following the first introduction of the purchaser to the property. The agent is entitled to commission in such a case as long as there is continuity between the introduction and the purchase. *Robertson v. Ball* (1996), 31 O.R. (3d) 30 (Gen. Div.).

EFFIGY. *n*. The representation of a person.

EFFLUENT. *n*. 1. A deleterious material flowing in or out of a drain, sewer, outfall, sewage disposal system or works. 2. The liquid discharge from water pollution control works. 3. All wastewaters deposited by a plant and includes process water, cooling water, tank drainage, storm water, wastes from water and wastewater treatment facilities and run-off from lands used for the storage or treatment or wastewater and sludges associated with the operation of a plant. See CONTAMINANT; MILL PROCESS ~; MINE WATER ~.

EFFLUENT GAS STREAM. The combination of gases and solids being emitted from a process or operation.

EFFLUENT IRRIGATION. The application of effluent to land for the purposes of effluent disposal and growing vegetation.

EFFORT. *n*. " . . . '[P]hysical' and 'mental' exertion. . ." *Pasqua Hospital v. Harmatiuk* (1987), 87 C.L.L.C. 17,021 at 16,251, 25 Admin. L.R. 157, 17 C.C.E.L. 121, [1987] 5 W.W.R. 98, 56 Sask. R. 241, 8 C.H.R.R. D/4242, 42 D.L.R. (4th) 134, 31 C.R.R. 174 (C.A.), Bayda C.J.S. See BEST ~S.

E-FILING. *n*. The filing of documents with government offices electronically. Electronic filing.

E.G. *abbr*. [L. exempli gratia] For instance.

EGALITARIAN CIVIL LIBERTIES. Those liberties which require equal treatment of persons under the law. These include equal access to employment, accommodation, education and benefits. The right to use either of the official languages and the rights of denominational or separate schools are included in this category of civil liberties as well.

EGALITY. *n*. Equality.

EGG. *n*. 1. An egg of a domestic hen in the shell. 2. An egg, i. of the domestic chicken of the species Gallis Domesticus or ii. of the domestic turkey of the species Meleagris Gallopavo, but does not include a partly formed egg that has been removed from a slaughtered domestic hen or domestic turkey. 3. Egg of a domestic hen other than hatching eggs. 4. The egg of a migratory bird and includes parts of such eggs.

EGG DRYER. Equipment used for converting liquid egg to dried egg by the extraction of moisture.

EGG-GRADING STATION. Premises for the grading, packing and marking of eggs.

EGGSHELL FRACTURE. The fracture of a flat bone which shows a quantity of intercommunicating fracture lines, whether or not fragments are displaced. F.A. Jaffe, *A Guide to Pathological Evidence*, 3d ed. (Toronto: Carswell, 1991) at 220.

EGG SOLID. Egg yolk or albumen, or a combination thereof, that contains no shell or water.

EGG STATION. Premises for the grading, packing and marking of eggs.

EGISTMENT. See AGISTMENT.

EGREGIOUS. *adj*. Extraordinarily or remarkably bad or undesirable.

EGRESS. See MEANS OF ~.

EI INCUMBIT PROBATIO, QUI DICIT, NON QUI NEGAT: CUM RERUM NATURAM FACTUM NEGANTIS PROBATIO NULLA SIT. [L.] The proof lies upon the one who affirms, not the one who denies; since, by the nature of things, one who denies a fact cannot prove it.

EI QUI AFFIRMAT, NON EI QUI NEGAT, INCUMBIT PROBATIO. [L.] The burden of proof lies on the one who affirms a fact, not on the one who denies it.

EJECIT INFRA TERMINUM. [L.] Ejected before the end of the term.

EJECTMENT. *n*. " . . . [A]n action for the recovery of land; . . ." *Point v. Dibblee Construction Co.*, [1934] O.R. 142 at 153, [1934] 2 D.L.R. 785 (H.C.), Armour J.

EJECTOR. *n*. A mechanism to expel an empty cartridge from a firearm after the round is fired. F.A. Jaffe, *A Guide to Pathological Evidence*, 3d ed. (Toronto: Carswell, 1991) at 217.

EJURATION. *n*. Resigning or renouncing one's place.

EJUSDEM GENERIS. [L. of the same kind] "Where there are general words following particular and specific words the general words must be confined to things of the same kind as those specified. The principle applies only where the special words are of the same nature and can be grouped together in the same genus; where there different genera the meaning of the general words is unaffected by their collocation with the special words and must be given their full and ordinary meaning." *Reg. v. Edmundson* (1859), 28 L.J.M.C. 213 at 215, Lord Campbell C.J.

EJUS EST INTERPRETARI CUJUS EST CONDERE. [L.] The one who establishes the law also interprets it.

EJUS NULLA CULPA EST CUI PARERE NECESSE.SIT. [L.] The one who is bound to obey is not at fault.

ELDER. *n*. An Aboriginal person who is a member of an Aboriginal community; and is recognized by the members of the Aboriginal community as having extensive knowledge of the culture and traditional practices of that community.

ELDER LAW. Law relating to mature individual clients: age discrimination, care-facility regulation, guardianship, substitute decision-makers, wills, estate planning, trust planning, powers of attorney.

ELDERLY PERSON. One who has reached the age of sixty-five years, and, in the absence of positive evidence of age, means a person who apparently has reached that age. *Family Services Act*, S.N.B. 1980, c. F2.2, s. 1.

ELDERLY PERSONS. (a) A single person of sixty-five or more years of age whose annual income, including assistance under the *Old Age Security Act* (Canada), does not exceed an amount equal to five times the annual rental for the accommodation that he occupies in an elderly persons' housing unit or a hostel, or (b) a person of 65 or more years of age whose annual income together with that of his or her spouse or common-law partner, including assistance under the *Old Age Security Act* (Canada), does not exceed an amount equal to five times the annual rental for the accommodation that the person and his or her spouse or common-law partner occupy in an elderly persons' housing unit or a hostel, or (c) a person who is the spouse or common-law partner of a person to whom clause (b) refers. *Elderly and Infirm Persons' Housing Act*, C.C.S.M., c. E20, s. 1.

ELDERLY PERSONS' HOUSING UNIT. Housing accommodation that has separate kitchen and bathroom facilities for either one or two elderly persons who are capable of living independently. *Elderly and Infirm Persons' Housing Act*, C.C.S.M., c. E20, s. 1.

ELDEST. *adj*. " . . . [I]n its ordinary and grammatical sense . . . is surpassing in years,' or is that person or thing which has existed the longest time, . . . But if applied to an individual having a particular character, it has a different meaning. The 'eldest' or 'senior magistrate' or 'officer' does not mean that magistrate or officer who has lived the greatest number of years, nor indeed always him who has filled the office for the longest time, for it may indicate rank only. . ." *Thellusson v. Lord Rendlesham* (1859), (*sub nom. Thellusson v. Thellusson*) 7 H.L. Cas. 429 at 520-21, 11 E.R. 172 (U.K.), Lord Wensleydale.

ELECT. *v.* To make a choice or decision between alternatives; to choose for office.

ELECTA UNA VIA, NON DATUR RECURSUS AD ALTERAM. [L.] Having elected to choose one way, recourse to the other way is not permitted.

ELECTED AUTHORITY. A council under the Municipal Government Act, or a board of trustees under the School Act. *Local Authorities Election Act*, R.S.A. 2000, c. L-21, s. 1.

ELECTION. *n.* 1. Making a choice. 2. Choosing a member or members to serve in the House of Commons, in a provincial legislature or on a municipal council. 3. In the context of choosing judicial review or appeal after having accepted an award, the essence of the doctrine of election is that a person is properly precluded from exercising a right that is fundamentally inconsistent with another right if he has consciously and unequivocally exercised the latter. In other words, one cannot have one's cake and eat it too, or one cannot blow hot and cold. *A.U.P.E. v. Lethbridge Community College*, 2002 ABCA 125, [2002] 8 W.W.R. 299 (C.A.). 3. [When a party] . . . not only determined to follow one of his remedies but has communicated it to the other side in such a way as to lead the opposite party to believe that he has made that choice, he has completed his election. . ." *Scarf v. Jardine* (1882), 7 App. Cas. 345 at 360 (U.K.), Lord Blackburn. See AT AN ~; BY-~; CANDIDATE AT AN ~; DURING AN ~; DURING THE ~; FIRST ~; GENERAL ~; NEW ~; REGULAR ~; STANDING COMMITTEE ON PRIVILEGES AND ~S; THROUGH AN ~; THROUGHOUT AN ~.

ELECTION ADVERTISING. The transmission to the public by any means during an election period of an advertising message that promotes or opposes a registered party or the election of a candidate, including one that takes a position on an issue with which a registered party or candidate is associated. For greater certainty, it does not include (a) the transmission to the public of an editorial, a debate, a speech, an interview, a column, a letter, a commentary or news; (b) the distribution of a book, or the promotion of the sale of a book, for no less than its commercial value, if the book was planned to be made available to the public regardless of whether there was to be an election; (c) the transmission of a document directly by a person or a group to their members, employees or shareholders, as the case may be; or (d) the transmission by an individual, on a non-commercial basis on what is commonly known as the Internet, of his or her personal political views. *Canada Elections Act*, S.C. 2000, c. 9, s. 319.

ELECTION ADVERTISING EXPENSE. An expense incurred in relation to (a) the production of an election advertising message; and (b) the acquisition of the means of transmission to the public of an election advertising message. *Canada Elections Act*, S.C. 2000, c. 9, s. 349.

ELECTION ASSISTANT. A person appointed by the clerk to assist in the conduct of an election.

ELECTION CLERK. A person appointed to assist the returning officer.

ELECTION COURT. A court to which a petition pursuant to The Controverted Elections Act may be made. *The Election Act, 1996*, S.S. 1996 c. E-6.01, s. 180(a).

ELECTION DAY. The day fixed for voting at an election.

ELECTION DOCUMENT. Any document or writing issued under the authority of an Act of Parliament or the legislature of a province with respect to an election held pursuant to the authority of that Act. *Criminal Code*, R.S.C. 1985, c. C-46, s. 377(2).

ELECTION DOCUMENTS. The following documents: (*a*) the writ with the return of the election endorsed on it; (*b*) the nomination papers filed by the candidates; (*c*) the reserve supply of undistributed blank ballot papers; (*d*) documents relating to the revision of the lists of electors; (*e*) the statements of the vote from which the validation of results was made; and (*f*) the other returns from the various polling stations enclosed in sealed envelopes, as required by Part 12, and containing (i) a packet of stubs and unused ballot papers, (ii) packets of ballot papers cast for the various candidates, (iii) a packet of spoiled ballot papers, (iv) a packet of rejected ballot papers, (v) a packet containing the list of electors used at the polling station, the written authorizations of candidates' representatives and the used transfer certificates, if any, and (vi) a packet containing the registration certificates. *Canada Election Act*, S.C. 2000, c. 9, s. 2(1).

ELECTION, ESTOPPEL BY. In general, election is the doctrine that if a person has a choice of one of two rights, but not both, where he chooses one, he cannot afterwards assert the other. Although an election must normally be communicated, detrimental reliance by a second party is not a necessary element. *Blueberry River Indian Band v. Canada (Department of Indian Affairs & Northern Development)*, 2001 CarswellNat 963, 2001 FCA 67, 6 C.P.C. (5th) 1, 201 D.L.R. (4th) 35, 274 N.R. 304 (C.A.), Rothstein, J.A. for the court.

ELECTION EXPENSES. (a) Amounts paid, (b) liabilities incurred, (c) the commercial value of goods and services donated or provided, other than volunteer labour, and (d) amounts that represent the differences between amounts paid and liabilities incurred for goods and services, other than volunteer labour, and the commercial value thereof where they are provided at less than their commercial value, (all of which are in this definition referred to as "the cost") for the purpose of promoting or opposing, directly and during an election, a particular registered party, or the election of a particular candidate, and without limiting the generality of the foregoing, includes (e) the cost of acquiring the right to the use of time on the facilities of any broadcasting undertaking, or of acquiring the right to the publication of an advertisement in any periodical publication, (f) the cost of acquiring the services of any person, including remuneration and expenses paid to the person or on behalf of the person, as an official agent or registered agent or otherwise, except where the services are donated or provided at materially less than their commercial value, (g) the cost of acquiring meeting space, of provision of light refreshment and of acquiring and distributing mailing objects, material or devices of a promotional nature, and (h) the cost of goods or services provided by a government, crown corporation or any other public agency, when those costs are incurred for a purpose set out in this definition.

ELECTION EXPENSES OF A CANDIDATE. Election expenses incurred or authorized, or deemed to have been incurred or authorized, by the official agent of that candidate.

ELECTION EXPENSES OF A REGISTERED POLITICAL PARTY. Election expenses incurred or authorized, or deemed to have been incurred or authorized, by the chief agent of that party.

ELECTION OF DOMICILE. The indication by a notary of the place where he intends to practise his profession. *Notarial Act*, 1977, c. N-2, s. 1.

ELECTION OFFICER. The Chief Electoral Officer, the Assistant Chief Electoral Officer and every returning officer, assistant returning officer, deputy returning officer, poll clerk, registrar of voters, election clerk enumerator, revising officer and revising agent and includes any person having any duty to perform pursuant to this act, to the faithful performance of which duty she or he may be sworn. *Elections acts.*

ELECTION OFFICIAL. Includes a returning officer, deputy returning officer, poll clerk, revising officer, nomination officer, enumerators and any other supervisory officers and assistants.

ELECTION PAPERS. The papers required under this Act to be transmitted by the returning officer to the Chief Electoral Officer after an election, and, without limiting the generality of the foregoing, include (i) writs of elections with the returns f the elections endorsed thereon (ii) nomination papers filed by candidates, (iii) enumerators' record books, (iv) statements of polls after the count by the deputy returning officers, (v) poll books used at polls, (vi) ballot papers, (vii) certified lists of electors used at polls, including any lists of additions thereto and (viii) any written oath required under this Act. *Elections acts.*

ELECTION PERIOD. 1. The period commencing on the day of issue of the writ instituting the holding of an election and ending on polling day, or on the day the writ is withdrawn or deemed to be withdrawn. 2. (*a*) In the case of a federal or provincial election or of a federal, provincial or municipal referendum, the period beginning on the date of the announcement of the election or referendum and ending on the date of the election or referendum; or (*b*) in the case of a municipal election, the period beginning two months before the date of the election and ending on the date of the election. *Broadcasting Distribution Regulations*, SOR/97-555, s. 1.

ELECTION PETITION. 1. A petition presented in pursuance of the Controverted Elections Act. 2. A petition complaining of an undue return or undue election of a member, or of no return, or of a double return, or of any unlawful act by any candidate not returned by which he is alleged to have become disqualified to sit in the assembly, or of the conduct of any returning or deputy returning officer. *The Controverted Elections Act*, C.C.S.M., c. C210, s. 1. 3. A petition complaining of an undue return or undue election of a member, of no return or a double return, of matters contained in a special return made or of any unlawful act by any candidate not returned by which she or he is alleged to have become disqualified to sit in the House of Commons or legislative assembly.

ELECTION SURVEY. An opinion survey of how electors voted or will vote at an election or respecting an issue with which a registered party or candidate is associated.

ELECTIO SEMEL FACTA ET PLACITUM TESTATUM NON PATITUR REGRESSUM. QUOD SEMEL PLACUIT IN ELECTIONIBUS AMPLIUS DISPLICERE NON POTEST. [L.] Once an election is made and a plea witnessed there is no recall. In elections whatever once pleased a person cannot displease after further consideration.

ELECTIVE INSURED HEALTH SERVICES. Insured health services other than services that are provided in an emergency or in any other circumstance in which medical care is required without delay. *Canada Health Act*, R.S.C. 1985, c. C-6, s. 11(3).

ELECTOR. *n*. 1. Person eligible to vote at an election. 2. A person entitled to vote at an election. 3. A person qualified to vote at an election. 4. Any person who is or who claims to be registered as an elector in the list of voters for any electoral district or who is, or claims to be, entitled to vote in any election. See CANADIAN FORCES ~; DEPENDANT ~; LIST OF ~S; MUNICIPAL ~S; PROPRIETARY ~; PUBLIC SCHOOL ~; PUBLIC SERVICE ~; QUALIFIED ~; RESIDENT ~; SEPARATE SCHOOL ~; VETERAN ~.

ELECTORAL DISTRICT. 1. An area entitled to elect a member to serve in a legislature. 2. The area from which a school board member is to be elected. See DISTRICT OR ~.

ELECTORAL DISTRICT ASSOCIATION. Of a political party means an association of members of the political party in an electoral district. *Canada Elections Act*, S.C. 2000, c. 9, s. 363.

ELECTORAL DIVISION. Any territorial division or district entitled to return a member. See POLLING DIVISION; URBAN ~.

ELECTORAL OFFICER. See CHIEF ~.

ELECTORAL PRECINCT. A territorial division effected in view of the election of a member to the Assemblée nationale du Québec.

ELECTRICAL CODE. See CANADIAN ~.

ELECTRICAL CONTRACTOR. Includes a person who installs electrical equipment for another person, and includes a utility corporation that installs electrical equipment for another person.

ELECTRICAL EQUIPMENT. Any apparatus, appliance, device, instrument, fitting, fixture, machinery, material or thing used, or capable of being used, in or for: (i) the generation, transformation, transmission, distribution, supply or utilization of electric power or energy; or (ii) the protection of buildings or premises from damage by lightning; and includes any assemblage or combination of materials or things used, or capable of being used or adapted, to serve or perform any purpose or function when connected to an electrical installation, notwithstanding that any of the materials or things may be mechanical, metallic or nonelectric in origin.

ELECTRICAL FACILITY. Any equipment, device, apparatus, wiring, conductor, assembly or part thereof that is employed for the generation, transformation, transmission, distribution, storage, control, measurement or utilization of electricial energy and that has an ampacity and voltage that is dangerous to employees.

ELECTRICAL INSTALLATION. 1. The wires, machinery, apparatus, appliances, devices, material and equipment used in, on or about a building, structure or premises by a supply authority or a consumer for the generation, receipt, distribution or use of electrical power or energy. 2. The wires, machinery, apparatus, appliances, devices, material and equipment used in, on or about a building, structure or premises by a consumer for the use of electrical power or energy, but does not include the wires, machinery, apparatus, appliances, devices, material and equipment used in the carrying out of any of the following work or services: (a) motor rewinding, (b) repairing radios and other electronic equipment, (c) installing or maintaining electrical conductors or equipment in aircrafts, ships, rolling stock or railways or automotive equipment, (d) generating or distributing electrical energy by a corporation or person as a principal business, (e) constructing or maintaining telephone, telegraph or other systems of communication, (f) installing a boiler that is within the scope of the Boiler and Pressure Vessel Act, or (g) installing an elevating device that is within the scope of the Elevators and Lifts Act. *Electrical Installation and Inspection Act*, S.N.B., c. E-4.1, s. 1. See WORK OF ~.

ELECTRICALLY SUPERVISED CONTROL VALVE. A valve permanently fitted with a mechanical device to actuate electrical contacts upon initiation of valve actuation. *Building Code Act*, R.R.O. 1980, Reg. 87, s. 1.

ELECTRICAL MOBILE EQUIPMENT. Equipment which during its operating cycle is required to move along the ground while energized and which receives its current through a trailing cable.

ELECTRICAL ROOM. A room that is intended for the exclusive installation of electrical equipment.

ELECTRICAL SAFETY CODE. A code established by the Canadian Standards Association.

ELECTRICAL SYSTEM. An assembly or any part of an assembly of electrical equipment or components used or intended to be used for the generation, transmission, distribution, control or utilization of electrical energy, but does not include any thing excluded by the regulations from the definition of electrical system. *Safety Codes Act*, R.S.A. 2000, c. S-1, s. 1(1).

ELECTRICAL TREATMENT. The administration of electricity to the foot or leg by means of electrodes, rays and the like, other than Xray unless used for diagnostic purposes.

ELECTRICAL UTILITY. A person or organization that, as its prime purpose performs one or more of the functions of generating, transmitting or distributing electric energy, otherwise than for consumption by such person or organization.

ELECTRICAL WORK. 1. The actual installation, repair and maintenance of cables, conduits, wiring, switchgear, transmission lines, transformers, motors and generators used for the production, transmission and utilization of electrical energy for light and power purposes. 2. Includes the installation of lightning rods.

ELECTRICAL WORKER. See QUALIFIED ~.

ELECTRIC BOILER. A boiler heated by electricity.

ELECTRIC DISTRIBUTION SYSTEM. Any system, works, plant, equipment or service for the delivery, distribution or furnishing of electric energy directly to the consumer, but does not include a power plant or transmission line.

ELECTRIC ELEVATOR. An elevator in which the motion of the car or platform is obtained through an electric motor applied directly to the elevator machinery.

ELECTRIC ENERGY. 1. Includes electric power that is produced, transmitted, distributed or furnished by a public utility. 2. In addition to its ordinary meaning includes (i) energy associated with an electromotive force, and (ii) power and reactive power and other electromagnetic effects associated with electric energy.

ELECTRICIAN. *n.* A person who, (i) lays out, assembles, installs, repairs, maintains, connects or tests electrical fixtures, apparatus, control equipment and wiring for systems of alarm, communication, light, heat or power in buildings or other structures, (ii) plans proposed installations from blueprints, sketches or specifications and installs panel boards, switch boxes, pull boxes and other related electrical devices, (iii) measures, cuts, threads, bends, assembles and installs conduits and other types of electrical conductor enclosures that connect panels, boxes, outlets and other related electrical devices, (iv) installs brackets, hangers or equipment for supporting electrical equipment, (v) installs in or draws electrical conductors through conductor enclosures, (vi) prepares conductors for splicing or electrical connections, secures conductor connections bar soldering or other mechanical means and reinsulates and protects conductor connections, or (vii) tests electrical equipment for proper function, but does not include a person who is permanently employed on an industrial plant at a limited purpose occupation in the electrical trade. See CONTRACTING ~; JOURNEYMAN ~; MASTER ~.

ELECTRICITY. *n.* Electric power, energy or current. See SURPLUS ~.

ELECTRICITY DISTRIBUTOR. Designates any person, partnership or corporation operating an undertaking for the production, sale or distribution of electric power.

ELECTRICITY SYSTEM. A system of lighting, heating or energy or power production by means of electricity.

ELECTRICITY UNDERTAKING. Any undertaking for the production, sale or distribution of electricity.

ELECTRIC POWER. The rate of transferring electric energy, expressed in units of kilowatts or megawatts.

ELECTRIC SYSTEM. See FARM ~; FUEL AND ~S MECHANIC.

ELECTRIC TRAMWAY. A railroad, railway or tramway for the conveyance of passengers or goods, or either of them, operated by electric motive power.

ELECTRIC UTILITY. A person who owns or operates equipment or facilities in the province for the production, generation, transmission, sale, delivery or furnishing of electrical power for compensation.

ELECTROCUTION. *n*. Death caused when an electric current passes through the body.

ELECTRODE. *n*. An electrically conductive element that interfaces with body tissue. See GROUND ~.

ELECTRO-MAGNETIC, ACOUSTIC, MECHANICAL OR OTHER DEVICE. 1. Any device or apparatus that is used or is capable of being used to intercept a private communication, but does not include a hearing aid used to correct subnormal hearing of the user to not better than normal hearing. 2. Any device or apparatus that is used or capable of being used to intercept any function of a computer system, but does not include a hearing aid used to correct subnormal hearing of the user to not better than normal hearing. *Criminal Code*, R.S.C. 1985, c. C-46, s. 342.1(2) as added by *Criminal Law Amendment Act*, R.S.C. 1985 (1st Supp.), c. 27, s. 45.

ELECTRONIC. *adj*. Created, recorded, transmitted or stored in digital or other intangible form by electronic, magnetic or optical means or by any other similar means.

ELECTRONIC AGENT. A computer program, or other electronic means, used to initiate an activity or to respond to electronic information, records or activities in whole or in part without review by an individual at the time of the response or activity;

ELECTRONIC DISCOVERY. The discovery of evidence in electronic format.

ELECTRONIC DOCUMENT. 1. Data that is recorded or stored on any medium in or by a computer system or other similar device and that can be read or perceived by a person or a computer system or other similar device. It includes a display, printout or other output of that data. *Federal statutes*. 2. Any form of representation of information or of concepts fixed in any medium in or by electronic, optical or other similar means and that can be read or perceived by a person or by any means.

ELECTRONIC DOCUMENTS SYSTEM. Includes a computer system or other similar device by or in which data is recorded or stored and any procedures related to the recording or storage of electronic documents. *Canada Evidence Act*, R.S.C. 1985, c. C-5, s. 31.8.

ELECTRONIC FILING. The filing of registry or court or other government documents electronically.

ELECTRONIC FORMAT. Includes an electronic format produced by making an electronic copy, image or reproduction of a written document. *Land Registration Reform Act*, R.S.O. 1990, c. L.4, s. 17.

ELECTRONIC HEARING. A hearing held by conference telephone or some other form of electronic technology allowing persons to hear one another.

ELECTRONIC SIGNATURE. 1. Information in electronic form that a person has created or adopted in order to sign a record and that is in, attached to or associated with the record. 2. A signature that consists of one or more letters, characters, numbers or other symbols in digital form incorporated in, attached to or associated with an electronic document.

ELECTROPHORESIS. *n*. A technique to separate various proteins using an electric current. F.A. Jaffe, *A Guide to Pathological Evidence*, 2d ed. (Toronto: Carswell, 1983) at 174 and 175.

ELEEMOSYNA. *n*. Alms.

ELEEMOSYNARY CORPORATION. A body corporate established to perpetually distribute free alms or its founder's gift.

ELEGIT. *n*. [L. one has chosen]. A writ of execution by which a judgment creditor is awarded the debtor's land to hold until the debt is satisfied. See WRIT OF ~.

ELEMENTARY PUPIL. A person enrolled in one of the grades from Grade 1 to Grade 7 in a public school and a person enrolled in a kindergarten class established in a public school under this Act. *School Act*, R.S.B.C. 1979, c. 375, s. 1.

ELEMENTARY SCHOOL. 1. A public school' in which accommodation and tuition are provided exclusively or mainly for elementary pupils. 2. A school in which instruction is given in some or all of the primary division, junior division and intermediate division but not in the senior division. *Education Act*, R.S.O. 1990, c. E.2, s. 1(1).

ELEMENT OF DESIGN. In respect of a vehicle or engine, (*a*) any control system, including computer software, electronic control systems and computer logic; (*b*) any control system calibrations; (*c*) the results of systems interaction; or (*d*) any hardware items. *On-Road Vehicle and Engine Emission Regulations*, SOR/2003-2, s. 1(1).

ELEMENTS. See COMMON ~.

ELEVATING DEVICE. A non-portable device for hoisting and lowering or moving persons or freight, and includes an elevator, dumbwaiter, escalator, moving walk, manlift, passenger ropeway, incline lift, construction hoist, stage lift, platform lift and stairway lift.

ELEVATION. See GEODETIC ~.

ELEVATOR. *n.* 1. Any mechanism equipped with a car or platform that moves in guides and that is used to transport persons or things from one level to another level and includes an escalator, a dumb-waiter, a hoist, a ski lift, a ski tow, and any other hoisting apparatus or appliance together with the mechanisms, equipment, controls, gates, loading and unloading thresholds signals and appurtenances of or to any of those things. 2. A rain elevator, warehouse or mill that has been declared by Parliament to be a work for the general advantage of Canada. *Canadian Wheat Board Act*, R.S.C. 1985, c. C-24, s. 2. 3. Any premises constructed for the purpose of handling and storing grain received directly from producers, otherwise than as a art of the farming operation of a particular producer, and into which grain may be received, at which grain may be weighed, cleaned, dried, elevated and stored and out of which grain may be discharged. 4. (*a*) any premises in the Western Division (i) into which grain may be received or out of which grain may be discharged directly from or to railway cars or ships, (ii) constructed for the purpose of handling and storing grain received directly from producers, otherwise than as a part of the farming operation of a particular producer, and

into which grain may be received, at which grain may be weighed, elevated and stored and out of which grain may be discharged, or (iii) constructed for the purpose of handling and storing grain as part of the operation of a flour mill, feed mill, seed cleaning plant, malt house, distillery, grain oil extraction plant or other grain processing plant, and into which grain may be received, at which grain may be weighed, elevated and stored and out of which grain may be discharged for processing or otherwise, (*b*) any premises in the Eastern Division, situated along Lake Superior, Lake Huron, Lake St. Clair, Lake Erie, Lake Ontario or the canals or other navigable waters connecting those Lakes or the St. Lawrence River or any tidal waters, and into which grain may be received directly from railway cars or ships and out of which grain may be discharged directly to ships, (*c*) the portion of any premises in the Eastern Division designated by regulation pursuant to subsection 116(3) that is used for the purpose of storing grain, (*d*) any premises in the Eastern Division constructed for the purpose of handling and storing grain received directly from producers, otherwise than as a part of the farming operation of a particular producer, and into which grain may be received, at which grain may be weighed, elevated and stored and out of which grain may be discharged, and (*e*) any premises in the Eastern Division constructed for the purpose of handling and storing grain as a part of the operation of a flour mill, feed mill, seed cleaning plant, malt house, distillery, grain oil extraction plant or other grain processing plant, and into which grain may be received, at which grain may be weighed, elevated and stored and out of which grain may be discharged for processing or otherwise, including any such premises owned or operated by Her Majesty in right of Canada or a province or any agent thereof. *Canada Grain Act*, R.S.C. 1985, c. G-10, s. 2. See CSA ~ CODE; ELECTRIC ~; GRAIN ~; MILL ~; PRIMARY ~; PROCESS ~; TERMINAL ~; TRANSFER ~.

ELEVATOR MACHINERY. The machinery and its equipment used in raising and lowering the elevator car or platform.

ELEVATOR RECEIPT. A document in prescribed form issued in respect of grain delivered to an elevator acknowledging receipt of the grain and, subject to any conditions contained therein or in this Act, entitling the holder of the document (a) to the delivery of grain of the same kind, grade and quantity as the grain referred to in the document, or (b) in the case of a document issued for specially binned grain, to delivery of the identical grain. *Canada Grain Act*, R.S.C. 1985, c. G-10, s. 2.

ELICIT. *v*. In the context of section 7 of the Charter, two sets of factors should be considered to determine whether the accused's statement was elicited. The first set of factors concerns the nature of the exchange between the accused and the state agent. Did the state agent actively seek out information such that the exchange could be characterized as akin to an interrogation, or did he or she conduct his or her part of the conversation as someone in the role the accused believed the informer to be playing would ordinarily have done? The focus should not be on the form of the conversation, but rather on whether the relevant parts of the conversation were the functional equivalent of an interrogation. The second set of factors concerns the nature of the relationship between the state agent and the accused. Did the state agent exploit any special characteristics of the relationship to extract the statement? Was there a relationship of trust between the state agent and the accused? Was the accused obligated or vulnerable to the state agent? Did the state agent manipulate the accused to bring about a mental state in which the accused was more likely to talk? In considering whether the statement in question was elicited, evidence of the instructions given to the state agent for the conduct of the conversation may be important. *R. v. Broyles*, [1991] 3 S.C.R. 595.

ELICITATION. *n*. Elicitation within the meaning of section 7 of the Charter is difficult to define. Two sets of factors are considered. See definition of "ELICIT", above.

ELIGIBLE. *adj*. Fit or proper to be chosen; deserving.

ELIGIBLE FINANCIAL CONTRACT. [As used in s. 11.1(1) of the *Companies' Creditors Arrangement Act*, R.S.C. 1985, c. C-36] includes spot contracts at (h), spot foreign exchange contracts at (c), and repurchase or reverse repurchase contracts at (g). These contracts can only be settled by physical delivery, never by financial payment. If eligible financial contracts require cash settlement, these terms are robbed of any meaning. Therefore an across-the-board interpretation of eligible financial contracts that excludes physically-settled transactions cannot stand. *Blue Range Resource Corp., Re*, 2000 ABCA 239, 20 C.B.R. (4th) 187, 266 A.R. 98 (C.A.).

ELIGIBILITY. *n*. Qualification.

ELISOR. *n*. Elector.

E.L.J. *abbr*. Education & Law Journal.

ELM TREE. A tree of the ulmus species. *Dutch Elm Disease Act*, R.S.M. 1987, c. D107, s. 1.

ELOIGNE. *v*. To distance; to go far away.

ELOIGNMENT. *n*. Removal; sending far away.

ELOINE. *v*. To distance; to go far away.

ELONGATA. *n*. A return made by a sheriff who found that goods had been eloigned.

ELONGATUS. *n*. A return to a writ stating that the person was out of the sheriff's jurisdiction.

E.L.R. *abbr*. Eastern Law Reporter, 1906-1914.

ELT. An emergency locator transmitter. *Canadian Aviation Regulations*, SOR/96-433, s. 101.01.

ELUDE. *v*. "[In s. 27(2)(f) of the Immigration Act, R.S.C. 1985, c. I-2] . . . has the connotation either of artifice or surreptitiousness, or of the intention to repudiate the obligation or escape the effect of the law in a general way . . ." *Rios v. Canada (Minister of Employment & Immigration)* (1990), 11 Imm. L.R. (2d) 122 at 126, 115 N.R. 394, [1990] 3 F.C. 632 (C.A.), MacGuigan J.A. (Pratte J.A. concurring).

E-MAIL. *v*. Electronic mail. To transmit a message from one person's computer, through his internet service provider, over the internet, to the intended recipient's internet service provider and then to the recipient's own computer.

E-MAIL. *n*. Electronic mail. A message sent from one person's computer to another person's computer over the internet. May also refer to multiple e-mails or to the body of messages one receives.

EMANATING. *adj*. Connotes active participation in the creation of the evidence. Requires that an accused was conscripted against himself and played a role in the creation of the evidence. *R. v. Borden* (1993), 84 C.C.C. (3d) 380 (N.S. C.A.).

EMANATION. *n*. That which issues or proceeds from some source. *International Railway v. Niagara Parks Commission*, [1941] 3 D.L.R. 385 at 393, [1941] A.C. 328, [1941] 2 All E.R. 456, 53 C.R.T.C. 1 (Ont. P.C.), the board per Luxmoore L.J. Use in the expression "emanation of the Crown" was disapproved.

EMBALM. *v.* To preserve and disinfect all or part of a dead human body by any means other than by refrigeration.

EMBALMER. *n.* Any person who preserves a dead human body, entire or in part.

EMBALMING. *n.* 1. The preservation of the dead human body, entire or in part, by the use of chemical substances, fluids or gases, either by outward application of such chemical substances, fluids or gases on the body or by the vascular introduction of the same into the body by vascular or hypodermic injection, or by direct application into the organs and cavities. 2. The preservation and disinfection of all or part of a dead human body by means other than by refrigeration.

EMBARRASSING. *adj.* 1. " . . . [P]leadings framed in such a confused or ambiguous manner as to cause real and undue embarrassment or prejudice." *Rogers v. Clark* (1900), 13 Man. R. 189 at 196 (K.B.), Killam C.J. 2. " . . . [B]ringing forward a defence which the defendant is not entitled to make use of: . . ." *Stratford Gas Co. v. Gordon* (1892), 14 P.R. 407 at 414 (Ont. H.C.), Armour C.J. 3. " . . . [T]he allegations are so irrelevant that to allow them to stand would involve useless expenses and would also prejudice the trial of the action by involving the parties in a dispute that is wholly apart from the issues." *London (Mayor) v. Ho Homer* (1914), 3 L.T.R. 512 at 514 (U.K.), Pickford L.J., cited in *Meyers v. Freeholders Oil Co.* (1956), 19 W.W.R. 546 at 549 (Sask. C.A.).

EMBARGO. *n.* Forbidding passage; an arrest, detention or stopping of a ship.

EMBASSAGE. *n.* 1. An ambassador's establishment. 2. The commission given by a nation to an ambassador, to deal with another nation.

EMBASSY. *n.* 1. An ambassador's establishment. 2. The commission given by a nation to an ambassador, to deal with another nation.

EMBEDDED. *adj.* Firmly attached within a surrounding structure.

EMBEZZLEMENT. *n.* Conversion to personal use of any chattel, money or valuable security received or taken into possession by an employee for, in the name or on account of the employer.

EMBLEM. *n.* "The word emblem [as found in s. 9(1)(n) of the Trade Marks Act, R.S.C. 1970,

c. T-10] does not have its origin in heraldic science but in its wider sense it is used as a symbol. It may be a figured object used symbolically . . ." *Insurance Corp of British Columbia v. Canada (Registrar of Trade Marks)* (1978), 44 C.P.R. (2d) 1 at 7, [1980] 1 F.C. 669 (T.D.), Cattanach J. See FLORAL ~ OF ONTARIO; OFFICIAL ~.

EMBLEMENTS. *n.* " . . . [T]he growing crops of those vegetable productions of the soil which are annually produced by the labour of the cultivator. They are a species of fructus industriales, but do not exhaust the genus." *Cochlin v. The Massey-Harris Co.* (1915), 8 Alta. L.R. 392 at 396, 8 W.W.R. 286, 23 D.L.R. 397 (C.A.), Beck J.A. (dissenting).

EMBOLI. *n.* The plural of embolus.

EMBOLISM. *n.* Clogging of a blood vessel by an embolus. F.A. Jaffe, *A Guide to Pathological Evidence*, 3d ed. (Toronto: Carswell, 1991) at 218. See AIR ~; AMNIOTIC FLUID ~; BONE MARROW ~; BULLET ~; FAT ~; PULMONARY~; TALCUM ~.

EMBOLUS. *n.* A mass of undissolved matter which plugs a vessel that is too narrow to permit it to pass. F.A. Jaffe, *A Guide to Pathological Evidence*, 3d ed. (Toronto: Carswell, 1991) at 218.

EMBRACEOR. *n.* A person who tries to influence a jury.

EMBRACERY. *n.* A common law offence of attempting to instruct or influence any jury member or giving a reward to a jury member for something done by that member.

EMBRYO. *n.* A human organism during the first 56 days of its development following fertilization or creation, excluding any time during which its development has been suspended, and includes any cell derived from such an organism that is used for the purpose of creating a human being. See ANIMAL ~.

EMBRYOLOGY. *n.* The study of human or animal development before birth.

EMBRYO TRANSFER BUSINESS. The business of collecting, acquiring, processing, storing, distributing or implanting embryos, as the case may be.

EMENDARE. *v.* [L.] To give compensation for some crime or trespass which has been committed.

EMENDATIO. *n*. [L.] The power to amend and correct abuses, following specified measures and rules.

EMERGENCY. *n*. 1. A present or imminent event that is or could affect the health, safety or welfare of people or could cause damage to property. 2. A sudden or unexpected, unusual or unforeseen occurrence. 3. War, invasion, riot or insurrection, real or apprehended. See ECONOMIC ~; ENVIRONMENTAL ~; INTERNATIONAL ~; PROVINCIAL ~; PUBLIC ORDER ~; PUBLIC WELFARE ~; WAR ~.

EMERGENCY ALERT MESSAGE. A warning to the public announcing an imminent or unfolding danger to life or property. *Broadcasting Distribution Regulations*, SOR/97-555, s. 1.

EMERGENCY AREA. The area in which an emergency exists.

EMERGENCY BRAKE. A mechanism designed to stop a vehicle after a failure of the service brake system. *Motor Vehicle Safety Regulations*, C.R.C., c. 1038, s. 2.

EMERGENCY HEALTH SERVICE. The provision of first aid or medical services in emergency situations.

EMERGENCY LIGHTING SYSTEM. A lighting system that will, in the event of the failure of the regular lighting system on any premises, provide dependable illumination to enable the carrying out of all emergency measures including the evacuation of all employees from those premises.

EMERGENCY LIGHTS. All lights required by law for the purpose of facilitating safe exit in case of fire or other emergency.

EMERGENCY-LOCKING RETRACTOR. A retractor incorporating adjustment hardware that has a locking mechanism that is activated by vehicle acceleration, webbing movement in relation to the vehicle, or other automatic action during an emergency and is capable when locked of withstanding restraint forces. *Motor Vehicle Safety Regulations*, C.R.C., c. 1038, s. 209.

EMERGENCY MEASURES. 1. Courses of action to be taken in the event of a disaster to save lives, to come to the assistance of persons in distress, to safeguard or to abate the effects of the disaster. 2. The planning, organization, establishment and operation of defensive, precautionary and safety measures, controls, facilities and services of all kinds other than those for which the military forces or other agencies of the Government of Canada are primarily responsible, necessary or desirable in the public interest for meeting, reducing, preventing and overcoming the effects of civil disaster or a war emergency and includes (i) the preparation and carrying out of all plans and measures necessary to ensure the survival and continuity of civil government in the province in times of civil disaster or war emergency, (ii) the preservation of law and order, (iii) the control of traffic, including the movement of persons and property and the maintenance, clearance and repair of roads, (iv) the establishment of areas in the province, and the provision of appropriate services in those areas, for the reception, accommodation and feeding of persons evacuated from other areas which have been or are likely to be subject to civil disaster, hostile action or enemy attack, (v) the organization of emergency medical services and public health and welfare measures, (vi) the organization of firefighting, rescue and salvage services and radioactive fallout detection services, (vii) the maintenance and repair of public utilities, (viii) assistance to municipalities in the development of emergency measures within their jurisdictions, (ix) liaison with the Government of Canada, other provinces of Canada and municipalities in the province in all matters relating to emergency planning, and (x) the institution of training and public information programs to ensure the existence of adequately trained and equipped forces to meet the emergency requirements of the province and to keep the civilian population fully informed of the measures which have been adopted and the action which they should take for their safety, welfare and well-being in times of civil disaster or war emergency. *Emergency Measures Act*, R.S. Nfld. 1990, c. E-8, s. 2.

EMERGENCY MEASURES PLAN. Any plan, program or procedure prepared by the Province or a municipality, as the case may be, that is intended to mitigate the effects of an emergency or disaster and to provide for the safety, health or welfare of the civil population and the protection of property in the event of such an occurrence. *Emergency Measures Act*, S.N.S. 1990, c. 8, s. 2.

EMERGENCY SECURITY CONTROL OF AIR TRAFFIC PLAN. The measures to be implemented by Her Majesty in right of Canada in accordance with the North American Aerospace Defence Command (NORAD) Agreement in the case of an air defence emergency. *Canadian Aviation Regulations*, SOR/96-433, s. 101.01(1).

EMERGENCY SERVICE AGENCIES. The public service and emergency service agencies operating within the Province, including all municipal police forces required to be maintained pursuant to the Police Act, including the Royal Canadian Mounted Police, all fire departments organized to serve any area of the Province, all ambulance services operating from time to time within the Province and such other emergency service agencies as may be approved by the Minister. *Emergency "911" Act*, S.N.S. 1992, c. 4, s. 3.

EMERGENCY SERVICE ZONE. A geographical area served by a common group of emergency service agencies. *Emergency "911" Act*, S.N.S. 1992, c. 4, s. 3.

EMERGENCY VEHICLE. 1. A vehicle used (i) for police duty, or (ii) by a fire department, or (iii) as an ambulance, or (iv) for purposes related to maintenance of a public utility and designated as an emergency vehicle by a traffic authority, or (v) under the authority of a municipality, as a fire-pumper, or (vi) by a volunteer fire-fighter responding to a fire or other emergency. 2. A cardiac arrest emergency vehicle operated by or under the authority of a hospital. See AUTHORIZED ~.

EMERGING CORPORATION. An eligible corporation the shares of which are (i) held by 25 or more shareholders at arms length, (ii) publicly traded, and (iii) not listed on a stock exchange. *Stock Savings Tax Credit Act*, R.S. Nfld. 1990, c. S-28, s. 2(1).

EMERITUS. *adj.* Retired but honoured. Retaining the same or similar status as prior to retirement.

EMIGRATION. *n.* The act of moving from one country to another with no intention of returning.

EMINENCE. *n.* The honorary title of a cardinal.

EMINENT DOMAIN. A government's right to take private property for public purposes, a doctrine which is American in origin. See EXPROPRIATION.

EMISSARY. *n.* One person sent on a mission as agent of another person.

EMISSION. *n.* That which is given off as a result of combustion or another process which creates fumes. See CRANKCASE ~S; EVAP-ORATIVE ~S; EXHAUST ~S; FUGITIVE ~; POINT OF ~; VISIBLE ~.

EMISSION CONTROL SYSTEM. A unique group of emission control devices, auxiliary emission control devices, engine modifications and strategies, and other elements of design used to control exhaust emissions from a vehicle. *On-Road Vehicle and Engine Emission Regulations*, SOR/2003-2, s. 1(1).

EMOLUMENTS. *n.* 1. " . . . '[T]he profit arising from office or employment,' and not merely the gross amount of salary, fees or perquisites, but the balance remaining after deduction of the necessary expenses paid out in earning the salary, fees or perquisites." *Lawless v. Sullivan* (1879), 3 S.C.R. 117 at 146, Henry J. 2. Includes fees, percentages and other payments made or consideration given, directly or indirectly, to a director as such, and the money value of any allowances or perquisites belonging to his office.

EMOTIONAL ABUSE. A pattern or behaviour the purpose of which is to deliberately undermine the mental or emotional well-being of a cohabitant. *C. (A.L.G.) v. Prince Edward Island* (1998), 157 D.L.R. (4th) 523 (P.E.I. T.D.).

EMPANEL. *v.* "[S]electing a new jury from the . . . jurors already summoned,. . ." *R. v. Gaffin* (1904), 8 C.C.C. 194 at 196 (N.S. C.A.), the court per Graham E.J. See IMPANEL; JURY.

EMPEROR. *n.* A sovereign, superior to a queen or king, who rules a large domain or territory.

EMPHYTEUSIS. *n.* 1. "[As defined in Art. 567-571 of the Quebec Civil Code] . . . 'carries with it' ownership full and complete of land and buildings in contradistinction to the common law . . ." *Reitman v. Minister of National Revenue*, [1967] C.T.C. 368 at 375, [1968] 1 Ex. C.R. 120, 67 D.T.C. 5253, Dumoulin J. 2. The right to enjoy all the fruits, and dispose at pleasure of another's property on condition a yearly rent is paid.

EMPIRE. *n.* An emperor's jurisdiction or dominion.

EMPIRIC. *n.* An experienced medical or surgical practitioner without legal or scientific qualification; a quack.

EMPIRICAL. *adj.* That which is based on experience, experiment or observation.

EMPLANE. *v.* To board an aircraft for a flight. *Air Transportation Tax Regulations*, C.R.C., c. 583, s. 2.

EMPLEAD. *v*. To accuse; to indict; to bring a charge against.

EMPLOY. *v*. " . . . [C]an be used in the sense of the common law master/servant relationship in which control is a principle factor in determining the existence of the relationship . . . common, and grammatically correct, . . . to use the word[s] in the sense of 'utilize'." *Pannu, Re* (1986), (*sub nom. Pannu v. Prestige Cab Ltd.*) 87 C.L.L.C. 17,003 at 16,010, 47 Alta. L.R. (2d) 56, [1986] 6 W.W.R. 617, 73 A.R. 166, 31 D.L.R. (4th) 338, 8 C.H.R.R. D/3911 (C.A.), the court per Laycraft J.A.

EMPLOY. *n*. " . . . '[E]mployment' . . . 'service; ' . . ." *Hirshman v. Beal* (1916), 38 O.L.R. 40 at 47, 28 C.C.C. 319, 32 D.L.R. 680 (C.A.), Meredith C.J.C.P.

EMPLOYED. *adj*. 1. Performing the duties of an office or employment. 2. " . . . '[O]ccupied or engaged'." *Might v. Minister of National Revenue*, [1948] Ex. C.R. 382 at 389, [1948] C.T.C. 144, [1949] 1 D.L.R. 250, O'Connor J. See CONTINUOUSLY ~; FULLY ~; REGULARLY ~.

EMPLOYED BY OR UNDER THE CROWN. Includes employed by or under any board, commission or other body established, organized or functioning as an administrative unit of the Province.

EMPLOYED IN A CONTINUOUS OPERATION. Employment in (a) any industrial establishment in which, in each seven day period, operations once begun normally continue without cessation until the completion of the regularly scheduled operations for that period; (b) any operations or services concerned with the running of trains, planes, ships, trucks and other vehicles, whether in scheduled or non-scheduled operations; (c) any telephone, radio, television, telegraph or other communication or broadcasting operations or services; or (d) any operation or service normally carried on without regard to Sundays or public holidays. *Canada Labour Code*, R.S.C. 1985, c. L-2, s. 191.

EMPLOYEE. *n*. 1. Any person employed by an employer and includes a dependent contractor and a private constable, but does not include a person who performs management functions or is employed in a confidential capacity in matters relating industrial relations. 2. Includes an officer. 3. Any person who is in receipt of or entitled to any compensation for labour or services performed for another. 4. Any person who performs duties and functions that entitle that person to compensation on a regular basis. 5. A person who is in receipt of or entitled to wages. 6. Includes an officer or director of a corporation or of an unincorporated organization and an agent acting for a principal on a substantially full-time basis. 7. Includes a dependent contractor. 8. A natural person who is employed by an employer. See ASSOCIATION OF ~S; CASUAL ~; CONTRACT ~; CONTRACTUAL ~; CORRECTIONS ~; CROWN ~; CUSTODIAL ~; FEMALE ~; FULL-TIME ~; HEAVY CONSTRUCTION ~S; LINE ~; MUNICIPAL ~; NON-OPERATING ~; PART-TIME ~; PERMANENT ~; PLANT PROTECTION ~; PROBATIONARY ~; PROFESSIONAL ~; PUBLIC ~; PUBLIC SECTOR ~; QUALIFIED ~; REDUNDANT ~; REGULAR ~; RELIEF ~; RETIRED ~; SEASONAL ~; SECURITY ~; SESSIONAL ~; STUDENT ~; TEMPORARY ~; TERM ~; UNIONIZED ~; WAGE ~.

EMPLOYEE BARGAINING AGENCY. An organization of affiliated bargaining agents that are subordinate or directly related to the same provincial, national or international trade union, and that may include the parent or related provincial, national or international trade union, formed for purposes that include the representation of affiliated bargaining agents in bargaining and which may be a single provincial, national or international trade union.

EMPLOYEE BENEFIT PLAN. A system to provide increased security to workers through schemes such as group insurance and cash benefits.

EMPLOYEE CONTRIBUTIONS. (i) Current service contributions, (ii) any contributions for prior service made by a participant, (iii) any part of a sum transferred into the Plan under a reciprocal agreement that is recognized by the Minister as employee contributions. *Pension Plan acts*, Alberta.

EMPLOYEE HANDBOOK. Book issued to employees to familiarize them with their work, the employers business, and company rules and policies.

EMPLOYEE ORGANIZATION. 1. Any organization of employees the purposes of which include the regulation of relations between the employer and its employees and includes, unless the context otherwise requires, a council of employee organizations. 2. A local or provincial organization or association of employees, or a local or provincial branch of a national or international organization or association of employees within the province and that has as one of its purposes the regulation in the province of relations between employers and employees through collective bargaining.

EMPLOYEE PERSONAL INFORMATION. Personal information about an individual that is collected, used or disclosed solely for the purposes reasonably required to establish, manage or terminate an employment relationship between the organization and that individual, but does not include personal information that is not about an individual's employment.

EMPLOYEE REPRESENTATIVE. 1. A person elected by employees who have no recognized bargaining agent to represent them in negotiations under this Act. 2. A person who is nominated by a person who has a grievance to act on his behalf in respect of the grievance.

EMPLOYEES' CHARITY TRUST. A registered charity that is organized for the purpose of remitting, to other registered charities, donations that are collected from employees bar an employer by means of Payroll deductions.

EMPLOYEES' MUTUAL BENEFIT SOCIETY. *var.* **EMPLOYEES MUTUAL BENEFIT SOCIETY**. A society incorporated by the officers or officers and employees of a corporation for the purpose of providing support and pensions to such of the officers or employees as become incapacitated or as cease to be employed by the corporation or for the purpose of pensions, annuities or gratuities to or for paying of such officers or employees or funeral benefits upon the death of such officers or employees. *Insurance acts.*

EMPLOYEES' ORGANIZATION. Includes an organization of employees formed for purposes that include the regulation of relations between employees and employers.

EMPLOYEES' REPRESENTATIVE. A person appointed as a member of a board who, in the opinion of the minister, represents the employees in respect of whom the board may or is required to make recommendations. *Construction Industry Wages Act*, R.S.M. 1987, c. C190, s. 1.

EMPLOYER. *n.* 1. Any person who employs one or more employees. 2. In relation to an officer, means the person from whom the officer receives remuneration. 3. Includes every person responsible for the payment of the wages of an employee under any act or law. 4. (a) Any person who employs one or more employees, and (b) in respect of a dependent contractor, such person as, in the opinion of the Board has a relationship with the dependent contractor to such extent that the arrangement that governs the performance of services by the dependent contractor for that person can be the subject of collective bargaining. *Canada Labour Code*, R.S.C. 1985, c. L- 2, s. 3. 5. Includes every person, firm, corporation, agent, manager, representative, contractor or subcontractor having control or direction of, or responsible, directly or indirectly, for the employment of an employee. 6. Includes every person having in service under a contract of hiring or apprenticeship, written or oral, express or implied, a person engaged in work in or about an industry, establishment, factory, office, shop, undertaking, work, trade or business. 7. Includes any person, partnership or corporation who has charge of all or part of an industrial or commercial establishment on his own account or on account of another person, partnership or corporation, as a contractor, subcontractor, manager, supervisor, foreman or agent, or otherwise. See APPROVED ~; PARTICIPATING ~; PROFESSIONAL ~; PUBLIC SECTOR ~; PUBLIC SERVICE ~; RECIPROCATING ~; SEPARATE ~; SUCCESSOR ~; UNIONIZED ~.

EMPLOYER BARGAINING AGENCY. An employers' organization or group of employers' organizations formed for purposes that include the representation of employers in bargaining.

EMPLOYER RIGHTS. Rights, such as hiring and price fixing, which management generally argues are not proper subjects of collective bargaining.

EMPLOYER'S AGENT. (i) A person or association acting on behalf of an employer; (ii) any officer, official, foreman or other representative or employee of an employer acting in any way on behalf of an employer with respect to the hiring or discharging any of the terms or conditions of employment of the employees of the employer.

EMPLOYERS' ASSOCIATION. A group organization of employers having as its objects the study and safeguarding of the economic interests of its members, and particularly assistance in the negotiation and application of collective agreements.

EMPLOYERS' LIABILITY INSURANCE. *var.* **EMPLOYER'S LIABILITY INSURANCE.** Insurance, not being insurance incidental to some other class of insurance defined by or under this Act, against loss to an employer through liability for accidental injury to or death of an employee arising out of or in the course of her or his employment, but does not include worker's compensation insurance. *Insurance acts.*

EMPLOYERS' ORGANIZATION. Organization of employers formed for purposes that include the regulation of relations between employers and employees. See ACCREDITED REPRESENTATIVE ~.

EMPLOYER'S PREMIUM. The amount that an employer of an insured person is required to pay under section 51 in respect of that insured person. *Unemployment Insurance Act*, R.S.C. 1985, c. U-1, s. 2.

EMPLOYMENT. *n.* 1. The performance of services under an express or implied contract of service or apprenticeship, and includes the tenure of an office. 2. The act of employing or the state of being employed. *Employment Insurance Act, 1996*, S.C. 1996, c. 23, s. 2(1). 3. Any activity for which a person receives or might reasonably be expected to receive valuable consideration. 4. The position of an individual in the service of some other person, including Her Majesty or a foreign state or sovereign. 5. The act of employing or the state of being employed. 6. " . . . '[A]ctivity' or 'occupation'." *Canada (Attorney General v. Skyline Cabs (1982) Ltd.* (1986), 11 C.C.E.L. 292 at 295, 45 Alta. L.R. (2d) 296, [1986] 5 W.W.R. 16, 86 C.L.L.C. 14,047, 70 N.R. 210 (Fed. C.A.), the court per MacGuigan J.A. See ACT WITHIN SCOPE OF ~; CASUAL ~; COMMON ~; COMMON ~ DOCTRINE: CONDITION OF ~; CONTRACT OF~; COURSE OF~; EQUIVALENT ~; EXCEPTED ~; FAIR ~ PRACTICE; FULL ~; FULL TIME ~; INCLUDED ~; INSURABLE ~; LONGSHORING ~; MULTI-EMPLOYER ~; PENSIONABLE ~; PERIOD OF ~; PLACE OF ~; PROVINCIAL ~; RE-~ LIST; SEASONAL ~; SELF~; SUITABLE ~; TERMINATION OF ~; TERMS OF ~; WORK SHARING ~; YEAR OF ~.

EMPLOYMENT AGENCY. 1. Includes a person who undertakes, with or without compensation, to procure employees for employers and a person who undertakes, with or without compensation, to procure employment for persons. *Human Rights codes.* 2. The business of procuring for a fee, reward or other remuneration, (a) persons for employment, or (b) employment for persons, and includes the business of counselling or testing persons for a fee, reward or other remuneration to assist them in securing employment. *Employment Agencies Act*, R.S.O. 1990, c. E.13, s. 1.

EMPLOYMENT AND IMMIGRATION CANADA. The federal ministry with mandate to develop and utilize human resources.

EMPLOYMENT CERTIFICATE. Permit issued by a school authority to allow work by children.

EMPLOYMENT CONTRACT. " . . . [A] contract whereby a person agrees to provide sales services in consideration of payment of salary and a commission on sales, . . ." *Prozak v. Bell Telephone Co. of Canada* (1984), 4 C.C.E.L. 202 at 219, 46 O.R. (2d) 385, 4 O.A.C. 12, 10 D.L.R. (4th) 382 (C.A.), the court per Goodman J.A.

EMPLOYMENT EXAMINATION. An examination conducted by the commission for positions in a particular class, admission to which is not limited to persons employed in the public service. *Public or Civil Service acts.*

EMPLOYMENT HISTORY. The ordinary meaning of "employment history" includes not only the list of positions previously held, places of employment, tasks performed and so on, but also, for example, any personal evaluations an employee might have received during his career. Such a broad definition is also consistent with the meaning generally given to that expression in the workplace. *Canada (Information Commissioner) v. Royal Canadian Mounted Police Commissioner*, 2003 SCC 8.

EMPLOYMENT INJURY. Personal injury, including disablement, caused by an industrial accident, occupational disease or employment hazard.

EMPLOYMENT INSURANCE. A contributory, federal insurance scheme for workers who are without work or unable to look for or to do work because of injury or illness.

EMPLOYMENT LIST. A list of persons who have passed an employment examination. *Civil Service acts.*

EMPLOYMENT PLAN. See ANNUAL ~.

EMPLOYMENT PREMISES. Residential premises provided by an employer to an employee to occupy during his employment.

EMPLOYMENT PURPOSES. The purposes of taking into employment, granting promotion, reassigning employment duties or retaining as an employee. *Consumer Reporting acts.*

EMPLOYMENT RECORD. Any document or record that is necessary in order to determine whether an employee is entitled to wages, overtime pay, entitlements or maternity benefits.

EMPLOYMENT STANDARD. A requirement or prohibition that applies to an employer for the benefit of an employee.

EMPORIUM. *n.* A place where trading takes place.

EMPOWER. *v.* " . . . '[T]o license or certify' . . ." *P.I.P.S. v. Northwest Territories (Commissioner)*, [1988] N.W.T.R. 223 at 228, [1989] 5 W.W.R. 684, 53 D.L.R. (4th) 530, 41 C.R.R. 230 (C.A.), the court per Kerans J.A.

EMPTIO REI SPERATAE. [L.] A conditional contract which binds the parties only if something comes into existence. G.H.L. Fridman, *Sale of Goods in Canada*, 3d ed. (Toronto: Carswell, 1986) at 55.

EMPTIO SPEI. [L.] The sale of a chance. G.H.L. Fridman, *Sale of Goods in Canada*, 3d ed. (Toronto: Carswell, 1986) at 55.

EMPTOR. *n.* A buyer.

EMPTY. *adj.* When used with reference to a container or tank for gasoline or an associated product, means voided of its contents as far as is practicable by suction or pouring.

EMPTY WEIGHT. In respect of an aircraft, means the total weight of the following parts or contents that are part of, or carried on board, the aircraft, namely, (*a*) the airframe, including the rotor in the case of a helicopter or gyroplane, (*b*) the power plant, (*c*) the fixed ballast, (*d*) the unusable fuel, (*e*) the maximum amount of normal operating fluids, including oil, power plant coolant, hydraulic fluid, de-icing fluid and anti-icing fluid but not including potable water, lavatory pre-charge fluid or fluid intended for injection into the engines, and (*f*) all of the installed equipment. *Canadian Aviation Regulations*, SOR/96-433, s. 101.01.

ENABLING STATUTE. A statute which gives power or authority.

ENACT. *v.* 1. To decree; to establish by law. 2. Includes to issue, make, establish or prescribe.

ENACTING CLAUSE. 1. In federal statutes, "Her Majesty, by and with the advice and consent of the Senate and House of Commons of Canada, enacts as follows:" A. Fraser, W.A. Dawson, & J. Holtby, eds., *Beauchesne's Rules and Forms of the House of Commons of Canada*, 6th ed. (Toronto: Carswell, 1989) at 193. 2. The formal portion of a by-law which describes the act or thing required to be done or forbidden. I.M. Rogers, *The Law of Canadian Municipal Corporations*, 2d ed. (Toronto: Carswell, 1971-) at 417.

ENACTMENT. *n.* 1. An act or a regulation or any portion of an act or regulation, and as applied to a territory of Canada, includes an ordinance of the territory. 2. An act of the legislature of a province or a regulation, bylaw or other instrument having the force of law made under the authority of an act.

EN AUTRE DROIT. [Fr.] In another's right.

EN BANC. [Fr.] As a bench. Used to describe the full court sitting together to hear an appeal.

EN BLOC VALUE. The aggregate value of an entire business. A. Bissett-Johnson & W.M. Holland, eds, *Matrimonial Property Law in Canada* (Toronto: Carswell, 1980) at V-8.

ENCEINTE. *adj.* [Fr.] Pregnant.

ENCLOSED. See WHOLLY ~.

ENCLOSED LAND. 1. Land that is surrounded by a natural or man made barrier sufficient to exclude or contain livestock. 2. Includes land in a rural area that is (a) surrounded by a lawful fence defined by or under this Act; (b) surrounded by a lawful fence and a natural boundary or by a natural boundary alone; or (c) being used for agricultural, pastoral or horticultural purposes, and at the corners, gates and points of access of which are posted notices prohibiting trespass.

ENCLOSED MOTORCYCLE. A motorcycle that (*a*) has steering handlebars that are completely constrained from rotating in relation to the axle of only one wheel in contact with the ground, (*b*) is designed to travel on two wheels in contact with the ground, (*c*) has a minimum seat height, when the vehicle is unladen, of 650 mm, and (*d*) has a structure partially or fully enclosing the driver and passenger that is an integral part of the vehicle chassis. *Motor Vehicle Safety Regulations*, C.R.C., c. 1038, s. 2(1).

ENCLOSED PANELBOARD. An assembly of buses and connections, over-current devices and control apparatus with or without switches, or other equipment, installed in a cabinet.

ENCLOSED WORKPLACE. An enclosed building or structure in which an employee works and includes a shaft, tunnel, caisson or similar enclosed space.

ENCLOSURE. *n.* Fencing in property in order to cultivate it. See HOISTWAY ~; PROTECTIVE ~.

ENCROACHMENT. *n.* An attempt to extend a right a person already possesses.

ENCRYPTED. *adj.* Treated electronically or otherwise for the purpose of preventing intelligible reception. *Broadcasting Act*, S.C. 1991, c. 11, s. 2(1).

ENCUMBER. *v.* To attach a burden, claim, lien or liability to property.

ENCUMBRANCE. *n.* 1. Any charge on land, created or effected for any purpose whatever, including mortgages, the hypothecation of a mortgage, a trust for securing money, mechanics' liens when authorized by statute or ordinance, and executions against lands, unless expressly distinguished. 2. "... [A] charge or liability to which land is subject..." *Seltor Holdings Ltd. v. Kettles* (1983) 29 R.P.R. 214 at 221, 43 O.R. (2d) 659, 3 C.L.R. 259, 2 D.L.R. (4th) 373 (Div. Ct.), Saunders J. 3. A claim of aboriginal title constitutes an encumbrance, an interest in land cognizable at law. *Haida Nation v. British Columbia (Minister of Forests)* (1997), 45 B.C.L.R. (3d) 80 (C.A.). See INCUMBRANCE.

ENCUMBRANCEE. *n.* The owner of an encumbrance.

ENCUMBRANCER. *n.* The owner of any land or of any estate or interest in land subject to any encumbrance and includes a person entitled to the benefit of an encumbrance, or to require payment or discharge of an encumbrance. See INCUMBRANCER; SUBSEQUENT ~.

ENCYCLOPEDIA. *n.* A collective work containing a series of articles by many contributors.

ENDANGER. *v.* "... [D]oes not have any special technical meaning. Among the ordinary meanings of that word are the concepts of exposing someone to danger, harm or risk, or putting someone in danger of something untoward occurring ..." *R. v. Thornton* (1991), 3 C.R.

(4th) 381 at 389, 1 O.R. (3d) 480, 42 O.A.C. 206 (C.A.), the court per Galligan J.A.

ENDANGERED SPECIES. 1. A wildlife species that is facing imminent extirpation or extinction. *Species at Risk Act*, S.C. 2002, c. 29, s. 2(1). 2. Any species or subspecies of fauna or flora threatened with extinction by reason of (a) the destruction of its habitat or a drastic modification or severe curtailment thereof, (b) disease, (c) over-exploitation, (d) predation, (e) the use of chemicals, or (f) any combination of the foregoing factors, and declared by regulation to be endangered.

ENDEAVOUR. *v.* To strenuously attempt or try to achieve an objective.

ENDEAVOURS. *n.* Strenuous efforts towards an objective.

END BOX. A container located on an end of a mercury cell that functions as a collection point for mercury, alkali metal amalgam and brine. *Chlor-Alkali Mercury National Emission Standards Regulations*, C.R.C., c. 406, s. 2.

ENDEMIC DISEASE. A disease which routinely occurs in a certain place and is due to lasting local causes.

ENDORSE. *v.* Imprinting a stamp on the face of articles or other document.

ENDORSED. *adj.* Written on any instrument or on any paper attached thereto by the registrar.

ENDORSEMENT. *n.* 1. Anything written by the registrar upon an instrument or upon a paper attached thereto. 2. An endorsement completed by delivery. *Bills of Exchange Act*, R.S.C. 1985, c. B-4, s. 2. 3. Includes entry, memorandum and notation. 4. An ordinary signature. I.F.G. Baxter, *The Law of Banking*, 3d ed. (Toronto: Carswell, 1981) at 96. 5. "... [I]n its literal sense means writing one's name of the back of the bill, ..." *Gorrie Co. v. Whitfield* (1920), 58 D.L.R. 326 at 329, 19 O.W.N. 336, 48 O.L.R. 605 (C.A.), Meredith C.J.O. (Magee and Hodgins JJ.A. concurring). 6. The inscribing of additional qualifications on a certificate. 7. A judge's writing on a document. See BLANK ~; INDORSEMENT.

ENDORSER. *n.* A person who, in the case of a depository bill, signs the depository bill otherwise than as drawer or acceptor, or in the case of a depository note, signs the depository note otherwise than as maker. *Depository Bills and Notes Act*, S.C. 1998, c. 13, s. 2(1).

ENDOW. *v.* To entitle to dower.

ENDOWMENT. *n.* 1. Assigning or giving dower. 2. Any kind of property belonging permanently to a charity. See INDOWMENT.

ENDOWMENT CARE. The preservation, improvement, embellishment and maintenance, in perpetuity and in a proper manner, of grave stones, grave markers, monuments, lots, plots, compartments, crypts or other space, in a cemetery, or of compartments in a columbarium or mausoleum.

ENDOWMENT CARE FUNDS. Funds and property received by an owner for the purpose of providing endowment care generally of a cemetery, columbarium or mausoleum, or of any particular part thereof.

ENDOWMENT INSURANCE. An undertaking to pay an ascertained or ascertainable sum at a fixed future date, if the person whose life is insured is then alive, or at the person's death if she or he dies before such date. *Insurance acts.*

ENDURING POWER OF ATTORNEY. (1) A power of attorney is an enduring power of attorney if (a) the donor is an individual who is an adult at the time of executing the power of attorney, and (b) the power of attorney meets at least the following requirements: (i) it is in writing, is dated and is signed (A) by the donor in the presence of a witness, or (B) if the donor is physically unable to sign an enduring power of attorney, by another person on behalf of the donor, at the donor's direction and in the presence of both the donor and a witness; (ii) it is signed by the witness in the presence of the donor; (iii) it contains a statement indicating that it either (A) is to continue notwithstanding any mental incapacity or infirmity of the donor that occurs after the execution of the power of attorney, or (B) is to take effect on the mental incapacity or infirmity of the donor. *Powers Of Attorney Act,* R.S.A. 2000, c. P-20, s. 2(1).

END USER. 1. " . . . [T]he last person in a specific chain of distribution." *Saugeen Indian Band v. R.* (1988), 18 C.E.R. 94 at 97, 89 D.T.C. 5010, [1989] 1 C.T.C. 86, Can. S.T.R. 80-039, 2 T.C.T. 4033, [1989] 3 F.C. 186, [1989] 1 C.N.L.R. 167, [1989] 1 T.S.T. 2073, 24 F.T.R. 1, Reed J. 2. The buyer of gas under a gas contract who purchases the gas for the purpose of using or consuming it. *Arbitration Amendment Act,* S.A. 1986, c. 10, s. 17(1).

ENEMY. *n.* Includes armed mutineers, armed rebels, armed rioters and pirates. *National Defence Act,* R.S.C. 1985, c. N-5, s. 2.

ENEMY ACTION OR COUNTERACTION AGAINST THE ENEMY. Includes marine hazards occasioned by the War and encountered by a ship engaged in the salt water fishing industry of Canada or Newfoundland, when it was employed on a voyage that in the opinion of the Minister was essential to the prosecution of the War on behalf of His Majesty or His Majesty's allies. *Civilian War-related Benefits Act,* R.S.C. 1985, c. C-31, s. 6.

ENEMY ALIEN. Any person, without regard to nationality, who willingly resides or carries on business within an area which is occupied by or belongs to a country with whom that person's nation is at war. J.G. McLeod, *The Conflict of Laws* (Calgary: Carswell, 1983) at 64.

ENERGY. *n.* 1. Electric power and energy. 2. As the context may require, (a) energy in any form and howsoever produced, generated or collected, but not including energy in the form of animal or human muscular power, or (b) the sources, fuels or processes, or any of them, that are or may be used to produce, generate or collect energy. 3. (a) Electricity, (b) heat which is supplied through a district heating system by hot water, hot air or steam, (c) manufacture gas liquified petroleum gas, natural gas, oil or any other combustible material which is supplied through a pipeline or any other distribution system directly to a customer. 4. Electricity, gas, steam and any other form of energy, hydraulic, thermic or other. See ATOMIC ~; ATOMIC ~ CONTROL BOARD; ATOMIC ~ OF CANADA LIMITED; ELECTRIC ~; FIRM ~; HEAT ~; HYDRO ~; INTERRUPTIBLE ~; NATIONAL ~ BOARD.

ENERGY COMMODITY. Oil and gas and any prescribed product resulting from the processing or refining of oil or gas and, where there is a designation in respect of coal, thorium and uranium, or any of those substances, under section 10, includes all those substances, or the designated substance, as the case maybe, and any prescribed product resulting from the processing or refining of the designated substance or substances. *Energy Monitoring Act,* R.S.C. 1985, c. E-8, s. 2.

ENERGY EFFICIENCY STANDARD. In respect of an energy-using product, means the standard, if any, prescribed for that product or for a class of energy-using products that includes that product. *Energy Efficiency Act, 1992,* S.C. 1992, c. 36, s. 2.

ENERGY ENTERPRISE. Any individual, corporation, partnership, trust or organization engaged in the exploration for, or the development, production, processing or refining of, any energy commodity in Canada. *Energy Monitoring Act*, R.S.C. 1985, c. E-8, s. 2.

ENERGY RESOURCE. 1. Any natural resource that can be used as a source of any form of energy. 2. Includes natural gas and oil, and all other natural forms of petroleum and hydrocarbon, both gaseous and in liquid form, coal and all other natural bituminous fuels, electrical power and all means of generation of electrical power, and all means by which energy is, or may be, generated.

ENERGY STORAGE FACILITY. A place where an energy resource is accumulated or stored in bulk as part of the process of being transported or distributed.

ENERGY TRANSHIPMENT TERMINAL. A place where an energy resource is accumulated or stored in bulk as part of the process of being transported or distributed.

ENERGY USE PROJECT. A mill, factory, plant, smelter, oil refinery, metal refinery or other undertaking or facility designed to use, convert or process an energy resource or coal, or any combination of them.

ENERGY UTILITY. A person, including his lessee, trustee, receiver or liquidator, who owns or operates in the Province equipment or facilities for the production, generation, storage, transmission, sale, delivery or furnishing of gas, electricity, steam or any other agency for the production of light, heat, cold or power to or for the public or any corporation for compensation.

ENERGY VECTOR. Any source, material or electromagnetic wave, field, plasma, pressure and any direct or indirect cause of transfer, storage or liberation of energy.

ENFEOFF. *v.* To give possession of lands or tenements.

ENFEOFFMENT. *n.* 1. Investing with a dignity or possession. 2. The deed or instrument by which one invests another with possessions.

ENFORCE. *v.* " . . . [T]o realize on an investment, not merely to protect it. . ." *MacDougall & Son Transport Ltd. v. Continental Bank of Canada* (1983), 23 B.L.R. 287 at 290 (Ont. Dist. Ct.), Scott Co. Ct. J.

ENFORCEABLE. *adj.* 1. "Refer[s] . . . to . . . [a] process . . . to enable measures to be taken to secure compliance . . ." *U.N.A. v. Alberta (Attorney General)* (1992), 71 C.C.C. (3d) 225 at 234, [1992] *3* W.W.R. 481, 1 Alta. L.R. (3d) 129, 13 C.R. (4th) 1, 89 D.L.R. (4th) 609, 135 N.R. 321, 92 C.L.L.C. 14,023, 9 C.R.R. (2d) 29, [1992] 1 S.C.R. 901, 125 A.R. 241, 14 W.A.C. 241, Sopinka J. (dissenting). 2. Refers to providing a penalty to induce obedience. *U.N.A. v. Alberta (Attorney General)* (1992), 71 C.C.C. (3d) 225 at 234, [1992] 3 W.W.R. 481, 1 Alta. L.R. (3d) 129, 13 C.R. (4th) 1, 89 D.L.R. (4th) 609, 135 N.R. 321, 92 C.L.L.C. 14,023, 9 C.R.R. (2d) 29, [1992] 1 S.C.R. 901, 125 A.R. 241, 14 W.A.C. 241, Sopinka J. (dissenting).

ENFORCEMENT. *n.* Seeking to prevent breaches of the law and finding and punishing those who break the law. See AUTOMATIC ~; LAW ~.

ENFORCEMENT AUTHORITY. In respect of a contravention, (a) any police officer or constable, including a special or auxiliary constable, (b) the minister responsible for administering the enactment creating the contravention, (c) any person, or member of a class of persons, designated by the minister responsible for administering the enactment creating the contravention, or (d) the corporation or other body that made or is responsible for administering the enactment creating the contravention. *Contraventions Act, 1992*, S.C. 1992, c. 47, s. 2.

ENFORCEMENT OFFICER. A member of the Royal Canadian Mounted Police, a municipal police officer, a wildlife officer, a fishery officer, a forest officer, a parks officer, a patrol officer, a conservation officer or a peace officer.

ENFORCEMENT SERVICE. See PROVINCIAL ~.

ENFRANCHISE. *v.* 1. To bestow a liberty; to make free. 2. To give someone the liberty to vote at an election.

ENGAGED. *adj.* 1. " . . . [E]mployed . . . hired . . ." *Knight v. Fairall* (1933), [1934] 1 W.W.R. 131 at 137-8, 48 B.C.R. 61 (S.C.), Fisher J. 2. " . . . [B]eing occupied . . ." *Munn v. City Lumber Co.* (1950), 58 Man. R. 26 at 31, [1950] 1 W.W.R. 823, 96 C.C.C. 365 (C.A.), Dysart J.A. (Coyne J.A. concurring).

ENGAGEMENT. *n.* Any promise or undertaking. See INTERMEDIATE ~; SHORT ~.

ENGAGING IN BUSINESS. Includes selling goods or services to or buying goods or services from.

ENGINE. *n.* 1. A steam or an internal combustion engine and includes the clutch, reduction gears, shaft, propeller, control and such accessories as properly form part of a mechanism for the propulsion of a fishing vessel. 2. Any steam locomotive, traction engine, logging, stationary or portable engine or other power producing plant or similar device. 3. A unit propelled by any form of energy, or a combination of such units operated from a single control, used in train or yard service. 4. Includes a turbine. See CRITICAL ~; INTERNAL COMBUSTION ~; MODEL ROCKET ~; PROPULSION ~; STATIONARY ~; TRACTION ~; VEHICLE ~; YARD ~.

ENGINEER. *n.* 1. A person who through specialized education, training and experience is skilled in the principles and practice of engineering. 2. A person who is in charge of the machinery of a ship whether or not the person holds an engineer certificate. *Shipping Regulations.*See CHIEF ~; FOREST ~; INSPECTING ~; MINE SAFETY ~; MUNICIPAL ~; PROFESSIONAL ~; SHIFT ~.

ENGINEERING. *n.* 1. The application of scientific principles and knowledge, to practical ends such as the investigation, design, construction, or operation of works and systems for the benefit of man. 2. The science and art of designing, investigating, supervising the construction, maintenance or operation of, making specifications inventories or appraisals of, and consultations or reports on: machinery, structures, works, plants, mines, mineral deposits, processes, transportation systems, transmission systems and communication systems or any other part thereof. See NATURAL SCIENCES AND RESEARCH COUNCIL OF CANADA; PRACTICE OF ~; PRACTICE OF PROFESSIONAL ~; PROFESSIONAL ~.

ENGINEERING RESEARCH OR FEASIBILITY STUDY. Includes work undertaken to facilitate the design or to analyse the viability of engineering technology, systems or schemes to be used in the exploration for or the development, production or transportation of petroleum.

ENGINEERING TECHNOLOGY. The application of technical knowledge and skill by certified engineering technicians and certified engineering technologists.

ENGINEERING WORK. Any work of construction or alteration or repair of a railway, harbour, dock, canal, sewer or system of water-works; and outside electrical construction of all kinds, including the alteration and repair of outside wires, cables, apparatus and appliances; and includes any other work for the construction, alteration or repair of which machinery driven by steam, water or other mechanical power is used.

ENGINEER-IN-TRAINING. *n.* A person who has fulfilled the academic requirements for registration and has enrolled with an association, but because of age or insufficient experience is not eligible for registration.

ENGINEER ON THE WATCH. (a) The senior engineer in charge of the entire watch, or (b) where there are two or more engineers on each regular watch, an assistant engineer on such watch.

ENGINEERS FIRM. A partnership or corporation (i) that (A) confines its practice to providing engineering consulting services, or (B) if it does not confine its practice to providing engineering consulting services, engages in a practice satisfactory to the Joint Board, and (ii) in which professional engineers (A) hold a majority interest, and (B) control the partnership or corporation, and that is otherwise entitled to engage in the practice of engineering under this Act. Alberta statutes.

ENGINEMAN. *n.* The employee in charge of and responsible for the operation of an engine. See STATIONARY ~.

ENGINE ROOM. All the main propelling machinery space of the ship.

ENGINE-ROOM ASSISTANT. A rating who is engaged as the assistant to an engineer. *Shipping Regulations.*

ENGINE-ROOM RATING. A rating who forms part of a watch in the engine room, but does not include (*a*) an engine-room assistant; (*b*) a rating who is in training; or (*c*) a rating whose duties while on watch are of an unskilled nature. *Shipping Regulations.*

ENGLISH LANGUAGE EDUCATION. A school program using English as the language of instruction.

ENGLISH REPORTS. The reprinted reports of English cases from 1220 to 1865.

ENGLISH RULE. " . . . [C]ited in *Henderson v. Merthyr Tydfil Urban District Council*, [1900] 1 Q.B. 434, where costs were allowed by the Court of Appeal to a solicitor employed at a fixed annual salary by the Council, for which he was to prosecute or defend all legal proceedings taken by or against the Council, in addition to his other duties." *Canadian Indemnity Co. v. British Columbia Hydro & Power Authority* (1975), 62 D.L.R. (3d) 524 at 528 (B.C. S.C.), Ruttan J.

ENGRAVINGS. *n*. Includes etchings, lithographs, woodcuts, prints and other similar works, not being photographs. *Copyright Act*, R.S.C. 1985, c. C-42, s. 2.

ENGROSS. *v*. 1. To type or write an agreement, deed or like document from a draft with all amounts, dates and words set out at length, and with the formal attestation and testatum clauses, so that the document is ready to be executed. 2. Formerly, to write in a particular script derived from the courthand in which records were written in ancient times.

ENHANCED RECOVERY. The increased recovery from a pool achieved by artificial means or by the application of energy extrinsic to the pool, which artificial means or application includes pressuring, cycling, pressure maintenance or injection to the pool of a substance or form of energy, but does not include the injection in a well of a substance or form of energy for the sole purpose of (i) aiding in the lifting of fluids in the well or (ii) stimulation of the reservoir at or near the well by mechanical, chemical, thermal or explosive means. *Oil and Gas Conservation Act*, R.S.A. 2000, c. O-6, s. 1(1).

ENJOIN. *v*. To prohibit by court order, the effect of an injunction.

ENJOYMENT. *n*. 1. The use or application of a right. 2. "Ordinarily . . . denotes the derivation of pleasure." *R. v. Phoenix* (1991), 64 C.C.C. (3d) 252 at 255 (B.C. Prov. Ct.), de Villiers Prov. J. 3. " . . . [A] different sense . . . in reference to [real] property . . . 'possession' . . ." *R. v. Phoenix* (1991), 64 C.C.C. (3d) 252 at 255 (B.C. Prov. Ct.), de Villiers Prov. J. See QUIET ∼.

ENLARGE. *v*. To lengthen time. To extend.

ENLISTMENT. *n*. 1. Enrolment in the armed forces. 2. Recruitment. See RECORDED ON MEDICAL EXAMINATION PRIOR TO ∼.

EN OWEL MAIN. [Fr.] In equal hand.

EN PASSANT. [Fr.] In passing.

ENQUIRY. See INQUIRY.

ENRG. *abbr*. Enregistre.

ENRICHMENT. *n*. A tangible benefit. See UNJUST ∼.

ENROL. *v*. 1. To cause any person to become a member of the Canadian Forces. *National Defence Act*, R.S.C. 1985, c. N-5, s. 2. 2. To enter or copy a document into an official record.

ENSEINT. [Fr.] Pregnancy.

ENSIENT. [Fr.] Pregnancy.

ENSLAVEMENT. *n*. The exercise of any or all of the powers attaching to the right of ownership over a person and includes the exercise of such power in the course of trafficking in persons, in particular women and children. *Rome Statute*, Article 7.

ENS LEGIS. [L.] A legal entity.

ENSURE. *v*. 1. " . . . [C]arries the connotation of a guarantee. . ." *R. v. Westeel-Rosco Ltd.* (1975), 10 O.R. (2d) 709 at 712, 27 C.C.C. (2d) 467 (Div. Ct.), the court per Reid J. 2. To make certain.

ENTAIL. *n*. An estate or interest in land which descends only to the grantee's issue.

ENTER. *v*. 1. When any part of his body or any part of an instrument that he uses is within anything that is being entered. *Criminal Code*, R.S.C. 1985, c. C-46, s. 350(a). 2. To come onto land. 3. To note, in a record or book, a transcript of a document or a transaction. See BREAK AND ∼.

ENTERAL. *adj*. Administration of a nutritional substance to a patient by means of a feeding tube into the gastrointestinal tract.

ENTER JUDGMENT. To deliver to the Registrar an order embodying a judgment or to cause the Registrar to make a formal record of a judgment.

ENTERPRISE. A business or undertaking. See AGRICULTURAL ∼; AIR TRANSPORT ∼; BUSINESS ∼; COMMERCIAL ∼; ECONOMIC ∼; ENERGY ∼; FISH BUSINESS OR ∼; FISHERY ∼; HAZARDOUS WASTE MANAGEMENT ∼; INDUSTRIAL MUNICIPAL ∼; SMALL BUSINESS ∼.

ENTERPRISE CRIME OFFENCE. For the purposes of the forfeiture provisions of the Code [*Criminal Code*, R.S.C. 1985, c. C-46], reference to an "enterprise crime offence" includes a "designated substance offence". *R. v. Marriott*, 2001 NSCA 84, 42 C.R. (5th) 339, (sub nom.

Stone Estate, Re) 155 C.C.C. (3d) 168, 194 N.S.R. (2d) 64 (C.A.).

ENTERTAINMENT. *n*. 1. Any contest, game, race, dance, apparatus, amusement, display, device, exhibition, attraction, performance, presentation, program, show or motion picture, operated either indoors or out of doors, in order to obtain money, or its equivalent, from the people who attend. 2. Includes a circus, contest, dance, exhibition, fair, game, movie-picture or stage performance. Newfoundland statutes. See PLACE OF ~.

ENTERTAINMENT HALL. (i) A hall, pavilion, place, premises, room, tent or structure of any kind kept or used for public concerts, carnival shows dances or other social gatherings, and (ii) includes a cafe, hotel or restaurant where facilities are supplied and used for public dancing.

ENTERTAINMENT LAW. The law relating to artists, actors, athletes, musicians and the film, television, music industries and sports activities.

ENTICEMENT. *n*. The deliberate inducement of a wife to leave her husband. The inducement must be made with knowledge of her marital status and with intent to interfere with the wife's duty to give consortium to her husband. John G. Flemin, *The Law of Torts*, 8th ed. (Sydney: The Law Book Company Limited, 1992) at 653-4.

ENTICING. *adj*. Soliciting, alluring.

ENTIRE AGREEMENT CLAUSE. Indicates that the document embodies all of the terms of the agreement between the parties.

ENTIRE ANIMAL. (i) A stallion over the age of 15 months, or (ii) a bull or jack over the age of nine months, or (iii) a ram, he-goat or boar over the age of five months.

ENTIRE TENANCY. Sole possession in one person.

ENTIRETY. See TENANCY BY THE ~.

ENTITLE. *v*. To bestow a right.

ENTITLED. *adj*. Clearly qualified; meeting all requirements.

ENTITLEMENT. *n*. A right to income, property or benefits.

ENTITY. *n*. 1. A body corporate, a trust, a partnership, a fund, an unincorporated association or organization, Her Majesty in right of Canada or of a province or an agency of Her Majesty in right of Canada or of a province and the government of a foreign country or any political subdivision or agency of the government of a foreign country. *Canada Pension Plan Investment Board Act*, S.C. 1997, c. 40, s. 2. 2. A person, group, trust, partnership or fund or an unincorporated association or organization. *Federal acts*. See AUTHORIZED ~; CROWN ~; FOREIGN ~; GOVERNMENT ENTITIES.

ENTOMOLOGY. *n*. The study of insects.

EN TOUTE JUSTICE. A journal published by Association canadienne d'assistance jurisique, d'information et de recherche des handicapes.

ENTRANCE. See MINE ~.

ENTRANCE FEE. Includes every charge made for seating accommodation, whether or not payment is required before entrance.

ENTRANCE RATE. The rate of pay an employee receives when first hired.

ENTRANT. *n*. Trespasser, licencee, invitee or one who has contracted to and paid for the right to enter premises, a contractual entrant.

ENTRANT AS OF RIGHT. A person who is empowered or permitted by law to enter premises without the permission of the occupier of those premises.

ENTRAPMENT. *n*. 1. "[Occurs] . . . when (a) the authorities provide a person with an opportunity to commit an offence without acting on a reasonable suspicion that this person is already engaged in criminal activity or pursuant to a bona fide inquiry; (b) although having such a reasonable suspicion or acting in the course of a bona fide inquiry, they go beyond providing an opportunity and induce the commission of an offence." *R. v. Mack* (1988), 37 C.R.R. 277 at 324, [1989] 1 W.W.R. 577, [1988] 2 S.C.R. 903, 67 C.R. (3d) 1, 90 N.R. 173, 44 C.C.C. (3d) 513, the court per Lamer J. 2. Entrapment is a unique area of the criminal law. In our view, it has been somewhat inappropriately referred to as an affirmative defence. In our opinion, that misdescribes it. A claim of entrapment is in reality a motion for a stay of proceedings based on the accused's allegation of an abuse of process. It does not rely on the underlying charge and does not affect the admissibility of any evidence which might influence the jury on the merits. In particular, unlike a claim of not criminally responsible on account of mental disorder, entrapment does not go to or involve *mens rea* or "criminal responsibility" in any way. Entrapment concerns the conduct of the police and the Crown. The question to be answered is not whether the accused is guilty, but whether his guilt was uncovered in a manner that shocks the conscience and offends the principle of decency and fair play. *R. v. Pearson*, 1998 CarswellQue 1079, 233 N.R. 367, 130 C.C.C. (3d) 293, 21 C.R. (5th) 106, [1998] 3 S.C.R. 620, Per Lamer, C.J.C. and Major, J. for the majority.

ENTRENCHED. *adj*. Capable of being altered solely through a constitutional amendment.

ENTRENCHMENT CLAUSE. Section 52(3) of the Constitution Act, 1982: "Amendments to the Constitution of Canada shall be made only in accordance with the authority contained in the Constitution of Canada."

ENTREPOT. *n*. [Fr.] A warehouse where goods already bought await resale.

ENTREPRENEUR. *n*. [Fr.] An individual who undertakes a business which employs others.

ENTRUSTED. *adj*. " . . . [I]n [an insurance] contract . . . a delivery or parting with possession coupled with real consent on the part of the insured, for a mutually understood purpose, on the condition that the recipient return or account for the property in given circumstances." *Hinks v. Canadian Home Assurance Co.* (1985), 12 C.C.L.I. 93 at 94, 39 Alta. L.R. (2d) 397, [1986] I.L.R. 1-1998 (Q.B.), Sulatycky J.

ENTRY. *n*. 1. Going onto land. 2. Setting down a record in a book. 3. Lawful permission to come into Canada as a visitor. *Immigration Act*, R.S.C. 1985, c. I-2, s. 2. 4. "[In the Canada Evidence Act, R.S.C. 1970, c. E-10, s. 29(1)] . . . an ordinary financial or bookkeeping entry, that is, the figures and the required explanation for such figures, in a ledger, book, card system or computer card system. . ." *Minister of National Revenue v. Furnasman Ltd.*, [1973] F.C. 1327 at 1333, [1973] C.T.C. 830, 73 D.T.C. 5599 (T.D.), Addy J. 5. Not only the record of a claim in the books of the mining recorder, but also the grant which may be issued for the claim. 6. Includes recording by photographic plate, microphotographic film or photocopy negative. *Judicature Act and Matrimonial Cause Act*, R.R.O. 1980, Reg. 540, s. 2. See DOUBLE ~; FORCIBLE ~; PORT OF ~; RE-~; RIGHT OF ~; SINGLE ~.

ENUMERATED GROUNDS. Those grounds of discrimination listed in s. 15(1) of the Charter: race, national or ethnic origin, colour, religion, sex, age, mental or physical disability.

ENUMERATION. *n*. A general residence to residence visitation to obtain or verify information respecting residence of voters and, where necessary, to obtain applications for registration for the purpose of updating or compiling new lists of voters. See GENERAL ~; SPECIAL ~.

ENUMERATION DATE. In respect of an election in an electoral district, the date for the commencement of the preparation of the preliminary lists of electors for that election.

ENUMERATION LIST. The most recent list of electors.

ENUMERATION YEAR. A calendar year in which a general enumeration takes place.

ENUMERATOR. *n*. 1. A person appointed to compile or revise a list of electors. 2. A person who takes a census.

ENURE. *v*. To take effect; to operate.

ENVELOPE. See INNER ~; OUTER ~.

EN VENTRE SA MÈRE. [Fr. in the mother's womb] Describes an unborn child.

ENVIRONMENT. *n*. 1. The air, land, water, plant life, animal life and ecological systems. *Environmental Bill of Rights, 1993*, S.O. 1993, c. 28, s.1. 2. The components of the Earth, and includes (a) land, water and air, including all layers of the atmosphere, (b) all organic and inorganic matter and living organisms, and (c) the interacting natural systems that include components referred to in paragraphs (a) and (b). *Federal acts*. 3. All the external conditions or influences under which human beings, animals and plants live or are developed. See NATURAL ~; POISONED ~ SEXUAL HARASSMENT; SMOKE-FREE ~.

ENVIRONMENTAL ACCIDENT. A release, leakage or spillage of a contaminant into the environment otherwise than in accordance with the provisions of this Act, its licences, orders and regulations or *The Environment Act*, its orders and regulations, or an incident which may or is likely to result in such a release, leakage or spillage, which, having regard to the environment in which the release, leakage or spillage takes place or may take place, and to the nature of the contaminant, creates or may create a hazard to human life or health, to other living organisms, or to the physical environment. *The Dangerous Goods Handling and Transportation Act*, R.S.M. 1987, c. D12, s. 1.

ENVIRONMENTAL ASSESSMENT. 1. A process by which the environmental impact of an undertaking is predicted and evaluated before the undertaking has begun or occurred. *Environmental Assessment acts*. 2. In respect of a project, an assessment of the environmental effects of the project that is conducted in accordance with this Act and the regulations. *Canadian Environmental Assessment Act*, S.C. 1992, c. 37, s. 2(1).

ENVIRONMENTAL ASSESSMENT REPORT. A report that presents the results of a complete environmental assessment.

ENVIRONMENTAL AUDIT. An internal evaluation by a company or government agency verifying its compliance with legal requirements, internal policies and standards as regards environmental concerns.

ENVIRONMENTAL EFFECT. In respect of a project, (a) any change that the project may cause in the environment, including any effect of any such change on health and socio-economic conditions, on physical and cultural heritage, on the current use of lands and resources for traditional purposes by aboriginal persons, or on any structure, site or thing that is of historical, archaeological, paleontological or architectural significance, and (b) any change to the project that may be caused by the environment, whether any such change occurs within or outside Canada. *Canadian Environmental Assessment Act, 1992*, S.C. 1992, c. 37, s.2.

ENVIRONMENTAL EMERGENCY. 1. An occurrence or natural disaster that affects the environment and includes (a) a flood, (b) a landslide, and (c) a spill or leakage of oil or of a poisonous or dangerous substance. 2. An environmental accident which creates an immediate or imminent hazard which requires the taking of prompt emergency measures to protect persons, property and the environment. *Dangerous Goods Handling and Transportation* Act, R.S.M. 1987, c. C12, s. 1. 3. An uncontrolled, unplanned or accidental release, or release in contravention of regulations made under this Part, of a substance into the environment; or the reasonable likelihood of such a release into the environment. *Canadian Environmental Protection Act, 1999*, S.C. 1999, c. 33, s. 193.

ENVIRONMENTAL HEALTH. 1. Those aspects of human health that are or can be affected by contaminants or changes in the environment. *Environmental Protection Act*, R.S.P.E.I. 1988, c. E-9, s. 1(h). 2. Those aspects of human health that are or can be affected by chemical or physical agents or the sanitary condition of water,

wastes or food. *Dangerous Goods Handling and Transportation Act*, R.S.M. 1987, c. D12, s. 1.

ENVIRONMENTAL IMPACT. Any change in the present or future environment that would result from an undertaking. *Environmental Assessment acts*.

ENVIRONMENTAL IMPACT ASSESSMENT. A process by which the environmental impact caused by or resulting from an undertaking is predicted and evaluated.

ENVIRONMENTAL IMPACT STATEMENT. A report that presents the results of a complete environmental assessment.

ENVIRONMENTAL LAW. The law governing the environment and natural resources.

ENVIRONMENTAL MONITORING. Analysis and sampling of the environment so that the concentration of a potentially hazardous substance and the degree of workers' exposure to it may be determined.

ENVIRONMENTAL QUALITY. I cannot accept that the concept of environmental quality is confined to the biophysical environment alone; such an interpretation is unduly myopic and contrary to the generally held view that the "environment" is a diffuse subject matter. The point was made by the Canadian Council of Resource and Environment Ministers, following the "Brundtland Report" of the World Commission on Environment and Development, in the Report of the National Task Force on Environment and Economy, September 24, 1987, at p. 2: Our recommendations reflect the principles that we hold in common with the World Commission on Environment and Development (WCED). These include the fundamental belief that environmental and economic planning cannot proceed in separate spheres. Long-term economic growth depends on a healthy environment. It also affects the environment in many ways. Ensuring environmentally sound and sustainable economic development requires the technology and wealth that is generated by continued economic growth. Economic and environmental planning and management must therefore be integrated. Surely the potential consequences for a community's livelihood, health and other social matters from environmental change are integral to decision-making on matters affecting environmental quality, subject, of course, to the constitutional imperatives. *Friends of the Oldman River Society v. Canada (Minister of Transport)*, 1992 CarswellNat 649, 84 Alta. L.R. (2d) 129,

[1992] 1 S.C.R. 3, [1992] 2 W.W.R. 193, 7 C.E.L.R. (N.S.) 1, 132 N.R. 321, 88 D.L.R. (4th) 1, 3 Admin. L.R. (2d) 1, 48 F.T.R. 160, La Forest for majority.

ENVIRONMENTAL STUDY. Work pertaining to the measurement or statistical evaluation of the physical, chemical and biological elements of the lands, oceans or coastal zones, including winds, waves, tides, currents, precipitation, ice cover and movement, icebergs, pollution effects, flora and fauna both onshore and offshore, human activity and habitation and any related matters.

ENVIRONMENT CANADA. The federal ministry responsible for managing and protecting migratory birds, providing information on climate, weather, sea and ice conditions and air quality, protecting and enhancing the natural environment (i.e. soil, water and air) and conserving renewable land, water and wildlife resources.

ENVOY. *n.* 1. A diplomatic agent sent to one nation from another. 2. The envoy of a foreign sovereign power accredited to Her Majesty in right of Canada.

ENZYME. *n.* A protein which acts as a catalyst in a chemical reaction. F.A. Jaffe, *A Guide to Pathological Evidence*, 3d ed. (Toronto: Carswell, 1991) at 218.

EODEM LIGAMINE QUO LIGATUM EST DISSOLVITUR. [L.] An obligation is ended the same way in which it was imposed.

EODEM MODO QUO QUID CONSTITUITUR, EODEM MODO DESTRUITUR. [L.] A thing is destroyed in the same way it was made.

E.O.E. *abbr.* Errors and omissions excepted.

EO INSTANTI. [L. at that moment] At the same moment; immediately.

EO NOMINE. [L.] By that name.

EPA. The United States Environmental Protection Agency.

EPA CERTIFICATE. A certificate of conformity to U.S. federal standards issued by the EPA. *On-Road Vehicle and Engine Emission Regulations*, SOR/2003-2, s. 1(1).

EPIDEMIC. *n.* The occurrence in a community of persons of a number of cases of a communicable disease in excess of normal expectations.

EPIDEMIC DISEASE. A disease generally occurring in a community or among a people at a particular time, and produced by peculiar causes not usually found in that locality.

EPIDEMIOLOGY. *n.* The study of the frequency and patterns of disease in populations and the study of prevention and control of disease within populations.

EPIDERMIS. *n.* Skin.

EPIDURAL HEMORRHAGE. A venous or arterial hemorrhage between the dura mater and the skull. F.A. Jaffe, *A Guide to Pathological Evidence*, 3d ed. (Toronto: Carswell, 1991) at 154.

EPIGLOTTIS. *n.* A structure at the base of the tongue which protects the opening of the larynx while one swallows. F.A. Jaffe, *A Guide to Pathological Evidence*, 3d ed. (Toronto: Carswell, 1991) at 218.

EPIGLOTTITIS. *n.* Inflammation of the epiglottis. F.A. Jaffe, *A Guide to Pathological Evidence*, 3d ed. (Toronto: Carswell, 1991) at 218.

EPILEPSY. *n.* A group of disorders characterized by episodic impairment or frequent convulsions and loss of consciousness. F.A. Jaffe, *A Guide to Pathological Evidence*, 3d ed. (Toronto: Carswell, 1991) at 218.

EPIPHYSEAL INJURY. Dislocation of a bone's epiphysis, often caused when an extremity is pulled too forcefully. F.A. Jaffe, *A Guide to Pathological Evidence*, 3d ed. (Toronto: Carswell, 1991) at 218.

EPIPHYSIS. *n.* The part of a bone which a layer of cartilage separates from the main part during childhood but which unites with the main part during adolescence or early adult life. F.A. Jaffe, *A Guide to Pathological Evidence*, 3d ed. (Toronto: Carswell, 1991) at 218-19.

EPISCOPATE. *n.* A bishop's jurisdiction.

EPISODE. See AIR POLLUTION ~.

EPISODIC. *adj.* Short-term.

EPOCH. *n.* The beginning of a new computation of time. See GREGORIAN ~.

EPOCHA. *n.* The beginning of a new computation of time.

EQUAL. *adj.* Subject to all requirements, qualifications and considerations that are not a prohibited ground of discrimination. *Human Rights Code*, R.S.O. 1990, c. H.19, s. 10(1).

EQUALITY. *n.* Can refer to the condition of same treatment of all persons. Interpreted to not necessarily mean identical treatment. Different treatment may be required to promote equality in some cases. Refers to the right to be free from discrimination based on membership in a group historically disadvantaged by prejudicial assumptions. See PROCEDURAL ~.

EQUALITY BEFORE AND UNDER THE LAW. " . . . [A] comparative concept, the condition of which may only be attained or discerned by comparison with the condition of others in the social and political setting in which the question arises. . . admittedly unattainable ideal should be that a law expressed to bind all should not because of irrelevant personal differences have a more burdensome or less beneficial impact on one than another." *Andrews v. Law Society (British Columbia)*, 56 D.L.R. (4th) 1 at 10-11, 10 C.H.R.R. D/5719, [1989] 2 W.W.R. 289, 25 C.C.E.L. 255, 91 N.R. 255, 34 B.C.L.R. (2d) 273, 36 C.R.R. 193, 56 D.L.R. (4th) 1, [1989] 1 S.C.R. 143, McIntyre J.

EQUALITY BEFORE THE LAW. "The guarantee . . . is designed to advance the value that all persons be subject to the equal demands and burdens of the law and not suffer any greater disability in the substance and application of the law than others. . ." *R v. Turpin* (1989), 39 C.R.R. 306 at 333, 69 C.R. (3d) 97, 48 C.C.C. (3d) 8, 96 N.R. 115, [1989] 1 S.C.R. 1296, 34 O.A.C. 115, the court per Wilson J.

EQUALITY IS EQUITY. When there is property to be divided among persons, the persons are entitled to equal shares unless there is sufficient reason to use another basis for division. P.V. Baker and P. St. J. Langan, eds., *Shell's Equity*, 29th ed. (London: Sweet & Maxwell, 1990) at 36.

EQUALITY RIGHTS. The rights provided by section 15 of the Charter. Section 15 states: (1) Every individual is equal before and under the law and has the right to the equal protection and equal benefit of the law without discrimination and, in particular, without discrimination based on race, national or ethnic origin, colour, religion, sex, age or mental or physical disability. (2) Subsection (1) does not preclude any law, program or activity that has as its object the amelioration of conditions of disadvantaged individuals or groups including those that are disadvantaged because of race, national or ethnic origin, colour, religion, sex, age or mental or physical disability.

EQUALIZATION LEVY. In the context of product marketing schemes, a pooling of proceeds, so that producers' returns are equalized even if the product was actually sold at different prices in different markets. P.W. Hogg, *Constitutional Law of Canada*, 3d ed. (Toronto: Carswell, 1992) at 650.

EQUALIZATION PAYMENT. Payment to a province to bring its share of tax rental payments up to the same per capita amount as the average capita yield in the two provinces with the highest yield. P.W. Hogg, *Constitutional Law of Canada*, 3d ed. (Toronto: Carswell, 1992) at 138.

EQUALIZED ASSESSMENT. The assessment upon which taxes are levied in the municipality or locality.

EQUAL PAY FOR EQUAL WORK. The same wage rate applied to jobs with no consideration of sex, race or other factors not related to ability to perform the work.

EQUILINGUALISM. *n.* " . . . [H]av[ing] an equal command of two languages. . ." *Assn. of Parents for Fairness in Education, Grand Falls District 50 Branch v.* Société *des Acadiens du Nouveau-Brunswick Inc.* (1986), 23 C.R.R. 119 at 188, [1986] 1 S.C.R. 549, 66 N.R. 173, 69 N.B.R. (2d) 271, 177 A.P.R. 271, 27 D.L.R. (4th) 406, Wilson J.

EQUINE. *n.* A horse, ass, mule or zebra.

EQUIP. *v.* In relation to a ship, includes the furnishing of anything that is used for the purpose of fitting or adapting the ship for the seas or for naval service.

EQUIPMENT. *n.* 1. Apparatus, device, mechanism, structure, machine, machinery, tool, device, contrivance or vehicle. 2. Goods that are not inventory or consumer goods. *Personal Property Security acts.* 3. Includes lifeboats, lifesaving equipment, apparatus for protection against fire, for detection and extinguishing of fire, fire-control plans, line-throwing apparatus, anchors, cables, pilot ladders, means of making sound signals and distress signals, compasses, lights, signals, navigating appliances and all other apparatus or equipment designed or required for safety of the ship or the protection of the passengers and crew, but does not include radio equipment other than radio equipment for survival craft. See AGRICULTURAL ~; AUTOMATIC TABULATING ~; BASIC ~; BEEHIVE ~; BEEKEEPING ~; CANADIAN ~; CAPITAL ~; DISTRIBUTION ~;

ELECTRICAL ~; ELECTRONIC ~; ESSEN-TIAL AIRCRAFT ~; FARM ~; FIRE DE-PARTMENT ~; FIRE-EXTINGUISHING ~; FISHING ~; FISHING ~ AND SUPPLIES; FOOD PREPARATION ~; FORESTRY ~; FUEL-BURNING ~; GAMING GAS ~; GE-OPHYSICAL ~; GROUNDING ~; HEAVY DUTY ~; IONIZING RADIATION ~; LUM-BERING ~; MATERIALS HANDLING ~; MILKING ~; MINING ~; MOBILE ~; NON-IONIZING RADIATION ~; OIL, NATURAL GAS, OR SALT PRODUCTION ~; PERMIS-SIBLE ~; PLUMBING ~; PORTABLE ~; PRESSURE ~; PROJECTION ~; PROTEC-TIVE BREATHING ~; PROTECTIVE ~; RADIATION ~; RAILWAY ~; RECORD-ING ~; SELF-PROPELLED ~; SHELTER ~; SPECIAL MOBILE ~; STORAGE ~; TRANSMISSION ~; TRANSPORTABLE ~; UTILIZATION ~; VENTILATION ~; WELDING ~; X-RAY ~.

EQUIPMENT TRUST. A means for a company to raise funds on the security of equipment, established by setting up a certificate or indenture. D.M.W. Waters, *The Law of Trusts in Canada*, 2d ed. (Toronto: Carswell, 1984) at 452.

EQUITABLE. *adj*. Fair; according to the rules of equity.

EQUITABLE CHARGE. A security for a debt which does not provide the lender with a legal estate in the charged property.

EQUITABLE DOCTRINE OF CON-STRUCTIVE NOTICE. Any equitable claim is good against a mortgagee who should have known of it by acting prudently, i.e., if the mortgagee had made the usual title search.

EQUITABLE ESTATE. A right relating to property which another person or the equitable owner in another capacity legally owns.

EQUITABLE ESTOPPEL. " . . . [W]here a representation is made by one party and relied upon by another to that person's detriment, the party making the representation will be estopped from following a contrary course of action. This concept has been modified to mean a basic sense of fairness and equity. One should not be able to say one thing, have it acted upon, and then behave differently than first represented." *Marchischuk v. Dominion Industrial Supplies Ltd.* (1989), 34 C.P.C. (2d) 181 at 182, 1989 3 W.W.R. 74, 58 Man. R. (2d) 56 (Q.B.), Kennedy J.

EQUITABLE EXECUTION. " . . . [T]he practice of granting an equitable substitute for execution at common law in respect of equitable property of the debtor by the appointment of a receiver. . ." *Fox v. Peterson Livestock Ltd.*, [1982] 2 C.N.L.R. 58 at 60, [1982] 2 W.W.R. 204, 17 Alta. L.R. (2d) 311, 35 A.R. 471, 131 D.L.R. (3d) 716 (C.A.), the court per Belzil J.A.

EQUITABLE FRAUD. " . . . [C]onduct which, having regard to some special relationship between the two parties concerned, is an unconscionable thing for the one to do towards the other." *Kitchen v. Royal Air Force Assn. et al.*, [1958] 1 W.L.R. 563 at 573 (U.K.), Lord Evershed M.R.

EQUITABLE INTEREST. A right relating to property which another person or the equitable owner in another capacity legally owns.

EQUITABLE LEASEHOLD MORTGAGE. A mortgage created when one agrees to make a lease or sub-lease, to assign a lease, to deposit title deeds or to do any other thing which creates an equitable charge of freehold.

EQUITABLE LIEN. 1. A lien not tied to possession. 2. " . . . [B]ased on the principle that if a person has acquired possession of property under a contract whereby he is obligated to pay for it, he will not be allowed to retain the property unless he does pay for it. It arises by operation of law and is an incident to the contract between the vendor and purchaser. . ." *Ahone v. Holloway* (1988), 30 B.C.L.R. (2d) 368 at 376 (C.A.), the court per McLachlin J.A. 3. An equitable right, such as an unpaid vendor's lien or a purchasers lien, which the law confers on one person in the form of a charge on the property of another person until particular claims are satisfied.

EQUITABLE LIMITATIONS. Refers to rules of equity developed to govern equitable claims. Originally statutes of limitations did not govern equitable claims. Limitation by analogy, laches, and acquiescence are types of equitable limitations.

EQUITABLE MORTGAGE. 1. Commonly, a charge or mortgage other than a statutory or registered mortgage. 2. A mortgage may be equitable either (1) because the interest mortgaged is future or equitable, or (2) because the mortgagor did not execute an instrument adequate to transfer the legal estate, e.g. a mortgage of the equity of redemption. Such a mortgage may also be created by depositing title deeds.

EQUITABLE SET-OFF. " . . . [I]s available where there is a claim for a money sum whether liquidated or unliquidated: . . . it is available where there has been an assignment. There is no requirement of mutuality." *Telford v. Holt* (1987), 37 B.L.R. 241 at 253, 21 C.P.C. (2d) 1, 78 N.R. 321, 54 Alta. L.R. (2d) 193, [1987] 6 W.W.R. 385, [1987] 2 S.C.R. 193, 46 R.P.R. 234, 81 A.R. 385, 41 D.L.R. (4th) 385, the court per Wilson J.

EQUITABLE SHARE. See JUST AND ~.

EQUITABLY. *adv*. Fairly.

EQUITY. *n*. 1. Fairness. 2. That part of the general law which provides remedies not available at common law in many cases. Prior to the late 1800s the courts administering equity were separate from the common law courts and were known as Chancery courts. By the Judicature Acts, the courts were united so that a judge might hear cases seeking equitable or common law remedies. 3. Equity of redemption. 4. In business, the excess of assets over liabilities. 5. The aggregate of (a) the share capital, (b) earned surplus, (c) contributed surplus, (d) other surplus or deficit accounts, (e) shareholders loans that are subordinated to all other liabilities, and (f) the proprietor's or partner capital accounts, less such accounts as unreasonably inflate the net worth of the applicant. Canada regulations. 6. " . . . Such interest as the seller has in property. *Bednarsky v. Weleschuk* (1961), 29 D.L.R. (2d) 270 at 272 (Alta. C.A.), the court per Johnson J.A. See ACCUMULATED NET RETAIL ~; ADJUSTED ~; BETTER ~; CLEAN HANDS DOCTRINE; DELAY DEFEATS EQUITIES; DIRECT ~ PERCENTAGE; EQUALITY IS ~; FORMAL ~; HE WHO COMES INTO ~ MUST COME WITH CLEAN HANDS; HE WHO SEEKS ~ MUST DO ~; INFORMAL ~; MAXIMS OF ~; NO MAN CAN BE ALLOWED TO DEROGATE FROM HIS OWN GRANT; NO MAN CAN TAKE ADVANTAGE OF HIS OWN WRONG; PAY ~; SHAREHOLDERS'~; TAX ~ OF A PARTNERSHIP.

EQUITY ACCOUNT. See VOLUNTARY ~.

EQUITY ACTS IN PERSONAM. Describes the procedure in equity.

EQUITY AIDS THE VIGILANT AND NOT THE INDOLENT. "[A] court of equity . . . has always refused its aid to stale demands where a party has slept upon his right and acquiesced for a great length of time. Nothing can call forth this court into activity, but conscience, good faith, and reasonable diligence; where these are wanting, the Court is passive, and does nothing." *Smith v. Clay* (1767), 3 Bro. C.C. 639n at 640n Lord Camden L.C.

EQUITY CAPITAL. Of a corporation, the amount of consideration paid in money for which the outstanding equity shares of the corporation have been issued.

EQUITY FOLLOWS THE LAW. Equity will interfere only in a case when an important aspect is ignored by the common law.

EQUITY IMPUTES AN INTENTION TO FULFIL AN OBLIGATION. An act other than that originally intended or required will be accepted as fulfillment of an obligation if the act is capable of being regarded a fulfillment of the obligation.

EQUITY LOOKS ON THAT AS DONE WHICH OUGHT TO BE DONE. A contract will be treated as completed in favour of persons who have a right to enforce that contract.

EQUITY LOOKS TO THE INTENT RATHER THAN TO THE FORM. "Courts of Equity make a distinction in all cases between that which is matter of substance and that which is matter of form; and if it find that by insisting on the form, the substance will be defeated, it holds it to be inequitable to allow a person to insist on such form, and thereby defeat the substance." *Parkin v. Thorold* (1852), 16 Beav. 59 at 466, Romilly M.R.

EQUITY OF A STATUTE. When a fact situation falls within a statute's spirit and intent, though apparently not its letter, it is within the equity of that statute.

EQUITY OF REDEMPTION. 1. A mortgagor's right to redeem a mortgage. 2. The interest remaining in a mortgagor after the execution of one or more mortgages upon any lands. 3. The amount by which a property's value exceeds the total charges, liens or mortgages against it. See CLOG ON ~.

EQUITY SECURITIES. Shares of any class of a corporation and any rights in connection therewith.

EQUITY SECURITY. Any security of an issuer that carries a residual right to participate in the earnings of the issuer and, upon the liquidation or winding up of the issuer, in its assets. *Securities acts*.

EQUITY SHARE. 1. A share of a class of shares of a corporation carrying voting rights under all circumstances and a share of a class of shares carrying voting rights by reason of the occurrence of a contingency that has occurred and is continuing. 2. A voting security and any security of an issuer that carries the residual right to participate in earnings of the issuer and in its assets on liquidation or winding up. 3. Any security other than a debt obligation of a corporation.

EQUITY SHARES. Shares of any class, whether or not preferred as to dividends or assets, which have unlimited dividend rights.

EQUITY WILL NOT SUFFER A WRONG TO BE WITHOUT A REMEDY. The maxim upon which the enforcement of uses and trusts was founded by the Court of Chancery. A wrong will not go unredressed if the courts are able to remedy it.

EQUIVALENCY. *n.* A principle which permits deviation from regulated requirements and specifications as long as the alternative designs, sizes, compositions or arrangements provide better or equal strength as well as heath and safety protection.

EQUIVALENT. See ACTUARIALLY ~; PENSION ~; WATER ~.

EQUIVALENT EMPLOYMENT. Employment of a similar nature to the employment held by the worker when he suffered the employment injury, from the standpoint of vocational qualifications required, wages, social benefits, duration and working conditions. *An Act Respecting Industrial Accidents and Occupational Diseases*, S.Q. 1985, c. 6, s. 2.

EQUIVALENT RATE. See CANADIAN ~.

EQUIVALENTS, DOCTRINE OF. It has been established that a patent owner has a remedy against an alleged infringer who does not take the letter of the invention but nevertheless appropriates its substance (or "pith and marrow"). This extended protection of the patentee is recognized in Anglo-Canadian law, and also finds expression in modified form in the United States under the doctrine of equivalents, which is said to be available against the producer of a device that performs substantially the same function in substantially the same way to obtain substantially the same result. The U.S. approach is to disaggregate the invention as described in the patent claims into its constituent parts, as we do, but instead of characterizing an element as essential or non-essential, they treat all elements as "material", *Free World Trust c. Électro Santé Inc.*, 2000 CarswellQue 2728, 2000 SCC 66, 194 D.L.R. (4th) 232, 263 N.R. 150, [2000] 2 S.C.R. 1024, 9 C.P.R. (4th) 168, Binnie, J.

EQUIVOCAL PRIVATIVE CLAUSE. One which fits into the overall process of evaluation of the factors to determine the legislator's intended degree of deference and does not have the preclusive effect of a full privative clause.

EQUIVOCATION. *n.* " . . . [W]here the meaning of the testator's words is neither ambiguous nor obscure, and . . . the devise is on the face of it perfect and intelligible, but, from some of the circumstances admitted in proof, an ambiguity arises, as to which of the two or more things, or which of the two or more persons (each answering the words in the will,) the testator intended to express." *Doe d. Hiscocks v. Hiscocks* (1839), 5 M. & W. 362 at 368-9, 151 E.R. 154 (U.K.).

ERECT. *v.* To build; construct; set up.

ERGONOMICS. *n.* The study of the relationship between a person and their working environment. An ergonomic practice assessment is designed to identify ergonomic compromises in the plaintiff's practice which may be increasing the risk for development of repetitive strain injuries. *Best v. Paul Revere Life Insurance Co.*, 2000 MBCA 81, [2000] 10 W.W.R. 441, 49 C.P.C. (4th) 38, 150 Man. R. (2d) 105 (C.A.).

EROTIC. See SERVICES DESIGNED TO APPEAL TO ~ OR SEXUAL APPETITES OR INCLINATIONS.

ERRANT. *adj.* Wandering.

ERRATA. *n.* [L.] Errors.

ERRATUM. *n.* [L.] Error.

ERRED IN LAW. " . . . [C]apable of several different meanings. . . [for example] the trial judge offended against case authority binding on him . . . the trial judge's conclusion is not in accord with the evidence." *Mallen v. Mallen* (1992), 40 R.F.L. (3d) 114 at 133, 65 B.C.L.R. (2d) 241, 11 B.C.A.C. 262, 22 W.A.C. 262 (C.A.), Gibbs J.A.

ERROR. *n.* 1. Incorrect information, and includes omission of information. *Vital Statistics acts.* 2. In old common law practice, a mistake in the proceeding which either the court in which it occurred or a superior court must correct. See ACCEPTANCE LIMITS OF ~; ARBI-

TRAL ~; CLERICAL ~; IN-SERVICE LIM-ITS OF ~; JURISDICTIONAL ~; MERE ~ OF LAW; OFFICIALLY INDUCED ~; RE-VIEWABLE ~; WRIT OF ~.

ERRORES AD SUA PRINCIPIA RE-FERRE, EST REFELLERE. [L.] To refute errors, go back to their origin.

ERROR FRUTATUS NUDA VERITATE IN MULTIS EST PROBABILIOR; ET SAEPE-NUMERO RATIONIBUS VINCIT VERI-TATEM ERROR. [L.] A well-dressed error often seems more probable than naked truth; it repeatedly conquers truth by reasoning.

ERROR IN DESIGN. A mistake in judgment based on an incorrect belief as to the existence of matters of fact. Does not necessarily imply negligence or other blameworthiness. *B.C. Rail Ltd. v. American Home Assurance Co.* (1991), 54 B.C.L.R. (2d) 228 (C.A.).

ERROR IN LAW." . . . [I]n construing a will, deed, contract, prospectus or other commercial document . . . it is an error in law to attribute a fixed meaning to a word of variable connotation by selecting one of alternative dictionary definitions without regard to the context of the paragraph or sentence in which the word is used." *R. v. Alberta Giftwares Ltd.* (1973) 11 C.P.R. (2d) 233 at 237, [1974] S.C.R. 584, [1973] 5 W.W.R. 458, 11 C.C.C. (2d) 513, 36 D.L.R. (3d) 321, the court per Ritchie J.

ERROR IN OBJECTO. See TRANSFERRED INTENT.

ERROR IN PRINCIPLE. Connotes, at least, failing to take into account a relevant factor, taking into account an irrelevant factor, failing to give sufficient weight to relevant factors, overemphasizing relevant factors and, more generally, it includes an error of law. *R. v. Rezaie* (1996), 31 O.R. (3d) 713 (C.A.), per Laskin J.A.

ERROR NOMINIS. [L.] A mistake as to a person's name.

ERROR OF LAW. 1. An error of law is defined as any decision that is an erroneous interpretation or application of the law. If an error deprives the accused of a fair trial, it constitutes a miscarriage of justice. *R. c. Arradi*, 2003 SCC 23. 2. " . . . [A]n error committed by an administrative tribunal in good faith in interpreting or applying a provision of its enabling Act, of another Act, or of an agreement or other document which it has to interpret and apply within the limits of its jurisdiction." *C.A.W. v. Nova Scotia Labour*

Relations Board (1988), 89 C.L.L.C. 14,003 at 12,017, 87 N.S.R. (2d) 61, 222 A.P.R. 61 (T.D.), Grant J. See MERE ~.

ERROR OF LAW ON THE FACE OF THE RECORD. The most authoritative definition of error of law on the face of the record is found in *Champsey Bhara & Co. v. Jivraj Balloo Spinning & Weaving Co.*, [1923] A.C. 480 (India P.C.) at p. 487: An error of law on the face of the record means that you can find in the award or a document actually incorporated therewith, as for instance a note appended by the arbitrator stating the reasons for judgment, some legal proposition which is the basis of the award and which you can then say is erroneous.

ERROR PERSONAE. [L.] Mistaken identity.

ERROR QUI NON RESTITUR, APPRO-BATUR. [L.] The one who is able to rectify a mistake but does not is deemed to have approved.

ERRORS AND OMISSIONS EXCEPTED. A phrase intended to excuse small mistakes or oversights in an account or document.

ERRORS AND OMISSIONS INSURANCE. Insurance which protects against defamation, invasion of privacy, violation of intellectual property rights.

ERRORS EXCEPTED. A phrase intended to excuse a small mistake or oversight in a stated account.

ESCALATION CLAUSE. 1. Clause in lease providing for increases in rent based on some factor such as tax increases. 2. Clause in wage contract or collective agreement providing for a raise in rate of pay based on a factor such as the Consumer Price Index.

ESCALATOR. *n.* 1. A moving, inclined, continuous stairway or runway used for raising or lowering passengers. 2. A power-driven, inclined, continuous stairway or runway affixed to a building or structure that is used for lifting or lowering persons and that serves two or more floors or permanent levels of the building or structure, and includes its hoistway enclosure.

ESCALATOR CLAUSE. See ESCALATION CLAUSE.

ESCAPE. *v.* Breaking prison, escaping from lawful custody or, without lawful excuse, being at large before the expiration of a term of imprisonment to which a person has been sentenced. *Criminal Code*, R.S.C. 1985, c. C-46, s. 149(2).

ESCAT PLAN. Emergency Security Control of Air Traffic Plan. *Canadian Aviation Regulations*, SOR/96-433, s. 101.01(1).

ESCHEAT. *n.* 1. The reversion of land or other property to the Crown when a company is dissolved or a person dies intestate without hers. 2. " . . . [A]n incident of tenure by which for the failure of heirs the feud falls back into the lord's hand by a termination of the tenure, . . ." *Ontario (Attorney General) v. Mercer* (1879), 5 S.C.R. 538 at 625, Ritchie C.J.

ESCROW. *n.* 1. Holding something in trust until a contingency happens or a condition is performed. " . . . [T]he delivery of a document in escrow is to render that document inoperative pending the conditions of the escrow being met. It is common ground that a delivery in escrow is not now confined to deeds, and it is also equally well established that the delivery need not be to a stranger. . ." *Draft Masonry (York) Co. v. PA Restoration Inc.* (1988), 48 R.P.R. 231 at 240, 29 C.L.R. 256 (Ont. Dist. Ct.), Hoilett D.C.J. See STOCK ~ TRUST.

ESPIONAGE. *n.* 1. Spying. 2. A method of information gathering—by spying, by acting in a covert way. Its use in the analogous term "industrial espionage" conveys the essence of the matter—information gathering surreptitiously. *Qu v. Canada (Minister of Citizenship & Immigration)*, 2000 CarswellNat 705, 5 Imm. L.R. (3d) 129, [2000] 4 F.C. 71 (T.D.).

ESQ. *abbr.* Esquire.

ESQUIRE. *n.* A title which confers dignity.

ESSENCE OF THE CONTRACT. Describes a provision in a contract which both parties agreed at the time they entered into the contract was so important that performance of the contract without strict compliance with that provision would be pointless.

ESSENTIAL ELEMENTS. Thus the elements of the invention are identified as either essential elements (where substitution of another element or omission takes the device outside the monopoly), or non-essential elements (where substitution or omission is not necessarily fatal to an allegation of infringement). For an element to be considered non-essential and thus substitutable, it must be shown either (i) that on a purposive construction of the words of the claim it was clearly *not* intended to be essential, or (ii) that at

the date of publication of the patent, the skilled addressees would have appreciated that a particular element could be substituted without affecting the working of the invention, i.e., had the skilled worker at that time been told of both the element specified in the claim and the variant and "asked whether the variant would obviously work in the same way", the answer would be yes: *Improver Corp. v. Remmington Consumer Products Ltd.* (1989), [1990] F.S.R. 181 (Eng. Patents Ct.), at p. 192. In this context, I think "work in the same way" should be taken for our purposes as meaning that the variant (or component) would perform substantially the same function in substantially the same way to obtain substantially the same result. *Free World Trust c. Électro Santé Inc.*, 2000 CarswellQue 2728, 2000 SCC 66, 194 D.L.R. (4th) 232, 263 N.R. 150, [2000] 2 S.C.R. 1024, 9 C.P.R. (4th) 168, Binnie, J.

ESSENTIAL PARTS. All integral and body parts of a vehicle of a type required to be registered hereunder, the removal, alteration or substitution of which would tend to conceal the identity of the vehicle or substantially alter its appearance, model, type or mode of operation.

ESSENTIAL POWERS. See STATUS AND ~.

ESSENTIAL QUALIFICATIONS. In relation to a position or class of positions, means the minimum factors or circumstances that are necessary having regard to the nature of the duties of the position or class of positions.

ESSENTIAL SERVICES. 1. " . . . [O]ne the interruption of which would threaten serious harm to the general public or to a part of the population. *Reference re Public Service Employee Relations Act (Alberta)* (1987), (*sub nom. A. U. P. E. v. Alberta (Attorney General)*) 28 C.R.R. 305 at 348, 87 C.L.L.C. 14,021, 38 D.L.R. (4th) 161, [1987] 1 S.C.R. 313, 51 Alta. L.R. (2d) 97, [1987] 3 W.W.R. 577, 74 N.R. 99, 78 A.R. 1, [1987] D.L.Q. 225, Dickson C.J.C. (dissenting) (Wilson J. concurring). 2. A class of services designated to be maintained during strikes; employees employed in such jobs have limited or no right to strike.

ESTABLISH. *v.* 1. " . . . [P]lace[s] a burden on an accused to prove the . . . elements delineated thereafter on a balance of probabilities . . ." *R. v. Wholesale Travel Group Inc.* (1991), 67 C.C.C. (3d) 193 at 222, 4 O.R. (3d) 799n, 8 C.R. (4th) 145, 84 D.L.R. (4th) 161, 130 N.R. 1, 38 C.P.R.

(3d) 451, 49 O.A.C. 161, [1991] 3 S.C.R. 154, 7 C.R.R. (2d) 36, Lamer C.J.C. (Sopinka, Gonthier, McLachlin, Stevenson and Iacobucci JJ. concurring). 2. " . . . '[T]o prove'. . ." *R. v. Oakes* (1986), 24 C.C.C. (3d) 321 at 332, [1986] 1 S.C.R. 103, 53 O.R. (2d) 719n, 50 C.R. (3d)1,14 O.A.C. 335,19 C.R.R. 308, 26 D.L.R. (4th) 200, 665 N.R. 87, Dickson C.J.C. (Chouinard; Lamer, Wilson and Le Dain JJ. concurring). 3. " . . . [I]n the educational statutes of Ontario. . . 'set up'." *Crawford v. Ottawa (City) Board of Education*, [1971] 2 O.R. 179 at 188, 17 D.L.R. (3d) 271 (C.A.), the court per Kelly J.A.

ESTABLISHED PLACE OF BUSINESS. A place actually occupied whether continuously or at regular periods by a dealer or manufacturer where books and records are kept and a large share of the business is transacted.

ESTABLISHMENT. *n*. A place of business or the place where an undertaking or a part thereof is carried on. See COMMERCIAL ~; DEFENCE ~; EDUCATIONAL ~; FUNERAL ~; FUNERAL SERVICES~; HATCHERY ~; HEAD OF ~; INDUSTRIAL ~; MINERAL PROCESSING ~; OUTPOST ~; PERMANENT ~; RETAIL BUSINESS ~; RETAIL ~; RIDING HORSE ~; SELF-CONTAINED DOMESTIC ~; TOURIST ~.

EST. & TR. J. *abbr*. Estates & Trusts Journal.

EST. & TR. Q. *abbr*. Estates & Trusts Quarterly.

ESTATE. *n*. 1. " . . . [I]n regard to its uses in conveyances, is properly defined to mean a property which one possesses, especially property in land. It is also understood as defining the nature and quantity of interests in lands, &c." *Macdonald v. Georgian Bay Lumber Co.* (1878), 2 S.C.R. 364 at 392, Henry. 2. " . . . [A]s applied to interests in land has a well recognized meaning due to the fact that under our law a person is not deemed to be the absolute owner of land but only of something which has for a long time been designated as an 'estate' in it." *Coleman (Town) v. Head Syndicate* (1917), 11 Alta. L.R. 314 at 317, [1917] 1 W.W.R. 1074 (C.A.), Harvey C.J. 3. All the property of which a testator or an intestate had power to dispose by will otherwise than by virtue of a special power of appointment, less the amount of funeral, testamentary and administration expenses, debts and liabilities, and succession duties payable out of the estate on death. 4. Includes both real and personal property. *Intestate Succession acts*. See EQUITABLE ~; EXECUTORY ~; EXPECTANT ~; FREEHOLD ~; FUTURE ~; HEIRS, NEXT OF KIN OR ~; INSOLVENT~; LEASEHOLD ~; LIFE ~; PARTICULAR~; PERSONAL ~; QUALITY OF ~; QUANTITY OF ~; REAL ~; SERVICE ~.

ESTATE AD REMANENTIAM. [L.] Property held in fee simple.

ESTATE AND PROPERTY. All the real and personal, tangible and intangible property of a collector or vendor, whether subject to liens, charges or encumbrances or whether free and clear of liens, charges or encumbrances. *Retail Sales Tax acts*.

ESTATE CERTIFICATE. (a) A grant of probate, administration or testamentary guardianship by the Ontario Court (General Division) or the Surrogate Court made before January 1, 1995, but not a grant of double probate, a cessate grant or a grant of administration de bonis non administratis by either of those courts before that date, or the Superior Court of Justice, (b) a certificate of appointment of estate trustee issued by the Ontario Court (General Division) after December 31, 1994, but not a certificate of succeeding estate trustee or a certificate of estate trustee during litigation issued by that court after that date. *Estate Administration Tax Act*, 1998, S.O. 1998, c. 34, Sched., s. 1.

ESTATE DUTY. A tax generally imposed on "property passing" when someone dies; its rate is based on the size of the estate.

ESTATE FREEZE. A transaction which replaces growth assets, i.e. common shares of an operating business corporation, with assets of limited growth potential, i.e. referred shares, so that a ceiling approximately preferred to the value at the date of the freeze is placed on the value of those assets for capital gain and succession duty purposes. Thus any future growth in the value of the assets usually benefits subsequent generations, who become common shareholders. W. Grover & F. Iacobucci, *Materials on Canadian Income Tax*, 4th ed. (Toronto: Richard De Boo Ltd., 1980) at 793.

ESTATE IN A MINERAL. An estate in fee simple in a mineral or an estate for a life or lives in being in a mineral.

ESTATE IN LAND. Includes a statutory right given or reserved to the Crown to enter any lands or premises for the purpose of doing any work, construction, repair or maintenance in, upon, through, over or under any such lands or premises. *Builders' Lien acts.*

ESTATE PLANNING. Arranging business and property interests to pass to heirs and successors in such a way as to receive maximum benefit of laws relating to wills, income tax, estate tax, succession duty, property, insurance, securities, and so on.

ESTATE PUR AUTRE VIE. [Fr.] A grant of property to one person for the life of another.

ESTATE REPRESENTATIVE. Includes, with respect to the estate of a deceased person, (a) an executor or administrator of the estate, (b) a person entitled to act in the capacity of executor or administrator of the estate, (c) a person appointed as guardian of a person who is a beneficiary of the estate of the deceased person or as guardian of the beneficiary's property, (d) an estate trustee, (e) an estate trustee with a will, and (f) an estate trustee without a will. *Estate Administration Tax Act, 1998*, S.O. 1998, c. 34, Sched., s.1.

ESTATE TAX. A tax levied on all a deceased person's property, irrespective of its location or who may inherit it.

ESTIMATE. *n.* 1. A representation as to the future price of a consumer transaction. 2. An estimate of the total cost of work on and repairs for a vehicle. See ~S; FINAL ~.

ESTIMATES. *n.* 1. Spending estimates of the Crown transmitted to the legislature and divided into classes, each one corresponding to a separate programme and each class divided into votes, on which the House committees may make separate decisions. A. Fraser, W.A. Dawson, & J. Holtby, eds., *Beauchesne's Rules and Forms of the House of Commons of Canada*, 6th ed. (Toronto: Carswell, 1989) at 259. 2. Refers to estimates of all sums required during the year for the municipality's purposes. Estimates do not include funds for capital expenditures, which are raised partly through borrowing or received as provincial subsidy. See ESTIMATE; SUPPLEMENTARY ~.

ESTOPPEL. *n.* 1. "The essential factors giving rise to an estoppel are . . . : (1) A representation or conduct amounting to a representation intended to induce a course of conduct on the part of the person to whom the representation is made. (2) An act or omission resulting from the representation, whether actual or by conduct, by the person to whom the representation is made. (3) Detriment to such person as a consequence of the act or omission." *Greenwood v. Martin's Bank Ltd.*, [1933] A.C. 51 at 57 (U.K. H.L.), Lord Tomlin. 2. . . . [W]here one party has, by his words or conduct, made to the other a promise or assurance which was intended to affect the legal relations between them and to be acted on accordingly, then, once the other party has taken him at his word and acted on it, the one who gave the promise or assurance cannot afterwards be allowed to revert to the previous legal relations . . . subject to the qualification which he himself has so introduced, even though it is not supported in point of law by any consideration, but only by his word." *Coombe v. Coombe*, [1951] 1 All E.R. 767 at 770 (U.K.), Denning L.J. 3. " . . . [A]n evidentiary rule." *Royal Bank v. McArthur* (1985), 3 C.P.C. (2d) 141 at 146, 51 O.R. (2d) 86, 10 O.A.C. 394, 19 D.L.R. (4th) 762 (Div. Ct.), the court per Montgomery J. 4. " . . . [H]as been sought to be limited by a series of maxims: estoppel is only a rule of evidence; estoppel cannot give rise to a cause of action; estoppel cannot do away with the need for consideration, and so forth. All these can now be seen to merge into one general principle shorn of limitations. When the parties to a transaction proceed on the basis of an underlying assumption (either of fact or law, and whether due to misrepresentation or mistake, makes no difference), on which they have conducted the dealings between them, neither of them will be allowed to go back on the assumption when it would be unfair or unjust to allow him to do so. If one of them does seek to go back on it, the courts will give the other such remedy as the equity of the case demands." *Amalgamated Investment & Property Co. Ltd. v. Texas Commerce Int'l. Bank Ltd.*, [1981] 3 All E.R. 577 at 5 84 (U.K. C.A.), Lord Denning M.R. See AGENCY BY ~; CAUSE OF ACTION ~; EQUITABLE ~; ISSUE ~; PROMISSORY ~; PROPRIETARY ~; QUASI-~.

ESTOPPEL BY DEED. A person cannot dispute his own deed or deny the recitals contained in his own deed.

ESTOPPEL BY REPRESENTATION. The following elements must be present before the doctrine of estoppel by representation can be applied: a representation of fact made with the intention that it be acted upon or that a reasonable person would assume that it was intended to be acted upon; that the representee acted upon the representation; that the representee altered his position in reliance upon the representation and thereby suffered a prejudice. *Lidder v. Canada (Minister of Employment & Immigration)*, [1992] 2 F.C. 621 (C.A.), at 630.

ESTOPPEL PER REM JUDICATAM. 1. " . . . [D]irected to the capacity of the parties to an action and, where it is properly applicable, it prevents those parties from relitigating either a cause of action or an issue that has previously been decided. . ." *Masunda v. Downing* (1986), 7 R.F.L. (3d) 26 at 37, 5 B.C.L.R. (2d) 113, 27 D.L.R. (4th) 268 (S.C.), Wood J. 2. " . . . [A] generic term which in modern law includes two species. The first species . . . 'cause of action estoppel', . . . prevents a party to an action from asserting or denying, as against the other party, the existence of a particular cause of action, the non-existence or existence of which has been determined by a court of competent jurisdiction in previous litigation between the same parties. . . The second species . . . 'issue estoppel', . . . If in litigation upon one such cause of action any of such separate issues as to whether a particular condition has been fulfilled is determined by a court of competent jurisdiction, either upon evidence or upon admission by a party to the litigation, neither party can, in subsequent litigation between one another upon any cause of action which depends upon the fulfillment of the identical condition, assert that the condition was fulfilled if the court has in the first litigation determined that it was not, or deny that it was fulfilled if the court in the first litigation determined that it was." *Thoday v. Thoday*, [1964] P. 181 at 197-8 (U.K. C.A.), Diplock L.J.

ESTOVER. *n.* Alimony.

ESTRAY. *n.* 1. An animal that is running at large. 2. An animal found on the premises of a person other than its owner.

ESTREAT. *n.* 1. Now used only in connection with forfeitures, fines and recognizances; if the condition of a recognizance is broken, the recognizance is forfeited and, when it is estreated, the cognisors become the Crown's debtors. 2. Formerly, a copy of a court record. A recognizance was estreated or extracted when a copy was made from the original and sent for the proper authority to enforce. *R. v. Creelman* (1893), 25 N.S.R. 404 at 418 (C.A.), Meagher J.A.

ESTREPEMENT. *n.* 1. Spoil or waste which prejudices a tenant for life in reversion made by that tenant on any land. 2. Formerly, the power to cut down trees without it being considered waste.

ET ADJORNATUR. [L.] And it is adjourned.

ET AL. *abbr.* 1. Et alii. 2. Et alius.

ET ALIT. [L.] And others.

ET ALIUS. [L.] And another.

ETHANE. *n.* In addition to its normal scientific meaning, a mixture mainly of ethane, which may ordinarily contain some methane or propane. Alberta statutes.

ETHNIC STATION. A station that is licensed as an ethnic station. *Broadcasting Distribution Regulations*, SOR/97-555, s. 1.

ETHNOGRAPHIC ART. See OBJECT OF ~.

ETHYL ALCOHOL. Any material or substance, whether in liquid or any other form, containing any proportion by mass or by volume of absolute ethyl alcohol (C_2H_5OH). See VOLUME OF ABSOLUTE ~.

E.T.R. *abbr.* Estates & Trusts Reports, 1977-.

ET SEQ. *abbr.* 1. Et sequentes. 2. Et sequentia.

ET SEQUENTES. [L.] And those following.

ET SEQUENTIA. [L.] And the following.

ET UX. *abbr.* Et uxor.

ET UXOR. [L.] And wife.

EUNDO, MORANDO, ET REDEUNDO. [L.] By going, remaining and returning.

EUNOMY. *n.* A constitution of good, well-administered laws.

EURO-DOLLAR. *n.* A United States dollar entry in the account of a bank or bank branch located outside the United States. I.F.G. Baxter, *The Law of Banking*, 3d ed. (Toronto: Carswell, 1981) at 163.

EUROPEAN COMMISSION OF HUMAN RIGHTS. A body which individuals in member states may petition to claim a violation of the European Convention on Human Rights.

EUROPEAN CONVENTION ON HUMAN RIGHTS. A convention which came into force in 1953 and has been observed by the United Kingdom and other European countries and which guarantees many of the same civil liberties as the Canadian Charter of Rights and Freedoms.

EUROPEAN COURT. The Court of Justice of the European Community.

EUROPEAN COURT OF HUMAN RIGHTS. The court to which the European Commission on Human Rights refers some petitions for decision.

EUTHANASIA. *n.* The deliberate infliction of an intended death upon an animal.

EVADE. *v.* " . . . [I]mplies something of an underhanded or deceitful nature. In other words a deliberate attempt to escape the requirement of paying tax on income that has been earned." *R. v. Branch*, [1976] C.T.C. 193 at 196, [1976] W.W.D. 78, 76 D.T.C. 6112 (Alta. Dist. Ct.), Medhurst J. See TAX EVASION.

EVADER. *n.* A person who (a) during World War I or World War II (i) served in the naval army or air forces of Canada or Newfoundland, (ii) served in the naval, army or air forces of His Majesty or any of the countries allied with His Majesty during World War I or World War II and was domiciled in Canada or Newfoundland at the time of his enlistment, or (iii) was a person referred to in any of paragraphs (a) to (e) of the definition "civilian prisoner of war" who was a civilian, (b) landed in or entered enemy or enemy occupied territory, (c) became separated from his unit other than a person who became separated while performing duties as a special agent, and (d) evaded capture during World War I or World War II or subsequent thereto. *Compensation for Former Prisoners of War Act*, R.S.C. 1985, c. F-31, s. 2.

EVALUATION. *n.* Judgment, appraisal, rating, interpretation.

EVALUATION WELL. A well that when being drilled, is expected by the Board to penetrate a pool or oil sands deposit and which is drilled for the sole purpose of evaluation. *Oil and Gas Conservation Act*, R.S.A. 1980, c. O-6, s. 1(1). See BITUMINOUS SHALE ~.

EVAPORATED MILK. Milk from which water has been evaporated, with or without, i. added vitamin D, or ii. disodium phosphate or sodium citrate, or both.

EVAPORATED PARTLY SKIMMED MILK. Evaporated skim milk from which only part of the milk-fat has been removed.

EVAPORATED SKIM MILK. Milk that has been concentrated to at least one-half of its original volume by the removal of water, and from which any of the milk-fat has been removed, with or without added vitamin D.

EVAPORATIVE EMISSIONS. Hydrocarbons emitted into the atmosphere from a vehicle, other than exhaust emissions and crankcase emissions. *On-Road Vehicle and Engine Emission Regulations*, SOR/2003-2, s. 1(1).

EVASION. *n.* The act of escaping by the use of artifice. See TAX ~.

EVASIVE. *adj.* Describes a pleading which answers the other party's pleading by a half-denial or a half-admission or fails to answer a substantial point.

EVENT. *n.* 1. An activity at which more than one thousand persons attend or are expected to attend on any single day. *Municipal Act*, S.M. 1971, c. 27, s. 46.2. "[In the context of an award of costs] . . . the outcome of the litigation, whether it be judgment for the applicant or a settlement in its favour." *RCP Inc. v. Minister of National Revenue* (1985), 10 C.E.R. 214 at 22, [1986] 1 F.C. 485 (T.D.), Rouleau J. See CPC ~; OUTDOOR ~; SPECIAL AVIATION ~.

EVENT OF DEFAULT. An event specified in a trust indenture on the occurrence of which (i) a security interest constituted by the trust indenture becomes enforceable, or (ii) the principal, interest or other money payable under the trust indenture become or may be declared to be payable before maturity, but the event is not an event of default until all conditions prescribed by the trust indenture in connection with that event for the giving of notice or the lapse of time or otherwise have been satisfied.

EVENTUS VARIOS RES NOVA SEMPER HABET. [L.] An innovation always produces varying results.

EVERY ONE *var.* **EVERYONE**. 1. "[In s. 7 of the Charter] . . . must be read in light of the rest of the section and defined to exclude corporations and other artificial entities incapable of enjoying life, liberty or security of the person, and include only human beings." *Irwin Toy Ltd. c. Québec (Procureur général)*, [1989] 1 S.C.R. 927 at 1004, 25 C.P.R. (3d) 417, 94 N.R. 167, 58 D.L.R. (4th) 577, 24 Q.A.C. 2, 39 C.R.R. 193, Dickson C.J.C., Lamer and Wilson JJ. 2. " . . . [I]ncludes every human being who is physically present in Canada and by virtue of such presence amenable to Canadian law." *Singh v. Canada (Minister of Employment & Immigration)* (1985), 14 C.R.R. 13 at 44, [1985] 1 S.C.R.

177, 12 Admin. L.R. 137, 17 D.L.R. (4th) 422, 58 N.R. 1, Wilson J. (Dickson C.J.C. and Lamer J. concurring). 3. " . . . [I]s an expression of the same kind as 'person' and therefore includes bodies corporate unless the context requires otherwise." *R. v. Union Colliery* Co. (1900), 31 S.C.R. 81 at 88, 21 C.L.T. 153, 4 C.C.C. 400, Sedgewick J. 4. Includes Her Majesty and public bodies, bodies corporate, societies, companies and inhabitants of counties, parishes, municipalities or other districts in relation to the acts and things that they are capable of doing and owning respectively. *Criminal Code*, R.S.C. 1985, c. 46, s. 2.

EVERY ORIGINAL LITERARY, DRAMATIC, MUSICAL AND ARTISTIC WORK. Includes every original production in the literary, scientific or artistic domain, whatever may be the mode or form of its expression, such as books, pamphlets and other writings, lectures, dramatic or dramatico-musical works or compositions with or without words, illustrations, sketches and plastic works relative to geography, topography, architecture or science. *Copyright Act*, R.S.C. 1985, c. C-42, s. 2.

EVICTION. *n*. 1. The act of dispossessing; recovering land through legal action. 2. The recovery of possession of rented premises by the landlord. See CONSTRUCTIVE ~; GROUP ~.

EVIDENCE. *n*. 1. The oral and written statements and information and any actual things produced in a proceeding, anything which may be used to prove a fact or support an assertion. 2. The body of law, the rules regarding the admission of information of all forms in proceedings before a court or tribunal. 3. "One of the hallmarks of the common law of evidence is that it relies on witnesses as the means by which evidence is produced in court. As a general rule, nothing can be admitted as evidence before the court unless it is vouched for viva voce by a witness. Even real evidence, which exists independently of any statement by any witness, cannot be considered by the court unless a witness identifies it and establishes its connection to the events under consideration. Unlike other legal systems, the common law does not usually provide for self-authenticating documentary evidence." *R. v. Schwartz* (1988), 55 D.L.R. (4th) 1 at 26, [1989] 1 W.W.R. 289, 66 C.R. (3d) 251, 88 N.R. 90, [1988] 2 S.C.R. 443, 45 C.C.C. (3d) 97, 56 Man. R. (2d) 92, 39 C.R.R. 260, Dickson C.J.C. (dissenting) 4. " . . . [P]art of the procedure which signifies those rules of law whereby, it is determined what testimony is to be admitted, and what rejected in each case, and what weight is to be given to the testimony admitted. . ." *Belisle v. Moreau* (1968), 5 C.R.N.S. 68 at 70, [1968] 4 C.C.C. 229, 69 D.L.R. (2d) 530, (N.B. C.A.), the court per Hughes J.A. 5. An assertion of fact, opinion, belief or knowledge, whether material or not and whether admissible or not. 6. Anything that has a significant rational tendency to make something manifest. *Military Rules of Evidence*, C.R.C., c. 1049, s. 2. See ADMISSIBLE ~; CIRCUMSTANTIAL ~; COMMISSION ~; CONSCIOUSNESS OF GUILT ~; CONSCRIPTIVE ~; CONTRADICTORY ~; DEMONSTRATIVE ~; DERIVATIVE ~; DIRECT ~; DOCUMENTARY ~; EXPERT ~; EXTRINSIC ~; FABRICATING ~; HEARSAY ~; INCRIMINATING ~; INDIRECT ~; INTRINSIC ~; ITEM OF ~; MINUTES OF PROCEEDINGS AND ~; ORIGINAL~; PAROL ~; PAROL ~ RULE; POSITIVE ~; PRESUMPTIVE ~; PRIMA FACIE ~; PRIMARY ~; REAL ~; REBUTTAL ~; RELEVANT ~; REPLY ~; SECONDARY ~; SIMILAR FACT ~; TESTIMONIAL ~; TRACE ~; WEIGHT OF ~.

EVIDENCE-BASED MEDICINE. The use of the current best evidence in a conscientious, explicit and judicious manner, to make decisions about the care of individual patients.

EVIDENTIAL BURDEN. " . . . [T]he requirement of putting an issue into play by reference to evidence before the court . . . The party with an evidential burden is not required to convince the trier of fact of anything, only to point out evidence which suggests that certain facts existed." *R. v. Schwartz* (1988), 39 C.R.R. 260 at 288, [1989] 1 W.W.R. 289, 66 C.R. (3d) 251, 88 N.R. 90, [1988] 2 S.C.R. 443, 45 C.C.C. (3d) 97, 56 Man. R. (2d) 92, 55 D.L.R. (4th) 1, Dickson C.J.C. (dissenting).

EVIDENCE-BASED MEDICINE. The use of the current best evidence in a conscientious, explicit and judicious manner, to make decisions about the care of individual patients.

EVIDENTIARY BURDEN. Used, in contrast to persuasive burden, to describe the effect of a statutory presumption which relieves the prosecution from leading evidence to prove a material fact and used to describe the burden imposed on the defence by a mandatory rebuttable presumption that they lead evidence to avoid certain conviction. P.K. McWilliams, *Canadian Criminal*

Evidence, 3d ed. (Aurora: Canada Law Book, 1988) at 25-2 and 25-3.

EVOCATION. *n*. Withdrawal of a case from an inferior court's cognizance.

EX ABUNDANTI CAUTELA. [L.] Out of abundant caution.

EXACTION. *n*. A form of extortion in which an officer of the law takes a fee or reward where none was due, takes more than was due or takes the fee or reward before it was due.

EXACTOR. *n*. A type of bet on a race to select, in the correct order, the first two horses in the official result.

EXACTOR REGIS. [L.] The sovereign's tax collector.

EX ADVERSO. [L.] On the opposing side.

EX AEQUO ET BONO. [L. out of what is equal and good] In equity and good conscience.

EXAMINATION. *n*. 1. The questioning of a person under oath. 2. Any procedure whereby an immigration officer determines whether a person seeking to come into Canada may be allowed to come into Canada or may be granted admission. *Immigration Act*, R.S.C. 1985, c. I-2, s. 2(1). 3. The examination of an unclothed body with or without the removal of body tissue or fluids for the purpose of toxicological examinations. See BAR ADMISSION ~; CLINICAL ~; COMMODITY SUPERVISORS' ~; CROSS-~ DIRECT ~; EMPLOYMENT ~; EXTERNAL ~; MEDICAL ~; NATIONAL COMMODITY FUTURES ~; PRELIMINARY ~; PROMOTIONAL ~; PROMOTION ~; RE-~; REGISTERED REPRESENTATIVE ~; SPECIAL ~.

EXAMINATION FOR DISCOVERY. 1. ". . . [E]mbraces two main elements: discovery of facts in the hands of an adversary and, the obtaining of admission for use in evidence. . ." *Minute Muffler Installations Ltd.* v. *Alberta* (1981), 23 C.P.C. 52 at 54, 16 Alta. L.R. (2d) 35, 23 L.C.R. 128, 30 A.R. 447 (C.A.), the court per Stevenson J.A. 2. ". . . [A]n examination of the opposite party or an opposite party. . . [and] is in the nature of a cross-examination . . ." *Stoikopoulous* v. *Remenda* (1985), 3 C.P.C. (2d) 303 at 305, 39 Sask. R. 58 (Q.B.), Estey J.

EXAMINATION IN AID OF EXECUTION. A creditor examining the judgment debtor or other people to determine the debtor's ability to settle the judgment.

EXAMINATION-IN-CHIEF. *n*. Questioning of a witness by the counsel for the party who called that witness to adduce evidence which supports the case of that party.

EXAMINED COPY. A copy proved to have been compared with the original and to correspond to it. *Military Rules Evidence* C.R.C., c. 1049, s. 2.

EXAMINER. *n*. 1. A person whom a court appoints to examine witnesses in an action. 2. A person appointed to examine into and pass upon the qualifications of a person applying for a driver's licence. 3. A functionary jurisdiction to enforce and conduct a examination, make an order or issue a warrant. See FINGERPRINT ~; MINE ~; OFFICIAL~; SPECIAL ~.

EXAMINER. *abbr*. Examiner (L'Observateur) (Que.).

EXAMINER (L'OBSERVATEUR). *abbr*. Examiner (L'Observateur) (1861).

EXAMINING BOARD. A body established for the purpose of assessing the vocational qualifications of adults in a trade or vocation.

EXAMINING WAREHOUSE. A warehouse for the safekeeping, examination and appraisal by customs of goods. See HIGHWAY FRONTIER ~.

EX ANTECEDENTIBUS ET CONSEQUENTIBUS FIT OPTIMA INTERPRETATIO. [L.] The best interpretation is made by referring to what goes before and to what comes after.

EX ASSENSU PATRIS. [L.] With the father's assent.

EXCAMBIATOR. *n*. A broker; one who exchanges lands.

EXCAMBIUM. *n*. An exchange; a place where traders meet to do business.

EX CATHEDRA. [L.] With the weight of authority.

EXCAVATE. *v*. Includes the preparation of land for excavation and removal of hills, sand dunes, knolls, stones and rocks other than metallic ores from the general surface of the ground.

EXCAVATION. *n*. The space created by the removal of soil, rock or fill for the purposes of construction.

EXCAVATION PIT. Any excavation in the ground opened for the purpose of searching for or removing clay, gravel, sand, shale, subsoil, topsoil, rock or any other surface or subterranean deposit, but does not include an excavation made within the boundaries of a highway.

EXCELLENCY. *n*. The title of the Governor General.

EXCEPTION. In a conveyance, refers to something in existence prior to the conveyance but which is not conveyed, remains in the transferor. See STATE OF MIND ~.

EXCEPTIONAL PUPIL. A pupil whose behavioural, communicational, intellectual, physical or multiple exceptionalities are such that he or she is considered to need placement in a special education program by a committee established under subparagraph iii of paragraph 5 of subsection 11(1), of the board, (a) of which the pupil is a resident pupil, (b) that admits or enrols the pupil other than pursuant to an agreement with another board for the provision of education, or (c) to which the cost of education in respect of the pupil is payable by the Minister. *Education Act*, R.S.O. 1990, c. E.2, s. 1(1).

EXCEPTIONAL CIRCUMSTANCES. [Allowing an arbitration board to adopt another penalty when reinstatement would otherwise be appropriate remedy] cannot be categorized or limited, but have been described as those that "total destroy" the viability of the employment relationship. These circumstances must be rare and truly exceptional . . . An examination of cases finding "extraordinary circumstances" shows that they usually involve an employee engaging in culpable behaviour, particularly theft or other deceit. There are very few cases of "extraordinary circumstances" where the conduct of the employee was non- culpable. *A.U.P.E. v. Lethbridge Community College*, 2002 ABCA 125, [2002] 8 W.W.R. 299 (C.A.).

EXCEPTIONS CLAUSE. A clause in a contract which excludes liability.

EXCEPTIO PROBAT REGULAM DE REBUS NON EXCEPTIS. [L.] An exception proves the rule concerning the unexceptional things.

EXCEPTIO SEMPER ULTIMA PONENDA EST. [L.] An exception should always be put last.

EXCEPTIS EXCIPIENDIS. [L.] Including all exceptions.

EXCERPTA. *n*. [L.] Extracts.

EXCERPT. *n*. An extract.

EXCESS COVERAGE. " . . . [C]overage whereby liability attaches only after a predetermined amount of primary coverage has been exhausted." *Privest Properties Ltd. v. Foundation Co. of Canada Ltd.*, [1991] I.L.R. 1-2737 at 1355, 57 B.C.L.R. (2d) 88, 6 C.C.L.I. (2d) 23 (S.C.), Drost J.

EXCESS INSURANCE. " . . . [I]nsurance in addition to the insurance which is first in order of liability for loss." *Canadian General Insurance Co. v. State Farm Mutual Automobile Insurance Co.*, [1957] O.R. 258 at 265, [1957] I.L.R. 1-260, 8 D.L.R. (2d) 257 (C.A.), Laidlaw J.A.

EXCESSIVE. *adj*. Extreme; out of the ordinary.

EXCESSIVE DISTRESS. Refers to a situation where the rent distrained for is due but good of a higher value are distrained and to the situation where distress is made for more rent than is due and goods of a value higher than the rent due or the amount distrained for are taken.

EXCESSIVE FORCE. 1. Every one who is authorized by law to use force is criminally responsible for any excess thereof according to the nature and quality of the act that constitutes the excess. *Criminal Code*, R.S.C. 1985, c. C-46, s. 26. 2. "Where excessive force in self-defence has been recognized as a substantive doctrine, it would appear that the following conditions, at least, are necessary to give rise to that qualified defence: (a) The accused must have been justified in using some force to defend himself against an attack, real or reasonably apprehended. (b) The accused must have honestly believed that he was justified in using the force he did. (c) The force used was excessive only because it exceeded what the accused could reasonably have considered necessary." *R. v. Trecroce* (1980), 55 C.C.C. (2d) 202 at 211 (Ont. C.A.), Martin J.A.

EXCESSIVE USER. An act done by the holder of a servient tenement which goes beyond the grant of easement to which he is entitled.

EXCESS OF LOSS REINSURANCE. "[T]he reinsurer agrees to indemnify the direct insurer against any loss under the direct policy in excess of an agreed amount and up to a limit of the reinsurance coverage. . . words having a technical meaning peculiar to the field of marine reinsurance." *Canadian International Marine Underwriters Ltd. v. Symonds General Insur-*

ance Co., [1986] I.L.R. 1-2042 at 7866 (Ont. H.C.), Griffiths J.

EXCHANGE. *n.* 1. When the consideration is giving other goods, it is a contract of barter or exchange. G.H.L. Fridman, *Sale of Goods in Canada*, 3d ed. (Toronto: Carswell, 1986) at 22. 2. " . . . [T]he act of giving or taking one thing for another. . ." *Deyell v. Deyell* (1991), 90 Sask. R. 81 at 87 (C.A.), Cameron J.A. 3. A building or location where agents, merchants, brokers, bankers and others meet at certain times to trade. 4. A group of persons formed for the purpose of exchanging reciprocal contracts of indemnity or inter-insurance with each other through the same attorney. 5. The value of one country's currency expressed in the terms of another. See BILL OF ~; COMMODITY ~; COMMODITY FUTURES ~; DRY ~; FILM ~; INTER-INSURANCE ~; LIVESTOCK ~; RATE OF ~; RECIPROCAL ~; RECIPROCAL OR INTER-INSURANCE ~; STOCK ~; TOBACCO AUCTION ~; VIDEO ~; WINNIPEG GRAIN AND PRODUCE ~ CLEARING ASSOCIATION LIMITED; WINNIPEG GRAIN ~.

EXCHANGE CONTRACT. A futures contract or an option that meets both of the following requirements: (a) its performance is guaranteed by a clearing agency; (b) it is traded on an exchange pursuant to standardized terms and conditions set forth in that exchange's bylaws, rules or regulatory instruments, at a price agreed on when the futures contract or option is entered into on the exchange, and includes another instrument or class of instruments that meets both of those requirements and is designated as an exchange contract in an order the commission may make for the purpose of this definition.

EXCHANGE SYSTEM. A system for issuing tickets on a daily double in which the holder of a winning ticket on the first race of the daily double is entitled to exchange it for a ticket on the second race of the daily double.

EXCHEAT. See ESCHEAT.

EXCHEQUER BILL. A bank-note, bond, note, debenture or security that is issued or guaranteed by Her Majesty under the authority of Parliament or the legislature of a province. *Criminal Code*, R.S.C. 1985, c. C-46, s. 321.

EXCHEQUER BILL PAPER. Paper that is used to manufacture exchequer bills. *Criminal Code*, R.S.C. 1985, c. C-46, s. 321.

EXCHEQUER COURT. The Exchequer Court of Canada, replaced by The Federal Court in 1971. See JUDGE OF THE ~; PRESIDENT OF THE ~.

EXCISE. See SUBJECT TO ~.

EXCISE DIVISION. The district or territory under the survey of the collector. *Excise Act*, R.S.C. 1985, c. E-14, s. 3.

EXCISE DUTY. A tax on the distribution or manufacture of goods.

EXCISE STAMP. A stamp prepared for the purposes of this Act pursuant to a direction of the Minister under section 60. *Excise Tax Act*, R.S.C. 1985, c. E-15, s. 2.

EXCISE TAXES. 1. The taxes imposed under the Excise Tax Act. 2. Taxes on the quantity of goods manufactured.

EXCISION. For greater certainty, in this section, "wounds" or "maims" includes to excise, infibulate or mutilate, in whole or in part, the labia majora, labia minora or clitoris of a person, except where (a) a surgical procedure is performed, by a person duly qualified by provincial law to practise medicine, for the benefit of the physical health of the person or for the purpose of that person having normal reproductive functions or normal sexual appearance or function; or (b) the person is at least eighteen years of age and there is no resulting bodily harm. *Criminal Code*, R.S.C. 1985, c. C-46, s. 268(1).

EXCLAMATION. See SPONTANEOUS ~.

EXCLUSION. *n.* 1. Of a witness is at the discretion of the trial judge who may, at any party's request, order that the witness stay out of the courtroom until called to give evidence 2. " . . . [A] term or provision of an insurance policy . . ." *Ben's Ltd. v. Royal Insurance Co.*, [1985] I.L.R. 1-1969 at 7574, 7 C.C.E.L. 57, 68 N.S.R. (2d) 379, 159 A.P.R. 379 (T.D.), MacIntosh J.

EXCLUSION CLAUSE. A clause that removes certain obligations from consideration or limits a party's liabilities for not performing or misperforming the contract. G.L. Fridman, *Sale of Goods in Canada*, 3d ed. (Toronto: Carswell 1986) at 282.

EXCLUSIVE ACCOUNTING PRACTICE. The performance of an audit or a review, but does not include activities related solely to record keeping, cost accounting or compilation services or the preparation of income tax information. Alberta statutes.

EXCLUSIVE AGENT. An agent with the sole right to act on the principal's behalf in regard of a particular transaction, type of transaction or property.

EXCLUSIVE BARGAINING RIGHT. The right of the union, which is designated as bargaining representative, to bargain collectively for all employees in the unit which it represents.

EXCLUSIVE DEALING. (a) Any practice whereby a supplier of a product, as a condition of supplying that product to a customer, requires that customer to (i) deal only or primarily in products supplied by or designated by the supplier or his nominee or (ii) refrain from dealing in a specified class or kind of product except as supplied by the supplier or his nominee, and (b) any practice whereby a supplier of a product induces a customer to meet a condition set out in subparagraph (a)(i) or (ii) by offering to supply the product to him on more favourable terms or conditions if the customer agrees to meet the condition set out in either of those subparagraphs. *Combines Investigation Act*, R.S.C. 1985, c. C-34, s. 39.

EXCLUSIVE DISTRIBUTOR. In relation to a book, a person who (a) has, before or after the coming into force of this definition, been appointed in writing, by the owner or exclusive licensee of the copyright in the book in Canada, as (i) the only distributor of the book in Canada or any part of Canada, or (ii) the only distributor of the book in Canada or any part of Canada in respect of a particular sector of the market, and (b) meets the criteria established by regulations made under section 2.6, and, for greater certainty, if there are no regulations made under section 2.6, then no person qualifies under this definition as an "exclusive distributor". *Copyright Act*, R.S.C. 1985, c. C-42, s. 2.

EXCLUSIVE ECONOMIC ZONE. 1. (a) In relation to Canada, means the exclusive economic zone of Canada as determined under the *Oceans Act* and includes the seabed and subsoil below that zone, and (b) in relation to any other state, means the exclusive economic zone of the other state as determined in accordance with international law and the domestic laws of that other state. *Interpretation Act*, R.S.C. 1985, c. I-21, s. 35(1). 2. The exclusive economic zone of Canada consists of an area of the sea beyond and adjacent to the territorial sea of Canada that has as its inner limit the outer limit of the territorial sea of Canada and as its outer limit (*a*) subject to paragraph (*b*), the line every point of which is at a distance of 200 nautical miles from the nearest point of the baselines of the territorial sea of Canada; or (*b*) in respect of a portion of the exclusive economic zone of Canada for which geographical coordinates of points have been prescribed pursuant to subparagraph 25(*a*)(iii), lines determined from the geographical coordinates of points so prescribed. *Oceans Act*, S.C. 1996, c. 31, s. 13.

EXCLUSIVE JURISDICTION CLAUSE. A clause which states that a tribunal has exclusive and unreviewable jurisdiction to decide issues before it.

EXCLUSIVE LISTING. An agreement in writing between a broker and a vendor of real estate, under which the broker has the exclusive right to negotiate a sale or lease of the real estate described therein.

EXCLUSIVE POSSESSION. The right to occupy premises without any interference by another person.

EXCLUSIVE RIGHT OF WAY. When used in connection with a bus service means a roadway, including entrances and exits, constructed for use by buses and upon which the public is not permitted to drive motor vehicles but not including accesses to stations and stops, or turning, storage and service facilities not otherwise associated with such a right of way, nor a reserved bus lane on an existing road.

EXCLUSIVE USE PORTION. A part of the common elements that is to be used by the owners of one or more designated units and not by all the owners.

EXCLUSIVITY. *n*. The constitutional doctrine which provides that each head of federal power grants power to the federal government and denies the same power to the provincial governments.

EXCOMMUNICATION. *n*. An ecclesiastical punishment in which a person is expelled from membership in the church.

EX CONCESSIS. [L. from what was conceded] Admittedly.

EX CONTRACTU. [L.] From contract.

EX. C.R. *abbr*. 1. Exchequer Court of Canada Reports. 2. Exchequer Court Reports of Canada, 1875-1922.

[] EX. C.R. *abbr*. Canada Law Reports Exchequer Court, 1923-1971.

EX. CT. *abbr*. Exchequer Court.

EXCULPATORY CONFESSION. A statement which relieves the person giving it of guilt or responsibility.

EXCULPATORY OPINION. An exculpatory opinion is called an "exclusion"; the suspect is excluded from the group of possible donors of the questioned sample. A difference of two base pairs or more [in mitochondrial DNA sequencing] is required by the FBI for an exclusion. *R. v. Murrin* (1999), 1999 CarswellBC 3015, 181 D.L.R. (4th) 320, 32 C.R. (5th) 97 (S.C.).

EX CURIA. [L.] Out of court.

EXCURSION BOAT. A boat which is used to transport the public on pleasure excursions.

EXCURSION CRAFT. See WATER ∼.

EXCUSABLE CONDUCT. Conduct which is acceptable, carries no legal consequences.

EXCUSAT AUT EXTENUAT DELICTUM IN CAPITALIBUS QUOD NON OPERATOR IDEM IN CIVILIBUS. [L.] In capital cases, a wrong is excused or diminished which would not be treated the same way in civil cases.

EXCUSE. *n*. "[In criminal theory] . . . concedes the wrongfulness of the action but asserts that the circumstances under which it was done are such that it ought not to be attributed to the actor. The perpetrator who is incapable, owing to a disease of the mind, of appreciating the nature and consequences of his acts, the person who labours under a mistake of fact, the drunkard, the sleepwalker: these are all actors of whose 'criminal' actions we disapprove intensely, but whom, in appropriate circumstances, our law will not punish." *R. v. Perka* (1984), 13 D.L.R. (4th) 1 at 12, [1984] 2 S.C.R. 232, [1984] 6 W.W.R. 289, 42 C.R. (3d) 113, 55 N.R. 1, 14 C.C.C. (3d) 385, Dickson J. See JUSTIFICATION; LAWFUL ∼.

EXCUSS. *n*. Distress.

EXCUSSION. *n*. Legal seizure.

EX. D. *abbr*. Law Reports, Exchequer Division, 1875-1890.

EX DEBITO JUSTITIAE. [L.] 1. The remedy to which an applicant is rightfully entitled. 2. " . . . To say in a case that the writ should issue ex debito justitiae simply means that the circumstances militate strongly in favour of the issuance of the writ rather than for refusal. . ." *Harelkin v. University of Regina* (1979), 96 D.L.R.

(3d) 14 at 41, [1979] 2 S.C.R. 561, 16 N.R. 364, [1979] 3 W.W.R. 676, Beetz J. (Martland, Pigeon and Pratte JJ. concurring).

EX DELICTO. [L.] From wrong or tort. See ACTION ∼.

EX DIUTURNITATE TEMPORIS OMNIS PRAESUNUNITUR ESSE RITE ET SOLEMNITUR ACTA. [L.] After the passage of time, all things are presumed to have been done correctly and customarily.

EX DIV. *abbr*. Ex dividend.

EX DIVIDEND. [L. without dividend] When selling stocks and shares on which a dividend was declared or is anticipated, ex div., the buyer may not claim the dividend.

EX DOLO MALO NON ORITUR ACTIO. [L.] 1. An action does not arise from a fraud. 2. " . . . No court will lend its aid to a man who founds his cause of action upon an immoral or an illegal act. . ." *Holman v. Johnson* (1775), 1 Cowp. 341, Lord Mansfield.

EXERT. [L.] Let the person go.

EXECUTE. *v*. 1. To carry into effect; to complete. 2. Of a deed, to sign, seal and deliver it. 3. Of a judgment or court order, to enforce it or carry it into effect. 4. Of a writ, to obey the instructions within it. 5. Of an affidavit, to swear or affirm the truth and sign of the affidavit's contents before a person empowered to take an affidavit.

EXECUTED. *adj*. Completed, done.

EXECUTED CONSIDERATION. Something done in exchange for a promise.

EXECUTED CONTRACT. 1. When nothing remains for either party to do, and the transaction is complete. 2. Documents amounting to a contract which have been finalized and signed and do not require any changes or signatures.

EXECUTED TRUST. A trust after the estate is conveyed to trustees for particular beneficiaries.

EXECUTIO EST EXECUTIO JURIS SECUN-DUM JUDICIUM. [L.] Execution is the functioning of the law according to the judgment.

EXECUTIO EST FINIS ET FRUCTUS LEGIS. [L.] Execution is the object and fruit of the law.

EXECUTIO JURIS NON HABET INJURIAM. [L.] The execution of a legal process does no harm.

EXECUTION. *n*. 1. The process of enforcing or carrying out a judgment. 2. A writ of fieri facias, and every subsequent writ for giving effect to a writ of fieri facias. 3. ". . . [I]n some situations means 'signed' and in other situations means 'signed, sealed and delivered'. . ." *Johnston, Re* (1982), 43 C.B.R. (N.S.) 39 at 40, 2 P.P.S.A.C. 150 (Ont. S.C.), Saunders J. 4. Includes a writ of seizure and sale and every subsequent writ for giving effect thereto. See EQUITABLE ~; EXAMINATION IN AID OF ~; LEGAL ~; SUBSISTING ~; WRIT OF ~.

EXECUTION CREDITOR. Includes a person in whose name or on whose behalf a writ of execution is issued on a judgment.

EXECUTION OF DEEDS. The signing, sealing, and delivery of documents.

EXECUTIVE. *n*. The Crown in its administrative role; the government. This includes government officials and departments directed by ministers of the Crown and the principal executive body, the Cabinet, headed by the Prime Minister. See CHIEF ~ OFFICER; SENIOR ~.

EXECUTIVE AUTHORITY. See GOVERNING ~.

EXECUTIVE COUNCIL. The premier and members of cabinet of a province.

EXECUTIVE GOVERNMENT. The Lieutenant-Governor and the Conseil exécutif du Québec. *Interpretation Act*, R.S.Q., c. I-16, s. 61.

EXECUTIVE OFFICER. The president, vice-president, secretary and treasurer of a corporation or association.

EXECUTIVE OFFICER OF A CORPORATION. The president of the corporation, the chairman of the board of directors of the corporation, a vice-president of the corporation, the secretary of the corporation, an assistant secretary of the corporation, the treasurer of the corporation, an assistant treasurer of the corporation, or a director of the corporation.

EXECUTOR. *n*. 1. A person appointed in a testator's will to carry out directions and requests set out there and to distribute property according to the will's provisions. 2. Where used in referring to the executor of a deceased includes an executor of the will of the deceased, an administrator of the estate of the deceased, and an executor de son tort of any property of the deceased. *Succession Duty Tax acts*. See ~ OF AN ~; LIMITED ~; SUBSTITUTED ~.

EXECUTOR DE SON TORT. " . . . [A] stranger [who] takes upon himself to act as executor or administrator without any just authority (as by intermeddling with the goods of the deceased), . . ." *Raiz v. Vaserbakh* (1986), 9 C.P.C. (2d) 141 at 144 (Ont. Dist. Ct.), Trotter D.C.J.

EXECUTOR LUCRATUS. [L.] An executor who has assets in hand.

EXECUTOR OF AN EXECUTOR. When an executor dies, any interest in a testator's estate and any effects vested in that executor devolve upon the executor's executor.

EXECUTOR'S YEAR. " . . . [A] year within which to gather in the estate before a legal entitlement to demand payment arises." *Cassidy, Re* (1985), 24 E.T.R. 299 at 303, 60 A.R. 92 (Surr. Ct.), Dea J.

EXECUTORY. *adj*. Still to be effected, in contrast to executed.

EXECUTORY CONSIDERATION. " . . . [A] promise to do or forbear from doing some act in the future." *Butt v. Humber* (1976), 6 R.P.R. 207 at 216, 17 Nfld. & P.E.I.R. 92, 46 A.P.R. 92 (Nfld. T.D.), Goodridge J.

EXECUTORY CONTRACT. A contract between a buyer and a seller for the purchase and sale of goods or services in respect of which delivery of the goods or performance of the services or payment in full of the consideration is not made at the time the contract is entered into.

EXECUTORY DEVISE. Legal limitation of a future interest in lands by a will.

EXECUTORY ESTATE. An interest dependant on some subsequent contingency or event for its enjoyment.

EXECUTORY INTEREST. A legal interest in the future.

EXECUTORY LIMITATION. A limitation, by will or deed, of a future interest.

EXECUTORY TRUST. An imperfect trust which requires some act to perfect it.

EXECUTRIX. *n*. A woman appointed by a testator to carry out the instructions in the will.

EXEMPLARY DAMAGES. 1. " . . . [O]r punitive damages may be awarded where the defendant's conduct is such as to merit punishment. This may be exemplified by malice, fraud or cruelty as well as other abusive and insolent acts toward the victim. The purpose of the award is to vindicate the strength of the law and to demonstrate to the offender that the law will not tolerate conduct which wilfully disregards the rights of others." *Warner v. Arsenault* (1982), 27 C.P.C. 200 at 205, 53 N.S.R. (2d) 146, 109 A.P.R. 146 (C.A.), the court per Pace J.A. 2. Damage awards which extend beyond the class of compensatory damages have found expression in a variety of terms but the most common of these are exemplary and punitive damages. The term "exemplary" was preferred by the House of Lords, while "punitive" is the term used in many Canadian Courts. These two terms are, in effect, interchangeable. Aggravated damages are in fact a form of compensatory damages which incorporates intangible aspects of the wrong. *Carrier Lumber Ltd. v. British Columbia*, 1999 CarswellBC 1741, 47 B.L.R. (2d) 50, 30 C.E.L.R. (N.S.) 219, [1999] B.C.T.C. 192 (S.C.), Parrett, J.

EXEMPLIFICATION. *n*. The official copy of a document made under a court's or public functionary's seal.

EXEMPLI GRATIA. [L. for example] For instance.

EXEMPT FROM. " . . . '[N]ot subject to'. . ." *Victoria Municipal Voters' List, Re* (1908), 7 W.L.R. 372 at 373 (B.C. S.C.), Clement J.

EXEMPTION. *n*. 1. Immunity; being free from duty or tax. "[May arise] . . . by virtue of having never been made liable to a law or by having been made liable and then excluded from its application." *Crown Forest Industries Ltd. v. British Columbia* (1991), 4 M.P.L.R. (2d) 267 at 274, 55 B.C.L.R. (2d) 250 (C.A.), the court per Hollinrake J.A. 2. Freedom from, not being subject to, a requirement generally applicable.

EXEMPTION CLAUSE. " . . . [G]enerally [has] the effect of excluding or limiting the liability of one party to a contract and . . . generally, but not always, appear[s] in standard form contracts widely used in commercial matters. . ." *Bauer v. Bank of Montreal* (1980), 10 B.L.R. 209 at 217, 33 C.B.R. (N.S.) 291, [1980] 2 S.C.R. 102, 110 D.L.R. (3d) 424, 32 N.R. 191, the court per McIntyre J.

EXEMPT OFFER. (i) An offer to purchase shares by way of private agreement with fewer than 15 shareholders and not made to shareholders generally, (ii) an offer to purchase shares to be effected through the facilities of a stock exchange or in the over-the-counter market, (iii) an offer to purchase shares in a private company, (iv) an offer exempted by order of the Commission or the Court. *Securities acts*.

EXEQUATOR. *n*. [L.] A permission given by the government of one country to the commercial agent or consul of another country to discharge his or her functions in the first-mentioned country.

EXERCISE. *v*. To use.

EXERCITORIAL POWER. The trust given to the master of a ship.

EXERCITOR NAVIS. [L.] The temporary charterer or owner of a ship.

EX FACIE. [L.] On the face of it.

EX FACTO ILLICITIO NON ORITUR ACTIO. [L.] See EX TURPI CAUSA NON ORITUR ACTIO.

EX FACTO JUS ORITUR. [L.] Law is grounded in fact.

EXFREDIARE. *v*. To breach the peace.

EX GRATIA. [L.] 1. Voluntary. 2. " . . . [U]sed simply to indicate . . . that the party agreeing to pay does not admit any pre-existing liability on his part; but he is certainly not seeking to preclude the legal enforceability of the settlement itself by describing the contemplated payment as 'ex gratia'." *Edwards v. Skyways Ltd.*, [1964] 1 All E.R. 494 at 500, [1964] 1 W.L.R. 349 (U.K. Q.B.), Megaw J.

EXHAUST DUCT. A duct through which air is conveyed from a room or space to the outdoors.

EXHAUST EMISSIONS. Substances emitted into the atmosphere from any opening downstream from the exhaust port of a vehicle's engine. *On-Road Vehicle and Engine Emission Regulations*, SOR/2003-2, s. 1(1).

EXHAUSTION DOCTRINE. A doctrine which requires an applicant to exhaust all administrative remedies before resorting to the courts to challenge the validity of an order or decision made by a statutory authority.

EXHIBIT. *v*. When used in respect of film or moving pictures, means to show film for viewing for direct or indirect gain or for viewing by the public.

EXHIBIT. *n*. A document or object admitted as evidence in court.

EXHIBITANT. *n.* One who exhibits something.

EXHIBITION. *n.* 1. Showing, projecting or otherwise displaying of film in a theatre to the public. 2. A boxing match. 3. Includes carnival, fair, regatta or exposition. See FAIR OR ~; PROFESSIONAL CONTEST OR ~; PUBLIC ~; TRAVELLING ~.

EXHIBITION CORPORATION. A corporation empowered pursuant to provincial law to hold an agricultural exhibition.

EXHIBITION FACILITIES. A building or a building complex or part of a building complex intended for use for agricultural exhibitions and other purposes that, in the opinion of the Minister, would be of benefit to the citizens of surrounding communities.

EXHIBITOR. *n.* A person who engages in exhibition of films on a continual and successive basis. See ITINERANT ~.

EXHUMATION. *n.* 1. The exposure of interred human remains for viewing or for examination, whether in or removed from the lot in which the human remains had been interred. 2. Disinterring a body from a grave in a burial ground or cemetery.

EX HYPOTHESI. [L.] From the hypothesis.

EXIGENCE. *n.* Need; want; demand.

EXIGENCY. *n.* Need; want; demand.

EXIGENT. *adj.* Requiring immediate action; demanding.

EXIGIBLE. *adj.* 1. Subject to execution. 2. Able to be demanded or required.

EXIGI FACIAS. [L.] That you cause to be demanded.

EXILE. *v.* " . . . [P]resupposes a positive action by the State to compel a person to leave or to banish him from his country." *Young v. Canada (Secretary of State)* (1982), 134 D.L.R. (3d) 545 at 549, [1982] 2 F.C. 541 (T.D.), Cattanach J.

EXILE. *n.* 1. Banishment. 2 The banished person.

EX IMPROVISO. [L.] Spontaneously.

EX-INMATE. *n.* A person who was an inmate of a penitentiary and who has completed his sentence and has been legally discharged.

EXISTING ABORIGINAL RIGHTS. In section 35 of the Charter, interpreted to permit the evolution of those rights over time. May have a larger content than those rights which existed in 1982 when the Charter came into force.

EXISTING SHIP. *A* ship that is not a new ship. Canada regulations.

EXISTING SURPLUS. The amount by which the estimated value of assets in a fund exceed the estimated value of all liabilities of the fund.

EXISTING USE. The use to which land has already been put.

EXIT. *n.* 1. That part of a means of egress that leads from the floor area it serves, including any doorway heading directly from a floor area, to a public thoroughfare or to an open space. 2. i. Includes aisles, doorways, corridors, hallways, passageways, stairways, ramps, lobbies, foyers, vestibules, but ii. does not include, A. escalators, elevators, slide escapes, turnstiles, revolving doors, overhead doors, sliding doors, folding doors and doorways to enclosed courts, B. ladders, hatches or windows, except where approved as an alternate means of egress from boiler, furnace mechanical service electrical service, or other service rooms, C. ramps with a gradient in excess of one in eight, and D. doorways and passageways leading the public through boiler rooms, furnace rooms, kitchens or other service rooms. *Hotel Fire Safety Act*, R.R.O. 1980, Reg. 505, s. 2. See ACCES TO ~; HORIZONTAL ~; MEANS OF ~.

EXIT INTERVIEW. A discussion between employer and employee when the employee is about to leave employment.

EXIT LEVEL. The lowest level in an exclosed exit stairway from which an exterior door provides access to a public thoroughfare or to an open space with access to a public thoroughfare at approximately the same level either directly or through a vestibule or exit corridor.

EXIT LIGHTS. All lights required by law for the purpose of facilitating safe exit in case of fire or other emergency.

EXIT STOREY. A storey from which an exterior door provides direct access at approximately the same level to a public thoroughfare or to an open space with access to a public thoroughfare.

EXITUS. *n.* [L. issue or offspring] 1. Annual rents and profits from lands and tenements. 2. A close of pleadings; a joinder of issue.

EXLEGALITICUS. *n.* [L.] One prosecuted as an outlaw.

EX LEX. *n*. An outlaw.

EX MALEFICIO NON ORITUR CON-TRAC-TUS. [L.] A contract cannot arise from an illegal act.

EX MERO MOTU. [L.] Of one's own accord.

EX MULTITUDINE SIGNORUM COLLI-GITUR IDENTITAS VERA. [L.] True identity is pieced together from many representations.

EX NECESSITATE LEGIS. [L.] From the necessity of law.

EX NECESSITATE REI. [L.] Out of the necessity of the thing or case.

EX NEW. Without the right to the new shares which will be issued.

EX NIHILO NIHIL FIT. [L.] Nothing comes out of nothing.

EX NON SCRIPTO JUS VENIT QUOD USUS COMPROBAVIT. [L.] A body of law which custom has validated comes into existence without anything being written.

EX NUDO PACTO NON ORITUR ACTIO. [L.] An action does not arise from an agreement with no consideration.

EX OFFICIO. [L.] By virtue of one's office.

EXONERATION. *n*. Relief from liability when that liability is thrown on another person.

EXONERETUR. [L.] Let the person be discharged.

EXOR. *abbr*. Executor.

EXORDIUM. *n*. [L.] The beginning part or introduction of a speech.

EXOTIC ANIMAL. An animal of a species or type that is not indigenous to a province and that in its natural habitat is usually found wild in nature.

EXOTIC FISH. Those species of fish which are not indigenous.

EXOTIC WILDLIFE. All birds, mammals and other vertebrates that are not indigenous to a province and that in their natural habitat are usually wild by nature, and includes any part of such birds mammals or other vertebrates.

EX PACTO ILLICITO NON ORITUR AC-TIO. [L.] No action can arise out of an illegal contract.

EXPANSIBLE FLUID. (i) Any vapour or gaseous substance, or (ii) any liquid under a pressure and at a temperature that is such that the liquid will change to a gas or vapour when the pressure is reduced to atmospheric pressure.

EXPANSION COILS. See DIRECT ~.

EXPANSION LINE. The addition to any part of a rural gas utility of a pipeline to provide gas service to a location that could have been but was not supplied with gas service from that part of the rural gas utility at the time that part was constructed. *Rural Gas Act*, R.S.A. 1980, c. R-19, s. 1.

EX PARTE. [L. on behalf of] 1. "[Refers to]. . . an order made at the instance of one party without the opposite party having had notice of the application." *Anderson v. Toronto-Dominion Bank* (1986), 9 C.P.C. (2d) 179 at 183, 70 B.C.L.R. (2d) 267 (C.A.), the court per Hutcheon J.A. 2. "[Used in British Columbia Supreme Court Rules, R. 52] . . . the absence of a party on the hearing of the application and not in the usual sense of an order made in the absence of service upon an interested person." *Dasmesh Holdings Ltd. v. McDonald* (1985), 49 C.P.C. 187 at 191, 60 B.C.L.R. 80 (C.A.), the court per Hutcheon J.A. 3. The Latin words *ex parte*, translated literally, mean from one side or party only. In a judicial sense the words *ex parte* refer to a proceeding granted at the instance of and for the benefit of one party only, without notice to, or contestation by, any person adversely affected. It has been held that the defining element of an *ex parte* proceeding is the absence of notice to the other party. *Society of Composers, Authors & Music Publishers of Canada v. 960122 Ontario Ltd.*, 2003 FCA 256, 26 C.P.R. (4th) 161, 307 N.R. 390 (C.A.).

EX PARTE MATERNA. [L.] Claiming through the mother's line.

EX PARTE PATERNA. [L.] Claiming through the father's line.

EXPATRIATION. *n*. Renouncing allegiance to one's native country when one becomes the citizen of a foreign country.

EXPECTANCY. See IN ~.

EXPECTANT. *adj*. Relating to; depending on.

EXPECTANT ESTATE. An interest one will possess and enjoy at some future time, i.e. a reversion or remainder.

EXPECTANT HEIR. " . . . [P]hrase used in England in reference to a person who expects from a person then living and who is not allowed, under the circumstances, to encumber the future estate by improvident bargains." *Hall v. Marshall*, [1938] 3 D.L.R. 419 at 423, 13 M.P.R. 112 (N.S. S.C.), Doull J.

EXPECTATION. See LEGITIMATE ~; REASONABLE ~.

EXPECTATION OF LIFE. The number of years which someone of a certain age may, given equal chances, expect to live. See LOSS OF ~.

EXPECTED CLAIMS RATIO. The claims ratio that the company expects to experience under policies issued by it with respect to a particular class of insurance during the unexpired terms of the policies. *Insurance acts*.

EXPEDIENT. *adj*. That which is suitable and appropriate to accomplish a specified object.

EXPEDIMENT. *n*. The total amount of a person's gods and chattels.

EXPEDITED. *adj*. Speedy, prompt.

EXPEDITION. See SCIENTIFIC OR EXPLORATORY ~.

EXPEDIT REIPUBLICAE NE SUA RE QUIS MALE UTATUR. [L.] It is in the public interest that one should not use one's own property badly.

EXPEDIT REIPUBLICAE UT FINIS SIT LITIUM. [L.] It is in the public interest that litigation end.

EXPEND. *v*. 1. To pay out. *Richer, Re* (1919), 46 O.L.R. 367 at 371, 50 D.L.R. 614, 17 O.W.N. 195 (C.A.), Meredith C.J.C.P. 2. "[Implies] . . . a recurring act of consumption. . ." *McFarland, Re*, [1963] 1 O.R. 273 at 275 (H.C.), Grant. J.

EXPENDITURE. *n*. 1. (i) Payment authorized by a supply vote, (ii) a reimbursement under the authority of one supply vote, of a payment charged against another supply vote, (iii) a payment authorized by a statutory appropriation, other than a statutory appropriation authorizing a payment to a revolving fund, or (iv) a payment from a revolving fund. 2. Any expense made for political purposes by a political party, an association or a candidate. See ALLOWABLE ~S; BASIC CARE ~S; CAPITAL ~; CURRENT ~; ELIGIBLE EXPLORATION ~S; PETTY CASH ~; TAX ~; WORKING ~.

EXPENSAE LITIS. [L. expenses of the cause] Costs.

EXPENSE. *n*. 1. Money laid out. 2. ". . . [W]ithin the meaning of paragraph s. 18(1)(a) of the Income Tax Act [R.S.C. 1952, c. 148 (as am. S.C. 1970-71-72, c. 63, s. 1)], is an obligation to pay a sum of money. . ." *R. v. Burnco Industries Ltd.*, [1984] 2 F.C. 218 at 218, 53 N.R. 393, [1984] C.T.C. 337, 84 D.T.C. 6348 (C.A.), the court per Pratte J.A. 3. Includes, in relation to the conducting of a trial with a jury, (i) the costs of summoning a jury panel and any costs incidental to the summoning, (ii) the fees and allowances paid to jurors, (iii) costs arising from the order of a judge to view evidence . . . (iv) costs for food, refreshments, accommodation and other requirements for a jury. *Jury Act*, S.a. 1982, c. J-2.1, s. 1. See ADMINISTRATIVE ~S; ADVERTISING ~S; CAMPAIGN ~; COMMON ~S; DRILLING OR EXPLORATION ~; ELECTION ~S; ELIGIBLE COST OR ~; ELIGIBLE EXPLORATION ~; FUNERAL ~S; GENERAL ~S; LABOUR ~; LIVING ~; LIVING ~S; OPERATING ~; PERSONAL ~S; PREPAID ~; REGULATION ~S; TRAVELLING ~S; WORKING ~S.

EXPENSE ACCOUNT. A list of obligations incurred while working on behalf of one's employer.

EXPENSES LEVY. Defrayal of expenses of administering a product marketing scheme. P.W. Hogg, *Constitutional Law of Canada*, 3d ed. (Toronto: Carswell, 1992) at 650.

EXPERIENCE. See WORK ~ PROGRAM.

EXPERIENCE GAIN. The increase in the value of the assets of a plan less the liabilities of the plan determined in a going concern valuation of the plan that is attributable to the difference between the experience anticipated in the most recent actuarial report, prepared on the basis of a going concern valuation and filed with the Superintendent in accordance with section 12 of the Act, and the actual experience that has emerged since that valuation. *Pension Benefits Standards Regulations, 1985*, SOR/87-19, s. 2(1), as am.

EXPERIENCE LOSS. The decrease in the value of the assets of a plan less the liabilities of the plan determined in a going concern valuation of the plan that is attributable to the difference between the experience anticipated in the most recent actuarial report, prepared on the basis of a going concern valuation and filed with the Superintendent in accordance with section 12 of the Act, and the actual experience that has emerged since that valuation. *Pension Benefits Standards Regulations, 1985*, SOR/87-19, s. 2(1), as am.

EXPERIENCE RATING. In insurance, a means of determining rates by using the experience of losses by the insured over a period of time.

EXPERIENTIAL INCREMENT. Salary recognition or wage increment offered to employees with certain experiential qualifications.

EXPERIMENTAL PROJECT. Work or activity involving the utilization of methods of equipment that are untried or unproven.

EXPERIMENTAL SCHEME. A scheme or operation (i) for the recovery of oil sands or crude bitumen, or (ii) for the processing of crude bitumen, derivatives of crude bitumen or declared oil sands not designed for commercial purposes, utilizing methods that may be untried or unproven in a particular application and includes, but is not limited to, test and pilot schemes.

EXPERIMENTAL TREATMENT. Any treatment that poses a significant risk of harm to the patient, other than one that is: (i) commonly accepted for treatment of the mental disorder involved or supported by widely accepted scientific studies; and (ii) provided by a qualified health professional. *Mental Health Services Act*, S.S. 1984-85-86, c. M-13.1, s. 2.

EXPERIMENTAL WELL. A well drilled or being drilled or operated pursuant to an experimental scheme.

EXPERIMENT EVIDENCE. A combination of sworn statements and the production of things.

EXPERT. *n*. 1. ". . . [G]enerally called to testify to provide information to enable the Court or a jury to understand technical and scientific issues raised in the litigation. They are also called upon to provide opinions and conclusions in areas where the Courts or jury are unable to make the necessary inferences from the technical facts presented. The role of the expert is circumscribed by his area of expertise. It is essential that the witness be shown to possess the necessary qualifications and skill in the area or field in which his opinion is sought. Those qualifications and skill can be based on or derived from academic study or practical experience." *Rieger v. Burgess* (1988), 45 C.C.L.T. 56 at 95, [1988]

4 W.W.R. 577, 66 Sask. R. 1 (C.A.), Tallis, Cameron and Vancise JJ.A. 2. Includes engineer, valuer, accountant, and any other person whose profession gives authority to a statement made by that person. *Companies acts*.

EXPERT EVIDENCE. 1. The admissible opinion of someone whose competency to form an opinion on some subject before the court was acquired by a special course of study or experience, e.g., in engineering, foreign law or medicine. 2. The test for the admissibility of expert evidence was consolidated. Four criteria must be met by a party which seeks to introduce expert evidence: relevance, necessity, the lack of any other exclusionary rule, and a properly qualified expert. Even where these requirements are met, the evidence may be rejected if its prejudicial effect on the conduct of the trial outweighs its probative value. *R. v. D. (D.)*, 2000 CarswellOnt 3255, 2000 SCC 43, 36 C.R. (5th) 261, 148 C.C.C. (3d) 41, 191 D.L.R. (4th) 60, 259 N.R. 156, 136 O.A.C. 201, [2000] 2 S.C.R. 275. See also necessity.

EXPERT WITNESS. "[F]unction . . . is to provide for the jury or other trier of fact an expert's opinion as to the significance of, or the inference which may be drawn from, proved facts in a field in which the expert witness possess special knowledge and experience going beyond that of the trier of fact. The expert witness is permitted to give such opinions for the assistance of the jury. . ." *R. v. Béland* (1987), 36 C.C.C. (3d) 481 at 493, 79 N.R. 263, 9 Q.A.C. 293, [1987] 2 S.C.R. 398, 60 C.R. (3d) 1, 43 D.L.R. (4th) 641, McIntyre J. (Dickson C.J.C., Beetz and Le Dain JJ. concurring).

EXPIRATION. *n*. The running out of a term or period by effluxion of time.

EXPIRATION DATE. 1. Any date prescribed by these Regulations as the expiration date and after which a drug is not recommended for use. *Food and Drug Regulations*, C.R.C., c. 870, s. C.01.001. 2. Of a device means the date after which the device is not recommended by the manufacturer for use. 3. A date designating the end of the period during which a veterinary biologic, when properly stored and handled, may be expected to be effective.

EXPIRATION OF BID. The later of: (i) the expiration of the period, including any extensions, during which securities may be deposited under a bid; and (ii) the time at which the offeror becomes obligated by the terms of the bid to take up or reject securities deposited under the bid. *Securities acts.*

EXPIRATIONS. *n.* "[I]n the insurance field . . . embodies the records of an insurance agency by which the agent has available a copy of the policy issued to the insured or records containing the date of the insurance policy, the name of the insured, the date of its expiration, the amount of insurance, premiums, property covered and terms of insurance. This information enables the agent to contact the insured before the existing contract expires . . ." *Economical Mutual Fire Insurance Co. v. Cherry & Sons* (1962), 36 D.L.R. (2d) 1 at 2, [1963] S.C.R. 93, the court per Ritchie J. adopting the definition of the U.S. Court of Appeals in *V.L. Phillips & Co. v. Pennsylvania Threshermen & Farmers' Mutual Casualty Ins. Co.* (1952), 199 F. (2d) 244 at 246.

EXPIRY DATE. The earlier of (*a*) the date, expressed at minimum as a year and month, up to and including which a natural health product maintains its purity and physical characteristics and its medicinal ingredients maintain their quantity per dosage unit and their potency, and (*b*) the date, expressed at minimum as a year and month, after which the manufacturer recommends that the natural health product should not be used. *Natural Health Products Regulations*, SOR/2003-196, s. 1(1).

EXPLANATORY NOTE. Technically not part of a bill and printed on the page across from the relevant clause. A. Fraser, W.A. Dawson, & J. Holtby, eds., *Beauchesne's Rules and Forms of the House of Commons of Canada*, 6th ed. (Toronto: Carswell, 1989) at 194.

EXPLANATORY PLAN. A plan that (a) is not based on a survey but on existing descriptions, plans or records of the land title office, and (b) is certified correct in accordance with the records of the land title office by a British Columbia land surveyor or by a person designated under section 121 (7) of the *Forest Act* or section 5 (3) of the *Highway Act* for the purposes of those sections. *Land Title Act*, R.S.B.C. 1996, c. 250, s. 1.

EXPLICIT KNOWLEDGE. Anything written or stored electronically in a form that is easy to reproduce and distribute, for example memoranda, books, videos.

EXPLOITATION. *n.* ". . . [T]he action of turning to account or utilizing for selfish purposes." *R. v. Cameron* (1966), 49 C.R. 49, at 78, [1966] 2 O.R. 777, [1966] 4 C.C.C. 273, 58 D.L.R. (2d)

486 (C.A.), Laskin J.A. (dissenting). See AGRICULTURAL ~.

EXPLORATION. *n.* Any operations on or over land or water to determine geologic or other conditions underlying the surface of land or water. See ADVANCED ~; GEOPHYSICAL ~; GEOTHERMAL ~; MINERAL ~.

EXPLORATION LICENCE. *var.* **EXPLORATION LICENSE.** 1. A licence to explore lands for the purpose of finding petroleum and natural gas there. 2. A license by which the holder thereof is granted the right to search and prospect for minerals on a designated area for a period of one year.

EXPLORATION OPERATIONS. Any work or acts done in connection with or incidental to exploration.

EXPLORATORY EXPEDITION. See SCIENTIFIC OR ~.

EXPLORATORY PROGRAM. A geological or geophysical study, investigation, reconnaissance or survey undertaken to establish the geological or physical settings of a mineral.

EXPLORATORY WELL. 1. A well other than a development well or delineation well. 2. A well drilled on a geological feature on which a significant discovery has not been made. 3. A well that is bored, drilled or deepened for the purpose of discovering a pool of oil or gas. *Petroleum Resources Act*, R.R.O. 1980, Reg. 752, s. 1.

EXPLORATORY WORK. Work in connection with or incidental to searching, drilling or testing for oil or gas and includes geological, geochemical or geophysical examinations.

EXPLORE. See TO PROSPECT AND TO ~.

EXPLOSION. *n.* "[I]mplies . . . a sudden expansion of a liquid substance, with the result that the gas generated by the expansion escapes with violence, usually causing a loud noise. . ." *Canadian General Electric Co. v. Liverpool & London & Globe Insurance Co.* (1980), 27 O.R. (2d) 401 at 407, [1980] I.L.R. 1-1201, 106 D.L.R. (3d) 750 (C.A.), the court per Wilson J.A. adopting the definition in *Bolich v. Provident Life & Accident Ins. Co.* (1933), 169 S.E. 826 at 828 (North Carolina S.C.).

EXPLOSION-HAZARD LOCATION. Any location where gasoline or an associated product that can produce a dangerous atmosphere is stored, or where leakage or spillage of the gasoline or associated products could occur and includes service stations, bulk plants, tank truck or tank car filling facilities, storage areas for packaged Class I or Class II gasoline or associated products, or empty containers and pump houses.

EXPLOSION INSURANCE. 1. Insurance against loss of or damage to property of any kind caused by explosion, bombardment, invasion, insurrection, riot, civil war or commotion or military or usurped power. 2. Insurance against loss of or damage to the property insured caused by explosion of steam boilers and pipes and engines and machinery connected therewith. 3. Insurance against the loss of, or damage to, property caused by explosion and includes insurance coming within the class of civil commotion insurance. See LIMITED OR INHERENT ~.

EXPLOSION-PROOF. *adj.* Enclosed in a case which is capable of withstanding without damage an explosion which may occur within it of a specific gas or vapour and which is also capable of preventing the ignition of a specified gas or vapour surrounding the enclosure from sparks, flashes or explosion of the specified gas or vapour within the enclosure.

EXPLOSIVE. *n.* Any thing that is made, manufactured or used to produce an explosion or a detonation or pyrotechnic effect, and includes any thing prescribed to be an explosive by the regulations, but does not include gases, organic peroxides or any thing prescribed not to be an explosive by the regulations. *Explosives Act*, R.S.C. 1985, c. E-17, s. 2. See AUTHORIZED ~; PLASTIC ~; UNMARKED PLASTIC ~.

EXPLOSIVE ACTUATED TOOL. A tool that is designed to be held in the hand and that is actuated by an explosive charge.

EXPLOSIVE OR OTHER LETHAL DEVICE. (a) An explosive or incendiary weapon or device that is designed to cause, or is capable of causing, death, serious bodily injury or substantial material damage; or (b) a weapon or device that is designed to cause, or is capable of causing, death, serious bodily injury or substantial material damage through the release, dissemination or impact of toxic chemicals, biological agents or toxins or similar substances, or radiation or radioactive material. *Criminal Code*, R.S.C. 1985, c. C-46, s. 431.2(1).

EXPLOSIVE SUBSTANCE. Includes (a) anything intended to be used to make an explosive substance, (b) anything, or any part thereof, used

or intended to be used, or adapted to cause, or to aid in causing an explosion in or with an explosive substance, (c) an incendiary grenade, fire bomb, molotov cocktail or other similar incendiary substance or device and a delaying mechanism or other thing intended for use in connection with such a substance or device. *Criminal Code*, R.S.C. 1985, c. C-46, s. 2.

EXPORT. *v.* 1. The transportation of goods from this to a foreign country. 2. ". . . [I]nvolves the idea of a severance of goods from the mass of things belonging to this country with the intention of uniting them with the mass of things belonging to some foreign country. It also involves the idea of transporting the thing exported beyond the boundaries of this country with the intention of effecting that. . ." *R. v. Carling Export Brewing & Malting Co.*, [1930] 2 D.L.R. 725 at 733, [1930] S.C.R. 351, Duff J. 2. Ship from Canada to any other country or from any province to any other province.

EXPORT. *n.* In order for there to be a sale for export, there must obviously be a person who exports. For there to be an exporter, there must be an importer. Put in a different way, a sale for export cannot exist without a corresponding purchase to import. *Deputy Minister of National Revenue v. Mattel Canada Inc.*, 2001 CarswellNat 1032, 2001 SCC 36, 29 Admin. L.R. (3d) 56, 199 D.L.R. (4th) 598, 270 N.R. 153, 12 C.P.R. (4th) 417. See COUNTRY OF ~.

EXPORT DEVELOPMENT CORPORATION. A federal corporation which offers bank guarantee and insurance services to Canadian exporters and encourages export trade by arranging credit for foreign buyers.

EXPORTED. *adj.* "A corporation is said to be 'exported' when it becomes a corporation in a different jurisdiction. . ." *Canada (Director appointed under s. 260 of the Business Corporations Act), Re* (1991), 1 B.L.R. (2d) 1 at 12, 3 O.R. (3d) 336 (Gen. Div.), Austin J.

EXPORT MARK. A trade mark used exclusively on goods which will be exported.

EXPORT MARKET. Any country to which goods of any kind are ordinarily exported from Canada.

EXPORT PERMIT. 1. A permit to export issued by a permit officer under this Act. 2. Includes any authorization in writing to remove game from a province issued by an authority thereto competent within that province.

EXPORT POWER GRID. A power grid in Canada from which electric energy may be exported.

EXPORT STANDARD SAMPLE. In respect of a grade of grain, a sample of grain of that grade designated by the Commission. *Canada Grain Act*, R.S.C. 1985, c. G-10, s. 2.

EXPORT TAX. A tax on goods to be exported.

EXPOSE. *v.* 1. To exhibit, to make visible. 2. Includes (a) a wilful omission to take charge of a child by a person who is under a legal duty to do so, and (b) dealing with a child in a manner that is likely to leave that child exposed to risk without protection. *Criminal Code*, R.S.C. 1985, c. C-46, s. 214.

EXPOSED. *adj.* Exhibited; made visible.

EXPOSED POSITION. A position that is (a) exposed to weather and sea, or (b) within a structure, so exposed, other than an enclosed superstructure.

EXPOSING BUILDING FACING. That part of the exterior wall of a building which faces one direction and is located between ground level and the ceiling of its top storey, or where a building is divided into fire compartments, the exterior wall of a fire compartment which faces one direction.

EXPOSURE THEORY. On this theory, from the first exposure to the condition or conditions which ultimately cause the property damage, that damage is inevitable, a certainty. As a result, the property damage is considered to have occurred on that first exposure so that the deterioration following that exposure is merely the manifestation of the damage that has already occurred requiring repair or replacement. *Alie v. Bertrand & Frère Construction Co.* (2002), 62 O.R. (3d) 345 (C.A.).

EXPOSITIO. *n.* [L.] A statement which explains.

EX POST FACTO. [L. by something done after] Describes a statute which, after the fact, either makes an act punishable which was not punishable when it was done, or which imposes punishment for an act which is different from what would have been inflicted when the act was done.

EXPOSURE CRITERIA. The concentration of any potentially harmful substance in the air above which a worker may or should not be exposed.

EXPOSURE RECORD. The record of a worker's exposure to harmful substances in the workplace.

EX PRAECEDENTIBUS ET CONSEQUENTIBUS EST OPTIMA INTERPRETATIO. [L.] The best interpretation comes from what precedes and follows.

EXPRESS. *adj.* 1. Clear; unambiguous. 2. Of some act showing intention, means done to communicate the intention directly, as opposed to by implication.

EXPRESS AGENCY. Agency deliberately created and limited by the agreement or contract terms.

EXPRESSA NON PROSUNT QUAE NON EXPRESSA PRODERUNT. [L.] If a benefit is produced without using certain words, then nothing is gained by using those words.

EXPRESS AUTHORITY. Actual express authority can be determined by consensual agreement and/or the contract of employment. Its scope is ascertained by applying ordinary principles of construction of contracts, including an proper implications from the express words used, the usages of the trade, or the course of business between the parties. Unless the authority is restricted, the appointment of a person to an executive or director position clothes that person with the authority which a person in his or her position normally has. *D. Fogell Associates Ltd. v. Esprit de Corp. (1980) Ltd. / Esprit de Corp. (1980) Ltée* (1997), 1997 CarswellBC 1131 (S.C.), Edwards, J.

EXPRESS CONDITION. A term specified in the agreement.

EXPRESS FREIGHT. Freight carried faster than ordinary freight.

EXPRESSIO EORUM QUAE TACIT INSUNT. [L] Expressing those things which are implicit.

EXPRESSIO EORUM QUAE TACITE INSUNT NIHIL OPERATUR. [L.] The expression of things which are tacitly implied accomplishes nothing.

EXPRESSION. *n.* "All activities which convey or attempt to convey meaning prima facie fall within the scope of the guarantee [of freedom of expression in s. 2(b) of the Charter]: . . ." *R. v. Keegstra* (1990), 61 C.C.C. (3d) 1 at 95, 1 C.R. (4th) 129, 77 Alta. L.R. (2d) 193, [1991] 2 W.W.R. 1, 117 N.R. 1, 114 A.R. 81, 3 C.R.R.

(2d) 193, [1990] 3 S.C.R. 697, McLachlin J. (dissenting) (La Forest and Sopinka JJ. concurring). See *Irwin Toy Ltd. v. Québec (Procureur général)* (1989), 58 D.L.R. (4th) 577 at 607, [1989] 1 S.C.R. 927, 25 C.P.R. (3d) 417, 94 N.R. 167, 24 Q.A.C. 2, 39 C.R.R. 193, Dickson C.J.C., Lamer and Wilson JJ. See COMMERCIAL SPEECH; FREEDOM OF ~; HATRED.

EXPRESSIO UNIUS EST EXCLUSIO ALTERIUS. [L.] 1. To express one thing is to exclude another. 2. "Often, . . . invoked to compare two provisions of the same statute. If section A prohibits certain individuals from participating in a decision while section B concerns decision-making but has no parallel prohibitions, it may be concluded that the law was intentionally silent, and that the individuals referred to in section A may participate in the decision provided for in section B." *Leblanc Estate v. Bank of Montreal* (1988), [1989] 1 W.W.R. 49 at 63, 69 Sask. R. 81, 54 D.L.R. (4th) 89 (C.A.), Sherstobitoff J.A.

EXPRESSIO UNIUS PERSONAE VEL REI, EST EXCLUSIO ALTERIUS. [L.] The express mention of one person or thing excludes another.

EXPRESSLY. *adv*. Leaving no doubt as to what is meant.

EXPRESS TERM. A term particularly mentioned, agreed on by the parties, and its character, content and form expressed when the contract was made.

EXPRESS TRUST. A trust which comes into existence because the settlor has expressed the intention to accomplish that effect.

EXPRESSUM FACIT CESSARE TACITUM. [L.] ". . . '[W]hat is expressed prevails over what is implied' . . ." *Alberta (Attorney General) v. Gares* (1976), 76 C.L.L.C. 14,016 at 87, 67 D.L.R. (3d) 635 (Alta. T.D.), McDonald J.

EXPRESSWAY. *n*. A divided arterial highway that is accessible only from intersecting arterial streets at intersections at grade that have been approved by the Minister, and, where required by the volume of traffic, at grade separated interchanges that have been approved by the Minister. *Public Transportation and Highway Improvement Act*, R.S.O. 1990, c. P.50, s. 98(1).

EXPROPRIATE. *v*. For an expropriating authority to take land without the consent of the owner in the exercise of its statutory powers.

EXPROPRIATED. *adj*. 1. Taken by the Crown under Part I. *Expropriation Act*, R.S.C. 1985, c. E-21, s. 2. 2. Said of minority shareholders when their right to cause a corporation to buy back their shares arises.

EXPROPRIATED INTEREST. Any right, estate or interest that has been lost, in whole or in part, by the registration of a notice of confirmation under Part I. *Expropriation Act*, R.S.C. 1985, c. E-21, s. 2.

EXPROPRIATING AUTHORITY. The Crown or an association or person empowered to acquire land by expropriation.

EXPROPRIATION. *n*. 1. The acquisition of title to land without the consent of the owner. 2. Taking without the consent of the owner. 3. " . E]xtinction of an interest in land must . . . be included. . ." *British Columbia v. Tener* (1985), 36 R.P.R. 291 at 301, [1985] 1 S.C.R. 533, [1985] 3 W.W.R. 673, 32 L.C.R. 340, 17 D.L.R. (4th) 1, 59 N.R. 82, 28 B.C.L.R. (2d) 241, Estey J. (Beetz, McIntyre, Chouinard and Le Dain JJ. concurring). 4. Derogation by Crown from its grant of a profit à prendre can amount to expropriation. *British Columbia v. Tener* (1985) 36 R.P.R. 291 at 319, [1985] 1 S.C.R. 533, [1985] 3 W.W.R. 673, 32 L.C.R. 340, 17 D.L.R. (4th) 1, 59 N.R. 82, 28 B.C.L.R. (2d) 241, Wilson J. (Dickson C.J.C. concurring).

EXPROPRIATION AUTHORITY. The Crown, a Minister of the Crown or any person or body that under or by virtue of an enactment has an expropriation owner.

EXPROPRIATION POWER. The power or authority granted by an enactment to enter upon, take and expropriate land without the consent of the owner of the land.

EX PROPRIO MOTU. [L.] Of one's own accord.

EX PROPRIO VIGORE. [L.] By its own strength.

EX PROVISIONE MARITI. [L.] From the husband's provision.

EXPUNGE. *v*. To strike out all or part of a document or pleading.

EXPUNGEMENT. *n*. The jurisdiction to amend or strike out any entry in the register because at the application date the entry as it appears on the register does not correctly define or express the existing rights of the person who appears to be the registered owner of the mark.

EXPURGATION. *n*. Cleansing; purging.

EXQ. *abbr.* Ex quay.

EX QUAY. *var.* **EX-QUAY**. Describes the contract in which a seller must make goods available to the buyer at the quay at a certain destination.

EX REL. *abbr.* Ex relatione.

EX RELATIONE. [L. from information or a narrative] On the information of a citizen called the relator.

EX RIGHTS. Without any right to the new issue of shares which will be made to shareholders.

EXS. *abbr.* Ex ship.

EXSANGUINATION. *n*. Death due to blood leaving the circulatory system.

EX SHIP. Describes the contract in which a seller must make goods available to the buyer on the ship at a certain destination.

EX-STORE. *adj.* Describes the contract in which the buyer must collect the goods from the store or works.

EX SUA NATURA. [L.] By its own nature.

EX TALI FACTO NON ORITUR ACTIO. [L.] Such facts will not support an action.

EXTANT. *adj.* Existing.

EXTENDED. See FULLY ~.

EXTENDED CARE. On-going treatment of a patient with little chance of recovery or a long-term illness.

EXTENDED CARE FACILITY. Includes a nursing home, home for the aged or other extended care facility.

EXTENDED COVERAGE. Insurance against (a) loss arising from the destruction in whole or in part of stands of fruit trees or perennial plants other than trees; or (b) loss arising when the seeding or planting of a crop is prevented by excess ground moisture, weather or other agricultural hazards. *Crop Insurance acts.*

EXTENDED FAMILY. When used in reference to a child means the persons to whom the child is related by blood, marriage or adoption.

EXTENDED HEALTH CARE SERVICES. The following services, as more particularly defined in the regulations, provided for residents of a province, namely, (a) nursing home intermediate care service, (b) adult residential care service, (c) home care service, and (d) ambulatory health care service. *Canada Health Act*, R.S.C. 1985, c. C-6, s. 2.

EXTENDED MEAT PRODUCT. A meat product to which a meat product extender has been added.

EXTENDED POULTRY PRODUCT. A poultry product to which a poultry product extended has been added.

EXTENDER. See MEAT PRODUCT ~; POULTRY PRODUCT ~.

EXTENDI FACIAS. [L. you cause to be extended] A writ of extent.

EXTENSION. *n*. 1. An indulgence by giving time to pay a debt or perform an obligation. 2. In reference to an agreement, refers to the prolonging of an agreement which already exists, not to renewal of the agreement. *Manulife Bank of Canada v. Conlin*, [1996] 3 S.C.R. 415. 3. [In the expression extension of credit] . . . according or granting or indeed opening of credit . . ." *R. v. Cohen* (1984), 15 C.C.C. (3d) 231 at 236, [1984] C.A. 408 (Que.), the court per Tyndale J.A.

EXTENSION INSURANCE. Automobile insurance that is in excess of the limits, or reduces the deductible amount or otherwise supplements one or more of the coverages, in a universal compulsory automobile insurance plan.

EXTENSION TRESTLE LADDER. A combination of a trestle ladder and a vertically-adjustable single ladder with suitable means for securely locking the ladders together.

EXTENSIVE INTERPRETATION. Interpretation which is liberal.

EXTENT. *n*. The special writ to recover debts owed to the Crown which at one time differed from an ordinary writ of execution because a debtor's land and goods could be taken all at once in order to force payment of the debt. See RE-~; WRIT OF ~.

EXTERIOR. *adj.* In direct contact with the weather.

EXTERIOR CLADDING. Those components of a building which are exposed to the outdoor environment and are intended to provide protection against wind, water or vapour.

EXTERMINATION. *n*. 1. Includes the intentional infliction of conditions of life, inter alia the deprivation of access to food and medicine, calculated to bring about the destruction of part of a population. *Rome Statute*, Article 7. 2.The destruction, prevention or control of a pest by means of a pesticide. *Agricultural Chemicals Act*, R.S.A. 1980, c. A-6, s. 1. See LAND ~; STRUCTURAL ~; WATER ~.

EXTERNAL APPLICATION. Application to the outer surface of the body.

EXTERNAL BALLISTICS. Studying the behaviour of projectiles in flight.

EXTERNAL EXAMINATION. The examination of an unclothed body with or without removal of body tissue or fluids for the purpose of a toxicological examination.

EXTERNALLY FINANCED TRANSACTION. Occurs when money to acquire a business interest comes from outside the business.

EXTERNAL SELF-DETERMINATION. A right to *external* self-determination (which in this case potentially takes the form of the assertion of a right to unilateral secession) arises in only the most extreme of cases and, even then, under carefully defined circumstances. External self-determination can be defined as in the following statement from the *Declaration on Friendly Relations, supra* [*Declaration on Principles of International Law Concerning Friendly Relations and Co-operation Among States in Accordance with the Charter of the United Nations*, GA Res. 2625 (XXV), 24 October 1970]. The establishment of a sovereign and independent State, the free association or integration with an independent State or the emergence into any other political status freely determined by a people constitute modes of implementing the right of self-determination by that people. *Reference re Secession of Quebec*, 1998 CarswellNat 1299, 161 D.L.R. (4th) 385, 228 N.R. 203, 55 C.R.R. (2d) 1, [1998] 2 S.C.R. 217 Per curiam.

EXTINCTIVE PRESCRIPTION. Limitation of an action because time has passed.

EXTINGUISHED. *adj*. Of a right or obligation, no longer existing.

EXTINGUISHMENT. *n*. The termination of a right.

EXTIRPATED SPECIES. A wildlife species that no longer exists in the wild in Canada, but exists elsewhere in the wild. *Species at Risk Act*, S.C. 2002, c. 29, s. 2(1).

EXTORTIO EST CRIMEN QUANDO QUIS COLORE OFFICII EXTORQUET QUOD NON EST DEBITUM, VEL SUPRA DEBI- **TUM, VEL ANTE TEMPUS QUOD EST DEBITUM**. [L.] Extortion is a crime committed when someone, through colour of office, demands something which is not due, something more than what is due or something before the time that it is due.

EXTORTION. *n*. Every one commits extortion who, without reasonable justification or excuse and with intent to obtain anything, by threats, accusation, menaces or violence induces or attempts to induce any person, whether or not he is the person threatened, accused or menaced or to whom violence is shown, to do anything or cause anything to be done. *Criminal Code*, R.S.C. 1985, c. C-46, s. 346(1).

EXTRA BILLING. The billing for an insured health service rendered to an insured person by a medical practitioner or a dentist in an amount in addition to any amount paid or to be paid for that service by the health care insurance plan of a province. *Canada Health Act*, R.S.C. 1985, c. C-6, s. 2.

EXTRACTING MACHINERY. Includes drilling machinery, excavating machinery, loading machinery, smelting machinery and refining machinery. Drilling holes on the working face of a mine so as to allow for the break up of the ore body though blasting is an integral part of the extraction process and the machinery used to perform this function is "extracting machinery" within the meaning of tariff item No. 9908.00.00. *Sandvik Tamrock Canada Ltd. v. Deputy Minister of National Revenue (Customs & Excise)*, 2001 FCA 340, 284 N.R. 183, 6 T.T.R. (2d) 302 (C.A.).

EXTRACRANIAL. *adj*. Not in the skull.

EXTRACT. See HOUSEHOLD ~S.

EXTRACTION. See METHANE ~.

EXTRACTION PLANT. Any plant or equipment, other than a well, used for the extraction of oil or other substances produced in association with oil from surface or subsurface deposits of oil sand, bitumen, bituminous sand, oil shale or other deposits from which oil may be extracted.

EXTRACTOR. *n*. A device which removes a fired cartridge from a firing chamber. F.A. Jaffe, *A Guide to Pathological Evidence*, 3d ed. (Toronto: Carswell, 1991) at 219.

EXTRACURRICULAR. *adj*. Outside a program of education.

EXTRADITION. *n*. ". . . [T]he surrender by one state to another, on request, of persons accused or convicted of committing a crime in the state seeking the surrender." *R. v. Schmidt* (1987), 28 C.R.R. 280 at 289, 76 N.R. 12, [1987] 1 S.C.R. 500, 58 C.R. (3d) 1, 20 O.A.C. 161, 39 D.L.R. (4th) 18, 33 C.C.C. (3d) 193, 61 O.R. (2d) 530, La Forest J. (Dickson C.J.C., Beetz, McIntyre and Le Dain JJ. concurring). See DISGUISED ~.

EXTRADITION ARRANGEMENT. A treaty, convention or arrangement that extends to Canada made by Her Majesty with a foreign state for the surrender of fugitive criminals. *Extradition Act*, R.S.C. 1985, c. E-23, s. 2.

EXTRADITION CRIME. 1. Any crime that, if committed in Canada, or within Canadian jurisdiction, would be one of the crimes described in Schedule I, and (b) in the application of this Act to the case of an extradition arrangement, any crime described in the arrangement, whether or not it is included in that Schedule. *Extradition Act*, R.S.C. 1985, c. E-23, s. 2. 2. An "extradition crime" is defined in s. 2 of the [Extradition Act, R.S.C. 1985, c. E-23] to mean any crime that if committed in Canada would be one of the crimes listed in the schedule to the Act or in the case of an extradition arrangement (a treaty) any crime described in such arrangement. Article 2 of the Canadian-United States Extradition Treaty no longer lists specific extradition offences. It provides that "extradition shall be granted for any offence punishable by the laws of both parties by imprisonment for a term exceeding one year or any greater punishment." It is not necessary that the Canadian offence established by the conduct be described by the same name or that it have the same legal elements as the offence charged in the requesting state. The protection afforded by the double criminality rule is ensured if the conduct that underlies the foreign charge constitutes any extradition crime under the laws of Canada. *D'Agostino, Re* (2000), 2000 CarswellOnt 465, (sub nom. *United States of America v. Commisso*) 47 O.R. (3d) 257, (sub nom. *United States of America v. Commisso*) 143 C.C.C. (3d) 158, (sub nom. *United States of America v. Commisso*) 129 O.A.C. 166, (sub nom. *United States of America v. Commisso*) 72 C.R.R. (2d) 198 (C.A.).

EXTRADITION HEARING. ". . . [D]oes not decide ultimate guilt or innocence but only if there is enough evidence adduced to justify surrendering the fugitive to the demanding State. . ." *Re U.S. v. Yue* (1983), 42 O.R. (2d) 651 at 658 (H.C.), White J.

EXTRADITION PARTNER. A State or entity with which Canada is party to an extradition agreement, with which Canada has entered into a specific agreement or whose name appears in the schedule. *Extradition Act*, S.C. 1999, c. 18, s. 2.

EXTRADURAL HEMORRHAGE. A venous or arterial hemorrhage located between the dura mater and the skull. F.A. Jaffe, *A Guide to Pathological Evidence*, 3d ed. (Toronto: Carswell, 1991) at 154.

EXTRAJUDICIAL. *var.* **EXTRA-JUDICIAL.** *adj.* Out of the usual conduct of legal procedure.

EXTRA-JUDICIAL COSTS. Fees or costs, whether provided for in the tariff or not, which an advocate may charge for professional services or in addition to judicial costs, and which arise from the practice of the profession of advocate. *Barreau du Québec Act*, R.S.Q. 1977, c. B-1, s. 1.

EXTRAJUDICIAL MEASURES. Measures other than judicial proceedings under this Act used to deal with a young person alleged to have committed an offence and includes extrajudicial sanctions. *Youth Criminal Justice Act*, S.C. 2002, c. 1, s. 2(1).

EXTRA-JUDICIAL SANCTION. A sanction that is part of a program referred to in section 10. May be used to deal with a young person alleged to have committed an offence only if the young person cannot be adequately dealt with by a warning, caution or referral because of the seriousness of the offence, the nature and number of previous offences committed by the young person or any other aggravating circumstances. *Youth Criminal Justice Act*, S.C. 2002, c. 1, ss. 2(1), 10(1).

EXTRA-JUDICIAL SERVICE. A judge of the Court of Appeal or Ontario Court (General Division) acts as an arbitrator, conciliator or referee or sits on a commission of inquiry authorized by an act of the legislature or an agreement made under an act (Courts of Justice Act, R.S.O. 1990, c. C.43, s. 84(1)). G.D. Watson & C. Perkins, eds., *Holmested & Watson: Ontario Civil Procedure* (Toronto: Carswell, 1984) at CJA-111.

EXTRA-JUDICIAL STATEMENT. In any proceedings of a court martial a hearsay statement that has been made by a declarant, other than in the course of those proceedings or in the course of taking evidence taken on commission for that court martial, and includes (a) words, oral or written, used by him, (b) the adoption, in some way, in whole or in part, of meaningful words uttered by another person as an accurate expression of the declarant's own observations or experience, and (c) the expression, in an intelligible manner, of the declarant's observation or experience. *Military Rules of Evidence*, C.R.C., c. 1049, s. 2.

EXTRA LEGEM POSITUS EST CIVILITER MORTUUS. [L.] One placed outside the law is dead civilly.

EXTRANEOUS DEFENCE. One which raises a new issue which oversteps the Crown's case.

EXTRAORDINARY. *adj*. Exceptional; not ordinary

EXTRAORDINARY REMEDY. A writ of mandamus, quo warranto or habeas corpus.

EXTRAORDINARY RESOLUTION. 1. A resolution passed by a majority of not less than three-fourths of the members of the company for the time being entitled to vote present in person or by proxy (in cases where by the act, charter, or instrument of incorporation, or the regulations of the company, proxies are allowed) at any general meeting of which notice specifying the intention to propose such resolution has been duly given. 2. A resolution passed by 2/3 of the members entitled to vote who are present in person at a general meeting of which notice specifying the intention to propose the resolution as an extraordinary resolution has been given.

EXTRA-PROVINCIAL. *adj*. Incorporated in another province and registered in the second province.

EXTRA-PROVINCIAL ACT. An Act of the Parliament of Canada, or an ct of a Legislature of another province, with objects similar to those of this Act. *Natural Products Marketing acts*.

EXTRA-PROVINCIAL AGENCY. A board, commission or other body constituted under an extra-provincial Act with objects similar to this Act. *The Natural Products Marketing Act*, R.S.S. 1978, c. N-3, s. 2.

EXTRA-PROVINCIAL BODY CORPORATE. A body corporate that is incorporated otherwise than by or under the authority of an Act of the Legislature or of the Parliament of Canada.

EXTRA-PROVINCIAL BUS TRANSPORT. The transport of passengers or passengers and

goods by means of an extra-provincial bus undertaking. *Motor Vehicle Transport Act, 1987*, R.S.C. 1985, c. 29 (3rd Supp.), s. 2(1).

EXTRA-PROVINCIAL BUS UNDERTAKING. A work or undertaking, for the transport of passengers or passengers and goods by bus, that connects a province with any other or others of the provinces, or extending beyond the limits of a province. *Motor Vehicle Transport Act, 1987*, R.S.C. 1985, c. 29 (3rd Supp.), s. 2(1)

EXTRA-PROVINCIAL COMPANY. *var*. **EXTRAPROVINCIAL COMPANY**. A company incorporated outside the province to which reference is made.

EXTRA-PROVINCIAL CORPORATION. 1. A body corporate incorporated otherwise than by or under the act of a legislature. 2. A company or certain class of companies incorporated in another jurisdiction which must become licensed or registered if they carry on business in a province.

EXTRA-PROVINCIAL INSURER. An insurer incorporated or legally constituted in a foreign jurisdiction other than an insurer which is registered and holds a certificate of registry under the Canadian and British Insurance Companies Act (Canada) or under the Foreign Insurance Companies Act (Canada).

EXTRA-PROVINCIALITY. *n*. ". . . [M]aking residence a criterion of exclusion." *Black v. Law Society of Upper Canada* (1989), 58 D.L.R. (4th) 317 at 339, [1989] 1 S.C.R. 591, 93 N.R. 266, 96 A.R. 352, [1989] 4 W.W.R. 1 66 Alta. L.R. (2d) 97, 38 C.R.R. 193, 37 Admin. L.R. 161, La Forest J. (Dickson C.J.C. and Wilson J. concurring).

EXTRA-PROVINCIAL LIMITED PARTNERSHIP. A limited partnership organized under the laws of a jurisdiction outside a province.

EXTRA-PROVINCIAL ORDER. *var*. **EXTRA-PROVINCIAL ORDER**. An order, or that part of an order, of an extraprovincial tribunal that grants to a person custody of or access to a child.

EXTRA-PROVINCIAL TRIBUNAL. *var*. **EXTRAPROVINCIAL TRIBUNAL**. A court or tribunal outside the province that has jurisdiction to grant to a person custody of or access to a child.

EXTRA-PROVINCIAL TRUCK TRANSPORT. The transport of goods by means of an extra-provincial truck undertaking. *Motor Vehicle Transport Act, 1987*, R.S.C. 1985, c. 29 (3rd Supp.), s. 2(1).

EXTRA-PROVINCIAL TRUCK UNDERTAKING. A work or undertaking, for the transport of goods by motor vehicle other than a bus, connecting a province with any other or others of the provinces or extending beyond the limits of a province. *Motor Vehicle Transport Act, 1987*, R.S.C. 1985, c. 29 (3rd Supp.), s. 2(1).

EXTRA PROVINCIAL UNDERTAKING. *var.* **EXTRA-PROVINCIAL UNDERTAKING.** A work or an undertaking for the transport of passengers or goods by motor vehicle, connecting a province with any of the other provinces or extending beyond the limits of a province. *Motor Vehicles Transport acts.*

EXTRA-REGIONAL TELEVISION STATION. In relation to a licensed area of a distribution undertaking, a licensed television station that has (*a*) a Grade A official contour or Grade B official contour that does not include any part of the licensed area; and (*b*) a Grade B official contour that includes any point located 32 km or less from the local head end of the licensed area. *Broadcasting Distribution Regulations*, SOR/97-555, s. 1.

EXTRA-TERRITORIAL. *adj.* Outside the territory of the jurisdiction which enacted the law in question.

EXTRATERRITORIALITY. *n.* The projection of a state's authority beyond the territory of the state.

EXTRA TERRITORIUM JUS DICENTI IMPUNE NON PARETUR. [L.] The sentence of a judge acting outside proper jurisdiction can be safely disobeyed.

EXTRA TRAIN. A train not authorized by a time table schedule.

EXTRA VIAM. [L.] Out of the way.

EXTRA VIRES. [L.] Beyond powers. See ULTRA VIRES.

EXTRICATE. *v.* To free oneself; release oneself.

EXTRINSIC EVIDENCE. ". . . [E]vidence which is not contained in the body of the document, agreement or contract which forms the, or a subject matter of the, issue under consideration and requiring determination. . ." *Saskatoon Market Mall Ltd. v. Macleod-Stedman Inc.* (1989), 78 Sask. R. 179 at 194 (Q.B.), Grotsky J.

EXTRINSIC FRAUD. Courts have drawn a distinction between "intrinsic fraud" and "extrinsic fraud" in an attempt to clarify the types of fraud that can vitiate the judgment of a foreign court. Extrinsic fraud is identified as fraud going to the jurisdiction of the issuing court or the kind of fraud that misleads the court, foreign or domestic, into believing that it has jurisdiction over the cause of action. Evidence of this kind of fraud, if accepted, will justify setting aside the judgment. The historic description of and the distinction between intrinsic and extrinsic fraud is of no apparent value and, because of its ability to both complicate and confuse, should be discontinued. *Beals v. Saldanha*, 2003 SCC 72, per Major, J.

EX TURPI CAUSA NON ORITUR ACTIO. [L.] ". . . [R]ule means . . . that the courts will not enforce a right which would otherwise be enforceable if the right arises out of an act committed by the person asserting the right (or by someone who is regarded in law as his successor) which is regarded by the court as sufficiently anti-social to justify the court's refusal to enforce that right." *Hardy v. Motor Insurers' Bureau*, [1964] 2 All E.R. 742 at 750-51 (U.K.), Lord Diplock.

EXUERE PATRIAM. [L.] To cast off one's citizenship; to expatriate oneself.

EX VISCERIBUS TESTAMENTI. [L.] From the contents of the will.

EX VI TERMINI. [L.] From the force of a term.

EX WAREHOUSE. A seller must pay all charges through discharge from a warehouse.

EX WHARF. A seller must pay all charges through delivery from a wharf.

EX WORKS. A seller has goods available at its factory or works so a buyer's responsibility begins there. I.F.G. Baxter, *The Law of Banking*, 3d ed. (Toronto: Carswell, 1981) at 136.

EYE-WITNESS. *n.* One who testifies about facts she or he has seen.

F. *abbr.* 1. Farad. 2. Femto. 3. Freeboard.

F.A.A. *abbr.* Free from all average. Used in marine insurance to mean an underwriter is not liable unless there is total loss of the insured property.

FABRIC. *n.* Any material woven, knitted, crocheted, knotted, braided, felted, bonded, laminated or otherwise produced from, or in combination with, a textile fibre. *Textile Labelling Act*, R.S.C. 1985, c. T-10, s. 2. See CANADIAN ~; IMPORTED ~; NARROW ~.

FABRICATE. *v.* To make up or concoct; to construct or manufacture.

FABRICATING EVIDENCE. Every one who, with intent to mislead, fabricates anything with intent that it shall be used as evidence in a judicial proceeding, existing or proposed, by any means other than perjury or incitement to perjury is guilty of an indictable offence and liable to imprisonment for a term not exceeding fourteen years. *Criminal Code*, R.S.C. 1985, c. C-46, s. 137.

FABRIQUE. *n.* A legal person constituted under this Act and consisting of the chairman, the pastor of a parish or the ministering cleric of a chapelry and the churchwardens of such parish or chapelry. *An Act Respecting Fabriques*, R.S.Q. 1977, c. F-1, s. 1.

FACE. *n.* The text of the document, not just the first page. See WORKING ~.

FACE VALUE. The nominal value printed or written on the face of a bond, debenture, note, share certificate or other document indicating its par value.

FACIALLY NEUTRAL. Adverse effect discrimination can only emanate from a law which is facially neutral. Facially neutral means that the provision, on its face, does not confer an advantage or impose a disadvantage on any group. The classic example is height and weight restrictions set by police forces as criteria for hiring. Such restrictions are neutral in that they apply equally to all people, although their effects may be felt unequally by men and women.

FACIAS. [L. that you cause] See FIERI FACIAS.

FACILITY. *n.* " . . . [S]omething built, installed or established to serve a particular function or to accomplish some end or provide a certain service." *R. v. McLaughlin* (1980), 18 C.R. (3d) 339 at 344, [1980] 2 S.C.R. 331, [1981] 1 W.W.R. 298, 32 N.R. 350, 23 A.R. 530, 53 C.C.C. (2d) 417, 113 D.L.R. (3d) 386, Laskin C.J.C. (Ritchie, Dickson and Lamer JJ. concurring). See APPROVED ~; AQUACULTURE ~; BURIED FACILITIES; CARE ~; CHILD CARE ~; CHILD CARING ~; COMMERCIAL ~; COMMON ~; COMMUNITY CARE ~; CORRECTIONAL ~; DAY CARE ~; ELECTRICAL ~; EXHIBITION FACILITIES; EXTENDED CARE ~; HAZARDOUS WASTE DISPOSAL ~; HAZARDOUS WASTE MANAGEMENT ~; HEALTH CARE ~; HEALTH ~; HOSPITAL FACILITIES; HYGIENE FACILITIES; IN-PATIENT ~; LOCKUP ~; NUCLEAR ~; OPTOMETRIC ~; OUTDOOR ADVERTISING FACILITIES; PORT ~; PRE-SCHOOL ~; PRODUCTION FACILITIES; PSYCHIATRIC ~; PUMP-OUT ~; RADIATION ~; RECREATION ~; REGIONAL COLLECTION ~; RESEARCH FACILITIES; RESEARCH ~; RESIDENTIAL CARE ~; RETAIL DISTRIBUTION FACILITIES; SANITARY ~; SERVICE FACILITIES; SERVICES AND FACILITIES; SEWAGE ~; SEWAGE TREATMENT ~; SOCIAL CARE ~; SUPPLY ~; SURFACE FACILITIES; TELECOMMUNICATION ~; TIMBER

F

PROCESSING ~; TRANSPORTATION ~; UNLOADING ~; VETERINARY ~; WASTE WATER TREATMENT ~; WOOD PROCESSING ~.

FACILITY ASSOCIATION. The unincorporated non-profit association of insurers known as a facility association, established for the purpose of allocating automobile insurance risks to ensure the availability of insurance to owners of automobiles.

FACIO UT DES. [L.] I do that you may give.

FACIO UT FACIAS. [L.] I do that you may do.

FACSIMILE. *n*. An accurate reproduction of a book, instrument, document or record and includes a print from microfilm and a printed copy generated by or produced from a computer record. *Land Titles Act*, R.S.O. 1990, c. L.5, s. 1.

FACT. *n*. " . . . [S]tatement, tale or news is an expression which, taken as a whole and understood in context, conveys an assertion of fact or facts and not merely the expression of opinion. . . Expression which makes a statement susceptible of proof and disproof is an assertion of fact; expression which merely offers an interpretation of fact which may be embraced or rejected depending on its cogency or normative appeal, is opinion." *R. v. Zundel* (1992), 75 C.C.C. (3d) 449 at 492, 95 D.L.R. (4th) 202 [1992] 2 S.C.R. 731, 140 N.R. 1, 56 O.A.C. 161, 16 C.R. (4th) 1, 10 C.R.R. (2d) 193, Cory and Iacobucci JJ. (dissenting) (Gonthier J. concurring). See ACCESSORY AFTER THE ~; ACCESSORY BEFORE THE ~; ADJUDICATIVE ~S; CAUSATION IN ~; CLUE ~; CONCLUSION OF ~; LEGISLATIVE ~S; MALICE IN ~; MATERIAL ~; MISTAKE OF ~; MIXED QUESTION OF LAW AND ~; PRESUMPTIONS OF ~; PRIMARY ~S; QUESTION OF SIMILAR ~ EVIDENCE.

FACTA PROBANDA. [L.] Facts which must be proved; facts in issue.

FACTA PROBANTIA. [L.] Facts given in evidence to prove facta probanda; evidentiary facts.

FACT FINDER. The person or body charged with determining which evidence is believed.

FACT IN ISSUE. A fact which the plaintiff must establish to succeed in proving his case and a fact which the defendant must prove in order to make out the defence.

FACTITIOUS. *adj*. Not real, genuine or natural.

FACTO. [L.] In fact.

FACTOR. *n*. 1. One who loans money on security of accounts receivable or merchandise and inventory or both, but who is in no way connected with selling them. I.F.G. Baxter, *The Law of Banking*, 3d ed. (Toronto: Carswell, 1981) at 190. 2. An agent who disposes of or sells products in the agent's control or possession. G.H.L. Fridman, *Sale of Goods in Canada*, 3d ed. (Toronto: Carswell, 1986) at 493. See CONNECTING ~; PROVINCIAL CONTENT ~; RHESUS ~; SIZE ~; TIME ~.

FACTORAGE. *n*. The commission which a factor receives.

FACTORING. *n*. A factoring of accounts receivable is based upon an absolute assignment of them. It is in effect a sale by a company of its accounts receivable at a discounted value to the factoring company for immediate consideration. Clearly a GABD does not meet the standard required for a factoring arrangement which requires an absolute transfer of the proprietary interest of the assignor in the book debts. *Canada Trustco Mortgage Corp. v. Port O'Call Hotel Inc.* (1996), (sub nom. *Pigott Project Management Ltd. v. Land-Rock Resources Ltd.*) 38 Alta. L.R. (3d) 1 (S.C.C.), per Cory, J. for majority.

FACTORING OF RECEIVABLES. Purchasing and discounting short-term accounts receivable.

FACTORY. *n*. A building, premises, workshop, structure, room or place where (a) any manufacturing process or assembling in connection with the manufacturing of products is carried on, (b) thermal, hydraulic, electrical or other form of energy or power is used to move or work any machinery or device in the preparing, inspecting, manufacturing or finishing, or in a process incidental to the preparing, inspecting, manufacturing, or finishing, of a product or is used to aid the manufacturing carried on there, or (c) manual labour is performed by way of trade or for purposes of gain in or incidental to the making of a product, or the altering, repairing, ornamenting, finishing, storing, cleaning, washing or adapting for sale of a product, and includes a facility used for the maintenance of aircraft, locomotives and motor vehicles.

FACTORY BUILT BUILDINGS. Buildings which are manufactured either wholly or in part, at an off-site location.

FACTORY-BUILT CHIMNEY. A chimney consisting entirely of factory made parts, each designed to be assembled with the other without requiring fabrication on site.

FACTORY-BUILT HOME. A manufactured home or a mobile home.

FACTORY BUILT HOUSING. Housing that is partly or totally built in a factory and then transported in sections or as a complete unit to a site where it is erected or stationed and provided with the necessary services to make it a habitable unit that, when occupied, is void of transport features such as wheels, tires, axles, brakes or lamps.

FACTORY SHIP. A ship in or on which whales or fish are treated whether wholly or in part.

FACTUAL CAUSATION. A causal link between any facts which constitute the breach of contract or tortious conduct and the loss or injury for which the plaintiff claims compensation. K.D. Cooper-Stephenson & I.B. Saunders, *Personal Injury Damages in Canada* (Toronto: Carswell 1981) at 637.

FACTUAL INFORMATION. Information on a subject as to name, age, place of residence, previous places of residence, marital status, spouse's name and age, number of dependents, particulars of education or professional qualifications, places of employment, previous places of employment, estimated income, paying habits, outstanding credit obligations, cost of living, outstanding obligations, matters of public record and any information voluntarily supplied by the subject of a personal investigation.

FACTUAL MATRIX. In relation to a commercial agreement, the background of relevant facts that the parties must clearly have been taken to have known and to have had in mind when they drafted the text of their agreement.

FACTUM. *n.* [L.] 1. A deed; an act. 2. A statement of facts and law which each party files in an application, appeal or motion.

FACTUM A JUDICE QUOD AD EJUS OFFICIUM NON SPECTAT NON RATUM EST. [L.] Anything which a judge does outside a judge's function is not valid just because that person is a judge.

FACULTAS PROBATIONUM NON EST ANGUSTANDA. [L.] The opportunity to prove should not be limited.

FACULTATIVE REINSURANCE. " . . . [A] separate reinsurance agreement between an orig-

inal insurer and a reinsurer, acquired in respect to the liability, or specific part of the liability, for a single risk." *Northern Union Insurance Co., Re* (1984), 55 C.B.R. (N.S.) 126 at 130, [1985] 2 W.W.R. 751, 33 Man. R. (2d) 81, [1985] I.L.R. 1-1899, 25 C.C.L.I. 112 (Q.B.), Kroft J.

FACULTY. *n.* 1. An ability, a capacity. 2. In a university, an administrative unit headed by a dean. 3. A faculty of a university and includes professors, associate professors, assistant professors, lecturers, instructors and all other persons engaged in the work of teaching or giving instruction at a university.

FACULTY MEMBER. A person employed by a university on a full time basis who serves as an instructor, lecturer, assistant professor, associate professor, professor, or in an equivalent designated position.

FAILURE. See CROP ~.

FAILURE OF ISSUE. Death without issue.

FAINT ACTION. An action which was feigned.

FAINT HOPE CLAUSE. Name given to s. 745.6 of the Criminal Code which provides that a person may apply, in writing, to the appropriate Chief Justice in the province in which their conviction took place for a reduction in the number of years of imprisonment without eligibility for parole if the person (a) has been convicted of murder or high treason; (b) has been sentenced to imprisonment for life without eligibility for parole until more than fifteen years of their sentence has been served; and (c) has served at least fifteen years of their sentence. (2) A person who has been convicted of more than one murder may not make an application under subsection (1), whether or not proceedings were commenced in respect of any of the murders before another murder was committed.

FAINT PLEADER. A collusive, false or fraudulent method of pleading.

FAIR. *n.* A gathering of people at which shows and entertainments of various sorts are presented.

FAIR. *adj.* 1. " . . . [R]easonable . . ." *Vanguard Coatings & Chemicals Ltd. v. R.* (1988), 30 Admin. L.R. 121 at 148, 88 D.T.C. 6374, Can. S.T.R. 80-020, [1988] 2 C.T.C. 178, 17 C.E.R. 71, 88 N.R. 241, 22 F.T.R. 80n, [1988] 3 F.C. 560, [1989] 1 T.S.T. 2025 (C.A.), MacGuigan J.A. (Urie J.A. concurring). 2. Impartial.

FAIR COMMENT. 1. In an action for libel or slander for words consisting partly of allegations of fact and partly of expression of opinion, the defence of fair comment. 2. " . . . An essential ingredient of that defence is that the comment was made on a matter of public interest and the customary form of pleading in this regard is to state that the words complained of 'were fair comment made in good faith and without malice upon a matter of public interest'. . . This defence is one which is available to every member of the public and relates exclusively to comments or opinions made upon facts which are shown to have been true. . ." *McLoughlin v. Kutasy* (1979), 8 C.C.L.T. 105 at 109, 26 N.R. 242, [1979] 2 S.C.R. 311, 97 D.L.R. (3d) 620, Ritchie J. (Martland, Pigeon, Beetz, Estey and Pratte JJ. concurring). 3. "As honesty of belief is an essential component of the defence of fair comment, that defence involves at least some evidence that the material complained of was published in a spirit of fairness." *Cherneskey v. Armadale Publishers Ltd.* (1978), 7 C.C.L.T. 69 at 87, [1979] 1 S.C.R. 1067, 24 N.R. 271, [1978] 6 W.W.R. 618, 90 D.L.R. (3d) 321, Ritchie J. (Laskin C.J.C., Pigeon and Pratte JJ. concurring).

FAIR EMPLOYMENT PRACTICE. Practice of offering equal employment opportunities to persons regardless of race, national origin, colour, religion, age, sex, marital status, physical handicap or conviction for which a pardon has been granted.

FAIRGROUND. *n.* An outdoor open space used for fairs.

FAIR HEARING. ". . . [T]he tribunal which adjudicates upon his rights must act fairly, in good faith, without bias and in judicial temper, and must give to him the opportunity adequately to state his case." *Duke v. R.*, [1972] S.C.R. 917 at 923, 18 C.R.N.S. 302, 7 C.C.C. (2d) 474, 28 D.L.R. (3d) 129, the court per Fauteux C.J.C.

FAIRLY. See ACT ~; DUTY TO ACT ~.

FAIR MARKET VALUE. 1. ". . . [T]he highest price available estimated in terms of money which a willing seller may obtain for the property in an open and unrestricted market from a willing knowledgeable purchaser acting at arm's length." *Minister of National Revenue v. Northwood Country Club* (1989), 89 D.T.C. 173 at 176, [1989] 1 C.T.C. 2230 (T.C.C.), Kempo T.C.J. 2. Of a security, means (i) in the case of a security listed or traded on a stock exchange in Canada, the quoted price at that time determined, (ii) in the case of a security that is a share of the capital stock of a mutual fund corporation, a unit of a mutual fund trust or an interest in a related segregated fund trust, the amount that would be received in respect of that share, unit or interest if it were redeemed or disposed of at that time.

FAIRNESS. *n.* The duty of an administrator to act fairly regarding procedure. Any administrator must, minimally let the party affected by her or his decision understand the case against that party and provide the party with a fair chance to answer it or to be heard. See ACT FAIRLY; DUTY TO ACT FAIRLY; PROCEDURAL ~.

FAIRNESS LETTER. This case turns largely on a letter dated May 3, 1999 that the visa officer sent to [the applicant], care of his lawyer in Toronto. It was the standard form letter sent in medical inadmissibility cases, and is generally known as the "fairness letter" because it provides an opportunity for visa applicants to submit additional material in support of their application and to respond to the concerns of the visa officer. *Khan v. Canada (Minister of Citizenship & Immigration)* (2001), 2001 FCA 345, 208 D.L.R. (4th) 265, 283 N.R. 173, [2002] 2 F.C. 413, 213 F.T.R. 56 (note) (C.A.).

FAIR OPPORTUNITY. Refers to the chance for accused persons to present their cases and to know the relevant evidence.

FAIR OR EXHIBITION. An event where agricultural or fishing products are presented or where activities relating to agriculture or fishing take place. *Criminal Code*, R.S.C. 1985, c. C-46, s. 206(3.1).

FAIR TRIAL. 1. One that is based on the law, the outcome of which is determined by the evidence, free of bias, real or apprehended. *R. v. S. (R.D.)*, [1997] 3 S.C.R. 484. 2. A trial that appears fair, both from the perspective of the accused and the perspective of the community. A fair trial must not be confused with the most advantageous trial possible from the accused's point of view: *R. v. L. (T.P.)*, [1987] 2 S.C.R. 309, at p. 362, per La Forest J. Nor must it be conflated with the perfect trial; in the real world, perfection is seldom attained. A fair trial is one which satisfies the public interest in getting at the truth, while preserving basic procedural fairness to the accused. *R. v. Harrer*, [1995] 3 S.C.R. 562, per McLachlin, J.

FAIR VALUE. 1. Value which is equitable and just in the circumstances; fair market value, intrinsic value or value to owner. 2. " . . . [F]air value and fair market value (or market value), are not necessarily synonymous. . ." *Whitehorse Copper Mines Ltd., Re* (1980), 10 B.L.R. 113 at 42 (B.C. S.C.), McEachern C.J.S.C. 3. Can be used to arrive at a value for a right which does not have a fair market value because it cannot be transferred. Fair value is a notional concept influenced by the nature of the property and the circumstances giving rise to the transaction. While fair value includes fair market value, other values included are investment value, value to owner, and liquidation value. Fair value allows adjustments to be made to recognize internal or external financing, liquidity discounts, and the reasonable expectations of the parties. *Standard Trust Ltd. (Trustee of) v. Standard Trust Co.* (1995), 26 O.R. (3d) 1 (C.A.). 4. The shares are simply to be priced at "fair value." The courts have interpreted "fair value" as something more than simply "fair market value." Although "fair value" is said to be what a prudent person would pay for the property in question (see *Woods Manufacturing Co. v. R.*, [1951] 2 D.L.R. 465 (S.C.C.).

FAIR WAGES. Such wages as are generally accepted as current for competent workers in the district in which the work is being performed for the character or class of work in which those workers are respectively engaged, but shall in all cases be such wages as are fair and reasonable.

FAIRWAY BUOY. A buoy marking the fairway.

FAIT. *n.* [Fr.] Writing; a deed.

FAIT ENROLLE. [Fr.] A deed enrolled.

FALL. *v.* To come into contact with the floor or ground; to cut down a tree.

FALLEN ANIMAL. A horse, goat, sheep, swine or head of cattle that has been disabled by disease, emaciation or other condition that is likely to cause death. *Dead Animal Disposal Act*, R.S.O. 1990, c. D.3, s. 1.

FALLING AIRCRAFT INSURANCE. Insurance against loss of or damage to the property insured caused by aircraft or objects falling from aircraft.

FALLOW. See SUMMER ~.

FALLOW-LAND. *n.* Land ploughed but not planted and, after a succession of crops, left uncultivated for a while.

FALL SESSION. A session of the Legislature that commences after the month of September in any year.

FALSA DEMONSTRATIO. [L.] Incorrect description.

FALSA DEMONSTRATIONE LEGATUM NON PERIMITUR. [L.] A legacy should not fail because of an incorrect description.

FALSA DEMONSTRATIO NON NOCET. [L.] A false description does make void.

FALSA ORTHOGRAPHIA NON VITIAT CONCESSIONEM; FALSA GRAMMATICA NON VITIAT CONCESSIONEM. [L.] Bad spelling or bad grammar do not invalidate a grant.

FALSE. *adj.* " . . . [S]hould be distinguished from the word inaccurate as the word 'false' implies an intention to mislead or deceive. . ." *Kinsdale Securities Co. v. Minister of National Revenue* (1974), [1975] C.T.C. 10 at 34, [1974] 2 F.C. 760, 74 D.T.C. 6674, 6 N.R. 240 (C.A.), Bastin D.J.A. (dissenting).

FALSE ALARM OF FIRE. Every one who wilfully, without reasonable cause, by outcry, ringing bells, using a fire alarm, telephone or telegraph, or in any other manner, makes or circulates or causes to be made or circulated an alarm of fire is guilty of an offence. *Criminal Code*, R.S.C. 1985, c. C-46, s. 437.

FALSE ARREST. 1. "A necessary element of false arrest . . . is that the arrest, . . . is made without foundation or probable cause." *Nicely v. Waterloo Regional Police Force* (1991), 7 C.C.L.T. (2d) 61 at 69, 47 C.P.C. (2d) 105, 2 O.R. (3d) 612, 79 D.L.R. (4th) 14, 44 O.A.C. 147 (Div. Ct.), the court per Rosenberg J. 2. The detention of a person without lawful authority and without the consent of the person arrested.

FALSE CONFLICT. In a conflict of laws case, it may not matter which system of law one applies because the relevant laws of all countries, including the forum, lead to identical conclusions or are the same in substance. J.G. McLeod, *The Conflict of Laws* (Calgary: Carswell, 1983) at 31.

FALSE DOCUMENT. 1. A document (a) the whole or a material part of which purports to be made by or on behalf of a person (i) who did not make it or authorize it to be made, or (ii) who did not in fact exist, (b) that is made by or on behalf of the person who purports to make it but is false in some material particular, (c) that is made in the name of an existing person, by him or under his authority, with a fraudulent intention that it should pass as being made by a person, real or fictitious, other than the person who makes it or under whose authority it is made. *Criminal Code*, R.S.C. 1985, c. C-46, s. 321. 2. " . . . [A]ny document that is false in some material particular . . . a document which is false in reference to the very purpose for which the document was created . . ." *R. v. Gaysek* (1971), 15 C.R.N.S. 345 at 348, 352, [1971] S.C.R. 888, 2 C.C.C. (2d) 545,18 D.L.R. (3d) 306, Ritchie J. (Judson and Spence JJ. concurring).

FALSEHOOD. *n.* A deliberate lie. See INJURIOUS ~.

FALSE IMPRISONMENT. Intentional restraint of a person's liberty without lawful authority by preventing the person from leaving a place or actively confining them.

FALSE INNUENDO. In the case of "popular or false innuendo", although it need not be separately pled, the plaintiff is required to show why a reader would reasonably import to the words complained of a defamatory character, different from the ordinary meaning that the words would otherwise import. Where the words complained of are susceptible to many interpretations, the onus rests on the plaintiff to set out the meaning or meanings the plaintiff alleges the words are capable of. *Moon v. Sher* (2003), 2003 CarswellOnt 2405 (S.C.J.).

FALSE NEWS. See SPREADING ~.

FALSE OR MISLEADING REPRESENTATION. 1. Includes (a) any representation in which expressions, words, figures depictions or symbols are used, arranged or sown in a manner that may reasonably be regarded as qualifying the declared net quantity of a prepackaged product or as likely to deceive a consumer with respect to the net quantity of a prepackaged product; (b) any expression, word, figure, depiction or symbol that implies or may reasonably be regarded as implying that a prepackaged product contains any matter not contained in it or does not contain any matter in fact contained in it; and (c) any description or illustration of the type, quality, performance, function, origin or method of manufacture or production of a prepackaged

product that may reasonably be regarded as likely to deceive a consumer with respect to the matter so described or illustrated. *Consumer Packaging and Labelling Act*, R.S.C. 1985, c. C-38, s. 7(2). 2. Include (a) any representation in which expressions, words, figures, depictions or symbols are arranged or shown in a manner that may reasonably be regarded as likely to deceive any person with respect to textile fibre content; (b) any expression, word, figure, depiction or symbol that implies or may reasonably be regarded as implying that a textile fibre product contains any fur or hair not contained in the product; and (c) any description of the type, quality, performance, origin or method of manufacture or production of a textile fibre product that may reasonably be regarded as likely to deceive any person with respect to the matter so described. *Textile Labelling Act*, R.S.C. 1985, c. T-10, s. 5(3).

FALSE PRETENCE. A representation of a matter of fact either present or past, made by words or otherwise, that is known by the person who makes it to be false and that is made with a fraudulent intent to induce the person to whom it is made to act upon it. *Criminal Code*, R.S.C. 1985, c. C-46, s. 361.

FALSE REPRESENTATION. A statement known to be untrue or intended to be misleading concerning something. See DECEIT; FALSE PRETENCE; MISREPRESENTATION; REPRESENTATION.

FALSEWORK. *n.* The structural supports, vertical or horizontal, for forms which are used to hold wet concrete until it dries.

FALSI CRIMEN. [L.] Fraudulently concealing or suborning in order to hide the truth, committed in words when a witness swears falsely; in writing when someone antedates a contract; or in doing something when a person sells using false weights and measures.

FALSUS IN UNO, FALSUS IN OMNIBUS. [L.] False in one, false in everything.

[] FAM. *abbr.* Law Reports, Family Division, 1972-.

FAM. CT. *abbr.* 1. Family Court. 2. Provincial Court (Family Division).

FAMILIA. *n.* [L. family] The servants of a certain master; land adequate to maintain a family.

FAMILY. *n.* 1. The husband, wife, child, step-child, parent, step-parent, brother, sister, half-brother, half-sister, step-brother, step-sister, in each case whether legitimate or illegitimate, of a person. 2. Includes a man and woman living together as husband and wife, whether or not married in a permanent relationship, or the survivor of either, and includes the children of both or either, natural or adopted or to whom either stands in loco parentis, and any person lawfully related to any of the aforementioned persons. 3. The parents and any children wholly or substantially maintained by those parents. See DEER ~; EXTENDED ~; FOSTER ~; HEAD OF A ~; HEAD OF ~; IMMEDIATE ~; MEMBER OF HIS OR HER ~; SAME-SEX PARTNERSHIP.

FAMILY ALLOWANCE. An amount payable in respect of a child pursuant to subsection 3(1) or (2), whichever is applicable. *Family Allowance Act*, R.S.C. 1985, c. F-1, s. 2.

FAMILY ALLOWANCE RECIPIENT. A person who received or is in receipt of an allowance or a family allowance pursuant to the Family Allowances Act, chapter F-1 of the Revised Statutes of Canada, 1970, as it read immediately before being repealed or the Family Allowances Act, for that period prior to a child reaching seven years of age, and such other persons as may be prescribed by regulation. *Canada Pension Plan*, R.S.C. 1985, c. C-8, s. 42.

FAMILY ARRANGEMENT. " . . . [A] transaction between members of the same family, which is for the benefit of the family generally, as, for example, one which tends to the preservation of the family property or to the peace and security of the family and the avoidance of family disputes and litigation." *Hall v. Marshall*, [1938] 3 D.L.R. 419 at 422, 13 M.P.R. 112 (N.S. S.C.), Doull J.

FAMILY ASSET. A matrimonial home and property owned by one spouse or both spouses and ordinarily used or enjoyed by both spouses or one or more of the children while the spouses are residing together for shelter or transportation or for household, educational, recreational, social or aesthetic purposes, and includes, (i) money in an account with a chartered bank, savings office, credit union or trust company where the account is ordinarily used for shelter or transportation or for household, educational, recreational, social or aesthetic purposes, (ii) where property owned by a corporation, partnership or trustee would, if it were owned by a spouse, be a family asset, shares in the corporation or an interest in the partnership or trust owned by the spouse having a market value equal to the value of the benefit the spouse has in respect of the property, (iii) property over which a spouse has, either alone or in conjunction with another person, a power of appointment exercisable in favour of himself or herself, if the property would be a family asset if it were owned by the spouse, and (iv) property disposed of by a spouse but over which the spouse has, either alone or in conjunction with another person a power to revoke the disposition or a power to consume, invoke or dispose of the property, if the property would be a family asset if it were owned by the spouse but does not include property that the spouses have agreed by a domestic contract is not to be included in the family assets.

FAMILY BUSINESS CORPORATION. A corporation in which, at the date of registration of any conveyance with respect to which the expression is being applied, all of the issued shares except for directors' qualifying shares are owned by a person or persons, each of whom is not a non-resident person and each of whom is a member of the family of each transferor of the land being conveyed, and where any of such persons is a corporation the provisions of clauses 3(1)(c) and (d) are applicable to such corporation. *Land Transfer Tax Act*, R.R.O. 1990, Reg. 697, s. 1.

FAMILY CEMETERY. A cemetery used for the burial of the remains of persons related by blood, marriage, or adoption to the person responsible for the cemetery. *Cemetery Companies Act*, R.S.N.B. 1973, c. C-1, s. 1.

FAMILY CORPORATION. A corporation in which all the voting shares are owned by (a) one natural person, or (b) one natural person plus one or any number of his father, mother, brother, sister, child, spouse or his spouse's mother, father or child. *Residential Tenancy Act*, S.B.C. 1984, c. C-1, s. 1.

FAMILY DEBT. " . . . [A] convenient term to designate a liability of either or both of the spouses which has been incurred during the marriage for a family purpose." *Mallen v. Mallen* (1992), 40 R.F.L. (3d) 114 at 121, 65 B.C.L.R. (2d) 241, 11 B.C.A.C. 262, 22 W.A.C. 262 (C.A.), Wood J.A. (dissenting).

FAMILY FARM. A farming enterprise managed by a farmer in respect of which the necessary labour is performed primarily by him and his family, if any. *The Family Farm Credit Act*, R.S.S. 1978, c. F-5, s. 2.

FAMILY FARM CORPORATION. A corporation (a) that is primarily engaged in the business of farming, (b) that is under the control in fact of farmers or eligible individuals related to farmers, or a combination of both, and (c) of which a majority of the issued and outstanding shares of each class of share are legally and beneficially owned by farmers or eligible individuals related to farmers. *Farm Lands Ownership Act*, R.S.M. 1987, c. F35, s. 1.

FAMILY FARMING CORPORATION. A corporation the principal object and business of which is farming or fishing and with respect to which: (i) at least 95% of the shares are owned wholly by persons related to one another by blood, marriage or adoption; and (ii) at least 51% of the shares are owned by a shareholder or shareholders principally occupied in the farming or fishing operations of the corporation. *Consumer Protection Act, 1996*, S.S. 1996, c. C-30.1, s. 39.

FAMILY FISHING CORPORATION. A corporation that is throughout the taxation year a corporation, (a) all shares of the capital stock of which that confer on the holder thereof the right to vote were owned by (i) an individual ordinarily resident in Canada or by that individual and a member or members of that individual's family ordinarily resident in Canada or by another family fishing corporation, (ii) another corporation all shares of the capital stock of which that confer on the holder thereof the right to vote were owned directly or indirectly by a person or persons referred to in subclause (i), (b) 75 per cent of the assets of which were fishing assets, and (c) which carried on the business of fishing in Ontario through the employment of a shareholder or a member of his or her family actually engaged in the operation of the business or, where subclause (a)(ii) applies, through the employment of the person or persons referred to in subclause (a)(ii). *Corporations Tax Act*, R.S.O. 1990, c. C.40, s. 1(2).

FAMILY HOME. The home which is the home of the owner held by him in fee simple or to which he holds the equity of redemption and is used by him for his family residence together with the land immediately appurtenant thereto not exceeding one and one-half acres and any immediately appurtenant outbuildings. *Expropriation Act*, R.S.N.S. 1989, c. 156, s. 3(1).

FAMILY HOUSING UNIT. A unit providing therein living, sleeping, eating, food preparation and sanitary facilities for one family, with or without other essential facilities shared with other family housing units.

FAMILY INCOME. See MONTHLY ~; RESIDUAL ~.

FAMILY IN NEED. A family whose monetary requirements for regularly recurring needs determined under the regulations exceed its income as determined under the regulations. *Family Benefits acts*.

FAMILY INSURANCE. 1. Insurance whereby the lives of the insured and one or more persons related to that person by blood, marriage or adoption are insured under a single contract between an insurer and the insured. 2. Insurance whereby the lives or well-being, or the lives and well-being, of the insured and one or more persons related to that person by blood, marriage or adoption are insured under a single contract between the insurer and the insured.

FAMILY LAW COMMISSIONER. One whom a judge directs to investigate and report on an issue relating to access, custody or maintenance.

FAMILY MATTER. A cause of action in respect of (a) the custody of, maintenance for, or access to a child by a parent or guardian; (b) the maintenance of a person by a spouse; or (c) the division or redistribution of real or personal property between members of a family, that is, under any Act, instituted or capable of being instituted in a court.

FAMILY NAME. 1. A surname that does not contain more than one word which may occur alone as a surname. 2. A family name which is a single unhyphenated word.

FAMILY OF LOW INCOME. A family that receives a total family income that, in the opinion of the housing authority, is insufficient to permit it to rent housing accommodation adequate for its needs at the current rental market in the area in which the family lives.

FAMILY ORDER. A custody and access order; a money order for support; a family property order.

FAMILY PROVISION. A support provision, a custody provision or an access right.

FAMILY STATUS. 1. Lamer C.J.C. quotes Marceau J.A. [from p. 35 [1991] 1 F.C.]: " 'Family' is not used in isolation in the Act [Canadian Human Rights Act, R.S.C. 1985, c. H-6] but rather coupled with the word 'status'. A status, to me, is primarily a legal concept which refers to the particular position of a person with respect to his or her rights and limitations as a result of his or her being a member of some legally recognized and regulated group. . . Even if we were to accept that two homosexual lovers can constitute 'sociologically speaking' a sort of family, it is certainly, not one which is now recognized by law as giving its members special rights and obligations." Lamer C.J. added at p. 582 that while the appeal was dismissed by the Supreme Court of Canada, "Nor should this decision be interpreted as meaning that homosexual couples cannot constitute a 'family' for the purposes of legislation other than the Canadian Human Rights Act. In this regard, each statute must be interpreted in its own context." *Canada (Attorney General) v. Mossop*, [1993] S.C.R. 554, Lamer C.J.C. affirming [1991] 1 F.C. 18, 32 C.C.E.L. 276, 71 D.L.R. (4th) 661, 90 C.L.L.C. 17,021, 12 C.H.R.R. D/355, 114 N.R. 241 (C.A.). 2. " . . . [S]ufficiently broad to include couples of the same sex that were living together in a long-term relationship . . ." *Canada (Attorney General) v. Mossop*, [1993] S.C.R. 554 at 648, Cory J. (dissenting). 3. The status of being in a parent and child relationship. *Human Rights acts*. 4. The status of an unmarried person or parent, a widow or widower or that of a person who is divorced or separated or the status of the children, dependants, or members of the family of a person. *Human Rights Act*, R.S.M. 1987, c. H175, s. 1. See SAME-SEX PARTNERSHIP STATUS.

FAMILY UNIT. An individual and his or her spouse, or any individuals occupying the same principal residence, whether or not they are related to each other. See COST OF CONSTRUCTION OF A ~.

FAM. L. REV. *abbr*. Family Law Review, 1978.

FAN. *n*. Any mechanical device used to circulate air through mine workings. See AUXILIARY ~; BOOSTER ~.

FAO. Food and Agriculture Organization of the United Nations.

FARAD. *n*. The capacitance of a capacitor between the equipotential surfaces of which there appears a difference of potential of one volt when the capacitor is charged by a quantity of electricity equal to one coulomb. *Weights and Measures Act*, S.C. 1970-71-72, c. 36, schedule 1.

FARE. *n*. Money paid for conveyance by any means. See PREMIUM ~.

FARM. *n*. 1. Land in Canada used for the purpose of farming, which term includes livestock raising, dairying, bee-keeping, fruit growing, the growing of trees and all tillage of the soil. 2. An area of land that is suitable for purposes of agricultural production, including a greenhouse, fur or tree farming operation. See BIG GAME ~; DAIRY ~; ECONOMIC ~; FAMILY ~; FUR ~; GAME ANIMAL PRODUCTION ~; GAME BIRD ~; LIVESTOCK ~; TOBACCO ~; WILD ANIMAL ~; WILDLIFE ~.

FARM BUILDING. A building or structure, other than a dwelling, situated on a farm and used or to be used on the actual farming operation.

FARM BUILDINGS. 1. Buildings situated on a parcel of land improved and used exclusively for the purpose of growing grain or forage crops, raising or keeping farm stock, growing horticultural crops including edible mushrooms, and the owner, tenant, lessee or occupant of the land derives income from the sale or disposal of the grain or forage, farm stock, horticultural crops or edible mushrooms raised, kept or grown on the land, and include farm residences on the land. *Revenue Act*, C.C.S.M., c. R150, s. 1.

FARM BULK TANK. A stationary storage tank used only for the holding and cooling of milk on the premises of a producer and includes fixtures thereto and the equipment required for the use of the tank. *Milk and Milk Products Act*, R.R.O. 1990, Reg. 761, s. 1.

FARM CORPORATION. A corporation (i) which is primarily engaged in the business of agriculture, and (ii) of which not less than 75% of all issued and voting shares are beneficially owned by bona fide farmers who are resident persons. *Prince Edward Island Lands Protection Act*, 1988, c. L-5, s. 1(1)(e).

FARM CREDIT CORPORATION CANADA. The federal body which helps farmers and people who want to become farmers to buy, develop and maintain viable farm businesses.

FARM ELECTRIC SYSTEM. All machinery, apparatus and appliances for the generation or distribution of electricity on a farm whether or not affixed to real property.

FARM EQUIPMENT MECHANIC. A person who, (i) inspects, disassembles, adjusts, repairs, overhauls, assembles or reassembles and tests farm equipment, (ii) inspects, tests, adjusts, and replaces components of self-contained coolers used on the farm exclusively for farm produce, and (iii) installs, inspects, maintains and removes automotive-type air-conditioning and heating systems for operator cabs on farm equipment. *Apprenticeship and Tradesmen's Qualification Act*, R.R.O. 1980, Reg. 33, s. 1.

FARMER. *n.* 1. Any individual, corporation, cooperative, partnership or other association of persons that is engaged in farming for commercial purposes. 2. A person whose chief occupation is farming and, (a) who is living upon and tilling his or her own land, or land to the possession of which he or she is for the time being entitled, or (b) who is a settler engaged in clearing land for the purpose of bringing it to a state of cultivation. *Fish and Wildlife Conservation Act, 1997*, S.O. 1997, c. 41, s. 1. 3. A person who is in possession of a farm and whose principal occupation consists of farming that farm. 4. A producer of primary agricultural products for sale. See ASPIRING ~; BONA FIDE ~; DAIRY ~; FULL-TIME ~; FUR ~; INSOLVENT ~; NECESSITOUS ~.

FARMERS ASSOCIATION. See PROVINCIAL ~.

FARM IMPLEMENT. Includes any implement, equipment, engine, motor, machine, combine, tractor or attachment used or intended for use in farming operations. See UNUSED ~; USED ~.

FARM IMPROVEMENT LOAN. A loan made by a lender to a farmer for the, purpose of financing (a) the purchase of, major repair to or major overhaul of agricultural implements or equipment for bee-keeping, (b) the purchase of livestock or bee-stock, (c) the purchase or installation of, major repair to or major overhaul of agricultural equipment or a farm electric system, (d) the alteration or improvement of a farm electric system, (e) the erection or construction of fencing or works of drainage on a farm, (f) the construction, repair or alteration of, or making additions to, any building or structure on a farm, (g) the purchase, by the owner of a farm, of additional land for the purpose of farming, or (h) any work for the improvement or development of a farm designated in the regulations. *Farm Improvement Loans Act*, R.S.C. 1985, c. F-3, s. 2.

FARM INCOME ASSURANCE PLAN. Any program, arrangement, or plan that provides in any way for the paying of moneys to, or guaranteeing or assuring of income for, such farmers or classes of farmers in the province as the Lieutenant Governor in Council may designate; and includes the Manitoba Beef Producers Income Assurance Plan. *Farm Income Assurance Plans Act*, C.C.S.M., c. F-38, s. 1.

FARM INCOME PLAN. Any programme, arrangement, proposal, plan, scheme, or similar measure, howsoever described, that provides in any way for the paying of moneys to, or guaranteeing or assuring of income for, such farmers or classes of farmers as the Lieutenant-Governor in Council designates. *Farm Income Assurance Act*, S.N.B., c. F-5.1, s. 1.

FARMING. *n.* (a) The production of field-grown crops, cultivated and uncultivated, and horticultural crops; (b) the raising of livestock, poultry and fur-bearing animals; (c) the production of eggs, milk, honey, maple syrup, tobacco, fibre, wood from woodlots and fodder crops; and (d) the production or raising of any other prescribed thing or animal. *Farm Debt Mediation Act, 1997*, S.C. 1997, c. 21 , s. 2.

FARMING ASSETS. (a) Cash, trade accounts receivable, supplies and inventory of commodities or things produced, raised or grown through farming, (b) land, buildings, equipment, machinery, and livestock that are used chiefly in the operation of the farm by the corporation, (c) any right or licence granted or issued under any Act of the Legislature that permits or regulates the production or sale of any commodity or thing produced, raised or grown through farming, (d) the building in which a shareholder or member or members of his or her family reside who are engaged in the operation of the farm if that building is on land that is used or is contiguous to land used by that shareholder or member or members of his or her family in the operation of the farm, (e) shares in another family farm corporation, (f) a mortgage taken by the family farm corporation as security for the balance of the sale price on its sale of farming assets referred to in clause (b), provided that the amount of the aggregate of its remaining farming assets referred to in clauses (a) to (e) exceeds 50 per cent of its assets. *Corporations Tax Act*, R.S.O. 1990, c. C.40, s. 1(2).

FARMING OPERATIONS. (i) The planting, growing and sale of trees, shrubs or sod, (ii) the raising or production of crops, livestock, game-production animals within the meaning of the Livestock Industry Diversification Act, fish, pheasants or poultry, (iii) fur production, or (iv) beekeeping. *Law of Property Act*, R.S.A. 2000, c. L-7, s. 47.

FARMING PURPOSES. Agricultural production and the pasturage and production of livestock.

FARM JOURNAL. A newspaper or periodical having broad distribution in the farm community. *Farm Products Marketing Act*, R.S.Q., c. M-35, s. 1.

FARM LABOUR CONTRACTOR. An employer whose employees do work in connection with the planting, cultivating or harvesting of any horticultural or agricultural product, for or under the direction of another person.

FARM LABOURER. A person who is employed by a farmer to work on a farm and whose chief occupation is farming.

FARM LAND. *var.* **FARMLAND**. 1. Land that is being farmed or is shortly to be farmed and includes buildings and other improvements thereon. 2. Land that is being used for crop production or animal husbandry. See TREE ~.

FARM MACHINERY. (i) A tractor, (ii) a farm implement powered by an internal combustion engine, whether it is self-propelled or not, (iii) a stationary engine located on a farm, or (iv) any vehicle, implement, machine or equipment designated as farm machinery. See UNUSED ~ AND EQUIPMENT; USED ~ AND EQUIPMENT.

FARM OPERATOR. Any physical person whose principal occupation is agriculture. Quebec statutes.

FARMOUT. *n*. A common agreement in the oil and gas industry under which one party does something on another party's land, for example drill a well, to earn an interest in that land. W. Grover & F. Iacobucci, *Materials on Canadian Income Tax*, 4th ed. (Toronto: Richard De Boo Ltd., 1980) at 1202.

FARM PRACTICE. See NORMAL ~.

FARM PRODUCE. Beans, corn, grain, grass seeds and oil seeds and all kinds thereof produced in Ontario. *Grain Elevator Storage Act*, R.S.O. 1990, c. G.10, s. 1.

FARM PRODUCT. 1. Those plants and animals useful to mankind and includes, but is not limited to, (i) forages and sod crops, grains and field crops, (ii) poultry and poultry products, (iii) livestock and livestock products, and (iv) fruits, vegetables, mushrooms, tobacco, nuts, flower and floral products, nursery products, apiaries and fur-bearing animal products. 2. An agricultural, horticultural, avicultural or forest product, in its raw state or partly or wholly processed by the producer, including, among other things, farm and farm-yard animals, live or slaughtered, the flesh of such animals, poultry, eggs, wool, dairy products, grain, fruits, vegetables, maple products, honey, tobacco, wood, beverages or foodstuffs derived from agricultural products and any other agricultural product or commodity desigated by the Government. *The Farm Producers Act*, R.S.Q. c. M-35, s. 1. 3. Animals, meats, eggs, poultry, wool, dairy products, grains, seeds, fruit, fruit products, vegetables, vegetable products, maple products, honey, tobacco, wood, or any class or part of any such product, and such articles of food or drink manufactured or derived in whole or in part from any such product, and such other natural products of agriculture as are designated in the regulations, and, for the purposes of this Act, fish shall be deemed to be a farm product. *Farm Products Marketing Act*, R.S.O. 1990, c. F.9, s. 1.

FARM PRODUCTS MARKETING COOPERATIVE. A cooperative association incorporated under the laws of Canada or a province for the purpose of processing, distributing or marketing on a cooperative basis the products of farming, each member or shareholder of which is a farmer. *Farm Improvement and Marketing Cooperatives Loans Act*, R.S.C. 1985, c. 25 (3rd Supp.), s. 2.

FARM PROPERTY. 1. The land and complementary buildings used for agricultural purposes but does not include any residential property in connection therewith. *Assessment Act*, S.N.S. 1989, c. 23, s. 2. 2. Arable land and complementary buildings, operated as a farm enterprise by a bona fide farmer and farm property includes land leased from the Crown and operated as part of a farm enterprise, but excludes land leased or rented from owners who are not bona fide farmers. *Real Property Assessment Act*, R.S.P.E.I. 1974, c. R-5, s. 4.

FARM RESIDENCE. The improvement used as a residence by a person who carries on farming operations.

FARM STATION. An experimental farm station established under this Act. *Experimental Farm Stations Act*, R.S.C. 1985, c. E-16, s. 2.

FARMSTEAD. *n*. The land on which farm buildings are situated and all adjacent land used or that may be used for shelterbelts, gardens, lawns, storage, shelter, traffic, water supply, water transmission, water storage, services and other facilities contributing to the beneficial use of farm buildings, and includes the buildings, vegetation and other developments or improvements pertaining to the land.

FARM STOCK. (a) Cattle, (b) sheep, (c) goats, (d) swine, (e) poultry, (f) fur-bearing animals kept in captivity for the production of fur, (g) bees, or (h) horses, other than horses boarded for another person or kept or raised for showing, riding, racing or amusement. *Revenue Act*, C.C.S.M. 1987, c. R150, s. 1.

FARM STRUCTURE. A structure used for agricultural or forestry production but does not include a structure used primarily for storage or human habitation. *Pesticides Act*, R.R.O. 1990, Reg. 914, s. 1.

FARM SUBSCRIBER. A person engaged in farming operations and receiving from a company, in his name, telephone service upon farm land. *The Rural Telephone Act*, R.S.S. 1978, c. R-27, s. 2.

FARM TRACTOR. A motor vehicle designed and used primarily as an implement of husbandry for drawing agricultural equipment.

FARM TRAILER. A trailer owned by an actual farmer and operated in the marketing of the produce, including livestock, of his own farm, or in the conveyance of property for use thereon. *The Highway Traffic Act*, C.C.S.M., c. H-60, s. 1.

FARM TRUCK. A truck owned by a farmer.

FARM USE. An occupation or use of land for farm purposes, including husbandry of land, plants and animals and any other similar activity.

FARM VEHICLE. A farm machine or other machine or equipment (i) that is identifiable by manufacturer's serial number cut, embossed or otherwise permanently marked or attached on it, (ii) that is used, or intended for use, in any type of farming operations, and (iii) that is not a motor vehicle. *Garage Keepers' Lien Act*, R.S.A. 2000, c. G-2, s. 1. See OVER-DIMENSIONAL ~.

F.A.S. *abbr*. Free alongside ship. A seller undertakes to deliver goods alongside a ship at the seller's own expense.

FASTENER. *n*. A device used to hold a thing in place.

FAT. *n*. Any fat or oil, whether of animal, vegetable, marine or mineral origin. See EXCESS PROPORTION OF ~; MILK ~.

FATAL ACCIDENT. An accident causing the death of a worker under circumstances that entitle that worker's dependents, if any, to compensation. *Workers' Compensation acts*.

FAT EMBOLISM. Obstruction by fat droplets of capillary blood vessels. F.A. Jaffe, *A Guide to Pathological Evidence*, 3d ed. (Toronto: Carswell, 1991) at 218.

FATETUR FACINUS QUI JUDICIUM FUGIT. [L.] One who flees judgment admits guilt.

FATHER. *n*. 1. The person named as the cause of the pregnancy. 2. A person who takes care of a child of whom he is the legitimate, natural or adoptive father, or the stepfather. See BIOLOGICAL ~; BIRTH ~; DEPENDENT ~; POSSIBLE ~; PUTATIVE ~.

FATHER OF A CHILD. In any one of the following circumstances: 1. The person is married to the mother of the child at the time of the birth of the child. 2. The person was married to the mother of the child by a marriage that was terminated by death or judgment of nullity within 300 days before the birth of the child or by divorce where the decree nisi was granted within 300 days before the birth of the child. 3. The person marries the mother of the child after the birth of the child and acknowledges that he is the natural father. 4. The person was cohabiting with the mother of the child in a relationship of some permanence at the time of the birth of the child or the child was born within 300 days after they ceased to cohabit. 5. The person and the mother of the child have filed a statutory declaration under subsection 6(8) of the Vital Statistics Act or a request under subsection 6(5) of that Act, or either under a similar provision under the corresponding Act in another jurisdiction in Canada. 6. The person has been found or recognized in his lifetime by a court of competent jurisdiction in Canada to be the father of the child.

FAUCES TERRAE. [L.] A gulf; a narrow inlet of a body of water.

FAUCET. *n*. A water tap.

FAULT. *n*. 1. " . . . [I]ncludes negligence, but it is much broader than that. Fault incorporates all intentional wrongdoing, as well as other types of substandard conduct." *Bell Canada v. Cope*

(Sarnia) Ltd. (1980), 11 C.C.L.T. 170 at 180 (Ont. H.C.), Linden J. 2. Wrongful act or default. *Sale of Goods acts.* 3. Blameworthiness. 4. In torts, includes negligence and intentional torts.

FAULTY. *adj*. Defective, unsound, imperfect, not up to a required standard.

FAULTY WORKMANSHIP. Error in design. Unsatisfactory physical effort or poor craftsmanship. May refer to negligence.

FAVORABILIA IN LEGE SUNT FISCUS, DOS, VITA, LIBERTAS. [L.] See CAUSAE DOTIS, VITAE, LIBERTATIS, FISCI, SUNT INTER FAVORABILIA, IN LEGE.

FAVORABILIORES REI POTIUS QUAM ACTORES HABENTUR. [L.] The law is on the defendant's side rather than the plaintiff's.

FAVORABILIORES SUNT EXECUTIONES ALIIS PROCESSIBUS QUIBUSCUNQUE. [L.] Executions are preferred more than all other process.

FBDB. *abbr*. Federal Business Development Bank.

F.C. *abbr*. 1. Federal Court. 2. Federal Court of Canada Reports.

[] F.C. *abbr*. Canada Federal Court Reports, 1971- (Recueil des arrêts de la Cour fédérale du Canada).

FCA. The English neutral citation for the Federal Court of Appeal.

F.C.A.D. *abbr*. Federal Court Appellate Division.

F.C.S. *abbr*. Free of capture and seizure. In marine insurance policies, indicates that the underwriter is not liable for capture or seizure of either the cargo or the ship.

FCT. The English neutral citation for the Federal Court, Trial Division.

F.C.T.D. *abbr*. Federal Court Trial Division.

FEALTY. *n*. 1. A mutual bond of obligation or special oath of fidelity between a lord and a tenant. 2. The general oath of allegiance of a subject to a sovereign.

FEASANCE. *n*. Executing or doing something. See MIS~; NON~.

FEASIBILITY STUDY. See ENGINEERING RESEARCH OR ~; RESEARCH OR ~.

FEATHERBEDDING. *n*. When payment is sought for work not done, work done with more workers than necessary or excess work.

FEATURE FILM. See CANADIAN ~.

FEATURE MOTION PICTURE. A motion picture film in excess of 60 minutes duration that has been produced for exhibition in a commercial motion picture theatre. *Cable Television Regulations*, C.R.C., c. 374, s. 2.

FEATURE POOL. The pool corresponding to the following types of bets, namely, a daily double, an exactor, a quinella, a triactor or any bet other than a win, place or show bet that an association is authorized to offer by its permit. *Pari-Mutuel Betting Supervision Regulations*, SOR/91-365, s. 2.

FED. *abbr*. Federal.

FED. C.A. *abbr*. Federal Court of Canada — Appeal Division.

FEDERAL. *adj*. 1. Refers to the government or a law of Canada as opposed to that of a province. 2. As applied to state documents, means of or pertaining to Canada. *Evidence acts*.

FEDERAL ACT. A law passed by the Parliament of Canada.

FEDERAL AIRPORT. Includes a military aerodrome. *Aeronautics Act*, R.S.C. 1985 (1st Supp.), c. 33, s. 5.4(1).

FEDERAL BENEFITS. Benefits payable under the Canada Pension Plan and to which any dependants are entitled as a result of the death, together with any benefits to which the dependent spouse is or becomes entitled under the Canada Pension Plan as a result of having retired or reached retirement age. *Workers Compensation Act*, R.S.B.C. 1996, c. 492, s. 17.

FEDERAL BOARD, COMMISSION OR OTHER TRIBUNAL. 1. Any body or any person or persons having, exercising or purporting to exercise jurisdiction or powers conferred by or under an Act of Parliament, other than any such body constituted or established by or under a law of a province or any such person or persons appointed under or in accordance with a law of a province or under section 96 of the Constitution Act, 1867. *Federal Court Act*, R.S.C. 1985, c. F-7, s. 2. 2. Any board, commission, tribunal or person that carries on regulatory activities and is expressly charged by or pursuant to an enactment of Parliament with the responsibility of making decisions or recommendations related directly or indirectly to the production, supply, acquisition or distribution of a product. *Competition Act*, R.S.C. 1985, c. C-34, s. 125.

FEDERAL BUSINESS DEVELOPMENT BANK. The bank, incorporated under the Federal Business Development Bank Act (Canada), which offers financial and management services to help businesses establish and develop themselves in Canada.

FEDERAL CHILD SUPPORT GUIDELINES. The objectives of these Guidelines are (a) to establish a fair standard of support for children that ensures that they continue to benefit from the financial means of both spouses after separation; (b) to reduce conflict and tension between spouses by making the calculation of child support orders more objective; (c) to improve the efficiency of the legal process by giving courts and spouses guidance in setting the levels of child support orders and encouraging settlement; and (d) to ensure consistent treatment of spouses and children who are in similar circumstances. *Federal Child Support Guidelines*, SOR/97-175, s. 1. See CHILD SUPPORT GUIDELINES

FEDERAL COMPANY. 1. A corporation incorporated or continued by or under an Act of Canada and not discontinued by or under an Act of Canada and includes the Governor and Company of Adventurers of England trading into Hudson's Bay. *Company Act*, R.S.B.C. 1996, c. 62, s. 1. 2. A company incorporated by or pursuant to an Act of the Parliament of Canada.

FEDERAL CONSERVATION AREA. An area that is (a) a national park; (b) public real property under the administration of the Minister of the Environment that is subject to measures imposed under the *Canada Wildlife Act* for the conservation of wildlife; or (c) a protection area for migratory birds prescribed under the *Migratory Birds Convention Act, 1994*. *Yukon Act, 2002*, S.C. 2002, c. 7, s. 2.

FEDERAL COURT. 1. The Federal Court of Canada. 2. " . . . [A] statutory court and its jurisdiction must be found in the Federal Court Act [R.S.C. 1970, (2d Supp.), c. 10] . . ." *Fiche v. Cold Lake Transmission Ltd.* (1979), [1981] 3 C.N.L.R. 78 at 85, [1980] 2 F.C. 369 (T.D.), Primrose D.J. 4. Any court, tribunal or other body that carries out adjudicative functions and is established by or pursuant to an Act of Parliament.

FEDERAL COURT OF APPEAL. That division of the Federal Court of Canada called the Federal Court—Appeal Division is continued as an additional court of law, equity and admiralty in and for Canada, for the better administration of the laws of Canada and as a superior court of record having civil and criminal jurisdiction. *Federal Courts Act*, R.S.C. 1985, c. F-7, s. 3.

FEDERAL CROWN. Her Majesty in right of Canada.

FEDERAL CUSTOMS LAWS.. Includes (a) Acts of Parliament, (b) regulations within the meaning of the *Statutory Instruments Act*, and (c) rules of law applicable in connection with those Acts or regulations, that relate to customs or excise, whether those Acts, regulations or rules come into force before or after June 30, 1983 and, for greater certainty but without restricting the generality of the foregoing, includes the following Acts, namely, the *Customs Act*, the *Customs Tariff*, the *Excise Act*, the *Excise Act, 2001*, the *Excise Tax Act*, the *Export and Import Permits Act*, the *Importation of Intoxicating Liquors Act* and the *Special Import Measures Act. Customs and Excise Offshore Application*, R.S.C. 1985, c. C-53, s. 2.

FEDERAL FINANCIAL INSTITUTION. (a) A bank, (b) a body corporate to which the *Trust and Loan Companies Act* applies, (c) an association to which the *Cooperative Credit Associations Act* applies or a central cooperative credit society for which an order has been made under subsection 473(1) of that Act, or (d) an insurance company or a fraternal benefit society incorporated or formed under the *Insurance Companies Act. Bank Act*, S.C. 1991, c. 46, s. 2.

FEDERAL GOVERNMENT. 1. A person or body which exercises power delegated to it by two or more independent states which have mutually agreed not to exercise certain sovereign powers but to delegate the exercise of those powers to the person or body they have chosen jointly. 2. The Governor General in Council.

FEDERAL INSTITUTION. Any of the following institutions of the Government of Canada: (a) a department, board, commission or council, or other body or office, established to perform a governmental function by or pursuant to an Act of Parliament or by or under the authority of the Governor in Council, and (b) a departmental corporation or Crown corporation as defined in section 2 of the *Financial Administration Act*.

FEDERALISM. 1. The system of government in Canada where legislative jurisdiction is divided between the provinces and the federal government under sections 91 and 92 of the Constitution Act. 2. In a federal system of government such as ours, political power is shared by two orders of government: the federal government on the one hand, and the provinces on the other. Each is assigned respective spheres of jurisdiction by the *Constitution Act, 1867* [(U.K.), 30 & 31 Vict., c. 3]. It is up to the courts "to control the limits of the respective sovereignties". In interpreting our Constitution, the courts have always been concerned with the federalism principle, inherent in the structure of our constitutional arrangements, which has from the beginning been the lodestar by which the courts have been guided. This underlying principle of federalism, then, has exercised a role of considerable importance in the interpretation of the written provisions of our Constitution. There can be little doubt that the principle of federalism remains a central organizational theme of our Constitution. Less obviously, perhaps, but certainly of equal importance, federalism is a political and legal response to underlying social and political realities. The principle of federalism recognizes the diversity of the component parts of Confederation, and the autonomy of provincial governments to develop their societies within their respective spheres of jurisdiction. The federal structure of our country also facilitates democratic participation by distributing power to the government thought to be most suited to achieving the particular societal objective having regard to this diversity. The principle of federalism facilitates the pursuit of collective goals by cultural and linguistic minorities which form the majority within a particular province. *Reference re Secession of Quebec*, 1998 CarswellNat 1299, 161 D.L.R. (4th) 385, 228 N.R. 203, 55 C.R.R. (2d) 1, [1998] 2 S.C.R. 217 Per curiam. See COOPERATIVE ~.

FEDERAL JURISDICTION. The legislative jurisdiction of the Parliament of Canada.

FEDERAL LAND. Land that belongs to Her Majesty in right of Canada, or that Her Majesty in right of Canada has the power to dispose of, and all waters on and airspace above that land; the internal waters of Canada and the territorial sea of Canada; and reserves and any other lands that are set apart for the use and benefit of a band under the *Indian Act*, and all waters on and airspace above those reserves and lands. *Species at Risk Act*, S.C. 2002, c. 29, s. 2.

FEDERAL OFFENCE. An offence as defined by the Young Offenders Act (Canada).

FEDERAL PARAMOUNTCY. A rule that in a case where there are validly provincial and federal enactments which conflict, the federal enactment will prevail.

FEDERAL PARLIAMENT. The parliament of Canada.

FEDERAL PROPERTY. (a) Real property and immovables owned by Her Majesty in right of Canada that are under the administration of a minister of the Crown, (b) real property and immovables owned by Her Majesty in right of Canada that are, by virtue of a lease to a corporation included in Schedule III or IV, under the management, charge and direction of that corporation, (c) immovables held under emphyteusis by Her Majesty in right of Canada that are under the administration of a minister of the Crown, (d) a building owned by Her Majesty in right of Canada that is under the administration of a minister of the Crown and that is situated on tax exempt land owned by a person other than Her Majesty in right of Canada or administered and controlled by Her Majesty in right of a province, and (e) real property and immovables occupied or used by a minister of the Crown and administered and controlled by Her Majesty in right of a province. *Payments in Lieu of Taxes Act*, R.S.C. 1985, c. M-13, s. 2. See PROVINCIALLY OCCUPIED ~.

FEDERAL REAL PROPERTY. Real property belonging to Her Majesty, and includes any real property of which Her Majesty has the power to dispose. *Federal Real Property and Federal Immovables Act, 1991*, S.C. 1991, c. 50, s. 2.

FEDERAL REFERENCE. The referral of a question to the Supreme Court of Canada by the cabinet for the purpose of obtaining an advisory opinion of the court. Authorized by the Supreme Court of Canada Act. See PROVINCIAL REFERENCE.

FEDERAL REGULATION. A regulation, as amended from time to time, made under the federal Act. *Income Tax acts*.

FEDERAL STATE. Canada is a federal state in which legislative powers are divided between the federal and provincial governments under sections 91 and 92 of the Constitution Act. Each individual is subject to the laws of a province or territory and the laws of Canada.

FEDERAL STATUTE. A law passed by the Parliament of Canada.

FEDERAL TERRITORY. By a procedure established under the Constitution Act, 1867 (U.K.), 30 & 31 Vict., c. 3, s. 146, the areas of Rupert's Land and the North-western Territory were admitted to Canada as areas under the authority of the federal Parliament. P.W. Hogg, *Constitutional Law of Canada*, 3d ed. (Toronto: Carswell, 1992) at 38-9.

FEDERAL WATERS. Other than in Yukon, waters under the exclusive legislative jurisdiction of Parliament and, in Yukon, waters in a federal conservation area within the meaning of section 2 of the Yukon Act. *Canada Water Act*, R.S.C. 1985, c. C-11, s. 2.

FEDERAL WORK, UNDERTAKING OR BUSINESS. Any work, undertaking or business that is within the legislative authority of Parliament, including, without restricting the generality of the foregoing, (a) a work, undertaking or business operated or carried on for or in connection with navigation and shipping, whether inland or maritime, including the operation of ships and transportation by ship anywhere in Canada, (b) a railway, canal, telegraph or other work or undertaking connecting any province with any other province, or extending beyond the limits of a province, (c) a line of ships connecting a province with any other province, or extending beyond the limits of a province, (d) a ferry between any province and any other province or between any province and any country other than Canada, (e) aerodromes, aircraft or a line of air transportation, (f) a radio broadcasting station, (g) a bank or an authorized foreign bank within the meaning of section 2 of the *Bank Act*, (h) a work or undertaking that, although wholly situated within a province, is before or after its execution declared by Parliament to be for the general advantage of Canada or for the advantage of two or more of the provinces, (i) a work, undertaking or business outside the exclusive legislative authority of the legislatures of the provinces, and (j) a work, undertaking or activity in respect of which federal laws within the meaning of section 2 of the *Oceans Act* apply pursuant to section 20 of that Act and any regulations made pursuant to paragraph 26(1)(k) of that Act. *Canada Labour Code*, R.S.C. 1985, c. L-2, s. 2.

FEDERATION. *n.* A composite state whose constitution distributes certain functions to a central authority and others to member states.

See ALLIED TRADES ~; FOUNDER ~; PROVINCIAL ~; SPECIALIZED ~.

FEDERATION OF COOPERATIVE CREDIT SOCIETIES. A federation, league or corporation incorporated or organized by or pursuant to an Act of Parliament or of the legislature of a province, the membership or the shareholders of which include two or more central cooperative credit societies.

FED. T.D. *abbr.* Federal Court of Canada—Trial Division.

FEE. *n.* 1. " . . . [I]ts technical common law meaning, i.e., an estate in land unrestricted as to time and capable of descending to the heir. . ." *Ameri-Cana Motel Ltd. v. Miller* (1983), 27 R.P.R. 75 at 79, [1983] S.C.R. 229, 46 N.R. 451, 143 D.L.R. (3d) 1, the court per Wilson J. 2. " . . . [I]n the context of s. 26 (now s. 29) of the Planning Act [R.S.O. 1970, c. 349] it was to be equated with the kind of interest in land which carries with it disposing power. . ." *Ameri-Cana Motel Ltd. v. Miller* (1983), 27 R.P.R. 75 at 79, [1983] S.C.R. 229, 46 N.R. 451, 143 D.L.R. (3d) 1, the court per Wilson J. 3. Recompense or reward for services. 4. An amount to be paid when filing documents. 5. The charge made by a service provider. In the case of law firms, generally refers to charges for legal services and for required disbursements. See ATTENDANCE ~; DETERMINABLE ~; ENTRANCE ~; ~ SIMPLE; ~ TAIL; FRANCHISE ~; INITIATION ~; LICENSE ~; MANAGEMENT ~S; MEMBERSHIP ~; MONTHLY ~S; OFFICIAL ~; OVERTIME ~S; PROVINCIAL TAX OR ~.

FEED. *v.* To offer additional support; to strengthen after the fact, i.e. a subsequently acquired interest feeds an estoppel.

FEED. *n.* Any substance or mixture of substances containing amino acids, anti-oxidants, carbohydrates, condiments, enzymes, fats, minerals, non-protein nitrogen products, proteins or vitamins, or pelletizing, colouring, foaming or flavouring agents and any other substance manufactured, sold or represented for use (a) for consumption by livestock, (b) for providing the nutritional requirements of livestock, or (c) for the purpose of preventing or correcting nutritional disorders of livestock, or any substance for use in any such substance or mixture of substances. *Fee Act*, R.S.C. 1985, c. F-9, s. 2. See AGRICULTURAL ~S; MEDICATED ~; MINERAL ~; TRACE-MINERAL-SALT ~.

FEEDER. *n.* A conductor or group of conductors which transmits electrical energy from a service supply, transformer, switchboard, distribution centre, generator, or other source of supply to the branch-circuit over-current devices. See LIVESTOCK ~.

FEEDER ASSOCIATION. An association incorporated under an Act of the Legislature and having for its object the assisting of its members to acquire livestock for growing and finishing. *Feeder Associations Guarantee Act*, R.S.A. 2000, c. F-11, s. 1.

FEEDER SCHOOL. A school from which all pupils are sent to a regional high school or to a central high school who are in the grades taught at that regional high school or central high school. *School Tax Act*, R.S. Nfld. 1990, c. S-10, s. 46(1).

FEEDER OR SPUR ROAD. A short, dead-end or circular road with a usable life-span of 1 operating season or less. *Forestry Act*, R.S. Nfld. 1990, c. F-23, s. 112.

FEED GRAIN. 1. Wheat, other than grades of wheat grown in the designated area and designated by regulation not to be feed grain for the purposes of this Act, oats and barley and such other grains and grain products as may be designated by regulation as feed grain for the purposes of this Act. *Livestock Feed Assistance Act*, R.S.C. 1985, c. L-10, s. 2. 2. Grain that is used or intended to be used for human or animal consumption. *New Brunswick Grain Act*, S.N.B. c. N-5.1, s. 1. 3. (a) In respect of wheat, wheat of the grade No. 3 Canada Western Red Spring or wheat of any equivalent or lower level of excellence, and (b) in respect of barley, feed barley of the grade Extra No. 1 Canada Western or barley of any lower level of excellence. *Canadian Wheat Board Regulations*, C.R.C. 397, s. 2. Canada regulations.

FEEDING THE ESTOPPEL. An interest in land is created by estoppel when the grantor has no legal estate or interest at the time of the grant. A title by estoppel is not good as against the world. It is good against the grantor who is estopped by his own deed. If the grantor later acquires legal title to the property which he has purported to grant that legal estate or interest feeds the estoppel. The original grant then takes effect as a grant in interest, not just estoppel. *Certain Titles to Land in Ontario, Re*, [1973] 2 O.R. 613 (C.A.).

FEED LOT. *var.* **FEEDLOT**. Land enclosed by a fence or other means on which stock is fed, or intended to be fed, in confinement.

FEED MILL OPERATOR. A person who purchases grain from producers and processes the grain into feed, for sale. *Western Grain Stabilization Regulations*, C.R.C., c. 1607, s. 2.

FEED STOCK. 1. Includes any form of flora or fauna given or intended to be given as food to aquacultural produce. *Fisheries and Coastal Resources Act, 1996*, S.N.S. 1996, c. 25 , s. 43. 2. Any controlled substance that is used and the molecular structure of which is transformed in the manufacture of another chemical substance. *Ozone-depleting Substances Regulations, 1998*, SOR/99-7, s. 1.

FEE GENERATING SERVICES. Those services which a solicitor would ordinarily render in civil matters on the understanding that he or she would receive no remuneration from the client except out of the proceeds generated through pursuing the matter. *Legal Aid Act*, S.S. 1983, c. L-9.1, s. 2.

FEE INDEMNITY INSURANCE. Insurance whereby an insurer undertakes to pay on behalf of a person, or to indemnify a person, for the payment of professional or other fees incurred by that person for services rendered .

FEE REVENUE. In respect of a licensee of a broadcasting undertaking, means the gross revenue derived during a return year from the licensed activity of the licensee, whether received by the licensee or by an associated corporation, and, without limiting the generality of the foregoing, includes (a) any revenue received in respect of all transmitters forming part of the undertaking, where the broadcasting undertaking consists of more than one transmitter; (b) the estimated annual revenue, based on the trends of the market in which the undertaking is licensed to operate, the previous financial performance of the undertaking, and, where applicable, the licensee's business plan for the first 12 months of operations, where the licensee has not filed a licence fee return covering 12 months of the most recently completed return year; and (c) revenue that is derived from the sale of air time of the broadcasting undertaking by the Corporation and paid by the Corporation to the licensee. This definition does not include any amount received by the licensee from another licensee, other than the amounts received from the Corporation for the sale of air time. *Broadcasting Licence Fee Regulations, 1997*, SOR/97-144, s. 1.

FEE SIMPLE. 1. " . . . [T]he largest estate in land in both time and status with a night of alienation and inheritability." *Saint John (City) v. McKenna* (1987), 45 R.P.R. 61 at 64, 78 N.B.R. (2d) 393, 198 A.P.R. 393, 37 D.L.R. (4th) 160 (C.A.), Hoyt J.A. (Ryan J.A. concurring). 2. An absolute estate in perpetuity. See REGISTERED OWNER IN ~.

FEE TAIL. An estate in land which is of smaller extent than an estate in fee simple. It is a grant to a person and his heirs. The estate is limited to the grantee's own issue.

FELLING AREA. An area where trees are being felled and into which they might fall.

FELLOWSHIP. *n.* A loan for educational and training purposes in respect of health to assist in the financing of a program of advanced study or research at a university or health institution approved by the Minister repayable by the performance of agreed upon services to the public. *Ministry of Health Act*, R.R.O. 1990, Reg. 780, s. 1.

FELO DE SE. [L.] A felon with respect to oneself] A person who commits suicide.

FELON. *n.* A person who was convicted of felony.

FELONIAE CEPIT ET ASPORTAVIT. [L.] One feloniously took and carried off.

FELONIA IMPLICATUR IN QUALIBET PRODITIONE. [L.] Felony is involved in every treason.

FELONY. *n.* Originally the condition of having forfeited goods and lands to the Crown when convicted of a certain offence; later the offence which caused such forfeiture, distinguished from misdemeanour, after conviction for which forfeiture did not follow. See MISPRISION OF ~.

FEMALE-DOMINATED CLASS. 1. A class of which 60% or more of the incumbents are women. *Pay Equity Act*, R.S.P.E.I. 1988, c. P-2, s. 1. 2. (i) A class in which there are 10 or more incumbents, as of the date any public sector employer is required to commence action to implement pay equity, of whom 70% or more are women, (ii) in the case of a public sector employer which employs 500 or more employees as of the date referred to in subclause (i), such other classes, irrespective of the number of incumbents and gender distribution, as the employer, bargaining agents and employee repre-

sentatives affected may agree should be considered female-dominated, and (iii) in the case of a public sector employer which employs less than 500 employees as of the date referred to in sub-clause (i), such other classes as may be further defined in the regulations. *The Pay Equity Act*, C.C.S.M., c. P13, s. 1.

FEMALE JOB CLASS. Except where there has been a decision that a job class is a male job class as described in clause (b) of the definition "male job class", (a) a job class in which 60 per cent or more of the members are female, (b) a job class that a review officer or the Hearings Tribunal decides is a female job class or a job class that the employer, with the agreement of the bargaining agent, if any, for the employees of the employer, decides is a female job class. *Pay Equity Act*, R.S.O. 1990, c. P.7, s. 1.

FEME. *n.* A woman; a wife.

FEME COVERT. A woman who is married.

FEME SOLE. A woman who is unmarried: spinster, widow or divorced.

FEMININE. *adj.* Relating to females.

FEMTO. *pref.* 10^{-15}. Prefix for multiples and submultiples of Basic, Supplementary and Derived Units of Measurement. *Weights and Measures Act*, S.C. 1970-71-72, c. 36, schedule 1, part V.

FENCE. *n.* Patent claims are frequently analogized to "fences" and "boundaries", giving the "fields" of the monopoly a comfortable pretence of bright line demarcation. Thus, in *Minerals Separation North American Corp. v. Noranda Mines Ltd.*, [1947] Ex. C.R. 306 (Can. Ex. Ct.), Thorson P. put the matter as follows, at p. 352: By his claims the inventor puts fences around the fields of his monopoly and warns the public against trespassing on his property. His fences must be clearly placed in order to give the necessary warning and he must not fence in any property that is not his own. The terms of a claim must be free from avoidable ambiguity or obscurity and must not be flexible; they must be clear and precise so that the public will be able to know not only where it must not trespass but also where it may safely go. In reality, the "fences" often consist of complex layers of definitions of different elements (or "components" or "features" or "integers") of differing complexity, substitutability and ingenuity. A matrix of descriptive words and phrases defines the monopoly, warns the public and ensnares the infringer. In some instances, the precise elements of the "fence" may be crucial or "essential" to the working of the invention as claimed; in others the inventor may contemplate, and the reader skilled in the art appreciate, that variants could easily be used or substituted without making any material difference to the working of the invention. The interpretative task of the court in claims construction is to separate the one from the other, to distinguish the essential from the inessential, and to give to the "field" framed by the former the legal protection to which the holder of a valid patent is entitled. *Free World Trust c. Électro Santé Inc.*, 2000 CarswellQue 2728, 2000 SCC 66, 194 D.L.R. (4th) 232, 263 N.R. 150, [2000] 2 S.C.R. 1024, 9 C.P.R. (4th) 168, Binnie, J. See LAWFUL ~; RAILWAY ~.

FENERATION. *n.* 1. Usury. 2. Interest on loaned money.

FEOD. See FEUD.

FEODAL. *adj.* Belonging to or of a feod.

FEODALITY. See FEALTY.

FEODAL SYSTEM. See FEUDAL SYSTEM.

FEODATORY. *n.* The tenant who holds an estate through feudal service.

FEOFFEE. *n.* One who is put in possession.

FEOFFMENT. *n.* Formerly, the transfer of freehold land by livery of seisin and word of mouth.

FEOFFOR. *n.* A person who makes a feoffment.

FERAE NATURAE. [L.] Having a wild nature.

FERIAE. *n.* [L.] Holidays.

FERIAL DAY. A holiday; feast.

FERRET. *n.* Any of the domesticated forms of the old world polecat (Putorius putorius) used for hunting. *Game and Fish Act*, R.S.O. 1990, c. G.1, s. 1.

FERRIAGE. *n.* A ferry fare.

FERROUS FOUNDRY. The part of a building, or premises, or the workshop, structure, room or place in which iron or any of its alloys is cast in moulds or where core-making, shake-out or cleaning of any casting or other dust-causing or odour-causing operation ancillary to the casting process is carried on. *Environmental Protection Act*, R.R.O. 1990, Reg. 336, s. 1.

FERRY. *n.* 1. A scow, barge or boat used to carry passengers, freight, vehicles or animals across a river, stream, lake or other body of water and includes any dock, cable and appliances used in connection with it. *Highway and Transportation Act, 1997*, S.S. 1997, c. H-3.01, s. 1. 2. Any and all methods and means of water transport including, but not limited to, ships, boats, vessels, barges, hydrofoils and hovercraft. *Ferry Corporation Act*, R.S.B.C. 1996, c. 137, s. 1. 3. At common law, a toll franchise granted by the Crown.

FERRY CABLE. Any ferry cable, rod, chain or other device put across, over, in or under any navigable water for working a ferry. *Navigable Waters Protection Act*, R.S.C. 1985, c. N-22, s. 29.

FERRY VESSEL. Any vessel, having provision only for deck passengers and for vehicles, that is operated on a short run on a schedule between two points over the most direct water route and offers a public service of a type normally attributed to a bridge or tunnel. *Hull Construction Regulations*, C.R.C., c. 1431, s. 2.

FERTILIZER. *n.* 1. Any substance or mixture of substances, containing nitrogen, phosphorus, potassium or other plant food, manufactured, sold or represented for use as a plant nutrient. 2. Includes agricultural lime, peat moss and similar soil conditioners. See CUSTOMER-FORMULA ~; MIXED ~; SPECIALTY ~.

FERTILIZER-PESTICIDE. *n.* Any fertilizer that contains a pesticide. *Fertilizers Regulations*, C.R.C., c. 666, s. 2.

FESANCE. *n.* An act.

FESTINATIO JUSTITIAE NOVERCA. [L.] The stepmother of justice is haste.

FESTINUM REMEDIUM. [L.] A prompt remedy.

FESTUM. *n.* [L.] A feast.

FETTERING OF DISCRETION. The general principle of law is that a tribunal which exercises a statutory discretion may not fetter the exercise of that discretion by the adoption of an inflexible policy. In every case the Tribunal must consider the merits of the particular application. It must have regard to any policies of the Board. But a policy is only a factor for the Tribunal's consideration. In this case, the Tribunal said it was obliged to follow and was bound by the policy. This indicates that the policy was applied without regard to the merits of the applicant's case. That amounts to a fettering of discretion. *Braden-Burry Expediting Services Ltd. v. Northwest Territories (Workers' Compensation Board)* (1998), 1998 CarswellNWT 170, 13 Admin. L.R. (3d) 232 (S.C.) Vertes J. See ON ITS MERITS; UNFETTERED DISCRETION.

FETTLER. *n.* An employee who makes minor repairs and puts things in order.

FETUS. *n.* 1. An unborn product of conception after the embryo stage. 2. A child developing in the uterus during the last two thirds of pregnancy. F.A. Jaffe, *A Guide to Pathological Evidence*, 3d ed. (Toronto: Carswell, 1991) at 219. See FOETUS.

FEUD. *n.* A grant of land made by a feudal lord or superior which is held by the grantee in return for services rendered.

FEUDAL SYSTEM. A peculiar system in which absolute or nominal ownership of land was in one feudal superior or lord while the occupation, use and benefit was in the feudal inferior or tenant who rendered the lord certain services.

FEUDATORY. *n.* The tenant who holds an estate through feudal service.

F.G.A. *abbr.* Free from general average. In marine insurance policies, means that the underwriters are not liable for general average losses.

FIAT. *n.* [L. let it be done] A decree; order or warrant made by a judge or public officer to allow certain processes.

FIAT JUSTITIA. [L.] Let justice be done.

FIAT JUSTITIA, RUAT COELUM. [L.] Let justice be done, even though the heavens fall.

FIAT QUOD PRIUS FIERI CONSUEVIT. [L.] Let what was usually done before be done.

FIAUNT. *n.* [L.] Warrant.

FIBRE. See ASBESTOS ~; CARBON ~S AND FILAMENTS; FLAX ~; MAN-MADE ~; TEXTILE ~; WOOD ~.

FIBRILLATION. See VENTRICULAR ~.

FICTIO LEGIS NON OPERATUR DAMNUM VEL INJURIAM. [L.] A legal fiction does not operate to cause loss or injustice.

FICTION. *n.* A rule of law which assumes something which is false is true, and will not allow it to be disproved. An assumption by law that something which is false is true. A statute may state that X is to be treated as Y. That a corporation is a person is sometimes said to be a legal fiction.

FICTITIOUS. *adj.* " . . . [W]here a person with signing authority writes a cheque to a named payee, but who is never intended to receive the amount drawn, the payee is treated as 'fictitious' within the meaning of s. 20(5) of the Bills of Exchange Act, [R.S.C. 1985, c. B-4] . . ." *Kelly Funeral Homes Ltd. v. Canadian Imperial Bank of Commerce* (1990), 72 D.L.R. (4th) 276 at 281 (Ont. H.C.), Walsh J.

FICTITIOUS IDENTIFICATION PLATE OR MARKER. An identification plate, sticker or marker which has not been issued under this Act or which has not been issued for the registration year in which it is used or which is attached to a vehicle other than that for which it was issued but does not include an identification plate, sticker or marker on a foreign vehicle lawfully operated in the province. *Highway Traffic Act*, R.S. Nfld. 1970, c. 152, s. 2.

FICTITIOUS NUMBER PLATE. A number plate or sticker that has not been issued under the Highway Traffic Act or that has not been issued for the registration year in which it is used or that is attached to a vehicle other than that for which it was issued, but does not include number plates or stickers on foreign vehicles lawfully operated in the province.

FICTITIOUS PAYEE. A person who is to receive money, but who does not exist. If the payee who is named, is never intended to receive the amount drawn, the payee is "fictitious" within the meaning of the *Bills of Exchange Act*. If the payee does not exist, the bill may be treated as payable to the bearer.

FICTITIOUS REGISTRATION PLATE. A registration plate not furnished and issued by the division or not furnished and issued for the current registration year, or that is attached to a vehicle other than that for which it was issued by the division but does not include registration plates on foreign vehicles lawfully operated in New Brunswick. *Motor Vehicle Act*, S.N.B., c. M-17, s. 1.

FIDEI-COMMISSUM. *n.* [L.] A disposition by will in which the testator obliges the receiver to transfer the object to a third person.

FIDE-JUSSOR. *n.* [L] A surety.

FIDELITY BOND. (a) A promise to make good financial loss resulting from the dishonesty of employees, or (b) a financial guarantee of the performance of an implied obligation.

FIDELITY INSURANCE. (a) Insurance against loss caused by the unfaithful performance of duties by a person in a position of trust; or (b) insurance whereby an insurer undertakes to guarantee the proper fulfilment of the duties of an office.

FIDUCIARY. *n*. 1. " . . . [W]here by statute, agreement, or perhaps by unilateral undertaking, one party has an obligation to act for the benefit of another, and that obligation carries with it a discretionary power, the party thus empowered becomes a fiduciary. . ." *Guerin v. R.* (1984), [1985] 1 C.N.L R. 120 at 137, [1984] 2 S.C.R. 335, 36 R.P.R. 1, 210 E.T.R. 6, [1984] 6 W.W.R. 481, 59 B.C.L.R. 301, 13 D.L.R. (4th) 321, 55 N.R. 161, Dickson J. (Beetz, Chouinard and Lamer JJ. concurring). 2. " . . . [U]se[d] in at least three distinct ways. . . [(a)] The focus is on the identification of relationships in which, because of their inherent purpose or their presumed factual or legal incidents, the Courts will impose a fiduciary obligation on one party to act or refrain from acting in a certain way. The obligation imposed may vary in its specific substance depending on the relationship, though compendiously it can be described as the fiduciary duty of loyalty and will most often include the avoidance of a conflict of duty and interest and a duty not to profit at the expense of the beneficiary. . . [(b)] a fiduciary obligation can arise as a matter of fact out of the specific circumstances of a relationship. As such it can arise between parties in a relationship in which fiduciary obligations would not normally be expected. . . [(c)] third usage of 'fiduciary' stems, it seems, from a perception of remedial inflexibility in equity. Courts have resorted to fiduciary language because of the view that certain remedies, deemed appropriate in the circumstances, would not be available unless a fiduciary relationship was present. In this sense, the label fiduciary imposes no obligations, but rather is merely instrumental or facilitative in achieving what appears to be the appropriate result." *International Corona Resources Ltd. v. LAC Minerals Ltd.* (1989), 35 E.T.R. 1 at 20, 21-2, 26 C.P.R. (3d) 97, 69 O.R. (2d) 287, 61 D.L.R. (4th) 14, [1989] 2 S.C.R. 574, 6 R.P.R. (2d) 1, 44 B.L.R. 1, 101 N.R. 239, 36 O.A.C. 57, La Forest J. (Lamer J. concurring). 3. "Relationships in which a fiduciary obligation have been imposed seem to possess three general characteristics: (1) The fiduciary has scope for the exercise of some discretion or power. (2) The

fiduciary can unilaterally exercise that power or discretion so as to affect the beneficiary's legal or practical interests. (3) The beneficiary is peculiarly vulnerable to or at the mercy of the fiduciary holding the discretion or power." *Frame v. Smith* (1987), [1988] 1 C.N.L.R. 152 at 155, 78 N.R. 40, 9 R.F.L. (3d) 225, 42 C.C.L.T. 1, [1987] 2 S.C.R. 99, 23 O.A.C. 84, 42 D.L.R. (4th) 81, Wilson J. (dissenting). 4. Any person acting in a fiduciary capacity and includes a personal representative of a deceased person. *Bank Act, 1991*, S.C. 1991, c. 46, s. 2. 5. A trustee, guardian, committee, curator, tutor, executor, administrator or representative of a deceased person, or any other person acting in a fiduciary capacity. *Canada Business Corporations Act*, R.S.C. 1985, c. C-44, s. 48.

FIDUCIARY DUTY. 1. One that arises in the context of a trust. 2. Certain relationships give rise to this type of duty: trustee and beneficiary, guardian and ward, principal and agent. 3. A duty by which the law seeks to protect vulnerable persons in transactions with others.

FIDUCIARY OBLIGATION. Arises in a relationship in which the fiduciary has a discretion or power to exercise, the fiduciary can unilaterally exercise this discretion or power, and the beneficiary is vulnerable to or at the mercy of the fiduciary.

FIEF. *n*. A fee; a manor.

FIELD. *n*. 1. In relation to oil or gas wells, (a) The surface area underlaid or appearing to be underlaid by one or more pools; and (b) the subsurface regions vertically beneath that surface area. 2. Patent claims are frequently analogized to "fences" and "boundaries", giving the "fields" of the monopoly a comfortable pretence of bright line demarcation. Thus, in *Minerals Separation North American Corp. v. Noranda Mines Ltd.*, [1947] Ex. C.R. 306 (Can. Ex. Ct.), Thorson P. put the matter as follows, at p. 352: By his claims the inventor puts fences around the fields of his monopoly and warns the public against trespassing on his property. His fences must be clearly placed in order to give the necessary warning and he must not fence in any property that is not his own. The terms of a claim must be free from avoidable ambiguity or obscurity and must not be flexible; they must be clear and precise so that the public will be able to know not only where it must not trespass but also where it may safely go. In reality, the "fences" often consist of complex layers of definitions of different elements (or "components" or "features" or "integers") of differing complexity, substitutability and ingenuity. A matrix of descriptive words and phrases defines the monopoly, warns the public and ensnares the infringer. In some instances, the precise elements of the "fence" may be crucial or "essential" to the working of the invention as claimed; in others the inventor may contemplate, and the reader skilled in the art appreciate, that variants could easily be used or substituted without making any material difference to the working of the invention. The interpretative task of the court in claims construction is to separate the one from the other, to distinguish the essential from the inessential, and to give to the "field" framed by the former the legal protection to which the holder of a valid patent is entitled. *Free World Trust c. Électro Santé Inc.*, 2000 CarswellQue 2728, 2000 SCC 66, 194 D.L.R. (4th) 232, 263 N.R. 150, [2000] 2 S.C.R. 1024, 9 C.P.R. (4th) 168, Binnie, J. See MUTUEL ~; OCCUPIED ~.

FIELD PRICE. See CONTRACT ~; REGULATED ~.

FIELD TRIAL. An activity, the objective of which is to test the hunting skills of a dog.

FIELD WORK. The work performed in the search for occurrences of placer or lode mineral deposits.

FIERI FACIAS. [L. that you cause to be made] A writ of execution used to levy a judgment debt. See WRIT OF ~.

FIERI FECI. [L. I have caused to be made] A return made by the sheriff who executed a writ of execution.

FIERI NON DEBUIT, SED FACTUM VALET. [L.] It should not have been done, but once done is binding.

FI. FA. *abbr*. Fieri facias.

FIFO. *abbr*. First in, first out.

FIFO METHOD OF INVENTORY VALUATION. In this method, it is assumed that the first items purchased as inventory are the first to be disposed of. The cost of inventory on hand at the end of a fiscal period is the cost of the items purchased most recently.

FIFTH FREEDOM. The privilege of a non-Canadian air carrier, where operating a charter flight, of embarking or disembarking in Canada passengers or goods destined for, or coming from, the territory of a country other than that of the non-Canadian air carrier; *Air Transportation Regulations*, SOR/88-58, s. 2.

FIFTH WHEEL ASSEMBLY. A coupling device having its lower-half mounted on the rear portion of a vehicle frame or the frame of a trailer converter dolly and its upper-half fastened to the underside of the forward portion of a semi-trailer for the purpose of supporting and towing the semi-trailer. *Highway Traffic Act*, R.R.O. 1990, Reg. 618, s. 1.

FIGHT. *n*. " . . . [A]n encounter in which one party intends to hurt the other." *Bithef v. Butler* (1920), 58 Que. S.C. 47 at 51, 54 D.L.R. 122, Archibald J. See PRIZE ~.

FIGURE. *n*. A numerical character.

FILE. *v*. 1. To leave with the appropriate office for keeping. 2. Register. 3. Requires actual delivery. A mailed document is not filed until received by the appropriate party.

FILE. *n*. All the information about a consumer recorded or retained by a credit reporting agency regardless of how the information is stored. See PERSONAL ~.

FILED SUBDIVISION PLAN. A plan of subdivision (a) approved by a development officer under this Act, or by the Provincial Planning Board or a commission under a previous Act, and filed in the registry office, or (b) filed in the registry office when there was no subdivision by-law or regulation under this or a previous Act applicable to the land comprised in the plan. *Community Planning Act*, S.N.B., c. C-12, s. 47.

FILE WRAPPER ESTOPPEL. In the United States, representations to the Patent Office were historically noted on the file cover or "wrapper", and the doctrine is thus known in that country as "file wrapper estoppel" or "prosecution history estoppel". In its recent decision in Warner-Jenkinson Co., [*Warner-Jenkinson Co. v. Hilton Davis Chemical Co.*, 520 U.S. 17 (Ohio, 1997)], the United States Supreme Court affirmed that a patent owner is precluded from claiming the benefit of the doctrine of equivalents to recapture ground conceded by limiting argument or amendment during negotiations with the Patent Office. The availability of file wrapper estoppel was affirmed, but it was narrowed in the interest of placing "reasonable limits on the doctrine of equivalents", per Thomas J., at p. 34. While prosecution history estoppel is still tied to amendments made to avoid the prior art, or otherwise to address a specific concern—such as obviousness—that arguably would have rendered the claimed subject matter unpatentable, the court placed the burden on the patentee to establish the reason for an amendment required during patent prosecution. Where no innocent explanation is established, the court will now presume that the Patent Office had a substantial reason related to patentability for including the limiting element added by amendment. In those circumstances, prosecution history estoppel bars the application of the doctrine of equivalents as to that element. The use of file wrapper estoppel in Canada was emphatically rejected by Thorson P. in *Lovell Manufacturing Co. v. Beatty Brothers Ltd.* (1962), 41 C.P.R. 18 (Can. Ex. Ct.), and our Federal Court has in general confirmed over the years the exclusion of file wrapper materials tendered for the purpose of construing the claims. No distinction is drawn in this regard between cases involving allegations of literal infringement and those involving substantive infringement. *Free World Trust c. Électro Santé Inc.*, 2000 CarswellQue 2728, 2000 SCC 66, 194 D.L.R. (4th) 232, 263 N.R. 150, [2000] 2 S.C.R. 1024, 9 C.P.R. (4th) 168, Binnie, J.

FILIAFAMILIAS. *n.* [L.] A daughter.

FILIATION. *n.* The relationship of a son to his father.

FILIATIO NON POTEST PROBARI. [L.] Filiation cannot be proved.

FILIBUSTER. *n.* A tactic used to delay legislative action.

FILING. *n.* 1. Registration; recording. 2. The entering in the daybook of any instrument. *Land Titles acts.*

FILIUSFAMILIAS. *n.* [L.] A son.

FILIUS MULIERATUS. [L.] The oldest legitimate son of a woman who was unlawfully connected with the father before marriage.

FILIUS NULLIUS. [L. son of no one] The child of unmarried parents.

FILIUS POPULL [L. son of the people] A bastard.

FILL. *n.* Earth, gravel, sand, rubbish, garbage or any other material, whether similar to or different from any of the aforementioned materials and whether originating on the site or elsewhere, used or capable of being used to raise or in any way affect the contours of the ground. See INERT ~.

FILL-AND-DRAW POOL. A pool so operated that the water is completely drained to waste intermittently and replaced by make-up water.

FILL-AND-DRAW SWIMMING POOL. A swimming pool so operated that the water is completely drained to waste intermittently and replaced by make-up water.

FILLER. *n.* 1. (a) Flour or meal prepared from grain or potato, but not from a legume, (b) processed wheat flour containing not less than the equivalent of 80 per cent dextrose as determined by the official method, (b) bread, biscuit or bakery products, but not those containing or made with a legume, (d) milk powder, skim milk powder, buttermilk powder or whey powder, and (e) starch. *Food and Drug Regulations*, C.R.C., c. 870. 2. (a) Flour or meal prepared from grain or potatoes, (b) processed wheat flour containing not less than the equivalent of 80 per cent dextrose, as determined by a method approved by the Minister, (c) bread, biscuit or bakery products, except those containing or made with a legume, or (d) milk powder, skim milk powder, buttermilk powder or whey powder. *Fish Inspection Regulations*, C.R.C., c. 802, s. 2. 3. A food added to a meat product to increase its bulk. *Meat Inspection Regulations*, C.R.C., c. 1032, s. 2.

FILLETS. *n.* (a) Slices of fish flesh of irregular size and shape that have been removed from the carcass of a fish by cuts made parallel to the backbone, or (b) slices of fish flesh described in paragraph (a) that have been cut into sections and from which all internal organs, head, fins, bones, except intramuscular or lateral bones, and all discoloured flesh have been removed. Canada regulations.

FILLING DENSITY. The percentage figure obtained when the maximum weight of anhydrous ammonia or of liquefied petroleum gas that may be in a container is divided by the water weight capacity of the tank and the result is multiplied by 100; all capacities shall be measured at a liquid temperature of 60°F. *Bulk Storage Regulations*, Canada regulations.

FILLING STATION. Any pump, tank, store, vehicle, place or premises, where or from which gasoline is sold at retail.

FILM. *n.* 1. Photographic film, pre-recorded video tapes, pre-recorded video discs and includes any other object or device on or within which there is recorded, by photographic, electronic or other means, the contents of a motion picture, and from which, by the use of a projector, machine or other appropriate technology, the motion picture may be viewed, exhibited or projected. 2. A work produced with the use of technical means resulting in a cinematographic effect, regardless of the medium, and includes a video. *An Act respecting the professional status and conditions of engagement of performing, recording and film artists,* R.S.Q., c. S-32.1, s. 1. See ADULT ~; CANADIAN ~; CINEMAT-OGRAPHIC ~; MINIATURE~; NA-TIONAL ~ BOARD; PHOTOGRAPHIC~; SAFETY ~; SILENT ~ SUBJECT; SOUND ~; SUBJECT; STANDARD ~; TELE~ CANADA; VIDEO~.

FILM ACTIVITY. Any activity relating to the production, distribution, projection or exhibition of films.

FILM DEPOT. Any building or premises in which film is assembled for shipment. *Theatres Act,* R.S.O. 1990, c. T-6, s. 1.

FILM DISTRIBUTOR. See ADULT ~.

FILM EXCHANGE. 1. The business of distributing film. 2. A place where film is stored, rented, sold, leased or supplied. See THEA-TRE ~.

FILM-MAKER. *n.* A person creatively engaged in film production.

FILM PRODUCTION. The creative, artistic and technical process of producing a film.

FILM RETAILER. See ADULT~.

FILM SOCIETY. A nonprofit cultural organization, membership of which is by annual subscription and limited to persons who are not less than 18 years of age and the objects of which are to encourage the appreciation of motion pictures as an art and a medium of information and education by exhibiting motion pictures to members only, and to discuss films exhibited and to provide its members with information respecting motion pictures.

FILM TECHNICIAN. A person engaged in the technical or administrative aspects of film production.

FILTER. *n.* Material placed in the useful beam to attenuate preferentially the lower energy radiations. *Radiation Emitting Devices Regulations,* C.R.C., c. 1370, s. 1.

FILUM AQUAE. See AD MEDIUM FILUM AQUAE.

FILUM VIAE. See AD MEDIUM FILUM VIAE.

FINAL. *v.* To put into final form. To conclude.

FINAL. *adj.* 1. Last; conclusive; terminated. 2. " . . . [N]ot subject to further appeal. . ." *Hi Rise Structures Inc. v. Scarborough (City)* (1992), 12 M.P.L.R. (2d) 1 at 11, 94 D.L.R. (4th) 385, 10 O.R. (3d) 299, 27 O.M.B.R. 443, 57 O.A.C. 287 (C.A.), the court per Carth J.A. 3. " . . . [A] judgment or order is . . . final . . . [if] it finally disposes of the rights of the parties. . ." *Kampus v. Bridgeford* (1982), 25 C.P.C. 169 at 171, 131 D.L.R. (3d) 612 (Ont. C.A.), the court per Brooke J.A. 4. Does not necessarily imply an intended restriction on judicial review. The opposite of interim. *C.J.A., Local 579 v. Bradco Construction Ltd.,* [1993] 2 S.C.R. 316.

FINAL ACT. A document which summarizes the work of, and any agreements reached at, an international conference.

FINAL AND BINDING. 1. This phrase has limited privative effect but signals that the court should exercise some restraint on judicial review. *Trent University v. T.U.F.A.* (1997), 102 O.A.C. 346 (C.A.). 2. At a minimum, reflects an intention to exclude a statutory right of appeal. *L.I.U.N.A., Local 183 v. Carpenters & Allied Workers, Local 27* (1997), 34 O.R. (3d) 472 (C.A.). See FINAL AND CONCLUSIVE.

FINAL AND CONCLUSIVE. 1. In the judgment of Weiler J.A., concurring in the result: "The words 'final and conclusive' do not in themselves imply a binding effect on another administrative tribunal. The words 'final and conclusive' in ss. 108(1) and (2) [Labour Relations Act, R.S.O. 1990, c. L.2] mean that 'the issue as between the parties has been settled and no further steps need be taken for the decision to qualify as a determination of the rights of the parties. In other words, the ruling is not an interim one.'" *C.U.P.E., Local 1394 v. Extendicare Health Services Inc.* (1993), 1993 CarswellOnt 887, 17 Admin. L.R. (2d) 27, 93 C.L.L.C. 14,052, 14 O.R. (3d) 65, 104 D.L.R. (4th) 8, 64 O.A.C. 126 (C.A.), Brooke, Doherty and Weiler JJ.A. 2. "On issues within jurisdiction, I do not attach the importance to the difference in the wording of 'final and conclusive' and 'final and binding' that Cory J. attributes to me. I do not believe that one is simply privative and the other not. The difference between these phrases is much less significant than that between either of them and the expansive privative clause in s. 108 [of the *Labour Relations Act*, R.S.O. 1980, c. 228] that protects decisions of the Labour Board. More importantly, this small distinction is more significant in determining whether a question is a jurisdictional one or within jurisdiction than in considering the standard of review for questions within jurisdiction. I cannot accept that courts should mechanically defer to the tribunal simply because of the presence of a 'final and binding' or 'final and conclusive' clause. These finality clauses can clearly signal deference, but they should also be considered in the context of the type of question and the nature and expertise of the tribunal." *Dayco (Canada) Ltd. v. C.A.W.*, 1993 CarswellOnt 883, 14 Admin. L.R. (2d) 1, 13 O.R. (3d) 164 (note), 152 N.R. 1, 63 O.A.C. 1, (sub nom. *Dayco v. N.A.W.*) C.E.B. & P.G.R. 8141, (sub nom. *Dayco v. C.A.W.*) 93 C.L.L.C. 14,032, [1993] 2 S.C.R. 230, 102 D.L.R. (4th) 609, Per La Forest J.

FINAL DISPOSITION. The [Manitoba Criminal Appeal Rules, SI/92-106] contemplate that an appeal may be launched only upon the final disposition of a matter. In the case of a finding of not guilty, nothing more need be done. That is the final disposition and the Crown may launch an appeal immediately upon the acquittal occurring. In the case of a finding of guilt, the matter is not finally disposed of until sentence is pronounced. Only then can the accused or the Crown launch an appeal. *R. v. Payne* (2002), 2002 MBCA 169, 170 C.C.C. (3d) 145, 170 Man. R. (2d) 102, [2003] 5 W.W.R. 76 (C.A. [In Chambers]).

FINAL DRAFT. In a publication contract, refers to a manuscript in publishable form after the completion of the editorial process.

FINALITY CLAUSE. A statement in a statute that the decisions of a tribunal are "final and conclusive" or "final and binding". See FINAL AND BINDING; FINAL AND CONCLUSIVE; PRIVATIVE CLAUSE.

FINAL JUDGMENT. 1. Any judgment, rule, order or decision that determines in whole or in part any substantive right of any of the parties in controversy in any judicial proceeding. *Supreme Court Act*, R.S.C. 1985, c. S-26, s. 2. 2. " . . . [A] judgment obtained in an action by which a previously existing liability of the defendant to the plaintiff is ascertained or established . . ." *Ex Parte Chinery* (1884), 12 Q.B.D. 342 at 345 (U.K.), Cotten L.J.

FINAL LICENCE. A licence authorizing the diversion, use or storage of water for power purposes, or the transmission and distribution of water-power. *Dominion Water Power Regulations*, C.R.C., c. 1603, s. 2.

FINALLY ACQUITTED. "[Refers to] . . . [a]n accused who is acquitted by a judgment containing no error . . . within the meaning of s. 11 (h) of the Charter. . ." *Thibault c. Corp. professionnelle des médicins (Québec)* (1988), 42 C.C.C. (3d) 1 at 10, 84 N.R. 247, 14 Q.A.C. 173, [1988] 1 S.C.R. 1033, 63 C.R. (3d) 273, the court per Lamer J.

FINAL ODDS. The odds that are calculated by an association after the close of betting on a race. *Pari-Mutuel Betting Supervision Regulations*, SOR/91-365, s. 2.

FINAL ORDER. 1. " . . . [F]inally disposes of the rights of the parties, . . . *Hendrickson v. Kallio*, [1932] 4 D.L.R. 580 at 585, [1932] O.R. 675 (C.A.), Middleton J.A. 2. An order made in a proceeding of which the claimant and respondent had proper notice and in which they had an opportunity to be present or represented and includes (a) the maintenance provisions in a written agreement between a claimant and a respondent where those provisions are enforceable in the state in which the agreement was made as if contained in an order of a court of that state, and (b) a confirmation order made in a reciprocating state. *Reciprocal Enforcement of Maintenance Orders acts.*

FINANCE. *v.* To fund; to arrange to pay for over time, on credit.

FINANCE. *n.* The management of money.

FINANCE COMPANY. Includes a corporation whose main or chief business is buying or selling and dealing in mortgages, conditional sales agreements, lien notes, bills or other similar obligations or property, or advancing or lending money and taking as security for the repayment thereof a mortgage of chattels. See SALES ~.

FINANCE CORPORATION. (a) A corporation designated as a finance corporation by its corporate name, or (b) a corporation, not being a chartered bank, which finances sales of goods and chattels sold upon deferred payments or whose businesses or one of whose businesses is to deal in or purchase or lend money on the security of (i) accounts receivable, (ii) agreements for the sale of goods or chattels upon deferred payments, or (iii) securities taken or given for the purpose of securing the performance of agreements for the sale and purchase of goods and chattels upon deferred payments. *Loan and Finance Corporations Licensing Act*, R.S. Nfld. 1990, c. L-24, s. 2.

FINANCIAL. *adj*. Concerning the management of money.

FINANCIAL ASSISTANCE. Includes assistance by way of grant, loan, loan guarantee, the purchase or guarantee of bonds, debentures, notes or other debt obligations, and the purchase or other acquisition of any common or preferred shares or other equity securities. See STUDENT ~.

FINANCIAL ASSURANCE. One or more of (a) cash, in the amount specified in the approval or order, (b) a letter of credit from a bank, in the amount and terms specified in the approval or order, (c) negotiable securities issued or guaranteed by the Government of Ontario or the Government of Canada in the amount specified in the approval or order, (d) a personal bond accompanied by collateral security, each in the form, terms and amount specified in the approval or order, (e) a bond or guarantee company approved under the Guarantee Companies Securities Act, in the form, terms and amount specified in the approval or order, (f) a bond of a guarantor, other than a guarantee company, accompanied by collateral security each in the form, terms and amount specified in the approval or order, (g) an agreement in the form and terms specified in the approval or order, and (h) an agreement, in the forms and terms prescribed by the regulations. *Environmental Protection Act*, R.S.O. 1990, c. E.19, s. 131.

FINANCIAL CENTRE. See INTERNATIONAL ~.

FINANCIAL INSTITUTION. 1. The Bank of Canada, the Federal Business Development Bank and any institution incorporated in Canada that accepts deposits of money from its members or the public, and includes a branch, agency or office of any such bank or institution. 2. (a) A bank or an authorized foreign bank, (b) a body corporate to which the *Trust and Loan Companies Act* applies, (c) an association to which the *Cooperative Credit Associations Act* applies or a central cooperative credit society for which an order has been made under subsection 473(1) of that Act, (d) an insurance company or a fraternal benefit society incorporated or formed under the *Insurance Companies Act*, (e) a trust, loan or

insurance corporation incorporated by or under an Act of the legislature of a province, (f) a cooperative credit society incorporated and regulated by or under an Act of the legislature of a province, (g) an entity that is incorporated or formed by or under an Act of Parliament or of the legislature of a province and that is primarily engaged in dealing in securities, including portfolio management and investment counselling, and (h) a foreign institution. *Bank Act*, S.C. 1991, c. 46, s. 2. See REGULATED ~.

FINANCIAL INTERMEDIARY. Includes a bank, trust company, loan company, insurance company, investment company and a body corporate carrying on business as a securities broker, dealer or underwriter. *Canada Business Corporations Regulations*, 2001, SOR/2001-512, s. 87.

FINANCIAL LEASE. A credit device which permits the lessee to have rights and obligations of ownership, while the lessor continues to be the technical owner. I.F.G. Baxter, *The Law of Banking*, 3d ed. (Toronto: Carswell, 1981) at 187.

FINANCIAL OFFICER. See CHIEF ~.

FINANCIAL ORGANIZATION. A trust corporation, a bank to which the Bank Act (Canada) applies, a loan corporation or a credit union. *Unclaimed Intangible Property Act*, R.S.O. 1990, c. U-1, s. 1.

FINANCIAL RESOURCES. With the exception of the exemptions specified in the regulations, any one or more of the following things: (a) all the real and personal property of an applicant, a recipient or a dependant of the applicant or recipient, including the net income from any such property, (b) allowances, pensions, insurance benefits, and income from business farming or any other source received by an applicant, recipient or a dependant of the applicant or recipient, (c) gifts and gratuities whether in cash or in kind received by an applicant, recipient or a dependent of the applicant or recipient on a one time basis or otherwise; (d) the value attributed by the director to free shelter, free board and free lodging, received by an applicant, recipient or a dependant of the applicant or recipient. *Employment and Income Assistance Act*, C.C.S.M., c. E.98, s. 1.

FINANCIAL RESPONSIBILITY. See PROOF OF ~.

FINANCIAL SECURITY. The essence of financial security is that the right to salary of a decision-maker must be established by law and there must be no way in which the Executive could interfere with that right. *Bell Canada v. C.T.E.A.* (2000), 2000 CarswellNat 2606, 2000 C.L.L.C. 230-043, 5 C.C.E.L. (3d) 123, 194 D.L.R. (4th) 499, 26 Admin. L.R. (3d) 253, (sub nom. *Bell Canada v. Canadian Telephone Employees Assn.*) 190 F.T.R. 42, (sub nom. *Bell Canada v. Canada (Human Rights Commission)*) [2001] 2 F.C. 392 (T.D.) Tremblay-Lamer J.

FINANCIAL STATEMENT. A summary of financial condition of a business or organization, usually a balance sheet and statement of profit and loss.

FINANCIAL SUPPORT ORDER. An order or judgment for maintenance, alimony or support, including an order or judgment for arrears of payments, made pursuant to the Divorce Act, or pursuant to the law of a province relating to family financial support.

FINANCIAL YEAR. The year in respect of which the accounts of the company or of the business are made up.

FINANCING. *n*. In the context of a labour dispute, . . . a voluntary, intentional act of contribution . . ." *Hills v. Canada (Attorney General)* (1988), 30 Admin. L.R. 187 at 225, 88 C.L.L.C. 14,011, 84 N.R. 86, [1988] 1 S.C.R. 513, 48 D.L.R. (4th) 193, L'Heureux-Dubé J. (Dickson C.J.C., Wilson and La Forest JJ. concurring). See BRIDGE ~; PERMANENT ~.

FIND. *v*. 1. To come across. 2. To make a judicial or quasi-judicial determination.

FINDING. *n*. The conclusion drawn after an inquiry of fact.

FINDING OF FACT. A determination that a thing exists, or that a thing has happened, or, is, or, will be happening.

FINDING OF GUILT. The plea of guilty by a defendant to an offence or the finding that a defendant is guilty of an offence made before or by a court that makes an order directing that the defendant be discharged for the offence either absolutely or on the conditions prescribed in a probation order, where (a) the order directing the discharge is not subject to further appeal; or (b) no appeal is taken in respect of the order directing the discharge. *Evidence acts*.

FINDINGS. *n*. 1. Of a court, the result of the court's deliberations in relation to a question of fact. 2. Of a medical practitioner, the factual information, including results of patient examination and testing, upon which the practitioner relies to make a diagnosis. 3. Any textile fibre products that (a) have been added to a consumer textile article for a functional purpose other than filling, stuffing or providing warmth, whether or not they also serve a decorative purpose, (b) differ in textile fibre content from the article to which they have been added, and (c) do not constitute a part of the outer surface of the article to which they have been added unless they are incorporated at or along an edge thereof, and without limiting the generality of the foregoing includes (d) belting, binding, tape, stiffening, facing, interfacing, thread, buttons, slide fasteners, hook and loop pile fasteners, garters, gussets, leg and wrist bands, waist bands and concealed pockets, (e) any lining (other than a laminated or bonded lining), interlining or padding incorporated primarily for structural purposes and not for warmth, and (f) any padding affixed to the underside of floor coverings, (g) elastic material inserted in or added to the consumer textile article, including elastic waist bands, elastic leg bands, elastic wrist bands and elastic smocking, and (h) elastic yarns used in a limited area in socks for the purpose of holding. *Textile Labelling and Advertising Regulations*, C.R.C., c. 1551, s. 25.

FINE. *n*. 1. A pecuniary penalty or other sum of money. *Criminal Code*. 2. A sum of money ordered to be paid to the Crown by an offender, as a punishment for the offence.

FINE FORCE. One does something de fine force when one is compelled and it is absolutely necessary.

FINFISH. *n*. Any of several species of fish having fins.

FINGERPRINT. *n*. The pattern in the skin on the finger tips, used to identify people.

FINGERPRINT EXAMINER. A person designated as such for the purposes of this section by the Solicitor General of Canada. *Criminal Code*, R.S.C. 1985, c. C-46, s. 667(5).

FINIS FINEM LITIBUS IMPONIT. [L.] A fine puts an end to an action.

FINIS LITIUM. [L.] The end of litigation.

FINIS REI ATTENDENDUS EST. [L.] One must bear in mind the awaited outcome.

FINIS UNIUS DIEI EST PRINCIPIUM AL-TERIUS. [L.] The end of one day is the start of another.

FINITIO. *n*. [L.] Death.

FIN WHALE. Any whale known by the name of common finback, common rorqual, finback, finner, fin whale, herring whale, razorback, or true fin whale.

FIRE. *n*. Combustion together with a visible glow or flame. C. Brown & J. Menezes, *Insurance Law in Canada*, 2d ed. (Toronto: Carswell 1991) at 182. See FALSE ALARM OF ~; FOREST ~; FOREST ~ AREA; STANDARD ~ TEST.

FIRE ALARM SIGNAL. An audible alarm or sound which is capable of notifying the occupants of a building.

FIRE ALARM SIGNALLING DEVICE. A sounding device that emits the fire alarm signal.

FIRE AND CASUALTY CORPORATION. A corporation incorporated under the laws of Canada or any province of Canada to undertake contracts of insurance other than contracts of life insurance.

FIREARM. *var*. **FIRE-ARM**. *n*. 1. A barrelled weapon from which any shot, bullet or other projectile can be discharged and that is capable of causing serious bodily injury or death to a person, and includes any frame or receiver of such a barrelled weapon and anything that can be adapted for use as a firearm. *Criminal Code*, R.S.C. 1985, c. C-46, s. 2. 2. Includes a device that propels a projectile by means of an explosion, compressed gas or spring and includes a rifle, shotgun, air gun, pistol, revolver, handgun or spring gun. 3. Crossbow or longbow. 4. A firearm must come within the definition of a weapon. A firearm is expressly designed to kill or wound. It operates with deadly efficiency in carrying out the object of its design. It followed that such a deadly weapon can, of course, be used for purposes of threatening and intimidating. Indeed, it is hard to imagine anything more intimidating or dangerous than a brandished firearm. A person waving a gun and calling 'hands up' can be reasonably certain that the suggestion will be obeyed. A firearm is quite different from an object such as a carving knife or an ice pick which will normally be used for legitimate purposes. A firearm, however, is always a weapon. No matter what the intention may be of the person carrying a gun, the firearm itself presents the ultimate threat of death to those in its presence." *R. v. Felawka*, 1993 CarswellBC 507, 25 C.R. (4th) 70, 159 N.R. 50, 33 B.C.A.C. 241, 54 W.A.C. 241, 85 C.C.C. (3d) 248, [1993] 4 S.C.R. 199, Cory, J. See ANTIQUE ~; AUTOMATIC ~; DEACTIVATED ~; IMITATION ~; LOADED ~; LOCAL REGISTRAR OF ~S; PIECE; REPLICA ~; RESTRICTED ~; RIFLE; SEALED ~.

FIREARMS OFFICER. (a) In respect of a province, an individual who is designated in writing as a firearms officer for the province by the provincial minister of that province, (b) in respect of a territory, an individual who is designated in writing as a firearms officer for the territory by the federal Minister, or (c) in respect of any matter for which there is no firearms officer under paragraph (*a*) or (*b*), an individual who is designated in writing as a firearms officer for the matter by the federal Minister. *Firearms Act, 1995*, S.C. 1995, c. 39, s. 2.

FIRE CHIEF. The person in charge of a fire department or fire brigade.

FIRE CODE. A set of safety standards for buildings and premises designed to prevent the outbreak of fire and to insure that emergency facilities and procedures to deal promptly with fires are available.

FIRE COMMISSIONER. A person appointed as a Fire Commissioner pursuant to a provincial statute. See DOMINION ~.

FIRE COMPARTMENT. An enclosed space in a building that is separated from all parts of the building by enclosing construction providing a fire separation having a required fire-resistance rating.

FIRE DAMPER. 1. A closure which consists of a normally held open damper installed in an air distribution system or in a wall or floor assembly, and designed to close automatically in the event of fire in order to maintain the integrity of the fire separation. 2. A blade or damper arranged to interrupt air flow through part of an air handling system, so as to restrict the passage of heat and smoke.

FIRE DEPARTMENT EQUIPMENT. Includes all fire hydrants, nozzles, hose, adapters, couplings, attachments and appliances ordinarily used by a fire department.

FIRE DEPARTMENT VEHICLE. Includes an emergency crash extrication vehicle owned and operated by a rescue organization approved by the Minister in writing for the purposes of this Part and a vehicle designated in writing by the Fire Marshal of Ontario as a "fire department vehicle". *Highway Traffic Act*, R.S.O. 1990, c. H.8, s. 61.

FIRE DOOR. *var*. **FIRE-DOOR**. A solid steel or hollow-steel or steel-clad door and frame or combination thereof or other approved door and frame that is self-closing and in which wired glass panels are permitted.

FIRED STEAM BOILER. A pressure vessel in which steam is generated by the application of heat resulting from the combustion of fuel in a solid, liquid or gaseous form. *Boilers and Pressure Vessels acts.*

FIRED VESSEL. A vessel that is directly heated by (a) a flame or the hot gases of combustion, (b) electricity, (c) rays from a radioactive source, or (d) molecular agitation arising from the process of fission. *Boilers and Pressure Vessels Act*, R.S.O. 1990, c. B.9, s. 1.

FIRE EXTINGUISHER. An appliance, container or apparatus containing any liquid, powder or gas, whether under pressure or not and designed, or purporting to be designed, for the purpose of extinguishing fire in its incipient stage.

FIRE EXTINGUISHER RATING. The rating of an extinguisher for extinguishing capacity and class of fire.

FIRE-EXTINGUISHING EQUIPMENT. A fire hose, an extinguisher or other similar equipment used to fight a fire.

FIRE FIGHTER. *n*. A person regularly employed on a salaried basis in a fire department and assigned to fire protection services and includes technicians but does not include a volunteer firefighter. *Fire Protection and Prevention Act, 1997*, S.O. 1997, c. 4, s.41. See FULLTIME ~; VOLUNTEER ~.

FIREFIGHTERS. *var*. **FIRE FIGHTERS**. 1. A trade union certified for a unit in which the majority of employees has as its principal duties the fighting of fires and the carrying out of rescue operations. 2. The persons, including officers and technicians, employed by a municipality and assigned exclusively to fire protection and fire prevention duties (which may include the performance of ambulance or rescue services).

FIRE FIGHTING. Includes controlling and extinguishing a fire.

FIRE HAZARD. A condition that will cause a fire to start or a condition that will increase the extent or severity of the fire.

FIRE HAZARD AREA. An area where a fire hazard may be created by smoking, matches or other means of producing heat or fire.

FIRE INSURANCE. 1. Insurance, not being insurance incidental to some other class of insurance defined by or under this Act, against loss of or damage to property through fire, lightning or explosion due to ignition. *Insurance acts.* 2. Insurance against the loss of, or damage to, property caused by fire, lighting, explosion due to ignition, smoke, and the breakage of or the leakage from a sprinkler or other fire protection or system. See BUSINESS OF ~ IN THE PROVINCE.

FIRE LOAD. The combustible contents of a room or floor area expressed in terms of the average weight of combustible materials per square foot and includes the furnishings, finished floor, wall and ceiling finishes, trim and temporary and movable partitions.

FIRE MARSHAL. A person appointed as Fire Marshal pursuant to a provincial statute.

FIRE PREVENTION. Includes fire inspections, determination of the cause of fire, measures for prevention of the spread of fire, fire protection and alarm systems, watchman's fire prevention services, minimization of damage subsequent to fire and protection of life. See NATIONAL ~ ASSOCIATION.

FIREPROOF. *adj*. Composed, constructed or made of fire resistant or incombustible materials.

FIRE PROTECTION. 1. Activities concerned with the prevention, detection and extinguishment, of fires in portions of the province that are not in an urban area; and includes the prevention of fire occurrence and of the spread of fire on lands not in an urban area where human life, property, protective vegetation, forage, or wild life, is endangered by the fire. 2. All aspects of fire safety including fire prevention, suppression, investigation, public education and information and training and advising.

FIRE PROTECTION INSTALLER. See SPRINKLER AND ~.

FIRE-PROTECTION RATING. The time in hours or fraction thereof that a closure, window assembly or glass block assembly will withstand the passage of flame when exposed to fire under specified conditions of test and performance criteria.

FIRE PROTECTION SERVICES. Includes fire suppression, fire prevention, fire safety education, communication, training of persons involved in the provision of fire protection services, rescue and emergency services and the delivery of all those services. *Fire Protection and Prevention Act, 1997*, S.O. 1997, c. 4, s.1.

FIRE RESISTANCE. The property of a material or assembly to withstand fire or give protection from it and when it is applied to elements or buildings, it is characterized by the ability to confine a fire or to continue to perform a given structural function, or both.

FIRE RESISTANCE RATING. *var.* **FIRE-RESISTANCE RATING**. 1. The rating assigned after a testing of the time of fire resistance of a representative specimen conducted by The National Research Council of Canada, Underwriters' Laboratories of Canada or any other approved testing laboratory. 2. The rating in hours or fraction thereof that a material or assembly of materials will withstand the passage of flame and the transmission of heat when exposed to fire.

FIRE RESISTING. As applied to buildings means constructed of masonry, reinforced concrete, or equivalent materials in accordance with the requirements of the fire underwriters.

FIRE RESISTIVE CONSTRUCTION. Having structural parts, in so far as walls, floors and partitions are concerned, constructed wholly of non-flammable materials, but structural parts do not include (a) any roof structure not forming in whole or in part the walls or ceiling of any room or rooms, (b) finished floors, (c) doors, doorframes and trim, (d) windows, window-frames and trim, or (e) base, handrails, mouldings, grounds and the like.

FIRE-RETARDANT TREATED WOOD. Wood or a wood product that has its surface-burning characteristics such as flame spread, rate of fuel contribution and density of smoke developed, reduced by impregnation with fire-retardant chemicals.

FIRE SEASON. The period in each year when a permit to burn is required before a fire may be set.

FIRE SEPARATION. 1. A barrier against the spread of fire and smoke. 2. A construction assembly that acts as a barrier against the spread of fire and that may or may not have a fire-resistance rating or a fire-protection rating.

FIRE SERVICES PERSONNEL. Persons regularly employed by a municipal fire department, appointed as auxiliary members of a fire department, or acting voluntarily as fire fighters.

FIRE STOP. A draft-tight barrier within or between construction assemblies that acts to retard the passage of smoke and flame.

FIRE STOP FLAP. A device intended for use in horizontal assemblies required to have a fire-resistance rating and incorporating protective ceiling membranes, which operates to close off a duct opening through the membrane in the event of a fire.

FIRE SUPPRESSION SYSTEM. An installation for the specific purpose of controlling a fire in a particular place.

FIREWALL. *var.* **FIRE WALL**. A type of fire separation of non-combustible construction that subdivides a building or separates adjoining buildings to resist the spread of fire and that has a fire-resistance rating prescribed under the Building Code Act and has structural stability to remain intact under fire conditions for the fire-resistance time for which it is rated. Ontario statutes.

FIRE WARDEN. A person who is an employee of a provincial government and whose duties include preventing and extinguishing forest fires.

FIREWORKS. *n.* Include cannon crackers, fireballs, fire crackers, mines, Roman candles, sky rockets, squibs, torpedoes and any other explosive designated as a firework by regulation. See HIGH HAZARD ~; LOW HAZARD ~; MANUFACTURED ~.

FIREWORKS COMPOSITION. Any chemical compound or mechanically mixed preparation of an explosive or inflammable nature that is used for the purpose of making any manufactured fireworks and is not included in any other class of explosives, and includes any star or coloured fire composition that is not manufactured fireworks. *Explosives Regulations*, C.R.C., c. 599, s. 2.

FIRING CHAMBER. The part of a firearm in which a cartridge rests in the position from which it can be fired. F.A. Jaffe, *A Guide to Pathological Evidence*, 3d ed. (Toronto: Carswell, 1991) at 219.

FIRING PIN. A device to strike and thus ignite the primer in a cartridge. F.A. Jaffe, *A Guide to Pathological Evidence*, 3d ed. (Toronto: Carswell, 1991) at 219.

FIRM. *n*. 1. (a) A person who is sole proprietor of a business carried on under a registered business name, or (b) the persons who are associated as partners in a business carried on by the partnership under a registered business name. 2. A sole practitioner or proprietorship, a partnership or a corporation. See ARCHITECTS ~; BROADCASTING ~; CABLECASTING ~; COMMISSION ~; ENGINEERS ~; JOINT ~; SUPPLY ~.

FIRM. *adj*. 1. Not soft, puffy, shrivelled or water soaked. 2. Not soft, flabby or shrivelled.

FIRMA. *n*. [L.] Provisions; rent.

FIRM ENERGY. Electric energy intended to be available at all times during a period covered by an agreement respecting the sale thereof.

FOR ET POTENTIOR EST OPERATIO LEGIS QUAM DISPOSITIO HOMINIS. [L.] The operation of law is stronger and more powerful than a human arrangement.

FIRM NAME. The name under which a business is carried on.

FIRM OF ACCOUNTANTS. A partnership, the members of which are accountants engaged in the practice of accounting, or a corporation incorporated under the laws of a province that is engaged in the practice of accounting.

FIRM POWER. Electric power or power-production capacity intended to be available at all times during a period covered by an agreement respecting the sale thereof.

FIRM PRICE CONTRACT. A contract that sets the total amount payable thereunder or pursuant to which the total amount payable is the product obtained by multiplying the number of identical units of work performed or identical items delivered by a predetermined fixed price for each unit or item. *Government Contracts Regulations*, C.R.C., c. 701, s. 2.

FIRST ADMISSION. Acceptance of a person who has no record of previous such care into a psychiatric inpatient facility.

FIRST-AID. *n*. Emergency or other treatment or care that conforms with recommended practice and is provided by an employer for any injury or illness of an employee arising from his work.

FIRST-AID ATTENDANT. A qualified person appointed by an employer to administer first-aid.

FIRST AID CERTIFICATE. A valid certificate of proficiency in first aid issued by the St. John Ambulance, the Canadian Red Cross Society, the Order of Malta or the Workers Compensation Board of British Columbia. *Marine Certification Regulations*, SOR/97-391, s. 1.

FIRST-AID ROOM. A room provided by an employer to be used exclusively for first-aid or medical purposes.

FIRST AID STATEMENT. A list of the hazardous ingredients in the chemical product; and a statement of the first aid treatment to be administered to anyone who has come into contact with a chemical product, such as through ingestion, absorption or inhalation, or information that may be helpful to someone who is assisting that individual. *Consumer Chemicals and Containers Regulations, 2001*, SOR/2001-269, s. 1.

FIRST-AID STATION. A place other than a first-aid room where first-aid supplies, instruments or equipment are stored for use.

FIRST CONVICTION. The earliest conviction.

FIRST CO-PILOT. A co-pilot assigned to duty as second-in-command of an aircraft during flight time.

FIRST DEALER. A person who sells under his own name or labels meat products prepared by some other person. Canada regulations.

FIRST DEGREE. See PRINCIPAL IN THE ~.

FIRST DEGREE MURDER. 1. Murder when it is planned and deliberate. *Criminal Code*, R.S.C. 1985, c. C-46, s. 231. 2. Irrespective of whether it is planned and deliberate (a) when the victim is a police officer or one of other named officials. *Criminal Code*, R.S.C. 1985, c. C-46, s. 231. 3. When death is caused while committing or attempting to commit hijacking an aircraft, sexual assault, sexual assault with a weapon, threats to a third party or causing bodily harm, aggravated sexual assault, kidnapping and forcible confinement or hostage taking. *Criminal Code*, R.S.C. 1985, c. C-46, s. 231.

FIRST FLOOR. The first floor above the basement and where no basement exists means the lowest floor of the building.

FIRST FRUITS. A term from feudal times for one year's profits of land after a tenant's death, which profits belonged to the monarch.

FIRST IMPRESSION. Describes a case which presents a new question of law for which there is no precedent.

FIRST IN, FIRST OUT. See FIFO.

FIRST INSPECTION. Inspection of a ship during construction and includes the initial inspection of a ship transferred from registry elsewhere than in Canada to Canadian registry. *Hull Inspection Regulations*, C.R.C., c. 1432, s. 2.

FIRST INSTANCE. Refers to the court which first hears a matter. See COURT OF ~.

FIRST ISSUE OF STOCK. All stock subscribed for and allotted prior to the first meeting of shareholders of the company for organization and election of directors, and upon which at least ten per cent has been paid. *Railway Act*, 1977, c. C-14, s. 6.

FIRST LOSS INSURANCE. ". . . [I]nsurance first in order of liability for loss,. . ." *Canadian General Insurance Co. v. State Farm Mutual Automobile Insurance Co.*, [1957] O.R. 258 at 265, [1957] I.L.R. 1-260, 8 D.L.R. (2d) 257 (C.A.), Laidlaw J.A.

FIRST MATE. The mate next to the master on board a ship in the line of authority. *Marine Certification Regulations*, SOR/97-391, s. 1.

FIRST MINISTERS' CONFERENCE. A federal-provincial conference of the federal Prime Minister and the provincial Premiers.

FIRST MORTGAGE. A mortgage which has priority over all other similar mortgages against the same land.

FIRST MORTGAGE BOND. A corporate obligation secured by a first mortgage on real estate.

FIRST NAME. Given name. In contrast to surname or family name.

FIRST NATION. An aboriginal governing body, however organized and established by aboriginal people within their traditional territory in British Columbia, that has been mandated by its constituents to enter into treaty negotiations on their behalf with Her Majesty in right of Canada and Her Majesty in right of British Columbia. *British Columbia Treaty Commission Act, 1995*, S.C. 1995, c. 45, s. 2.

FIRST NATION LAND. Reserve land to which a land code applies and includes all the interests in and resources of the land that are within the legislative authority of Parliament. *First Nations Land Management Act, 1999*, S.C. 1999, c. 24, s. 2.

FIRST NATION LAW. The council of a first nation has, in accordance with its land code, the power to enact laws respecting (a) interests in and licences in relation to first nation land; (b) the development, conservation, protection, management, use and possession of first nation land; and (c) any matter arising out of or ancillary to the exercise of that power. *First Nations Land Management Act, 1999*, S.C. 1999, c. 24, s. 20. See LAND CODE.

FIRST NATIONS GOVERNMENT. The government of a "band" as defined in the *Indian Act* (Canada). *Ont. Regs.*

FIRST OFFENDER. One who was convicted for the first time.

FIRST OPEN WATER. Describes water immediately after ice breaks up so that navigation is possible.

FIRST-PARTY INSURANCE. Insurance which indemnifies the insured without reference to fault. John G. Fleming, *The Law of Torts*, 8th ed. (Sydney: The Law Book Company Limited, 1992) at 395.

FIRST PROCESSING. The first change in the form of materials such as agricultural products.

FIRST READING. A purely formal stage of parliamentary deliberation decided without amendment or debate, coupled with an order to print the bill. A. Fraser, W.A. Dawson, & J. Holtby, eds., *Beauchesne's Rules and Forms of the House of Commons of Canada*, 6th ed. (Toronto: Carswell, 1989) at 195.

FIRST REFUSAL. See RIGHT OF ~.

FIRST STOREY. The storey with its floor closest to grade and having its ceiling more than 1.8 m. above grade. *Building Code, 1992* O. Reg. 403/97, s. 1.1.3.

FISCAL. *adj*. Relating to revenue.

FISCAL AGENT. A fiscal agent appointed under Part IV and includes the Bank of Canada. *Financial Administration Act*, R.S.C. 1985, c. F-11, s. 2.

FISCAL CAPACITY. The capacity of a province to raise taxes.

FISCAL PERIOD. The period for which the accounts of the business of the taxpayer have been ordinarily made up and accepted for purposes of assessment under the Income Tax Act.

FISCAL YEAR. 1. When used to mean the fiscal year of the government means the period from April 1 in one year to March 31 in the next year. 2. The period for which the business accounts of a corporation or a business of a taxpayer are made up and accepted for the purposes of the Income Tax Act. See PREVIOUS ~.

FISH. *v.* 1. To catch or take or attempt to catch or take fish by any method. 2. Includes shellfish, crustaceans and marine animals. *Bankruptcy and Insolvency Act.*

FISH. *n.* 1. Includes (a) parts of fish, (b) shellfish, crustaceans, marine animals, and any parts of shellfish, crustaceans or marine animals and (c) the eggs, sperm, spawn, larvae, spat and juvenile stages of fish, shellfish, crustaceans and marine animals. *Fisheries Act*, S.C. 1991, c. 1, s. 1(2). 2. Includes shellfish, crustaceans and marine animals. See BAIT ~; COARSE ~; COMMERCIAL ~; DOG~; EXOTIC ~; FIN~; GROUND~; GUIDE FOR ~; PROCESSING OF ~; SPORT ~; UNCLEAN ~; WATER FREQUENTED BY ~; WILD ~.

FISH ARROW. An arrow with retractable or detachable barbs.

FISH-BREEDING PLANT. An establishment in which the commercial production or breeding of fish, amphibians, echinoderms, crustaceans or shellfish or their eggs, sexual products or larvae is carried on for consumption or stocking purposes. *Aquaculture Credit Act*, S.Q. 1984, c. 1, s. 1.

FISH BUYING STATION. (a) A building, structure, machinery, appurtenances, appliances and apparatus; (b) a vehicle; and (c) a vessel, scow, barge or float, within British Columbia or its coastal waters, with or without installed propulsion machinery, used in the business of buying, collecting, assembling, eviscerating, transporting, conveying, packing or carrying fish direct from a fisherman. *Fisheries Act*, R.S.B.C. 1996, c. 149, s. 12.

FISH COLD STORAGE PLANT. A building, structure, machinery, appurtenances, appliances and apparatus occupied and used in the business of freezing fish or storing frozen fish, either alone or in conjunction with any other business, but excludes (a) a fish buying station as defined in this section; (b) a licensed fishing vessel engaged in fishing, eviscerating and freezing on board the product of its catch, or while delivering that catch; or (c) a building, equipment or plant occupied or used by a person for storing fish for the purpose only of resale by him at retail in the Province. *Fisheries Act*, R.S.C. 1996, c. 149, s. 12.

FISH CURING. See BY-PRODUCTS OF ~.

FISH DEALER. A person who sells or barters fish or offers fish for sale or barter or has in his possession fish for sale or barter, and includes a person who goes from house to house selling or bartering fish or offering fish for sale or barter or soliciting orders for fish for future delivery, but does not include a person who sells or barters fish or offers fish for sale or barter or has in his possession fish for sale or barter by retail sale only.

FISHER. *n.* A person who is engaged in the catching and taking of fish from the sea.

FISHERIES. *n.* 1. The business of catching, harvesting, raising, cultivating and handling of fish directly or indirectly by a fisherman. 2. Any fishery, including the sealfishery, which fishermen regularly carry on as a means of making a livelihood and includes the catching of fish and every other phase of fishery production. See ATLANTIC ~; CANADIAN ~ WATERS; FISHERY.

FISHERIES AND OCEANS. The federal ministry which oversees coastal and inland fisheries, hydrography, marine sciences and small craft harbours.

FISHERIES PRODUCT. Any natural product of the commercial fisheries of Canada.

FISHERMAN. *n.* 1. Every person who takes, attempts to take, or assists in taking fish or shellfish from the sea. 2. A person whose business consists in whole or in part of fishing. *Bank Act*, S.C. 1991, c. 46, s. 425. 3. (a) A person who has or intends to acquire a prescribed interest in a fishing vessel or a proprietary share in a fishing vessel, or (b) a person who has a prescribed interest in a weir, or similar fish catching or trapping device, that is affixed to the ground, or a proprietary share in such a weir or similar fish catching or trapping device, and whose principal occupation is participation in a primary fishing enterprise. *Fisheries Improvement Loans Act*, R.S.C. 1985, c. F-22, s. 2. 4. (a) The holder of a commercial fishing licence, (b) a hired hand who derives all or a substantial portion of his income from employment as such on a fishing vessel, (c) a fishing vessel owner who derives all or a substantial portion of his income from the rental of fishing vessels to holders of commercial fishing licences, and (d) a person who derives all or a substantial portion of his income from the handling of fish on shore directly after the landing thereof from fishing vessels, but does not include a person engaged in the processing of fish. *Canada Shipping Act*, R.S.C. 1985, c. S-9, s. 654. See COMMERCIAL ~; INDEPENDENT BOAT-OWNER ~; YEAR-ROUND ~.

FISHERMAN'S LICENCE. See ZONE ~.

FISHERY. *n*. 1. " . . . [T]he right of catching fish in the sea, or in a particular stream of water; . . . also . . . used to denote the locality where such right is exercised." *R. v. Fowler* (1980), 9 C.E.L.R. 115 at 121, [1980] 2 S.C.R. 213, [1980] 5 W.W.R. 511, 113 D.L.R. (3d) 513, 53 C.C.C. (2d) 97, 32 N.R. 230, the court per Martland J. 2. Includes the area, locality, place or station in or on which a pound, seine, net, weir or other fishing appliance is used, set, placed or located, and the area, tract or stretch of water in or from which fish may be taken by the said pound, seine, net, weir or other fishing appliance, and also the pound, seine, net, weir, or other fishing appliance used in connection therewith. *Fisheries Act*, R.S.C. 1985, c. F-14, s. 2. 3. Includes the area, locality, place or station in or on which a pound, seine, net, weir or other fishing appliance is used, set, placed or located, and the area, tract or stretch of water in or from which fish may be taken by the said pound, seine, net, weir or other fishing appliance, and also the pound, seine, net, weir, or other fishing appliance used in connection therewith. *Fisheries Act*, R.S.C. 1985 (1st Supp.), c. 35, s. 5. See FISHERIES.

FISHERY ENTERPRISE. Any person that is engaged directly or indirectly in, or controls or is controlled by a person that is engaged directly or indirectly in, the Atlantic Fisheries. *Atlantic Fisheries Restructuring Act*, R.S.C. 1985, c. A-14, s. 2.

FISHERY GUARDIAN. A person appointed as a fishery guardian pursuant to subsection 5(3). *Fisheries Act*, R.S.C. 1985, c. F-14, s. 2.

FISHERY LEASE. A lease conferring for a term therein mentioned, upon the lessee therein named, the right to take and keep, for the purpose of fishing, under and subject to the provisions of this Act and of all regulations made hereunder,

the exclusive or other possession of any Crown lands therein described, with the exclusive or other right to fish in any waters flowing over or covering the same, at such time, and in such manner, and with such restrictions, and subject to such regulations as may be permitted, regulated or prescribed by any lawful authority in that behalf. *Fisheries Act*, R.S.N.B. 1973, c. F-15, s. 1.

FISHERY OFFICER. A person appointed as a fishery officer pursuant to subsection 5(1) or designated as a fishery officer pursuant to subsection 5(5). *Fisheries Act*, R.S.C. 1985, c. F-14, s. 2.

FISHERY PRODUCTS. Any fishery resources and any products derived from fishery resources.

FISHERY RESOURCES. 1. Includes fish, molluscs, crustaceans, marine mammals and marine plants. *Fisheries Development Act*, R.S.C. 1985, c. F-21, s. 2. 2. Includes all vertebrate and invertebrate animals and all plants which spend all or part of their life in the aquatic and marine environment. *Fisheries Act*, R.S.N.S. 1989, c. 173, s. 3.

FISH HABITAT. Spawning grounds and nursery, rearing, food supply and migration areas on which fish depend directly, or indirectly in order to carry out their life processes. *Fisheris Act*, R.S.C. 1985, c. F-14, s. 3.

FISHING. *n*. 1. " . . . [A] continuous process beginning from the time when the preliminary preparations are being made for the taking of the fish and extending down to the moment when they are finally reduced to actual and certain possession. . ." *"Frederick Gerring Jr." (The) v. R.* (1897), 27 S.C.R. 271 at 280, Sedgewick J. 2. Fishing for, catching or attempting to catch fish by any method. *Fisheries Act*, R.S.C. 1985, c. F- 4, s. 2. See BOW ~; COMMERCIAL ~; DOMESTIC ~; FAMILY ~ CORPORATION; FLY ~; FOOD ~; ICE ~; LAWFULLY ~; RECREATIONAL ~; SKIN-DIVING ~; SPORT ~; VESSEL ENGAGED IN ~; WINTER ~.

FISHING ASSETS. (a) Cash, trade accounts receivable, supplies and inventory used in the fishing business, (b) land, buildings, boats, ships, equipment, machinery and nets that are used chiefly in the operation of the fishing business by the corporation, (c) any right or licence granted or issued under any Act of the Legislature that permits or regulates the catching or sale of fish, and (d) shares in another family fishing corporation. *Corporations Tax Act*, R.S.O. 1990, c. C.40, s. 1(2).

FISHING EQUIPMENT. Equipment of a prescribed class or kind used in connection with a primary fishing enterprise but does not include a shore installation. *Fisheries Improvement Loans Act*, R.S.C. 1985, c. F-22, s. 2. See MECHANIZED ~.

FISHING GEAR. Any net, line or other gear used for catching fish. *Fishing Gear Marking Regulations*, C.R.C., c. 813, s. 2.

FISHING INDUSTRY. Includes the catching, harvesting, raising, handling, processing, marketing and distributing of fisheries resources and products and includes aquaculture.

FISHING LICENCE. A licence granting the right to fish. It may be restricted as to time, place, species or quantity. See DOMESTIC ~; PERSONAL COMMERCIAL ~.

FISHING LICENSEE. A person licensed to fish.

FISHING LODGE. See HUNTING OR ~.

FISHING OPERATION. An operation in which a vessel is used for (a) the capture of fish or the harvesting of a marine resource for profit, (b) the treatment of fish or a marine resource, (c) the transporting of fish or a marine resource from any fishing apparatus, vessel or collection centre of fish, or (d) the enforcement of any regulation made under the Fisheries Act. *Fishing Vessel Insurance Regulations*, C.R.C., c. 325, s. 2.

FISHING OR RECREATIONAL HARBOUR. (a) Any harbour, wharf, pier, breakwater, slipway, marina or part thereof, together with machinery, works, land and structures related or attached thereto, and (b) any other facility, installation, works or part thereof located on or adjacent to water where accommodation or services are provided principally for fishing or recreational vessels or the occupants thereof. *Fishing and Recreational Harbours Act*, R.S.C. 1985, c. F-24, s. 2.

FISHING POND. A body of water containing exclusively breeding fish, closed on all sides to hold the fish captive, and used for angling.

FISHING PORTS. Harbours, ports, coves, heads, points, bays, inlets and communities which are used by fishing vessels or in which fishery products are off-loaded or processed and, so as not to limit the generality of the foregoing,

as the regulations may prescribe. *Fisheries Act*, R.S.N.S. 1989, c. 173, s. 3.

FISHING PRESERVE. An artificial body of water lying wholly within the boundaries of privately-owned land, containing water from surface run-off, natural springs, ground water or water diverted or pumped from a stream or lake but not being composed of natural streams, ponds or lakes or water impounded by the damming of natural streams and in which fish under a licence or fish taken under propagated commercial fishing licence are released for angling purposes. *Game and Fish Act*, R.S.O. 1990, c. G.10, s. 1. See PRIVATE ~; PUBLIC ~.

FISHING SHIP. A ship engaged in deep-sea fishing, sealing or whaling. Canada regulations.

FISHING STATION. A building or place where fish are collected from commercial fishermen.

FISHING VESSEL. 1. Any ship or boat or any other description of vessel for use in fishing and equipment, apparatus and appliances for use in the operation thereof and forming part thereof, or any share or part interest therein. *Bank Act*, S.C. 1991, c. 46, s. 425. 2. Any vessel used, outfitted or designed for the purpose of catching, processing or transporting fish. *Fisheries Act*, R.S.C. 1985, c. F-14, s. 2. See CANADIAN ~; COMMERCIAL ~; FOREIGN ~; FRENCH ~; HERRING ~; UNITED STATES ~.

FISHING VOYAGE, CLASS I. A voyage in the course of which a fishing vessel may proceed anywhere in the world. *Crewing Regulations*, SOR/97-390, s. 1.

FISHING VOYAGE, CLASS II. A voyage in the course of which a fishing vessel may proceed anywhere within the area around North America bounded by the meridians of longitude 30°00'W and 180°00'W and north of the parallel of latitude 6°00'N. *Crewing Regulations*, SOR/97-390, s. 1.

FISHING VOYAGE, CLASS III. A voyage in the course of which a fishing vessel may proceed anywhere in the coastal waters of North America that is within 200 miles of the shore or within the waters of the continental shelf, whichever distance is farther. *Crewing Regulations*, SOR/97-390, s. 1.

FISH LIVER REDUCTION PLANT. A building, structure, machinery, appurtenances, appliances and apparatus occupied and used in the business of producing fish oil from fish livers. *Fisheries Act*, R.S.B.C. 1996, c. 149, s. 12.

FISH OFFAL REDUCTION PLANT. A building, structure, machinery, appurtenances, appliances and apparatus occupied and used in the business of producing oil, fish meal, fish scrap, chicken feed or fertilizer from fish offal. *Fisheries Act*, R.S.B.C. 1996, c. 149, s. 12.

FISH PLANT. Buildings, structures, machinery, appurtenances, appliances, apparatus and chemicals occupied or used: (a) to prepare, cut or otherwise process any type of salt fish or fishery product for sale whether or not further treated by smoking, cutting or drying and whether or not in barrels, butts, tubs, or other containers and whether or not sold in such containers; (b) to prepare fish or shellfish for sale by icing, cutting, shucking or any other method or combination of methods and whether or not smoked or otherwise processed; (c) to freeze fish or shellfish for sale; (d) to store or handle fish or shellfish or to store or handle fish or shellfish on behalf of any other person; (e) to prepare fertilizer, animal or poultry food, meal, vitamin concentrates or glue by the drying, cooking or other treatment of fish or shellfish; (f) to prepare fish oils whether such oils are refined or not; but does not include buildings, structures, machinery, appurtenances, appliances, apparatus and chemicals occupied or used by (g) a fisherman who prepares, stores or handles fish or shellfish caught only by himself; (h) a person who prepares, stores or handles fish or shellfish for the purpose only of resale by him at retail or for his personal and occasional use. *Fisheries Act*, R.S.N.S. 1967, c. 109, s. 1.

FISH POND. See COMMERCIAL ~; PRIVATE ~; RAINBOW TROUT ~.

FISH PROCESSING PLANT. (a) A building, structure, machinery, appurtenances, appliances and apparatus; and (b) a vessel, scow, barge or float, within coastal waters, with or without installed propulsion machinery, either ashore or afloat, occupied and used in the business of processing fish. *Fisheries Act*, R.S.B.C. 1996, c. 149, s. 12.

FISHWHEEL. *n.* An implement set in a river or stream to catch fish by utilizing the water flow.

FISLO. *abbr.* Free in stow, liner out.

FISSIONABLE SUBSTANCE. Any prescribed substance that is, or from which can be obtained, a substance capable of releasing atomic energy by nuclear fission.

FIT. *adj.* Just and equitable.

FITNESS. *n.* The physical and mental condition of an individual that enables that person to function at their best in society. See PRESUMPTION OF ~.

FITTER. *n.* A person who (a) reads and interprets drawings, specifications and bills of material, reference charts and tables, (b) selects mechanical measuring, checking, layout tools and devices, (c) assembles metal plates and metal sections to form a complete unit, to the limits of accuracy shown in the shop drawings, connecting components by tack welding or bolting, (d) performs measuring, checking, layout operations and selects work piece materials and is familiar with the operation of straightening machines and equipment, and (e) safely turns and handles individual pieces or complete assemblies using cranes or other lifting equipment, but does not include a person or class of persons in a limited purpose occupation that, in the opinion of the Director, does not equate with the definition of fitter (structural steel/platework). *Apprenticeship and Tradesmen's Qualification Act*, R.R.O. 1980, Reg. 34, s. 1. See GAS ~.

FITTING. *n.* A safety valve, stop valve, automatic stop-and-check valve, a blow-down valve, reducing valve, water gauge, gauge cock, pressure gauge, injector, test cock, fusible plug, regulating or controlling device, and pipe fittings, attached to or used in connection with a boiler, pressure vessel or plant. See GAS-~.

FITTING-OUT. *n.* The time spent preparing the machinery of a ship for operation, during which it is possible to train an engineer or electrician. *Marine Certification Regulations*, SOR/97-391, s. 1.

FIT-UP. *n.* Leasehold improvements undertaken by a tenant with respect to the space it usually occupies exclusively. *Martel Building Ltd. v. R.*, 2000 CarswellNat 2678, 2000 SCC 60, 36 R.P.R. (3d) 175, 193 D.L.R. (4th) 1, 262 N.R. 285, 3 C.C.L.T. (3d) 1, 5 C.L.R. (3d) 161, 186 F.T.R. 231 (note), [2000] 2 S.C.R. 860, Per Iacobucci and Major JJ. for the court.

FIX. *v.* To determine; to ascertain.

FIX. *n.* A usually intravenous injection of a narcotic. F.A. Jaffe, *A Guide to Pathological Evidence*, 3d ed. (Toronto: Carswell, 1991) at 219.

FIXED. *adj*. Determined; ascertained.

FIXED ASSET. Property used in a business which will not be used or converted into cash during the current fiscal year. See NET ~S.

FIXED CAPITAL. That which a company retains, in the shape of assets upon which the subscribed capital has been expended, and which assets either themselves produce income independent of any further action of the company, or being retained by the company are made use of to produce income or a profits. *Ammonia Soda Company Ltd. v. Chamberlain*, [1918] 1 Ch. 266.

FIXED CARGO GEAR. Ships' cranes, winches and other hoisting appliances, derrick booms, derricks and mast bands, goose-necks, eyebolts and all other permanent attachments to any part of a ship used in connection with the processes, also shore cranes and other shore based appliances employed in loading or unloading a ship.

FIXED CHARGE. A security interest similar to the charge which a typical real property mortgage creates. It is a charge on specific property, contrasted to a floating charge.

FIXED COLLISION BARRIER. A device that (a) consists of (i) a structure with a flat, vertical, unyielding impact surface that is of a size sufficient to ensure that no portion of a vehicle striking the surface projects or passes beyond the surface and (ii) a horizontal approach surface that does not impede vehicle motion during impact and that is of a size sufficient to ensure that a vehicle will be able to attain a stable attitude during its approach to the impact surface, and (b) does not absorb any significant portion of the kinetic energy of a vehicle striking the impact surface. *Motor Vehicle Safety Regulations*, C.R.C., c. 1038, s. 100.

FIXED COMMERCIAL FISHING UNIT. A salmon trap net, mackerel trap net, sea fish trap net or herring weir that is fixed and is used in commercial fishing.

FIXED COSTS. Costs set as a lump sum without being regulated by tariffs.

FIXED DATE. Includes any numbered day, or any Monday, Tuesday, or as the case may be, numbered, alternate or recurring, of a stated month or months. *Insurance acts*.

FIXED PLATFORM. An artificial island or a marine installation or structure that is permanently attached to the seabed for the purpose of exploration or exploitation of resources or for other economic purposes. *Criminal Code*, R.S.C. 1985, c. C-46, s. 78.1.

FIXED PRICE CONTRACT. Contract in which the price is preset regardless of actual cost. Contemplates extra work or deletions from the work, resulting in variation from the stated contract price.

FIXED SERVICE. A radiocommunication service that provides for communications between fixed stations or between fixed stations and space stations. *Radiocommunication Regulations*, SOR/96-484.

FIXED-SHIFT. *n*. The same working hours set for a period of time.

FIXED SIGNAL. A signal of fixed location indicating a condition affecting the movement of a train or engine.

FIXED STATION. A radio station authorized to operate at a fixed point. *Radiocommunication Regulations*, SOR/96-484.

FIXED TERM TENANCY AGREEMENT. A tenancy agreement with a predetermined expiry date.

FIXTURE. *n*. 1. An object or thing which by its degree of attachment to the land has come in law to form part of the land. 2. A receptacle or equipment that receives water, liquids or sewage and discharges water, liquids or sewage directly into drainage piping.

FIXTURES. *n*. 1. Personal chattels connected with or fastened to land. 2. All appurtenances; furniture, furnishing, equipment, fixtures services and facilities supplied or to be supplied by a landlord to a tenant under a tenancy agreement. 3. Goods that are installed in or affixed to a mobile home. See PRODUCT HOLDING ~; TRADE ~.

FIXTURE TRAP. A trap integral with or serving a fixture and includes an interceptor serving as a trap for a fixture.

FLAG. *n*. A banner; ensign; standard. See LAW OF ~; PILOT ~.

FLAGMAN. *n*. 1. A person employed by a traffic authority, or a contractor doing work on behalf of a traffic authority, for the purpose of directing the movement of traffic on any portion of a highway under construction, or where repair work or other work is being carried on. 2. Includes a brakeman or other trainman on a train of a railway who, in connection with the operation of the train, is warning people on a highway.

FLAG OF CONVENIENCE. Refers to practice of registering ships in countries with favourable laws.

FLAGRANT. *adj.* 1. " . . . [G]laring, scandalous or conspicuously wrongful: . . ." *R. v. Harris* (1987), 35 C.C.C. (3d) 1 at 25, 20 O.A.C. 26, 57 C.R. (3d) 356 (C.A.), the court per Martin J.A. 2. " . . . [C]lear or obvious . . . scandalous . . ." *R. v. Nelson* (1987), 35 C.C.C. (3d) 347 at 350, [1987] 3 W.W.R. 144, 46 M.V.R. 145, 45 Man. R. (2d) 68, 29 C.R.R. 80 (C.A.), Huband J.A. (Hall J.A. concurring).

FLAGRANTE DELICTO. [L. while the crime is glaring] While committing the offence charged.

FLAG STATE. Of a foreign fishing vessel means the state in which the vessel is registered or, where the vessel is not registered the state whose flag the vessel is entitled to fly. Canada regulations.

FLAME ARRESTOR. A device consisting of a group of parallel metal plates, tubes, fins or screens or a similar device with a large surface area for heat dissipation, which is designed to prevent the entrance of flame into a storage tank through a vent or similar opening.

FLAME PROJECTION. The flame resulting from the ignition of a chemical product discharged from a spray container when tested in accordance with the procedure set out in Schedule 1. *Consumer Chemicals and Containers Regulations, 2001*, SOR/2001-269, s. 1.

FLAME-RETARDANT. *adj.* When applied to a material means that the material will not burn for more than a specified period of time and will not permit flame to travel or extend beyond a specified distance. *Power Corporation Act*, R.R.O. 1980, Reg. 794, s. 0.

FLAME-SPREAD RATING. *var.* **FLAME SPREAD RATING**. An index or classification indicating the extent of spread-of-flame on the surface of a material or an assembly of materials as determined in a standard fire test.

FLAMMABLE. *adj.* Capable of being easily set on fire.

FLAMMABLE LIQUID. 1. Any liquid that has a flash point of twenty-one degrees Celsius or less as determined by a Tagliabue or equivalent closed-cup device. *Motor Vehicle Act*, S.N.B., c. M-17, s. 1. 2. A liquid having a flash point below 37.8° Celsius, and a vapour pressure below 275 kilopascals absolute at 37.8° Celsius. 3. Any liquid with a flash point below 175°F, as determined by Tagliabue's Open Cup Tester, and having a Reid vapour pressure not exceeding 40 psi absolute at 100°F or any liquid with a flash point of 175°F or above when it is heated by artificial means to a temperature not less than its flash point temperature. *Flammable Liquids Bulk Storage Regulations*, C.R.C., c. 114, s. 2.

FLAMMABLE PRODUCT. A chemical product that is capable of (a) spontaneous combustion; (b) becoming flammable when in contact with air; or (c) having a flash point below 60°C or a flame projection greater than 15 cm or exhibiting a flashback. *Consumer Chemicals and Containers Regulations, 2001*, SOR/2001-269, s. 1.

FLANGE TAPS. Small diameter pipes tapped into the flanges between which the orifice plate is fitted so as to permit the measurement of the pressure on the up-stream and down-stream sides of the orifice. *Gas and Gas Meters Regulations*, C.R.C., c. 876, s. 25.

FLANK. *n.* The longer side of a regularly-shaped corner lot except where the lot is square, in which case it means the side designated by the assessor as the flank. *The Local Improvements Act*, R.S.S. 1978, c. L-33, s. 2.

FLASHBACK. *n.* 1. The part of a flame projection that extends from the point of ignition back to the spray container when a chemical product is tested in accordance with the procedure set out in Schedule 1. *Consumer Chemicals and Containers Regulations, 2001*, SOR/2001-269, s. 1. 2. An experience of reliving momentarily a past distressing experience.

FLASH POINT. *var.* **FLASHPOINT.** The minimum temperature at which a substance gives off a vapour in sufficient concentration to ignite under test conditions. *Consumer Chemicals and Containers Regulations, 2001*, SOR/2001-269, s. 1.

FLAT. *n.* A self-contained separate residence.

FLAT-RATE PENSION PLAN. Provides a fixed amount of pension regardless of wages or years of service.

FLAT ROOF. A roof that is horizontal or has a vertical rise of not more than one foot for each six feet measured horizontally. *Lightning Rods Act*, R.R.O. 1980, Reg. 577, s. 1.

FLAVOUR. See NORMAL ~ AND AROMA; NORMAL ~ AND ODOUR.

FLAX FIBRE. The scutched product of retted flax straw that may be used in spinning.

FLEA MARKET. A place where five or more persons or one or more organizations, or a combination thereof, sell for a non-profit purpose, seventy-five per cent or more of which goods are second hand or used. *Lord's Day (Nova Scotia) Act*, S.N.S. 1974, c. 40, s. 1.

FLEET MAIL OFFICE. A military post office operated by the Canadian Forces Postal Services to provide postal facilities for Canadian naval ships on cruise to a place in Canada, the United States, any possession of the United States or any other foreign country. Canada regulations.

FLEXIBLE SCHEDULE. Work hours and period are not fixed but vary with product requirements.

FLEX TIME. Work hours per work period are fixed but the number of hours worked per day may be varied.

FLIGHT. *n.* 1. The act of flying or moving through the air. *Criminal Code*, R.S.C. 1985, c. C-46, s. 7(8). 2. The movement of an aircraft from the point of take-off to the first point of landing. 3. Air transportation between two or more airports. 4. ". . . '[A]ction of running away from danger,' . . ." *Rowe v. R.* (1951), 100 C.C.C. 97 at 103, [1951] S.C.R. 713,12 C.R. 148, [1951] 4 D.L.R. 238, Kellock J. 5. Every one commits an offence who, operating a motor vehicle while being pursued by a peace officer operating a motor vehicle, fails, without reasonable excuse and in order to evade the peace officer, to stop the vehicle as soon as is reasonable in the circumstances. *Criminal Code* R.S.C. 1985, c. C-46, s. 249.1. See ACROBATIC ~; ATLANTIC ~; BACK-TO-BACK ~S; DOMESTIC ~; IFR ~; IN ~; INTERNATIONAL ~; NON-SCHEDULED ~; POLAR ~; POSITIONING ~; SCHEDULED ~; SONIC ~; SUPERSONIC ~; TRANS-OCEANIC ~; VFR ~.

FLIGHT ATTENDANT. A crew member, other than a flight crew member, who has been assigned duties to be performed in the interest of the passengers in a passenger-carrying aircraft. *Canadian Aviation Regulations* SOR 96-433, s. 101.01.

FLIGHT AUTHORITY. A certificate of airworthiness, special certificate of airworthiness, flight permit or validation of a foreign document attesting to an aircraft's fitness for flight, issued under Subpart 7 of Part V, or a foreign certificate of airworthiness that meets the requirements of Article 31 of the Convention. *Canadian Aviation Regulations* SOR 96-433, s. 101.01.

FLIGHT CREW MEMBER. A crew member assigned to act as pilot or flight engineer of an aircraft during flight time. *Canadian Aviation Regulations* SOR 96-433, s. 101.01.

FLIGHT CREW MEMBER ON CALL. A flight crew member who has been designated by an air operator to be available to report for flight duty on notice of one hour or less. *Canadian Aviation Regulations*, SOR/96-433, s. 101.01(1)

FLIGHT CREW MEMBER ON STANDBY. A flight crew member who has been designated by an air operator or private operator to remain at a specified location in order to be available to report for flight duty on notice of one hour or less. *Canadian Aviation Regulations*, SOR/96-433, s. 101.01(1).

FLIGHT DECK DUTY TIME. The period spent by a flight crew member at a flight crew member position in an aeroplane during flight time. *Canadian Aviation Regulations* SOR/96-433, s. 101.01(1).

FLIGHT DUTY TIME. The period that starts when a flight crew member reports for a flight, or reports as a flight crew member on standby, and finishes at "engines off" or "rotors stopped" at the end of the final flight, except in the case of a flight conducted under Supart 4 or 5 of Part VII, in which case the period finishes 15 minutes after "engines off" or "rotors stopped" at the end of the final flight, and includes the time required to complete any duties assigned by the air operator or private operator or delegated by the Minister prior to the reporting time and includes the time required to complete aircraft maintenance engineer duties prior to or following a flight. *Canadian Aviation Regulations*, SOR/96-433, s. 101.01(1).

FLIGHT ELEMENT. A Space Station element provided by Canada or by a Partner State under the Agreement and under any memorandum of understanding or other implementing arrangement entered into to carry out the Agreement concerning the space station. *Criminal Code*, R.S.C. 1985, c. C-46, s. 7.

FLIGHT INFORMATION REGION. An airspace of defined dimension extending upwards from the surface of the earth within which flight information service and alerting service is provided. *Air Regulations*, C.R.C., c. 2, s. 101.

FLIGHT INFORMATION SERVICES. (a) the dissemination of aviation weather information and aeronautical information for departure, destination and alternate aerodromes along a proposed route of flight, (b) the dissemination of aviation weather information and aeronautical information to aircraft in flight, (c) the acceptance, processing and activation of flight plans and flight itineraries and amendments to and cancellations of flight plans and flight itineraries, (d) the exchange of flight plan information with domestic or foreign governments or agencies or foreign air traffic services units, and (e) the dissemination of information concerning known ground and air traffic. *Canadian Aviation Regulations* SOR 96-433, s. 101.01.

FLIGHT INSPECTION. The operation of an aircraft for the purpose of (a) calibrating air navigation aids, (b) monitoring or evaluating the performance of air navigation aids, or (c) obstacle assessment. *Canadian Aviation Regulations* SOR 96-433, s. 101.01.

FLIGHT ITINERARY. The information required to be filed in the form of a flight itinerary pursuant to Division III of Subpart 2 of Part VI. *Canadian Aviation Regulations* SOR 96-433, s. 101.01.

FLIGHT LEVEL. The altitude, expressed in hundreds of feet, indicated on an altimeter set to 29.92 inches of mercury or 1 013.2 millibars. Canada regulations.

FLIGHT LINE. A predetermined directional line of flight within a flying display area. *Special Aviation Events Safety Order*, C.R.C., c. 66, s. 2.

FLIGHT PLAN. The information that is required to be filed in the form of a flight plan pursuant to Division III of Subpart 2 of Part VI. *Canadian Aviation Regulations* SOR 96-433, s. 101.01. See DVFR ~; OPERATIONAL ~.

FLIGHT SERVICE STATION. A ground station established to provide air traffic advisory services, flight information services and emergency assistance services for the safe movement of aircraft. *Canadian Aviation Regulations* SOR 96-433, s. 101.01.

FLIGHT TIME. The time from the moment an aircraft first moves under its own power for the purpose of taking off until the moment it comes to rest at the end of the flight. *Canadian Aviation Regulations* SOR 96-433, s. 101.01.

FLIGHT TRAINING. A training program of ground instruction and airborne training that is conducted in accordance with the flight instructor guide and flight training manual applicable to the aircraft used. *Canadian Aviation Regulations* SOR 96-433, s. 101.01.

FLIGHT TRAINING SERVICE. A commercial air service that is operated for the purpose of conducting flight training. *Canadian Aviation Regulations* SOR 96-433, s. 101.01.

FLIGHT TRAINING UNIT. (a) in the case of an aeroplane or helicopter, the holder of a flight training unit operator certificate, or (b) in the case of a glider, balloon, gyroplane or ultra-light aeroplane, a club, school or other organization that conducts flight training. *Canadian Aviation Regulations* SOR 96-433, s. 101.01.

FLIGHT VISIBILITY. The visibility forward from the cockpit of an aircraft in flight. *Canadian Aviation Regulations* SOR 96-433, s. 101.01.

FLIGHT WATCH SYSTEM. A system described in the operations manual for the monitoring of an aeroplane during flight time.

FLOAT. *n.* 1. A floating structure designed for the mooring or berthing of vessels and includes a floating wharf. 2. A non-self-propelled vehicle of a semi-trailer type designed for the purpose of being towed and of carrying construction equipment or other heavy equipment or material.

FLOATER. *n.* A body decomposing in water. F.A. Jaffe, *A Guide to Pathological Evidence*, 3d ed. (Toronto: Carswell, 1991) at 219.

FLOATING ALLOWANCE. A payment in addition to regular wages to compensate for increases in cost of living.

FLOATING CAPITAL. Capital available to meet current expenditure.

FLOATING CHARGE. 1. " . . . [A]n equitable charge on the assets, for the time being, of a going concern. It does not specifically affect any particular assets until some event occurs or some act is done on the part of the mortgagee which causes the security to crystallize into a fixed security. Until the security is crystallized the charge is an equitable one and the legal title to the goods remains in the mortgagor." *Meen v. Realty Development Co.* (1953), [1954] O.W.N. 193 at 194, [1954] 1 D.L.R. 649 (C.A.), the court per MacKay J.A. 2. "A floating security is not a future security; it is a present security, which presently affects all the assets of the company expressed to be included in it. On the other hand, it is not a specific security; the holder cannot affirm that the assets are specifically mortgaged to him. The assets are mortgaged in such a way that the mortgagor can deal with them without the concurrence of the mortgagee. A floating security is not a specific mortgage of the assets, plus a licence to the mortgagor to dispose of them in the course of his business, but a floating mortgage applying to every item comprised in the security, but not specifically affecting any item until some event occurs or some act on the part of the mortgagee is done which causes it to crystallize into a fixed security." *Evans v. Rival Granite Quarries Ltd*, [1910] 2 K.B. 979 at 999 (U.K. C.A.), Buckley L.J. 3. The opposite of a specific charge. If assets can be disposed of free from the charge, it is a floating charge, otherwise a fixed or specific charge.

FLOATING CHEST. A chest unstable because of multiple rib fractures in which loose rib fragments inhibit inhalation. F.A. Jaffe, *A Guide to Pathological Evidence*, 3d ed. (Toronto. Carswell, 1991) at 219.

FLOATING GAME. A gambling game which takes place in several successive locations, by design, in order to avoid police raids.

FLOATING POLICY. A policy of insurance which covers all goods ascertainable at the time of loss, up to a certain amount.

FLOATING RATE. A rate of interest that bears a specified mathematical relationship to a public index.

FLOOD. *v*. See RIGHT TO ~.

FLOOD. *n*. The temporary covering, bar water of land or all or a portion of buildings or structures caused by the overflow of a watercourse or standing body of water. *The Water Resources Management Act*, R.S.S. 1978, c. W-7, s. 2.

FLOODABLE LENGTH. In relation to any portion of a ship at any draught, means the maximum length of that portion having its centre at a given point in the ship that, at that draught and under such of the assumptions of permeability set forth in Schedule I as are applicable in the circumstances, can be flooded without submerging any part of the ship's margin line when the ship has no list. *Hull Construction Regulations*, C.R.C., c. 1431, s. 2.

FLOOD CONTROL WORKS. Water control works used for the purpose of preventing or controlling floods. *The Water Resources Management Act*, R.S.S. 1978, c. W-7, s. 2.

FLOOD DRAIN. A drain to receive water from a floor of a building, and in its simplest form shall consist of a strainer or grate set flush with the upper surface of a floor so that water passing down through the strainer or grate enters a connected drainage pipe and without limiting the generality of the foregoing shall include, when located between the strainer and the connected pipe or nipple, any ancillary part such as a floor drain body, water stop, trap, backwater valve or primer connection. *Ontario Water Resources Act*, R.R.O. 1980, Reg. 736, s. 1.

FLOODGATES ARGUMENT. The argument that the acceptance of the plaintiff's or applicant's claim will lead to a multitude of similar claims by others.

FLOOD HAZARD AREA. See SPECIAL ~.

FLOOD LEVEL. The level at which water begins to overflow the top or rim of a fixture. *Ontario Water Resources Act*, R.R.O. 1980, Reg. 736, s. 1.

FLOOD LEVEL RIM. The top edge of a receptacle from which water overflows. *Ontario Water Resources Act*, R.R.O. 1980, Reg. 736, s. 1.

FLOOD PROOFING. The use of devices, equipment, construction, materials, measures or practices to protect buildings, structures or land from damage due to flooding. *The Water Resources Management Act*, R.S.S. 1978, c. W-7, s. 2.

FLOOR. *n*. 1. A lower limit, as on rates of pay. 2. A storey; a set of rooms and spaces on the same level in a building. See CELLULAR ~; FIRST ~; GROUND ~.

FLOOR AREA. The space on any storey of a building between exterior walls and required firewalls, including the space occupied by interior walls and partitions, but not including exits and vertical spaces that pierce the storey. *Building Code, 1992* O. Reg. 403/97, s. 1.1.3. See TOTAL ~.

FLOOR SPACE. The superficial area of every floor in the building in which business is carried on, and includes the superficial area of any land not forming the site of a building but occupied or used for the purpose of or incidental to the exercise or carrying on of a business.

FLOOR TRADER. An individual who is employed by a dealer for the purpose of entering into contracts on the floor of a securities or commodity futures exchange on behalf of such dealer.

FLORAL EMBLEM OF ONTARIO. The flower known botanically as the trillium grandiflorum and popularly known as the white trillium.

FLOTSAM. *n*. Goods afloat on the surface of the sea.

FLOUNDER. See WINTER ~; WITCH ~; YELLOWTAIL ~.

FLOUT. *v*. To treat with disdain; to mock; to express contempt for.

FLOW. See BACK ~.

FLOWING. *adj*. Warping or overflowing the land with water for the manurance or building up of the same. *Marsh Act*, R.S.N.S. 1989, c. 273, s. 2.

FLOWING WELL. A well that has a static water level above the surface of the ground.

FLOW LINE. 1. A pipe for (a) the transmission of fluids from an oil well or wells to a tank, battery or common pipeline manifold, or (b) the transmission of water obtained from oil or gas for disposal to other than an underground formation 2. A pipeline serving to interconnect wellheads with separators, treaters, dehydrators, field storage tanks or field storage batteries.

FLOW RATE. See MAXIMUM ~.

FLOW-THROUGH SHARE. A share (other than a prescribed share) of the capital stock of a principal-business corporation that is issued to a person under an agreement in writing entered into between the person and the corporation after February 1986, under which the corporation agrees for consideration that does not include property to be exchanged or transferred by the person under the agreement in circumstances in which section 51, 85, 85.1, 86 or 87 applies (a) to incur, in the period that begins on the day the agreement was made and ends 24 months after the end of the month that includes that day, Canadian exploration expenses or Canadian development expenses in an amount not less than the consideration for which the share is to be issued, and (b) to renounce, before March of the first calendar year that begins after that period, in prescribed form to the person in respect of the share, an amount in respect of the Canadian exploration, Canadian exploration expenses or Canadian development expenses so incurred by it not exceeding the consideration received by the corporation for the share, and includes a right of a person to have such a share issued to that person and any interest acquired in such a share by a person pursuant to such an agreement. *Income Tax Act*, R.S.C. 1985, c.1 (5th Supp.), s. 66(15).

FLOW-THROUGH SWIMMING POOL. A swimming pool in which during any time when the pool is in use the water is undergoing continuous displacement to waste by make-up water only.

F.L.R.A.C. *abbr*. Family Law Reform Act Cases, 1980-.

FLUCTUATING WORKWEEK. Employee's hours of work vary from week to week.

FLUE. *n*. An enclosed passageway for conveying flue gases.

FLUE COLLAR. The portion of a fuel-fired appliance designed for the attachment of the flue pipe or breeching.

FLUE PIPE. The pipe connecting the flue collar of an appliance to a chimney.

FLUID. *n*. See AMNIOTIC ~; BRAKE~; CEREBROSPINAL ~; EXPANSIBLE ~.

FLUID. *adj*. " . . . [M]oving freely . . ." *Amoco Canada Resources Ltd. v. Potash Corp. of Saskatchewan* (1991), 86 D.L.R. (4th) 700 at 706, 93 Sask. R. 300, 4 W.A.C. 300, [1992] 2 W.W.R. 313, the court per Cameron J.A.

FLUID DRAM. 1/8 fluid ounce. *Weights and Measures Act*, S.C. 1970-71-72, c. 36, schedule II.

FLUID MILK. Raw, pasteurized milk or sterilized whole milk for sale to consumers.

FLUID MILK PRODUCTS. The classes of milk and milk products processed from Grade A milk and designated as fluid milk products in the regulations. *Milk Act*, R.S.O. 1990, c. M.12, s. 1.

FLUID OUNCE. 1/160 gallon. *Weights and Measures Act*, S.C. 1970-71-72, c. 36, schedule II.

FLUMINA ET PORTUS PUBLICA SUNT, IDEOQUE JUS PISCANDI OMNIBUS COMMUNE EST. [L.] Navigable rivers and ports are public; therefore all have a common right to fish there.

FLUORIDATION SYSTEM. A system comprising equipment and materials for the addition of a chemical compound to release fluoride ions into a public water supply.

FLUORINATION DEVICE. A system which may be installed in a filtration plant, permitting the control of fluorine concentration in the water treated by such plant.

FLUSH DECK SHIP. A ship with no superstructure on the freeboard deck.

FLUSH VALVE. A valve for flushing a sanitary unit.

FLY. See ARTIFICIAL ~; WEIGHTED ~.

FLY-ASH. *n*. Particulate matter removed from combustion flue gases.

FLYER. *n*. An item of householder mail not enclosed in an envelope.

FLY FISHING. 1. To cast upon water and retrieve in the usual and ordinary manner an unbaited, unweighted artificial fly attached to a line to which no extra weight has been added, but does not include trolling. 2. Angling by the use of an artificial fly or flies that are attached to a line or to a leader that is attached to a line.

FLY-IN. *n*. A prearranged meeting of a number of aircraft at a specified aerodrome (a) for the purpose of competitive flying, or (b) to which the public is invited.

FLYING SCHOOL. See COMMERCIAL ~.

F.M. *abbr.* Frequency modulation.

FMCS. The Federal Mediation and Conciliation Service.

FMO. *abbr.* Fleet Mail Office.

FM STATION. A station that broadcasts in the FM frequency band of 88 to 108 MHz. It does not include a carrier current undertaking or a transmitter that only rebroadcasts the radiocommunications of another station. *Broadcasting Distribution Regulations*, SOR/97-555, s. 1. See LOCAL ~; REGIONAL ~.

FOAL. *n*. A young horse. *Riding Horse Establishments Act*, R.S.O. 1990, c. R.3 2, s. 1.

FOAMING AGENT. Any chemical that is added to any plastic during the process of manufacturing plastic foam so that gas cells are formed throughout the plastic. *Ozone-depleting Substances Regulations, 1998*, SOR/99-7, s. 1.

F.O.B. *abbr.* 1. Free on board. 2. " . . . [T]he seller is obliged to put the goods on the truck but thereafter the goods are at the risk of the buyer and the buyer alone is responsible for the freight and insurance . . ." *George Smith Trucking Co. v. Golden Seven Enterprises Inc.* (1989), 55 D.L.R. (4th) 161 at 174, 34 B.C.L.R. (2d) 43, [1989] 3 W.W.R. 544 (C.A.), Hutcheon J.A. (dissenting).

FOCAL SPOT. The section at which the anode of an X-ray tube intercepts the electron beam. *Radiation Emitting Devices Regulations*, C.R.C., c. 1370, s. 1. See EFFECTIVE ~.

FOCUS GROUP. A group of about ten people who are led in a discussion by a moderator. The moderator obtains the views of these people concerning an issue or topic.

FODDER. *n*. Hay or other material ordinarily used for animal food. See GRAZING AND ~ ASSOCIATION.

FOENERATION. *n*. Making money available for usury.

FOETUS. *n*. [L.] 1. An unborn product of conception after the embryo stage. 2. A human organism during the period of its development beginning on the fifty-seventh day following fertilization or creation, excluding any time during which its development has been suspended, and ending at birth. See FETUS.

FOG. See DE~.

FOI. Freedom of Information.

FOI REQUEST. A request for disclosure of information held by a government body.

FOLIO. *n*. 1. One hundred words. *Interpretation acts*. 2. Ninety words. *Interpretation Act*, R.S.N.S. 1989, c. 235, s. 7(1).

FONTANELLE. *n*. A soft spot between the skull bones of an infant or fetus. F.A. Jaffe, *A Guide to Pathological Evidence*, 3d ed. (Toronto: Carswell, 1991) at 219.

FOOD. *n*. 1. Any article manufactured, sold or represented for use as food or drink for man, chewing gum, and any ingredient that may be mixed with food for any purpose whatever. 2. Every article that (a) is used by human or animal for food, drink, confectionery or condiment, or (b) enters into the composition of the same, whether simple, blended, mixed or compound. See ANIMAL ~, CANNED ~S; HAZARDOUS ~; INFANT ~; JUNIOR ~; LOCAL ~;

MEDICINAL ~; PRE-PACKAGED ~; SPE-CIALTY ~; STRAINED ~; TEST MAR-KET ~; UNFIT FOR ~; UNSTANDARDI-ZED ~.

FOOD ADDITIVE. Any substance, including any source of radiation, the use of which results, or may reasonably be expected to result in it or its by-products becoming part of or affecting the characteristics of a food, but does not include (a) any nutritive material that is used, recognized or commonly sold as an article or ingredient of food; (b) vitamins, mineral nutrients and amino acids; (c) spices, seasonings, flavouring preparations, essential oils, oleoresins and natural extractives; (d) agricultural chemicals; (e) food packaging materials and components thereof; and (f) drugs recommended for administration to animals that may be consumed as food. *Food and Drug Regulations*, C.R.C., c. 870, s. B.01.001.

FOOD ANIMAL. Bovine animals, swine, horses, sheep, goats, whales, bison, domestic rabbit, deer, elk, moose or birds.

FOOD COLOUR. 1. Those colours permitted for use in or upon food by Division 6. *Food and Drug Regulations*, C.R.C., c. 870, c. B.O1.001. 2. Beta-carotene.

FOOD CONTACT SURFACE. Any surface with which food comes in contact during its preparation, processing, packaging, service or storage.

FOOD FISHING. Catching fish for personal consumption but not for sale or barter.

FOOD PREMISE. A premises where food or milk is manufactured, processed, prepared, stored, handled, displayed, distributed, transported, sold or offered for sale, but does not include a private residence. *Health Protection and Promotion Act*, R.S.O. 1990, c. H.7, s. 1(1).

FOOD PREPARATION EQUIPMENT. The following classes of tangible personal property: blenders and mixers, bowls, pots, pans and tins for cooking and baking, broilers and grills, ovens, kitchen ranges and food warming equipment, coffee makers, dishwashers, flatware, dishes, glasses, serving trays and kitchen utensils, food choppers, slicers and grinders, free-standing kitchen refrigerators, toasters, but does not include food wrapping and storage equipment, mobile buffets and mobile cooking units, refrigerated displays, table linens, waste disposal equipment and compactors, fixtures or drink or ice cream dispensers or parts for the maintenance and repair of tangible personal property described in this paragraph.

FOOD SERVICE PREMISES. Any food premises where meals or meal portions are prepared for immediate consumption or sold or served in a form which will permit immediate consumption on the premises or elsewhere, but does not include retail or wholesale grocery premises where facilities are not provided for eating on the premises.

FOODSTUFFS. *n.* All food used for human consumption.

FOOT. *n.* 1. 1/3 yard. *Weights and Measures Act*, S.C. 1970-71-72, c. 36, schedule II. 2. 12.789 inches. Unit of measurement to describe certain land in Quebec. *Weights and Measures Act*, S.C. 1970-71-72, c. 36, schedule III. See BOARD ~; CUBIC ~; RATE PER ~; SQUARE ~.

FOOT FRONTAGE. The lineal measurement in feet of a frontage.

F.O.R. *abbr.* Free on rail.

FOR. *prep.* 1. " . . . [W]ith the intention of . . ." *R. v. Chow*, [1938] 2 D.L.R. 332 at 333, [1938] 1 W.W.R. 458, 70 C.C.C. 150, 52 B.C.R. 467 (C.A.), the court per Sloan J.A. 2. " . . . '[W]ith the object or purpose of . . ." *Blackstock v. Insurance Corp. of British Columbia*, [1983] I.L.R. 1-1630 at 6264, [1983] 3 W.W.R. 282, 20 M.V.R. 293, 143 D.L.R. (3d) 743 (B.C. S.C.), Macdonell J. 3. In to work for, pursuant to a contractual relationship.

FORAGE. See PERENNIAL ~.

FORBID. *v.* " . . . '[P]rohibit' . . ." *Krautt v. Paine* (1980), 17 R.P.R. 1 at 21, [1980] 6 W.W.R. 717, 118 D.L.R. (3d) 625, 25 A.R. 390 (C.A.), the court per Laycraft J.A.

FOR CAUSE. In relation to employee or office-holder, connotes misconduct or dishonesty, behaviour inconsistent with the employment or office.

FORCE. *n.* 1. Violence. 2. The Royal Canadian Mounted Police. 3. The members of a police department. See ARMED ~S; EXCESSIVE ~; FINE ~; HER MAJESTY'S ARMED ~; IN ~; LABOUR ~; MEMBER OF A ~; MEMBER OF THE ~; POLICE ~; REASONABLE ~; REGULAR ~; RESERVE ~; SERVICE IN THE ~; SPECIAL ~; VISITING ~.

FORCED-AIR FURNACE. A furnace equipped with a fan that provides the primary means for circulation of air. *Building Code, 1992* O. Reg. 403/97, s. 1.1.3.

FORCED PREGNANCY. The unlawful confinement of a woman forcibly made pregnant, with the intent of affecting the ethnic composition of any population or carrying out other grave violations of international law. This definition shall not in any way be interpreted as affecting national laws relating to pregnancy. *Rome Statute*, Article 7.

FORCED SALE. 1. " . . . [I]mplies that there is available less than the normal time within which to find a purchaser. . ." *Canada Permanent Trust Co. v. King Art Developments Ltd.* (1984), 12 D.L.R. (4th) 161 at 217, [1984] 4 W.W.R. 587, 32 Alta. L.R. (2d) 1, 54 A.R. 172 (C.A.), Laycraft J.A. (McGillivray C.J.A. concurring). 2. " . . . [N]ot . . . a voluntary one, . . ." *Bocz v. Spiller* (1905), 1 W.L.R. 366 at 368 (N.W.T. S.C.), Newlands J.

FORCE MAJEURE. [Fr.] Irresistible urge.

FORCE MAJEURE CLAUSE. " . . . [G]enerally operates to discharge a contracting party when a supervening, sometimes supernatural, event, beyond the control of either party, makes performance impossible. The common thread is that of the unexpected, something beyond reasonable human foresight and skill. *Atlantic Paper Stock Ltd. v. St. Anne-Nackawic Pulp & Paper Co.* (1975), 10 N.B.R. (2d) 513 at 516, [1976] 1 S.C.R. 580, 4 N.R. 539, 56 D.L.R. (3d) 409, the court per Dickson J. See ACT OF GOD.

FORCE OF LAW. Of a rule, must be unilateral and have binding legal effect. *Reference re Language Rights*, [1992] 1 S.C.R. 212.

FORCES. *n.* 1. Except in the definition of "regular force", means the naval, army or air forces of His Majesty or of any of the Allies of His Majesty during World War I or World War II. *Public Service Superannuation Act*, R.S.C. 1985, c. P-36, s. 3. 2. In the case of World War II, any of His Majesty's naval, army or air forces, the Royal Canadian Mounted Police, the Corps of (Civilian) Canadian Fire Fighters for Service in the United Kingdom, the armed forces of the United States, the Fighting French forces and any other force designated by the Governor in Council for the purposes of this Part. *Public Service Superannuation Act*, R.S.C. 1985, c. P-36,

s. 6(2). See ARMED ~; CANADIAN ~; MAJESTY'S ~; MEMBER OF THE ~.

FORCES CANTEEN. A mess or canteen operated in connection with a component unit of the Canadian Forces, both regular and reserve, or the Royal Canadian Mounted Police Force, in a camp, armoury, barracks, base, or station, of any one or more of these units or establishments in New Brunswick.

FORCIBLE CONFINEMENT. Use of physical restraint, contrary to the wishes of the person restrained, but to which the victim submits unwillingly, thereby depriving the person of liberty to move from one place to another.

FORCIBLE DETAINER. 1. Refusal to restore goods to another though sufficient means were tendered. 2. A person commits forcible detainer when, being in actual possession of real property without colour of right, he detains it in a manner that is likely to cause a breach of the peace or reasonable apprehension of a breach of the peace, against a person who is entitled by law to be in possession of it. *Criminal Code*, R.S.C. 1985, c. C-46, s. 72(2).

FORCIBLE ENTRY. Of a dwelling house occurs when entry is made with such threats and show of force as would, if resisted, cause a breach of the peace, even though no actual force was used. *R. v. Walker* (1906), 12 C.C.C. 197 at 199-200, 4 W.L.R. 288, 6 Terr. L.R. 276 (N.W.T. C.A.), Scott J. (Sifton C.J., Wetmore, Prendergast and Newlands JJ. concurring).

F.O.R. CONTRACT. A seller undertakes to deliver goods into railway cars at the station at personal expense. G.H.L. Fridman, *Sale of Goods in Canada*, 3d ed. (Toronto: Carswell, 1986) at 485.

FORE. *n.* The direction in which the occupant of a seat faces when seated normally in such seat.

FORECASTLE. *n.* A continuous superstructure extending aft from the bow. *Hull Construction Regulations*, C.R.C., c. 1431, s. 100.

FORECLOSURE. *n.* 1. An action brought by a mortgagee when a mortgagor is in default asking that a day be fixed on which the mortgagor is to pay off the debt, and that in default of payment the mortgagor may be foreclosed of, that is deprived of her or his right to redeem, the equity of by redemption. 2. A proceeding, commenced by a vendor under an agreement for sale, in which the relief claimed is an order for one or more of the following: (a) specific performance of the agreement, (b) cancellation of the agreement, or (c) determination of the agreement. *Law Reform Act*, S.B.C. 1985, c. 10, s. 16.1. 3. " . . . [T]erm of art to describe Albertan procedure for the enforcement of the remedies of a mortgagee." *Co-operative Centre Credit Union Ltd. v. Greba* (1984), 33 R.P.R. 71 at 75, [1984] 3 W.W.R. 481, 32 Alta. L.R. (2d) 389, 10 D.L.R. (4th) 449, 55 A.R. 176 (C.A.), the court per Kerans J.A. See DECREE OF ~.

FORECLOSURE ORDER. " . . . [N]ot a final order disposing of a proceeding; it merely fixes the amount due on a mortgage and forecloses the right of a mortgagor to redeem the property, unless the amount due on the mortgage plus costs is paid . . ." *Golden Forest Holdings Ltd. v. Bank of Nova Scotia* (1990), 43 C.P.C. (2d) 16 at 19, 98 N.S.R. (2d) 429, 263 A.P.R. 429 (C.A.), the court per Hallett J.A.

FOREGOER. *n.* A royal purveyor.

FOREGONE. *adj.* Gone without.

FOREIGN. *adj.* 1. Out of a certain nation's jurisdiction. 2. At any time, of a taxpayer resident in Canada means a non-resident corporation in which, at that time, (a) the taxpayer's equity percentage is not less than 1%, and (b) the total of the equity percentages in the corporation of the taxpayer and of each person related to the taxpayer (where each such equity percentage is determined as if the determinations under paragraph (b) of the definition "equity percentage" in subsection 95(4) were made without reference to the equity percentage of any person in the taxpayer or in any person related to the taxpayer) is not less than 10%, except that a corporation is not a foreign affiliate of a non-resident-owned investment corporation. *Income Tax Act*, R.S.C. 1985, c. 1 (5th Supp.), s. 95(1)(d). " . . . [I]n a private international law (conflicts) sense, namely, a territory which does not share precisely the same law . . ." *Canadian Commercial Bank v. McLaughlan* (1990), 73 D.L.R. (4th) 678 at 685, 39 E.T.R. 54, 75 Alta. L.R. (2d) 40, 107 A.R. 232 (C.A.), Bracco and Stevenson JJ.A. and Forsyth J. (ad hoc).

FOREIGN AFFILIATE. 1. At any time, of a taxpayer (other than a non-resident-owned investment corporation) resident in Canada means a corporation (other than a corporation resident in Canada), in which, at that time, the taxpayer's equity percentage was not less than 10%. *Income Tax Act*, R.S.C. 1952, c. 148 (as am. S.C. 1974-

75-76, c. 26, s. 59), s. 95(1)(d). 2. In relation to an insured, a corporation carrying on business outside Canada that, directly or indirectly, (a) is controlled by the insured; (b) controls the insured; or (c) is controlled by a person who directly or indirectly controls the insured. *Export Development Act*, R.S.C. 1985, c. E-20, s. 25.

FOREIGN BANK. Subject to section 12, means an entity incorporated or formed by or under the laws of a country other than Canada that (a) is a bank according to the laws of any foreign country where it carries on business, (b) carries on a business in any foreign country that, if carried on in Canada, would be, wholly or to a significant extent, the business of banking, (c) engages, directly or indirectly, in the business of providing financial services and employs, to identify or describe its business, a name that includes the word "bank", "banque", "banking" or "bancaire", either alone or in combination with other words, or any word or words in any language other than English or French corresponding generally thereto, (d) engages in the business of lending money and accepting deposit liabilities transferable by cheque or other instrument, (e) engages, directly or indirectly, in the business of providing financial services and is affiliated with another foreign bank, (f) controls another foreign bank, or (g) is a foreign institution, other than a foreign bank within the meaning of any of paragraphs (a) to (f), that controls a bank incorporated or formed under this Act, but does not include a subsidiary of a bank named in Schedule I as that Schedule read immediately before the day section 184 of the *Financial Consumer Agency of Canada Act* comes into force, unless the Minister has specified that subsection 378(1) no longer applies to the bank. *Bank Act*, S.C. 1991, c. 46, s. 2. See NON-BANK AFFILIATE OF A ~.

FOREIGN BILL. A bill that is neither drawn in Canada upon a person resident in Canada nor drawn and payable in Canada. I.F.G. Baxter, *The Law of Banking*, 3d ed. (Toronto: Carswell, 1981) at 117.

FOREIGN BROADCASTING UNDERTAKING. A network operation or a broadcasting transmitting undertaking located outside Canada or on a ship or aircraft not registered in Canada.

FOREIGN COMPANY. 1. A company formed or incorporated by or under the laws of any country other than Canada. 2. A company incorporated otherwise than by or under the act of a legislature and includes a dominion company.

FOREIGN CONTROLLED CORPORATION. A corporation that is effectively controlled directly or indirectly by a person who is not a resident of Canada.

FOREIGN CORPORATION. A corporation incorporated otherwise than under a law of Canada or a province.

FOREIGN COUNTRY. Any country other than the designated province, whether a kingdom, empire, republic, commonwealth, state, dominion, province, territory, colony, possession or protectorate or a part thereof. *Foreign Judgments acts*. See INVESTMENT IN A ~.

FOREIGN COURT. "In Canada, the courts of one province are, with respect to the courts of the other provinces, foreign courts." *Brand v. National Life Assurance Co.* (1918), 44 D.L.R. 412 at 420, [1918] 3 W.W.R. 858 (Man. K.B.), Mathers C.J.K.B.

FOREIGN DUTY FREE SHOP. A retail store that is located in a country other than Canada and that is authorized under the laws of that country to sell goods free of certain duties and taxes to individuals who are about to leave that country;

FOREIGN ECONOMIC ENTITY. A foreign state or a group of foreign states, or an entity that is controlled, in law or in fact, or is substantially owned, by a foreign state or a group of foreign states. *Security of Information Act*, R.S.C. 1985, c. O-5, s. 2.

FOREIGN ENTITY. A foreign power, a group or association of foreign powers, or of one or more foreign powers and one or more terrorist groups, or a person acting at the direction of, for the benefit of or in association with a foreign power or a group or association referred to above. *Security of Information Act*, R.S.C. 1985, c. O-5, s. 2.

FOREIGN FISHING VESSEL. A fishing vessel that is not a Canadian fishing vessel.

FOREIGN-GOING. *adj*. When used with reference to a ship, means employed on foreign voyages. *Canada Shipping Act*, R.S.C. 1985, c. S-9, s. 2.

FOREIGN GRAIN. Any grain grown outside Canada and includes screenings from such a grain and every grain product manufactured or processed from such a grain.

FOREIGN GRANT. A grant of probate or administration or other document purporting to be of the same nature granted by a court in (a) a province or territory of Canada, (b) the United Kingdom or any British possession, colony or dependency, or (c) a member nation of the British Commonwealth.

FOREIGN IMMOVABLE RULE. The courts in one jurisdiction do not have jurisdiction to adjudicate on the right and title to lands not within that jurisdiction's boundaries. Only the courts in which the land is situate may adjudicate the right and title to lands.

FOREIGN INSTITUTION. An entity that is (a) engaged in the business of banking, the trust, loan or insurance business, the business of a cooperative credit society or the business of dealing in securities or is otherwise engaged primarily in the business of providing financial services, and (b) incorporated or formed otherwise than by or under an Act of Parliament or of the legislature of a province. *Bank Act*, S.C. 1991, c. 46, s. 2.

FOREIGN INTELLIGENCE. Information or intelligence about the capabilities, intentions or activities of a foreign individual, state, organization or terrorist group, as they relate to international affairs, defence or security.

FOREIGN JUDGMENT. 1. " . . . [J]udgments from another country." *Morguard Investments Ltd. v. De Savoye* (1988), 29 C.P.C. (2d) 52 at 59, 27 B.C.L.R. (2d) 155, [1988] 5 W.W.R. 650 (C.A.), the court per Seaton J.A. 2. A judgment or order of a court of a foreign country, whether heretofore or hereafter obtained, whereby a sum of money is with or without costs made payable or whereby costs only are made payable. *Foreign Judgments acts*.

FOREIGN JURISDICTION. A province, state, country or other jurisdiction outside the province enacting the legislation.

FOREIGN LAW. The law of another jurisdiction.

FOREIGN LIFE CORPORATION. A corporation incorporated outside Canada to undertake contracts of life insurance.

FOREIGN NATIONAL. A person who is not a Canadian citizen or a permanent resident, and includes a stateless person. *Immigration and Refugee Protection Act, 2001*, S. C. 2001, c. 27, s. 2.

FOREIGN NON-RESIDENT. Any person who is not a resident and is domiciled outside Canada.

FOREIGN OFFENDER. A citizen or a national of a foreign state, irrespective of age, who has been found guilty of a criminal offence and is subject to supervision either in confinement or at large by reason of parole, probation or any other form of supervision without confinement, in Canada. *Transfer of Offenders Act*, R.S.C. 1985, c. T-15, s. 2.

FOREIGN ORGANIZATION. A corporation whose head office is outside Canada or an association that is not incorporated and has members who are not residents of Canada but does not include a Canadian branch of any such association.

FOREIGN PETROLEUM. Petroleum other than domestic petroleum. *Energy Administration Act*, R.S.C. 1985, c. E-6, s. 56.

FOREIGN POWER. The government of a foreign state, an entity exercising or purporting to exercise the functions of a government in relation to a territory outside Canada regardless of whether Canada recognizes the territory as a state or the authority of that entity over the territory, or a political faction or party operating within a foreign state whose stated purpose is to assume the role of government of a foreign state. *Security of Information Act*, R.S.C. 1985, c. O-5, s. 2.

FOREIGN RACE INTER-TRACK BETTING. Pari-mutuel betting at one or more satellite tracks on a foreign race, where the money bet on each pool at each satellite track is combined with the money bet on the corresponding pool that is operated by the organization holding the foreign race to form one pool, from which the pay-out price is calculated and distributed. *Pari-Mutuel Betting Supervision Regulations*, SOR/91-365, s. 2.

FOREIGN RACE SEPARATE POOL BETTING. Separate pool betting in Canada on a foreign race. *Pari-Mutuel Betting Supervision Regulations*, SOR/91-365, s. 2.

FOREIGN SHIP. A ship other than a British ship. *Canada Shipping Act*, R.S.C. 1985, c. S-9, s. 2.

FOREIGN STATE. 1. Includes every dominion other than the United Kingdom of Great Britain and Northern Ireland, Canada or a British possession. *Evidence acts*. 2. Any state other than Canada. 3. A state other than Canada, a province, state or other political subdivision of a state other than Canada, or a colony, dependency, possession, protectorate, condominium, trust territory or any territory falling under the jurisdiction of a state other than Canada. *Security of Information Act*, R.S.C. 1985, c. O-5, s. 2. 4. A state, the name of which is set out in the schedule with which Canada has entered into a treaty on the transfer of offenders. *Transfer of Offenders Act*, R.S.C. 1985, c. T-15, s. 2. See AGENCY OF A ~.

FOREIGN TRADE LAW. A law of a foreign jurisdiction that directly or indirectly affects or is likely to affect trade or commerce between (a) Canada, a province, a Canadian citizen or a resident of Canada, a corporation incorporated by or under a law of Canada or a province or a person carrying on business in Canada, and (b) any person or foreign state. *Foreign Extraterritorial Measures Act*, R.S.C. 1985, c. F-29, s. 2.

FOREIGN TRIBUNAL. A tribunal of a foreign state or of an organization of states.

FOREIGN TRUST. A trust that is not resident in Canada in a taxation year and of which a beneficiary, at any time in the year, is a person resident in Canada, a corporation or trust with which such a person is not dealing at arm's length or a controlled foreign affiliate of such a person.

FOREIGN VEHICLE. A motor vehicle, trailer or semi-trailer which is brought into a province otherwise than in the ordinary course of business by or through a manufacturer or dealer and which has not been registered in that province.

FOREIGN VESSEL. A vessel that is not a Canadian vessel or a pleasure craft. *Canada Shipping Act, 2001*, S.C. 2001, c. 26, s. 2.

FOREIGN VOYAGE. A voyage extending beyond the area of a home-trade voyage and not being an inland or minor waters voyage. *Canada Shipping Act*, R.S.C. 1985, c. S-9, s. 2.

FOREIGN WARSHIP. A ship of war, a military transport or military supply ship owned, operated or controlled by the government of any country other than Canada.

FOREIGN YACHT. A ship registered in a country other than Canada and used exclusively for pleasure purposes.

FOREJUDGER. *n*. A judgment which deprives someone of something in question.

FOREMAN. *n.* 1. The member of a jury who speaks for that body. 2. A supervisory employee. See SENIOR ~.

FORENSIC. *adj.* Applied to the law; belonging to law courts.

FORENSIC DNA ANALYSIS. In relation to a bodily substance, means forensic DNA analysis of the bodily substance. *DNA Identification Act, 1998*, S. C. 1998, c. 37, s. 2.

FORENSIC MEDICINE. 1. Legal medicine. 2. Medical skills and knowledge which may be used to solve legal problems. F.A. Jaffe, *A Guide to Pathological Evidence* 3d ed. (Toronto: Carswell, 1991) at 1. 3. Jurisprudence of medicine.

FORENSIC ODONTOLOGY. The study of the teeth of an unidentified body during autopsy. F.A. Jaffe, *A Guide to Pathological Evidence*, 3d ed. (Toronto: Carswell, 1991) at 33.

FORENSIC PSYCHIATRY. Includes psychiatric consultation, assessment, therapy or treatment services provided to the courts or to other components of the administration of justice.

FORESCHOKE. *adj.* Abandoned; disclaimed.

FORESEEABILITY. *n.* A reasonable person's ability to anticipate the consequences of his or her action.

FORESEEABLE. *adj.* A risk is foreseeable when a reasonable person would consider it real and not fanciful or far-fetched. John G. Fleming, *The Law of Torts*, 8th ed. (Sydney: The Law Book Company Limited, 1992) at 115.

FORESHORE. *n.* The land between the low water mark and the highest high water mark.

FOREST. *n.* 1. Land in Canada covered with timber stands or that, formerly so covered, is not put to any use inconsistent with forestry, and includes a sugar bush. 2. The plant cover on any forest land whether standing, dead trees or scrub plants or grass. 3. A plant association consisting predominantly of trees. Nova Scotia statutes. 4. Includes wood, barren or tract covered by underwood or any dry vegetable matter. *Fire Prevention Act*, S.P.E.I. 1983, c. 16, s. 1. 5. Land containing timber, shrubs, slash or peat. *Forest Act*, R.S.B.C. 1979, c. 140, s. 108. See LAKE, ~ AND FUR ASSOCIATION; PRODUCTIVE ~; PRODUCTS OF THE ~; PROTECTION ~; PROVINCIAL ~; PUBLIC ~.

FOREST ACCESS ROAD. A road whether permanent or temporary that is used primarily for the harvesting of timber, the conduct of silviculture or forest protection activities.

FORESTALL. *v.* To forcibly obstruct the way.

FOREST AREA. Any uncultivated land that, by reason of the existence of trees, grass or other vegetation thereon, possesses timber, forage, recreational, wildlife or other value.

FOREST CONCESSION. Any licence, lease, contract of lease and hire or of farming-out or agreement of any kind granting to any person, firm or corporation, under any law, the right to cut wood on any land or lands of the public domain of Québec. *Forest Resources Utilization Act*, R.S.Q. 1977, c. U-2, s. 1.

FOREST ENGINEER. Any person practising the profession of engineer and qualified to give advice upon or supervise, execute, or direct the execution of the following works: the inventory, classification and valuation of the soil and crops of forest, the preparation of maps and topographical plans of forests; the management, maintenance, conservation, lumbering, reforestation and protection of woods and forests, silviculture; forest photogrammetry; logging and transportation of woods, the exploitation of forests and other forest resources; the application of forest engineering sciences to economical wood utilization; the preparation of maps, estimates and specifications, working plans and reports concerning forest management and any engineering work relating to the execution of the above-mentioned purposes and the preparation of plans in connection with such works. *Forest Engineers Act*, R.S.Q. 1977, c. I-10, s. 2.

FOREST FIRE. A fire burning on forest land or threatening forest land.

FOREST INDUSTRIES. All persons or corporations engaged in the manufacturing or processing of primary forest products.

FOREST INDUSTRY. All operations in or incidental to the production or manufacture of articles produced from wood.

FOREST INDUSTRY OPERATION. The harvesting and transporting of trees, including Christmas trees, and the processing of trees into logs or lumber and includes employment incidental to the above operations or immediately connected therewith.

FOREST LAND. 1. Any uncultivated land in a province on which trees or shrubs are growing or standing; any barren, dry marsh, or bog, whether the land is owned by the Crown or by private persons, or held under lease from the Crown. 2. Land bearing forest growth or land from which the forest has been removed but which shows surface evidence of past forest occupancy and is not now in other use. Nova Scotia statutes. 3. Any land lying outside the boundaries of a city or town and not cultivated for agricultural purposes, on which trees, shrubs, plants or grass are growing, together with roads thereon, other than public highways.

FOREST MANAGEMENT. The practical application of scientific, economic and social principles to the administration of forest land for specified objectives. The manipulation of forest land at any stage of the life cycle of the trees occupying it in such a manner that the stand of trees on an area of forest land is replaced by a stand of trees of equivalent or higher quality. See SUSTAINED YIELD ~.

FOREST MANAGEMENT BERTH. Any area for which a forest management licence is granted under this Act for the purpose of providing timber in a sustained yield basis to a wood-using industry.

FOREST MANAGEMENT PLAN. A master plan prepared for the proper management of an area of forest land for the continuous production of timber therefrom.

FOREST MANAGEMENT PROGRAM. A program designed to provide for more effective management of Crown lands and to encourage and assist private landowners to manage their land more effectively by providing professional and technical advice and assistance, training programs and suitable financial incentives.

FOREST MANAGEMENT UNIT. An area which may be subject to a separate management plan, and from which sustained yield is sought as the object of management.

FOREST OWNER. A physical person having full ownership of his forest except one engaged in wood processing otherwise than on a small scale industrial basis, as defined by regulation. *Forest Credit Act*, R.S.Q. 1977, c. C-8, s. 1.

FOREST PLANTATION. A young artificially forested area established by planting or by direct seeding.

FOREST PRODUCT. 1. Wood in its raw state or transformed into pulp or wood-pulp by mechanical, chemical or other processes. 2. A type of product harvested from a tree and includes but is not limited to logs, pulp, fuelwood (either round or chips), maple sap and its derivatives, Christmas trees, fence posts, stakes, rails, and box wood. See PRIMARY ~; SECONDARY ~.

FOREST PRODUCTS. 1. Includes logs, bolts and billets of wood for the manufacture of lumber, pulp, etc., and also pit props, hewn ties, poles, piling, posts, fuelwood, and any other such products of trees in the form in which they are to be used. *Scalers Act*, R.S.N.B. 1973, c. S-4, s. 1. 2. Includes pulp, pulpwood, paper, veneer, plywood, lumber, timber, poles, posts, chips and other products accruing from a forest harvesting operation. *Prairie and Forest Fires Act*, S.S. 1982-83, c. P-22.1, s. 2. 3. Logs, even if they are flatted, wood chips, railway ties and spoolwood. *Taxation Act*, R.S.Q. 1977, c. I-3, s. 1176. See SPECIAL ~.

FOREST PROPERTY. Any lot of land, excluding any buildings or structures thereon, not used for agricultural purposes that is not used or intended to be used for residential or commercial or industrial purposes or any combination of such purposes.

FOREST ROAD. 1. A road on Crown Lands to the fullest extent of the right-of-way of such road and includes the bridges thereon but does not include a highway as defined in the Highway Act, or a logging road. *Crown Lands and Forests Act*, S.N.B. 1980, c. C-38.1, s. 1. 2. A road or part of a road on a Public land under the jurisdiction of the Minister of Lands and Forests. *Lands and Forests Act*, R.S.Q. 1977, c. T-9, s. 98.

FORESTRY. *n*. For a fee or remuneration, performing or directing works, services or undertakings which, because of their scope and forest management implications, require specialized knowledge, training and experience equivalent to that required for a professional forester under this Act, and includes the following: (a) managing forests or forest land for the integration and optimum realization of their total forest resource values; (b) assessing the impact of planned activities on forests and forest land; (c) designing, specifying or approving methods for or directing the undertaking of (i) the classification and inventory of forests and forest land, (ii) silvicultural prescriptions and treatments of forest stands and forest land including timber harvesting, (iii) the protection of forest resources, (iv) the valuation of forest land, and (v) research pertaining to the management of forests and forest land; (d) planning, locating and approving forest transportation systems, including forest roads; (e) examining and verifying forest management performance. See PRACTICE OF PROFESSIONAL ~; PROFESSIONAL ~.

FORESTRY IMPLEMENTS. Tools, implements, apparatus, appliances and machines, of any kind not usually affixed to real property, for use in forestry, and includes vehicles for use in forestry. *Bank Act*, S.C. 1991, c. 46, s. 425.

FORESTRY PRODUCER. A person whose business consists in whole or in part of forestry and includes a producer of maple products. *Bank Act*, S.C. 1991, c. 46, s. 425.

FORESTRY PURPOSES. Includes the production of wood and wood products, provision of proper environmental conditions for wild life, protection against floods and erosion, recreation, and protection and production of water supplies. Ontario statutes.

FOREST TREE PEST. Any vertebrate or invertebrate animal or any virus, fungus, or bacterium or other organism that is injurious to trees commonly found growing in a forest or windbreak or the products from such trees. *Forestry Act*, R.S.O. 1990, c. F-26, s. 1.

FORFEIT. *v.* 1. " . . . '[T]o lose by some breach of condition; to lose by some offence.' . . ." *R. v. Premier Cutlery Ltd.* (1980), 55 C.P.R. 134 at 154 (2d) (Ont. Prov. Ct.), Bernard Prov. J. 2. To forfeit to Her Majesty in right of Canada. *Customs Act*, R.S.C. 1985 (2d Supp.), c. 1, s. 2.

FORFEIT. *adj.* See APPEARANCE ~.

FORFEITURE. *n.* 1. The surrender of goods or chattels to punish someone for a crime, for failure to comply with terms of a recognizance or pay duty or fulfil some obligation and to compensate the person to whom they were forfeited for any injury. 2. Section 98 [of the Courts of Justice Act, R.S.O. 1990, c. C.43] speaks of relief from penalties and forfeitures. Each word lends meaning to the other. "Penalties" is derived from penal and connotes punishment. "Forfeiture" is a giving up of a right or property and when allied with "penalties" suggests something of the nature of goods being forfeited to customs officials. Neither penalties nor forfeitures are compensatory and both connote an added element to any money damages when associated with a breach of a contract. The failure to pay premiums on a term life insurance policy and the consequent lapse of that policy engage none of the above considerations. The premium is the payment for coverage for the next term. Subject to the grace provision, there is no coverage for that term when a payment is not made and the insurer arranges its commercial affairs accordingly. In these circumstances, the contract terminates on its own terms and not by a breach. There is no forfeiture in the sense of a loss of property. To be sure, the coverage has been lost, but it wasn't paid for in the first place. *Pluzak v. Gerling Global Life Insurance Co.* (2001), 2001 CarswellOnt 10 (C.A.). See RELIEF AGAINST ~.

FORGED DOCUMENT. See UTTERING ~.

FORGED PASSPORT. See UTTERING ~.

FORGERY. *n.* Making a false document, knowing it to be false, with intent (a) that it should in any way be used or acted upon as genuine, to the prejudice of any one whether within Canada or not, or (b) that some person should be induced, by the belief that it is genuine, to do or to refrain from doing anything, whether within Canada or not. *Criminal Code*, R.S.C. 1985, c. C-46, s. 366.

FORGERY INSURANCE. Insurance against loss sustained by reason of forgery.

FORGERY OF PASSPORT. Everyone who, while in or out of Canada, (a) forges a passport, or (b) knowing that a passport is forged (i) uses, deals with or acts upon it, or (ii) causes or attempts to cause any person to use, deal with, or act upon it, as if the passport were genuine, is guilty of an offence. *Criminal Code*, R.S.C. 1985, c. C-46, s. 57.

FORJUDGE. *v.* To deprive someone of some thing or right by judgment.

FORM. *n.* 1. The contents or structure of a document distinguished from its substance. 2. A temporary structure or mould used to support concrete while it is drying. See BEARER ~; COMMON ~ BUSINESS; DOSAGE ~; EQUITY LOOKS TO THE INTENT RATHER THAN TO THE ~; FULLY REGISTERED ~; ORDER ~; PROPER ~; REGISTERED ~.

FORMAL ADMISSION. A judicial admission. An admission made by a party in pleadings.

FORMAL CONTRACT. A deed; a contract under seal.

FORMA LEGALIS FORMA ESSENTIALIS. [L.] Legal form is the essential form.

FORMAL EQUITY. (a) With respect to a corporation, any share of the corporation, other than a share excluded by the regulations, that is, or is deemed under the regulations to be, issued and outstanding, (b) with respect to a partnership, any interest or right in the capital or income, or both, of the partnership, (c) with respect to a trust, any beneficial interest in the property of the trust, and (d) with respect to any other person, such interest or right in respect of that person as is prescribed. *Canadian Ownership and Control Determination*, R.S.C. 1985, c. C-20, s. 2.

FORMA PAUPERIS. See IN ~.

FORMAT. In relation to a book, means (a) the type or quality of binding; (b) the typeface or size of print; (c) the type or quality of paper; or (d) the content, including whether the book is abridged or unabridged, or illustrated. *Book Importation Regulations*, SOR/99-324, s. 1. See ALTERNATIVE ~; FOREGROUND ~; GRAMOPHONE ~; MOSAIC ~; ROLLING ~.

FORMER MEMBER. In relation to a pension plan, an employee or former employee who has terminated membership or commenced a pension or whose plan has been terminated, and who retains a present or future entitlement to receive a benefit under the plan.

FORM OF MARRIAGE. Includes a ceremony of marriage that is recognized as valid (a) by the law of the place where it was celebrated, or (b) by the law of the place where an accused is tried, notwithstanding that it is not recognized as valid by the law of the place where it was celebrated. *Criminal Code*, R.S.C. 1985, c. C-46, s. 214.

FORM OF PROXY. A written or printed form that, upon completion and execution by or on behalf of a shareholder, security holder or member becomes a proxy.

FORMS OF ACTION. The common law procedural devices compliance with which was necessary to seek a remedy before the courts, ex. assumpsit, trespass on the case.

FORMULA. See FULTON-FAVREAU ~; INFANT ~; NETBACK PRICING ~; RAND ~; VANCOUVER ~.

FORMULARY. *n*. 1. A precedent; a form. 2. The formulary established pursuant to section 4. *The Prescription Drugs Act*, R.S.S. 1978, c. P-23, s. 2.

FORMULATION. *n*. The preparation of a bill for introduction into the legislature.

FORNICATION. *n*. Voluntary sexual intercourse between two people not married to each other.

FORSPEAKER. *n*. In a proceeding, an advocate or attorney.

FORTHWITH. *adv*. 1. Immediately, or as soon as possible in the circumstances. 2. Within a reasonable time, considering the circumstances and the object.

FORTIFIED WINE. Wine having an alcohol content of more than 14.9 per cent but less than 20 per cent by volume that is made by adding to wine or grape product in fermentation brandy or fruit spirit, or alcohol derived from alcoholic fermentation of a food source that is distilled to not less than 94 per cent alcohol by volume.

FORTIOR EST CUSTODIA LEGIS QUAM HOMINIS. [L.] Legal custody is stronger than personal.

FORTIOR ET POTENTIOR EST DISPOSITIO LEGIS QUAM HOMINIS. [L.] A legal arrangement is stronger and more powerful than a personal one.

FORTIUS CONTRA PROFERENTEM. [L.] More strongly against those using them. Refers to the construction of documents. See CONTRA PROFERENTEM.

FORTUITOUS. *adj*. " . . . [C]arries the connotation that the cause of the loss will not have been intentional or inevitable . . ." *C.C.R. Fishing Ltd. v. Tomenson Inc*. (1990), (*sub nom. C.R.R. Fishing Ltd. v. British Reserve Insurance Co*.) 43 C.C.L.I. 1 at 8, [1990] 3 W.W.R. 501, [1990] I.L.R. 1-2582, 45 B.C.L.R. (2d) 145, [1990] 1 S.C.R. 814, 69 D.L.R. (4th) 112, 109 N.R. 1, the court per McLachlin J.

FORTUNE-TELLING. *n*. Fraudulently undertaking, for a consideration, to tell fortunes is an offence. *Criminal Code*, R.S.C. 1985, c. C-46, s. 365.

FORTY-HOUR WEEK. Overtime must be paid for longer work hours; an historic goal of the labour movement.

FORUM. *n*. [L. a place] The place where legal remedies can be sought, a court. See CONVENIENT ~; NATURAL ~.

FORUM CAN. GRIM. *abbr*. Le Forum canadien de criminologie (Canadian Criminology Forum).

FORUM CONVENIENS. **[L.]** " ' . . . [F]orum which is the more suitable for the ends of justice'." *United Oilseed Products Ltd. v. Royal Bank* (1988), 29 C.P.C. (2d) 28 at 38, 60 Alta. L.R. (2d) 73, [1988] 5 W.W.R. 181, 87 A.R. 337 (C.A.), the court per Stevenson J.A.

FORUM NON CONVENIENS. [L.] 1. A doctrine which a court may apply to decline jurisdiction in a particular case. Another forum is considered more appropriate. 2. ". . . [T]wo conditions must be satisfied: (a) . . . (the defendant) must satisfy the court that there is another forum to whose jurisdiction he was amenable and in which justice can be done between the parties at substantially less inconvenience and expense; (b) if the first condition is met, the plaintiff may still prevent a stay being granted if he can show that a stay would deprive him of a legitimate personal or juridical advantage which would be available to him if he invoked the jurisdiction of the court where the stay is sought." *Avenue Properties Ltd. v. First City Development Co.* (1986), 7 B.C.L.R. (2d) 5 at 51-52, [1987] 1 W.W.R. 249, 32 D.L.R. (4th) 40 (C.A.), McLachlin J.A.

FORUM ORIGINIS. [L.] The court of the place of a person's domicile by birth.

FORUM REI. [L.] The court of the place where the subject thing or person is situated.

FORWARD COMMODITY CONTRACT. Is a financial hedge and risk management tool. Interpreting them in the context of the rest of the section requires that they share certain traits. The contracts listed in s. 11.1(1) of the *Companies' Creditors Arrangement Act*, R.S.C. 1985, c. C-36] deal with units that are the equivalent of any other unit. Therefore commodities must be interchangeable, and readily identifiable as fungible commodities capable of being traded on a futures exchange or as the underlying asset of an over-the-counter derivative transaction. Commodities must trade in a volatile market, with a sufficient trading volume to ensure a competitive trading price, in order that forward commodity contracts may be "marked to market" and their value determined. This removes from the ambit of s. 11.1(1)(h) contracts for commercial merchandise and manufactured goods which neither trade on a volatile market nor are completely interchangeable for each other. *Blue Range Resource Corp., Re*, 2000 ABCA 239, 20 C.B.R. (4th) 187, 266 A.R. 98 (C.A.).

FORWARD CONTROL CONFIGURATION. A configuration in which more than half of the engine length is rearward of the foremost point of the windshield base and the steering wheel hub is in the forward quarter of the vehicle. *Motor Vehicle Safety Regulations*, C.R.C., c. 1038, s. 2.

FORWARDER. See FREIGHT ~.

FORWARDING AGENT. One who accepts and forwards goods, paying the cost of transportation and receiving in return compensation from the owners. The agent has no concern in the vehicles or vessels by which the goods are transported and no interest in the freight itself.

FORWARD PERPENDICULAR. A vertical line intersecting the point where the foreside of the stem of a ship crosses the waterline on which the length is measured. Canada regulations.

FORWARD SORTATION AREA CODE. The first three characters of a postal code. *Mail Preparation Regulations*, C.R.C., c. 1281, s. 2.

FOSSIL. *n.* Includes (a) natural casts; (b) preserved tracks, coprolites and plant remains; and (c) the preserved shells and exoskeletons of invertebrates and the eggs, teeth and bones of vertebrates. *Nunavut Archaeological and Palaeontological Sites Regulations* SOR/2001-220, s. 1. See INVERTEBRATE ~; PLANT ~; VERTEBRATE ~; VERTEBRATE TRACE ~.

FOSSIL AMBER. Fossil resin with or without inclusions.

FOSTER CARE. The provision of residential care to a child, by and in the home of a person who, (a) receives compensation for caring for the child, except under the Family Benefits Act, the General Welfare Assistance Act, or the regulations made under either of them, and (b) is not the child's parent or a person with whom the child has been placed for adoption under Part VII. *Child and Family Services Act*, R.S.O. 1990, c. 11, s. 3.

FOSTER CHILD. A child whose parents are unable, in the opinion of the provincial authority, to support him and who is cared for (by a person or persons standing in loco parentis to him) in a private home approved as a suitable place of care by a child welfare authority or by a person designated for that purpose.

FOSTER FAMILY. A family which takes charge of one or several adults or children.

FOSTER HOME. 1. A home, other than the home of the child's parent, in which a child is placed for care and supervision but not for the purposes of adoption. 2. With respect to a child who lacks normal parental relations, means a home other than that of parents or relatives, in which such child may be placed to be treated as a member of the family. See GROUP ~.

FOSTER PARENT. 1. An adult who as part of his family, cares for a child on behalf of the Minister. *Child and Family Services and Family Relations Act*, S.N.B. 1980, c. C-2.1, s. 1. 2. Any person who conducts, maintains, operates, or manages a foster home.

FOSTER PARENT AGREEMENT. An agreement entered into between a foster parent and the Minister transferring all or part of the care, custody and control of the child.

F.O.T. *abbr.* Free on truck. Describing a seller's responsibility to have the goods placed on a truck.

FOUL HOOKING. Fishing with a hook or hooks attached to a line manipulated in such a manner as to pierce a fish in any part of its body other than its mouth.

FOULING. *n.* Placement of powder and lubricant residue on the inside of a firearm barrel or on skin surrounding the entrance wound of a bullet. F.A. Jaffe, *A Guide to Pathological Evidence*, 3d ed. (Toronto: Carswell, 1991) at 219.

FOUNDATION. *n.* 1. A corporation established to receive, hold, administer and apply any property or the income from it for purposes or objects in connection with a hospital, other public or charitable purpose. 2. A system or arrangement of foundation units through which the loads from a building are transferred to supporting soil or rock. See CHARITABLE DEEP ~; SHALLOW ~.

FOUNDATION DRAIN. A drain installed below the surface of the ground to collect and convey water from the foundation of a building or other structure.

FOUNDATION UNIT. One of the structural members of the foundation of a building such as a footing, raft or pile.

FOUNDER. *n.* 1. A person who has signed the memorandum of association or who has been admitted as a member at the time of the organization meeting. *Cooperative Associations Act*, R.S.Q. 1977, c. A-24, s. 1. 2. A person who has signed the founding memorandum of a union or was admitted as a member at the organization meeting. *Savings and Credit Unions Act*, R.S.Q. 1977, c. C-4, s. 1.

FOUNDER FEDERATION. The federation upon whose application the security fund corporation has been incorporated. *An Act respecting security fund corporations*, S.Q. 1979, c. 53, s. 1.

FOUND IN. Present in; discovered in the premises. Refers to a person found in a bawdy house or at a gaming location.

FOUNDRY. *n.* The part of a building or premises or the workshop, structure, room or place in which base metals or their alloys are cast in moulds, other than permanent moulds, or where core-making, shakeout or cleaning or any casting or other dust-causing operation ancillary to the casting process is carried on. See FERROUS ~.

FOUR AXLE GROUP. Four consecutive axles, not including the front axle of a motor vehicle, (a) that are entirely within either a motor vehicle or trailer or semi-trailer, and (b) in which the spacings between the consecutive axles do not exceed 2.5 metres. *Highway Traffic Act*, R.S.O. 1990, c. H.8, s. 114.

4-H PROGRAM. A program designed for the education and training of farm boys and girls through local 4-H clubs.

FOURTH FREEDOM. The privilege of a non-Canadian air carrier, where operating a charter flight, of embarking in Canada passengers or goods destined for the territory of the country of the non-Canadian air carrier and includes the privilege of disembarking such passengers in Canada on return from that territory. *Air Transportation Regulations*, SOR/88-58, s. 2.

FOUR TRIGGER THEORIES. Four approaches have been developed in the U.S. and Canadian jurisprudence for determining the timing of property damage which is latent, or developing over time, and which does not become apparent immediately. The "Exposure Theory", the "Manifestation Theory", the "Injury in Fact Theory" and the "Continuous Trigger or Triple Trigger Theory". *Alie v. Bertrand & Frère Construction Co.* (2002), 62 O.R. (3d) 345 (C.A.).

F.O.W. *abbr.* First open water. Describes water immediately after ice breaks up so that navigation is possible.

FOWL. *n.* 1. A domestic hen more than twenty weeks of age. 2. Domesticated fowl.

FOX PAT. C. *abbr.* Fox's Patent, Trade Mark, Design and Copyright Cases, 1940-1971.

F.P.A. *abbr*. Free from particular average. In marine insurance, means an underwriter is liable only for total loss, either actual or constructive.

F.P.R. *abbr*. Fisheries Pollution Reports.

FRA. *abbr*. Family Relations Act.

FRACTIONEM DIEI NON RECIPIT LEX. [L.] The law does not recognize a fraction of a day.

FRACTION OF A DAY. The portion of a day recognized only in cases of necessity and for judicial purposes.

FRACTURE. *n*. The break in a bone. See BUMPER ~; COMMINUTED ~; COMPOUND ~; CONTRE COUP ~; DEPRESSED ~; EGGSHELL ~; GREENSTICK ~; HAIRLINE ~; RADIATING ~.

FRAME. *v*. To fabricate false evidence so it appears someone else committed an offence.

FRAME. *n*. See SPACE ~.

FRAMEWORK AGREEMENT. The Framework Agreement on First Nation Land Management concluded between Her Majesty in right of Canada and the first nations on February 12, 1996, and includes any amendments to the Agreement made pursuant to its provisions. *First Nations Land Management Act, 1999*, S.C. 1999, c. 24, s. 2.

FRANC. See GOLD ~.

FRANCHISE. *n*. 1. At common law, a royal privilege. 2. An agreement whereby the right to supply electricity, natural gas or natural gas liquids to the residents of a defined area is given. 3. A method of distributing or marketing a service or product through a system. The franchisor grants the franchisee the right to carry on the business in this particular way, according to this system. 4. A right to engage in a business where the franchisee is required by contract or otherwise to make a payment or continuing payments, whether direct or indirect, or a commitment to make such payment or payments, to the franchisor, or the franchisor's associate, in the course of operating the business or as a condition of acquiring the franchise or commencing operations and, (a) in which, (i) the franchisor grants the franchisee the right to sell, offer for sale or distribute goods or services that are substantially associated with the franchisor's, or the franchisor's associate's, trade-mark, service mark, trade name, logo or advertising or other commercial symbol, and (ii) the franchisor or the franchisor's

associate exercises significant control over, or offers significant assistance in, the franchisee's method of operation, including building design and furnishings, locations, business organization, marketing techniques or training, or (b) in which, (i) the franchisor, or the franchisor's associate, grants the franchisee the representational or distribution rights, whether or not a trade-mark, service mark, trade name, logo or advertising or other commercial symbol is involved, to sell, offer for sale or distribute goods or services supplied by the franchisor or a supplier designated by the franchisor, and (ii) the franchisor, or the franchisor's associate, or a third person designated by the franchisor, provides location assistance, including securing retail outlets or accounts for the goods or services to be sold, offered for sale or distributed or securing locations or sites for vending machines, display racks or other product sales displays used by the franchisee. *Arthur Wishart Act (Franchise Disclosure), 2000*, S.O. 2000, c. 3, s. 1. See AREA ~; PYRAMID ~; PYRAMID SALES ~; SPECIAL ~.

FRANCHISE AGREEMENT. Any agreement that relates to a franchise between, (a) a franchisor or franchisor's associate, and (b) a franchisee. *Arthur Wishart Act (Franchise Disclosure), 2000*, S.O. 2000, c. 3, s. 1.

FRANCHISEE. *n*. 1. A person to whom a franchise is granted. 2. A person to whom a franchise is granted and includes, (a) a subfranchisor with regard to that subfranchisor's relationship with a franchisor, and (b) a subfranchisee with regard to that subfranchisee's relationship with a subfranchisor. *Arthur Wishart Act (Franchise Disclosure), 2000*, S.O. 2000, c. 3, s. 1.

FRANCHISE FEE. A direct or indirect payment to purchase a franchise or to operate a franchised business, but does not include (a) a purchase of or an agreement to purchase a reasonable amount of goods at a reasonable bona fide wholesale price, (b) a purchase of or an agreement to purchase a reasonable amount of services at a reasonable bona fide price, or (c) a payment of a reasonable service charge to the issuer of a credit or debit card by an establishment accepting the credit or debit card, as the case may be franchise fee means a direct or indirect payment to purchase a franchise or to operate a franchised business, but does not include (d) a purchase of or an agreement to purchase a reasonable amount of goods at a reasonable bona fide wholesale price, (e) a purchase of or an agreement to purchase a reasonable amount of services at a reasonable bona fide price, or (f) a payment of a reasonable service charge to the issuer of a credit or debit card by an establishment accepting the credit or debit card, as the case may be. *Franchises Act*, R.S.A. 2000, c. F-23, s. 1.

FRANCHISE SYSTEM. Includes, (a) the marketing, marketing plan or business plan of the franchise, (b) the use of or association with a trade-mark, service mark, trade name, logo or advertising or other commercial symbol, (c) the obligations of the franchisor and franchisee with regard to the operation of the business operated by the franchisee under the franchise agreement, and (d) the goodwill associated with the franchise. *Arthur Wishart Act (Franchise Disclosure), 2000*, S.O. 2000, c. 3, s. 1.

FRANCHISOR. *n.* 1. A person who grants a franchise. 2. One or more persons who grant or offer to grant a franchise and includes a subfranchisor with regard to that subfranchisor's relationship with a subfranchisee. *Arthur Wishart Act (Franchise Disclosure), 2000*, S.O. 2000, c. 3, s. 1.

FRANCHISOR'S ASSOCIATE. A person, (a) who, directly or indirectly, (i) controls or is controlled by the franchisor, or (ii) is controlled by another person who also controls, directly or indirectly, the franchisor, and (b) who, (i) is directly involved in the grant of the franchise, (A) by being involved in reviewing or approving the grant of the franchise, or (B) by making representations to the prospective franchisee on behalf of the franchisor for the purpose of granting the franchise, marketing the franchise or otherwise offering to grant the franchise, or (ii) exercises significant operational control over the franchisee and to whom the franchisee has a continuing financial obligation in respect of the franchise. *Arthur Wishart Act (Franchise Disclosure), 2000*, S.O. 2000, c. 3, s. 1.

FRANGIBLE. *adj.* Brittle, easily broken.

FRATER CONSANGUINEUS. [L.] A brother by the father's side.

FRATER FRATRI UTERINO NON SUCCEDET IN HAEREDITATE PATERNA. [L.] A brother may not succeed a brother by the mother's side in a paternal inheritance.

FRATERNAL BENEFIT SOCIETY. 1. A corporation having a representative form of government and incorporated for fraternal, benev-

olent or religious purposes among which purposes is the insuring of the members, or the spouses or children of the members thereof, exclusively, against accident, sickness, disability or death and includes a corporation incorporated for those purposes on the mutual plan for the purpose of so insuring the members, or the spouses or children of the members thereof, exclusively. 2. A body corporate (a) that is without share capital, (b) that has a representative form of government, and (c) that was incorporated for fraternal, benevolent or religious purposes, including the provision of insurance benefits solely to its members or the spouses, common-law partners or children of its members. *Insurance Companies Act, 1991*, S.C. 1991, c. 47, s. 2.

FRATERNAL CLUB. A chartered branch of an established fraternal organization.

FRATERNAL OR SORORAL BENEFIT SOCIETY. A society, order or voluntary association incorporated or formed to carry on for the purpose of making with its members only and not for profit contracts of life, accident or sickness insurance under which benefits may be paid only to its members or their beneficiaries in accordance with its constitution and laws and the laws of the province.

FRATERNAL SOCIETY. A society, order or association incorporated for the purpose of making with its members only, and not for profit, contracts of life, accident or sickness insurance in accordance with its constitution, by-laws and rules and the governing statute.

FRATERNIA. *n.* [L.] A brotherhood, fraternity.

FRATER NUTRICIUS. [L.] A bastard brother.

FRATER UTERINUS. [L.] A brother by the mother's side.

FRATRES CONJURATI. [L.] Sworn brothers.

FRATRICIDE. *n.* The murder of a sibling.

FRAUD. *n.* 1. The essential elements of fraud are dishonesty, which can include nondisclosure of important facts, and deprivation or risk of deprivation. *R. v. Cuerrier*, [1998] 2 S.C.R. 371, per Cory, J. 2. "Fraud is false representation of fact, made with a knowledge of its falsehood, or recklessly, without belief in its truth, with the intention that it should be acted upon by the complaining party, and actually inducing him to act upon it." *Parna v. G. & S. Properties Ltd.*, [1971] S.C.R. 306 at 316, 15 D.L.R. (3d) 336, the court per Spence J., adopting a quotation from Anson on Contract. 3. (a) Every one who, by deceit, falsehood or other fraudulent means whether or not it is a false pretence within the meaning of this Act defrauds the public or any person whether ascertained or not, of any property, money or valuable security, is guilty of an offence. (b) Every one who, by deceit, falsehood or other fraudulent means, whether or not it is a false pretence within the meaning of this Act, with intent to defraud, affects the public market price of stocks, shares, merchandise or anything that is offered for sale to the public, is guilty of an offence. *Criminal Code*, R.S.C. 1985, c. C-46, s. 380 in part. 4. The elements of fraud, in the context of an application for insurance are: a representation of a material fact, in writing on the application, which judged objectively, was false at the time it was made, and upon which there was reliance to the prejudice or harm of the insurer. *35445 Alberta Ltd. v. Transamerica Life Insurance Co. of Canada* (1996), 40 Alta. L.R. (3d) 44 (Q.B.), affirmed (1998), 61 Alta. L.R. (3d) 215 (C.A.). See BADGES OF ~; CONSTRUCTIVE ~; EQUITABLE ~; EXTRINSIC ~; INTRINSIC ~; STATUTE OF ~S.

FRAUDULENT ACT. 1. In connection with a trade in real estate: (a) any intentional misrepresentation by word, conduct or manner of a material fact, present or past, and an intentional omission to disclose such a material fact; (b) a promise or representation as to the future that is beyond reasonable expectation and that is not made in good faith; (c) the failure, within a reasonable time, properly to account for or pay over to the person entitled thereto any moneys received; (d) the failure on the part of a broker or salesman to disclose to all parties concerned whether he or she is acting as a principal or as an agent in the trade; (e) any course of conduct or business calculated or put forward with intent to deceive the public or the purchaser or the vendor as to the value of any real estate; (f) the failure on the part of a broker or salesman to disclose to a vendor of any real estate for whom he or she acts directly or indirectly any offer to purchase same, received by the broker or salesman; (g) the gaining of, or attempt to gain, a commission, fee or gross profit so large and so exorbitant as to be unconscionable and unreasonable; (h) generally, any artifice, agreement, device, scheme, course of conduct or business,

to obtain money, profit or property by any of the means hereinbefore set forth or otherwise contrary to law, or by wrongful or dishonest dealing, and anything specifically defined in the regulations as coming within the meaning of this definition. 2. (a) Any fictitious or pretended trade in any security; (b) the gaining or attempt to gain, directly or indirectly, through a trade in any security, a commission, fee or gross profit so large and exorbitant as to be unconscionable and unreasonable; (c) any course of conduct or business which is calculated or put forward with intent to deceive the public or the purchaser or the vendor of any security as to the nature of any transaction or as to the value of such security. 3. (a) The making of any material false statement in any application, registration statement, prospectus, information, material or evidence submitted, or given to the Minister, the Minister's representative, or to the Registrar under this Act, or the regulations; (b) the violation of any provision relating to trading securities; (c) the failure on the part of a broker, manager or salesman to disclose to all parties concerned whether he or she is acting as a principal or as an agent in the trade.

FRAUDULENT CONVEYANCE. A conveyance which defrauds, delays or hinders creditors and others. *Toronto Dominion Bank v. Miller* (1990), (*sub nom. Miller, Re*) 3 C.B.R. (3d) 285 at 288, 1 O.R. (3d) 528 (Gen. Div.), Steele J.

FRAUDULENT MISREPRESENTATION. " . . . [O]ne (a) which is untrue in fact; (b) which defendant knows to be untrue or is indifferent as to its truth; (c) which was intended or calculated to induce the plaintiff to act upon it; and (d) which the plaintiff acts upon and suffers damage . . ." *Francis v. Dingman* (1983), 23 B.L.R. 234 at 253, 43 O.R. (2d) 641, 2 D.L.R. (4th) 244 (C.A.), Goodman J.A. (Zuber J.A. concurring).

FRAUDULENT PREFERENCE. " . . . [A]n act by which one creditor obtained an advantage over the others when two things concurred: first, that the act was voluntary on the part of the debtor; and secondly, that it was done in contemplation of bankruptcy. . ." *Stephens v. McArthur* (1891), 19 S.C.R. 446 at 462, 6 Man. R. 496, Patterson J.

FRAUS DANS LOCUM CONTRACTUI. [L.] A fraud inducing a contract.

FRAUS EST CELARE FRAUDEM. [L.] To conceal fraud is fraud.

FRAUS EST ODIOSA ET NON PRAESU-MENDA. [L.] Fraud is hateful and not to be undertaken.

FRAUS ET DOLUS NEMINI PATROCI-NARI DEBENT. [L.] Fraud and deceit ought not to provide a defence to anyone.

FRAUS ET JUS NUNQUAM COHABI-TANT. [L.] Fraud and justice never dwell together.

FRAUS LEGIS. [L. fraud of the law] The use of legal proceedings with fraudulent intent.

FRAUS OMNIA CORRUMPIT. Fraud invalidates all.

FRAY. See AFFRAY.

FREE. *adj*. 1. "In the context of s. 121 [of the Constitution Act, 1867 (30 & 31 Vict.), c. 3] . . . without impediment related to the traversing of a provincial boundary." *Murphy v. Canadian Pacific Railway* (1958), 15 D.L.R. (2d) 145 at 150, [1958] S.C.R. 626, 77 C.R.T.C. 322, Rand J. 2. When applied to any goods described in Schedule II, means that the goods may be imported and taken out of the warehouse for consumption in Canada, without duty. *Customs Tariff*, R.S.C. 1985, c. C-54, s. 2. 3. Without impediment. 4. Without cost. 5. Without limitation.

FREE AND DEMOCRATIC SOCIETY. " . . . [T]he values and principles essential to a free and democratic society . . . embody, to name but a few, respect for the inherent dignity of the human person, commitment to social justice and equality, accommodation of a wide variety of beliefs, respect for cultural and group identity, and faith in social and political institutions which enhance the participation of individuals and groups in society . . ." The underlying values and principles of a free and democratic society are the genesis of the rights and freedoms guaranteed by the Charter and the ultimate standard against which a limit on a right or freedom must be shown, despite its effects, to be reasonable and demonstrably justified. *R. v. Oakes* (1986), 19 C.R.R. 308 at 334, [1986] 1 S.C.R. 103, 50 C.R. (3d) 1,14 O.A.C. 335, 24 C.C.C. (3d) 321, 26 D.L.R. (4th) 200, 65 N.R. 98, Dickson C.J.C. (Chouinard, Lamer, Wilson and Le Dain JJ. concurring).

FREE ALONGSIDE SHIP. A seller undertakes to deliver goods alongside a ship at the seller's own expense.

FREEBOARD. *n*. 1. The vertical distance amidships from the subdivision load water line to the margin line. *Hull Construction Regulations*, C.R.C., c. 1431, Schedule 1, s. 11. 2. A distance that is calculated in respect of a ship in accordance with these Regulations and measured vertically downwards from a position coinciding with the midpoint of the upper edge of the deck line. *Load Line Regulations*, Canada regulations. See DEPTH FOR ~.

FREE CAPITAL. See NET ~.

FREE COMPETITION. " . . . [A]s judicially understood, affirmatively may be stated, as a situation in which the freedom of any individual or firm to engage in legitimate economic activity is not restrained by (a) agreements or conspiracies between competitors, or (b) by predatory practices of a rival, contrary to The Combines Investigation Act. And 'free competition' thus understood is quite compatible with the presence of monopoly elements as understood by economists, in the economic sense of the word monopoly, for the antithesis of the economic conception of monopoly is not 'free competition', as understood by the courts, but 'pure competition'." *R. v. Canadian Coat & Apron Supply Ltd.* (1967), 2 C.R.N.S. 62 at 77 (Ex. Ct.), Gibson J.

FREEDOM. *n*. 1. " . . . [I]n a broad sense embraces both the absence of coercion and constraint, and the right to manifest beliefs and practices. Freedom means that, subject to such imitations as are necessary to protect public safety, order, health, or morals or the fundamental rights and freedoms of others, no one is to be forced to act in a way contrary to his beliefs or his conscience." Freedom can primarily be characterized by the absence of coercion or constraint. If a person is compelled by the state or the will of another to a course of action or inaction which he would not otherwise have chosen, he is not acting of his own volition and he cannot be said to be truly free. Coercion includes not only such blatant forms of compulsion as direct commands to act or refrain from acting on pain of sanction, coercion includes indirect forms of control which determine or limit alternative courses of conduct available to others. *R. v. Big M Drug Mart* (1985), 13 C.R.R. 64 at 97, [1985] 1 S.C.R. 295, [1985] 3 W.W.R. 481, 37 Alta. L.R. (2d) 97, 58 N.R. 81, 18 C.C.C. (3d) 385, 60 A.R. 161, 18 D.L.R. (4th) 321, 85 C.L.L.C. 14,023, Dickson C.J.C. (Beetz, McIntyre, Chouinard and Lamer JJ. concurring). 2. " . . . [I]s defined by determining first the area which is regulated. The freedom is then what exists in the unregulated area — a sphere of activity within which all acts are permissible. It is a residual area in which all acts are free of specific legal regulation and the individual is free to choose . . ." *R. v. Zundel* (1987), 56 C.R. (3d) 1 at 23, 18 O.A.C. 161, 58 O.R. (2d) 129, 31 C.C.C. (3d) 97, 35 D.L.R. (4th) 338, 29 C.R.R. 349 (C.A.), Howland C.J.O., Brooke, Martin, Lacourcière, and Houlden JJ.A. See FIFTH ~; FOURTH ~; FUNDAMENTAL ~; LIBERTY; RIGHT; THIRD ~.

FREEDOM OF ASSOCIATION. 1. " . . . [T]he freedom to combine together for the pursuit of common purposes or the advancement of common causes. It is one of the fundamental freedoms guaranteed by the Charter, a sine qua non of any free and democratic society, protecting individuals from the vulnerability of isolation and ensuring the potential of effective participation in society. . ." *Reference re Public Service Employee Relations Act (Alberta)* (1987), 38 D.L.R. (4th) 161 at 173, [1987] 1 S.C.R. 313, 87 C.L.L.C. 14,021, 51 Alta. L.R. (2d) 97, [1987] 3 W.W.R. 577, 74 N.R. 99, 28 C.R.R. 305, 78 A.R. 1, [1987] D.L.Q. 225, Dickson C.J.C. 2 . Three elements of freedom of association are summarized, along with a crucial fourth principle, in the oft-quoted words of Sopinka J. in *P.I.P.S. v. Northwest Territories (Commissioner)*, [1990] 2 S.C.R. 367 ("*PIPSC*"), at pp. 401-2: Upon considering the various judgments in the *Alberta Reference*, I have come to the view that four separate propositions concerning the coverage of the s. 2(*d*) guarantee of freedom of association emerge from the case: *first, that s. 2(d)* protects the freedom to establish, belong to and maintain an association; *second,* that s. 2(*d*) does not protect an activity solely on the ground that the activity is a foundational or essential purpose of an association; third, that s. 2(*d*) protects the exercise in association of the constitutional rights and freedoms of individuals; and fourth, that s. 2(*d*) protects the exercise in association of the lawful rights of individuals. In addition to the four-part formulation in *PIPSC, supra,* an enduring source of insight into the content of s. 2(*d*) is the purpose of the provision. This purpose was first articulated in the labour trilogy and has accordingly been used to define both the "positive" freedom to associate as well as the "negative" freedom not to (see *Alberta Reference, supra*; *Lavigne v. O.P.S.E.U.*, [1991] 2 S.C.R. 211, at p. 318; *R. c. Advance Cutting & Coring Ltd.*,

2001 SCC 70). While freedom of association like most other fundamental rights has no single purpose or value, at its core rests a rather simple proposition: the attainment of individual goals, through the exercise of individual rights, is generally impossible without the aid and cooperation of others. The purpose of s. 2(*d*) commands a single inquiry: has the state precluded activity *because* of its associational nature, thereby discouraging the collective pursuit of common goals? In my view, while the four-part test for freedom of association sheds light on this concept, it does not capture the full range of activities protected by s. 2(*d*). In particular, there will be occasions where a given activity does not fall within the third and fourth rules, but where the state has nevertheless prohibited that activity solely because of its associational nature. These occasions will involve activities which (a) are not protected under any other constitutional freedom, and (b) cannot, for one reason or another, be understood as the lawful activities of individuals. Such activities may be *collective* in nature, in that they cannot be performed by individuals acting alone. The prohibition of such activities must surely, in some cases, be a violation of s. 2(*d*). There will, however, be occasions when no analogy involving individuals can be found for associational activity, or when a comparison between groups and individuals fails to capture the essence of a possible violation of associational rights. . . *The overarching consideration remains whether a legislative enactment or administrative action interferes with the freedom of persons to join and act with others in common pursuits.* The legislative purpose which will render legislation invalid is the attempt to preclude associational conduct because of its concerted or associational nature. In sum, a purposive approach to s. 2(*d*) demands that we "distinguish between the associational aspect of the activity and the activity itself". Such an approach begins with the existing framework which enables a claimant to show that a group activity is permitted for individuals in order to establish that its regulation targets the association *per se*. Where this burden cannot be met, however, it may still be open to a claimant to show, by direct evidence or inference, that the legislature has targeted associational conduct because of its concerted or associational nature. *Dunmore v. Ontario (Attorney General)*, [2001] 3 S.C.R. 1016. 3. " . . . [I]nclude[s] freedom from forced association . . ." *Lavigne v. O.P.S.E.U.* (1991), 4 C.R.R. (2d) 193 at 212, 91 C.L.L.C. 14,029, 3 O.R. (3d) 511n, 81 D.L.R. (4th) 545, 126 N.R. 161, 40

O.A.C. 241, [1991] 2 S.C.R. 211, La Forest J. (Sopinka and Gonthier JJ. concurring).

FREEDOM OF CONSCIENCE AND RELIGION. 1. " . . . [B]roadly construed to extend to conscientiously-held beliefs whether grounded in religion or in a secular morality. . ." *R. v. Morgentaler* (1988), 37 C.C.C. 449 at 560, 82 N.R. 1, [1988] 1 S.C.R. 30, 63 O.R. (2d) 281n, 62 C.R. (3d) 1, 26 O.A.C. 1, 44 D.L.R. (4th) 385, 31 C.R.R. 1, Wilson J. 2. " . . . [W]hatever else freedom of conscience and religion [in s. 2(*a*) of the Charter] may mean, it must at the very least mean this: government may not coerce individuals to affirm a specific religious belief or to manifest a specific religious practice for a sectarian purpose . . . freedom from compulsory religious observance . . ." *R. v. Big M Drug Mart* (1985), 18 C.C.C. (3d) 385 at 426-7, 85 C.L.L.C. 14,023, [1985] 1 S.C.R. 295, [1985] 3 W.W.R. 481, 37 Alta. L.R. (2d) 97, 58 N.R. 81, 13 C.R.R. 64, 60 A.R. 161, 18 D.L.R. (4th) 321, Dickson C.J.C. (Beetz, McIntyre, Chouinard and Lamer JJ. concurring).

FREEDOM OF CONTRACT. The parties to contracts are left by the court to use their own discretion and to make their own agreements.

FREEDOM OF EXPRESSION. 1. " . . . [P]urpose of the guarantee is to permit free expression to the end of promoting truth, political or social participation, and self-fulfilment. That purpose extends to the protection of minority beliefs which the majority regard as wrong or false: . . ." *R. v. Zundel* (1992), 5 C.C.C. (3d) 449 at 506, 95 D.L.R. (4th) 202, [1992] 2 S.C.R. 731, 140 N.R. 1, 56 O.A.C. 161, 16 C.R. (4th) 1, 10 C.R.R. (2d) 193, McLachlin J. (La Forest, L'Heureux-Dubé and Sopinka JJ. concurring). 2. " . . . [I]ncludes the freedom to express oneself in the language of one's choice. . ." *Devine v. Quebec (Attorney General)* (1989), 10 C.H.R.R. D/5610 at D/5624, 90 N.R. 48, 19 Q.A.C. 33, [1988] 2 S.C.R. 790, 36 C.R.R. 64, 55 D.L.R. (4th) 641, Dickson C.J.C., Beetz, McIntyre, Lamer and Wilson JJ. 3. . . . [I]s not, however, a creature of the Charter. It is one of the fundamental concepts that has formed the basis for historical development of the political, social and educational institutions of western society. Representative democracy, as we know it today, which is in great part the product of free expression and discussion of varying ideas, depends upon its maintenance and protection." *Dolphin Delivery Ltd. v. R.WD.S.U., Local 580* (1986), 38 C.L.L.T. 184 at 196, 71 N.R. 83, [1986] 2 S.C.R. 573, 9 B.C.L.R. (2d) 273, 87 C.L.L.C. 14,002, [1987] 1 W.W.R. 577, 33 D.L.R. (4th) 174, 25 C.R.R. 321, [1987] D.L.Q. 69n, McIntyre J. (Dickson C.J.C., Estey, Chouinard and Le Dain JJ. concurring). 4. The values which underlie the protection of freedom of expression relate to the search for truth, participation in the political process, and individual self-fulfilment. *R. v. Butler*, 1992 CarswellMan 100, [1992] 2 W.W.R. 577, [1992] 1 S.C.R. 452, 11 C.R. (4th) 137, 70 C.C.C. (3d) 129, 134 N.R. 81, 8 C.R.R. (2d) 1, 89 D.L.R. (4th) 449, 78 Man. R. (2d) 1, 16 W.A.C. 1 per Sopinka, J. 5. Freedom of expression is fundamental to freedom. It is the foundation of any democratic society. It is the cornerstone of our democratic institutions and is essential to their functioning. *K Mart Canada Ltd. v. U.F.C.W., Local 1518*, 1999 CarswellBC 1909, (sub nom. *United Food & Commercial Workers, Local 1518 v. KMart Canada Ltd.*) 99 C.L.L.C. 220-064, [1999] 9 W.W.R. 161, 245 N.R. 1, 176 D.L.R. (4th) 607, 66 B.C.L.R. (3d) 211, 66 C.R.R. (2d) 205, 128 B.C.A.C. 1, 208 W.A.C. 1, [1999] 2 S.C.R. 1083, Cory, J. for the court.

FREEDOM OF INFORMATION. Refers to legislation governing access to government documents and records.

FREEDOM OF RELIGION. " . . . The essence of the concept of freedom of religion is the right to entertain such religious beliefs as a person chooses, the right to declare religious beliefs openly and without fear of hindrance or reprisal, and the right to manifest religious belief by worship and practice or by teaching and dissemination. But the concept means more than that. . . Freedom means that, subject to such limitations as are necessary to protect public safety, order, health, or morals or the fundamental rights and freedoms of others, no one is to be forced to act in a way contrary to his beliefs or his conscience." *R. v. Big M Drug Mart* (1985), 13 C.R.R. 64 at 97, [1985] 1 S.C.R. 295, [1985] 3 W.W.R. 481, 37 Alta. L.R. (2d) 97, 58 N.R. 81, 18 C.C.C. (3d) 385, 60 A.R. 161, 18 D.L.R. (4th) 321, 85 C.L.L.C. 14,023, Dickson C.J.C. (Beetz, McIntyre, Chouinard and Lamer JJ. concurring).

FREEDOM OF SPEECH. 1. Speech limited by the laws against defamation, sedition, blasphemy and other prohibited forms of speech. 2. A privilege and fundamental right of any member of Parliament on the House floor and in committee. A. Fraser, W.A. Dawson, & J. Holtby, eds., *Beauchesne's Rules and Forms of the*

House of Commons of Canada, 6th ed. (Toronto: Carswell, 1989) at 22. See FREEDOM OF EXPRESSION.

FREEDOM OF THE PRESS. 1. " . . . [R]efers to the dissemination of expression of thought, belief or opinion through the medium of the press." *Reference re s 12(1) of the Juvenile Delinquents Act (Canada)* (1983), 6 C.R.R. 1 at 9, 146 D.L.R. (3d) 408, 3 C.C.C. (3d) 515, 41 O.R. (2d) 113, 33 R.F.L. (2d) 279, 34 C.R. (3d) 27 (C.A.), the court per MacKinnon A.C.J.O. 2. That the right of the public to information relating to court proceedings, and the corollary right to put forward opinions pertaining to the courts, depend on the freedom of the press " to transmit this information is fundamental to an understanding of the importance of that freedom. The full and fair discussion of public institutions, which is vital to any democracy, is the *raison d'être* of the s. 2(*b*) guarantees. Debate in the public domain is predicated on an informed public, which is in turn reliant upon a free and vigorous press. The public's entitlement to be informed imposes on the media the responsibility to inform fairly and accurately. This responsibility is especially grave given that the freedom of the press is, and must be, largely unfettered. The significance of the freedom and its attendant responsibility lead me to the second issue relating to s. 2(*b*). Essential to the freedom of the press to provide information to the public is the ability of the press to have access to this information. *Canadian Broadcasting Corp. v. New Brunswick (Attorney General)*, 1996 CarswellNB 462, 2 C.R. (5th) 1, 110 C.C.C. (3d) 193, [1996] 3 S.C.R. 480, 139 D.L.R. (4th) 385, 182 N.B.R. (2d) 81, 463 A.P.R. 81, 39 C.R.R. (2d) 189, 203 N.R. 169, La Forest, J. for the court. 3. In *Société Radio-Canada c. Lessard*, (sub nom. *Canadian Broadcasting Corp. v. Lessard*) [1991] 3 S.C.R. 421, I [La forest, J.]noted that freedom of the press not only encompassed the right to transmit news and other information, but also the right to gather this information. At pp. 429-30, I stated, "There can be no doubt, of course, that it comprises the right to disseminate news, information and beliefs. This was the manner in which the right was originally expressed, in the first draft of s. 2(*b*) of the *Canadian Charter of Rights and Freedoms* before its expansion to its present form. However, the freedom to disseminate information would be of little value if the freedom under s. 2(*b*) did not also encompass the right to gather news and other information without undue governmental interference. 4. Cory J. stated in *Société Radio-Canada c. Nouveau-Brunswick (Procureur général)*, (sub nom. *Canadian Broadcasting Corp. v. New Brunswick (Attorney General)*) [1991] 3 S.C.R. 459, at p. 475: The media have a vitally important role to play in a democratic society. It is the media that, by gathering and disseminating news, enable members of our society to make an informed assessment of the issues which may significantly affect their lives and well-being.

FREE FROM GENERAL AVERAGE. In marine insurance policies, means that the underwriters are not liable for general average losses.

FREE FROM PARTICULAR AVERAGE. In marine insurance policies, means that an underwriter is liable only for total loss, either actual or constructive.

FREEHOLD. *n.* 1. Free tenure. 2. An estate the maximum duration of which is unknown.

FREEHOLD CONDOMINIUM CORPORATION. A corporation in which all the units and their appurtenant common interests are held in fee simple by the owners. *Condominium Act, 1998*, S.O. 1998, c. 19, s. 1.

FREEHOLDER. *n.* One who possesses a freehold estate.

FREEHOLD ESTATE. An interest in land by which the freeholder is entitled to hold the land for an unfixed and uncertain period of time.

FREEHOLD GAS. All gas (a) produced from freehold lands; or (b) allocated to freehold lands, or to the holder of any right thereto or interest therein, under a voluntary pooling arrangement, a pooling order, an agreement for unit operation or a unit operation order.

FREEHOLD LANDS. All lands in a province, and all rights thereto and interests therein, that are not Crown lands, and, for greater certainty, includes all Crown-acquired lands.

FREEHOLD MINERAL INTEREST. The estate or interest of a person, other than the Province, in a mineral on or below the surface of mineral land whether or not that estate or interest is registered as a charge against the title of that land.

FREE IN STOW, LINER OUT. In a ship's bill of lading, indicates the shipper has the obligation to load and stow the goods with the cost of discharge included in the ocean freight. *Olbert Metals Sales Ltd. v. Cerescorp Inc.* (1996), [1997] 1 F.C. 899 (T.D.).

FREE OF CAPTURE AND SEIZURE. In marine insurance policies, indicates that the underwriter is not liable for capture or seizure of either the cargo or the ship.

FREE ON BOARD. 1. " . . . [T]he seller, and not the shipper, shall pay the cost of loading the cargo on board, where it is stipulated that the price shall be for a stipulated sum f.o.b. . . ." *Johnson v. Logan* (1899), 32 N.S.R. 28 at 42 (C.A.), McDonald C.J. 2. "If, upon an order for undetermined goods to be shipped f.o.b., the seller delivers to the designated common carrier, goods which answer the order, without more, the property passes forthwith to the purchaser — and this is the case also if a bill of lading is taken, and taken in the name of the purchaser. If, however, the bill of lading is taken in the name of the seller, prima facie he retains the disposing power over and property in the goods. He may, indeed, endorse it over to the purchaser forthwith, and send it forward for delivery to the purchaser; in that case the taking of the bill of lading to his own order is a mere form, and the transaction is equivalent to taking the bill of lading in the name of the purchaser. The seller may endorse in blank and send forward to his agent, bank, etc., for delivery to the purchaser upon payment for the goods, acceptance of a draft, or performance of some other condition — in that case, the goods remain in the control and are the property of the seller, at least until the condition is fulfilled or the purchaser offers to fulfil it and demands the bill of lading . . ." *Vipond v. Sisco* (1913), 20 O.L.R. 200 at 203, 14 D.L.R. 129 (C.A.), Riddell J.A. (Sutherland, Leitch and Clute JJ.A. concurring).

FREE ON RAIL. Describes the situation where the seller is responsible to have goods placed on a train at her expense.

FREE ON TRUCK. Describing a seller's responsibility to have the goods placed on a truck.

FREE RIDER. A non-union worker who benefits from the gains made by union activities.

FREE SOCIETY. " . . . [O]ne which can accommodate a wide variety of beliefs, diversity of tastes and pursuits, customs and codes of conduct. A free society is one which aims at equality with respect to the enjoyment of fundamental freedoms and I say this without any reliance upon s. 15 of the Charter. Freedom must surely be founded in respect for the inherent dignity and the inviolable rights of the human person." *R. v. Big M Drug Mart* (1985),13 C.R.R. 64 at 97, [1985] 1 S.C.R. 295, [1985] 3 W.W.R. 481, 37 Alta. L.R. (2d) 97, 58 N.R. 81, 18 C.C.C. (3d) 385, 60 A.R. 161, 18 D.L.R. (4th) 321, 85 C.L.L.C. 14,023, Dickson C.J.C. (Beetz, McIntyre, Chouinard and Lamer JJ. concurring).

FREE TIME. In respect of goods, means a period of time during which goods may be kept on a wharf without the payment of storage charges thereon. Canada regulations.

FREE TRADE AGREEMENT. NAFTA, CCFTA or CIFTA.

FREE TRADE PARTNER. A NAFTA country, Chile, or Israel or another CIFTA beneficiary.

FREE VOTE. A parliamentary division on a question for which party lines are ignored. A. Fraser, W.A. Dawson, & J. Holtby, eds., *Beauchesne's Rules and Forms of the House of Commons of Canada*, 6th ed. (Toronto: Carswell, 1989) at 93.

FREEWAY. *n.* A divided arterial highway that is accessible only from intersecting arterial streets at grade separated interchanges that have been approved by the Minister. *Public Transportation and Highway Improvement Act*, R.S.O. 1990, c. P.50, s. 98(1).

FREEZE. See ESTATE ~; QUICK ~.

FREIGHT. *n.* 1. Includes the profit derivable by ship owners from the employment of their ships to carry their own goods or movables as well as freight payable by a third party, but does not include passage-money. *Insurance acts.* 2. Cargo. 3. Transport from one place to another. 4. . . . [T]he reward which the law entitles a person to recover for bringing goods lawfully on a lawful voyage. It is the price to be paid for the actual carriage of the goods. . ." *Edmonstone v. Young* (1862), 12 U.C.C.P. 437 at 442, Draper J. See DEAD EXPRESS ~; PACKAGE ~.

FREIGHT CAPACITY. See GROSS ~.

FREIGHT TO PRICE RATIO. In respect of any calendar year, means an amount equal to the quotient, expressed as a percentage, obtained by dividing the average cost to the shipper of moving one tonne of grain in that calendar year by the weighted average price for that calendar year. *Western Grain Tranportation Act*, R.S.C. 1985, c. W-8, s. 61.

FREIGHT VEHICLE. A vehicle operated by or on behalf of any person carrying on upon any highway the business of a carrier of freight for gain. *Motor Carrier Act*, R.S.N.S. 1989, c. 292, s. 2. See LIMITED ~; PRIVATE ~; PUBLIC ~.

FRENCH LANGUAGE EDUCATION. A school program using French as the language of instruction.

FRENCH-LANGUAGE INSTRUCTIONAL UNIT. A class, group of classes or school in which French is the language of instruction.

FRENCH-SPEAKING PERSON. A child of a person who has the right under subsection 23(1) or (2), without regard to subsection 23(3), of the Canadian Charter of Rights and Freedoms to have his or her children receive their primary and secondary school instruction in the French language in Ontario. *Education Act*, R.S.O. 1990, c. E.2, s. 288.

FRENCH-SPEAKING RATEPAYER. A person who is entitled to vote at an election of members of the board and who has the right under subsection 23(1) or (2), without regard to subsection 23(3), of the Canadian Charter of Rights and Freedoms to have his or her children receive their primary and secondary school instruction in the French language in Ontario. *Education Act*, R.S.O. 1990, c. E.2, s. 288.

FREQUENT FLYER PLAN. A contract between an airline and a member of the plan. Membership is open to individuals who benefit from the plan by acquiring points which may be redeemed, subject to rules of the plan.

FREQUENTIA ACTUS MULTUM OPERATUR. [L.] The frequency of an act is of great effect.

FRESH. *adj*. In relation to (a) a meat product other than sausages, means untreated except by refrigeration, and (b) sausages, means prepared from meat that is untreated except by refrigeration. *Meat Inspection Regulations*, C.R.C., c. 1032, s. 2.

FRESH CATCH. A catch that is not cured or processed.

FRESHET. *n*. The flood state of a river caused by rain or snow melt.

FRESH EVIDENCE. The traditional test for the admission of fresh evidence on appeal was stated by this Court in *R. v. Palmer* (1979), [1980] 1 S.C.R. 759, at p. 775: (a) The evidence should generally not be admitted if, by due diligence, it could have been adduced at trial provided that this general principle will not be ap-

plied as strictly in a criminal case as in civil cases: see *R. v. McMartin*, [1964] S.C.R. 484. (b) The evidence must be relevant in the sense that it bears upon a decisive or potentially decisive issue in the trial. (c) The evidence must be credible in the sense that it is reasonably capable of belief, and (d) It must be such that if believed it could reasonably, when taken with the other evidence adduced at trial, be expected to have affected the result. *Public School Boards' Assn. (Alberta) v. Alberta (Attorney General)*, 2000 CarswellAlta 678, 2000 SCC 2, [2000] 1 S.C.R. 44, 182 D.L.R. (4th) 561, 251 N.R. 1, 250 A.R. 314, 213 W.A.C. 314, [2000] 10 W.W.R. 187, 82 Alta. L.R. (3d) 211, 9 C.P.C. (5th) 36, Binnie J.

FRESHWATER MARSH. An inland area, lying between dry land and a lake, pond, river or stream, where the water table is ordinarily near or above the surface of the land and which is characterized by aquatic and grass-like vegetation.

FRESH WATER PRODUCT. Any fish, shellfish or crustacean unable to live in a marine environment and any batrachian, including parts of such animals and the products or by-products derived therefrom.

FRIABLE. *adj*. Easily crumbled or powdered.

FRICTION HOIST. The type of hoist where the rope passes over or around a driving pulley, and where the rope is driven by the friction between it and the pulley tread material.

FRIEND. See ALIEN ~; AMICUS CURIAE; NEXT ~; ~ OF THE COURT.

FRIENDLY SOCIETY. A society, order, association or company formed or incorporated and operated for the purpose of making with its members only, and not for profit, contracts under which (a) sickness, accident and disability benefits, or any one or more of them, not exceeding five dollars per week, or (b) funeral benefits not exceeding one hundred and fifty dollars, or all of those benefits may be paid only to its members or their beneficiaries in accordance with its charter and this Act. *Insurance acts*.

FRIENDLY SUIT. A suit brought which parties mutually arrange to bring to obtain a decision on a point which interests both.

FRIEND OF THE COURT. Any person who, with leave of a judge or at the invitation of a presiding judge or master, and without becoming a party to the proceeding, intervenes to render assistance to the court by way of argument (Ontario, Rules of Civil Procedure, r. 13.02). G.D. Watson & C. Perkins, eds., *Holmested & Watson: Ontario Civil Procedure* (Toronto: Carswell, 1984) at 13-2.

FRINGE BENEFIT. 1. An employment benefit such as a pension, paid holidays, health insurance. Granted by the employer at the employer's cost without affecting wage rates. 2 . ". . . [P]art of an employee's wages and are a proper consideration in computing damages for wrongful dismissal." *Zylawy v. Edmonton (City)* (1985), 8 C.C.E.L. 93 at 101, 60 A.R. 259 (Q.B.), Stratton J.

FRINGE GROUP. Employees whose activities are on the borderline so far as application of a statute is concerned or who perform tasks connected with but not identical to work performed by bargaining unit members.

FRINGE TIME. Time spent in preparatory or winding-up activities.

FRISK SEARCH. The patting down of outside clothing, examining of pocket contents, lasting briefly, to determine if the person has a weapon or contraband on their person.

FRIVOLOUS. *adj.* " . . . '[L]acking in substance' . . ." *Halliday v. Gouge* (1919), 14 Alta. L.R. 296 at 303, [1919] 1 W.W.R. 359 (C.A.), Walsh J.A.

FRIVOLOUS AND VEXATIOUS. Said of a pleading which is hopeless factually and plainly cannot succeed in its purpose.

FRIVOLOUS OR VEXATIOUS ACTION. See VEXATIOUS ACTION.

FROM. *conj.* 1. In relation to geography, signifies a starting point. 2. Depending on the context, may include or exclude the date referred to in a phrase beginning with this word. *Independent Order of Foresters, Lethbridge Local 2 v. Afaganis*, [1949] 1 W.W.R. 314 at 319, [1949] 2 D.L.R. 209 (Alta. Dist. Ct.), Sissons J.

FRONTAGE. *n.* When used in reference to a lot abutting directly on a work, means that side or limit of the lot that abuts directly on the work. See ACTUAL ~; FOOT ~; TAXABLE ~; TOTAL ACTUAL ~; TOTAL TAXABLE ~.

FRONTAGE TAX. Any tax levied on the owners of real property or immovables that is computed by applying a rate to all or part of the assessed dimension of the property and includes any tax levied on the owners of real property or immovables that is in the nature of a local improvement tax, a development tax or a redevelopment tax, but does not include a tax in respect of mineral rights. *Payments in Lieu of Taxes Act, 2000*, R.S.C. 1985, c. M-13, s. 2.

FRONT AND REAR TOWNSHIP. 1. One where the usual practice in the original survey was to survey the boundaries, base lines, if any, and the side lines of the lots and establish the corners of the lots and make road allowances between each concession and along the side lines between each second lot. *Surveys Act*, R.R.O. 1980, Reg. 928, Meth. 1. 2. A lot with an area of 100 acres and dimensions of 50 chains by 20 chains. B.J. Reiter, B.N. McLellan & P.M. Perell, *Real Estate Law*, 4th ed. (Toronto: Emond Montgomery, 1992) at 535.

FRONT AXLE WEIGHT. (a) For a single front axle, that part of the gross vehicle weight transmitted to the highway by the front axle, (b) for a dual front axle, one-half of that part of the gross vehicle weight transmitted to the highway by the front axle, and (c) for a triple front axle, one-third of that part of the gross vehicle weight transmitted to the highway by the front axle.

FRONT-END PAYMENT. A payment made by an owner pursuant to a front-ending agreement, which may be in addition to a development charge that the owner is required to pay under a development charge by-law, to cover the net capital costs of the services designated in the agreement that are required to enable the land to be developed. *Development Charges Act*, R.S.O. 1990, c. D.9, s. 1.

FRONTIER. See HIGHWAY ~ EXAMINING WAREHOUSE.

FRONTIER LANDS. Lands that belong to Her Majesty in right of Canada, or in respect of which Her Majesty in right of Canada has the right to dispose of or exploit the natural resources, and that are situated in (a) the Yukon Territory, the Northwest Territories or Sable Island, or (b) those submarine areas, not within a province, adjacent to the coast of Canada and extending throughout the natural prolongation of the land territory of Canada to the outer edge of the continental margin or to a distance of two hundred nautical miles from the baselines from which the breadth of the territorial sea of Canada is measured, whichever is the greater. Canada statutes.

FRONTING. *adj.* Includes abutting .

FRONTS. See BROKEN ~.

FROST. See DE~.

FROST ACTION. The phenomenon that occurs when water in soil is subjected to freezing which, because of the water ice phase change or ice lens growth, results in a total volume increase or the build-up of expansive forces under confined conditions or both and the subsequent thawing that leads to loss of soil strength and increased compressibility.

FROZEN. *adj.* 1. Refers to a trust in which the trustee is required only to hold the original assets and return them to the settlor when the trust ends. D.M.W. Waters, *The Law of Trusts in Canada*, 2d ed. (Toronto: Carswell, 1984) at 438. 2. Preserved by freezing temperature and does not include any surface freezing that may occur during holding and transportation.

FROZEN FOOD LOCKER PLANT. A business that provides individual lockers to store frozen food for human consumption.

FROZEN SENIORITY. Seniority protected but not allowed to increase during a period of layoff.

FROZEN TRUST. A trust for an office holder in which the trustee retains original assets and simply transfers them back to the settlor when the trust ends.

FRUCTUS AUGENT HAEREDITATEM. [L.] A yearly increase enriches an inheritance.

FRUCTUS INDUSTRIALES. [L.] Crops like wheat, barley and potatoes, which includes both emblements (crops produced annually by agriculture) and industrial growing crops (products of the soil which are not permanent, like artificial grass and clover). See EMBLEMENT.

FRUCTUS NATURALES. [L.] Natural product of land.

FRUIT. *n.* Fruit known botanically as such of any kind grown in Canada.

FRUIT TREE DISEASE. Any disease or injury of a fruit tree that is caused by an insect, virus, fungus, bacterium or other organism. *Abandoned Orchards Act*, R.S.O. 1990, c. A.1, s. 1.

FRUIT TREES. (a) Apple trees, (b) cherry trees, (c) grape vines, (d) peach trees, (e) pear trees, (f) plum trees, and (g) such other fruit-producing trees, shrubs or vines as are designated in the regulations. *Abandoned Orchards Act*, R.S.O. 1990, c. A.1, s. 1.

FRUSCA TERRAE. [L.] Wasteland; desert land.

FRUSTRA FIT PER PLURA, QUOD FIERI POTEST PER PAUCIORA. [L.] It is useless to employ many agents when fewer will suffice.

FRUSTRA LEGIS AUXILIUM QUAERIT QUI IN LEGEM COMMITTIT. [L.] It is vain for one who commits an offence against the law to seek the help of the law.

FRUSTRA PROBATUR QUOD PROBATUM NON RELEVAT. [L.] To prove anything which does not improve your case is useless.

FRUSTRATION. *n.* 1. The authoritative definition of frustration was stated by Lord Radcliffe in *Davis Contractors Ltd. v. Fareham Urban District Council*, [1956] A.C. 696 (U.K. H.L.) at 728-29, [1956] 2 All E.R.145 (H.L.): So perhaps it would be simpler to say at the outset that frustration occurs whenever the law recognizes that without default of either party a contractual obligation has become incapable of being performed because the circumstances in which performance is called for would render it a thing radically different from that which was undertaken by the contract. Non haec in foedera veni. It was not this that I promised to do. It has been adopted and applied in Canada. See *Capital Quality Homes Ltd. v. Colwyn Construction Ltd.* (1975), 9 O.R. (2d) 617, 61 D.L.R. (3d) 385 (C.A.) at 623 [O.R.]. *Lockhart v. Chrysler Canada Ltd.* (1984), 1984 CarswellBC 814, 7 C.C.E.L. 43, 16 D.L.R. (4th) 392 (C.A.), Taggart, Macdonald and Hutcheon JJ.A. 2. " . . . [O]ccurs whenever the law recognizes that without default of either party a contractual obligation has become incapable of being performed because the circumstances in which performance is called for would render it a thing radically different from that which was undertaken by the contract. Non haec in foedera veni. It was not this that I promised to do . . . It is not hardship or inconvenience or material loss itself which calls the principle of frustration into play. There must be as well such a change in the significance of the obligation that the thing undertaken would, if performed, be a different thing from that contracted for." *Davis Contractors Ltd. v. Fareham Urban Dist. Council*, [1956] A.C. 696 at 729, Lord Radcliffe. 3. In order to find that the contract at issue has been frustrated the following criteria would have to be satisfied. The event in question must have occurred after the formation of the contract and cannot be self-induced. The contract must, as a result, be totally different from what the parties had intended. This difference must take into account the distinction between complete fruitlessness and mere inconvenience. The disruption must be permanent, not temporary or transient. The change must totally affect the nature, meaning, purpose, effect and consequences of the contract so far as concerns either or both parties. Finally, the act or event that brought about such radical change must not have been foreseeable. *Folia v. Trelinski* (1997), 1997 CarswellBC 2325, 32 R.F.L. (4th) 209, 14 R.P.R. (3d) 5, 36 B.L.R (2d) 108 (S.C.) Sigurdson J. 4. " . . . [O]f a contract takes place when there supervenes an event (without default of either party and for which the contract makes no sufficient provision) which so significantly changes the nature (not merely the expense or onerousness) of the outstanding contractual rights and/or obligations from what the parties could reasonably have contemplated at the time of its execution that it would be unjust to hold them to the literal sense of its stipulations in the new circumstances; in such case the law declares both parties to be discharged from further performance." *National Carriers Ltd. v. Panalpina (Northern) Ltd.*, [1981] A.C. 675 at 700 (U.K. H.L.), Lord Simon.

FRUSTRUM TERRAE. [L.] A parcel or piece of land.

FSA. *abbr.* Forward sortation area.

FSA CODE. See RURAL ~; URBAN ~.

FTAA. *abbr.* Free Trade Agreement of the Americas.

F.T.R. *abbr.* Federal Trial Reports.

FUEL. *n.* Any form of matter that, in its primary use, is combusted or oxidized for the generation of energy. See ALTERNATIVE ~; AVIATION ~; AVIATION ~ IN BULK; BLENDED ~; BUNKER ~; CLEAR ~; COLOURED ~; DIESEL ~; LOCOMOTIVE ~; MARKED ~; MIXED~; MOTIVE~; TAXABLE ~; TRANSPORTATION ~.

FUEL AND ELECTRIC SYSTEMS MECHANIC. A person engaged in the repair and maintenance of motor vehicles who, (a) repairs and adjusts fuel systems, (b) installs, repairs and removes ignition systems, generators, alternators, starters, coils, panel instruments, wiring and other electrical systems and equipment, (c) performs a complete tune-up of an engine, and (d) installs, inspects, maintains and removes motor vehicle air-conditioning systems.

FUEL-BURNING EQUIPMENT. *var.* **FUEL BURNING EQUIPMENT**. Any equipment, apparatus, device, mechanism or structure that burns solid, liquid or gaseous fuel for the purpose of vehicle transportation, heating, drying, generating power, processing steam or any combination thereof.

FUEL CONSUMPTION. The quantity of fuel used by a motor vehicle when driven a given distance. *Motor Vehicle Fuel Consumption Standards Act*, R.S.C. 1985, c. M-9, s. 2.

FUEL CONSUMPTION NUMBER. A number that represents the fuel consumption of a motor vehicle under controlled test conditions. *Motor Vehicle Fuel Consumption Standards Act*, R.S.C. 1985, c. M-9, s. 2.

FUEL CONSUMPTION STANDARD. A standard prescribed pursuant to section 3. *Motor Vehicle Fuel Consumption Standards Act*, R.S.C. 1985, c. M-9, s. 2.

FUEL IN BULK. Fuel transported or transferred by any means other than a fuel tank of a motor vehicle in which fuel for generating power in the motor vehicle is kept.

FUEL METERING DEVICE. The carburetor, fuel injector, fuel distributor or fuel injection pump. *Motor Vehicle Safety Regulations*, C.R.C., c. 1038, s. 2.

FUEL OIL. 1. The liquid derived from petroleum or natural gas, and any other liquid, by whatever name known or sold, containing any derivative of coal, petroleum or natural gas used to produce a flame for heating, cooking or raising steam, but does not include gasoline. 2. Furnace oil, stove oil, bunker fuel oil and diesel fuel oil. See COLOURED ~.

FUEL PETROLEUM PRODUCT. (a) Any liquid product that is obtained or recovered from petroleum, natural gas or coal, whether by distillation, condensation, absorption or otherwise; (b) any combination of liquid products that are so obtained or recovered; or (c) any natural gas or manufactured gas; that, by combustion, develops the power required for the purpose of operating internal combustion engines, and includes crude oil and every other liquid product and combination of liquid products, whether or not obtained or recovered from petroleum, that is capable of fulfilling the same purpose by means of combustion.

FUEL SPILLAGE. The fall, flow or run of fuel from a vehicle but does not include wetness resulting from capillary action. *Motor Vehicle Safety Regulations*, C.R.C., c. 1038, s. 2.

FUEL SYSTEM. With reference to anything powered by an internal combustion engine, includes a fuel tank, carburetor, fuel filter, fuel injection system, pipes or any other thing in physical association with the engine that contains fuel oil or through which fuel oil passes during the operation of the engine.

FUEL TANK. A tank or container that is (a) originally provided by the manufacturer of a motor vehicle to carry the fuel required to propel it, or (b) carried in or upon a motor vehicle and capable of being easily connected to its fuel system. See VEHICLE ~.

FUGACIOUS. *adj*. Wandering, refers to substances which are not fixed in a certain place, for example, oil and gas.

FUGAM FECIT. [L.] One fled.

FUGITIVE. *n.* " . . . The [definition of fugitive in the Extradition] Act seems to make every one who has ever been convicted [a] fugitive for life. That cannot be. The Act must contemplate that there is sentence left to be served. . ." *Reutcke v. Pre-trial Services Centre* (1984), (*sub nom Reutcke v. R.*) 11 C.C.C. (3d) 386 at 387, [1985] 1 W.W.R. 11 (B.C. C.A.), the court per Seaton J.A.

FUGITIVE EMISSION. A dust, fog, fume, gas, liquid, mist, solid or vapour which escapes from emission control equipment, process equipment or from a product.

FUGITIVE'S GOODS. The goods of a person which were forfeited because the person fled.

FULFIL. See EQUITY IMPUTES AN INTENTION TO ~ AN OBLIGATION.

FULL AGE. Age of majority.

FULL ANSWER AND DEFENCE. "[In the Charter] . . . entitle[s] the accused to put forward all defences, regardless of whether they are based on a technicality or not. Indeed the adjective 'full' permits no other conclusion. The right to make a full answer and defence cannot be diminished to the right to make non-technical answer and defence." *R. v. Garafoli* (1990), 60 C.C.C. (3d) 161 at 210, 80 C.R. (3d) 317, 116 N.R. 241, 43 O.A.C. 1, [1990] 2 S.C.R. 1421, 50 C.R.R. 206, 36 Q.A.C. 161, McLachlin J. (dissenting) Dubs J. concurring).

FULL COMMUNITY. All immovables and movables acquired during marriage over which

the husband has wide powers of administration. J.G. McLeod, *The Conflict of* Laws (Calgary: Carswell, 1983) at 371.

FULL COSTS. 1. Party-and-party costs. *Williams v. Crow* (1884), 10 O.A.R. 301 at 306 (C.A.), Hagarty C.J.O. 2. In expropriation cases, costs as between client and solicitor. *Bronson v. Canada Atlantic Railway* (1890), 13 P.R. 440 at 441 (H.C.), Boyd C.

FULL COURT. A court with all judges present. For example, when all nine judges of the Supreme Court of Canada hear a case, the case is heard by the full court.

FULL DISCLOSURE. The provision of the cost of borrowing in terms of annual rate of interest and in dollar terms.

FULL EMPLOYMENT. Work available to all persons willing and able to work.

FULL FAITH AND CREDIT. Doctrine under which the courts of one province are under a constitutional obligation to recognize the decisions of the courts of another province. Constitutional rule inferred but not expressed. *R. v. Campbell* (1997), (sub nom. *Reference re Public Sector Pay Reduction Act (P.E.I.), s. 10*) 150 D.L.R. (4th) 577 (S.C.C.).

FULL PAROLE. The authority granted to an offender by the Board or a provincial parole board to be at large during the offender's sentence. *Corrections and Conditional Release Act, 1992*, S.C. 1992, c. 20, s. 99.

FULL-TIME BASIS. In relation to an employee of a particular class, means engaged to work, throughout the year, all or substantially all of the normally scheduled hours of work established for persons in that class of employees.

FULL TIME EMPLOYMENT. *var.* **FULL-TIME EMPLOYMENT**. Employment requiring continuous service in an office or position, where the employee is normally required to work the minimum number of hours prescribed by the person having authority to establish the hours of such employment.

FULL-TIME FIRE FIGHTER. *var.* **FULL-TIME FIRE-FIGHTER**. 1. A person regularly employed in the fire department on a full-time salaried basis and assigned exclusively to fire protection or fire prevention duties, and includes officers and technicians. 2. A person regularly employed in the fire department on a full-time salaried basis and assigned exclusively to fire protection or fire prevention duties but does not include the fire chief or a deputy fire chief or any other person having authority to employ or discharge a full-time fire-fighter or regularly acting in a confidential capacity on behalf of the fire chief or the city or any board commission or other body established to manage, control and operate the fire department.

FULL TRAILER. A vehicle that is towed by another vehicle and is so designed and used that the whole of its weight and load is carried on its own axles and includes a combination consisting of a semi-trailer and a trailer converter dolly.

FULLY DILUTED EARNINGS PER SHARE. The amount of income attributable to each share that would, if all potential conversions, exercises and contingent issuances had occurred during the period, be outstanding and have as an incident of ownership the right to participate in earnings to an unlimited degree, calculated in the manner prescribed in the regulations.

FULLY FUNDED. When applied to a pension means a pension plan that at any particular time has assets that will provide for the payment of all pension and other benefits required to be paid under the terms of the plan in respect of service rendered by employees and former employees prior to that time, and has no unpaid initial unfunded liabilities or experience deficiencies.

FULLY PAID. With reference to any share, means a share on which there remains no liability, actual or contingent, to the issuing corporation.

FULLY REGISTERED FORM. Of bonds or debentures with both principal and interest payable to the registered holders.

FULLY-SECRET TRUST. Arises when a testatrix gives property to a person apparently beneficially, but has communicated to that person during his lifetime certain trusts on which the property is to be held. Arises out of a will. The trust obligation undertaken is hidden from view and revealed only by extrinsic evidence. *Jankowski v. Pelek Estate* (1995), [1996] 2 W.W.R. 457 (Man. C.A.).

FULMINATE. *n*. Any chemical compound or mechanical mixture, whether included in the foregoing classes or not, that by reason of its great susceptibility to detonation is suitable for employment in percussion caps or any other appliances for developing detonation, or that by

reason of its extreme sensibility to explosion and its great instability (that is to say readiness to undergo decomposition from very slight exciting causes) is essentially dangerous. Canada regulations.

FULTON-FAVREAU FORMULA. A constitutional amending procedure which required the unanimous consent of all provincial Legislatures and the federal Parliament for significant amendments. P.W. Hogg, *Constitutional Law of Canada*, 3d ed. (Toronto: Carswell, 1992) at 65.

FUME. *n*. Solid particles in the air that are generated by condensation from the vapour of a solid material. *Consumer Chemicals and Containers Regulations, 2001*, SOR/2001-269, s. 1.

FUMES. *n*. In the context of the information that must be displayed on a container, means a vapour or a fume or both that may be given off by a chemical product under normal conditions of use or storage. *Consumer Chemicals and Containers Regulations, 2001*, SOR/2001-269, s. 1.

FUMIGANT. *n*. A pesticide that is or that produces a gas, vapour, fume or smoke and that operates as a pesticide exclusively or primarily by the action of the gas, vapour, fume or smoke.

FUMIGATION. *n*. Treatment of any plant or other matter that is infested, or likely to be infested, with a pesticide in such a concentration, at such a temperature and for such a period of time as is necessary to ensure that the plant or other matter is no longer infested.

FUNCTION. *n*. 1. An object, power or duty or group of them. 2. Includes logic, control, arithmetic, deletion, storage and retrieval and communication or telecommunication to, from or within a computer system. *Criminal Code*, R.S.C. 1985, c. C-46, s. 342.1(2) as added by *Crimina2l Law Amendment Act*, R.S.C. 1985 (1st Supp.), c. 27, s. 45. 3. The purpose for which one uses a trade mark. 4. " ... [T]he act of performing and is defined as the kind of action belonging to the holder of an office, hence the function is the performance of the duties of that office. By the performance of the duties of an office the holder thereof can be said to fulfil his function. Functions are therefore the powers and duties of an office." *Mudarth v. Canada (Minister of Public Works)* (1988), 27 C.C.E.L. 310 at 314-15, 22 F.T.R. 312, [1989] 3 F.C. 371 (T.D.), Addy J. See FUND-RAISING ~.

FUNCTIONAL APPROACH. " ... [R]ather than attempting to set a value on lost happiness, attempts to assess the compensation required to provide the injured person with reasonable solace for his misfortune. Money is awarded not because lost faculties have a dollar value but because money can be used to substitute other enjoyments and pleasures for those that have been lost." *Lindal v. Lindal* (1981), 19 C.C.L.T. 1 at 28, [1982] 1 W.W.R. 433, 34 B.C.L.R. 273, 129 D.L.R. (3d) 263, 39 N.R. 261, [1981] 2 S.C.R. 529, the court per Dickson J.

FUNCTIONALITY, DOCTRINE OF. A thing that is primarily functional cannot be a trademark. Intended to prevent a person from obtaining a patent through the guise of a trademark. *Kirkbi AG v. Ritvik Holdings Inc. / Gestions Ritvik Inc.*, 2003 FCA 297 (C.A.)

FUNCTIONARY. *n*. A person who functions in a specific capacity, especially in government, an official, civil servant or bureaucrat.

FUNCTUS. [L.] Having pronounced judgment; having made a decision. Refers to FUNCTUS OFFICIO.

FUNCTUS OFFICIO. [L. having discharged one's duty] . 1. " . . . [B]ased . . . on the policy ground which favours finality of proceedings rather than the rule which was developed with respect to formal judgments of a Court whose decision was subject to a full appeal. . . its application must be more flexible and less formalistic in respect to the decisions of administrative tribunals which are subject to appeal only on a point of law. Justice may require the reopening of administrative proceedings in order to provide relief which would otherwise be available on appeal." *Chandler v. Assn. of Architects (Alberta)* (1989), 36 C.L.R. 1 at 14, [1989] 6 W.W.R. 521, [1989] 2 S.C.R. 848, 70 Alta. L.R. (2d) 193, 40 Admin. L.R. 128, 62 D.L.R. (4th) 577, 99 N.R. 277, 101 A.R. 321, Sopinka J. (Dickson C.J.C. and Wilson J. concurring). 2. " . . . [A]n adjudicator, be it an arbitrator, an administrative tribunal or a court, once it has reached its decision cannot afterwards alter its award except to correct clerical mistakes or errors arising from an accidental slip or omission . . ." *Chandler v. Assn. of Architects (Alberta)*, [1989] 2 S.C.R. 848 at 867, 70 Alta. L.R. (2d) 193, 40 Admin. L.R. 128, 36 C.L.R. 1, 62 D.L.R. (4th) 577, 99 N.R. 277, 101 A.R. 321, [1989] 6 W.W.R. 521, L'Heureux-Dubé J. (dissenting) (La Forest J. concurring). 3. " . . . [A] trial judge sitting without a jury is not functus officio until he has finally disposed of the case. Where the accused is acquitted the trial judge will have

exhausted his jurisdiction when the accused is discharged and the trial judge cannot then reopen the case. Following a finding of guilt, however, the judge's duties are not spent until after a sentence is imposed. . . The state of the case-law until now is as follows. [In a case heard by judge and jury, even] after discharge, a jury can be reconvened to correct an improper or incomplete transmission or registration of a verdict, but cannot reconsider a verdict or complete its deliberations with a view to handing down additional verdicts on counts or on included offences it has not finally determined prior to that discharge; nor can anyone go behind the verdict or make inquiries as regards the nature of the deliberations." *R. v. Head* (1986), 30 C.C.C. (3d) 481 at 491, 495, [1987] 1 W.W.R. 673, 70 N.R. 364, [1986] 2 S.C.R. 684, 55 C.R. (3d) 1, 53 Sask. R. 1, 35 D.L.R. (4th) 231, Lamer J.

FUND. *n*. 1, A sum of money available to pay or discharge liabilities. 2. Capital, as opposed to income or interest. See ACCIDENT ~; ASSURANCE ~; BLENDED ~; CAPITAL ~; CARE ~; CONSOLIDATED ~; DISTRESS ~; ~S; GUARANTEED ~; INJURY ~; INSURANCE ~; LIEN ~; MAINTENANCE ~; MAJOR LIEN ~; MUTUAL ~; NO-LOAD ~; PENSION ~; POOLED ~; REGULATED ~; RENT REDUCTION ~; RESERVE~; RETIREMENT INCOME ~; REVENUE ~; REVOLVING ~; SEGREGATED ~; SINKING SPECIAL ~; SPECIAL PURPOSE ~; STRIKE ~; SUPERANNUATION ~; TRUST ~.

FUNDAMENTAL BREACH. "[Occurs] . . . where the event resulting from the failure by one party to perform a primary obligation has the effect of depriving the other party of substantially the whole benefit which it was the intention of the parties that he should obtain from the contract." *Syncrude Canada Ltd. v. Hunter Engineering Co.* (1989), 57 D.L.R. (4th) 321 at 369, [1989] 1 S.C.R. 426, [1989] 3 W.W.R. 385, 35 B.C.L.R. (2d) 145, 92 N.R. 1, Wilson J.

FUNDAMENTAL FREEDOM. " . . . [T]he freedom of the individual to take action to do something, to manifest and express himself, to make what he wants of his own individual skills, talents and abilities, to seek self-realization." *Reference re Public Service Employee Relations Act (Alberta)* (1985), 85 C.L.L.C. 14,027 at 12,163, 35 Alta. L.R. (2d) 124, [1985] 2 W.W.R. 289, 16 D.L.R. (4th) 359, 57 A.R. 268 (C.A.), Belzil J.A.

FUNDAMENTAL JUSTICE. 1. Not synonymous with natural justice. *Reference re s. 94(2) of the Motor Vehicle Act (British Columbia)* (1985), 23 C.C.C. (3d) 289 at 301-3, 310, [1985] 2 S.C.R. 486, 36 M.V.R. 240, 69 B.C.L.R. 145, 48 C.R. (3d) 289, 63 N.R. 266, 24 D.L.R. (4th) 536, 18 C.R.R. 30, [1986] 1 W.W.R. 481, Lamer J. (Dickson C.J.C., Beetz, Chouinard and Le Dain JJ. concurring). 2. " . . . [N]ot a right, but a qualifier of the right not to be deprived of life, liberty and security of the person; its function is to set the parameters of that right. Sections 8 to 14 [of the Charter] address specific deprivations of the right to life, liberty and security of the person in breach of the principles of fundamental justice, and as such, violations of s. 7. They are therefore illustrative of the meaning, in criminal or penal law, of 'principles of fundamental justice'; they represent principles which have been recognized by the common law, the international conventions and by the very fact of entrenchment in the Charter, as essential elements of a system for the administration of justice which is founded upon a belief in the dignity and worth of the human person and the rule of law. Consequently, the principles of fundamental justice are to be found in the basic tenets and principles, not only of our judicial process, but also of the other components of our legal system. . . those words cannot be given any exhaustive content or simple enumerative definition, but will take on concrete meaning as the courts address alleged violations of s. 7." *Reference re s 94(2) of the Motor Vehicle Act (British Columbia)* (1985), 23 C.C.C. (3d) 289 at 301-3, 310, [1985] 2 S.C.R. 486, 36 M.V.R. 240, 69 B.C.L.R. 145, 48 C.R. (3d) 289, 63 N.R. 266, 24 D.L.R. (4th) 536, 18 C.R.R. 30, [1986] 1 W.W.R. 481, Lamer J. (Dickson C.J.C., Beetz, Chouinard and Le Dain JJ. concurring). See PRINCIPLES OF ~.

FUNDAMENTAL MISTAKE. Occurs in a situation where both parties to an agreement make the same mistake about an underlying and fundamental fact. The error goes to the root of the contract and eliminates the subject of the contract.

FUNDAMENTAL RIGHTS ACT. *An Act respecting the exercise of the fundamental rights and prerogatives of the Québec People and the Québec State.* Statute of Quebec which received Royal Assent on December 13, 2000 and came into effect on April 1, 2001. Quebec enacted this statute in response to the federal government's Clarity Act.

FUNDAMENTAL TERM. 1. Something which must be performed, regardless of any clause in the contact which relieves a party from performing other terms or from being liable for breaching those terms. G.H.L. Fridman, *Sale of Goods in Canada*, 3d ed. (Toronto: Carswell, 1986) at 284-285. 2. " . . . '[S]omething which underlies the whole contract so that, if it is not complied with, the performance becomes something totally different from that which the contract contemplates' . . ." *Murray v. Sperry Rand Corp.* (1979), 5 B.L.R. 284 at 295, 23 O.R. (2d) 456, 96 D.L.R. (3d) 113 (H.C.), Reid J.

FUNDED. See FULLY ~; PROVISIONALLY ~.

FUNDED BENEFITS PLAN. A plan, including a multi-employer benefits plan, which gives protection against risk to an individual that could otherwise be obtained by taking out a contract of insurance, whether the benefits are partly insured or not, and which comes into existence when the premiums paid into a fund out of which benefits will be paid exceed amounts required for payment of benefits foreseeable and payable within thirty days after payment of the premium. *Retail Sales Tax Act*, R.S.O. 1990, c. R-31, s. 1.

FUNDI PATRIMONIALES. [L.] Lands belonging to an inheritance.

FUND-RAISING FUNCTION. *var.* **FUND RAISING FUNCTION**. Includes events or activities held for the purpose of raising funds for the political party, constituency association, candidate or leadership contestant by whom or on whose behalf the function is held. *Election Finances acts.*

FUNDS. *n.* Moneys or any other consideration. See ENDOWMENT CARE ~; FUND; PERPETUAL CARE ~; PUBLIC TRUST ~.

FUND UNION. A local or joint board with which an employer has contracted to contribute to the employees' pension fund.

FUNDUS. [L.] *n.* The bottom; the foundation.

FUNERAL. *n.* A rite or ceremony in connection with the death of a person where the body is present. See PREARRANGED ~ PLAN; PREPAID ~ CONTRACT.

FUNERAL DIRECTOR. 1. Any person who takes charge of a dead body for the purpose of burial, cremation, removal or other disposition. 2. A person who takes charge of the body of a still-born child or a deceased person for the purpose of burial, cremation or other disposition. *Vital Statistics Act*, R.S.O. 1990, c. V-4, s. 1. See INCAPACITATED ~; LAY ~.

FUNERAL ESTABLISHMENT. Premises where funeral services are supplied.

FUNERAL EXPENSES. Expenses permitted before all other debts and charges against an estate.

FUNERAL GOODS. Those items of merchandise sold or offered for sale directly to the public which will be used in connection with a funeral or an alternative or final disposition of human remains.

FUNERAL HOME. A facility or establishment, by whatever name called, offering or providing funeral merchandise or services to the public.

FUNERAL PROVIDER. A person who owns, controls or manages a funeral home.

FUNERAL SERVICES. Any services and commodities usual in the preparation for burial and the burial of the dead other than the supplying of lots, burial vaults, grave markers, vases and services rendered or to be rendered at the cemetery. See PREARRANGED ~ PLAN.

FUNERAL SUPPLIES. Goods that are used in connection with the care and preparation of dead human bodies or the disposition of dead human bodies.

FUNGIBLE. *n.* In relation to securities, securities of which any unit is, by nature or usage of trade, the equivalent of any other like unit.

FUNGIBLE GOODS. Goods of which any unit is, from its nature or by mercantile custom, treated as the equivalent of any other unit.

FUR. *n.* 1. The pelt or skin, or any part thereof, of any fur-bearing animal. 2. The skin of any animal, whether fur-bearing, hair-bearing or wool-bearing, that is not in the unhaired condition. See LAKE, FOREST AND ~ ASSOCIATION.

FURANDI ANIMUS. [L.] The intention to steal.

FUR ANIMAL. 1. Includes all animals wild by nature whose skins or pelts are commonly used for the manufacture of clothing or rugs, and are of marketable value, and also includes the parts of such animals.

FUR-BEARER. *n.* Includes beaver, muskrat, mink, otter, lynx, wildcat, fox, wolf, raccoon, weasel, fisher, marten, squirrel, skunk and any other animal valuable for its fur.

FUR-BEARING ANIMAL. *var.* **FUR BEARING ANIMAL**. 1. Any animal that is wild by nature and whose pelt or skin is commonly used for commercial purposes. 2. Beaver, bobcat, badger, cougar, fisher, fox, hare, lynx, marten, mink, muskrat, otter, rabbit, raccoon, skunk, squirrel or weasel or ermine, wildcat, bear, wolverine, wolf, coyote and chinchilla.

FUR-BEARING ANIMAL RANCH. An area where fur bearing animals are raised and kept in their natural habitat and under the direct supervision of any person.

FUR BUYER. A person engaged in the business of buying, selling or trading in pelts or skins of fur-bearing animals or other wildlife designated by the Governor in Council. *Wildlife Act*, R.S.N.S. 1989, c. 504, s. 3(1).

FUR DEALER. A person who carries on or who is engaged in any manner in trafficking in the skins or pelts, or parts thereof, of fur-bearing animals or fur-bearing carnivores.

FUR FARM. *var.* **FUR-FARM**. 1. Any place where fur bearing animals are kept in captivity for the purpose of propagation or for sale, gain or profit. 2. A place where fur-bearing animals are kept in captivity.

FUR FARMER. A person whose occupation is operating a premises on which fur-bearing animals are kept in captivity for sale or for the purpose of selling their pelts.

FUR GARMENT. Any coat, jacket, cape, detached cuff, detached collar, scarf, cap, hat, glove or muff, the whole or part of the outer surface of which is trimmed with fur or consists of fur.

FURIOSI NULLA VOLUNTAS EST. [L.] Mad people have no free will.

FURIOSUS SOLO FURORE PUNITUR. [L.] A mad person is punished only by the madness.

FURIOSUS STIPULARE NON POTEST, NEC ALIQUID NEGOTIUM AGERE, QUIA NON INTELLIGIT QUOD ALIT. [L.] An insane person cannot enter into a contract or transact business because mad people do not know what they are doing.

FURLONG. *n.* 220 yards. *Weights and Measures Act*, S.C. 1970-71-72, c. 36, schedule II.

FURLOUGH. *n.* Temporary halt of employment.

FURNACE. *n.* A space-heating appliance using warm air as the heating medium and usually having provision for the attachment of ducts. See FORCED-AIR ~; REVERBERATORY ~.

FURNISH. *v.* To provide. *W. & B. Construction Ltd. v. Mahaney* (1978), 4 R.P.R. 5 at 11, 25 N.S.R. (2d) 361, 85 D.L.R. (3d) 425, 36 A.P.R. 361 (C.A.), the court per Coffin J.A.

FURNITURE. See UPHOLSTERED ~.

FURNITURE AND HOUSEHOLD EFFECTS. Removable furniture and effects that are commonly found in the home.

FUR RANCH. Premises on which fur bearing animals are kept, raised, bred or propagated, or any combination thereof, in captivity for sale or for the purpose of selling their pelts.

FURRIER. *n.* A person who buys or otherwise acquires the raw skins or pelts, or parts thereof, of fur-bearing animals or fur-bearing carnivores for the purpose of manufacture.

FURTHERANCE. *n.* Helping forward, advancement, aid.

FURTHER ASSURANCE. See COVENANT FOR ~.

FUR TRADER. A person who is engaged in the business of buying, selling or trading in pelts or skins of fur bearing animals or other wildlife prescribed for the purpose of this definition, whether as principal, agent or employee, and whether the pelts or skins were obtained, taken or trapped by the fur trader or another person.

FURTUM. [L.] *n.* Theft, robbery.

FURTUM EST CONTRECTATIO REI ALIENAE FRAUDULENTA, CUM ANIMO FURANDI, INVITO ILLO DOMINO CUJUS RES ILLA FUERAT. [L.] Theft is wrongfully appropriating another person's property, without consent, and with the intent to steal it.

FURTUM NON EST UBI ITITIUM HABET DETENTIONIS PER DOMINUM REI. [L.] There is no theft where one has possession of the goods with the consent of the owner.

FUSE. *n.* A device capable of automatically opening a circuit under predetermined overload conditions by the fusing of metal. See CAPPED ~; DETONATING ~; SAFETY ~.

FUTILITY. *n.* State of being of no practical effect.

FUTURE ADVANCE. The advance of money, credit or other value secured by a security agreement whether or not such advance is given pursuant to commitment.

FUTURE CARE. See COST OF ~.

FUTURE CONSIDERATION. A promise to something later.

FUTURE DAMAGES. Damages to compensate for pecuniary losses to be incurred, or expenditures to be made, after the date of the trial judgment in a proceeding.

FUTURE ESTATE. An expectancy; a reversion; a remainder.

FUTURE GOODS. Goods to be manufactured or acquired by the seller, after the making of the contract of sale. *Sale of Goods acts.*

FUTURE INTEREST. See FUTURE ESTATE.

FUTURE PERFORMANCE AGREEMENT. A consumer agreement in respect of which delivery, performance or payment in full is not made when the parties enter the agreement. *Consumer Protection Act, 2002*, S.O. 2002, c. 30, Sched. A.

FUTURE RIGHT. " . . . [I]s inchoate in that while it does not now exist, it may arise in the future. . ." *Elias v. Hutchison* (1981), 14 Alta. L.R. (2d) 268 at 275, 37 C.B.R. (N.S.) 149, 27 A.R. 1, 121 D.L.R. (3d) 95 (C.A.), the court per McGillivray C.J.A.

FUTURES. *n.* " . . . [S]peculative transactions, in which there is a nominal contract of sale for future delivery, but where in fact none is ever intended or executed. . . a mere speculative contract, in which the parties speculate in the rise or fall of prices, and imply a contract in relation to the prices of the article, and not the article itself." *Betcherman v. E.A. Pierce & Co.*, [1933] 3 D.L.R. 99 at 111, [1933] O.R. 505 (C.A.), the court per Latchford C.J. See COMMODITY ~ CONTRACT; GRAIN ~.

FUTURES CONTRACT. A contract to make delivery or take delivery on a specified date or during a specified period of (a) a specified cash equivalent of the subject matter of the contract, or (b) a specified asset.

FUTURE SERVICES. See CONTRACT FOR ~.

G

G. *abbr.* Giga.

GAAP. *abbr.* Generally accepted accounting principles.

GAAR. *abbr.* General anti-avoidance rule.

GAAS. *abbr.* Generally accepted auditing standards.

GABD. General assignment of book debts.

GABEL. *n.* Excise, a tax on movables; a custom, rent or service. See LAND ~.

GABULUS DENARIORUM. [L.] Rent paid with money.

GAGE. *n.* [Fr.] Pledge or pawn; anything given as security.

GAGER DE DELIVERANCE. [Fr.] Pledge that a person, being sued, would deliver cattle he or she had distrained.

GAGER DEL LEY. [Fr.] Wager of law.

GAIN. *n.* " . . . [A] benefit, profit, or advantage, . . . " *R. v. James* (1903), 6 O.L.R. 35 at 38, 7 C.C.C. 196 (C.A.), Osler J.A. See ACOUSTIC ~; AIR-TO-AIR ~; CAPITAL ~; MAXIMUM ACOUSTIC ~; MAXIMUM AIR-TO-AIR ~; TOLL, ~ OR COMPENSATION.

GAINAGE. *n.* The profit raised by cultivating planted or tilled land.

GAIN OR REWARD. Any payment, consideration, compensation or gratuity, directly or indirectly charged, demanded, received or collected for the use of a vehicle by a person who, as owner, lessee, hirer, chauffeur, driver or otherwise, has possession of or control over the vehicle or has directed the movement of the vehicle. *Highway Traffic acts.*

GALE. *n.* A periodic rent payment.

GALE-DAY. *n.* Rent-day.

GALLERY. *n.* 1. Of the parliamentary chamber, consists of a press gallery, visitors galleries called the public gallery, galleries for the diplomatic corps and departmental officials and private galleries. A. Fraser, W.A. Dawson, & J. Holtby, eds., *Beauchesne's Rules and Forms of the House of Commons of Canada*, 6th ed. (Toronto: Carswell, 1989) at 37. 2. The seating for visitors or the press in a legislature.

GALLINACEOUS BIRD. Includes all species of grouse, partridge, pheasant, quail, ptarmigan, wild turkey and the eggs of all such species. *Wildlife acts.*

GALLON. *n.* 1. 454 609/100 000 000 cubic metre. *Weights and Measures Act*, S.C. 1970-71-72, c. 36, schedule II. 2. A Canadian gallon.

GALLOWS. *n.* A beam laid over a post or posts from which prisoners were hanged.

GAMBLE. *v.* " . . .[A]nother form of the word 'game',. . ." *R. v. Shaw* (1891), 7 Man. R. 518 at 530 (C.A.), Bain J.A.

GAMBLING. *n.* Wagering or betting. Must involve a chance of gain and risk of loss. See GAMING.

GAME. *n.* 1. A game of chance or mixed chance and skill. *Criminal Code*, R.S.C. 1985, c. C-46, s. 197. 2. Fur bearing animals, game animals and game birds, and also includes all species of animals and birds that are wild by nature. 3. A game animal, game bird or fur-bearing animal, and includes any part of such animal. See BIG ~; CONFIDENCE ~; MIXED ~ OF CHANCE AND SKILL; SMALL ~.

GAME ANIMAL. Any animal, except a fur-bearing animal, protected by this Act, and includes any part of such animal. *Game and Fish Act*, R.S.O. 1990, c. G.1, s. 1.

GAME BIRD. 1. An upland game bird or a migratory game bird. 2. Any bird protected by this Act or the Migratory Birds Convention Act, (Canada), and includes any part of such bird. *Game and Fish* Act, R.S.O. 1990, c. G.1, s. 1. See MIGRATORY ~ S; UPLAND ~.

GAME BIRD FARM. A place on which game birds are kept for the purposes of propagation, or for sale, gain, profit or pleasure. *Wildlife Act*, R.S.A. 1970, c. 391, s. 2.

GAME BIRD HUNTING PRESERVE. Any area in which pheasants or other game birds propagated under a licence are released for hunting purposes. *Game and Fish* Act, R.S.O. 1980, c. 182, s. 1.

GAME FARM. See PROVINCIAL ~.

GAME OF CHANCE. 1. " . . . [O]ne which is determined entirely, or in part, by luck, and in which judgment, practice, skill or adroitness has either no office at all, or is thwarted by chance, thus dividing games into games of chance, games of skill, and mixed games of chance and skill." *R. v. Fortier* (1903), 13 Que. K.B. 308 at 311, 7 C.C.C. 417, the court per Wurtele J. 2. " . . . [W]ithin the definition of the criminal law, is one in which hazard entirely predominates; . . ." *R. v. Fortier* (1903), 13 Que. K.B. 308 at 313, 7 C.C.C. 417, the court per Wurtele J.

GAME OFFICER. A person declared by subsection 5(1) to be a game officer. *Game Export Act*, R.S.C. 1985, c. G-1, s. 2. See CHIEF ~.

GAME-PRODUCTION ANIMAL. A wildlife animal of a prescribed species that does not belong to the Crown, that is identified and registered and that is in captivity in Alberta for the purpose or the ultimate purpose of reproduction, sale as breeding stock or as meat or the sale of prescribed parts of it, of for any combination of those purposes. *Livestock Industry Diversification Act*, S.A. 1990, c. L-22.7, s. 1(1).

GAME RANCHING. Raising big game for the purpose of selling its meat for human consumption. *Wildlife Act*, S.A. 1984, c. W-9.1, s. 1.

GAME SANCTUARY. A game sanctuary established pursuant to this Section and any part of the Province heretofore designated by the Governor in Council in which it shall be unlawful to hunt, take or kill or attempt to take or kill any game. *Lands and Forests Act*, R.S.N.S. 1967, c. 163, s. 161.

GAMETE. *n*. A reproductive cell.

GAMETES OR EMBRYOS CONSERVATION CENTRE. Premises outside a facility maintained by an institution operating a hospital centre, designed for the collection, conservation or distribution of human gametes or embryos with a view to using the gametes or embryos for medical or scientific purposes. *Medical laboratories, organ, tissue, gamete and embryo conservation, and the disposal of human bodies, An Act respecting*, R.S.Q. L-0.2, s. 1.

GAMING. *n*. 1. " . . . [I]nvolves wagering or betting. . . takes place where there is the chance not only of winning but of losing; in other words where some stake has been hazarded." *R. v. Di Pietro* (1986), 14 O.A.C. 387 at 398-9, [1986] 1 S.C.R. 250, 50 C.R. (3d) 266, 25 C.C.C. (3d) 100, 26 D.L.R. (4th) 412, 65 N.R. 245, the court per Lamer J. quoting from *Ellesmere (Earl) v. Wallace*, [1929] 2 Ch. 1 at 28 (U.K. C.A.) and *McCollom v. Wrightson*, [1968] A.C. 522 at 528 (U.K. H.L.). 2. " . . . [A] contract between two or more persons by which they agree to risk money on a chance, and to play by certain rules at cards, dice or some contrivance, and that one or several of them may be the winner, or winners, and the other, or others, the loser, or losers. To constitute gaming it is necessary that the game which is played should contain a controlling element of chance or hazard. . ." *R. v. Fortier* (1903), 13 Que. K.B. 308 at 311, 7 C.C.C. 417, the court per Wurtele J.

GAMING EQUIPMENT. Anything that is or may be used for the purpose of playing games or for betting. *Criminal Code*, R.S.C. 1985, c. C-46, s. 197.

GAMING HOUSE. See COMMON ~.

GANGRENE. *n*. The death of a portion of an organ or limb in a living body. F.A. Jaffe, A *Guide to Pathological Evidence*, 3d ed. (Toronto: Carswell, 1991) at 220.

GANG-HOOK. *n*. A combination of two or more hooks used as a unit. *National Parks Fishing Regulations*, C.R.C., c. 1120, s. 2.

GANG TRAPPED. That the waste piping from a group of two or more fixtures or other drainage openings is so arranged that all the fixtures or other drainage openings drain to a common trap, but the term shall not apply when the trap is a secondary trap such as a building trap or the trap of a fixture that receives waste from one or more indirect waste pipes. *Ontario Water Resources Act*, R.R.O. 1980, Reg. 736, s. 1.

GANGWAY. *n*. A defined passageway between a metal melting unit and a metal pouring area. *Occupational Health and Safety Act,* R.R.O. 1980, Reg. 692, s. 1.

GAOL. *n.* 1. Prison; place to confine offenders. 2. A provincial institution where lesser offences are punished.

GAOL DELIVERY. The commission of general gaol delivery given to judges or commissioners of assize authorizing them to try, and to discharge from custody if acquitted, every prisoner in gaol for an alleged crime when they arrived at the circuit town.

GAOLER. *n.* One who keeps a prison.

GAP. See AIR ~.

GARAGE. *n.* A place or premises where motor vehicles are received for housing, storage or repairs for compensation. See PRIVATE ~; PUBLIC ~; REPAIR ~; REPAIRMAN'S ~; STORAGE ~.

GARAGE KEEPER. 1. A person, firm, or corporation, who or which renders service upon a motor vehicle in a garage for or at a charge, price, or consideration, in the ordinary course of business and as the principal employment or one of the principal employments of that person, firm, or corporation. 2. Any person who keeps a place of business for the sale of motor accessories or for the storage or repair of motor vehicles, aircraft, boats or outboard motors. *Repairers Lien Act,* R.S.B.C. 1996, c. 404, s. 1.

GARAGEMAN. *n.* A person who keeps a place of business for the housing, storage or repair of a motor vehicle and who receives compensation for such housing, storage or repair.

GARAGE OPERATOR. The person who operates an establishment where road vehicles are maintained or repaired, and receives payment therefor. *Highway Safety Code,* R.S.Q. 1986, c. C-24.2, s. 661.

GARAGIST. *n.* The holder of a garage licence within the meaning of the Highway Code, as well as a person who operates an establishment where repairs are made to the body of the vehicle only, without any alteration being made therein, and where automobiles are not stored at the same time. *Automobile Insurance Act,* R.S.Q. 1977, c. A-25, s. 1.

GARBAGE. *n.* All kinds of victual, domestic and operational waste.

GARBAGE GRINDER. See ON-SITE ~.

GARD. *n.* [Fr.] Care, custody, wardship.

GARDENING. See MARKET ~.

GARMENT. *n.* Any article of wearing apparel *National Trade Mark Garment Sizing Regulations,* C.R.C., c. 1139, s. 2. See FUR ~.

GARNISH. *v.* 1. To attach a debt. 2. To warn.

GARNISHABLE MONEYS. Moneys authorized to be paid by Her Majesty by or under such Acts of Parliament or provisions thereof or programs thereunder as are designated by the regulations. *Family Orders and Agreements Enforcement Assistance Act,* R.S.C. 1985, c. 4, (2nd Supp.), s. 23.

GARNISHEE. *n.* The person who owes a judgment debtor money and against whom the court issues garnishment process.

GARNISHEE ORDER. " . . . [G]ives to the garnishor certain statutory rights enabling him to prevent the garnishee paying money to the original creditor and also to give a valid discharge of that original creditor's claim. It does not confer any right by way of equitable assignment or otherwise in the original debt." *MacKay & Hughes (1973) Ltd v. Martin Potatoes Inc.* (1984), 4 P.P.S.A.C. 107 at 113, 46 O.R. (2d) 304, 51 C.B.R. (N.S.) 1, 4 O.A.C. 1, 9 D.L.R. (4th) 439 (C.A.), the court per Blair J.A.

GARNISHEE SUMMONS. 1. First step in a garnishment proceeding. C.R.B. Dunlop, *Creditor-Debtor Law* in *Canada* (Toronto: Carswell, 1981) at 268. 2. Includes any document or court order of like import.

GARNISHMENT. *n.* 1. A way to enforce a judgment by which money owed by the garnishee to the judgment debtor is attached to pay off the judgment debtor's debt to a judgment creditor. 2. Includes attachment. See ATTACHMENT; ATTACHMENT OF WAGES; CONTINUING ~; PROVINCIAL ~ LAW.

GARNISTURE. *n.* Furnishing; providing.

GAROFOLI HEARING. " . . . [A] hearing before the trial judge to determine the compliance of the authorization [of a wiretap] with s. 8 of the Charter . . ." *R. v. Garofoli* (1990), 60 C.C.C. (3d) 161 at 182, 80 C.R. (3d) 317, 116 N.R. 241, 43 O.A.C. 1, [1990] 2 S.C.R. 1421, 50 C.R.R. 206, 36 Q.A.C. 161, Sopinka J. (Dickson C.J.C., Lamer C.J.C., La Forest and Gonthier JJ. concurring).

GARRANTY. See GUARANTEE.

GARROTTING. *n.* Asphyxia caused when a ligature is twisted around the neck. F.A. Jaffe, *A*

Guide to Pathological Evidence, 3d ed. (Toronto: Carswell, 191) at 220.

GAS. *n*. 1. Any hydrocarbon or mixture of hydrocarbons that, at a temperature of 15°C and a pressure of 101.325 kPa, is in a gaseous state. Canada statutes. 2. Natural gas or any fluid hydrocarbon, other than a hydrocarbon that is a liquid in its naturally occurring state, recovered from a natural reservoir in Canada. Canada statutes. 3. Natural gas whether or not produced in association with oil, and includes all liquid hydrocarbons resulting from the condensation of natural gas. 4. Raw gas or marketable gas or any constituent of raw gas, condensate or crude oil that is recovered in processing and that is gaseous at the conditions under which its volume is measured or estimated. 5. Natural gas, manufactured gas, liquified petroleum gas or any mixtures of such gases. 6. A gaseous mixture consisting primarily of methane. 7. Natural gas, manufactured gas, any variety or any mixture of either, liquified petroleum gas or any mixture of liquified petroleum gas and air, conveyed or distributed by tubing. Quebec statutes. 8. All natural gas, both before and after it has been subjected to absorption, purification, scrubbing or other treatment or process, and includes all fluid hydrocarbons not herein defined as oil or condensate. 9. Any gas, including casing-head gas, and any hydrocarbon other than oil. See COAL ~; COMMODITY VALUE OF ~; COMPRESSED ~; COMPRESSED INFLAMMABLE ~; FREEHOLD ~; ILLEGAL ~; LEVIABLE ~; LIQUEFIED PETROLEUM ~; LIQUID PETROLEUM ~; MANUFACTURED ~; MARKETABLE ~; NATURAL ~; NETBACK ~; OIL AND ~; OIL OR ~; PINTSCH ~; PRODUCTION OF OIL [OR] ~; PUTREFACTIVE ~ES; RAW ~; RURAL ~ CO-OPERATIVE ASSOCIATION; WARNING ~.

GAS COMPANY. A person engaged in the sale or distribution of gas in the Province. *Gas Safety Act*, R.S.B.C. 1996, c. 169, s. 1.

GAS CONTRACT. A contract under which gas is sold and delivered by a seller to a buyer, and includes an agreement that varies or amends that contract and an arbitration award that relates to that contract. Alberta statutes.

GAS DISCHARGE TUBE. An electronic tube in which glow discharges or X-rays or both may be produced by the acceleration of electrons or ions. *Radiation Emitting Devices Regulations*, C.R.C., c. 1370, s. 1.

GAS DISTRIBUTION SYSTEM. A system (a) that includes the works, structures, erections, equipment, pipes, machinery, tools, appliances, compression stations, gate valves, check valves, gasometers, regulator stations, terminal facilities, appurtenances and other things that are used on or in connection with the system; and (b) that is used for the distribution, delivery, furnishing, or sale of natural or manufactured gas directly to consumer inhabitants of a municipal corporation; but does not include (c) a pipeline; or (d) a building, plant, warehouse, or storage yard used for the purpose of obtaining and producing natural gas underlying the surface of the land or (e) a building, plant, warehouse, or storage yard used for the manufacture, refining or marketing of gas; or (f) similar equipment, machinery, pipes, tools or appliances stored in such a building, plant, warehouse or storage yard. Manitoba statutes.

GAS EQUIPMENT. Includes machinery, equipment, appliances and devices of every kind and description used or intended to be used in the transmission, distribution, supply or use of gas.

GAS EXPORT COMPANY. Any person that holds a permit under the *Gas Resources Preservation Act* for the removal of gas from Alberta. *Gas Utilities Act*, R.S.A. 2000, c. G-5, s. 29.

GAS FITTER. *var*. **GAS-FITTER**. A person who installs, repairs or alters any gas installation or gas equipment.

GAS-FITTING. *n*. The installing, removing, altering or repairing of all gas piping from the gas meter to the point of consumption of the gas, of appliances, and of any device that is attached to or forms a part of any gas piping or gas venting system, including electrical apparatus and wiring, where work on combination gas and electrical fixtures or appliances is involved. *National Parks Natural Gas Regulations*, C.R.C., c. 1129, s. 2.

GAS INSTALLATION. 1. The installation of a system of gas piping in or on any land, building or premises from the meter or regulator where gas is delivered therein or thereon up to the point or points where the gas can be consumed or used therein or thereon by any gas consuming equipment and includes the connection of any such gas piping with any of that equipment and any part of the gas system, and the alteration, extension and repair of that gas piping, but does not include any electrical installation. 2. A facility or system, including fittings, that is owned or operated by a gas company and that is used for storing, conveying, measuring or regulating gas. *Gas Safety Act*, R.S.B.C. 1996, c. 169, s. 1.

GASKET. *n*. A gasket made of butyl rubber or neoprene and containing no adulterants or reclaimed material and having a compression set after twenty-four hours at 158 ° Fahrenheit of not more than 15 per cent. *Ontario Water Resources Act*, R.R.O. 1980, Reg. 736, s. 72.

GAS LINE. 1. A pipe for the transmission of gas from a secondary line or storage facility to a distribution centre or storage facility and includes installations in connection with that pipe, but does not include a multiphase line, secondary line, flow line or distribution line. *Pipeline Act*, R.S.A. 1980, c. P-8, s. 1. 2. A pipe for the transmission of gas and any accompanying liquids and includes installations in connection therewith but does not include a secondary line, flow line, distribution line or private line. *Pipe Line Act*, S.N.B. 1976, c. P-8.1, s. 1.

GAS METER. See ORIFICE ~; POSITIVE DISPLACEMENT ~.

GASOHOL. *n*. A blend of gasoline and denatured ethanol. See UNLEADED ~.

GAS OIL RATIO. *var.* **GAS-OIL RATIO**. The ratio of the number of standard cubic feet of natural gas produced to the number of barrels of oil produced.

GASOLINE. *n*. Gasoline type fuels for use in internal combustion engines other than aircraft engines. See AIRCRAFT ~; BULK ~; LEADED ~; UNLEADED ~.

GASOLINE IN BULK. Gasoline stored, transported or transferred by any means other than in a fuel tank of a motor vehicle in which gasoline for generating power in the motor vehicle is kept. *Gasoline Tax Act*, R.S.O. 1990, c. G.5, s. 1.

GASOLINE PUMP. A tank or receptacle of not less than fifty gallon or two hundred and twenty-seven litre capacity used or intended to be used for the storage of gasoline or motive fuel and equipped with a pump for dispensing such gasoline or motive fuel. *Gasoline and Motive Fuel* Tax Act S.N.B. 1976, c. 26, s. 1.

GASOLINE SERVICE STATION. Any building, portion of a building, booth, stall, gasoline pump, or place, where, or by means of which gasoline is offered for sale by retail for use in internal combustion engines or dispensed in sale by retail for such use, and the premises occupied or used in connection therewith, or any part of such premises that may be specified in a municipal by-law. *Shops Regulation Act*, R.S.M. 1987, c. S 110, s. 1.

GAS OR OIL LEASE. Includes any agreement, whether by way of option, lease, grant or otherwise, granting the right to operate lands for the production and removal of natural gas or oil, or both, except a grant to so operate where the amount or payment of the consideration therefor is not dependent upon the operation of such lands or upon the production of gas or oil or upon the amount of gas or oil produced. *Gas and Oil Leases Act*, R.S.O. 1990 c. G.3, s. 1.

GASPÉ PENINSULA. That portion of the Gaspé region of the Province of Quebec that extends to the western border of Kamouraska County and includes the Magdalen Islands. *Income Tax Act*, R.S.C. 1952, c. 148 (as am. S.C. 1985, c. 45, s. 72(5)), s. 127(9).

GASPESIA REGION. That part of the Province of Quebec consisting of the following parishes: St-Fidèle de Restigouche, St-Conrad, Ste-Anne de Restigouche, Pointe à la Garde, Escuminac, St-Jean l'Evangéliste, St-Jean de Brébeuf, St-Louis de Gonzague, Carleton, Maria, New Richmond, St-Edgar, Paspébiac, St-Godefroi, Port Daniel, Gascons, Newport, Pellegrin, Chandler, Ste-Adélaïde de Pabos, Grande Rivière, Ste-Thérèse, St-Gabriel de Rameau, Caplan, St-Alphonse, St-Siméon, Bonaventure, St-Elzéar, New Carlisle, St-Jogues, Cap d'Espoir, Val d'Espoir, Percé, Barachois, St-Georges de Malbaie, Douglastown, Canne des Roches.

GAS PIPE. Any tubing or pipe used or intended for the conveyance or distribution of gas, except the connecting piping of an apparatus.

GAS PIPELINE. *var.* **GAS PIPE LINE**. 1. A pipe line for the transportation, transmission, or conduct of gas and includes all property, real and personal, required for the purposes thereof, and, without restricting the generality of the foregoing, further includes any system, works, plant, pipe line, or equipment for the production, transmission, delivery, or furnishing of gas, directly or indirectly, to the public, and a gas transmission line as herein defined. *Gas Pipe Line Act*, R.S.M. 1987, c. G50, s. 1. 2. A pipe or any system or arrangement of pipes wholly within Alberta whereby gas is conveyed from a wellhead or other place where it is stored, processed or treated to any other place, (a) includes all property of any kind used for the purpose of, or in connection with, or incidental to the operation of a gas pipeline in the gathering, transporting, handling and delivery of gas and (b) without restricting the generality of the foregoing, includes tanks, surface reservoirs, pumps, racks, storage and loading facilities, compressors, compressor stations, pressure measuring and controlling equipment and fixtures, flow controlling and measuring equipment and fixtures, metering equipment and fixtures and heating, cooling and dehydrating equipment and fixtures, but (c) does not include any pipe or any system or arrangement of pipes that constitutes a distribution system for the distribution of gas to ultimate consumers. *Gas Utilities Act*, R.S.A. 2000, c. G-5, s. 1.

GAS PLANT. See COMPRESSED~.

GAS PROCESSING PLANT. A plant for the extraction from gas of hydrogen sulphide, helium, ethane, natural gas liquids or other substances, but does not include a well-head separator, treater or dehydrator.

GAS PRODUCER. A person who has the right to take or remove gas from a natural reservoir in Canada.

GAS-PROOF ROOM. A room so constructed and maintained that combustible gases or fumes cannot enter the room.

GAS REPROCESSING PLANT. An installation in Canada at which natural gas liquids are removed from marketable pipeline gas and at which those liquids and the remaining marketable pipeline gas are not further processed.

GAS SALES CONTRACT. A contract for the sale and delivery of gas in Alberta under which the producer of the gas is the seller. Alberta statutes.

GAS SOURCE. A point at which gas is supplied to a rural gas utility or an individual tap. *Rural Gas Act*, R.S.A. 1980, c. R-19, s. 1.

GAS SYSTEM. 1. Any equipment or installation used or intended to be used in or in conjunction with the processing, transmission, storage, distribution, supply or use of gas but does not include any thing excluded by the regulations from the definition of gas system. *Safety Codes Act*, R.S.A. 2000, c. S-1, s. 1. 2. A system of gas equipment that (a) is installed in premises and is downstream of an outlet of a gas company's meter, (b) utilizes liquefied petroleum gas and is downstream of a second stage regu-

lator, (c) is installed other than by or on behalf of a gas company and is upstream of the outlet of a meter or upstream of a second stage regulator, or (d) is installed at a propane bulk plant, and includes a vehicle gas system. *Gas Safety Act*, R.S.B.C. 1996, c. 169, s. 1.

GAS TRANSMISSION LINE. A gas pipe line that is used and operated for the transportation, transmission, or conduct of gas to a distribution system and that has been so designated by the board under section 13. Gas *Pipe Line Act*, R.S.M. 1987, c. G50, s. 2.

GAS UTILITY. 1. A corporation which owns or operates in the Province equipment or facilities for the production, generation, storage, transmission, sale, delivery or furnishing of gas for the production of light, heat, cold or power to or for the public or any corporation for compensation, but does not include a company within the meaning of that word as defined in the National Energy Board Act (Canada). *Gas Utility Act*, R.S.B.C. 1996, c. 170, s. 1.2. (a) Any gas pipeline, (b) any system, works, plant, pipes, equipment or service for the production, gathering, conveying, transmission, transporting, delivery, furnishing or supplying of gas by retail or wholesale, either directly or indirectly, to or for the public or any member of the public, whether an individual or a corporation, other than the transportation, delivery, furnishing or supplying by retail or wholesale, either directly or indirectly, of liquified petroleum gas (except propane and butanes) by means of tank car, tank wagon, cylinder or vessel, (c) any absorption plant or scrubbing plant, and (d) any system, well, works, plant, equipment or service for the production of gas or capable of producing gas which may be declared by the Energy Resources Conservation Board to be a gas utility. *Gas Utilities Act*, R.S.A. 2000, c. G-5, s. 1. See OWNER OF A ~; RURAL ~.

GAS VENT. That portion of a venting system designed to convey vent gases vertically to the outside air from the vent connector of a gas-fired appliance, or directly from the appliance when a vent connector is not used and includes any offsets. *Building Code Act*, R.R.O. 1980, Reg. 87, s. 1.

GAS WELL. 1. A well in which casing is run and that, in the opinion of the commission, is producing or is capable of producing from a natural gas bearing zone. *Petroleum and Natural Gas Act*, R.S.B.C. 1996, c. 361, s. 1. 2. A well (a) that produces natural gas not associated or blended with oil at the time of production, (b) that produces more than 30,000 cubic feet of natural gas to each barrel of oil from the same producing horizon, (c) wherein the gas producing stratum has been successfully segregated from the oil and the gas is produced separately, or (d) that is classified as a gas well by the Minister for any reason. *Canada Oil and Gas Drilling and Production Regulations*, C.R.C., c. 1517, s. 2. See COMMERCIAL ~.

GATE. See CITY ~; GROUND ~S.

GATE RECEIPTS. See GROSS ~.

GATHERING LINE. A pipe line used for the collection of oil or gas within a field. *The Pipe Lines Act*, R.S.S. 1978, c. P-12, s. 2.

GATINEAU VALLEY REGION. That part of the Province of Quebec consisting of the parishes of Grand Remous, Bois-Franc, Montcerf, Ste-Famille d'Aumond, Ste-Thérèse de Gatineau, Lac Ste-Marie, Maniwaki, Messines, Bouchette, Blue Sea Lake and Gracefield. *Gatineau Wood Order*, C.R.C., c. 262, s. 2.

GATING. *n*. " . . . [A] practice of releasing inmates on mandatory supervision . . . but in the case of inmates considered to be dangerous, of rearresting them immediately upon their release and detaining them in the institution from which they had just been released . . ." *Ross v. Kent Institution* (1987), 34 C.C.C. (3d) 452 at 454, 12 B.C.L.R. (2d) 145, 57 C.R. (3d) 79 (B.C. C.A.), the court per Hinkson J.A.

GATT. *abbr*. General Agreement on Tariffs and Trade, a multi-lateral international agreement regarding tariffs.

GAUGE. *n*. 1. A measure of the diameter of wire or the thickness of sheet metal in accordance with the American Wire Gauge or Brown and Sharpe, Gauge Standards. 2. A measure of shotgun bore diameter. 3. Of railways, the measure of their width. See B-S ~; NOMINAL ~; STANDARD ~; VOLUME-PRESSURE ~.

GAVEL. *n*. Rent, tribute, payment to someone higher in rank.

GAWR. *abbr*. Gross axle weight rating.

GAZETTE. *n*. 1. A government's official newspaper. 2. Journal published by the Law Society of Upper Canada. See OFFICIAL ~.

GEAR. See CLASS A ~; CLASS B ~; FISHING ~; FIXED CARGO ~.

GELD. *n*. A compensation, mulct, payment, price, tax, tribute, value.

GELDABLE. *adj*. Taxable.

GELLING AGENT. Gelatin, agar and carrageenan. *Food and Drug Regulations*, C.R.C., c. 870, s. B.01.001.

GEN. *abbr*. General.

GENE. *n*. The basic unit of heredity. A sequence of nucleotides along a segment of DNA. Leads to expression of hereditary characteristics.

GENEALOGY. *n*. A family history; specification of descendants in order of succession; pedigree.

GENEARCH. *n*. The chief person in a family.

GENERAL ACCEPTANCE. A general acceptance assents without qualification to the order of the drawer. *Bills of Exchange Act*, R.S.C. 1985, c. B-4, s. 37.

GENERAL ACREAGE QUOTA. Any permission given by the Board to deliver grain, either under a permit book or otherwise. *Prairie Grain Advance Payment Act*, R.S.C. 1985, c. P-18, s. 2.

GENERAL ADJUSTMENT. A wage increase given to all employees.

GENERAL ADVANTAGE OF CANADA. See WORKS FOR THE ~.

GENERAL AGENT. 1. A person or corporation directly representing an insurance company and who can issue policies, interim receipts and give oral coverage. 2. A person acting under authority from an insurer to supervise and appoint agents, inspect risks and otherwise transact business for, or as a representative of, such insurer. *The Saskatchewan Insurance Act*, R.S.S. 1978, c. S-26, s. 2.

GENERAL ASSEMBLY. All the sessions of the Legislative Assembly held subsequent to a general provincial election until the dissolution of the Legislature by the Lieutenant Governor. *Legislature and Executive Pensions Act*, S.P.E.I. 1994, c. 35, s. 1.

GENERAL AVERAGE. In maritime law, an apportionment of loss which was caused by intentional damage to a ship, or sacrifice of cargo to secure the general safety of the ship and cargo. Contribution is made by the owners in proportion to the value of their respective interests. See FREE FROM ~.

GENERAL AVERAGE ACT. Occurs where any extraordinary sacrifice or expenditure is voluntarily and reasonably made or incurred in time of peril for the purpose of preserving the property imperilled in the common adventure. *Insurance (Marine) Act*, R.S.B.C. 1996, c. 230, s. 67.

GENERAL AVERAGE CONTRIBUTION. A rateable contribution from the other parties interested in a general average loss. *Insurance (Marine) Act*, R.S.B.C. 1996, c. 230, s. 67.

GENERAL AVERAGE LOSS. A loss caused by or directly consequential on a general average act. It includes a general average expenditure as well as a general average sacrifice. The party on whom it falls is entitled, subject to the conditions imposed by maritime law, to a rateable contribution from the other parties interested, and that contribution is called a general average contribution. *Insurance (Marine) Act*, R.S.B.C. 1996, c. 230, s. 67.

GENERAL CARGO. All cargo not carried in bulk, that is, all cargo not carried loose or in mass.

GENERAL CENSUS. The census taken by the Government of Canada. *Election Act*, R.S.Q. 1977, c. E-3, s. 2.

GENERAL CONTRACTOR. A contractor whose principal activity consists of organizing or coordinating construction work entrusted to persons under his orders or to contractors to execute. *Building Contractors Vocational Qualifications Act*, R.S.Q. 1977, c. Q-1, s. 53.

GENERAL COURT MARTIAL. May try any person who is liable to be charged, dealt with and tried on a charge of having committed a service offence. A General Court Martial is composed of a military judge and a panel of five members.

GENERAL COURT OF APPEAL. The words "general court of appeal" in s. 101 [of the *Constitution Act, 1867* (U.K.), 30 & 31 Vict., c. 3] denote the status of the Court within the national court structure and should not be taken as a restrictive definition of the Court's functions. In most instances, this Court acts as the exclusive ultimate appellate court in the country, and, as such, is properly constituted as the "general court of appeal" for Canada. Moreover, it is clear that an appellate court can receive, on an exceptional basis, original jurisdiction not incompatible with its appellate jurisdiction. *Reference re Secession of Quebec*, 1998 CarswellNat 1299, 161 D.L.R. (4th) 385, 228 N.R. 203, 55 C.R.R. (2d) 1, [1998] 2 S.C.R. 217. Per Curiam.

GENERAL DAMAGES. 1. " . . . [T]hose which, upon the breach of a legal duty, the law itself presumes to arise, and they can be shown by general evidence of matters which are accepted as affected by such a breach. . ." *Rowlett v. Karas*, [1944] S.C.R. 1 at 10, [944] 1 D.L.R. 241, Rand J. (Duff C.J. concurring). 2. " . . . [S]uch as the law will presume to be the direct, natural, or probable consequence of the act complained of; . . ." *Graham v. Saville*, [1945] 2 D.L.R. 489 at 492, [1945] O.R. 301 (C.A.), Laidlaw J.A. (dissenting in part).

GENERAL DENIAL. In a pleading, a contradiction of each of the allegations of the plaintiff in the statement of claim or petition.

GENERAL DETERRENCE. A sentence which will discourage others who may be inclined to commit the same or a similar offence.

GENERALE DICTUM GENERALITER EST INTELLIGENDUM. [L.] A general dictum should be comprehended in a general sense.

GENERAL ELECTION. 1. An election in respect of which election writs are issued for all electoral districts. 2. An election that is held in respect of each constituency on the same day. 3. An election held for all the members of an elected authority to fill vacancies caused by the effluxion of time.

GENERALE NIHIL CERTI IMPLICAT. [L.] A general statement implies nothing definite.

GENERALE NIHIL PONIT. [L.] A general statement says nothing.

GENERAL ENUMERATION. An enumeration of electors in all electoral divisions. *Election Act*, R.S.A. 1980, c. E-2, s. 1.

GENERALE TANTUM VALET IN GENERALIBUS QUANTUM SINGULARE IN SINGULIS. [L.] General words should be taken in a general sense, just as particular words refer only to particular things.

GENERAL EXPENSES. The direct and indirect costs, charges and expenses of producing and selling goods for export, other than the costs, charges and expenses referred to in paragraph (2)(a) and subsection (3) . *Customs Act*, R.S.C. 1985 (2d Supp.), c. 1, s. 52(4).

GENERAL HOLIDAY. 1. New Year's Day, Good Friday, Victoria Day, Canada Day, Labour Day, Thanksgiving Day, Remembrance Day, Christmas Day and Boxing Day and includes any day substituted for any such holiday pursuant to section 195. *Canada Labour Code*, R.S.C. 1985, c. L-2, s. 166. 2. New Year's Day, Good Friday, National Aboriginal Day, Canada Day, the first Monday in August, Labour Day, Thanksgiving Day, Remembrance Day, Christmas Day, and the day fixed by the Governor General for observance of the birthday of the reigning sovereign, and includes any day substituted for any such holiday pursuant to section 23 or 25. *Labour Standards Act*, R.S.N.W.T. 1988, c. L-1, s. 1.

GENERAL HOSPITAL. 1. A hospital in which diagnostic services and medical, surgical and obstetrical treatment are provided to persons having various illness, disabilities, injuries or other conditions. *The Hospital Standards Act*, R.S.S. 1978, c. H-10, s. 2. 2. A hospital providing diagnostic services and facilities for medical or surgical treatment in the acute phase for adults and children and obstetrical care or any of them. *Hospitals Act*, R.S.A. 2000, c. H-12, s. 1.

GENERALIA SPECIALIBUS NON DERO-GANT. [L.] 1. The general does not detract from the specific. 2. " . . . [W]here there are general words in a later Act capable of reasonable and sensible application without extending them to subjects specially dealt with by earlier legislation, you are not to hold that earlier and special legislation indirectly repealed, altered or derogated from merely by force of such general words, without any indication of a particular intention to do so." *Seward v. The Vera Cruz* (1884), 10 App. Cas. 59 at 68 (U.K. H.L.), Lord Selborne.

GENERALIA VERBA SUNT GENERALITER INTELLIGENDA. [L.] General words should be comprehended generally.

GENERALIBUS SPECIALIA DERO-GANT. [L.] The special derogates from the general.

GENERAL INTENT. " . . . [O]ne in which the only intent involved relates solely to the performance of the act in question with no further ulterior intent or purpose . . ." *R. v. Bernard*, [1988] 2 S.C.R. 833 at 863 67 C.R. 3d 113, 90 N.R. 321, 45 C.C.C. (3d) 1, 32 O.A.C. 161, 38 C.R.R. 82, McIntyre J.

GENERAL INTENT OFFENCE. One in which the actor's intent is solely to perform the act in question.

GENERALIS CLAUSULA NON PORRI-GITUR AD EA QUAE ANTEA SPECIALITER SUNT COMPREHENSA. [L.] A general clause does not extend to things which were included in prior special words.

GENERALIS REGULA GENERALITER EST INTELLIGENDA. [L.] A general rule should be comprehended generally.

GENERAL JURISDICTION. Unrestricted and unlimited authority in any matter of substantive law, criminal or civil. S.A. Cohen, *Due Process of Law* (Toronto: Carswell, 1977) at 344.

GENERAL LEGACY. Describes a legacy which does not bequeath a specified item. P.V. Baker and P. St. J. Langan, eds., *Snells' Equity*, 29th ed. (London: Sweet and Maxwell, 1990) at 360.

GENERAL LIEN. A lien on personal property for an account due or general debt to the one who claims it, which operates as a form of floating charge on any of the debtor's personal property in the lien claimant's hands. D.N. Macklem & D.I. Bristow, *Construction and Mechanics' Liens in Canada*, 5th ed. (Toronto: Carswell, 1985) at 579.

GENERAL LISTING. " . . . [T]hat the understanding, express or implied between the parties, is that if the agent procures a purchaser who is willing to buy at a price and upon terms which the vendor is willing to accept, the agent shall be entitled to his commission; the price and terms specified in the listing being considered simply as a basis of negotiations." *Hunt Real Estate Corp. v. Meck Developments Ltd.* (1980), 25 A.R. 99 at 102 (Q.B.), Medhurst J.

GENERALLY. *adv.* On the whole, in those cases.

GENERALLY ACCEPTED. For a practice to be generally accepted, it does not have to be a practice that everyone does or that everyone necessarily agrees with. It is simply a practice which is permissible or legitimate under the circumstances. *Lloyds Bank Canada v. Alberta Opportunity Co.* (1989), 1989 CarswellAlta 197, 71 Alta. L.R. (2d) 257, 101 A.R. 294, [1990] 2 W.W.R. 692, 46 B.L.R. 236 (Q.B.).

GENERALLY ACCEPTED ACCOUNTING PRINCIPLES. Conventions, rules and procedures that set out accepted accounting practice, usually the principles established by the Canadian Institute of Chartered Accountants.

GENERALLY ACCEPTED AUDITING STANDARDS. Standards concerning an auditor's conduct in carrying out examinations.

GENERALLY ACCEPTED BANKING PRACTICES. Can be interpreted as meaning that anything that is permissible or legitimate as a bona fide exercise of sound banking judgment constitutes an accepted banking practice. This general definition allows the bank to carry out a number of different procedures and practices in any given situation or circumstance. The failure to carry out specific practices or procedures does not mean that the plaintiff did not act in accordance with generally accepted practices. *Lloyds Bank Canada v. Alberta Opportunity Co.* (1989), 1989 CarswellAlta 197, 71 Alta. L.R. (2d) 257, 101 A.R. 294, [1990] 2 W.W.R. 692, 46 B.L.R. 236 (Q.B.).

GENERAL MACHINIST. A person who (a) sets up and operates to prescribed tolerances engine lathes and milling, grinding, drilling, sawing and boring machines, (b) reads and interprets blueprints, operation and product-related reference charts and tables and elects mechanical measuring and checking and layout tools and devices, and (c) performs measuring, checking and layout operations and selects work piece materials and the required cutting tools and abrasives for metal removal operations, but does not include a person or class of persons in a limited purpose occupation that, in the opinion of the Director, does not equate with the definition of general machinist. *Apprenticeship and Tradesmen's Qualification Act*, R.R.O. 1980, Reg. 38 , s. 1.

GENERAL MANAGER. The chief executive officer of a corporation who has supervision over and directs the work of the staff of the corporation.

GENERAL MEASUREMENT POINT. In respect of any accommodation space, means (a) a point midway between two adjacent lamps; (b) a point midway between a lamp and any position on the boundary of the space; and (c) the central point of part of a space that is available for free movement where that part is shaded from the direct rays of a lamp by a reentrant angle formed in the boundary of the space. *Towboat Crew Accommodation Regulations*, C.R.C., c. 1498, Schedule IV, s. 1.

GENERAL MEETING. Any annual, regular, special or class meeting of an organization. See ANNUAL ∼.

GENERAL ORDER NO. 448. General Order No. 448 of the Board of Railway Commissioners for Canada dated Friday the 26th day of August 1927 . *Western Grain Transportation Act*, R.S.B.C . 1985, c. W-8, s. 2.

GENERAL PARTNER. Person associated with one or more other persons in an enterprise and assuming personal liability. See LIMITED PARTNERSHIP.

GENERAL PERMIT. A permit to export issued by the Minister under section 17. *Cultural Property Export and Import Act*, R.S.C. 1985, c. C-51,s. 2.

GENERAL POWER. 1. Includes any power or authority enabling the donee or other holder thereof either alone or jointly with or, with the consent, of any other person to appoint, appropriate or dispose of property as she or he sees fit whether exercisable by instrument inter vivos or by will, or both, but does not include (a) any power exercisable in a fiduciary capacity under a disposition not made by the donee except to the extent that having regard to the fiduciary restrictions imposed upon the donee under the disposition it is reasonable to regard the donee or holder of the power as capable of conferring the property or any part thereof upon herself or himself for her or his own benefit, or (b) any power exercisable as a mortgagee, or (c) any power exercisable jointly with, or with the consent of, any other person (i) who has a substantial interest in the property to which the power relates, and (ii) whose interest in that property would be adversely affected by the exercise of the power in favour of the donee or holder. 2. The power of a donee to appoint property to anyone, including her or himself. D.M.W. Waters, *The Law of Trusts in Canada*, 2d ed. (Toronto: Carswell, 1984) at 72.

GENERAL PRACTITIONER. A physician who does not hold a specialist's certificate.

GENERAL PROPERTY TAX. (a) A tax that is levied on the assessment, as shown on the assessment roll of the municipality, for municipal, school or hospital purposes; (b) where levied, a local improvement tax under The Local Improvements Act shown on the tax notice; and (c) where levied, a conservation and development tax under The Conservation and Development Act, shown on the tax notice. Saskatchewan statutes.

GENERAL REGISTER. An index of documents that do not affect any particular piece of land such as wills and powers of attorney which, when registered, are allotted a number and stored.

GENERAL REVIEW. In relation to the construction, enlargement or alteration of a building, means an examination of the building to determine whether the construction, enlargement or alteration is in general conformity with the design governing the construction, enlargement or alteration, and reporting thereon.

GENERAL STRIKE. Cessation of work by all union members in a geographical area.

GENERAL TAX. A tax levied upon the taxable assessments in a municipality or local improvement district. *The Heath Services Act*, R.S.S. 1978, c. H-1, s. 2.

GENERAL USE SWITCH. A switch intended for use in general distribution and branch-circuits and which is rated in amperes and capable of interrupting its rated current at rated voltage. *Power Corporation Act*, R.R.O. 1980, Reg. 794, s. 0.

GENERAL VERDICT. A jury's decision for either the defendant or the plaintiff generally.

"GENERAL WELFARE" CLAUSE. In municipal statutes, the source of local police power or municipalities. Authority over public health, nuisances and the regulation of trades is included in this power. See POLICE POWER.

GENERAL WORDS. Words added to the description of a parcel of land in a conveyance or mortgage, words which describe every kind of appurtenance, easement or privilege, fixtures and produce of the land.

GENERATE. *v.* 1. With respect to electricity, means to produce electricity or provide ancillary services, other than ancillary services provided by a transmitter or distributor through the operation of a transmission or distribution system. *Electricity Act, 1998*, S.O. 1998, c. 15, Sched. A, s. 2. 2. To cause or allow to cause, by virtue of ownership, management, operation or control, the creation or storage of hazardous waste. *Dangerous Goods Handling and Transportation Act*, R.S.M. 1987, c. D 12, s. 1.

GENERATING CAPABILITY. See NET ~.

GENERATION. *n.* 1. With respect to electricity, means to produce electricity or provide ancillary services, other than ancillary services provided by a transmitter or distributor through the operation of a transmission or distribution system. *Electricity Act, 1998*, S.O. 1998, c. 15, Sched. A, s. 2. 2. Production by hydraulic, electrical, pneumatic, steam, internal combustion engine, gas, oil, atomic or any other process.

GENERATION AND SALE FOR DISTRIBUTION TO THE PUBLIC. Generation and sale (a) to a person or persons with whom the vendor deals at arms length, or (b) to a person or persons with whom the vendor does not deal at arm's length for resale directly or indirectly to persons with whom the vendor does deal at arm's length. *Public Utilities Income Tax Transfer Act*, R.S.C. 1985, c. P-37, s. 2.

GENERATION FACILITY. A facility for generating electricity or providing ancillary services, other than ancillary services provided by a transmitter or distributor through the operation of a transmission or distribution system, and includes any structures, equipment or other things used for that purpose. *Electricity Act, 1998*, S.O. 1998, c. 15, Sched. A, s. 2.

GENERATOR. *n.* A person who owns or operates a generation facility. *Electricity Act, 1998*, S.O. 1998, c. 15, Sched. A, s. 2. See PULSE ~; RADIONUCLIDE ~; X-RAY ~.

GENERIC. *adj.* 1. Relating to a group or class. 2. Chemical name of a drug.

GENERIC DRUG. Drug that is therapeutically equivalent to and contains the same quantities of active medicinal ingredients as a drug already marketed in Canada that is a brand-name drug. *Apotex Inc. v. Canada (Attorney General)* (1996), 123 F.T.R. 161 (T.D.).

GENERIC DRUG COMPANY. A company which manufactures and sells generic drugs, drugs discovered or invented by others, under compulsory licence arrangements provided in the *Patent Act*.

GENERIC PREJUDICE. A form of juror prejudice which arises from a juror's stereotypical attitudes toward the defendant, victim, witnesses or the nature of the crime itself.

GENETIC MARKER. An inherited characteristic used in a forensic investigation or paternity study. F.A. Jaffe, *A Guide to Pathological Evidence*, 3d ed. (Toronto: Carswell, 1991) at 220.

GENETIC TESTING. The analysis of DNA, RNA or chromosomes for purposes such as the prediction of disease or vertical transmission risks, or monitoring, diagnosis or prognosis. *Medical Devices Regulations* SOR/98-282, s. 1.

GENEVA CONVENTIONS. Agreements to ameliorate the condition of wounded and sick members of the armed forces in the field, to ameliorate the condition of sick, wounded and ship-wrecked members of the armed forces at sea, to treat prisoners of war and civilian persons in time of war in particular ways.

GENOCIDE. *n.* 1. Any of the following acts committed with intent to destroy in whole or in part any identifiable group, namely, (a) killing members of the group, or (b) deliberately inflicting on the group conditions of life calculated to bring about its physical destruction. *Criminal Code*, R.S.C. 1985, c. C-46, s. 318(2). 2. Any of the following acts committed with intent to destroy, in whole or in part, a national, ethnical, racial or religious group, as such: (a) killing members of the group; (b) causing serious bodily or mental harm to members of the group; (c) deliberately inflicting on the group conditions of life calculated to bring about its physical destruction in whole or in part; (d) imposing measures intended to prevent births within the group; (e) forcibly transferring children of the group to another group. *Rome Statute*, Article 6. 3. An act or omission committed with intent to destroy, in whole or in part, an identifiable group of persons, as such, that, at the time and in the place of its commission, constitutes genocide according to customary international law or conventional international law or by virtue of its being criminal according to the general principles of law recognized by the community of nations, whether or not it constitutes a contravention of the law in force at the time and in the place of its commission. *Crimes Against Humanity and War Crimes Act, 2000*, S.C. 2000, c. 24, s. 4. See IDENTIFIABLE GROUP.

GENOME. *n.* The totality of the deoxyribonucleic acid sequence of a particular cell.

GENS. *n.* [L.] Great family; nation; race.

GENUINE. *adj.* 1. " . . . '[N]ot spurious' . . ." *Irving Ungennan Ltd v. Galanis* (1991),1 C.P.C. (3d) 248 at 255, 4 O.R. (3d) 545, 20 R.P.R. (2d) 49n, 83 D.L.R. (4th) 734, 50 O.A.C. 176 (C.A.), the court per Morden A.C.J.O. 2. The obverse of false. *R. v. Nuosci* (1991), 10 C.R. (4th) 332 at 345, 6 O.R. (3d) 316, 69 C.C.C. (3d) 64, 51 O.A.C. 41 (C.A.), the court per Morden A.C.J.O. 3. Free of forgery or counterfeit.

GENUINE GUN COLLECTOR. An individual who possesses or seeks to acquire restricted weapons that are related or distinguished by historical, technological or scientific characteristics, has knowledge of those characteristics, has consented to the periodic inspection, conducted in a reasonable manner and in accordance with the regulations, of the premises in which the restricted weapons are to be kept and has complied with such other requirements as are prescribed by regulation respecting knowledge, secure storage and the keeping of records in respect of the restricted weapons. *Criminal Code*, S.C. 1991, c. 40, s. 2(5).

GENUINE INTEREST. A prerequisite for public interest standing. Belongs to a person likely to gain some advantage other than the satisfaction of righting a wrong, upholding a principle or winning a contest if his action succeeds and who will suffer some disadvantage other than a sense of grievance and a debt for costs if his action fails. *Finlay v. Canada (Minister of Finance)*, [1986] 2 S.C.R. 607.

GENUINE TRADE MARK. A trade mark that is true, real, authentic, not counterfeit or not spurious. H.G. Fox, *The Canadian Law of Trade Marks and Unfair Competition*, 3d ed. (Toronto: Carswell, 1972) at 671.

GENUS. *n.* [L.] A universal idea or quality common to a whole class, which differentiates every member of that class from all other classes.

GEODESIST. See DOMINION ~.

GEODETIC ELEVATION. 1. An elevation designated by a regulation of the Surveyor General based on the Canadian Geodetic Datum, authorized by O/C 630 of the Privy Council of Canada, dated March 11, 1935, and derived from a numbered precise bench mark established from it, and appearing in an official publication of the Geodetic Survey of Canada. *Land Title Act*, R.S.B.C. 19 9, c. 219, s. 135.

GEOGRAPHICAL POSITIONING SYSTEM. A series of data bases co-ordinated by the Director that contain the geographical positions of survey control markers, land survey monuments and photogrammetric control points. *Surveys Act*, R.S.A. 2000, c. S-26, s. 1.

GEOGRAPHIC WAGE DIFFERENTIAL. Difference in wages dependent on location of work.

GEO-IDENTIFICATION SOFTWARE. Computer software which detects an internet user's geographic location, limiting access to users from one or more geographic areas.

GEOLOGIST. See PROFESSIONAL ~.

GEOLOGICAL WORK. Work involving direct collection, examination, processing or other analysis, in the field or laboratory, of lithological, paleontological or geochemical materials recovered from surface outcrops or the sea-floor or subsurface and includes the analysis and interpretation of mechanical well logs.

GEOLOGY. See PRACTICE OF ~; PROFESSIONAL ~.

GEOPHYSICAL EQUIPMENT. Equipment used for or in connection with or preparatory to geophysical exploration. *Oil and Natural Gas Act*, R.S.P.E.I. 1988, c. O-5, s. 1.

GEOPHYSICAL EXPLORATION. Any investigation of the subsurface of the land and includes (a) seismic operations, (b) gravimetric operations, (c) magnetic operations, (d) electrical operations, (e) geochemical operations, (f) test drilling, and (g) any other operation employed to determine geologic or other subsurface conditions.

GEOPHYSICAL OPERATION. An operation conducted on or over land to determine geologic or other conditions in the subsurface for the purpose of locating reservoirs, and includes (a) a seismic program, (b) a gravity, magnetic, electrical, radioactivity or geochemical survey, and (c) a hole that is 150 m or less in depth drilled through sedimentary rock to obtain information respecting structure, stratigraphy or lithology. *The Oil and Gas Act*, S.M. 1993, c. 4, s. 1.

GEOPHYSICAL SURVEY. Any investigation carried out on the surface of the ground to determine the nature and structure of the subsurface. *Territorial Land Use Regulations*, C.R.C., c. 1524, s. 2.

GEOPHYSICAL WORK. Work involving the indirect measurement of the physical properties of rocks in order to determine the depth, thickness, structural configuration or history of deposition thereof and includes the processing, analysis and interpretation of material or data obtained from that work.

GEOPHYSICIST. See PROFESSIONAL ~.

GEOPHYSICS. See PRACTICE OF ~; PROFESSIONAL ~.

GEORGIAN BAY AND ST. LAWRENCE PORTS. The ports of Midland, Port McNicoll, Collingwood, Owen Sound, Goderich, Sarnia, Windsor, Port Colborne, Toronto, Kingston, Prescott, Montreal, Sorel, Trois-Rivières and Quebec City. *Feed Grain Reserve Stock Regulations*, C.R.C., c. 324, s. 2.

GEOSCIENCE. See PRACTICE OF ~; PROFESSIONAL GEOSCIENCE.

GEOTECHNICAL WORK. Work, in the field or laboratory, undertaken to determine the physical properties of materials recovered from the surface or subsurface or the seabed or its subsoil of any frontier lands. Canada statutes.

GEOTHERMAL EXPLORATION. Investigation of the subsurface of land for the presence of a geothermal resource by means of (a) seismic, gravimetric, magnetic, radiometric, electric, geological or geochemical operations, (b) well drilling or test hole drilling, or (c) any other method approved by the division head. *Geothermal Resources Act*, R.S.B.C. 1996, c. 171, s. 1.

GEOTHERMAL RESOURCE. The natural heat of the earth and all substances that derive an added value from it, including steam, water and water vapour heated by the natural heat of the earth and all substances dissolved in the steam, water or water vapour obtained from a well, but does not include (a) water that has a temperature less than 80°C at the point where it reaches the surface, or (b) hydrocarbons. *Geothermal Resources Act*, R.S.B.C. 1996, c. 171, s. 1.

GEOTHERMAL WELL. A well in which casing is run and that the minister considers is producing or capable of producing a geothermal resource from a geothermal resource bearing zone. *Geothermal Resources Act*, R.S.B.C. 1996, c. 171, s. 1.

GERIATRIC. *adj.* Relating to aged persons. Aged.

GERIATRIC CENTRE. Includes a nursing home, supervisory care home, sheltered care home or other institution used primarily for the purpose of providing supervisory care, personal care and nursing care for persons who by reason of need, age, infirmity or blindness are unable to care for themselves. *The Election Act*, R.S.S. 1978, c. E-6, s. 2.

GERMAN. *n.* A brother; one related as closely as a brother.

GERRYMANDER. *v.* To manipulate boundaries of constituencies unfairly in order to secure a disproportionate influence in an election for one party or candidate.

GESTATION. *n.* The period of development of a mammal in the womb.

GET. *n.* A bill of divorce under Hebraic law.

GETTLER-YAMAKAMI TEST. A test for blood chloride levels. F.A. Jaffe, *A Guide to Pathological Evidence*, 3d ed. (Toronto: Carswell, 1991) at 110.

GET-UP. *n.* Of products, in passing-off actions, refers to their whole visible external appearance in the form in which they are likely to be seen by the public before purchase. If the goods are packaged, their get-up means the appearance of the package taken as a whole. *Ciba-Geigy Canada Ltd. v. Apotex Inc.*, [1992] 3 S.C.R. 120.

GHOST WRITER. A writer who writes a story based on material supplied by a well-known person. H.G. Fox, *The Canadian Law of Copyright and Industrial Designs*, 2d ed. (Toronto: Carswell, 1967) at 246-247.

GIBBET. *n.* A beam laid over a post or posts from which prisoners were hanged.

GIBLETS. *n.* The liver from which the bile sac has been removed, the heart from which the pericardial sac has been removed and the gizzard from which the contents and lining have been removed. *Dressed and Eviscerated Poultry Regulations*, C.R.C., c. 283, s. 2.

GIFT. *n.* 1. " . . . [T]o constitute a 'gift', it must appear that the property transferred was transferred voluntarily and not as the result of a contractual obligation to transfer it and that no advantage of a material character was received by the transferor by way of return." *Commissioner of Taxation of the Commonwealth v. McPhail* (1967), 41 A.L.J.R. 346 at 348, Owen J., cited with approval in *R. v. McBurney*, [1985] 2 C.T.C. 214 at 218, 85 D.T.C. 5433, 20 E.T.R. 283, 62 N.R. 104 (Fed. C.A.), Heald, Urie and Stone JJ.A. 2. " . . . [C]onstituted by two things—the words giving (not merely expressing a promise or intention) and possession in the donee . . ." *Standard Trust Co. v. Hill* (1922), 68 D.L.R. 722 at 723, [1922] 2 W.W.R. 1003, 18 Alta. L.R. 137 (C.A.), Beck J.A. (Stuart and Hyndman JJ.A. concurring). 3. In its usual meaning, a gift is a voluntary transfer of personal property without consideration. *Birce v. Birce*

(2001), 2001 CarswellOnt 3481 (C.A.). See CLASS ~; DEED OF ~; INTER VIVOS ~.

GIFT INTER VIVOS. A gift made by a living person to another living person.

GIFT MORTIS CAUSA. " . . . [A] gift conditioned upon the death of the donor . . . *McIntyre v. Royal Trust Co.*, [1945] 3 D.L.R. 71 at 75, [1945] 2 W.W.R. 364, 53 Man. R. 353 (K.B.), Dysart J. See DONATIO MORTIS CAUSA.

GIFT TAX. Tax imposed on the transfer of property by gift.

GIGA. *pref.* 10^9. Prefix for multiples and submultiples of basic, supplementary and derived units of measurement. *Weights and Measures Act*, S.C. 1970-71-72, c. 36, schedule I.

GILD. *n.* 1. A tax; tribute. 2. A society formed for mutual benefit and protection.

GILDABLE. *adj.* Legally bound to pay gild.

GILDA MERCATORIA. [L.] A guild merchant; an assembly or meeting of merchants.

GILL. *n.* 1 /32 gallon. *Weights and Measures Act*, S.C. 1970-71-72, c. 36, schedule II.

GILL NET. 1. A net that is used to catch fish by enmeshing them and that does not enclose an area of water. *Fishery Regulations*, Canada regulations. 2. A floating gill net that is neither anchored nor staked but floats freely with the tide or current. *Pacific Commercial Salmon Fishery Regulations*, C.R.C., c. 823, s. 2.

GILT-EDGED SECURITY. An investment of the highest class.

GIRL. See YOUNG ~.

GISTMENT. *n.* Agistment.

GIVE. *v.* To transfer property without compensation.

GIVEN NAME. 1. " . . . [A] name given at birth to distinguish it from the surname, family or ancestral name." *Wilson, Re* (1984), 51 C.B.R.(N.S.) 85 at 87, 46 O.R. (2d) 28, 8 D.L.R. (4th) 271, 4 P.P.S.A.C. 69, 26 B.L.R. 271 (S.C.), Saunders J. 2. Includes a given name, Christian name or baptismal name. 3. Includes an initial.

GIVE TIME. For a creditor to enter into a binding contract which permits a debtor to defer the payment of money or to do something after the time it was originally agreed the act should be done.

GIVE-WAY VESSEL. A vessel that is required by these Regulations to keep out of the way of another vessel. *Collision Regulations*, C.R.C., c. 1416, s. 2.

GLASS. *n*. Refers to glass in the doors, windows, side wings, or windshield, of a motor vehicle, but does not refer to the glass in frost shields or in storm windows installed on the outside of a bus. *The Highway Traffic* Act, S.M. 1985-86, c. 3, s. 52(1). See LAMINATED ~; PLATE ~ INSURANCE; SAFETY ~; TEMPERED ~; WIRED ~.

GLASS SCREEN. See WIRED~.

GLAZIER AND METAL MECHANIC. Person who (a) performs layout, fabrication, assembly and installation of extruded frames, hardware, store fronts, wall facings, manual sliding doors, window sashes, manual door closers, automatic door operators and curtain walls, (b) performs layout, fabrication, assembly and installation of suspended glass fronts, stuck glass fronts, auto glass, art glass, aquariums and similar special products, (c) cuts, fits and installs glass in wood and metal frames for windows, skylights, store fronts and display cases, or on building fronts, interior walls, ceilings, tables and similar surfaces by means of mastic, screws or decorative moldings, and (d) reads and understands design drawings, manufacturers' literature and installation diagrams. *Apprenticeship and Tradesmen's Qualification Act*, R.R.O. 1980, Reg. 39, s. 1.

GLEBE. *n*. The land held as part of an ecclesiastical benefice.

GLIDER. *n*. A non-power-driven heavier-than-air aircraft that derives its lift in flight from aerodynamic reactions on surfaces that remain fixed during flight. *Canadian Aviation Regulations*, SOR/96-433, s. 101.01.

GLOBAL INFORMATION INFRASTRUCTURE. Includes electromagnetic emissions, communications systems, information technology systems and networks, and any data or technical information carried on, contained in or relating to those emissions, systems or networks.

GLOBAL SUM. An award in which no specific amount is allocated under separate heads of damage.

GLOSS. *n*. Interpretation consisting of an annotation, explanation or comment on any passage in a text. See SPECULAR ~.

GLOTTIS. *n*. The vocal cords including the space between. F.A. Jaffe, *A Guide to Pathological Evidence*, 3d ed. (Toronto: Carswell, 1991) at 220.

GLOW. See AFTER~.

GLUESTOCK. *n*. The hair, bones, hoofs, horns, fleshings, hide cuttings or parings of an animal or any other part of an animal that may be used in the manufacture of glue. *Animal Disease and Protection Regulations*, C.R.C., c. 296, s. 2.

G.M.A.C. *abbr*. General Motors Acceptance Corporation.

GNP. *abbr*. Gross national product.

GOB. *n*. The space in a mine from which coal has been mined and that has been allowed to subside or fall in. *Coal Mines (CBDC) Safety Regulations*, C.R.C., c. 1011, s. 2.

GOD. See ACT OF ~ CLAUSE.

GODSON. *abbr*. Godson, Mining Commissioner's Cases (Ont.), 1911-1917.

GOING CONCERN. A business operating in the usual and ordinary way as it was intended to operate.

GOING CONCERN ASSETS. The value of the assets of a plan, including income due and accrued, determined on the basis of a going concern valuation. *Pension Benefits Standards Regulations, 1985*, SOR/87-19, s. 2, as am.

GOING CONCERN LIABILITIES. The present value of the accrued benefits of a plan, including amounts due and unpaid, determined on the basis of a going concern valuation. *Pension Benefits Standards Regulations, 1985*, SOR/87-19, s. 2, as am.

GOING CONCERN VALUATION. A valuation of the assets and liabilities of a plan using actuarial assumptions and methods that are in accordance with accepted actuarial practice for the valuation of a plan that is not expected to be terminated or wound up. *Pension Benefits Standards Regulations, 1985*, SOR/87-19, s. 2, as am.

GOING-CONCERN VALUE. The worth of an established business or plant with its earning power already entirely or partly matured. A. Bissett-Johnson & W.M. Holland, eds., *Matrimonial Property Law in Canada* (Toronto: Carswell, 1980) at V-10.

GOING PRIVATE TRANSACTION. 1. Re-organization of a corporation in such a way as to eliminate its minority shareholders and convert to private company status. 2. An amalgamation, arrangement, consolidation or other transaction carried out under this Act by a corporation that would cause the interest of a holder of a participating security of the corporation to be terminated without the consent of the holder and without the substitution therefor of an interest of equivalent value in a participating security that, (a) is issued by the corporation, an affiliate of the corporation or a successor body corporate, and (b) is not limited in the extent of its participation in earnings to any greater extent than the participating security for which it is substituted, but does not include, (c) an acquisition under section 188, (d) a redemption of, or other compulsory termination of the interest of the holder in, a security if the security is redeemed or otherwise acquired. in accordance with the terms and conditions attaching thereto or under a requirement of the articles relating to the class of securities or of this Act or (e) a proceeding under Part XVI. *Business Corporations Act*, R.S.O. 1990, c. B.16, s. 190.

GOING RATE. The prevailing rate of wages.

GOLD BEARING QUARTZ. All gold bearing rock in situ. *Mines Act*, R.S.N.S. 1967, c. 185, s. 1.

GOLD CLAUSE OBLIGATION. Any obligation incurred before, on or after the 3rd day of June, 1939 (including any such obligation that has, at any time before, on or after that date, matured or been repudiated) that purports to give to the creditor a right to require payment in gold or in gold coin or in an amount of money measured thereby, and includes any such obligation of the Government of Canada or of any province. *Gold Clauses Act*, R.S.C. 1970, c. G-4, s.2.

GOLD CLAUSES ACT. An act which declares any gold clause obligation, wherever payable, contrary to public policy. J.G. McLeod, *The Conflict of Laws* (Calgary: Carswell, 1983) at 516.

GOLDEN HANDSHAKE. A termination payment provided to a senior executive or manager.

GOLDEN PARACHUTE. When a change in control of a business occurs, a provision in the employment contract of senior officers guaranteeing several years salary if they lose or choose to leave their jobs as a result of the change. S.M. Beck *et al.*, *Cases and Materials on Partnerships and Canadian Business Corporations* (Toronto: The Carswell Company Limited, 1983) at 416.

GOLDEN RULE. When construing a statute, the ordinary meaning of the words and the ordinary rules of grammatical construction should be used unless that produces a result contrary to the intent of the legislators or leading to obvious repugnance or absurdity. P.St.J. Langan, ed., *Maxwell on The Interpretation of Statutes*, 12th ed. (Bombay: N.M. Tripathi,1976) at 43.

GOLDEN THREAD. " . . . [T]he presumption of innocence, . . ." *R. v. Chaulk* (1990), 2 C.R. (4th) 1 at 27, 119 N.R. 161, [1991] 2 W.W.R. 385, 69 Man. R. (2d) 161, 62 C.C.C. (3d) 193, 1 C.R.R. (2d) 1, [1990] 3 S.C.R. 1303, Lamer C.J.C. (Dickson C.J.C., La Forest and Cory JJ. concurring).

GOLD FRANC. A unit consisting of sixty-five and one-half milligrams of gold of millesimal fineness nine hundred. *Canada Shipping Act*, R.S.C. 1985, c. S-9, s. 584.

GONZALES TEST. See PARAFFIN TEST.

GOOD. *adj.* 1. When describing pleading, sound or valid. 2. Satisfactory, adequate, having positive qualities.

GOOD BEHAVIOUR. The standard necessary to remain in office. Requirement of a level of integrity necessary to maintain public confidence in the institution and the process of appointment to office.

GOOD CAUSE. 1. " . . . [F]air and just . . ." *Vernon (City) v. British Columbia Public Utilities Commission* (1953), 9 W.W.R. (N.S.) 384 at 384 (B.C. C.A.), the court per O'Halloran J.A. 2. "[In s. 73 of the County Courts Act, R.S.B.C. 1924, c. 53] . . . means something that would bring the case out of the ordinary, . . ." *Goldie v. Colquhoun* (1930), 42 B. R. 356 at 357, [1930] 1 W.W.R. 624, [1930] 2 D.L.R. 1002 (C.A.), Martin J.A. 3. "[In Saskatchewan King's Bench Rule of Court 672(3)] . . . includes not only misconduct or oppression on the part of the successful party, but anything, which would make it just and reasonable, that there should be a departure from the rule that costs should follow the event. Forster v. Farquhar, [1893] 1 Q.B. 564 [(U.K.)] . . . *Dominion Fire Insurance Co. v. Thomson* (1923), 17 Sask. L.R. 527 at 531, [1923] 3 W.W.R. 1265, [1923] 4 D.L.R. 903 (C.A.), Lamont J.A. (Haultain C.J.S. and McKay J.A. concurring). 4. " . . . [I]ncludes (a) misconduct of the party, (b) miscarriage in the procedure; (c) oppressive and vexatious conduct of the proceedings. Also, anything which would make it just and reasonable that the party be deprived of costs." *Welk v. Saskatchewan (Social Services Appeal Board)* (1985), 21 Admin. L.R. 78 at 93, 44 Sask. R. 252, 23 D.L.R. (4th) 698, [1986] 2 W.W.R. 333 (Q.B.), Grotsky J.

GOOD CONSIDERATION. 1. " . . . '[V]aluable [consideration]' . . ." *China Software Corp. v. Leambigler* (1990), 49 B.L.R. 173 at 177 (B.C. S.C.), Drake J. 2. " . . . [T]here must be a real and honest bargain, and not one which is so made that it is manifest that the form which it took was in reality a sham, or was intended to be and was a fraud. There may be overvaluation and yet an honest bargain. The test is honesty, and if that is present the Court will not inquire into the adequacy or inadequacy of the consideration. . ." *Hood v. Caldwell* (1921), 64 D.L.R. 442 at 456, 20 O.W.N. 251, 50 O.L.R. 397 (C.A.), Hodgins J.A.

GOOD FAITH. 1. " . . . [A] bona fide belief in the existence of a state of facts which, had they existed, would have justified him in acting as he did. . . The contrast is with an act of such a nature that it is wholly wide of any statutory or public duty, i.e., wholly unauthorized and where there exists no colour for supposing that it could have been an authorized one. In such case there can be no question of good faith or honest motive." *Chaput v. Romain* (1955), 1 D.L.R. (2d) 241 at 261, [1955] S.C.R. 834, 114 C.C.C. 170, Kellock J. (Rand J. concurring). 2. " . . . In the context of s. 8 of the Charter, good faith has come to mean that state of mind which relies upon express statutory authority to support the lawfulness of a search . . ." *R. v. Klimchuk* (1991), 67 C.C.C. (3d) 385 at 419, 8 C.R. (4th) 327, 32 M.V.R. (2d) 202, 4 B.C.A.C. 26, 9 W.A.C. 26, 9 C.R.R. (2d) 153 (C.A.), Wood J.A. 3. "[In the clause] . . . 'any amount payable under the contract which has not been paid by the owner under the contract in good faith' . . . [means] without knowledge that a lien claim had been registered. . ." *Red Deer College v. W. W Construction (Lethbridge) Ltd.*, [1989] 56 D.L.R. (4th) 204 at 206, 32 C.L.R. 155, [1988] 3 W.W.R. 1987, 65 Alta. L.R. (2d) 1, 93 A.R. 393 (C.A.), the court per Bracco J.A. 4. . . [R]efers to the quality of his belief as to the intoxication of the person in question (when taken into custody) and of his recovery (when released from custody). If it also applies to his conduct towards the person during the period of custody, then I believe it must be taken to require a reasonable standard

of conduct towards the detainee similar to that required by the common law. One could be said to act in good faith in the use of force only if the force reasonably relates to the performance of the duties imposed by law." *Rumsey v. R*, [1984] 5 W.W.R. 585 at 592, 32 Alta. L.R. (2d) 364, 12 D.L.R. (4th) 44 (Fed. T.D.), Strayer J. 5. Honesty in fact in the conduct of the transaction concerned. *Bank Act, 1991* S.C. 1991, c. 46, s. 81. 6. Honestly whether done negligently or not. 7. Good faith has been established in situations where the violation stemmed from police reliance upon a statute or from the following of a procedure which was later found to infringe the Charter. *R. v. Wise*, [1992] 1 S.C.R. 527. See IN ~; UBERRIMAE FIDES.

GOOD FAITH PURCHASER. A purchaser for value, in good faith and without notice of any adverse claim, (a) who takes delivery of a security certificate in bearer form or order form or of a security certificate in registered form issued to the purchaser or endorsed to the purchaser or endorsed in blank, (b) in whose name an uncertified security is registered or recorded in records maintained by or on behalf of the issuer as a result of the issue or transfer of the security to the purchaser, or (c) who is a transferee or pledgee as provided in section 85. *Business Corporations Act*, R.S.O. 1990, c. B.16, s. 53.

GOODS. *n.* 1. Chattels personal other than things in action or money, and includes emblements, industrial growing crops and things attached to or forming part of the land that are agreed to be severed before sale or under the contract of sale. 2. Includes tokens, coupons or other documents or things issued or sold by a seller to a buyer that are exchangeable or redeemable for goods or services. *Consumer Protection acts*. 3. Anything that is the subject of trade or commerce. *Criminal Code*, R.S.C. 1985, c. C-46, s. 379. 4. Any article that is or may be the subject of trade or commerce, but does not include land or any interest therein. *Bills of Exchange Act*, R.S.C. 1985, c. B-4, s. 188. 5. Includes all personal property other than vessels. 6. For greater certainty, includes conveyances and animals. *Customs Act*, R.S.C. 1985 (2d Supp.), c. 1, s. 2. 7. "[In the Customs Act, R.S.C. 1970, c. C-40] . . . must . . . be taken to include all movable effects of any kind. . . In the Customs Tariff . . . the word 'goods' is given a general meaning to include all personal effects, and not merely to include strictly items of commerce. . ."" *Ladakis v. R.* (1985), 10 C.E.R. 95

at 102 (Fed. T.D.), Collier J. 8. Includes wares and merchandise. *Factor acts*. 9. Personal property. *Consumer Protection acts* 10. "Coin is not money . . . when it is not used as a means of exchange, or in its aspect as money. . . antique coins that are bought and sold in retail shops are treated as wares or merchandise and are goods . . ." *R. v. Vanek*, [1969] 2 O.R. 724 at 727, [1970] 1 C.C.C. 111, 6 D.L.R. (3d) 591 (H.C.), Osler J. quoting with approval the lower court judge. 11. Tangible personal property other than chattel paper, documents of title, instruments, money and securities, and includes fixtures, growing crops, the unborn young of animals, timber to be cut, and minerals and hydrocarbons to be extracted; *Personal Property Security Act*, R.S.O. 1990, c. P-10, s. 1. See ABANDONED ~; ASCERTAINED ~; BONDED ~; BULK ~; CANADIAN ~; CONSUMER ~; CONTAINERIZED ~; DANGEROUS ~; DISPLAY ~; DOCUMENT OF TITLE TO ~; FUGITIVE'S ~; FUNERAL ~; FUNGIBLE ~; FUTURE ~; HEALTH ~; HOT ~; HOUSEHOLD ~; IDENTICAL ~; INCINERATOR ~; LIKE~; OBSOLETE OR SURPLUS ~; PRE-PACKAGED ~; QUALITY OF ~; SALE OF ~; SECOND-HAND ~; SHOP ~; SIMILAR ~; SLANDER OF ~; SPECIFIC ~; SUBSIDIZED ~; SYSTEM ~; TRESPASS TO ~; UNASCERTAINED ~; UNITIZED ~; UNSOLD ~; UNSOLICITED ~.

GOOD SAMARITAN LAW. 1. A statute which protects those who render assistance in emergencies from liability where their assistance increases the injury to the one they seek to rescue or assist. 2. Despite the rules of common law, a person described (health care professional or person who provides first aid) in subsection (2) who voluntarily and without reasonable expectation of compensation or reward provides the services described in that subsection is not liable for damages that result from the person's negligence in acting or failing to act while providing the services, unless it is established that the damages were caused by the gross negligence of the person. *Good Samaritan Act, 2001*, S.O. 2001, c. 2, s. 2.

GOODS AND CHATTELS. 1. Things personal. 2. In addition to the things usually understood thereby, any movable property of any kind whatsoever which may be left with a keeper of a storage warehouse for storage. *Storage Warehouse Keepers Act*, R.S.N.S. 1989, c. 447, s. 2. 3. Includes shares and dividends of a stockholder

in any incorporated company in New Brunswick having transferable joint stock. *Memorials and Executions Act*, R.S.N.B. 1973, c. M-9, s. 23.

GOODS AND SERVICES TAX. The federal tax imposed on the consumption of goods and services, including imports into Canada. Applied to the consideration paid or payable for goods or services.

GOOD SCIENTIFIC PRACTICES. For the development of test data, conditions and procedures similar to those set out in the OECD Test Guidelines; for laboratory practices, practices similar to those set out in the OECD Principles of Good Laboratory Practice; and for human experience data, a peer-reviewed study of clinical cases. *Consumer Chemicals and Containers Regulations, 2001*, SOR/2001-269, s. 1.

GOODS CONTRACT. A contract for the purchase of articles, commodities, equipment, goods, materials or supplies and includes (a) a contract for printing or for the reproduction of printed matter, and (b) a contract for the construction or repair of a vessel. *Government Contracts Regulations*, SOR 87-402, s. 2.

GOODS IN BULK. The following goods laden or freighted in ships and, except as otherwise provided in this definition, not bundled or enclosed in bags, bales, boxes, cases, casks, crates or any other container: (a) grain and grain products, including flour and mill feeds in bulk or in sacks, (b) ores and minerals (crude, screened, sized, refined or concentrated, but not otherwise processed), including ore concentrates in sacks, sand, stone and gravel, coal and coke, and liquids, (c) pulpwood, woodpulp, poles and logs, including pulpwood and woodpulp in bales, and (d) waste paper loaded as full ship's cargo, iron and steel scrap and pig iron. Transport Act, R.S.C. 1985, c. T-17, s. 2.

GOODS OF A DANGEROUS NATURE. Goods that by reason of their nature, quantity or mode of stowage are either singly or collectively liable to endanger the lives of the passengers or imperil the ship, and includes all substances determined by the Governor in Council, in regulations made by him, to be dangerous goods. *Canada Shipping Act*, R.S.C. 1985, c. S-9, s. 2.

GOODS OF THE SAME CLASS OR KIND. In relation to goods being appraised, means imported goods that (a) are within a group or range of imported goods produced by a particular industry or industry sector that includes identical goods and similar goods in relation to the goods being appraised, and (b) for the purposes of (i) section 51, were produced in any country and exported from any country, and (ii) section 52, were produced in and exported from the same country as the country in and from which the goods being appraised were produced and exported. *Customs Act*, R.S.C. 1985 (2d Supp.), c. 1, s. 45.

GOODS OR SERVICES. See CEME-TERY ~.

GOOD STANDING. See MEMBER IN ~.

GOODS, WARES AND MERCHANDISE. Includes products of agriculture, products of aquaculture, products of the forest, products of the quarry and mine, products of the sea, lakes and rivers, and all other articles of commerce. *Bank Act*, S.C. 1991, c. 46, s. 425.

GOODWILL. *n.* " . . . [T]he benefit and advantage of the good name, reputation and connection of a business. It is the attractive force which brings in custom." *Inland Revenue Commissioners v. Muller & Co.'s Margarine Ltd.*, [1901] A. C. 217 at 223-4, Lord Macnaghten.

GOOF BALL. See BARBITURATE.

GOON. *n.* A person who engages in violence during a strike.

GOOSE FLESH. See CUTIS ANSERINA.

GO PUBLIC. To issue shares of a corporation to the general public for the first time.

GORE. *n.* A parcel of land in the shape of a wedge.

GOVERNING AUTHORITY. See LO-CAL ~.

GOVERNING EXECUTIVE AUTHORITY. The executive committee, executive board, management committee, grand executive committee, or such other board, committee or body as is charged under the constitution, bylaws and rules of a fraternal society with its general management between general meetings. *Insurance acts.*

GOVERNMENT. *n.* 1. " . . . [I]n its generic sense—meaning the whole of the governmental apparatus of the state. . ." *Dolphin Delivery Ltd. v. R.W.D.S.U., Local 580* (1986), [1987] 1 W.W.R. 577 at 597, 38 C.C.L.T. 184, 71 N.R. 83, [1986] 2 S.C.R. 573, 9 B.C.L.R. (2d) 273, 87 C.L.L.C. 14,002, 33 D.L.R. (4th) 174, 25 C.R.R. 321, [1987] D.L.Q. 69, McIntyre J. (Dickson C.J.C., Estey, Chouinard and Le Dain JJ. concurring). 2. " . . . [T]he executive or ad-

ministrative branch of a government. This is the sense in which one generally speaks of the Government of Canada or of a province . . ." *Dolphin Delivery Ltd. v. R.W.D.S.U., Local 580* (1986), [1987] 1 W.W.R. 577 at 597, 38 C.C.L.T. 184, 71 N.R. 83, [1986] 2 S.C.R. 573, 9 B.C.L.R. (2d) 273, 87 C.L.L.C. 14,002, 33 D.L.R. (4th) 174, 25 C.R.R. 321, [1987] D.L.Q. 69, McIntyre J. (Dickson C.J.C., Estey, Chouinard and Le Dain JJ. concurring). 3. In a political sense, the members of Parliament and the Senate, federally, or the legislature, provincially, who support the current Prime Minister or Premier. 4. The government of Canada or of any province and includes any department, commission, board or branch of any such government. *Canada Evidence Act*, R.S.C. 1985, c. C-5, s. 31. 5. (a) The Government of Canada, (b) the government of a province, or (c) Her Majesty in right of Canada or a province. *Criminal Code*, R.S.C. 1985, c. C-46, s. 118. 6. (i) Her Majesty in right of Canada or of a province, or (ii) the government of a foreign state or of a political subdivision of a foreign state. See AGENCY OF ~; AGENCY OF THE ~; ASSOCIATED ~; CABINET ~; CHIEF ~ WHIP; EXECUTIVE ~; FEDERAL ~; FOREIGN ~; HOST ~; LOCAL ~; MUNICIPAL ~; PARLIAMENTARY ~; RESPONSIBLE ~; SOVEREIGN ~.

GOVERNMENT AGENCY. 1. (a) A department of the government, (b) a corporation that is an agent of the Crown in right of a province, or (c) any corporation, commission, board or other body empowered to exercise quasi-judicial or governmental functions and whose members are appointed by an act of a legislature, a Lieutenant Governor in Council or a member of any executive council or any combination thereof. 2. Any board, commission or body, whether incorporated or not, all the members of which or all the members of the governing board of which (a) are appointed by an Act of a legislature or by a Lieutenant Governor in Council, or (b) if not so appointed are, in the discharge of their duties, public officers or servants of the Crown or, for the proper discharge of their duties, are directly or indirectly responsible to the Crown.

GOVERNMENTAL ORGANIZATION. A Ministry, commission, board or other administrative unit of the Government of Ontario, and includes any agency thereof. *Ombudsman Act*, R.S.O. 1990, c. 0.6, s. 1.

GOVERNMENT ASSISTANCE. Assistance from a government, municipality or other public authority whether as a grant, subsidy, forgivable loan, deduction from tax, investment allowance or as any other form of assistance other than as a deduction under subsection (5) or (6). *Income Tax Act*, R.S.C. 1952, c. 148 (as am. S.C. 1985, c. 45, s. 72(5)), s. 127(9).

GOVERNMENT BILL. A bill approved by cabinet and introduced into a legislature by a minister.

GOVERNMENT BODY. The Legislative Assembly, or a department or division of the Government of the Northwest Territories and includes the office of any commission, board, bureau or other branch of the public service of the Northwest Territories. *Archives Act*, S.N.W.T. 1981 (3d Sess.), c. 2, s. 2.

GOVERNMENT BUOY. A buoy maintained by Her Majesty in right of Canada or in right of any province or any agent thereof, or by a municipal corporation or by a corporation that is owned or controlled by Her Majesty in right of Canada. *Private Buoy Regulations*, C.R.C., c. 1460, s. 2.

GOVERNMENT CONTRACT. A contract entered into with the Crown for any purpose, and includes any contract for: (a) the supply to or by the Crown of any goods or services; (b) the sale, lease or other disposition of any real property to or by the Crown; (c) the construction of any public work for the Crown; (d) the determination of compensation or damages with respect to real property taken, damaged or purchased by the Crown; (e) the determination of compensation or damages to be paid by the Crown in cases not provided for in clause (d); or (f) the lending of moneys to or by the Crown. *The Members' Conflict of Interest Act*, S.S. 1993, c. M-11.11, s. 15.

GOVERNMENT DISTRICT. See LOCAL ~.

GOVERNMENT GUARANTEED BOND. A bond of the Government of Canada or a bond unconditionally guaranteed as to principal and interest by the Government of Canada that is (a) payable to bearer, (b) hypothecated to the Receiver General in accordance with the Domestic Bonds of Canada Regulations, or (c) registered in the name of the Receiver General. *Government Contracts Regulations*, C.R.C., c. 701, s. 2.

GOVERNMENT HOUSE. 1. Name given to house where the Lieutenant Governor resides. 2. The building at 12845-102 Avenue in the City of Edmonton commonly known as "Government House". *Government House Act*, R.S.A. 2000, c. G-9, s. 1.

GOVERNMENT HOUSE LEADER. The member of the government, responsible to the Prime Minister, who arranges government business in the House of Commons. A. Fraser, W.A. Dawson, & J. Holtby, eds., *Beauchesne's Rules and Forms of the House of Commons of Canada*, 6th ed. (Toronto: Carswell, 1989) at 56.

GOVERNMENT INCENTIVE SECURITY. A security designed to enable the holder thereof to receive a grant or other monetary benefit, such as a right to a credit against taxes or a deduction in the determination of income for tax purposes, pursuant to provisions of a statute or a regulation of Canada or a province of Canada.

GOVERNMENT INSTITUTION. Any department, branch, office, board, agency, commission, corporation or body for the administration or affairs of which a Minister of the Crown is accountable to the Parliament of Canada. *Emergency Preparedness Act*, S.C. 1988, c. 11. s. 2.

GOVERNMENT ISSUE. Machinery, machine tools, equipment or defence supplies furnished by the Minister or by an agent of Her Majesty on behalf of Her Majesty or on behalf of an associated government or acquired or purchased on behalf of Her Majesty or on behalf of an associated government with funds provided by the Minister or by an agent of Her Majesty or by an associated government. *Defence Production Act*, R.S.C. 1985, c. D-1, s. 2.

GOVERNMENT NEGOTIATOR. The President of the Treasury Board, established in accordance with any Act of the province governing financial administration, or such other person authorized by her or him to bargain collectively under her or his control and supervision on behalf of the employer.

GOVERNMENT OF ALBERTA. Her Majesty in right of Alberta.

GOVERNMENT OF CANADA. 1. Her Majesty in right of Canada, that is, the Crown. *Formea Chemicals Ltd v. Polymer Corp.*, [1968] S.C.R. 754 at 758, 38 Fox Pat. C. 116, 55 C.P.R. 38, 64 D.L.R. (2d) 114, the court per Martland J. 2. The Crown in right of Canada, every corporation and agency thereof and the Governor General in Council. 3. " . . . [M]ay be interpreted and read as the Cabinet, which by convention is a committee of Parliament." *Operation Disman-tle Inc. v. R.* (1983), 39 C.P.C. 120 at 128, [1983] 1 F.C. 429 (C.A.), Cattanach J.A.

GOVERNMENT OF ONTARIO. 1. . . . [T]he Crown (Her Majesty the Queen in right of Ontario) . . . *Mai v. Mississauga (City)* (1990), 67 D.L.R. (4th) 138 at 145, 72 O.R. (2d) 97, 47 C.P.C. (2d) 1 (H.C.), Farley J. 2. Includes every ministry thereof and every commission or board created by any Act of the Legislature. *Government Contracts Hours and Wages Act*, R.S.O. 1990, c. G.8, s. 1.

GOVERNMENT OF PRINCE EDWARD ISLAND. Her Majesty in right of the province. *Interpretation Act*, S.P.E.I. 1981, c. 18, s. 26.

GOVERNMENT OF SASKATCHEWAN. The Crown in right of Saskatchewan, every corporation and agency thereof and the Lieutenant Governor in Council. Saskatchewan statutes.

GOVERNMENT OR PUBLIC FACILITY. A facility or conveyance, whether permanent or temporary, that is used or occupied in connection with their official duties by representatives of a state, members of a government, members of a legislature, members of the judiciary, or officials or employees of a state or of any other public authority or public entity, or by officials or employees of an intergovernmental organization. *Criminal Code*, R.S.C. 1985, c. C-46, s. 2.

GOVERNMENT PLAN. A plan of a government, other than the Government of Canada that provides insurance for surgical and medical expenses and in which participation is compulsory. *Public Service Health Insurance Regulations*, C.R.C., c. 339, s. 2.

GOVERNMENT PROPERTY. Property owned or occupied by Her Majesty in right of Canada. *Government Property Traffic* Regulations, C.R.C., c. 887, s. 2.

GOVERNMENT PUBLICATION. Any document prepared by or for a department and reproduced for distribution or sale outside the government.

GOVERNMENT PUBLIC UTILITY. A public utility owned and operated by Her Majesty the Queen in right of a province.

GOVERNMENT RELATED AGENCY. Includes Ontario Hydro, the Ontario Transportation Development Corporation, the Ontario Food Terminal Board, any public institution that is assisted by money appropriated by the Leg-islature and a corporation with or without share capital, the controlling interest of which is owned by the Crown in right of Ontario or whose bonds or debentures are guaranteed by the Crown in right of Ontario. *Ministry of Government Services Act*, R.S.O. 1990, c. M.25, s. 1.

GOVERNMENT SECURITIES. 1. Bonds, debentures, notes or other evidences of indebtedness of, or guaranteed by, the Government of Canada or the government of any province. *Co-operative Credit Associations Act*, R.S.C. 1985, c. C-41, s. 49. 2. Notes, bonds, debentures or interest-bearing or non-interest-bearing treasury bills issued by the Crown or any other securities under which the Crown is the debtor. *Financial Administration Act*, R.S.A. 2000, c. F-12, s. 55(1).

GOVERNMENT SHIP. A ship or vessel that is owned by and is in the service of Her Majesty in right of Canada or of any province or is, while so employed, wholly employed in the service of Her Majesty in that right. *Canada Shipping Act*, R.S.C. 1985, c. S-9, s. 2.

GOVERNMENT STORE. A store established or authorized under this Act by the Board for the sale of spirits, beer or wine. *Liquor Control* Act, R.S.O. 1990, c. L.18, s. 1.

GOVERNMENT VESSEL. A vessel that is owned by and is in the service of Her Majesty in right of Canada or a province or that is in the exclusive possession of Her Majesty in that right. *Canada Shipping Act, 2001*, S.C. 2001, c. 26, s. 2.

GOVERNOR. *n.* 1. The Governor of the Bank or the person acting for the Governor pursuant to this Act. *Bank of Canada Act*, R.S.C. 1985, c. B-2, s. 2. 2. A member of a board. 3. The Lieutenant Governor of the Province or the chief executive officer or administrator carrying on the Government of the Province on behalf and in the name of the Sovereign by whatever title he is designated. *Interpretation Act*, R.S.N.S. 1989, c. 235, s. 7(1). See BOARD OF ~S; LIEUTENANT ~.

GOVERNOR GENERAL. *var.* **GOVERNOR-GENERAL.** The Governor General of Canada or other chief executive officer or administrator carrying on the government of Canada on behalf and in the name of the Sovereign, by whatever title that person is designated.

GOVERNOR GENERAL IN COUNCIL. *var.* **GOVERNOR-GENERAL IN COUN-**

CIL. The Governor General or person administrating the government of Canada, acting by and with the advice of, or by and with the advice and consent of, or in conjunction with the Queen's Privy Council for Canada.

GOVERNOR IN COUNCIL. 1. The Governor General of Canada acting by and with the advice of, or by and with the advice and consent of, or in conjunction with the Queen's Privy Council for Canada. 2. The Lieutenant Governor acting by and with the advice of the Executive Council of the Province. See LIEUTENANT ~.

GOVERNOR OF CANADA. The Governor General of Canada or other chief executive officer or administrator carrying on the Government of Canada on behalf of and in the name of the Sovereign, by whatever title that officer is designated. *Interpretation Act*, R.S.C. 1985, c. I-21, s. 35.

GOVT. *abbr.* Government.

GO WITHOUT DAY. Formerly when a ,proceeding was dismissed, the plaintiff was said to go without day, i.e., the case was not adjourned to a day in the future.

GOWN. See SILK ~; STUFF ~.

GR. *abbr.* Upper Canada Chancery (Grant), 1849-1922.

GRAB SAMPLE. A quantity of undiluted effluent collected at any given time. *Metal Mining Liquid Effluent Regulations*, C.R.C., c. 819, s. 2.

GRACE. *n.* Dispensation; licence. See DAYS OF ~.

GRADE. *n.* 1. The lowest of the average levels of finished ground adjoining each exterior wall of a building, but does not include localized depressions such as for vehicle or pedestrian entrances. 2. The classification of any livestock or livestock product, fruit, vegetable or other product according to prescribed standards. 3. Includes standard. 4. The percentage content of total nitrogen, available acid and soluble potash stated in that sequence. *Fertilizers Regulations*, C.R.C., c. 666, s. 2. See CANADA PEDIGREED ~;   PAY ~;   SECONDARY SCHOOL~.

GRADED. *adj.* When used with reference to a pipe, means its slope with reference to the true horizontal. *Ontario Water Resources Act*, R.R.O. 1980, Reg. 736, s. 1.

GRADE NAME. 1. Any mark, description or designation of a grade. 2. The name, or name

and number, assigned to any grade of grain established by or under this Act and includes any abbreviation prescribed for that grade name. *Canada Grain Act*, R.S.C. 1985, c. G-10, s. 2. 3. (a) The name, or name and number, assigned to a grade of grain established bar or pursuant to the Canada Grain Act, and (b) a name, or name and number, so nearly resembling any such name, or name and number, as to be calculated or likely to cause confusion. *Grain Buyers Licensing Act*, R.S.A. 1980, c. G-9, s. 1.

GRADE OF PAY. A series of rates of remuneration for a class that provides for a minimum rate, a maximum rate, and such intermediate rates as may be considered necessary to permit periodic increases in remuneration. *Civil Service Act*, R.S.M. 1970, c. C110, s. 2.

GRADER. *n.* A person appointed or designated as a grader pursuant to legislation.

GRADE SEPARATION. A subway or an overhead bridge. *Railway Grade Separations Regulations*, C.R.C., c. 1191, s. 2.

GRADE SIGNAL. A stop and proceed signal equipped with a marker displaying the letter "G". *Regulations No. 0-8, Uniform Code of Operating Rules*, C.R.C., c. 1175, Part III, s. 2.

GRADIENT. *n.* The deviation between the inclination of a road or railway and a level surface.

GRADING. See OFFICIAL ~.

GRADING STATION. A place, other than the premises of a producer grader, where dressed or eviscerated poultry or both dressed and eviscerated poultry is graded and packed. *Dressed and Eviscerate Poultry Regulations* C.R.C., c. 283, s. 2.

GRADING STATION OPERATOR. A person who operates a station at which eggs are graded. *Canadian Egg Licensing Regulations*, C.R.C., c. 655, s. 2.

GRADUATE. *n.* A scholar who takes a university degree.

GRADUS. *n.* [L.] Degree; step.

GRADUS PARENTELAE. [L.] A pedigree; a family tree.

GRAFFER. *n.* A scrivener; a notary.

GRAFFIUM. *n.* A register; a writing-book.

GRAIN. *n.* 1. Includes wheat, oats, barley, rye, corn, buckwheat, flax, beans, peas and all kinds of seeds. 2. 1/7 000 pound. *Weights and Meas-*

ures Act, S.C. 1970-71-72, c. 36, schedule II. 3. Includes the seed of any cereal, legume, grass or fibre. *Seed Grain Purchase Act*, R.S.A. 1980, c. S-10, s. 1. 4. Wheat, barley, oats, corn, rye, Faba beans, soybeans, field peas or colza, or any other substance designated as grain by regulation. *Grain Act*, S. Q. 1979, c. 84, s. 1. See CASH ~; COARSE~; DAMP ~; DRIED ~; EASTERN ~; FEED ~; FOREIGN ~; MIXED ~; SEED ~; SIX ~S; SPRING ~; TOUGH ~; WESTERN ~.

GRAIN ALCOHOL. Alcohol manufactured from grain. See PURE ~.

GRAIN BUYER. A person who carries on or transacts the business of buying grain, either as principal or agent, and either for cash or under any form of contract with respect to delivery or payment, but does not include (a) a person who buys grain for seed, feed or otherwise for his own personal use, (b) a person who is the holder of licence for flour milling or feed milling issued under the Licensing of Trades and Businesses Act and who buys grain that is to be milled, or used for manufacturing purposes, in the mill or mills of the licensee within Alberta, or (c) the employee of either of those persons. *Grain Buyers Licensing Act*, R.S.A. 1980, c. G-9, s. 1.

GRAIN CARGO. A cargo of which the portion consisting of grain is more than one-quarter of the dead weight carrying capacity of the ship carrying it. *Canada Shipping Act*, R.S.C. 1985, c. S-9, s. 2.

GRAIN CORN. Shelled corn or ear corn. *Crop Insurance Act*, R.R.O. 1980, Reg. 205, s. 3.

GRAIN DEALER. A person who, for self or on behalf of another person, receives grain to store, sell, resell, manufacture or process it.

GRAIN DRIER. Any producer or other person who dries grain by artificial means.

GRAIN ELEVATOR. Any building, container, structure or receptacle in which farm produce is received for storage, but does not include, (a) premises where a producer receives or stores farm produce as farm feed for the producer's own live stock or poultry, (b) premises where a producer stores and sells farm produce actually produced by that producer, or (c) premises where a terminal transfer or processor grain elevator is licensed under any Act of the Parliament of Canada. *Grain Elevator Storage Act*, R.S.O. 1990, c. G.10, s. 1.

GRAIN FUTURES. Contracts negotiated by members of The Winnipeg Grain Exchange under the conditions and terms set forth in its by-laws or rules, as principals or agents, for the purchase or sale of grain to be accepted or delivered during future months in respect of which facilities for trading in grain futures have been provided by The Winnipeg Grain Exchange, but does not include contracts for the purchase or sale of cash grain. *Grain Futures Act*, R.S.C. 1985, c. G-11, s. 2.

GRAIN OR CROPS. Wheat, oats, barley, flax, rye, corn, peas, seed of alfalfa, seed of crested wheat grass, seed of brome grass, seed of clover, seed of sunflowers, seed of rape and seed of all commercial grasses. *The Local Improvement Districts Act*, R.S.S. 1978, c. L-31, s. 2.

GRAIN PRODUCT. Any product that is produced by processing or manufacturing any grain alone or with any other grain or substance and that may be presented for storage or handling at an elevator.

GRAIN RECEIPT. A document in prescribed form issued in respect of grain delivered to a process elevator or grain dealer acknowledging receipt of the grain and entitling the holder of the document to payment by the operator of the elevator or the grain dealer for the grain. *Canada Grain Act*, R.S.C. 1985, c. G-10, s. 2.

GRAIN SPIRIT. An alcoholic distillate, obtained from a mash of cereal grain or cereal grain products saccharified by the diastase of malt or by other natural enzyme and fermented by the action of yeast, and from which all or nearly all of the naturally occurring substances other than alcohol and water have been removed. *Food and Drug Regulations*, C.R.C., c. 870, c. B.02.002.

GRAIN STANDARDS COMMITTEE. (a) In the case of western grain, means the Western Grain Standards Committee; and (b) in the case of eastern grain, means the Eastern Grain Standards Committee. *Canada Grain Act*, R.S.C. 1985, c. G-10, s. 24(3).

GRAIN STORAGE RECEIPT. A receipt as prescribed by the regulations that is to be issued a grain elevator operator or authorized representative to the owner of farm produce.

GRAMMATICA FALSA NON VITIAT CHARTAM. [L.] Bad grammar does not invalidate a deed.

GRANDCHILD. *n*. 1. The child of a child. *Succession Law Reform Act*, R.S.O. 1990, c. S.26, s. 1(1). 2. Includes the child of an adopted child. *Insurance acts*. 3. Includes any child or other lineal descendant of a child of the deceased. *Fatal Accidents Act*, R.S.P.E.I. 1988, c. F-5, s. 1(h).

GRAND DISTRESS. Distress which extends to all the goods and chattels which the distrained party has within the county.

GRANDFATHER. *n*. The father of one's parent.

GRANDFATHER CLAUSE. May now be called grandparent clause.

GRAND JURY. An inquisition which sits, receives indictments and hears evidence from the prosecution; any finding is only an accusation, to be tried afterwards.

GRANDMOTHER. *n*. The mother of one's parent.

GRANDPARENT. The mother or father of one's parent. See GRANDCHILD.

GRANDPARENTING. *adj*. Traditionally this has been referred to as a grandfathering. The continuation of existing rights or privileges under new legislation which would do away with them but for a grandparent(ing) provision in the legislation. See GRANDFATHER CLAUSE.

GRANT. *v*. To transfer; to sell; to dispose of.

GRANT. *n*. 1. " . . . [T]he strongest and widest word of gift and conveyance known to the law. . ." *Toronto (City) Board of Education v. Doughty* (1934), [1935] 1 D.L.R. 290 at 294, [1935] O.R. 85 (H.C.), Middleton J.A. 2. Any grant of Crown land, whether by letters patent under the Great Seal, a notification or any other instrument whether in fee or for years, and whether direct from Her Majesty or by or pursuant to any statute. 3. A right created or transferred by the Crown, for example the grant of a charter, franchise, patent or pension. 4. Public money devoted to a special purpose. 5. (a) A grant of probate, (b) a resealed grant of probate or administration, (c) a grant of administration, or (d) a grant of letters of guardianship of the person or estate, or both, of a minor. 6. In respect of a franchise, includes the sale or disposition of the franchise or of an interest in the franchise and, for such purposes, an interest in the franchise includes the ownership of corporation that owns the franchise. *Arthur Wishart Act (Franchise Disclosure), 2000*, S.O. 2000, c. 3, s. 1. 7. Letters patent under the Great Seal, a notification and any other instrument by which territorial lands may be granted in fee simple or for an equivalent estate. See CROWN ~; DEED OF ~; FOREIGN ~; LEGISLATIVE ~; NO ONE CAN BE ALLOWED TO DEROGATE FROM HIS OWN ~; PROPERTY IMPROVEMENT ~; RECOVERABLE ~; RE ~.

GRANTED. *adj*. 1. "[A divorce] . . . decree [is] granted when it has been pronounced in open court and endorsed on the record." *Chant v. Chant* (1976), 30 R.F.L. 72 at 74, 13 O.R. (2d) 581, 71 D.L.R. (3d) 643 (H.C.), Fanjoy L.J.S.C. 2. "Before a decree nisi can be said to be granted it must be pronounced, drawn up, initialled by the judge (or on his behalf), signed by the Registrar and sealed." *Sawers v. Sawers* (1972), 10 R.F.L. 198 at 199, [1973] 1 W.W.R. 287, 30 D.L.R. (3d) 511 (B.C. S.C.), Seaton J.

GRANTEE. *n*. 1. A person to whom one makes a grant. 2. The person to whom real property is transferred by deed for value or otherwise. 3. Includes the bargainee, assignee, transferee, mortgagee or other person to whom a bill of sale is made.

GRANT OF ADMINISTRATION. The grant made when the proper court issues administration. See DE BONIS NON ADMINISTRATIS.

GRANT OF ADMINISTRATION WITH WILL ANNEXED. The grant made if the deceased leaves a will naming no executor or if the named executor declines to act. J.G. McLeod, *The Conflict of Laws* (Calgary: Carswell, 1983) at 400.

GRANT OF PROBATE. The grant made when the proper court issues probate.

GRANTOR. *n*. 1. A person who makes a grant. 2. Includes the bargainor, assignor, transferor, mortgagor, or other person by whom a bill of sale is made. *Bills of Sale acts*. See CREDIT ~.

GRAPE MUST. Grapes that have been destemmed and crushed leaving grape skins pulp and seeds. *Wine Content Act* .S.O. 1990, c. W.9, s. 1.

GRAPE PRODUCT. Grape concentrate, grape juice, grape must or wine. *Wine Content and Labelling Act, 2000*, S.O. 2000, c. 26, Sched. P, s. 2.

GRAPHIC MATERIAL. Books, manuscripts, records, documents, photograph positives or negatives, cinematographic film, maps or any designs or material whose primary object is the communication of information in a visual form other than written or printed language. *Canadian Cultural Property Export Control List*, C.R.C., c. 448, s. 1.

GRAPHIC MEDIUM. A model, map, diagram, photograph or other pictorial or graphic mode of description and includes a record of data, experience, communications or events made by accurate, mechanical, electrical or other scientific methods. *Military Rules of Evidence*, C.R.C., c. 1049, s. 82.

GRAPHIC REPRESENTATION. A representation produced by electrical, electronic, photographic, hand-drawn, or printing methods, and includes a representation produced on a video display terminal.

GRASS. *n*. Slang for marijuana. See LAWN ~ MIXTURE; TURF ~ MIXTURE.

GRASS-ROOTS COMMUNICATION. Appeals to members of the public through the mass media or by direct communication that seek to persuade members of the public to communicate directly with a public office holder in an attempt to place pressure on the public office holder to endorse a particular opinion. *Lobbyists Registration Act, 1998*, S.O. 1998, c. 27, Sched, s. 1.

GRATIS. *adj*. [L.] Without reward or recompense.

GRATIS DICTUM. [L.] A mere assertion; a voluntary statement.

GRATUITOUS. *adj*. Without reward or recompense.

GRATUITOUS AGENCY. The assumption of specific agency tasks, without a fee, along with the assumption of fiduciary duties associated with the trust imposed by the agency.

GRATUITOUS BAILMENT. Bailment without recompense. Three forms are: gratuitous deposit of a chattel with the bailee who is to keep the chattel for the bailor; delivery of a chattel to the bailee, who is to do something without reward for the bailee to or with the chattel; and, gratuitous loan of a chattel by the bailor to the bailee for the bailee's use.

GRATUITOUS PROMISE. Promise made without consideration.

GRATUITY. *n*. 1. A tip. *Canada (Attorney General) v. Canadian Pacific Ltd.* (1986), 86 C.L.L.C. 14,032 at 12,158, [1986] 1 S.C.R. 678, 11 C.C.E.L. 1, 66 N.R. 321, 27 D.L.R. (4th) 1, La Forest J. (Dickson C.J.C., Lamer and Le Dain JJ. concurring). 2. A reward for services rendered. *C. v. Minister of National Revenue* (1950), 2 Tax A.B.C. 6 at 10 (Can. App. Bd.), Graham (Chair) (Monet K.C. concurring).

GRAVAMEN. *n*. The essence of the complaint or grievance. The substantial complaint; the cause or matter.

GRAVE. *n*. Includes a place within a building or structure for the permanent placement of human remains. *Cemetery and Funeral Services Act*, R.S.N.S. 1989, c. 62, s. 2.

GRAVE CRIME. Any offence created by an Act of Parliament for which an offender may be sentenced to imprisonment for five years or more. *Diplomatic and Consular Privileges and Immunities Act*, R.S.C. 1985, c. P-22, s. 4.

GRAVE MARKER. A granite upright headstone, or a granite or bronze marker, which is of the standard established by the Department. *Veterans Burial Regulations*, C.R.C., c. 1583, s. 2.

GRAVEL. *n*. A soil consisting of particles smaller than 3 in. (76 mm), but retained on a No. 4 sieve. *Building Code Act*, R.R.O. 1980, Reg. 87, s. 4.2.1.4.

GRAVE RISK. More than ordinary risk, something greater than normally expected. A weighty risk. One of substantial harm.

GRAY WHALE. Any whale known by the name of whale, California gray, devil fish, hard head, mussel digger, gray back, rip sack. *Whaling Convention Act*, R.S.C. 1970, c. W-8, Schedule, s. 18.

GRAZE. *n*. Abrasion caused when skin contacts a rough surface. F.A. Jaffe, *A Guide to Pathological Evidence*, 3d ed. (Toronto: Carswell, 1991) at 220.

GRAZING AND FODDER ASSOCIATION. Includes an association incorporated or registered under this Act having as its principal objects, or any of them, the operation and maintenance of land for the grazing of livestock or the production of feed and fodder for livestock required by members and patrons in livestock production or rendering to members and patrons as producers services ancillary to such principal objects or any of them. *The Co-operative Production Associations Act*, R.S.S. 1978, c. C-37, s. 59.

GRAZING LEASE. A hybrid form of document which encompasses attributes of both a common law lease and a profit a prendre.

GRAZING SEASON. A period during which livestock may graze on Crown land under a grazing licence or grazing permit. *Range Act*, S.B.C. 1979, c. 355, s. 1.

GREATER TORONTO AREA. The regional municipalities of Durham, Halton, Peel and York and The Municipality of Metropolitan Toronto. *Commercial Concentration Tax Act*, R.S.O. 1990, c. C.16, s. 1.

GREAT LAKES. 1. Lakes Ontario, Erie, Huron (including Georgian Bay), Michigan and Superior, and their connecting waters. *Canada Shipping Act*, R.S.C. 1985,c. S-9, s. 2. 2. Lakes Ontario, Erie, Huron, including Georgian Bay, and Superior and their connecting waters and includes the St. Lawrence River and its tributaries as far seaward as the west end of the Island of Orleans. *Transport Act*, R.S.C. 1985, c. T-17, s. 2. See NORTH AMERICAN ~ ZONE.

GREAT LAKES BASIN. The waters of the Great Lakes, their connecting and tributary waters and the St. Lawrence River as far as the lower exit of the St. Lambert Lock at Montreal in the Province of Quebec. *Crewing Regulations*, SOR/97-390, s. 1.

GREAT LAKES PORT. Any port on the Great Lakes or their connecting waters west of the Port of Cornwall. Canada regulations.

GREAT LAKES SHIP. A ship of not less than 50 tons register tonnage (a) engaged in trade on the Great Lakes and traversing foreign waters, or (b) proceeding directly from a Great Lakes port to any port in Canada east of and including the Port of Cornwall, Ontario, or vice versa. Canada regulations.

GREAT SEAL. 1. The Great Seal of Canada. *Interpretation Act*, R.S.C. 1985, c. I-21, s. 35. 2. The Great Seal of a province.

GREAT SEAL OF THE REALM. The Great Seal of the United Kingdom of Great Britain and Northern Ireland for which provision was made in Article XXIV of An Act for an Union of the two Kingdoms of England and Scotland, 5 Anne, 1706, chapter VIII [Statutes at Large, Volume IV], and includes the wafer seal. *Seals Act*, R.S.C. 1985, c. S-6, s. 2.

GREENBELT LAND. Land preserved in its natural state as a buffer around a developed area.

GREEN CIRCLING. An employee is reassigned to a lower paying position but retains the rate of pay of his old position and receives increases in pay that he would have received had he not been reassigned.

GREEN CLAUSE. A clause endorsed on a commercial letter of credit in coloured ink which authorizes a bank to pay or accept drafts in return for an undertaking that a bill of lading and other documents will be provided when the goods are shipped. I.F.G. Baxter, *The Law of Banking*, 3d ed. (Toronto: Carswell, 1981) at 156.

GREEN HEAD. Any fresh untanned head of deer or moose. *Fish and Wildlife Act*, S.N.B. 1980, c. F-14.1, s. 1.

GREEN HIDE. Any fresh untanned hide or pelt. *Wildlife acts.*

GREENHOUSE CUCUMBERS. Cucumbers that have been grown in artificial conditions under glass or other protective covering. *Fresh Fruit and Vegetable Regulations*, C.R.C., c. 285, s. 1.

GREENHOUSE TOMATOES. Tomatoes that have been grown in artificial conditions under glass or other protective covering. *Fresh Fruit and Vegetable Regulations*, C.R.C., c. 285, s. 1.

GREENHOUSE VEGETABLES. Tomatoes, cucumbers and lettuce produced in the Province of Ontario in a greenhouse or any other enclosure under glass, plastic or other material used for the purpose of controlling temperature and providing protection for growing plants. Canada regulations.

GREENLAND HALIBUT. A fish of the species Reinhardtius hippoglossus (Walb.). *Northwest Atlantic Fisheries Regulations*, C.R.C., c. 860, s. 2.

GREENSPOND AREA. The waters of Newfoundland adjacent to that part of the coast in the vicinity of Greenspond between a line drawn due east in the district of Bonavista North from the northern point of Loo Cove on the north and a line drawn due east from the southern point of Shoe Cove Point on the south. *Newfoundland Fishery Regulations*, C.R.C., c. 846, s. 344.

GREENSTICK FRACTURE. A fracture seen in children in which a long bone is partly broken and partly bent. F.A. Jaffe, *A Guide to Pathological Evidence*, 3d ed. (Toronto: Carswell., 1991) at 220.

GREGORIAN EPOCH. The Gregorian calendar reckoning which commenced in 1582.

GRENADIER. See ROUNDNOSE ~.

GREVE. *n.* A word of authority or power.

GREY RING. A grey discolouration around an entrance wound caused by bullet lubricant or by the metal of the bullet. F.A. Jaffe, *A Guide to*

Pathological Evidence, 3d ed. (Toronto: Carswell, 1991) at 220.

GRID. See POWER ~.

GRID ROAD. A road or any portion thereof in: (a) a municipality; or (b) a local improvement district; that is designated as a grid road under section 5. *The Municipal Road Assistance Authority Act*, R.S.S. 1978, c. M-33, s. 2.

GRIEVANCE. *n.* 1. Includes any disagreement between the parties to a collective bargaining agreement with respect to the meaning or application of a collective agreement or any violation of a collective bargaining agreement 2. A complaint made in writing setting forth the reasons for the complaint in respect of dismissal, working conditions or terms of employment. *Public Service Act*, R.R.O. 1980, Reg. 881, s. 36. 3. A complaint in writing presented in accordance with the governing act by an employee personally or on behalf of the employee and one or more other employees, except that (a) for the purposes of any of the provisions of the governing act respecting grievances, a reference to an "employee" includes a person who would be a employee but for the fact that the person is employed in a managerial or confidential capacity, and (b) for the purposes of any of the provisions of the governing act respecting grievances with respect to disciplinary action resulting in discharge or suspension, a reference to an "employee" includes a former employee or a person who would be a former employee but for the fact that at the time of the discharge or suspension of that person the person was employed in a managerial or confidential capacity. See CONTINUING ~; GROUP ~; INDIVIDUAL ~; POLICY ~; UNION ~.

GRIEVANCE ARBITRATION. An adjudicative process by which disputes over the application or operation of a collective agreement are resolved. D.J.M. Brown and D.M. Beatty, *Canadian Labour Arbitration*, 3d ed. (Aurora: Canada Law Book, 1988-) at 1-1.

GRIEVANCE SETTLEMENT PROVISION. A provision for final settlement without stoppage of work, by arbitration or otherwise, of all differences between the parties to or persons bound by a collective agreement or on whose behalf it was entered into, concerning its meaning or violation. *Canada Labour Code Act*, R.S.C. 1970, c. L-1, s. 25.

GRIEVOR. *n.* 1. A person who has a grievance. 2. Person who has made a complaint in writing

concerning dismissal from employment, working conditions or terms of employment.

GRIEVOUS BODILY HARM. The injury need not be "either permanent or dangerous, if it be such as seriously to interfere with the comfort or health, it is sufficient . . ." *R. v. Ashman* (1858), 175 E.R. 638, Willes J., cited with approval in *R. v. Martineau* (1990), 79 C.R. (3d) 129 at 151, [1990] 6 W.W.R. 97, 58 C.C.C. (3d) 353, 112 N.R. 83, 76 Alta. L.R. (2d) 1, [1990] 2 S.C.R. 633, 109 A.R. 321, 50 C.P.R. 110, L'Heureux-Dubé J. (dissenting).

GRILSE. *n.* 1. A young salmon. *Fisheries Act*, R.S.N.B. 1973, c. F-15, s. 1. 2. Salmon of 3 pounds in weight or less undressed. *British Columbia Fishery (General) Regulations*, C.R.C., c. 840, s. 2.

GRINDING. *n.* The treatment of waste by uniformly reducing the waste to particles of controlled maximum size. *Environmental Protection Act*, R.R.O. 1980, Reg. 309, s. 1.

GROCERY. *n.* An establishment the main object of which is to sell foodstuffs. *An Act Respecting the Commission de Contrôle des Permis d'Alcool*, R.S.Q. 1977, c. C-33, s. 20.

GROOVE. *n.* The space between two adjacent tread ribs of a tire. Canada regulations.

GROOVES. See RIFLING.

GROSS. *n.* See IN ~.

GROSS. *adj.* Entire; absolute.

GROSS AREA. The total area of all floors above grade measured between the outside surfaces of exterior walls or, where no access or building service penetrates a firewall, between the outside surfaces of exterior walls and the centre line of firewalls but in a residential occupancy where access or a building service penetrates a firewall, the measurement may be taken to the centre line of the firewall. Ontario statutes.

GROSS AXLE WEIGHT RATING. The value specified by the vehicle manufacturer as the load-carrying capacity of a single axle system, as measured at the tire-ground interfaces. *Motor Vehicle Safety Regulations*, C.R.C., c. 1038, s. 2.

GROSS DEBT SERVICE RATIO. (a) In the case of a loan on a one-family dwelling, the ratio of the annual mortgage charges for principal, interest and taxes to the estimated gross annual income of the home owner or home purchaser, and (b) in the case of a loan on a home-owner duplex or a home-owner semi-detached house, the ratio of the annual mortgage charges for principal, interest and taxes to the estimated gross annual income of the home owner or home purchaser excluding rental derived from the housing unit not occupied by the home owner. *National Housing Loan Regulations*, C.R.C., c. 1108, s. 2.

GROSS FREIGHT CAPACITY. The aggregate obtained by multiplying the weight or mass of freight carried by the corporation by the distance the freight is carried. *Corporatins Tax Act*, R.R.O. 1980, Reg. 191, s. 306.

GROSS GATE RECEIPTS. All money collected in respect of a boxing match including all television and film royalties or money collected to obtain the rights to represent the boxing match or exhibition in any form. *Boxing Authority Act*, R.S.N.S. 1989, c. 43, s. 2.

GROSS INDECENCY. A marked departure from decent conduct expected of the average Canadian in the circumstances that existed. *R. v. Quesnel* (1979), 51 C.C.C. (2d) 270 (Ont. C.A.).

GROSS INTEREST INCOME. Income received as interest and dividends from loans, deposits and investments, less interest rebates. *Credit Union Act*, R.S.N.S. 1989, c. 111, s. 2.

GROSS MASS. See MAXIMUM ~.

GROSS NATIONAL PRODUCT. See PER CAPITA ~.

GROSS NEGLIGENCE. 1. Conduct in which if there is not conscious wrongdoing, there is a very marked departure from the standards by which responsible and competent people in charge of motor cars habitually govern themselves. *Walker v. Coates*, [1968] S.C.R. 599, per Ritchie, J. 2. "[In the Municipal Act, R.S.O. 1914, s. 192] . . . The circumstances giving rise to the duty to remove a dangerous condition, including notice, actual or imputable, of its existence, and the extent of the risk which it creates—the character and the duration of the neglect to fulfil that duty, including the comparative ease or difficulty of discharging it—these elements must vary in infinite degree; and they seem to be important, if not vital, factors in determining whether the fault (if any) attributable to the municipal corporation is so much more than merely ordinary neglect that it should be held to be very great, or gross negligence . . ." *Holland v. Toronto (City)*, [1927] 1

D.L.R. 99 at 102, [1927] S.C.R. 242, 59 O.L.R. 628, the court per Anglin C.J.C. 3. ". . . [A] high or serious degree of negligence." *British Columbia Telephone Co. v. Quality Industries Ltd.* (1984), 49 C.P.C. 224 at 227, 59 B.C.L.R. 68 (C.A.), the court per Esson J.A. 4. Very great negligence. *Kingston (City) v. Drennan* (1897), 27 S.C.R. 46, Sedgewick J.

GROSS PROCEEDS. The actual price obtained at a sale where all charges on sale are paid by the sellers. *Maritime Insurance acts*.

GROSS PROFIT. " . . . [F]or income tax purposes . . . in the case of a business which consists of acquiring property and reselling it, is the excess of sale price over cost, subject only to any modification effected by the 'cost or market whichever is lower' rule . . ." *Irwin v. Minister of National Revenue*, [1964] C.T.C. 362 at 364, [1964] S.C.R. 662, 64 D.T.C. 5227, 46 D.L.R. (2d) 717, the court per Abbott J.

GROSS REGISTERED TONS. The gross tonnage stated in the certificate of registry of a ship or, where the ship has more than one gross registered tonnage, means the largest gross registered tonnage of that ship. Canada regulations.

GROSS REVENUE. As applied to a fiscal period of a business enterprise, means the aggregate of all amounts received in the period or receivable in the period, depending on the method regularly followed in computing the profit from the enterprise, otherwise than as or on account of capital. *Small Business Loans Act*, R.S.C. 1985, c. S-11, s. 2. See GROSS SALES OR ~.

GROSS REVENUE INSURANCE PROGRAM. A program that combines the protection offered by a crop insurance program and the protection offered by a revenue insurance program. *Farm Income Protection Act*, S.C. 1991, c. 22, s. 2.

GROSS ROYALTY TRUST. A trust under the terms of which the trustee receives a percentage of gross proceeds, less taxes, from the producer. D.M.W. Waters, *The Law of Trusts in Canada*, 2d ed. (Toronto: Carswell, 1984) at 448.

GROSS SALES. The total dollar volume of sales.

GROSS TONNAGE. The gross tonnage stated in the certificate of registry of a ship, or, where a ship is not registered, the figure found in accordance with the rules for the time being in force for the measurement of ships in respect of tonnage. *Canada Shipping Act*, R.S.C. 1985, c. S-9, s. 2. See REGISTERED ~.

GROSS-UP. *n*. The practice of increasing lump sum awards for future care costs and pecuniary losses in personal injury cases (other than loss of future income) and for pecuniary losses in fatal accident cases to take into account the impact of taxation on the income generated by lump sum awards in respect of those heads of damages. It has been accepted at common law as a proper head of damages to be included in a lump sum award at trial. *McErlean v. Sarel* (1987), 61 O.R. (2d) 396 (C.A.).

GROSS VALUE. The wholesale price or, if there is no wholesale price, the estimated value, with, in either case, freight, landing charges and duty paid beforehand, except that in the case of goods or merchandise customarily sold in bond, the bonded price is deemed to be the gross value. *Marine Insurance acts.*

GROSS VEHICLE WEIGHT. 1. The manufacturer's gross weight rating for a vehicle. 2. The combined weight of the commercial vehicle and its load. *Commercial Transport Act*, R.S.B.C. 1979, c. 55, s. 1. 3. The total weight in kilograms transmitted to the highway by a vehicle, or combination of vehicles and load. *Highway Traffic* Act, R.S.O. 1980, c. 198, s. 97.

GROSS VEHICLE WEIGHT RATING. The value specified by the vehicle manufacturer as the loaded weight of a single vehicle. Canada regulations.

GROSS WEIGHT. 1. The combined weight of vehicle and load. 2. With respect to any equipment, means the total weight of the equipment as specified by its manufacturer. *Airport Traffic Regulations*, C.R.C. c. 886, s. 52. See MAXIMUM ~; REGISTERED ~.

GROUND. *n*. A connection to earth of electrical equipment by means of a ground electrode. See PHEASANT SHOOTING ~; SAFETY ~; VOLTAGE TO ~.

GROUND DISTURBANCE. Any work, operation or activity that results in a disturbance of the earth including, without limitation, excavating, digging, trenching, plowing, drilling, tunneling, augering, backfilling, blasting, topsoil stripping, land leveling, peat removing, quarrying, clearing and grading, but does not include, (a) except as otherwise provided in subclause (b), a disturbance of the earth to a depth of less than 30 centimetres that does not result in a re-duction of the earth cover over the pipeline to a depth that is less than the cover provided when the pipeline was installed, (b) cultivation to a depth of less than 45 centimetres below the surface of the ground, or (c) any work, operation or activity that is specified in the regulations not to be a ground disturbance. *Pipeline Act, 1991*,R.S.A. 2000, c. P-15, s. 1.

GROUNDED. *adj*. Connected to the mass of the earth through a conductor and earth contact of adequately low resistance for the desired purpose.

GROUND ELECTRODE. A metallic water-piping system, or a metallic object or device buried in, or driven into, the earth so as to make intimate contact therewith, to which a grounding conductor is electrically and mechanically connected. *Power Corporation Act*, R.R.O. 1980, Reg. 794, s. 0.

GROUND FAULT CIRCUIT INTERRUPTER. A device which will interrupt, within a predetermined time, the electrical circuit to the load when a current to ground exceeds some predetermined value that is less than that required to operate the overcurrent protection device of the supply circuit. *Power Corporation Act*, R.R.O. 1980, Reg. 794, s. 0. See PORTABLE ~.

GROUNDFISH. *n*. 1. Demersal species of fish and includes flatfish, grey cod, ling cod, rockfish, black cod, hake, sea perch, pollock, skate and ratfish. *Pacific Fishery Registration and Licensing Regulations*, C.R.C., c. 824, s. 2. 2. Cod, haddock, hake, pollock, plaice, flounder or halibut. *Quebec Fishery Regulations*, C.R.C., c. 852, s. 2.

GROUNDFISH NET. A gill net used for the purpose of catching demersal species of fish. *Fishery regulations*, Canada regulations.

GROUND FLOOR. The lowest floor in a building.

GROUND GATES. Any arrangement of horizontal bars placed in a gateway upon the ground.

GROUNDING. *n*. The portion of a conductor underground that makes electrical contact with the earth. See AUXILIARY ~; INDEPENDENT ~; MAIN ~; SAFETY ~.

GROUNDING CONDUCTOR. A path of copper or other suitable metal specially arranged as a means whereby electrical equipment is electrically connected to a ground electrode. *Power Corporation Act*, R.R.O. 1980, Reg. 794, s. 0.

GROUNDING EQUIPMENT. A permanent connection to ground of non-current carrying parts of apparatus which are insulated from the system. *Coal Mines Regulation Act*, R.S.N.S. 1989, c. 73, s. 85(1) .

GROUNDING NETWORK. A grounded system of conductors to facilitate effective grounding. *Coal Mines Regulation Act*, R.S.N.S. 1989, c. 73, s. 85(1).

GROUNDING SYSTEM. All those cables and other conductors, clamps, ground clips and ground plates or rods by means of which the electrical installation is grounded.

GROUND LANDLORD. The owner of the freehold of land, whether built upon or not, or who receives rent for land exclusive of the buildings which may be erected upon it. *City of Corner Brook Act*, R.S. Nfld. 1990, c. C-17, s. 2.

GROUND LEASE. 1. Lease of bare land or land exclusive of any building on it. 2. A registered lease of land (a) granted by a leasehold landlord for the purposes of this Part, and (b) to which a model strata lot lease is attached; *Strata Property Act*, S.B.C. 1998, c. 43, s. 199.

GROUND-RENT. *n*. Rent, usually for many years, generally rent payable for land on which the lessee erects buildings under a building lease.

GROUND-ROD. *n*. A solid rod of copper, copper-clad steel or galvanized steel that is used as a grounding. *Lightning Rods Act*, R.R.O. 1980, Reg. 577, s. 1.

GROUNDS. *n*. Reasons. See ENUMERATED

GROUND STATION. A location on the ground equipped with radio transmitting and receiving equipment capable of two-way voice communications with an aircraft. *Canadian Aviation Regulations* SOR 96-433, s. 101.01.

GROUND VISIBILITY. In respect of an aerodrome, means the visibility at that aerodrome as contained in a weather observation reported by (a) an air traffic control unit, (b) a flight service station, (c) a community aerodrome radio station, (d) an AWOS used by the Department of Transport, the Department of National Defence or the Atmospheric Environment Service for the purpose of making aviation weather observations, or (e) a radio station that is ground-based and operated by an air operator. *Canadian Aviation Regulations* SOR 96-433, s. 101.01.

GROUND WATER. *var*. **GROUNDWATER**. 1. Water beneath the surface of the land. 2. " . . .

[P]ercolating water . . ." *Schneider v. Olds (Town)* (1970), 71 W.W.R. 380 at 380, 8 D.L.R. (3d) 680 (Alta. T.D.), Milvain C.J.T.D. 3. A free standing body of water in the ground. *Building Code Act*, R.R.O. 1980, Reg. 87, s. 1. 4. All water in a zone of saturation beneath the land surface regardless of its origin and quality. *Northern Inland Waters Regulations*, C.R.C., c. 1234, s. 2. See PERCHED ~.

GROUNDWATER LEVEL. The top surface of a free standing body of water in the ground. *Building Code Act*, R.R.O. 1980, Reg. 87, s. 1.

GROUP. *n*. A number of persons travelling together as an entirety pursuant to a contract. *Air Carrier Regulations*, C.R.C., c. 3, s. 83. See ADULT TEST ~; BLOOD ~S; COMMODITY ~; DESIGNATED ~; DETROIT RIVER ~; ELECTORAL ~; EMPLOYEE-ASSOCIATIONS ~; FRINGE ~; IDENTIFIABLE ~; INCLUSIVE TOUR ~; RELATED ~; RESEARCH ~; SEALING ~; SELLING~; SHIPPER ~; UNRELATED ~; VOTING ~; YOUTH ~.

GROUP ACCIDENT INSURANCE. Accident insurance, other than creditor's group accident insurance, whereby the lives or well-being or the lives and well-being of a number of persons are insured severally under a single contract between an insurer and an employer or other person contracting with the insurer. *Insurance acts*. See CREDITOR'S ~.

GROUP ADVERTISING. Display advertising consisting of individual business names of a number of franchisees or distributors of a common logo or trademark.

GROUP BONUS. Wage incentive paid to some workers who are jointly responsible for maintaining an aspect of output.

GROUP CONTRACT. 1. A master contract of insurance arranged between an insurer and a party such as an employer, union, or association. C. Brown and J. Menezes, *Insurance Law in Canada*, 2d ed. (Toronto: Carswell, 1991) at 16. 2. A contract of insurance whereby two or more persons other than members of the same family are insured severally under a single contract of insurance. *Hospital Insurance acts*.

GROUP CREDITORS' INSURANCE. Form of group insurance under which a lender institution insures the collective lives of the borrowers.

GROUP FOSTER HOME. A home where not less than four or more than eight children are placed by a child caring agency for full time care and supervision in a family setting. *Child Welfare Act*, S.M. 1974, c. 30, s. 1.

GROUP GRIEVANCE. A collection of individual grievances concerning similar matters. The individual grievances are joined in one application or are determined at the same time.

GROUP HOME. " . . . [A] semi-institutional home. It is an arrangement whereby a number of individuals, usually limited to six or eight persons, agree to live together as a single household unit in order to enjoy the benefits and assume the responsibilities of living in a residential neighbourhood. In the case of convalescent, disabled persons or rehabilitated prisoners, the choice of the individual is rather limited since he or she is sent there by another body or agency. The premises or homes are organized by an association or organization, staffed, maintained and operated by it. An individual either qualifies or does not, is either welcomed or not in the group home. If qualified and welcomed, he or she enjoys the benefits of living in a residential neighbourhood under full-time or part-time staff supervision. In some of the homes there is no permanent resident staff. The individuals work or report to various agencies for work activities." *Alcoholism Foundation of Manitoba v. Winnipeg (City)* (1990), 49 M.P.L.R. 1 at 9, 1 C.R.R. 2d 275, 69 D.L.R. (4th) 697, 65 Man. R. (2d) 81, [1990] 6 W.W.R. 232 (C.A.), Monnin C.J.M. (Lyon C.J. concurring in part).

GROUP INSURANCE. 1. A policy of insurance that covers, under a master policy, the participants of a specified group or of a specified group and other persons. 2. Insurance other than creditor's group insurance and family insurance, whereby the lives or well-being, or the lives and well-being, of a number of persons are insured severally under a single contract between an insurer and an employer or other person. *Insurance acts*. 3. Insurance, other than creditor's group insurance and family insurance, whereby the lives of a number of persons are insured severally under a single contract between an insurer and an employer or other person. *Insurance acts*. See CREDITOR'S ~.

GROUP LIFE INSURED. A person whose life is insured by a contract of group insurance but does not include a person whose life is insured under the contract as a person dependent upon, or related to, the insured. *Insurance acts*.

GROUP MAIL BOX SYSTEM. A privately owned group of lock boxes in an apartment building or office complex designed for the receipt of the mail of all occupants of the building or complex and so constructed that each owner or tenant has an individual compartment that may be kept locked. *Mail Receptacles Regulations*, C.R.C., c. 1282, s. 2.

GROUP MANAGEMENT VENTURE. A co-operative or company formed for the purpose of implementing forest management activities on land of any of the members of the co-operative or company. *Forests Act*, R.S.N.S. 1989, c. 179 , s. 3.

GROUP PERSON INSURED. A person who is insured under a contract of group insurance and upon whom a right is conferred by the contract, but does not include a person who is insured thereunder as a person dependent upon or related to the insured. *Insurance acts*.

GROUP PLAN. A contract for the provision of services under this Act, under which an association provides services to insure severally the well-being of a number of individuals under a single contract between the association and an employer or other person. *Prepaid Hospital and Medical Services Act*, R.S.O. 1990, c. P.21, s. 1.

GROUP SICKNESS INSURANCE. Sickness insurance, other than creditor's group sickness insurance, whereby the lives or well-being or the lives and well-being of a number of persons are insured severally under a single contract between an insurer and an employer or other person contracting with the insurer. *Insurance* acts. See CREDITOR'S ~.

GROUP SYSTEM. A system by which a weighted average rate of depreciation is calculated for a particular group of plant accounts, a plant account, or a group of assets within a plant account, and established in recognition of the fact that some part of the investment in a group of assets may be recovered through salvage realization and that there will be variations in the service lives of the assets constituting the group, even among assets of the same class. *Oil Pipeline Uniform Accounting Regulations*, Canada regulations.

GROUP TERM LIFE INSURANCE POLICY. A group life insurance policy under which the only amounts payable by the insurer are (a) amounts payable on the death or disability of individuals whose lives are insured in respect of, in the course of or because of, their office or employment or former office or employment, and (b) policy dividends or experience rating refunds. *Income Tax Act*, R.S.C. 1985, c. 1 (5th Supp.), s. 248.

GROWER. *n*. Any person owning, leasing or otherwise occupying land who farms that land.

GROWING CROP. Any plant growth, other than weeds, having a commercial value.

GROWTH REGULATOR. See PLANT ~.

G.R.P. *abbr*. Glass reinforced plastic. *Life Saving Equipment Regulations*, C.R.C., c. 1436, s. 74.

GRUB-STAKING. *n*. " . . . [P]arol agreements for an interest in a mining, claim entered into prior to the staking out . . ." *Paquette v. Chubb* (1988), 31 C.P.C. (2d) 87 at 103, 65 O.R. (2d) 321, 29 O.A.C. 243, 52 D.L.R. (4th) 1 (C.A.), the court per Finlayson J.A.

G.S.P. *abbr*. General Sessions of the Peace.

G.S.T. The federal Goods and Services Tax.

G.T.P. *abbr*. Grand Trunk Pacific.

G.T.R. *abbr*. Grand Trunk Railway.

GUARANTEE. *n*. 1. " . . . [A] contract between a guarantor and a lender. The subject of the guarantee is a debt owed to the lender by a debtor. In the contract of guarantee, the guarantor agrees to repay the lender if the debtor defaults. The exact nature of the obligation owed by the guarantor to the lender depends on the construction of the contract of guarantee, but the liability of the guarantor is usually made coterminous with that of the principal debtor . . ." *Communities Economic Development Fund v. Canadian Pickles Corp*. (1991), 8 C.B.R. (3d) 121 at 143, [1992] 1 W.W.R. 193, 85 D.L.R. (4th) 88, 121 N.R. 81, [1991] 3 S.C.R. 388, 76 Man. R. (2d) 1, 10 W.A.C. 1, the court per Iacobucci J. 2. A promise to answer for another's obligation. *Schell v. McCallum & Vannatter* (1918), 42 D.L.R. 563 at 571-2, 57 S.C.R. 15, [1918] 2 W.W.R. 735, Brodeur J. (dissenting). 3. A written agreement under which a person agrees to answer for the default or act or omission of another person. Usually refers to payment of a debt. Payment is contingent on the default of the principal debtor. See CONTRACT OF ~; INCREMENTAL LOAN ~; PERFORMANCE ~; WAGE ~.

GUARANTEE BOND. A promise to perform an agreement or contract or to discharge a trust, duty or obligation upon default of a person liable for that performance or discharge.

GUARANTEE COMPANY. An incorporated company empowered to grant guarantees, bonds policies or contracts for the integrity and fidelity of employed persons, or in respect of any legal proceedings, or for other like purposes.

GUARANTEED. See GOVERNMENT ~ BOND.

GUARANTEED INCOME SUPPLEMENT. The guaranteed income supplement payable pursuant to the Old Age Security Act. Canada regulations.

GUARANTEED INSTRUMENT. An instrument, the payment of which is guaranteed by the Corporation under this Act or the former Act. *Export Development Act*, R.S.C. 1985, c. E-20, s. 23.

GUARANTEED INVESTMENT CERTIFICATE. A certificate issued by a trust company in evidence of the deposit of guaranteed trust money and the guarantee thereof by the company. *Trust Companies Act*, R.S.C. 1985, c. T-20, s. 2.

GUARANTEED LOAN. A loan to a borrower made and guaranteed by a financial institution.

GUARANTEED PORTION. The portion of a guaranteed loan repayment which is guaranteed by the province pursuant to this Act. *The Cooperative Guarantee Act*, R.S.S. 1978, c. C-35, s. 2.

GUARANTEED RATE. The amount a worker will receive regardless of achieving or exceeding a standard or quota.

GUARANTEED TRUST MONEY. Money received by a trust company in trust for investment subject to a guarantee by the company in respect of the payment of interest or the repayment of principal.

GUARANTEE INSURANCE. 1. The undertaking to perform an agreement or contract or to discharge a trust, duty or obligation upon default of the person liable for such performance or discharge or to pay money upon such default or in lieu of such performance or discharge, or where there is loss or damage through such default, but does not include credit insurance. *Insurance acts*. 2. The undertaking to perform an agreement or contract or to discharge a trust, duty or obligation upon default of the person liable for such performance or discharge or to pay money upon such default or in lieu of such performance or discharge or where there is loss or damage through such default, and includes insurance against loss or liability for loss due to the invalidity of the title to any property or of any instrument or to any defect in such title or instrument, but does not include credit insurance. *Insurance acts.*

GUARANTEE OF ISOLATION. In respect of an electrical facility, a guarantee by the person in control of the facility that it is isolated. *Canada Electrical Safety Regulations*, C.R.C., c. 998, s. 2.

GUARANTEE OF SIGNATURE. A guarantee signed by or on behalf of a person reasonably believed by the issuer to be responsible.

GUARANTOR. *n.* 1. A surety, a person who is bound by a guarantee. 2. A person who undertakes under a bond, upon the default of the bondee in paying a debt or a debt of a class of debts specified in the bond, to pay a sum of money or to pay the debt. *Guarantors' Liability Act*, R.S.M. 187, c. G120, s. 1.

GUARANTY. *n.* A promise to pay another's debt or to perform another's obligation.

GUARD. *n.* 1. A protective barrier. 2. " . . . [I]ndividual must exercise monitoring functions of a quasi-supervisory character with respect to other employees in the bargaining unit . . . they must perform duties . . . which clearly place them in a conflict of interest with those employees . . ." *Therrian v. S.E.I.U., Local 204*, [1986] O.L.R.B. Rep. 152 at 153, MacDowell (Vice-Chair), Stamp and Ballentine (Members). 3. A person employed to watch over property or persons. See MACHINE ~; PLANT PROTECTION EMPLOYEE; PRIVATE ~; SECURITY ~.

GUARD AGENCY. See SECURITY ~.

GUARDAGE. *n.* Keeping; wardship.

GUARD DOG. A dog used for the purpose of protecting persons or property.

GUARDED. *adj.* 1. Protected in a manner designed to prevent a person (a) from falling through an opening or from one level to another, or (b) from making contact with a dangerous machine or other object. *Canada Building Safety Regulations*, C.R.C., c. 995, s. 2. 2. In respect of an electrical facility, that the facility is covered, shielded, fenced, enclosed or inaccessible by location or otherwise protected in a manner that will prevent or reduce, to the extent that is reasonably practicable, danger to any person who might touch or go near that facility. *Electrical Safety Regulations*, C.R.C., c. 998, s. 2. 3. When applied to electrical equipment means that the electrical equipment is so covered, shielded, fenced, enclosed, or otherwise protected by means of suitable covers, casings, barriers, rails, screens, mats or platforms as to remove the likelihood of dangerous contact or approach by persons or objects. *Power Corporation Act*, R.R.O. 1980 Reg. 794, s. 0. 4. (a) In relation to a plant that every boiler, compressor or engine in the plant is guarded, and (b) in relation to a boiler, compressor or engine, as the case may be, that the boiler, compressor or engine is provided with such device in good operating condition as will ensure that the boiler, compressor or engine may be operated safely, notwithstanding that the operating engineer or operator in charge of the plant may be absent from the boiler room, compressor room or engine room, as the case may be or, where the boiler, compressor or engine is not enclosed in a room, from the immediate vicinity. *Operating Engineers Act*, R.R.O. 1980, Reg. 740, s. 1.

GUARDED PLANT. A plant that is equipped with fail-safe controls and audio and visual alarm systems and that is approved by the chief inspector. *The Boiler and Pressure Vessel Act*, R.S.S. 1978, c. B-5, s. 2.

GUARDIAN. *n.* 1. Includes any person who has in law or in fact the custody or control of another person. *Criminal Code*, R.S.C. 1985, c. C-46, s. 150. 2. Includes a person who has in law or in fact custody or control of a child. *Criminal Code*, R.S.C. 1985, c. C-46, s. 214. 3. In respect of a child, any person, other than a parent of the child, who is under a legal duty to provide for the child or who has, in law or in fact, the custody or control of the child. *Royal Canadian Mounted Police Act*, S.C. 1986, c. 11, s. 2(1). 4. A parent or other person who is under a legal duty to provide for a child. *Children's Residential Services Act*, R.R.O. 1980, Reg. 101, s. 1. 5. Includes a person acting *in loco parentis* to a child. See CHILDREN'S ~; FIRE ~; FISHERY ~; LEGAL ~; LITIGATION ~; OFFICIAL ~.

GUARDIAN AD LITEM. A person who sues on behalf of an infant. Formerly referred to as a "next friend". Also known as litigation guardian.

GUARDIANSHIP. *n.* 1. " . . . [T]he full bundle of rights and duties voluntarily assumed by an adult regarding an infant akin to those naturally arising from parenthood . . . Guardianship implies the voluntary assumption of a duty to maintain, protect and educate the ward. It includes the power to correct, to grant or withhold consent to marriages and, if the guardian is also the parent, to delegate parental authority. . . the full bundle of parental personal rights, including necessarily the entitlement to physical possession of the child. . ." *Anson v. Anson* (1987), 10 B.C.L.R. (2d) 357 at 361-2 (Co. Ct.), Huddart Co. Ct. J. 2. The responsibilities associated with custody, other than physical or day to day care and control, are the rights and obligations embodied in the phrase "guardian of the person". *Abbott v. Abbott*, 2001 CarswellBC 420, 2001 BCSC 323, 13 R.F.L. (5th) 233, 89 B.C.L.R. (3d) 68 (S.C.), Pitfield J. 3. The relationship between a person and a child whereby the person has, by a written decision of the competent authority of the country where the child resides, been entrusted with the legal responsibility for the child and is authorized to act on their behalf.

GUARDIANSHIP AGREEMENT. An agreement permanently transferring from the parent the guardianship of the child, including the custody, care and control of, and all parental rights and responsibilities with respect to, the child.

GUARDIANSHIP ORDER. 1. An order which transfers the guardianship of the child, including the custody, care and control of, and all parental rights and responsibilities with respect to, the child. 2. Any order of a court appointing a person as a guardian.

GUEST. *n.* 1. "To be a guest one must be willingly in the vehicle . . ." *King v. Hommy* (1962), 39 W.W.R. 209 at 213, 34 D.L.R. (2d) 770 (Alta. C.A.), the court per Johnson J.A. 2. A person permitted to stay on premises belonging to another; person to whom hospitality is extended.

GUEST STATUTE. A statute which imposes liability in respect of any gratuitous passenger on the driver of a car solely in a case of misconduct or gross negligence which is wanton, wilful or reckless. John G. Fleming, *The Law of Torts*, 8th ed. (Sydney: The Law Book Company Limited, 1992) at 23.

GUIDANCE. *n.* " . . . [E]ducation, training, discipline, moral teaching, . . ." *Schmidt, Re* (1981), (*sub nom. Thornborrow v. MacKinnon*) 16 C.C.L.T. 198 at 206, 32 O.R. (2d) 740, 123 D.L.R. (3d) 124 (H.C.), Linden J. See LOSS OF ~.

GUIDE. *n.* 1. " . . . [O]ne who accompanies another over unfamiliar terrain being ready to point the way, being ready to give advice, . . ."

R. v. Kurth (1990), 72 Alta. L.R. (2d) 300 at 303,103 A.R. 75 (Q.B.), Veit J. 2. A person who, for compensation or reward received or promised, accompanies and assists another person to hunt wildlife or angle for fish. 3. A person who for gain or reward accompanies or assists another person in any outdoor recreational activity. See ANGLING ~; DOG ~; MASTER STREET ADDRESS ~.

GUIDE ANIMAL. An animal used by a person with a disability to avoid hazards or to assist in compensating for the disability.

GUIDED LAND TRANSPORT. Includes transport systems propelled by electric, hydraulic, mechanical, electromechanical or other power and mechanical, electrodynamic, electromagnetic or air-cushion levitated transport, linked or not to a network, and operated on rails or other guideways. *An Act to ensure safety in guided land transport*, R.S.Q., chapter S-3.3, s. 1.

GUIDED LAND TRANSPORT WORKS. Includes, in particular, level crossings, railway tracks, including subway or monorail tracks, and any other guideway as well as the infrastructures, structures and permanent structures. *An Act to ensure safety in guided land transport*, R.S.Q., chapter S-3.3, s. 1.

GUIDE DOG. A dog which is trained to assist a person who is disabled or has a disease which causes the person to require assistance. See HEARING DOG.

GUIDE FOR FISH. A person who, for compensation or reward received or promised, (a) accompanies another person and assists that person to angle, (b) attends another person at or near an angling site in a manner that, directly or indirectly, assists that person to angle, or (c) transports, for the purposes of angling, another person to, from or between angling sites.

GUIDELINE. *n.* 1. Form of administrative directive which cannot confer enforceable rights, but can be written to be mandatory. 2. Set of expectations for performance. 3. "The word 'guidelines' cannot be construed in isolation; s. 6 [of the Department of the Environment Act, R.S.C. 1985, c. E-10] must be read as a whole. When so read it becomes clear that Parliament has elected to adopt a regulatory scheme that is 'law', and thus amenable to enforcement through prerogative relief." *Friends of the Oldman River Society v. Canada (Minister of Transport)* (1992), 3 Admin. L.R. (2d) 1 at 36, [1992]

2 W.W.R. 193, [1992] 1 S.C.R. 3, 84 Alta. L.R. (2d) 129, 7 C.E.L.R. (ICS.) 1, 132 N.R. 321, 88 D.L.R. (4th) 1, 48 F.T.R. 160n, La Forest J. (Lamer C.J.C., L'Heureux-Dubé Sopinka, Gonthier, Cory, McLachlin and Iacobucci JJ. concurring). 2. "[Guidelines issued by the Superintendent of Bankruptcy] . . . are just that: they have no force of statute, but purport to indicate to bankruptcy trustees throughout Canada as appropriate level of payment that one would expect when one of low income makes a declaration of bankruptcy." *Westmore v. McAfee* (1988), 49 D.L.R. (4th) 401 at 412, 23 B.C.L.R. (2d) 273, [1988] 3 W.W.R. 593, 67 C.B.R. (N.S.) 209 (C.A.), the court per Locke J.A.

GUIDE POST. See WOODEN ~.

GUILD. *n*. A company, corporation or fraternity formed for a commercial purpose.

GUILT. *n*. The state of having committed a crime or offence or being subject to punishment. See FINDING OF ~.

GUILTY. *adj*. 1. Having committed a tort or crime. 2. The word used by a prisoner entering a plea and by a convicting jury. 3. "With respect to an accused who has pleaded guilty, such a plea is ordinarily regarded as an admission that the matters alleged in the information are true." *R. v. Rapien* (1954), 18 C.R. 168 at 170, 11 W.W.R. 529, 108 C.C.C. 198 (Alta. C.A.), the court per MacDonald J.A. See NOT ~.

GUILTY PLEA. An admission that the accused has committed the crime charged and a consent to a conviction being entered without any trial.

GUINEAS. *n*. Guinea chickens and guinea fowl. *Meat Inspection Regulations*, C.R.C., c. 1032, s. 135.

GUISE. See DISTINGUISHING ~.

GULF AREA. All the waters of the St. Lawrence River, Chaleur Bay, Northumberland Strait, and the Gulf of St. Lawrnece bounded on the north by a straight line drawn from the lighthouse at Amour Point to the lighthouse on Flowers Island in Flowers Cove, Newfoundland and all the waters of Cabot Strait and of the Atlantic Ocean seaward thereof and seaward of the east coast of Nova Scotia and bounded on the north by a straight line drawn due east from Cape Race,

Newfoundland. *Seal Protection Regulations*, C.R.C., c. 833, s. 2.

GULF OF ST. LAWRENCE. 1. The area bounded on the east by the west coast of the Island of Newfoundland, on the north by a line joining Flowers Island and Point Amour, Newfoundland and on the southeast by a line Joining Port aux Basques, Newfoundland, and Sydney, Nova Scotia. *Life Saving Equipment Regulations*, C.R.C., c. 1436, s. 2. 2. That area of the sea adjacent to the coast of Canada described as Zone 1 in the schedule to the Fishing Zones of Canada (Zones 1, 2 and 3) Order. *Atlantic Fishery Regulations*, C.R.C., c. 807, s. 2.

GUM SPIRITS OF TURPENTINE. A liquid obtained by steam-distillation of the gum of coniferous trees. *Turpentine Labelling Regulations*, C.R.C., c. 1140, s. 2.

GUN. *n*. 1. A firearm. F.A. Jaffe, *A Guide to Pathological Evidence*, 3d ed. (Toronto: Carswell, 1991) at 220. 2. A syringe. F.A. Jaffe, *A Guide to Pathological Evidence*, 3d ed. (Toronto: Carswell, 1991) at 220. 3. Any barrelled weapon from which any shot, bullet or other missile can be discharged and that is capable of causing serious injury or death to game, and includes anything that can be readily adopted for use as a gun or firearm. *Game Act*, R.S.N.B. 1973, c. G-1, s. 1. See STUD ~.

GUN COLLECTOR. See GENUINE ~.

GUTTER. See AUXILIARY ~.

GVWR. *abbr*. 1. Gross vehicle weight rating. 2. The gross vehicle weight rating specified by a manufacturer as the maximum design loaded weight of a single vehicle. *On-Road Vehicle and Engine Emission Regulations*, SOR/2003-2, s. 1.

GYNAECOCRACY. *n*. Government by women.

GYNARCY. *n*. Government by women.

GYPSUM. *n*. Includes any gypsum-bearing substance removed from a mine. *Gypsum Mining Income Tax Act*, R.S.N.S. 1989, c. 190, s. 2.

GYROPLANE. *n*. A heavier-than-air aircraft that derives its lift in flight from aerodynamic reactions on one or more non-power-driven rotors on substantially vertical axes. *Canadian Aviation Regulations*, SOR/96-433, s. 101.01.

H. *abbr.* 1. Hour. 2. Henry. 3. Hecto.

HABEAS CORPUS. [L. that you have the body]1. " . . . [T]he writ of habeas corpus is available to any subject detained or imprisoned, not to hear and determine the case upon the evidence, but to immediately and in a summary way test the validity of his detention or imprisonment. It matters not whether the basis for the detention or imprisonment be criminal or civil law . . ." *Storgoff, Re, (sub nom. R. v. Storgoff)* [1945] 3 D.L.R. 673 at 733, [1945] S.C.R. 526, 84 C.C.C. 1, Estey J. 2. Acts as a check on the jurisdiction of the convicting court or tribunal to order the detention of the applicant. If the court or tribunal has exceeded its jurisdiction in ordering imprisonment of the accused, resort may be had to habeas corpus to secure the release of the person. Will lie to discharge a prisoner from prison when the prisoner's sentence has expired. See HABEAS CORPUS AD SUBJICIENDUM.

HABEAS CORPUS AD SUBJICIENDUM. [L.] An order that a person arrested be brought into a court or before a judge to determine if the imprisonment is lawful.

HABEMUS OPTIMUM TESTEM CONFITENTEM REUM. [L.] We hold that an accused who pleads guilty is the best possible witness.

HABENDUM. *n.* [L. having] 1. The first word of a clause which follows a legal description of land which is being granted. 2. "[Part of a deed which] . . . is intended to include the designation of the estate or interest to be conveyed in the property described in the premises of the deed such as a term of years, a term for life, a fee simple or the interest remainder." *Wheeler v. Wheeler No. 2* (1979), 25 N.B.R. (2d) 376 at 378, 51 A.P.R. 376 (C.A.), Limerick, Bugold and Ryan JJ.A.

HABERE FACIAS POSSESSIONEM. [L. that you cause to have possession] A writ

awarded to a plaintiff successful in an ejectment action.

HABILITATION AND CARE. The maintenance, training, and other necessary care of a patient. *Hospital Schools Act*, R.S.N.B. 1973, c. H-8, s. 1.

HABIT. *n.* A specific repeated response to a particular situation.

HABITAT. *n.* 1. That kind of place or situation in which a human being, animal or plant lives. 2 In respect of aquatic species, spawning grounds and nursery, rearing, food supply, migration and any other areas on which aquatic species depend directly or indirectly in order to carry out their life processes, or areas where aquatic species formerly occurred and have the potential to be reintroduced; and in respect of other wildlife species, the area or type of site where an individual or wildlife species naturally occurs or depends on directly or indirectly in order to carry out its life processes or formerly occurred and has the potential to be reintroduced. *Species at Risk Act*, S.C. 2002, c. 29, s. 2(1). See CRITICAL ~; FISH ~; WILDLIFE ~.

HABITAT CONSERVATION STAMP. A stamp issued for the purposes of Wildlife Habitat Canada for that period beginning on the day of issue and ending on March 10th next following the day of issue. *Migratory Birds Regulations*, C.R.C., c. 1035,s. 2(1).

HABITUAL CRIMINAL. The term used for a repeat offender prior to the enactment of the current Criminal Code provisions concerning dangerous offenders.

HABITUAL RESIDENCE. 1. " . . . [R]efers to the quality of residence. Duration may be a factor depending on the circumstances. It requires an animus less than that required for domicile; it is a midpoint between domicile and residence. . ." *Adderson v. Adderson* (1987), 51 Alta. L.R. (2d) 193 at 198, 7 R.F.L. (3d) 185, 77 A.R. 256, 36 D.L.R. (4th) 361 (C.A.), the court per Laycraft J.A. 2. A regular, lasting physical presence. A. Bissett-Johnson & W.M. Holland, eds., *Matrimonial Property Law in Canada* (Toronto: Carswell, 1980) at A-9.

HABITUÉ. *n.* [Fr.] An alcoholic or drug habitue. *Private Sanitaria Act*, R.S.O. 1980, c. 391, s. 1.

HACK. *n.* A horse-drawn vehicle used to transport passengers for compensation. *Motor Vehicle Act*, R.S.N.S. 1989, c. 293, s. 2.

HAD AND RECEIVED. See MONEY ~.

HADDOCK. *n.* A fish of the species Melano grammus aeglefinus (L.). *Northwest Atlantic Fisheries Regulations*, C.R.C., c. 860, s. 2.

HAEREDES PROXIMI. [L.] Offspring, children.

HAEREDES REMOTIORES. [L.] Heirs which were not offspring.

HAEREDIPETA. *n.* The next heir to property.

HAEREDITAS, ALIA CORPORALIS, ALIA INCORPORALIS; CORPORALIS EST, QUAE TANGI POTEST ET VIDERI; INCORPORALIS QUAE TANGI NON POTEST NEC VIDERI. [L.] Sometimes an inheritance is corporeal, sometimes incorporeal; a corporeal inheritance is visible and tangible; an incorporeal inheritance is invisible and intangible.

HAEREDITAS NIHIL ALIUD EST QUAM SUCCESSIO IN UNIVERSUM JUS QUOD DEFUNCTUS HABUERIT. [L.] Heirship is nothing but succession to everything a deceased possessed.

HAEREDITAS NUNQUAM ASCENDIT. [L.] Inheritance never ascends.

HAEREDUM APPELLATIONE VENIUNT HAEREDES HAEREDUM IN INFINITUM. [L.] Under the title of "heirs" come the heirs of heirs for ever.

HAERES. *n.* [L.] An heir.

HAERES EST AUT JURE PROPRIETATIS, AUT JURE REPRAESENTATIONIS. [L.] One is an heir by right of property, or by right of representation.

HAERES EST NOMEN JURIS, FILIUS EST NOMEN NATURAE. [L.] Heir is a label of law, child is a label of nature.

HAERES FACTUS. [L.] A chosen heir.

HAERES LEGITIMUS EST QUEM NUPTIAE DEMONSTRANT. [L.] The lawful heir is one whom wedlock shows so to be.

HAERES NATUS. [L.] A born heir.

HAGUE CONVENTION ON ADOPTION. The Convention on the Protection of Children and Co-operation in respect of Inter-Country Adoption that was concluded on May 29, 1993 and came into force on May 1, 1995.

HAGUE CONVENTIONS. Agreements on rules of international law relating to matters such as the peaceful settlement of international disputes and the conduct of war.

HAIL INSURANCE. 1. Insurance against loss of or damage to crops caused by hail. 2. Insurance against loss of or damage to growing crops caused by hail. 3. Insurance against loss of or damage to crops in the field, whether growing or cut, caused by hail. *Insurance Act*, R.S.O. 1990, c. I.8, s. 1. 4. Insurance against loss of or damage to property caused by hail. *Insurance Act*, R.S.B.C. 1979, c. 200, s. 1. See LIMITED ~.

HAIR. See LANUGO ~S; RAW WOOL, ~ OR BRISTLES.

HAIRDRESSER. *n.* Unless the context otherwise requires, means any person who for fee, gain or reward (i) with the hands or by the use of any mechanical application or appliance engages in the occupation of cutting, bleaching, colouring, dressing, curling, waving, permanently waving, cleansing or similar work upon the hair of any person, (ii) with the hands or by the use of any mechanical application or appliance, or by the use of cosmetic preparations, creams or similar preparations or compounds, engages in any one or more or any combination of the following practices, to wit, manicuring the nails or massaging, cleansing or beautifying the scalp, face, neck or arms of any person.

HAIRLINE FRACTURE. A barely visible linear bone fracture in which no bone fragments are displaced. F.A. Jaffe, *A Guide to Pathological Evidence*, 3d ed. (Toronto: Carswell, 1991) at 220.

HAKAPIK. *n.* A metal ferrule that weighs at least 340 g with a slightly bent spike not more than 14 cm in length on one side of the ferrule and a blunt projection not more than 1.3 cm in length on the opposite side of the ferrule and that is attached to a wooden handle that measures not less than 105 cm and not more than 153 cm in length and not less than 3 cm and not more than 5.1 cm in diameter. *Marine Mammal Regulations*, SOR/93-56, s. 28.

HAKE. See RED ~; SILVER ~; WHITE ~.

HALF-BLOOD. *n*. One related through one parent only.

HALF BROTHER. A brother by only one parent's side.

HALF-LIFE. *n*. The period it takes the concentration of a substance to be reduced by half, by transformation, in a medium. *Persistence and Bioaccumulation Regulations*, SOR/2000-107, s. 1.

HALF-SECRET TRUST. A legatee is identified in a will as a trustee but the terms of the trust are not spelled out in the will. Extrinsic evidence is admissible to establish the missing terms of the trust.

HALF SISTER. A sister by only one parent's side.

HALFWAY HOUSE. A group home for persons having recently left a penal or psychiatric institution.

HALIBUT. *n*. The species of fish known as hippoglossus. *Northern Pacific Halibut Fisheries Convention Act*, R.S.C. 1985, c. F-19, s. 2. See GREENLAND ~.

HALL. See DANCE ~; ENTERTAINMENT ~; HIRING ~; PUBLIC ~.

HALLIDAY ORDER. Named after *Halliday v. McCulloch* (1986), 1 B.C.L.R. (2d) 194 (C.A.). In the *Halliday* case an application was made for the disclosure of the hospital records of the plaintiff. The plaintiff objected on the grounds that some of the documents may be subject to litigation privilege. Mr. Justice Lambert set out what he called a "set of mechanics" for the disclosure of hospital records over which the plaintiff had claimed there may be a privilege. That procedure contemplates that the documents will first be disclosed to the plaintiff's solicitor. They would be reviewed by the solicitor and a list made in the normal course of those documents that would be disclosed and those over which privilege was claimed. Towards the end of his reasons Lambert J.A. said the following: "I have suggested that the order should permit decisions with respect to relevance to be made in the first instance by the patient-litigant, subject to being disputed by adverse parties. I have done so because it permits the patient-litigant to avoid disclosing embarrassing or confidential material that is completely irrelevant or that can be made completely irrelevant if he wishes, by amending his pleadings before the time for delivery of the documents to adverse parties. But if that method of disputing relevance were to be abused, in any particular case, then there should be some recognition of that abuse in an award of costs. And if that method of disputing relevance were to be shown to be impractical, then the mechanics I have suggested should be modified." This procedure has come to be followed in cases involving personal injuries where medical records are sought to be produced by the defendant.

HALLMARK. *n*. A stamp affixed to articles of gold or silver as evidence of genuineness.

HALLMARK CASE. Another crime allegedly committed by the accused which is admissible because it bears a hallmark or characteristic in common with the crime for which the accused is being tried. P.K. McWilliams, *Canadian Criminal Evidence*, 3d ed. (Aurora: Canada Law Book, 1988) at 11-15.

HALLUCINATION. *n*. An illusory sensory perception. F.A. Jaffe, *A Guide to Pathological Evidence*, 3d ed. (Toronto: Carswell, 1991) at 220.

HALLUCINOGENIC DRUG. A drug producing hallucination such as lysergic acid diethylamide (L.S.D.) or mescaline.

HAM. *n*. Meat from the hind leg of a pig. *Meat Inspection Regulations*, C.R.C., c. 1032, s. 2.

HAMBURGER POLL. During an election a poll relating to the election conducted by matching goods to political candidates or parties. The sales of each item are then considered to match public sentiment concerning the candidates or parties.

HAMLET. *n*. An unincorporated community.

HAMPERED SHIP. A ship that, to the knowledge of and so declared by the Authority, is unable to be navigated in a normal fashion because of excessive list, excessive trim by the head or stern, shifted deckloads, damage, faulty steering, faulty engines, lack of normal navigational aid equipment, faulty navigational aid equipment or other unseaworthy conditions. Canada regulations.

HANDBOOK. See EMPLOYEE ~.

HANDGUN. A firearm that is designed, altered or intended to be aimed and fired by the action of one hand, whether or not it has been redesigned or subsequently altered to be aimed and fired by the action of both hands. *Criminal Code*, R.S.C. 1985, c. C-46, s. 84(1).

HANDICAP. See BECAUSE OF ~; DEVELOPMENTAL ~; EMPLOYMENT ~; PHYSICAL ~; PHYSICAL OR MENTAL ~.

HANDICAPPED CHILDREN. Children who have a physical or mental impairment.

HANDICAPPED PERSON. 1. A person limited in the performance of normal activities who is suffering, significantly and permanently, from a physical or mental deficiency, or who regularly uses a prosthesis or an orthopedic device or an other means of the handicap. 2. person who (a) is permanently dependent on a wheelchair, (b) has suffered loss of a limb, (c) has suffered the complete and permanent functional loss of the lower limbs. 3. A person who is handicapped visually or aurally. See PHYSICALLY ~; VISUALLY ~.

HANDICRAFT. *n.* " . . . [A]n article generally manually created by the author alone; his concepts, manual craftsmanship, expertise and creativity. It is an article conceived, designed and worked and finished by essentially the one individual." *R. v. Magder* (1983), 4 C.C.C. (3d) 327 at 330, 41 O.R. (2d) 281 (C.A.), the court per Grange J.A. adopting the words of Purvis Prov. Ct. J. in *R. v. United Cigar Stores*, unreported, May 9, 1979 at p. 5.

HANDLE. *v.* Includes use, store, treat, manufacture, generate, manufacture, mix, package, process, reprocess, sell, offer for sale and dispose.

HANDLING. *n.* 1. Loading, packing or placing, unloading, unpacking or removing or reloading, repacking or replacing dangerous goods in or from any container, packaging or means of transport or at any facility for the purposes of, in the course of or following transportation and includes storing dangerous goods in the course of transportation. 2. The storing, transmitting, transporting or distributing of gasoline or an associated product, and includes putting gasoline or an associated product into the fuel tank of a motor vehicle, motor boat or other water craft or into a container. *Gasoline Handling Act*, R.S.O. 1990, c. G.4, s. 1.

HANDLING CHARGE. 1. A charge on goods for their receipt at and stowage in the warehouse and delivery to the warehouse handling floor. *Montreal Cold Storage Warehouse Tariff By-law*, C.R.C., c. 1076, s. 2. 2. A charge for moving goods between ordinary places of rest and vessel slings. Canada regulations. See CONTAINER ~.

HANDLING RATES. Rates imposed for moving freight to or from ships' slings and includes rates imposed for ordinary sorting, piling and trucking in a shed. *Port Alberni Assembly Wharves By-law*, C.R.C., c. 913, s. 2.

HAND PICKED. That the fruit shows no evidence of rough handling or of having been on the ground. *Fresh Fruit and Vegetable Regulations*, C.R.C., c. 285, s. 1.

HAND TOOL. A tool that is designed to be held in the hand and that is operated by manual power. *Canada Hand Tools Regulations* C.R.C., c. 1002, s. 2.

HANDWRITING. *n.* The form of writing peculiar to a person.

HANG. *v.* To suspend an animal by one or more legs. *Humane Slaughter Regulations*, C.R.C., c. 937, s. 2.

HANG GLIDER. A glider that is designed to carry not more than two persons and has a launch weight of 45 kg (99.2 pounds) or less. *Canadian Aviation Regulations*, SOR/96-433, s. 101.01(1).

HANGING. *n.* Ligature strangulation caused by gravity. F.A. Jaffe, *A Guide to Pathological Evidence*, 3d ed. (Toronto: Carswell 1991) at 220.

HANG UP. A tree that has not fallen to the ground after being (i) partly or wholly separated from its stump or (ii) displaced from its natural position. *Occupational Health and Safety* Act, R.R.O. 1980, Reg. 692, s. 107.

HANSARD. *n.* A record of speeches made in the House of Commons and answers to written questions from the Order Paper. 2. Also refers to the similar record of debates in a legislative assembly or legislature.

HAPTOGLOBIN. *n.* A protein in blood plasma. F.A. Jaffe, *A Guide to Pathological Evidence*, 3d ed. (Toronto: Carswell, 1991) at 220-21.

HARASS. *v.* 1. " . . . '[A]nnoy'." *R. v. Sabine* (1990), 57 C.C.C. (3d) 209 at 212, 78 C.R. (3d) 34, 107 N.B.R. (2d) 73, 267 A.P.R. 73 (Q.B.), Stevenson J. 2. Includes worry, exhaust, fatigue, annoy, plague, pester, tease or torment, but does not include the lawful hunting, trapping or capturing of wildlife. *Wildlife Act*, S.B.C. 1982, c. 57, s. 1. 3. To engage in a course of vexatious comment or conduct that is known or ought reasonably to be known to be unwelcome. *Human Rights Code*, R.S. Nfld. 1990, c. H-14, s. 1. 4. Means more than to annoy, to vex. Implies being tormented, troubled, worried continually and chronically, being plagued, bedeviled and badgered. In addition, the conduct of the accused must be shown to have caused the complainant reasonably to fear for her safety or the safety of anyone known to her. *R. v. Sillipp* (1997), 55 Alta. L.R. (3d) 263 (C.A.). See SEXUALLY ~.

HARASSMENT. *n*. 1. Engaging in a course of vexatious comment or conduct that is known or ought reasonably to be known to be unwelcome. *Human Rights Code*, R.S.O. 1990, c. H.19, s. 10(1). 2. Persistently annoying . See CRIMINAL ~; POISONED ENVIRONMENT SEXUAL ~; QUID PRO QUO SEXUAL ~; SEXUAL ~.

HARBOUR. *v*. To give refuge to, to shelter.

HARBOUR. *n*. Harbours and places properly so called whether proclaimed public harbours or not, and whether natural or artificial, to which ships may resort for shelter or to ship or unship goods or passengers. *Canada Shipping Act*, R.S.C. 1985, c. S-9, s. 2. See PUBLIC ~; SCHEDULED~.

HARBOUR DUES. 1. A charge on a vessel entering the harbour. Canada regulations. 2. The rates payable in respect of a vessel using the harbour. Canada regulations.

HARBOUR TOLL. Every rate, toll and charge established or proposed to be established by any Act of Parliament or by, or with the approval of, the Governor in Council in respect of ships entering, using or leaving any harbour in Canada, the passengers thereof or goods loaded, unloaded, shipped, transhipped, moved in transit or stored in any harbour in Canada or on or in any wharf, dock, pier, warehouse or other facility within the limits of any such harbour or situated on lands appurtenant thereto. *Transport Act*, R.S.C. 1985, c. T-17, s. 2.

HARD. *adj*. Rock comparable to concrete with a compressive strength greater than 6,000 psi. *Building Code Act*, R.R.O. 1980, Reg. 87, s. 4.2.1.10. See MEDIUM ~.

HARD BARGAINING. " . . . [T]he adoption of a tough position in the hope and expectation of being able to force the other side to agree to one's terms. . . there is a genuine intention to continue collective bargaining and to reach agreement. . ." *Nova Scotia (Labour Relations Board) v. C U.P.E.* (1983), 83 C.L.L.C. 14,069 at 12,360, 49 N.R. 107, 60 N.S.R. (2d) 369, 128 A.P.R. 369, 1 D.L.R. (4th) 1, [1983] 2 S.C.R. 311, Laskin C.J.C.

HARDSHIP. *n*. Suffering or privation.

HARD SWELL. A can with both ends bulging as a result of spoilage from gas-producing organisms. *Processed Fruit and Vegetable Regulations*, C.R.C. c. 291, s. 2.

HARD TO SERVE PUPIL. A pupil who, under this section, is determined to be unable to profit by instruction offered by a board due to a mental handicap or a mental and one or more additional handicaps. *Education Act*, R.S.O. 1990, c. E.2, s. 35(1).

HARDWARE. *n*. 1. Any metal or rigid plastic part designed to secure a person in a vehicle in conjunction with straps or webbing. *Motor Vehicle Safety Regulations*, C.R.C., c. 1038, s. 209. 2. Any metal or rigid plastic part of an occupant restraint assembly or product restraint assembly. *Children's Car Seats and Harnesses Regulations*, C.R.C., c. 921, s. 2. See ADJUSTMENT ~; ATTACHMENT ~; PANIC ~.

HARD WATER. Water which holds mineral salts in solution and is not useful for washing purposes.

HARDWOOD. *adj*. Non-coniferous. *Crown Timber Act*, R.R.O. 1980, Reg. 234, s. 1.

HARM. *v*. To injure; to affect adversely.

HARM. *n*. 1. Connotes an adverse effect on the child's upbringing that is more than transitory. The impugned exercise by the access parent must be shown to create a substantial risk that the child's physical, psychological or moral well-being will be adversely affected. Exposure to new experiences and ideas may upset children and cause them considerable discomfort. *Young v. Young*, 1993 CarswellBC 264, 84 B.C.L.R. (2d) 1, [1993] 8 W.W.R. 513, 49 R.F.L. (3d) 117, 160 N.R. 1, 34 B.C.A.C. 161, 56 W.A.C. 161, 108 D.L.R. (4th) 193, [1993] 4 S.C.R. 3, 18 C.R.R. (2d) 41, [1993] R.D.F. 703, Per Sopinka, J. 2. Any contamination or degradation and includes harm caused by the release of any solid, liquid, gas, odour, heat, sound, vibration or radiation. *Environmental Bill of Rights, 1993*, S.O. 1993, c. 28, s. 1(1). See BODILY ~; IR-

REPARABLE ~; SERIOUS BODILY ~; SERIOUS ~.

HARMFUL INTERFERENCE. An adverse effect of electromagnetic energy from any emission, radiation or induction that (a) endangers the use or functioning of a safety-related radiocommunication system, or (b) significantly degrades or obstructs, or repeatedly interrupts, the use or functioning of radio apparatus or radio-sensitive equipment. *Radiocommunication Act*, R.S.C. 1985, c. R-2, s. 2.

HARMONIZATION. The objectives of harmonization of federal legislation with the civil law of Quebec are to ensure that federal legislation is fully consistent with the new civil law concepts and institutions, that federal legislation employs correct and precise terminology, and that amendments to federal legislation take into account French common law terminology. Let me be clear that Harmonization Act, Bill S-4 does not create substantive rights or enshrine any new individual or collective rights. *Schreiber v. Canada (Attorney General)*, [2002] 3 S.C.R. 269.

HARMONIZED SALES TAX. Three provinces, Nova Scotia, New Brunswick, and Newfoundland and Labrador, have harmonized their provincial sales tax with GST to create HST. HST applies at a rate of 15% to the same base of goods and services that are taxable at **7%** under GST. HST follows the same general rules as GST.

HARMONIZED SYSTEM CODE. In respect of goods, the numeric identifier set out for those goods in the *Harmonized Commodity Description and Coding System* published by the World Customs Organization.

HARM PRINCIPLE. The State has no right to interfere with the personal freedom and liberty of an individual unless that individual causes harm to other persons or to society in general. The harm principle is not the constitutional standard for what conduct may or may not be the subject of the criminal law for the purposes of s. 7. The 'harm principle' is better characterized as a description of an important state interest rather than a normative 'legal' principle. There is nevertheless a state *interest* in the avoidance of harm to those subject to its laws which may justify parliamentary action. Avoidance of harm is a 'state interest' within the rule against arbitrary or irrational state conduct. *R. v. Malmo-Levine*, 2003 SCC 74.

HARMONY PLEDGE. Clause in which employer and union agree to co-operate on a particular subject.

HARNESS. See SAFETY ~.

HARNESS RACING. Horse racing in which the horses participating are harnessed to a sulky, carriage or similar vehicle. *Harness Racing Commission Act*, R.S.N.S. 1967, c. 124, s. 1.

HARPOON. *n.* An apparatus equipped with one or more points that is capable of catching fish by piercing or impaling them. *Quebec Fishery Regulations*, C.R.C., c. 852, s. 2.

HARR. & HODG. *abbr.* Harrison & Hodgins' Municipal Reports (Ont.), 1845-1851.

HARVEST. *v.* Cut, take, dredge, rake or otherwise obtain. *Fisheries Act*, R.S.C. 1985, c. F-14, s. 47. See RIGHT TO ~.

HARVESTER. *n.* A person in possession of or in charge of a harvesting machine. *Noxious Weeds Act*, R.S.M. 1987, c. N110, s. 1.

HARVESTING. *n.* 1. Includes gathering, raking, dragging, cutting, pumping, transporting, or by any other means acquiring sea plants or sea plant products whether on the foreshore or in the water, or whether attached to the solum or loose-lying, whether biologically living or not living. 2. Includes pasturing. *Crop Insurance Act (Ontario)*, R.R.O. 1980, Reg. 211, s. 3.

HARVESTING ADVANCES. The necessary goods supplied or services rendered to a farmer in connection with the cutting, harvesting or threshing of his crop by reason of which any of the following claims arise: (a) the claim of an employee for wages for work done in connection with the cutting or harvesting of any crop, including work done on or about any threshing machine; (b) the claim of the vendor of binder twine or fuel oil for the amount remaining unpaid of the purchase price of the binder twine or fuel oil in connection with the cutting, harvesting or threshing of any crop; (c) the claim of a person for the amount remaining unpaid for repairs carried out in connection with the cutting, harvesting or threshing of any crop; (d) the claim of the owner, operator or person for the time being entitled to the possession of any machinery for amount owing for the rent of the machinery provided in connection with the cutting, harvesting or threshing of any crop; and includes all money advanced to the farmer to enable him to discharge any of the claims set out in clauses (a) to (d). *Harvesting Liens Act*, R.S.A. 1980, c. H-2, s. 1.

HARVESTING MACHINE. A machine that while moving or stationary harvests, threshes, or processes any forage or cereal crop, root crop, or the residue thereof. *Noxious Weeds Act*, R.S.M. 1987, c. N110, s. 1.

HARVESTING OF CROPS. Includes the cutting, swathing, combining, threshing, division into their respective shares as between landlord and tenant, and the removal, delivery and sale of such crops. *The Agricultural Leaseholds Act*, R.S.S. 1978, c. A-12, s. 2.

HASH. *n.* " . . . [A] colloquial term for hashish." *R. v. O'Brien* (1987), 41 C.C.C. (3d) 86 at 88, 10 Q.A.C. 135, the court per McCarthy J.A.

HASHISH. *n.* A resinous juice found in the upper leaves and the flowering tops of the plant Cannabis sativa. F.A. Jaffe, *A Guide to Pathological Evidence*, 3d ed. (Toronto: Carswell, 1991) at 221.

HATCH. *n.* An opening in a deck used for the purpose of the processes or for trimming or ventilation. *Tack Regulations*, C.R.C., c. 1494, s. 2.

HATCHERY. *n.* Any place, buildings or premises equipped with an incubator capacity of one thousand or more eggs and used for incubation purposes.

HATCHERY ESTABLISHMENT. Any establishment in which the rearing of fish takes place. *Quebec Fishery Regulations*, C.R.C. c. 852, s. 2 .

HATCHERYMAN. *n.* Any person who operates a hatchery. *Livestock and Livestock Products Act*, R.S.C. 1985, c. L-9, s. 42.

HATCHING EGGS. 1. Eggs of a domestic hen produced for the purpose of hatching into chicks. 2. The fertilized eggs of poultry. *Animal Disease and Protection Regulations*, C.R C. c. 296, s. 2.

HATCHWAY. *n.* The whole space within the square of the hatches, from the top deck to the bottom of the hold. *Tackle Regulations*, C.R.C., c. 1494, s. 2.

HATE PROPAGANDA. 1. Any writing, sign or visible representation that advocates or promotes genocide or the communication of which by any person would constitute an offence under section 319. *Criminal Code*, R.S.C. 1985, c. C-46, s. 320(8) as am. 2. " . . . [E]xpression intended or likely to create extreme feelings of opprobrium and enmity against a racial or religious group,. . ." *R. v. Keegstra* (1990), 61 C.C.C. (3d) 1 at 18, 1 C.R. (4th) 129, 77 Alta. L.R. (2d) 193, [1991] 2 W.W.R. 1, 117 N.R. 1, 114 A.R. 81, 3 C.R.R. (2d) 193, [1990] 3 S.C.R. 697, Dickson C.J.C. (Wilson, L'Heureux-Dubé and Gonthier JJ. concurring).

HATRED. *n.* 1. "[In s. 319(2) of the Criminal Code, R.S.C. 1985, c. C-46] . . . connotes emotion of an intense and extreme nature that is clearly associated with vilification and detestation. . . a most extreme emotion that belies reason; an emotion, that, if exercised against members of an identifiable group, implies that those individuals are to be despised, scorned, denied respect and made subject to ill-treatment on the basis of group affiliation." *R. v. Keegstra* (1990), 3 C.R.R. (2d) 193 at 249, 1 C.R. (4th) 129, 77 Alta. L.R. (2d) 193, [1991] 2 W.W.R. 1, 61 C.C.C. (3d) 1, 117 N.R. 1, 114 A.R. 81, [1990] 3 S.C.R. 697, Dickson C.J.C. (Wilson, L'Heureux-Dubé and Gonthier JJ. concurring). 2. As referred to in human rights legislation, extreme ill-will and an emotion which allows for no redeeming qualities in the persons to whom it is directed; and unusually strong and deep-felt emotions of detestation, calumny and vilification. *Canada (Human Rights Commission) v. Taylor*, [1990] 3 S.C.R. 892, 75 D.L.R. (4th) 577, 13 C.H.R.R. D/435, 3 C.R.R. (2d) 116, 117 N.R. 191, at 928 [S.C.R.], per Dickson, C.J.C. See COMMERCIAL SPEECH; FREEDOM OF EXPRESSION; PROMOTE ~.

HAULED LIQUID INDUSTRIAL WASTE. Liquid waste, other than hauled sewage, that results from industrial processes or manufacturing or commercial operations and that is transported in a tank or other container for treatment or disposal, and includes sewage residue from sewage works that are subject to the provisions of the Ontario Water Resources Act. *Environmental Protection Act*, R.R.O. 1980, Reg. 309, s. 1.

HAULED SEWAGE. Waste removed from, (i) a cesspool, (ii) a septic tank system, (iii) a privy vault or privy pit, (iv) a chemical toilet, (v) a portable toilet, or (vi) a sewage holding tank. *Environmental Protection Act*, R.R.O. 1980, Reg. 309, s. 1.

HAUL ROAD. A road, other than a highway as defined in the Highway Traffic Act, on which vehicles used to haul logs are operated. *Occupational Health and Safety Act*, R.R.O. 1980, Reg. 692, s. 107.

HAVE. *v*. " . . . '[P]ossess'." *R. v. Theriault* (1951), 28 M.P.R. 412 at 417, 101 C.C.C. 233 (N.B. C.A.), Harrison J.A. See TO ~ AND TO HOLD.

HAVE AND TO HOLD. See TO HAVE AND TO HOLD.

HAVE CHARGE OF. In relation to a plant, to have at all times while the plant is in operation general supervision of the operation and maintenance of the plant and of the power engineers operating the plant.

HAVEN. *n*. A harbour or port; any place which contains or holds ships.

HAVE NO ISSUE. A want or failure of issue in the lifetime or at the time of death of that person, and not an indefinite failure of issue unless a contrary intention appears by the will. *Wills acts.*

HAVE-NOT PROVINCE. A province entitled to an equalization grant from the federal government.

HAVING. *v*. Controlling; possessing; giving birth to.

HAWKER. *n*. " . . . [A] man who goes through the streets or roads of the city or country calling out his wares for sale . . ." *R. v. Phillips* (1898), 35 N.B.R. 393 at 395-6 (C.A.), Tuck C.J.

HAY. *n*. The harvested, cured, unthreshed herbage of those kinds of forage plants that have recognized feeding value.

HAZARD. *n*. A danger. A risk. See AVOIDABLE ~; FIRE ~; HEALTH~; MORAL~; NUCLEAR ENERGY ~.

HAZARD CATEGORY. A category into which a chemical product or container is classified, in particular: (*a*) Category 1, toxic products set out in Part 1; (*b*) Category 2, corrosive products set out in Part 2; (*c*) Category 3, flammable products set out in Part 3; (*d*) Category 4, quick skin-bonding adhesives set out in Part 4; and (*e*) Category 5, pressurized containers set out in Part 5. *Consumer Chemicals and Containers Regulations, 2001*, SOR/2001-269, s. 1(1).

HAZARDOUS FOOD. Any food capable of supporting the growth of pathogenic organisms or the production of the toxins of such organisms. *Food Premises Act*, R.R.O. 1990, Reg. 562, s. 1(1).

HAZARDOUS INGREDIENT. (*a*) A pure chemical product; (*b*) an ingredient present in a chemical product in a concentration of 1% or more that is taken into consideration when classifying the product and that (i) is a chemical product, (ii) the supplier believes on reasonable grounds may be harmful to humans, (iii) has toxicological properties that are not known to the supplier, or (iv) derives from a reaction between precursor constituents and the hazards associated with the chemical product are not known to the supplier; or (*c*) a complex mixture present in a chemical product in a concentration of 1% or more that is taken into consideration when classifying the product and that (i) is a chemical product, (ii) the supplier believes on reasonable grounds may be harmful to humans, or (iii) has toxicological properties that are not known to the supplier. *Consumer Chemicals and Containers Regulations, 2001*, SOR/2001-269, s. 1(1).

HAZARDOUS MATERIAL. A biological or chemical agent named or described in the regulations as a hazardous material. *Occupational Health and Safety Act*, R.S.O. 1990, c. O.1, s. 1(1).

HAZARDOUS OCCUPATION. A job classified as dangerous.

HAZARDOUS PRODUCT. Any prohibited product, restricted product or controlled product. *Hazardous Products Act*, R.S.C. 1985, c. H-3, s. 2.

HAZARDOUS ROOM. A room in a factory or similar place where something is present which may ignite easily or explode, causing a fire or an imminently hazardous atmosphere. D. Robertson, *Ontario Health and Safety Guide* (Toronto: Richard De Boo Ltd., 1988) at 5-200.

HAZARDOUS SITUATION. A condition, which in the opinion of an inspector or environment officer will or may result in imminent risk of serious injury or damage to the health or safety of a person, the environment, or plant or animal life. *Dangerous Goods Handling and Transportation Act*, R.S.M. 1987, c. D12, s. 1.

HAZARDOUS SUBSTANCE. Includes a controlled product and a chemical, biological or physical agent that, by reason of a property that the agent possesses, is hazardous to the safety or health of a person exposed to it. *Canada Labour Code*, R.S.C. 1985, c. L-2, s. 122(1).

HAZARDOUS WASTE. A waste that is a, (a) hazardous industrial waste, (b) acute hazardous waste chemical, (c) hazardous waste chemical,

(d) severely toxic waste, (e) ignitable waste, (f) corrosive waste, (g) reactive waste, (h) radioactive waste, except radioisotope wastes disposed of in a landfilling site in accordance with the written instructions of the Canadian Nuclear Safety Commission or the Atomic Energy Control Board, (i) pathological waste, (j) leachate toxic waste, or (k) PCB waste as defined in Regulation 362 of the Revised Regulations of Ontario, 1990, but does not include, (l) hauled sewage, (m) waste from the operation of a sewage works subject to the Ontario Water Resources Act where the works, (i) is owned by a municipality, (ii) is owned by the Crown subject to an agreement with a municipality under the Ontario Water Resources Act, or (iii) receives only waste similar in character to the domestic sewage from a household, (n) domestic waste, (o) incinerator ash resulting from the incineration of waste that is neither hazardous waste nor liquid industrial waste, (p) waste that is a hazardous industrial waste, hazardous waste chemical, ignitable waste, corrosive waste, leachate toxic waste or reactive waste and that is produced in any month in an amount less than five kilograms or otherwise accumulated in an amount less than five kilograms, (q) waste that is an acute hazardous waste chemical and that is produced in any month in an amount less than one kilogram or otherwise accumulated in an amount less than one kilogram, (r) an empty container or the liner from an empty container that contained hazardous industrial waste, hazardous waste chemical, ignitable waste, corrosive waste, leachate toxic waste or reactive waste, (s) an empty container of less than twenty litres capacity or one or more liners weighing, in total, less than ten kilograms from empty containers, that contained acute hazardous waste chemical, (t) the residues or contaminated materials from the clean-up of a spill of less than five kilograms of waste that is a hazardous industrial waste, hazardous waste chemical, ignitable waste, corrosive waste, leachate toxic waste or reactive waste, or (u) the residues or contaminated materials from the clean-up of a spill of less than one kilogram of waste that is an acute hazardous waste chemical. *General — Waste Management Act*, R.R.O. 1990, Reg. 347, s. 1(1).

HAZARDOUS WASTE DISPOSAL FACILITY. A facility or place operated in whole or in part for the purpose of treatment, disposal or bulk storage of hazardous waste but does not include a facility or place approved by the director (i) that treats, stores or disposes of hazardous wastes on the generation site, or (ii) that treats or stores hazardous wastes as part of a process for the recycling, reuse or reclamation of hazardous wastes. *The Dangerous Goods Handling and Transportation Act*, R.S.M. 1987, c. D12, s. 1.

HAZARDOUS WASTE MANAGEMENT FACILITY. A facility for the reception, collection, movement, examination, storage, treatment or disposal of hazardous waste.

HAZARD SYMBOL. 1. Includes any design, mark, pictogram, sign, letter, word, number, abbreviation or any combination thereof that is to be displayed on a controlled product or container in which a controlled product is packaged in order to show the nature of the hazard of the controlled product. *Hazardous Products Act*, S.C. 1987, c. 30, s. 11(1). 2. A pictograph and its frame as set out in Schedule 2. *Consumer Chemicals and Containers Regulations, 2001*, SOR/2001-269, s. 1(1).

H.C. *abbr.* 1. High Court of Justice. 2. Haute Cour.

HCFC. A hydrochlorofluorocarbon each molecule of which contains one, two or three carbon atoms and at least one atom each of hydrogen, chlorine and fluorine. *Ozone-depleting Substances Regulations, 1998*, SOR/99-7, s. 1.

HEAD. *n.* 1. In respect of a government institution, means (a) in the case of a department or ministry of state, the member of the Queen's Privy Council for Canada presiding over that institution, or (b) in any other case, the person designated by order in council to be the head of that institution. Canada statutes. 2. The Minister of the Crown in charge of a department. 3. (i) When used in respect of a fire-tube boiler, the plate into which the ends of the tubes are fitted, (ii) when used in respect of a water-tube boiler, the plate closing the ends of the drum, and (iii) when used in respect of a pressure vessel, the plate closing the part in which the gas, vapour or liquid is under pressure. *Boilers and Pressure Vessels Act*, R.R.O. 1980, Reg. 84, s. 1. See DEPARTMENT ~; DEPUTY ~; GREEN ~; PERMANENT ~; PIT ~.

HEAD END. An antenna positioned to receive signals from satellites or from television-broadcasting stations in the area.

HEAD IMPACT AREA. The non-glazed surfaces of the interior of the vehicle that are capable of being contacted statically by the head form of a measuring device in accordance with the following procedure or its graphic equivalent: (*a*) at each designated seating position, by placing the pivot point of the measuring device, (i) for seats that are adjustable fore and aft, at (A) the seating reference point, and (B) a point 130 mm (five inches) horizontally forward of the seating reference point displaced vertically 20 mm (0.75 inches) or a distance equal to the rise that results from a 130 mm (five inches) forward adjustment of the seat, and (ii) for seats that are not adjustable fore and aft, at the seating reference point, (*b*) with the pivot point to top-of-head dimension at each adjustment allowed for the measuring device by the interior dimension of the vehicle, by determining all contact points above the lower windshield glass line and forward of the seating reference point, and (*c*) beginning with the head form of the measuring device at each contact point referred to in paragraph (*b*) and with the measuring device in a vertical position if no contact point exists for a particular adjusted length, by pivoting the measuring device forward and downward through all arcs in vertical planes to 90° each side of the longitudinal plane through the seating reference point until the head form contacts an interior surface or until it is tangent to a horizontal plane 25 mm (1 inch) above the seating reference point, whichever occurs first. *Motor Vehicle Safety Regulations*, C.R.C. c. 1038, s. 201(1).

HEADING. *n*. 1. A text prefixed to a section or group of sections in a modern statute. P.St.J. Langan, ed., *Maxwell on The Interpretation of Statutes*, 12th ed. (Bombay: N.M. Tripathi, 1976) at 11. 2. The direction in which the longitudinal axis of an aircraft is pointed, usually expressed in true, magnetic or grid degrees from North. *Canadian Aviation Regulations*, SOR/96-433, s. 101.01(1).

HEADLAMP CONCEALMENT DEVICE. A device, including the operating system and components thereof, that provides concealment of one or more headlamps when it is not in use and includes a movable headlamp cover and a headlamp that is displaced for concealment purposes. *Motor Vehicle Safety Regulations*, C.R.C., c. 1038, s. 114.

HEAD LEASE. A contract under which (a) Her Majesty in right of Canada or a province grants, or (b) an owner in fee simple, other than Her Majesty in right of Canada or a province, grants for a period of not less than 10 years, any right, licence or privilege to explore for, drill for or take petroleum, natural gas or related hydrocarbons in Canada or to prospect, explore, drill or mine for minerals in a mineral resource in Canada. *Income Tax Act*, R.S.C. 1952, c. 148 (as am. S.C. 1986, c. 55, s. 73), s. 209(1).

HEADLESS DRAWN WEIGHT. The weight of a fish after the head, gills and entrails have been removed without cutting the belly. *Manitoba Fishery Regulations*, C.R.C., c. 843, s. 2.

HEADLESS DRESSED WEIGHT. The weight of the fish after the head, gills and entrails have been removed and the belly has been cut. *Manitoba Fishery Regulations*, C.R.C., c. 843, s. 2.

HEAD MONEY. Poll tax.

HEADNOTE. *n*. In law reports, a summary of what the author considers to be the critical factual findings, analysis and conclusions of the judge who wrote the reasons. The Headnotes are intended to inform the reader, quickly and efficiently, whether the judicial reasons are relevant to the reader's purposes, so that if they are, the reasons may then be read. *CCH Canadian Ltd. v. Law Society of Upper Canada*, 2002 FCA 187, 18 C.P.R. (4th) 161, 212 D.L.R. (4th) 385, 289 N.R. 1, [2002] 4 F.C. 213, 224 F.T.R. 111 (note) (C.A.).

HEAD OF A DEPARTMENT. (i) In the case of an unincorporated Crown agency, the minister charged with the administration of the Act under which the agency is established; (ii) in the case of an incorporated Crown agency, the chief executive officer of the agency, and (iii) in all other cases, the minister charged with the administration of the department. *The Freedom of Information Act*, S.M. 1985-86, c. 6, s. 1. See DEPARTMENT HEAD.

HEAD OF A FAMILY. 1. A person who has charge of a household and who has one or more dependants therein. 2. The member of a family who habitually is the chief provider for the needs of such family. *Social Aid Act*, R.S.Q. 1977, c. A-16, s. 1. See HEAD OF FAMILY.

HEAD OF COUNCIL. Includes a chairman of the board of an improvement district. *Emergency Plans Act, 1983*, S.O.1983, c. 30, s.1. See HEAD OF THE COUNCIL.

HEAD OF ESTABLISHMENT. Includes any person, partnership or corporation who has charge of all or part of an industrial or commercial establishment on his own account or on account of another person, partnership or corporation, as a contractor, subcontractor, manager, supervisor, foreman or agent, or otherwise. *Industrial and Commercial Establishments Act*, R.S.Q. 1977, c. E-15, s. 2.

HEAD OF FAMILY. The person in the family upon whom the other members are mainly dependent for support. *Immigration Act*, R.S.C. 1970, c. I-2, s. 2. See HEAD OF A FAMILY.

HEAD OFFICE. 1. The principal office or place of business of a corporation. 2. The place where the chief executive officer of an insurer carries on business. *Insurance acts*. 3. The place where the chief executive officers of the corporation transact its business. *Trust Corporations acts*.

HEAD OF MISSION. (a) An ambassador, high commissioner or consul-general of Canada; or (b) any other person appointed to represent Canada in another country or a portion of another country or at an international organization or diplomatic conference and designated head of mission by the Governor in Council. *Department of Foreign and International Trade Affairs Act*, R.S.C. 1985, c. E-22, s. 13(1).

HEAD OF THE COUNCIL. The mayor of a city or town, the overseer of a village or the reeve of a rural municipality. *The Tax Enforcement Act*, R.S.S. 1978, c. T-2, s. 2. See HEAD OF COUNCIL.

HEAD OF THE DEPARTMENT. The member of the Executive Council presiding over a department of government. See DEPARTMENT HEAD.

HEAD RESTRAINT. A device that limits rearward angular displacement of the occupant's head relative to his torso. Canada regulations.

HEAD SPACE. That space between the top edge or rim of the container and the upper level of the contents. *Processed Fruit and Vegetable Regulations*, C.R.C., c. 291, s. 2.

HEALTH. *n*. 1. " . . . [N]ot merely . . . the absence of disease and infirmity, but . . . a state of physical, mental and social well-being." *R. v. Morgentaler* (1988), 62 C.R. (3d) 1 at 29-30, 82 N.R. 1, [1988] 1 S.C.R. 30, 63 O.R. (2d) 281n, 26 O.A.C. 1, 44 D.L.R. (4th) 385, 31 C.R.R. 1, 37 C.C.C. (3d) 449, Dickson C.J.C. (Lamer J. concurring). 2. A state of complete physical, mental and social well-being. See BOARD OF ~; ENVIRONMENTAL ~; MEDICAL OFFICER OF ~; MINISTER OF ~; OCCUPATIONAL ~; RADIATION ~; SAFETY

AND ~ COMMITTEE; SAFETY AND ~ REPRESENTATIVE.

HEALTH AGENCY. The regional board of a health region established pursuant to The Health Services Act or a non-profit association, corporation or other organization whose sole purpose and object is the payment for medical services and related services to and for its members or subscribers. *The Saskatchewan Medical Care Insurance Act*, R.S.S. 1978, c. S-29, s. 2.

HEALTH AND SAFETY REPRESENTA-TIVE. A health and safety representative elected by the employees at a place of employment. *Occupational Health and Safety acts*.

HEALTH AND WELFARE CANADA. The federal ministry with mandate to promote and preserve Canadians' health, social welfare and social security.

HEALTH CARE. 1. Includes (i) any examination, diagnosis, procedure or treatment undertaken to prevent any disease or ailment, (ii) any procedure undertaken for the purpose of preventing pregnancy, (iii) any procedure undertaken for the purpose of an examination or a diagnosis, (iv) any medical, surgical, obstetrical or dental treatment, and (v) anything done that is ancillary to any procedure, treatment, examination or diagnosis. *Dependent Adults Act*, R.S.A. 2000, c. D-11, s. 1. 2. Medical, surgical, obstetrical, optical, dental and nursing services, and includes drugs, dressings, prosthetic appliances and any other items or health services necessary to or commonly associated with the provision of any such specified services, but does not include any part of such items and health services payable under the Ontario Health Insurance Plan under the Health Insurance Act. *Developmental Services Act*, R.R.O. 1980, Reg. 242, s. 1.

HEALTH CARE FACILITY. A facility that provides diagnostic or therapeutic services to patients.

HEALTH CARE INSURANCE PLAN. In relation to a province, a plan or plans established by the law of the province to provide for insured health services. *Canada Health Act*, R.S.C. 1985, c. C-6, s. 2.

HEALTH CARE PRACTITIONER. A person lawfully entitled under the law of a province to provide health services in the place in which the services are provided by that person. *Canada Health Act*, R.S.C. 1985, c. C-6, s. 2.

HEALTH CARE PROFESSIONAL. A person who is entitled under the laws of a province to provide health services in the province.

HEALTH CARE SERVICES. Medical, surgical, obstetrical, optical, dental and nursing services, and includes drugs, dressings, prosthetic appliances and any other items or health services necessary to or commonly associated with the provision of any such specified services. See EXTENDED ~.

HEALTH CARE UNIONS. A trade union certified for a unit in which the majority of employees has as its principal duties the health care of patients or operation and maintenance of a hospital. *Essential Service Disputes Act*, R.S.B.C. 1979, c. 113, s. 1.

HEALTH CERTIFICATE. 1. A statement that a worker is fit to return to work after a period of absence or that the worker is unfit to work due to illness or other health issue. 2. In respect of any plant or other matter means a certificate signed by an official of the country of origin of the plant or other matter who has been authorized by the government of that country to sign certificates as to the health of plants or other matter. *Plant Quarantine Regulations*, C.R.C., c. 1273, s. 5.

HEALTH CLUB. A health club is generally understood to mean a facility where people sign up as members for a fee, giving them access to the facilities for a defined period of time, usually measured in months or all or part of a year. The facilities include, as a predominant feature, weight machines, exercise machines and other apparatus and facilities designed for the development of physical fitness. It is customary to have change and shower facilities on the premises. A health club could also include features such as a steam room, a sauna, a spa and perhaps even swimming facilities. Therapeutic massage would normally be considered as an appropriate component of a health club. *1423107 Ontario Inc. v. Woodstock (City)* (2001), 2001 CarswellOnt 1204, 200 D.L.R. (4th) 175, 19 M.P.L.R. (3d) 256 (S.C.J.), Heeney, J.

HEALTH FACILITY. 1. An ambulance service, a nursing home, a private hospital, a laboratory, a specimen collection centre, a hospital, health centre or other health program or service.

HEALTH GOODS. Any material, substance, mixture, compound or preparation, of whatever composition or in whatever form, sold or represented for use in the diagnosis, treatment, mitigation or prevention of a disease, a disorder, an abnormal physical state or the symptoms thereof in human beings or animals or for use in restoring, correcting or modifying organic functions in human beings or animals. *Excise Tax Act*, R.S.C. 1985 (2d Supp.), c. 7, s. 1(4).

HEALTH HAZARD. (a) A condition of a premises, (b) a substance, thing, plant or animal other than man, or (c) a solid, liquid, gas or combination of any of them, that has or that is likely to have an adverse effect on the health of any person. *Health Protection and Promotion Act*, R.S.O. 1990, c. H.7, s. 1(1).

HEALTH INSURANCE OR BENEFIT PLAN. Includes a plan, fund or arrangement provided, furnished or offered by an employer to an employee that provides benefits to an employee, a spouse or dependant of an employee or deceased employee for medical, hospital, nursing, drug or dental expenses or other similar expenses. *Employment Standards Act*, R.R.O. 1980, Reg. 282, s. 1.

HEALTH LAW. The law governing the healing professions and hospitals and other care-giving facilities.

HEALTH L. CAN. *abbr*. Health Law in Canada.

HEALTH OFFICER. A medical health officer appointed for the enforcement of this Act or of any other Act of the Province relating to public health. *Health Act*, R.S.B.C. 1979, c. 161, s. 1.

HEALTH PRACTITIONER. Any person who provides health care or treatment to any person. *Public Health Act*, S.A. 1984, c. P-27.1, s. 1.

HEALTH PROTECTION. See RADIOLOGICAL ~.

HEALTH RESOURCES. (i) Community health facilities including health practitioners and personnel through which health services can be provided to persons in a community, and (ii) the operation of a mobile vision van by a non-profit organization to provide eye care in underserviced areas in Ontario. *Ministry of Health Act*, R.R.O. 1980, Reg. 658, s. 1.

HEALTH SERVICES. Services provided by a hospital or services provided by a licensed medical practitioner or dentist, a registered nurse or any other qualified person, and includes drugs, appliances and treatment prescribed by such medical practitioner or dentist or other qualified person. *The Health Services Act*, R.S.S. 1978,

c. H-1, s. 2. See BASIC ~; EMERGENCY HEALTH SERVICE; INSURED ~; LIVE-STOCK ~; PUBLIC ~.

HEALTH TRAINING FACILITY. A school, hospital or other institution, or any portion thereof, (a) for the training of persons in the health professions or in occupations associated with the health professions, or (b) for the conducting of research in the health fields, but does not include residential accommodation. *Health Resources Fund Act*, R.S.C. 1970, c. H-4, s. 2.

HEALTHY. *adj.* Fresh and natural in appearance. *Farm Products Grades and Sales Act*, R.R.O. 1980, Reg. 331, s. 1.

HEARD. *v.* 1. Refers to a hearing on the merits. 2. Heard and disposed of.

HEARING. *n.* 1. " . . . [N]ormally . . . an oral hearing. But . . . a statutory board, acting in an administrative capacity, may . . . [hear applications] on written evidence and arguments,. . ." *Knight v. Indian Head School Division No. 19* (1990), 43 Admin. L.R. 157 at 189, 30 C.C.E.L. 237, [1990] 3 W.W.R. 289, [1990] 1 S.C.R. 653, 106 N.R. 17, 83 Sask. R. 81, 69 D.L.R. (4th) 489, 90 C.L.L.C. 14,010, L'Heureux-Dubé J. (Dickson C.J.C., La Forest and Cory JJ. concurring) quoting and agreeing with H.W.R. Wade, *Admninistrative Law*, 5th ed. (Oxford: Clarendon Press, 1982) at 482-3. 2. The right to be heard by the decision-maker with a full opportunity to lay before him all the pertinent facts supporting his side of the issue. 3. Generic label to describe trials, appeals, and interlocutory proceedings. 4. Need not be an auditory event. Evidence can be in written form. See COSTS OF THIS ~; DE NOVO ~; ELECTRONIC ~; EXTRADITION ~; FAIR ~; GAROFOLI ~; ORAL ~; PRELIMINARY ~; PUBLIC ~; RE~; STATUS ~; WRITTEN ~.

HEARING AID. A wearable instrument or device designed for or offered for aiding or compensating for impaired human hearing and parts or accessories for the instrument, including an earmould, but not including batteries and cords.

HEARING AID DEALER. Any person engaged in (a) testing or measuring human hearing by audiometer or any other means for the purpose of selecting, adapting, recommending or selling hearing aids, or (b) selling or offering for sale hearing aids, or (c) making impressions for earmoulds to be used in connection with hearing aids. See PRACTICE OF A ~ AND CONSULTANT.

HEARING DE NOVO. " . . . [I]s . . . an altogether fresh or new hearing and not limited to an inquiry to determine if the tribunal acted properly and correctly on the evidence and material before it . . ." *Newterm Ltd., Re* (1988), 38 M.P.L.R. 17 at 19, 70 Nfld. & P.E.I.R. 216, 215 A.P.R. 216 (Nfld. T.D.), Steele J.

HEARING DOG. A dog trained as a guide for a deaf person.

HEARING ROLL. Identifies the parties and nature of the case to be heard by reference to a section of a statute or regulation or by a short description.

HEARSAY. *n.* 1. Evidence of something that was said by another person. 2. Gossip. See RULE AGAINST ~.

HEARSAY EVIDENCE. 1. "Evidence of a statement made to a witness by a person who is not himself called as a witness may or may not be hearsay. It is hearsay and inadmissible when the object is to establish the truth of what is contained in the statement. It is not hearsay and is admissible when it is proposed to establish by the evidence, not the truth of the statement, but the fact it was made. The fact that the statement was made, quite apart from its truth, is frequently relevant in considering the mental state and conduct thereafter of the witness or of some other person in whose presence the statement was made." *Subramaniam v. Public Prosecutor*, [1956] 1 W.L.R. 965 at 970 (Malaya P.C.). 2. Is defined not by the nature of the evidence *per se*, but by the use to which that evidence is sought to be put: namely, to prove that what is asserted is true . . . Narrative is not considered hearsay as it is not given for the truth of its contents. *R. v. Magloir*, 2003 NSCA 74, 216 N.S.R. (2d) 257 (C.A.).

HEARSAY RULE. Evidence of the written, oral or communicative conduct of a person who is not testifying is inadmissible as proof of the truth of the statements or as proof of the implied assertions contained in the statements. 2. A hearsay statement will be admissible for the truth of its contents if it meets the separate requirements of "necessity" and "reliability". These two requirements serve to minimize the evidentiary dangers normally associated with the evidence of an out-of-court declarant, namely the absence of an oath or affirmation, the inability of the trier of fact to assess the demeanour of the declarant, and the lack of contemporaneous cross-examination. *R. v. Hawkins*, [1996] 3 S.C.R. 1043.

HEART INFARCT. Occurs when a part of the heart muscle suffers local cellular breakdown as a result of inadequate blood supply. F.A. Jaffe, *A Guide to Pathological Evidence*, 2d ed. (Toronto: Carswell, 1983) at 46.

HEAT. See DEAD ~.

HEAT DETECTOR. A device for sensing an abnormally high air temperature or an abnormal rate of heat rise and automatically initiating a signal indicating this condition. *Building Code Act*, R.R.O. 1980, Reg. 87, s. 1.

HEAT ENERGY. Energy that is conveyed in the medium of steam, hot water, or hot air and that is produced for sale. *Power Corporation Act*, R.S.O. 1990, c. P.18, s. 1(1).

HEATER. See SERVICE WATER ~; SPACE ~; STORAGE-TYPE WATER ~; UNIT ~.

HEAT EXCHANGER. A pressure vessel under pressure of more than fifteen pounds used exclusively for transferring heat from one substance to another. *Boilers and Pressure Vessels Act*, R.R.O. 1980, Reg. 84, s. 1.

HEAT EXHAUSTION. A state of collapse caused by loss of electrolytes and body fluids after exposure to high temperature. F.A. Jaffe, *A Guide to Pathological Evidence*, 2d ed. (Toronto: Carswell, 1983) at 177 and 178.

HEATING BOILER. A boiler in which gas or vapour is generated, approved to carry a working pressure of 100 kilopascals or less; or a hot weater heating or hot water supply boiler approved to carry a working pressure of 1100 kilopascals or less and temperature not exceeding 120° Celsius. *Boiler, Pressure Vessel and Compressed Gas Act*, R.S. Nfld. 1990, c. B-5, s. 2.

HEATING PLANT. 1. A steam plant used to generate steam for heating purposes. *Operating Engineers and Firemen Act*, R.S.M. 1970, c. 050, s. 2. 2. (i) Any one or more boilers in which steam or other vapour may be generated at a pressure not exceeding 103 (or 100) kilopascals and a temperature not exceeding 121 degrees Celsius, or (ii) any one or more boilers in which water or other liquid may be heated to a pressure not exceeding 1100 kilopascals and a temperature not exceeding 121 degrees Celsius at or near the outlet of the boiler, or (iii) any system or arrangement of boilers referred to in subclause (i) or (ii), and the engines, turbines, pressure vessels, pressure piping system, machinery or ancillary equipment of any kind used in connection therewith. See HIGH PRESSURE ~; LOW PRESSURE ~; TEMPORARY ~.

HEATING SURFACE. 1. The area of a boiler or pressure vessel that transfers heat. 2. Any part of the surface of a fired pressure vessel that is in contact with the fluid under pressure on one side and the products of combustion on the other side. *Boilers and Pressure Vessels acts*.

HEATING SYSTEM. See THERMAL LIQUID ~.

HEAT PUMP. A machine whose principal use is extracting heat from an area outside the building to heat that building.

HEAT RECOVERY UNIT OR DEVICE. A machine which extracts heat from water, air or gases that are not intended to be reused or recycled in any manufacturing or production process, or otherwise.

HEAT SOURCE. The flame or gases produced during the combustion process of any liquid, solid or gaseous fuel, but does not include the heat source of an electric boiler, which is the electrical energy consumed by the heating elements. *Power Engineers Act*, R.S.P.E.I. 1988, c. P-15, s.1.

HEAT TREATMENT. Either annealing or normalizing as described in Schedule II. *Tackle Regulations*, C.R.C., c. 1494, s. 2.

HEAVIER-THAN-AIR AIRCRAFT. An aircraft supported in the atmosphere by lift derived from aerodynamic forces. *Canadian Aviation Regulations*, SOR/96-433, s. 101.01.

HEAVY CONSTRUCTION EMPLOYEES. (i) Employees employed in the construction industry as operators of heavy construction equipment, and (ii) employees employed in the construction industry to do work that is necessarily incidental to work done by heavy construction equipment and who are not within the building construction trades. *Construction Industry Wages Act*, R.S.M. 1970, c. C190, s. 2.

HEAVY CRUDE OIL. A naturally occurring viscous mixture that consists mainly of hydrocarbons heavier than pentane, that may contain sulphur compounds and that in its naturally occurring state has a density of more than 900 kilograms per cubic metre. Alberta statutes.

HEAVY DIESEL OIL. Diesel oil, other than those distillates of which more than 50 per cent by volume distills at a temperature not exceeding

340°C when tested by the American Society for Testing and Materials, Standard Method D.86/59. *Oil Pollution Prevention Regulations*, C.R.C., c. 1454, s. 2.

HEAVY-DUTY ENGINE. An engine designed to be used for motive power in a heavy-duty vehicle, other than a medium-duty passenger vehicle or a complete heavy-duty vehicle. *On-Road Vehicle and Engine Emission Regulations*, SOR/2003-2, s. 1(1).

HEAVY DUTY EQUIPMENT. Any mobile equipment and attachments thereto, used for building construction, engineering construction, logging, mining and farming operations. *Apprenticeship and Tradesmen's Qualification Act*, R.R.O. 1980, Reg. 42, s. 1.

HEAVY DUTY VEHICLE. An on-road vehicle that has a GVWR of more than 3,856 kg (8,500 pounds), a curb weight of more than 2,722 kg (6,000 pounds) or a basic vehicle frontal area in excess of 4.2 m² (45 square feet). *On-Road Vehicle and Engine Emission Regulations*, SOR/2003-2, s. 1.

HEAVY HAULER TRAILER. A trailer that has (a) brake lines designed to adapt to separation or extension of the vehicle frame, or (b) a body that consists of only a platform the primary cargo-carrying surface of which is not more than 101.6 cm (40 inches) above the ground in an unloaded condition, but may include sides that are designed for easy removal and a permanent front end structure. *Motor Vehicle Safety Regulations*, C.R.C., c. 1038, s. 2.

HEAVY-LIFT CHARGE. A charge on goods for crane service consisting of a single, direct vertical lift. Canada regulations.

HEAVY LIGHT-DUTY TRUCK. A light-duty truck having a GVWR of more than 2,722 kg (6,000 pounds). *On-Road Vehicle and Engine Emission Regulations*, SOR/2003-2, s. 1(1).

HEAVY OIL. A naturally occurring viscous mixture, other than crude bitumen, that consists mainly of hydrocarbons heavier than pentane, that may contain sulphur compounds and that in its naturally occurring state has a density of more than 920 kilograms per cubic metre. *Environmental Protection and Enhancement Act* R.S.A. 2000, c. E-12, s. 1.

HEAVY OIL SITE. A location at which a facility exists or is to be developed for recovering heavy oil by drilling and includes any injection or pumping facilities and any associated infrastructures and pipelines. *Environmental Protection and Enhancement Act* R.S.A. 2000, c. E-12, s. 1.

HEAVY PACK. A pack in which a minimum amount of water required for proper processing is used as the packing media. *Processed Fruit and Vegetable Regulations*, C.R.C., c. 291, s. 2.

HEAVY TIMBER CONSTRUCTION. 1. That type of combustible construction in which a degree of fire safety is attained by placing limitations on the sizes of wood structural members and on thickness and composition of wood floors and roofs, by avoidance of concealed spaces under floors and roofs and by use of required fastenings, construction details and adhesives for structural members. *Building Code Act*, R.R.O. 1980, Reg. 87, s. 1. 2. An approved type of wood construction in which a degree of fire endurance is attained by placing limitations on the minimum sizes of wood structural assemblies. *Hotel Fire Safety* Act, R.R.O. 1980, Reg. 505, s. 2.

HEAVY TURKEY. A turkey that is more than 103 days old and less than 161 days old. *Canadian Turkey Marketing Quota Regulations*, C.R.C., c. 661, s. 2.

HEAVY VEHICLE. A vehicle that has a gross weight exceeding 5000 kilograms, or a vehicle or combination of vehicles that transmits to the highway a weight in excess of 5000 kilograms. *St. Lawrence Parks Commission Act*, R.R.O. 1980, Reg. 909, s. 11.

HECKLING. *n*. Interruption of a speaker by a loud or audible words or noises directed at the issue upon which the speaker is speaking.

HECTARAGE. See TOBACCO~.

HECTARE. *n*. A metric measure of area equivalent to 100 acres or 10,000 square metres (approximately equal to 2.471 acres).

HECTO. *pref*. 10². Prefix for multiples and sub-multiples of basic, supplementary and derived units of measurement. *Weights and Measures Act*, S.C. 1970-71-72, c. 36, Schedule I.

HEDGER. *n*. A person who carries on agricultural, mining, forestry, processing, manufacturing or other commercial activities and, as a necessary part of those activities, becomes exposed to a risk attendant on fluctuations in the price of a commodity and offsets that risk through trading in commodity contracts for the commodity or related commodities whether or not a particular trade is effected for that purpose, but the person is a hedger only with respect to these trades.

HEDGING. *n.* The fixing of a price for a mineral commodity before delivery by means of a forward sale or a futures contract on a recognized commodity exchange, or the purchase or sale forward of a foreign currency related directly to the proceeds of the sale of the processed product of the mineral output, but does not include speculative currency hedging except to the extent that any one of these transactions determine the final price and proceeds for the product.

HEIGHT. *n.* 1. With reference to a building, the vertical distance of a building measured from the average level of the grade along the front of the building to (a) the parapet, in the case of a flat roof, (b) the deck line, in the case of a mansard roof, or (c) the mean height level between eaves and ride, in the case of a gable, hip or gambrel roof. Canada regulations. 2. Of a letter, means the height of an upper case letter where words appear in upper case and the height of the lower case letter "o" when words appear in lower case or in a mixture of upper and lower case. Canada regulations. See BUILDING ~. STUMP ~.

HEIGHT ABOVE THE HULL. Height above the uppermost continuous deck. *Collision Regulations*, C.R.C., c. 1416, Annex I, s. 1.

HEIGHT OF SUPERSTRUCTURE. The least vertical height measured at the side from the top of the superstructure deck beams to the top of the freeboard deck beams. *Load Line Regulations (Inland)*, C.R.C., c. 1440, s. 1.

HEIR. *n.* 1. " . . . [T]he party to which by the operation of law alone or by the will of man, the estate, rights and liabilities of the deceased are transmitted." *Levesque v. Turcotte* (1931), 12 C.B.R. 290 at 297, 69 Que. S.C. 148, Lemieux J. 2. Includes a person beneficially entitled to property of an intestate. See EXPECTANT ~; JOINT ~; LAST ~; PRESUMPTIVE ~; ULTIMATE ~.

HEIR APPARENT. One whose right of inheritance is indisputable provided the ancestor dies first; the eldest son of the sovereign.

HEIRDOM. *n.* Succession through inheritance.

HEIRESS. *n.* A female heir.

HEIRLOOM. *n.* Originally personal chattels like evidences of title, deeds and charters which went to an heir along with the inheritance.

HEIR PRESUMPTIVE. A person likely to be heir if the ancestor dies immediately but who could be displaced if a nearer heir is born.

HEIRS. *n.* " . . . [T]he person or persons to whom the land of another person descends by operation of law, when that other person dies intestate." *Sparks v. Wolff* (1898), 25 O.A.R. 326 at 334, (C.A.), MacLennan J.A.

HEIRSHIP. *n.* The condition or quality of being an heir; the relation between an heir and an ancestor.

HEIRS, NEXT OF KIN OR ESTATE. *var.* **HEIRS, NEXT-OF-KIN OR ESTATE.** Or the use of words of like import in a designation, shall be deemed to be a designation of a personal representative. *Insurance acts.*

HELD. *v.* 1. Decided, as in "The court held that X owed Y a sum of money". 2. Maintained; possessed of; having title to. See HOLD.

HELD. *adj.* Decided.

HELICOPTER. *n.* A power-driven heavier-than-air aircraft that derives its lift in flight from aerodynamic reactions on one or more power-driven rotors on substantially vertical axes. *Canadian Aviation Regulations*, SOR/96-433, s. 101.01(1).

HELIPORT. *n.* An aerodrome used or intended to be used for the arrival, landing, take-off or departure of aircraft capable of vertical take-off and landing. *Canadian Aviation Regulations*, SOR/96-433, s. 101.01(1).

HELIUM. *n.* In addition to its normal scientific meaning, a mixture mainly of helium which ordinarily may contain some nitrogen and methane.

HELPER. *n.* 1. A person, other than an apprentice, who is employed to assist the holder of a licence. 2. A person who was employed and paid by Canadian Legion War Services Inc., The National Council of the Young Men's Christian Association of Canada, Knights of Columbus Canadian Army Huts or Salvation Army Canadian War Services to assist supervisors and who proceeded from Canada for attachment to (a) the Canadian naval forces under the authority of the Chief of Naval Personnel, (b) active units and formations of the Canadian army forces under the authority of the Adjutant-General, or (c) active units and formations of the Canadian air forces under the authority of the Air Member for Personnel. *Civilian War Pensions and Allow-*

ances Act, R.S.C. 1985, c. C-31, s. 16. See MINER'S ~.

HEMATOCRIT. *n*. The volume of blood cells. F.A. Jaffe, *A Guide to Pathological Evidence*, 2d ed. (Toronto: Carswell, 1983) at 84.

HEMISPHERE. See WESTERN ~.

HEMOCONCENTRATION. *n*. The thickening of blood. F.A. Jaffe, *A Guide to Pathological Evidence*, 3d ed. (Toronto: Carswell, 1991) at 107.

HEMODILUTION. *n*. Blood thinning. F.A. Jaffe, *A Guide to Pathological Evidence*, 2d ed. (Toronto: Carswell, 1983) at 80.

HEMOLYSIS. *n*. Red blood cell breakdown. F.A. Jaffe, *A Guide to Pathological Evidence*, 3d ed. (Toronto: Carswell, 1991) at 107.

HEMOPERITONEUM. *n*. Free blood being present in the abdominal cavity. F.A. Jaffe, *A Guide to Pathological Evidence*, 3d ed. (Toronto: Carswell, 1991) at 221.

HEMORRHAGE. *n*. Blood escaping from the heart or a blood vessel. F.A. Jaffe, *A Guide to Pathological Evidence*, 3d ed. (Toronto: Carswell, 1991) at 221. See EPIDURAL ~; EXTRADURAL ~; INTRACEREBRAL ~; PETECHIAL ~; SUBARACHNOID ~; SUBDURAL ~.

HEMOSIDERIN. *n*. Healing; a reaction of white blood cells. F.A. Jaffe, *A Guide to Pathological Evidence*, 3d ed. (Toronto: Carswell, 1991) at 44.

HEMOTHORAX. *n*. Free blood being present in the chest cavity. F.A. Jaffe, *A Guide to Pathological Evidence*, 3d ed. (Toronto: Carswell, 1991) at 221.

HEMP. *n*. Cannabis. See INDUSTRIAL ~.

HEN. *n*. The hen of any class of the domestic chicken belonging to the species Gallus Domesticus. Canada regulations. See DOMESTIC ~.

HENCHMAN. *n*. Originally an attendant, a page.

HENRY. *n*. The inductance of a closed circuit in which an electromotive force of one volt is produced when the electric current in the circuit varies uniformly at a rate of one ampere per second. *Weights and Measures Act*, S.C. 1970-71-72, c. 36, Schedule I.

HENRY VIII CLAUSE. A clause in a statute permitting the executive to amend the statute by

regulation or to make regulations inconsistent with the statute.

H.E.P.C. *abbr*. Hydro-Electric Power Commission.

HERALD. *n*. An English official who registers genealogies or adjusts coats of arms.

HERALDRY. *n*. The knowledge or field of study of a herald.

HERALDS' COLLEGE. The British College of Arms which grants coats of arms.

HERBICIDE. *n*. Any substance or mixture of substances used for the destruction or control of vegetation. See HORMONE TYPE ~; SELECTIVE ~.

HERD. *n*. A number of cattle or sheep. See TUBERCULOSIS-ACCREDITED ~.

HERDER. *n*. A person who has charge of a number of domestic animals grazing or travelling together.

HERD OF ORIGIN. The flock or herd of which an animal was a member, where the animal was a member of that flock or herd for not less than 60 days immediately preceding its importation into Canada and in any other case means the flock or herd in which it was born. *Animal Disease and Protection Regulations*, C.R.C., c. 296, s. 2.

HEREAFTER. *adv*. Referring to the time after the commencement of the enactment containing that *word*. *Interpretation Act*, S.P.E.I. 1981, c. 18, s. 26. See NOW, NEXT, HERETOFORE AND ~.

HEREDITAMENT. *n*. Any kind of property which may be inherited. *Tomkins v. Jones* (1889), 22 Q.B.D. 599 at 602 (U.K. C.A.), Bowen L.J. See CORPOREAL ~; INCORPOREAL ~; LANDS, TENEMENTS AND ~S.

HEREIN. *adv*. 1. Used in any section shall be understood to relate to the whole enactment, and not to that section only. *Interpretation Act*, R.S.C. 1985, c. I-21, s. 35. 2. Used in a section or part of an enactment, shall be construed as referring to the whole enactment and not to that section, provision or part only.

HEREINAFTER. *prep*. Later in the same document.

HEREINBEFORE. *prep*. Earlier in the same document.

HEREOF. *adv*. Used in any section shall relate to the whole enactment and not only that section. *Interpretation Act*, R.S.N.B. 1973, c. I-13, s. 38.

HERETOFORE. *prep*. Earlier in the same document. See NOW, NEXT, ~ AND HEREAFTER.

HEREUNDER. *prep*. Later in the same document.

HERITAGE. *adj*. Of historic, architectural, archaeological, palaeontological or scenic significance to the Province or a municipality.

HERITAGE CHARACTER. The overall effect produced by traits or features which give property or an area a distinctive quality or appearance.

HERITAGE LANGUAGE. A language, other than one of the official languages of Canada, that contributes to the linguistic heritage of Canada. *Canadian Heritage Languages Institute Act*, S.C. 1991, c. 7, s. 2.

HERITAGE OBJECT. 1. An archaeological object, a palaeontological object, a natural heritage object, and an object designated as a heritage object. 2. Personal property of heritage significance. See NATURAL ~.

HERITAGE PROPERTY. 1. Property, whether a work of nature or of man, that is primarily of interest for its archaeological, historical, cultural, scientific or aesthetic value, and includes, but is not limited to, a site where archaeological, historical, cultural or scientific property is found. *The Saskatchewan Heritage Act*, R.S.S. 1978, c. S-22, s. 2. 2. Property that has sufficient heritage value or heritage character to justify its conservation. See MUNICIPAL ~; PROVINCIAL ~.

HERITAGE RESOURCE. Includes (i) a heritage site, (ii) a heritage object, and (iii) any work or assembly of works of nature or of human endeavour that is of value for its archaeological, palaeontological, pre-historic, historic, cultural, natural, scientific or aesthetic features, and may be in the form of sites or objects or a combination thereof. *The Heritage Resources Act*, S.M. 1985-86, c. 10, s. 1.

HERITAGE RESOURCE IMPACT ASSESSMENT. A written assessment showing the impact that proposed work, activity or development or a project, as described in section 12, is likely to have upon heritage resources or human remains. *The Heritage Resources Act*, S.M. 1985-86, c. 10, s. 1.

HERITAGE RIVER. A river designated as a heritage river and subject to a management plan.

HERITAGE SITE. Land, including land covered by water, of heritage significance.

HERITAGE VALUE. The historical, cultural, aesthetic, scientific or educational worth or usefulness of property or an area.

HER MAJESTY. 1. Her Majesty in right of Canada or of a province. 2. The Sovereign of the United Kingdom, Canada and Her other Realms and Territories, and Head of the Commonwealth. See GOVERNMENT OR ~; OFFICE UNDER ~; SHIPS BELONGING TO ~; SUBJECT OF ~.

HER MAJESTY'S CANADIAN SHIP. Any vessel of the Canadian Forces commissioned as a vessel of war. *National Defence Act*, R.S.C. 1985, c. N-5, s. 2.

HER MAJESTY'S DOMINIONS. The Commonwealth. *Interpretation Act*, R.S.M. 1970, c. 180, s. 23.

HER MAJESTY'S FORCES. The naval, arm and air forces of Her Majesty wherever raised, and includes the Canadian Forces.

HER MAJESTY'S REALMS AND TERRITORIES. All realms and territories under the sovereignty of Her Majesty. *Interpretation Act*, R.S.C. 1985, c. I-21, s. 35.

HERMENEUTICS. *n*. The art of construction and interpretation.

HERMETICALLY SEALED. In respect of a container, that it is so constructed and secured that it is for practical purposes airtight and will maintain its airtightness under all usual conditions. *Dangerous Goods Shipping Regulations*, C.R.C., c. 1419, s. 2.

HEROIN. *n*. Diacetyl morphine, a partly-synthetic narcotic analgesic derived from morphine. F.A. Jaffe, *A Guide to Pathological Evidence*, 3d ed. (Toronto: Carswell, 1991) at 185.

HERRING. *n*. Fish of the species Clupea harengus or Clupea pallasii.

HERRING CANNERY. A building, structure, machinery, appurtenances, appliances and apparatus occupied and used in the business of herring canning, or of converting the natural herring into canned herring. *Fisheries Act*, R.S.B.C. 1996, c. 149, s. 12.

HERRING DRY SALTERY. A building, structure, machinery, appurtenances, appliances and apparatus occupied and used in the business of dry salting herring, or of converting the natural herring into dry salted herring, where the herring are not kept or shipped in a brine solution after being processed. *Fisheries Act*, R.S.B.C. 1996, c. 149, s. 12.

HERRING FISHING VESSEL. Any ship or other description of vessel used in or equipped for the commercial fishing, transporting or processing of herring and includes pumpers and carriers. *Atlantic Coast Herring Regulations*, C.R.C., c. 804, s. 2.

HERRING REDUCTION PLANT. A building, structure, machinery, appurtenances, appliances and apparatus occupied and used in the business of oil, fish meal, fish scrap, chicken feed or fertilizer from herring. *Fisheries Act*, R.S.B.C. 1996, c. 149, s. 12.

HERRING WEIR. A fixed trap net consisting of one or more compartments each of which is constructed of stakes attached to the soil, held together with one or more sets of ribbands and surrounded by brush, twine or wire netting, into which fish are guided by one or more fixed leaders. Canada regulations.

HERTZ. *n*. The frequency of a periodic phenomenon of which the periodic time is one second. *Weights and Measures Act*, S.C. 1970-71-72, c. 36, Schedule I.

HESITATION WOUND. Stabs or cuts which are tentative and made by a suicide before inflicting the deadly wound on himself or herself. F.A. Jaffe, *A Guide to Pathological Evidence*, 3d ed. (Toronto: Carswell, 1991) at 229.

HETEROSEXUALITY. *n*. The state of being sexually attracted to members of the opposite sex.

HE WHO COMES INTO EQUITY MUST COME WITH CLEAN HANDS. When a plaintiff seeks the assistance of a court of equity, that plaintiff must be prepared to act fairly and properly and must be able to show that past behaviour regarding the transaction is beyond reproach. P.V. Baker and P. St. J. Langan, eds., *Snell's Equity*, 29th ed. (London: Sweet & Maxwell, 1990) at 31-2. See CLEAN HANDS DOCTRINE.

HE WHO SEEKS EQUITY MUST DO EQUITY. " . . . In many instances this contains a pun on the word 'equity' and means nothing more than that, 'he who seeks the assistance of a Court of Equity must in the matter in which he so asks assistance do what is just as a term of receiving such assistance.' 'Equity' means 'Chancery' in one instance and 'right' or 'fair dealing' in the other." *Richards v. Collins* (1912), 27 O.L.R. 390 at 398, 9 D.L.R. 249 (Div. Ct.), Riddell J. (Falconbridge C.J. and Lennox J. concurring).

HIDE. *n*. The untanned skin of livestock. *Livestock Brand Act*, S.B.C. 1980, c. 25, s. 1. See GREEN ~; RAW ~.

HIERARCHY. *n*. A body of persons organized according to authority, position or rank.

HIGHEST AND BEST USE. In expropriation law, the use which supports the highest value for the property provided it is physically possible, appropriately supported and financially feasible.

HIGH HAZARD FIREWORKS. Those Division 2 fireworks that, in the opinion of the Chief Inspector, present a special hazard to persons. *Explosives Regulations*, C.R.C. c. 599, s. 14.

HIGH LEVEL AIRSPACE. Airspace at or above 18,000 feet ASL that is within Canadian Domestic Airspace. *Canadian Aviation Regulations*, SOR/96-433, s. 101.01.

HIGH-LEVEL LANGUAGE. " . . . [H]as symbols and rules that correspond closely enough to ordinary mathematics and English (or other common language) that it may be read and understood with relative ease. Examples are languages such as BASIC, COBOL, PASCAL and FORTRAN." *Apple Computer Inc. v. Mackintosh Computers Ltd.* (1986), 10 C.P.R. (3d) 1 at 7, 8 C.I.P.R. 153, 3 F.T.R. 118, [1987] 173, 28 D.L.R. (4th) 178 (T.D.), Reed J.

HIGHNESS. *n*. A title authorized by British letters patent of December 11, 1917 to apply to the children of any sovereign, the children of the sovereign's sons, and the eldest living son of the eldest son of any Prince of Wales. The Duke of Edinburgh may also be called Royal Highness.

HIGH PRESSURE BOILER. 1. A boiler designed to carry and to operate at a working pressure of more than fifteen pounds. 2. A boiler designed to carry a working pressure of more than one hundred kilopascals but does not include such boiler if it is equipped with a safety valve that is set to relieve at more than one hundred kilopascals. *The Boiler and Pressure Vessel Act*, R.S.S. 1978, c. B-5, s. 2.

HIGH PRESSURE HEATING PLANT. A boiler or two or more boilers on the same premises having a safety valve setting of more than fifteen pounds per square inch (one hundred and three kilopascals) when the boiler is used for producing steam, or a safety valve setting of more than one hundred and sixty pounds per square inch (one thousand one hundred kilopascals) when the boiler is used for producing hot water or when the temperature of the hot water produced is in excess of two hundred and fifty degrees Fahrenheit (one hundred and twenty degrees Celsius).

HIGH-RISE HOTEL. A hotel six or more storeys in height.

HIGH SCHOOL. 1. One or more rooms or departments maintained exclusively for pupils above grade eight. *The School Act*, R.S.S. 1978, c. S-36, s. 2. 2. Includes collegiate institute. *The Secondary Education Act*, R.S.S. 1978, c. S-41, s. 2. See JUNIOR ~.

HIGH SEAS. 1. The area of the ocean beyond territorial waters. 2. Any body of water, or frozen surface thereof, that is not within the territorial waters of any state. *Canadian Aviation Regulations* SOR/96-433, s. 101.01. 2. Any body of water, or frozen surface thereof, that is not within the territorial waters of any state. *Canadian Aviation Regulations*, SOR/96-433, s. 101.01(1).

HIGH STICKING. *n.* In hockey, striking an opponent's head with an uplifted stick.

HIGH TREASON. Anyone commits high treason in Canada who kills or attempts to kill Her Majesty, or does her any bodily harm tending to death or destruction, maims or wounds her or imprisons or restrains her; levies war against Canada or does any act preparatory thereto; or assists an enemy at war with Canada, or any armed forces against whom Canadian Forces are engaged in hostilities whether or not a state of war exists between Canada and the country whose forces they are, and a Canadian citizen or person who owes allegiance to Her Majesty in right of Canada commits high treason who does any of these acts while in or out of Canada. *Criminal Code*, R.S.C. 1985, c. C-46, s. 46(1) and (3).

HIGH WATER MARK. 1. " . . . [T]he medium high tide line between the spring and the neap tides . . ." *Turnbull v. Saunders* (1921), 60 D.L.R. 666 at 670, 48 N.B.R. 502 (C.A.), the court per Hazen C.J. 2. " . . . [T]he average height of the river after the great flow of the spring had abated, and the river is in its ordinary state: . . ." *Plumb v. McGannon* (1871), 32 U.C.Q.B. 8 at 14, the court per Wilson J. See NORMAL ~.

HIGHWAY. *n.* 1. " . . . [A] public road or way open equally to everyone for travel, and includes the public streets of an urban district equally with connecting roads between urban districts." *Consumers' Gas Co. v. Toronto (City)*, [1940] 4 D.L.R. 670 at 672, [1941] O.R. 175, 52 C.R.T.C. 98 (C.A.), Robertson C.J.O. 2. A road to which the public has the right of access, and includes bridges over which or tunnels through which a road passes. *Criminal Code*, R.S.C. 1985, c. C-46, s. 2. 3. Includes a common and public highway, street, avenue, parkway, driveway, square, place, bridge, viaduct or trestle, any part which is intended for or used by the general public for the passage of vehicles and includes the area between the lateral lines thereof. 4. Any thoroughfare, street, property road, trail, avenue, parkway, driveway, viaduct, lane, alley, square, bridge, causeway, trestleway or other place, whether publicly or privately owned, any apart of which the public is ordinarily entitled or permitted to use for the passage or parking of vehicles and includes a sidewalk (including boulevard portion of the sidewalk), if a ditch lies adjacent to and parallel with the roadway, the ditch, and if a highway right of way is contained between fences or between a fence and one side of the roadway, all the land between the fences, or all the land between the fence and the edge of the roadway, as the case may be. See ARTERIAL ~; CONTROLLED-ACCESS ~; ~S; LANED ~; LIMITED ACCESS ~; ONE-WAY ~; PROVINCIAL ~; PUBLIC ~; THROUGH~.

HIGHWAY AND ROAD. A common and public highway or any part thereof, and includes a street, bridge, and any other structure incidental thereto or any part thereof. Ontario statutes.

HIGHWAY AUTHORITY. The public authority having legal jurisdiction to open and maintain for the public highways in the area under its jurisdiction.

HIGHWAY COACH. A passenger vehicle of a design commonly known in the transportation industry as a highway coach, an intercity coach or an intercity motor bus, whether the vehicle is used or intended for use on scheduled routes or for charters, tours, sightseeing trips or other purposes, but does not include a passenger vehicle incapable of being fitted with more than thirty passenger seats. *Highway Coach Moratorium Act*, R.S.N.S. 1989, c. 200, s. 2(1).

HIGHWAY MOTOR VEHICLE OPERA-TOR. A motor vehicle operator who is not a bus operator or a city motor vehicle operator. *Motor Vehicle Operators Hours of Work Regulations*, C.R.C., c. 990, s. 2.

HIGHWAY OR ROAD. 1. (i) Means land used or surveyed for use as a public highway or road, and (ii) includes a bridge forming part of a public highway or road and any structure incidental to the public highway or road or bridge. 2. Includes any highway, road, road allowance, street, lane, or thoroughfare, dedicated to the public use as a highway or opened or made as a highway under this or any other Act of the Legislature, and any bridge, floodway, pier, ferry, square or public place dedicated to the use as a highway and any highway improvements or works thereon or appurtenant thereto. *Highway Department Act*, R.S.M. 1970, c. H40, s. 2.

HIGHWAYS. *n*. Highways, docks, ferries, wharfs, parking lots in connection therewith, land held to provide clear view at road junctions and railroad crossings, and land acquired and held for future highways. *Municipal Tax Assistance Act*, R.S.O. 1990, c. M.59, s.1 . See HIGHWAY.

HIJACKING. *n*. 1. Unlawfully, by force or threat thereof, or by any form of intimidation, seizing or exercising control of an aircraft with intent (a) to cause any person on board the aircraft to be confined or imprisoned against his will, (b) to cause any person on board the aircraft to be transported against his will to any place other than the next scheduled place of landing of the aircraft, (c) to hold any person on board the aircraft for ransom or to service against his will, or (d) to cause the aircraft to deviate in a material respect from its flight plan. *Criminal Code*, R.S.C. 1985, c. C-46, s. 76. 2. The gravity of the crime of hijacking is obvious; it is universally condemned and punished severely. [. . .] Hijacking may combine, in one act, numerous offences, including kidnapping, unlawful confinement, theft, assault, extortion, and potentially murder. It entails the violation of individual human rights, such as the right to life, personal security and freedom of movement. It financially damages airlines, associated industries and the economy as a whole. Hijacking is not the mere seizure of an aircraft for its own sake; it exploits control over the aircraft "as a weapon of psychological coercion and extortion directed against governments" (see P. Wilkinson, *Terrorism and the Liberal State* (London:

MacMillan Press, 1977), at 207). 3. Moreover, the victims of this crime are not limited to those persons unfortunate enough to be physically affected, nor are the effects of hijacking limited to one government. Hijacking terrorizes all nations and society as a whole. *Saini v. Canada (Minister of Citizenship & Immigration)* (2001), 2001 FCA 311, 206 D.L.R. (4th) 727, 278 N.R. 127, [2002] 1 F.C. 200, 214 F.T.R. 320 (note) (C.A.).

HILL. *n*. A natural elevation of land rising up above the level of the surrounding land.

HILL CLAIM. A claim situate on a hillside or adjoining a creek claim.

HILL PRINCIPLE. 1. Principle sanctions the imposition of a life sentence for offenders who have committed a very serious offence and who appear to represent a continuing danger to the community. *R. v. Hill* (1974), 15 C.C.C. (2d) 145 (Ont. C.A.), affirmed (1975), [1977] 1 S.C.R. 827. 2. The dominant feature in these cases is the horrific nature of the very offence for which the accused is being sentenced. Often, there is also some expert evidence demonstrating that the offender suffers from a mental disorder that shows he or she represents a continuing danger to the public and that there is little likelihood of successful treatment during the course of a fixed sentence. In these cases, the life sentence is justified on the theory that the parole board will be in the best position to decide when to release the very dangerous offender who is capable of inflicting the gravest type of harm and where at the time of sentencing the possibility of successful rehabilitation is at least uncertain and at best lies many years in the future. *R. v. Edwards* (2001), 54 O.R. (3d) 737 (C.A.).

HIMALAYA CLAUSE. 1. The bill of lading expressly extended the benefit of a limitation of liability on third parties [to those it employed] such as stevedores, which is the essence of a "Himalaya clause." *London Drugs Ltd. v. Kuehne & Nagel International Ltd.*, 1992 CarswellBC 315, 73 B.C.L.R. (2d) 1, [1992] 3 S.C.R. 299, (sub nom. *London Drugs Ltd. v. Brassart*) 143 N.R. 1, Per Iacobucci, J. for the majority. 2. " . . . [A] bill of lading contained an exemption from liability clause as between the shipper of the goods and the carrier. The clause expressly provided that the same exemption from liability extended to the carrier's servants, agents, and independent contractors though they were not parties to the contract. Such clauses have come to be called 'Himalaya' clauses, after the ship in *Alder v. Dickson*, [1955] 1 Q.B. 15 8

... ." *London Drugs Ltd. v. Keuhne & Negel International Ltd.* (1990), 2 C.C.L.T. (2d) 161 at 217, 31 C.C.E.L. 67, 45 B.C.L.R. (2d) 1, [1990] 4 W.W.R. 289, 70 D.L.R. (4th) 51 (C.A.), Lambert J.A.

HIRE. *n.* 1. A bailment for compensation or a reward; hiring something to use; labour and work, services and care to be bestowed or performed on the thing delivered, or the carriage of goods from one place to another. 2. Any payment, consideration, gratuity or benefit, directly or indirectly charged, demanded, received or collected by any person for the use of an aircraft. *Aeronautics Act*, R.S.C. 1985, c. A-2, s. 3. See CRANE ~ CHARGE.

HIRE OR REWARD. Any payment, consideration, gratuity or benefit, directly or indirectly charged, demanded, received or collected by any person for the use of an aircraft. *Aeronautics Act*, R.S.C. 1985 (1st Supp.), c. 33, s. 3.

HIRE-PURCHASE AGREEMENT. An agreement under which the hirer can, at the end of the term of the agreement, terminate the agreement or purchase the goods governed by the agreement. See RETAIL HIRE-PUR-CHASE.

HIRER. *n.* The person who requests services.

HIRING. *n.* The act of recruiting for employment. See PREFERENTIAL ~; REFERRAL ~ SYSTEM.

HIRING HALL. 1. " ... [P]ool of workers competent to do the job in hand." *I.U.O.E., Local 901 v. Hydro Projects Management Assn.* (1977), 77 C.L.L.C. 14,100 at 242 (Man. Q.B.), Wilson J. 2. An office operated by a union to fill requests for employees. See CENTRAL ~; JOINT ~.

HIS MAJESTY. The Sovereign of the United Kingdom, Canada and His other Realms and Territories, and Head of the Commonwealth.

HIS TESTIBUS. [L. these being witnesses] A phrase which used to be added to deeds.

HISTORIAN. *n.* A person who writes history as opposed to a chronicler. A scholar of the human past.

HISTORICAL OBJECT. An object or specimen of historic significance and includes an archaeological object and a palaeontological object.

HISTORIC CHARGE. A criminal charge dealing with incidents which took place some time in the past.

HISTORIC COMPROMISE. In workers compensation law the compromise by which workers lost the right to sue their employers in return to entitlement to compensation for work-related injuries which was not dependent on the employer's fault or the employer's ability to pay.

HISTORIC DISTRICT. 1. A group or collection of buildings and their environs, in urban or rural areas, that are considered by the Minister to be of historic or architectural significance and designated to be an historic district by the Minister. *Historic Sites Protection Act*, S.N.B. 1976, c. 30, s. 1. 2. A territory designated as such by the Government because of the concentration of historic monuments or sites found there. *Cultural Property Act*, R.S.Q., c. B-4, s. 1.

HISTORIC MONUMENT. An immoveable which has historic interest because of its use or architecture. *Cultural Property Act*, R.S.Q. 1977, c. B-4, s. 1.

HISTORIC OBJECT. Any object of historical significance to or connected with archaeology.

HISTORIC PLACE. A site, building or other place of national historic interest or significance, and includes buildings or structures that are of national interest by reason of age or architectural design. *Historic Sites and Monuments Act*, R.S.C. 1915, c. H-4, s. 2.

HISTORIC PROPERTY. Any manuscript, printed item, audio-visual document or man-made object whose conservation is of historic interest, excluding an immoveable. *Cultural Property Act*, R.S.Q., c. B-4, s. 1.

HISTORIC RESOURCE. Any work of nature or of man that is primarily of value for its palaeontological, archaeological, prehistoric, historic, cultural, natural, scientific or aesthetic interest including, but not limited to, a palaeontological, archaeological, prehistoric, historic or natural site, structure or object. *Historical Resources acts*.

HISTORIC SITE. 1. Any, building, structure, object or area that is significant in the history or culture of a province. 2. A place where events have occurred marking the history of Québec or an area containing historic property or monuments. *Cultural Property Act*, R.S.Q., c. B-4, s. 1.

HISTORIC TRADEOFF. In workers compensation law the compromise by which workers lost the right to sue their employers in return to entitlement to compensation for work-related injuries which was not dependent on the employer's fault or the employer's ability to pay.

HISTORIC VEHICLE. A motor vehicle, (i) that is at least thirty years old, (ii) that is operated on a highway for the purpose of exhibition, tours or similar functions organized by a properly constituted automobile club or for purposes of parades, repair, testing or demonstrations for parades, (iii) that is substantially unchanged or unmodified from the original manufacturer's product. Ontario regulations.

HISTORY. See LEGISLATIVE ~.

HIT AND RUN. "[A case] . . . where, with the intent to escape civil or criminal liability, the driver of a motor vehicle involved in a motor vehicle accident fails to stop and give his name and address and where necessary to offer assistance." *Leggett v. Insurance Corp. of British Columbia* (1991), 50 C.C.L.I. 246 at 254 (B.C. S.C.), Harvey J.

HITCH. See TRAILER ~.

HIVE. *n*. Any cavity in which bees have constructed honeycomb.

H.L. *abbr*. House of Lords.

H.O. *abbr*. Hearing Officer, Trade Marks.

HOARD. *v*. To acquire and keep goods not reasonably necessary to the person.

HOARDING. *n*. Fence set up around construction site.

HODG. *abbr*. Hodgins, Elections (Ont.), 1871-1879.

HODGES'S CASE. See RULE IN~.

HOG. *n*. Any member of the species Sus Scrofa L. (domestic pig). Canada regulations.

HOIST. *n*. A drum or friction hoist used for transporting persons or materials in an underground mine. See AUTOMATIC ~; CONTRUCTION ~; DRUM ~; FRICTION ~; SIX MONTHS'~.

HOISTING PLANT. A hoist equipped with, (i) a drum and a hoisting rope or chain, or (ii) an hydraulic pump, that is driven by a prime mover or movers other than steam and that is used for raising, lowering or swinging material. See MINE ~; STEAM ~.

HOISTING ROPE. A steel wire rope manufactured in accordance with the most recent standard of the Canadian Standards Association for steel wire rope for mine hoisting and haulage purposes or any equivalent standard acceptable to the chief inspector. *Mining Regulation Act*, R.S.B.C. 1979, c. 265, s. 140.

HOIST OPERATOR. A stationary engineer who is designated by a mine manager to operate a hoist for the raising or lowering of persons or material in a mine. *Coal Mines (CBDC) Safety Regulations*, C.R.C., c. 1011, s. 2.

HOISTWAY. *n*. A shaftway, hatchway, well hole, or other vertical opening or space in which an elevator, escalator or dumb-waiter operates or is intended to operate.

HOISTWAY ENCLOSURE. Any structure which separates the hoistway, either wholly or in part, from the floors or landings through which the hoistway extends.

HOLD. *v*. 1. To be possessed of; to have title to; to have; to occupy. 2. Of a judge, to pronounce a legal opinion. See TO HAVE AND TO ~.

HOLD. *n*. 1. Any space within the main hull of a ship. 2. A compartment below the deck of a ship suitable for the stowage of cargo.

HOLDBACK. *var*. **HOLD BACK**. Amount required under a builders or construction lien act to be deducted from payments made under a contract or a sub-contract and retained for a period prescribed.

HOLDBACK ACCOUNT. An interest bearing account in a bank, trust company or credit union in the joint names of the owner and the contractor. *The Builders' Liens Act*, R.S.M. 1987, c. B91, s. 1.

HOLDBACK PAY. Wages withheld by the employer; the amount earned between the end of a pay period and pay day.

HOLDER. *n*. 1. A person in possession of a security issued or endorsed to that person, to bearer or in blank. 2. The payee or endorsee of a bill or note who is in possession of it, or the bearer thereof. *Bills of Exchange Act*, R.S.C. 1985, c. B-4, s. 2. 3. As applied to a negotiable receipt, means a person who has possession of the receipt and a right of property therein, and, as applied to a non-negotiable receipt, means a person named therein as the person to whom the goods are to be delivered or that person's transferee. *Warehouse Receipts acts*. 4. When used in relation to a permit, means the person in whose name the plate portion of a permit is issued. *Highway Traffic acts.* 5. A person or corporation deriving title from a mineral claim. 6. In relation to any document that entitles the person to whom it is delivered to the payment of money or the delivery of grain, means the person who, from time to time, is so entitled by virtue of (a) the issue or endorsement to him of the document, or (b) the delivery to him of the document after it has been endorsed in blank. *Canada Grain Act,* R.S.C. 1985, c. G-10, s. 2. 7. The person to whom a credit card is issued. *Consumer Protection acts.* 8. In respect of an interest or a share therein, the person indicated, in the register maintained pursuant to Part VIII, as the holder of the interest or the share. *Canada Petroleum Resources Act,* R.S.C. 1985 (2d Supp.), c. 36, s. 2. 9. In relation to any Canada lands the registered holder of an interest or share in an interest in respect of those Canada lands including, where applicable, Her Majesty in right of Canada holding through the appropriate Minister or a designated Crown corporation. *Oil and Gas Act,* R.S.C. 1985, c. O-6, s. 2. 10. In relation to any Nova Scotia Lands, the registered holder of an interest or share in an interest in respect of those Nova Scotia Lands including, where applicable, Her Majesty holding through the appropriate minister or a designated Crown corporation. *Offshore Oil and Gas Act,* S.N.S. 1984, c. 8, s. 2. See CO-~; CONTRACT ~; CO-OPERATIVE INTEREST ~; INTEREST ~; INTERMENT RIGHTS ~; LAMP~; LAND~; LIEN~; LIMIT~; PERMIT ~; PLAN ~; QUOTA ~; SECURITY ~; SURFACE ~.

HOLDER FOR VALUE. Someone who gives valuable consideration for a bill, who has a lien on it, or who claims through another holder for value. E.L.G. Tyler & N.E. Palmer, eds., *Crossley Vaines' Personal Property*, 5th ed. (London: Butterworths, 1973) at 232.

HOLDER IN DUE COURSE. A holder in due course is a holder who has taken a bill, complete and regular on the face of it, under the following conditions, namely, (a) that he became the holder of it before it was overdue and without notice that it had been previously dishonoured, if such was the fact; and (b) that he took the bill in good faith and for value, and that at the time the bill was negotiated to him he had no notice of any defect in the title of the person who negotiated it. *Bills of Exchange Act,* R.S.C. 1985, c. B-4, s. 55(1).

HOLDER IN THE PROVINCE. In respect of an issuer, a holder of securities of the issuer whose last address as shown in the books of the issuer is in the province.

HOLDER OF A LOCATION. A permittee, licensee, lessee or holder of a drilling reservation.

HOLDFAST. *n.* That portion of a marine plant by which it is attached to the ocean floor. *Atlantic Coast Marine Plant Regulations*, C.R.C., c. 805, s. 2.

HOLD HARMLESS. To assume liability in a situation and relieve the other party of responsibility.

HOLDING. *n.* 1. Refers to property owned, usually in the form of shares or other securities. 2. Land rented to a tenant. 3. Sometimes used to refer to the decision of a court or tribunal especially on a particular issue. See LAND ~; MAXIMUM AGGREGATE ~S; MAXIMUM INDIVIDUAL ~S; MINERAL ~.

HOLDING BODY CORPORATE. A body corporate is the holding body corporate of any entity that is its subsidiary.

HOLDING COMPANY. 1. A company the primary purpose of which is owning shares of one or more other companies. 2. A company is the holding company of another if, but only if, the other is its subsidiary. *Companies acts.* See INVESTMENT ~.

HOLDING CORPORATION. Includes any corporation as hereinbefore defined which is formed for the purpose of acquiring and holding all the shares or a controlling interest therein of other companies, and which actually does acquire or hold all such shares or a controlling interest therein, and which does not otherwise engage in any trade or business. *Corporations Registration Act,* R.S.N.S. 1989, c. 101, s. 2.

HOLDING OUT. 1. Representing oneself as qualified and properly authorized to practise a profession or trade. 2. Representing oneself as, lending one's credit to, a business or firm.

HOLDING TANK. A tank used for the collection and storage of sewage for eventual disposal. *Great Lakes Sewage Pollution Prevention Regulations*, C.R.C., c. 1429, s. 2.

HOLDING TRUST. The trustee retains assets until required under an independent agreement to transfer the assets to specific persons. D.M.W.

Waters, *The Law of Trusts in Canada*, 2d ed. (Toronto: Carswell, 1984) at p. 101.

HOLD ORDER. A written instruction prohibiting the movement, transfer, transport, sale or disposal of a dangerous good until such time as the hold order is withdrawn. *Dangerous Goods Handling and Transportation Act*, R.S.M. 1987, c. D12, s. 1.

HOLD OVER. For a lessee to keep possession of land after the lease has expired.

HOLDS OUT. " . . . [P]resents himself . . ." *British Columbia (Attorney General) v. Cowen*, [1939] 1 D.L.R. 288 at 290, [1939] S.C.R. 20, Kerwin J.

HOLD-UP. *n*. A robbery.

HOLE. See SHOT ~; TEST ~.

HOLIDAY. *n*. Any of the following days, namely, Sunday; New Year's Day; Good Friday, Easter Monday; Christmas Day; the birthday or the day fixed by proclamation for the celebration of the birthday of the reigning Sovereign; Victoria Day; Canada Day; the first Monday in September, designated Labour Day; Remembrance Day; any day appointed by proclamation to be observed as a day of general prayer or mourning or day of public rejoicing or thanksgiving; and any of the following additional days, namely, (a) in any province, any day appointed by proclamation of the lieutenant governor of the province to be observed as a public holiday or as a day of general prayer or mourning or day of public rejoicing or thanksgiving within the province, and any day that is a non-juridical day by virtue of an Act of the legislature of the province, and (b) in any city, town, municipality or other organized district, any day appointed to be observed as a civic holiday by resolution of the council or other authority charged with the administration of the civic or municipal affairs of the city, town, municipality or district. *Interpretation Act*, R.S.C. 1985, c. I-21, s. 35. See CIVIC ~; GENERAL ~; PUBLIC ~; SPECIAL ~.

HOLOGRAPH. *n*. A deed or writing written completely by the grantor.

HOLOGRAPH WILL. A will written entirely in the testator's own hand.

HOME. *n*. 1. A private dwelling occupied by persons who live as a household. 2. A home for the use of senior citizens. 3. (i) A self-contained one-family dwelling, detached or attached to one or more others by a common wall, (ii) a building composed of two self-contained, one-family dwellings under one ownership, or (iii) a condominium one-family dwelling unit, including the common interests appurtenant thereto. 4. A farm, ranch or other land on which a dwelling house is situated. *Names of Homes* acts. 5. A house, multiple-family dwelling or housing project or a building consisting of business premises and family housing units, where the repairs, alterations and additions may be fairly considered to be primarily for the benefit of the housing units, but does not include a building used as a hotel or summer residence or a building used for seasonal occupancy. *National Housing Loan Regulations*, C.R.C., c. 1108, s. 78. See APPROVED ~; BOARDING ~; DAY CARE ~; DETENTION ~; FACTORY-BUILT ~; FAMILY ~; FOSTER ~; FUNERAL ~; GROUP ~; JOINT ~; MANUFACTURED ~; MARITAL ~; MATERNITY ~; MATRIMONIAL ~; MOBILE ~; MODULAR ~; MOTOR ~; NURSING ~; OWNER-OCCUPIED ~; PERSONAL CARE ~; PERSON AT ~; PRIVATE-SERVICE ~; RECEIVING ~; SPECIAL CARE ~; TEMPORARY ~.

HOME BUYER. A person who buys the interest of an owner in a premises that is a home, whether built or not at the time of the agreement of purchase and sale in respect thereof is entered into, provided, (a) not more than 30 per cent of the purchase price, excluding money held in trust under section 53 of the Condominium Act, is paid prior to the conveyance, and (b) the home is not conveyed until it is ready for occupancy, evidenced in the case of a new home by the issuance of a municipal permit authorizing occupancy or the issuance under the Ontario New Home Warranties Plan Act of a certificate of completion and possession. *Construction Lien Act*, R.S.O. 1990, c. C.30, s. 1(1).

HOME CARE SERVICES. Services provided to any person who, because of illness or disability, requires care and support while living in the community and, without limiting the generality of the foregoing, includes: (i) assessment services and care co-ordination services; (ii) nursing services; (iii) home-making services; (iv) meal services; (v) home maintenance services.

HOME DAY CARE. Day care provided on a regular basis, for a consideration, by a natural person in a private residence.

HOME EXTENSION LOAN. A loan or a purchase of obligations representing loans or advances of money made before July 1, 1956 by a bank or approved instalment credit agency for the purpose of financing the alteration of, or the making of additions to, an existing home to add one or more family housing units thereto, but does not include a farm improvement loan as defined in the Farm Improvement Loans Act. *National Housing Act*, R.S.C. 1985, c. N-11, s. 45(2).

HOME FOR SPECIAL CARE. 1. A residential welfare institution that is of a kind prescribed for the purposes of this Act as a home for special care and that is listed in a schedule to an agreement under section 4, but does not include a hospital, correctional institution or institution whose primary purpose is education, other than that part of a hospital that is used as a residential welfare institution and that is listed in a schedule to an agreement under section 4. *Canada Assistance Plan*, R.S.C. 1985, c. C-1, s. 2 . 2. A home for the care of persons requiring nursing, residential or sheltered care. *Homes or Special Care Act*, R.S.O. 1990, c. H.12, s. 1.

HOME HEATING OIL. Includes the refined petroleum products commercially known as kerosene, stove oil, furnace oil, gas oil, distillate heating oil and number one, two and three fuel oils, and any other refined petroleum product declared by the Lieutenant-Governor in Council to be home heating within the meaning of this Act. *Gasoline Diesel Oil and Home Heating Oil Pricing Act*, S.N.B. 1987, c. G-3.1, s. 1.

HOME IMPROVEMENTS. Improvements to the home of a farmer situated on a farm and includes (i) water systems, sewage systems, central heating systems, insulation, concrete basements, new floors, new roofs, new siding, painting, interior decorating and remodelling, and (ii) additions to the home when the addition is a bathroom or provides for a bathroom, but does not include household furnishings, electrical appliances or other things not affixed to the home. *Farm Home Improvements Act*, R.S.A. 1980, c. F-3, s. 1.

HOME INVASION. Entering a home for purposes of committing theft or robbery. The home is entered even though residents are present. If present, the residents are forcibly confined while theft is committed.

HOMEMAKER. *n*. 1. A person who performs housekeeping services including cleaning, other than as a sitter only. *Employment Agencies Act*, R.R.O. 1980, Reg. 280, s. 1. 2. A person who provides homemaker services. *Family and Child Services acts*. 3. A person managing, maintaining and controlling an independent, domestic establishment and who neither: (i) engages in a definite regular occupation for wages or for profit; nor (ii) reports regularly to a place of employment apart from his residence. *Automobile Accident Insurance Amendment Act, 1981*, S.S. 1980-81, c. 34, s. 3. 4. A person approved by the local director or a Director and who remains or is placed on a premises for the purpose of caring for a child. *Child Welfare Act*, R.S.O. 1980, c. 66, s. 23.

HOMEMAKER SERVICES. 1. The tasks normally performed by a mother which have been assumed by a visiting homemaker within a *family*. *Family and Child Services Act*, R.S.P.E.I. 1988, c. F-2, s. 1(1)(o). 2. Includes (i) the care of a child or adult, (ii) the purchase and preparation of meals and special diets, (iii) housekeeping duties, exclusive of heavy or seasonal cleaning, (iv) laundry and mending of clothing, (v) simple bedside care under the direction of a physician or visiting nurse, and (vi) training recipients in housekeeping and homemaking skills. *Day Care and Homemaker Services Act*, R.S. Nfld. 990, c. D-2, s. 2.

HOMEMAKING SERVICES. Housekeeping services including, (i) the care of a child or children, (ii) meal planning, marketing and the preparation of nourishing meals, and the preparation of special diets where required, (iii) light housekeeping duties, exclusive of heavy or seasonal cleaning, (iv) light laundry, ironing and essential mending of clothing, (v) personal care, including assistance in walking, climbing or descending stairs, getting into or out of bed, eating, dressing, bathing and other matters of personal hygiene, (vi) simple bedside care, where required, under the direction of a physician or nurse, but not including nursing services, and (vii) training and instruction in household management and the care of children, provided in accordance with section 6 of the Act by a homemaker qualified under this Regulation. *Homemakers and Nurses Services Act*, R.R.O. 1980, Reg. 499, s. 1.

HOME NE SERRA PUNY PUR SUER DES BRIEFES EN COURT LE ROY, SOIT IL A DROIT OU A TORT. [Fr.] A person should not be punished for commencing an action in a sovereign's court, whether or not that person has a cause of action.

HOME OCCUPATION. An occupation conducted for gain or reward within a dwelling as a secondary use of that dwelling. Canada regulations.

HOME OWNER. The owner of a principal residence that is subject to a mortgage and includes that person's heirs, successors or assigns. Saskatchewan statutes.

HOME-OWNER DUPLEX. A house containing two family housing units (one of which is to be occupied by the owner) built one above the other, with separate entrances. *National Housing Loan Regulations*, C.R.C., c, 1108, s. 2.

HOMEOWNER POLICY. See MULTI-PERIL POLICY.

HOME-OWNER SEMI-DETACHED HOUSE. A house containing two family housing units (one of which is to be occupied by the owner) built side by side, with separate entrances. *National Housing Loan Regulations*, C.R.C., c. 1108, s. 2.

HOME OWNERSHIP SAVINGS PLAN. An arrangement entered into by an individual and a depositary under which payment is made by the individual to the depositary of an amount of money as a payment under the arrangement to be used, invested or otherwise applied by the depositary for the purpose of providing to the individual as the planholder under the arrangement an amount of money to be used by the individual for the purchase by him or her of a qualifying eligible home. *Ontario Home Ownership Savings Plan Act*, R.S.O. 1990, c. 0.20, s. 1(1). See REGISTERED ~.

HOME OWNERS PACKAGE. A fire insurance policy to which other risks have been added to provide an insurance policy attractive to home owners. C. Brown and J. Menezes, *Insurance Law in Canada*, 2d ed. (Toronto: Carswell, 1991) at 86.

HOME PURCHASE LOAN. That portion of any loan received or debt otherwise incurred by an individual in the circumstances described in subsection (1) that is used to acquire, or to repay a loan or debt that had been received or incurred to acquire, a dwelling for the habitation of (i) the individual by virtue of whose office or employment the loan is received or the debt is incurred, (ii) a specified shareholder of the corporation by virtue of whose services the loan is received or the debt is incurred, or (iii) a person related to a person described in subparagraph (i) or (ii), or

that is used to repay a home purchase loan. *Income Tax Act*, R.S.C. 1952, c. 148 (as am. S.C. 1984, c. 45, s. 25(3)), s. 80.4(7)(a).

HOME RELOCATION LOAN. A loan received by an individual or his spouse in circumstances where he had commenced employment at a location in Canada (in this definition referred to as his "new work location") and by reason thereof has moved from the residence in Canada at which, before the move, he ordinarily resided (in this definition referred to as his "old residence") to a residence in Canada at which, after the move, he ordinarily resided (in this definition referred to as his "new residence") if (a) the distance between his old residence and his new work location is at least 40 kilometres greater than the distance between his new residence and his new work location, (b) the loan is used to acquire a dwelling for the habitation of the individual that is his new residence, (c) the loan is received in the circumstances described in subsection 80.4(1), and (d) the loan is designated by the individual to be a home relocation loan, but in no case shall more than one loan in respect of a particular move, or more than one loan at any particular time, be designated as a home relocation loan by the individual. *Income Tax Act*, R.S.C. 1952, c. 148 (as am. S.C. 1986, c. 6, s. 126(4)), s. 248(1).

HOMES FOR SPECIAL CARE. Nursing homes, hostels for indigent transients, homes for the aged, poor houses, alms houses, and hostel facilities provided for the aged within housing projects constructed under the National Housing Act. *Unemployment Assistance Act*, R.S.C. 1970, c. U-1, s. 4.

HOMESTEAD. *n.* 1. A farmer's dwelling-house together with the land upon which it sits and the appurtenances attached to it. 2. parcel of land (i) on which the dwelling house occupied by the owner of the parcel as his residence is situated, and (ii) that consists of (A) not more than 4 adjoining lots in one block in a city, town or village as shown on a plan registered in the land titles office, or (B) not more than one quarter section of land other than land in a city, town or village. *Dower Act*, R.S.A. 1980, c. D-38, s. 1. 3. Land, whether leasehold or freehold, together with erections or buildings, with their rights, members and appurtenances, registered as a homestead; and an erection or building on a homestead, whether or not affixed to the soil, shall be taken to be land and part of the homestead. *Homestead Act*, R.S.B.C. 1979, c. 173, s. 1.

HOMESTEAD LAW. Legislation to protect a home against execution creditors. A. Bissett-Johnson & W.M. Holland, eds., *Matrimonial Property Law in Canada* (Toronto: Carswell, 1980) at I-47.

HOMESTEAD LEASE. See CROP SHARE ~.

HOME STUDY COURSE. Any course, text or matter for study offered by any person, whereby such person teaches or undertakes or proposes to teach or prepare students to study a trade or subjects through the use of the mail, express or other common carrier or by private carriers or by an other means of communication. *Trade Schools Regulation Act*, R.S.N.S. 1989, c. 474, s. 2.

HOME TERMINAL. Of a motor vehicle operator means the place of business of a motor carrier to which the operator normally reports for work. *Canada Motor Vehicle Operators Hours of Service Regulations*, C.R.C., c. 1005, s. 2.

HOME-TRADE SHIPS. Ships engaged in home-trade voyages. *Canada Shipping Act*, R.S.C. 1985, c. S-9, s. 2.

HOME-TRADE VOYAGE. A voyage, not being an inland or minor waters voyage, between places within the area following, namely, Canada, the United States other than Hawaii, St. Pierre and Miquelon, the West Indies, Mexico, Central America and the northeast coast of South America, in the course of which a ship does not go south of the sixth parallel of north latitude. *Canada Shipping Act*, R.S.C. 1985, c. S-9, s. 2.

HOMEWORK. *n*. The doing of any work in the manufacture, preparation, improvement, repair, alteration, assembly or completion of any article or thing, or any part thereof in premises occupied primarily as living accommodation.

HOMEWORKER. *n*. 1. An individual who performs work for compensation in premises occupied by the individual primarily as residential quarters but does not include an independent contractor. *Employment Standards Act, 2000*, S.O. 2000, c. 41, s. 1. 2. A person who for wages in the performance of work in his residence provides labour only. *Workplace Act*, S.B.C. 1985, c. 34, s. 5.

HOMICIDE. *n*. Directly or indirectly, by any means, causing the death of a human being. *Criminal Code*, R.S.C. 1985, c. C-46, s. 222(1).

See CULPABLE ~; JUSTIFIABLE ~; MURDER ; NON CULPABLE ~.

HOMOGENIZED. *adj*. It has been treated in such a manner as to break up the fat lobules to such an extent that after forty-eight hours of storage no visible cream separation occurs in the milk and the fat percentage of the top one hundred millilitres of milk in a quart bottle, or of proportionate volumes in containers of other sizes, does not differ by more than five per cent from the fat percentage of the remaining milk as determined after thorough mixing. *Public Health Act*, R.S.N.S. 1967, c. 247, s. 122.

HOMOLOGATION. *n*. In civil law, a judicial confirmation of an arbitration award.

HOMO POTEST ESSE HABILIS ET IN-HABILIS DIVERSIS TEMPORIBUS. [L.] A person may be capable and incapable at differing times.

HOMOSEXUALITY. *n*. The state of being sexually attracted to members of one's own sex.

HONEST BELIEF. A belief held in good faith.

HONEST MISTAKE. Bona fide error in judgment. Connotes an action which is wrong but made without mental awareness of its being wrong on the part of the actor.

HONEY. *n*. The edible product of bees. See COMB ~.

HONEYCOMB. *n*. A structure of cells used for, or capable of being used by bees for, the storage of honey.

HONEYMOON CONTRACT. An initial contract between an employer and union when the union accepts most or all of the employer's terms.

HONEY SUBSTITUTE. A product other than pure honey manufactured or derived in whole or in part from a farm product and prepared for the same uses as honey and resembling honey in appearance. *Farm Products Grades and Sales Act*, R.R.O. 1980, Reg. 337, s. 1.

HONORARIUM. *n*. 1. " . . . (. . . [W]hich really means a gift on assuming an office, is now often used as equivalent to 'salary' by those who do not like to think they receive wages)." *Lavere v. Smith's Falls Public Hospital* (1915), 26 D.L.R. 346 at 347, 35 O.L.R. 98 (C.A.), Riddell J.A. 2. " . . . [A] compensation for services rendered, it is nevertheless not a payment for which the recipient, if not paid, could sue in a Court of law.

It is thus in the nature of an ex gratia or gratuitous payment, unlike a salary or wage or other contracted remuneration . . ." *Vladicka v. Calgary Board of Education* (1974), 45 D.L.R. (3d) 442 at 453, [1974] 4 W.W.R. 149 (Alta. T.D.), McDonald J.

HONOUR. *v.* 1. For a drawee to accept a bill of exchange. 2. For the maker of a note or the acceptor of a bill to pay it.

HONOUR. *n.* A title applied to judges and other officials.

HONOURABLE. *adj.* A title applied to judges and ministers of the Crown.

HOOD. *n.* Any exterior movable body panel forward of the windshield that is used to cover an engine, luggage, storage or battery compartment. *Motor Vehicle Safety Regulations*, C.R.C., c. 1038, s. 115.

HOOK. *n.* 1. In respect of angling, a single, double or treble pointed hook on a common shank or shaft. *Fishery regulations.* 2. (a) A single, double or multiple pointed hook on a common shaft, or (b) an artificial pad or lure having one or more hooks attached as part of it. *Alberta Fishery Regulations*, C.R.C. c 838, s. 2. 3. When used with reference to angling, means (a) a single, double or multiple hook on a common shaft, or (b) an artificial bait or lure that is not spring loaded and that has one or more hooks attached as a part of it. *Manitoba Fishery Regulations*, C.R.C., c. 843, s. 2.

HOOKED. *adj.* Addicted.

HOOKING. See FOUL ~.

HOOKTENDER. *n.* On a logging crew, lead hand responsible for the protection and safety of the crew.

HOOP NET. 1. A box-shaped or funnel-shaped device that is made of netting or wire mesh fastened to hoops or frames and that is used to catch fish without enmeshing them. *Fishery regulations*, Canada regulations. 2. A net that (a) is stretched over frames, (b) has one or more pots, and (c) is secured in place by posts or other means. *Manitoba Fishery Regulations*, C.R.C., c. 843, s. 2. See DOUBLE ~; SINGLE~.

HORIZONTAL AMALGAMATION. An amalgamation of two or more subsidiaries of the same holding corporation.

HORIZONTAL BRANCH. That part of a waste pipe that is horizontal and installed to convey the discharge from more than one fixture.

HORIZONTAL CONTROL SYSTEM. A survey method based on a network of monuments, among which the angles and distances are measured with great accuracy. To locate any point in or near the network, one specifies co-ordinates derived from distances among the monuments and a co-ordinate axis. B.J. Reiter R.C.B. Risk & B.N. McLellan, *Real Estate Law*, 3d ed. (Toronto: Emond Montgomery, 1986) at 641.

HORIZONTAL EXIT. An exit from one building to another by means of a doorway, vestibule, walkway, bridge or balcony. *Building Code, 1992*, O. Reg. 403/97, s. 1.1.3.2(1).

HORIZONTAL SERVICE SPACE. A space such as an attic, duct, ceiling, roof or crawl space oriented essentially in a horizontal plane, concealed and generally inaccessible through which building service facilities such as pipes, ducts and wiring may pass. *Building Code, 1992*, O. Reg. 403/97, s. 1.1.3.

HORIZONTAL UNION. Union the members of which belong to different crafts or work for different employers.

HORMONE. *n.* A natural or synthetic biochemical compound which regulates tissues of the body of a plant or animal. See SEX ~.

HORMONE DISRUPTING SUBSTANCE. A substance having the ability to disrupt the synthesis, secretion, transport, binding, action or elimination of natural hormones in an organism, or its progeny, that are responsible for the maintenance of homeostasis, reproduction, development or behaviour of the organism. *Canadian Environmental Protection Act, 1999*, S.C. 1999, c. 33, s. 43.

HORMONE TYPE HERBICIDE. Any pesticide containing, (i) 2,4-D, (ii) 2,4-DB, (iii) 2,4,5,-T, (iv) mecoprop, (v) fenoprop, (vi) MCPA, (vii) MCPB, (viii) dichlorprop, (ix) dicamba; (x) TBA, (xi) fenac, or (xii) picloram. *Pesticides Act*, R.R.O. 1980, Reg. 751, s. 1.

HORNBOOK. *n.* A primer.

HORN RULE. Owners cannot recover disturbance or incidental damages arising from the loss of certain lands where the owner has been compensated for loss of the same lands on the basis that its highest and best use is a better use than the existing use. *Horn v. Sunderland Corp.*, [1941] 2 K.B. 26 (Eng. C.A.).

HORS DE LA LOI. [Fr.] Outlawed.

HORS DE SON FEE. [Fr. out of one's fee] Describing land beyond the compass of a person's fee.

HORSE. *n.* 1. A stallion, mare, gelding, filly, colt, ass or mule. 2. Any animal of the equine species. *Riding Horse Establishment Act*, R.S.O. 1990, c. R.32, s.1. See RIDING ~ ESTABLISHMENT; SADDLE ~.

HORSEPOWER. *var.* **HORSE POWER.** 1. The capacity of any engine or plant or the standard by which that capacity is measured. See BOILER ~; BRAKE ~; NOMINAL ~.

HORSE RACING. Any race in which horses participate.

HORSE STABLE. A building, the whole or any part of which is used for the accommodation of horses.

HORSETAIL. *n.* A red marine plant of the species Furcellaria fastigiata. *Atlantic Coast Marine Plant Regulations*, C.R.C. c. 805, s. 2.

HORTICULTURAL OPERATION. See SPECIALIZED ~.

HORTICULTURE. *n.* 1. " . . . [G]ardening . . ." *Cedarvale Tree Services Ltd. v. L.I.U.N.A., Local 183* (1971), 5 C.L.L.C. 214 at 216, [1971] 3 O.R. 832, 22 D.L.R. (3d) 40 (H.C.), Wright J. 2. " . . . [I]ncludes the care, treatment and cultivation of trees." *Cedarvale Tree Services Ltd. v. L.I.U.N.A., Local 183* (1971), 5 C.L.L.C. 377 at 380, [1971] 1 O.R. 383, 15 D.L.R. (3d) 413 (C.A.), Arnup J.A. 3. (a) The operations relating to the propagating, producing, raising or harvesting of (i) legumes, flowers, shrubs or ornamental grasses, and (ii) seeds, seedlings, grafts and cuttings of legumes, flowers, shrubs or ornamental grasses, and (b) the operations relating to landscape gardening where the landscape gardening is incident to the carrying on of (i) any of the operations described in paragraph (a), or (ii) agriculture, and includes all the services incident to the carrying on of any of the operations described in paragraph (a) if those services are performed at the place where the operations are carried on. Canada regulations.

HOSE. See STANDARD ~.

HOSE SYSTEM. See STANDPIPE AND ~.

HOSPITAL. *n.* 1. Any hospital, sanitarium, sanatorium, nursing home or other institution operated for the observation, care or treatment of persons afflicted with or suffering from any physical or mental illness, disease or injury or for the observation, care or treatment of convalescent or chronically ill persons. 2. " . . . [T]he most basic component of a hospital [is] the element of overnight and continuous care and treatment." *Co-operative Health Centre v. Prince Albert (City)* (1987), 58 Sask. R. 281 at 292, 42 D.L.R. (4th) 706 (C.A.), Wakeling J.A. (dissenting). 3. Any establishment that admits or treats persons or animals for disease, infirmity or injury. 4. A hospital in which diagnostic services and medical surgical and obstetrical treatment are provided to persons having various illnesses, disabilities, injuries or other conditions. 5. Any facility or portion thereof that provides hospital care, including acute, rehabilitative or chronic care, but does not include (a) a hospital or institution primarily for the mentally disordered, or (b) a facility or portion thereof that provides nursing home intermediate care service or adult residential care service, or comparable services for children. *Canada Health Act*, R.S.C. 1985, c. C-6, s. 2. See ACCREDITED ~; APPROVED ~; AUXILIARY ~; CONTRACT ~; DEPARTMENTAL ~; FEDERAL ~; GENERAL ~; MATERNITY ~; NON-DISTRICT ~; PRIVATE ~; PUBLIC ~; TEACHING ~.

HOSPITAL CENTRE. Facilities to which persons are admitted for preventive purposes, medical diagnosis, medical treatment, physical or mental rehabilitation.

HOSPITAL FACILITIES. Includes laboratories, laundries and things, services and premises used or supplied in conjunction with a hospital or hospitals. See GOVERNMENT HOSPITAL FACILITY.

HOSPITALITY INDUSTRY. Every corporation, partnership, organization or individual providing accommodation, camping, food, beverage, information, entertainment, recreation and related services and facilities to persons travelling.

HOSPITALIZATION. *n.* 1. " . . . [A] hospital. . . supplies board and lodging to those undergoing medical treatment together with incidentals required resulting from such treatment . . ." *Hotel Dieu de Sherbrooke v. Caron*, [1945] Que. K.B. 149 at 151 (C.A.), Mackinnon J. (ad hoc). 2. The admission of a patient to a hospital. 3. The period of time during which a patient remains in hospital. See STANDARD WARD ~.

HOSPITAL MEDICAL STAFF REVIEW COMMITTEE. Any committee appointed by the board of an approved hospital or by the medical staff (a) to evaluate and control clinical practice in the hospital on a continuing basis for the purpose of maintaining and improving the safety and quality of patient care, or (b) to perform any functions in relation to the appraisal and control of the quality of patient care in the hospital. *Hospitals Act*, R.S.A. 2000, c. H-12, s. 16.

HOSPITAL SCHOOL. A facility or portion thereof for the habilitation and care of persons presenting evidence of general retardation, specific learning disabilities, or any other related condition for which admission to a hospital school will be beneficial. *Hospital Schools Act*, R.S.N.B. 1973, c. H-8, s. 1.

HOSPITAL SERVICES. Any of the following services provided to in-patients or out-patients at a hospital, if the services are medically necessary for the purpose of maintaining health, preventing disease or diagnosing or treating an injury, illness or disability, namely, (a) accommodation and meals at the standard or public ward level and preferred accommodation if medically required, (b) nursing service, (c) laboratory, radiological and other diagnostic procedures, together with the necessary interpretations, (d) drugs, biologicals, and related preparations when administered in the hospital, (e) use of operating room, case room and anaesthetic facilities, including necessary equipment and supplies, (f) medical and surgical equipment and supplies, (g) use of radiotherapy facilities, (h) use of physiotherapy facilities, and (i) services provided by persons who receive remuneration therefor from the hospital, but does not include services that are excluded by the regulations. *Canada Health Act*, R.S.C. 1985, c. C-6, s. 2.

HOSPITIUM. *n*. [L. hospitality] The shelter provided by an inn.

HOST. See PLANT INDICATOR ~.

HOSTAGE. *n*. A person held in exchange for certain behaviour.

HOSTAGE TAKING. Every one takes a person hostage who (a) confines, imprisons, forcibly seizes or detains that person, and (b) in any manner utters, conveys or causes any person to receive a threat that the death of, or bodily harm to, the hostage will be caused or that the confinement, imprisonment or detention of the hostage will be continued with intent to induce any person, other than the hostage, or any group of persons or any state or international or intergov-ernmental organization to commit or cause to be committed any act or omission as a condition, whether express or implied, of the release of the hostage. *Criminal Code*, R.S.C. 1985, c. C-46, s. 279.1(1).

HOSTEL. *n*. An institution for the temporary care of transient or homeless persons.

HOSTEL ACCOMMODATION. A hostel or dormitory type dwelling having shared food preparation or bathroom facilities.

HOSTELER. *n*. An innkeeper.

HOSTEL UNIT. A unit of housing accommodations of which the occupant shares one or more of the facilities of sleeping, eating, food preparation or sanitary facilities, such facility being necessarily provided exclusively within the housing unit, and may include personal service or light nursing care. *Housing Corporation Act*, R.S P.E.I. 1988, c. H-11, s. 1(k).

HOSTES SUNT QUI NOBIS VEL QUIBUS NOS BELLUM DECERNIMUS; CAETERI PRODITORES VEL PRAEDONES SUNT. [L.] An enemy is one with whom we are at war; others are either traitors or robbers.

HOSTILE. *adj*. " .. : [N]ot giving her evidence fairly and with a desire to tell the truth because of a hostile animus toward the [party who called the witness] . . ." *R. v. Coffin*, [1956] S.C.R. 191 at 213, 23 C.R. 1, 114 C.C.C. 1, Kellock J. (Rand and Fauteux JJ. concurring).

HOSTILE ACTIVITIES. See SUBVERSIVE OR ~.

HOSTILE ENVIRONMENT. In the context of sexual harassment occurs when employees have to endure sexual gestures and posturing in the workplace. *Janzen v. Platy Enterprises Ltd.*, [1989] 1 S.C.R. 1252.

HOSTILE POSSESSION. See ADVERSE POSSESSION.

HOSTILE WITNESS. A witness whose demeanour, general attitude and evidence are such while under examination that the side which called that witness may, with the judge's leave, cross-examine.

HOSTILITIES. *n*. Acts of war.

HOT CARGO. Material shipped from a business the employees of which are on strike.

HOTCHPOT. *n*. A blend or mix of chattels and lands.

HOT DECLARATION. " . . . [A]n employer may be declared 'hot' in an effort to persuade persons to cease doing business with that employer and . . . to persuade customers of that employer to find an alternative to the services or products supplied by the employer . . . a hot declaration might involve the pronouncement that a certain product is 'hot'. The purpose of such an edict would be to persuade customers of that product to find some alternative . . . the purpose of the hot declaration is to exert a form of economic pressure upon an employer or employers embroiled in a labour dispute." *Pulp & Paper Industrial Relations Bureau v. I.W.A.* (1986) 13 C.L.R.B.R. N.S. 196 at 203 (B.C.), Hall (Vice-Chair), Richardson and Lippert (Members).

HOTEL. *n.* " . . [P]remises where not only rooms are supplied but the ordinary needs of the traveller for meals or food are also forthcoming:. . ." *R. v. Zinburg* (1953), 16 C.R. 424 at 425, [1953] O.W.N. 601, 106 C.C.C. 141 (C.A.), the court per Aylesworth J.A. See HIGHRISE ~; MOTOR ~; PUBLIC ~.

HOTELKEEPER. *n.* The person who has the management and control of a hotel. *Hotel Fire Safety Act*, R.S.O. 1990, s. H.16, s. 1.

HOTEL SHIP. A ship designed to carry passengers in which berthed accommodation is available to persons for other than the purpose of a voyage. *Hull Construction Regulations*, C.R.C., c. 1431, s. 2.

HOT GOODS. Goods which workers refuse to handle because the producer of the goods is engaged in a labour dispute with other workers.

HOT PRODUCT. A product which workers refuse to handle because the producer of the product is engaged in a labour dispute with other workers.

HOT PURSUIT. 1. Continuous pursuit conducted with reasonable diligence so that pursuit and capture along with the commission of the offence may be considered as forming part of a single transaction. *R. v. Macooh*, [1993] 2 S.C.R. 802. 2. A coastal state may pursue a foreign merchant ship which committed an offence against its local law within that state's territorial or national waters into the high seas.

HOT-ROLLED OR COLD-ROLLED. When applied to shapes, sections, bars, rods, plates, sheets or strips of iron or steel, includes stapes, sections, bars, rods, plates, sheets or strips that have been annealed, tempered, pickled, limed or polished. *Customs Tariff*, R.S.C. 1985, c. C-54, s. 2.

HOT SHOT. 1. Of a narcotic, an accidental fatal overdose. F.A. Jaffe, *A Guide to Pathological Evidence*, 3d ed. (Toronto: Carswell, 1991) at 221. 2. A narcotic to which poison was added. F.A. Jaffe, *A Guide to Pathological Evidence*, 3d ed. (Toronto: Carswell, 1991) at 221.

HOT TUB. See PUBLIC ~.

HOT WATER BOILER. A boiler connected in a closed type hot water heating system. *Boiler and Pressure Vessel Act*, R.S.B.C. 1979, c. 30, s. 1.

HOT-WATER HEATING SYSTEM. See CLOSED-TYPE ~; OPEN-TYPE ~.

HOT WATER PLANT. See LOW PRESSURE ~.

HOT WATER STORAGE TANK. A pressure vessel used for the storage of hot water.

HOT WATER SYSTEM. See CLOSED TYPE ~.

HOT WORK. Welding, burning, rivetting, drilling, grinding, chipping or any other work where flame is used or sparks are produced. *Safe Working Practices Regulations*, C.R.C., c. 1467, s. 2.

HOUR. *n.* 3,600 seconds. *Weights and Measures Act*, S.C. 1970-71-72, c. 36, Schedule I. See CLOCK ~; KILOWATT~; MAN-~; MAXIMUM ~S; PROHIBITED ~S; QUARTER ~ BLOCK; REGULAR ~S; SCHEDULE OF ~S OF LABOR; THERM ~; WORKING ~S.

HOURS OF THE DAY. This and all other references to time relate to local time.

HOURS OF WORK. The period of time during which an employee works for an employer.

HOUSE. *n.* 1. A building, together with the land on which it is situated, intended for human habitation comprising not more than two family housing units. 2. Includes school, church, hall, railway passenger station, factory, and any other building, hut or tent used for human habitation or work whether it is permanent or temporary and whether stationary or movable, and includes the curtilage thereof. 3. The portion, situated within the territory of Quebec, of any building, construction, shelter, penthouse, shed or other erection, under whatever name known or designated, attached to the ground or portable, built, erected or placed on the surface or above or underground, permanently or temporarily, partly on the territory of Quebec and partly on that of one of the United States of America or of another province of Canada. *Disorderly Houses Act*, R.S.Q. 1977, c. M-2, s. 13. 4. The House of Assembly. Nova Scotia statutes. 5. The Legislative Assembly. *Crown Corporation Reporting Act*, R.S.B.C. 1979, c. 84, s. 1. 6. The House of Commons. See ALMS~; BAWDY ~; BOARDING ~; CLEARING ~; CUSTOM-~; DISORDERLY ~; DWELLING ~; GOVERNMENT ~; HALFWAY ~; LODGING ~; MOBILE ~; PUBLIC ~; REFRESHMENT ~; ROOMING ~; ROW ~; SUPPLY ~; TENT ~; VICTUALLING ~.

HOUSE-BOAT. *n.* A boat designed, fitted or employed as a dwelling whether temporary or permanent. *Provincial Parks Act*, R.R.O. 180, Reg. 822, s. 1.

HOUSEBREAKING. See BREAK AND ENTER.

HOUSEBREAKING INSTRUMENT. An instrument used to break in.

HOUSE COUNSEL. A lawyer employed by and acting as lawyer for a corporation or public entity.

HOUSE-DRAIN. *n.* A drain used for the drainage of a house or premises and made merely for the purpose of communicating therefrom with a private sewage disposal system or other like receptacle for sewage, or with a sewer in a street. *Public Health Act*, R.S.A. 1970, c. 294, s. 2.

HOUSEHOLD. *n.* 1. ". . . [I]s of flexible meaning. In the general understanding it is associated and at times identical with what is connoted by 'family' or 'domestic establishment'. . . a collective group living in a home, acknowledging the authority of a head, the members which, with few exceptions, are bound by marriage, blood, affinity or other bond, between whom there is an intimacy and by whom there is felt a concern with an interest in life and that gives a unity." *Wawanesa Mutual Insurance Co. v. Bell*, [1957] S.C.R. 581 at 583-4, [1957] I.L.R. 1-273, 8 D.L.R. (2d) 577, Rand J. 2. A parcel of land separately assessed under paragraph 2 of subsection 14 (2) of the Assessment Act according to the last returned assessment roll that is used or intended to be used as a residence, except that in respect of a Canadian Forces Base, "household" means a self-contained living unit consisting of two or more rooms in which the occupants usually sleep and prepare and serve meals. *Ontario Unconditional Grants Act*, R.S.O. 1990, c. 0.38, s. 1. See HOUSE OR ~.

HOUSEHOLD APPLIANCE. A kitchen range, a refrigerator, a freezer, a dishwasher, a clothes washer, a clothes dryer or a television set. *Consumer Protection Act*, S.Q. 1978, c. 9, s. 182.

HOUSEHOLD ARTICLE. See PERSONAL OR ~.

HOUSEHOLD EFFECTS. See FURNITURE AND ~.

HOUSEHOLDER. *n.* The person in charge of any premises whether as owner, tenant, agent or otherwise. *Public Health acts.*

HOUSEHOLD EXTRACTS. Flavouring preparations manufactured for sale to the general public for use as a flavouring extract. *Manufacturers in Bond Regulations*, C.R.C., c . 575, s. 2.

HOUSEHOLD GOODS. 1. Personal property (i) that is owned by one or both spouses, and (ii) that was ordinarily used or enjoyed by one or both spouses or one or more of the children residing in the matrimonial home for transportation, household, educational, recreational, social or aesthetic purposes. 2. Furniture, equipment, appliances and effects owned by one spouse or both spouses and ordinarily used or enjoyed by both spouses or by one or more of their children within or about a marital home while the spouses are or were cohabiting. New Brunswick statutes.

HOUSEKEEPER. *n.* Of the House of Commons, the Sergeant-at-Arms who is responsible for committee rooms, buildings, and all moveables. A. Fraser, W.A. Dawson, & J. Holtby, eds., *Beauchesne's Rules and Foms of the House of Commons of Canada*, 6th ed. (Toronto: Carswell, 1989) at 61.

HOUSEKEEPING UNIT. One or more habitable rooms for use as a unit for dwelling purposes by one family and containing separate facilities for the preparation of food. Canada regulations.

HOUSE LEADER. The designated member of parliament responsible for arranging the business of the House of Commons or the legislature. See GOVERNMENT ~; OPPOSITION ~.

HOUSE OF COMMONS. The lower house of the bicameral legislature which governs Canada. The members of the House are elected from each of the federal ridings in the country. The upper house is known as the Senate. See CLERK OF THE ~.

HOUSE OF COMMONS PROGRAMMING SERVICE. The programming service of an undertaking required by the Commission to cover the entire proceedings of the House of Commons. *Broadcasting Distribution Regulations*, SOR/97-555, s. 1.

HOUSE OF DETENTION. For the purposes of this act, means any place, other than a penitentiary, in which persons charged with offences are usually kept and detained in custody. *Summary Convictions Act*, R.S.Q. 1977, c. P-15, s. 1.

HOUSE OF LORDS. The body of lords spiritual and temporal who constitute the second branch of the British Parliament and act as a supreme court of appeal from the British Court of Appeal.

HOUSE ORGAN. A company publication.

HOUSE OR HOUSEHOLD. Includes a dwelling house, lodging house and hotel, and also includes a students' residence, fraternity house or other building in which any person in attendance as a student, pupil or teacher or employed in any capacity in or about a university, college, school or other institution of learning resides or is lodged. *Public Health Act*, R.S.O. 1980, c. 409, s. 1.

HOUSE PIPING. The gas piping in any premises beyond the outlet of the meter and the gas piping in any premises ahead of the meter which is not installed by or on behalf of the gas company.

HOUSE TRAILER. 1. A vehicle capable of being attached to and drawn by a motor vehicle and designed, constructed or equipped as a dwelling place, living abode or sleeping place. *Highway Traffic acts*. 2. A vehicle used or intended to be used as living quarters. *The Conditional Sales Act*, R.S.S. 1978, c. C-25, s. 2.

HOUSEWIFE. *n*. A woman managing, maintaining and controlling an independent domestic establishment, who does not either: (i) engage in a definite regular occupation for wages or for profit; or (ii) report regularly to a place of employment apart from her residence. *The Automobile Accident Insurance Act*, R.S.S. 1978, c. A-35, s. 2.

HOUSING. *n*. 1. Any buildings or structures suitable for human habitation and which are primarily used for that purpose. 2. Any unit, building or mobile home that provides in it living, sleeping, eating, food preparation and sanitary facilities for one or more persons, with or without essential facilities shared with other units, buildings or mobile homes. See CANADA MORTGAGE AND ~ CORPORATION; FACTORY BUILT ~; LOW INCOME ~; PROTECTIVE ~; PUBLIC ~; STUDENT ~; SUBSIDIZED PUBLIC ~.

HOUSING ACCOMMODATION. 1. Any place of dwelling and includes any place where other services are provided in addition to accommodation, but does not include a place of dwelling that is part of a building in which the owner or his family resides and where the occupant of the place of dwelling is required to share a bathroom or kitchen facility with the owner or his family. *Humans Rights Code acts*. 2. Any place of dwelling, except a place of dwelling that is part of a building in which the owner or his family or both, reside where the occupants of the place of dwelling are required to share (a) a bathroom or kitchen facility, or (b) a common entrance, except in a duplex, apartment building or condominium, with the owner of the dwelling or his family or both. *Human Rights Act*, R.S.M. 1987, c. H175, s. 1. See SERVICED ~.

HOUSING ACTS. The National Housing Act, chapter N-10 of the Revised Statutes of Canada, 1970, the National Housing Act, 1954, and the National Housing Act, chapter 188 of the Revised Statutes of Canada, 1952. *Canada Mortgage and Housing Corporation Act*, R.S.C. 1985, c. C-7, s. 2.

HOUSING ASSOCIATION. 1. (i) An association that builds or otherwise acquires housing accommodation and leases it to its members; (ii) an association that builds or otherwise acquires housing accommodation and sells it to its members for their individual ownership and use; (iii) an association that provides services to achieve or maintain the objectives described in subclause (i) or (ii); (iv) an association of corporate bodies of which at least eighty per cent of the members are housing associations and cooperative associations incorporated or registered under this Act and which has as its objectives any or all of those described in subclause (i), (ii) or (iii). *The Cooperative Associations Act*, R.S.S. 1978, c. C-34, s. 86. 2. Any society, body of trustees or company established for the purpose of, or amongst whose objects or powers are included those of constructing, improving or managing or facilitating or encouraging the construction or improvement of houses. *Housing Association (Loans) Act*, R.S. Nfld. 1970, c. 161, s. 2. See COOPERATIVE ~.

HOUSING COMPANY. A limited-dividend housing company (within the meaning of that expression as defined in section 2 of the National Housing Act), all or substantially all of the business of which is the construction, holding or management of low-rental housing projects. *Income Tax Act*, R.S.C. 1952, c. 148 (as am. S.C. 1979, c. 5, s. 51), s. 149(1)(n).

HOUSING COMPLEX. Several immoveables situated near one another if such immoveables are administered jointly by the same person or by related persons.

HOUSING PROJECT. A project consisting of one or more houses, one or more multiple-family dwellings, housing accommodation of the hostel or dormitory type, one or more condominium units or any combination thereof, together with any public space, recreational facilities, commercial space and other buildings appropriate to the project, but does not include a hotel. See COMMUNITY ~; COOPERATIVE ~; LOW-RENTAL ~; RENTAL ~; STUDENT ~.

HOUSING UNIT. A unit that provides therein living, sleeping, eating, food preparation and sanitary facilities for one or more persons, with or without essential facilities shared with other housing units. See ELDERLY PERSONS'~; FAMILY ~.

HOWEVER. *adv.* Yet, regardless, nevertheless.

H.S.T. *abbr.* Harmonized sales tax.

HUB. *n.* A rotating member that provides for mounting of disc wheels. *Motor Vehicle Safety Regulations*, C.R.C., c. 1038, s. 2.

HUDSON'S BAY COMPANY. The company incorporated by British royal charter in 1670 as "The Governor and Company of Adventurers of England trading into Hudson's Bay".

HUE AND CRY. In the old common law, pursuing felons and those who had wounded another with horn and voice.

HULL. *n.* The body of a vessel including the masts and rigging and all parts of its structure. *Canada Shipping Act*, R.S.C. 1985, c. S-9, s. 2. See HEIGHT ABOVE THE ~.

HUMAN BEING. A child becomes a human being within the meaning of this Act when it has completely proceeded, in a living state, from the body of its mother, whether or not (*a*) it has breathed; (*b*) it has an independent circulation; or (*c*) the navel string is severed. *Criminal Code*, R.S.C. 1985, c. C-46, s. 223(1).

HUMAN CLONE. An embryo that, as a result of the manipulation of human reproductive material or an *in vitro* embryo, contains the same nuclear deoxyribonucleic acid sequence as is found in the cell of a living or deceased human being, foetus or other embryo.

HUMAN CONSUMPTION. See PRODUCT FOR ~.

HUMAN DIGNITY. 1. The fundamental attributes of a human being, the intrinsic value which a person has. The respect to which every person is entitled simply because he or she is a human being and the respect that a person owes to himself or herself. *Québec (Curateur public) c. Syndicat national des employés de l'hôpital St-Ferdinand*, 1996 CarswellQue 916, 202 N.R. 321, (sub nom. *Quebec (Public Curator) v. Syndicat national des employés de l'hôpital St-Ferdinand*) 138 D.L.R. (4th) 577, 1 C.P.C. (4th) 183, [1996] 3 S.C.R. 211. L'Heureux-Dube for the court. 2. The idea of human dignity finds expression in almost every right and freedom guaranteed in the *Charter*. Individuals are afforded the right to choose their own religion and their own philosophy of life, the right to choose with whom they will associate and how they will express themselves, the right to choose where they will live and what occupation they will pursue. These are all examples of the basic theory underlying the *Charter*, namely that the state will respect choices made by individuals and, to the greatest extent possible, will avoid subordinating these choices to any one conception of the good life. *R. v. Morgentaler*, [1988] 1 S.C.R. 30, per Wilson, J. 3. Human dignity means that an individual or group feels self-respect and self-worth. It is concerned with physical and psychological integrity and empowerment. Human dignity is harmed by unfair treatment premised upon personal traits or circumstances which do not relate to individual needs, capacities, or merits. It is enhanced by laws which are sensitive to the needs, capacities, and merits of different individuals, taking into account the context underlying their differences. Human dignity is harmed when individuals and groups are marginalized, ignored, or devalued, and is enhanced when laws recognize the full place of all individuals and groups within Canadian society. *Law v. Canada*

(Minister of Employment & Immigration), [1999] 1 S.C.R. 497 at 530, Iacobucci J. for the court.

HUMANE SOCIETY. A corporation that has as its principal object, the prevention of cruelty to animals and that is designated as such for the purposes of this Part. *Animal Husbandry Act*, R.S.M. 1987, c. A90, s. 64.

HUMAN EXPERIENCE DATA. Data, collected in accordance with good scientific practices, that demonstrates that injury to or poisoning of a human has or has not resulted from (*a*) exposure to a chemical product; or (*b*) the reasonably foreseeable use of a chemical product or container by a consumer, including, in particular, the consumption of the product by a child. *Consumer Chemicals and Containers Regulations, 2001*, SOR/2001-269, s. 1(1).

HUMANITIES. See SOCIAL SCIENCES AND ~ RESEARCH COUNCIL OF CANADA.

HUMANITY. See CRIME AGAINST ~.

HUMAN PATHOGEN. An infectious substance, the toxin of an infectious substance, or any diagnostic specimen or other material that contains, or that its importer has reasonable grounds to believe contains, an infectious substance or the toxin of an infectious substance. *Human Pathogens Importation Regulations*, SOR/94-558, s. 2.

HUMAN REMAINS. A dead human body and includes a cremated human body.

HUMAN REPRODUCTIVE MATERIAL. A sperm, ovum or other human cell or a human gene, and includes a part of any of them.

HUMAN RIGHTS. The subject of Human Rights Codes in the provinces and federally. Refers mainly to equality rights. See CANADIAN ~ COMMISSION; EUROPEAN COMMISSION OF ~; EUROPEAN CONVENTION ON ~; EUROPEAN COURT OF ~; INTERNATIONAL BILL OF ~; UNIVERSAL DECLARATION OF ~.

HUMAN RIGHTS LEGISLATION ... [I]s of a special nature and declares public policy regarding matters of general concern. It is not constitutional in nature in the sense that it may not be altered, amended or repealed by the Legislature. It is, however, of such nature that it may not be altered, amended, or repealed, nor may exceptions be created to its provisions, save by clear legislative pronouncements. . ." *Craton v. Winnipeg School Division No. 1* (1985), 8 C.C.E.L. 105 at 111, [1985] 2 S.C.R. 150, 15 Admin. L.R. 177, [1985] 6 W.W.R. 166, 85 C.L.L.C. 17,020, 61 N.R. 241, 6 C.H.R.R. D/ 3014, 21 D.L.R. (4th) 1, 38 Man. R. (2d) 1, the court per McIntyre J.

HUMPBACK WHALE. Any whale known by the name of hunch, humpback, humpback whale, humpbacked whale, hump whale, or hunchbacked whale. *Whaling Convention Act*, R.S.C. 1970, c. W-8, Schedule, s. 18.

HUNDREDWEIGHT. *n*. 100 pounds. *Weights and Measures Act*, S.C. 1970-71-72, c. 36, Schedule II.

HUNG JURY. A jury unable to reach a unanimous decision in a criminal case.

HUNT. *v*. To kill, injure, seize, capture or trap, or to attempt to do so, and includes to pursue, stalk, track, search for, lie in wait for or shoot at for any of those purposes. *Canada National Parks Act*, S.C. 2000, c. 32, s. 26(5).

HUNT. *abbr*. Hunter's Torrens Cases (Can.).

HUNTER'S CERTIFICATE. The document issued by the Minister, establishing that a person is recognized competent in the handling of firearms for hunting purposes. *Wild-life Conservation Act*, S.Q. 1978, c. 65, s. 1.

HUNTING. *n*. 1. Includes, (a) lying in wait for, searching for, being on the trail of, pursuing, chasing or shooting at wildlife, whether or not the wildlife is killed, injured, captured or harassed, or (b) capturing or harassing wildlife, except that "hunting" does not include, (c) trapping, or (d) lying in wait for, searching for, being on the trail of or pursuing wildlife for a purpose other than attempting to kill, injure, capture or harass it, unless the wildlife is killed, injured, captured or harassed as a result. *Fish and Wildlife Conservation Act, 1997*, S.O. 1997, c. 41, s. 1(1). 2. Chasing, driving, flushing, attracting, pursuing, worrying, following after or on the trail of, searching for, trapping, attempting to trap, snaring or attempting to snare, shooting at, stalking or lying in wait for any wildlife whether or not the wildlife is then or subsequently captured, killed, taken or wounded, but does not include stalking, attracting, searching for or lying in wait for any wildlife by an unarmed person solely for the purpose of watching or taking pictures of it. *Wildlife acts*. See SPORT ~.

HUNTING OR FISHING LODGE. An establishment erected in a hunting or fishing territory and equipped for lodging and meals.

HUNTING PRESERVE. See GAME BIRD ~; PHEASANT ~.

HUNTING TROPHY. A dead animal or a part or derivative of one that an individual acquired and possessed through legal hunting. *Wild Animal and Plant Trade Regulations*, SOR/96-263, s. 14.

HUSBAND. *n*. A man who has entered into a marriage. See SPOUSE.

HUSBAND OR WIFE. The legal spouse of an insured or, if the insured did not have a legal spouse at the time of his death who had an enforceable claim for benefits under this Act, the person who, at the time of the death of an insured and during the two years immediately preceding the accident out of which the claim arose, lived and manifested an intention of continuing to live together permanently with the insured as husband and wife even though they were not married. *The Automobile Accident Insurance Act*, R.S.S. 1978, c. A-35, s. 2.

HUSBANDRY. *n*. Farming. See IMPLEMENT OF ~.

HUSH-MONEY. *n*. A bribe to keep someone silent.

HUSKY DOG. Any dog of the breed or type to which that name is commonly applied, and in particular includes an Eskimo dog, an Alaskan Malamute, and a Siberian Husky (also known as a Samoyede), and also includes a dog that is partly of one of those breeds or strains, and the young of any such dog. *Animal Husbandry Act*, R.S.M. 1987, c. A90, s. 28.

HUSTINGS. *n*. A temporary wooden platform from which parliamentary candidates formerly addressed electors.

HUTESIUM ET CLAMOR. [L.] Hue and cry.

HYBRID. *n*. 1. (*a*) A human ovum that has been fertilized by a sperm of a non-human life form; (*b*) an ovum of a non-human life form that has been fertilized by a human sperm; (*c*) a human ovum into which the nucleus of a cell of a non-human life form has been introduced; (*d*) an ovum of a non-human life form into which the nucleus of a human cell has been introduced; or (*e*) a human ovum or an ovum of a non-human life form that otherwise contains haploid sets of chromosomes from both a human being and a

non-human life form. 2. Being born the first generation of a cross between two or more inbred lines or their combinations including single crosses, double crosses and three way crosses. *Seeds Regulations*, C.R.C., c. 1400, s. 19.

HYBRID OFFENCE. Term applied to a criminal offence which may be tried by summary conviction procedure or by indictment at the option of the prosecutor. A hybrid offence is an indictable offence until the Crown elects to proceed by way of summary conviction.

HYBRID PROMOTION CLAUSE. A clause which enables management to consider applicants' seniority, qualifications, abilities, and other relevant factors in hiring but requires that the employer invoke seniority as the governing factor in the case of equally rated applicants.

HYDRAULIC DEVICE. A fishing device used for the harvesting of shellfish by which the shellfish are lifted from the bottom of the water by the use of water under pressure. *Fishery* regulations.

HYDRAULICKING PURPOSE. The use of the water under head to move earth, sand, gravel or rock, except when the moving is done or proposed to be done in order to get mineral from it. *Water Act*, R.S.B.C. 1996, c. 483, s. 1.

HYDRAULIC SYSTEM MINERAL OIL. A mineral-oil-based fluid designed for use in motor vehicle brake systems in which none of the components contacting the fluid are SBR, EPDM, neoprene or natural rubber. *Motor Vehicle Safety Regulations*, C.R.C., c. 1038, s. 2.

HYDREMIA. *n*. The increase of water content of the blood and is distinguished by a watery and edematous condition of the subcutaneous tissues and body cavities. *Meat Inspection Regulations*, C.R.C., c. 1032, s. 46.

HYDROBROMOFLUOROCARBON. *n*. A hydrobromofluorocarbon each molecule of which contains one, two or three carbon atoms and at least one atom each of hydrogen, bromine and fluorine. *Ozone-depleting Substances Regulations, 1998*, SOR/99-7, s. 1.

HYDROCARBON. *n*. 1. A chemical compound of hydrogen and carbon used as a fuel, either liquid or gaseous. *Energy Act*, R.S.O. 1990, c. E.16, s. 1. 2. Does not include coal. Canada statutes.

HYDROCARBONS. *n*. 1. Solid, liquid and gaseous hydrocarbons and any natural gas whether consisting of a single element or of two or more elements in chemical combination or uncombined and, without restricting the generality of the foregoing, includes oil-bearing shale, tar sands, crude oil, petroleum, helium and hydrogen sulphide. *Bank Act*, S.C. 1991, c. 46, s. 425(1). 2. Reside in sub-surface containers in three forms: oil reservoirs, gas reservoirs and mixed reservoirs. In mixed reservoirs, before the reservoir is penetrated by drilling, the percentage of liquid and gaseous hydrocarbons is fixed. *Anderson v. Amoco Canada Oil & Gas*, 2002 ABCA 162, 214 D.L.R. (4th) 272 (C.A.).

HYDROCHLOROFLUOROCARBON. A hydrochlorofluorocarbon each molecule of which contains one, two or three carbon atoms and at least one atom each of hydrogen, chlorine and fluorine. *Ozone-depleting Substances Regulations, 1998*, SOR/99-7, s. 1.

HYDRO DEVELOPMENT. (i) Means a project for the furnishing of hydro energy to a power plant, and (ii) includes dams, diversion works, water conduits and all structures, machinery, appliances, fixtures and equipment, and all appurtenances and lands and rights of way required in connection with that project. *Hydro and Electric Energy Act*, R.S.A. 1980, c. H-13, s. 1.

HYDRO-ELECTRIC COMMISSION. A hydro-electric commission or public utility commission or public utilities commission entrusted with the control and management of works for the retail supply of power.

HYDROELECTRIC POWER PLANT. A facility for the generation of electricity, from the motion of water.

HYDRO ENERGY. Energy associated with the motion or the position and potential motion of water.

HYDROGEN SWELL. A can with one or both ends bulging as a result of hydrogen gas produced inside the can from the reaction of the product on the metal of the container. *Processed Fruit and Vegetable Regulations*, C.R.C., c. 291, s. 2.

HYDROSTATIC TEST. A flotation test in which the buoyancy of lung tissue on water is observed to recognize live birth. F.A. Jaffe, *A Guide to Pathological Evidence*, 3d ed. (Toronto: Carswell, 1991) at 221.

HYGIENE. See DENTAL ~.

HYGIENE FACILITIES. Facilities for cleaning, washing and eating. D. Robertson, *Ontario Health and Safety Guide* (Toronto: Richard De Boo Ltd., 1988) at 5-214.

HYGIENIST. See DENTAL ~.

HYMEN. *n.* A roughly circular, thick membrane around the vaginal opening. F.A. Jaffe, *A Guide to Pathological Evidence*, 3d ed. (Toronto: Carswell, 1991) at 165.

HYOID BONE. A U-shaped bone above the larynx in the neck. F.A. Jaffe, *A Guide to Pathological Evidence*, 3d ed. (Toronto: Carswell, 1991) at 221.

HYPERKALEMIA. *n.* A marked increase in blood potassium. F.A. Jaffe, *A Guide to Pathological Evidence*, 2d ed. (Toronto: Carswell, 1983) at 80.

HYPERSENSITIVITY REACTION. A side effect or adverse reaction with an allergic or immunological basis. F.A. Jaffe, *A Guide to Pathological Evidence*, 3d ed. (Toronto: Carswell, 1991) at 81.

HYPERTHERMIA. *n.* Heat stroke. F.A. Jaffe, *A Guide to Pathological Evidence*, 3d ed. (Toronto: Carswell, 1991) at 46.

HYPERVOLEMIA. *n.* Greater blood volume. F.A. Jaffe, *A Guide to Pathological Evidence*, 2d ed. (Toronto: Carswell, 1983) at 80.

HYPNOTIC. *n.* A drug which brings on sleep.

HYPNOTISM. *n.* A process or act intended to put any person into induced sleep or trance in order to make that person's mind more susceptible to direction or suggestion.

HYPOPHARYNX. *n.* The part of the pharynx below the palate. F.A. Jaffe, *A Guide to Pathological Evidence*, 3d ed. (Toronto: Carswell, 1991) at 224.

HYPOSTASIS. *n.* Blood settling into dependent parts of the body after death. F.A. Jaffe, *A Guide to Pathological Evidence*, 3d ed. (Toronto: Carswell, 1991) at 221.

HYPOSTATIC OR CONGESTION LIVIDITY. Lividity of the skin appearing a half hour after death when blood distends the capillary blood vessels. F.A. Jaffe, *A Guide to Pathological Evidence*, 3d ed. (Toronto: Carswell, 1991) at 6.

HYPOTHEC. *n.* 1. "In Mutual Life Assurance Co. v. Douglas [(1918)], 57 S.C.R. 243 . . . Fitzpatrick C.J.C., said at pp. 224-45 . . . 'Speaking generally I see very little practical difference at the present time between the mortgage of the English law and the hypothec of the civil law . . . the real owner of the land is the mortgagor; and the mortgage is a mere security for the debt or obligation."' *Saint John (City) v. McKenna* (1987), (*sub nom. Saint John* (City) *v.* Saab) 45 R.P.R. 61 at 64, 78 N.B.R. (2d) 393, 198 A.P.R. 393, 37 D.L.R. (4th) 160 (C.A.), Hoyt J.A. (Ryan J.A. concurring). 2. "Throughout the years, the rules of equity developed a tendency to conceptualize the mortgage in terms of civil law, as an hypothec. The distinction is well summarized by Harrison C.J. in Mann v. English (1876), 38 U.C.Q.B. 240 at 245 (C.A.): 'Courts of law at one time construed the conveyance of land by mortgage as a conveyance of the legal estate, leaving the mortgagor no right except that of regaining the estate on performance of the condition. Courts of equity, on the contrary, treated the mortgage as a mere security for the debt, and held that the debt was the principal and the land the incident." *Saint John (City) v. McKenna* (1987), (*sub nom. Saint John (City) v. Saab*) 45 R.P.R. 61 at 66, 78 N.B.R. (2d) 393, 198 A.P.R. 393, 37 D.L.R. (4th) 160 (C.A.), Angers J.A. (dissenting).

HYPOTHECATION. *n.* Pledging something as security for a demand or debt without giving up that thing.

HYPOTHERMIA. *n.* A condition of unusually low body temperature. F.A. Jaffe, *A Guide to Pathological Evidence, 3d ed.* (Toronto: Carswell, 1991) at 221.

HYPOTHETICAL. *adj.* Depending on an assumption of fact which may or may not be provable or true. Robert J. Sharpe, ed., *Charter Litigation* (Toronto: Butterworths, 1987) at 335.

HYPOTHETICAL OR NOTIONAL MARKET. The valuation mechanism when there is no contemplated or actual open market transaction on the valuation date(s). A. Bissett-Johnson & W.M. Holland, eds., *Matrimonial Property Law in Canada* (Toronto: Carswell, 1980) at V-7.

HYPOVOLEMIA. *n.* Decreased blood volume. F.A. Jaffe, *A Guide to Pathological Evidence*, 2d ed. (Toronto: Carswell, 1983) at 81.

HYPOXIA. *n.* Being without enough oxygen. F.A. Jaffe, *A Guide to Pathological Evidence*, 3d ed. (Toronto: Carswell, 1991) at 221.

HZ. *abbr.* Hertz.

I.A.B. *abbr*. Immigration Appeal Board.

I.A.C. *abbr*. Immigration Appeal Cases, 1970-1976.

IATROGENIC. *adj*. Describes an injury or illness caused by a physician or medical treatment.

IATROGENIC ARTEFACT. A foreign object left in the patient's body accidentally after surgical or medical treatment.

IBID. *abbr*. Ibidem.

IBIDEM. *adv*. [L.] In the same place.

I.B.M. *abbr*. International Business Machines.

I.C.B.C. *abbr*. Insurance Corporation of British Columbia.

ICE. *n*. The ice used for the preparation or preservation of food. *An Act to Amend the Agricultural Products, Marine Products and Food Act*, S.Q. 1983, c. 53, s. 1.

ICE ANGLING. Angling in ice-covered waters.

ICE BREAKER. *var*. **ICE-BREAKER**. *var*. **ICEBREAKER**. A ship designed and constructed for the purpose of assisting the passage of other ships through ice.

ICE CREAM. The frozen food that is made from ice cream mix by freezing, with or without the addition of cocoa or chocolate syrup, fruit, nuts or confections.

ICE CREAM FACTORY. Any building where the milk or cream of cows is manufactured into ice cream or where any stage in the manufacture thereof is carried on.

ICE CREAM PLANT. A place where ice cream, ice cream mix, milk shake mix, sherbet or any frozen dessert made wholly or mainly from milk is prepared, processed or manufactured for the purpose of sale to retail distributors.

ICE FISHING. Fishing or attempting to fish through the ice in inland waters.

ICE SHELTER. Any structure that is located on or over ice over any water for more than one day and that is or may be used for shelter, privacy or the storage or sale of any thing. *Environmental Protection Act*, R.S.O. 1990, c. E.19, s. 24(1).

ID. *abbr*. Idem.

ID CERTUM EST QUOD CERTUM REDDI POTEST. [L.] What is certain is what can be made certain.

IDEM. [L.] The same.

IDEM AGENS ET PATIENS ESSE NON POTEST. [L.] It is impossible to do better than to suffer the same thing.

IDEM EST FACERE ET NON PROHIBERE CUM POSSIS; ET QUI NON PROHIBET CUM PROHIBERE POSSIT IN CULPA EST. [L.] It is the same thing to do an act as not to prevent it when prevention is possible; whoever has the power but does not prevent the commission of an offence is at fault.

IDEM EST NIHIL DICERE ET INSUFFICIENTER DICERE. [L.] It is the same to say nothing as to say what is insufficient.

IDEM EST NON ESSE ET NON APPARERE. [L.] In law, not to exist and not to appear to exist are the same.

IDEM PER IDEM. [L. the same for the same] Describes an illustration which adds nothing new to the question being considered.

IDEM SEMPER ANTECEDENTI PROXIMO REFERTUR. [L.] The word "idem" always refers to the closest antecedent.

IDEM SONANS. [L. sounding alike] 1. Sounding to the same effect. 2. Similar in sound. H.G. Fox, *The Canadian Law of Trade Marks and Unfair Competition*, 3d ed. (Toronto: Carswell, 1972) at 160.

IDEM RE ET SENSU. [L.] In the same matter and meaning (in reference to words in a document or conveyance).

IDEM SYLLABIS SEU VERBIS. [L.] In the very same syllables and words (in reference to words in a document or conveyance).

IDENTICAL. *adj.* One and the same.

IDENTICAL GOODS. In relation to goods being appraised, means imported goods that (a) are the same in all respects, including physical characteristics, quality and reputation, as the goods being appraised, except for minor differences in appearance that do not affect the value of the goods, (b) were produced in the same country as the country in which the goods being appraised were produced, and (c) were produced by or on behalf of the person by or on behalf of whom the goods being appraised were produced, but does not include imported goods where engineering, development work, art work, design work, plans or sketches undertaken in Canada were supplied, directly or indirectly, by the purchaser of those imported foods free of charge or at a reduced cost for use in connection with the production and sale for export of those imported goods. *Customs Act*, R.S.C. 1985 (2d Supp.), c. 1, s. 45.

IDENTICAL PROPERTY. A property which is the same in all material respects, so that a potential buyer would not prefer one as opposed to another.

IDENTIFIABLE. *adj.* The court adopted Professor Donovan Waters' description of the distinction between "identifiable" and "traceable" property as set out in "Trusts in the Setting of Business, Commerce, and Bankruptcy" (1983), 21 Alta. Law Rev. 395. He stated at pp. 431-34 that: "identifiable" refers to the ability to point to the particular property obtained by the debtor as a result of the dealing with the collateral, while "traceable" refers to the situation where the collateral is commingled with other property so that its identity is lost. *Transamerica Commercial Finance Corp. Canada v. Royal Bank*, [1990] 4 W.W.R. 673 (Sask. C.A.).

IDENTIFIABLE GROUP. Any section of the public distinguished by colour, race, religion or ethnic origin. *Criminal Code*, R.S.C. 1985, c. C-46, s. 318(4).

IDENTIFICATION. *n.* 1. Showing that some person or thing is the person or thing in question. 2. The knowledge of officers of a corporation can be attribute to the corporation so that the corporation can be notionally aware of conflicts of interest and therefore breach of duties owed to plaintiff. G.H.L. Fridman, *Restitution*, 2d ed. (Toronto: Carswell, 1992) at 379. See VALID ~.

IDENTIFICATION BRAND. An identification impressed or affixed on or within the body of livestock for a purpose other than to indicate ownership. *Livestock Identification Act*, R.S.B.C. 1996, c. 271, s. 1.

IDENTIFICATION DOCTRINE. In criminal law, the concept that the board of directors and anyone to whom governing executive authority is delegated by the board of directors merge with the corporation for the purpose of giving it a directing mind. The conduct of any of the merged entities is attributed to the corporation.

IDENTIFICATION TAG. A tag used to mark a corner of a claim and made of a substance and of a size approved by the Minister and issued as one of a set of four by the Mining Recorder. *Canada Mining Regulations*, C.R.C., c. 1516, s. 2.

IDENTIFICATION THEORY. In criminal law, the concept that the board of directors and anyone to whom governing executive authority is delegated by the board of directors merge with the corporation for the purpose of giving it a directing mind. The conduct of any of the merged entities is attributed to the corporation.

IDENTIFIED. *adj.* " . . . [R]equires no more than that the [breath test] solution used be described so as to be capable of later recognition for the purpose of further investigation. . ." *R. v. Genero*, [1980] 2 W.W.R. 182 at 186, 5 M.V.R. 78, 50 C.C.C. (2d) 312 (B.C. S.C.), Taylor J.

IDENTIFIER. *n.* 1. A label on a map that corresponds to a description contained in the mapping system. *Land Titles Act*, R.S.A. 2000, c. S-26, s. 1. 2. A unique series of letters or numbers or any combination of these or a bar code that is assigned to a medical device by the manufacturer and that identifies it and distinguishes it from similar devices. *Medical Devices Regulations* SOR/98-282, s. 1.

IDENTIFY. *v.* To use one's trade mark in order to or intending to distinguish one's wares or services from those of others. H.G. Fox, *The Canadian Law of Trade Marks and Unfair Competition*, 3d ed. (Toronto: Carswell, 1972) at 18.

IDENTITAS VERA COLLIGITUR EX MULTITUDINE SIGNORUM. [L.] True identity is derived from many signs.

IDENTITY. *n*. 1. " . . . [C]an be established not only by the name but also by a physical description of the person and other more sophisticated forensic methods such as fingerprints or voiceprints. . ." *R. v. Khela* (1991), 68 C.C. (3d) 81 at 85, 9 C.R. (4th) 380 (Que. C.A.), Proulx J.A. (Tourignay J.A. concurring). 2. " . . . [I]nvolves all the ingredients by which a person purports to identify himself." *Francey v. Wawanesa Mutual Insurance Co.* (1990), 46 C.C.L.I. 240 at 254, 75 Alta. L.R. (2d) 257, [1990] 6 W.W.R. 329, 108 A.R. 82, 72 D.L.R. (4th) 544, [1990] I.L.R. 1-2652 (Q.B.), Fraser J. 3. " . . . [S]omething different from 'name and address', though name and address are sufficient to establish identity, . . ." *R. v. Lloyd* (1980), 16 C.R. (3d) 221 at 240, 53 C.C.C. (2d) 121 (B.C. C.A.), Hinkson J.A.

IDENTITY DOCTRINE. " . . . [M]erges the board of directors, the managing director, the superintendent, the manager or anyone else delegated by the board of directors to whom is delegated the governing executive authority of the corporation, and the conduct of any of the merged entities is thereby attributed to the corporation . . ." *R. v. McNamara (No. 1)* (1985), (*sub nom. Canadian Dredge & Dock Co. v. R.*) 45 C.R. (3d) 289 at 312, [1985] 1 S.C.R. 662, 9 O.A.C. 321, 19 C.C.C. (3d) 1, 19 D.L.R. (4th) 314, 59 N.R. 241, the court per Estey J.

ID EST. [L. that is] That is to say.

IDIOPATHY. *n*. A disease or condition without a known cause.

IDIOSYNCRACY. *n*. An individual or unusual reaction, usually to drugs. F.A. Jaffe, *A Guide to Pathological Evidence*, 3d ed. (Toronto: Carswell, 1991) at 221.

IDLE POSITION. The position of the throttle at which it first comes in contact with an engine idle speed control appropriate for existing conditions according to the manufacturers' recommendations respecting engine speed adjustments for a cold engine, air conditioning, emission control and throttle setting devices. *Motor Vehicle Safety Regulations*, C.R.C., c. 1038, s. 2.

IDLE TIME. Non-productive time caused by waiting for work or repairs to equipment.

IDONEUM SE FACERE, IDONEARE SE. [L.] To atone oneself by oath for a crime of which one was accused.

IDONEUS HOMO. [L.] A proper person.

ID POSSUMUS QUOD DE JURE POSSUMUS. [L.] We can do what law permits us to do.

ID QUOD COMMUNE EST, NOSTRUM ESSE DICITUR. [L.] Whatever is common is said to be ours.

ID QUOD NOSTRUM EST SINE FACTO NOSTRO AD ALIUM TRANSFERRI NON POTEST. [L.] Whatever is ours may not be transferred to another except by our own action.

I.E. *abbr.* Id est.

IF. *prep.* On the condition that; on the supposition that.

IFR. *abbr.* Instrument flight rules. *Canadian Aviation Regulations*, SOR/96-433, s. 101.01.

IFR AIRCRAFT. An aircraft operating in IFR flight. *Canadian Aviation Regulations*, SOR/96-433, s. 101.01.

IFR AIR TRAFFIC CONTROL MESSAGE. A message that contains an air traffic control clearance or instruction, a position report or procedure related to the conduct of an IFR flight. *Canadian Aviation Regulations*, SOR/96-433, s. 101.01.

IFR FLIGHT. A flight conducted in accordance with the instrument flight rules. *Canadian Aviation Regulations*, SOR/96-433, s. 101.01.

IGNETEGIUM. *n*. [L.] A curfew.

IGNITEGIUM. *n*. [L.] A curfew.

IGNITION COMPOUND. The chemical compound used to make the striking tip of a match. *Hazardous Products (Matches) Regulations*, C.R.C., c. 929, s. 2.

IGNORAMUS. [L.] We are ignorant.

IGNORANCE OF THE LAW. Ignorance of the law by a person who commits an offence is not an excuse for committing that offence. *Criminal Code*, R.S.C. 1985, c. C-46, s. 19.

IGNORANTIA EORUM QUAE QUIS SCIRE TENETUR NON EXCUSAT. [L.] Ignorance of things which everyone should know is no excuse.

IGNORANTIA FACTI EXCUSAT; IGNORANTIA JURIS NON EXCUSAT. [L.] Ignorance of fact is excusable; ignorance of the law is no excuse.

IGNORANTIA JUDICIS FORET CALAMITAS INNOCENTIS. [L.] A judge's ignorance would mean calamity for the innocent.

IGNORANTIA JURIS NEMINEM EXCUSAT. [L.] Ignorance of the law excuses no one.

IGNORANTIA JURIS NON EXCUSAT. [L.] Ignorance of the law is no excuse.

IGNORANTIA JURIS HAUD EXCUSAT. "In Cooper v. Phibbs [(1867), L.R. 2 H.L. 149 (U.K.) at 170], Lord Westbury says: 'It is said "Ignorantia juris haud excusat," but in that maxim the word "jus" is used in the sense of denoting general law, the ordinary law of the country. But when the word "jus" is used in the sense of denoting a private right that maxim has no application;' and in Earl Beauchamp v. Winn [(1873), L.R. 6 H.L. (U.K.) at 234], Lord Chelmsford says: 'The rule ignorantia etc., applies where the alleged ignorance is that of a well known rule of law, but not where there is a matter of law arising upon the doubtful construction of a grant.'" *Hobbs v. Esquimalt & Nanaimo Railway* (1897), 6 B.C.R. 228 at 237 (S.C.), Davis C.J.

IGNORANTIA JURIS QUOD QUISQUE SCIRE TENETUR NON EXCUSAT. [L.] Ignorance of a law which everyone should know offers no excuse.

IGNORANTIA LEGIS NEMINEM EXCUSAT. [L.] Ignorance of law offers no one an excuse.

IJC. *abbr*. International Joint Commission.

ILLEGAL. *adj*. Forbidden by law. Infringing on public policy. Infringing on the terms or object of an enactment. See UNLAWFUL.

ILLEGAL CONTRACT. 1. A contract is illegal as to formation when it is prohibited by statute. It is illegal as performed if, though lawful in its formation, it is performed by one of the parties in a manner prohibited by statute. *Still v. Minister of National Revenue* (1997), [1998] 1 F.C. 549 (C.A.). 2. An agreement to do anything forbidden either by statute or by the common law.

ILLEGAL GAS. Gas produced from any well in the province in violation of this Act or any regulation or order made under the authority thereof. *The Oil and Gas Conservation Act*, R.S.S. 197 8, c. O-2, s. 2.

ILLEGALITY. *n*. 1. " . . . [A] generic term covering any act not in accordance with the law. . ." *Immeubles Port Louis Ltée c. Lafontaine (Village)* (1991), 5 M.P.L.R. (2d) 1 at 55, [1991] 1 S.C.R. 326, 78 D.L.R. (4th) 15, 121 N.R. 323, 38 Q.A.C. 253, the court per Gonthier J. 2. A contract prohibited by statute or for an illegal purpose will be declared void even it conforms to all other requirements of a valid transaction. 3. By 'illegality' as a ground for judicial review I mean that the decision-maker must understand correctly the law that regulates his decision-making power and must give effect to it. Whether he has or not is par excellence a justiciable question to be decided, in the event of dispute, by those persons, the judges, by whom the judicial power of the state is exercisable. *Council of Civil Service Unions v. Minister for Civil Service* (1984), [1985] 1 A.C. 374, [1984] 3 All E.R. 935 (H.L.), at pp. 410 and 411 [A.C.], Lord Diplock.

ILLEGALLY ENLISTED PERSON. A person who has accepted or agreed to accept, or is about to leave Canada with intent to accept, any commission or engagement, or who has been induced to go on board a conveyance under a misapprehension or false representation of the service in which the person is to be engaged with the intention or in order that the person may accept or agree to accept any commission or engagement contrary to this Act. *Foreign Enlistment Act*, R.S.C. 1985, c. F-28, s. 2.

ILLEGAL OR UNLAWFUL MEANS. The case law reflects two different views of "illegal or unlawful means," one narrow, the other broad. The narrow view confines illegal or unlawful means to an act prohibited by law or by statute. The broader view, however, extends illegal or unlawful means to an act the defendant "is not at liberty to commit"—in other words, an act without legal justification. *Reach M.D. Inc. v. Pharmaceutical Manufacturers Assn. of Canada* (2003), 65 O.R. (3d) 30, 172 O.A.C. 202 (C.A.).

ILLEGAL PRACTICES. Acts in relation to elections that are declared to be illegal practices by the Canada Elections Act.

ILLEGAL PRODUCT. A product derived in whole or in part from illegal oil or illegal gas. *The Oil and Gas Conservation* Act, R.S.S. 1978, c. O-2, s. 2.

ILLEGAL STRIKE. Strike called in violation of the law.

ILLEGITIMATE CHILD. Obsolete expression used to refer to a child born out of wedlock, that is when the parents were not married to each other.

ILLEVIABLE. *adj.* Describes a duty or debt which ought or cannot be levied.

ILL HEALTH. See NOTIFIABLE CONDITION OF ~.

ILLICIT. *adj.* 1. " . . . '[U]nlawful' . . ." *R. v. Deutsch* (1986), 18 O.A.C. 1 at 14, 52 C.R. (3d) 305, [1986] 2 S.C.R. 2, 68 N.R. 321, 27 C.C.C. (3d) 385, 30 D.L.R. (4th) 435, Le Dain J. (Beetz, McIntyre and Wilson JJ. concurring). 2. " . . . [R]eferring to sexual intercourse not authorized or sanctioned by lawful marriage." *R. v. Deutsch* (1986), 18 O.A.C. 1 at 14, 52 C.R. (3d) 305, [1986] 2 S.C.R. 2, 68 N.R. 321, 27 C.C.C. (3d) 385, 30 D.L.R. (4th) 435, Le Dain J. (Beetz, McIntyre and Wilson JJ. concurring).

ILLICIT DRUG. A controlled substance or precursor the import, export, production, sale or possession of which is prohibited or restricted pursuant to the Controlled Drugs and Substances Act. *Criminal Code*, R.S.C. 1985, c. C-46, s. 462.1.

ILLICIT DRUG USE. The importation, exportation, production, sale or possession of a controlled substance or precursor contrary to the Controlled Drugs and Substances Act or a regulation made under that Act. *Criminal Code*, R.S.C. 1985, c. C-46, s. 462.1. See INSTRUMENT FOR ~; LITERATURE FOR ~.

ILLICIT SEXUAL INTERCOURSE. Sexual intercourse which is not authorized or sanctioned by lawful marriage. *R. v. Deutsch* (1986), 18 O.A.C. 1 (S.C.C.).

ILLICITUM COLLEGIUM. [L.] An unlawful corporation.

ILLNESS. *n.* Incapacitation; inability to work because of the state of one's health. See MENTAL ~; OCCUPATIONAL ~.

ILLOCABLE. *adj.* Incapable of being hired or rented.

ILLUMINATION. See LEVEL OF ~.

ILLUS QUOD ALIAS LICITUM NON EST NECESSITAS FACIT LICITUM; ET NECESSITAS INDUCIT PRIVILEGIUM QUOD JURE PRIVATUR. [L.] Necessity permits what otherwise is not permitted; and necessity establishes a privilege which is justly removed.

I.L.O. *abbr.* International Labour Organization.

I.L.R. *abbr.* 1. Canadian Insurance Law Reports. 2. Insurance Law Reporter (Can.).

IMC. Instrument meteorological conditions. *Canadian Aviation Regulations*, SOR/96-433, s. 101.01.

I.M.C.O. CODE. The International Maritime Dangerous Goods Code published by the Inter-Governmental Maritime Consultative Organization. *National Harbours Board Operating By-law*, C.R.C., c. 1064, s. 106.

IMITATION. See COLOURABLE ~.

IMITATION FIREARM. 1. Any thing that imitates a firearm, and includes a replica firearm; *Criminal Code*, R.S.C. 1985, c. C-46, s. 84(1). 2. Parliament intended that an object which resembles a firearm, and is used to facilitate a robbery, satisfies the requirements of s. 85(2) [of the Criminal Code, R.S.C. 1985, c. C-46]. To require the Crown to go on and prove that it is in fact not a "firearm" defeats the purpose of the section. Furthermore, an unordinary meaning must be ascribed to the term "imitation firearm" to achieve the purpose of the section. Firearms that are capable of causing serious bodily harm (i.e. real firearms) must be included so that the intention of Parliament is not defeated. Such an interpretation of "imitation firearm" is also mandated by the so-called "golden rule" of statutory interpretation, since absurdities would arise in firearms case if the Crown is required to prove that a firearm is not a real firearm. *R. v. Scott*, 2000 CarswellBC 840, 2000 BCCA 220, 222 W.A.C. 161 (C.A.), Per Braidwood J.A. 3. Imitation is being contrasted with the original. . . I find it inconceivable that Parliament intended the definition of "imitation firearm" to include the real thing. If Parliament had intended the definition of "imitation firearm" to include "firearm", it could have said so by simply including firearm in the definition, as for example, it did in including "firearm" within the definition of "weapon", and "replica firearm" within the definition of "imitation firearm". Instead, Parliament chose to define "firearm" and "imitation firearm" separately and to create separate offences in relation to each of them. *R. v. Scott*, 2000 CarswellBC 840, 2000 BCCA 220, 222 W.A.C. 161 (C.A.). 4. In my view, "imitation" in the English version of section 85(2) may usefully and properly be read as making it illegal for a person to use an object that appears to be a firearm in the commission of an indictable offence. I have no difficulty concluding that something that appears to be a gun, whether or not it is a gun, can nevertheless be an imitation of a gun for the purposes of s. 85(2). This is particularly so when the object is used as a gun is commonly used, as in a robbery where it is used or displayed for threatening or coercive purposes. *R. v. Scott*, 2000 CarswellBC 840, 2000 BCCA 220, 222 W.A.C. 161 (C.A.). Per McEachern, C.J.B.C. concurring in the result.

IMITATION MILK PRODUCT. Any food substance other than milk or a manufactured milk product, of whatever origin, source or composition, that is manufactured for human consumption and for the same use as or in semblance of milk or a manufactured milk product, and that is manufactured wholly or in part from any fat or oil other than that of milk. *Milk Industry Act*, R.S.B.C. 1996, c. 289, s. 1.

IMMATERIAL AVERMENT. A statement which is not necessary.

IMMATERIAL ISSUE. An issue on some point which will not decide the outcome of an action.

IMMATURE. *adj.* Not fully developed; not yet adult.

IMMEDIATE. *adj.* 1. Stronger than the expression "within a reasonable time" and implies prompt, vigorous action, without any delay. *Reg. v. Justices of Berkshire*, [1878] 4 Q.B.D. 469 at 471 (U.K.), Cockburn C.J. 2. The word "imminent" used in the French version and the word "immediate" in the English version can be easily reconciled. Both words must mean, in the context of the subsection, that the serious danger must occur soon or within a short time. However, as to what constitutes a short time or soon in a given case must be determined on the facts of that case. *Atomic Energy of Canada Ltd. v. Chalk River Professional Employees Group* (2002), 2002 FCA 489, 2003 C.L.L.C. 220-020, 298 N.R. 285, [2003] 3 F.C. 313 (C.A.).

IMMEDIATE ANNUITY. An annuity that becomes payable to the contributor immediately when the contributor becomes entitled. *Superannuation acts.*

IMMEDIATE CONTAINER. The container that is in direct contact with a natural health product. *Natural Health Products Regulations*, SOR/2003-196, s. 1.

IMMEDIATE FAMILY. 1. When used to indicate a relationship with any person, means (i) any spouse, son or daughter of that person who has the same home as that person, or (ii) any other relative of that person or of that person's spouse who has the same home as that person. 2. The husband, wife, son, daughter, brother, sister, mother, father or grandparent of an individual.

IMMEDIATE LIFE ANNUITY. A life annuity that (a) commences periodic payments within one year after its purchase, (b) provides for equal periodic payments or periodic payments that have been varied by reference to (i) the amount of any pension payable under the Old Age Security Act, (ii) the amount of any pension payable under either the Canada Pension Plan or a provincial pension plan as defined in section 3 of the Canada Pension Plan, (iii) the Consumer Price Index for Canada as published by Statistics Canada under the authority of the Statistics Act, or (iv) the value of the assets held in a segregated fund, and (c) is issued by a person authorized to carry on a life insurance business in Canada. *Pension Benefits Standards Regulations, 1985*, SOR/87-19, s. 2, as am.

IMMEDIATELY. *adv.* Within reasonable time; without delay; at once.

IMMEDIATE PENSION. A pension that becomes payable to a person immediately on his becoming entitled thereto.

IMMEDIATE PENSION BENEFIT. A pension benefit that is to commence within one year after the member becomes entitled to it. *Pension Benefits Standards Act*, R.S.C. 1985 (2d Supp.), c. 32, s. 2.

IMMEMORIAL. *adj.* Beyond the memory of the law.

IMMEMORIAL USAGE. A very long-held practice; a custom.

IMMIGRANT. *n.* A person who seeks landing. *Immigration Act*, R.S.C. 1985, c. I-2, s. 2.

IMMIGRANT CHILD. A child who has been brought into a province for the purpose of settlement in a province, and who does not reside in the home of a parent within a province.

IMMIGRATION. *n.* Entering a country for the purpose of establishing permanent residence in it. See EMPLOYMENT AND ~ CANADA.

IMMIGRATION APPEAL BOARD. A federal body which acts as an independent court to hear appeals of people ordered deported from Canada, whose relatives have been refused admission into Canada or those with refugee claims.

IMM. L.R. (2d). *abbr*. Immigration Law Reporter (Second Series) 1987—.

IMMORAL CONTRACT. A contract based on consideration contra bonos mores and considered void.

IMMOVABLE. *n*. A thing which can be touched but which cannot be moved. Includes a chattel real.

IMMOVABLE BY NATURE. " . . . [T]he structures . . . must participate in the fixity or immobility of the land, which is the ultimate measure of whether a thing is immovable by nature. This principle is observed as long as a structure participates in the immovable nature of the land, by adhering directly to it or to another structure, which in turn adheres to the land. In either case the structure is immovable by nature because it is naturally immobile." *Cablevision Montreal Inc. v. Quebec.* [1978] 2 S.C.R. 64 at 73, 19 N.R. 121, the court per Beetz J.

IMMOVABLE PROPERTY. Includes real property and any leasehold or other interest in land. *Wills Act*, R.S.N.W.T. 1974, c. W-3, s. 2.

IMMOVEABLE. *n*. 1. An immoveable by nature within the meaning of the Civil Code or a moveable object placed by anyone for a permanency in or on an immoveable by nature. *An Act respecting municipal taxation and providing amendments to certain legislation*, S.Q. 1979, c. 72, s. 1. 2. " . . . [C]omprises everything which could be regarded as real estate for the purposes of the taxation by-laws and resolutions . . . and while it may not be so clear that such immovables as the pipes, poles, wires and transformers in question are real estate and real property, the weight of authority certainly favours that view . . . the real property of English law is not entirely co-extensive with the immovables of the civil law, . . ." *Montreal Light, Heat & Power Consolidated v. Westmount (Town)*, [1926] S.C.R. 515 at 523, [1926] 3 D.L.R. 466, Anglin C.J.C. (Duff, Mignault, Newcombe and Rinfret JJ. concurring). 3. Includes any land or premises that may be occupied separately. *Real Estate Assessment Act*, R.S.Q. 1977, c. E-16, s. 29. 4. Includes any edifice, building, house, premises, enclosed or unenclosed ground, in Québec, or any part of such edifice, building, house, premises or ground. *Physical Contests Act*, R.S.Q. 1977, c. C-52, s. 2.

IMMOVEABLE BY DESTINATION. Any moveable thing placed for a permanency by any person on or in an immoveable by nature. *Real Estate Assessment Act*, R.S.Q. 1977, c. E-16, s. 1.

IMMUNITY. *n*. The state of being free or exempt. See CROWN ~; JUDICIAL ~; PUBLIC INTEREST ~; RESTRICTIVE SOVEREIGN ~; SOVEREIGN ~.

IMMUNIZATION. *n*. The administration of a biological agent to a person to increase that person's resistance to the effect of an infectious agent or its toxic products. *Public Health Act*, R.S.A. 2000, c. P-37, s. 1.

IMMUNIZING AGENT. A vaccine or combination of vaccines administered for immunization against diptheria, tetanus, poliomyelitis, pertussis, measles, rubella, hepatitis B, rabies, Haemophilus influenzae b infections, influenza or a prescribed disease. *Health Protection and Promotion Act*, R.S.O. 1990, c. H.7, s. 38(1).

IMPACT. See ENVIRONMENTAL ~; HEAD ~ AREA; PELVIC ~ AREA.

IMPACT ASSESSMENT. See HERITAGE RESOURCE ~.

IMPACT BY VEHICLES INSURANCE. Insurance against loss of or damage to the property insured caused by vehicles or objects falling from them.

IMPACT STATEMENT. A statement which specifies in detail the expected effect of a proposed development.

IMPAIR. *v*. To make worse, to lessen the value of, to weaken.

IMPAIRED. *adj*. Ability adversely affected by drugs, alcohol, disease or condition.

IMPAIRMENT. *n*. A physical or functional abnormality or loss (including disfigurement) which results from an injury and any psychological damage arising from the abnormality or loss. *Workplace Safety and Insurance Act, 1997*, S.O. 1997, c. 16, Sched. A, s. 2. See PERMANENT ~.

IMPANEL. *v*. " . . . [S]ometimes means to enroll upon a panel or list for jury duty, and sometimes to draw from that panel and select a jury for a particular case." *R. v. Gaffin* (1904), 8 C.C.C. 194 at 196 (N.S. S.C.), the court per Graham E.J. See EMPANEL; JURY.

IMPARTIAL CHAIRMAN. The third, neutral member of a tripartite labour arbitration panel.

IMPARTIAL. *adj.* " . . . [C]onnotes absence of bias, actual or perceived." *R. v. Valente (No. 2)* (1985), 23 C.C.C. (3d) 193 at 201, [1985] 2 S.C.R. 673, 52 O.R. (2d) 779, 37 M.V.R. 9, 49 C.R. (3d) 97, 24 D.L.R. (4th) 161, 64 N.R. 1, 14 O.A.C. 79,19 C.R.R. 354, [1985] D.L.Q. 85n, the court per Le Dain J.

IMPARTIALITY. 1. [I]mpartiality can be described—perhaps somewhat inexactly—as a state of mind in which the adjudicator is disinterested in the outcome, and is open to persuasion by the evidence and submissions. *R. v. S. (R.D.)*, 1997 CarswellNS 301, 151 D.L.R. (4th) 193, 118 C.C.C. (3d) 353, 10 C.R. (5th) 1, 218 N.R. 1, 161 N.S.R. (2d) 241, 477 A.P.R. 241, [1997] 3 S.C.R. 484, 1 Admin. L.R. (3d) 74, per Cory, J. 2. Impartiality refers first and foremost to an absence of prejudice or bias, actual or perceived, on the part of a judge in a particular case, but like independence it includes an institutional aspect. If the system is structured in such a way as to create a reasonable apprehension of bias at the institutional level, the requirement of impartiality is not met. *R. c. Lauzon* (1998), 1998 CarswellNat 1810, 18 C.R. (5th) 288, (sub nom. *R. v. Lauzon*) 230 N.R. 272, 56 C.R.R. (2d) 30, (sub nom. *R. v. Lauzon*) 129 C.C.C. (3d) 399, 8 Admin. L.R. (3d) 33 (Can. Ct. Martial App. Ct.). 3. Is not the same as neutrality. Impartiality does not require that the juror's mind be a blank slate. Nor does it require jurors to jettison all opinions, beliefs, knowledge and other accumulations of life experience as they step into the jury box. Jurors are human beings, whose life experiences inform their deliberations. *R. v. Find*, 2001 CarswellOnt 1702, 2001 SCC 32, 42 C.R. (5th) 1, 154 C.C.C. (3d) 97, 199 D.L.R. (4th) 193, 269 N.R. 149, 146 O.A.C. 236 McLachlin C.J.C., for the court. See INSTITUTIONAL ~.

IMPASSE. *n.* A breakdown in collective bargaining when neither side will change its position.

IMPEACH. *v.* " . . . [T]o call into question the veracity of evidence given by a witness by calling evidence to contradict, challenge or impugn the witness's prior testimony." *Machado v. Berlet* (1986), 15 C.P.C. (2d) 207 at 217, 57 O.R. (2d) 207, 32 D.L.R. (4th) 634 (H.C.), Ewaschuk J.

IMPEACHMENT. *n.* Attack on a patent by questioning its validity.

IMPECUNIOSITY. *n.* The state of destitution and the inability to raise money required from other sources.

IMPECUNIOUS. *adj.* Lacking sufficient assets for a purpose and unable to raise the moneys required from other sources.

IMPEDIMENT. See DIRIMENT~.

IMPEDIMENT TO MARRIAGE. Marriage is not possible if (a) a prior marriage continues, (b) the parties are related in a prohibited degree, (c) if the marriage is arranged by error, force or fraud, (d) if either party is not old enough or is mentally or physically disabled.

IMPEDITIVE VOTER. A voter otherwise qualified under this Part who is or will be unable to vote because of his or her being (a) in service in the merchant marine of Canada or of another country; (b) a fisher in the course of his or her occupation; (c) a hunter or trapper in the course of his or her occupation; (d) a patient in a hospital as defined by the Hospital Act but including similar hospitals owned or operated by the Crown in right of Canada or an agency of the Crown in right of Canada; (e) a full-time student at an educational institution situated within or outside the province; (f) a worker employed at a construction site; or (g) a person who is certified by a medical practitioner to be so ill or infirm as to be unable to vote at a polling booth. *Municipalities Act*, R.S. Nfld. 1990, c. M-23, s. 542.

IMPERFECT OBLIGATION. A moral duty which the law cannot enforce.

IMPERFECT TRUST. An executory trust which is not sufficiently constituted or declared.

IMPERIAL. *adj.* As applied to state documents, means of or pertaining to the United Kindom of Great Britain and Northern Ireland and includes any kingdom that included England, whether known as the United Kingdom of Great Britain and Ireland or otherwise. *Evidence acts.*

IMPERIAL ACTS. The laws passed by the Imperial Parliament.

IMPERIALISM. *n.* Domination of one nation by another, whether direct or indirect.

IMPERIAL PARLIAMENT. The parliament of the United Kingdom of Great Britain and Northern Ireland, as at present constituted, or any former kingdom that included England, whether known as the United Kingdom of Great Britain and Ireland or otherwise. *Evidence acts.*

IMPERIAL STATUTES. The laws passed by the Imperial Parliament.

IMPERIAL UNITS: Units of measurement in feet and decimals of a foot.

IMPERITIA CULPAE ADNUMERATUR. [L.] Lack of skill is counted as a fault.

IMPERIUM. *n.* [L.] Entitlement to command, attributed to executive power.

IMPERIUM IN IMPERIO. [L.] Power within a power.

IMPERSONATION. *n.* The act of representing that one is someone else, whether dead or living, fictitious or real.

IMPERTINENCE. *n.* Irrelevance.

IMPLANT. *n.* A device that has been inserted into, over, through or under the jawbone for the purpose of supporting a dental prosthesis.

IMPLEAD. *v.* 1. " . . . [A]sserting jurisdiction against the opposition of the parties sought to be sued." *Canadian Commercial Bank v. Mc-Laughlan* (1990), 73 D.L.R. (4th) 678 at 685, 39 E.T.R. 54, 75 Alta. L.R. (2d) 40 (C.A.), Bracco and Stevenson JJ.A. and Forsyth J. 2. To institute legal proceedings against a person.

IMPLEMENT. *n.* Any implement, equipment or machine that is used or intended for use on a farm. See AGRICULTURAL ~(S); FARM ~; FORESTRY ~S; UNUSED FARM ~; USED ~.

IMPLEMENT OF HUSBANDRY. A vehicle designed and adapted primarily for agricultural, horticultural or livestock raising operations. See SELF-PROPELLED ~.

IMPLICATION. *n.* An inference which is necessary or may be presumed and arises out of words or acts in evidence.

IMPLIED AUTHORITY. 1. Authority which may be read into an agent's express authority. 2. Actual implied authority is found to exist where an officer exceeds the authority usually attached to the position and does so with the knowledge and acquiescence of the corporation. *D. Fogell Associates Ltd. v. Esprit de Corp (1980) Ltd. / Esprit de Corp (1980) Ltée* (1997), 1997 CarswellBC 1131 (S.C.), Edwards J.

IMPLIED CONDITION. In some circumstances a court has a right to conclude that everything the parties agreed is not contained in their oral statements or in the written documents which appear to constitute the contract. The additional term is said to exist in the agreement though unspecified; a statute may imply it. G.H.L. Fridman, *The Law of Contract in Canada*, 2d ed. (Toronto: Carswell, 1986) at 448.

IMPLIED CONSENT. In relation to team sports, the players are deemed to consent to forms of intentional bodily contact which are inherent in and incidental to the game.

IMPLIED CONTRACT. A contract which law concludes does exist from an act, circumstance or relationship.

IMPLIED GRANT. An easement arises by implication under a grant where the intention to grant the easement can properly be inferred. The intention may be inferred on the basis of several different rules.

IMPLIED MALICE. One presumes that the malice needed to support a cause of action exists when someone publishes a defamatory remark. R.E. Brown, *The Law of Defamation in Canada* (Toronto: Carswell, 1987) at 730.

IMPLIED POWERS. Of a corporation include those which are necessary to carry out express powers, those implied to permit more complete execution of implied powers, those naturally implicit in an express power and those inferred logically from and consonant with the purposes and functions of the corporation. I.M. Rogers, *The Law of Canadian Municipal Corporations*, 2d ed. (Toronto: Carswell, 1971) at 359.

IMPLIED TERM. 1. " . . . [T]here may be cases where obviously some term must be implied if the intention of the parties is not to be defeated, some term of which it can be predicated that 'it goes without saying,' some term not expressed but necessary to give the transaction such business efficacy as the parties must have intended." *Luxor (Eastbourne) Ltd. v. Cooper*, [1941] A.C. 108 at 137 (U.K. H.L.), Lord Wright. 2. . . . "[S]ometimes . . . denotes some term which does not depend on the actual intention of the parties but on a rule of law, such as the terms, warranties or conditions which, if not expressly excluded, the law imports, as for instance under the Sale of Goods Act, . . ." *Luxor (Eastbourne) Ltd. v. Cooper*, [1941] A.C. 108 at 137 (U.K. H.L.), Lord Wright.

IMPLIED TRUST. A trust which comes about when an equitable interpretation is put on the conduct of the parties, for example where one person voluntarily transfers property to another person or pays for property and has that property put into another person's name.

IMPLIED UNDERTAKING. Documents and other information obtained through the discovery process in litigation will not be used for collateral or ulterior purposes.

IMPLIED WARRANTY. See IMPLIED CONDITION.

IMPLIED WARRANTY OF FITNESS. A warranty that upon completion a house will be fit for habitation and that the work will have been carried out in a good and workmanlike manner.

IMPLIED WARRANTY OF HABITATION. A warranty that upon completion a house will be fit for habitation and that the work will have been carried out in a good and workmanlike manner.

IMPLOSION. *n.* A bursting inward of a vessel or of a building.

IMPORT. *v.* 1. Import into Canada. *Customs Act,* R.S.C. 1985 (2d Supp.), c. 1, s. 2. 2. " . . . [T]o bring into the country or to cause to be brought into the country." *R. v. Bell* (1983), 8 C.C.C. (3d) 97 at 110, 36 C.R. (3d) 289, 3 D.L.R. (4th) 385, 50 N.R. 172, [1983] 2 S.C.R. 471, McIntyre J. (Beetz, Estey and Chouinard JJ. concurring). 3. With reference to gas or oil, to bring into Canada through pipelines, by railway tank car, by tank truck or by tanker. *National Energy Board Act,* R.S.C. 1985, c. N-7, s. 2. 4. To bring into any province of Canada from any other country or any other province of Canada. Canada regulations. See CANADIAN ~ TRIBUNAL.

IMPORTANCE. *n.* In addition to the factors set out in s. 2(3)(a)(b) and (c) [of Rules of Court], "importance" means important to the public at large or at least to other litigation of a similar nature. Difficult issues of fact and law are to be taken into account. To find a matter of unusual difficulty, the question is whether the collection and proof of the difficult facts were uncommon, remarkable, or exceptional events. *M. (F.S.) v. Clarke,* 2000 CarswellBC 878, 2000 BCSC 432 (S.C.).

IMPORTATION. *n.* Bringing goods and merchandise into a country from overseas. See PORT OF ~; TIME OF ~.

IMPORT CONTROL LIST. A list of goods established under section 5. *Export and Import Permits Act,* R.S.C. 1985, c. E-19, s. 2.

IMPORTED FABRIC. A fabric that has been woven in any country other than Canada, whether or not it contains Canadian materials, but does not include (a) a fabric imported free of duty, or (b) a fabric that would qualify for a drawback under any other regulations. *Customs Drawback Shirting Fabrics Regulations,* C.R.C., c. 487, s. 2.

IMPORTER. *n.* A person engaged in the business of importing goods into Canada. See CASUAL ~; DESIGNATED ~.

IMPORTS. *n.* Produce or goods brought from abroad into a country.

IMPOSITION. *n.* Contribution; tax.

IMPOSSIBILITY. *n.* Something either physical, legal or logical: physical when it is unnatural, legal when a rule of law makes it not possible to do and logical when it goes against the essential qualities of the transaction.

IMPOSSIBILIUM NULLA OBLIGATIO EST. [L.] There is no obligation to do the impossible.

IMPOST. *n.* A rate, charge, fee, tariff, rent, royalty, levy, tax, or any other payment payable under, regulated under or subject to control or approval under an act.

IMPOTENCE. *n.* Physical inability of any person to perform sexual intercourse.

IMPOTENTIA EXCUSAT LEGEM. [L.] When one is unable to do something one may plead the law as an excuse.

IMPOUND. *v.* To place in legal custody.

IMPOUNDMENT. *n.* The confining or holding of a stray animal by a poundkeeper for a period of time.

IMPRACTICABLE. *adj.* Difficult to put into practice; unmanageable.

IMPRESCRIPTABLE RIGHT. A right which people may or may not use as they please, since it cannot be taken away bar anyone else whose claim is founded on prescription.

IMPRIMATUR. [L.] Let it be printed.

IMPRISONED. *adj.* Held in prison, penitentiary or lock up.

IMPRISONMENT. *n.* 1. " . . . [C]arries with it a complete lack of choice. There must be an involuntary element to the confinement before it can be said to be a restraint on the personal liberty or freedom . . ." *R. v. Degan* (1985), 20 C.C.C. (3d) 293 at 299, 38 Sask. R. 234 (C.A.), the court per Vancise J.A. 2. Includes imprisonment in default of payment of a fine or penalty in money. See FALSE ~; TERM OF ~.

IMPROPER. *adj.* Not in accordance with truth, fact, reason or rule; unsuitable.

IMPROPER CONDUCT. Includes wilful disobedience of orders, wilful self-inflicted wounding and vicious or criminal conduct. *Pension Act*, R.S.C. 1985, c. P-6, s. 3.

IMPROPERLY. *adv*. Incorrectly, unsuitably, in an unbecoming manner.

IMPROPER PURPOSE. In an administrative law sense, these words ['bad faith' and 'improper purpose'] are not necessarily pejorative. A purpose may be improper merely because the actor is misguided. If an extraneous purpose—no matter how laudable—enters in, it will be considered an improper one and the act will have become tainted. In this sense, the terms are judicially taken to mean 'the making of regulations for any purpose other than one authorized by the parent statute'. 'Motive' addresses that which prompts one to act in a certain way or that determines volition, and speaks to the goal or object of one's actions. 'Purpose' addresses the reason for which something exists, and speaks to the practical result, effect or advantage obtained. *Morgentaler v. Prince Edward Island (Minister of Health & Social Services)* (1995), 1995 CarswellPEI 61, 32 Admin. L.R. (2d) 205, 126 Nfld. & P.E.I.R. 240, 393 A.P.R. 240, 122 D.L.R. (4th) 728 (T.D.).

IMPROPRIETY. *n*. An irregularity; an improper action. See APPREHENSION OF ~; PROCEDURAL ~.

IMPROVE A ROAD. To gravel, stone or macadamize a road, or to cover the surface thereof with a layer of materials welded by means of cement, bitumen or mechanical pressure; or to harden the surface thereof with a mixture of sand and clay, following a process approved by the Minister of Transport. *Roads Act*, R.S.Q., c. V-8, s. 23.

IMPROVED LAND. 1. A parcel of land separately assessed that has a building thereon, and includes any land in actual use for agricultural purposes, although there is no building thereon. Ontario statutes. 2. Includes enclosed pasture lands.

IMPROVED REAL ESTATE. Real estate (i) on which there exists a building used or capable of being used for residential, financial commercial, industrial, educational, professional, institutional, religious, charitable or recreational purposes, (ii) on which such a building is being or is about to be constructed, (iii) which is provided with the utilities necessary to serve such a building with electric power, water and sewers but only when the land is being mortgaged for the purpose of financing the construction of such a building, (iv) on which actual farming or ranching operations are being conducted, or (v) that is restricted by law in its use to commercial, industrial or residential purposes by zoning or otherwise.

IMPROVEMENT. *n*. 1. "... [O]rdinary meaning ... includes buildings, structures and all things which become attached to the land, but does not include buildings, structures or fixtures which merely rested on the land and which could be removed at will without changing the character of the land itself,. . ." *Beloit Sorel Walmsley Ltd. v. New Brunswick* (1976), 10 L.C.R. 373 at 376, 71 D.L.R. (3d) 240 (N.B. C.A.), the court per Limerick J.A. 2. In the leases, the word "improvement" is used to refer to things other than buildings. Clause 8(a), for example, refers to "any buildings and such other improvements, including construction of roads, water, sewer, electricity and/or gas systems". Improvements include services, and conversely "unimproved" means without services. The internal coherence of the rent review clause also supports the view that "unimproved" means unserviced. The leases were signed before any buildings were built, so the word "unimproved" would have added nothing to the phrase "unimproved lands in the same state as they were on the date of this agreement" unless it referred to the pre-existing servicing. *Musqueam Indian Band v. Glass* (2000), 2000 CarswellNat 2405, 2000 SCC 52, [2000] 11 W.W.R. 407, 36 R.P.R. (3d) 1, 192 D.L.R. (4th) 385, 82 B.C.L.R. (3d) 199, 261 N.R. 296, 186 F.T.R. 248 (note), [2000] 2 S.C.R. 633, [2001] 1. See CAPITAL ~; COMMUNITY ~; DRIVER ~ PROGRAM; HOME ~S; INTERNATIONAL RIVER ~; LAND ~ ASSOCIATION; LAND ~ PURPOSE; LOCAL ~; LOCAL ~S; PERMANENT ~; PROPERTY ~ GRANT; PUBLIC ~; RIVER ~ PURPOSE; ROAD ~ LINE; ROADSIDE ~.

IMPROVEMENT PLAN. See COMMUNITY ~.

IMPROVEMENT PROJECT. See COMMUNITY ~ AREA.

IMPROVER. *n*. A person who has been employed in a designated trade for a length of time not less than the term of apprenticeship specified in the appropriate apprenticeship standards, and, except for seasonal employment is regularly employed in that trade and who is eligible for training to qualify as a journeyman in that trade.

IMPROVIDENT. *adj*. Unreasonable in the circumstances.

IMPROVING LAND. The doing of any work which improves the character of the land and without limiting the generality of the foregoing includes (a) clearing the land of timber or scrub, (b) landscaping the land, (c) fencing the land, and (d) demolishing structures on the land, but does not include tilling, seeding, cultivating or mowing the land for agricultural or forest production or the harvesting of a crop from the land or the cutting of timber from the land for sale. *The Builders Lien Act*, R.S.M. 1987, c. B91, s. 1.

IMPUNITAS SEMPER AD DETERIORA INVITAT. [L.] Leaving a crime unpunished always invites worse crimes to be committed.

IMPUTED INCOME. Income with two salient qualities: (1) it is income in kind or non-cash income and (2) it originates outside of the market place. A.F. Sheppard, "The Taxation of Imputed Income and the Rule in *Sharkey v. Wernher*" (1973) Can. Bar Rev. 617 at 617-618.

IMPUTED INCOME FROM PROPERTY. The increase to a person's economic power if the person owns property which produces goods or services that the person or the person's family may enjoy. W. Grover & F. Iacobucci, *Materials on Canadian Income Tax*, 4th ed. (Toronto: Richard De Boo Ltd., 1980) at 157.

IN. *prep*. Expresses the relation of inclusion, position, existence within limits of space, time, condition or circumstances.

INABILITY. *n*. The condition of being unable; lack of ability, power or means.

INACCESSIBLE. *adj*. When applied to a room or compartment means that the room or compartment is sufficiently remote from access or so placed or guarded that unauthorized persons cannot inadvertently enter the room or compartment, and when applied to electrical equipment means that the electrical equipment is covered by the structure or finish of the building in which it is installed or maintained or is sufficiently remote from access or so placed or guarded that unauthorized persons cannot inadvertently touch or interfere with the equipment.

INACCURACY. *n*. Incorrectness.

INACTIVE DOCUMENT. A document no loner used for administrative or legal purposes.

INACTIVITY. *n*. That advanced exploration, mine production and mining operations on a site have been suspended indefinitely in accordance with a closure plan and although protective measures are in place on the site, the site is no longer being monitored by the proponent on a continuous basis. *Mining Act*, R.S.O. 1990, c. M.14, s. 139(1).

INADVERTENCE. *n*. 1. "[A]ccidental or unintentional." *Guimond v. Sornberger* (1980), 13 Alta. L.R. (2d) 228 at 242, 13 M.P.L.R. 134, 25 A.R. 18, 115 D.L.R. (3d) 321 (C.A.), Clement J.A. 2. " . . . [I]nvolves oversight, inattention, carelessness and the like." *Campbell v. Dowdall* (1992), 12 M.P.L.R. (2d) 27 at 37 (Ont. Gen. Div.), Rutherford J.

IN AEQUALI JURE MELIOR EST CONDITIO POSSIDENTIS. [L.] Where all parties' rights are equal, the actual possessor's claim is stronger.

IN AETERNUM. [L.] For ever.

INALIENABLE. *adj*. Not able to be transferred.

IN ALIENO SOLO. [L.] On another person's land.

IN ALIO LOCO. [L.] In some other place.

IN ALTA PRODITIONE NULLUS POTEST ESSE ACCESSORIUS SED PRINCIPALIS SOLUMMODO. [L.] In high treason no one can be an accessory but certainly one can be a principal.

IN AMBIGUA VOCE LEGIS EA POTIUS ACCIPIENDA EST SIGNIFICATIO QUAE VITIO CARET, PRAESERTIM CUM ETIAM VOLUNTAS LEGIS EX HOC COLLIGI POSSIT. [L.] Where the words of a statute are ambiguous, it is better to accept an interpretation which lacks defects, especially if one may see the intention of the act within it.

IN AMBIGUIS ORATIONIBUS MAXIME SENTENTIA SPECTANDA EST EJUS QUI EAS PROTULISSET. [L.] When dealing with ambiguous words one should especially regard the intention of the one who used them.

IN ANGLIA NON EST INTERREGNUM. [L.] There is no interregnum in England.

IN ARBITRIO JUDICIS. [L.] At the judge's discretion.

IN ARREARS. Payment is overdue.

IN ARTICULO MORTIS. [L.] At the moment of death.

IN ATROCIORIBUS DELICTIS, PUNITUR AFFECTUS LICET NON SEQUATUR EFFECTUS. [L.] In the case of more horrible crimes, one punishes the intent even though there may be no effect.

INAUGURATION. *n.* Solemn induction into office.

IN AUTER DROIT. [Fr.] In the right of another.

IN AUTRE DROIT. [Fr.] In the right of another.

IN BANC. See BANC.

IN BANCO. [L.] As a bench (of judges). Refers to the court sitting as a whole. See BANCO.

IN BANK. See BANC; BANCO.

IN BEING. 1. Living or en ventre sa mere. *Perpetuities acts.* 2. Living or conceived but unborn.

IN BONAM PARTEM. [L.] A word should prima facie be taken in its lawful and rightful sense. P. St. J. Langan, ed., *Maxwell on The Interpretation of Statutes*, 12th ed. (Bombay: N.M. Tripathi, 1976) at 274.

IN BOND. Subject to customs control. Canada regulations.

INBRED LINE. Being a relatively homozygous line produced by inbreeding and selection. *Seeds Regulations*, C.R.C., c. 1400, s. 19.

IN BULK. 1. In respect of a sale of gasoline or diesel fuel, means (a) in a quantity of five hundred litres or more, where the gasoline or diesel fuel is delivered to the purchaser at a retail outlet of the vendor, and (b) in any quantity, in any other case. *Excise Tax Act*, R.S.C. 1985 (2d Supp.), c. 7, s. 69. 2. For the purposes of subsection (5), means confined by the permanent structures of a ship or vessel, without intermediate containment or packaging. *Transportation of Dangerous Goods Act*, R.S.C. 1985, c. T-19, s. 3(6). 3. In relation to any pollutant carried on board a ship whether as cargo or otherwise, means in a quantity that exceeds a quantity prescribed by the Governor in Council with respect to that pollutant by any regulation made pursuant to paragraph 657(1)(p). *Canada Shipping Act*, R.S.C. 1985, c. S-9, s. 654. 4 . In relation to oil carried on board a ship, whether as a cargo or otherwise, means in a quantity that exceeds 1,000 tons. *Maritime Pollution Claims Fund Regulations*, C.R.C., c. 1444, s. 2. See AVIATION FUEL ~.

INC. *abbr.* 1. Incorporated. 2. Incorporé.

IN CAMERA. [L.] " . . . '[W]ithout publicity, privately and, if possible, in the private office of the judge or a private room'. . ." *R. v. B. (C.)* (1981), 23 C.R. (3d) 289 at 294, 62 C.C.C. (2d) 107, 38 N.R. 451, [1981] 6 W.W.R. 701, 24 R.F.L. (2d) 225, 12 Man. R. (2d) 361, [1981] 2 S.C.R. 480, 127 D.L.R. (3d) 482, the court per Chouinard J.

INCAPABLE. *adj.* Unable because of death, illness, absence from the province or otherwise. *Vital Statistics acts.*

INCAPACITATED. *adj.* In a condition of physical or mental illness or disability of such a nature as to make a person incapable of maintaining himself or herself or his or her family. *Social Assistance Act*, R.S.Nfld. 1990, c. S-17, s. 2.

INCAPACITATED FUNERAL DIRECTOR. A funeral director suffering from a physical or mental condition or disorder of a nature and extent making it desirable in the interests of the public or the funeral director that he no longer be permitted to engage in the practice of a funeral director or that his practice be restricted. *Funeral Services Act*, R.S.O. 1980, c. 180, s. 14.

INCAPACITATED LICENSEE. A licensee suffering from a physical or mental condition or disorder of a nature and extent making it desirable in the interests of the public or the licensee that he or she no longer be permitted to practise or that his or her practice be restricted. *Denture Therapists Act*, R.S.O. 1990, c. D.7, s. 12(1).

INCAPACITATED MEMBER. 1. A member of a professional body suffering from a physical or mental condition or disorder of a nature and extent making it desirable in the interests of the public or the member that the member no longer be permitted to practise or that that practice be restricted. 2. A member suffering from a physical or mental condition, emotional disturbance or excessive use of alcohol or drugs, of a nature and extent making it desirable in the interests of the public or the member that he not be permitted to remain a member of the Institute, or that restrictions be imposed upon his membership. *Chartered Accountants' Act, 1986*, S.N.B. 1986, c. 87, s. 2.

INCAPACITY. *n.* 1. Lack of ability. 2. Referring to the capacity to form an intent to commit a crime, in criminal law, a quality attributed to people with severe mental disorders and young children and, on occasion, to those who are intoxicated. 2. A physical or mental condition or disorder suffered by a member of a professional body of such nature and extent that it is desirable in the interests of the public or the member that the member no longer be permitted to practice. See LEGAL ~.

INCARCERATE. *v*. To imprison.

INCARCERATION. *n*. Imprisonment.

IN CASU EXTREMAE NECESSITATIS OMNIA SUNT COMMUNIA. [L.] In the case of extreme necessity, all things are common.

INCAUTE FACTUM PRO NON FACTO HABETUR. [L.] Something done per incuriam is considered to have not been done at all.

INCB. The International Narcotics Control Board.

INCENDIARISM. *n*. Deliberate setting of fire to property. See ARSON.

INCENTIVE. *n*. A grant, loan, payment or other financial concession made to encourage an activity. See DEVELOPMENT ~; INDIRECT ~ PLAN.

INCENTIVE PROGRAM. A program to encourage an activity

INCENTIVE WAGE PLAN. A wage payment plan under which extra pay is provided for extra work, perfect attendance or the like.

INCERTA PRO NULLIS HABENTUR. [L.] Uncertain things are treated as nullities.

INCERTA QUANTITAS VITIAT ACTUM. [L.] Uncertainty about quantity makes a deed invalid.

INCERTUS. [L.] Uncertain.

INCEST. *n*. Knowing that another person is by blood relationship his or her parent, child, brother, sister, grandparent or grandchild, as the case may be, having sexual intercourse with that person. *Criminal Code*, R.S.C. 1985, c. C-46, s. 155.

INCH. *n*. 1/36 yard. *Weights and Measures Act*, S.C. 1970-71-72, c. 36, Schedule II. See CUBIC ~; SQUARE ~.

INCHARTARE. To transfer using a written deed.

IN CHIEF. Describes the examination of a witness by the person who called that witness.

INCHMAREE CLAUSE. In maritime insurance, a clause covering losses due to special causes not properly covered by the general clause, namely losses due solely to negligence of the master, mariners, engineers, or pilots, provided "no want of due diligence by the assured, the owners or managers of the vessel" had been involved. Extends the cover to loss of or damage caused by any latent defect in the machinery or hull.

INCHOATE. *adj*. Commenced but not finished.

INCHOATE OFFENCE. A preparatory offence, such as conspiracy, complete upon agreement of the parties and does not require the acts agreed upon to be carried out.

INCIDENT. *n*. 1. Something which follows or appertains to another thing. 2. An event; a happening. See NUCLEAR ~.

INCIDENTAL. *adj*. In its simplest formulation, the plain meaning of "incidental" is "connected with in a meaningful way" and includes an activity that is subordinate to a principal activity. The ordinary sense of "incidental" does not imply or import a temporal connection between the two related activities. *Bank of Nova Scotia v. British Columbia (Superintendent of Financial Institutions)*, 2003 BCCA 29, 11 B.C.L.R. (4th) 206 (C.A.).

INCIDENTAL CATCH. A catch of fish of a species other than a species toward which the fishing effort of a vessel is primarily directed.

INCIDENTAL MOTION. A motion which is connected with and arises out of other motions. A. Fraser, W.A. Dawson, & J. Holtby, eds., *Beauchesne's Rules and Forms of the House of Commons of Canada*, 6th ed. (Toronto: Carswell, 1989) at 173-4.

INCIDENTAL QUESTION. An issue which presents itself while the main question before the court is being decided and which must be solved before the main question can be answered. J.G. McLeod, *The Conflict of Laws* (Calgary: Carswell, 1983) at 50-51.

INCIDENT TO ARREST. The second requirement before a strip search incident to arrest may be performed is that the search must be *incident* to the arrest. What this means is that the search must be related to the reasons for the arrest itself. *R. v. Golden*, 2001 SCC 83.

INCINERATION. *n.* The treatment of waste by controlled burning.

INCINERATOR. *n.* Any equipment, apparatus, device or mechanism that is used for the burning of garbage, wood waste, refuse or other waste materials. See ON-SITE ~.

INCINERATOR ASH. The ash residue, other than fly-ash, resulting from incineration.

INCINERATOR GOODS. (a) Materials for use exclusively in the construction of, or (b) machinery or apparatus, including equipment to be installed in a chimney or smoke stack, and repair and replacement parts therefor, for use directly and exclusively in the operation of an incinerator owned or to be owned by a municipality and used or to be used primarily for the incineration of waste for the municipality, but does not include motor vehicles, attachments therefor or office equipment. *Excise Tax Act,* R.S.C. 1985 (2d Supp.), c. 7, s. 68.27.

INCINERATOR WASTE. The residue from incineration, other than incinerator ash and fly-ash.

INCIPITUR. [L.] It begins.

INCITE. *v.* To arouse, provoke, encourage.

INCIVILE EST NISI TOTA SENTENTIA PERSPECTA DE ALIQUA PARTE JUDI-CARE. [L.] It is unreasonable to judge some part of a decision unless one considers the entire decision.

INCIVISM. *n.* Hostility to a country or government by one of its citizens.

INCLINE. *n.* An excavation that is driven in the earth or strata of an underground mine at an angle with the plane of the horizon and that is or may be used, (i) for ventilation or drainage, or (ii) for the ingress or egress of men, animals or material to or from the mine or part thereof. *Coal Mines Regulation Act,* R.S.A. 1970, c. 52, s. 2.

INCLINED PLANE. Includes slope. *Coal Mines Regulation Act,* R.S.N.S. 1989, c. 73, s. 4.

INCLINE LIFT. A mechanism having a power driven rope, belt or chain, with or without handholds or seats, for lifting or lowering persons or freight on an incline, and includes a ski lift and ski tow. *Elevators and Lifts acts.*

INCLOSURE. *n.* Fencing in property in order to cultivate it.

INCLUDE. *v.* 1. " . . . [G]enerally used in interpretation clauses in order to enlarge the meaning of words or phrases occurring in the body of a statute . . ." *Dilworth v. New Zealand Commissioner of Stamps,* [1899] A.C. 99 at 105 (New Zealand P.C.), Lord Watson. 2. " . . . It may be equivalent to 'mean and include', and in that case it may afford an exhaustive explanation of the meaning . . ." *Dilworth v. New Zealand Commissioner of Stamps,* [1899] A.C. 99 at 105 (New Zealand P.C.), Lord Watson. 3. When used in a definition indicates that the definition is not intended to be exhaustive. Those things listed in the definition and, in addition, things of like import.

INCLUDED EMPLOYMENT. Employment, other than excepted employment, on or in connection with the operation of any work, undertaking or business that is within the legislative authority of the Parliament of Canada, including, without restricting the generality of the foregoing, (a) any work, undertaking or business operated or carried on or in connection with navigation and shipping, whether inland or maritime, including the operation of a ship and transportation by ship anywhere in Canada; (b) any railway, canal, telegraph or other work or undertaking connecting a province with another province or extending beyond the limits of a province; (c) any line of steam or other ships connecting a province with another province or extending beyond the limits of a province; (d) any ferry between a province and another province or between a province and a country other than Canada; (e) any aerodrome, aircraft or line of air transportation; (f) any radio broadcasting station; (g) any bank or authorized foreign bank within the meaning of section 2 of the Bank Act; (h) any work, undertaking or business that, although wholly situated within a province, is before or after its execution declared by the Parliament of Canada to be for the general advantage of Canada or for the advantage of two or more provinces; and (i) any work, undertaking or business outside the exclusive legislative authority of provincial legislatures, and any work, undertaking or business of a local or private nature in Yukon, the Northwest Territories or Nunavut. *Pension Benefits Standards Act,* R.S.C. 1985 (2d Supp.), c. 32, s. 4(4).

INCLUDED OFFENCE. 1. An offence which has the same basic elements as the principal offence with which a person is charged. 2. " . . . [P]art of the main offence. The offence charged, either as described in the enactment creating the offence or as charged in the count, must contain the essential elements of the offence said to be included . . . the offence charged, either as described in the enactment creating the offence or as charged in the count, must be sufficient to inform the accused of the included offences which he must meet." *R. v. Simpson* (1981), 20 C.R. (3d) 36 at 49, 50, 58 C.C.C. (2d) 308 (Ont. C.A.), the court per Martin J.A.

INCLUDED PROVINCE. A province other than Yukon, the Northwest Territories or Nunavut, except a province providing a comprehensive pension plan unless at the time in respect of which the description is relevant there is in force an agreement entered into under subsection 4(3) with the government of that province. *Canada Pension Plan*, R.S.C. 1985, c. C-8, s. 114.

INCLUDES. *v.* When used in a definition indicates that the definition is not intended to be exhaustive. Those things listed in the definition and, in addition, things of like import.

INCLUDIBLE BOOK. In the case of a publisher, a book published by him which is not a book published at the author's expense and in the case of an accredited bookseller, a new book owned by him. *An Act Respecting the Guarantee of Certain Loans to Publishers and Booksellers*, R.S.Q. 1977, c. G-1, s. 1.

INCLUSIO UNIUS EST EXCLUSIO ALTERIUS. [L.] Where the law stipulates as to certain cases which it lists, the law is presumed to exclude the other cases.

INCLUSIVE TOUR. A round or circle trip performed in whole or in part by aircraft for an inclusive tour price for the period from the time of departure of the participants from the starting point of the journey to the time of their return to that point. *Air Transportation Regulation*, SOR/88-58, s. 2.

INCLUSIVE TOUR CHARTER. A passenger flight operated according to the conditions of a contract entered into between an air carrier and one or more tour operators that requires the tour operator or tour operators to charter the entire passenger seating capacity of an aircraft for resale by them to the public at an inclusive tour price per seat. *Air Transportation Regulation*, SOR/88-58, s. 2.

INCLUSIVE TOUR PRICE. Includes, for a participant in an inclusive tour, charges for transportation, accommodation and, where applicable, tour features. *Air Transportation Regulation*, SOR/88-58, s. 2.

INCOMBUSTIBLE MATERIAL. Material that neither burns nor gives off flammable vapours in sufficient quantity to ignite at a pilot-flame.

INCOME. *n.* 1. The gross amount received as the product of labour, business or capital. 2. The net receipts over disbursements in the taxation year in the totality of the taxpayer's business as an ongoing concern other than capital expenditures, gifts and the like. *Premium Iron Ores Ltd. v. N.R.*, [1966] 1 S.C.R. 685, [1966] C.T.C. 311, 66 D.T.C. 5280. 2. Includes (i) the gross amount received or receivable as the product of capital, labour, industry, or skill, (ii) all moneys earned and all gratuities and annuities, (iii) all income, fees, revenue rent, interest, dividends, or profits arising from any source, including the Dominion, provincial, and municipal governments. *Mining Tax acts.* See GROSS ~; GROSS INTEREST ~; IMPUTED ~; LOW ~; MAXIMUM BENEFIT ~; MONTHLY ~; NET ~; NET ~ OR REVENUE; ORDINARY ~; PERSONAL ~; RESIDUAL ~ OF THE SURVIVING SPOUSE; RESOURCE ~; TAXABLE ~.

INCOME APPROACH. In valuing a business, uses an estimation of the cash flow of the business and its profitability. The profitability is converted to value by the application of a capitalization or discount rate. Various factors are taken into account in setting the appropriate rate.

INCOME ASSURANCE PLAN. See FARM ~.

INCOME INTEREST. Of a taxpayer in a trust means a right (whether immediate or future and whether absolute or contingent) of the taxpayer as a beneficiary under a personal trust to, or to receive, all or any part of the income of the trust and, after 1999, includes a right (other than a right acquired before 2000 and disposed of before March 2000) to enforce payment of an amount by the trust that arises as a consequence of any such right *Income Tax Act*, R.S. C. 1985, c. 1 (5th Supp.), s. 108.

INCOME SUPPLEMENT. See GUARANTEED ~.

INCOME TAX. 1. Tax on net income, i.e., income after deducting expenses incurred in order to earn the income. 2. " . . . [A] charge upon the profits; the thing which is taxed is the profit that is made. . ." *Ashton Gas Co. v. Attorney-General* (1905), [1906] A.C. 10 at 12 (U.K. H.L.), Earl of Halsbury L.C. See CORPORATION~; PROVINCIAL ~; TERRITORIAL ~.

INCOME TAX STATUTE. With reference to an agreeing province, the law of that province that imposes a tax similar to the tax imposed under the federal Income Tax Act. *Income Tax acts.*

IMCOMMODUM NON SOLVIT ARGU-MENDUM. [L.] Inconvenience does not spoil an argument.

IN COMMON. The definition of "band" uses the term "in common" in relation to the interest that the members of the band have in the reserve. The term "in common" connotes a communal, as opposed to a private, interest in the reserve, by the members of the band. In other words, an individual member of a band has an interest in association with, but not independent of, the interest of the other members of the band. *Blueberry River Indian Band v. Canada (Department of Indian Affairs & Northern Development),* 2001 CarswellNat 963, 2001 FCA 67, 6 C.P.C. (5th) 1, 201 D.L.R. (4th) 35, 274 N.R. 304 (C.A.), Rothstein, J.A. for the court.

INCOMPETENCE. *n.* Acts or omissions of the part of a member of a professional body, in that member's occupation, that demonstrate a lack of knowledge, skill or judgment, or disregard for the interests of the recipient of the services of such a nature and to such an extent as to render that member unfit to carry on the occupation.

INCOMPETENCY. *n.* Absence of reasonable skill. See MENTAL ~.

INCOMPETENT. *n.* A person who lacks reasonable skill. See MENTAL ~.

INCOMPETENT. *adj.* Lacking reasonable skill.

IN CONCERT. ". . . [P]resupposes some form of active participation rather than passive consent to a decision taken by another person. . ." *Vaskevitch v. Minister of National Revenue,* [1969] C.T.C. 47 at 55, 69 D.T.C. 5062 (Can. Ex. Ct.), Cattanach J. See ACTING JOINTLY OR ~.

IN CONJUNCTIVIS OPORTET UTR-UMQUE, IN DISJUNCTIVIS SUFFICIT ALTERAM PARTEM ESSE VERAM. [L.] In conjunctives both should be true; in disjunctives it is enough that one is true.

IN CONSIMILI CASU. [L.] In a similar case.

IN CONSIMILI CASU, CONSIMILE DE-BET ESSE REMEDIUM. [L.] In a similar case the remedy should be similar.

INCONSISTENT. *adj.* 1. "[In the context of constitutional law] . . . refers to a situation where two legislative enactments cannot stand together. . ." *Friends of the Oldman River Society v. Canada (Minister of Transport)* (1992), 3 Admin. L.R. (2d) 1 at 37, [1992] 2 W.W.R. 193, [1992] 1 S.C.R. 3, 84 Alta. L.R. (2d) 129, 7 C.E.L.R. (N.S.) 1, 132 N.R. 321, 88 D.L.R. (4th) 1, 48 F.T.R. 160n, La Forest J. (Lamer C.J.C., L'Heureux-Dubé, Sopinka, Gonthier, Cory, McLachlin and Iacobucci JJ. concurring). 2. "Two laws are deemed to be inconsistent when 'compliance with one law involves breach of the other', see Smith v. R., [1960] S.C.R. 776 at 800 . . . per Martland J., or if resort to one statute from a practical point of view precludes the other from having any application: see Multiple Access Ltd. v. McCutcheon (1978), 19 O.R. (2d) 516 . . . (C.A.). . ." *James v. Lockhart* (1981), 24 R.F.L. (2d) 333 at 335-6 (Ont. Co. Ct.), Flanigan Co. Ct. J.

IN CONSUETUDINIBUS NON DIUTUR-NITAS TEMPORIS SED SOLIDITAS RA-TIONIS EST CONSIDERANDA. [L.] In the case of customs, one should consider not the length of time but the entirety of the reason.

INCONTESTABILITY. *n.* The quality of registration of a trade mark which may be attacked only upon the ground of prior use. H.G. Fox, *The Canadian Law of Trade Marks and Unfair Competition,* 3d ed. (Toronto: Carswell, 1972) at 252.

IN CONTRACTIS, BENIGNA; IN TESTA-MENTIS, BENIGNIOR; IN RESTITU-TIONIBUS, BENIGNISSIMA INTERPRE-TATIO FACIENDA EST. [L.] The interpretation of contracts should be liberal, of wills more liberal, and of restitutions most liberal.

IN CONTRACTIS TACITE INSUNT QUAE SUNT MORIS ET CONSUETUDINIS. [L.] In contracts, clauses in accord with custom and usage are implied.

IN CONVENTIONIBUS CONTRAHEN-TIUM VOLUNTAS POTIUS QUAM VERBA SPECTARI PLACUIT. [L.] In construing agreements, one should consider the parties' intention instead of the words actually used.

INCORPORATED. *adj.* One of the words which must be used as part of the name of a corporation. See CORPORATION ~ IN CANADA.

INCORPORATING INSTRUMENT. The special Act, letters patent, instrument of continuance or other constating instrument by which a body corporate was incorporated or continued and includes any amendment to or restatement of the constating instrument.

INCORPORATION. *n*. 1. The formation of a group of people into a corporation or body politic. 2. Merger of one thing with another so that the two constitute one whole. See ARTICLES OF ~; CERTIFICATE OF ~; INSTRUMENT OF ~; PRE- ~CONTRACT.

INCORPORATOR. *n*. 1. A person who signs articles of incorporation. 2. In relation to a company, means a person who applied for letters patent to incorporate the company.

INCORPOREAL. *adj*. Not capable of being possessed physically.

INCORPOREAL CHATTEL. An incorporeal right attached to chattels.

INCORPOREAL HEREDITAMENT. 1. "[A right] . . . in land, which [includes] such things as rent charges, annuities, easements, profits à prendre, and so on." *Pegg v. Pegg* (1992), 38 R.F.L. (3d) 179 at 184, 21 R.P.R. (2d) 149, 1 Alta. L.R. (3d) 249, 128 A.R. 132 (Q.B.), Agrios J. 2. Property which is not tangible but can be inherited. See PROFIT.

INCORPORÉ. *adj*. One of the words which must be used as part of the name of a corporation.

INCOTERMS. *n*. Rules for the interpretation of major terms used in international trade contracts published by the International Chamber of Commerce. I.F.G. Baxter, *The Law of Banking*, 3d ed. (Toronto: Carswell, 1981) at 135 and 136.

INCREASE. See INCREMENT ~; LENGTH-OF-SERVICE ~; MERIT ~; STATUTORY ~; SUBSEQUENT ~.

INCREASED COSTS. Increased costs will only be awarded if there is some unusual feature in the case or misconduct in addition to a significant disparity between ordinary and special costs which justifies greater indemnity than provided by ordinary costs. *Rieta v. North American Air Travel Insurance Agents Ltd.* (1998), 52 B.C.L.R. (3d) 114 (C.A.).

INCREMENT. *n*. In respect of a job or position, means the difference between the compensation payable for a rate in the scale or rates applicable to the job or position and the next higher rate in that scale. See EXPERIENTIAL ~.

INCREMENTAL PRODUCTION ROYALTY. The amount, if any, by which a produc-

tion royalty in respect of the production of old oil exceeds the amount that would be the production royalty in respect thereof if the old oil were valued at its old oil base price.

INCREMENTAL RESOURCE ROYALTY. The amount, if any, by which a resource royalty in respect of the production of old oil exceeds the amount that would be the resource royalty in respect thereof if the old oil were valued at its old oil base price.

INCREMENTUM. *n*. [L.] Improvement; increase.

IN CRIMINALIBUS PROBATIONES DEBENT ESSE LUCE CLARIORES. [L.] In criminal cases, proof ought to be more clear than light.

IN CRIMINALIBUS SUFFICIT GENERALIS MALITIA INTENTIONIS CUM FACTO PARIS GRADUS. [L.] When it is accompanied by the right act, what may be generally described as malice may be sufficient to constitute a crime.

INCRIMINATE. *v*. "In this context, the word 'incriminate' need not be equated with 'tending to prove guilt of a criminal offence'. The history of the various aspects of the principle against self-incrimination shows that the word 'incriminate' was not thus limited in this context. It extended, for example, to evidence having the tendency to expose the individual to a penalty or a forfeiture . . ." *R. v. Jones*, 1994 CarswellBC 580, 30 C.R. (4th) 1, 166 N.R. 321, 43 B.C.A.C. 241, 69 W.A.C. 241, 89 C.C.C. (3d) 353, [1994] 2 S.C.R. 229, 114 D.L.R. (4th) 645, 21 C.R.R. (2d) 286 Lamer, C.J.C. for minority. See PRINCIPLE AGAINST SELF-INCRIMINATION; PRIVILEGE AGAINST SELF-INCRIMINATION.

INCRIMINATING EVIDENCE. Any evidence which the Crown tenders as part of its case against an accused.

INCROACHMENT. See ENCROACHMENT.

INCULPATORY CONFESSION. A statement which incriminates the maker.

INCULPATORY OPINION. An inculpatory opinion is to the effect that the accused, because a [mitochondrial DNA ("mtDNA")] sequence matching his was found at the crime scene, "cannot be excluded" from the group of people who could have deposited the questioned sample there. Any other person with the same mtDNA sequence could also have done so. *R. v. Murrin* (1999), 1999 CarswellBC 3015, 181 D.L.R. (4th) 320, 32 C.R. (5th) 97 (S.C.).

INCUMBRANCE. *n.* 1. A charge or liability to which land is subject. 2. "By generally accepted definition . . . it comprehends 'every right to or interest in land which may subsist in third persons to the diminution of the value of land but consistent with the passing of the fee by the conveyance' . . ." *Wotherspoon v. Canadian Pacific Ltd.* (1987), (*sub nom. Eaton Retirement Annuity Plan v. Canadian Pacific Ltd.*) 45 R.P.R. 138 at 192, 76 N.R. 241, 21 O.A.C. 79, [1987] 1 S.C.R. 952, 39 D.L.R. (4th) 169, the court per Estey J. 2. A claim that secures the payment of money or the performance of any other obligation, and includes a charge, a mortgage and a lien. See ENCUMBRANCE.

INCUMBRANCER. *n.* Includes every person entitled to the benefit of an incumbrance, or to require payment or discharge thereof. See ENCUMBRANCER.

INCUR. *v.* " . . . '[L]iable to' or 'subject to'." *R. v. Allen* (1979), 45 C.C.C. (2d) 524 at 529 (Ont. C.A.), the court per Lacourcière J.A.

IN CURIA. [L.] In an open court.

INCURRED. *v.* 1. Rendered liable to. 2. Having become necessary. 3. Said of expenses, current or future, known with certainty.

IN CUSTODIA LEGIS. [L.] In legal custody.

INDEBITATUS ASSUMPSIT. [L. the indebted undertook] A kind of action of assumpsit.

INDECENT. *adj.* 1. A performance is indecent if the social harm engendered by the performance, having made reference to the circumstances in which it took place, is such that the community would not tolerate it taking place. *R. v. Mara*, [1997] 2 S.C.R. 630, per Sopinka, J. 2. " . . . [S]uch as would shock or disgust the average member of the Canadian contemporary community." *Priape Enrg. c. Sous-Ministre du Revenu national* (1979), (*sub nom. Priape Enrg. v. Deputy Minister of National Revenue (Customs & Excise)*) 24 C.R. (3d) 66 at 71, [1980] C.S. 86, 52 C.C.C. (2d) 44, 2 C.E.R. 169 (Qué. S.C.), Hugessen A.C.J.S.C.

INDECENT ASSAULT. " . . . [A]n assault that is committed in circumstances of indecency, or, as sometimes described, an assault with acts of indecency . . ." *R. v. Swietlinski* (1980), 18 C.R.

(3d) 231 at 243, 34 N.R. 569, 55 C.C.C. (2d) 481, 117 D.L.R. (3d) 285, [1980] 2 S.C.R. 956, the court per McIntyre J.

INDEFEASIBLE. *adj.* Not able to be voided.

INDEFEASIBLE TITLE. An estate in fee simple held under a good marketable title.

INDEFENSUS. *n.* [L.] A person who was impleaded and refused to answer.

INDEFINITUM AEQUIPOLLET UNIVERSALI. [L.] What is indefinite is equivalent to universal.

INDEMNIFICATION. *n.* Making good.

INDEMNIFY. *v.* To make good the loss which someone suffered through another's act or default; to grant an indemnity; to agree to indemnify.

INDEMNITY. *n.* 1. Indemnity may arise by contract, by statute, or by the nature of the relationship itself. An obligation to indemnify means an obligation to protect against or keep free from loss, to repay for what has been lost or damaged, to compensate for a loss. Contribution, on the other hand, is *only* available when a co-debtor has paid more than his equal share of the debt. Contribution among co-debtors is an equitable concept, and a co-debtor, while liable to the creditor for the full amount, is only liable as among the co-debtors for his or her share. *Lafrentz v. M & L Leasing Ltd. Partnership* (2000), 2000 CarswellAlta 1121, 2000 ABQB 714, 8 B.L.R. (3d) 219, [2001] 1 W.W.R. 629, 85 Alta. L.R. (3d) 233, 275 A.R. 334 (Q.B.), Perras J. 2. " . . . [T]he concept of indemnity has central to it the idea of compensation, of making good, or paying moneys to a person, to reimburse them for losses sustained . . ." *Arklie v. Haskell* (1986), 25 C.C.L.I. 277 at 284, 33 D.L.R. (4th) 458, [1987] I.L.R. 1-2176 (B.C. C.A.), McLachlin J.A. (Hutcheon and MacFarlane JJ.A. concurring). 3. "In a contract of indemnity, the indemnified assumes a primary obligation to repay the debt, and is liable regardless of the liability of the principal debtor. An indemnifier will accordingly be liable even if the principal debt is void or otherwise unenforceable." *Communities Economic Development Fund v. Canadian Pickles Corp.* (1991), 8 C.B.R. (3d) 121 at 143, [1992] 1 W.W.R. 193, 85 D.L.R. (4th) 88, 131 N.R. 81, [1991] 3 S.C.R. 388, 76 Man. R. (2d) 1, 10 W.A.C. 1, the court per Iacobucci J. 4. The sessional pay authorized by a legislature to be paid to members. 5. " . . . [D]escribes a situation where the wrong-doer who has paid all of the plaintiff's damages is entitled to receive payment of this amount from the other wrong-doer whose conduct has contributed to or caused the injury to the plaintiff . . ." *Peter v. Anchor Transit Ltd.*, [1979] 4 W.W.R. 150 at 153, 100 D.L.R. (3d) 37 (B.C. C.A.), the court per Craig J.A. See CONTRACT OF ~; DOUBLE ~ INSURANCE; MONTH OF ~; REPLACEMENT ~; SESSIONAL ~.

INDEMNITY, ACTION FOR. This action was brought against M & L Leasing to indemnify the partners for the payment they made to satisfy the judgment. An action for indemnity or contribution is not the appropriate means for partners to seek indemnity; the proper remedy is an action for the taking of accounts. *Lafrentz v. M & L Leasing Ltd. Partnership* (2000), 2000 CarswellAlta 1121, 2000 ABQB 714, 8 B.L.R. (3d) 219, [2001] 1 W.W.R. 629, 85 Alta. L.R. (3d) 233, 275 A.R. 334 (Q.B.), Perras J.

INDEMNITY INSURANCE. The distinction between indemnity and non-indemnity insurance is well-recognized in the insurance industry. The following definitions, which I adopt here, were used by the 1988 *Report of Inquiry into Motor Vehicle Accident Compensation in Ontario* (the Osborne Commission), at p. 429: An indemnity payment is one which is intended to compensate the insured in whole or in part for a pecuniary loss . . . A non-indemnity payment is a payment of a previously determined amount upon proof of a specified event, whether or not there has been pecuniary loss. Perhaps the best example of non-indemnity insurance is that of life insurance. The beneficiary under a life insurance policy collects a set amount upon the death of the policy holder without reference to any pecuniary loss. Pensions are also considered to be non-indemnity payments. *Cooper v. Miller*, 1994 CarswellBC 121, (sub nom. *Cunningham v. Wheeler*) 88 B.C.L.R. (2d) 273, (sub nom. *Cunningham v. Wheeler*) [1994] 4 W.W.R. 153, (sub nom. *Cunningham v. Wheeler*) 20 C.C.L.T. (2d) 1, [1994] 1 S.C.R. 359, (sub nom. *Cunningham v. Wheeler*) 113 D.L.R. (4th) 1, (sub nom. *Cunningham v. Wheeler*) 23 C.C.L.I. (2d) 205, (sub nom. *Cooper v. Miller (No. 1)*) 164 N.R. 81, (sub nom. *Cooper v. Miller (No. 1)*) 41 B.C.A.C. 1, (sub nom. *Cooper v. Miller (No. 1)*) 66 W.A.C. 1, (sub nom. *Cunningham v. Wheeler*) 2 C.C.P.B. 217. See FEE ~.

INDEMNITY PAYMENT. One which is intended to compensate the insured in whole or in part for a pecuniary loss. *Cooper v. Miller*, (sub nom. *Cunningham v. Wheeler*) [1994] 1 S.C.R. 359.

INDENT. *v*. To cut the top of the first sheet or page of a document in a wavy or toothed line.

INDENTURE. *n*. A deed which two or more parties made. See DEED-POLL; NON-TRUST ~; TRUST ~.

INDENTURED APPRENTICESHIP. A long term apprenticeship agreement.

INDEPENDENCE. *n*. 1. The state of not being dependent on another or others. 2. Independence is based on the existence of a set of objective conditions or guarantees which ensure judges have the complete freedom to try the cases before them. It is more concerned with the status of the Court in relation to the other branches of government and bodies which can exercise pressure on the judiciary through power conferred on them by the state. *R. c. Lauzon* (1998), 1998 CarswellNat 1810, 18 C.R. (5th) 288, (sub nom. *R. v. Lauzon*) 230 N.R. 272, 56 C.R.R. (2d) 30, (sub nom. *R. v. Lauzon*) 129 C.C.C. (3d) 399, 8 Admin. L.R. (3d) 33 (Can. Ct. Martial App. Ct.). See COLLECTIVE ~; INSTITUTIONAL ~; JUDICIAL ~.

INDEPENDENT. *n*. An independent member of the legislature, that is a member of the legislature not a member of one of the party caucuses represented in the legislature.

INDEPENDENT. *adj*. "[In s. 11(d) of the Charter] . . . reflects or embodies the traditional constitutional value of judicial independence. As such, it connotes not merely a state of mind or attitude in the actual exercise of judicial functions, but a status or relationship to others, particularly to the Executive Branch of government, that rests on objective conditions or guarantees." *R. v. Valente (No. 2)* (1985), 23 C.C.C. (3d) 193 at 201, [1985] 2 S.C.R. 673, 52 O.R. (2d) 779, 37 M.V.R. 9, 49 C.R. (3d) 97, 24 D.L.R. (4th) 161, 64 N.R. 1, 14 O.A.C. 79, 19 C.R.R. 354, [1985] D.L.Q. 85n, the court per Le Dain J.

INDEPENDENT ADVICE. " . . . [M]ay cover the situation in which a lawyer explains, independently, the nature and consequences of an agreement . . . It may extend, as it does in cases of undue influence, to the need to give informed advice. . ." *Brosseau v. Brosseau* (1989), 23 R.F.L. (3d) 42 at 46, 63 D.L.R. (4th) 111, 100 A.R. 15, 70 Alta. L.R. (2d) 247, [1990] 2 W.W.R. 34 (C.A.), Stevenson, Stratton and Irving JJ.A.

INDEPENDENT ADOPTION. An adoption in which the child is placed for adoption by a birth parent.

INDEPENDENT BOAT-OWNER FISHERMAN. A fisherman who is a self-employed boat owner engaged in fishing for gain. *Fisherman's Association Act*, R.S.N.S. 1989, c. 175, s. 2.

INDEPENDENT CANDIDATE. A person, other than a candidate of an authorized party, whose nomination paper has been received by a returning officer.

INDEPENDENT CONTRACTOR. A person who undertakes with another person to produce a given result but so that, in the actual execution of the work he is not under the orders or control of the person for whom he does it, and may use his own discretion in things not specified beforehand. *Employment Standards Act*, R.S.M. 1987, c. E110, s. 1.

INDEPENDENT MEMBER. A member of a legislature who does not belong to a caucus.

INDEPENDENT OPERATOR. 1. " . . . [M]ay be an employer engaged in an independent business, or may be someone who is not an employer but who is engaged in an independent business." *IPX International Ltd. v. British Columbia (Workers' Compensation Board)* (1988), 25 B.C.L.R. (2d) 273 at 279, 49 D.L.R. (4th) 86 (C.A.), the court per Macfarlane J.A. 2. A natural person who carries on work for her or his own account, alone or in partnership, and does not employ any worker.

INDEPENDENT PRODUCTION FUND. A production fund, other than the Canadian production fund, that meets the criteria listed in the Commission's Public Notice entitled *Contributions to Canadian Programming by Broadcasting Distribution Undertakings*, as amended from time to time. *Broadcasting Distribution Regulations*, SOR/97-555, s. 1.

INDEPENDENT QUALIFIED APPRAISER. A qualified appraiser who is not in full-time employment of the insurer whose fund is being valued or any associate or affiliated companies of the insurer.

INDEPENDENT SCHOOL. A school that (a) is not a public school; (b) is maintained and operated in the Province by an authority; and (c) functions as an elementary school, secondary school or both.

INDEPENDENT TORTFEASORS. See SEVERAL TORTFEASORS.

INDEPENDENT UNION LOCAL. A union not affiliated with any other labour organization.

IN DERNIER RESORT. [Fr.] As a last resort.

INDETERMINATE. *adj.* Not fixed in extent or amount; of uncertain size; indefinite.

INDETERMINATE SENTENCE. Imprisonment of undetermined length.

INDEX. *n.* [L.] 1. An alphabetical list of separate subjects or items contained in a book, writing or similar thing. 2. A ratio or other number based on a series of observations and used as a standard. See AIR POLLUTION ~; CONSUMER PRICE ~; COST OF LIVING ~; DEVELOPMENT ~; PENSION ~.

INDEX ANIMI SERMO EST. [L.] Words are indicators of intent.

INDEXING. *n.* The process by which tax rate brackets under the Income Tax Act are adjusted to reflect any increase in the cost of living index.

INDIAN. *n.* 1. " . . . '[A]borigines.' . . ." *Reference re whether the Term "Indians" in s. 91(24) of the Constitution Act 1867, includes Eskimo Inhabitants of Quebec*, [1939] S.C.R. 104 at 111, [1939] 2 D.L.R. 417, Duff C.J. 2. A person who pursuant to this Act is registered as an Indian or is entitled to be registered as an Indian. *Indian Act*, R.S.C. 1985, c. I-5, s. 2. 3. The extent of federal jurisdiction over Indians has not been definitively addressed by this Court. We have not needed to do so because the *vires* of federal legislation with respect to Indians, under the division of powers, has never been at issue. The cases which have come before the Court under s. 91(24) [Constitution Act, 1867 (U.K.), 30 & 31 Vict., c. 3] have implicated the question of jurisdiction over Indians from the other direction—whether provincial laws which on their face apply to Indians intrude on federal jurisdiction and are inapplicable to Indians to the extent of that intrusion. The Court has held that s. 91(24) protects a "core" of Indianness from provincial intrusion, through the doctrine of interjurisdictional immunity. It follows, at the very least, that this core falls within the scope of federal jurisdiction over Indians. That core encompasses aboriginal rights, including the rights that are recognized and affirmed by s. 35(1) [*Constitution Act, 1982*, being Schedule B to the *Canada Act 1982* (U.K.), 1982, c. 11]. Laws which purport to extinguish those rights therefore touch the core of Indianness which lies at the heart of s. 91(24), and are beyond the legislative competence of the provinces to enact. The core of Indianness encompasses the whole range of aboriginal rights that are protected by s. 35(1). Those rights include rights in relation to land; that part of the core derives from s. 91(24)'s reference to "Lands reserved for the Indians". But those rights also encompass practices, customs and traditions which are not tied to land as well; that part of the core can be traced to federal jurisdiction over "Indians". Provincial governments are prevented from legislating in relation to both types of aboriginal rights. *Delgamuukw v. British Columbia* (1997), 153 D.L.R. (4th) 193, 220 N.R. 161, 99 B.C.A.C. 161, 162 W.A.C. 161, [1997] 3 S.C.R. 1010, [1998] 1 C.N.L.R. 14, [1999] 10 W.W.R. 34, 66 B.C.L.R. (3d) 285, Per Lamer C.J.C. (Cory and Major JJ. concurring). See MENTALLY INCOMPETENT ~; STATUS ~.

INDIAN AGENCY. The reserves over which an Indian superintendent has jurisdiction. *The Vital Statistics Act*, R.S.S. 1978, c. V-7, s. 2.

INDIAN AND NORTHERN AFFAIRS CANADA. The federal ministry responsible for the Indian and Inuit people of Canada and for managing natural resources in the Northwest Territories and Yukon Territory.

INDIAN BAND. 1.An unincorporated association of first nations persons created by statute. 2. The definition of "band" does not constitute an Indian Band as a legal entity. Rather, I take it from the definition of "band", and other provisions of the Indian Act, that in relation to rights to an Indian reserve, a band is a distinct population of Indians for whose use and benefit, in common, a reserve has been set aside by the Crown. *Blueberry River Indian Band v. Canada (Department of Indian Affairs & Northern Development)*, 2001 CarswellNat 963, 2001 FCA 67, 6 C.P.C. (5th) 1, 201 D.L.R. (4th) 35, 274 N.R. 304, [2001] 3 C.N.L.R. 72, [2001] 4 F.C. 451, 2001 CarswellNat 3104, 203 F.T.R. 320 (note), [2001] F.C.J. No. 725 (C.A.). See BAND.

INDIAN BAND COUNCIL. " . . . [A]n elected public authority, dependent on Parliament for its existence, powers and responsibilities, whose essential function it is to exercise municipal and government power—delegated to it by Parliament — in relation to the Indian reserve whose inhabitants have elected it; as such, it is to act from time to time as the agent of the minister and the representative of the band with respect to the administration and delivery of certain federal programs for the benefit of Indians on Indian reserves, and to perform an advisory, and in some cases a decisive, role in relation to the exercise by the minister of certain of his statutory authority relative to the reserve." *Whitebear Band v. Carpenters Provincial Council (Saskatchewan)* [1982] 3 C.N.L.R. 181 at 186, [1982] 3 W.W.R. 554, 15 Sask. R. 37, 135 D.L.R. (3d) 128 (C.A.), the court per Cameron J.A.

INDIAN LANDS. Lands reserved for the Indians, including any interests therein, surrendered in accordance with the Indian Act and includes any lands or interests in lands described in any grant, lease, permit, licence or other disposition referred to in section 5. *Indian Oil and Gas Act*, R.S.C. 1985, c. I-7, s. 2.

INDIAN MONEYS. All moneys collected, received or held by Her Majesty for the use and benefit of Indians or bands. *Indian Act*, R.S.C. 1985, c. 1-5, s. 2.

INDIAN REGISTER. The register of persons that is maintained under section 5. *Indian Act*, R.S.C. 1985 (1st Supp.), c. 32, s. 1.

INDIAN RESERVE. 1. Lands conveyed or assigned to the Crown in right of Canada for the use of Indians. 2. The setting apart and appropriating of land is not the entire matter; the Crown must also manifest an intent to make the land so set apart a reserve. The use of the words "as may be necessary" implies a separation in time between the appropriation of the lands and the fulfilment of the treaty obligations. In other words, once the land is appropriated, it does not yet have the legal status of a reserve; something more is required to accomplish that end. This requirement reflects the nature of a process which is political, at least in part. Given the consequences of the creation of a reserve for government authorities, for the bands concerned and for other non-native communities, the process will often call for some political assessment of the effect, circumstances and opportunity of setting up a reserve, as defined in the *Indian Act*, in a particular location or territory. Thus, in the Yukon Territory as well as elsewhere in Canada, there appears to be no single procedure for creating reserves, although an Order-in-Council has been the most common and undoubtedly best and clearest procedure used to create reserves. (See: *Canadian Pacific Ltd. v. Paul*, [1988] 2 S.C.R. 654, at pp. 674-75) Whatever method is employed, the Crown must have had an intention to create a reserve. This intention must be possessed by Crown agents holding sufficient authority to bind the Crown. For example, this intention may be evidenced either by an exercise of executive authority such as an Order in Council, or on the basis of specific statutory provisions creating a particular reserve. Steps must be taken in order to set apart land. The setting apart must occur for the benefit of Indians. And, finally, the band concerned must have accepted the setting apart and must have started to make use of the lands so set apart. Hence, the process remains fact-sensitive. The evaluation of its legal effect turns on a very contextual and fact-driven analysis. Thus, this analysis must be performed on the basis of the record. It should be noted that the parties did not raise, in the course of this appeal, the impact of the fiduciary obligations of the Crown. It must be kept in mind that the process of reserve creation, like other aspects of its relationship with First Nations, requires that the Crown remain mindful of its fiduciary duties and of their impact on this procedure, and taking into consideration the *sui generis* nature of native land rights: see the comments of Lamer C.J. in *St. Mary's Indian Band v. Cranbrook (City)*, [1997] 2 S.C.R. 657, at paras. 14-16. *Ross River Dena Council Band v. Canada*, [2002] 2 S.C.R. 816. See RESERVE.

INDIANS AND LANDS RESERVED FOR INDIANS. [Since 1871, the exclusive power to legislate in relation to "Indians, and Lands reserved for Indians" has been vested with the federal government by virtue of s. 91(24) of the Constitution Act, 1867 [(U.K.) 30 & 31 Vict., c. 3]. That head of jurisdiction encompasses within it the exclusive power to extinguish aboriginal rights, including aboriginal title. *Delgamuukw v. British Columbia* (1997), 153 D.L.R. (4th) 193, 220 N.R. 161, 99 B.C.A.C. 161, 162 W.A.C. 161, [1997] 3 S.C.R. 1010, [1998] 1 C.N.L.R. 14, [1999] 10 W.W.R. 34, 66 B.C.L.R. (3d) 285, per Lamer C.J.C. (Cory and Major JJ. concurring).

INDIAN SETTLEMENT. Any group of Indians living in a district that is not an Indian reserve.

INDIAN TITLE. ". . . [A] legal right to occupy and possess certain lands, the ultimate title to which is in the Crown. While their interest does not, strictly speaking, amount to beneficial ownership, neither is its nature completely exhausted by the concept of a personal right. It is true that the sui generis interest which the Indians have in the land is personal in the sense that it cannot be transferred to a grantee, but it is also true, as will presently appear, that the interest gives rise

upon surrender to a distinctive fiduciary obligation on the part of the Crown to deal with the lands for the benefit of the surrendering Indians. . ." *Guerin v. R.* (1984), [1985] 1 C.N.L.R. 120 at 136, [1984] 2 S.C.R. 335, 36 R.P.R. 1, 20 E.T.R. 6, [1984] 6 W.W.R. 481, 59 B.C.L.R. 301, 13 D.L.R. (4th) 321, 55 N.R. 161, Dickson J. (Beetz, Chouinard and Lamer JJ. concurring).

INDIAN TREATY. An agreement between the Crown and an Indian nation with the features described in the cases of Simon v. The Queen (1985) [R. v. Simon (sub nom. Simon v. R.) [1985] 2 S.C.R. 387, 62 N.R. 366, 23 C.C.C. (3d) 238, 71 N.S.R. (2d) 15, 171 A.P.R. 15, [1986] 1 C.N.L.R. 153, 24 D.L.R. (4th) 390] and R. v. Sioui (1990) [(Sioui v. Quebec (Attorney General)) [1990] 1 S.C.R. 1025, 109 N.R. 22, 56 C.C.C. (3d) 225, 70 D.L.R. (4th) 427, [1990] 3 C.N.L.R. 127, 30 Q.A.C. 280]. The parties are the Crown and an Indian nation. The signatories must have authority to bind the parties for whom they act. Legally binding obligations must be intended by the parties. The agreement must be a bargain with both parties assuming obligations. "A certain measure of solemnity" must exist. P.W. Hogg, *Constitutional Law of Canada*, 3d ed. (Toronto: Carswell, 1992) at 684.

INDICATING SWITCH. A switch designed or marked to show readily whether the switch is in an "On" or "Off" position.

INDICATION. *n.* A signal lens display that is activated by internal illumination. *Highway Traffic Act*, R.S.O. 1990, c. H.8, s. 133. See SIGNAL ~.

INDICIA. *n.* [L.] 1. Marks; signs. 2. Facts which cause inferences to be made.

INDICTABLE OFFENCE. A criminal offence which is triable by way of indictment. The most serious criminal offences are indictable offences. Murder, for example, is an indictable offence. Some offences may be tried by indictment or by summary conviction, hybrid offences.

INDICTABLE ONLY OFFENCE. A criminal offence which can only be tried by way of indictment.

INDICTED. *adj.* Charged with a criminal offence in an indictment.

INDICTEE. *n.* The person who is presented with an indictment.

INDICTIO. *n.* [L.] An indictment.

INDICTMENT. *n*. 1. The formal legal document containing the alleged indictable offences upon which an accused will be tried. 2. Includes (a) information or a count therein, (b) a plea, replication or other pleading, and (c) any record. *Criminal Code*, R.S.C. 1985, c. C-46, s. 2. 2. Includes an information or charge in respect of which a person has been tried for an indictable offence under Part XIX. *Criminal Code*, R.S.C. 1985, c. C-46, s. 673. See BILL OF ~; PREFERRED ~.

INDICTOR. *n*. The one who indicts another person for an offence.

INDIFFERENT. *adj*. Not having any interest which may prevent impartial judgment.

INDIGENT. *n*. 1. " . . . [A] person possessed of some means but such scanty means that he is needy and poor." *National Sanitarium Association v. Mattawa (Town)* (1925), 56 O.L.R. 474 at 477, [1925] 2 D.L.R. 491 (C.A.), the court per Mulock C.J.O. 2. In law, the word "indigent" does not mean a person without any means, namely a pauper, but a person possessed of some means but such scanty means that he or she is needy and poor. *Hopkins v. Hill*, 2000 CarswellBC 1021, 2000 BCSC 637 (S.C.).

INDIGENT PERSON. A person who is actually destitute of means from personal resources of obtaining food, clothing, shelter, medical advice or attention and hospital care necessary for the immediate personal wants or those of any dependants.

INDIGNITY. *n*. The ordinary sense of "indignity" clearly does not require any physical contact with a body. It should be noted that the French text does not include physical interference: "commet tout outrage, indécence ou indignité." This makes my claim that physical contact is not necessary even stronger. The words "whether buried or not" also reveal that physical contact is a sufficient but not a necessary element of this offence. Parliament clearly contemplated the offering of indignities taking place when the body or human remains were buried. That is, Parliament contemplated the offering of indignities to human remains separated from an accused by six feet of dirt. *R. v. Moyer*, 1994 CarswellOnt 95, 32 C.R. (4th) 232, 170 N.R. 1, 92 C.C.C. (3d) 1, [1994] 2 S.C.R. 899, 73 O.A.C. 243, per Lamer, C.J.C. for the court.

INDIRECT CONTRIBUTION. Financial contributions to property are examples of direct contributions. Homemaking or household management services are an example of indirect contributions. *Sanders v. Tomei*, 2000 CarswellBC 1032, 2000 BCSC 696, 9 R.F.L. (5th) 376 (S.C.).

INDIRECT DISCRIMINATION. Occurs when the effect of a law or practice is to discriminate on one of the prohibited grounds even though that was not the intention of the law or practice. See MEIORIN TEST.

INDIRECT EVIDENCE. Proof of related circumstances from which a controversial fact, not directly proved by documents or witnesses, may be inferred. See CIRCUMSTANTIAL EVIDENCE.

INDIRECTLY. See YOU CANNOT DO ~ WHAT YOU CANNOT DO DIRECTLY.

INDIRECT SERVICE WATER HEATER. A service water heater that derives its heat from a heating medium such as warm air, steam or hot water.

INDIRECT TAX. " . . . [T]hat which is demanded from one person in the expectation and with the intention that he shall indemnify himself at the expense of another." *Reference re Grain Futures Taxation Act (Manitoba)*, [1925] 2 D.L.R. 691 at 694, [1925] 2 W.W.R. 60, [1925] A.C. 561 (Can. P.C.), the board per Viscount Haldane.

INDIRECT TAXATION. The method of taxation where the tax is demanded from one person in the expectation that he will indemnify himself at the expense of another person. Customs and excise are indirect taxes when imposed on businesses.

INDIRECT WASTE. Waste that is not discharged directly into drainage piping. *Ontario Water Resources Act*, R.R.O. 1980, Reg. 736, s. 1.

INDIRECT WASTE PIPE. A waste pipe that does not connect directly with drainage piping, but discharges into it through a trapped fixture.

INDIVIDUAL. *n*. 1. A natural person. *Rudolf Wolf & Co. v. Canada* (1990), 46 C.R.R. 263 at 69, 43 Admin. L.R. 1, 41 C.P.C. (2d) 1, [1990] 1 S.C.R. 695, 106 N.R. 1, 69 D.L.R. (4th) 392, 39 O.A.C. 1, the court per Cory J. 2. A human being as opposed to a corporation. 3. In our view, the use of the word "individual" in s. 12 relates to a sole proprietorship. If it was the intention of the Legislature to engulf citizens in their personal capacity, outside a sole proprietorship, and outside the corporate veil, in what is little short of confiscatory legislation, they must do so in clear, unambiguous language. We conclude that the Legislature did not use clear enough language to denote such personal responsibility. *550551 Ontario Ltd. v. Framingham* (1991), 1991 CarswellOnt 184, 5 C.B.R. (3d) 204, 91 C.L.L.C. 14,031, 4 O.R. (3d) 571, 49 O.A.C. 376, 4 B.L.R. (2d) 75, (sub nom. *550551 Ontario Ltd. v. Ontario (Employment Standards Officer)*) 82 D.L.R. (4th) 731 (Div. Ct.) Montgomery, J. for the court. 4. An individual of a wildlife species, whether living or dead, at any developmental stage and includes larvae, embryos, eggs, sperm, seeds, pollen, spores and asexual propagules. *Species at Risk Act*, S.C. 2002, c. 29, s. 2. 5. A natural person, but does not include a partnership, unincorporated association, unincorporated syndicate, unincorporated organization, trust, or a natural person in the capacity of trustee, executor, administrator or other legal representative. 6. A person who is not a corporation. 7. Any person who is not a member of a family. See RELATED ~.

INDIVIDUAL BARGAINING. The right of an individual to present grievances not contrary to an existing union contract with the unit to which that individual belongs.

INDIVIDUAL GRIEVANCE. One in which the substance of the complaint directly affects the rights of an individual employee under the collective agreement.

INDIVIDUALLY. *adv*. Separately; one by one.

INDIVIDUALLY MEASURED COMMODITY. A commodity that is measured by a device that (a) records the measurement, or (b) is operated by a person who observes or records the measurement of each quantity of commodity measured by the device. *Weights and Measures Regulations*, C.R.C., c. 1605, s. 45.

INDIVIDUAL RATE. The actual rate of pay received by a person; a rate of pay based on each employee's qualifications.

INDIVIDUAL TAP. A connection made into a pipeline transmitting gas in order to provide gas service to a rural consumer outside the service area of a rural gas utility.

INDOLENT. See EQUITY AIDS THE VIGILANT AND NOT THE ~.

INDOOR POOL. A swimming pool where the pool and deck are totally or partially enclosed within a building or structure covered by a roof.

INDORSEE. *n*. The individual to whom a bill of exchange, bill of lading or promissory note, for example, is assigned by indorsing it.

INDORSEMENT. *n*. Anything printed or written on the back of a document or deed. See ENDORSEMENT; QUALIFIED ~; RESTRICTIVE ~.

INDORSER. *n*. The person who indorses the holder or payee by writing her or his name on the back of a bill of exchange.

INDOWMENT. *n*. 1. Assigning or giving dower. 2. Any kind of property belonging permanently to a charity. See ENDOWMENT.

IN DUBIO. [L.] In a state of doubt; doubtful.

IN DUBIO HAEC LEGIS CONSTRUCTIO QUAM VERBA OSTENDUNT. [L.] In a doubtful situation, the construction which the words indicate is the legal construction.

INDUCE. *v*. To lead or bring about another person by persuasion or influence.

INDUCEMENT. *n*. 1. Incitement to do something. 2. " . . . '[P]ersuade or influence'." *Canadian Imperial Bank of Commerce v. Dorey* (1991), 110 N.S.R. (2d) 432 at 437, 299 A.P.R. 432 (T.C.), MacDonald J. 3. The confessions rule stipulates that a statement will be excluded as evidence if it is the product of an inducement that raises a reasonable doubt as to voluntariness. What then is an inducement within the meaning of the confessions rule? In its modern formulation the confessions rule postulates that any statement by an accused to a person in authority will be disallowed as evidence on the basis of an inducement negating voluntariness if there is a reasonable doubt about whether the quid pro quo offer that it conveys caused the will of the accused to be overborne. *R v. Tessier*, 2001 NBCA 34, 153 C.C.C. (3d) 361, 41 C.R. (5th) 242, 245 N.B.R. (2d) 1, 636 A.P.R. 1 (C.A.)

INDUCEMENT PAYMENT. A contractual payment made by a landlord for the purpose of persuading a tenant to enter into a long term lease.

INDUCING BREACH OF CONTRACT. A concise statement of the tort of inducing breach of contract was provided by Lord Morris in D.C. Thomson & Co. v. Deakin, [1952] Ch. 646 (Eng. C.A.), at page 702: The breach of contract must be brought about or procured or induced by some act which a man is not entitled to do, which may take the form of direct persuasion to break the contract or the intentional bringing about of a breach by indirect methods involving wrongdoing. *923087 N.W.T. Ltd. v. Anderson Mills Ltd.*, 1997 CarswellNWT 36, 35 B.L.R. (2d) 1, 13 C.P.C. (4th) 357, [1997] N.W.T.R. 212, 40 C.C.L.T. (2d) 15 (S.C.), Vertes J.

INDUCTIVE METHOD. Deduction of a general rule from a particular instance.

INDUST. L.J. *abbr.* Industrial Law Journal.

INDUSTRIAL ACCIDENT. A sudden and unforeseen event, attributable to any cause, which happens to a person, arising out of or in the course of his work and resulting in an employment injury to him. *An Act Respecting Industrial Accidents and Occupational Diseases*, S.Q. 1985, c. 6, s. 2.

INDUSTRIAL ACTION. (a) A strike, (b) picketing. *Labour Code Amendment Act*, S.B.C. 1984, c. 24, s. 3. See UNLAWFUL ~.

INDUSTRIAL AGGREGATE. In relation to an adjustment year is the average weekly earnings for all employees in Prince Edward Island for that year as published by Statistics Canada under the authority of the Statistics Act (Can) R.S.C. 1970, c. S-16. *An Act to Amend the Legislative Assembly Act*, S.P.E.I. 1986, c. 2, s. 1.

INDUSTRIAL CLEANING. The use of a solvent for cold cleaning or vapour degreasing, whether for electrical or electronic equipment cleaning, metal cleaning or precision cleaning, and excludes wipe cleaning and cleaning during the maintenance of equipment. *Ozone-depleting Substances Regulations, 1998*, SOR/99-7, s. 1.

INDUSTRIAL COMPANY. A company other than a company recognized by the Board as a mining company or investment company. *Security Frauds Prevention Act*, R.S.N.B. 1973, c. S-6, s. 1.

INDUSTRIAL COMPOSITE. For an adjustment year means the average weekly wages and salaries of the Industrial Composite in Canada as published by Statistics Canada under the authority of the Statistics Act (Canada) as amended from time to time.

INDUSTRIAL CONTRACT. A contract of life insurance for an amount not exceeding $2000, exclusive of any benefit, surplus, profit, dividend or bonus also payable under the contract, and that provides for payment of premiums at fortnightly or shorter intervals, or, if the premiums are usually collected at the home of the insured, at monthly intervals. *Insurance acts.*

INDUSTRIAL CROP. A crop produced by human industry.

INDUSTRIAL CUSTOMER. A person purchasing electricity for the operation of a manufacturing, mining or processing plant or operation that is served with electricity at 60kV or higher. *Industrial Electricity Rate Discount Act*, S.B.C. 1985, c. 49, s. 1.

INDUSTRIAL DESIGN. 1. Features of shape, configuration, pattern or ornament and any combination of those features that, in a finished article, appeal to and are judged solely by the eye. *Industrial Design Act*, R.S.C. 1985, c. I-9, s. 2. 2. " . . . [A] design to be 'applied' to 'the ornamenting' of an article . . . something that determines the appearance of an article, or some part of an article, because ornamenting relates to appearance. And it must have as its objective making the appearance of an article more attractive because that is the purpose of ornamenting. . ." *Cimon Ltd. v. Bench Made Furniture Co.* (1964), 48 C.P.R. 31 at 49, [1965] Ex. C.R. 811, 30 Fox Pat. C. 77 (Ex. Ct.), Jackett P.

INDUSTRIAL DISEASE. 1. Includes, (a) a disease resulting from exposure to a substance relating to a particular process, a trade, or occupation in an industry, (b) a disease peculiar to or characteristic of a particular industrial process, trade or occupation, (c) a medical condition that in the opinion of the Board requires a worker to be removed either temporarily or permanently from exposure to a substance because the condition may be a precursor to an industrial disease, or (d) any of the diseases mentioned in Schedule 3 or 4. *Workers' Compensation Act*, R.S.O. 1990, c. W.11, s. 1(1). 2. Any disease in respect of which compensation is payable under the law of the province where the employee is usually employed respecting compensation for workmen and the dependants of deceased workmen. *Government Employees Compensation Act*, R.S.C. 1985, c. G-5, s. 2. 3. Silicosis and any other disease that the Lieutenant Governor in Council may by Order declare to be an industrial disease. *Industrial Safety Act*, R.S.N.B. 1973, c. I-5, s. 1.

INDUSTRIAL DISPUTE. Any dispute or difference or apprehended dispute or difference between an employer and one or more employees or a bargaining agent acting on behalf of the employees, as to matters or things affecting or relating to terms or conditions of employment or work done or to be done by the employee or employees or as to privileges, rights and duties of the employer, the employee or employees.

INDUSTRIAL ESPIONAGE. See ESPIONAGE.

INDUSTRIAL ESTABLISHMENT. 1. A building or part of a building in which any manufacturing process, assembling or handling of materials in connection with the manufacturing, preparing, treating or finishing of any goods or products, is carried on. 2. An office building, factory, arena, shop or office, and any land buildings and structures appertaining thereto 3. Any federal work, undertaking or business and includes such branch section or other division of a federal work, undertaking or business as is designated as an industrial establishment by regulations made under paragraph 264(b). *Canada Labour Code*, R.S.C. 1985, c. L-2, s. 166.

INDUSTRIAL HEMP. The plants and plant parts of the genera *Cannabis*, the leaves and flowering heads of which do not contain more than 0.3% THC w/w, and includes the derivatives of such plants and plant parts. It also includes the derivatives of non-viable cannabis seed. It does not include plant parts of the genera *Cannabis* that consist of non-viable cannabis seed, other than its derivatives, or of mature cannabis stalks that do not include leaves, flowers, seeds or branches, or of fibre derived from those stalks. *Industrial Hemp Regulations*, SOR/98-156, s. 1.

INDUSTRIAL MILK PLANT. A cheese factory, concentrated milk plant, creamery or milk receiving station.

INDUSTRIAL OCCUPANCY. Occupancy for assembling, fabricating, manufacturing, processing, repairing or storing of goods or materials or for producing, converting, processing or storing of energy, waste or natural resources. Ontario statutes.

INDUSTRIAL OPERATION. Any work within or upon forest land in which more than two people are engaged. *Forest Fires Act*, R.S.N.B. 1973, c. F-20, s. 1.

INDUSTRIAL OVEN. An oven used to bake and dry materials.

INDUSTRIAL PLANT. Includes any factory or industry, and all works, plants and processes incidental to it.

INDUSTRIAL PROPERTY. 1. Copyright, industrial design, patent and trade mark matters.

2. All patents of invention, copyrights, industrial designs, and any other intellectual or industrial property rights in every country where the same exist from time to time, all applications therefor arising from or acquired in connection therewith and all right to make such applications. 3. Land that is constructed to be used for the assembling, processing or manufacturing of finished or partially finished products from raw materials or fabricated parts. *Commercial Concentration Tax Act*, R.S.O. 1990, c. C.16, s. 1.

INDUSTRIAL PURPOSES. The operation of railways, factories, stores or warehouses but does not include the sale or barter of water for any of those purposes. *Water Resources acts*.

INDUSTRIAL RADIOGRAPHY. Radiography for industrial purposes involving the use of radioactive prescribed substances or particle accelerators.

INDUSTRIAL RADIOLOGICAL TECHNICIAN. A person who operates an x-ray machine or uses radioactive isotopes for the examination or treatment of things other than living persons.

INDUSTRIAL RAILWAY. Any railway operated by or for an industry served thereby.

INDUSTRIAL RELATIONS. The interactions among unions, management, government, employees, and employers.

INDUSTRIAL RESTRUCTURING. Includes technological change. *Labour Adjustment Benefits Act*, R.S.C. 1985, c. L-1, s. 2.

INDUSTRIAL ROAD. A road constructed or existing for transportation by motor vehicle of (a) natural resources, raw or manufactured, or (b) machinery, materials or personnel, and includes all bridges, wharves, log dumps and works forming a part of the road, but does not include (c) a public road, street, lane or other public communication, (d) a privately owned road used by a farmer or resident for the person's own purposes, (e) a road used exclusively for the construction and maintenance of electric power lines, telephone lines or pipe lines, or (f) roads and yards within manufacturing plants, industrial sites, storage yards, airports and construction sites; tote roads, cat roads and access roads. *Highway (Industrial) Act*, R.S.B.C. 1996, c. 189, s. 1.

INDUSTRIAL SOURCE. Any facility, equipment, action, operation or treatment, that may be a source of an air contaminant, involving or relating to physical, chemical, industrial or manufacturing processes but does not include fuel-burning equipment or incinerators.

INDUSTRIAL STANDARDS SCHEDULE. A document which fixes the hours and wages for employees in various industries in a province.

INDUSTRIAL STRUCTURE. See MOBILE INDUSTRIAL OR COMMERCIAL STRUCTURE.

INDUSTRIAL UNDERTAKING. Any establishment, work, or undertaking in or about any industry, business, trade, or occupation. 2. Includes (i) mines, quarries, and other works for the extraction of minerals from the earth, (ii) industries in which articles are manufactured, altered, cleaned, repaired, ornamented, finished, adapted for sale, broken up or demolished, or in which minerals are transformed, including ship-building, and the generation, transformation, and transmission of electricity and motive power of any kind, (iii) construction, reconstruction, maintenance, repair, alteration or demolition of any building, railway, tramway, harbour, dock, pier, canal, inland waterway, road, tunnel, bridge, viaduct, sewer, drain, well, telegraphic or telephonic installation, electrical undertaking, gas work, waterwork, or other work of construction, as well as the preparation for or laying the foundation of any such work or structure, and (iv) transport of passengers or goods by road or rail or inland waterways, including the handling of goods at docks, quays, wharves, and warehouses, but excluding transport by hand.

INDUSTRIAL UNION. A group whose members includes employees in a particular industry regardless of the actual nature of their work.

INDUSTRIAL UNION COUNCIL. See CITY ~.

INDUSTRIAL UNIT. A bargaining group made up of production and maintenance employees.

INDUSTRIAL WASTE. Any liquid, solid or other waste or any combination thereof, resulting from any process of industry or manufacture or the exploration for, or development of, a natural resource and includes (a) storm water that has been contaminated through contact with useful or waste materials as a result of human activity, and (b) useful or waste material from a danger of pollution that becomes a contaminant. See LIQUID ~.

INDUSTRIAL WASTE WATER. Waste water carrying solid, liquid or gaseous residue from (a) an industrial, manufacturing, commercial or institutional process or establishment, or any other process or establishment of the same nature; or (b) the development, recovery or processing of raw material.

INDUSTRY. *n.* 1. An establishment, undertaking, trade or business, whether it is carried on in conjunction with other occupations or separately. 2. Includes any business, calling, trade, profession, work or occupation. See AGRICULTURAL ~; AMBULANCE SERVICE ~; CONSTRUCTION ~; CONTINUOUS ~; CRITICAL ~; FISHING ~; FOREST INDUSTRIES; FOREST ~; HOSPITALITY ~; INTEGRATED ~; LOGGING ~ ; METALLIFEROUS MINING ~; PETROLEUM ~; REGULATED INDUSTRIES DOCTRINE; RENEWABLE RESOURCE ~; RESOURCE-BASED ~; RETAIL GASOLINE SERVICE ~; SEASONAL ~; TRADE, ~ OR PROFESSION.

INDUSTRY-WIDE AGREEMENT. A collective agreement affecting all employees of an industry in a geographic area.

INDUSTRY-WIDE BARGAINING. Bargaining in respect of all employers and employees of an industry in a geographic area.

INEBRIATE. *n.* An intoxicated person.

INEDIBLE. *adj.* Unfit for food.

IN EO QUOD PLUS SIT, SEMPER INEST ET MINUS. [L.] The less is always part of the greater.

INEQUITABLE. *adj.* 1. Unfair; unjust. 2. In determining whether a transaction is inequitable, "courts should consider all the circumstances of the transaction including such factors as the risk involved, the harshness of the terms, and whether the terms are much harsher than those available to like debtors at the time the transaction was entered into". *Vencer Mortgage Investments Ltd. v. Batley* (1984), 1984 CarswellBC 194, 54 B.C.L.R. 374, 27 B.L.R. 255 (S.C.), Lander J.

INEQUITY. *n.* An injustice, an unfair situation or result. See INTER-PLANT ~.

INERT. *adj.* In relation to atmosphere or gas, means that the atmosphere or gas is so deficient in oxygen as to be incapable of propagating flame. *Fire Detection and Extinguishing Equipment Regulations*, C.R.C., c. 1422, s. 10.

INERT FILL. Earth or rock fill that contains no putrescible materials or soluble or decomposable chemical substances.

IN ESSE. [L.] Which actually exists; in being.

IN ESSE VIDENTUR. In seeming existence.

INEVITABILITY DOCTRINE. " ... [R]epresents a happy judicial compromise between letting no one who has suffered damage as a consequence of the statutorily authorized activities of public bodies recover and letting everyone so suffering damage recover. Recovery will be allowed unless it is shown that the interference with the plaintiff's rights was permitted by either (1) express language in the statute ... or (2) necessary implication from the language of the statute ..." *Tock v. St John's (City) Metropolitan Area Board* (1984), 64 D.L.R. (4th) 620 at 629, 47 M.P.L.R. 113, [1989] 2 S.C.R. 1181, 1 C.C.L.T. (2d) 113, 104 N.R. 241, 82 Nfld. & P.E.I.R. 181, 257 A.P.R. 181, Wilson J. (Lamer and L'Heureux-Dubé JJ. concurring).

INEVITABLE. *adj.* " ... Damage is said to be 'inevitable' when the body responsible for it establishes to the satisfaction of the Court that it was demonstrably impossible to avoid the damage inasmuch as it had carried out its operations with a degree of skill and care commensurate with current scientific and technical knowledge, but with due allowance for practical considerations bearing on time and expense." *Tock v. St. John's (City) Metropolitan Area Board* (1989), 47 M.P.L.R. 113 at 145, [1989] 2 S.C.R. 1181, 1 C.C.L.T. (2d) 113, 64 D.L.R. (4th) 620, 104 N.R. 241, 82 Nfld. & P.E.I.R. 181, 257 A.P.R. 181, La Forest J. (Dickson C.J.C. concurring).

INEVITABLE ACCIDENT. 1. Pleading that the injuries caused were not caused by or contributed to by negligence of the defendant. 2. An accident which could not have been avoided with ordinary care, caution or skill on the part of the party charged with responsibility. 3. A collision which could not possibly have been prevented by the exercise of ordinary care, caution and maritime skill on the part of the captain.

INEVITABLE DAMAGE. Established where the public body responsible for it shows that it was impossible to avoid the damage exercising the degree of skill and care commensurate with current scientific and technical knowledge with allowance for practical considerations of time and expense.

IN EXPECTANCY. Executory, relating to some future thing. See INTEREST ~.

IN EXTENSO. [L.] From start to finish; omitting nothing.

IN EXTREMIS. [L.] 1. At the very last. 2. Close to death.

IN FACIENDO. [L.] In feasance; in doing.

INFAMOUS CONDUCT. More serious than unprofessional conduct. Must be evidence of moral turpitude to constitute infamous conduct. *N. v. College of Physicians & Surgeons (British Columbia)* (1997), 30 B.C.L.R. (3d) 390 (C.A.).

INFAMY. *n.* Disgrace in public; complete loss of character.

INFANT. *n.* 1. A person under the age of eighteen years. 2. Any person under the age of 19 years. *Public Trustee Act*, R.S.B.C. 1979, c. 348, s. 1. 3. Person who is unmarried and under the age of nineteen years, and includes a child who is unborn at the death of its father. *Guardianship Act*, R.S.N.S. 1989, c. 189, s. 2. 4. A person who is under the age of one year. *Food and Drug Regulations*, C.R.C., s. 870, c. B.25.001 5. person under 3 years of age. *Aircraft Seat, Safety Belts and Safety Harnesses Order*, C.R.C., c. 28, s. 2. See SUDDEN ~ DEATH SYNDROME.

INFANT CHILD. A child who has not attained the age of majority. *Change of Name Act*, R.S.N.S. 1989, c. 66, s. 2.

INFANT FOOD. A food that is sold or is labelled or advertised for consumption by infants. *Food and Drug Regulations*, C.R.C. c. 870, s. B.25.001.

INFANT FORMULA. A food that is sold or is labelled or advertised as a substitute for human milk in meeting the nutritional requirements of (a) infants with normal dietary needs, or (b) infants with special dietary needs, and that is of such consistency that when ready to serve, it passes freely through a nursing bottle nipple. *Food and Drug Regulations*, C.R.C., c. 870, s. B.25.001.

INFANTICIDE. *n.* 1. The murder of a child by its mother. 2. A female person commits infanticide when by a wilful act or omission she causes the death of her newly-born child, if at the time of the act or omission she is not fully recovered from the effects of giving birth to the child and by reason thereof or of the effect of lactation consequent on the birth of the child her mind is then disturbed. *Criminal Code*, R.S.C. 1985, c. C-46, s. 233.

INFANT OR MINOR. A person under eighteen years of age. Saskatchewan statutes.

INFANTS' IMMUNITY. Rule of law exempting infants from discovery by way of documents or interrogatories.

INFARCT. *n*. The death of part of an organ in a living body because its blood supply is suddenly obstructed. F.A. Jaffe, *A Guide to Pathological Evidence*, 3d ed. (Toronto: Carswell, 1991) at 221. See BRAIN ~.

IN FAVOREM LIBERTATIS. [L.] In favour of liberty.

IN FAVOREM VITAE, LIBERTATIS ET INNOCENTIAE OMNIA PRAESUMUNTUR. [L.] In partiality to life, liberty and innocence all things are presumed.

INFECTED. *adj*. Infected with the causal organisms of a disease. Having a venereal disease in a communicable stage.

INFECTION. *n*. The entry and multiplication of an infectious agent in the body of a person or animal.

INFECTIOUS. *adj*. Communicable in any manner, even at a distance.

INFECTIOUS AGENT. An organism or micro-organism that is capable of producing a communicable disease.

INFECTIOUS DISEASE. 1. Includes a reportable disease. Any disease included in the schedule. *Quarantine Act*, R.S.C. 1985, c. Q-1, s. 2.

INFECTIOUS SUBSTANCE. A micro-organism or parasite that is capable of causing human disease, or an artificially produced hybrid or mutant micro-organism that contains genetic components of any micro-organism capable of causing human disease. *Human Pathogens Importation Regulations*, SOR/94-558, s. 2.

INFERENCE. *n*. 1. " . . . [I]n the legal sense . . . is a deduction from the evidence, and if it is a reasonable deduction it may have the validity of legal proof. The attribution of an occurrence to a cause is, I take it, always a matter of inference. . ." *Jones v. Great Western Rwy. Co.* (1930), 47 T.L.R. 39 at 45, Lord Macmillan, cited with approval in *Gwyllt, Re*, [1944] O.W.N. 212 at 213 (C.A.), Henderson J.A. 2. Facts sufficient that a particular conclusion may be drawn from them. 3. This court, in its judg-

ment on appeal in Willard Miller [Newfoundland (Workers' Compensation Commission) v. Miller (1998), 167 Nfld. & P.E.I.R. 115 (Nfld. T.D.)] . . . has stressed that an inference is different from speculation . . . Drawing an inference amounts to a process of reasoning by which a factual conclusion is deduced as a logical consequence from other facts established by the evidence. Speculation on the other hand is merely a guess or conjecture; there is a gap in the reasoning process that is necessary, as a matter of logic, to get from one fact to the conclusion sought to be established. Speculation, unlike an inference, requires a leap of faith. *Osmond v. Newfoundland (Workers' Compensation Commission)*, 2001 NFCA 21, 200 Nfld. & P.E.I.R. 202, 603 A.P.R. 202, 10 C.C.E.L. (3d) 56, [2001] N.J. No. 111, 2001 CarswellNfld 119 (C.A.). See ADVERSE ~.

INFERIOR COURT. 1. A court which is subject to the control of a higher court. 2. "[A court] . . . in which provincially appointed judges sat . . ." *Reference re s. 6 of Family Relations Act, 1978 (British Columbia)* (1982), 26 R.F.L. (2d) 113 at 141, [1982] 1 S.C.R. 62, [1982] 3 W.W.R. 1, 36 B.C.L.R. 1, 131 D.L.R. (3d) 257, 40 N.R. 206, Estey J. 3. A court staffed by justices of the peace or magistrates which has jurisdiction over minor criminal offences and small civil claims.

INFESTATION. *n*. An actual or potential infestation or infection by a forest tree pest. *Forest Tree Pest Control Act*, R.S.O. 1990, c. F.25, s. 1.

INFESTED. *adj*. 1. Containing any injurious, noxious or troublesome insect or animal pest. 2. Contaminated with a pest or so exposed to a pest that contamination can reasonably be expected to exist. *Plant Quarantine Act*, R.S.C. 1985, c. P-15, s. 2.

IN FICTIONE JURIS SEMPER AEQUITAS EXISTIT. [L.] Equity is always manifested in legal fiction.

INFIDELITY. *n*. " . . . [U]nfaithfulness or disloyalty. . ." *Smetana v. Manitoba Public Insurance Corp.* (1986), 21 C.C.L.I. 95 at 106, 41 Man. R. (2d) 100 (Q.B.), Kroft J.

INFIELD. *n*. The area of a race course surrounded by the racing strip.

IN FIERI. [L.] While something was being accomplished.

INFIRM. *adj*. As applied to any person, has reference to any mental or physical infirmity rendering that person incapable ordinarily of pursuing any substantially gainful occupation.

INFIRMITY. *n*. " . . . [P]hysical weakness, debility, frailty or feebleness of body resulting from constitutional defect." *Tomlinson v. Prudential Insurance Co*., [1954] O.R. 508 at 516, [1954] I.L.R.1-144 (C.A.), the court per Laidlaw J.A.

INFIRM PERSON. 1. A person who because of mental or physical disability is certified by a duly qualified medical practitioner as a person unable to provide or care for herself or himself and needs to be under the care or supervision of another person. 2. An institutionalized person whose age or health is such that they require institutional care or treatment.

IN FLAGRANTE DELICTO. [L.] In the actual act.

INFLAMMABLE. *adj*. And flammable are deemed to be synonymous. *Dangerous Goods Shipping Regulations*, C.R.C., c. 1419, s. 2.

INFLAMMABLE LIQUID. Any liquid that gives off inflammable vapours (as determined the flash point from Tagliabue's open cup tester, as used for test of burning oils) at or below a temperature of 80°F. *Electric Sparks Prevention Regulations*, C.R.C., c. 1181, s. 3.

INFLAMMABLE MATERIAL. Trees, timber, brush, slash, grass, debris or other vegetation or things of a similar nature.

INFLAMMABLE PETROLEUM PRODUCTS. Any products obtained or recovered from petroleum, whether by distillation, condensation, absorption, or otherwise, that have a flash point below one hundred and seventy-five degrees Fahrenheit according to the Tagliabue Closed Cup Tester, and include any combination of such products.

INFLATION. The decrease in the exchange value of a dollar over time due to the increasing valuation placed on goods and services See ANTI-~ ACT (CANADA).

INFLATION PRESSURE. See MAXIMUM PERMISSIBLE ~.

INFLICT. *v*. " . . . [C]ause another to suffer or incur, . . ." *R. v. Neil*, [1957] S.C.R. 685 at 687-8, 26 C.R. 281, 119 C.C.C. 1, 11 D.L.R. (2d) 545, Kerwin C.J. (Abbott J. concurring).

IN FLIGHT. From the time when all external doors are closed following embarkation until the later of (a) the time at which any such door is opened for the purpose of disembarkation, and (b) where the aircraft makes a forced landing in circumstances in which the owner or operator thereof or a person acting on behalf of either of them is not in control of the aircraft, the time at which control of the aircraft is restored to the owner or operator thereof or a person acting on behalf of either of them. *Criminal Code*, R.S.C. 1985, c. C-46, s. 7(8).

INFLUENCE. *v*. To persuade.

INFLUENCE. *n*. Power, particularly power to persuade. The ability of one person to dominate the will of another. See UNDUE ~.

IN FORCE. 1. " . . . [E]ffectively enacted . . ." *Lord's Day Alliance of Canada v. Manitoba (Attorney General)* (1924), [1925] 1 D.L.R. 561 at 565, [1925] 1 W.W.R. 296, [1925] A.C. 384, 43 C.C.C. 185 (Man. P.C.), the board per Lord Blanesburgh. 2. Currently valid.

INFORMAL. *adj*. Lacking proper legal form.

INFORMAL CONTRACT. A parol or simple contract.

INFORMAL EQUITY. Subject to the regulations, any interest or right to participate in or benefit from, either currently or in the future, other than by way of formal equity, the assets, revenues or business activities of another person. *Canadian Ownership and Control Determination Act*, R.S.C. 1985, c. C-20, s. 2.

INFORMALITY. *n*. Lack of legal form.

INFORMAL PATIENT. A person who is a patient in a psychiatric facility under the authority of a parent, guardian or committee of the person appointed for the patient under the Mental Incompetency Act. *Mental Health Act*, R.S.O. 1990, c. M.7, s. 1.

INFORMANT. *n*. A person who lays an information. *Criminal Code*, R.S.C. 1985, c. C-46, s. 785.

IN FORMA PAUPERIS. [L. in the form of a poor person] A litigant allowed to proceed in this way is not liable to pay court costs.

INFORMATION. *n*. 1. A document which alleges that an accused person has committed an offence. The laying of an information before a justice is the means to commence a criminal proceeding by way of indictment. An information is usually laid before a justice or sworn before a justice by a peace officer. However, a member of the public also can lay an information. 2. Includes (a) a count in an information, and (b) a complaint in respect of which a justice is authorized by an Act of Parliament or an enactment made thereunder to make an order. *Criminal Code*, R.S.C. 1985, c. C-46, s. 785. 3. Information respecting a consumer's identity, residence, dependents, marital status, employment, borrowing and repayment history, income, assets and liabilities, credit worthiness, education, character, reputation, health, physical or personal characteristics or mode of living. *Consumer Reporting Act*, R.S.N.S. 1989, c. 93, s. 2(1). See CONFIDENTIAL ~; CONSUMER ~; CONTACT ~; CREDIT ~; DESIGNATED ~; EMPLOYEE PERSONAL ~; LAYING AN ~; EXPERIMENT ~; FACTUAL ~; FLIGHT ~ REGION; INVESTIGATIVE ~; LAYING AN ~; MEDICAL ~; PERSONAL ~; PRIVILEGED ~; PROPRIETARY ~; STATISTICAL ~; SUFFICIENT ~.

INFORMATION BANK. See PROVINCIAL ~.

INFORMATION BULLETIN. In respect of an area to be navigated by a ship, means the chart catalogue for that area published by the Canadian Hydrographic Service. *Charts and Publication's Regulations*, C.R.C., c. 1415, s. 2.

INFORMATION BUREAU. See TOURIST ~.

INFORMATION CENTRE. A place that is held out to the public as being available for or engaged in furnishing travel information to the public whether for hire or reward or otherwise. *Tourism Act*, R.S.O. 1990, c. T.16, s. 1. See TOURIST ~.

INFORMATION CIRCULAR. An information circular prepared in accordance with the regulations. *Securities acts.*

INFORMATION COMMISSIONER. The Commissioner appointed under section 54. *Access to Information Act*, R.S.C. 1985, c. A-1, s. 3.

INFORMATION COMMISSIONER OF CANADA. A federal official appointed to hear complaints of government failure to comply with the rights provided by the Access to Information Act.

INFORMATION MANAGEMENT SYSTEM. A system of software and hardware components and related technology that interact and operate to integrate reception, creation, collection, recording, filing, analysis, reporting, transmission, storing, sending, reproduction and dissemination of information and data.

INFORMATION OF INTRUSION. A prerogative remedy which was used to eject person wrongfully in possession of Crown lands and to recover lost rents and profits and damages for waste committed during the wrongful possession. *Alberta v. Buys*, [1989] 4 W.W.R. 636 (Alta. C.A.).

INFORMATION SYSTEM. A system used to generate, send, receive, store, or otherwise process an electronic document. Federal Statutes. See LAND-RELATED ~ S NETWORK.

INFORMATUS NON SUM. [L. I am not informed] I have been given no instructions.

INFORMED CONSENT. Every individual has the right to know what risks are involved in undergoing or foregoing medical treatment and the concomitant right to make meaningful decisions based on a full understanding of those risks. *Hollis v. Birch*, (sub nom. *Hollis v. Dow Corning Corp.*) [1995] 4 S.C.R. 634.

INFORMER. *n*. The one who commences an action or takes some other steps to recover a penalty. See POLICE ~ PRIVILEGE.

INFORMER PRIVILEGE. 1. A subset of public interest immunity. The value of reliable informers to the administration of justice has been recognized for a long time, so much so that it too is a class privilege. This explains why the high standard of showing that the innocence of the accused is at stake before permitting invasion of the privilege is necessary. Should the privilege be invaded, the State then generally provides for the protection of the informer through various safety programs, again illustrating the public importance of that privilege. *R. v. McLure*, [2001] 1 S.C.R. 445. 2. Is an ancient and hallowed protection which plays a vital role in law enforcement. It is premised on the duty of all citizens to aid in enforcing the law. The discharge of this duty carries with it the risk of retribution from those involved in crime. The rule of informer privilege was developed to protect citizens who assist in law enforcement and to encourage others to do the same. Informer privilege is of such importance that once found, courts are not entitled to balance the benefit enuring from the privilege against countervailing considerations, as is the case, for example, with Crown privilege or privileges based on Wigmore's four-part test. Informer privilege prevents not only disclosure of the name of the informant, but of any information which might implicitly reveal his or her identity. *R. v. Leipert*, [1997] 1 S.C.R. 281.

IN FORO CONSCIENTIAE. [L.] In the forum of conscience, before the court of conscience.

INFRA. [L. under, underneath, below] In a document, reference to a later part or page of the document.

INFRA ANNUM LUCTUS. [L.] Within the mourning period.

INFRACTION. See PARKING ~.

INFRASTRUCTURE FACILITY. A publicly or privately owned facility that provides or distributes services for the benefit of the public, including services relating to water, sewage, energy, fuel and communications. *Criminal Code*, R.S.C. 1985, c. C-46, s. 431.2 (1).

INFRINGEMENT. *n.* 1. The right of the owner of a registered trade-mark to its exclusive use shall be deemed to be infringed by a person not entitled to its use under the Trade-marks Act who sells, distributes or advertises wares or services in association with a confusing trade-mark or trade-name. 2. Of a patent is any act that "interferes with the full enjoyment of the monopoly granted": Lishman v. Eron Roche Inc. (1996), 68 C.P.R. (3d) 72 (Fed. T.D.) . . . [T]he definition of infringement as stated in Lishman is intended to reflect the idea that what constitutes infringement in a particular case is a function of the scope of the statutory monopoly, so that any act that impairs the statutory monopoly is by definition "infringement". . . Thus, to determine whether a certain act amounts to an infringement, the scope of the statutory monopoly must be determined by construing the claims of the patent. *Monsanto Canada Inc. v. Schmeiser* (2002), 218 D.L.R. (4th) 31, 293 N.R. 340, [2003] 2 F.C. 165, 231 F.T.R. 160 (note), 21 C.P.R. (4th) 1 (C.A.) 3. Of copyright, the exercise of a right which only the owner of the copyright is entitled to exercise. 4. Of copyright in a musical work, there must be sufficient objective similarity for the infringing work to be described as a reproduction or adaptation of the copyright work and the copyright work must be the source from which the infringing work is derived, directly or indirectly. See PATENT ~.

INFRINGEMENT BY EQUIVALENCY. In patent law, refers to the taking of the essential elements of an invention with the introduction of a non-essential equivalent element substituted for one of the elements of the invention.

INFRINGING. *adj.* In relation to a work in which copyright subsists, any copy, including any colourable imitation, made or dealt with in contravention of this Act, in relation to a performer's performance in respect of which copyright subsists, any fixation or copy of a fixation of it made or dealt with in contravention of this Act, in relation to a sound recording in respect of which copyright subsists, any copy of it made or dealt with in contravention of this Act, or in relation to a communication signal in respect of which copyright subsists, any fixation or copy of a fixation of it made or dealt with in contravention of this Act. The definition includes a copy that is imported in the circumstances set out in paragraph 27(2)(e) and section 27.1 but does not otherwise include a copy made with the consent of the owner of the copyright in the country where the copy was made. *Copyright Act*, R.S.C. 1985, c. C-42, s. 2.

IN FUTURO. [L.] In future.

IN GENERALIBUS LATET ERROR. [L.] In generalities error lurks.

IN GOOD FAITH. A thing is deemed to be done "in good faith" when it is in fact done honestly, whether it be done negligently or not. *Sale of Goods acts.*

INGREDIENT. *n.* An individual unit of food that is combined as an individual unit of food with one or more other individual units of food to form an integral unit of food. Canada regulations. See ACTIVE ~; MEDICATING~; SWEETENING ~.

IN GREMIO LEGIS. [L.] In the bosom of the law.

INGRESS. *n.* Entry.

IN GROSS. Not appendant, appurtenant, or otherwise annexed to land. See EASEMENT ~.

INGROSS. *v.* To write a fair copy of an instrument or deed so that parties may formally execute it.

INHABITANT. *n.* 1. " . . . [A] dweller, or one who dwells or resides permanently in a place, or who has a fixed residence, as distinguished from an occasional lodger or visitor. . ." *Smith, Ex parte* (1874), 15 N.B.R. 147 at 148 (C.A.), the court per Ritchie C.J. 2. A permanent resident or a temporary resident having a permanent dwelling within the locality. *Municipal Act*, R.S.O. 1990, c. M.45, s. 10(1).

IN HAEC VERBA. [L.] In these actual words.

INHERENT. *adj*. Intrinsic; permanently part of.

INHERENT DEFECT. An intrinsic fault or problem.

INHERENT DEFENCE. A defence such as lawful purpose, innocent intent or mistake of fact which simply denies the mens rea which must be proved by the prosecution. P.K. McWilliams, *Canadian Criminal Evidence*, 3d ed. (Aurora: Canada Law Book, 1988) at 25-8.

INHERENT JURISDICTION. 1. That which enables a court to exercise its powers by regulating the practice before the court and preventing abuse of process and punishing for contempt. 2. Operates to ensure that there will always be a court which has the power to vindicate a legal right independent of any statutory grant of jurisdiction. 3. The inherent jurisdiction of the court is traditionally invoked as an adjunct or aid to an existing common law or other right and that in such circumstances its effect is in the nature of a procedural remedy. This, in my opinion, is not its exclusive role. Its use can also be justified in novel circumstances where the failure to do so will adversely impact upon the court's ability "to administer justice according to law" (Master Jacob, at p. 52). It is in this sense that the existence of an amorphous, indefinable residual power in a superior court becomes not a weakness, but a strength. This is because it is truly impossible to define with any sense of finality (and undesirable to attempt to do so) the circumstances in which this essential reserve of judicial powers should be utilized on a principled basis in the interests of justice. *Gillespie v. Manitoba (Attorney General)*, 2000 MBCA 1, 185 D.L.R. (4th) 214, 144 C.C.C. (3d) 193, [2000] 6 W.W.R. 605, 41 C.P.C. (4th) 199, 145 Man. R. (2d) 229 (C.A.). 4. ". . . The inherent jurisdiction of a superior court is derived not from any statute or rule of law but from the very nature of the court as a superior court: . . . Utilizing this power, superior courts, to maintain their authority and to prevent their processes from being obstructed or abused, have amongst other things punished for contempt of court, stayed matters that are frivolous and vexatious and regulated their own processes. . ." *R. v. Unnamed Person* (1985), 20 C.R.R. 188 at 190-91, 10 O.A.C. 305, 22 C.C.C. (3d) 284 (C.A.), the court per Zuber J.A.

INHERENT POWER. 1. A power vested in a court that is not derived from statutory authority. 2. The power a judge may draw upon to assist or help him or her in the exercise of the ordinary jurisdiction of the court. It does not generally stand alone waiting to be exercised on the judge's own initiative without a suit or application or without parties. *Gillespie v. Manitoba (Attorney General)*, 2000 MBCA 1, 185 D.L.R. (4th) 214, 144 C.C.C. (3d) 193, [2000] 6 W.W.R. 605, 41 C.P.C. (4th) 199, 145 Man. R. (2d) 229 (C.A.). 3. Authority, possessed by a corporation, not obtained from statute or a charter, e.g. the power to own land the right of perpetual succession.

INHERENT VICE. A condition inherent in an insured property which causes it to be damaged when exposed to normal conditions. *University of Saskatchewan v. Fireman's Fund Insurance Co. of Canada* (1997), 158 Sask. R. 223 (C.A.).

INHERITABLE. *adj*. Able to inherit.

INHERITANCE. *n*. What descended to the heir of the owner who died intestate, formerly a hereditament. See SEVERAL ~.

INHERITANCE TAX. Succession duty calculated upon the inheritance received by any beneficiary. P.W. Hogg, *Constitutional Law of Canada*, 3d ed. (Toronto: Carswell, 1992) at 746.

INHIBITOR. *n*. Any antibiotic, medicine or chemical preparation that can be detected in milk. *Milk Act*, R.R.O. 1980, Reg. 629, s. 1.

IN HIS QUAE DE JURE COMMUNI OMNIBUS CONCEDUNTUR, CONSUETUDO ALICUJUS PATRIAE VEL LOCI NON EST ALLEGANDA. [L.] In those things which common right concedes to all, the custom of a particular country or place should not be brought forward.

IN HIS QUAE SUNT FAVORABILIA ANIMAE, QUAMVIS SUNT DAMNOSA REBUS, FIAT ALIQUANDO EXTENSIO STATUTI. [L.] In things favourable to the spirit, though they may be injurious to things, the extension of a statute is sometimes made.

IN-HOME SERVICES. Services provided for a child, (a) in the child's own home, or (b) in a place other than the child's own home where the child is receiving residential care. *Day Nurseries Act*, R.S.O. 1990, c. D.2, s. 1.

IN-HOUSE LOBBYIST. An individual who is employed by a person or organization and a significant part of whose duties as an employee is to lobby on behalf of the employer, or if the employer is a corporation, on behalf of any subsidiary of the employer or any corporation of which the employer is a subsidiary. *Lobbyists Registration Act, 2001*, s. B.C. 2001, c. 42. 2. A person employed by an organization whose duties include communicating with public office holders on behalf of the organization in an attempt to influence the development of legislative proposals, the introduction, amendment or passage of legislation or resolutions in the legislature.

IN INVIDIAM. [L.] In order to stir up prejudice.

IN INVITUM. [L.] Against one who is unwilling.

INIQUUM EST ALIQUEM REI SUAE ESSE JUDICEM. IN PROPRIA CAUSA NEMO JUDEX SIT. [L.] It is wrong for a person to judge his or her own cause. In certain cases no one can be a judge.

INITIAL. *n*. The first letter of a name.

INITIAL PROCESSING OPERATION. An operation the product of which is a fuel or a material mainly used for further processing or manufacturing.

INITIAL UNFUNDED LIABILITY. The increase on or after January 1, 1987 in the going concern liabilities of a plan or the decrease on or after January 1, 1987 in the going concern assets of a plan as a result of (*a*) the establishment of the plan, (*b*) an amendment to the plan, (*c*) a change in the methods or bases of valuation of the plan, or (*d*) an experience loss. *Pension Benefits Standards Regulation, 1985*, SOR/87-19, s. 9.

INITIATE. *v*. To commence; to set in motion.

INITIATION FEE. 1. A sum charged when one becomes a member of a union or society. 2. A one-time fee in addition to a membership fee.

INITIATIVE PETITION. A petition to have a proposed law introduced into the Legislative Assembly. A legislative proposal may be made with respect to any matter within the jurisdiction of the Legislature. A registered voter may apply to the chief electoral officer for the issuance of a petition to have a legislative proposal introduced into the Legislative Assembly in accordance with this Act. If satisfied that the requirements of section 3 have been met, the chief electoral officer must (a) notify the proponent that the application has been approved in principle, (b) publish notice of the approval in principle in the Gazette and in at least one newspaper circulating in British Columbia, and (c) issue the petition 60 days after the notice is published in the Gazette. *Recall and Initiative Act*, R.S.B.C. 1996, c. 398.

IN JEOPARDY. At risk of being convicted of a criminal offence.

IN JUDICIIS MINORI AETATE SUCCURRITUR. [L.] In the courts' decisions, a minor is aided.

IN JUDICIO NON CREDITOR NISI JURATIS. [L.] In a trial no one's evidence is accepted unless that person has been sworn.

INJUNCTION. *n*. 1. An equitable remedy in the form of an order of a court requiring a party either to do a specific act or acts or to refrain from doing a specific act or acts. 2. Recognizes that coercive measures may be required to protect a plaintiff's entitlement to some specific right. See INTERIM ~; INTERLOCUTORY ~; MANDATORY ~; MAREVA ~; PERMANENT ~; PERPETUAL ~; PROHIBITORY ~.

INJUNCTION QUIA TIMET. The injunction which a court awards to prevent an act which is threatened or feared.

INJURE. *v*. 1. To cause harm to. 2. To deprive one of what is in one's best interests.

INJURED. *adj*. 1. Bodily harm, and includes mental or nervous shock and pregnancy. *Criminal Injury Compensation acts*. 2. In respect of live stock or poultry means injured by wounding, worrying or pursuing.

IN JURE, NON REMOTA CAUSA SED PROXIMA SPECTATOR. [L.] In law one regards the proximate, not the remote, cause.

IN JURE OMNIS DEFINITIO PERICULOSA EST. [L.] In law, all definition is hazardous.

INJURIA. *n*. [L.] 1. Wrong. 2. An act which encroaches on some right.

INJURIA ABSQUE DAMNO. [L.] Injury or wrong without damage.

INJURIA NON EXCUSAT INJURIUM. [L.] Wrong does not justify wrong.

INJURIA NON PRAESUMITUR. [L.] One should not presume wrongdoing.

INJURING LIABILITY. The part of the cost of the construction, improvement, maintenance or repair of a drainage works required to relieve the owners of any land or road from liability for injury caused by water artificially made to flow from such land or road upon any other land or road. *Drainage Act*, R.S.O. 1990, c. D.17, s. 1.

INJURIOUS AFFECTION. 1. "The conditions required to give rise to a claim for compensation for injurious affection to a property, when no land is taken are now well established . . . These conditions are: (1) the damage must result from an act rendered lawful by statutory powers of the person performing such act; (2) the damage must be such as would have been actionable under the common law, but for the statutory powers; (3) the damage must be an injury to the land itself and not a personal injury or an injury to business or trade; (4) the damage must be occasioned by the construction of the public work, not by its user." *R. v. Loiselle* (1962), 35 D.L.R. (2d) 274 at 275, [1962] S.C.R. 624, the court per Abbott J. 2. (i) Where a statutory authority acquires part of the land of an owner, (A) the reduction in market value thereby caused to the remaining land of the owner by the acquisition or by the construction of the works thereon or by the use of the works thereon or any combination of them, and (B) such personal and business damages, resulting from the construction or use, or both, of the works as the statutory authority would be liable for if the construction or use were not under the authority of a statute, (ii) where the statutory authority does not acquire part of the land of an owner, (A) such reduction in the market value of the land of the owner, and (B) such personal and business damages, resulting from the construction and not the use of the works by the statutory authority, as the statutory authority would be liable for if the construction were not under the authority of a statute. *Expropriation acts.*

INJURIOUS FALSEHOOD. Tort of injurious falsehood consists of the publication of false statements, whether oral or written, concerning the plaintiff or his property. The statements are calculated to induce others not to deal with him.

INJURIS ILLATA JUDICI, SEU LOCUM TENENTI REGIS, VIDETUR IPSI REGI ILLATA, MAXIME SI FIAT IN EXERCENTE OFFICIUM. [L.] An injury to a judge, that is, a person representing the monarch, is considered an injury to the very monarch, especially if it is done in the exercise of an office.

INJURY. *n.* 1. " . . . The broadest acceptable sense of the word 'injury' is 'interference with a right'. . ." *Guest v. Bonderove & Co.* (1988), 59 Alta. L.R. (2d) 86 at 87, 28 C.P.C. (2d) 202, 88 A.R. 277 (C.A.), the court per Kerans J.A. 2. " . . . [B]odily injury." *Guest v. Bonderove & Co.* (1988), 59 Alta. L.R. (2d) 86 at 88, 28 C.P.C. (2d) 202, 88 A.R. 277 (C.A.), the court per Kerans J.A. 3. Actual bodily harm and includes pregnancy and mental or nervous shock. *Criminal Injuries Compensation acts.* 4. Disrupting tissue by violence. F.A. Jaffe, *A Guide to Pathological Evidence*, 3d ed. (Toronto: Carswell, 1991) at 221. 5. [For the purposes of interpretation of s. 272(1)(a) of the *Criminal Code*, R.S.C. 1985, c. C-46, dealing with sexual assault with a weapon.] The expression "injury" in s. 2 is not synonymous with "bodily harm". Sexual assault causing bodily harm is the object of a separate offence, provided for by s. 272(1)(c). The expression "bodily harm", which is broadly used in the context of assaults, is defined in s. 2 to mean "any hurt or injury to a person *that interferes with the health or comfort of the person and that is more than merely transient or trifling in nature* " (emphasis added). This in itself is sufficient to establish that the acquittal of the respondent on the charge of sexual assault causing bodily harm is not dispositive of the question of whether he used an object "in causing . . . injury" so as to make that object a weapon. One cannot go as far as the appellant argues, and conclude that because all cases of sexual assault cause injury (physical or psychological), that therefore if an object is used in the course of any sexual assault, the charge of sexual assault with a weapon is automatically made out. On the other hand, if an object is used in inflicting injury, be it physical or psychological, in the commission of a sexual assault, it is not necessary that the injury amount to bodily harm to trigger the application of s. 272(1)(a). *R. c. Lamy*, [2002] 1 S.C.R. 860. 6. Refers to the initial physical or mental impairment of the plaintiff's person as a result of the sexual assault, while "loss" refers to the pecuniary or non-pecuniary consequences of that impairment. *Blackwater v. Plint*, 2001 CarswellBC 1468, 2001 BCSC 997, 93 B.C.L.R. (3d) 228 (S.C.), Brenner C.J.S.C. See APPEARANCE OF THE ~ OR DISEASE; BIRTH ~; BODILY ~; COMPENSABLE ~; COMPRESSION ~; CONTRECOUP ~; CRITICAL ~; DISABLING ~; EMPLOYMENT ~; EPIPHYSEAL ~; MATERIAL ~; MINOR ~; PERSONAL ~; SEAT BELT ~; SERIOUS ~;

SHEARING ~; STEERING WHEEL ~; WAR SERVICE ~; WHIPLASH ~; WORK ~.

INJURY FUND. The fund providing for the payment of compensation, medical aid, outlay and expenses under a worker's compensation act.

INJURY IN FACT THEORY. A policy responds if in fact there was damage which actually occurred during the policy period, whether or not anyone was aware of it or could have been aware of it. Where property damage is ongoing or continuous, every policy in effect while the damage continues to occur is triggered to respond to the loss. *Alie v. Bertrand & Frère Construction Co.* (2002), 62 O.R. (3d) 345 (C.A.).

INJUSTUM EST NISI TOTA LEGE INSPECTA UNA ALIQUA PARTICULA PROPOSITA JUDICARE VEL RESPONDERE. [L.] Unless the entire statute has been inspected, it is unreasonable to judge or respond to any particular thing set out in it.

IN JUS VOCARE. [L.] To take legal proceedings against someone.

INLAND BILL. A bill that is, or on the face of it purports to be, (a) both drawn and payable within Canada; or (b) drawn within Canada upon some person resident therein. *Bills of Exchange Act*, R.S.C. 1985, c. B-4, s. 24.

INLAND NOTE. A note that is, or on the face of it purports to be, both made and payable within Canada. *Bills of Exchange Act*, R.S.C. 1985, c. B-4, s. 177.

INLAND TRANSPORTATION INSURANCE. Insurance, other than marine insurance, against loss of or damage to property: (i) while in transit or during delay incidental to transit; or (ii) where, in the opinion of the superintendent, the risk is substantially a transit risk. *Insurance acts.*

INLAND VOYAGE. A voyage, not being a minor waters voyage, on the inland waters of Canada together with such part of any lake or river forming part of the inland waters of Canada as lies within the United States or on Lake Michigan. *Canada Shipping Act*, R.S.C. 1985, c. S-9, s. 2.

INLAND WATERS. All the rivers, lakes and other fresh waters in Canada and includes the St. Lawrence River as far seaward as the straight lines drawn (a) from Cape-des-Rosiers to the westernmost point of Anticosti Island, and (b) from Anticosti Island to the north shore of the St. Lawrence River along the meridian of longitude sixty-three degrees west.

INLAND WATERS OF CANADA. All the rivers, lakes and other navigable fresh waters within Canada, and includes the St. Lawrence River as far seaward as the straight line drawn (a) from Cape-des-Rosiers to the west point of Anticosti Island, and (b) from Anticosti Island to the north shore of the St. Lawrence River along the meridian of longitude sixty-three degrees west.

INLAND WATERS SHIP. A ship employed on an inland voyage. *Canada Shipping Act*, R.S.C. 1985, c. S-9, s. 2.

IN LIEU OF. Instead of.

IN LIMINE. [L.] At the beginning; preliminary.

IN LOCO PARENTIS. [L.] 1. In the place of the parent. 2. "A person in loco parentis to a child is one who has acted so as to evidence his intention of placing himself towards the child in the situation which is ordinarily occupied by the father for the provision of the child's pecuniary wants." *Shtitz v. Canadian National Railway* (1926), [1927] 1 D.L.R. 951 at 959, [1927] 1 W.W.R. 193, 21 Sask. L.R. 345 (C.A.), Turgeon J.A.

IN MAJORE SUMMA CONTINETUR MINOR. [L.] The small sum is contained in the greater.

IN MALAM PARTEM. [L.] In a bad aspect.

IN MALEFICIIS VOLUNTAS, NON EXITUS, SPECTATOR. [L.] In the case of criminal acts one must regard the intention, not the result.

INMATE. *n.* 1. A person who is in a penitentiary pursuant to (i) a sentence, committal or transfer to penitentiary, or (ii) a condition imposed by the National Parole Board in connection with day parole or statutory release, or a person who, having been sentenced, committed or transferred to penitentiary, (i) is temporarily outside penitentiary by reason of a temporary absence or work release authorized under this Act, or (ii) is temporarily outside penitentiary for reasons other than a temporary absence, work release, parole or statutory release, but is under the direction or supervision of a staff member or of a person authorized by the Service. *Corrections and Conditional Release Act, 1992*, S.C. 1992, c. 20(1). 2. A person admitted to a correctional facility pursuant to a committal order. 3. A person sentenced to a term of imprisonment in or detained in a correctional institution. 4. "[Of a common bawdy-house is] . . . the prostitute who works on the premises with some regularity but is not responsible for any of the organizational duties involved in running the business as a business . . ." *R. c. Corbeil* (1991), 64 C.C.C. (3d) 272 at 292, 5 C.R. (4th) 62, 124 N.R. 241, [1991] 1 S.C.R. 830, 40 Q.A.C. 283, L'Heureux-Dubé J. (dissenting). See DISCHARGED ~; EX-~; PAROLED ~.

IN MEDIAS RES. [L. in the heart of the subject] Without any introduction or preface.

IN MEDIO. [L.] In the middle.

IN MITIORI SENSU. [L.] In a milder sense.

IN MORA. [L.] In delay.

IN MERCY. At the direction of.

IN MORTUO. [L.] In a dead body. F.A. Jaffe, *A Guide to Pathological Evidence*, 3d ed. (Toronto: Carswell, 1991) at 221.

INN. *n.* 1. Includes hotel, inn, tavern, public house or other place of refreshment, the keeper of which is by law responsible for the goods and property of the guests. 2. A building or structure in which accommodation or lodging, with or without food, is furnished for a price to travelers and includes a cabin, a cottage, a housekeeping unit, a hotel, a lodge, a motel, a motor hotel, and a tourist home.

IN NEED OF PROTECTION. 1. In relation to a child, that he is (a) abused or neglected so that his safety or well being is endangered, (b) abandoned, (c) deprived of necessary care through the death, absence or disability of his parent, (d) deprived of necessary medical attention, or (e) absent from his home in circumstances that endanger his safety or well being. 2. Requiring legally authorized protective intervention in order to preserve essential security and well-being, the necessity for which arises because, owing to physical or mental infirmity or disability or other incapacity to remedy the situation himself, the person in need, being an adult, continually or repeatedly (i) is a victim of abuse or neglect by, or otherwise put in danger by the behaviour or way of life of, someone having recognized supervisory responsibility for the persons well-being, (ii) is incapable of fending for himself and is unable to make provision for necessary care, aid or attention, or (iii) refuses, delays or fails to arrange for or comply with necessary care, aid or attention. See ADULT ~; CHILD ~.

INNER ENVELOPE. The plain envelope supplied by the Chief Electoral Officer in which a ballot paper is to be enclosed after the ballot paper has been marked by an elector and before the ballot paper is transmitted to a special returning officer in an outer envelope. *Special Voting Rules*, R.S.C. 1985, c. E-2, Schedule II, s. 2.

INNER LABEL. 1. A label on or affixed to the immediate container of a cosmetic. *Cosmetic Regulations*, C.R.C., c. 869, s. 2. 2. The label on or affixed to an immediate container of a food or drug. *Food and Drug Regulations*, C.R.C., c. 870, s. A.01.010. 3. A label on, affixed to or impressed upon the outer surface of a device. *Medical Devices Regulations*, C.R.C., c. 871, s. 2.

INNERLINER. *n.* The layers that contain the inflating medium within a tire and form the inside surface of a tubeless tire. *Motor Vehicle Tire Safety Regulations, 1995*, SOR/95-148, s. 2.

INNERLINER SEPARATION. The parting of the innerliner from the cord. *Motor Vehicle Tire Safety Regulations, 1995*, SOR/95-148, s. 2.

INNER PACKAGE. A substantial case, bag, canister, covering, or other suitable container, made and closed so as to prevent any explosive from escaping.

INNKEEPER. *n.* 1. The keeper of an inn. 2. A person who is by law responsible for the property of guests and includes a keeper of a hotel, motel, auto court, cabin or other place or house who holds out that to the extent of the available accommodation the keeper will provide lodging to any person who comes as a guest, who appears able and willing to pay a reasonable sum for the services and facilities offered and who is in a fit state to be received.

INNOCENCE. *n.* Lack of guilt or knowledge. See PRESUMPTION OF ~.

INNOCENCE AT STAKE EXCEPTION. Exception to informer privilege. In order to raise the "innocence at stake" exception to informer privilege, there must be a basis on the evidence for concluding that disclosure of the informer's identity is necessary to demonstrate the innocence of the accused. *R. v. Leipert*, [1997] 1 S.C.R. 281.

INNOCENT. *adj.* Not guilty; not negligent. See RIGHT TO BE PRESUMED ~.

INNOCENT AGENCY. At common law, the doctrine that a person who committed an offence by means of an innocent agent was deemed to be the actual perpetrator. This doctrine of innocent agency has survived the codification of criminal law in Canada. Thus a person who commits an offence by means of an instrument "whose movements are regulated" by him, actually commits the offence himself. *R. v. Berryman* (1990), 48 B.C.L.R. (2d) 105 (C.A.).

INNOCENT DISSEMINATION. Someone can escape liability if the individual can show that the work was disseminated in the ordinary course of business and that he was innocent of any knowledge of the libel contained in the work disseminated by him, that there was nothing in the work or the circumstances under which it came to him or was disseminated by him which ought to have led him to suppose that it contained a libel, and that, when the work was disseminated by him, it was not by any negligence on his part that he did not know that it contained the libel, then, although the dissemination of the work by him was *prima facie* publication of it, he may, nevertheless, on proof of the before-mentioned facts, be held not to have published it. *Menear v. Miguna* (1996), 30 O.R. (3d) 602 (Gen. Div.).

INNOCENT MISREPRESENTATION. A misstatement which the party making it did not know was such. G.H.L. Fridman, *Sale of Goods in Canada*, 3d ed. (Toronto: Carswell, 1986) at 153.

INNOCENT PASSAGE. The right of a foreign ship to cross territorial waters.

IN NOVO CASU, NOVUM REMEDIUM APPONENDUM EST. [L.] In a new case a new remedy ought to be applied.

IN NUBIBUS. [L.] In the clouds.

INNUENDO. *n*. Occurs when then defamatory meaning of words arises from inference or implication. See FALSE ~; LEGAL ~; POPULAR ~; TRUE ~.

IN ODIUM SPOLIATORIS OMNIA PRAESUMUNTUR. [L.] Everything possible should be presumed against a wrongdoer.

IN OMNIBUS [L.] In all things.

IN OMNIBUS QUIDEM, MAXIME TAMEN IN JURE, AEQUITAS SPECTANDA SIT. [L.] In all things, but particularly in law, equity should be regarded.

INOPERATIVE. *adj*. 1. Having ceased to have effect. 2. In relation to an item, component or system, that the item, component or system malfunctions to the extent that it does not accomplish its intended purpose or is not consistently functioning within its designed operating limits or tolerances.

INORDINATE. *adj*. Excessive; outside reasonable bounds.

IN PACATO SOLO. [L.] In a place which is at peace.

IN PAIS. [Fr.] In the country. Describes a legal transaction which took place without legal proceedings.

IN PARI CAUSA POSSESSOR POTIOR HABERI DEBET. [L.] When two persons each having equally strong claims to property, the one in possession of the property should be preferred.

IN PARI DELICTO. [L.] Equally to blame; equally at fault.

IN PARI DELICTO MELIOR EST CONDITIO POSSIDENTIS. [L.] In a situation of equal guilt, the condition of possessing is better.

IN PARI DELICTO, POTIOR EST CONDITIO DEFENDENTIS. [L.] Where each party is equally at fault the defendant's position is superior.

IN PARI DELICTO, POTIOR EST CONDITIO POSSIDENTIS. [L.] Unless the parties are unequal, the one in possession has the advantage.

IN PARI MATERIA. [L.] 1. In an analogous situation. 2. Relating to the same subject matter.

IN-PATIENT. *var*. INPATIENT. *n*. A person admitted to a hospital for care and treatment and to whom the hospital has assigned a bed for overnight stay.

IN-PATIENT FACILITY. A facility with provision for continuous care of patients.

IN-PATIENT SERVICES. All of the following services to in-patients, namely, (a) accommodation and meals at the standard or public ward level, (b) necessary nursing service, (c) laboratory, radiological and other diagnostic procedures together with the necessary interpretations for the purpose of maintaining health, preventing disease and assisting in the diagnosis and treatment of any injury, illness or disability, (d) drugs, biologicals and related preparations as provided in an agreement when administered in the hospital, (e) use of operating room, case room and anaesthetic facilities, including necessary equipment and supplies, (f) routine surgical supplies, (g) use of radiotherapy facilities where available, (h) use of physiotherapy facilities where available, (i) services rendered by persons who receive remuneration therefor from the hospital.

IN PERPETUITY. Forever.

IN PERPETUUM. [L.] Forever.

IN PERSONAM. [L. in person] Describes an action the only purpose of which is to affect the rights of any parties to that action inter se. See ACTION ~; EQUITY ACTS ~; JURA ~; JUS ~.

IN PLACE. Where used in reference to mineral means in the place or position where originally formed in the solid rock as distinguished from being in loose, fragmentary or broken rock, boulders, float, beds or deposits of gold or platinum bearing sand, earth, clay or gavel, or placer.

IN PLENO LUMINE. [L.] In daylight; in common knowledge; in public.

IN POENALIBUS CAUSIS BENIGNIUS INTERPRETANDUM EST. [L.] In relation to penalties, interpretation should be more lenient.

IN POENAM. [L.] By way of penalty.

IN POSSE. Describes something which does not actually exist, but which may come to exist.

IN PRAESENTI. [L.] For the present time.

IN PROMPTU. [L.] At hand; in readiness.

IN PROPRIA PERSONA. [L.] In one's own proper person.

INQUEST. *n.* An inquiry held before a coroner by a jury regarding the death of a person who was killed or died under suspicious circumstances or suddenly. Inquisitorial investigation conducted into the death of an individual and held before a coroner and jury. No lis exists and no parties' rights are affected directly by the inquest.

INQUIRE. *v.* To seek knowledge; to ask about.

INQUIRY. *n.* 1. An investigation; a hearing. 2. The minister presiding over any ministry of the public service of British Columbia may at any time, under authority of an order of the Lieutenant Governor in Council, appoint one or more commissioners to inquire into and to report on (a) the state and management of the business, or any part of the business, of that ministry, or of any branch or institution of the executive government of British Columbia named in the order, whether inside or outside that ministry, and (b) the conduct of any person in the service of that ministry or of the branch or institution named, so far as it relates to the person's official duties. See COMMISSION OF ~; PUBLIC ~.

INQUISATORIAL SYSTEM. Proceedings in which the judge, not the parties, adduces evidence in contrast to the adversarial system.

IN QUO QUIS DELINQUIT, IN EO DE JURE EST PUNIENDUS. [L.] In that in which one offends, in that one should be punished according to law.

IN RE. [L.] In the matter of, regarding.

IN RE DUBIA MAGIS INFICIATIO QUAM AFFIRMATIO INTELLIGENDA. [L.] In a questionable case, the negative should be understood more than the affirmative.

IN REM. [L.] 1. Something done or directed with reference to no person in particular, and therefore with reference to or against anyone it might concern or the whole world. 2. Describes an action to determine the rights or interests of everyone with respect to a particular res, even though the action may involve only two people. J.G. McLeod, *The Conflict of Laws* (Calgary: Carswell, 1983) at 60. See ACTION ~; JUDGMENT ~; JURA ~; QUASI ~.

IN REPUBLICA MAXIME CONSERVANDA SUNT JURA BELLI. [L.] Rights recognised in war should be preserved to the fullest in the state.

IN RERUM NATURA. [L.] In the nature of things.

IN RESPECT OF. 1. " . . . '[I]n relation to', 'with reference to' and 'in connection with'. The phrase 'in respect of' is probably the widest of any expression intended to convey some connection between two related subject matters." *Nowegijick v. R.*, [1983] 2 C.N.L.R. 89 at 96, [1983] 1 S.C.R. 29, [1983] C.T.C. 20, 46 N.R. 1, 144 D.L.R. (3d) 193, 83 D.T.C. 5041, the court per Dickson J. 2. Concerning; with reference to; in connection with; in relation to; relating to.

IN RESTITUTIONEM, NON IN POENAM HAERES SUCCEDIT. [L.] An heir succeeds to a restitution, not to a penalty.

INS. *abbr.* Insurance.

INSANE. *adj.* Incapable because of mental disorder of conforming conduct to the limits imposed by criminal law. A person who is insane is not legally responsible for his or her action. See LOCAL ASYLUM FOR HARMLESS ~.

INSANE DELUSION. A belief that has no basis in reason and which cannot be dispelled by argument.

INSANE PERSON. Includes a person, not an infant, who is incapable from infirmity of mind of managing his own affairs. *Incompetent Persons Act*, R.S.N.S. 1989, c. 218, s. 2.

INSANITARY CONDITION. A condition or circumstance (a) that is offensive; or (b) that is, or may be, or might become injurious to health; or (c) that prevents or hinders the suppression of disease; or (d) that contaminates or pollutes, or may contaminate or pollute food, air, or water; or (e) that might render food, air, or water injurious to the health of any person; and includes a nuisance and any circumstance or condition declared to be an insanitary condition under the regulations. *Public Health Act*, R.S.M. 1987, c. P210, s. 1.

INSANITY. *n.* 1. "The definition of 'legal insanity', or insanity which will preclude a criminal conviction, is found in subss. 16(2) and 16(3) of the [Criminal Code, R.S.C. 1985, c. C-46]." *R. v. Chaulk* (1990), 2 C.R. (4th) 1 at 18, 119 N.R. 116, [1991] 2 W.W.R. 385, 69 Man. R. (2d) 161, 62 C.C.C. (3d) 193, 1 C.R.R. (2d) 1, [1990] 3 S.C.R. 1303, Lamer C.J.C. (Dickson C.J.C., La Forest and Cory JJ. concurring). Criminal Code: S. 16(2) For the purposes of this section, a person is insane when the person is in a state of natural imbecility or has disease of the mind to an extent that renders the person incapable of appreciating the nature and quality of an act or omission or of knowing that an act or omission is wrong. 16(3) A person who has specific delusions, but is in other respects sane, shall not be acquitted on the ground of insanity unless the delusions caused that person to believe in the existence of a state of things that, if it existed, would have justified or excused the act or omission of that person. S. 16 now amended by S.C. 1991, c. 43, s. 2 to read in part: S. 16(1) No person is criminally responsible for an act committed or an omission made while suffering from a mental disorder that rendered the person incapable of appreciating the nature and quality of the act or omission or of knowing that it was

wrong . . . 2. " . . . Under s. 615 [of the Criminal Code, R.S.C. 1985, c. C-46], insanity includes any 'illness, disorder or abnormal condition which impairs the human mind or its functioning'." *R. v. Steele* (1991), 63 C.C.C. (3d) 149 at 181, 4 C.R. (4th) 53, 36 Q.A.C. 47, the court per Fish J.A. See DISEASE OF THE MIND.

INSCRIBE. *v.* To enter; to record.

INSECTIVOROUS BIRDS. See MIGRATORY ~.

INSEMINATING BUSINESS. A person who provides an artificial insemination service for domestic animals.

INSEMINATION. See ARTIFICIAL ~.

INSEMINATOR. *n.* A person who engages in the process of artificial insemination. *Artificial Insemination of Live Stock Act*, R.S.O. 1990, c. A.29, s. 1.

IN SERVICE. For the purpose of this section and section 77, an aircraft shall be deemed to be in service from the time when pre-flight preparation of the aircraft by ground personnel or the crew thereof begins for a specific flight until (a) the flight is cancelled before the aircraft is in flight, (b) twenty-four hours after the aircraft, having commenced the flight, lands, or (c) the aircraft having commenced the flight, ceases to be in flight, whichever is the latest. *Criminal Code*, R.S.C. 1985, c. C-46, s. 7(9).

IN-SERVICE LIMITS OF ERROR. The limits of error that apply to a device when the performance of the device is tested at any time other than a time referred to in the definition of "acceptance limits of error". *Weights and Measures Regulations*, C.R.C., c. 1605, s. 2.

INSHORE TRAFFIC ZONE. A routing measure that is a designated area between the landward boundary of a traffic separation scheme and the adjacent coast that is intended for local traffic. *Collision Regulations*, C.R.C., c. 1416, s. 2.

INSIDER. *n.* With respect to a corporation, (i) the corporation, (ii) an affiliate of the corporation, (iii) a director or officer of the corporation, (iv) a person who beneficially owns, directly or indirectly, more than 10 per cent of the voting securities of the corporation or who exercises control or direction over more than 10 per cent of the votes attached to the voting securities of the corporation, (v) a person employed or retained by the corporation, or (vi) a person who receives specific confidential information from a person described in this clause or elsewhere, including a person described in this subclause, and who has knowledge that the person giving the information is a person described in this clause or elsewhere, including a person described in this subclause, (vii) every director or senior officer of a company that is itself an insider or subsidiary of an issuer, (viii) an issuer where it has purchased, redeemed or otherwise acquired any of its securities, for so long as it holds any of its securities.

INSIDER INTEREST. The direct or indirect beneficial ownership of or control or direction over capital securities of a corporation. *Securities Act*, R.S.Q., c. V-1, s. 157.

INSIDER TRADING. " . . . [T]he purchase or sale of the securities of a company by a person who, by reason of his position in the company, has access to confidential information not known to other shareholders or the general public. . ." *Multiple Access Ltd. v. McCutcheon* (1982), 18 B.L.R. 138 at 142, [1982] 2 S.C.R. 161, 138 D.L.R. 93d) 1, 44 N.R. 181, Dickson J. (Laskin C.J.C., Martland, Ritchie, McIntyre and Lamer JJ. concurring).

INSIDE WIRE. The wire that is used by a distribution undertaking for the distribution of programming services that extends from the demarcation point to one or more terminal devices inside a subscriber's residence or premises. It includes the outlets, splitters and faceplates that are attached or connected to the wire but does not include a secured enclosure that is used to house the wire and that is attached to the exterior wall of a subscriber's premises, an amplifier, a channel converter, a decoder or a remote control unit. *Broadcasting Distribution Regulations*, SOR/97-555, s. 1.

INSIGNIA. *n.* [L.] Arms, ensigns.

IN SIMILI MATERIA. [L.] Dealing with similar or related subject-matter.

INSINUATION. *n.* Of a will, lodging it with a registrar to obtain probate.

IN SITU. [L.] In place; in the position originally held.

IN SITU OPERATION. (i) A scheme or operation ordinarily involving the use of well production operations for the recovery of crude bitumen from oil sands, or (ii) a scheme or operation designated by the Board as an in situ operation but does not include a mining opera-

tion. *Oil Sands Conservation Act*, R.S.A. 2000, c. O-7, s. 1.

IN SITU OPERATION SITE. An area within which an in situ operation is being conducted or that is the subject of an approval under this Act for an in situ operation, and includes a discard site and any area within which any facilities or equipment used in connection with the in situ operation are located. *Oil Sands Conservation Act*, R.S.A. 2000, c. O-7, s. 1.

IN SOLIDO. [L.] Completely.

IN SOLIDUM. [L.] For the entire sum.

INSOLVENCY. *n.* 1. "In a general sense, . . . inability to meet one's debts or obligations; in a technical sense, it means the condition or standard of inability to meet debts or obligations, upon the occurrence of which the statutory law enables a creditor to intervene, with the assistance of a Court, to stop individual action by creditors and to secure administration of the debtor's assets in the general interest of creditors; the law also generally allows the debtor to apply for the same administration." *British Columbia (Attorney General) v. Canada (Attorney General)*, [1937] A.C. 391 at 402, 18 C.B.R. 217, [1937] 1 W.W.R. 320, [1937] 1 D.L.R. 695 (B.C. P.C.), the board per Lord Thankerton. 2. A broader term than bankruptcy that contemplates measures dealing with the property of debtors unable to pay their debts and other arrangements. Composition and voluntary assignment are devices which may avoid technical bankruptcy without great prejudice to creditors and hardship to the debtor. See BANKRUPTCY AND ~.

INSOLVENT. *adj.* 1. Unable to meet obligations as they come due in the ordinary course of business. 2. Either ceasing to pay one's debts in the ordinary course of business or unable to pay one's debts as they become due. 3. As applied to a corporation, means a corporation (i) that is, for any reason, unable to meet its liabilities to its creditors, as they generally become due, or (ii) the aggregate of the value of the assets of which is not, at a fair valuation, sufficient to enable it to meet all its liabilities to its creditors due or accruing due.

INSOLVENT ESTATE. The real and personal estate of a deceased person which is not sufficient for the payment in full of the debts and liabilities of the deceased person.

INSOLVENT PERSON. A person who is not bankrupt and who resides or carries on business in Canada, whose liabilities to creditors provable as claims under this Act amount to one thousand dollars, and (a) who is for any reason unable to meet his obligations as they generally become due, (b) who has ceased paying his current obligations in the ordinary course of business as they generally become due, or (c) the aggregate of whose property is not, at a fair valuation, sufficient, or, if disposed of at a fairly conducted sale under legal process, would not be sufficient to enable payment of all his obligations, due and accruing due. *Bankruptcy and Insolvency Act*, R.S.C. 1985, c. B-3, s. 2.

IN SPECIE. [L. in its own form] 1. In money or coin. 2. In kind.

INSPECT. *v.* Includes test, survey, photograph, measure and record.

INSPECTING ENGINEER. An engineer who is directed to examine any railway or works, and includes two or more engineers, when two or more are so directed.

INSPECTION. *n.* 1. Critical examination; close scrutiny. 2. Includes an audit, examination, survey, test and inquiry. *Pesticides Act*, R.S.O. 1990, c. P.11, s. 1(1). 3. An examination of real or personal property ordered by a court when an examination is necessary to determine an issue in a proceeding. See FIRST ~: OFFICIAL ~; SHOP ~.

INSPECTION AUDIT. An examination of accounting records. *Audit Act*, R.S.O. 1990, c. A.35, s. 1.

INSPECTION MARK. A mark that is made by an inspector after an inspection of a device and that consists of a symbol for the time being used by inspectors and the date of the inspection. *Weights and Measures Regulations*, C.R.C., c. 1605, s. 2.

INSPECTION OF DOCUMENTS. The disclosure of documents relevant to the issue prior to trial.

INSPECTION POINT. Any place at which the Commission has made provision for the inspection of grain. *Canada Grain Act*, R.S.C. 1985, c. G-10, s. 2.

INSPECTION RECORD. See VEHICLE ~.

INSPECTION SIGN. See VEHICLE ~.

INSPECTION STATION. See OFFICIAL ~; VEHICLE ~.

INSPECTION STICKER. See VEHICLE ~.

INSPECTOR. *n.* 1. One who examines and reports. 2. A person appointed or designated under an act to carry out inspections or other duties prescribed. See BUILDING ~; CHIEF ~; CIVIL AVIATION ~; DISTRICT ~.

INSPECTOR GENERAL. The Inspector General appointed pursuant to subsection 30(1). *Canadian Security Intelligence Service*, R.S.C. 1985, c. C-23, s. 2.

INSPEXIMUS. [L.] We have inspected.

INSTALL. *v.* Includes placing an appliance in position for temporary use, venting an appliance and connecting piping to an appliance. *Energy Act*, R.S.O. 1990, c. E.16, s. 1.

INSTALLATION. *n.* 1. (i) Any equipment, apparatus, mechanism, machinery or instrument incidental to the operation of a pipeline, and (ii) any building or structure that houses or protects anything referred to in subclause (i), but does not include a refinery, processing plant, marketing plant or manufacturing plant. 2. The ceremony in which a person is inducted or invested with a charge, rank or office. See ELECTRICAL ~; GAS ~; IONIZING RADIATION ~; NON-IONIZING RADIATION ~; NUCLEAR ~; PIPING ~; POSTAL ~; PUBLIC UTILITY ~; RADIATION ~; SHORE ~; TEMPORARY ~.

INSTALLED. *adj.* That the boiler is so placed and so equipped that in the opinion of the chief officer it is ready for use. *Operating Engineers Act*, R.S.O. 1990, c. O.42, s. 10(1).

INSTALLER. *n.* A person who places or installs a boiler or pressure vessel in position for operation and use, or connects a boiler or pressure vessel with other machinery or equipment for operation and use. *Steam and Pressure Plants Act*, R.S.M. 1970, c. S210, s. 2. See INSULATION ~; SPRINKLER AND FIRE PROTECTION ~.

INSTALMENT. *n.* 1. Part payment. 2. Episode. 3. One part of a debt.

INSTALMENT METHOD. The instalment system takes into income for the year only the gross profit content of the instalments actually received in the year, that is to say, the full amount of such payments less the cost of the merchandise content proportionate to them. *Publishers Guild of Canada v. M.N.R.*, [1957] C.T.C. 1, 57 D.T.C. 1017 (Exch. Ct.).

INSTANCE. *n.* An urgent solicitation.

INSTANS EST FINIS UNIUS TEMPORIS ET PRINCIPIUM ALTERIUS. [L.] An instant ends one period of time and begins another.

INSTANTER. *adv.* [L.] At once, immediately.

INSTAR. *n.* A stage through which insect larvae develop. F.A. Jaffe, *A Guide to Pathological Evidence*, 3d ed. (Toronto: Carswell, 1991) at 221.

IN STATU QUO. [L.] In its former condition.

IN STIPULATIONIBUS CUM QUAERITUR QUID ACTUM SIT VERBA CONTRA STIPULATOREM INTERPRETANDA SUNT. [L.] When questioning what is done in agreements, words should be interpreted against the person who uses them.

INSTITUTE. *v.* To commence.

INSTITUTE. *n.* 1. An organization, body. 2. A treatise; a commentary. See RESEARCH ~.

INSTITUTION. *n.* 1. A bank, credit union, trust company, treasury branch or other similar person, a public school, college, hospital, gaol, penitentiary, correctional institution. 2. "... [B]ears ... the concept of it having a public object. . ." *Ontario (Attorney General) v. Tufford Rest Home* (1980), 30 O.R. (2d) 636 at 640 (Co. Ct.), Kovacs Co. Ct. J. 3. A law, rite or ceremony imposed by authority, as a permanent rule of government or conduct. 4. An institution that is publicly owned and is operated solely for the benefit of the public, that is established for educational or cultural purposes and that conserves objects and exhibits them or otherwise makes them available to the public. *Cultural Property Export and Import Act*, R.S.C. 1985, c. C-51, s. 2. See CERTIFIED ~; CHARITABLE ~; CHILD CARING ~; CHILDREN'S ~; CORRECTIONAL ~; CREDIT ~; DEPOSIT ~; EDUCATIONAL ~; FEDERAL ~; FINANCIAL ~; GOVERNMENT~; GOVERNMENT SUPPORTED ~; ~S; LENDING ~; MEMBER ~; PENAL ~; POST SECONDARY ~; PRIVATE TRAINING ~; PROVINCIALLY ADMINISTERED ~; PROVINCIALLY OWNED ~; PUBLIC ~; REFORMATORY ~; RESIDENTIAL ~; UNIVERSITARIAN ~.

INSTITUTIONAL BIAS. The test developed by the courts for identifying this situation was: would an informed person viewing the matter realistically and practically, and having thought the matter through, have a reasonable apprehension of bias in a large number of cases arising before one particular tribunal. *Therrien c. Québec (Ministre de la justice)*, 2001 SCC 35.

INSTITUTIONAL BUILDING. A building used for purposes such as medical or care of persons suffering from physical or mental illness disease or infirmity, for the care of infants convalescents or aged persons, orphanages, and for penal or corrective purposes which provide sleeping facilities for the occupants. *Fire Prevention Act*, R.S.N.S. 1989, c. 171, s. 2.

INSTITUTIONAL CONSULTATION. Consultation among members of a tribunal including those not actually hearing a case. Considered appropriate to ensure consistency in decision-making within a tribunal.

INSTITUTIONAL DELAY. Delay in handling criminal cases expeditiously caused by lack of judges, courtrooms or adequate case management methods.

INSTITUTIONAL IMPARTIALITY. "The test for institutional impartiality is the same as the test adopted in [R. v. Valente (1985), 24 D.L.R. (4th) 161] with respect to the issue of judicial independence, that is the apprehension of an informed person, viewing the matter realistically and practically, and having thought the matter through. . ." *Alex Couture Inc. c. Canada (Procureur general)* (1991), (*sub nom. Alex Couture Inc. v. Canada (Attorney General)*) 38 C.P.R. (3d) 293 at 388, 83 D.L.R. (4th) 577, 41 Q.A.C. 1, [1991] R.J.Q. 2534, the court per Rousseau-Houle J.A. See IMPARTIAL.

INSTITUTIONAL INDEPENDENCE. 1. Elements are security of tenure, financial security and administrative control. Essential elements are summed as judicial control over the administrative decisions that bear directly and immediately on the exercise of the judicial function. *2747-3174 Québec Inc. c. Québec (Régie des permis d'alcool)*, [1996] 3 S.C.R. 919. 2. "Judicial control over . . . assignment of judges, sittings of the court, and court lists . . . as well as the related matters of allocation of courtrooms and direction of the administrative staff engaged in carrying out these functions, has generally been considered the essential and minimum requirement . . ." *R. v. Valente (No. 2)* (1985), 19 C.R.R. 354 at 368, 372, 376, 379-80, [1985] 2 S.C.R. 673, 52 O.R. (2d) 779, 37 M.V.R. 9, 49 C.R. (3d) 97, 23 C.C.C. (3d) 193, 24 D.L.R. (4th) 161, 64 N.R. 1, 14 O.A.C. 79, [1985] D.L.Q. 85n, the court per Le Dain J.

INSTITUTIONAL LANDS. Lands owned by the Crown, or by a university, (i) that are used as the site of an educational institution; and (ii) that are exempt from municipal taxation; and includes also (iii) any lands to which sub-clauses (i) and (ii) apply that are leased by the Crown or a university, to any college or other educational institution; (iv) such lands as are appurtenant to lands hereinbefore in this clause described and are necessarily or reasonably used for the purposes of a university, college, or other educational institution, including use as a campus or for recreational purposes; and (v) lands owned by a university that are used or occupied by any person under lease or permit for grazing or hay making purposes, or under a general permit for use or occupancy; and includes any building on any land heinbefore in this clause described. *Municipal Act*, S.M. 1970, c. 100, s. 795.

INSTITUTIONAL OCCUPANCY. Occupancy for the harbouring, housing or detention of persons who require special care or treatment on account of their age or mental or physical limitations or who are involuntarily detained. Ontario statutes.

INSTITUTIONS. *n.* A person who (i) grants degrees, (ii) provides a program of post-secondary study leading to a degree, or (iii) sells, offers for sale or, provides by agreement for a fee, reward or other remuneration, a degree, and includes a natural person, an association of natural persons, a partnership or a corporation that carries on any activity referred to in subclauses (i) to (iii). *Degree Granting Act*, S.N.S. 1983, c. 5, s. 2. See INSTITUTION.

INSTRUCT. *v.* 1. For a client to convey information to a solicitor. 2. For a client to authorize a solicitor to appear on their behalf.

INSTRUCTION. *n.* 1. Teaching. 2. Direction. 3. Imparting of knowledge. 4. A motion which gives a committee power to do something otherwise impossible, or to direct it to do something otherwise impossible. A. Fraser, W.A. Dawson, & J. Holtby, eds., *Beauchesne's Rules and Forms of the House of Commons of Canada*, 6th ed. (Toronto: Carswell, 1989) at 203. See AIR TRAFFIC CONTROL ~; APRON TRAFFIC CONTROL ~; FULL-TIME ~; MARINE TRAFFIC ~; PART-TIME ~; PROGRAM OF ~; TECHNICAL ~.

INSTRUCTIONAL DAY. A school day that is designated as an instructional day on a school calendar and upon which day an instructional program that may include examinations is provided for each pupil whose program is governed by such calendar.

INSTRUCTIONAL UNIT. See FRENCH-LANGUAGE ~.

INSTRUCTOR. *n.* A person who operates a motor vehicle for the purpose of instructing another person with regards to the skill and knowledge necessary for the safe operation of a motor vehicle. See DRIVER ~; DRIVING ~.

INSTRUCTORS ASSOCIATION. An organization recognized by the department and a college board concerned as the official body representing the instructional staff of a college. *The Community Colleges Act*, R.S.S. 1978, c. C-19, s. 2.

INSTRUMENT. *n.* 1. " . . . [A] word of very wide signification in our language and embraces, inter alia, such objects as implements or tools, a contrivance which produces sounds, as a musical instrument, or even a legal document." *R. v. Hayes* (1958), 29 C.R. 235 at 238, [1958] O.W.N. 449 (C.A.), the court per Schroeder J.A. 2. A formal legal document. 3. " . . . '[W]ritten document,' . . ." *R. v. Evans* (1962), 37 W.W.R. 610 at 611, 37 C.R. 341, 132 C.C.C. 271 (B.C. C.A.), the court per Tysoe J.A. 4. Any grant, certificate of title, conveyance, assurance, deed, map, plan, will, probate or exemplification of probate of will, letters of administration or an exemplification thereof, mortgage or encumbrance, or any other document in writing relating to or affecting the transfer of or other dealing with land or evidencing title thereto. *Land Titles Act*, R.S.C. 1985, c. L-5, s. 2. 5. A promissory note, bill of exchange or other negotiable instrument payable by a foreign customer or a bond, debenture or other evidence of indebtedness issued or given by a foreign customer and includes an agreement to pay. *Export Development Act*, R.S.C. 1985, c. E-20, s. 23. 6. Any instrument for measuring a line or angle. *Provincial Land Surveyors Act*, R.S.N.S. 1967, c. 243, s. 1. 7. Includes a statute. *Trustee Act*, R.S.N.S. 1989, c. 479, s. 2. See ACKNOWLEDGEMENT OF ~; APPROVED ~; AUTHORIZING ~; BANKING ~; CONSTATING ~; GUARANTEED ~; HOUSEBREAKING ~; NEGOTIABLE ~; PRIMARY ~ OF INDEBTEDNESS; PRIORITY PAYMENT ~; ROYAL ~; SCIENTIFIC~; SECURITY ~; SELLING ~; STATUTORY ~; TESTAMENTARY ~.

INSTRUMENTA. *n.* [L.] Documents not under seal.

INSTRUMENTALITY. *n*. "...An agent..." *Medicine Hat (City) v. Canada (Attorney General)* (1985), 29 M.P.L.R. 165 at 175, 37 Alta. L.R. (2d) 208, [1985] 4 W.W.R. 367, 85 D.T.C. 5365, 18 D.L.R. (4th) 428, 59 A.R. 355 (C.A.), the court per Prowse J.A.

INSTRUMENT APPROACH. The orderly positioning of an IFR aircraft from the enroute phase to a position and altitude from which a landing may be completed or a missed approach procedure may be initiated. *Canadian Aviation Regulations*, SOR/96-433, s. 101.01.

INSTRUMENT APPROACH PROCEDURE. In respect of an aircraft on an instrument approach to a runway or aerodrome, a procedure for an instrument approach determined by the pilot-in-command of the aircraft on the basis of the information specified in the Canada Air Pilot Act for an IFR approach to that runway or aerodrome or, where no such information is specified in the Canada Air Pilot Act, the information specified in (*a*) the air operator certificate or the private operator certificate, or (*b*) the route and approach inventory, where the aircraft is operated pursuant to Part VII or Subpart 4 of Part VI. *Canadian Aviation Regulations*, SOR 96-433, s. 101.01.

INSTRUMENT FOR ILLICIT DRUG USE. Anything designed primarily or intended under the circumstances for consuming or to facilitate the consumption of an illicit drug, but does not include a "device" as that term is defined in section 2 of the Food and Drugs Act. *Criminal Code*, R.S.C. 1985, c. C-46, s. 462.1.

INSTRUMENT OF INCORPORATION. Original or restated letters patent of incorporation, letters patent of amalgamation, letters patent of continuance and any supplementary letters patent issued and any special act or charter incorporating a body corporate and any amendments to the special act or charter.

INSTRUMENT METEOROLOGICAL CONDITIONS. Meteorological conditions less than the minima specified in Division VI of Subpart 2 of Part VI for visual meteorological conditions, expressed in terms of visibility and distance from cloud. *Canadian Aviation Regulations*, SOR 96-433, s. 101.01.

INSTRUMENT RECORD. A book, file, micrograph, electronic or other storage means for recording the receipt of instruments at a land titles office. *Land Titles Act*, S.N.S. 1978, c. 8, s. 4.

INSTRUMENT REQUIRING TO BE STAMPED. Includes all matters, proceedings, memoranda, deeds, instruments, documents and papers, subject to the control of the Legislature and which, under this act, or any order-in-council, require to have any stamp attached thereto or impressed thereon, and also all letters patent, commissions, licenses, permits, certificates and instruments, whether originals, exemplifications or copies, which, under this act or any other act of the Legislature, or under any order-in-council founded on or recognized by any such act, require to have any stamp attached thereto or impressed theron. *Stamp Act*, R.S.Q. 1977, c. T-10, s. 4.

INSUBORDINATION. *n*. Failure to obey the lawful order of an employer. There must be a clear order understood by the worker and given by a person in authority and the order must be disobeyed.

IN SUBSIDIUM. [L.] Supporting.

IN SUBSTANTIALIBUS. [L.] In substance.

INSUFFICIENT. *adj*. To describe an answer or affidavit not complying with formal requirements.

INSULATED. *adj*. 1. Covered with insulating materials or insulated from ground and from other live parts of a system in a manner adequate and consistent with safe and reliable performance under the conditions of operation. 2. Separated from other conducting surfaces by a dielectric material or air space having a degree of resistance to the passage of current and to disruptive discharge sufficiently high for the condition of use.

INSULATING. *adj*. As applied to non-conducting substances means that they are capable of bringing about the condition defined as insulated.

INSULATION. *n*. Material the chief purpose of which is to prevent heat from escaping from a building and which is not essential for the support or enclosure of the building, or for the finishing of the interior of the building.

INSULATION CONTRACT. A contract, whether verbal or written, between an owner and an insulation installer providing for the installation of insulation, or insulation and energy conserving material, in an eligible residence.

INSULATION INSTALLER. An individual, firm or corporation that installs insulation for others.

INSULATION MATERIALS. See THER-MAL ~.

INSULIN. *n.* The active principle of the pancreas that affects the metabolism of carbohydrates in the animal body and that is of value in the treatment of diabetes mellitus. *Food and Drug Regulations*, C.R.C., s. 870, c. C.03.050.

INSULT. *n.* In the context of the defence of provocation, an act or the action of attacking or assailing; an open and sudden attack or assault without formal preparations; injuriously contemptuous speech or behaviour; scornful utterance or action intended to wound self-respect; an affront; indignity. Must be one which could, in light of the past history of the relationship between the accused and the deceased, deprive an ordinary person, of the same age, and sex, and sharing with the accused such other factors as would give the act or insult in question a special significance, of the power of self-control. *R. v. Thibert*, [1996] 1 S.C.R. 37.

INSURABLE ACREAGE. The acreage seeded or to be seeded for harvest to any insurable crop with respect to each insurance unit, as reported by the insured person or as determined by the board in accordance with the regulations. *The Saskatchewan Crop Insurance Act*, R.S.S. 1978, c. S-12, s. 2.

INSURABLE CROP. Wheat, oats, barley or any other agricultural crop declared by the regulations to be an insurable crop for the purposes of this act. *Crop Insurance acts*.

INSURABLE EARNINGS. The total amount of the earnings, as determined in accordance with Part IV, that an insured person has from insurable employment. *Employment Insurance Act, 1996*, S.C. 1996, c. 23, s. 2. See MAXI-MUM ~.

INSURABLE EMPLOYMENT. (1) Subject to subsection (2), insurable employment is (*a*) employment in Canada by one or more employers, under any express or implied contract of service or apprenticeship, written or oral, whether the earnings of the employed person are received from the employer or some other person and whether the earnings are calculated by time or by the piece, or partly by time and partly by the piece, or otherwise; (*b*) employment in Canada as described in paragraph (*a*) by Her Majesty in right of Canada; (*c*) service in the Canadian Forces or in a police force; (*d*) employment included by regulations made under subsection (4) or (5); and (*e*) employment in Canada of an in-

dividual as the sponsor or co-ordinator of an employment benefits project. *Employment Insurance Act, 1996*, S.C. 1996, c. 23, s. 5.

INSURABLE INTEREST. 1. " . . . [I]f an insured can demonstrate . . . 'some relation to, or concern in the subject of the insurance, which relation or concern by the happening of the perils insured against may be so affected as to produce a damage, detriment or prejudice to the person insuring', . . . To 'have moral certainty of advantage or benefit, but for those risk[s] or dangers', or 'to be so circumstanced with respect to [the subject matter of the insurance] as to have benefit from its existence, prejudice from its destruction'. . ." *Kosmopoulos v. Constitution Insurance Co. of Canada* (1987), (*sub nom. Constitution Insurance Co. of Canada v. Kosmo*poulos) 36 B.L.R. 233 at 255, [1987] 1 S.C.R. 2, 22 C.C.L.I. 296, [1987] I.L.R. 1-2147, 74 N.R. 360, 21 O.A.C. 4, 34 C.L.R. (4th) 208, Wilson J. (Beetz, Lamer, Le Dain and La Forest JJ. concurring). 2. A person has an insurable interest in his own life and well-being and in the life and well-being of, (a) his child or grandchild; (b) his spouse; (c) any person upon whom he is wholly or in part dependent for, or from whom he is receiving, support or education; (d) his officer or employee; and (e) any person in whom he has a pecuniary interest. *Insurance acts*.

INSURABLE PERSON. An operator of a farm who has an insurable interest in an insurable crop seeded or to be seeded thereon.

INSURABLE STATUS. The status by which a premium rate is determined for an insured person.

INSURANCE. *n.* 1. The undertaking by one person to indemnify another person against loss or liability for loss in respect of a certain risk or peril to which the object of the insurance may be exposed, or to pay a sum of money or other thing of value upon the happening of a certain event. *Insurance acts*. 2. Insurance on the life or health of a borrower or buyer, or on property charged to secure payment of the indebtedness of a borrower or buyer to a lender or seller. *Consumer Protection acts*. 3. Accident insurance, sickness insurance, or accident and sickness insurance. *Insurance acts*. 4. Life insurance. *Insurance acts*. See ACCIDENTAL DEATH ~; ACCIDENT ~; AIRCRAFT ~; ALL-RISK ~; AUTOMOBILE ~; BLANKET ~; BOILER AND MACHINERY ~; BOILER ~; BURGLARY ~; BUSINESS OF ~; CIVIL COMMOTION ~; COMPRE-

HENSIVE ~; CONTINGENCY ~; CONTRACT OF ~; CONTRACT OF MARINE ~; CREDIT~; CROP ~; DEPOSIT ~; DEPRECIATION ~; DISABILITY ~; DOUBLE INDEMNITY ~; DOUBLE ~; EARTHQUAKE ~; EMPLOYMENT ~; EMPLOYERS' LIABILITY ~; ENDOWMENT ~; ERRORS AND OMISSIONS ~; EXCESS ~; EXPLOSION ~; EXTENSION ~; FALLING AIRCRAFT ~; FAMILY ~; FIDELITY ~; FIRE ~; FIRST LOSS ~; FIRST PARTY ~; FORGERY ~; GROUP ACCIDENT ~; GROUP ~; GUARANTEE ~; HAIL ~; IMPACT BY VEHICLES ~; INDEMNITY ~; INLAND TRANSPORTATION ~; KEY MAN ~; LEGAL EXPENSE ~; LIABILITY ~; LIFE~; LIMITED ~; LIVESTOCK ~; LOSS ~; LOST OR NOT LOST ~; MACHINERY ~; MARINE ~; MARITIME ~; MORTGAGE ~; MOTOR VEHICLE ~; MUTUAL ~; NO-FAULT ~; NO-FAULT AUTO-ACCIDENT ~; NON-INDEMNITY ~; OVER- ~; PERSONAL ACCIDENT ~; PERSONAL PROPERTY ~; PLATE GLASS ~; PLEASURE CRAFT ~; POLICY OF ~; PROPERTY DAMAGE ~; PROPERTY ~; PUBLIC LIABILITY ~; REAL PROPERTY ~; RE~; REPLACEMENT COST ~; SICKNESS ~; SPRINKLER LEAKAGE ~; STEAM BOILER ~; SUM ~; SUPERINTENDENT OF ~; SURETY ~; THEFT ~; THIRD PARTY LIABILITY ~; TITLE ~; UNDER- ~; UNEMPLOYMENT~; VARIABLE ~; WATER DAMAGE ~; WEATHER ~; WINDSTORM ~; WORKERS' COMPENSATION ~.

INSURANCE AGENCY. A company which for compensation solicits on behalf of an insurer or transmits for a person other than itself an application for or a policy of insurance to or from the insurer or offers or acts or assumes to act in the solicitation for and negotiation of the insurance or in negotiating its continuance or renewal.

INSURANCE AGENT. An employee of an insurer who represents the insurer.

INSURANCE BROKER. A middle person between an insured and an insurer who solicits insurance from the public and places it with a company selected by the broker or the insured. Not an employee of any insurance company.

INSURANCE BUSINESS. The business of (a) undertaking or offering to undertake to indemnify another person against loss or liability for loss in respect of a certain risk or peril to which the object of the insurance may be exposed, (b) soliciting or accepting any risk, (c) soliciting an application for a contract of insurance, (d) issuing or delivering a (i) receipt for any contract of insurance, or (ii) contract of insurance, (e) in consideration of any premium or payment, granting an annuity on a life or lives, (f) collecting or receiving any premium for a contract of insurance, (g) adjusting any loss covered by a contract of insurance, or (h) advertising for any business described in paragraphs (a) to (g).

INSURANCE CARD. (a) A Motor Vehicle Liability Insurance Card in form approved by the Commissioner, (b) a policy of automobile insurance or a certificate of a policy in the form approved by the Commissioner, or (c) such evidence of insurance as is prescribed by the regulations. *Compulsory Automobile Insurance Act*, R.S.O. 1990, c. C-25, s. 1(1).

INSURANCE CHARGE. The cost of insuring the risk assumed by the person who advances or is to advance credit under an agreement or arrangement, where the face amount of the insurance does not exceed the credit advanced. *Criminal Code*, R.S.C. 1985, c. C-46, s. 347(2).

INSURANCE COMPANY. 1. (a) An insurer, and (b) a Lloyd's association but does not include a fraternal society. 2. A company transacting the business of insurance and includes any unincorporated association or reciprocal exchange transacting that business. See CAPTIVE ~; CASH-MUTUAL ~; CO-OPERATIVE ~; PROVINCIAL ~; PUBLIC ~; PURE CAPTIVE ~.

INSURANCE CONTRACT. Any contract under which one party, the insurer, assumes the risk of an uncertain event, which is not within its control, happening at a future time and in which event the other party, the insured, has an interest. The insurer is bound to pay money or provide its equivalent if the uncertain event occurs. See VARIABLE ~.

INSURANCE FUND. As applied to a fraternal society or as applied to any corporation not incorporated exclusively for the transaction of insurance, includes all money, securities for money and assets appropriated by the rules of the society or corporation to the payment of insurance liabilities or appropriated for the management of the insurance ranch or department or division of the society, or otherwise legally available for insurance liabilities but does not include funds of a trade union appropriated to or applicable for the voluntary assistance of wage earners unemployed or upon strike. *Insurance acts.*

INSURANCE MONEY. The amount payable by an insurer under a contract, and includes all benefits, surplus, profits, dividends, bonuses and annuities payable under the contract. *Insurance acts.*

INSURANCE OF DEBTS. A creditor may insure the payment of an existing or contemplated debt.

INSURANCE ON THE CASH PLAN. Any insurance that is not mutual insurance.

INSURANCE PLAN. See HEALTH CARE ~; SELF-~.

INSURANCE POLICY. A contract under which one party, the insurer, assumes the risk of an uncertain event, which is not within its control, happening at a future time and in which event the other party, the insured, has an interest. The insurer is bound to pay money or provide its equivalent if the uncertain event occurs.

INSURANCE PRACTICE. See UNFAIR ~.

INSURANCE SALESMAN. A person who is employed by an insurance agent to solicit, obtain or take an application for insurance other than life insurance, or to negotiate for or procure insurance other than life insurance, or to collect or receive a premium.

INSURANCE UNIT. All or any part of the insurable acreage in respect of which an insured person has an interest in the crop seeded or to be seeded theron. *The Saskatchewan Crop Insurance Act,* R.S.S. 1978, c. S-12, s. 2.

INSURED. *n.* 1. (a) In the case of group insurance means, in the provision of this Part relating to the designation of beneficiaries or of personal representatives as recipients of insurance money and their rights and status, the group or person insured, and (b) in all other cases means the person who makes a contract with an insurer. *Insurance acts.* 2. A person insured by a contract whether named or not. *Insurance* acts. 3. A person who makes a contract with an insurer. *Insurance acts.* 4. Includes (i) a person to or in respect of whom or to whose dependants benefits are payable if bodily injuries are sustained by him as a result of one of the perils mentioned in section 22 whether he is named in a certificate or not; (ii) a person to whom insurance money

is payable if loss of or damage to a vehicle results from one of the perils mentioned in section 38; and (iii) a person to whom or on whose behalf insurance money is payable if bodily injury to or the death of others, or loss of or damage to the property of others, for which he is legally liable results from one of the perils mentioned in section 42 whether he is named in an owner's certificate or not. *The Automobile Accident Insurance Act,* R.S.S. 1978, c. A-35, s. 2. See NAMED ~.

INSURED. *adj.* See PERSON ~; SOPHISTICATED ~; CAPTIVE INSURANCE COMPANY ~; SUM ~.

INSURED HEALTH SERVICES. Hospital services, physician services and surgical-dental services provided to insured persons, but does not include any health services that a person is entitled to and eligible for under any other Act of Parliament or under any Act of the legislature of a province that relates to workers' or workmen's compensation. *Canada Health Act,* R.S.C. 1985, c. C-6, s. 2. See ELECTIVE ~.

INSURED MOTOR VEHICLE. A motor vehicle the owner of which is insured.

INSURED OFF-HIGHWAY VEHICLE. An off-highway vehicle the owner of which is insured by a policy of insurance.

INSURED PERSON. 1. A person who enters into a subsisting contract of insurance with an insurer and includes (a) a person insured by a contract whether named or not; and (b) a person to whom or for whose benefit all or part of the proceeds of a contract of insurance is payable; and (c) a person entitled to have insurance money applied toward satisfaction of his judgment in accordance with the Insurance Act. *Insurance acts.* 2. A person who has entered into a contract. *Crop Insurance acts.* 3. In relation to a province, a resident of the province other than (a) a member of the Canadian Forces, (b) a member of the Royal Canadian Mounted Police who is appointed to a rank therein, (c) a person serving a term of imprisonment in a penitentiary as defined in the Penitentiary Act, or (d) a resident of the province who has not completed such minimum period of residence or waiting period, not exceeding three months, as may be required by the province for eligibility for or entitlement to insured health services. *Canada Health Act,* R.S.C. 1985, c. C-6, s. 2. 4. A person who is or has been employed in insurable employment. *Employment Insurance, 1996,* S.C. 1996, c. 23, s. 2.

INSURED PLAN. A plan in which all benefits are paid by means of an annuity or insurance contract issued by a person authorized to carry on a life insurance business in Canada and under which the person is obligated to pay all the benefits set out in the plan. *Pension Benefits Standards Regulations, 1985*, SOR/87-19, s. 2, as am.

INSURER. *n.* 1. The person, corporation, underwriter, partnership, fraternal or other society, association, or syndicate who undertakes or agrees or offers to undertake a contract. *Insurance acts.* 2. Any corporation incorporated for the purpose of carrying on the business of insurance, any association of persons formed on the plan known as Lloyds whereby each associate underwriter becomes liable for a stated, limited or proportionate part of the whole amount insured under a contract of insurance, and any exchange. *Excise Tax Act*, R.S.C. 1985, c. E-15, s. 3. See AUTHORIZED ~; EXTRAPROVINCIAL ~; LIABILITY ~; LIFE ~; PROVINCIAL ~; RE~; SELF ~.

INSURGENT. *n.* Someone acting just short of belligerently, often a revolutionary.

INSURRECTION. *n.* Actions taken with an intention to overthrow the government or usurp its powers.

INT. *abbr.* International.

INTACT. *adj.* Without openings.

IN TALI CONFLICTU MAGIS EST UT JUS NOSTRUM QUAM JUS ALIENUM SERVEMUS. [L.] When there is such a conflict, own law serves us better than that of a foreign jurisdiction.

INTANGIBLE. *n.* All personal property, including choses in action, that is not goods, chattel paper, documents of title, instruments or securities. *Personal Property Security acts.*

INTANGIBLE PROPERTY. A right of ownership over any personal property that is not a chattel or a mortgage, and includes without limiting the generality of the foregoing, (a) money, a cheque, a bank draft, a deposit, a dividend and income, (b) a credit balance, a customer overpayment, a gift certificate, a security deposit, a refund, a credit memo, an unpaid wage and an unused airline ticket, (c) a share or any other intangible ownership interest in a business organization, (d) money deposited to redeem a share, a bond, a coupon or other security, or to make a distribution, (e) an amount due and payable by the insurer under the terms of an insurance policy, and (f) an amount distributable from a trust or custodial fund established under a plan to provide education, health, welfare, vacation, severance, retirement, death, share purchase, profit sharing, employee savings, supplemental unemployment insurance or similar benefits. *Unclaimed Intangible Property Act*, R.S.O. 1990, c. U.1, s. 1.

INTEGRAL. *adj.* Essential to completeness; constituent.

INTEGRATED CIRCUIT PRODUCT. A product, in a final or intermediate form, that is intended to perform an electronic function and in which the elements, at least one of which is an active element, and some or all of the interconnections, are integrally formed in or on, or both in and on, a piece of material. *Integrated Circuit Topography Act, 1990*, S.C. 1990, c. 37, s. 2.

INTEGRATED INDUSTRY. An industry in which a manufacturer controls production from beginning to end.

INTEGRITY. *n.* 1. Soundness of moral principles; probity; honesty; uprightness. 2. In respect of any device or equipment, the ability of the device or equipment to retain all of the qualities essential to its safe, reliable and adequate performance. *Canada Protective Clothing and Equipment Regulations*, C.R.C., c. 1007, s. 2.

INTELLECTUAL PROPERTY. Refers to property which is subject to copyright, patent, trade-mark, industrial design or integrated circuit topography legislation. See INDUSTRIAL PROPERTY; INDUSTRIAL AND ~.

INTELLIGIBLE. *adj.* Under s. 6 of the Canada Evidence Act [R.S.C. 1985, c. C-5]: "[a] witness who is unable to speak may give his evidence in any other manner in which he can make it intelligible". Although there does not appear to be any case law on the meaning of intelligible, to render the section meaningful it must include that a witness is able to communicate to the Court in a manner which accurately and comprehensively conveys their testimony on a particular matter. To accomplish this, the manner of giving evidence must not only convey the witness' testimony to the Court, but also the questions of counsel to the witness. As long as a witness' testimony can be communicated to the Court, the fact that that witness uses a unique method of communication or language does not render the evidence inadmissible. *R. v. Carlick* (1999), 1999 CarswellBC 1104 (S.C.).

INTEND. *v.* To plan; to have in mind as a purpose or goal.

INTENT. *n.* 1. The exercise of free will to use particular means to produce a particular result. 2. In relation to legislation, refers to the state of mind of the legislators at the time of enactment. See CERTAINTY OF ~; EQUITY LOOKS TO THE ~ RATHER THAN TO THE FORM; GENERAL ~; LETTER OF ~; SPECIFIC ~; TRANSFERRED ~.

INTENTIO CAECA MALA. [L.] A secret intention is bad.

INTENTIO INSERVIRE DEBET LEGIBUS, NOT LEGES INTENTIONI. [L.] Intention ought to serve the laws, not the laws' intention.

INTENTION. Of a legislature, can only be ascertained from the express words of the enactment or by reasonable and necessary implication from them. See CERTAINTY OF ~; EQUITY IMPUTES AN ~ TO FULFIL AN OBLIGATION.

INTENTIONAL INDUCEMENT OF BREACH OF CONTRACT. Liability arises where, knowing of the contract and with intent to prevent or hinder its performance, the defendant induces one party not to perform his part of the contract or the defendant commits a wrongful act to prevent the performance of the contract. John G. Fleming, *The Law of Torts*, 8th ed. (Sydney: The Law Book Company Limited, 1992) at 690.

INTENTIONAL INFLICTION OF NERVOUS SHOCK. An overt act by the defendant intended to produce the harm which is produced in the form of a provable illness.

INTENTIONALLY UNDER-EMPLOYED. The parent required to pay [child support] is intentionally under-employed if that parent chooses to earn less than he or she is capable of earning. *Drygala v. Pauli* (2002), 61 O.R. (3d) 711 (C.A.).

INTENTIONALLY UNEMPLOYED. That parent [required to pay child support] is intentionally unemployed when he or she chooses not to work when capable of earning an income. *Drygala v. Pauli* (2002), 61 O.R. (3d) 711 (C.A.).

INTENTIONAL TORT. A tort in which the wrongdoer either wishes to accomplish the result or believes the result will follow from his act and the result is an injury to the plaintiff.

INTENTION IN COMMON. Between a party and a principal to an offence, refers to both parties having in mind the same unlawful purpose. May also refer to a shared intention to carry out the action or purpose for the same motives.

INTENT TO DEFEND. See NOTICE OF ~.

INTER. *v.* The burial of human remains and includes the placing of human remains in a lot. *Cemeteries Act (Revised)*, R.S.O. 1990, c. C.4, s. 1.

INTER ALIA. [L.] Among other things.

INTER ARMA LEGES SILENT. [L.] In war, laws stay silent.

INTERCEPT. *v.* 1. Includes listen to, record or acquire a communication or acquire the substance, meaning or purport thereof. 2. Includes listen to or record a function of a computer system, or acquire the substance, meaning or purport thereof. *Criminal Code*, R.S.C. 1985, c. C-46, s. 342.1(2) as added by *Criminal Law Amendment Act*, R.S.C. 1985 (2nd Supp.) c. 27, s. 45.

INTERCEPTOR. *n.* A receptacle to prevent oil, grease, sand or other materials from passing into drainage piping.

INTERCHANGE. *n.* A place where the line of a railway company connects the line of another railway company and where loaded or empty cars may be stored until delivered or received by that other company. *Canada Transportation Act*, S.C. 1996, c. 10, s. 111.

INTERCHANGEABLE DRUG. A drug of equal quality that contains, in the same dosage form, the same amount of the same active ingredients as the drug prescribed.

INTERCHANGEABLE PHARMACEUTICAL PRODUCT. A product containing a drug or drugs in the same amount, of the same active ingredients and in the same dosage form as that directed by a prescription.

INTERCHANGEABLE PRODUCT. A drug or combination of drugs identified by a specific product name or manufacturer and designated as interchangeable with one or more other such products. *Prescription Drug Cost Regulation Act*, R.S.O. 1990, c. P.23, s. 1.

INTERCONNECTED RADIO-BASED TRANSMISSION FACILITY. Any radio apparatus that is used for the transmission or reception of intelligence to or from anywhere on a public switched network. *Radiocommunications Regulations*, SOR/96-484, s. 2.

INTERCOUNTRY ADOPTION. An adoption to which the Convention on Protection of Children and Co-operation in respect of Intercountry Adoption applies, or any other adoption of a child who is habitually resident outside Canada, by an Ontario resident, (i) that is intended to create a permanent parent-child relationship, and (ii) that is finalized in the child's country of origin. *Intercountry Adoption Act, 1998*, S.O. 1998, c. 29, s. 1.

INTER-DELEGATION. *n.* The delegation of provincial power to the federal level or of federal power to the provinces.

INTERDICTED PERSON. 1. Person to whom the sale of liquor is prohibited by order under this act. *Liquor Control acts.* 2. A person who is prohibited from having or consuming liquor by an order under this act. *Liquor acts.*

INTERDICTION. *n.* The declaration of any person incapable by reason of habitual drunkenness of the management of his own business or affairs. *Inebriates Guardianship Act*, R.S.N.S. 1989, c. 227, s. 2.

INTERESSE TERMINI. [L.] An executory interest which is a right of entry that a lessee acquires in land through a demise.

INTEREST. *n.* 1. Something which a person has in a thing when that person has advantages, duties, liabilities, losses or rights connected with it, whether ascertained or potential, present or future. 2. In the law of insurance, something which a person has in the life of a person or in property when the death of the person or destruction or damage to the property would expose that person to pecuniary liability or loss. 3. Charge or compensation for the use of or retention of money. 4. The aggregate of all charges and expenses, whether in the form of a fee, fine, penalty, commission or other similar charge or expense or in any other form, paid or payable for the advancing of credit under an agreement, by or on behalf of the person to whom the credit is or is to be advanced, irrespective of the person to whom any such charges and expenses are or are to be paid or payable, but does not include any repayment credit advanced or any insurance charge, official fee, overdraft charge, required deposit balance or, in the case of a mortgage transaction, any amount required to be paid on account of property taxes. *Criminal Code*, R.S.C. 1985, c. C-46, s. 347(2). See ABSOLUTE ~; ADVERSE IN ~; AGAINST ~; BENEFICIAL ~; BEST ~S OF THE CHILD; CAPITAL ~; COMMON ~; COMPOUND ~; CONFLICT OF ~; CONTROLLING ~; DIRECT PECUNIARY ~; EQUITABLE ~; EXECUTORY ~; EXPROPRIATED ~; FINANCIAL ~; INCOME ~; INSIDER ~; INSURABLE ~; LICENSEE WITH AN ~; LIFE ~; LOGGING ~; MATERIAL ~; MEMBERSHIP ~; MINERAL ~; OPEN ~; OWNERSHIP ~; PECUNIARY ~; PERFECTED SECURITY ~; POLICY PROOF OF ~; POST-JUDGMENT ~; PRE-JUDGMENT ~; PRIVATE ~; PUBLIC ~; RESIDUAL ~; REVERSIONARY ~; ROYALTY ~; SECURITY ~; SIGNIFICANT SUBSTANTIAL ~; SUCCESSIVE LEGAL ~; TIME SHARE ~; UNDIVIDED ~; UNENCUMBERED ~; VOTING ~; WORKING ~.

INTEREST ARBITRATION. 1. " ... [A] means of resolving collective bargaining impasses by having outstanding matters in dispute resolved by an arbitrator, or board of arbitration. . ." *Haldimand-Norfolk Health Unit v. O. N. A.* (1981), 81 C.L.L.C. 14,085 at 76, 120 D.L.R. (3d) 101, 31 O.R. (2d) 730 (C.A.), Goodman J.A. (Howland C.J.O., Lacourcière, Houlden and Morden JJ.A. concurring). 2. A type of dispute resolution by which an arbitrator determines the conditions, terms and rules which govern an employer-union-employee relationship.

INTEREST BUY-DOWN. A way a vendor arranges mortgage financing at less than the current market rate when interest rates are high through prepayment of part of the interest that the mortgagee requests so that the annual rate during the term is reduced. D.J. Donahue & P.D. Quinn, *Real Estate Practice in Ontario*, 4th ed. (Toronto: Butterworths, 1990) at 227.

INTEREST DISPUTE. A dispute arising between the employer and the employee as to the content of a collective agreement.

INTERESTED PARTY. Charge or compensation for the use of or retention of money. One who has an economic, pecuniary, or proprietary interest in the subject matter of a trust.

INTERESTED PERSON. 1. Includes (a) an offeree whether or not he deposits shares pursuant to a take-over bid; (b) an offeree corporation; (c) an offeror; and (d) a rival offeror. *Can-*

ada Business Corporations Act, R.S.C. 1985, c. C-44, s. 205(4). 2. (a) A director of the Corporation or a member of a Council, (b) the spouse or a child, brother, sister or parent of a director or a member of a Council, or (c) the spouse of a child, brother, sister or parent of a director or a member of a Council. *Federal Business Development Bank Act*, R.S.C. 1985, c. F-6, s. 36. 3. Any person who is or would be affected by an order made under this act and includes (a) the next of kin of the person in respect of whom an order is made or for whom an order is applied and (b) a person who holds property of the person in respect of whom an order is made or for whom an order is applied. *Presumption of Death acts*. 4. Not restricted to persons who stand to benefit financially from a matter or transaction. See PERSON INTERESTED.

INTEREST HOLDER. 1. In respect of an interest or a share therein, the person indicated, in the register maintained pursuant to Part VIII, as the holder of the interest or the share. *Canada Petroleum Resources Act*, R.S.C. 1985 (2nd Supp.), c. 36, s. 2. 2. In relation to any Canada lands, the registered holder of an interest or share in an interest in respect of those Canada lands including, where applicable, Her Majesty in right of Canada holding through the appropriate Minister or a designated Crown corporation. *Oil and Gas Act*, R.S.C. 1985, c. O-, s. 2. See CO-OPERATIVE ~.

INTEREST INCOME. See GROSS ~.

INTEREST IN EXPECTANCY. Includes an estate or interest in remainder or reversion and any other future interest whether vested or contingent, but does not include a reversion expectant on the determination of a lease.

INTEREST IN LAND. (a) Any estate in land less than an estate in fee simple, and (b) any interest, right, easement, or right-of-way, in, to, or over, land other than the interest of the estate in fee simple. *Land Acquisition Act*, R.S.M. 1987, c. L40, s. 1.

INTEREST IN THE PREMISES. An estate or interest of any nature, and includes a statutory right given or reserved to the Crown to enter any lands or premises belonging to any person or public authority for the purpose of doing any work, construction, repair or maintenance in, upon, through, over or under any lands or premises. *Construction Lien Act*, R.S.O. 1990, c. C.30, s. 1(1).

INTEREST OF A MEMBER. Includes his shares in the association, if any; loan capital due to him and any other amount held to his credit by the association. *The Co-operative Production Associations Act*, R.S.S. 1978, c. C-37, s. 2.

INTEREST OWNER. The interest holder who holds an interest or the group of interest holders who hold all of the shares in an interest. See WORKING ~.

INTEREST PREJUDICE. A form of juror prejudice which arises when a juror has a direct stake in the trial due to his or her relationship with the defendant, victim, witnesses or the outcome.

INTEREST RATE. See POSTJUDGEMENT ~; PREJUDGEMENT ~; SPECIFIED ~.

INTEREST REIPUBLICAE NE MALEFICIA REMANEANT IMPUNITA. [L.] It is a concern of the state that wrongdoings do not go unpunished.

INTEREST REIPUBLICAE NE SUA QUIS MALE UTATUR. [L.] It is a concern of the state that people not wrongfully use their own property.

INTEREST REIPUBLICAE QUOD HOMINES CONSERVENTUR. [L.] It is a concern of the state that people are kept safe.

INTEREST REIPUBLICAE RES JUDICATAS NON RESCINDI. [L.] It is a concern of the state that judgments are not rescinded.

INTEREST REIPUBLICAE SUPREME HOMINUM TESTAMENTA RATA HABERI. [L.] It is a concern of the state that a person's last will be considered valid.

INTEREST REIPUBLICAE UT SIT FINIS LITIUM. [L.] It is a concern of the state that lawsuits be concluded.

INTEREST UPON INTEREST. Compound interest.

INTERFACE. See POOLING ~.

INTER FAUCES TERRAE. [L.] Within the mouth of the land.

INTERFERE. *v*. To obstruct; to disrupt.

INTERFERENCE. *n*. Disruption; obstruction. See UNLAWFUL AND INTENTIONAL ~; UNLAWFUL ~ WITH CONTRACTUAL RELATIONS.

INTERFERENCE WITH CONTRACTUAL RELATIONS. A tort in which there must be direct and deliberate interference with the performance of a contract.

INTERGOVERNMENTAL AGREEMENT. An agreement between Her Majesty in right of a province and one or more of Her Majesty in right of Canada, Her Majesty in right of any other province and any other sovereign government.

INTERGOVERNMENTAL AFFAIRS. Any relationship between governments.

INTER-GOVERNMENTAL DISPUTES. An appeal lies to the Court from a decision of the Federal Court of Appeal in the case of a controversy between Canada and a province or between two or more provinces. *Supreme Court Act*, R.S.C. 1985, c. S-26, s. 35.1.

INTERIM. *adj.* 1. " . . . '[I]n the meantime', . . . 'for the time being'. . . ." *Bell Canada v. Canada (Canadian Radio-Television & Telecommunications Commission)* (1987), 43 D.L.R. (4th) 30 at 46, 79 N.R. 58, [1988] 1 F.C. 296 (C.A.) Marceau J.A. 2. Not permanent or final.

INTERIM AGREEMENT. A collective bargaining agreement which covers a period between the lapse of one contract and the completion of negotiations on another.

INTERIM COSTS. Inherent jurisdiction of the courts to grant costs to a litigant, in rare and exceptional circumstances, prior to the final disposition of a case and in any event of the cause. The party seeking the order must be impecunious to the extent that, without such an order, that party would be deprived of the opportunity to proceed with the case. The claimant must establish a *prima facie* case of sufficient merit to warrant pursuit. And there must be special circumstances sufficient to satisfy the court that the case is within the narrow class of cases where this extraordinary exercise of its powers is appropriate. *British Columbia (Minister of Forests) v. Okanagan Indian Band*, 2003 SCC 71.

INTERIM DEVELOPMENT CONTROL. A form of land use control exercised by granting of permits at the discretion of the granting body. Used when an official plan is pending. I.M. Rogers, *The Law of Canadian Municipal Corporations*, 2d ed. (Toronto: Carswell, 1971) at 801.

INTERIM DIVIDEND. A dividend paid during a company's financial year.

INTERIM INJUNCTION. A species of interlocutory injunction granted for a very brief period until application for an interlocutory injunction is made.

INTERIM ORDER. 1. " . . . [I]nterim decisions may be reviewed and modified in a retrospective manner by a final decision. It is inherent in the nature of interim orders that their effect, as well as any discrepancy between the interim order and the final order, may be reviewed and remedied by the final order . . ." *Bell Canada v. Canada (Canadian Radio-Television & Telecomunications Commission)* (1989), 38 Admin. L.R. 1 at 30, [1989] 1 S.C.R. 1722, 60 D.L.R. (4th) 682, 97 N.R. 15, the court per Gonthier J. 2. " . . . [A] temporary decision that does not finally dispose of the case before the tribunal." *Bell Canada v. Canada (Canadian Radio-Television & Telecommunications Commission)* (1987), 43 D.L.R. (4th) 30 at 33, 79 N.R. 58, [1988] 1 F.C. 296 (C.A.) Pratte J.A. 3. " . . . [Governs] the rights of the parties from the time it is granted until the issue is resolved finally at trial. . ." *Janssen v. Janssen* (1979), 11 R.F.L. (2d) 274 at 278, 25 O.R. (2d) 213, 1 F.L.R.A.C. 455 (Co. Ct.), Borins Co. Ct. J.

INTERIM RECEIVER. A person appointed under The Bankruptcy Act between filing a petition and making an order judging that the debtor is bankrupt. The property does not vest in the interim receiver. The receiver's function is to preserve the assets of the business. He is not to interfere with the rights of the debtor and he is not to interfere with the debtor carrying on the business in the usual course.

INTERIM RELEASE. See JUDICIAL ~.

INTERIM RELIEF. 1. " . . . [T]emporary relief which is granted pending determination of the application for final or permanent relief. An interim order terminates upon an order being made at trial." *St. Cyr v. Lechkoon* (1991), 36 R.F.L. (3d) 203 at 206 (Ont. Gen. Div.), Kozak J. 2. Interim custody, interim support and interim support pending confirmation or provisional variation. *Divorce Act, 1985*, S.C. 1986, c. 4, ss. 15-19.

INTERIM SUPPLY. A measure to provide a government with money to meet any obligations before its main estimates are approved. A. Fraser, W.A. Dawson, & J. Holtby, eds., *Beauchesne's Rules and Forms of the House of Commons of Canada*, 6th ed. (Toronto: Carswell, 1989) at 260.

INTERIM TERM INSURANCE. Insurance subject to the terms and conditions of the policy for which application is made, in respect of a period of less than one month commencing at such time as the first monthly premium is paid and terminating upon the due date of such premium.

INTER-INSURANCE EXCHANGE. A group of subscribers exchanging reciprocal contracts of indemnity or inter-insurance with each other through the same attorney. See RECIPROCAL OR ~.

INTERIOR. *adj.* Not in direct contact with the weather. *Hull Construction Regulations,* C.R.C., c. 1431, s. 100.

INTERIOR COMPARTMENT DOOR. Any door in the interior of a vehicle installed by the manufacturer as a cover for storage space normally used for personal effects. *Motor Vehicle Safety Regulations,* C.R.C., c. 1038, s. 201.

INTERIOR DESIGN. Carrying out the practice of those functions which have as their object the design of interior space.

INTERIOR DESIGNER. See PROFESSIONAL ~.

INTERIOR LOT. A lot other than a corner lot. Canada regulations.

INTERJURISDICTIONAL CARRIER. A person who engages in the commercial transportation of goods or passengers and who operates for such purpose, (a) one or more motor vehicles licensed or required to be licensed under the Highway Traffic Act and operating inside and outside Ontario, (b) one or more motor vessels operating under the Canada Shipping Act, or (c) railway equipment operated on rails in connection with and as part of a public transportation system. *Fuel Tax Act,* R.S.O. 1990, c. F.35, s. 1.

INTERJURISDICTIONAL IMMUNITY. The . . . constitutional doctrine of interjurisdictional immunity . . . is an exception to the general rule that a valid provincial enactment of general application may apply to and affect federal matters or entities . . . The doctrine renders a valid provincial enactment of general application constitutionally inapplicable to a federal matter if . . . "the effect of the provincial law would be to . . . affect a vital part of a federally-regulated enterprise." The doctrine addresses the issue of the applicability of the provincial law; it does not address the question of its validity, which for the purpose of analysis is assumed. *DFS Ventures Inc. v. Manitoba (Liquor Control Commis-*

sion), 2003 MBCA 33, 225 D.L.R. (4th) 59, 173 Man. R. (2d) 76, [2003] 8 W.W.R. 200, 293 W.A.C. 76 (C.A.).

INTER-JURISDICTIONAL WATERS. Any waters, whether international, boundary or otherwise, that, whether wholly situated in a province or not, significantly affect the quantity or quality of waters outside the province. *Canada Water Act,* R.S.C. 1985, c. C- 11, s. 2.

INTERLINEATION. *n.* Inserting anything into a document after it has been executed.

INTERLINING. A process whereby several carriers participate in the supply of a freight transportation service in the course of a continuous freight movement from the shipper's premises to the customers' premises. The supply of freight transportation services by one carrier of property to a second carrier of the same property (interlining) is a zero rated service for the purposes of the Excise Tax Act [R.S.C. 1985, c. E-15], where the services are part of a continuous freight movement and the second carrier is neither the shipper nor the consignee of the property being transported. *482733 Ontario Inc. v. R.,* 2003 FCA 43, [2003] G.S.T.C. 29, 300 N.R. 54, 2003 G.T.C. 1571 (C.A.).

INTERLOCK. *n.* A component or set of components that prevents the generation of microwave power when access to a cavity is possible. *Radiation Emitting Devices Regulations,* C.R.C., c. 1370, s. 1. See SAFETY ~.

INTERLOCKING. *n.* An arrangement of signals and signal appliances so interconnected that their movements must succeed each other in proper sequence and for which interlocking rules are in effect. It may be operated manually or automatically. *Regulations No. O-8, Uniform Code of Operating Rules,* C.R.C., c. 1175, Part III, s. 2.

INTERLOCKING LIMITS. The tracks between the extreme or outer opposing interlocking signals of an interlocking. *Regulations No. O-8, Uniform Code of Operating Rules,* C.R.C., c. 1175, Part III, s. 2.

INTERLOCKING SIGNAL. A fixed signal at the entrance to or within interlocking limits to govern the use of the routes. *Regulations No. 08, Uniform Code of Operating Rules,* C.R.C., c . 1175, Part III, s. 2.

INTERLOCKING STATION. A place from which an interlocking is operated. *Regulations*

No. O-8, Uniform Code of Operating Rules, C.R.C., c. 1175, Part III, s. 2.

INTERLOCUTORY. *adj.* 1. Incidental to the major intent of an action. 2. Temporary, provisional, not final. 3. ". . . [E]mployed to designate steps in an action intermediate between the initial and final proceeding, and merely leading towards the proceeding which finally terminates the litigation, . . ." *Whiting v. Hovey* (1885), 12 O.A.R. 119 at 125 (C.A.), Patterson J.A. 4. Refers to an order or judgement which does not finally dispose of the rights of the parties.

INTERLOCUTORY APPLICATION. An application in a pending proceeding. *Rules of the Supreme* Court, S. Nfld. 1986, r. 1, s. 1.03.

INTERLOCUTORY INJUNCTION. 1. An order intended to ensure that certain specified acts do not take place until the rights of the parties are finally determined by the court. 2. ". . . [A]n extraordinary and discretionary remedy and one which will not be granted unless the court is satisfied that it is a proper case in which to exercise its discretion. A tripartite test has evolved through the jurisprudence to assist the court in making a decision: (1) has the applicant shown a prima facie/serious issue to be tried; (2) is there a danger of irreparable harm to the applicant, and; (3) does the balance of convenience lie with the applicant." *Imperial Chemical Industries PLC v. Apotex* Inc. (1989), 23 C.P.R. (3d) 1 at 15, 22 C.I.P.R. 201, [1989] 2 F.C. 608, Rouleau J.

INTERLOCUTORY ORDER. "[An order which does not] . . . finally dispose of the rights of the parties . . ." *Hockin v. Bank of British Columbia* (1989), 35 C.P.C. (2d) 250 at 253, 37 B.C.L.R. (2d) 139 (C.A.), Wallace J.A.

INTERLOPER: *n.* Someone who intercepts another persons's trade.

INTERMEDDLE. *v.* To interfere wrongly without any justification.

INTERMEDIARY. See CHEMICAL ~; FINANCIAL ~.

INTERMEDIATE DIVISION. The division of the organization of a school comprising the first four years of the program of studies immediately following the junior division. *Education Act*, R.S.O. 1990, c. E.2, s. 1(1).

INTERMEDIATE ENGAGEMENT. A fixed period of service of a member of the regular force of such duration as is prescribed by regulation. *Canadian Forces Superannuation Act*, R.S.C. 1985, c. C-17, s. 2.

INTERMEDIATE NURSING CARE. Nursing and personal care given by or under the supervision of a registered nurse or registered nursing assistant under the direction of a physician to a resident for less than one and one-half hours per day. Ontario regulations.

INTERMEDIATE PROVINCE. A province (other than Quebec) having a population greater than its population determined according to the results of the penultimate decennial census but not more than two and a half million and not less than one and a half million. *Constitution Act, 1974*, S.C. 1974-75-76, c. 13 reprinted as R.S.C. 1985, App. Document No. 40.

INTERMEDIATE-RUN FERRY. A ship that operates in waters of home-trade voyages or inland voyages, between terminals that are not more than seven miles apart. *Marine Certification Regulations*, SOR/97-391, s. 1.

INTERMEDIATE VOYAGE. A voyage, not being a local voyage or minor waters voyage, that is within the area bounded by meridians of longitude 180°00'W and 30°00'W and the parallel of latitude 6°00'N. *Marine Certification Regulations*, SOR/97-391, s. 1.

INTERMENT. *n.* 1. Burial. 2. Includes cremation. 3. Disposition by (a) burial of human remains or cremated remains in a cemetery, (b) entombment of human remains in a mausoleum, or (c) inurnment of cremated remains in a columbarium. See RIGHT OF ~.

INTERMENT RIGHTS HOLDER. A person with interment rights with respect to a lot and includes a purchaser of interment rights.

INTERMITTENT DUTY. A requirement of service that demands operation for definitely specified alternate intervals of, (i) load and no load, (ii) load and rest, or (iii) load, no load and rest.

INTERMITTENT SENTENCE. Where the court imposes a sentence of imprisonment of ninety days or less on an offender convicted of an offence, whether in default of payment of a fine or otherwise, the court may, having regard to the age and character of the offender, the nature of the offence and the circumstances surrounding its commission, and the availability of appropriate accommodation to ensure compliance with the sentence, order that the sentence be served intermittently at such times as are specified in the order; and that the offender comply with the conditions prescribed in a probation order when not in confinement during the period that the sentence is being served and, if the court so orders, on release from prison after completing the intermittent sentence. *Criminal Code*, R.S.C. 1985, c. C-46, s. 732.

INTERNAL BALLISTICS. The behaviour of a projectile inside the weapon from which it was fired. F.A. Jaffe, *A Guide to Pathological Evidence*, 3d ed. (Toronto: Carswell, 1991) at 213.

INTERNAL COMBUSTION ENGINE. Includes a turbine engine that generates power by the use of fuel.

INTERNAL FLIGHT ALTERNATIVE. In immigration and refugee law, description of the fact situation where a person may be in danger or persecution in one part of his own country but not in another.

INTERNALLY FINANCED TRANSACTION. A buyer purchases assets or shares of a business (a business interest) using that interest or assets to generate enough money to fund a major part or all of the purchase price. A. Bissett-Johnson & W.M. Holland, eds., *Matrimonial Property Law in Canada* (Toronto: Carswell, 1980) at V-12.

INTERNAL NECESSITIES TEST. Assesses whether the exploitation of sex has a justifiable role in advancing the plot or the theme, and in considering the work as a whole, does not merely represent "dirt for dirt's sake" but has a legitimate role when measured by the internal necessities of the work itself. *R. v. Butler*, [1992] 1 S.C.R. 452.

INTERNAL SELF-DETERMINATION. The recognized sources of international law establish that the right to self-determination of a people is normally fulfilled through *internal* self-determination—a people's pursuit of its political, economic, social and cultural development within the framework of an existing state. *Reference re Secession of Quebec*, 1998 CarswellNat 1299, 161 D.L.R. (4th) 385, 228 N.R. 203, 55 C.R.R. (2d) 1, [1998] 2 S.C.R. 217 Per curiam.

INTERNAL USE. 1. Ingestion by mouth or application for systemic effect to any part of the body in which the drug comes into contact with mucous membrane. *Food and Drug Regulations*, C.R.C., c. 870, s. C.01.001. 2. Local or systemic absorption upon introduction into the body or by parenteral route or through a body

orifice. *Health Disciplines Act*, R.R.O. 1980, Reg. 451, s. 1.

INTERNAL WATERS. In relation to Canada, means the internal waters of Canada as determined under the Oceans Act and includes the airspace above and the bed and subsoil below those waters, and in relation to any other state, means the waters on the landward side of the baselines of the territorial sea of the other state. *Interpretation Act*, R.S.C. 1985, c. I-21, s. 35.

INTERNATIONAL AIRCRAFT. An aircraft operating internationally in the transportation of passengers or goods for reward. Canada regulations.

INTERNATIONAL ARBITRATION AGREEMENT. An arbitration agreement in respect of a legal relationship, (a) that involves property that is outside Canada, (b) that envisages substantial performance or enforcement outside Canada, or (c) at least one party to which is domiciled or ordinarily resident outside Canada.

INTERNATIONAL ARBITRATION LAW. The Model Law on International Commercial Arbitration, adopted by the United Nations Commission of International Trade Law on June 21, 1985, as set out in Schedule B.

INTERNATIONAL BILL OF HUMAN RIGHTS. The Universal Declaration of Human Rights and its three supplementary agreements dated December 16, 1966: the International Covenant on Economic, Social and Cultural Rights, the International Covenant on Civil and Political Rights and the Optional Protocol to the International Covenant on Civil and Political Rights which had the effect of extending and elaborating the rights expressed in the Universal Declaration and establishing mechanisms for enforcement through the United Nations.

INTERNATIONAL BORDER PRICE. Of any gas means the price of that gas at the point it crosses the international boundary of Canada as specified in the licence of the National Energy Board authorizing the removal of that gas from Canada or as otherwise prescribed by the Government of Canada. *Natural Gas Price Administration Act*, R.S.A. 1980, c. N-3, s. 13.

INTERNATIONAL BRIDGE. A bridge or tunnel, including the approaches or facilities connected therewith, over or under any waterway being or running along or across the boundary between Canada and any foreign country. *Railway Act*, R.S.C. 1985, c. R-3, s. 9(3).

INTERNATIONAL COMITY. Rules of conduct which are observed in relations between states on account of courtesy.

INTERNATIONAL COURT OF JUSTICE. A judicial body created by the Charter of the United Nations.

INTERNATIONAL CRIMINAL COURT. The International Criminal Court established by the Rome Statute.

INTERNATIONAL CRUISE SHIP. A passenger ship that is suitable for continuous ocean voyages of at least forty-eight hours duration, but does not include such a ship that is used or fitted for the primary purpose of transporting cargo or vehicles. *Criminal Code*, R.S.C. 1985, c. C-46, s. 207.1.

INTERNATIONAL DOCUMENTARY CREDIT. " . . . [I]ntended to give the exporter an assurance of some sort from the banking community that he will, upon proof of performance of his obligations, receive the purchase price, and need not rely on his foreign buyer's willingness or ability to pay for the goods. The assurance is in the form of an undertaking by a bank or banks, in either or both countries, to pay either then or at a later date upon presentation by the seller of documentary proof of shipment in accordance with the contract of sale. The nature of the documentary proof required is precisely stipulated by the terms of the credit." *Michael Doyle & Associates Ltd. v. Bank of Montreal* (1982), 19 B.L.R. 62 at 64, [1982] 6 W.W.R. 24, 39 B.C.L.R. 186, 140 D.L.R. (3d) 596 (S.C.), Taylor J.

INTERNATIONAL EMERGENCY. An emergency involving Canada and one or more other countries that arises from acts of intimidation or coercion or the real or imminent use of serious force or violence and that is so serious as to be a national emergency. *Emergencies Act*, R.S.C., 1985, c. 22 (4th Supp.), s. 27.

INTERNATIONAL FINANCIAL CENTRE. Any business or part of a business (a) that is operated by a corporation; (b) all the activities of which are related to prescribed international transactions; (c) wherein the management of activities leading to such transactions is entirely carried on at Montréal; (d) the activities of which are grouped together in a place separate from that where the other activities of the corporation are conducted, where such is the case; (e) in respect of which the corporation keeps a separate accounting of its operations attributable thereto; (f) in respect of which the corporation holds a certificate in force, issued by a prescribed authority; and (g) that fulfils any other prescribed requirement. *An Act to Amend Various Fiscal Laws and Other Legislation*, S.Q. 1986, c. 15, s. 112.

INTERNATIONAL FLIGHT. A flight between Canada and a place outside of Canada.

INTERNATIONAL JOINT COMMISSION. A body established by the 1909 Boundary Waters Treaty to prevent and solve disputes along the Canada-United States border. It also conducts investigations of issues relating to the 1978 Great Lakes Water Quality Agreement.

INTERNATIONAL LABOUR ORGANIZATION. A United Nations agency dealing with labour conditions and related matters.

INTERNATIONAL LAW. 1. Of two kinds: public international law, a code of rules which controls the conduct of independent nations in their relations with one another and private international law, a branch of municipal law which determines before what nation's courts a certain action or suit ought to be brought and by what nation's law it should be settled. 2. The Model Law on International Commercial Arbitration adopted by the United Nations Commission on International Trade Law on June 21, 1985. *International Commercial Arbitration acts*. See CONVENTIONAL ~; CUSTOMARY ~; PRIVATE ~.

INTERNATIONALLY PROTECTED PERSON. (a) A head of state, including any member of a collegial body that performs the functions of a head of state under the constitution of the state concerned, a head of a government or a minister of foreign affairs, whenever that person is in a state other than the state in which he holds that position or office, (b) a member of the family of a person described in paragraph (a) who accompanies that person in a state other than the state in which that person holds that position or office, (c) a representative or an official of a state or an official or agent of an international organization of an intergovernmental character who, at the time when and at the place where an offence referred to in subsection 7(3) is committed against his person or any property referred to in section 431 that is used by him, is entitled, pursuant to international law, to special protection from any attack on his person freedom or dignity, or (d) a member of the family of a representative, official or agent described in paragraph (c) who forms part of his household, if the representative, official or agent, at the time when and at the place where any offence referred to in subsection 7(3) is committed against the member of his family or any property referred to in section 431 that is used by that member, is entitled, pursuant to international law, to special protection from any attack on his person, freedom or dignity. *Criminal Code*, R.S.C. 1985, c. C-46, s. 2.

INTERNATIONAL MORALITY. A code of conduct which nations may be bound ethically, but not legally, to observe.

INTERNATIONAL ORGANIZATION. 1. Any intergovernmental organization of which two or more states are members. *Foreign Missions and International Organizations Act*, S.C. 1991, c. 41, s. 2. 2. (a) Any specialized agency of which Canada is a member that is brought into relationship with the United Nations in accordance with Article 63 of the Charter of the United Nations, and (b) any international organization of which Canada is a member, the primary purpose of which is the maintenance of international peace or the economic or social well-being of a community of nations. Canada regulations.

INTERNATIONAL PERSONALITY. The status of a person or thing which has duties and rights under international law.

INTERNATIONAL POWER LINE. Facilities constructed or operated for the purpose of transmitting power from or to a place in Canada to or from a place outside Canada. *National Energy Board Act*, R.S.C. 1985, c. N-7, s. 2.

INTERNATIONAL PUBLIC POLICY. A doctrine which states that basic rules of international law override any treaty which is incompatible with them.

INTERNATIONAL RIVER. Water flowing from any place in Canada to any place outside Canada. *International River Improvement Act*, R.S.C. 1985, c. I-20, s. 2.

INTERNATIONAL RIVER IMPROVEMENT. A dam, obstruction, canal, reservoir or other work the purpose or effect of which is (a) to increase, decrease or alter the natural flow of an international river, or (b) to interfere with, alter or affect the actual or potential use of the international river outside Canada. *International River Improvement Act*, R.S.C. 1985, c. I-20, s. 2.

INTERNATIONAL SERVICE. An air service between Canada and a point in the territory of another country. *Canada Transportation Act*, S.C. 1996, c. 10, s. 55.

INTERNATIONAL STANDARD CLASSIFICATION OF OCCUPATIONS. The booklet entitled "International Standard Classification of Occupations" that is published and revised from time to time by the International Labour Organization. *The Occupational Health and Safety Act*, R.S.S. 1978, c. O-1, s. 2.

INTERNATIONAL UNION. A union with locals in both the United States and Canada.

INTERNATIONAL VOYAGE. (a) When used with reference to Load Line Convention ships, means a voyage, not being an inland voyage, from a port in one country to a port in another country, either of those countries being a country to which the Load Line Convention applies, and (b) when used with reference to Safety Convention ships, means a voyage, not being an inland voyage, from a port in one country to a port in another country, either of those countries being a country to which the Safety Convention applies, and, for the purposes of this definition, every territory for the international relations of which a country to which the appropriate Convention applies is responsible or for which the United Nations is the administering authority shall be deemed to be a separate country. *Canada Shipping Act*, R.S.C. 1985, c. S-9, s. 2. See SHORT ~.

INTERNATIONAL WATERS. Waters of rivers that flow across the international boundary between the United States and Canada. *Canada Water Act*, R.S.C. 1985, c. C-11, s. 2.

INTERNATIONAL WILL. A will that has been made in accordance with the rules regarding an international will set out in the annex to the convention regarding international wills.

INTERNEE. See PROTECTED ~.

INTERNET. The decentralized global network connecting networks of computers and similar devices to each other for the electronic exchange of information using standardized communication protocols. *Consumer Protection Act, 2002*, S.O. 2002, c. 30, Sched. A., s. 20.

INTERNET AGREEMENT. A consumer agreement formed by text-based internet communications. *Consumer Protection Act, 2002*, S.O. 2002, c. 30, Sched. A., s. 20.

INTERNUNCIO. *n*. [L.] One who carries a message from one party to another; a representative of the Pope in another country.

INTERNUNCIUS. *n*. [L.] One who carries a message from one party to another; a representative of the Pope in another country.

INTER PARTES. [L.] Between the parties.

INTER-PLANT INEQUITY. An inequality in pay rates between two plants where the same work is done.

INTERPLEADER. *n*. The process by which a person who expects to be or is sued by two or more parties with adverse claims to foods or a debt in the first person's hands, but in which the first person has no interest, obtains relief by arranging that the other parties try their rights between themselves. See STAKEHOLDER.

INTERPOLATE. *v*. To insert words in a finished document.

INTERPOLATION. *n*. The act of interpolating; the words which are inserted.

INTER PONTEM ET FONTEM. [L.] Between the bridge and the stream.

INTERPRETARE ET CONCORDARE LEGES LEGIBUS EST OPTIMUS INTERPRETANDI MODUS. [L.] To interpret and to reconcile laws with other laws is the best method of interpretation.

INTERPRETATIO CHARTARUM BENIGNE FACIENDA EST UT RES MAGIS VALEAT QUAM PEREAT. [L.] The construction of deeds should be made liberally so that the thing fares well instead of coming to nothing.

INTERPRETATIO FIENDA EST UT RES MAGIS VALEAT QUAM PEREAT. [L.] Interpretation should be made so that the thing fares well instead of coming to nothing.

INTERPRETATION. *n*. 1. Construction of a document or statute. 2. Oral translation. 3. A basic rule of interpretation is set out in the Interpretation Acts in the following, or similar, words: Every enactment is deemed remedial, and shall be given such fair, large and liberal construction and interpretation as best ensures the attainment of its objects. 4. It is well accepted that the *Charter* should be given a generous and expansive interpretation and not a narrow, technical, or legalistic one (*Canada (Director of Investigation & Research, Combines Investigation Branch) v. Southam Inc.*, (sub nom. *Hunter v. Southam Inc.*) [1984] 2 S.C.R. 145; *R. v. Big M Drug Mart Ltd.*, [1985] 1 S.C.R. 295; *Reference re s. 94(2) of the Motor Vehicle Act (British Columbia)*, [1985] 2 S.C.R. 486; *Reference re Provincial Electoral Boundaries*, [1991] 2 S.C.R. 158; *Vriend v. Alberta*, [1998] 1 S.C.R. 493). The need for a generous interpretation flows from the principle that the Charter ought to be interpreted purposively. While courts must be careful not to overshoot the actual purposes of the Charter's guarantees, they must avoid a narrow, technical approach to Charter interpretation which could subvert the goal of ensuring that right holders enjoy the full benefit and protection of the Charter. *Doucet-Boudreau v. Nova Scotia (Department of Education)*, 2003 SCC 62, per Iacobucci and Arbour, JJ. 4. Primarily concerned with the spoken word as opposed to the written text. Interpretation as required by the Charter, defined by reference to a number of criteria aimed at helping to ensure that persons with language difficulties have the same opportunity to understand and be understood as if they were conversant in the language being employed in the proceedings. These criteria include, and are not necessarily limited to, continuity, precision, impartiality, competency and contemporaneousness. *R. v. Tran*, [1994] 2 S.C.R. 951. See AMBIGUITY; ASSOCIATED WORDS RULE; COHERENCE, PRESUMPTION OF; CONSECUTIVE ~; CONTEMPORANEOUS ~; CONTEXTUAL APPROACH; EJUSDEM GENERIS; EXTENSIVE ~; GOLDEN RULE; LIMITED CLASS RULE; LIVING TREE APPROACH; MODERN RULE OF ~; PLAIN MEANING RULE; PRESUMPTION AGAINST ABSURDITY; PRESUMPTION AGAINST EXPROPRIATION OF PROPERTY; PRESUMPTION AGAINST IMPLIED REPEAL; PRESUMPTION AGAINST INTERNAL CONFLICT; PRESUMTPION AGAINST INTESTACY; PRESUMPTION AGAINST TAUTOLOGY; PRESUMPTION OF COHERENCE; PRESUMPTION OF CONSISTENT EXPRESSION; PRESUMPTION OF CONSTITUTIONAL VALIDITY; PRESUMPTION OF CONSTITUTIONALITY; PRESUMPTION OF CONTINUANCE; PRESUMPTION OF IMPLIED EXCLUSION; PRESUMPTION OF KNOWLEDGE AND COMPETENCE; PRESUMPTION OF LEGISLATIVE COHERENCE; PRESUMPTION OF LEGITIMACY; PRESUMPTION OF LINGUISTIC COMPETENCE; PURPOSIVE ~;

RESTRICTIVE ~; SHARED MEANING RULE; SIMULTANEOUS ~.

INTERPRETATION CLAUSE. A clause which sets out the meanings of particular words used in that statute.

INTERPRETATION SECTION. A section which sets out the meanings of particular words used in that statute.

INTERPRETER. *n.* At a trial, someone sworn to interpret the evidence of someone else who speaks a language which is not that of the proceedings, a mute or a hearing impaired person.

INTERPROVINCIAL. *adj.* Between provinces.

INTER-REGIONAL ABC (DOMESTIC). *abbr.* Inter-regional advance booking charter (domestic).

INTER-REGIONAL TRANSIT SYSTEM. A transit system that is principally operated, (i) in more than one regional area, and (ii) within the area of jurisdiction of the Authority. *Toronto Area Transit Operating Authority Act,* R.S.O. 1980, c. 505, s. 1.

INTERREGNUM. *n.* [L.] A time when a throne is vacant.

INTERROGATION. *n.* The conduct of an inquiry; the asking of questions particularly in an atmosphere of oppression.

INTERROGATORY. *n.* A written question addressed to one party on behalf of the other party to a cause.

IN TERROREM. [L.] By way of threat. Terrifying.

INTERRUPTIBLE ENERGY. Electric energy made available under an agreement that permits curtailment or cessation of delivery at the option of the supplier.

INTERRUPTIBLE POWER. Electric power made available under an agreement that permits curtailment or cessation of availability at the option of the supplier. *National Energy Board Part VI Regulations,* C.R.C., c. 1056, s. 2.

INTERRUPTIO MULTIPLEX NON TOLLIT PRAESCRIPTIONEM SEMEL OBTENTAM. [L.] Frequent interruption does not remove a prescription which was already obtained.

INTERRUPTION. *n.* Breaking the continued enjoyment of a right. See POSTAL ~.

INTERRUPTION OF EARNINGS. An interruption that occurs in the earnings of an insured person at any time and in any circumstances determined by the regulations. *Employment Insurance Act, 1996,* S.C. 1996, c. 23, s. 2.

INTERSATELLITE SERVICE. A radiocommunication service that provides for communications between space stations. *Radiocommunications Regulations,* SOR/96-484, s. 2.

INTER SE. [L.] Between themselves.

INTERSECTION. *n.* 1. The area embraced within the prolongation or connection of the lateral curb lines or, if none, then of the lateral boundary lines of two or more highways which join one another at an angle, whether or not one highway crosses the other. 2. Includes any portion of a highway indicated by markings on the surface of the roadway as a crossing place for pedestrians. *Highway Traffic Act,* R.S.O. 1990, c. H.8, s. 144(1). See CENTRE POINT OF AN ~; POINT OF ~.

INTERSWITCH. *v.* To transfer traffic from the lines of one railway company to the lines of another railway company in accordance with regulations. *Canada Transportation Act,* S.C. 1996, c. 10, s. 111.

INTER-TRACK BETTING. Pari-mutuel betting at one or more satellite tracks or in one or more places in one or more foreign countries on a race that is held at a host track, where the money bet on each pool at each satellite track or place is combined with the money bet on the corresponding pool at the host track to form one pool from which the pay-out price is calculated and distributed.

INTER-UNION DISPUTE. A conflict between unions with regard to which one should represent a group of employees or as to which one's members should perform work of a certain kind.

INTER-UTILITY TRANSFER. A transfer of any of the following classes, namely, (a) a sale transfer, being a transfer of electric power and energy under a contract of sale, (b) an equi-change transfer, being an interchange of equal quantities of electric power or energy within a stated period, (c) a storage transfer, being an electric energy transfer "banked" for the time being in the form of water in reservoir space of another electrical utility, in the expectation that equivalent electric energy will be returned at a later time, (d) an adjustment transfer, being an electric power or energy transfer for purposes such as to adjust electric energy account balances, to compensate for services rendered, to deliver output entitlements, or to deliver upstream or downstream benefits, or (e) a carrier transfer, being a transfer of electric power or energy wheeled from one electrical utility through circuits of another electrical utility that acts as a carrier for delivery to a third party or to the originating utility. *National Energy Board Part VI Regulations*, C.R.C., c. 1056, s. 2.

INTER-UTILITY TRANSFER POINT. A stated point at which electric power and energy pass from the circuits of one electrical utility into the circuits of another electrical utility. *National Energy Board Part VI Regulations*, C.R.C., c. 1056, s. 2.

INTERVAL. See ESCAPE ~; LUCID ~; PULSE ~.

INTER-VEHICLE-UNIT DISTANCE. For a combination of vehicles means, (i) the distance measured between the centres of the last axle of the tractor and the first axle of the first trailer or semi-trailer, or (ii) the distance measured between the centres of the last axle of the first trailer or semi-trailer and the first axle of the second trailer or semi-trailer, whichever is smaller.

INTERVENANT. *n*. 1. Someone who intervenes in a suit in which he or she was not originally involved. 2. A person or association permitted to make representations in proceedings which do not determine the person's or association's own rights.

INTERVENE. *v*. A person who is not a party to a . . . claims (a) an interest in the subject matter of the proceeding; (b) that the person may be adversely affected by a judgment in the proceeding; or (c) that there exists between the person and one or more of the parties to the proceeding a question of law or fact in common with one or more of the questions in issue in the proceeding . . . (Ontario, Rules of Civil Procedure, r. 13.01).

INTERVENER. *n*. 1. A person who files an intervention or who intervenes. 2. A person or association permitted to make representations in proceedings which do not determine the person's or association's own rights. See INTERVENOR; LOCAL ~.

INTERVENING PARCEL. (a) Any land in an existing district which lies between the point of diversion of water on an irrigation works of the board of that district and an irrigable parcel, and in respect of which the board does not have and did not at any time prior to May 2, 1968 acquire, any legal estate or interest or right permitting it to use that land for the purpose of delivering water from the point of diversion of water on the irrigation works of the board to the irrigable parcel, or (ii) any land, inside or outside the district, on or within which there exists any irrigation works or natural channels or features that from time to time during the 10-year period immediately preceding May 2, 1968 were used by the board of the district for the purpose of carrying water from any irrigation works of the board to any other place, whether or not the board had any legal estate or interest or right permitting it to do so. *Irrigation Act*, R.S.A. 1980, c. I-11, s. 191.

INTERVENOR. *n*. 1. " . . . [D]escribe persons or associations that are permitted to participate in proceedings to promote their own views, though the proceedings will not determine their legal rights." *Canada (Attorney General) v. Aluminum Co. of Canada* (1987), 35 D.L.R. (4th) 495 at 505, 26 Admin. L.R. 18, 15 C.P.C. (2d) 289, 10 B.C.L.R. (2d) 371, [1987] 3 W.W.R. 193 (C.A.), Seaton J.A. (Hinkson J.A. concurring). 2. A newsletter of the Canadian Environmental Law Association. See INTERVENER.

INTERVENTION. See PROTECTIVE~.

INTERVIEW. See EXIT ~.

INTER VIVOS. [L.] Between living people. See GIFT ~.

INTER VIVOS GIFT. A gratuitous transfer of property from the owner (donor) to another person (donee) with the intention that the transfer will take effect immediately and the title to the property will rest in the donee.

INTER VIVOS TRUST. Created by writing, a deed or oral declaration, a trust which is to take effect during the lifetime of the trust's creator. D.M.W. Waters, *The Law of Trusts in Canada*, 2d ed. (Toronto: Carswell, 1984) at 29.

INTESTACY. *n*. The condition or state of dying without a valid will.

IN TESTAMENTIS PLENIUS TESTATORIS INTENTIONEM SCRUTAMUR. [L.] In the case of wills, we examine the testator's intention even more fully.

INTESTATE. *n*. A person owning property who dies without a will.

INTESTATE. *adj*. See PERSON DYING ~.

INTIMIDATION. *n*. 1. Every one who, wrongfully and without lawful authority, for the purpose of compelling another person to abstain from doing anything that he has a lawful right to do, or to do anything that he has a lawful right to abstain from doing, (a) uses violence or threats of violence to that person or his spouse or common-law partner or children, or injures his property, (b) intimidates or attempts to intimidate that person or a relative of that person by threats that, in Canada or elsewhere, violence or other injury will be done to or punishment inflicted on him or a relative of his, or that the property of any of them will be damaged, (c) persistently follows that person about from place to place, (d) hides any tools, clothes or other property owned or used by that person, or deprives him of them or hinders him in the use of them, (e) with one or more other persons, follows that person, in a disorderly manner, on a highway, (f) besets or watches the dwelling-house or place where that person resides, works, carries on business or happens to be, or (g) blocks or obstructs a highway, is guilty of an offence punishable on summary conviction. *Criminal Code*, R.S.C. 1985, c. C-46, s. 423. 2. "The essential ingredients of the tort [of intimidation] are: 1. A threat by one person to use unlawful means (such as violence, or a tort or a breach of contract) so as to compel another to obey his wishes. 2. The person so threatened must comply with the demand rather than risk the threat being carried into execution." *Roth v. Roth* (1991) 9 C.C.L.T. (2d) 141 at 152, 4 O.R. (3d) 740, 34 M.V.R. (2d) 228 (Gen. Div.), Mandel J. 3. Every person is guilty of an offence who (a) by intimidation or duress, compels a person to vote or refrain from voting or to vote or refrain from voting for a particular candidate at an election; or (b) by any pretence or contrivance, including by representing that the ballot or the manner of voting at an election is not secret, induces a person to vote or refrain from voting or to vote or refrain from voting for a particular candidate at an election. *Canada Elections Act, 2000*, S.C. 2000, c. 9, s. 482.

INTOL AND UTTOL. A custom or toll paid for something exported or imported.

INTOLERABLE. *adj*. The circumstances in which a court may refuse to order the return of a child under Article 13 [of the Hague Convention on the Civil Aspects of International Child Abduction, 1980, C.T.S. 1983/35; 19 I.L.M. 1501] are exceptional. The risk of physical or psychological harm or, as alleged in this case, an intolerable situation must be, as set out in Article 13, "grave". The use of the term "intolerable" speaks to an extreme situation, a situation that is unbearable; a situation too severe to be endured. *Jabbaz v. Mouammar* (2003), 38 R.F.L. (5th) 103 (Ont. C.A.).

IN TOTIDEM VERBIS. [L.] In so many words.

IN TOTO. [L.] Completely, entirely, wholly.

IN TOTO ET PARS CONTINETUR. [L.] A part is contained within the whole.

INTOXICANT. *n*. Includes alcohol, alcoholic, spirituous, vinous, fermently malt or other intoxicating liquor or combination of liquors and mixed liquor a part of which is spirituous, vinous, fermented or otherwise intoxicating and all drinks, drinkable liquids, preparations or mixtures capable of human consumption that are intoxicating.

INTOXICATED. *adj*. Under the influence of alcohol to the extent that a person's physical and mental functioning is substantially impaired. *Treatment of Intoxicated Persons Act*, R.S.N.B. 1973, c. T-11.1, s. 1.

INTOXICATING LIQUOR. 1. Includes every spirituous or malt liquor, and every wine, and any and every combination of liquors or drinks that is intoxicating, and any mixed liquor capable of being, used as a beverage, and part of which is spirituous or otherwise intoxicating. *Export Act*, R.S.C. 1985, c. E-18, s. 6(2). 2. Any liquor that is, by the law of the province for the time being in force, deemed to be intoxicating liquor and that it is unlawful to sell or have in possession without a permit or other authority of the government of the province or any board, commission, officer or other governmental agency authorized to issue the permit or grant the authority. *Importation of Intoxicating Liquors Act*, R.S.C. 1985, c. I-3, s. 2. 3. Any fermented, spirituous, beer or malt liquor or combination of such liquors that contain more than 2 1/2 per cent proof spirits. *Air Regulations*, C.R.C., c. 2, s. 82.

INTOXICATING VAPOUR. Any gas, vapour, fume or liquid that is emitted, given off or produced from a regulated matter.

INTOXICATION. *n*. The state of being under the influence of alcohol to the extent that physical and mental functioning is impaired. See INVOLUNTARY ~; SELF-INDUCED ~.

INTRACARDIAL. *adj*. Delivered into the heart. *Animals for Research Act*, R.R.O. 1980, Reg. 18, s. 1.

INTRACEREBRAL HEMORRHAGE. Bleeding into the tissue of the brain. F.A. Jaffe, *A Guide to Pathological Evidence*, 2d ed. (Toronto: Carswell, 1983) at 46.

INTRACRANIAL. *adj*. Within the skull. F.A. Jaffe, *A Guide to Pathological Evidence*, 3d ed. (Toronto: Carswell, 1991) at 154.

IN TRADITIONIBUS SCRIPTORUM, NON QUOD DICTUM EST SED QUOD GESTUM EST INSPICITUR. [L.] In the delivery of deeds, what is regarded is not what was said but what was done.

INTRA FAMILIAM. [L.] Within the family.

IN TRANSIT. Under way, moored to a buoy, secured in a lock or at anchor. Canada regulations.

IN-TRANSIT PASSENGER. A person who arrives by aircraft at a Canadian airport from any country for the sole purpose of reboarding their flight or boarding a connecting flight departing from that airport to a country other than Canada.

IN-TRANSIT PRECLEARANCE PASSENGER. An in-transit passenger who is subject to a preclearance procedure in accordance with the *Preclearance Act*.

IN TRANSITU. [L.] During a passage.

INTRAPERITONEAL. *adj*. Delivered into the abdominal cavity. *Animals or Research Act*, R.R.O. 1980, Reg. 18, s. 1.

INTRATHORACIC. *adj*. Delivered into the thoracic cavity. *Animals for Research Act*, R.R.O. 1980, Reg. 18, s. 1.

INTRA-VEHICLE-UNIT DISTANCE. For a five or six axle vehicle without trailer or semi-trailer means, (i) the distance measured between the centres of the second and the third axles from the front of the vehicle, or (ii) the distance measured between the centres of the third and the fourth axles from the front of the vehicle, whichever is greater.

INTRAVENOUS. *adj*. Delivered into a vein.

INTRA VIRES. [L.] 1. Within the range of authority or power. 2. Said of a law found to be valid because it was enacted under powers allocated to the legislative body which enacted it, by the Constitution.

INTRINSIC. *adj*. Internal; inherent; essential to the nature of.

INTRINSIC EVIDENCE. In libel, relates to the libel itself and to the circumstances of its publication.

INTRINSICALLY SAFE. As applied to electrical equipment or electrical installation means that any sparking that may occur either in the normal use of the electrical equipment or installation or the use of the same under any condition of fault likely to occur therein in practice, is safe, such as to be incapable of causing an ignition of flammable gas, vapour or dust. *Power Corporation Act*, R.R.O. 1980, Reg. 794.

INTRINSIC FRAUD. Courts have drawn a distinction between "intrinsic fraud" and "extrinsic fraud" in an attempt to clarify the types of fraud that can vitiate the judgment of a foreign court. Intrinsic fraud is fraud which goes to the merits of the case and to the existence of a cause of action. The extent to which evidence of intrinsic fraud can act as a defence to the recognition of a judgment has not been as clear as that of extrinsic fraud. The historic description of and the distinction between intrinsic and extrinsic fraud is of no apparent value and, because of its ability to both complicate and confuse, should be discontinued. *Beals v. Saldanha*, 2003 SCC 72, per Major, J.

INTRINSIC VALUE. The price which a piece of property will command in the open market.

INTRODUCED. *adj*. 1. " . . . '[P]resented, tendered or offered'." *Maritime Construction Ltd. v. R.* (1988), [1989] 1 C.T.C. 306 at 307, 93 N.B.R. (2d) 438, 238 A.P.R. 438 (Q.B.), McLellan J. 2. Said of a bill on first reading in a legislature. 3. Said of evidence proffered in a hearing or at trial.

INTRUSION. See INFORMATION OF ~.

INTRUSIVE PROCEDURE. (a) A mechanical means of controlling behaviour, (b) an aversive stimulation technique, or (c) any other procedure that is prescribed as an intrusive procedure. *Child and Family Services Act*, R.S.O. 1990, c. C.11, s. 112.

INUIT. Those persons enrolled from time to time under the terms of Article 35 of the Agreement and includes, in the case of the jointly owned lands referred to in section 0.2.8 of the Agreement, the Inuit of northern Quebec. The agreement is the land claims agreement between the Inuit of the Nunavut Settlement Area and

Her Majesty the Queen in right of Canada that was ratified, given effect and declared valid by the Nunavut Land Claims Agreement Act, which came into force on July 9, 1993. *Nunavut Waters and Nunavut Surface Rights Tribunal Act*, S.C. 2002, c. 10.

INUIT OF NORTHERN QUEBEC. The Inuit of northern Quebec within the meaning of the James Bay and Northern Quebec Agreement that was approved, given effect and declared valid by the *James Bay and Northern Quebec Native Claims Settlement Act*, S.C. 1976-77, c. 32.

INUK. *n.* 1. A person who is a direct descendant of a person who is or was of the race of aborigines commonly referred to as Eskimos and possesses at least one-quarter of Inuk blood. Canada regulations. 2. An individual member of the group of persons referred to in the definition of "Inuit" in subsection 2(1). *Nunavut Waters and Nunavut Surface Rights Tribunal Act*, S.C. 2002, c. 10, s. 152.

INURE. *v.* 1. To come to the benefit of. 2. To take effect.

INUTILIS LABOR ET SINE FRUCTUS NON EST EFFECTUS LEGIS. [L.] Law does nothing useless and fruitless.

IN VACUO. [L.] In a vacuum. Without aim or goal.

INVADIARE. To mortgage or pledge land.

INVADIATUS. *n.* A person who gave surety to appear to answer a charge awaiting settlement.

IN VADIO. [L.] In pledge; in gage.

INVALID. *adj.* 1. Void, having no effect. 2. Physically or mentally incapable of earning financial remuneration.

INVASIVE DEVICE. A medical device that is intended to come into contact with the surface of the eye or penetrate the body, either through a body orifice or through the body surface. *Medical Devices Regulations*, SOR/98-282, s. 1.

INVECTA ET ILLATA. [L.] Ordinary equipment on the premises such as stock-in-trade and furniture which are covered by a landlord's hypothec.

INVENTION. *n.* 1. I conclude that Parliament did not intend to include higher life forms within the definition of invention found in the Patent Act [R.S.C. 1985, c. P-4]. In their grammatical and ordinary sense alone, the words "manufacture" and "composition of matter" are somewhat imprecise and ambiguous. However, it is my view that the best reading of the words of the Act supports the conclusion that higher life forms are not patentable. A higher life form such as the oncomouse is [not] easily understood as either a "manufacture" or a "composition of matter". For this reason, I am not satisfied that the definition of "invention" in the Patent Act is sufficiently broad to include higher life forms. The definition of invention in s. 2 of the *Patent Act* lists five categories of invention: art (*réalisation*), process (*procédé*), machine (*machine*), manufacture (*fabrication*) or composition of matter (*composition de matières*). The first three, "art", "process" and "machine", are clearly inapplicable when considering claims directed toward a genetically engineered non-human mammal. If a higher life form is to fit within the definition of invention, it must therefore be considered to be either a "manufacture" or a "composition of matter". In drafting the Patent Act, Parliament chose to adopt an exhaustive definition that limits invention to any "art, process, machine, manufacture or composition of matter". Parliament did not define "invention" as "anything new and useful made by man". By choosing to define invention in this way, Parliament signalled a clear intention to include certain subject matter as patentable and to exclude other subject matter as being outside the confines of the Act. This should be kept in mind when determining whether the words "manufacture" and "composition of matter" include higher life forms. *Harvard College v. Canada (Commissioner of Patents)*, [2002] 4 S.C.R. 45, Bastarache, J. for the majority. 2. The definition of invention [Patent Act, R.S.C. 1985, c. P-4, s. 2] should be read as a whole and expansively with a view to giving protection to what is novel and useful and unobvious. *Harvard College v. Canada (Commissioner of Patents)*, [2002] 4 S.C.R. 45 (Binnie J. (dissenting) (McLachlin C.J.C., Major and Arbour JJ. concurring)). 2. Any new and useful art, process, machine, manufacture or composition of matter, or any new and useful improvement in any art, process, machine, manufacture or composition of matter.

INVENTIONES. *n.* [*L.*] A treasure-trove.

INVENTOR. *n.* The person who applies for a patent and who invented the thing alone, not because another suggested it or because the person read about it. H.G. Fox, *The Canadian Law and Practice Relating to Letters Patent for Inventions*, 4th ed. (Toronto: Carswell, 1969) at 225.

INVENTORY. *n*. 1. Goods that are held by a person for sale or lease, or that are to be furnished or have been furnished under a contract of service, or that are raw materials, work in process or materials used or consumed in a business or profession. *Personal Property Security acts*. 2. A schedule or list which accurately describes goods and chattels. 3. A stock taking.

INVENTORY VALUATION. See FIFO METHOD OF ~.

IN VENTRE SA MÈRE. [Fr.] In one's mother's womb. See EN VENTRE SA MÈRE.

IN VERBIS NON VERBA SED RES ET RATIO QUAERENDA EST. [L.] In interpreting words, one should look not at their literal meaning but at the intention and the reason of the user.

INVERTEBRATE FOSSIL. The fossilized remains of an animal that did not possess a backbone. *Canadian Cultural Property Export Control List*, C.R.C., c. 448, s. 1.

INVEST. *v*. 1. To transfer possession. 2. To contribute money. 3. To place money in hopes of receiving an increase in the capital or income on the money.

INVESTIGATED PERSON. A person, corporation or other entity with respect to whose conduct a hearing by a review panel is being held or may be held. *Acts regulating professions*.

INVESTIGATION. *n*. 1. The action of investigation. Examining systematically; searching and inquiring. 2. An investigation that (a) pertains to the administration or enforcement of an Act of Parliament; (b) is authorized by or pursuant to an Act of Parliament; or (c) is within a class of investigations specified in the regulations. *Access to Information Act*, R.S.C. 1985, c. A-1, s. 16(4). 3. An investigation related to (i) a breach of agreement, (ii) a contravention of an enactment of Alberta or Canada or of another province of Canada, or (iii) circumstances or conduct that may result in a remedy or relief being available at law, if the breach, contravention, circumstances or conduct in question has or may have occurred or is likely to occur and it is reasonable to conduct an investigation. *Personal Information Protection Act*, S.A. 2003, c. P-6.5, s. 1. See ARCHAEOLOGICAL ~; PERSONAL ~; SUBSURFACE ~.

INVESTIGATIVE INFORMATION. Information respecting a consumer's character, general reputation, personal characteristics or mode of living that is obtained through personal interviews with neighbors, friends or associates of the consumer or with others to whom the consumer is known. *The Credit Reporting Agencies Act*, R.S.S. 1978, c. C-44, s. 2.

INVESTIGATOR. *n*. The person appointed to conduct an investigation. See PERSONAL INFORMATION ~; PRIVATE ~.

INVESTITURE. *n*. 1. The free transfer of possession or seisin. 2. The formal bestowal of office or honour.

INVESTMENT. *n*. 1. A purchase of a security of an issuer or a loan or advance to a person, but does not include a loan or advance, whether secured or unsecured, that is (a) made by mutual fund, its mutual fund manager or its mutual fund distributor, and (b) merely ancillary to the main business of the mutual fund, its manager or its distributor. 2. (a) An investment in a corporation by way of purchase of bonds, debentures, notes or other evidences of indebtedness thereof or shares thereof, or (b) a loan to a person or persons. See AUTHORIZED ~; BUSINESS OF ~; DOWNSTREAM ~; POOLED ~ TRUST; REGISTERED ~; TRUSTEE ~S; UNAUTHORIZED ~ OR LOAN.

INVESTMENT CONTRACT. 1. Investment of money in a common enterprise with profits to come from the efforts of others. 2. A contract, agreement, certificate, instrument or writing containing an undertaking by an issuer to pay the holder thereof, or the holder's assignee or personal representative or other person, a stated or determinable maturity value in cash or its equivalent on a fixed or determinable date and containing optional settlement, cash surrender or loan values prior to or after maturity, the consideration for which consists of payments made or to be made to the issuer in instalments or periodically, or of a single sum, according to a plan fixed by the contract, whether or not the holder is or may be entitled to share in the profits or earnings of, or to receive additional credits or sums from the issuer, but does not include a contract within the meaning of the Insurance Act.

INVESTMENT CO-OPERATIVE. A co-operative: (i) that is incorporated pursuant to The Co-operatives Act; (ii) that has as one of its principal objects, as stated in its articles of incorporation, the investment of its equity capital in accordance with this Act; and (iii) all of whose members are employees of the same employer. *Labour-Sponsored Venture Capital Corporation Act*, S.S. 1986, c. L-0.2, s. 2.

INVESTMENT CORPORATION. A corporation that is approved by the Governor in Council for the purposes of section 146 of the Income Tax Act (Canada) and that issues investment contracts as described in that section.

INVESTMENT COUNSEL. Any person or company that engages in or holds herself, himself or itself out as engaging in the business of advising others as to the advisability of investing in or purchasing or selling specific securities and that is primarily engaged in giving continual advice as to the investment of funds on the basis of the individual needs of each client.

INVESTMENT DEALER. Any person or company that is a member, branch office, or associate member of the Investment Dealers Association of Canada or any person or company recognized by a commission as an investment dealer that engages either for the whole or part of her, his or its time in the business of trading in securities in the capacity of an agent or principal.

INVESTMENT FINANCE COURSE. See CANADIAN ~.

INVESTMENT FUNDS COURSE. See CANADIAN ~.

INVESTMENT PLAN. See INDEXED SECURITY ~.

INVESTMENT SHARE. A share in the capital of a cooperative that is not a membership share. *Canada Cooperatives Act*, S.C. 1998, c. 1, s. 2.

INVESTMENT TRUST. A trust which collects, retains and invests funds for multiple purposes. D.M.W. Waters, *The Law of Trusts in Canada*, 2d ed. (Toronto: Carswell, 1984) at 101. See REAL ESTATE ~.

INVESTOR. *n.* One who invests money in property or in a business venture. See RESIDENT ~.

INVIOLABILITY. *n.* Section 1 of the Charter [of Human Rights and Freedoms, R.S.Q., c. C-12] guarantees the right to personal "inviolability". The common meaning of the word 'inviolability' [pursuant to s. 1 of the Charter] suggests that the interference with that right must leave some marks, some sequelae which, while not necessarily physical or permanent, exceed a certain threshold. The interference must affect the victim's physical, psychological or emotional equilibrium in something more than a fleeting manner. *Québec (Curateur public) c. Syndicat national des employés de l'hôpital St-Ferdinand*, 1996 CarswellQue 916, 202 N.R. 321, (sub nom. *Quebec (Public Curator) v. Syndicat national des employés de l'hôpital St-Ferdinand*) 138 D.L.R. (4th) 577, 1 C.P.C. (4th) 183, [1996] 3 S.C.R. 211, L'Heureux-Dubé for the court.

IN VIRIDI OBSERVANTIA. [L.] Present to people's minds, and fully in force and operation.

INVITATION TO TREAT. A statement which indicates general commercial intent, the wish of that party to contract with another party if they can make suitable arrangements.

INVITEE. *n.* One who is either impliedly or expressly invited to an occupier's premises for some purpose connected indirectly or directly with the occupier's business. In law, a guest is a licensee, not an invitee.

INVITO BENEFICIUM NON DATUR. [L.] A benefit is not given to anyone who did not ask for it.

INVITOR. *n.* A person who invites another to her or his premises for business purposes.

IN VITRO. [L. in glass] In a test tube. F.A. Jaffe, *A Guide to Pathological Evidence*, 3d ed. (Toronto: Carswell, 1991) at 221.

IN VITRO DIAGNOSTIC DEVICE. A medical device that is intended to be used *in vitro* for the examination of specimens taken from the body. *Medical Devices Regulations*, SOR/98-282, s. 1.

IN VITRO EMBRYO. An embryo that exists outside the body of a human being.

IN VIVO. [L.] In a living body. F.A. Jaffe, *A Guide to Pathological Evidence*, 3d ed. (Toronto: Carswell 1991) at 221.

INVOICE. *n.* A written account of the particulars of goods shipped or sent to a purchaser or for labour or services provided.

INVOLUNTARY INTOXICATION. Intoxication which is not self-induced.

INVOLUNTARY PATIENT. A person who is detained in a psychiatric facility.

INVOLVING. *adj.* Including; related to.

IN WRITING. Printing, lithography and other modes of reprinting, or reproducing words in visible form.

IONIZING RADIATION. Any atomic or subatomic particle or electromagnetic wave emitted or produced directly or indirectly by a machine or radioactive isotope and having sufficient kinetic or quantum energy to produce ionization.

IONIZING RADIATION EQUIPMENT. A device capable of emitting ionizing radiation, but does not include: (i) equipment operated at less than 15 kilovolts and not designed principally to produce useful radiation; (ii) equipment that is in storage, in transit or not being used or equipment operated in such a manner that it cannot produce radiation; (iii) any radioactive substance; or (iv) any other equipment or class of equipment specified in the regulations. *Radiation Health and Safety Act*, S.S. 1984-85-86, c. R-1.1, s. 2.

IONIZING RADIATION INSTALLATION. The whole or any part of a building or other place in which ionizing radiation equipment is manufactured, used or placed or installed for use, and includes that ionizing radiation equipment. *Radiation Health and Safety Act*, S.S. 1984-85-86, c. R-1.1, s. 2.

IOTA. *n*. The smallest possible quantity.

IOU. *abbr*. I owe you. The written admission or expression of a debt.

IP. *abbr*. Intellectual property.

IPEA. *abbr*. International Preliminary Examining Authority (under PCT).

IPIC. *abbr*. Intellectual Property Institute of Canada.

I.P.J. *abbr*. Intellectual Property Journal.

IPSE DICIT. [L.] He says it himself.

IPSE DIXIT. [L. one said it oneself] A simple assertion.

IPSISSIMA VERBA. [L.] The very same words.

IPSO FACTO. [L.] By the very same act; by the same fact.

IPSO JURE. [L.] By the very law.

I.R.B. *abbr*. 1. Immigration and Refugee Board. 2. Industrial Relations Board.

IRE AD LARGUM. [L. to go at large] To be set free; to escape.

IRHD. *abbr*. International Rubber Hardness Degrees as referred to in ASTM D 1415-1968, Standard Test Method of International Hardness of Vulcanized Natural and Synthetic Rubbers.

Motor Vehicle Safety *Regulations*, C.R.C., c.1038, s. 2.

IRISH MOSS. The red seaweeds Chondrus, Gigartina and Furcellaria.

IRON BAR. An iron or steel bar five-eighths of an inch square and two feet long pointed at one end and planted in the ground so that the top of the bar is flush with the ground level. *Surveys Act*, R.R.O. 1980, Reg. 927, s. 1. See SHORT STANDARD ~; STANDARD ~.

IRON POST. 1. (i) A pointed iron tube at least thirty-six inches long and three-quarters of an inch in diameter, having the top four inches squared and weighing, at least two and one-half pounds, termed a standard iron post; (ii) solid iron, round or square, at least thirty inches long and three-quarters of an inch in diameter; provided that solid rock the length may be reduced to six inches. *The Land Surveys Act*, R.S.S. 1978, c. L-4, s. 2. 2. An iron or steel tube one and one-quarter inches inside diameter and thirty inches long filled with concrete, fitted with an iron or steel foot plate and a bronze identification cap on the top and planted so that the identification cap is flush with the ground level. *Surveys Act*, R.R.O. 1980, Reg. 927, s. 1.

IRONWORKER. *n*. A person who, (i) in the field, fabricates, assembles, installs, hoists, erects, dismantles, reconditions, adjusts, alters, repairs or services all structural ironwork, precast or prestressed concrete, concrete reinforcing materials, ferrous and non-ferrous materials in curtain wall, ornamental and miscellaneous metal work and all other materials used in lieu thereof and applies sealants where applicable thereto, and moves and places machinery and heavy equipment, and (ii) reads and understands all shop and field drawings, including those taken from original architectural and engineering drawings, that are related to the work operations contained in subclause (i), but does not include a person employed as a shop-man on the fabrication and assembly of materials in an industrial manufacturing plant. *Apprenticeship and Tradesmen's Qualification* Act, R.R.O. 1980, Reg. 44, s. 1.

IRRATIONALITY. *n*. By 'irrationality' I mean what can by now be succinctly referred to as 'Wednesbury unreasonableness' (Associated Provincial Picture Houses Ltd. v. Wednesbury Corp. (1947), [1948] 1 K.B. 223 (Eng. C.A.)). It applies to a decision which is so outrageous in its defiance of logic or of accepted moral standards that no sensible person who had applied his mind to the question to be decided could have arrived at it. Whether a decision falls within this category is a question that judges by their training and experience should be well equipped to answer, or else there would be something badly wrong with our judicial system. To justify the court's exercise of this role, resort I think is today no longer needed to Viscount Radcliffe's ingenious explanation in *Edwards v. Bairstow* (1955), [1956] A.C. 14 (U.K. H.L.) of irrationality as a ground for a court's reversal of a decision by ascribing it to an inferred though unidentifiable mistake of law by the decision-maker. 'Irrationality' by now can stand upon its own feet as an accepted ground on which a decision may be attacked by judicial review. *Council of Civil Service Unions v. Minister for Civil Service* (1984), [1985] 1 A.C. 374, [1984] 3 All E.R. 935 (H.L.), at 410 and 411 [A.C.], Lord Diplock.

IRREBUTTABLE. *adj*. Not rebuttable; not capable of disproof.

IRREFRAGABLE. *adj*. Indisputable; inviolable; undeniable.

IRREGULARITY. *n*. 1. Informality, not according to form. 2. A minor defect.

IRREGULAR LOT. A township lot whose boundaries according to the original plan do not conform within one degree to the bearings shown for the corresponding boundaries of the majority of the lots in the tier in which the lot occurs. *Surveys Act*, R.S.O. 1990, c. S.30, s. 1.

IRREGULARLY-SHAPED LOT. A lot that is not rectangular. *The Local Improvements Act*, R.S.S. 1979, c. L-33, s. 2.

IRRELEVANT. *adj*. 1. Not relevant. 2. Not related to the issue at hand.

IRREPARABLE HARM. 1. A test used in determining whether to grant interlocutory relief. "Irreparable" refers to the nature of the harm suffered rather than its magnitude. It is harm which either cannot be quantified in monetary terms or which cannot be cured, usually because one party cannot collect damages from the other. 2. "[The injury] . . . must be material and one which cannot be adequately remedied by damages . . ." *Spooner Oils Ltd. v. Turner Valley Gas Conservation Board*, [1932] 2 W.W.R. 641 at 646, [1932] 4 D.L.R. 681 (Alta. C.A.), McGillivary J.A.

IRREPLEVIABLE. *adj*. Unable to be replevied.

IRREPLEVISABLE. *adj*. Unable to be replevied.

IRREVOCABLE. *adj*. 1. Not able to be revoked. 2. Of a cheque, can no longer be prevented or recalled by the unilateral action of the payer.

IRREVOCABLE BENEFICIARY. A designation by an insured of a beneficiary. The designation may not be altered or revoked without the consent of the beneficiary during his or her lifetime.

IRREVOCABLE CREDIT. The credit which an issuing bank agrees to consider irrevocable.

IRREVOCABLE LETTER OF CREDIT. " . . . [W]hen a letter of credit is issued and confirmed by a bank, the bank must pay it if the documents are in order and the terms of the credit are satisfied. Any dispute between buyer and seller must be settled between themselves. The bank must honour the credit . . ." *Edward Owen Enrg. Ltd. v. Barclays Bank Internat. Ltd*, [1978] 1 All E.R. 976 at 981 (U.K. C.A.), Lord Denning M.R.

IRRIGABLE UNIT. Land in a district having the same owner and consisting of (a) a quarter-section, a part of a quarter-section described in a certificate of title or a surveyed lot, or (b) lands designated as an irrigable unit by the board pursuant to subsection (2). *Irrigation Act*, R.S.A. 1980, c. I-11, s. 58.

IRRIGATION. See EFFLUENT ~.

IRRIGATION PURPOSE. The use of water for frost protection of grapevines by sprinkling during the growing season is within the statutory definition of "irrigation purpose" in the Water Act [R.S.B.C. 1996, c. 483, s. 1]. *Wagner v. Oliver (Town)*, 2003 BCCA 38, 36 M.P.L.R. (3d) 237, 179 B.C.A.C. 293 (C.A.).

IRRIGATION RATE. The rate imposed per irrigation acre pursuant to a bylaw made under section 118. *Irrigation Districts Act*, R.S.A. 2000, c. I-11, s. 1.

IRRIGATION WORKS. Any structure, device, contrivance or thing or any artificial body of water or watercourse used or to be used by a district and includes, without limitation, (i) any dike, dam, weir, breakwater, drainage works, ditch, basin or reservoir, (ii) any canal, tunnel, bridge, culvert, embankment, headwork, aqueduct, pipe, pump or floodgate, (iii) any contrivance for measuring water, and (iv) any building or fence or other works in any way used in or in relation to the carrying out by a district of its obligations or responsibilities to supply water. *Irrigation Districts Act*, R.S.A. 2000, c. I-11, s. 1.

ISA. *abbr*. International Searching Authority (under PCT).

ISCHEMIA. *n*. The condition of insufficient blood supply to tissue or an organ. F.A. Jaffe, *A Guide to Pathological Evidence*, 3d ed. (Toronto: Carswell, 1991) at 221.

ISLAND. *n*. All land comprising an island, and includes surrounding land attached to and extending from an island, whether or not water flows over or under it. See ARTIFICIAL ~; PUMP ~.

ISOCYANATE. *n*. A substance designated under the Ontario Occupational Health and Safety Act. D. Robertson, *Ontario Health and Safety Guide* (Toronto: Richard De Boo Ltd., 1988) at 5-223.

ISOLATED. *adj*. In respect of an electrical facility, that the facility is separated or disconnected from every source of electrical, hydraulic, pneumatic or other kind of energy that is capable of making the facility dangerous. *Canada Electrical Safety Regulations*, C.R.C., c. 998, s. 2.

ISOLATED WORK PLACE. Any work place that, under normal travel conditions and using the fastest means of transportation that is readily available for emergency use, is more than 2 hours travel time from a physician or hospital. *Canada First-Aid Regulations*, C.R.C., c. 1001, s. 2.

ISOLATING SWITCH. A switch intended for isolating a circuit or electrical equipment from the source of supply of electrical power or energy, but does not include a switch intended for establishing or interrupting the flow of current in a circuit.

ISOLATION. *n*. The separation of a person or animal infected with a communicable disease from other persons or animals for the period of infectivity in a place and under conditions that will prevent the direct or indirect conveyance of the infectious agent from the infected person or animal to a susceptible person or animal. See GUARANTEE OF ~.

ISOLATION ROOM. See SECURE~.

ISP. *abbr*. Internet service provider.

ISSUE. *v*. 1. In respect of an award, means make and publish to the parties to the arbitration. 2. With reference to a disposition that is required to be executed by the holder, means to mail or deliver 2 or more copies of the disposition to the intended holder for execution by him. 3. To release shares, securities or documents. 4. To release stamps.

ISSUE. *n*. 1. A matter in dispute. 2. The first delivery of a bill or note, complete in form, to a person who takes it as a holder. *Bills of Exchange Act*, R.S.C. 1985, c. B-4, s. 2. 3. "... [T]echnical meaning [is] 'descendants' ..." *Davidson, Re* (1926), 59 O.L.R. 643 at 644 (C.A.), the court per Latchford C.J. 4. One who is no longer the child of his or her biological parent can no longer be the issue. *Benefield v. Hrenko Estate*, 2001 CarswellAlta 353, 2001 ABQB 242, [2001] 7 W.W.R. 402, 38 E.T.R. (2d) 175, 92 Alta. L.R. (3d) 168, 287 A.R. 33 (Surr. Ct.), Bensler J. 5. Generally the word "issue" when used in a will is a technical term meaning "all lineal descendants" "of the remotest degree" unless the context of the will displaces this primary meaning and "makes it clear" that "issue" means "children" only. *Acreman Estate, Re*, 2001 CarswellBC 1027, 2001 BCSC 678, 38 E.T.R. (2d) 159 (S.C.), Edwards J. 6. The first delivery of a depository bill or note, complete in form, to the person to whom it is payable. *Depository Bills and Notes Act*, S.C. 1998, c. 13, s. 2. 7. The first release of shares or securities or postal stamps. See DIE WITHOUT ~; DIE WITHOUT LEAVING ~; DYING WITHOUT ~; FAILURE OF ~; FIRST ~ OF STOCK; GOVERNMENT ~; HAVE NO~; IMMATERIAL ~; JOINDER OF ~; MALE ~; OVER~; SUBSTANTIAL ~.

ISSUED. *adj*. Describes an originating process which a registrar dates, signs, seals with the seal of the court and to which a court file number is assigned.

ISSUED CAPITAL. The quantity of shares allotted and issued.

ISSUED TO THE PUBLIC. Merely by placing them on sale, inviting the public to acquire copies; it is unnecessary to advertise or inform the public that publication was made. H.G. Fox, *The Canadian Law of Copyright and Industrial Designs*, 2d ed. (Toronto: Carswell, 1967) at 70.

ISSUE ESTOPPEL. 1. A subcategory of res judicata, and refers to the principle that precludes a party to litigation from seeking a judicial determination of a point of fact that has been determined with finality in another proceeding. *Connaught Laboratories Ltd. v. Medeva Pharma Ltd.* (1999), 1999 CarswellNat 2809, 4 C.P.R. (4th) 508, 179 F.T.R. 200 (T.D.). 2. " . . . [P]revents [the prosecution] from raising again any of the separate issues of fact which the jury have decided, or are presumed to have decided, in reaching their verdict in the accused's favour. . ." *R. v. Greeno* (1983), 6 C.C.C. (3d) 325 at 328, 58 N.S.R. (2d) 261, 123 A.P.R. 261 (C.A.), the court per Macdonald J.A. 3. "The requirements of issue estoppel still remain (1) that the same question has been decided; (2) that the judicial decision which is said to create the estoppel was final; and, (3) that the parties to the judicial decision or their privies were the same persons as the parties to the proceedings in which the estoppel is raised or their privies." *Carl-Zeiss-Stiftung v. Rayner & Keeler Ltd. (No. 2)*, [1967] 1 A.C. 853 at 935, [1966] 2 All E.R. 536 (U.K. H.L.), Lord Guest.

ISSUE MALE. Words which restrict gifts to descendants in the male line.

ISSUE OF OUR MARRIAGE. Words which restrict gifts to the first generation only, children of the marriage.

ISSUER. *n.* 1. A person or company who has outstanding, issues or proposes to issue, a security or a body corporate, (i) that is required to maintain a securities register, (ii) that directly or indirectly creates fractional interests in its rights or property and issues security certificates or uncertified securities as evidence of the fractional interests, (iii) that places or authorizes the placing of its name on a security certificate, otherwise than as an authenticating trustee, registrar or transfer agent, or that otherwise authorizes the issue of a security certificate or an uncertificated security evidencing a share, participation or other interest in its property or in an enterprise or evidencing its duty to perform an obligation, or (iv) that becomes responsible for or in place of any other person described as an issuer. 2. The person who issues a credit card. 3. An issuer of marriage licences. See OFFEREE ~; PRIVATE ~; REPORTING~; SECURITY ~.

ISSUER BID. An offer made by the issuer to acquire or an offer to redeem securities of an issuer, other than debt securities that are not convertible into equity securities.

ITA UTERE TUO UT ALIENUM NON LAEDAS. [L.] Use your own property so that you do not injure your neighbours.

ITC. *abbr.* Inclusive tour charter.

ITEM. *n.* 1. That portion of a vote used for a specific program purpose. *Financial Administration acts.* 2. " . . . [A]ny separate fact or statement . . ." *Goddard v. Barker* (1951), 4 W.W.R. (N.S.) 433 at 437 (B.C. C.A.), O Halloran J.A. 3. " . . . [A] paragraph or a short article. . ." *Goddard v. Barker* (1951), 4 W.W.R. (N.S.) 433 at 437 (B.C. C.A.), O'Halloran J.A. See LETTER-POST ~S; OPTIONAL ~S; PAYMENT ~.

ITINERANT. *adj.* Travelling, on circuit.

ITINERANT EXHIBITOR. A person travelling from one place to another with a moving picture or cinematograph machine or similar apparatus, for the purpose of giving moving picture or cinematograph exhibitions. *The Theatres and Cinematographs Act*, R.S.S. 1978, c. T-11, s. 2.

ITINERANT MACHINE. A motor vehicle, aircraft, trailer or oil well drilling equipment. Alberta statutes.

ITINERANT MERCHANT. A merchant who, personally or through a representative, elsewhere than at his address, (a) solicits a particular consumer for the purpose of making a contract; or (b) makes a contract with a consumer.

ITINERANT SALESMAN. (i) A person who as vendor or agent for the vendor, such vendor not having his principal place of business in the city, goes about from place to place within the city selling goods or offering the same for sale directly to the consumer, or soliciting orders from the consumer for goods, or (ii) a person who goes about from place to place within the city taking orders for goods to be made, grown or completed, in whole or in part, outside the city by any person not having his principal place of business in the city.

ITINERANT SELLER. A seller whose business includes the sale or offering for sale of goods or soliciting of orders for goods at a place other than the seller's permanent place of business, whether personally or by the seller's agent or employee.

ITINERANT VENDOR. Any vendor who, elsewhere than at his address, solicits the signing of a contract of sale from a specified consumer or makes a similar contract with a consumer.

IVDD. A medical device that is intended to be used *in vitro* for the examination of specimens taken from the body. *Medical Devices Regulations*, SOR/98-282, s. 1.

J. *abbr*. 1. Justice. 2. Joule.

J.A. *abbr*. Justice of appeal.

JACKET. *n*. The partial or complete shell of hard metal which surrounds a bullet's soft metal core. F.A. Jaffe, *A Guide to Pathological Evidence*, 3d ed. (Toronto: Carswell, 1991) at 221. See LIFE ~.

JACTITATION. *n*. A false pretension to marry.

JACTIVUS. *adj*. [L.] Lost by default; tossed away.

JACTUS. *n*. [L.] Throwing goods away.

JAIL. *n*. 1. A prison or gaol. 2. Includes a common jail and also includes a jail farm or correctional institution. See COMMON ~; GAOL; MUNICIPAL ~.

JAIL DELIVERY. See GAOL DELIVERY.

JAILER. See GAOLER.

J. BUS. L. *abbr*. Journal of Business Law.

J. CAN. STUDIES. *abbr*. Journal of Canadian Studies (Revue d'études canadiennes).

JDR. *abbr*. Judicial Dispute Resolution.

J.E. *abbr*. Jurisprudence Express.

JELLING AGENT. Gelatin, agar or carrageein.

JEOPARDY. *n*. 1. In the state of being at risk of being convicted of an offence. 2 At risk of self incrimination. See DOUBLE ~; IN ~.

JET-POWERED AIRCRAFT. Any aircraft that, on landing or taking off, is powered by one or more jet engines of the turbo jet, fan jet or any other type of jet engine, but, for greater certainty, does not include an aircraft that, on landing or taking off, is powered by one or more turbo-prop engines. *Toronto Harbour Commissioners' Act, 1985*, S.C. 1986, c. 10, s. 2(1).

JETSAM. *n*. Goods thrown into the sea which sink and stay under water.

JETTISON. *v*. To throw goods overboard to lighten a vessel during a storm, to prevent capture or for any other good reason.

JEWEL. *n*. In respect of a designated article, a part formed of polished natural corundum or synthetic corundum that is incorporated in the mechanism of the article to bear the friction of a moving part or to transmit motion impulses between parts. *Watch Jewels Marking Regulations*, C.R.C., c. 1141, s. 2.

JEWELLER. *n*. Includes watchmaker. *Liens on Goods and Chattels Act*, R.S.N.B. 1973, c. L-6. s. 1.

J.I.B.C. *abbr*. Justice Institute of British Columbia.

JIGGING. *n*. Fishing for, catching or killing fish with a hook or hooks manipulated so as to pierce and hook a fish in any part of the body other than the mouth.

JIGS. *n*. Devices used in the accurate machining of goods in process which hold the goods firmly and guide the working tools.

JITNEY TRANSACTION. A trade made by a brokerage which had no trading privileges on the stock exchange using another firm which has such privileges.

JJ. *abbr*. Judges or Justices.

JJ. A. *abbr*. Judges or Justices of Appeal Court.

J. JUGES PROV. *abbr*. Journal des juges provinciaux (Provincial Judges Journal).

J.L. & SOCIAL POL'Y. *abbr*. Journal of Law and Social Policy (Revue des lois et des politiques sociales).

J

J.M.V.L. *abbr.* Journal of Motor Vehicle Law.

JOB. *n.* A specific assignment of work; a full-time work position.

JOB ACTION. Action taken to enforce a union contract.

JOBBER. *n.* Someone who buys and sells goods wholesale and who sells goods on commission.

JOB CLASS. Those positions in an establishment that have similar duties and responsibilities and require similar qualifications, are filled by similar recruiting procedures and have the same compensation schedule, salary grade or range of salary rates. *Pay Equity Act*, R.S.O. 1990, c. P.7, s. 1(1). See FEMALE ~, MALE ~.

JOB CLASSIFICATION. The rating of jobs based on skills and other requirements.

JOB CONTENT. The actual duties and functions which make up a job.

JOB CREATION PROJECT. A project that is approved by the Commission for the purposes of this section under a designed program primarily to create employment and conducted by the Government of Canada pursuant to any Act of Parliament. *Unemployment Insurance Act*, R.S.C. 1985, c. U-1, s. 25.

JOB DESCRIPTION. A statement of the duties, conditions and purpose of a job.

JOB RATE. 1. The rate of pay for a job. 2. The highest rate of compensation for a job class. *Pay Equity Act*, R.S.O. 1990, c. P.7, s. 1(1).

JOB-SITE STEWARD. A union member representing workers in settlement of disputes arising on job-sites in the construction industry.

JOHN DOE. A made-up name used in legal proceedings for an imagined or unnamed plaintiff.

JOINDER. *n.* Coupling of matters, proceeding together. See MIS~; NON~.

JOINDER OF CAUSES OF ACTION. The coupling of several matters in one proceeding or suit.

JOINDER OF ISSUE. Occurs when, at their time to plead, a party denies one particular part or every part of the previous pleading and does not allege any new facts to a support their case so that the pleadings end completely or to some extent.

JOINDER OF PARTIES. The coupling of people as plaintiffs or defendants.

JOINDER SIMPLICITER. A charge, in the same indictment, of conspiracy to commit an offence and the commission of that offence. M.R. Goode, *Criminal Conspiracy in Canada* (Toronto: Carswell, 1975) at 170.

JOINT. *adj.* Combined; shared between many; possessed by the same party.

JOINT ACTOR. In relation to a person, an associate or affiliate of that person or a person acting jointly or in concert with that person.

JOINT ADDRESS. A House of Commons and Senate resolution which was passed by both Houses of Parliament. P.W. Hogg, *Constitutional Law of Canada*, 3d ed. (Toronto: Carswell, 1992) at 62-3.

JOINT ADVENTURE. A species of partnership which may lack a firm name, may be limited as to time and may restrict the authority of a joint adventurer to pledge the credit of the adventure or the co-adventurers.

JOINT AND SEVERAL. Describes the obligation of two or more persons when all are liable jointly and each is liable severally.

JOINT AND SURVIVOR PENSION. A pension payable during the joint lives of the person entitled to the pension and his or her spouse or same-sex partner and thereafter during the life of the survivor of them. *Pension Benefits Act*, R.S.O. 1990, c. P-8, s. 1.

JOINT AND SURVIVOR PENSION BENEFIT. An immediate pension benefit that continues at least until the death of the member or former member or the death of the survivor of the member or former member, whichever occurs later. *Pension Benefits Standards Act*, R.S.C. 1985, c. 32 (2nd Supp.), s. 2.

JOINT AUTHORSHIP. A collaborative work of two or more authors in which one author's contribution is indistinct from the contribution of any other. H.G. Fox, *The Canadian Law of Copyright and Industrial Designs*, 2d ed. (Toronto: Carswell, 1967) at 244. See WORK OF ~.

JOINT BANK ACCOUNT. An account in the names of two or more persons who have equal rights to it with a right of survivorship.

JOINT BORROWERS. Several physical persons to whom a loan is granted jointly, who jointly operate an economic farm constituted of the aggregate of the farms of which they are the owners or lessees while sharing, according to the proportions determined among them, the income from the aggregate of such farms, provided that not less than sixty per cent of the aggregate of the interests in such farm are owned by one or several farmers. Quebec statutes.

JOINT COMMISSION. See INTERNATIONAL ~.

JOINT COMMITTEE. 1. A group consisting of members of both houses of Parliament, usually with an investigative or administrative purpose. A. Fraser, W.A. Dawson, & J. Holtby, eds., *Beauchesne's Rules and Forms of the House of Commons of Canada*, 6th ed. (Toronto: Carswell, 1989) at 222. 2. A committee appointed by the minister consisting of employers or their representatives and employees or their bargaining agents engaged in the trade in question. *The Apprenticeship and Tradesmen's Qualification Act*, R.S.S. 1978, c. A-23, s. 2.

JOINT CONTRIBUTORY PERIOD. The period commencing on January 1, 1966 or with the month in which the elder of the two spouses reached eighteen years of age, whichever is later, and ending, (a) where both spouses are contributors, with the month in which the later of their respective contributory periods ends, or (b) where only one spouse is a contributor, with the later of (i) the month in which the contributor's contributory period ends, and (ii) the earlier of the month in which the non-contributor reaches seventy years of age and the month in which an application for an assignment of a retirement pension is approved, but excluding, where subsection (6) applies, any month that is excluded from the contributory period of both spouses pursuant to 49(c) or (d). *Canada Pension Plan*, R.S.C. 1985 (2nd Supp.), c. 30, s. 65.1(8).

JOINT CUSTODY. 1. " . . . [S]hared parental responsibility. A joint custody award gives legal custody to both parents, with care and control to one and liberal access to the other." *Baker v. Baker* (1978), 3 R.F.L. (2d) 193 at 196, 95 D.L.R. (3d) 529, 1 Fam. L. Rev. 266 (Ont. H.C.), Boland J. 2. A sharing of power or control over the course of a child's life, both physically and emotionally.

JOINT DEPOSIT. See JOINT BANK ACCOUNT.

JOINT EARNINGS PLAN. Profits are divided between employees and shareholders.

JOINT HEIR. A co-heir.

JOINT HIRING HALL. A place or service sponsored by employers and union for purposes of filling requests for workers.

JOINT INSURED BOND. A bond under which a company is insured jointly with one or more corporations affiliated with the company. Canada regulations.

JOINT INTEREST. 1. Being personally and directly interested in the result of a proceeding along with another person. 2. The admission of any one party cannot be produced in evidence against another party unless that second party has a joint interest with the party making an admission.

JOINT LINE MOVEMENT. Any rail traffic that passes over any continuous route in Canada operated by two or more railway companies. *Western Grain Transportation Act*, R.S.C. 1985, c. W-8, s. 49(2).

JOINTLY. *adv*. 1. " . . . '[T]ogether with'. . ." *Grieve McClory Ltd. v. Dome Lumber Co.*, [1923] 2 D.L.R. 154 at 156, [1923] 1 W.W.R. 989 (S.C.C.), Davies C.J. 2. Can refer to property held by persons as tenants in common or as joint tenants. See ACTING ~ OR IN CONCERT.

JOINTLY AND SEVERALLY. Describes parties who are liable separately or all together.

JOINT OPERATORS. Several natural persons who jointly operate an economic farm constituted of the aggregate of the farms of which they are the owners or lessees while sharing, according to the proportions determined among them, the income from the aggregate of such farms, provided that not less than sixty per cent of the aggregate of the interests in such farm are owned by one or several farmers. Quebec statutes.

JOINT PRACTICE BOARD. Joint Practice Board established to deal with questions relating to the practice of architecture and engineering.

JOINT STOCK COMPANY. In English law, an unincorporated company or large partnership with transferable shares formed in the nineteenth century.

JOINT TARIFF. A tariff that applies to through service by two or more air carriers. *Air Carrier Regulations*, C.R.C., c. 3, s. 2.

JOINT TENANCY. 1. For a joint tenancy to exist there must be four unities, the unity of title, of interest, of time and of possession. 2. " . . . [C]reated where the same interest in real or personal property is passed by the same conveyance to two or more persons in the same right or by construction or operation of law jointly, with a right of survivorship, ie. the right of the survivor or survivors to the whole property." *R. v. Uniacke*, [1944] 4 D.L.R. 297 at 301, 3 W.W.R. 232, 82 C.C.C. 247 (Sask. C.A.), the court per Martin C.J.S.

JOINT TENANT. One who holds an undivided equal interest in the entire property; after death, the survivor acquires the deceased's interest.

JOINT TOLL. A toll that applies to through service by two or more air carriers. *Air Carrier Regulations*, C.R.C., c. 3, s. 2.

JOINT TORT. 1. A breach of duty committed jointly by two or more persons. 2. " . . . [A] common wrongful act by several persons, in which there is but one injuria, giving rise to a joint and several liability by all, and in which each is liable for the whole damage. . ." *Lambert v. Roberts Drug Stores Ltd. (No. 1)*, [1933] 4 D.L.R. 193 at 194-5, [1933] 2 W.W.R. 508, 41 Man. R. 322 (C.A.), the court per Trueman J.A.

JOINT TORTFEASOR. One who is the principal of or vicariously responsible for the other; persons who have a duty imposed jointly upon them which is not performed; when they act in concert toward a common end. To be considered joint tortfeasors the persons must combine mentally together for a purpose except in the case of nonfeasance in breach of a joint duty.

JOINT TRAINING COMMITTEE. A committee formed for the purpose of training apprentices in a designated trade that: (i) consists of employers in the designated trade or their representatives and employees in the designated trade or their bargaining agents; and (ii) is recognized by the minister pursuant to section 24. *Apprenticeship and Trade Certification Act*, S.S. 1984-85-86, c. A-22.1, s. 2.

JOINTURE. *n*. A provision a husband makes to support his wife after he dies.

JOINT VENTURE. 1. An association of two or more person or entities, where the relationship among those associated persons or entities does not, under the laws in force in Canada, constitute a corporation, a partnership or a trust and where, in the case of an investment to which this Act applies, all the undivided ownership interests in the assets of the Canadian business or in the voting interests of the entity that is the subject of the investment are or will be owned by all the persons or entities that are so associated. *Invest-*

ment Canada Act, R.S.C. 1985 (1st Supp.), c. 28, s. 3. 2. I refer to pp. 563-5 of *Williston on Contracts*, 3d ed., (N.Y., 1959). and in particular to p. 563: *Besides the requirement that a joint venture must have a contractual basis*, the courts have laid down certain additional requisites deemed essential for the existence of a joint venture . . . the following factors must be present: (a) A contribution by the parties of money, property, effort, knowledge, skill or other asset to a common undertaking; (b) A joint property interest in the subject matter of the venture; (c) A right of mutual control or management of the enterprise; (d) Expectation of profit, or the presence of "adventure," as it is sometimes called; (e) A right to participate in the profits; (f) Most usually, limitation of the objective to a single undertaking or ad hoc enterprise. . . I regard the foregoing when read with the 1993 supplement as a reasonable and compendious statement of the characteristics of a joint venture. *Canlan Investment Corp. v. Gettling* (1997), 1997 CarswellBC 1380, 37 B.C.L.R. (3d) 140, 10 R.P.R. (3d) 180, 95 B.C.A.C. 16, 154 W.A.C. 16, [1998] 2 W.W.R. 431, 36 B.L.R. (2d) 117 (C.A.), Goldie, J. A. for the court.

JOINT WILL. " . . . [A] will made by two or more testators contained in the same document duly executed by testator and testatrix disposing either of their separate properties or their joint property. It operates on the death of each testator as his will disposing of his separate property and is, in effect, two or more wills . . ." *Ohorodnyk, Re* (1979), 4 E.T.R. 233 at 244, 24 O.R. (2d) 228, 97 D.L.R. (3d) 502 (H.C.), Hollingworth J. See MUTUAL WILLS.

JOIST. See ROOF ~.

JOULE. *n*. The work done when the point of application of a force of one newton is displaced a distance of one metre in the direction of the force. *Weights and Measures Act*, S.C. 1970-71-72, c. 36, Schedule I.

JOURNAL. *n*. A diary or day-book of transactions. See FARM ~.

JOURNALS. *n*. The official and permanent record of proceedings in the House of Commons. A. Fraser, W.A. Dawson, & J. Holtby, eds., *Beauchesne's Rules and Forms of the House of Commons of Canada*, 6th ed. (Toronto: Carswell, 1989) at 299.

JOURNEYMAN. *n*. A tradesman who holds a journeyman's certificate.

JOURNEYMAN ELECTRICIAN. A person who has completed his apprenticeship and holds a certificate of qualification.

JOURNEYMAN PLUMBER. A person who has been issued a certificate of qualification in the trade of plumber under the Trades Qualification Act. *Municipal Act*, R.S.O. 1990, c. M.45, s. 236(12).

JOYRIDE. *v.* " . . . [T]he unauthorized taking of a motor vehicle with the intent to drive or use it temporarily . . ." *Lafrance v. R.* (1973), 23 C.R.N.S. 100 at 115, 13 C.C.C. (2d) 289, 39 D.L.R. (3d) 693, [1975] 2 S.C.R. 201, Laskin J. (dissenting) (Hall and Spence JJ. concurring).

J.P. *abbr.* Justice of the peace.

J. PLAN. & ENV. L. *abbr.* Journal of Planning and Environmental Law.

J. SOCIAL WELFARE L. *abbr.* Journal of Social Welfare Law.

JUDEX AD QUEM. [L.] A judge to whom one makes an appeal.

JUDEX AEQUITATEM SEMPER SPECTARE DEBET. [L.] A judge should always bear equity in mind.

JUDEX A QUO. [L.] A judge from whom one makes an appeal.

JUDEX EST LEX LOQUENS. [L.] A judge is the law speaking.

JUDEX NON REDDIT PLUS QUAM QUOD PETENS IPSE REQUIRIT. [L.] A judge does not give more than what the very plaintiff requests.

JUDGE. *n.* 1. The person authorized to determine any question or cause in a court. 2. Includes any person lawfully presiding in a court. See ASSOCIATE CHIEF ~; CHIEF ~; CITIZENSHIP ~; NO MAN SHALL BE ~ IN HIS OWN CAUSE; PRESIDING~; PROVINCIAL COURT ~; SENIOR COUNTY COURT ~; SENIOR ~; TERRITORIAL ~; TRIAL ~S; YOUTH COURT ~.

JUDGE ADVOCATE GENERAL. The Judge Advocate General acts as legal adviser to the Governor General, the Minister, the Department and the Canadian Forces in matters relating to military law. The Judge Advocate General has the superintendence of the administration of military justice in the Canadian Forces.

JUDGE-MADE LAW. The common law which includes the interpretation of statutes and

subordinate legislation by the courts. Contrasted to statute law.

JUDGE OF THE EXCHEQUER COURT. The President or a puisne judge of that Court. *Admiralty Act*, R.S.C. 1970, c. A-1, s. 2.

JUDGE SHOPPING. Using the Crown's scheduling privilege to get the case before a judge of its own choosing. *R. v. Regan*, [2002] 1 S.C.R. 297 [Per Binnie J. (dissenting) (Iacobucci, Major, Arbour JJ. concurring)].

JUDGE'S NOTES. Notes usually taken by a judge when evidence is given viva voce.

JUDGES' RULES. Procedures devised in England which govern the taking of statements by police.

JUDGMENT. *n.* 1. A judicial decision; the determination of a court; a court's sentence or decision on the major question in a proceeding. 2. Includes orders. *Muzak Corp. v. C.A.P.A.C.*, [1953] 2 S.C.R. 182 at 196-7, 13 Fox Pat. C. 168, 19 C.P.R. 1, Cartwright J. 3. The reasons a court gives for a decision. 4. A judgment or an order of a court in any civil proceedings whereby any sum of money is payable, and includes an award in proceedings on an arbitration if the award has, in pursuance of the law in force in the province or territory where it was made, become enforceable in the same manner as a judgment given by a court therein. 5. Any decision, however described (judgment, order and the like), given by a court in a civil or commercial matter, and includes an award in proceedings on an arbitration if the award has become enforceable in the territory of origin in the same manner as a 'judgment' given by a court in that territory. *Reciprocal Enforcement of Judgment (U.K.) acts*: 6. When used with reference to the court appealed from, includes any judgment, rule, order, decision, decree, decretal order or sentence thereof, and when used with reference to the Supreme Court, includes any judgment or order of that Court. *Supreme Court Act*, R.S.C. 1985, c. S-26, s. 2. See AMOUNT DUE ON THE ~; CONSENT ~; DECLARATORY ~; DEFAULT ~; ENTER ~; FINAL ~; FOREIGN ~; MERGER INTO ~; MOTION FOR ~; PECUNIARY ~; SUMMARY ~.

JUDGMENT CREDITOR. 1. The person by whom the judgment was obtained, and includes the executors, administrators, successors and assigns of that person. 2. The person in whose favour the judgment was given, and includes that person's executors, administrators, successors and assigns. 3. A person in whose favour an order for maintenance has been made. See REGISTERED ~.

JUDGMENT DEBT. A sum of money or any costs, charges or expenses made payable by or under a judgment in a civil proceeding.

JUDGMENT DEBTOR. 1. Includes a party required to make a payment of money and costs, or either, under an order, and any executor, administrator or assignee of a judgment debtor. 2. The person against whom the judgment was given and includes any person against whom the judgment is enforceable under the law of the territory of origin. 3. The person liable for the payment of money payable under a judgment or order. 4. A person against whom a maintenance order has been given. 5. A person named in a garnishee summons in respect of whom garnishable moneys are sought to be garnisheed under this Part. *Family Orders and Agreements Enforcement Assistance Act*, R.S.C. 1985, c. 4, s. 23.

JUDGMENT FIRST GIVEN. (a) Shall, in a case where a judgment is reversed on appeal, be construed as a reference to the judgment first given that is not so reversed, and (b) shall, in a case where a judgment is varied on appeal, be construed as a reference to that judgment as so varied. *Tort-Feasors acts.*

JUDGMENT IN PERSONAM. One which determines the rights, liabilities and interests of the parties to the litigation only.

JUDGMENT IN REM. 1. " . . . [A]n adjudication pronounced upon the status of some particular subject matter by a tribunal having competent authority for that purpose. Such an adjudication being a solemn declaration from the proper and accredited quarter that the status of the thing adjudicated upon is as declared, concludes all persons from saying that the status of the thing adjudicated upon as not such as declared by the adjudication." *Sleeth v. Hurlbert* (1896), 25 S.C.R. 620 at 630, 3 C.C.C. 197, Sedgewick J. (Gwynne, King and Girouard JJ. concurring). 2. Examples of these are an action in maritime law concerning the status of a ship, a divorce decree, a bankruptcy adjudication, a judgment concerning the validity of a patent, a declaration of mental incapacity, a grant of administration. Such a judgment is notice to all who deal with a person or thing on which the court has pronounced concerning the status of that person or thing. See IN REM.

JUDGMENT ORDER. Includes any sum of money or any costs, charges or expenses made payable by or under any judgment of a court in any civil proceeding. *Judgment Interest Act*, S. Nfld. 1983, c. 81, s. 2.

JUDGMENT SUMMONS. An order requiring a judgment debtor to appear to be examined in front of a judge or court officer.

JUDICES NON TENENTUR EXPRIMERE CAUSAM SENTENTIAE SUAE. [L.] Judges are not required to explain the reason for their decisions.

JUDICIA IN CURIA REGIS REDDITA NON ADNIHILENTUR, SED STENT IN SUO ROBORE, QUOUSQUE PER ERROR AUT ATTINCTAM ADNULLENTUR. [L.] Judgments given in the monarch's court should not be thought of as nothing, but should stand in full force until they are reversed through error or attaint.

JUDICIA IN DELIBERATIONIBUS CREBRO MATURESCUNT, IN ACCELERATO PROCESSU NUNQUAM. [L.] Judgments often ripen through deliberation, never in a hurried process.

JUDICIAL. *adj.* 1. Relating to judges. 2. Having the quality of being judge-like. 3. " . . . [T]he question of whether any particular function is 'judicial' is not to be determined simply on the basis of procedural trappings. The primary issue is the nature of the question which the tribunal is called upon to decide. Where the tribunal is faced with a private dispute between parties, and is called upon to adjudicate through the application of a recognized body of rules in a manner consistent with fairness and impartiality, then normally, it is acting in a 'judicial capacity' . . . the judicial task involves questions of 'principle', that is consideration of the competing rights of individuals or groups. This can be contrasted with questions of 'policy' involving competing views of the collective good of the community as a whole . . ." *Reference re Residential Tenancies Act* (1981), (*sub nom. Residential Tenancies Act of Ontario, Re*) 123 D.L.R. (3d) 554 at 571, [1981] 1 S.C.R. 714, 37 N.R. 158, Dickson J.

JUDICIAL ACT. " . . . [A]n act done by competent authority upon consideration of acts and circumstances, and imposing liability or affecting the rights of others." *The Queen v. Corporation of Dublin* (1878), 2 L.R. Ir. 371 at 377, May C.J.

JUDICIAL ADMISSION. A formal admission. An admission made by a party in pleadings.

JUDICIAL CENTRE. A judicial centre of the Trial Division established pursuant to this Act. *Judicature Act*, S. Nfld. 1986, c. 42, s. 2.

JUDICIAL COMMITTEE. A committee of the Privy Council of the United Kingdom made up of Privy Councillors who are judges. They advise the Queen how to dispose of each appeal, and their advice is considered to be a binding judgment. Historically, this was the final court of appeal for Canada.

JUDICIAL COMMITTEE OF THE PRIVY COUNCIL. The final appeal court from every colonial court. It continues as a Commonwealth court for Commonwealth nations which have retained that appeal.

JUDICIAL COSTS. Costs provided for in the tariff, and taxable by the competent officer of a court. *Barreau du Québec Act*, R.S.Q. 1977, c. B-1, s. 1.

JUDICIAL COUNCIL. See CANADIAN ~; ONTARIO ~.

JUDICIAL DECISION. Determined by the identity of the person making the decision, the fact that the rights of persons are affected by the decision, and by the duty on the decision-maker to act judicially.

JUDICIAL DEFERENCE. The degree to which a court will refrain from interfering with a decision of an administrative tribunal or a lower court. Factors such as public interest, expertise of the tribunal, the courts' treatment of a tribunal historically and the existence and type of privative clause in place are important in determining which standard of deference will be applied. See CORRECTNESS; PATENTLY UNREASONABLE; STANDARD OF REVIEW; UNREASONABLE.

JUDICIAL DICTA. " . . . [C]onsist of considered enunciations of the judges opinions of the law on some point which does not arise for decision on the facts of the case before him, and so is not part of the ratio decidendi . . ." *Richard West & Partners (Inverness) Ltd. v. Dick* (1968), [1969] 1 All E.R. 289 at 292 (U.K. Ch.), Megarry J.

JUDICIAL DISCRETION. During a trial, the freedom of a judge to summarily decide certain matters which cannot afterwards be questioned.

JUDICIAL DISPUTE RESOLUTION. A term used in Alberta to refer to alternate dispute resolution (ADR). Abbreviated as JDR. Refers to a range of procedures from variations within the pre-trial conference process to mini-trials.

JUDICIAL DISTRICT. A territory, county or district in respect of which a judge has been appointed to exercise judicial functions. *Canada Elections Act*, R.S.C. 1985, c. E-2, s. 2.

JUDICIAL IMMUNITY. " . . . [A] judge of a superior court is protected when he is acting in the bona fide exercise of his office and under the belief that he has jurisdiction, though he may be mistaken in that belief and may not in truth have any jurisdiction . . ." *Sirros v. Zoore*, [1974] 3 All E.R. 776 at 784 (U.K.), Lord Denning M.R.

JUDICIAL INDEPENDENCE. 1. " . . . [T]he generally accepted core of the principle of judicial independence has been the complete liberty of individual judges to hear and decide the cases that come before them: no outsider—be it government, pressure group, individual or even another judge—should interfere in fact or attempt to interfere with the way in which a judge conducts his or her case and makes his or her decision." *R. v. Beauregard (sub nom. Beauregard v. Canada)*, [1986] 2 S.C.R. 56 at 69, 73, 70 N.R. 1, 30 D.L.R. (4th) 481, 26 C.R.R. 59, Dickson C.J. (Estey J. and Laskin JJ. concurring). 2. Three conditions that are prerequisites for judicial independence. These are security of tenure, financial security and institutional independence with respect to matters of administration bearing directly on the exercise of the court's judicial function. *Lippé c. Charest* (1990), (*sub nom. R. c. Lippé*) [1991] 2 S.C.R. 114, per Le Dain J. 3. " . . . [I]ncludes both independence from government and independence from the parties to the litigation." *Lippé v. Charest* (1991), 5 M.P.L.R. (2d) 113 at 152, 64 C.C.C. (3d) 513, 128 N.R. 1, 39 Q.A.C. 241, 5 C.R.R. (2d) 31 (S.C.C.), Gonthier J. (La Forest, L'Heureux-Dubé and McLachlin JJ. concurring). 4. " . . . Security of tenure . . . financial security. . . the institutional independence of the tribunal with respect to matters of administration bearing directly on the exercise of its judicial function . . ." *R. v. Valente No. 2* (1985), 19 C.R.R. 354 at 368, 372, 376, 379-80, [1985] 2 S.C.R. 673, 52 O.R. (2d) 779, 37 M.V.R. 9, 49 C.R. (3d) 97, 23 C.C.C. (3d) 193, 24 D.L.R. (4th) 161, 64 N.R. 1, 14 O.A.C. 79, [1985] D.L.Q. 85n, the court per Le Dain J. See INSTITUTIONAL INDEPENDENCE.

JUDICIAL INTERIM RELEASE. 1. Bail. 2. The judge's setting free the accused between committal for trial and the trial's completion.

JUDICIAL KNOWLEDGE. Refers to documents which the court knows or suspects exist and which the court would likely consult on its own initiative. *Quebec (Attorney General). v. Eastmain Band,* (sub nom. *Eastmain Band v. Canada (Federal Administrator))* [1992] 3 F.C. 800 (C.A.).

JUDICIAL LEGISLATION. Growth or advancement of law through a judicial decision.

JUDICIALLY. *adv.* The expression most often used in the Federal Court is that a discretion must be exercised "judicially". That term is taken to mean that if a decision were made in bad faith, that is for an improper purpose or motive, in a discriminatory manner, or the decision-maker ignored a relevant factor or considered an irrelevant one, then the decision must be set aside. [Whether or not a factor is relevant may be in issue.] The same fate awaits a decision based on a mistaken principle of law or a misapprehension of the facts (as opposed to inferences drawn from accepted facts) or what is commonly referred to as a "palpable and overriding error". *Suresh v. Canada (Minister of Citizenship & Immigration),* 2000 CarswellNat 25, 183 D.L.R. (4th) 629, 5 Imm. L.R. (3d) 1, 252 N.R. 1, 18 Admin. L.R. (3d) 159, [2000] 2 F.C. 592, 180 F.T.R. 57 (note) (C.A.) Robertson J.A. for the court.

JUDICIAL NOTICE. 1. The acceptance of a fact without proof. It applies to two kinds of facts: facts which are so notorious as to not be the subject of dispute among reasonable persons; and facts that are capable of immediate and accurate demonstration by resorting to readily accessible sources of indisputable accuracy. *R. v. Williams,* [1998] 1 S.C.R. 1128. 2. One classic statement of the content and purpose of the doctrine is outlined in Varcoe v. Lee, 181 P. 223 (U.S. Cal., 1919), at p. 226: The three requirements . . . that the matter be one of common and general knowledge, that it be well established and authoritatively settled, be practically indisputable, and that this common, general, and certain knowledge exist in the particular jurisdiction—all are requirements dictated by the reason and purpose of the rule, which is to obviate the formal necessity for proof when the matter does not require proof. *Moge v. Moge,* [1992] 3 S.C.R. 813, per L'Heureux-Dube, J.

JUDICIAL OFFICE. The office of a judge of a superior or county court or of the Tax Court of Canada. *Judges Act,* R.S.C. 1985, c. J-1, s. 42(4).

JUDICIAL OFFICER. See BRIBERY OF ~.

JUDICIAL OR QUASI-JUDICIAL PROCEEDING. "It is possible . . . to formulate several criteria for determining whether a decision or order is one required by law to be made on a judicial or quasi-judicial basis. The list is not intended to be exhaustive. (1) Is there anything in the language in which the function is conferred or in the general context in which it is exercised which suggests that a hearing is contemplated before a decision is reached? (2) Does the decision or order directly or indirectly affect the rights and obligations of persons? (3) Is the adversary process involved? (4) Is there an obligation to apply substantive rules to many individual cases rather than . . . in a broad sense?" *Minister of National Revenue v. Coopers & Lybrand,* [1979] 1 S.C.R. 495 at 504, 92 D.L.R. (3d) 1, [1978] C.T.C. 829, 78 D.T.C. 6258, the court per Dickson J.

JUDICIAL PROCEEDING. 1. A proceeding (a) in or under the authority of a court of justice, (b) before the Senate or House of Commons or a committee of the Senate or House of Commons, or before a legislative council, legislative assembly or house of assembly or a committee thereof that is authorized by law to administer an oath, (c) before a court, judge, justice, provincial court judge or coroner, (d) before an arbitrator or umpire, or a person or body of persons authorized by law to make an inquiry and take evidence therein under oath, or (e) before a tribunal by which a legal right or legal liability may be established, whether or not the proceeding is invalid for want of jurisdiction or for any other reason. *Criminal Code,* R.S.C. 1985, c. C-46, s. 118 as am. by R.S.C. 1985 (1st Supp.), c. 27, s. 15. 2. Includes any action, suit, cause, matter or other proceeding in disposing of which the court appealed from has not exercised merely a regulative, administrative or executive jurisdiction. *Supreme Court Act,* R.S.C. 1985, c. 26, s. 2. 3. A proceeding of a court of record. *Judicature Act,* R.S.O. 1980, c. 223, s. 67.

JUDICIAL REVIEW. 1. The right of a court to investigate and question the validity of any legislation enacted by a Canadian legislative body. 2. The power of the court to review the actions and decisions of administrative decision-makers. It is not an investigation into the appropriateness of the result, but is an investigation into the propriety of the processes which brought about that result. 3. Refers to any relief that the applicant would be entitled to in any one or more of the following: Proceedings by way of application for an order in the nature of mandamus, prohibition or certiorari. Proceedings by way of an action for a declaration or for an injunction, or both, in relation to the exercise, refusal to exercise or proposed or purported exercise of a statutory power. *Judicial Review Procedure Act*, R.S.O. 1990, c. J-1, s. 2. 4. The control of the executive action by the courts.

JUDICIAL SEPARATION. A decree which does not affect status of a married couple but simply acknowledges the deterioration of a union. J.G. McLeod, *The Conflict of Laws* (Calgary: Carswell, 1983) at 702.

JUDICIAL STAY. A stay of prosecution granted by a court. Amounts to an acquittal. The court effectively brings the proceedings to a final conclusion in favour of the accused. The accused has the right not to have the judicially stayed allegations raised as similar fact evidence in subsequent proceedings.

JUDICIA POSTERIORA SUNT IN LEGE FORTIORA. [L.] In law, later decisions are stronger.

JUDICIARY. *n*. The bench, the judges collectively.

JUDICIA SUUM EFFECTUM HABERE DEBENT. [L.] Judgments ought to have their own effect.

JUDICI OFFICIUM SUUM EXCEDENTI NON PARETUR. [L.] One does not give effect to the decision of a judge who exceeded jurisdiction.

JUDICIS EST JUS DICERE, NON DARE. [L.] It is a judge's duty to declare existing law, not to make new law.

JUDICIS OFFICIUM EST OPUS DIEI IN DIE SUO PERFICERE. [L.] It is a judge's duty to finish each day's work during that day.

JUDICIS OFFICIUM EST UT RES ITA TEMPORA RERUM QUAERERE. [L.] It is a judge's duty to query both the time of things and things themselves.

JUDICIUM A NON SUO JUDICE DATUM NULLIUS EST MOMENTI. [L.] A judgment given with no proper jurisdiction has no effect in law.

JUDICIUM NON DEBET ESSE ILLUSORIUM. [L.] A judgment should not be considered to be mocking.

JUDICIUM REDDITUR IN INVITUM. [L.] Judgment is pronounced against one, willing or not.

JUDICIUM SEMPER PRO VERITATE ACCIPITUR. [L.] A judgment is always accepted as truth.

JULIENNE. *adj*. Means potatoes cut into straight cut strips that are predominantly 1/4 by 1/4 inch or less in cross-sectional dimensions. *Processed Fruit and Vegetable Regulations*, C.R.C., c. 291, Schedule I, s. 44.

JUMP PRINCIPLE. The proposition that successive sentences to an offender should be increased gradually rather than by "jumps." *R. v. M. (A.)* (1996), 30 O.R. (3d) 313 (C.A. [In Chambers]).

JUNIOR. *n*. A person who is at least thirteen years of age but who has not yet attained the age of eighteen years. *Ontario Place Corporation Act*, R.R.O. 1980, Reg. 732, s. 1.

JUNIOR. *adj*. Younger; of lower rank.

JUNIOR DEPARTMENT STORE. A retailing entity which sells the same wide range of goods that are sold in traditional, major department stores and which is popularly called a discount operation.

JUNIOR DIVISION. The division of the organization of an elementary school comprising the first three years of the program of studies immediately following the primary division. *Education Act*, R.S.O. 1990, c. E.2, s. 1(1).

JUNIOR FOOD. A food that normally contains particles of a size to encourage chewing by infants, but may be readily swallowed by infants without chewing. *Food and Drug Regulations*, C.R.C., c. 870, s. B.25.001.

JUNK. *n*. 1. Unserviceable, discarded or junked motor vehicles or other machinery, and includes bodies, engines or other component parts thereof. *Highway Act*, R.S.N.B. 1973, c. H-5, s. 58. 2. Narcotics. F.A. Jaffe, *A Guide to Pathological Evidence*, 3d ed. (Toronto: Carswell, 1991) at 222.

JUNK MAIL. Third class mail, flyers and unaddressed advertisements.

JUNKIE. *n*. An addict to narcotics. F.A. Jaffe, *A Guide to Pathological Evidence*, 3d ed. (Toronto: Carswell, 1991) at 222.

JUNKIE'S LUNG. Lungs exhibiting microscopic spots of chronic inflammation caused by intravenously injecting insoluble material like talcum powder or starch granules. F.A. Jaffe, *A Guide to Pathological Evidence*, 3d ed. (Toronto: Carswell, 1991) at 222.

JUNK YARD. See AUTOMOBILE ~.

JURA EODEM MODO DESTITUUNTUR QUO CONSTITUUNTUR. [L.] Laws are abrogated in the same way as they are made.

JURA IN PERSONAM. [L.] Contractual rights. G.H.L. Fridman, *Sale of Goods in Canada*, 3d ed. (Toronto: Carswell, 1986) at 29.

JURA IN REM. [L.] Property rights. G.H.L. Fridman, *Sale of Goods in Canada*, 3d ed. (Toronto: Carswell, 1986) at 29-30.

JURAMENTUM EST INDIVISIBLE, ET NON EST ADMITTENDUM IN PARTE VERUM ET IN PARTE FALSUM. [L.] An oath may not be divided and may not be admitted as in part true and in part false.

JURA NATURAE SUNT IMMUTABILIA. [L.] The laws of nature are immutable.

JURA NOVIT CURIA. [L.] The court knows the law.

JURA PERSONARUM. [L.] The right of people.

JURA PUBLICA ANTEFERENDA PRIVATIS. [L.] Public rights should be put before private.

JURA PUBLICA EX PRIVATO PROMISCUE DECIDI NON DEBENT. [L.] Public rights should not to be decided obiter out of a private transaction.

JURARE EST DEUM IN TESTEM VOCARE, ET EST ACTUS DIVINI CULTUS. [L.] To swear is to call a deity to witness, and is an act of religious worship.

JURA REGALIA. [L.] Rights of a sovereign.

JURA REGIS SPECIALIA NON CONCEDUNTUR PER GENERALIA VERBA. [L.] No special rights are conceded to a monarch by general words.

JURA RERUM. [L.] The rights which someone may acquire in things.

JURA SANGUINIS NULLO JURE CIVILI DIRIMI POSSUNT. [L.] The rights of blood cannot be brought to naught by any right which arises out of law.

JURA SUB IMPERII. [L.] The supreme rights of sovereignty or control.

JURAT. *n*. [L.] A clause at the bottom of an affidavit which states where, when and before whom that affidavit was sworn.

JURATION. *n*. Swearing; administering an oath.

JURATO CREDITUR IN JUDICIO. [L.] At a trial, a sworn statement is credited.

JURATOR. *n*. [L.] A juror.

JURATORES DEBENT ESSE VICINI, SUFFICIENTES, ET MINUS SUSPECTI. [L.] Jurors should be neighbours of adequate estate, and beyond suspicion of partiality.

JURATORES SUNT JUDICES FACTI. [L.] Jurors are the judges of fact.

JURE CORONAE. [L.] In the right of the Crown.

JURE DIVINO. [L.] By sacred right.

JURE EMPHYTEUTICO. [L.] By the law relating to rents and services.

JURE MARITI. See JUS MARITI.

JURE NATURAE AEQUUM EST NEMINEM CUM ALTERIUS DETRIMENTO ET INJURIA FIERI LOCUPLETIOREM. [L.] By the law of nature, it is fair that no one be enriched by loss or injury to another.

JURE UXORIS. [L.] In right of the wife.

JURICERT. An online professional authentication service which creates a digital credential for each lawyer to use when carrying out electronic filing in government or court offices.

JURIDICAL. *adj*. Relating to the administration of justice.

JURIDICAL DAY. A day on which one may transact legal business.

JURI NON EST CONSONUM QUOD ALIQUIS ACCESSORIUS IN CURIA REGIS CONVINCATUR ANTEQUAM ALIQUIS DE FACTO FUERIT ATTINCTUS. [L.] It is not lawful that some accessory should be convicted in the monarch's court before anyone else has been affected by the deed.

JURISDICTION. *n*. 1. " . . . [R]efers to the power of the court to hear a particular matter

..." *Tolofson v. Jensen* (1992), 9 C.C.L.T. (2d) 289 at 293, 4 C.P.C. (3d) 113, 65 B.C.L.R. (2d) 114, [1992] 3 W.W.R. 743, 89 D.L.R. (4th) 129, 11 B.C.A.C. 94, 22 W.A.C. 94, the court per Cumming J.A. 2. A province or territory of Canada or a state outside Canada having sovereign power. 3. The authority of an administrative tribunal over a particular subject matter which is found in the tribunal's authorizing statute. 4. The scope of the authority of a government in terms of subject matter or territory. See ANCILLARY ~; APPELLATE ~; CONCURRENT ~; CONTENTIOUS ~; COURT OF COMPETENT ~; DOMESTIC ~; EXCLUSIVE ~ CLAUSE; FEDERAL ~; FOREIGN ~; GENERAL ~; INHERENT ~; LOCAL ~; ORIGINAL ~; PENDENT ~; RECIPROCATING ~; STATUTORY ~; SUMMARY ~.

JURISDICTIONAL DISPUTE. A dispute between two or more trade unions or councils of trade unions or between an employer and one or more trade unions or councils of trade unions over the assignment of work.

JURISDICTIONAL ERROR. 1. An error on an issue with respect to which, according to the outcome of the pragmatic and functional analysis, the tribunal must make a correct interpretation and to which no deference will be shown. *Pushpanathan v. Canada (Minister of Employment & Immigration)*, [1998] 1 S.C.R. 982. 2. The refusal by a body to exercise a power 3. The purported exercise of a power which the body does not have 4. The exercise of the wrong power in the circumstances. 5. " . . . [R]elates generally to a provision which confers jurisdiction, that is, one which describes, lists and limits the powers of an administrative tribunal, or which is [translation] 'intended to circumscribe the authority' of that tribunal, as Pigeon J. said in Komo Construction v. Commmission des relations du travail du Quebec [R. v. Quebec (Labour Relations Board), [1968] S.C.R. 172, 1 D.L.R. (3d) 125, 68 C.L.L.C. 14,108]. A jurisdictional error results generally in an excess of jurisdiction or a refusal to exercise jurisdiction, whether at the start of the hearing, during it in the findings or in the order disposing of the matter. Such an error, even if committed in the best possible good faith, will result nonetheless in the decision containing it being set aside, . . ." *Syndicat des employés de production du Québec & de l'Acadie v. Canada (Labour Relations Board)*, [1984] 2 S.C.R. 412 at 420-21, 84 C.L.L.C. 14,069, 14 Admin. L.R. 72, 55 N.R.

321, 14 D.L.R. (4th) 457, Beetz J. 6. " . . . [I]f a tribunal answers the wrong question which is not before it instead of answering the right question which is before it, that is a jurisdictional error (sometimes called declining jurisdiction). . ." *I.A.F.F., Local 2130 v. St Albert (City)* (1990), 90 C.L.L.C. 14,043 at 12,370, 109 A.R. 161 (C.A.), Bracco, Irving and Côté JJ.A.

JURISDICTIONAL STRIKE. A work stoppage resulting from a jurisdictional dispute between unions.

JURISDICTION OVER. Includes possession and control. *City of Winnipeg Act*, S.M. 1971, c. 105, s. 1.,

JURIS EFFECTUS IN EXECUTIONE CONSISTIT. [L.] The effect of law is given by execution.

JURIS ET DE JURE. [L. of law and from law] Describes a presumption which is a conclusive presumption.

JURIS PRAECEPTA SUNT HAEC; HONESTE VIVERE, ALTERUM NON LAEDERE, SUUM CUIQUE TRIBUERE. [L.] The precepts of law are these: to live honestly, to hurt no one and to give every person their due.

JURISPRUDENCE. *n.* 1. The philosophy or science of law which ascertains the principles which are the basis of legal rules. 2. A body of law. See MEDICAL ~.

JURISPRUDENTIA EST DIVINARUM ATQUE HUMANARUM RERUM NOTITIA, JUSTI ATQUE INJUSTI SCIENTIA. [L.] Jurisprudence is knowledge of things sacred and human, a science of right and wrong.

JURIST. *n.* A civil lawyer; an eminent legal theorist; a civilian.

JURISTIC REASON. 1. A recognized legal or equitable justification which supports the transfer of a benefit and corresponding detriment between parties in circumstances in which the transfer should not be considered unjust. 2. But even if the principles of unjust enrichment are applicable, the law is clear that "a contract" can constitute a juristic reason for the enrichment. As a recent example of this, see the decision of this Court in Hill Estate v. Chevron Standard Ltd. (1992), 83 Man. R. (2d) 58 (C.A.) (at p. 70): Decided cases are of little assistance in determining what is meant by "juristic reason." It simply comes down to this: if there is an explanation based upon law for the enrichment of one at the detriment of another, then the enrichment will not be considered unjust and no remedy, whether by constructive trust or otherwise, will be available. For example, there might be a contract between the parties under the terms of which an enrichment by one at the expense of the other is contemplated or justified. *Rillford Investments Ltd. v. Gravure International Capital Corp.*, 118 Man. R. (2d) 11, [1997] 7 W.W.R. 534 (C.A.), Scott, C.J. M. for the court.

JUROR. *n*. [L.] A person who serves on a jury.

JUROR PREJUDICE. Four types of juror prejudice have been identified: interest, specific, generic and conformity. See CONFORMITY PREJUDICE; GENERIC PREJUDICE; INTEREST PREJUDICE; SPECIFIC PREJUDICE.

JURORS' LIST. The list of names of the persons summoned by a sheriff to serve as jurors at a sitting of the court. *Jury Act*, R.S.M. 1987, c. J30, s. 1.

JURORS' PRIVILEGE. Jurors are privileged against disclosing deliberations in a jury room. Section 649 of the Criminal Code, R.S.C. 1985, c. C-46 makes disclosing such information an offence. P.K. McWilliams, *Canadian Criminal Evidence*, 3d ed. (Aurora: Canada Law Book, 1988) at 35-74.

JURORS' ROLL. A jurors roll prepared for a district by the Chief Sheriff by a random jury selection from appropriate lists. *Jury Act*, R.S.M. 1987, c. J30, s. 1.

JURY. *n*. 1. A group of people sworn to deliver a verdict after considering evidence delivered to them concerning the issue. 2. The jury is a judicial organ of the criminal process. It accomplishes a large part of the function exercised by judges in non-jury criminal cases. In a jury trial, the jury is the "judge" of the facts, while the presiding judge is the "judge" of the law. They, judge and jury together, produce the judgment of the court. The jury hears all the evidence admitted at trial, receives instructions from the trial judge as to the relevant legal principles, and then retires to deliberate. It applies the law to the facts in order to arrive at a verdict. *R. v. Pan*, 2001 CarswellOnt 2261, 2001 SCC 42, 155 C.C.C. (3d) 97, 200 D.L.R. (4th) 577, 43 C.R. (5th) 203, 147 O.A.C. 1, 85 C.R.R. (2d) 1, 270 N.R. 317, Arbour, J. for the court. See CHARGE THE ~; EMPANEL; GRAND ~; HUNG ~; IMPANEL.

JURY DISTRICT. An area of the province described under section 8 as a jury district in respect of a judicial centre. *Jury Act*, R.S.M. 1987, c. J30, s 1.

JURY LIST. The permanent list of jurors drawn up in accordance with this act. *Jurors Act*, R.S.Q. 1977, c. J-2, s. 1.

JURY NOTICE. A request by one party to an action that the damages be assessed or the issues of fact be tried, or both, by a jury.

JURY PANEL. Those persons summoned from amongst whom a jury will be selected.

JURY SECRECY. The common law rule of jury secrecy, which prohibits the court from receiving evidence of jury deliberations for the purpose of impeaching a verdict, . . . reflects a desire to preserve the secrecy of the jury deliberation process and to shield the jury from outside influences. . . A proper interpretation of the modern version of Lord Mansfield's rule is as follows: Statements made, opinions expressed, arguments advanced and votes cast by members of a jury in the course of their deliberations are inadmissible in any legal proceedings. In particular, jurors may not testify about the effect of anything on their or other jurors' minds emotions or ultimate decision. On the other hand, the common law rule does not render inadmissible evidence of facts, statements or events extrinsic to the deliberation process, whether originating from a juror or from a third party, that may have tainted the verdict. *R. v. Pan*, 2001 CarswellOnt 2261, 2001 SCC 42, 155 C.C.C. (3d) 97, 200 D.L.R. (4th) 577, 43 C.R. (5th) 203, 147 O.A.C. 1, 85 C.R.R. (2d) 1, 270 N.R. 317 Arbour, J. for the court. See LORD MANSFIELD'S RULE.

JURY TRIAL. The trial of an action or issue which is to be tried with a jury and the trial of a criminal matter and proceeding with a jury. *Jury Act*, R.S.M. 1987, c. J30, s. 1.

JUS. *n*. [L.] Law; right; equity; rule; authority. See IGNORANTIA JURIS HAUD EXCUSAT.

JUS ACCRESCENDI. [L.] The right of survivorship. A feature of joint tenancy.

JUS ACCRESCENDI PRAEFERTUR ONERIBUS. [L.] The right of survivorship is put before encumbrances.

JUS ACCRESCENDI PRAEFERTUR ULTIMAE VOLUNTATI. [L.] The right of survivorship is put before a last will.

JUS AD REM. [L.] The right to claim against the whole world.

JUS AESNECIAE. [L.] The right of the first born.

JUS CANONICUM. [L.] Canon law.

JUS CIVILE. [L.] Local law.

JUS CIVITATIS. [L.] The right of citizenship.

JUS COMMUNE. [L.] Common law.

JUS CONSTITUI OPORTET IN HIS QUAE UT PLURIMUM ACCIDUNT, NON QUAE EX INOPINATO. [L.] Law should be made for situations which happen most often, and not for the unexpected.

JUS CORONAE. [L.] The Crown's right.

JUS CREDITI. [L.] A creditor's right.

JUS DESCENDIT, ET NON TERRA. [L.] Right and not the land descends.

JUS DISPONENDI. [L.] The right to dispose.

JUS DIVIDENDI. [L.] The right to dispose of realty by will.

JUS DUPLICATUM. [L.] The right to possess as well as the right of property in something.

JUS EST NORMA RECTI; ET QUICQUID EST CONTRA NORM RECTI EST INJURIA. [L.] A legal right is the rule of right; and whatever goes against the rule of right is a wrong.

JUS EX INJURIA NON ORITUR. [L.] Right does not arise out of a wrong.

JUS FIDUCIARIUM. [L.] A trust.

JUS GENTIUM. [L.] Customary law.

JUS HABENDI. [L.] The right to actually possess property.

JUS HAEREDITATIS. [L.] The right to inherit.

JUS IN PERSONAM. [L.] A right which gives the one holding it power to help another person to do or not to do, to gain or give anything.

JUS IN RE. [L.] A full and complete right; a real right or a right to have something to the exclusion of everyone else.

JUS JURANDI FORMA VERBIS DIFFERT, RE CONVENIT; HUNC ENIM SENSUM HABERE DEBET: UT DEUS INVOCETUR. [L.] Oaths differ in the pattern of their words but come to the same conclusion; every oath must call on their deity to witness.

JUS JURANDUM INTER ALIOS FACTUM NEC NOCERE NEC PRODESSE DEBET. [L.] An oath others made in another proceeding should neither hurt nor benefit.

JUS MARITI. [L.] The right of a husband to chattels of a woman which, because there was no special provision, her husband acquired when they married.

JUS NATURALE. [L.] Natural law.

JUS NATURALE EST QUOD APUD OMNES HOMINES EANDEM HABET POTENTIAM. [L.] Natural law has the same force among all people.

JUS NON HABENTI TUTE NON PARETUR. [L.] It is safe to disobey one who has no legal right.

JUS NON PATITUR UT IDEM BIS SOLVATUR. [L.] Law does not allow the same thing to be paid twice.

JUS NON SCRIPTUM. [L.] Unwritten law.

JUS POSSESSIONIS. [L.] The right to possess.

JUS PRECARIUM. [L.] A right by sufferance or courtesy which could be remedied only by request or entreaty.

JUS PRESENTATIONIS. [L.] The right to present.

JUS PRIVATUM. [L.] The municipal or civil law.

JUS PUBLICUM. [L.] The law concerning public affairs.

JUS PUBLICUM PRIVATORUM PACTIS MUTARE NON POTEST. [L.] Public law should not be superseded by private agreements.

JUS RECUPERANDI. [L.] The right to recover.

JUS REGALE. [L.] A right of the King.

JUS RELICTAE. [L.] The right of a widow (relict).

JUS RESPICIT AEQUITATEM. [L.] Law is mindful of equity.

JUS SANGUINIS. [L.] A principle that one's parentage determines nationality by birth.

JUS SOLI. [L.] A principle that the territory where the birth takes place determines nationality by birth.

JUS SUPERVENIENS AUCTORI AC-CRESCIT SUCCESSORI. [L.] A right invested in a former owner of land descends to the successor.

JUST. *adj.* 1. Conforming to law. According to the rules of law and equity. 2. " . . . [A] just remedy in the context of the criminal law is one which, while furthering the object of the right guaranteed by the [Charter] that has been infringed, nevertheless does that, as far as possible, in a way that does not offend the reasonable expectations of the community for the enforcement of the criminal law." *R. v. Germain* (1984), (*sub nom. Germain v. R.*) 10 C.R.R. 232 at 341, 53 A.R. 264 (Q.B.), McDonald J.

JUST AND EQUITABLE SHARE. Of a producer of a developed unit, unless otherwise agreed upon by the interested persons, means that part of the allowable production for the pool that is substantially in the same proportion that the quantity of recoverable oil and gas in each developed unit of the tract or tracts concerned in the pool bears to the recoverable oil or gas in the total developed area of the pool, subject to reasonable measures for the prevention of waste and to reasonable adjustment by reason of structural position, and that, if produced, will minimize reasonably avoidable drainage from each developed unit and will enable the producer to utilize his fair share of the reservoir energy. *The Oil and Gas Conservation Act*, R.S.S. 1978, c. 0-2, s. 2.

JUST CAUSE. 1. "If an employee has been guilty of serious misconduct, habitual neglect of duty, incompetence, or conduct imcompatible with his duties, or prejudicial to the employer's business, or if he has been guilty of wilful disobedience to the employer's orders in a matter of substance, the law recognizes the employer's right summarily to dismiss the delinquent employee." *Port Arthur Shipbuilding Co. v. Arthurs*, [1967] 2 O.R. 49 at 55, 62 D.L.R. (2d) 342, 67 C.L.L.C. 14,024 (C.A.), Schroeder J.A. (dissenting), approved on appeal [1969] S.C.R. 85. 2. Journal published by Canadian Legal Advocacy, Information and Research Association of the Disabled.

JUST DISMISSAL. " . . . [D]ismissal based on an objective, real and substantial cause, independent of caprice, convenience or purely personal disputes, entailing action taken exclusively to ensure the effective operation of the business . . ." *Canadian Imperial Bank of Commerce v. Boisvert* (1986), 13 C.C.E.L. 264 at 291, [1986]

2 F.C. 431, 68 N.R. 355 (C.A.), Marceau J.A. (MacGuigan and Lacombe JJ.A. concurring).

JUS TERTII. [L.] Third party right.

JUSTICE. *n.* 1. The principle of giving every person her or his due. 2. A judge of certain courts. 3. A justice of appeal. 4. A justice of the peace. 5 A justice of the peace or a provincial court judge, and includes two or more justices where two or more justices are, by law, required to act or, by law, act or have jurisdiction. *Criminal Code*, R.S.C. 1985, c. C-46, s. 2 as am. by R.S.C. 1985 (1st Supp.), c. 27, s. 2. See ADMINISTRATION OF ~; CHIEF ~; COURSE OF ~; DEPARTMENT OF ~ CANADA; FUNDAMENTAL ~; INTERNATIONAL COURT OF ~; NATURAL ~; OBSTRUCTING ~; PREVENTIVE ~; REVISING ~; TRAFFIC ~.

JUSTICEMENT. *n.* Any thing pertaining to justice.

JUSTICE OF THE PEACE. A judicial officer who has authority to deal with the initiation of criminal proceedings and to try minor criminal or quasi-criminal offences.

JUSTICE REP. *abbr.* Justice Report.

JUSTICESHIP. *n.* The office or rank of a justice.

JUSTICE SHOULD NOT ONLY BE DONE BUT SHOULD MANIFESTLY AND UNDOUBTEDLY BE SEEN TO BE DONE. A rule enunciated in *R. v. Sussex Justices, Ex parte McCarthy*, [1924] 1 K.B. 256 at 259 (U.K. Div. Ct.), Lord Hewart C.J.

JUSTICE SYSTEM. See CRIMINAL ~.

JUSTICE SYSTEM PARTICIPANT. A member of the Senate, of the House of Commons, of a legislative assembly or of a municipal council, and a person who plays a role in the administration of criminal justice, including the Solicitor General of Canada and a Minister responsible for policing in a province, a prosecutor, a lawyer, a member of the Chambre des notaires du Québec and an officer of a court, a judge and a justice, a juror and a person who is summoned as a juror, an informant, a prospective witness, a witness under subpoena and a witness who has testified, a person employed in the administration of a court, an employee of the Canada Customs and Revenue Agency who is involved in the investigation of an offence under an Act of Parliament, an employee of a federal or provincial correctional service, a parole supervisor and any other person who is involved in the administration of a sentence under the supervision of such a correctional service and a person who conducts disciplinary hearings under the Corrections and Conditional Release Act, and an employee and a member of the National Parole Board and of a provincial parole board. *Criminal Code*, R.S.C. 1985, c. C.46, s. 2 as am.

JUSTICIABLE. *adj*. 1. Proper to be examined in a court of justice, triable. 2. "[In The Fatal Accidents Act, R.S.S. 1920, c. 62, s. 3] . . . must have reference to legal justification, and an act or neglect which is neither actionable nor punishable cannot be said to be otherwise than justifiable . . ." *Walpole v. Canadian Northern Railway* (1922), 70 D.L.R. 201 at 205, [1922] 3 W.W.R. 900, [1923] A.C. 113, 28 C.R.C. 237 (P.C.), Viscount Cave. 3. The notion of justiciability is linked to the notion of appropriate judicial restraint. In exercising its discretion whether to determine a matter that is alleged to be non-justiciable, the Court's primary concern is to retain its proper role within the constitutional framework of our democratic form of government. Thus the circumstances in which the Court may decline to answer a reference question on the basis of "non-justiciability" include: (i) if to do so would take the Court beyond its own assessment of its proper role in the constitutional framework of our democratic form of government or (ii) if the Court could not give an answer that lies within its area of expertise: the interpretation of law. *Reference re Secession of Quebec*, 1998 CarswellNat 1299, 161 D.L.R. (4th) 385, 228 N.R. 203, 55 C.R.R. (2d) 1, [1998] 2 S.C.R. 217, per curiam.

JUSTIFIABLE HOMICIDE. Homicide which is not culpable, the killing of a human being when no legal guilt is incurred.

JUSTIFICATION. *n*. 1. "[In criminal theory, in contrast to excuse] . . . challenges the wrongfulness of an action which technically constitutes a crime. The police officer who shoots the hostage-taker, the innocent object of an assault who uses force to defend himself against his assailant, the good Samaritan who commandeers a car and breaks the speed laws to rush an accident victim to the hospital, these are all actors whose actions we consider rightful, not wrongful. . ." *R. v. Perka* (1984),13 D.L.R. (4th) 1 at 12, [1984] 2 S.C.R. 232, [1984] 6 W.W.R. 289, 42 C.R. (3d) 113, 55 N.R. 1, 14 C.C.C. (3d) 385, Dickson J. (Ritchie J. concurring). 2. Truth, a complete defence to a defamation action. R.E. Brown, *The Law of Defamation in Canada* (Toronto: Carswell, 1987) at 361. See PUTATIVE ~.

JUSTIFICATOR. *n*. *A* kind of compurgator.

JUSTIFIED. *adj*. Authorized. Proper. See REASONABLE AND DEMONSTRABLY ~.

JUSTIFY BAIL. To prove the sufficiency of sureties or bail.

JUSTINIANIST. *n*. A person who studies the civil law; a civilian.

JUSTITIA. *n*. [L.] A law, statute or ordinance; the office of a judge or a jurisdiction.

JUSTITIA DEBET ESSE LIBERA, QUIA NIHIL INIQUIS VENALI JUSTITIA; PLENA, QUIA JUSTITIA NON DEBET CLAUDICARE; ET CELERIS, QUIA DILATIO EST QUAEDAM NEGATIO. [L.] Justice should be free, because nothing is worse than venal justice; full, for justice should not be wanting; and swift, for delay is almost denial.

JUSTITIA EST DUPLEX, VIZ: SEVERE PUNIENS ET VERE PRAEVENIENS. [L.] Justice is double: it punishes severely and is truly preventive.

JUSTITIA FIRMATUR SOLIUM. [L.] The throne is strengthened by justice.

JUSTITIA NEMINI NEGANDA EST. [L.] Justice should be denied to no one.

JUSTITIA NON EST NEGANDA, NON DIFFERENDA. [L.] Justice should not be denied nor delayed.

JUSTITIA PIEPOUDROUS. [L.] Swift justice.

JUS VENANDI ET PISCANDI. [L.] The right to hunt and fish.

JUV. CT. *abbr*. Juvenile Court.

JUVENILE. *n*. 1. A person who has not attained his sixteenth birthday. *The Saskatchewan Health Insurance Act*, R.S.S. 1978, c. S-21, s. 2. 2. Includes every child apparently or actually under the age of seventeen years. *Juveniles Act*, R.S. Nfld. 1970, c. 190, s. 27.

JUVENILE APPLICANT. An applicant under the age of eighteen years. *Legal Aid Services Society of Manitoba Act*, S.M. 1971, c. 76, s. 1.

JUVENILE COURT. The equivalent of Youth Court prior to the enactment of the Young Offenders Act. See YOUTH COURT.

JUVENILE DELINQUENT. 1.The term used to describe a Young Offender prior to the enactment of the Young Offenders Act. 2. Any child who violates any provision of the Criminal Code or of any federal or provincial statute, or of any by-law or ordinance of any municipality, or who is guilty of sexual immorality or any similar form of vice, or who is liable by reason of any other act to be committed to an industrial school or juvenile reformatory under any federal or provincial statute. *Juvenile Delinquents Act*, R.S.C. 1970, c. J-3, s. 2.

JUXTA FORMAM STATUTI. [L.] According to the statute's form.

K. *abbr*. 1. Kilo. 2. Kelvin.

K.B. *abbr*. 1. King's Bench. 2. Court of King's Bench. See QUEEN'S BENCH.

K.C. *abbr*. King's Counsel. See QUEEN'S COUNSEL.

KEELAGE. *n*. A toll paid by a ship when it enters a harbour.

KEEP. v. To maintain in possession; to have available for use.

KEEPER. *n*. 1. A person who (a) is an owner or occupier of a place, (b) assists or acts on behalf of an owner or occupier of a place, (c) appears to be, or to assist or act on behalf of an owner or occupier of a place, (d) has the care or management of a place, or (e) uses a place permanently or temporarily, with or without the consent of the owner or occupier thereof. Crim*inal Code*, R.S.C. 1985, c. C-46, s. 197. 2. "In terms of what it means to be a 'keeper' of a common bawdy-house, an element of participation in the wrongful use of the place is a minimum requirement: R. v. Kerim, [1963] S.C.R. 124 . . ." *Reference re ss. 193 & 195.1(1)(c) of the Criminal Code (Canada)*, [1990] 4 W.W.R. 481 at 510, 77 C.R. (3d) 1, 56 C.C.C. (3d) 65, [1990] 1 S.C.R. 1123, 109 N.R. 81, 68 Man. R. (2d) 1, 48 C.R.R. 1, Lamer J. 3. Includes owner, lessee and proprietor. See BEE~; DAM~; GARAGE ~; HOTEL~; INN~; LIVERY STABLE ~; POUND ~; STABLE ~; WAREHOUSE ~.

KEEPER OF A STORAGE WAREHOUSE. Includes the proprietor, keeper or manager of a warehouse, building shed, storehouse, yard, wharf or other place for the storage of goods, chattels, wares or merchandise delivered to him as bailee for hire, whether the person is engaged in other business or not. *Storage Warehouse Keepers Act*, R.S.N.S. 1967, c. 293, s. 1.

KEEP THE PEACE. To prevent or avoid breaches of the peace.

KELVIN. *n*. The unit for the measurement of thermodynamic temperature, being the fraction 1/273.16 of the thermodynamic temperature of the triple point of water. *Weights and Measures Act*, S.C. 1970-71-72, c. 36, Schedule I.

KENNEL. *n*. Traditionally limited to housing dogs. One aspect of a "kennel" use is the boarding of the animal. "Boarding" suggests to me that the owner of the animal makes an arrangement to leave it in the care of the boarding facility. Includes facilities for the breeding of dogs. *Woodman v. Capital (Regional District)* (1999), 1999 CarswellBC 2193, 6 M.P.L.R. (3d) 128 (S.C.).

KERB. *n*. An alternate spelling of curb. See, for example, *Highways Protection Act*, R.S.M. 1987, c. H50, s. 1.

KEROSINE. See 1-K ~.

KEY. See RESTRICTED ~.

KEY MAN INSURANCE. Life or disability insurance held by a business on a valued employee or officer of the business.

KG. *abbr*. Kilogram.

KICKBACK. *n*. 1. A payment for help or a favour in business matters. 2. Payment back to a seller or employer of a portion of purchase price or wages of an employee.

KIDNAP. *v*. 1. " . . . The crime is complete when the person is picked up and then transported by fraud to his place of confinement. . ." *R. v. Metcalfe* (1983), 10 C.C.C. (3d) 114 at 118 (B.C. C.A.), the court per Nemetz C.J.B.C. 2. " . . . [A] case in which the parties had been separated for some time and the mother snatches the child from the matrimonial home or from some other place where the child has been placed... a situation where the mother, in defiance of a court order in some other province or in the face of litigation pending in some other province, has removed the child from the province having original jurisdiction to Ontario..." *Lussier v. Lussier* (1977), 3 R.F.L. (2d) 335 at 336 (Ont. Div. Ct.), the court per Evans C.J.H.C.

KIENAPPLE PRINCIPLE. "Multiple convictions are only precluded under the Kienapple principle [named after Kienapple v. R., [1975] 1 S.C.R. 729] if they arise from the same 'cause' 'matter', or 'delict', and if there is sufficient proximity between the offences charged. This requirement of sufficient proximity between offences will only be satisfied if there is no additional and distinguishing element contained in the offence for which a conviction is sought to be precluded by the Kienapple principle." *R. v. Wigman* (1987), 33 C.C.C. (3d) 97 at 103, [1987] 4 W.W.R. 1, 56 C.R. (3d) 289, [1987] 1 S.C.R. 246, 75 N.R. 51, 38 D.L.R. (4th) 530, Dickson C.J.C., Beetz, McIntyre, Chouinard, Lamer, Le Dain and La Forest JJ.

KILL. *n.* The number of individuals of a given species or population thereof, killed or permitted to be killed during a given period. *An Act respecting hunting and fishing rights in the James Bay and New Québec territories*, S.Q. 1978, c. 92, s. 78.

KILLING AND DRESSING STATION. A place where poultry is killed, dressed and graded. *Dressed and Eviscerated Poultry Regulations*, C.R.C., c. 283, s. 2.

KILO. *pref.* 10^3. Prefix for multiples and submultiples of basic, supplementary and derived units of measurement. *Weights and Measures Act*, S.C. 1970-71-72, c. 36, Schedule 1.

KILOGRAM. *n.* The unit for the measurement of mass, being a mass equal to the mass of the international prototype of the kilogram established in the year 1889 by the First General Conference of Weights and Measures and deposited at the International Bureau of Weights and Measures. *Weights and Measures Act*, S.C. 1970-71-72, c. 36, Schedule 1.

KILOMETRE. *n.* A thousand metres. See POLE ~; ROAD ~S.

KILOPASCAL. *n.* Measure of barometric pressure. Abbreviated kPa.

KILOWATT. *n.* One thousand watts.

KILOWATT-HOUR. *n.* For electrical energy, the "kilowatt-hour", which is the energy supplied by a power of one thousand watts operating for one hour. *Electrical and Photometric Units Act*, R.S.C. 1970, c. E-3, s. 2.

KIMBERLEY PROCESS. The international understanding among participants that was recognized by Resolution 55/56 adopted by the General Assembly of the United Nations on December 1, 2000, as that understanding is amended from time to time. Deals with manner of handling rough diamonds. *Export and Import of Rough Diamonds Act*, S.C. 2002, c. 25, s. 2.

KIN. *n.* Relatives by blood. See NEXT OF ~.

KIND. *n.* Either (a) a refillable glass container; (b) a nonrefillable glass container; (c) a nonrefillable metal container; or (d) a plastic container. *Litter Act*, R.S.B.C. 1979, c. 239, s. 1. See DONATION IN ~; EARNED INCOME IN ~; GOODS OF THE SAME CLASS OR ~; PAYMENT IN ~.

KINDERGARTEN. *n.* Any class recognized as such by the Minister of Education, to which children are admitted for one year of study immediately preceding the first year of the elementary course. *Grants to School Boards Act*, R.S.Q. 1977, c. S-36, s. 1.

KINDRED. *n.* Relations by blood.

KINEMATOGRAPH. *n.* A moving picture machine.

KING. *n.* A male sovereign of the United Kingdom, Canada and other Realms and Territories, and Head of the Commonwealth. See THE ~ CAN DO NO WRONG.

KING'S BENCH. Title of what is now the court of Queen's Bench during the reign of a King.

KING'S COUNSEL. Honourary title given to senior barristers, equivalent to Queen's Counsel, during the reign of a King. See QUEEN'S COUNSEL.

KING'S PRINTER. Name of a government printing office during the reign of a King. See QUEEN'S PRINTER.

KING'S PROCTOR. Name of the Queen's Proctor during the reign of a King. See QUEEN'S PROCTOR.

KINSFOLK. *n.* Relatives; members of the same family.

KINSMAN. *n.* A man of the same family or race.

KINSWOMAN. *n*. A woman of the same family or race.

KIT. *n*. A complete or substantially complete number of parts that can be assembled to construct a finished article. *Industrial Design Act*, R.S.C. 1985, c. I-9, s. 2. See TEST ~.

KITING. *n*. " . . . [A] term used with regard to obtaining money by cheques passed through banks without value being deposited against the cheque—that is, kiting is an effort to obtain the use of money during the process of a cheque passing through one bank or through a clearing house to another, and perhaps through many more." *Corp. Agencies Ltd. v. Home Bank of Canada*, [1927] 2 D.L.R. 1 at 2, [1927] 1 W.W.R. 1004, [1927] A.C. 318 (Can. P.C.), the board per Lord Wrenbury.

KLEPTOMANIA. *n*. An uncontrollable inclination to steal.

KM. *abbr*. Knowledge management.

KNIFE-RIBBING. *n*. To cut the side of a carcass midway between the 11th and 12th ribs, beginning at the backbone, continuing towards the plate side and severing the costal cartilages but not severing the backbone. *Beef Carcass Grading Regulations*, C.R.C., c. 282, s. 2.

KNOB. See DUAL ~.

KNOT. *n*. A unit of speed equal to one nautical mile per hour.

KNOW. *v*. 1. " . . . [H]as a positive connotation requiring a bare awareness, the act of receiving information without more. . ." *R. v. Barnier*, [1980] 1 S.C.R. 1124 at 1137, 109 D.L.R. (3d) 257, 13 C.R. (3d) 129 (Eng.), 19 C.R. (3d) 371 (Fr.), [1980] 2 W.W.R. 659, 31 N.R. 273, 51 C.C.C. (3d) 193, the court per Estey J. 2. Refers to true knowledge. One cannot say that one knows something that is not so.

KNOW-HOW. *n*. Technical knowledge or expertise.

KNOWING ASSISTANCE. The only basis upon which the Bank may be held liable as a constructive trustee is under the "knowing receipt" or "knowing receipt and dealing" head of liability. Under this category of constructive trusteeship it is generally recognized that there are two types of cases. First, although inapplicable to the present case, there are strangers to the trust, usually agents of the trustees, who receive trust property lawfully and not for their own benefit but then deal with the property in a

manner inconsistent with the trust. These cases may be grouped under the heading "knowing dealing". Secondly, there are strangers to the trust who receive trust property for their own benefit and with knowledge that the property was transferred to them in breach of trust. In all cases it is immaterial whether the breach of trust was fraudulent. The second type of case, which is relevant to the present appeal, raises two main issues: the nature of the receipt of trust property and the degree of knowledge required of the stranger to the trust. In "knowing assistance" cases, which are concerned with the furtherance of fraud, there is a higher threshold of knowledge required of the stranger to the trust. Constructive knowledge is excluded as the basis for liability in "knowing assistance" cases. *Citadel General Assurance Co. v. Lloyds Bank Canada* (1997), 1997 CarswellAlta 823, 152 D.L.R. (4th) 411, (*sub nom. Citadel General Life Assurance Co. v. Lloyds Bank Canada*) 206 A.R. 321, (*sub nom. Citadel General Life Assurance Co. v. Lloyds Bank Canada*) 156 W.A.C. 321, 19 E.T.R. (2d) 93, 35 B.L.R. (2d) 153, 47 C.C.L.I. (2d) 153, [1997] 3 S.C.R. 805, 219 N.R. 323, [1999] 4 W.W.R. 135, 66 Alta. L.R. (3d) 241, per La Forest, J.

KNOWING DEALING. Under this category of constructive trusteeship it is generally recognized that there are two types of cases. First, although inapplicable to the present case, there are strangers to the trust, usually agents of the trustees, who receive trust property lawfully and not for their own benefit but then deal with the property in a manner inconsistent with the trust. These cases may be grouped under the heading "knowing dealing". *Air Canada v. M & L Travel Ltd.*, [1993] 3 S.C.R. 787, at pp. 811-13. *Citadel General Assurance Co. v. Lloyds Bank Canada* (1997), 1997 CarswellAlta 823, 152 D.L.R. (4th) 411, (*sub nom. Citadel General Life Assurance Co. v. Lloyds Bank Canada*) 206 A.R. 321, (*sub nom. Citadel General Life Assurance Co. v. Lloyds Bank Canada*) 156 W.A.C. 321, 19 E.T.R. (2d) 93, 35 B.L.R. (2d) 153, 47 C.C.L.I. (2d) 153, [1997] 3 S.C.R. 805, 219 N.R. 323, [1999] 4 W.W.R. 135, 66 Alta. L.R. (3d) 241, per La Forest, J.

KNOWINGLY. *adv*. "The general principle of criminal law is that accompanying a prohibited act there must be an intent in respect of every element of the act, and that is ordinarily conveyed in statutory offences by the word 'knowingly'." *R. v. Rees* (1956), 24 C.R. 1 at 8, [1956]

S.C.R. 640, 115 C.C.C. 1, 4 D.L.R. (2d) 406, Rand J. (Locke J. concurring).

KNOWING RECEIPT. In "knowing receipt" cases, which are concerned with the receipt of trust property or one's own benefit, there should be a lower threshold of knowledge required of the stranger to the trust. More is expected of the recipient, who, unlike the accessory, is necessarily enriched at the plaintiff's expense. Because the recipient is held to this higher standard, constructive knowledge (that is, knowledge of facts sufficient to put a reasonable person on notice or inquiry) will suffice as the basis for restitutionary liability. *Citadel General Assurance Co. v. Lloyds Bank Canada* (1997), 1997 CarswellAlta 823, 152 D.L.R. (4th) 411, (*sub nom. Citadel General Life Assurance Co. v. Lloyds Bank Canada*) 206 A.R. 321, (*sub nom. Citadel General Life Assurance Co. v. Lloyds Bank Canada*) 156 W.A.C. 321, 19 E.T.R. (2d) 93, 35 B.L.R. (2d) 153, 47 C.C.L.I. (2d) 153, [1997] 3 S.C.R. 805, 219 N.R. 323, [1999] 4 W.W.R. 135, 66 Alta. L.R. (3d) 241, per La Forest, J. See KNOWING ASSISTANCE; KNOWING DEALING.

KNOWING THAT THE ACT WAS WRONG. [Referring to these words in s. 16 of the Criminal Code], the rule focuses not on a general capacity to understand right and wrong in some abstract sense, but on the particular capacity of the accused to understand that his or her act was wrong *at the time of committing the act*. The crux of the inquiry is whether the accused lacks the capacity to rationally decide whether the act is right or wrong and hence to make a rational choice about whether to do it or not. The inability to make a rational choice may result from a variety of mental disfunctions. *R. v. Oommen*, 1994 CarswellAlta 121, 19 Alta. L.R. (3d) 305, 30 C.R. (4th) 195, [1994] 7 W.W.R. 49, 168 N.R. 200, [1994] 2 S.C.R. 507, 91 C.C.C. (3d) 8, 155 A.R. 190, 73 W.A.C. 190, McLachlin, J. for the court.

KNOWLEDGE. *n*. 1. The condition of knowing something. 2. For legal purposes, is true belief. Knowledge therefore has two components—truth and belief—and of these, only belief is mental or subjective. Truth is objective, or at least consists in the correspondence of a proposition or mental state to objective reality. Accordingly, truth, which is a state of affairs in the external world that does not vary with the intention of the accused, cannot be a part of *mens rea*. The truth of an actor's belief that certain monies are the proceeds of crime is something different from the belief itself. That the belief be true is one of the attendant circumstances that is required if the *actus reus* is to be completed. In other words, the act of converting the proceeds of crime presupposes the existence of some money that is in truth the proceeds of crime. *United States v. Dynar*, 1997 CarswellOnt 1981, [1997] 2 S.C.R. 462, Cory and Iacobucci, JJ. for the majority. See COMMON ~; EXPLICIT ~; TACIT ~.

KNOWLEDGE MANAGEMENT. The collection, organization, and dissemination of explicit and tacit knowledge of members of a legal firm for use by other members of the firm.

KN. P.C. *abbr*. Knapp, Privy Council, 1829-1836.

KORAN. *n*. The sacred scripture of Islam.

KOREAN WAR. The military operations undertaken by the United Nations to restore peace in the Republic of Korea, and the period denoted by the term "Korean War" is the period from June 25, 1950 to July 27, 1953, inclusive.

KPA. *abbr*. Kilopascal. Measure of barometric pressure.

KUSARI. *n*. A length of rope, cord, wire or chain fastened at each end to a hexagonal or other geometrically shaped hard weight or hand-grip. *Prohibited Weapons Order No. 2*, C.R.C., c. 434, s. 2.

L. *abbr.* 1. Litre. 2. Length. 3. Length in metres. *Oil Pollution Prevention Regulations*, C.R.C., c. 1454, Schedule III, c. 1. 4. Linnaeus. *Weed Control Act*, R.R.O. 1980, Reg. 944, s. 1.

LABEL. *n.* 1. Any label, mark, sign, device, imprint, stamp, brand, ticket or tag. 2. Any legend, word or mark attached to, included in, belonging to or accompanying any food, drug, cosmetic, device or package. *Food and Drugs Act*, R.S.C. 1985, c. F-27, s. 2. 3. Includes any mark, sign, device, stamp, seal, sticker, ticket, tag or wrapper. *Hazardous Products Act*, S.C. 1987, c. 30, s. 11(1). See BALLOT ~; DESCRIPTIVE ~; DISCLOSURE ~; INNER ~; OUTER ~ REPRESENTATION ~; UNION ~.

LABORATORY. *n.* 1. A medical diagnostic laboratory where examinations of specimens of blood, spinal fluid, sputum, stool, urine, gastric washings, exudate or other specimen or discharge derived from a body are made for the purpose of determining the presence or absence of an infectious agent. *Public Health Act*, R.S.A. 2000, c. P-37, s. 1. 2. A place outside an establishment equipped for manufacturing or repairing ortheses or prosthetic devices, main medical biology examinations, particularly in the fields of biochemistry, haematology, bacteriology, immunology, histopathology and virology, for making radioisotope or radiology examinations for purposes of and treatment of disease prevention in humans or for making examinations in the fields of toxicology, audiology and the physiology of respiration. *Public Health Protection Act*, S.Q. 1979, c. 63, s. 297. See DENTAL ~; DIAGNOSTIC ~; VETERINARY ~.

LABORATORY AND X-RAY FACILITIES. Mechanical, electrical, laboratory, and other facilities and equipment necessary or useful in the diagnosis of disease and other abnormal conditions of the human body. *Health Services Act*, R.S.M. 1987, c. H30, s. 1.

LABORATORY DIRECTOR. A person who is responsible for the administration of the scientific and technical operation of a laboratory including the supervision of tests and the reporting of the results of the tests. *Laboratories Act*, R.R.O. 1990, Reg. 682, s. 1.

LABORATORY SUPERVISOR. A person who under the general supervision of a laboratory director supervises laboratory personnel and who may perform tests requiring special scientific skills. *Laboratories Act*, R.R.O. 1990, Reg. 682, s. 1.

LABORATORY TECHNICIAN. A person who under direct supervision performs laboratory tests which require limited technical skill and responsibilities. *Laboratories Act*, R.R.O. 1990, Reg. 682, s. 1.

LABORATORY TECHNOLOGIST. A person who under general supervision performs tests which require the exercise of independent judgment. *Laboratories Act*, R.R.O. 1990, Reg. 682, s. 1.

LABOUR. *v.* Of a jury, to tamper with that jury.

LABOUR. *n.* 1. Work. 2. Physical work. 3. Includes cutting, skidding, felling, hauling, scaling, rossing, banking, driving, running, rafting or booming any logs or timber and any work done by cooks, blacksmiths, artisans and others usually employed in connection therewith. W*oodmen's Lien acts*. See CHILD ~; COST OF ~; SEMI-SKILLED ~; SKILLED ~; STATUTE ~; UNSKILLED ~; VOLUNTEER ~.

LABOUR ADJUSTMENT BENEFITS. The benefits payable under this Act. *Labour Adjustment Benefits Act*, R.S.C. 1985, c. L-1, s. 2.

LABOUR AND MATERIAL BOND. " . . . [G]uarantee to the owner that the principal will pay all sums due for labour and materials provided the claimant has a direct contract with the principal . . ." *Johns-Manville Canada Inc. v. John Carlo Ltd.* (1980), (*sub nom. Canadian Johns-Manville Co. v. John Carlo Ltd.*) 12 B.L.R. 80 at 87, 29 O.R. (2d) 592,113 D.L.R. (3d) 686 (H.C.), R.E. Holland J. See CONTRACT BOND; PERFORMANCE BOND.

LABOUR ARBITRATION. The hearing and determination of labour disputes. Includes grievance and interest arbitration.

LABOUR ASSOCIATION. (a) A labour organization as defined in The Trade Union Act; (b) a corporation incorporated or continued pursuant to The Non-profit Corporations Act all of whose shareholders are employees of the same employer; (c) an investment co-operative; or (d) any other association of employees or class of association of employees that is prescribed in the regulations. *Labour-Sponsored Venture Capital Corporation Act*, S.S. 1986, c. L-0.2, s. 2.

LABOUR CANADA. The federal ministry empowered to maintain balanced legislation concerning industrial relations in federal jurisdiction, to help parties overcome industrial disputes, to set standards for wages, employment conditions and occupational health and safety, to set non-legislative programs to foster cooperative understanding be between business and labour and to act for Canada to improve labour conditions worldwide.

LABOUR CONGRESS. See CENTRAL ~.

LABOUR COUNCIL. See LOCAL ~.

LABOUR DISPUTE. 1. Any dispute between employers and employees, or between employees and employees, that is connected with the employment or non-employment, or the terms or conditions of employment, of any persons. *Employment Insurance Act*, S.C. 1996, c. 23, s. 2. 2. A dispute or difference concerning terms, tenure or conditions of employment or concerning the association or representation of persons in negotiating, fixing, maintaining, changing or seeking to arrange terms or conditions of employment, regardless of whether the disputants stand in the proximate relation of employer and employee.

LABOURER. *n.* 1. A person employed for wages in any kind of labour whether employed under a contract of service or not. 2. Includes every mechanic, artisan, machinist, miner, builder or other person doing labour for wages. *Mechanics' Lien Act*, R.S.N.W.T. 1974, c. M-8, s. 2. See DAY ~; FARM ~.

LABOUR EXPENSE. Of a corporation for a taxation year is the aggregate of all wages, salaries and management fees paid by the corporation in the taxation year.

LABOUR FORCE. All members of the population of employable age who are employed or unemployed. See NEW ENTRANT OR RE ENTRANT TO THE ~.

LABOUR-MANAGEMENT DISPUTE. 1. Any dispute or difference affecting employees represented by a bargaining agent, the employer of the employees, or the bargaining agent. Nova Scotia statutes. 2. Any dispute or difference between an employer and one or more of his employees or a trade union with respect to: (a) matters or things affecting or relating to work done or to be done by the employee or employees or trade union; or (b) the privileges, rights, duties, terms and conditions, or tenure of, employment or working conditions of the employee or employees or trade union. *The Trade Union Act*, R.S.S. 1988, c. T-17, s. 2.

LABOUR MARKET. The market for workers offering their services and employers offering jobs.

LABOUR MARKET AREA. The geographic area beyond which employees do not usually seek work and employers do not usually seek employees.

LABOUR ORGANIZATION. An organization of employees, not necessarily employees of one employer, that has bargaining collectively among its purposes. *The Trade Union Act*, R.S.S. 1978, c. T-17, s. 2.

LABOUR RELATIONS. All matters concerning the worker-employer relationship. See CANADA ~ BOARD.

LABOUR UNION. Any organization of employees that has as one of its purposes the regulation of relations between employers and employees and that has a constitution setting out its objectives and its conditions for membership. *Corporations and Labour Unions Returns Act*, R.S.C. 1985, c. C-43, s. 2. See CERTIFICATION OF ~.

LABRADOR. *n.* 1. The Coast of Labrador as delimited in the report delivered by the Judicial

Committee of His Majesty's Privy Council on the first day of March, 1927, and approved by His Majesty in His Privy Council on the twenty-second day of March, 1927, together with the islands adjacent to the said Coast of Labrador. *Labrador (Rehabilitation and Recreation) Act*, S. Nfld. 1973, c. 141, s. 4. 2. All that part of the Province situated on the mainland of Canada. Newfoundland statutes. 3. Includes all of the islands forming part of the province that are located wholly north of Cape Bauld. Newfoundland statutes. See NORTHERN ~.

L.A.C. *abbr.* Labour Arbitration Cases.

LACERATION. *n.* An injury to tissue involving a tearing or crushing.

L.A.C. (4TH). *abbr.* Labour Arbitration Cases (Fourth Series).

LACHES. *n.* [Fr.] 1. Negligent or unreasonable delay in pursuing a remedy. 2. "Unreasonable delay simipiciter is not sufficient to allow a party to succeed in the defence of laches. The defendants must establish that the consequences flowing from the unreasonable delay are such that, having regard to the relative positions of the parties presently, granting injunctive relief would lead to inequitable results." *Institut national des appellations d'origine des vins & eaux-de-vie v. Andres Wines* Ltd. (1987), 16 C.P.R. (3d) 385 at 446, 41 C.C.L.T. 94, 60 O.R. (2d) 316, 14 C.I.P.R. 138, 40 D.L.R. (4th) 239 (H.C.), Dupont J.

L.A.C. (2D). *abbr.* Labour Arbitration Cases (Second Series), 1973-1981.

L.A.C. (3D). *abbr.* Labour Arbitration Cases (Third Series), 1982-.

LACUNA. *n.* Gap.

LACUNAE. Plural of lacuna. Gaps.

LADING. *n.* Cargo. See BILL OF ~.

LAGAN. *n.* Goods fastened to a buoy and submerged in the sea.

LAID OPEN DATE. There remains, however, a choice between the date of issuance of the patent and the date of its publication because under the former Act [*Patent Act*, R.S.C. 1985, c. P-4] the date of issue and the date of publication were the same. Now, as a result of the obligations assumed by Canada under the *Patent Cooperation Treaty 1970* implemented by s. 10 of the new Act (S.C. 1993, c. 15, s. 28), the patent specification is "laid open" 18 months after the effective date of the Canadian patent application. In my view, the same logic that favoured the date of issuance/publication as the critical date for claims construction under the former Act, favours the choice of the "laid open" date under the new act. On that date, the invention is disclosed to the public, those interested have some ability to oppose the grant of the patent applied for, and the applicant for the patent is eventually allowed to claim reasonable compensation (s. 55(2)), provided the patent is ultimately granted, from and after the "laid open" date. The public, the patentee, its competitors and potential infringers all have an interest and/or concern from that date forward. The notional skilled addressee has a text available for interpretation. In summary, public disclosure and the triggering of legal consequences on the "laid open" date, as well as the policy considerations that underpinned the earlier case law, favour that date over the other possibilities as the critical date for the purpose of claims construction. *Free World Trust c. Électro Santé Inc.*, 2000 CarswellQue 2728, 2000 SCC 66, 194 D.L.R. (4th) 232, 263 N.R. 150, [2000] 2 S.C.R. 1024, 9 C.P.R. (4th) 168, Binnie, J.

LAISSER-FAIRE. *n.* [Fr.] A policy permitting unrestricted action, free of state planning.

LAKE. *n.* 1. " . . . [A] body of water of considerable depth surrounded by a well-defined beach or bank and with a reasonable permanent nature where one can swim if the water is not too cold. . ." *Alberta v. Very* (1983), 149 D.L.R. (3d) 688 at 703, 29 R.P.R.179, [1983] 6 W.W.R. 143, 27 Alta. L.R. (2d) 119 (Q.B.), Egbert J. 2. Includes a pond. *Lakes and Rivers Improvement Act*, R.S.O. 1990, c. L.3, s. 1. See PRODUCTS OF THE SEA, ~S AND RIVERS.

LAKE AND RIVER NAVIGATION. Includes all the rivers, lakes and other navigable waters within Canada. *Inland Water Freight Rates Act*, R.S.C. 1985, c. I-10, s. 2.

LAKE, FOREST AND FUR ASSOCIATION. Includes an association having as its principal objects, or any of them, the production or utilization of the products of forest, lake or river, or of other natural resources, on behalf of its members and patrons, or rendering services to members and patrons as producers, ancillary to such principal objects, or any of them. *The Cooperative Production Associations Act*, R.S.S. 1978, c. C-37, s. 63.

LAKE SHORE AREA. That portion of land lying within twenty-five metres above and twenty-five metres below the normal high water mark of any lake, and includes any bed, bank, beach, shore, bar, flat, mud flat or sand dune associated with the lake whether or not it lies within that portion of land. *An Act to Amend the Trespass Act*, S.N.B. 1985, c. 70, s. 1.

LAKE STURGEON. A fish of the species Acipenser fulvescens. *Quebec Fishery Regulations*, C.R.C., c. 852, s. 2.

LAKE TROUT. (Salvelinus namaycush, Walbaum) includes common lake trout, Great Lakes trout, grey trout, Makinaw trout, siscowet and splake (a cross breed of brook trout and lake trout). *Ontario Fishery Regulations*, C.R.C., c. 849, s. 2.

LAMB CARCASS. The carcass of an animal of the ovine species, of either sex, up to and including 12 months of age, having four well defined, relatively soft ridges at the break join of the forelegs. *Lamb and Mutton Carcass Grading Regulations*, C.R.C., c. 288, s. 2.

LAMINATED GLASS. Two or more sheets of glass bonded to an intervening layer or layers of plastic material. *Safety Glass Regulations*, C.R.C., c. 933, s. 2.

LAMP. *n.* A device for producing light. See AUXILIARY ~; FOG ~; SAFETY ~.

L.A.N. *abbr.* Labour Arbitration News.

LAND. *n.* 1. " . . . [I]n the great majority of cases, where the context does not require a special and technical meaning, . . . it means something quite concrete and tangible, something distinguished from water as a rule, or it may be from movable property . . ." *Murph Estate, Re* (1955), 37 M.P.R. 107 at 111, [1955] 5 D.L.R. 768 (Nfld. C.A.), Winter J.A. 2. " . . . [I]s not, in law, the soil we touch, but the rights attached to it. Such rights include the right to work the soil, to mine beneath the surface and build in the airspace above it and the incorporeal rights to light, support and the use of water flowing across land."' *Trizec Manitoba Ltd. v. Winnipeg City Assessor* (1986), 34 M.P.L.R. 9 at 12, 41 R.P.R. 176, [1986] 5 W.W.R. 97, 42 Man. R. (2d) 98 (C.A.), Twaddle J.A. (Huband J.A. concurring). 3. " . . . [I]n its primary meaning refers to corporeal hereditaments: . . ." *Wiener v. Elgin (County)*, [1947] 2 D.L.R. 346 at 348, 194 O.W.N. 360 (H.C.), Urquhart J. 4. Lands, messuages, tenements and hereditaments, corporeal and incorporeal, of every nature and description, and every estate or interest therein, whether the estate or interest is legal or equitable, together with all paths, passages, ways, watercourses, liberties, privileges, easements, mines, minerals and quarries appertaining thereto, and all trees and timber thereon and thereunder lying or being, unless specially excepted. 5. The solid part of the earth's surface and includes the foreshore and land covered by water. 6. When land is sold, "land" refers to "a right to receive a good title in fee simple" unless the agreement states otherwise. "Land" is not given a special meaning in the leases; in particular, it is *not* defined as a 99-year leasehold interest in the property under the lease. *Musqueam Indian Band v. Glass* (2000), 2000 CarswellNat 2405, 2000 SCC 52, [2000] 11 W.W.R. 407, 36 R.P.R. (3d) 1, 192 D.L.R. (4th) 385, 82 B.C.L.R. (3d) 199, 261 N.R. 296, 186 F.T.R. 248 (note), [2000] 2 S.C.R. 633, [2001] 1 C.N.L.R. 208, Per Gonthier J. (Major, Binnie and LeBel JJ. concurring). 7. Land, tenements, hereditaments and appurtenances and any estate or interest therein. 8. Includes land covered by water and any building erected on land and any estate, interest, right or easement in or over any land or building. See ADJACENT ~; ADJOINING ~; AGRICULTURAL ~; ALLOCATED ~; ARABLE ~; COAL ~; CONSERVATION AUTHORITY ~; CONSERVATION ~; CONTIGUOUS ~; CONVEYANCE OF ~; CROWN ~; CULTIVATED ~; DEVELOPED ~; ENCLOSED ~; ESTATE IN ~; FALLOW~; FARM ~; FEDERAL ~; FOREST ~; GREENBELT~; IMPROVED ~; IMPROVING ~; INTEREST IN ~; ~S; MARSH~; MINERAL ~; OCCUPIED ~; ORIGINAL COST OF THE ~; PARCEL OF ~; PARK~; PICK OF ~; PRIVATE ~; PRIVATELY OWNED ~; PROVINCIAL ~; PUBLIC ~; RATEABLE ~; RECREATIONAL ~; RESERVED ~; RESIDENTIAL ~; RUN WITH THE ~; RURAL ~; SERVICED VACANT ~; SHORE~; SUBAQUATIC ~; SUBDIVIDED ~; TIMBER ~; TRACT OF ~; TRESPASS TO ~; UNCULTIVATED ~; UNRESTRICTED ~; USE OF ~; VACANT ~; WET~; WILD ~.

LAND AGENT. (a) A person who (i) on behalf of his employer, (ii) as an agent on behalf of another person, or (iii) on his own behalf, negotiates for or acquires an interest in land, or (b) a person who for a fee gives or offers advice to an owner or his agent with respect to negotiations for or acquisition of an interest in land.

Land Agents Licensing Act, R.S.A. 2000, c. L-2, s. 1.

LAND AIRCRAFT. An aircraft that is not capable of normal operations on water; *Canadian Aviation Regulations*, SOR/96-433, s. 101.01(1).

LAND ASSEMBLY. The development of land for any purpose or project permitted by this Act or related to a purpose or project permitted by this Act, including the acquisition, assembly, planning, servicing, sale, conveyance, leasing or other disposal of the land. *Housing Development acts.*

L. & C. *abbr*. Lefroy & Cassels' Practice Cases (Ont.), 1881-1883.

LAND CLAIMS AGREEMENT. A land claims agreement within the meaning of section 35 of the *Constitution Act, 1982*. An agreement which resolves a claim to land by an aboriginal group.

LAND CODE. A first nation that wishes to establish a land management regime in accordance with the Framework Agreement and this Act shall adopt a land code applicable to all land in a reserve of the first nation, which land code must include the following matters: (a) a legal description of the land that will be subject to the land code; (b) the general rules and procedures applicable to the use and occupancy of first nation land, including use and occupancy under (i) licences and leases, and (ii) interests in first nation land held pursuant to allotments under subsection 20(1) of the Indian Act or pursuant to the custom of the first nation; (c) the procedures that apply to the transfer, by testamentary disposition or succession, of any interest in first nation land; and related matters. *First Nations Land Management Act*, S.C. 1999, c. 24, s. 6(1).

LAND CO-OPERATIVE. A parcel of land that is owned by a corporation exclusively for the benefit of its shareholders who (a) have a right to occupy a portion of the parcel, and (b) own shares or shares and other securities in the corporation that have a value equivalent to the value of the portion in relation to the value of the parcel. *Home Owner Grant Act*, R.S.B.C. 1996, c. 194, s. 1.

LAND DRAINAGE. Storm, surface, overflow, subsurface, or seepage waters or other drainage from land, but does not include wastewater.

LAND DRAINAGE SEWER. A sewer that carries storm water and surface water, street wash and other wash waters or drainage but excludes domestic wastewater and industrial wastes. *City of Winnipeg Act*, S.M. 1971, c. 105, s. 453.

LANDED. *adj*. Having lawful permission to establish permanent residence in Canada.

LANDED IMMIGRANT. One who lawfully has permanent resident status in Canada.

LAND EXTERMINATION. The destruction, prevention or control in, on or over land of a pest or pests by the use of a pesticide but does not include a structural extermination, a water extermination or the destruction, prevention or control of termites. *Pesticides Act*, R.S.O. 1990, c. P.11, s. 1(1).

LANDFILL. *n*. A waste management facility at which waste is disposed of by placing it on or in land.

LANDFILLING. *n*. The disposal of waste by deposit, under controlled conditions, on land or on land covered by water, and includes compaction of the waste into a cell and covering the waste with cover materials at regular intervals. *Environmental Protection Act*, R.R.O. 1990, Reg. 347, s. 1.

LAND FOR PUBLIC PURPOSES. Land, other than streets, for the recreational or other use or enjoyment of the general public, such as (a) an access to a lake, river, stream, sea or other body of water, (b) a beach or scenic area along the shore of a lake, river, stream, sea or other body of water, (c) a conservation area, (d) land adjoining a school for joint recreational purposes, (e) land for a community hall, public library, recreational use or other similar community facility, (f) open space, to provide air and light, to afford a view to or from a development or to a lake, river, stream, sea or other body of water, or for other purposes, (g) a park, green belt or buffer area dividing developments, parts of a highway or a development and a highway, (h) a pedestrian way to a school, recreational area or other facility, (i) a protection area for a water course, stream, marsh, water supply lake or other body of water, (j) a public park, playground or other recreational use, (k) a visual feature, or (l) a wooded area, slope area or a site giving view to a scenic area to provide diversity. *Community Planning Act*, R.S.N.B., c. 12, s. 1.

LAND GABEL. A rent or tax which issues out of land.

LAND HOLDING. *var*. **LANDHOLDING**. 1. An interest conferring the right to possession, occupation or use of land in the province but does not include land or an interest in land acquired by a bank, trust company or other financial institution in the ordinary course of its business by way of security for a debt or other obligation. *Prince Edward Island Lands Protection Act*, R.S.P.E.I. 1988, c. L-5, s. 1(1)(g). 2. Includes (a) any interest in land held under an agreement to purchase the land that may directly or indirectly result in the vesting of title or confer the right to possession of that land, or confer a right or control ordinarily accruing to an owner of land, (b) any lease of land that would vest in the lessee possession and control of the land, (c) land legally or beneficially owned by a corporation whose shares or securities of a kind or class designated in the regulations for the purposes of this clause are owned or held by ineligible persons, (d) any interest in land, other than those specified in subclauses (a) and (b) but does not include any land or an interest in land held by way of security for a debt or other obligation. *An Act to Amend the Agricultural Lands Protection Act*, S.M.1980-81, c. 36, s. 2. See AGGREGATE ~; TENURIAL FORM OF ~.

LAND IMPROVEMENT ASSOCIATION. Includes an association incorporated or registered under this Act having as its principal objects or any of them the conservation of land against erosion from wind or water, conservation of water resources, irrigation, the planting and maintenance of trees as shelter belts or the conservation of other natural resources required by members and patrons engaged in the production of agricultural products or other products, or rendering to the members and patrons as producers, services ancillary to such principal objects, or any of them. *The Co-operative Production Associations Act*, R.S.S. 1978, c. C-37, s. 61.

LAND IMPROVEMENT PURPOSE. The diversion or impounding of water to protect property, to facilitate the development of a park or the reclamation, drainage or other improvement of land or to carry out a project of a similar nature. *Water Act*, R.S.B.C. 1996, c. 483, s. 1.

LANDING. *n*. 1. Lawful permission to establish permanent residence in Canada. *Immigration Act*, R.S.C. 1985, c. I-2, s. 2. 2. (a) In respect of an aircraft other than an airship, the act of coming into contact with a supporting surface, and includes the acts immediately preceding and following the coming into contact with that surface, and (b) in respect of an airship, the act of bringing the airship under restraint, and includes the acts immediately preceding and following the bringing of the airship under restraint. *Canadian Aviation Regulations*, SOR/96-433, s. 101.01(1). See TECHNICAL ~.

LANDING AREA. A cleared area where trees or logs are stored, measured, processed, unloaded or loaded and includes a log dump. *Industrial Establishments Act*, R.R.O. 1990, Reg. 851, s. 103.

LANDING DISTANCE AVAILABLE. The length of a runway at an aerodrome that the aerodrome operator declares available and suitable for the ground run of an aeroplane that is landing. *Canadian Aviation Regulations*, SOR/96-433, s. 101.01(1).

LANDING NET. A fishing gear that is made of a small net that is mounted on a frame fixed to a handle and that is ordinarily used to bag fish caught by a hook. *Quebec Fishery Regulations*, C.R.C., c. 852, s. 2.

LAND LEASE COMMUNITY. The land on which one or more occupied land lease homes are situate and includes the rental units and the land, structures, services and facilities of which the landlord retains possession and that are intended for the common use and enjoyment of the tenants of the landlord. *Tenant Protection Act, 1997*, S.O. 1997, c. 24, s.1.

LAND LEASE HOME. A dwelling, other than a mobile home, that is a permanent structure where the owner of the dwelling leases the land used or intended for use as the site for the dwelling. *Tenant Protection Act, 1997*, S.O. 1997, c. 24, s. 1(1).

LANDLOCKED. *adj*. Describes a piece of land which belongs to one person and is surrounded by land which belongs to other people, so that the single owner cannot approach her or his own parcel except over the other's land.

LANDLORD. *n*. 1. Includes lessor, owner or the person giving or permitting the occupation of the premises in question and the heirs, assigns and legal representatives thereof. 2. A person who rents land to another person for a share of the crop or of the proceeds of the crop produced on such land. *The Saskatchewan Insurance Act*, R.S.S. 1978 ,c. S-12, s. 2. See GROUND ~.

LANDMARK. *n*. An object which fixes the boundary of property or an estate.

LAND MOBILE SERVICE. A radiocommunication service that provides for communications between mobile stations and (a) fixed stations, (b) space stations, or (c) other mobile stations. *Radiocommunication Regulations*, SOR/96-484, s. 2.

LAND-OWNING PARISHIONER. A parishioner who has possessed as proprietor for at least six months an immoveable situated in the parish or chapelry. *An Act Respecting Fabriques*, R.S.Q. 1977, c. F-1, s. 1.

LAND PEST CONTROL. The destruction, prevention or control of pests in, on or over land by the use of a pest control product, but does not include structural pest control. *Pest Control Products (Nova Scotia) Act*, S.N.S. 1986, c. 16, s. 3.

LANDPLANE. *n*. An aircraft other than a seaplane. *Life-saving Equipment Order*, C.R.C., c. 50, s. 2.

LAND REGISTRAR. A land registrar appointed under the Registry Act, in whose land titles division land affected or intended to be affected by any proceeding, instrument, application or plan is or may be registered or deposited. *Land Titles Act*, R.S.O. 1990, c. L.5, s. 1.

LAND REGISTRATION DISTRICT. See NORTH ALBERTA ~.

LAND REGISTRY. A land titles office.

LAND-RELATED INFORMATION SYSTEMS NETWORK. A series of data bases coordinated by the Director that contain information on land or related to land and that are compatible because all the data bases (a) contain geographically positioned data elements, and (b) adhere to common design standards. *Surveys Act*, R.S.A. 2000, c. S-26, s. 1.

LANDS. *n*. 1. Lands the acquiring, taking or using of which is authorized by this Act or a Special Act, and includes real property, messuages, lands, tenements and hereditaments of any tenure, and any easement, servitude, right, privilege or interest in, to, on, under, over or in respect of the same. Canada statutes. 2. Include water (and the frozen surface thereof) and any other supporting surface. *Aeronautics Act*, R.S.C. 1985 (1st Supp.), c. 33, s. 5.4. 3. Includes all granted or ungranted, wild or cleared, public or private lands, all real property, messuages, lands, tenements and hereditaments of any tenure, all real rights, easements and servitudes and all other things for which compensation is to be paid by the Crown. *Government Railways Act*, R.S.C. 1985, c. G-7, s. 2. 4. The inner surface

areas of a firearm barrel between the rifling grooves. F.A. Jaffe, *A Guide to Pathological Evidence*, 3d ed. (Toronto: Carswell, 1991) at 222. See ALLODIAL ~; CANADA ~; CROWN ~; CUT-OFF ~; DOCUMENT OF TITLE TO ~; FREEHOLD ~; FRONTIER ~; INDIAN ~; INSTITUTIONAL ~; LAND; MATURE~; MINERAL ~; MINING ~; NOVA SCOTIA ~; OCCUPIED ~; PATENTED ~; PRIVATE ~; PRODUCTIVE ~; PUBLIC ~; SEVERANCE ~; SURRENDERED ~; TAKE ~; TERRITORIAL ~; UNPRODUCTIVE ~.

LANDS AND PREMISES. 1. Buildings, lands, hereditaments and easements of any tenure. *Public Health Act*, R.S.A. 1970, c. 294, s. 2. 2. Includes messuages, buildings, lands and easements of any tenure. *City of St. John's Act*, R.S. Nfld. 1970, c. 40, s. 2.

LANDSCAPE CONSTRUCTION. Any clearing, breaking, grading, fertilizing or cultivation of an area or the construction of an outdoor ground surface for games or athletics or the establishment thereon of trees, shrubs, flowers, grass or other forms of vegetative growth or outdoor furniture, including seating of a type suitable for a garden or park but not for an audience or assembly of spectators, or any functional or aesthetic feature contributing to the general landscape design of the area, and includes the provision of such machines, equipment and tools as is requisite for all or any of such matters.

LANDSCAPE MAINTENANCE. The sustaining of landscape construction and includes the provision of such machines, equipment and tools as is requisite therefor.

LANDS, TENEMENTS AND HEREDITAMENTS. A traditional description of real property, considered the most comprehensive.

LAND SURVEY. The establishment, location or definition on the ground of any boundary, limit or angle of any land, size, location, parcel, claim, common, easement, road, street, lane, district, municipality, county or township.

LAND SURVEYING. The determination of any point or of the direction or length of any line required in measuring, laying off, or dividing land for the purpose of establishing boundaries or title to land. See PRACTICE OF ~; PRACTICE OF PROFESSIONAL ~; PROFESSIONAL ~.

LAND SURVEYOR. See ALBERTA ~; PRO-VINCIAL ~.

LAND TAX. A tax that is imposed on land against the owner and assessed as a percentage of the value of the land. Generally a direct tax.

LAND TITLE OFFICE. The registry office of the land title district in which land is situate.

LAND TITLES. See REGISTRAR OF ~.

LAND TITLES ASSURANCE FUND. A fund available for those who suffer a loss as a result of the operation of a land titles system.

LAND TITLES SYSTEM. A system of registration of ownership of and interests in land. The government makes a brief, simple statement concerning the ownership of land and all outstanding interests or claims so that the purchaser need not be concerned, as in a registry system, with the history of the transactions which affected that land.

LAND TREATMENT. The controlled application of a substance on the soil surface and incorporation of the substance into the upper soil zone in such a manner that physical, chemical or biological degradation of the substance takes place. *Activities Designation Regulation*, Alta. Reg. 276/2003, s. 2.

LAND USE CONTROL LAW. Any Act of the Legislature, and any regulation, plan or by-law made under the authority of an Act of the Legislature that restricts or prescribes the use to which land or premises may be put or the nature of businesses or activities that may be carried on on any land or premises. *Agricultural Operation Practices Act*, S.N.B. 1986, c. A-5 .2, s. 1.

LAND USE DISTRICT. An area of land that is within a reservoir development area or special flood hazard area and that is designated by regulation as a land use district within which specified uses and limitations on uses are imposed. *The Water Resources Management Act*, R.S.S. 1978, c. W-7, s. 2.

LAND USE PLAN. A plan for the control of land within a defined area proposing that parts of the land may be used only for industry, commerce, government, recreation, transportation, hospitals, schools, churches, residences, homes for the elderly or for other purposes or classes of users, with or without subdivisions of the various classes. *Roadway Relocation and Crossing Act*, R.S.C. 1985, c. R-4, s. 17.

LANE. n, 1. A public highway vested in the Crown as a secondary level or access to a site.

The Planning and Development Act, R.S.S. 1978, c. P-13, s. 2. 2. A street not over twenty feet in width. *City of Winnipeg Act*, S.M. 1971, c. 105, s. 1. 3. A public thoroughfare not over 33 feet in width that affords a secondary means of access to a lot. Canada regulations. See BACK ~; PARKING ~; PUBLIC ~; TRAFFIC ~.

LANED HIGHWAY. A roadway that is divided into two or more clearly marked lanes for vehicular traffic. *Motor Vehicle Act* R.S.N.B. 1973, c. M-17, s. 1.

LANED ROADWAY. A roadway which is divided into two or more clearly marked lanes for vehicular traffic.

LANGUAGE. *n*. The means of communication of a person, part of the person's identity and culture and the means by which persons understand themselves and their surroundings. See ABORIGINAL ~; ASSEMBLY ~; COMPUTER ~; HERITAGE ~; HIGH-LEVEL ~; MACHINE ~; OFFICIAL ~.

LANGUAGE TRAINING. Basic training, at public expense, in one of the official languages, the nature, duration and location of which is prescribed on an individual basis.

LANUGO HAIRS. Fine hairs appearing at the end of the sixth month which covers the fetus during the seventh and eighth months of gestation. F.A. Jaffe, *A Guide to Pathological Evidence*, 3d ed. (Toronto: Carswell, 1991) at 222.

LAPARASCOPY. *n*. Surgery performed through an illuminated instrument inserted through a body cavity while the operative area is projected onto a screen for the surgeon to visualize the site.

LAPAROTOMY. *n*. Surgery performed through a surgical incision across the abdominal wall.

LAP DANCING. Dance by an employee which may include touching of patrons during the performance including sexual touching.

LAPSE. *v*. To fail, said of a bequest or devise of property which goes into residue as if the gift had not been made when the person to whom the property was bequeathed or devised dies before the testator.

LAPSE. *n*. 1. Error; failure in duty. 2. Occurs when a gift fails because the donee of the gift predeceases the donor-testator.

LAPSE DATE. (a) In the case of a prospectus, the date on which a prospectus ceases to be valid for the distribution of securities for which the prospectus was filed, and (b) in the case of a summary statement, the date on which a summary statement ceases to be valid for the distribution of securities for which the summary statement was filed.

LAPSING. See TIME OF ~.

LAPSUS CALAMI. [L.] A clerical error; a slip.

LAPSUS PENNAE. [L.] A drafting or printing slip.

LARCENY. *n*. Theft.

LA REINE LE VEULT. [Fr.] The Queen wishes it.

LA REINE N'EST LIÉ PAR AUCUN STATUT SI ELLE NE FUT EXPRESSÉMENT NOMMÉE. [Fr.] The Queen is not bound by any statute if not expressly named in it.

LA REINE REMERCIE SES BONS SUJETS, ACCEPTE LEUR BÉNÉVOLENCE ET AINSI LE VEUT. [Fr.] The Queen is grateful to her loyal subjects, accepts their benevolence, and wishes it this way.

LA REINE S'AVISERA. [Fr.] The Queen will consider this.

LARGE. *adj*. "The term 'large' which appears in [the Interpretation Act, R.S.C. 1985, c. 1-21, s. 12] is not one in modern use in the sense in which it is used there. Its meaning is synonymous with broad." *R. v. Myers* (1991), 65 C.C.C. (3d) 135 at 139, 91 Nfld. & P.E.I.R. 37, 286 A.P.R. 37 (Nfld. C.A.), Goodridge C.J.N. (Steele J.A. concurring).

LARGE AEROPLANE. An aeroplane with an MCTOW of more than 5 700 kg (12,566 pounds). *Canadian Aviation Regulations*, SOR/96-433, s. 101.01.

LARGE-CAPACITY CARTRIDGE MAGAZINE. Any device or container from which ammunition may be fed into the firing chamber of a firearm. *Criminal Code*, S.C. 1991, c. 40, s. 2(5).

LARGE-MESH TRAWL NET. A trawl net having a cod end the mesh size of which is 2 inches or more extension measure. *Ontario Fishery Regulations*, C.R.C., c. 949, s. 2.

LARGE PROVINCE. A province (other than Quebec) having a population greater than two

and a half million. *Constitution Act 1974*, S.C. 1974-75-76, c. 13, reprinted as R.S.C. 1985, App. Document No. 40.

LARVA. *n*. [L.] A stage between egg and pupa in the metamorphosis of an insect.

LARYNX. *n*. A hollow, cartilaginous and muscular structure which is lined with mucous membrane, located between the trachea and the hyoid bone and contains the vocal cords.

LASER. *n*. Any device that can be made to produce light primarily by the process of stimulated emission. *Emitting Devices Regulations*, C.R.C., c. 1370, s. 1.

LASER RADIATION. All electromagnetic radiation generated by a laser that is coherent and propagates collinearly through space. *Radiation Emitting Devices Regulations*, C.R.C., c. 1370, s. 1. See SCANNED ~.

LASING MEDIUM. A material that emits laser radiation by virtue of stimulated transitions between specific electronic or molecular energy levels. *Radiation Emitting Devices Regulations*, C.R.C., c. 1370, s. 1.

LAST. *adj*. Farthest.

LAST ASCERTAINABLE SIDE LINE. A line in a broken concession established from the front of the concession on the course of a side line of a lot from the lot corner nearest the end of the part of the concession so broken. *Surveys Act*, R.S.O. 1990, c. S.30, s. 1.

LAST CHANCE AGREEMENT. An employee agrees as a condition of continued employment that she will abide by all company rules and policies.

LAST CHANCE SETTLEMENT. The parties to a grievance agree that certain conduct of the employee will constitute a final incident giving the employer the right to terminate the employee.

LAST CLEAR CHANCE DOCTRINE. Assigns responsibility for a loss to a negligent party who had the 'last clear chance' to avert the loss which was sustained by another party.

LAST HEIR. Any person to whom land comes when there are no other heirs.

LAST-IN, FIRST-OUT METHOD OF INVENTORY VALUATION. A method of valuing inventory in which it is assumed that the items most recently acquired are the ones disposed of first. The inventory value at the end of the period amounts to the cost of the items which were acquired first.

LASTING IMPROVEMENT. 1. An addition to property consisting of more than mere repair or replacement of waste. 2. Preparation of farm land for cultivation by clearing trees and rock picking.

LAST RESORT. Describes a court from which there is no further appeal. Generally speaking, in each of the provinces it is the court of appeal and in Canada as a whole it is the Supreme Court of Canada. See COURT OF ~.

LATA CULPA DOLO AEQUIPARATUR. [L.] Gross negligence is on a par with fraud.

LATENT. *adj*. Concealed, hidden; secret.

LATENT AMBIGUITY. " . . . [W]here the language is equivocal, or if unequivocal but its application to the facts is uncertain or difficult, a latent ambiguity is said to be present. The term 'latent ambiguity' seems now to be applied generally to all cases of doubtful meaning or application." *Leitch Gold Mines Ltd. v. Texas Gulf Sulphur Co.* (1968), 3 D.L.R. (3d) 161 at 216, [1969] 1 O.R. 469 (H.C.), Gale C.J.O.

LATENT DEFECT. 1. One not discoverable on casual inspection and not observable. A defect which a reasonably careful inspection will not reveal. 2. " . . . 'Not discernible by adequate inspection' . . ." *Scottish Metropolitan Assurance Co. v. Canada Steamship Lines Ltd*, [1930] S.C.R. 262 at 279, [1930] 1 D.L.R. 201, Anglin C.J.C. (Rinfret and Lamont JJ. concurring).

LATERAL. *adj*. Towards the side.

LATERAL DRAIN. A drain that is designed for the drainage of one property and that begins and ends on the same property. *Drainage Act*, R.S.O. 1990, c. D.17, s. 1.

LATERAL TRANSFER. A change in an employee's job to one with similar duties.

LATE SCRATCH. A horse that is withdrawn from a race after betting on that race has begun. *Pari-Mutuel Betting Supervision Regulations*, SOR/91-365, s. 2.

LATHER. *n*. A person who, (a) plans proposed installations from blueprints, sketches, specifications, building standards and codes, (b) installs by tying, nailing, clipping, screwing or welding wire, metal or wood lath, drywall gypsum board or other materials in the construction or repair of walls, partitions, ceilings or arches in any structure, (c) erects light metal studs, metal furring components, acoustical ceilings systems and accessories to receive drywall gypsum board, wire and metal lath, (d) reads and understands design drawings, manufacturers' literature and installation diagrams, but does not include a person engaged in the manufacture of equipment or the assembly of a unit, prior to delivery to a building structure or site. *Apprenticeship and Tradesmen's Qualification Act*, R.R.O. 1980, Reg. 45, s. 1.

LATIN. *n*. The language of ancient Rome. Law Latin includes both good Latin, familiar to lawyers and classical grammarians, and words of art or lawyers' latin, familiar to the legal profession but not to grammarians.

LAUNCH. *n*. A steamship in which the passengers are carried in an open cockpit or in a cockpit that is covered by a light trunk cabin. Canada regulations.

LAUNCH WEIGHT. The total weight of a hang glider or an ultra-light aeroplane when it is ready for flight, including any equipment, instruments, fuel or oil, but not including (a) the weight of the occupants, (b) the weight of any float equipment to a maximum of 34 kg (74.93 pounds), or (c) the weight of any ballistic parachute installation. *Canadian Aviation Regulations*, SOR/96-433, s. 101.01(1).

LAUNDERING PROCEEDS OF CRIME. Every one commits an offence who uses, transfers the possession of, sends or delivers to any person or place, transports, transmits, alters, disposes of or otherwise deals with, in any manner and by any means, any property or any proceeds of any property with intent to conceal or convert that property or those proceeds, knowing or believing that all or a part of that property or of those proceeds was obtained or derived directly or indirectly as a result of (a) the commission in Canada of a designated offence; or (b) an act or omission anywhere that, if it had occurred in Canada, would have constituted a designated offence. *Criminal Code*, R.S.C. 1985, c. C-46, s. 462.31. See MONEY LAUNDERING.

LAUNDRY. *n*. A building or part of a building used for the washing, ironing or pressing of clothes, linens or other fabrics and material where such work is carried on as a trade or business. *The Public Health Act*, R.S.S. 1978, c. P-37, s. 2. See PUBLIC ~.

LAW. *n*. 1. A rule to govern action. 2. An enactment. 3. Includes an Act of the Parliament of

Canada or of the Legislature and includes a proclamation, regulation, order in council, a decree or an ordinance made under the authority of any Act. 4. In its general sense, refers to all the rules which govern society and are enforceable through the judicial or administrative systems. Law in this general sense is comprised of the written and unwritten Constitution, federal and provincial statutes and the "judge-made" common law and equity. See ABORIGINAL ~; ACT IN THE ~; ACT OF THE ~; ADJECTIVE ~; ADMINISTRATIVE ~; ADMIRALTY ~; ANTITRUST~; BLUE-SKY ~; BY-~; CANON ~; CASE ~; CHOICE OF ~; CIVIL ~; COLONIAL ~; COMMERCIAL ~; COMMON ~; CONCLUSION OF ~; CONSTITUTIONAL ~; CONSUETUDINARY ~; CONTRACT ~; CRIMINAL ~; ECCLESIASTICAL ~; ELDER ~; ENTERTAINMENT ~; ENVIRONMENTAL ~; EQUALITY BEFORE AND UNDER THE ~; EQUALITY BEFORE THE ~; EQUITY FOLLOWS THE ~; ERRED IN ~; ERROR IN ~; ERROR OF ~; FAMILY~ COMMISSIONER; FISCAL ~; HOMESTEAD ~; INTERNAL ~; INTERNATIONAL ARBITRATION ~; INTERNATIONAL ~; JUDGE-MADE ~; LAND USE CONTROL ~; MALICE IN ~; MARITIME ~; MARTIAL ~; MEDIA ~; MERCANTILE ~; MERE ERROR OF ~; MILITARY ~; MISTAKE OF ~; MIXED ~; MIXED QUESTION OF ~ AND FACT; MUNICIPAL ~; NATURAL ~; NEW ~; OLD ~; PENAL ~; POLITICAL ~; POSITIVE ~; PRACTICE OF ~; PRESCRIBED BY ~; PRESUMPTION OF ~; PRIVACY ~; PRIVATE ~; PROCEDURAL ~; PROPER ~; PROPERTY ~; PROVISION OF ~; PUBLIC ~; QUESTION OF ~; RESTATEMENT OF ~; REVENUE ~; RIGHT-TO-WORK ~; RULE OF ~; SUBSTANTIVE ~; SUMPTUARY ~; SUNDAY CLOSING ~.

LAW CLERK AND PARLIAMENTARY COUNSEL. An official appointed by Letters Patent under the Great Seal whose principal duty is to provide comprehensive legal advice to the Speaker, officers of the House of Commons and Board of Internal Economy and who helps members of Parliament draft legislation. A. Fraser, W.A. Dawson, & J. Holtby, eds., *Beauchesne's Rules and Forms of the House of Commons of Canada*, 6th ed. (Toronto: Carswell, 1989) at 61.

LAW COMMISSION. The purpose of the Commission is to study and keep under system-atic review, in a manner that reflects the concepts and institutions of the common law and civil law systems, the law of Canada and its effects with a view to providing independent advice on improvements, modernization and reform that will ensure a just legal system that meets the changing needs of Canadian society and of individuals in that society, including (a) the development of new approaches to, and new concepts of, law; (b) the development of measures to make the legal system more efficient, economical and accessible; (c) the stimulation of critical debate in, and the forging of productive networks among, academic and other communities in Canada in order to ensure cooperation and coordination; and (d) the elimination of obsolete laws and anomalies in the law. *Law Commission of Canada Act*, S.C. 1996, c. 9, s. 3. Some provinces have similar bodies with similar purposes.

LAW ENFORCEMENT. (a) Policing, (b) investigations or inspections that lead or could lead to proceedings in a court or tribunal if a penalty or sanction could be imposed in those proceedings, and (c) the conduct of proceedings referred to in clause (b). Ontario statutes.

LAWFUL. *adj.* 1. Authorized by law. *R. v. Robinson* (1948), 6 C.R. 343 at 346, [1948] O.R. 857, 92 C.C.C. 223 (C.A.), Laidlaw J.A. 2. Not in contravention of any law. 3. Legal.

LAWFUL ADMISSION. Compliance with all requirements to gain admission to Canada.

LAWFUL EXCUSE. 1. " . . . [N]ormally includes all of the defences which the common law considers sufficient reason to excuse a person from criminal liability. It can also include excuses specific to particular offences . . ." *R. v. Holmes* (1988), 34 C.R.R. 193 at 200, 85 N.R. 21, 27 O.A.C. 321, [1988] 1 S.C.R. 914, 64 C.R. (3d) 97, 41 C.C.C. (3d) 497, Dickson C.J.C. (Lamer J. concurring). 2. " . . . [I]ncludes any honest and reasonable belief in a state of facts which, if they had been as the accused believed them to be, would have made his act innocent . . ." *R. v. Ireco Canada II Inc.* (1988), 17 C.E.R. 245 at 258, 65 C.R. (3d) 160, 43 C.C.C. (3d) 482, 29 O.A.C. 161 (C.A.), Martin, Cory and Finlayson JJ.A. 3. (a) The ability to prove that fish in possession during the close time therefor at the place of possession were legally caught, or (b) the unintentional or incidental catching of any fish that may not then be taken, when legally fishing for other fish. *Fisheries Act*, R.S.C. 1985, c. F-14, s. 2.

LAWFUL FENCE. 1. A substantial fence not less than four feet high and consisting of not less than four strands of ordinary fence wire, the lower wire being not more than twelve inches above the ground, the posts in such fences to be placed not more than twenty-seven feet apart. *The Saskatchewan Railway Act*, R.S.S. 1978, c. S-33, s. 2. 2. A substantial fence of a height of not less than four feet above the level of the ground, constructed of woven wire, barbed wire or rails, boards or slabs, of a size and structure that will suitably confine animals under normal circumstances, and fastened to posts not more than sixteen feet apart. *Herd and Fencing Act*, R.S.N.W.T. 1974, c. H-1, s. 8.

LAWFULLY. *adv.* (a) In accordance with this Act and the Canadian Wheat Board Act, and (b) in respect of (i) the offering of grain for delivery to or storage in a primary elevator, (ii) the delivery of grain to a terminal elevator, transfer elevator or process elevator or to a consignee at a destination other than an elevator, or (iii) the delivery of grain to a public carrier for carriage to any elevator or consignee referred to in subparagraph (ii), deliverable by the owner of the grain, receivable by the public carrier for carriage to the elevator or consignee and receivable by the operator of the elevator or consignee, in accordance with this Act and the Canadian Wheat Board Act. *Canada Grain Act*, R.S.C. 1985, c. G-10, s. 2. See PERSON ~ IN POSSESSION OF THE BODY.

LAWFULLY FISHING. Fishing in accordance with the game laws of the Province and the laws of the Dominion of Canada and any regulations made thereunder for the purpose of sport, and includes the taking and carrying away of any fish lawfully caught. *Angling Act*, R.S.N.S. 1989, c. 14, s. 2.

LAWFUL PICKETING. The giving of information by picketers with the objective of persuading or soliciting support from third persons who can lawfully give such support.

LAWFUL RIGHT. In the context of the Radiocommunications Act, the concept of "lawful right" refers to the person who possesses the regulatory rights through proper licensing under the *Act*, the authorization of the Canadian Radio-television and Telecommunications Commission as well as the contractual and copyrights necessarily pertaining to the content involved in the transmission of the encrypted subscription programming signal or encrypted network feed.

Bell ExpressVu Ltd. Partnership v. Rex, [2002] 2 S.C.R. 559.

LAWFUL WORK. Any work not contrary to the laws in force at the place of construction of the work at the time of its construction. *Navigable Waters Protection Act*, R.S.C. 1985, c. N-22, s. 3.

LAW LIST. A listing of all persons who are practicing as barristers or solicitors and any other lawyers.

LAW LORDS. In England, the Lord Chancellor, the Lords of Appeal in Ordinary, former Lord Chancellors and other peers who held high judicial offices.

LAW MERCHANT. The law which governs any mercantile transaction.

LAW OF AGENCY. The law concerning the relationships between those who act for others on their behalf.

LAW OF CANADA. 1. In s. 101 of the Constitution Act, 1867 (30 & 31 Vict.), c. 3 includes federal common law. *Wewayakum Indian Band v. Canada* (1989), 3 R.P.R. (2d) 1 at 8, 13, 16, 92 N.R. 241, 25 F.T.R. 161, [1989] 3 W.W.R. 117, 35 B.C.L.R. (2d) 1, 57 D.L.R. (4th) 197, [1979] 1 S.C.R. 322, [1989] 2 C.N.L.R. 146, the court per Wilson J. 2. In Part I means an Act of the Parliament of Canada enacted before of after the coming into force of this Act, any order, rule or regulation thereunder, and any law in force in Canada or in any part of Canada at the commencement of this part that is subject to be repealed, abolished or altered by the Parliament of Canada. *Canadian Bill of Rights*, 8-9 Elizabeth II, c. 44 (Canada). 3. A law enacted by the Parliament of Canada. See LAWS OF CANADA.

LAW OF CONTRACT. The law governing agreements concerning promises to be performed.

LAW OFFICER. The Minister of Justice of Québec. *Interpretation Act*, R.S.Q. 1977, c. I-16, s. 61.

LAW OFFICER OF THE CROWN. 1. An Attorney-General; a Solicitor-General. 2. The Minister of Justice of Québec. *Interpretation Act*, R.S.Q. 1977, c. I-16, s. 61.

LAW OF FLAG. The law of the country of the flag of which a ship is flying.

LAW OF NATIONS. Public international law.

LAW OF ONTARIO. Includes any law of the former Province of Canada or of Upper Canada, continued as the law of Ontario, or consolidated or incorporated with the Law of Ontario. *Loan and Trust Corporations Act*, R.S.O. 1980, c. 249, s. 1.

LAW OF PRIVACY. The law relating to the storage, retrieval and manipulation of personal information.

LAW OF THE PROVINCE. A law of a province or municipality not inconsistent with this Act. *Motor Vehicle Transport Act*, R.S.C. 1985, c. M-12, s. 2.

LAW REFORM COMMISSION. See LAW COMMISSION.

LAW REFORM COMMISSION OF CANADA. A body established by the federal government in 1972 permanently to review the laws of Canada continuously and systematically. See LAW COMMISSION.

LAW REPORT. 1. The published account of any legal proceeding. 2. The report of a judgment of a court on points of law, published so that it may be used as a precedent.

LAW REPR. *abbr*. The Law Reporter (Ramsay & Morin) (Que.), 1854.

LAW SOCIETY. A provincial body charged, by the legislature, with governing the legal profession and regulating the conduct of members of the profession.

LAWS OF CANADA. The same meaning as those words have in section 101 of the Constitution Act, 1867. *Federal Court Act*, R.S.C. 1985, c. F-7, s. 2. See LAW OF CANADA.

LAW STUDENT. A person enrolled in any law course approved by the Law Society or in the Bar Admission Course during the time he is in attendance at the teaching period thereof. *Legal Aid Act*, R.R.O. 1980, Reg. 575, s. 1.

LAW SUIT. Litigation; an action.

LAWYER. *n*. 1. In the Province of Quebec, an advocate, lawyer or notary and, in any other province, a barrister or solicitor. 2. A person qualified to practise law. 3. A graduate of a law school.

LAY. *adj*. Not professional, belonging to the general population in contrast to a certain profession.

LAY ASSISTANT. A person trained to carry out specific veterinary procedures. *Veterinary Profession Act*, R.S.P.E.I. 1974, c. V-4, s. 2.

LAY CORPORATION. A body politic created for charitable or business purposes.

LAY-DAY. *var*. **LAY DAY**. 1. A day of work with pay to which an employee becomes entitled by working on board a ship for a number of days. Canada regulations. 2. The time to load and unload ships.

LAY DISPENSER. A person who is authorized by a Medical Health Officer, appointed pursuant to the Public Health Act, to administer emergency first aid in a community which is without a resident nurse. *Mental Health Act*, S.N.W.T. 1985 (2d Sess.), c. 6, s. 2.

LAYER. *n*. A female chicken over six months of age that may produce eggs. *Saskatchewan Egg Marketing Levies Order*, C.R.C. c. 270, s. 2. See ACTIVE ~.

LAY FUNERAL DIRECTOR. Any person other than a funeral director who takes charge of a dead body for the purpose of burial, cremation or other disposition. *Vital Statistics Act*, R.S.M. 1987, c. V60, s. 1.

LAYING-UP. *n*. The time spent preparing the machinery of a ship for periods of inactivity. *Marine Certification Regulations*, SOR/97-391, s. 1(1).

LAY OFF. *v*. To terminate employment. To terminate work with an expectation of a return at a later date.

LAY-OFF. *var*. **LAYOFF**. *n*. While in common parlance the term "layoff" is sometimes used synonymously with termination of the employment relationship, its function in the lexicon of the law is to define a cessation of employment where there is the possibility or expectation of a return to work. The expectation may or may not materialize. But because of this expectation, the employer-employee relationship is said to be suspended rather than terminated. The suspension of the employer-employee relationship contemplated by the term "layoff" arises as a result of the employer's removing work from the employee. It follows that for there to be a lay-off, there must be a cessation of work. *Canada Safeway Ltd. v. R.W.D.S.U., Local 454* (1998), 1998 CarswellSask 298, [1998] L.V.I. 2938-1, (sub nom. *Retail, Wholesale & Department Store Union, Local 454 v. Canada Safeway Ltd.*) 98 C.L.L.C. 220-042, (sub nom. *Canada Safeway Ltd. v. Retail, Wholesale & Department Store Union, Local 454*) 226 N.R. 19, 160 D.L.R. (4th) 1, (sub nom. *Canada Safeway Ltd.*

v. Retail, Wholesale & Department Store Union, Local 454) 168 Sask. R. 104, (sub nom. *Canada Safeway Ltd. v. Retail, Wholesale & Department Store Union, Local 454*) 173 W.A.C. 104, [1998] 1 S.C.R. 1079, 10 Admin. L.R. (3d) 1, [1999] 6 W.W.R. 453, Cory and McLachlin JJ. (Gonthier, Iacobucci, Major and Bastarache JJ. concurring). See EFFECTIVE DATE OF ~; TEMPORARY ~; WEEK OF ~.

LAY PERSON. A person other than a person registered or licensed under one of the acts governing professions.

L.C.B. *abbr.* Land Compensation Board.

L.C.J. *abbr.* Lord Chief Justice.

L.C. JUR. *abbr.* Lower Canada Jurist, 1857-1891.

L.C. JURIST. *abbr.* Lower Canada Jurist (1848-1891).

L.C.L.J. *abbr.* Lower Canada Law Journal (1865-1868).

L.C.R. *abbr.* 1. Land Compensation Reports, 1971-. 2. Lower Canada Reports, 1851-1867 (Déecisions des Tribunaux du Bas-Canada).

L.C. REP. *abbr.* Lower Canada Reports.

LDA. Landing distance available.

LEAD. *v.* To call or adduce evidence.

LEAD. *n.* The element lead. See SECONDARY ~ SMELTER.

LEAD ALLOY. An alloy of lead that contains 40 per cent or more of lead, by weight. *Secondary Lead Smelter National Emission Standards Regulations*, C.R.C., c. 412, s. 2.

LEADED GASOLINE. 1. Gasoline that contains more than (a) 0.06 grams of lead per Imperial gallon (0.013 grams per litre), or (b) 0.006 grams of phosphorous per Imperial gallon (0.0013 grams per litre). *Motor Vehicle Safety Regulations*, C.R.C., c. 1038, s. 2. 2. A gasoline, other than aircraft gasoline, which contains tetraethyl lead. *The Gasoline Tax Act*, C.C.S.M., c. G40, s. 1.

LEADER. *n.* 1. An individual who is recognized by the members of an Aboriginal community as their representative. 2. A fixed vertical panel attached to the front of a fishing net in order to lead fish towards the opening in the net. *Quebec Fishery Regulations*, C.R.C., c. 852, s. 2. See LOSS ~; RAIN WATER ~.

LEADER OF A RECOGNIZED POLITICAL PARTY. A member of the Legislative Assembly other than the Premier or Leader of the Official Opposition, who is the leader in the Legislative Assembly of an affiliation of electors comprised in a political organization whose prime purpose is the fielding of candidates for election to the Legislative Assembly and that is represented in the Legislative Assembly by 4 or more members. *Constitution Act*, R.S.B.C. 1996, c. 66, s. 1.

LEADER OF THE OPPOSITION. 1. A member of Parliament or a legislature recognized by the Speaker as the leader of Her Majesty's loyal opposition. 2. The member of the House of Commons who is presently leader of the party opposing the Government and who has certain special rights regarding the questioning of Ministers. A. Fraser, W.A. Dawson & J. Holtby, eds., *Beauchesne's Rules and Forms of the House of Commons of Canada*, 6th ed. (Toronto: Carswell, 1989) at 55-6. 3. The leader of the political party which has the second largest number of seats in the legislature, provided the leader is recognized as leader of the opposition.

LEADER OF THE THIRD PARTY. The member who is the recognized leader of two or more members constituting the second largest group sitting in the Assembly in opposition to the Government. *Legislative Assembly and Executive Council Act*, S.S. 1979, c. L-11.1, s. 2(1).

LEADERSHIP CONTESTANT. A person seeking election as leader of a registered party at a leadership convention called by that party for the purpose. *Election Finances Act*, R.S.O. 1990, c. E.7, s. 1(1).

LEADERSHIP CONTEST PERIOD. The period commencing with the date of the official call for a leadership convention as set forth in the statement filed by a registered party under subsection 14(2) and terminating two months after the date of the leadership vote. *Election Finances Act*, R.S.O. 1990, c. E.7, s. 1(I).

LEADERSHIP VOTE. The date on which polling takes place to elect a leader of a registered party at a leadership convention. *Election Finances Act*, R.S.O. 1990, c. E.7, s. 1(1).

LEADING CASE. A judicial precedent or decision which settled the principles in a certain branch of law.

LEADING QUESTION. A question which suggests the answer required of that witness.

LEAGUE. *n*. 1. A treaty allying different nations or parties. 2. A corporation incorporated as a credit union league or federation under this Act or a predecessor of this Act. *Credit Unions and Caisses Populaires Act*, R.S.O. 1990, c. C.44, s. 1(1). 3. A distance of three miles.

LEAGUE OF NATIONS. An international assembly established in 1920 and superseded after World War II by the United Nations Organization.

LEAKAGE. *n*. Escape of water under pressure through a hole or crack.

LEAKAGE RADIATION. 1. All radiation, except the useful beam, coming from within the housing of an energized X-ray tube. *Radiation Emitting Devices Regulations*, C.R.C. c. 1370, s. 1. 2. An radiation transmitted outside the external surface. *Radiation Emitting Devices Regulations*, C.R.C., c. 1370, s. 1.

LEAKER. *n*. 1. A can of fish that has not been properly sealed or has developed a leak. *Fish Inspection Act*, R.S. Nfld. 1970, c. 132, s. 12. 2. An egg that is cracked with the inner membrane ruptured and from which the contents are leaking. Ontario regulations.

LEAP-YEAR. *n*. A calendar year, called bissextile and consisting of 366 days, which occurs every fourth year.

LEARNED INTERMEDIATE RULE. Manufacturers of drugs are required to warn physicians of propensities of drugs. The physicians, the learned intermediaries, who prescribe them are expected to bring their expertise and knowledge of their patients to bear on the process of prescribing the drugs. A rule intended to equitably distribute tort liability among manufacturer, physician, and patient.

LEARNER. *n*. A person who, although not under a contract of service or apprenticeship, becomes subject to the hazards of an industry to which the act applies for the purpose of undergoing testing, training or probationary work preliminary to employment in an industry to which the act applies. *Workers' Compensation acts*.

LEASE. *n*. 1. " . . . [U]sed in various senses: it is sometimes applied to term or estate created, and sometimes to the conveyance creating the estate. To constitute a lease, however, the possession of the lessee must be exclusive . . . under a lease the lessee's right to possession is exclusive until the expiration of the term agreed upon . . ." *Johnston v. British Canadian Insurance Co.*, [1932] 4 D.L.R. 281 at 284, [1932] S.C.R. 680, Lamont J. 2. Every agreement in writing, and every parol agreement whereby one person as landlord confers upon another person as tenant the right to occupy land, and every sublease and every agreement for a sublease and every assurance whereby any rent is secured by condition. 3. In leasing a vehicle or piece of equipment, includes agreement for a lease. 4. Long term rental of a vehicle or piece of equipment or other chattel. 5. " . . . [M]ay be a security agreement; it becomes so when it in substance is intended to have and has the effect of permitting the lessee to acquire title to the chattel leased by a series of time payments expressed as rental which will, over the term, discharge the purchase debt and give him title, or will do so on a final optional payment that is nominal and cannot reasonably be refused. . ." *Corporate Leasing Inc v. William Day Construction Ltd.* (1986), 6 P.P.S.A.C. 188 at 200 (Ont. H.C.), Henry J. 6. An oil and gas lease. See ANCIENT ~; BUILDING ~; CROWN ~; DRY ~; FINANCIAL ~; FISHERY ~; GROUND ~; HEAD ~; MINING ~; NET ~; OPERATING ~; PROPRIETARY ~; REGISTERED LONG TERM ~; RENEWABLE ~; REVERSIONARY ~; SURFACE ~; UNDER ~; WET ~.

LEASE AREA. The land covered by a mining lease. *Mining Act*, S.N.B. 1985, c. M-14.1, s. 1.

LEASEBACK. *var*. **LEASE BACK**. An arrangement in which land or property is sold and then leased back to the vendor. See SALE-~.

LEASED PARCEL. See MULTI DWELLING ~.

LEASEHOLD. *n*. 1. The area demised by a lease. 2. A holding or estate distinguished from a freehold because its duration is certain and both its beginning and its end are defined.

LEASEHOLD CONDOMINIUM CORPORATION. A corporation in which all the units and their appurtenant common interests are subject to leasehold interests held by the owners. *Condominium Act, 1998*, S.O. 1998, c. 19, s. 1.

LEASEHOLD ESTATE. In contrast to a freehold estate, an estate of fixed duration. The tenant is the owner of the leasehold estate.

LEASEHOLD STRATA PLAN. A strata plan in which the land shown on the strata plan is subject to a ground lease; *Strata Property Act*, S.B.C. 1998, c. 43, s. 199.

LEASEHOLD TENANT. A person, including an owner developer, registered in the land title office as a tenant under a strata lot lease, whether entitled to it in the person's own right, in a representative capacity or otherwise, and includes a subtenant. *Strata Property Act*, S.B.C. 1998, c. 43, s. 199.

LEASE TERM. The period during which the lessee is entitled to retain possession of the leased goods. *Consumer Protection Act, 2002*, S.O. 2002, c. 30, s. 86.

LEASING CORPORATION. A corporation (a) that is incorporated or continued under an Act of Parliament, (b) the activities of which are limited to the financial leasing of personal property and such related activities as are prescribed by the regulations and conform with such restrictions and limitations thereon as are so prescribed, and (c) that, in conducting its activities that are financial leasing of personal property and any other prescribed activities related thereto, does not (i) direct its customers or potential customers to particular dealers in the leased property or to the lease, (ii) enter into lease agreements with persons in respect of any motor vehicle having a gross vehicle weight, as that expression is defined in the regulations, of less than twenty-one metric tonnes, or (iii) enter into lease agreements with individuals in respect of personal household property, as that expression is defined by the regulations. *Bank Act*, R.S.C. 1985, c. B-1, s.193.

LEAVE. *n*. 1. Permission. 2. Permission from an employer for an employee to be absent from work. 3. Period of time permitted by terms of employment during which an employee is absent from work. See ABSENCE WITHOUT ~; BEREAVEMENT ~; MATERNITY ~; SABBATICAL ~; SICK ~.

LEAVE AND LICENCE. A defence to a trespass action in which the defendant claims that plaintiff consented to the act complained of.

LEAVE OF ABSENCE. A period of time during which an employee is permitted to be absent from work, usually without pay.

LEAVING. *v*. Departing; dropping off. See DATE OF ~.

LECTURE. *n*.. Includes address, speech and sermon. *Copyright Act*, R.S.C. 1985, c. C-42, s. 2.

LECTURER. *n*. One who instructs.

LEDGER. *n*. An account book.

LEFT. *adj*. In reference to a highway or the position of traffic thereon means the left when facing or moving in the direction of travel.

LEFT HAND. *var*. **LEFT-HAND**. In reference to a highway or the position of traffic thereon means the left when facing or moving in the direction of travel.

LEGABLE. *adj*. Able to be bequeathed.

LEGACY. *n*. 1. The means by which personal property is disposed of by will. 2. A personal gift as opposed to a "bequest" to charity. *Smith v. Chatham (City) Home of the Friendless*, [1932] 4 D.L.R. 173 at 174, [1932] S.C.R. 713, Duff J. See CONTINGENT ~; CUMULATIVE ~; DEMONSTRATIVE ~; GENERAL ~; SPECIFIC ~.

LEGAL. *adj*. 1. According to law, lawful. 2. Not in contravention of any law. 3. Relating to the law or lawyers. See MEDICO~.

LEGAL ADVICE. Not confined to merely telling the client the state of the law. It includes advice as to what should be done in the relevant legal context. It must, as a necessity, include ascertaining or investigating the facts upon which the advice will be rendered. *Gower v. Tolko Manitoba Inc.*, 2001 MBCA 11, 7 C.C.E.L. (3d) 1, 196 D.L.R. (4th) 716, 153 Man. R. (2d) 20, 238 W.A.C. 20, [2001] 4 W.W.R. 622, 2 C.P.C. (5th) 197 (C.A.).

LEGAL ADVISER. (a) A defending officer, counsel or adviser qualified under QR&O 111.60; and (b) a solicitor. *Military Rules of Evidence*, C.R.C., c. 1049, s. 77.

LEGAL AGE. 1. The age of majority. 2. May, in a particular context, mean the age at which a person is permitted to engage in the regulated action or activity, for example, driving or consuming alcohol or tobacco.

LEGAL AID. Legal advice and services available or furnished under a legal aid act. Intended to assist those who are financially unable to retain a lawyer privately.

LEGAL BURDEN OF PROOF. The burden of establishing a case, an issue, or a fact to the standard required in the context.

LEGAL CAUSATION. In the context of negligence claims, encompasses such concepts as novus actus interveniens, proximity, remoteness, and causa causans. All of these concepts share in the explanation of and attribution of responsibility for negligence.

LEGAL CIVIL LIBERTIES. These are the liberties relating to legal proceedings: freedom from unlawful search and seizure, imprisonment, arrest, cruel and unusual punishment, and unfair process.

LEGAL CLINIC. An office run by students or staff to supply legal services concerning a particular issue or issues or to provide legal services to those unable to afford or obtain advice from a lawyer in private practice. See CLINIC; CLINIC LAW.

LEGAL CORNER POST. A post or cairn that has been placed and marked in accordance with the regulations, and that establishes the point from which the location of a claim is determined. *Mineral Tenure Act*, R.S.B.C. 1996, c. 292, s. 1.

LEGAL COUNSEL. In the Province of Quebec, an advocate or a notary and, in any other province, a barrister or solicitor.

LEGAL CUSTODY. 1. Any restraint of a person that is authorized by law. 2. Refers to the person who has been awarded custody of a child under a custody order.

LEGAL DESCRIPTION. "Normally. . . used to indicate the exact boundaries of a piece of land . . ." *Edkar Construction Ltd. v. Thompson (City) Board of Revision*, [1992] 6 W.W.R. 563 at 568, 8 Admin. L.R. (2d) 278, 82 Man. R. (2d) 118 (Q.B.), Morse J.

LEGAL EFFECT. Refers to how legislation as a whole affects rights and liabilities of those subject to its terms. The effect is determined by the legislation itself.

LEGAL EXECUTION. Seizure of property, for purposes of satisfying a judgment, under the common law process of writ of fieri facias or equivalent process.

LEGAL EXPENSE INSURANCE. Insurance against the cost incurred by a person for specified legal services, including fees and other costs incurred relative to the provision of those services. *Insurance Act*, R.S.M. 1987, c. I40, s. 1.

LEGAL FICTION. An assumption by law that something which is false is true. A statute may state that X is to be treated as Y. That a corporation is a person is sometimes said to be a legal fiction. See FICTION.

LEGAL GUARDIAN. A person appointed or recognized as the guardian of a child.

LEGAL INCAPACITY. 1. Mental infirmity of such a nature as would, but for this Act, invalidate or terminate a power of attorney. *Powers of Attorney Act*, R.S.O. 1990, c. P.20, s. 1. 2. Mental disability of a nature (a) such that were a person to engage in an action he or she would be unable to understand its nature and effect, and (b) that would, but for this Act, invalidate or terminate a power of attorney. *Enduring Powers of Attorney Act*, R.S. Nfld. 1990, c. E-11, s. 2(1). See CAPACITY.

LEGAL INFORMATION INSTITUTE. Institutes in various countries which promote and support free access to public legal information throughout the world, principally via the Internet; cooperate in order to achieve these goals and, in particular, to assist organisations in developing countries to achieve these goals, recognising the reciprocal advantages that all obtain from access to each other's law; help each other and to support, within their means, other organisations that share these goals with respect to: promotion, to governments and other organisations, of public policy conducive to the accessibility of public legal information; technical assistance, advice and training; development of open technical standards; academic exchange of research results. See CANADIAN ~.

LEGAL INNUENDO. Requires the pleading of extrinsic facts or special knowledge of the persons to whom the words were spoken so as to import to the words spoken the defamatory character alleged. *Moon v. Sher* (2003), 2003 CarswellOnt 2405 (S.C.J.).

LEGAL INTEREST. An interest arising by operation of law or an interest enforceable at law. See SUCCESSIVE ~.

LEGALISATION. *var.* **LEGALIZATION**. *n.* The transformation of a prima facie illegal act into a legal act. Refers to the passing of a law to legalize a formerly illegal act.

LEGALISE. *var.* **LEGALIZE**. *v.* To transform a prima facie illegal act into a legal act. Refers to passing a law to legalize a formerly illegal act.

LEGALIS HOMO. [L. a lawful person] Someone not an outlaw.

LEGALIS MONETA ANGLIAE. [L.] The lawful money of England.

LEGAL LIEN. Confers on a person rightfully in possession of another person's property the passive right to detain that property until the debt owing by the owner of the property is paid to the person detaining it.

LEGALLY QUALIFIED. Used in connection with a tradesman or a trade, the expression includes a tradesman in that trade who holds a valid subsisting certificate of proficiency in that trade. *Apprenticeship and Tradesmen's Qualification Act*, R.S.P.E.I. 1974, c. A-13, s. 1.

LEGAL MEDICINE. The application of medical principles and knowledge to legal problems. See FORENSIC MEDICINE.

LEGAL MED. Q. *abbr.* Legal Medical Quarterly.

LEGAL MONUMENT. A device planted by a surveyor.

LEGAL MORTGAGE. Transfer of the legal estate to create a mortgage.

LEGAL N. *abbr.* Legal News (1878-1897).

LEGAL PERSON. Any entity having juridical personality. The most obvious example of a legal person is a corporation which has the legal qualities of a person for at least some purposes.

LEGAL POSSESSION. Something more than a mere right to be on the land in question. Refers to entitlement close to an interest in land. Includes enjoying some benefit from the land.

LEGAL POST. 1. A stake having a diameter throughout of not less than 5 inches, standing not less than 4 feet above the ground and flatted on two sides for at least 1 foot from the top, each of the sides so flatted measuring at least 4 inches across the face, and includes a stump or tree cut off and flatted or faced to that height and size. *Yukon Placer Mining Act*, R.S.C. 1985, c. Y-3, s. 2. 2. A stake or post of any kind of sound timber of sufficient length so that when firmly planted in the ground in an upright position, not less than 4 feet of such post is above ground, and the post must be of such diameter that when squared or faced for 18 inches from the top end, each face of the squared or faced portion is not less than 4 inches in width across the face for the full 18 inches or, if a tree of suitable size is found in position, it may be made into a post by cutting the tree off not less than 4 feet from the ground and squaring and facing the upper 18 inches, each face of the portion so squared or faced to be not less than 4 inches in width, and, whether a post is planted or a stump of a tree is made into a post, a mound of stones or earth shall be erected around the base of the post, which mound of earth or stones shall be not less than 3 feet in diameter on the ground and not less than 18 inches high, cone-shaped and well constructed. *Yukon Quartz Mining Act*, R.S.C. 1985, c. Y-4, s. 2. 3. A post, tree, mound of earth or stone used for making a claim in accordance with section 14. *Canada Mining Regulations*, C.R.C., c. 1516, s. 2.

LEGAL POWER. Enables its holder to perform tasks such as conveying an estate. D.M.W. Waters, *The Law of Trusts in Canada*, 2d ed. (Toronto: Carswell, 1984) at 71.

LEGAL PROCEEDING. Any civil or criminal proceeding or inquiry in which evidence is or may be given, and includes an arbitration. *Evidence acts.*

LEGAL PROFESSIONAL PRIVILEGE. 1. The ability to claim that a document should not be introduced in evidence in a proceeding because it was prepared in contemplation of litigation or for the purpose of seeking legal advice. Where legal advice has been sought communications made to the adviser in confidence by the client are at the client's instance permanently protected from disclosure by himself or his adviser unless the protection is waived. 2. In Waugh v. British Railways Board, [1979] 2 All E.R. 1169 it was decided that under that authority a party need not produce a document otherwise subject to production if the dominant purpose for which the document was prepared was submission to a legal advisor for advice and use in litigation (whether in progress or as contemplated). Such documents are shielded from production by what is usually described as legal professional privilege. . . the legal professional privilege should only be applied when there is a significant connection between the preparation of the document and the anticipation of litigation. This leads to the introduction of the 'dominant purpose' test." *Nova, An Alberta Corporation v. Guelph Engineering Co.* (1984), 80 C.P.R. (2d) 93 at 95, 97, [1984] 3 W.W.R. 314, 42 C.P.C. 194, 30 Alta. L.R. (2d) 183, 5 D.L.R. (4th) 755, 50 A.R. 199 (C.A.), the court per Stevenson J.A. See DOMINANT PURPOSE TEST; SOLICITOR-CLIENT PRIVILEGE.

LEGAL PROCESS. ". . . [D]oes not mean 'by lawful means'. It means 'by a process available through the operation of law', such as by seizure under a writ of execution. . ." *Rogerson Lumber Co. v. Four Seasons Chalet Ltd.* (1980),12 B. L. R. 93 at 102, 29 O.R. (2d) 193, 36 C.B.R. (N.S.)

141, 1 P.P.S.A.C. 160, 113 D.L.R. (3d) 671 (C.A.), Arnup J.A.

LEGAL RATE. Of interest means the rate from time to time payable under the Interest Act (Canada) on liabilities on which interest is payable but on which no other rate is fixed. *Consumer Protection Act*, R.S.M. 1987, c. C200, s. 1.

LEGAL REPRESENTATIVE. 1. An executor, an administrator, a judicial trustee of the estate of a deceased person or a guardian of the person or estate, or both, of a minor. 2. Includes heirs, executors, administrators, guardians, curators, tutors, assigns and all other persons claiming through or under applicants for patents and patentees of inventions. *Patent Act*, R.S.C. 1985, c. P-4, s. 2. 3. Includes heirs, executors, administrators, successors and assigns, or agents or attorneys who are thereunto duly authorized in writing. *Copyright Act*, R.S.C. 1985, c. C-42, s. 2. 4. The executor, administrator, guardian, trustee, liquidator, receiver or other person upon whom an interest in a mineral right has devolved by operation of law, legal process or order of a court of competent jurisdiction. *Mineral Resources Act*, S.N.S. 1990, c. 18, s. 2.

LEGAL REQUIREMENT. In this Act, a reference to a legal requirement includes a reference to a provision of law, (a) that imposes consequences if writing is not used or a form is not used, a document is not signed or an original document is not provided or retained; or (b) by virtue of which the use of writing, the presence of a signature or the provision or retention of an original document leads to a special permission or other result. *Electronic Commerce Act, 2000*, S.O. 2000, c. 17, s. 1(2).

LEGAL RESIDENCE. That a person (a) is or was lawfully in Canada pursuant to the immigration laws of Canada in force on that day; (b) is or was a resident of Canada and is or was absent from Canada, but (i) is deemed, pursuant to subsection 21(4) or (5) or under the terms of an agreement entered into under subsection 40(1) of the Act, not to have interrupted the person's residence in Canada during that absence, and (ii) was lawfully in Canada pursuant to the immigration laws of Canada immediately prior to the commencement of the absence; or (c) is not or was not resident of Canada but is deemed, pursuant to subsection 21(3) or under the terms of an agreement entered into under subsection 40(1) of the Act, to be or to have been resident in Canada. *Old Age Security Regulations*, C.R.C., c. 1246, s. 22.

LEGAL RESPONSIBILITY. Civil or criminal responsibility.

LEGAL RIGHT. "[In s. 215(3) of the Criminal Code, R.S.C. 1970, c. C-34] . . . a right which is sanctioned by law, for example, the right to use lawful force in self-defence, as distinct from something that a person may do without incurring any legal liability. . ." *R. v. Haight* (1976), 30 C.C.C. (2d) 168 at 175 (Ont. C.A.), the court per Martin J.A.

LEGAL RIGHTS. Sections 7 to 14 of the Charter of Rights and Fundamental Freedoms sets out legal rights which are provided to persons within the criminal justice system concerning trial procedure, arrest, search and seizure, and imprisonment.

LEGAL SET-OFF. 1. The netting out of a debt owed by one person to a second person against the debt owed to the first person by the second. 2. " . . . '[R]equires the fulfilment of two conditions. The first is that both obligations must be debts. The second is that both debts must be mutual cross obligations. Both conditions must be fulfilled at the same time': . . ." *Canadian Commercial Bank (Liquidator of) v. Parlee McLaws* (1989), 72 C.B.R. (N.S.) 39 at 43, 64 Alta. L.R. (2d) 218 (Q.B.), Wachowich J.

LEGAL STANDING. A party's right to seek a remedy apart from the substantive merits of the case. There must be a serious issue, a genuine interest, and lack of any other reasonable and effective means to test the law in order for a person to have legal standing.

LEGAL TENDER. 1. A tender of payment of money is a legal tender if it is made (a) in coins that are current and (b) in notes issued by the Bank of Canada pursuant to the *Bank of Canada Act* intended for circulation in Canada. 2. A payment in coins referred to in subsection 1 is a legal tender for no more than the following amounts for the following denominations of coins: (a) forty dollars if the denomination is two dollars or greater but does not exceed ten dollars; (b) twenty-five dollars if the denomination is one dollar; (c) ten dollars if the denomination is ten cents or greater but less than one dollar; (d) five dollars if the denomination is five cents; and (e) twenty-five cents if the denomination is one cent. (2.1) In the case of coins of a denomination greater than ten dollars, a payment referred to in subsection (1) may consist of not more than one coin, and the payment is a legal tender for no more than the value of a single coin of that denomination. 3. For the purposes of subsections (2) and (2.1), where more than one amount is payable by one person to another on the same day under one or more obligations, the total of those amounts is deemed to be one amount due and payable on that day. (4) A coin that has been called in is not legal tender. *Currency Act*, R.S.C. 1985, c. C-52, s. 8.

LEGATARY. *n*. One to whom a legacy is left.

LEGATE. *n*. An ambassador; a deputy; a nuncio of the Pope.

LEGATEE. *n*. 1. One to whom a legacy is left. *Smith v. Chatham (City) Home of the Friendless*, [1931] 4 D.L.R. 173 at 174, [1932] S.C.R. 713, Duff J. 2. Includes a devisee. *Probate Courts Act*, R.S.N.B. 1973, c. P-17, s. 1. See RESIDUARY ~.

LEGATION. *n*. A mission; an embassy.

LEGATOR. *n*. One who makes a will leaving legacies.

LEGATUS REGIS VICE FUNGITUR A QUO DESTINATUR ET HONORANDUS EST SICUT ILLE CUJUS VICEM GERIT. [L.] An ambassador takes the place of the monarch who sent that ambassador and should be honoured just as the person in whose place the ambassador stands.

LEGEM FACERE. [L.] To institute legal proceedings or make law on oath.

LEGEM HABERE. [L.] To be able to give evidence or institute legal proceedings upon oath.

LEGES EXTRA TERRITORIUM NON OBLIGANT. [L.] Laws are not binding outside their own territory.

LEGES POSTERIORES PRIORES CONTRARIAS ABROGANT. [L. later laws repeal prior laws which were contrary] The later section of a statute prevails over an earlier one if the two provisions are repugnant.

LEG-HOLD TRAP. A trap designed to capture an animal by seizing and holding the animal by the leg or foot. *Game and Fish Act*, R.S.O. 1990, c. G.1, s. 1.

LEGIS CONSTRUCTIO NON FACIT INJURIAM. [L.] The construction of law does not work a wrong.

LEGISLATION. *n*. 1. The creation of law by passing bills into law in a legislature. 2. A collection of laws or statutory instruments or by-laws. See CONSUMER PROTECTION ~; HUMAN RIGHTS ~; JUDICIAL ~; PLANNING ~; SUBORDINATE ~.

LEGISLATIVE ACT. An action or decision which imposes a general rule of conduct. Contrasted with decisional or judicial act which concerns a particular case.

LEGISLATIVE ASSEMBLY. 1. The legislative assembly of a province. 2. Includes the Lieutenant Governor in Council and the Legislative Assembly of the Northwest Territories, as constituted before September 1, 1905, the Legislature of Yukon, the Commissioner in Council of the Northwest Territories, and the Legislature for Nunavut. *Interpretation Act*, R.S.C. 1985, c. I-21, s. 35(1).

LEGISLATIVE ASSEMBLY OFFICE. The office of the clerk of a legislative assembly.

LEGISLATIVE COMMITTEE. Appointed by the House to consider a specific bill and amendments; its existence ends when the bill is reported back to the House. A. Fraser, W.A. Dawson & J. Holtby, eds., *Beauchesne's Rules and Forms of the House of Commons of Canada*, 6th ed. (Toronto: Carswell, 1989) at 222.

LEGISLATIVE COUNCIL. Includes the Lieutenant Governor in Council and the Legislative Assembly of the Northwest Territories, as constituted before September 1, 1905, the Legislature of Yukon, the Commissioner in Council of the Northwest Territories, and the Legislature for Nunavut. *Interpretation Act*, R.S.C. 1985, c. I-21, s. 35(1).

LEGISLATIVE COUNSEL. The office attached to the legislature which is responsible for the drafting of legislation in co-operation with individual ministries and agencies.

LEGISLATIVE FACTS. 1. " . . . [T]wo categories of facts in constitutional litigation: 'adjudicative facts' and 'legislative facts'. . . Legislative facts are those that establish the purpose and background of legislation, including its social, economic and cultural context. Such facts are of a more general nature and are subject to less stringent admissibility requirements . . ." *Danson v. Ontario (Attorney General)* (1990), 50 C.R.R. 59 at 69, 43 C.P.C. (2d) 165, 73 D.L.R. (4th) 686, [1990] 2 S.C.R. 1086, 41 O.A.C. 250, 74 O.R. (2d) 763n, 112 N.R. 362, the court per Sopinka J. 2. Legislative facts are traditionally directed to the validity or purpose of a legislative scheme under which relief is being sought. Such background material was originally put before the courts of the United States in constitutional litigation through what became known as the Brandeis brief. Legislative facts are those that establish the purpose and background of legislation, including its social, economic and cultural context. Such facts are of a more general nature, and are subject to less stringent admissibility requirements. The usual vehicle for reception of legislative fact is judicial notice, which requires that the "facts" be so notorious or uncontroversial that evidence of their existence is unnecessary. Legislative fact may also be adduced through witnesses. The concept of "legislative fact" does not, however, provide an excuse to put before the court controversial evidence to the prejudice of the opposing party without providing a proper opportunity for its truth to be tested. *Public School Boards' Assn. (Alberta) v. Alberta (Attorney General)*, 2000 CarswellAlta 678, 2000 SCC 2, [2000] 1 S.C.R. 44, 182 D.L.R. (4th) 561, 251 N.R. 1, 250 A.R. 314, 213 W.A.C. 314, [2000] 10 W.W.R. 187, 82 Alta. L.R. (3d) 211, 9 C.P.C. (5th) 36, Binnie J.

LEGISLATIVE GRANT. The school grant payable by the Department of Education in respect of the operation of a school. *The Larger School Units Act*, R.S.S. 1978, c. L-7, s. 2.

LEGISLATIVE HISTORY. The history of a statute from its conception through enactment.

LEGISLATIVE LIBRARY. A library situated in or adjacent to a legislature and providing library and research services to members of the legislature and to the government generally.

LEGISLATIVE MATERIALS. The annual Statutes of the Province, a consolidation or revision of such Statutes, the Bills, the Journals and the Debates and Proceedings of the House of Assembly, reports, documents and papers of any Committee of the House of Assembly, departmental and other reports and documents to be laid before the House of Assembly, the Royal Gazette, books, forms and other papers required to conduct an election to elect a member to serve in the House of Assembly, and any other reports, books, documents, forms and other papers that the Speaker designates. *Queen's Printer Act*, S.N.S. 1978-79, c. 6, s. 2.

LEGISLATIVE UNION. The uniting of two or more states or provinces into one new state so that the original states or provinces are subjected to the power of the newly created state.

LEGISLATOR. *n.* A member of a legislature; a lawmaker.

LEGISLATURE. *n.* 1. The body exercising legislative power in a province. 2. Includes any legislative body or authority competent to make laws for a dominion. *Evidence acts*. 3. The Lieutenant Governor acting by and with the advice and consent of the legislative assembly of a province. 4. Includes the Lieutenant Governor in Council and the Legislative Assembly of the Northwest Territories, as constituted before September 1, 1905, the Commissioner in Council of the Yukon Territory, the Commissioner in Council of the Northwest Territories, and the Legislature for Nunavut. *Interpretation Act*, R.S.C. 1985, c. I-21, s. 35. See PROVINCIAL ~.

LEGITIMATE. *adj.* Lawful; describing children who were born in wedlock.

LEGITIMATE EXPECTATION. 1. ". . . [A] part of the rules of procedural fairness which can govern administrative bodies. Where it is applicable, it can create a right to make representations or to be consulted. It does not fetter the decision following the representations or consultation. . ." *Reference re Canada Assistance Plan (Canada)* (1991), 1 Admin. L.R. (2d) 1 at 32, 58 B.C.L.R. (2d) 1, [1991] 6 W.W.R. 1, [1991] 2 S.C.R. 525, 127 N.R. 161, 1 B.C.A.C. 241, 1 W.A.C., 241, the court per Sopinka J. 2. ". . . [M]ay arise either from an express promise given on behalf of a public authority or from the existence of a regular practice which the claimant can reasonably expect to continue." *Council of Civil Service Unions v. Minister for Civil Service* (1984), [1985] A.C. 374 at 401, [1984] 3 All E.R. 935 (U.K. H.L.), Lord Fraser of Tullybelton. 3. Legitimate expectations are capable of including expectations which go beyond enforceable legal rights, provided they have some reasonable basis. The justification for it is primarily that, when a public authority has promised to follow a certain procedure, it is in the interest of good administration that it should act fairly and should implement its promise, so long as implementation does not interfere with its statutory duty. The principle is also justified by the further consideration that, when the promise was made, the authority must have considered that it would be assisted in discharging its duty fairly by any representations from interested parties and as a general rule that is correct. *Hong Kong (Attorney General) v. Ng*, [1983] 2 A.C. 629, [1983] 2 All E.R. 346 (Hong Kong P.C.), at 636-638 [A.C.]. Lord Fraser of Tullybelton. See REASONABLE EXPECTATION.

LEGITIMATION. *n.* 1. The making legal of something otherwise not. 2. The act by which one makes a person born illegitimate legitimate. See DATE OF ~.

LEGITIME IMPERANTI PARERE NECESSE EST. [L.] It is necessary to obey the person who gives an order lawfully.

LENDER. *n.* 1. A bank, credit union or other institution designated which grants a loan. 2. A person who extends credit. See APPROVED ~; MONEY~; MORTGAGE ~.

LENDING INSTITUTION. 1. A person who lends money in the ordinary course of business or operations. 2. A loan, insurance, trust or other company or corporation, a trustee of trust funds, a credit union authorized to lend money on the security of real or immovable property, a bank or a treasury branch.

LENDING VALUE. 1. The value for lending purposes of the house or housing project determined by the Corporation. *National Housing Act*, R.S.C. 1985, c. N-11, s. 2. 2. In relation to real estate, means the market value of the real estate reduced by those amounts that are attributable to contingencies or assumptions the occurrence of which is remote and that have increased the market value of the real estate, multiplied by the lesser of (a) seventy-five per cent, and (b) such percentage less than seventy-five per cent as the company has determined in accordance with its prudent investment standards to be appropriate in the circumstances. *Loan and Trust Companies acts.*

LENGTH. *n.:* 1. The measure of size of a thing along the longest axis; the measure of time taken by or for an event. 2. In the case of a ship that is registered or required by the act to be registered, (a) the distance from the fore part of the uppermost end of the stem to the aft side of the head of the stern post, except that if a stern post is not fitted to the ship the measurement shall be taken to the foreside of the head of the rudder stock, (b) if the ship has no rudder stock or has a rudder stock situated outside of the hull at the stern, the distance from the foreside of the foremost permanent structure to the aft side of the aftermost permanent structure of the ship not including guards or rubbing strakes, or (c) if the ship is double-ended, the distance from the aft side of the forward rudder stock to the foreside of the after rudder stock. Canada regulations. See

BASE ~; DEVELOPED ~; FLOODABLE ~; OVERALL ~; REGISTERED ~; TOTAL ~.

LENGTH-OF-SERVICE INCREASE. An automatic pay increase granted periodically to an employee.

LENGTH OF STAY. The length of time spent in any institution from the admission date to the date of official separation.

LENGTH OF SUPERSTRUCTURE. The length of those parts of the superstructure that lie within the length (L) and extend athwartship in a straight line from side to side of the ship or to within four per cent of the breadth (B) of the ship's side. *Load Line Regulations (Inland)*, C.R.C., c. 1440, s. 1.

LENGTH OVERALL. 1. The length of a vessel from the forward part of the stern to the after side of the rim timbers. Newfoundland statutes. 2. The horizontal distance measured between perpendiculars erected at the extreme ends of the main hull of a vessel. Canada regulations.

LENS. *n.* The part of the eye through which light is concentrated or dispersed; a glass or plastic object through which light is concentrated or dispersed. See OPHTHALMIC ~.

LE ROY LE VEULT. [Fr.] The King wishes it.

LE ROY N'EST LIÉ PAR AUCUN STATUT S'IL NE FUT EXPRESSÉMENT NOMMÉ. [Fr.] The King is not bound by any statute if not expressly named in it.

LE ROY REMERCIE , SES BONS SUJETS, ACCEPTE LEUR BÉNÉVOLENCE ET AINSI LE VEUT. [Fr.] The King is grateful to his loyal subjects, accepts their benevolence and wishes it this way.

LE ROY S'AVISERA. [Fr.] The King will consider this.

LESION. *n.* An unusual change in a tissue's structure. F.A. Jaffe, *A Guide to Pathological Evidence*, 3d ed. (Toronto: Carswell, 1991) at 222.

LES LOIS NE SE CHARGENT DE PUNIR QUE LES ACTIONS EXTÉRIORS. [Fr.] Laws do not charge themselves with punishing anything but overt acts.

LESSEE. *n.* 1. The person to whom one makes or gives a lease. 2. The holder of a lease. 3. Includes an original or derivative under-lessee and the heirs, executors, administrators and assigns of a lessee and a grantee under such a grant and the grantee's heirs and assigns. *Landord and Tenant Act*, R.S.O. 1990, c. L.7, s. 19(1). 4. Tenant. See NEW ~.

LESSER OFFENCE. " . . . [A] 'part of the offence' which is charged, and it must necessarily include some element of the 'major offence', but be lacking in some of the essentials, without which the major offence would be incomplete." *Fergusson v. R.* (1961), [1962] S.C.R. 229 at 233, 36 C.R. 271,132 C.C.C. 112, the court per Taschereau J. For example, manslaughter is a lesser offence in relation to murder.

LESSER PLANT NUTRIENT. Any plant nutrient other than nitrogen, phosphorus and potassium. *Fertilizers Regulations*, C.R.C., c. 666, s. 2.

LESSOR. *n*. 1. The person who makes or gives anything to someone else by lease. 2. Includes an original or derivative under-lessor and the heirs, executors, administrators and assigns of a lessor and a grantor under such a grant and the grantor's heirs and assigns. *Landlord and Tenant Act*, R.S.O. 1990, c. L.7, s. 19(1). 3. Landlord.

LESS PUNISHMENT. Any one or more of the punishments lower in the scale of punishments than the specified punishment. *National Defence Act*, R.S.C. 1985, c. N-5, s. 139(2).

LET. *v*. 1. To lease. 2. To permit. 3. To award a contract.

LETHAL WEAPON. A weapon capable of killing.

LETTER. *n*. A statement in writing that is capable of being transmitted by mail. See CALDERBANK ~; COMMITMENT ~; DEMAND ~; POST ~; ROGATORY ~ S; UNDELIVERABLE ~.

LETTER CHUTE. An enclosed rectangular shaped metal tube extending through each storey of a building in a continuous vertical line leading directly to a mail dispatching facility at the bottom of the chute. *Mail Receptacles Regulations*, C.R.C., c. 1282, s. 2.

LETTER OF CREDIT. 1. " . . . [A] proposal or request to the person named therein, or, in the case of an open letter, to persons generally, to advance money on the faith of it, and the advance constitutes an acceptance of the proposal, thus making a contract between the giver of the letter of credit and the person cashing or negotiating the draft, by which the former is bound to honour the draft." *Kingsway Electric Co. v. 330604 Ontario Ltd*. (1979), 9 B.L.R. 316 at 322, 27 O.R. (2d) 541, 11 R.P.R. 96, 33 C.B.R. (N.S.) 137, 107 D.L.R. (3d) 172 (H.C.), Lovekin L.J.S.C. 2. " . . . [I]n effect, a guarantee by the bank that upon presentation of predetermined documentation, the bank will pay the beneficiary named in the letter. . ." *Canadian Pioneer Petroleums Inc. v. Federal Deposit Insurance Corp*. (1984), 25 B.L.R. 1 at 3, [1984] 2 W.W.R. 563, 30 Sask. R. 315 (Q.B.), Halvorson J. See COMMERCIAL ~; CONFIRMED ~; DOCUMENTARY ~; IRREVOCABLE ~.

LETTER OF EXCHANGE. A bill of exchange.

LETTER OF INTENT. 1. " . . . [U]sed by businessmen and contractors as an initial means of establishing a contractual relationship and at the same time, not committing themselves to legally binding commitments until details are negotiated to conclusion." *Marathon Realty Co. v. Toulon Construction Corp*. (1987), 45 R.P.R. 23 at 255, 80 N.S.R. (2d) 390, 200 A.P.R. 390 (T.D.), Davison J. 2. "[In labour law] . . . documents that clarify the meaning of provisions in the main document containing the collective agreement . . . documents which create obligations not contained in the main agreement. . ." *Hiram Walker & Sons Ltd. v. Canadian Union of Distillery Workers, Local 1* (1976), 13 L.A.C. (2d) 417 at 421 (Ont.), Beck.

LETTER-POST ITEMS. Includes letters, postcards, printed papers, literature for the blind or small packets .

LETTERS OF ADMINISTRATION. 1. An instrument, granted by a Surrogate Court, giving authority to an administrator to manage and distribute the estate of a person who died without making a will. Granted when there is no provable will of the deceased person whose estate the administrator will administer. 2. Include letters probate, letters of administration or other legal documents purporting to be of the same legal nature granted by a court in another jurisdiction and resealed in a particular province. See LETTERS OF ADMINISTRATION WITH WILL ANNEXED; LETTERS PROBATE; PROBATE AND~.

LETTERS OF ADMINISTRATION WITH WILL ANNEXED. Special letters of administration used when the executor named in the will is unwilling or unable to serve, or when no executor was named in the will.

LETTERS OF REQUEST. A request from one judge to another, in another jurisdiction, that the second judge cause the conduct of an examination of a witness.

LETTERS OF SAFE-CONDUCT. A document by which the subject of a nation at war with any country can, under the law of nations, come into that country, travel on the high seas or send goods and merchandise from one place to another without fearing that the subject or the goods will be seized.

LETTERS PATENT. 1. A document sealed with the Great Seal by which a company or person may do something or enjoy privileges not otherwise possible. The document is so called because it is open, with seal affixed, ready to be exhibited to confirm the grant. 2. When used with respect to public lands, includes any instrument by which such lands or any interest therein may be granted or conveyed. *Exchequer Court Act*, R.S.C. 1970, c. E-11, s. 2. 3. A means of incorporating a corporation upon application to the responsible Minister by the applicants for incorporation, the acceptance of the application, and the granting of the letters patent under the seal of the incorporating jurisdiction. See SUPPLEMENTARY ~.

LETTERS PATENT JURISDICTION. A jurisdiction in which incorporation takes place by application for and issue of letters patent. The issue of the letters patent is at the discretion of the Minister responsible.

LETTERS PATENT OF 1947. A document which outlines the office of Governor General, reprinted in the Appendix to the R.S.C. 1985.

LETTERS PROBATE. 1. An instrument, granted by a Surrogate Court, giving authority to an executor to carry out the provisions of a person's will. 2. Include letters probate, letters of administration or other legal documents purporting to be of the same legal nature granted by a court in another jurisdiction and resealed in a particular province.

LETTERS ROGATORY. " . . . [S]ometimes known as letters of request. They constitute a request from one Judge to another asking for the examination of a witness by commission in the jurisdiction which is foreign to the requesting Court . . ." *A-Dec Inc. v. Dentech Products Ltd.* (1988), 32 C.P.C. (2d) 290 at 294, 31 B.C.L.R. (2d) 320 (S.C.), Bouck J. See COMMISSION EVIDENCE; COMMISSION ROGATORY; PERPETUATE TESTIMONY; ROGATORY; ROGATORY LETTERS.

LETTRE DE CHANGE. [Fr.] A bill of exchange. I.F.G. Baxter, *The Law of Banking*, 3d ed. (Toronto: Carswell, 1981) at 60.

LEUCOCYTE. *n.* A white blood cell.

LEVARI FACIAS. [L.] A writ of execution by which a sheriff levied a judgment debt on a debtor's goods and land by seizing and selling those goods and taking any rent and profit from the land until the debt is satisfied.

LEVEL. *n.* A substantially horizontal excavation in the ground or in strata of an underground mine used or usable for (a) drainage or ventilation, or (b) the ingress or egress of men or materials to or from a mine or part thereof. *Coal Mines Safety Act*, R.S.A. 1980, c. C-15, s. 1. See ACTION ~; EXIT ~; FLIGHT ~; FLOOD~; GROUNDWATER ~; SAFE ~; SOUND ~.

LEVEL ACCESS. In respect of a polling station, means a polling station that is so located in a building that a person may reach the polling station from the street or roadway and enter the station without going up or down any step, stairs or escalator. *Canada Elections Act*, R.S.C. 1985, c. E-2, s. 2.

LEVEL CROSSING. The intersection of a railway with a public highway or with a private road open to general vehicular traffic within the meaning of the *Highway Safety Code* (c. C-24.2). *An Act to ensure safety in guided land transport*, R.S.Q., c. S-3.3, s. 1.

LEVEL OF ASSESSMENT. That level of valuation which is in accordance with an assessment manual that is approved by the agency, as amended from time to time. *Assessment Management Agency Act*, S.S. 1986, c. A-28.1, s. 2.

LEVY. *v.* 1. " . . . [T]o take all the necessary steps to enforce payment, that is, such steps as under the particular circumstances of the case would be reasonable and proper." *Bayview Estates Ltd*, Re (1980), 28 Nfld. & P.E.I.R. 225 at 243, 79 A.P.R. 225 (Nfld. T.D.), Mahoney J. 2. " . . . [S]ignifies the execution of legislative power which charges on person or property the obligation of or liability for a tax." *Vancouver (City) v. British Columbia Telephone Co.*, [1951] S.C.R. 3 at 6, [1950] 4 D.L.R. 289, Rand J. (Rinfret C.J.C. concurring).

LEVY. *n.* 1. A payment which results directly or indirectly from a seizure under execution. 2.

A tax or duty. See ADJUSTENT ~; CONTINGENCY ~; EQUALIZATION ~; EXPENSES ~; GENERAL COUNTY ~; GENERAL DISTRICT ~; LOCAL MUNICIPALITY ~; NET REGIONAL ~; PROVINCIAL SCHOOL ~; SEIZURE; SPECIAL ~; SPECIAL REGIONAL ~; TELEPHONE ~.

LEX. *n*. [L.] Law.

LEX ACTUS. [L.] The proper law of a transfer. G.H.L. Fridman, *Sale of Goods in Canada*, 3d ed. (Toronto: Carswell, 1986) at 475.

LEX ANGLIAE EST LEX MISERICORDIAE. [L.] English law is a law of mercy.

LEX ANGLIAE SINE PARLIAMENTO MUTARI NON POTEST. [L.] English law can be changed only by Parliament.

LEX BENEFICIALIS REI CONSIMILI REMEDIUM PRAESTAT. [L.] A beneficial law offers a remedy for any case on the same footing.

LEX CAUSAE. [L.] The law governing an issue according to the choice of law rules.

LEX CITIUS TOLERARE VULT PRIVATUM DAMNUM QUAM PUBLICUM MALUM. [L.] The law more easily tolerates private loss than public evil.

LEX CONVENTIONALIS. [L. conventional law] The law which the parties agree is to govern.

LEX CRESCIT ET DEBET CRESCERE. [L.] The law continues to grow and must grow.

LEX DERAISNIA. [L.] The proof of something which a person denies to have done, defeating an adversary's assertion that it was done and showing the thing was unreasonable or improbable.

LEX DILATIONES SEMPER EXHORRET. [L.] The law always detests delays.

LEX DOMICILII. [L.] The law of the country where someone is domiciled.

LEX EST DICTAMEN RATIONIS. [L.] Law is the pronouncement of reason.

LEX EST EXERCITUS JUDICUM TUTISSIMUS DUCTOR. [L.] The law is a judge's safest guide.

LEX EST RATIO SUMMA, QUAE JUBET QUAE SUNT UTILIA ET NECESSARIA, ET CONTRARIA PROHIBET. [L.] Law is a supreme science which prescribes what is useful and necessary and forbids the contrary.

LEX EST SANCTIO JUSTA, JUBENS HONESTA, ET PROHIBENS CONTRARIA. [L.] Law is a sacred sanction prescribing what is proper and forbidding the contrary.

LEX EST TUTISSIMA CASSIS, SUB CLYPEO LEGIS NEMO DECIPITUR. [L.] The law is the safest helmet; under the law's shield no one is misled on purpose.

LEX ET CONSUETUDO PARLIAMENTI. [L.] The law and custom of Parliament.

LEX FINGIT UBI SUBSISTIT AEQUITAS. [L.] The law can resort to fictions when the resources of equity are exhausted.

LEX FORI. [L. law of the forum] The law of the jurisdiction where a legal proceeding is commenced and heard. *243930 Alberta Ltd. v. Wickham* (1990), 14 R.P.R. (2d) 95 at 98, 73 D.L.R. (4th) 474, 75 O.R. (2d) 289, 40 O.A.C. 367 (C.A.), Lacourciére J.A.

LEX FORI REI. [L.] The law of the matter's forum.

LEX INJUSTA NON EST LEX. [L.] An interpretation of the law by which law works injustice is bad law.

LEX INTENDIT VICINUM VICINI FACTA SCIRE. [L.] The law asserts that one neighbour should know another's deeds.

LEX LOCI. [L.] The law of a place.

LEX LOCI ACTUS. [L.] The law of the jurisdiction where an act took place.

LEX LOCI CELEBRATIONIS. [L.] The law of the jurisdiction in which a marriage was celebrated. J.G. McLeod, *The Conflict of Laws* (Calgary: Carswell, 1983) at 779.

LEX LOCI CONTRACTUS. [L.] 1. The law of the jurisdiction in which the contract was made. 2. The law of the jurisdiction where the last necessary act to make a contract took place.

LEX LOCI DELICTI. [L.] The law of the place where the wrong occurred.

LEX LOCI REGIS ACTUM. [L.] The law of the jurisdiction where the benefit was received.

LEX LOCI REI SITAE. [L.] The law of the jurisdiction where the thing is located.

LEX LOCI SOLUTIONIS. [L.] The law of the jurisdiction in which a debt will be paid, a contract be performed or another obligation met.

LEX MERCATORIA. [L.] Law merchant.

LEX MONETAE. [L.] The law of the jurisdiction whose currency expresses the debt.

LEX NECESSITATIS EST LEX TEMPORIS, SCILICET, INSTANTIS. [L.] The law of necessity is the law at the time, namely, for the moment.

LEX NEMINEM COGET AD VANA SEU INUTILIA. [L.] The law does not require anyone to do that which is in vain or useless.

LEX NEMINEM COGIT OSTENDERE QUOD NESCIRE PRAESUMITUR. [L.] The law forces no one to reveal what it is presumed that person does not know.

LEX NIL FRUSTRA FACIT. [L.] The law does nothing without cause.

LEX NON A REGE EST VIOLANDA. [L.] The law may not be violated by the monarch.

LEX NON COGIT AD IMPOSSIBILIA. [L.] The law does not require the impossible.

LEX NON CURAT DE MINIMIS. [L.] The law does not heed trifles.

LEX NON DEBET DEFICERE CONQUERENTIBUS IN JUSTITIA EXHIBENDA. [L.] The law should not fail to dispense justice to those seeking it.

LEX NON DEFICIT IN JUSTITIA EXHIBENDA. [L.] The law does not fail in dispensing justice.

LEX NON FAVET DELICATORUM VOTIS. [L.] The law does not favour the wishes of the scrupulous.

LEX NON INTENDIT ALIQUID IMPOSSIBILE. [L.] The law does not assert anything which is impossible.

LEX NON PRAECIPIT INUTILIA. [L.] The law does not demand useless things.

LEX NON REQUIRIT VERIFICARI QUOD APPARET CURIAE. [L.] The law does not consider it necessary to verify what is apparent to a court.

LEX NON SCRIPTA. [L. unwritten law] The common law.

LEX PATRIAE. [L.] The law of the country to which one owes allegiance.

LEX PERSONALIS. [L. personal law] An inclusive term of which lex patriae and lex domicilii are examples.

LEX PLUS LAUDATUR QUANDO RATIONE PROBATUR. [L.] The law is most praiseworthy when it is proved by reason.

LEX POSTERIOR DEROGAT PRIORI. [L.] A later act repeals an earlier one.

LEX PROSPICIT NON RESPICIT. [L.] The law looks forward; it does not look backward.

LEX PUNIT MENDACIUM. [L.] The law punishes a lie.

LEX REJICIT SUPERFLUA, PUGNANTIA, INCONGRUA. [L.] The law rejects the unnecessary, inconsistent and incongruous.

LEX REPROBAT MORAM. [L.] The law condemns delay.

LEX RESPICIT AEQUITATEM. [L.] The law has regard for equity.

LEX SCRIPTA. [L. written law] Statutory law.

LEX SCRIPTA SI CESSET, ID CUSTODIRI OPORTET QUOD MORIBUS ET CONSUETUDINE INDUCTUM EST; ET SI QUA IN RE HOC DEFECERIT, TUNC ID QUOD PROXIMUM ET CONSEQUENS EI EST; ET SI ID NON APPAREAT, TUNC, JUS QUO URBS ROMANA UTITUR SERVARI OPORTET. [L.] If written law is silent, one should observe what is inferred from manners and custom; and if that is defective in any way, then whatever is closest and follows from it; and if that is not obvious, then, one should follow the law used by Rome.

LEX SEMPER DABIT REMEDIUM. [L.] The law will always provide a remedy.

LEX SEMPER INTENDIT QUOD CONVENIT RATIONI. [L.] The law always asserts whatever goes along with reason.

LEX SITUS. [L.] The law of the place where land is situate.

LEX SPECIALIS DEROGAT GENERALI [L.] A special statute repeals a general one.

LEX SPECTAT NATURAE ORDINEM. [L.] The law has regard for natural order.

LEX SUCCURRIT IGNORANTI. [L.] The law aids the ignorant.

LEX TERRAE. [L.] The law of the land.

LEX UNO ORE OMNES ALLOQUITUR. [L.] The law addresses everyone with a single voice.

LEX VALIDATIS. [L.] The law of the jurisdiction which validated a transaction or act.

LEZE-MAJESTY. *n*. An offence against sovereignty; treason.

LIABILITIES. *n*. 1. Of a corporation at any particular time means the aggregate of all debts owing by the corporation, and all other obligations of the corporation to pay an amount, that were outstanding at that time. *Income Tax Act*, R.S.C. 1952, c. 8 (as am. S.C. 1973-74, c. 49, s. 18(1)), s. 130.1(9)(a). 2. All current, long term, and other liabilities and includes all accounts payable, loans payable, trust liabilities or other debts or financial responsibilities of the Territories other than contingent or unproven claims. *Financial Administration Act*, S.N.W.T. 1982, c. 2, s. 2. 3. Includes duties. *Companies acts*. See CONTINGENT ~.

LIABILITY. *n*. 1. The situation in which one is potentially or actually subject to some obligation. 2. The term 'liability' is a broad term and is most often used to describe an unliquidated or unspecified legal obligation which arises due to negligence, breach of contract, etc. *Royal Trust Co. v. H.A. Roberts Group Ltd.*, 1995 CarswellSask 7, 31 C.B.R. (3d) 207, [1995] 4 W.W.R. 305, 17 B.L.R. (2d) 263, 44 R.P.R. (2d) 255, 129 Sask. R. 161 (Q.B.), Baynton J. 3. [In actions arising out of construction projects] can be used in different senses. It may refer simply to whether or not there was a breach of contract. But it may also refer to particular items of loss. To give a simple example, if a contractor does not install a roof according to specifications and the roof leaks, the contractor is liable, that is to say he was in breach of contract, and the damages would ordinarily be the cost of bringing the roof to specification, but the trier of fact may also have to address questions of whether the contractor is "liable" for consequential loss. For instance, is he liable for damage to the plaintiff's grand piano from the leaking if the plaintiff, although knowing the roof was leaking, failed to move the piano to a place of safety? Such an issue is characterized as one of avoidable loss or mitigation. In British Columbia, if a defendant wishes to allege that the plaintiff ought to have avoided some part of what the plaintiff says is his loss, he must so plead. [T]he issue of mitigation is one of "damages" and not "liability", at least in the narrow sense of that word. *JJM Construction Ltd. v. Sandspit Harbour Society*, 2000 CarswellBC 622, 2000 BCCA 208 (C.A.). See ACCRUED ~; ALTERNATIVE ~; CON-

TINGENT ~; CURRENT ~; DEMAND ~; INJURING ~; LONG-TERM~; NON-PERSONAL ~; OCCUPIERS'~; OUTLET ~; PRODUCT ~; STRICT ~; STRICT ~ OFFENCE; TORT ~; VICARIOUS ~.

LIABILITY INSURANCE. Covers the insured for loss or damage incurred by a third party for which the insured person is liable. See BODILY INJURY ~; EMPLOYERS' ~; PROPERTY DAMAGE ~; PUBLIC ~.

LIABILITY INSURER. A person regularly engaged in the business of undertaking risks in respect of negligence. Newfoundland statutes.

LIABILITY POLICY. See MOTOR VEHICLE ~.

LIABLE. *adj*. Obliged; accountable.

LIBEL. 1. The making of a defamatory statement in a visible and permanent form. 2. Defamatory words in a newspaper or in a broadcast shall be deemed to be published and to constitute libel. *Libel and Slander Act*, R.S.O. 1990, c. L.12, s. 2. See DEFAMATORY ~; SEDITIOUS ~.

LIBERATA PECUNIA NON LIBERAT OFFERENTEM. [L.] The freeing of money does not free the one who offers.

LIBERATION. See CONDITIONAL ~.

LIBER HOMO. [L.] A free person.

LIBERTAS. *n*. [L.] Freedom.

LIBERTAS EST NATURALIS FACULTAS EJUS QUOD CUIQUE FACERE LIBET, NISI QUOD DE JURE AUT VI PROHIBETUR. [L.] Freedom is a power given by nature to do whatever one pleases, unless that thing is prohibited by the law or by force.

LIBERTAS EST RES INESTIMABILIS. [L.] Freedom is something priceless.

LIBERTICIDE. *n*. One who destroys liberty.

LIBERTIES. See CIVIL ~.

LIBERTINUM INGRATUM LEGES CIVILES IN PRISTINAM SERVITUTEM REDIGUNT; SED LEGES ANGLIAE SEMEL MANUMISSUM SEMPER LIBERUM JUDICANT. [L.] Civil laws bring back one who was freed but is ungrateful to original servitude, but English laws adjudge one who was freed as always free.

LIBERTY. *n*. 1. [T]he right to liberty enshrined in s. 7 of the Charter protects within its ambit

the right to an irreducible sphere of personal autonomy wherein individuals may make inherently private choices free from state interference. [T]he autonomy protected by the s. 7 right to liberty encompasses only those matters that can properly be characterized as fundamentally or inherently personal such that, by their very nature, they implicate basic choices going to the core of what it means to enjoy individual dignity and independence. *Godbout c. Longueuil (Ville)* (1997), 1997 CarswellQue 883 (S.C.C.), Per La Forest J. (L'Heureux-Dubé and McLachlin JJ. Concurring). 2. Does not mean unconstrained freedom and does not mean merely freedom from physical restraint. Refers to the personal autonomy to live one's own life and to make decisions that are of fundamental personal importance. 3. " . . . [T]he right of liberty contained in s. 7 [of the Charter] guarantees to every individual a degree of personal autonomy over important decisions intimately affecting their private lives. . ." *R. v. Morgentaler* (1988), 62 C.R. (3d) 1 at 107, 82 N.R. 1, [1988] 1 S.C.R. 30, 63 O.R. (2d) 281n, 26 O.A.C. 1, 44 D.L.R. (4th) 385, 31 C.R.R. 1, 37 C.C.C. (3d) 449, Wilson J. 4. " . . . [N]ot confined to mere freedom from bodily restraint. It does not, however, extend to protect property or pure economic rights. It may embrace individual freedom of movement, including the right to choose one's occupation and where to pursue it, subject to the right of the state to impose, in accordance with the principles of fundamental justice, legitimate and principles reasonable restrictions on the activities of individuals. . ." *Wilson v. British Columbia (Medical Services Commission)* (1988), 41 C.R.R. 276 at 295, 30 B.C.L.R. (2d) 1, 34 Admin. L.R. 235, [1989] 2 W.W.R. 1, 53 D.L.R. (4th) 171 (C.A.), Nemetz C.J.B.C., Carrothers, Hinkson, Macfarlane and Wallace JJ.A. 5. The most obvious engagement of the "liberty" interest is imprisonment. In *Reference re s. 94(2) of the Motor Vehicle Act (British Columbia)*, [1985] 2 S.C.R. 486 at 515, the Supreme Court of Canada stipulated that when there is a threat of imprisonment, the "liberty" interest under s. 7 [of the Canadian Charter of Rights and Freedoms] is automatically engaged. When there is not a threat of imprisonment, courts must consider more closely whether the actions in question engage the liberty interest. The issue can be boiled down to essentially the question: is the activity of "fundamental personal importance"? *R. v. Malmo-Levine*, 2000 CarswellBC 1148, 2000 BCCA 335, 145 C.C.C. (3d) 225, 34 C.R. (5th) 91, 74 C.R.R. (2d) 189, 138 B.C.A.C. 218,

226 W.A.C. 218 (C.A.), Per Braidwood J.A. (Rowles J.A. concurring). See FREEDOM; RIGHT.

LIBERTY TO APPLY. An order by a master or judge which enables parties to come to court again without formally applying.

LIBERUM TENEMENTUM. [L.] A freehold.

LIBR. Lowest intermediate balance rule.

LIBRA PENSA. [L.] A pound, by weight, of money.

LIBRARIAN. See CHIEF ~.

LIBRARY. *n.* 1. A collection of books, periodicals, newspapers, film, recordings and other articles and objects of educational or artistic value for circulation or reference and includes branch libraries, mobile units and reading rooms established or used in connection with a library. 2. The National Library. *National Library Act*, R.S.C. 1985, c. N-12, s. 2. See LEGISLATIVE ~; NATIONAL ~; NATIONAL ~ OF CANADA; PUBLIC SCHOOL ~.

LIBRARY BOARD. A board appointed under this Act to have the administration, management, supervision, charge, or control, of a library or to exercise any powers and discharge any duties herein granted to, or charged on, a municipal or regional library board. *Public Libraries Act*, C.C.S.M.c. P220, s. 1.

LIBRARY OF PARLIAMENT. A large staff and collection of documents and books for parliamentarians' research and information.

LICENCE. *n.* 1. The permission given to do something which would otherwise be unlawful. 2. A permit, certificate, approval, registration or similar form of permission required by law. 3. An instrument issued conferring upon the holder the privilege of doing the things set forth in it, subject to the conditions, limitations and restrictions contained in it. 4. " . . . [U]nder a licence the licensee has no exclusive possession, and his right both to the possession and the use may be revoked at any time by the licensor, unless the licence is coupled with an interest or the circumstances raise equitable considerations to which the court will give effect." *Johnson v. British Canadian Insurance Co.*, [1932] 4 D.L.R. 281 at 284, [1932] S.C.R. 680, Lamont J. 5. Permission to occupy land and perhaps to carry out specified activities there. See BEER~; BROADCASTING ~; COMPULSORY ~; CONDITIONAL~; DEVELOPMENT ~;

DRIVER'S ~; EXPLORATION ~; FINAL ~; FISHING ~; INTERIM ~; LEAVE AND ~; MINING ~; OPERATOR'S ~; OPTION ~; OPTOMETRIC DRUG ~; REVOCABLE ~; SPORT FISHING ~; STATION ~; TIMBER ~; WELL ~; ZONE COMMERCIAL ~; ZONE FISHERMAN'S ~; ZONE RECREATIONAL FISHING ~,

LICENCE AREA. An area in respect of which the right, exclusive or otherwise, to cut or remove Crown timber has been or is granted to any person by a management licence, timber permit, timber sale or timber agreement. *The Forest Act*, R.S.S. 1978, c. F-19, s. 2.

LICENCE PLATE. A licence plate issued by the administrator pursuant to The Vehicle Administration Act for a snowmobile, on which there is an imprint or to which there is attached a validation sticker or stickers showing the year and month in which the licence period expires. *Highway Traffic Consequential Amendment Act*, S.S. 1986, c. 33, s. 2.

LICENCE PERIOD. Period for which a certificate of registration for a motor vehicle, trailer or semi-trailer or a licence to drive is issued.

LICENSE. *v*. 1. The act of permitting; granting a licence. 2. Var. of licence *n*. See DEVELOPMENT ~; DRIVER'S ~; LICENCE.

LICENSED AREA. An area for which a licensee has been licensed to carry on a distribution undertaking. *Broadcasting Distribution Regulations*, SOR/97-555, s. 1.

LICENSED DEALER. A dealer who is the holder of a licence.

LICENSED PHARMACIST. A pharmacist who is the holder of a valid licence entitling him to practise and to exercise all the privileges, rights, and authorities of a licensed pharmacist under this Act. *The Pharmaceutical Act*, S.M. 1980-81, c. 12, s. 1.

LICENSED PILOT. A person who holds a valid licence as pilot issued by a Pilotage Authority under the Pilotage Act. *Canada Shipping Act*, R.S.C. 1985, c. S-9, s. 2.

LICENSED PREMISES. The premises in respect of which a licence has been issued and is in force. *Liquor Control acts*.

LICENSED STUDENT. A person registered hereunder as a student holding a valid licence issued under section 31. *Pharmacy Act*, S.N.B. 1983, c. 100, s. 2.

LICENSED TRUST COMPANY. A trust company or any other body corporate licensed as a trust company under this Act. *Loan and Trust Companies acts*.

LICENSED TRUSTEE. A person who is licensed or appointed under this Act. *Bankruptcy Act*, R.S.C. 1985, c. B-3, s. 2.

LICENSED WHOLESALER. Any wholesaler, jobber of other dealer licensed under this Part. *Excise Tax Act*, R.S.C. 1985, c. E-15, s. 42.

LICENSEE. *n*. 1. A person who holds a subsisting licence. 2. " . . . [A] person who is neither a passenger, servant nor trespasser, and not standing in any contractual relation with the owner of the premises, and is permitted to come upon the premises for his own interest, convenience, or gratification." *Smiles v. Edmonton (Board of Education)* (1918), (*sub nom. Smiles v. Edmonton School District*) 43 D.L.R. 171 at 180, [1918] 3 W.W.R. 673, 14 Alta. L.R. 351 (C.A.), Hyndman J.A. See BARE ~; FISHING ~; INCAPACITATED ~; MILL ~; WELL ~.

LICENSE FEE. Includes any provincial license, registration, filing or other fee imposed upon corporations or any class or classes thereof or any individual corporation, or upon any person or partnership carrying on a class of business and it also includes a license fee or other fee or tax for specific rights, benefits or franchises granted by the province. *Licensing Act*, R.S.P.E.I. 1974, c. L-15 s 1.

LICENSING AUTHORITY. A body which may grant or refuse to grant a licence.

LICENSING POWER. A power in municipal or local governments to enact licensing bylaws. Also known as police power. It is derived from the province's jurisdiction over property and civil rights under the Constitution. See POLICE POWER.

LICENTIATE. *n*. A person who has a licence to practise any art or skill.

LICET. [L. it is permitted] Although.

LICET DISPOSITIO DE INTERESSE FUTURO SIT INUTILIS, TAMEN FIERI POTEST DECLARATIO PRAECEDENS QUAE SORTIATUR EFFECTUM, INTERVENIENTE NOVO ACTU. [L.] Though to grant a future interest is useless, it may still become a declaration precedent to take effect when some new act intervenes.

LICITA BENE MISCENTUR, FORMULA NISI JURIS OBSTET. [L.] Things which are permitted are properly combined unless a rule of law stands in the way.

LICITATION. *n*. Exposure for sale to the highest bidder.

LIE. *v*. Of an action, to be, on the facts of the case, able to be properly begun or continued. For example, "An action lies against one who has negligently harmed another".

LIE DETECTOR TEST. An analysis, examination, interrogation or test taken or performed by means of or in conjunction with a device, instrument or machine, whether mechanical, electrical, electromagnetic, electronic or otherwise, and that is taken or performed for the purpose of assessing or purporting to assess the credibility of a person.

LIEGE. *n*. One bound by a feudal tenure; a subject.

LIEGE-LORD. *n*. A superior lord; a sovereign.

LIEGEMAN. *n*. One who owes allegiance to another.

LIEGES. *n*. An ambassador who is resident.

LIEN. *n*. 1. "In law, a lien is a right to retain possession of property until a debt due to the person detaining the property is satisfied. . ." *Montreal Lithographing Ltd. v. Deputy Minister of National Revenue Customs & Excise* (1984), 12 C.E.R. 1 at 3, [1984] 2 F.C. 22, 8 C.R.R. 299 (T.D.), Cattanach J. 2. "Originally a lien was a possessory interest, but a lien was later recognized under some circumstances in equity, notwithstanding that the holder of it had surrendered possession. Sometimes a lien was an interest in specific property, whilst at other times it was an interest in all of the debtor's property. The one characteristic which each lien had in common was that it was an interest which a person had in property belonging to another." *John Deere Ltd. v. Firdale Farms Ltd. Receiver* of) (1987), 8 P.P.S.A.C. 52 at 82, [1988] 2 W.W.R. 406, 45 D.L.R. (4th) 641, 50 Man. R. (2d) 45 (C.A.), Twaddle J.A. (Hall J.A. concurring). 3. The right in one man to retain that which is in his possession belonging to another, till certain demands of him the person in possession are satisfied. *Hammonds v. Barclay* (1802), 2 East 227, 102 E.R. 356 (K.B.), at 235 [East], at 359 [E.R.], Grose J. A right which accrues to a worker or artisan who repairs, adds to, or improves a chattel for another. See AGENT'S ~; BUILDER'S ~; CONSTRUCTION ~; CREATION OF ~; EQUITABLE ~; GENERAL ~; MECHANICS' ~; OPERATOR'S ~; PARTICULAR ~; PERSON HAVING A ~; POSSESSORY ~; PURCHASER'S ~; STATUTORY ~; UNPAID SELLER'S ~; VENDOR'S ~.

LIEN CLAIMANT. 1. A person having a preserved or perfected lien. 2. A person who is entitled to claim a lien.

LIEN FUND. The fund which is created by an owner of property upon whose property work has been performed or materials furnished by workers. The fund is the holdback of a portion of the amount otherwise owing to the contractor for the work and materials. See MINOR ~.

LIENHOLDER. *n*. Any person having a lien.

LIEU. *n*. [Fr.] A room; a place. See IN LIEU OF.

LIEUTENANT. *n*. A deputy; a rank in the army or navy.

LIEUTENANT GOVERNOR. *var*. **LIEUTENANT-GOVERNOR**. The lieutenant governor or other chief executive officer or administrator carrying on the government of the province indicated by the enactment, by whatever title that officer is designated, and in Yukon in the Northwest Territories and Nunavut means the Commissioner. *Interpretation Act*, R.S.C. 1985, c. I-21, s. 35(1).

LIEUTENANT GOVERNOR IN COUNCIL. *var*. **LIEUTENANT-GOVERNOR IN COUNCIL**. The lieutenant governor acting by and with the advice of, or by and with the advice and consent of, or in conjunction with the executive council of the province indicated by the enactment and, in relation to the Yukon Territory, the Northwest Territories or Nunavut, means the Commissioner thereof. *Interpretation Act*, R.S.C. 1985, c. I-21, s. 35.

LIEUT. GOV. *abbr*. Lieutenant Governor.

LIFE. *n*. The law presumes that any given state of facts continues unless it is demonstrated either that inevitably it must end or it did end. Once it is established that life existed on a given date, the law presumes it will continue and does not presume that a human life must end within a certain period. See DETERMINED ~; DURABLE ~; EXPECTATION OF ~; NECESSARIES OF ~; SERVICE ~; WRONGFUL ~.

LIFE ANNUITY. 1. A yearly payment while any particular life or lives continues. 2. An annuity that continues for the duration of the life of the annuitant, whether or not it is thereafter continued to some other person. See DEFERRED ~.

LIFE BENCHER. A bencher who holds that office during his or her lifetime because of prior office-holding or other honour.

LIFE COMPANY. A company or a provincial company that is permitted to insure risks falling within the class of life insurance, other than a company or a provincial company that is also permitted to insure risks falling within any other class of insurance other than accident and sickness insurance, accident insurance, personal accident insurance, sickness insurance and loss of employment insurance. *Insurance Companies Act*, S.C. 1991, c. 47, s. 2(1).

LIFE CORPORATION. See FOREIGN ~.

LIFE ESTATE. The grant of an estate, an interest in property, for the length of the life of the person to whom the estate is granted.

LIFEGUARD. *n.* A person appointed by the owner or operator to maintain surveillance over the bathers while they are on the deck or in the pool and to supervise bather safety. *Public Pools Act*, R.R.O. 1990, Reg. 565, s. 1.

LIFE INSURANCE. 1. " . . . [I]n its characteristic forms involves, as its essence, a risk in a specified payment of money absolute from the moment the contract takes effect. That constitutes the security sought by the insured, the premiums for which in turn furnish the consideration to the insurer." *Gray v. Kerslake* (1957), 11 D.L.R. (2d) 225 at 227, [1957] I.L.R. 1-279, [1958] S.C.R. 3, Rand J. 2. Insurance whereby an insurer undertakes to pay insurance money: (a) on death; (b) on the happening of an event or contingency dependent on human life; (c) at a fixed or determinable future time; or (d) for a term dependent on human life; and, without limiting the generality of the foregoing, includes: (e) accidental death insurance; (f) disability insurance; and (g) an undertaking given by an insurer to provide an annuity or what would be an annuity except that the periodic payments may be unequal in amount; but does not include accident insurance.

LIFE INSURANCE PLAN. A plan, fund or arrangement, provided, furnished or offered by an employer to an employee that provides upon the death of the employee a benefit either in a lump sum or by periodic payments to a benefi-

ciary, survivor or dependant of the employee, and includes accidental death and dismemberment insurance.

LIFE INSURANCE POLICY. Includes an annuity contract and a contract all or any part of the insurer's reserves for which vary in amount depending upon the fair market value of a specified group of assets. *Income Tax Act*, R.S.C. 1952, c. 148 (as am. S.C. 1980-81-82-83, c. 140, s. 96(7)), s. 138(12)(f). See PARTICIPATING ~; REGISTERED ~.

LIFE INSURED. The person upon whose life insurance is placed. The person whose death will result in payment of a life policy. See GROUP ~.

LIFE INSURER. 1. Includes a person who is licensed or otherwise authorized under a law of Canada or a province to issue contracts that are annuity contracts. 2. Any body corporate licensed to transact the business of life insurance or annuities.

LIFE INTEREST. An interest for another's life (pur autre vie) or one's own life.

LIFEJACKET. *n.* A personal flotation device that provides buoyancy adequate to keep a worker's head above water, face up, without effort by the worker. *Occupational Health and Safety Act*, R.R.O. 1980, Reg. 691, s. 1.

LIFE-LIMITED PART. A part that, as a condition of the type of certificate, may not exceed a specified time, or number of operating cycles, in service. *Canadian Aviation Regulations*, SOR/96-433, s. 101.01.

LIFE-SAVING APPLIANCES. See RULES FOR ~.

LIFE SUPPORT SERVICE. See ADVANCED ~.

LIFE TENANT. One who beneficially holds property as long as she or he lives.

LIFETIME. *n.* As applied to a work means the lifetime of the work as estimated by the engineer.

LIFO. *abbr.* Last-in, first-out.

LIFT. See INCLINE ~.

LIFTING DEVICE. A device that is used to raise or lower any material or object and includes its rails and other supports but does not include a device to which the Elevating Devices Act applies. *Industrial Establishments Act*, R.R.O. 1990, Reg. 851, s. 1.

LIFTING MACHINERY. Any fixed cargo gear used in hoisting or lowering. *Tackle Regulations* C.R.C., c. 1494, s. 2.

LIFTING THE CORPORATE VEIL. To ignore the corporate entity to make directors liable or responsible for corporate wrongs or actions.

LIGAN. *n*. Goods fastened to a cork or buoy so that they can be retrieved and sunk in the sea.

LIGATURE. *n*. A long and slender object which constricts and is applied around some part of the body. F.A. Jaffe, *A Guide to Pathological Evidence*, 3d ed. (Toronto: Carswell, 1991) at 222.

LIGATURE STRANGULATION. Strangulation caused when a ligature is applied around the neck. F.A. Jaffe, *A Guide to Pathological Evidence*, 3d ed. (Toronto: Carswell, 1991) at 222.

LIGEANCE. *n*. The faithful and true obedience of a subject to a sovereign; the territory and dominion of a liege-lord.

LIGEANTIA EST VINCULUM FIDEI; LIGEANTIA EST LEGIS ESSENTIA. [L.] Ligeance is the bond of faithfulness; ligeance is the indispensable element of the law.

LIGHT. *n*. A point source of light radiation. *Aerodrome Minimum Lighting Order*, C.R.C., c. 18, s. 2. See ALL-ROUND ~; AUXILIARY ~; BLUE ~; DAY~; EMERGENCY ~S; EXIT ~S; FLASHING ~; FOG ~; MASTHEAD ~; RED ~; SIDE ~S; STERN ~; TOWING ~; TRAFFIC CONTROL~.

LIGHT BEER. Beer containing not more than 2.5 per cent absolute alcohol by volume. *Brewery Departmental Regulations*, C.R.C., c. 566, s. 2.

LIGHT DUTY MOTOR VEHICLE. A motor vehicle having a gross vehicle weight of 2,720 kilograms or less, but does not include a motorcycle. *Environmental Protection Act*, R.R.O. 1980, Reg. 311, s. 1.

LIGHT-DUTY TRUCK. An on-road vehicle that has a GVWR of 3,856 kg (8,500 pounds) or less, a curb weight of 2,722 kg (6,000 pounds) or less and a basic vehicle frontal area of 4.2 m² (45 square feet) or less and that (a) is designed primarily for the transportation of property or that is a derivative of a vehicle that is designed for that purpose; (b) is designed primarily for the transportation of persons and has a desig-

nated seating capacity of more than 12 persons; or (c) is available with special features that enable it to be operated and used off-road, the special features being four-wheel drive and at least four of the following characteristics, that are calculated when the vehicle is at curb weight and on a level surface with the front wheels parallel to the vehicle's longitudinal centreline and the tires are inflated to the manufacturer's recommended pressure, namely, (i) an approach angle of not less than 28 degrees, (ii) a break-over angle of not less than 14 degrees, (iii) a departure angle of not less than 20 degrees, (iv) ground clearances of not less than 17.8 cm (7 inches) under the front and rear axles, and (v) a ground clearance of not less than 20.3 cm (8 inches) under any point other than the front or rear axle. *On-Road Vehicle and Engine Emission Regulations*, SOR/2003-2, s. 1(1).

LIGHT DUTY VEHICLE. An on-road vehicle that is designed primarily for the transportation of persons and has a designated seating capacity of not more than 12 persons. *On-Road Vehicle and Engine Emission Regulations*, SOR/2003-2, s. 1(1).

LIGHTER CHARGE. A charge for renting or leasing a lighter for use in connection with crane service. *Montreal Floating Crane No. 1 HeavyLift Tariff By-law*, C.R.C., c. 1077, s. 2.

LIGHTER-THAN-AIR AIRCRAFT. An aircraft supported in the atmosphere by its buoyancy. *Canadian Aviation Regulations*, SOR/96-433, s. 101.01.

LIGHTING. *n*. The overall illumination of an area. The system used to provide illumination for an area. See EMERGENCY ~ SYSTEM; OUTLINE ~.

LIGHTING FIXTURE RACEWAY. A raceway which may or may not be a part of a lighting fixture and which is designed to support or suspend the lighting fixture or to hold conductors supplying power to the lighting fixture. *Power Corporation Act*, R.R.O. 1980, Reg. 794, s. 0.

LIGHTING SYSTEM. That part of an electrical system designed to provide illumination in an area normally occupied by an employee in the performance of his work. *Canada Safe Illumination Regulations*, C.R.C., c. 1008, s. 2.

LIGHT LIGHT-DUTY TRUCK. A light-duty truck that has a GVWR of 2,722 kg (6,000 pounds) or less. *On-Road Vehicle and Engine Emission Regulations*, SOR/2003-2, s. 1(1).

LIGHT METAL ALLOY. An alloy that includes aluminum, magnesium or titanium, either singly or in combination, in which the total content of any or all of those constituents exceeds 15% by weight, or in which the content of magnesium and titanium together exceeds 10% by weight. *Coal Mine Regulation Act*, R.S.B.C. 1979, c. 52, s. 1.

LIGHTNING. *n.* 1. The discharge of electric energy between the earth and the atmosphere or within the atmosphere with accompanying flash of light. 2. Is deemed to include other electrical currents. *Insurance Act*, S.N.W.T. 1975 (3d Sess.), c. 5, s. 67.

LIGHTNING PROTECTION SYSTEM. A complete system of air terminals, conductors, ground terminals, interconnecting conductors, arresters and other conductors or fittings required to complete the system. *An Act to Amend the Electrical Installation and Inspection Act*, S.N.B. 1983, c. 28, s. 1.

LIGHTNING ROD. Includes any apparatus, material, appliance, or device used or intended or purporting to be used for the protection of a building or its contents from damage from lightning.

LIGHTNING RODS. The points, cables, groundings and other apparatus installed or to be installed to protect buildings and structures from damage by lightning. *Lightning Rods Act*, R.S.O. 1990, c. L-14, s. 1.

LIGHTNING ROD SYSTEM. All materials, apparatus and equipment installed or designed to be installed on a building or structure to act as a conductor to divert lightning from a building or structure to the ground. *Lightning Rod Act*, R.S.P.E.I. 1988, c. L-12, s. 1(c).

LIGHT TRUCK TIRE. A tire designed by its manufacturer for use on lightweight trucks or multipurpose passenger vehicles. *Motor Vehicle Tire Safety Regulations, 1995*, SOR /95-148, s. 2.

LIGHT TURBULENCE. Turbulence that momentarily causes slight, erratic changes in altitude or attitude or turbulence that causes slight, rapid and somewhat rhythmic bumpiness without appreciable changes in altitude or attitude. *Canadian Aviation Regulations*, SOR/96-433, s. 101.01(1).

LIGHT WINE. Wine having an alcohol content of more than 6.5 per cent but less than 8.5 per cent by volume.

LIGULA. *n.* [L.] A transcript or copy of a deed or court-roll.

LIKE GOODS. In relation to any other goods, means (a) goods that are identical in all respects to the other goods, or (b) in the absence of any goods described in paragraph (a), goods the uses and other characteristics of which closely resemble those of the other goods. *Special Imports Measures Act*, R.S.C. 1985, c. S-15, s. 2.

LIKELY. *adj.* " . . . '[A]t least more probable than not."' *Sayle v. Jevco Insurance Co.* (1985), 16 C.C.L.I. 309 at 310 (B.C. C.A.), the court per Lambert J.A.

LIKELY. *adv.* " . . . [P]robably . . ." *R. v. K C. Irving Ltd.* (1975), 20 C.P.R. (2d) 193 at 210, 11 N.B.R. (2d) 181, 23 C.C.C. (2d) 479, 62 D.L.R. (3d) 157 (C.A.), the court per Limerick J.A.

LIMBING. *n.* The act of removing limbs from a tree before or after felling.

LIMESTONE. Calcium carbonate or calcite found in sedimentary formation with varying amounts of calcium, magnesium, iron and other minerals. See AGRICULTURAL ~.

LIMIT. See AUTHORIZED ~; BAG ~; INTERLOCKING ~S; MAXIMUM ACCEPTABLE ~; MAXIMUM DESIRABLE ~; MAXIMUM TOLERABLE ~; POSSESSION ~; REASONABLE ~S; TIMBER ~; YARD ~S.

LIMITATION. *n.* 1. Of an interest or estate, the designation of the greatest period during which it will continue. 2. Includes any provision whereby property or any interest is disposed of, created or conferred. *Perpetuities acts*. See EXECUTORY ~; STATUTE OF ~S; WORDS OF ~.

LIMITATION BY ANALOGY. A statutory limitation period applicable to a legal claim may be applied by analogy to an equitable claim if the equitable claim and the legal claim are sufficiently similar. The equitable doctrine of application by analogy cannot apply in the presence of an applicable statutory limitation period for the equitable claim. Limitation by analogy is most applicable in the case of concurrent actions in law and equity. Actions arising solely in equity will rarely be comparable to a common law analogue. Even if an analogy can be drawn, the limitation period by analogy does not necessarily apply. There is a discretion to determine this. *M. (K.) v. M. (H.)*, (sub nom. *M. c. M.*) [1992] 3 S.C.R. 6.

LIMITATION OF ACTION. A fixed period of time within which proceedings must be begun or an action commenced. After the period of time has passed the action or proceedings cannot be commenced. The action then is said to be out of time. See EQUITABLE LIMITATIONS; LIMITATION BY ANALOGY; ULTIMATE LIMITATION PERIOD.

LIMITATIONS PERIOD. The time period specified by a statute and within which an action must be brought or a complaint filed.

LIMITED. *adj*. 1. One of the words required as part of every corporate name. Refers to the limited liability of a corporation. 2. May be used in the firm name of a limited partnership but only in the expression "Limited Partnership". *Limited Partnership Act*, S.N.B. 1984, c. L-9.1, s. 6(3).

LIMITED ACCESS HIGHWAY. A public highway that may be entered or left only at specially provided entrances or exits.

LIMITED ADMINISTRATION. The temporary and special administration of a testator's or intestate's designated particular effects.

LIMITED CLASS RULE. Known as the ejusdem generis rule. In an enactment or document, where a class of things is followed by general wording, the general wording is restricted to things of the same type or genus as the listed items.

LIMITED COMMON PROPERTY. Common property designated for the exclusive use of the owners of one or more strata lots; *Strata Property Act*, S.B.C. 1998, c. 43, s. 1(1).

LIMITED COMPANY. Includes a company limited by shares, a company limited by guarantee and a specially limited company. *Companies Act*, R.S.A. 2000, c. C-21, s. 1. See SPECIAL ~; SPECIALLY ~; SPECIFICALLY ~.

LIMITED-DIVIDEND HOUSING COMPANY. *var*. **LIMITED DIVIDEND HOUSING COMPANY**. A company incorporated to construct, hold and manage a low-rental housing project, whose dividends payable are limited by the terms of its charter or instrument of incorporation to 5 per cent per annum or less.

LIMITED EXECUTOR. An executor with an appointment which is limited in time or place or subject-matter.

LIMITED FIRE PROTECTION UNIT. A fire protection unit without motorized pump-equipped vehicles. *Fire Prevention Act*, R.S.N.S. 1989, c. 171, s. 2.

LIMITED HAIL INSURANCE. Insurance against loss of or damage to property other than crops caused by hail.

LIMITED INSURANCE. Insurance against a loss in production of apples caused by an insured peril in which a reduction in grade or quality is not taken into account in evaluating the loss. *Crop Insurance Act (Ontario)*, R.R.O. 1980, Reg. 198, s. 3.

LIMITED LIABILITY COMPANY. A business entity that (a) was organized in a jurisdiction other than British Columbia, (b) is recognized as a legal entity in the jurisdiction in which it was organized, (c) is not a corporation, and (d) is not a partnership or a limited partnership. *Business Corporations Act*, S.B.C. 2002, c. 57, s. 1(1).

LIMITED LIABILITY PARTNERSHIP. A partner in a limited liability partnership is not liable, by means of indemnification, contribution, assessment or otherwise, for debts, obligations and liabilities of the partnership or any partner arising from negligent acts or omissions that another partner or an employee, agent or representative of the partnership commits in the course of the partnership business while the partnership is a limited liability partnership. This does not affect the liability of a partner in a limited liability partnership for the partner's own negligence or the negligence of a person under the partner's direct supervision or control. A limited liability partnership may carry on business in Ontario only for the purpose of practising a profession governed by an Act and only if, (a) that Act expressly permits a limited liability partnership to practise the profession; (b) the governing body of the profession requires the partnership to maintain a minimum amount of liability insurance; and (c) the partnership complies with section 44.3 if it is not an extra-provincial limited liability partnership or section 44.4 if it is an extra-provincial limited liability partnership. *Partnerships Act*, R.S.O. 1990, c. P-5, as am.

LIMITED OR INHERENT EXPLOSION INSURANCE. Insurance against loss of or damage to the property insured caused by the explosion of dust, gas or any substance, where the explosion arises out of hazards inherent in the business conducted on the premises.

LIMITED OWNER. A tenant for life, by the curtesy or in tail, or any person who does not have a fee simple absolutely.

LIMITED PARTNERSHIP. Partnership in which the liability of some partners is limited to their capital contribution and in which these limited partners do not exercise management functions with respect to the business of the partnership. See EXTRA-PROVINCIAL ~; PARTNERSHIP.

LIMITÉE. *adj.* [Fr.] One of the words which must form part of every corporate name. Refers to the limited liability of a corporation.

LIMIT HOLDER. The holder of the right to cut timber or the owner of the land or the holder of the cutting licence when that person has not assigned the cutting rights to a third party.

LIMITING DISTANCE. The distance from an exposing building face to a property line, the centre line of a street, lane or public thoroughfare, or to an imaginary line between two buildings or fire compartments on the same property, measured at right angles to the exposing building face. *Building Code* O. Reg. 403/97, s. 1.1.3.2(1).

LIMIT STATES. Those conditions of a building structure in which the building ceases to fulfil the function for which it was designed. *Building Code Act*, R.R.O. 1980, Reg. 87, s. 4.1.4.1. See SERVICEABILITY ~; ULTIMATE ~.

LIMOUSINE. *n.* A commercial passenger vehicle, other than a taxicab not provided with a taxi meter, having a seating capacity of not less than five and not more than 10 persons including a uniformed driver, and used for transportation of passengers on a zone fare basis. *Government Airport Concession Operations Regulations*, C.R.C., c. 1565, s. 2.

LINE. *n.* 1. An ordered series of relatives. 2. Includes the space between a transmitter and a receiver of telecommunications and any other channel of transmission of telecommunications. 3. A boundary. 4. A route used to give surface access to any land for the purpose of carrying out a geophysical, geological or engineering survey. *Territorial Land Use Regulations*, C.R.C., c. 1524, s. 2. See BASE ~; BILGE BOUNDARY ~; BONDING ~; BOUNDARY ~; BRANCH ~; BUILDING ~; CENTRE ~; COMMUNICATION ~; CONTROL ~; CREDIT ~; DECK ~; DISTRIBUTION ~; EXPANSION~; FLIGHT ~; FLOW ~; FLU-

IDS ~; GAS ~; GATHERING ~; IN-BRED ~; ~S; LOAD ~; LOCATION ~; LONG~; MARGIN ~; MINERAL ~; MORNING ~; MULTIPHASE ~; NIGHT-~; OIL ~; OVERHEAD ~; PICKET ~; PIPE~; POVERTY ~; PRIVATE ~; PROOF ~; ROAD IMPROVEMENT ~; ROAD ~; SECONDARY ~; SEPARATION ZONE OR ~; SERVICE ~; SET- ~; SOLIDS ~; SUPPLY~; TELECOMMUNICATION ~; TELEPHONE ~; TRANSMISSION ~; UTILITY ~.

LINEAGE. *n.* A family, progeny or race in either ascending or descending order.

LINEAL CONSANGUINITY. The relationship which exists between people descended from each other in a line, e.g. grandparent, parent, child, grandchild.

LINEAL DESCENT. The proper bequest of an estate from an ancestor to an heir.

LINEA RECTA SEMPER PRAEFERTUR TRANSVERSALI. [L.] A direct line is always preferred to a collateral one.

LINE EMPLOYEE. An employee who produces and distributes the employer's products.

LINE MAKE. Line make as defined in the individual dealer agreement failing which it shall be defined according to the standards and the practices of the industry. *Motor Vehicle Franchise Act*, S.N.B. 1987, c. 70, s. 1.

LINEMAN. *n.* A person who, (a) operates, maintains and services power lines used to conduct electricity from generating plants to consumers, and (b) constructs or assembles a system of power lines used to conduct electricity from generating plants to consumers. *Apprenticeship and Tradesmen's Qualification Act*, R.R.O. 1980, Reg. 46, s. 1.

LINER. See CHIMNEY ~; INNER ~.

LINES. *n.* The wire, cables or other conductors used for the purpose of conveying or distributing power for telegraph, telephone or power purposes. See EASTERN ~; LINE; LOAD ~.

LINE-UP. *n.* The presentation of a group of persons including a suspect for identification by a witness.

LINE WORK. (a) A line or railway, including any structure supporting or protecting that line of railway or providing for drainage thereof, (b) a system of switches, signals or other like devices that facilitates railway operations, or (c) any other structure built across, beside, under or over a line of railway, that facilitates railway operations, but does not include a crossing work. *Railway Safety Act*, S.C. 1988, c. 40, s. 4(1).

LING COD. A fish of the species Ophiodon elongatus commonly known as ling cod. *British Columbia Fishery General Regulations*, C.R.C., c. 840, s. 2.

LINK. *n.* 1. A measure used by surveyors in the past equal to 7.92 inches. 2. 1/100 chain. *Weights and Measures Act*, S.C. 1970-71-72, c. 36, schedule II. See BUILDING ~.

LIQUEFIED GAS TANKER. A ship constructed and used for the carriage in bulk of any liquefied gas listed in Chapter 19 of the *International Code for the Construction and Equipment of Ships Carrying Liquefied Gases in Bulk*, published by the International Maritime Organization, as amended from time to time. *Crewing Regulations*, SOR/97-390, s. 1(1).

LIQUEFIED PETROLEUM GAS. 1. Includes any matter or substance that is composed predominantly of any of the following hydrocarbons or mixtures of them, namely, propane, propylene, butane (normal or isobutane) or butylenes. 2. Gases derived from petroleum or natural gas; they are in the gaseous state at normal atmospheric temperature and pressure, but may be maintained in a liquid state by the application of moderate pressure; the following gases are those most commonly handled as liquefied petroleum gases: propane, normal butane, propylene, isobutane, butylenes.

LIQUID. See FLAMMABLE ~; INFLAMMABLE ~; NATURAL GAS ~; PLANT ~S; THERMAL ~ HEATING SYSTEM.

LIQUID ASSETS. Cash or property which can be easily realized.

LIQUIDATE. *v.* To change assets into cash.

LIQUIDATED. *adj.* Ascertained, fixed.

LIQUIDATED DAMAGES. 1. "The essence of liquidated damages is a genuine covenanted pre-estimate of damage . . ." *Canadian General Electric Co. v. Canadian Rubber Co.* (1915), 27 D.L.R. 294 at 295, 52 S.C.R. 349, Fitzpatrick C.J. 2. In *Dunlop Pneumatic Tyre Co. v. New Garage & Motor Co.* (1914), [1915] A.C. 79 (U.K. H.L.), Lord Dunedin is quoted at 86 as follows: The essence of a penalty is a payment of money stipulated as in terrorem of the offend-

ing party; the essence of liquidated damages is a genuine covenanted pre-estimate of damage. More recently, in *H.F. Clarke Ltd. v. Thermidaire Corp.* (1974), 54 D.L.R. (3d) 385 (S.C.C.), Chief Justice Laskin suggested at p. 397 that a sum would be held to be a penalty if it is "extravagant and unconscionable in amount in comparison with the greatest loss that could conceivably be proved to have followed from the breach." An emphasis on the need to show oppression is apparent. *32262 B.C. Ltd. v. See-Rite Optical Ltd.*, 1998 CarswellAlta 239, 216 A.R. 33, 175 W.A.C. 33, 60 Alta. L.R. (3d) 223, [1998] 9 W.W.R. 442, 39 B.L.R. (2d) 102 (C.A.), Per Hunt, J.A.

LIQUIDATED DEMAND. 1. "[A demand] . . . the amount of which had been ascertained or settled by agreement of the parties. . ." *Logistique & Transport Internationaux Ltée v. Armada Lines Ltd.* (1991), 50 F.T.R. 21 at 23, Dubé J. 2. The operative test as to what constitutes a liquidated demand is expressed in *Standard Oil Co. of British Columbia v. Wood* (1964), 47 W.W.R. 494 (B.C. Co. Ct.) at p. 497: A liquidated demand in the nature of a debt, i.e., a specific sum of money due and payable under or by virtue of a contract. Its amount must either be already ascertained or capable of being ascertained as a mere matter of arithmetic. If the ascertainment of a sum of money, even though it be specified or named as a definite figure, requires investigation, beyond mere calculation, then the sum is not a 'debt or liquidated demand,' but constitutes 'damages.' This claim can otherwise be a liquidated demand only if it is a "specific sum" which is either "already ascertained or capable of being ascertained as a mere matter of arithmetic". *Busnex Business Exchange Ltd. v. Canadian Medical Legacy Corp.* (1999), 1999 CarswellBC 218, 119 B.C.A.C. 78, 194 W.A.C. 78 (C.A.).

LIQUIDATING TRADE. Effecting settlement of a commodity futures contract, (a) in relation to a long position, by assuming an offsetting short position in relation to a contract entered into on the same commodity futures exchange for a like quantity and quality, grade or size of the same commodity deliverable during the same designated future month, (b) in relation to a short position, by assuming an offsetting long position in relation to a contract entered into on the same commodity futures exchange for a like quantity and quality, grade or size of the same commodity deliverable during the same designated future month. *Commodity Futures Act*, R.S.O. 1990, c. C.20, s. 1(1) as am.

LIQUIDATION. *n.* " . . . [A] winding up of the affairs of the company by getting in all its assets and distributing the proceeds to those entitled. . . *Linder v. Rutland Moving & Storage Ltd.*, [1991] 4 W.W.R. 355 at 362, 54 B.C.L.R. (2d) 98, 78 D.L.R. (4th) 755, [1991] 1 C.T.C. 517 (C.A.), the court per Hollinrake J.A.

LIQUIDATION PROCEEDINGS. Any proceedings pursuant to which all or any substantial portion of the property in the control or possession of a collector is taken or released from his control or possession for the purposes of receivership proceedings, sale or repossession by a secured creditor, winding-up proceedings or for the purpose of distribution to creditors. *Department Revenue & Financial Services Amendment Act*, S.S. 1984-85-86, c. 62, s. 48.

LIQUIDATOR. *n.* 1. ". . . [A] person appointed to carry out the winding up of a company whose duty is to get in and realize the property of the company, to pay its debts and to distribute the surplus (if any) among the shareholders." *Minister of National Revenue v. Parsons* (1983), 4 Admin. L.R. 64 at 79, [1983] C.T.C. 321, 83 D.T.C. 5329 (Fed. T.D.), Cattanach J. 2. On his appointment, shall take into his custody or under his control all the property, effects and choses in action to which the company is or appears to be entitled, and shall perform such duties with reference to winding-up the business of the company as are imposed by the court or by this Act. A court may appoint, at any time when found advisable, one or more inspectors, whose duty it is to assist and advise a liquidator in the liquidation of a company. *Winding-up and Restructuring Act*, R.S.C. 1985, c. W-11, ss. 33, 41.

LIQUID CAPITAL. The amount by which active assets exceed the sum of total liabilities.

LIQUID INDUSTRIAL WASTE. Liquid waste that results from industrial processes, manufacturing or commercial operations. See HAULED ~.

LIQUID PETROLEUM GAS. A substance that is composed predominantly of any of the following hydrocarbons, or a mixture of them: (a) propane; (b) propylene; (c) butane (normal or isobutane); (d) butylene. *Fuel Tax Act*, R.S.A. 2000, c. F-28, s. 1.

LIQUOR. *n.* 1. " . . . [A]lcoholic spiritous liquids if distilled or fermented, . . . peculiarly ap-

plicable to distilled drink as distinguished from a fermented beverage; . . ." *R. v. Foxton* (1920), 48 O.L.R. 207 at 208, 34 C.C.C. 9 (H.C.), Middleton J. 2. Spirits, wine and beer or any combination thereof and includes any alcohol in a form appropriate for human consumption as a beverage, alone or in combination with any other matter. See ALCOHOLIC ~; INTOXICATING ~; MALT ~.

LIQUOR STORE. 1. A government liquor store, government beer store or government wine store, or a liquor store operated by a vendor.

LIS. *n.* [L.] An action or suit; a controversy or dispute.

LIS ALIBI PENDENS. [L. a suit pending somewhere else] 1. A plea that an action in one forum should be postponed until litigation begun elsewhere is concluded. C.R.B. Dunlop, *Creditor-Debtor Law in Canada* (Toronto: Carswell, 1981) at 484. 2. " . . . [U]sed to describe a situation in which the defendant may have instituted his own action against the plaintiffs in a foreign jurisdiction . . . the applicant must establish that the foreign jurisdiction is the more appropriate natural forum to try the actions in the sense that the foreign jurisdiction has the most real and substantial connection with the lawsuit." *Galatco Redlaw Castings Corp. v. Brunswick Industrial Supply Co.* (1989), 69 O.R. (2d) 478 at 482, 36 C.P.C. (2d) 225 (H.C.), Gray J.

LIS MOTA. [L.] Anticipated or existing litigation.

LIS PENDENS. [L. a pending suit] To register a lis pendens is to give intending mortgagees or purchasers notice of the litigation. Gives notice that the pending litigation affects an interest in the land against which the lis pendens is registered.

LIST. *n.* 1. An employment list, a promotion list or a re-employment list. *Public Service acts*. 2. A list of persons made for a particular purpose such as voting or employment. See APPROPRIATE ~; ASSESSMENT ~; BAND ~; BLACK ~; COMMERCIAL ~; CONTROL ~; CREW ~; ELECTION ~; ELIGIBLE ~; EMPLOYMENT ~; ENUMERATION ~; EXPORT CONTROL ~; JURORS' ~; JURY ~; LAW ~; MINIMUM EQUIPMENT ~; ~ OF ELECTORS; POLLING ~; PRICE ~; PROMOTION ~; RE-EMPLOYMENT ~; VOTERS ~.

LISTED. *adj.* 1. Refers to an appliance shown in a list published by a testing agency. 2. Certified for its intended use as having been produced under the certification program of Underwriters' Laboratories of Canada or Canadian Standards Association. *Building Code Act*, R.R.O. 1980, Reg. 87, s. 1. 3. Listed on the list of Wildlife Species at Risk. *Species at Risk Act*, S.C. 2002, c. 29, s. 2(1).

LISTED DRUG PRODUCT. A drug or combination of drugs identified by a specific product name or manufacturer and designated as a listed drug product. *Ontario Drug Benefits Act*, R.S.O. 1990, c. 0.10, s. 1.

LISTED PERSONAL PROPERTY. Of a taxpayer means his personal-use property that is all or any portion of, or any interest in or right to, any (a) print, etching, drawing, painting, sculpture, or other similar work of art, (b) jewellery, (c) rare folio, rare manuscript, or rare book, (d) stamp, or (e) coin. *Income Tax Act*, R.S.C. 1952, c. 148 (as am. S.C. 1970-71-72, c. 63), c. 54(e).

LISTED STOCK. A security admitted for trading on a stock exchange.

LISTING. *n.* An agreement between an agent or broker and a vendor for the agent or broker to offer the vendor's property for sale upon terms agreed. See CO-OPERATIVE ~; EXCLUSIVE ~; GENERAL ~; MULTIPLE ~; OPEN ~.

LISTING AGREEMENT. An agreement between an agent or broker and a vendor for the agent or broker to offer the vendor's property for sale upon terms agreed. During the term of the agreement, the vendor is required to pay the agent or broker the commission for any sale or transfer of the property.

LIST OF ELECTORS. The list showing the surname, given names, civic address and mailing address of every elector in a polling division. See OFFICIAL ~; PRELIMINARY ~.

LIST PRICE. The price for a book that is set out in a catalogue or printed on the cover or jacket of the book. *Book Importation Regulations*, SOR/99-324, s. 1.

LITEM LITE RESOLVERE. [L.] To solve one problem by raising another; to resolve one action by pursuing another.

LITERAL PROOF. Evidence in writing.

LITERARY AGENT. A person who acts on behalf of an author to place a manuscript for publication and to negotiate the terms of the publishing contract.

LITERARY WORK. 1. Includes tables, computer programs, and compilations of literary works. *Copyright Act*, R.S.C. 1985, c. C-42, s. 2. 2. The computer programme in its source code form (i.e., as written by the programmer in a programming language readable by other people) met the test set out in the jurisprudence regarding the meaning of "literary work". The computer programme in such form was an expression of thought in an original form. A literary work need not be "literature". If the idea expressed by the computer programme was capable of various modes of expression, then the programme was copyrightable. *IBM Corp. v. Ordinateurs Spirales Inc./Spirales Computers Inc.* (1984), 1984 CarswellNat 15, 27 B.L.R. 190, 80 C.P.R. (2d) 187, 2 C.I.P.R. 56, 12 D.L.R. (4th) 351 (Fed. T.D.), Reed, J. See EVERY ORIGINAL LITERARY, DRAMATIC, MUSICAL AND ARTISTIC WORK.

LITERATURE. The creation and the translation of original literary works such as novels, stories, short stories, dramatic works, poetry, essays or any other written works of the same nature. *An Act respecting the professional status of artists in the visual arts, arts and crafts and literature, and their contracts with promoters*, R.S.Q., c. S-32.01, s. 2.

LITERATURE FOR ILLICIT DRUG USE. Any printed matter or video describing or depicting, and designed primarily or intended under the circumstances to promote, encourage or advocate the production, preparation or consumption of illicit drugs. *Criminal Code*, R.S.C. 1985, c. C-46, s. 462.1.

LITIGANT. *n.* 1. A person who engages in a lawsuit. 2. Refers to a lawyer, a barrister, whose main work is representing clients in proceedings in the courts or before tribunals.

LITIGATION. *n.* 1. A law suit and all the related proceedings. 2. May refer to any proceeding before a court or tribunal.

LITIGATION ADMINISTRATOR. An administrator appointed for the purposes of conducting litigation on behalf of an estate of a deceased person. Formerly known as an administrator ad litem.

LITIGATION GUARDIAN. A person who acts on behalf of a child or person incapable of acting on their own behalf during the course of litigation. Known as a next friend or guardian ad litem in some jurisdictions and in some circumstances.

LITIGATION PRIVILEGE. Attaches to correspondence and other material prepared in anticipation of litigation. It provides the right to claim privilege over these documents, that is to refuse to produce the documents during proceedings.

LITIS AESTIMATIO. [L.] The assessment of damages.

LITIS NOMEN OMNEM ACTIONEM SIGNIFICAT, SIVE RE REM, SIVE IN PERSONAM SIT. [L.] The term "lis" applies to every action, whether it is in rem or in personam.

LITRE. *n*. 1. 1 / 1 000 cubic metre. *Weights and Measures Act*, S.C. 1970-71-72, c. 36, schedule I. 2. (a) With respect to fuel in liquid form, one cubic decimetre, or (b) with respect to fuel in the form of liquefied petroleum gas, 0.5 kg. *Motor Fuel Tax Act*, S.B.C. 1985, c. 76, s. 1. When it applies to propane gas, butane gas or liquefied petroleum gas, is equivalent to 0.50887 kg. *Fuel Tax Act*, S.Q. 1978, c. 28, s. 1. See NTP ~.

LITTER. *v*. To throw, drop, or deposit or cause to be deposited any glass bottle, glass, nails, tacks, cans or scraps of metals or any rubbish, refuse or waste.

LITTER. *n*. 1. (a) Rubbish, garbage or waste materials, including containers, packages, bottles, cans or parts of them; or (b) any abandoned or discarded article, product of goods manufacture; but not including wastes of the primary processes of mining, logging, sawmilling, farming or manufacturing. 2. Includes material left or abandoned in a place other than a receptacle or place intended or approved for receiving such material.

LIVABLE FLOOR AREA. (a) In the case of a one-family dwelling or semi-detached dwelling, the aggregate of all floor areas measured from the outside faces of enclosing walls, less any area that does not form an integral part of the habitable accommodation, and (b) in the case of a multiple-family dwelling, the aggregate of the area of the building at grade level, plus the areas of any other floors above or below grade level, designed and usable as living quarters, all measured from the outside faces of enclosing walls. *National Housing Loan Regulations* C.R.C., c. 1108, s. 2.

LIVE. *adj*. 1. In respect of an electrical facility, that the electrical facility (a) produces, contains, stores or is electrically connected to a source of alternating or direct current of an ampacity and voltage that is dangerous to employees, or (b) contains any hydraulic, pneumatic or other kind of energy that is capable of making the facility dangerous to employees. *Canada Electrical Safety Regulations*, C.R.C., c. 998, s. 2. 2. Electrically connected to a source of potential difference, or electrically charged so as to have a potential different from that of the earth. *Power Corporation Act*, R.R.O. 1980, Reg. 794, s. 0.

LIVE-IN CAREGIVER. A person who resides in and provides child care, senior home support care or care of the disabled without supervision in the private household in Canada where the person being cared for resides.

LIVELIHOOD. *n*. 1. In our view, taking into account the purposes of s. 6, any attempt by residents of an origin province to create wealth, whether by production, marketing, or performance in a destination province constitutes "the gaining of a livelihood in any province" and satisfies the requirement of mobility implied by the title of the section. *Canadian Egg Marketing Agency v. Richardson*, [1998] 3 S.C.R. 157, Bastarache and Iacobucci, for the majority. 2. Means of support or subsistence.

LIVE LOAD. The load other than dead load to be assumed in the design of the structural members of a building and includes loads resulting from snow, rain, wind, earthquake and those due to occupancy. *Building Code*, O. Reg. 403/97, s. 1.1.3.2(1).

LIVERY. *n*. 1. Delivery; giving possession or seisin. 2. A motor vehicle with the capacity to carry several people which operates on a regular schedule.

LIVERY OF SEISIN. In times past, the public act needed to transfer an immediate freehold estate in tenements or lands.

LIVERY STABLE KEEPER. A person who carries on the business of letting or hiring out (a) carriages, sleighs or other vehicles, or (b) horses or other animals, whether with or without a carriage, sleigh or other vehicle, and whether accompanied by an employee of the livery stable keeper or not, for a money consideration or the equivalent.

LIVESTOCK. *var*. **LIVE STOCK**. 1. Includes (a) horses and other equines, (b) cattle, sheep, goats and other ruminants, and (c) swine, poultry, bees and fur-bearing animals. 2. Horses, cattle, sheep, goats, swine, foxes, fish, mink, rabbits, and poultry and includes such other creatures as may be designated by regulation as livestock for the purposes of this Act. *Feeds Act*, R.S.C. 1985, c. F-9, s. 2. 3. Wild animals and birds, whether captive or not, and domestic animals and birds, but does not include fish or reptiles. *Livestock Health Act*, R.S. Nfld. 1990, c. L-22. s. 2. See AFFECTED ~; BASIC HERD ~; PEDIGREED ~.

LIVESTOCK ASSOCIATION. Includes an association incorporated or registered under this Act having as its principal objects or any of them the breeding, raising, feeding, finishing, acquiring and selling of livestock, poultry, fur-bearing animals raised in captivity and bees, by or through the association on behalf of its members and patrons, or rendering to members and patrons as producers, services ancillary to such principal objects or any of them. *The Cooperative Production Associations Act*, R.S.S. 1978, c. C-37, s. 57.

LIVESTOCK AUCTION MARKET. A place where animals are sold by public auction. *The Stray Animals Act*, R.S.S. 1978, c. S-60, s. 2.

LIVESTOCK DEALER. *var.* **LIVE STOCK DEALER.** Any person who buys cattle from a producer or who acts as an agent of a producer for the sale of cattle, and includes drovers and auctioneers. *Cattle Producers Association Act*, S.M. 1978, c. 15, s. 1.

LIVESTOCK ENTERPRISE. See SPECIALIZED ~.

LIVESTOCK EXCHANGE. *var.* **LIVE STOCK EXCHANGE.** An organization composed of persons engaged in the business of buying and selling, or buying or selling, livestock at a stockyard.

LIVESTOCK FEEDER. A person who raises livestock in Eastern Canada, British Columbia, the Yukon Territory or the Northwest Territories. *Livestock Feed Assistance Act*, R.S.C. 1985, c. L-10, s. 2.

LIVESTOCK HEALTH SERVICES. The professional services of veterinarians to livestock owners. *Livestock Health Services Act*, R.S.N.S. 1989, c. 262, s. 2.

LIVESTOCK INSURANCE. *var.* **LIVE STOCK INSURANCE.** 1. Insurance, not being insurance incidental to some other class of insurance defined by or under this Act, against loss through the death or sickness of or accident to an animal. *Insurance acts.* 2. Insurance against loss of or damage to animals caused by injury,

sickness or death. *Insurance Act*, R.S.B.C. 1979, c. 200, s. 1.

LIVESTOCK LOAN. *var.* **LIVE STOCK LOAN.** 1. A loan made to a farmer by a lender for the purpose of purchasing female cattle, female sheep or such other animals as may be designated by the Lieutenant Governor in Council. 2. A loan made to a farmer by a lender for the purpose of purchasing animals as are designated by the Lieutenant-Governor in Council.

LIVE STOCK OPERATION. See INTENSIVE ~.

LIVESTOCK OWNER. Includes a person who has possession of livestock for farming purposes. *Livestock Health Services Act*, R.S.N.S. 1989, c. 262, s. 2.

LIVE STOCK PRODUCTION. Live stock raising and the production of live stock products. *The Agricultural Incentives Act*, R.S.S. 1978, c. A-11, s. 2.

LIVESTOCK PRODUCTS. *var.* **LIVE STOCK PRODUCTS.** Meat, raw hides, raw furs, dressed poultry, eggs, wool, honey in any form, hay and cordwood.

LIVESTOCK SALE. See PUBLIC ~.

LIVIDITY. *n.* A bluish red or dark red discoloration of the surface of the extremities of the body when the blood stops flowing after death. F.A. Jaffe, *A Guide to Patholo ical Evidence*, 3d ed. (Toronto: Carswell, 1991) at 222. See CONGESTION ~; DIFFUSION ~; HYPOSTATIC OR CONGESTION ~.

LIVING EXPENSE. Reasonable charges incurred for sleeping accommodation and meals while on duty away from home.

LIVING EXPENSES. Expenses of a continuing nature including expenses for food, clothing, shelter, utilities, household sundries, household maintenance, medical and dental services and life insurance premiums.

LIVING ROOM. The principal habitable room of a dwelling, not being a dining room, sleeping room, library, den, sewing room or sunroom. Canada regulations.

LIVING TREE APPROACH. Approach to constitutional interpretation was developed in *Edwards v. Canada (Attorney General)*. "The British North America Act planted in Canada a living tree capable of growth and expansion within its natural limits". *Edwards v. Canada*

(Attorney General) (1929), [1930] A.C. 124 (Canada P.C.), per Lord Sankey at p. 136. This approach eschews narrow technical interpretation. The past plays a critical but not exclusive role in determining interpretation but the approach must be capable of growth to meet the future.

L.J. *abbr*. 1. Law Journal Reports. 2. Lord Justice of Appeal.

LL.B. *abbr*. Bachelor of Laws.

LL.D. *abbr*. Doctor of Laws.

L. LIB. *abbr*. Law Librarian.

LL.M. *abbr*. Master of Laws.

LLP. *var*. **L.L.P.** *abbr*. Limited liability partnership.

LLOYD'S ASSOCIATION. An association of individuals formed on the plan known as Lloyd's, whereby each associate underwriter becomes liable for a stated, limited or proportionate part of the whole amount insured by a contract. *Insurance acts*.

LM. *abbr*. Lumen.

LOAD. *n*. 1. Everything conveyed by a motor vehicle. 2. In reference to the ammunition of a rifled weapon, the propellant's weight. F.A. Jaffe, *A Guide to Pathological Evidence*, 3d ed. (Toronto: Carswell, 1991) at 222. 3. In reference to ammunition for a shotgun, the combined weight of propellant and shot. F.A. Jaffe, *A Guide to Pathological Evidence*, 3d ed. (Toronto: Carswell, 1991) at 222. See ALLOWABLE ~; AXLE ~; DEAD ~; DESIGN ~; FIRE ~; LIVE ~; MAXIMUM ~; MAXIMUM SAFE ~; NORMAL ~; OCCUPANT ~; PEAK ~; ROAD ~; WORKING ~.

LOADBEARING. *adj*. As applying to a building element means subjected to or designed to carry loads in addition to its own dead load, excepting a wall element subjected only to wind or earthquake loads in addition to its own dead load. *Building Code* O. Reg. 403/97, s. 1.1.3.2(1).

LOADED CONDITION. The sum of the weight of the lifeboat or life raft, equipment, blocks and falls, and the number of persons with which the lifeboat or life raft is required to be lowered, each person being considered to weigh 75 kg. *Life Saving Equipment Regulations*, C.R.C., c. 1436, s. 1.

LOADED FIREARM. Includes, (a) in the case of a breech-loading firearm, a firearm carrying shells or cartridges in the breech or in a magazine attached to the firearm; (b) in the case of a percussion muzzle-loading firearm, a firearm charged with powder and projectile when the percussion cap is in place on the firearm; and (c) in the case of a flint-lock muzzle-loading firearm, a firearm the barrel of which is charged with powder and projectile and the frizzen or pan of which is charged with powder.

LOADED TRUCK. A truck having on or in it goods or a passenger or passengers. *The Vehicles Act*, R.S.S. 1978, c. V-3, s. 2.

LOADING. See DATE OF ~.

LOADING CHARGE. A charge for loading goods from an ordinary place of rest onto closed railway cars or closed motor transport vehicles and for all necessary labour and equipment other than that required for bracing and securing. Canada regulations.

LOADING SPACE. A space (a) on the same lot with a building or contiguous to a group of buildings, (b) intended for the temporary parking of a commercial vehicle while loading or unloading merchandise or materials, and (c) that abuts upon a street, lane or other means of access. Canada regulations.

LOAD LINE. *var*. **LOADLINE**. The imaginary line on the side of a ship below which that ship should not sink when it is loaded. See DEEPEST SUBDIVISION ~; ~S; TIMBER ~.

LOAD LINE CONVENTION. The International Convention respecting Load Lines together with the Final Protocol signed at London on July 5, 1930. *Canada Shipping Act*, R.S.C. 1985, c. S-9, s. 2.

LOAD LINE CONVENTION CERTIFICATE. A certificate indicating that a ship has been surveyed and marked with load lines in accordance with Part V and complies with the conditions of assignment to the extent required in its case. *Canada Shipping Act*, R.S.C. 1985, c. S-9, s. 2.

LOAD LINE CONVENTION SHIP. A Load Line ship belonging to a country to which the Load Line Convention applies. *Canada Shipping Act*, R.S.C. 1985, c. S-9, s. 2.

LOAD LINE REGULATIONS. The regulations made pursuant to section 375 to carry out and give effect to the provisions of the International Convention on Load Lines, 1966. *Canada Shipping Act*, R.S.C. 1985, c. S-9, s. 2.

LOAD LINE RULES. The rules made by the Governor in Council for the purpose of giving effect to Articles 6 to 10 of the Load Line Convention and Annex I and Annex II thereto. *Canada Shipping Act*, R.S.C. 1985, c. S-9, s. 2.

LOAD LINES. The marks indicating the several maximum depths to which a ship can be safely loaded in the various circumstances prescribed by the Load Line Rules and Load Line Regulations applicable to that ship. *Canada Shipping Act*, R.S.C. 1985, c. S-9, s. 2.

LOAD LINE SHIP. A ship of the kind described in section 353 that is not exempt under subsections (2) and (3) of that section from the provisions of Part V relating to load lines. *Canada Shipping Act*, R.S.C. 1985, c. S-9, s. 2.

LOAD RATING. The maximum load a tire is rated to carry at a given inflation pressure. Canada regulations.

LOAN. *n.* 1. Anything given or lent to someone on condition that it be repayed or returned. 2. " . . . [T]he lending of money with the expectation that the money will be repaid. . ." *Canada Deposit Insurance Corp. v. Canadian Commercial Bank* (1990), 73 Alta. L.R. (2d) 230 at 244, [1990] 4 W.W.R. 445, 105 A.R. 368 (Q.B.), Wachowich J. 3. The term 'debt' is a narrower term and means a specific kind of obligtion for a liquidated or certain sum incurred pursuant to an agreement. The term 'loan' is even narrower and means a specific type of debt. *Royal Trust Co. v. H.A. Roberts Group Ltd.*, 1995 CarswellSask 7, 31 C.B.R. (3d) 207, [1995] 4 W.W.R. 305, 17 B.L.R. (2d) 263, 44 R.P.R. (2d) 255, 129 Sask. R. 161 (Q.B.), Baynton J. See APPROVED ~; BASE ~; BUSINESS IMPROVEMENT ~; COMPLETION ~; CONSOLIDATED ~; CONSTRUCTION ~; COST OF ~; COST OF THE ~; CURRENT ~; DEED OF ~; DOUBTFUL~; EQUITY ~; FARM IMPROVEMENT ~; FOREST ~; GUARANTEED ~; HOME EXTENSION ~; HOME IMPROVEMENT ~; HOME PURCHASE ~; HOME RELOCATION ~; INSURABLE ~; INSURED ~; LIVESTOCK ~; MEMBER ~; PATRONAGE ~; POLICY ~; PROTECTED ~; SECURED ~; STUDENT ~; SUBORDINATED SHAREHOLDER ~; TERM ~; UNAUTHORIZED INVESTMENT OR ~; UNSECURED ~.

LOAN AGREEMENT. A document or memorandum in writing (a) evidencing a loan, (b) made or given as security for a loan, or (c) made or given as security for a past indebtedness arising under a previous loan agreement or time sale agreement, and made or given in substitution for the previous agreement, and includes a mortgage of real property. See REVOLVING ~.

LOAN AMOUNT. The amount lent. The principal amount of a loan.

LOAN BROKER. A person who carries on the business of providing services or goods to a consumer to assist the consumer in obtaining a loan of money from another person.

LOAN BROKERING. Services or goods that are intended to assist a consumer in obtaining a loan of money, including obtaining a loan of money from the loan broker's own funds. *Consumer Protection Act, 2002*, S.O. 2002, c. 30, Sched. A, s. 1.

LOAN CAPITAL. 1. Includes a sum contributed to an association by a member, in his capacity as member, (a) by way of contributions to capital otherwise than by the purchase of shares or the making of loans under Section 35, or (b) by allocation or payment pursuant to Section 38 or pursuant to an enactment, of net earnings or other sums available for distribution to members. *Cooperative Associations Act*, R.S.N.S. 1989, c. 98, s. 2. 2. A loan with a prescribed rate of interest and with a repayment term of more than one year. *The Heritage Fund (Saskatchewan) Act*, R.S.S. 1978, c. H-2.1, s. 2.

LOAN COMMITMENT. A document setting out the undertaking to loan money and the conditions under which a lender agrees to loan money to a borrower.

LOAN COMPANY. 1. A body corporate that accepts deposits transferable by order to a third party and that (a) carries on the business of a loan company under the Loan Companies Act, or (b) carries on, under an Act of the legislature of a province or a constating instrument issued under provincial jurisdiction, the business of a loan company within the meaning of the Loan Companies Act. *Canadian Payments Association Act*, R.S.C. 1985, c. C-21, s. 2. 2. A body corporate incorporated or operated for the purpose of receiving deposits from the public and lending or investing those deposits, but does not include a bank, an insurance corporation, a trust company or a credit union. 3. A company incorporated for the purpose of lending money on the security of freehold real estate, or investing money in mortgages or hypothecs upon freehold real estate, either with or without other objects or powers. See SMALL LOANS COMPANY.

LOAN CORPORATION. An incorporated company, association or society, constituted, authorized or operated for the purpose of accepting deposits or issuing debentures, notes and like obligations and of lending money on the security of real estate or investing money in mortgages, charges or hypothecs upon real estate or for those and any other purposes. See FOREIGN ~; MORTGAGE ~; TRUST AND ~; TRUST OR ~.

LOAN GUARANTEE. See SHARED-RISK ~.

LOAN OFFICER. A person appointed pursuant to clause 5(2)(d) to consider applications and grant or deny loans and credit out of the funds of the Authority. *Lending Authority Act*, S.P.E.I. 1980, c. 34, s. 1.

LOAN SOCIETY. A corporation or a company authorized to do business as trust, insurance, loan, building or finance companies having its head office or a place of business in Québec and authorized by the Gouvernement to make building loans for the purposes of this act. *Family Housing Act, R.S.Q.* 1977, c. H-1, s. 1.

LOANS RECEIVABLE. Includes (a) receivables arising from factoring activities, (b) receivables arising bar reason of financial lease contracts and, without duplication, the value of the personal property to which such contracts relate, and (c) receivables arising by reason of the purchase of conditional sales agreements and, without duplication, the value of the personal property to which such agreements relate. *Bank Act*, R.S.C. 1985, c. B-1, s. 193.

LOAN VALUE. The market value of securities less the applicable margin requirements.

LOBBY. *v.* To communicate with a public office holder in an attempt to influence the development of any legislative proposal by the government or by a member of Parliament or the Legislative Assembly, the introduction of any bill or resolution, the making or amendment of any regulations or statutory instruments, the development, amendment or termination of any program or policy of the government, or the awarding of any contract or financial benefit by or on behalf of the government, to influence a decision concerning transfer of an asset from the Crown or to have the private sector supply goods or services to the public or to the Crown, to influence the awarding of any contract by or on behalf of the Crown, and to arrange a meeting between a public office holder and any other person.

LOBBYING MAIL. Third class advertising and flyers which is left in apartment building lobbies for residents to pick up if they choose.

LOBBYIST. *n.* A person engaged to represent the interests of a certain group in dealings with the government.

LOBSTER COCKTAIL. Lobster canned in combination with cod, haddock, hake or cusk or any combination thereof. *Fish Inspection Regulations*, C.R.C., c. 802, s. 2.

LOBSTER SHIFT. Night shift; a shift which starts late at night or in early morning hours.

LOBSTER TRAP. See MODIFIED ~.

LOC. *abbr.* Local.

LOCAL. *n.* Of an international or national union, is a union which is affiliated with the international or national union. See DIRECTLY CHARTERED ~.

LOCAL. *adj.* When it qualifies the words "municipality", "corporation", "council" or "councillor", refers, as the case may be, to rural or village councils, councillors, corporations or municipalities. *An Act to Amend Various Legislative Provisions Respecting Municipalities*, S.Q. 1982, c. 2, s. 4.

LOCAL ACCEPTANCE. Payment at a specified, particular place only. E.L.G. Tyler & N.E. Palmer, eds., *Cross Vaines' Personal Property*, 5th ed. (London: Butterworths, 1973) at 236.

LOCAL ACT. An act which deals with a matter relating to a particular area, usually a municipality.

LOCAL ADVERTISING. Advertising aimed at stimulating demand for a product at a particular location.

LOCAL AM STATION. In relation to a licensed area of a distribution undertaking, a licensed AM station that has its principal studio located within 32 km of the local head end of the licensed area. *Broadcasting Distribution Regulations*, SOR/97-555, s. 1.

LOCAL AUTHORITY. 1. Any public organization created by an act of a legislature and exercising jurisdiction or powers of a local nature. 2. The council of a municipality.

LOCAL AUTONOMY. The power vested in a local union to determine what it will negotiate.

LOCAL BOARD. Any board, commission, committee, body or local authority of any kind established to exercise or exercising any power or authority under any general or special act with respect to any of the affairs or purposes of a municipality or parts thereof or of two or more municipalities or parts thereof, or to which a municipality or municipalities are required to provide funds.

LOCAL CARRIER. 1. A person who operates a local undertaking. *Motor Vehicle Transport Act*, R.S.C. 1985, c. M-12, s. 2. 2. A railway company that moves traffic to or from an interchange on a continuous route from the point of origin or to the point of destination that is served exclusively by the railway company. *Canada Transportation Act*, S.C. 1996, c. 10, s. 111.

LOCAL COMMUNITY SERVICE CENTRE. Facilities other than a professional's private consulting office in which sanitary and social preventive and action services are ensured to the community, in particular by receiving or visiting persons who require current health services or social services for themselves or their families, by rendering such services to them, counselling them or, if necessary, by referring them to the establishments most capable of assisting them. *Health Services and Social Services Act*, R.S.Q. 1977, c. S-5, s. 1.

LOCAL COOPERATIVE CREDIT SOCIETY. A cooperative credit society incorporated by or under an Act of the legislature of a province (a) whose members consist substantially of individuals, and (b) whose principal purpose is to receive deposits from, and make loans to, its members. *Canadian Payments Act*, R.S.C. 1985, c. C-21, s. 2(1).

LOCAL COUNCIL. (a) The council of a city or town, (b) the commissioners of an incorporated village, (c) a community improvement committee, (d) the trustees or directors of an area improvement district, or (e) in any regional administrative unit which is not within a city, town, incorporated village or area improvement district and does not have a community improvement committee, the trustees of a regional administrative unit. *Recreation Development Act*, R.S.P.E.I. 1974, c. R-9, s. 1.

LOCAL CTS. & MUN. GAZ. *abbr.* Local Courts' and Municipal Gazette (1865-1872).

LOCAL DIGITAL RADIO STATION. In relation to a licensed area of a distribution undertaking, a licensed digital radio station that has a digital service area that includes any part of the licensed area. *Broadcasting Distribution Regulations*, SOR/97-555, s. 1.

LOCAL EDUCATION AUTHORITY. Includes a community education council for an education district within an education division or a Divisional Board of Education where an education division is comprised of one education district. *Education Act*, S.N.W.T. 1985 (3d Sess.), c. 3, s. 4.

LOCAL FM STATION. In relation to a licensed area of a distribution undertaking, a licensed FM station that has a 500 μV/m official contour that includes any part of the licensed area. *Broadcasting Distribution Regulations*, SOR/97-555, s. 1.

LOCAL FOOD. A food that is manufactured, processed, produced or packaged in a local government unit and sold only in (a) the local government unit in which it is manufactured, processed or packaged, (b) one or more local government units that are immediately adjacent to the one in which it is manufactured, processed, produced or packaged, or (c) the local government unit in which it is manufactured, processed, produced or packaged and in one or more local government units that are immediately adjacent to the one in which it is manufactured, processed, produced or packaged. *Food and Drug Regulations*, C.R.C., c. 870, c. B.01.012.

LOCAL GOVERNING AUTHORITY. A council in the case of a municipality, the Minister of Municipal Affairs in the case of a local improvement district and the Minister of Northern Saskatchewan in the case of the Northern Saskatchewan Administration District. Saskatchewan statutes.

LOCAL GOVERNMENT. 1. A system of government by which administration of local affairs is entrusted to local authority. 2. A municipal government at any level.

LOCAL GOVERNMENT DISTRICT. Includes a school district in unorganized territory that is not in a local government district, and a reference to the resident administrator of a local government district shall, where the context so requires, be deemed to include the board of trustees of such a school district. *Health Services Act*, R.S.M. 1970, c. H30, s. 88. See FOUNDATION ~.

LOCAL GOVERNMENT UNIT. A city, metropolitan government area, town, village, municipality or other area of local government but does not include any local government unit situated within a bilingual district established under the Official Languages Act. Canada regulations.

LOCAL HEAD END. In respect of (a) a licensed area of a cable distribution undertaking, means the specific location at which a licensee receives the majority of the programming services that are transmitted by local television stations or, if there are no such stations, by regional television stations, and that are distributed by the licensee in the licensed area; and (b) a radiocommunication distribution undertaking, means the licensee's transmitter site. *Broadcasting Distribution Regulations*, SOR/97-555, s. 1.

LOCAL IMPROVEMENT. A work or service intended to be paid for or maintained wholly or partly by special assessments against the land benefitted thereby. Usually, the improvement is carried out by a local government and consists of improvements to facilities or services which will benefit property owners in the immediate neighbourhood.

LOCAL IMPROVEMENT DISTRICT. A local improvement district heretofore or hereafter constituted under any Local Improvement Districts Act. Saskatchewan statutes.

LOCAL IMPROVEMENTS. Any expenditure of public funds upon any street or locality by which such street or locality is benefitted. *City of St. John's Act*, R.S. Nfld. 1970, c. 40, s. 2.

LOCAL IMPROVEMENT TAX. Includes betterment charges and all taxes and charges imposed, defraying any part of the cost of any of the works, improvements or services which may be undertaken as a local improvement project. *Dartmouth City Charter Act*, S.N.S. 1978, c. 43A, s. 2.

LOCAL INTERVENER. A person or a group or association of persons who, in the opinion of the Board, (a) has an interest in, or (b) is in actual occupation of or is entitled to occupy land that is or may be directly and adversely affected by a decision of the Board in or as a result of a proceeding before it, but, unless otherwise authorized by the Board, does not include a person or group or association of persons whose business includes the trading in or transportation or recovery of any energy resource. *Energy Re-*

sources Conservation Amendment Act, 1981, S.A. 1981, c. 47, s. 31.

LOCALITY. *n.* 1. A part of territory without municipal organization that is deemed to be a district municipality for the purposes of a divisional board or of a district combined separate school board. *Education Act*, R.S.O. 1990, c. E.2, s. 1(1). 2. A public school section, a separate school zone or a secondary school district that comprises or includes territory without municipal organization and includes the board of any of them. *Assessment Act*, R.S.O. 1990, c. A.31, s. 1. 3. An area where, in the opinion of an employment officer, all points are within commuting distance of the place in relation to which the term is used. *Manpower Mobility Regulations*, C.R.C., c. 331, s. 2.

LOCALITY OF DEBTOR. The principal place (a) where the debtor has carried on business during the year immediately preceding his bankruptcy, (b) where the debtor has resided during the year immediately preceding his bankruptcy, or (c) in cases not coming within paragraph (a) or (b), where the greater portion of the property of the debtor is situated. *Bankruptcy Act*, R.S.C. 1985, c. B-3, s. 2.

LOCAL JURISDICTION. A municipality, a hospital district as defined in the Hospitals Act, a district as defined in the Nursing Homes Act or a district or division as defined in the School Act, as the case may be. *Local Authorities Election Act*, S.A. 1983, c. L-27.5, s. 1.

LOCAL LABOUR COUNCIL. A federation of labour organizations within a city.

LOCAL MASTER. A local master of Her Majesty's Court of Queen's Bench, and includes a judge of the District Court lawfully performing the duties of a local master of Her Majesty's Court of Queen's Bench. *The Queen's Bench Act*, R.S.S. 1978, c. Q-1, s. 2.

LOCAL MUNICIPALITY. 1. A municipality wholly or partly within the National Capital Region. *National Capital Act*, R.S.C. 1985, c. N-4, s. 2. 2. A city, town, village and township. Ontario statutes. 3. Any city, town, village or rural municipality, governed by a municipal council. *Education Act*, R.S.Q. 1977, c. I-14, s. 1.

LOCAL MUNICIPALITY LEVY. The amount required for local municipality purposes under section 162 including the sums required for any board commission or other body, but excluding those amounts required to be raised for county and school purposes. *Municipal Act*, R.S.O. 1990, c. M.45, s. 375(1).

LOCAL OFFICE. An office established to serve an area comprising a part but not the whole of Canada. *Public Service Employment Act*, R.S.C. 1985, c. P-33, s. 2.

LOCAL OPTION AREA. A local option area established pursuant to section 33. *Liquor Licensing Act*, R.S.S. 1978, c. L-21, s. 32.

LOCAL OPTION BY-LAW. A by-law of a municipality forbidding the local sale of liquor in the municipality. *Liquor Control Act*, R. S. M. 1970, c. L160, s. 260.

LOCAL PORT CORPORATION. A corporation established under section 25. *Canada Ports Corporation Act*, R.S.C. 1985, c. C-9, s. 2.

LOCAL PRODUCT. A prepackaged product that is manufactured, processed, produced or packaged in a local government unit and sold only in (a) the local government unit in which it is manufactured, processed, produced or packaged, (b) one or more local government units that are immediately adjacent to the one in which it is manufactured, processed, produced or packaged, or (c) the local government unit in which it is manufactured, processed, produced or packaged and in one or more local government units that are immediately adjacent to the one in which it is manufactured, processed, produced or packaged. Canada regulations.

LOCAL RADIO STATION. A local AM station, a local FM station or a local digital radio station. *Broadcasting Distribution Regulations*, SOR/97-555, s. 1.

LOCAL REGISTRAR. The local registrar or deputy local registrar of a court.

LOCAL REGISTRAR OF FIREARMS. Any person who has been designated in writing as a local registrar of firearms by the Commissioner or the Attorney General of a province or who is a member of a class of police officers or police constables that has been so designated. *Criminal Code*, R.S.C. 1985, c. C-46, s. 84.

LOCAL ROAD. Any road, trail or path situated within the boundaries of a park, historical site, natural area or wilderness area. *Provincial Parks Act*, R.S.A. 1970, c. 288, s. 2.

LOCAL SERVICES. Services of a type that may be provided in a municipality at the expense, either wholly or partly, of a municipality or of a school district, school division, or school area, and without limiting the generality of the foregoing includes (a) water supply and water distributon systems, (b) sewage systems and sewage disposal plants, (c) garbage and waste disposal facilities, (d) local roads and sidewalks, (e) local drains and drainage systems, (f) fire and police protection, (g) street lighting, (h) planning, (i) recreation facilities including parks, (j) transportation facilities including ferries, wharves, docks and facilities for the landing of aircraft, (k) libraries, (l) weed control, and (m) schools. *Northern Affairs Act*, S.M. 1974, c. 56, s. 1.

LOCAL STANDARD. Any standard designated by the Minister under section 13. *Weights and Measures Act*, R.S.C. 1985, c. W-6, s. 2.

LOCAL STATUTE. A statute which deals with a matter relating to a particular area, usually a municipality. See LOCAL ACT.

LOCAL TARIFF. A tariff containing the local tolls of each air carrier named therein. *Air Carrier Regulations*, C.R.C., c. 3, s. 2.

LOCAL TAXATION. Taxation of any kind whatsoever imposed by or under any Act or law of the province for the benefit of a city, a municipality, local schools, or any municipal area whatsoever. *Crown Corporations (Local Taxation) Act*, R.S. Nfld. 1970, c. 69, s. 2.

LOCAL TELEVISION STATION. In relation to a licensed area of a distribution undertaking, means a licensed television station that (a) has a Grade A official contour that includes any part of the licensed area; or (b) has, if there is no Grade A official contour, a transmitting antenna that is located within 15 km of the licensed area. *Broadcasting Distribution Regulations*, SOR/97-555, s. 1.

LOCAL TIME. In relation to any place, means the time observed in that place for the regulation of business hours. *Interpretation Act*, R.S.C. 1985, c. I-21, s. 35.

LOCAL TOLL. A toll that applies between places served by one air carrier. *Air Carrier Regulations*, C.R.C., c. 3, s. 2.

LOCAL TRANSPORT. The transport of passengers or goods by motor vehicle otherwise than by means of an extra-provincial undertaking. *Motor Vehicle Transport Act*, R.S.C. 1985, c. M-12, s. 2.

LOCAL UNDERTAKING. A work or an undertaking, not being an extra-provincial undertaking, for the transport of passengers or goods by motor vehicle. *Motor Vehicle Transport Act*, R.S.C. 1985, c. M-12, s. 2.

LOCAL UNION. The lowest structural unit of a union that elects its own slate of officers. *Corporations and Labour Unions Returns Act*, R.S.C. 1985, c. C-43, s. 12(4).

LOCAL VOYAGE. A voyage, other than a minor waters voyage, that is between places that are no further south than the port of New York, New York or Portland, Oregon and (a) is on any lake, river, harbour or canal in North America; or (b) does not extend farther than 200 miles from the shore or beyond the continental shelf, whichever is farther. *Marine Certification Regulations*, SOR/97-391, s. 1(1).

LOCAL WARD. A ward established for the purpose of electing a councillor or councillors to the council of an area municipality. *Municipality of Metropolitan Toronto Act*, R.S.O. 1990, c. M.62, s. 1.

LOCAL WARRANT. For the purpose of determining a municipality's fiscal effort, means the difference between the net municipal budget of a municipality for the previous year and the amount of unconditional grant plus any transitional adjustment payments computed for that municipality for the previous year. *An Act to Amend the Municipal Assistance Act*, S.N.B. 19 86, c. 58, s. 1.

LOCATIO. *n*. [L.] Hire, renting out. See CONTRACT OF ~ ET CONDUCTIO.

LOCATIO CONDUCTIO. [L.] Goods left with a bailee which the bailee may rent out. E.L.G. Tyler & N.E. Palmer, eds., *Crossley Vaines' Personal Property*, 5th ed. (London: Butterworths, 1973) at 85.

LOCATIO CUSTODIAE. [L.] The receipt of goods deposited for reward.

LOCATIO MERCIUM VEHENDARUM. , [L.] A contract to carry goods for hire.

LOCATION. *n*. The area described in, and in respect of which rights are given by, a permit or lease to mine. See ACCESSIBLE ~; DAMP ~; EXPLOSION-HAZARD ~; HAZARDOUS ~; HOLDER OF A ~; MINERAL ~; ORDINARY ~; WET ~.

LOCATION LINE. A straight line opened or indicated throughout No. 1 and No. 2 location posts of a mineral claim and joining them. *Yukon Quartz Mining Act*, R.S.C. 1985, c. Y-4, s. 2.

LOCATIO OPERIS. [L.] The renting out of services and labour.

LOCATIO OPERIS FACIENDI. [L.] A delivery to convey or otherwise manage, for a consideration paid to a bailee, something for someone who exercises a public function, or is a private person. E.L.G. Tyler & N.E. Palmer, eds., *Cross Vaines' Personal Property*, 5th ed. (London: Butterworths, 1973) at 85.

LOCATIO REI. [L.] The renting out of something.

LOCATOR. *n*. 1. A licensee who enters on land, prospects for minerals, locates a claim or has a claim located for him. *Canada Mining Regulations*, C.R.C., c. 1516, s. 2. 2. One who lets out things or services for hire.

LOC. CIT. *abbr*. Loco citato. At the quoted passage.

LOC. CT. GAZ. *abbr*. Local Courts & Municipal Gazette (Ont.), 1865-1872.

LOCK. See AIR ~; ANTI- ~; SYSTEM; ELECTRIC SWITCH ~; MEDICAL ~.

LOCK BOX. A numbered compartment in a post office that is kept locked and to which the boxholder and the postmaster have access.

LOCKED-IN REGISTERED RETIREMENT SAVINGS PLAN. A registered retirement savings plan, as defined in subsection 146(1) of the *Income Tax Act*, that meets the requirements set out in section 20. *Pension Benefits Standards Regulations, 1985*, SOR/87-19, s. 2(1), as am.

LOCKE KING'S ACT. A British statute of 1854 which reversed the rule that, when a mortgagor of real property died, any mortgage debt of that person was payable out of her or his general personal estate. As far as any beneficiaries of a deceased mortgagor's estate are concerned, any mortgage debt is chargeable prima facie against mortgaged land. W B. Rayner & R.H. McLaren, *Falconbridge on Mortgages*, 4th ed. (Toronto: Canada Law Book ,1977) at 341 and 342.

LOCKER PLANT. Any food premises in which individual lockers are rented or offered for rent to the public for the storage of frozen foods. See FROZEN FOOD ~.

LOCKMASTER. *n*. A person actually on duty in charge of a lock. *Canal Regulations*, C.R.C., c. 1564, s. 2.

LOCKOUT: *var.* **LOCK-OUT**. *n.* Includes the closing of a place of employment, a suspension of work by an employer or a refusal by an employer to continue to employ some employees, done to compel the employees, or to aid another employer to compel those employees, to a agree to certain terms or conditions of employment.

LOCK SEAL TAG. Any type of locking or sealing tag supplied with a hunting or angling licence that is made of cardboard, paper, plastic, metal or any other material. *Fish and Wildlife Act*, S.N.B. 1980, c. F-14.1, s. 1.

LOCKSMITH. *n.* A person who (a) makes, services, repairs, codes or recodes locks, (b) cuts, makes, sells or otherwise provides restricted keys, (c) cuts, makes, sells or otherwise provides keys from numerical or alphabetical codes or both, (d) sells, services or repairs safes, vaults or strongboxes, other than common strongboxes, or (e) is a member of a class of persons designated by the Lieutenant Governor in Council as locksmiths for the purposes of this Act, but a person is not a locksmith by reason only that he (f) codes or recodes locks of which he is the owner, or that he has sold, or (g) cuts, makes, sells or otherwise provides a key from a numerical or alphabetical code or both, if the key is intended for use with a lock he has sold and the key is sold or provided to the owner of the lock. *Private Investigators and Security Agencies Act*, R.S.B.C. 1996, c. 374, s. 1.

LOCK TENDER. A person who continuously supervises the controls of an air lock when workers are in it or about to enter it. D. Robertson, *Ontario Health and Safety Guide* (Toronto: Richard De Boo Ltd., 1988) at 5-239.

LOCK-UP. *n.* A jail. Usually refers to holding cells for brief stays by prisoners. See LOCKUP FACILITY.

LOCK-UP FACILITY. A police or court facility for the custody of an offender upon arrest, pending a transfer to a correctional facility or ending a court hearing. *Corrections Act*, S.N.S. 1989, c. 103, s. 3.

LOCO CITATO. [L.] At the quoted passage.

LOCOMOTIVE. *n.* The motor unit or car of a train.

LOCOMOTIVE BOILER. A high pressure boiler that may be used to furnish motivating power for travelling on rails. *Boilers and Pressure Vessels Act*, R.R.O. 1980, Reg. 84, s. 1.

LOCOMOTIVE FUEL. Fuel for use in an internal combustion engine in any rolling stock or other vehicle run on rails.

LOCUM TENENS. [L.] A person who lawfully executes another person's office, a deputy.

LOCUS IN QUO. [L. a place in which] A place where.

LOCUS POENITENTIAE. [L.] The power to draw back from an agreement before anything is done to confirm it legally.

LOCUS REGIT ACTUM. [L.] The law of the country where the act took place which governs its form. J.G. McLeod, *The Conflict of Laws* (Calgary: Carswell, 1983) at 779.

LOCUS SIGILLI. [L. the place of the seal] The place at the bottom of a document which requires a seal.

LOCUS SOLUTIONIS. [L.] The place where a payment should be made. J.G. McLeod, *The Conflict of Laws* (Calgary: Carswell, 1983) at 510.

LOCUS STANDI. [L. a place to stand] The right to be heard or appear during a proceeding.

LODE. See VEIN OR ~.

LODGE. *v.* To file or leave documents.

LODGE. *n.* Includes a primary subordinate division, by whatever name known, of a fraternal society. *Insurance acts*. See HUNTING OR FISHING ~.

LODGED. *adj.* When used is respect of a tree, means that by reason of other than natural causes the tree does not fall to the ground after being, (a) partly or wholly separated from its stump, or (b) displaced from its natural position. *Crown Timber Act*, R.R.O. 1980, Reg. 234, s. 1.

LODGER. *n.* A person who occupies rooms in a house.

LODGING. *n.* The provision of a room and meals.

LODGING HOUSE. *var.* **LODGING-HOUSE**. A house in which sleeping accommodation is let to transient lodgers.

LOG. *n.* 1. A record kept by the master of a ship. 2. Includes logs, timbers, boards, deals, scantlings or laths, telegraph poles, railway ties, pit-props, shingle bolts or staves, fence posts, cordwood, piles, poles, pulplogs, pulpwood, sawlogs, spars, wood chips and other cut timber of whatever length, whether round or flatted. See MERCHANTABLE ~; SAW ~S.

LOGGER. *n*. (a) A person engaged in the cutting, trimming, peeling, hauling, skidding, driving, piling, handling or loading of pulpwood, pitprops or other forms of timber or in any other work connected with a logging operation, whether of the foregoing kinds or not, or (b) a person engaged in the preparation of meals, cleaning or providing other services in a logging camp or on the site of logging operations.

LOGGING. *n*. The felling, limbing, bucking and marking of trees, construction of logging roads, off-highway transportation of logs to a millpond or mill yard, log salvaging and reforestation.

LOGGING CAMP. A structure of any kind which a logger occupies or uses while he is working as a logger or in which loggers are provided with sleeping accommodation or meals or both, other than (a) a restaurant, hotel or boarding-house which is licensed or subject to inspection under any other statute, or (b) a private residence, and includes the land surrounding and the buildings, structures or installations adjacent to a logging camp. *Logging Camps Act*, R.S. Nfld. 1970, c. 222, s. 2.

LOGGING INDUSTRY. Includes the cutting, driving, rafting, booming, transportation or sawing of logs, timber, pulpwood, firewood , pitprops, railroad ties or sleepers and also includes any employment incidental thereto or immediately connected therewith. *Logging Camps Act*, R.S.N.B. 1973, c. L-12, s. 1.

LOGGING INTEREST. A right of any kind held to an area of land or to trees growing on the land for the purpose of cutting timber thereon or otherwise producing timber therefrom commercially and whether received or held under grant, lease, licence, permit, contract or assignment of any of them or otherwise. *Logging Camps Act*, R.S. Nfld. 1970, c. 222, s. 2.

LOGGING OPERATION. The felling, cutting into logs, barking in the forest, cartage, piling, driving, loading and highway transportation of timber but not its processing outside the forest.

LOGGING OPERATOR. The holder of a forest management permit to supply a wood processing plant issued under the Forest Act (1986 , chapter 108), or a forest producer supplying a wood processing plant from a private woodlot. *Forest Act*, S.Q. 1986, c. 108, s. 242.

LOGGING ROAD. A temporary road within a timber harvesting area on Crown Lands to the fullest extent of the right-of-way, built solely for the extraction of timber, and includes a landing and other works associated with the harvesting operation. *Crown Lands and Forests Act*, S.N.B. 1980, c. C-38.1, s. 1.

LOGGING TAX. A tax imposed by the legislature of a province that is declared by regulation to be a tax of general application on income from logging operations. *Income Tax Act*, R.S.C. 1952, c. 148 (as am. S.C. 1970-71-72, c. 63), c. 127(2)(b).

LOGICALLY PROBATIVE. Tending to make the existence of a fact in issue more or less probable.

LOIR. Lost opportunity for an interdependent relationship. Head of pecuniary loss in personal injury law.

LOITER. *v*. 1. " . . . '[H]anging around' . . ." *R. v. Andsten* (1960), 32 W.W.R. 329 at 331, 33 C.R. 213 (B.C. C.A.), the court per Davey J.A. 2. In s. 179(1)(*b*) [of the *Criminal Code*, R.S.C. 1985, c. C-46] should be given its ordinary meaning, namely to stand idly around, hang around, linger, tarry, saunter, delay, dawdle, etc. This is consistent with the meaning given to the word as used elsewhere in the Code, and with the context and purpose of s. 179(1)(*b*). *R. v. Heywood*, 1994 CarswellBC 592, 34 C.R. (4th) 133, 174 N.R. 81, 50 B.C.A.C. 161, 82 W.A.C. 161, [1994] 3 S.C.R. 761, 94 C.C.C. (3d) 481, 24 C.R.R. (2d) 189, 120 D.L.R. (4th) 348, Cory, J. for the majority.

LOITERER. *n*. " . . . [A]n individual who is wandering about, apparently without precise destination, who does not have, in his manner of moving, a purpose or reason to do so other than to pass the time, who is not looking for anything identifiable and who often is merely motivated by the whim of the moment . . ." *R. v. Cloutier* (1991), 66 C.C.C. (3d) 149 at 154, 51 Q.A.C. 143, the court per Chevalier J.A.

L.O.M.J. *abbr*. Law Office Management Journal.

LONGA POSSESSIO PARIT JUS POSSIDENDI ET TOLLIT ACTIONEM VERO DOMINO. [L.] Prolonged possession creates a right of possession, and removes any right of action from the real owner.

LONGBOW. *n*. Includes a longbow, recurve bow and a compound bow.

LONG-BUTT. *v.* To cut a log of any length from a tree or from a log, and to not utilize it. *Crown Timber Act*, R.R.O. 1980, Reg. 234, s. 1.

LONGLINE. *n.* A line to which hooks are attached at intervals and that rests wholly on the bottom. *Quebec Fishery Regulations*, C.R.C., c. 852, s. 2.

LONG POSITION. Where used in relation to a commodity futures contract, means to be under an obligation to take delivery.

LONG SERVICE MEDAL. The Royal Canadian Mounted Police Long Service Medal as approved by royal warrant, hereinafter referred to as the "Long Service Medal", may be awarded to (a) a regular member who completes 20 years of qualifying service and meets the requirements set out in section 93; and (b) a retired regular member who has completed 20 years of qualifying service prior to his discharge from the Force and meets the requirements set out in section 93. *Royal Canadian Mounted Police Regulations*, C.R.C., c. 1391, s. 92.

LONGSHORING EMPLOYMENT. Employment in the loading or unloading of ship's cargo and in operations related to the loading or unloading of ship's cargo. *Canada Labour Standards Regulations*, C.R.C., c. 986, s. 19.

LONG TERM AVERAGE YIELD. As applied to a crop in a risk area means the weighted average yield for that crop, in that risk area as determined on the basis of available records during a period of not more than twenty-five continuous years next preceding the crop year in which any such determination is made. *Crop Insurance Act*, S.M. 1970, c. 30, s. 2.

LONG-TERM BONDS OF CANADA. Marketable bonds issued by the Government of Canada payable in Canadian currency and due to mature in not less than 10 years. *N.H.A. Maximum Interest Rates Regulations*, C.R.C., c. 1107, s. 3.

LONG-TERM DEBT. (a) In the case of a corporation that is a bank, indebtedness evidenced by bank debentures, within the meaning assigned by the Bank Act or the Quebec Savings Bank Act, and (b) in the case of a corporation that is not a bank subordinate indebtedness evidenced by obligations issued for a term of not less than five years. *Income Tax Act*, R.S.C. 1952, c. 148 (as am. S.C. 1986, c. 6, s. 100), s. 190(1).

LONG TERM DISABILITY PLAN. Insurance to provide benefits to employees who are unable to work because of illness or injury. The pre-condition to receipt of benefits is total disability.

LONG TERM LEASE. See REGISTERED ~.

LONG-TERM LIABILITY. A debt which is due over a long period of time, over a year.

LONG TERM OFFENDER. The court may, on application made following the filing of an assessment report, find an offender to be a long-term offender if it is satisfied that (a) it would be appropriate to impose a sentence of imprisonment of two years or more for the offence for which the offender has been convicted; (b) there is a substantial risk that the offender will reoffend; and (c) there is a reasonable possibility of eventual control of the risk in the community. *Criminal Code*, R.S.C. 1985, c. C-46, s. 753.1(1).

LONG-TERM SUPERVISION. Long-term supervision ordered provisions of the *Criminal Code*, dealing with long term offenders. The offender is subject to supervision after completing any sentence. *Corrections and Conditional Release Act, 1992*, S.C. 1992, c. 20, s. 2(1).

LONG-TERM UNIT. An inpatient unit to provide treatment services regular medical assessment and continuing nursing care to patients.

LONG TITLE. A description which sets out the purposes of a bill or statute in general terms. Contrast with the short title which is the name by which the statute is known and cited.

LONGUM TEMPUS ET LONGUS USUS, QUI EXCEDIT MEMORIAM HOMINUM, SUFFICIT, PRO JURE. [L.] Long time and long use, which surpass human memory, are sufficient in law.

LONG VACATION. The months July and August when the courts traditionally did not sit. D. Sgayias *et al., Federal Court Practice 1988* (Toronto: Carswell, 1987) at 253.

LOOP VENT. A branch vent that functions for two or more traps and loops back or extends to a stack vent from a point in front of the last connection of a fixture to a horizontal branch. *Ontario Water Resources Act*, R.R.O. 1980, Reg. 736, s. 1.

LOOSE. *adj.* 1. If it is possible for a man of average weight to push a wooden picket 8 in. or more into the soil. *Building Code Act*, R.R.O. 1980, Reg. 87, s. 4.2.1.5. 2. When it requires between 4 and 10 blows per foot in a penetration test. *Building Code Act*, R.R.O. 1980, Reg. 87, s. 4.2.1.5.

LOOSE TOBACCO. Loose, fine-cut manufactured tobacco for use in making cigarettes. *Excise Tax Act*, S.C. 1991, c. 42, s. 29.

LOQUITUR UT VULGUS. [L.] Following the common interpretation and agreed on meaning of the term. St. J. Langan, ed., *Maxwell on The Interpretation of Statutes*, 12th ed. (Bombay: N.M. Tripathi, 1976) at 81.

LORD. *n.* 1. Title given to a Supreme Court Judge. 2. Traditionally, in relation to real property, the person whose land another holds as tenant. See HOUSE OF ~S; LAW ~S; LIEGE~; MESNE ~.

LORD MANSFIELD'S RULE. The common law rule of jury secrecy, which prohibits the court from receiving evidence of jury deliberations for the purpose of impeaching a verdict, similarly reflects a desire to preserve the secrecy of the jury deliberation process and to shield the jury from outside influences. The common law rule, also referred to as Lord Mansfield's rule, can be traced back to the case of *Vaise v. Delaval* (1785), 1 Term Rep. 11, 99 E.R. 944 (K.B.), in which Lord Mansfield ruled that the court could not receive affidavits from jurors attesting to their own misconduct in reaching a verdict by lot. The rule was explicitly adopted by this Court is *Danis v. Saumure*, [1956] S.C.R. 403, in the context of a civil jury trial. *R. v. Pan*, 2001 CarswellOnt 2261, 2001 SCC 42, 155 C.C.C. (3d) 97, 200 D.L.R. (4th) 577, 43 C.R. (5th) 203, 147 O.A.C. 1, 85 C.R.R. (2d) 1, 270 N.R. 317, Arbour, J. for the court. See JURY SECRECY.

LORD'S DAY. The period of time that begins at midnight on Saturday night and ends at midnight on the following night.

LORD'S DAY ACT. Legislation respecting Sunday observance which requires businesses to close and regulates certain other activities.

LOSS. *n.* 1. Includes the happening of an event or contingency by reason of which a person becomes entitled to a payment under a contract of insurance of money other than a refund of unearned premiums. *Insurance acts*. 2. " . . . [T]he inverse of profit . . ." *Mountain Park Coals Ltd. v. Minister of National Revenue*, [1952] Ex. C.R. 560 at 568, [1952] C.T.C. 392, [1952] D.T.C. 1221, Thorson P. 3. "Injury" refers to the initial physical or mental impairment of the plaintiff's person as a result of the sexual assault, while "loss" refers to the pecuniary or non-pecuniary consequences of that impairment. *Blackwater v. Plint*, 2001 CarswellBC 1468, 2001 BCSC 997, 93 B.C.L.R. (3d) 228 (S.C.), Brenner C.J.S.C. See ACTUAL ~; ACTUAL ~ OR DAMAGE; ECONOMIC ~; EXCESS OF ~ INSURANCE; FINANCIAL ~; MONETARY ~; NON-PECUNIARY ~; OPERATING ~; PARTIAL ~; PECUNIARY ~; PROFIT AND ~; PROSPECTIVE ~ OF EARNINGS OR PROFITS; RELATIONAL ~; TOTAL ~.

LOSS ANALYSIS. " . . . [T]he investigation which becomes necessary to study the claim of a beneficiary to the supplementary indemnity for accidental death." *Metropolitan Life Insurance Co. v. Frenette*, [1992] I.L.R. 1778 at 1784, 89 D.L.R. (4th) 653, [1992] 1 S.C.R. 647, 46 Q.A.C. 161, [1992] R.R.A. 466, L'Heureux-Dubé J.

LOSS INSURANCE. An agreement under which the insurer agrees to make good a loss specified in the agreement. John G. Fleming, *The Law of Torts*, 8th ed. (Sydney: The Law Book Company Limited, 1992) at 395.

LOSS LEADER. " . . . [S]elling at less than cost; . . . *R. v. Philips Appliances Ltd.* (1966), (*sub nom. R. v. Philips Electronics Industries Ltd.*) 52 C.P.R. 224 at 227 (Ont. H.C.), Morand J.

LOSS OF ACCUMULATED WEALTH. The loss of capital assets which dependants can recover and which they would have received if the deceased had not died. K.D. Cooper-Stephenson & I.B. Saunders, *Personal Injury Damages in Canada* (Toronto: Carswell, 1981) at 440.

LOSS OF AMENITIES. A physical disability the victim sustained in an accident, and the effect that disability has on all the victim's activities. A loss for which the victim may be compensated by damages. In expropriation, refers to substantially diminished enjoyment.

LOSS OF CHANCE. " . . . [T]he damage which results from the loss of an opportunity either to realize a benefit or to avoid an injury. . . the damage is future or hypothetical and clearly not certain. It is distinguished by the fact that it is contingent, or dependent on an element of chance which must be evaluated in terms of probabilities. This contingent or probabilistic aspect provides the potential for ascertainment of damages in the present. . ." *Laferriée v. Lawson* (1991), 6 C.C.L.T. (2d) 119 at 196, 123 N.R. 325, 38 Q.A.C. 161, [1991] R.R.A. 320, [1991]

1 S.C.R. 541, 78 D.L.R. (4th) 609, Gonthier J. (Lamer, L'Heureux-Dubé, Sopinka, Cory and McLachlin JJ. concurring).

LOSS OF DEPENDENCY ON INCOME. The part of the deceased's revenue which would have benefitted all that person's statutory dependants during a certain period of their dependency. K.D. Cooper-Stephenson & I.B. Saunders, *Personal Damages in Canada* (Toronto: Carswell, 1981) at 423.

LOSS OF DEPENDENCY ON VALUABLE SERVICES. The deceased's many activities which, though not directly revenue-producing, are still of value to the claimants. K.D. Cooper-Stephenson & I.B. Saunders, *Personal Injury Damages in Canada* (Toronto: Carswell, 1981) at 431.

LOSS OF EXPECTATION OF LIFE. Shortening of the length of the victim's life. A loss for which the victim may be compensated by damages.

LOSS OF GUIDANCE. A loss for which the victim may be compensated by damages. Refers to loss of a parent or person standing in the place of a parent.

LOSS OF PROSPECT. In expropriation, refers to substantially diminished enjoyment.

LOSS OF PUBLICITY. " . . . [L]oss of the opportunity for the enhancement or maintenance of his reputation. . ." *Multivision Films Inc. v. McConnell Advertising Co.* (1983), 69 C.P.R. (2d) 1 at 36 (Ont. H.C.), Henry J.

LOSS OF SERVICES. A claim by a husband against a person who injured his wife wrongfully or a claim by a parent for loss occasioned the wrongful injury of his or her child or a claim by a master in respect of an injury to her or his servant. John G. Fleming, *The Law of Torts*, 8th ed. (Sydney: The Law Book Company Limited, 1992) at 658, 660, 684.

LOST. *adj.* " . . . [T]he location of the person or thing is unknown or uncertain. In other usages, 'lost' may mean mislaid and not found after reasonably diligent search." *Gagnon v. Northwest Territories (Registrar of Vehicles)*, [1983] N.W.T.R. 289 at 292 (C.A.), the court per Laycraft J.A..

LOST CIRCULATION ZONE. A zone within a geological formation generally known by this name and into which wastes can be discharged without positive injection pressure at the surface.

Environmental Protection Act, R.R.O. 1980, Reg. 303, s. 1.

LOST CORNER. A corner established during an original survey or during a survey of a plan of subdivision where the original post no longer exists or never existed and which cannot be reestablished from the field notes of either of such surveys or by evidence under oath.

LOST MONUMENT. A monument which has disappeared entirely and the position of which cannot be established by evidence. *Surveys acts.*

LOST OPPORTUNITY FOR AN INTERDEPENDENT RELATIONSHIP. Head of pecuniary loss in personal injury law.

LOST OR NOT LOST INSURANCE. Normally, in order to recover under a contract for a loss, the insured must have an insurable interest in the subject-matter insured at the time of the loss, but need not have such an interest when the contract is concluded. However, where the subject-matter is insured "lost or not lost", the insured may recover in respect of an insurable interest in the subject-matter acquired after a loss unless, at the time the contract was concluded, the insured was aware of the loss and the insurer was not. *Marine Insurance Act*, S.C. 1993, c. 22, s. 7(1), (2).

LOST TIME. Time not used productively at work.

LOT. *n.* 1. A parcel of land, described in a deed or other document legally capable of conveying land, or shown as a lot or block on a registered plan of subdivision. 2. The method of determining the candidate to be excluded or the candidate to fill the vacancy, as the case may be, by placing the names of the candidates on equal size pieces of paper placed in a box and one name being drawn by a person chosen by the clerk. *Municipal Act*, R.S.O. 1990, c. M.45, s. 45(6). 3. A parcel of land containing or which may contain one or more graves and includes a space within a building or structure which contains or may contain one or more places for the permanent placement of human remains. 4. That quantity of produce that for any reason is considered separately from other produce. Canada regulations. See BOARD ~; BROKEN ~; CORNER ~; FEED ~; INTERIOR ~; IRREGULAR ~; IRREGULARLY-SHAPED ~; MASTER ~; REGULAR ~; STRATA ~; SURVEYED ~; THROUGH ~; TOT ~; UNBROKEN ~; WATER ~.

LOT AREA. The horizontal area within the boundary lines of a lot.

LOT DEPTH. The horizontal distance of a lot between the front and rear lot lines, measured along the median between the side lot lines. Canada regulations.

LOT LINE. The line dividing one parcel of land from another. See REAR ~; SIDE ~.

LOT NUMBER. Any combination of letters, figures, or both, by which a natural health product can be traced in manufacture and identified in distribution. *Natural Health Products Regulations*, SOR/2003-196, s. 1(1).

LOTTERY. *n*. A game of chance; a division and sharing of prizes by chance or lot.

LOTTERY SCHEME. 1. A game or any proposal, scheme, plan, means, device, contrivance or operation described in any of paragraphs 206(1)(a) to (g), whether or not it involves betting, pool selling or a pool system of betting other than (a) a dice game, three-card monte, punch board or coin table; (b) bookmaking, pool selling or the making of recording or bets, including bets made through the agency of a pool or pari-mutuel system, on any race or fight, or on a single sport event or athletic contest; or (c) for the purposes of paragraphs (1)(b) to (f), a game or proposal, scheme, plan, means, device, contrivance or operation described in any of paragraphs 206(1)(a) to (g) that is operated on or through a computer, video device or slot machine, within the meaning of section 198(3). *Criminal Code*, R.S.C. 1985, c. C-46, s. 207(4) as am. 2. Includes a game of chance and a game of mixed chance and skill.

LOT WIDTH. The horizontal distance of a lot between the side lot lines, measured at right angles to the median between those lines at a point on the median that is midway between the front lot line and the rear lot line or 40 feet from the street it faces, whichever is the lesser. Canada regulations.

LOUNGE. *n*. (a) Part of a licensed hotel or motel, or (b) premises not part of a licensed hotel or motel, provided with special accommodations, facilities or equipment prescribed in the regulations, where in consideration of payment, beer, wine or spirits are served. *Liquor Control Act*, R.S. Nfld. 1990, c. L-18, s. 2. See AIRPORT ~.

LOW. CAN. R. *abbr*. Lower Canada Reports, 1851-1867.

LOWER CANADA. That part of Canada which heretofore constituted the Province of Lower Canada, and means now the Province of Quebec. *Interpretation Act*, R.SQ. 1977, c. I-16, s. 61.

LOWER CHURCHILL BASIN. The waters of the Churchill River downstream of the point of intersection of the Churchill River with the meridian of 63°40' West of Greenwich and between that point and the intersection of the Churchill River with the meridian of 60°46' West of Greenwich and within the catchment area of the Churchill River between those two points, but the expression "Lower Churchill Basin" does not include any rivers in the said catchment area other than the Churchill River, whether or not such other rivers are tributary to the said Churchill River. *Lower Churchill Development Act*, R.S. Nfld. 1990, c. L-27, Schedule A, s. 1.

LOWER TIER MUNICIPALITY. A municipality that forms part of an upper-tier municipality for municipal purposes. *Ont. Statutes*.

LOWEST INTERMEDIATE BALANCE RULE. The "lowest intermediate balance rule" states that a claimant to a mixed fund cannot assert a proprietary interest in that fund in excess of the smallest balance in the fund during the interval between the original contribution and the time when a claim with respect to that contribution is being made against the fund. Descendant of the Rule in Clayton's case. Originally articulated by Sargant J. in *James Roscoe (Bolton) Ltd. v. Winder* (1914), [1915] 1 Ch. 62 (Eng. Ch. Div.). *Law Society of Upper Canada v. Toronto Dominion Bank* (1998), 42 O.R. (3d) 257 (C.A.).

LOW HAZARD FIREWORKS. Those Division 2 fireworks that, in the opinion of the Chief Inspector, are relatively innocuous in themselves and are not liable to explode violently or all at once. *Explosives Regulations*, C.R.C., c. 599, s. 14.

LOW INCOME. An income that is insufficient to allow an individual or family with that income to obtain adequate housing. See FAMILY OF ~; PERSON OF ~.

LOW INCOME HOUSING. Housing for individuals or families of low income.

LOW-LEVEL AIR RACE. A competitive flight during which aircraft are flown at altitudes lower than minimal altitudes specified in the Air Regulations. *Special Aviation Events Safety Order*, C.R.C., c. 66, s. 2.

LOW LEVEL AIRSPACE. Airspace below 18,000 feet ASL that is within Canadian Domestic Airspace; *Canadian Aviation Regulations*, SOR/96-433, s. 101.01(1).

LOW PRESSURE BOILER. A boiler in which gas or vapour is generated, approved to carry a working pressure of 15 pounds or less, or a hot-water heating or hot-water supply boiler approved to carry a working pressure of 160 pounds or less per square inch and temperature not exceeding 250 degrees Fahrenheit, or a closed-type hot-water heating system approved to carry a working pressure of 30 pounds or less per square inch.

LOW PRESSURE DISTRIBUTION PIPE-LINE. A pipeline that (a) is used for transmitting gas for domestic, commercial or industrial purposes, (b) is designed or intended to operate at a maximum pressure of 700 kilopascals or less, and (c) is not part of a rural gas utility. *Gas Distribution Act*, R.S.A. 2000, c. G-3, s. 1.

LOW PRESSURE HEATING PLANT. A boiler or two or more boilers on the same premises having a safety valve setting of not more than 15 pounds per square inch (103 kilopascals) when the boiler is used for producing steam, or a safety valve setting of not more than 160 pounds per square inch (1100 kilopascals) when the boiler is used for producing hot water at a temperature of not more than 250 degrees Fahrenheit (120 degrees Celsius).

LOW PRESSURE HOT WATER PLANT. An assembly of hot water boilers that operate at a temperature of 121°C or less and at a pressure of 1 100 kPa or less and includes a pressure plant that is connected to the assembly of boilers. *Power Engineers and Boiler and Pressure Vessel Safety Act*, R.S.B.C. 1996, c. 368, s. 1.

LOW PRESSURE ORGANIC FLUID PLANT. An assembly of organic fluid boilers that (a) operate at a temperature of 343°C or less and (b) have no valves or other obstruction to prevent circulation between the boiler and an expansion tank that is fully vented to the atmosphere and includes a pressure plant that is connected to the assembly of boilers. *Power Engineers and Boiler and Pressure Vessel Safety Act*, S.B.C. 1996, c. 368, s. 1.

LOW-PRESSURE STATIONARY PLANT. An installation comprised of one or more boilers, (a) containing, steam at a pressure of 15 or less, or (b) containing water at a temperature at any boiler outlet of more than 212°F. and up to and including 250°F., and in addition a low-pressure stationary plant may have one or more compressors and one or more refrigeration compressors, and the total Therm-hour rating of all such boilers and compressors is more than 50. *Operating Engineers Act*, R.S.O. 1990, c. 0.42, s. 1.

LOW PRESSURE STEAM PLANT. An assembly of boilers that operate at a steam or other vapour pressure of 103 kPa or less and includes a pressure plant that is connected to the assembly of boilers. *Power Engineers and Boiler and Pressure Vessel Safety Act*, R.S.B.C. 1996, c. 368, s. 1.

LOW-RENTAL HOUSING PROJECT. *var.* **LOW RENTAL HOUSING PROJECT**. A housing project undertaken to provide decent, safe and sanitary housing accommodation, complying with standards approved by the Corporation, to be leased to families of low income or to such other persons as the Corporation, (a) in its discretion, in the case of a housing project owned by it, or (b) under agreement with the owner, in the case of a housing project not owned by it, designates, having regard to the existence of a condition of shortage, overcrowding or congestion of housing. *National Housing Act*, R.S.C. 1985, c. N-11, s. 2.

LOYALTY. *n.* Faithfulness.

LOYALTY CONTRACT. A contract between a shipper of goods and the members of a conference whereby the shipper agrees, in return for certain advantages, to offer to those members for transportation by them all goods, all goods of certain classes or a portion only of all goods or of all goods of certain classes shipped by that shipper. *Shipping Conferences Exemption Act, 1987*, S.C. 1987, c. 22, s. 2(1).

L.Q. REV. *abbr*. Law Quarterly Review.

L.R. *abbr*. Law Reports.

L.R.B. *abbr*. Labour Relations Board.

L.R. 1 A. & E. *abbr*. Law Reports, Admiralty and Ecclesiastical Cases, 1865-1875.

L.R. 1 C.C.R. *abbr*. Law Reports, Crown Cases Reserved, 1865-1875.

L.R. 1 CH. *abbr*. Law Reports, Chancery Appeals, 1865-1875.

L.R. 1 C.P. *abbr*. Law Reports, Common Pleas, 1865-1875.

L.R. 1 EQ. *abbr*. Law Reports, Equity Cases, 1865-1875.

L.R. 1 EX. *abbr*. Law Reports, Exchequer, 1865-1875.

L.R. 1 H.L. *abbr*. Law Reports, House of Lords Cases, 1865-1875.

L.R. 1 P. & D. *abbr*. Law Reports, Probate and Divorce, 1865-1875.

L.R. 1 P.C. *abbr*. Law Reports, Privy Council Cases, 1865-1875.

L.R. 1 Q.B. *abbr*. Law Reports, Queen's Bench, 1865-1875.

L.R. 1 SC. & DIV. *abbr*. Law Reports, Scottish and Divorce.

L.R.P.C. *abbr*. Law Reports Privy Council Appeals.

L.S. *abbr*. Locus sigilli. The place for the seal.

L.S.D. *abbr*. The hallucinogenic drug lysergic acid diethylamide. F.A. Jaffe, *A Guide to Pathological Evidence*, 3d ed. (Toronto: Carswell, 1991) at 222.

L. SOC. GAZ. *abbr*. Law Society Gazette (Law Society of Upper Canada).

L.S.U.C. *abbr*. Law Society of Upper Canada.

L.T. *abbr*. Law Times Reports.

LTD. *abbr*. Limited. One of the words or abbreviations which is required as part of a company's name.

LTÉE. *abbr*. Limitée. One of the words or abbreviations which is required as part of a company's name.

LTO. *abbr*. Land Titles Office.

LUCID INTERVAL. A period of sanity between two periods of insanity.

LUCRI CAUSA. [L.] With the intent of gain.

LUMBER. *n*. 1. Timber, mast, spar, shingle bolt, sawlog or lumber of any description. *Criminal Code*, R.S.C. 1985, c. C-46, s. 339(6). 2. The products of logs or timber after the same have been sawn or manufactured in a saw mill. *Woodsmen's Lien Act*, R.S.N.B. 1973, c. W-12, s. 1. See PACKAGED ~; SOFTWOOD ~.

LUMBERING. *n*. The milling of timber into lumber or boards when carried on in a forest, on a woodlot or on a tree farm.

LUMBERING EQUIPMENT. Includes a boom chain, chain, line and shackle. *Criminal Code*, R.S.C. 1985, c. C-46, s. 339(6).

LUMBER PRODUCT. Any part of a log or piece of lumber, and without derogating from the generality of the foregoing, includes a tie, post, beam, plank, board, siding, lath or shingle.

LUMEN. *n*. The luminous flux emitted in a solid angle of one steradian by a point source having an intensity of one candela. *Weights and Measures Act*, S.C. 1970-71-72, c. 36, schedule I.

LUMINOUS SIGN. Any device for lighting a poster by electricity or gas and any luminous poster or poster covered with a reflecting paint or coating.

LUNATIC. *n*. 1. Any person found by any competent tribunal or commission de lunatico inquirendo, to be a lunatic. 2. Includes an idiot and a person of unsound mind. 3. Includes a person, not an infant, who is incapable from infirmity of mind of managing his own affairs. *Incompetent Persons Act*, R.S.N.S. 1989, c. 218, s. 2.

LUNCH ROOM. A room that is used by employees for the purpose of eating or preparing meals or lunches.

LUNG. See JUNKIE'S ~.

LURE CROP AREA. An area of crop land that, pursuant to an agreement between the Government of Canada and the government of a province, remains unharvested for the purpose of luring migratory birds away from other unharvested crops and that is designated as such an area by poster, notice or sign. *Migratory Birds Regulations*, C.R.C., c. 1035, s. 2(1).

LURING A CHILD. Using the internet to attract a child or children for the purposes of committing certain offences.

LUX. *n*. The illuminance produced by a flux of one lumen uniformly distributed over one square metre. *Weights and Measures Act*, S.C. 1970-71-72, c. 36, schedule 1.

L.V.A.C. *abbr*. Land Value Appraisal Commission.

LX. *abbr*. Lux.

LYING IN WAIT. The waiting of a vessel, during the season of navigation, for a berth.

LYING-UP. *n*. The occupying by a vessel, during the season of navigation, of a berth.

M. *abbr*. 1. Mega. 2. Metre. 3. Micro. 4. Milli.

MACE. *n*. 1. The symbol of authority of the House of Commons or a legislature. 2. Spray used to subdue persons.

MACHINE. *n*. The mechanical embodiment of any mode or function of operation intended to accomplish something particular. H.G. Fox, *The Canadian Law and Practice Relating to Letters Patent for Inventions*, 4th ed. (Toronto: Carswell, 1969) at 17. See AIR-BLAST ~; AMUSEMENT ~; DRILLING ~; HARVESTING ~; ITINERANT ~; MEASURING ~; MOTION PICTURE ~; MOVING PICTURE ~; ROAD BUILDING ~; SLOT ~; WEIGHING ~; X-RAY ~.

MACHINE GUARD. A device that (a) is installed on a machine to prevent a person or any part of his body or his clothing from becoming engaged in (i) any rotating, moving, electrically charged, hot or otherwise dangerous part of a machine, or (ii) the material that the machine is processing, transporting or handling, or (b) makes the machine inoperative if a person or any part of his clothing is in or near a part of the machine that can cause injury.

MACHINE LANGUAGE. 1. "A third level of [computer] language, the lowest, is sometimes referred to as machine language or object code. There are two versions of machine language relevant for the purposes of this case: a system of hexadecimal notation and a system of binary notation." *Apple Computer Inc. v. Mackintosh Computers Ltd.* (1986), 10 C.P.R. (3d) 1 at 7, 8 C.I.P.R. 153, 3 F.T.R. 118, [1987] 1 F.C. 173, 28 D.L.R. (4th) 178 (T.D.), Reed J. 2. Since the computer only responds to machine language, a computer programme written in another language must be translated. The language in which the programme is written is called the source code and the language into which it is translated

is called the object code. Object code in many instances, and in the jurisprudence, I notice, is used as synonymous with machine language and I will adopt that usage. *I.B.M. Corp. v. Ordinateurs Spirales Inc./Spirales Computers Inc.* (1984), 27 B.L.R. 190, 80 C.P.R. (2d) 187, 2 C.I.P.R. 56, 12 D.L.R. (4th) 351 (Fed. T.D.), Reed J. See OBJECT CODE.

MACHINERY. *n*. 1. Includes the propelling engines, boilers, pumps, steering engines, windlasses and all similar apparatus required for the safety and operation of a ship. *Canada Shipping Act*, R.S.C. 1985, c. S-9, s. 2. 2. Includes steam and other engines, boilers, furnaces, milling and crushing apparatus, hoisting and pumping equipment, chains, trucks, tramways, tackles, blocks, ropes and tools, and all appliances used in or about or in connection with a mine. See ELEVATOR ~; FARM ~; LIFTING ~; SELF-LUBRICATING ~; TRADE ~.

MACHINERY ASSOCIATION. Includes an association incorporated or registered under this Act having as its principal objects or any of them the purchasing, leasing or otherwise acquiring, maintaining and operating of farm machinery or other equipment for use by or on behalf of the members and patrons thereof in the production of agricultural products or other products, and rendering to the members and patrons as producers services ancillary to such principal objects or any of them. *The Co-operative Production Associations Act*, R.S.S. 1978, c. C-37, s. 53.

MACHINERY INSURANCE. Insurance against (a) liability arising out of (i) bodily injury to, or the death of, a person, or (ii) the loss of, or damage to, property, or (b) the loss of, or damage to, property, caused by breakdown of machinery. *Classes of Insurance Regulations*, C.R.C., c. 977, s. 25.

MACHINERY SPACE. Any space within the main hull of a ship that contains the propelling or auxiliary machinery, including pumping units, boilers when installed, and all permanent coal bunkers. Canada regulations.

MACHINE TOOL, METAL CUTTING. A power driven device, not portable by hand, used for the purpose of removing metal in the form of chips.

MACHINE TOOL, METAL FORMING. A power driven machine not portable by hand, used to press, forge, emboss, hammer, blank or shear metals.

MACHINIST. See AUTOMOTIVE ~; GENERAL ~.

MACKEREL. *n.* A fish of the species Scomber scombrus.

MACNAUGHTON'S CASE. See MCNAGHTEN'S CASE.

MADE. *adj.* 1. [In relation to an order,] " . . . [R]efers to pronouncement, not entry: . . . *Levesque v. Levesque* (1992), 41 R.F.L. (3d) 96 at 98, 3 Alta. L.R. (3d) 193, 131 A.R. 106, 25 W.A.C. 106 (C.A.), Côté J.A. 2. " . . . [P]ronouncement [or] . . . signed or entered in court . . ." *Harvey v. Harvey* (1989), 23 R.F.L. (3d) 53 at 55, 60 Man. R. (2d) 302 (C.A.), Helper J.A. 3. Of an application, the date when the application is heard by the court. 4. Of a claim under an insurance policy, the time when the person asserting the claim brings it to the attention of or notifies the person against whom it is asserted. 5. Of an arbitral award, to have done everything necessary to perfect it.

MAG. *abbr.* Magistrate(s).

MAGAZINE. *n.* 1. Any building, storehouse, structure or place in which any explosive is kept or stored, but does not include (a) a place where an explosive is kept or stored exclusively for use at or in a mine or quarry in a province in which provision is made by the law of that province for efficient inspection and control of explosives stored and use at or in mines and quarries, (b) a vehicle in which an authorized explosive is being conveyed in accordance with this Act, (c) the structure or place in which is kept for private use, and not for sale, an authorized explosive to an amount not exceeding that authorized by regulation, (d) any store or warehouse in which are stored for sale authorized explosives to an amount not exceeding that authorized by regulation, or (e) any place at which the blending or assembling of the inexplosive component arts of an authorized explosive is allowed under section 8. *Explosives Act*, R.S.C. 1985, c. E-17, s. 2. 2. Any building, storehouse, structure or place in which any explosive is kept or stored, whether in or about a mine and includes detonator storage buildings, detonator and fuse houses, explosives storage boxes and thawing houses. 3. In a firearm, the part where unfired cartridges are kept. F.A. Jaffe, *A Guide to Pathological Evidence*, 3d ed. (Toronto: Carswell, 1991) at 222. See LARGE-CAPACITY ~; CARTRIDGE ~.

MAGAZINES AND PERIODICALS. Includes bound magazines and periodicals, bound trade magazines, employees' house organs, unbound literary and technical papers and employees' newsletters and club information bulletins issued at intervals not less frequent than four times a year.

MAG. CT. *abbr.* Magistrate's Court.

MAGIS DE BONO QUAM DE MALO LEX INTENDIT. [L.] The law favours good instead of bad construction.

MAGISTER. *n.* [L.] A ruler; a master.

MAGISTER LITIS. [L.] The master of the action.

MAGISTER NAVIS. [L.] The master of the ship.

MAGISTER RERUM USUS. [L.] Experience is the master of things.

MAGISTER SOCIETATIS. [L.] The manager of the partnership.

MAGISTRACY. *n.* The group of officials who administer the law; the office of magistrate.

MAGISTRATE. *n.* A provincial or territorial judge authorized to accept informations to commence criminal proceedings and to hear and determine regulatory and lesser criminal offences.

MAGNA CARTA. A charter or collection of statutes based largely on Saxon common law granted by the British King John in 1215 to confirm certain liberties.

MAGNUM. *adj.* Of ammunition, especially large or powerful. F.A. Jaffe, *A Guide to Pathological Evidence*, 3d ed. (Toronto: Carswell, 1991) at 222.

MAHR. *n.* In Islamic law, an obligatory gift or contribution made by the husband-to-be to his wife-to-be for her exclusive property.

MAIL. *v.* Refers to the deposit of the matter to which the context applies in the Canada Post Office at any place in Canada, postage prepaid, for transmission by post, and includes deliver. *Interpretation Act*, R.S.B.C. 1996 c. 238, s. 29. See POST.

MAIL. *n.* Mailable matter from the time it is posted to the time it is delivered to the addressee thereof. *Canada Post Corporation Act*, R.S.C. 1985, c. C-10, s. 2. See ADDRESS ~; CERTIFIED ~; REDIRECTED ~; REGISTERED ~; REQUEST ~; SERVICE BY ~; UNDELIVERABLE ~.

MAILABLE MATTER. Any message, information, funds or goods that may be transmitted by post. *Canada Post Corporation Act*, R.S.C. 1985, c. C-10, s. 2.

MAIL BAG. Any container or covering in which mail is transmitted, whether it contains mail or not. *Canada Post Corporation Act*, R.S.C. 1985, c. C-10, s. 2.

MAIL BOX. A privately owned mail receiving facility designed for indoor or outdoor use in an urban area.

MAIL CONTRACTOR. A person who has entered into a contract with the Corporation for the transmission of mail, which contract has not expired or been terminated. *Canada Post Corporation Act*, R.S.C. 1985, c. C-10, s. 2.

MAIL CONVEYANCE. Any physical, electronic, optical or other means used to transmit mail. *Canada Post Corporation Act*, R.S.C. 1985, c. C-10, s. 2.

MAIN. *n.* A tank, storage unit or pipe for the storage, transmission, delivery or furnishing of gas. See DISTRIBUTION ~.

MAIN DECK. The uppermost weathertight deck extending from side to side of the ship and includes any stepped portions thereof, but does not include any part of a superstructure deck where the deck next beneath the superstructure deck extends from side to side of the ship, is weathertight and is not stepped down inside the superstructure. *Hull Construction Regulations*, C.R.C., c. 1431, s. 100.

MAINLINE. *v.* To intravenously inject a drug.

MAINPERNOR. *n.* The surety or pledge to whom a person is handed over.

MAINPRISE. *n.* Handing over a person to a surety or pledge who agrees to produce that person some time in the future.

MAINTAIN. *v.* 1. "[To provide] . . . financial or other material support . . ." *Desjarlais v. Macdonell Estate* (1988), 31 E.T.R. 18 at 24, [1988] 3 W.W.R. 534, 23 B.C.L.R. (2d) 195 (C.A.), Anderson J.A. (Esson and McLachlin JJ.A. concurring). 2. " . . . [M]ay mean either to bring or institute an action or proceeding or to continue or further prosecute an action already commenced. . ." *Komnick System Sandstone Brick Machinery Co. v. B.C. Pressed Brick Co.* (1918), 56 S.C.R. 539 at 549, 41 D.L.R. 423, [1918] 2 W.W.R. 564, Anglin J. 3. " . . . [T]o keep in being, to keep up and to repair. . . *Red Lake (Township) v. Drawson*, [1964] 1 O.R. 324 at 328, 42 D.L.R. (2d) 121 (H.C.), Ferguson J.

MAINTAINABLE EARNINGS. What a business entity earns and what cash flow should follow the valuation date. A. Bissett-Johnson & W.M. Holland, eds., *Matrimonial Property Law in Canada* (Toronto: Carswell, 1980) at V-13.

MAINTAINOR. *n.* A person who, by assisting either party, supports or seconds a cause in which she or he is not interested.

MAINTENANCE. *n.* 1. " . . . [I]n the ordinary sense, mean[s] 'keep in repair'; . . ." *Canadian Pacific Railway v. Grand Trunk Railway* (1914), 20 D.L.R. 56 t 63, 49 S.C.R. 525, 17 C.R.C. 300, Brodeur J. 2. Pecuniary support including support or alimony to be paid to someone who is not a spouse. C.R.B. Dunlop, *Creditor-Debtor Law in Canada*, Second Cumulative Supplement (Toronto: Carswell, 1986) at 209. 3. "The law of maintenance as I understand it upon the modern constructions, is confined to cases where a man improperly and for the purpose of stirring up litigation and strife, encourages others either to bring actions or to make defences which they have no right to make." *Findon (Finden) v. Parker* (1843), 152 E.R. 976 at 979 (U.K. Ex.), Lord Abinger, C.B. 4. Includes preserving works or machines and keeping them in good repair for proper operation. 5. Includes shelter, clothing, nursing support, medical treatment, necessary training, instruction and transportation. 6. The preservation and keeping in repair of a public highway, and includes the removal of snow and the doing of any work and the supplying of any materials in connection therewith. *Public Highways Act*, R.S.N.S. 1989, c. 371, s. 2. See CAPITAL ~; LANDSCAPE ~.

MAINTENANCE COSTS. All expenditures required specifically in relation to the operation or maintenance of an approved project. *Conservation Authorities Act*, R.S.O. 1990, c. C.27, s. 1.

MAINTENANCE DEBTOR. A person who is required under a maintenance order to pay maintenance to or for the benefit of another person.

MAINTENANCE FEE. A patentee of a patent issued by the Patent Office under this Act after the coming into force of this section shall, to maintain the rights accorded by the patent, pay to the Commissioner such fees, in respect of such periods, as may be prescribed. *Patent Act*, R.S.C. 1985, c. P-4, s. 46.

MAINTENANCE FUND. A fund established for the upkeep and repair of a cemetery, mausoleum or columbarium.

MAINTENANCE ORDER. An order for the periodical payment of money as alimony or as maintenance for a wife or former wife or reputed wife or a child or any other dependant of the person against whom the order was made.

MAINTENANCE WORK. The work of keeping equipment, apparatus or appliances in good working order or repair.

MAIN TRACK. A track extending through yards and between stations upon which trains are operated by time-table or train order, or both, or the use of which is governed by block signals or other method of control.

MAJESTY. *n*. A title of a sovereign. See LEZE-~.

MAJOR ALTERATION. Any alteration of a building where the plans and specifications for the alteration are required by law to be approved by the building authority.

MAJOR ATTACHMENT CLAIMANT. A claimant who qualifies to receive benefits and has 600 or more hours of insurable employment in their qualifying period. *Employment Insurance Act*, S.C. 1996, c. 23, s. 6.

MAJOR BURDEN. " . . . [T]he burden of establishing a case . . ." *R v. Schwartz* (1988), 45 C.C.C. (3d) 97 at 115, [1989] 1 W.W.R. 289, 66 C.R. (3d) 251, 88 N.R. 90, [1988] 2 S.C.R. 443, 56 Man. R. (2d) 92, 55 D.L.R. (4th) 1, Dickson C.J.C. (dissenting).

MAJOR HAEREDITAS VENIT UNICUIQUE NOSTRUM A JURE ET LEGIBUS

QUAM A PARENTIBUS. [L.] A greater inheritance comes to each of us through legal right and laws than from our parents.

MAJORITY. *n*. 1. Age of maturity. 2. The largest number. See AGE OF ~; RELIGIOUS ~.

MAJOR LIEN FUND. (i) Where a certificate of substantial performance is not issued, the amount required to be retained under section 18(1) or (1.1) plus any amount payable under the contract (A) that is over and above the 10% referred to in section 18(1) or (1.1), and (B) that has not been paid by the owner in good faith while there is no lien registered; (ii) where a certificate of substantial performance is issued, the amount required to be retained under section 18(1) or (1.1) plus any amount payable under the contract (A) that is over and above the 10% referred to in section 18(1) or (1.1), and (B) that, with respect to any work done or materials furnished before the date of issue of the certificate of substantial performance, has not been paid by the owner in good faith while there is no lien registered. *Builders' Lien Act*, R.S.A. 2000, c. B-7, s. 1.

MAJOR OCCUPANCY. The principal occupancy for which a building or part thereof is used or intended to be used.

MAJOR PERILS. The perils of fire, lightning, smoke, windstorm, hail, explosion, water escape, strikes, riots or civil commotion, impact by aircraft and vehicles, vandalism and malicious mischief. *Condominium Act*, R.S.O. 1990, c. C.26, s. 27(11).

MAJOR PLANT NUTRIENT. Nitrogen (N), phosphoric acid (P_2O_5) or potash (K_2O). *Fertilizers Regulations*, C.R.C., c. 666, s. 2.

MAJOR REPAIRS. Repairs that may affect the strength of a boiler, pressure vessel or plant. *Boilers and Pressure Vessels acts*.

MAJOR SEXUAL ASSAULT. An assault in which the perpetrator by violence or threat of violence forces an adult victim to submit to sexual activity of a sort that a reasonable person would know that the victim likely would suffer a lasting emotional or psychological injury whether or not there was a physical injury. May include rape, attempted rape, buggery, cunnilingus, and fellatio.

MAJOR SHAREHOLDER. A person or group of persons is deemed a major shareholder of a corporation or company if that person or group controls, directly or indirectly, more than ten or twenty or thirty per cent of the voting shares in that corporation or company.

MAJUS CONTINET MINUS. [L.] Greater contains less.

MAJUS DIGNUM TRAHIT AD SE MINUS DIGNUM. [L.] The more worthy brings the less worthy along with it.

MAJUS EST DELICTUM SEIPSUM OC-CIDERE QUAM ALIUM. [L.] To kill one's self is a greater crime than to kill another.

MAKE. See LINE ~.

MAKER. *n.* 1. The person who signs the promise in a promissory note. 2. The person who makes a depository note. *Depository Bills and Notes Act*, S.C. 1998, c. 13, s. 2. 3. In relation to a cinematographic work, the person by whom the arrangements necessary for the making of the work are undertaken, or in relation to a sound recording, the person by whom the arrangements necessary for the first fixation of the sounds are undertaken. *Copyright Act*, R.S.C. 1985, c. C-42, s. 2. See BOOK~; MARKET~; MOULD ~.

MAKE-UP WATER. Water added to a swimming pool from an external source.

MAKE-WORK PRACTICE. A procedure requiring the expansion or spreading of available work.

MAKING WAY. The state of being under way on the surface of the water and having a velocity relative to such surface.

MAL. *pref.* Wrong; bad; fraudulent.

MALA FIDE. [L.] In bad faith.

MALA FIDES. [L.] Bad faith, contrasted to bona fides, good faith.

MALA GRAMMATICA NON VITIAT CHARTAM. SED IN EXPOSITIONE IN-STRUMENTORUM MALA GRAMMA-TICA QUOAD FIERI POSSIT EVITANDA EST. [L.] Bad grammar does not invalidate a deed. But in the interpretation of documents, bad grammar should be avoided as much as possible.

MALA IN SE. [L.] "[At] common law . . . truly criminal conduct . . . [was designated] mala in se . . . today [such] prohibited acts are . . . classified as . . . crimes . . ." *R. v. Wholesale Travel Group Inc.* (1991), 8 C.R. (4th) 145 at 159, 67 C.C.C. (3d) 193, 4 O.R. (3d) 799n, 84 D.L.R.

(4th) 161, 130 N.R. 1, 38 C.P.R. (3d) 451, 49 O.A.C. 161, [1991] 3 S.C.R. 154, 7 C.R.R. (2d) 36, Cory J. (L Heureux-Dubé J. concurring).

MALA MENS. [L.] An malevolent mind.

MALA PRAXIS. For a medical practitioner to injure a patient through lack of skill, neglect or by experiment.

MALA PROHIBITA. [L.] "[At] common law . . . conduct, otherwise lawful, which is prohibited in the public interest . . . today . . . [such] prohibited acts are . . . classified as . . . regulatory offences." *R. v. Wholesale Travel Group Inc.* (1991), 8 C.R. (4th) 145 at 159, 67 C.C.C. (3d) 193, 4 O.R. (3d) 799n, 84 D.L.R. (4th) 161,130 N.R. 1, 38 C.P.R. (3d) 451, 49 O.A.C. 161, [1991] 3 S.C.R. 154, 7 C.R.R. (2d) 36, Cory J. (L Heureux-Dubé J. concurring).

MALE. See ~ ISSUE.

MALECREDITUS. *n.* A person who has bad credit.

MALEDICTA EST EXPOSITIO QUAE CORRUMPIT TEXTUM. [L.] It is bad definition which corrupts a text.

MALEDICTION. *n.* A curse.

MALE-DOMINATED CLASS. 1. (i) A class in which there are 10 or more incumbents, as of the date any public sector employer is required to commence action to implement pay equity, of whom 70% or more are men, (ii) in the case of a public sector employer which employs 500 or more employees as of the date referred to in subclause (i), such other classes, irrespective of the number of incumbents and gender distribution, as the employer, bargaining agents and employee representatives affected may agree should be considered male-dominated, and (iii) in the case of a public sector employer which employs less than 500 employees as of the date referred to in sub-clause (i), such other classes as may be further defined in the regulations. *The Pay Equity Act*, C.C.S.M. c. P13, s. 1. 2. A class of which 60% or more of the incumbents are men. *Pay Equity Act*, R.S.P.E.I. 1988, c. P-2, s. 1.

MALEFACTION. *n.* An offence; a crime.

MALEFACTOR. *n.* A person who commits a malum in se.

MALEFICIA NON DEBENT REMANERE IMPUNITA; ET IMPUNITAS CONTIN-UUM AFFECTUM TRIBUIT DELIN-

QUENDI. [L.] Evil deeds should not remain unpunished; and impunity offers continual inducement to commit crime.

MALEFICIA PROPOSITIS DISTINGUUNTUR. [L.] Evil deeds differ from evil purposes.

MALEFICIUM. *n*. [L.] Damage; injury; waste.

MALE ISSUE. Descendants in the male line. T. Sheard, R. Hull & M.M.K. Fitzpatrick, *Canadian Forms of Wills*, 4th ed. (Toronto: Carswell, 1982) at 191.

MALE JOB CLASS. Except where there has been a decision that a job class is a female job class as described in clause (b) of the definition of "female job class", (a) a job class in which 70 per cent or more of the members are male, or (b) a job class that a review officer or the Hearings Tribunal decides is a male job class or a job class that the employer, with the agreement of the bargaining agent, if any, for the employees of the employer, decides is a male job class. *Pay Equity Act*, R.S.O. 1990, c. P.7, s. 1(1).

MALEVOLENT. *adj*. Desirous of evil to others; disposed to ill will; actuated by ill will.

MALFEASANCE. *n*. The commission of an unlawful act. See MISFEASANCE.

MALFUNCTION. *n*. Faulty function.

MALICE. *n*. 1. "Malice has been described as 'improper purpose.' Lamer J. in Nelles [*Nelles v. Ontario* (1989), 41 Admin. L.R. 1 (S.C.C.)], supra, at p. 22, referred to John G. Fleming, The Law of Torts, 5th ed. (Sydney: Law Book Company, 1977), at p. 609, where Fleming stated that malice has a 'wider meaning than spite, ill-will or a spirit of vengeance, and includes any other improper purpose, such as to gain a private collateral advantage.'" *Falloncrest Financial Corp. v. Ontario* (1995), 1995 CarswellOnt 1064, 33 Admin. L.R. (2d) 87 (Gen. Div.), Ground, J. 2. Malice is commonly understood, in the popular sense, as spite or ill- will. However, it also includes, as Dickson J. pointed out in dissent in *Cherneskey*, supra, at p. 1099, "any indirect motive or ulterior purpose" that conflicts with the sense of duty or the mutual interest which the occasion created. See also *Taylor v. Despard*, [1956] O.R. 963 (C.A.). Malice may also be established by showing that the defendant spoke dishonestly, or in knowing or reckless disregard for the truth. *Hill v. Church of Scientology of Toronto*, [1995] 2 S.C.R. 1130. 3. [In the tort of malicious prosecution] the core meaning of malice is the use of the criminal justice system for an improper purpose, the proper use of it being to bring before the court a person whom the prosecutor has reasonable and probable cause to believe has committed a criminal offence. As the authorities indicate, malice has a "wider meaning than spite, ill-will or a spirit of vengeance, and includes any other improper purpose". *Oniel v. Metropolitan Toronto (Municipality) Police Force* (2001), 141 O.A.C. 201 (C.A.) Per Borins J.A. (Sharp J.A. concurring). 4. "[In defamation] . . . not limited to spite or ill will, although these are its most obvious instances. Malice includes any indirect motive or ulterior purpose, and will be established if the plaintiff can prove that the defendant was not acting honestly when he published the comment. . ." *Cherneskey v. Armadale Publishers Ltd.*, [1979] 1 S.C.R. 1067 at 1099, 24 N.R. 271, [1978] 6 W.W.R. 618, 7 C.C.L.T. 69, 90 D.L.R. (3d) 321, Dickson J. (dissenting) (Spence and Estey JJ. concurring). See IMPLIED ~.

MALICE AFORETHOUGHT. 1. ". . . [W]as . . . adopted to distinguish murder from manslaughter, which denoted all culpable homicides other than murder. . . was not limited to its natural and obvious sense of premeditation, but would be implied whenever the killing was intentional or reckless. In these instances, the malice was present and it is the premeditation which was implied by law." *R. v. Vaillancourt* (1987), 60 C.R. (3d) 289 at 321, 81 N.R. 115, [1987] 2 S.C.R. 636, 68 Nfld. & P.E.I.R. 281, 209 A.P.R. 281, 10 Q.A.C. 161, 39 C.C.C. (3d) 118, 47 D.L.R. (4th) 399, 32 C.R.R. 18, Lamer J. (Dickson C.J.C. and Wilson J. concurring). 2. " . . . [A]t least in modern usage, is misleading, but it has come to be a comprehensive term to describe the various forms of mens rea or the various mental elements which must be present to justify a conviction for murder . . . has been greatly broadened in modern times. . ." *R. v. Switelinski* (1980), 18 C.R. (3d) 231 at 246, 248, 34 N.R. 569, 55 C.C.C. (2d) 481, 117 D.L.R. (3d) 285, [1980] 2 S.C.R. 956, the court per McIntyre J.

MALICE IN FACT. " . . . [I]s indicated where a party was actuated either by spite or ill-will towards an individual, or by indirect and improper motives, though these may be wholly unconnected with any uncharitable feeling towards anybody: . . ." *Owsley v. Ontario* (1983), 34 C.P.C. 96 at 99 (Ont. H.C.), DuPont J.

MALICE IN LAW. " . . . [E]stablished by a wrongful act done intentionally without just cause or excuse, but it does not necessarily require ill-will against a particular person: . . ." *Owsley v. Ontario* (1983), 34 C.P.C. 96 at 99 (Ont. H.C.), DuPont J.

MALICIOUS FALSEHOOD. A tort designed to provide a remedy for a falsehood which causes monetary harm.

MALICIOUSLY. *adv*. With an intent to cause harm or while being reckless about whether that harm will occur.

MALICIOUS PROSECUTION. " . . . [F]our necessary elements which must be proved for a Plaintiff to succeed in an action for malicious prosecution: (a) the proceedings must have been initiated by the defendant; (b) the proceedings must have terminated in favour of the plaintiff; (c) the absence of reasonable and probable cause; (d) malice, or a primary purpose other than that of carrying the law into effect." *Nelles v. Ontario* (1989), 37 C.P.C. (2d) 1 at 21, 49 C.C.L.T. 217, [1989] 2 S.C.R. 170, 71 C.R. (3d) 358, 60 D.L.R. (4th) 609, 98 N.R. 321, 69 O.R. (2d) 448n, 35 O.A.C. 161, 42 C.R.R. 1, 41 Admin. L.R. 1, Lamer J. (Dickson C.J.C. and Wilson J. concurring).

MALIGNARE. [L.] To slander, to malign.

MALITIA PRAECOGITATA. [L.] Predetermined malice.

MALITIA SUPPLET AETATEM. [L.] Malice makes up for lack of age.

MALLORY-WEISS SYNDROME. Vomiting blood caused by a tear in the esophagus. F.A. Jaffe, *A Guide to Pathological Evidence*, 2d ed. (Toronto: Carswell, 1983) at 184 and 185 .

MALPRACTICE. *n*. 1. " . . . [B]ad or unskilful practice by a physician or surgeon, whereby the health of the patient is injured . . ." *Town Archer* (1902), 4 O.L.R. 383 at 387, 1 O.W.R. 391 (H.C.), Falconbridge C.J. 2. The negligent or careless act of a professional.

MALT. *n*. Any substance prepared by steeping grain or leguminous seeds in water, allowing the grain or seeds to germinate, and checking the germination by drying. *Excise Act*, R.S.C. 1985, c. E-14, s. 4. See PEAT-DRIED ~.

MALT LIQUOR. 1. Any beverage, other than beer, obtained by the alcoholic fermentation of an infusion or decoction of barley, malt and hops in drinkable water. *The Liquor Act*, R.S.S. 1978, c. L-18, s. 2. 2. All fermented liquor brewed in whole or in part from malt, grain or any saccha-

rine matter without any process of distillation. *Excise Act*, R.S.C. 1985, c. E-14, s. 4.

MALT-WINE. *n*. An alcoholic distillate obtained by pot-still distillation from a mash of cereal grain or cereal grain products saccharified by the diastase of malt and fermented by the action of yeast. *Food and Drug Regulations*, C.R.C., c. 870, s. B.02.002.

MALUM IN SE. [L.] See MALA IN SE.

MALUM NON PRAESUMITUR. [L.] One does not presume evil.

MALUM PROHIBITUM. [L.] See MALA PROHIBITA.

MALUM QUO COMMUNIUS EO PEJUS. [L.] The more common the evil the worse it is.

MALUS ANIMUS. [L.] Malevolent intent.

MALUS USUS EST ABOLENDUS, QUIA IN CONSUETUDINIBUS NON DIUTURNITAS TEMPORIS, SED SOLIDITAS RATIONIS EST CONSIDERANDA. [L.] A bad usage should be abolished, because with customs it is not the length of time that they have been observed but the totality of the reasoning behind them which must be considered.

MAMMAL. *n*. A vertebrate of the class Mammalia.

MAMMALIAN PEST. Any rat, mouse, raccoon, rabbit, porcupine, squirrel, ground-hog, mole or skunk.

MAMMOGRAM. *n*. A radiological examination of the breast.

MAN. *abbr*. Manitoba.

MANACLE. *n*. A chain used to bind the hands; a shackle.

MANAGEMENT. See FOREST ~; HAZARDOUS WASTE ~ ENTERPRISE; KNOWLEDGE ~; PORTFOLIO ~; RECORDS ~; STANDING COMMITTEE ON ~ AND MEMBERS' SERVICES; WASTE ~; WASTE ~ POWER; WATER ~ PROJECT; WATER QUALITY ~; WILDLIFE ~.

MANAGEMENT AREA. See WATER ~.

MANAGEMENT COMPANY. A person or company that provides investment advice under a management contract.

MANAGEMENT CONTRACT. A contract under which, for valuable consideration, a mutual fund is provided with investment advice, alone or together with administrative or management services.

MANAGEMENT CORPORATION. See MUTUAL FUND SALES OR ~.

MANAGEMENT FEES. Of a corporation means those fees paid to a person for services performed by an individual that could, had the corporation hired individuals as employees for that purpose, have been performed by those employees.

MANAGEMENT FUNCTION. Actions such as the preparation of a budget, decisions as to organization of the enterprise and staffing levels, representation of the employer in collective bargaining or in contract administration, formulation of corporate policy, hiring, firing, promoting, and disciplining of employees, and authorizing leave.

MANAGEMENT RIGHTS. Rights which an employer retains such as hiring, contracting and price fixing.

MANAGER. *n*. 1. A person who has significant administrative responsibilities and exercises powers of independent action, autonomy, and discretion. 2. In relation to companies in financial distress, one who displaces the board of directors and operates the commercial aspects of the debtor's business. See AIRPORT ~; CITY ~; GENERAL ~; MINE ~; MUTUAL FUND ~; MUTUEL ~; PORTFOLIO ~; RECEIVER AND ~; TOTALIZATOR ~; UNDERGROUND ~.

MANAGERIAL CAPACITY. See PERSON EMPLOYED IN A MANAGERIAL OR CONFIDENTIAL CAPACITY.

MANAGING AGENT. A person or corporation directly representing an insurance company and who can issue policies, interim receipts and give oral coverage.

MANAGING DIRECTOR. 1. " . . . [A] director having the management of affairs." *Claudet v. Golden Giant Mines Ltd.* (1910), 13 W.L.R. 348 at 350, 15 B.C.R. 13 (C.A.), Galliher J.A. (Macdonald C.J.A. concurring). 2. " . . . [A]n ordinary director entrusted with some special powers: . . ." *Standard Construction Co. v. Crabb* (1914), 7 W.W.R. 719 at 721, 30 W.L.R. 151, 7 Sask. L.R. 365 (C.A.), the court per Lamont J.A.

MANAGING TRUSTEE. A trustee responsible for managing the trust while the title to the trust property is in another's name, the custodian trustee's name.

MAN. & SASK. TAX R. *abbr*. Manitoba & Saskatchewan Tax Reports.

MAN. BAR N. *abbr*. Manitoba Bar News.

MANCIPATE. *v*. To bind; to enslave; to tie.

MANDAMUS. *n*. [L. we command] "[An extraordinary remedy which] . . . lies to secure the performance of a public duty in the performance of which the applicant has sufficient legal interest. The applicant must show that he demanded the performance of the duty and that performance of it has been refused by the authority obliged to discharge it . . . Another principle is that a mandamus will not be issued to order a body as to how to exercise its jurisdiction or discretion." *Turmel v. Canada (Canadian Radio-Television & Telecommunications Commission)* (1980), 60 C.P.R. (2d) 37 at 38, 117 D.L.R. (3d) 697, [1981] 2 F.C. 411 (T.D.), Walsh J.

MANDANT. *n*. The principal party in a contract of mandate.

MANDATA LICITA STRICTAM RECIPIUNT INTERPRETATIONEM, SED ILLICITA LATAM ET EXTENSAM. [L.] Lawful orders receive strict interpretation, but unlawful ones broad and extensive interpretation.

MANDATARIUS TERMINOS SIBI POSITOS TRANSGREDI NON POTEST. [L.] A mandatary cannot exceed limitations imposed on her or him.

MANDATARY. *n*. A person to whom someone gives a charge, commandment or mandate.

MANDATE. *n*. 1. A request; a directive. 2. A bailment of goods, without recompense, to have something done in connection with them or to be transported from one place to another.

MANDATOR. *n*. A director.

MANDATORY. *adj*. 1. Imperative. 2. Refers to a provision which must be followed. If not complied with, the action performed or completed will be invalid.

MANDATORY ALLOCATION PROGRAM. A program established to control the allocation of supplies of an energy product at the level of the suppliers and wholesale customers thereof. When the Governor in Council is of the opinion that a national emergency exists by reason of actual or anticipated shortages of petroleum or disturbances in the petroleum markets that affect or will affect the national security and welfare and the economic stability of Canada, and that it is necessary in the national interest to conserve the supplies of petroleum products within Canada, the Governor in Council may, by order, so declare and by that order authorize the establishment of a program for the mandatory allocation of petroleum products within Canada in accordance with this Act. *Energy Supplies Emergency Act*, R.S.C. 1985, c. E-9.

MANDATORY INJUNCTION. An injunction to restrain the continuance of some wrongful omission, that is, requiring action.

MANDATORY ORDER. Includes equitable remedies resulting from imperative or peremptory orders such as an order for specific performance. Includes orders such as mandamus.

MANDATORY PRESUMPTION. 1. ". . . [R]equires that the inference [which flows from the facts] be made." *R. v. Oakes* (1986), 24 C.C.C. (3d) 321 at 330, [1986] 1 S.C.R. 103, 53 O.R. (2d) 719, 50 C.R. (3d) 1, 14 O.A.C. 335, 19 C.R.R. 308, 26 D.L.R. (4th) 200, 65 N.R. 87, Dickson C.J.C. (Chouinard, Wilson and Le Dain JJ. concurring). 2. " . . . [R]equires the trier of fact to find the presumed fact upon proof of the fact giving rise to the presumption, in the absence of some countering evidence." *R. v. Oakes* (1983), 3 C.R.R. 289 at 308, 40 O.R. (2d) 660, 2 C.C.C. (3d) 339, 32 C.R. (3d) 193, 145 D.L.R. (3d) 123 (C.A.), the court per Martin J.A.

MANDATUM. *n*. [L.] When a mandatary agrees, without reward, to do something about things which have been bailed or simply to transport them. E.L.G. Tyler & N.E. Palmer, eds., *Crossley Vaines' Personal Property*, 5th ed. (London: Butterworths, 1973) at 85.

MAN-DAY. *n*. The amount of work which can be accomplished by one person in one day.

MAN-HOUR. *n*. The amount of work which can be accomplished by one person in one hour.

MANIFEST. *v*. To become apparent; to become evident.

MANIFEST. *n*. 1. The document designed to identify the quantity, composition, origin and destination of hazardous waste during transportation and the persons consigned, transporting and accepting that waste. 2. Of a merchant ship, a list of the goods which comprise her cargo.

MANIFEST. *adj*. Evident.

MANIFESTA PROBATIONE NON INDIGENT. [L.] Obvious things need not be proved.

MANIFESTATION THEORY. On this theory, damage only occurs when it becomes known (on one formulation, to the insured, and on another, to the third party whose property is affected). Therefore, coverage is triggered when the insured or third party first becomes or could have become aware of the damage. *Alie v. Bertrand & Frère Construction Co.* (2002), 62 O.R. (3d) 345 (C.A.).

MANIFESTLY UNLAWFUL. An overt violation of the law; a certain and obvious unlawfulness.

MANIFESTO. *n*. The public declaration by a government, sovereign or person of what the intend to do or how they intend to behave. See ANTI~.

MANIFEST UNFAIRNESS. There must be a rational connection between the deprivation of life, liberty or security of the person and the purpose of the law [being challenged under s. 7 of the Canadian Charter of Rights and Freedoms]. In [*Rodriguez v. British Columbia (Attorney General)*, [1993] 3 S.C.R. 519] . . . , Sopinka J. stated at p. 596 that if the deprivation of the right "does little or nothing to enhance the State's purpose, then the deprivation is not in accordance with the principles of fundamental justice." Courts have often used the term "manifest unfairness" to describe such situations. *R. v. Malmo-Levine*, 2000 CarswellBC 1148, 2000 BCCA 335, 145 C.C.C. (3d) 225, 34 C.R. (5th) 91, 74 C.R.R. (2d) 189, 138 B.C.A.C. 218, 226 W.A.C. 218 (C.A.) Per Braidwood J.A. (Rowles J.A. concurring).

MANIPULATION. *n*. A calculated procedure, force or thrust designed to move one structure in relation to another, particularly of the spinal column to remove subluxations or fixations and to mobilize the affected structures for the purpose of restoring or maintaining health.

MANIPULATIVE TREATMENT. The use of the hand or machinery in the operation or working on the foot or its articulations.

MANLIFT. n, A mechanism having a power driven endless belt with platforms or footholds for lifting or lowering persons in a substantially vertical direction and includes its hoistway enclosure.

MAN. L.J. *abbr*. Manitoba Law Journal.

MAN. L.R. *abbr.* Manitoba Law Reports (First Series).

MAN-MADE FIBRE. A staple fibre or filament produced by manufacturing processes, wholly or in part of organic polymers but does not include rubber. *Customs Tariff*, R.S.C. 1985, c. C-54, s. 2.

MAN-MADE LANDSCAPE. An area established to protect the biodiversity of an inhabited area of water or land whose landscape and natural features have been shaped over time by human activities in harmony with nature and present outstanding intrinsic qualities the conservation of which depends to a large extent on the continuation of the practices that originally shaped them. *Natural Heritage Conservation Act*, R.S.Q., c. C-61.01, s. 2.

MANNER. *n.* The mode or method in which something is done or happens or one acts.

MANNER OF DEATH. The mode or method of death whether natural, homicidal, suicidal, accidental or undeterminable.

MANOEUVRE. See VESSEL RESTRICTED IN HER ABILITY TO ~.

MANOEUVRING AREA. That part of an aerodrome, other than an apron, that is intended to be used for the take-off and landing of aircraft and for the movement of aircraft associated with take-off and landing. *Canadian Aviation Regulations*, SOR/96-433, s. 101.01.

MAN OF STRAW. See STRAMINEUS HOMO.

MANPOWER REQUIREMENT. A requirement for the movement of employees into or out of an industry, or from one type of employment within an industry to another type of employment within that industry, where the requirement arises from (a) a technological or other industrial change that renders the employees' skills or aptitudes superfluous to the needs of the industry or the type of employment from which the employees are moved, or (b) an expansion of the industry to which the employees are moved.

MAN. R. *abbr.* Manitoba Reports, 1883-1961.

MANRIKIGUSARI. *n.* A length of rope, cord, wire or chain fastened at each end to a hexagonal or other geometrically shaped hard weight or hand-grip.

MAN. R. (2D). *abbr.* Manitoba Reports (Second Series), 1979-.

MAN. R. TEMP. WOOD. *abbr.* Queen's Bench, temp. Wood (Man.), 1875-1883.

MANSION HOUSE. Means a dwelling house. Dwelling-house does not mean a separate, single-family building. It means any place a person dwells. *R. v. Kutschera*, 1999 CarswellBC 2751, 1999 BCCA 748, 141 C.C.C. (3d) 254, 131 B.C.A.C. 120, 214 W.A.C. 120 (C.A.). Per Southin J. dissenting).

MANSLAUGHTER. *n.* 1. Culpable homicide that is not murder or infanticide. *Criminal Code*, R.S.C. 1985, c. C-46, s. 234. 2. Culpable homicide that otherwise would be murder may be reduced to manslaughter if the person who committed it did so in the heat of passion caused by sudden provocation. *Criminal Code*, R.S.C. 1985, c. C-46, s. 232(1). 3. " . . . [A]n ulawful killing without proof of the existence of the required specific intent has always been characterized as manslaughter." *R. v. Switelinski* (1980), 18 C.R. (3d) 231 at 248, 34 N.R. 569, 55 C.C.C. (2d) 481, 117 D.L.R. (3d) 285, [1980] 2 S.C.R. 950, the court per McIntyre J.

MANSUETAE NATURAE. [L.] Harmless animals. Of a tame disposition.

MANTICULATE. To pick pockets.

MANUAL. See RATE ~.

MANUALIS OBEDIENTIA. [L.] Submission under oath; sworn obedience.

MANUAL STRANGULATION. Strangling with one or both hands which sometimes injures the thyroid cartilage or hyoid bone. F.A. Jaffe, *A Guide to Pathological Evidence*, 3d ed. (Toronto: Carswell, 1991) at 226.

MANUCAPTOR. *n.* A person who stands bail for another person.

MANUFACTORY. *n.* 1. " . . . [W]ork-shop . . ." *Toronto (City) v. Foss* (1913), 10 D.L.R. 627 at 628, 27 O.L.R. 612, 4 O.W.N. 597 (C.A.), the court per Meredith J.A. 2. " . . . '[F]actory' . . ." *R. v. Ferguson* (1906), 13 O.L.R. 479 at 481 (H.C.), Falconbridge C.J. See BONDED~; CIGAR~; TOBACCO ~.

MANUFACTURE. *v.* To manufacture is to fabricate. It is the act or process of making articles for use. It is the operation of making goods or wares of any kind. It is the production of articles produced from raw or prepared material by giving to these materials new forms, qualities and properties or combinations whether by hand or machine. *Minister of National Revenue v. Do-*

minion Shuttle Co. (1933), 72 C.S. 15 (Que. S.C.)

MANUFACTURE. *n.* 1. This word does not include higher forms of life. As a result a mouse was not patentable. Commonly understood to denote a non-living mechanistic product or process. *Harvard College v. Canada (Commissioner of Patents)*, 2002 SCC 76, Bastarache, J. for the majority. 2. However, the tradition of patent jurisprudence has been expansive, not restrictive. By 1851 the learned text *Godson on Patents* (2nd ed.) noted that the word "manufactures" had received from the English courts "very extended signification. It has not, as yet, been accurately defined; for the objects which may possibly come within the spirit and meaning of that act, are *almost infinite*" (p. 35). We should not encourage the Commissioner to try to circle each of the five definitional words with tight language that creates arbitrary gaps between, for example, "manufacture" and "composition of matter" through which useful inventions can fall out of the realm of patentability. To do so would conflict with this Court's earlier expression of a "judicial anxiety to support a really useful invention". The definition of invention should be read as a whole and expansively with a view to giving protection to what is novel and useful and unobvious. *Harvard College v. Canada (Commissioner of Patents)*, [2002] 4 S.C.R. 45 Per Binnie J. (dissenting) (McLachlin C.J.C., Major and Arbour JJ. concurring). 3. " . . . [A] large-scale production of the article and/or the production of the article by combining the efforts or creations of two or more contributions by subcontract or otherwise. Thus the components might be made by several different persons and the final product might be assembled or produced for marketing by the manufacturer. . . might be applied to a person who physically or actually makes, fabricates or assembles nothing, but who, as the 'general contractor' is the coordinator of all the contributing makers of components or sub-assemblies. . ." *Compo Co. v. Blue Crest Music Inc.* (1979), 45 C.P.R. (2d) 1 at 16, [1980] 1 S.C.R. 357, 105 D.L.R. (3d) 249, 29 N.R. 296, the court per Estey J. 4. The process of assembling or altering a motor vehicle in order to complete that motor vehicle for the purpose of sale of that motor vehicle to the first purchaser at the retail level. *Motor Vehicles Safety Act*, R.S.C. 1985, c. M-10, s. 2. 4. Includes the production, refining or compounding of fuel.

MANUFACTURED ARTICLE. Any article that is formed to a specific shape or design during manufacture.

MANUFACTURED FIREWORKS. Explosives of any class and any fireworks composition that is enclosed in any case or contrivance, or is otherwise manufactured or adapted for the production of pyrotechnic effects, pyrotechnic signals or sound signals. *Explosives Regulations*, C.R.C., c. 599, s. 2.

MANUFACTURED GAS. Any artificially produced fuel gas, except acetylene and any other gas used principally in welding or cutting metals. *Ontario Energy Board Act*, R.S.O. 1990, c. 0.13, s. 1(1).

MANUFACTURED GOODS. See PARTLY ~.

MANUFACTURED HOME. A structure, whether or not ordinarily equipped with wheels, that is designed, constructed or manufactured to be moved from one place to another by being towed or carried, and used or intended to be used as living accommodation.

MANUFACTURED HOME PARK. The parcel or parcels, as applicable, on which one or more manufactured home sites that the same landlord rents or intends to rent and common areas are located.

MANUFACTURED HOME SITE. A site in a manufactured home park, which site is rented or intended to be rented to a tenant for the purpose of being occupied by a manufactured home.

MANUFACTURED TOBACCO. Every article, other than a cigar or packaged raw leaf tobacco, that is manufactured in whole or in part from raw leaf tobacco by any process. *Excise Act, 2001*, S.C. 2002, c. 22, s. 1.

MANUFACTURER. *n.* 1. Any person who manufactures or produces by hand, art, process or mechanical means any goods, wares and merchandise and a person who packs, freezes or dehydrates any goods, wares and merchandise. 2. Includes one who makes, prepares, alters, repairs, renovates, services, dyes, cleans, ornaments, prints, finishes, packs, or assembes the parts of and adapts for use or sale any raw material, goods, article or commodity. 3. A person who manufactures or assembles motor vehicles. See AFFIDAVIT OF ~; BONDED ~; CIGAR ~; PRODUCER OR ~; TOBACCO ~.

MANUFACTURING. *n*. Includes making, preparing, altering, repairing, renovating, servicing, dyeing, cleaning, ornamenting, printing, finishing, packing or assembling the parts of and adapting for use or sale any raw materials, goods, articles or commodities.

MANUFACTURING ASSOCIATION. Includes an association incorporated or, registered under this Act having as its principal objects, or any of them, producing, preparing, adapting, processing and manufacturing goods, wares and merchandise from raw materials derived chiefly from the products of agriculture, forest, lake, river or the utilization for such purposes of products of other natural resources, or for use or sale primarily by its members or for use or sale by or through the association. *The Co-operative Production Associations Act*, R.S.S. 1978, c. C-37, s. 65.

MANUFACTURING LOCATION. See INTERDEPENDENT ~.

MANUFACTURING OR PROCESSING ACTIVITY. An activity whereby any footwear or leather (a) is made, fabricated, processed or refined out of any raw material or other substance or combination thereof and includes the tanning of any raw material or other substance or combination thereof, or (b) is made by causing any raw material or other substance to undergo a significant chemical, bio-chemical or physical change including any change that preserves or improves the keeping qualities of that raw material or other substance but excluding any change by growth or decay. Canada regulations.

MANUFACTURING PLANT. A plant that utilizes a mineral or a substance recovered from a mineral as a component of a product manufactured by the plant. See DAIRY ~; MILK ~.

MANU FORTI. [L.] With a strong hand.

MANUMISSION. *n*. The act of freeing slaves.

MANU OPERA. [L.] Goods held by a thief caught in the act of stealing them.

MANUS. *n*. [L.] An oath.

MANUSCRIPT. *n*. " . . . [I]ncludes more than what is written in the author's hand. I believe it embraces all material from an author that is neither printed for general distribution nor given permanent form on paper . . ." *University of Winnipeg v. Deputy Minister of National Revenue (Customs & Excise)* (1988), 16 C.E.R. 14 at 20, 13 T.B.R. 5 8 (T.B.), Beauchamp. See WRITING, ~.

MANUSCRIPT, RECORD OR DOCUMENT. Textual material, other than a printed book, pamphlet or serial consisting of one or more pages bound, stitched or fastened together or in loose format that clearly forms a single unit of information. *Canadian Cultural Property Export Control List*, C.R.C., c. 448, s. 1.

MAP. *n*. A document that is a cartographic representation and includes a topographic, hydrographic, military, cadastral, aeronautic or survey map, cartogram, chart or plan. *Canadian Cultural Property Export Control List*, C.R.C. c. 448, s. 1.

MAPLE PRODUCT. Any product or preparation reared directly or indirectly from the sap of the maple.

MAPLE PRODUCT SUBSTITUTE. A product other than a pure maple product manufactured or derived in whole or in part from a farm product and prepared for the same uses as a maple product and resembling a maple product in appearance.

MAPLE SUGAR. A solid product resulting from the evaporation of maple sap or male syrup, and may be either in solid blocks or in a more or less pulverized form.

MAPLE SYRUP. Syrup made by the evaporation of maple sap or by the solution of maple sugar in water.

MAPPING. *n*. The planning, co-ordination, generation, procurement, maintenance and distribution of maps and mapping materials and includes activities connected with topographic, thematic and cadastral mapping in photographic, cartographic and digital formats.

MAPPING SYSTEM. A series of data bases coordinated by the Director that cover a range of accuracy and detail levels, that contain at least the positions of points, lines and areas and their identifiers, and that depict the survey control, land survey system, hydrographic features, relief features, municipal boundaries and transportation features. *Land Titles Act*, R.S.A. 2000, c. S-26, s. 1.

MARBLING. *n*. The visibility of the patterns of blood vessels on skin after death. F.A. Jaffe, *A Guide to Pathological Evidence*, 3d ed. (Toronto: Carswell, 1991) at 223.

MARCHIONESS. *n*. In England, a female marquess.

MAREVA INJUNCTION. 1. Originally a prejudgment remedy intended to freeze assets until judgment was obtained and a writ of execution issued which was named after the case *Mareva Compania Naviera S.A. v. Int. Bulkcarriers S.A.*, [1980] 1 All E.R. 213 (U.K. C.A.). C.R.B. Dunlop, *Creditor-Debtor Law in Canada*, Second Cumulative Supplement (Toronto: Carswell, 1986) at 88. 2. "The gist of the Mareva action is the right to freeze exigible assets when found within the jurisdiction, wherever the defendant may reside, providing, of course, there is a cause between the plaintiff and the defendant which is justiciable in the Courts of England. However, unless there is a genuine risk of disappearance of assets, either inside or outside the jurisdiction, the injunction will not issue. This generally summarizes the position in this country . . . " *Aetna Financial Services Ltd. v. Feigelman* (1985), 29 B.L.R. 5 at 25, [1985] 1 S.C.R. 2, [1985] 2 W.W.R. 97, 55 C.B.R. (N.S.) 1, 56 N.R. 241, 15 D.L.R. (4th) 161, 4 C.P.R. (3d) 145, 32 Man. R (2d) 241, the court per Estey J. 3. A remedy designed to (1) obtain something like security, at least by ensuring that there are funds available to meet any judgment, and (2) put pressure on a defendant to provide proper security for any claim. However, it has been held that such an injunction does not create a proprietary right in the enjoined property; it merely prevents dealing with that property in particular ways. C.R.B. Dunlop, *Creditor-Debtor Law in Canada* (Toronto: Carswell, 1981) at 190.

MARGARINE. *n.* Includes oleo, oleomargarine, butterine, and any substitute for butter of whatever origin, source, or composition, that is prepared for the same uses as butter and is manufactured wholly or in part from any fat or oil other than that of milk.

MARGIN. *n.* The difference between the cost and selling price of a commodity. See BUY ON ~; RETAILER ~.

MARGIN ACCOUNT. An account agreement with a securities' dealer permitting the purchase of securities on credit.

MARGINAL NOTE. Something printed beside the section of an act which summarizes the effect of that section.

MARGIN DEPOSIT. A payment, deposit or transfer to a clearing house under the rules of the clearing house to assure the performance of the obligations of a clearing member in connection with security transactions, including, without limiting the generality of the foregoing, transactions respecting futures, options or other derivatives or to fulfil any of those obligations. *Bankruptcy and Insolvency Act*, R.S.C. 1985, c. B-3, s. 95.

MARIHUANA. *n.* Cannabis sativa L.

MARINA. *n.* Any premises at which gasoline or an associated product is sold and is put into the fuel tanks of motor boats and other water craft or into portable containers. See COMMERCIAL ~.

MARINARIUS. *n.* [L.] A mariner, sailor.

MARINE. *adj.* Relating to naval matters.

MARINE ADVENTURE. Any situation where insurable property is exposed to maritime perils, and includes any situation where (a) the earning or acquisition of any freight, commission, profit or other pecuniary benefit, or the security for any advance, loan or disbursement, is endangered by the exposure of insurable property to maritime perils, and (b) any liability to a third party may be incurred by the owner of, or other person interested in or responsible for, insurable property, by reason of maritime perils. *Marine Insurance Act*, S.C. 1993, c. 22, s. 2.

MARINE AREA. The sea-bed and subsoil of any area covered by sea water.

MARINE BUNKER FUEL. (a) Bunker oil, or (b) a combination of fuels including bunker oil that has a viscosity not lower than 20 centistokes when measured at a temperature of 50°C and is used in a ship as fuel for an internal combustion engine, steam engine or steam turbine.

MARINE CHEMIST. A person who (a) has graduated from an educational institution approved by the Board and has completed (i) courses in chemical engineering, or (ii) a general course with a major in chemistry, or (b) has obtained a fellowship in the Chemical Institute of Canada, and thereafter has had at least three years experience in chemical or engineering work, of which a minimum of 150 working hours has been gained under proper supervision in ship board work involving the testing and inspection of tank vessels and other vessels in the application of gas hazard control standards prescribed by the Board. *Safe Working Practices Regulations*, C.R.C., c. 1467, s. 2.

MARINE CRAFT WASTE DISPOSAL SYSTEM. A waste disposal system operated by a person or a municipality for the receiving of waste from marine craft for deposit in holding tanks.

MARINE DIESEL FUEL. Diesel fuel for use in a ship as fuel for an internal combustion engine.

MARINE INSTALLATION OR STRUCTURE. Includes (*a*) any ship and any anchor, anchor cable or rig pad used in connection therewith, (*b*) any offshore drilling unit, production platform, subsea installation, pumping station, living accommodation, storage structure, loading or landing platform, dredge, floating crane, pipelaying or other barge or pipeline and any anchor, anchor cable or rig pad used in connection therewith, and (*c*) any other work or work within a class of works prescribed. *Oceans Act*, S.C. 1996, c. 31, s. 2.

MARINE INSURANCE. 1. A contract of marine insurance is a contract whereby the insurer undertakes to indemnify the insured, in the manner and to the extent agreed in the contract, against (a) losses that are incidental to a marine adventure or an adventure analogous to a marine adventure, including losses arising from a land or air peril incidental to such an adventure if they are provided for in the contract or by usage of the trade; or (b) losses that are incidental to the building, repair or launch of a ship. Subject to the Act, any lawful marine adventure may be the subject of a contract. *Marine Insurance Act*, S.C. 1993, c. 22, s. 6. 2. Insurance against, (i) liability arising out of, (A) bodily injury to or death of a person, or (B) the loss of or damage to properties; or (ii) the loss of or damage to property, occurring during a voyage or marine adventure at sea or on an inland waterway or during delay incidental thereto, or during transit otherwise than by water incidental to such a voyage or marine adventure. See CONTRACT OF ~.

MARINE PLANT. 1. Includes Irish moss, kelp and other salt water plants, and any products or by-products thereof. *Fish Inspection Act*, R.S.C. 1985, c. F-12, s. 2. 2. Includes all benthic and detached algae, marine flowering plants, brown algae, red algae, green algae and phytoplankton. *Fisheries Act*, R.S.C. 1985, c. F-14, s. 47.

MARINE POLLUTION. The introduction by humans, directly or indirectly, of substances or energy into the sea that results, or is likely to result, in (a) hazards to human health; (b) harm to living resources or marine ecosystems; (c) damage to amenities; or (d) interference with other legitimate uses of the sea. *Canadian Environmental Protection Act, 1999*, S.C. 1999, c. 33, s. 120.

MARINE PRODUCT. Any fish, shellfish or crustacean able to live in a marine environment and any echinoderm, including parts of such animals and the products or by-products derived therefrom.

MARINER. *n.* A person who is serving on a ship or boat within the province, and includes a fisherman.

MARINE RISK. A hazard of the sea, a condition of sea, weather, or accident of navigation producing a result which would not have occurred but for these conditions.

MARINE SANITATION DEVICE. Any equipment installed on board a ship that is designed to receive, retain, store, treat or discharge sewage and any process to treat such sewage. *Great Lakes Sewage Pollution Prevention Regulations*, C.R.C., c. 1429, s. 2.

MARINE SECTION. The water transport and personnel of the Force. *Royal Canadian Mounted Police Pension Contribution Act*, R.S.C., 1970, R-10, s. 2.

MARINE SURVEY. The inspection of a vessel.

MARITAL. *adj.* Pertaining to the state of marriage; relating to a husband.

MARITAL DEBTS. The indebtedness of either or both spouses to another person (a) for the purpose of facilitating, during cohabitation, the support, education or recreation of the spouses or one or more of their children; or (b) in relation to the acquisition, management, maintenance, operation or improvement of marital property.

MARITAL HOME. Property in which one or both spouses have an interest and that is or has been occupied as their family residence, and where property that includes a marital home is used for a purpose in addition to a family residence, that marital home is that portion of the property that may reasonably be regarded as necessary to the use and enjoyment of the family residence.

MARITAL PROPERTY. (a) Family assets; (b) property owned by one spouse or by both spouses that is not a family asset and that was acquired while the spouses cohabited, or in contemplation of marriage, except (i) a business asset, (ii) property that was a gift from one spouse to the other, including income from that property, (iii) property that was a gift, devise, or bequest from any other person to one spouse only, including income from that property, (iv) property that represents the proceeds of disposition of property that was not a family asset and was not acquired while the souses cohabited or in contemplation of marriage, or that was acquired in exchange for or was purchased with the proceeds of disposition of such property or that represents insurance proceeds with respect to loss of or damage to such property; and (v) property that represents the proceeds of disposition of property referred to in sub-paragraphs (ii) and (iii) or that was acquired in exchange for or was purchased with the proceeds of disposition of such property or that represents insurance proceeds with respect to loss of or damage to such property; and (c) property that was acquired by one spouse after the cessation of cohabitation and that was acquired through the disposition of property that would have been marital property had the disposition not occurred; but does not include property that the spouses have agreed by a domestic contract is not to be included in marital property.

MARITAL REGIME. See STANDARD ~.

MARITAL RIGHTS. A husband's rights. See now CONJUGAL RIGHTS.

MARITAL STATUS. 1. The status of being single, engaged to be married, married, separated, divorced, widowed or a man and woman living in the same household as if they were married. *Human Rights Act*, S.N.S. 1991, c. 12, s. 3. 2. " . . . [I]n the Canadian Human Rights Act, S.C.1976-77, c. 33 does not mean the status of a married person but, rather, the status of a person in relation to marriage, namely, whether that person is single, married, divorced or widowed." *Schaap v. Canada (Canadian Armed Forces)* (1988), 27 C.C.E.L. 1 at 8, 56 D.L.R. (4th) 105 (Fed. C.A.), Pratte J.A. (concurring). 3. The status of being married, single, widowed, divorced or separated and includes the status of living with a person of the opposite sex in a conjugal relationship outside marriage. *Human Rights Code*, R.S.O. 1990, c. H-19, s. 10 as am. 4. [In s. 1(a) of Regulations under *The Saskatchewan Human Rights Code*, S.S. 1979, c. S-24.1, *General Regulations*, Sask. Reg. 216/79, now s. 2(1)(i.01) of *The Saskatchewan Human Rights Code*, S.S. 1979, c. S-24.1] can refer to being or not being married or how you live your life together with your life partner; or it can be to whom you are married. *Ennis v. Prince Albert Elks Club Inc.*, 2002 SKCA 106, (sub nom. *Saskatchewan Human Rights Commission v. Prince Albert Elks Club Inc.*) 2002 C.L.L.C. 230-035, 20 C.C.E.L. (3d) 98 (C.A.). See MARRIAGE STATUS; SAME-SEX PARTNERSHIP STATUS.

MARITIME INSURANCE. Insurance against marine losses; that is to say, the losses incident to marine adventure, and may be the express terms of a contract or by usage of trade extend so as to protect the insured against losses on inland waters or by land or air which are incidental to any sea voyage.

MARITIME LAW. The law relating to ships, harbours and mariners. See CANADAN ~.

MARITIME PERILS. The perils consequent on or incidental to the navigation of the sea, that is to say, perils of the seas, fire, war perils, pirates, rovers, thieves, captures, seizures, restraints, and detainments of princes and peoples, jettisons, barratry, and any other perils, either of the like kind or which may be designated by the policy. *Insurance acts*.

MARITIME PROVINCES. The Provinces of Nova Scotia, New Brunswick, Prince Edward Island and Newfoundland.

MARITIME SERVICE. A radiocommunication service that provides for the safety and navigation and other operations of ships or vessels, and that may also include the exchange of ship-to-shore messages on behalf of the public. *Radiocommunications Regulations*, SOR/96-484.

MARITIME TORT. A tort committed on water as opposed to one committed on land.

MARK. *n.* 1. A mark, brand, seal, wrapper or design used by or on behalf of (a) the government of Canada or a province, (b) the government of a state other than Canada, or (c) any department, board, commission or agent established by a government mentioned in paragraph (a) or (b) in connection with the service or business of that government. *Criminal Code*, R.S.C. 1985, c. C-46, s. 376. 2. Any mark, sign, device, imprint, stamp, brand, label, ticket, letter, word or figure. *Precious Metals Marking Act*, R.S.C. 1985, c. P-19, s. 2. 3. "To constitute a mark, there must be a pictorial representation or design, or something which marks or distinguishes it in some way and allows it to be recognized. . ." *Ingle v. Canada (Registrar of Trade Marks)* (1973), 12 C.P.R. (2d) 75 at 77 (Fed. T.D.), Addy J. 4. A brand or any permanent mark applied to the exterior of an animal or any device implanted beneath the skin or within the body of an animal, but does not include any mark registered under the authority of the Livestock Pedigree Act (Canada). *The Animals Identification Act*, R.S.S. 1978, c. A-20.1, s. 2. See CERTIFICATION ~; CODE ~; DISTINGUISHING ~; EX-PORT ~; INSPECTION ~; LAND~; PLIM-SOLL ~; QUALITY ~; SAFETY ~; SER-VICE ~; TRADE- ~.

MARKED. *adj.* Marked by a specific dye as required by the regulations. *Gasoline Tax acts.*

MARKED DEPARTURE. A significant, important or notable departure.

MARKED FUEL. Fuel that is coloured or identified.

MARKER. *n.* A plaque or monument of metal, concrete, stone or other material installed or to be installed in a cemetery, columbarium or mausoleum in memory of a deceased person. See CONTROL SURVEY ~; FICTITIOUS IDEN-TIFICATION PLATE OR ~; FICTITIOUS ~; GENETIC ~; GRAVE ~.

MARKET. *n.* 1. An area of rivalry between suppliers of goods and services who vie with each other for the patronage of consumers of the goods and services. 2. " . . . [T]he action or business of buying and selling commodities." *Schecter v. Bluestein* (1981), 23 C.R. (3d) 39 at 45, [1981] C.S. 477, 121 D.L.R. (3d) 345, 58 C.C.C. (2d) 208 (Que. S.C.), Malouf J. 3. " . . . [D]efined by a certain number of properties which establish equivalence of price, of goods and of availability. It is often in relation to a geographic place which may be local, regional, national or international, depending upon the clientele. Often, and more and more frequently, a market will depend on a network such as in the case of currency or electronics . . ." *Alex Couture Inc. c. Canada (Procureur général)* (1990), (*sub nom. Alex Couture Inc. v. Canada (Attorney General)*) 30 C.P.R. (3d) 486 at 514, 69 D.L.R. (4th) 635 (Qué. C.S.), Philippon J. 4. A stockyard, abbatoir or auction market and includes a feedlot where livestock is held for sale or slaughter. See AFTER-~; AVAILABLE ~; COM-MON ~; EURO-CURRENCY ~; EX-PORT ~; FLEA ~; HYPOTHETICAL OR NOTIONAL ~; LABOUR ~; MUNICI-PAL ~; OVER-THE-COUNTER ~; PUB-LISHED ~.

MARKETABLE GAS. A mixture mainly of methane originating from raw gas, if necessary, through the processing of the raw gas for the removal or partial removal of some constituents, that meets specifications for use as a domestic, commercial or industrial fuel or as an industrial raw material.

MARKETABLE SECURITY. A security which may be sold on a stock market.

MARKET APPROACH. In relation to the valuation of a business, involves looking at the value of comparable properties which have sold on the open market and then making adjustments to take into account the special features of the business being evaluated.

MARKET DEMAND. The amount of oil or gas reasonably needed for current consumption, use, storage and working stocks.

MARKET GARDENING. The occupation of using land for growing, vegetables, fruit, and flowers for sale.

MARKETING. *n.* 1. Buying, selling, shipping for sale or offering for sale. 2. In relation to any farm product that is not a regulated product, includes selling and offering for sale and buying, pricing, assembling, packing, processing, transporting, storing and any other act necessary to prepare the product in a form or to make it available at a place and time for purchase for consumption or use and, in relation to a regulated product, includes only such of the above acts as are specified in the marketing plan relating to the regulated product. 3. Includes bartering, advertising, packing, processing, storing, shipping, and transporting, for the purposes of sale or in anticipation of sale. See BLACK ~.

MARKETING AGENCY. A marketing agency of Canada that is authorized to exercise powers of regulation in relation to the marketing of a regulated product in interprovincial or export trade and that has been granted authority to regulate the marketing of the regulated product locally within Ontario. *Commodity Boards and Marketing Agencies Act*, R.S.O. 1990, c. C.19, s. 1.

MARKETING CONTRACT. See COOPER-ATIVE ~.

MARKETING COOPERATIVE. See FARM PRODUCTS ~.

MARKETING PLAN. A plan relating to the promotion, regulation and control of the marketing of any regulated product in interprovincial or export trade that includes provision for all or any of the following: (a) the determination of those persons engaged in the growing or production of the regulated product for interprovincial or export trade and the exemption of any class of persons so engaged from the marketing plan or any aspect thereof, (b) the specification of those acts that constitute the marketing of the regulated product and of those persons engaged in its marketing, as so specified, in interprovincial or export trade, and for the exemption of any class of persons so engaged from the marketing plan or any aspect thereof, (c) the marketing of the regulated product on a basis that enables the agency that is implementing the plan to fix and determine the quantity, if any, in which the regulated product or any variety, class or grade thereof may be marketed in interprovincial or export trade by each person engaged in the marketing thereof and by all persons so engaged, and the price, time and place at which the regulated product or any variety, class or grade thereof may be so marketed, (d) the pooling of receipts from the marketing of the regulated product or any variety, class or grade thereof, in interprovincial or export trade and the operation of pool accounts including provision for the system of initial, interim and final payments to producers and deduction from the pool of the expenses of the operation thereof, (e) a system for the licensing of persons engaged in the growing or production of the regulated product for, or the marketing thereof in, interprovincial or export trade, including provision for fees, other than fees related to the right to grow the regulated product, payable to the appropriate agency by any such person in respect of any licence issued to such person and for the cancellation or suspension of any such licence where a term or condition thereof is not complied with, and (f) the imposition and collection by the appropriate agency of levies or charges from persons engaged in the growing or production of the regulated product or the marketing thereof and for such purposes classifying those persons into groups and specifying the levies or charges, if any, payable by the members of each group. 2. A plan for the marketing in interprovincial or export trade of grain produced and delivered to elevators or grain dealers licensed under the Canada Grain Act by producers who have agreed to participate in the plan and whose permit books are endorsed to that effect that include provision for the pooling or averaging of all or part of the receipts from the sale of the grain and a system of initial payments to those producers and deduction from the pool of the operational expenses thereof. *Canadian Wheat Board Act*, R.S.C. 1985, c. C-24, s. 48.

MARKETING PLANT. Any plant used for the marketing or distribution of any product obtained from the refining, processing or purifying of oil, gas or minerals.

MARKET-MAKER. *n*. A trading representative registered with the Commission des valeurs mobilières du Quebec to carry on his activity for his own account or as the employee of a clearing member on the trading floor of the Montreal Stock Exchange and appointed by the Exchange to maintain the market of the listed stocks. *An Act to Amend Taxation Act and Other Fiscal Legislation*, S.Q. 1985, c. 25, s. 143.

MARKET ORDER. A direction by a client to sell or buy a security immediately at the best possible price.

MARKET OVERT. An open, public, and legally constituted market.

MARKET PRICE. 1. The highest price for which an owner can sell property under conditions prevalent in that market. A. Bissett-Johnson & W.M. Holland, eds., *Matrimonial Property Law in Canada* (Toronto: Carswell, 1980) at V-11. 2. As to securities to which there is a published market, the price at any particular date determined in accordance with regulations. See MARKET VALUE.

MARKET RENTAL VALUE. A rental amount which the current rental market would bear assuming willing participants.

MARKET RESTRICTION. Any practice whereby a supplier of a product, as a condition of supplying the product to a customer, requires that customer to supply any product only in a defined market, or exacts a penalty of any kind from the customer if he supplies any product outside a defined market. *Combines Investigation Act*, R.S.C. 1985 (2d Supp.), c. 19, s. 77.

MARKET VALUE. 1. " ... '[R]ealizable money value'. . ." *R. v. Thomas Lawson & Sons Ltd.*, [1948] Ex. C.R. 44 at 82, [1948] 3 D.L.R. 334, 62 C.R.T.C. 277, Thorson P. 2. The amount in terms of cash that would probably be realized for property in an arm's length sale in an open market under conditions requisite to a fair sale, the buyer and seller each acting knowledgeably and willingly. *Loan and Trust Companies acts*. 3. The value actually or theoretically ascertained by the test of competition between a free and willing vendor and a free and willing purchaser. 4. Market price. A. Bissett-Johnson & W.M. Holland, eds., *Matrimonial Property Law in*

Canada (Toronto: Carswell, 1980) at V-11. 5. Where used with respect to, (i.) a commodity futures contract means the settlement price on the relevant date or last trading day prior to the relevant date, (ii.) a security means, A. where the security is listed and posted for trading on a stock exchange, (1.) the bid price, or (2.) if the security is sold short, the ask price, as shown on the exchange quotation sheets as of the close of business on the relevant date or last trading date prior to the relevant date, as the case may be, subject to an appropriate adjustment where an unusually large or unusually small quantity of securities is being valued. See FAIR ~.

MARKMAN ORDER. Named after 1996 U.S. case. Noel, J. in Realsearch Inc. v. Valon Kone Brunette 2003 FCT 669 has given first one in Canada. The order requires the parties to proceed with a separate determination of claim construction prior to trial for patent infringement.

MARKSMAN. *n.* An illiterate person who makes the mark X when signing a document.

MARK-UP. *n.* 1. The amount added to cost in determining the selling price to cover overhead and profit. 2. A margin of profit that the retailer adds to the value of a commodity sold.

MARQUEE. *n.* Any roof-like structure constructed as permanent part of the building over an entrance thereto and projecting more than twelve inches (12") from the exterior wall of any building.

MARQUESS. *n.* In England, the second order of nobility, below a duke.

MARQUIS. *n.* In England, the second order of nobility, below a duke.

MARRIAGE. *n.* 1. " . . . [T]he classic definition of marriage is provided by Lord Penzance in Hyde v. Hyde (1866), L.R. 1 P. & D. 130, as [at p. 133]: 'the voluntary union for life of one man and one woman, to the exclusion of all others.'" *Keddie v. Currie* (1991), 44 E.T.R. 61 at 76 (B.C. C.A.), Cumming J.A. (Legg J.A., concurring). 2. The common law definition of marriage is inconsistent with the *Charter* to the extent that it excludes same-sex couples. The remedy that best corrects the inconsistency is to declare invalid the existing definition of marriage to the extent that it refers to "one man and one woman", and to reformulate the definition of marriage as "the voluntary union for life of two persons to the exclusion of all others". This remedy achieves the equality required by s. 15(1) of the *Charter* but ensures that the legal status of marriage is not left in a state of uncertainty. *Halpern v. Toronto (City)* (2003), (sub nom. *Halpern v. Canada (Attorney General)*) 172 O.A.C. 276 (C.A.). 3. For civil purposes, the lawful union of two persons to the exclusion of all others. See BANNS OF ~; CELEBRATION OF ~; CHILD OF THE ~; COMMON LAW ~; CONTEMPLATION OF ~; CONVENTIONAL ~; FORM OF ~; IMPEDIMENT TO ~; ISSUE OF OUR ~; NULLITY OF ~; RESTRAINT OF ~; SOLEMNIZATION OF ~; TRADITIONAL ~.

MARRIAGE COMMISSIONER. A person who is not a clergyman who is appointed or authorized to solemnize marriage.

MARRIAGE CONTRACT. 1. An agreement two people enter into before their marriage, during their marriage or while cohabiting which may deal with almost any marital right or obligation, whether it arises during marriage, on separation, when a marriage is dissolved or annulled or upon death. A. Bissett-Johnson & W.M. Holland, eds., *Matrimonial Property Law in Canada* (Toronto: Carswell, 1980) at NB-38. 2. A man and a woman who are married to each other or intend to marry may enter into an agreement in which they agree on their respective rights and obligations under the marriage or on separation, on the annulment or dissolution of the marriage or on death, including, (a) ownership in or division of property; (b) support obligations; (c) the right to direct the education and moral training of their children, but not the right to custody of or access to their children; and (d) any other matter in the settlement of their affairs. *Family Law Act*, R.S.O. 1990, c. F-3, s. 52, as am.

MARRIAGE LICENCES. See ISSUER OF ~.

MARRIAGE SETTLEMENT. Any indenture, contract, agreement, covenant or settlement entered into in consideration of marriage whereby one of the parties agrees to pay a sum or sums of money to or for the benefit of self or the other party or any other person or the issue of the marriage, and whereby that party settles, grants, conveys, transfers, mortgages, or charges, or agrees to settle, grant, convey, transfer, mortgage or charge, real or personal property of any description upon or to or in favour of any person for the benefit of self or the other party or any other person or the issue of the marriage.

MARRIAGE STATUS. " . . . [A] description of a person's relation to another. It is simply a social position recognized by the law. It emanates from the choice of two persons, both of whom wish to have a legal relationship with the other." *Qually v. Qually*, [1987] 2 W.W.R. 553 at 560, 5 R.F.L. (3d) 365, 56 Sask. R. 165 (Q.B.), Dickson J. See MARITAL STATUS.

MARRIED PERSON. An adult person other than a single person.

MARRIED WOMAN. 1. A woman lawfully married to a living husband. 2. Includes a woman who, within the period of gestation prior to the birth of the child in respect of whose birth an application for registration is made under this Act, was lawfully married. *Vital Statistics acts.*

MARRIED WOMEN'S PROPERTY ACT. An act most provinces passed to give a wife the right to acquire and hold property in her own name.

MARSH. *n.* A tract of low, wet land. See FRESHWATER ~; SALTWATER ~.

MARSHAL. *v.* 1. Marshalling is an equitable remedy that may arise when you have two creditors of the same debtor, with one creditor, sometimes referred to as the senior creditor, having the right to resort to two funds of the debtor for payment of the debt, and the other creditor, the junior creditor, has the right to resort to one fund only. The court can "marshal" or arrange the funds so that both creditors are paid to the greatest possible extent. Equity will be invoked to protect the junior creditor, make the senior creditor realize on assets in such a way that the senior creditor will not wipe out assets that would only be available to the junior creditor. The junior creditor will be subrogated and will have a charge on the second or subsequent funds. *Bockhold v. Lawson Lundell Lawson & McIntosh* (1999), 1999 CarswellBC 989, 10 C.B.R. (4th) 90 (S.C.). 2. "The doctrine of marshalling, in its application to mortgages or charges upon two estates or funds, may be stated as follows: If the owner of two estates mortgages them both to one person, and then one of them to another, either with or without notice, the second mortgagee may insist that the debt of the first mortgagee shall be satisfied out of the estate not mortgaged to the second, so far as that will extend. This right is always subject to two important qualifications: first, that nothing will be done to interfere with the paramount right of the first mortgagee to pursue his remedy against either of the two estates; and, second, that the doctrine will not be applied to the prejudice of third parties: . . ." *Ernst Brothers v. Canada Permanent Mortgage Corp.* (1920), 47 O.L.R. 362 at 367 (H.C.), Orde J.

MARSHAL. *n.* An ex officio court officer; every sheriff of the Federal Court. See DEPUTY ~; FIRE ~; PROVOST~.

MARSHLAND. *n.* (i) Land forming part of the sea coast or the bank of a tidal river below the level of the highest tide; and (ii) land that is poorly drained or subject to periodic flooding.

MARSHLAND TRACT. An area of marshland which may be effectively dealt with as a unit in the construction and maintenance of works.

MART. *n.* A market, a place of public traffic or sale.

MARTIAL LAW. 1. Military law. 2. The replacement of ordinary law and the temporary government of a nation or area by a military council if this is done following a government proclamation or notice by military authorities.

MARY CARTER AGREEMENT. Named after *Booth v. Mary Carter Paint Co.*, 202 So. 2d 8 (U.S. Fla. Ct. App. 2 Dist., 1967). An agreement with the following characteristics: the plaintiff and one of multiple defendants agree; the contracting defendant guarantees the plaintiff a certain amount and the exposure of the defendant is "capped" at a certain amount; the contracting defendant remains a party to the action; the contracting defendant's liability is decreased in direct proportion to the increase in the non-contracting defendant's liability; the agreement is kept secret.

MASK. See QUICK DONNING ~.

MASON. See BRICK AND STONE ~; CEMENT~.

MASONRY. *n.* A method of construction. See PLAIN ~; REINFORCED ~.

MASS. See AXLE ~; CURB ~; MAXIMUM GROSS ~; TOTAL LOADED ~.

MASSAGE. *n.* The kneading, rubbing or massaging of the human body, whether with or without steam baths, vapour baths, fume baths, electric light baths or other appliances, and hydrotherapy or any similar method taught in schools of massage.

MASSAGE THERAPY. 1. The kneading, rubbing or massaging of the human body, whether with or without steam baths, vapour baths, fume baths, electric light baths or other appliances, and hydrotherapy or any similar method taught in schools of massage approved under the former *Physiotherapists Act*, but does not include any form of medical electricity. B.C. Reg. 2. The practice of massage therapy is the assessment of the soft tissue and joints of the body and the treatment and prevention of physical dysfunction and pain of the soft tissues and joints by manipulation to develop, maintain, rehabilitate or augment physical function, or relieve pain. *Massage Therapy Act, 1991*, S.O. 1991, c. 27, s. 3.

MASS DISTRIBUTION. See SAMPLES FOR ~.

MASTER. *n.* 1. A judicial officer of the Supreme Court who may decide certain matters before or after trial. 2. The person in immediate charge or control of a vehicle. 3. Includes every person having command or charge of a ship but does not include a pilot. 4. The Master of the Mint. *Royal Canadian Mint Act*, R.S.C. 1985, c. R-9, s. 2. 5. A person who has completed an apprenticeship and worked as a journeyman for a period of time. See LOCAL ~; LOCK~.

MASTER AGREEMENT. 1. A contract between a union and the leading employer in an industry. 2. A model agreement.

MASTER AND SERVANT. " . . . [T]he relationship imports the existence of power in the employer not only to direct what work the servant is to do, but also the manner in which it is to be done. . ." *Atlas Industries Ltd. v. Goertz* (1985), 4 C.P.C. (2d) 187 at 193, [1985] 4 W.W.R. 598, 38 Sask. R. 294 (Q.B.), Grotsky J. See now EMPLOYER and EMPLOYEE.

MASTER ELECTRICIAN. Any person who: (a) does business as an electrical contractor; (b) advertises as such; (c) undertakes to carry out or to cause to be carried out or carries out, as such and for his profit, electrical installation work or the renewing, altering or repairing of electrical installations, whether such work is done for payment or free of charge, whether the remuneration, if any, is by the hour, day or for lump sum, and whether such work is carried out under any oral, written, expressed or implied agreement; (d) prepares estimates, makes or submits tenders, either personally or by a person interposed, with a view to carrying out such work for profit; (e) prepares plans at his expense.

MASTER FRANCHISE. A franchise which is a right granted by a franchisor to a subfranchisor to grant or offer to grant franchises for the su-

bfranchisor's own account. *Arthur Wishart Act (Franchise Disclosure), 2000*, S.O. 2000, c. 3, s. 1.

MASTER KEY. See AUTOMOBILE ~.

MASTER OF THE MINT. The Master of the Mint and such other persons as constitute the Board of Directors of the Mint are hereby incorporated as a body corporate under the name of the Royal Canadian Mint. The objects of the Mint are to mint coins in anticipation of profit and to carry out other related activities. *Royal Canadian Mint Act*, R.S.C. 1985, c. R-9, s. 3.

MASTER OF THE ROLLS. In England, a judge of the Court of Appeal who retains the non-judicial role of custodian of the records.

MASTER PIPE-MECHANIC. Any person who: (a) does business as a contractor for the installation of piping; (b) undertakes to carry out, or to cause to be carried out or carries out as such and for his profit the work of installation of piping, whether such work is done for payment or free of charge, whether the remuneration, if any, is by the hour, by the day or for a lump sum, and whether such work is carried out under an oral or written, expressed or implied agreement; (c) prepares estimates, makes or submits tenders, either personally or by a person interposed, with a view to carrying out such work for his profit; (d) prepares plans at his expense, but solely for his own use and that of the board of examiners, with a view to obtaining and carrying out such work for his profit; (e) employs apprentices or journeymen.

MASTER PLAN. 1. Also known as official plan or municipal or community planning scheme, it provides a framework for the control of land use in a municipality. 2. A program and policy, or any part thereof, prepared from time to time in respect of a provincial park or proposed provincial park and includes the maps, texts and other material describing such program and policy. *Provincial Parks Act*, R.S.O. 1990, c. P.34, s. 1.

MASTER PLUMBER. A person who is skilled in the planning, superintending and installing of plumbing, is familiar with the laws, rules and regulations governing the same and who alone or by supervising journeymen plumbers performs plumbing work.

MASTER POLICY. " . . . The group [insurance] policy is known as the 'master policy' to distinguish it from the certificate issued to the employee. . . The master policy is in effect, merely an agreement by the [insurer] with the [employer] to insure the individual employees who are eligible, on the terms specified in the master policy . . . the master policy is incorporated in, and made part of, each individual certificate of insurance. . ." *Lawton, Re* (1945), 53 Man. R. 155 at 193, 195, [1945] 2 W.W.R. 529, 12 I.L.R. 210, [1945] 4 D.L.R. 8 (C.A.), Bergman J.A. (Richards J.A. concurring).

MASTER STREET ADDRESS GUIDE. A database that correlates civic numbers and street, road or highway names or other identifiers with emergency service zones.

MASTHEAD LIGHT. A white light placed over the fore and after centreline of the vessel showing an unbroken light over an arc of the horizon of 225 degrees and so fixed as to show the light from right ahead to 22.5 degrees abaft the beam on either side of the vessel. *Collision Regulations*, C.R.C., c. 1416, Rule 3.

MATCH. See WOOD ~ES.

MATE. *n.* In respect of a ship, means a person, other than the master, or a pilot or rating, who has charge of the navigation, manoeuvring, operation or security of the ship. *Marine Certification Regulations*, SOR/97-391, s. 1.

MATERIA. [L.] Subject matter.

MATERIAL. *n.* Every kind of movable property. See ADVERTISING ~; AGGREGATE ~; AIRCRAFT ~; COMBUSTIBLE ~; CORROSION-RESISTANT ~; ELECTION ~; FINE ~; FOREIGN ~; GRAPHIC ~; HAZARDOUS ~; INCOMBUSTIBLE ~; INFLAMMABLE ~; ~S; NEW ~; NUCLEAR ~; QUARRY ~; RADIOACTIVE ~; RECYCLABLE ~; REJECTED ~; SECOND-HAND ~; TEXTILE ~; TEXTUAL ~; VIDEO ~; WASTE ~.

MATERIAL. *adj.* 1. Important; essential. 2. ". . [T]hat which goes to the foundation of the decision or which goes to the crux of a central issue before the court. . ." *International Corona Resources Ltd. v. Lac Minerals Ltd.* (1988), 54 D.L.R. (4th) 647 at 658, 66 O.R. (2d) 610 (H.C.), Osborne J. 3. In relation to an insurance policy a matter that is concealed or misrepresented is material when, if it had been truly disclosed, the circumstances would have influenced a reasonable insurer to decline the risk or require a higher premium.

MATERIAL ALTERATION. "An instrument is altered in a material particular if the rights and obligations of the parties under it, if effect were given to it in its altered condition, would be different from that which the law would imply if no alteration had taken place. . ." *McCoy v. Hop*, [1923] 3 D.L.R. 873 at 876, [1923] 2 W.W.R. 801, 17 Sask. L.R. 278 (C.A.), the court per Lamont J.A.

MATERIAL BOND. See LABOUR AND ~.

MATERIAL CHANGE. 1. In relation to spousal support payments means one that had it been known earlier would likely have resulted in different terms. 2. Where used in relation to the affairs of an issuer means a change in the business, operations or capital of the issuer that would reasonably be expected to have a significant effect on the market price or value of any of the securities of the issuer and includes a decision to implement such a change made by the board of directors of the issuer or by senior management of the issuer who believe that confirmation of the decision by the board of directors is probable. *Securities acts.*

MATERIAL DISCOMFORT. In relation to environmental protection, requires that the complainant subjectively suffered a material discomfort and that it was objectively material to the complainant.

MATERIAL FACT. 1. One that is necessary to formulate a complete cause of action. 2. In tort, the damage sustained by the plaintiff and the damage resulting from the injury and the conduct of the defendant which caused the injury. 3. In relation to insurance, a fact which, if it had been truthfully and fully disclosed, would upon a fair consideration of the evidence, have caused a reasonable insurer to refuse to insure the risk or to have required a higher premium to take the risk. 4. Where used in relation to securities issued or proposed to be issued, a fact that significantly affects, or would reasonably be expected to have a significant effect on the market price or value of those securities.

MATERIAL INJURY. In respect of the dumping or subsidizing of any goods, material injury to the production in Canada of like goods, and includes, in respect only of the subsidizing of an agricultural product, an increase in the financial burden on a federal or provincial government agricultural support program in Canada. *Special Imports Measures Act*, R.S.C. 1985, c. S-15, s. 2.

MATERIAL INTEREST. Where used to refer to the material interest in a person means (i) the relationship of spouse, parent, child, grandparent, grandchild, brother or sister of the person or of the spouse of the person or the relationship of the spouse of the parent, child, grandparent, grandchild, brother or sister of the person, or (ii) the relationship of a creditor of the person for a debt that is in excess of $2,000.00, or (iii) the relationship of a guarantor of the debt or obligation of the person in an amount that is in excess of $2,000.00, or (iv) where the person is a body corporate, the ownership or beneficial ownership of not less than 20% of any class of voting or preferred shares of the corporation, or (v) where the person is a partnership or association, membership in the partnership or association. *Credit Unions and Caisses Populaires Act*, S.M. 1980, c. 20, s. 7.

MATERIALITY. *n.* 1. " . . . The objective test for materiality is whether, if the matters concealed or misrepresented had been truly disclosed, they would, on a fair consideration of the evidence, have influenced a reasonable insurer to decline the risk or stipulate for a higher premium: Mutual Life Insurance Co. v. Ont. Metal Products Co. (1924) . . . [1925] 1 D.L.R. 583 at 588 (P.C.) . . ." *V.K Mason Construction Management Inc. v. Hanover Insurance Co.* (1988), 35 C.C.L.I. 56 at 65, 63 Alta. L.R. (2d) 277, 91 A.R. 186 (Q.B.), Virtue J. 2. The essential ingredients or elements of an offence which must be proved, not the evidence which proves them in any particular case. P.K. McWilliams, *Canadian Criminal Evidence*, 3d ed. (Aurora: Canada Law Book, 1988) at 3-3.

MATERIAL MAN. A person who supplies or rents material that is intended to become part of the improvement or to be used in the making of it or to facilitate the making of it, which material has been delivered to the land on which the improvement is placed or situate. *Builders' Lien Amendment Act*, S.B.C. 1984, c. 17, s. 1.

MATERIAL RISK. " . . . [S]ignificant risks that pose a real threat to the patients life, health or comfort. In considering whether a risk is material or immaterial, one must balance the severity of the potential result and the likelihood of its occurring. Even if there is only a small chance of serious injury or death, the risk may be considered material. On the other hand, if there is a significant chance of slight injury this too may be held to be material. . ." *White v. Turner* (1981), 15 C.C.L.T. 81 at 99, 31 O.R. (2d) 773,

5 L. Med. Q. 119, 120 D.L.R. (3d) 269 (H.C.), Linden J.

MATERIALS. *n.* 1. Includes every kind of movable property. *Builders' Lien acts*. 2. Every kind of movable property that becomes or is intended to become, part of the improvement, or that is used to facilitate directly the making of the improvement. *Builders' Lien* acts. Includes books, periodicals, pamphlets, newspapers, photographic reproductions, paintings, films, filmscripts, sheet music and sound recordings. *Libraries Act*, R.S.N.B. 1973, c. L-5, s. 1. See BUILDING ~; CONVENTION ~; LEGISLATIVE ~; MATERIAL; QUARRY ~; REFRACTORY ~.

MATERIAL SAFETY DATA SHEET. A document providing certain required information concerning the nature of, effects of and remedies for exposure to hazardous products.

MATERIALS HANDLING EQUIPMENT. Any machine, equipment or mechanical device used to transport, lift, move or position or to assist in transporting, lifting, moving or positioning materials, goods, articles, persons or things, and includes any crane, derrick, loading tower, powered industrial truck, hand-truck, conveyor, hoist, earth-moving equipment, rope, chain, sling, dock, ramp, storage rack, container, pallet and skid.

MATERIALS MANAGEMENT SYSTEM. See REJECTED ~.

MATERIAL WAVE. A line or surface propagated by shock or vibration of gaseous, liquid or solid matter including infrasounds (0 to 16 Hertz), sounds (16 Hz to 16KHz) including shock waves, ultrasounds (16KHz to MHz), and any mechanical oscillation. *Environment Quality Act*, R.S.Q. 1977, c. Q-2, s. 1.

MATERIAL WITNESS. A person whose evidence is important in the prosecution or defence of a case.

MATERIEL. *n.* All public property, other than real property, immovables and money, provided for the Canadian Forces or for any other purpose under this Act, and includes any vessel, vehicle, aircraft, animal, missile, arms, ammunition, clothing, stores, provisions or equipment so provided. *National Defence Act*, R.S.C. 1985, c. N-5, s. 2.

MATERNAL. *adj.* Belonging to or coming from the mother.

MATERNITY. *n.* The state of motherhood.

MATERNITY HOME. A house in which one or more pregnant women receive nursing or other care during the confinement period.

MATERNITY HOSPITAL. A private hospital for the reception and care of patients in or in respect of child-birth.

MATERNITY LEAVE. A leave of absence allowed to a worker who is pregnant or who has given birth.

MATRICIDE. *n.* The slaying of a mother; a person who slays a mother.

MATRICULATE. *v.* To enter university.

MATRIMONIAL. *adj.* Relating to the act of marrying or to the state of being married.

MATRIMONIAL ASSETS. The matrimonial home or homes and all other real and personal property acquired by either or both spouses before or during their marriage, with the exception of (a) gifts, inheritances, trusts or settlements received by one spouse from a person other than the other spouse except to the extent to which they are used for the benefit of both spouses or their children; (b) an award or settlement of damages in court in favour of one spouse; (c) money paid or payable to one spouse under an insurance policy; (d) reasonable personal effects of one spouse; (e) business assets; (f) property exempted under a marriage contract or separation agreement; (g) real and personal property acquired after separation unless the spouses resume cohabitation. *Matrimonial Property Act*, R.S.N.S. 1989, c. 275, s. 4.

MATRIMONIAL DISPUTE. There is no statutory definition of the term "matrimonial dispute" and the question is whether "matrimonial" was intended to encompass only matters arising out of legal marriages or can be interpreted to include marriage-like common-law relationships. In the case at bar, the petitioner co-habited with the proposed defendant for over twenty years, and she used his surname, but they were not legally married. I conclude that the petitioner's contingent fee agreement is not in respect of a matrimonial dispute. *Legal Profession Act (British Columbia), Re*, 2000 CarswellBC 971, 2000 BCSC 690, 74 B.C.L.R. (3d) 302, (sub nom. *Legal Profession Act Section 67(4) (Re)*) 187 D.L.R. (4th) 167 (S.C.).

MATRIMONIAL HOME. 1. Property that is owned or leased by one or both spouses that is or has been occupied by the spouses as their family home. 2. The dwelling and real property occupied by a person and that person's spouse as their family residence and in which either or both of them have a property interest other than a leasehold interest. *Matrimonial Property Act*, R.S.N.S. 1989, c.275, s. 3(1).

MATRIMONIAL OFFENCE. (a) Adultery; (b) cruelty; (c) desertion (i) for two years or upward without reasonable cause, or (ii) constituted by the fact that the wife or husband, as the case may be, has failed to comply with a judgment for restitution of conjugal rights; or (d) sodomy or bestiality, or an attempt to commit either offence. *Domestic Relations Act*, R.S.N.W.T. 1974, c. D-9, s. 6.

MATRIMONIUM. *n.* [L.] Property inherited through the mother's side.

MATRIMONY. *n.* Marriage.

MATRON. *n.* 1. A woman who is married. 2. A woman superintendent.

MATTER. *n.* 1. Includes every proceeding in the court not in a cause. 2. Includes every proceeding in the court not in an action. *Judicature Act*, R.S.P.E.I. 1974, c. J-3, s. 1. 3. "The content or subject matter" of the law. *Reference re Anti-Inflation Act, 1975 (Canada)*, [1976] 2 S.C.R. 373 at 450, 9 N.R. 541, 68 D.L.R. (3d) 452, Beetz J. 4. Of a law, its leading feature or true character, its pith and substance, its dominant or most important characteristic. 5. My colleague, Bastarache J., quotes from the *Oxford English Dictionary* (2nd ed. 1989) vol. IX, at p. 480, the entry that "matter" is a "[p]hysical or corporeal substance in general . . ., contradistinguished from immaterial or incorporeal substance (spirit, soul, mind), and qualities, actions, or conditions", but this, of course, depends on context. "Matter" is a most chameleon-like word. The expression "grey *matter*" refers in everyday use to "intelligence"—which is about as incorporeal as "spirit" or "mind". Indeed, the same Oxford editors define "grey matter" as "intelligence, brains" (*New Shorter Oxford English Dictionary* (1993), vol. 1, p. 1142). The *primary* definition of matter, according to the *Oxford English Dictionary*, is "[t]he substance, or the substances collectively, out of which a physical object is made or of which it consists; constituent material" (at p. 479). The definition of "*matière*" in *Le Grand Robert*, quoted by my colleague, is to the same effect. The question, then, is what, in the Commissioner's view, is the "constituent material" of the oncomouse as a physical entity? If the oncomouse is not composed of matter, what, one might ask, are such things as oncomouse "minds" composed of? The Court's mandate is to approach this issue as a matter (that slippery word in yet another context!) of law, not murine metaphysics. In the absence of any evidence or expert assistance, the Commissioner now asks the Court to take judicial notice of the oncomouse, if I may use Arthur Koestler's phrase, as a "ghost in a machine" but this pushes the scope of judicial notice too far. With respect, this sort of literary metaphor (or its dictionary equivalent) is an inadequate basis on which to narrow the scope of the *Patent Act* [R.S.C. 1985, c. P-4], and thus to narrow the patentability of scientific invention at the dawn of the third Millennium. *Harvard College v. Canada (Commissioner of Patents)*, [2002] 4 S.C.R. 45, Per Binnie J. (dissenting)(McLachlin C.J.C., Major and Arbour JJ. concurring). See ADVERTISING ~; CIVIL ~; CRIMINAL ~; DISCIPLINARY ~; FAMILY ~; INERT ~; MAILABLE ~; ORGANIC ~; PLANT OR OTHER ~; TESTAMENTARY ~S AND CAUSES; TOTAL SUSPENDED ~.

MATTERS AND CAUSES TESTAMENTARY. Includes all matters and causes relating to the grant and revocation of probate of wills or letters of administration. See TESTAMENTARY MATTERS AND CAUSES.

MATURE. *adj*. That the produce has reached such stage of development as ensures completion of the ripening process.

MATURITY. *n*. 1. The date on which a note, loan or obligation becomes due. 2. The date fixed under a retirement savings plan for the commencement of any retirement income the payment of which is provided for by the plan. See DATE OF ~.

MATURITY DATE. The date, excluding days of grace, on which the debt will be fully paid if every payment is made according to the original terms of the security agreement.

MAUSOLEUM. *n*. A building or structure, other than a columbarium, used as a place for the interment of the human remains in sealed crypts or compartments.

MAVERICK. *n*. An unmarked reindeer. *Northwest Territories Reindeer Regulations*, C.R.C., c. 1238, s. 2.

MAXIM. *n*. A general principle; an axiom.

MAXIMS OF EQUITY. These include: equity will not allow a wrong to exist without a remedy; equity looks to intent rather than to form; equity considers what ought to be done as having been done; an equitable remedy is discretionary; delay defeats equity; one who comes to equity must come with clean hands; one who seeks equity must do equity; equity never lacks a trustee. These are not rigid rules but principles to be applied in particular situations.

MAXIMUM CAPACITY. The number of persons or the weight that an elevating device can carry safely as determined under the regulations.

MAXIMUM FLOW RATE. The maximum volume of commodity per unit time that can be measured by a measuring machine as set out in the notice of approval. *Weights and Measures Regulations*, C.R.C., c. 1605, s. 57.

MAXIMUM GROSS MASS. In reference to a commercial motor vehicle, the curb mass together with the load, including the mass of the driver and of other persons carried, and, in reference to a bus or school bus, the curb mass together with the mass of the driver and of the number of passengers for which the vehicle is licensed, and for the purposes of a regulation unless otherwise provided in the regulation, the mass of a person shall be taken as 70 kilograms. *Highway Traffic Act*, R.S. Nfld. 1990, c. H-3, s. 2.

MAXIMUM GROSS WEIGHT. In reference to a commercial motor vehicle, the curb weight together with the load, including the weight of the driver and of any other persons carried, and, in reference to a bus, the curb weight together with the weight of the driver and of the number of passengers for which the vehicle is licensed, and for the purposes of any regulations, unless otherwise provided therein, the weight of a person shall be taken as one hundred and fifty pounds. *Highway Traffic Act*, R.S.Nfld. 1970, c. 152, s. 2.

MAXIMUM HOURS. The number of hours that a worker may be required to work without overtime compensation.

MAXIMUM LOAD RATING. The load rating at the maximum permissible inflation pressure for that tire. Canada regulations.

MAXIMUM PERMISSIBLE INFLATION PRESSURE. The maximum cold inflation pressure to which a tire may be inflated. Canada regulations.

MAXIMUM RETIREMENT AGE. 1. The age of 65 years or an age prescribed by the Lieutenant Governor in Council as the maximum retirement age applicable to any employee or group or class of employees. 2. The age of 65 years or the age at which the officer retires, whichever is greater.

MAXIMUM SAFE LOAD. With respect to any materials handling equipment or any floor, dock or other structure used in handling materials, means (a) the maximum load that such equipment or structure was designed and constructed to handle or support safely, or (b) the maximum load that such equipment or structure is guaranteed in writing by the manufacturer to handle or support safely, whichever is the lesser. *Canada Materials Handling Regulations* C.R.C., c. 1004, s. 2.

MAY. *v.* 1. ". . . [C]ommonly used to denote a discretion . . ." *R. c. Potvin*, [1989] 1 S.C.R. 525 at 547, 93 N.R. 42, 68 C.R. (3d) 193, 47 C.C.C. (3d) 289, 21 Q.A.C. 258, La Forest J. and Dickson C.J. 2. ". . . [P]ermissive and empowering and confers an 'area of discretion'." *Charles v. Insurance Corp. of British Columbia* (1989), 34 B.C.L.R. (2d) 331 at 337 (C.A.), the court per Lambert J.A. 3. ". . . [S]hould not be construed as imperative unless the intention that it should be so construed is clear from the context. . ." *Heare v. Insurance Corp. of British Columbia* (1989), 34 B.C.L.R. (2d) 324 at 327 (C.A.), the court per Lambert J.A. See SHALL, MUST, MAY.

MAYOR. *n.* The chief elected officer of a municipality.

MAYORALTY. *n.* The office of mayor.

MBCA. The neutral citation for the Manitoba Court of Appeal.

M.B.M. *abbr.* Thousand feet board measure.

MBQB. The neutral citation for the Manitoba Court of Queen's Bench.

M.C. *abbr.* Master's Chambers.

MCF. *abbr.* 1,000 cubic feet of natural gas, measured at 14.73 psia pressure and 60°F. *Natural Gas Prices Regulations*, C.R.C., c. 1259, s. 2.

MCGILL L.J. *abbr.* McGill Law Journal (Revue de droit de McGill).

MCMURRAY FORMATION. The stratigraphic formation lying above the upper Devonian carbonate sediments and below the Clearwater formation. *Mines and Minerals Act*, R.S.A. 1980, c. M-15, s. 121.

MCNAGHTEN'S CASE. R. v. McNaghten or M'Naghten or Macnaughton (1843) 4 St.Tr. (N.S.) 847, a British case which established the law relating to insanity with special reference to criminal responsibility.

M.C.R. *abbr.* Montreal Condensed Reports, 1854-1884.

M.D.A. *abbr.* Methylenedioxyamphetamine, a more common euphorigenic amphetamine. F.A. Jaffe, *A Guide to Pathological Evidence*, 3d ed. (Toronto: Carswell, 1991) at 91.

MEAL. *n.* Food sufficient to constitute a person's breakfast, lunch or dinner.

MEAL PERIOD. The time during which a worker is permitted to eat.

MEAN. *v.* 1. Where a definition uses the word "means" and not "includes" " . . . the definition is to be construed as being exhaustive." *Yellow Cab Ltd. v. Alberta (Industrial Relations Board)*, [1980] 2 S.C.R. 761 at 768, 14 Alta. L.R. (2d) 39, 24 A.R. 275, 80 C.L.L.C. 14,066, 33 N.R. 585, 114 D.L.R. (3d) 427, the court per Ritchie J. 2. " . . . Normally construed as comprehending that which is specifically described or defined . . ." *R. v. Hauser* (1979), 98 D.L.R. (3d) 193 at 213, [1979] 1 S.C.R. 984, 26 N.R. 541, [1979] 5 W.W.R. 1, 46 C.C.C. (2d) 481,16 A.R. 91, 8 C.R. (3d) 89 (Eng.), 8 C.R. (3d) 281 (Fr.), Dickson J. (dissenting) (Pratte J. concurring).

MEAN. *n.* A point midway between two extremes.

MEANING. See SECONDARY ~.

MEANS. *v.* When used in a definition, the definition is construed as being comprehensive and including that which is specifically described or listed. To be contrasted with "includes".

MEANS. *n.* 1. " . . . [T]he historical interpretation of the term as including all pecuniary resources, capital assets, income from employment or earning capacity, and other sources from which the person receives gains or benefits." *Strang v. Strang* (1992), 3 Alta. L.R. (3d) 1 at 7, 137 N.R. 203, 39 R.F.L. (3d) 233, 125 A.R. 331,14 W.A.C. 331, 92 D.L.R. (4th) 762, [1992] 2 S.C.R. 112, the court per Cory J. 2. Includes (a) the administration of a drug or other noxious thing; (b) the use of an instrument; and (c) manipulation of any kind. *Criminal Code*, R.S.C.

1985, c. C-46, s. 287(3). 3. In my view, the phrase "accidental means" conveys the idea that the consequences of the actions and events that produced death were unexpected. Reference to a set of consequences is therefore implicit in the word "means". "Means" refers to one or more actions or events, seen under the aspect of their causal relation to the events they bring about. *Martin v. American International Assurance Life Co.*, 2003 SCC 16. See ACCIDENTAL ~; DISCONNECTING ~.

MEANS OF EGRESS. 1. A continuous path of travel provided by a doorway, hallway, corridor, exterior passageway, balcony, lobby, stair, ramp or other egress facility or combination thereof, for the escape of persons from any point in a building floor area, room or contained open space to a public thoroughfare or other open space and includes exits and access to exits. Ontario regulations. 2. A way or ladder leading to an exit from a building, structure, excavation or other part of a project.

MEANS OF EXIT. A continuous path of travel provided by a doorway, hallway, corridor, exterior passageway, balcony, lobby, stair, ramp or other exit facility, or a combination of them, for the escape of persons from any point in a building, floor area, room or contained open space to a public thoroughfare or other unobstructed open space and includes exits and access to exits.

MEANS OF TRANSPORT. 1. Any road or railway vehicle, aircraft, water-borne craft, pipeline or any other contrivance that is or may be used to carry persons or goods whether or not the goods are in packaging or containers. *Transportation of Dangerous Goods Act*, R.S.C. 1985, c. T-19, s. 2. 2. Anything used for conveyance from one place to another.

MEASURE. *v.* Includes weigh. *Weights and Measures Act*, R.S.C. 1985, c. W-6, s. 2.

MEASURE. *n.* 1. Includes weight. *Weights and Measures Act*, R.S.C. 1985, c. W-6, s. 2. 2. With respect to a linear or volume measuring device, means a static measure having no moving parts incorporated therein, but includes a roller tape-measure of any material. *Weights and Measures Act*, R.S.C. 1970, c. W-7, s. 2. See ALTERNATIVE ~S; EMERGENCY ~S; EXTENSION ~; PROTECTIVE ~S; SAFETY ~; STATIC ~.

MEASUREMENT. See GENERAL ~ POINT.

MEASURE OF DAMAGES. A test to determine the amount of damages which should be given.

MEASURES. See ALTERNATIVE ~.

MEASURING CUP. See STANDARD ~.

MEASURING MACHINE. Any machine that measures length, area, volume or capacity, temperature or time and has a moving or movable part that has or can have an effect on the accuracy of the machine. *Weights and Measures Act*, R.S.C. 1985, c. W-6, s. 2.

MEAT. *n.* The flesh of any animal or any product of it intended for human consumption in primary or processed form.

MEAT ANIMAL. A bull, cow, ox, heifer, steer or calf.

MEAT BINDER. A substance added to a meat product to hold its ingredients together.

MEAT BY-PRODUCT. An edible part of a food animal other than meat.

MEAT MEAL. The rendered and dried carcass or part of the carcass of an animal.

MEAT PLANT. An abbatoir, slaughterhouse or place or premises where animals are slaughtered and includes a place or premises where meat or a meat product is processed, prepared, handled or stored.

MEAT PROCESSING PLANT. A plant where meat is processed or used in the production of a manufactured meat product.

MEAT PRODUCT. 1. (a) A carcass, (b) the blood of an animal or a product or by-product of a carcass, or (c) a product containing anything described in paragraph (b). 2. Meat, meat by-product, prepared meat or prepared meat by-product. *Food and Drug Regulations*, C.R.C., c. 870, c. B.01.001. See EXTNDED ~; MANUFACTURED ~; PREPARED ~; SIMULATED ~.

MEAT PRODUCT EXTENDER. A food that is a source of protein and that is represented as being for the purpose of extending meat products. *Food and Drug Regulations*, C.R.C., c. 870, c. B.01.001.

MECHANIC. *n.* A person who has a minimum of four years work experience directly related to the work assigned to him or her and who has full knowledge of this Act and the regulations and of the codes applicable to the elevating device upon which he or she is assigned to work. See ALIGNMENT AND BRAKES ~; DENTAL ~; FARM EQUIPMENT ~; FUEL AND ELECTRIC SYSTEMS ~; MOTORCYCLE ~; MOTOR VEHICLE INSPECTION ~; MOTOR VEHICLE ~; REFRIGERATION AND AIR CONDITIONING ~; TICKET ISSUING MACHINE ~.

MECHANICAL. See ELECTRO-MAGNETIC, ACOUSTIC, ~ OR OTHER DEVICE.

MECHANICAL BREAKDOWN. A functional or operational defect which may represent a manifestation of or effect of an underlying error in design.

MECHANICALLY CONTROLLED SEAL. Any device in a trap whereby the water seal of the trap is replenished by the action of moving parts.

MECHANICAL SEALING. The closing and sealing of the loading door of a compartment in a controlled-atmosphere storage plant by the operator so as to be sufficiently air-tight for the purpose of controlled-atmosphere storage.

MECHANICAL TREATMENT. The application of a mechanical appliance to the foot or in the shoe to treat a disease deformity or ailment.

MECHANICS' LIEN. 1. A lien in favour of a mechanic or other person who conferred skill, money and materials on a chattel. 2. A lien against land given to a supplier of the labour and material which benefitted that land. 3. A right in the form of a lien on any money paid by the owner of land to a contractor given to a worker or supplier of materials.

MECHANISM. *n*. Of death, whatever disturbance in vital function was initiated by the cause of death. F.A. Jaffe, *A Guide to Pathological Evidence*, 3d ed. (Toronto: Carswell, 1991) at 12.

MECHANIZED FISHING EQUIPMENT. A gurdy, danish seine winch, dragging winch, power flock or other proved power equipment for fishing which is suitable to the tonnage of a particular ship and complies with the regulations. *Fishing Ships Bounties Act*, R.S. Nfld. 1990, c. F-19, s. 2.

MECONIUM. *n*. The feces of a newborn. F.A. Jaffe, *A Guide to Pathological Evidence*, 3d ed. (Toronto: Carswell, 1991) at 223.

MEDAL. See LONG SERVICE ~.

MEDIA. *n*. Any means of communication, and, without limiting the foregoing, includes radio, television, billboards, newspapers, magazines, handbills, pamphlets and flyers.

MEDIAL. *adj*. Towards the middle.

MEDIA LAW. The law concerning the press and broadcast media. Deals with telecommunications law, regulation of the media, intellectual property issues, defamation, journalistic sources and the like.

MEDIAN. *n*. A physical barrier or area that separates traffic travelling in one direction from traffic travelling in the opposite direction on a highway.

MEDIAN AMOUNT. An amount that is half way between one amount and another amount.

MEDIAN STRIP. The portion of a highway so constructed as to separate traffic travelling in one direction from traffic travelling in the opposite direction by a physical barrier or an unpaved strip of ground.

MEDIATION. *n*. The reconciliation of a dispute by a third party.

MEDIATOR. *n*. 1. One who resolves disputes by mediation. 2. "The status of a mediator allows its holder to decide on the basis of equity, without being bound by substantive or procedural rules of law, except of course for rules of public order such as those of natural justice which provide for impartiality, opportunity for the parties to be heard, reasons to be given for the award, and so on. Mediation is not, as such, a legal concept distinct from that of arbitration. Rather, the mediator is an arbitrator who is exempted from compliance with the rules of law as provided in art. 948 [of the Code of Civil Procedure, R.S.Q. 1977, c. C-25] . . . The mediator is in fact only the 'bon père de famille' of the Civil Code transposed to arbitration matters. Mediation is a departure from the law of arbitration. Like any exception it must, if it is not expressly provided for, at least result from a clear and umambiguous intent . . ." *Zittrer c. Sport Maska Inc.* (1988), 38 B.L.R. 221 at 310, 83 N.R. 322, [1988] 1 S.C.R. 564, 13 Q.A.C. 241, L'Heureux-Dubé J. (Lamer, Wilson and Le Dain JJ. concurring).

MEDICAL. *adj*. ". . . [H]as two meanings. The first is the science and art concerned with the cure, alleviation and prevention of disease, and with the restoration and preservation of health. Psychiatric services would come within that meaning. So would surgical services. The second meaning is the science and art of restoring and preserving health by means of remedial substances and the regulation of diet and habits. This second meaning distinguishes medicine from surgery and from obstetrics . . ." *Baart v. Kumar* (1985), 20 C.C.L.R. 232 at 263, 66 B.C.L.R. 61, 4 C.P.C. (2d) 211, 21 D.L.R. (4th) 705 (C.A.), Lambert J.A. (dissenting).

MEDICAL AID. Medical, surgical and dental aid, hospital and skilled nursing services and a prothesis or apparatus and the repairing and replacement of them, transportation and other matters and things that the commission may authorize or provide.

MEDICAL CARE. 1. Care provided by a general practitioner, and excludes major surgery. 2. The provision of any blood transfusion or transfusions or injection or injections.

MEDICAL CARE SERVICES. See INSURED ~.

MEDICAL CERTIFICATE. A written statement containing the signature of a physician.

MEDICAL CONTROL. Medical orders issued by a physician either prospectively through the development of protocols or directly by verbal or written orders.

MEDICAL DEPARTMENT. A division of the medical staff of a hospital for the provision of a specified type of medical diagnosis or treatment. *Public Hospitals Act*, R.S.O. 1990, c. P.40, s. 1.

MEDICAL DEVICE. A device within the meaning of the Act, but does not include any device that is intended for use in relation to animals. *Medical Devices Regulations* SOR/98-282, s. 1.

MEDICAL DEVICE FAMILY. A group of medical devices that are made by the same manufacturer, that differ only in shape, colour, flavour or size, that have the same design and manufacturing process and that have the same intended use. *Medical Devices Regulations* SOR/98-282, s. 1.

MEDICAL DEVICE GROUP. A medical device comprising a collection of medical devices, such as a procedure pack or tray, that is sold under a single name. *Medical Devices Regulations* SOR/98-282, s. 1.

MEDICAL DEVICE GROUP FAMILY. A collection of medical device groups that are made by the same manufacturer, that have the same generic name specifying their intended use, and that differ only in the number and combination of products that comprise each group. *Medical Devices Regulations* SOR/98-282, s. 1.

MEDICAL EXAMINATION. Includes a mental examination, a physical examination and medical assessment of records respecting a person.

MEDICAL GROUNDS. In relation to refusal to provide a breath sample, a danger to the health of the accused by the performance of the test or as a result of his required attendance for medical treatment during the time period when the police officer wished to have the test performed.

MEDICAL HISTORY. The history of illness, treatment, and surgeries which an individual has had during his life.

MEDICAL INFORMATION. Any information obtained with the consent of a subject from licensed physicians, medical practitioners, chiropractors, qualified psychologists, psychiatrists or hospitals, clinics or other medically related facilities in respect of the physical or mental health and attitude of the subject.

MEDICAL JURISPRUDENCE. The part of the law related to the practice of medicine.

MEDICAL LABORATORY TECHNOLOGY. The practice of medical laboratory technology is the performance of laboratory investigations on the human body or on specimens taken from the human body and the evaluation of the technical sufficiency of the investigations and their results. *Medical Laboratory Technology Act, 1991*, S.O. 1991, c. 28, s. 3.

MEDICAL LOCK. A chamber in which persons may be subjected to changes in air pressure for medical purposes.

MEDICAL MONITORING. Examining and testing workers in danger of exposure to a toxic substance so that an affected worker may be removed from exposure when necessary.

MEDICAL OFFICER IN CHARGE. The physician appointed to be in charge of the care and treatment being provided to the patients of an institution, psychiatric centre, psychiatric ward, mental health clinic or other facility.

MEDICAL OXYGEN. A volume of 1 litre of gas at a temperature of 20°C and at a pressure of 760 millimetres of mercury. *Medical Devices Regulations*, C.R.C., c. 871, s. 1.

MEDICAL PRACTITIONER. 1. A person lawfully entitled to practise medicine in the place in which the practice is carried on by that person. 2. A person lawfully entitled to practise medicine or dentistry in the jurisdiction where he practises and includes a medical or dental officer of the Canadian Armed Forces. *Evidence Act*, S.N.B. 1980, c. 18, s. 1. 3. A person who is authorized by law to practise medicine in the place where such person is so practising and includes a person skilled in the art of healing who is authorized by law to practise the art of healing in the place where such person is so practising. *Workers' Compensation Act*, R.S.N.W.T. 1974, c. W-4, s. 2. See DULY QUALIFIED ~; PHYSICIAN; QUALIFIED ~.

MEDICAL RADIATION TECHNOLOGY. The practice of medical radiation technology is the use of ionizing radiation and other forms of energy prescribed under subsection 12 (2) to produce diagnostic images and tests, the evaluation of the technical sufficiency of the images and tests, and the therapeutic application of ionizing radiation. *Medical Radiation Technology Act, 1991*, S.O. 1991, c. 29, s. 3.

MEDICAL RADIOLOGICAL TECHNICIAN. A person who operates an x-ray machine or uses radioactive isotopes for the examination or treatment of living persons. *Radiological Technicians Act*, R.S.A. 1980, c. R-3, s. 1.

MEDICAL RADIOLOGICAL TECHNOLOGY. The act, process, science or art of carrying out on humans for medical purposes, the technical aspects of radiological-diagnoses or radiological-therapeutics.

MEDICAL RESEARCH COUNCIL OF CANADA. A federal body which offers scholarships and grants in the health sciences.

MEDICAL SERVICES. Includes surgical, dental, optical, optometrical and nursing services, and the furnishing of health appliances, optical and pharmaceutical supplies.

MEDICAL SERVICE UNIT. A building containing offices and treatment rooms for physicians and other health personnel and includes any building or part of a building used as a residence for medical practitioners and other health personnel.

MEDICAL STAFF. The medical practitioners to whom the board has granted the privilege of diagnosing, prescribing for and treating patients in the hospital. *Public Hospitals Act*, R.R.O. 1980, Reg. 865, s. 1.

MEDICAL STAFF COMMITTEE. A committee established or approved by a board of

management of a hospital for (a) evaluating, controlling and reporting on clinical practice in a hospital to continually maintain and improve the safety and quality of patient care in the hospital; or (b) performing a function for the appraisal and control of the quality of patient care in the hospital.

MEDICAL-SURGICAL SERVICES AGREEMENT. An agreement made between one or more employers and a trade union or trade unions representing his or their employees to establish a plan for providing such employees with medical and surgical care and treatment to be operated by the employer or employers and representatives of such employees.

MEDICAL TREATMENT. 1. Includes (a) surgical and dental treatment, (b) any procedure undertaken for the purpose of diagnosis, (c) any procedure undertaken for the purpose of preventing any disease or ailment, and (d) any procedure that is ancillary to any treatment as it applies to that treatment. 2. Treatment of any sick or injured person through the performance of cardiopulmonary resuscitation, cardiac monitoring, defibrillation, airway or gastric intubation, pneumothorax relief and the administration of drugs and intravenous fluids. 3. The application to, or prescription for, the foot of medicines, pads, adhesives, felt, plasters or a medicinal agency. See RELATED ~.

MEDICAMENT. *n.* A substance or a mixture of substances that may be used to diagnose, cure, reduce or prevent an ailment, a disorder, an abnormal physical or psychological condition or symptoms hereof in human beings or in animals or to restore, correct or alter their organic functions.

MEDICARE. *n.* A medical care programme which makes hospital and doctors' services universally available.

MEDICATED FEED. 1. A mixed feed containing (a) a medicating ingredient at a therapeutic or prophylactic level, (b) a hormone the function of which is to promote growth in the animal body, (c) a medicating ingredient for use in effecting oestrus synchronization in livestock, or (d) a medicating ingredient the purpose of which is to promote growth or feed efficiency in the presence of a specific disease or specific stress condition. 2. An animal feed that contains a veterinary drug.

MEDICATED WINE. Any product containing an alcoholic beverage and medicine, provided that the quantity of alcoholic beverage therein is no more than is strictly necessary for purposes of solution or preservation and that the quantity of medicine is sufficient to render the product unsuitable for use as an alcoholic beverage.

MEDICATION. *n*. Any substance or mixture of substances which may be used: (i.) for the diagnosis, treatment, remission or prevention of any disease, ailment, any abnormal physical or mental condition, or their symptoms in man or animal; or (ii.) to restore, rectify, or change organic functions in man or animal. See SAFE ~.

MEDICINAL FOOD. A mixture of substances intended for use without processing for the feeding of animals and containing a medicinal premix or a nutriment and a medication, as the case may be.

MEDICINE. *n*. 1. Includes all drugs for internal or external use of humans, animals, or fowl, and any substance or mixture of substances intended to be used for the treatment, mitigation or prevention of disease in humans, animals, or fowl. 2. Includes surgery and obstetrics, but does not include homeopathy, osteopathy, veterinary surgery or veterinary medicine. 3. The practice of medicine is the assessment of the physical or mental condition of an individual and the diagnosis, treatment and prevention of any disease, disorder or dysfunction. *Medicine Act, 1991*, S.O. 1991, c. 30, s. 3. See DRUGS AND ~S, FORENSIC ~; NUCLEAR ~ TECHNOLOGIST; PRACTICE OF ~; PRACTISE ~; PROPRIETARY ~; VETERINARY ~.

MEDICO-LEGAL. *adj*. Concerning the law relating to medical issues.

MEDIUM. See GRAPHIC ~; LASING ~.

MEDIUM-DUTY PASSENGER VEHICLE. A heavy-duty vehicle that has a GVWR of less than 4,536 kg (10,000 pounds) and that is designed primarily for the transportation of persons but does not include any vehicle that (*a*) is a truck that is incomplete because it does not have a primary load carrying device or container attached; (*b*) has a seating capacity of more than 12 persons; (*c*) is designed to seat more than 9 persons behind the driver; or (*d*) is equipped with an open cargo area (for example, a pick-up truck box or bed) of 183 cm (72.0 inches) in interior length or more or with a covered box not readily accessible from the passenger compartment. *On-Road Vehicle and Engine Emission Regulations*, SOR/2003-2, s. 1.

MEDIUM HARD. Rock comparable to concrete with a compressive strength greater than 2,500 psi.

MEDIUM SAND. A soil consisting of particles passing a No. 10 sieve but retained on a No. 40 sieve.

MEETING. *n*. A gathering of people to decide, by proper voting procedure, whether something should be done. See CLASS ~; CREDITORS' ~; GENERAL ~; PUBLIC ~; RACE ~; RACING ~; SERIES ~.

MEETING OF DIRECTORS. Includes a meeting of an executive committee of the directors.

MEETING OF MEMBERS. Any meeting of members, a class of members or a subdivision of members that does not constitute a separate class of members of a corporation for the purpose of: (i) electing or removing directors; (ii) considering financial statements or any auditor's report; (iii) appointing an auditor or reappointing an incumbent auditor; (iv) making any fundamental change under Division XIV of Part I; (v) determining liquidation and dissolution under Division XVI I of Part I; and for any purpose where the articles or bylaws of the corporation require the approval of the members. *Non-profit Corporations Act*, S.S. 1979, c. N-4.1, s. 2.

MEGA. *pref*. 10[6]. Prefix for multiples and submultiples of basic, supplementary and derived units of measurement. *Weights and Measures Act*, S.C. 1970-71-72, c. 36, schedule I.

MEGATRIAL. *n*. A criminal trial involving multiple accused and multiple charges lasting for a lengthy period.

MEIORIN TEST. The Meiorin test was developed in the employment context, it applies to all claims for discrimination under the B.C. Human Rights Code. Meiorin announced a unified approach to adjudicating discrimination claims under human rights legislation. The distinction between direct and indirect discrimination has been erased. *British Columbia (Superintendent of Motor Vehicles) v. British Columbia (Council of Human Rights)* (1999), 1999 CarswellBC 2730, [2000] 1 W.W.R. 565, 47 M.V.R. (3d) 167, 249 N.R. 45, 70 B.C.L.R. (3d) 215, 181 D.L.R. (4th) 385, 36 C.H.R.R. D/129, [1999] 3 S.C.R. 868, 131 B.C.A.C. 280, 214 W.A.C. 280, McLachlin for the court. See BONA FIDE OCCUPATIONAL REQUIREMENT.

MELIOREM CONDITIONEM SUAM FACERE POTEST MINOR, DETERIOREM

NEQUAQUAM. [L.] A minor may make her or his condition better, by no means worse.

MELIOR EST CONDITIO DEFENDENTIS. [L.] The stronger position is the defendant's.

MELIOR EST CONDITIO POSSIDENTIS ET REI QUAM ACTORIS. [L.] The possessor's position is better; and the defendant's is better than the plaintiff's.

MELIOR EST CONDITIO POSSIDENTIS, UBI NEUTER JUS HABET. [L.] The possessor's position is better, where neither has clear title.

MELIOR EST JUSTITIA VERE PRAE-VENIENS, QUAM SEVERE PUNIENS. [L.] Justice which truly prevents is better than justice which punishes severely.

MELIUS EST OMNIA MALA PATI QUAM MALO CONSENTIRE. [L.] It is better to endure all evil than to agree to evil.

MELIUS EST PETERE FONTES QUAM SECTARI RIVULOS. [L.] It is better to go to the source than to follow tributaries.

MEMBER. *n.* 1. A subscriber of the memorandum of a company, and includes every other person who agrees to become a member of a company and whose name is entered in its register of members or a branch register of members. 2. In relation to a pension plan, means a person who has become a member of the pension plan and has neither ceased membership in the plan nor retired from the plan. *Pension Benefits Standards Act, 1985*, R.S.C. 1985, c. 32 (2nd Supp.), s. 2. 3. A member of the House of Commons. 4. A member of the Legislative Assembly. 5. "...[A]s used in the War Veterans Allowance Act [R.S.C. 1970, c. W-5] has a broad meaning. It is broad enough to include soldiers, sailors and airmen and the officers of all three branches of the forces. But in my view it is not necessarily confined to those categories. . ." *Canada (Attorney General) v. MaCLaren* (1987), 26 Admin. L.R. 146 at 150, 79 N.R. 1, 41 D.L.R. (4th) 41 (Fed. C.A.), the court per Thurlow C.J.F.C. See BOARD ~; CIVILIAN ~ OF OVERSEAS AIR CREW; CLEARING ~; CLUB ~; CREW ~; DECEASED~; EXECUTIVE~; FACULTY~; FORMER ~; FUTURES ~; IN-ACTIVE ~; INCAPACITATED ~; INDE-PENDENT ~; INTEREST OF A ~; MEET-ING OF ~S; MUNICIPAL ~; NAME A ~; NON-COMMISSIONED ~; NON-VOT-ING ~; PROBATIONARY ~; PROFES-SIONAL ~; PROPERTY OF A ~; PUBLIC ~; REGULAR ~; RESIDENT ~; SPONSOR ~; UNFIT ~; VOTING ~.

MEMBER IN GOOD STANDING. A member who is not in default for fees, dues or costs payable and who is not under suspension.

MEMBER INSTITUTION. A corporation any of whose deposits are insured by the Corporation pursuant to this Act. *Canada Deposit Insurance Corporation Act*, R.S.C. 1985, c. C-3, s. 2.

MEMBER LOAN. A loan required by the co-operative from its members as a condition of membership or to continue membership in the cooperative. *Canada Cooperatives Act*, S. C. 1998, c. 1, s. 2.

MEMBER OF A BAND. A person whose name appears on a Band List or who is entitled to have his name appear on a Band List. *Indian Act*, R.S.C. 1985, c. I-5, s. 2.

MEMBER OF A CLUB. A person: (i) who, whether as a charter member or admitted in accordance with the bylaws or rules of a club, has become a member thereof; (ii) who maintains his membership by payment of his regular periodic dues in the manner provided by the bylaws or rules; and (iii) whose name and address are entered on the list of members supplied to the commission at the time of the application for a club licence under this Act or are subsequently supplied if admitted thereafter. *The Liquor Licensing Act*, R.S.S. 1978, c. L-21, s. 2.

MEMBER OF A CONGREGATION. An adult, living with the members of the congregation, who conforms to the practices of the religious organization of which the congregation is a constituent part whether or not he has been formally accepted into the organization, and a child, other than an adult, of such adult, if the child lives with members of the congregation. *Income Tax Acts*.

MEMBER OF A CREW. Any person, including a master, who is employed on board or forms part of the staff or crew of a vehicle. *Immigration Act*, R.S.C. 1985, c. I-2, s. 2.

MEMBER OF A FAMILY. 1. A worker's spouse, parent, grandparent, step-parent, child, grandchild step-child, brother, sister, half-brother, half-sister and a person who stands in loco parentis to the worker or to whom the worker stands in loco parentis (whether or not there is any degree of consanguinity between such person and the worker) and includes an illegitimate grandchild of the worker and the parents and of a worker who is an illegitimate child. 2. A wife or husband, father, mother, grandfather, grandmother, stepfather, stepmother, son, daughter, grandson, granddaughter, stepson, stepdaughter, brother, sister, half brother, half sister, adopted child, foster parent. See MEMBER OF HIS OR HER FAMILY.

MEMBER OF A FORCE. A member of (a) the Canadian Forces; or (b) the naval, army or air forces of a state other than Canada that are lawfully present in Canada. *Criminal Code*, R.S.C. 1985, c. C-46, s. 62(2). See MEMBER OF THE FORCES.

MEMBER OF AN ORDER. Any person who holds a permit issued by an order and who is entered on the roll of the latter. *Professional Code*, R.S.Q., chapter C-26, s. 1.

MEMBER OF HIS OR HER FAMILY. Any person connected with a member by blood relationship, marriage or adoption, and (i) persons are connected by blood relationship if one is the child or other descendant of the other or one is the brother or sister of the other, (ii) persons are connected by marriage if one is married to the other or to a person who is connected by blood relationship to the other, and (iii) persons are connected by adoption if one has been adopted, either legally or in fact, as the child of other or as the gild of a person who is so connected by blood relationship (otherwise than as a brother or sister) to the other. See MEMBER OF A FAMILY.

MEMBER OF THE FAMILY. See MEMBER OF A FAMILY, MEMBER OF HIS OR HER FAMILY.

MEMBER OF THE FORCE. A member of the Force, as defined in the Royal Canadian Mounted Police Act, holding a rank in the Force, and any other member of the Force as defined therein, of a class designated in accordance with the regulations for the purposes of this Part. *Royal Canadian Mounted Police Act*, R.S.C. 1985, c. R-11, s. 3.

MEMBER OF THE FORCES. (*a*) A person who has served in the Canadian Forces at any time since the commencement of World War I, and (*b*) a Canadian merchant mariner of World War I, World War II or the Korean War, as described in section 21.1. *Pension Act*, R.S.C. 1985, c. P-6, s. 3. See MEMBER OF A FORCE.

MEMBER OF THE LEGISLATIVE ASSEMBLY. See DUTY OF A ∼.

MEMBER OF THE OVERSEAS HEADQUARTERS STAFF. A person who is not a supervisor or helper and who was a member of the Headquarters Staff of, and was employed and paid by, Canadian Legion War Services Inc., The National Council of the Young Men's Christian Association of Canada, Knights of Columbus Canadian Army Huts or Salvation Army Canadian War Services and who proceeded from Canada under the authority of the Chief of Naval Personnel, the Adjutant-General or Air Member for Personnel. *Civilian War-related Benefits Act*, R.S.C. 1985, c. C-31, s. 16.

MEMBER OF THE PUBLIC. Any section or segment of the public without regard to the numbers thereof.

MEMBER OF THE REGULAR FORCE. An officer or man of the regular force. *Canadian Forces Superannuation Act*, R.S.C. 1985, c. C-17, s. 2.

MEMBER OF THE VOLUNTARY AID DETACHMENT. A member of the Nursing Auxiliary Canadian Red Cross Corps or the Nursing Division of the St. John Ambulance Brigade of Canada who, with the approval of the Adjutant-General, served with the Royal Canadian Army Medical Corps during the War. *Civilian War-related Benefits Act*, R.S.C. 1985, c. C-31, s. 43.

MEMBER OF THE WOMEN'S ROYAL NAVAL SERVICES. A person who (a) enrolled in the Women's Royal Naval Service, (b) enrolled in Queen Alexandra's Royal Naval Nursing Service or the reserve therefor, or (c) enrolled as a medical or dental practitioner employed with the Medical Branch or Dental Branch of the Royal Navy with naval status for general service. *Public Service Employment Act*, R.S.C. 1985, c. P-33, Sched.

MEMBERSHIP. *n*. 1. A state of being one of a group of individuals composing a group. 2. Includes a share of a credit union. 3. Includes a share of a corporation.

MEMBERSHIP CORPORATION. A corporation incorporated or continued to carry on activities that are primarily for the benefit of its members.

MEMBERSHIP INTEREST. The rights, privileges, restrictions and conditions conferred or imposed on a member of each class of members of a corporation in accordance with the provisions of its articles or bylaws. *Non-profit Corporations Act*, S.S. 1995, c. N-4.2, s. 2.

MEMBERSHIP SHARE. A cooperative with membership shares must have one class of membership shares, designated as such in the articles. Membership shares may be issued only to members, each of whom must hold the minimum number of membership shares prescribed by the by-laws. Subject to Parts 20 and 21, the membership shares of a cooperative confer on their holders equal rights, including equal rights to (a) receive dividends declared on membership shares; and (b) subject to the articles, receive the remaining property of the cooperative on dissolution. *Canada Cooperatives Act, 1998*, S. C. 1998, c. 1, s. 117 and 118.

MEMBERS' SERVICES. See STANDING COMMITTEE ON MANAGEMENT AND ~.

MEMENTO. See OFFICIAL ~.

MEMORANDUM. *n. 1*. The memorandum of association of a company, as originally framed or as altered in pursuance of this Act. *Companies Act*, R.S.N.S. 1989, c. 81, s. 2. 2. The *Companies* Act, of association for incorporation of a society incorporated under this Act. *Societies Act*, R.S.N.S. 1989, c. 435, s. 2. 3. The endorsement on the certificate of title and on the duplicate copy thereof of the particulars of any instrument presented for registration. *Land Titles acts*. 4. A document summarizing the state of the law on a particular issue. See OFFERING ~.

MEMORANDUM OF AGREEMENT. A written, ratified and signed document which frequently precedes a formal collective agreement. Usually when the collective agreement is executed, the memorandum is merged. D.J.M. Brown and D.M. Beatty, *Canadian Labour Arbitration*, 3d ed. (Aurora: Canada Law Book 1988-) at 4-2.

MEMORANDUM OF ASSOCIATION. An incorporating document in some jurisdictions. It contains the name, capital structure and proposed business of the company. S.M. Beck *et al., Cases and Materials on Partnerships and Canadian Business Corporations* (Toronto: The Carswell Company Limited, 1983) at 159.

MEMORIAL. *n. 1*. A memorial, marker, monument, headstone, footstone, tombstone, plaque, tablet or plate marking a grave and includes an inscription of lettering or ornamentation, or both, on or on the front of a space within a building or structure for the permanent placement of human remains. *Cemetery and Funeral Services Act*, R.S.N.S. 1989, c. 62, s. 2. 2. Whatever contains the details of a deed. 3. A record of a judg-

ment signed by the Registrar or clerk, as the case may be, containing the names of the parties, the sum recovered, or the amount ordered to be paid as alimony or otherwise, as the case may be, and the date of signing the judgment or of the decree, as the case may be, and verified by affidavit.

MENHADEN. *n*. A fish of the species Brevoortia tyrannus.

MENIAL. *adj*. Domestic.

MENINGES. *n*. Three membranes which enclose the brain and spinal cord. F.A. Jaffe, *A Guide to Pathological Evidence*, 3d ed. (Toronto: Carswell, 1991) at 223.

MENSA ET THORO. [L.] From bed and board.

MENS REA. [L.] 1. A mental state, the subjective element of a crime. The intent to commit the offence in question. Does not encompass the objective truth of a proposition which the accused believes. knowledge, for legal purposes, is true belief. Knowledge therefore has two components—truth and belief—and of these, only belief is mental or subjective. Truth is objective, or at least consists in the correspondence of a proposition or mental state to objective reality. Accordingly, truth, which is a state of affairs in the external world that does not vary with the intention of the accused, cannot be a part of *mens rea*. *United States v. Dynar*, [1997] 2 S.C.R. 462. 2. " . . . [A] basis for the imposition of liability. Men's rea focuses on the mental state of the accused and requires proof of a positive state of mind such as intent, recklessness or wilful blindness." *R. v. Wholesale Travel Group Inc.* (1991), 8 C.R. (4th) 145 at 176, 67 C.C.C. (3d) 193, 4 O.R. (3d) 799n, 84 D.L.R. (4th) 161, 130 N.R. 1, 38 C.P.R. (3d) 451, 49 O.A.C. 161, [1991] 3 S.C.R. 154, 7 C.R.R. (2d) 36, Cory J. (L'Heureux-Dubé J. concurring). 3. ". . . [A complex concept having different meanings in different contexts, but is most frequently used to describe the minimum necessary mental element required for criminal liability where a particular mental element is not expressly made a constituent element of the offence. The minimum mental element required for criminal liability for most crimes is knowledge of the circumstances which make up the actus reus of the crime and foresight or intention with respect to any consequence required to constitute the actus reus of the crime." *R. v. Metro News Ltd.* (1986), 23 C.R.R. 77 at 95, 16 O.A.C. 319, 56 O.R. (2d) 321, 53 C.R. (3d) 289, 29 C.C.C. (3d) 35, 32

D.L.R. (4th) 321 (C.A.), the court per Martin J.A.

MENS TESTATORIS IN TESTAMENTIS SPECTANDA EST. [L.] In construing wills the testator's intention must be regarded.

MENTAL DEFECTIVE. A person in whom there is a condition of arrested or incomplete development of mind, whether arising from inherent causes or induced by disease or injury, and who requires care, supervision and control for his or her own protection or welfare or for the protection of others. *Interpretation Act*, R.S.O. 1990, c. I.11, s. 29(1).

MENTAL DEFICIENCY. The condition of mind of a mental defective. *Interpretation Act*, R.S.O. 1990, c. I.11, s. 29(1).

MENTAL DISABILITY. (i) A condition of mental retardation or impairment, (ii) a learning disability, or a dysfunction in one or more of the processes involved in understanding or using symbols or spoken language, or (iii) a mental disorder. See PHYSICAL DISABILITY OR ~.

MENTAL DISORDER. 1. *A disease of the mind. Criminal Code*, R.S.C. 1985, c. C-46, s. 2. 2. A substantial disorder of thought, mood, perception, orientation or memory, any of which grossly impairs judgment, behaviour, capacity to recognize reality or ability to meet the ordinary demands of life but mental retardation or a learning disability does not of itself constitute a mental disorder. 3. No person is criminally responsible for an act committed or an omission made while suffering from a mental disorder that rendered the person incapable of appreciating the nature and quality of the act or omission or of knowing that it was wrong. *Criminal Code*, R.S.C. 1985, c. C-46, s. 16. See VERDICT OF NOT CRIMINALLY RESPONSIBLE ON ACCOUNT OF ~.

MENTAL HANDICAP. See PHYSICAL OR ~.

MENTAL HEALTH CENTRE. A place where services are provided to in-patients and outpatients. See CHILDREN'S ~.

MENTAL HEALTH CLINIC. A place where services are provided to out-patients and not to in-patients and that is designated by the minister as a mental health clinic.

MENTAL ILLNESS. A disorder of mind, other than psychoneurosis and psychopathic disorder, that results in such a change in the behaviour and judgment of a person as to require medical treatment, or in respect of which disorder of mind, treatment, care, and supervision, of the person are necessary for the protection or welfare of the person and others.

MENTAL INCOMPETENCY. The condition of mind of a mentally incompetent person.

MENTAL INCOMPETENT. A person, (i) in whom there is such a condition of arrested or incomplete development of mind, whether arising from inherent causes or induced by disease or injury, or (ii) who is suffering from such a disorder of the mind, that that person requires care, supervision and control for self protection and the protection of that person's property.

MENTALLY CAPABLE. Able to understand the information that is relevant to making a decision concerning the subject-matter and able to appreciate the reasonably foreseeable consequences of a decision or lack of decision. *Long-Term Care Act, 1994*, S.O. 1994, c. 26, s. 2.

MENTALLY COMPETENT. Having the ability to understand the subject matter in respect of which consent is requested and the ability to appreciate the consequences of giving or withholding consent.

MENTALLY DEFECTIVE PERSON. A person in whom there is a condition of arrested or incomplete development of mind, whether arising from inherent causes or induced by disease or injury, and who requires care, supervision and control for his or her own protection or welfare or for the protection of others. *Interpretation Act*, R.S.O. 1990, c. I.11, s. 29(1).

MENTALLY DISABLED PERSON. A person (i) in whom there is such a condition of arrested or incomplete development of mind, whether arising from inherent causes or induced by disease or injury, or (ii) who is suffering from a disorder of the mind, requiring care, supervision and control for the protection of his or her property, whether or not he or she has been committed to the hospital under the Mental Health Act. *Mentally Disabled Persons' Estates Act*, R.S. Nfld. 1990, c. M-10, s. 2.

MENTALLY DISORDERED PERSON. A person who is suffering from mental illness, mental retardation or any other disorder or disability of the mind.

MENTALLY ILL PERSON. A person, other than a mental defective, who is suffering from such a disorder of the mind that that person requires care, supervision and control for self protection or welfare, of for the protection of others.

MENTALLY INCAPABLE. 1. Unable to understand the information that is relevant to making a decision concerning the subject-matter or unable to appreciate the reasonably foreseeable consequences of a decision or lack of decision. *Ont. Statutes*. 2. Not mentally capable. *Long-Term Care Act, 1994*, S.O. 1994, c. 26, s. 2.

MENTALLY INCOMPETENT INDIAN. An Indian who, pursuant to the laws of the province in which he resides, has been found to be mentally defective or incompetent for the purposes of any laws of that province providing for the administration of estates of mentally de defective or incompetent persons. *Indian Act*, R.S.C. 1985, c. I-5, s. 2.

MENTALLY INCOMPETENT PERSON. 1. A person (a) in whom there is such a condition of arrested or incomplete development of mind, whether arising from inherent causes or induced by disease or injury, or (b) who is suffering from such a disorder of the mind, that that person requires care, supervision and control for self protection or welfare or for the protection of others or for the protection of that person's property. 2. A person, (i) in whom there is such a condition of arrested or incomplete development of mind, whether arising from inherent causes or induced by disease or injury, or (ii) who is suffering from such a disorder of the mind, that that person requires care, supervision and control for self protection and the protection of that person's property.

MENTAL RETARDATION. A condition of arrested or incomplete development of mind whether arising from inherent causes or induced by disease or injury.

MENTIO UNIUS EXCLUSIO ALTERIUS. [L.] To mention one thing excludes another.

MENTIRI EST CONTRA MENTEM IRE. [L.] To lie is to go against conscience.

MERA NOCTIS. [L.] Midnight.

MERCABLE. *adj*. Able to be bought or sold.

MERCANTILE. *adj*. Includes manufacturing; relating to merchants or their trade; commercial.

MERCANTILE AGENT. 1. A person having, in the customary course of business as an agent, authority either to sell goods or to consign goods for the purpose of sale, or to buy goods or to raise money on the security of goods. 2. Includes a broker or agent to negotiate and make contracts for the sale of products of which he is not entrusted with the possession or control; a factor or agent to sell or dispose of products of which he is entrusted with the possession or control; and a jobber, or person whose normal business is to buy or sell products in wholesale quantities, when handling or disposing of products on commission; and an agent of such broker, factor or jobber. *The Sales on Consignment Act*, R.S.S. 1978, c. S-4, s. 2.

MERCANTILE BUILDING. A building used for the display and sale of merchandise.

MERCANTILE LAW. The law concerning matters like bills of exchange, marine insurance and contracts of affreightment.

MERCANTILE OCCUPANCY. Occupancy or use for displaying or selling retail goods, wares or merchandise.

MERCATIVE. *adj*. Pertaining to trade.

MERCATURE. *n*. The act of buying and selling.

MERCHANDISE. *n*. " . . . [C]ommodities or goods for sale." *R. v. Robert Simpson Co.* (1964), 43 C.R. 366 at 371, [1964] 2 O.R. 227, [1964] 3 C.C.C. 318 (H.C.), Landreville J. See FUNERAL ~ OR SERVICES; GOODS, WARES AND ~.

MERCHANT. *n*. 1. 1. " . . . [O]ne who buys and sells commodities as a business and for profit; who has a place of sale and stock of goods and is generally a trader in a large way. . ." *R. v. Wells* (1911), 2 O.W.N. 1232 at 1235, 24 O.L.R. 77, 18 C.C.C. 377 (H.C.), Middleton J. 2. Includes any person doing business or extending credit in the course of his business. 3. Does not include a person who has a recognized retail store if more than fifty per cent of the goods and services sold by that person in the Province are sold by direct sale. *Direct Sellers' acts*. See COMMISIONER ~; ITINERANT ~; WHOLESALE ~.

MERCHANTABLE. *adj*. " . . . [W]hatever else merchantable may mean, it does mean that the article sold, if only meant for one particular use in ordinary course, is fit for that use; . . ." *Grant v. Australian Knitting Mills Ltd.* (1935), [1936] A.C. 85 at 99, [1936] 1 W.W.R. 145, 105 L.J.P.C. 6, [1932] All E.R. 209 (Australia P.C.), the board per Lord Wright.

MERCHANTABLE QUALITY. Of a quality and in a condition that a reasonable person would, after a full examination, accept it under the circumstances in performance of the person's offer to buy it, whether the person is buying it for the person's own use or for resale.

MERCHANTABLE TIMBER. 1. For an old temporary tenure or a timber licence, trees that (a) on January 1, 1975 were older than 75 years; and (b) are on an area of Crown land in quantities determined by the regional manager to be sufficient to be commercially valuable at the time when a timber cruise submitted under section 57 is made. *Forest Act*, R.S.B.C. 1979, c. 140, s. 1. 2. " . . . [N]ot including the roots or stumps, which would be left in the ordinary course of logging . . ." *MacCrimmon v. Smith* (1907), 12 B.C.R. 377 at 382 (C.A.), Hunter C.J.A.

MERCHANT SEAMAN. Any person who served during World War II as Master, Officer or member of the crew of (a) a ship registered in Canada, (b) a United Kingdom ship registered in Canada or elsewhere, or (c) a registered ship of one of the countries allied with His Majesty during World War II if, in the case of a person who served on other than a ship registered in Canada, that person was born or domiciled in Canada or Newfoundland, or was an ordinary resident in Canada or Newfoundland at anytime during the period between September 9, 1929 and the date on which he commenced to so serve. *Memorial Cross Order (World War II)*, C.R.C., c. 1623, s. 2.

MERCHANT SHIPPING ACTS. The Merchant Shipping Act, 1894 of the Parliament of the United Kingdom, 57-58 Victoria, chapter 60, and all Acts adding to or amending that Act. *Canada Shipping Act*, R.S.C. 1985, c. S-9, s. 2.

MERCIAMENT. *n*. Fine; penalty.

MERCURY. *n*. 1. Elemental mercury and all chemical forms thereof. *Chlor-Alkali Mercury Liquid Effluent Regulations*, C.R.C., c. 811, s. 2. 2. A substance designated under the Ontario Occupational Health and Safety Act.

MERCURY CELL. Any device utilizing mercury as a cathode. *Chlor-Alkali Mercury National Emission Standards Regulations*, C.R.C., c. 406, s. 2.

MERCY. *n*. Compassion or forbearance. See PARDON; RECOMMENDATION TO ~.

MEREDITH MEM. LECT. *abbr*. Meredith Memorial Lectures (Conférences commémoratives Meredith).

MERE ERROR OF LAW. " . . . [A]n error committed by an administrative tribunal in good faith in interpreting or applying a provision of its enabling Act, of another Act, or of an agreement or other document which it has to interpret and apply within the limits of its jurisdiction. A mere error of law is to be distinguished from one resulting from a patently unreasonable interpretation of a provision which an administrative tribunal is required to apply within the limits of its jurisdiction. . . A mere error of law should also be distinguished from a jurisdictional error." *Syndicat des employés de production du Québec et de l'Acadie v. Canada (Labour Relations Board)*, [1984] 2 S.C.R. 412 at 420, 14 Admin. L.R. 72, 84 C.L.L.C. 14,069, 55 N.R. 321, 14 D.L.R. (4th) 457, Beetz J.

MERGE. *v*. Of original cause of action, to include in the judgment of a domestic court of record if the plaintiff succeeds. J.G. McLeod, *The Conflict of Laws* (Calgary: Carswell, 1983) at 606.

MERGED. *adj*. 1. Of the rights and duties created by a contract for the sale of land, subsumed by a deed. 2. Of original remedies for a debt subsumed in a higher security, when that security is taken or obtained for the debt.

MERGER. *n*. 1. " . . . [I]n real estate law merger occurs when two estates coalesce through a vesting in the same person at the same time in the same right. . ." *Fraser-Reid v. Droumtsekas* (1979), 9 R.P.R. 121 at 139, [1980] 1 S.C.R. 720, 103 D.L.R. (3d) 385, 29 N.R. 424, Dickson J. (Martland, Estey and McIntyre JJ. concurring). 2. The acquisition or establishment, direct or indirect, by one or more persons, whether by purchase or lease of shares or assets, by amalgamation or by combination or otherwise, of control over or significant interest in the whole or a part of a business of a competitor, supplier, customer or other person. *Competition Act*, R.S.C., c. C-34, s. 91. 3. " . . . [T]hat branch of res judicata which is known as merger: [is described as follows] all claims which the plaintiff might have had against the defendants . . . have merged in the judgment . . . and the maxim nemo debet bis vexari pro una et eadem causa applies." *Thornton v. Tittley* (1985), 4 C.P.C. (2d) 13 at 19, 51 O.R. (2d) 315 (H.C.), Scott L.J.S.C. See DELAWARE ~; NON-~.

MERGER INTO JUDGMENT. A theory that once a creditor begins an action against a debtor which is carried to judgment, the original obligation is transformed into a judgment debt.

MERIT. *n*. "[Includes] . . . not only inherent, internal elements of credit, meritorious characteristics, achievements of the candidate and so on, but also external characteristics which would include the suitability or usefulness of the candidate in the office or position in question. That is to say, merit might on the one hand embrace only inherent or intrinsic values as discerned in the nature, personality, character, training and experience of the candidate, or it might additionally include the extra-natural or man-made attributes such as usefulness, suitability or incapacities created in the community and not intrinsic in the candidate. . ." *Evans v. Canada (Public Service Commission)* (1983), 1 Admin. L.R. 16 at 25, [1983] 1 S.C.R. 582, 83 C.L.L.C. 14,038, 47 N.R. 255, 146 D.L.R. (3d) 1, Estey J. (Ritchie, McIntyre, Chouinard and Lamer JJ. concurring).

MERIT INCREASE. An increase in pay awarded to employees for performance or service.

MERITO BENEFICIUM LEGIS AMITTIT, QUI LEGEM IPSAM SUBVERTERE INTENDIT. [L.] One who intends to subvert the law itself justly loses benefit of the law.

MERITORIOUS CONSIDERATION. A factor based on a moral obligation.

MERITORIOUS CONTRIBUTION. (i) Performance at an unusually high level over an extended period of time; (ii) the successful completion, in a manner beyond what could normally be expected by management, of a major project, special assignment or research study; (iii) the performance of duties under abnormal circumstances in a manner which constitutes a contribution of unusual merit to the Public Service. W. Grover & F. Iacobucci, *Materials on Canadian Income Tax*, 4th ed. (Toronto: Richard De Boo Ltd., 1980) at 216-217.

MERITORIOUS DEFENCE. 1. " . . . [A] defence of a character which would entitle a defendant to have the matter inquired into by the Court . . ." *Straton v. Saskatoon (City)* (1908), 1 Sask. L.R. 426 at 427, 9 W.L.R. 136 (S.C.), Wetmore C.J. 2. " . . . [A] substantial and not a formal or technical defence to the charge." *R. v. Cronin* (1875), 36 U.C.Q.B. 342 at 345 (C.A.), the court per Richards C.J.

MERIT PAY. Compensation related directly to work performance and given at management's discretion.

MERIT PRINCIPLE. When there is an opportunity for promotion, the most meritorious person should be promoted.

MERITS. *n*. 1. Used to describe a good cause of action or defence when it is based, not on technical grounds, but on the real issues in question. *R. v. Cronin* (1875), 36 U.C.Q.B. 342 at 345 (C.A.), the court per Richards C.J. 2. Of a cause of action or defence, the substance, elements or grounds. See AFFIDAVIT OF ~.

MERO MOTU. [L.] Of one's own motion. See EX ~.

MESCALINE. *n*. A hallucinogenic drug obtained from peyote cactus. F.A. Jaffe, *A Guide to Pathological Evidence*, 3d ed. (Toronto: Carswell, 1991) at 223.

MESH. *n*. Netting.

MESH SIZE. 1. The distance between opposite angles of a single mesh pulled tightly and measured inside and between the knots. Canada regulations. 2. The size of a single mesh of net determined by measuring, without straining the twine, the inside diagonal distance between the knots after immersion in water for not less than 1/2 hour. *Yukon Territory Fishery Regulations*, C.R.C., c. 854, s. 2.

MESNE. *adj*. Intermediate. E.L.G. Tyler & N.E. Palmer, eds., Crossley *Vaines' Personal Property*, 5th ed. (London: Butterworths, 1973) at 4.

MESNE LORD. A lord who holds something on behalf of a higher lord, and on whose behalf an inferior lord or tenant holds something.

MESNE PROCESS. 1. Pre-judgment. C.R.B. Dunlop, *Creditor-Debtor Law in Canada* (Toronto: Carswell, 1981) at 198. 2. In an action or suit, writs which come between the beginning and end.

MESNE PROFIT. An action for damages suffered when possession of land has been withheld improperly. *Mortimer v. Shaw* (1922), 66 D.L.R. 311 at 312, [1922] 2 W.W.R. 562, 15 Sask. L.R. 476 (C.A.), Lamont J.A. (McKay J.A. concurring).

MESS. See MILITARY ~.

MESSAGE. See COMMERCIAL ~.

MESSAGES. *n*. Includes signs, signals, writing, images, sounds or intelligence of any nature.

MESSENGER. *n*. One who carries an errand; one who goes before.

MESSIS SEMENTEM SEQUITUR. [L.] Reaping follows seeding.

MESSUAGE. *n.* A dwelling-house including any out-buildings, adjacent land and curtilage assigned to its use.

META-ANALYSIS. *n.* A medical or scientific study which manipulates and considers the data from all available studies of a particular issue. The combination of the data from various studies may be considered more reliable than the data from individual studies.

METACHRONISM. *n.* A mistake in calculation of time.

METAGE. *n.* The act of determining size or quantity.

METAL. *n.* Includes antimony, bismuth, cadmium, cobalt, copper, chromium, gold, iron, lead, magnesium, mercury, molybdenum, nickel, niobium, silver, tantalum, tin, thorium, titanium, tungsten, uranium and zinc. *Metal Mining Liquid Effluent Regulations*, C.R.C., c. 819, s. 2. See ALKALI ~ AMALGAM; PRECIOUS ~; UNWROUGHT ~.

METAL CHIMNEY. A single-wall chimney of metal constructed on site.

METAL-CLAD. *adj.* Having sides made of or covered with metal.

METAL CUTTING. See MACHINE TOOL, ~.

METAL FORMING. See MACHINE TOOL, ~.

METALLIC COVERING. An iron or steel wire armoring applied to cables. *Coal Mines Regulation Act*, R.S.N.S. 1989, c. 73, s. 85(1).

METALLIC TUBING. See ELECTRICAL ~.

METAL MECHANIC. See GLAZIER AND ~.

METAL-ROOFED. *adj.* Having a roof made of or covered with metal. *Lightning Rods Act*, R.R.O. 1980, Reg. 577, s. 1.

METAL SEAL. A metal seal furnished by the Chief Electoral Officer to seal a ballot box.

METAL SHIELD. A shield not less than .008 of an inch thick made of stainless steel or other metal equal in tensile strength and corrosion resistance to stainless steel. *Ontario Water Resources Act*, R.R.O. 1980, Reg. 736, s. 72.

METAL TIRE. Every tire the surface of which in contact with the roadway is wholly or partly of metal or other hard, nonresilient material.

METAL WORKER. See SHEET ~.

METEORITE. *n. Any* naturally-occurring object of extraterrestrial origin. *Canadian Cultural Property Export Control List*, C.R.C., c. 448, s. 1.

METER. *n.* An electric or gas meter and includes any apparatus used for the purpose of making measurements of, or obtaining the basis of a charge for, electricity or gas supplied to a purchaser. See PARKING ~; PO TAGE ~; SOUND LEVEL ~; VERIFIED ~.

METER USER. A person who pays postage by means of a postage meter. *Postage Meter Setting Service Regulations*, C.R.C., c. 1286, s. 2.

METES AND BOUNDS. The description of land's boundaries beginning at a fixed point and then outlining the borders in north, south, west and east directions and in degrees, minutes and seconds.

METHANE. *n.* In addition to its normal scientific meaning, a mixture mainly of methane, which may ordinarily contain some ethane, nitrogen, helium or carbon dioxide. Alberta statutes.

METHANE EXTRACTION. Any process approved by the Minister by which methane gas is extracted or manufactured from coal. *Petroleum Resources Act*, R.S.N.S. 1989, c. 342, s. 2.

METHOD. *n.* The system or procedure followed. See ANNUITY ~; ARITHMETICAL OR ACTUARIAL ~; CASH ~; COMPARISON ~; COMPLETED CONTRACT ~; DEVEOPMENT COST ~; INDUCTIVE ~; INSTALMENT ~; MULTIPLIER ~; STANDARD ~S; SUBSTITUTION ~.

METIS. *n.* 1. A person of aboriginal ancestry who identifies with Metis history and culture. 2. A person of mixed Aboriginal and European heredity.

METIS SETTLEMENT. Any lands set aside for occupation by a settlement association under The Metis Betterment Act, Alberta. *Alberta Fishery Regulations*, C.R.C., c. 838, s. 2.

METRE. *n.* The unit for the measurement of length, being, a length equal to 1 650 763.73 wavelengths in vacuum of the radiation corresponding to the transition between the levels $2p_{10}$

and 5d$_5$ of the krypton 86 atom. *Weights and Measures Act*, S.C. 1970-71-72, c. 36, schedule I. See CUBIC ~; CUBIC ~ (SOLID); CUBIC ~ (STACKED).

METRIC SYSTEM. 1. A measurement system in which any basic unit is divided or multiplied by ten. 2. All units of measurement used in Canada shall be determined on the basis of the International System of Units established by the General Conference of Weights and Measures. *Weights and Measures Act*, R.S.C. 1985, c. W-6, s. 4.

METRIC UNITS. Units of measurement in metres and decimals of a metre.

METRO. *abbr*. Metropolitan.

METROPOLIS. *n*. The main city; the seat of government.

METROPOLITAN AREA. A city together with one or more adjacent municipalities in close economic relationship with the city.

MEZZANINE. *n*. An intermediate floor between the floor and ceiling of any room or storey.

M FT. *abbr*. One thousand feet board measure. *Customs Tariff*, R.S.C. 1985, c. C-54, s. 2.

M.G.M. *abbr*. Maximum gross mass.

M.G.W. *abbr*. Maximum gross weight.

MICRO. *pref*. 10^{-6}. Prefix for multiples and submultiples of basic, supplementary and derived units of measurement. *Weights and Measures Act*, S.C. 1970-71-72, c. 36, schedule I.

MICROCURIE. *n*. That quantity of a radioactive isotope that is disintegrating at the rate of 37,000 disintegrations per second. *Atomic Energy Control Regulations*, C.R.C., c. 365, schedule I.

MICROGRAPHICS. *n*. All processes, techniques and methods of micro-reproduction on film of printed or other graphic matter regardless of the composition thereof. *Public Printing Act*, S.M. 1979, c. 17, s. 1.

MICRO-ORGANISM. *n*. A microscopic plant or animal and includes bacteria, viruses, fungi, algae and protozoa. *Pest Control Products (Nova Scotia) Act*, S.N.S. 1986, c. 16, s. 3.

MICROWAVE. *n*. An electromagnetic wave with frequency in the range 0.010 GHz to 300 GHz. *Radiation Emitting Devices Regulations*, C.R.C., c. 1370, s. 1.

MICROWAVE OVEN. Any apparatus or device for heating food or material by absorption of electromagnetic radiation in the range of electromagnetic frequencies from 890 megahertz to 6,000 megahertz. *Public Health Act*, R.S.O. 1980, c. 409, s. 49.

MIDDLE-MAN. *n*. An intermediary between a wholesale merchant and a retail dealer; one who distributes from producer to consumer.

MIDWATER TRAWL. A trawl net that is designed so as not to come into contact with the sea-bed while in operation. Canada regulations.

MIDWIFE. *n*. A person whose profession is the delivery of children.

MIDWIFERY. *n*. The practice of midwifery is the assessment and monitoring of women during pregnancy, labour and the post-partum period and of their newborn babies, the provision of care during normal pregnancy, labour and postpartum period and the conducting of spontaneous normal vaginal deliveries. *Midwifery Act, 1991*, S.O. 1991, c. 31. s. 3.

MIGRATORY BIRD. A migratory bird referred to in the Convention for the protection of migratory birds in Canada and the United States and includes the sperm, eggs, embryos, tissue cultures and parts of the bird. *Migratory Birds Convention Act, 1994*, S.C. 1994, c. 22.

MIGRATORY BIRDS. Migratory game birds, migratory insectivorous birds and migratory non-game birds as defined in the Act, and includes any such birds raised in captivity that cannot readily be distinguished from wild migratory birds by their size, shape or colour, and any part or parts of such birds. *Migratory Birds Regulations*, SOR/98-282, s. 2.

MIGRATORY GAME BIRDS. (a) Anatidae or waterfowl, including brant, wild ducks, geese and swans, (b) Gruidae or cranes, including little brown, sandhill and whooping cranes, (c) Rallidae or rails, including coots, gallinules and sora and other rails, (d) Limicolae or shorebirds, including avocets, curlew, dowitchers, godwits, knots, oyster catchers, phalaropes, plovers, sandpipers, snipe, stilts, surf birds, turnstones, willet, woodcock, and yellowlegs, and (e) Columbidae or pigeons, including doves and wild pigeons. *Migratory Birds Convention Act, 1994*, S.C. 1994, c. 22, Article 1.

MIGRATORY INSECTIVOROUS BIRDS. Bobolinks, catbirds, chickadees, cuckoos, flickers, fly-catchers, grosbeaks, hummingbirds, kinglets, martins, meadowlarks, nighthawks or bull bats, nuthatches, orioles, robins, shrikes, swallows, swifts, tanagers, titmice, thrushes, vireos, warblers, waxwings, whippoorwills, woodpeckers and wrens, and all other perching birds that feed entirely or chiefly on insects. *Migratory Birds Convention Act, 1994*, S.C. 1994, c. 22, Article 1.

MIGRATORY NONGAME BIRDS. Auks, auklets, bitterns, fulmars, gannets, grebes, guillemots, gulls, herons, jaegers, loons, murres, petrels, puffins, shearwaters and terns. *Migratory Birds Convention Act, 1994*, S.C. 1994, c. 22, Article 1.

MIGRATORY WORKER. A person who moves from one work site to another doing the same kind of work.

MILE. *n*. 1. 1 760 yards. *Weights and Measures Act*, S.C. 1970-71-72, c. 36, schedule II. 2. The international nautical mile of 1 852 metres. Canada regulations. 3. A nautical mile measuring 6,080 feet. Canada regulations. See REVENUE ~S; ROUTE ~; SQUARE ~.

MILEAGE. *n*. Travelling expenses which sheriffs, witnesses and others may claim.

MILITARY. *adj*. 1. Relating to all or any part of the Canadian Forces. 2. With respect to any aircraft or facility, an aircraft or facility operated by or on behalf of the Department of National Defence, the Canadian Forces or a visiting force. 3. Relating to any warlike force. *Canadian Cultural Property Export Control List*, C.R.C., c. 448, s. 1.

MILITARY CANTEEN. A mess or canteen operated in connection with a unit or establishment of the Royal Canadian Navy, the Canadian Army, the Royal Canadian Air Force, or the Royal Canadian Mounted Police Force, in a camp, armoury, barracks, post, station, or ship.

MILITARY FORCES OF A STATE. The armed forces that a state organizes, trains and equips in accordance with the law of the state for the primary purpose of national defence or national security, and every person acting in support of those armed forces who is under their formal command, control and responsibility.

MILITARY JUDGE. Military judges preside at courts martial and perform other judicial duties under this Act that are required to be performed by military judges. The Governor in Council may designate a military judge to be the Chief Military Judge. The Chief Military Judge assigns military judges to preside at courts martial and to perform other judicial duties under this Act.

MILITARY LAW. 1. "[In s. 11(f) of the Charter means] . . . a system of law administered by the military itself and the most important institution of which has always been the General Court Martial." *R. v. Genereux* (1990), 60 C.C.C. (3d) 536 at 543, 70 D.L.R. (4th) 207, 114 N.R. 321, 4 C.R.R. (2d) 307, (Can. Ct. Martial Appeal Ct.), Pratte J. 2. Includes all laws, regulations or orders relating to the Canadian Forces. *Criminal Code*, R.S.C. 1985, c. C-46, s. 2.

MILITARY MESS. Includes a canteen and an institute in a building or camp used for the accommodation of the active or reserve units of the naval, military or air forces of Canada. *Liquor Control Act*, R.S.Nfld. 1990, c. L-18, s. 2.

MILITARY OFFENCE. An offence recognized by a military court, e.g. insubordination.

MILITARY SERVICE. Service as a member of the armed forces. See ACTIVE ~.

MILITARY VEHICLE. A vehicle that is designed to be used in combat or in a combat support role.

MILITIAMAN. *n*. A non-commissioned officer or private of the force. *Defence Services Pension Continuation Act*, R.S.C. 1970, c. D-3, s. 2.

MILK. *n*. 1. The normal secretion from the mammary gland of a cow, goat or sheep. 2. Includes whole milk and such products of milk as are supplied, processed, distributed or sold in any form including but not so as to restrict the generality of the foregoing, cream, butter, cheese ice cream and condensed, evaporated or powdered milk.

MILK CONDENSERY. Any building where milk, cream or any dairy by-product is dehydrated and converted into a concentrated dairy product.

MILK DEALER. A person who as a principal, purchases or receives milk or cream for the purpose of processing or selling milk or cream.

MILK FAT. The fat of cow's milk.

MILKING PARLOUR. An area used solely for the milking of animals.

MILK MANUFACTURING PLANT. A plant in which milk is processed or handled including a pasteurization plant, and every building, machine, apparatus, equipment and appurtenance employed in, or necessary for storing, cooling, processing, packaging or handling of milk and milk products and forming a part of, or connected with the plant.

MILK PLANT. See INDUSTRIAL ~.

MILK POWDER. Dried milk that contains not less than, (i.) 95 per cent milk solids, and (ii.) 26 per cent milk-fat, with or without added vitamin D.

MILK PRODUCT. Any product processed or derived in whole or in part from milk, and includes cream, butter, cheese, cottage cheese, condensed milk, milk powder, dry milk, ice cream, ice cream mix, casein, malted milk, sherbet and such other products that are designated as milk products in the regulations.

MILK PRODUCTION. The quantity of pounds of fat or milk which a producer markets or is authorized to market during a year.

MILK RECEIVING STATION. A place suitably equipped with the necessary washing, steaming, grading, sampling and cooling equipment at which milk is received for the purpose of being transported to a cheese factory, concentrated milk plant, creamery or dairy.

MILK SOLIDS. The solids consisting of butter fat, casein, albumen, sugar and ash in milk.

MILK TEETH. The first set of a young child's teeth which are eventually replaced by permanent teeth. F.A. Jaffe, *A Guile to Pathological Evidence*, 3d ed. (Toronto: Carswell, 1991) at 217.

MILK TRANSFER STATION. Premises at which milk is received for the purpose of being transported to a plant for processing. *Milk Act*, R.S.O. 1990, c. M.12, s. 1.

MILK VENDOR. A person who, as a principal, purchases or receives milk or cream from a milk dealer for reselling or distributing to consumers but does not include a storekeeper.

MILL. *n*. 1. A plant in which logs or wood-bolts are initially processed, and includes a saw mill and a pulp mill. 2. ". . . [A]ny premise fitted with machinery for the purpose of either mixing, separating, treating or cleaning grain . . ." *Ammeter v. Slywchuk*, [1971] 4 W.W.R. 70 at 73 (Sask. Dist. Ct.), Maher D.C.J. See FEED ~ OPERATOR.

MILL CONSTRUCTION. As applied to a building means one in which walls are of masonry or reinforced concrete and an interior framing of wood, with plank or laminated wood floors and roofs, and in which the interior structural elements are arranged in heavy solid masses and smooth flat surfaces assembled to avoid thin sections, sharp projections, and concealed or inaccessible spaces, but the interior framing may be partly or entirely of protected steel or concrete and the floors and roofs may be constructed in whole or in part of incombustible material.

MILLED MONEY. Money with regularly marked edges; coins.

MILLI. *pref*. 10⁻³. Prefix for multiples and sub-multiples of basic, supplementary and derived units of measurement. *Weights and Measures Act*, S.C. 1970-71-72, c. 36, schedule I.

MILLING. *n*. The crushing or grinding of ore.

MILLION. See PARTS PER ~.

MILLIRAD. *n*. A submultiple of a unit of dose equal to .001 rad.

MILL PROCESS EFFLUENT. Includes tailing slurries and all other effluent discharged from a milling operation.

MILL RATE. See REQUISITION ~.

MIN. *abbr*. 1. Minister. 2. Ministry. 3. Minute.

MINATUR INNOCENTIBUS, QUI PARCIT NOCENTIBUS. [L.] Whoever spares the guilty threatens the innocent.

MIND. *n*. The mental faculties of reason, memory, and understanding. See DISEASE OF THE ~; INSANITY; STATE OF ~ EXCEPTION.

MINE. *v*. 1. " . . . [T]he initial recovery of the gold from ground in its virgin state as it passed through the dredge:" *Olsen v. Canadian Klondyke Mining Co.* (1917), 34 D.L.R. 529 at 532, [1917] 2 W.W.R. 640, 24 B.C.R.114 (C.A.), McPhillips J.A. 2. Includes any mode or method of working whereby the soil or earth or any rock, stone or mineral-bearing substance may be disturbed, removed, washed, sifted, leached, roasted, smelted, refined, reduced, crushed, or dealt with for the purpose of obtaining any mineral therefrom whether the same may have been previously disturbed or not, and any mode or method of excavation or rehabilitation of shafts, tunnels, or chambers for industrial purposes.

MINE. *n*. 1. A munition designed, altered or intended to be placed under, on or near the ground or other surface area and to be exploded by the presence, proximity or contact of a person or a vehicle. *Anti-Personnel Mines Convention Implementation Act*, S.C. 1997, c. 33, s. 2. 2. Any opening or excavation in, or working of, the ground for the purpose of winning any mineral or mineral bearing substance. 3. Any work or undertaking for the purpose of opening up, proving, removing or extracting any metallic or non-metallic mineral or mineral bearing substance, rock, earth, clay, sand or gravel. 4. Any opening or excavation in, or working of the ground for the purpose of winning, opening up or proving any mineral or mineral-bearing substance, and any ore body, mineral deposit, stratum, rock earth, clay, sand or gravel, or place where mining is or may be carried on, and all ways, works machinery, plant, buildings and premises below or above ground belonging to or used in connection with the mine, and also any quarry, excavation or opening of the ground made for the purpose of searching for or removal of mineral rock, stratum, earth, clay, sand or gravel and any roasting or smelting furnace, concentrator, mill, work or place used for or in connection with washing, crushing, sifting, reducing, leaching, roasting, smelting, refining, treating or research on any of such substances. See ABANDONED ~; ANTI-PERSONNEL ~; CLOSED ~; COAL ~; ENERGY, ~S AND RESOURCES CANADA; GOLD ~; NEW ~; OPEN PIT ~; OPERATION OF ~; POTASH ~; PRODUCTS OF THE QUARRY AND ~; SMALL ~; STRIP ~; SURFACE ~; UNDERGROUND ~.

MINE EXAMINER. A person who is possessed of a certificate of competency as such under this or some former Act and who is appointed to inspect the working places of a mine and approaches thereto, the airways and other accessible parts of a mine, and to see that such are safe before a shift is allowed to enter such workings or other parts of the mine; and to examine as to the safety of using and to supervise the use of the explosives used in breaking coal. *Coal Mines Regulation Act*, R.S.N.S. 1989, c. 73, s. 4.

MINE HOISTING PLANT. A hoist for an underground mine and includes the prime mover, transmission equipment, head-frame, sheaves, ropes, shaft, shaft conveyances, shaft sinking equipment, shaft furnishings, hoist controls, counterweight, signalling and communications equipment and any other equipment used in connection with a hoist.

MINE MANAGER. The chief officer of a mine who holds a certificate as a mine manager.

MINER. *n*. 1. Any person working upon a mine or mining claim or in connection therewith. 2. A person employed in an underground mine to cut, shear, break or loosen coal or rock. See COAL ~.

MINERAL. *n*. 1. Any natural, solid, inorganic or fossilized organic substance. 2. Any nonliving substance formed by the processes of nature which occurs in, on or under land, of any chemical or physical state, but does not include oil, earth, surface water and ground water. 3. ". . . [M]ineral substances and . . . petroleum and natural gas . . ." *Crows Nest Pass Coal Co. v. R.*, [1961] S.C.R. 750 at 761, 36 W.W.R. 513, 82 C.R.T.C. 10, 30 D.L.R. (2d) 93, the court per Locke J. 4. ". . . '[M]ining rights' . . ." *Tisdale (Township) v. Cavana*, [1942] 4 D.L.R. 65 at 68, [1942] S.C.R. 384, the court per Kerwin J. 5. Includes base and precious metal, coal, salt and every other substance that is an article of commerce obtained from the earth by any method of extraction, but does not include a hydrocarbon or any animal or vegetable substance other than coal. See CROWN~; ESTATE IN A ~; PLACER ~; QUARRIABLE ~; SUBSURFACE ~S; UNIT OF ~S; VALUABLE IN PLACE.

MINERAL ACID. Includes hydrochloric acid, sulphuric acid, nitric acid, phosphoric acid and any combination thereof. *Hazardous Products (Hazardous Substances) Regulations*, C.R.C., c. 926, s. 2.

MINERAL CLAIM. 1. A plot of ground staked out or acquired. 2. A claim to the minerals within an area which has been located or acquired by a method set out in the regulations.

MINERAL EXPLORATION. Prospecting or exploring for a mineral resource.

MINERAL HOLDING. All the estates, titles, interests or rights of whatever kind in or to minerals generally or to specific minerals in a mineral area of 1 hectare or more, held directly or indirectly from the Crown, whether (i) as an incident of a fee simple or leasehold estate in land or minerals, (ii) as an interest in or to the minerals situated in that area, or (iii) as a right to obtain the minerals in that area exclusive of an exempt mineral interest within the mineral area and of the area of a mine within the mineral area not exceeding 2,000 hectares in respect of which mining operations, as defined in the Mining and Mineral Rights Tax Act, are being carried out. *Mineral Holdings Impost Act*, R.S. Nfld. 1990, c. M-14, s. 2.

MINERAL INTEREST. (i) The ownership of, title to, or an interest in, or (ii) a right, a licence other than a licence issued by the Crown, or an option, to drill for, take, win, or gain, and remove from land, oil or gas, whether acquired by way of instrument commonly called a lease or otherwise, and includes a grant or assignment of a profit à prendre in respect of any oil or gas; but does not include the ownership of, title to, or an interest in oil or gas purchased or otherwise acquired by any person as a result of that person's purchase or other acquisition of land or interest in land the title to which includes the mines and minerals in, under, or upon the land. See FREEHOLD ~.

MINERAL INTEREST BROKER. A person or company who or that is engaged in the business of (i) purchasing or acquiring any mineral interest on his own behalf, or (ii) negotiating, on behalf of another person or company, the purchase or acquisition of any mineral interest, or (iii) otherwise trading in any mineral interest.

MINERAL LAND. Land, other than Crown land and land comprising a right of way, station ground, yard or terminal of a railway, in respect of which (a) a mineral is, or may be, situated; or (b) a person has the right to work, win or carry away a mineral.

MINERAL LANDS. Includes lands and mining rights under disposition and lands or mineral rights located, staked out, used or intended to be used for mining purposes. See CROWN ~.

MINERAL LEASE BROKER. A person who or company that is engaged in the business of: (i) purchasing or acquiring an mineral interest on his behalf; or (ii) negotiating, on behalf of another person or company, the purchase or acquisition of any mineral interest. *Securities Act*, S.S. 1984-85-86, c. S-42.1, s. 145.

MINERAL LINE. A pipe for the transmission of a mineral whether in solution, suspension or other state and includes installations in connection therewith, but does not include a gas line, oil line, secondary line, flow line, distribution line or private line.

MINERAL LOCATION. A tract of Crown land containing minerals or land upon or under

which minerals have been reserved to the Crown and in respect of which a grant has been made for the purpose of mining, and includes a boring claim, a mining claim, a placer claim, and a quarrying claim, and an oil and natural gas tract. *Mines Act*, R.S.M. 1987, c. M160, s. 1.

MINERAL NUTRIENT. Any of the following chemical elements whether alone or in a compound with one or more other chemical elements: (a) calcium; (b) phosphorus; (c) iron; (d) sodium; (e) potassium; (f) iodine; (g) zinc; (h) copper; (i) magnesium; (j) manganese; (k) chlorine; and (1) fluorine. *Food and Drug Regulations*, C.R.C., c. 870, c. D.02.001. ,

MINERAL OIL. See HYDRAULIC SYSTEM ~.

MINERAL ORE. Includes unprocessed minerals or mineral bearing substances. See NEW ~; PROBABLE ~; PROVEN ~.

MINERAL PRODUCT. 1. A product derived from the operation of a mine. 2. A product derived from mineral bearing substances processed in a mineral processing establishment of an operator including those mined, milled, smelted, refined recrystallized or otherwise beneficiated to a state of purity suitable for (a) sale to a person with whom the operator is dealing at arms length for further processing, or (b) fabrication by manufacturing, or (c) acceptance by the Royal Canadian Mint.

MINERAL RECOVERY. The taking of mineral water or the recovery from mineral water by artificial means of all minerals, including mineral salts, either in solution or suspense. *The Water Rights Act*, R.S.S. 1978, c. W-8, s. 2.

MINERAL RESOURCE. (a) A base or precious metal deposit, (b) a coal deposit, (c) a bituminous sands deposit, oil sands deposit or oil shale deposit, or (d) a mineral deposit in respect of which (i) the Minister of Energy, Mines and Resources has certified that the principal mineral extracted is an industrial mineral contained in a non-bedded deposit, (ii) the principal mineral extracted is sylvite, halite, gypsum or kaolin, or (iii) the principal mineral extracted is silica that is extracted from sandstone or quartzite. *Income Tax Act*, R.S.C. 1952, c. 148 (as am. S.C. 1988, c. 55, s. 188(5)), s. 248(1).

MINERAL RIGHT. An estate in fee simple in a mineral located in a tract.

MINERAL RIGHTS. 1. The right to enter upon or use lands for the sole purpose of exploring, drilling for, winning, taking, removing or raising the minerals situate therein and includes such easements, rights of way or other similar rights of access as are incidental to winning, taking, removing or raising the minerals situate therein. 2. The right to explore for, work and use natural mineral substances situated within the volume formed by the vertical projection of the perimeter of a parcel of land, including the right to explore for underground reservoirs or to develop or use them for the storage or permanent disposal of any mineral substance or of any industrial product or residue. *Mining Act*, R.S.Q. 1977, c. M-13, s. 1.

MINERAL SPECIMEN. See DE-SCRIBED ~; TYPE ~.

MINERAL SUBSTANCE. Every type and kind of ore, rock and mineral and tailings whether organic or inorganic, but does not include diatomaceous earth, limestone, marl, peat, clay, building stone, stone for ornamental or decorative purposes, non-auriferous sand or gravel, or natural gas or petroleum, or sodium chloride recovered by solution method. *Mining Tax Act*, R.S.O. 1990, c. M.15, s. 1(1). See MINES AND MINERALS.

MINERAL TITLE. A claim or a lease.

MINERAL TRADING PURPOSE. 1. The sale, barter or exchange of natural mineral water in bottles or other containers, or the utilization of the waters in sanatoriums or for other purposes. 2. Bottling, distributing, using and dealing in water so impregnated with foreign ingredients as to give it medicinal properties, or water of a temperature that gives it a commercial value.

MINERAL WATER. Water containing in its natural state, either in solution or suspense, more than one per cent of minerals or mineral salts.

MINERAL WATER PURPOSES. The purpose of a public bath house or public swimming pool, for medicinal purposes or purposes of sale, trade or barter.

MINE RESCUE CORPS. All mine rescue personnel under the supervision of a mine rescue station superintendent.

MINE RESCUE TEAM. A group of not less than five men especially trained in mine rescue work and first aid.

MINER'S HELPER. A person employed in an underground mine to work under the supervision of a miner.

MINE SAFETY ENGINEER. A safety officer.

MINES AND MINERALS. Include any strata or seam of minerals or substances in or under any land and powers of working and getting the same, but not an undivided share thereof.

MINE SITE. 1. A location at which a facility for extracting coal by underground, strip or open pit operations exists or is to be developed, and includes (i) a coal processing plant, storage facility or discard disposal facility which exists or is to be developed in connection with a mine, and (ii) all connected access roads. 2. An area within which mining operations are being conducted.

MINE SURVEYOR. 1. A person responsible for (i) surveying the workings of a mine, and (ii) preparing the plans required under this Act or the Coal Conservation Act. *Coal Mines Safety Act*, R.S.A. 1980, c. C-15, s. 1. 2. Any person who possesses a certificate of competency as a mine surveyor issued under this or some former Act and who does surveying work in or about a mine. *Coal Mines Regulation Act*, R.S.N.S. 1989, c. 73, s. 4.

MINE WATER EFFLUENT. Water pumped or flowing out of any underground workings or open pit.

MINIATURE BOILER. A boiler approved to carry a working pressure of not more than 700 kilopascals that has a shell with an inside diameter not greater than 400 millimetres and an overall length of not more than 1000 millimetres from outside to outside of the heads and a water heating capacity of not more than 70 kilowatts. *Boiler, Pressure Vessel and Compressed Gas Act*, R.S. Nfld. 1990, c. B-5, s. 2.

MINIATURE FILM. Photographic moving picture film which is sixteen millimetres or less in width.

MINIBIKE. *var.* **MINI-BIKE.** *n.* A vehicle having steering handlebars completely constrained from rotating in relation to the axle of one wheel in contact with the ground, designed to travel on not more than three wheels in contact with the ground and having (a) a minimum seat height unladen of less than 711 mm (28 inches), (b) a wheel rim diameter of less than 254 mm (10 inches), (c) a wheelbase of less than 1 016 mm (40 inches), or (d) a braking system operating on one wheel only. Canada regulations.

MINIBUS. *n.* A motor vehicle of the small van type designed for the transportation, for a fare, óf more than seven occupants at a time or for the group transportation of handicapped persons.

MINIME MUTANDA SUNT QUAE CERTAM HABENT INTERPRETATIONEM. [L.] Whatever has an interpretation which has been settled should be changed as little as possible.

MINIMENT. *n*. Documentary evidence of title.

MINIMUM DESCENT ALTITUDE. The altitude ASL specified in the *Canada Air Pilot* or the route and approach inventory for a non-precision approach, below which descent shall not be made until the required visual reference to continue the approach to land has been established. *Canadian Aviation Regulations*, SOR/96-433, s. 101.01.

MINIMUM ENROUTE ALTITUDE. The lowest altitude ASL that is specified in the *Designated Airspace Handbook* for a designated area or between fixes on airways or air routes, that assures acceptable navigational signal coverage and that meets the obstruction clearance criteria. *Canadian Aviation Regulations*, SOR/96-433, s. 101.01.

MINIMUM OBSTRUCTION CLEARANCE ALTITUDE. The altitude ASL that will ensure that an IFR aircraft will be clear of the highest obstacle within an airway or air route. *Canadian Aviation Regulations*, SOR/96-433, s. 101.01.

MINIMUM OVERTIME RATE. A rate of wages one-and-one-half times as great as the minimum rate prescribed.

MINIMUM REST PERIOD. A period during which a flight crew member is free from all duties, is not interrupted by the air operator or private operator, and is provided with an opportunity to obtain not less than eight consecutive hours of sleep in suitable accommodation, time to travel to and from that accommodation and time for personal hygiene and meals. *Canadian Aviation Regulations*, SOR/96-433, s. 101.01.

MINIMUM WAGE. The lowest compensation established by statute.

MINING. *n*. 1. The extracting of minerals from a mineral resource, the processing of ore, other than iron ore, from a mineral resource to the prime metal state or its equivalent, the processing of iron ore from a mineral resource to the pellet state or its equivalent and the restoration of strip-mined land to a usable condition, but does not include activities related to the exploration for or development of a mineral resource. *Excise Tax*, R.S.C. 1985 (2d Supp.), c. 7, s. 69. 2. " . . . [I]nclude[s] the sinking of the working shafts, installation of machinery, construction of the necessary lateral passages, and other underground workings preparatory to the actual removal of minerals." *Patrick Harrison & Co. v. Manitoba (Attorney General)* (1966), 56 D.L.R. (2d) 256 at 262, 61 W.W.R. 521 (Man. Q.B.), Wilson J. 3. Includes diamond drilling and any mode or method of working whereby any soil, earth, rock, stone, quartz, clay, or gravel may be disturbed, removed, carted, carried, washed, sifted, crushed, roasted, smelted, refined or dealt with for the purpose of obtaining any minerals or metal therefrom, whether the same may have been previously disturbed or not, and all operations and workings in a mine. 4. Any mode or method of working whereby the earth or any rock, stratum, stone or mineral-bearing substance may be disturbed, removed, washed, sifted, leached, roasted, smelted, refined, crushed or dealt with for the purpose of obtaining any mineral therefrom, whether it has been previously disturbed or not. See PLACER ~.

MINING AREA. An area in which the holder of a permit may conduct a mining operation.

MINING ASSETS. The plant, equipment, machinery and buildings acquired for the purpose of the extraction of mineral substances from the ground and ancillary activities, but does not include processing assets or social assets. *Mining Tax Act*, R.S.O. 1990, c. M.15, s. 1(1).

MINING CLAIM. 1. A parcel of land staked out and to which the holder thereof has exclusive right to prospect, under authority of a prospecting licence, for minerals the ownership of which is vested in the Crown, and which ownership has not been alienated. 2. A plot of Crown land containing a mineral and staked out for mining purposes, other than that contained in a boring claim. See UNPATENTED ~.

MINING COMPANY. A company that for the time being carries on as its principal business the business of operating any producing mining properties owned or controlled by it.

MINING CONCESSION. A mining property sold out of the public domain for the purpose of operating mining rights.

MINING LANDS. Includes lands and mining rights leased under or by authority of any statute, regulation or order in council, respecting mines, minerals or mining, and also lands or mining rights located, staked out, used or intended to be used for mining purposes.

MINING LEASE. A lease, grant or licence for mining purposes, including the searching for, working, getting, making merchantable, smelting or otherwise converting or working for the purposes of any manufacture, carrying away or disposing of mines or minerals, and substances in, on or under the land, obtainable by underground or by surface working or purposes connected therewith.

MINING LICENCE. A licence by which the holder thereof is granted the right to prospect, develop, or mine on a designated area for a period of one year.

MINING OPERATION. 1. All the work whereby mineral substances are explored for in view of being extracted or extracted for the purpose of obtaining a commercial product. 2. The extraction or production, transportation, distribution and sale of the output of mineral ore from a mine.

MINING PLAN. An approved plan for the operation of a mine and the reclamation of a disturbed area.

MINING PLANT. Any roasting or smelting furnace, concentrator, mill or place used for or in connection with washing, crushing, grinding, sifting, reducing, leaching, roasting, smelting, refining, treating or research on any substance mentioned in the definition of "mine". *Occupational Health and Safety Act*, R.S.O. 1990, c. 0.1, s. 1(1).

MINING PROPERTY. 1. A right to prospect, explore or mine for minerals or a property the principal value of which depends upon its mineral content. 2. Includes every mineral claim, lease, ditch or water right used for mining purposes, and all other things belonging to a mine or used in the working thereof. 3. Land in which a vein or lode or rock in place or natural stratum or bed of earth, gravel or cement is mined for gold or other precious minerals or stones or for any base mineral or mineral bearing substance, including coal, petroleum and natural gas. 4. Includes a mineral claim, 2 post claim, leasehold and real and personal property pertaining to a mine or used in the working of it.

MINING PURPOSES. The making, excavating or sinking of a mine and the working of a mine and searching for, winning, opening up, removing, proving, or storing underground, any mineral or mineral-bearing substance and the erection of buildings and the execution of engineering and other works suitable for those purposes.

MINING RIGHT. A mining or mineral claim, a mining licence or lease.

MINING RIGHTS. 1. " . . . '[M]inerals' . . ." *Banner Coal Co. v. Gervais (No. 1)* (1922), 18 Alta. L.R. 535 at 541, 70 D.L.R. 206, [1922] 3 W.W.R. 564 (C.A.), the court per Beck J.A. 2. Includes the right to the minerals and mines upon or under the surface of the land.

MINISTER. *n.* 1. A member of the Cabinet. 2. A member of the Queen's Privy Council for Canada as is designated by the Governor in Council. 3. A member of the Executive Council appointed as a Minister who is responsible for the enactment or its subject matter or the department to which its context refers. 4. Includes any priest, rabbi, elder, evangelist, missionary or commissioned officer ordained or appointed by the religious body to which he belongs. See APPROPRIATE ~; CABINET ~; DEPUTY ~; INCUMBENT ~; PRIME ~.

MINISTERIAL. *adj.* Describes the discharge of a duty without discretion or independent judgment or the issue of a formal instruction determined beforehand. S.A. DeSmith, Judicial *Review of Administrative Action*, 4th ed. by J.M. Evans (London: Stevens, 1980) at 70.

MINISTERIAL DUTY. A duty involved in operating a trust, i.e., keeping of accounts or hiring an agent like a solicitor or valuer. D.M.W. Waters, *The Law of Trusts in Canada*, 2d ed. (Toronto: Carswell, 1984) at 28.

MINISTERIAL OFFICE. Any office in or under the ministries, branches and institutions of the Executive Government of the Province, other than a record office.

MINISTERIAL RECORD. A record of a member of the Queen's Privy Council for Canada who holds the office of a Minister and that pertains to that office, other than a record that is of a personal or political nature or that is under the control of a government institution.

MINISTERING CLERIC. The cleric appointed to administer a chapelry. Quebec statutes.

MINISTER OF HEALTH. (a) In the Provinces of Ontario, Quebec, New Brunswick, Prince Edward Island, Manitoba and Newfoundland, the Minister of Health, (b) in the Provinces of Nova Scotia and Saskatchewan, the Minister of Public Health, and (c) in the Province of British Columbia, the Minister of Health Services and Hospital Insurance, (d) in the Province of Alberta, the Minister of Hospitals and Medical Care, (e) in the Yukon and the Northwest Territories and Nunavut the Minister of Health. *Criminal Code*, R.S.C. 1985, c. C-46, s. 287(6).

MINISTER OF THE CROWN. A member of the Queen's Privy Council for Canada in that member's capacity of managing and directing or having responsibility for a department.

MINISTER WITHOUT PORTFOLIO. A member of the cabinet not in charge of a department.

MINISTRY. *n.* A department of government.

MINISTRY OF STATE. Where it appears to the Governor in Council that the requirements for formulating and developing new and comprehensive policies in relation to any matter or matters coming within the responsibility of the Government of Canada warrant the establishment of a special portion of the public service of Canada presided over by a minister charged with responsibility for the formulation and development of such policies, the Governor in Council may, by proclamation, establish a ministry of State for that purpose.

MINKE WHALE. Any whale of the species Balaenoptera acutorostrata, B. davidsoni, B. huttoni, commonly known as lesser rorqual, little piked whale, minke whale, pike-headed whale or sharp-headed finner. *Whaling Regulations*, C.R.C., c. 1608, s. 2.

MINNOW TRAP. An impounding apparatus used to catch small fish. *Manitoba Fishery Regulations*, C.R.C., c. 843, s. 2.

MINOR. *n.* 1. A person who has not attained the age of majority. 2. A person who has not attained the age of eighteen years. 3. A person who has not attained, in British Columbia, the age of 19 and in all other provinces and territories, the age of 18. See INFANT OR ~.

MINOR ANTE TEMPUS AGERE NON POTEST IN CASU PROPRIETATIS, NEC ETIAM CONVENIRE; DIFFERETUR USQUE AETATEM; SED NON CADIT BREVE. [L.] In the case of property, a minor before majority cannot act, not even to consent;

this should be deferred until majority; but the writ is not faulty.

MINORA REGALIA. [L.] The Crown's revenue in contrast to its power and dignity.

MINOR ATTACHMENT CLAIMANT. A claimant who qualifies to receive benefits and has fewer than 600 hours of insurable employment in their qualifying period *Employment Insurance Act, 1996*, S.C. 1996, c. 23, s. 6.

MINOR CHILD. A child ceases to be a minor child after the last day of the month in which the child attains the age of seventeen years. *Excise Tax Act*, R.S.C. 1985 (1st Supp.), c. 16, s. 5(7.1).

MINORITY. *n.* 1. The situation of being under the age of majority. 2. The smaller part or smaller number. See RELIGIOUS ~.

MINORITY OPINION. The decision and reasons of the minority of three or more judges who heard and decided a case.

MINOR JURARE NON POTEST. [L.] A minor is not able to swear.

MINOR LIEN FUND. The amount required to be retained under section 23(1) or (1.1) plus any amount payable under the contract (i) that is over and above the 10% referred to in section 23(1) or (1.1), and (ii) that, with respect to any work done or materials furnished on and after the date of issue of a certificate of substantial performance, has not been paid by the owner in good faith while there is no lien registered. *Builders' Lien Act*, R.S.A. 2000, c. B-7, s. 1.

MINOR MINOREM CUSTODIRE NON DEBET; ALIOS ENIM PRAESUMITUR MALE REGERE QUI SEIPSUM REGERE NESCIT. [L.] A minor may not be a minor's guardian; for one who does not know how to control oneself is presumed to control others badly.

MINOR, QUI INFRA AETATEM XII ANNORUM FUERIT, UTLAGARI NON POTEST, NEC EXTRA LEGEM PONI, QUIA ANTE TALEM AETATEM NON EST SUB LEGE ALIQUA. [L.] A minor, under twelve years old, cannot be outlawed, nor placed outside the law, because before that age one is not under any law at all.

MINOR VARIANCE. " . . . The term is a relative one and should be flexibly applied: . . . No hard and fast criteria can be laid down, the question whether a variance is minor must in each case be determined in the light of the particular facts and circumstances of the case. . ." *McNamara Corp. v. Colekin Investments Ltd.* (1977), 2 M.P.L.R. 61 at 64, 15 O.R. (2d) 718, 76 D.L.R. (3d) 609 (Div. Ct.), the court per Robins J.

MINOR WATERS OF CANADA. All inland waters of Canada other than Lakes Ontario, Erie, Huron, including Georgian Bay, and Superior and the St. Lawrence River east of a line drawn from Father Point to Point Orient, and includes all bays, inlets and harbours of or on those lakes and Georgian Bay and such sheltered waters on the sea-coasts of Canada as the Minister may specify. *Canada Shipping Act*, R.S.C. 1985, c. S-9, s. 2.

MINOR WATERS SHIP. A ship employed on a minor waters voyage. *Canada Shipping Act*, R.S.C. 1985, c. S-9, s. 2.

MINOR WATERS VOYAGE. A voyage within the following limits, namely, the minor waters of Canada together with such part of any lake or river forming part of the minor waters of Canada as lies within the United States. *Canada Shipping Act*, R.S.C. 1985, c. S-9, s. 2.

MINT. *n*. 1. A place where money in coined. 2. The Royal Canadian Mint established by this Act. The objects of the Mint are to mint coins in anticipation of profit and to carry out other related activities. *Royal Canadian Mint Act*, R.S.C. 1985, c. R-9, ss. 2, 3. See ROYAL CANADIAN ~.

MINT. *adj*. New; in fine condition.

MINTAGE. *n*. Whatever is stamped or coined.

MINUTE. *n*. 1. A record or note of a transaction. 2. 60 seconds. *Weights and Measures Act*, S.C. 1970-71-72, c. 36, schedule I. 3. Of arc, (/10 800 radian. *Weights and Measures Act*, S.C.1970-71-72, c. 36, schedule I.

MINUTES OF PROCEEDINGS AND EVIDENCE. Of legislative and standing committees, a record of the proceedings of a committee prepared and signed by the clerk of that committee. A. Fraser. W.A. Dawson, & J. Holtby, eds., *Beauchesne's Rules and Forms of the House of Commons of Canada*, 6th ed. (Toronto: Carswell, 1989) at 233.

MINUTES OF SETTLEMENT. A document filed with a court which sets out terms by which the parties have agreed to settle the dispute.

MIRANDA WARNING. Named after *Miranda v. Arizona*, 384 U.S. 436 (S.C., 1966)] and given in the following terms: You have the right to remain silent. Anything you say can and will be used against you in a court of law. You have the right to talk to a lawyer before you are questioned and to have him present with you while you're being questioned. If you cannot afford to hire a lawyer, one will be appointed to represent you before questioning if you wish one. You can decide at any time to exercise these rights, not to answer any questions or make any statements. Okay, do you understand each of the rights I've read to you? *R. v. Terry*, [1996] 2 S.C.R. 207.

MISADVENTURE. *n*. Accident, mischance.

MISALLEGE. *v*. To claim falsely as an argument or proof.

MISAPPROPRIATION. *n*. ". . . [Dishonest or fraudulent appropriation of] money or other property entrusted to or received by [a person] whether to his own use or to the use of a third party." *Pay v. Law Society (British Columbia)* (1987), 36 D.L.R. (4th) 313 at 318, [1987] 3 W.W.R. 659, 11 B.C.L.R. (2d) 246 (C.A.), the court per Hinkson J.A.

MISAPPROPRIATION OF PERSONALITY. The common law tort of misappropriation of personality was first articulated by Estey J.A. in the Court of Appeal in *Krouse v. Chrysler Canada Ltd.* (1973), 40 D.L.R. (3d) 15 (Ont. C.A.). While no formal definition of the tort was offered, he stated at pp. 30-1: there may well be circumstances in which the Courts would be justified in holding a defendant liable in damages for appropriation of a plaintiff's personality, amounting to an invasion of his right to exploit his personality by the use of his image, voice, or otherwise with damage to the plaintiff. *Gould Estate v. Stoddart Publishing Co.* (1996), 30 O.R. (3d) 520 (Gen Div.). See RIGHT OF PUBLICITY.

MISBEHAVIOUR. *n*. "[In relation to an office] . . . improper exercise of the functions appertaining to the office, or non-attendance or neglect of or refusal to perform the duties of the office." *Chesley v. Lunenburg (Town)* (1916), 28 D.L.R. 571 at 572, 50 N.S.R. 85 (C.A.), Harris J.A. (Graham C.J. concurring).

MISC. *abbr*. Miscellaneous.

MISCARRIAGE. *n*. 1. " . . . [S]uch departure from the rules which permeate all judicial procedure as to make that which happened not in the proper use of the word judicial procedure at all." *Robins v. National Trust Co.*, [1927] 1 W.W.R. 692 at 695, [1927] A.C. 515, [1927] 2

D.L.R. 97, [1927] All E.R. Rep. 73 (Ont. P.C.), Viscount Dunedin. 2. " . . . Proof of actual prejudice resulting from an error of law is not requisite to a finding that a 'miscarriage of justice' has occurred. It may be enough that an appearance of unfairness exists: . . ." *R. v. Duke* (1985), 39 Alta. L.R. (2d) 313 at 319, [1985] 6 W.W.R. 386, 62 A.R. 204, 22 C.C.C. (3d) 217 (C.A.), the court per McClung J.A. 3. The expulsion of a fetus, usually in the second third of a pregnancy. F.A. Jaffe, *A Guide to Pathological Evidence*, 3d ed. (Toronto: Carswell, 1991) at 223. See PROCURING A ~.

MISCARRIAGE OF JUSTICE. An error of law is defined as any decision that is an erroneous interpretation or application of the law. If an error deprives the accused of a fair trial, it constitutes a miscarriage of justice within the meaning of s. 686(1)(*a*)(iii) of the Criminal Code. *R. c. Arradi*, 2003 SCC 23.

MISCHIEF. *n.* 1. Wilfully destroying or damaging property; rendering property dangerous, useless, inoperative or ineffective; obstructing, interrupting or interfering with the lawful use, enjoyment or operation of property; or obstructing, interrupting or interfering with any person in the lawful use, enjoyment or operation of property. *Criminal Code*, R.S.C. 1985, c. C-46, s. 430(1). 2. Wilfully destroying or altering data, rendering data meaningless, useless or ineffective, obstructing, interrupting or interfering with the lawful use of data; or obstructing, interrupting or interfering with any person in the lawful use of data or denying access to data to any person who is entitled to access thereto. *Criminal Code*, R.S.C. 1985, c. C-46, s. 430(1.1) as added by R.S.C. 1985, c. 27 (1st Supp.), s. 57. 3. " . . . [R]efers to the misuse of confidential information by a lawyer against a former client." *MacDonald Estate v. Martin* (1990), 48 C.P.C. (2d) 113 at 125, [1991] 1 W.W.R. 705, 121 N.R. 1, 77 D.L.R. (4th) 249, 70 Man. R. (2d) 241, [1990] 3 S.C.R. 1235, Sopinka J. (Dickson C.J.C., La Forest and Gonthier JJ. concurring). See PUBLIC ~.

MISCHIEF RULE. 1. It is the duty of every judge to always construe a situation to suppress mischief and advance the remedy. *Heydon's Case* (1584), 3 Co. Rep. 7a at 7b, 76 E.R. 637 (U.K.). 2. A test of the purpose or object of a statute. " . . . [R]e uires the court to consider the evil or defect the law was meant to remedy and to see that the decision reached reinforces the remedy and does not compound the mischief."

Vijendren v. Hopkins (1987), 11 R.F.L. (3d) 132 at 135 (Ont. Prov. Ct.), Campbell Prov. J.

MISCHIEVOUS. *adj.* 1. " . . . '[M]ischievous' in this context [Animals Act, R.S.B.C. 1979, c. 16, s. 20] is affected by its association with 'vicious' and that it involves and denotes the concept of fierce, ferocious, dangerous, attacking, causing harm or injury. It does not, in my opinion, include such ideas as playful, boisterous, demonstrative or excitable." *Kirk v. Trerise* (1981), 17 C.C.L.T. 121 at 125, [1981] 4 W.W.R. 677, 28 B.C.L.R. 165, 122 D.L.R. (3d) 642 (C.A.), McFarlane J.A. (Hutcheon J.A. concurring). 2. As applied to animals means any cross or dangerous animal or an animal which has been shown to have trespassed upon land enclosed by a lawful fence by breaking or jumping over the fence. *Livestock Act*, R.S.Nfld. 1990, c. L-20, s. 2.

MISCOGNISANT. *adj.* Unacquainted with; ignorant of.

MISCONDUCT. *n.* 1. Wilful disobedience. 2. "[A servant] . . . not being able to perform, in a due manner, his duties [to his master], or of not being able to perform his duty in a faithful manner, . . ." *Pearce v. Foster* (1885), 17 Q.B. 536 at 539 (U.K. C.A.), Lord Esher M.R. 3. " . . . [A]s in most other arbitration statutes the only ground stated permitting the Court to set aside or remit an award if for 'misconduct' . . . In Canada . . . the word 'misconduct' is given a very wide meaning going beyond any sense of moral culpability and including an error in law on the face of the award. That which would be mere regrettable error, if done by a Judge, earns for the arbitrator the opprobrium of misconduct' . . ." *Mijon Holdings Ltd. v. Edmonton (City)* (1980), 15 C.P.C. 5 at 11, 12 Alta. L.R. (2d) 88, 109 D.L.R. (3d) 383, 23 A.R. 215 (C.A.), the court per Laycraft J.A. 4. Serious digression from recognized or established standards or rules of conduct in a profession. 5. Failure to perform a duty. 6. The commission of an offence by a member of the forces. 7. "[In reference to a deputy sheriff] . . . includes active misconduct in office also includes a failure through negligence or want of adequate precautions to properly conduct or carry out the duties assigned to the official." *Higgins v. MacDonald*, [1928] 4 D.L.R. 241 at 248, [1928] 3 W.W.R. 115, 50 C.C.C. 353, 40 B.C.R. 150 (C.A.), MacDonald J.A. See PROFESSIONAL ~; STRIKE-RELATED ~.

MISCONTINUANCE. *n.* Stoppage; pause.

MISDELIVERY. *n.* "[Occurs when the goods are received by someone who] . . . had no right to possession either derivatively . . . or otherwise . . ." *Premier Lumber Co. v. Grand Trunk Pacific Railway*, [1923] 1 D.L.R. 649 at 654, [1923] 1 W.W.R. 473, [1923] S.C.R. 84, [1923] C.R.C. 144, Duff J.

MISDEMEANOUR. *n.* A lesser offence than a felony.

MISDESCRIPTION. *n.* An incorrect description.

MISDIRECTION. *n.* 1. An error in law made when a judge charges a jury or when a judge sitting alone puts the wrong questions forward to answer. 2. Failure to refer to a specific piece of evidence will amount to misdirection by a judge requiring a new trial only where that item is the foundation of the defence. *R. v. Demeter* (1975), 25 C.C.C. (2d) 417 (Ont. C.A.), affirmed on other grounds (1977), 34 C.C.C. (2d) 137 (S.C.C.).

MISERA EST SERVITUS, UBI JUS EST VAGUM AUT INCERTUM. [L.] Obedience to law is a hardship, where that law is vague or uncertain.

MISERERE. [L.] Have mercy.

MISERICORDIA. *n.* An arbitrary punishment or amerciament one imposes on someone for an offence.

MISFEASANCE. *n.* The improper execution of a lawful act, e.g. to be guilty of negligence in fulfilling a contract.

MISFEASANCE IN PUBLIC OFFICE. A tort which consists of the elements that the defendants were acting either with malice or with a knowledge that they had no power to do what they were doing, that the defendants' actions were deliberately calculated to injure the plaintiff, and that damage resulted from those actions.

MISJOINDER. *n.* The erroneous involvement of someone as a plaintiff or defendant in an action.

MISLEAD. *v.* "To withhold truthful, relevant and pertinent information may very well have the effect of 'misleading' just as much as to provide, positively, incorrect information." *Hilario v. Canada (Minister of Manpower & Immigration)* (1978), 18 N.R. 529 at 530, [1978] 1 F.C. 697 (C.A.), the court per Heald J.A.

MISLEADING REPRESENTATION. See FALSE OR ~.

MISNOMER. *n.* 1. Naming wrongly. 2. "The test . . . must be: How would a reasonable person receiving the document take it? If, in all the circumstances of the case and looking at the document as a whole, he would say to himself: 'Of course it must mean me, but they have gotten my name wrong', then there is a case of mere misnomer. If, on the other hand, he would say: 'I cannot tell from the document itself whether they mean me or not and I shall have to make inquiries', then it seems to me that one is getting beyond the realm of misnomer. One of the factors which must operate on the mind of the recipient of a document, and which operates in this case, is whether there is or is not another entity to whom the description on the writ might refer." *Davies v. Elsby Bros. Ltd.*, [1960] 3 All E.R. 672 at 676 (U.K. C.A.), Devlin L.J.

MISPLEADING. *n.* Omission of anything essential to a defence or action.

MISPRISION. *n.* Negligence, neglect, oversight.

MISPRISION OF FELONY. For someone who knows that another person committed a felony to conceal or bring about the concealment of that knowledge.

MISPRISION OF TREASON. For someone who knows that another person committed high treason not to inform an appropriate authority within a reasonable time.

MISRECITAL. *n.* A faulty recital.

MISREPRESENT. *v.* " . . . [A]lways connotes a positive act. One cannot misrepresent without positively representing, either by words or conduct, a material circumstance, which circumstance does not truly accord with the representation. . ." *Taylor v. London Assurance Corp.*, [1934] O.R. 273 at 279, [1934] O.W.N. 199, [1934] 2 D.L.R. 657 (C.A.), Masten J.A. (dissenting).

MISREPRESENTATION. *n.* 1. " . . . [M]ay consist just as well in the concealment of that which should be disclosed as in the statement of that which is false for misrepresentation unquestionably may be made by concealment. If the non-disclosure of a material fact which the representor is bound to communicate is deliberate the misrepresentation is a fraudulent one; if it is unintentional it is none the less a misrepresentation though an innocent one." *Stearns v.*

Stearns (1921), 56 D.L.R. 700 at 708, [1921] 1 W.W.R. 40 (Alta. T.D.), Walsh J. 2. " . . . [M]ay be made by silence when either the representee or a third person in his presence, or to his knowledge, states something false which indicates to the representor that the representee either is being, or will be, misled unless the necessary correction is made. Silence under the circumstances is either a tacit adoption by the party of another's misrepresentation as his own or a tacit confirmation of another's error as true." *Toronto Dominion Bank v. Leigh Instruments Ltd. (Trustee of)* (1991), 40 C.C.E.L. 262 at 289, 51 D.A.C. 321, 4 B.L.R. (2d) 220 (Div. Ct.), the court per Rosenberg J. 3. " . . . [A]s used in the relevant sections [of the Income Tax Act (Canada)] must be construed to mean any representation which was false in substance and in fact at the material date and it includes both innocent and fraudulent representations." *Hawrish v. Minister of National Revenue*, [1975] C.T.C. 446 at 453, 75 D.T.C. 5314 (Fed. T.D.), Heald J. 4. (a) An untrue statement of a material fact, or (b) an omission to state a material fact that is (i) required to be stated, or (ii) necessary to prevent a statement that is made from being false or misleading in the circumstances in which it was made. *Securities acts.* 5. An untrue statement of material fact or an omission to state a material fact. See FRAUDULENT ~; INNOCENT ~; NEGLIGENT ~.

MISSED APPROACH PROCEDURE. The procedure to be followed if, for any reason after conducting an instrument approach, a landing is not effected. *Canadian Aviation Regulations*, SOR/96-433, s. 101.01.

MISSING PERSON. 1. A person who cannot be found and whose present place of abode is unascertainable. 2. A person who cannot be found after all reasonable efforts have been made to locate him and includes a person who dies intestate or intestate as to some part of his estate without leaving any known heir-at-law living in the Province or any heir-at-law who can be readily communicated with living elsewhere or where the only heir-at-law is an infant or where Her Majesty in the right of the Province has an interest in the estate or proceeds thereof. *Public Trustee Act*, R.S.N.S. 1989, c. 379, s. 2.

MISSION. See HEAD OF ~.

MIST. *n.* Droplets of liquid suspended in air that are produced by the condensation of a vapourized liquid or by the dispersion of a liquid by a spray container. *Consumer Chemicals and Containers Regulations, 2001*, SOR/2001-269, s. 1.

MISTAKE. *n.* 1. Misunderstanding about the existence of something which arises either from a false belief or ignorance. 2. " . . . [A] written instrument does not accord with the true intention of the party who prepared it. . ." *Farbwerke Hoechst A.G. Vormals Meister Lucius & Bruning v. Canada (Commissioner of Patents)* (1966), 33 Fox Pat. C. 99 at 108, [1966] S.C.R. 604, 50 C.P.R. 220, the court per Martland J. See UNILATERAL ~.

MISTAKE OF FACT. 1. " . . . [A] defence-where, . . . where it prevents an accused from having the mens rea which the law requires for the very crime with which he is charged. Mistake of fact is more accurately seen as a negation of guilty intention than as the affirmation of a positive defence. It avails an accused who acts innocently, pursuant to a flawed perception of the facts, . . ." *R. v. Pappajohn (sub nom. Pappajohn v. R.)* (1980), 52 C.C.C. (2d) 481 at 494, [1980] 2 S.C.R. 120, 14 C.R. (3d) 243, 19 C.R. (3d) 97, [1980] 4 W.W.R. 387, 111 D.L.R. (3d) 1, 32 N.R. 104, Dickson J. 2. A misunderstanding about the existence of some fact or about the existence of a right which depends on questions of mixed fact and law.

MISTAKE OF LAW. 1. An error, not in the actual facts, but relating as to their legal consequence, relevance or significance. D. Stuart, *Canadian Criminal Law: a Treatise*, 2d ed. (Toronto: Carswell, 1987) at 299. 2. An error regarding some general rule of law. 3. Examples of mistakes of law which a statutory decision maker may make include " . . . addressing his or her mind to the wrong question, applying the wrong principle, failing to apply a principle he or she should have applied, or incorrectly applying a legal principle." *Fraser v. Canada (Treasury Board, Department of National Revenue)* (1985), (*sub nom. Fraser v. Public Service Staff Relations Board*) 9 C.C.E.L. 233 at 242, [1985] 2 S.C.R. 455, 18 Admin. L.R. 72, 86 C.L.L.C. 14,003, 63 N.R. 161, 23 D.L.R. (4th) 122, 19 C.R.R. 152, [1986] D.L.Q. 84n, the court per Dickson C.J.C.

MISTAKE OF TITLE. " . . . '[T]he belief that the land is his own.' If the land turns out not to be the property of the person occupying it, and that belief is bona fide, then that is a mistake of title." *Robertson v. Saunders* (1977), 75 D.L.R. (3d) 507 at 512 (Man. Q.B.), Hamilton J.

MISTRESS. *n*. The title of the wife of a gentleman or an esquire.

MISTRIAL. *n*. An incorrect trial.

MISUSER. *n*. The abuse of any benefit or liberty which results in forfeit.

MITIGATE. *v*. To lessen the effect of. See DUTY TO ~.

MITIGATION. *n*. 1. Reduction. 2. A duty or requirement that one who has suffered a loss seek to reduce the damages suffered as a result of the loss. The defendant in an action for breach of contract cannot be called upon to pay for avoidable losses which would result in a larger quantum of damages to be awarded to the plaintiff. 3. [T]he issue of mitigation is . . . one of "damages" and not "liability", at least in the narrow sense of that word. *JJM Construction Ltd. v. Sandspit Harbour Society*, 2000 CarswellBC 622, 2000 BCCA 208 (C.A.).

MITIGATION CONTINGENCY. In relation to claims for damages for death of a family member, an event which will reduce the size of loss experienced because of the family member's death. The two most common events are remarriage and adoption.

MITIGATION OF DAMAGES. " . . . [T]he defendant cannot be called upon to pay for avoidable losses which would result in an increase in the quantum of damages payable to the plaintiff. . . may recover] depend on whether he has taken reasonable steps to avoid their unreasonable accumulation." *Michaels v. Red Deer College*, [1976] 2 S.C.R. 324 at 330-1, [1975] 5 W.W.R. 575, 5 N.R. 99, 75 C.L.L.C. 14,280, 57 D.L.R. (3d) 386, Laskin C.J.C.

MITOCHONDRIAL DNA. Is inherited only from the mother. Although no two people (with the exception of identical twins) have the same nuclear DNA sequence, all maternally related individuals will (in the absence of a mutation) have the same mtDNA sequence. This fact can be both an advantage and a limitation. On the one hand, it is possible to infer the mtDNA sequence of a subject by obtaining and analyzing a blood sample from, for example, her brother or father. On the other hand, mtDNA analysis is capable only of suggesting that the suspect, or any other person related to her in the maternal line, could have left the identifying material at the crime scene. There is a much higher probability of two people possessing the same mtDNA sequence [than nuclear DNA sequence], so the danger that the jury will accept the opinion of the expert as, in effect, deciding the ultimate issue largely disappears. Mitochondrial DNA evidence is just another link in the chain of evidence tending to prove identity. It is not a "genetic fingerprint". *R. v. Murrin* (1999), 1999 CarswellBC 3015, 181 D.L.R. (4th) 320, 32 C.R. (5th) 97 (S.C.).

MIXED FUEL. Fuel that consists of a combination of fuel oil and oxygenate.

MIXED GAME OF CHANCE AND SKILL. " . . . [O]ne in which the element of hazard prevails, notwithstanding the skill and adroitness of the gamesters, and the combinations brought to bear by their understanding and ability. The character of a game does not, however, depend, on the one hand, on the ability and skill of the player, or on the other hand, on his inexperience; it depends entirely on the intrinsic nature of the game or of the contrivance on which it is played. . ." *R. v. Fortier* (1903), 13 Que. K.B. 308 at 313, 7 C.C.C. 417 the court per Wurtele J.

MIXED LAW. A law which concerns both property and people.

MIXED PROPERTY. A combination of personalty and realty.

MIXED QUESTION. A question which arises when foreign and domestic laws conflict. See ~ OF LAW AND FACT.

MIXED QUESTION OF LAW AND FACT. A case in which a jury finds the particular facts, and the court must decide on the legal quality of those facts using established rues of law, without general inferences or conclusions drawn by the jury.

MIXTURE. *n*. A combination of two or more products, materials or substances that do not undergo a chemical change as a result of their interaction. *Consumer Chemicals and Containers Regulations, 2001*, SOR/2001-269, s. 1.

M.L. DIG. & R. *abbr.* Monthly Law Digest and Reporter (Que.), 1892-1893.

M.L.R. (Q.B.). *abbr.* Montreal Law Reports (Queen's Bench), 1885-1891.

M.L.R. (S.C.). *abbr.* Montreal Law Reports (Superior Court), 1885-1891.

M.M.C. *abbr.* Martin's Mining Cases (B.C.), 1853-1908.

M'NAGHTEN'S CASE. See MCNAGHTEN'S CASE.

M'NAUGHTEN'S CASE. See MCNAGH-TEN'S CASE.

M.N.R. *abbr.* Minister of National Revenue.

MOBILE EQUIPMENT. (i) Machinery or equipment capable of being moved to its place of use under its own power or by being towed, pulled or carried and not intended to be affixed to land, and (ii) includes equipment for the purposes of seismographic exploration and, without restricting the generality of the foregoing includes (A) seismographic recording equipment and all appurtenances thereto, (B) conductor cables and cable reels, geophones, amplifiers and cameras, (C) explosive and detonating equipment, (D) drilling units and all the component parts and appurtenances thereof, and (E) water tanks and pumping equipment. See ELECTRICAL ~; SPECIAL ~.

MOBILE HOME. 1. A trailer coach: (i) that is used as a dwelling all the year round; (ii) that has water faucets and shower or other bathing facilities that may be connected to a water distribution system; and (iii) that has facilities for washing and a water closet or other similar facility that may be connected to a sewerage system. 2. A dwelling unit designed to be mobile and to be used, and that is being used, as a permanent or temporary residence. 3. Includes any trailer that is affixed to real property and is designed for or intended to be equipped with wheels, whether or not it is equipped with wheels, and (i) that is constructed or manufactured to provide a residence for one or more persons, whether or not it is in use for that purpose, or (ii) that is used for the conducting of any business.

MOBILE HOME DEALER. A person who acquires, disposes of, exchanges, trades, leases or otherwise deals in mobile homes in the ordinary course of business or pursuant to a scheme or plan for profit.

MOBILE HOME PAD. Land rented as space for and on which a tenant, under a tenancy agreement, is entitled to bring a mobile home.

MOBILE HOME PARK. 1. An area of land designed to provide services, including roads, streets, sidewalks, water, electrical, sewage, gas, communication or other services or facilities, to mobile homes. 2. Land used or occupied by a person for the purpose of providing space for the accommodation of one or more mobile homes and for imposing a charge or rental for the use of that space. 3. The land on which one or more occupied mobile homes are located and includes the rental units and the land, structures, services and facilities of which the landlord retains possession and that are intended for the common use and enjoyment of the tenants of the landlord. *Tenant Protection Act, 1997*, S.O. 1997, c. 24, s.1.

MOBILE HOME SITE. Land rented or intended to be rented as a site for the purpose of being occupied by a mobile home where (i) the mobile home is used for residential purposes, and (ii) the owner of the mobile home is not the same person as the owner of the site on which the mobile home is to be located.

MOBILE HOME SPACE. A plot of ground within a mobile home park designed to accommodate one mobile home.

MOBILE HOUSE. A vehicle that (i) is so constructed as to be capable of being attached to, and drawn on highways by, a motor vehicle, or which can be propelled by a motor vehicle engine installed therein or thereon; and (ii) is intended to be used and is used by persons for living, sleeping, eating, or business purposes, or any one or more of all of those purposes.

MOBILE INDUSTRIAL OR COMMERCIAL STRUCTURE. A portable structure other than a mobile home constructed to be towed on its own chassis designed for use without a permanent foundation on a temporary or permanent basis and which has provision for connection to a supply service.

MOBILE MACHINE. See SPECIAL ~.

MOBILE POLLING STATION. A polling station established for the purpose of taking the vote of electors who are residents of treatment centres or patients in public hospitals.

MOBILE PREMISES. A vehicle or other itinerant food premises from which food is offered for sale to the public but in which no food is prepared other than hot beverages and french fried potatoes.

MOBILE PREPARATION PREMISES. A vehicle or other itinerant food premises from which food prepared therein is offered for sale to the public.

MOBILE STATION. A radio station intended to be used while in motion and during stops; *Radiocommunications Regulations*, SOR 96-484.

MOBILE UNIT. 1. Any structure, whether ordinarily equipped with wheels or not, that is (i) constructed or manufactured to be moved from one location to another by being towed or carried, and (ii) used to provide living or business accommodation or other use for one or more persons. 2. (a) A vacation trailer or house trailer or relocatable trailer, or (ii) a structure whether ordinarily equipped with wheels or not, that is constructed or manufactured to be moved from one point to another by being towed or carried and to provide living accommodation or other use by one or more persons. See MULTIPLE SECTION ~.

MOBILIA SEQUUNTUR PERSONAM. [L.] 1. Movables follow a person. J.G. McLeod, *The Conflict of Laws* (Calgary: Carswell, 1983) at 779. 2. " . . . [F]or certain limited purposes we deal with 'mobilia' (or leave them to be dealt with) under the law governing their owner as though they were situate in his country instead of ours, and, in return, foreign countries generally do the like with regard to English movables situated abroad." *R. v. Lovitt* (1911), [1912] A.C. 212 at 221, 28 T.L.R. 41, 10 E.L.R. 156 (Ca. P.C.), the board per Lord Robson. 3. " . . . [I]s used as a convenient statement of the rule of private international law with reference to the descent of personal property. The law of the domicile, the personal law, is to apply to those who take upon the death of the testator. In the same connection a situs is attributed to things that cannot have any real situs." *Lunness, Re* (1919), 46 O.L.R. 30 at 336, 51 D.L.R. 114, 17 O.W.N. 186 (C.A.), Middleton J.A. (Latch ford J.A. concurring). See MOVABLE.

MOBILITY. See SELF ~.

MOBILITY AID. See MOTORIZED ~.

MOBILITY RIGHTS. 1. "[In s. 6 of the Charter] . . . [R]ights of the person to move about, within and outside the national boundaries." *Skapinker v. Law Society of Upper Canada,* [1984] 1 S.C.R. 357 at 377, 9 D.L.R. (4th) 161, 8 C.R.R. 193, 53 N.R. 169, 3 O.A.C. 321, 11 C.C.C. (3d) 481, 20 Admin. L.R. 1, the court per Estey J. 2. " . . . Section 6(2) [of the Charter] touches only (a) the right to move freely from one province to another; (b) the right to take up residence in the province of one's choice; and (c) the right to work in any province, whether resident there or not." *Reference re Lands Protection Act (Prince Edward Island)* (1987), 48 R.P.R. 92 at 110, 64 Nfld. & P.E.I.R. 249, 197 A.P.R. 249, 40 D.L.R. (4th) 1 (P.E.I. C.A.), McQuaid J.A. (Carruthers C.J.P.E.I. concurring).

MOBILITY VEHICLE. A device or vehicle which is specifically manufactured or modified for operation by a physically handicapped person and which has a maximum speed capability of more than 15 kilometres per hour but not more than 50 kilometres per hour. *The Highway Traffic Act,* C.C.S.M., c. H60, s. 1.

MOCA. Minimum obstruction clearance altitude. means the altitude ASL that will ensure that an IFR aircraft will be clear of the highest obstacle within an airway or air route; *Canadian Aviation Regulations,* SOR/96-433, s. 101.01.

MODE. *n.* Of death, not a strict medical term but a reference to the legal context in which that death occurred: natural or unnatural and, if the latter, accidental, homicidal or suicidal. F.A. Jaffe, *A Guide to Pathological Evidence,* 3d ed. (Toronto: Carswell, 1991) at 12.

MODEL. *n.* 1. Includes design, pattern and specimen. *Official Secrets Act,* R.S.C. 1985, c. O-5, s. 2. 2. Equipment identified by, and permanently marked with, a unique brand, trade name, symbol or logo and an identification code, comprised of letters, numbers or a combination thereof. *Radiocommunications Regulations,* SOR/96-484. See PATENT ~; PROTOTYPE ~; SCALE ~.

MODEL AGREEMENT. See MASTER AGREEMENT.

MODEL AIRCRAFT. An aircraft, the total weight of which does not exceed 35 kg (77.2 pounds), that is mechanically driven or launched into flight for recreational purposes and that is not designed to carry persons or other living creatures. *Canadian Aviation Regulations,* SOR/96-433, s. 101.01.

MODEL DESIGNATION. Any combination of letters or figures or both letters and figures by which a device that bears that designation is claimed to have characteristics and design features that are uniform. Canada regulations.

MODEL ROCKET. A rocket (*a*) equipped with model rocket engines that will not generate a total impulse exceeding 80 newton-seconds, (*b*) of a gross weight, including engines, not exceeding 500 g (1.1 pounds), and (*c*) equipped with a parachute or other device capable of retarding its descent. *Canadian Aviation Regulations,* SOR/96-433, s. 101.01.

MODEL YEAR. The year, as determined under section 5, that is used by a manufacturer to designate a model of vehicle or engine. *On-Road*

Vehicle and Engine Emission Regulations, SOR/2003-2, s. 1.

MODERATOR. *n*. Chairman; president.

MODERN PRINCIPLE. " . . . [A] contextual interpretation, which E.A. Driedger terms 'the modern principle' of statutory construction, which he defines as follows (Construction of Statutes (2nd ed., 1983), p. 87): 'Today there is only one principle or approach, namely, the words of an Act are to be read in their entire context and in their grammatical and ordinary sense harmoniously with the scheme of the Act, the object of the Act, and the intention of Parliament.'" *Crupi v. Canada (Employment & Immigration Commission)* (1986), 10 C.C.E.L. 286 at 312, 66 N.R. 93 (Fed. C.A.), MacGuigan J.A. (dissenting).

MODERN RULE OF INTERPRETATION. The meaning of legislation must be determined in its total context, having regard to its purpose, the consequences of proposed interpretations, the presumptions and rules of interpretation and admissible external evidence. The courts must consider and take into account all admissible factors which indicate the meaning. The court then must adopt an appropriate interpretation that can be justified in terms of plausibility that it complies with the words of the legislation, efficacy in promotion of the legislative purpose, and acceptability in producing a reasonable and just result.

MODIFIED UNION SHOP. A place of work where the employer and union agree that all present members and those who join later must remain members of the union but those not members at the time of the agreement need not join.

MODIFY. *v*. To enlarge, extend, decrease, change.

MOD. L. REV. *abbr*. Modern Law Review.

MODO ET FORMA. [L.] In manner and form.

MODU. A mobile offshore unit that is designed or fitted for drilling operations beneath the seabed for the exploration for, or exploitation of, resources such as liquid or gaseous hydrocarbons, sulphur or salt. *Marine Certification Regulations*, SOR/97-391, s. 1.

MODULAR BUILDING UNIT. A building component or unit, the manufacture and assembly of which is completed or substantially completed before delivery to a construction site, that is designed for installation on a foundation and is composed of at least one room or area with finished walls, a finished floor and a finished ceiling, including installed plumbing, heating and electrical equipment appropriate to that room or area, and that, when installed on a foundation at the site with or without other similarly manufactured and assembled components or units, forms a complete residential, commercial, educational, institutional or industrial building, but does not include any freestanding appliances or furniture sold with the unit. *Excise Tax Act*, R.S.C. 1985 (2d Supp.), c. 7, s. 1(4).

MODULAR HOME. 1. A house that is intended for residential purposes and that is constructed by assembling manufactured modular units each of which comprises at least one room or living area and has been manufactured to comply with the standards set out in the National Building Code of Canada. *Revenue Tax Act*, R.S.P.E.I. 1988, c. R-14, s. 1. 2. A house that is intended for residential purposes and that is constructed by assembling manufactured modular units each of which comprises at least one room or living area, has been manufactured to comply with the A277 series of standards prescribed by the Canadian Standards Association and bears the seal of that association attesting to such compliance. *Retail Sales Tax Act*, R.S.O. 1990, c. R.31, s. 1.

MODU/INLAND. A MODU/self-elevating or MODU/surface that is capable of operating in the inland waters of Canada or the minor waters of Canada. *Marine Certification Regulations*, SOR/97-391, s. 1.

MODUS. *n*. [L.] Manner; method.

MODU/SELF-ELEVATING. A MODU with movable legs that is capable of raising its hull above the surface of the sea. *Marine Certification Regulations*, SOR/97-391, s. 1.

MODUS ET CONVENTIO VINCUNT LEGEM. [L.] Custom and agreement override law.

MODUS LEGEM DAT DONATIONI. [L.] Custom makes a donation legal.

MODUS OPERANDI. [L.] Method of operating.

MODUS PROCEDENDI. [L.] Method of proceeding.

MODUS TENENDI. [L.] Manner of holding.

MODUS TRANSFERRENDI. [L.] Manner of transferring.

MODU/SURFACE. A MODU with a ship- or barge-type displacement hull of single or multiple hull construction intended for operation in the floating condition. *Marine Certification Regulations*, SOR/97-391, s. 1.

MODUS VACANDI. [L.] Manner of vacating.

MODUS VIVENDI. [L.] Way of living.

MOIETY. *n.* A half; any fraction.

MOLASSES SPIRIT. An alcoholic distillate, obtained from sugar-cane by-products fermented by the action of yeast, from which all or nearly all of the naturally occurring substances other than alcohol and water have been removed. *Food and Drug Regulations*, C.R.C., c. 870, c. B.02.002.

MONARCHY. *n.* A government in which a single person holds supreme power.

MONETANDI JUS COMPREHENDITUR IN REGALIBUS QUAE NUNQUAM A REGIO SCEPTRO ABDICANTUR. [L.] The right to coin money is included in those royal rights which are never distinct from the royal sceptre.

MONETARY CONTRIBUTION. An amount of money provided that is not repayable.

MONETARY LOSS. Does not include pain and suffering, physical inconvenience and discomfort, social discredit, injury to reputation, mental suffering, injury to feelings, loss of amenities and of expectation of life or loss of society of spouse or child. *Judgment Debts Instalments Act*, R.S. Nfld. 1990, c. J-2, s. 2.

MONEY. *n.* 1. " . . . [A]s commonly understood is not necessarily legal tender. Any medium which by practice fulfils the function of money and which everybody will accept in payment of a debt is money in the ordinary sense of the words even though it may not be legal tender . . ." *Reference re Alberta Legislation*, [1938] 2 D.L.R. 81 at 92, [1938] S.C.R. 100, Duff C.J.C. (Davis J. concurring). 2. " . . . [W]hen used in a will means money in its strict sense unless there is a context which is sufficient to show that the testator used it in a more extended sense . . ." *Lubeck, Re*, [1927] 1 W.W.R. 980 at 981 (Alta. C.A.), Clarke J.A. 3. " . . . [I]n the strict sense includes cash in hand and in the bank and any money for which at the time of his death the testator might have claimed immediate payment: . . ." *Couperthwaite v. Couperthwaite*, [1950] 2 W.W.R. 58 at 63, [1950] 3 D.L.R. 229 (Sask.

C.A.), the court per Martin C.J.S. 4. Includes currency, government or bank notes, cheques, drafts, post office, express and bank money orders. 5. Includes negotiable instruments. 6. A medium of exchange authorized by the Parliament of Canada or authorized or adopted by a foreign government as part of its currency. *Personal Property Security Act*, S.A. 1988, c. P-4.05, s. 1(1). 7. "[In the Jury Act, S.A. 1982, c. J-2.1, s. 17(1)] . . . should be interpreted to mean money or money's worth." *Sayers v. Shell Canada Resources Ltd.* (1984), 64 A.R. 319 at 320 (C.A.), the court per Kerans J.A. See ATTENDANCE ~; CONDUCT ~; COUNTERFEIT ~; GARNISHABLE ~S; GUARANTEED TRUST ~; HEAD ~; HUSH-~; INDIAN ~S; INSURANCE ~; MILLED ~; MORTGAGE ~; OFFICE ~; PAPER ~; PRINCIPAL ~; PUBLIC ~; PURCHASE ~; QUANTITY THEORY OF ~; SCHOOL ~S; SHARE~; TRUST ~.

MONEY BILL. A bill to impose, repeal, remit, alter or regulate taxation, to impose charges on a consolidated fund to pay debt or for other financial purposes or to supply government requirements.

MONEY BROKER. A person who raises or lends money for or to other people.

MONEY BY-LAW. 1. A by-law for contracting a debt or obligation or for borrowing money. 2. A by-law which must be advertised and may be required to be submitted to a vote of the proprietary electors. Alberta statutes.

MONEY HAD AND RECEIVED. Money a defendant has received and which for reasons of equity the defendant should not retain. See ACTION FOR ~.

MONEY LAUNDERING. Occurs when money produced through criminal activity is converted into "clean money", the criminal origins of which are obscured. See LAUNDERING PROCEEDS OF CRIME.

MONEY-LENDER. *var.* **MONEY LENDER**. A person who carries on the business of money lending or advertises or claims in any way to carry on that business, but does not include a registered pawn broker as such.

MONEY LENT. Includes money advanced or credit granted to or on account of any person in any transaction that, whatever its form may be, is substantially one of money-lending or credit granting or securing the repayment of money so advanced or extended in the way of credit and includes a mortgage or real or personal property, or both.

MONEY MARKET DEALERS. Those resident controlled dealers approved by the Bank of Canada from time to time as money market dealers. *Securities Act*, R.R.O. 1980, Reg. 910, s. 84.

MONEY OF ACCOUNT. The currency in which one expresses or calculates a debt.

MONEY OF PAYMENT. The currency in which one discharges an obligation. J.G. McLeod, *The Conflict of Laws* (Calgary: Carswell, 1983) at 517.

MONEY ORDER. An order to pay money which may be purchased at a bank or post office.

MONEY PAID TO THE PROVINCE FOR A SPECIAL PURPOSE. Includes all money paid to a public officer under a statute, trust, treaty, undertaking or contract, to be disbursed for a purpose specified in such statute, trust, treaty, undertaking or contract.

MONEY PRIZE. A sum of money payable as the result of the selection of a winning ticket under a lottery scheme.

MONGER. *n*. A seller, dealer.

MONIMENT. *n*. A memorial, record or superscription.

MONITOR. *n*. A person appointed by a security holder to review and report on the cash flow, accounts payable and assets of a debtor's business if that security holder is unsure that the business is presently viable. F. Bennett, *Receiverships* (Toronto: Carswell, 1985) at 4. See ALARM ~.

MONITORING. *n*. Obtaining and analyzing samples. *Clean Environment Act*, S.N.B. 1975, c. 12, s. 1. See ENVIRONMENTAL ~; MEDICAL ~.

MONOCRACY. *n*. Government by a single person.

MONOFILAMENT. *n*. Any single filament having more than 50 deniers, that is weighing more than 50 grams per 9 000 metres of filament. *Fishery regulations*.

MONOGAMY. *n*. The marriage of one wife to one husband.

MONOGRAPH. See PRODUCT ~.

MONOPOLY. *n*. A situation where one or more persons either substantially or completely control throughout Canada or any area thereof the class or species of business in which they are engaged and have operated that business or are likely to operate it to the detriment or against the interest of the public, whether consumers, producers or others, but a situation shall not be deemed a monopoly within the meaning of this definition by reason only of the exercise of any right or enjoyment of any interest derived under the Patent Act or any other Act of Parliament. *Combines Investigation Act*, R.S.C. 1985, c. C-34, s. 2.

MONSTRANS DE DROIT. [Fr.] The display or plea of a right.

MONSTRANS DE FAITS OU RECORDS. [Fr.] The display of deeds or records.

MONTH. *n*. 1. A calendar month. 2. A period calculated from a day in one month to a day numerically corresponding to that day in the following month. 3. Includes part of a month. 4. Thirty days. 5. The period commencing on a date in one calendar month and terminating on the day immediately preceding the same date in the next calendar month or, if there is no corresponding date in the next calendar month, terminating on the last day of such calendar month. Canada regulations. See ANIMAL UNIT ~; ANNIVERSARY ~; CALENDAR ~; TENANCY ~.

MONTH OF TENANCY. The monthly period on which the tenancy is based and not necessarily a calendar month and, unless otherwise specifically agreed upon, the month shall be deemed to begin on the day upon which rent is payable. *Landlord and Tenant acts*.

MONTREAL DECLARATION ON PUBLIC ACCESS TO LAW. Legal information institutes of the world, meeting in Montreal, declare that: Public legal information from all countries and international institutions is part of the common heritage of humanity. Maximizing access to this information promotes justice and the rule of law; Public legal information is digital common property and should be accessible to all on a non-profit basis and, where possible, free of charge; Independent non-profit organizations have the right to publish public legal information and the government bodies that create or control that information should provide access to it so that it can be published. See CANADIAN LEGAL INFORMATION INSTITUTE; LEGAL INFORMATION INSTITUTE.

MONUMENT. *n*. 1. An iron post, wooden post, mound, pit or trench, or anything else used to mark a boundary corner or line by a qualified surveyor. 2. A monumental stone placed above the level of the surrounding ground at the head of a grave or plot. *National Parks Cemetery Regulations*, C.R.C., c. 1117, s. 2. See BOUNDARY ~; CO-ORDINATE ~; HISTORIC ~; LEGAL ~; LOST ~; OBLITERATED ~; ORIGINAL ~; OUTLINE ~.

MONUMENTA QUAE NOS RECORDA VOCAMUS SUNT VERITATIS ET VETUSTATIS VESTIGIA. [L.] The writing we call records are footprints of truth and tradition.

MOONLIGHT. *v*. To hold more than one job for more than one employer.

MOO. P.C. *abbr*. Moore, Privy Council.

MOO. P.C. (N.S.). *abbr*. Moore (N.S.) Privy Council.

MOOT. *n*. An exercise in which students plead and argue doubtful questions and cases.

MOOT. *adj*. A case is moot when something occurs after proceedings are commenced which eliminates the issue between the parties.

MOOTNESS. *n*. 1. " . . . [A]n aspect of a general policy or practice that a court may decline to decide a case which raises merely a hypothetical or abstract question. The general principle applies when the decision of the court will not have the effect of resolving some controversy which affects or may affect the rights of the parties. If the decision of the court will have no practical effect on such rights, the court will decline to decide the case. This essential ingredient must be present not only when the action or proceeding is commenced but at the time when the court is called upon to reach a decision. Accordingly if, subsequent to the initiation of the action or the proceeding, events occur which affect the relationship of the parties so that no present live controversy exists which affects the rights of the parties, the case is said to be moot." *Borowski v. Canada (Attorney General)* (1989), 38 C.R.R. 232 at 239, [1989] 3 W.W.R. 97, 33 C.P.C. (2d) 105, 47 C.C.C. (3d) 1, 57 D.L.R. (4th) 231, 92 N.R. 110, [1989] 1 S.C.R. 342, 75 Sask. R. 82, the court per Sopinka J. 2. The criteria for courts to consider in exercising discretion to hear a moot case (at pp. 358-63) are: (1) the presence of an adversarial context; (2) the concern for judicial economy; and (3) the need for the Court to be sensitive to its role as the adjudicative branch in our political framework. Sopinka, J. in *Borowski v. Canada*, cited above.

MOPED. *n*. 1. A motor vehicle which (i) has 2 tandem wheels or 3 wheels, each of which is more than 410 millimetres in diameter, (ii) has a set or saddle having a minimum unladen height of 700 millimetres, when measured from the ground level to the top of the forwardmost part of the seat or saddle, (ii) is capable of being driven at all times by pedals only, by motor only, or both, and the motor has a piston displacement of not more than 50 cubic centimetres, or is an electric motor neither of which is capable of enabling the moped to attain a speed greater than 50 kilometres per hour. 2. A passenger vehicle having two or three wheels and a net mass not in a excess of 60 kg, provided with a motor having a piston displacement of not over 50 cm³ and equipped with an automatic transmission, as well as a three-wheel passenger vehicle designed for the transportation of a handicapped person which meets the criteria established by regulation for recognition as a moped by the Régie. *Highway Safety Code*, S.Q. 1986, c. 91, s. 4. See MOTOR ASSISTED PEDAL BICYCLE.

MORA. *n*. [L.] Delay.

MORA DEBITORIS NON DEBET ESSE CREDITORI DAMNOSA. [L.] Delay by the one who owes should not be injurious to the one to whom the thing is owed.

MORAL ACTION. A situation in which a person has knowledge for guidance and will to choose freely.

MORAL CERTAINTY. Proof beyond a reasonable doubt is equivalent to proof beyond a moral certainty. The general standard of proof in criminal law.

MORAL CULPABILITY. In sentencing, examination of the intentional risks taken by the offender, the harm caused, and the degree of deviation from acceptable standards of behaviour the conduct constitutes.

MORAL HAZARD. Factors such as solvency, past record of claims, any record of fraud or arson convictions in respect of which an insurer may assess an applicant for insurance. M.G. Baer & J.A. Rendall, eds., *Cases on the Canadian Law of Insurance*, 4th ed. (Toronto: Carswell, 1988) at 7.

MORALITY. *n*. Section 76(2) of the *School Act* clearly distinguishes between "the highest morality" and religious dogmas or creeds. That morality, while it may originate in religious reflection, must stand independently of its origins to maintain the allegiance of the whole of society including the plurality of religious adherents and those who are not religious. In this context, the highest morality is public virtue in a truly free society. Public virtue upholds the dignity of the individual, the first principle which underlies the Charter and informs all of public life in a truly free society. That highest morality includes non-discrimination on grounds of sexual orientation. *Chamberlain v. Surrey School District No. 36*, 2000 CarswellBC 2009, 80 B.C.L.R. (3d) 181, [2000] 10 W.W.R. 393, 191 D.L.R. (4th) 128, 143 B.C.A.C. 162, 235 W.A.C. 162, 26 Admin. L.R . (3d) 297 (C.A.), Esson, Mackenzie, Proudfoot JJ.A. See INTERNATIONAL ~.

MORAL OBLIGATION. "[Considering oneself] . . . compelled to [do something] by what [one] thought was the right thing to do." *Norman v. Norman* (1972), 11 R.F.L. 105 at 106, 32 D.L.R. (3d) 262 (N.S. T.D.), Bissett J.

MORAL PREJUDICE. Moral prejudice has been defined as including loss of enjoyment of life, esthetic prejudice, physical and psychological pain and suffering, inconvenience, loss of amenities, and sexual prejudice. *Québec (Curateur public) c. Syndicat national des employés de l'hôpital St-Ferdinand*, 1996 CarswellQue 916, 202 N.R. 321, (sub nom. *Quebec (Public Curator) v. Syndicat national des employés de l'hôpital St-Ferdinand*) 138 D.L.R. (4th) 577, 1 C.P.C. (4th) 183, [1996] 3 S.C.R. 211. L'Heureux-Dube for the court.

MORAL RIGHTS. The rights the author of a work has, subject to the *Copyright Act*, the right to the integrity of the work and, in connection with an act, the right, where reasonable in the circumstances, to be associated with the work as its author by name or under a pseudonym and the right to remain anonymous. *Copyright Act*, R.S.C. 1985, c.C-42, s. 14.1(1).

MORAL RISK. " . . . [T]wo main categories of risk which concern an insurer in its decision as to whether or not it will accept a particular application for insurance. . . [one] is what is known as the moral risk. The risk relates to the insured person himself." *Chernier v. Madill* (1973), 43 D.L.R. (3d) 28 at 32, 2 O.R. (2d) 361, [1974] I.L.R. 1-585 (H.C.), Galligan J.

MORALS. See CORRUPTING ~.

MORAL TURPITUDE. Baseness or depravity in private or social duties, contrary to the customary rules of behaviour among persons.

MORA REPROBATUR IN LEGE. [L.] In law, delay is not approved.

MORATORIUM. *n*. The authorized delay in paying a debt.

MORE OR LESS. 1. A phrase used to compensate for slight inaccuracies in description in a contract for the sale of land or conveyance. 2. " . . . '[A]bout' . . . words of general import and the excess or deficiency, as the case may be, which they cover bears a very small proportion to the amount named. . ." *Canada Law Book Co. v. Boston Book Co.* (1922), 64 S.C.R. 182 at 200-201, 66 D.L.R. 209, Anglin J. (Mignault J. concurring).

MORGUE. See PRIVATE ~; PUBLIC ~.

MORPHINE. *n*. The main alkaloid in opium, an analgesic and narcotic.

MORS DICITUR ULTIMUM SUPPLICIUM. [L.] Death is called the ultimate penalty.

MORS IN TABULA. [L. death on the table] Death in the operating room. F.A. Jaffe, *A Guide to Pathological Evidence*, 3d ed. (Toronto: Carswell, 1991) at 223.

MORS OMNIA SOLVIT. [L.] Death settles all differences.

MORTGAGE. *v*. To convey as security for a debt.

MORTGAGE. *n*. 1. The conveyance of land as a security for the discharge of an obligation or the payment of a debt, a security which may be redeemed when the obligation or debt is discharged or paid. B.J. Reiter, B.N. McLellan & P.M. Perell, *Real Estate Law*, 4th ed. (Toronto: Emond Montgomery, 1992) at 813. 2. Any charge on real property or chattels real for securing money or moneys worth and includes a part of a mortgage or an interest in a mortgage and a mortgage of a mortgage. 3. Includes (i) an assignment, transfer, conveyance, declaration of trust without transfer or other assurance of chattels intended to operate as a mortgage or pledge of chattels, (ii) a power or authority or licence to take possession of chattels as security, and (iii) an agreement, whether intended or not to be followed by the execution of any other instrument, by which a right in equity to charge or security on any chattels is conferred, but does not include (iv) a mortgage or charge, whether specific or floating, of chattels, created by a corporation, and contained (A) in a trust deed or other like instrument to secure bonds, debentures, or debenture stock of the corporation, (B) in any bonds, debentures, or debenture stock of the corporation, as well as in the trust deed or other like instrument securing the bonds, debentures or debenture stock, or (C) in any bonds, debentures, or debenture stock or any series of bonds or debentures of the corporation and not secured by any trust deed or other like instrument, (v) security taken by a bank under section 88 of the Bank Act, (Canada), or (vi) a power of distress contained in a mortgage of real property. *Bills of Sale acts.* See BANK ~ SUBSIDIARY; BLANKET ~; BUILDER'S ~; CANADA ~ AND HOUSING CORPORATION; CHATTEL ~; CONVERTIBLE ~; DERIVATIVE ~; EQUITABLE LEASEHOLD ~; EQUITABLE ~; FIRST ~; GRADUATED PAYMENT ~; LEGAL LEASEHOLD ~; LEGAL ~; PARTICIPATION ~; PURCHASE-MONEY ~; SECOND ~; SUB ~; UNIT ~; VARIABLE RATE ~; VENDOR TAKE-BACK ~; WELSH ~; WRAP-AROUND ~.

MORTGAGE BACK. In a sale of a property, the vendor receives a mortgage on the property in exchange for loaning part of the purchase price.

MORTGAGE BOND. A corporate debt security in which the indenture is a mortgage on property of the corporation and the indenture trustee is mortgagee on behalf of the bondholders. See FIRST ~.

MORTGAGE BROKER. A person who, (i) directly or indirectly, carries on the business of lending money on the security of real estate, whether the money is personal or that of another person; (ii) carries on the business of dealing in mortgages; or (ii) represents or, by an advertisement, notice or sign, claims to be a mortgage broker or a person who carries on the business of dealing in mortgages. See CARRY ON BUSINESS AS A ~.

MORTGAGE COMMITMENT. A document issued by a lender to a borrower when, based on a credit report and property appraisal, the lender decides to go ahead with the loan.

MORTGAGE DEALER. A person who (a) either directly or indirectly arranges for the investment by another person, in a mortgage, whether that investment is effected, or is intended to be effected, by making a loan secured by a mortgage, by selling a mortgage to that other person or by buying a mortgage for that other person, (b) lends money on mortgages and sells mortgages securing the loans, (c) as principal, buys and sells mortgages or who acts as an agent in the purchase or sale of a mortgage, (d) arranges or places mortgages for other whether by obtaining loans for borrowers or by finding mortgage investments for lenders, or both, (e) registers a mortgage, a mortgage of a mortgage, or a transfer of a mortgage in the mortgage dealer's name where another person or other persons have contributed mortgage moneys or are entitled to share the proceeds of the mortgage, or both, (f) for a reward or hope or promise thereof, administers a mortgage for or on behalf of any other person, or (g) holds himself or herself out as doing any of the things mentioned in sub-clauses (a) to (f). *The Mortgage Dealers Act,* C.C.S.M., c. M210, s. 1.

MORTGAGE DEBENTURE. ". . . [F]orm of security, a debenture which is both an obligation for the payment of the money which is payable by the terms of it, and a mortgage on the property of the company by which it is issued, or some part of it, or secured by such a mortgage, . . ." *Farmers Loan & Savings Co., Re* (1898), 20 O.R. 337 at 354 (C.A.), Meredith J.A.

MORTGAGEE. *n.* 1. The owner of a mortgage. 2. The person who assumes a mortgage to secure a loan. 3. Includes chargee. 4. Includes a vendor under an agreement for the sale of land. 5. Includes a person from time to time deriving title under the original mortgage. 6. Includes a trustee for holders of bonds, debentures, notes or other evidences of indebtedness. See SUBSEQUENT PURCHASER OR ~.

MORTGAGEE IN POSSESSION. A mortgagee who, in right of the mortgage, has entered into and is in possession of the mortgaged property.

MORTGAGE INSURANCE. Insurance against loss caused by default on the part of a borrower under a loan secured by a mortgage upon real property, a hypothec upon immovable property or an interest in real or immovable property.

MORTGAGE LENDER. A person who carries on the business of lending money on the security of land, whether the money is his or her own or that of another person.

MORTGAGE MONEY. Money or money's worth secured by a mortgage. *Casson v. Westmorland Investment Ltd.* (1961), 27 D.L.R. (2d) 674 at 677, 33 W.W.R. 28 (B.C. C.A.), the court per Tysoe J.A.

MORTGAGE TRANSACTION. The borrowing of money on the security of real property or the assignment of a mortgage for consideration.

MORTGAGE TRUST. A trustee holds mortgaged assets on behalf of multiple lenders on the same mortgage security. D.M.W. Waters, *The Law of Trusts in Canada*, 2d ed. (Toronto: Carswell, 1984) at 450.

MORTGAGOR. *n.* 1. One who borrows on security of property. 2. A person who gives a mortgage to secure a loan. 3. The owner or transferee of land or of any estate or interest in land pledged as security for a debt or loan. 4. Includes chargor. See ORIGINAL ~.

MORTIS CAUSA. See DONATIO ~; GIFT~.

MORTIS CAUSA DONATIO. See DONATIO MORTIS CAUSA.

MORTMAIN. *n.* [Fr. dead hand] 1. The state of possession of land which makes it inalienable. 2. Refers to a corporation's owning of real property. R. Megarry and H.W.R. Wade, *The Law of Real Property*, 5th ed. (London: Stevens, 1984) at cxxvi. See ALIENATION IN ~.

MORTMAIN ACT. An act which forbade the conveyance of land into the "dead hand" of the church or another corporation because a lord might thus be deprived of the benefits of tenure which arose in the lord's favour when the tenant died, because such conveyance prevented free alienation. Under these acts, the Crown always had the power to regulate the holding of land and there were significant statutory exceptions to these rules. E.L.G. Tyler & N.E. Palmer, eds., *Crossley Vaines' Personal Property*, 5th ed. (London: Butterworths, 1973) at 16.

MORTUARY. *n.* A place where dead bodies are received before interment.

MORTUUM VADIUM. [L.] Dead pledge; mortgage.

MOST-FAVOURED NATION CLAUSE. In a treaty, the provision that one party grants to the other party the same treatment granted to the most-favoured nation.

MOTEL. *n.* A tourist establishment that (i) consists of one or more than one building containing attached accommodation units accessible from the exterior only, (ii) may or may not have facilities for serving meals, and (ii) is designed to accommodate the public for whom the automobile is the principal means of transportation.

MOTHER. *n.* 1. "... [A] person who has borne a child." *Bear v. Winnipeg North (Director of Walfare)* (1978), 3 R.F.L. (2d) 59 at 60 (Man. C.A.), the court per Monnin J.A. 2. "... [A] woman in relation to her child—a female parent; and in broad sense it means that which is a source of anything—a generatrix—in which sense it refers to the origin, cause, or root of anything. . ." *Rutherford, Re* (1917), 40 O.L.R. 266 at 268 (H.C.), Kelly J. 3. A person who takes care of a child of whom she is the legitimate, natural or adoptive mother, or the stepmother. 4. Includes a grandmother. 5. (i) A woman who (A) has, while single, been delivered of an illegitimate child, (B) being single, is pregnant and likely to be delivered of an illegitimate child, (C) was single at the time of her conception of a child, who if its mother continued single would be an illegitimate child, whether or not its mother is single at the time of the birth of such child, or (D) is single at the date of her illegitimate child's birth, whether or not she is single at the date of the commencement of affiliation proceedings, or (ii) a married woman who (A) is living apart from her husband and has been delivered of an illegitimate child, or (B) is pregnant and likely to be delivered of an illegitimate child and was living apart from her husband at the time of the conception of the child. See BIOLOGICAL ~; BIRTH ~; WIDOWED ~.

MOTHER OF PARLIAMENTS. The Parliament of the United Kingdom.

MOTHER TONGUE. The first language learned and still understood at the relevant time.

MOTION. *n.* An oral or written application that the court rule or make an order before, during or after a trial. See DILATORY ~; INCIDENTAL ~; NOTICE OF ~; ORIGINATING ~; PRIVILEGED ~; SUBSIDIARY ~; SUBSTANTIVE ~; SUPERSEDING ~; WAYS AND MEANS ~.

MOTION FOR DIRECTED VERDICT. An application for a decision by a trial judge that there is no case to put to the jury. P.K. McWilliams, *Canadian Criminal Evidence*, 3d ed. (Aurora: Canada Law Book, 1988) at 27-28.

MOTION FOR JUDGMENT. The plaintiff may request judgment in any action in which the parties did not sign a default judgment.

MOTION PICTURE. Includes a television or other audio visual production whether on cinematographic film, videotape, video-disc or other medium. See ADULT ~; FEATURE ~.

MOTION PICTURE DISTRIBUTOR. A person who distributes a film to a proprietor, lessee, manager or employee of a theatre or who contracts respecting films with any of those persons or with any other motion picture distributor.

MOTION PICTURE MACHINE. Includes a cinematograph or other similar apparatus used for the showing of films or slides.

MOTION PICTURE THEATRE. Includes a theatre, hall, building, premises, room or place, including an open air place commonly known as a drive in theatre.

MOTIVE. *n.* 1. " . . . [T]hat which precedes and induces the exercise of the will. . . in criminal law sense [means] 'ulterior intention' . . ." *R. v. Lewis* (1979), 98 D.L.R. (3d) 111 at 120-1, [1979] 2 S.C.R. 821, 27 N.R. 451, 10 C.R. (3d) 299 (Eng.), 12 C.R. (3d) 315 (Fr.), 47 C.C.C. (2d) 24, the court per Dickson J. 2. " . . . [R]efers to an emotion or inner feeling such as hate or greed which is likely to lead to the doing of an act. The word 'motive' is also used, however, to refer to external events, for example, a previous quarrel, which is likely to excite the relevant feeling." *R. v. Malone* (1984), 11 C.C.C. (3d) 34 at 43, 2 O.A.C. 321 (C.A.), Martin J.A. (Lacourcière and Goodman JJ.A. concurring).

MOTIVE FUEL. 1. (a) Diesel fuel, or (b) a combination of fuels including diesel fuel, for use in propelling a motor vehicle. 2. Fuel for an internal combustion engine, and, without restricting the generality of the foregoing, includes gasoline, distillate, and diesel fuel and also includes oil and grease for the lubrication of such an engine or of agricultural machinery. 3. An gas fuel or liquid fuel that is not gasoline and that can be used for moving or operating any internal combustion engine or machine, or for heating and without restricting the generality of the foregoing includes kerosene, propane, crude oil, distillate and other motor fuel, but does not include natural gas or manufactured gas that is used as a fuel. See BULK ~.

MOTOR. *n.* An internal combustion engine used in a vehicle. *Environmental Protection Act*, R.S.O. 1990, c. E.19, s. 21. See MULTI-WINDING ~; PART-WINDING START ~.

MOTOR ASSISTED BICYCLE. A bicycle, (a) that is fitted with pedals that are operable at all times to propel the bicycle, (b) that weighs not more than fifty-five kilograms, (c) that has no hand or foot operated clutch or gear box driven by the motor and transferring power to the driven wheel, (d) that has an attached motor driven by electricity or having a piston displacement of not more than fifty cubic centimetres, and (e) that does not have sufficient power to enable the bicycle to attain a speed greater than 50 kilometres per hour on level ground within a distance of 2 kilometres from a standing start. *Highway Traffic Act*, R.S.O. 1990, c. H.8, s. 1(1).

MOTOR ASSISTED PEDAL BICYCLE. A vehicle that (i) is provided with an electric motor or a motor having a piston displacement no greater than fifty cubic centimeters, (ii) is not capable of obtaining speed of greater than 50 km/h on the level when driven by a person weighing 60 kg, and (iii) has no more than three wheels in contact with the ground. *Highway Traffic Act*, R.S.P.E.I. 1988, c. H-5, s. 1(k.2). See MOPED.

MOTOR BOAT. Includes every vessel propelled by machinery and not more than 65 feet in length, other than vessels towing, the length to be measured from end to end, over the deck, excluding sheer. *Rules of the Road for the Great Lakes*, C.R.C., c. 1464, s. 2.

MOTOR CARRIER. 1. A person operating, whether alone or with another, a motor vehicle with or without trailer attached, as a public passenger vehicle or as a freight vehicle. 2. A person that operates or causes to be operated a public motor bus or a public motor truck. 3. A person operating a public service vehicle or a commercial truck.

MOTOR-CIRCUIT SWITCH. A fused or unfused manually-operated knife or snap switch rated in horsepower.

MOTORCYCLE. *var.* **MOTOR CYCLE**. An on-road vehicle with a headlight, taillight and stoplight that has two or three wheels and a curb weight of 793 kg (1,749 pounds) or less, but does not mean a vehicle that has an engine displacement of less than 50 cm³ (3.1 cubic inches), or that, with an 80 kg (176 pound) driver (*a*) cannot start from a dead stop using only the engine; or (*b*) cannot exceed a speed of 40 km/h (25 miles per hour) on a level paved surface. *On-Road Vehicle and Engine Emission Regulations*, SOR/2003-2, s. 1. See COMPETITION ~; POWER ~; USED ~.

MOTORCYCLE MECHANIC. A person who services, repairs, overhauls and inspects motorcycles, and tests them for faults or road-worthiness.

MOTOR DEALER. A person who, in the course of business, (a) engages in the sale of motor vehicles, whether for his own account or for the account of another person, or who holds himself out as engaging in the sale of motor vehicles; or (b) with or without remuneration acts as a motor vehicle broker or, as an agent, sells motor vehicles on commission.

MOTOR DREDGE. A dredge, the primary power plant of which consists of internal combustion engines.

MOTOR DRIVEN CYCLE. 1. A motor vehicle having a seat or saddle for the use of the rider and designed to travel on not more than three wheels and propelled by a motor not to exceed fifty cubic centimetres in size and includes a motor scooter, tricycle or bicycle with such a motor attached. 2. A vehicle having steering handlebars completely constrained from rotating in relation to the axle of one wheel in contact with the ground, designed to travel on not more than three wheels in contact with the ground, and having a motor that produces five brake horsepower or less. Canada regulations.

MOTOR HOME. 1. A motor vehicle designed and constructed as an integral unit to provide permanent living accommodation and which is equipped with one or more beds and a stove or refrigerator or washing and toilet facilities, and is so designed that there is direct access from the living quarters to the driver's seat. 2. A motor vehicle designed or used primarily for accommodation during travel or recreation, but does not include a motor vehicle that has attached to it a structure (a) designed or used primarily for accommodation during travel or recreation; and (b) designed or intended to be detachable.

MOTOR HOTEL. A tourist establishment that, (i) consists of one or more than one building containing four or more accommodation units grouped under one roof and accessible from the interior or partially from the exterior, (ii) may or may not have facilities for serving meals, and (iii) is designed to accommodate the public for whom the automobile is the principal means of transportation.

MOTORIST. *n.* One who uses or operates a motor vehicle.

MOTORIZED MOBILITY AID. A device which is specifically manufactured or modified for operation by a physically handicapped person and which has (a) a maximum speed capability of not more than 15 kilometres per hour,

(b) a maximum width of not more than 81.2 centimetres, and (c) a maximum mass of not more than 226 kilograms, and includes a motorized wheel chair. *The Highway Traffic Act*, C.C.S.M., c. H60, s. 1.

MOTORIZED SNOW VEHICLE. A self-propelled vehicle designed to be driven exclusively or chiefly on snow or ice or both, whether or not it is capable of being driven elsewhere.

MOTORIZED VEHICLE. A motorcycle, minibike, motorbike, moped, trail bike or dune buggy.

MOTOR SHIP. A ship the propulsive power of which is derived from an internal combustion engine. *Marine Certification Regulations*, SOR/ 97-391, s. 1.

MOTOR TRACTOR. Any mechanically propelled vehicle, other than a farm tractor, designed for traction purposes on the highway. *Motor Carrier Act*, R.S.P.E.I. 1988, c. M-10, s. 1(1)(e).

MOTOR VEHICLE. 1. " . . . [A] vehicle which is capable of being and is ordinarily self propelled by power generated within itself, as distinct, for example, from a horse drawn vehicle, or from one that is propelled by the application of externally generated power." *R. v. Thornton* (1950), 25 M.P.R. 10 at 148, 96 C.C.C. 323 (N.S. C.A.), Parker J.A. (Hall, MacQuarrie and Ilsley JJ.A. concurring). 2. A vehicle that is drawn, propelled or driven by any means other than by muscular power, but does not include a vehicle of a railway that operates on rails. 3. A vehicle that is propelled or driven by means of an internal combustion or turbine engine. 4. A vehicle that is designed to be self propelled. 5. (a) A vehicle propelled by any power other than muscular power, and (ii) includes an airplane, but (iii) does not include a motor vehicle that runs only on rails. See ABANDONED ~; ANTIQUE ~; COMMERCIAL ~; DANGEROUS OPERATION OF ~S; DERELICT ~; DRIVE-YOURSELF ~; HIGHWAY ~ OPERATOR; INSURED ~; LIGHT DUTY ~; NEW ~; PUBLIC TRANSIT ~; REGISTRAR OF ~S.

MOTOR VEHICLE DEALER. A person who carries on the business of buying or selling motor vehicles, whether for the person's own account or the account of any other person, or who holds himself, herself or itself out as carrying on the business of buying or selling motor vehicles. *Motor Vehicle Dealers Act*, R.S.O. 1990, c. M.42, s. 1. See NEW ~.

MOTOR VEHICLE INSPECTION ME-CHANIC. A person who certifies by means of a safety standards certificate that a motor vehicle complies with the equipment and performance standards prescribed by the regulations. *Highway Traffic Act*, R.S.O. 1990, c. H.8, s. 88.

MOTOR VEHICLE INSPECTION STA-TION. Any premises maintained or operated for the inspection of motor vehicles and the issuance of safety standards certificates or vehicle inspection stickers in respect of the motor vehicles. *Highway Traffic Act*, R.S.O. 1990, c. H.8, s. 88.

MOTOR VEHICLE INSURANCE. Insurance against liability for loss or damage to persons or property caused by a motor vehicle or the use or operation thereof, and against loss of or damage to a motor vehicle.

MOTOR VEHICLE LIABILITY POLICY. A policy or part of a policy evidencing a contract insuring: (a) the owner or driver of an automobile; or (b) a person who is not the owner or driver thereof where the automobile is being used or operated by that person's employee or agent or any other person on that person's behalf; against liability arising out of bodily injury to or the death of a person or loss or damage to property caused by an automobile or the use or operation thereof. *Insurance acts.*

MOTOR VEHICLE MECHANIC. A person engaged in the servicing, repairing, overhauling, diagnosing or inspecting of motor vehicles who, (i) disassembles, adjusts, repairs and reassembles engines, transmissions, clutches, rear ends, differentials, brakes, drive shafts, axles and other assemblies, (ii) tests, diagnoses and corrects faulty alignment of wheels and steering mechanisms, manual or power, (iii) diagnoses faults, repairs or replaces suspension systems, including shock absorbers and spring assemblies, (iv) diagnoses faults, installs, repairs and removes ignition systems, generators, alternators, starters, coils, panel instruments, wiring and other electrical systems and equipment, (v) diagnoses faults, repairs and adjusts fuel systems, (vi) performs complete engine tune-ups, and (vii) diagnoses faults, installs, insects, maintains and removes motor vehicle air-conditioning and refrigeration systems, but does not include a person who is permanently employed for the limited purpose of, (viii) removing and replacing auto glass, (ix) removing and replacing exhaust systems, (x) removing and replacing radiators, or (xi) removing and replacing shock absorbers or springs that do not require the realignment of the front or rear suspension.

MOTOR VEHICLE PRIVILEGE. (a) Registration of a motor vehicle under this Act, (b) a licence issued under this Act, (c) the privilege of operating a motor vehicle in the Province under section 80, and (d) the privilege of an owner of a motor vehicle registered in his name in another province, state or country to have the vehicle operated in the Province. *Motor Vehicle Act*, R.S.N.B. 1973, c. M-17, s. 272.

MOTOR VESSEL. Any vessel, ship, boat or watercraft that is designed to move in or through water, and that is powered by fuel.

MOULDED DEPTH. Subject to paragraphs (a) to (d), the vertical distance measured from the top of the keel to the top of the freeboard deck beam at side, but (a) in vessels of other than metal construction, the distance is measured from the lower edge of the keel rabbet, (b) where the form at the lower part of the midship section is of a hollow character, or where thick garboards are fitted, the distance is measured from the point where the line of the flat of the bottom continued inwards cuts the side of the keel, (c) in ships having rounded gunwales, the distance is measured to the point of intersection of the moulded lines of the deck and sides, the lines extending as though the gunwale were of angular design, (d) where the freeboard deck is stepped and the raised part of the deck extends over the point at which the moulded depth is to be determined, the moulded depth shall be measured to a line of reference extending from the lower part of the deck along a line parallel with the raised part. Canada regulations.

MOULD MAKER. A person who, (i) sets up and operates to prescribed tolerances engine lathes and milling, grinding, drilling, sawing and boring machines, (ii) reads and interprets blueprints, operation or product related reference charts and tables and selects mechanical measuring and checking and layout tools and devices, (iii) performs measuring, checking and layout operations and selects work piece materials and the required cutting tools and abrasives for metal removal operations, (iv) performs metal removal operations using hand and power tools and selects work piece clamping and holding devices and product-related components, (v) performs hand finishing and polishing operations on moulds, and (vi) assembles and tests moulds for application purposes.

MOULDS. *n*. Hollow forms into which materials are placed to produce desired shapes, matrices or cavities which shape or form goods in process, and cores, pins, inserts, bushings and similar parts for moulds.

MOUND. See STONE ~.

MOUNTAIN STANDARD TIME. The time that is seven hours behind Greenwich time.

MOVABLE. *n. A* type of property distinguished in civil law. J.G. McLeod, *The Conflict of Laws* (Calgary: Carswell, 1983) at 55.

MOVABLE PROPERTY. 1. Includes personal property other than a leasehold or other interest in land. 2. All property which is not considered immovable by the laws of Québec, and includes gas, electricity, telephone service, and lighting service. *Retail Sales Tax Act*, R.S.Q., c. I.1, s. 2.

MOVABLES. *n*. Any movable tangible property, other than the ship, and includes money, valuable securities, and other documents. *Insurance acts*.

MOVAGE. *n*. 1. The moving of a ship within a pilotage area, whether the ship is moved from one berth to another or is returned to the same berth, but does not include, unless a pilot is employed, the warping of a ship from one berth to another solely by means of mooring lines attached to a wharf, to the shore or to a mooring buoy. Canada regulations. 2. The moving of a ship wholly within a harbour or port from one anchored or moored position to another or back to the same position, but does not include the warping of a ship from one berth to another solely by means of mooring lines unless a pilot is employed, and includes anchoring of a ship while en route between one harbour, port or pilot boarding station and another due to stress of weather, tidal conditions, safety of the ship or crew, waiting berth availability or waiting due to minor engine or equipment repairs performed by ship's personnel that are considered reasonable engine or equipment maintenance. Canada regulations.

MOVEMENT. See BACK-TO-WORK ~; INWARD ~; JOINT LINE ~; OUTWARD ~; SOIL ~.

MOVEMENT AREA. A part of an aerodrome that is intended to be used for the surface movement of aircraft, and includes the manoeuvring area and aprons; *Canadian Aviation Regulations*, SOR/96-433, s. 101.01.

MOVER. See PRIME ~.

MOVING PICTURE MACHINE. A machine or device in which film is used and that is operated by or with the aid of electricity and adapted or used to project pictorial representations on a screen or other surface.

MOVING PICTURE THEATRE. Any theatre, concert hall, premises, room, place, house, building or structure of any kind where a cinematograph, moving picture machine or other similar apparatus is operated and to which the public is admitted.

M.P.I.C. *abbr*. Manitoba Public Insurance Corporation.

M.P.L.R. *abbr*. Municipal and Planning Law Reports, 1976-.

M.P.R. *abbr*. Maritime Provinces Reports, 1929-1968.

M.R. *abbr*. Master of the Rolls.

M.R.N. *abbr*. Ministre du Revenu national.

MSDS. *abbr*. Material safety data sheet. A summary of the hazards of a toxic material or product.

MSG. *abbr*. The Manufacturer's Standard Gauge for uncoated steel.

MTDNA. *abbr*. [written mtDNA] Mitochondrial DNA.

M.T.R. *abbr*. Maritime Tax Reports.

MUGGING. *n*. Strangling by throwing the arm around a victim's neck from behind. F.A. Jaffe, *A Guide to Pathological Evidence*, 3d ed. (Toronto: Carswell, 1991) at 223.

MULCT. *n*. A fine; a penalty.

MULE. *n*. Slang term for a person recruited to transport contraband.

MULIER. *n*. A wife; a woman; a legitimate child.

MULTA CONCEDUNTUR PER OBLI-QUUM, QUAE NON CONCEDUNTUR DE DIRECTO. [L.] Many things are permitted indirectly which are not permitted directly.

MULTA IN JURE COMMUNI, CONTRA RATIONEM DISPUTANDI, PRO COMMUNI UTILITATE INTRODUCTA SUNT. [L.] Many things in the common law that are illogical were incorporated for the public good.

MULTA MULTO EXERCITATIONE FA- CILIUS QUAM REGULIS PERCIPIES. [L.] There are many things you will understand more easily from much practice than from rules.

MULTICRAFT UNION. A union which represents workers in more than one craft.

MULTICULTURAL HERITAGE. Section 27 of the Charter recognizes the multi-cultural heritage of Canadians in the following terms: This Charter shall be interpreted in a manner consistent with the preservation and enhancement of the multicultural heritage of Canadians.

MULTICULTURALISM. *n*. The preservation and development of the multicultural composition of the province and, without limiting the generality of the foregoing, includes the recognition of the right of every community, whose common history spans many generations, to retain its distinctive group identity, and to develop its relevant language and its traditional arts and sciences, without political or social impediment and for the mutual benefit of all citizens. *The Saskatchewan Multicultural Act*, R.S.S. 1978, c. S-31, s. 2.

MULTI-EMPLOYER BARGAINING. Collective bargaining between a union and more than one employer.

MULTI-EMPLOYER EMPLOYMENT. As more particularly defined by the regulations, means employment in any occupation or trade in which, by custom of that occupation or trade, any or all employees would in the usual course of a working month be ordinarily employed by more than one employer. *Canada Labour Code*, R.S.C. 1985, c.L-2, s. 203.

MULTI-EMPLOYER PENSION PLAN. 1. A pension plan organized and administered for employees of two or more employers who contribute to the plan pursuant to an agreement, by-law or statute, where the pension plan provides pension benefits that are determined by periods of employment with any or all of the participating employers, but does not include a pension plan where more than ninety-five per cent of the plan members are employed by participating employers who are incorporated and are affiliates within the meaning of the Canada Business Corporations Act. *Pension Benefit Standards Act*, R.S.C. 1985 (2d Supp.) c. 32, s. 2. 2. A pension plan established and maintained for employees of two or more employers who contribute or on whose behalf contributions are made to a pension fund by reason of agreement, municipal by-law or statute to provide a pension benefit that is determined by employment with one or more of the employers, but does not include a pension plan where all the employers are affiliates within the meaning of the Business Corporations Act. *Pension Benefits Act*, S.N.B., c. P-5.1, s. 1.

MULTI-ENGINE AIRCRAFT. An aircraft having two or more engines that is capable of maintaining flight in the event of failure of the critical engine.

MULTI-FAMILY RESIDENTIAL. See MEDIUM DENSITY ~.

MULTI-FARM OPERATION. Two or more farm units operated by two or more different participants as a joint undertaking.

MULTILATERAL. *adj*. Concerning more than two nations.

MULTI-LEVEL MARKETING PLAN. A plan for the supply of a product whereby a participant in the plan receives compensation for the supply of the product to another participant in the plan who, in turn, receives compensation for the supply of the same or another product to other participants in the plan. *Competition Act*, R.S.C. 1985, c. C-34, s. 55(1).

MULTI-OUTLET ASSEMBLY. A surface or flush enclosure carrying conductors for extending one 2-wire or multi-wire branch circuit to two or more receptacles of the grounding type that are attached to the enclosure.

MULTIPARTITE. *adj*. Divided into many parts.

MULTI-PERIL POLICY. A policy of insurance which insures against loss from several causes. A typical homeowner policy is a multi-peril policy.

MULTIPHASE LINE. A pipe for the transmission of effluent consisting of oil, gas and water in any combination from one or more oil wells and includes installations in connection with that pipe. *Pipeline Act*, R.S.A. 1980, c. P-8, s. 1.

MULTI-PLANT BARGAINING. Collective bargaining involving the employees of more than one plant owned by the same employer.

MULTIPLE DWELLING. A building or buildings located on a lot and containing two or more dwelling units.

MULTIPLE-FAMILY DWELLING. A building containing three or more family housing units. *Housing acts.*

MULTIPLE LISTING. 1. An agreement between a vendor and one broker authorizing other brokers to sell the property for a portion of the commission agreed. 2. Property listed through a real estate board's multiple listing service.

MULTIPLE SECTION MOBILE UNIT. A structure formed by the mechanical and electrical coupling together of two or more mobile units.

MULTIPLE SUFFICIENT CAUSATION. Two legally relevant causes, each alone sufficient to cause an injury or loss and each required (in a but for sense) if the other were absent, combine to originate an injury or loss. K.D. Cooper-Stephenson & I.B. Saunders, *Personal Injury Damages in Canada* (Toronto: Carswell, 1981) at 653.

MULTIPLE UNIT DWELLING. A building so constructed, altered or used as to provide accommodation for more than one family to dwell in separately; and includes, (i) flats, (ii) semi-detached housing, (iii) duplex and multiplex housing, (iv) row housing, (v) condominium housing, and (vi) residence apartment buildings.

MULTIPLICATA TRANSGRESSIONE, CRESCAT POENAE INFLICTIO. [L.] As wrongdoing multiplies, the inflicting of punishment increases.

MULTIPLICITY. *n.* Excessive division or fracture of one cause or suit.

MULTIPLIER METHOD. Calculation of loss by multiplying the number of years a loss will last (the multiplier) by lost annual income (the multiplicand). K.D. Cooper-Stephenson & I.B. Saunders, *Personal Injury Damages in Canada* (Toronto: Carswell, 1981) at 72.

MULTI-PURPOSE PASSENGER VEHICLE. A vehicle that has a seating capacity of 10 or less and is constructed on a truck-chassis or with special features for off-highway operation, but does not include an air cushion vehicle, an all terrain vehicle, a passenger car or a truck.

MULTI-SERVICE ARTICLE. Any container or eating utensil that is intended for repeated use in the service of food. *Public Health Act*, R.R.O. 1980, Reg. 840, s. 1.

MULTI-STAKEHOLDER CO-OPERATIVE. A co-operative, (a) the articles of which provide that it is a multi-stakeholder co-operative for the purposes of this Act, (b) the articles of which provide for the division of its members into two or more stakeholder groups, (c) the articles of which set out the method of determining the number of directors each stakeholder group may elect, and (d) for which the requirements that each member of the co-operative belongs to a stakeholder group; and that no member of a co-operative belongs to more than one stakeholder group at the same time are satisfied. *Co-operative Corporations Act*, R.S.O. 1990, c. C.35, s. 1 as am.

MULTITUDINEM DECEM FACIUNT. [L.] Ten constitutes a multitude.

MULTITUDO ERRANTIUM NON PARIT ERRORI PATROCINIUM. [L.] That many people make a mistake does not excuse the error.

MULTITUDO IMPERITORUM PERDIT CURIAM. [L.] A crowd of masters ruins a court.

MULTI-UNION BARGAINING. Collective bargaining involving more than one union.

MULTI-UNIT RESIDENTIAL BUILDING. " . . . [P]rovided investors with 'soft cost' write-offs against income for certain categories of expenses associated with getting real estate projects off the ground. In addition to the attraction provided by the immediate write-offs against income, there was the added attraction of a long-term investment." *Hodgkinson v. Simms* (1989), 43 B.L.R. 122 at 128 (B.C. S.C.), Prowse J.

MULTI-WINDING MOTOR. A motor having multiple windings or tapped windings, or both, designed for connection or reconnection in more than one configuration to operate at speeds and voltages respective to the configurations.

MULTI-WIRE BRANCH CIRCUIT. A branch circuit consisting of two or more ungrounded conductors having a voltage difference between them, and an identified grounded conductor having equal voltage between it and each ungrounded conductor with the identified grounded conductor connected to the neutral conductor.

MULTI-YEAR CONTRACT. An agreement which covers a period of two or more years.

MULTIZONE WELL. A well that may be used for segregated production from, or segregated injection to, more than one zone or pool through the same well.

MUMMIFICATION. *n.* Exposure of a dead body or its parts to a warm, dry environment so that it dries to a leathery, brown parchment-like condition. F.A. Jaffe, *A Guide to Pathological Evidence*, 3d ed. (Toronto: Carswell, 1991) at 223.

MUN. *abbr.* 1. Municipal. 2. Municipality.

MUN. CT. *abbr.* Municipal Court.

MUNICIPAL. *adj.* Related to a municipal corporation.

MUNICIPAL ADMINISTRATOR. See URBAN ~.

MUNICIPAL ASSISTANCE. Assistance provided by a municipality to a person in need who is a resident of, or found in, the municipality. *Municipal Act*, S.M. 1972, c. 42, s. 17.

MUNICIPAL AUTHORITY. A municipal corporation or commission.

MUNICIPAL BUDGET. See NET ~.

MUNICIPAL CLERK. 1. The clerk of a municipality. 2. The clerk of a city or town or the secretary treasurer of a village.

MUNICIPAL COMMISSION. 1. A hydroelectric commission or public utilities commission, entrusted with the control and management of works for the retail distribution and supply of power. 2. Municipal corporation or municipal commission or the trustees of a police village supplying power that is supplied to it or them by the Corporation. *Power Corporation Amendment Act, 1981 (No. 2)*, S.O. 1981, c. 41, s. 2.

MUNICIPAL CORPORATION. 1. The legal entity established under legislation which is distinct from residents, ratepayers or members of municipal council and which transacts the business of a municipality. 2. " . . . [A] public corporation created by the government for political purposes and having subordinate and local powers of legislation. It can exercise its corporate powers only within its defined limits. It does not own its defined territorial area, but is limited thereto as to its jurisdiction." *Hatch v. Rathwell* (1909), 12 W.L.R. 376 at 377, 19 Man. R. 465 (C.A.), the court per Cameron J.A. 3. Any body entrusted with the administration of a territory for municipal purposes. Quebec statutes.

MUNICIPAL CORRUPTION. Every one who (*a*) gives, offers or agrees to give or offer to a municipal official, or (*b*) being a municipal official, demands, accepts or offers or agrees to accept from any person, a loan, reward, advantage or benefit of any kind as consideration for the official (*c*) to abstain from voting at a meet-

ing of the municipal council or a committee thereof, (*d*) to vote in favour of or against a measure, motion or resolution, (*e*) to aid in procuring or preventing the adoption of a measure, motion or resolution, or (*f*) to perform or fail to perform an official act, is guilty of an indictable offence. *Criminal Code*, R.S.C. 1985, c. C-46, s. 123.

MUNICIPAL COUNCIL. The council of a municipality.

MUNICIPAL ELECTORS. The persons entitled to vote at a municipal election. *Municipal Act*, R.S.O. 1990, c. M.45, s. 1(1).

MUNICIPAL EMPLOYEE. A person who is in receipt of or entitled to any remuneration for labour or services performed for a northern municipality.

MUNICIPAL ENTERPRISE. Any body corporate the borrowings of which are or may be guaranteed by a municipality, any body corporate to which a municipality may lend money, and any body corporate the deficit of which is or may be paid by a municipality. *Municipal Finance Corporation Act*, R.S.N.S. 1989, c. 301, s. 2.

MUNICIPAL GOVERNMENT. A body subordinate to national and provincial authority with legislative power over a local territory.

MUNICIPAL GRANT BASE. See UNADJUSTED ~.

MUNICIPAL HERITAGE PROPERTY. A building, streetscape or area registered in a municipal registry of heritage property.

MUNICIPALITY. *n.* 1. A locality the inhabitants of which are incorporated. 2. Includes the corporation of a city, town, village, county, township, parish or other territorial or local division of a province, the inhabitants of which are incorporated or are entitled to hold property collectively for a public purpose. *Criminal Code*, R.S.C. 1985, c. C-46, s. 2. 3. An incorporated city, metropolitan authority, town, village, township, district or rural municipality or other incorporated municipal body however designated, and includes any other local government body that is established by or under a law of a province. 4. An area under the jurisdiction of a municipal council. See AREA ~; COUNTY ~; DISTRICT ~; DIVIDED ~; FOUNDATION ~; LOCAL ~; LOWER TIER ~; MEMBER ~; REGIONAL ~; RU-

RAL ~; SCHOOL ~; SINGLE TIER ~; UPPER TIER ~; URBAN ~.

MUNICIPAL JAIL. A place of confinement for the custody of persons sentenced to imprisonment for infractions of the bylaws of a municipality or charged with such infractions. *Jails Act*, R.S.P.E.I. 1988, c. J-1, s. 1(f).

MUNICIPAL LAW. 1. Law relating to municipal corporations and their government. 2. Law relating exclusively to the citizens and inhabitants of a country, differing thus from the law of nations and political law.

MUNICIPAL LICENSING POWER. See LICENSING POWER.

MUNICIPAL MARKET. Any public market maintained by a municipal corporation. Canada regulations.

MUNICIPAL OFFICER. One who holds a responsible permanent position with definite duties and rights prescribed by statute or by-law. In contrast to a servant, an appointed officer has discretionary authority and responsibility to perform important duties. The class includes executive and administrative positions established by the legislature and subject to municipal council control e.g. clerk, treasurer, council head, manager, assessor, tax collector, auditor. I.M. Rogers, *The Law of Canadian Municipal Corporations*, 2d ed. (Toronto: Carswell, 1971-) at 281-2.

MUNICIPAL ORGANIZATION. See TERRITORY WITHOUT ~.

MUNICIPAL PLANNING SCHEME. See MASTER PLAN.

MUNICIPAL POLICE POWER. See POLICE POWER.

MUNICIPAL PROPERTY. See TAXABLE ~.

MUNICIPAL PUBLIC UTILITY. A public utility owned and operated by a municipality. *Municipal Act*, R.S.O. 1990, c. M.45, s. 194(1).

MUNICIPAL PURPOSE. 1. " . . . [A]reas of activity specifically attributed to municipal corporations in the interests of the community" *Leiriao v. Val-Bélair (Ville)* (1991), 46 L.C.R. 161 at 166, [1991] 3 S.C.R. 349, 7 M.P.L.R. (2d) 1, 129 N.R. 188, L'Heureux-Dubé J. (dissenting). 2. A household and sanitary purpose, the watering of animals, streets, walks, paths, boulevards, lawns and gardens, fire protection and the flushing of sewers, and includes the construction of buildings and of civic works, and other purposes usually served by water within a city, town or village.

MUNICIPAL PURPOSES. Are determined by reference to not only those that are expressly stated but those that are compatible with the purpose and objects of the enabling statute. *Shell Canada Products Ltd. v. Vancouver (City)*, 1994 CarswellBC 115, 88 B.C.L.R. (2d) 145, [1994] 3 W.W.R. 609, 20 M.P.L.R. (2d) 1, 110 D.L.R. (4th) 1, 163 N.R. 81, [1994] 1 S.C.R. 231, 41 B.C.A.C. 81, 66 W.A.C. 81, 20 Admin. L.R. (2d) 202, per Sopinka, J. for the majority.

MUNICIPAL QUESTION. One which deals with municipal governance or the structure of the municipal government, a question which may be submitted to the electorate by plebiscite.

MUNICIPAL SECURITIES. Bonds, debentures, notes or other evidences of indebtedness of or guaranteed by any municipal corporation in Canada.

MUNICIPAL SERVICE. The water, sewer, police, fire protection, recreation, cultural activities, roads, garbage removal and disposal, lighting, snow removal or septic tank cleaning service supplied by a municipality or a municipal corporation.

MUNICIPAL SERVICES. Roads, sidewalks, boulevards, parks, open spaces, sewers, water service, street lighting and other electrical services.

MUNICIPAL SEWERAGE CORPORATION. A corporation established for the purpose of constructing and operating facilities for the collection and treatment of sewage from one or more municipalities.

MUNICIPAL TAX. 1. " . . . [T]axes imposed by the governing body of a municipality for the purposes of the municipality., . . ." *Canadian Pacific Railway v. Winnipeg (City)* (1900), 30 S.C.R. 558 at 564, the court per Sedgewick J. 2. All taxes assessed against lands and levied by or through a municipality.

MUNICIPAL TELEPHONE SYSTEM. A telephone system, other than a public utility, established by by-law of a municipality under a predecessor of this Act. *Telephone Act*, R.S.O. 1990, c. T.4, s. 1.

MUNICIPAL UNIT. A city, town, municipality or village.

MUNICIPAL UTILITY. Any water lines, sanitary or storm sewer lines, or water, waste management or sanitary or storm sewerage plants or facilities that are owned by a municipality or jointly owned by 2 or more municipalities.

MUNICIPAL WASTE MANAGEMENT SYSTEM. A waste management system, or any part thereof, of which a municipality is the owner.

MUNIMENT. *n.* A record; defence; a written document upon which one establishes a right or claim and depends; evidence.

MUNITIONS OF WAR. Arms, ammunition, implements or munitions of war, military stores or any articles deemed capable of being converted thereinto or made useful in the production thereof. *Security of Information Act*, R.S.C. 1985, c. O-5, s. 2.

MURAL THROMBUS. A thrombus attached to the heart chamber or a blood vessel's wall. F.A. Jaffe, *A Guide to Pathological Evidence*, 3d ed. (Toronto: Carswell, 1991) at 228.

M.U.R.B. *abbr.* Multi-unit residential building.

MURDER. *n.* 1. "The classic definition of murder is that of Sir Edward (Chief Justice) Coke . . . 'Murder is when a man . . . unlawfully killeth . . . any reasonable creature in rerum natura under the king's peace, with malice aforethought, either expressed by the party, or implied by law, so as the party wounded, or hurt , etc., die of the wound, or hurt, etc. within a year and a day after the same.' . . . Murder requires, positively, the mental element traditionally known as 'malice aforethought', and, negatively, the absence of certain mitigating circumstances that would turn the case into one of manslaughter. . . the law has consistently required that murder be an offence of specific intent. The specific intents have generally been clearly described in Canada in statutory form, and an unlawful killing without proof of the existence of the required specific intent has always been characterized as manslaughter. On all the authorities, the mental element—the 'malice aforethought' of ancient usage—must always be demonstrated in order to procure a conviction of murder." *R. v. Swietlinski* (1980), 18 C.R. (3d) 231 at 247-9, 34 N.R. 569, 55 C.C.C. (2d) 481, 117 D.L.R. (3d) 285, [1980] 2 S.C.R. 956, the court per McIntyre J. 2. Culpable homicide is murder (a) where the person who causes the death of a human being (i) means to cause his death, or (ii) means to cause him bodily harm that he knows is likely to cause his death, and is reckless whether death ensues or not; (b) where a person, meaning to cause death to a human being or meaning to cause him bodily harm that he knows is likely to cause his death, and being reckless whether death ensues or not, by accident or mistake causes death to another human being, notwithstanding that he does not mean to cause death or bodily harm to that human being; or (c) where a person, for an unlawful object, does anything that he knows or ought to know is likely to cause death, and thereby causes death to a human being, notwithstanding that he desires to effect his object without causing death or bodily harm to any human being. *Criminal Code*, R.S.C. 1985, c. C-46, s. 229. 3. Culpable homicide is murder when committed while committing or attempting to commit certain offences if certain conditions are met. *Criminal Code*, R.S.C. 1985, c. C-46, s. 230. See CAPITAL ~; CLASSIFICATION OF ~; FIRST DEGREE ~; ~ IN COMMISSION OF OFFENCES; NON-CAPITAL ~; SECOND DEGREE ~; SELF-~.

MURDER IN COMMISSION OF OFFENCES. Culpable homicide is murder where a person causes the death of a human being while committing or attempting to commit high treason or treason or sabotage, piracy, hijacking an aircraft, escape or rescue from prison or lawful custody, assaulting a peace officer, resisting lawful arrest, sexual assault, kidnapping, forcible confinement, hostage taking, breaking and entering, robbery, or arson whether or not the person means to cause death to any human being and whether or not he knows that death is likely to be caused to any human being, if (a) he means to cause bodily harm for the purpose of (i) facilitating the commission of the offence, or (ii) facilitating his flight after committing or attempting to commit the offence, and the death ensues from the bodily harm; (b) he administers a stupefying or overpowering thing for a purpose mentioned in paragraph (a), and the death ensues therefrom; (c) he wilfully stops, by any means, the breath of a human being for a purpose mentioned in paragraph (a), and the death ensues therefrom; or (d) he uses a weapon or has it upon his person (i) during or at the time he commits or attempts to commit the offence, or (ii) during or at the time of his flight after committing or attempting to commit the offence, and the death ensues as a consequence. *Criminal Code*, R.S.C. 1985, c. C-46, s. 230.

MUSEUM. *n.* An institution that, (i) is established for the purpose of conserving, studying, interpreting, assembling and exhibiting to the public for its instruction and enjoyment objects and specimens of educational and cultural value including historical, technological, anthropological or scientific material or (ii) an art museum. See NATIONAL ~S OF CANADA; PUBLIC ~.

MUSICAL WORK. Any work of music or musical composition, with or without words, and includes any compilation thereof. *Copyright Act*, R.S.C. 1985, c. C-42, s. 2. See EVER ORIGINAL LITERARY, DRAMATIC, MUSICAL AND ARTISTIC WORK.

MUST. *v.* 1. Shall. 2. An imperative, expresses command, obligation, duty. 3. "... [A] common imperative... In its present or future tense it expresses command, obligation, duty [,] necessity and inevitability..." *U.A.W. v. Massey-Ferguson Industries Ltd.* (1979) 79 C.L.L.C. 14,228 at 237, 23 O.R. (2d) 56, 94 D.L.R. (3d) 743, 22 L.A.C. (2d) 16n (Div. Ct.), Reid J. See SHALL, MUST, MAY.

MUST. *n.* See GRAPE ~.

MUTATIS MUTANDIS. [L.] With needed changes in the details. *R. v. Century 21 Ramos Realty Inc.* (1987), 56 C.R. (3d) 150 at 181-2, 87 D.T.C. 5158, 19 O.A.C. 25, 32 C.C.C. (3d) 353, 37 D.L.R. (4th) 649, 29 C.R.R. 320, [1987] 1 C.T.C. 340, 58 O.R. (2d) 737 (C.A.), Martin, Houlden and Tarnopolsky JJ.A.

MUTILATION. *n.* Depriving of any necessary part or limb.

MUTINY. *n.* Collective insubordination or a combination of two or more persons in the resistance of lawful authority in any of Her Majesty's Forces or in any forces cooperating therewith. *National Defence Act*, R.S.C. 1985, c. N-5, s. 2.

MUTTON CARCASS. The carcass of an animal of the sheep species, of either sex, more than twelve months of age, having two smooth hard white ridges where the feet are severed at the ankle (spool) joint and bones somewhat whiter and harder than those in a lamb carcass.

MUTUAL ASSOCIATION. A mutual insurance association and a mutual benefit association.

MUTUAL BENEFITS. Amounts paid to or benefits conferred upon persons who are members of a group or to or upon members of their families in case of misfortune, sickness, accident or death, out of the premiums, assessments, gifts or subscriptions from persons who are members of that group.

MUTUAL BENEFIT SOCIETY. A mutual company formed for the purpose of providing sick and funeral benefits for its members or for this and any other purposes necessary or incidental thereto except life insurance. See EMPLOYEES' ~.

MUTUAL COMPANY. A company empowered solely to transact mutual insurance.

MUTUAL CORPORATION. A corporation without share capital that is empowered to undertake mutual insurance exclusively. *Insurance Act*, R.S.O. 1990, c. I-8, s. 1.

MUTUAL DEBTS. 1. "... [D]ebts or claims due from one to another which are ascertainable and which are in the same right..." *McMahon v. Canada Permanent Trust Co.* (1979), 6 E.T.R. 43 at 47, 8 B.L.R. 143, [1980] 2 W.W.R. 438, 32 C.B.R. (N.S.) 258, 17 B.C.L.R. 193, 108 D.L.R. (3d) 71 (C.A.), the court per Bull J.A. 2. Cross obligations.

MUTUAL FUND. 1. Includes an issuer of a security that entitles the holder to receive on demand, or within a specified period after demand, an amount computed by reference to the value of a proportionate interest in the whole or in a part of the net assets, including a separate fund or trust account, of the issuer of the security. 2. A form of investment in which investors pool their assets in order to achieve economies of scale, spread their risks, and diversify their portfolios. 3. A fund established by a corporation duly authorized to operate a fund in which moneys from two or more depositors are accepted for investment and where shares allocated to each depositor serve to establish at any time the proportionate interest of each depositor in the assets of the fund. *Pension Benefits Standards Regulations*, C.R.C., c. 1252, s. 2. See OPEN-END ~; PRIVATE ~; RELATED ~S.

MUTUAL FUND CORPORATION. A company that offers public participation in an investment portfolio through the issue of one or more classes of mutual fund shares.

MUTUAL FUND IN THE PROVINCE. A mutual fund that is (a) a reporting issuer, or (b) organized under the laws of the province, but does not include a private mutual fund.

MUTUAL FUND SHARE. A share having conditions attached thereto that include conditions requiring the company issuing the share to accept, at the demand of the holder thereof and at prices determined and payable in accordance with the conditions, the surrender of the share, or fractions or parts thereof, that are fully paid.

MUTUAL INSURANCE. 1. A contract of insurance, in which the consideration is not fixed or certain at the time the contract is made but is to be determined at the termination of the contract or at fixed periods during the term of the contract according to the experience of the insurer in respect of all similar contracts whether or not the maximum amount of such consideration is predetermined. *Insurance acts*. 2. Insurance whereby two or more persons mutually agree to insure one another against marine losses. *Marine Insurance Act, 1993*, S.C. 1993, c. 22, s. 89.

MUTUAL INSURANCE COMPANY. 1. A company without share capital or with guarantee capital stock subject to repayment by the company, in respect of which the dividend rate is limited by its charter which is empowered to undertake mutual insurance exclusively. *Insurance Companies Act*, R.S.Nfld. 1990, c. I-10, s. 2. 2. A corporation without share capital that provides insurance on the mutual plan.

MUTUAL INSURANCE CORPORATION. A corporation without share capital or with guarantee capital stock subject to repayment by the corporation, in respect of which the dividend rate is limited by its Act or instrument of incorporation, that is empowered to undertake mutual insurance exclusively.

MUTUALITY OF ASSENT. Regarding the main or necessary part of any agreement, for each party to intend the same thing and to know what the other will do.

MUTUALITY OF OBLIGATION. For each party to an agreement to be bound to do something.

MUTUALITY OF REMEDY. For each party to an agreement to be able to enforce that agreement against the other.

MUTUAL PROMISES. Simultaneous considerations which support each other.

MUTUAL WILLS. " . . . [T]hey confer mutual benefits upon two or more testators and there must be something in the nature of a contract, that is one contracting party agrees to confer certain benefits by will, the other contracting party will confer reciprocal benefits by his will. The situation should be one in which one party would not make his will unless the other one also made a will conferring similar benefits. . ." *Ohorodnyk, Re* (1979), 4 E.T.R. 233 at 244, 97 D.L.R. (3d) 502, 24 O.R. (2d) 228 (H.C.), Hollingworth J.

MUTUEL FIELD. Two or more horses in a race that, for the purpose of making a bet, are treated as one horse because the number of horses in the race exceeds the number that can be dealt with individually by the pari-mutuel system. *Pari-Mutuel Betting Supervision Regulations*, SOR/91-365, s. 2.

MUZZLE. *v*. To secure a dog's mouth in such a fashion that it cannot bite anything.

MUZZLE. *n*. The front end of a firearm's barrel.

MUZZLE VELOCITY. The speed, expressed in feet or meters per second, at which a projectile leaves a firearms barrel. F.A. Jaffe, *A Guide to Pathological Evidence*, 3d ed. (Toronto: Carswell, 1991) at 223.

M.V.R. *abbr*. Motor Vehicle Reports, 1979-1988.

M.V.R. (2D). *abbr*. Motor Vehicle Reports (Second Series), 1988-.

MYCOTIC ANEURYSM. An aneurysm caused when a blood vessel wall is weakened by infection. F. A. Jaffe, *A Guide to Pathological Evidence*, 3d ed. (Toronto: Carswell, 1991) at 212.

MYOCARDITIS. *n*. Inflammation of the muscle tissue of the heart.

N. *abbr.* 1. Newton. 2. Nano.

NAC. *abbr.* National Arts Centre.

NAFTA. The North American Free Trade Agreement.

NAKED CONTRACT. A contract which lacks consideration.

NAM. *n.* The seizure or distraint of another person's goods.

NAME. *n.* A given name and surname. See BUSINESS ~; CHANGE OF ~; CHRISTIAN ~; CORPORATE ~; FAMILY ~; FIRM GIVEN ~; GIVEN ~S; GRADE ~; NUMBER ~; PROPER ~; REGISTERED ~; SUR~ AND CHRISTIAN ~S; TRADE-~.

NAME A MEMBER. The Speaker of the House, by naming a mamber, requires that they remove themselves from the House for the rest of that sitting. A. Fraser, W.F. Dawson & J.A. Holtby, eds., *Beauchesne's Rules and Forms of the House of Commons of Canada*, 6th ed. (Toronto: Carswell, 1989) at 54.

NAMED INSURED. A person specified in a contract of insurance as the one protected by the contract.

NAMED PRINCIPAL. A party whose name was revealed by the agent to the third party.

NAME SIGN. A sign (a) that is erected on land adjacent to a highway; (b) that is not more than 2 feet in height and not more than 3 feet in width; and (c) that does not display or indicate any information or advertising thereon other than the name of the occupant of the land, his address and his trade, business, profession or calling. *Highways Protection Act*, C.C.S.M., c. H50, s. 1.

NAMIUM. *n.* 1. Distress. 2. The seizure or distraint of another person's goods.

NAMIUM VETITUM. The unjust seizure of another's cattle bar driving them to an illegal place and pretending they had done damage.

NANNY. *n.* A person employed to rear a child who is a member of the household where the person is considered to be qualified to do so because of formal training or experience equivalent to formal training.

NANO. *pref.* 10^{-9}. Prefix for multiples and sub-multiples of basic, supplementary and derived units of measurement. *Weights and Measures Act*, S.C. 1970-71-72, c. 36, schedule I.

NARCOTIC. *n.* A drug which controls pain, induces sleep and stupor. Formerly controlled under the Narcotics Control Act and more recently under the *Controlled Drugs and Substances Act, 1996*, S.C. 1996, c. 19. See ORAL PRESCRIPTION ~.

NARWHAL. *n.* A cetacean (Monodon monoceros) of the dolphin family that inhabits the Arctic seas.

NARWHAL CALF. A narwhal that is light in colour and less than 1.8 m in length, measured from the point of the upper jaw to the notch between the tail flukes. *Marine Mammals Regulation*, SOR/93-56, s. 2.

NASOPHARYNX. *n.* The part of the pharynx above the palate. F.A. Jaffe, *A Guide to Pathological Evidence*, 3d ed. (Toronto: Carswell, 1991) at 224.

NAT. BANKING L. REV. *abbr.* National Banking Law Review.

NAT. CREDITOR/DEBTOR REV. *abbr.* National Creditor/Debtor Review.

NAT. INSOLVENCY REV. *abbr.* National Insolvency Review.

NATION. *n.* People distinct from other people, usually because of language or government. See

COMITY OF ~S; INTERNATIONAL LAW; LAW OF ~S; LEAGUE OF ~S.

NATIONAL. *n*. 1. An individual possessing the nationality of a state. 2. Any legal person, partnership and association deriving its status as such from the law in force in a state.

NATIONAL ANTHEM. The words and music of the song "O Canada" are designated as the national anthem of Canada.

NATIONAL ARTS CENTRE. A federal corporation which operates the National Arts Centre in Ottawa and develops performing arts in the National Capital Region.

NATIONAL ASSEMBLY. The legislative assembly of the province of Quebec.

NATIONAL AVERAGE RATE OF TAX. In respect of a revenue source it is the quotient obtained by dividing the aggregate of the revenues to be equalized for a revenue source for all provinces for a fiscal year by the revenue base for that revenue source for all provinces for that fiscal year. *Federal-Provincial Fiscal Arrangements Act*, R.S.C. 1985, c. F-8, s. 4(2).

NATIONAL BUILDING CODE OF CANADA. The National Building Code issued by the National Research Council.

NATIONAL CAPITAL COMMISSION. A federal body which promotes public use and enjoyment of land it controls in the National Capital Region. A corporation, called the National Capital Commission, consisting of a Chairperson, a Vice-Chairperson and thirteen other members. The objects and purposes of the Commission are to (a) prepare plans for and assist in the development, conservation and improvement of the National Capital Region in order that the nature and character of the seat of the Government of Canada may be in accordance with its national significance; and (b) organize, sponsor or promote such public activities and events in the National Capital Region as will enrich the cultural and social fabric of Canada, taking into account the federal character of Canada, the equality of status of the official languages of Canada and the heritage of the people of Canada. The Commission shall, in accordance with general plans prepared under the National Capital Commission Act, coordinate the development of public lands in the National Capital Region.

NATIONAL CAPITAL REGION. The seat of the Government of Canada and its surrounding area.

NATIONAL COMMODITY FUTURES EXAMINATION. An examination relating to the commodity futures industry that has been prepared by the Chicago Board of Trade and is administered in the United States of America by the National Association of Securities Dealers, Inc. and is administered in Canada by the Canadian Securities Institute.

NATIONAL CONCERN. Features of the doctrine are: 1.The national concern doctrine is separate and distinct from the national emergency doctrine of the peace, order and good government power, which is chiefly distinguishable by the fact that it provides a constitutional basis for what is necessarily legislation of a temporary nature; 2. The national concern doctrine applies to both new matters which did not exist at Confederation and to matters which, although originally matters of a local or private nature in a province, have since, in the absence of national emergency, become matters of national concern; 3. For a matter to qualify as a matter of national concern in either sense it must have a singleness, distinctiveness and indivisibility that clearly distinguishes it from matters of provincial concern and a scale of impact on provincial jurisdiction that is reconcilable with the fundamental distribution of legislative power under the Constitution; 4. In determining whether a matter has attained the required degree of singleness, distinctiveness and indivisibility that clearly distinguishes it from matters of provincial concern it is relevant to consider what would be the effect on extra-provincial interests of a provincial failure to deal effectively with the control or regulation of the intra-provincial aspects of the matter. *R. v. Crown Zellerbach Canada Ltd.*, [1988] 1 S.C.R. 401, per Le Dain, J.

NATIONAL DAY OF REMEMBRANCE. On December 6, 1989, fourteen women died as a result of a massacre at the University of Montreal. Throughout Canada, in each and every year, 6th day of December shall be known under the name of "National Day of Remembrance and Action on Violence Against Women".

NATIONAL DEBT. Money which a national government owes and on which interest is paid.

NATIONAL DNA DATA BANK. The Solicitor General of Canada shall, for criminal identification purposes, establish a national DNA data bank, consisting of a crime scene index and a convicted offenders index, to be maintained by the Commissioner of the R.C.M.P. *DNA Identification Act, 1998*, S. C. 1998, c. 37, s. 5.

NATIONAL EMISSIONS MARK. A mark established by regulation for use in respect of emissions from vehicles, engines or equipment and which may be applied by a company authorized to do so. *Canadian Environmental Protection Act, 1999*, S.C. 1999, c. 33, s. 149, 151.

NATIONAL ENERGY BOARD. A federal body which regulates certain areas of the gas, oil and electrical industry and advises government on developing and using energy resources.

NATIONAL FILM BOARD. A federal body which produces and distributes films which interpret Canada for Canadians and non-Canadians.

NATIONAL FIRE PREVENTION ASSO-CIATION. A standards setting body in the United States some of whose standards are referred to or have been adopted in Ontario statutes, e.g., the Fire Code under the Fire Marshals Act. D. Robertson, *Ontario Health and Safety Guide* (Toronto: Richard De Boo Ltd., 1988) at 5-278.

NATIONALITY. *n.* The character or quality which originates in a person belonging to a particular nation and which determines that individual's political status. See DUAL ~.

NATIONALIZATION. *n.* The acquisition of a business by government.

NATIONAL LIBRARY. 1. Continued under the National Library Act. The publisher of a book published in Canada shall, at the publisher's own expense and within one week after the date of publication, send two copies of the book to the National Librarian, who shall give to the publisher a written receipt therefor. 2. The Bibliothèque nationale du Québec. *An Act Respecting the Bibliothèque Nationale du Québec*, R.S.Q. 1977, c. B-2, s. 1.

NATIONAL LIBRARY OF CANADA. A federal body with mandate to acquire, preserve and make available the published heritage of Canada and to help all Canadian people share the country's library resources.

NATIONAL MOBILITY AGREEMENT. An agreement among law societies to permit members of one society to practise in another jurisdiction on a temporary basis.

NATIONAL MUSEUMS OF CANADA. A federal body with mandate to display the products of nature and the work of people with special though not exclusive reference to Canada.

NATIONAL OCCUPATIONAL CLASSI-FICATION. The *National Occupational Classification* published by the Department of Human Resources Development, as amended from time to time.

NATIONAL ORIGIN. 1. Includes nationality and ancestry. 2. The national origin of an ancestor.

NATIONAL PARK. A national park established and maintained under the *Canada National Parks Act*. See PROPOSED ~.

NATIONAL PAROLE BOARD. A federal body with authority to grant unescorted temporary absence from a federal correctional institution and to grant, terminate, or revoke parole for inmates of federal institutions and for inmates of provincial institutions in the Atlantic and Prairie provinces.

NATIONAL RATE OF UNEMPLOY-MENT. The rate of unemployment as determined by Statistics Canada for the whole of Canada.

NATIONAL RESEARCH COUNCIL OF CANADA. The federal body which carries out applied and basic research, studies topics of long-term national concern, offers laboratory support in important technological areas, manages programs of industrial development, administers national facilities for the scientific community and coordinates a national network for scientific and technological information.

NATIONAL SAFETY MARK. The expression "Canada Motor Vehicle Safety Standard" or "Norme de sécurité des véhicules automobiles du Canada", the abbreviation "CMVSS" or "NSVAC".

NATIONAL STANDARD. A standard recognized by the National Standards System of the Standards Council of Canada.

NATIONAL TRADE-MARK. Certain national trade-marks established by legislation.

NATIONAL TREATMENT. Dealing with a foreigner in the same way as a national of one's own country.

NAT. LABOUR REV. *abbr.* National Labour Review.

NAT'L BANKING L. REV. *abbr.* National Banking Law Review.

NAT'L INSOLV. REV. *abbr.* National Insolvency Review.

NAT. PROPERTY REV. *abbr.* National Property Review.

NATURAE VIS MAXIMA. [L.] Natural force is very great.

NATURAL AFFECTION. The love which someone has for kin, held to be not a valuable but a good consideration in certain circumstances.

NATURAL AREA. A parcel of land designated as such under section 3 that (i) contains natural ecosystems or constitutes the habitat of rare, endangered or uncommon plant or animals species, (ii) contains unusual botanical, zoological, geological, morphological, or palaeonto-logical features, (iii) exhibits exceptional and diversified scenery, (iv) provides haven for seasonal concentration of birds and animals, or (v) provides opportunities for scientific and educational programs in aspects of the natural environment. *Natural Areas Protection Act*, R.S.P.E.I. 1988, c. N-2, s. 1(b).

NATURAL-BORN SUBJECT. A person born within the Crown's dominion and the sovereign's allegiance.

NATURAL BOUNDARY. The visible high water mark of any lake, river, stream or other body of water where the presence and action of the water are so common and usual, and so long continued in all ordinary years, as to mark on the soil of the bed of the body of water a character distinct from that of its banks, in vegetation, as well as in the nature of the soil itself. *Land* Act, R.S.B.C. 1996, c. 245, s. 1.

NATURAL CHILD. A child of one's body; a child in fact.

NATURAL DISASTER. Major damage caused by certain elements or disturbances in nature, such as: (i) droughts, hurricanes, tornadoes, violent winds, earthquakes, landslides, electrical storms, excessive rains, floods, hail, frost, sleet and heavy snowstorms; (ii) uncontrollable fire of any origin; (iii) an insect plague beyond normal control seriously affecting production; and (iv) plant and animal diseases, when their spread reaches epidemic proportions and seriously affects production.

NATURAL DISTRICT. A territory designated as such by the Government because of the aesthetic, legendary or scenic interest of its natural setting. *Cultural Property Act*, R.S.Q., chapter B-4, s. 1.

NATURALE EST QUIDLIBET DISSOLVI EO MODO QUO LIGATUR. [L.] It is natural for something to be loosened the same way it was tied.

NATURAL ENVIRONMENT. Any part or combination of the air, land and water. See ENVIRONMENT; RESTORE THE ~.

NATURALES LIBERI. [L.] Natural children.

NATURAL FORUM. 1. " . . . [T]hat forum in which, a person 'with nothing but common sense to guide him', would say that the action 'ought to be tried':. . ." *General Dynamics Corp. v. Velitis* (1985), 7 C.P.C. (2d) 169 at 174, 53 O.R. (2d) 371 (H.C.), White J. 2. The place where the tort occurred or operates, the usual or significant residence of the parties, convenience in relation to the availability of evidence required by the parties are considerations in determining the natural forum for a dispute.

NATURAL GAS. A mixture, consisting principally of hydrocarbons that may contain non-hydrocarbon gases such as carbon dioxide, hydrogen sulphide, nitrogen or other elements, which mixture is recoverable from an underground reservoir and is in the gaseous phase or in solution with crude oil in the reservoir. See OIL, ~, OR SALT PRODUCTION EQUIPMENT.

NATURAL GAS LIQUID. Ethane, propane and butane, and any mixture of two or more thereof, that are produced at a gas processing plant or a gas reprocessing plant.

NATURAL HEALTH PRODUCT. A substance set out in Schedule 1 or a combination of substances in which all the medicinal ingredients are substances set out in Schedule 1, a homeopathic medicine or a traditional medicine, that is manufactured, sold or represented for use in (*a*) the diagnosis, treatment, mitigation or prevention of a disease, disorder or abnormal physical state or its symptoms in humans; (*b*) restoring or correcting organic functions in humans; or (*c*) modifying organic functions in humans, such as modifying those functions in a manner that maintains or promotes health. However, a natural health product does not include a substance set out in Schedule 2, any combination of substances that includes a substance set out in Schedule 2 or a homeopathic medicine or a traditional medicine that is or includes a substance set out in Schedule 2. *Natural Health Products Regulations*, SOR/2003-196, s. 1.

NATURAL HERITAGE OBJECT. A work of nature consisting of or containing evidence of flora or fauna or geological processes. *The Heritage Resources Act*, C.C.S.M., c. H391, s. 43.

NATURALIZATION. *var.* **NATURALISATION**. *n.* 1. The act of becoming the subject of a nation. 2. " . . . [S]eems prima facie to include the power of enacting what shall be the consequences of naturalization, or, in other words, what shall be the rights and privileges pertaining to residents in Canada after they have been naturalized . . ." *Union Colliery & Co. British Columbia v. Bryden*, [1899] A.C. 580 at 586, 15 T.L.R. 598, 1 M.M.C. 337 (B.C. P.C.), the board per Lord Watson. See CERTIFICATE OF ~.

NATURAL JUSTICE. 1. " . . . [T]wo main components, the right to be heard and the right to a hearing from an unbiased tribunal, . . ." *Wark v. Green* (1985), (*sub nom. Wark v. C. U.P.E.*) 66 N.B.R. (2d) 77 at 83, 169 A.P.R. 77, 86 C.L.L.C. 14,020, 23 D.L.R. (4th) 594 (C.A.), Hoyt J.A. 2. "The concept of natural justice is an elastic one, that can and should defy precise definition. The application of the principle must vary with the circumstances. How much or how little is encompassed by the term will depend on many factors; to name a few, the nature of the hearing, the nature of the tribunal presiding, the scope and effect of the ruling made." *Tandy Electronics Ltd. v. U.S.W.A.* (1979), 79 C.L.L.C. 14,216 at 170, 26 O.R. (2d) 68, 102 D.L.R. (3d) 126 (Div. Ct.), the court per Cory J.

NATURAL LAW. The code of rules which originates with the divine, nature or reason in contrast to laws people make.

NATURAL OBLIGATION. A duty with a definite purpose which is not necessarily governed by legal obligation.

NATURAL PERSON. A human being.

NATURAL PRODUCT. A product of agriculture or of the forest, sea, lake or river and an article of food or drink wholly or partly manufactured or derived from such product.

NATURAL RESOURCES. 1. Land, plant life, animal life, water and air. 2. Land, water and atmosphere, their mineral, vegetable and other components, including flora and fauna.

NATURAL RESOURCES AGREEMENT. An agreement made between Canada and one of the three prairie provinces which were granted constitutional status by amendment to the Constitution Act in 1930. P.W. Hogg, *Constitutional Law of Canada*, 3d ed. (Toronto: Carswell, 1992) at 678.

NATURAL SCIENCES AND ENGINEERING RESEARCH COUNCIL OF CANADA. The federal agency which offers financial support for advanced research and development in natural science and engineering at Canadian universities and encourages cooperation between industry and these institutions.

NATURAL USER. The use of land for most residential, recreational and industrial purposes. See NON-~.

NATURAL WATER. Includes water that has been treated for the control of impurities in the interest of public health, but does not include water that is sold in bottles and other containers each containing one litre or less. *Retail Sales Tax Act*, R.R.O. 1990, c. 1013, s. 1.

NATURAL WINE. Any alcoholic beverage obtained by the fermentation of the natural sugar content of fruits or other agricultural products, and that does not contain more than 14 per cent alcohol by volume. *Liquor Control Act*, R.S.M. 1970, c. L160, s. 2.

NATURA NON FACIT SALTUM; ITA NEC LEX. [L.] Nature does not leap; nor does the law.

NATURA NON FACIT VACUUM, NEC LEX SUPERVACUUM. [L.] Nature does nothing worthless, nor does the law do anything useless.

NATURE. See IMMOVABLE BY ~; STATE OF ~.

NATURE CONSERVANCY AREA. A roadless area, in a park, retained in a natural condition for the preservation of its ecological environment and scenic features, and designated as a nature conservancy area under this Act. *Park Act*, R.S.B.C. 1979, c. 309, s. 1.

NATURE RESERVE. Land under private ownership recognized as a nature reserve because it has significant biological, ecological, wildlife, floristic, geological, geomorphic or landscape features that warrant preservation. *Natural Heritage Conservation Act*, R.S.Q. c. C-61.01, s. 2

NATUROPATH. *n.* A person who practises naturopathy. *Naturopathy Act*, R.S.A. 1970, c. 257, s. 2.

NATUROPATHIC MEDICINE. The art of healing by natural methods or therapeutics, including the first aid treatment of minor cuts, abrasions and contusions, bandaging, taking of blood samples, and the prescribing or administering of authorized preparations and medicines.

NATUROPATHY. *n*. A drugless system of therapy that treats human injuries, ailments, or diseases, by natural methods, including any one or more of the physical, mechanical, or material, forces or agencies of nature, and employs as auxiliaries for such purposes the use of electrotherapy, hydro-therapy, body manipulations or dietetics.

NAULAGE. *n*. The freight belonging to a ship's passengers.

NAVAL COURT. Any officer who commands a ship belonging to Her Majesty on any foreign station or any consular officer may hold such a court when a complaint which requires immediate investigation arises, when the owner's interest in any Canadian ship or cargo seems to require it or when a Canadian ship is abandoned, wrecked or lost. R.M. Fernandes & C. Burke, *The Annotated Canada Shipping Act* (Toronto: Butterworths, 1988) at 213.

NAVIGABLE. *adj*. 1. " . . . [T]he legal test of navigability adopted by Canadian Courts, (including the law of Quebec) that is, navigability in fact, by any mode of craft and capability of use as a highway for trade and commerce. . ." *Coleman v. Ontario (Attorney General)* (1983), 27 R.P.R. 107 at 113, 12 C.E.L.R. 104, 143 D.L.R. (3d) 608 (Ont. H.C.), Henry J. 2. . . [I]n Ontario, navigability in law ought to be determined according to a less restrictive test in the light of modern conditions which, in recent years, have seen extensive use of lakes, rivers and streams for non-commercial purposes. . . I conclude therefore that if the stream is navigable in fact for the purposes of transportation or travel, or is floatable, whether for large or small craft of shallow draft, it is navigable in law without the necessity of applying the test of its usefulness for trade and commerce, a test which may well have been apt when the country was developing in the course of settlement, but is now no longer realistic in the light of modern conditions." *Coleman v. Ontario (Attorney General)* (1983), 27 R.P.R. 107 at 113, 119, 12 C.E.L.R. 104, 143 D.L.R. (3d) 608 (Ont. H.C.), Henry J.

NAVIGABLE WATER. Includes a canal and any other body of water created or altered as a resin of the construction of an work. *Navigable*

Waters Protection Act, R.S.C. 1985, c. N-22, s. 2.

NAVIGATION. *n*. The direction of movement of vessels on navigable waters. See AID TO ~; LAKE AND RIVER ~; SEASON OF ~.

NAVIGATION AND SHIPPING. Head of power in section 91(1) of the Constitution Act refers to traffic on navigable waters and the use to which such waters are put. Includes the commercial shipping and pleasure craft.

NAVIGATION SEASON. The annual period designated by the authority and the corporation, which is appropriate to weather and ice conditions or vessel traffic demands, during which the seaway is open for navigation. *Seaway Regulations*, C.R.C., c. 1397, s. 2.

NAVY. *n*. A fleet, a group of ships.

N.B. *abbr*. 1. New Brunswick. 2. [L. nota bene] Observe.

NBC. *abbr*. National Building Code of Canada.

NBCA. Neutral citation for New Brunswick Court of Appeal.

N.B. EQ. *abbr*. New Brunswick Equity Reports, 1894-1912.

N.B.L.L.C. *abbr*. New Brunswick Labour Law Cases.

N.B.R. *abbr*. New Brunswick Reports, 1825-1929.

N.B.R. (2d). *abbr*. New Brunswick Reports (Second Series), 1969-.

N.C.C. *abbr*. National Capital Commission.

NCR. *abbr*. Not criminally responsible on account of mental disorder, verdict in a criminal trial.

NEAR. *adj*. In proximity.

NEAR PATIENT IVDD. An *in vitro* diagnostic device that is intended for use outside a laboratory, for testing at home or at the point of care, such as a pharmacy, a health care professional's office or the bedside. *Medical Devices Regulations* SOR/98-282, s. 1.

NEAR PATIENT IN VITRO DIAGNOSTIC DEVICE. An *in vitro* diagnostic device that is intended for use outside a laboratory, for testing at home or at the point of care, such as a pharmacy, a health care professional's office or the bedside. *Medical Devices Regulations* SOR/98-282, s. 1.

NEAREST RELATIVE. The person first described in this clause who is mentally competent and available: (i) the spouse; (ii) a son or daughter who has attained the age of majority; (iii) a parent or guardian; (iv) a brother or sister who has attained the age of majority; (v) any other of the next-of-kin who has attained the age of majority.

NEAR RELATIVE. 1. One of the following persons, namely, the wife, father, mother, grandfather, grandmother, child, grandchild, brother or sister of the seaman. *Canada Shipping Act*, R.S.C. 1985, c. S-9, s. 191. 2 A grandfather, grandmother, father, mother, son, daughter, husband, wife, brother, sister, half brother or half sister, friend, caregiver or companion designated by patient and includes the legal guardian of a minor and a representative under an agreement made under the *Representation Agreement Act* and a committee having custody of the person of a patient under the *Patients Property Act*. *Mental Health Act*, R.S.B.C. 1996, c. 288, s. 1.

NEAT. See NET.

N.E.B. *abbr*. National Energy Board.

NECATION. *n*. Killing.

NECESSARIES. *n*. Goods suitable to the condition of life of infant or minor or other person, and to his or her actual requirements at the time of the sale and delivery. *Sale of Goods acts.*

NECESSARIES OF LIFE. 1. " . . . In order to establish that the articles are necessaries, it must be shown that they are necessary to maintain the person in the station in life in which he finds himself." *Consumers Gas Co. v. Stewart* (1980), 31 O.R. (2d) 559 at 561, 36 C.B.R. (N.S.) 136, 119 D.L.R. (3d) 286 (Div. Ct.), Southey J. 2. " . . . Medicine and medical treatment where it was reasonable and proper that they should be provided: . . . Education suitable to an infant's prospects in life has been held to be a necessary for which he can bind himself: . . . Education in a trade with a view to making an infant a useful citizen has also been held to be a necessary:. . ." *Peel (Regional Municipality) v. A. (T.O.)* (1982), 26 R.F.L. (2d) 351 at 357-8, 35 O.R. (2d) 260, 17 M.P.L.R. 94, 131 D.L.R. (3d) 297, 64 C.C.C. (2d) 289 (C.A.), the court per Howland C.J.O. 3. Food, clothing, lodging and other means that at the time of death of an insured are available to the person claiming to be dependent upon the insured and reasonably necessary to the maintenance of life and to the continuation of the degree of health then enjoyed by the person so claiming. *The Automobile Accident Insurance Act*, R.S.S. 1978, c. A-35, s. 2.

NECESSARY. *adj*. 1. Useful; probative of an issue. 2. Hearsay evidence is considered necessary and admissible when the declarant is unavailable to testify at trial and the party presenting the evidence is unable to obtain it from another source of similar quality.

NECESSARY CAUSE. A cause without which the loss or injury would not have happened.

NECESSARY IMPLICATION. The Crown may be bound by a statute by its express terms or by necessary implication. Necessary implication exists where it is manifest from the terms of the statute that the legislature intended the Crown to be bound or where it is apparent from the terms of the statute when it was passed and received royal assent that its beneficial purpose would be wholly frustrated if the Crown were not bound.

NECESSITAS EST LEX TEMPORIS ET LOCI. [L.] Necessity is a law of time and place.

NECESSITAS INDUCIT PRIVILEGIUM QUOAD JURA PRIVATA. [L.] Necessity introduces privilege with respect to private rights.

NECESSITAS NON HABET LEGEM. [L.] Necessity does not submit to law.

NECESSITAS PUBLICA MAJOR EST QUAM PRIVATA. [L.] A public necessity is more important than a private one.

NECESSITAS QUOD COGIT DEFENDIT. [L.] Necessity defends whatever it collects.

NECESSITATED. *adj*. Required as a matter of physical necessity or inevitability; appropriate, suitable, proper.

NECESSITOUS FARMER. A farmer who by reason of circumstances beyond his control is unable out of his own resources to provide himself with any of the commodities that may be furnished to him pursuant to this Act. *Agricultural Relief Advances Act*, R.S.A. 1980, c. A-10, s. 1.

NECESSITY. *n*. 1. "The [defence of necessity] doctrine exists as an excusing defence, operating in very limited circumstances, when conduct that would otherwise be illegal and sanctionable is excused and made unsanctionable because it is properly seen as the result of a 'morally involuntary' decision . . ." *R. v. Goltz*, [1991] 3 S.C.R. 485 at 519, 8 C.R. (4th) 82, 31 M.V.R. (2d) 137,

61 B.C.L.R. (2d) 145, 67 C.C.C. (3d) 481, 131 N.R. 1, 7 C.R.R. (2d) 1, 5 B.C.A.C. 161, 11 W.A.C. 161, Gonthier J. (La Forest, L'Heureux-Dubé, Sopinka, Cory and Iacobucci JJ. concurring). 2. " . . . [R]efers to the necessity of the hearsay evidence to prove a fact in issue. . . the criterion of necessity must be given a flexible definition, capable of encompassing diverse situations. What these situations will have in common is that the relevant direct evidence is not, for a variety of reasons, available." *R. v. Smith* (1992), 75 C.C.C. (3d) 257 at 271, 15 C.R. (4th) 133, 139 N.R. 323, 94 D.L.R. (4th) 590, 55 O.A.C. 321, [1992] 2 S.C.R. 915, the court per Lamer C.J.C. 3. [In the context of admissibility of expert evidence] The second requirement of the analysis exists to ensure that the dangers associated with expert evidence are not lightly tolerated. Mere relevance or "helpfulness" is not enough. The evidence must also be *necessary*. I agree with the Chief Justice that some degree of deference is owed to the trial judge's discretionary determination of whether the requirements have been met on the facts of a particular case, but that discretion cannot be used erroneously to dilute the requirement of necessity. Mere helpfulness is too low a standard to warrant accepting the dangers inherent in the admission of expert evidence. *A fortiori*, a finding that some aspects of the evidence "might reasonably have assisted the jury" is not enough. As stated by Sopinka et al., expert evidence must be necessary in order to allow the fact finder: (1) to appreciate the facts due to their technical nature, or; (2) to form a correct judgment on a matter if ordinary persons are unlikely to do so without the assistance of persons with special knowledge. (J. Sopinka, S. N. Lederman and A. W. Bryant, *The Law of Evidence in Canada* (2nd ed. 1999), at p. 620.) *R. v. D. (D.)*, 2000 CarswellOnt 3255, 2000 SCC 43, 36 C.R. (5th) 261, 148 C.C.C. (3d) 41, 191 D.L.R. (4th) 60, 259 N.R. 156, 136 O.A.C. 201, [2000] 2 S.C.R. 275 Per Major, J. for majority. 4. When it comes to necessity, the question is whether the expert will provide information which is likely to be outside the ordinary experience and knowledge of the trier of fact: B. (R.H.), *supra*; Mohan, *supra*; *R. v. Lavallee*, [1990] 1 S.C.R. 852; *R. v. Abbey*, [1982] 2 S.C.R. 24 (S.C.C.); *Kelliher (Village) v. Smith*, [1931] S.C.R. 672. "Necessity" means that the evidence must more than merely "helpful", but necessity need not be judged "by too strict a standard": Mohan, *supra*, at p. 23. Absolute necessity is not required. *R. v. D. (D.)*, 2000 CarswellOnt 3255, 2000 SCC 43, 36 C.R. (5th) 261, 148 C.C.C. (3d) 41, 191 D.L.R. (4th) 60, 259 N.R. 156, 136 O.A.C. 201, [2000] 2 S.C.R. 275 Per McLachlin J. for minority. 5. In terms of admissibility of hearsay evidence, hearsay evidence will be necessary in circumstances where the declarant is unavailable to testify at trial and where the party is unable to obtain evidence of a similar quality from another source. Consistent with a flexible definition of the necessity criterion, there is no reason why the unavailability of the declarant should be limited to closed, enumerated list of causes. *R. v. Hawkins*, [1996] 3 S.C.R. 1043. 6. If all members of a tribunal competent to determine a matter are subject to disqualification they may be authorized to hear and determine a matter by virtue of necessity. See AGENCY OF ~; BASIC NECESSITIES.

NEC PER VIM, NEC CLAM, NEC PRECARIO. [L.] Neither by violence, nor stealth nor by request.

NECROPSY. *n*. An autopsy.

NECROSIS. *n*. The death of cells in an organism which is alive.

NEC TEMPUS NEC LOCUS OCCURRIT REGI. [L.] Neither time nor place oppose the monarch.

NEC VENIAM, EFFUSO SANGUINE, CASUS HABET. [L.] If blood is spilled, the case is unforgivable.

NEC VI, NEC CLAM, NEC PRECARIO. [L.] Neither by violence, nor stealth nor by request.

NEED. See FAMILY IN ~; PERSON IN ~; REASONABLE ~S; SPECIAL ~.

NE EXEAT. [L.] Let him not go forth.

NE EXERT PROVINCIA. [L.] A writ restraining a debtor from leaving the province.

NE EXERT REGNO. [L.] A writ preventing a person from leaving the country without the court's leave.

NEGATIO CONCLUSIONIS EST ERROR IN LEGE. [L.] In law, the negation of a conclusion is an error.

NEGATIO DESTRUIT NEGATIONEM, ET AMBO FACIUNT AFFIRMATIVUM. [L.] Negative destroys negative, and together they make an affirmative.

NEGATIVE. *n*. Denial.

NEGATIVE DAMAGE. The removal of desirable things: amenities, earnings, enjoyment and expectation of life. K.D. Cooper-Stephenson & I.B. Saunders, *Personal Injury Damages in Canada* (Toronto: Carswell, 1981) at 52.

NEGATIVE EASEMENT. One which involves a right to prohibit the commission of certain acts on the servient tenement, acts which the servient owner otherwise would be entitled to commit.

NEGATIVE OPTION SCHEME. An arrangement between a buyer and a seller under which the seller will, from time to time; (a) on notice to the buyer, supply the buyer with goods described in the notice, unless the buyer notifies the seller that he does not want to be supplied with the goods described in the notice; or (b) pursuant to the arrangement, supply the buyer with certain goods and the buyer will be deemed to have accepted the goods unless the buyer returns the goods to the seller. *Consumer Protection Act*, R.S.B.C. 1979, c. 65, s. 39.

NEGATIVE PREGNANT. In pleading, an evasive answer to something alleged, a literal answer but not an answer to substance.

NEGLECT. *n.* 1. A lack or failure to provide necessary care, aid, guidance or attention which causes or is reasonably likely to cause the victim severe physical or psychological harm or significant material loss to his estate. *Adult Protection Act*, R.S.P.E.I. 1988, c. A-5, s. 1(k). 2. Any failure to provide necessary care, assistance, guidance or attention to an adult that causes, or is reasonably likely to cause within a short period of time, the adult serious physical, mental or emotional harm or substantial damage to or loss of assets, and includes self neglect. *Adult Guardianship Act*, R.S.B.C. 1996, c. 6, s. 1.

NEGLECTED ADULT. An adult: (i) who is incapable of caring properly for himself or herself by reason of physical or mental infirmity, (ii) who is not suitable to be in a treatment facility under The Mental Health Act, (iii) who is not receiving proper care and attention, and (iv) who refuses, delays or is unable to make provision for proper care and attention for himself or herself. *Neglected Adults Welfare Act*, R.S. Nfld. 1990, c. N-3, s. 2.

NEGLECTED CHILD. A child in need of protection and without restricting the generality of the foregoing includes any child who is within one or more of the following descriptions: (i) a child who is not being properly cared for; (ii) a child who is abandoned or deserted by the person in whose charge that child is or who is an orphan who is not being properly cared for; (iii) a child when the person in whose charge that child is cannot, by reason of disease, infirmity, misfortune, incompetence or imprisonment, or any combination thereof, care properly for the child; (iv) a child who is living in an unfit or improper place; (v) a child found associating with an unfit or improper person; (vi) a child found begging in a public place; (vii) a child who, with the consent or connivance of the person in whose charge the child is, commits any act that renders the child liable to a penalty under an Act of Canada or of the Legislature, or under a municipal by-law; (viii) a child who is misdemeanant by reason of inadequacy of the control exercised by the person in whose charge the child is, or who is being allowed to grow up without salutory parental control or under circumstances tending to make the child idle or dissolute; (ix) a child who without sufficient cause, habitually is away from home or school; (x) a child where the person in whose charge the child is neglects or refuses to provide or obtain proper medical, surgical or other medical care or treatment necessary for the child's health or well-being, or refuses to permit that care or treatment to be supplied to the child when it is recommended by a physician; (xi) a child whose emotional or mental development is endangered because of emotional rejection or deprivation of affection by the person in whose charge the child is; (xii) a child whose life, health or morals may be endangered by the conduct of the person in whose charge the child is; (xiii) a child who is being cared for by and at the expense of someone other than the child's parents and in circumstances which indicate that the child's parents are not performing their parental duties; (xiv) a child who is not under proper guardianship or who has no parent (A) capable of exercising, (B) willing to exercise, or (C) capable of exercising and willing to exercise, proper parental control over the child; (xv) a child whose parent wishes to be rid of parental responsibilities toward the child.

NEGLIGENCE. *n.* 1. An independent tort which consists of breach of a legal duty to take care which results in damage, undesired by the defendant, to the plaintiff. 2. Conduct which creates an objectively unreasonable risk of harm. 3. The concept of fault in the Negligence Act, [R.S.O. 1990, c. N.1, s. 1] includes negligence, but is much broader than negligence. It incorporates all intentional wrongdoing as well as other types of substandard conduct. *Alpha Tire Corp. v. South China Industries (Canada) Inc.*

(2000), 2000 CarswellOnt 178 (S.C.J.). 4. " . . . [M]easures the conduct of the accused on the basis of an objective standard, irrespective of the accused's subjective mental state. Where negligence is the basis of liability, the question is not what the accused intended, but rather whether the accused exercised reasonable care." *R. v. Wholesale Travel Group* Inc. (1991), 8 C.R. (4th) 145 at 176, 67 C.C.C. (3d) 193, 4 O.R. (3d) 799n, 84 D.L.R. (4th) 161, 130 N.R. 1, 38 C.P.R. (3d) 451, 49 O.A.C. 161, [1991] 3 S.C.R. 154, 7 C.R.R. (2d) 36, Cory J. (L'Heureux-Dubé J. concurring). See ACTION FOR ~; ADVERTENT ~; CONCURRENT ~; CONTRIBUTORY ~; CRIMINAL ~; GROSS ~; MINOR ~; PENAL ~; SYSTEMIC ~.

NEGLIGENT BATTERY. Concerned with the physical consequences of one's actions. Accordingly, negligent battery will only be properly pleaded when it is alleged that the defendant negligently harmed the plaintiff by disregarding a foreseeable risk of physical contact. *S. (J.A.) v. Gross*, 2002 ABCA 36, [2002] 5 W.W.R. 54, 100 Alta. L.R. (3d) 310 (C.A.).

NEGLIGENT DRIVING. A continuum from momentary lack of attention giving rise to civil responsibility to dangerous driving under the Criminal Code.

NEGLIGENTIA SEMPER HABET INFORTUNIUM COMITEM. [L.] Negligence always has the companion misfortune.

NEGLIGENT MISREPRESENTATION. 1. Five general requirements to establish the cause of action are: (1) there must be a duty of care based on a "special relationship" between the representor and the representee; (2) the representation in question must be untrue, inaccurate, or misleading; (3) the representor must have acted negligently in making said misrepresentation; (4) the representee must have relied, in a reasonable manner, on said negligent misrepresentation; and (5) the reliance must have been detrimental to the representee in the sense that damages resulted. *Queen v. Cognos Inc.*, [1993] 1 S.C.R. 87, per Iacobucci, J. 2. "An action for negligent misrepresentation is made out where there is: (a) a negligent misrepresentation; (b) made carelessly and in breach of a duty owed by the representor to the representee to take reasonable care to ensure that the representation is adequate; which (c) causes loss which was the foreseeable consequence of the misrepresentation at the time it was made to the representee." *Rainbow Industrial Caterers Ltd. v. Canadian Na-*

tional Railway (1991), 8 C.C.L.T. (2d) 225 at 238, 59 B.C.L.R. (2d) 129, [1991] 6 W.W.R. 385, 84 D.L.R. (4th) 291, 126 N.R. 354, 3 B.C.A.C. 1, 7 W.A.C. 1, [1991] 3 S.C.R. 3, McLachlin J. (dissenting).

NEGLIGENT OPERATION. Includes the operation of a vessel in a manner that unnecessarily or unreasonably interferes with the free and proper use of the waters by other craft or other persons, or that endangers other craft. *Hamilton Harbour Commissioners' General By-law*, C.R.C., c. 894, s. 20.

NEGLIGENT TORT. A tort in which the wrongdoer as a reasonable person should have foreseen that her or his conduct involved a risk which was foreseeable though not certain.

NEGOTIABILITY. *n.* Capable of being exchanged for currency, money.

NEGOTIABLE INSTRUMENT. 1. Something which: (i) if payable to bearer, is transferable by delivery alone, or if payable to order, by delivery together with indorsement: (ii) presumes the giving of consideration; (iii) permits a transferee to take in good faith and for value to acquire good title despite lack of or defects in the transferor's title. E.L.G. Tyler & N.E. Palmer, eds., *Crossley Vaines' Personal Property*, 5th ed. (London: Butterworths, 1973) at 208. 2. Includes any cheque, draft, traveller's cheque, bill of exchange, postal note, money order, postal remittance and any other similar instrument.

NEGOTIABLE RECEIPT. A receipt in which it is stated that the goods therein specified will be delivered to bearer or to the order of a named person. *Warehouse Receipts acts*.

NEGOTIATE. *v.* 1. To transfer for value, by indorsement or delivery, a bill of exchange or other negotiable instrument. 2. To bargain in good faith with a view to the conclusion of an agreement or the revision or the renewal of an existing agreement.

NEGOTIATE IN GOOD FAITH. A party may commence negotiations by presenting an extreme position but in a series of meetings gradually withdraws to a more reasonable position.

NEGOTIATING RANGE. The limits within which a negotiator will make demands or concessions.

NEGOTIATION. *n.* 1. Transference of a bill from one person to another so that the transferee becomes the holder of the bill. E.L.G. Tyler & N.E. Palmer, eds., *Crossley Vaines' Personal Property*, 5th ed. (London: Butterworths, 1973) at 222. 2. Deliberation and discussion upon the terms of a proposed agreement, and includes conciliation and arbitration. See PLEA ~.

NEGOTIATOR. See GOVERNMENT ~.

NEGOTIORUM GESTIO. [L.] Interference in someone else's affairs out of kindness but with no authority.

NEIGHBOURHOOD IMPROVEMENT AREA. An area of a municipality for which the corporation has approved the implementation of a program to improve the quality of neighbourhood amenities and the housing and living conditions of persons of the area.

NEIGHBOURING RIGHTS. Musical performers' and record manufacturers' entitlement to compensation whenever qualifying sound recordings in which they hold rights are performed in public.

NEIGHBOUR TEST. The test of proximity between defendant and plaintiff in a negligence suit per Lord Atkin in *Donoghue v. Stevenson*, [1931] A.C. 562, 580: "You must take reasonable care to avoid acts or omissions which you can reasonably foresee would be likely to injure your neighbour. Who, then, in law is my neighbour? The answer seems to be — persons who are so closely and directly affected by my act that I ought reasonably to have them in contemplation as being so affected when I am directing my mind to the acts or omissions which are called in question."

NE JUDEX ULTRA PETITA PARTIUM. [L.] No judge should award more than the party sought to obtain.

NEM. CON. *abbr*. [L. nemine contradicente] Without anyone saying otherwise.

NEM. DIS. *abbr*. [L. nemine dissentiente] Without dissent.

NEMINE OPORTET ESSE SAPIENTIOREM LEGIBUS. [L.] No one should be wiser than the laws.

NEMO ADMITTENDUS EST INHABILITARE SEIPSUM. [L.] No one should be allowed to incapacitate oneself.

NEMO AGIT IN SEIPSUM. [L.] No one initiates proceedings against oneself.

NEMO ALIQUAM PARTEM RECTE INTELLIGERE POTEST ANTEQUAM TO-TUM ITERUM ATQUE ITERUM PERLEGIT. [L.] No one can properly understand any part before one has read the whole thing over and over again.

NEMO ALLEGANS TURPITUDINEM SUAM EST AUDIENDUS. [L.] No one who pleads one's own guilt will be heard.

NEMO COGITUR REM SUAM VENDERE, ETIAM JUSTE PRETIIO. [L.] No one is compelled to sell one's property, even for a fair price.

NEMO CONTRA FACTUM SUUM PROPRIUM VENIRE POTEST. [L.] No one can contradict one's very own deed.

NEMO DAT QUI NON HABET. [L.] No one who does not possess gives.

NEMO DAT QUOD NON HABET. [L.] No one gives what one does not possess.

NEMO DEBET BIS PUNIRI PRO UNO DELICTO. [L.] No one should be punished twice for one mistake. An accused cannot be convicted twice for precisely the same offence arising out of the same act. Once an accused is found guilty of the principle offence, this is a bar against further convictions being entered for included offences in the same proceeding or in a subsequent one where the accused can plead autrefois acquit.

NEMO DEBET BIS VEXARI, SI CONSTAT CURIAE QUOD SIT PRO UNA ET EADEM CAUSA. [L.] No one should be harassed twice, if the court agrees that it is for one and the same cause.

NEMO DEBET ESSE JUDEX IN PROPRIA CAUSA. [L.] No one should judge one's own cause.

NEMO DEBET LOCUPLETARI ALIENA JACTURA. [L.] No one should be enriched by another's loss.

NEMO DE DOMO SUA EXTRAHI DEBET. [L.] No one should be dragged out of one's own house.

NEMO EST HAERES VIVENTIS. [L.] No one is the heir of a living person.

NEMO EX ALTERIUS INCOMMODI DEBET LOCUPLETARI. [L.] No one should be enriched by another's misfortune.

NEMO EX DOLO SUO PROPRIO RELEVETUR, AUT AUXILIUM CAPIAT. [L.] No one is relieved or receives help out of one's very own fraud.

NEMO EX PROPRIO DOLO CONSEQUITUR ACTIONEM. [L.] No one pursues a cause of action out of one's very own fraud.

NEMO EX SUO DELICTO MELIOREM SUAM CONDITIONEM FACERE POTEST. [L.] No one can achieve a better personal position from one's own wrongdoing.

NEMO JUDEX IN CAUSA SUA DEBET ESSE. [L.] " . . . No one ought to be a Judge in his own cause. . ." *Barry v. Alberta Securities Commission* (1989), 3 Admin. L.R. 1 at 10, 93 N.R. 1, 65 Alta. L.R. (2d) 97, [1989] 3 W.W.R. 456, 57 D.L.R. (4th) 458, [1989] 1 S.C.R. 301, 96 A.R. 241, the court per L'Heureux-Dubé J.

NEMO PATRIAM IN QUA NATUS EST EXUERE NEC LIGEANTIAE DEBITUM EJURARE POSSIT. [L.] No one can cast away the country where one was born, nor forswear the allegiance owed to the sovereign.

NEMO PLUS JURIS TRANSFERE POTEST QUAM SE IPSE HABET. [L.] No one can confer a greater right on another than she has herself.

NEMO POTEST CONTRA RECORDUM VERIFICARE PER PATRIAM. [L.] No one can assume the verdict of a jury in any decision is correct.

NEMO POTEST ESSE SIMUL ACTOR ET JUDEX. [L.] No one can be suitor and judge at the same time.

NEMO POTEST ESSE TENENS ET DOMINUS. [L.] No one can be tenant and lord.

NEMO POTEST EXUERE PATRIAM. [L.] No one can shed his homeland.

NEMO POTEST FACERE PER ALIUM, QUOD PER SE NON POTEST. [L.] No one can do through another what it is not possible to do alone.

NEMO POTEST MUTARE CONSILIUM SUUM IN ALTERIUS INJURIAM. [L.] No one can change intention to the wrong of another.

NEMO POTEST PLUS JURIS AD ALIUM TRANSFERRE QUAM IPSE HABET. [L.] No one can give another a greater right than one oneself has.

NEMO PRAESUMITUR ALIENAM POSTE RITATEM SUAE PRAETULISSE. [L.] No one is presumed to have preferred another's descendants to one's own.

NEMO PRAESUMITUR ESSE IMNEMOR SUAE AETERNAE SALUTIS, ET MAXIME IN ARTICULO MORTIS. [L.] No one is presumed to be forgetful of one's own eternal wellbeing, and especially at the moment of death.

NEMO PRAESUMITUR MALUS. [L.] No one is considered bad in advance.

NEMO PROHIBETUR PLURIBUS DEFENSIONIBUS UTI. [L.] No one is prohibited from using many defences.

NEMO PUNITUR PRO ALIENO DELICTO. [L.] No one is punished for another's fault.

NEMO PUNITUR SINE INJURIA, FACTO, SEU DEFALTA. [L.] No one is punished except for a wrong, deed or default.

NEMO REUS EST NISI MENS SIT REA. [L.] No one is guilty unless she has a guilty mind.

NEMO SIBI CAUSAM POSSESSIONIS MUTARE POTEST. [L.] No one can change the reason of his possession for himself.

NEMO SIBI ESSE JUDEX VEL SUIS JUS DICERE DEBET. [L.] No one should be one's own judge, or decide matters of personal interest.

NEMO TENETUR AD IMPOSSIBILIA. [L.] No one is bound to do the impossible.

NEMO TENETUR ARMARE ADVERSARIUM CONTRA SE. [L.] No one is bound to arm an adversary against oneself.

NEMO TENETUR PRODERE SEIPSUM. [L.] No one is bound to betray oneself.

NEMO TENETUR SEIPSUM ACCUSARE. [L.] No one is bound to accuse herself. " . . . [T]he privilege of a witness not to answer a question which may incriminate him. That is all that is meant by the Latin maxim, nemo tenetur seipsum accusare, often incorrectly advanced in support of a much broader proposition. . ." *Marcoux v. R.* (1975), 60 D.L.R. (3d) 119 at 122, [1976] 1 S.C.R. 763, 29 C.R.N.S. 211, 4 N.R. 64, 24 C.C.C. (2d) 1, Dickson J. See PRIVILEGE AGAINST SELF-INCRIMINATION.

NEONATAL DEATH. The death of a child before the end of the six hundred and seventy-second hour after the birth of the child. *Hospital Management Act*, R.R.O. 1990, Reg. 965, s. 1.

NEPHEW. *n*. The son of a sister or brother, a half-sister or half-brother.

NEPOTISM. *n*. The practice of favouring relatives of the employer or management in hiring, in giving benefits or promotions.

NE RELESSE PAS. [Fr.] One did not release.

NERVOUS AILMENTS. See PRIVATE HOSPITAL FOR ~.

NERVOUS SHOCK. 1. " . . . [T]he claimant [must] show through the application of the relevant principles of negligence law that the negligent conduct of the defendant caused injuries to others whose suffering was seen and heard by the plaintiff, who was shocked by the experience and, as a result, developed a recognizable psychiatric or emotional illness. The plaintiff must show he suffers from some medically recognizable psychiatric or emotional illness, but damages will only be awarded if he shows the negligent conduct of the defendant caused the illness." *Beecham v. Hughes* (1988), 45 C.C.L.T. 1 at 18-19, 27 B.C.L.R. (2d) 1, [1988] 6 W.W.R. 33, 52 D.L.R. (4th) 635 (C.A.), Taggart J.A. (Carrothers J.A. concurring). 2. A legal label for types of mental or psychological injury which courts have recognized as worthy of an award of damages. Grief and sorrow are not included. See INTENTIONAL INFLICTION OF ~.

NET. *n*. 1. The weight of the commodity without its container. 2. In accounting, an amount of money after all specified expenditures or deductions are deducted.

NET. *adj*. Obtained after adjustments and deductions have been made.

NET ANNUAL INCOME. The annual receipts from sales less expenditures and depreciation.

NETBACK GAS. Marketable gas sold and delivered pursuant to producer-shipper contracts under which the same shipper is the buyer, where the price payable to the producers for as so delivered is calculated in accordance with a netback pricing formula, but does not include marketable gas sold and delivered pursuant to a producer-shipper contract under which the producer's obligation to deliver gas under the contract is preconditioned on his consent to the actual resale price or prices used in the netback pricing formula. *Natural Gas Marketing Act*, R.S.A. 2000, c. N-1, s. 9.

NETBACK PRICING FORMULA. A formula or method under which the actual price payable by the shipper for marketable gas sold and delivered pursuant to a producer-shipper contract is calculated wholly or partly by reference to a price or prices payable to the shipper on the resale of gas by him, whether the formula or method is contained in or incorporated by reference in the producer-shipper contract. *Natural Gas Marketing Act*, R.S.A. 2000, c. N-1, s. 9.

NET BOOK VALUE. The amount of assets less liabilities as recorded on a financial statement.

NET COUNTY LEVY. The amount required for county purposes including the sums required for any board, commission or other body, apportioned to each lower tier municipality by the county. *Ontario Unconditional Grants Act*, R.S.O. 1990, c. 0.38, s. 9(1).

NET EARNINGS. 1. Of a worker, means his average earnings while employed in the industry in which the worker was injured, less the total of: (i) employment insurance contributions for those earnings; (ii) Canada Pension Plan contributions for those earnings; and (iii) probable income tax deductions for those earnings based on tables produced by CCRA.

NET EDUCATION CAPITAL COST. The education capital cost reduced by any capital grants and subsidies paid or that may be paid to the board in respect of such education capital cost. *Development Charges Act*, R.S.O. 1990, c. D.9, s. 29(1).

NET EQUITY. Net proceeds less sales commission, legal fees and any penalties.

NET FACTOR. The difference between one and the sum of the legal percentages that an association deducts from the value of each bet made on a pool, expressed as a fraction. *Pari-Mutuel Betting Supervision Regulations*, SOR/91-365, s. 2.

NET FAMILY PROPERTY. The value of all the property, except property described in subsection (2), that a spouse owns on the valuation date, after deducting: (a) the spouse's debts and other liabilities; and (b) the value of property, other than a matrimonial home, that the spouse owned on the date of the marriage, after deducting the spouse's debts and other liabilities calculated as of the date of the marriage. *Family Law Act*, R.S.O. 1990, c. F.3, s. 4(1).

NET FIXED ASSETS. The value of the net investment in fixed assets for the purposes of a balance sheet. S.M. Beck *et al., Cases and Materials on Partnerships and Canadian Business* Corporations (Toronto: The Carswell Co., 1983), at 778.

NET GENERATING CAPABILITY. With reference to power, means the net capacity available from the generating facilities being referred to, with all the equipment available, at the time of the annual firm power peak load on the power grid, and, with reference to electric energy, means the net energy output available for a period of specified duration from such facilities.

NET INCOME. Income less expenses and an amount for anticipated income tax.

NET LEASE. " . . . [T]ype of lease, wherein the lessor undertakes to pay certain expenses . . ." *Boots Drug Stores (Canada) Ltd. v. Ritt* (1980), 12 R.P.R. 114 at 116 (Ont. H.C.), Callaghan J.

NET MUNICIPAL BUDGET. The total expenditure of a municipality less any non-tax revenue. *An Act to Amend the Municipal Assistance Act*, S.N.B. 1986, c. 58, s. 1.

NET NET LEASE. " . . . [L]ease under which a tenant pays all such costs and the landlord rents the premises in an 'as is' state without covenanting to pay any costs attendant upon the maintenance or operation of the leasehold premises. . ." *Boots Drug Stores (Canada) Ltd. v. Ritt* (1980), 12 R.P.R. 114 at 116 (Ont. H.C.), Callaghan J.

NET POOL. That portion of a pool remaining after deduction of the legal percentages. *Pari-Mutuel Betting Supervision Regulations*, SOR/91-365, s.2.

NET PROCEEDS. The amount remaining from a sale of property after deduction of expenses of the sale.

NET PROFIT. Clear profit after every deduction.

NET SALE PROCEEDS. The amount remaining after payment of commission and taxes.

NET SALVAGE VALUE. Salvage value minus any removal costs. Canada regulations.

NETTING. *n.* Setting the current capital gains and income of the taxation year off against the losses for that year.

NET VALUE. The value of the estate, wherever situate, both within and without the province, after payment of the charges thereon and the debts, funeral expenses, expenses of administra-

tion, succession duty and estate tax. *Intestate Succession acts*.

NETWORK. *n.* Includes any operation where control over all or any part of the programs or program schedules of one or more broadcasting undertakings is delegated to another undertaking or person. *Broadcasting Act*, S.C. 1991, c. 11, s. 2(1). See DISTRIBUTION ~; GROUNDING ~; LAND-RELATED INFORMATION SYSTEMS ~.

NETWORK FEED. Any radiocommunication that is transmitted (*a*) by a network operation to its affiliates, (*b*) to a network operation for retransmission by it to its affiliates, or (*c*) by a lawful distributor to a programming undertaking. *Radiocommunication Act*, R.S.C. 1985, c. R-2, s. 2.

NETWORK OPERATOR. Any person to whom permission has been granted by the Canadian Radio-television and Telecommunications Commission to form and operate a network. *Canada Elections Act, 2000*, S.C. 2000, c. 9, s. 319.

NET WORTH. The value of assets less liabilities.

NET WORTH TAXATION. A tax on personal wealth calculated on an individual's total assets minus any liabilities.

NE UNQUES. [Fr.] Never.

NE UNQUES ACCOULPÉ. [Fr.] A plea which denies there was a marriage.

NE UNQUES EXECUTOR. [Fr.] Never an executor.

NE UNQUES INDEBITATUS. [Fr.] Never in debt.

NE UNQUES SON RECEIVER. [Fr.] Never one's receiver.

NEUTRAL CITATION STANDARD. The neutral citation is consists of three (3) principal elements : (1) style of cause ; (2) core of the citation ; (3) optional elements. The core of the citation is constituted of three important elements : (i) the year ; (ii) the tribunal identifier ; (iii) the ordinal number of the decision.

NEUTRAL CONDUCTOR. That conductor of a polyphase circuit, or of a single-phase 3-wire circuit having an approximately uniform potential difference and an equal spacing in phase with each of the other conductors.

NEUTRALISATION. *n*. By treaty, exclusion of some territory from a region at war so that the territory has neutral status.

NEUTRALITY. *n*. A situation in which a territory is allied to neither side of a war.

NE VARIETUR. [L.] Let it not be varied.

NEVERTHELESS. *prep. or conj.* In spite of; notwithstanding. Creates an exclusion from or a diminution of the ambit of immediately preceding words.

NEW. *adj*. Not previously existing.

NEW EVIDENCE. Evidence which did not previously exist. Can also mean evidence not available previously even though a diligent search was carried out for it. See FRESH EVIDENCE.

NEWLY-BORN CHILD. A child under the age of 1 year. *Criminal Code*, R.S.C. 1985, c. C-46, s. 2.

NEWS-AGENT. *n*. A person, firm, or corporation, who sells by retail only all or any of the following: newspapers, magazines, periodicals, pamphlets, books, writing material, playing cards, picture cards, and souvenirs.

NEWSCASTS. *n*. Includes news headlines, reports of news events and summaries of the news.

NEWSPAPER. *n*. 1. Any paper, magazine or periodical containing public news, intelligence or reports of events, or any remarks or observations thereon, printed for sale and published periodically or in parts or numbers, at intervals not exceeding 31 days between the publication of any two such papers, parts or numbers, and any paper, magazine or periodical printed in order to be dispersed and made public, weekly or more often, or at intervals not exceeding 31 days, that contains advertisements, exclusively or principally. *Criminal Code*, R.S.C. 1985, c. C-46, s. 297. 2. A paper containing news, intelligence, occurrences, pictures or illustrations or remarks or observations thereon, printed for sale and published periodically, or in parts or numbers, at intervals not exceeding 31 days between the publication of any two of such papers, parts or numbers. *Defamation acts.* 3. In a provision requiring publication in newspaper, means a printed publication in sheet form, intended for general circulation, published regularly at intervals of not longer than a week, consisting in greater part of news of current events of general interest and sold to the public and to regular subscribers. *Interpretation Act*, R.S.O. 1990, c.I.11, s. 29(1). See CONSTRUCTION TRADE ~; WEEKLY CANADIAN ~.

NEWSPAPER RULE. " . . . [A] very limited form of protection has been extended to journalists by some Courts, but only at the pre-trial stage. This rule characterized or known as the 'newspaper rule' enables the Court to exercise its discretion and hold that during the discovery stage of a defamation action in which the press are defendants, they cannot be compelled to identify sources of this information even though the information is relevant. But if the matter proceeds to trial and the identity of the source is still a relevant issue disclosure may be made at that stage." *Wasylyshen v. Canadian Broadcasting Corp.* (1989), 48 C.C.L.T. 1 at 18, 32 C.P.C. (2d) 237, 73 Sask R. 295 (C.A.), Tallis, Vancise and Sherstobitoff JJ.A.

NEWSREEL. *n*. A film of one reel in length giving news of recent events and items of public interest.

NEWS REPORTING. Includes interviews, commentaries or other works prepared for and published by any newspaper, magazine or other periodical publication or broadcast on the facilities of any broadcasting undertaking without charge to any political party, constituency association or candidate registered under this Act. *Election Finances Act*, R.S.O. 1990, c. E.7, s. 1(1). See BONA FIDE ~.

NEWTON. *n*. The force that, when applied to a body having a mass of 1 kilogram, gives the body an acceleration of 1 metre per second. *Weights and Measures Act*, S.C. 1970-71-72, c. 36, schedule I.

NEW TRIAL. Application to the court for this is the only remedy when there is any defect in judgment through entirely extrinsic causes or something outside the record.

NEXT. See NOW AND ~; NOW, ~, HERETOFORE AND HEREAFTER; NOW OR ~.

NEXT FRIEND. The person who intervenes to bring an action on behalf of an infant. See LITIGATION GUARDIAN.

NEXT OF KIN. *var*. **NEXT-OF-KIN**. 1. The mother, father, children, brothers, sisters, spouse and common law spouse of a deceased person, or any of them. 2. (a) Means the spouse and children of the deceased person; or (b) if there is no spouse or children, means the persons who are entitled to share under the Intestate Succession Act in the estate of the deceased person. 3. In relation to a patient, means (i) the husband or wife of that patient, or (ii) where there is no husband or wife of that patient, a descendant, ascendant or collateral, in either case over 18 years old, in that order of priority who is nearest in blood to the patient, and where if two or more persons in the class of relationship are of equal blood to the patient, the elder or oldest of the persons in that class. *Mental Health Act*, R.S. Nfld. 1990, c. M-9, s. 2. See HEIRS, ~ OR ESTATE.

NEXUS. *n*. Refers to a causative relationship. Bond, connection, chain.

NFB. *abbr*. National Film Board.

NFCA. The neutral citation for the Newfoundland Court of Appeal.

NFLD. *abbr*. Newfoundland.

NFLD. & P.E.I.R. *abbr*. Newfoundland and Prince Edward Island Reports, 1971-.

NFLD. R. *abbr*. Newfoundland Reports, 1817-1949.

NFLD. SEL. CAS. *abbr*. Tucker's Select Cases (Nfld.), 1817-1828.

NFPA. *abbr*. National Fire Prevention Association.

NIECE. *n*. The daughter of a sister or brother.

NIENT COMPRISE. [Fr. not contained] An objection to a petition on grounds that the desired thing is not contained in the proceeding or deed which is the foundation of the petition.

NIENT CULPABLE. [Fr.] Not guilty.

NIENT DEDIRE. [Fr.] Permitting judgment by neither opposing nor denying it.

NIENT LE FAIT. [Fr.] Not that person's deed. See NON EST FACTUM.

NIGHT. *n*. 1. The period between 9 p.m. and 6 a.m. of the following day. *Criminal Code*, R.S.C. 1985, c. C-46, s. 2. 2. The period from one-half hour after sunset to one-half hour before sunrise. 3. The period beginning one half-hour after sunset and ending one half-hour before sunrise and, in respect of any place where the sun does not rise or set daily, the period during which the centre of the sun's disc is more than six degrees below the horizon.

NIGHT COURT. A court held by a judge between the hours of 5 o'clock and 11 o'clock in the afternoon. *Night Courts Act*, R.S.N.S. 1989, c. 310, s. 2.

NIGHT PREMIUM. A higher rate of pay for work at night.

NIGHT TIME. *var*. **NIGHT-TIME**. 1. That period commencing 1 hour after sunset and ending 1 hour before the following sunrise. 2. Includes all that portion of the day extending from one-half hour after sunset until one-half hour before sunrise.

NIGHT VFR. A flight conducted in accordance with VFR during the hours of night.

NIGHTWALKER. *n*. A person who sleeps during the day and walks at night.

NIHIL AD REM. [L.] Not to the point.

NIHIL ALIUD POTEST REX QUAM QUOD DE JURE POTEST. [L.] The King cannot do anything he cannot do lawfully.

NIHIL CAPIAT. [L.] Let her take nothing.

NIHIL CAPIAT PER BREVE. [L.] That one takes nothing by one's writ.

NIHIL CONSENSUI TAM CONTRARIUM EST QUAM VIS ET METUS. [L.] Nothing is more antithetical to agreement than force and fear.

NIHIL DAT QUI NON HABET. [L.] One who has nothing gives nothing.

NIHIL DICIT. [L.] One says nothing.

NIHIL FACIT ERROR NOMINIS CUM DE CORPORE CONSTAT. [L.] A mistake about a name means nothing when there is no mistake about the person meant.

NIHIL HABET FORUM EX SCENA. [L.] The court has no concern with things which are not before it.

NIHIL INFRA REGNUM SUBDITOS MAGIS CONSERVAT IN TRANQUILLITATE ET CONCORDIA QUAM DEBITA LEGUM ADMINISTRATIO. [L.] Nothing keeps those subject to royal authority more tranquil and peaceful than due administration of the law.

NIHIL IN LEGE INTOLERABILIUS EST, QUAM EANDEM REM DIVERSO JURE CENSERI. [L.] Nothing is more intolerable in law than that a similar case is decided upon a different construction of the law.

NIHIL PRAESCRIBITUR NISI QUOD POSSIDETUR. [L.] Nothing can be acquired by prescription except in respect of what is possessed.

NIHIL PROBETUR NISI ALLEGATUM. [L.] Nothing is to be proved unless it is alleged.

NIHIL QUOD EST CONTRA RATIONEM EST LICITUM. [L.] Nothing contrary to reason is lawful.

NIHIL QUOD INCONVENIENS ET LICITUM EST. [L.] Nothing inconvenient is lawful.

NIHIL SIMUL INVENTUM EST ET PERFECTUM. [L.] Nothing is both invented and perfected at the same time.

NIHIL TAM CONVENIENS EST NATURALI AEQUITATI QUAM UNUMQUODQUE DISSOLVI EO LIGAMINE QUO LIGATUM EST. [L.] Nothing agrees more with natural justice than that anything bound should be freed by the same means.

NIHIL TAM CONVENIENS EST NATURALI AEQUITATI QUAM VOLUNTATEM DOMINI VOLENTIS REM SUAM IN ALIUM TRANSFERRE RATAM HABERE. [L.] Nothing agrees more with natural justice than to honour the intent of an owner who wants to transfer property to another.

NIHIL TAM PROPRIUM IMPERIO QUAM LEGIBUS VIVERE. [L.] Nothing is more characteristic of royal power than that it is exercised under the law.

NIHIL TEMERE NOVANDUM. [L.] Avoid rash innovations.

NIL. *n.* [L.] Nothing.

NIL ASSESSMENT. An assessment which shows that no tax is owed.

NIL DEBET. [L.] One owes nothing.

NIL FACET ERROR NOMINIS CUM DE CORPORE VEL PERSONA CONSTAT. [L.] An error in a name is of no effect as long as there is certainty as to the identity of the person.

NIMIA SUBTILITAS IN JURE REPROBATUR. [L.] In law too much subtlety is rejected.

NIMIUM ALTERCANDO VERITAS AMITTITUR. [L.] By arguing too much the truth is lost.

1968 CONVENTION. The Convention September 27, 1968 on Jurisdiction and the Enforcement of Judgments in Civil and Commercial Matters as amended. *Civil and Commercial Judgments Convention*, R.S.C. 1985, c. C-30, s. 1.

NISEI. *n.* A second generation resident or citizen of Japanese origin.

NISI. [L.] Describes an order effective only when the affected party fails to respond to it by a certain time. See DECREE ~; RULE~.

NISI PRIUS. [L.] Unless before.

NISI PRIUS JUDGMENT. Judgment given in circumstances where the exigencies require an immediate decision without the opportunity to fully consider the authorities.

NITRATE MIXTURE. Any preparation, other than gunpowder, formed by the mechanical mixture of a nitrate with any form of carbon or with any carbonaceous substance not possessed of explosive properties, whether or not the preparation contains sulphur and whether or not such preparation is mechanically mixed with any other non-explosive substance.

NITRO-COMPOUND. *n.* Any chemical compound that has explosive properties, or is capable of combining with metals to form an explosive compound, and is produced by the chemical action of nitric acid (whether mixed or not with sulphuric acid) or of a nitrate mixed with sulphuric acid upon any carbonaceous substance, whether such compound is mechanically mixed with other substances or not. Canada regulations.

NITROGEN. *n.* Elemental nitrogen (N). See OXIDES OF ~; WATER-INSOLUBLE~.

NITRO-GLYCERINE. See LOW FREEZE ~.

N.L. *abbr.* [L.] Non liquet. It is not evident.

NO. *abbr.* Number.

NOBILIORES ET BENIGNIORES PRESUMPTIONES IN DUBIIS SUNT PRAEFERENDAE. [L.] In doubtful cases, more generous and favourable presumptions should be preferred.

NOBILITY. *n.* In England, the division of the population consisting of barons, dukes, earls, marquesses and viscounts.

NOBIS DICERE NON DARE. [L.] It is for judges (us) to state the law not to give it (make it).

NOC. *abbr.* Notice of compliance.

NOCENT. *adj*. Criminal; guilty.

NO-CERTIORARI CLAUSE. A clause in a statute governing an administrative tribunal which provides that certiorari and any similar remedy is not available to judicially review a decision of the tribunal.

NO-FAULT DIVORCE. Divorce based on grounds other than a matrimonial offence, i.e. adultery or cruelty.

NO-FAULT INSURANCE. No-fault means that the respondent's liability to pay benefits occurs when injury arises out of the ownership, use or operation of a vehicle, regardless of the presence or absence of fault. The injury must still arise out of the ownership, use or operation. *Amos v. Insurance Corp. of British Columbia*, [1995] 3 S.C.R. 405, Major, J. for the court.

NOISE. *n*. Loud, unpleasant or unwanted sound.

NOISE RESTRICTED RUNWAY. Airport at which air operations are restricted by maximum noise levels permitted to be made by a particular type of aircraft.

NOLENS VOLENS. [L.] Unwilling or willing.

NO LIMIT ORDER. An order to buy or sell securities with no stipulation as to price.

NOLLE PROSEQUI. [L.] 1. To be not willing to prosecute. 2. A stay of proceedings.

NO-LOAD FUND. A mutual fund which charges little or no fee in the sale of its shares.

NO MAN CAN TAKE ADVANTAGE OF HIS OWN WRONG. ". . . [M]axim . . . recognized by Courts of law and of equity, . . ." *Houghton v. May* (1910), 22 O.L.R. 434 at 439 (H.C.), Clute J. A basic maxim of the law. See CLEAN HANDS DOCTRINE.

NO MAN SHALL BE JUDGE IN HIS OWN CAUSE. See *House Repair & Service Co. v. Miller* (1921), 49 O.L.R. 205 at 212-13, 64 D.L.R. 115 (C.A.), the court per Hodgins J.A.

NOM DE PLUME. [Fr.] Pen name.

NOMEN COLLECTIVUM. [L. a collective name] The description of members of a particular class.

NOMEN GENERALISSIMUM. [L.] The most general term.

NOMETHETICAL. *adj*. Relating to legislation.

NOMINAL CAPITAL. The number of shares or the aggregate par value of shares which a company is authorized to issue, fixed in the company's memorandum or articles of incorporation or letters patent.

NOMINAL DAMAGES. " . . . [A] technical phrase which means that you have negatived anything like real damage, but that you are affirming by your nominal damages that there is an infraction of a legal right which, though it gives you no right to any real damages at all, yet gives you a right to the verdict or judgment because your legal right has been infringed . . ." *Mediana (The)*, [1900] A.C. 113 at 116 (U.K. H.L.), Lord Halsbury L.C.

NOMINAL FUEL TANK CAPACITY. The volume of the fuel tank specified by the manufacturer to the nearest three eighths of a litre (one tenth of a U.S. gallon). *On-Road Vehicle and Engine Emission Regulations*, SOR/2003-2, s. 1.

NOMINALISTIC PRINCIPLE. A debtor must pay the debt's nominal amount in whatever tender is legal. J.G. McLeod, *The Conflict of Laws* (Calgary: Carswell, 1983) at 513.

NOMINAL PARTNER. A person who does not have any actual interest in a business, trade or its profits but appears to have an interest because her or his name is used in the trade or business.

NOMINAL PLAINTIFF. 1. " . . . [O]ne who merely represents others . . ." *U.F.C.W. Local 1252, Fishermen's Union v. Cashin* (1987), 6 Nfld. & P.E.I.R. 181 at 185, 204 A.P.R. 181 Md. T.D.), Cameron J. 2. " . . . [A] plaintiff is only a nominal plaintiff within the meaning of [Ontario Rules of Practice] R. 373(f) if he has no interest whatever in the result of the action." *Lincoln Terrace Restaurant Ltd. v. Bray* (1980), 19 C.P.C. 290 at 292 (Ont. Master), Garfield (Master).

NOMINAL SECTION. Measures 259 hectares or 640 acres.

NOMINAL VALUE. (a) The mass or weight shown on a local standard of mass or weight; (b) the length shown between any two graduations, whether or not successive graduations, on a local standard of length; (c) in the case of a cylindrical graduated standard the maximum volume or capacity shown on the cylindrical graduated standard; and (d) in the case of a narrow-neck metal standard or a narrow-neck glass standard, the volume or capacity shown on that standard. *Weights and Measures Regulations*, C.R.C., c. 1605, s. 53.

NOMINAL VOLUME. The approximate volume of product put in a container by the manufacturer.

NOMINA SUNT MUTABILIA, RES AUTEM IMMOBILES. [L.] Names are changeable but things remain unchanged.

NOMINATIM. [L. by name] Mentioned one at a time.

NOMINATED. See OFFICIALLY ~.

NOMINATION. *n.* A mention by name. See DAY OF ~; OFFICIAL ~.

NOMINATION DAY. 1. The day upon which nominations close. 2. The last day for filing nominations.

NOMINEE. *n.* One who is designated to act as representative of an other. May refer to an agent or trustee.

NOMINE POENAE. [L.] Under a penalty's description.

NOMINIS UMBRA. [L. the shadow of a name] A one-person company.

NON AD IDEM. [L.] Not in agreement.

NOMOGRAPHER. *n.* A person who writes about laws.

NON-ABILITY. *n.* Inability.

NON-ACCEPTANCE. *n.* The refusal to accept.

NON ACCEPTAVIT. [L.] One did not accept.

NON-ACCESS. *n.* Though one presumes access during wedlock, one may counter this presumption by proving that sexual intercourse did not occur at a time when the husband could be the father.

NON ACCIPI DEVENT VERBA IN DEMONSTRATIONEM FALSAM QUAE COMPETUNT IN LIMITATIONEM VERAM. [L.] Words which comprise a clearly intended limitation should not be interpreted as a false description.

NON ACCREVIT INFRA SEX ANNOS. [L.] It did not accrue within 6 years.

NOMOGENIC. *adj.* Of subjective symptoms, an absence of organic causes, not genuine, motivated by desire for pecuniary gain.

NON-AGE. *n.* The state of being a minor.

NON ALIO MODO PUNIATUR ALIQUIS, QUAM SECUNDUM QUOD SE HABET CONDEMNATIO. [L.] A person should not be punished in any way except according to the sentence.

NON ALITER A SIGNIFICATIONE VERBORUM RECEDI OPORTET QUAM CUM MANIFESTUM EST ALIUD SENSISSE TESTATOREM. [L.] There should be no deviation in any way from the usual meaning of words unless it is obvious that the testator meant something else.

NON-APPEARANCE. *n.* The failure to appear in a timely and proper manner.

NON ASSUMPSIT. [L.] One did not promise.

NON ASSUMPSIT INFRA SEX ANNOS. [L.] One did not promise within 6 years.

NON BIS IN IDEM. [L.] Not tried twice for the same offence.

NON-BUSINESS DAYS. Days observed as legal holidays or non-juridicial days.

NON-CANADIAN. *n.* An individual, a government or an agency thereof or an entity that is not Canadian.

NON-CANADIAN SHIP. A ship registered elsewhere than in Canada. See CERTIFIED ~.

NON-CANADIAN TELEVISION STATION. A television station that has a transmitter site located outside Canada. *Broadcasting Distribution Regulations*, SOR/97-555, s. 1.

NON-CAPITAL MURDER. All murder other than capital murder. *Criminal Code*, R.S.C. 1970, c. C-34, s. 214. See now SECOND DEGREE MURDER.

NON CEPIT MODO ET FORMA. [L.] One did not take in the alleged manner and form.

NON-CERTIFICATED SECURITY. Includes a security for which no certificate is issued and a certificated security held within a security clearing and settlement system in the custody of a custodian or nominee. *Financial Administration Act*, R.S.C. 1985, c. F-11, s. 2.

NON-CHEQUABLE DEPOSITS. Deposits not subject to withdrawal by bill of exchange, including cheque, or other negotiable order. *Credit Union Act*, R.S.N.S. 1989, c. 111, s. 2.

NON-CIRCULATION COIN. A coin composed of base metal, precious metal or any combination of those metals that is not intended for circulation.

NON-COMBATANT. *n*. A civilian.

NONCOMBUSTIBLE. *var*. **NON-COM-BUSTIBLE**. *adj*. 1. As applied to a material or combination of materials, means material that will pass an approved test for determination of noncombustibility in building materials conducted by: (i) The Canadian Standards Association Testing Laboratories; (ii) The National Research Council of Canada; (iii) Underwriters' Laboratories of Canada; or (iv) any other approved testing laboratory. 2. Incapable of sustaining combustion in air, either when ignited or when subjected to and maintained at a high temperature.

NONCOMBUSTIBLE BUILDING. A building in which all load-bearing walls, columns, partitions, floors and roofs are constructed of concrete, brick, tile, steel or other noncombustible material or combination of materials.

NONCOMBUSTIBLE CONSTRUCTION. That type of construction in which a degree of fire safety is attained by the use of noncombustible materials for structural members and other building assemblies.

NON-COMMISSIONED MEMBER. Any person, other than an officer, who is enrolled in, or who pursuant to law is attached or seconded otherwise than as an officer to, the Canadian Forces. *National Defence Act*, R.S.C. 1985, c. N-5, s. 2.

NON-COMPELLABILITY. *n*. The provision of section 11(c) of the Charter that anyone charged with an offence cannot be compelled to be a witness against herself or himself. P.W. Hogg, *Constitutional Law of Canada*, 3d ed. (Toronto: Carswell, 1992) at 1096.

NON COMPOS MENTIS. [L.] Not sound in mind.

NON CONCESSIT. [L.] One did not grant.

NON-CONFORMING BUILDING. A building (i) that is lawfully constructed or lawfully under construction at the date of first publication of an official notice of a proposal to pass a zoning by-law affecting the land on which the building is situated and (ii) that does not or will not conform to the requirements of the zoning by-law when it becomes effective.

NON-CONFORMING USE. Use of land or buildings in a manner or for a purpose "lawful when it commenced and lawful prior to a change in a government land use by-law. . ." *Mehta v. Truro (Town)* (1991), 5 M P.L.R. (2d) 216 at 218, 104 N.S.R. (2d) 440, 283 A.P.R. 440 (C.A.), Hallett J.A.

NON CONSTAT. [L.] It does not follow; it is not clear.

NON-CONTENTIOUS. *adj*. Not disputed.

NON-CONTRIBUTORY PENSION PLAN. A plan financed by the employer only.

NON CULPABILIS. [L.] Not guilty.

NON-CULPABLE CONDUCT. Conduct which an employee cannot change such as incompetence or inability to perform duties of his employment.

NON CULPABLE HOMICIDE. Homicide that is not culpable is not an offence. *Criminal Code*, R.S.C. 1985, c. C-46, s. 222(3).

NONCUMULATIVE DIVIDEND. A dividend which need not be paid in a subsequent year if it was not paid in an earlier year.

NON DAMNIFICATUS. [L.] Not injured.

NON DAT QUI NON HABET. [L.] One who does not have cannot give.

NON DEBEO MELIORIS CONDITIONIS ESSE QUAM AUCTOR MEUS A QUO JUS IN ME TRANSIT. [L.] I should not be in a better position than my assignor from whom a right passes to me.

NON DEBET ALTERI PER ALTERUM INIQUA CONDITIO INFERRI. [L.] An unjust condition should not be imposed on one person by another.

NON DEBET CUI PLUS LICET QUOD MINUS EST NON LICERE. [L.] It should be lawful to do something less if one is entitled to do something more.

NON DECIPITUR QUI SCIT SE DICIPI. [L.] One who realizes the deception is not deceived.

NON DEFINITUR IN JURE QUID SIT CONATUS. [L.] What an attempt is is not defined in law.

NON-DELEGABLE DUTY RULE. A person cannot escape liability for the negligence by delegating the performance of the duty to a contractor.

NON-DELIVERY. *n*. Neglect or failure to deliver goods on the part of a bailee, carrier, or other expected to deliver.

NON DEMISIT. [L.] One did not demise.

NON-DEROGATION CLAUSE. A clause in a statute which provides that nothing in the statute abrogates or derogates from aboriginal or treaty rights.

NONDESTRUCTIVE TEST. The examination of a part without subjecting it to physical distortion, damage or destruction.

NON DETINET. [L.] One does not detain.

NON DIFFERUNT QUAE CONCORDANT RE TAMETSI NON IN VERBIS IISDEM. [L.] Things which agree in substance though not in words do not differ from each other.

NON-DIRECTION. *n*. The failure of a judge to draw the jury's attention to a necessary legal point.

NON-ENTRY ORDER. The powers of a court to prevent a spouse from entering his or her home so that the other spouse or children of the marriage are not harassed.

NON-EQUITY SHARE. A share in a credit union that (a) evidences indebtedness of the credit union to the holder of the share, and (b) does not represent an equity interest in the credit union. British Columbia statutes.

NON-ESSENTIAL ELEMENTS. Thus the elements of the invention are identified as either essential elements (where substitution of another element or omission takes the device outside the monopoly), or non-essential elements (where substitution or omission is not necessarily fatal to an allegation of infringement). For an element to be considered non-essential and thus substitutable, it must be shown either (i) that on a purposive construction of the words of the claim it was clearly *not* intended to be essential, or (ii) that at the date of publication of the patent, the skilled addressees would have appreciated that a particular element could be substituted without affecting the working of the invention, i.e., had the skilled worker at that time been told of both the element specified in the claim and the variant and "asked whether the variant would obviously work in the same way", the answer would be yes: *Improver Corp. v. Remmington Consumer Products Ltd.* (1989), [1990] F.S.R. 181 (Eng. Patents Ct.), at p. 192. In this context, I think "work in the same way" should be taken for our

purposes as meaning that the variant (or component) would perform substantially the same function in substantially the same way to obtain substantially the same result. *Free World Trust c. Électro Santé Inc.*, 2000 CarswellQue 2728, 2000 SCC 66, 194 D.L.R. (4th) 232, 263 N.R. 150, [2000] 2 S.C.R. 1024, 9 C.P.R. (4th) 168, Binnie, J.

NON EST ARCTIUS VINCULUM INTER HOMINES QUAM JUSJURANDUM. [L.] There is nothing more binding between people than an oath.

NON EST DISPUTANDUM CONTRA PRINCIPIA NEGANTEM. [L.] One cannot dispute with a person who denies first principles.

NON EST FACTUM. [L.] 1. It is not that person's deed. 2. " . . . [A] form of mistake, where the mistake does to the very nature of the document which is being signed. Where such a mistake is established, it is invariably a fundamental mistake causing the contract to be void." *Granville Savings & Mortgage Corp. v. Slevin* (1992), 12 C.C.L.T. (2d) 275 at 297, [1992] 5 W.W.R. 1, 24 R.P.R. (2d) 185, 93 D.L.R. (4th) 268, 6 B.L.R. (2d) 192, 78 Man. R. (2d) 241, 16 W.A.C. 241 (C.A.), O'Sullivan J.A. (dissenting in part). 3. Where a document was executed as a result of a misrepresentation as to its nature and character and not merely its contents the defendant was entitled to raise the plea of non est factum on the basis that his mind at the time of the execution of the document did not follow his hand. In such a circumstance the document was void ab initio. Any person who fails to exercise reasonable care in signing a document is precluded from relying on the plea of non est factum as against a person who relies upon that document in good faith and for value. *Marvco Color Research Ltd. v. Harris*, 1982 CarswellOnt 142, 20 B.L.R. 143, [1982] 2 S.C.R. 774, 26 R.P.R. 48, 45 N.R. 302, 141 D.L.R. (3d) 577 Per Estey, J.

NON EST INVENTUS. [L.] One is not found.

NON EST RECEDENDUM A COMMUNI OBSERVANTIA. [L.] There should be no deviation from ordinary usage.

NON EST REGULA QUIN FALLET. [L.] A rule does not exist without exceptions.

NON FACIAS MALUM UT INDE FIAT BONUM. [L.] You do not do evil so that good may come of it.

NONFEASANCE. *n*. The failure or neglect to do something which a person ought to do.

NONGAME BIRDS. See MIGRATORY ~.

NON HAEC IN FOEDERA VENI. [L.] I did not make this agreement.

NON IMPEDIT CLAUSULA DEROGA-TORIA QUO MINUS AB EODEM POTES-TATE RES DISSOLVANTUR A QUA CON-STITUUNTUR. [L.] A derogatory clause does not keep something from being destroyed by the same power which created it.

NON-INCENDIVE CIRCUIT. A circuit or part of a circuit in which any sparking that may be produced by normally arcing parts is incapable, under normal operating conditions, of causing an ignition of flammable gas or vapour.

NON-INDEMNITY INSURANCE. The distinction between indemnity and non-indemnity insurance is well-recognized in the insurance industry. The following definitions, which I adopt here, were used by the 1988 *Report of Inquiry into Motor Vehicle Accident Compensation in Ontario* (the Osborne Commission), at p. 429: An indemnity payment is one which is intended to compensate the insured in whole or in part for a pecuniary loss. A non-indemnity payment is a payment of a previously determined amount upon proof of a specified event, whether or not there has been pecuniary loss. Perhaps the best example of non-indemnity insurance is that of life insurance. The beneficiary under a life-insurance policy collects a set amount upon the death of the policy holder without reference to any pecuniary loss. Pensions are also considered to be non-indemnity payments: *Cooper v. Miller*, (sub nom. *Cunningham v. Wheeler*) [1994] 1 S.C.R. 359, MacLachlin, J. dissenting.

NON-INDEMNITY PAYMENT. A payment of a previously determined amount upon proof of a specified event, whether or not there has been pecuniary loss. *Cooper v. Miller*, (sub nom. *Cunningham v. Wheeler*) [1994] 1 S.C.R. 359, MacLachlin, J. dissenting. Life insurance and fixed sum accident benefits are examples.

NON-INDUSTRIAL ACCIDENT. Personal injury to an employee that does not arise out of and in the course of his employment and for which the employer is not liable to provide or to pay compensation under the Worker's Compensation Act.

NON INFREGIT CONVENTIONEM. [L.] One did not breach the covenant.

NON IN LEGENDO SED IN INTELLI-GENDO LEGES CONSISTUNT. [L.] The laws are determined not by reading but by understanding them.

NON-INSTRUCTIONAL DAY. A day on which pupils are excused from tuition and instruction and during which teachers are subject to the direction of the board.

NON-INSTRUCTIONAL PERSONNEL. School bus drivers, janitors, clerical staff and such other persons as the regional school board designates.

NON-IONIZING RADIATION. Electromagnetic energy that is not capable of ionizing atoms, but that may cause photochemical, heating or other effects.

NON-IONIZING RADIATION EQUIP-MENT. Equipment that is capable of emitting non-radiation.

NON-IONIZING RADIATION INSTAL-LATION. The whole or any part of a building or other place in which non-ionizing radiation equipment is manufactured, used or placed or installed for use, and includes that non-ionizing radiation equipment.

NON-ISSUABLE PLEA. A plea which, if decided, would not settle the action upon its merits, e.g., a plea in abatement.

NON-JOINDER. *n*. The omission of someone from an action who should be made party.

NON JURIDICAL DAY. A day on which no business is normally done in the civil courts.

NON JUS, SED SEISINA, FACIT STIPI-TEM. [L.] Not right, but seisin, makes the family tree.

NON LIQUET. [L.] It is not evident.

NON-MERGER. *n*. In Anglo-Canadian law a foreign judgment does not extinguish a cause of action nor is the original cause merged into the foreign court's judgment. J.G. McLeod, *The Conflict of Laws* (Calgary: Carswell, 1983) at 606-607.

NON MI RICORDO. [L.] I do not remember.

NON-NATURAL USER. Special use bringing with it increased danger to others and not the ordinary use of land or a use which is suitable for the general benefit of the community.

NON-NEGOTIABLE RECEIPT. A receipt in which it is stated that the goods therein specified will be delivered to the holder thereof. *Warehouse Receipts acts*.

NON NISI JURATUS IN LITE CREDITUR. [L.] No one is believed at trial unless he is sworn.

NON OBSERVATA FORMA INFERTUR ADNULLATIO ACTUS. [L.] By not observing prescribed formalities, the proceeding is invalidated.

NON OBSTANTE. [L.] Notwithstanding.

NON OBSTANTE CLAUSE. In reference to the Charter, refers to a provision in federal or provincial legislation permitted by section 33 which states: (1) Parliament or the legislature of a province may expressly declare in an Act of Parliament or of the legislature, as the case may be, that the Act or a provision thereof shall operate notwithstanding a provision included in section 2 or sections 7 to 15 of this Charter. (2) An Act or a provision of an Act in respect of which a declaration made under this section is in effect shall have such operation as it would have but for the provision of this Charter referred to in the declaration. (3) A declaration made under subsection (1) shall cease to have effect five years after it comes into force or on such earlier date as may be specified in the declaration. (4) Parliament or the legislature of a province may re-enact a declaration made under subsection (1). (5) Subsection (3) applies in respect of a re-enactment made under subsection (4).

NON OBSTANTE VEREDICTO. [L.] The verdict notwithstanding.

NON OFFICIT AFFECTUS NISI SEQUATUR EFFECTUS. [L.] An intention is not hurtful unless a result follows.

NON OMITTAS. [L.] That you do not omit.

NON OMNE QUOD LICET HONESTUM EST. [L.] Not everything which is lawful is honourable.

NON OMNIUM QUAE A MAJORIBUS NOSTRIS CONSTITUTA SUNT RATIO REDDI POTEST. [L.] A reason cannot be offered for all the laws which our ancestors established.

NON-OPERATING EMPLOYEE. A clerical or maintenance worker.

NON-OWNER'S POLICY. A motor vehicle liability policy insuring a person solely in respect of the use or operation by her or him or on her or his behalf of an automobile that is not owned by her or him. *Insurance acts.*

NON-PECUNIARY LOSS. 1. Compensation for suffering and pain, for loss of enjoyment of life and amenities, and for shortened expectation of life. *Reekie v. Messervey* (1989), 48 C.C.L.T. 217 at 235, 36 B.C.L.R. (2d) 316, 59 D.L.R. (4th) 481, 17 M.V.R. (2d) 94 (C.A.), Lambert J.A. 2. Includes loss of care and guidance from a parent or loss generally of guidance, care and companionship.

NON-PILOTED AIRCRAFT. A power-driven aircraft, other than a model aircraft, that is operated without a flight crew member on board; *Canadian Aviation Regulations* SOR 96-433, s. 101.01.

NON PLACET. [L.] It is not accepted.

NON PLEVIN. Failure to replevy land within the allotted time.

NON POSSESSORI INCUMBIT NECESSITAS PROBANDI POSSESSIONES AD SE PERTINERE. [L.] The possessor need not prove that the possessions belong to her or him.

NON POTEST ADDUCI EXCEPTIO EJUSDEM REI CUJUS PETITUR DISSOLUTIO. [L.] It is not possible to plead the same thing one takes exception to when one seeks to upset it.

NOT POTEST PROBARI QUOD PROBATUM NON RELEVAT. [L.] It is not possible to prove what is immaterial if proved.

NON POTEST REX GRATIAM FACERE CUM INJURIA ET DAMNO ALIORUM. [L.] A monarch cannot favour one person to the injury and damage of all the others.

NON-PRECISION APPROACH. An instrument approach by an aircraft using azimuth information; *Canadian Aviation Regulations* SOR 96-433, s. 101.01.

NON-PROFIT. *adj.* Having a purpose to promote a specific goal rather than to generate profit.

NON-PROFIT AGENCY. A corporation without share capital that has objects of a charitable nature and, (a) to which Part III of the Corporations Act applies, or (b) that is incorporated by or under a general or special Act of the Parliament of Canada. *Child and Family Services* Act, R.S.O. 1990, c. C.11, s. 192.

NON-PROFIT CO-OPERATIVE HOUSING CORPORATION. A corporation incorporated without share capital under the Co-operative Corporations Act or any predecessor thereof or under similar legislation of Canada or any province, the main purpose and activity of which is the provision of housing for its members and the charter or by-laws of which provide that, (a) its activities shall be carried on without the purpose of gain for its members, (b) on dissolution, its property after payment of its debts and liabilities shall be distributed to non-profit or charitable organizations, (c) housing charges, other charges similar to rent, or any other charges payable by members are decided by a vote of the members or of a body duly elected or appointed by the members, or a committee thereof, (d) termination of occupancy rights may be brought about only by a vote of the members or of a body duly elected or appointed by the members, or a committee thereof, and that the member whose occupancy rights are terminated has a right to appear and make representations prior to such vote. *Residential Rent Regulation* Act, R.S.O. 1990, c. R.29, s. 1.

NON-PROFIT CORPORATION. A corporation, no part of the income of which is payable to or is otherwise available for the personal benefit of any proprietor, member or shareholder thereof.

NON-PROFIT ORGANIZATION. 1. An organization (i) wholly owned by the Government, by a municipality or by any agency of either of them; or (ii) constituted exclusively for charitable or benevolent purposes where no part of the income is payable to or otherwise available for the personal benefit of any proprietor, member or shareholder. 2. A corporate or unincorporated body carrying on an activity the preponderant purpose of which is a purpose other than the making of a profit. *Real Property Assessment Act*, R.S.P.E.I. 1988, c. R-4, s. 1.

NON PROS. *abbr*. Non prosequitur.

NON PROSEQUITUR. [L.] One does not follow up.

NON QUOD DICTUM EST, SED QUOD FACTUM EST, IN JURE INSPICITUR. [L.] In law, not what is said, but what is done, is considered.

NON QUOD VOLUIT TESTATOR, SED QUOD DIXIT IN TESTAMENTO INSPICITUR. [L.] In construing a will, not what the testator wished, but what was said, is considered.

NON-QUOTA FISHERY. The parties were involved in a non-quota fishery in the Spiller Channel. In such a fishery, fishing vessels travel to the opening's location to await word from the Department of Fisheries and Oceans ("DFO")

that the fishery has opened. These vessels compete for a school of fish, often within very close confines. A non-quota fishery can last for as little as several minutes before the DFO closes it down. By contrast, a quota fishery can last for several days or weeks, thus eliminating the need for fishing vessels to compete within close confines. *North Ridge Fishing Ltd. v. "Prosperity" (The)*, 2000 CarswellBC 982, 2000 BCCA 283, 74 B.C.L.R. (3d) 383, 186 D.L.R. (4th) 374 (C.A.), Per Cumming J.A. (Prowse and Saunders JJ.A. concurring).

NON REFERT AN QUIS ASSENSUM SUUM PRAEFERT VERBIS, AUT REBUS IPSIS ET FACTIS. [L.] It does not matter whether one offers agreement in words, or by the acts and deeds themselves.

NON REFERT QUID NOTUM SIT JUDICI, SI NOTUM NON SIT IN FORMA JUDICII. [L.] It does not matter what is noted by the judge, if it is not noted judicially.

NON-RENEWABLE RESOURCE. Any naturally occurring inorganic substance.

NON-RESIDENT. *var*. **NON RESIDENT**. *var*. **NONRESIDENT**. 1. (a) An individual who is not ordinarily resident in Canada; (b) a corporation incorporated, formed or otherwise organized elsewhere than in Canada; (c) a corporation that is controlled directly or indirectly by nonresidents as defined in paragraph (a) or (b); (d) a trust established by a non-resident as defined in paragraph (a), (b) or (c), or a trust in which non-residents as so defined have more than 50 per cent of the beneficial interest, or (e) a corporation that is controlled directly or indirectly by a trust mentioned in paragraph (d). 2. A person who is not a resident of the province, and for certain purposes a person who resides in the province for any period not exceeding 90 days shall with respect o that period be deemed to be a non-resident. See ASSOCIATES OF THE ~; CANADIAN ~; FOREIGN ~.

NON-RESIDENT ALIEN. *var*. **NON RESIDENT ALIEN**. 1. A person who is neither a resident nor a non resident. 2. A person who is neither a Canadian citizen or a resident.

NON-RESIDENT CANADIAN. A Canadian citizen who is not a resident.

NON-RESIDENT CONTRACTOR. In the case of a natural person, one who is not domiciled in the province, and in the case of a company, a company which was not incorporated in the province.

NON-RESIDENT CORPORATION. A corporation which is not resident in Canada.

NON-SECTARIAN. *adj*. 1. The dual requirements that education be "secular" and "non-sectarian" refer to keeping the schools free from inculcation or indoctrination in the precepts of any religion and do not prevent persons with religiously based moral positions on matters of public policy from participating in deliberations concerning moral education in public schools. *Chamberlain v. Surrey School District No. 36*, [2002] 4 S.C.R. 710. 2. Must now be extended to include other religious traditions as well as those who do not adhere to any religious faith or tradition. The section precludes the teaching of religious doctrine associated with any particular faith or tradition (except in a context which is intended to educate students generally about the various religious traditions for the purpose of advancing religious tolerance and understanding and does not advance any particular doctrinal position over others). *Chamberlain v. Surrey School District No. 36* (2000), 80 B.C.L.R. (3d) 181 (C.A.).

NON-SEGREGATED PROPERTY. Of an insurer means its property other than property included in a segregated fund. *Income Tax Act*, R.S.C. 1952, c. 148 (as am. S.C. 1980-81-82-83, c. 140, c. 96(7)), s. 138(12)(j).

NON SEQUITUR. [L.] It does not follow.

NON SOLENT QUAE ABUNDANT VITIARE SCRIPTURAS. [L.] Excess does not usually make what is written void.

NON SUI JURIS. [L.] Not able to manage one's own affairs; with no legal capacity.

NONSUIT. *n*. The judgment ordered when a plaintiff cannot establish any legal cause of action or cannot support pleadings with any evidence.

NON-SUIT MOTION. A motion that there is no evidence or no evidence upon an essential element of the plaintiff's case or a motion to weigh the evidence that there is and determine that it is not of sufficient strength to establish a prima facie case.

NON SUM INFORMATUS. [L. I am not informed] I have not been instructed to defend.

NON SUNT PROBANDA NISI SECUNDUM ALLEGATA. [L.] Facts should not be proven unless they have been alleged.

NON-TRUST INDENTURE. A simple indenture used when a small number of lenders make a loan to a corporation and secure it by way of a floating charge. No trust is set up.

NON-USER. *n*. One who no longer exercises a right.

NON VALET CONFIRMATIO, NISI ILLE, QUI CONFIRMAT, SIT IN POSSESSIONE REI VEL JURIS UNDE FIERI DEBET CONFIRMATIO; ET EODEM MODO, NISI ILLE CUI CONFIRMATIO FIT, SIT IN POSSESSIONE. [L.] Confirmation has no effect unless the very person who confirms either possesses the thing or the right of which confirmation should be made, and, likewise, unless the very person to whom confirmation is made has possession.

NON-VENTILATED CABLETROUGH. A cabletrough in which there are no ventilating openings in the bottom or sides.

NON VIDENTUR QUI ERRANT CONSENTIRE. [L.] Those who are mistaken are not considered to consent.

NON VIDETUR CONSENSUM RETINUISSE SI QUIS EX PRAESCRIPTO MINANTIS ALIQUID IMMUTAVIT. [L.] One is not deemed to have retained consent if one changed anything on order of someone threatening.

NON VIDETUR QUISQUAM ID CAPERE, QUOD EI NECESSE EST ALII RESTITUERE. [L.] No one is deemed to take what must be given up to another.

NO ONE CAN BE ALLOWED TO DEROGATE FROM HIS OWN GRANT. See *Keewatin Power Co. v. Keewatin Flour Mills Ltd*, [1928] 1 D.L.R. 32 at 53, 61 O.L.R. 363 (H.C.), Grant J. See CLEAN HANDS DOCTRINE.

NO ORDER AS TO COSTS. Neither party will pay the other any costs. M.M. Orkin, *The Law of Costs*, 2d ed. (Aurora: Canada Law Book, 1987) at 1-12.

N.O.P. *abbr*. Not otherwise provided for. *Customs Tariff*, R.S.C. 1985, c. C-54, s. 2.

NO PAR VALUE. Describes shares which have no nominal value but represent some portion of a company's net assets.

NORMAL. *adj*. Usual, in contrast to exceptional.

NORMAL ATMOSPHERIC PRESSURE. An absolute pressure of 101.324 kPa at 20°C.

NORMAL COURSE. In relation to a trade mark, evidence of a single transaction is not evidence of the normal course of trade. Normal course refers to a functioning business.

NORMAL CUBIC METRE. The quantity of gas occupying a volume of 1 cubic metre at 25 degrees Celsius and at a pressure of 760 millimetres of mercury.

NORMAL DATE OF RETIREMENT. The first day of the month next following the day on which an employee attains the age of 65 years.

NORMAL FARM PRACTICE. A practice that, (a) is conducted in a manner consistent with proper and acceptable customs and standards as established and followed by similar agricultural operations under similar circumstances, or (b) makes use of innovative technology in a manner consistent with proper advanced farm management practices. *Farming and Food Production Protection Act, 1998*, S.O. 1998, c. 1, s. 1.

NORMAL FORM OF PENSION. An annuity under which payments are made during the lifetime of the annuitant and terminate on his death.

NORMAL FULL-TIME COURSE LOAD. The number of courses in an approved program of study that an approved institution requires a student to take in any year in order to obtain a certificate, diploma or degree in a minimum length of time.

NORMAL HIGH WATER MARK. The visible high water mark of a lake or river where the presence and action of water are so usual and so long continued in ordinary years as to mark upon the bed of the lake or river a character distinct from that of the bank thereof with respect to vegetation and the nature of the soil itself.

NORMALLY. *adj*. Regularly.

NORMAL OFFICE HOURS. Those days and hours that an office is open to the public.

NORMAL PENSIONABLE AGE. The date or age specified in a pension plan at which an employee can retire from his employment and receive the regular pension benefit provided by the pension plan, whether such date is the day upon which the employee attains a given age or upon which the employee has completed a given period of employment.

NORMAL RETIREMENT AGE. Sixty-five years of age.

NORMAL RETIREMENT DATE. The first day of the month immediately following the month in which normal retirement age is attained.

NORMAN-FRENCH. *n*. In England, the language of legal procedure until the statute 1362, 36 Edw. 3, c. 15. The language has remained the same since the Conquest so that it differs from modern French.

NORTH AMERICAN FREE TRADE AGREEMENT. Commonly referred to as NAFTA. The North American Free Trade Agreement entered into between the Government of Canada, the Government of the United Mexican States and the Government of the United States of America and signed on December 17, 1992, and includes any rectifications thereto made prior to its ratification by Canada.

NORTH AMERICAN GREAT LAKES ZONE. Lake Ontario, Lake Erie, Lake Huron (including Georgian Bay), Lake Michigan, Lake Superior, the waters connecting those lakes, the St. Lawrence Seaway and the St. Lawrence River west of the Victoria Bridge in Montreal. *General Load Line Rules*, C.R.C., c. 1425, s. 2.

NORTHERN AFFAIRS. See INDIAN AND ~ CANADA.

NOSCITUR A SOCIIS. [L.] 1. One is known by one's associates. The meaning of a particular word or expression may be determined by its association with other words. 2. " . . . [W]here general words are closely associated with preceding specific words the meaning of the general words must be limited by reference to the specific words." *Insurance Corp. of British Columbia v. Canada (Registrar of Trade Marks)* (1978), 44 C.P.R. (2d) 1 at 11, [1980] 1 F.C. 669 (T.D.), Cattanach J.

NOSCITUR EX SOCIO, QUI NON COGNOSCITUR EX SE. [L.] One who cannot be known from the self is known from an associate.

NOSCUNTUR A SOCIIS. [L.] They are known by their companions (refers to words). When one joins words which could have analogous meaning, one is using them in their cognate sense. P. St. J. Langan, ed., *Maxwell on The Interpretation of Statutes*, 12th ed. (Bombay: N.M. Tripathi, 1976) at 289. See NOSCITUR A SOCIIS.

NO SHOOTING AREA. An area in which the discharge of a firearm is prohibited.

NOSTRUM EST JUDICARE SECUNDUM ALLEGATA ET PROBATA. [L.] It is our role to judge by pleadings and proofs.

NOTA BENE. [L.] Note well.

NOTAM. A notice to airmen concerning the establishment or condition of, or change in, any aeronautical facility, service or procedure, or any hazard affecting aviation safety, the knowledge of which is essential to personnel engaged in flight operations; *Canadian Aviation Regulations*, SOR/96-433, s. 101.01.

NOTARIAL. *adj*. Includes prothonotarial. *Registry Act*, R.S.O. 1990, c. R.20, s. 1.

NOTARIAL ACT. 1. A notary's written authentication or certification, under official seal or signature, of any entry or document. 2. Any attestation, certificate or instrument which a notary executes.

NOTARIAL CERTIFICATE. An instrument which certifies the authenticity of the document to which it is attached.

NOTARY. *n*. 1. One who attests a deed or document to make it authentic in another jurisdiction. 2. In Quebec, notaries are legal practitioners and public officers whose chief duty is to draw up and execute deeds and contracts to which the parties are bound or desire to give the character of authenticity attached to acts of the public authority and to assure the date thereof. Their duties shall also include the preservation of the deposit of the deeds executed by them en minute, the giving of communication thereof and the issuing of authentic copies thereof or extracts therefrom. *Notarial Act*, R.S.Q., c. N-2, s. 2. See RECORDS OF A ~.

NOTARY PUBLIC. One who attests a deed or document to make it authentic in another jurisdiction and is empowered to take affidavits and declarations and to perform various other acts relating to legal matters.

NOT AT ARM'S LENGTH. ". . . [A] transaction 'not at arm's length' is one in respect of which unrelated persons are, in the eyes of the law, in the same position as persons related by blood or marriage. In other words, if a transaction between unrelated persons has the same essential characteristics as one between related persons, i.e., the parties are influenced in their bargaining by something other than individual self-interest, those unrelated persons are said not to deal at arm's length." *Skalbania (Trustee of) v. Wedgewood Village Estates Ltd.* (1989), 44 C.R.R. 341 at 346, 37 B.C.L.R. (2d) 88, 74 C.B.R. (N.S.) 97, [1989] 5 W.W.R. 254, 60 D.L.R. (4th) 43 (C.A.), Esson J.A. (Southin J.A. concurring).

NOTATION. *n*. Any addition to, or alteration of, a registration in the records of the Registrar General or a division registrar. *Vital Statistics Act*, R.S.O. 1990, c. V.4, s. 1.

NOTE. *v*. 1. Of a dishonoured foreign bill, for a notary public to record her or his initials, the day, month, year and reason, if given, for non-payment. 2. To note up a case is to find references to it in later cases.

NOTE. *n*. 1. A promissory note. *Bills of Exchange Act*, R.S.C. 1985, c. B-4, s. 2. 2. Any corporate obligation, unsecured or secured. H. Sutherland, D.B. Horsley & J.M. Edmiston, eds., *Fraser's Handbook on Canadian Company Law*, 7th ed. (Toronto: Carswell, 1985) at 310. See BANK-~; CIRCULAR ~; COVER ~; CREDIT ~; DEBIT ~; DEMAND ~; EXPLANATORY ~; INLAND ~; MARGINAL ~; POST~; PREMIUM ~; PROMISSORY ~; SUBORDINATED ~; TREASURY ~.

NOTED CONSPICUOUSLY. Written so that the person against whom words appear to operate should reasonably notice them.

NOTE OF HAND. A promissory note.

NOTES. *n*. Notes of the Bank intended for circulation in Canada. *Bank of Canada Act*, R.S.C. 1985, c. B-2, s. 2. See JUDGE'S ~.

NOT GUILTY. The plea appropriate to an indictment when the accused chooses to raise a general issue, *i.e.*, to deny everything and let the prosecution prove whatever they can.

NOTHINGS. *n*. Business expenditures which are not recognized in the tax system. W. Grover & F. Iacobucci, *Materials on Canadian Income Tax*, 4th ed. (Toronto: Richard De Boo Ltd., 1980) at 339.

NOTICE. *n*. 1. Cognisance; knowledge. 2. Judicial notice. 3. To give someone notice of a fact is to bring that fact to the person's attention. 4. A document which informs or advises someone that that person's interests are involved in a proceeding or which informs the person of something which that person has a right to know. 5. ". . . [S]omething which is in a form calculated to attract attention." *Montreal Trust v. Canadian Pacific Airlines Ltd.*, [1977] 2 S.C.R. 793 at 802, 12 N.R. 408, 72 D.L.R. (3d) 257, Ritchie J. (Laskin C.J.C., Spence and Dickson JJ. concurring). See ACTUAL ~; ADEQUATE ~; ADMINISTRATIVE ~; APPEARANCE ~; CONSTRUCTIVE ~; DEPARTURE ~; JUDI-

CIAL ~; JURY ~; OFFICIAL ~; SECURITY ~; STATUS ~; STRIKE ~.

NOTICE OF ACTION. A document containing a short statement about the nature of the claim which may commence any action other than a divorce action when there is not enough time to prepare a full statement of claim (Ontario Rules of Civil Procedure, r. 14.03(2)). G.D. Watson & C. Perkins, eds., *Holmested & Watson: Ontario Civil Procedure* (Toronto: Carswell, 1984) at 14-3.

NOTICE OF APPEAL. A document by which an appeal is commenced.

NOTICE OF APPLICATION. The first step in commencing an application.

NOTICE OF CLAIM. In insurance law, informs the insurer of the possibility of a future action, allows the insurer time to investigate the merits and to negotiate a settlement.

NOTICE OF COMPLIANCE. A document issued when the safety and efficacy of a medicine has been approved. A prerequisite to sale of prescription medicine in Canada. A notice of compliance is issued under section C.08.004 of the *Food and Drug Regulations*, C.R.C. 870.

NOTICE OF DISHONOUR. Subject to this Act, when a bill has been dishonoured by non-acceptance or by non-payment, notice of dishonour must be given to the drawer and each endorser, and any drawer or endorser to whom the notice is not given is discharged. *Bills of Exchange Act*, R.S.C. 1985, c. B-4, s. 95.

NOTICE OF INTENT TO DEFEND. In Ontario practice, the document which a defendant who intends to defend an action delivers and which gives that defendant more days to file a statement of defence.

NOTICE OF MOTION. In Ontario practice, the document which initiates a motion and notifies other parties of the motion, used unless the circumstances or the nature of the motion make it unnecessary.

NOTICE OF READINESS FOR TRIAL. In Ontario practice, the document, formerly called a certificate of readiness, which the party who is ready for trial and who wishes to set the action down for trial serves on every other party to the action.

NOTICE PAPER. A document by which members of Parliament give notice that they intend to introduce bills, seek answers to written questions or move a motion as Private Members' business. A. Fraser, W.A. Dawson, & J. Holtby, eds., *Beauchesne's Rules and Forms of the House of Commons of Canada*, 6th ed. (Toronto: Carswell, 1989) at 300.

NOTICE TO QUIT. The notice required for either a landlord or a tenant to terminate a tenancy without the other's consent when that tenancy runs from year to year or for some other indefinite period.

NOTIFIABLE DISEASE. A disease the presence of which must pursuant to this Act or the regulations, be made known to the director of a health unit, a medical health officer, a board of health or other officer. *Health Act*, R.S.N.S. 1989, c. 195, s. 2.

NOTIFICATION. *n.* A direction.

NOTIFY. *v.* 1. " . . . [M]eans, in its everyday sense, to inform expressly', and in law: . . . 'to make known, to give notice, to inform'." *Brière v. Canada (Employment & Immigration Commission)* (1988), 89 C.L.L.C. 14,05 at 12,203, 93 N.R. 115, 25 F.T.R. 80n, 57 D.L.R. (4th) 402 (C.A.), Lacombe J.A. 2. To take such steps as are reasonably required to give information to the person to be notified so that (i) it comes to her or his attention; or (ii) it is directed to such person at her or his customary address or at her or his place of residence, or at such other place as is designated by her or him over her or his signature. *Personal Property Security acts*.

NOTING. *n.* A notary's record on a bill at the time it is dishonoured. I.F.G. Baxter, *The Law of Banking*, 3d ed. (Toronto: Carswell, 1981) at 117.

NOTORIOUS. *adj.* In evidence, describes a matter which need not be proved.

NOTWITHSTANDING. *conj.* Although.

NOTWITHSTANDING. *prep.* Despite.

NOTWITHSTANDING CLAUSE. In reference to the Charter, refers to a provision in federal or provincial legislation permitted by section 33 which states: (1) Parliament or the legislature of a province may expressly declare in an Act of Parliament or of the legislature, as the case may be, that the Act or a provision thereof shall operate notwithstanding a provision included in section 2 or sections 7 to 15 of this Charter. (2) An Act or a provision of an Act in respect of which a declaration made under this section is in effect shall have such operation as it would have but for the provision of this Charter referred to in the declaration. (3) A declaration made under subsection (1) shall cease to have effect five years after it comes into force or on such earlier date as may be specified in the declaration. (4) Parliament or the legislature of a province may re-enact a declaration made under subsection (1). (5) Subsection (3) applies in respect of a re-enactment made under subsection (4).

NO-UNION VOTE. A ballot rejecting all unions participating in a representation vote of workers.

NOVA CAUSA INTERVENIENS. [L.] A new cause intervenes. *Emerson v. Skinner* (1906), 12 B.C.R. 154 at 155, 4 W.L.R. 255 (C.A.), Hunter C.J.A.

NOVA CONSTITUTIO FUTURIS FORMAM IMPONERE DEBET NON PRAETERITIS. [L.] A new law should regulate the future not the past.

NOVA CUSTOMA. [L.] Duty; imposition.

NOVATIO. *n.* [L.] The remaking or renewing of an extant obligation.

NOVATION. *n.* " . . . [A] trilateral agreement by which an existing contract is extinguished and a new contract brought into being in its place. Indeed, for an agreement to effect a valid novation the appropriate consideration is the discharge of the original debt in return for a promise to perform some obligation. The assent of the beneficiary (the creditor or mortgagee) of those obligations to the discharge and substitution is crucial. The Courts have established a three part test for determining if novation has occurred. It is set out in Polson v. Wulffsohn (1890), 2 B.C.R. 39 at 43 (S.C.) as follows: ' . . . first, the new debtor must assume the complete liability; second, the creditor must accept the new debtor as a principal debtor, and not merely as an agent or guarantor; and third, the creditor must accept the new contract in full satisfaction and substitution for the old contract . . .'" *National Trust Co. v. Mead* (1990),12 R.P.R. (2d) 165 at 180, [1990] 2 S.C.R. 410, [1990] 5 W.W.R. 459, 71 D.L.R. (4th) 488, 112 N.R. 1, Wilson J. (Lamer C.J.C., La Forest, L'Heureux-Dubé, Gonthier and Cory JJ. concurring).

NOVATIO NON PRAESUMITUR. [L.] One does not presume a novation.

NOVEL DISSEISIN. Recent disseisin.

NOVELTY. *n.* 1. In the context of constitutional law refers to legislation which responds to new societal interest and approach concerning the subject matter of the legislation, legislation based on principles of law distinct from similar legislation and legislation where there is an identifiable social policy different from the policy goals of analogous legislation. *Reference re Act to Amend Chapter 401 of the Revised Statutes, 1989, the Residential Tenancies Act, S.N.S. 1992, c. 31,* (sub nom. *Reference re Amendments to the Residential Tenancies Act*) [1996] 1 S.C.R. 186. 2. In the context of patent law, something completely new. A lack of novelty is a ground for an attack on a patent. See OBJECTION FOR WANT OF ~.

NOVITAS NON TAM UTILITATE PRODEST QUAM NOTITATE PERTURBAT. [L.] Something new does not benefit by its utility as much as it disturbs with its novelty.

NOVITER AD NOTITIAM PERVENTA. [L.] Things which recently came to a party's knowledge.

NOVUM JUDICIUM NON DAT JUS NOVUM, SED DECLARAT ANTIQUUM; QUIA JUDICIUM EST JURIS DICTUM ET PER JUDICIUM JUS EST NOVITER REVELATUM QUOD DIU FUIT VELATUM. [L.] A new judgment does not create new law, but clarifies old law; because a judgment is a statement of the law and through a judgment law which was previously obscure is newly clarified.

NOVUS ACTUS INTERVENIENS. [L.] 1. A new act intervenes. 2. " . . . [A] ' . . . conscious act of human origin intervening between a negligent act or omission of a defendant and the occurrence by which the plaintiff suffers damage . . . ' . . . The important element in the defence 'novus actus interveniens' is that the intervening act must be one which the party defending could not reasonably [sic] forsee. . ." *Mercantile Bank of Canada v. Carl B. Potter Ltd.* (1979), 7 B.L.R. 54 at 77-8, 31 N.S.R. (2d) 402, 52 A.P.R. 402 (C.A.), Coffin J.A. 3. " . . . One such case is where, although an act of the accused constitutes a cause sine qua non of (or necessary condition for) the death of the victim, nevertheless the intervention of a third person may be regarded as the sole cause of the victim's death, thereby relieving the accused of criminal responsibility. Such intervention, if it has such an effect, has often been described by lawyers as a novus actus interveniens." *R. v. Pagett* (1983), 76 Cr. App.

R. 279 at 288 (U.K. C.A.), the court per Lord Goff.

NOVUS HOMO. [L.] A discharged insolvent; a pardoned criminal.

NOW. *adv*. Shall be construed as referring to the time of commencement of the enactment containing the word. *Interpretation acts*.

NOX. Oxides of nitrogen, which is the sum of nitric oxide and nitrogen dioxide contained in a gas sample as if the nitric oxide were in the form of nitrogen dioxide. *On-Road Vehicle and Engine Emission Regulations*, SOR/2003-2, s. 1.

NOXA SEQUITUR CAPUT. [L.] Guilt follows the individual.

NOXIOUS WEED. A plant that is designated as a noxious weed.

N.P.B. *abbr*. National Parole Board.

N.P.L. *abbr*. Non-personal liability. Part of the name of a specially limited company in B.C. H. Sutherland, D.B. Horsley & J.M. Edmiston eds., *Fraser's Handbook on Canadian Company Law*, 7th ed. (Toronto: Carswell, 1985) at 438.

N.R. *abbr*. National Reporter, 1974-.

NRC. *abbr*. National Research Council of Canada.

NRCC. Neighbouring rights collective of Canada

N.S. *abbr*. Nova Scotia.

NSCA. The neutral citation for the Nova Scotia Court of Appeal.

N.S.F. *abbr*. Not sufficient funds.

N.S. L. NEWS. *abbr*. Nova Scotia Law News.

N.S.R. *abbr*. Nova Scotia Reports, 1834-1929.

N.S.R. (2d). *abbr*. Nova Scotia Reports (Second Series), 1970-.

NSSC. The neutral citation for the Nova Scotia Supreme Court.

NUCJ. The neutral citation for the Nunavut Court of Justice.

NUCLEAR ENERGY. Any form of energy released in the course of nuclear fission or nuclear fusion or of any other nuclear transmutation.

NUCLEAR ENERGY HAZARD. The radioactive, toxic, explosive or other hazardous properties of prescribed substances under the Atomic Energy Control Act (Canada). *Insurance Acts*.

NUCLEAR ENERGY WORKER. A person who is required, in the course of the person's business or occupation in connection with a nuclear substance or nuclear facility, to perform duties in such circumstances that there is a reasonable probability that the person may receive a dose of radiation that is greater than the prescribed limit for the general public. *Nuclear Safety and Control Act, 1997*, S.C. 1997, c. 9, s. 2.

NUCLEAR FACILITY. Any of the following facilities, namely, (*a*) a nuclear fission or fusion reactor or subcritical nuclear assembly, (*b*) a particle accelerator, (*c*) a uranium or thorium mine or mill, (*d*) a plant for the processing, reprocessing or separation of an isotope of uranium, thorium or plutonium, (*e*) a plant for the manufacture of a product from uranium, thorium or plutonium, (*f*) a plant for the processing or use, in a quantity greater than 10^{15} Bq per calendar year, of nuclear substances other than uranium, thorium or plutonium, (*g*) a facility for the disposal of a nuclear substance generated at another nuclear facility, (*h*) a vehicle that is equipped with a nuclear reactor, and (*i*) any other facility that is prescribed for the development, production or use of nuclear energy or the production, possession or use of a nuclear substance, prescribed equipment or prescribed information, and includes, where applicable, the land on which the facility is located, a building that forms part of, or equipment used in conjunction with, the facility and any system for the management, storage or disposal of a nuclear substance. *Nuclear Safety and Control Act, 1997*, S.C. 1997, c. 9, s. 2.

NUCLEAR FUEL WASTE. Irradiated fuel bundles removed from a commercial or research nuclear fission reactor. *Nuclear Fuel Waste Act*, S.C. 2002, c. 23.

NUCLEAR INSTALLATION. A structure, establishment or place, or two or more structures, establishments or places at a single location, coming within any of the following descriptions and designated as a nuclear installation for the purposes of this Act by the Atomic Energy Control Board, namely: (a) a structure containing nuclear material in such an arrangement that a self-sustaining chain process of nuclear fission can be maintained therein without an additional source of neutrons, including any such structure that forms part of the equipment of a ship, aircraft or other means of transportation; (b) a factory or other establishment that processes or reprocesses nuclear material; or (c) a place in which nuclear material is stored other than incidentally to the carriage of the material. *Nuclear Liability Act*, R.S.C. 1985, c. N-28, s. 2.

NUCLEAR MATERIAL. 1. (a) Any material other than thorium or natural or depleted uranium uncontaminated by significant quantities of fission products, that is capable of releasing energy by a self-sustaining chain process of nuclear fission; (b) radioactive material produced in the production or utilization of material referred to in paragraph (a); and (c) material made radioactive by exposure to radiation consequential on or incidental to the production or utilization of material referred to in paragraph (a), but does not include radioactive isotopes that are not combined, mixed or associated with material referred to in paragraph (a). 2. (a) Plutonium, except plutonium with an isotopic concentration of lutonium-238 exceeding 80 per cent; (b) uranium-233; (c) uranium containing uranium-233 or uranium-235 or both in such an amount that the abundance ratio of the sum of those isotopes to the isotope uranium-238 is greater than 0.72 per cent; (d) uranium with an isotopic concentration equal to that occurring in nature; and (e) any substance containing anything described in paragraphs (a) to (d), but does not include uranium in the form of ore or ore-residue. *Criminal Law Amendment Act*, R.S.C. 1985, c. C-46, s. 2.

NUCLEAR MEDICINE TECHNOLOGIST. A medical radiation technologist who is registered as a member of the Canadian Association in the discipline of nuclear medicine and who utilizes radionuclides, radio-pharmaceuticals and radiation detecting devices in the practice of medical radiation technology.

NUCLEAR SHIP. A ship fitted with a nuclear power plant.

NUCLEAR SUBSTANCE. (*a*) Deuterium, thorium, uranium or an element with an atomic number greater than 92; (*b*) a derivative or compound of deuterium, thorium, uranium or of an element with an atomic number greater than 92; (*c*) a radioactive nuclide; (*d*) a substance that is prescribed as being capable of releasing nuclear energy or as being required for the production or use of nuclear energy; (*e*) a radioactive by-product of the development, production or use of nuclear energy; and (*f*) a radioactive substance or radioactive thing that was used for the development or production, or in connection with the use, of nuclear energy. *Nuclear Safety and Control Act, 1997*, S.C. 1997, c. 9, s. 2.

NUCLEOTIDES. *n*. Those nucleotides that can be represented using the symbols set out in section 115 and such nucleotides when they have been modified. *Patent Rules* SOR/96-423, s. 2.

NUCLEOTIDE SEQUENCE. An unbranched sequence of 10 or more contiguous nucleotides. *Patent Rules* SOR/96-423, s. 2.

NUDA PACTIO OBLIGATIONEM NON PARIT. [L.] A simple promise does not create an obligation.

NUDE. *adj*. " . . . '[C]ompletely bare', without reference to public decency or order." *R. v. Verrette* (1978), 3 C.R. (3d) 132 at 140, [1978] 2 S.C.R. 838, 40 C.C.C. (2d) 273, 21 N.R. 571, 85 D.L.R. (3d) 1, the court per Beetz J.

NUDI CONSENSUS OBLIGATIO CONTRARIO CONSENSU DISSOLVITUR. [L.] The binding force of a contract made with no consideration is dissolved by an agreement to the contrary.

NUDUM PACTUM. [L. a bare agreement] An agreement made with no consideration.

NUDUM PACTUM EST UBI NULLA SUB EST CAUSA PRAETER CONVENTIONEM; SED UBI SUBEST CAUSA, FIT OBLIGATIO, ET PARIT ACTIONEM. [L.] A contract is naked where there is no consideration except the agreement; but where there is consideration, an obligation arises and creates a cause of action.

NUISANCE. *n*. 1. An unreasonable interference with a person's use and enjoyment of property. 2. A condition that is or that might become injurious or dangerous to the public health or that might hinder in any manner the prevention or suppression of disease. 3. Anything which is injurious to the health or indecent, or offensive to the senses, or an obstruction to the free use of property so as to interfere with the comfortable enjoyment of life or property. 4. Includes and shall be deemed to include any condition, existing in any locality, which is or may become injurious or dangerous to health, or prevent or hinder in any manner the suppression of disease; and without restricting the generality of the aforegoing, for greater particularity the following shall be deemed nuisances within the meaning of this Act, if in such a state, or so situated, as to be injurious or dangerous to health: (a) any premises improperly constructed or in a state of disrepair; (b) any house of part of a house so over-crowded as to be injurious or dangerous to the health of the inmates, or in which insufficient air space is allowed for each inmate as required by the regulations; (c) any accumulation or deposit of refuse, wherever situate; (d) a street, pool, ditch, gutter, water-course, sink, cistern, water or earth closet, privy, urinal, cesspool, drain, dung pit or ash pit in a foul condition; (e) a well, spring or other water supply; and (f) a burial ground, cemetery, crematorium, columbariuum or other place of sepulchre located or so overcrowded or otherwise so arranged or managed as to be offensive, or injurious or dangerous to health. *Health Act*, R.S.N.B. 1973, c. H- 2, s. 1. 5. An animal, bird, insect, plant or disease declared to be a nuisance under section 2. *Agricultural Pests Act*, S.A. 1984, c. A-8.1, s. 1. See ABATEMENT OF ~; COMMON ~; PRIVATE ~; PUBLIC ~.

NUISANCE SEAL. A seal that represents a danger (*a*) to fishing equipment despite deterrence efforts, or (*b*) based on a scientific recommendation, to the conservation of anadromous or catadromous fish stocks because it inflicts great damage to them along estuaries and in rivers and lakes during the migration of those species. *Marine Mammal Regulations*, SOR/93-56, s. 2.

NULLA BONA. [L. no goods] The proper return of a writ when the judgment debtor has no goods in the sheriff's bailiwick or there are no proceeds available to satisfy the writ.

NULLA CRIMEN SINE LEGE, NULLA POENA SINE LEGE. [L.] There can be no crime or punishment unless it is in accordance with law that is certain, unambiguous and not retroactive.

NULLA CURIA QUAE RECORDUM NON HABET POTEST IMPONERE FINEM, NEQUE ALIQUEM MANDARE CARCERI; QUIA ISTA SPECTANT TANTUMMODO AD CURIAS DE RECORDO. [L.] No court which does not have a record can impose a fine, or sentence any person to prison; because those powers only belong to courts of record.

NULLA EST INJURIA QUAE IN VOLENTEM FIT. [L.] No wrongdoing is done to a willing person.

NULLA IMPOSSIBILIA AUT INHONESTA SUNT PRAESUMENDA; VERA AUTEM ET HONESTA ET POSSIBILIA. [L.] One should not presume things which are impossible or shameful, but instead things which are true seemly and possible.

NULL AND VOID. Not legally binding.

NULLA PACTIONE EFFICI POTEST UT DOLUS PRAESTETUR. [L.] By no contract is it possible to arrange that someone be indemnified against their own fraud.

NULLA POENA SINE LEGE. [L.] 1. There can be no punishment unless it is in accordance with law that is certain, unambiguous and not retroactive. 2. An accused's silence in the face of a police accusation can be considered a particular example of the liberty to do that which is not prohibited embodied in this maxim.

NULLIS EXCEPTIS. [L.] There were no exceptions made.

NULLITY. *n*. 1. Something which has no legal effect. 2. A charge may be quashed as a nullity if it refers to an offence not known to law or it is so badly drawn not to give the accused notice of the charge.

NULLITY OF MARRIAGE. The total invalidity of an attempted, pretended or supposed marriage which was void from the beginning because the parties lacked consent or capacity to marry or which was voidable or liable to annulment later because one spouse was unable to consummate the marriage.

NULLIUS FILIUS. [L. the son of no one] A bastard.

NULLIUS HOMINIS AUCTORITAS APUD NOS VALERE DEBET, UT MELIORA NON SEQUEREMUR SI QUIS ATTULERIT. [L.] The authority of no one should prevail with us so that we would not adopt better things if someone else brought them.

NULLI VENDEMUS, NULLI NEGABIMUS AUT DIFFEREMUS, RECTUM AUT JUSTICIAM. [L.] " . . . [T]o none will we sell, to none will we deny or delay, right or justice . . ." *R. v. Toronto Railway* (1911), 2 O.W.N. 681 at 682, 23 O.L.R. 186, 18 C.C.C. 417 (H.C.), Riddell J.

NULLUM ARBITRIUM. [L.] There is no such award.

NULLUM CRIMEN SINE LEGS. [L.] There should be no crime except according to predetermined, fixed law. D. Stuart, *Canadian Criminal Law: a Treatise*, 2d ed. (Toronto: Carswell, 1987) at 15.

NULLUM CRIMEN SINE POENA. [L.] There should be no crime without a penalty.

NULLUM EXEMPLUM EST IDEM OMNIBUS. [L.] No example is the same to everyone.

NULLUM FECERUNT ARBITRIUM. [L.] They submitted to no arbitration.

NULLUM INIQUUM EST IN JURE PRAESUMENDUM. [L.] In law, the doing of something contrary to justice should not be presumed.

NULLUM SIMILE EST IDEM. [L.] Something similar to something else is not the same thing.

NULLUM TEMPUS AUT LOCUS OCCURRIT REGI. [L.] No time or place affects a monarch.

NULLUM TEMPUS OCCURRIT REGI. [L.] ". . . [N]o lapse of time bars the King . . ." *Alberta v. Buys* (1989), 24 C.P.C. (2d) 125 at 129, 66 Alta. L.R. (2d) 361, [1989] 4 W.W.R. 636, 95 A.R. 248, 59 D.L.R. (4th) 677 (C.A.), the court per Foisy J.A. Separate from the prerogative of not being bound by a statute. The Crown is considered to be preoccupied with the business of government and should not suffer from negligence of its officers.

NULLUS COMMODUM CAPERE POTEST DE INJURIA SUA PROPRIA. [L.] No one can gain advantage by her or his very own wrong. ". . . [N]o devisee [can] take under the will of a testator whose death has been caused by the criminal and felonious act of the devisee himself, . . ." *MacKinnon v. Lundy* (1895), (*sub nom. Lundy v. Lundy*) 24 S.C.R. 650 at 651, Strong C.J.

NULLUS VIDETUR DOLO FACERE QUI SUO JURE UTITUR. [L.] No one who merely avails herself or himself of a legal right is considered to be a wrongdoer.

NUL PRENDRA ADVANTAGE DE SON TORT DEMESNE. [Fr.] No person shall profit by the wrong that person does.

NUL TIEL AGARD. No such award.

NUL TIEL RECORD. No such record.

NUL TORT. No wrong has been done.

NUMBER. *n.* See CODE ~; CORPORATION ~; FUEL CONSUMPTION ~; REGISTER ~; REGISTRATION ~; SERIAL ~.

NUMBER NAME. The name of a corporation that consists only of its corporation number followed by the word "Ontario" and one of the words or abbreviations provided for in subsection 10 (1). *Business Corporations Act*, R.S.O. 1990, c. B.16, s. 1.

NUMBER PLATE. 1. Includes any proof of registration issued and required to be affixed to a motor vehicle or trailer. 2. Validation decals for attachment to number plates. See FICTITIOUS ~; IDENTIFICATION ~.

NUMBER RECORDER. Any device that can be used to record or identify the telephone number or location of the telephone from which a telephone call originates, or at which it is received or is intended to be received. *Criminal Code*, R.S.C. 1985, c. C-46, s. 492.2.

NUNAVUT. *n.* A territory of Canada consisting of (*a*) all that part of Canada north of the sixtieth parallel of north latitude and east of the boundary described in Schedule I that is not within Quebec or Newfoundland; and (*b*) the islands in Hudson Bay, James Bay and Ungava Bay that are not within Manitoba, Ontario or Quebec. A Legislature for Nunavut consisting of the Commissioner and the Legislative Assembly of Nunavut is established. There is established a Legislative Assembly of Nunavut, each member of which is elected to represent an electoral district in Nunavut.

NUNCHAKU. *n.* Two hard non-flexible sticks, clubs, pipes or rods connected by a rope, cord, wire or chain and designed to be used in connection with the practice of a system of self-defence such as karate. *Prohibited Weapons Order, No. 2*, C.R.C., c. 434, s. 2.

NUNCIO. *n.* [L.] A messenger; the Pope's envoy.

NUNC PRO TUNC. [L. now for then] 1. The order of a court that a proceeding be dated with an earlier date than the date it actually took place, or that the same effect be produced as if the proceeding had happened at an earlier date. 2. " . . . [U]sed to refer to the common law power of the Court to permit that to be done now which ought to have been done before. . ." *Krueger v. Raccah* (1981), 24 C.P.C. 14 at 17, 12 Sask. R. 130, 128 D.L.R. (3d) 177 (Q.B.), Cameron J.

NUNCUPATE. *v.* To declare solemnly and publicly.

NUNCUPATIVE WILL. " . . . [A] will made by a soldier under circumstances in which it is presumed he would not be able to have a proper will drawn and properly witnessed." *Smith v.*

Hubbard, [1917] 1 W.W.R. 1237 at 1238 (B.C. S.C.), Macdonald J.

NUNDINATION. *n*. Traffic at a fair or market; any buying and selling.

NUNQUAM CRESCIT EX POST FACTO PRAETERITI DELICTI AESTIMATIO. [L.] The seriousness of an offence, once committed, never increases subsequently.

NUNQUAM INDEBITATUS. [L.] Never in debt.

NUPTIAE. *n*. [L.] Marriage.

NUPTIAL. *adj*. Related to marriage. See ANTE-NUPTIAL.

NUPTIAS NON CUNCUBITUS SED CONSENSUS FACIT. [L.] Not cohabitation but consent makes a marriage.

NURSE. *n*. Any person who is possessed of the qualifications required and is authorized to offer service for the care of the sick and to give care intended for the prevention of disease and to receive remuneration therefor. See DENTAL ~; PRACTICAL ~; PSYCHIATRIC ~; REGISTERED ~.

NURSE PRACTITIONER. A nurse with special training to permit him or her to work in a remote area without the presence of a physician.

NURSERY. *n*. Any place where fruit trees, fruit stock or ornamental plants are propagated for sale. See DAY ~.

NURSERY-MAN. *n*. Any person who cultivates, for their increase and sale, trees, shrubs, bushes or fruit-bearing, ornamental or other plants.

NURSERY SCHOOL. Day-care services provided in an establishment that receives at least 10 children from 2-5 years of age on a regular basis for periods of up to 3 hours a day.

NURSERY STOCK. Coniferous or hardwood seedlings, transplants, grafts or trees propagated or grown in a nursery and having the roots attached and includes cuttings having or not having roots attached.

NURSING. *n*. The practice of nursing is the promotion of health and the assessment of, the provision of care for and the treatment of health conditions by supportive, preventive, therapeutic, palliative and rehabilitative means in order to attain or maintain optimal function. *Nursing Act, 1991*, S.O. 1991, c. 32, s. 3. See PRACTI-

CAL ~; PRACTICE OF ~; PSYCHIATRIC ~.

NURSING AIDE. A person who, being neither a registered nurse nor a person in training to be a registered nurse at an approved school of nursing, undertakes the care of patients for remuneration.

NURSING ASSISTANT. A person who is trained to care for convalescent, subacutely ill and chronically ill patients, and to assist nurses in the care of acutely ill patients. See REGISTERED ~.

NURSING CARE. The use of methods, procedures and techniques employed in providing nursing care by persons with technical nursing training beyond the care that an untrained person can adequately administer. *Homes for Special Care Act*, R.S.N.S. 1989, c. 203, s. 2(1). See INTERMEDIATE ~; SKILLED ~.

NURSING EDUCATION PROGRAM. A program approved by the Board and which is a prerequisite for a person to have completed prior to the taking by that person of examinations as may be prescribed from time to time by a board to qualify as a registered nurse.

NURSING HOME. Any house, building or structure in which accommodation, meals and nursing services are provided to residents for compensation.

NURSING HOME CARE. Provides the following services to patients: (i) accommodation, meals and laundry; (ii) personal services such as help and supervision in cleanliness, mobility, safety, feeding and dressing; (iii) special diets when necessary; (iv) routine drugs and dressings as ordered by the attending physician; (v) recreational, diversional and re-activational activities; and any other services prescribed by the regulations. *Nursing Homes Act*, R.S.A. 1980, c. N-14, s. 1.

NUTRIENT. *n*. 1. Any substance or combination of substances that, if added to any waters in sufficient quantities, provides nourishment that promotes the growth of aquatic vegetation in those waters to such densities as to (a) interfere with their use by human beings or by any animal, fish or plant that is useful to human beings; or (b) degrade or alter or form part of a process of degradation or alteration of the quality of those waters to an extent that is detrimental to their use by human beings or by any animal, fish or plant that is useful to human beings. *Canadian*

Environmental Protection Act, S.C. 1988, c. 22, s. 49. 2. Fertilizers, organic materials, biosolids, compost, manure, septage, pulp and paper sludge, and other material applied to land for the purpose of improving the growing of agricultural crops or for the purpose of a prescribed use, but does not include any material that the regulations specify does not come within the definition of "nutrient". *Nutrient Management Act, 2002*, S.O. 2002, c. 4, s. 2. See MINERAL ~.

NUTRIENT MANAGEMENT PLAN. A plan for the management of materials containing nutrients that may be applied to lands, which plan is prepared in accordance with the regulations. *Nutrient Management Act, 2002*, S.O. 2002, c. 4, s. 2.

NUTRIENT MANAGEMENT STRATEGY. A plan prepared by a municipality or generator of prescribed materials to ensure the prescribed materials generated in the municipality or by the generator are appropriately managed and may include one or more nutrient management plans. *Nutrient Management Act, 2002*, S.O. 2002, c. 4, s. 2.

N.W.T. *abbr.* 1. Northwest Territories. 2. North West Territories Reports, 1887-1898.

[] **N.W.T.R.** *abbr.* Northwest Territories Reports, 1983-.

NWTSC. The neutral citation for the Northwest Territories Supreme Court.

NWTTC. The neutral citation for the Northwest Territories Territorial Court.

O

O.A.C. *abbr*. Ontario Appeal Cases.

O.A.R. *abbr*. Ontario Appeal Reports, 1876-1900.

OATH. *n*. 1. " . . . [A]n appeal to a Supreme Being in whose existence the person taking the oath believes to be a rewarder of truth and an avenger of falsehood: . . . The purpose of the oath is to bind the conscience of the witness. . ." *R*. *v*. *Deli*, [1932] 1 W.W.R. 545 at 546, 57 C.C.C. 401, 26 Alta. L.R. 134 (C.A.), the court per McGillivray J.A. 2. ". . . Canada's emerging multi-cultural society requires an acknowledgement in the courts that the Judaic-Christian form of oath is not necessarily the only form of religious oath to be administered, and that persons of other religious persuasions should not automatically be given affirmation as the only alternative." *R*. *v*. *Kalevar* (1991), 4 C.R. (4th) 114 at 117 (Ont. Gen. Div.), Haley J. 3. Includes affirmation and statutory declaration. 4. Includes a solemn affirmation in cases in which, by the law of Canada, or of a province, as the case may be, a solemn affirmation is allowed instead of an oath. See CORPORAL ~.

OATH-HELPING. 1. Evidence adduced to prove that a witness is truthful. It is not admissible. 2. The actual credibility of a particular witness is not generally the proper subject of opinion evidence. This is known as the rule against oath-helping. *R*. *v*. *D*. *(D.)*, 2000 CarswellOnt 3255, 2000 SCC 43, 36 C.R. (5th) 261, 148 C.C.C. (3d) 41, 191 D.L.R. (4th) 60, 259 N.R. 156, 136 O.A.C. 201, [2000] 2 S.C.R. 275 Per McLachlin C.J.C. (dissenting) (L'Heureux-Dubé, Gonthier JJ. concurring).

OATH OF ALLEGIANCE. The words of the oath are: I, ———, do swear that I will be faithful and bear true allegiance to Her Majesty Queen Elizabeth the Second Queen of Canada Her Heirs and Successors. So help me God.

Oaths of Allegiance Act, R.S.C. 1985, c. O-1, s. 2(1).

OATH OR AFFIDAVIT. In the case of persons for the time being allowed or required by law to affirm or declare instead of swearing, includes affirmation and declaration.

OATH OR AFFIRMATION OF CITIZENSHIP. The words of the oath are: I swear (or affirm) that I will be faithful and bear true allegiance to Her Majesty Queen Elizabeth the Second Queen of Canada Her Heirs and Successors, and that I will faithfully observe the laws of Canada and fulfill my duties as a Canadian citizen. *Citizenship Act*, R.S.C. 1985, c. C-29, Schedule.

OAT PRODUCT. Any substance produced by processing or manufacturing oats.

OBEDIENTIA EST LEGIS ESSENTIA. [L.] Obedience is the indispensable element of law.

OBITER DICTA. [L.]1. " . . . [M]ere passing remarks of the judge . . ." *Richard West Partners Inverness Ltd*. *v*. *Dick* (1968), [1969] 1 All E.R. 289 at 292 (U.K. Ch.), Megarry J. 2. As Green J.A. observed in para. 34 of his judgment in *R*. *v*. *Hynes* (1999), 177 Nfld. & P.E.I.R. 232 (Nfld. C.A.), a reading of *R*. *v*. Sellars, [1980] 1 S.C.R. 527 and authorities from which it drew indicates the Sellars' direction should be interpreted as saying: *obiter* statements of legal principle in majority judgments of the Supreme Court of Canada will be regarded as declaratory of the law, and binding on lower courts, where from a reading of the judgment, it appears that: (i) the Court considered it desirable to express its opinion on the matter; (ii) the matter was fully argued; and (iii) accordingly, the comments are the fully-considered opinion of the Court. Although Green J.A. wrote these words in dissent, no exception is taken with this passage as an accurate synopsis of the criteria for attributing binding effect to *obiter* pronounced in the Supreme Court of Canada. One important rider must be attached to the endorsement of the foregoing passage from Green J.A.'s judgment in *Hynes* as representative of the law regarding the authoritative effect of Supreme Court *obiter*, however. This is that it will be very much the exception, rather than the rule, that it will be possible to demonstrate the criterion of "fully-considered opinion" requisite for authoritative *obiter* was not fulfilled. In other words, very rare will be the instances where the circumstances will afford latitude for lower courts to treat *obiter* emanating from the Supreme Court of Canada as other than binding legal principle. *Newfoundland Assn. of Provincial Court Judges v. Newfoundland*, 2000 CarswellNfld 266, 2000 NFCA 46, 191 D.L.R. (4th) 225, 50 C.P.C. (4th) 1, 27 Admin. L.R. (3d) 1 (C.A.), Per Marshall J.A., dissenting.

OBITER DICTUM. [L. a remark in passing] 1. An opinion not required in a judgment and so not a binding precedent. 2. " . . . [T]he time is past . . . when the language of a conclusion is minutely scrutinized regardless of the underlying reasons and the conclusions sought in the action, and everything not echoed in the conclusion [is] necessarily regarded as an obiter dictum." *Celliers du Monde Inc. c. Dumont Vins & Spiriteux Inc.* (1992), 42 C.P.R. (3d) 197 at 204, 139 N.R. 357, [1992] 2 F.C. 634 (C.A.), the court per Decary J.A.

OBJECT. *v*. To take issue with.

OBJECT. *n*. 1. Goal or purpose. 2. A tangible item.

OBJECT CODE. 1. Both "application" and "operating system" programs can be expressed in what is known as "source code" or in "object code". Most programs are essentially created in "source code" and converted into "object code". "Object code" is more difficult to read or understand by a programmer, because it is a series of 0's and 1's and, to a layman at least, could be described as the language of a computer. *Apple Computer Inc. v. Macintosh Computers Ltd.* 3 C.I.P.R. 133, 3 C.P.R. (3d) 34, F.C.T.D. Cullen J. 2. Since the computer only responds to machine language, a computer programme written is called the source code and the language into which it is translated is called the object code. Object code in many instances, and in the jurisprudence, I notice, is used as synonymous with machine language and I will adopt that usage.

International Business Machines Corp. v. Ordinateurs Spirales Inc./Spirales Computers Inc. 27 B.L.R. 190, 80 C.P.R. (2d) 187, 2 C.I.P.R. 56, 12 D.L.R. (4th) 351 F CT D., Reed J. 3. "A third level of [computer] language, the lowest, is sometimes referred to as machine language or object code. There are two versions of machine language relevant for the purposes of this case: a system of hexadecimal notation and a system of binary notation." *Apple Computer Inc. v. Mackintosh Computers Ltd.* (1986), 10 C.P.R. (3d) 1 at 7, 8 C.I.P.R. 153, 3 F.T.R. 118, [1987] 1 F.C. 173, 28 D.L.R. (4th) 178 (T.D.), Reed J. See MACHINE LANGUAGE.

OBJECTION FOR WANT OF NOVELTY. Used to describe an objection to a patent because the invention is not new or original.

OBJECTIVE. *n*. Aim, intended end.

OBJECTIVE. *adj*. Reasoned; impersonal; observed.

OBJECTIVE EVIDENCE. Information that can be proved true, based on facts obtained through observation, measurement, testing or other means, as set out in the definition "objective evidence" in section 2.19 of International Organization for Standardization standard ISO 8402:1994, *Quality management and quality assurance—Vocabulary*, as amended from time to time. *Medical Devices Regulations*, SOR/98-282, s. 1.

OBJECTIVELY. *adv*. Having an evidentiary base.

OBJECTIVE RATIONALE. The principle that no matter where committed, the court has jurisdiction to try an offence which threatens the society in its own territory. M.R. Goode, *Criminal Conspiracy in Canada* (Toronto: Carswell, 1975) at 162.

OBJECTIVES. *n*. In relation to a parent Crown corporation, means the objectives of the corporation as set out in a corporate plan or an amendment to a corporate plan that has been approved pursuant to section 122. *Financial Administration Act*, R.S.C. 1985, c. F-11, s. 120.

OBJECT OF A POWER. A person in whose favour one may exercise a power of appointment.

OBJECT OF ETHNOGRAPHIC ART. An art product, commonly known as primitive art, or other artifact and includes a military, scientific or technological object, that is (a) made by an aboriginal person; (b) an expression of indigenous culture developed outside the centre of civilization as traditionally viewed by western culture; which may (c) incorporate features reflecting contact with non-indigenous cultures; and (d) be a single object or an object together with its component parts that form a single unit. *Canadian Cultural Property Export Control List*, C.R.C., c. 448, s. 1.

OBJECTOR. See CONSCIENTIOUS ~.

OBJECTS. *n.* The purposes of a corporation. The purposes of a trust. See CERTAINTY OF ~.

OBLIGATION. *n.* 1. " . . . [R]efers to something in the nature of a contract, such as a covenant, bond or agreement . . ." *Stokes v. Leavens* (1918), 40 D.L.R. 23 at 24, [1918] 2 W.W.R. 188, 28 Man. R. 479 (C.A.), Perdue J.A. 2. "[Not restricted] to a duty arising out of contract [but] . . . also includes a duty or liability arising from an actionable tort." *Smith v. Canadian Broadcasting Corp.*, [1953] O.W.N. 212 at 214, [1953] 1 D.L.R. 510 (H.C.), Judson J. 3. " . . . [T]hat which constitutes legal duty and which renders one liable to coercion for neglecting it — an act which binds a person to some performance." *Ging, Re* (1890), 20 O.R. 1 at 5 (H.C.), Robertson J. 4. "[In the definition of property in the Bankruptcy Act, R.S.C. 1970, c. B-3, s. 2] . . . an asset owing to the bankrupt as an obligee . . ." *Targa Holdings Ltd. v. Whyte* (1974), 21 C.B.R. (N.S.) 54 at 71, [1974] 3 W.W.R. 632, 44 D.L.R. (3d) 208 (Alta. C.A.), Clement J.A. 5. Includes duty and liability. 6. The total amount payable when the contract was entered into. *Consumer Protection Act*, R.R.O. 1980, Reg. 181, s. 22. 7. Includes requirement, restriction, limitation, condition and duty. *Water Act*, R.S.B.C. 1979, c. 429, s. 1. 8. Bonds, debentures, notes or other evidences of indebtedness. *Trust Companies Act*, R.S.A. 1980, c. T-9, s. 111. See DEBT ~; EQUITY IMPUTES AN INTENTION TO FULFIL AN ~; FUNDED ~; GOLD CLAUSE ~; IMPERFECT ~; MORAL ~; MUTUALITY OF ~; NATURAL ~; PRINCIPAL ~; TOTAL ~.

OBLIGATION IN SOLIDUM. The purpose of the concept is to organize the manner in which more than one debt relating to a single object may coexist. Reiterates the fundamental elements of the institution of joint and several liability. When two debts relate to the same object, it allows the creditor to look to any one of the debtors for payment. The debtor who has paid is then subrogated in the rights of the creditor against its co-debtor. *Perras c. Immeubles Les Castels de Greenfield Park inc.*, (sub nom. *Prévost-Masson v. General Trust of Canada*) [2001] 3 S.C.R. 882.

OBLIGATION SECURED. When determining the amount payable under a lease that secures payment or performance of an obligation, (i) the amount originally contracted to be paid under the lease, (ii) any other amounts payable pursuant to the terms of the lease, and (iii) any other amount required to be paid by the lessee to obtain full ownership of the collateral, less any amount paid prior to the determination. *Personal Property Security Act*, R.S.A. 2000, c. P-7, s. 1(1).

OBLIGEE. *n.* 1. The person in whose favour a bond or other security is furnished and by whom the bond or security is held. 2. (i) In the case of a bid bond, the person requesting bids for the performance of a contract; and (ii) in the case of a payment bond or performance bond, the person who has contracted with a principal for the completion of the contract and to whom the obligation of the surety runs in the event of a breach by the principal of the conditions of a payment bond or performance bond. *Business Loans, Guarantees and Indemnities Act*, S.N.W.T. 1983 (1st Sess.), c. 1, s. 3. 3. A creditor; the person in whose favour one enters into a bond or obligation.

OBLIGOR. *n.* A debtor; the one who enters into a bond or obligation.

OBLITERATED BOUNDARY. A boundary established during an original survey or during a survey of a plan of subdivision registered under the Land Titles Act or the Registry Act where the original posts or blazed trees no longer exist and which cannot be re-established from the field notes of either of such surveys or by evidence under oath. *Surveys Act*, R.S.O. 1990, c. S.30, s. 1.

OBLITERATED MONUMENT. A monument the position of which can be ascertained beyond reasonable doubt either by traces of the original monument or by other evidence, although the monument itself has partly or entirely disappeared.

OBSCENE. *adj.* 1. Any publication whose dominant characteristic is the undue exploitation of sex, or of sex and any one or more of the following subjects, namely: crime, horror, cruelty and violence, shall be deemed to be obscene. *Criminal Code*, R.S.C. 1985, c. C-46, s. 163(8).

2. In determining whether the exploitation of sex is "undue", three tests are considered: the "community standards test" is concerned not with what Canadians would not tolerate being exposed to themselves, but what they would not tolerate *other* Canadians being exposed to; the "degradation or dehumanization test" considers degrading or dehumanizing materials place women (and sometimes men) in positions of subordination, servile submission or humiliation. They run against the principles of equality and dignity of all human beings; the "internal necessities test" assesses whether the exploitation of sex has a justifiable role in advancing the plot or the theme, and in considering the work as a whole, does not merely represent "dirt for dirt's sake" but has a legitimate role when measured by the internal necessities of the work itself. *R. v. Butler*, [1992] 1 S.C.R. 452.

OBSCURITAS PACTI NOCET El QUI APERTIUS LOQUI POTUIT. [L.] Obscurity in a contract harms the one who could have spoken more directly.

OBSERVATION UNIT. A public hospital or a part of it designated by the minister as an observation unit. *Mental Health Act*, R.S.B.C. 1996, c. 288, s. 1.

OBSIGNATORY. *adj*. Confirming, ratifying.

OBSOLESCENCE. *n*. " . . . [A] type or classification of depreciation for which an allowance may be made when there is a loss in value resulting from various causes. . ." *Royalite Oil Co., Re* (1957), 23 W.W.R. (N.S.) 328 at 337, 11 D.L.R. (2d) 527 (B.C. S.C.), Lett C.J.S.C.

OBSOLETE. *adj*. 1. Invalid because it was discontinued. 2. Discarded; no longer used.

OBSOLETE OR SURPLUS GOODS. Goods that are (a) found to be obsolete or surplus to requirements by (i) their importer or owner, in the case of imported goods; or (ii) their manufacturer, producer or owner, in any other case; (b) not used in Canada for any purpose; (c) destroyed in such manner as the Minister directs; and (d) not damaged before their destruction. *Duties Relief Act*, R.S.C. 1985 (2d Supp.), c. 21, s. 32.

OBSTRICTION. *n*. Bond; obligation.

OBSTRUCT. *v*. To do any act which makes it more difficult for the police to carry out their duties.

OBSTRUCTING JUSTICE. 1. Every one who wilfully attempts in any manner to obstruct, pervert or defeat the course of justice in a judicial proceeding, (a) by indemnifying or agreeing to indemnify a surety, in any way and ether in whole or in part; or (b) where he is a surety, by accepting or agreeing to accept a fee or any form of indemnity whether in whole or in part from or in respect of a person who is released or is to be released from custody. *Criminal Code*, R.S.C. 1985, c. C-46, s. 139(1). 2. Every one shall be deemed wilfully to attempt to obstruct, pervert or defeat the course of justice who in a judicial proceeding, existing or proposed, (a) dissuades or attempts to dissuade a person by threats, bribes or other corrupt means from giving evidence; (b) influences or attempts to influence by threats, bribes or other corrupt means a person in his conduct as a juror; or (c) accepts or obtains, agrees to accept or attempts to obtain a bribe or other corrupt consideration to abstain from giving evidence, or to do or to refrain from doing anything as a juror. *Criminal Code*, R.S.C. 1985, c. C-46, s. 139(3).

OBSTRUCTION. *n*. 1. " . . . [A]ny act, not necessarily an unlawful act, including a concealment, which frustrates or makes more difficult the execution of a peace officer's duty. . ." *R. v. Moore* (1977), 40 C.R.N.S. 93 at 105, [1977] 5 W.W.R. 241, 36 C.C.C. (2d) 481 (B.C. C.A.), Carrothers J.A. 2. Any slide, dam or other obstruction impeding the free passage of fish. *Fisheries Act*, R.S.C. 1985, c. F-14, s. 2. 3. Every person is guilty of an offence who, with the intention of delaying or obstructing the electoral process. *Canada Elections Act*, S.C. 2000, c. 9, s. 480(1). Every person is guilty of an offence who, at any time between the issue of a writ and the day after polling day at the election, acts, incites others to act or conspires to act in a disorderly manner with the intention of preventing the transaction of the business of a public meeting called for the purposes of the election. *Canada Elections Act*, S.C. 2000, c. 9, s. 480(2).

OBTAIN. *v*. To acquire, procure, get, have granted to.

OBTEMPERANDUM EST CONSUETUDINI RATIONABILI TANQUAM LEGI. [L.] One must obey reasonable custom as if it were law.

OBTEST. *v*. To express disagreement or disapproval.

OBTURATION. *n*. The sealing of powder gases between the walls of the finny chamber and cartridge case and the barrel and the bullet.

F.A. Jaffe, *A Guide to Pathological Evidence*, 3d ed. (Toronto: Carswell, 1991) at 223.

OBVIATE. *v*. To do away with.

OBVIOUS. *adj*. 1. In the law of patents, something is obvious when it would occur directly to an ordinary person skilled in the relevant art or subject searching for something normal without serious thought, research or experiment. 2. When used with reference to a disability or disabling condition of a member of the forces at the time he became a member, means that the disability or disabling condition was apparent at that time or would have been apparent to an unskilled observer on examination of the member at that time. *Pensions Act*, R.S.C. 1985, c. P-6, s. 21(12).

OBVIOUSNESS. *n*. An attack on a patent based on its lack of inventiveness. Obviousness alleges that "any fool could have done that", while anticipation alleges that "your invention, though clever, was already known." *SmithKline Beecham Pharma Inc. v. Apotex Inc.* (2002), 2002 FCA 216, 21 C.P.R. (4th) 129, 219 D.L.R. (4th) 124, [2003] 1 F.C. 118, 226 F.T.R. 144 (note) (C.A.).

O.C. *abbr*. Order in Council.

OCCASION. *v*. Cause. *Jackson Brothers Grain Co. v. United States Fidelity & Guaranty Co.* (1934), 42 Man. R. 469 at 471, [1934] 3 W.W.R. 485 (K.B.), Adamson J.

OCCASION. *n*. An event; occurrence. See SOCIAL ~.

OCCASIONAL. *adj*. Limited to specific occasions.

OCCASIONAL SKILLED CARE. Nursing or other services rendered intermittently or periodically to a person by a formally trained person under an arrangement approved by the inspector, in an amount or to a degree or with a frequency which, in the opinion of the, inspector, is less than that which would necessitate the individual being lodged in a nursing home or hospital in order to be properly cared for. *Hospital Act*, R.S.B.C. 1996, c. 200, s. 5(1).

OCCASIONAL TEACHER. A teacher, employed to teach as a substitute for a permanent, probationary, continuing education or temporary teacher who has died during the school year or who is absent from his or her regular duties for a temporary period that is less than a school year and that does not extend beyond the end of a school year. *Education Act*, R.S.O. 1990, c. E.2, s. 1(1).

OCCIPUT. *n*. The back of the skull or head. F.A. Jaffe, *A Guide to Pathological Evidence*, 3d ed. (Toronto: Carswell, 1991) at 223.

OCCUPANCY. *n*. The use or intended use of a building or part thereof for the shelter or support of persons, animals or property. *Building Code*, O. Reg. 403/97, s. 1.1.3.2(1). See ASSEMBLY ~; BUSINESS ~; CLASS OF ~; INDUSTRIAL ~; INSTITUTIONAL ~; MAJOR ~; MERCANTILE ~; PERSONAL SERVICES ~; RESIDENTIAL ~.

OCCUPANCY DUTY. In occupiers' liability, a duty based on occupancy.

OCCUPANCY PERMIT. A permit, certificate or other document issued by a municipality or an official thereof in respect of a building indicating that the building or a part thereof may be occupied.

OCCUPANT. *n*. 1. The owner, lessee, or other person having possession of or control over lands. 2. "To be an 'occupant' of premises, as that word is understood in law, a person must have control of them." *Stinson v. Middleton (Township)*, [1949] O.R. 237 at 252, [1949] 2 D.L.R. 328 (C.A.), Robertson C.J.O. 3. ". . . [I]n a wide sense means 'one who occupies, resides in or is at the time in a place'." *Stinson v. Middleton (Township)*, [1949] 2 D.L.R. 328 at 333, [1949] O.R. 237 (C.A.), Laidlaw J.A. 4. Includes the person in charge of a house, building or premises or under whose care they are, and a person apparently in charge thereof or exercising control or authority thereover. 5. Includes the resident occupier of and or, if there is no resident occupier, the person entitled to the possession thereof, a leaseholder and a person having or enjoying in any way for any purpose the use of land otherwise than as owner, whether or not the land or part thereof is in an unsurveyed area, and also includes a squatter. 6. A person who occupies an immoveable otherwise than as owner. *An Act respecting municipal taxation and providing amendments to certain legislation*, S.Q. 1979, c. 2, s. 1. 7. Any person who occupies an immoveable in his own name, otherwise than as proprietor, usufructuary or institute, and who enjoys the revenues derived from such immoveable. *Cities and Towns Act*, R.S.Q. 1977, c. C-19, s. 6. 8. Under an automobile insurance policy, a person driving, being carried in or upon or entering or getting onto or alighting from an automobile. See PASSIVE ~ PROTECTION; RESIDENT ~.

OCCUPANT DISTRIBUTION. The distribution of occupants in a vehicle in a manner specified in the third column of the table to this section. *Motor Vehicle Safety Regulations*, C.R.C., c. 1038, s. 111.

OCCUPANT LOAD. The number of persons for which a building or part thereof is designed. See HIGH ~.

OCCUPANT RESTRAINT ASSEMBLY. Any harness, including webbing, buckles and hardware, that is used or to be used to secure or restrain an occupant in a product. *Children's Car Seats and Harnesses Regulations*, C.R.C., c. 921, s. 2.

OCCUPANT SPACE. The space directly above the seat and footwell, bounded vertically by the ceiling and horizontally by the normally positioned seat back and the nearest obstruction of occupant motion in the direction the seat faces. *Motor Vehicle Safety Regulations*, C.R.C., c.1038, s. 2.

OCCUPATILE. *adj*. Left by the proper owner and now possessed by someone else.

OCCUPATION. *n*. 1. An employment, business, calling, pursuit, trade, vocation or profession. 2. The act of possessing. 3. " .. [T]hat which engages the time and attention. . ." *Northern Trusts Co. v. Eckert*, [1942] 3 D.L.R. 121 at 124, 23 C.B.R. 387, [1942] 2 W.W.R. 382 (Alta. C.A.), Ewin J.A. (Hawsen J.A. concurring). See DUST EXPOSURE ~; HAZARDOUS ~; HOME ~; INTERNATIONAL STANDARD CLASSIFICATION OF ~S; USE AND ~.

OCCUPATIONAL ASSOCIATION. An organization, other than a trade union or employers' organization, in which membership is a prerequisite to carrying on a trade, occupation or profession.

OCCUPATIONAL CATEGORY. Any of the following categories of employees, namely, (a) scientific and professional; (b) technical; (c) administrative and foreign service; (d) administrative support; (e) operational; and (f) any other occupationally-related category of employees determined by the Board to be an occupational category. *Public Service Staff Relations Act*, R.S.C. 1985, c. P-35, s. 2.

OCCUPATIONAL CLASSIFICATION. (i) Classification of employees on the basis of the performance of similar work or duties and the exercise of a similar type and degree of skill or (ii) where only one employee is employed by an employer to perform work or duties of a particular kind or to exercise a particular type particular and degree of skill, the job or position of that employee. *The Labour Standards Act*, R.S.S. 1978, c. L-1, s. 2.

OCCUPATIONAL DISABILITY PENSION. A private pension plan which provides benefits in the event that a participant becomes disabled from employment.

OCCUPATIONAL DISEASE. 1. Any disease or illness or departure from normal health arising out of, or in the course of, employment in a workplace and includes an industrial disease. 2. A disease contracted out of or in the course of work and characteristic of that work or directly related to the risks peculiar to that work. 3. Includes, (a) a disease resulting from exposure to a substance relating to a particular process, trade or occupation in an industry, (b) a disease peculiar to or characteristic of a particular industrial process, trade or occupation, (c) a medical condition that in the opinion of the Board requires a worker to be removed either temporarily or permanently from exposure to a substance because the condition may be a precursor to an occupational disease, or (d) a disease mentioned in Schedule 3 or 4. *Workplace Safety and Insurance Act, 1997*, S.O. 1997, c. 16, Sched. A, s. 2(1).

OCCUPATIONAL HEALTH. (i) The promotion and maintenance of the highest degree of physical, mental and social well-being of workers; (ii) the prevention among workers of ill health caused by their working conditions; (iii) the protection of workers in their employment from factors adverse to their health; and (iv) the placing and maintenance of workers in occupational environments which are adapted to their individual physiological and psychological conditions. *The Occupational Heath and Safety Act*, R.S.S. 1978, c. O-1, s. 2.

OCCUPATIONAL HEALTH SERVICE. A service organized in or near a place of employment for the purpose of (i) protecting workers against any health or safety hazard that may arise out of their work or the conditions under which it is carried on; (ii) contributing to the workers' physical and mental adjustment in their employment and their assignment to jobs for which they are suited; and (iii) contributing to the establishment and maintenance of a high degree of physical and mental well-being in the workers. *The Occupational Health and Safety Act*, R.S.S. 1978, c. O-1, s. 2.

OCCUPATIONAL ILLNESS. A condition that results from exposure in a workplace to a physical, chemical or biological agent to the extent that the normal physiological mechanisms are affected and the health of the worker is impaired thereby and includes an industrial disease as defined in the Worker's Compensation Act. *Occupational Health and Safety Act*, R.S.O. 1990, c. 0.1, s. 1(1).

OCCUPATIONAL QUALIFICATION. See BONA FIDE ~.

OCCUPATIONAL REQUIREMENT. 1. The Supreme court has established a new test, the unified approach or Meiorin test: Having considered the various alternatives, I propose the following three-step test for determining whether a prima facie discriminatory standard is a BFOR. An employer may justify the impugned standard by establishing on the balance of probabilities: (1) that the employer adopted the standard for a purpose rationally connected to the performance of the job; (2) that the employer adopted the particular standard in an honest and good faith belief that it was necessary to the fulfilment of that legitimate work-related purpose; and (3) that the standard is reasonably necessary to the accomplishment of that legitimate work-related purpose. To show that the standard is reasonably necessary, it must be demonstrated that it is impossible to accommodate individual employees sharing the characteristics of the claimant without imposing undue hardship upon the employer. *British Columbia (Public Service Employee Relations Commission) v. B.C.G.E.U.*, 1999 CarswellBC 1907, 99 C.L.L.C. 230-028, 1999] 10 W.W.R. 1, 176 D.L.R. (4th) 1, 244 N.R. 145, 66 B.C.L.R. (3d) 253, 127 B.C.A.C. 161, 207 W.A.C. 161, 46 C.C.E.L. (2d) 206, 35 C.H.R.R. D/257, 68 C.R.R. (2d) 1, [1999] 3 S.C.R. 3, McLachlin, J. for the court. 2. " . . . [A] requirement for the occupation, not a requirement limited to an individual. It must apply to all members of the employee group concerned because it is a requirement of general application concerning the safety of employees. The employee must meet the requirement in order to hold the employment. It is, by its nature, not susceptible to individual application." *Bhinder v. Canadian National Railway*, [1985] 2 S.C.R. 561 at 558-9, 9 C.C.E.L. 135, 17 Admin. L.R. 111, 86 C.L.L.C.

17,003, 7 C.H.R.R. D/3093, 23 D.L.R. (4th) 481, 63 N.R. 185, McIntyre J. See BONA FIDE ~.

OCCUPATIONAL THERAPY. The practice of occupational therapy is the assessment of function and adaptive behaviour and the treatment and prevention of disorders which affect function or adaptive behaviour to develop, maintain, rehabilitate or augment function or adaptive behaviour in the areas of self-care, productivity and leisure. *Occupational Therapy Act, 1991*, S.O. 1991, c. 33, s. 3. See PRACTICE OF ~.

OCCUPATIONAL TRAINING. 1. Includes manual, pre-vocational, vocational and supplementary training and training for the purpose of developing broader and more remunerative skill and capacity. 2. Any instruction, other than university instruction, that provides a person with skills for, or improves a person's skills in, an occupation. *National Training Act*, R.S.C. 1985, c. N-19, s. 2.

OCCUPATIONAL TRAINING PROGRAM. Any course or program of study (a) provided to a person (i) to enhance that person's employability in an occupation; or (ii) to improve that person's ability to carry out a present or future occupation; and (b) for which fees are paid to a training organization by the person or charged to a third party on the person's behalf. *An Act to Amend the Trade Schools Act*, S.N.B. 1987, c. 60, s. 1.

OCCUPATION RENT. Compensation to a joint owner of a residence or other asset before receipt of that person's share of the joint property when that person is out of possession and must pay for rent and other expenses. A. Bissett-Johnson & W.M. Holland, eds., *Matrimonial Property Law in Canada* (Toronto: Carswell, 1980) at PEI-22.

OCCUPATIO PACIFICA. [L.] Taking possession, with its consent, of another nation's territory in peacetime.

OCCUPATIVE. *adj*. Employed; possessed; used.

OCCUPIED FIELD. Refers to the notion that if Parliament has enacted constitutionally valid legislation and it conflicts with provincial legislation, Parliament's legislation prevails since it is considered to have occupied the field.

OCCUPIED LAND. Privately-owned land, upon or adjoining which the owner or occupant is actually residing.

OCCUPIED PUBLIC LAND. Public land held by a person under a disposition from the Crown. *Forest and Prairie Protection Act*, R.S.A. 2000, c. F-19, s. 1.

OCCUPIED WATER PRIVILEGE. A mill privilege, or water power, that has been or is in use for mechanical, manufacturing, milling or hydraulic purposes, or for the use of which for any of such purposes the necessary works are in course of construction. *Lakes and Rivers Improvement Act*, R.S.O. 1990, c. L.3, s. 90.

OCCUPIER. *n.* 1. The person occupying any dwelling, and includes the person having the management or charge of any public or private institution where persons are cared for or confined and the proprietor, manager, keeper or other person in charge of a hotel, inn, apartment, lodging house or other dwelling or accommodation. *Vital Statistics acts.* 2. A person having a sufficient degree of control over premises that he ought to realize that any failure to take care may result in injury to a person coming lawfully onto the premises.

OCCUPIERS' LIABILITY. An area of the law of negligence concerning the duty owed by a person having control over premises such that he should realize that any failure to take care may result in injury to a person coming lawfully onto the premises. See ACTIVITY DUTY; OCCUPANCY DUTY.

OCCUR. *v.* To happen.

OCCURRENCE. A happening; an event. See AVIATION ~.

OCCURRENCE POLICY. Every insurance policy must provide a mechanism for determining the claims for which the insurer is liable in a temporal sense. The traditional way has been to focus on the occurrence giving rise to the claim. For example, most automobile insurance liability policies provide coverage for accidents caused by the insured's negligence during the policy period. Provided that the negligent act occurred in the policy period, the insurer is required to indemnify the insured for all loss arising from it, regardless of when a claim is made against the insured for that loss. This type of insurance policy is called an "occurrence" policy. *Reid Crowther & Partners Ltd. v. Simcoe & Erie General Insurance Co.*, [1993] 1 S.C.R. 252, McLachlin, J. for the court.

OCEAN. See FISHERIES AND ~S; PACIFIC ~.

OCEAN CARRIER. An owner, lessee or charterer of a vessel who is engaged in the business of the transportation of goods by water. *Shipping Conferences Exemption Act, 1987*, S.C. 1987, c. 22, s. 2(1).

OCEAN SHIP. (a) An ocean-going ship of not less than 50 tons register tonnage; or (b) an ocean-doing towing or salvage tug. Canada regulations.

OCEAN SHORE AREA. That portion of land lying within the ordinary low tide mark and 300 metres above the ordinary high tide mark of any ocean or any inlet thereof, and includes any bed, bank, beach, shore, bar, flat, mud flat or sand dune associated with the ocean or inlet whether or not it lies within that portion of land. *The Trespass Act*, S.N.B. 1983, c. T-11.2, s. 1.

OCHLOCRACY. *n. A* form of government in which citizens have all the power and administration in their own hands.

O.C.M. *abbr.* Ontario Corporation Manual.

OCTANOL-WATER PARTITION COEFFICIENT. The ratio of the concentration of a substance in an octanol phase to the concentration of the substance in the water phase of an octanol-water mixture. *Persistence and Bioaccumulation Regulations*, SOR/2000-107, s. 1.

OCULIST. *n.* A physician who specializes in diseases of the eyes and whose services include, in addition to the examination of the eyes and treatment of diseases pertaining to sight, the prescription of lasses or spectacles where necessary. *General Act*, R.R.O. 1990, Reg. 1013, s. 1.

OCULOS HABENT ET NON VIBEBUNT. [L.] Having eyes and not seeing.

ODAS. *n.* Any object, other than a ship, on or in the water that is designed to collect, store or transmit samples or data relating to the marine environment or the atmosphere or the uses thereof. *Collision Regulations*, C.R.C., c. 1416, s. 2.

ODDS. *n.* The probable pay-out price in the win pool or the ratio that represents that pay-out price. *Pari-Mutuel Betting Supervision Regulations*, SOR/91-365, s. 2. See APPROXIMATE ~; FINAL ~.

ODIOSA ET INHONESTA NON SUNT IN LEGE PRAESUMENDA; ET IN FACTO QUOD IN SE HABET ET BONUM ET MALUM, MAGIS DE BONO QUAM DE MALO PRAESUMENDUM EST. [L.] Odious and dishonest things should not be presumed in law; and in an act which contains both good and bad, one should presume more of the good than the bad.

ODIOUS TAINT. Of a foreign judgment, having been obtained by fraud, or through a procedure offensive to natural justice, or the enforcement of which would be contrary to public policy in the jurisdiction where the action is brought to enforce it.

ODOMETER. *n*. A device which measures the distance which a wheel travels.

ODONTOLOGY. *n*. Knowledge of the development, function and structure of the teeth and pathological processes which involve them. F.A. Jaffe, *A Guide to Pathological Evidence*, 3d ed. (Toronto: Carswell 1991) at 223. See FORENSIC ~.

ODOUR.. *n*. Aroma.

OF. *prep*. From; through; under.

OF COURSE. Describes a step in a proceeding or action which a court or its officers may not refuse provided that the proper formalities were observed.

OFFENCE. *n*. 1. " . . . The rights guaranteed by s. 11 of the Charter are available to persons prosecuted by the state for public offences involving punitive sanctions, i.e., criminal, quasi-criminal and regulatory offences, either federally or provincially enacted. . . a true penal consequence which would attract the application of s. 11 is imprisonment or a fine which by its magnitude would appear to be imposed for the purpose of redressing the wrong done to society at large rather than to the maintenance of internal discipline within the limited sphere of activity." *R. v. Wigglesworth* (1987), 37 C.C.C. (3d) 385 at 397, 401, [1988] 1 W.W.R. 193, 61 Sask. R. 105, 60 C.R. (3d) 193, 81 N.R. 161, 28 Admin. L.R. 294, [1987] 2 S.C.R. 541, 24 O.A.C. 321, 45 D.L.R. (4th) 235, 32 C.R.R. 219, Wilson J. (Dickson C.J.C., Beetz, McIntyre, Lamer and La Forest JJ. concurring). 2. " . . . [T]hree categories of offences . . . 1. Offences in which mens rea, consisting of some positive state of mind such as intent, knowledge, or recklessness, must be proved by the prosecution either as an inference from the nature of the act committed, or by additional evidence. 2. Offences in which there is no necessity for the prosecution to prove the existence of mens rea; the doing of the prohibited act prima facie imports the offence, leaving it open to the accused to avoid liability by proving that he took all reasonable care. This involves consideration of what a reasonable man would have done in the circumstances. The defence will be available if the accused reasonably believed in a mistaken set of facts which, if true, would render the act or omission innocent, or if he took all reasonable steps to avoid the particular event. These offences may properly be called offences of strict liability. 3. Offences of absolute liability where it is not open to the accused to exculpate himself by showing that he was free of fault. Offences which are criminal in the true sense fall in the first category. Public welfare offences would prima facie be in the second category. They are not subject to the presumption of full mens rea. An offence of this type would fall in the first category only if such words as 'wilfully', 'with intent', 'knowingly' or 'intentionally' are contained in the statutory provision creating the offence. On the other hand, the principle that punishment should in general not be inflicted on those without fault applies. Offences of absolute liability would be those in respect of which the Legislature had made it clear that guilt would follow proof merely of the proscribed act. The overall regulatory pattern adopted by the Legislature, the subject matter of the legislation, the importance of the penalty, and the precision of the language used will be primary in determining whether the offence falls into the third category." *R. v. Sault Ste. Marie (City)* (1978), 7 C.E.L.R. 53 at 70, [1978] 2 S.C.R. 1299, 3 C.R. (3d) 30, 21 N.R. 295, 40 C.C.C. (2d) 353, 85 D.L.R. (3d) 161, the court per Dickson J. 3. An offence created by an act or by any regulation or by-law made under an act or a municipal by-law. 4. The contravention of an enactment. 5. "[The] . . . context and circumstance of the word 'offence' appearing in s. 54.1 of the Police Act [R.S.B.C. 1979, c. 331 (en. 1982, c. 62, s. 6)] especially as applicable to an infraction of a provincial regulation, compels me to construe offence' as extending and having application to a 'disciplinary default' under the Police (Discipline) Regulations [B.C. Reg. 330/75]." *Matsqui Police Board v. Matsqui Police Assn. Local 7* (1987), 14 B.C.L.R. (2d) 88 at 96, 39 D.L.R. (4th) 676 (C.A.), Carrothers J.A. 6. " . . . [D]oes not become an offence until the occurrence results in a conviction." *Gill v. Ontario (Registrar of Motor Vehicles)* (1984), 12 C.C.C. (3d) 23 at 27 (Ont. H.C.), Smith J. See CONTINUING ~; CRIMINAL ~; FEDERAL ~; HYBRID ~; INCLUDED ~; INDICTABLE ~; INDICTABLE ONLY ~; LESSER ~; MATRIMO-

NIAL ~; MILITARY ~; PARTIES TO AN ~; PRESUMPTIVE ~; PUBLIC WELFARE~; RECORD OF ~S; REGULATORY ~; SECOND OR SUBSEQUENT ~; SERIOUS CRIMINAL ~; SERIOUS PERSONAL INJURY ~; SERIOUS VIOLENT ~; SERVICE ~; STATUS ~; STRICT LIABILITY ~; SUBSEQUENT ~; SUMMARY CONVICTION~; SUMMARY ~.

OFFENCE-RELATED PROPERTY. Any property, within or outside Canada, (a) by means or in respect of which an indictable offence under this Act is committed, (b) that is used in any manner in connection with the commission of an indictable offence under this Act, or (c) that is intended for use for the purpose of committing an indictable offence under this Act. *Criminal Code*, R.S.C. 1985, c. C-46, s. 2.

OFFENDER. *n*. 1. A person who has been determined by a court to be guilty of an offence, whether on acceptance of a plea of guilty or on a finding of guilt. *Criminal Code*, R.S.C. 1985, c. C-46 s. 2 as amended by *Criminal Law Amendment Act*, R.S.C. 1985 (1st Supp.), c. 27, s. 2. 2. (a) An inmate, or (b) a person who, having been sentenced, committed or transferred to penitentiary, is outside penitentiary (i) by reason of parole or statutory release, (ii) pursuant to an agreement with an aboriginal community, or (iii) pursuant to a court order. *Corrections and Conditional Release Act*, S.C. 1992, c. 20, s. 2(1). See CANADIAN ~; FIRST ~; FOREIGN ~.

OFFENSIVE WEAPON. Has the same meaning as "weapon". *Criminal Code*, R.S.C. 1985, c. C-46, s. 2 as amended by *Criminal Law Amendment Act*, R.S.C. 1985 (1st Supp.), c. 27, s. 2.

OFFER. *n*. 1. The indication by one person that the person is willing to enter into an agreement with another person. 2. " . . . [A]n offer to sell or deliver a narcotic is complete once the offer is put forward by the accused in a serious manner intending to induce [the offeree] to act upon it and accept it as an offer." *R. v. Sherman*, [1977] 5 W.W.R. 283 at 283, 39 C.R.N.S. 255, 36 C.C.C. (2d) 207 (B.C. C.A.), the court per McFarlane J.A. 3. Includes an invitation to make an offer. 4. An invitation to treat. *Saskatchewan Human Rights Code*, S.S. 1979, v. S-24.1, s. 2. See CONDITIONAL ~; COUNTER ~; DATE OF THE ~; EXEMPT ~.

OFFEREE. *n*. A person to whom a take-over bid is made. See DISSENTING ~.

OFFEREE COMPANY. A company whose shares are the subject of a take-over bid.

OFFEREE CORPORATION. *var.* **OFFEREE-CORPORATION**. A corporation whose shares are the object of a take-over bid.

OFFEREE ISSUER. An issuer whose securities are the subject of an offer to acquire.

OFFER FOR TRANSPORT. Presenting, placing, positioning, or otherwise preparing goods for transportation on a highway. *Dangerous Goods Handling and Transportation Act*, R.S.M. 1987, c. D12, s. 1.

OFFERING. *n*. 1. Putting up for sale. 2. Presenting. See SHARE ~ DOCUMENT.

OFFERING CORPORATION. A corporation that is offering its securities to the public within the meaning of subsection (6) and that is not the subject of an order of the Commission deeming it to have ceased to be offering its securities to the public. *Business Corporations Act*, R.S.O. 1990, c. B.16, s. 1.

OFFERING MEMORANDUM. A document that: (i) sets forth information concerning the business and affairs of an issuer; and (ii) has been prepared primarily for prospective purchasers to assist those purchasers to make an investment decision with respect to securities being sold pursuant to a trade that is made in reliance on an exemption.

OFFEROR. *n*. 1. A person, other than an agent, who makes a take-over bid, and includes two or more persons who, directly or indirectly, (a) make take-over bids jointly or in concert; or (b) intend to exercise jointly or in concert voting rights attached to shares for which a take-over bid is made. 2. A person who makes an offer to acquire or an issuer bid. 3. (i) A person or company, other than an agent, who makes a take-over bid or an issuer bid; or (ii) an issuer who accepts from a security holder an offer to sell securities of the issuer other than debt securities that are not convertible into voting securities.

OFFEROR'S PRESENTLY-OWNED SECURITIES. *var.* **OFFEROR'S PRESENTLY OWNED SECURITIES**. Voting securities or rights to voting securities of an offeree company beneficially owned directly or indirectly, on the date of a take-over bid by the offeror or associates of the offeror and if 2 or more persons or companies make offers (i) jointly or in concert, or (ii) intending to exercise jointly or in concert any voting rights attaching to the securities acquired through the offers, includes the voting securities and rights to voting securities owned by all of the persons or companies and their associates.

OFFEROR'S PRESENTLY-OWNED SHARES. *var.* **OFFEROR'S PRESENTLY OWNED SHARES.** 1. Equity shares of an offeree company beneficially owned, directly or indirectly, on the date of a take-over bid by the offeror or an associate of the offeror. 2. Voting-shares of an offeree company beneficially owned, directly or indirectly, on the date of a take-over bid by the offeror or a person related to him. *Securities Act*, R.S.Q. 1977, c. V-1, s. 131.

OFFEROR'S SECURITY. The security of an offeree issuer beneficially owned, or over which control or direction is exercised, on the date of an offer to acquire by the offeror and the offeror's joint actors.

OFFER TO ACQUIRE. (i) An offer to purchase, or a solicitation of an offer to sell, securities; (ii) an acceptance of an offer to sell securities, whether or not that offer to sell has been solicited, and the person or company accepting that offer to sell is deemed to be making an offer to acquire; or (iii) any combination of the foregoing.

OFFER TO SETTLE. In the context of litigation, an admission of limited liability and an offer to pay a certain amount or a denial of liability and an offer to pay something to end the dispute.

OFFER TO THE PUBLIC. In the case of a company (other than a private company), with relation to securities issued or to be issued by it, every attempt or offer to dispose of, or solicitation of a subscription or application for, or solicitation of an offer to subscribe or apply for any of its securities or any interest in such securities, made by or on behalf of the company, and every such attempt or offer or solicitation made by any underwriter, as hereinafter defined, shall be deemed to have been made by or on behalf of the company, but "offer to the public" does not include (a) preliminary negotiations or preliminary agreements between the company and an underwriter, or (b) any offer of securities of the company to a director or directors of such company only. *Canada Corporations Act*, R.S.C. 1970, c. C-32, s. 74.

OFF-HIGHWAY VEHICLE. Any motorized vehicle designated for cross-country travel on land, water, snow, ice, marsh or swamp land or on other natural terrain and, without limiting the generality of the foregoing, includes, when designed for such travel, (i) 4-wheel drive or low pressure tire vehicles; (ii) motor cycles and related 2-wheel vehicles; (iii) amphibious machines; (iv) all terrain vehicles; (v) miniature motor vehicles; (vi) snow vehicles; (vii) mini-bikes; and (viii) any other means of transportation which is propelled by any power other than muscular power or wind, but does not include (ix) motor boats. See INSURED ~.

OFFICE. *n.* 1. " . . . [A] position of duty, trust or authority in the public service or is a service under constituted authority. . ." *R. v. Sheets* (1971), 15 C.R.N.S. 232 at 236, [1971] S.C.R. 614, [1971] 1 W.W.R. 672, 1 C.C.C. (2d) 508, 16 D.L.R. (3d) 221, the court per Fauteux C.J.C. 2. A room, building or other place where business is conducted. 3. Includes (a) an office or appointment under the government; (b) a civil or military commission; and (c) a position or an employment in a public department. *Criminal Code*, R.S.C. 1985, c. C-46, s. 118. 4. The position of an individual entitling him to a fixed or ascertainable stipend or remuneration and includes a judicial office, the office of a Minister of the Crown, the office of a member of the Senate or House of Commons of Canada, a member of a legislative assembly or a member of a legislative or executive council and any other office, the incumbent of which is elected by popular vote or is elected or appointed in a representative capacity and also includes the position of a corporation director. *Income Tax Act*, R.S.C. 1952, c. 148 (as am. S.C. 1970-71-72, c. 63), s. 248(1). See BRANCH ~; COLOUR OF ~; CUSTOMS ~; FLEET MAIL ~; HEAD ~; JUDICIAL ~; LAND TITLE ~; LEGISLATIVE ASSEMBLY ~; LOCAL ~; MINISTERIAL ~; PERMANENT ~ OF AN AUTHORIZED PARTY; POST ~; PUBLIC ~; RECORD ~; REGIONAL ASSESSMENT ~; REGISTERED ~; REGISTRY ~; REPRESENTATIVE ~.

OFFICE BUILDING. A building used for the transaction of business, other than those included within the definition of mercantile building, for keeping accounts and records and similar purposes. *Fire Prevention Act*, R.S.N.S. 1989, c. 171, s. 2.

OFFICE COMPLEX. A building that is (a) an office building; or (b) a building used for an office and some other purpose, and contains at least three offices. *Mail Receptacles Regulations*, C.R.C., c. 1282, s. 2.

OFFICE HOURS. See NORMAL ~.

OFFICE MONEY. Money received by and for the benefit and use of a broker whether before or after services have been rendered. *Real Estate Brokers Act*, R.S.M. 1987, c. R20, s. 1.

OFFICE OF THE COURT. The office of the prothonotary or of the clerk of any court to which the provision is applicable. *Code of Civil Procedure*, R.S.Q. 1977, c. C-25, s. 4.

OFFICER. *n*. 1. A person holding the position entitling that person to a fixed or ascertainable stipend or remuneration and includes a judicial office, the office of a minister of the Crown, the office of a lieutenant governor, the office of a member of the Senate or House of Commons, a member of a legislative assembly or a member of a legislative or executive council and any other office the incumbent of which is elected by popular vote or is elected or appointed in a representative capacity, and also includes the position of a corporation director. 2. In relation to the Crown, includes a minister of the Crown and any servant of the Crown. 3. Includes a trustee, director, manager, treasurer, secretary or member of the board or committee of management of an insurer and a person appointed by the insurer to sue and be sued in its behalf. 4. A person employed in connection with the administration and management of a department. 5. The chairman and any vice-chairman of the board of directors, the president, any vice-president, the secretary, any assistant secretary, the treasurer, any assistant treasurer, the general manager and any other person designated an officer by by-law or by resolution of the directors, and any other individual who performs functions for a company similar to those normally performed by an individual occupying any of those offices. 6. (a) A person who holds Her Majesty's commission in the Canadian Forces, (b) a person who holds the rank of officer cadet in the Canadian Forces, and (c) any person who pursuant to law is attached or seconded as an officer to the Canadian Forces. *National Defence Act*, R.S.C. 1985, c. N-5, s. 2(1). 7. (a) The chairman, president, vice-president, secretary, treasurer, comptroller, general counsel, general manager, managing director or any other individual who performs functions for a corporation similar to those normally performed by an individual occupying any such office; and (b) each of the five highest paid employees of a corporation including any individual mentioned in paragraph (a). *Canada Business Corporations Act*, R.S.C. 1985, c. C-44, s. 126. 8. A commissioned officer of the R.C.M.P. Force. 9. A peace officer or public officer. *Criminal Code*, R.S.C. 1985, c. C-46, s. 488.1(1) as added by *Criminal Law Amendment Act*, R.S.C. 1985 (1st Supp.), c. 27, s. 71. 10. (a) A person who holds Her Majesty's commission in the Canadian Forces; (b) a person who holds the rank of officer cadet in the Canadian Forces; and (c) any person who pursuant to law is attached or seconded as an officer to the Canadian Forces. *National Defence Act*, R.S.C. 1985, c. N-5, s. 2. 11. Wherever used in this Act, will include all prothonotaries, clerks of appeals, sheriffs, coroners, clerks of the Crown, clerks of the peace, clerks of Provincial Courts, clerks of judges of the sessions, criers, assistant criers, tipstaffs, clerks of commissioners' courts, and registrars. *Stamp Act*, R.S.Q. 1977, c. T-10, s. 5. See ADMITTING ~; AFTER CARE ~; ASSESSMENT ~; BRIBERY OF ~S; CHIEF EXECUTIVE ~; CHIEF FINANCIAL ~; CHIEF ~; CLASSIFICATION ~; CONCILIATION ~; CONSULAR ~; CUSTOMS ~; DECK WATCH ~; DIPLOMATIC OR CONSULAR ~; ELECTION ~; ENFORCEMENT ~; EXECUTIVE ~; FIREARMS ~; FISHERY ~; FOREIGN SERVICE ~; GAME ~; HEALTH ~; IMMIGRATION ~; LAW ~; LOAN ~; MEDICAL ~; MUNICIPAL ~; PEACE ~; PLEBISCITE ~; POLICE ~; PRESIDING ~; PROBATION~; PROPER ~; PROTECTION ~; PUBLIC ~; RESPONSIBLE ~ OF THE BANK; RETURNING ~; REVENUE ~; REVISING ~; SECURITY ~; SENIOR ~; SENIOR POLICE ~; SHERIFF'S ~; STATUTORY ~; SUBORDINATE ~; SUPERIOR ~; TRUANT ~; UTILITIES ~; VISA ~; WILDLIFE ~.

OFFICER-DIRECTOR. *n*. In respect of a parent Crown corporation, means (a) the chairman and the chief executive officer of the corporation; and (b) in the case of a parent Crown corporation established by an Act of Parliament, any person who holds an office in the corporation that is established by the Act and the holder of which by a provision in the Act, is to be appointed by the Governor in Council and is declared to be a director of the corporation. *Financial Administration Act*, R.S.C. 1985, c. F-11, s. 105(10).

OFFICER DOWN CALL. An emergency call by police indicating that an officer is in difficulty and requires assistance.

OFFICER IN CHARGE. 1. The officer for the time being in command of the police force responsible for the lock-up or other place to which an accused is taken after arrest or a peace officer designated by him for the purposes of this Part who is in charge of that place at the time an accused is taken to that lace to be detained in custody. *Criminal Code*, R.S.C. 1985, c. C-46, s. 493. 2. The officer who is responsible for the administration and management of a psychiatric facility. *Mental Health Act*, R.S.O. 1980, c. 262, s. 1. 3. The police officer who at any particular time, while on duty, is in charge of and responsible for, the proper functioning of a police facility. *Metropolitan Toronto Police Force Complaints Act*, S.O. 1984, c. 63, s. 1. 4. The person other than the master in charge of a ship. Canada regulations. See MEDICAL ~.

OFFICER OF A BANK. (a) The chairman of the board of directors, chief executive officer, president, vice-president, chief general manager, secretary, chief accountant, comptroller, general counsel and general manager of the bank; (b) any individual designated an officer of the bank by by-law or by resolution of the directors; and (c) any individual who performs functions for the bank similar to those performed by an individual occupying an office referred to in paragraph (a) individual referred to in paragraph (b). *Bank Act*, R.S.C. 1985, c. B-1, s. 168.

OFFICERS OF EDUCATION. Every person holding a teacher's diploma or certificate and teaching in a school under the control of school commissioners or trustees, or who has the direction, administration or supervision thereof; school inspectors, and professors and teachers of normal schools, but they do not include members of the clergy or of religious communities or professors in universities. *Education Act*, R.S.Q. 1977, c. I-14, s. 1.

OFFICE SERVICES. Printing, copying, recoding and related services that a public agency requires to transact its business and includes services connected with drawing, illustrating, filming, photographing, recording, addressing, printing, duplicating, micro-photographing, photocopying and typesetting.

OFFICE SPACE. See RENTAL ~.

OFFICE SUPPLIES. Includes stationery, computers, word processing equipment, type-writers, calculators, recorders, projectors and photographic equipment.

OFFICE UNDER HER MAJESTY. Includes any office or employment in or under any department or branch of the government of Canada or of any province, and any office or employment in, on or under any board, commission, corporation or other body that is an agent of Her Majesty in right of Canada or any province. *Official Secrets Act*, R.S.C. 1985, c. O-5, s. 2.

OFFICIAL. *n*. 1. Includes president, vice-president, secretary, treasurer, managing director, general manager, department manager, branch office manager and every person acting in a similar capacity whether so designated or not. 2. Any person employed in, or occupying a position of responsibility in, the service of Her Majesty and includes any person formerly so employed or formerly occupying such a position. 3. Includes an examiner, judge, master of ceremonies, legally qualified medical practitioner, referee and timekeeper. *Athletics Control Act*, R.S.O. 1990, c. A.34, s. 1. 4. A person who (a) holds an office, or (b) is appointed to discharge a public duty. *Criminal Code*, R.S.C. 1985, c. C-46, s. 118. See AUTHORIZED ~; ELECTION ~; MINE ~; MUNICIPAL ~; PUBLIC ~; SENIOR ~.

OFFICIAL. *adj*. Authorized; formal.

OFFICIAL AGENT. 1. An official agent of a party or of a candidate in an election. 2. A person appointed by a candidate to represent the candidate during an election. 3. The official agent of a candidate is responsible for administering the candidate's financial transactions for his or her electoral campaign and for reporting on those transactions in accordance with the provisions of this Act. *Canada Elections Act*, S.C. 2000, c. 9, s. 436.

OFFICIAL CANDIDATE. A candidate of an authorized party whose nomination paper has been received by the returning officer.

OFFICIAL COMMUNITY PLAN. A master plan of community development and land utilization prepared by a local planning authority and legally adopted by or on behalf of a municipality. *National Housing Act*, R.S.C. 1985, c. N-11, s. 2.

OFFICIAL CONTOUR. A service contour marked for a licensed television station, licensed AM station or licensed FM station on the map most recently published under the *Department* *of Industry Act* by the Minister of Industry and that pertains to that station. *Broadcasting Distribution Regulations*, SOR/97-555, s. 1.

OFFICIAL DRUG. Any drug (a) for which a standard is provided in these Regulations, or (b) for which no standard is provided in these Regulations but for which a standard is provided in any of the publications mentioned in schedule B to the Act. *Food and Drug Regulations*, C.R.C., c. 870, c. C.01.001.

OFFICIAL EMBLEM. Any bird, tree, mineral, flag, flower or other item designated as an official emblem of a jurisdiction. An emblem used in connection with the official business of the jurisdiction.

OFFICIAL EXAMINER. The officer of a court who presides over examinations for discovery, cross-examinations on affidavits and other examinations.

OFFICIAL FEE. A fee that is required to be paid by or under a statute of a province or Canada.

OFFICIAL GAZETTE. The Canada Gazette and the gazette published under the authority of the government of the province where the proceedings for the winding-up of the business of a company are carried on, or used as the official means of communication between the lieutenant governor of that province and the people, and if no such gazette is published in the province, any newspaper published in the province and designated by a court for publishing the notices required by this Act. *Winding-up Act*, R.S.C. 1985, c. W-11, s. 2.

OFFICIAL GRADING. The grading by an inspector of a sample of grain that has not been taken from a parcel of grain by an inspector. *Canada Grain Regulations*, C.R.C., c. 889, s. 2.

OFFICIAL GUARDIAN. The provincial official who is charged with acting on behalf of minors or persons incapable of managing their own affairs. May manage the estates of such persons.

OFFICIAL INSPECTION. The sampling and grading of a parcel of grain by an inspector. *Canada Grain Act*, R.S.C. 1985, c. G-10, s. 2.

OFFICIAL INSPECTION STATION. A place of business registered to provide inspection services in connection with motor vehicle legislation.

OFFICIAL LANGUAGE. The English language or the French language. Section 16 of the Charter provides: English and French are the official languages of Canada and have equality of status and equal rights and privileges as to their use in all institutions of the Parliament and government of Canada. See COMMISSIONER OF ~S.

OFFICIAL LIST OF ELECTORS. The list of persons eligible to vote.

OFFICIALLY INDUCED ERROR. 1. "The defence of 'officially induced error', exists where the accused, having adverted to the possibility of illegality, is led to believe, by the erroneous advice of an official, that he is not acting illegally." *R. v. Cancoil Thermal Corp.* (1986), 23 C.R.R. 257 at 265, 11 C.C.E.L. 219, 14 O.A.C. 225, 52 C.R. (3d) 188, 27 C.C.C. (3d) 295 (C.A.), the court per Lacourcière J.A. 2. Occurs when an accused is led to believe by erroneous advice of an official responsible for enforcement of a regulatory statute that he is not acting illegally.

OFFICIALLY NOMINATED. Describes a candidate who files a nomination paper and deposit with the returning officer at any time between the date of the proclamation and the hour fixed for the close of nominations on nomination day.

OFFICIAL MARK. A mark adopted and used by a public authority and protected under the Trade Marks Act from use by other persons.

OFFICIAL MEMENTO. Any item of public property of a distinctly Canadian character and manufacture, including contemporary arts and crafts and articles, representative of all or part of the Canadian Forces or of Canadian culture or Canadian manufacturing. *National Defence Official Mementos Regulations*, C.R.C., c. 716, s. 2.

OFFICIAL NOMINATION. The filing of a nomination paper and deposit by a candidate with the returning officer at any time between the date of the proclamation and the hour fixed for the close of nominations on nomination day.

OFFICIAL NOTICE. The power of a tribunal to take notice of publicly available information which amounts to general knowledge. Equivalent of judicial notice.

OFFICIAL OPPOSITION. Known as Her Majesty's Loyal Opposition.

OFFICIAL PLAN. Sets out the goals, objectives and policies established to manage and direct physical change and its effects on the social, economic and natural environment of a municipality or part of it, or an area that is without municipal organization. See MASTER PLAN.

OFFICIAL RECEIVER. A person delegated by the Superintendent to accept debtors' assignments in bankruptcy and generally supervise trustees' administration of bankrupt estates. F. Bennett, *Receiverships* (Toronto: Carswell, 1985) at 3.

OFFICIAL REPORT. The publication of reports of cases directed by statute or a court itself.

OFFICIAL REPORT OF DEBATES. Hansard, a record of speeches made in the House of Commons and verbatim answers to written questions from the Order Paper. A. Fraser, W.A. Dawson, & J. Holtby, eds., *Beauchesne's Rules and Forms of the House of Commons of Canada*, 6th ed. (Toronto: Carswell, 1989) at 300.

OFFICIAL RESULT. The order of finish of the horses in a race as declared by the stewards or judges, as the case may be. *Pari-Mutuel Betting Supervision Regulations*, SOR/91-365, s. 2.

OFFICIAL SAMPLE. 1. A sample taken from a parcel of grain by a person authorized by the Commission to take the sample. *Canada Grain Act*, R.S.C. 1985, c. G-10, s. 2. 2. A sample of blood, urine or other bodily substance that is, by means of approved paraphernalia, collected from a horse and packaged and sealed by or under the supervision of a test inspector. *Pari-Mutuel Betting Supervision Regulations*, SOR/91-365, s. 2.

OFFICIAL SIGN. A sign, pavement marking, barricade or object that the minister or an officer or employee of the department with the written authority of the minister authorizes to be erected, placed or painted upon the roadway or right of way of a public highway for the legal control, warning, guidance, direction or information of traffic on the highway.

OFFICIAL TAG. 1. A tag issued by the Plant Products Division of the Department in respect of seed of Canadian origin having pedigreed status. *Seeds Regulations*, C.R.C., c. 1400, s. 2. 2. A tag or label issued under the authority of the Minister for the purpose of identifying seed potatoes. *Seeds Regulations*, C.R.C., c. 1400, s. 45.

OFFICIAL TOWN PLAN. A master plan of land use and community development prepared by or on behalf of a municipality and legally adopted by a municipality.

OFFICIAL TRAFFIC SIGNALS. Signals not inconsistent with this Act, placed or erected by authority of an official having jurisdiction, for the purpose of directing, warning or regulating traffic. *Highway Traffic acts*.

OFFICIAL TRAFFIC SIGNS. Signs, markings and devices, not inconsistent with this Act, placed or erected by authority of an official having jurisdiction, for the purpose of guiding, directing, warning or regulating traffic. *Highway Traffic acts*.

OFFICIAL TRUSTEE. The title for the public trustee in some provinces.

OFFICIAL VACCINATE. A female bovine vaccinated with Brucella abortus strain 19 vaccine, of a potency approved by the Minister, not less than 2 months and not more than 8 months after the birth of the animal. *Animal Disease and Protection Regulations*, C.R.C., c. 296, s. 2.

OFFICIAL WEIGHING. The weighing of grain by a person authorized by the Commission to weigh the grain. *Canada Grain Act*, R.S.C. 1985, c. G-10, s. 2.

OFFICIO. See EX ~.

OFFICIT CONATUS SI EFFECTUS SEQUATUR. [L.] An attempt is detrimental if an effect follows.

OFFICIUM NEMINI DEBET ESSE DAMNOSUM. [L.] An office should be harmful to no one.

OFF-PREMISES SALE. Sale of packaged liquor to be consumed in a place other than the premises where it was sold.

OFF-ROAD UTILITY VEHICLE. A vehicle having a gross vehicle weight of 6,000 pounds or less, designed for carrying persons, property or a work-performing structure and that incorporates special features for off-road operations. *Motor Vehicle Safety Regulations*, C.R.C., c.1038 , s. 1100.

OFF-ROAD VEHICLE. A vehicle propelled or driven otherwise than by muscular power or wind and designed to travel, (a) on not more than three wheels, or (b) on more than three wheels and being of a prescribed class of vehicle. *Off-Road Vehicles Act*, R.S.O. 1990, c. 0.4, s. 1.

OFFSET. *v*. Offset is a business or an accounting term. I do not agree that offset means the same as the legal term set-off, which normally refers to an amount claimed by a defendant as a counter-claim or cross claim against a plaintiff arising out of the same subject matter. *Belliveau v. Royal Bank* (2000), 224 N.B.R. (2d) 354, 574 A.P.R. 354 (C.A.), Turnbull, J.A. for the court.

OFFSET. *n*. When used with reference to piping, means a pipe or a bend of pipe or both that takes one section of the piping out of line with, but parallel to, another section. *Ontario Water Resources Act*, R.R.O. 1980, Reg. 736, s. 1.

OFFSHORE AREA. Sable Island or any area of land not within a province that belongs to Her Majesty in right of Canada or in respect of which Her Majesty in right of Canada has the right to dispose of or exploit the natural resources and that is situated in submarine areas in the internal waters of Canada, the territorial sea of Canada or the continental shelf of Canada. *Energy Administration Act*, R.S.C. 1985, c. E-6, s. 20.

O.H.I.P. *abbr*. Ontario Health Insurance Plan.

OHM. *n*. The electrical resistance between two points of a metallic conductor, when a constant difference of potential of one volt, applied between these two points, produces in the conductor a current of one ampere and the conductor itself is not the seat of any electromotive force. *Weights and Measures Act*, S.C. 1970-71-72, c. 36, schedule I.

OIL. *n*. 1. Crude petroleum oil and any other hydrocarbon, regardless of gravity, in liquid form. 2. (i) Crude petroleum regardless of gravity produced at a well head in liquid form, and (ii) any other hydrocarbons, except coal and gas, including hydrocarbons that may be extracted or recovered from surface or subsurface deposits, including deposits of oil sand, bitumen, bituminous sand, oil shale and other types of deposits. See CROWN ~; CRUDE ~; DIESEL ~; FREEHOLD ~; FUEL ~; HOME HEATING ~; ILLEGAL ~; NEW ~; OLD ~; PERSISTENT ~; PRODUCTION OF ~ [OR] GAS; REFINED ~S; SYNTHETIC CRUDE ~.

OIL AND GAS. Includes petroleum, natural gas, hydrocarbons, sulphur compounds, nitrogen, carbon dioxide and helium, where naturally occurring separately or as a mixture and where recovered or recoverable at a well from an underground reservoir, but excludes substances that can be extracted only by destructive distillation from coal, bituminous shales and other

stratified deposits. *Oil and Gas Rights Act*, S.N.S. 1971-72, c. 12, s. 1.

OIL AND GAS DEALER. Any person or association of persons who supplies, transports or stores oil, gas or petroleum products and includes, without limiting the generality of the foregoing, any exporter, importer, refiner, processor, wholesale marketer, jobber, distributor, terminal operator or broker who supplies oil, gas or petroleum products. *Energy Monitoring Act*, R.S.C. 1985, c. E-8, s. 2.

OIL AND GAS RIGHT. An estate in fee simple in any or all oil, petroleum, natural gas, all other hydrocarbons, except coal and valuable stone, all other gases and minerals and substances, whether liquid or solid and whether hydrocarbon or not, occurring in association with any of the foregoing and the spaces or formations occupied formerly occupied thereby in all producing tracts in a province.

OIL AND GAS ROYALTY TRUST. A trust of a fraction of reserved royalty rights conveyed to a third party for a lump sum. The trustee has the right to receive the total amount of any assigned regular royalty payment; the beneficiary is the one who purchased the fraction. Such fractional interests can be bought and sold, like any other property. D.M.W. Waters, *The Law of Trusts in Canada*, 2d ed. (Toronto: Carswell, 1984) at 447.

OIL FIELD BRINE. Brine produced in association with oil and gas drilling.

OIL HANDLING FACILITY. A facility, including an oil terminal, that is used in the loading or unloading of petroleum in any form, including crude oil, fuel oil, sludge, oil refuse and refined products, to or from vessels. *Canada Shipping Act, 2001*, S.C. 2001, c. 26, s. 2.

OIL LEASE. See GAS OR ~.

OIL LINE. A pipe for the transmission of oil from a secondary line, storage facility or processing plant to a terminal or storage facility and includes installations in connection with that pipe, but does not include a secondary line or flow line.

OIL OR GAS. Mineral oil, petroleum, natural gas and related hydrocarbons or any of them.

OIL OR GAS WELL. Any well drilled for the purpose of producing petroleum or natural gas or of determining the existence, location, extent or quality of a petroleum or natural gas deposit.

OIL PIPELINE. *var.* **OIL PIPE LINE.** A pipe or any system or arrangement of pipes whereby oil is conveyed from any place at which it is produced to any other place, or from any place where it is stored, processed or treated to any other place.

OIL POLLUTION DAMAGE. In relation to any ship, loss or damage outside the ship caused by contamination resulting from the discharge of oil from that ship. *Canada Shipping Act*, S.C. 1987, c. 7, s. 746.

OIL POLLUTION INCIDENT. An occurrence, or a series of occurrences having the same origin, that results or is likely to result in a discharge of oil. *Canada Shipping Act, 2001*, S.C. 2001, c. 26, s. 185.

OIL REVENUE. See INCREMENTAL ~.

OIL SAND. Sand or other petroliferous substance from which oil sand products can be produced.

OIL SAND PRODUCTS. Petroleum or natural gas and all other minerals and substances that can be produced from oil sand or oil shale.

OIL SANDS. 1. Sands and other rock materials which contain crude bitumen and includes all other mineral substances in association therewith. 2. (i) Sands and other rock materials containing crude bitumen; (ii) the crude bitumen contained in those sands and other rock materials; and (iii) any other mineral substances in association with that crude bitumen or those sands and other rock materials, but does not include petroleum or natural gas that in its natural state is recoverable by conventional methods.

OIL SANDS DEPOSIT. A natural reservoir containg or appearing to contain an accumulation of oil sands separated or appearing to be separated from any other such accumulation.

OIL SANDS PROCESSING PLANT. A plant for the recovery from oil sands of crude bitumen, sand and other substances, or the extraction from crude bitumen of crude oil, natural gas and other substances.

OIL SANDS PRODUCT. Any product derived from oil sands and includes crude bitumen and residue sand.

OIL SANDS RIGHTS. (i) The right to mine, quarry, work, remove, treat or process oil sands; and (ii) the right to dispose of the oil sands and any products recovered therefrom.

OIL SANDS SITE. An in situ operation site, a mine site or a processing plant, or any one or more of them. *Oil Sands Conservation Act*, R.S.A. 2000, c. 0-7, s. 1.

OIL SEED PROCESSING PLANT. A plant for the commercial production of edible oil products.

OIL SHALE. Shale or other petroliferous substance from which oil shale products can be produced.

OIL SHALE PRODUCTS. Petroleum or natural gas and all other minerals and substances that can be produced from oil sand or oil shale in association with the production of petroleum or natural gas.

OIL TANKER. A cargo ship constructed and used for the carriage of petroleum or petroleum products in bulk. *Marine Certification Regulations*, SOR/97-391, s. 1(1).

OIL WELL. Any well capable of producing oil and is not a gas well. *Canada Oil and Gas Drilling and Production Regulations*, C.R.C., c. 1517, s. 2. See WELL OR ~.

OILY MIXTURE. A mixture with any oil content. *Pollution Prevention regulations*.

OLD AGE. See STATUTORY ~.

OLD AGE SECURITY PENSION. Old age security pension payable pursuant to the Old Age Security Act.

OLD OIL. (a) Crude or heavy oil recovered after 1981 from a natural reservoir in Canada that was known, before January 1, 1981, to be capable of production in commercial quantities; and (b) the prescribed percentage of petroleum produced from a mine in a bituminous sands deposit that came into production in reasonable commercial quantities before January 1, 1976, but does not include (c) the incremental production of petroleum, determined in such manner as may be prescribed, that is recovered from a natural reservoir or portion thereof under a project that commenced operation after December 31, 1980, that is a prescribed tertiary oil recovery project; (d) petroleum produced from a prescribed experimental plant; or (e) prescribed petroleum produced after May 31, 1984. *Petroleum and Gas Revenue Tax Act*, R.S.C. 1985, c. P-12, s. 2.

OLD OIL BASE PRICE. In respect of old oil of a particular quality from a well or mineral resource, means such amount as is prescribed to be the base price of that quality of oil. *Petroleum and Gas Revenue Tax Act*, R.S.C. 1985, c. P-12, s. 2.

OLEOMARGARINE. *n*. 1. Any food substance other than butter, of whatever origin, source or composition that is prepared for the same uses as butter and that is manufactured wholly or in part from any fat or oil other than that of milk. *Oleomargarine Act*, R.S.O. 1990, c. 0.5, s. 1. 2. Any food substance other than butter, of whatever origin, source or composition that is prepared for the same uses as butter, but does not include any substance consisting of a blend of butterfat and edible oils. *Oleomargarine Act*, S.N.B. 1977, c. 37, s. 1. See DIET ~; REGULAR ~.

OLIGARCHY. *n*. A form of government in which a few people administer affairs.

OLIGOSPERMIA. *n*. An unusually small quantity of sperm cells in semen. F.A. Jaffe, *A Guide to Pathological Evidence*, 3d ed. (Toronto: Carswell, 1991) at 223.

O.L.R. *abbr*. Ontario Law Reports, 1901-1931.

O.L.R.B. *abbr*. Ontario Labour Relations Board.

O.L.R.B. REP. *abbr*. Ontario Labour Relations Board Reports, 1974-.

O.M.B. *abbr*. Ontario Municipal Board.

O.M.B.R. *abbr*. Ontario Municipal Board Reports, 1973-.

OMBUDSMAN. *n*. A person appointed to consider and investigate complaints of members of the public concerning the administration of the government.

OMISSION. *n*. 1. " . . . [M]eans the failure to do something which it is one's duty to do, or which a reasonable man would do." *Greenlaw v. Canadian Northern Railway* (1913), 12 D.L.R. 402 at 405, [1913] 4 W.W.R. 847, 15 C.R.C. 329, 23 Man. R. 410, 24 W.L.R. 509 (C.A.), Perdue J.A. (Howell C.J.M., Cameron and Haggart JJ.A. concurring). 2. Includes a deliberate choice to leave something out. See ACT OR ~.

OMITTANCE. *n*. Omission.

OMNE CRIMEN EBRIETAS ET INCENDIT ET DETEGIT. [L.] Drunkenness kindles and exposes every crime.

OMNE JUS AUT CONSENSUS FECIT AUT NECESSITAS CONSTITUIT AUT FIR-

MAVIT CONSUETUDO. [L.] Mutual consent made, necessity established, or custom fixed, every rule of law.

OMNE MAJUS CONTINET IN SE MINUS. [L.] Every greater thing contains the less. See *Granger v. Fotheringham* (1894), 3 B.C.R. 590 at 597 (S.C.), Crease J.

OMNE QUOD SOLO INAEDIFICATUR SOLO CEDIT. [L.] Everything built into the ground is merged with it.

OMNE SACRAMENTUM DEBET ESSE DE CERTA SCIENTIA. [L.] Every oath should spring from certain knowledge.

OMNES LICENTIAM HABENT HIS, QUAE, PRO SE INDULTA SUNT, RENUNCIARE. [L.] All people have liberty to renounce things which were granted for their benefit.

OMNES SUBDITI SUNT REGIS SERVI. [L.] All subjects are the servants of the monarch.

OMNE TESTAMENTUM MORTE CON. SUMMATUM EST. [L.] Every will is completed in death.

OMNIA DELICTA IN APERTO LEVIORA SUNT. [L.] All offences are less serious when committed openly.

OMNIA PRAESUMUNTUR CONTRA SPOLIATOREM. [L.] The maxim should only apply where the wrongdoer's acts make it difficult or impossible for the innocent party to prove its loss or where the facts needed to prove the loss are known only to the wrongdoer and the wrongdoer does not disclose those facts to the innocent party.

OMNIA PRAESUMUNTUR IN ODIUM SPOLIATORIS. [L.] All is presumed against the person who destroyed evidence. A rebuttable presumption is raised that the person who destroyed a document is adversely affected by the document or the document is not favourable to the person.

OMNIA PRAESUMUNTUR LEGITIME FACTA DONEC PROBETUR IN CONTRARIUM. [L.] All things are presumed to have been done legitimately until it is proved to the contrary.

OMNIA PRAESUMUNTUR RITE ACTA ESSE. [L.] " . . . [W]here acts are of an official nature or require the concurrence of official persons a presumption arises in favour of their due execution." *Kane v. University of British Columbia* (1980), 31 N.R. 214 at 229, [1980] 2 S.C.R. 1105, 18 B.C.L.R. 124, [1980] 3 W.W.R. 125, 110 D.L.R. (3d) 311, Ritchie J. (dissenting).

OMNIA PRAESUMUNTUR RITE ET SOLEMNITER ESSE ACTA. [L.] All things are presumed to be done correctly and solemnly. See *Davidson v. Garrett* (1899), 30 O.R. 653 at 660, 5 C.C.C. 200 (C.A.), Rose J.A.

OMNIA PRAESUMUNTUR RITE ET SOLEMNITER ESSE DONEC PROBETUR IN CONTRARIUM. [L.] "[The] . . . presumption of the proper and due performance of administrative acts, until the contrary is proved . . ." *Ettershank v. Owen* (1981), 26 C.P.C. 228 at 233 (Ont. Prov. Ct.), Vogelsang Prov. J.

OMNIA QUAE JURE CONTRAHUNTUR, CONTRARIO JURE PEREUNT. [L.] All things accomplished by a law come to naught with a contradictory law.

OMNIBUS. *n*. A motor vehicle owned by a city designed for the transportation of passengers and regularly operated by the city for compensation, on a fixed route either within the city or within the city and such additional area as may be permitted by the Lieutenant Governor in Council, for the purpose of taking up and setting down passengers at fixed points. *The Fuel Petroleum Products Act*, R.S.S. 1978, c. F-23, s. 2.

OMNIBUS ACCOUNT. An account carried by a dealer for another dealer in which the transactions of two or more persons or companies are combined and effected in the name of the second mentioned dealer without disclosure of the identity of such persons or companies. *Commodity Futures Act*, R.R.O. 1980, Reg. 114, s. 7.

OMNIBUS POENALIBUS JUDICIIS ET AETATI EST IMPRUDENTIAE SUCCURRITUR. [L.] In all criminal proceedings, age and ignorance are aided.

OMNIS ACTIO EST LOQUELA. [L.] Each action is a complaint.

OMNIS CONCLUSIO BONI ET VERI JUDICII SEQUITUR EX BONIS ET VERIS PRAEMISSIS ET DICTIS JURATORUM. [L.] Each conclusion showing good and proper judgment is drawn from premises which the jury members properly and reasonably found.

OMNIS CONSENSUS TOLLIT ERROREM. [L.] Each consent removes error.

OMNIS INNOVATIO PLUS NOVITATE PERTURBAT QUAM UTILITATE PROD- **EST.** [L.] Each innovation causes more confusion by its novelty than good by its usefulness.

OMNIS INTERPRETATIO SI FIERI POTEST ITA FIENDA EST IN INSTRUMENTIS, UT OMNES CONTRARIETATES AMOVEANTUR. [L.] If possible in the case of deeds, every interpretation should be made so that all inconsistencies are removed.

OMNIS NOVA CONSTITUTIO FUTURIS TEMPORIBUS FORMAM IMPONERE DEBET, NON PRAETERITIS. [L.] Each new law should regulate future time, not the past.

OMNIS PRIVATIO PRAESUPPONIS HABITUM. [L.] Each deprivation presupposes possession.

OMNIS QUERELA ET OMNIS ACTIO INJURIARUM LIMITATA EST INFRO CERTA TEMPORA. [L.] Each complaint and each action for damages is limited within set times.

OMNIS RATIHABITIO RETRITRAHITUR ET MANDATA PRIORI AEQUIPARATUR. [L.] Each ratification of something already done has a retroactive effect and is like an earlier request to do it.

OMNIUM. *n*. [L.] The total of designated portions of different stocks in a public fund.

OMNIUM CONTRIBUTIONE SARCIATUR QUOD PRO OMNIBUS DATUM EST. [L.] The sum total which was provided for all is perfected by distribution.

ON. *prep*. Situated over or supported by another.

ON-CALL TIME. The hours during which an employee may be called to work.

ON CONSIGNMENT. For payment by the consignee after sale by him.

ON DECK. Above deck, as opposed to under deck. *Dangerous Goods Shipping Regulations*, C.R.C., c. 1419, s. 2.

ON DECK ONLY. In an uncovered space, though special deckhouses having doors which can be continuously open (except in heavy weather) may be used, but does not include stowage in a shelter deck space. *Dangerous Goods Shipping Regulations*, C.R.C. c. 1419, s. 2.

ONE. See EVERY ~.

O.N.E. *abbr*. Office national de l'énergie.

ONE DAY. The period beginning 2 hours before sunrise and ending 2 hours after sunset. *Fishery regulations*.

ONE-ENGINE-INOPERATIVE TAKE-OFF DISTANCE. The distance from the start of the take-off roll to the point at which the aeroplane reaches 35 feet above the runway elevation, where failure of the critical engine is recognized at V_1. *Canadian Aviation Regulations*, SOR/96-433, s. 101.01(1).

ONE-ENGINE-INOPERATIVE TAKE-OFF RUN. The distance from the start of the take-off roll to the point midway between the lift-off point and the point at which the aeroplane reaches 35 feet above the runway elevation, where failure of the critical engine is recognized at V_1. *Canadian Aviation Regulations*, SOR/96-433, s. 101.01(1).

ONE-FAMILY DWELLING. A house consisting of one family housing unit not attached to or forming part of any other house. *National Housing Act*, R.S.C. 1985, c. N-11, s. 2.

ONEROUS. *adj.* Describes an obligation which outweighs or exceeds its advantage.

ONE-WAY HIGHWAY. A highway designated as such by signs on or erected or posted along the highway directing traffic to proceed in only one direction. *Highway Traffic Act*, S.S. 1986, c. H-3.1, s. 2.

ONE-WAY ROADWAY. A roadway designated and marked by a traffic authority as a roadway upon which vehicles may be operated in one direction only.

ONE-WAY STREET. A highway designated and marked by a department or traffic authority upon which vehicles may be operated in one direction only.

ON ITS MERITS. The general principle of law is that a tribunal which exercises a statutory discretion may not fetter the exercise of that discretion by the adoption of an inflexible policy. What is essential is that each case be considered individually on its own merits. The legislation clearly intends that the Tribunal make independent decisions. Its only obligation is to apply, where applicable, Board policies. But, it must surely also enjoy the power to decide when a policy should not apply. That is what is meant by deciding a case on its merits. *Braden-Burry Expediting Services Ltd. v. Northwest Territories (Workers' Compensation Board)* (1998), 1998 CarswellNWT 170, 13 Admin. L.R. (3d) 232 (S.C.), Vertes J.

ONLY. *adv.* "Where a power of activity is described in language which extends to such and such terms 'only', the significance of that word is to emphasize the limits of what is prescribed, . . ." *Solvanson v. Manitoba Public Insurance Corp.* (1976), 1 D.L.R. (3d) 277 at 280, [1976] 6 W.W.R. 690, [1977] I.L.R. 1-856 (Man. Q.B.), Wilson J.

ON OR ABOUT. 1. Within some period of time. 2. On but not inside a person.

ON POINT. Cases which decide a point of law, not cases in which the facts resemble the case before the court.

ON-PREMISES SALE. The sale of a beverage intended for consumption on the premises on which it is sold.

ON-ROAD VEHICLE. A self-propelled vehicle designed for or capable of transporting persons, property, material or permanently or temporarily affixed apparatus on a highway, but does not mean a vehicle that (*a*) cannot exceed a speed of 40 km/h (25 miles per hour) on a level paved surface; (*b*) lacks features customarily associated with safe and practical highway use such as a reverse gear, unless the vehicle is a motorcycle, a differential, or safety features required by federal or provincial laws; (*c*) exhibits features that render its use on a highway unsafe, impractical, or highly unlikely, such as tracked road contact means or inordinate size; or (*d*) is a military vehicle designed for use in combat or combat support. *On-Road Vehicle and Engine Emission Regulations*, SOR/2003-2, s. 1(1).

ON-SITE ROAD. A road for the movement of vehicles and equipment within a site.

ONT. *abbr.* Ontario.

ONTARIO CONTRACT. A subsisting contract of insurance that (a) has for its subject, (i) property that at the time of the making of the contract is in Ontario or is in transit to or from Ontario, or (ii) the life, safety, fidelity or insurable interest of a person who at the time of the making of the contract is resident in Ontario or of an incorporated company that has its head office in Ontario, or (b) makes provision for payment thereunder primarily to a resident of Ontario or to an incorporated company that has its head office in Ontario.

ONTARIO JUDICIAL COUNCIL. A body reporting to the Attorney General which receives and investigates complaints against and considers proposed appointments of provincial judges.

ONTARIO SECURITIES COMMISSION. " . . . [A] statutory tribunal charged by the Legislature with the administration of the Act [Securities Act, R.S.O. 1980, c. 466]. It has extensive powers to regulate, control and investigate trading in securities. It comprises an adjudicative body which is an autonomous statutory tribunal and a large staff concerned with the day-to-day operations of the Commission." *Ontario (Securities Commission) v. Biscotti* (1988), 40 B.L.R. 160 at 161 (Ont. H.C.), Anderson J.

ONTARIO WINE. (a) Wine produced from grapes, cherries, apples or other fruits grown in Ontario or the concentrated juice thereof and includes Ontario wine to which is added herbs, water, honey, sugar or the distillate of Ontario wine or cereal grains grown in Ontario, (b) wine produced by the alcoholic fermentation of Ontario honey, with or without the addition of caramel, natural botanical flavours or the distillate of Ontario honey wine, or (c) wine produced from the combination of, (i) apples grown in Ontario or the concentrated juice thereof to which is added herbs, water, honey, sugar or the distillate of Ontario wine or cereal grains grown in Ontario, and (ii) the concentrated juice of apples grown outside of Ontario, in such proportion as is prescribed. *Liquor Licence Act*, R.S.0. 1990, c. L.19, s. 1.

ONT. CASE LAW DIG. *abbr*. Ontario Case Law Digest.

ONT. CORPS. LAW GUIDE. *abbr*. Ontario Corporations Law Guide.

ONT. DIV. CT. *abbr*. Supreme Court of Ontario, High Court of Justice (Divisional Court).

ONT. ELEC. *abbr*. Ontario Election Cases, 1884-1900.

ONT. H.C. *abbr*. Supreme Court of Ontario, High Court of Justice (including Family Law Division).

ONT. PROV. CT. (CIV. DIV.). *abbr*. Ontario Provincial Court, Civil Division.

ON-TRACK ACCOUNT BETTING. Pari-mutuel betting conducted at a race-course or in a betting theatre of an association otherwise than by buying a ticket, and in accordance with sections 84.1 to 84.9. *Pari-Mutuel Betting Supervision Regulations*, SOR/91-365, s. 2.

ON-TRACK ACCOUNT BETTING SYSTEM. The services, facilities and equipment used for conducting on-track account betting. *Pari-Mutuel Betting Supervision Regulations*, SOR/91-365, s. 2.

ONT. R.E.L.G. *abbr*. Ontario Real Estate Law Guide.

ONT. S.C. *abbr*. Supreme Court of Ontario (in Bankruptcy).

ONT. TAX R. *abbr*. Ontario Tax Reports.

ONT. W.C.A.T. *abbr*. Ontario Workers' Compensation Appeals Tribunal.

ONUS. *n*. [L.] Burden. See CIVIL ~; CRIMINAL ~.

ONUS OF PROOF. ". . . [S]hould be restricted to the persuasive burden, since an issue can be put into play without being proven." *R. v. Schwartz* (1988), 45 C.C.C. (3d) 97 at 115, [1989] 1 W.W.R. 289, 66 C.R. (3d) 251, 99 N.R. 90, [1988] 2 S.C.R. 443, 56 Man. R. (2d) 92, 55 D.L.R. (4th) 1, Dickson C.J.C.

ONUS PROBANDI. [L. the burden of proving] "The strict meaning of the term onus probandi is this, that if no evidence is given by the party on whom the burden is cast, the issue must be found against him." *Barry v. Butlin* (1838), 2 Moo. P.C. 480 at 484 Parke B.

ONWSIAT. The neutral citation for the Ontario Workplace Safety and Insurance Appeals Tribunal.

OPACITY. *n*. 1. (i) The color of a visible emission in shades of grey to black; or (ii) the degree to which a visible emission obstructs the passage of light. *Environmental Protection Act*, 1980, Reg. 308, s. 1. 2. The fraction of a beam of light, expressed as a percentage, that fails to penetrate the exhaust emission. *Motor Vehicle Safety Regulations*, C.R.C., c. 1038, s. 1100.

OP. CIT. *abbr:* [L.] Opere citato.

OPEC. *abbr*. Organization of Petroleum Exporting Countries.

OPEN ACCOUNT. An account which the parties have not stated or settled.

OPEN AIR. The atmosphere outside a building.

OPEN BODY OF WATER. A river, stream, watercourse, bay, estuary, open municipal reservoir, farm pond, dugout, or other body of water, whether it contains water continuously or intermittently.

OPEN COMMODITY CONTRACT. An outstanding obligation under a commodity contract for which settlement has not been effected by the tender and receipt of the commodity, by the tender and receipt of an instrument evidencing title or the right to that commodity, or by a liquidating trade.

OPEN COMMODITY FUTURES CONTRACT. An outstanding obligation under a commodity futures contract for which settlement has not been effected by the tender and receipt of the commodity or of an instrument evidencing title or the right to that commodity or by a liquidating trade.

OPEN COMPETITION. A competition that is open to employees as well as to persons who are not employees.

OPEN CONSTRUCTION. With respect to a fishing vessel, means a fishing vessel other than one of closed construction. *Small Fishing Vessel Inspection Regulations*, C.R.C., c. 1486, s. 2.

OPEN COURT. " . . . [T]he Court must be open to any who may present themselves for admission. The remoteness of the possibility of any public attendance must never by judicial action be reduced to the certainty that there will be none." *McPherson v. McPherson*, [1936] 1 D.L.R. 321 at 327 (Alta. P.C.), Lord Blanesborough.

OPEN CREDIT. Credit under a credit agreement that, (a) anticipates multiple advances to be made as requested by the borrower in accordance with the agreement, and (b) does not define the total amount to be advanced to the borrower under the agreement, although it may impose a credit limit. *Consumer Protection Act, 2002*, S.O. 2002, c. 30 Sched. A, s. 1.

OPEN CUSTODY. Custody in (a) a community residential centre, group home, child care institution, or forest or wilderness camp, or (b) any other like place or facility designated by the Lieutenant Governor in Council of a province or his delegate as a place of open custody for the purposes of this Act, and includes a place or facility within a class of such places or facilities so designated. *Young Offenders Act*, R.S.C. 1985 (2d Supp.), c. 24, s. 24.1. See PLACE OF ~.

OPENED. *adj*. Not closed; uncovered; unconfined. See FULLY ~.

OPEN-END MUTUAL FUND. A corporation that makes a distribution to the public of its shares and that carries on only the business of investing the consideration it receives for the shares it issues, and all or substantially all of those shares are redeemable upon the demand of a shareholder.

OPEN FIELDS DOCTRINE. In American constitutional law, there is no constitutionally protected right of privacy in open spaces.

OPENING. *n*. Gap, aperture. See CLEAR ~; EFFECTIVE ~; UNPROTECTED ~.

OPENING A ROAD. " . . . [L]aying it out on the ground by survey in the usual manner, and declaring that as so laid out it is a public highway; . . ." *Palmatier v. McKibbon* (1894), 21 O.A.R. 441 at 451 (C.A.), MacLennan J.A.

OPEN INTEREST. Where used in relation to commodity futures contracts, means the total outstanding long positions or the total outstanding short positions, for each delivery month and in aggregate, in commodity futures contracts relating to a particular commodity entered into on a commodity futures exchange. *Commodity Futures Act*, R.S.O. 1990, c. C-20, s. 1(1) as am.

OPEN LISTING. Authority, given to a single or multiple agents, which usually implies or states that a commission will be paid only when a sale is consummated and in which the vendor usually retains a right to sell the property without reference to any agent. B.J. Reiter, R.C.B. Risk & B.N. McLellan, *Real Estate Law*, 3d ed. (Toronto: Emond Montgomery, 1986) at 74 and 75.

OPEN MARKET. A market of willing sellers and willing buyers.

OPEN ORDER. An order, which remains valid until cancelled by the customer, to buy securities at, above or below a named price. *Ussher v. Simpson* (1909), 13 O.W.R. 285 at 286 (Div. Ct.), the court per Magee J.

OPEN PERIOD. With respect to a municipality and a bargaining agent (i) if no collective agreement is in effect, any time; or (ii) if a collective agreement is in effect, any time after notice to commence collective bargaining is served.

OPEN PIT. A surface opening, quarry or excavation in, or working of, the ground for the purpose of searching for, winning, opening up, removal of or proving any mineral-bearing substance.

OPEN PIT MINE. A mine worked by removal of overlying strata and subsequent excavation of exposed coal in terrain that is not flat or substantially flat.

OPEN POLICY. An insurance policy in which the value of goods or a ship insured will be calculated in the event of loss.

OPEN RING NET. A net whose bottom is closed to form a bag and that is hung on a ring or metal frame attached to a line or rope. *Pacific Shellfish Regulations*, C.R.C., c. 826, s. 2.

OPEN SEASON. A specified period of time during which a species of wildlife may be hunted or taken or fishing may take place.

OPEN SHOP. A business in which union membership is not required as a condition of employment.

OPEN SPLICE. Any parting at any junction of tread, sidewall or innerliner that extends to the cord. *Motor Vehicle Tire Safety Regulations*, C.R.C., c. 1039, s. 2.

OPEN TEMPORARY DETENTION. See PLACE OF ~.

OPEN-TYPE HOT-WATER HEATING SYSTEM. A system in which water is heated and circulated and where there are no intervening valves between the boiler and the expansion tank, and which is vented to the atmosphere. *Boiler and Pressure Vessel Act*, R.S. Nfld. 1970, c. 24, s. 2.

OPEN UNION. A union lacking restrictive membership conditions.

OPEN WATER. Water that is not ice-covered. *Manitoba Fishery Regulations*, C.R.C., c. 843, s. 2.

OPERATE. *v.* 1. " . . . '[U]se' . . ." *Hudson v. Insurance Corp. of British Columbia* (1991), 2 C.C.L.I. (2d) 157 at 163, 57 B.C.L.R. (2d) 183, 83 D.L.R. (4th) 377, [1992] I.L.R. 1-2792, 8 B.C.A.C. 13, 17 W.A.C. 13 (C.A.), the court per Locke J.A. 2. " . . . [T]o superintend, or conduct, or manage, or direct." *O'Reilly v. Canada Accident & Fire Assurance Co.*, [1928] 4 D.L.R. 415 at 417, 62 O.L.R. 654 (H.C.), Kelly J. 3. To have the management and control. 4. To carry on the activity permitted by a licence. *Health Facilities Special Orders Act, 1983*, S.O. 1983, c. 43, s. 1. 5. (a) Means, in respect of a motor vehicle, to drive the vehicle; and (b) includes in respect of a vessel or an aircraft, to navigate the vessel or aircraft. *Criminal Code*, R.S.C. 1985, c. C-46, s. 214 as amended by *Criminal Law Amendment Act*, R.S.C. 1985 (1st Supp.), c. 27, s. 33. 6. When used in relation to a heating plant or a power plant, means to operate, manipulate, observe and check manual, mechanical, automatic and remote controls and equipment in connection with a heating plant or power plant, but does not include "have charge of" a heating plant

or power plant. 7. Having physical control of a vehicle.

OPERATING. *adj.* Maintaining; functioning; carrying on; repairing; keeping going.

OPERATING AGREEMENT. See UNIT ~.

OPERATING AUTHORITY. A written authorization of the Commission conferring the right to operate over such routes, to carry such commodities, in such vehicles and subject to such limitations or conditions, as are therein specified, and includes a temporary operating authority and a temporary permit. *Motor Carrier Act*, S.P.E.I. 1984, c. 26, s. 1.

OPERATING BALANCE. The amount of the balance to the credit of the Canada Pension Plan Account less the balance in the Canada Pension Plan Investment Fund. *Canada Pension Plan*, R.S.C. 1985, c. C-8, s. 110.

OPERATING BASE. With respect to an air craft, means an aerodrome (a) that is frequently used by the aircraft; (b) at which shelter and means of sustaining life are available; and (c) at which there is a responsible person with whom the pilot-in-command may leave information concerning any proposed flight. *Sparsely Settled Areas Order*, C.R.C., c. 65, s. 2.

OPERATING BUSINESS. A business undertaking in Canada to which employees employed in connection with the undertaking ordinarily report for work. *Combines Investigation Act*, R.S.C. 1985 (2d Supp.), c. 19, s. 108.

OPERATING CORPORATION. A municipal corporation or commission or a company or individual operating or using a telephone or telegraph service, or transmitting, distributing or supplying electricity or artificial or natural gas for light, heat or power and includes Ontario Hydro. *Public Service Works on Highways Act*, R.S.O. 1990, c. P.49, s. 1.

OPERATING COSTS. The cost of the furnishings, equipment, supplies, salaries and transportation for a nursing service, and such other expenses as may be approved by the Minister. *Nursing Service* Act, R.S.A. 1980, c. N-15, s. 1.

OPERATING ENGINEER. See CHIEF ~.

OPERATING EXPENSE. An expenditure for administration or management.

OPERATING FUND. A fund for common expenses that usually occur either once a year or more often than once a year. *Strata Property Act*, S.B.C. 1998, c. 43, s. 1(1).

OPERATING LEASE. The authorization to produce petroleum and natural gas. *Mining Act*, R.S.Q. 1977, c. M-13, s. 1.

OPERATING LOSS. With respect to any fiscal year of the city, means the excess of the aggregate amount of all operating expenses resulting from the operation of the transit system over the aggregate amount of all operating revenue derived from that operation, for that fiscal year. *City of Winnipeg Act*, S.M. 1971, c. 105, s. 565.

OPERATING MIND. In relation to confessions, a test requiring an accused to possess a limited degree of cognitive ability to understand what she is saying and to comprehend that the evidence may be used against her. *R. v. Whittle*, [1994] 2 S.C.R. 914.

OPERATING PROFIT. With respect to any fiscal year, means the excess of the aggregate amount of all operating revenues over the aggregate amount of all operating expenses. See ADJUSTED ~S.

OPERATING REVENUES. All revenues from the operation of all plants and properties. See GROSS OPERATING REVENUE.

OPERATING SYSTEM PROGRAM. Designed primarily to facilitate the operation of "application programs" and perform tasks common to any "application program", such as reading and writing data to a disk. Without them, each "application program" would need to duplicate its functions. *Apple Computer Inc. v. Macintosh Computers Ltd.* (1985), 3 C.I.P.R. 133, 3 C.P.R. (3d) 34 (Fed. T.D.) Cullen J.

OPERATION. *n.* 1. " . . . [M]ay be given two distinct meanings — a wider meaning when used figuratively (as where a person 'operates' a fleet of vehicles by organizing a system of activity, without necessarily driving any of the vehicles himself), and a more narrow meaning restricted to the physical acts or omissions of the operator of a vehicle while it is being driven." *R. v. Twoyoungmen* (1979), 48 C.C.C. (2d) 550 at 559, 16 A.R. 413, [1979] 5 W.W.R. 712, 3 M.V.R. 186, 101 D.L.R. (3d) 598 (C.A.), the court per Prowse J.A. 2. " . . . [O]f a vessel connotes a captain or a person in charge and by extension further connotes the possibility of a crew or other persons who assist in the operation of the vessel under the direction of the person in charge. To my mind any or all of these persons are involved in the operation of the vessel, whether in the role of directing its operation by commanding others or by the actual working of the mechanisms or procedures which control the boat or enable it to function." *R. v. Turbide* (1986), 76 N.B.R. (2d) 138 at 140, 192 A.P.R. 138 (Q.B.), Creaghan J. 3. (a) In relation to a facility, the manufacturing or processing operation of which the facility constitutes the necessary components, and (b) in relation to a commercial facility, the commercial undertaking of which the commercial facility constitutes the necessary components. 4. " . . . [R]efers to the working of the railway — how the cars should be run — control of the tracks, motive power and equipment . . ." *Ottawa Electric Railway v. Nepean (Township)* (1920), 54 D.L.R. 468 at 487, 60 S.C.R. 216, Anglin J. See AGRICULTURAL ~; BASE OF ~S; CADASTRAL ~; CAESAREAN ~; CONTINUOUS ~; DANGEROUS ~ OF AIRCRAFT; EXPLORATION ~S; FARMING ~S; FISHING ~; FOREST INDUSTRY ~; FORESTRY ~; GEOPHYSICAL ~; GROUP ~; INDUSTRIAL ~; INDUSTRIAL OR COMMERCIAL~; IN SITU ~; LOGGING ~; MINING ~; MULTI-FARM ~; NEGLIGENT ~; NORMAL ~S; PRODUCTION ~S; SPECIAL PURPOSE ~; SUBSIDIARY CONTROLLED ~; TRANSFER ~; UNITIZED ~; WASTEFUL ~.

OPERATIONAL. *adj.* Describes a " . . . function of government [which] . . . involves the use of governmental powers for the purpose of implementing, giving effect to or enforcing compliance with the general or specific goals of a policy decision." *Just v. British Columbia* (1985), 33 C.C.L.T. 49 at 52, 34 M.V.R. 124, 64 B.C.L.R. 349, [1985] 5 W.W.R. 570 (S.C.), McLachlin J.

OPERATIONAL CONTROL. In respect of a flight, means the exercise of authority over, or the initiation, continuation, diversion or termination of, a flight. Canada regulations.

OPERATIONAL DECISION. The operational area is concerned with the practical implementation of the formulated policies, it mainly covers the performance or carrying out of a policy. Operational decisions will usually be made on the basis of administrative direction, expert or professional opinion, technical standards or general standards of reasonableness. *Brown v. British Columbia (Minister of Transportation & Highways)*, [1994] 1 S.C.R. 420.

OPERATIVE PART. In a mortgage, lease, conveyance or other formal instrument, the part which expresses the main object of that instrument.

OPERATIVE WORD. A word which contributes to the origin or transfer of an estate.

OPERATOR. *n*. 1. In relation to any work, undertaking or business, means the person having the charge, management or control of the work, undertaking or business whether on that person's own account or as the agent of any other person. 2. A person who drives a motor vehicle on a public highway. 3. A person who uses or operates or is in actual physical control of an all-terrain vehicle. 4. A person having direct control of the starting, stopping and speed of an amusement ride. 5. A person who uses or controls the use of any radiation equipment. 6. A person (i) who operates a race course; (ii) who conducts a race meeting; or (iii) who is in any manner the custodian or depositary of money that is staked or deposited in the making of a bet on any race during the actual progress of a race meeting conducted by that person on races being run on a race course or at a race meeting. 7. In respect of an aircraft, means the person that has possession of the aircraft as owner, lessee or otherwise. *Canadian Aviation Regulations*, SOR/96-433, s. 101.01(1). See ASSEMBLY YARD ~; CHIEF ~; CITY MOTOR VEHICLE ~; COD TRAP ~; CONCESSION ~; CONTAINER~; CREAMERY ~; CUSTOM ~; DRIVER OR ~; FAN ~; FARM ~; FEED MILL ~; FOREST GARAGE ~; GRADING STATION~; HIGHWAY MOTOR VEHICLE ~; HOIST ~; INDEPENDENT ~; JOINT ~S; LICENSED ~; LOGGING ~; MARKET ~; NETWORK ~; OWNER~; SEED COMPANY ~; SHIFT ~; SUGAR BUSH ~; TOUR ~; TRACK ~; UNIT WELDING ~.

OPERATOR OF A PHARMACY. (a) The holder of a certificate of accreditation for the operation of a pharmacy under section 139 of the Health Disciplines Act, or (b) the operator of a pharmacy operated in or by a hospital that is a public hospital under the Public Hospitals Act. *Ontario Drug Benefits Act*, R.S.O. 1990, c. 0.10, s. 1.

OPERATOR'S CERTIFICATE. A certificate of insurance issued to a person holding a licence or other permit to drive a motor vehicle under The Vehicles Act, or The Snowmobile Act. *The Automobile Accident Insurance Act*, R.S.S. 1978, c. A-35, s. 2.

OPERATOR'S LICENCE. A valid licence issued under this Ordinance to a person to operate or manipulate a motion picture machine in a theatre. *Motion Pictures Act*, R.S.N.W.T. 1974, c. M-14, s. 2.

OPERATOR'S LIEN. Any charge on or right in relation to an interest or a share in an interest (a) that arises under a contract (i) to which the interest owner or holder of the interest or share is a party; (ii) that provides for the operator appointed thereunder to carry out any work or activity related to the exploration for or the development or production of petroleum in the frontier lands to which the interest or share applies; and (iii) that requires the interest owner or holder to make payments to the operator to cover all or part of the advances made by the operator in respect of the costs and expenses of such work or activity; and (b) that secures the payments referred to in subparagraph (a)(iii). *Petroleum Resources Act*, R.S.C. 1985 (2d Supp.), c. 36, s. 84.

OPERE CITATO. [L.] In the work just cited.

OPHTHALMIC APPLIANCE. Lenses, spectacles, eyeglasses, frames, contact lenses, artificial eyes or other specified devices, for the relief, prevention or correction of visual or other anomalies of the eyes.

OPHTHALMIC DISPENSER. A person who (a) prepares and dispenses lenses, including contact lenses, spectacles, eyeglasses, and appurtenances thereto, or any of those things, to the intended wearers thereof, on the written prescriptions of duly qualified medical practitioners or of the holders of certificates of registration under The Optometry Act; and (b) in accordance with such prescriptions interprets, measures, adapts, fits, and adjusts, such lenses, including contact lenses, spectacles, eye-glasses and appurtenances thereto or any of those things, to the human face for the aid of vision or the correction of visual or ocular anomalies of human eyes. *Ophthalmic Dispensers Act*, R.S.M. 1987, c. 045, s. 1.

OPHTHALMIC DISPENSING. (i) Supplying, preparing and dispensing ophthalmic appliances; (ii) interpreting prescriptions of legally qualified medical practitioners and optometrists; and (iii) the fitting, adjusting and adapting of ophthalmic appliances to the human face and eyes in accordance with the prescriptions of legally qualified medical practitioners and optometrists.

OPHTHALMIC DISPENSING SERVICE. The measuring, adjusting or adapting of ophthalmic appliances to the needs of the intended wearer, whether or not for hire, gain or reward. *The Ophthalmic Dispensers Act*, R.S.S. 1978, c. O-5, s. 2.

OPHTHALMIC LENS. Any spherical, cylindrical, or prismatic lens to aid vision.

OPHTHALMOLOGIST. *n*. A person legally qualified to practise as a physician under The Medical Profession Act and recognized as a specialist in ophthalmology by The College of Physicians and Surgeons of the Province of Saskatchewan. *The Ophthalmic Dispensers Act*, R.S.S. 1978, c. O-5, s. 2.

OPINION. *n*. 1. The advice a counsel gives on the facts of a case. 2. Any inference from observed fact. 3. A statement which may be admissible as evidence. The opinion of an expert witness is called expert evidence. 4. " . . . [Statement, tale or news is an expression which, taken as a whole and understood in context, conveys an assertion of fact or facts and not merely the expression of opinion. . . Expression which makes a statement susceptible of proof and disproof is an assertion of fact; expression which merely offers an interpretation of fact which may be embraced or rejected depending on its cogency or normative appeal, is opinion." *R. v. Zundel* (1992), 75 C.C.C. (3d) 449 at 492, 95 D.L.R. (4th) 202, [1992] 2 S.C.R. 731, 140 N.R. 1, 56 O.A.C. 161, 16 C.R. (4th)1, 10 C.R.R. (2d) 193, Cory and Iacobucci JJ. (dissenting) (Gonthier J. concurring). 5. "In section 742 [of the Criminal Code, S.C. 1892, c. 29] the word 'opinion' must be construed as meaning the decision or judgment of the court . . ." *R. v. Viau* (1898), 2 C.C.C. 540 at 544, 29 S.C.R. 90, the court per Strong C.J. See ADVISORY ~; ASSERTION ~; CONCURRING ~; DICTUM; DISSENTING ~; EXPERT EVIDENCE; MINORITY ~; OBITER DICTUM.

OPINION SURVEY. A poll.

OPIUM. *n*. Juice containing the alkaloids morphine and codeine from unripe seed capsules of the plant Papaver somniferum. F.A. Jaffe, *A Guide to Pathological Evidence*, 3d ed. (Toronto: Carswell 1991) at 84.

OPIUM POPPY. Papaver somniferum L. *Narcotic Control Act*, R.S.C. 1985, c. N-1, s. 2.

OPORTET QUOD CERTA RES DEDUCATUR IN JUDICIUM. [L.] It is necessary that what is certain be brought to judgment.

OPP. BD. *abbr*. Opposition Board.

OPPORTUNITY. *n*. 1. A possibility of doing something; a chance to do something. 2. A requirement for the finding of guilt in relation to commission of a crime. The accused must have been capable of being at the scene of the crime at the relevant time. See FAIR ~.

OPPORTUNITY COST. A form of overhead which accounts for the fact that but for the disruption people would be able to do other things valuable to their contractual interests if they did not have to deal with the effects of the disruption.

OPPOSING DIRECTION. The direction that is displaced from the facing direction by 180 angular degrees. *Children's Car Seats and Harnesses Regulations*, C.R.C., c. 921, s. 2.

OPPOSITE. *n*. One who opposes.

OPPOSITE. *adj*. Placed or lying on the other or farther side.

OPPOSITE PARTY. 1. " . . . [A] party on the other side of the record to the applicant, or a party on the same side between whom and the applicant there is some right to be adjusted in the action. . ." *Rose & Laflamme Ltd. v. Campbell Wilson & Strathdee Ltd.*, [1923] 2 W.W.R. 1067 at 1068-9, [1923] 4 D.L.R. 92, 17 Sask. L.R. 332 (C.A.), the court per Lamont J.A. 2. Includes the owner of land to be taken under this Act and a person having a registered interest in or right or privilege with regard to the land. *The Expropriation Act*, R.S.S. 1978, c. E-15, s. 2.

OPPOSITION. *n*. 1. In a legislature, the members who are not members of the government caucus. 2. An objection to the registration of a trademark. See LEADER OF THE ~; OFFICIAL ~.

OPPOSITION CAUCUS. The group of members who constitute the largest group sitting in the Assembly in opposition to the Government and who belong to the same political party.

OPPOSITION HOUSE LEADER. A member of the Official Opposition designated by its Leader to discuss with the Government House Leader business arrangements for the House and to reach compromise on the length of debate on each item. A. Fraser W.A. Dawson, & J. Holtby, eds., *Beauchesne's Rules and Forms of the House of Commons of Canada*, 6th ed. (Toronto: Carswell, 1989) at 56.

OPPOSITION PARTY. A party other than the governing party in the legislature. See RECOGNIZED ~.

OPPRESSION. *n.* 1. The state from which a minority shareholder may claim relief. A majority exercises " . . . [I]ts authority in a manner 'burdensome, harsh, wrongful'. . ." *Scottish Co-operative Wholesale Society v. Meyer*, [1959] A.C. 324 at 342, [1958] 3 All E.R. 66 (U.K. H.L.), Viscount Simonds. Suggests " . . . [A] lack of probity and fair dealing in the affairs of a company to the prejudice of some portion of its members." *Scottish Co-operative Wholesale Society v. Meyer*, [1959] A.C. 324 at 364, [1958] 3 All E.R. 66 (U.K. H.L.), Lord Keith. 2. The broad outlines of the legal concept of "oppression", as it relates to the confessions rule, are sketched in the following excerpt from Justice Iacobucci's opinion in [*R. v. Oickle*, [2000] 2 S.C.R. 3], at paras. 58-62: Oppression clearly has the potential to produce false confessions. If the police create conditions distasteful enough, it should be no surprise that the suspect would make a stress-compliant confession to escape those conditions. Alternately, oppressive circumstances could overbear the suspect's will to the point that he or she comes to doubt his or her own memory, believes the relentless accusations made by the police, and gives an induced confession. Without trying to indicate all the factors that can create an atmosphere of oppression, such factors include depriving the suspect of food, clothing, water, sleep, or medical attention; denying access to counsel; and excessively aggressive, intimidating questioning for a prolonged period of time. A final possible source of oppressive conditions is the police use of non-existent evidence. . . The use of false evidence is often crucial in convincing the suspect that protestations of innocence, even if true, are futile. *R v. Tessier*, 2001 NBCA 34, 153 C.C.C. (3d) 361, 41 C.R. (5th) 242, 245 N.B.R. (2d) 1, 636 A.P.R. 1 (C.A.).

OPPRESSION ACTION. A remedy for minority shareholders to protect them from unfairly prejudicial activity by the corporaton. See OPPRESSION REMEDY

OPPRESSION REMEDY. The oppression remedy is designed to afford a remedy when a corporation acts in an oppressive, unfair or prejudicial manner towards a minority shareholder or creditor or in a manner that unfairly disregards their interests. Important underpinnings of the oppression remedy are the expectations, intentions and understandings of the minority shareholder and creditor. Against these are to be balanced the extent to which the acts complained of were unforeseeable or the extent to which the creditor and minority shareholder could reasonably have protected itself from the acts about which complaint is now made. *Bank Leu AG v. Gaming Lottery Corp.* (2003), 175 O.A.C. 143, 37 B.L.R. (3d) 1, 231 D.L.R. (4th) 251 (C.A.).

OPPRESSIVE. *adj.* 1. " . . . [B]urdensome, harsh and wrongful . . ." *Scottish Co-operative Wholesale Society v. Meyer*, [1959] A.C. 324 at 342, [1958] 3 All E.R. 66 (U.K. H.L.), Viscount Simonds. 2. The word oppressive has been legally defined as usually referring to deliberate acts of moral, although not necessarily legal, delinquency such as an unfair abuse of power by the stronger party in order that a weaker party may be put in difficulties in obtaining his just rights. *Whitehead v. Taber* (1983), 1983 CarswellAlta 379, 46 A.R. 14 (Q.B.), Crossley, J.

OPTICAL APPLIANCE. Lenses, spectacles, eyeglasses, artificial eyes, contact lenses or appurtenances thereto for the aid or correction of visual or ocular anomalies of the eyes.

OPTICAL DISPENSING. (i) Supplying, preparing and dispensing optical appliances; (ii) interpreting prescriptions of legally qualified medical practitioners and optometrists; and (iii) the fitting, adjusting and adapting of optical appliances to the human face and eyes in accordance with the prescriptions of legally qualified medical practitioners and optometrists.

OPTICIAN. *n.* Any person who supplies ophthalmic lenses, spectacles, eyeglass mountings, etc., in accordance with the prescription of an optometrical or medical practitioner, or by duplication, and any person who is engaged in the manufacture of ophthalmic lenses, frames, mountings or parts thereof. See DISPENSING ~.

OPTICIANRY. *n.* The practice of opticianry is the provision, fitting and adjustment of subnormal vision devices, contact lenses or eye glasses. *Opticianry Act, 1991*, S.O. 1991, c. 34, s. 3.

OPTIMACY. *n.* 1. People of the highest rank. 2. In England, the nobility.

OPTIMA EST LEGIS INTERPRES CONSUETUDO. [L.] The best interpreter of the law is custom.

OPTIMA EST LEX QUAE MINIMUM RELINQUIT ARBITRIO JUDICIS; OPTIMUS JUDEX QUI MINIMUM SIBI. [L.] The best system of law is that which leaves the least to a judge's discretion; the best judge is one who leaves the least to one's own discretion.

OPTIMA LEGUM INTERPRES EST CON-SUETUDO. [L.] The best interpreter of the law is custom.

OPTIMA STATUTI INTERPRETATRIX EST (OMNIBUS PARTICULIS EJUSDEM INSPECTIS) IPSUM STATUTUM. [L.] The best interpreter of a statute (all separate parts having been considered) is the statute itself.

OPTIMUS INTERPRES RERUM USUS. [L.] Usage is the best interpreter of things.

OPTIMUS INTERPRETANDI MODUS EST SIC LEGES INTERPRETARI UT LEGES LEGIBUS CONCORDANT. [L.] The best way to interpret laws is so they agree with other laws.

OPTIMUS LEGUM INTERPRES CON-SUETUDO. [L.] The best interpreter of the law is custom.

OPTION. *n.* 1. " . . . [A] right acquired by contract to accept or reject a resent offer within a limited, or, it may be a present time in the future." *Paterson v. Houghton* (1909), 19 Man. R. 168 at 175 (C.A.), Cameron J.A. 2. A privilege, acquired by consideration, to call or to make delivery or both, within a certain time, of some specified article or stock at a certain price. 3. "The obligation to hold an offer open for acceptance, until the expiration of a specified time, . . ." *Day v. M.N.R.*, [1971] Tax A.B.C. 1050 at 1054, 71 D.T.C. 723. 4. An option does not create a security interest. An option is a right; it is not a payment or an obligation. *Kaak v. Bank of Montreal* (2003), 2003 CarswellOnt 3490 (C.A.). See COMMODITY FUTURES ~; COMMODITY ~; PRODUCTION ~S WEIGHT; RIGHT OF FIRST REFUSAL; STOCK ~; SURFACE RIGHTS ~; WORK ~.

OPTIONAL ITEMS. Automatic transmission, power steering, power brakes, power windows, power seats, radio and heater. *Motor Vehicle Safety Regulations*, C.R.C., c. 1038, s. 111.

OPTION LICENCE. A licence issued for the purpose of survey and investigation of the timber resources of a selection area. *Forest Act*, R.S.M. 1987, c. F150, s. 1.

OPTION TO PURCHASE. An option gives to the optionee, at the time it is granted, a right, which he may exercise in the future, to compel the optionor to convey to him the optioned prop-erty. The essence of an option to purchase is that, forthwith upon the granting of the option, the optionee upon the occurrence of certain events solely within his control can compel a conveyance of the property to him. *Canadian Long Island Petroleums Ltd. v. Irving Wire Products* (1974), [1975] 2 S.C.R. 715, per Martland J. at pp. 731-732.

OPTOMETRIC DRUG LICENCE. A licence for the use of topically administered drugs for diagnostic purposes. *Optometry Act*, R.S.M. 1987, c. O45, s. 1.

OPTOMETRIC FACILITY. A place in which the practice of optometry is carried on.

OPTOMETRIST. *n.* 1. A person who employs any means other than drugs, medicines and surgery for the measurement of the power of vision and the adaptation of lenses and prisms for the correction and aid thereof. 2. A person who through specialized education, training and experience is skilled in the principles and practice of optometry.

OPTOMETRY. *n.* 1. The employment of any means other than the use of drugs, medicines and surgery for the measurement of the powers of vision and the adaptation of lenses and prisms for the correction and aid of the vision of human beings. 2. The practice of optometry is the assessment of the eye and vision system and the diagnosis, treatment and prevention of, (a) disorders of refraction; (b) sensory and oculomotor disorders and dysfunctions of the eye and vision system; and (c) prescribed diseases. *Optometry Act, 1991,* S.O. 1991, c. 35, s. 3. See PRACTICE OF ~.

O.R. *abbr.* Ontario Reports, 1882-1900.

[] O.R. *abbr.* Ontario Reports, 1931-1973.

ORAL. *adj.* Conveyed by mouth; not in writing.

ORAL ARGUMENT. The presentation of an argument before a court.

ORAL CONTRACT. A contract whose terms are not written down.

ORAL HEARING. A hearing at which the parties or their counsel or agents attend before the court or tribunal in person.

ORAL LD50 VALUE. The amount of a chemical that, when administered orally, will kill 50 per cent of test animals under the specified conditions of test. *Science Education Sets Regulations*, C.R.C., c. 934, s. 2.

ORAL QUESTION. A question put to the government by a member of the legislature during question period in the legislature. Used to deal with urgent business.

ORATOR. *n*. One who brings a petition.

ORBATION. *n*. Depriving one of one's parent or child; poverty.

ORCHARD. *n*. 1. An area of land of at least one-fifth hectare on which there are at least 13 fruit trees and on which the number of fruit trees bears a proportion to the area of at least 65 fruit trees per hectare. 2. Includes any land on which any apple tree is growing. *Agriculture and Marketing Act*, R.S.N.S. 1989, c. 6, s. 110. See ABANDONED ~.

ORDER. *n*. 1. The direction of a court or judge which commands a party to do or not to do something in particular. 2. " . . . [A] proposal in the nature of an offer which invites, without more, some form of acceptance intended to lead to an obligation; that acceptance, according to the nature of the order, may be by promise or by some act as, say, the delivery of goods to a carrier." *Canadian Atlas Diesel Engines Co. v. McLeod Engines Co.*, [1952] 2 S.C.R. 122 at 129, [1952] 3 D.L.R. 513, Rand J. (dissenting) (Cartwright J. concurring). 3. " . . . [A] proper term for describing an act of the Governor-in-council by which he exercises a law-making power, whether the power exist as part of the prerogative or devolve upon him by statute." *Gray, Re* (1918), 57 S.C.R. 150 at 167, [1918] 3 W.W.R. 111, 42 D.L.R. 1, Duff J. 4. . . [A] ruling which a tribunal is specifically authorized to make by statute and which takes immediate effect to force the doing or not doing of something by somebody . . ." *Canadian Pacific Air Lines Ltd. v. C.A.L.P.A.* (1988), 30 Admin. L.R. 277 at 281, 84 N.R. 81 (Fed. C.A.), the court per Hugessen J.A. 5. Includes a judgment, decree rule award and declaration. 6. An order or determination of a court providing for the payment of money as maintenance by the respondent named in the order for the benefit of the claimant named in the order, or the maintenance provisions of an order or determination that includes other matters. 7. Any professional order listed in Schedule I to this Code or constituted in accordance with this Code. *Professional Code*, R.S.Q., c. C-26, s. 1. 8. Includes any directive to the trade issued by the Commission. *Canada Grain Act*, R.S.C. 1985, c. G-10, s. 2. See ACCESS ~; AFFILI-ATION ~; ANTON PILLER ~; BAS-TARDY ~; "BULLOCK" ~; CHARGING ~;

COMMITTAL ~; COMMUNITY SER-VICE ~; COMPENSATION ~; COMPLI-ANCE ~; CONFIRMATION ~; CON-TROL ~; CONVEYANCE ~; CUSTODY ~; DATE OF THE ~; DECLARATORY ~; DEMOLITION ~; DEPORTATION ~; DE-TENTION ~; DISTRIBUTIVE ~ FOR COSTS; EXCLUSION ~; EXTRA-PROVIN-CIAL ~; FAMILY ~; FINAL ~; FORECLO-SURE ~; GARNISHEE ~; GENERAL ~ NO. 448; GENERAL ~S; GUARDIANSHIP ~; HOLD ~; INTERIM ~; INTERLOCU-TORY~; JUDGMENT ~; MAINTE-NANCE ~; MATRIMONIAL PROPERTY ~; MONEY ~; NO LIMIT ~; NON-ENTRY ~; NO ~ AS TO COSTS; OPEN ~; PAYABLE TO ~; PREROGATIVE ~; PROBATION ~; PROVISIONAL ~; QUEENS REGULA-TIONS AND ~S; QUESTION OF ~; QUIET-ING ~; RECEIVING ~; REGISTERED ~; REJECTION ~; REMOVAL ~; RESTITU-TION ~; RESTRAINING ~; RETROAC-TIVE ~; RETROSPECTIVE ~; RICE ~; RIGHT OF ENTRY ~; SANDERSON ~; SESSIONAL ~; SHOW CAUSE ~; SPE-CIAL ~; STANDING ~; STANDING, SES-SIONAL AND SPECIAL ~; STOP ~; STOP WORK ~; SUPERVISION ~; SUPPORT ~; TRANSPORT ~; TRAP ~; VARIATION~; VERBAL ~; VESTING ~; WINDING-UP ~; WRITTEN ~.

ORDER ABSOLUTE. A complete rule or order, with full effect, as opposed to a rule or order nisi.

ORDER FOR COSTS. See DISTRIBU-TIVE ~.

ORDER FORM. A security is in order form where the security is not a share and, by its terms, it is payable to the order or assigns of any person therein specified with reasonable certainty or to the person or the person's order. *Bank Act*, S.C. 1991, c. 46, s. 83.

ORDER FOR THE RECOVERY OF PER-SONAL PROPERTY. See REPLEVIN.

ORDER IN COUNCIL. *var*. **ORDER-IN-COUNCIL**. An order made by the Lieutenant Governor or Governor General by and with the advice of the Executive or Privy Council sometimes under statutory authority or sometimes by virtue of royal prerogative.

ORDER OF COURSE. An order, made on an ex parte application, which a party is rightfully entitled to on that party's own statement and at that party's own risk.

ORDER OF THE DAY. A proceeding which may be considered only as the result of a previous order made in the House itself, except for a measure requiring immediate consideration such as the successive stages of a bill. A. Fraser, W.A. Dawson, & J. Holtby, eds., *Beauchesne's Rules and Forms of the House of Commons of Canada*, 6th ed. (Toronto: Carswell, 1989) at 110-11.

ORDER PAPER. The official agenda which lists every item which may be brought forward during that day's sitting. A. Fraser, W.A. Dawson, J. Holtby, eds., *Beauchesne's Rules and Forms of the House of Commons of Canada*, 6th ed. (Toronto: Carswell, 1989) at 300.

ORDER TO CONTINUE. An order obtained by someone entitled to carry on the proceedings or someone not already a party on whom the interest devolved, e.g., the personal representative of a plaintiff who is deceased. G.D. Watson & C. Perkins eds., *Holmested & Watson: Ontario Civil Procedure* (Toronto: Carswell, 1984) at 1115.

ORDINANCE. *n.* 1. Includes an ordinance of the Territories passed before, on or after April 1, 1955. *Northwest Territories Act*, R.S.C. 1985, c. N-27, s. 2. 2. Includes an ordinance of the Territory passed before, on or after April 1, 1955. *Yukon Act*, R.S.C. 1985, c. Y-2, s. 2. 3. An enactment of the Regional Government which applies within the municipalities under its jurisdiction or to the inhabitants of these municipalities, except where the enactment itself expressly provides otherwise. *An Act concerning Northern Villages and the Kativik Regional Government*, S.Q. 1978, c. 87, s. 2.

ORDINANDI LEX. [L.] The law of procedure, in contrast to substantive law.

ORDINARILY RESIDENT. 1. " . . . [O]ne is 'ordinarily resident' . . . in the place where in the settled routine of his life he regularly, normally or customarily lives." *Thomson v. Minister of National Revenue*, [1946] 1 D.L.R. 689 at 707, [1946] S.C.R. 206, [1946] C.T.C. 51, Estey J. 2. " . . . [R]esidence in the course of the customary mode of life of the person concerned, and it is contrasted with special or occasional or casual residence. . ." *Thomson v. Minister of National Revenue*, [1946] S.C.R. 209 at 224, [1946] 1 D.L.R. 689, [1946] C.T.C. 51, Rand J.

ORDINARILY RESIDENT IN CANADA. If, at the time the expression is being applied, (a) he or she has sojourned in Canada during the next preceding 24 months for a period of, or periods the aggregate of which is, 366 days or more; (b) he or she is a member of the Canadian Forces required to reside outside Canada; (c) he or she is an ambassador, minister, high commissioner, officer or servant of Canada, or is an agent-general, officer or servant of a province of Canada, and resided in Canada immediately prior to appointment or employment by Canada or a province of Canada or is entitled to receive representation allowances; (d) he or she is performing services in a country other than Canada under an international development assistance program of the Government of Canada that is prescribed for the purposes of paragraph 250(1)(d) of the Income Tax Act (Canada), and resided in Canada at any time in the 3-month period preceding the day on which such services commenced; or (e) he or she resides outside Canada and is the spouse or child of, and is living with, an individual described in clause (b), (c) or (d). *Land Transfer Tax Act*, R.S.O. 1990, c. L.6, s. 1(5).

ORDINARIUS ITA DICITUR QUIA HABET ORDINARIAM JURISDICTIONEM, IN JURE PROPRIO, ET NON PROPTER DEPUTATIONEM. [L.] The ordinary is called that because one has ordinary jurisdiction, in one's own right, and not through being deputized.

ORDINARY BY-LAW. A by-law of an association that is not subject to the approval of the Minister. *Canada Cooperative Associations Act*, R.S.C. 1985, c. C-40, s. 3.

ORDINARY COURSE OF BUSINESS. The regular transactions in which people in that business engage.

ORDINARY COURT. The court that would, but for this Act, have jurisdiction in respect of an offence alleged to have been committed. *Young Offenders Act*, R.S.C., 1985, c. Y-1, s. 2.

ORDINARY INCOME. Income from a source other than from capital.

ORDINARY LOCATION. A dry location in which at normal atmosphere pressure and under normal conditions of use, electrical equipment is not unduly exposed to injury from mechanical causes, excessive dust, moisture, or extreme temperatures, and in which electrical equipment is entirely free from the possibility of injury through corrosive, flammable or explosive atmospheres.

ORDINARY MEANING. The meaning understood, in the context, by a competent user of the language. Can refer to the meaning in the vernacular of a particular special community.

ORDINARY MEANING RULE. The ordinary meaning of an enactment prevails in the absence of a reason to reject it. Even if the meaning appears clear, the court must consider the purpose and scheme of the enactment and the consequences of adopting the proposed meaning. After considering these other factors, the court may adopt a modified meaning which must be plausible and one which the words are reasonably capable of bearing.

ORDINARY PERSON. In relation to the provocation defence, must be a person of the same age and sex and share with the accused such other factors as would give the act or insult in question a special significance and have experienced the same series of acts or insults as those experienced by the accused. *R. v. Thibert*, [1996] 1 S.C.R. 37.

ORDINARY POLLING DAY. The day fixed for holding the poll at an election.

ORDINARY PRACTICE OF SEAMEN. As applied to any case, means the ordinary practice of skilful and careful persons engaged in navigation in like cases. *Canada Shipping Act*, R.S.C. 1985, c. S-9, s. 2.

ORDINARY REMUNERATION. The remuneration paid to an employee on a pay day in respect of employment in the relevant pay period and includes fees paid to a director of a corporation if no other remuneration is payable to the director by the corporation. *Canada Pension Plan Regulations*, C.R.C., c. 385, s. 3.

ORDINARY RESIDENCE. With major regard to intention, the country that one regards as one's "real home", the place where one regularly lives and the place from which one may be temporarily absent, intending all the while to return. J.G. McLeod, *The Conflict of Laws* (Calgary: Carswell, 1983) at 183 . See PLACE OF ~.

ORDINARY RESOLUTION. 1. A resolution passed by a majority of the votes cast by or on behalf of the shareholders who voted in respect of that resolution. 2. (a) A resolution passed by the members of a company in general meeting by a simple majority of the vote cast in person or by proxy; or (b) a resolution that has been submitted to the members of a company who would have been entitled to vote on it in person

or by proxy at a general meeting of the company and that has been consented to in writing by such members of the company holding shares carrying less than 3/4 of the votes entitled to be cast on it; and a resolution so consented to shall be deemed to be an ordinary resolution passed at a general meeting of the company. *Company Act*, R.S.B.C.1996, c. 62, s. 1. 3. (a) a resolution passed in a general meeting by the members of a society by a simple majority of the votes cast in person or, if proxies are allowed, by proxy, (b) a resolution that has been submitted to the members of a society and consented to in writing by 75% of the members who would have been entitled to vote on it in person or by proxy at a general meeting of the society, and a resolution so consented to is deemed to be an ordinary resolution passed at a general meeting of the society, or (c) if a society has adopted a system of indirect or delegate voting or voting by mail, a resolution passed by a simple majority of votes cast in respect of the resolution. *Society Act*, R.S.B.C. 1996, c. 433, s. 1.

ORDINARY RETIREMENT. A retirement of depreciable plant that results from causes reasonably assumed to have been anticipated or contemplated in prior depreciation or amortization provisions. *Pipeline Uniform Accounting regulations*; Canada regulations.

ORDINARY USE. Use which is commonplace, customary, normal, regular or usual in the course of everyday life and part of the life of a family. A. Bissett-Johnson & W.M. Holland, eds., *Matrimonial Property Law in Canada* (Toronto: Carswell, 1980) at NB-12.

ORDINARY WITNESS. A witness who testifies to facts observed or experienced by him, but who is not testifying as an expert in the matter concerned. *Military Rules of Evidence*, C.R.C., c. 1049, s. 2.

ORDINARY WORKMAN. In the context of a specification refers to the hypothetical person who possesses ordinary knowledge and skill of the particular art to which an invention relates and a mind ready to understand any specification addressed to her or him. H.G. Fox, *The Canadian Law and Practice Relating to Letters Patent for Inventions*, 4th ed. (Toronto: Carswell, 1969) at 184.

ORDNANCE. See HAND CARRIED WEAPON OR PIECE OF ~.

ORE. *n*. 1. A mineral substance in natural deposit of such size, composition and situation as to allow reasonable hope of extracting therefrom, at present or in the future, products which may be sold at a profit. 2. Includes ore from a mineral resource that has been processed to any stage that is prior to the prime metal stage or its equivalent. *Income Tax Regulations*, C.R.C., c. 945, s. 1104. See MININERAL ~; PROBABLE ~; PROVEN ~.

ORE REDUCTION WORKS. Includes mines, smelters, ore roasters, ore concentrators and metal refineries, and all works, plants and processes incidental to them. *Industrial Operation Compensation Act*, R.S.B.C. 1979, c. 195, s. 1.

ORE TENUS. [L. by mouth] Verbally.

ORGAN. *n.* A means of action; an instrument; a person or body of persons by which some purpose is carried out or function performed.

ORGAN AND TISSUE BANK. A place outside a hospital centre equipped for keeping organs or tissues taken from human bodies, in view of the utilization of such organs or tissues for medical or scientific purposes. *Public Health Protection Act*, R.S.Q. 1977, c. P-35, s. 1.

ORGANIC ACID. Includes acetic acid, trichloracetic acid, lactic acid, formic acid and any combination thereof. *Hazardous Products (Hazardous Substances) Regulations*, C.R.C., c. 926, s. 2.

ORGANIC FLUID PLANT. See LOW PRESSURE ~.

ORGANIC MATTER. That substance of animal or vegetable origin remaining after removal of the moisture and total ash fractions. *Fertilizers Regulations*, C.R.C., c. 666, s. 2.

ORGANIC SOIL CONDITIONING. The incorporation of processed organic waste in the soil to improve its characteristics for crop or ground cover growth. *General — Waste Management Act*, R.R.O. 1990, Reg. 347, s. 1(1).

ORGANIC WASTE. See PROCESSED ~.

ORGANIZATION. *n.* 1. Includes a trade union or other unincorporated association. 2. (a) Any specialized agency of which Canada is a member that is brought into relationship with the United Nations in accordance with Article 63 of the Charter of the United Nations; (b) any international organization of which Canada is a member, the primary purpose of which is the maintenance of international peace or the economic or social well-being o the community of nations; and (c) any organization specified in Schedule II. *Privileges and Immunities Act*, R.S.C. 1985, c. P-23, s. 3. 3. An institution, association, society, body or other organization, the income and assets of which are not available for the personal benefit of any 'proprietor, member or shareholder. See AGRICULTURAL ~; BUSINESS ~; CENTRAL POLITICAL PARTY ~; COMPANY DOMINATED ~; CONSUMER ~; CROWN-CONTROLLED EMPLOYEE ~; EMPLOYEES' ~; EMPLOYER ~; EMPLOYERS' ~; FINANCIAL ~; FOREIGN ~; GOVERNMENTAL ~; INTERNATIONAL LABOUR ~; INTERNATIONAL ~; LABOUR ~; NON-PROFIT ~; NON-RESIDENT ~; NOT-FOR-PROFIT ~; POLITICAL ~; PRODUCER ~; PROMOTIONAL ~; RELIGIOUS ~; RE~; RESIDENT ~; SELF-REGULATORY ~.

ORGANIZED MARKET. A recognized exchange for a class of securities or a market that regularly publishes the price of that class of securities in a publication that is generally available to the public.

ORGANIZER. *n.* A person who solicits workers to become members of a union.

ORIENTATION. See SEXUAL ~.

ORIGIN. *n.* 1. Of a grievance, the point at which the union became aware of the company's position in relation to the type of grievance presented. 2. The place from which a thing comes. See COUNTRY OF ~; DOMICILE OF ~; FLOCK OF ~; HERD OF ~; NATIONAL ~; TERRITORY OF ~.

ORIGINAL. *n.* The document actually prepared, not a copy. See DUPLICATE ~.

ORIGINAL. *adj.* 1. For a compilation of data to be original, it must be a work that was independently created by the author and which displays at least a minimal degree of skill, judgment and labour in its overall selection or arrangement. *Tele-Direct (Publications) Inc. v. American Business Information Inc.* (1997), [1998] 2 F.C. 22 (C.A.). 2. To determine whether or not the materials in issue are "original" works, a principled and reasoned approach based upon evidence is required, not reliance on a particular word or phrase that merely seeks to explain the concept of originality. *CCH Canadian Ltd. v. Law Society of Upper Canada*, 2002 FCA 187, 18 C.P.R. (4th) 161, 212 D.L.R. (4th) 385, 289 N.R. 1, [2002] 4 F.C. 213, 224 F.T.R. 111 (note) (C.A.). 3. " . . . [C]ontemplates that the person has originated something, that by the exercise of intellectual activity he has started an idea which had not occurred to any one before, that a particular pattern or shape or ornament may be rendered applicable to the particular article to which he suggests that it shall be applied. . ." *Dover, Limited v. Nurnberger Celluloidwaren Fabrik Gebruder Wolff*, [1910] 2 Ch. 25 at 29, (U.K.), Buckley L.J. 4. ". . . [D]oes not in this connection mean that the work must be the expression of original or inventive thought. Copyright Acts are not concerned with the originality of ideas, but with the expression of thought, and, in the case of 'literary work,' with the expression of thought in print or writing. The originality which is required relates to the expression of the thought. But the Act does not require that the expression must be in an original or novel form, but that the work must not be copied from [sic] another work — that it should originate from the author." *University of London Press, Ltd. v. University Tutorial Press, Ltd.*, [1916] 2 Ch. 601 at 608-9 (U.K.), Peterson J.

ORIGINAL CLAIMANT. The person from whom title must be traced in order to establish a right or claim to letters patent for the lands in question. *Exchequer Court Act*, R.S.C. 1970, c. E-11, s. 2.

ORIGINAL COURT. 1. In relation to any judgment means the court by which the judgment was given. 2. The court in which the foreign judgment was obtained. *Foreign Judgments acts*. 1. The court by which the judgment was given and in relation to an award or order made by a statutory authority, includes the statutory authority. *Reciprocal Enforcement of Judgments Act*, R.S.M. 1987, c. J20, s. 1.

ORIGINAL DOCUMENT RULE. The original of a document is preferred, as evidence, to a copy. Wherever possible, the original should be produced as evidence.

ORIGINAL DOMINION POST. Any post planted to define a survey of an original allotment of land made by or under authority of the Government of Canada. *Surveys Act*, R.S.M. 1987, c. S240, s. 1.

ORIGINAL EVIDENCE. Evidence offered to prove that a statement was made, either in a document or orally, not that the statement is true. P.K. McWilliams, *Canadian Criminal Evidence*, 3d ed. (Aurora: Canada Law Book, 1988) at 113.

ORIGINALITY. *n*. The characteristic of distinctive trade marks in Canada is that they actually distinguish the wares or services of the owner from the wares or services of others or are adapted to distinguish them. *Union Carbide Corp. v. W.R. Grace & Co.* (1987), 1987 CarswellNat 657, 14 C.I.P.R. 59, 14 C.P.R. (3d) 337, 78 N.R. 124 (Fed. C.A.) Urie, J.A. for the court.

ORIGINAL JURISDICTION. Conferred on or inherent in a court and enabling it to proceed at first instance.

ORIGINAL MAXIMUM BENEFIT PERIOD. In relation to a contract of group insurance, the maximum period provided under that contract for the payment of any benefit payable thereunder in respect of loss of income.

ORIGINAL MONUMENT. A mound, post, mark or monument marked, erected, placed or planted lawfully to mark the boundaries of a township, range, section or other legal subdivision, block, gore, lot, common or other parcel of land, under this or another enactment *Land Survey Act*, R.S.B.C. 1996, c. 247, s. 11.

ORIGINAL MORTGAGOR. Any person who by virtue of privity of contract with the mortgagee is personally liable to the mortgagee to pay the whole or any part of the moneys secured by the mortgage. *Mortgages Act*, R.S.O. 1990, c. M.40, s. 20(1).

ORIGINAL PLAN. A plan certified by the Surveyor General as being the original plan of an original survey. *Surveys Act*, R.S.O. 1980, c. 493, s. 1.

ORIGINAL POST. Any object that defines a point and that was placed, planted or marked during the original survey or during a survey of a plan of subdivision registered under the Land Titles Act or the Registry Act. *Surveys Act*, R.S.O. 1990, c. S.30, s. 1.

ORIGINAL SURVEY. 1. Any original or first survey of land made by or under the authority of the Government of Canada, or any survey of land of which a plan has been or is, before or after the coming into force of the Revised Statutes, filed or registered under The Real Property Act or The Registry Act in any land titles office or registry office in Manitoba. *Surveys Act*, R.S.M. 1987, c. S240, s. 1. 2. A survey made under competent authority. *Surveys Act*, R.S.O. 1990, c. S.30, s. 1.

ORIGINATING DOCUMENT. A writ of summons, counter-claim, petition for divorce, counter-petition for divorce or originating notice that initiates an application, an originating application or a statement of claim that commences a proceeding.

ORIGINATING DRUG COMPANY. A company which engages in original research, development and marketing of pharmaceutical products.

ORIGINATING PROCESS. The document by which a proceeding is commenced. A writ of summons, a petition, and a notice of application are examples.

ORIGINATING SUMMONS. A summons by which proceedings are commenced without writ. *The Queen's Bench Act*, R.S.S. 1978, c. Q-1, s. 2.

ORIGINATOR. *n.* A person who made remarks or a series of remarks which the Crown wants to offer as evidence. P.K. McWilliams, *Canadian Criminal Evidence*, 3d ed. (Aurora: Canada Law Book, 1988) at 13-4 and 13-5.

ORIGINE PROPRIA NEMINEM POSSE VOLUNTATE SUA EXIMI MANIFESTUM EST. [L.] It is obvious that no one can, by will, get rid of one's own origin.

ORIGO MALI. [L.] The origin of malevolence.

ORNAMENTAL CONTAINER. A container that, except on the bottom, does not have any promotional or advertising material thereon, other than a trade mark or common name and that, because of any design appearing on its surface or because of its shape or texture, appears to be a decorative ornament and is sold as a decorative ornament in addition to being sold as the container of a product. Canada regulations.

ORNAMENTATION. *n.* A textile fibre or yarn that (a) is present in a textile fibre product as an integral part thereof for a decorative purpose; and (b) is or is made from a textile fibre other than the textile fibre from which the remainder of the product is made. *Textile Labelling and Advertising Regulations*, C.R.C., c. 1551, s. 25.

ORNITHOPTER. *n.* A heavier-than-air aircraft supported in flight chiefly by the reactions of the air on planes to which a flapping motion is imparted. *Canadian Aviation Regulations*, SOR/96-433, s. 101.01(1).

ORPHAN. *n.* 1. " . . . [G]enerally applied to a child who has lost both its parents, although . . . it has been held to apply to a child bereft of either. . ." *Hunter v. Dow*, [1917] 3 W.W.R. 132

at 135 (Man. K.B.), Mathers C.J.K.B. 2. A child whose parents are deceased; a child born out of wedlock is deemed an orphan if the mother is deceased. *Children's Protection Act*, R.S.P.E.I. 1974, c. C-7, s. 1. 3. With respect to a contributor, means a dependent child of a contributor who has died. 4. (a) A child who is bereft by death of his parents; (b) a child who is bereft by death of one parent and whose surviving parent has, in the opinion of the Minister or the Board, abandoned or deserted the child; or (c) a child of divorced, separated or unmarried parents who is bereft by death of his father and whose father was, at the time of his death, receiving an additional allowance in respect of that child, and which child, not being the child of any other recipient; is (d) under the age of 17 years; (e) under the age of 25 years and following and making satisfactory progress in a course of instruction approved by the Minister; (f) under the age of 21 years and prevented by physical or mental incapacity from earning a livelihood; or (g) over the age of 21 years and prevented by physical or mental incapacity from earning a livelihood, where the incapacity occurred before the child attained the age of twenty-one years or after the age of twenty-one years while following and making satisfactory progress in a course of instruction approved by the Minister. *War Veterans Allowance Act*, R.S.C. 1985, c. W-3, s. 2.

O.R. (2d). *abbr.* Ontario Reports (Second Series), 1974-.

ORTHESIS. *n.* A device fitted to a human being and intended to ensure the proper functioning of one of his members or organs or to restore proper functioning, make up for the limitations or improve the physiological capacity of one of his members or organs that has ceased to function, has never become fully developed or suffers from a congenital abnormality. *An Act respecting medical laboratories, organ, tissue, gamete and embryo conservation, and the disposal of human bodies*, R.S.Q., c. L-0.2, s. 1.

ORTHOPAEDIC APPLIANCES. Include trusses and parts, surgical supports and appliances and parts, spinal braces, sacro-iliac belts and supports, surgical weight elastic support hosiery and orthotic devices and custom-made corrective footwear, but does not include shoulder braces, athletic supports, suspensories, arch, ankle, knee and like supports, including bracer and sporter types. *General Act*, R.R.O. 1990, Reg. 1013, s. 1.

O.S. *abbr.* 1. Old Series. 2. Upper Canada, Queen's Bench Old Series, 1831-1444.

O.S.C. *abbr.* Ontario Securities Commission.

O.S.C.B. *abbr.* Ontario Securities Commission Bulletin.

OS DEMONSTRAT QUOD COR RUMINAT. [L.] The mouth divulges what the heart is thinking.

OSGOODE HALL L.J. *abbr.* Osgoode Hall Law Journal.

OSSIFICATION. *n.* The transformation of fibrous tissue or cartilage into bone. F.A. Jaffe, *A Guide to Pathological Evidence*, 3d ed. (Toronto: Carswell, 1991) at 223. See CENTRE OF ~.

OSTENSIBLE. *adj.* Apparent; professed.

OSTENSIBLE AUTHORITY. 1. " . . . [A] legal relationship between the principal and the contractor created by a representation, made by the principal to the contractor, intended to be and in fact acted upon by the contractor, that the agent has authority to enter on behalf of the principal into a contract of a kind within the scope of the 'apparent' authority, so as to render the principal liable to perform any obligations imposed upon him by such contract. To the relationship so created the agent is a stranger. He need not be (although he generally is) aware of the existence of the representation but he must not purport to make the agreement as principal himself." *Freeman & Lockyer v. Buckhurst Park Properties (Magnal) Ltd.*, [1964] 2 Q.B. 480 at 503 (U.K. C.A.), Diplock L.J. 2. Ostensible authority is the authority of an agent as it appears to others. Ostensible authority is concerned with what the outsider thinks while negotiating with the agent. *D. Fogell Associates Ltd. v. Esprit de Corp (1980) Ltd. / Esprit de Corp. (1980) Ltée* (1997), 1997 CarswellBC 1131 (S.C.), Edwards J.

OSTEOLOGY. *n.* Knowledge of the development, function and structure of bones. F.A. Jaffe, *A Guide to Pathological Evidence*, 3d ed. (Toronto: Carswell, 1991) at 223.

OSTEOPATH. *n.* Any person who practises or advertises or holds himself out in any way as practising the treatment by diagnosis, including all diagnostic methods, direction, advice, written or otherwise, of any ailment, disease, defect or disability of the human body, by methods taught in colleges of osteopathy and approved by the

Board. *Drugless Practitioners Act*, R.R.O. 1980, Reg. 250, s. 1.

OSTEOPATHY. *n.* The practice of the healing art as taught and practised in the recognized associated colleges of osteopathy. *Osteopathic Practice Amendment Act, 1979*, S.S. 1979, c. 50, s. 3.

O.T.C. *abbr.* Over the counter.

OTC CORPORATION. The Canadian Dealing Network Inc. *Toronto Stock Exchange Act*, R.S.O. 1990, c. T-15, s. 1.

OTC QUOTATION AND TRADE REPORTING SYSTEM. The quotation and trade reporting system operated by the OTC Corporation. *Toronto Stock Exchange Act*, R.S.O. 1990, c. T-15, s. 1.

OTHER ATTRIBUTE. Includes (a) in relation to a tax levy for the purpose of financing all or part of the capital cost of a service to real property; (i) the actual or estimated cost of constructing a new building (ii) the number of rooms, living units or beds in a building; or (iii) the number of persons in occupancy of a building; and (b) in relation to a tax levy for the purposes of financing all or part of the operating cost of a service to real property, such criteria as are prescribed. *Municipal Grants Act*, R.S.C. 1985, c. M-13, s. 2.

OTHER COUNSEL. The term "other counsel" in ss. 30 and 69(1) [of the *Immigration Act*, R.S.C. 1985, c. I-2] cannot be a simple repetition or another way of expressing the concept of lawyers. It is plain from the structure of the Act that this expression is used in contradistinction to the terms "barrister and solicitor." Lawyers are either barristers or solicitors, so "other counsel" must mean non- lawyers. *Law Society (British Columbia) v. Mangat*, [2001] 3 S.C.R. 113.

OTHER FRAUDULENT MEANS. In the context of fraud under section 380(1) of the Criminal Code, has been used to support convictions in a number of situations where deceit or falsehood cannot be shown. These situations include, to date, the use of corporate funds for personal purposes, non-disclosure of important facts, exploiting the weakness of another, unauthorized diversion of funds, and unauthorized arrogation of funds or property. Fraud by "other fraudulent means" does not require that the accused subjectively appreciate the dishonesty of his or her acts. The accused must knowingly, i.e. subjectively, undertake the conduct which constitutes the dishonest act, and must subjectively appreciate that the consequences of such conduct could be deprivation, in the sense of causing another to lose his or her pecuniary interest in certain property or in placing that interest at risk. *R. v. Zlatic*, [1993] 2 S.C.R. 29.

OTHER PROCEEDINGS. In the context of section 13 of the Charter which guarantees a witness protection from the use of incriminating evidence in other proceedings, a retrial of the same offence would be an example of an other proceeding.

OTTAWA L. REV. *abbr.* Ottawa Law Review (Revue de droit d'Ottawa).

OTTER OR OTHER TRAWL OF A SIMILAR NATURE. Includes a Danish seine and Scottish seine. *Fisheries Act*, R.S.C. 1985, c. F-14, s. 64(2).

OTTER TRAWL. Any large bag-type net that is dragged in the sea by a vessel or vessels for the purpose of catching fish, and includes midwater purpose and any nets of a similar nature. Canada regulations.

OTTO-CYCLE ENGINE. A type of engine that has operating characteristics that are significantly similar to those of the theoretical Otto combustion cycle. The use of a throttle during normal operation is indicative of an Otto-cycle engine. *On-Road Vehicle and Engine Emission Regulations*, SOR/2003-2, s. 1(1).

OTTO-CYCLE HEAVY-DUTY VEHICLE. A heavy-duty vehicle that is powered by an Otto-cycle engine. *On-Road Vehicle and Engine Emission Regulations*, SOR/2003-2, s. 1(1).

OUNCE. *n.* 1/16 pound or 437 1/2 grains. *Weights and Measures Act*, S.C. 1970-71-72, c. 36, schedule II. See FLUID ~; TROY ~.

OUST. *v.* To put out of possession.

OUSTER. *n.* Wrongfully being put out of possession.

OUTBOARD DESIGNATED SEATING POSITION. A designated seating position where a longitudinal vertical plane tangent to the outboard side of the seat cushion is less than 305 mm from the innermost point on the inside surface of the vehicle, which point is located vertically between the seating reference point and the shoulder reference point and longitudinally between the front and rear edges of the seat cushion. *Motor Vehicle Safety Regulations*, C.R.C., c. 1038, s. 100.

OUTDOOR ADVERTISING FACILITIES. Facilities, other than radio and television and newspapers, magazines and other periodical publications, of any person or corporation that is in the business of providing such facilities on a commercial basis for advertising purposes. *Election Finances Act*, R.S.O. 1990, c. E.7, s. 1(1).

OUTDOOR EVENT. An event held out of doors for a period of 12 consecutive hours or more for the provision of entertainment, sports or other such purpose. *Public Health Act*, R.S.P.E.I. 1988, c. P-30, s. 1.

OUTDOOR RECREATIONAL ACTIVITY. Any outdoor leisure time pursuit involving the use of natural resources and includes hunting, fishing and camping. *Travel and Tourism Act*, S.N.W.T. 1983 (1st Sess.), c. 15, s. 2.

OUTER BAR. The area outside the bar where junior barristers plead in contrast to Queen's Counsel, who plead within the bar.

OUTER DOORS. The doors intended to allow persons to obtain egress through and beyond the outside walls or structure of any public building after leaving any audience room therein. *Public Buildings Act*, R.S.M. 1970, c. P200, s. 2.

OUTER ENVELOPE. An envelope supplied by the Chief Electoral Officer for transmission to a special returning officer of the ballot paper of an elector after the ballot paper has been marked and enclosed in an inner envelope. *Special Voting Rules*, R.S.C. 1985, c. E-2, Schedule II, s. 2.

OUTER LABEL. The label on or affixed to the outside of a package. Canada regulations.

OUTER PACKAGE. A box, barrel, case or cylinder of wood, metal or other solid material, of such strength, construction and character that it will not be broken or accidentally opened, nor become defective or insecure while being conveyed, and will not allow any explosive to escape. Canada regulations.

OUTER SURFACE. An imaginary surface located above and in the immediate vicinity of the airport, which outer surface is more particularly described in the schedule. *Airport Zoning regulations*.

OUTFITTER. *n.* 1. Any individual or corporate body who provides equipment to be used in connection with an outdoor recreational activity or provides guides or guiding services or both. 2.

A person, association or organization that for money or reward operates or maintains an establishment to provide sleeping or food services to hunters or fishermen. *Game Act*, R.S.N.B. 1973, c. G-1, s. 1. 3. A person who carries on commercial river rafting.

OUTFITTER ESTABLISHMENT. See TOURIST ~.

OUTHOUSE. *n.* A building belonging to and adjacent to a dwelling-house.

OUTLAW. *n.* A person put outside the law or deprived of legal benefits by a judgment of outlawry.

OUTLAW MOTORCYCLE GANG. Term now commonly used to describe motorcycle clubs around the world which have adopted a fairly stereotyped lifestyle which the members themselves consider that of a 'righteous outlaw'. The term 'outlaw' is intended to differentiate such bikers from those who are law-abiding. *Brown v. Durham Regional Police Force* (1996), 19 M.V.R. (3d) 207 (Ont. Gen. Div.).

OUTLAWRY. *n.* A declaration which permitted the confiscation of a defendant's property, including debts owed to that person. Originally this property went to the Crown if the defendant failed to appear, and the confiscated property and debts were paid directly to creditors. A series of statutes passed in the 19th century replaced outlawry with a fairer and simpler process against debtors who are absent. C.R.B. Dunlop, *Creditor-Debtor Law in Canada* (Toronto: Carswell, 1981) at 195-196.

OUTLAY. *n.* The expending of a sum of money. See ANNUAL ~.

OUTLAY COST. A cash disbursement.

OUTLET. *n.* Any station, shop, establishment or other place in which gasoline is sold or kept for sale, by retail. See CONSUMER ~; RETAIL ~; SUFFICIENT ~; VIDEO ~; WHOLESALE ~.

OUTLET LIABILITY. The part of the cost of the construction, improvement or maintenance of a drainage works that is required to provide such outlet or improved outlet. *Drainage Act*, R.S.O. 1980, c. 126, s. 1.

OUTLINE. *n.* A summary; a precis; a drawing showing the exterior limit. See PRODUCT ~.

OUTLINE LIGHTING. An arrangement of incandescent lamps or electric discharge tubing, outlining or accentuating, certain features of buildings. *Power Corporation Act*, R.R.O. 1980, Reg. 794, s. 0.

OUTLINE MONUMENT. All survey monuments planted to define any special survey made under The Special Survey Act on the principle of a block-out-line survey; all monuments of a permanent character planted in accordance with subsection 112(4) of The Real Property Act; all monuments placed on offset lines to evidence block corners in subdivision surveys, and all monuments defining any road or main highway. *Surveys Act*, R.S.M. 1987, c. S240, s. 1.

OUT-PATIENT. *var.* **OUTPATIENT**. *n.* 1. A person who is received in a hospital for examination or treatment or both, but who is not admitted as a patient. 2. A patient who is not an inpatient. 3. A patient who is not an inpatient who is admitted to a hospital for necessary diagnostic or treatment services, but who is not assigned to a bed in the hospital.

OUTPOST CAMP. Any fixed or portable rental unit that is remote from a base of operations and accessible only by air, water or forest trails, and is used for commercial purposes. *Tourism Act*, R.R.O. 1990, Reg. 1037, s. 1.

OUTPOST ESTABLISHMENT. A tourist establishment consisting of one or more outpost camps being used for commercial purposes. *Tourism Act*, R.R.O. 1990, Reg. 1037, s. 1.

OUTPUT. *n.* 1. The act or fact of turning out; production. 2. The minerals taken or gained from the mine, and the mineral products derived from the processing of those minerals.

OUTSIZED VEHICLE. (a) A road vehicle or a combination of road vehicles the axle load, the total loaded mass, or one dimension of which does not conform to the standards established by regulation; or (b) a combination of road vehicles made up of more than four motorized road vehicles or chassis of motor vehicles, or of more than three vehicles, a detachable axle supporting a semi-trailer not being considered when calculating the number of vehicles making up the combination. *Highway Safety Code*, R.S.Q., c. C-24.2, s. 462.

OUTSTANDING. *adj.* Not yet paid; not yet claimed.

OUTSTANDING TICKET. A winning ticket that has not been cashed before the end of the racing day for which it was issued. *Pari-Mutuel*

Betting Supervision Regulations, SOR/91-365, s. 2.

OUTWORKER. *n*. A person to whom articles or materials are given out to be made up, cleaned, washed, altered, ornamented, finished, repaired or adapted for sale in that person's own home or on other premises not under the control or management of the person who gave out the articles or materials.

OVEN. See INDUSTRIAL ~; MICROWAVE ~.

OVER. *adj*. Describes a limitation whose effect is continent on a prior estate failing. See JURISDICTION ~; RELIEF ~.

OVERAGE. *n*. The amount by which the aggregate of the quantity of grain of any grade discharged from an elevator in a period between two consecutive weigh-overs of grain of that grade in the elevator and the quantity of grain of that grade in storage in the elevator at the end of that period exceeds the aggregate of the quantity of grain of that grade in storage in the elevator at the beginning of that period and the quantity of grain of that grade received into the quantity during that period. *Canada Grain Act*, R.S.C. 1985, c. G-10, s. 2.

OVERALL ASSESSMENT PER CAPITA. The quotient resulting from dividing the total of the municipal assessment bases of all municipalities by the total population of all municipalities. *Municipal Assistance Act*, R.S.N.B. 1973, c. M-19, s. 1.

OVERALL ASSESSMENT PER ROAD KILOMETRE. The quotient resulting from dividing the total of the municipal assessment bases of all municipalities by the total road kilometres of all municipalities. *Metric Conversion Act*, S.N.B. 1977, c. M-11.1, s. 18.

OVERALL LENGTH. 1. With respect to a vessel, means the horizontal distance measured between perpendiculars erected at the extreme ends of the outside of the main hull of the vessel. 2. With respect to herring, the length from the tip of the nose to the end of the caudal fin. *Atlantic Coast Herring Regulations*, C.R.C., c. 804, s. 2.

OVERALL WIDTH. 1. The nominal design dimension of the widest part of the vehicle with doors and windows closed and wheels in the straight ahead position, exclusive of signal lamps, marker lamps, outside rearview mirrors, flexible fender extensions and mud flaps. *Motor*

Vehicle Safety Regulations, C.R.C., c. 1038, s. 2. 2. The linear distance between the exteriors of the sidewalls of an inflated tire, including elevations due to labelling, decorations or protective bands. Canada regulations.

OVERBREADTH. *n*. Overbreadth and vagueness are different concepts, but are sometimes related in particular cases. [T]he meaning of a law may be unambiguous and thus the law will not be vague; however, it may still be overly broad. Where a law is vague, it may also be overly broad, to the extent that the ambit of its application is difficult to define. Overbreadth and vagueness are related in that both are the result of a lack of sufficient precision by a legislature in the means used to accomplish an objective. In the case of vagueness, the means are not clearly defined. In the case of overbreadth the means are too sweeping in relation to the objective. Overbreadth analysis looks at the means chosen by the state in relation to its purpose. In considering whether a legislative provision is over broad, a court must ask the question: are those means necessary to achieve the State objective? If the State, in pursuing a legitimate objective, uses means which are broader than is necessary to accomplish that objective, the principles of fundamental justice will be violated because the individual's rights will have been limited for no reason. The effect of overbreadth is that in some applications the law is arbitrary or disproportionate. Reviewing legislation for overbreadth as a principle of fundamental justice is simply an example of the balancing of the State interest against that of the individual. *R. v. Heywood*, 1994 CarswellBC 592, 34 C.R. (4th) 133, 174 N.R. 81, 50 B.C.A.C. 161, 82 W.A.C. 161, [1994] 3 S.C.R. 761, 94 C.C.C. (3d) 481, 24 C.R.R. (2d) 189, 120 D.L.R. (4th) 348 Cory, J. for the majority.

OVERBURDEN. *n*. All material which overlies an ore body and which must be removed before ore can be extracted.

OVERCHARGE. *v*. To charge a more serious offence than it seems is justified by the facts or to charge an offence with a fixed minimum penalty. S.A. Cohen, *Due Process of Law* (Toronto: Carswell, 1977) at 182.

OVER CURRENT DEVICE. Any device capable of automatically opening an electric circuit both under predetermined overload and short-circuit conditions, either by fusing of metal or by electro-mechanical means. *Power Corporation Act*, R.R.O. 1980, Reg. 794, s. 0.

OVERDENTURE. *n*. A dental prosthesis which replaces natural teeth, is removable by the patient and is attached to or supported by implants, or attached to, supported by or covers retained roots or natural teeth.

OVER-DIMENSIONAL FARM VEHICLE. A farm tractor, self-propelled implement of husbandry, implement of husband or any combination of them having a weight, width, length or height in excess of the limits provided in this Part or Part VII. *Highway Traffic Act*, R.S.O. 1990, c. H.8, s. 108.

OVERDOSE. *n*. Any amount of a drug taken which exceeds the maximum therapeutic dose for that particular type of person. F.A. Jaffe, A *Guide to Pathological Evidence*, 3d ed. (Toronto: Carswell, 1991) at 81.

OVERDRAFT. *n*. 1. " . . . [A]ny adverse balance in the customer's general account, whether this balance was created by charging up cheques of the customer or debiting past due bills and notes to that account. The resulting debit balance against the customer would be an 'overdraft,' . . ." *Cox v. Canadian Bank of Commerce* (1911), 18 W.L.R. 568 at 574, 21 Man. R. 1 (C.A.), Perdue J.A. 2. A situation where withdrawals exceed the amount of unencumbered deposits and approved lines of credit. *Credit Union Act*, S.S. 1984-85-86, c. C-45.1, s. 2.

OVERDUE. *adj*. Past the time a payment should be made.

OVEREXPOSURE. *n*. Exposure of a person, other than a patient undergoing medical examination or treatment, to radiation in excess of the maximum exposure limit of that form of radiation. *Radiation Protection Act*, R.S.A. 2000, c. R-2, s. 1.

OVERGRADE. *n*. An egg that meets the requirements for a higher grade than the one at which it is set. *Egg Regulations*, C.R.C., c. 284, s. 2.

OVERHAUL. *n*. A restoration process that includes the disassembly, inspection, repair or replacement of parts, reassembly, adjustment, refinishing and testing of an aeronautical product, and ensures that the aeronautical product is in complete conformity with the service tolerances specified in the applicable instructions for continued airworthiness. *Canadian Aviation Regulations*, SOR/96-433, s. 101.01(1).

OVERHEAD. *n*. The costs of operating an enterprise, costs which cannot be assigned to a particular business activity, such as rent, electricity, heating.

OVERHEAD BRIDGE. A structure, including the approaches thereto, that carries a highway across and over the railway. *Railway Grade Separations Regulations*, C.R.C., c. 119, s. 2.

OVERHEAD LINE. An overhead telephone, telegraph, telecommunication or electric power line or any combination thereof constructed across a pipeline. *Pipeline Overhead Crossing Order*, C.R.C., c. 1060, s. 2.

OVERHOLDING TENANT. A person who was a tenant of premises and who does not vacate the premises after the tenancy has expired or been terminated. *Landlord and Tenant Amendment Act, 1991*, S.A. 1991, c. 18, s. 3.

OVER-INSURANCE. *n*. On a vessel and the electronic equipment thereon means insurance on the vessel and electronic equipment in an amount exceeding the appraised value of the vessel and electronic equipment. *Fishing Vessel Insurance Regulations*, C.R.C., c. 325, s. 2.

OVER-INSURED. *adj*. An insured is over-insured by double insurance if two or more marine policies are effected by or on behalf of the insured on the same marine adventure and interest or part thereof and the sums insured exceed the indemnity allowed by this Act. *Marine Insurance Act*, S.C. 1993, c. 22, s. 86(1).

OVERISSUE. *var*. **OVER-ISSUE**. *n*. The issue of securities in excess of any maximum number of securities that the issuer is authorized by its articles or a trust indenture to issue.

OVERLAY. *v*. The action of an adult accidentally smothering a small child in a bed by rolling over onto the child.

OVERLOAD. *n*. The larger of the following: (a) the number of kilograms derived by subtracting from the gross vehicle weight of a commercial vehicle the licensed gross vehicle weight; (b) the number of kilograms derived by subtracting from the weight on any one axle or combination of axles of a commercial vehicle the weight authorized by regulation to be carried on the axle or combination of axles. *Commercial Transport Act*, R.S.B.C. 1996, c. 58, s. 1.

OVERLOAD DEVICE. A device affording protection from excess current, but not necessarily short-circuit protection, and capable of automatically opening an electric circuit either by the fusing of metal or by electro-mechanical means. *Power Corporation Act*, R.R.O. 1980, Reg. 794, s. 0.

OVERMAN. *n*. Any person who is in charge of any mine or any portion of a mine, whose authority is next to the underground manager.

OVERPAYMENT. *n*. The aggregate of all amounts paid by a person as tax or as interest or penalties, less the aggregate of all amounts payable by that person as tax, interest or penalties, or any amount so paid where no amount is so payable.

OVERRIDE. *v*. 1. Under section 33, for Parliament or a legislature to disregard a provision of the Charter included in section 2 or sections 7 to 15. This is accomplished by having the statute expressly declare that this statute will operate notwithstanding that provision. P.W. Hogg, *Constitutional Law of Canada*, 3d ed. (Toronto: Carswell, 1992) at 304-5. 2. In reference to the Charter, refers to a provision in federal or provincial legislation permitted by section 33 which states: (1) Parliament or the legislature of a province may expressly declare in an Act of Parliament or of the legislature, as the case may be, that the Act or a provision thereof shall operate notwithstanding a provision included in section 2 or sections 7 to 15 of this Charter; (2) An Act or a provision of an Act in respect of which a declaration made under this section is in effect shall have such operation as it would have but for the provision of this Charter referred to in the declaration; (3) A declaration made under subsection (1) shall cease to have effect five years after it comes into force or on such earlier date as may be specified in the declaration; (4) Parliament or the legislature of a province may re-enact a declaration made under subsection (1); (5) Subsection (3) applies in respect of a re-enactment made under subsection (4).

OVERRIDING ERROR. An error by the court which either did or may have altered the result at trial.

OVERRIDING ROYALTY. An overriding royalty or a gross overriding royalty is a royalty granted normally by the owner of a working interest to a third party in exchange for consideration which could include, but is not limited to, money or services (e.g., drilling or geological surveying). G. J. Davies, "The Legal Characterization of Overriding Royalty Interests in Oil and Gas" (1972), 10 *Alta. L. Rev.* 232, at p. 233. The rights and obligations of the two types of royalties are identical. The only difference is to

whom the royalty was initially granted. *Bank of Montreal v. Dynex Petroleum Ltd.*, [2002] 1 S.C.R. 146.

OVERRULE. *v*. To set aside an earlier decision's authority.

OVERSEAS AIR CREW. See CIVILIAN MEMBER OF ~.

OVERSEAS HEADQUARTERS STAFF. See MEMBER OF THE ~.

OVERSEAS SERVICE. Any service involving duties required to be performed outside the western hemisphere and includes service involving duties required to be performed outside Canada and the United States and the territorial waters thereof in aircraft or anywhere in a ship or other vessel, service in which is classed as "sea time" for the purpose of advancement of naval ratings, or which would be so classed were the ship or other vessel in the service of the naval forces of Canada. *War Service Grants Act*, R.S.C. 1970, c. W-4, s. 2.

OVERSEAS VETERAN. A person who has served in an active theatre of war in the armed forces, the auxiliary forces or the merchant marine of Canada or any of her allies, and who was honourably discharged therefrom. *Civil Service Act*, S.P.E.I. 1983, c. 4, s. 1.

OVERSEAS WELFARE WORKER. A person who, under the auspices of the Canadian Red Cross Society or the St. John Ambulance Brigade of Canada proceeded from Canada to serve as a welfare worker, nursing aid, ambulance or trapsport driver or member of the Overseas Headquarters Staff or in any other capacity and includes Orthopaedic Nurses selected by the Canadian Red Cross Society for service overseas with the Scottish Ministry of Health. *Civilian War Pensions and Allowances*, R.S.C. 1985, c. C-31, s. 48.

OVERSIZE. *n*. The amount derived by subtracting from the outside width, height or length of a commercial vehicle with its load, if any, the permissible outside width, height or overall length prescribed under this Act and the regulations made under it. *Commercial Transport Act*, R.S.B.C. 1996, c. 58, s. 1.

OVER-SNOW VEHICLE. A vehicle that is capable of being propelled or driven otherwise than by muscular power, that runs on tracks or skis or on tracks and skis and that is designed for operation on snow or ice. Canada regulations.

OVERT. *adj*. Open. See MARKET ~.

OVERT ACT. An act done in the open.

OVER-THE-COUNTER MARKET. Includes all trading in securities other than trades in securities that are listed and posted for trading on any stock exchange.

OVERTIME. *n*. Hours of work in excess of standard hours of work. See CLOCK ~.

OVERTIME CHARGE. An additional charge for services performed at any time other than during normal working hours.

OVERTIME RATE. A rate of pay not less than 1.5 times the regular wages of an employee. See MINIMUM ~.

OVERTURE. *n*. An opening; a proposal.

OVERT WORD. A word whose meaning is beyond doubt and clear.

OWE. *v*. Of a sum of money, to be under the obligation to pay it.

OWELTY. *n*. Equality.

OWING. *adj*. 1. Due. *Smith v. McIntosh* (1893), 3 B.C.R. 26 at 28 (S.C.), Crease J. 2. Required to be paid.

OWING OR ACCRUING. Money that is earned or owing, although not yet due or payable. *Small Claims Courts Act*, R.S.O. 1980, c. 476, s. 141.

OWN. *v*. (i) Owning in a representative capacity, such as executor, administrator or trustee; (ii) holding an option to purchase; and (iii) purchasing by way of agreement for sale.

O.W.N. *abbr*. Ontario Weekly Notes, 1909-1932.

[]O.W.N. *abbr*. Ontario Weekly Notes, 1933-1962.

OWNED. *adj*. 1. Having an interest in. 2. Beneficially owned. See CANADIAN-~; WHOLLY ~.

OWNER. *n*. 1. " . . . [H]as no definite meaning. It may refer to owners having either the whole or partial interests. It is not a legal term but must be understood from its ordinary use. It may be taken to mean any parties who have any interest. . ." *Royal Bank v. Port Royal Pulp & Paper Co.*, [1937] 4 D.L.R. 254 at 257, 12 M.P.R. 219 (N.B. C.A.), the court, per Baxter C.J. 2. "Ordinarily the word 'owner' of land means the person who holds it in fee simple, though it may be used to include one who is not the actual owner or who has an interest less than a fee simple. In the latter cases the subject matter dealt with, and the context in connection with which it is used, extend its ordinary meaning to cover other situations in particular instances; but it does not (unless possibly in special connection) mean a person without any interest in the land who is neither occupant nor in possession." *Springhill (Town) v. McLeod* (1929), 60 N.S.R. 272 at 277, [1929] 1 D.L.R. 882 (C.A.), Graham J.A. (Harris C.J., Chisholm, Jenks and Paton JJ.A. concurring). 3. Any person or body corporate entitled to any freehold or other estate or interest in land, at law or in equity, in possession, in futurity or in expectancy. 4. A person having an estate or interest in land at whose request, express or implied; and (i) on whose credit; (ii) on whose behalf; (iii) with whose privity and consent; or (iv) for whose direct benefit, work is done on or material is furnished for an improvement to the land and includes all persons claiming under that person whose rights are acquired after the commencement of the work or the furnishing of the material. 5. A person entitled to convey land and whose interest in the land is defined and whose name is specified in an instrument registered in the proper land registry office. 6. Any person who holds an immoveable as owner, usufructuary, institute of a substitution or emphyteutic lessee, or occupies Crown land under a promise of sale occupation license or location ticket. *Real Estate Assessment Act*, R.S.Q. 1977, c. E-16, s. 1. 7. Includes a person who is in possession of a motor vehicle under a contract by which that person may become the owner of the motor vehicle on full compliance with the terms of the contract. 8. In relation to a certification mark, means the person by whom the defined standard has been established. *Trade-marks Act*, R.S.C. 1985, c. T-13, s. 2. 9. Includes Her Majesty and public bodies, bodies corporate, societies, companies and inhabitants of counties, parishes, municipalities or other districts in relation to the acts and things that they are capable of doing and owning respectively. *Criminal Code*, R.S.C. 1985, c. C-46, s. 2. 10. Includes the agent, charterer by demise or master of a vessel. Canada regulations. 11. Includes (a) in respect of a vessel, the agent, charterer by demise or master of the vessel and (b) in respect of goods, the agent sender, consignee or bailee of the goods as well as the carrier of the goods to, upon, over or from a small vessel facility. Canada regulations. 12. In respect of an aircraft, means the person who has legal custody and control of the aircraft. *Canadian Aviation Regulations*, SOR/96-433, s. 101.01(1). See AMUSEMENT ~; ASSESSED ~; BENEFICIAL ~; CATTLE ~; CO-~; FOREST ~; HOME ~; INTEREST ~; LIMITED ~; LIVESTOCK ~; PART~; PROPERTY~; REAL ~; REGISTERED ~; REGISTERED ~ IN FEE SIMPLE; RESIDENT ~; ROYALTY ~; VALUE TO ~; WORKING INTEREST ~.

OWNER-BUILDER. *n*. Any person who, for personal account, carries out or has carried out building work.

OWNER DEVELOPER. (a) A person (i) who, on the date that application is made to the registrar for deposit of the strata plan, is registered in the land title office as (A) the owner of the freehold estate in the land shown on the strata plan, or (B) in the case of a leasehold strata plan as defined in section 199, the lessee of the ground lease of the land, or (ii) who acquires all the strata lots in a strata plan from the person referred to in subparagraph (i), and (b) a person who acquires all of the interest of a person who is an owner developer under paragraph (a) in more than 50% of the strata lots in a strata plan. *Strata Property Act*, S.B.C. 1998, c. 43, s. 1(1).

OWNER-OCCUPIED HOME. Of an individual is a housing unit in Canada that is owned in a taxation year or within 60 days after the end of the taxation year by the individual, whether alone or jointly with another person, and that was inhabited by the individual at any time in that year or within 60 days after the end of that year. If a housing unit in Canada is owned by a housing cooperative, "owner-occupied home" also includes a share of the capital stock of the cooperative that is owned in the taxation year or within 60 days after the end of the taxation year by the individual, whether alone or jointly with another person, if the share was acquired by the individual for the sole purpose of acquiring the right to inhabit the housing unit and that housing unit was inhabited by the individual at any time in that year or within 60 days after the end of that year. *Taxation Act*, L.R.Q., c. I-3, s. 943.

OWNER OF A COPYRIGHT. Includes the owner of the right to publish in serial form as distinct and separate from other rights of publication. *Copyright Act*, R.S.C. 1985, c. C-42, s. 24.

OWNER-OPERATOR. *n*. 1. A person who has an ownership interest in a business she operates. 2. A commercial driver who has an ownership interest in the vehicle that he drives. 3. An individual who owns and operates a commercial fishing vessel.

OWNER'S CERTIFICATE. A certificate of insurance issued to a person in respect of the ownership of a vehicle.

OWNERSHIP. *n*. 1. The most far-ranging right in rem the law allows to a person: to deal with something to the exclusion of everyone else or of everyone except one or more designated people. 2. A patentee who makes a patented article has his monopoly as patent owner and also has ownership of the thing, the right to possess. See BENEFICIAL ~; CANADIAN ~ RATE; TRANSFER OF ~.

OWNERSHIP INTEREST. In relation to a corporation, means a direct or indirect entitlement, in the event of the dissolution of the corporation, to a determinable person of the net assets thereof. *Export Development Act*, R.S.C. 1985, c. E-20, s. 36(2).

OWNERSHIP PLAN. See TIME SHARE ~.

OWNERS OF A DOCK OR CANAL. Includes any person or authority having the control and management of any dock or canal, and any ship repairer using the dock or canal, as the case may be. *Canada Shipping Act*, R.S.C. 1985, c. S-9, s. 578(4).

OWNER'S PERMIT. A permit issued to a registered owner of a motor vehicle.

OWNER'S POLICY. A motor vehicle liability policy insuring a person in respect of the ownership, use or operation of an automobile owned by her or him and within the description or definition thereof in the policy and, if the contract so provides, in respect of the use or operation of any other automobile. *Insurance acts.*

OWNER'S PORTION OF THE COST. That part or portion of the cost of a work that is to be specially assessed upon the land abutting directly on the work or upon land immediately benefited by the work.

OWNER'S SHARE OF THE COST. That portion of the cost of a work that is to be specially assessed upon the lots abutting directly on the work or upon lots benefited by the work. *The Local Improvements Act*, R.S.S. 1978, c. L-33, s. 2.

OWNER TO USES. A transferee registered under a transfer to uses.

O.W.R. *abbr.* Ontario Weekly Reporter, 1902-1916.

OXIDES OF NITROGEN. The sum of the nitric oxide and nitrogen dioxide be contained in a gas sample as if the nitric oxide were in the form of nitrogen dioxide. *On-Road Vehicle and Engine Emission Regulations*, SOR/2003-2, s. 1(1).

OXYGEN. See MEDICAL ~.

OXYGEN DEFICIENCY. With respect to the atmosphere in a confined space, means a concentration of oxygen by volume in the atmosphere that is less than 17 per cent. *Canada Confined Spaces Regulations*, C.R.C., c. 996, s. 2.

OYER. [Fr.] To hear.

OYER AND TERMINER. [Fr.] To hear and decide.

OYER DE RECORD. [Fr.] To hear the record.

OYEZ. [Fr. hear ye] Pay attention.

OYSTER-FISHING. See PUBLIC ~ AREA.

OZONE DEPLETING SUBSTANCE. A chlorofluorocarbon, a halon or any other substance that has the potential to destroy ozone in the stratosphere. *Environmental Protection Act*, R.S.O. 1990, c. E.19, s. 56.

P. *abbr.* 1. President, chief judge or chief justice of a court (Exchequer Court in Canada). 2. Pico.

[] P. *abbr.* Law Reports, Probate, 1891-1971.

PACEMAKER. *n.* A device which usually is implanted under the skin and which controls the beating of the heart by transmitting electrical impulses to the heart through an insulated wire or wires which are inserted through an artery into the heart and affixed to the heart muscle. See CARDIAC ~.

PACIFIC BLOCKADE. A blockade used as a reprisal in peacetime.

PACIFIC OCEAN. "[In the British Columbia Act, 1866 (29 & 30 Vict.), c. 67, s. 7] . . . the waters off the west coast of Vancouver Island . . ." *Canada (Attorney General) v. British Columbia (Attorney General)*, [1984] 4 W.W.R. 289 at 311, [1984] 1 S.C.R. 388, 8 D.L.R. (4th) 161, 52 N.R. 335, 54 B.C.L.R. 97, Dickson J. (Beetz, Estey and Chouinard JJ. concurring).

PACIFIC SALMON. Includes coho salmon, chinook salmon, kokanee salmon, pink salmon and any member of the genus Oncorhynchus.

PACK. *n.* Two or more dogs that are running at large.

PACKAGE. *n.* 1. Includes wrapper, carton, box, tub, crock, crate or other covering or container. 2. An inner or outer receptacle or covering used for containing, packing, wrapping or covering an agricultural product. 3. A bottle, jug, jar, keg, cask, barrel or other container or receptacle used for holding liquor. 4. Includes any container or holder ordinarily associated with wares at the time of the transfer of the property in or possession of the wares in the course of trade. *Trade-marks Act*, R.S.C. 1985, c. T-13, s. 2. See CATCHWEIGHT ~; CLOSED ~; HOME-OWNERS ~; INNER ~; OUTER ~.

PACKAGE BARGAINING. Collective bargaining in which the union or employer covers groups of proposals.

PACKAGE CHEESE. Process cheese or the product resulting from the comminuting and mixing of one or more lots of cheese without the aid of heat or emulsifying agents.

PACKAGED. See PRE-~ FOOD; PRE-~ GOODS; PRE~ PRODUCT.

PACKAGED LUMBER. Lumber of uniform lengths that are in unit loads and properly arranged and strapped for handling by mechanical means.

PACKAGE FREIGHT. Goods bagged, baled, boxed, bundled, crated, wrapped, enclosed or bound for transportation.

PACKAGING. *n.* Any receptacle or enveloping material used to contain or protect goods, but does not include a container or a means of transport.

PACKER. *n.* 1. Any person, partnership or corporation engaged in the business of slaughtering livestock. 2. A person who owns or operates an abbatoir, slaughterhouse, packing plant or other premises used for the purpose of preparing cattle for human consumption. 3. Any person who packs and grades honey for sale. 4. A vessel used only for the purpose of collecting, holding, storing or transporting fish. See TOBACCO ~.

PACKER'S YARD. Any enclosed place owned, controlled or operated by any packer or his agent and used in connection with receiving, holding or weighing livestock for slaughter or for marketing or for shipment for slaughter.

PACKET. *n.* A container for documents relating to an application made pursuant to Criminal Code section 185 or subsections 186(6) or 196(2). These documents are confidential and,

except for the authorization, are placed in this container and sealed by the judge to whom the application is made as soon as the application is determined. This packet is kept in the court's custody in a place to which the public does not have access or in any other place authorized by the judge. The packet may not be (a) opened or its contents removed except (i) to deal with an application for renewal of the authorization; or (ii) pursuant to the order of a superior court judge or a judge described in section 552. P.K. McWilliams, *Canadian Criminal Evidence*, 3d ed. (Aurora: Canada Law Book, 1988) at 1348. See MONEY ~; SMALL ~.

PACKING AND BAILING. The treatment of waste by its compression into blocks or bales and binding or sheathing the blocks with wire, metal, plastic or other material.

PACKING DEVICE. A device that, as part of a mechanical packaging system, measures a predetermined quantity of commodity without recording the measurement of each quantity of commodity measured by the device or without being operated by a person who observes or records the measurement of each quantity of commodity measured by the device. *Weights and Measures Regulations*, C.R.C., c. 1605, s. 2.

PACKING PLANT. 1. A building or place, other than a processing plant, where fish are received from commercial fishermen for the purpose of packing or assembling the fish for shipment to a market. 2. Premises in which honey is packed or graded by a packer. 3. A plant in which maple products are graded and packed.

PACT. *n.* Bargain; contract; covenant.

PACTA CONVENTA QUAE NEQUE CONTRA LEGES NEQUE DOLO MALO INITA SUNT OMNIMODO OBSERVANDA SUNT. [L.] Agreements which are neither illegal nor originate out of fraud must be observed in every respect.

PACTA DANT LEGEM CONTRACTUI. [L.] Agreements establish the law of contract.

PACTA PRIVATA JURI PUBLICO DEROGARE NON POSSUNT. [L.] Private agreements cannot restrict public right.

PACTA QUAE CONTRA LEGES CONSTITUTIONESQUE VEL CONTRA BONOS MORES FIUNT NULLAM VIM HABERE INDUBITATI JURIS EST. [L.] It is unquestioned law that agreements which go against laws and constitutions or against good morals have no force.

PACTA QUAE TURPEM CAUSAM CONTINENT NON SUNT OBSERVANDA. [L.] Agreements which contain a disgraceful cause should not be observed.

PACTA SUNT SERVANDA. [L.] Contracts should be kept.

PACTA TERTIIS NEC NOCENT NEC PROSUNT. [L.] Contracts neither impose burdens nor confer benefits on third parties.

PACTIO. *n.* Bargain; contract; covenant.

PACTIS PRIVATORUM JURI PUBLICO NON DEROGATUR. [L.] An agreement between individuals is not restricted by public right.

PACTO ALIQUOD LICITUM EST, QUOD SINE PACTO NON ADMITTITUR. [L.] By special agreement something not otherwise allowed is permitted.

PACTUM. See NUDUM ~.

PACTUM DE CONTRAHENDO. [L.] An agreement to negotiate or complete a contract.

PAD. See MOBILE HOME ~.

PAEDOPHILIA. *n.* The sexual desire or fantasies of an adult for a child; sexual behaviour of an adult with a child.

PAID. *adj.* ". . . [P]ayment is made to some one, . . ." *Western Power Co. of Canada v. Matsqui (District)*, [1934] A.C. 322 at 327, [1934] 1 W.W.R. 483, [1934] 2 D.L.R. 81 (B.C. P.C.), the board per Lord Wright. See FULLY ~.

PAID BREAK. A period when employees travel, rest, clean up or eat their meals and during which time they are generally not expected to perform any service but are paid under a provision of a collective agreement.

PAID IN. As applied to the capital stock of a company or to any of its shares, means the amount paid to it on its shares, including the premium, if any, paid on the shares, whether the shares are or are not fully paid.

PAID IN CAPITAL STOCK. As applied to a provincial company having common shares without par value, means the amount paid in on the common shares of the company.

PAID OUT. See AMOUNT ~.

PAID UP. *var.* **PAID-UP.** When applied to the capital of a company, means capital stock or shares on which there remains no liability, actual or contingent, to the issuing company.

PAID-UP CAPITAL EMPLOYED IN CANADA. The paid-up capital employed by a non-resident corporation as at the close of a fiscal year.

PAIN AND SUFFERING. Non-pecuniary general damages for every kind of emotional distress which a victim feels and which was caused by a personal injury.

PAINTER. *n.* A person who: (i) prepares and performs interior and exterior work to plaster, wallboard, wood, metal, concrete, masonry, stucco and allied materials; (ii) erects scaffolding including swing stage; (iii) prepares and performs work by steam wallpaper stripping machines and applies wall coverings, wallpaper, grass cloth, wood veneer, vinyl fabrics and allied materials; (iv) prepares and performs work by mechanical processes, blow torches, spray guns and sandblasting. See AUTOMOTIVE ~.

PAINTING. *n.* A unique artistic representation or work executed in oil-base pigments or other media such as fresco, collage, tempera or encaustic on a support such as stretched canvas, mounted paper, cardboard or other manufactured board, metal, glass, wood or silk.

PAIR. *v.* For two members with opposite opinions to agree to be absent from the House of Commons for voting during a given period or on a particular division.

PAIS. *n.* Nation. See ACT IN ~.

PALAEONTOLOGICAL OBJECT. The remains or fossil or other object indicating the existence of extinct or prehistoric animals, but does not include human remains.

PALAEONTOLOGICAL RESOURCE. A work of nature consisting of or containing evidence of extinct multicellular beings.

PALAEONTOLOGICAL SITE. A site where a fossil is found.

PALLETS. *n.* Small portable platforms upon which goods may be consolidated into individual loads for transportation or storage. *Wharfage Charges By-law*, C.R.C., c. 1066, s. 2.

PALMISTRY. *n.* Telling peoples' fortunes from lines on the palms of their hands.

PALM PRINT. An impression made on some surface by the palm of a person's hand used to identify that person.

PALPABLE ERROR. An error which can be plainly seen. *Housen v. Nikolaisen*, [2002] 2 S.C.R. 235.

PAMPHLET. See PRINTED BOOK OR ~.

PANEL. *n.* 1. A page or schedule which contains the names of jurors called to serve. 2. A list of consultants or authoritative people from whom one might seek a decision or advice. 3. The members of a tribunal who are charged with conducting a hearing or giving a decision. See CONTROL ~; DISPLAY ~; JURY ~.

PANELBOARD. *n.* An assembly of buses and connections, over-current devices and control apparatus with or without switches, or other equipment, constructed for installation as a complete unit in a cabinet. See ENCLOSED ~.

PANEL WALL. A non-loadbearing exterior masonry wall having bearing support at each storey.

PANIC HARDWARE. An approved bar or panel listed by Underwriters' Laboratories of Canada or any other approved laboratory or an approved bar or panel extending not less than two-thirds the width of the door, placed at heights suitable for the service required, and designed to cause the door to open when a pressure not in excess of 20 pounds is applied to the bar or panel in the direction of egress.

PANNELLATION. *n.* The act of assembling a jury panel.

PAPER. See BALLOT ~S; BOOKS AND ~S; BOOKS OR ~S; CHATTEL ~; COMMAND ~S; COMMERCIAL ~; ELECTION ~S; EXCHEQUER BILL ~; NOTICE ~; ORDER ~; PULP AND ~; REVENUE ~; STAMPED ~; WHITE ~.

PAPERBACK. *n.* Any printed matter other than a periodical that is published for general distribution to the public and that is not bound in a hard cover, and includes paperback books. *Paperback and Periodical Distributors Act*, R.S.O. 1990, c. P.1, s. 1(1).

PAPER BLOCKADE. A blockade which a belligerent declares but cannot or does not actually enforce.

PAPER CARRIER. A natural person who carries out home delivery of a daily or weekly newspaper for a remuneration.

PAPER MONEY. Bills of exchange, bank notes and promissory notes.

PAR. *n*. State of equality; equal value. See ABOVE ~; BELOW ~.

PARADOXICAL EFFECT. An effect caused by a drug which is opposite what was expected, e.g. excitement after taking a sedative. F.A. Jaffe, *A Guide to Pathological Evidence*, 3d ed. (Toronto: Carswell, 1991) at 81.

PARAFFIN TEST. A test, no longer considered as specific enough, for the nitrites and nitrates of gunpowder residues on skin. F.A. Jaffe, *A Guide to Pathological Evidence*, 3d ed. (Toronto: Carswell, 1991) at 223-4.

PARAGE. *n*. Equality of blood, dignity or name.

PARAGIUM. *n*. Equality of blood, dignity or name.

PARAGRAPH. *n*. 1. A section or part of an affidavit, contract, pleading, statute or will. 2. In a statute, part of a subsection.

PARALEGAL. n. A non-lawyer who, under a lawyer's supervision, performs tasks essential to the provision of legal services to clients. Usually specialized in one area of practice. Conveyancers, law clerks, and litigation clerks may be referred to as paralegals.

PARALLELISM. See CONSCIOUS ~.

PARAMOUNT. *adj*. Superior; of the highest jurisdiction.

PARAMOUNTCY. *n*. "There can be a domain in which provincial and Dominion legislation may overlap in which case neither legislation will be ultra vires if the field is clear, but if the field is not clear and the two legislations meet the Dominion legislation must prevail . . ." *Reference re Fisheries Act, 1914 (Canada), (sub nom. Canada (Attorney General) v. British Columbia (Attorney General))* [1930] A.C. 111 at 118, [1929] 3 W.W.R. 449, [1930] 1 D.L.R. 194 (P.C.), Lord Tomlin. See FEDERAL ~.

PARAMOUNT OCCUPANCY. The principle of paramount occupancy holds that when two persons occupy or use the same land at the same time assessability depends on who has the paramount occupancy or use of the land for its business. The court must determine which of the two competing occupants had the greater business interest in using the land. Three main considerations bear on this determination: first, an oc-cupant's physical presence on the land, second, any controls imposed by one occupant on the other occupant's use of the land and the purpose and effect of those controls and third, the relative significance of the activities carried out on the land to the primary business of each of the competing occupants. *Gottardo Properties (Dome) Inc. v. Toronto (City)* (1998), 111 O.A.C. 272 (C.A.).

PARAMOUNT PURPOSE TEST. " . . . [A] claim to privilege should be denied when litigation was merely one of several purposes of equal or similar importance intended to be served by the material sought to be withheld from disclosure. . . in order to have it privileged it must be shown that the document was brought into existence to be used in legal proceedings as the paramount or dominant purpose . . ." *Sgambelluri v. Canadian Indemnity Co.* (1983), 37 C.P.C. 174 at 180 (Ont. S.C.), Shea L.J.S.C.

PARAPUBLIC SECTORS. See PUBLIC AND ~.

PARAS FORMULA. General objectives of child support had previously been examined in detail by Kelly J.A. of the Ontario Court of Appeal in *Paras v. Paras* (1970), [1971] 1 O.R. 130 (C.A.). The ratio of this decision, which has become known as the "*Paras* formula," suggests that a court calculate the appropriate quantum of child support by, firstly, arriving at a sum which would be adequate to care for, support, and educate the children, and, secondly, dividing this sum in proportion to the respective incomes and resources of the parents. This formula has subsequently been used as a guideline for the determination of the amount of child support payable by a spouse after separation or divorce. *Willick v. Willick*, [1994] 3 S.C.R. 670, per L'Heureux-Dubé, J.

PARCEL. *n*. Any lot, block or other area in which land is held or into which land is divided or subdivided. See ABUTTING ~; AIR SPACE ~; INTERVENING ~; RESIDENTIAL ~; RUN-OFF ~; TAXABLE ~.

PARCEL OF LAND. 1. A lot or block within a registered plan of subdivision. 2. A quarter section of land or any smaller area owned by one person. 3. Area owned by one person, or by more persons than one as tenants in common or as joint tenants.

PARCENARY. *n*. The tenure of land by a parcener.

PARCENER. *n.* A person who, with one or more others, equally shares an estate inherited from a common ancestor.

PARCHMENT. *n.* The skin of sheep specially prepared as a surface on which to write.

PARDON. *v.* For the Crown to release a person from the punishment that person incurred for some offence.

PARDON. *n.* A pardon granted or issued by the National Parole Board. The Board may grant a pardon for certain offences prosecuted by indictment or certain service offences if the Board is satisfied that the applicant, during the period of five years, (*a*) has been of good conduct; and (*b*) has not been convicted of an offence under an Act of Parliament or a regulation made under an Act of Parliament. A pardon for certain offences punishable on summary conviction or for certain service offences shall be issued if the offender has not been convicted of an offence under an Act of Parliament or a regulation made under an Act of Parliament during the period of three years. See PLEA OF ~.

PARENS EST NOMEN GENERALE AD OMNE GENUS COGNATIONIS. [L.] Parent is the general name for every kind of blood relationship.

PARENS PATRIAE. [L.] 1. A residual jurisdiction of the court, based on necessity, which may be invoked in the best interests of a person who cannot act on his own behalf. May be relied upon where legislation fails to address an issue concerning the best interests of a child or other person needing the court's protection. 2. "As parens patriae the Sovereign is the constitutional guardian of children, but that power arises in a community in which the family is the social unit. No one would . . . suggest that the power ever extended to the disruption of that [unit] by seizing any of its children at the whim or for any public or private purpose of the Sovereign or for any other purpose than that of the welfare of one unable because of infancy to care for himself . . ." *Hepton v. Maat*, [1957] 1 S.C.R. 606 at 607, 10 D.L.R. (2d) 1, Rand J.

PARENT. *n.* 1. The father or mother of a child and includes an adoptive parent. 2. Includes, in respect of another person, any person who is under a legal duty to provide for that other person or any person who has, in law or in fact, the custody or control of that other person. 3. A person who has demonstrated a settled intention to treat a child as a member of his or her family whether or not that person is the natural parent of the child. 4. Includes a person with whom a child resides and who stands in place of the child's father or mother. 5. Includes a father, mother, grandfather, grandmother, stepfather, stepmother, a person who adopted a child, and a person who stood in loco parentis to a deceased person. 6. " . . . [T]he word 'parent' has no precise meaning in the law of companies. One can readily understand if one company is a wholly owned subsidiary of another company that the latter could be said to be the parent company. But that does not necessarily mean that the parent company controls the activities of the subsidiary. . . Before the parent is liable in law for the acts and omissions of the subsidiary, one must show that control existed and was exercised." *Hunt v. T & N plc* (1989), 38 C.P.C. (2d) 1 at 3-4, 41 B.C.L.R. (2d) 269 (C.A.), the court per Hutcheon J.A. See BIRTH ~; CHILD; DEPENDENT ~; FOSTER ~.

PARENTAGE. See COMMON ~.

PARENTAL CARE. The care and supervision of a child in the child's own home whether or not the care and supervision is provided by the child's parents.

PARENT COMPANY. A company is deemed to be another's parent company if, but only if, that other is its subsidiary.

PARENT CORPORATION. 1. A corporation that controls another corporation. 2. A corporation whose officers establish or take proceedings to establish a pension fund society under this Act. *Pension Fund Societies Act*, R.S.C. 1985, c. P-8, s. 2.

PARENT CROWN CORPORATION. A corporation that is wholly owned directly by the Crown, but does not include a departmental corporation. *Financial Administration Act*, R.S.C. 1985, c. F-11, s. 83.

PARENTERAL. *adj.* Administration of a substance to a patient directly into the blood stream.

PARENTERAL USE. Administration of a drug by means of a hypodermic syringe, needle or other instrument through or into the skin or mucous membrane.

PARENTHESIS. *n.* Any part of a sentence which, if omitted, would not harm the grammatical construction of the rest of that sentence.

PARENTICIDE. *n.* A person who murders a parent.

PARENTIS. See IN LOCO ~.

PARENT MODEL RESIDENCE. *var.* **PAR-ENT-MODEL RESIDENCE**. A building, group of buildings or part of a building where not more than two adult persons live and provide care for children on a continuous basis. *Child and Family Services Act*, R.S.O. 1990, c. C.11, s. 192.

PARES. *n.* [L.] A person's peer or equal.

PARIBUS SENTENTIIS REUS ABSOLVITUR. [L.] If opinions are equal, the defendant is acquitted.

PARI-MUTUEL DEPARTMENT. (*a*) The facilities of an association in which the pari-mutuel system is situated, and (*b*) the operations of an association related to the pari-mutuel system. *Pari-Mutuel Betting Supervision Regulations*, SOR/91-365, s. 2.

PARI-MUTUEL SYSTEM. 1. A pari-mutuel system of betting through the agency of which bets may be placed and recorded and tickets or other documents showing the amount of money bet by a bettor issued to the bettor. *Pari-Mutuel Tax Act*, R.S.M. 1987, c. P12, s. 1. 2. The manual, electro-mechanical or computerized system and all software, including the totalizator, the telephone account betting system, the on-track account betting system and the inter-track betting equipment, that are used to record bets and to transmit betting data. *Pari-Mutuel Betting Supervision Regulations*, SOR/91-365, s. 2.

PAR IN PAREM IMPERIUM NON HABET. [L.] An equal has no control over an equal.

PARI PASSU. [L.] Equally; with no preference.

PARISH. *n.* 1. Any territory erected into a parish by civil authority. *Education Act*, R.S.Q. 1977, c. I-14, s. 1. 2. A territory canonically erected as a parish or quasi-parish for the purposes of the Roman Catholic religion and the benefit of the faithful of such religion. *An Act Respecting Fabriques*, R.S.Q., c. F-1, s. 1.

PARISHIONER. *n.* A person of full age of the Roman Catholic religion who belongs to a parish or chapelry and is not a cleric assigned to administer to that parish or chapelry. *An Act Respecting Fabriques*, R.S.Q., c. F-1, s. 1. See LAND-OWNING ~.

PARK. *v.* 1. The standing of a vehicle, whether occupied or not, except when standing temporarily for the purpose of and while engaged in loading or unloading. 2. The standing of an aircraft, whether occupied or not.

PARK. *n.* 1. " . . . [A]n extended area with trees, shrubs and lawns and in itself is admirably suited for outdoor pleasures and recreation. . ." *Winnipeg (City) v. St. Vital (Rural Municipality)* (1945), [1946] 1 D.L.R. 497 at 501, [1946] S.C.R. 101, [1946] C.T.C. 123, Hudson J. 2. Any public or privately owned area that is set aside for recreational use by the public. 3. "[Land . . . thrown open by the city to the public for recreational purposes." *McErlean v. Sarel* (1987), 42 D.L.R. (4th) 577 at 591, 42 C.C.L.T. 78, 61 O.R. (2d) 396, 22 O.A.C. 186 (C.A.), Howland C.J.O., Houlden, Morden, Robins and Tarnopolsky JJ.A. See AMUSEMENT ~; CONSERVATION ~; MOBILE HOME ~; NATIONAL ~; PROVINCIAL ~; PUBLIC ~; RECREATIONAL ~; TRAILER ~; WAYSIDE ~S.

PARKING. *n.* The standing of a vehicle whether occupied or not, upon a roadway, otherwise than temporarily for the purpose of and while actually engaged in loading or unloading, or in obedience to traffic signs or signals. See PUBLIC ~ AREA.

PARKING BRAKE. A mechanism designed to prevent the movement of a stationary vehicle.

PARKING CONTROL DEVICE. A sign, marking or device, including a parking meter, used for the purpose of regulating or prohibiting the stopping, standing or parking of vehicles.

PARKING INFRACTION. Any unlawful parking, standing or stopping of a vehicle that constitutes an offence.

PARKING LANE. That portion of a primary highway between (i) the edge of the roadway to the right of the direction of traffic; and (ii) the nearest solid white line (not being the centre line) marked on the roadway.

PARKING LOT. See COMMERCIAL ~.

PARKING METER. A mechanical appliance or device placed or installed at or near a parking space for the purpose of timing, indicating, regulating and controlling the use and occupation by vehicles of such parking space.

PARKING SPACE. A space that is provided for the parking of vehicles and for which a parking meter is installed.

PARKING ZONE. A street or portion of a street or a parking lot or parking facility approved by the council for the purpose of parking vehicles and on or in which parking meters are installed and maintained to collect a fee for the use and occupation of a parking space. *Municipalities Act*, R.S.N.B. 1973, c. M-22, s. 164.

PARKLAND. *n.* Crown land constituted pursuant to this Act as a provincial park, protected area, recreation site or historic site.

PARK USE PERMIT. A licence authorizing an activity or a course of behaviour or conduct, or the occupancy, use, development, exploitation or extraction of a natural resource on or in a park.

PARK WARDEN. 1. Any official whose duties include the enforcement of regulations for the protection of forests and game. 2. A person designated by the Minister under the *Parks Canada Agency Act*, whose duties include the enforcement of the Canada National Parks Act, to be park wardens for the enforcement of this Act and the regulations in any part of Canada and for the preservation and maintenance of the public peace in parks, and for those purposes park wardens are peace officers within the meaning of the *Criminal Code. Canada National Parks Act, 2000*, S.C. 2000, c. 32, s. 18.

PARLIAMENT. *n.* 1. The Queen, the House of Commons and the Senate. 2. The Parliament of Canada. *Interpretation Act*, R.S.C. 1985, c. I-21, s. 35. 3. In Canada, this title is limited to the federal parliament. 4. A period between the Governor General's summons after a general election and dissolution by the Crown before a general election which does not exceed 5 years. A. Fraser, W.A. Dawson, & J. Holtby, eds., *Beauchesne's Rules and Forms of the House of Commons of Canada*, 6th ed. (Toronto: Carswell, 1989) at 65. See ACT OF ~; CONTEMPT OF ~; FEDERAL ~; IMPERIAL ~; LIBRARY OF ~; MOTHER OF ~S; SITTING DAY OF ~.

PARLIAMENTARY AGENT. A person who promotes private bills and conducts proceedings upon petitions against such bills. A. Fraser, W.A. Dawson & J. Holtby, eds., *Beauchesne 's Rules and Forms of the House of Commons of Canada*, 6th ed. (Toronto: Carswell, 1989) at 296.

PARLIAMENTARY COMMITTEE. A committee of the whole House, a standing or joint committee.

PARLIAMENTARY COUNSEL. See LAW CLERK AND ~.

PARLIAMENTARY GOVERNMENT. Government in which Prime Minister or Premier selects members of her or his own party elected to Parliament and perhaps others to be Ministers of the Crown. This group collectively form the Cabinet, the policy-making arm of government. The Ministers and Cabinet are responsible to Parliament for the conduct of the government. The government remains in power so long as it has the confidence of a majority of the House of Commons or the Legislature. In theory, the Privy Council or Executive Council advises the formal head of state (the Governor General or Lieutenant Governor) though, in fact, the Committee of Council, known as the Cabinet, carries out this function in most situations.

PARLIAMENTARY PRECINCTS. By tradition and practice the buildings themselves, principally the East and West Blocks, Centre Block, and the Wellington and Confederation Building. A. Fraser, W.A. Dawson, & J. Holtby, eds., *Beauchesne's Rules and Forms of the House of Commons of Canada*, 6th ed. (Toronto: Carswell, 1989) at 34.

PARLIAMENTARY PRIVILEGE. A necessary immunity provided to members of Parliament and the legislatures in order to permit those legislators to do their work. Ensures that members and the bodies themselves are free from outside interference which might prohibit them from carrying out their functions. Also provided to persons taking part in proceedings in Parliament or a legislature. The authority and power of both Houses of Parliament and of the legislatures to enforce the immunity.

PARLIAMENTARY SECRETARY. A Parliamentary Secretary to a Minister of the Crown. *Parliamentary Secretaries Act*, S.Nfld. 1982, c. 10, s. 2.

PARLIAMENT BUILDINGS. The Centre, East and West Blocks, Confederation and Wellington buildings, other nearby buildings and their parts which house office space for members, support facilities and committee rooms. A. Fraser, W.A. Dawson, & J. Holtby, eds., *Beauchesne's Rules and Forms of the House of Commons of Canada*, 6th ed. (Toronto: Carswell, 1989) at 33.

PARLIAMENT OF CANADA. The Queen, an upper house styled the Senate and the House of Commons. *Constitution Act, 1867* (U.K.), 30 & 31 Vict., c. 3, s. 17. See ACT OF THE ~.

PARLOUR. See ADULT ENTERTAIN-MENT ~; BODY-RUB ~; MILKING ~.

PAROCHIAL BODY. A fabrique as well as a body holding a church or a public chapel used for Roman Catholic worship. *Roman Catholic Cemetery Corporations Act*, R.S.Q. 1977, c. C-69, s. 1.

PARODY. *n*. A new literary, musical, or artistic work which mimics and mocks the style and ideas of an original.

PAROL. *adj*. Verbal, oral.

PAROL AGREEMENT. An oral agreement.

PAROL CONTRACT. An oral contract.

PAROLE. *n*. System to allow release of prisoners before the expiration of their full sentence on a part-time or full-time basis. Federal and provincial parole boards make the decisions regarding granting of parole. 2. Full parole or day parole. *Corrections and Conditional Release Act, 1992*, S.C. 1992, c. 20, s. 2. See DAY ~.

PAROLE. *adj*. [Fr.] Oral.

PAROLE BOARD. See NATIONAL ~; PROVINCIAL ~.

PAROLED INMATE. A person to whom parole has been granted.

PAROLEE. *n*. An inmate who has been granted parole.

PAROLE SUPERVISOR. A person charged with the guidance and supervision of a paroled inmate or of an inmate who is subject to mandatory supervision.

PAROL EVIDENCE. Oral testimony by a witness.

PAROL EVIDENCE RULE. " . . . [I]f there be contract which has been reduced into writing, verbal evidence is not allowed to be given of what passed between the parties, either before the written instrument was made, or during the time that it was in the state of preparation, so as to add to or subtract from, or in any manner to vary or qualify the written contract; but after the agreement has been reduced into writing, it is competent to the parties, at any time before breach of it, by a new contract not in writing, either altogether to waive, dissolve, or annul the former agreements, or in any manner to add to, or subtract from, or vary or qualify the terms of it, and thus to make a new contract; which is to be proved, partly by the written agreement, and partly by the subsequent verbal terms engrafted upon what will be thus left of the written agreement. . ." *Goss v. Lord Nugent* (1833), 5 B. & Ad. 58 at 64-5, 110 E.R. 713 at 716 (U.K.), Denman C.J.

PARRICIDE. *n*. The murder of a father.

PARS PRO TOTO. [L.] The name of one part which represents the whole.

PARS RATIONABILIS. [L.] A rational part.

PARS SOLI. [L.] Part of the soil.

PART. *n*. 1. A portion of a whole. 2. A class into which parties to a formal instrument are divided according to their interests or estates in the subject-matter. See CONSTITUENT ~; COUNTER~; ESSENTIAL ~S; MOVING ~S; OPERATIVE ~; UNUSED ~.

PARTIAL. *adj*. 1. Less than total or less than whole. 2. Not indifferent.

PARTIAL ACCEPTANCE. Willingness to pay only a part of the amount of a bill.

PARTIAL DENTURE. A dental prosthesis which is removable by the patient, restores one or more natural teeth or associated structures, and is supported in part by natural teeth, crowns, or mucosa.

PARTIAL DISABILITY. Unable to perform all of one's duties as those duties existed prior to injury or disease.

PARTIAL DISCHARGE. See DISCHARGE AND ~.

PARTIALITY. *n*. 1. Section 638(1)(*b*) of the [*Criminal Code*, R.S.C. 1985, c. C-46] permits a party to challenge for cause on the ground that "a juror is not indifferent between the Queen and the accused". Lack of indifference may be translated as "partiality". Both terms describe a predisposed state of mind inclining a juror prejudicially and unfairly toward a certain party or conclusion. *R. v. Find*, 2001 CarswellOnt 1702, 2001 SCC 32, 146 O.A.C. 236, McLachlin C.J.C., for the court. 2. Has both an attitudinal and a behavioural component, referring to one who has biases and who will allow those biases to affect his or her verdict.

PARTIAL LOSS. 1. " . . . [O]ne in which the insurers are liable to pay an amount less than that insured for damage happening to the subject, or expense incurred and occasioned by the perils insured against." *Mowat v. Boston Marine Insurance Co.* (1895), 33 N.B.R. 108 at 121 (C.A.),

Tuck J.A. 2. Of insured property means any loss of the property that is less than total loss thereof.

PARTIALLY SMOOTH WATERS. Minor waters of Canada, and waters of a home-trade voyage, Class IV within the meaning of the *Home-Trade, Inland and Minor Waters Voyages Regulations. Marine Certification Regulations*, SOR/97-391, s. 1.

PARTIAL MEDICAL TEACHING HOSPITAL. A hospital which provides a post-graduate education program in at least one medical specialty.

PARTIAL PRIVATIVE CLAUSE. One which fits into the overall process of evaluation of the factors to determine the legislator's intended degree of deference and does not have the preclusive effect of a full privative clause.

PARTICEPS CRIMINIS. [L.] "...[O]ne who shares or co-operates in a criminal offence..." *R. v. Morris*, (1979) 10 C.R. (3d) 259 at 281, [1979] 2 S.C.R. 1041, 26 N.B.R. (2d) 273, 55 A.P.R. 273, 27 N.R. 313, 47 C.C.C. (2d) 257, 99 D.L.R. (3d) 420, Spence J. (dissenting) (Laskin C.J.C., Dickson and Estey JJ. concurring).

PARTICEPS FRAUDIS. [L.] One who shares in fraud.

PARTICIPANT. *n.* 1. A person who is entitled to designate another person to receive a benefit payable under a plan on the participant's death. 2. A person who is participating in a plan established by an employer or a trust company and who in the case of a plan established by an employer (i) is or has been employed by the employer; or (ii) is an agent or former agent of the employer. 3. Any person against whom proceedings have been instituted under this Act and in the case of a prosecution means any accused and any person who, although not accused, is alleged in the charge or indictment to have been a co-conspirator or otherwise party or privy to the offence charged. *Competition Act*, R.S.C. 1985, c. C-34, s. 69. See AGENT OF A ~; CONDITIONAL ~; PUBLIC SERVICE ~; REGULAR FORCE ~; SYSTEM ~.

PARTICIPANT SURVEILLANCE. See CONSENT SURVEILLANCE.

PARTICIPATE. *v.* "...[T]o take part or share..." *Graham, Re*, [1945] 3 W.W.R. 713 at 717, [1946] 1 D.L.R. 357 (Alta. C.A.), the court per Harvey C.J.A.

PARTICIPATED. *v.* Within the context [of the Canada Agricultural Products Act] means took part in or was privy to. *R. v. A & A Foods Ltd.* (1997), 1997 CarswellBC 2541, 120 C.C.C. (3d) 513 (S.C.).

PARTICIPATING EMPLOYER. In relation to a multi-employer pension plan, means an employer who is required to contribute to that plan. *Pension Benefits Standards Act*, R.S.C. 1985 (2d Supp.), c. 32, s. 2.

PARTICIPATING LIFE INSURANCE POLICY. A life insurance policy under which the policyholder is entitled to share (other than by way of an experience rating refund) in the profits of the insurer other than profits in respect of property in a segregated fund. *Income Tax Act*, R.S.C. 1985, c. 1 (5th Supp.), s. 138(12)(k).

PARTICIPATING POLICY. A policy issued by a company that entitles its holder to participate in the profits of the company. *Insurance Companies Act, 1991*, S.C. 1991, c. 47, s. 2.

PARTICIPATING PROVINCE. A province in respect of which there is in force a reciprocal taxation agreement entered into with the government of that province. *Federal-Provincial Fiscal Arrangements Act*, R.S.C. 1985, c. F-8, s. 31.

PARTICIPATING SECURITY. A security issued by a body corporate other than a security that is, in all circumstances, limited in the extent of its participation in earnings and includes, (a) a security currently convertible into such a security, and (b) currently exercisable warrants entitling the holder to acquire such a security or such a convertible security. *Business Corporations Act*, R.S.O. 1990, c. B.16, s. 190.

PARTICIPATION. See TRACT ~.

PARTICIPATION AGREEMENT. An agreement by a bank making a large loan to syndicate the loan to other banks to spread the risk.

PARTICIPATION MORTGAGE. A mortgage in which the lender shares in any increased value of the property over the term or shares income from the property with the borrower. D.J. Donahue & P.D. Quinn, *Real Estate Practice in Ontario*, 4th ed. (Toronto: Butterworths, 1990) at 233.

PARTICLE ACCELERATOR. Equipment that is capable of imparting high kinetic energy to charged particles through interaction with electric or magnetic fields and is primarily designed to produce or use in its operation atomic energy and prescribed substances.

PARTICULA. *n*. [L.] A small parcel of land.

PARTICULAR AGENT. " . . . [O]ne who is given authority to deliver a particular message or buy a particular thing on one occasion or do some special thing, and has no implied authority aliunde from his position or the nature of his business. . ." *McLaughlin v. Gentles* (1919), 46 O.L.R. 477 at 485, 51 D.L.R. 383, 17 O.W.N. 245 (C.A.), the court per Hodgins J.A.

PARTICULAR AVERAGE. See FREE FROM ~.

PARTICULAR ESTATE. An estate carved out of fee simple.

PARTICULARITY. *n*. In an affidavit or pleading, the allegation of details or particulars.

PARTICULAR LIEN. A right to retain the chattels upon which materials and labour have been expended until all charges incurred are paid.

PARTICULARS. *n*. 1. In a pleading, the details of an allegation which are ordered (1) to define any issues; (2) to prevent surprise; (3) to enable the parties to get ready for trial and (4) to facilitate a hearing. *Fairbairn v. Sage* (1925), 56 O.L.R. 462 at 470 (C.A.), Ferguson J.A. 2. "The function of particulars in a criminal trial is twofold. Primarily their function is to give such exact and reasonable information to the accused respecting the charge against him as will enable him to establish fully his defence. The second purpose is to facilitate the adminstration of justice: . . ." *R. v. Canadian General Electric Co.* (1974), 16 C.P.R. (2d) 175 at 184, 17 C.C.C. (2d) 433 (Ont. H.C.), Pennell J. 3. " . . . [G]iven to supplement paragraphs of a statement of claim or a defense as the case may be and should stand by themselves in connection with the paragraphs which they particularize without any reference to the evidence supporting them. *Cercast Inc. v. Shellcast Foundaries Inc. (No. 3)* (1973), 9 C.P.R. (2d)18 at 29, [1973] F.C. 28 (T.D.), Walsh J.

PARTICULAR SOCIAL GROUP. In the context of convention refugees, three possible categories are: (1) groups defined by an innate or unchangeable characteristics; (2) groups whose members voluntarily associate for reasons so fundamental to their human dignity that they should not be forced to forsake the association; and (3) groups associated by a former voluntary status, unalterable due to its historical permanence. The first category would embrace individuals fearing persecution on such bases as gender, linguistic background and sexual orientation, while the second would encompass, for example, human rights activists. The third branch is included more because of historical intentions, although it is also relevant to the antidiscrimination influences, in that one's past is an immutable part of the person. *Ward v. Canada (Minister of Employment & Immigration)*, (sub nom. *Canada (Attorney General) v. Ward*) [1993] 2 S.C.R. 689.

PARTICULAR TENANT. The one who owns a particular estate.

PARTICULATE. *n*. Solid particles.

PARTICULATE COLLECTION EFFICIENCY. The amount of solid particles that is removed from the effluent gas stream, expressed as a percentage of the total particulate in the uncontrolled effluent gas stream on a weight basis. *Environmental Protection Act*, R.R.O. 1990, Reg. 336, s. 1.

PARTIES. *n*. 1. In any act or deed, the people concerned; litigants. 2. (a) In relation to collective bargaining or arbitration of a dispute, the employer and a bargaining agent, and (b) in relation to a grievance, the employer and the employee who presented the grievance. 3. (a) In relation to the entering into, renewing or revising of a collective agreement and in relation to a dispute, the employer and the bargaining agent that acts on behalf of his employees; (b) in relation to a difference relating to the interpretation, application, administration or alleged contravention of a collective agreement, the employer and the bargaining agent; and (c) in relation to a complaint to the Board under this Part, the complainant and any person or organization against whom or which a complaint is made. *Canada Labour Code*, R.S.C. 1985, c. L-2, s. 3. See CHANGE OF ~; JOINDER OF ~; PARTY.

PARTIES TO AN OFFENCE. 1. Every one is a party to an offence who actually commits it, does or omits to do anything for the purpose of aiding any person to commit it, or abets any person in committing it. *Criminal Code*, R.S.C. 1985, c. C-46, s. 21. 2. Each person who is one of two or more persons who formed an intention in common to carry out an unlawful purpose when an offence is committed by any one of them in carrying out the unlawful purpose and the person knew or ought to have known that the commission of the offence would be a probable consequence of carrying out the common purpose is a party to any offence. *Criminal Code*, R.S.C. 1985, c. C-46, s. 21.

PARTISAN POLITICAL CHARACTER. Intended to favour one candidate or party in an election over another or others.

PARTITION. *n*. 1. Division. 2. A proceeding involving dividing real property, previously owned by tenants in common or joint tenants, into different parts. 3. An interior wall one storey or part-storey in height that is not loadbearing. *Building Code Act, 1992*, O. Reg. 403/97, s. 1.1.3.

PARTITION OR SALE. The name of a proceeding concerning division of land.

PARTLY MANUFACTURED GOODS. (a) Goods that are to be incorporated into or form a constituent or component part of an article that is subject to the consumption or sales tax; or (b) goods that are to be assembled, blended, mixed, cut to size, diluted, bottled, packaged, repackaged or otherwise prepared for sale as an article that is subject to the consumption or sales tax, other than goods that are so prepared in a retail store for sale in that store exclusively and directly to consumers, and the Minister is the sole judge as to whether or not goods are partly manufactured goods. *Excise Tax Act*, R.S.C. 1985, c. E-15, s. 42.

PARTLY PROCESSED TIMBER. Timber which has not undergone all the treatments or all the phases of processing necessary to make it suitable for the use for which it is intended.

PARTNER. *n*. A member of a partnership. See GENERAL ~; NOMINAL ~; SILENT ~.

PARTNERS', DIRECTORS' AND SENIOR OFFICERS' QUALIFYING EXAMINATION. An examination prepared and conducted by the Canadian Securities Institute and so designated by that Institute.

PARTNERSHIP. *n*. 1. A contractual relationship, an agreement, between two or among more persons to run a business together in order to make a profit. Only persons who intend to or by their conduct can be seen to have intended to can become partners. 2. ". . . [T]here should be some common profit or gain to be derived from it. Whether or not the element of division or distribution of the common profit or gain among the members is an essential, need not be discussed; but there must be . . . a community of interest in the benefits accruing from the joint activity of the partners. If that community of interest is lacking, there is no partnership. . ." *Ottawa Lumbermen's Credit Bureau v. Swan*, [1923] 4 D.L.R. 1157 at 1163, 53 O.L.R. 135 (C.A.), Orde J.A. See AGRICULTURAL OPERATIONS ~; LIMITED ~; LIMITED LIABILITY ~; QUASI ~.

PARTNERSHIP PROPERTY. Property and rights and interests in property originally brought into the partnership stock, or acquired, whether by purchase or otherwise, on account of the firm, or for the purposes of and in the course of the partnership business.

PART-OWNER. *n*. A person entitled to property in common, jointly or in coparcenary.

PART PAYMENT. ". . . [P]ayment . . . made on account of a greater debt, . . ." *Stark v. Sommerville* (1918), 41 D.L.R. 496 at 496, 41 O.L.R. 591 (C.A.), the court per Meredith C.J.C.P.

PART PERFORMANCE. In relation to a contract, partial completion.

PART-TIME. *adj*. 1. In relation to an employee, means engaged to work on other than a full-time basis. 2. Employed for irregular hours of duty or for specific intermittent periods or both 3. Employed to work less than the full number of regular working hours or less than the full number of regular working days per week.

PART-TIME BASIS. In relation to an employee, means engaged to work on other than a full-time basis. *Pension Benefits Standards Act*, R.S.C. 1985 (2d Supp.), c. 32, s. 2.

PART-TIME EMPLOYEE. *var.* **PART TIME EMPLOYEE**. 1. A person employed for irregular hours of duty or for specific intermittent periods, or both, during a day, week, month or year and whose services are not required for the normal work day, week, month or year, as the case may be. 2. A person who is regularly employed to work less than the full number of working hours in each working day or less than the full number of regular working days in each month.

PARTUS SEQUITUR VENTREM. [L.] The offspring follow the dam. Offspring of all domestic animals belong to the owner of the mother.

PART-WINDING START MOTOR. A motor whose starting entails the energizing of part of its primary winding as a first step and the energizing of the remainder of this winding as the next step or steps.

PARTY. *n*. 1. A person by or against whom a legal suit is brought. 2. A political party registered under an Election Act. 3. A person whose rights will be varied or affected by the exercise of a statutory power or by an act or thing done pursuant to that power. 4. A person bound by a collective agreement, or involved in a dispute. See ACCOMMODATION ~; ACT OF THE ~; ADVERSE ~; CHARTER ~; CONTRACTING ~; INTERESTED ~; OPPOSITE ~; PARTIES; PERMANENT OFFICE OF AN AUTHORIZED ~; POLITICAL ~; RECOGNIZED ~; REGISTERED ~; RESPONDING ~; RESTRICTED ~; SECURED ~; THIRD ~.

PARTY-AND-PARTY COSTS. *var.* **PARTY AND PARTY COSTS**. 1. "The fundamental principle of party and party costs has always been that they are given as an indemnity to the party entitled to them." *Kendall v. Hunt No. 2* (1979), 12 C.P.C. 264 at 267, 16 B.C.L.R. 295, 106 D.L.R. (3d) 277 (C.A.), Craig J.A. 2. These represent only a partial indemnity, calculated from a prescribed tariff designed to strike the proper balance between the burden of costs which must be borne by a successful litigant, and the risk of putting litigation beyond the reach of a potential loser. *Holloway v. Holloway*, 2001 NFCA 17, 199 Nfld. & P.E.I.R. 1, 600 A.P.R. 1, 6 C.P.C. (5th) 34 (C.A.).

PARTY AUTHORITY. The organization of a political party at the level of an electoral division, of a region or of Québec.

PARTY UNDER DISABILITY. A general term which includes those declared by a court incapable of managing their affairs, minors, absentees and mental incompetents whether or not declared so by a court.

PARTY WALL. 1. " . . . [M]ay . . . be used in four different senses. First, a wall of which the two adjoining owners are tenants in common . . . that is the most common and the primary meaning of the term. [Secondly,] a wall divided longitudinally into two strips, one belonging to each of the neighbouring owners. . . thirdly, . . . a wall which belongs entirely to one of the adjoining owners, but is subject to an easement or right in the other to have it maintained as a dividing wall between the two tenements; [and fourthly,] a wall divided longitudinally into two moieties, each moiety being subject to a cross easement in favour of the owner of the other moiety." *Watson v. Gray* (1880), 14 Ch. D. 192 at 195 (U.K.), Fry J. 2. A wall jointly owned and jointly used by 2

parties under easement agreement or by right in law, and erected at or upon a line separating 2 parcels of land each of which is, or is capable of being, a separate real-estate entity. *Building Code Act, 1992*, O.Reg. 403/97, s. 1.1.3.

PARUM DIFFERUNT QUAE RE CONCORDANT ET CUM ADSUNT TESTIMONIA RERUM QUID OPUS EST VERBIS? [L.] Things which agree substantially differ too little, and when the witnesses to the facts agree, what is the use for words?

PARUM EST LATAM ESSE SENTENTIAM NISI MANDETUR EXECUTIONI. [L.] It is not enough that a judgment be proclaimed if it is not carried out.

PARUM PROFICIT SCIRE QUID FIERI DEBET SI NON COGNOSCAS QUOMODO SIT FACTURUM. [L.] It is not enough to know what should be done if you do not know how to do it.

PAR VALUE. 1. The face value of a share or security, as opposed to its market or selling price. 2. An arbitrary value placed on a share at the time of issue. See NO ~; SHARES WITHOUT ~.

PASS. *v*. 1. To transfer or to be transferred. 2. To change hands. *Wagstaff, Re*, [1941] O.R. 71 at 77, [1941] D.L.R. 108 (H.C.), Roach J. 3. For a legislature to give final approval to an act. 4. To bring into court an account for approval. 5. Of a by-law, to deliberate on the merits of a proposal framed as a draft by-law and finally to adopt it as the law of the municipal corporation. A by-law is considered passed when the enacting is finished and the presiding officer announces that the motion for final reading has been carried. I.M. Rogers, *The Law of Canadian Municipal Corporations*, 2d ed. (Toronto: Carswell, 1971-) at 458. See PROPERTY ~ING ON THE DEATH.

PASS. *n*. A written authorization or permit issued by an issuing authority permitting the person named therein to enter upon or into a property.

PASSAGE. *n*. 1. " . . . [C]oming into operation. . ." *Winnipeg (City) v. Brock* (1911), 20 Man. R. 669 at 683, 18 W.L.R. 28 (C.A.), Perdue J.A. (Cameron J.A. concurring). 2. The easement to pass over a body of water. See INNOCENT ~.

PASS AN ACCOUNT. For a court to approve an account.

PASS BOOK. See BANK ~.

PASSENGER. *n*. 1. A person carried on a vessel by the owner or operator, other than the crew. 2. The word "passenger", [in s. 224(1) of the *Insurance Act*, R.S.O. 1990, c. I.8] like the word "driver" identifies a status rather than a physical activity. . . It does not follow that the person is *only* to be considered a passenger while he or she is *actually* being conveyed. *McIntyre Estate v. Scott* (2003), 178 O.A.C. 44 (C.A.). 3. A person, other than a crew member, who is carried on board an aircraft; *Canadian Aviation Regulations* SOR 96-433, s. 101.01.

PASSENGER CAR. A motor vehicle that has a seating capacity of 10 or less.

PASSENGER CHARGE. A toll imposed on an ocean-going vessel in respect of a passenger of the vessel.

PASSENGER SERVICE. See RAILWAY ~;

PASSENGER SHIP. A ship carrying passengers. *Canada Shipping Act*, R.S.C. 1985, c. S-9, s. 2.

PASSENGER SPACE. Space provided for the use of passengers.

PASSENGER STEAMSHIP. (a) In the case of a Safety Convention ship, a steamship that carries more than 12 passengers, and (b) in the case of any other ship, a steamship that carries any number of passengers. Canada regulations.

PASSENGER TRADE. See SPECIAL ~.

PASSENGER TRANSPORT. The transportation of passengers for reward by bus or by any other means of transportation except taxi.

PASSENGER VEHICLE. A motor vehicle, other than a minibus, designed for the transportation of not more than nine occupants at a time. See COMMERCIAL ~; LIMITED ~; MULTI-PURPOSE ~; PRIVATE ~; PUBLIC ~.

PASSIM. *adv*. [L.] In different places.

PASSING OFF. Every one commits an offence who, with intent to deceive or defraud the public or any person, whether ascertained or not, (a) passes off other wares or services as and for those ordered or required; or (b) makes use, in association with wares or services, of any description that is false in a material respect regarding (i) the kind, quality, quantity or composition, (ii) the geographical origin, or (iii) the mode of the manufacture, production or performance of those wares or services. *Criminal Code*, R.S.C. 1985, c. C-46, s. 408.

PASSIVE ACQUIESCENCE. Occurs when the aggrieved parent allows enough time to pass without insisting on summary return. *Katsigiannis v. Kottick-Katsigiannis* (2001), 55 O.R. (3d) 456 (C.A.).

PASSIVE TRUST. A trust for which a trustee need perform no active duty.

PASSIVE USE. Permissive use.

PASS OFF. 1. " . . . [T]he gist of the action of 'passing off' is that the defendant is attempting to sell its wares, services or business under a description which would mislead customers of the plaintiff into thinking that they were buying the plaintiff's wares or doing business with the plaintiff." *Westfair Foods Ltd. v. Jim Pattison Industries Ltd.* (1990), 30 C.P.R. (3d) 174 at 179, 45 B.C.L.R. (2d) 253, 68 D.L.R. (4th) 481, [1990] 5 W.W.R. 484 (C.A.), the court per Wallace J.A. 2. "To succeed in a passing-off action, the plaintiff must first establish that there is a distinguishing feature to his goods and that his goods are known and have acquired a reputation by reason of that distinguishing feature. Secondly, the plaintiff must show that the defendant passed off his goods for those of the plaintiff: . . ." *Ayerst, McKenna & Harrison Inc. v. Apotex Inc.* (1983), 72 C.P.R. (2d) 57 at 66, 41 O.R. (2d) 366, 146 D.L.R. (3d) 93 (C.A.), the court per Cory J.A. 3. Where goodwill or reputation is attached to the plaintiff's wares or services and identifies the plaintiff's name with the wares or services, to misrepresent the facts in a manner that leads or is likely to lead the public to believe that the wares or services are those of the plaintiff or the plaintiff's authorized representative and to cause damage to the plaintiff or create a situation which is likely to cause damage to the plaintiff.

PASSPORT. *n*. A document issued by or under the authority of the Minister of Foreign Affairs for the purpose of identifying the holder thereof. *Criminal Code*, R.S.C. 1985, c. C-46, s. 57 (5). See FORGERY OF ~; UTTERING FORGED ~.

PASSWORD. See COMPUTER ~.

PAST CONSIDERATION. Consideration for services already performed which do not support a promise or create a contract which may be enforced. G.H.L. Fridman, *The Law of Contract in Canada*, 2d ed. (Toronto: Carswell, 1986) at 96.

PAST COST OF INSURED SERVICES. The total cost of the insured services made necessary as the result of an injury and provided to a patient up to and including the date of settlement or, where there is no settlement, the first day of trial. *Health Insurance Act*, R.S.O. 1990, c. H.6, s. 1.

PAST DEBT. A debt which existed before some legal act relating to it was passed.

PASTEURIZATION. *n*. Subjecting every particle of milk in such manner as is required by the regulations to a temperature and for a time prescribed by the regulations.

PASTEURIZED. *adj*. 1. In relation to dairy products, means the treatment for the purpose of the destruction of harmful bacteria. 2. In relation to honey, means treated in a registered pasteurizing plant by the controlled application of heat so that the honey is free of viable sugar-tolerant yeasts.

PASTEURIZING. *n*. The treatment of extracted honey by the controlled application of heat to a point where it is free of viable sugar-tolerant yeasts.

PASTOR. *n*. The cleric entrusted with the administration of a parish.

PAST SERVICE CREDIT. A credit toward a pension given to an employee for a period of employment prior to implementation of a pension plan.

PASTURE. *n*. An area of land fenced for the purpose of grazing animals. See COMMON OF ~; COMMUNITY ~; HAY AND ~.

PAT. APP. BD. *abbr*. Patent Appeal Board.

PAT. COMMR. *abbr*. Commissioner of Patents.

PAT DOWN SEARCH. The patting down of outside clothing, examining of pocket contents, lasting briefly, to determine if the person has a weapon or contraband on their person.

PATENT. *n*. 1. A method by which inventive solutions to practical problems are coaxed into the public domain by the promise of a limited monopoly for a limited time. *Apotex Inc. v. Wellcome Foundation Ltd*., [2002] 4 S.C.R. 153. 2. Letters patent for an invention. Every patent granted under this Act shall contain the title or name of the invention, with a reference to the specification, and shall, subject to this Act, grant to the patentee and the patentee's legal representatives for the term of the patent, from the granting of the patent, the exclusive right, privilege and liberty of making, constructing and using the invention and selling it to others to be used, subject to adjudication in respect thereof before any court of competent jurisdiction. *Patent Act*, R.S.C. 1985, c. P-4, *ss*. 2 and 42. 3. A grant from the Crown in fee simple or for a less estate under the Great Seal. See LETTERS ~.

PATENT AGENT. 1. A register of patent agents shall be kept in the Patent Office on which shall be entered the names of all persons and firms entitled to represent applicants in the presentation and prosecution of applications for patents or in other business before the Patent Office. *Patent Act*, R.S.C. 1985, c. P-4, s. 15. 2. A person knowledgeable in the technology of the patents they draft and in legal issues relating thereto.

PATENT AMBIGUITY. Something clearly doubtful in the text of an instrument.

PATENT APPLICATION. The Commissioner shall grant a patent for an invention to the inventor or the inventor's legal representative if an application for the patent in Canada is filed in accordance with this Act and all other requirements for the issuance of a patent under this Act are met. The prescribed application fee must be paid and the application must be filed in accordance with the regulations by the inventor or the inventor's legal representative and the application must contain a petition and a specification of the invention. *Patent Act*, R.S.C. 1985, c. P-4, s. 27.

PATENT DEFECT. A defect which a purchaser is likely to discover if she inspects the subject property with ordinary care.

PATENTED ARTICLE. Includes articles made by a patented process. *Patent Act*, R.S.C. 1985, c. P-4, s. 65(5).

PATENTED LANDS. Those tracts of land in the Province in respect of which Canada accepted surrenders of their rights and interests therein from the Indians entitled to the use and occupation thereof and in respect of which grants were made by Letters Patent issued under the Great Seal of Canada. *Indian Lands Act*, R.S.N.S. 1989, c. 219, Schedule, s. 1.

PATENTEE. *n*. 1. The person for the time being entitled to the benefit of a patent. *Patent Act*, R.S.C. 1985, c. P-4, s. 3. 2. Includes grantee.

PATENT INFRINGEMENT. 1. The correct test is: whether persons with practical knowledge and experience of the kind of work in which the invention was intended to be used, would understand that strict compliance with a particular descriptive word or phrase appearing in a claim was intended by the patentee to be an essential requirement of the invention so that any variant would fall outside the monopoly claimed, even though it could have no material effect upon the way the invention worked. (formulated by Lord Diplock in *Catnic Components Ltd. v. Hill & Smith Ltd.* (1981), [1982] R.P.C. 183 (U.K. H.L.)) *Bourgault Industries Ltd. v. Flexi-Coil Ltd.* (1998), 141 F.T.R. 268, 80 C.P.R. (3d) 1 (T.D.). 2. Any act that "interferes with the full enjoyment of the monopoly granted": *Lishman v. Erom Roche Inc.* (1996), 68 C.P.R. (3d) 72 (Fed. T.D.) . . . [T]he definition of infringement as stated in Lishman is intended to reflect the idea that what constitutes infringement in a particular case is a function of the scope of the statutory monopoly, so that any act that impairs the statutory monopoly is by definition "infringement". . . Thus, to determine whether a certain act amounts to an infringement, the scope of the statutory monopoly must be determined by construing the claims of the patent. *Monsanto Canada Inc. v. Schmeiser*, 218 D.L.R. (4th) 31, 293 N.R. 340, [2003] 2 F.C. 165, 231 F.T.R. 160 (note), 21 C.P.R. (4th) 1 (C.A.).

PATENTLY UNREASONABLE. 1. "Refers to an error in interpretation of 'a provision which an administrative tribunal is required to apply within the limits of its jurisdiction.' This kind of error amounts to a fraud on the law or a deliberate refusal to comply with it. As Dickson J. (as he then was) described it, speaking for the whole court in *Canadian Union Public Employees Local 963 v. New Brunswick Liquor Corporation*, [1979] 2 S.C.R. 227 at p. 237, it is ' . . . so patently unreasonable that its construction cannot be rationally supported by the relevant legislation and demands intervention by the court upon review . . .' An error of this kind is treated as an act which is done arbitrarily or in bad faith and is contrary to the principles of natural justice." *Syndicat des Employés de production de Québec et de l'Acadie v. Canada (Labour Relations Board)*, [1984] 2 S.C.R. 412 at 420, 14 Admin. L.R. 72, 84 C.L.L.C. 14,069, 55 N.R. 321, 14 D.L.R. (4th) 457, the court per Beetz J. 2. At the patently unreasonable end of the spectrum, the tribunal is protected by a true privative clause, is deciding a matter within its jurisdiction and there is no statutory right of appeal. *Syndicat national des employés de la commission scolaire*

régionale de l'Outaouais v. U.E.S., local 298, (sub nom. *Union des employés de service, local 298 v. Bibeault*) [1988] 2 S.C.R. 1048 at p. 1089, and *Domtar Inc. c. Québec (Commission d'appel en matière de lésions professionnelles)*, [1993] 2 S.C.R. 756.

PATENT MEDICINE. See PROPRIETARY OR ~.

PATENT MODEL. The model constructed for the purpose of obtaining a patent for an invention, discovery or process.

PATER EST QUEM NUPTIAE REMONSTRANT. [L.] The father is the one whom marriage indicates.

PATER ET MATER NON SUNT DE SANGUINE PUERORUM. [L.] A father and a mother are not of their children's blood.

PATERFAMILIAS. *n.* [L.] A person who is sui juris and the head of the family.

PATERNITY. *n.* The relationship of a father.

PATERNITY AGREEMENT. If a man and a woman who are not spouses enter into an agreement for, (a) the payment of the expenses of a child's prenatal care and birth; (b) support of a child; or (c) funeral expenses of the child or mother, on the application of a party, or a children's aid society, to the Ontario Court (Provincial Division) or the Unified Family Court, the court may incorporate the agreement in an order, and Part III (Support Obligations) applies to the order in the same manner as if it were an order made under that Part. *Family Law Act*, R.S.O. 1990, c. F-3, s. 59, as am.

PATHOLOGICAL GAMBLING. Continuous or periodic loss of control over gambling, a preoccupation with gambling and with obtaining money with which to gamble, and a continuation of this behaviour without regard to the consequences.

PATHOLOGIST. *n.* A duly qualified medical practitioner who specializes in laboratory medicine. See SPEECH-LANGUAGE ~.

PATHOLOGY. *n.* The branch of medicine which studies any tissue changes caused by aging, disease, poisons or violence. See SPEECH-LANGUAGE ~.

PATIENT. *n.* 1. A person received at or in a hospital. 2. A person who receives investigation, diagnosis, treatment or other services at or in a hospital. 3. A recipient of health care services.

4. A recipient of dental care services. 5. A person who requires ambulance services because of illness, injury or incapacity. 6. A person receiving psychiatric care or treatment, or diagnostic services for the purpose of determining the existence of a mental disorder. See DAY-~; FORMAL ~; INFORMAL ~; IN-~; INVOLUNTARY ~; OUT-~; PERSON BOUND TO PROVIDE OR CARE FOR A ~.

PATIENT ABUSE. Improper treatment of patients.

PATIENT-DAY. *n*. The period an inpatient is served between the census-taking hours on two successive days.

PATR. ELEC. CAS. *abbr*. Patrick, Contested Elections (Ont.), 1824-1849.

PATRIA. *n*. [L.] A nation.

PATRIA LABORIBUS ET EXPENSIS NON DEBET FATIGARI. [L.] A jury should not be harassed by chores and expenses.

PATRIA POTESTAS. [L.] The power of a father.

PATRIATION. *n*. The bringing of the Constitution to Canada. The ending of the United Kingdom's control over Canada's constitution.

PATRIATION REFERENCE (1981). The Supreme Court was asked to clarify whether the past practice of securing provincial consent to a constitutional amendment affecting provincial powers was a convention (as eight provinces argued) or a usage (as the federal government and two provinces argued). P.W. Hogg, *Constitutional Law of Canada*, 3d ed. (Toronto: Carswell, 1992) at 22.

PATRICIDE. *n*. 1. Killing a father. 2. One who kills a father.

PATRIMONY. *n*. An hereditary right or estate handed down from ancestors.

PATROL. See SECURITY ~.

PATRON. *n*. A person who uses the services provided by a business or service-provider.

PATRONAGE. *n*. The right to make appointments to an office.

PATRONAGE ALLOCATION. An amount that an association allocates among and credits or pays to its members or to its member and non-member patrons based on the business done by them with or through the association, and includes (a) a patronage refund, and (b) an allo-

cation in proportion to borrowing. *Cooperative Credit Associations Act, 1991*, S.C. 1991, c. 48, s. 2.

PATRONAGE DIVIDEND. An amount that is allocated among and credited or paid by a cooperative to its members, or to its members and non-member patrons, based upon the business done by each of them with or through the cooperative.

PATRONAGE LOAN. A loan by a member to a cooperative of all or part of a patronage dividend.

PATRONAGE REFUND. An amount allocated or paid in proportion to patronage to the members or members and patrons out of savings or surpluses arising from the operations of a cooperative.

PATRONAGE RETURN. An amount that the cooperative allocates among and credits or pays to its members or to its member and non-member patrons based on the business done by them with or through the cooperative. *Canada Cooperatives Act, 1998*, S. C. 1998, c. 1, s. 2.

PATTERN. *n*. Includes the instructions for the knitting or crocheting of a garment. See SERVICE ~.

PATTERN BARGAINING. Collective bargaining by a union with distinct employers attempting to achieve the same terms and conditions.

PATTERNS. *n*. (a) Reproductions of goods to be processed that serve to shape moulds for making such goods; (b) models for dies, jigs, fixtures and moulds that are to be used in the manufacture of goods; (c) the first finished printed motion picture film (also referred to as the negative of the exposed film) for exhibition in a public theatre or for broadcast to the public on television, if such film is used exclusively for the purpose of making reproductions thereof for sale; (d) masters, inter-masters and running masters of video or audio magnetic recording tapes produced by and used in the television and sound recording industries in making reproductions for sale or for the use of the person making the reproduction; and (e) typesetting and composition, metal plates, cylinders, matrices, film artwork, designs, photographs, rubber material, plastic material and paper material when impressed with or displaying or carrying an image for reproduction, made by or imported by or sold to a manufacturer, and used by him exclusively for the purposes of reproduction in the printing and publishing industries.

PAUPER. *n*. A person who sues or defends an action in forma pauperis.

PAVEMENT. *n*. Any type of street surfacing.

PAVING. *n*. 1. Includes laying down or constructing any description of pavement with or without curbing. 2. Macadamizing and the laying down or construction of any description of pavement or curbing. 3. Includes macadamizing, planking and the laying down or construction of any description of pavement or roadway and the construction of a curbing.

PAWN. *n*. A pledge, a kind of bailment in which a debtor delivers goods to the creditor for the creditor to keep until the debt is discharged.

PAWNBROKER. *n*. 1. A person whose business is taking any article as a pawn or pledge for the repayment of money lent against that article. 2. A person who engages in the business of granting credit to individuals for personal, family or household purposes and who takes and perfects security interests in consumer goods by taking possession of them, or who purchases consumer goods under agreements or undertakings, express or implied, that the goods may be repurchased by the sellers. *Personal Property Security acts.*

PAWNEE. *n*. The person with whom one deposits a pawn.

PAWNER. *n*. A person who delivers an article to a pawnbroker for pawn.

PAWNING. *n*. Within the meaning of this division, is the lending of money or anything convertible into money or having a pecuniary value, for a profit, either impliedly or expressly stipulated, in favor of the lender, and the taking of a pledge to secure the return of the money or thing lent, with or without the profit. *Licences Act*, R.S.Q. 1977, c. L-3, s. 100.

PAWNOR. *n*. A person who deposits a pawn.

PAX REGIS. [L.] The monarch's peace.

PAY. *v*. " . . . Means primarily to discharge a debt by money." *McIntosh Re*, [1923] 2 W.W.R. 605 at 607 (Man. K.B.), Dysart J.

PAY. *n*. 1. Remuneration in any form. 2. Wages due or paid to an employee and compensation paid or due to an employee but does not include deductions from wage that may lawfully be made by an employer. See ANNUAL HOLI-DAY ~; BACK ~; CALL-BACK ~; CALL-IN ~ OR PREMIUM; DISMISSAL ~; EQUAL ~ FOR EQUAL WORK; GRADE OF ~; HOLDBACK ~; MERIT ~; PREMIUM ~; REPORTING~; RETROACTIVE ~; SHOW-UP ~; SICK ~; STRAIGHT-TIME ~; TAKE-HOME ~; VACATION ~.

PAYABLE. *adj*. 1. Requiring to be paid; due. 2. Describes a sum of money when someone is obliged to pay it. See ACCOUNT ~; PRICE PAID OR ~.

PAYABLE TO ORDER. Describes a cheque or bill of exchange payable to the person named on it or in any way directed by an endorsement.

PAY AGENCY. The Department of Supply and Services or such other appropriate agency, office or person that is charged with the duty or that performs the function of paying remuneration to a person. Canada regulations.

PAY-AS-YOU-GO PENSION PLAN. A plan in which the employer pays benefits from earnings instead of from a pension fund.

PAY AUDIO SERVICE. The programming service provided by a person licensed to carry on a pay audio programming undertaking. *Broadcasting Distribution Regulations*, SOR/97-555, s. 1.

PAY DAY. The day on which remuneration ordinarily is paid to an employee. *Canada Pension Plan Regulations*, C.R.C., c. 385, s. 3.

PAYEE. *n*. One to whom a cheque, bill of exchange or promissory note is payable. See FICTITIOUS ~.

PAY EQUITY. A compensation practice which is based primarily on the relative value of the work performed, irrespective of the gender of employees, and includes the requirement that no employer shall establish or maintain a difference between the wages paid to male and female employees, employed by that employer, who are performing work of equal or comparable value.

PAYER. *n*. The owner, contractor or subcontractor who is liable to pay for the services or materials provided to an improvement under a contract or subcontract.

PAY GRADE. A series of rates of remuneration for a class that provides for a minimum rate, a maximum rate, and such intermediate rates as may be considered necessary to permit periodic increases in remuneration.

PAY IN LIEU. A term used to mean the damages paid in compensation for the breach of the employment contract where the employer has failed to give reasonable notice. . .To limit entitlement to benefits where there has been "payment in lieu", would be tantamount to giving the company the power to circumscribe benefits during the notice period where notice is provided. In the absence of such a power having been expressly reserved in the termination policy itself, it follows that the phrase "or similar employment benefits" should be construed broadly so as to equate "payment in lieu" as closely as possible with the "notice" alternative. *Gilchrist v. Western Star Trucks Inc.*, 2000 CarswellBC 2136, 2000 BCSC 1523, 82 B.C.L.R. (3d) 99, 25 C.C.P.B. 22 (S.C.).

PAYMENT. *n.* 1. Remuneration in any form. 2. " . . . [A] sum expressly applicable in reduction of the particular demand on which it is made; that demand is therefore reduced by the extent of the payment. . ." *Miron v. McCabe* (1867), 4 P.R. 171 at 174 (H.C.), Wilson J. 3. Includes the set-off of any amount against indebtedness incurred. 4. Delivery to another person, voluntarily or otherwise, of a sum of money or thing. 5. Not restricted to money. *Nelson v. Rentown Enterprises Inc.* (1992), 1992 CarswellAlta 145, 5 Alta. L.R. (3d) 149, 96 D.L.R. (4th) 586, [1993] 2 W.W.R. 71, 7 B.L.R. (2d) 319, 134 A.R. 257 (Q.B.), Hunt J. See ADVANCE ~; BALLOON ~; BLENDED ~; CANADIAN ~S ASSOCIATION; CAVEAT ~; COVENANT FOR ~; DOWN ~; EQUALIZATION ~; EXCESS ~; FRONT-END ~; INITIAL ~; INVOLUNTARY ~; MONEY OF ~; MORTGAGE PROTECTION ~S; OTHER ~ REQUISITION; OVER~; PART ~; PERIODIC ~; PROGRESS ~; STABILIZATION ~; TERMINATION ~; UNAUTHORIZED ~.

PAYMENT BOND. A bond held as security for the payment of certain classes of persons performing labour or services, or supplying materials in connection with a contract.

PAYMENT BY RESULT. Remuneration dependent upon output.

PAYMENT CERTIFIER. An architect, engineer or any other person on whose certificate payments are made under a contract or subcontract.

PAYMENT IN KIND. Remuneration in the form of goods or services.

PAYMENT INTO COURT. The deposit of money with a court official in connection with proceedings commenced in that court.

PAYMENT QUARTER. A period of 3 months commencing on the first day of April, July, October or January in a fiscal year.

PAYMENT REQUISITION. A cheque requisition or another payment requisition.

PAYMENTS SYSTEM. A mechanism by which debit and credit positions between banks are ascertained and the cheques are sorted. The balances are settled by making transfers in the Chartered Banks' accounts with the Bank of Canada.

PAYOR. *n.* A person liable for payment.

PAY-OUT PRICE. In respect of a pool, means the amount of money that is payable to the holder of a winning ticket or to an account holder who has made a winning bet, for each dollar bet by the holder or account holder, as the case may be, calculated in accordance with Part IV. *Pari-Mutuel Betting Supervision Regulations*, SOR/91-365, s. 2.

PAY PERIOD. 1. The period of employment established by an employer for the computation of wages, overtime pay or time off in place of overtime pay. 2. In respect of any particular person, the period commencing on the day following the day that that person's salary cheque is normally dated and ending on the day that that person's next salary cheque is normally dated.

PAY-PER-VIEW SERVICE. A scheduled programming service that is provided to subscribers on a pay-per-view basis. *Broadcasting Distribution Regulations*, SOR/97-555, s. 1.

PAY RANGE. A series of rates of remuneration for a class that provides for a minimum rate, a maximum rate, and such intermediate rates as may be considered necessary to permit periodic increases in remuneration.

PAYROLL. *n.* 1. In respect of an employer, means the aggregate of the remuneration in any calendar year of workers employed by the employer in any industry in the year. 2. In respect of an employer, the greater of (a) the wages earned by employees in the twelve-month period ending on the last day of the last fiscal year established by the employer that ended prior to the termination of an employee's employment, (b) the wages earned by employees in the twelve-month period ending on the last day of the second last fiscal year established by the employer that ended prior to the termination of an employee's employment, or (c) the wages earned by employees in the four weeks that ended with the last day of the last pay period completed prior to the termination of an employee's employment, multiplied by 13. *Employment Standards Act*, R.S.O. 1990, c. E.14, s. 1. See TOTAL ~.

PAYS. *n*. [Fr.] A nation.

PAY TELEVISION SERVICE. The programming service, other than the pay-per-view service, provided by a person licensed to carry on a pay television programming undertaking. *Broadcasting Distribution Regulations*, SOR/ 97-555, s. 1.

PAY WEEK. A period of 7 consecutive days that ends, or any one of two or more such periods that are contiguous, the last of which ends, on the employer's payroll ending date.

P.C. *abbr*. 1. Privy Council. 2. Privy Councillor. 3. Police constable. 4. In any one of the tariff columns in Schedule II, means per cent ad valorem. *Customs Tariff*, R.S.C. 1985, c. C-54, s. 2.

PCT. *abbr*. Patent Cooperation Treaty.

P.D. *abbr*. Law Reports, Probate, Divorce and Admiralty Division, 1875-1890.

PEACE. *n*. 1. Quiet behaviour towards the sovereign and the sovereign's subjects. 2. The condition of international relations in which a nation does not bring military force against another. See BREACH OF THE ~; CLERK OF THE ~; COMMISSION OF THE ~; JUSTICE OF THE ~; KEEP THE ~; PUBLIC ~.

PEACE BOND. A written promise made to a court to keep the peace.

PEACE OFFICER. Includes (*a*) a mayor, warden, reeve, sheriff, deputy sheriff, sheriff's officer and justice of the peace, (*b*) a member of the Correctional Service of Canada who is designated as a peace officer pursuant to Part I of the *Corrections and Conditional Release Act*, and a warden, deputy warden, instructor, keeper, jailer, guard and any other officer or permanent employee of a prison other than a penitentiary as defined in Part I of the *Corrections and Conditional Release Act*, (*c*) a police officer, police constable, bailiff, constable, or other person employed for the preservation and maintenance of the public peace or for the service or execution of civil process, (*d*) an officer or a person having the powers of a customs or excise officer when performing any duty in the administration of the *Customs Act* or the *Excise Act*, (*e*) a person designated as a fishery guardian under the *Fisheries Act* when performing any duties or functions under that Act and a person designated as a fishery officer under the *Fisheries Act* when performing any duties or functions under that Act or the *Coastal Fisheries Protection Act*, (*f*) the pilot in command of an aircraft (i) registered in Canada under regulations made under the *Aeronautics Act*, or (ii) leased without crew and operated by a person who is qualified under regulations made under the *Aeronautics Act* to be registered as owner of an aircraft registered in Canada under those regulations, while the aircraft is in flight, and (*g*) officers and non-commissioned members of the Canadian Forces who are (i) appointed for the purposes of section 156 of the *National Defence Act*, or (ii) employed on duties that the Governor in Council, in regulations made under the *National Defence Act* for the purposes of this paragraph, has prescribed to be of such a kind as to necessitate that the officers and non-commissioned members performing them have the powers of peace officers. *Criminal Code*, R.S.C. 1985, c. C-46, s. 2.

PEACE, ORDER AND GOOD GOVERN-MENT. 1. "[Under s. 91 of the Constitution Act, 1867 (30 & 31 Vict.), c. 3 includes] . . . federal competence [based] on the existence of a national emergency; . . . federal competence [may arise] because the subject-matter did not exist at the time of Confederation and clearly cannot be put into the class of matters of merely local or private nature; [or] . . . Where the subject-matter 'goes beyond local or provincial concern or interests and must, from its inherent nature be the concern of the Dominion as a whole' . . ." *Labatt Breweries of Canada Ltd. v. Canada (Attorney General)* (1979), 9 B.L.R. 181 at 208, [1980] 1 S.C.R. 914, 30 N.R. 496, Estey J. (Martland, Dickson, Beetz and Pratte JJ. concurring). 2. ". . . [T]he true test must be found in the real subject matter of the legislation; if it is such that it goes beyond local or provincial concern or interests and must from its inherent nature be the concern of the Dominion as a whole . . . then it will fall within the competence of the Dominion Parliament as a matter affecting the peace, order and good government of Canada [contained in s. 91 of the Constitution Act, 1867 (30 & 31 Vict.), c. 3], though it may in another aspect touch on matters specially reserved to the provincial legislature." *Reference* re *Canada Tem-*

perance Act, [1946] A.C. 193 at 205, 1 C.R. 229, [1946] 2 W.W.R. 1, 85 C.C.C. 225, [1946] 2 D.L.R. 1 (Ont. P.C.), the board per Viscount Simon. See NATIONAL CONCERN; RESIDUARY POWER.

PEACETIME DISASTER. A disaster, real or apprehended, resulting from fire, explosion, flood, earthquake, landslide, weather, epidemic, shipping accident, mine accident, transportation accident, electrical power failure, nuclear accident and any other disaster not attributable to enemy attack, sabotage or other hostile action whereby injury or loss is or may be caused to persons or property.

PEAK CRUSH RESISTANCE. The greatest force recorded over the entire 457 mm crush. *Motor Vehicle Safety Regulations*, C.R.C., c. 1038, s. 214.

PEAK LOAD. Unless otherwise specified, means the annual maximum electric power load as averaged for 1 hour.

PEAT. *n*. A highly organic soil consisting chiefly of more or less fragmented remains of vegetable matter sequentially deposited.

PEAT-DRIED MALT. Barley malt that has been kilned over fires of peat with or without a mixture of other fuels.

PEAT OPERATION. Any opening or excavation in, or working of, the surface or subsurface of the ground for the purpose of working, recovering, opening up or proving any peat or peaty substance.

PECCATA CONTRA NATURAM SUNT GRAVISSIMA. [L.] The most serious crimes are those against nature.

PECCATUM PECCATO ADDIT QUI CULPAE QUAM FACIT PATROCINIUM DEFENSIONIS ADJUNGIT. [L.] Whoever adds defence of a wrong committed to guilt adds crime to crime.

PECK. *n*. 2 gallons. *Weights and Measures Act*, S.C. 1970-71-72, c. 36, schedule II.

PECULATUS. *n*. [L.] Embezzlement of public funds.

PECUNIA. *n*. [L.] Money.

PECUNIARY. *adj*. Concerning money.

PECUNIARY INTEREST. " . . . [S]omething that could monetarily affect land, giving either an advantage or a disadvantage in terms of financial impact. . . an interest that can be measured pecuniarily." *Edmonton (City) v. Purves* (1982), 18 M.P.L.R. 221 at 232, 19 Alta. L.R. (2d) 319, 37 A.R. 376, 136 D.L.R. (3d) 340 (Q.B.), Moshansky J. See DIRECT ~.

PECUNIARY JUDGMENT. " . . . [A] judgment which can be enforced by a writ of seizure and sale—the modern equivalent of a writ of fi. fa." *S.G. & S. Investments (1972) Ltd. v. Golden Boy Foods Inc*. (1991), 3 B.L.R. (2d) 80 at 95, 60 B.C.L.R. (2d) 305, 84 D.L.R. (4th) 751, 4 B.C.A.C. 105, 9 W.A.C. 105, the court per Southin J.A.

PECUNIARY LOSS. 1. Consists of the support, services, and contributions which the claimant might reasonably have expected to receive. 2. " . . . As applied to a dependent's loss from death the term has been interpreted to mean 'the reasonable expectation of pecuniary benefit from the continued life of the deceased' . . . In a later decision Mason v. Peters (1982), 139 D.L.R. (3d) 104 . . . Robins J.A. . . said at p. 109: 'Pecuniary loss may consist of the support, services or contributions which the claimant might reasonably have expected to receive from the deceased had he not been killed.' Thus, the courts have recognized that the child of a deceased mother may recover, as pecuniary loss, an amount to compensate for the loss of a mother's care and moral training . . ." *Harris Estate v. Roy's Midway Transport Ltd.* (1989), 60 D.L.R. (4th) 99 at 103, 50 C.C.L.T. 67 (N.B. C.A.), the court per Stratton C.J.N.B. 3. Does not include loss arising from pain and suffering, physical inconvenience and discomfort, social discredit, injury to reputation, mental suffering, injury to feelings, loss of amenities and of expectation of life or loss of society of spouse or child.

PEDAL BICYCLE. See MOTOR ASSISTED ~.

PEDDLE. See TO ~.

PEDDLER. *n*. Anyone who carries on one's person, or who transports with one, goods, wares or merchandise, with intent to sell the same within the limits of a local municipality. See HAWKER AND ~; PEDLAR.

PEDDLING. *n*. Having on one's person or transporting with one goods and selling or intending to sell them.

PEDESTRIAN. *n*. 1. A person afoot. 2. A person afoot, or a person in a wheelchair or a child's carriage or physically handicapped person operating a motorized mobility-aid. 3. A person on foot, an invalid in a wheelchair or a child in a carriage or sleigh.

PEDESTRIAN CONTROL SIGNAL. A traffic control signal directed to pedestrians.

PEDESTRIAN CORRIDOR. A crosswalk, at an intersection or elsewhere, that has been designated as a pedestrian corridor by the proper traffic authority and that is illuminated and distinctly indicated for pedestrian crossing by (i) such lights and other traffic control devices on the highway; and (ii) such lines or other markings on the surface of the roadway, as are prescribed in regulations made by the traffic board.

PEDESTRIAN CROSSOVER. Any portion of a roadway, designated by by-law of a municipality, at an intersection or elsewhere, distinctly indicated for pedestrian crossing by signs on the highway and lines or other markings on the surface of the roadway.

PEDESTRIAN DECK. A bridge, platform or deck in a street provided for the use of pedestrians as a place of public resort or as a means of public thoroughfare, together with the places and means of access thereto and exit therefrom.

PEDIATRIC. *adj*. Diagnosing and treating patients, most of whom are 14 years old or younger.

PEDIGREE. *n*. In relation to an animal, means genealogical information showing the ancestral line of descent of the animal. *Animal Pedigree Act*, R.S.C. 1985, c. 8 (4th Supp.), s. 2.

PEDIGREED STATUS. With respect to seed, means that the seed is of foundation status, registered status or certified status.

PEDIS POSSESSIO. [L. foothold] Something actually possessed.

PEDLAR. *n*. Any person who, whether as principal or agent, (i) goes from house to house selling or offering for sale any merchandise or service, or both, to any person, and who is not a wholesale or retail dealer in that merchandise or service, and not having a permanent place of business in the municipality, (ii) offers or exposes for sale to any person by means of samples, patterns, cuts or blueprints, merchandise or a service, or both, to be afterwards delivered in and shipped into the municipality, or (iii) sells merchandise or a service, or both, on the streets or roads or elsewhere than at a building that is his permanent place of business, but does not include any person selling (A) meat, fruit or other farm produce that has been produced, raised or grown by himself, or (B) fish of his own catching. See PEDDLER.

PEER. *n*. 1. An equal, a person of the same rank. 2. In England, a member of the House of Lords.

PEERAGE. *n*. In England, barons, dukes, earls, marquises and viscounts.

PEERESS. *n*. In England, the wife of a peer, the unmarried widow of a peer or a woman who is herself a peer.

PEER REVIEW. The process of submitting one's hypothesis, methods and conclusions to the scrutiny of other, independent experts in the field. Publication in a refereed journal of wide circulation in the field is a major, although not the only, method of inviting peer review. When a scientific conclusion has been published and a reasonable time has elapsed without any meritorious criticism of it, the publication and peer review process provides a circumstantial guarantee of trustworthiness. *R. v. Murrin* (1999), 1999 CarswellBC 3015, 181 D.L.R. (4th) 320, 32 C.R. (5th) 97 (S.C.).

P.E.I. *abbr*. 1. Prince Edward Island. 2. Haszard & Warburton's Reports, 1850-1872.

PELAGIC SEALING. The killing, taking or hunting in any manner whatever of fur seals at sea.

PELLET. See SHOT ~.

PELT. *n*. The untanned skin of a fur bearing animal. See RAW ~; UNPRIME ~.

PELVIC IMPACT AREA. That area of the door or body side panel adjacent to any outboard designated seating position that is bounded by: (*a*) horizontal planes 180 mm (seven inches) above and 100 mm (four inches) below the seating reference point, and (*b*) vertical transverse planes 200 mm (eight inches) forward and 50 mm (two inches) rearward of the seating reference point. *Motor Vehicle Safety Regulations*, C.R.C., c. 1038, s. 201.

PELVIC RESTRAINT. A seat belt assembly or portion thereof intended to restrain movement of the pelvis. *Motor Vehicle Safety Regulations*, C.R.C., c. 1038, s. 2.

PENAL. *adj*. 1. " . . . [A]n accurate and convenient way of describing provincial 'criminal' proceedings." *Trumbley v. Metropolitan Toronto Police Force (sub nom. Trumbley v. Fleming)*

(1986), 21 Admin. L.R. 232 at 254, 55 O.R. (2d) 570, 29 D.L.R. (4th) 557, 24 C.R.R. 333, 15 O.A.C. 279 (C.A.), the court per Morden J.A. 2. Inflicting punishment.

PENAL CONSEQUENCE. See TRUE ~.

PENAL INSTITUTION. Includes jail, prison, lockup, or adult reformatory institution.

PENAL LAW. Laws in favour of the state for the recovery of pecuniary penalties for violation of statutes for the protection of revenue and other statutes.

PENAL NEGLIGENCE. Negligence in a criminal setting which unlike negligence under civil law, which is concerned with the apportionment of loss, is concerned with the punishment of moral blameworthiness. Incorporates the particular frailties of the accused, if any, because he or she could not have acted other than they did in the circumstances. Does not involve the fault element of criminal negligence. *R. c. Gosset*, [1993] 3 S.C.R. 76.

PENAL SERVITUDE. Punishment of an offender by confining and compelling that person to work.

PENAL STATUTE. A law which imposes a penalty or punishment for the offence committed.

PENAL SUM. A sum of money to be paid as punishment or an equivalent for some injury.

PENALTY. *n.* 1. " . . . [A] sum of money the purpose of which is not to compensate, but to discourage certain conduct." *Bank of Nova Scotia v. Dunphy Leasing Enterprises Ltd.* (1987), 51 Alta. L.R. (2d) 324 at 328, 77 A.R. 181, 38 D.L.R. (4th) 575 (C.A.), Prowse J.A. 2. (a) A fine; or (b) a term of imprisonment including a term of imprisonment in default of payment or satisfaction of a fine. 3. Includes any forfeiture or pecuniary penalty imposed or authorized to be imposed by any Act of Parliament for any contravention of the laws relating to the collection of the revenue, or to the management of any public work producing tolls or revenue, notwithstanding that part of such forfeiture or penalty is payable to the informer or prosecutor, or to any other person. 4. Includes any forfeiture or pecuniary penalty imposed or authorized to be imposed by any Act of Parliament for any contravention of the laws relating to the collection of the revenue, or to the management of any public work producing tolls or revenue, notwithstanding that part of such forfeiture or penalty is payable to the informer or prosecutor, or to any other person. *Financial Administration Act*, R.S.C. 1985, c. F-11, s. 23. 5. Section 98 [of the Courts of Justice Act, R.S.O. 1990, c. C.43] speaks of relief from penalties and forfeitures. Each word lends meaning to the other. "Penalties" is derived from penal and connotes punishment. "Forfeiture" is a giving up of a right or property and when allied with "penalties" suggests something of the nature of goods being forfeited to customs officials. Neither penalties nor forfeitures are compensatory and both connote an added element to any money damages when associated with a breach of a contract. The failure to pay premiums on a term life insurance policy and the consequent lapse of that policy engage none of the above considerations. The premium is the payment for coverage for the next term. Subject to the grace provision, there is no coverage for that term when a payment is not made and the insurer arranges its commercial affairs accordingly. In these circumstances, the contract terminates on its own terms and not by a breach. There is no forfeiture in the sense of a loss of property. To be sure, the coverage has been lost, but it wasn't paid for in the first place. *Pluzak v. Gerling Global Life Insurance Co.* (2001), 2001 CarswellOnt 10 (C.A.). 6. In *Dunlop Pneumatic Tyre Co. v. New Garage & Motor Co.* (1914), [1915] A.C. 79 (U.K. H.L.), Lord Dunedin is quoted at 86 as follows: The essence of a penalty is a payment of money stipulated as in terrorem of the offending party; the essence of liquidated damages is a genuine covenanted pre-estimate of damage. More recently, in *H.F. Clarke Ltd. v. Thermidaire Corp.* (1974), 54 D.L.R. (3d) 385 (S.C.C.), Chief Justice Laskin . . . suggested at 397 . . . that a sum would be held to be a penalty if it is "extravagant and unconscionable in amount in comparison with the greatest loss that could conceivably be proved to have followed from the breach." An emphasis on the need to show oppression is apparent. *32262 B.C. Ltd. v. See-Rite Optical Ltd.*, 1998 CarswellAlta 239, 216 A.R. 33, 175 W.A.C. 33, 60 Alta. L.R. (3d) 223, [1998] 9 W.W.R. 442, 39 B.L.R. (2d) 102 (C.A.), Per Hunt, J.A.

PENDENT. *adj.* Describes an action, arbitration or proceeding after it is begun and before the final award or judgment is given.

PENDENTE LITE. [L.] During litigation.

PENDENTE LITE NIHIL INNOVETUR. [L.] During litigation nothing should be altered.

PENDENT JURISDICTION. If a federal court in the United States has jurisdiction over a certain case, then that court has jurisdiction to decide all of the questions presented by the case, including "state" issues over which a federal court has no independent jurisdiction. P.W. Hogg, *Constitutional Law of Canada*, 3d ed. (Toronto: Carswell, 1992) at 178.

PENDING. *adj.* During; commenced but not completed.

PENES QUEM SOLUM ARBITRIUM ET JUST ET POTESTAS CREANDI. [L.] In whom rests the sole right of judgment, law, and power to create.

PENETRATING WOUND. A wound which has an entrance opening only and extends into tissue or an organ. F.A. Jaffe, *A Guide to Pathological Evidence*, 3d ed. (Toronto: Carswell, 1991) at 229.

PENITENTIAL COMMUNICATION. A confession of culpable conduct made secretly and in confidence by a person to a clergyman or priest in the course of the discipline or practice of the church or religious denomination or organization of which the person making the penitential communication is a member. *Military Rules of Evidence*, C.R.C., c. 1049, s. 78.

PENITENTIARY. *n.* A facility of any description, including all lands connected therewith, that is operated, permanently or temporarily, by the Corrections Service for the care and custody of inmates, and any prison or hospital declared to be a penitentiary.

PENITENTIARY SERVICE. The body now called the Canadian Corrections Service.

PENNY STOCK. A share less than $1 in price.

PENOLOGY. *n.* The study of prison management and rehabilitation of inmates.

PENSION. *n.* 1. A pension right arises as an *asset* or a contingent bundle of rights to a future *income* stream. After retirement, when the pension produces an income, the pension asset is, in a sense, being liquidated. This has caused debate about whether a pension is property (a capital asset) or income (a maintenance asset), or a combination of both. *Boston v. Boston*, 2001 CarswellOnt 2432, 2001 SCC 43, 201 D.L.R. (4th) 1, 17 R.F.L. (5th) 4, 271 N.R. 248, 149 O.A.C. 50, Per Major, J. 2. " . . . [A] pension is the fruit, through insurance, of all the money which was set aside in the past in respect of his past work." *Parry v. Cleaver*, [1970] A.C. 1 at 16 (U.K. H.L.), Lord Reid. 3. " . . . [I]ncludes periodic money payments payable on involuntary retirement due to disability occasioned by illness or injury as well as retirement due to age. . ." *Webb v. Webb* (1985), 49 R.F.L. (2d) 279 at 285, 70 B.C.L.R. 15 (S.C.), Lysyk J. 4. An annual allowance made to a person, usually in consideration of past services. 5. A series of payments that continues for the life of a former member of a pension plan, whether or not it is thereafter continued to any other person. See COMMUTED ~; DEFERRED ~; IMMEDIATE ~; JOINT AND SURVIVOR ~; OCCUPATIONAL DISABILITY ~; OLD AGE SECURITY ~; PORTABLE ~; SURVIVOR ~.

PENSIONABLE AGE. In relation to a member, means the earliest age (taking into account the period of employment with the employer or the period of membership in the pension plan, if applicable) at which a pension benefit, other than a benefit in respect of a disability (as defined in the regulations), is payable to the member under the terms of the pension plan without the consent of the administrator and without reduction by reason of early retirement. *Pension Benefits Standards Act*, R.S.C. 1985 (2d Supp.), c. 32, s. 2. See NORMAL ~.

PENSIONABLE EMPLOYMENT. Employment in respect of which a person is eligible for superannuation under a superannuation act. See PERIOD IN ~.

PENSIONABLE SALARY. 1. A person's average annual salary in the 5 consecutive years of pensionable service over which that person's average salary was the highest. 2. The annual average of salary received from public funds for the last 3 years of pensionable service. 3. The salary paid to an employee in the course of 1 year.

PENSIONABLE SERVICE. 1. Service in respect of which contributions have been made to a pension plan. 2. Service which may be taken into account in determining whether an employee has qualified for the award of a pension and the amount of a pension.

PENSION APPEALS BOARD. The federal body which hears appeals under the Canada Pension Plan and some provincial pension plans.

PENSION BENEFIT. 1. The aggregate annual, monthly or other periodic amounts to which an employee will become entitled upon retirement or to which any other person is entitled by virtue of death after retirement under a pension plan. 2. A periodic amount to which, under the terms of a pension plan, a member or former member, or the spouse, common-law partner, survivor or other beneficiary or estate or succession of a member or former member, is or may become entitled. *Pension Benefits Standards Act, 1985*, R.S.C. 1985, c. 32 (2nd Supp.), s. 2. See CONTRIBUTORY ~; DEFERRED ~; IMMEDIATE ~; JOINT AND SURVIVOR ~; NET ~.

PENSION BENEFIT CREDIT. The value at a particular time of the pension benefits and any other benefits provided under the pension plan to which an employee has become entitled.

PENSION CREDIT. The value at a particular time of any pension, benefit or reimbursement provided for under a supplemental plan, to which a person has become entitled.

PENSIONER. *n.* A person who has been awarded a pension.

PENSION FUND. The fund maintained to provide benefits under or related to a pension plan. See REGISTERED ~ OR PLAN.

PENSION FUND SOCIETY. The president, vice-president, general manager, assistant general manager, or the person acting as such, and the cashier, assistant cashier and inspector of any corporation legally transacting business in Canada under any Act of Parliament, or any two of those officers, with any other of the superior officers, may establish a pension fund society in connection with the administration of the corporation under the regulations and subject to the supervision and control designated in this Act, and thereupon they and the employees of the corporation who join the society and those who replace them from time to time are and shall be designated as the pension fund society of the corporation, and under that name are a body corporate. *Pension Fund Societies Act*, R.S.C. 1985, c. P-8, s. 3.

PENSION INDEX. For any one year, the average of the consumer price index over a 12-month period.

PENSION PLAN. 1. A superannuation or other plan organized and administered to provide pension benefits to employees employed in included employment (and former employees) and to which the employer is required under or in accordance with the plan to contribute, whether or not provision is also made for other benefits or for benefits to other persons, and includes a sup-

plemental pension plan, whether or not the employer is required to make contributions under or in accordance with the supplemental pension plan. 2. A superannuation or other plan organized and administered to provide pension benefits to employees employed in included employment (and former employees) and to which the employer is required under or in accordance with the plan to contribute, whether or not provision is also made for other benefits or for benefits to other persons, and includes a supplemental pension plan, whether or not the employer is required to make contributions under or in accordance with the supplemental pension plan, but does not include (*a*) an employees' profit sharing plan or a deferred profit sharing plan as defined in sections 144 and 147, respectively, of the *Income Tax Act*; (*b*) an arrangement to provide a "retiring allowance" as defined in subsection 248(1) of the *Income Tax Act*; or (*c*) any other prescribed arrangement. *Pension Benefits Standards Act, 1985*, R.S.C. 1985, c. 32 (2nd Supp.), s. 4. See BONA FIDE ~; CANADA ~; CONTRIBUTORY ~; DEFINED BENEFIT ~; FLAT RATE ~; INSURED ~; MULTI-EMPLOYER ~; NON-CONTRIBUTORY ~; ,PAY-AS-YOU-GO ~; PROVINCIAL ~; QUEBEC ~; REGISTERED PENSION FUND OR PLAN; REGISTERED ~; SUPPLEMENTAL ~.

PENSION TRUST. A trust established by an employer to provide payments to employees after their retirement.

PENSIONS ADVOCATE. See CHIEF ~.

PENTANES PLUS. A mixture mainly of pentanes and heavier hydrocarbons which ordinarily may contain some butanes and which is obtained from the processing of raw gas, condensate or crude oil.

PENULTIMATE DECENNIAL CENSUS. The decennial census that preceded the then most recent decennial census. *Constitution Act, 1974*, S.C. 1974-75-76, c. 13, reprinted as R.S.C. 1985, App. Document No. 40.

PEOPLE. *n.* The inhabitants of a country, province, town or other area.

PEOPLES. *n.* International law grants the right to self-determination to "peoples". Accordingly, access to the right requires the threshold step of characterizing as a people the group seeking self-determination. However, as the right to self-determination has developed by virtue of a combination of international agreements and conventions, coupled with state practice, with little formal elaboration of the definition of "peoples", the result has been that the precise meaning of the term "people" remains somewhat uncertain. It is clear that "a people" may include only a portion of the population of an existing state. The right to self-determination has developed largely as a human right, and is generally used in documents that simultaneously contain references to "nation" and "state". The juxtaposition of these terms is indicative that the reference to "people" does not necessarily mean the entirety of a state's population. *Reference re Secession of Quebec*, [1998] 2 S.C.R. 217 Per curiam.

PEPPERCORN RENT. A rent far below actual value.

PER. *prep*. For each; for every.

PERAMBULATE. *v*. To walk around the limits of an area of land.

PER ANNUM. [L.] By year.

PER AUTRE VIE. [Fr.] For the length of someone else's life.

PER CAPITA. [L. by heads] In equal shares. See MUNICIPAL ASSESSMENT ~; PER STIRPES.

PER CAPITA REVENUE. See NATIONAL ~; PROVINCIAL ~.

PER CAPITA YIELD. In respect of a province for a revenue source for a fiscal year is the quotient obtained by dividing the product of the national average rate of tax for that revenue source and the province's revenue base for that revenue source for the fiscal year by the population of the province for that fiscal year. *Federal-Provincial Fiscal Arrangements Act*, R.S.C. 1985, c. F-8, s. 4(2).

PER CENT. *abbr*. [L.] Per centum. By one hundred.

PERCENTAGE. Describes a relationship between two numbers. The proportion one is to another. See DIRECT EQUITY ~; PRIME RATE ~.

PERCENTAGE RATE. See ANNUAL ~.

PERCENTAGE TRUST. A guarantee that a would-be "income" beneficiary will regularly receive a fixed percentage on the value of the trust property. D.M.W. Waters, *The Law of Trusts in Canada*, 2d ed. (Toronto: Carswell, 1984) at 867.

PER CENTUM. [L.] By one hundred.

PERCEPTUAL DISABILITY. A disability that prevents or inhibits a person from reading or hearing a literary, musical, dramatic or artistic work in its original format, and includes such a disability resulting from (a) severe or total impairment of sight or hearing or the inability to focus or move one's eyes, (b) the inability to hold or manipulate a book, or (c) an impairment relating to comprehension. *Copyright Act*, R.S.C. 1985, c. C-42, s. 2.

PERCH. *n*. 1. As a measure of area, 324 square feet (French measure). Units of measurement to describe certain land in Quebec. *Weights and Measures Act*, S.C. 1970-71-72, c. 36, schedule III. 2. As a measure of length, 18 feet (French measure). Units of measurement to describe certain land in Quebec. *Weights and Measures Act*, S.C. 1970-71-72, c. 36, schedule III. 3. 5 1/2 yards. *Weights and Measures Act*, S.C. 1970-71-72, c. 36 schedule II. 4. Yellow perch, Perca flavescens Lacepede. *Ontario Fishery Regulations*, C.R.C., c. 849, s. 2.

PERCHED GROUNDWATER. A free-standing body of water in the ground extending to a limited depth. *Building Code Act, 1992*, O. Reg. 403/97, s. 1.1.3.

PERCHED POND. A pond resulting from a pit or quarry or a wayside pit or quarry excavation.

PERCOLATION TIME. The average time in minutes that is required for water to drop one centimetre during a percolation test or as determined by a soil evaluation or analysis. *Building Code Act, 1992*, O. Reg. 403/97, s. 1.1.3.

PER CUR. *abbr*. [L.] Per curiam. By a court.

PER CURIAM. [L.] By a court.

PERCUSSIVE DRILLING METHOD. This method entails the formation of a drill hole by breaking the rock into fragments by means of a great force or energy on a continual basis until the proper depth has been reached. This energy is transmitted from the rock drilling machine to the rock via the drill string, which consists of the drill rods and coupling sleeves, with a drill bit at the end of the drill string against the rock face. Once the percussion drills achieve the required depth, an explosive charge is placed in the hole and detonated. The force from the charge breaks up the material being mined from the rock face. *Sandvik Tamrock Canada Ltd. v. Deputy Minister of National Revenue (Customs & Excise)*,

2001 FCA 340, 284 N.R. 183, 6 T.T.R. (2d) 302 (C.A.).

PER DIEM. [L.] By day.

PERDURABLE. *adj*. Describes an estate which lasts very long or forever.

PEREMPTION. *n*. Nonsuit; quashing.

PEREMPTORY. *adj*. Determinate, final and, concerning statutes, obligatory in contrast to permissive.

PEREMPTORY CHALLENGE. " . . . [A]llows a party to dismiss a person from serving on [a] jury without providing a reason. . . *R. v. Bain* (1992), 10 C.R. 4th 257 at 274, [1992] 1 S.C.R. 91, 69 C.C.C. (3d) 481, 87 D.L.R. (4th) 449, 133 N.R. 1, 51 O.A.C. 161, 7 C.R.R. (2d) 193, Stevenson J.

PERENNIAL FORAGE. All clovers (except sweet clover), sainfoin, trefoil, alfalfa and perennial grasses.

PER EUNDEM. [L.] By the same thing.

PERFECT. *v*. To register.

PERFECTED SECURITY INTEREST. " . . . [A]n interest the protection of which against third parties has been accomplished by the doing of whatever was necessary to achieve such in the jurisdiction from which the debtor has moved." *Juckes (Trustee of) v. Holiday Chevrolet Oldsmobile (1983) Ltd*. (1990), 82 Sask. R. 303 at 307, 68 D.L.R. (4th) 142, 79 C.B.R. (N.S.) 143 (Q.B.), Armstrong J.

PERFECTION. *n*. 1. " . . . [O]f a security interest deals with those steps legally required to give the secured party an interest in the property against the grantor's creditors. An instrument such as a debenture or mortgage is said to become perfected when it is recorded or registered in the appropriate registry as a matter of record, and that recording or registration renewed and kept current and subsisting so that notice to the grantor's debtors does not lapse." *First City Capital Ltd. v. Ampex Canada Inc*. (1989), 75 C.B.R. (N.S.) 109 at 140, 97 A.R. 256 (Q.B.), Yanosik J. 2. " . . . A security interest, even though it may be registered, cannot be perfected until it has attached. . ." *Canadian Imperial Bank of Commerce v. Otto Timm Enterprises Ltd*. (1991), 2 P.P.S.A.C. (2d) 58 at 74, 79 D.L.R. (4th) 67 (Ont. Gen. Div.), Donnelly J.

PERFLUOROCARBON. *n*. A fully fluorinated fluorocarbon each molecule of which contains only carbon and fluorine atoms.

PERFORATING WOUND. A wound with both entrance and exit openings which completely crosses an organ or tissue. F.A. Jaffe, *A Guide to Pathological Evidence*, 2nd ed. (Toronto: Carswell, 1983) at 187.

PERFORM. *v*. To carry out an action; to achieve; to execute an action.

PERFORMANCE. *n*. 1. " . . . [T]he equitable doctrine of performance [is] expressed in the maxim 'equity imputes an intention to fulfil an obligation'. According to this doctrine a man under an obligation, who does an act which is suitable to be the means of performing the obligation, will be presumed in equity to have done the act with that intention. . . The difference between performance and satisfaction is that whereas the former does not, the latter does, depend upon intention." *Northern Trust Co. v. Coldwell* (1914), 18 D.L.R. 512 at 514, 516, 6 W.W.R. 1165, 25 Man. R. 120, 28 W.L.R. 625 (K.B.), Mathers C.J. 2. Any acoustic or visual representation of a work, performer's performance, sound recording or communication signal, including a representation made by means of any mechanical instrument, radio receiving set or television receiving set. *Copyright Act*, R.S.C. 1985, c. C-42, s. 2. *Copyright Act*, R.S.C. 1985, c. C-42, s. 2. See PART ~; SPECIFIC ~; SUBSTANTIAL ~.

PERFORMANCE BOND. 1. A bond that is conditioned upon the completion by the principal of a contract in accordance with its terms. 2. " . . . [G]uarantee to the owner that the contractor will perform the terms of the contract." *Johns-Manville Canada Inc. v. John Carlo Ltd*. (1980), (*sub nom. Canadian Johns-Manville Co. v. John Carlo Ltd*.) 12 B.L.R. 80 at 87, 29 O.R. (2d) 592, 113 D.L.R. (3d) 686 (H.C.), R.E. Holland J. See CONTRACT BOND; LABOUR AND MATERIAL BOND.

PERFORMER'S PERFORMANCE. Any of the following when done by a performer: (a) a performance of an artistic work, dramatic work or musical work, whether or not the work was previously fixed in any material form, and whether or not the work's term of copyright protection under this Act has expired, (b) a recitation or reading of a literary work, whether or not the work's term of copyright protection under this Act has expired, or (c) an improvisation of a dramatic work, musical work or literary work, whether or not the improvised work is based on a pre-existing work. *Copyright Act*, R.S.C. 1985, c. C-42, s. 2.

PERFORMING ARTS. The arts of the theatre and the concert hall, including the creating, staging and performing of drama, music and dance.

PERFORMING RIGHT. In the case of a work that has not been performed in public before January 1, 1924, includes the right at common law, if any, to restrain the performance thereof in public. *Copyright Act*, R.S.C. 1985, c. C-42, s. 71.

PERFORMING RIGHTS SOCIETY. A business which acquires the performing rights in a copyrighted work and licenses others the right to perform it in public. H.G. Fox, *The Canadian Law of Copyright and Industrial Designs*, 2d ed. (Toronto: Carswell, 1967) at 525.

PERICARDIUM. *n*. The membranous sac which surrounds the heart.

PERICULOSUM EST RES NOVAS ET IN-USITATAS INDUCERE. [L.] It is dangerous to introduce new and untried things.

PERICULUM REI VENDITAE, NONDUM TRADITAE, EST EMPTORIS. [L.] Something sold and not yet delivered is at the purchaser's risk.

PERIL. *n*. 1. A risk of unavoidable misfortune. 2. Danger arising from failure to be duly circumspect. See ALL OTHER ~S; DESIGNATED ~S; MAJOR ~S; MARITIME ~S.

PERILS OF THE SEAS. 1. "Where there is an accidental incursion of seawater into a vessel at a part of the vessel and in a manner where seawater is not expected to enter in the ordinary course of things and there is consequent damage to the thing insured, there is prima facie a loss by perils of the sea... It is the fortuitous entry of the seawater which is the peril of the sea in such cases..." *Canada Rice Mills v. Union Marine & General Insurance Co.* (1940), [1941] 1 D.L.R. 1 at 9, [1941] A.C. 55, [1941] 3 W.W.R. 401, [1940] 4 All E.R. 169, 8 I.L.R. 1 (P.C.), Lord Wright for their Lordships. 2. Refers only to fortuitous accidents or casualties of the seas. It does not include the ordinary action of the winds and waves. *Marine Insurance acts*.

PER INCURIAM. [L.] Through inadvertence or by overlooking an applicable principle.

PER INFORTUNIUM. [L.] Through bad luck.

PERIOD. *n*. 1. An interval of time. 2. A space of time. 3. Any length of time. See ACCOUNTING ~; BENFIT ~; BILLING ~; CAMPAIGN ~; CANDIDACY ~; CONTINU-OUS ~; COOLING-OFF ~; CRITICAL ~; DOWN~; ELECTION ~; FISCAL ~; JOINT CONTRIBUTORY ~; LEADERSHIP CONTEST~; LICENCE ~; LIMITATIONS ~; MEAL ~; NOTICE ~; OPEN ~; PAYMENT REVIEW ~; PAY ~; PERPETUITY ~; POOL ~; REDEMPTION ~; REFERENDUM ~; REFRACTORY RENT ~; RENTAL PAYMENT ~; RENTAL~; REPORTING ~; REST ~; RESTRAINT ~; SUMMER ~; WAITING ~; WINTER ~.

PERIODICAL. *n*. Any printed matter that is published for general distribution to the public and that purports to be a copy of one publication in a series of publications at regular intervals, and that is not bound in a hard cover but does not include a periodic publication that is devoted primarily to conveying current news. *Paperback and Periodical Distributors Act*, R.S.O. 1990, c. P.1, s. 1(1). See MAGAZINES AND ~S; REGISTRAR'S ~.

PERIODICAL PUBLICATION. (a) Any paper, magazine or periodical that contains public news, intelligence or reports of events, or any remarks or observation thereon and that is printed for sale and published periodically, or in parts or numbers, at intervals not exceeding 31 days between the publication of any two such papers, parts or numbers and (b) any paper, magazine or periodical that contains advertisements, exclusively or principally, and that is printed in order to be disbursed and made public weekly or more often, or at intervals not exceeding 31 days. *Canada Elections Act*, R.S.C. 1985, c. E-2, s. 2.

PERIODIC DUTY. A type of intermittent duty in which the load conditions are regularly recurrent.

PERIODIC PAYMENT. 1. "... [I]n order to constitute periodic payments there is no requirement that the time elapsing between each payment be of equal duration, the time between each payment may vary and be quite unpredictable, yet, the payments may still be characterized as periodic. Periodic indicates something which recurs from time to time but not necessarily at precise or regular intervals..." *R. v. Guay*, [1975] C.T.C. 88 at 93, 75 D.T.C. 5044, 27 R.F.L. 76 (Fed. T.D.), Addy J. 2. "... 'Payments which are made periodically, recurring at fixed times, not at variable periods, not in the exercise of the discretion of one or more individuals, but from the antecedent obligation': ..." *Supreme*

Legion Select Knights of Canada, Re (1898), 29 O.R. 708 at 715 (H.C.), Boyd C .

PERIODIC TENANCY. 1. Tenancy from week to week, month to month or year to year. 2. (i) A tenancy under a residential tenancy agreement that is renewed or continued without notice, and (ii) with respect to a fixed term tenancy that contains a provision allowing for renewal or continuation of the tenancy without notice, that part of the tenancy that arises after the end of the fixed term tenancy.

PERIOD OF EMPLOYMENT. The period of time from the last hiring of an employee by an employer to his discharge by that employer and includes time on lay-off or suspension, of less than twelve consecutive months.

PERIOD OF PROBATION. A period during which a person convicted of an offence was directed by the court that convicted him (a) to be released on his own recognizance to keep the peace and be of good behaviour; or (b) to be released on or comply with the conditions prescribed in a probation order. *Criminal Act*, R.S.C. 1985, c. C-47, s. 2.

PERIOD OF SERVICE. Time served on active service in the forces, excluding therefrom any period of absence without leave or leave of absence without pay, or time served while undergoing sentence of penal servitude, imprisonment or detention, or period of service in respect of which pay is forfeited.

PERIOD OF STUDIES. A period of studies at a specified educational institution in a course that is recognized by that educational institution and the appropriate authority for the province to be equivalent to a course that may be taken by a full-time student at that institution as part of a program of studies of at least 12 consecutive weeks duration. *Canada Student Loan Act*, R.S.C. 1985, c. S-23, s. 2.

PERIPHERAL CLAIMING PRINCIPLE. The *Patent Act* [R.S.C. 1985, c. P-4] requires the letters patent granting a patent monopoly to include a specification which sets out a correct and full "disclosure" of the invention, i.e., "correctly and fully describes the invention and its operation or use as contemplated by the inventor" (s. 34(1)(*a*)). The disclosure is followed by "a claim or claims stating distinctly and in explicit terms the things or combinations that the applicant regards as new and in which he claims an exclusive property or privilege" (s. 34(2)). It is the invention thus claimed to which the patentee receives

the "exclusive right, privilege and liberty" of exploitation (s. 44). These provisions, and similar provisions in other jurisdictions, have given rise to two schools of thought. One school holds that the claim embodies a technical idea and claims construction ought to look to substance rather than form to protect the inventive idea underlying the claim language. This is sometimes called the "central claims drafting principle" and is associated with the German and Japanese patent systems [. . .] . The other school of thought supporting what is sometimes called the "peripheral claiming principle" emphasizes the language of the claims as defining not the underlying technical idea but the legal boundary of the state-conferred monopoly. Traditionally, for reasons of fairness and predictability, Canadian courts have preferred the latter approach. *Free World Trust c. Électro Santé Inc.*, 2000 CarswellQue 2728, 2000 SCC 66, 194 D.L.R. (4th) 232, 263 N.R. 150, [2000] 2 S.C.R. 1024, 9 C.P.R. (4th) 168 Binnie, J.

PERIPHRASIS. *n.* Using many words to express a simple sense.

PERISH. *v.* For some existing thing to cease to exist.

PERITONEUM. *n.* The membrane which lines the inside surface of the abdominal walls and wraps the abdominal organs. F.A. Jaffe, *A Guide to Pathological Evidence*, 3d ed. (Toronto: Carswell, 1991) at 224.

PERITONITIS. *n.* Inflammation of the peritoneum.

PERITUS VIRTUTE OFFICII. [L.] Experienced because of her office.

PERJURY. *n.* With intent to mislead, making before a person who is authorized by law to permit it to be made before him a false statement under oath or solemn affirmation, by affidavit, solemn declaration or deposition or orally, knowing that the statement is false. *Criminal Code*, R.S.C. 1985, c. C-46, s. 131(1).

PERMAFROST. *n.* That condition under which earth material exists at a temperature at or below 32°F continuously for a period of 2 years of more. *Gas Pipeline Regulations*, C.R.C., c. 1052, s. 2.

PERMANENT. *adj.* 1. Intended to remain in place while useful. 2. Not occasional. 3. prolonged. 4. Where used in the expression "total and permanent disability" or the expression "partial and permanent disability " means prolonged in the sense that the disability is likely to be long continued and of indefinite duration, or likely to result in death. 5. ". . . [A] relative term which does not necessarily involve remaining in the same state and place forever or for an indefinitely long period. It is used in contradistinction to 'occasional'. If the thing is intended to remain in place so long as it serves its purpose, that satisfies the element of permanency." *Boomars Plumbing & Heating Ltd. v. Marogna Brothers Enterprises Ltd.* (1988), 27 B.C.L.R. (2d) 305 at 317, 50 R.P.R. 81, [1988] 6 W.W.R. 289, 51 D.L.R. (4th) 13 (C.A.), the court per Esson J.A.

PERMANENT ARBITRATOR. A person appointed to determine disputes arising during a period of time or during the life of a collective agreement.

PERMANENT CAVITY. A track left in tissue by a projectile passing through. The passage's diameter is usually greater than the projectile's. F.A. Jaffe, *A Guide to Pathological Evidence*, 3d ed. (Toronto: Carswell, 1991) at 224.

PERMANENT DECK COVERING. A deck covering adhering to, or permanently attached to the deck and shall include any combination of decking material such as underlayments and surface material. *Hull Construction Regulations*, C.R.C., c. 1431, s. 76.

PERMANENT EMPLOYEE. A person who has completed the probationary period and is employed on a full-time basis to hold office without reference to any specified date of termination of service.

PERMANENT ESTABLISHMENT. A fixed place of business.

PERMANENT FINANCING. The advance of the whole amount, minus costs, of a mortgage loan by a lender to a borrower when construction of the borrower's new building is completed; the lender has inspected the building and is satisfied. D.J. Donahue & P.D. Quinn, *Real Estate Practice in Ontario*, 4th ed. (Toronto: Butterworths, 1990) at 224-225.

PERMANENT IMPAIRMENT. Impairment that continues to exist after the worker reaches maximum medical recovery. *Workplace Safety and Insurance Act, 1997*, S.O. 1997, c. 16, Sched. A, s. 2.

PERMANENT INJUNCTION. An injunction to finally settle and enforce the rights of disputing parties.

PERMANENTLY UNEMPLOYABLE PERSON. A person who is unable to engage in remunerative employment for a prolonged period of time as verified by objective medical findings accepted by the medical advisory board.

PERMANENT RESIDENT. 1. A person who has acquired permanent resident status and has not subsequently lost that status under section 46. *Immigration and Refugee Protection Act*, S.C. 2001, c. 27, s. 2. A person who (a) has been granted landing, (b) has not become a Canadian citizen, and (c) has not ceased to be a permanent resident pursuant to section 24 or 25.1, and includes a person who has become a Canadian citizen but who has subsequently ceased to be a Canadian citizen under subsection 10(1) of the Citizenship Act, without reference to subsection 10(2) of that Act. *Immigration Act*, R.S.C. 1985, c. I-2, s. 2.

PERMANENT SHARES. All stock or all shares of permanent or fixed capital not liable to be withdrawn from or repaid by the corporation.

PERMANENT STOCK. All stock or all shares of permanent or fixed capital not liable to be withdrawn from or repaid by the corporation.

PERMANENT TOTAL DISABILITY. Without restricting the generality of the term, includes the loss of both eyes, both hands, both feet, or one hand and one foot.

PERMANENT X-RAY LOCATION. An enclosure, room or localized space within the bounds of which the owner of an X-ray machine confines or intends to confine its use.

PERMEABILITY. *n*. In relation to a space, means the percentage of that space below the ship's margin line that, on the assumption that it is in use for the purpose for which it is appropriated can be occupied by water. *Hull Construction Regulations*, C.R.C., c. 1431, s. 2.

PER MENSEM. [L.] By month.

PERMISSIBLE EQUIPMENT. Apparatus of a special design and construction suitable for use in a mine where methane gas or coal dust (or in special cases, other explosive gases) may be present in the atmosphere in dangerous proportions, and which is identical with similar apparatus which has been investigated and certified by an acceptable explosion testing and certifying authority.

PERMISSIVE OCCUPATION. A situation in which the occupier has a mere permission or licence from the person who is otherwise entitled to occupy the property.

PERMISSIVE PRESUMPTION. "[Leaves] . . . it optional as to whether the inference of the presumed fact is drawn following proof of the basic fact." *R. v. Oakes* (1986), 24 C.C.C. (3d) 321 at 330, [1986] 1 S.C.R. 103, 50 C.R. (3d) 1, 14 O.A.C. 335,19 C.R.R. 308, 26 D.L.R. (4th) 200, 65 N.R. 87, Dickson C.J.C. (Chouinard, Lamer, Wilson and Le Dain JJ. concurring).

PERMISSIVE WASTE. 1. " . . . [W]aste is either voluntary or permissive . . . Permissive waste involves the failure or omission to take some precaution which results in damage to the property." *Prior v. Hanna* (1987), 55 Alta. L.R. (2d) 276 at 282, 82 A.R. 3, 43 D.L.R. (4th) 612 (Q.B.), Miller A.C.J.Q.B. 2. Neglect to make needed repairs.

PERMIT. *v.* To allow. To authorize.

PERMIT. *n.* 1. An authorization, a written authority. 2. Any permission, whether termed approval, permit, licence or certificate or other term. 3. A permit issued which allows the exclusive practice of the profession mentioned therein. 4. A permit issued under this Code and the Charter of the French language which allows the exclusive practice of the profession mentioned therein and the use of a title reserved to the professionals practising such profession or only allows the use of a title reserved to the members of the order issuing the permit, subject to entry of the holder of such permit on the roll of that order. *Professional Code*, R.S.Q., chapter C-26, s. 1. See BUILDING ~; BURIAL ~; COLOURING ~; DEVELOPMENT ~; EXPORT ~; FEDERAL RESEARCH ~; GENERAL~; OCCUPANCY~; OWNER'S ~; PARK USE ~; PROVISIONAL ~; PUBLIC TRANSIT ~; REGISTRATION ~; RESOURCE USE ~; TIMBER ~; TRANSPORT ~; USE ~.

PERMIT AREA. The tract of land or location described in a permit. Canada regulations.

PERMIT HOLDER. A person who holds a permit.

PERMIT PREMISES. Premises or parts of premises where an activity for which a permit is required is conducted.

PERMITTED USE. The use of a registered trade-mark by a registered user thereof in accordance with the terms of his registration as such in association with wares or services manufac-tured, sold, leased, hired or performed by him, or the use of a proposed trade-mark as provided in subsection 40(2) by a person approved as a registered user thereof. *Trade-marks Act*, R.S.C. 1985, c. T-13, s. 50(2).

PERMITTEE. *n.* 1. A person who is the holder of a permit. 2. The person named in a permit.

PERMUTATION. *n.* Barter, exchanging one movable object for another.

PER MY ET PER TOUT. [Fr.] Not of a part but of all.

PERNANCY. *n.* Acceptance or receipt of anything.

PERNOR. *n.* A person who receives the profits of land.

PER ORA. [L.] Through the mouth.

PER PAIS. See TRIAL ~.

PERPARS. *n.* Part of an inheritance.

PERPENDICULAR. See AFTER ~; AFT ~; FORWARD~.

PERPENDICULARS. *n.* 1. Perpendiculars are taken at the extreme ends of the subdivision load water line. *Hull Construction Regulations*, C.R.C., c.1431, Schedule 1, s. 11. 2. The forward and after perpendiculars shall be taken at the forward and after ends of the length (L). The forward perpendicular shall coincide with the foreside of the stem on the water line on which the length is measured. *Load Line Regulations (Sea)*, C.R.C., c. 1441, s. 3.

PERPETUAL CARE. The preservation, improvement, embellishment and maintenance in perpetuity in a proper manner of markers, lots, compartments, crypts or other space in a cemetery, columbarium or mausoleum. See CEMETERY OR ~ TRUST.

PERPETUAL CARE FUNDS. The funds and property received by an owner for the purpose of providing perpetual care generally of a cemetery, mausoleum or columbarium or of any particular part thereof.

PERPETUAL DURATION. See RULE AGAINST ~.

PERPETUA LEX EST, NULLAM LEGEM HUMANAM AC POSITIVAM PERPETUAM ESSE, ET CLAUSULA QUAE ABROGATIONEM EXCLUDIT, AB INITIO NON VALET. [L.] It is a universal law that no human and positive law lasts forever, and a clause which excludes formal repeal is invalid from the beginning.

PERPETUAL INJUNCTION. An injunction to finally settle and enforce the rights of disputing parties.

PERPETUAL SUSTAINED YIELD. Continuous management of a resource to maintain a steady yield or harvest by keeping annual growth or increase at least as high as annual yield or harvest.

PERPETUATE TESTIMONY. To reserve and perpetuate evidence which is likely to be lost because the witness is old, infirm or going away before the matter it relates to can be investigated judicially so that justice does not fail. See COMMISSION EVIDENCE; COMMISSION ROGATORY; LETTERS ROGATORY; ROGATORY; ROGATORY LETTERS.

PERPETUITY. *n*. 1. Time without limit. 2. The term "perpetuity" literally means something that lasts forever, but as used in [the] context [of the rule against perpetuities] it is generally used to refer to limitations of contingent future interests which may or will not vest beyond the period prescribed by the rule. In this context a perpetuity is a limitation upon the common law right of every person to dispose of his land to any other person at his or her discretion. *Taylor v. Scurry-Rainbow Oil (Sask) Ltd.*, 2001 SKCA 85, 203 D.L.R. (4th) 38, 207 Sask. R. 266, 247 W.A.C. 266, [2001] 11 W.W.R. 25 (C.A.).

PERPETUITY PERIOD. The period within which at common law as modified by this Act an interest must vest. *Perpetuities Acts*.

PERPETUITY RULE. Limits the time during which a grantor may withdraw property granted from commerce or effectively control the use of property by future generations, by making the property subject to a series of successive interests. D.M.W. Waters, *The Law of Trusts in Canada*, 2d ed. (Toronto: Carswell, 1984) at 282. See RULE AGAINST PERPETUITIES.

PER PRO. By procuring. "[These words] . . . in the acceptance or endorsement of a bill of exchange or promissory note amount to an express statement that the party so accepting or endorsing the bill or note has only a special and limited authority, and therefore, that a person who takes a bill or note so accepted or endorsed is bound at his peril to inquire into the extent of the agent's authority . . ." *Bryant, Powis and Bryant Ltd. v. Banque du peuple*, [1893] A.C. 170 at 177 (P.C.), Lord Macnaghten.

PER PROC. By procuring.

PER PROCURATION. " . . . [W]here a bill or note upon the face of it purports to be accepted or made per procuration, it is a notice to all the world that the person who signed it has but a limited authority, and that whoever takes it does so at his own peril . . ." *Cooper v. Blacklock* (1880), 5 O.A.R. 535 at 539 (C.A.), Burton J.A.

PERQUISITE. *n*. An emolument, privilege or incidental profit resulting from one's position or employment in addition to regular salary.

PERQUISITIO. *n*. Acquiring anything except through inheritance.

PERQUISITION. *n*. Acquiring anything except through inheritance.

PER QUOD. [L.] Whereby; sometimes used to refer to an action per quod servitium amisit.

PER QUOD CONSORTIUM AMISIT. [L.] Whereby one lost the benefit of the other's society.

PER QUOD SERVITIUM AMISIT. [L.] Whereby one lost the benefit of the other's service. An action founded on an employer's right to recover damages against a wrongdoer who injured the servant and deprived the employer of the servant's services.

PER SALTUM. [L.] At a leap.

PER SE. [L. by itself] Alone.

PERSISTENT OIL. Crude oil, fuel oil, heavy diesel oil and lubricating oil.

PERSECUTION. *n*. 1. The intentional and severe deprivation of fundamental rights contrary to international law by reason of the identity of the group or collectivity. *Rome Statute* Article 7. 2. Harassing or afflicting with repeated acts of cruelty or annoyance.

PERSON. *n*. 1. "The scope of 'person' as set out in s. 2 of the [Criminal Code, R.S.C. 1985, c. C-46] extends somewhat beyond the individual, covering additionally public bodies, corporations, societies and companies, but groups having common characteristics such as race, religion, colour and ethnic origin are not included in the definition." *R. v. Keegstra* (1990), 61 C.C.C. (3d) 1 at 19, 1 C.R. (4th 129, 77 Alta. L.R. (2d)193, [1991] 2 W.W.R. 1, 117 N.R. 1, 114 A.R. 81, 3 C.R.R. (2d) 193, [1990] 3 S.C.R. 697, Dickson C.J.C. (Wilson, L'Heureux-Dubé and Gonthier JJ. concurring). 2. " . . . [T]he term, as used in s. 203 of the Criminal Code, R.S.C.

1970, c. C-34 is synonymous with the term 'human being' [as used in s. 206]." *R. v. Sullivan* (1991), 3 C.R. (4th) 277 at 288, 122 N.R. 166, 63 C.C.C. (3d) 97, 55 B.C.L.R. (2d) 1, [1991] 1 S.C.R. 489, Lamer C.J.C. (Wilson, La Forest, Sopinka, Gonthier, Cory, McLachlin and Stevenson JJ. concurring). 3. " . . . [I]n the context of s. 11(b) of the Charter includes corporations." *R. v. C.I.P. Inc.* (1992), 12 C.R. (4th) 237 at 250, 71 C.C.C. (3d) 129, 135 N.R. 90, 52 O.A.C. 366, [1992] 1 S.C.R. 843, 9 C.R.R. (2d) 62, 7 C.O.H.S.C. 1, the court per Stevenson J. 4. " . . . [A]ny being that is capable of having rights and duties, and is confined to that. Persons are of two classes only—natural persons and legal persons. A natural person is a human being that has the capacity for rights or duties. A legal person is anything to which the law gives a legal or fictional existence or personality, with capacity for rights and duties. The only legal person known to our law is the corporation—the body corporate." *Hague v. Cancer Relief & Research Institute*, [1939] 4 D.L.R. 191 at 193, [1939] 3 W.W.R. 160, 47 Man. R. 325 (K.B.), Dysart J. 5. " . . . [I]n the Charter refers to a human being and must include the parts that constitute the whole; certainly the parts which are so individual as to identify the whole." *R. v. Legere* (1988), 43 C.C.C. (3d) 502 at 513, 89 N.B.R. (2d) 361, 226 A.P.R. 361 (C.A.), the court per Angers J.A. 6. A natural person. 7. Includes a body corporate or politic. 8. An individual, partnership, unincorporated association, unincorporated organization, syndicate, trustee, executor, administrator or other legal personal representative. 9. Includes: (i) the Government of Canada and of any province of Canada and any department, commission, board or branch of any such government; (ii) a corporation, its successors and assigns; and (iii) the heirs, executors, administrators or other legal representatives of a person. *Evidence Acts*. 10. Includes any lawful trade union and any lawful association engaged in trade or business or the promotion thereof, and the administrative authority of any country, state, province, municipality or other organized administrative area. *Trade-marks Act*, R.S.C. 1985, c. T-13, s. 2. 11. Includes any body corporate or association, syndicate, trust or other body and the heirs, executors and administrators thereof, and the curators and assigns or other legal representatives of that person according to the law of that part of Canada to which the context extends. 12. Includes Her Majesty and public bodies, bodies corporate, societies, companies and inhabitants of countries, parishes, municipalities or other districts in relation to the acts and things that they are capable of doing and owning respectively. *Criminal Code*, R.S.C. 1985, c. C-46, s. 2. See ABORIGINAL ~; ACCUSED ~; ADULT ~; APPROPRIATE ~; ARTIFICIAL ~; ASSOCIATED ~S; AUTHORIZED ~; BLIND ~; CHRONICALLY ILL ~; CLASS OF ~S; COMPETENT ~; CONTROL ~; CONVALESCENT ~; CUSTODIAL ~; DEAF ~; DECEASED ~; DISABLED ~; DISADVANTAGED ~; DURESS OF THE ~; ELDERLY ~; ELDERLY ~S; FEEBLE-MINDED ~; FRENCH-SPEAKING ~; HANDICAPPED ~; ILLEGALLY ENLISTED ~; INDIGENT ~; INFIRM ~; INSANE ~; INSOLVENT ~; INSURABLE ~; INSURED ~; INTERDICTED ~; INTERESTED ~; INTERNATIONALLY PROTECTED ~; INVESTIGATED ~; LAY ~; LEGAL ~; MARRIED ~; MENTALLY DEFECTIVE ~; MENTALLY DISABLED ~; MENTALLY ILL ~; MENTALLY INCOMPETENT ~; MISSING ~; NATIVE ~; NATURAL -,~; NON-ELIGIBLE ~; NON-RESIDENT ~; PHYSICALLY DISABLED ~S; PROFESSIONAL ~; PSYCHOTIC ~; QUALIFIED ~; RATABLE ~; REASONABLE ~; RELATED ~; RELATED ~ OR COMPANY; RELATED ~S; RESIDENT ~; RESPONSIBLE ~; SECURITY OF THE ~; SELF-EMPLOYED ~; SINGLE ~; TRADES~; UNEMPLOYABLE ~; UNEMPLOYED ~; YOUNG ~.

PERSONA. *n*. [L.] Anybody who can have and become subject to rights.

PERSONABLE. *adj*. Describes someone or something which has the status of a person and is therefore able to bring an action in a court.

PERSONA CONJUNCTA AEQUIPARATUR INTERESSE PROPRIO. [L.] A related person is considered to be the same as the person.

PERSONA DESIGNATA. [L.] 1. Someone described or designated as an individual, in contrast to someone who is the member of a class or represents a particular characteristic. 2. "The concept of persona designata came from the courts and it can be modified or abolished by the courts. In my view, I think this court should declare that whenever a statutory power is conferred upon a judge or officer of a court, the power should be deemed exercisable in official capacity as representing the court unless there is express provision to the contrary." *Herman v. Canada (Deputy Attorney General)* (1978), 5

C.R. (3d) 242 at 264, [1978] 1 S.C.R. 729, 23 N.R. 235, 91 D.L.R. (3d) 3, [1978] C.T.C. 744, 78 D.T.C. 6456, Laskin C.J.C. 3. "Prima facie, Parliament should be taken to intend a Judge to act qua Judge whenever by statute it grants powers to a Judge. He who alleges that a Judge is acting in the special capacity of persona designata must find in the specific legislation provisions which clearly evidence a contrary intention on the part of Parliament. The test to be applied in considering whether such a contrary intention appears in the relevant statute can be cast in the form of a question: Is the Judge exercising the peculiar, and distinct, and exceptional jurisdiction, separate from and unrelated to the tasks which he performs from day-to-day as a Judge, and have nothing in common with the Court of which he is a member? . . ." *Herman v. Canada (Deputy Attorney General)* (1978), 91 D.L.R. (3d) 3 at 13, 18, 5 C.R. (3d) 242 at 264, [1978] 1 S.C.R. 729, 23 N.R. 235, [1978] C.T.C. 744, 78 D.T.C. 6456, Dickson J. (Martland, Ritchie, Pigeon, Beetz and Pratte JJ. concurring).

PERSONA EXTRANEA. [L.] Someone outside of one's family.

PERSON AGGRIEVED. A person adversely affected.

PERSONA GRATA. [L.] An acceptable person.

PERSONAL. *adj*. Referring to an individual's person. See CHATTELS ~.

PERSONAL ACCIDENT INSURANCE. Insurance against loss or damage caused by bodily injury to or death of the person or persons insured arising out of an accident or the agreement to pay a certain sum or sums on the happening of these contingencies.

PERSONAL ACTION. "The general, indeed the invariable, rule is: that a personal action is one brought for the specific recovery of goods and chattels, or for damages or other redress for breach of contract, or other injuries, of whatever description, the specific recovery of lands, tenements, and hereditament only excepted . . ." *McConnell v. McGee* (1917), 39 O.L.R. 460 at 463, 37 D.L.R. 486 (C.A.), Meredith C.J.C.P. (Lennox J.A. concurring).

PERSONAL BELONGINGS. Clothes, jewellery, personal effects, household furnishings. *Re Stanner's Estate* (1984), 28 Man. R. (2d) 64 (Man. Q.B.) at 65, 66.

PERSONAL BODY CORPORATE. A body corporate that is not actively engaged in any financial, commercial or industrial business and that is controlled by an individual or a group of individuals, each member of which is connected by blood relationship, adoption or marriage or by cohabiting with another member in a conjugal relationship.

PERSONAL CARE. 1. Assistance with the performance of the personal functions and activities necessary for daily living that one is unable to perform efficiently for oneself. 2. Room and board, assistance with some of the activities of daily living, nonprofessional care and supervision and a planned program of social and recreational activities.

PERSONAL CARE HOME. A building used for accommodation of persons who in the opinion of a duly qualified medical practitioner require continual or intensive assistance and supervision in their daily living.

PERSONAL CHATTELS. Automobiles and accessories, domestic animals, garden effects, household or personal articles for use or ornament, furniture, books, pictures, prints, paintings and other works of art, jewellery, video or audio reproductive equipment, musical and scientific instruments and apparatus, wines, liquors, consummable stores and other articles of personal property not amounting to an interest in land.

PERSONAL COMMERCIAL FISHING LICENCE. A licence authorizing a person to engage in commercial fishing.

PERSONAL CONTACT. Face-to-face contact.

PERSONAL DAMAGE. Any serious permanent damage, whether physical or mental, including death.

PERSONAL DEVELOPMENT SERVICES. (a) Services provided for, (i) health, fitness, diet or matters of a similar nature, (ii) modelling and talent, including photo shoots relating to modelling and talent, or matters of a similar nature, (iii) martial arts, sports, dance or similar activities, and (iv) other matters as may be prescribed, and (b) facilities provided for or instruction on the services referred to in clause (a) and any goods that are incidentally provided in addition to the provision of the services. *Consumer Protection Act, 2002*, S.O. 2002, c. 30, Sched. A, s. 20.

PERSONAL DIGNITY. The fundamental entitlement of every human being to be respected as a human being by others and to respect himself or herself.

PERSONAL EMPLOYEE INFORMATION. In respect of an individual who is an employee or a potential employee, personal information reasonably required by an organization that is collected, used or disclosed solely for the purposes of establishing, managing or terminating (i) an employment relationship, or (ii) a volunteer work relationship between the organization and the individual but does not include personal information about the individual that is unrelated to that relationship; *Personal Information Protection Act*, S.A. 2003, c. P-6.5, s. 1.

PERSONAL ESTATE. Includes leasehold estates and other chattels real, and also money, shares of government and other funds, securities for money (not being real estate), debts, choses in action, rights, credits, goods, and all other property, except real estate, that by law devolves upon the executor or administrator, and any share or interest therein.

PERSONAL EXPENSES. 1. With respect to the expenditure of any candidate in relation to any election at which he is a candidate, includes and any reasonable amount incurred by the candidate in respect of such travel living and other related expenses as the Chief Electoral Officer may designate. 2. Includes the following: 1. Reasonable and ordinary rent for hire of halls or other places used by the candidate in which to address public meetings personally of voters, and the expenses incurred in heating, lighting and cleaning such halls or other places; 2. Reasonable and ordinary travelling and living expenses of the candidate; 3. Reasonable and ordinary travelling and living expenses of one speaker for each meeting who accompanies the candidate and travels with her or him for the purpose of speaking at public meetings to be addressed by the candidate; 4. Reasonable and ordinary charges for the hire of conveyances for the use of the candidate; 5. Reasonable and ordinary charges for use by the candidate personally of not more than one conveyance on the polling day.

PERSONAL FILE. Any collection or repository of information obtained from others in the course of making a personal investigation whether the information is stored in written, photographic, electronic or any other form. *Personal Investigations Act*, R.S.M. 1987, c. P34, s. 1.

PERSONAL HARASSMENT. Objectionable comments or conduct directed toward a specific person or persons which serves no legitimate work purpose and which creates an intimidating, humiliating, hostile or offensive workplace.

PERSONAL HEALTH INFORMATION. With respect to an individual, whether living or deceased, means (a) information concerning the physical or mental health of the individual; (b) information concerning any health service provided to the individual; (c) information concerning the donation by the individual of any body part or any bodily substance of the individual or information derived from the testing or examination of a body part or bodily substance of the individual; (d) information that is collected in the course of providing health services to the individual; or (e) information that is collected incidentally to the provision of health services to the individual. *Personal Information Protection and Electronic Documents Act*, S.C. 2000, c. 5, s. 2.

PERSONAL INCOME. The sum of (1) the market value of rights one exercises in consumption and (2) the change in value of the accumulated property rights between the beginning and end of a certain period of time. W. Grover & F. Iacobucci, *Materials on Canadian Income Tax*, 4th ed. (Toronto: Richard De Boo Ltd., 1980) at 40.

PERSONAL INCOME TAX RATE. See PROVINCIAL ~.

PERSONAL INFORMATION. 1. Information about an identifiable individual. 2. Information other than credit information about a consumer's character, reputation, health, physical or personal characteristics or mode of living or about any other matter concerning the consumer. 3. Information respecting a person's identity, dependents, marital status, employment, borrowing and repayment history, income, assets and liabilities, credit worthiness, education, character, reputation, health, physical or personal characteristics or mode of living. 4. Information that can be identified with a person, including (i) information relating to the race, national or ethnic origin, colour, religion, age, sex, sexual orientation or matrimonial or family status of the person, (ii) information relating to the education or the medical, psychiatric, psychological, criminal or employment history of the person, the person's income, assets, liabilities and credit worthiness or information relating to financial transactions in which the person has been involved, (iii) an identifying number, symbol or other particular assigned to the person, (iv) the address, telephone number, finger prints or blood type of the person, (v) correspondence sent to a department by the person that is implicitly or explicitly of a private or confidential nature, and replies to that correspondence that would reveal the contents of the original correspondence, (vi) the persons name where it appears with other personal information relating to the person or where disclosure of the name would reveal other personal information about the person. *Freedom of Information Act*, S.N.S. 1990, c. 11, s. 2.

PERSONAL INFORMATION BANK. A collection or grouping of personal information.

PERSONAL INFORMATION INVESTIGATOR. A person who obtains or reports personal information to a consumer reporting agency for hire or reward. *Consumer Reporting acts*.

PERSONAL INJURY. 1. Bodily or physical injury. K.D. Cooper-Stephenson & I.B. Saunders, *Personal Injury Damages in Canada* (Toronto: Carswell, 1981) at 5. 2. [T]he civil law concepts of "préjudice corporel—bodily injury", despite their flexibility, incorporate an inner limitation to the potential ambit of s. 6(*a*) of the Act, requiring some form of interference with physical integrity. Although the terms "death" or "personal injury" found in the English version allow the possibility of non-physical injury to be captured within the s. 6(*a*) exception, the civil law concept of "dommages corporels" found in the French version of s. 6(*a*) does not. As the French version is the clearer and more restrictive version of the two, it best reflects the common intention of the legislator found in both versions. Therefore, the guiding principle in the interpretation of the s. 6(*a*) exception, more consonant with the principles of international law and with the still important principle of state immunity in international relations, is found in the French version of the provision. It signals the presence of a legislative intent to create an exception to state immunity which would be restricted to a class of claims arising out of a physical breach of personal integrity, consistent with the Quebec civil law term "préjudice corporel". This type of breach could conceivably cover an overlapping area between physical harm and mental injury, such as nervous stress; however, the mere deprivation of freedom and the normal consequences of lawful imprisonment, as framed by the claim, do not allow the appellant to claim an exception to the *State Immunity Act*. *Schreiber v. Canada (Attorney General)*, [2002] 3 S.C.R. 269.

PERSONAL INJURY OFFENCE. See SERIOUS ~.

PERSONAL INVESTIGATION. Any inquiry by any person to obtain factual or investigative information from any source other than the subject with a view to entering into or amending an agreement with the subject for credit, insurance, employment or tenancy, whether the information is transmitted immediately in a personal report or compiled in a personal file. *Personal Investigations Act*, R.S.M. 1987, c. P34, s. 1.

PERSONALITY. See INTERNATIONAL~.

PERSONAL KNOWLEDGE. Actual knowledge or knowledge of the affairs of a business based on perusal of the business' records.

PERSONAL NEEDS. Refers to items such as grooming supplies, toiletries, tobacco.

PERSONAL PREROGATIVE. Power which the Governor General may exercise at personal discretion, *i.e.* the power to select or dismiss a Prime Minister. P.W. Hogg, *Constitutional Law of Canada*, 3d ed. (Toronto: Carswell, 1992) at 246-9.

PERSONAL PROPERTY. 1. " . . . [G]oods, wares, merchandise, or effects [but not land] . . ." *Merritt v. Toronto (City)* (1895), 22 O.A.R. 205 at 213 (C.A.), MacLennan J.A. (Hagarty C.J.O. and Burton J.A. concurring). 2. Chattel paper, documents of title, goods, instruments, intangibles, money and securities and includes fixtures but does not include building materials that have been affixed to real property. *Personal Property Security Act*, R.S.O. 1990, c. P.10, s. 1. 3. Includes all property other than land, an interest in land or anything attached to it. See LISTED ~; TANGIBLE ~; VALUE OF ~.

PERSONAL PROPERTY INSURANCE. Insurance against loss of or damage to movable or personal property.

PERSONAL PROPERTY SECURITY ACT. Legislation, based on Article 9 of the United States Uniform Commercial Code, to reform and make the law concerning security interests in goods uniform.

PERSONAL PROTECTIVE EQUIPMENT. Any clothing, equipment or device worn or used by a person to protect himself from the dangers of his employment.

PERSONAL REPORT. Any report, whether written or oral, of information obtained from others in the course of making a personal investigation. *Personal Investigations Act*, R.S.M. 1987, c. P34, s. 1.

PERSONAL REPORTER. Any person who conducts a personal investigation but where the personal investigation is conducted by an employee of a user, or an employee of a personal reporting agency, in the course of his duties, the employer shall be deemed to be the personal reporter. *Personal Investigations Act*, R.S.M. 1987, c. P34, s. 1.

PERSONAL REPORTING AGENCY. Any person whose main business is to regularly conduct personal investigations for the purpose of supplying personal reports or the contents of personal files to others for gain. *Personal Investigations Act*, R.S.M. 1987, c. P34, s. 1.

PERSONAL REPRESENTATIVE. 1. An executor, an administrator, and an administrator with the will annexed. 2. A person who stands in place of and represents another person and, without limiting the generality of the foregoing, includes, as the circumstances require, a trustee, an executor, an administrator, a committee, a guardian, a tutor, a curator, an assignee, a receiver, an agent or an attorney of any person.

PERSONAL REQUIREMENTS. Items of a minor nature, other than the ordinary requirements of food, shelter, clothing, fuel, utilities and household supplies, that are necessary in day-to-day living to a person's health or well-being, and, without limiting the generality of the foregoing, includes items relating to (a) personal care, cleanliness and grooming; (b) the observance of religious obligations; and (c) recreation.

PERSONAL RESIDENCE. The residence ordinarily inhabited by the owner.

PERSONAL SERVICE. 1. " . . . Hogg J.A. stated in Re Avery, [1952] 2 D.L.R. 413 at p. 415 . . . (C.A.): 'Personal service has been said to be service made by delivering the process into the defendants hands or by seeing him and bringing the process to his notice.' Modern cases stress that the question of whether the purpose of giving notice to the person being served has been achieved is the relevant question [in satisfying the requirement of being 'served person-

ally' within the meaning of the Federal Court Rules, C.R.C. 1978, c. 663, s. 355(4)]. In Re Consiglio, [1971] 3 O.R. 798 (Master's Ch.) . . . the court held that personal service was satisfied if it appeared that the document came to the knowledge or into possession of the person to be served either directly or indirectly from a third party. Then, in *Rupertsland Mortgage Investment Ltd. v. City of Winnipeg* (1981), 25 Man. R. (2d) 29 . . . (Co. Ct.) . . . It was held that . . . personal service will be effected if it can be shown that the person to be served actually received the document and was apprised of the contents whether directly or through an intermediary." *Polo Ralph Lauren Corp. v. Ashby* (1990), 31 C.P.R. (3d) 129 at 137, 36 F.T.R. 81, [1990] F.C. 541, Reed J. 2. On any individual except a disabled person, to leave a copy of the document with that individual. On a corporation, to leave a copy of the document with an agent, director or officer of the corporation, or with someone at that corporation's place of business who appears to be in management or control of that place of business.

PERSONAL SERVICE ROOM. A change room, toilet room, wash room, shower room, lunch room or any combination thereof.

PERSONAL SERVICES. The regular performance for a resident of, or significant assistance with the performance by a resident of, personal functions necessary for daily living, such as grooming and hygiene.

PERSONAL SERVICE SHOP. A building or part of a building in which services, other than repair services, are provided to individuals.

PERSONAL SERVICES OCCUPANCY. Occupancy for the rendering or receiving of professional or personal services.

PERSONAL SUPERVISION. Direct supervision by a licensed pharmacist who is physically present. *Pharmacy acts.*

PERSONALTY. *n*. Personal property.

PERSON AT HOME. A person, having or not having a spouse, whose chief occupation consists in attending to the usual occupations of a person who stays at home for the benefit of that person's household.

PERSONATING POLICE OFFICER. Falsely representing oneself to be a peace officer or public officer, or using a badge or article of uniform or equipment in a manner that is likely to cause persons to believe that one is a peace officer or a public officer. *Criminal Code*, R.S.C. 1985, c. C-46, s. 130.

PERSONATION. *n.* 1. The act of representing that one is someone else, whether dead or living, fictitious or real. 2. Every one who fraudulently personates any person, living or dead, (a) with intent to gain advantage for himself or another person, (b) with intent to obtain any property or an interest in any property, or (c) with intent to cause disadvantage to the person whom he personates or another person, is guilty of an indictable offence or an offence punishable on summary conviction. *Criminal Code*, R.S.C. 1985, c. C-46, s. 403.

PERSON CONNECTED. When used in relation to another person, means an employee, agent, partner or associate of the other person and, where the other person is a corporation, includes a director, officer, shareholder or member of the corporation. *Discriminatory Business Practices Act*, R.S.O. 1990, c. D.12, s. 1.

PERSON DYING INTESTATE. A person owning property who dies without a will.

PERSON EMPLOYED IN A MANAGERIAL OR CONFIDENTIAL CAPACITY. Any person who (a) is employed in a position confidential to the person occupying the recognized position of Speaker of the Senate, Speaker of the House of Commons, Clerk of the Senate, Clerk of the House of Commons, Administrator of the House of Commons, Gentleman Usher of the Black Rod, Sergeant-at-Arms or Law Clerk and Parliamentary Counsel of either House; (b) is employed as parliamentary counsel in either House or as legal counsel to a committee of either or both Houses; or (c) is employed by an employer and, in connection with an application for certification of a bargaining agent for a bargaining unit, is designated by the Board, or, in any case where a bargaining agent for a bargaining unit has been certified by the Board, is designated in prescribed manner by the employer or by the Board on objection thereto by the bargaining agent, to be a person (i) who has executive duties and responsibilities in relation to the development and administration of employer programs; (ii) whose duties include those of a personnel administrator or who has duties that cause the person to be directly involved in the process of collective bargaining on behalf of the employer; (iii) who is required by reason of the duties and responsibilities of that person to deal formally on behalf of the employer with a grievance presented in accordance with the grievance process provided by this Part; (iv) who is employed in a position confidential to any person described in paragraph (b) or subparagraph (i), (ii) or (iii); or (v) who is not otherwise described in subparagraph (i), (ii), (iii) or (iv) but who, in the opinion of the Board, should not be included in a bargaining unit by reason of his duties and responsibilities to the employer. *Public Service Staff Relations Act*, R.S.C. 1985 (2d Supp.), c. 33, s. 3. 2. A person who: (i) is involved in the formulation of organization objectives and policy in relation to the development and administration of programs of the employer or in the formulation of budgets of the employer; (ii) sends a significant portion of his time in the supervision of employees; (iii) is required by reason of his duties or responsibilities to deal formally on behalf of the employer with a grievance of an employee; (iv) is employed in a position confidential to any person described in subclauses (i), (ii) or (iii), (v) is employed in a confidential capacity in matters relating to employee relations; (vi) is not otherwise described in subclauses (i) to (v) but who should not be included in a bargaining unit by reason of his duties and responsibilities to the employer.

PERSON IN AUTHORITY. Someone formally involved in the arrest, detention, examination or prosecution of the accused, and whom the accused believes to have such authority. In other words, the proper test for "persons in authority" begins with an objective threshold test and then subsequently examines the subjective belief of the accused. *R. v. Wells* (1998), 1998 CarswellBC 1931, 230 N.R. 183, 127 C.C.C. (3d) 500, 163 D.L.R. (4th) 628, 18 C.R. (5th) 181, 112 B.C.A.C. 101, 182 W.A.C. 101, [1998] 2 S.C.R. 517, 57 B.C.L.R. (3d) 104, [1999] 5 W.W.R. 331 Per L'Heureux-Dubé J. (dissenting) (Bastarache J. concurring).

PERSON IN CHARGE. 1. Person over the age of 21 years with whom a child lives or who controls or is in a position to control or has the apparent charge of a child. 2. A qualified person appointed by his employer to ensure the safe and proper conduct of an operation or of the work of employees.

PERSON IN CHARGE OF THE DECK WATCH. A person who has immediate charge of the navigation, manoeuvring, operation or security of a ship, but does not include a pilot. *Crewing Regulations*, SOR/97-390, s. 1.

PERSON IN NEED. (a) A person who, by reason of inability to obtain employment, loss of the principal family provider, illness, disability, age or other cause of any kind acceptable to the provincial authority, is found to be unable, on the basis of a test established by the provincial authority that takes into account the budgetary requirements of that person and the income and resources available to that person to meet those requirements, to provide adequately for himself, or for himself and his dependants or any of them; or (b) a person under the age of 21 years who is in the care or custody or under the control or supervision of a child welfare authority, or a person who is a foster-child as defined by regulation. *Canada Assistance Plan*, R.S.C. 1985, c. C-1, s. 2.

PERSON IN RECEIPT OF A PENSION BY REASON OF WAR SERVICE. A person who (a) is in receipt of a pension (i) by reason of service in World War I; or (ii) by reason of service only in World War II, and who at the commencement of such service was domiciled in Canada or Newfoundland; (b) has, from causes attributable to that service lost capacity for physical exertion to an extent that makes the person unfit to pursue efficiently the vocation that the person was pursuing before the war; and (c) has not been successfully re-established in any other vocation. *Public Service Employment Act*, R.S.C. 1985, c. P-33, Sched. II, s. 1.

PERSON INSURED. A person in respect of an accident to whom, or in respect of whose sickness, benefits are payable under a contract. See GROUP ~.

PERSON INTERESTED. Includes any person who is affected or reasonably apprehends that he may be affected by any entry in the register, or by any act or omission or contemplated act or omission under or contrary to this Act, and includes the Attorney General of Canada. *Trademarks Act*, R.S.C. 1985, c. T-13, s. 2.

PERSON LAWFULLY IN POSSESSION OF THE BODY. Does not include (i) a constable, coroner or medical examiner in possession of a body for the purposes of an autopsy or other post-mortem examination; (ii) an embalmer or funeral director in possession of a body for the purpose of its burial, cremation or other disposition; or (iii) the superintendent of a crematorium in possession of the body for the purpose of its cremation. *Human Tissue Acts*.

PERSONNEL. *n*. Workers; employees. See FIRE SERVICES ~; NON-INSTRUCTIONAL ~; SCHOOL ~; TEACHING ~.

PERSONNEL AGENCY. An intermediary in the labour market who supplies businesses with the services of employees. A three-party relationship results among the agency, the employee, and the person contracting with the agency for services.

PERSON OF LOW INCOME. A person who receives a total income, that, in the opinion of a housing commission, is insufficient to permit that person to obtain adequate housing accommodation at the current rentals or prices in the area in which the person lives.

PERSON OF MIXED BLOOD. A person of (a) mixed Indian and non-Indian blood who is at least one-quarter Indian; or (b) mixed Inuk and non-Inuk blood who is at least one-quarter Inuk. *Northwest Territories Fisheries Regulations*, C.R.C., c. 847, s. 2.

PERSON OF UNSOUND MIND. In the context of the Limitations Act, a person is of unsound mind when he or she, by reason of mental illness, is incapable of managing his or her affairs as a reasonable person would do in relation to the incident, or event, which entitles the person to bring an action. *Bisoukis v. Brampton (City)* (1999), 46 O.R. (3d) 417 (C.A.).

PERSON RESPONSIBLE. When used with reference to a pesticide, substance or thing, means: (i) the owner; (ii) the person having the charge, management or control of the handling, storage, use, disposal, transportation or display; or (iii) the person having the charge, management or control, of the pesticide, substance or thing.

PERSONS WITH DISABILITIES. Persons who have a long-term or recurring physical, mental, sensory, psychiatric or learning impairment and who (a) consider themselves to be disadvantaged in employment by reason of that impairment, or (b) believe that an employer or potential employer is likely to consider them to be disadvantaged in employment by reason of that impairment, and includes persons whose functional limitations owing to their impairment have been accommodated in their current job or workplace. *Employment Equity Act*, S.C. 1995, c. 44, s. 3.

PERSON UNDER DISABILITY. A person who is a minor or a mentally incompetent person.

PERSON WITH A DISABILITY. A person who is apparently blind or otherwise disabled and is dependent on a guide animal or white cane.

PERSPICUA VERA NON SUNT PROBANDA. [L.] Evident truths do not need to be proved.

PER STIRPES. [L. according to stocks] " . . . [M]eans 'by roots' or 'by stocks'. When used in the context of a gift to issue, it indicates that the gift will be divided among a certain number of 'stirpes' on the date that the gift vests, and will be distributed within each stirpe according to generation. Children never take concurrently with their parents in a stirpital distribution. Instead, all generations of descendants represent their ancestors and take the share to which those ancestors have been entitled had they survived until the distribution date." *Fraser Estate, Re* (1986), 23 E.T.R. 57 at 66 (Ont. H.C.), White J. See PER CAPITA.

PERSUASION. See BURDEN OF ~.

PERSUASIVE AUTHORITY. A judgment or other origin of law whose intrinsic value takes strength from something other than its being binding in character.

PERSUASIVE BURDEN. "[Refers] . . . to the requirement of proving a case or disproving defences, . . . The party who has the persuasive burden is required to persuade the trier of fact, to convince the trier of fact that a certain set of facts existed. Failure to persuade means that the party loses. . ." *R. v. Schwartz* (1988), 55 D.L.R. (4th) 1 at 19, [1989] 1 W.W.R. 289, 66 C.R. (3d) 251, 88 N.R. 90, [1988] 2 S.C.R. 443, 45 C.C.C. (3d) 97, 56 Man. R. (2d) 92, Dickson C.J.C. (dissenting).

PER SUBSEQUENS MATRIMONIUM. [L.] By a later marriage.

PER TOTAM CURIAM. [L. by the whole court] A unanimous decision.

PER VARIOS ACTUS LEGEM EXPERIENTIA FECIT. [L.] By various acts experiences have made the law.

PERVERSE. *adj*. Contrary to the weight of evidence.

PERVERSE VERDICT. 1. A verdict in which a jury refuses to follow the judge's direction on a point of law. 2. " . . . [O]ne, for instance, in which it appears that the jury have not confined themselves to the terms of the issue and to the evidence legitimately brought before them, but have allowed extraneous topics to be introduced

into the jury box." *Evenden v. Merchants Casualty Insurance Co.*, [1935] 2 W.W.R. 484 at 490, 2 I.L.R. 288 (Sask. C.A.), Turgeon J.A. 3. One which is wholly contrary to the evidence.

PESCAD. The neutral citation for the Prince Edward Island Supreme Court, Appeal Division.

PESCTD. The neutral citation for the Prince Edward Island Supreme Court, Trial Division.

PESSIMI EXEMPLI. [L.] Of the worst example.

PESSURABLE WARES. Merchandise which takes up a lot of room in a ship.

PEST. *n*. 1. Any injurious, noxious or troublesome plant or animal life other than human or plant or animal life on or in human beings and includes any injurious, noxious or troublesome organic function of a plant or animal. 2. Any injurious, noxious or troublesome plant or animal life and includes any injurious, noxious or troublesome organic function of a plant or animal. 3. Any injurious, noxious or troublesome insect, fungus, bacterial organism, virus, weed, rodent or other plant or animal pest, and includes any injurious, noxious or troublesome organic function of a plant or animal. *Pest Control Products Act*, R.S.C. 1985, c. P-9, s. 2. See CATTLE ~; FOREST TREE ~; MAMMALIAN ~.

PEST CONTROL. See LAND ~; STRUCTURAL ~; WATER ~.

PESTICIDE. *n*. Any organism, substance or thing that is manufactured, represented, sold or used as a means of directly or indirectly controlling, preventing, destroying, mitigating, attracting or repelling any pest or of altering the growth, development or characteristics of any plant life that is not a pest and includes any organism, substance or thing registered under the Pest Control Products Act (Canada). *Pesticides Act*, R.S.O. 1990, c. P.11, s. 1. See FERTILIZER-~.

PESTICIDE RESIDUE. The residue of any pesticide or degradation product thereof. *Pesticide Residue Compensation Act*, R.S.C. 1985, c. P-10, s. 2.

PET BOARDING. A "pet boarding facility" covers one aspect of a "kennel" use—that is the boarding of the animal. "Boarding" suggests to me that the owner of the animal makes an arrangement to leave it in the care of the boarding facility. A "pet boarding facility" extends to include all domesticated animals, whereas a "kennel" seems to be traditionally limited to housing dogs. *Woodman v. Capital (Regional District)* (1999), 1999 CarswellBC 2193, 6 M.P.L.R. (3d) 128 (S.C.).

PETECHIAE. *n.* Very small bleeding points in the skin or membranes. F.A. Jaffe, *A Guide to Pathological Evidence*, 3d ed. (Toronto: Carswell, 1991) at 224.

PETECHIAL HEMORRHAGE. A very small bleeding point in the membranes of the body or skin. F.A. Jaffe, *A Guide to Pathological Evidence*, 3d ed. (Toronto: Carswell, 1991) at 141.

PETERS. *abbr.* Peters' Reports (P.E.I.), 1850-1872.

PETITIO. *n.* [L.] A count; a declaration.

PETITION. *n.* 1. The process which originates a divorce action. 2. A petition for a receiving order. *Bankruptcy Rules*, C.R.C., c. 368, s. 60. 3. An inferior's supplication to a superior who has jurisdiction to grant redress. 4. A written document by which an ordinary citizen asks the Crown and Parliament for redress, presented through a member following conditions laid down in the Standing Orders of the House. A. Fraser, W.A. Dawson, & J. Holtby, eds., *Beauchesne's Rules and Forms of the House of Commons of Canada*, 6th ed. (Toronto: Carswell , 1989) at 277. See COUNTER~; ELECTION ~; PRAYER.

PETITION DE DROIT. [Fr.] A common law method to obtain possession or restitution of real or personal property from the Crown or damages to compensate for breach of a contract. P.W. Hogg, *Constitutional Law of Canada*, 3d ed. (Toronto: Carswell, 1992) at 263.

PETITIONER. *n.* 1. One who brings a petition. 2. Any person applying to court no matter what the formal document used to make the application is called.

PETITIONING CREDITOR. A person who requests a receiving order in bankruptcy against a debtor.

PETITION OF RIGHT. A common law method to obtain possession or restitution of real or personal property from the Crown or damages to compensate for breach of a contract. Such a petition could proceed to hearing only if the monarch consented by endorsing it "fiat justitiae" (let right be done). P.W. Hogg, *Constitutional Law of Canada*, 3d ed. (Toronto: Carswell, 1992) at 263.

PETITIO PRINCIPII. [L.] Begging the question.

PETROLEUM. *n.* 1. Oil or gas. 2. Any hydrocarbon or mixture of hydrocarbons other than gas. 3. In addition to its ordinary meaning, any mineral oil or relative hydrocarbon and any natural gas, including coal gas, existing in its natural condition in strata, but does not include coal or bituminous shales or other stratified deposits from which oil can be extracted by destructive distillation. See CROWN ~; CRUDE ~; DOMESTIC ~; FOREIGN ~; PRIVATELY OWNED ~.

PETROLEUM GAS. See LIQUID ~.

PETROLEUM INDUSTRY. Includes the carrying on in a province of any of the following industries or businesses: (a) distillation, refining or blending of petroleum; (b) manufacture, refining, preparation or blending of products obtained from petroleum; (c) storage of petroleum or petroleum products; and (d) wholesale or retail distribution or selling of petroleum products.

PETROLEUM PRODUCT. 1. Crude oil or other hydrocarbon or mixture of hydrocarbons recovered in liquid or solid state from a natural reservoir, any hydrocarbon or mixture thereof, in liquid or solid state, that results from the processing or refining of crude oil or other hydrocarbon, and natural gasoline or condensate resulting from the production, processing or refining of natural gas or a derivative of natural gas. 2. Petroleum, gasoline, naphtha, benzene, kerosene lubricating oils, stove oil, fuel oil, furnace oil, paraffin, aviation fuels, butane, propane and other liquified petroleum gas, and all derivatives of a petroleum and any product obtained from petroleum, whether or not blended with or added to other things. See FUEL ~; INFLAMMABLE ~S; REFINED ~.

PETROLEUM RIGHT. An exploration licence, an exploration agreement, a production lease or a coal gas agreement granted pursuant to this Act or the regulations and includes any right arising from exploration licence, exploration agreement, production lease or coal gas agreement. *Petroleum Resources Act*, R.S.N.S. 1989, c. 342, s. 2.

PETROLEUM WELL. A well in which casing is run and that, in the opinion of the minister, is producing or is capable of producing from a petroleum bearing zone. See COMMERCIAL ~.

PETTIFOGGER. *n*. A lawyer who is not honest.

PETTY CASH EXPENDITURE. A disbursement made out of an accountable advance held in a department in cash. *Accountable Advances Regulations*, C.R.C., c. 668, s. 2.

PEW. *n*. In a church, an enclosed seat.

PFRA. *abbr*. Prairie Farm Rehabilitation Administration.

P.G. *abbr*. Procureur général.

PHARMACEUTICAL. *n*. See APPROVED DRUG AND ~; RADIO ~.

PHARMACEUTICAL. *adj*. Relating to a pharmacy.

PHARMACEUTICAL CHEMIST. A person who is legally qualified to practise pharmacy and who is the holder of a valid and subsisting licence entitling him to practise his profession under this Act. *Pharmacy acts*.

PHARMACEUTICAL PREPARATION. Includes (a) any substance or mixture of substances manufactured, sold or represented for use in (i) the diagnosis, treatment, mitigation or prevention of a disease, disorder or abnormal physical state, or the symptoms thereof, in humans or animals; or (ii) restoring, correcting or modifying organic functions in humans or animals; and (b) any substance to be used in the preparation or production of any substance or mixture of substances described in paragraph (a), but does not include any such substance or mixture of substances that is the same or substantially the same as a substance or mixture of substances that is a proprietary medicine within the meaning from time to time assigned to that expression by regulations made pursuant to the Food and Drugs Act. *Trade-Marks Act*, R.S.C. 1985, c. T-13, s. 51(3).

PHARMACEUTICAL PRODUCT. See INTERCHANGEABLE ~.

PHARMACIST. *n*. 1. A person who is registered, licensed or authorized under the law of any province to carry on the business of preparing, manufacturing, compounding or dispensing, for sale to a consumer, medicines and pharmaceutical preparations, and does in fact carry on business as a retail pharmacist. *Excise Act*, R.S.C. 1985, c. E-14, s. 136. 2. A person holding a licence, signifying entitlement to practise pharmacy. See LICENSED ~.

PHARMACY. *n*. 1. The custody, compounding and dispensing of drugs, the provision of non-prescription drugs, health care aids and devices and the provision of information related to drug use. 2. When referring to a facility means any place where pharmacy is practised. 3. A place where prescriptions, drugs, medicines, chemicals and poisons are compounded, dispensed, sold by retail, or distributed, and includes a dispensary, drug store, drug department, or a hospital dispensary. 4. A place where prescriptions, medicines, drugs, chemicals and poisons are compounded or prepared or sold by retail. See OPERATOR OF A ~; PARTICIPATING ~; PRACTICE OF ~.

PHARYNX. *n*. A tube of muscle and membranes which connects the cavities of the nose and mouth with the larynx and esophagus. F.A. Jaffe, *A Guide to Pathological Evidence*, 3d ed. (Toronto: Carswell, 1991) at 224. See HYPO~; NASO~.

PHASED STRATA PLAN. A strata plan that is deposited in successive phases under Part 13; *Strata Property Act*, S.B.C. 1998, c. 43, s. 1.

PHEASANT. *n*. Any of the species Phasianus colchicus Linnaeus. *Game and Fish Act*, R.S.O. 1990, c. G.1, s. 1.

PHEASANT HUNTING PRESERVE. An area in which pheasants propagated under license are released for hunting purposes.

PHEASANT RESERVE. An area licensed by the Minister for the propagation and hunting of pheasants.

PHEASANT SHOOTING GROUND. A parcel of land on which pen-reared pheasants are released for hunting.

PHILANTHROP. *abbr*. The Philanthropist (Le Philanthrope).

PHILANTHROPIC. *adj*. " . . . '[B]enevolent' . . ." *Brewer v. McCauley*, [1954] S.C.R. 645 at 647, [1955] 1 D.L.R. 415, Rand J.

PHILLIPS V. EYRE. See RULE IN ~.

PHOBIA. *n*. An irrational fear.

PHOSPHORIC ACID. Phosphorus pentoxide (P_2O_5). *Fertilizers Regulations*, C.R.C., c. 666, s. 2.

PHOTOGRAPH. *n*. 1. Includes photo-lithograph and any work produced by any process analogous to photography. *Copyright Act*, R.S.C. 1985, c. C-42, s. 2. 2. Includes film, prints, reductions and enlargements, microphotographic film and photocopies. 3. A reproduction made by any process that makes an exact copy of the original and includes any photographic plate, microphotographic film, photostatic negative, autopositive and any photographic print made therefrom. See PRINTED BOOK OF ~S.

PHOTOGRAPHER. *n*. Anyone using a photographic process that involves the formation of images directly or indirectly by action of light or other forms of radiation on sensitive surfaces.

PHOTOGRAPHIC FILM. Includes any photographic plate, microphotographic film and photostatic negative. *Evidence acts.*

PHOTOGRAPHIC RECORD OR DOCUMENT. (a) Photographs attached or mounted to form a unit, other than a printed book such as a photograph album; or (b) loose or unattached photographs that clearly form a single unit of visual information.

PHOTOGRAPHIC SLIDE. A stationary photographic slide or other similar device used in conjunction with a motion picture.

PHYSICAL ABUSE. Improper use of the body of another person. Maltreatment.

PHYSICAL DEFECT. A problem such as cracked walls, sunken floors, rotten rafters, leaky roofs or basements. B.J. Reiter, B.N. McLellan & P.M. Perell, *Real Estate Law*, 4th ed. (Toronto: Emond Montgomery, 1992) at 201.

PHYSICAL DISABILITY. Any degree of disability, infirmity, malformation or disfigurement of a physical nature caused by bodily injury, illness or birth defect and, without limiting the generality of the foregoing, includes any disability resulting from any degree of paralysis or from diabetes mellitus, epilepsy, amputation, lack of physical co-ordination, blindness or visual impediment, deafness or hearing impediment, muteness or speech impediment, or physical reliance on a guide dog or on a wheelchair, cane, crutch or other remedial device or appliance.

PHYSICAL DISABILITY OR MENTAL DISABILITY. An actual or perceived (i) loss or abnormality of psychological, physiological or anatomical structure or function, (ii) restriction or lack of ability to perform an activity, (iii) physical disability, infirmity, malformation or disfigurement, including, but not limited to, epilepsy and any degree of paralysis, amputation, lack of physical coordination, deafness, hardness of hearing or hearing impediment, blindness or visual impediment, speech impairment or impediment or reliance of a hearing-ear dog, a guide dog, a wheelchair or a remedial appliance or device, (iv) learning disability or a dysfunction in one or more of the processes involved in understanding or using symbols or spoken language, (v) condition of being handicapped or impaired, (vi) mental disorder, or (vii) previous dependency on drugs or alcohol. *Human Rights Act*, S.N.S. 1991, c. 12, s. 3 .

PHYSICAL HANDICAP. A physical disability, infirmity, malformation or disfigurement that is caused by bodily injury, birth defect or illness and includes epilepsy, but is not limited to, any degree of paralysis, amputation, lack of physical co-ordination, blindness or visual impediment, deafness or hearing impediment, muteness or speech impediment, or physical reliance on a guide dog, wheelchair or other remedial appliance or device.

PHYSICAL IMPEDIMENT. A material hindrance, obstruction or obstacle.

PHYSICALLY DISABLED PERSONS. Persons who are subject to physiological defect or deficiency, regardless of cause, nature or extent and whether they are ambulatory or use a wheelchair. *Buildings Accessibility Act*, R.S. Nfld. 1990, c. B-10, s. 2.

PHYSICALLY HANDICAPPED PERSON. A person who is subject to a physiological defect or deficiency regardless of its cause, nature or extent, and includes all such persons whether ambulatory or confined to a wheelchair. *Building Access Act*, R.S.N.S. 1989, c. 45, s. 2.

PHYSICAL OR MENTAL HANDICAP. A previous or existing disability, infirmity, malformation or disfigurement, whether of a physical or mental nature, that is caused by injury, birth defect or illness, and includes but is not limited to epilepsy, any degree of paralysis, amputation, lack of physical coordination, blindness or visual impediment, deafness or hearing impediment, muteness or speech impediment, or physical reliance on a guide dog, wheelchair or other remedial device. *Human Rights Act*, R.S.P.E.I. 1988, c. H-12, s. 1(1)(1).

PHYSICAL THERAPIST. A physiotherapist.

PHYSICAL THERAPY. The application of professional physical therapy knowledge in the assessment and treatment of the human body in order to obtain, regain and maintain optimal function by the use of any suitable medium of therapeutic exercise, massage and manipulation or by radiant, mechanical and electrical energy.

PHYSICIAN. *n*. 1. A legally qualified medical practitioner. 2. Someone who practises an art of healing. See ATTENDING ~; COLLEGE OF ~S AND SURGEONS; CONTRACT ~; JAIL ~; MEDICAL PRACTITIONER.

PHYSICIAN-PATIENT RELATIONSHIP. A fiduciary relationship giving rise to a duty of care, the breach of which constitutes negligence. Includes a duty not to touch the patient without consent, breach of which constitutes battery.

PHYSICIAN SERVICES. Any medically required services rendered by medical practitioners.

PHYSIOTHERAPIST. *n*. A person who practises physiotherapy. See REGISTERED ~.

PHYSIOTHERAPY. *n*. The assessment of physical function and the treatment, rehabilitation and prevention of physical dysfunction, injury or pain, to develop, maintain, rehabilitate or augment function or to relieve pain. See PRACTICE OF ~; PROGRAM OF ~.

PIA MATER. The deepest of the three membranes which surround the spinal cord and brain. F.A. Jaffe, *A Guide to Pathological Evidence*, 3d ed. (Toronto: Carswell, 1991) at 224.

PICKED. See HAND ~.

PICKET. *n*. A barrier. A person on a picket line.

PICKETING. *n*. 1. An organized effort of people carrying placards in a public place at or near a business premises. The act of picketing involves an element of physical presence, which in turn incorporates an expressive component. *Pepsi-Cola Canada Beverages (West) Ltd.* v. *R.W.D.S.U., Local 558*, [2002] 1 S.C.R. 156. 2. Attending at or near a person's place of business, operations or employment for the purpose of persuading or attempting to persuade anyone not to (a) enter that place of business, operations or employment, (b) deal in or handle that person's products, or (c) do business with that person, and a similar act at such a place that has an equivalent purpose. *Labour Relations Code*, R.S.B.C. 1996, c. 244, s. 1. See CHAIN ~; CROSS ~; PUBLICITY ~; SECONDARY ~.

PICKET LINE. An area in which picketing is carried on.

PICK OF LAND. The narrow piece of land which runs into a corner.

PICK-POCKET. *var*. **PICKPOCKET**. *n*. A person who steals by secretly putting hands into another person's pocket or purse.

PICK-PURSE. *n*. A person who steals by secretly putting hands into another person's pocket or purse.

PICNIC. See GROUP ~ AREA.

PICNIC GROUNDS. See PUBLIC ~.

PICO. *pref*. 10^{-12}. Prefix for multiples and submultiples of basic, supplementary and derived units of measurement. *Weights and Measures Act*, S.C. 1970-71-72, c. 36 schedule I.

PICTORIAL RECORD OR DOCUMENT. (a) A bound or attached collection of designs such as a sketch book; or (b) loose or unattached designs that clearly form a single unit of visual information such as a set of architectural plans or blueprints.

PICTURE. See PRINTED BOOK OF ~S OR DESIGNS.

PICTURE SHOW. See TRAVELLING ~.

PIECE. *n*. 1. A firearm held in the hand. F.A. Jaffe, *A Guide to Pathological Evidence*, 3d ed. (Toronto: Carswell, 1991) at 224. 2. Something which contains drugs. F.A. Jaffe, *A Guide to Pathological Evidence*, 3d ed. (Toronto: Carswell, 1991) at 224. See BY THE ~; FIREARM; RIFLE.

PIECE RATE. See DIFFERENTIAL ~.

PIECE WORK RATE. A rate of pay calculated upon a unit of work performed.

PIER. *n*. A deep foundation unit, made of materials such as wood, steel or concrete or combination thereof, which is either premanufactured and placed by driving, jacking, jetting or screwing, or cast-in-place in a hole formed by driving, excavating or boring.

PIERAGE. *n*. The toll which a vessel pays for the use of a pier.

PIERCE CORPORATE VEIL. To find corporate officers or directors liable or responsible for acts where the existence of the corporation would ordinarily shield them from liability or responsibility.

PIERRINGER SETTLEMENT. A *Pierringer* agreement arises from the 1963 decision of the

Wisconsin Supreme Court in *Pierringer v. Hoger*, 124 N.W.2d 106 (U.S. Wis. S.C., 1963). Like a *Mary Carter* agreement, a *Pierringer* settlement is an agreement between the plaintiff and one of several joint tortfeasors. However, the contracting tortfeasor does not remain a party to the action. The key aspects of a *Pierringer* settlement are therefore: (a) segregation of the contracting defendant's liability; (b) satisfaction of the contracting defendant's liability to the credit of all parties to the litigation; (c) the plaintiff's ability to continue with the action against the remaining defendants; (d) the plaintiff's agreement that it will indemnify the contracting defendant for any contribution it pays to the other defendants and covenants to satisfy any judgment against the contracting defendant. *Hudson Bay Mining & Smelting Co. v. Fluor Daniel Wright* (1997), 120 Man. R. (2d) 214 (Q.B.).

PIGGYBACKING. *n.* " . . . [O]ne sovereign authority (federal) might make it a criminal offence to breach a [statute] of another sovereign authority (provincial), . . ." *R. v. Clement* (1981), 23 C.R. (3d) 193 at 197, [1981] 2 S.C.R. 468, [1981] 6 W.W.R. 735, 23 R.F.L. (2d) 255, 10 Man. R. (2d) 92, 61 C.C.C. (2d) 449, 38 N.R. 302, the court per Estey J.

PIGNORATIVE. *adj.* Pawning, pledging.

PIGNUS. See CONTRACT OF ~.

PIKE. *n.* With respect to fish, includes northern pike, (Esox lucius, Linnaeus), great northern pike, grass pike and jackfish. *Ontario Fishery Regulations*, C.R.C., c.1849, s. 2.

PILE. *n.* A slender deep foundation unit, made of materials such as wood, steel or concrete or combination thereof, which is either premanufactured and placed by driving, jacking, jetting or screwing, or cast-in-place in a hole formed by driving, excavating or boring. *Building Code Act*, R.R.O. 1992, O. Reg. 403/97, s. 1.1.3. See COMPOSITE ~.

PILFERER. *n.* Someone who steals small things.

PILLORY. *n.* A framework which an offender was made to stand behind, with head and hands protruding through its holes.

PILOT. *n.* I . Any person not belonging to a ship who has the conduct thereof. 2. " . . . [A] person who operates the controls of an aircraft in motion." *Holmes v. Sun Life Assurance Co. of Canada*, [1977] I.L.R. 1-904 at 770, 6 A.R. 171 (T.D.), Moore J. 3. An employee assigned to a train when the engineman or conductor, or both, are not fully acquainted with the physical characteristics or rules of the railway, or portion of the railway, over which the train is to be moved. *Regulations No. O-8, Uniform Code of Operating Rules*, C.R.C., c. 1175, Part III, s. 2. See APPRENTICE ~; CO-~; LICENSED ~; REGISTERED ~.

PILOTAGE. *n.* 1. The guidance which a pilot provides. 2. The remuneration provided to a pilot. See COMPULSORY ~.

PILOTAGE DUES. The remuneration payable in respect to pilotage.

PILOT BOARDING STATION. A place used for the purpose of embarking or disembarking pilots.

PILOT FLAG. A flag of large dimensions compared with the size of a pilot vessel, and of two colours, the upper horizontal half, white, and the lower horizontal half, red, or such other flag as may hereafter at any time be adopted as and for a pilot flag. *Canada Shipping Act*, R.S.C. 1970, c. S-9, s..

PILOT-IN-COMMAND. *n.* In relation to an aircraft, the pilot having responsibility and authority for the operation and safety of the aircraft during flight time. *Aeronautics Act*, R.S.C. 1985 (1st Supp.), c. 33, s. 3.

PILOT WHALE. Any whale of the species Globicephala melaena or G. scammonic, commonly known as pothead whale or blackfish. *Whaling Regulations*, C.R.C., c. 1608, s. 2.

PINBALL MACHINE. A mechanical or electronic device in which a ball propelled by a plunger scores points as it rolls down a slanting surface among pins and targets.

PINK SALMON. The species known as Orcorhynchus gorbuscha.

PINT. *n.* 1 /8 gallon. *Weights and Measures Act*, S.C. 1970-71-72, c. 36 schedule II.

PINTSCH GAS. The product obtained by "cracking" oil and compressing the oil gas to 10 to 14 atmospheres. *Railway Cars Gas Fuel Systems Regulations*, C.R.C., c. 1165, s. 2.

PIPE. *n.* 1. Includes tube and tubing other than copper tube or tubing and includes fittings. 2. Any tubing or pipe used or intended for the conveyance or distribution of gas, except the connecting piping of an apparatus. 3. A large vein into which one may inject a narcotic. F.A. Jaffe,

A Guide to Pathological Evidence, 3d ed. (Toronto: Carswell, 1991) at 224. See DISTRIBUTING ~; FLUE ~; GAS ~; WASTE ~.

PIPEDA. *Personal Information Protection and Electronic Documents Act, 2000*, S.C. 2000, c. 5.

PIPEFITTER. See STEAMFITTER-~ TRADE.

PIPELINE. *var.* **PIPE LINE**. 1. (i) A pipe for the transmission of any substance, and installations in connection with that pipe; or (ii) a sewer or sewage system and installations in connection with that sewer or sewage system. 2. A flow line, gas line, oil line, mineral line, secondary line, distribution line or private line. 3. Any pipe or any system or arrangement of pipes by which oil, gas or water incidental to the drilling for or production of oil or gas is conveyed from any well-head or other place at which it is produced to any other place, or from any place where it is stored, processed or treated to any other place, and includes all property of any kind used for the purpose of, or in connection with or incidental to, the operation of a pipeline in the gathering, transporting, handling and delivery of oil or gas, and, without restricting the generality of the foregoing, includes offshore installations or vessels, tanks, surface reservoirs, pumps, racks, storage and loading facilities, compressors, compressor stations, pressure measuring and controlling equipment and fixtures, flow controlling and measuring equipment and fixtures, metering equipment and fixtures, and heating, cooling and dehydrating equipment and fixtures, but does not include any pipe or any system or arrangement of pipes that constitutes a distribution system for the distribution of gas to consumers. See COMBINED ~; COMMODITY ~; COMPANY ~; GAS ~; MAJOR ~; SECONDARY LINE; TRANSMISSION ~.

PIPE LINE COMPANY. *var.* **PIPELINE COMPANY**. Every person, firm, partnership, association or corporation owning or operating a pipe line.

PIPE LINE CORPORATION. A person owning or operating a pipe line, all or any part of which is situate in the province, for the purpose of gathering or transporting natural gas, petroleum or petroleum products.

PIPELINE GAS. See MARKETABLE ~.

PIPE-MECHANIC. See MASTER ~.

PIPE TAPS. Small diameter pipes tapped into the wall of the pipe at a specified number of main pipe diameters away from the orifice plate, so as to permit the measurement of the gas pressure on the up-stream and down-stream sides of the orifice. *Gas and Gas Meters Regulations*, C.R.C., c. 876, s. 25.

PIPING. *n.* 1. Includes tube and tubing other than copper tube or tubing and includes fittings. 2. Tubes, conduits and fittings, the sole purpose of which is the conveyance of a gas, vapour or liquid and the control of the flow or a gas, vapour or liquid between two points. See DRAINAGE ~; HOUSE ~; PRESSURE ~; ROUGH ~; STORM DRAINAGE ~.

PIPING INSTALLATION. The installing of any or all of the following systems, to wit: (a) heating systems used for producing motive power or heat in any form whatsoever, in any building or construction; such systems including among others gravity or forced hot water systems, and high, low or vacuum steam systems and likewise any firing system; (b) refrigerating systems for cooling air, chilling substances or making ice; (c) plumbing systems, in any building or construction, including piping and all accessories used for drainage or draining; for back air vent; for supplying hot or cold water or gas; (d) oil or natural gas burner systems but not propane gas burner systems; (e) automatic sprinkler systems utilized to prevent and fight fires in any building or construction.

PIPING SYSTEM. An assembly of pipe, pipe fittings and valves, together with any pumps, compressors and other fixed equipment to which it is connected, that is used for transferring a liquid or gaseous dangerous substance from one location to another. *Canada Dangerous Substances Regulations*, C.R.C., c. 997, s. 2.

PIRACY. *n.* 1. Acts of violence and robbery at sea. 2. Every one commits piracy who does any act that, by the law of nations, is piracy. *Criminal Code*, R.S.C. 1985, c. C-46, s. 74(1). See PIRATICAL ACTS.

PIRACY EX JURE GENTIUM. Piracy defined by the law of nations, in contrast to offences which a statute declares to be piracy.

PIRATA EST HOSTIS HUMANI GENERIS. [L.] A pirate is the enemy of the human race.

PIRATE. *v.* To encourage employees to change employers by offering higher wage rates.

PIRATES. *n* Passengers on the insured ship who mutiny and persons who attack the ship from land. *Marine Insurance Act*, S.C. 1993, c. 22, Sched., s. 1.

PIRATICAL ACTS. (a) Stealing a Canadian ship; (b) stealing or without lawful authority throwing overboard, damaging or destroying anything that is part of the cargo, supplies or fittings in a Canadian ship; (c) doing or attempting to do a mutinous act on a Canadian ship or (d) counselling a person to do anything mentioned in paragraph (a), (b) or (c). *Criminal Code*, R.S.C. 1985, c. C-46, s. 75 as am. by R.S.C. 1985 (1st Supp.), c. 27, s. 7(3).

PISCARY. *n*. A right of freedom to fish. See COMMON OF ~.

PIT. *n*. A place where unconsolidated gravel, stone, sand, earth, clay, fill, mineral or other material is being or has been removed by means of an open excavation to supply material for construction, industrial or manufacturing purposes. See COCK ~; EXCAVATION ~; OPEN ~; WAYSIDE ~.

PITH AND SUBSTANCE. Though pith and substance may be described in different ways, the expressions "dominant purpose" or "true character" used in *R. v. Morgentaler*, [1993] 3 S.C.R. 463, at pp. 481-82, or "the dominant or most important characteristic of the challenged law" used in *Whitbread v. Walley*, [1990] 3 S.C.R. 1273, at p. 1286, and in *Oldman River, supra*, at p. 62, appropriately convey the meaning to be attached to the term. *Canada (Procureure générale) c. Hydro-Québec*, (sub nom. *R. v. Hydro-Québec*) [1997] 3 S.C.R. 213, 24 C.E.L.R. (N.S.) 167 La Forest, J. for the majority.

PIT HEAD. A landing at the top of a shaft or slope or at any other surface entrance in an underground mine. *Coal Mines Regulation Act*, R.S.A. 1970, c. 52, s. 2.

PIT'S MOUTH. The loading point at ground level of the conveyor or other transportation facility that delivers a mineral substance to the pick-up point for shipment from the mine property to market or that delivers it to the processing plant. *Mining Tax Act*, R.R.O. 1980, Reg. 639, s. 1.

PL. *abbr*. [L.] Placitum. Any point decided in a judgment summarized by the reporter.

PLACARD. *n*. An advertisement; declaration; edict; public notice.

PLACART. *n*. An advertisement; declaration; edict; public notice.

PLACE. *v*. To transfer a child from the care and control of one person or agency to another person or agency.

PLACE. *n*. 1. "[In s. 10(1)(a) of the Narcotic Control Act, R.S.C. 1970, c. N-1] . . . includes places of fixed location such as offices or ships or gardens as well as vehicles, vessels and aircraft. It does not, however, include public streets, or other public places: . . . when found in a statute is usually associated with other words which control its meaning. . ." *R. v. Rao* (1984), 12 C.C.C. (3d) 97 at 125, 46 O.R. (2d) 80, 40 C.R. (3d) 1, 4 O.A.C. 162, 9 D.L.R. (4th) 542, 10 C.R.R. 275 (C.A.), the court per Martin J.A. 2. (a) A dwelling-house; (b) a building or structure or any part thereof, other than a dwelling-house; (c) a railway vehicle, a vessel, an aircraft or a trailer; or (d) a pen or an enclosure in which fur-bearing animals are kept in captivity for breeding or commercial purposes. 3. A type of bet on a race to select a horse to finish first or second in the official result. *Pari-Mutuel Betting Supervision Regulations*, SOR/91-365, s. 2. See HISTORIC ~; IN ~; NON-CONFORMING ~; POLLING ~; PRIVATE ~; PROHIBITED ~; PUBLIC ~; REGULATED~; WORKING ~; WORK~.

PLACEBO. *n*. An inert substance used for comparison purposes in a controlled study of an active substance, that is, a drug.

PLACEBO FACTOR. One which influences a patient's response to treatment independent of the pharmacological effect of a drug.

PLACED. *adj*. The key factor in determining whether machines or structures have been so "placed" as to render them assessable as "improvements", although not in law "fixtures", is simply whether they have been given "some permanency of position". *British Columbia Assessment Commissioner v. Woodwards Stores Ltd.*, 1982 CarswellBC 180, 38 B.C.L.R. 152, [1982] 4 W.W.R. 686 (S.C.), Taylor J.

PLACEMENT. *n*. Transferring a child from the custody of one person or agency to the custody of another. See DIRECT ~; PRIVATE ~.

PLACEMENT AGENCY. Includes any person or organization that is engaged in the business of placing individuals in employment or of securing employment for individuals for a fee, reward or other remuneration.

PLACENTA. *n*. A flat, round organ where the embryo is implanted which contains both fetal and maternal blood vessels and through which an embryo receives nourishment and oxygen. F.A. Jaffe, *A Guide to Pathological Evidence,* 3d ed. (Toronto: Carswell, 1991) at 224.

PLACE OF ABODE. The place where one resides. See USUAL ~.

PLACE OF AMUSEMENT. A building, hall, pavilion, place, premises, room, tent or structure of any kind or park, field or grounds where an amusement takes place for which an admission price is charged or collected, whether within the premises or elsewhere, in cash or by means of tickets or otherwise, and includes (i) a theatre, travelling picture show, open air theatre, amusement hall, entertainment hall, music hall or concert hall; (ii) a hall, pavilion, place, premises, room, tent or structure of any kind kept or used for public concerts, carnival shows, dances or other social gatherings; (iii) a dance hall, dance pavilion, hotel, restaurant or café in which facilities are supplied and used for public dancing; (iv) a circus, menagerie, midway, grandstand, race track, race course or place where a pari mutuel system of betting is operated; (v) a hockey rink, skating rink or roller skating rink, or a park, field or grounds used for athletics, baseball, football or other games; and (vi) a hall or grounds used for a boxing or wrestling contest.

PLACE OF ASSEMBLY. Includes a building or structure, or a portion thereof, and a tent or awning with walls or side curtains designed, used or intended to be used to accommodate 50 or more persons at the same time for the purpose of meetings, entertainment, instruction, worship, recreation, drill, or the viewing or purchasing of goods. *Fire Prevention Act,* R.S.N.B. 1973, c. F-13, s. 1.

PLACE OF BUSINESS. A place where an undertaking or activity, including a function of government, is carried on, whether or not carried on for gain or profit. *Employer Health Tax Act,* R.S.O. 1990, c. E.11, s.1(1). See ESTABLISHED ~.

PLACE OF CUSTODY. A place designated as a place of open custody.

PLACE OF DOMICILE. The place in which one has one's home or in which one resides or to which one returns as one's place of permanent abode and does not mean a place in which one stays for a mere special or temporary purpose.

PLACE OF EMPLOYMENT. Any building, structure, premises, water or land where work is carried on by one or more employees, and includes a project site and a mine.

PLACE OF ENTERTAINMENT. 1. Includes a theatre, cinema, amusement premises, concert hall, pool hall, circus, race course, baseball park, athletic ground, fairground, skating rink, dance hall, a place where there are coin operated games or a hotel, restaurant, club or cafe in which facilities are supplied for and used by the public for dancing or other places as the council may declare to be places of entertainment. *Municipalities Act,* R.S. Nfld. 1990, c. M-23, s. 245. 2. Any building, structure, tent, enclosure or area used in the entertainment of the people who attend thereat.

PLACE OF ORDINARY RESIDENCE. Generally, the place that has always been, or that he has adopted as, the place of his habitation or home, to which he intends to return when he is away from it and, where a person usually sleeps in one place and has his meals or is employed in another place, the place of his ordinary residence is where the person sleeps.

PLACE OF PUBLIC RESORT. A building used, or constructed or adapted to be used, either ordinarily or occasionally, as a church, chapel or other place of public worship (not being merely a dwelling-house so used), or as an orphanage, school, theatre, public hall, public concert room, public ballroom, public lecture room, or public exhibition room, or as a public place of assembly for persons admitted thereto by tickets or by payment, or used or constructed or adapted to be used either ordinarily or occasionally, for any other public purpose, but shall not include a private dwelling house used occasionally or exceptionally for any of those purposes.

PLACE OF PUBLIC USE. Those parts of land, a building, street, waterway or other location that are accessible or open to members of the public, whether on a continuous, periodic or occasional basis, and includes any commercial, business, cultural, historical, educational, religious, governmental, entertainment, recreational or other place that is accessible or open to the public on such a basis. *Criminal Code,* R.S.C. 1985, c. C-46, s. 431.2 (1).

PLACE OF SAFETY. Any place used for the emergency temporary care and protection of a child.

PLACER MINERAL. 1. Gold, platinum, precious stones, cassiterite or other valuable minerals occurring in unconsolidated superficial deposits. 2. Ore of metal and every natural substance that can be mined and that is either loose, or found in fragmentary or broken rock that is not talus rock and occurs in loose earth, gravel and sand, and includes rock or other materials from placer mine tailings, dumps and previously mined deposits of placer minerals.

PLACER MINING. Includes every mode and method of working whatever whereby earth, soil, gravel or cement may be removed, washed, shifted or refined or otherwise dealt with, for the purpose of obtaining gold or other precious minerals or stones, but does not include the working of rock on the site.

PLACES OF PUBLIC ACCOMMODATION. Public hotels, boarding houses, restaurants, sample rooms and rest and reading rooms.

PLACIT. *n.* A decree; a decision.

PLACITA CORONAE. [L.] The Crown's pleas.

PLACITARE. [L.] To plead.

PLACITATOR. *n.* One who pleads.

PLACITORY. *adj.* Relating to a pleading or plea.

PLACITUM. *n.* [L.] Any point decided in a judgment summarized by the reporter.

PLACITUM ALIUD PERSONALE, ALIUD REALE, ALIUD MIXTUM. [L.] A plea is either personal, real or mixed.

PLACITUM NOMINATUM. [L.] The day designated for an accused person to appear, plead and defend.

PLAGIARISM. *n.* The act of publishing the thought or writing of someone else as one's own.

PLAGIARIST. *n.* One who publishes the thought or writing of someone else as one's own.

PLAGUE. *n.* Pestilence; a malignant, contagious fever.

PLAICE. See AMERICAN ~.

PLAINANT. *n.* A plaintiff.

PLAIN LANGUAGE. Refers to the use of ordinary, not technical, words and writing style in legal documents.

PLAIN MASONRY. Masonry without steel reinforcement.

PLAIN MEANING RULE. If the words of a statute are ambiguous on their face then one may go beyond them to ascertain their meaning but if the precise words used are plain and unambiguous, they are to be construed in their ordinary sense according to the intent of Parliament.

PLAINT. *n.* The written statement of a cause of action.

PLAINTIFF. *n.* 1. A person who commences an action. 2. A person at whose instance a summons is issued. 3. Includes every person asking for any relief, otherwise than by way of counterclaim as a defendant, against any other person by any form of proceeding. 4. Includes a person asking any relief against any other person in an action. 5. Includes a defendant counterclaiming. See NOMINAL ~.

PLAIN VIEW DOCTRINE. Officers may seize evidence which is in plain view even though the evidence is not specified in the search warrant.

PLAN. *n.* 1. The map of a piece of real property divided into lots and parcels. 2. "... [D]esign is the concept of the project when finally completed. A plan is a description of that design set out graphically..." *Bird Construction Co. v. United States Fire Insurance Co.* (1985), 45 Sask. R. 96 at 99,18 C.L.R. 115, [1987] I.L.R. 1-2047, 24 D.L.R. (4th) 104,18 C.C.L.I. 92 (Sask. C.A.), Vancise J.A. 3. (i) A map, including any profile or section, of a mine or part of a mine, certified by the mine surveyor to be correct; or (ii) a reproduction of such a map. 4. Includes any drawn or written description, illustration or explanation of any construction. 5. A pension, retirement, welfare, or profit-sharing fund, trust, scheme, arrangement, or other plan established for the purpose of providing pensions, retirement allowances, annuities, or sickness, death, or other benefits to, or for the benefit of, employees, former employees, agents, and former agents of an employer, or any of them, and for the widows, dependants, or other beneficiaries of any of them. 6. A plan to provide for the control and regulation of the marketing of a farm product. See ACTION AREA ~; ASSIGNED RISK ~; BENEFITS ~; CANADA ASSISTANCE ~; CANADA PENSION ~; CIVIL EMERGENCY ~; CLOSURE ~; COMPENSATION ~; CONDOMINIUM ~; CONSTANT WAGE ~; CONTRACTUAL ~; COOPERATIVE ~; DEFINED CONTRIBUTION ~; DEVELOPMENT ~; DISABILITY ~; DISTRICT ~; DUPLICATE ~; ECONOMIC ~; EMERGENCY MEASURES ~; EMPLOYEE SHARE OWNERSHIP ~; EX-

PLANATORY ~; FARM INCOME ~; FOREST MANAGEMENT ~; GOVERNMENT ~; INDIRECT INCENTIVE ~; INSURED ~; JOINT EARNINGS ~; LAND USE ~; LIFE INSURANCE ~; MANAGEMENT ~; MARKETING ~; MASTER ~; MINING ~; MONEY ACCUMULATION ~; MONEY PURCHASE ~; MULTI-EMPLOYER ~; MULTIPLE USE ~; OFFICIAL ~; ORIGINAL ~; PENSION ~; PRE-ARRANGED FUNERAL ~; PREARRANGED FUNERAL SERVICES ~; PRENEED CEMETERY ~; PRENEED CEMETERY SERVICES ~; PROFIT SHARING ~; REDEVELOPMENT ~; REFERENCE ~; REGIONAL ~; REPLACEMENT ~; SIMILAR ~; SKETCH ~; STOCK SAVINGS ~; STRUCTURAL ~S; SUPPLEMENTAL ~; TRANSPORTATION ~.

PLANE. See GYRO~; INCLINED ~; LAND~.

PLANNED. *adj.* 1. " ... [M]eans that the scheme was conceived and carefully thought out before it was carried out . . ." *R. v. Nygaard* (1989), 51 C.C.C. (3d) 417 at 432, [1989] 2 S.C.R. 1074, [1990] 1 W.W.R. 1, 70 Alta. L.R. (2d) 1, 72 C.R. (3d) 257, 101 N.R.108, 102 A.R. 186, Cory J. 2. . . [A]rranged beforehand. . . *R. v. Nakoneshny* (1989), 73 Sask. R. 205 at 214, 47 C.C.C. (3d) 423, 41 C.R.R. 205 (C.A.), the court per Cameron J.A.

PLANNED UNIT DEVELOPMENT. 1. Development of land by a method of subdividing land whereby the land is specifically subdivided for the uses and purposes specified in the proposed plan of subdivision, as approved. *The Planning and Development Act*, R.S.S. 1978, c. P-13, s. 2. 2. A land development project planned as an entity in accordance with a unitary site plan which permits flexibility in siting of building, mixture of housing types and land uses, usable open spaces, and the preservation of significant natural features. *Planning Act*, R.S.M. 1987, c. P80, s. 1.

PLANNING. *n.* ". . . [E]ssential to orderly development of a municipality. Generally, a plan is developed for the municipality, and zoning by-laws implement the plan. . ." *Zive Estate v. Lynch* (1989), 47 M.P.L.R. 310 at 314, 7 R.P.R. (2d) 180, 94 N.S.R. (2d) 401, 247 A.P.R. 401 (C.A.), the court per Macdonald J.A. See EMERGENCY ~ CANADA; ESTATE ~.

PLANNING LEGISLATION. Considers overall planning for an entire municipality. Its subject matter is the control of the use of buildings and land. I.M. Rogers, *The Law of Canadian Municipal Corporations*, 2d ed. (Toronto: Carswell, 1971-) at 769.

PLANNING OFFICE. See COMMUNITY -,~.

PLANNING SCHEME. A statement of policy with respect to the use and development of land and the use, erection, construction, relocation and enlargement of buildings within a defined area.

PLAN OF DEVELOPMENT. See COMPREHENSIVE ~.

PLAN OF SUBDIVISION. A plan by which the owner of land divides the land into areas designated on the plan.

PLANT. *n.* 1. Any establishment, works, or undertaking, in or about any industry. 2. An organism usually deriving part of its sustenance by photosynthesis and part by root sorption and includes parasitic plants, trees, shrubs, weeds, grasses, ferns, mosses and micro-organisms. 3. An installation of any combination of boilers and pressure vessels, together with pipes, fittings, machinery and other equipment that is used to contain a gas, vapour or liquid under pressure. 4. A premises where cattle are slaughtered. 5. The premises on which are situated the fixtures, implements, machinery or apparatus used in carrying on any activity of a manufacturer. 6. Any tree, shrub, vine, tuber, bulb, corm, rhizome or root, or the fruit or any other part of any of them. See ABSORPTION ~; ANIMAL FOOD ~; AQUACULTURAL ~; AQUATIC ~; AQUATIC ~S OR ANIMALS; ASPHALT PAVING ~; BOILER ~; BULK ~; COLD STORAGE ~; COMPRESSED-AIR ~; COMPRESSED GAS ~; COMPRESSOR ~; CONCENTRATED MILK ~; CONTINUOUSLY-OPERATING ~; CONTROLLED-ATMOSPHERE STORAGE ~; DAIRY ~; EXTRACTION ~; FISHBREEDING ~; FISH ~; GUARDED ~; HEATING ~; HOISTING ~; INDUSTRIAL LOCKER ~; MANUFACTURING ~; MARINE ~; MARKETING ~; MEAT ~; MINING ~; PACKING ~; POWER ~; PRESSURE ~; PROCESSING ~; RECEIVING ~; REFRIGERATING ~; REFRIGERATION ~; REFRIGERATOR ~; RENDERING ~; SCRUBBING ~; SEA ~; SEMI-FABRICATING ~; STEAM ~; STEAM-POWERED ~; TRANSPORTATION ~; USED BOILER, PRESSURE VESSEL OR ~.

PLANTATION. *n*. A British colony in North America or in the West Indies. See FOREST ~.

PLANT BREEDER. A person who is recognized as a plant breeder pursuant to the circular entitled *Regulations and Procedures for Pedigreed Seed Crop Production*, as amended from time to time, published by the Canadian Seed Growers' Association. *Industrial Hemp Regulations*, SOR/98-156, s. 1.

PLANT DISEASE. Any disease or injury of a plant that is caused by an insect, virus, fungus, bacterium or other organism and that is designated a plant disease in the regulations. *Plant Diseases acts*.

PLANT FOSSIL. The fossilized remains of vegetable matter.

PLANT GROWTH REGULATOR. A substance or mixture of substances that, through physiological action, accelerates or alters the behaviour of plants, but does not include a plant nutrient, a trace element plant inoculant or a soil amendment. *Pesticides Control Act*, R.S. Nfld. 1990, c. P-8, s. 2.

PLANT INDICATOR HOST. Any plant that may indicate a virus or other pathogenic infection after inoculation by sap, vector, scion graft or other means from a plant being tested. Seeds *Regulations*, C.R.C., c. 1400, s. 45.

PLANTING. See RE ~.

PLANT NUTRIENT. See LESSER ~; MAJOR ~.

PLANT PROTECTION EMPLOYEE. A security guard. See GUARD.

PLANT SYSTEM. The series of pipes and fittings, prime movers, machinery and other equipment for the transfer or conversion of heat ever produced by a boiler. *Power Engineers Act*, R.S.P.E.I. 1988, c. P-15, s. 1.

PLANT UNIT. A plant-wide unit for collective-bargaining purposes.

PLASMA. *n*. A state of matter characterized by disorganization of atoms at a very high temperature and which may exhibit a particular behaviour in an electric or magnetic field.

PLASTERER. *n*. A person who, (i) applies plaster and stucco to the walls and ceilings, whether interior or exterior, of a structure; (ii) applies plaster and stucco on lath, masonry and rigid insulation; and (iii) tapes gyprock and wallboard.

PLASTIC EXPLOSIVE. An explosive that (a) is formulated with one or more high explosives that in their pure form have a vapour pressure less than 10-4 Pa at a temperature of 25oC, (b) is formulated with a binder material, and (c) is, when mixed, malleable or flexible at normal room temperature. *Explosives Act*, R.S.C. 1985, c. E-17, s. 2.

PLASTIC FOAM. A plastic the weight per unit of volume of which is decreased substantially by the use of a foaming agent during the manufacturing process. *Ozone-depleting Substances Regulations, 1998*, SOR/99-7, s. 1.

PLATE. *n*. 1. Includes (a) any stereotype or other plate, stone, block, mould, matrix, transfer or negative used or intended to be used for printing or reproducing copies of any work, and (b) any matrix or other appliance used or intended to be used for making or reproducing sound recordings, performer's performances or communication signals. *Copyright Act*, R.S.C. 1985, c. C-42, s. 2. 2. When applied to iron or steel, means a flat-rolled product of any shape (a) having a width of more than 8 inches but not more than 48 inches, and a thickness of .23 inch or more; or (b) having a width of more than 48 inches and a thickness of .18 inch or more. *Customs Tariff*, R.S.C. 1985, c. C-54, s. 2. See DEALER'S ~; LICENCE ~; NUMBER ~; REGISTRATION ~.

PLATE COUNT. See STANDARD ~.

PLATED ARTICLE. An article composed of any substance on the surface of which a layer or plating of a precious metal is deposited or plated by means of a chemical, electrical, mechanical or metallurgical process or by means of a combination of any of those processes, and an article composed of an inferior metal to the surface of which a covering or sheeting of a precious metal is fixed by brazing, soldering or by any mechanical means, *Precious Metals Marking Act*, R.S.C. 1985, c. P-19, s. 2.

PLATE GLASS INSURANCE. Insurance, not being insurance incidental to some other class of insurance defined by or under an act, against loss of or damage to plate, sheet or window glass, whether in place or in transit.

PLATFORM. See DIVING ~; PRODUCTION ~.

PLAYGROUND ZONE. A zone on a highway identified by a traffic control device as an area where children (a) may be expected to be on the highway; or (b) are permitted to cross the highway at a designated point along the highway. *Highway Traffic Act*, R.S.A. 1980, c. W-7, s. 72.

PLEA. *n*. 1. An action or suit. 2. A way to put forward a defence in certain proceedings. 3. A defendant's factual answer to a plaintiff's declaration. See NON-ISSUABLE ~; ROLLED UP ~.

PLEA BARGAIN. For an accused person to agree to plead guilty, or to give material information or testimony in exchange for an apparent advantage which the prosecutor offers, acting within the scope of a prosecutor's seeming authority. The advantage for which the accused bargains is conviction on a lesser offence than the greater one with which the accused was charged originally or a shorter or lesser sentence.

PLEAD. *v*. 1. To allege something in a cause. 2. To argue a case in court. 3. To answer to an offence charged in criminal court.

PLEADER. *n*. One who elaborates a plea. See FAINT ~.

PLEADING. *n*. 1. The process in which parties to an action alternately present written statements of their contentions, each one responding to the preceding statement, and each statement attempting to better define the controversial areas. 2. ". . . [A] statement in writing, in summary form, of material facts on which a party to a dispute relies in support of a claim or defence. . ." *Zavitz Technology Inc. v. 146732 Canada Inc.* (1991), 49 C.P.C. (2d) 26 at 38 (Ont. Gen. Div.), Isaac J. 3. Includes a petition or summons, other than a writ of summons, and also the statement in writing of the claim or demand of a plaintiff, and of the defence or the counterclaim of a defendant thereto, and of the reply of the plaintiff to a defence or counterclaim of a defendant, and of the defendant's rejoinder to such reply. See CLOSE OF ~S; MIS~; RULES OF ~.

PLEAD OVER. To reply to an opponent's pleading but to overlook a defect to which one might have taken exception.

PLEA IN ABATEMENT. Such a plea must point out the plaintiff's error and show how it may be corrected and furnish material for avoiding the same mistake in another action in regard to the same subject matter.

PLEA NEGOTIATION. For an accused person to agree to plead guilty, or to give material information or testimony in exchange for an apparent advantage which the prosecutor offers, acting within the scope of a prosecutor's seeming authority. S.A. Cohen, *Due Process of Law* (Toronto: Carswell, 1977) at 179.

PLEA OF PARDON. A plea that a pardon is a bar to an indictment, after the verdict is a bar to a judgment, or after the judgment is a bar to execution. S. Mitchell, P.J. Richardson & D.A. Thomas, eds., *Archbold Pleading, Evidence and Practice in Criminal Cases*, 43d ed. (London: Sweet & Maxwell, 1988) at 368.

PLEA OF THE CROWN. In criminal law, an offence triable only in the monarch's courts.

PLEASURE. See DISMISSABLE AT ~.

PLEASURE BOAT. A boat used primarily for the carriage of a person or persons for pleasure, whether on charter or not, and whether for compensation or not, and includes a boat used on water for living purposes.

PLEASURE CRAFT. A vessel that is used for pleasure and does not carry passengers.

PLEASURE CRAFT INSURANCE. (a) Personal property insurance in respect of pleasure craft; and (b) insurance against liability arising out of (i) bodily injury to or the death of a person; or (ii) loss of or damage to property caused by a pleasure craft or the use or operation of it.

PLEASURE VEHICLE. Equipped for the transportation of persons, not more than seven at a time, effects such transportation without any pecuniary consideration, and includes a motorcycle, with or without a side-car.

PLEASURE VESSEL. A vessel being used for pleasure and not carrying persons or goods for hire or reward and includes a vessel chartered or hired by or on behalf of the persons carried thereon.

PLEASURE YACHT. A ship however propelled that is used exclusively for pleasure and does not carry passengers. *Canada Shipping Act*, R.S.C. 1985, c. S-9, s. 2.

PLEBISCITE. *n*. The referral of an issue to the population to decide by vote.

PLEBISCITE OFFICER. The returning officer, assistant returning officer, deputy returning officer, poll clerk and enumerator and, except for the Chief Plebiscite Officer and the Deputy Chief Plebiscite Officer, includes every person who has a duty to perform pursuant to an act.

PLEDGE. *n*. 1. "Delivery is necessary to constitute a pledge, and the pledgee's right or special property is to hold the goods as security for the debt and on default to sell the goods as needed. . ." *N. M. Patterson & Co. v. Carnduff* [1931] 2 W.W.R. 221 at 227 (Sask. C.A.), Martin J.A. 2. Includes any contract pledging, or giving a lien or security on goods, whether in consideration of an original advance or of any further or continuing advance, or of any pecuniary liability. 3. An article pawned with a pawnbroker. 4. A debtor's bailment of goods, to be kept until the debt is paid, to a creditor. 5. A promise to contribute money to a charity. 6. A movable hypothec with delivery, which is commonly called a "pledge" (see art. 2665, para. 2 [of the *Civil Code of Quebec*, S.Q. 1991, c. 64], enables a creditor and a debtor to grant a hypothec on a property without the hypothec having to be registered in the registry in order for it to be set up against third persons. The hypothec is granted by handing over the property to the creditor, and the holding of the property by the creditor is sufficient to publish the hypothec. *Blouin, Re*, (sub nom. *Caisse Populaire Desjardins de Val-Brillant v. Blouin*) 2003 SCC 31, Per Gonthier J. (Iacobucci, Bastarache, Arbour JJ. concurring). See DEAD ~; HARMONY ~.

PLEDGEE. *n*. A person who receives a pledge; a pawnee.

PLEDGERY. *n*. The state of being a surety.

PLEDGOR. *n*. A person who offers a pledge; a pawner.

PLEGII DE PROSEQUENDO. Promises to prosecute in order to effect an action of replevin.

PLEGII DE RETORNO HABENDO. Promises to return something which was distrained, if the right is determined against the party who brought the action of replevin.

PLENA FORISFACTURA. [L.] The forfeiture of all of someone's possessions.

PLENARY. *adj*. 1. Complete, full. 2. Describes a proceeding with formal steps and gradations, in contrast to summary.

PLENE ADMINISTRAVIT. [L. one has fully administered] An executor's or administrator's defence that that person fully administered all the assets which that person received.

PLENE ADMINISTRAVIT PRAETER. [L. one has fully administered, except] An executor's or administrator's defence that that person fully administered all the assets which that person received with some exceptions.

PLENIPOTENTIARY. *n*. One who has complete power and authority to do anything.

PLENO LUMINE. See IN ~.

PLENUM. *n*. An air compartment or chamber which may have one or more ducts connected to it and which forms part of an air distribution system.

PLEURA. *n*. A membrane which lines the chest interior and covers the lungs. F.A. Jaffe, *A Guide to Pathological Evidence*, 3d ed. (Toronto: Carswell, 1991) at 224.

PLEURAL. *adj*. Of the chest. F.A. Jaffe, *A Guide to Pathological Evidence*, 3d ed. (Toronto: Carswell, 1991) at 21.

PLIGHT. *n*. An estate, with the quality of land; it included rent-charge and possible dower.

PLIMSOLL MARK. The mark or load line on the side of a ship which marks the depth to which she may sink when loaded with her proper cargo.

PLOT. *n*. 1. A lot as numbered and shown on the plan of survey by which the cemetery has been subdivided. 2. Two or more lots in which the rights to inter have been sold as a unit. *Cemeteries Act (Revised)*, R.S.O. 1990, c. C.4, s. 1.

PLOTTAGE. *n*. In expropriation, the advantage of a large holding in organizing an assembly for development.

P.L.T.C. Professional Legal Training Course, the bar admission course administered by the Law Society and the Continuing Legal Education Society of B.C.

PLUMBER. *n*. A person who, (i) lays out, assembles, installs, maintains or repairs in any structure, building or site, piping, fixtures and appurtenances for the supply of water for any domestic or industrial purpose or for the disposal of water that has been used for any domestic or industrial purpose; (ii) connects to piping any appliance that uses water supplied to it or disposes of waste, (iii) installs the piping for any process, including the conveyance of gas or any tubing for a pneumatic or handling system; (iv) makes joints in piping; or (v) reads and understands design drawings, manufacturers' literature and installation diagrams for piping and appliances connected thereto, but does not include a person engaged in: (vi) the manufacture of equipment or the assembly of a unit prior to delivery to a building, structure or site; (vii) the laying of metallic or non-metallic pipe into trenches to form sanitary or storm sewers, drains or water mains; or (viii) the repair and maintenance of the installations in an operating industrial plant. See JOURNEYMAN ~; MASTER ~; QUALIFIED ~.

PLUMBING. *n*. A drainage system, a venting system and a water system or parts thereof.

PLUMBING CONTRACTOR. A person who for reward undertakes by verbal or written agreement or otherwise to supply a plumbing service.

PLUMBING SERVICE. Any work with respect to the installation, repair or renewal of a plumbing system, together with piping and other materials forming part of the system.

PLUMBING SYSTEM. A drainage system, a venting system and a water system.

PLUNDERAGE. *n*. Embezzling goods while they are on board ship.

PLURAL. *adj*. Referring to more than one.

PLURALITY. *n*. A greater number.

PLURES COHAEREDES SUNT QUASI UNUM CORPUS PROPTER UNITATEM JURIS QUOD HABENT. [L.] Several co-heirs are almost one body because of the unity of right they hold.

PLURES PARTICIPES SUNT QUASI UNUM CORPUS, IN EO QUOD UNUM JUS HABENT. [L.] Several people sharing are almost one body, in that they hold one right.

PLURIES WRIT. A third or subsequent writ.

PLUS VALET QUOD AGITUR QUAM QUOD SIMULATE CONCIPITUR. [L.] What is done is worth more than what is pretended.

PLUS VALET UNUS OCULATUS TESTIS QUAM AURITI DECEM. [L.] One eyewitness is worth more than ten witnesses who report hearsay only.

PLUS VALET VULGARIS CONSUETUDO QUAM REGALIS CONCESSIO. [L.] Common custom is worth more than a royal grant.

PLY. *n*. A layer of rubber-coated parallel cords. Canada regulations.

PLY SEPARATION. The parting of the rubber compound between adjacent plies of a tire. Canada regulations.

P.M. *abbr*. 1. Post-meridiem, afternoon. 2. Prime Minister. 3. " . . . Police Magistrate. . ." *R. v. Linder*, [1924] 3 D.L.R. 505 at 507, [1924]

2 W.W.R. 646, 42 C.C.C. 289, 20 Alta. L.R. 415 (C.A.), the court per Becker J.A.

P.N.E. *abbr*. Pacific National Exhibition.

PNEUMATIC TIRE. 1. Every tire that is designed to support a load by compressed air. 2. A device made of rubber, chemicals, fabric or steel or other materials that, when mounted on an automotive wheel, provides traction and contains the gas or fluid that sustains the load. *Motor Vehicle Safety Regulations*, C.R.C., c.1038, s. 110.

PNEUMOCONIOSIS. *var*. **PNEUMONO-CONIOSIS**. *n*. A diseased condition characterized by generalized changes in the fibres in the lungs caused by breathing air containing siliceous dust. This term includes the diseases called "silicosis" and "asbestosis". See COAL MINERS' ~.

PNEUMOTHORAX. *n*. Air in the cavity of the chest. F.A. Jaffe, *A Guide to Pathological Evidence*, 3d ed. (Toronto: Carswell, 1991) at 224.

P.O. *abbr*. Post office.

POACH. *v*. To unlawfully take or destroy game on another person's land.

PODIATRIST. *n*. A person who practises or advertises or holds himself out in any way as practising podiatry and massage in connection therewith.

PODIATRY. *n*. (i) Means the branch of the healing arts that treats all ailments, diseased conditions, deformities and injuries of the human foot and the leg muscles controlling the foot; and (ii) includes the examination, diagnosis and treatment of those ailments, conditions, deformities or injuries; but (iii) does not include the treatment of systemic diseases of bones, muscles or ligaments, or the use of X-ray equipment for purposes other than diagnostic, or the use of anaesthetics other than local.

POENA. *n*. [L.] A punishment, a penalty.

POENAE POTIUS MOLLIENDAE QUAM EXASPERANDAE SUNT. [L.] Punishments should be softened more than aggravated.

POENA EX DELICTO DEFUNCTI, HAERES TENERI NON DEBET. [L.] An heir should not be penalized for a wrong done by a defunct.

P.O.G.G. *abbr*. Peace, order and good government. See RESIDUARY POWER.

POINT. *n*. In respect of a unit toll commercial air service, means the city, town or place specified in a licence that an air carrier is authorized to serve by such licence and that is identified where necessary by reference to latitude and longitude and that, (a) in respect of a point in a Class 1 licence, comprises an area 25 miles in radius measured from the main post office of such point or from the latitude and longitude of such point; and (b) in respect of a point in a Class 2 licence comprises an area 10 miles in radius measured from the main post office of such point or from the latitude and longitude of such point. *Air Carrier Regulations*, C.R.C., c. 3, s. 2. See ASCERTAINABLE ~; CENTRE ~ OF AN INTERSECTION; DEMERIT ~; DYE-~; FLASH ~; GENERAL MEASUREMENT ~; H-~; INLAND ~; INSPECTION ~; POSTAL CONSOLIDATION ~; REFERENCE ~; SHIPPING ~; UNDISPUTED ~.

POINTED. *adj*. As applied to fur, means that hairs from any other peltry have been attached individually or in small groups to such fur.

POINT OF EMISSION. The point at which a contaminant enters the natural environment.

POINT OF INTERSECTION. The point at which the centre lines of such roads or highways intersect, and in the case of a road or highway intersecting with a railroad the point of intersection is the point at which the centre line of the road intersects with the centre line of the railroad.

POISON. *n*. Drugs or chemicals, or compounds thereof, that are dangerous to human or animal health or life.

POISONED ENVIRONMENT SEXUAL HARASSMENT. " . . . The line of sexual harassment is crossed only where the conduct may be reasonably construed to create, as a condition of employment, a work environment which demands an unwarranted intrusion upon the employee's sexual dignity as a man or woman. . ." *University of Manitoba v. C.A.I.M.A.W., Local 9* (1989), 6 L.A.C. (4th) 182 at 213-14 (Man.), Chapman.

POISONED WORK ENVIRONMENT. One which exhibits an atmosphere of prejudice which makes work difficult or impossible for the worker.

POISONING. *n*. The presence, in a body, of any harmful substance which, indirectly or directly, caused death. F.A. Jaffe, *A Guide to Path-ological Evidence*, 3d ed. (Toronto: Carswell, 1991) at 79.

POLAR FLIGHT. A flight traversing that part of Canada between 75° and 115° west longitude and 49° and 85° north latitude. *National Defence Aerodrome Fees Regulations*, C.R.C., c. 714, s. 2.

POLARIS. *abbr*. Province of Ontario Land Registration and Information Service.

POLAR REGIONS. When used in relation to Canada, means all regions north of sixty degrees north latitude and all regions north of the southern limit of the discontinuous permafrost zone and, when used generally or in an international context, means the circumpolar regions including the continent of Antarctica. *Canadian Polar Commission Act*, S.C. 1991, c. 6, s. 2.

POLE. *n*. 5 1/2 yards. *Weights and Measures Act*, S.C. 1970-71-72, c. 36, schedule II. See CATCH~; FAIR START ~; SPRING ~.

POLE KILOMETRE. A lineal kilometre in a telephone system necessarily occupied by telephone poles strung with one or more wires for the use of the telephone system.

POLE TRAILER. A vehicle without motive power that is designed to be drawn by another vehicle and to be attached to the towing vehicle by means of a reach or pole, or by being boomed or otherwise secured to the towing vehicle and is ordinarily used for transporting poles, pipes, structural members or other long or irregularly shaped loads which are capable of sustaining themselves as beams between the supporting connections.

POLICE. *n*. A force of people charged with maintenance of public order, detection, and prevention of crime. See BRIDGE ~; ROYAL CANADIAN MOUNTED ~.

POLICE ASSOCIATION. An association of either (i) the police officers of a municipal police force who hold the rank of inspector or higher, excluding the chief constable and deputy chief constables; or (ii) the police officers or a municipal police force who hold ranks lower than that of inspector that is limited to members of one municipal police force and has collective bargaining among its objects.

POLICE COMMISSIONER. "[The board of police commissioners] . . . are a separate department of the civic government, possessing special statutory powers and subject to the performance of certain duties independently of the municipal council, but dependent for their maintenance upon the council. Any property which they control they do not own, but merely hold and administer in the interest of the municipality." *Aikens v. Kingston (City)* (1922), 53 O.L.R. 41 at 43, [1923] 3 D.L.R. 869 (H.C.), Orde J.

POLICE COURT. The court of a magistrate.

POLICE FORCE. 1. " . . . [A] body of police. . ." *R. v. Gendron* (1985), 22 C.C.C. (3d) 312 at 321, 10 O.A.C. 122 (C.A.), Grange J.A. (dissenting). 2. Includes the chief officer, police officers and the necessary personnel, equipment, furnishings, vehicles and facilities.

POLICE INFORMANT PRIVILEGE. Protects from disclosure the identity of an informer whose assistance to the police is important in the investigation and detection of crime.

POLICE INFORMER PRIVILEGE. "[Protects] . . . from disclosure the identity of informers whose assistance is important in the investigation and detection of crime. . ." *Inquiry into Confidentiality of Health Records in Ontario, Re* (1981), 23 C.P.C. 99 at 128, 23 C.R. (3d) 338, 128 D.L.R. (3d) 193, 38 N.R. 588, 62 C.C.C. (2d) 193, [1981] 2 S.C.R. 494, Laskin C.J.C. (dissenting) (Dickson J. concurring).

POLICEMEN'S UNION. A trade union certified for a unit in which the majority of employees is engaged in police duties.

POLICE OFFICER. 1. A peace officer who is a member of a police force with authority to enforce federal and provincial statutes. 2. A member of a police force in a province. 3. The member of a police force appointed for policing duties and duties incidental to those duties. See PERSONATING ~; SENIOR ~.

POLICE POWER. A licensing power to enact by-laws which allows a municipality to govern, control and regulate licensed trades or businesses and those engaged in them. See "GENERAL WELFARE" CLAUSE; LICENSING POWER.

POLICY. *n*. 1. The instrument evidencing a contract. *Insurance acts*. 2. A government commitment to the public to follow an action or course of action in pursuit of approved objectives. *Public Service Act*, S.N.W.T. 1983 (1st Sess.), c. 12, s. 1. 3. " . . . [D]ecisions concerning budgetary allotments for departments or government agencies will be classified as policy decisions." *Just v. British Columbia* (1989), 1 C.C.L.T. (2d) 1 at 18, [1989] 2 S.C.R. 1228, 18 M.V.R. (2d) 1, [1990] 1 W.W.R. 385, 41 B.C.L.R. (2d) 350, 103 N.R. 1, 64 D.L.R. (4th) 689, 41 Admin. L.R. 161, [1990] R.R.A. 140n, Cory J. (Dickson C.J.C., Wilson, La Forest, L'Heureux-Dubé and Gonthier JJ. concurring). 4. " . . . [R]efers to a decision of a public body at the planning level involving the allocation of scarce resources or balancing such factors as efficiency and thrift . . . One hallmark of a policy as opposed to an operational, decision is that it involves planning. . . A second characteristic of a policy decision as opposed to an operational function is that a policy decision involves allocating resources and balancing factors such as efficiency or thrift . . . A third criterion is found in the suggestion that the greater the discretion conferred on the decision-making body, the more likely the resultant decision is to be a matter of policy rather than operational . . . Fourthly, it has been suggested that where there are standards against which conduct can be evaluated, a decision may move into the operational area and immunity should not be granted: . . . The setting of a standard is a policy function; its implementation is an operational function. . . the fact the person or body making the decision is working in the field does not prevent it from being a policy decision . . ." *Just v. British Columbia* (1985), 33 C.C.L.T. 49 at 52-4, 34 M.V.R. 124, 64 B.C.L.R. 349, [1985] 5 W.W.R. 570 (S.C.), McLachlin J. 5. "[In s. 34(1)(c) of the Combines Investigation Act, R.S.C. 1970, c. C-23] . . . a planned and deliberate course of conduct by responsible employees of the company. . ." *R. v. Hoffman-La Roche Ltd. (Nos. 1 & 2)* (1980), 109 D.L.R. (3d) 5 at 35, 28 O.R. (2d) 164, 14 C.R. (3d) 289, 48 C.P.R. (2d) 145, 53 C.C.C. (2d) 1 (H.C.), Linden J. 6. Any written contract of insurance or reinsurance whether contained in one or more documents and, in the case of insurance in a fraternal benefit society, any contract of insurance whether evidenced by a written document or not and any certificate of membership relating in any way to insurance, and includes any annuity contract. *Insurance Companies Act*, S.C. 1991, c. 47, s. 2. See CLAIMS MADE ~; DECLARATION ~; DRIVER'S ~; FLOATING ~; LIFE INSURANCE ~; MASTER ~; NONOWNER'S ~; OPEN ~; OWNER'S ~; PUBLIC LIABILITY INSURANCE ~; PUBLIC SEGREGATED FUND ~; TIME ~; TRANSIT ~; UNVALUED ~; VALUED ~; VOYAGE ~; WITH PROFITS ~.

POLICY DECISION. Generally made by a person at a high level of authority and is identified by its nature. Decisions concerning budget allotment are policy decisions.

POLICY GRIEVANCE. " . . . [T]he subject-matter of the grievance is of general interest and . . . individual employees may, or may not be affected at the time that the grievance is filed; . . ." *New Brunswick (Treasury Board) v. C.U.P.E., Local 2745* (1985), 64 N.B R. (2d) 91 at 106, 165 A.P.R. 91 (Q.B.), Daigle J. quoting from *Canadian Broadcasting Corp. v. N.A.B.E.T.* (1973), 4 L.A.C. (2d) 263 at 65-6 (Ont.).

POLICYHOLDER. *n*. A person who owns an insurance policy.

POLICYHOLDER IN CANADA. The legal holder for the time being of a policy in Canada.

POLICY IN CANADA. (a) With respect to life insurance, a policy on the life of a person resident in Canada at the time the policy was issued, (b) with respect to fire insurance, a policy on property in Canada, and (c) with respect to any other class of insurance, a policy where the risks covered by the policy were ordinarily in Canada at the time the policy was issued. *Insurance Companies Act*, S.C. 1991, c. 47, s. 2.

POLICY LOAN. An amount advanced at a particular time by an insurer to a policyholder in accordance with the terms and conditions of a life insurance policy in Canada.

POLICY OF DEPOSIT INSURANCE. The instrument evidencing a contract of deposit insurance with a provincial institution. *Canada Deposit Insurance Corporation Act*, R.S.C. 1985, c. C-3, s. 2.

POLICY OF INSURANCE. The writing whereby any contract of insurance is made or is evidenced.

POLICY PROOF OF INTEREST. A policy requires no proof of interest except the insurance contract itself. C. Brown and J. Menezes, *Insurance Law in Canada*, 2d ed. (Toronto: Carswell, 1991) at 4.

POLITIAE LEGIBUS NON LEGES POLITIIS ADAPTANDAE. [L.] Politics should be adapted to the laws, not laws to politics.

POLITICAL ADVERTISEMENT. Any matter promoting or opposing any registered political party or the election of any registered candidate for which a fee is paid, but does not include any bona fide news reporting.

POLITICAL ADVERTISING. Any matter promoting or opposing any registered political party or the election of any registered candidate or which a fee is paid, but does not include any bona fide news reporting.

POLITICAL AFFILIATION. With respect to a candidate, means affiliation with a political party.

POLITICAL ASYLUM. The granting of falls within the Crown's prerogative. To be contrasted with a political refugee whose status is determined by the Immigration and Refugee Board.

POLITICAL CIVIL LIBERTIES. Include freedom of assembly, association, religion and speech, the right to be a candidate for elected office and vote, the freedom to leave and enter Canada and move between provinces.

POLITICAL CRIME. Determination of what is a political crime involves the proportionality to a legitimate political objective.

POLITICAL LAW. The interdisciplinary study of the interaction among law, public policy and administration, and politics, and with the *influence* of law on the other types of instruments of democratic governance. It incorporates elements of constitutional and administrative law with public administration and political science. It deals specifically with topics such as: the factors motivating the choice of instruments for governing, the balance of law and politics in the legislative process, the precedence of law and its accommodation with other types of instruments in government management, the legal value to be ascribed to political and campaign promises, as well as with the relative weight of legal, administrative and political influences in the adjudication of political disputes on issues of public governance. The Quebec Secession reference was the most fundamental and the most comprehensive political law judgment to arise from the Canadian judiciary since Confederation. Gregory Tardi, *The Latest Phase in the Sovereignty Debate: A Feud of Statutes*.

POLITICAL ORGANIZATION. (i) Before the closing of nominations on nomination day, means (A) a political organization which advises a returning officer in writing that it has or intends to sponsor a candidate in the electoral district at the election, or (B) a person, not sponsored by a political organization, who advises a returning officer in writing that he has been or intends to be officially nominated as a candidate in the electoral district at the election, or (ii) after the close of nominations on nomination day, means (A) the political organization whose candidate has been officially nominated as a candidate in the electoral district, or (B) a person, not sponsored by a political organization, who has been officially nominated as a candidate in the electoral district. *Elections Act*, R.S.N.S. 1989, c. 140, s. 3. See AFFILIATED ~.

POLITICAL PARTY. 1. An association, organization or affiliation of voters comprising a political organization whose prime purpose is the nomination and support of candidates at elections. 2. A group of persons comprised in a political organization by which: (i) money or effort is expended; (ii) money is solicited or received; for the purpose of promoting, opposing, endorsing or supporting the platform of the group, of any recognized political party or candidate nominated at an election. *The Election Act*, R.S.S. 1978, c. E-6, s. 2. See CENTRAL ~ ORGANIZATION; RECOGNIZED ~.

POLITICAL SUBDIVISION. Any province, state, territory, dependency or any other similar subdivision of a state. *Foreign Missions and International Organizations Act*, S.C. 1991, c. 41, s. 2.

POLITY. *n*. A form or process of government; civil constitution.

POLL. *v*. 1. At an election, to give a vote or to receive a vote. 2. To take the votes of everyone entitled to vote.

POLL. *n*. See ADVANCE ~.

POLL BOOK. The book in which the name and other particulars of every person applying to vote are consecutively entered by the poll clerk. See WRITE-IN BALLOT ~.

POLL CLERK. A person appointed under this Act to assist a deputy returning officer. *Municipal Elections Act*, R.S.N.S. 1989, c. 300, s. 2(1).

POLLING. See DAY OF ~.

POLLING BOOTH. The building or place where polling is authorized by law to take place.

POLLING DAY. The day fixed for taking the votes of the electors. See ADVANCE ~; ORDINARY ~.

POLLING DISTRICT. Includes a ward or a town which is not divided into wards. *Municipal Elections Act*, R.S.N.S. 1989, c. 300, s. 2(1).

POLLING DIVISION. Any division, subdivision, district, sub-district or other territorial area fixed by the returning officer, for which a list of electors is prepared and for which one or more polling stations is or are established for the taking of the vote on polling day. See ELECTORAL DIVISION; RURAL ~; URBAN ~.

POLLING LIST. The list of electors for each polling subdivision revised and certified by the clerk.

POLLING PLACE. A place where electors vote at an election.

POLLING STATION. Premises secured by a returning officer for the taking of the vote of the electors on polling day and to which the whole or a portion of the official list of electors for a polling division is allotted. See MOBILE ~.

POLLING SUBDIVISION. *var*. **POLLING-SUBDIVISION**. 1. That area of an electoral division so designated by the returning officer to enable the efficient conduct of an election. 2. A territorial division for which a separate electoral list must be made or in which a polling station may be established. See RURAL ~; URBAN ~.

POLLOCK. *n*. A fish of the species saithe or Pollachius virens (L.). *Northwest Atlantic Fisheries Regulations*, C.R.C., c. 860, s. 2.

POLL-TAX. *n*. A tax on every person.

POLLUTANT. *n*. 1. (a) A substance that, if added to any waters, would degrade or alter or form part of a process of degradation or alteration of the quality of the waters to an extent that is detrimental to their use by humans or by an animal or a plant that is useful to humans; and (b) any water that contains a substance in such a quantity or concentration, or that has been so treated, processed or changed, by heat or other means, from a natural state, that it would, if added to any waters, degrade or alter or form part of a process of degradation or alteration of the quality of the waters to an extent that is detrimental to their use by humans or by an animal or a plant that is useful to humans. It includes oil and any substance or class of substances that is prescribed to be a pollutant. *Canada Shipping Act, 2001*, S.C. 2001, c. 26, s. 165. 2. A contaminant other than heat, sound, vibration, or radiation, and includes any substance from which a pollutant is derived. *Environmental Protection Act*, R.S.O. 1990, c. E.19, s. 91(1). See OWNER OF THE ~.

POLLUTION. *n*. 1. The presence in the environment of substances or contaminants that substantially alter or impair the usefulness of the environment. 2. Alteration of the physical, chemical, biological or aesthetic properties of the environment including the addition or removal of any contaminant that will render the environment harmful to the public health, that is unsafe or harmful for domestic, municipal, industrial, agricultural, recreational or other lawful uses or that is harmful to wild animals, birds or aquatic life. See AIR ~; DANGER OF ~; OIL ~ DAMAGE; WATER ~.

POLLUTION DAMAGE. In relation to any ship, loss or damage outside the ship caused by contamination resulting from the discharge of a pollutant from that ship. *Canada Shipping Act*, S.C. 1987, c. 7, s. 746.

POLYANDRY. *n*. Polygamy in which one woman has several husbands.

POLYCENTRIC ISSUE. An issue which deals with a number of interwoven and interacting interests and considerations.

POLYCENTRICITY. *n*. The broad principle of "polycentricity" well known to academic commentators who suggest that it provides the best rationale for judicial deference to non-judicial agencies. A "polycentric issue is one which involves a large number of interlocking and interacting interests and considerations" (P. Cane, An Introduction to Administrative Law (3rd ed. 1996), at p. 35). While judicial procedure is premised on a bipolar opposition of parties, interests, and factual discovery, some problems require the consideration of numerous interests simultaneously, and the promulgation of solutions which concurrently balance benefits and costs for many different parties. Where an administrative structure more closely resembles this model, courts will exercise restraint. The polycentricity principle is a helpful way of understanding the variety of criteria developed under the rubric of the "statutory purpose". The purpose of the Convention [Convention Relating to the Status of Refugees, [1969] C.T.S. 6] and particularly that of the exclusions contained in Article 1F is clearly not the management of flows of people, but rather the conferral of minimum human rights' protection. The context in which the adjudicative function takes place is not a "polycentric" one of give-and-take between different groups, but rather the vindication of a set of relatively static human rights, and ensuring that those who fall within the prescribed categories are protected. *Pushpanathan v. Canada (Minister of Employment & Immigration)*, 1998 CarswellNat 830, 226 N.R. 201, (sub nom. *Pushpanathan v. Canada (Minister of Citizenship & Immigration)*) 160 D.L.R. (4th) 193, [1998] S.C.J. No. 46, (sub nom. *Pushpanathan v. Canada (Minister of Citizenship & Immigration)*) [1998] 1 S.C.R. 982, 43 Imm. L.R. (2d) 117, 11 Admin. L.R. (3d) 1, Bastarache J. for the majority.

POLYGAMY. *n*. 1. The state of having many wives or husbands. 2. It is an offence (a) to practise or enter into or in any manner agree or consent to practise or enter into (i) any form of polygamy, or (ii) any kind of conjugal union with more than one person at the same time, whether or not it is by law recognized as a binding form of marriage; or (b) celebrate, assist or be a party to a rite, ceremony, contract or consent that purports to sanction a relationship mentioned in subparagraph (a)(i) or (ii). *Criminal Code*, R.S.C. 1985, c. C-46, s. 293(1).

POLYGARCHY. *n*. Government by many people.

POLYGRAPH. *n*. A lie detector; an apparatus which records physiological changes in the body.

POND. See BREEDING ~; FISHING ~; PERCHED ~; TREATMENT ~.

PONDERANTUR TESTES, NON NUMERANTUR. [L.] The weight of the evidence not mere numbers. Refers to giving weight to evidence as opposed to counting the number of witnesses in favour of one view.

PONY. *n*. A horse of a breed that, when mature, does not normally attain a height in excess of 58 inches measured at the withers. *Riding Horse Establishments Act*, R.R.O. 1980, Reg. 905, s. 1.

PONY AXLE. One which is designed to carry load only under certain conditions.

POOL. *n*. 1. " . . . [I]n order to constitute a 'pool' there must be an 'aggregation of interest or property' or throwing of revenue or property into one common fund or a sharing of interest in that fund by all on an equal or previously agreed basis." *Canadian Fur Auction Sales Co. (Que.) v. Neely* (1954), 11 W.W.R. (N.S.) 254 at 265, 62 Man.

R. 148, [1954] 2 D.L.R. 154 (C.A.), the court per Beaubien J.A. 2. " . . . [T]he source of a group of individuals from which individuals can be drawn as required for a particular job. . ." *Bradson Mercantile Canada Inc. v. PersonnelPool of America Inc.* (1981), 64 C.P.R. (2d) 260 at 271 (T.M. Opp. Bd.), Partington (Chair). 3. Includes billiards, bagatelle and any other similar game. *Places of Amusement Regulations*, C.R.C., c. 962, s. 2. 4. A natural underground reservoir containing or appearing to contain an accumulation of oil or gas or both oil and gas and being separated or appearing to be separated from any other accumulation. 5. In respect of each type of bet that may be made on a race, means the total amount of money bet on the race. *Pari-Mutuel Betting Supervision Regulations*, SOR/91-365, s. 2. See CALCULATING ~; FEATURE ~; FILL-AND-DRAW ~; INDOOR ~; MORTGAGE ~; NET ~; NON-CONFORMING ~; PLACE ~; PROMOTIONAL ~; PUBLIC ~; SALMON ~; SHOW ~; SWIMMING ~; WIN ~.

POOL CAR OPERATOR. A freight forwarder who consolidates freight for transportation by boxcar.

POOLED FUND. A fund established by a corporation duly authorized to operate a fund in which moneys from two or more depositors are accepted for investment and where shares allocated to each depositor serve to establish at any time the proportionate interest of each depositor in the assets of the fund. *Pension Benefits Standards Regulations*, C.R.C., c. 1252, s. 2.

POOLED INVESTMENT TRUST. A trust which combines and invests the funds of several estates and trusts into a common trust fund.

POOLED SPACING UNIT. The area that is subject to a pooling agreement or a pooling order.

POOLED TRACT. The portion of a pooled spacing unit defined as a tract in a pooling agreement or a pooling order.

POOLING. *n.* The joining or combining of all the various interests within a spacing unit for the purpose of drilling and subsequent producing of a well.

POOLING AGREEMENT. An agreement to pool the interests of owners in a spacing unit and to provide for the operation or the drilling and operation of a well thereon.

POOLING SYSTEM. See DEBT ~.

POOL PERIOD. 1. A crop year. *Canadian Wheat Board Act*, R.S.C. 1985, c. C-24, s. 31. 2. In respect of a marketing plan, the period set as the pool period for the plan by the order establishing the plan. 3. Such period or periods, not exceeding one year, as the Governor in Council may prescribe as a pool period or pool periods in respect of that wheat. *Canadian Board Act*, R.S.C. 1985, c. C-24, s. 40.

POOLROOM. *n.* A room or rooms in a building, house, shed, tent or other place in which a pool table is set up for hire or gain and includes an annex, addition or extension thereto over which the owner has control. *Places of Amusement Regulations*, C.R.C., c. 962, s. 2.

POPPY. See OPIUM ~.

POPULAR INNUENDO. In the case of "popular or false innuendo", although it need not be separately pled, the plaintiff is required to show why a reader would reasonably import to the words complained of a defamatory character, different from the ordinary meaning that the words would otherwise import. Where the words complained of are susceptible to many interpretations, the onus rests on the plaintiff to set out the meaning or meanings the plaintiff alleges the words are capable of. *Moon v. Sher* (2003), 2003 CarswellOnt 2405 (S.C.J.).

POPULAR VOTE. The total counted ballots cast in favour of all candidates in an electoral district and does not include any rejected, cancelled, declined or unused ballot. *Election Finances Act*, R.S.O. 1990, c. E.7, s. 44(8).

POPULATION. *n.* 1. As used in reference to a municipality, means the number of persons resident in the municipality. 2. Population as determined in accordance with the latest census taken pursuant to the Statistics Act (Canada). See VOTER ~.

PORNOGRAPHY. *n.* " . . . [C]an be usefully divided into three categories: (1) explicit sex with violence; (2) explicit sex without violence but which subjects people to treatment that is degrading or dehumanizing, and (3) explicit sex without violence that is neither degrading nor dehumanizing. Violence in this context includes both actual physical violence and threats of physical violence. . ." *R. v. Butler* (1992), 11 C.R. (4th) 137 at 163, [1992] 2 W.W.R. 577, [1992] 1 S.C.R. 452, 70 C.C.C. (3d) 129, 134 N.R. 81, 8 C.R.R. (2d) 1, 89 D.L.R. (4th) 449,

78 Man. R. (2d) 1, 16 W.A.C. 1, Sopinka J. (Lamer C.J.C., La Forest, Cory, McLachlin, Stevenson and Iacobucci JJ. concurring).

PORT. *n.* 1. A place where vessels or vehicles may discharge or load cargo. 2. The navigable waters under the jurisdiction of a port authority and the real property that the port authority manages, holds or occupies as set out in the letters patent. *Canada Marine Act, 1998*, S. C. 1998, c. 10, s. 5. 3. In respect of a vessel, means the left side of the vessel looking forward. See CUSTOMS ~; EAST COAST ~; EASTERN ~; FISHING ~S; FRONTIER ~; GREAT LAKES ~; INTERMEDIATE ~; NON-CORPORATE ~; QUARANTINE ~.

PORTABILITY. *n.* Of a mortgage, refers to the carrying of a mortgage's terms, such as penalties and rate, to a new mortgage on the same property or to a new mortgage on another property.

PORTABLE. *adj.* 1. In respect of any plan referred to therein, means that benefits to which an employee covered thereby is entitled and the rate of premium he is required to pay while employed by an employer will remain equivalent if he becomes employed by any other employer. 2. The equipment is specifically designed not to be used in a fixed position and receives current through the medium of a flexible cord or cable, and usually a detachable plug.

PORTABLE CONTAINER. A container that has a capacity of 10 gallons or less, that is designed, manufactured and used or to be used for the storage or conveyance of gasoline or an associated product. *Gasoline Handling Act*, R.S.O. 1990, c. G.4, s. 1.

PORTABLE CYLINDERS. Containers designed to hold propane or butane and designed in such a manner that they may readily be removed from equipment on which they are used as a fuel source for purposes of refilling with propane or butane.

PORTABLE EQUIPMENT. Electrically operated equipment which is usually held in the hands while being worked.

PORTABLE GROUND FAULT CIRCUIT INTERRUPTER. A ground fault circuit interrupter which is specifically designed to receive current by means of a flexible cord or cable and an attachment plug cap, and which incorporates one or more receptacles for the connection of electrical equipment which is provided with a flexible cord cable and an attachment plug cap.

PORTABLE PENSION. A pension scheme which permits an employee to move to another employer without forfeiting any accrued pension rights.

PORTABLE POWER TOOL. A tool that is designed to be held in the hand and that is operated by any source of power other than manual power.

PORTABLE PRIVY. A portable latrine in which the receptacle for human body waste and the superstructure are combined structurally into one unit.

PORTABLE SIGN. A sign or advertising device that is not permanently attached to the ground, a building or a structure that is designed to be moved from place to place. *Public Transportation and Highway Improvement Act*, R.S.O. 1990, c. P.50, s. 34(1).

PORTAL TIME. Time spent by workers on incidental activities before or after their regular work.

PORT AUTHORITY. A port authority established under the Canada Marine Act. The Minister may issue letters patent of incorporation for a port authority without share capital for the purpose of operating a particular port in Canada if the Minister is satisfied that the port (*a*) is, and is likely to remain, financially self-sufficient; (*b*) is of strategic significance to Canada's trade; (*c*) is linked to a major rail line or a major highway infrastructure; and (*d*) has diversified traffic. *Canada Marine Act*, S.C. 1998, c. 10, s. 2 and 8.

PORT-CALL-TONNAGE. *n.* The aggregate of the products obtained by multiplying, for each ship operated by the corporation, the number of calls made in the year by that ship at ports by the number of tons of the registered net tonnage of that ship. Canada regulations.

PORT FACILITY. A wharf, pier, breakwater, terminal, warehouse or other building or work located in, on or adjacent to navigable waters used in connection with navigation or shipping and includes all land incidental to their use. *Canada Marine Act*, S.C. 1998, c. 10, s. 2. See PUBLIC ~.

PORTFOLIO. See MINISTER WITHOUT ~.

PORTFOLIO MANAGEMENT. The investment or control, in any way that involves an element of discretionary judgment by the person engaging therein, of money or securities that (a) are not owned by that person, or (b) are not moneys deposited with that person in the ordinary course of that person's business.

PORTFOLIO MANAGER. An adviser who manages the investment portfolio of clients through discretionary authority granted by one or more clients.

PORTFOLIO SECURITY. Where used in relation to a mutual fund, a security held or proposed to be purchased by the mutual fund.

PORT HAND BUOY. A buoy that is located on the port side (left hand) of the channel when the vessel is proceeding (a) with the flood tide on the sea coast; (b) against the current of a river; or (c) away from the outlet towards the head of a lake.

PORTION. *n*. One of the usual cuts derived from a carcass, such as sides, quarters, shoulders, hams and bellies and also entire organs, including tongues, livers and hearts. See EXCLUSIVE USE ~; GUARANTEED ~; OWNER'S ~ OF THE COST; RATEABLE ~; TRAVELLED ~.

PORT OF ENTRY. The port or office at which cargo is presented for release by a customs officer.

PORT OF IMPORTATION. The port or place at which cargo is required to be reported pursuant to the Customs Act. Canada regulations.

PORTORIA. *n*. [L.] Duties paid on merchandise in a port.

PORTRAIT. *n*. A likeness, still or moving, and includes a likeness of another deliberately disguised to resemble the plaintiff, and a caricature.

PORT WARDEN. An official who arbitrates certain disputes regarding shipping matters.

POSITION. *n*. " . . . [T]he identification and definition . . . of functions to be performed and of the qualifications required for such performance [result] . . . in the creation of a position within the meaning of the [Public Service Employment Act, R.S.C. 1970, c. P-32]." *Canada v. St-Hilaire* (1987), (*sub nom. Doré v. Canada*) 45 D.L.R. (4th) 135 at 141, 87 C.L.L.C. 14,056, 81 N.R. 77, [1987] 2 S.C.R. 503, 29 Admin L.R. 81, the court per Le Dain J. See BILINGUAL ~; CLASS OF ~S; DOMINANT ~; EXPOSED ~; IDLE ~; LONG ~; SHORT ~.

POSITIONING. See GEOGRAPHICAL ~; SYSTEM.

POSITIONING FLIGHT. The flight of an aircraft that has no payload.

POSITION OF AUTHORITY. In relation to the consent defence to a charge of sexual touching, does not necessarily entail just the exercise of a legal right over the young person, but also a lawful or unlawful power to command which the adult may acquire in the circumstances. *R. c. Audet*, [1996] 2 S.C.R. 171.

POSITION OF TRUST. In relation to the consent defence to a charge of sexual touching, where the nature of the relationship between an adult and a young person is such that it creates an opportunity for all of the persuasive and influencing factors which adults hold over children and young persons to come into play, and the child or young person is particularly vulnerable to the sway of these factors, the adult is in a position where those concepts of reliability and truth and strength are put to the test. Taken together, all of these factors combine to create a 'position of trust' towards the young person. *R. c. Audet*, [1996] 2 S.C.R. 171.

POSITIVE DAMAGE. The acquisition of something undesirable such as pain and suffering or extra expense. K.D. Cooper-Stephenson & I.B. Saunders, *Personal Injury Damages in Canada* (Toronto: Carswell, 1981) at 52.

POSITIVE DISPLACEMENT GAS METER. Any gas meter whose primary metering mechanism displaces a definite volume per cycle. *Gas and Gas Meters Regulations*, C.R.C., c. 876, s. 21.

POSITIVE EASEMENT. Confers a right on its holder to commit an act or acts upon the servient easement.

POSITIVE EVIDENCE. Proof of a particular fact.

POSITIVE LAW. Rules of conduct set down and enforced with the sanction of authority.

POSSE. *n*. [L.] A possibility. Something in posse is something which possibly may be; something in esse is something which actually is.

POSSE COMITATUS. [L.] The sheriff of a county traditionally could summon it to defend that county against enemies of the Crown, to pursue felons, to keep the peace or to enforce a royal writ.

POSSESSED. *adj*. 1. Applies to receipt of income of, and to any vested estate less than a life estate, legal or equitable, in possession or in expectancy, in any land. *Trustee acts*. 2. Is applicable to any vested estate less than a life estate, in law or in equity, in possession or in expectancy, in any land.

POSSESSIO. *n*. [L.] Possession.

POSSESSION. *n*. 1. In relation to land, primarily connotes physical control. Used to refer to present use and enjoyment as opposed to future or contingent interests. 2. For the purposes of this Act, (a) a person has anything in possession when he has it in his personal possession or knowingly (i) has it in the actual possession or custody of another person, or (ii) has it in any place, whether or not that place belongs to or is occupied by him, for the use or benefit of himself or of another person; and (b) where one of two or more persons, with the knowledge and consent of the rest, has anything in his custody or possession, it shall be deemed to be in the custody and possession of each and all of them. *Criminal Code*, R.S.C. 1985, c. C-46, s. 4(3). 3. The right of control or disposal of any article, irrespective of the actual possession or location of such article. 4. " . . . [W]ithin the meaning of the criminal law . . . where . . . there is manual handling of a thing, it must be co-existent with knowledge of what the thing is, and both these elements must be co-existent with some act of control (outside public duty). . . *R. v. Hess (No. 1)* , [1949] 1 W.W.R. 577 at 579, 8 C.R. 42, 94 C.C.C. 48 (B.C. C.A.), O'Halloran J.A. 5. When applied to persons claiming title to land, includes the reception of the rents and profits thereof. 6. In the context of section 283(1) of the Criminal Code does not refer solely to the physical control of a child exercised by the deprived parent at the time of taking but extends to the ability of the deprived parent to exercise control over the child. *R. v. Dawson*, [1996] 3 S.C.R. 783. See ACTUAL ~; ADVERSE ~; BRITISH ~; CHANGE OF ~; CHOSE IN ~; CONSTRUCTIVE ~; DATE OF ~; DE FACTO ~; EXCLUSIVE ~; LEGAL ~; MORTGAGEE IN ~; PERSON LAWFULLY IN ~ OF THE BODY; RECENT ~; REDUCTION INTO ~; RE~; VACANT ~; WRIT OF ~.

POSSESSION LIMIT. The maximum number of a wildlife species that may be possessed by a hunter, trapper or fisherman for any time period specified.

POSSESSORY. *adj*. Describes something arising out of or concerned with possession.

POSSESSORY LIEN. A common law lien which arises from an express or implied agreement and which can be extinguished when the amount due is tendered and can be lost by an express or implied waiver. It continues only as long as one retains actual possession.

POSSESSORY TITLE. The claimant must have actual possession, the intention to exclude the true owner from possession and to have effectively excluded the true owner from possession.

POSSIBILITY. *n*. 1. A future event, which may or may not happen. 2. In real property, an interest in land which depends on such an event happening.

POSSIBILITY OF REVERTER. A future interest dependant on a conditional or determinable fee simple, the possibility of acquiring an interest in land some time in the future. A limitation on the grant in fee simple.

POSSIBLE. *adj*. " . . . [C]ould in some circumstances be coloured by context to mean more likely than not. But in the case at bar it is coupled with words indicating that the prognosis is 'uncertain'." *Bola v. Canada (Minister of Employment & Immigration)* (1990), 107 N.R. 311 at 316 (Fed. C.A.), MacGuigan J.A.

POSSIBLE FATHER. Includes any one or more persons who have had sexual intercourse with a single woman who is the mother of a child and by whom it is possible she was pregnant. *Family Maintenance Act*, R.S.N.S. 1989, c. 160, s. 2.

POST. *v*. To leave in a post office or with a person authorized by the Corporation to receive mailable matter. *Canada Post Corporation Act*, R.S.C. 1985, c. C-10, s. 2.

POST. *n*. 1. An office of a department or other portion of the public service of Canada located outside Canada and, without restricting the generality of the foregoing, includes every embassy, office of a high commissioner, permanent delegation to an international organization, consulate general, consulate, trade commissioner's office and immigration office. *Special Voting Rules*, R.S.C. 1985, c. E-2, Schedule II, s. 2. 2. A vertical member of shoring and timbering that acts as a spacer between wales. 3. An office or employment to which an employee is or may be appointed. 4. A place where a member is stationed for duty, either permanently or temporarily. *Royal Canadian Mounted Police Regula-*

tions, C.R.C., c. 1391, s. 2. See HEAD OF ~; IRON ~; LEGAL ~; ORIGINAL DOMIN-ION ~; ORIGINAL ~; REFERENCE ~; ROCK ~; SEND BY ~; TRANSMIT BY ~; WITNESS ~; WOODEN GUIDE ~.

POST. *adv.* [L.] After.

POSTAGE. *n.* The charge or surcharge payable for the collection, transmission and delivery by the Corporation of messages, information, funds or goods and for insurance or other special services provided by the Corporation in relation thereto. *Canada Post Corporation Act*, R.S.C. 1985, c. C-10, s. 2.

POSTAGE INDICIA IMPRESSION DIE. The part of a postage meter including the manufacturer's identification and the postage meter serial number that prints an impression showing the denomination of postage that has been prepaid. *Postage Meters Regulations*, C.R.C., c. 1287, s. 2.

POSTAGE METER. 1. A machine for the making or printing of postage impressions. Canada regulations. 2. A mechanical device that is used for printing prepaid postage. *Postage Meters Regulations*, C.R.C., c. 1287, s. 2.

POSTAGE STAMP. Any stamp, postage impression or postage meter impression authorized by the Corporation for the purpose of paying postage. *Canada Post Corporation Act*, R.S.C. 1985, c. C-10, s. 2.

POSTAGE SUPPLIES. Post cards, envelopes or letter forms with postage printed thereon. *Methods of Payment of Postage Regulations*, C.R.C., c. 1284, s. 2.

POSTAL CODE. A six character alpha-numeric combination assigned to one or more postal addresses that designates a specific delivery area. *Mail Preparation Regulations*, C.R.C., c. 1281, s. 2.

POSTAL CONSOLIDATION POINT. A postal facility designated for the receipt of bundled or bagged mail for a specific area. *Mail Preparation Regulations*, C.R.C., c. 1281, s. 2.

POSTAL INSTALLATION. The main post office, a postal station or letter carrier depot. *Third Class Mail Regulations*, C.R.C., c. 1297, s. 2.

POSTAL INTERRUPTION. A cessation of normal public postal service in Canada or in any part of Canada that is or may reasonably be expected to be of more than 48 hours' duration.

POSTAL REMITTANCE. Any instrument authorized by the Corporation for the remittance of funds. *Canada Post Corporation Act*, R.S.C. 1985, c. C-10, s. 2.

POST AUDIT CUSTOMS CONTROL SYSTEM. An independent control system exercised by periodic audits of accountable revenue documents covering goods in bond carried by transportation companies approved by the Deputy Minister. *Cargo Container (Customs) Regulations*, C.R.C., c. 452, s. 2.

POSTDATE. *v.* To give a bill, note or cheque a date after its date of issue in order to delay the payment date.

POSTDATED CHEQUE. One which is dated after its date of issue in order to delay payment.

POST DIEM. [L.] After a day.

POST-DISASTER BUILDING. A building essential to provide services in the event of a disaster, and includes hospitals, fire stations, police stations, radio stations, telephone exchanges, power stations, electrical substations, pumping stations (water and sewage) and fuel depot buildings. *Building Code Act*, R.R.O. 1992, O. Reg. 403/97, s. 1.1.3.

POSTER. *n.* Any printing, writing, drawing, painting, lithograph or representation by any process whatsoever, placed so as to be seen by the public and used for notices, announcements, advertisements or publicity.

POSTERIOR. *adj.* Dorsal, behind, in the rear of, facing backwards.

POSTERIORITY. *n.* Comparing and relating tenure, the opposite of priority.

POSTERITY. *n.* Generations which follow.

POSTHUMOUS CHILD. A child born after the father's death.

POST-JUDGMENT INTEREST. Interest payable on the amount awarded under a judgment including costs calculated from the date of the order calculated at the postjudgment interest rate.

POSTJUDGMENT INTEREST RATE. The bank rate at the end of the first day of the last month of the quarter preceding the quarter in which the date of the order falls, rounded to the next higher whole number where the bank rate includes a fraction, plus 1 per cent. *Courts of Justice Act*, R.S.O. 1990, c. C.43, s. 127(1).

POST LITEM MOTAM. [L.] After the beginning of litigation.

POSTMARK IMPRESSION DIE. The part of a postage meter that prints an impression showing the name of the city or town and province from which the mail is despatched together with the date of mailing. *Postage Meters Regulations*, C.R.C., c. 1287, s. 2.

POSTMASTER. *n.* 1. Includes the manager of a postal station 2. A postmaster within the meaning of the Canada Post Corporation Act (Canada).

POSTMORTEM. *n.* An autopsy.

POST MORTEM ARTEFACT. A mark or lesion inflicted after death. F.A. Jaffe, *A Guide to Pathological Evidence*, 3d ed. (Toronto: Carswell, 1991) at 16.

POST MORTEM CHANGE. A physical and chemical process which commences immediately after death. F.A. Jaffe, *A Guide to Pathological Evidence*, 3d ed. (Toronto: Carswell, 1991) at 224.

POST MORTEM CLOT. A clot which forms in a heart chamber, blood vessel or the site of a hemorrhage after death. F.A. Jaffe, *A Guide to Pathological Evidence*, 3d ed. (Toronto: Carswell, 1991) at 215.

POST MORTEM INTERVAL. The period between death and the body being examined. F.A. Jaffe, *A Guide to Pathological Evidence*, 3d ed. (Toroto: Carswell, 1991) at 224.

POST-NOTE. *n.* A bank-note payable on a specified date in the future.

POST-OBIT. *n.* A money bond required to be paid at or after some person beside the giver of the bond dies.

POST OFFICE. Includes any place, receptacle, device or mail conveyance authorized by the Corporation for the posting, receipt, sorting, handling, transmission or delivery of mail. *Canada Post Corporation Act*, R.S.C. 1985, c. C-10, s. 2. See CANADA ~; CANADIAN FORCES ~; DEPOSIT AT A ~.

POSTPONEMENT. *n.* A document which subordinates a separate document to another separate document.

POST-SECONDARY EDUCATION. Education in courses and subjects normally offered by universities and colleges.

POST SECONDARY INSTITUTION. Includes a community college, institute, private vocational school, university.

POSTERIORA PRIORIBUS DEROGANT. [L.] Later derogate from prior. Later statutes amend earlier ones.

POST HOC ERGO PROPTER HOC. [L.] It was after therefore it was caused by. The argument that something happened after an event and therefore was caused by it.

POST TERMINUM. [L.] After the end of a term.

POST TIME. The time that is set for the start of a race. *Pari-Mutuel Betting Supervision Regulations*, SOR/91-365, s. 2.

POT. See BLACKCOD ~.

POTABLE. *adj.* Fit for human consumption.

POTABLE WATER. 1. Water fit for human consumption. 2. Water that is microbiologically and chemically safe for human consumption.

POTABLE WATER SYSTEM. 1. The plumbing that conveys potable water. 2. The equipment used on a conveyance for handling, treating, storing and distributing potable water.

POTASH. *n.* 1. Any non-viable substance formed by the processes of nature that contains the element potassium. 2. Potassium salts and the ores thereof. 3. Potassium oxide (K_2O). See PRIMARY PRODUCTION OF ~.

POTATO CYST NEMATODE. Potato cyst nematode Heterodera rostochiensis/Woll. and H. Pallida Stone. *Plant Quarantine Regulations*, C.R.C., c. 1273, s. 2.

POTATO WART. Potato wart Synchytrium endobioticum (Schilb.) Perc. *Plant Quarantine Regulations*, C.R.C., c. 1273, s. 2.

POTENTIAL PROPERTY. Something which is the expected increase or natural product of something which the seller already owns or possesses. G.H.L. Fridman, *Sale of Goods in Canada*, 3d ed. (Toronto: Carswell, 1986) at 54.

POTENTIA PROPINQUA. [L.] A frequent possibility which one may expect will happen.

POTENTIA REMOTA. [L.] An unlikely possibility which one does not expect to happen.

POTESTAS SUPREME SEIPSAM DISSOLVERE POTEST, LIGARE NON POTEST.

[L.] A supreme power may loose itself, but it cannot bind.

POTIOR EST CONDITIO DEFENDENTIS. [L.] The better condition is the defendant's.

POTIOR EST CONDITIO POSSIDENTIS. [L.] The better condition is the possessor's.

POULTRY. *n.* 1. Domestic fowl and pigeons and includes any bird that is in captivity. 2. Domestic or wild fowl or birds. 3. A turkey, goose, duck, cock, hen, capon, guinea fowl or pheasant.

POULTRY PRODUCT. Poultry meat, prepared poultry meat, poultry meat by-product or prepared poultry meat by-product. *Food and Drug Regulations*, C.R.C., c. 870, c. B.01.001.

POULTRY PRODUCT EXTENDER. A food that is a source of protein and that is represented as being for the purpose of extending poultry products. *Food and Drug Regulations*, C.R.C., c. 870, c. B.01.001.

POULTRY PRODUCTS. Eggs, dressed poultry and live poultry.

POUND. *n.* 1. .45359237 of a kilogram. *Weights and Measures Act*, S.C. 1970-71-72, c. 36, schedule II. 2. Premises where stray animals are confined. 3. An enclosure, building or piece of land where a distrainor places goods which have been seized as distress.

POUNDAGE. *n.* A fee owed to a court officer or to the public revenue for services which that officer performed.

POUND-BREACH. *n.* The act of removing goods from a pound before the distrainor's claim is satisfied.

POUND KEEPER. *var.* **POUNDKEEPER.** The person for the time being in the authorized charge of any pound.

POUND NET. 1. An impounding net (a) that is held in place by stakes driven into the water bed, and (b) the main part of which, including the crib and bent wings, commonly known as the "heart", extends to the surface of the water. Canada regulations. 2. A net that is set to enclose an area of water into which fish are guided through an opening or openings by one or more leaders.

POURING AISLE. A passageway leading from a gangway where metal is poured into a mould or box.

POURVEYANCE. *n.* The provision of necessaries for a sovereign.

POURVEYOR. *n.* One who buys; the person who provided for a royal household.

POVERTY LINE. There is no official measure which is equated to the poverty line. Several agencies publish income measurements which are referred to as the poverty line, the line between poor persons and others.

POWDER STIPPLING. Tattoo. F.A. Jaffe , *A Guide to Pathological Evidence*, 3d ed. (Toronto: Carswell, 1991) at 224.

POWER. *n.* 1. A right or privilege. 2. Jurisdiction. 3. " . . . [T]he description of an authority in respect to property or an interest in property which does not itself belong to the person holding the power. Even when a power to dispose of property is wide enough to enable the holder of the power to exercise it in favour of himself the power itself, in the absence of any exercise of it is not regarded as equivalent to ownership of the property. . ." *Montreal Trust Co. v. Minister of National Revenue* (1960), 60 D.T.C. 1183 at 1185, [1960] C.T.C. 308, [1960] Ex. C.R. 543, Thurlow J. 4. Rule 212(1) [of the Saskatchewan *Queen's Bench Rules*] requires disclosure of documents in the "possession" or "power" of the litigant. . . If the litigant has the right to direct the third party to produce the document, it would follow that the document is in his power. *Spencer v. Canada (Attorney General)* (2000), 2000 SKCA 96, 199 Sask. R. 127, 232 W.A.C. 127, [2001] 7 W.W.R. 476, 7 C.P.C. (5th) 280 (C.A.). 5. Includes hydraulic, electrical, steam or other power and also includes energy. 6. Includes energy, light and heat however developed or produced, and includes electricity and natural, manufactured or mixed gas, or liquified petroleum gas. See COMPULSORY ~; DECLARATORY ~; DISTRIBUTION OF ~S; ELECTRIC ~; EXERCITORIAL ~; EXPROPRIATION ~; FIRM ~; GENERAL ~; IMPLIED ~S; INHERENT ~; INTERRUPTIBLE ~; LEGAL ~; LICENSING ~; MEDIUM ~; OBJECT OF A ~; POLICE ~; PRISONER OF WAR OF ANOTHER ~; PROTECTING ~; RESERVE ~; RESIDUARY ~; SMALL ~; SOVEREIGN ~; SPECIAL ~; SPENDING ~; STATUS AND ESSENTIAL ~S; STATUTORY ~; STATUTORY ~ OF DECISION; TRANSMITTER ~; TRUST ~; WASTE MANAGEMENT ~; WATER ~.

POWER BICYCLE. A vehicle that (i) may be propelled by muscular or mechanical power; (ii) is fitted with pedals that are continually operable to propel it; (iii) weighs not more than 35 kilograms; (iv) has a motor that produces not more than 750 watts and that is driven by electricity or has an engine displacement of not more than 50 cubic centimetres; (v) has no hand-operated or foot-operated clutch or gearbox driven by the motor that transfers power to the driven wheel; and (vi) does not have sufficient power to enable it to attain a speed greater than 35 kilometres per hour on level ground within a distance of 2 kilometres from a standing start.

POWER BOAT. *var*. **POWER-BOAT**. 1. A boat, raft or barge of any kind that is being driven, drawn or propelled by any means other than human muscular power. 2. Any boat, canoe or yacht equipped with an electric, gasoline, oil or steam motor as a means of propulsion.

POWER BOILER. A boiler designed to carry and operate at a working pressure of more than 100 kilopascals gauge. *Boiler, Pressure Vessel and Compressed Gas Act*, R.S. Nfld. 1990, c. B-5, s. 2.

POWER CIRCUIT. See EXTRA-LOW-VOLTAGE ~; LOW-ENERGY ~.

POWER-DRIVEN. *adj*. Propelled by machinery.

POWER-DRIVEN VESSEL. Any vessel propelled by machinery.

POWERED GLIDER. An aeroplane that, with engines inoperative, has the flight characteristics of a glider; *Canadian Aviation Regulations*, SOR/96-433, s. 101.01.

POWER GRID. The network of interconnected power circuits owned or controlled by a single electrical utility and operated as a unit for the bulk transmission and distribution of power. See EXPORT ~.

POWER MOTOR CYCLE. A motor vehicle mounted on two or three wheels and includes those motor vehicles known to the trade as scooters and power bicycles, but does not include motor cycles.

POWER OF APPOINTMENT. 1. The power of a donee or appointor to appoint by will the people who will succeed to property after the person to whom the power is given dies. This power is given by a donor using an instrument such as a trust inter vivos, marriage settlement or will. J.G. McLeod, *The Conflict of Laws* (Calgary: Carswell, 1983) at 428. 2. Includes any discretionary power to transfer a beneficial interest in property without the furnishing of valuable consideration.

POWER OF ATTORNEY. Authority for a donee or donees to do on behalf of a donor or principal anything which that donor can lawfully do through an attorney. G.H.L. Fridman, *The Law of Agency*, 6th ed. (London: Butterworths, 1990) at 55-6.

POWER OF DISTRESS. The right that a person has to enforce the payment of any claim against, or the taking of any goods or chattels out of the possession of, another person by the taking of a personal chattel out of the possession of that last mentioned person otherwise than by the authority of a writ of execution or other process of a similar nature.

POWER OF THE COUNTY. See POSSE COMITATUS.

POWER PLANT. 1. A facility for the generation of electric energy from any energy source. 2. A boiler or two or more boilers on the same premises together with the accessories thereto, from which the steam produced is used to provide motive power for an engine or turbine or two or more engines or turbines or any combination thereof. See HYDROELECTRIC ~; STATIONARY ~; THERMAL ELECTRIC ~.

POWER PROJECT. Includes any charter, franchise, privilege or other right, or land, buildings, plant, machinery or equipment acquired, or proposed to be acquired, by a person with a view to the generation or supply of power, or any plans, surveys or data made or assembled with a view to the generation or supply of power.

POWER PURPOSE. The use of water in the production of electricity or other power.

POWER RATING. (i) When used in respect of a compressed-air plant or compressed-gas plant, the total horse-power of the machinery-units driving the compressors; (ii) when used in respect of an electric boiler in a steam plant, the quotient obtained by dividing the total maximum capacity of the heating elements in kilowatts by ten; or (iii) when used in respect of a boiler in a steam plant, other than an electric boiler, the quotient obtained by dividing the total heating surface of the boiler in square feet by ten. *Boilers and Pressure Vessels Act*, R.R.O. 1980, Reg. 84, s. 1.

POWER SITE. Includes any land, or any lake, river, stream, watercourse, or body of water, water licence or privilege, or reservoir, dam, water storage, sluice, canal, raceway, tunnel, or aqueduct, that is used or that might be used for or in connection with the development or generation of power.

POWER SUPPLY CORD. A length of flexible cord or power supply cable with an attachment at one end.

POWER TOOL. See PORTABLE ~.

POWER TRANSFER. The power transmitted through an inter-utility transfer point.

POWER UNIT. 1. A motor vehicle used solely for the purpose of drawing a semi-trailer. 2. That part of a motor vehicle over which a motor vehicle operator has direct control and, where the power unit and the rest of the motor vehicle are permanently joined together, means the entire motor vehicle.

POWER UTILITY. An energy utility that generates, transmits or distributes electrical energy for sale, or that sells or otherwise deals in electrical energy.

POWER VESSEL. Any vessel that uses machinery in whole or in part for its propulsion or is equipped with such machinery.

P.P. *abbr.* Per pro., by procurating.

P.P.I. *abbr.* Policy proof of interest.

PPSA. *abbr.* Personal Property Security Act.

P.P.S.A.C. *abbr.* Personal Property Security Act Cases, 1980-.

P.R. *abbr.* Practice Reports (Ont.), 1848-1900.

PRACTICABLE. *adj.* 1. " . . . [W]hen it is capable of being done, having regard to all the circumstances 'feasible'." *R. v. Cambrin* (1982), 1 C.C.C. (3d) 59 at 61, [1983] 2 W.W.R. 250, 18 M.V.R.160 (B.C. C.A.), Craig J.A. 2. Capable of being effected or accomplished. *Environmental Protection Act*, R.S.O. 1990, c. E.19, s. 91(1).

PRACTICAL. *adj.* " . . . [C]apable of being done usefully or at not too great a cost . . ." *Crédit foncier franco-canadien v. McGuire* (1979), 12 C.P.C. 103 at 105, 14 B.C.L.R. 281 (S.C.), van der Hoop L.J.S.C.

PRACTICAL COMPULSION. The probability, or even certainty, that if money requested is not paid, the payer will be in economic or some similar danger because a legal process is invoked which might jeopardise the payer's current fiscal

status. G.H.L. Fridman, *Restitution*, 2d ed. (Toronto: Carswell, 1992) at 129.

PRACTICALLY. *adv.* " . . . [A]lmost or very nearly . . ." *Meivre v. Steine* (1912), 2 D.L.R. 106 at 108, 5 Sask. L.R. 235, 20 W.L.R. 687 (S.C.), the court per Newlands J.

PRACTICAL NURSE. A person who, being neither a registered nurse nor a person in training to be a registered nurse at a school of nursing undertakes nursing for remuneration.

PRACTICE. *n.* 1. " . . . [T]hose legal rules which direct the course of proceedings to bring parties into court, and the course of the court after they are brought in . . ." *Delisle v. Moreau* (1968), 5 C.R.N.S. 68 at 70, [1968] 4 C.C.C. 229, 69 D.L.R. (2d) 530, (N.B. C.A.), the court per Hughes J.A. 2. "' . . . [I]n its larger sense,' says Lord Justice Lush in Payser v. Minors, (1881), 7 Q.B.D. 329 at 333 (C.A.), 'denotes the mode of proceeding by which a legal right is enforced as distinguished from the law which gives or defines the right.' Where used in its ordinary and common sense, it denotes the rules that make or guide the cursus curiae and regulate procedure within the walls or limits of the Court itself: Attorney-General v. Sillem, 33 L.J. Ex. 209." *Morris Provincial Election, Re* (1907), 6 W.L.R. 742 at 748 (Man. K.B.), Mathers J. 3. " . . . [T]he exercise of [a] profession or calling frequently, customarily or habitually: . . ." *R. v. Mills* (1963), [1964] 1 O.R. 74 at 76 (C.A.), the court per McLennan J.A. 4. " . . . [T]he accepted 'way of doing things'; [the parties in collective bargaining] uniform and constant response to a recurring set of circumstances: . . ." *Dominion-Consolidated Truck Lines Ltd. v. I.T.B., Local 141* (1980), 28 L.A.C. (2d) 45 at 49 (Ont.), Adams, McRae and Fosbery. 5. For a fee or remuneration, performing or directing works, services or undertakings which, because of their scope and implications, require specialized knowledge, training and experience. See AREA ~; CORRUPT ~; DECEPTIVE ACT OR ~; EXCLUSIVE ACCOUNTING ~; FAIR EMPLOYMENT ~; GENERALLY ACCEPTED BANKING ~S; ILLEGAL ~S; MAKE-WORK ~; NORMAL FARM ~; ORDINARY ~ OF SEAMEN; PRIVATE ~; RULES OF ~; UNFAIR ACTS OR ~S; UNFAIR INSURANCE ~; UNFAIR ~S.

PRACTICE AND PROCEDURE. " . . . [I]n s. 19(1)(a) of the Divorce Act [R.S.C. 1970, c. D-8] means 'the mode or proceeding by which a legal right is enforced, as distinguished from the law which gives or defines the right' (Poyser v. Minors [1880-1] 7 Q.B.D. 329 at 333 (U.K. C.A.)). . ." *Joe v. Joe* (1984), 39 R.F.L. (2d) 444 at 447, 46 O.R. (2d) 764, 10 D.L.R. (4th) 472 (C.A.), the court per Morden J.A.

PRACTICE OF A HEARING AID DEALER AND CONSULTANT. (a) Testing human hearing by audiometer or other means for the purpose of selecting, adapting, recommending or selling hearing aids; (b) selecting, adapting, recommending, selling or offering for sale hearing aids; or (c) making impressions for ear-moulds to be used in connection with hearing aids..

PRACTICE OF ARCHITECTURE. (i) The preparation or provision of a design to govern the construction, enlargement or alteration of a building; (ii) evaluating, advising on or reporting on the construction, enlargement or alteration of a building; or (iii) a general review of the construction, enlargement or alteration of a building.

PRACTICE OF CADASTRAL SURVEYING. Advising on, reporting on, conducting or supervising the conducting of surveys to establish, locate, define or describe lines, boundaries or corners of parcels of land or land covered with water. *Surveyors Act*, R.S.O. 1990, c. S.29, s. 1.

PRACTICE OF DENTISTRY. Any professional service usually performed by a dentist or dental surgeon and includes (a) the diagnosis or treatment of, and the prescribing, treating and operating for the prevention, alleviation or correction of any injury, disease, pain, deficiency, deformity, defect, lesion, disorder or physical condition of, to in or from any human tooth, mandible or maxilla or associated structures or tissues, including the prescribing, treating and administering of x-rays, anaesthetics, drugs and medicines in connection therewith; (b) the making, producing, reproducing, constructing, fitting, furnishing, supplying, altering, or repairing, prescribing or advising the use of any prosthetic denture, bridge, appliance or thing for any of the purposes indicated in paragraph (a) or to replace, improve or supplement any human tooth, or to prevent, alleviate, correct or improve any condition in the human oral cavity, or to be used in, upon or in connection with any human tooth, jaw or associated structure or tissue, or in the treatment of any condition thereof; (c) the taking or making, or the giving of advice or assistance or the providing of facilities for the taking or making of an impression, bite or cast and design preparatory to, or for the purpose of,

or with a view to making, producing, reproducing, constructing, fitting, furnishing, supplying, altering or repairing any such prosthetic denture, bridge, appliance or thing; (d) any specialty of dentistry; (e) the dental procedures performed by a dental hygienist or dental assistant.

PRACTICE OF DENTURE TECHNOLOGY. (i) The taking of impressions or bite registrations for the purpose of or with a view to the making, producing, reproducing, constructing, furnishing, supplying, altering or repairing of any complete upper or complete lower prosthetic denture, or both, to be fitted to an edentulous arch or arches, (ii) the fitting of any complete upper or complete lower prosthetic denture, or both, to an edentulous arch or arches, and includes the making, producing, reproducing, constructing, furnishing, supplying, altering and repairing complete upper or complete lower prosthetic dentures in respect of which a service is performed under subclause (i) or (ii). *Denturist acts*.

PRACTICE OF DENTURE THERAPY. (a) The taking of impressions or bite registrations for the purpose of, or with a view to, the making, producing, reproducing, constructing, furnishing, supplying, altering or repairing of any complete upper or complete lower prosthetic denture, or both, to be fitted to an edentulous arch, (b) the fitting of any complete upper or complete lower prosthetic denture or both, to an edentulous arch, and (c) the making, producing, reproducing, constructing, furnishing, supplying, altering and repairing complete upper or complete lower prosthetic dentures or both in respect of which a service is performed under clause (a) or (b). *Denture Therapists Act*, R.S.O. 1990, c. D.7, s. 1.

PRACTICE OF DENTUROLOGY. (a) The making, fitting, constructing, altering, reproducing or repairing of a complete upper or lower prosthetic denture or both, the furnishing or supplying of such a denture directly to a person or advising on the use of any such denture; (b) the taking, making, or giving of advice, assistance or facilities respecting the taking or making of any impression, bite, cast or design preparatory to, or for the purpose of making, constructing, fitting, furnishing, supplying, altering, repairing or reproducing any such complete upper or complete lower removable prosthetic denture, or both; (c) the demanding by a denturist from any person to whom he provided the services mentioned in subclauses (a) and (b) and the recovering as a debt in any court of competent juris-diction of reasonable charges for the services provided. *Denturists' Act*, S.N.B. 1986, c. 90, s. 2.

PRACTICE OF DIETETICS. The translation and application of the scientific knowledge of foods and human nutrition toward the attain-ment, maintenance or promotion of the health of individuals, groups and the community and in-cludes the following: (i) administering food ser-vice systems; (ii) assessing nutritional needs of individuals and developing and implementing nutritional care plans based on the assessments; (iii) establishing and reviewing the principles of nutrition and guidelines for health and ill people throughout their lives; (iv) assessing the overall nutritional needs of a community in order to establish priorities and influence policies which provide the nutritional component of preventa-tive programs, and implementing and evaluating those programs; (v) interpreting and evaluating, for consumer protection, information on nutri-tion that is available to the public; (vi) consulting with individuals, families and groups on the principles of food and nutrition and the practical application of those principles; (vii) planning, conducting and evaluating educational pro-grams on nutrition for registered dietitians and other professionals and supporting occupations; (viii) conducting basic and applied research in food, nutrition and food service systems.

PRACTICE OF ENGINEERING. Reporting on, advising on, evaluating, designing, preparing plans and specifications for or directing the con-struction, technical inspection, maintenance or operation of any structure, work or process (A) that is aimed at the discovery, development or utilization of matter, materials or energy or in any other way designed for the use and conven-ience of people; and (B) that requires in the re-porting, advising, evaluating, designing, prepa-ration or direction the professional application of the principles of mathematics, chemistry, physics or any related applied subject.

PRACTICE OF GEOLOGY. (i) Reporting, advising, evaluating, interpreting, geological surveying, sampling or examining related to any activity (A) that is aimed at the discovery or development of oil, natural gas, coal, metallic or non-metallic minerals, precious stones, other natural resources or water or that is aimed at the investigation of geological conditions; and (B) that requires in that reporting, advising, evalu-ating, interpreting, geological surveying, sam-

pling or examining, the professional application of the principles of the geological sciences; or (ii) teaching geology at a university.

PRACTICE OF GEOPHYSICS. (i) Reporting on, advising on, acquiring, processing, evaluat-ing or interpreting geophysical data, or geo-physical surveying that relates to any activity (A) that is aimed at the discovery or development of oil, natural gas, coal, metallic or non-metallic minerals, precious stones, other natural re-sources or water or that is aimed at the investi-gation of sub-surface conditions in the earth; and (B) that requires in that reporting, advising, eval-uating, interpreting, or geophysical surveying, the professional application of the principles of the geophysical sciences; or (ii) teaching geo-physics at a university.

PRACTICE OF GEOSCIENCE. Reporting on, advising on, evaluating, interpreting, proc-essing, geological and geophysical surveying, exploring, classifying reserves or examining ac-tivities related to the earth sciences or engineer-ing-geology (a) that is aimed at the discovery or development of oil, natural gas, coal, metallic or nonmetallic minerals or precious stones, water or other natural resources or that is aimed at the investigation of geoscientific conditions, and (b) that requires in the reporting, advising, evaluat-ing, interpreting, processing, geoscientific sur-veying, exploring, reserve classifying or exam-ining the professional application of mathematics, chemistry or physics through the application of the principles of geoscience, and includes providing educational instruction on the matters contained in this paragraph to a stu-dent at an educational institution. *Engineers and Geoscientists Act*, R.S. Nfld. 1990, c. E-12, s. 2.

PRACTICE OF LAND SURVEYING. (i) The survey of land to determine or establish bound-aries; (ii) the survey of land to determine or es-tablish the boundaries of any right or interest in land or in air space; (iii) the survey of air space to determine or establish boundaries; (iv) the survey of land to determine the location of an-ything relative to a boundary for the purpose of certifying the location of the thing; (v) the survey of lakes, rivers or watercourses to establish or determine their boundaries; (vi) the survey by any means, including photogrammetric, elec-tronic or astronomic methods, of land, water or air space for the purpose of preparing maps, plans and documents connected in any way with the establishment or determination of bounda-ries delineating any right or interest in land, water or air space; (vii) cadastral operations and compiling and recording information related to the matters specified in subclauses (i) to (vi); (viii) establishing and maintaining a network of geodetic points of any order of precision and establishing photogrammetric controls for the purposes of the work specified in subclauses (i) to (v), including the preparation of maps, plans and documents and giving advice with respect to any other specified matters.

PRACTICE OF LAW. Includes (a) appearing as counsel or advocate, (b) drawing, revising or settling (i) a petition, memorandum or articles under the Company Act, or an application, statement, affidavit, minute, resolution, bylaw or other document relating to the incorporation, registration, organization, reorganization, dissolution or winding up of a corporate body, (ii) a document for use in a proceeding, judicial or extra-judicial, (iii) a will, deed of settlement, trust deed, power of attorney or a document relating to any probate or letters of administration or the estate of a deceased person, (iv) a document relating in any way to proceedings under a statute of Canada or the Province, or (v) an instrument relating to real or personal estate which is intended, permitted or required to be registered, recorded or filed in a registry or other public office, (c) doing any act or negotiating in any way for the settlement of, or settling, a claim or demand for damages, (d) agreeing to place at the disposal of another person the services of a barrister or solicitor, (e) giving legal advice, (f) the making of an offer to do anything referred to in paragraphs (a) to (e), and (g) the making of a representation by a person that the person is qualified or entitled to do anything referred to in paragraphs (a) to (e), but it does not include (h) any of those acts if it is not done for or in the expectation of a fee, gain or reward, direct or indirect, from the person for whom the acts are performed, (i) the drawing or preparing of an instrument by a public officer in the course of his duty, (j) the lawful practice of a notary public, (k) the usual business carried on by an insurance adjuster.

PRACTICE OF MEDICINE. The carrying on for hire, gain or hope of gain or reward, either directly or indirect, of the healing art or any of its banches.

PRACTICE OF NURSING. Representing oneself as a registered nurse while carrying out the practice of those functions which, directly or indirectly in collaboration with a client and with other health workers, have as their objective, promotion of health, prevention of illness, alleviation of suffering, restoration of health and maximum development of health potential and without restricting the generality of the foregoing includes (a) collecting data relating to he health status of an individual or groups of individuals, (b) interpreting data and identifying health problems, (c) setting care goals, (d) determining nursing approaches, (e) implementing care, supportive or restorative of life and well-being, (f) implementing, care relevant to medical treatment, (g) assessing outcomes, and (h) revising plans. *Registered Nurses Act*, R.S.M. 1987, c. R40, s. 1.

PRACTICE OF OCCUPATIONAL THERAPY. The provision of services that focus on self-care, work and leisure through the identification or assessment of human physical, emotional, developmental or cognitive dysfunction from whatever cause in order to alleviate the dysfunction, restore, improve or maintain optimal function or develop latent ability, and may include (i) the application and interpretation of selected evaluative procedures and assessments, (ii) the planning, administration and evaluation of restorative, developmental, preventive, educational and health maintenance programs, and (iii) the provision of consultative, advisory, research and other professional services to complement or implement the services referred to in this clause. *Occupational Therapy Profession Act*, S.A. 1987, c. O-2.5, s. 1.

PRACTICE OF OPTOMETRY. The application of the science of assessing the oculo-visual state, the correction and treatment of any defects by the prescribing and dispensing of corrective lenses, appliances and procedures and making use of any such instruments or devices designed therefor, and of differentiating between the normal and pathologically abnormal eye and adnexa. *Optometry Act*, R.S.P.E.I. 1988, c. O-6, s. 1.

PRACTICE OF PHARMACY. (i) Responsibility for preparing, distributing and controlling drugs in a pharmacy, (ii) compounding a drug, (iii) dispensing a drug, (iv) selling a drug by retail, (v) disseminating information on the safe and effective use of a drug when dispensing or selling the drug, (vi) subdividing or breaking up a manufacturer's original package of a drug for the purpose of re-packaging the drug in larger or smaller quantities for re-distribution or sale by retail, (vii) operating a pharmacy insofar as the operation relates to the practice of pharmacy, or (viii) supervising the practice of pharmacy. *Pharmaceutical Profession Act*, S.A. 1988, c. P-7.1, s. 1(1).

PRACTICE OF PHYSIOTHERAPY. The services usually performed by a physiotherapist in the identification, assessment, prevention and alleviation of physical dysfunction or pain, from whatever cause, and the restoration and maintenance of optimal function, and includes (a) the assessment in consultation with the patient's physician leading to the determination of the nature and degree of physical dysfunction, and of potential level of function and the application and interpretation of selected evaluative procedures, (b) the planning, administration and evaluation of remedial treatment programs of physiotherapy in communication with the patient's physician, (c) the planning, administration and evaluation of preventative and health maintenance programs of physiotherapy, (d) the provision of consultative, educational, advisory, research and other professional services as may be required. *The Physiotherapists Act*, R.S.M. 1987, c. P65, s. 1.

PRACTICE OF PROFESSIONAL CHEMISTRY. The practice for gain of any branch of chemistry, pure or applied, including, without limiting the generality of the foregoing, organic, inorganic, physical, metallurgical, biological, clinical, analytical and industrial chemistry, but does not include the execution of chemical or physical tests based on known methods to determine the quality of a product or to control a manufacturing process. *Professional Chemists Act*, R.S.Q. 1977, c. C-15, s. 1.

PRACTICE OF PROFESSIONAL COMMUNITY PLANNING. The preparation of comprehensive plans of development, including the preparation of such plans for one or more communities or regions.

PRACTICE OF PROFESSIONAL ENGINEERING. 1. Any act of designing, composing, evaluating, advising, reporting, directing or supervising wherein the safeguarding of life, health, property or the public welfare is concerned and that requires the application of engineering principles, but does not include practising as a natural scientist. *Professional Engineers Act*, R.S.O. 1990, c. P.28, s. 1. 2. The carrying on of any branch of chemical, civil, electrical, forest, geological, mechanical, metallurgical, mining or structural engineering, including the reporting on, designing, or directing the construction of any works that require for their design, or the supervision of their construction, or the supervision of their maintenance, such experience and technical knowledge as are required by or under an act for the admission by examination to membership in an association. 3. Reporting on, advising on, valuing, measuring for, laying out, designing, directing, constructing or inspecting any of the works or processes set forth in a schedule, or such works or processes omitted therefrom as are similar to those set forth therein by reason of their requiring the skilled application of the principles of mathematics, physics, mechanics, aeronautics, hydraulics, electricity, physics, chemistry or geology in their development and attainment; and includes the reporting, advising, valuing, measuring for, laying out, designing, directing, constructing or inspecting by any person under the general supervision of a professional engineer; but does not include the execution or supervision of works as contractor, foreman, superintendent, inspector, road master, superintendent of maintenance, technical assistant, student or engineer in training where the work has been designed by and is done under the responsible supervision of a professional engineer.

PRACTICE OF PROFESSIONAL FORESTRY. Advising, planning, reporting on and supervising any phase of the administration or management of forests or forest land including the valuation, maintenance, improvement, conservation and protection of forest land and the regeneration of forests.

PRACTICE OF PROFESSIONAL LAND SURVEYING. The determination of natural and artificial features of the surface of the earth and the storage and representation of such features on a chart, map, plan or graphic representation, and includes the practice of cadastral surveying. *Surveyors Act*, R.S.O. 1990, c. S.29, s. 1.

PRACTICE OF PSYCHOLOGY. Includes, for a fee or reward, monetary or otherwise, (a) the provision, to individuals, groups, organizations or the public, of any service involving the application of principles, methods and procedures of understanding, predicting and influencing behaviour, including the principles of learning, perception, motivation, thinking, emotion and interpersonal relationships, (b) the application of methods and procedures of interviewing, counselling, psychotherapy, behaviour therapy, behaviour modification, hypnosis or research, or (c) the construction, administration and interpretation of tests of mental abilities, aptitudes, interests, opinions, attitudes, emotions, personality characteristics, motivations and psychophysiological characteristics, and the assessment or diagnosis of behavioural, emotional and mental disorder. *Health Professions Act, Psychologists Regulation*, B.C. Reg. 442/99.

PRACTICE OF RESPIRATORY TECHNOLOGY. A person shall be deemed to be practising respiratory technology who by advertisement, sign, or statement of any kind, written or oral, alleges or implies or states that that person is, or claims to be qualified, able or willing to assist any individual or individuals by way of medically supervised and co-ordinated treatment by medical gases, aerosols, oxygen, compressed air, or other therapeutic medical gas mixtures applied directly or indirectly to the airways.

PRACTICE OF SUPERVISED DENTURE THERAPY. (a) The taking of impressions or bite registrations for the purpose of, or with a view to, the making, producing, reproducing, constructing, furnishing, supplying, altering or repairing of any removable prosthetic denture, (b) the fitting of any removable prosthetic denture, and (c) the making, producing, reproducing, constructing, furnishing, supplying, altering and repairing removable prosthetic dentures in respect of which a service is performed under clause (a) or (b). *Denture Therapists Act*, R.S.O. 1990, c. D.7, s. 1.

PRACTICE OF SURVEYING. (i) The determination, establishment or recording by any means of the positions of points or natural or man-made features on, over or under the surface of the earth; (ii) the determination of the form of the earth; (iii) the practice of land surveying, and includes the preparation of maps, plans, systems and documents and the giving of advice with respect to any of the matters referred to in this clause.

PRACTICE OF THE PROFESSION OF CHIROPODY. That specialty of the healing arts that treats of ailments or diseased conditions or deformities or injuries of the human foot, and includes examining or diagnosing or prescribing for or treating such disabilities and massage or adjustment in connection therewith.

PRACTICE OF VETERINARY MEDICINE. Any service usually performed by a veterinarian, including (i) the application of surgery or medicine to animals, (ii) prescribing, treating, manipulating, or operating for the prevention, alleviation or correction of any disease, injury, pain, deficiency, deformity, defect, lesion, disorder or physical condition of animals with or without the use of instruments, appliances, medicine, drugs, preparations or anaesthetics, (iii) the giving of advice in respect of any of the matters mentioned in subclauses (i) and (ii) with the view of obtaining a fee or salary, but not including (iv) the furnishing, without remuneration, of first aid or temporary assistance to an animal in an emergency, (v) the treatment of an animal by its owner, by a member of the owner's household or by a person regularly employed by the owner in agricultural or domestic work, (vi) the treatment of an animal by an employee of a licensed member under the supervision of the member, (vii) the castration of calves, pigs and lambs and the caponizing of poultry, (viii) the dehorning of cattle, (ix) the artificial insemination of any species of animal, (x) the non-surgical implantation of an embryo, other than synchronization of donor and recipient animals, superovulation and the collection, evaluation and processing of embryos, (xi) the dispensing of medicines pursuant to the Pharmacy Act, (xii) the drawing of blood from animals by trained technical personnel employed by the Province or the Government of Canada, (xiii) the use of an animal in research which is carried out using acceptable veterinary procedures if the use of the animal has been approved by an appropriate animal care committee of which at least one member is a licensed veterinarian, (xiv) the study, prevention and treatment of fish diseases. *Veterinary Medical Act*, R.S.N.S. 1989, c. 490, s. 2.

PRACTISE AGROLOGY. To teach or demonstrate the science or art of agriculture or advise or conduct scientific experiments and research in relation thereto as a chief occupation.

PRACTISE MEDICINE. To offer or undertake by any means or method to diagnose, treat, operate, or prescribe for any human disease, pain, injury, disability or physical condition or to hold oneself out as being able to diagnose, treat, operate or prescribe for any human disease, pain, injury, disability or physical condition.

PRACTISING. *v*. Carrying on a practice. It means the ongoing activity customarily and usually employed in the treatment of patients. It does not include the acquisition of a practice. One cannot be "practising" before one has a practice. *Sandilands v. Powell*, 2003 ABCA 162, 34

C.P.C. (5th) 81, 35 B.L.R. (3d) 1, 330 A.R. 92, [2003] 11 W.W.R. 618, 299 W.A.C. 92 (C.A.).

PRACTISING. *adj.* " . . . [M]eans a person who is living in accordance with the teachings of his church. . ." *Caldwell v. Stuart* (1982), 3 C.H.R.R. D/785 at D/788, 35 B.C.L.R. 97, 132 D.L.R. (3d) 79, 82 C.L.L.C. 17,008 (C.A.), Seaton J.A.

PRACTITIONER. *n.* 1. One who exercises or employs any art or profession. 2. A person who is registered and entitled under the laws of a province to practise in that province the profession of medicine, dentistry or veterinary medicine. 3. A chiropractor, dental mechanic, dental surgeon, ophthalmic dispenser, optometrist, osteopath, physician or podiatrist or other person who provides a basic health service or an extended health service. *Alberta Health Care Insurance Act*, R.S.A. 1980, c. A-24, s. 1. 4. A person other than a physician entitled to render insured services in the place where they are rendered. *Health Insurance acts*. See DRUGLESS ~; GENERAL ~; HEALTH CARE ~; HEALTH ~; MEDICAL ~; NATUROPATHIC ~; NURSE ~; RESTRICTED ~.

PRAECIPE. *n.* [L.] 1. A requisition. 2. " . . . [I]nstructions to the Registrar to issue the writ. In old times it was the name given to the writ itself; now it is nothing more than instructions to the officer. . ." *Kimpton v. McKay* (1895), 4 B.C.R. 196 at 211 (C.A.), Drake J.A. (Walkem J.A. concurring). 3. A piece of paper on which one party to a proceeding specifies what document that party wishes to have prepared or issued and the particulars of the document.

PRAECOGNITA. *n.* [L.] Things known previously so that something later can be understood.

PRAEDA BELLI. [L.] Property taken in wartime.

PRAEDIAL SERVITUDE. A servitude which affects land.

PRAENOMEN. *n.* [L.] The given name of a person, as opposed to a family name.

PRAESCRIPTIO EST TITULUS EX USU ET TEMPORE SUBSTANTIAM CAPIENS AD AUCTORITATE LEGIS. [L.] Prescription is a title arising from use and time which takes its substance from legal authority.

PRAESENTIA CORPORIS TOLLIT ERROREM NOMINIS; ET VERITAS NOM-

INIS TOLLIT ERROREM DEMONSTRATIONIS. [L.] The presence of a body removes error from a name; and the truth of a name removes error from a description.

PRAESTAT CAUTELA QUAM MEDELA. [L.] Caution is superior to cure.

PRAESUMPTIO. *n.* [L.] 1. Intrusion. 2. The unlawful seizure of something.

PRAESUMPTIO VIOLENTA VALET IN LEGE. [L.] Strong presumption prevails in law.

PRAIRIE PROVINCES. The provinces of Manitoba, Saskatchewan and Alberta.

PRANK. *n.* A practical joke.

PRAXIS. *n.* Practice, use.

PRAYER. *n.* The conclusion of a petition to Parliament which expresses the petitioners' particular object. A. Fraser, W.A. Dawson & J. Holtby, eds., *Beauchesne's Rules and Forms of the House of Commons of Canada*, 6th ed. (Toronto: Carswell, 1989) at 278. See PETITION.

PRAYER FOR RELIEF. The portion of a statement of claim requesting damages or an order of the court.

P.R.B. *abbr.* Pension Review Board.

PREAMBLE. *n.* A preface which states the reasons for and intended effects of legislation.

PRE-APPRENTICE. *n.* A person who is a full-time or part-time student registered in an approved program of study from which the person is to receive training and instruction in a designated occupation in preparation for qualification under this Act. *An Act to Amend the Industrial Training and Certification Act*, S.N.B. 1987, c. 27, s. 2.

PREARRANGED CEMETERY CONTRACT. A contract or agreement whereby, in consideration of payment therefor in advance, by a lump sum or instalments, a person undertakes to provide lots, compartments, crypts or other space in a cemetery, columbarium or mausoleum, or cemetery services or cemetery supplies, for a person alive at the time the agreement is made. *The Cemeteries Act*, R.S.S. 1978, c. C-4, s. 2.

PREARRANGED FUNERAL PLAN. *var.* **PRE-ARRANGED FUNERAL PLAN**. An agreement where, in consideration of payment in advance by lump sum or instalments, a person contracts to provide funeral merchandise or services when required for one or more individuals alive at the time the agreement is entered into.

PREARRANGED FUNERAL SERVICES PLAN. A contract where, in consideration of payment made in advance, either in whole or in part, a funeral provider contracts to provide future funeral services for one or more persons who are alive at the time the contract is entered into.

PREARRANGEMENT. *n.* An arrangement for the provision of specific funeral services, supplies or transportation of a dead human body on the death of a person who is alive at the time the arrangement is made. *Funeral Directors and Establishments Act*, R.S.O. 1990, c. F.36, s. 1.

PREAUDIENCE. *var.* **PRE-AUDIENCE**. *n.* One person's right to be heard before another; the usual order of precedence is the Attorney-General, Queen's Counsel, and junior barristers, usually in the order in which they were called to the bar.

PREBENDA. *n.* [L.] Goods provided.

PRECATORY CLAUSE. In a will, expresses the testator's hope or wish that another party will do something.

PRECATORY TRUST. Created when a gift or bequest to a charitable corporation is combined with a moral obligation to use the property in a certain way. The moral obligation is expressed in words of expectation, desire, or purpose.

PRECATORY WORDS. An expression in a will which indicates a wish, desire or request that something be done.

PRECEDENCE. *n.* The state or act of going first.

PRECEDENT. *n. 1.* A decision or judgment of a court of law which is cited as the authority for deciding a similar situation in the same manner, on the same principle or by analogy. 2. Decisions of the courts in the common law system are governed by precedent, the prior decisions of equal or higher courts. 3. Standard contracts or other agreements or documents used as examples for later documents. Law offices develop their own sets of precedents for various types of agreements or documents. Also available commercially. See STARE DECISIS.

PRECEDENT CONDITION. Something which must be performed or happen before an interest can vest or grow or an obligation be performed.

PRECEDING. *adj.* Coming before in time; happening or existing before.

PRECEPT. *n.* Direction, order.

PRECEPTOR. *n.* A professional who trains others in his or her profession.

PRECINCT. *n. 1.* The immediate environs of a court. 2. The district of a constable. See ELECTORAL ~; PARLIAMENTARY ~S.

PRECINCTS OF THE BUILDING. The space enclosed by the walls of the building.

PRECIOUS METAL. Gold, palladium, platinum and silver and an alloy of any of those metals and any other metal and an alloy thereof that is designated by the regulations as a precious metal for the purposes of this Act. *Precious Metals Marking Act*, R.S.C. 1985, c. P-19, s. 2.

PRECIOUS METAL ARTICLE. An article wholly or partly, or purporting to be wholly or partly, composed of a precious metal and includes a plated article. *Precious Metals Marking Act*, R.S.C. 1985, c. P-19, s. 2.

PRECIOUS METAL COIN. A coin at least fifty per cent of the composition of which is gold, silver or platinum or of the platinum group of metals. *Royal Canadian Mint Act*, S.C. 1987, c. 43, s. 1(3).

PRECIPE. See PRAECIPE.

PRECISION APPROACH. An instrument approach by an aircraft using azimuth and glide path information; *Canadian Aviation Regulations*, SOR/96-433, s. 101.01.

PRECONISATION. *n.* A proclamation.

PREDATOR. *n. 1.* A coyote, fox, timber wolf, or bear, and includes a pup or cub of any of them. 2. An animal which preys upon livestock. *Livestock Insurance Act*, R.S. Nfld. 1990, c. L-23, s. 2.

PREDATORY ANIMAL. Coyote and wolf. *Game Act*, R.S.N.W.T. 1974, c. G-1, s. 2.

PREDECEASE. *v.* " . . . [D]ie before. . ." *Conn, Re* (1916), 28 D.L.R. 805 at 806, 10 O.W.N. 5 (H.C.), Lachford J.

PREDECESSOR. *n.* One person who preceded another.

PREDECESSOR IN TITLE. Refers to a person separate from and going before the applicant for a trade mark.

PRE-DEVELOPMENT. *n.* Any act or deed relating to surveys and research in the field for a limited period of time for the purpose of gathering information with a view to deciding whether or not development will take place. *An Act respecting the land regime in the James Bay and New Quebec territories*, S.Q. 1979, c. 25, s. 50.

PRE-DISPOSITION REPORT. *var.* **PRE-DISPOSITION REPORT**. A report on the personal and family history and present environment of a young person.

PREDOMINATE. *adj.* Main.

PREEMPTIVE RIGHT. The right to purchase shares or other securities to be issued or subjected to rights or options to purchase, as such right is defined in this section. *Loan and Trust Companies Act*, S.N.B. 1987, c. L-11.2, s. 74.

PRE-EMPTIVE RIGHTS. In a non-offering company, a requirement that new shares be offered to existing shareholders first before offering them to other persons.

PRE-EXISTING CONTRACT. A sales contract that has been replaced by another sales contract.

PRE-EXISTING OR UNDERLYING CONDITION. A condition of the worker which existed or was discernible as an underlying condition before the accident.

PREFABRICATED TRENCH SUPPORT SYSTEM. A trench box, trench-shield or similar structure composed of members connected to one another, capable of being moved as a unit, and designed to resist the pressure from the walls of a trench.

PREFATORY AVERMENT. An old term from common law pleading for particulars of facts and circumstances, including any special knowledge which listeners might possess prepared by the plaintiff. R.E. Brown, *The Law of Defamation in Canada* (Toronto: Carswell, 1987) at 156.

PREFER. *v.* 1. To move for, to apply. 2. To place before the court for consideration and action. 3. " . . . [T]o bear or carry before, or to give the object of the preference a place before some other. . . conveys the idea of giving one creditor a position more advanced than the others, or precedence in relation to the payment of his debt debt. . ." *Stephens v. McArthur* (1891), 19 S.C.R. 446 at 464-5, 6 Man. R. 496, Patterson J.

PREFER A CHARGE. " . . . [D]one by reading to him, as it appears from the information and complaint laid against him upon which he was committed for trial (as well as such additional charges as may by leave of the Judge be preferred by the prosecuting officer under sec. 834 [of the Criminal Code, S.C. 1892, c. 29]), and when this is done the preferring of the charge is complete and constitutes the first part of the arraignment . . ." *R. v. Goon* (1916), 25 C.C.C. 415 at 421, 28 D.L.R. 374, 10 W.W.R. 24, 22 B.C.R. 381 (C.A.), Martin J.A. (McPhillips J.A. concurring).

PREFERENCE. *n.* " . . . [O]f one creditor over another . . . consists . . . in the voluntary disposition by an insolvent of some portion of his property so as to confer greater benefit upon one or more of his creditors than upon others, when unable to pay all in full. To constitute a preference it must have been given by the insolvent of his own mere motion, and as a favour or bounty proceeding voluntarily from himself." *Molsons Bank v. Halter* (1890), 18 S.C.R. 88 at 102, Gwynne J. See FRAUDULENT ~.

PREFERENCE SHARE. " . . . [S]hares which carry a preference may properly be denominated preference shares, though in certain respects they may be shorn of rights which belong to common shares . . ." *Rubas v. Parkinson* (1929), 64 O.L.R. 87 at 93, 56 O.W.N. 133, [1929] 3 D.L.R. 558 (C.A.), Masten J.A. (Latchford C.J., Orde, Fisher and Riddell JJ.A. concurring). See CUMULATIVE ~.

PREFERENTIAL HIRING. A system by which employers agree to hire union members as long as there are enough members to fill the employers' requirements.

PREFERRED. *adj.* 1. " . . . [A]n indictment based upon a committal for trial without the intervention of a grand jury is not 'preferred' against an accused until it is lodged with the trial court at the opening of the accused's trial, with a court ready to proceed with the trial." *R. v. Chabot* (1980), 18 C.R. (3d) 258 at 271, [1980] 2 S.C.R. 985, 22 C.R. (3d) 350, 34 N.R. 361, 55 C.C.C. (2d) 385, 117 D.L.R. (3d) 527, the court per Dickson J. 2. Having an advantage over another.

PREFERRED BENEFICIARY. Under a trust for a particular taxation year of the trust means a beneficiary under the trust at the end of the particular year who is resident in Canada at that time if (*a*) the beneficiary is (i) an individual in respect of whom paragraphs 118.3(1)(a) to (b) apply for the individual's taxation year (in this definition referred to as the "beneficiary's year") that ends in the particular year, or (ii) an individual (A) who attained the age of 18 years before the end of the beneficiary's year, was a dependant (within the meaning assigned by subsection 118(6)) of another individual for the beneficiary's year and was dependent on the other individual because of mental or physical infirmity, and (B) whose income (computed without reference to subsection 104(14)) for the beneficiary's year does not exceed the amount used under paragraph (c) of the description of B in subsection 118(1) for the year, and (*b*) the beneficiary is (i) the settlor of the trust, (ii) the spouse or common-law partner or former spouse or common-law partner of the settlor of the trust, or (iii) a child, grandchild or great grandchild of the settlor of the trust or the spouse or common-law partner of any such person. *Income Tax Act*, R.S.C. 1985, c.1 (5th Supp.), s. 108(1).

PREFERRED CREDITOR. A creditor whom the common law or legislation gives some advantage over other claimants.

PREFERRED INDICTMENT. "... [L]odged by the Attorney-General against an accused..." *R. v. Biernacki* (1962) 37 C.R. 226 at 235 (Que. S.P.), Trottier J.S.P. See PREFERRED.

PREFERRED SHARE. 1. A share other than a common share. 2. A share in the capital stock of an association that is not a co-op share. *Canada Cooperative Associations Act*, R.S.C. 1985, c. C-40, s. 3. See PREFERENCE SHARE.

PREGNANCY. *n*. The state of having a child in utero.

PRE-HEARING VOTE. A vote taken prior to determination of the appropriate bargaining unit at an application for certification by a labour relations board.

PRE-INCORPORATION CONTRACT. *var.* **PREINCORPORATION CONTRACT**. A contract entered into by a contractor in the name of or on behalf of a corporation before its incorporation.

PRE-JUDGMENT INTEREST. An award which compensates the plaintiff for the loss and use of the value of a monetary award until it is paid.

PREJUDGMENT INTEREST RATE. The bank rate at the end of the first day of the last month of the quarter preceding the quarter in which the proceeding was commenced, rounded to the nearest tenth of a percentage point. *Courts of Justice Act*, R.S.O. 1990, c. C.43, s. 127(1).

PREJUDICE. *n*.1. An injury. 2. Being denied the right to which one is entitled. 3. Unjustly made to suffer. 4. Based on stereotypes formed with incomplete and inaccurate information. See ACTUAL ~; CONFORMITY ~; DISMISSAL WITHOUT ~; GENERIC ~; JUROR ~; INTEREST ~; SPECIFIC ~; WITHOUT ~.

PREJUDICED. *adj*. 1. "[In Mechanics' Lien Act, S.A. 1906, s. 21, s. 14] ... I think must be taken to mean 'unjustly made to suffer' ..." *Rendall, MacKay, Michie Ltd. v. Warren & Dyett* (1915), 8 W.W.R. 113 at 118, 21 D.L.R. 801 (Alta. T.D.), Beck J. 2. "... [S]uffered a pecuniary loss or damage ..." *Gray-Campbell v. Jamieson*, [1923] 3 D.L.R. 845 at 847, [1923] 3 W.W.R. 478, 17 Sask. L.R. 405 (K.B.), Maclean J.

PREJUDICIAL. *adj*. Causing harm. See UNFAIRLY ~.

PRELIMINARY HEARING. The hearing, held in accordance with procedure set out in Part XVIII of the Criminal Code, in which a justice determines whether there is sufficient evidence to commit an accused for trial.

PRELIMINARY INQUIRY. 1. The procedure conducted by a provincial court or equivalent judge to determine whether the Crown has sufficient evidence to warrant a full trial of the accused. The Crown's evidence against the accused is heard in part or in its entirety at the hearing. 2. There is substantial body of jurisprudence to the effect that the sole purpose of the preliminary inquiry provisions of the Criminal Code [R.S.C. 1985, c. C- 46] is to establish a charge screening device. The proceedings are oriented towards the determination of whether there is sufficient evidence to force the accused to stand trial ... In this sense, the purpose of the preliminary inquiry is directed squarely at the accused who is subject of the proceedings. While the [accused] is a compellable witness to give evidence at a preliminary inquiry, it is unfair to use that process for the predominate purpose of compelling the [accused] to incriminate himself for the purpose of creating new evidence against him from another witness. *R. v. Z. (L.)* (2001), 54 O.R. (3d) 97 (C.A.). See PRELIMINARY HEARING.

PRELIMINARY LIST OF ELECTORS. The lists of electors prepared by enumerators.

PRELIMINARY QUESTION. 1. A question collateral to the merits or the heart of an inquiry but which is not the major question to be decided. S.A. DeSmith, *Judicial Review of Administrative Action*, 4th ed. by J.M. Evans (London: Stevens, 1980) at 114. 2. "The current tendency is . . . to limit the concept of a 'preliminary question' as far as possible. Even those who favour retaining this concept limit it to questions concerning jurisdiction in the strict sense, of the initial power to proceed with an inquiry . . . These questions are identified by the fact that they fall outside the limits of the enabling legislation itself, and are not usually within the area of expertise of the administrative tribunal . . ." *Blanchard c. Control Data Canada Ltée* (1984), 14 Admin. L.R. 133 at 170, [1984] 2 S.C.R. 476, 84 C.L.L.C. 14,070, 55 N.R. 194, 14 D.L.R. (4th) 289, Lamer J. (McIntyre J. concurring).

PREMATURE. *adj*. In relation to an application to court, anticipated circumstances have not materialized or there are existing reasons to defer the application.

PREMIER. *n*. 1. A minister of the Crown holding the recognized position of first Minister. 2. The Prime Minister.

PREMISES. *n*. 1. " . . . [A]lthough in popular language it is applied to buildings, in legal language means 'a subject or thing previously expressed';. . ." *Beacon Life Assurance & Fire Co. v. Gibb* (1862), 7 L.C. Jur. 57 at 61, 15 E.R. 630, 1 Moo. P.C. (N.S.) 73, 8 R.U.R.Q. 476, 13 Low. Can. R. 81 (P.C.), their Lordships per Lord Chelmsford. 2. " . . . [I]n the ordinary acceptation of the term, means the grounds immediately surrounding a house." *Martin v. Martin* (1904), 8 O.L.R. 462 at 466 (C.A.), Falconbridge C.J. 3. Lands and structures, or either of them, and includes trailers and portable structures designed or used for residence, business or shelter. 4. Lands and structures, or either of them, and includes: (i) water; (ii) ships and vessels; (iii) trailers and portable structures designed or used for residence, business or shelter; (iv) trains, railway cars, vehicles and aircraft. See ACCESS TO COMPANY ~; BUSINESS ~; BUYER'S ~; CARETAKER'S ~; EMPLOYMENT ~; FOOD PREMISE; FOOD SERVICE ~; INTEREST IN THE ~; LANDS AND ~; LICENSED ~; MOBILE ~; MOBILE PREPARATION ~; OFF-~; SALE; ON-~ SALE; PERMIT ~; RESIDENTIAL ~; ROADSIDE ~.

PREMISES OF A DEED. 1. "It is customary to include in the premises [of a deed] the effectual date of the transfer; the names of the parties to the transfer of title as grantor and grantees, the recitals, the words of grant and the description of the property transferred." *Wheeler v. Wheeler (No. 2)* (1979), 25 N.B.R. (2d) 376 at 378 (C.A.), Limerick, Bugold and Ryan JJ.A. 2. " . . . [A]ll the foreparts of a deed before the habendum, and the office of this part of the deed is rightly to name the grantor and grantee, and to comprehend the certainty of the thing granted, and herein is sometimes (though improperly) set down, the estate . . ." *Jamieson v. London & Canadian Loan & Agency Co.* (1896), 23 O.A.R. 602 at 619 (C.A.), Burton J.A.

PREMIUM. *n*. 1. The single or periodical payment to be made for insurance and includes dues and assessments. 2. Any goods, services, rebate or other benefit offered or given at the time of the sale of goods or the lease of services, which may be granted or obtained immediately or in a deferred manner, from the merchant, manufacturer or advertiser, either gratuitously or on conditions explicitly or implicitly presented as advantageous. 3. Where used in relation to a commodity futures option, means the consideration for which the option is acquired. 4. The excess value of the consideration received from the issue or resale of securities over the par or stated value of the securities. *Pipeline Uniform Accounting regula*tions. See ACCELERATING ~; BASIC ~; CALL-IN PAY OR ~; EMPLOYEE'S ~; EMPLOYER'S ~; NET ~S; NIGHT ~.

PREMIUM NOTE. An instrument given as consideration for insurance whereby the maker undertakes to pay such sum or sums as may be legally demanded by the insurer, but the aggregate of those sums does not exceed an amount specified in the instrument.

PREMIUM PAY. The pay which an employee is entitled to receive for employment on a public holiday or a day that is deemed to be a public holiday.

PREMIUM RATE. The rate of pay to which an employee is entitled for each hour of employment on a public holiday, or a day that is deemed to be a public holiday.

PRE MORTEM. Occurring or present before death. F.A. Jaffe, *A Guide to Pathological Evidence*, 3d ed. (Toronto: Carswell, 1991) at 224.

PRENDER. *n.* The right or power to seize anything before it is offered.

PRE-NEED CEMETERY PLAN. An agreement where, in consideration of payment in advance by a lump sum or instalments, a cemetery or crematorium contracts to provide cemetery goods or services when required for one or more individuals alive at the time the agreement is entered into. *Cemetery and Funeral Services Act*, R.S.N.S. 1989, c. 62, s. 2.

PRENEED CEMETERY SERVICES PLAN. A contract where, in consideration of payment made in advance, either in whole or in part, an operator contracts to provide future cemetery services for one or more persons who are alive at the time the contract is entered into.

PRE-NEED SUPPLIES OR SERVICES. Cemetery supplies or services that are not required to be provided until the death of a person alive at the time the arrangements are made. *Cemeteries Act (Revised)* R.S.O. 1990, c. C.4, s. 1, as am.

PRE-PACKAGED FOOD. Food which is packaged at a premises other than the place at which it is offered for sale.

PRE-PACKAGED GOODS. Goods packaged in a wrapper or container ready for retail sale; and, if goods packaged in a wrapper or container are found in premises where such goods are packaged or kept for sale, they shall prima facie be deemed to be packaged ready for retail sale. *Weights and Measures Act*, R.S.C. 1970, c. W-7, s. 2.

PREPACKAGED PRODUCT. Any product that is packaged in a container in such a manner that it is ordinarily sold to or used or purchased by a consumer without being re-packaged.

PREPAID CONTRACT. An agreement whereby a person contracts with a purchaser to provide or make provision for funeral services, funeral supplies, or both, or for the transportation of a dead human body, including disbursements, upon the death of a beneficiary, if any payment for the contract is made prior to the death of the beneficiary or the purchaser enters into an insurance contract or plan under which a licensee is to receive directly or indirectly the proceeds of the insurance policy upon the death of the beneficiary. *Funeral Directors and Establishments Act*, R.S.O. 1990, c. F.36, s. 1.

PREPAID EXPENSE. An expenditure or outlay which a taxpayer makes or incurs, the benefit of which extends beyond the end of a taxation year.

PREPAID FUNERAL CONTRACT. Any contract or agreement, or series or combination of contracts or agreements, other than a contract of insurance issued by an insurer licensed pursuant to The Saskatchewan Insurance Act, pursuant to which: (i) for a specified monetary consideration paid in advance of death in a lump sum or by instalments, a contract seller promises to furnish or make available or provide funeral services or funeral goods for use at a time determinable by the death of the contract beneficiary, and includes: (A) prepaid, pre-arranged deposit contracts, where funds are left with the contract seller and are to be used toward the eventual costs of funeral goods and funeral services on behalf of the contract beneficiary; and (B) prepaid, pre-arranged trust contracts, where the contract buyer and the contract seller have a fixed agreement for the provision, on behalf of the contract beneficiary, of funeral goods and funeral services specified in the contract; or (ii) for monetary consideration, a contract seller provides counselling or advice to any person with respect to funeral services or funeral goods. *Prepaid Funeral Service Act*, S.S. 1986, c. P-22.3, s. 2.

PREPARATION. *n.* 1. A drug that contains a controlled drug and one or more active medicinal ingredients, in a recognized therapeutic dose, other than a controlled drug. *Food and Drug Regulations*, C.R.C., c. 870, c. G.O1.001. 2. A preparation of one or more synthetic colours containing less than 3 per cent dye and sold for household use. *Food and Drug Regulations*, C.R.C., c. 870, c. B.06.001. See FOOD ~ EQUIPMENT; PHARMACEUTICAL ~.

PREPARED MEAT PRODUCT. A meat product to which has been added any ingredient permitted by these Regulations, other than meat, or that has been preserved, canned or cooked. *Meat Inspection Regulations*, C.R.C., c. 1032, s. 2.

PREPAYMENT PRIVILEGE. The right to prepay all or part of mortgage or loan principal without paying a penalty.

PREPENSE. *adj.* Thought of in advance, preconceived, planned beforehand.

PREPONDERANCE. *n.* " ... [T]he most weight . . ." *Snider v. Harper* (1922), 66 D.L.R. 149 at 158, [1922] 2 W.W.R. 417, 18 Alta. L.R.

82 (C.A.), Hyndman J.A. (Beck J.A. concurring).

PRE-PRODUCTION. *n.* In relation to mining or oil and gas recovery, things which take place in advance of production or in advance of any tangible result from industry and labour.

PREPRODUCTION DEVELOPMENT COSTS. Aggregate expenses incurred by the operator of a mine in the development of the ore body from the date of acquiring the mine to the date production from the mine begins, and that are essential to the production of the output of the mine.

PREROGATIVA REGIS. [L.] The royal prerogative.

PREROGATIVE. *n.* An exceptional power, privilege or pre-eminence which the law grants to the Crown. See PERSONAL ~; ROYAL ~.

PREROGATIVE ORDER. An act by which a superior court prevents a subordinate tribunal from exceeding jurisdiction, from making errors of law on the face of its judgments and from denying natural justice. Examples are writs of habeas corpus or prohibition.

PREROGATIVE RIGHTS OF THE CROWN. The body of special common law rules which apply to Her Majesty.

PREROGATIVE WRIT. A writ of certiorari, habeas corpus, mandamus, prohibition or quo warranto.

PRE-SCHOOL FACILITY. A place other than an institution, boarding home, foster home or group foster home licensed under this act for the provision of services to children of preschool age.

PRESCRIBE. *v.* 1. In a modern act of Parliament, to regulate the details after the general nature of the proceedings is indicated. This is done by regulations made pursuant to the Statutory Instruments Act, R.S.C. 1985, c. S-22, s. 2. In the provinces this is done by regulation or equivalent. 2. Concerning a levy, includes the power to fix the amount payable and to impose the legal obligation to pay that amount. 3. To write or determine a formula or prescription other than for drugs for the relief or correction of a visual or muscular error or defect of the eye. *Optometry Act*, R.S. Nfld. 1990, c. O-7, s. 2.

PRESCRIBED. *adj.* 1. Prescribed by an act, by the rules of court, by regulation, by-law or other rules. 2. When used with reference to a drug or mixture of drugs, means that a prescriber has directed the dispensing of the drug or mixture of drugs to a named person.

PRESCRIBED BY LAW. "The limit will be prescribe by law within the meaning of s. 1 [of the Charter] if it is expressly provided for by statute or regulation, or results by necessary implication from the terms of a statute or regulation or from its operating requirements. The limit may also result from the application of a common law rule." *R. v. Therens*, [1985] 1 S.C.R. 613 at 645, [1985] 4 W.W.R. 286, 32 M.V.R. 153, 45 C.R. (3d) 97, 38 Alta. L.R. (2d) 99, 18 C.C.C. (3d) 481, 13 C.R.R. 193, 40 Sask. R. 122, 18 D.L.R. (4th) 655, 59 N.R. 122, Le Dain J.

PRESCRIBED DAY OF REST. (a) New Year's Day; (b) Good Friday; (c) Victoria Day; (d) Canada Day; (e) New Brunswick Day; (f) Labour Day; (g) Thanksgiving Day; (h) Remembrance Day; (i) Christmas Day; (j) Boxing Day; and (k) any day appointed by any statute in force in the province or by proclamation of the Governor General or Lieutenant-Governor as a general holiday within the province.

PRESCRIBED SUBSTANCES. Uranium, thorium, plutonium, neptunium, deuterium, their respective derivatives and compounds and such other substances as the Board may by regulation designate as being capable of releasing atomic energy or as being requisite for the production, use or application of atomic energy. *Atomic Energy Control Act*, R.S.C. 1985, c. A-16, s. 2.

PRESCRIBED TIME PERIOD. In relation to a contract of group insurance, a continuous period of 6 months following the termination of the contract or benefit provision therein or such longer continuous period as may be provided in that contract instead of the 6-month period. *Insurance acts.*

PRESCRIBER. *n.* A person who is authorized to give a prescription within the scope of the practice of a health discipline or profession.

PRESCRIPTION. *n.* 1. A common law doctrine extended by statute whereby profits and easements can be acquired over others' land. It is fundamentally a rule of evidence which presumes that the owner granted the land so that title is derived from her or him. R. Megarry and H.W.R. Wade, *The Law of Real Property*, 5th ed. (London: Stevens, 1984) at 1030. 2. A direction from a person authorized to prescribe drugs within the scope of his or her practice of a health discipline directing the dispensing of a drug or mixture of drugs for a specified person. *Drug Interchangeability and Dispensing Fee Act*, R.S.O. 1990, c. P.23, s. 1. 3. The direction of a medical practitioner directing a physiotherapist to treat a named person. *Practice of Physiotherapy Act*, R.S.P.E.I. 1974, c. P-16, s. 1. 4. A written and dated authorization signed by a dentist or a qualified medical practitioner, directing that a service be performed that a dental laboratory technician may be licensed under this Act to perform, for the purpose specified in the authorization. *Dental Technicians Act*, R.S.B.C. 1979, c. 91, s. 1. 5. In respect of a controlled drug, an authorization given by a practitioner that a stated amount of the controlled drug be dispensed for the person named therein. *Food and Drugs Act*, R.S.C. 1985, c. F-27, s. 38 as am. by *Criminal Law Amendment Act*, R.S.C. 1985 (1st Supp.), c. 27, s. 193. 6. In respect of a narcotic, an authorization given by a practitioner that a stated amount of the narcotic be dispensed for the person named therein. *Narcotic Control Act*, R.S.C. 1985, c. N-1, s. 2 as am. by *Criminal Law Amendment Act*, R.S.C. 1985 (1st Supp.), c. 27, s. 196. 7. " . . . [D]elegated legislation containing rules that, along with the rules in the statute, must be applied in the computation of 'value for duty' [in s. 47(1)(a) of the Customs Act, R.S.C. 1970, c. C-40] or 'normal value' [in s. 11 of the Anti-Dumping Act, R.S.C. 1970, c. A-15]." *Canada (Tariff Board) v. Danmour Shoe Co.* (1974), (*sub nom. Danmour Shoes Co., Re*) 1 F.C. 22 at 24-5, 1 N.R. 422 (C.A.), Jackett, Pratte and Hyde JJ.A. See ACQUISITIVE ~; EXTINCTIVE ~; ORAL ~ NARCOTIC.

PRESCRIPTION DRUG. A drug that may be dispensed by a pharmacist only upon the direction of a prescriber.

PRESCRIPTIVE EASEMENT. To establish the easement the claimant must demonstrate a use and enjoyment of the right of way under a continuous, uninterrupted, open and peaceful claim of right for the prescribed period of time immediately prior to the commencement of the action making claim to the easement.

PRESENT. *v.* To offer; to tender.

PRESENT CONSIDERATION. A consideration exchanged at time of contract formation.

PRE-SENTENCE REPORT. 1. A report prepared before sentencing containing information concerning the offender's history to be used in assisting the court in passing sentence. 2. A report on the personal and family history and present environment of a young person. *Youth Criminal Justice Act*, S.C. 2002, c. 1, s. 2.

PRESENTMENT. *n.* 1. Subject to this Act, a bill must be duly presented for payment. If a bill is not duly presented for payment, the drawer and endorsers are discharged. Where the holder of a bill presents it for payment, he shall exhibit the bill to the person from whom he demands payment. *Bills of Exchange Act*, R.S.C. 1985, c. B-4, s. 84. 2. A species of report given by a jury. 3. "The public return of the bill of indictment in open court was termed the presentment of the indictment." *R. v. Chabot* (1980), 18 C.R. (3d) 258 at 265, [1980] 2 S.C.R. 985, 22 C.R. (3d) 350, 34 N.R. 361, 55 C.C.C. (2d) 385, 117 D.L.R. (3d) 527, the court per Dickson J.

PRESENTS. *n.* In a deed, the term which refers to the deed itself.

PRESENT VALUE. An amount that is actuarially equivalent to a payment or payments that become due in the future. See NET ~.

PRESERVATION. *n.* The duty of a secured party to hold and preserve property that has been pledged. In the case of intangible property, the secured party must preserve the rights against parties liable secondarily on the instrument.

PRESERVE. See FISHING ~; SHOOTING ~.

PRESERVED. *adj.* In relation to a meat product, means salted, pickled, corned, cured, dried or smoked. *Meat Inspection Regulations*, C.R.C., c. 1032, s. 2.

PRE-SHIPMENT APPLICATION. The treatment, with methyl bromide, within 21 days prior to export, of a commodity or product that is to be entirely exported to another country, or of a means of conveyance, where such treatment is required by the importing country or in support of Canada's sanitary or phytosanitary export programs. *Ozone-depleting Substances Regulations, 1998*, SOR/99-7, s. 1.

PRESIDENT. *n.* 1. A person placed in authority over other people; a person in charge of others. 2. One who exercises chief executive functions. 3. A Chief Justice or Chief Judge. 4. Includes the chairman, governor, manager or other principal officers of a company.

PRESIDENT OF THE ASSEMBLÉE NATIONALE. The President of the Assemblée nationale and, when the office of President is vacant or when the President is absent from Québec or unable to act, the Secretary of the Assemblée nationale. *An Act Respecting Provincial Controverted Elections*, R.S.Q. 1977, c. C-65, s. 2.

PRESIDENT OF THE EXCHEQUER COURT. Now the Chief Justice of the Federal Court of Canada.

PRESIDING JUDGE. The judge of the Court appointed by the President or Chief to preside at any sitting of the Court in his place.

PRESIDING OFFICER. The Deputy Speaker and Chairman of Committees and a Deputy Chairman and an Assistant Deputy Chairman of Committees appointed under S.O. 8, who, whenever the Chairman is absent from the Chair, may exercise all the powers of the Chairman of Committees, including the powers of Deputy Speaker when the Speaker is unavoidably absent. A. Fraser. W.A. Dawson, & J. Holtby, eds., *Beauchesne's Rules and Forms of the House of Commons of Canada*, 6th ed. (Toronto: Carswell, 1989) at 53-4.

PRESIDING STEWARD. The person who acts as spokesman for the stewards.

PRESS. *n*. 1. The print media. 2. Read in the contemporary manner, includes radio and television as well as the print media. See FREEDOM OF THE ~.

PRESSURE. *n*. 1. Pressure in pounds per square inch measured above prevailing atmospheric pressure. 2. Pressure in kilopascals as measured by a pressure gauge. *Boiler, Pressure Vessel and Compressed Gas Act*, R.S. Nfld. 1990, c. B-5, s. 2. See ALLOWABLE BEARING ~; BURSTING ~; DESIGN BEARING ~; DESIGNED~; DESIGN ~; MAXIMUM ALLOWABLE ~; RATED MAXIMUM SOUND ~; STANDARD ~ REGION; VAPOUR ~; WORKING ~.

PRESSURE ALTITUDE. See CABIN ~.

PRESSURE COMPONENT. Any internal component of the brake master cylinder or master control unit, wheel brake cylinder, brake line, brake hose, or equivalent, except vacuum assist components. *Motor Vehicle Safety Regulations*, C.R.C., c. 1038, s. 105.

PRESSURE EQUIPMENT. A thermal liquid heating system and any containment for an expansible fluid under pressure, including, but not limited to, fittings, boilers, pressure vessels and pressure piping systems.

PRESSURE PIPING. Pipes, tubes, conduits, fittings, gaskets, bolting and all systems containing any arrangement of components thereof, the sole purpose of which is the conveyance of an expansible fluid under pressure and the control of the flow of an expansible fluid under pressure between two points.

PRESSURE PIPING SYSTEM. Pipe, tubes, conduits, fittings, gaskets, bolting and other components making up a system the sole purpose of which is the conveyance of an expansible fluid under pressure and the control of the flow of an expansible fluid under pressure between two or more points.

PRESSURE PLANT. 1. Any one or more pressure vessels or any system or arrangement of pressure vessels and the engines, turbines, pressure piping system, machinery and ancillary equipment of any kind used in connection therewith. 2. An installation of a boiler, pressure vessel, refrigerating system or compressed gas system or combination of them as a unit under the same owner and management and includes all engines, turbines, compressors, piping, appliances, machinery or equipment attached to them or used in connection with them, whether the unit is portable, automotive or permanently attached to a solid base. *Boiler, Pressure Vessel and Compressed Gas Act*, R.S. Nfld. 1990, c. B-5, s. 2.

PRESSURE SYSTEM. A boiler, pressure vessel or pressure plant. *Boiler, Pressure Vessel and Compressed Gas Act*, R.S. Nfld. 1990, c. B-5, s. 2.

PRESSURE VESSEL. 1. Any receptacle of a capacity exceeding .0425 cubic metres that contains or is intended to contain an expansible fluid under pressure. 2. An unfired vessel other than a boiler which may be used for containing, storing, distributing, transferring, distilling or otherwise handling any gas, vapour or liquid under pressure, and includes a pipe, fitting and other equipment attached to it. 3. Any receptacle intended to contain a gas whether inflammable or not, or any pressurized liquid, a boiler and any equipment necessary to their operation. 4. A vessel that is heated or its contents are heated by: (i) a flame or the hot gases of combustion; (ii) electricity; or (iii) a liquid. 5. Includes boilers, air receivers and other vessels subject to pressure. Canada regulations. See USED BOILER, ~ OR PLANT.

PRESSURIZED AIRCRAFT. An aircraft the pressure in the cabin of which is controlled by mechanical means.

PRESUME. *v*. To assume to be true; to take for granted. See RIGHT TO BE ~ED INNOCENT.

PRESUMPTIO JURIS ET DE JURE. [L.] A presumption of law and by law.

PRESUMPTION. *n*. 1. Presumptions can be classified into two general categories: presumptions *without* basic facts and presumptions *with* basic facts. A presumption without a basic fact is simply a conclusion which is to be drawn until the contrary is proved. A presumption with a basic fact entails a conclusion to be drawn upon proof of the basic fact. Basic fact presumptions can be further categorized into permissive and mandatory presumptions. A permissive presumption leaves it optional as to whether the inference of the presumed fact is drawn following proof of the basic fact. A mandatory presumption requires that the inference be made. Presumptions may also be either rebuttable or irrebuttable. If a presumption is rebuttable, there are three potential ways the presumed fact can be rebutted. First, the accused may be required merely to raise a reasonable doubt as to its existence. Secondly, the accused may have an evidentiary burden to adduce sufficient evidence to bring into question the truth of the presumed fact. Thirdly, the accused may have a legal or persuasive burden to prove on a balance of probabilities the non-existence of the presumed fact. Finally, presumptions are often referred to as either presumptions of law or presumptions of fact. The latter entail "frequently recurring examples of circumstantial evidence", while the former involve actual legal rules. *R. v. Oakes*, [1986] 1 S.C.R. 103. 2. " . . . [A]n evidentiary technique by which the elements of a cause of action may be established; it cannot itself stand as an element of a cause of action." *Machtinger v. HOJ Industries* (1992), 40 C.C.E.L. 1 at 20, 7 O.R. (3d) 480n, 92 C.L.L.C. 14,022, 91 D.L.R. (4th) 491, [1992] 1 S.C.R. 986, 136 N.R. 40, 53 O.A.C. 200, McLachlin J. 3. " . . . [E[]ffect is to impose a duty on the party against whom they operate to adduce some evidence . . ." *Powell v. Cockburn* (1976), 22 R.F.L. 155 at 161, [1977] 2 S.C.R. 218, 8 N.R. 215, 68 D.L.R. (3d) 700, Dickson J. (Laskin C.J., Spence and Beetz JJ. concurring). See COMPELLING ~; CONCLUSIVE ~; MANDATORY ~; PERMISSIVE ~.

PRESUMPTION AGAINST ABSURDITY. The interpretation which leads to an unreasonable or absurd result should be rejected where there are two possible interpretations of a provision.

PRESUMPTION AGAINST EXPROPRIATION OF PROPERTY. The legislature or Parliament is presumed not to intend to take away private property rights unless the intention is clearly indicated.

PRESUMPTION AGAINST IMPLIED REPEAL. There is a presumption against the implied repeal of one statute by another. An interpretation which reconciles the two provisions is preferred.

PRESUMPTION AGAINST INTERNAL CONFLICT. The court presumes that legislative provisions in a statute are intended to work together as a whole.

PRESUMTPION AGAINST INTESTACY. The court prefers an interpretation of a will which will avoid intestacy.

PRESUMPTION AGAINST TAUTOLOGY. It is presumed that the legislature avoids superfluous or meaningless words.

PRESUMPTION OF ADVANCEMENT. 1. An exception to ordinary equitable rules relating to resulting trusts, in which property paid for by a husband and conveyed into the name of his wife or child is presumed to be a gift by the husband. A. Bissett-Johnson & W.M. Holland, eds., *Matrimonial Property Law in Canada* (Toronto: Carswell, 1980) at I-13. 2. " . . . [A]s abolished by s. 21 [of the Matrimonial Property Act, S.N.S. 1980, c. 9] is the presumption of law that a spouse who purchases property and puts it in the other spouse's name or voluntarily transfers property to the marriage partner intends to make a gift and it is for the spouse making the transfer to the other spouse to prove there was no such intention." *Levy, Re* (1981), 25 R.F.L. (2d) 149 at 159, 131 D.L.R. (3d) 15, 50 N.S.R. (2d) 14, 98 A.P.R. 14 (T.D.), Hallett J.

PRESUMPTION OF COHERENCE. A presumption against internal conflict within a statute. See PRESUMPTION OF LEGISLATIVE COHERENCE.

PRESUMPTION OF CONSISTENT EXPRESSION. Words within the same statute have the same meaning and different words have different meanings.

PRESUMPTION OF CONSTITUTIONAL VALIDITY. 1. An impugned statute should be construed, if possible, in a way which makes it conform to the Constitution. 2. The onus on establishing that legislation contravenes the Charter is on the person who challenges the statute.

PRESUMPTION OF CONSTITUTIONALITY. An impugned statute should be construed, if possible, in a way which makes it conform to the Constitution.

PRESUMPTION OF CONTINUANCE. An evidentiary inference that when an issue exists, evidence of action by a particular person at a previous time is some evidence of action by that same person at a later time.

PRESUMPTION OF FITNESS. An accused is presumed fit to stand trial unless the court is satisfied on the balance of probabilities that the accused is unfit to stand trial. *Criminal Code*, R.S.C. 1985, c. C-46, s. 672.22.

PRESUMPTION OF IMPLIED EXCLUSION. When legislation expresses one thing, it excludes another. Failure to mention something indicates an intention to exclude it.

PRESUMPTION OF INNOCENCE. 1. The provision in section 11(d) of the Charter of Rights that any person charged with an offence has the right to be presumed innocent until proven guilty according to law in a fair and public hearing by an independent and impartial tribunal. P.W. Hogg, *Constitutional Law of Canada*, 3d ed. (Toronto: Carswell, 1992) at 1100. 2. "' . . . [A]n accused is innocent until proven guilty in accordance with established procedure, and secondly, that guilt must be proven beyond a reasonable doubt.' . . . the presumption of innocence is maintained 'as long as the prosecution has the final burden of establishing guilt, on any element of the offence charged, beyond a reasonable doubt' . . ." *R. v. Oakes* (1986), 19 C.R.R. 308 at 328, [1986] 1 S.C.R. 103, 53 O.R. (2d) 719n, 50 C.R. (3d) 1, 14 O.A.C. 335, 24 C.C.C. (3d) 321, 26 D.L.R. (4th) 200, 65 N.R. 87, Dickson C.J.C. (Chouinard, Lamer, Wilson and Le Dain JJ. concurring).

PRESUMPTION OF KNOWLEDGE AND COMPETENCE. The legislature is presumed to know the existing statutory and common law and to understand the functioning of the courts and tribunals.

PRESUMPTION OF LAW. 1. "[Their] . . . influence on the resolution of the issue is limited to the burden of proof. Text writers and courts are divided on whether presumptions of law affect only the evidential burden or both the evidential and the legal burden. This Court, in Circle Film Enterprises Inc. v. Canadian Broadcasting Corp., [1959] S.C.R. 602 . . . adopted the former or evidentiary burden view,

. . ." *Goodman, Estate v. Geffen* (1991), 42 E.T.R. 97 at 136, [1991] 5 W.W.R. 389, 80 Alta. L.R. (2d) 293,125 A.R. 81, 14 W.A.C. 81, 81 D.L.R. (4th) 211, [1991] 2 S.C.R. 353, Sopinka J. 2. " . . . [I]nvolves actual legal rules." *R v. Oakes* (1986), 24 C.C.C. (3d) 321 at 331, [1986] 1 S.C.R. 103, 53 O.R. (2d) 719n, 50 C.R. (3d) 1, 14 O.A.C. 335, 19 C.R.R. 308, 26 D.L.R. (4th) 200, 65 N.R. 87, Dickson C.J.C. (Chouinard, Lamer, Wilson and Le Dain JJ. concurring). See REBUTTABLE~.

PRESUMPTION OF LEGISLATIVE COHERENCE. 1. When a legislature enacts two statutes and the provisions are in conflict in that compliance with one necessitates violation of the other, the courts will attempt to interpret the statutes to resolve this conflict. 2. A presumption against internal conflict within a statute.

PRESUMPTION OF LEGITIMACY. A child borne of a married woman is presumed to be a child of that marriage.

PRESUMPTION OF LINGUISTIC COMPETENCE. There is a presumption that the legislature knew what it intended and knew the language of enactment and expressed its meaning accurately.

PRESUMPTION OF RESULTING TRUST. " . . . [A] presumption of a (resulting) trust arises 'where a person transfers his property into another's name gratuitously', but that presumption is rebuttable by the transferee: Goodfriend v. Goodfriend, [1972] S.C.R. 640." *Fediuk v. Gluck* (1990), 26 R.F.L. (3d) 454 at 459 (Man. Q.B.), Wright J.

PRESUMPTION OF SURVIVORSHIP. Where two or more people die in the same accident it is presumed that the younger survived.

PRESUMPTIONS OF FACT. " . . . A natural inference which has become standardized and which may be drawn by the tribunal of fact, although it is not obliged to draw the inference." *R. v. Boyle* (1983), 5 C.C.C. (3d) 193 at 205, 41 O.R (2d) 713, 35 C.R. (3d) 34, 148 D.L.R. (3d) 449, 5 C.R.R. 218 (C.A.), the court per Martin J.A.

PRESUMPTION WITH A BASIC FACT. " . . . [E]ntails a conclusion to be drawn upon proof of the basic fact . . ." *R. v. Oakes* (1986), 19 C.R.R. 308 at 319, [1986] 1 S.C.R. 103, 53 O.R. (2d) 719n, 50 C.R. (3d) 1, 14 O.A.C. 335, 24 C.C.C. (3d) 321, 26 D.L.R. (4th) 200, 65 N.R. 87, Dickson C.J.C. (Chouinard, Lamer, Wilson and Le Dain JJ. concurring).

PRESUMPTION WITHOUT A BASIC FACT. " . . . [A] conclusion that is to be drawn until the contrary is proved. . ." *R. v. Oakes* (1986), 19 C.R.R. 308 at 319, [1986] 1 S.C.R. 103, 53 O.R. (2d) 719n, 50 C.R. (3d) 1, 14 O.A.C. 335, 24 C.C.C. (3d) 321, 26 D.L.R. (4th) 200, 65 N.R. 87, Dickson C.J.C. (Chouinard, Lamer, Wilson and Le Dain JJ. concurring).

PRESUMPTIVE EVIDENCE. Evidence which implies the large probability if not the certainty that the facts and the inference are related. P.K. McWilliams, *Canadian Criminal Evidence*, 3d ed. (Aurora: Canada Law Book, 1988) at 1-12 and 1-13. See now CIRCUMSTANTIAL EVIDENCE.

PRESUMPTIVE HEIR. The person who would have been their heir if the ancestor had died immediately, but whose right to inherit might be supplanted by a nearer heir being born.

PRESUMPTIVE OFFENCE. An offence committed, or alleged to have been committed, by a young person who has attained the age of fourteen years, or, in a province where the lieutenant governor in council has fixed an age greater than fourteen years under section 61, the age so fixed, under one of the following provisions of the *Criminal Code*: (i) section 231 or 235 (first degree murder or second degree murder within the meaning of section 231), (ii) section 239 (attempt to commit murder), (iii) section 232, 234 or 236 (manslaughter), or (iv) section 273 (aggravated sexual assault); or (*b*) a serious violent offence for which an adult is liable to imprisonment for a term of more than two years committed, or alleged to have been committed, by a young person after the coming into force of section 62 (adult sentence) and after the young person has attained the age of fourteen years, or, in a province where the lieutenant governor in council has fixed an age greater than fourteen years under section 61, the age so fixed, if at the time of the commission or alleged commission of the offence at least two judicial determinations have been made under subsection 42(9), at different proceedings, that the young person has committed a serious violent offence. *Youth Criminal Justice Act*, S.C. 2002, c. 1, s. 2.

PRESUMPTIVE POSSESSION. See CONSTRUCTIVE POSSESSION.

PRESUMPTIVE RELEASE DATE. In respect of an inmate, the earliest day on which the inmate may be entitled to be released from imprisonment. *Parole and Penitentiary Act*, R.S.C. 1985 (2d Supp.), c. 34, s. 21.2.

PRÊT À USAGE. [Fr.] Loan to be used.

PRETENCE. *n.* Pretext; excuse; show of intention. See FALSE ~.

PRETERITION. *n.* The complete omission of a child's name from its parent's will.

PRETIUM SUCCEDIT IN LOCUM REI. [L.] The price takes the place of the thing.

PRE-TRIAL CONFERENCE. A meeting to consider possibly settling any or all of the issues in a proceeding, simplifying the issues, possibly obtaining admissions which would facilitate the hearing, allocation of liability or any other matter that might assist in a just, efficient and inexpensive disposition of that proceeding.

PREVAILING WAGE. The level of remuneration common in a locality for a particular type of work.

PREVARICATION. *n.* 1. Conspiracy between an informer and a defendant to feign prosecution. 2. Secret abuse committed in a public or private office. 3. Wilfully concealing or misrepresenting truth by giving equivocating or evasive evidence.

PREVENIENT ARRANGEMENT. " . . . [L]inks together what would otherwise appear to be a series of contracts by a preliminary understanding whereby the supplier agrees to supply materials as ordered from time to time on terms then agreed upon or to be fixed later as the materials are supplied. The 'preliminary understanding' may be sufficiently informal that it is not, itself, a binding contact, nor need it contain all the terms upon which the material is to be supplied. Nevertheless, the informal understanding serves to link together the later series of transactions into one continuing contract or open account." *Tage Davidsen Drywall Supplies Ltd. v. Alberta Natural Gas Co.* (1991), 46 C.L.R. 233 at 236, 82 D.L.R. (4th) 1, 117 A.R. 143, 2 W.A.C. 143 (C.A.), the court per Laycraft C.J.A.

PREVENTER. See BACKFLOW ~.

PREVENTION. See FIRE ~.

PREVENTIVE DETENTION. Detention in a penitentiary for an indeterminate period. *Criminal Code*, R.S.C. 1970, c. C-34, s. 687.

PREVENTIVE JUSTICE. ". . . [M]easures to protect the public, or indeed the accused himself, from the possibility of a repetition of . . . unfortunate occurrences. . . control could be exercised by means of the common law power to make an order to keep the peace vested in any judge or magistrate. This power of 'preventive justice' has been recognized in England for centuries . . ." *R. v. Parks* (1992), 75 C.C.C. (3d) 287 at 299, 140 N.R. 161, 55 O.A.C. 241, 95 D.L.R. (4th) 27, 15 C.R. (4th) 289, [1992] 2 S.C.R. 871, Lamer C.J.C. (La Forest, L'Heureux-Dubé, Sopinka, Gonthier, Cory, McLachlin and Iacobucci JJ. concurring).

PREVIEW. See ENVIRONMENTAL ~ REPORT.

PREVIOUS FISCAL YEAR. The fiscal year ending next before the current fiscal year.

PREY. See BIRD OF ~.

PRICE. *n.* 1. A consideration in money. 2. Includes rate or charge for any service. See ADMINISTERED ~; ADMISSION ~; ALBERTA BORDER ~; ALLOWANCE~; BARGAIN ~; BASE ~; CASH ~; CONTRACT ~; FIRM ~ CONTRACT; FIXED ~ CONTRACT; FREIGHT TO ~ RATIO; INCLUSIVE TOUR ~; INTERNATIONAL BORDER ~; INVOICE ~; LEASE ~; MARKET ~; PAY-OUT ~; PURCHASE ~; SALE ~; SETTLEMENT ~; STRIKING ~; WHOLESALE ~.

PRICE. *abbr.* Price's Mining Commissioner's Cases (Ont.), 1906-1910.

PRICE CLUB. A large open warehouse offering its customers, who are members paying a membership fee, a wide variety of products at retail and at wholesale.

PRICE LEVEL ADJUSTED ACCOUNTING. Modification of accounting data based on historic costs by adjusting the price levels of non-monetary assets and liabilities according to appropriate general price indexes. W. Grover & F. Iacobucci, *Materials on Canadian Income Tax*, 4th ed. (Toronto: Richard De Boo Ltd., 1980) at 602.

PRICE LIST. Numerical or alphabetical enumeration of goods, wares, merchandise items or services, quoting wholesale or retail prices or both and printed on cards, or sheets of paper presented in loose-leaf form, stapled, stitched or bound.

PRICE MAINTENANCE AGREEMENT. An agreement between a manufacturer and a retailer in which the retailer contracts not to sell the manufacturer's goods at less than a specified price.

PRICE OF ADMISSION. Any payment made to attend to take part in any amusement. See ADMISSION PRICE.

PRICE OF AIR-TIME. The total amount payable for the broadcast of an advertisement.

PRICE PAID OR PAYABLE. In respect of the sale of goods for export to Canada, means the aggregate of all payments made or to be made, directly or indirectly, in respect of the goods by the purchaser to or for the benefit of the vendor. *Customs Act*, R.S.C. 1985 (2nd Supp.), c. 1, s. 45.

PRICING. See DELIVERED ~.

PRIMAE IMPRESSIONIS. [L.] Of the first impression.

PRIMA FACIE. [L.] At first glance; on the surface.

PRIMA FACIE CASE. " . . . [I]n this context [adverse effect discrimination] is one which covers the allegations made and which, if they are believed, is complete and sufficient to justify a verdict in the complainant's favour in the absence of an answer from the respondent-employer." *Ontario (Human Rights Commission) v. Simpsons-Sears Ltd.* (1985), 7 C.R.H.H. D/3102 at D/3108, 9 C.C.E.L. 185, 17 Admin. L.R. 89, 86 C.L.L.C. 17,002, 64 N.R. 161, 23 D.L.R. (4th) 321, 12 O.A.C. 241, [1985] 2 S.C.R. 536, the court per McIntyre J.

PRIMA FACIE DUTY OF CARE. A duty of care arises, prima facie, when a loss is caused as a foreseeable consequence of a defendant's act or omission. This is subject to restrictions or exclusions based on considerations of policy, fairness, or reasonableness in the circumstances of the case.

PRIMA FACIE EVIDENCE. " . . . [H]as two meanings as described by authors such as Dean Wigmore and Sir Rupert Cross, namely: 1. Where the Crown evidence is so strong that no reasonable man would fail to convict. (This is the mandatory sense in which the term is used and compels conviction if there is no evidence to displace the prima facie case). 2. Where the Crown evidence is sufficiently strong to entitle a reasonable man to find the accused guilty although as a matter of common sense he is not obliged to do so. (This is the permissive and usual sense in which the term is used). . ." *R. v. Pye* (1984), 11 C.C.C. (3d) 64 at 68, 38 C.R. (3d) 375, 62 N.S.R. (2d) 10, 136 A.P.R. 10, 7

D.L.R. (4th) 275 (C.A.), the court per Macdonald J.A.

PRIMAL CUT. 1. One of the portions into which a carcass is subdivided for commercial purposes. *Meat Inspection Regulations*, C.R.C., c. 1032, s. 2. 2. A short hip, steak piece, short loin, rib or chuck cut.

PRIMARILY. *adv*. " . . . [A]s used in the [Manitoba Public Insurance Corporation Act, R.S.M. 1970, c. A180—Man. Reg. 333/74, s. 29(e) means] 'mostly, chiefly, principally, or in the main' . . ." *Fleisher, Re* (1981), (*sub nom. Dil v. Manitoba Public Insurance Corp.*) [1981] I.L.R. 1-1380 at 278, 9 M.V.R. 287, 13 Man. R. (2d) 448 (Q.B.), Huband J.A.

PRIMARY. *adj*. 1. Original or foundational. 2. Of major importance.

PRIMARY BREEDING FLOCK. A flock of poultry, comprising one or more generations of poultry, that is being maintained for the purpose of establishing, continuing or improving parent lines and from which multiplier breeding flocks may be produced. *Hatchery Regulations*, C.R.C., c. 1023, s. 2.

PRIMARY BURDEN. "The burden of establishing a case . . ." *R. v. Schwartz* (1988), 45 C.C.C. (3d) 97 at 115, [1989] 1 W.W.R. 289, 66 C.R. (3d) 251, 88 N.R. 90, [1988] 2 S.C.R. 443, 56 Man. R. (2d) 92, 55 D.L.R. (4th) 1, Dickson C.J.C. (dissenting).

PRIMARY DISTRIBUTION TO THE PUBLIC. Used in relation to trading in securities, means: (i) trades that are made for the purpose of distributing to the public securities issued by a company and not previously distributed; or (ii) trades in previously issued securities for the purpose of distributing such securities to the public where the securities form all or a part of or are derived from the holdings of any person, company or any combination of persons or companies holding a sufficient number of any of the securities of a company to materially affect the control of such company; whether such trades are made directly to the public or indirectly to the public through an underwriter or otherwise; and includes any transaction or series of transactions involving a purchase and sale or a repurchase and resale in the course of or incidental to such distribution.

PRIMARY DIVISION. The division of the organization of an elementary school comprising junior kindergarten, kindergarten and the first 3 years of the program of studies immediately following kindergarten. *Education Act*, R.S.O. 1990, c. E.2, s. 1(1).

PRIMARY ELEVATOR. An elevator whose principal use is the receiving of grain directly from producers for storage or forwarding or both. *Canada Grain Act*, R.S.C. 1985, c. G-10, s. 2.

PRIMARY EVIDENCE. The best evidence, in contrast to secondary evidence. For example the original of a document is preferred to a copy. The witness' own recollection is preferred to another's evidence about what he told the other person he remembered.

PRIMARY FACTS. " . . . [F]acts which are observed by witnesses and proved by oral testimony or facts proved by the production of a thing itself, such as original documents. Their determination is essentially a question of fact for the tribunal of fact, and the only question of law that can arise on them is whether there was any evidence to support the finding." *British Launderers' Research Association v. Hendon Rating Authority*, [1949] 1 K.B. 462 at 471 (U.K. C.A.), Denning L.J.

PRIMARY FISHING ENTERPRISE. 1. An enterprise that is carried on for the purpose of catching or trapping fish for sale, and does not include the processing of fish except as prescribed. *Fisheries Improvement Loans Act*, R.S.C. 1985, c. F-22, s. 2. 2. The processing of fish that may be carried on in any area is the preparation of fish or the making of fishery products to the extent that the preparation or making is (a) normally carried out by fishermen in that particular area; or (b) carried out for the purpose of making fish into a saleable product to meet a particular marketing situation. *Fisheries Improvement Loans Regulations*, C.R.C., c. 864, s. 6.

PRIMARY FOREST PRODUCT. 1. Everything resulting from the processing, treating, manufacturing or breaking down of logs, their by-products or wastes. 2. Wood cut and prepared primarily for processing into wood pulp, paper, paper products, lumber, compressed board or any product manufactured from wood fibre, including Christmas trees, sawmill chips, pulpwood chips, fuel chips and any wood fibre intended for use in heat or power generation. *Primary Forest Products Marketing Act*, R.S.N.S. 1989, 355, s. 3.

PRIMARY INSTRUMENT OF INDEBT-EDNESS. A security evidencing the amount of indebtedness constituting a loan but does not include a debenture or other security taken as collateral security only.

PRIMARY PRODUCTION. A mineral produced from a mineral resource that is: (i) in the form in which it exists on its recovery or severance from its natural state; or (ii) any product resulting from processing or refining that mineral, other than a manufactured product or a product resulting from refining crude oil, refining upgraded heavy crude oil, refining gases or liquids derived from coal or refining a synthetic equivalent of crude oil.

PRIMARY PRODUCTION OF POTASH. (i) Potash that is in the form in which it exists upon its recovery or severance from its natural state; and (ii) any product containing the element potassium resulting from processing or refinishing potash, other than a manufactured product.

PRIMARY SHOCK. A temporary loss of consciousness caused by violent emotion or fear. F.A. Jaffe, *A Guide to Pathological Evidence*, 3d ed. (Toronto: Carswell, 1991) at 226.

PRIMARY X-RAY BEAM. That X-radiation emitted directly from the target of the X-ray tube and emerging through the window of the X-ray generator. *Radiation Emitting Devices Regulations*, C.R.C., c. 1370, s. 1.

PRIME CONTRACTOR. The person with whom the obligee has contracted to perform the contract.

PRIME MINISTER. The minister with power to select, promote, demote or dismiss other ministers, who is personally responsible for advising the Governor General about when Parliament should be dissolved for an election and when the elected parliament should be called into session and who enjoys special authority because she or he was selected as the leader of a political party which was victorious in the previous election. See PREMIER.

PRIME MOVER. An initial source of motive power.

PRIMER. *n*. A small charge placed within the main charge to initiate an explosion.

PRIME RATE. The lowest rate of interest quoted by a bank to its most credit-worthy borrowers for prime business loans.

PRIME RATE PERCENTAGE. The prime rate of the chartered bank that has the highest prime rate on the relevant day expressed as a percentage only, without the addition on of the words "per annum".

PRIMER CARTRIDGE. A cartridge into which a hole is punched and a detonator inserted for firing the charge either by fuse or electric current.

PRIME TIME. In the case of a radio station, means the time between the hours of 6 a.m. and 9 a.m., noon and 2 p.m. and 4 p.m. and 7 p.m., and, in the case of a television station, means the hours between 6 p.m. and midnight. *Canada Elections Act, 2000*, S.C. 2000, c. 9, s. 319.

PRIMO EXCUTIENDA EST VERBI VIS, NE SERMONIS VITIO OBSTRUETUR ORATIO, SIVE LEX SINE ARGUMENTIS. [L.] First, the meaning of the word should be examined so that the meaning of the sentence will not be obscured by verbal error nor the law be obscured by not being argued.

PRIMOGENITO FILIO. [L.] By the first-born son.

PRIMOGENITURE. *n*. 1. Seniority; the status of being born first. 2. A rule of inheritance by which the oldest of two or more males of the same degree succeeds to an ancestor's land, excluding all the others.

PRIMUM DECRETUM. [L.] A provisional decree.

PRIMUS ACTUS JUDICII EST JUDICIS APPROBATORIUS. [L.] The first step taken by a party to an action is to concede that the court has jurisdiction in that action.

PRIMUS INTER PARES. [L.] First among equals. Said of the Chief Judge of a court in relation to the other judges of the same court.

PRINCE. *n*. A sovereign; a chief ruler, either female or male.

PRINCIPAL. *n*. 1. A chief; a head. 2. A capital amount of money loaned at interest. 3. A teacher who is appointed to be in charge of a school. 4. . . . [I]n this context [Real Estate Act, R.S.B.C. 1979, c. 356, s. 37(1)] means the party responsible for the sale occurring, as opposed to any agency by, or through, which effect is given to that decision." *Higginson v. Kelowna Pines Golf Course Ltd.* (1981), 121 D.L.R. (3d) 449 at 457, 26 B.C.L.R. 89 (S.C.), Taylor J. 5. The lawyer to whom a law student is articled. See DEALER ~; DISCLOSED ~; NAMED ~; UNDISCLOSED ~; VICE~.

PRINCIPAL AMOUNT. In relation to any obligation means the amount that, under the terms of the obligation or any agreement relating thereto, is the maximum amount or maximum aggregate amount, as the case may be, payable on account of the obligation by the issuer thereof, otherwise than as or on account of interest or as or on account of any premium payable by the issuer conditional upon the exercise by the issuer of a right to redeem the obligation before the maturity thereof. *Income Tax Act*, R.S.C. 1985, c. 1 (5th Supp.), s. 248.

PRINCIPAL AND AGENT. A principal is one who, being sui juris and competent to do any act for one's own benefit on one's own account, employs the agent to do it.

PRINCIPAL AND SURETY. The principal or principal debtor owes a debt for which the surety is liable in case the principal defaults in paying it.

PRINCIPAL CONTRACTOR. 1. The owner or any other person who, on a construction site, is responsible for the carrying out of all the work. 2. A person, partnership or group of persons who, pursuant to a contract, an agreement or ownership, directs the activities of 1 or more employers involved in work at a work site.

PRINCIPAL DEBTOR. The person whose liability a surety guarantees.

PRINCIPAL IN THE FIRST DEGREE. " . . . [R]efers to someone who actually committed the offence . . ." *R. v. Thatcher* (1987), 32 C.C.C. (3d) 481 at 510, [1987] 4 W.W.R. 193, 57 C.R. (3d) 97, [1987] 1 S.C.R. 652, 75 N.R. 198, 57 Sask. R. 113, 39 D.L.R. (4th) 275, Dickson C.J.C.

PRINCIPAL IN THE SECOND DEGREE. " . . . ([S]omeone who was actually or constructively present but who only aided and abetted in the commission of the offence) . . ." *R. v. Thatcher* (1987), 32 C.C.C. (3d) 481 at 510, [1987] 4 W.W.R. 193, 57 C.R. (3d) 97, [1987] 1 S.C.R. 652, 75 N.R. 198, 57 Sask. R. 113, 39 D.L.R. (4th) 275, Dickson C.J.C.

PRINCIPALLY. *adv*. Chiefly, for the most part.

PRINCIPAL MONEY. The amount lent, in contrast to interest or other money owed.

PRINCIPAL RESIDENCE. Residential premises that constitute a person's normal or permanent place of residence and to which, when that person is absent, that person has the intention of returning.

PRINCIPAL TAXPAYER. An individual who, on the 31st day of December in the taxation year, occupies and inhabits a principal residence except when that individual, on the 31st day of December in the taxation year, occupies and inhabits a principal residence with his spouse, in which case, "principal taxpayer" means that spouse who has the higher taxable income for the taxation year.

PRINCIPAL UNDERWRITER. A person (i) to whom a company makes an allotment or agrees to make an allotment of shares or debentures of the company with a view to all or any of the shares or debentures being offered for sale to the public; and (ii) who sells or agrees to sell to any other person such shares or debentures with a view to all or any part of such shares or debentures being offered for sale to the public by that other person.

PRINCIPAL USE. The use of land that is most extensive in the area occupied.

PRINCIPIORUM NON EST RATIO. [L.] First principles do not need to be proved.

PRINCIPLE. *n*. Something which, unlike a rule, does not set out legal consequences which follow automatically if certain conditions are met. S.A. Cohen, *Due Process of Law* (Toronto: Carswell, 1977) at 203. See CO-OPERATIVE ~S; GENERALLY ACCEPTED ACCOUNTING ~S; KIENAPPLE ~; MERIT ~; MODERN ~; NOMINALISTIC ~S.

PRINCIPLE AGAINST SELF-INCRIMINATION. 1. It is now well-established that there exists, in Canadian law, a principle against self-incrimination that is a principle of fundamental justice under s. 7 of the [Canadian Charter of Rights and Freedoms]. The principle against self-incrimination is that an accused is not required to respond to an allegation of wrongdoing made by the state until the state has succeeded in making out a prima facie case against him or her. *R. v. White*, [1999] 2 S.C.R. 417. 2. "It should therefore be made clear here that I distinguish between the *principle* against self-incrimination and the *privilege* against self-incrimination . . . The *privilege* is the narrow traditional common law rule relating only to testimonial evidence at trial. Much of the confusion around such issues as silence, non-compellability, and self-incrimination has, I believe, arisen as a result of the failure to distinguish between these two levels of protection against self-incrimination. The *principle* is a general organizing principle of criminal law from which particular rules can be derived (for example, rules about non-compellability of the accused and admissibility of confessions). The *privilege* is merely one rule that has been derived from the principle. When the protection against self-incrimination is limited to the privilege against self-incrimination, then the underlying rationale for the various common law rules protecting against self-incrimination is lost and principled decisions about particular cases as they arise become impossible." (2) "The principle against self-incrimination, in its broadest form, can be expressed in the following manner: the individual is sovereign and proper rules of battle between government and individual require that the individual not be conscripted by his opponent to defeat himself. Or, put another way, nemo tenetur seipsum accusare and nemo tenetur seipsum prodere and nemo tenetur armare adversarium contra se—no one shall be required to accuse or betray or arm his enemy against himself." *R. v. Jones*, [1994] 2 S.C.R. 229, Lamer, C.J.C. for minority.

PRINCIPLE IN LISTER V. DUNLOP. The principle in *Ronald Elwyn Lister Ltd. v. Dunlop Canada Ltd.*, [1982] 1 S.C.R. 726, is that a person from whom a seizure is being made under a security instrument is entitled to receive such notice of the proposed seizure as is reasonable in the circumstances. The principle may also apply to other seizures but it is not necessary in this case to determine whether that is so. It is possible for the principle in *Lister v. Dunlop* to be limited, modified or eliminated by constitutionally enacted legislation. Subject to that, the principle applies to the realization of all security interests where a person's property is being taken away by the security holder. *Waldron v. Royal Bank* (1991), 53 B.C.L.R. (2d) 294 (C.A.).

PRINCIPLES OF FUNDAMENTAL JUSTICE. 1. " . . . [R]eflect the fundamental tenets on which our legal system is based. Those tenets include, but are not limited to, the rules of natural justice and the duty to act fairly that have been developed over the years in the administrative law context. . . included in these fundamental principles is the concept of a procedurally fair hearing before an impartial decision-maker. . ." *Pearlman v. Law Society (Manitoba)* (1991), 6 C.R.R. (2d) 259 at 268, [1991] 6 W.W.R. 289, 2 Admin. L.R. (2d) 185, 84 D.L.R. (4th) 105, 130 N.R. 121, 75 Man. R. (2d) 81, 6 W.A.C. 81, [1991] 2 S.C.R. 869, the court per Iacobucci J.

2. Include the right to make full answer in defence, procedural fairness, right to a fair trial, accused's right to an interpreter in a trial, right of defence to control his own defence in a criminal trial, and the privilege against self incrimination. 3. " . . . [P]rinciples that govern the justice system. They determine the means by which one may be brought before or within the justice system, and govern how one may be brought within the system and, thereafter, the conduct of judges and other actors once the individual is brought within it. Therefore, the restrictions on liberty and security of the person that s. 7 [of the Charter] is concerned with are those that occur as a result of an individual's interaction with the justice system, and its administration. . ." *Reference re ss. 193 and 195(1)(c) of the Criminal Code (Canada)* (1990), 56 C.C.C. (3d) 65 at 102, 77 C.R. (3d) 1, [1990] 1 S.C.R. 1123, [1990] 4 W.W.R. 481, 109 N.R. 81, 68 Man. R. (2d) 1, 48 C.R.R. 1, Lamer J. 4. " . . . Have both a substantive and a procedural component . . ." *R. v. Morgentaler* (1988), 37 C.C.C. (3d) 449 at 471, 82 N.R. 1, [1988] 1 S.C.R. 30, 63 O.R. (2d) 281n, 62 C.R. (3d) 1, 26 O.A.C. 1, 44 D.L.R. (4th) 385, 31 C.R.R. 1, Dickson C.J.C. (Lamer J. concurring). 5. [Within the meaning of s. 7 of the Canadian Charter of Rights and Freedoms] has at least three qualities: 1. it is a legal principle; 2. it is precise; and 3. there is a consensus among reasonable people that it is vital to our system of justice. The phrase "in accordance with the principles of fundamental justice" [in s. 7 of the Canadian Charter of Rights and Freedoms] should be restricted to principles and rules that are central to our legal system. *R. v. Malmo-Levine*, 2000 BCCA 335, 145 C.C.C. (3d) 225 (C.A.), Per Braidwood J.A. (Rowles J.A. concurring). See PRINCIPLE AGAINST SELF INCRIMINATION.

PRINCIPLES OF SENTENCING. The fundamental purpose of sentencing is to contribute, along with crime prevention initiatives, to respect for the law and the maintenance of a just, peaceful and safe society by imposing just sanctions that have one or more of the following objectives: (a) to denounce unlawful conduct; (b) to deter the offender and other persons from committing offences; (c) to separate offenders from society, where necessary; (d) to assist in rehabilitating offenders; (e) to provide reparations for harm done to victims or to the community; and (f) to promote a sense of responsibility in offenders, and acknowledgment of the harm done to victims and to the community.

Criminal Code, R.S.C. 1985, c. C-46, s. 718. Proportionality is another principle of sentencing which must be applied by the Court. In addition the following principles are applied in sentencing: (a) a sentence should be increased or reduced to account for any relevant aggravating or mitigating circumstances relating to the offence or the offender, and, without limiting the generality of the foregoing, (i) evidence that the offence was motivated by bias, prejudice or hate based on race, national or ethnic origin, language, colour, religion, sex, age, mental or physical disability, sexual orientation, or any other similar factor, (ii) evidence that the offender, in committing the offence, abused the offender's spouse or common-law partner or child, (iii) evidence that the offender, in committing the offence, abused a position of trust or authority in relation to the victim, or (iv) evidence that the offence was committed for the benefit of, at the direction of or in association with a criminal organization, or (v) evidence that the offence was a terrorism offence shall be deemed to be aggravating circumstances; (b) a sentence should be similar to sentences imposed on similar offenders for similar offences committed in similar circumstances; (c) where consecutive sentences are imposed, the combined sentence should not be unduly long or harsh; (d) an offender should not be deprived of liberty, if less restrictive sanctions may be appropriate in the circumstances; and (e) all available sanctions other than imprisonment that are reasonable in the circumstances should be considered for all offenders, with particular attention to the circumstances of aboriginal offenders. *Criminal Code*, R.S.C. 1985, c. C-46, s. 718.2. Balancing of these goals is required to fashion a sentence that is just and appropriate and that reflects the culpability of the offender and the circumstances of the offence. See GENERAL DETERRENCE; PROPORTIONALITY; RETRIBUTION; SPECIFIC DETERRENCE; TOTALITY PRINCIPLE. SENTENCING.

PRINT. *n*. An artistic representation or work usually on paper or vellum, executed in media such as woodcut, metalcut, wood engraving, engraving, etching, drypoint, mezzotint, aquatint, soft ground, lithography, monotype, clichéverre or silk sceen. See FINGER~; PALM ~.

PRINTED. *adj*. Includes lithographed or reproduced by any mechanical, electrostatic or photostatic means.

PRINTED ATLAS OR CARTOGRAPHIC BOOK. A bound work with an established date of printing and includes each volume of a set of bound works issued under a single title. *Canadian Cultural Property Export Control List*, C.R.C., c. 448, s. 1.

PRINTED BOOK OF PHOTOGRAPHS. A bound work with an established date of printing and includes each volume of a set of bound works issued under a single title. *Canadian Cultural Property Export Control List*, C.R.C., c. 448, s. 1.

PRINTED BOOK OF PICTURES OR DESIGNS. A bound work with an established date of printing and includes each volume of a set of bound works issued under a single title. *Canadian Cultural Property Export Control List*, C.R.C., c. 448, s. 1.

PRINTED BOOK OR PAMPHLET. A work of at least five pages, exclusive of cover pages, made up of sheets bound, stitched or fastened together so as to form a material whole under an established date of printing, and includes each work in a set issued under a single title. *Canadian Cultural Property Export Control List*, C.R.C., c. 448, s. 1.

PRINTER. See QUEEN'S ~.

PRINTING. *n*. 1. Shall include reproduction by set type, the offset process, the stencil process, or any facsimile reproduction process, provided however that the reproduced copy shall throughout be clear and legible, notwithstanding the state of the original, and shall be on paper of good quality and suitable for the process used. 2. All processes, techniques and methods of publication, duplication or reproduction, whether by type, photographic, offset, electrostatic, micrographing or other process, of written or graphic matter. 3. Includes any means of reproducing the written word. *Municipal Act*, R.S.B.C. 1979, c. 290, s. 1. 4. Includes words written, painted, engraved, lithographed, photographed or represented or reproduced by any mode of representing or reproducing words in a visible form. *Election acts*. See PREPARATORY ASPECTS OF ~.

PRIORITY. *n*. When two or more competing claims which arose at different times against the same parcel of land are asserted, the one who is entitled to exercise rights to the exclusion of the others is said to have priority.

PRIORITY OF EVIDENCE RULE. Rule used in order to determine the best evidence of the location of the boundary. This rule requires that evidence must be considered in the following order: (1) natural boundaries; (2) original monuments; (3) fences or occupation which can reasonably be related back to the time of the original survey; (4) the lines and courses of an adjoining grant, if these are called for in a deed; (5) courses and distances. *Richmond Hill Furriers Ltd. v. Clarissa Developments Inc.* (1996), 31 O.R. (3d) 529 (Div. Ct.).

PRIORITY PAYMENT INSTRUMENT. A money order, bank draft or similar instrument issued, directly or indirectly, by a member other than a money order, bank draft or similar instrument issued by a member to another member for the purpose of effecting a payment between those members. *Canadian Payments Association Act*, R.S.C. 1985, c. C-21, s. 31.

PRIOR PETENS. [L.] The person who applies first.

PRIOR SERVICE. Any service other than that for which current service contributions are made. *Pension Plan acts.*

PRIOR TEMPORE POTIOR JURE. [L.] The person first in time is preferred in right.

PRIOR USE. Use which takes place over a longer period than what the statute permits or which discloses the invention to the public.

PRISON. *n.* 1. Includes a penitentiary, common jail, public or reformatory prison, lock-up, guard-room or other place in which persons who are charged with or convicted of offences are usually kept in custody. *Criminal Code*, R.S.C. 1985, c. C-46, s. 2. 2. A place of confinement other than a penitentiary. See BREACH OF ~; CIVIL ~; SERVICE ~.

PRISON BREACH. Every one who (a) by force or violence breaks a prison with intent to set at liberty himself or any person confined therein; or (b) with intent to escape forcibly breaks out of, or makes any breach in, a cell or other place within a prison in which he is confined. *Criminal Code*, R.S.C. 1985, c. C-46, s. 144.

PRISONER. *n.* A person under arrest, remand or sentence who is confined in a correctional centre according to law. See REMAND ~.

PRISONERS' REPRESENTATIVE. In relation to a protected prisoner of war, means the person elected or recognized as that prisoner's representative pursuant to Article 79 of the Ge-

neva Convention set out in Schedule III. *Geneva Convention Act*, R.S.C. 1985, c. G-3, s. 4.

PRIVACY. *n.* 1. This Court has most often characterized the values engaged by privacy in terms of liberty, or the right to be left alone by the state. For example, in *R. v. Dyment*, [1988] 2 S.C.R. 417 at p. 427, La Forest J. commented that "privacy is at the heart of liberty in a modern state". In *R. v. Edwards*, [1996] 1 S.C.R. 128 at para. 50, *per* Cory J., privacy was characterized as including "[t]he right to be free from intrusion or interference". This interest in being left alone by the state includes the ability to control the dissemination of confidential information. As La Forest J. stated in *R. v. Sanelli*, [1990] 1 S.C.R. 30 at pp. 53-54: . . . it has long been recognized that this freedom not to be compelled to share our confidences with others is the very hallmark of a free society. Yates J., in *Millar v. Taylor* (1769), 4 Burr. 2303, 98 E.R. 201 (K.B.), states, at p. 2379 and p. 242: It is certain every man has a right to keep his own sentiments, if he pleases: he has certainly a right to judge whether he will make them public, or commit them only to the sight of his friends. These privacy concerns are at their strongest where aspects of one's individual identity are at stake, such as in the context of information "about one's lifestyle, intimate relations or political or religious opinions": *Thomson Newspapers, supra*, at pp. 517-18, *per* La Forest J., cited with approval in *Baron, supra*, at pp. 444-45. The significance of these privacy concerns should not be understated. Many commentators have noted that privacy is also necessarily related to many fundamental human relations. *R. v. Mills*, [1999] 3 S.C.R. 668 [Per McLachlin and Iacobucci JJ. for the court.] 2. " . . . [M]ay be defined as the right of the individual to determine for himself when, how, and to what extent he will release personal information about himself, . . ." *R. v. Sanelli* (1990), (*sub nom. R. v. Duarte*) 45 C.R.R. 278 at 290, 74 C.R. (3d) 281, 103 N.R. 86, 37 O.A.C. 322, [1990] 1 S.C.R. 30, 53 C.C.C. (3d) 1, 65 D.L.R. (4th) 240, 71 O.R. (2d) 575, La Forest J. (Dickson C.J.C., L'Heureux-Dubé, Sopinka, Gonthier and McLachlin JJ. concurring). See LAW OF~.

PRIVACY COMMISSIONER. The Commissioner appointed under section 53. *Privacy Act*, R.S.C. 1985, c. P-21, s. 3.

PRIVACY COMMISSIONER OF CANADA. The federal official who investigates complaints of government failure to comply with rights to personal information provided by the Privacy Act.

PRIVACY LAW. The law regarding the collection and storage of and access to personal information.

PRIVATE. *adj*. Not public. Personal.

PRIVATE AIRCRAFT. A civil aircraft other than a commercial aircraft or state aircraft.

PRIVATE ARCHIVES. Archives other than public archives.

PRIVATE BILL. 1. A bill relating to matters of particular interest or benefit to an individual or group. A. Fraser, W.A. Dawson, & J. Holtby, eds., *Beauchesne's Rules and Forms of the House of Commons of Canada*, 6th ed. (Toronto: Carswell, 1989) at 192. 2. A bill relating to a particular person, institution or locality which is often introduced by a private member and enacted by a different and simpler procedure, not requiring government sponsorship. P.W. Hogg, *Constitutional Law of Canada*, 3d ed. (Toronto: Carswell, 1992) at 244.

PRIVATE BUOY. A buoy other than a government buoy.

PRIVATE CARRIER. " . . . [O]ne who under takes to carry goods in a particular case, but is not engaged in the business of so carrying as a public employment and does not undertake to carry goods for persons generally." *Tri-City Drilling Co. Ltd. v. Velie* (1960), 30 W.W.R. 61 at 64, 82 C.R.T.C. 69 (Alta. T.D.), Riley J.

PRIVATE COLLEGE. A college in Alberta, other than a public college, that is in affiliation with a university and provides instruction in courses acceptable to that university as constituting a full year's work toward a degree. *Colleges Act*, R.S.A. 1980, c. C-18, s. 1.

PRIVATE COMMUNICATION. Any oral communication, or any telecommunication, that is made by an originator who is in Canada or is intended by the originator to be received by a person who is in Canada and that is made under circumstances in which it is reasonable for the originator to expect that it will not be intercepted by any person other than the person intended by the originator to receive it, and includes any radio-based telephone communication that is treated electronically or otherwise for the purpose of preventing intelligible reception by any person other than the person intended by the originator to receive it. *Criminal Code*, R.S.C. 1985, c. C-46, s. 183.

PRIVATE COMPANY. A company that by its memorandum or articles, special act, letters patent or other incorporating document: (i) restricts the right to transfer its shares; (ii) limits the number of its members to 50 or less, the number so limited being, unless the memorandum or articles otherwise provide, exclusive of persons who are in the employment of the company and of persons who are members while in the employment of the company and continue to be members after the termination of the employment, but where two or more persons hold one or more shares in the company jointly they shall be counted as a single member; and (iii) prohibits any invitation to the public to subscribe for shares or debentures of the company.

PRIVATE CONSTABLE. A person appointed as a constable under Part III of the *Canada Transportation Act*. *Canada Labour Code*, R.S.C. 1985, c. L-2, s. 3.

PRIVATE CORPORATION. A corporation resident in Canada at that time, not a public corporation and not controlled directly or indirectly in any manner whatever by a public corporation. See CANADIAN-CONTROLLED ~.

PRIVATE COTTAGE. A seasonal residence used primarily for the personal use of the owner and immediate family and whose owners hold a valid lease or freehold title to the land.

PRIVATE DRIVEWAY. A driveway not open to the use of the public for purposes of vehicular traffic.

PRIVATE DYKE. A dyke built on private property without public funds to protect only the property of the person owning the private dyke.

PRIVATEER. *n*. A ship commissioned to exercise general reprisals.

PRIVATE FISHING PRESERVE. Land or water that is privately owned and maintained and on which, or part of which, fish have been reared or stocked for the purpose of angling and are designated as private fishing preserves in the regulations. *Fish and Game Protection Act*, R.S.P.E.I. 1988, c. F-12, s. 1 (bb).

PRIVATE FISH POND. An artificially constructed pond which is used by the owner or his guests solely for pleasure.

PRIVATE FREIGHT VEHICLE. A motor vehicle, other than a public vehicle or a limited vehicle, that is operated at any time on a highway for the transportation of freight, and includes any motor vehicle which is operated for the (a) transportation of freight bona fide the property of the owner of the motor vehicle; (b) transportation of freight used or subjected to a process or treatment by the owner of the motor vehicle in the course of a regular trade or occupation or established business of the owner, when the transportation is incidental to his trade, occupation or business; (c) delivery or collection of freight sold or purchased, or agreed to be sold or purchased, or let on hire by the owner of the motor vehicle, otherwise than as agent, in the course of a regular trade or established business of that owner.

PRIVATE GARAGE. A subordinate building or portion of a main building used for the parking or temporary storage of the motor vehicles of the occupants of the main building. Canada regulations.

PRIVATE GUARD. A person who for hire or reward (i) provides security services with respect to persons or property, including the services of a guard dog, (ii) accompanies a guard dog while the dog is guarding or patrolling. *Private Investigators and Private Guards Act*, R.S.N.S. 1989, c. 356, s. 2.

PRIVATE-HOME DAY CARE. *var.* **PRIVATE HOME DAY CARE**. The temporary care for reward or compensation of five children or less who are under 10 years of age where such care is provided in a private residence, other than the home of a parent or guardian of any such child, for a continuous period not exceeding 24 hours. *Day Nurseries Act*, R.S.O. 1990, c. D.2, s. 1.

PRIVATE-HOME DAY CARE AGENCY. A person who provides private-home day care at more than one location. *Day Nurseries Act*, R.S.O. 1990, c. D.2, s. 1.

PRIVATE HOSPITAL. A house in which two or more patients are received and lodged at the same time.

PRIVATE INTEREST. Does not include an interest in a decision (a) that is of general public application, (b) that affects a member as one of a broad class of electors, or (c) that concerns the remuneration and benefits of a member or an officer or employee of the Legislative Assembly. *Members' Conflict of Interest acts.*

PRIVATE INTERNATIONAL LAW. Or conflict of laws, the part of a country's law that is concerned with resolving legal disputes which involve one or more foreign elements.

PRIVATE INVESTIGATOR. A person who, for hire or reward, investigates and provides information, and includes a person who (i) searches for and provides information as to the personal character or actions of a person, or the character or kind of business or occupation of a person, (ii) searches for offenders against the law, (iii) searches for missing persons or property, (iv) performs shopping or other services in civilian or plain clothes for a client for the purpose of reporting to the client upon the conduct, integrity or trustworthiness of his or her employees, or (v) provides services in civilian or plain clothes for the prevention or detection of shoplifting. *Private Investigations and Security Services Act*, R.S. Nfld. 1990, c. P-24, s. 2. See BUSINESS OF A ~.

PRIVATE ISSUER. An issuer, other than a mutual fund, in whose articles of incorporation, limited partnership agreement, unit-holders' agreement, declaration of trust or other instrument legally constituting such issuer (i) the right to transfer shares or units is restricted; (ii) the number of its shareholders or unit-holders, exclusive of individuals who are in its employment or the employment of an affiliate and exclusive of individuals, who, having been formerly in the employment of the issuer or the employment of an affiliate, were, while in that employment, and have continued after termination of that employment to be shareholders or unit-holders of the issuer, is limited to not more than 50, two or more individuals who are the joint registered owners of one or more shares or units being counted as one shareholder or unit-holder; and (iii) any invitation to the public to subscribe for its securities is prohibited.

PRIVATE LAND. Land other than land vested in the Crown.

PRIVATE LANDS. 1. Lands other than Crown Lands and other lands vested in Her Majesty. *Crown Lands and Forests Act*, S.N.B. 1980, c. C-38.1, s. 1. 2. All lands conceded or alienated by the Crown except mining concessions, lands conceded as such and, on Crown lands, lands under mining lease, operating lease, storage lease or disposal licence. *Mining Act*, R.S.Q. 1977, c. M-13, s. 1.

PRIVATE LAW. All law relating to persons; used in distinction to public law.

PRIVATE LINE. A pipe used for transmitting gas from a gas line, secondary line, distribution line or a well to be used for domestic, commercial or industrial purposes on land owned or leased by the owner of the pipe, and includes the installations in connection therewith but does not include any pipe or installation on, within or under a building.

PRIVATELY-OWNED LAND. (i) Land held under a certificate of title by a person other than the Crown; (ii) land held under an agreement for sale under which the Crown is the seller; or (iii) land or classes of land held under leases or other dispositions from the Crown that are prescribed to be privately-owned land.

PRIVATELY-OWNED PETROLEUM. Petroleum or any right, title or interest therein which is held by any person other than Her Majesty in right of the province.

PRIVATE MEMBER'S BILL. A bill, either public or private, introduced by a private member. P.W. Hogg, *Constitutional Law of Canada*, 3d ed. (Toronto: Carswell, 1992) at 244.

PRIVATE MORGUE. A place where bodies are customarily retained before their disposition, other than a public morgue. *Anatomy Act*, R.S.O. 1990, c. A.21, s. 1.

PRIVATE MUTUAL FUND. A mutual fund that is (i) operated as an investment club; where (A) its shares or units are held by not more than 50 persons and its indebtedness has never been offered to the public; (B) it does not pay or give any remuneration for investment advice or in respect of trades in securities, except normal brokerage fees; and (C) all of its members are required to make contributions in proportion to the shares or units each holds for the purpose of financing its operations; (ii) a pooled fund maintained solely to serve registered pension funds or plans or deferred profit sharing plans registered under the Income Tax Act (Canada); (iii) a pooled fund maintained by a trust company in which moneys belonging to various estates and trusts in its care are comingled, pursuant to a power conferred by or under the law governing the same or by the will or trust instrument, for the purpose of facilitating investment where no general solicitations are made with a view to promoting participation in the pooled fund.

PRIVATE NUISANCE. Substantial and unreasonable interference which damages the enjoyment by its occupier of land. *Pugliese v. Canada (National Capital Commission)* (1979), 8 C.E.L.R. 68 at 74, [1979] 2 S.C.R. 104, 8 C.C.L.T. 69, 25 N.R. 498, 97 D.L.R. (3d) 631, the court per Pigeon J.

PRIVATE OWNER. An owner of land that has been granted by the Crown, or that is held under homestead entry, pre-emption record, lease or purchase agreement from the Crown.

PRIVATE PASSENGER VEHICLE. 1. A motor vehicle designed and used primarily for the transportation of persons without remuneration and does not include a bus or taxicab. 2. A vehicle used solely for personal transportation; (i) including the transportation of goods which are the property of the owner and intended for the use or enjoyment of himself or members of his household; but (ii) not including the transportation of goods in connection with any line of business except that of a salesman conveying sample cases or display goods which are not for delivery or resale.

PRIVATE PLACE. (i) A private dwelling; and (ii) privately-owned land, whether or not it is used in connection with a private dwelling.

PRIVATE PLACEMENT. Any distribution of securities with respect to which no prospectus is required to be filed, accepted or otherwise approved by or pursuant to a law enacted in Canada for the supervision or regulation of trading in securities and includes a distribution of securities with respect to which a prospectus would be required to be filed, accepted or otherwise approved except for an express exemption contained in or given pursuant to such a law.

PRIVATE PRACTICE. The offering of professional services for fee or remuneration expected and accepted.

PRIVATE PROSECUTION. A prosecution commenced by a member of the public, as opposed to a peace officer, laying an information.

PRIVATE RECEIVER. A receiver appointed by a letter or similar instrument by one who holds security over a debtor's assets according to the powers specified in the security instrument. F. Bennett, *Receiverships* (Toronto: Carswell, 1985) at 2.

PRIVATE RECORD. Any record, held by a third party, in respect of which a reasonable expectation of privacy exists.

PRIVATE RIGHT. A right at common law or created by statute the infringement of which gives rise to a cause of action for tort, breach of contract or trust or other cause. *Finlay v. Canada (Minister of Finance)* (1986), 17 C.P.C. (2d) 289 at 301, [1986] 1 W.W.R. 603, [1986] 2 S.C.R. 607, 71 N.R. 338, 23 Admin. L.R. 197, 33

D.L.R. (4th) 321, 8 C.H.R.R. D/3789, the court per Le Dain J.

PRIVATE ROAD. A road not open to the use of the public for purposes of vehicular traffic.

PRIVATE ROADWAY. Any private road, lane, ramp or other means of vehicular access to or egress from a building or structure and it may include part of a parking lot.

PRIVATE SCHOOL. An institution at which instruction is provided at any time between the hours of 9 a.m. and 4 p.m. on any school day for five or more pupils who are of or over compulsory school age in any of the subjects of the elementary or secondary school courses of study and that is not a school as defined in this section. *Education Act*, R.S.O. 1990, c. E.2, s. 1(1).

PRIVATE SECTOR. Those employers and employees whose labour relations are within the exclusive jurisdiction of the Legislature to regulate, but does not include the public sector.

PRIVATE SEWAGE DISPOSAL SYSTEM. All types of sewage disposal systems not directly connected to a municipal or approved central sewage system, including a privy and septic tank with a disposal field.

PRIVATE SHOOTING PRESERVE. Land that is privately owned and maintained and on which, or part of which, game birds that have been raised in captivity are kept in captivity or released for the purpose of hunting and are designated as private shooting reserves in the regulations.

PRIVATE STREET. A street, road, lane or track that is not vested in the Crown or a municipality.

PRIVATE TRACK. A track outside of a carrier's right-of-way, yard or terminals, and of which the carrier does not own either the rails, ties, roadbed or right-of-way, or a track or portion of a track which is devoted to the purpose of its user, either by lease or written agreement, in which case the lease or written agreement will be considered as equivalent to ownership. Canada regulations.

PRIVATE TRAINING INSTITUTION. A person who, for remuneration, provides instruction to a person for the purpose of allowing that person to obtain, or enhancing his possibilities of obtaining, employment in a skill or occupation.

PRIVATE TRANSACTION. An arranged or negotiated transaction that is not generally available on identical terms to all holders of a class of securities.

PRIVATE TRUST. A trust whose objects are specific, ascertainable people.

PRIVATE VOCATIONAL SCHOOL. A school or place at which instruction in the skill and knowledge requisite for employment in any vocation is offered or provided by class room instruction or by correspondence.

PRIVATE WASTE MANAGEMENT SYSTEM. A waste management system, or any part thereof, whose owner is a person rather than a municipality.

PRIVATE WOODLOT. Forest land owned by anyone other than the Crown or corporations whose principal business involves dealing in primary forest products.

PRIVATE WORKS. Includes private roadways, crossings, openings, signs or other advertising devices and other structures constructed, erected, installed or maintained on a highway for the use or benefit of owners or occupants of property adjoining or connected therewith.

PRIVATION. *n*. Removal; withdrawal.

PRIVATIS PACTIONIBUS NON DUBIUM EST NON LAEDI JUS CAETERORUM. [L.] There is no doubt that the rights of others are not damaged by private agreements.

PRIVATIVE CLAUSE. One that declares that decisions of a tribunal are final and conclusive and from which no appeal lies and excludes all forms of judicial review. See EQUIVOCAL ~; FINALITY CLAUSE ~ PARTIAL ~.

PRIVATORUM CONVENTIO JURI PUBLICO NON DEROGAT. [L.] A statutory requirement imposed in the public interest cannot be waived. P. St. J. Langan, ed., *Maxwell on The Interpretation of Statutes*, 12th ed. (Bombay: N.M. Tripathi, 1976) at 330.

PRIVATUM COMMODUM PUBLICO CEDIT. [L.] Private good gives way to public good.

PRIVATUM INCOMMODUM PUBLICO BONO PENSATUR. [L.] Private loss is counterbalanced by public good.

PRIVIES. Those who have an interest in an action by blood, title or pecuniary interest. Includes persons who participate in an act. A director is a privy to the company.

PRIVILEGE. *n.* 1. An exceptional advantage or right; an exemption to which certain people are entitled from an attendance, burden or duty. 2. ". . . [A]n exclusionary rule of evidence which is appropriately asserted in court. . ." *Thomson Newspapers Ltd. v. Canada (Director of Investigation & Research)* (1990), 47 C.R.R. 1 at 94, 76 C.R. (3d) 129, 72 O.R. (2d) 415n, 54 C.C.C. (3d) 417, 67 D.L.R. (4th) 161, 29 C.P.R. (3d) 97, [1990] 1 S.C.R. 425, 39 O.A.C. 161, 106 N.R. 161, Sopinka J. (dissenting in part). 3. Acts as an exception to the truth finding process of trials. All relevant evidence is presumed admissible but some probative and trustworthy evidence is excluded in order to serve other overriding social interests. Similarly, some communications arising out of defined relationships are exempt from disclosure in judicial proceedings. See ABSOLUTE ~; BREACH OF ~; CASE-BY-CASE ~; CLASS ~; COMMON INTEREST ~; CROWN ~; DIPLOMATIC ~; DOCTOR-PATIENT~; DOMINANT PURPOSE TEST; DRIVING ~; INFORMER ~; JURORS' ~; LEGAL PROFESSIONAL ~; LITIGATION ~; MOTOR VEHICLE ~; OCCUPIED WATER ~; PARLIAMENTARY ~; POLICE INFORMER ~; PREPAYMENT ~; QUALIFIED ~; QUESTION OF ~; RELIGIOUS COMMUNICATIONS ~; SOLICITOR-CLIENT ~; SPOUSAL ~; SPOUSAL COMMUNICATIONS ~; STANDING COMMITTEE ON ~S AND ELECTIONS; THERAPEUTIC ~.

PRIVILEGE AGAINST SELF-INCRIMINATION. 1. ". . . [O]ften used as a general term embracing aspects of the right to remain silent . . . in modern usage, the privilege against self-incrimination is limited to the right of an individual to resist testimony as a witness in a legal proceeding. A privilege is an exclusionary rule of evidence which is appropriately asserted in court. A modern statement of the privilege emphasizing its application in juridicial proceedings is contained in the judgement of Goddard L.J. in Blunt v. Park Lane Hotel Ltd. . . [1942] 2 K.B. 253 [(U.K. C.A.)]. He stated, at p. 257: ' . . . the rule is that no one is bound to answer any question if the answer thereto would, in the opinion of the judge, have a tendency to expose the deponent to any criminal charge, penalty or [in a criminal case] forfeiture which the judge regards as reasonably likely to be referred or sued for.'" *Thomson Newspapers Ltd. v. Canada (Director of Investigation & Research)* (1990), 47 C.R.R. 1 at 94, 76 C.R. (3d) 129, 72 O.R. (2d) 415n, 54 C.C.C. (3d) 417, 67 D.L.R. (4th) 161, 29 C.P.R. (3d) 97, [1990] 1 S.C.R. 425, 39 O.A.C. 161, 106 N.R. 161, Sopinka J. (dissenting in part). 2. ". . . [T]he privilege of a witness not to answer a question which may incriminate him. That is all that is meant by the Latin maxim, nemo tenetur seipsum accusare, often incorrectly advanced in support of a much broader proposition. . . As applied to witnesses generally, the privilege must be expressly claimed by the witness when the question is put to him in the witness box, Canada Evidence Act, R.S.O. 1970, c. E-10, s. 5. As applied to an accused the privilege is the right to stand mute. An accused cannot be asked, much less compelled, to enter the witness-box or to answer incriminating questions. If he chooses to testify, the protective shield, of course, disappears. In short, the privilege extends to the accused qua witness and not qua accused, it is concerned with testimonial compulsion specifically and not with compulsion generally . . ." *Marcoux v. R.* (1975), 60 D.L.R. (3d) 119 at 112-3, [1976] 1 S.C.R. 763, 29 C.R.N.S. 211, 4 N.R. 64, 24 C.C.C. (2d) 1, Dickson J. 3. "It should therefore be made clear here that I distinguish between the *principle* against self-incrimination and the *privilege* against self-incrimination . . . The *privilege* is the narrow traditional common law rule relating only to testimonial evidence at trial. Much of the confusion around such issues as silence, non-compellability, and self-incrimination has, I believe, arisen as a result of the failure to distinguish between these two levels of protection against self-incrimination. The *principle* is a general organizing principle of criminal law from which particular rules can be derived (for example, rules about non-compellability of the accused and admissibility of confessions). The *privilege* is merely one rule that has been derived from the principle. When the protection against self-incrimination is limited to the privilege against self-incrimination, then the underlying rationale for the various common law rules protecting against self-incrimination is lost and principled decisions about particular cases as they arise become impossible." *R. v. Jones*, [1994] 2 S.C.R. 229, Lamer, C.J.C. for minority. See PRINCIPLE AGAINST SELF INCRIMINATION.

PRIVILEGE CLAUSE. In construction contracts, reserves conditionally to the owner the privilege to decide not to proceed with the work by indicating that the lowest or any bid will not necessarily be accepted.

PRIVILEGED COMMUNICATION. 1. A communication which one cannot compel a witness to divulge. 2. "In slander or libel the term 'privileged communication' comprehends all cases of communications made bona fide in pursuance of a duty, or with a fair and reasonable purpose of protecting the interest of the party uttering the defamatory matter: . . . Privileged communications are of four kinds, viz.: (1). When the publisher of the alleged slander acted in good faith in the discharge of a public or private duty, legal or moral or in prosecution of his own rights or interests. (2). Anything said or written by a master concerning the character of a servant who has been in his employment. (3). Words used in the course of a legal or judicial proceeding. (4). Publications duly made in the ordinary mode of parliament: Clarke v. Molyneux (1877), 3 Q.B.D. 237." *Trafton v. Deschene* (1917), 36 D.L.R. 433 at 435, 44 N.B.R. 552 (C.A.), Grimmer J.A.

PRIVILEGED DOCUMENT. "A document which was produced or brought into existence with either the dominant purpose of its author, or of the person or authority under whose direction, whether particular or general, it was produced or brought into existence, of using it or its contents in order to obtain legal advice or to conduct or aid in the conduct of litigation, at the time of its production in reasonable prospect, should be privileged and excluded for inspection." *Voth Brothers Construction (1974) Ltd. v. North Vancouver School District No. 44*, [1981] 5 W.W.R. 91 at 94, 29 B.C.L.R. 114 (C.A.), Nemetz J.A. adopting the test of Barwick C.J. Aust. in *Grant v. Downs* (1976), 135 C.L.R. 674 at 677 (H.C.).

PRIVILEGED INFORMATION. Any information concerning a material fact not yet known to the public that could affect the value or the market price of securities of an issuer. *Securities Act*, S.Q. 1982, c. 48, s. 5.

PRIVILEGED MOTION. A way to deal with a situation arising from the debate on or the subject-matter of an original question either following or preceding a vote or because a new proceeding is needed. A. Fraser, W.A. Dawson, & J. Holtby, eds., *Beauchesne's Rules and Forms of the House of Commons of Canada*, 6th ed. (Toronto: Carswell, 1989) at 173.

PRIVILEGED OCCASION. An occasion when the person who makes a communication has an interest or a legal, social, or moral duty to make it to the person to whom it is made and the person to whom it is made has a corresponding interest or duty to receive it.

PRIVILEGED WILL. A will executed by a member of the military or a seaman or mariner and not meeting the general formality requirements.

PRIVILEGIUM EST BENEFICIUM PERSONALE, ET EXTINGUITUR CUM PERSONA. [L.] Privilege is a personal benefit, and it dies with the person.

PRIVILEGIUM EST QUASI PRIVATA LEX. [L.] A privilege is almost a private law.

PRIVILEGIUM NON VALET CONTRA REPUBLICAM. [L.] A privilege does not prevail against the state.

PRIVITY. *n.* 1. The doctrine of privity of contract has been stated by many different authorities sometimes with varying effect. Broadly speaking, it stands for the proposition that a contract cannot, as a general rule, confer rights or impose obligations arising under it on any person except the parties to it. *London Drugs Ltd. v. Kuehne & Nagel International Ltd.*, [1992] 3 S.C.R. 299, Per Iacobucci, J. for the majority. 2. The direct connection between the one to pay the money being sought in an action for recovery and the one to receive such money. G.H.L. Fridman, *Restitution*, 2d ed. (Toronto: Carswell, 1992) at 65. 3. Knowledge.

PRIVITY OF CONTRACT. The doctrine of privity of contract has been stated by many different authorities sometimes with varying effect. Broadly speaking, it stands for the proposition that a contract cannot, as a general rule, confer rights or impose obligations arising under it on any person except the parties to it. *London Drugs Ltd. v. Kuehne & Nagel International Ltd.*, [1992] 3 S.C.R. 299, Per Iacobucci, J. for the majority.

PRIVY. *n.* 1. Someone who partakes or has an interest in some action or thing. 2. Someone related to another person. 3. A place for the purpose of urination or defecation that is not a flush toilet. *Tourism Act*, R.R.O. 1980, Reg. 936, s. 1.

PRIVY. *adj.* Participating in some act.

PRIVY COUNCIL. 1. In Canada, the Queen's Privy Council for Canada including cabinet ministers and other people as well. P.W. Hogg, *Constitutional Law of Canada*, 3d ed. (Toronto: Carswell, 1992) at 234. 2. In the United Kingdom, a large body which now exercises formal functions only. The Queen, on the advice of the Prime Minister, appoints its members. P.W. Hogg, *Constitutional Law of Canada*, 3d ed. (Toronto: Carswell, 1992) at 202. See JUDICIAL COMMITTEE OF THE ~; QUEEN'S ~ FOR CANADA.

PRIVY SEAL. The seal adopted by the Governor General or the Administrator for the sealing of official documents that are to be signed by him or with his authority by his deputy, and that do not require to be sealed with the Great Seal. *Formal Documents Regulations*, C.R.C., c. 1331, s. 2.

PRIZE. *n.* " . . . [S]omething striven for in a competition, in a contest, . . . *R. v. McLaughlin*, [1978] C.T.C. 602 at 603, [1979] 1 F.C. 470, 78 D.T.C. 6406 (T.D.), Marceau J. See MONEY ~.

PRIZE COURT. The Federal Court of Canada has and shall exercise, subject to the Canada Prize Act, jurisdiction in all matters of prize in Canada. The Court shall, subject to this section, take cognizance of and judicially proceed upon all, and all manner of, captures, seizures, prizes and reprisals made under the authority of Her Majesty in right of Canada of all ships, aircraft or goods, and shall hear and determine the same and, according to the Course of Admiralty and the Law of Nations, adjudge and condemn all such ships, aircraft or goods as belong to any enemy country or the citizens or subjects thereof or any other persons inhabiting any of the countries, territories or dominions of any enemy country or that are otherwise condemnable as prize. *Canada Prize Act*, R.S.C. 1970, c. P-24.

PRIZE FIGHT. An encounter or fight with fists or hands between two persons who have met for that purpose by previous arrangement made by or for them, but a boxing contest between amateur sportsmen, where the contestants wear boxing gloves of not less than one hundred and forty grams each in mass, or any boxing contest held with the permission or under the authority of an athletic board or commission or similar body established by or under the authority of the legislature of a province for the control of sport within the province, shall be deemed not to be a prize fight. *Criminal Code*, R.S.C. 1985, c. C-46, s. 83(2).

PRO. *prep.* [L.] For, in respect of.

PROBABILIS CAUSA LITIGANDA. [L.] A credible cause for litigation.

PROBABILITY. *n.* A mathematical expression in the form of a fraction which expresses the chance of a particular event happening. See BALANCE OF PROBABILITIES; SIMPLE ~.

PROBABLE CAUSE. Grounds which are reasonable. *Archibald v. McLaren* (1892), 21 S.C.R. 588 at 594, Strong J. (Fournier J. concurring). See REASONABLE AND ~.

PROBANDA. *n.* Goods provided.

PROBANDI NECESSITAS INCUMBIT ILLI QUI AGIT. [L.] The need to prove rests upon the person who commences proceedings.

PROBATA SECUNDUM ALLEGAT. [L.] Proven according to what was alleged.

PROBATE. *n.* A process to prove the originality and validity of a will. 2. Includes letters of verification issued in the Province of Quebec. See COURT OF ~; GRANT OF ~; LETTERS ~.

PROBATE DUTY. A tax on the gross value of a deceased testator's personal property.

PROBATE VALUE. When used in reference to any property held in trust by an executor or trustee, means the total value of all such property, at the date of death, over and above all mortgages, liens, and encumbrances thereon, plus any income received by the executor or trustee; and when used in the case of a petition for administration de bonis non means the amount of the estate that will pass for administration by the new appointee; and in all other cases shall be taken to mean the outside total value of the estate of the deceased at the date of death over and above all mortgages, liens or encumbrances thereon, and without allowing for other debts due by the deceased.

PROBATION. *n.* 1. The disposition of a court authorizing a person to be at large subject to the conditions of a probation order or community service order. 2. Temporarily appointing a person to an office until that person has, by conduct, proved to be fit to fill it. 3. " . . . [A] testing to determine character and qualification. It is a judicial act of grace and clemency (as indeed, are most of the dispositions under the Juvenile Delinquents Act [R.S.C. 1970, c. J-3] under which the execution of a harsher sentence is suspended and a milder one is substituted on the very clear understanding that the harsher one will be reimposed if the person being tested fails to honour certain terms and conditions." *R. v. M. (D.)* (1982), 144 D.L.R. (3d) 98 at 108, 30 C.R. (3d) 210, 32 C.C.C. (3d) 296 (Ont. Fam. Ct.), Beaulieu Sr. Prov. J. See PERIOD OF ~.

PROBATIONARY EMPLOYEE. A person who is employed on a full-time basis but who has worked less than the probationary period.

PROBATIONARY MEMBER. A member with less than 2 years of service in the RCMP. *Royal Canadian Mounted Police Act*, R.S.C. 1985 (2d Supp.), c. 8, s. 45.19(11).

PROBATIONARY PERIOD. The period of time at the beginning of employment with a new employer during which the employer has an opportunity to determine the suitability of the employee.

PROBATIONER. *n*. A convicted person who is placed on probation by a court or a person who is discharged conditionally by a probation order of a court.

PROBATION OFFICER. The person who supervises another person placed on probation.

PROBATION ORDER. An order made in respect of a particular individual and so long as it remains in force, it attaches to that individual wherever he or she may go. Orders of disposition and probation orders are not identical. All dispositions under s. 20(1) of the [*Young Offenders Act*, R.S.C. 1985, c. Y-1], including custodial or probation dispositions, are subject to the requirements of s. 20(6). In contrast, s. 23 is specific to probation orders. It identifies the required and optional contents of a probation order and provides statutory rules designed to ensure that the conditions of a probation order are read to, and understood by, the affected young person and, further, are brought to the attention of the parent of the young person, if the parent is in attendance at the proceedings against the young person. Accordingly, the scope of s. 20(6) is wider than that of s. 23. *R. v. H. (J.)* (2002), 161 C.C.C. (3d) 392, 155 O.A.C. 146, [2002] O.J. No. 268, 2002 CarswellOnt 156 (C.A.).

PROBATIS EXTREMIS PRAESUMUNTUR MEDIA. [L.] Once the extremes are proved, the means are presumed.

PROBATIVE. *adj.* ". . . [R]aising a likelihood, affording some measure of proof; . . . others may take it as meaning only consistency, rather than roof." *R. v. Stanger* (1983), 6 C.R.R. 257 at 272, [1983] 5 W.W.R. 331, 26 Alta. L.R. (2d) 193, 7 C.C.C. (3d) 337, 2 D.L.R. (4th) 121, 46 A.R. 242, 10 W.C.B. 237 (C.A.), Stevenson J.A. (Harradence J.A. concurring).

PROBATIVE VALUE. "To have probative value the evidence must be susceptible of an inference relevant to the issues in the case other than the inference that the accused committed the offence because he or she has a disposition to the type of conduct charged . . . As in the case of relevance, evidence can be logically probative but not legally probative. When the term 'probative value' is employed in the cases, reference is made to legally probative value." *R. v. R. (C.R.)* (1990), 55 C.C.C. (3d) 1 at 7, [1990] 3 W.W.R. 385, 73 Alta. L.R. (2d) 1, [1990] 1 S.C.R. 717, 107 N.R. 241, 109 A.R. 81, Sopinka J.

PROBATOR. *n*. One who examines; one who accuses, approves or undertakes to prove the crime with which another is charged.

PROBATUM EST. [L.] It is tried; it is proved.

PROB. CT. *abbr*. Probate Court.

PROBI ET LEGALES HOMINES. [L.) Good and lawful people.

PROBIOTIC. *n*. A monoculture or mixed-culture of live micro-organisms that benefit the microbiota indigenous to humans. *Natural Health Products Regulations*, SOR/2003-196, s. 1.

PRO BONO PUBLICO. [L.] For the public good. Often shortened to "pro bono". See PRO BONO SERVICES.

PRO BONO SERVICES. Legal services donated to individuals or to groups.

PROC. *abbr*. Procuration.

PROCEDENDO. *n*. [L.] The writ which issued when the judge of a subordinate court delayed the parties by not giving judgment.

PROCEDURAL EQUALITY. Equality of application of the law without necessarily treating persons equally.

PROCEDURAL FAIRNESS. ". . . [R]equires that the complainant be provided with an opportunity to make submissions, at least in writing, before any action is taken on the basis of the report; however, a hearing is not necessarily required. . . in order to ensure that such submissions are made on an informed basis, it must, prior to its decision, disclose the substance of the case against the party." *Radulesco v. Canada (Canadian Human Rights Commission)* (1984), 9 C.C.E.L. 6 at 9, [1984] 2 S.C.R. 407, 9 Admin. L.R. 261, 84 C.L.L.C. 17,029, 14 D.L.R. (4th) 78, 55 N.R. 384, 6 C.H.R.R. D/2831, the court per Lamer J.

PROCEDURAL IMPROPRIETY. I have described the third head as 'procedural impropriety' rather than failure to observe basic rules of natural justice or failure to act with procedural fairness towards the person who will be affected by the decision. This is because susceptibility to judicial review under this head covers also failure by an administrative tribunal to observe procedural rules that are expressly laid down in the legislative instrument by which its jurisdiction is conferred, even where such failure does not involve any denial of natural justice. But the instant case is not concerned with the proceedings of an administrative tribunal at all. *Council of Civil Service Unions v. Minister for Civil Service* (1984), [1985] 1 A.C. 374, [1984] 3 All E.R. 935 (H.L.) at pp. 410 and 411 [A.C.], Lord Diplock.

PROCEDURAL LAW. 1. " . . . [T]he vehicle providing the means and instruments by which those ends [the ends which the administration of justice seeks to attain] are attained. It regulates the conduct of Courts and litigants in respect of the litigation itself . . ." *Sutt v. Sutt*, [1969] 1 O.R. 169 at 175, 2 D.L.R. (3d) 33 (C.A.), Schroeder J.A. (McGillivray J.A. concurring). 2. "The types of laws which have generally been considered to be procedural are, first, evidentiary rules such as admissibility, the requirements of written evidence, the competency or compellability of witnesses, the burden of proof, etc; second, the question of who are the appropriate parties to a lawsuit; and third, questions of how a judgment may be executed." *243930 Alberta Ltd. v. Wickham* (1990), 14 R.P.R. (2d) 95 at 111, 73 D.L.R. (4th) 474, 75 O.R. (2d) 289, 40 O.A.C. 367 (C.A.), McKinlay J.A. (Blair J.A. concurring).

PROCEDURE. *n.* 1. "The concept of procedure, too, is . . . a comprehensive one, including process and evidence, methods of execution, rules of limitation affecting the remedy and the course of the Court with regard to the kind of relief that can be granted to a suitor. . ." *Livesley v. E. Clemens Horst Co.* (1924), [1925] 1 D.L.R. 159 at 161, [1924] S.C.R. 605, the court per Duff J. 2. " . . . [P]roperly means neither the machinery nor the product, but rather the rules set forth by the managers of the machine, showing not who have the right to use it, but how those who have the right are to behave. If the machine exists for you, if there is a Court of Appeal in criminal matters, these shall be the rules by which you shall approach the machine to obtain our result. . ." *R. v. Johnson* (1892), 2 B.C.R. 87 at 88 (C.A.), Begbie C.J.A. (Drake J.A. concurring). 3. " . . . [W]hen used in a statute such as the

Bankruptcy Act [R.S.C. 1970, c. B-3] refers to the mode or method by which a litigant secures his rights. . ." *Eisler, Re* (1984), 54 C.B.R. (N.S.) 235 at 239 (B.C. S.C.), Murray J. 4. "[In s. 91(27) of the Constitution Act, 1867 (30 & 31 Vict.), c. 3] . . . means the steps to be taken in prosecutions or other criminal proceedings . . ." *Clement, Re* (1919), 48 D.L.R. 237 at 238, [1919] 3 W.W.R. 115, 33 C.C.C. 119, 27 B.C.R. 361 (C.A.), MacDonald C.J.A. 5. " . . . [P]leading, evidence and practice . . ." *Delisle v. Moreau* (1968), 5 C.R.N.S. 68 at 70, [1968] 4 C.C.C. 229, 69 D.L.R. (2d) 530, (N.B. C.A.), the court per Hughes J.A. See CIVIL ~; CRIMINAL ~; INTRUSIVE ~; PRACTICE AND~; WELDING ~.

PROCEED. *v.* Includes "carry on". *Environmental Assessment Act*, R.S.O. 1990, c. E.18, s. 1.

PROCEEDING. *v.* " . . . [A] vessel—or as here a vehicle—is 'proceeding' so long as there is no 'discontinuance' of the intended journey. Halting for a proper and reasonable act such as awaiting tides, loading coal, turning left safely, does not discontinue a journey. . ." *Wigton v. Ratke* (1984), 6 C.C.L.I. 50 at 55, 55 A.P. 154, 9 D.L.R. (4th) 464, [1984] I.L.R. 1-777 (Q.B.), Wachowich J.

PROCEEDING. *n.* 1. " . . . [O]ne of those words of very wide import that must be interpreted according to the context in which it is used. . ." *I.W.A., Local 1-324 v. Wescana Inn Ltd.* (1978), 27 C.B.R. (N.S.) 201 at 206, [1978] 1 W.W.R. 679, 82 D.L.R. (3d) 368 (Man. C.A.), O'Sullivan J.A. (Freedman C.J.M. concurring). 2. " . . . [C]apable of including every species of activity in matters legal, from an interlocutory application in Chambers to an appeal in a Court of last resort." *Ontario (Attorney General) v. Palmer* (1979), 108 D.L.R. (3d) 349 at 358-9, 28 O.R. (2d) 35, 15 C.P.C. 125, [1980] I.L.R. 1-1196 (C.A.), Anderson J.A. (dissenting). 3. " . . . [R]efers to the whole event, from the commencement of action by the issuance of a writ to the conclusion of the trial, no matter how many causes of action are raised by way of pleadings in either the statement of claim or in the counterclaim." *Hughes v. O'Sullivan* (1986), 12 C.P.C. (2d) 62 at 66 (B.C. S.C.), Toy J. 4. A matter, cause or action, whether civil or criminal, before the court. 5. "' . . . [A] step in an action.'" *Hannah v. Flagstaff*, [1926] 4 D.L.R. 470 at 473, [1926] 3 W.W.R. 301 (Alta. T.D.), Simmons C.J. 6. " . . . [T]he form and manner of conducting judicial business before a Court or judicial officer rather than all possible steps in an action from its commencement to the execution of Judgment." *Carlson v. Loraas Disposal Services Ltd.* (1988), 30 C.P.C. (2d) 181 at 187, 70 Sask. R. 161 (Q.B.), Walker J. 7. The [*Companies' Creditors Arrangement Act*, R.S.C. 1985, c. C-36] has consistently been read as authorizing a stay of proceedings beyond the narrowly judicial. The word "proceeding" includes ". . .judicial or extra-judicial conduct against the debtor company the effect of which is, or would be, seriously to impair the ability of the debtor company to continue in business during the compromise or arrangement negotiating period." *Quintette Coal Ltd. v. Nippon Steel Corp.* (1990), 51 B.C.L.R. (2d) 105 (C.A.) at 113. . . Unlike the United States Code, which specifically exempts governmental regulatory enforcement proceedings from the stay (11 USC para. 362(b)(4)), the [*Companies' Creditors Arrangement Act*, R.S.C. 1985, c. C-36] does not so limit the powers of the Court. *Toronto Stock Exchange Inc. v. United Keno Hill Mines Ltd.* (2000), 2000 CarswellOnt 1770, 48 O.R. (3d) 746, 7 B.L.R. (3d) 86, 19 C.B.R. (4th) 299 (S.C.J. [Commercial List]) Lane J. 8. Includes an action, application or submission to any court or judge or other body having authority by law or by consent to make decisions as to the rights of persons. See ADMIRALTY ~; AFFILIATION ~; BASTARDY ~; COROLLARY RELIEF ~; COSTS OF THIS ~; CRIMINAL ~; DEFECT IN THE ~S; DIVORCE ~; JUDICIAL OR QUASI-JUDICIAL ~; JUDICIAL ~; LEGAL ~; LIQUIDATION ~S; MINUTES OF ~S AND EVIDENCE ~; RECORD OF THE ~; REPRESENTATIVE ~; VARIATION ~; VEXATIOUS ~.

PROCEEDING AGAINST THE CROWN. Includes a claim by way of set-off or counterclaim raised in proceedings by the Crown, interpleader proceedings to which the Crown is a party, and a proceeding in which the Crown is a garnishee.

PROCEEDINGS. *n.* 1. " . . . [S]hould be given a large and liberal interpretation so as to cover any kind of proceeding, whether adjudicative or investigative. This would be consistent with the principle of Charter interpretation that we construe rights guaranteed in the Charter so as to provide maximum protection to the citizen . . ." *Thomson Newspapers Ltd. v. Canada (Director of Investigation & Research, Combines Investigation Branch)* (1990), (*Thomson Newspapers*

v. Canada (Director of Investigation & Research, Restrictive Trade Practices Commission)) 29 C.P.R. (3d) 97 at 137, 76 C.R. (3d) 129, 72 O.R. (2d) 415n, 54 C.C.C. (3d) 417, 67 D.L.R. (4th) 161, [1990] 1 S.C.R. 425, 39 O.A.C. 161, 106 N.R. 161, 47 C.R.R. 1, Wilson J. (dissenting). 2. " . . . [M]eans in a criminal case all judicial steps taken upon one charge to resolve and reach a final conclusion of the issue therein raised between the same party and the Crown. This would include the preliminary hearing, the trial, and an appeal and a new trial. . . *R. v. Dubois* (1985), 18 C.R.R. 1 at 29, [1985] 2 S.C.R. 350, [1986] 1 W.W.R. 193, 41 Alta. L.R. (2d) 97, 48 C.R. (3d) 193, 22 C.C.C. (3d) 513, 23 D.L.R. (4th) 503, 62 N.R. 50, 66 AS.R. 202, [1986] D.L.Q. 87n, McIntyre J. (dissenting). See PROCEEDING; STAY OF ~.

PROCEEDS. *n.* 1. The amount, sum or value of any land, goods or investments sold or converted into cash. 2. Identifiable or traceable personal property in any form derived directly or indirectly from any dealing with collateral or proceeds therefrom, and includes any payment representing indemnity or compensation for loss of or representing to the collateral or proceeds therefrom. *Personal Property Security Act*, R.S.O. 1990, c. P.1, s. 1.1(1). See GRAIN SALE ~; GROSS ~; NET ~.

PROCEEDS OF CRIME. Any property, benefit or advantage, within or outside Canada, obtained or derived directly or indirectly as a result of (a) the commission in Canada of a designated offence, or (b) an act or omission anywhere that, if it had occurred in Canada, would have constituted a designated offence. *Criminal Code*, R.S.C. 1985, c. C-46, s. 462.3. See LAUNDERING ~.

PROCEEDS OF SALE. Includes (i) the purchase price or consideration payable to the vendor, or passing from the purchaser to the vendor, on a sale in bulk; and (ii) the money realized by a trustee under a security or by the sale or other disposition of any property coming into his or her hands as the consideration or part of the consideration for the sale. *Bulk Sales acts*.

PROCESS. *n.* 1. Includes, with respect to goods, the adjustment, alteration, assembly, manufacture, modification, production or repair of the goods. 2. " . . . [A]s a legal term is a word of comprehensive signification. In its broadest sense it is equivalent to 'proceedings' or 'procedure' and may be said to embrace all the steps and proceedings in a case from its commencement to its conclusion. 'Process' may signify the means whereby a Court compels a compliance with its demands. Every writ is of course, a process, and in its narrowest sense the term 'process' is limited to writs or writings issued from or out of a Court under the seal of the Court and returnable to the Court. . ." *Selkirk, Re* (1961), 27 D.L.R. (2d) 615 at 621, [1961] O.R. 391 (C.A.), Schroeder J.A. (McGillivray J.A. concurring). 3. " . . . [A] writ or other judicial order: . . ." *R. v. Landry* (1986), 50 C.R. (3d) 55 at 72, [1986] 1 S.C.R. 145, 54 O.R. (2d) 512n, 65 N.R. 161, 25 C.C.C. (3d) 1, 14 O.A.C. 241, 26 D.L.R. (4th) 368, La Forest J. (dissenting). 4. Includes a writ, petition, warrant or order issued under the seal of the court, a judge's summons or order, a notice, subpoena and other proceeding at law or otherwise. 5. A mode or method of operation, by which chemical action, the application or operation of some power or element of nature, or some substance produces a result or effect on another thing or the performance of an operation or use of a method to produce a certain result. H.G. Fox, *The Canadian Law and Practice Relating to Letters Patent for Inventions*, 4th ed. (Toronto: Carswell, 1969) at 17. 6. In relation to a meat product, includes cutting, cooking, canning, comminuting, preserving, dressing, dehydrating, rendering, fractionating, defibrinating and treating, but does not include chilling or freezing. *Meat Inspection Regulations*, C.R.C., c. 1032, s. 2. 7. Any part of the work of dressing or eviscerating poultry. *Dressed and Eviscerated Poultry Regulations*, C.R.C., c. 283, s. 2. 8. Includes breaking eggs, filtering, blending, pasteurizing, stabilizing, mixing, cooling , freezing and drying processed eggs. *Processed Egg Regulations*, C.R.C., c. 290, s. 2. See ABUSE OF ~; DUE ~; LEGAL ~; MESNE ~; ORIGINATING ~; PAY EQUITY ~; SERVICE OF ~.

PROCESS BUTTER. Creamery butter that has been melted or clarified or refined and remanufactured into butter. *Farm Products Grades and Sales Act*, R.R.O. 1980, Reg. 327, s. 1.

PROCESS CATEGORY. See COMPONENT ~.

PROCESS CHEESE. The food product that is produced by comminuting or mixing one or more lots of cheese with the aid of heat and emulsifying agents into a homogeneous mass.

PROCESSED. *adj.* Canned, cooked, dehydrated or otherwise prepared for food to assure preservation of a food product.

PROCESSED ORGANIC WASTE. Waste that is predominantly organic in composition and has been treated by aerobic and anaerobic digestion, or other means of stabilization, and includes sewage residue from sewage works.

PROCESSED WOOD. Secondary wood products manufactured from timber in a wood processing facility.

PROCESS ELEVATOR. An elevator the principal use of which is the receiving and storing of grain for direct manufacture or processing into other products. *Canada Grain Act*, R.S.C. 1985, c. G-10, s. 2.

PROCESS FOR RESOLUTION OF A DISPUTE. Either of the following processes for the resolution of a dispute, namely: (a) by the referral of the dispute to arbitration; or (b) by the referral thereof to a conciliation board. *Public Service Staff Relations Act*, R.S.C. 1985, c. P-35, s. 2.

PROCESSING. *n.* 1. " . . . [T]he treatment must make the goods more marketable and . . . there must be some change in the nature or appearance of the goods." *Tenneco Canada Inc. v. R.*, [1988] 2 F.C. 3 at 9, [1987] 2 C.T.C. 231, 87 D.T.C. 5434, 15 F.T.R. 315, Dubé J. 2. Includes changing the nature, form, size, shape, quality or condition of a natural product by mechanical, chemical or any other means. 3. With respect to mineral substances, any form of beneficiation, concentrating, smelting, refining or semi-fabricating, or any combination thereof. 4. Changing the nature or form of an agricultural product and includes, in the case of animals, the killing of them. 5. Includes cleaning, filleting, icing, packing, canning, freezing, smoking, salting, cooking, pickling, drying or preparing fish for market in any other manner. 6. Heating, pasteurizing, evaporating, drying, churning, freezing, packaging, packing, separating into component parts, combining with other substances by any process or otherwise treating milk or cream or milk products in the manufacture or preparation of milk products or fluid milk products. See DATA ~; DATA ~ SERVICES; FIRST ~; MANUFACTURING OR ~ ACTIVITY; MINERAL ~ ESTABLISHMENT.

PROCESSING ASSETS. Processing plants, machinery, equipment and structures acquired for the purpose of processing mineral substances and ancillary activities, but does not include, (a) the value of spare parts held in inventory for such assets, (b) stockpiles or inventories of processed mineral substances, (c) assets used for the transportation of processed mineral substances to market, or (d) mining assets or social assets. *Mining Tax Act*, R.S.O. 1990, c. M.15, s. 1(1).

PROCESSING FACILITY. See TIMBER ~; WOOD ~.

PROCESSING OF FISH. Includes the cleaning, filleting, smoking, salting, icing, packing, freezing, cooking, or drying of fish or the preparing of fish for market in any other manner.

PROCESSING OPERATION. See INITIAL ~.

PROCESSING PLANT. 1. A plant for the extraction from gas of hydrogen sulphide, helium, ethane, natural gas liquids or other substances, but does not include a well head separator, treater, or dehydrator. 2. A plant used in processing, smelting or refining of metals. 3. A facility (i) for obtaining crude bitumen from oil sands that have been recovered; or (ii) for obtaining oil sands products from oil sands, crude bitumen or derivatives of crude bitumen that have been recovered. 4. A fish cannery or a fish processing or fish curing establishment and includes a building or other structure and a floating barge or vessel connected with or used in connection with the cannery or establishment. 5. An installation for improving the quality of the coal or producing a marketable solid fuel from it and includes a coal storage or handling facility directly connected with the installation.

PROCESSOR. *n*. A person engaged in the preparation or conversion of an agricultural product for marketing.

PROCESS STOCK. Beer in any process of manufacture prior to duty assessment.

PROCHEIN AMY. *var.* **PROCHEIN AMI**. [Fr.] With respect to a child, a next friend or next-of-kin who manages the infant's affairs.

PROCHRONISM. *n*. A mistake in chronology; dating something before it happened.

PROCLAMATION. *n*. 1. Authorized publication. 2. A proclamation under the Great Seal. See ROYAL ~ OF 1763.

PROCLAMATION DATE. The date on which a statute is proclaimed in force when the statute provides that it will come into force when proclaimed.

PRO CONFESSO. [L.] By confession.

PROCTOR. See QUEEN'S ~.

PROCURATION. *n*. An agency, the administering of another's business. See PER ~.

PROCURATIONEM ADVERSUS NULLA EST PRAESCRIPTIO. [L.] There is no limitation of procuration.

PROCURATOR. *n*. One to whom someone commits a charge; an agent.

PROCURE. *v*. " . . . [I]n the context in which is used is s. 422 [of the Criminal Code, R.S.C. 1970, c. C-34] means to instigate, persuade or solicit." *R. v. Gonzague* (1983), 4 C.C.C. (3d) 505 at 508, 34 C.R. (3d) 169 (Ont. C.A.), the court per Martin J.A.

PROCURING. *n*. " . . . [W]here the services of any agency include intermediary services to bring together the natural mother and the proposed adopting parents so that the mother has an opportunity to select parents for her child, such conduct constitutes assistance in finding, introducing and, in the result, procuring a child within the meaning of s. 7 of the [Child Welfare Act., S.A. 1984, c. 8.1]. . ." *S. (R.G.J.) v. P. (B.L.)* (1987), 75 A.R. 287 at 291, 7 R.F.L. (3d) 58 (Q.B.), Berger J.

PROCURING A MISCARRIAGE. "[In s. 251 of the Criminal Code, R.S.C. 1970, c. C-34] . . . '[P]erfoming an abortion'. . ." *R. v. Morgentaler* (1988), 31 C.R.R. 1 at 111, 82 N.R. 1, [1988] 1 S.C.R. 30, 63 O.R. (2d) 281n, 62 C.R. (3d) 1, 26 O.A.C. 1, 44 D.L.R. (4th) 385, 37 C.C.C. (3d) 449, McIntyre J. (dissenting) (La Forest J. concurring).

PRO DEFECTU JURATORUM. [L.] For failure of jurors.

PRODITION. *n*. Treachery, treason.

PRODITOR. *n*. One who commits treason.

PRODITORIE. *adv*. Treacherously.

PRODUCE. *v*. 1. Includes grow, manufacture and mine. 2. Extract or obtain from the earth. *Geothermal Resources Act*, S.B.C. 1982, c. 14, s. 1.

PRODUCE. *n*. Livestock, furbearing animals raised in captivity, poultry, eggs, fruit, vegetables, honey. See AQUACULTURAL ~; FARM ~; FRUIT AND ~.

PRODUCED. *adj*. 1. " . . . A thing is produced if what a person does has the result of producing something new; and a thing is new when it can perform a function that could not be preformed by the things which existed previously." *Enseig-*

nes Imperial Signs Ltée v. Minister of National Revenue (1990), 3 T.C.T. 5389 at 5390 (Eng.), 3 T.C.T. 5113 (Fr.), [1991] 1 C.T.C. 229, Can. S.T.R. 80-074, 116 N.R. 235, 43 F.T.R. 239n, (C.A.), Pratte J.A. 2. All the visual and sound components of the commercial message have been assembled into a composite whole.

PRODUCER. *n.* 1. A producer of grain, livestock, or poultry. 2. A person engaged in the production of honey, fruit or vegetables and includes a person engaged in the handling, packing, processing, shipping, transporting, purchasing or selling of honey, fruit or vegetables. 3. A producer actually engaged in the production of grain and any person entitled, as landlord, vendor or mortgagee, to the grain grown by a producer actually engaged in the production of grain or to any share therein. 4. The owner of a well that is capable of producing oil or gas. 5. Any person who sells or delivers milk or cream to a plant. Canada regulations. 6. A person or partnership who or which retains the services of artists in view of producing or presenting to the public an artistic work in an artistic endeavour. See ACTUAL ~; ASSOCIATION OF ~S; CANADIAN ~; DAIRY ~; FORESTRY ~; GAS ~; PRIMARY ~; QUALIFIED ~; SERVICES TO ~S.

PRODUCER ORGANIZATION. An organization of producers that is engaged in marketing a crop.

PRODUCER-PROVINCE. *n.* 1. A province in which the quantities of crude oil ordinarily produced, extracted or recovered in that province in a month are such that a significant quantity of that crude oil is normally available for use outside that province in each month. *Energy Administration Act*, R.S.C. 1985, c. E-6, s. 20. 2. A province in which the quantities of gas ordinarily produced, extracted, recovered or manufactured in that province in a month are such that a significant quantity of that gas is normally available for use outside that province in each month. *Energy Administration Act*, R.S.C. 1985, c. E-6, s. 36.

PRODUCERS' BOARD. The body entrusted with implementation and administration of a joint plan to market farm products.

PRODUCER-SHIPPER CONTRACT. A gas contract relating to the first sale and delivery of (i) gas after it is first recovered from a well, if the gas is marketable gas at the time it is so recovered; or (ii) gas after it first becomes marketable gas, in any other case.

PRODUCING. *adj.* 1. Planting, growing, harvesting, curing or preparing for sale. *Farm Products Marketing Act*, R.S.O. 1990, c. F.9, s. 20(1). 2. (a) In the case of chicks-for-placement, the provision of housing, feed, water or care therefor and the preparation thereof for sale or for use as fowl, and (b) in the case of eggs and hatching eggs, the provision of housing, feed, water or care for the fowl that lay such eggs or hatching eggs and the preparation of the eggs or hatching eggs for sale or for hatching, as the case may be. *Farm Products Marketing Act*, R.S.O. 1990, c. F.9, s. 21(1).

PRODUCING TRACT. A drainage unit, as defined in The Oil and Gas Conservation Act: (i) in which or in respect of which is situate a well from which oil: (A) is being produced or is capable of being produced; or (B) is, by virtue of an order of the Lieutenant Governor in Council, deemed to be produced; or (ii) the whole or a portion of which is included in an area in respect of which there exists: (A) a plan; (B) a unit operation agreement; or (C) any other arrangement or agreement for the production of oil or oil and natural gas or for the allocation of royalty on that production; under which oil is being produced or is capable of being produced from the drainage unit. Saskatchewan statutes.

PRODUCING WELL. A well that, in the opinion of the Minister, is capable of producing (i) petroleum in paying quantity from a zone in which petroleum rights are granted under the lease; or (ii) natural gas in paying quantity from a zone in which natural gas rights are granted under the lease. *Mines and Minerals Amendment Act*, S.A. 1985, c. 39, s. 6.

PRODUCT. *n.* Any article that is or may be the subject of trade or commerce but does not include land or any interest therein. *Consumer Packaging and Labelling Act*, R.S.C. 1985, c. C-38, s. 2. 2. Includes an article and a service. See AERONAUTICAL ~; AGRICULTURAL ~; ANIMAL ~; ASSOCIATED ~; BAKERY ~; BARLEY ~; CATCH WEIGHT ~; CONSUMER ~; CONTROLLED ~; CONTROL ~; CORROSIVE ~; DAIRY ~; EDIBLE OIL ~; FARM ~; FINISHED ~; FISHERIES ~; FISHERY ~S; FLUID MILK ~S; FOOD ~; FOOD ~S; FOREST ~; FOREST ~S; FRESH WATER ~; GRAIN~; GRAPE ~; HAZARDOUS ~; HOT ~; ILLEGAL ~; INTERCHANGEABLE ~; LIVESTOCK ~S; LOCAL ~; LUMBER ~; MANITOBA ~S; MANUFACTURED ~;

MAPLE ~; MARINE ~; MARKETED ~; MEAT ~; MILK ~; MINERAL ~; NATURAL ~; OAT ~; OIL SANDS ~; OIL SHALE ~S; PEST CONTROL ~; PETROLEUM ~; POULTRY ~; POULTRY ~S; PREPACKAGED ~; REGULATED ~; SPECIALTY ~; TEST MARKET ~; TEXTILE FIBRE ~; TIMBER ~S; TOBACCO ~S; WHALE ~S; WHEAT ~; WOOD ~.

PRODUCT FOR HUMAN CONSUMPTION. Includes every substance, whether a solid or a liquid, used or intended to be used for human consumption and any article intended to enter into or to be used in preparation or composition of such substance including confectionery, flavouring or colouring matter and condiments, but does not include a drug.

PRODUCT HOLDING FIXTURES. Devices for holding the goods in process while the working tools are in operation and are usually held securely in the machine while the operation is in progress, but which do not contain any special arrangement for guiding the working tools.

PRODUCTION. *n*. 1. In court, the exhibition of a document. 2. " . . . [T]he production of existing evidence, [or] the production or creation of new evidence [if it] is necessary or expedient to obtain full information or evidence for the purposes of litigation." *Peck v. Glendinning* (1985), 9 C.P.C. (2d) 132 at 136, 68 B.C.L.R. 264, 23 D.L.R. (4th) 472 (C.A.), Lambert J.A. (dissenting). 3. " . . . [T]he bringing forth or into existence natural resources from underground . . ." *Commissioner of Northwest Territories v. Pine Point Mines Ltd.*, [1981] 5 W.W.R. 420 at 437 (N.W.T. S.C.), Greschuk J. 4. Mining for the purposes of sale, barter or stockpiling. *Mining Act*, S.N.B. 1985, c. M-14.1, s. 1. See ALLOCATED ~; ALLOWABLE ~; COMMERCIAL ~; COST OF ~; FILM ~; GAME ANIMAL~ FARM; LIMITED ~; LIVE STOCK ~; MILK ~; NORMAL ~; PRIMARY ~; PROVINCE OF ~; STANDARD OF ~; SYNTHETIC ~.

PRODUCTION BOYCOTT. A strike.

PRODUCTION DAY. In respect of any brewery, a day not exceeding 24 consecutive hours during which beer is produced. Canada regulations.

PRODUCTION DEVELOPMENT COSTS. The aggregate expenses incurred by the operator of a mine, other than those claimed as eligible exploration expenditures, on the mining right from the date of acquiring the mining right to the date of commencement of production.

PRODUCTION FACILITIES. Production equipment and apparatus at the field site and separating, treating and processing facilities and includes such other equipment or facilities as are required in support of production operations, including airstrips, helicopter landing areas, storage or tank facilities and living quarters for personnel.

PRODUCTION OF OIL [OR] GAS. The bringing forth or into existence and human realization, from underground, of a basic substance containing gas, and at the same time, other matter. *Texaco Exploration Inc. v. The Queen*, [1975] C.T.C. 404; 75 D.T.C. 5288 (F.C.).

PRODUCTION OPERATIONS. All the operations involved in the assembling, processing or conditioning of goods, resulting in other goods different in nature or characteristics from the former, or the reconditioning or repair of moveable property by its owner, and includes the operations of a business engaged in farming, logging, the extraction or treatment of mineral resources, or fisheries, but does not include construction, meal preparation, or any other prescribed operation. See BITUMINOUS SHALE ~.

PRODUCTION PLATFORM. The main production structure and equipment located offshore and any structure or equipment associated therewith.

PRODUCTION ROYALTY. An amount computed by reference to the amount or value of production of petroleum or gas, including any minimum or advance royalty payment with respect to the amount or value of production but does not include (a) a resource royalty; or (b) an amount to which paragraph 7(e) applies paid to a person referred to therein. See INCREMENTAL ~.

PRODUCTION SERVICE ASSOCIATION. Includes an association incorporated or registered under this Act having as its principal objects, or any of them, providing services to assist its members and patrons to become established as producers of agricultural products, goods, wares, merchandise or services for sale or to assist its members and patrons to improve their efficiency and income as producers. *The Cooperative Production Associations Act*, R.S.S. 1978, c. C-37, s. 67.

PRODUCTION SPACING UNIT. That area designated by the appropriate provincial authority for the production of oil or gas where distinction is made between the areas assigned for production and for drilling purposes.

PRODUCTION TRACT. A parcel or group of parcels, whether or not a parcel is contiguous with another, from which a designated mineral is or has at any time been produced.

PRODUCTION WORKER. An employee who actually makes the goods or performs the service.

PRODUCTIVE FOREST. An area of forest producing or capable of producing, at rotation age and under natural conditions, a forest stand containing a minimum merchantable timber volume of 30 m3 (solid) per hectare. *Forestry Act*, R.S. Nfld. 1990, c. F-23, s. 2.

PRODUCTIVE LANDS. Lands that are not rock barrens, muskeg or lands covered with water. *Crown Timber Act*, R.S.O. 1990, c. C.51, s. 1.

PRODUCTIVITY AGREEMENT. A collective agreement including terms relating to physical work conditions, methods and level of production.

PRODUCT LIABILITY. Liability of manufacturers and sellers to buyers and others for damages suffered because of defects in the goods manufactured or sold.

PRODUCT MONOGRAPH. Upon attaining government approval, a drug manufacturer receives a NOC [notice of compliance] together with a product monograph. The product monograph, among other things, sets out what the indications are for the drug product—the uses for which the government has approved a product. Therefore, a product monograph limits indications, and is available on the Compendium of Pharmaceutical Specialities (CPS). *AB Hassle v. Canada (Minister of National Health & Welfare)*, 2002 FCA 421, 22 C.P.R. (4th) 1, 298 N.R. 323 (C.A.).

PRODUCT OUTLINE. A detailed description of (a) the process followed in preparing a veterinary biologic and any diluent to be used therewith; (b) the methods and procedures to be employed in handling, storing, administering and testing a veterinary biologic and any diluent to be used therewith; and (c) the tests used to establish the purity, safety, potency and efficacy of a veterinary biologic, and the purity and safety of any diluent to be used therewith, and the results of all such tests.

PRODUCT RESTRAINT ASSEMBLY. Any webbing, buckle, hardware or combination thereof that is designed to secure or restrain a product in a vehicle.

PRODUCTS OF AGRICULTURE. Includes (a) grain, hay, roots, vegetables, fruits, other crops and all other direct products of the soil; and (b) honey, livestock (whether alive or dead), dairy products, eggs and all other indirect products of the soil. *Bank Act*, S.C. 1991, c. 46, s. 425.

PRODUCTS OF AQUACULTURE. Includes all cultivated aquatic plants and animals. *Bank Act*, S.C. 1991, c. 46, s. 425.

PRODUCTS OF COMBUSTION DETECTOR. A device for sensing the presence of visible or invisible particles produced by combustion and automatically initiating a signal indicating this condition. *Building Code Act*, R.R.O. 1980 Reg. 87, s. 1.

PRODUCTS OF THE FOREST. Includes (a) logs, pulpwood, piling, spars, railway ties, poles, pit props and all other timber; (b) boards, laths, shingles, deals, staves and all other lumber, bark, wood chips and sawdust and Christmas trees; (c) skins and furs of wild animals; and (d) maple products. *Bank Act*, S.C. 1991, c. 46, s. 425.

PRODUCTS OF THE QUARRY AND MINE. Includes stone, clay, sand, gravel, metals, ores, coal, salt, precious stones, metalliferous and non-metallic minerals and hydrocarbons, whether obtained by excavation, drilling otherwise. *Bank Act*, S.C. 1991, c. 46, s. 425.

PRODUCTS OF THE SEA, LAKES AND RIVERS. Includes fish of all kinds, marine and freshwater organic and inorganic life and any substances extracted or derived from any water, but does not include products of aquaculture. *Bank Act*, S.C. 1991, c. 46, s. 425.

PRO EADEM CAUSA. [L.] For the same cause.

PRO EO QUO. [L.] For this thing which.

PROFER. *v.* To produce.

PROFERT. One produces.

PROFESSION. *n.* A vocation or calling; divinity, law and medicine are called learned professions. See DESIGN ~; TRADE, INDUSTRY OR ~.

PROFESSIONAL. *n.* 1. Relating to an occupation requiring special training in the liberal arts and sciences. Involving mutual or intellectual labour or skill rather than physical or manual labour and skill. 2. Any person who holds a permit issued by an order and who is entered on the roll of the latter. *Professional Code*, R.S.Q., c. C-26, s. 1. See HEALTH CARE ~; NON-PARTICIPATING ~.

PROFESSIONAL ARBITRATOR. An arbitrator who is by profession a barrister, solicitor, architect, Dominion land surveyor or Alberta land surveyor. *Arbitration Act*, R.S.A. 1980, c. A-43, s. 1.

PROFESSIONAL ASSOCIATION. An organization of persons that by an enactment, agreement or custom has power to admit, suspend, expel, or direct persons in the practice of any occupation or calling.

PROFESSIONAL CHEMISTRY. See PRACTICE OF ~.

PROFESSIONAL COMMUNITY PLANNING. See PRACTICE OF ~.

PROFESSIONAL CONTEST OR EXHIBITION. A professional contest or exhibition of baseball, bicycle riding, boxing, dancing, golf, hockey, jaialai, lacrosse, motorcycle riding, physical prowess whether by contortion or otherwise, rowing, rugby, running, skating whether speed skating or figure skating, tennis, wrestling or any professional contest or exhibition of any other sort or game designated by the Lieutenant Governor in Council. *Athletics Control Act*, R.S.O. 1990, c. A.34, s. 1.

PROFESSIONAL CORPORATION. A corporation that is the holder of a subsisting permit or is entered in the register under a statute governing a profession.

PROFESSIONAL EMPLOYEE. 1. An employee who (a) is, in the course of employment, engaged in the application of specialized knowledge ordinarily acquired by a course of instruction and study resulting in graduation from a university or similar institution; and (b) is, or is eligible to be, a member of a professional organization that is authorized by statute to establish the qualifications for membership in the organization. 2. An employee of an institution who provides educational services to students and includes an employee who is a librarian or an administrator.

PROFESSIONAL EMPLOYER. 1. An employer who habitually has employees in his employ for any kind of work which is the object of a decree. *Collective Agreement Decrees Act*, R.S.Q. 1977, c. D-2, s. 1. 2. An employer who habitually has one or more employees in his employ for any kind of work which is the object of an ordinance. *Minimum Wage Act*, R.S.Q. 1977, c. S-1, s. 1. 3. An employer whose main activity is to do construction work and who habitually employs employees for any kind of work which is the object of a decree, or, failing a decree, of a collective agreement. *Construction Industry Labour Relations Act*, R.S.Q. 1977, c. R-20, s. 1.

PROFESSIONAL ENGINEER. A person who, by reason of knowledge of mathematics, the physical and social sciences and the principles of engineering, is qualified to engage in the practice of professional engineering and who is registered as a Professional engineer.

PROFESSIONAL ENGINEERING. Any act of designing, composing, evaluating, advising, reporting, directing or supervising wherein the safeguarding of life, health, property or the public welfare is concerned and that requires the application of engineering principles, but does not include practising as a natural scientist. See PRACTICE OF ~.

PROFESSIONAL FORESTRY. The practice of professional forestry is the provision of services in relation to the development, management, conservation and sustainability of forests and urban forests. See PRACTICE OF ~.

PROFESSIONAL GEOLOGY. Reporting, advising, evaluating, interpreting, geological surveying, sampling or examining related to any activity (i) that is aimed at the discovery or development of oil, natural gas, coal, metallic or non-metallic minerals or precious stones, or other natural resources or water or that is aimed at the investigation of geological conditions; and (ii) that requires in that reporting, advising, evaluating, interpreting, geological surveying, sampling or examining the professional application of the principles of the geological sciences or any related subject including, without limiting the generality of the foregoing, the geological field of mineralogy, palaeontology, structural geology, stratigraphy, sedimentation, petrology, geomorphology, photogeology and the like, but does not include any of the above activities that are normally associated with the business of prospecting when carried on by a prospector.

PROFESSIONAL GEOPHYSICS. Reporting, advising, evaluating, interpreting or geophysical surveying related to any activity (i) that is aimed at the discovery or development of oil, natural gas, coal, metallic or non-metallic minerals or precious stones or other natural resources or water or that is aimed at the investigation of subsurface conditions in the earth; and (ii) that requires in that reporting, advising, evaluating, interpreting or geophysical surveying, the professional application of the principles of one or more of the subjects of physics, mathematics or any related subject including, without limiting the generality of the foregoing, principles of elastic wave propagation, gravitational, magnetic and electrical fields, natural radio activity, and the like, but does not include the routine maintenance or operation of geophysical instruments, or if carried out under the responsible supervision of a professional geophysicist, the routine reduction or plotting of geophysical observations.

PROFESSIONAL GEOSCIENCE. An individual practises professional geoscience when he or she performs an activity that requires the knowledge, understanding and application of the principles of geoscience and that concerns the safeguarding of the welfare of the public or the safeguarding of life, health or property including the natural environment.

PROFESSIONAL LAND SURVEYING. The advising on, reporting on, the supervising of or the conducting of surveys to establish, locate, define or describe the lines, boundaries or corners of parcels of land or land covered with water.

PROFESSIONAL LIABILITY CLAIM. A claim against a licensed member, registered practitioner or professional corporation for an amount of money that the licensed member, registered practitioner or professional corporation is legally obligated to pay as damages, which claim arises out of the performance of professional services for a person by the licensed member, registered practitioner or professional corporation, or by another person for whose acts the licensed member, registered practitioner or professional corporation is legally liable.

PROFESSIONAL MEMBER. A professional engineer, professional geologist or professional geophysicist registered as a member of the Association pursuant to this Act. *Engineering, Geological and Geophysical Professions Act*, S.A. 1981, c. E-11.1, s. 1.

PROFESSIONAL MISCONDUCT. 1. " . . . [C]onduct which would be reasonably regarded as disgraceful, dishonourable, or unbecoming of a member of the profession by his well respected brethren in the group—persons of integrity and good reputation amongst the membership." *Law Society (Manitoba) v. Savino* (1983), 6 C.R.R. 336 at 343, [1983] 6 W.W.R. 538, 23 Man. R. (2d) 293, 1 D.L.R. (4th) 285 (C.A.), Monnin C.J.M. 2. " . . . [S]omething improper, disgraceful, or professionally inappropriate." *Forster v. Saskatchewan Teachers' Federation* (1992), 89 D.L.R. (4th) 283 at 286, [1992] 2 W.W.R. 651, 97 Sask. R. 98, 12 W.A.C. 98 (C.A.), the court per Gerwing J.A. 3. " . . . [F]or which a solicitor may be held personally responsible in costs to an opposite party need not be criminal and need not involve dishonesty. A mere mistake or error of judgment is not generally sufficient. It need not involve obliquity. It is conduct which involves a failure on the part of solicitor to fulfil his duty to the court and to realize his duty to aid in promoting in his own sphere the cause of justice." *Sonntag v. Sonntag* (1979), 11 C.P.C. 13 at 16, 24 O.R. (2d) 473 (H.C.), Vannini J. 4. On the part of a solicitor, conduct involving a failure to fulfill his duty to the court or to realize his duty to aid in promoting the cause of justice in his own sphere. A failure to observe the duty owed by the members of the profession to the public at large and to the state.

PROFESSIONAL ORDER. Any professional order listed in Schedule I to this Code or constituted in accordance with this Code; *Professional Code*, R.S.Q., chapter C-26, s. 1.

PROFESSIONAL PERSON. A physician, nurse, dentist or other health or mental health professional, a hospital administrator, a school principal, school teacher or other teaching professional, a social work administrator, social worker or other social service professional, a child care worker in any day care center or child caring institution, a police or law enforcement officer, a psychologist, a guidance counsellor, or a recreational services administrator or worker, and includes any other person who by virtue of his employment or occupation has a responsibility to discharge a duty of care towards a child. *Child and Family Services and Family Relations Act*, S.N.B. 1980, c. C-2.1, s. 30.

PROFESSIONAL PRIVILEGE. See LEGAL ~.

PROFESSIONAL SERVICES. Those services for which professional training is required as a prerequisite to performance.

PROFESSIONAL STRIKEBREAKER. A person who is not involved in a dispute and whose primary object, in the board's opinion, is (i) to prevent, interfere with or break up a lawful strike; or (b) to assist an employer in a lockout.

PROFESSIONAL SYNDICATE. 15 persons or more, Canadian citizens, engaged in the same profession, the same employment or in similar trades, or doing correlated work having for object the establishing of a determined product, may make and sign a memorandum setting forth their intention of forming an association or professional syndicate. *Professional Syndicates Act*, R.S.Q., c. S-40, s. 1.

PROFILING. See DNA ~.

PROFIT. *n.* 1. " . . . [T]he profit of a trade or business is the surplus by which the receipts from the trade or business exceed the expenditure necessary for the purpose of earning those receipts." *Russell v. Town & Country Bank* (1888), 13 App. Cas. 418 at 424 (U.K.) Lord Herschell. 2. The difference between the receipts of a trade or business and the expenditures made to earn those receipts. See ACCUMU-LATED ~S; GROSS ~; INCORPOREAL HEREDITAMENT; ~S; MESNE ~; NET ~; OPERATING ~; ~S; PROSPECTIVE LOSS OF EARNINGS OR ~S; SECRET ~.

PROFIT AND LOSS. The gain or loss which results when goods are bought or sold or when any other business is carried on.

PROFIT À PRENDRE. [Fr.] 1. " . . . [A] right to take something off the land of another person. . . more fully defined as a right to enter on the land of another person and take some profit of the soil such as minerals, oil, stones, trees, turf, fish or game, for the use of the owner of the right. It is an incorporeal hereditament, and unlike an easement it is not necessarily appurtenant to a dominant tenement but may be held as a right in gross, and as such may be assigned and dealt with as a valuable interest according to the ordinary rules of property." *Cherry v. Petch*, [1948] O.W.N. 378 at 380 (H.C.), Wells J. 2. " . . . [I]t is the right of severance which results in the holder of the profit à prendre acquiring title to the thing severed. The holder of the profit does not own the minerals in situ. They form part of the fee. What he owns are mineral claims and the right to exploit them . . ." *British Columbia v. Tener* (1985), 36 R.P.R. 291 at 309, [1985] 1 S.C.R. 533, [1985] 3 W.W.R. 673, 32 L.C.R. 340, 17 D.L.R. (4th) 1, 59 N.R. 82, 28 B.C.L.R.

(2d) 241, Wilson J. (dissenting) (Dickson C.J. concurring).

PROFIT A PRENDRE IN ALIENO SOLO. [FR. and L.] The right to take something from the soil of another.

PROFITS. *n.* " . . . [T]hat surplus in the taxation period by which the receipts from trade or business exceed the expenditures necessary for the purpose of earning those receipts." *Canada (Minister of National Revenue) v. Anaconda American Brass Ltd*, [1954] C.T.C. 335 at 349, [1954] S.C.R. 737, 54 D.T.C. 1179, [1955] 1 D.L.R. 529, Estey J. See PROFIT.

PROFIT SHARING PLAN. An arrangement under which payments computed by reference to an employer's profits from the employer's business, or by reference to those profits and the profits, if any, from the business of a corporation with which the employer does not deal at arm's length, are or have been made by the employer to a trustee in trust for the benefit of employees or former employees of that employer. *Income Tax Act*, R.S.C. 1985, c.1 (5th Supp.), s. 147(1). See DEFERRED ~.

PRO FORMA. [L.] In order to observe proper form.

PROGNOSIS. *n.* Only a doctor's representations about real and substantial future possibilities to the particular patient, which are factually based on a patient's existing condition, may be the foundation for a claim in negligent misrepresentation. Generally speaking, a doctor's opinion on a patient's prognosis need not include more. *Kelly v. Lundgard*, [2001] 9 W.W.R. 399, 2001 ABCA 185 (C.A.).

PROGRAM. *n.* 1. A plan of individual intervention or provision of safe shelter and appropriate counselling to residents in need. 2. A series or group of courses leading to a statement of standing. 3. Sounds or visual images, or a combination of sounds and visual images, that are intended to inform, enlighten or entertain, but does not include visual images, whether or not combined with sounds, that consist predominantly of alphanumeric text. *Broadcasting Act*, S.C. 1991, c. 11, s. 2(1). See AMBULANCE SERVICES ~; APPLICATION ~; APPRENTICESHIP ~; COMPUTER ~; DRIVER IMPROVEMENT ~; EXPLORATORY ~; FOREST MANAGEMENT ~; INCENTIVE ~; JOB TRAINING ~; MANAGEMENT ~; MANDATORY ALLOCATION ~; MANPOWER ~S AND SERVICES; NON-

PROFIT ~ OF CAMPING; OCCUPATIONAL TRAINING ~; RATIONING ~; RECREATION ~; REHABILITATION ~; RESEARCH ~; SCHOOL ~; SERVICES AND ~S; TRAINING ~; TREATMENT ~; WORK EXPERIENCE ~.

PROGRAMMING. *n.* 1. "[In s. 3(d) of the Broadcasting Act, R.S.C. 1970, c. B-11] . . . extends to more than the mere words which go out over the air but the total process of gathering, assembling and putting out the programmes generally . . ." *R. v. CKOY Ltd.* (1978), 40 C.P.R. (2d) 1 at 10, [1979] 1 S.C.R. 1, 43 C.C.C. (2d) 1, 90 D.L.R. (3d) 1, 24 N.R. 254, Spence J. (Ritchie J. concurring). 2. Audio signals or visual signals, or both, or the provision of such signals, were the signals are directed to the public at large by means of telecommunication facilities and (i) are designed to inform, enlighten or entertain; or (ii) that, in nature, character or substance, are similar to signals normally provided by television or radio broadcasting. 3. The ordered arrangement of programmes composing the schedule of a broadcasting station or of a cablecasting channel. See CABLECAST ~; COMMUNITY ~; EDUCATIONAL. ~; NON-~.

PROGRAMMING SERVICE. 1. Any broadcast of sound or visual matter by radio or television stations that is designed to inform, enlighten or entertain. 2. A program that is distributed by a licensee. *Broadcasting Distribution Regulations*, SOR/97-555, s. 1.

PROGRAMMING UNDERTAKING. An undertaking for the transmission of programs, either directly by radio waves or other means of telecommunication or indirectly through a distribution undertaking, for reception by the public by means of broadcasting receiving apparatus. *Broadcasting Act*, S.C. 1991, c. 11, s. 2(1).

PROGRAM OF INSTRUCTION. A course of instruction in a vocation, trades, technical or technological field of education or a related general course of instruction, a course taught in a school or institute for instruction of apprentices, correspondence study courses, study courses for disabled persons and study of practical courses for vocational, trades, technical or technological teachers.

PROGRAM OF PHYSIOTHERAPY. A program planned, administered and evaluated by a physiotherapist and may include the use of such mediums as exercise, massage, manipulations, hydrotherapy, radiant, mechanical and electrical energy. *The Physiotherapists Act*, R.S.M. 1987, c. P65, s. 1.

PROGRAM OF STUDY. See APPROVED ~.

PROGRAM TIME. Any period longer than two minutes during which a broadcaster does not normally present commercial messages, public service announcements or station or network identification. *Canada Elections Act*, S.C. 2000, c. 9, s. 344.

PROGRESS ADVANCES. The instalments of an approved loan advanced by the approved lender as the building construction progresses. *National Housing Loan Regulations*, C.R.C., c. 1108, s. 2.

PROGRESSIVE DISCIPLINE. Discipline in the workplace for violations. Describes proceeding by first warning, orally or in writing, then giving increasingly long suspensions and resorting last to termination to punish violations.

PROGRESSIVE REHABILITATION. Rehabilitation done continually and sequentially, within a reasonable time, during the entire period that the project continues. *Mining Act*, R.S.O. 1990, c. M.14, s. 139(1).

PROGRESSIVE TAX RATE STRUCTURE. A system in which the percentage of income paid in taxes increases with the taxpayer's income.

PROGRESSIVE WAGE INCREASE. A scheduled or periodic increment which is neither work nor performance related, in contrast to a merit raise.

PROGRESS PAYMENT. A payment made by or on behalf of Her Majesty under the terms of a contract after the performance of the part of the contract in respect of which the payment is made but before the performance of the whole contract. *Government Contracts Regulations* C.R.C., c. 701, s. 2.

PRO HAC VICE. [L.] For this particular occurrence.

PROHIBIT. *v.* " . . . '[F]orbid' . . ." *Krautt v. Paine* (1980), 17 R.P.R. 1 at 21, [1980] 6 W.W.R. 717, 118 D.L.R. (3d) 625, 25 A.R. 390 (C.A.), the court per Laycraft J.A.

PROHIBITED ACT. An act or omission that (a) impairs the efficiency or impedes the working of any vessel, vehicle, aircraft, machinery, apparatus or other thing; or (b) causes property, by whomever it may be owned, to be lost, damaged or destroyed. *Criminal Code*, R.S.C. 1985, c. C-46, s. 52(2).

PROHIBITED AMMUNITION. Ammunition, or a projectile of any kind, that is prescribed to be prohibited ammunition. *Criminal Code*, R.S.C. 1985, c. C-46, s. 84(1).

PROHIBITED DEGREE. The prohibited degrees of marriage. Subject to the exceptions listed, persons related by consanguinity, affinity or adoption are not prohibited from marrying each other by reason only of their relationship. No person shall marry another person if they are related (a) lineally by consanguinity or adoption; (b) as brother and sister by consanguinity, whether by the whole blood or by the half-blood; or (c) as brother and sister by adoption. *Marriage (Prohibited Degrees) Act*, S.C. 1990, c. 46. See AFFINITY.

PROHIBITED DEVICE. (*a*) Any component or part of a weapon, or any accessory for use with a weapon, that is prescribed to be a prohibited device, (*b*) a handgun barrel that is equal to or less than 105 mm in length, but does not include any such handgun barrel that is prescribed, where the handgun barrel is for use in international sporting competitions governed by the rules of the International Shooting Union, (*c*) a device or contrivance designed or intended to muffle or stop the sound or report of a firearm, (*d*) a cartridge magazine that is prescribed to be a prohibited device, or (*e*) a replica firearm; *Criminal Code*, R.S.C. 1985, c. C-46, s. 84(1).

PROHIBITED FIREARM. (*a*) A handgun that (i) has a barrel equal to or less than 105 mm in length, or (ii) is designed or adapted to discharge a 25 or 32 calibre cartridge, but does not include any such handgun that is prescribed, where the handgun is for use in international sporting competitions governed by the rules of the International Shooting Union, (*b*) a firearm that is adapted from a rifle or shotgun, whether by sawing, cutting or any other alteration, and that, as so adapted, (i) is less than 660 mm in length, or (ii) is 660 mm or greater in length and has a barrel less than 457 mm in length, (*c*) an automatic firearm, whether or not it has been altered to discharge only one projectile with one pressure of the trigger, or (*d*) any firearm that is prescribed to be a prohibited firearm. *Criminal Code*, R.S.C. 1985, c. C-46, s. 84(1).

PROHIBITED HOURS. The hours during which the hunting of a specified species of wildlife in a locality is prohibited.

PROHIBITED MARK. A mark adopted and used by a public authority and protected under the Trade Marks Act from use by other persons.

PROHIBITED PLACE. (a) Any work of defence belonging to or occupied or used by or on behalf of Her Majesty, including arsenals, armed forces establishments or stations, factories, dockyards, mines, minefields, camps, ships, aircraft, telegraph, telephone, wireless or signal stations or offices, and places used for the purpose of building, repairing, making or storing any munitions of war or any sketches, plans, models or documents relating thereto, or for the purpose of getting any metals, oil or minerals for use in time of war; (b) any place not belonging to Her Majesty where any munitions of war or any sketches, plans, models or documents relating thereto are being made, repaired, obtained or stored under contract with, or with any person on behalf of, Her Majesty or otherwise on behalf of Her Majesty; and (c) any place that is for the time being declared by order of the Governor in Council to be a prohibited place on the ground that information with respect thereto or damage thereto would be useful to a foreign power. *Official Secrets Act*, R.S.C. 1985, c. O-5, s. 2.

PROHIBITED WEAPON. (*a*) A knife that has a blade that opens automatically by gravity or centrifugal force or by hand pressure applied to a button, spring or other device in or attached to the handle of the knife, or (*b*) any weapon, other than a firearm, that is prescribed to be a prohibited weapon. *Criminal Code*, R.S.C. 1985, c. C-46, s. 84(1).

PROHIBITION. *n*. 1. An order of the court which lies to prevent a tribunal from acting or continuing to act in excess of its jurisdiction or contrary to the rules of natural justice. 2. An order to prevent a person from driving a motor vehicle. See WRIT OF ~.

PROHIBITION ORDER. An order made under this Act or any other Act of Parliament prohibiting a person from possessing any firearm, cross-bow, prohibited weapon, restricted weapon, prohibited device, ammunition, prohibited ammunition or explosive substance, or all such things. *Criminal Code*, R.S.C. 1985, c. C-46, s. 84(1).

PROHIBITORY INJUNCTION. An injunction restraining the doing or continuance of a wrongful act.

PRO INDIVISO. [L.] As not divided.

PRO INTERESSE SUO. [L.] In respect of one's own interest.

PROJECT. *n*. A place where the building, construction, improvement, repair, alteration, reconstruction, demolition or excavating of any building structure, road, bridge, pipeline, wharf or marine structure, excavation or tunnel is being carried on. See ABATEMENT ~; BUILDING ~; CONDOMINIUM ~; CONSTRUCTION ~; DEFENCE ~S; DEMONSTRATION OR RESEARCH ~; EDUCATIONAL ~; ENERGY USE ~; EXPERIMENTAL ~; FOREST INDUSTRY ~; HIGHWAY ~ AREA; HOSPITAL ~; HOUSING ~; JOB CREATION ~; POWER ~; PUBLIC HOUSING ~; REGULATED ~; SELF-LIQUIDATING ~; SEWAGE TREATMENT ~; SEWERAGE ~; SPECIAL ~; TANKER~; TURNKEY ~; WATER MANAGEMENT ~; WATER SUPPLY ~; WORK ACTIVITY ~.

PROJECTION EQUIPMENT. The equipment necessary or used for the transducing from a film to moving images, including equipment for accompanying sound. *Theatres Act*, R.S.O. 1990, c. T.6, s. 1.

PROJECTIONIST. *n*. 1. A person who operates projection equipment. *Theatres Act*, R.S.O. 1990, c. T.6, s. 1. 2. A person, employee or otherwise, who operates or manipulates a kinematograph in a theatre.

PROJECTION ROOM. The room in which projection equipment is located while in use. *Theatres Act*, R.S.O. 1990, c. T.6, s. 1.

PROJECTOR. *n*. The equipment necessary or used for the transducing from a film to moving images, including equipment for accompanying sound. *Theatres Act*, R.S.O. 1990, c. T.6, s. 1.

PROJECT SITE. Any building, structure, premises, water or land where construction is carried on.

PRO LAESIONE FIDEI. [L.] For breach of faith.

PROLEM ANTE MATRIMONIUM NATAM, ITA UT POST LEGITIMAM, LEX CIVILIS SUCCEDERE FACIT IN HAEREDITATE PARENTUM; SED PROLEM, QUAM MATRIMONIUM NON PARIT, SUCCEDERE NON SINIT LEX ANGLORUM. [L.] Civil law permits offspring born before marriage, as long as they are afterwards legitimised, to be their parents' heirs; but English law does not permit offspring not produced by marriage to succeed.

PROLES. *n*. [L.] Offspring.

PROLICIDE. *n*. The killing of human offspring.

PROLIXITY. *n*. " . . . [A]pplied to pleadings . . . taken to imply length and wordiness; diffuseness, discussion at great length; tediousness. . ." *Maclean v. Kingdon Printing* Co. (1908), 9 W.L.R. 370 at 371, Cameron J.

PROLONGED DISABILITY. See SERIOUS OR ~.

PROMISE. *n*. An undertaking as to future conduct; agreeing to act or refrain from acting in a certain way in order to benefit another person. See BREACH OF ~ TO MARRY; CONTRACTUAL ~; DONATIVE ~; GRATUITOUS ~; MUTUAL ~S.

PROMISEE. *n*. One to whom one makes a promise.

PROMISE TO APPEAR. A promise in Form 10 given to an officer in charge. *Criminal Code*, R.S.C. 1985, c. C-46, s. 493.

PROMISOR. *n*. One who makes a promise.

PROMISSORY ESTOPPEL. " . . . The party relying on the doctrine must establish that the other party has, by words or conduct, made a promise or assurance which was intended to affect their legal relationship and to be acted on. Furthermore, the representee must establish that, in reliance on the representation, he acted on it or in some way changed his position. . ." *Manacle v. Travellers Indemnity Co. of Canada* (1991), 50 C.P.C. (2d) 213 at 220, I.L.R. 1-2728, 125 N.R. 294, 3 O.R. (3d) 510n, 80 D.L.R. (4th) 652, 3 C.C.L.I. (2d) 186, 47 O.A.C. 333, [1991] 2 S.C.R. 50, the court per Sopinka J.

PROMISSORY NOTE. An unconditional promise in writing made by one person to another person, signed by the maker, engaging to pay, on demand or at a fixed or determinable future time, a sum certain in money to, or to the order of, a specified person or to bearer. *Bills of Exchange Act*, R.S.C. 1985, c. B-4, s. 176. See CONSUMER NOTE.

PROMOTE. *v*. " . . . [I]ndicates active support or instigation. . ." *R. v. Keegstra* (1990), 61 C.C.C. (3d) 1 at 59, 1 C.R. (4th) 129, 77 Alta. L.R. (2d) 193, [1991] 2 W.W.R. 1, 117 N.R. 1, 114 A.R. 81, 3 C.R.R. (2d) 193, [1990] 3 S.C.R.

697, Dickson C.J.C. (Wilson, L'Heureux-Dubé and Gonthier JJ. concurring).

PROMOTE HATRED. 1. "[In s. 319(2) of the Criminal Code, R.S.C. 1985, c. C-46] . . . indicates active support or instigation. Indeed, the French version of the offence uses the verb 'fomenter', which in English means to foment or stir up. In 'promotes' we thus have a word that indicates more than simple encouragement or advancement. The hatemonger must intend or foresee as substantially certain direct and active stimulation of hatred against an identifiable group." *R. v. Keegstra* (1990), 3 C.R.R. (2d) 193 at 249, 1 C.R. (4th) 129, 77 Alta. L.R. (2d) 193, [1991] 2 W.W.R. 1, 61 C.C.C. (3d) 1, 117 N.R. 1, 114 A.R. 81, [1990] 3 S.C.R. 697, Dickson C.J.C. (Wilson, L'Heureux-Dubé and Gonthier JJ. concurring). 2. " . . . [T]o instill detestation, enmity, ill-will and malevolence in another. . ." *R. v. Andrews* (1988), 39 C.R.R. 36 at 56, 28 O.A.C. 161, 65 C.R. (3d) 320, 65 O.R. (2d) 161, 43 C.C.C. (3d) 193 (C.A.), Cory J.A.

PROMOTER. *n*. 1. When used in relation to an issuer, a person who (a) acting alone or in concert with one or more other persons, directly or indirectly, takes the initiative in founding, organizing or substantially reorganizing the business of the issuer; or (b) in connection with the founding, organization or substantial reorganization of the business of the issuer, directly or indirectly receives, in consideration of services or property or both, 10% or more of a class of the issuer's own securities or 10% or more of the proceeds from the sale of a class of the issuer's own securities of a particular issue but does not include a person who (c) receives securities or proceeds referred to in paragraph (b) solely (i) as underwriting commissions; or (ii) in consideration for property; and (d) does not otherwise take part in founding, organizing or substantially reorganizing the business. 2. A person named in the application or petition for incorporation. 3. An individual who enters into a contract on behalf of a company not yet, but about to be, incorporated.

PROMOTION. *n*. A change of employment from one class to another having a higher maximum salary. See TOURISM ~.

PROMOTIONAL AGENCY. All persons and firms carrying on business or acting as agents or otherwise, to promote, further, organize, develop, manage, administer, or otherwise control or assist in the promotion, organization, development or management of any undertaking whatsoever. *Charities Endorsement Act*, R.S.M. 1987, c. C60, s. 1.

PROMOTIONAL DISTRIBUTION. The provision by a person to another person of tangible personal property that is, in the opinion of the commissioner, provided for one or more of the following purposes: (a) to describe, promote or encourage the purchase, consumption or use of tangible personal property; (b) to furnish or distribute to a person a catalogue, directory, listing or compilation of persons, places, prices, services, commodities or places of business in respect of the purchase, consumption or use of tangible personal property; or (c) for a purpose, function or use prescribed by the Lieutenant Governor in Council as a promotional distribution.

PROMOTIONAL DISTRIBUTOR. Any person who, within a province, provides, by way of promotional distribution to another person, goods whose fair value (i) exceeds the amount of the payment specifically made therefor by the person to whom the goods are provided; or (ii) is not specifically charged to and required to be paid by the person to whom the goods are provided.

PROMOTIONAL POOL. A swimming pool used solely for commercial display and demonstration purposes.

PROMOTION LIST. A list of persons who have passed a promotion examination for a particular class. *Civil Service acts*.

PROMPT. *adj*. " . . . '[I]mmediately' . . . 'with alacrity. . ." *Filiatrault v. Zurich Insurnace Co.*, [1981] I.L.R. 1-1440 at 511, 126 D.L.R. (3d) 555 (B.C. S.C.), Esson J.

PROMPTLY. *adv*. "[In s. 10(a) of the Charter] . . . immediately or forthwith." *R. v. Vautour* (1987), 62 Nfld. & P.E.I.R. 143 at 145, 190 A.P.R. 143, 20 C.R.R. 268 (Nfld. C.A.), the court per Morgan J.A.

PROMULGATION. *n*. The act of publishing.

PROMUTUUM. *n*. A quasi-contract, by which the person who received a certain sum of money or a certain quantity of fungible items by mistake agrees to restore them.

PRONOTARY. *n*. The first notary.

PRONOUNCED. *adj*. "If the judicial opinion, oral or written, is not pronounced or delivered in open Court, then it cannot be said to be pronounced or delivered until the parties are notified of it." *Fawkes v. Swayzie* (1899), 31 O.R. 256 at 261 (C.A.), the court per Armour C.J.

PROOF. *n*. 1. Testimony; evidence. 2. Of a will, obtaining probate of it. 3. The strength of spirits, obtained by multiplying the percentage of alcohol by volume by 1.75 in Britain and Canada and by 2 in the United States. So, pure alcohol is 175 British and Canadian proof, 200 U.S.A. proof. F.A. Jaffe, *A Guide to Pathological Evidence*, 3d ed. (Toronto: Carswell, 1991) at 96. See BURDEN OF ~; LITERAL ~; ONUS OF ~; POLICY ~ OF INTEREST; STANDARD OF ~; TESTIMONIAL ~; UPON ~.

PROOF LINE. A line surveyed across one or more concessions in the original survey of a single front township or of a double front township to govern the course of a side line of a lot. *Surveys Act*, R.S.O. 1990, c. S.30, s. 1.

PROOF OF FINANCIAL RESPONSIBILITY. A certificate of insurance, a bond or a deposit of money or securities given or made.

PROOF OF SERVICE. Proof provided by the affidavit of the person who served it, by a certificate of service or by a solicitor's written admission or acceptance of the service or in accordance with rules regarding document exchanges.

PROOFREADING. *n*. The examination and correction of typographical details or of illustrations on sheets printed from type or plates and includes the verification of numbers contained in tables and documents. *Translation Bureau Regulations*, C.R.C., c. 1561, s. 2.

PROPAGANDA. Information used to support a doctrine or interest. See HATE ~.

PROPANE. *n*. 1. In addition to its normal scientific meaning, a mixture mainly of propane, which may ordinarily contain some ethane or butanes. 2. A hydrocarbon consisting of 95 per cent or more of propane, propylene, butane or butylene, or any blend thereof. *Ontario Energy Board Act*, R.S.O. 1990, c. 0.13, s. 1(1).

PROPANE BULK PLANT. A facility that is used primarily for the storage of liquefied petroleum gas before distribution to persons outside the facility or other places.

PROPANE IN BULK. Propane stored, transported or transferred by any means other than in a fuel tank of a motor vehicle in which propane for generating power in the motor vehicle is kept. *Gasoline Tax Act*, R.S.O. 1990, c. G.5, s. 1.

PROP. COMP. BD. *abbr*. Property Compensation Board.

PROPELLANT. n, The powder in a cartridge which the primer ignites and which propels a projectile. F.A. Jaffe, *A Guide to Pathological Evidence*, 3d ed. (Toronto: Carswell, 1991) at 224.

PROPER. *adj*. Correct, fit, suitable.

PROPER CAUSE. A nexus or reasonable relationship between an employee's misconduct and the employer's response by way of discipline or termination of the employee.

PROPER FORM. Regular on its face with regard to all formal matters.

PROPER LAW. 1. The system of law which the parties intend to govern the contract, or, if their intention is not expressed or inferred from their circumstances, the system of law with which the transaction is most closely and really connected. G.H.L. Fridman, *Sale of Goods in Canada*, 3d ed. (Toronto: Carswell, 1986) at 473. 2. What determines the lex causae by referring to every fact in the individual case. J.G. McLeod, *The Conflict of Laws* (Calgary: Carswell, 1983) at 195.

PROPERLY PACKED. That the produce is not slack, overpressed or otherwise in a condition likely to result in permanent damage during handling or in transit.

PROPER MAINTENANCE AND SUPPORT. In relation to a person not having made adequate provision for a spouse in a will, that which is adequate in light of the standard of living to which the spouse is entitled and proper in light of the obligations which the law would impose on the deceased if he were alive. The word "proper" requires a reflection of society's expectations of what a judicious person would do in the circumstances, having reference to contemporary community standards.

PROPER NAME. In respect of an ingredient of a natural health product, one of the following: (*a*) if the ingredient is a vitamin, the name for that vitamin set out in item 3 of Schedule 1; (*b*) if the ingredient is a plant or a plant material, an alga, a bacterium, a fungus, a non-human animal material or a probiotic, the Latin nomenclature of its genus and, if any, its specific epithet; and (*c*) if the ingredient is other than one described in paragraphs (*a*) or (*b*), the chemical name of the ingredient. *Natural Health Products Regulations*, SOR/2003-196, s. 1.

PROPER QUESTION. 1. In relation to a cross-examination on an affidavit, a question which is relevant to the issue in relation to which the affidavit was given or to the credibility of the witness, is fair, and is asked with the intention that it be directed at the issue in the case or the credibility of the witness. 2. Relevant to the issues raised and allegations made in the pleadings.

PROPERTY. *n*. 1. "The plain and ordinary meaning of 'property' is legal title and not a contingent future equitable right to reacquire property which one does not presently hold." *Canada Trustco Mortgage Corp. v. Port O'Call Hotel Inc.*, (sub nom. *Alberta (Treasury Branches) v. Minister of National Revenue*) [1996] 1 S.C.R. 963, Major J. (dissenting) (Iacobucci J. concurring). 2. " . . . [I]n its ordinary sense may include both personalty and realty. But in any partricular case its meaning must be gathered from the whole of the instrument." *London Guarantee & Accident Co. v. George* (1906), 3 W.L.R. 236 at 238, 16 Man. R. 132 (K.B.), Richards J. 3. " . . . [E]ven in its widest sense, is limited to things which are capable of ownership and which are transferable or assignable. It does not include purely personal rights such as the right to personal safety . . . the right to privacy or the right to be free from physical restraint. None of these are considered subject to ownership in the ordinary sense. . ." *Marr v. Marr Estate* (1989), 71 Alta. L.R. (2d) 168 at 176, 63 D.L.R. (4th) 500, 101 A.R. 43, [1990] 2 W.W.R. 638 (Q.B.), O'Leary J. 4. " . . . [A] broad term which embraces choses in action. . ." *Herchuk v. Herchuk* (1983), 35 R.F.L. (2d) 327 at 336, [1983] 6 W.W.R. 474 (Alta. C.A.), the court per Stevenson J.A. 5. " . . . [I]mports the right to exclude others from the enjoyment of, interference with or appropriation of a specific legal right. . . *National Trust Co. v. Bouckhuyt* (1987), 38 B.L.R. 77 at 86, 46 R.P.R. 221, 21 C.P.C. (2d) 226, 7 P.P.S.A.C. 273, 23 O.A.C. 40, 61 O.R. (2d) 640, 43 D.L.R. (4th) 543 (C.A.), the court per Cory J.A. 6. " . . . [A] word of wide signification and certainly includes money." *R. v. Ruggles* (1973), 21 C.R.N.S. 39 at 360, 12 C.C.C. (2d) 65 (Ont. C.A.), the court per Schroeder J.A. See AFTER-ACQUIRED ~; AGRICULTURAL ~; ARCHAEOLOGICAL ~; ASSESSABLE ~; BUSINESS ~; CAPITAL ~; COMMERCIAL ~; COMMON ~; COMMUNAL ~; COMMUNITY ~; CONSULAR ~; CORPOREAL ~; CROWN -,~; CULTURAL ~; DEFENCE ~; DESIGN ~; DURESS OF ~; ESTATE AND ~; ESTATE OR ~; FAMILY ~; FARM ~; FEDERAL ~; FOREST ~; GOVERNMENT ~; HERITAGE ~; HISTORIC ~; IDENTICAL ~; IMPUTED INCOME FROM ~; INCLOSED ~; INCOME FROM A BUSINESS (OR ~); INCOME FROM ~; INDUSTRIAL AND INTELLECTUAL ~; INDUSTRIAL ~; INTANGIBLE ~; MARITAL ~; MARRIED WOMEN'S ~ ACT; MATRIMONIAL ~; MINING ~; MIXED ~; MOVABLE ~; MOVEABLE ~; NON-PUBLIC ~; NON-SEGREGATED ~; OIL AND GAS ~; OTHER ~; PARTNERSHIP ~; PERISHABLE ~; PERSONAL ~; POTENTIAL ~; PROTECTED ~; PROVINCIAL ~; PUBLIC ~; QUALIFIED ~; RATEABLE ~; REAL ~; RECREATIONAL ~; RENTAL ~; REPLACEMENT ~; RESIDENTIAL ~; RESOURCE ~; SPECIAL ~; TANGIBLE ~; TAXABLE MUNICIPAL ~; TAXABLE ~; UNSIGHTLY ~.

PROPERTY AND CASUALTY COMPANY. A company or a provincial company that is not a life company. *Insurance Companies Act*, S.C. 1991, c. 47, s. 2.

PROPERTY AND CIVIL RIGHTS. A subject in relation to which provincial legislatures have power to make laws under section 92(13) of the Constitution Act, 1867.

PROPERTY DAMAGE. Damage caused in an accident to an automobile or to other property.

PROPERTY DAMAGE INSURANCE. Insurance against loss or damage to property that is not included in or incidental to some other class of insurance defined by or under this Act. *Insurance acts*.

PROPERTY DIMENSION. The frontage, area, other dimension or other attribute that, in the opinion of the Minister, would be established by an assessment authority in respect of federal property as the basis for computing the amount of any frontage or area tax that would be applicable to that property if it were taxable property.

PROPERTY INSURANCE. Insurance against the loss of, or the damage to, property but does not include insurance coming within the class of aircraft insurance, automobile insurance, or hail insurance.

PROPERTY LAW. Law which deals with ownership, rights and interests in property. See PROVINCIAL ~.

PROPERTY LIABLE. See VALUE OF THE~.

PROPERTY OF A MEMBER. Anything, wherever situated, kept by, acquired by or given to a member by or for a client or other person where such thing in any way relates to his practice or former practice as a barrister or solicitor or the business or affairs of his clients or former clients, and whether or not such thing was acquired before or after he ceased to practise as a barrister or solicitor and, without restricting the generality of the foregoing, includes ledgers, books of account, records, files, documents, papers, securities, shares, trust money in cash or on deposit, negotiable instruments, corporate seals and chattels. *Barristers and Solicitors acts.*

PROPERTY OF THE DECEASED. All property the value of which is included in computing the aggregate net value of the property of the deceased for the purposes of this Act, and includes any property acquired by the executor of the deceased by one or more transactions effecting one or more substitutions. *Succession Duty acts.*

PROPERTY-OWNER. *var.* **PROPERTY OWNER**. Any person who possesses immoveable property in his own name as owner, as usufructuary, or as institute in cases of substitutions, or as possessor of Crown Lands with a promise of sale. Quebec statutes.

PROPERTY RIGHT. 1. Any estate, interest, power or other right in or with respect to land. *Quieting Titles Act*, R.S.N.S. 1989, c. 382, s. 2. 2. Any right or power in respect to any kind of property including things in action. *Conveyancing Act*, R.S.N.S. 1989, c. 97, s. 9(2).

PROPERTY TAX. Tax levied on property. *Petrofina Canada Ltd. v. Markland Developments Ltd.* (1977), 3 R.P.R. 33 at 37, 29 N.S.R. (2d) 158, 45 A.P.R. 158 (T.D.), Hallett J. See GENERAL ~.

PROPINQUI ET CONSANGUINEI. [L.] The nearest relative of a deceased person.

PROPINQUITY. *n.* Parentage; kindred.

PROPONENT. *n.* 1. A person who, (i) carries out or proposes to carry out an undertaking; or (ii) is the owner or person having charge, management or control of an undertaking. *Environmental Assessment acts.* 2. The holder of an unpatented mining claim or licence of occupation or an owner as defined in section 1. *Mining Act*, R.S.O. 1990, c. M.14, s. 139(1).

PROPORTION. See RATEABLE ~.

PROPORTIONALITY. *n.* Principle of sentencing expressed in the Criminal Code as follows: A sentence must be proportionate to the gravity of the offence and the degree of responsibility of the offender. *Criminal Code*, R.S.C. 1985, c. C-46, s. 718.1.

PROPORTIONALITY ANALYSIS. Used in assessing whether discriminatory legislation is demonstrably justified in a free and democratic society. The proportionality analysis comprises three branches. First, the connection between the goal and the discriminatory distinction is examined to ascertain if it is rational. Second, the law must impair the right no more than is reasonably necessary to accomplish the objective. Finally, if these two conditions are met, the court must weigh whether the effect of the discrimination is proportionate to the benefit thereby achieved. *Miron v. Trudel*, [1995] 2 S.C.R. 418.

PROPORTIONALITY TEST. "There are . . . three important components of a proportionality test. First, the measures adopted . . . must be rationally connected to the objective. Second, the means, even if rationally connected to the objective in this first sense, should impair 'as little as possible' the right or freedom in question . . . Third, there must be a proportionality between the effects of the measures which are responsible for limiting the Charter right or freedom, and the objective which has been identified as of 'sufficient importance'." *R. v. Oakes*, [1986] 1 S.C.R. 103 at 139, 50 C.R. (3d) 1, 14 O.A.C. 335, 19 C.R.R. 308, 24 C.C.C. (3d) 321, 26 D.L.R. (4th) 200, 65 N.R. 87, Dickson C.J.C. (Chouinard, Lamer, Wilson and Le Dain JJ. concurring).

PROPORTIONALLY. *adv.* In due proportion; corresponding in degree or amount.

PROPORTIONAL TAX RATE STRUCTURE. A system whereby the percentage of income paid in taxes does not vary with the taxpayer's income.

PROPORTIONATE TERMS. For the purposes of this section, an allowance is offered on proportionate terms only if (a) the allowance offered to a purchaser is in approximately the same proportion to the value of sales to him as the allowance offered to each competing purchaser is to the total value of sales to that competing purchaser; (b) in any case where advertising or other expenditures or services are exacted in return therefor, the cost thereof required to be incurred by a purchaser is in approximately the same proportion to the value of sales to him as the cost of the advertising or other expenditures or services required to be incurred by each competing purchaser is to the total value of sales to that competing purchaser; and (c) in any case where serices are exacted in return therefor, the requirements thereof have regard to the kinds of services that competing purchasers at the same or different levels of distribution are ordinarily able to perform or cause to be performed. *Competition Act*, R.S.C. 1985, c. C-34, s. 51(3).

PROPOSAL. *n.* 1. " . . . [B]asically a contract between the debtor and his creditors which gives the debtor as much or as little freedom over his actions as is agreed upon in such contract. In Dinovitzer v. Waiss (1957), 37 C.B.R. 160, Collins J. of the Quebec Superior Court in Bankruptcy said (p. 162): 'A proposal constitutes an offer made by an insolvent person to his creditors which they are free to accept or reject. If it is accepted, it becomes binding on them in accordance with its terms when it is approved by the Court.'" *Bruce v. Neiff Joseph Land Surveyors Ltd.* (1977), (*sub nom. Neiff Joseph Land Surveyors Ltd. v. Bruce*) 23 C.B.R. (N.S.) 258 at 270 (N.S. C.A.), the court per Macdonald J.A. 2. (*a*) In any provision of Division I of Part III, a proposal made under that Division, and (*b*) in any other provision, a proposal made under Division I of Part III or a consumer proposal made under Division II of Part III and includes a proposal or consumer proposal, as the case may be, for a composition, for an extension of time or for a scheme or arrangement. *Bankruptcy and Insolvency Act*, R.S.C. 1985, c. B-3, s. 2. 3. An application for an insurance contract which particularizes any risks the applicant wants the insurer to undertake. Raoul Colinvaux, *The Law of Insurance*, 5th ed. (London: Sweet & Maxwell, 1984) at 18. See COUNTER ~.

PROPOSED TRADE-MARK. *var.* **PROPOSED TRADE MARK**. A mark that is proposed to be used by a person for the purpose of distinguishing or so as to distinguish wares or services manufactured, sold, leased, hired or performed by him from those manufactured, sold, leased, hired or performed by others. *Trade-Marks Act*, R.S.C. 1985, c. T-13, s. 2.

PROPOSED UNIT. Land described in an agreement of purchase and sale that provides for delivery to the purchaser or a deed or transfer capable of registration after a declaration and description have been registered in respect of the land. *Condominium acts.*

PROPOSITION. *n.* One logical sentence.

PROPOSITUS. *n.* [L. the one proposed] The person from whom one traces descent.

PROPOUND. *v.* With respect to a will, to offer as authentic.

PROPRIETARY. *n.* One who has property.

PROPRIETARY. *adj.* Owned by a private organization or an individual and operated for profit.

PROPRIETARY CHARGE. The charge a province levies to exercise proprietary rights over its public property, i.e. a licence fee, rent or royalty paid to exploit provincially-owned natural resources or a charge for the sale of books, electricity, liquor, rail travel or any goods or services the province supplies in a commercial way. P.W. Hogg, *Constitutional Law of Canada*, 3d ed. (Toronto: Carswell, 1992) at 749.

PROPRIETARY ESTOPPEL. Estoppel by encouragement or acquiescence. Arises where one party knowingly encourages another to act or acquiesces in the other's actions to his detriment and infringing his rights. The party who encouraged or acquiesced cannot later complain about the infringement or detriment he suffered.

PROPRIETARY LEASE. A lease, agreement or arrangement by which a person acquires: (i) a tenancy, or an extension of an existing tenancy, of residential premises; and (ii) a direct or indirect ownership interest in residential premises through any agreement or arrangement that includes the acquisition of shares of, or a membership interest in, a corporation, other than a co-operative incorporated or continued pursuant to The Co-operatives Act, 1989. *Condominium Property Act, 1993*, S.S. 1993, c. C-26.1, s. 13.

PROPRIETARY MEDICINE. A drug that (i) is in a form in which it is ready for use by the consumer according to the directions for use recommended by the manufacturer without requiring any further manufacturing or processing; and (ii) is sold for use in respect of humans in accordance with the provisions of the Food and Drugs Act (Canada).

PROPRIETARY RIGHT. 1. Concerning information, entitlement to access to it. 2. An interest as owner or lessee or an interest under an agreement authorizing the right to use, distribute or exhibit a film.

PROPRIETAS DEDUCTA USUFRUCTU. [L.] Ownership with no usufruct.

PROPRIETAS NUDA. [L.] Bare ownership.

PROPRIETAS VERBORUM EST SALUS PROPRIETATUM. [L.] The proper signification of words is the salvation of property.

PROPRIETOR. *n.* 1. The owner, lessee or other person in lawful possession of any property. 2. In relation to a business enterprise, means the person by whom the enterprise is carried on or is about to be carried on, whether as sole proprietor or in association or partnership with any other person having a proprietary interest therein, but does not include Her Majesty or an agent of Her Majesty in right of Canada or a province, a municipality or a municipal or other public body that performs a function of government. *Small Business Loans Act*, R.S.C. 1985, c. S-11, s. 2. 3. The author of any design unless that person executed the design for another person in exchange for a good or valuable consideration. H.G. Fox, *The Canadian Law of Copyright and Industrial Designs*, 2d ed. (Toronto: Carswell, 1967) at 673. See HOSPITAL ~.

PROPRIETORSHIP. *n.* One who carries on business under a name other than one's own. See SOLE ~.

PROPRIO MOTU. [L.] On his own motion.

PROPRIO MOTU, NUNC PRO TUNC, EX POST FACTO. [L.] Of its own motion, now as of the previous date, for something done after.

PROPRIO VIGORE. [L.] By its own strength.

PRO PRIVATO COMMODO. [L.] For private advantage.

PROPTER. *prep.* [L.] Because of.

PROPTER DEFECTUM SANGUINIS. [L.] Because of the failing of the bloodline.

PROPTER DELICTUM TENENTIS. [L.] Because of the wrong of the tenant.

PROPTER SAEVITIAM. [L.] Because of cruelty.

PROPTER SUSPICIONEM MORTIS. [L.] Because of a suspicion of death.

PROPULSION ENGINE. Any internal combustion engine which can directly or indirectly generate propulsion.

PROPULSIVE POWER. The power in kilowatts that is specified in a ship's certificate of registry. Canada Regulations.

PRO QUER. *abbr.* Pro querente.

PRO QUERENTE. [L.] For the plaintiff.

PRO RATA. [L.] In proportion, according to a certain percentage or rate.

PRO RATA EVALUATION. In marriage breakdown, a method to divide a spouse's pension based on the ratio of number of years of cohabitation to the number of years of service accumulated in the pension plan.

PRO RATA PARTE. [L.] Proportionately.

PRORATED. *adj.* Proportional.

PRO RE NATA. [L.] To meet some emergency, as an occasion arises.

PROROGATION. *n.* 1. Prolongation or postponement until another day. 2. The termination of a session of Parliament. A. Fraser, W.A. Dawson, & J. Holtby, eds., *Beauchesne's Rules and Forms of the House of Commons of Canada*, 6th ed. (Toronto: Carswell, 1989) at 66.

PROROGUE. *v.* To terminate a session of Parliament.

PROSECUTE. *v.* To commence proceedings and to carry the proceedings through to their ultimate conclusion including pursuing any available appeal rights.

PROSECUTION. *n.* 1. " . . . [I]mplies 'suit', but that is only one meaning of the word in its legal sense because it is just as much attributable to a pressing of claims without suit. . ." *Taylor v. Mackintosh*, [1924] 3 D.L.R. 926 at 932, [1924] 3 W.W.R. 97, 42 C.C.C. 327, 34 B.C.R. 56 (C.A.), Martin J.A. 2. The putting of an offender on trial. 3. "[In s. 45(2) of the Combines Investigation Act, R.S.C. 1970, c. C-23] . . . may be used to designate the presentation of the Crown's case as distinguished from evidence offered by the defence." *R v. Anthes Business Forms Ltd.* (1974), 16 C.P.R. (2d) 216 at 227, 19 C.C.C. (2d) 394 (Ont. H.C.), Grant J. See MALICIOUS ~; SUCCESSIVE ~.

PROSECUTION HISTORY ESTOPPEL. In the United States, representations to the Patent Office were historically noted on the file cover or "wrapper", and the doctrine is thus known in that country as "file wrapper estoppel" or "prosecution history estoppel". In its recent decision in *Warner-Jenkinson Co.*, [*Warner-Jenkinson Co. v. Hilton Davis Chemical Co.*, 520 U.S. 17 (Ohio, 1997)], the United States Supreme Court affirmed that a patent owner is precluded from claiming the benefit of the doctrine of equivalents to recapture ground conceded by limiting argument or amendment during negotiations with the Patent Office. The availability of file wrapper estoppel was affirmed, but it was narrowed in the interest of placing "reasonable limits on the doctrine of equivalents", *per* Thomas J., at p. 34. While prosecution history estoppel is still tied to amendments made to avoid the prior art, or otherwise to address a specific concern—such as obviousness—that arguably would have rendered the claimed subject matter unpatentable, the court placed the burden on the patentee to establish the reason for an amendment required during patent prosecution. Where no innocent explanation is established, the court will now presume that the Patent Office had a substantial reason related to patentability for including the limiting element added by amendment. In those circumstances, prosecution history estoppel bars the application of the doctrine of equivalents as to that element. The use of file wrapper estoppel in Canada was emphatically rejected by Thorson P. in *Lovell Manufacturing Co. v. Beatty Brothers Ltd.* (1962), 41 C.P.R. 18 (Can. Ex. Ct.), and our Federal Court has in general confirmed over the years the exclusion of file wrapper materials tendered for the purpose of construing the claims: see, e.g., *P.L.G. Research Ltd. v. Jannock Steel Fabricating Co.* (1991), 35 C.P.R. (3d) 346 (Fed. T.D.), at p. 349. No distinction is drawn in this regard between cases involving allegations of literal infringement and those involving substantive infringement. *Free World Trust c. Électro Santé Inc.*, [2000] 2 S.C.R. 1024, Binnie, J.

PROSECUTOR. *n*. 1. The Attorney General or, where the Attorney General does not intervene, means the person who institutes proceedings to which this Act applies, and includes counsel acting on behalf of either of them. *Criminal Code*, R.S.C. 1985, c. C-46, s. 2. 2. The Attorney General or, where the Attorney General does not intervene, the informant, and includes counsel or an agent acting on behalf of either of them. *Criminal Code*, R.S.C. 1985, c. C-46, s. 785. 3. The Attorney General or, where the Attorney General does not intervene, means the person who issues a certificate or lays an information and includes counsel or agent acting on behalf of either of them. *Provincial Offences Act*, R.S.O. 1990, c. P. 33, s. 1(1).

PROSECUTORIAL DISCRETION. Without being exhaustive, we believe the core elements of prosecutorial discretion encompass the following: (a) the discretion whether to bring the prosecution of a charge laid by police; (b) the discretion to enter a stay of proceedings in either a private or public prosecution, as codified in the *Criminal Code*, R.S.C. 1985, c. C-46, ss. 579 and 579.1; (c) the discretion to accept a guilty plea to a lesser charge; (d) the discretion to withdraw from criminal proceedings altogether: *R. v. Osborne* (1975), 25 C.C.C. (2d) 405 (N.B. C.A.); and (e) the discretion to take control of a private prosecution: *Osiowy v. Linn* (1989), 50 C.C.C. (3d) 189 (Sask. C.A.). While there are other discretionary decisions, these are the core of the delegated sovereign authority peculiar to the office of the Attorney General. Significantly, what is common to the various elements of prosecutorial discretion is that they involve the ultimate decisions as to *whether* a prosecution should be brought, continued or ceased, and *what* the prosecution ought to be for. Put differently, prosecutorial discretion refers to decisions regarding the nature and extent of the prosecution and the Attorney General's participation in it. Decisions that do not go to the nature and extent of the prosecution, i.e., the decisions that govern a Crown prosecutor's tactics or conduct before the court, do not fall within the scope of prosecutorial discretion. Rather, such decisions are governed by the inherent jurisdiction of the court to control its own processes once the Attorney General has elected to enter into that forum. It is a constitutional principle in this country that the Attorney General must act independently of partisan concerns when supervising prosecutorial decisions. This side of the Attorney General's independence finds further form in the principle that courts will not interfere with his exercise of executive authority, as reflected in the prosecutorial decision-making process. *Krieger v. Law Society (Alberta)*, [2002] 3 S.C.R. 372.

PROSPECT. *v*. To search for valuable mineral and includes any mode of working whereby soil or rock is disturbed, removed, washed or otherwise tested for the purpose of finding, identifying or determining the extent of any mineral therein.

PROSPECT AND TO EXPLORE. See TO ~.

PROSPECTING. *n*. 1. Includes trenching, stripping and drilling and performing geological, geophysical and geochemical surveys. 2. The investigating of, or searching for, minerals. *Mining* Act, R.S.O. 1990, c. M.14, s. 1.

PROSPECTING COMPANY. A company incorporated for the purpose of prospecting for a mineral or minerals.

PROSPECTIVE. *adj*. Governing the future and affecting vested rights.

PROSPECTIVE ADJUDICATION. A challenge to the employer's formulation of a rule or policy without an incident having occurred to trigger the operation of the rule or policy.

PROSPECTIVE BUYER. A prospective buyer is someone who has a prospect or expectation of buying something in the future. *Rosling Real Estate (Nelson) Ltd. v. Robertson Hilliard Cattell Realty Co.* (1999), 1999 CarswellBC 1554 (S.C.).

PROSPECTIVE LOSS OF EARNINGS OR PROFITS. A financial gain, primarily of wage or income, which the plaintiff would have made and which the plaintiff will now not be able to make because of injury. K.D. Cooper-Stephenson & I.B. Saunders, *Personal Injury Damages in Canada* (Toronto: Carswell, 1981) at 52.

PROSPECTOR. *n*. One who prospects or explores for minerals or develops a property for minerals on behalf of oneself, on behalf of oneself and others or as an employee.

PROSPECTUS. *n*. A document published by a corporation or persons acting on its behalf describing the nature and objects of an issue of shares or other securities of the company and inviting persons to subscribe for those shares or securities. See OFFERING MEMORANDUM ~; SHELF ~.

PROSTHESIS. *n*. A device intended to replace the whole or part of an organ or member of a human being. *Public Health Protection Act*, R.S.Q. 1977, c. P-35, s. 1.

PROSTHETIC APPLIANCE. Includes any artificial device necessary to support or take the place of a part of the body or to increase the efficiency of a sense organ.

PROSTHETIC SERVICE. See DENTAL ~.

PROSTITUTE. *n*. A person of either sex who engages in prostitution.

PROSTITUTION. *n*. " . . . [T]he exchange of sexual services of one person in return for payment by another." *Reference re ss. 193 & 195.1(1)(c) of the Criminal Code (Canada)* (1990), 48 C.R.R. 1 at 30, 77 C.R. (3d) 1, 56 C.C.C. (3d) 65, [1990] 4 W.W.R. 481, [1990] 1 S.C.R. 1123, 109 N.R. 81, 68 Man. R. (2d) 1, Lamer J.

PRO TANTO. [L. for so much] To such an extent.

PROTECTED. *adj*. 1. As applied to electrical equipment means the equipment is constructed so that the electrical parts are protected against damage from foreign objects. *Power Corporation Act*, R.R.O. 1980, Reg. 794, s. 0. 2. As applied to wildlife, means protected throughout the year, or for any open or closed season, pursuant to this Act or the regulations. *Wildlife Act*, R.S.N.S. 1989, c. 504, s. 3(1).

PROTECTED AREA. 1. A geographically defined expanse of land or water established under a legal and administrative framework designed specifically to ensure the protection and maintenance of biological diversity and of related natural and cultural resources. *Natural Heritage Conservation Act*, R.S.Q., c. C-61.01, s. 2. 2. An area surrounding a classified historic monument whose perimeter is determined by the Minister. *An Act to Amend the Cultural Property Act and Other Legislation*, S.Q. 1985, c. 24, s. 2.

PROTECTED INTERNEE. A person interned in Canada who is protected by the Geneva Convention set out in Schedule IV. *Geneva Conventions Act*, R.S.C. 1985, c. G-3, s. 4.

PROTECTED LOAN. A loan in respect of which protection is provided by contract under subsection 65(1). *National Housing Act*, R.S.C. 1985, c. N-11, s. 64.

PROTECTED PRISONER OF WAR. A prisoner of war who is protected by the Geneva Convention set out in Schedule III. *Geneva Conventions Act*, R.S.C. 1985, c. G-3, s. 4.

PROTECTED PROPERTY. Any property that has been designated protected property under this Act. *The Saskatchewan Heritage Act*, R.S.S. 1978, c. S-22, s. 2.

PROTECTED SPECIES. A species or type of animal listed in Division 6 of Schedule A or declared by the regulations to be a protected species, or any part thereof. *Wildlife Act*, S.M. 1980, c. 73, s. 1.

PROTECTING POWER. (a) In relation to a protected prisoner of war, the country or organization that is carrying out, in the interests of the country of which that prisoner is a national or of whose forces that prisoner is or was a member at the time of his being taken prisoner of war, the duties assigned to protecting powers under the Geneva Convention set out in Schedule III; and (b) in relation to a protected internee, the country or organization that is carrying out, in the interests of the country of which that internee is or was a national at the time of his internment, the duties assigned to protecting powers under the Geneva Convention set out in Schedule IV. *Geneva Convention Act*, R.S.C. 1985, c. G-3, s. 4.

PROTECTION. *n*. 1. Of the lien, to register a claim for lien, to shelter under a certificate of action or to give notice of the lien to certain people. 2. In respect of a protectee, may include relocation, accommodation and change of identity as well as counselling and financial support for those or any other purposes in order to ensure the security of the protectee or to facilitate the protectee's re-establishment or becoming self-sufficient. *Witness Protection Program Act*, S.C. 1996, c. 15, s. 2. See CONSUMER ~; LEGIS-LATION; DIPLOMATIC ~; FIRE ~; IN NEED OF ~; LOW-VOLTAGE ~; PASSIVE OCCUPANT ~; RESOURCE ~ AND DE-VELOPMENT SERVICE; STATION ~ SIG-NAL.

PROTECTION OFFICER. (a) A fishery officer within the meaning of the Fisheries Act; (b) an officer of the Royal Canadian Mounted Police.

PROTECTION OF MINORITIES. The fourth underlying constitutional principle we address here concerns the protection of minorities. There are a number of specific constitutional provisions protecting minority language, religion and education rights. Some of those provisions are, as we have recognized on a number of occasions, the product of historical compromises. However, we highlight that even though those provisions were the product of negotiation and political compromise, that does not render them unprincipled. Rather, such a concern reflects a broader principle related to the protection of minority rights. We emphasize that the protection of minority rights is itself an independent principle underlying our constitutional order. *Reference re Secession of Quebec*, [1998] 2 S.C.R. 217 Per curiam.

PROTECTION OF PUBLIC AUTHORI-TIES. A provision which protects justices of the peace, constables, tribunal members or other public authorities from actions for anything done pursuant to a statute.

PROTECTIO TRAHIT SUBJECTIONEM, ET SUBJECTIO PROTECTIONEM. [L.] Protection includes subjugation, and subjugation protection.

PROTECTIVE BREATHING EQUIP-MENT. Equipment designed to cover the eyes, nose and mouth of the wearer, or the nose and mouth where accessory equipment is provided to protect the eyes, and to protect the wearer from the effects of smoke, carbon dioxide or other harmful gases; *Canadian Aviation Regulations*, SOR/96-433, s. 101.01.

PROTECTIVE CARE. A service which provides an immediate safeguard for a child's security and development. *Child and Family Services and Family Relations Act*, S.N.B. 1980, c. C-2.1, s. 1.

PROTECTIVE CUSTODY. A period not exceeding 7 days during which a child is under the care of the director pending his return to his parents or his apprehension. *Child Welfare Act*, R.S.N.B. 1973, c. C-4, s. 1.

PROTECTIVE EQUIPMENT. Any piece of equipment or clothing designed to be used to protect the health or safety of an employee. See PERSONAL ~.

PROTECTIVE HOUSING. A structure that encloses the components of a laser and prevents the emission of laser radiation except through an exit aperture.

PROTECTIVE INTERVENTION. An intervention, on the authority of a court order under this Act, to assist or protect a person found to be in need of assistance or protection. *Adult Protection Act*, R.S.P.E.I. 1988, c. A-5, s. 1(n).

PROTECTIVE MEASURES. Steps taken in accordance with the prescribed standards to prevent personal injury or property damage that is reasonably forseeable as a result of closure commencing. *Mining Act*, R.S.O. 1990, c. M.14, s. 139(1).

PROTECTIVE SERVICE. The two police forces of Parliament who maintain order and control the conduct of people admitted to the precincts. A. Fraser, W.A. Dawson, & J. Holtby, eds., *Beauchesne's Rules and Forms of the House of Commons of Canada*, 6th ed. (Toronto: Carswell, 1989) at 21.

PRO TEM. *abbr*. Pro tempore.

PRO TEMPORE. [L. for the time being] Temporarily.

PROTEST. *n*. 1. The solemn declaration that a bill is dishonoured. I.F.G. Baxter, *The Law of Banking*, 3d ed. (Toronto: Carswell, 1981) at 117. 2. A serious declaration of opinion, usually dissent. 3. The express declaration by someone doing something that the act does not imply what it might.

PROTESTANT. *adj.* 1. " . . . Christians [who] . . . accept what are generally regarded as the principles and doctrines of the Reformation of the 16th century. . ." *Hirsch v. P.S.B.G.M,* [1926] S.C.R. 246 at 255, [1926] 32 D.L.R. 8, the court per Anglin C.J.C. 2. Includes the Christian religious denominations other than Roman Catholic. *Child Welfare Act,* R.S.A. 1970, c. 45, s. 34.

PROTHONOTARY. *n.* Of the Federal Court, a barrister or advocate from any province who is needed for the Court to work efficiently and whose powers are set out in the rules. See SPECIAL ~.

PROTOCOL. *n.* 1. The rules concerning ceremony observed in the official relations between nations and their representatives. 2. The minutes of a deliberative gathering of representatives of different countries. 3. The original drafts or copy of any document. 4. Guidelines for the design, operation and maintenance of complex equipment or processes.

PROTOTYPE. *n.* An original thing; trial model; preliminary version.

PROTOTYPE MODEL. Any original working model on which subsequent production was based.

PROUT PATET PER RECORDUM. [L.] Just as it appears in the record.

PROV. *abbr.* 1. Provincial. 2. Province.

PROVABLE CLAIM. A claim which is recoverable by legal process.

PROV. CT. *abbr.* 1. Provincial Court. 2. Provincial Court (Criminal Division).

PROV. CT. CIV. DIV. *abbr.* Provincial Court Civil Division.

PROV. CT. CRIM. DIV. *abbr.* Provincial Court Criminal Division.

PROV. CT. FAM. DIV. *abbr.* Provincial Court Family Division.

PROVE. *v.* 1. To establish. *R. v. Whyte* (1988), 35 C.R.R. 1 at 9, 6 M.V.R. (2d) 138, [1988] 45 W.W.R. 26, 86 N.R. 328, 64 C.R. (3d) 123, 42 C.C.C. (3d) 97, [1988] 2 S.C.R. 8, 29 B.C.L.R. (2d) 273, 51 D.L.R. (4th) 481, the court per Dickson C.J.C. 2. " . . . [I]n criminal law [re-

quires] . . . convincing proof, at least on the balance of probabilities. *R. v. Whyte* (1988) 35 C.R.R. 1 at 9, 6 M.V.R. (2d) 1, [1988] 45 W.W.R. 26, 86 N.R. 328, 64 C.R. (3d) 123, 42 C.C.C. (3d) 97, [1988] 2 S.C.R. 8, 29 B.C.L.R. (2d) 273, 51 D.L.R. (4th) 481, the court per Dickson C.J.C. 3. With respect to a will, to obtain probate.

PRO VERTITATE ACCEPITUR. [L.] Taken for the truth.

PROVIDE. *v.* " . . . [T]o 'supply' or 'furnish' . . ." *Toronto (City) v. 421311 Ontario Ltd.* (1985), 38 R.P.R. 83 at 89 (Ont. H.C.), Griffiths J. See TO ~.

PROVIDER. See FUNERAL ~; SERVICE ~.

PROVIDING THAT. " . . . [O]rdinarily signify or denote a limitation upon something preceeding, or a condition on the performance or nonperformance of which the validity of the instrument may depend. That is not invariably so. It may also affirm that a proposition of fact is true and take effect as a warranty." *Fraser-Reid v. Droumtsekas* (1980), 103 D.L.R. (3d) 385 at 392, [1980] 1 S.C.R. 720, 29 N.R. 424, 9 R.P.R. 121, Dickson J. (Martland, Estey and McIntyre JJ. concurring).

PROVINCE. *n.* 1. A province of Canada. 2. A field of duty. 3. Her Majesty the Queen in right of the Province. 4. A province of Canada, and includes Yukon, the Northwest Territories and Nunavut. *Interpretation Act,* R.S.C. 1985, c. I-21, s. 35. See AGREEING ~; ATLANTIC ~S, ATTORNEY GENERAL OF THE ~; CIVIL RIGHTS IN THE ~; DESIGNATED ~; HAVE-NOT ~; HOLDER IN THE ~; INCLUDED ~; INTERMEDIATE ~; LARGE ~; LAW OF THE ~; MARITIME ~S; MONEY PAID TO THE ~ FOR A SPECIAL PURPOSE; MUTUAL FUND IN THE ~; PARTICIPATING HOSPITAL ~; PARTICIPATING MEDICAL ~; PARTICIPATING ~; PRODUCER-~; RECIPROCATING ~; RECIPROCATING ~ OR TERRITORY; RESIDENT OF THE ~; RESIDES IN THE ~; SMALL ~.

PROVINCIAL. *adj.* As applied to state documents, means of or pertaining to a province or territory within Canada.

PROVINCIAL ACT. In relation to any province, means that Act of the legislature of the province.

PROVINCIAL ANALYST. Any analyst appointed by the government of any province and having authority to make any analysis for any public purpose.

PROVINCIAL AUDITOR. The officer charged by law with the audit of the accounts of the government of a province.

PROVINCIAL COMPANY. 1. A company incorporated under the laws of any province of Canada of Newfoundland or any former province of British North America now forming part of Canada, other than the former Province of Canada, for the purpose of carrying on the business of insurance. *Canadian and British Insurance Companies Act*, R.S.C. 1985, c. I-12, s. 2. 2. A loan company or a trust company incorporated or continued pursuant to this Act and includes a loan company, trust company or any other body corporate authorized to execute the office of executor, administrator, trustee or guardian of a minor's estate or a mentally incompetent person's estate, incorporated pursuant to a special Act of the Legislature after the commencement of this Act, whether or not it is licensed pursuant to this Act. *Loan and Trust Companies acts.*

PROVINCIAL CONTENT. The dollar value attributed to a bid as a result of consideration, as prescribed, of the provincial overhead allowance, the provincial labour content and the provincial material content in that bid, as calculated in accordance with the prescribed method. *Provincial Preference Act*, R.S. Nfld. 1990, c. P-33, s. 2.

PROVINCIAL CONTENT FACTOR. In relation to an examined bidder is the difference between (i) the provincial content of the examined bid, and (ii) the provincial content of the lowest bid divided by the difference between (iii) the bid price of the examined bidder, and (iv) the bid price of the lowest bidder. *Provincial Preference Act*, R.S. Nfld. 1990, c. P-33, s. 2.

PROVINCIAL COOPERATIVE ASSOCIATION. A cooperative association that is not a federal cooperative association. *Canada Cooperative Association Act*, R.S.C. 1985, c. C-40, s. 129.

PROVINCIAL CORPORATION. A corporation that is incorporated by or under the act of a legislature.

PROVINCIAL COURT. 1. Under section 92(14) of the Constitution Act, 1867 the body which a provincial legislature constitutes, maintains, and organizes to administer justice in the province. P.W. Hogg, *Constitutional Law of Canada*, 3d ed. (Toronto: Carswell, 1992) at 660. 2. " . . . [C]ourts which, as to their jurisdiction are primarily subjects of provincial legislation and whose process in civil matters, save in certain exceptional cases which will be adverted to, does not run beyond the limits of the province." *Reference re Privy Council Appeals (1940), (sub nom. Reference re Supreme Court Act Amendment)* [1940] S.C.R. 49 at 56, [1940] 1 D.L.R. 289, Duff C.J. 3. With respect to a province in which a claim sought to be enforced under this Part arises, means (a) in the province of Quebec, the Provincial Court; and (b) in any other province, the county or district court that would have jurisdiction if the claim were against a private person of full age and capacity, or if there is no such county or district court in the province or the county or district court in the province does not have that jurisdiction, the superior court of the province. *Crown Liability Act*, R.S.C. 1985, c. C-50, s. 21.

PROVINCIAL COURT (CIVIL DIVISION). Formerly in Ontario, a small claims court.

PROVINCIAL COURT (FAMILY DIVISION). In Ontario formerly included the youth court.

PROVINCIAL COURT JUDGE. A person appointed or authorized to act by or pursuant to an Act of the legislature of a province, by whatever title that person may be designated, who has the power and authority of two or more justices of the peace and includes the lawful deputy of that person. *Criminal Code*, R.S.C. 1985, c. C-46, s. 2.

PROVINCIAL DIRECTOR. A person, a group or class of persons or a body appointed or designated by or under an Act of the legislature of a province or by the lieutenant governor in council of a province or his or her delegate to perform in that province, either generally or in a specific case, any of the duties or functions of a provincial director under this Act. *Youth Criminal Justice Act*, S.C. 2002, c. 1, s. 2.

PROVINCIAL EMERGENCY. An emergency occurring in a province if the province or a local authority in the province has the primary responsiblity for dealing with the emergency. *Emergency Preparedness Act*, R.S.C. 1985, c. 6, s. 2.

PROVINCIAL ENFORCEMENT SERVICE. Any service, agency or body designated in an agreement with a province under section 3 that is entitled under the laws of the province to enforce family provisions. *Family Orders and Agreements Enforcement Assistance Act*, R.S.C. 1985 (2d Supp.), c. 4, s. 2.

PROVINCIAL FEDERATION. A provincial organization whose members are the members of a labour congress in that province.

PROVINCIAL GARNISHMENT LAW. 1. The law of a province relating to garnishment as it applies to the enforcement of support orders and support provisions. *Family Orders and Agreements Enforcement Assistance Act*, R.S.C. 1985 (2d Supp.), c. 4, s. 23. 2. The law of general application of a province relating to garnishment that is in force at the time in question. *Garnishment, Attachment and Pension Diversion Act*, R.S.C. 1985, c. G-2, s. 2.

PROVINCIAL HIGHWAY. 1. A public highway. 2. A highway outside the limits of a city or incorporated town. *Motor Vehicle Act*, R.S.N.S. 1989, c. 293, s. 2. 3. A highway built and maintained by or under the supervision of the Department of Transportation whether or not such highway lies within the geographical boundaries of a local authority. *An Act to Amend the Motor Vehicle Act, S.N.B.* 1985, c. 34, s. 1.

PROVINCIAL INCOME TAX. That part of money paid by utility companies as income tax or estimated income tax under the Alberta Income Tax Act or the Alberta Corporate Income Tax Act for the 1966 and any subsequent taxation year that is attributable to the utility companies' gross revenue for the year from (i) the distribution and sale to the public in Alberta, or the generation and sale in Alberta for distribution to the public in Alberta, of electrical energy or steam; or (ii) the distribution and sale of gas to the public in Alberta. *Utility Companies Income Tax Rebates Act*, R.S.A. 1980, c. U-10, s. 1.

PROVINCIAL INFORMATION BANK. A source of information designated in an agreement made under section 3. *Family Orders and Agreements Enforcement Assistance Act*, R.S.C. 1985 (2d Supp.), c. 4, s. 2.

PROVINCIAL LAND. Land vested in the Crown in right of a province.

PROVINCIAL LEGISLATURE. Any legislative body other than the Parliament of Canada.

PROVINCIAL PARK. 1. An historic park, a recreation park, a natural environment park or a wilderness park. 2. Includes provincial camp grounds, provincial picnic grounds and provincial camp and picnic grounds. *Provincial Parks Act*, R.S.O. 1990, c. P.34, s. 1.

PROVINCIAL PAROLE BOARD. The Ontario Board of Parole, la Commission québécoise des libérations conditionnelles, the Board of Parole for the Province of British Columbia or any other parole board established by the legislature or the lieutenant governor in council of a province. *Corrections and Conditional Release Act*, S.C. 1992, c. 20, s. 99. A provincial parole board for a province shall exercise jurisdiction in accordance with this Part in respect of the parole of offenders serving sentences in provincial correctional facilities in that province, other than (*a*) offenders sentenced to life imprisonment as a minimum punishment; (*b*) offenders whose sentence has been commuted to life imprisonment; or (*c*) offenders sentenced to detention for an indeterminate period. (2) A provincial parole board may, but is not required to, exercise its jurisdiction under this section in relation to day parole.

PROVINCIAL PROPERTY. All property of Her Majesty in the right of the Province.

PROVINCIAL PROPERTY LAW. Includes all statutory and common law that affects the property rights between parties in a spousal relationship.

PROVINCIAL RAILWAYS. Railways situate wholly within a province and under the exclusive control of the Provincial legislature. *Montreal v. Montreal Street Railway Co.*, [1912] A.C. 333, [1912] 1 D.L.R. 681 at 683 (P.C.).

PROVINCIAL REFERENCE. Each province has enacted legislation which permits the provincial government to send a reference to its provincial court of appeal.

PROVINCIAL SECURITIES. Securities issued and payable by the government.

PROVINCIAL SERVICE. Service under a provincial government that may be counted for superannuation or pension purposes under a provincial scheme. *Public Service Superannuation Act*, R.S.C. 1985, c. P-36, s. 34.

PROVINCIAL SUPERIOR COURT. 1. " . . . They are descendants of the Royal Courts of Justice as Courts of general jurisdiction. They cross the dividing line, as it were, in the federal-provincial scheme of division of jurisdiction, being organized by the provinces under s. 92(15) of the [Constitution Act, 1867 (30 & 31 Vict.), c. 3] and are presided over by Judges appointed and paid by the federal government (ss. 96 and 100 of the Constitution Act, 1867). . ." *Canada (Attorney General) v. Law Society (British Columbia)* (1982), 19 B.L.R. 234 at 257, [1982] 2 S.C.R. 307, 37 B.C.L.R. 145, [1982] 5 W.W.R. 289, 43 N.R. 451, 137 D.L.R. (3d) 1, 66 C.P.R. (2d) 1, the court per Estey J. 2. "They are not mere local courts for the administration of the local laws passed by the Local Legislatures of the Provinces in which they are organized. They are the courts which were established courts of the respective Provinces before Confederation . . . They are the Queen's Courts, bound to take cognizance of and execute all laws, whether enacted by the Dominion Parliament or the Local Legislatures." *Valin v. Langlois* (1879), 3 S.C.R. 1 at 19-20, Ritchie C.J.C.

PROVINCIAL TAX OR FEE. (a) Any tax of general application payable on a value, price or quantity basis by the purchaser, lessee, user or consumer of tangible personal property or services subject to the tax in respect of the sale, rental, consumption or use of the property or services, except to the extent that the tax is payable in respect of property or services acquired for resale, lease or sub-lease; (b) any fee of general application payable by the owner, user or lessee or any vehicle or item of mobile equipment drawn, propelled or driven by any kind of power in respect of the registration of the vehicle or item or the licensing or certification thereof or in respect of the transfer or renewal of any registration permit, licence or certificate issued for the use of the vehicle or item; and (c) any tax of a like nature to a tax described in a paragraph (a) or any fee of a like nature to a fee described in paragraph (b) that is from time to time prescribed. *Federal-Provincial Fiscal Arrangements Act*, R.S.C. 1985, c. F-8, s. 31.

PROVINCIAL TRANSPORT BOARD. A board, commission or other body or person having, under the law of a province, authority to control or regulate the operation of a local undertaking. *Motor Vehicles Transport Act*, R.S.C. 1985, c. M-12, s. 2.

PROVINCIAL TRUST COMPANY. A trust company that is a provincial corporation. *Loan and Trust Corporations Act*, R.S.O. 1980, c. 249, s. 1.

PROVINCIAL WATER-POWERS. *var.* **PROVINCIAL WATER POWERS.** Any water-powers on provincial land, or any other water-powers that are the property of the Crown or

are placed under the control and management of a minister.

PROVINCIAL WELFARE PROGRAM. A welfare program administered by the province, by a municipality in the province or privately, to which public money of the province is or may be contributed and that is applicable or available generally to residents of the province. *Canada Assistance Plan*, R.S.C. 1985, c. C-1, s. 10.

PROVING A WILL IN SOLEMN FORM. Proving the will in open Court upon notice to all interested parties.

PROVISION. *n.* 1. In a legal document, a clause. 2. The act of providing, supplying. See CUSTODY ~; DEFINED CONTRIBUTION ~; FAMILY ~; SUCCESSOR ~; SUPPORT ~.

PROVISIONALLY. *adv.* Conditionally.

PROVISIONAL ORDER. 1. An order that has no effect until it is confirmed by another court. 2. An order made by a court which does not have personal jurisdiction over the person against whom the order is made.

PROVISIONAL PERMIT. A permit authorizing the permittee to proceed on the conditions set out in the permit prior to the issuance of a final permit.

PROVISO. *n.* [L.] 1. A clause in a document which sets a condition, limits, qualifies or covenants, as the case may be. 2. "[Something] . . . which, according to the ordinary rules of construction, the effect must be to except out of the earlier part of the section something which, but for the proviso, would be within it." *Duncan v. Dixon* (1890), 38 W.R. 700 at 701 (U.K. Ch. D.), Kekewich J. 3. " . . . [A] proviso, joined with words of convenant, make it a condition . . ." *McIntosh v. Samo* (1875), 24 U.C.C.P. 625 at 630 (Ont.), Hagarty C.J.

PROVISO EST PROVIDERE PRAESENTIA ET FUTURA NON PRAETERITA. [L.] A proviso is to provide for the present and future not the past.

PROVISO FOR REDEMPTION. The condition in a mortgage by which the mortgagee must reconvey the mortgaged property to the mortgagor at any time the mortgagor requests if the mortgagor pays the mortgagee on specified day costs plus the principal, interest and any other moneys which the mortgage secured.

PROVISOR. *n.* A buyer.

PROV. JUDGES J. *abbr.* Provincial Judges Journal (Journal des juges provinciaux).

PROVOCATION. *n.* 1. A wrongful act or insult that is of such a nature as to be sufficient to deprive an ordinary person of the power of self-control is provocation for the purposes of this section if the accused acted upon it on the sudden and before there was time for his passion to cool. *Criminal Code*, R.S.C. 1985, c. C-46, s. 232(2). 2. " ... [T]wo key elements to a defence of provocation reducing what would otherwise be culpable murder to manslaughter [under s. 215 of the Criminal Code, R.S.C. 1970, c. C-34]. The person causing death must have done so (i) in the 'heat of passion', caused by (ii) 'sudden provocation'. Whether the accused was provoked to lose his self-control is a question of fact for the jury." *R. v. Faid* (1983), 33 C.R. (3d) 1 at 12, [1983] 1 S.C.R. 265, [1983] 3 W.W.R. 673, 25 Alta. L.R. (2d) 1, 2 C.C.C. (3d) 513, 145 D.L.R. (3d) 67, 46 N.R. 461, 42 A.R. 308, the court per Dickson J. 3. The two concepts [of automatism and provocation] are quite distinct and their application depends on the nature of the impact on an accused of the triggering event. The key distinction between the two concepts is that automatism relates to a lack of voluntariness in the accused, an essential element of the offence, while provocation is a recognition that an accused who "voluntarily" committed all the elements of murder may nevertheless have been provoked by a wrongful act or insult that would have been sufficient, on an objective basis, to deprive an ordinary person of the power of self-control. Provocation simply operates, where applicable, to reduce murder to manslaughter. Thus, while evidence relating to the events preceding the commission of an offence may raise questions about both automatism and provocation, very different proof of facts must be made before either one of these issues can be left with the jury. *R. v. Stone*, 1999 CarswellBC 1064, [1999] 2 S.C.R. 290. See SUDDEN ~.

PROVOST-MARSHAL. *n.* An officer of the royal forces in charge of military prisoners.

PROWL. *v.* " ... [I]nspires a pejorative reaction. The verb includes a notion of evil; it depreciates in his eyes the person who is involved in the action that it presents. The prowler does not act without a purpose like the loiterer his actions lead one to believe that he has something in mind and that this thing is not commendable. To see him acting so, one can properly say that he is eventually going to do some specific act, which will be such to attract the reprobation of honest people, even if it is not otherwise specifically prohibited by the Criminal Code. . ." *R. v. Cutter* (1991), 66 C.C.C.(3d) 149 at 154-5, 51 Q.A.C. 143 (C.A.), the court per Chevalier J.A.

PROX. *abbr.* Proximo.

PROXENETA. *n.* One who arranges marriages.

PROXIMAL. *adj.* Near the origin; near the trunk. F.A. Jaffe, *A Guide to Pathological Evidence*, 3d ed. (Toronto: Carswell, 1991) at 225.

PROXIMATE. *adj.* " ... '[D]irect' ..." *Accidental Insurance Co. of North America v. Young* (1892), 20 S.C.R. 280 at 295, Patterson J.

PROXIMATE CAUSE. 1. " ... [A]n expression referring to the efficiency as an operating factor upon the result. Where various factors or causes are concurrent, and one has to be selected, the matter is determined as one of fact, and the choice falls upon the one to which may be variously ascribed the qualities of reality, predominance, efficiency. The true efficient cause never loses its hold. The result is produced, a result attributable in common language to the casualty as a cause, and this result, proximate as well as continuous in its efficiency, properly meets, whether under contract or under the statute, the language of the expression 'proximately caused.'" *Leyland Shipping Co., Ltd. v. Norwich Union Fire Ins. Society, Ltd.*, [1918] A.C. 350 at 370-71 (U.K. H.L.), Lord Shaw of Dunfermline. 2. " ... [E]ffective cause ..." *Boulay v. Rousselle* (1984), 30 C.C.L.T. 149 at 164, 57 N.B.R. (2d) 235, 148 A.P.R. 235 (Q.B.), Meldrum J. See CAUSA CAUSANS.

PROXIMITY. *n.* " ... [B]efore the law will impose liability there must be a connection between the defendant's conduct and [the] plaintiff's loss which makes it just for the defendant to indemnify the plaintiff . . . In tort, [this] notion is proximity. Proximity may consist of various forms of closeness – physical, circumstantial, causal or assumed—which serve to identify the categories of cases in which liability lies. . . Proximity is the controlling factor which avoids the spectre of unlimited liability." *Canadian National Railway v. Norsk Pacific Steamship Co.* (1992), 11 C.C.L.T. (2d) 1 at 26, 137 N.R. 241, 91 D.L.R. (4th) 289, [1992] 1 S.C.R. 1021, 53 F.T.R. 79n, McLachlin J. (L'Heureux-Dubé and Cory JJ. concurring).

PROXIMO. *adv.* [L.] Next month.

PROXY. *n.* 1. " ... [U]sed in two senses. It may be used to designate the person appointed by a shareholder (or a limited partner) to vote his shares in the company (or his interest in a limited partnership). It may also be used to designate the instrument by which a person is appointed to vote the shares (or interest) of another." *Beatty v. First Exploration Fund (1987) & Co.* (1988), 40 B.L.R. 90 at 95, 25 B.C.L.R. (2d) 377 (S.C.), Hinds J. 2. A completed and executed form of proxy by means of which a security holder has nominated a person or company to attend and act on her or his behalf at a meeting of security holders. See FORM OF ~; SPECIAL ~ CERTIFICATE.

PROXYHOLDER. *n.* The person appointed by proxy to attend and act on behalf of a shareholder at a meeting of shareholders.

PRUDENTER AGIT QUI PRAECEPTO LEGIS OBTEMPERAT. [L.] One acts prudently who complies with the precept of the law.

P.S. *abbr.* Post script.

P.S.A.B. *abbr.* Public Service Adjudication Board.

P.S.B.G.M. *abbr.* Protestant School Board of Greater Montreal.

P.S.C.A.B. *abbr.* Public Service Commission Appeal Board.

PSEUDOGRAPH. *n.* Supposed but not real writing.

PSEUDONYM. *n.* A nom de plume.

P.S.I. *abbr.* Pounds per square inch gauge pressure. *Boiler and Pressure Vessel acts.*

PSIG. *abbr.* 1. Pounds per square inch above atmospheric pressure. *Occupational Health and Safety Act*, R.R.O. 1980, Reg. 691, s. 240. 2. Pounds per square inch gauge. *Gasoline Handling Act*, R.R.O. 1980, Reg. 439, s. 1.

P.S.L.R. ADJUD. *abbr.* Public Service Labour Relations Act Adjudicator.

P.S.L.R.B. *abbr.* Public Service Labour Relations Board.

P.S.S.R.B. *abbr.* Public Service Staff Relations Board.

PSYCHIATRIC CLINICAL EXAMINATION. An examination held to determine if the state of mental health of a person requires that he be placed under close treatment.

PSYCHIATRIC DISORDER. Any disease or disability of the mind and includes alcoholism and drug addiction. *Hospitals Act*, R.S.N.S. 1989, c. 208, s. 2.

PSYCHIATRIC FACILITY. A facility for the observation, care and treatment of persons suffering mental disorder, and designated as such the regulations.

PSYCHIATRIC NURSING. The nursing care of mentally disordered persons under the direction and supervision of a duly qualified medical practitioner.

PSYCHIATRIST. *n.* A duly qualified medical practitioner who is duly certified as a specialist in psychiatry by the Royal College of Physicians and Surgeons of Canada, or who has practical experience and training in the diagnosis and treatment of mental disorders that is a equivalent to such a certificate. See ATTENDING ~.

PSYCHIATRY. See FORENSIC ~.

PSYCHIC. *adj.* Mental, in contrast to physical. K.D. Cooper-Stephenson & I.B. Saunders, *Personal Injury Damages in Canada* (Toronto: Carswell, 1981) at 555.

PSYCHOLOGICAL HARM. A psychological condition that (a) interferes with the health or comfort of a person, and (b) is more than merely transient or trifling in nature. *Crime Victim Assistance Act*, S.B.C. 2001 c. 38, s. 1.

PSYCHOLOGY. *n.* The practice of psychology is the assessment of behavioural and mental conditions, the diagnosis of neuropsychological disorders and dysfunctions and psychotic, neurotic and personality disorders and dysfunctions and the prevention and treatment of behavioural and mental disorders and dysfunctions and the maintenance and enhancement of physical, intellectual, emotional, social and interpersonal functioning. *Psychology Act, 1991*, S.O. 1991, c. 38, s. 3. See PRACTICE OF ~.

PSYCHONEUROSIS. *n.* A severe or persistent emotional disturbance of a person, other than mental illness or psychopathic disorder, that results in marked impairment of social adaptation and adjustment. *Mental Health Act*, R.S.M. 1987, c. M110, s. 1.

PSYCHOPATHIC DISORDER. A persistent disorder or disability of mind other than mental illness that results in abnormally aggressive or serious socially disruptive conduct on the part of a person.

PSYCHOSURGERY. *n.* Any procedure that by direct access to the brain removes, destroys or interrupts the normal connections of the brain for the primary purpose of treating a mental disorder or involves the implantation of electrodes, but does not include neurosurgical procedures designed to treat reliably diagnosed organic brain conditions or epilepsy.

PSYCHOTIC PERSON. A person who suffers from a psychosis.

PUB. *n*. A place arranged for the consumption of beer and weak cider.

PUBERTY. *n*. The age at which persons become capable of bearing or begetting children.

PUBLIC. *n*. 1. "... [A] term of uncertain import it must be limited in every case by the context in which it is used..." *Jennings v. Stephens*, [1936] 1 Ch. 469 at 476 (U.K.), Lord Wright, M.R. 2. Does not include (i) close personal friends; (ii) business associates; (iii) customers with whom the person who calls for the purpose of trading securities has completed at least five trades in the past in the course of regular business in the sale of or obtaining subscriptions for securities; (iv) any person who has received a prospectus and who subsequently makes a request in writing, signed by himself, or further information with respect to the securities described in the prospectus. *Securities Act*, R.S.N.W.T. 1974, c. S-5, s. 29. 3. "... [A]ppropriate to denote those outside the immediate circle of those who control the company. *Morrisons Holdings Ltd. v. Inland Revenue Commissioners*, [1966] 1 All E.R. 789 at 798 (U.K. Ch. D.), Pennycuick J. See DISTRIBUTION TO THE~; ISSUED TO THE ~; MEMBER OF THE ~; OFFER TO THE ~; PRIMARY DISTRIBUTION TO THE ~.

PUBLIC. *adj*. See GO ~.

PUBLIC ACCESS TO LAW. Legal information institutes of the world, meeting in Montreal, declare that: Public legal information from all countries and international institutions is part of the common heritage of humanity. Maximizing access to this information promotes justice and the rule of law; Public legal information is digital common property and should be accessible to all on a non-profit basis and, where possible, free of charge; Independent non-profit organizations have the right to publish public legal information and the government bodies that create or control that information should provide access to it so that it can be published. See CANADIAN LEGAL INFORMATION INSTITUTE; LAW INFORMATION; LEGAL INFORMATION IN-STITUTE; MONTREAL DECLARATION ON ~.

PUBLIC ACCOUNTANCY. The investigation and audit of accounting records and preparation and reporting on balance sheets, profit and loss accounts and financial statements. *Public Accountants Act*, R.S.N.S. 1989, c. 369, s. 2(1).

PUBLIC ACCOUNTANT. A person who either alone or in partnership engages for reward in public practice involving, (a) the performance of services which include causing to be prepared, signed, delivered or issued any financial, accounting or related statement, or (b) the issue of any written opinion, report or certificate concerning any such statement, where, by reason of the circumstances or of the signature, stationery or wording employed, it is indicated that such person or partnership acts or purports to act in relation to such statement, opinion, report or certificate as an independent accountant or auditor or as a person or partnership having or purporting to have expert knowledge in accounting or auditing matters, but does not include a person who engages only in bookkeeping or cost accounting or in the installation of bookkeeping, business or cost systems or who performs accounting or auditing functions exclusively in respect of, (c) any public authority or any commission, committee or emanation thereof, including a Crown company, (d) any bank, loan or trust company, (e) any transportation company incorporated by Act of the Parliament of Canada, or (f) any other publicly-owned or publicly-controlled public utility organization. *Public Accountancy Act*, R.S.O. 1990, c. P.37, s. 1.

PUBLIC ACCOUNTING AND AUDITING. The investigation or audit of accounting records or the preparation of, or reporting on, balance sheets, profit and loss accounts and other financial statements, but does not include bookkeeping, cost accounting, or the exercise by accountants and auditors in the employ of the governments of the province or Canada of their functions as such. *Public Accounting and Auditing Act*, R.S.P.E.I. 1988, c. P-28, s. 1.

PUBLIC ACCOUNTS. The accounts of a country's or province's expenditures.

PUBLIC ACT. See ACT OF PARLIAMENT.

PUBLIC ADVERTISEMENT. An advertisement in the public press.

PUBLIC AFFAIRS PROGRAMMING SERVICE. The programming service of a person licensed to carry on a programming undertaking of which 100% of the programming provided represents categories 3 (reporting and actualities) and 12 (filler programming), as referred to in column I of item 6 of Schedule I to the *Specialty Services Regulations, 1990. Broadcasting Distribution Regulations*, SOR/97-555, s. 1.

PUBLIC AGENCY. An agency, board, commission or corporation, including any wholly-owned subsubsidiary corporation, established or controlled by the Crown.

PUBLIC AND PARAPUBLIC SECTORS. The Government and the government departments and those government agencies and bodies whose personnel is appointed or remunerated in accordance with the Civil Service Act, as well as the colleges, school boards and establishments contemplated in the Act respecting management and union party organization in collective bargaining in the sectors of education, social affairs, and government agencies (R.S.Q., chapter O-7.1). *An Act to Amend the Labour Code, the Code of Civil Procedure and Other Legislation*, S.Q. 1982, c. 37, s. 111.2.

PUBLIC ARCHIVES. 1. Include all books, papers and records vested in the Province by virtue of the Public Records Act or such other property of the province as, from time to time, the Governor in Council declares to be Public Archives, and all documents, records, structures, erections, monuments, objects, materials, articles or things of historic, artistic, scientific or traditional interest acquired by the Board under this Act. *Public Archives Act*, R.S.N.S. 1967, c. 246, s. 1. 2. The archives of public bodies. *Archives Act*, S.Q. 1983, c. 38, s. 2.

PUBLIC ARCHIVES CANADA. A federal research institution which acquires important records of Canadian life and the nation's development and which also provides facilities and services to make these records accessible to all Canadians.

PUBLIC ARENA. An area traditionally open to use for the exercise of freedom of expression, whether the public is admitted as of right or not, where the activities are compatible with the intended use of the property, and where the property may be symbolically significant for the message.

PUBLIC ART. Art placed on public land or property and in areas of private development which are open to the public such as an atrium or square in a building complex.

PUBLICATION. *n*. 1. " . . . [A]ny act of communication from one to another: . . ." *Peel Board of Education v. B. (W.)* (1987), 36 M.P.L.R. 95 at 103, 24 Admin. L.R. 164, 59 O.R. (2d) 654, 38 D.L.R. (4th) 566 (H.C.), Reid J. 2. (a) In relation to works, (i) making copies of a work available to the public, (ii) the construction of an architectural work, and (iii) the incorporation of an artistic work into an architectural work, and (b) in relation to sound recordings, making copies of a sound recording available to the public, but does not include (c) the performance in public, or the communication to the public by telecommunication, of a literary, dramatic, musical or artistic work or a sound recording, or (d) the exhibition in public of an artistic work. *Copyright Act*, R.S.C. 1985, c. C-42, s. 2. 3. Use in this section means any words legibly marked upon any substance or any object signifying the matter otherwise than by words, exhibited in public or caused to be seen or shown or circulated or delivered with a view to its being seen by any person. *Defamation Act*, R.S.M. 1970, c. C20, s. 19. 4. Includes a newspaper or a broadcast. *Defamation Act*, R.S. Nfld. 1990, c. D-3, s. 2. 5. For a document to qualify as a "publication", it must: (1) have become generally available, without restriction, to members of the public, (2) the person or persons receiving the document, to be categorized as members of the public, must have no special relationship to the author of the so-called publication. *Xerox of Canada Ltd. v. IBM Canada Ltd.* (1977), 33 C.P.R. (2d) 24 (Fed. T.D.) at 85, Collier J. See GOVERNMENT ~; PERIODICAL ~; RE~.

PUBLICATION BAN. In assessing whether to issue common law publication bans, therefore, in my opinion, a better way of stating the proper analytical approach for cases of the kind involved herein would be: A publication ban should only be ordered when: (a) such an order is necessary in order to prevent a serious risk to the proper administration of justice because reasonably alternative measures will not prevent the risk; and (b) the salutary effects of the publication ban outweigh the deleterious effects on the rights and interests of the parties and the public, including the effects on the right to free expression, the right of the accused to a fair and public trial, and the efficacy of the administration of justice. This reformulation of the *Dagenais* test aims not to disturb the essence of that test, but to restate it in terms that more plainly recognize, as Lamer C.J. himself did in that case, that publication bans may invoke more interests and rights than the rights to trial fairness and freedom of expression. This version encompasses the analysis conducted in *Dagenais*, and Lamer C.J.'s discussion of the relative merits of publication bans remains relevant. *R. v. Mentuck*, [2001] 3 S.C.R. 442.

PUBLICATION CONTEMPT. Canadian courts have consistently applied a definition [of publication contempt] which finds its origins in Lord Russell's commentary [in *R. v. Gray*, [1900] 2 Q.B. 36 (Eng. Q.B.)]. "The gravamen of the matter [is] the interference with the administration of justice by publishing articles that [pose] a real risk of prejudice to the accused". The current test requires that the court be satisfied beyond a reasonable doubt that the publication of the material constituted a real and substantial risk of prejudice to the administration of justice. The definition of criminal contempt of court by publication cannot be re-written so as to eliminate all restrictions to freedom of the press and freedom of expression without risking the elimination of the contempt of court power. *R. v. Edmonton Sun*, 2003 ABCA 3, 320 A.R. 217 (C.A.).

PUBLIC AUTHORITIES. See PROTECTION OF~.

PUBLIC AUTHORITY. 1. Her Majesty in right of Canada or a province, an agent of Her Majesty in either such right, a municipality in Canada, a municipal or public body performing a function of government in Canada or a corporation performing a function or duty on behalf of Her Majesty in right of Canada or a province. *Cultural Property Export and Import Act*, R.S.C. 1985, c. C-51, s. 2. 2. A provincial or municipal authority or a public educational authority. *National Training Act*, R.S.C. 1985, c. N-19, s. 2.

PUBLIC BILL. A bill relating to public policy matters. A. Fraser, W.A. Dawson, & J. Holtby, eds., *Beauchesne's Rules and Forms of the House of Commons of Canada*, 6th ed. (Toronto: Carswell, 1989) at 192.

PUBLIC BODY. (i) The government of Canada or a province; (ii) a crown corporation, board, commission or agency of a government; (iii) a municipality; (iv) a body elected or appointed under an act: (A) to develop, administer or regulate schools, hospitals, health facilities libraries, water utilities, drainage and irrigation works, sewerage works, local improvements or public utilities; or (B) to levy and collect taxes.

PUBLIC BUILDING. 1. Any building to which the public has a right of access. 2. A place of public resort or amusement. See OWNER OF A ~.

PUBLIC CAMP GROUND. An area in a park designated for use by the public for camping purposes.

PUBLIC CARRIER. Any railway company, any federal carrier within the meaning of the Motor Vehicle Transport Act and any owner or operator of a ship. *Canada Grain Act*, R.S.C. 1985, c. G-10, s. 2.

PUBLIC COMMERCIAL VEHICLE. A commercial motor vehicle as defined in the Highway Traffic Act or a dual-purpose vehicle or the combination of a commercial motor vehicle and trailer or trailers drawn by it, operated by the holder of an operating licence. *Public Commercial Vehicles Act*, R.S.O. 1980, c. 407, s. 1.

PUBLIC COMMUNICATIONS. Any telecommunication that is available to the public. *The Teleglobe Canada Act*, R.S.C. 1985, c. T-4, s. 2.

PUBLIC COMPANY. 1. A company that is not a private company. 2. A company (a) that has outstanding any of its securities in respect of which a prospectus or a document of a similar nature has been filed with and accepted by a public authority; (b) any of the shares of which are listed or posted for trading on any recognized stock exchange in Canada. 3. A company that (a) is a reporting issuer, (b) is a reporting issuer equivalent, (c) has registered its securities under the *Securities Exchange Act* of 1934 of the United States of America, (d) has any of its securities, within the meaning of the *Securities Act*, traded on or through the facilities of a securities exchange, or (e) has any of its securities, within the meaning of the *Securities Act*, reported through the facilities of a quotation and trade reporting system. *Business Corporations Act*, S.B.C. 2002, c. 57, s. 1.

PUBLIC COMPLAINT. A complaint having a public aspect, that is, made by a member of the public, initiated by a public official or resulting in a public hearing.

PUBLIC CORPORATION. 1. (a) A body corporate that is, by reason of its shares, a reporting issuer within the meaning of the Securities Act or that has, by reason of its shares, a status comparable to a reporting issuer under the law of any other jurisdiction, (b) a body corporate that issues shares that are traded on any market if the prices at which they are trade on that market are regularly published in a newspaper or business or financial publication of general and regular paid circulation, or (c) subject to subsection (2), a body corporate that is, within the meaning of subsections 1(1) and (2), clause 1(3)(a) and subsections 1(4), (5) and (6) of the Securities Act, controlled by or is a subsidiary of a body corporate or two or more bodies corporate described in clause (a) or (b). *Education Act*, R.S.O. 1990, c. E.2, s. 113(1) in part. 2. Includes a municipal and quasi-municipal corporation as either is created for public, not private, purposes. I.M. Rogers, *The Law of Canadian Municipal Corporations*, 2d ed. (Toronto: Carswell, 1971-) 13.

PUBLIC CORRIDOR. A corridor that provides access to exit from individually rented rooms, suites of rooms or dwelling units.

PUBLIC DEBT. Direct debt obligations of the government.

PUBLIC DEPARTMENT. A department of the Government of Canada or a branch thereof or a board, commission, corporation or other body that is an agent of Her Majesty in right of Canada. *Criminal Code*, R.S.C. 1985, c. C-46, s. 2.

PUBLIC DISTURBANCE. "[In s. 175(1)(a) of the Criminal Code, R.S.C. 1985, c. C-46] . . . must be an externally manifested disturbance of the public peace, in the sense of interference with the ordinary and customary use of the premises by the public . . . The disturbance may consist of the impugned act itself, as in the case of a fight interfering with the peaceful use of barroom, or it may flow as a consequence of the impugned act, as where shouting and swearing produce a scuffle." *R. v. Lohnes* (1991), 69 C.C.C. (3d) 289 at 290, 10 C.R. (4th) 125, [1992] 1 S.C.R. 167, 132 N.R. 297, 109 N.S.R. (2d) 145, 297 A.P.R. 145, the court per McLachlin J.

PUBLIC DOCUMENT. 1. " . . . (1) [T]hat a judicial or semi judicial inquiry was . . . held . . . (2) that the inquiry in fact held . . . was held with the object that his report should be made public; or (3) that the report was in fact at all times open to public inspection or that an inference to this effect should be drawn from the act that it was produced in evidence without objection by the . . . authorities. . ." *Thrasyvoulos Iannou v. Papa Christoforos Demetriou*, [1952] A.C. 84 at 94 (Cyprus P.C.), Lord Tucker for the Judicial Committee. 2. Includes certificates under the Great Seal of a province, legal documents, vouchers, cheques, accounting records, correspondence, maps, photographs and all other documents created in the administration of public affairs. 3. Must have a public purpose or objective, be retained and be open for inspection by interested parties, prepared pursuant to a public duty, and may be required to determine the truth of the facts recorded in the document.

PUBLIC DOMAIN. The sphere in which the public operates. Something is in the public domain if it is generally known to the public.

PUBLIC EATING ESTABLISHMENT. (i) A building, structure or enclosure or any part thereof where food or drink is prepared or kept and served or sold to the public for immediate consumption; (ii) a restaurant, hotel dining room, coffee shop, cafeteria, luncheonette, sandwich shop, milk bar, dairy bar, soda fountain, soft drink stand, outlet within the meaning of The Liquor Licensing Act, and another eating or drinking establishment; (ii) a kitchen and any other place in which food or drink is prepared for sale for immediate consumption elsewhere. *The Public Health Act*, R.S.S. 1978, c. P-37, s. 2.

PUBLIC EATING PLACE. A place where food or drink is offered for sale to the public for consumption on the premises and includes a hotel, inn, restaurant, public transport, eating house and lunch counter.

PUBLIC EMPLOYEE. An employee of (i) any of the departments of government; (ii) any agency; or (iii) any commission, board, corporation, authority or other body.

PUBLIC ENEMIES. Refers to situations of war or rebellion, not to groups of citizens breaking the law.

PUBLIC EXHIBITION. A display of goods open to the general public.

PUBLIC FACILITY. See GOVERNMENT OR ~.

PUBLIC FISHING PRESERVE. Land or water that is Crown owned, leased or developed with Crown funds, on which or part of which, fish have been reared or stocked for the purpose of angling and are designated as public fishing preserves in the regulations. *Fish and Game Protection Act*, R.S.P.E.I. 1988, c. F-12, s. 1(jj).

PUBLIC FOREST. A state-owned forest. *Forestry Credit Act*, R.S.Q. 1977, c. C-78, s. 1.

PUBLIC FORUM. A place which constitute a favourable platform for the public to exercise its right of freedom of expression.

PUBLIC FREIGHT VEHICLE. A motor vehicle, other than a limited freight vehicle, that is operated at any time on a highway by, for or on behalf of any person who charges or collects compensation for the transportation of freight in or on the motor vehicle.

PUBLIC FUNDS. Money from the treasury of the federal, provincial or municipal government. *Les Soeurs de la Visitation d'Ottawa v. Ottawa*, [1952] O.R. 61 at 71, 72.

PUBLIC GARAGE. A building for the care, repair or equipping of motor vehicles or for the parking or storing of motor vehicles for remuneration, hire or sale. Canada regulations.

PUBLIC HALL. 1. A building, including a portable building or tent with a seating capacity for over 100 persons that is offered for use or used as a place of public assembly, but does not include a theatre within the meaning of the Theatres Act or a building, except a tent, used solely for religious purposes. *Public Halls Act*, R.S.O. 1990, c. P.39, s. 1. 2. A hall, pavilion, place or building, except such as used in connection with churches or owned and conducted by municipal authorities, in which public concerts, dances and other social gatherings are held. *The Theatres and Cinematographs Act*, R.S.S. 1978, c. T-11, s. 2.

PUBLIC HARBOUR. 1. Any harbour under the control and management of the Minister by virtue of section 9. *Public Harbours and Port Facilities Act*, R.S.C. 1985, c. P-29, s. 2. 2. " . . . [N]ot merely a place suited by its physical characteristics for use as a harbour, but a place to which on the relevant dates the public had access as a harbour and which they had actually used for that purpose. . ." *Canada (Attorney General) v. Ritchie Contracting & Supply Co.* (1919), 48 D.L.R. 147 at 150, [1919] 3 W.W.R. 347, [1919] A.C. 999 (Can. P.C.), the board per Lord Dunedin.

PUBLIC HEALTH SERVICES. Preventive health services.

PUBLIC HEARING. 1. " . . . [O]ne in open court which the public including representatives of the media are entitled to attend." *Canadian Newspapers Co. v. Canada (Attorney General)* (1985), 14 C.R.R. 276 at 302, 49 O.R. (2d) 557, 17 C.C.C. (3d) 385,16 D.L.R. (4th) 642, 44 C.R.

(3d) 97, 7 O.A.C. 161, the court per Howland C.J.O. 2. A hearing of which public notice is given, which is open to the public, and at which any person who has an interest in a matter may be heard.

PUBLIC HIGHWAY. Any part of a bridge, road, street, place, square or other ground open to public vehicular traffic.

PUBLIC HOLIDAY. Includes New Year's Day, Good Friday, Labour Day, Christmas Day.

PUBLIC HOSPITAL. A building, premises, or place that is established and operated for the lodging and treatment or the treatment of persons afflicted with or suffering from sickness, disease, or injury and includes a maternity hospital, a nurses residence and all buildings and equipment used for the purposes of the hospital.

PUBLIC HOTEL. Includes every hotel, motel, common lodging house and place of public accommodation, other than a boarding house, supplying lodging to the public.

PUBLIC HOT TUB. A hot tub that is available for use by the general public.

PUBLIC HOUSE. A place arranged for the consumption of beer and weak cider.

PUBLIC HOUSING. One or more houses or multiple-family dwellings or housing accommodation of the hostel or dormitory type or any combination thereof, together with the land upon which it is situated, acquired, constructed, held, maintained and managed by the corporation or a municipality, or a housing authority, or a housing and renewal authority, under an agreement with such parties as may have an interest in the housing accommodation, for leasing to persons or families of low income in need of decent, safe, and sanitary housing or to such other persons as the corporation designates, having regard to the shortage, overcrowding or congestion of housing accommodation. See SUBSIDIZED ~.

PUBLIC HOUSING AGENCY. A corporation that is wholly owned by (a) the government of a province, or any agency thereof; (b) one or more municipalities in a province; or (c) the government of a province or an agency thereof and one or more municipalities in that province and that has power to acquire and develop land for a public housing project or to construct or acquire and operate a public housing project. *National Housing Act*, R.S.C. 1985, c N-11, s. 78.

PUBLIC HOUSING PROJECT. 1. A project, together with the land on which it is situated, consisting of a housing project or housing accommodation of the hostel or dormitory type or any combination thereof, that is undertaken to provide decent, safe and sanitary housing accommodation in compliance with standards approved by the corporation and that is intended to be leased to individuals or families of low income. *National Housing Act*, R.S.C. 1985, c. N-11, s. 78. 2. Any housing project constructed, held, maintained, and managed by the corporation jointly with (i) any municipality; (ii) any housing authority; (iii) any agency of Canada; or (iv) any municipality, housing authority and an agency of Canada.

PUBLIC INFORMATION SERVICE. A radiocommunication service that provides for communications in which the transmissions are intended for the public, but does not include transmissions by a broadcasting undertaking; *Radiocommunications Regulations*, SOR/96-484.

PUBLICI JURIS. [L.] Of public right.

PUBLIC IMPROVEMENT. 1. Anything for the purpose of which an authority may expropriate land. *The Expropriation Procedure Act*, R.S.S. 1978, c. E-16, s. 2. 2. Public highways, culverts, bridges, aerodromes, air services, public transit systems, private transit systems when considered by the minister to be a public benefit, railways, ditches, drains, ferries, wells and public fire-guards; dams, reservoirs or other works constructed for the storage of water, water towers and works connected therewith; lands, streams, water courses and property, real and personal, heretofore or hereafter acquired for any public improvement or land required for securing material in connection with road construction; and any matter or thing done or to be done in connection with any such public improvement under this Act. *The Highways Act*, R.S.S. 1978, c. H-3, s. 2.

PUBLIC INQUIRY. The Governor in Council may, whenever the Governor in Council deems it expedient, cause inquiry to be made into and concerning any matter connected with the good government of Canada or the conduct of any part of the public business thereof. Where an inquiry is not regulated by any special law, the Governor in Council may, by a commission, appoint persons as commissioners by whom the inquiry shall be conducted. A Lieutenant Governor in Council has similar powers to establish an inquiry.

PUBLIC INSTITUTION. An institution owned or operated by the government of a province.

PUBLIC INSURANCE COMPANY. A company that (i) does not restrict the right to transfer any of its shares; (ii) does not limit the number of its shareholders to 50 or less, with persons who are joint registered owners of one or more shares in the company being counted as one shareholder; and (iii) does not prohibit any invitation to the public to subscribe for any of the shares of the company.

PUBLIC INTEREST. 1. "In R. v. Collins, [(1987), 33 C.C.C. (3d) 1 (S.C.C.)], . . . at p. 18 . . . Lamer J. (now C.J.C.) writing for the Supreme Court of Canada, set out one of the criteria that a judge must take into consideration when dealing with public interest: 'It serves as a reminder to each individual judge that his discretion is grounded in community values and in particular long term community values.'" *R. v. Shah* (1991), 7 C.R. (4th) 102 at 115 (Ont. Gen. Div.), Caswell J. 2. Includes matters broader than the mere protection of the public and includes the public's perception of and confidence in the administration of justice. 3. "[In the Securities Act, R.S.O. 1980, c. 466] . . . not only the interest of residents of Ontario, but the interest of all persons making use of Ontario capital markets." *Asbestos Corp., Re* (1992), (*sub nom. Sa Majesté du chef du Québec v. Ontario (Securities Commission)*) 15 O.S.C.B. 4973 at 4999, 58 O.A.C. 277, 97 D.L.R. 144, 10 O.R. (3d) 577 (C.A.), McKinlay J.A. 4. The term 'public interest' in s. 25(1)(b) [of the Freedom of Information and Protection of Privacy Act, S.B.C. 1992, c. 61] cannot be so broad as to encompass anything that the public may be interested in learning. The term is not defined by the various levels of public curiosity. The public is, however, truly 'interested' in matters that may affect the health or safety of children." *Clubb v. Saanich (District)* (1996), 1996 CarswellBC 231, 46 C.R. (4th) 253, 35 Admin. L.R. (2d) 309, 35 C.R.R. (2d) 325 (S.C.), Melvin J. 5. Includes concerns of society generally and the particular interests of identifiable groups in the context of weighing the balance of convenience on an application for an interlocutory injunction.

PUBLIC INTEREST GROUP. An organization without personal, proprietary or pecuniary interest in the outcome of proceedings which has as its object the taking of public initiative, including litigation, to affect policy in relation to matters of interest to the group and to enforce constitutional, statutory and common law rights in relation to these matters.

PUBLIC INTEREST IMMUNITY. 1. Rule of evidence which permits the Crown to exclude evidence, records of Cabinet discussions and planning documents, in order to ensure the proper functioning of the executive branch of government. 2. " . . . [W]hat the Crown has and may assert in relation to such documents is neither a 'privilege' nor an 'immunity', but rather, more accurately, a claim for protection on the ground of a specified public interest, being that upon which the Crown relies to support its claim. The right which the Crown has to assert such a claim is a right which our law clearly recognizes and which our Courts must respect, but it is no more than the right to claim the protection sought and thus to place in issue in judicial proceedings a matter which the Courts must decide." *R. v. Carey* (1983), 38 C.P.C. 237 at 277, 43 O.R. (2d) 161, 3 Admin. L.R. 158, 7 C.C.C. (3d) 193, 1 D.L.R. (4th) 498 (C.A.), the court per Thorson J.A.

PUBLIC-INTEREST STANDING. "[In order to be entitled to public-interest standing] three criteria must be met: (1) there must be a serious issue; (2) the plaintiff must have a genuine interest as a citizen [in the issue] and (3) there must be no other reasonable and effective manner in which the issue may be brought before the court." *Canadian Council of Churches v. R.* (1990), 10 Imm. L.R. (2d) 81 at 88, 106 N.R. 61, 68 D.L.R. (4th) 197, 46 C.R.R. 290, 44 Admin. L.R. 56, [1990] 2 F.C. 534 (C.A.), the court per MacGuigan J.A.

PUBLIC INTERNATIONAL LAW. See INTERNATIONAL LAW.

PUBLICIST. *n*. One who writes about the law of nations.

PUBLICITY. See LOSS OF ~.

PUBLICITY CONTEST. A contest, a lottery scheme, a game, a plan or an operation which results in the awarding of a prize, carried on for the object of promoting the commercial interests of the person for whom it is carried on.

PUBLICITY PICKETING. Picketing intended to inform the public of the existence of a labour dispute.

PUBLIC LAND. Land belonging to Her Majesty the Queen in right of a province. See OCCUPIED ~; UNOCCUPIED ~.

PUBLIC LANDS. 1. Lands belonging to Her Majesty in right of Canada and includes lands of which the Government of Canada has power to dispose. 2. Lands belonging to Her Majesty in right of Canada or of which Government of Canada has, subject to the terms of any agreement between the Government of Canada and the government of the province in which the lands are situated, power to dispose, including waters on or flowing through, and the natural resources of, those lands. *National Parks Act*, R.S.C. 1985, c. N-14, s. 2. 3. Real property or any interest therein, under the control and management of a department. *National Capital Act*, R.S.C. 1985, c. N-4, s. 2.

PUBLIC LAUNDRY. Any shop, dwelling or building whatsoever in which linen, brought or sent there by the public, is washed or ironed for profit.

PUBLIC LAW. All law dealing with relations between an individual and the state or between states and the organization of government, i.e., criminal, administrative, constitutional and international law.

PUBLIC LAW OF QUEBEC. " . . . [C]onsists of statute law and the common law as it applies to public bodies." *Laurentide Motels Ltd. c. Beauport (Vine)* (1989), 45 M.P.L.R. 1 at 11, 94 N.R. 1, [1989] 1 S.C.R. 705, 23 Q.A.C. 1, Beetz J. (McIntyre, Lamer, Wilson and La Forest JJ. concurring).

PUBLIC LEGAL INFORMATION. Legal information produced by public bodies that have a duty to produce law and make it public. It includes primary sources of law, such as legislation, case law and treaties, as well as various secondary (interpretative) public sources, such as law reform reports, and reports from boards of inquiry. See CANADIAN LEGAL INFORMATION INSTITUTE; LEGAL INFORMATION INSTITUTE; MONTREAL DECLARATION ON PUBLIC ACCESS TO LAW; PUBLIC ACCESS TO LAW.

PUBLIC LENDING RIGHT. A right which entitles an author to receive payments from time to time for books they authored which were lent out to the public by libraries.

PUBLIC LIABILITY INSURANCE. Insurance against loss or damage to the person or property of others that is not included in or incidental to some other class of insurance defined by or under this Act. *Insurance acts*.

PUBLIC LIABILITY INSURANCE POLICY. A policy or that part of a policy which insures a person against loss of or damage to the person or property of others where the insurance is not included in or incidental to some other class of insurance.

PUBLIC LIBRARY. 1. Any municipal library, regional library or community library. 2. A library where services are available without charge to residents of the Province.

PUBLIC LIVESTOCK SALE. Any place where livestock is offered for sale to the public.

PUBLICLY-TRADED SECURITIES. (i) Securities of a corporation that are listed or posted for trading on a recognized stock exchange, or (ii) securities of a corporation that has more than 15 shareholders and any of whose issued securities were part of a distribution to the public.

PUBLICLY-TRADED SHARES. (i) Shares of a corporation that are listed or posted for trading on a recognized stock exchange in Canada or the United States of America; or (ii) shares of a corporation that has more than 15 shareholders and any of whose issued shares, or securities which may or might be exchanged for or converted into shares, were part of a distribution to the public.

PUBLIC MEETING. 1. A meeting bona fide and lawfully held for a lawful purpose and for the furtherance or discussion of any matter of public concern, whether admission thereto is general or restricted. Defamation acts. 2. In examining these submissions it is helpful to recognize that section 4 of the British Columbia Libel and Slander Act [R.S.B.C. 1996, c. 263] is substantially similar to section 7 of the English Defamation Act, 1952 [15 & 16 Geo. 6 & 1 Eliz. S.c.66]. In its structure, however, the British Columbia legislation sets out within section 4 the types of meetings and reports entitled to the statutory privilege where the English legislation describes those matters in schedules to the legislation. Gatley on Libel and Slander, 8th ed. (London: Sweet & Maxwell, 1981) reviews the legislative history of this statutory privilege. In describing the nature of a "public meeting" covered by the privilege the author states at p. 281: It is submitted that the mere fact that admission to a meeting is restricted to those members of the public who purchase a ticket does not prevent it from being a public meeting within the meaning of the Act, unless the price of the ticket is so exorbitant as to exclude the general public. But if admission to a meeting can only be obtained by virtue of some personal qualification, it is not a "public meeting." Cassidy v. Abbotsford (City) Police Department (1999), 1999 CarswellBC 2887 (S.C. [In Chambers]).

PUBLIC MEMBER. A person representing the public, the state, on an arbitration panel or board as opposed to a member representing a particular interest.

PUBLIC MISCHIEF. With intent to mislead, causes a peace officer to enter upon or continue an investigation by (a) making a false statement that accuses some other person of having committed an offence; (b) doing anything that is intended to cause some other person to be suspected of having committed an offence that the person has not committed, or to divert suspicion from himself; or (c) reporting that an offence has been committed when it has not been committed; or (d) reporting or in any other way making it known or causing it to be made known that he or some other person has died when he or that other person has not died. *Criminal Code*, R.S.C. 1985, c. C-46, s. 140.

PUBLIC MONEY. 1. All money belonging to Canada received or collected by the Receiver General or any other public officer in his official capacity or any person authorized to receive or collect such money, and includes (a) duties and revenues of Canada; (b) money borrowed by Canada or received through the issue or sale of securities; (c) money received or collected for or on behalf of Canada; and (d) all money that is paid to or received or collected by a public officer under or pursuant to any Act, trust, treaty, undertaking or contract, and is to be disbursed for a purpose specified in or pursuant to that Act, trust, treaty, undertaking or contract. *Financial Administration Act*, R.S.C. 1985, c. F-11, s. 2. All public money shall be deposited to the credit of the Receiver General. The Receiver General may establish, in the name of the Receiver General, accounts for the deposit of public money. 2. All money belonging to the province received or collected by a minister or any public officer in an official capacity or any person authorized to receive or collect such money, and includes (i) revenues of a province; (ii) money borrowed by the province or received through the sale of securities; (iii) money received or collected for or on behalf of the province; and (iv) money aid to the province for a special purpose. 3. "[In s. 4 of the Highway Act, R.S.B.C. 1979, c. 167] . . . refers to money expended by departments of the provincial, municipal and other governments for highway purposes, and does not include money spent by autonomous, or 'quasi-autonomous', Crown corporations such as the Hydro Authority . . ." *British Columbia v. Hilyn Holdings Ltd.* (1991), 78 D.L.R. (4th) 27 at 35 (B.C.C.A.), the court per Taylor J.A. See RECIPIENT OF ~S.

PUBLIC MONEYS. All revenue and moneys arising from whatever source belonging or payable to the government. Manitoba statutes.

PUBLIC MORGUE. A place under the control and management of a municipal corporation where bodies are retained before their disposition. *Anatomy Act*, R.S.O. 1990, c. A.21, s. 1.

PUBLIC MOTOR BUS. A motor vehicle operated by or on behalf of a person carrying on upon any highway the business of a public carrier of passengers, or passengers and freight for gain.

PUBLIC MOTOR TRUCK. A motor vehicle carrying or used to carry goods or chattels, exclusive of express freight as carried on a public motor bus, for hire.

PUBLIC MUSEUM. Includes buildings used, or to be used, for the preservation of a collection of paintings or other works of art, or of objects of natural history, or of mechanical, scientific or philosophical inventions, instruments, models or designs, and dedicated or to be dedicated to the recreation of the public, together with any libraries, reading rooms, laboratories and other offices and premises used or to be used in connection therewith.

PUBLIC NUISANCE. 1. Activity which unreasonably interferes with the interest, of the public or a class of the public, in health, safety, morality, comfort, or convenience. 2. " . . . [O]ne which affects citizens generally as opposed to a private nuisance which only affects particular individuals, but a normal and legitimate way of proving a public nuisance is to prove a sufficiently large collection of similar private nuisances: . . ." *British Columbia (Attorney General) v. Couillard* (1984), 31 C.C.L.T. 26 at 32, 42 C.R. (3d) 273, 59 B.C.L.R. 102, 11 D.L.R. (4th) 567, 14 C.C.C. (3d) 169 (S.C.), McEachern C.J.

PUBLIC OFFICE. Has a meaning corresponding to that of Public Official and a person shall be deemed to be serving in a Public Office during such time as he is entitled to receive the salary annexed to that Public Office. *Diplomatic Ser-*

vice Superannuation Act, R.S.C. 1985, c. D-2, s. 2.

PUBLIC OFFICER. 1. " . . . [E]very one who is appointed to discharge a public duty, and receives a compensation in whatever shape, whether from the crown or otherwise, is constituted a public officer . . ." *Henly v. Mayor and Burgesses of Lyme* (1828), 5 Bing. 91 at 107, 130 E.R. 995 at 1001, Best C.J. 2. Includes any person in the public service (i) who is authorized by or under an enactment to do or enforce the doing of an act or thing or to exercise a power; or (ii) upon whom a duty is imposed by or under an enactment. 3. Includes a minister of the Crown and any person employed in the public service. 4. Includes (a) an officer of customs or excise; (b) an officer of the Canadian Forces; (c) an officer of the Royal Canadian Mounted Police; and (d) any officer while the officer is engaged in enforcing the laws of Canada relating to revenue, customs, excise, trade or navigation. *Criminal Code*, R.S.C. 1985, c. C-46, s. 2. 5. A person having a legal duty or authority to make official statements which duty or authority is expressly imposed by or given in a statute, regulation or specific instruction, or implied from the nature of the office because he is an official of the Government of Canada, the government of a Canadian province, a Canadian municipality, or because he is a member of the Canadian Forces. *Military Rules of Evidence*, C.R.C., c. 1049, s. 2.

PUBLIC OFFICIAL. 1. A person appointed to an office or employment by or under the Government. 2. An ambassador, minister, high commissioner or consul-general of Canada to another country and such other person of comparable status serving in another country in the public service of Canada as the Governor in Council may designate. *Diplomatic Service Superannuation Act*, R.S.C. 1985, c. D-2, s. 2.

PUBLIC ORDER EMERGENCY. An emergency that arises from threats to the security of Canada and that is so serious as to be a national emergency. *Emergencies Act*, S.C. 1988, c. 29, s. 16.

PUBLIC PARK. Includes any park, garden, or other land dedicated or to be dedicated to the recreation of the public.

PUBLIC PARKING AREA. A structure or an open area, other than a street, used for the temporary parking of more than four automobiles and available for public use without charge or for compensation or as an accommodation for clients or customers.

PUBLIC PASSENGER TRANSPORTA-TION SYSTEM. A public system for the transportation of passengers and goods operated under an annual operating agreement.

PUBLIC PASSENGER VEHICLE. 1. A motor vehicle operated by or on behalf of a person carrying on upon any highway the business of a public carrier of passengers, or passengers and freight, for gain and includes a school bus. *Motor Carrier Act*, R.S.N.S. 1989, c. 292, s. 2. 2. A motor vehicle that is available for use by the public and is operated at any time on a highway over a regular route or between fixed terminating points and on a regular time schedule by, for or on behalf of any person who charges or collects compensation for the transportation of passengers in or on the motor vehicle. *Motor Carrier Act*, R.S.B.C. 1979, c. 286, s. 1.

PUBLIC PEACE. " . . . [M]ay be taken as equivalent to the 'King's Peace' in its broader and later signification. The King's Peace is 'the legal name of the normal state of society.' (Stephens' History of Criminal Law, vol. 1, p. 185)." *R. v. Magee*, [1923] 3 W.W.R. 55 at 57, 17 Sask. L.R. 501, 40 C.C.C. 10 (C.A.), Haultain C.J.S.

PUBLIC PICNIC GROUNDS. An area in a park for use by the public for picnic purposes.

PUBLIC PLACE. 1. Includes any place to which the public have access as of right or by invitation, express or implied. *Criminal Code*, R.S.C. 1985, c. C-46, s. 150. 2. Includes any place, building or convenience to which the public has, or is permitted to have, access, and any highway, street, lane, park or place of public resort or amusement. 3. Includes any place in which the public has an interest arising out of the need to safeguard the public health. 4. A place to which ordinary members of the public have access by right or otherwise. 5. Includes (i) a place or building to which the public has access; (ii) a place of public resort; and (iii) any vehicle in a public place, but does not include a location off a highway that is reasonably remote from any settlement and that is used for picnicking, sport fishing or other outdoor recreational activity, does not include an premises licensed pursuant to Ordinance. *Liquor Act*, S.N.W.T. 1983 (1st Sess.), c. 26, s. 2. See ENCLOSED ~.

PUBLIC POLICY. 1. A highly indefinite moral value, usually resorted to as a principle of judicial legislation or interpretation based on the per-

ceived needs of the community. It is not usually dependent on evidence, but on judicial impression of what is or is not in the public interest. *Simpson v. Chiropractors' Assn. (Saskatchewan)*, 2001 SKCA 22, 31 Admin. L.R. (3d) 87 (C.A.), Cameron, J.A. for the court. 2. " . . . [A]n action [will be barred] on the ground of public policy only if we could say it was contrary to 'essential public or moral interest' or 'contrary to our conceptions of essential justice and morality.'" *Block Brothers Realty Ltd. v. Mollard* (1981), 122 D.L.R. (3d) 323 at 330, [1981] 4 W.W.R. 65, 27 B.C.L.R. 17 (C.A.), the court per Craig J.A. 3. " . . . [F]ederal and provincial statutes and public law may be resorted to as a guide to public policy . . ." *Seneca College of Applied Arts & Technology v. Bhadauria* (1979), 9 B.L.R. 117 at 125, 27 O.R. (2d) 142, 11 C.C.L.T. 121, 105 D.L.R. (3d) 707, 80 C.L.L.C. 14,003 (C.A.), the court per Wilson J.A. 4. The use of the defence of public policy to challenge the enforcement of a foreign judgment involves impeachment of that judgment by condemning the foreign law on which the judgment is based. It is not a remedy to be used lightly. The expansion of this defence to include perceived injustices that do not offend our sense of morality is unwarranted. The defence of public policy should continue to have a narrow application. *Beals v. Saldanha*, 2003 SCC 72, per Major, J. See INTERNATIONAL ~.

PUBLIC POOL. A structure, basin, chamber or tank containing or intended to contain an artificial body of water for swimming, water sport, water recreation or entertainment, but does not include, (a) one that is located on a private residential property under the control of the owner or occupant and that is limited to use for swimming or bathing by the owner or occupant, members of their family and their visitors, or (b) one that is used solely for commercial display and demonstration purposes. *Health Protection and Promotion Act*, R.S.O. 1990, c. H.7 s. 1(1).

PUBLIC PORT FACILITY. Any port facility under the control and management of the Minister by virtue of section 9. *Public Harbours and Port Facilities Act*, R.S.C. 1985, c. P-29, s. 2.

PUBLIC PROMISSORY ESTOPPEL. The requirements of public law promissory estoppel are the same as private law promissory estoppel except that legislative intent will be considered. *St. Anthony Seafoods Ltd. Partnership v. Newfoundland (Minister of Fisheries & Aquaculture)* (2003), 227 Nfld. & P.E.I.R. 310 (N.L. T.D.).

PUBLIC PROPERTY. 1. Property, immovable or movable, real or personal, belonging to Her Majesty in right of a province and includes property belonging to an agency of government. 2. All property, other than money, belonging to Her Majesty in right of Canada. *Financial Administration Act*, R.S.C. 1985, c. F-11, s. 2 . 3. All money and property of Her Majesty in right of Canada. *National Defence Act*, R.S.C. 1985, c. N-5, s. 2. 4. All property belonging to the government.

PUBLIC PURPOSES. See LAND FOR ~.

PUBLIC RECORD. A record created by or received by a department in the conduct of its affairs except the copy of a record created only for convenience of reference and surplus copies of mimeographed, multilithed, printed or processed circulars or memoranda.

PUBLIC RECREATIONAL FACILITY. A recreational facility available to any individual who wishes to use it for its intended purposes.

PUBLIC REGULATORY AGENCY. Any ministry, agency, board, commission or corporation established or controlled by the Crown which approves, establishes, regulates, recommends or requires particular prices, user charges or fees to be charged for any product or service.

PUBLIC REPRESENTATIVE. A person appointed as a member of a board who, in the opinion of the minister, is impartial respecting the interests of the employees in respect of whom the board may be or is required to make recommendations and the interests of the employers of such employees. *Construction Industry Wages Act*, R.S.M. 1970, c. 190, s. 2.

PUBLIC RESERVE. Land which vests in a municipality and which is dedicated to the public. *An Act to Amend the Real Property Act*, S.M. 1980-81, c. 10, s. 2.

PUBLIC RESORT. See PLACE OF ~.

PUBLIC REVENUE. All revenue and public moneys, from whatever source arising, whether the revenues and moneys belong to the province, or are held by the province, or collected or held by officers of the province for or on account of or in trust for any other province, or for Canada or for the Imperial Government or for any other party or person.

PUBLIC ROOMS. Includes halls, dining rooms, bars, smoke rooms, lounges, recreation rooms, nurseries and libraries. *Hull Construction Regulations*, C.R.C., c. 1431, s. 2.

PUBLIC SAFETY. See PRIMARY ~ ANSWERING POINT.

PUBLIC SAFETY ANSWERING POINT. A communication centre that functions to receive emergency calls and to dispatch such calls to the appropriate emergency service agency. See SECONDARY ~.

PUBLIC SALE. A sale either by public auction or public tender conducted in accordance with this Act and the prescribed rules. *Municipal Tax Sales Act*, R.S.O. 1990, c. M.60, s. 1(1).

PUBLIC SALE YARD. A place of business where livestock is sold, offered for sale or kept for sale.

PUBLIC SAUNA. A sauna that is available for use by the general public and includes a sauna located in a hotel, motel, campground, university or a residential property containing more than four living units.

PUBLIC SCHOOL. A school operated by a school board and receiving grants from public funds of the province provided for education.

PUBLIC SECTOR. The civil service, Crown entities and external agencies. See PROVINCIAL ~.

PUBLIC SECTOR EMPLOYEE. A person employed by a public sector employer.

PUBLIC SECTOR EMPLOYER. (a) The government; (b) a corporation or an unincorporated board, commission, council, bureau, authority or similar body that has: (i) on its board of management or board of directors, a majority of members who are appointed by an act, a minister or the Lieutenant Council; or (ii) employees appointed under a Public Service act; (c) a municipality; (d) a board of school trustees; (e) a university; (f) a community care facility; (g) a hospital.

PUBLIC SERVANT. 1. Any person employed in a department, and includes a member of the Canadian Forces or the Royal Canadian Mounted Police. *Public Servants Inventions Act*, R.S.C. 1985, c. P-32, s. 2. 2. A person appointed under this Act to the service of the Crown by the Lieutenant Governor in Council, by the Commission or by a minister. *Public Service Act*, R.S.O. 1990, c. P.47, s. 1. 3. In my opinion, however, the balance of the evidence favours the conclusion that, as ordinarily understood, the term "public servants" does not include judges but approximates to "civil servants" or "government employees", not independent office holders. It does not include members of the judicial branch of government which performs its work independently of the executive and legislative branches. *Crowe v. R.*, 2003 FCA 191, 2003 D.T.C. 5288, [2003] 3 C.T.C. 271, 303 N.R. 305 (C.A.).

PUBLIC SERVICE. 1. The several positions in or under any department or other portion of the public service of Canada specified in Schedule I. *Public Service Staff Relations Act*, R.S.C. 1985, c. P-35, s. 2. 2. The several positions in or under any department or portion of the executive government of Canada, and, for the purposes of this Part, of the Senate and House of Commons, the Library of Parliament and any board, commission, corporation or portion of the public service of Canada specified in Schedule I. *Public Service Superannuation Act*, R.S.C. 1985, c. P-36, s. 3. 3. All ministries or any part thereof.

PUBLIC SERVICE COMMISSION. The body which staffs the federal public service.

PUBLIC SERVICE EMPLOYER. (i) The Government of Canada; (ii) the government of a province or territory of Canada; (iii) a university.

PUBLIC SERVICE STAFF RELATIONS BOARD. The federal body which, under the Public Service Staff Relations Act, oversees collective bargaining, grievances and adjudication for the federal public service.

PUBLIC SERVICE VEHICLE. A motor vehicle or trailer that is operated by or on behalf of any person for gain or reward.

PUBLIC SHOOTING PRESERVE. Land that is Crown owned, leased or developed with Crown funds, on which, or part of which, game birds that have been raised in captivity or released for the purpose of hunting and are designated as public shooting preserves in the regulations. *Fish and Game Protection Act*, R.S.P.E.I. 1988, c. F-12, s. 1(kk).

PUBLIC'S RIGHT TO KNOW. The right of members of the public to be informed about the operations of government and public officials.

PUBLIC STOCKYARD. An area of land used as a public market for purchasing and selling livestock, with the buildings situated thereon and used in connection therewith. *The Brand and Brand Inspection Act*, R.S.S. 1978, c. B-7, s. 2.

PUBLIC STORES. Includes any personal property that is under the care, supervision, administration or control of a public department or of any person in the service of a public department. *Criminal Code*, R.S.C. 1985, c. C-46, s. 2.

PUBLIC SWIMMING POOL. A swimming pool that is available for use by the general public and includes a swimming pool located in a hotel, motel, campground, university or a residential property containing more than four living units.

PUBLIC SWITCHED TELEPHONE NETWORK. A telecommunication facility the primary purpose of which is to provide a land line-based telephone service to the public for compensation.

PUBLIC TRAIL. The whole of any motorized snow vehicle trail established and maintained in whole or in part by public funds.

PUBLIC TRANSIT MOTOR VEHICLE. Any motor vehicle operated by, for or on behalf of the municipality, or any other municipality.

PUBLIC TRANSIT PERMIT. A permit that is valid and in force issued by the Commission authorizing its holder to provide a bus transport service for passengers, and their baggage, where such is the case, for direct or indirect remuneration, on a regular route and on a fixed time-schedule. *Municipal and Intermunicipal Transit Corporations Act*, R.S.Q. 1977, c. C-70, s. 1.

PUBLIC TRANSIT SYSTEM. A system of providing passenger transportation.

PUBLIC TRANSPORTATION. Any service for which a fare is charged for transporting the public bar vehicles operated by or on behalf of a municipality or a local board thereof, or under an agreement between a municipality and a person, firm or corporation.

PUBLIC TRANSPORTATION SERVICE. A service provided by vehicles operated either underground, above ground or on highways or rights-of-way on the ground surface for the transportation for compensation of passengers, or passengers and express freight that may be carried in such vehicles.

PUBLIC TRANSPORTATION SYSTEM. A publicly or privately owned facility, conveyance or other thing that is used in connection with publicly available services for the transportation of persons or cargo. *Criminal Code*, R.S.C. 1985, c. C-46, s. 431.2 (1).

PUBLIC TRUCK. A commercial motor vehicle or the combination of a commercial motor vehicle and trailer or trailers drawn by it, operated by the holder of an operating licence. *Truck Transportation Act*, R.S.O. 1990, c. T.22, s. 1(1).

PUBLIC TRUST. A trust established to benefit the public or a section of it.

PUBLIC TRUSTEE. Public official who attends to matters relating to persons who are mentally incompetent, especially to property.

PUBLIC USE. The phrase "public use" in s. 914(2) [Local Government Act, R.S.B.C. 1996, c. 323] is used in contradistinction to "private use" . . . the words "public use" mean that the lands may be freely used by the public at large subject only to restrictions imposed by one of the three levels of government or are used by a public institution owned by one of the three levels of government. To have privately owned property restricted to a public use, the general public would have to be given a right to use the property for a particular purpose and the owner of the property would have to be compelled by statute or bylaw to permit such use by the public. The words "public use" are [not] sufficiently broad to include any use which involves the public being given general access to the lands. For example, a restriction of the use of property to the use of a department store would not amount to a restriction to a public use. Although the public has general access to a department store, the owner of the store has the right to control access to the public and the purpose of operating the store is to make a profit for the benefit of a private institution. Similarly with a railway, the owner of the railway has the right to control access to the public and is entitled to generate a profit by imposing charges on persons who wish to use the railway. *535534 British Columbia Ltd. v. White Rock (City)*, 2001 CarswellBC 2159, 2001 BCSC 1381 (S.C.), Tysoe J.

PUBLIC UTILITIES COMMISSION. A commission established by by-law by any municipality to control and manage works for the production or supply of a public utility. Where a commission already exists, it may be entrusted with any other public utility.

PUBLIC UTILITY. 1. Any person or association of persons that owns, operates or manages an undertaking (a) for the supply of petroleum or petroleum products by pipeline; (b) for the supply, transmission or distribution of gas, electricity, steam or water; (c) for the collection and disposal of garbage or sewage or for the control of pollution; (d) for the transmission, emission, reception or conveyance of information by any telecommunication system; or (e) for the provision of postal services. *Statistics Act*, R.S.C. 1985, c. S-19, s. 17(3). 2. "[In s. 2(j), Public Utilities Board Act, R.S.A. 1970, c. 302] . . . a concept embracing physical plant and nonphysical service elements." *Atco Ltd. v. Calgary Power Ltd.* (1982), 20 B.L.R. 227 at 232, [1982] 2 S.C.R. 557, [1983] 1 W.W.R. 385, 23 Alta. L.R. (2d) 1, 41 A.R. 1, 45 N.R. 1, 140 D.L.R. (3d) 193, Estey J. (Beetz, Chouinard and Lamer JJ. concurring). See GOVERNMENT ~; MUNICIPAL ~; OWNER OF A ~.

PUBLIC UTILITY INSTALLATION. Any pole, tower, overhead or underground conduit, any other supporting or sustaining structure, and any trench, together with accessories, susceptible of use for the supply or distribution of electrical, telephone, telegraph, cable delivery or signalling service or any other similar service.

PUBLIC UTILITY UNDERTAKING. A water works or water supply system, sewage works, electrical power or energy generating transmission or distribution system, street lighting system, natural or artificial gas works or supply system, and a transportation system, and includes any lands, buildings or equipment required for the administration or operation of any such system. *Municipal Act*, R.S.O. 1990, c. M.45, s. 5 8.

PUBLIC VEHICLE. A motor vehicle operated on a highway by, for, or on behalf of any person who receives compensation either directly or indirectly for the transportation therein of passengers and express freight which might be carried on a passenger vehicle.

PUBLIC WASHROOM. Any room that contains one or more sanitary units and to which (i) employees of a business or institution, (ii) patrons of, or visitors to, a place of business, (iii) students, patients, inmates or visitors of an institution, (iv) the travelling or transient public, or (v) all tenants of an apartment building or condominium, would expect to have the right of access without any special permission from management.

PUBLIC WATER SUPPLY. Includes water being supplied or to be supplied for human consumption to (a) ten or more households; or (b) any business, public building or place of assembly.

PUBLIC WAY. A sidewalk, street, highway, square or other open space to which the public has access, as of right or by invitation, expressed or implied.

PUBLIC WELFARE EMERGENCY. An emergency that is caused by a real or imminent (a) ire, flood drought, storm, earthquake or other natural phenomenon, (b) disease in human beings, animals or plants, or (c) accident or pollution and that results or may result in a danger to life or property, social disruption or a breakdown in the flow of essential goods, services or resources, so serious as to be a national emergency. *Emergencies Act*, S.C. 1988, c. 29, s. 5.

PUBLIC WELFARE OFFENCE. 1. A form of offence, the legislative object of which is to regulate some activities in the interests of the public as a whole. 2. " . . . [B]elong in a category between those where guilt flows from mere proof of the actus reus and full mens rea offences. . ." *R. v. Ellis-Don Ltd.* (1990), 34 C.C.E.L. 130 at 149, 2 C.R. (4th) 118, 1 O.R. (3d) 193, 76 D.L.R. (4th) 347, 61 C.C.C. (3d) 423, 42 O.A.C. 49 (C.A.), Carthy J.A. (dissenting). 3. " . . . [N]ot criminal in the true sense and it is therefore not subject to the presumption of full mens rea. . . An accused may absolve himself on proof that he took all the care which a reasonable man might have been expected to take in all the circumstances or, in other words, that he was in no way negligent." *R. v. Chapin* (1979), 8 C.E.L.R. 151 at 157, 159, [1979] 2 S.C.R. 121, 7 C.R. (3d) 225 (Eng.), 26 N.R. 289, 45 C.C.C. (2d) 333, 95 D.L.R. (3d) 13, 10 C.R. (3d) 371 (Fr.), the court per Dickson J.

PUBLIC WHIRLPOOL. A whirlpool that is available for use by the general public and includes a whirlpool located in a hotel, motel, campground, university or a residential property containing more than four living units. *An Act to Amend the Health Act*, S.N.B. 1987, c. 24, s. 1.

PUBLIC WORK. 1. Any work or property under the management, charge and direction or the administration and control of the Minister. *Public Works Act*, R.S.C. 1985, c. P-38, s. 3. 2. "[In Exchqeuer Court Act, R.S.C. 1927, c. 34] . . . means a physical thing having a definite area. . . designates a physical thing, and not a public service." *R. v. Dubois*, [1935] 3 D.L.R. 209 at 215, 221, [1935] S.C.R. 378, Duff C.J.C. 3. " . . . Not merely some building or other erection or structure belonging to the public, but any operations undertaken by or on behalf of the Government in constructing, repairing or maintaining public property." *R. v. Compagnie Generale d'Enterprises Publiques* (1971), 57 S.C.R. 527 at 532, Anglin J. 4. Includes all work and properties acquired, made, built, constructed, erected, extended, enlarged, repaired, improved, formed, or excavated, at the expense of the government. 5. Any undertaking carried out by the Crown.

PUBLIC WORKING CIRCLE. An area of land within the forest land under a forest management plan wherein the cutting of Crown timber thereon is authorized by a timber permit or timber sale. *The Forest Act*, R.S.S. 1978, c. F-19, s. 2.

PUBLIC WORKS CANADA. The federal ministry which manages public works and federal real estate in Canada.

PUBLISH. *v.* 1. With respect to a libel, when he (a) exhibits it in public; (b) causes it to be read or seen; or (c) shows or delivers it, or causes it to be shown or delivered, with intent that it should be read or seen by the person whom it defames or by any other person. *Criminal Code*, R.S.C. 1985, c. C-46, s. 299. 2. Transmission, emission, dissemination or the making public of writings, signs, signals, symbols, pictures and sounds of all kinds, from or by a newspaper or from or by broadcasting. *Defamation Act*, R.S.M. 1987, c. D20, s. 1.

PUBLISHED. *adj.* 1. Published in a daily or weekly newspaper that, in the opinion of the clerk of the municipality, has circulation within the municipality as to provide reasonable notice to those affected thereby. *Municipal Act*, R.S.O. 1990, c. M.45, s. 1(1). 2. Released for public distribution or sale. 3. Communicated to someone else besides the plaintiff. R.E. Brown, *The Law of Defamation in Canada* (Toronto: Carswell, 1987) at 247.

PUBLISHED IN CANADA. Released in Canada for public distribution or sale. The publisher of a book published in Canada shall, at the publisher's own expense and within one week after the date of publication, send two copies of the book to the National Librarian, who shall give to the publisher a written receipt therefor.

PUBLISHED MARKET. In respect of a class of securities, a market on which securities of that class are traded if the prices at which they have been traded on that market are regularly published in a bona fide newspaper, news magazine or business or financial publication that is of general and regular paid circulation.

PUBLISHER. *n*. 1. " . . . [O]ne who participates in the preparation and/or publication of an article, . . ." *Munro v. Toronto Sun Publishing Corp.* (1982), 21 C.C.L.T. 261 at 298, 39 O.R. (2d) 100 (H.C.), Holland J. 2. " . . . [T]he publisher of the newspaper is the proprietor of the business of publishing the paper and in that sense is necessarily the proprietor of the paper. . ." *Scown v. Herald Publishing Co.* (1917), 38 D.L.R. 43 at 44, 12 Alta. L.R. 127, [1917] 3 W.W.R. 925 (C.A.), Harvey C.J. (Beck and Walsh JJ.A. concurring). 3. Any person whose main or secondary activity in Québec is the selection and production of a manuscript or a text in the form of a book, its distribution and its putting on sale. *An Act respecting the development of Quebec firms in the book industry*, S.Q. 1979, c. 68, s. 1.

P.U. (C.) BD. *abbr*. Public Utilities (Commissioners') Board.

PUFF. *n*. A statement which praises a seller's goods but which an ordinary, reasonable buyer does not usually regard as important. G.H.L. Fridman, *Sale of Goods in Canada*, 3d ed (Toronto: Carswell, 1986) at 149-150.

PUFFER. *n*. A person appointed to bid on the part of the seller. *Conveyancing and Law of Property Act*, R.S.O. 1990, c. C.34, s. 1(1).

PUFFERY. *n*. Exaggeration or embellishment of the qualities of goods by the seller.

PUISNE. *adj*. [Fr.] Junior, of lower rank. Used to describe a judge or justice other than the chief judge or justice of a court.

PULLORUM TEST OR BLOOD TEST. A test for pullorum disease. *Livestock and Livestock Products Act*, R.S.C. 1985, c. L-9, s. 42.

PULMONARY EDEMA. Escape of circulatory fluid into the lungs. F.A. Jaffe, *A Guide to Pathological Evidence*, 3d ed. (Toronto: Carswell, 1991) at 107.

PULMONARY EMBOLISM. Blockage of the main artery in a lung or its branches by an embolus. F.A. Jaffe, *A Guide to Pathological Evidence*, 3d ed. (Toronto: Carswell, 1991) at 218.

PULP AND PAPER. Includes all forms of processed or manufactured wood pulp, whether ultimately manufactured into paper or otherwise. *Logging Tax Act*, R.S.B.C. 1979, c. 248, s. 1.

PULPWOOD. *n*. The raw material intended to be processed by a pulp mill.

PULPWOOD BERTH. Any area leased for the cutting of pulpwood.

PULSARE. [L.] To accuse; to lay a complaint against.

PULSATOR. *n*. An actor or plaintiff; a prosecutor or complainant.

PULSE. *n*. An intermittent emission.

PULSE AMPLITUDE. The zero to peak, peak to peak or other specified magnitude of variation of a pulse. *Medical Devices Regulations*, C.R.C., c. 871, s. 1.

PULSE DURATION. 1. The time interval of the wave shape measured in milliseconds at specified reference points. *Medical Devices Regulations*, C.R.C., c. 871, s. 1. 2. The time interval measured between the half-peak power points on the leading and trailing edges. *Radiation Emitting Devices Regulations*, C.R.C., c. 1370, s. 1.

PULSE GENERATOR. That portion of a cardiac pacemaker that produces a periodical electrical pulse and includes the power source and electronic circuit. *Medical Devices Regulations*, C.R.C., c. 871, s. 1.

PULSE INTERVAL. The time between the leading edges of successive pulse generator pulses. *Medical Devices Regulations*, C.R.C., c. 871, s. 1.

PUMP. See CONSUMER ~; GASOLINE ~; HEAT ~; MOTIVE FUEL ~.

PUMPER. *n*. A vessel that is used only for the purpose of pumping fish from a fishing vessel or from fishing gear.

PUMPING WELL. A chamber, manhole, or other structure used for the installation of portable or temporary pumping equipment.

PUMP-OUT FACILITY. A device or equipment for removing sewage from a pleasure boat in which a toilet is installed by the use of hose or pipe connected to a pump or equipment designed to create suction and located other than on the boat from which the sewage is to be removed.

PUNCTURE. A wound greater in depth than in width, said to be penetrating. F.A. Jaffe, *A Guide to Pathological Evidence*, 3d ed. (Toronto: Carswell, 1991) at 167.

PUNISHABLE. *adj*. Subject to punishment.

PUNISHMENT. *n.* 1. A penalty for breaking the law. *R. v. Johnson* (1972), 17 C.R.N.S. 254 at 256, [1972] 3 W.W.R. 145, 6 C.C.C. (2d) 380 (B.C. C.A.), the court per Bull J.A. 2. A deprivation of property or right. 3. In [*Rodriguez v. British Columbia (Attorney General)*, [1993] 3 S.C.R. 519, 85 C.C.C. (3d) 15], the Supreme Court considered the applicability of s. 12 [of the Canadian Charter of Rights and Freedoms] in the context of a Criminal Code provision that had the effect of imposing cruel and unusual punishment on someone other than an accused person. Sopinka J., for the majority of the Court, held that the negative effects of a Criminal Code provision upon a person not facing a criminal charge could not amount to being subjected by the state to any form of punishment within the meaning of s. 12. *Canadian Foundation for Children, Youth & the Law v. Canada (Attorney General)* (2000), 2000 CarswellOnt 2409, 146 C.C.C. (3d) 362, 188 D.L.R. (4th) 718, 49 O.R. (3d) 662, 36 C.R. (5th) 334, 76 C.R.R. (2d) 251 (S.C.J.). See ARBITRARY ~; CAPITAL ~; CRUEL AND UNUSUAL ~; LESS ~; SCALE OF ~S.

PUNITIVE DAMAGES. 1. " . . . [A]warded to punish the defendant and to make an example of him or her in order to deter others from committing the same tort: . . ." *Norberg v. Wynrib* (1992), 12 C.C.L.T. (2d) 1 at 29, [1992] 4 W.W.R. 577, 68 B.C.L.R. (2d) 29, 138 N.R. 81, 8 B.C.A.C. 1, 19 W.A.C. 1, 92 D.L.R. (4th) 449, [1992] 2 S.C.R. 226, La Forest J. (Gonthier and Cory JJ. concurring). 2. " . . . [M]ay only be employed in circumstances where the conduct giving the cause for complaint is of such nature that it merits punishment. . . may only be awarded in respect of conduct which is of such nature as to be deserving of punishment because of its harsh, vindictive, reprehensible and malicious nature . . . in any case where such an award is made the conduct must be extreme in its nature and such that by any reasonable standard it is deserving of full condemnation and punishment . . ." *Vorvis v. Insurance Corp. o f British Columbia* (1989), 58 D.L.R. (4th) 193 at 201-2, 205-9, [1989] 1 S.C.R. 1085, [1989] 4 W.W.R. 193, 25 C.C.E.L. 81, 90 C.L.L.C. 14,035, 36 B.C.L.R. (2d) 273, 94 N.R. 321, 42 B.L.R. 111, McIntyre J. (Beetz and Lamer JJ. concurring). 3. Punitive damages may be awarded in situations where the defendant's misconduct is so malicious, oppressive, and high-handed that it offends the court's sense of decency. Punitive damages bear no relation to what the plaintiff should receive by way of compensation. Their aim is not to compensate the plaintiff, but rather to punish the defendant. It is the means by which the jury or judge expresses its outrage at the egregious conduct of the defendant. They are in the nature of a fine, which is meant to act as a deterrent to the defendant and to others from acting in this manner. *Hill v. Church of Scientology of Toronto*, [1995] 2 S.C.R. 1130.

PUPA. *n.* The stage of rest between the larva and the adult form during the metamorphosis of certain insects. F.A. Jaffe, *A Guide to Pathological Evidence*, 3d ed. (Toronto: Carswell, 1991) at 225.

PUPIL. *n.* 1. "A . . . connotation of childhood attaches to the word 'pupil' used in s. 43 [of the Criminal Code R.S.C. 1970, c. C-34], which, unlike the more neutral 'student' has overtones of immaturity or youthful . . . the term 'pupil' as used in s. 43 must be limited, as it was at common law, to a child taking instruction." *R. v. Ogg-Moss* (1984), 11 D.L.R. (4th) 549 at 564, [1984] 2 S.C.R. 173, 54 N.R. 81, 14 C.C.C. (3d) 116, 5 O.A.C. 81, 6 C.H.R.R. D/2498, 41 C.R. (3d) 297, the court per Dickson J. 2. " . . . [O]ne who is taught by another within the context of the educational system." *Maw v. Scarborough Board of Education* (1983) 43 O.R. (2d) 694 at 697 (Div. Ct.), the court per Osborne J. 3. A person who is enrolled in a school or private school and includes any person who is of compulsory school age. 4. A person to whom education is given for a direct or indirect remuneration. See CANADA SUPPORTED ~; ELEMENTARY ~; EXCEPTIONAL ~; HALF-TIME ~; HARD TO SERVE ~; QUALIFYING ~; RESIDENT ~; RESIDENT ~S; SECONDARY ~.

PUPIL RECORD. A record in respect of a pupil that is established and maintained by the principal of a school in accordance.

PUR AUTRE VIE. [Fr.] For or during the life of another. R. Megarry and H.W.R. Wade, *The Law of Real Property*, 5th ed. (London: Stevens, 1984) at cxxvii. See ESTATE ~.

PUR CAUSE DE VICINAGE. By reason of neighbourhood.

PURCHASE. *v.* See OFFER TO ~; TO ~.

PURCHASE. *n.* 1. Contract, conveyance or assignment under or by which any beneficial interest in any kind of property may be acquired. 2. Includes taking by sale, lease, negotiation, mortgage, pledge, lien, gift or any other consensual transaction creating an interest in personal property. *Personal Property Security acts.* See CASH ~ TICKET; COMPULSORY ~; CONSUMER ~; HOME ~ LOAN; SHARE ~ WARRANT.

PURCHASE AGREEMENT. 1. An agreement for the sale and purchase of residential premises. 2. An agreement for the purchase of a prearranged funeral plan, a pre-need cemetery plan or a cemetery lot for use at a future date or the right to use such a lot. *Cemetery and Funeral Services Act*, R.S.N.S. 1989, c. 62, s. 2.

PURCHASE FINANCING TRANSAC-TION. The extension of credit to a borrower by a creditor where the creditor knows or ought to know that the credit proceeds will be used by the borrower to purchase goods or services from a seller.

PURCHASE FOR CANCELLATION. In relation to mutual fund shares of the company, be deemed to be a reference to acceptance by the company of the surrender of those shares.

PURCHASE MONEY. Includes the consideration for a lease. *Companies acts.*

PURCHASE-MONEY MORTGAGE. A mortgage given by a purchaser of land to the vendor of the land or the vendor's nominee as security for the payment of all or part of the consideration for the sale.

PURCHASE-MONEY SECURITY INTER-EST. *var.* **PURCHASE MONEY SECURITY INTEREST**. A security interest taken or reserved in collateral to secure payment of all or part of its price, or a security interest taken by a person who gives value for the purpose of enabling the debtor to acquire rights in or to collateral to the extent that the value is applied to acquire the rights, but does not include a transaction of sale by and lease back to the seller. *Personal Property Security Acts*.

PURCHASE PRICE. 1. "[In a contract for commission means] . . . the actual price or sum at which the property was sold . . ." *George v. Howard* (1913), 16 D.L.R. 468 at 469, 5 W.W.R. 1152, 49 S.C.R. 75, 27 W.L.R. 425, Davies J. 2. The entire consideration for the purchase, delivery and installation of a property and, without restricting the generality of the foregoing, includes the value of property given in exchange or trade and outstanding obligations or liabilities cancelled assumed or satisfied. *Assessment Act*, S.N.S. 1986, c. 22, s. 9. 3. The total value of the consideration or such part thereof as has been paid by the consumer to the retail seller or his assignee for a consumer product and includes such finance charges or other credit costs that the consumer has reasonably incurred respecting the product. *The Consumer Products Warranties Act*, R.S.S. 1978, c. C-30, s. 2. 4. The price for which accommodation is purchased, including the price in money, the value of services rendered, and other considerations accepted by the operator in return for the accommodation provided. *Hotel Room Tax Act*, R.S.B.C. 1979, c. 183, s. 1. 5. The total obligation payable by the buyer under an executory contract. *Consumer Protection Act*, R.S.O. 1990, c. C.31, s. 1. 6. Includes a price in money and also the value of services rendered, the actual value of the thing exchanged and other considerations accepted by the seller or person from whom the property passes as price or on account of the price of the thing covered by the contract, sale or exchange, and includes (i) customs and excise; (ii) charges for installation of the thing sold, for interest, for finance, for service and for transportation, unless such charges are shown separately, on the invoice or in the contract with the purchaser.

PURCHASER. *n.* 1. A person who buys or agrees to buy goods or services. 2. A person who takes by sale, mortgage, hypothec, pledge, issue, reissue, gift or any other voluntary transaction creating an interest in a security. 3. Includes a lessee, a mortgagee and an intending purchaser, lessee or mortgagee, or other person, who, for valuable consideration, takes or deals for any property. *Conveyancing acts.* 4. Includes a person who barters or exchanges property whether real or personal with any other person for stock in bulk. *Bulk Sales acts.* 5. Includes mortgagee and pledgee. *Warehouse Receipts acts.* See BONA FIDE ~; DOMESTIC ~; GOOD FAITH ~; INTERMEDIATE ~; RETAIL ~; SUBSEQUENT ~; SUBSEQUENT ~ OR MORTGAGEE; TAX ~.

PURCHASER FOR VALUE. " . . . [O]ne who obtains a property for a valuable, as distinguished from a merely good, consideration; and where there is no question of bona fides involved . . . the question of the adequacy of the consideration cannot be inquired into." *Crosseit v. Haycock* (1904), 7 O.L.R. 655 at 657 (Div. Ct.), Street J. (Falconbridge C.J. concurring).

PURCHASER FOR VALUE WITHOUT NOTICE. One who purchased property bona fide for a valuable, even if inadequate, consideration without notice of any prior title or right that, if upheld, would restrict or limit the title which the purchaser supposedly acquired.

PURCHASER'S COST OF A SHARE. The price paid for a share plus any reasonable expenses and fees for that purchase.

PURCHASER'S LIEN. A lien which protects the deposit and any other money that a person who agreed to purchase land paid on account of the purchase price, as well as costs and interest. B.J. Reiter, B.N. McLellan & P.M. Perell, *Real Estate Law*, 4th ed. (Toronto: Emond Montgomery, 1992) at 777.

PURCHASING COMMISSION. The commission must do the following: (a) acquire supplies required by the government and, on request, supplies required by government institutions; (b) direct the establishment, maintenance and operation of depots or warehouses in which supplies of the government and government institutions may be stored and from which they may be distributed; (c) supervise the distribution of supplies for the government and, on request, supervise the distribution of supplies for government institutions; (d) provide advice and assistance to the government and, on request, to government institutions in order that (i) supplies and services of the most advantageous and suitable type on an economically effective and environmentally sound basis may be utilized, and (ii) uniformity in supplies and services may be attained if desirable; (e) create and arrange opportunities for the government and government institutions to acquire supplies and services at rates and on terms and conditions conducive to the economic and environmental well-being of British Columbia; (f) in conjunction with the performance of its other duties and with the exercise of its powers, arrange, encourage and facilitate other transactions conducive to the economic and environmental well-being of British Columbia; (g) recommend to the government policies to be applied in the acquisition and disposition of supplies.

PURCHASING OFFICE. Every one who purports to purchase or gives a reward or profit for the purported purchase of any such appointment, resignation or consent, or agrees or promises to do so, is guilty of an indictable. *Criminal Code*, R.S.C. 1985, c. C-46, s. 124.

PURE. *adj.* " . . . [N]ot . . . defiled, corrupted or impaired, . . ." *Jay-Zee Food Products v. Deputy*

Minister of National Revenue (Customs & Excise), [1965] C.T.C. 336 at 338, [1966] Ex. C.R. 307, 65 D.T.C. 5179 (Ex. Ct.), Gibson J.

PURE-BRED. *var.* **PUREBRED**. *adj.* In relation to an animal of a distinct breed, means an animal that is a purebred of the breed as determined by the by-laws of the association authorized to register animals of that breed.

PURE-BRED CATTLE. Cattle registered in the Canadian National Livestock Records or in any records recognized by the Canadian National Livestock Record Committee.

PURE CAPTIVE INSURANCE COMPANY. An insurance company incorporated under the Company Act to insure the risks of its parent, the parent's affiliated corporations or their or its officers, directors, employees, agents or independent contractors in accordance with section 5. *Insurance (Captive Company) Act*, S.B.C. 1987, c. 9, s. 1.

PURE ECONOMIC LOSS. "[Usually refers to] . . . a diminution of worth incurred without any physical injury to any asset of the plaintiff . . ." *Ontario (Attorney General) v. Fatehi* (1984), 31 M.V.R. 301 at 307, [1984] 2 S.C.R. 536, 31 C.C.L.T. 1, 56 N.R. 62, 6 O.A.C. 270, 15 D.L.R. (4th) 132, the court per Estey J.

PURE GRAIN ALCOHOL. Absolute alcohol manufactured from grain.

PURE TAX HAVEN. A country, often an island, which imposes minimal taxes to get not only the benefits of active business but spin off benefits like financial institutions and greater numbers of professional jobs. W. Grove & F. Iacobucci, *Materials on Canadian Income Tax*, 4th ed. (Toronto: Richard De Boo Ltd., 1980) at 712.

PURE WATER AREAS. Waters approved by the Department of National Health and Welfare for the taking of shellfish. *Fishery regulations*.

PURGE. *v.* With respect to contempt, to make amends for or clear oneself of contempt of court.

PURIFICATION SYSTEM. Includes any plant or installation used, or designed to be used, for the improvement of the physical, chemical, biological or aesthetic properties of land, air, or water.

PURIFICATION WORKS. A sewer, a sewer system, a waste water pumping station, a water purification station or any other works used to collect, receive, carry, treat or drain waste water, or a part of any such equipment. *An Act to Amend the Act Respecting the Communauté Urbaine de Montréal and Other Legislation*, S.Q. 1985, c. 31, s. 11. See WATER ~.

PURPARTY. *n*. A portion or share; to hold land in purparty with someone is to hold it jointly with that person.

PURPORT. *n*. The substance of an instrument as it appears on the instrument's face.

PURPOSE. *n*. 1. The word "purpose" in s. 258(1)(a) [of the *Criminal Code*, R.S.C. 1985, c. C-46] refers to intent and not ability. *R. v. MacAulay*, 2002 PESCAD 24, 169 C.C.C. (3d) 321, 218 Nfld. & P.E.I.R. 312, 8 C.R. (6th) 109, 30 M.V.R. (4th) 263, 653 A.P.R. 312 (P.E.I. C.A.) 2. Object. 3. Reason for which something exists. See ADMINISTRATIVE ~; BASE ~; CHARITABLE ~; CONSERVATION ~; CONVEYING ~; DOMESTIC ~; DOMINANT ~ TEST; EMPLOYMENT ~S; FARMING ~S; FORESTRY ~S; HYDRAULICKING ~; INDUSTRIAL ~S; IRRIGATION ~; LAND IMPROVEMENT ~; MINERAL TRADING ~; MINERAL WATER ~S; MINING ~; MINING ~S; MUNICIPAL ~; PARAMOUNT ~ TEST; POWER ~; RIVER IMPROVEMENT ~; SUBSTANTIAL ~ TEST; UNLAWFUL ~.

PURPOSIVE INTERPRETATION. Remedies provisions must be interpreted in a way that provides "a full, effective and meaningful remedy for *Charter* violations" since "a right, no matter how expansive in theory, is only as meaningful as the remedy provided for its breach". A purposive approach to remedies in a *Charter* context gives modern vitality to the ancient maxim *ubi jus, ibi remedium*: where there is a right, there must be a remedy. More specifically, a purposive approach to remedies requires at least two things. First, the purpose of the right being protected must be promoted: courts must craft *responsive* remedies. Second, the purpose of the remedies provision must be promoted: courts must craft *effective* remedies. *Doucet-Boudreau v. Nova Scotia (Department of Education)*, 2003 SCC 62, per Iacobucci and Arbour, JJ.

PURPRESTURE. *n*. [Fr.] Anything which annoys or harms the Crown's demesnes or highways by enclosing, building or endeavouring to make private something which should be public.

PURSE. *n*. The money or other prize that is paid to the owners of horses that compete in a race.

PURSE SEINE NET. A net that is weighted at the bottom and mounted with rings through which a line is run, floated at the top, cast from a boat so as to enclose an area of water and then closed at the bottom by the line through the rings to form a purse or bag. *Fishery regulations*.

PURSUANT. *adv*. 1. " . . . '[W]ithin the limits of' or 'as circumscribed by' . . ." *R. v. Melford Developments Inc.*, [1981] 2 F.C. 627 at 634, 36 N.R. 9, [1981] C.T.C. 30, 81 D.T.C. 5020 (C.A.), Urie J.A. (Thurlow C.J. concurring). 2. " . . . '[B]y reason of' . . ." *Canada (Minister of National Revenue) v. Armstrong*, [1954] C.T.C. 236 at 240, [1954] Ex. C.R. 529, 54 D.T.C. 1104, Potter J.

PURSUANT TO. Following upon; consequent upon; in consequence of.

PURSUE. *v*. Of an authority or warrant, to execute or carry it out.

PURSUIVANT. *n*. A royal messenger.

PURVEYANCE. *n*. The provision of necessaries for a sovereign.

PURVEYOR. *n*. One who buys; the person who provided for a royal household. See WATER ~.

PURVIEW. *n*. The policy or scope of a statute.

PUSH-OUT WINDOW. A vehicle window designed to open outward to provide for emergency egress.

PUT. *v*. With respect to a question, to read a motion or amendment from the Chair, seeking the House's pleasure. A. Fraser, W.A. Dawson, & J. Holtby, eds., *Beauchesne's Rules and Forms of the House of Commons of Canada*, 6th ed. (Toronto: Carswell, 1989) at 93.

PUT. *n*. 1. An option transferable by delivery to deliver a specified number or amount of securities at a fixed price within a specified time. 2. " . . . [A] 'put' option is one to sell a specific quantity of stock at a fixed price for a stipulated period of time. . ." *Posluns v. Toronto Stock Exchange*, [1964] 2 O.R. 547 at 553, 46 D.L.R. (2d) 210 (H.C.), Gale J.

PUTATIVE. *adj*. Supposed, reputed.

PUTATIVE FATHER. A person alleged to have caused the pregnancy whereby a woman has become a mother.

PUTATIVE JUSTIFICATION. A situation in which an accused genuinely believes that the act was justified in law but, on the facts as the accused believed them, no such legal justification exists. D. Stuart, *Canadian Criminal Law: a treatise*, 2d ed. (Toronto: Carswell, 1987) at 392.

PUTREFACTION. *n*. The disintegration of the tissues caused by bacterial action. F.A. Jaffe, *A Guide to Pathological Evidence*, 3d ed. (Toronto: Carswell, 1991) at 225.

PUTREFACTIVE GASES. Gases which develop during putrefaction, especially hydrogen sulphide, ammonia, methane and carbon dioxide. F.A. Jaffe, *A Guide to Pathological Evidence*, 3d ed. (Toronto: Carswell, 1991) at 225.

PYKE. *abbr*. Pyke's Reports, King's Bench (Que.), 1809-1810.

PYRAMID. *v*. For an employee to work during certain hours which seem to attract premium rates under two different provisions of a collective agreement. Most frequently this occurs when an employee claims both a shift premium and an overtime premium for the same hours worked or when overtime pay is computed so that it includes work performed on a weekend or holiday. D.J.M. Brown and D.M. Beatty, *Canadian Labour Arbitration*, 3d ed. (Aurora: Canada Law Book, 1988-) at 8-19.

PYRAMID DISTRIBUTOR. Any person who distributes for valuable consideration goods or services through a marketing scheme involving independent agents, contractors or distributors, at different levels, where participants in the marketing scheme may or are required to recruit other participants, and where commissions or other consideration are or may be paid or allowed as a result of the sale of those goods or services to others or the recruitment, actions or performances of additional participants.

PYRAMID FRANCHISE. An agreement or arrangement, expressed or implied, oral or written, between two or more persons by which a franchisee upon paying a franchise fee or upon purchasing goods is granted the right: (i) to offer to sell, sell or distribute goods; and (ii) to recruit one or more persons who upon paying a franchise fee or upon purchasing goods are granted the same or similar purchasing rights; under a marketing plan or system, organized, directed, prescribed or controlled, in substantial part, by a franchisor.

PYRAMIDING. *n*. The provision of two or more employment benefits for the same period of time.

PYRAMID SALES FRANCHISE. A scheme, arrangement, device or other means whereby a participant pays a franchise fee and (i) is required or receives the right to recruit one or more other persons as participants who are subject to a similar requirement or who obtain a similar right; and (ii) has the right to receive money, credits, discounts, goods or any other right or thing of value the amount of which is dependent on the number of participants.

PYRAMID SELLING. See SCHEME OF ~.

Q.A.C. *abbr.* Causes en appel au Québec (Quebec Appeal Cases).

Q.B. *abbr.* 1. Queen's Bench. 2. Court of Queen's Bench. 3. Supreme Court, Queen's Bench Division.

[] Q.B. *abbr.* Law Reports, Queen's Bench, 1891-.

Q.B.D. *abbr.* 1. Queen's Bench Division. 2. Law Reports, Queen's Bench Division, 1875-1890.

QCTP. The neutral citation for the Tribunal des professions du Quebec.

Q.C. *abbr.* Queen's Counsel.

Q.L.R. *abbr.* Quebec Law Reports, 1875-1891 (Rapports judiciaires du Québec).

QR & O. *abbr.* Queen's Regulations and Orders.

QUA. *adv.* [L.] As, in the aspect of.

QUACUNQUE VIA DATA. [L.] Whichever way is given.

QUADACTOR. *n.* A betting transaction in which a purchaser of a ticket undertakes to select, in the exact order of finish, the first four horses to finish in the race on which that feature is operated. *Race Track Supervision Regulations*, C.R.C., c. 441, s. 2.

QUADRANT. *n.* 1. A measure of a 90 degree angle. 2. An instrument used in navigation and astronomy.

QUADRIPARTITE. *adj.* Having four parts or parties.

QUAE AB INITIO INUTILIS FUIT INSTITUTIO, EX POST FACTO CONVALESCERE NON POTEST. [L.] What was a useless institution from the beginning cannot be strengthened by anything done after.

QUAE ACCESSIONUM LOCUM OBTINENT EXTINGUUNTUR CUM PRINCIPALES RES PEREMPTAE FUERINT. [L.] Things which are incidental are extinguished when the principal things are extinguished.

QUAE AD UNUM FINEM LOQUUTA SUNT, NON DEBENT AD ALIUM DETORQUERI. [L.] Things which are said for one purpose should not be distorted to another.

QUAE COMMUNI LEGE DEROGANT STRICTE INTERPRETANTUR. [L.] Things which detract from the common law should be interpreted narrowly.

QUAE CONTRA RATIONEM JURIS INTRODUCTA SUNT, NON DEBENT TRAHI IN CONSEQUENTIAM. [L.] Things introduced which contradict a rule of law should not be drawn into precedent.

QUAE DUBITATIONIS TOLLENDAE CAUSA INSERUNTUR, COMMUNEM LEGEM NON LAEDUNT. [L.] Things inserted to remove doubt do not harm the common law.

QUAE EST EADEM. [L.] Which is the same.

QUAE IN CURIA REGIS ACTA SUNT RITE AGI PRAESUMUNTUR. [L.] Things done in a sovereign's court are presumed to be done correctly.

QUAE IN TESTAMENTO ITA SUNT SCRIPTA, UT INTELLIGI NON POSSINT, PERINDE SUNT AC SI SCRIPTA NON ESSENT. [L.] Things in a will which were written so that they cannot be understood are just as if they had not been written.

QUAE IPSO USU CONSUMUNTUR. [L.] That which is consumed in its own use.

QUAELIBET CONCESSIO FORTISSIME CONTRA DONATOREM INTERPRE-

TANDA EST. [L.] Every grant should be construed in the strongest way against the grantor.

QUAELIBET POENA CORPORALIS, QUAMVIS MINIMA, MAJOR EST QUALIBET POENA PECUNIARIA. [L.] Whatever the corporal punishment and however slight, it is greater than any fine.

QUAE MALA SUNT INCHOATA IN PRINCIPIO VIX BONO PERANGUNTUR EXITU. [L.] Things bad in the beginning can hardly be brought to a good end.

QUAE NON VALEANT SINGULA JUNCTA JUVANT. [L.] Words which have no effect alone are effective when combined.

QUAE PLURA. [L.] Of what more.

QUAERE. [L.] Inquire.

QUAE SUNT EADEM. [L.] Those which are the same.

QUALIFICATION. *n*. 1. An ability, quality or attribute that fits a person to perform a particular task or function. 2. Limitation; diminishing. 3. Of an expert witness, ability to be an expert established after hearing evidence for and against, and after cross-examination. P.K. McWilliams, *Canadian Criminal Evidence*, 3d ed. (Aurora: Canada Law Book, 1988) at 9-10. See BONA FIDE OCCUPATIONAL ~; DESIRABLE ~S; ESSENTIAL ~S.

QUALIFICATIONS. *n*. " . . . [A] wider [than 'aptitude'] though connected concept relating to [translation] 'mental and intellectual attributes rewired by the employment.' " *Brossard (Town) v. Quebec (Commission des droits de la personne)* (1989), 10 C.H.R.R. D/5515 at D/5530, 88 C.L.L.C. 17,031, [1988] 2 S.C.R. 297, 88 N.R. 321, 18 Q.A.C. 164, 53 D.L.R. (4th) 609, Beetz J. (McIntyre, Lamer and La Forest JJ. concurring).

QUALIFIED. *adj*. 1. Suggests that certain conditions must be met as a precondition. 2. Limited, modified, restricted in some aspect. 3. Possessed of capacity or ability to perform a job or task. See DULY ~; LEGALLY ~.

QUALIFIED ACCEPTANCE. 1. An acceptance with some change in the effect of the bill as originally drawn. 2. In express terms varies the effect of the bill as drawn and, in particular, an acceptance is qualified that is (a) conditional, that is to say, that makes payment by the acceptor dependent on the fulfilment of a condition therein stated; (b) partial, that is to say, an ac-

ceptance to pay part only of the amount for which the bill is drawn; (c) qualified as to time; or (d) the acceptance of one or more of the drawees, but not of all. *Bills of Exchange Act*, R.S.C. 1985, c. B-4, s. 37(3).

QUALIFIED APPRAISER. A person who: (a) is a member in good standing for a continuous period of not less than 2 years, of (i) The Appraisal Institute of Canada and has been designated as a member (C.R.A.) or accredited member (A.A.C.I.); (ii) The Royal Institute of Chartered Surveyors (Britain) and has been designated A.R.I.C.S. or F.R.I.C.S. under its Valuation Subdivision; (iii) The American Institute of Real Estate Appraisers and has been designated M.A.I.; (iv) The Society of Residential Appraisers; or (v) Corporation des Evaluateurs Agréé du Québec; or (b) has been employed or in public practice primarily as a property appraiser for a period of not less than 5 years. *Insurance Act*, R.R.O. 1980, Reg. 536, s. 1. See INDEPENDENT ~.

QUALIFIED ASSETS. 1. (a) Cash; (b) first mortgages on improved real estate and first mortgages made under the National Housing Act, or any predecessor thereof; (c) bonds, debentures, stocks and other securities of the classes authorized under the Canadian and British Insurance Companies Act (Canada) for the investments of the funds of companies registered thereunder; (d) real property acquired by foreclosure or in satisfaction of a debt and held for a period of less than 7 years; and (e) any other investments or securities designated by the regulations. *Investment Contracts Acts*. 2. (a) Cash; (b) bonds, debentures, stocks, other evidences of indebtedness and other securities, in which or on the security of which an issuer is authorized by this Act to invest or lend its funds; (c) real property which an issuer is authorized to acquire and hold pursuant to this Act; when valued under section 28. *The Investment Contracts Act*, R.S.S. 1978, c. I-14, s. 2.

QUALIFIED AUDITOR. A professional auditor or a firm of professional auditors. *Provincial Auditor's Act*, S.M. 1979, c. 12

QUALIFIED BID. A bid that meets the specifications of the tender. *Provincial Preference Act*, R.S. Nfld. 1990, c. P-33, s. 2.

QUALIFIED ELECTOR. A person qualified under the Act to vote in a polling division at a general election. *Canada Elections Act*, R.S.C. 1970 (1st Supp.), c. 14, Schedule IV, s. 2.

QUALIFIED ELECTRICAL WORKER. A person who is the holder of a valid electrician's certificate issued in the Territories or in a province, or such other person as may be approved by the Chief Inspector pursuant to section 5. *Electrical Protection Act*, S.N.W.T. 1975 (3d Sess.), c. 3, s. 2.

QUALIFIED EMPLOYEE. An employee who has been determined by the Commission pursuant to this Act to be qualified to receive labour adjustment benefits. *Labour Adjustment Benefits Act*, R.S.C. 1985, c. L-1, s. 2.

QUALIFIED INDORSEMENT. An indorsement with no recourse to the indorser for payment.

QUALIFIED INVESTIGATOR. A person who is a member in good standing of a professional association of persons entitled under the laws of a province to provide health care in the province and who is designated, by the ethics committee of the health care facility at which investigational testing is to be conducted, as the person to conduct the testing. *Medical Devices Regulations*, SOR/98-282, s. 1.

QUALIFIED MEDICAL DOCTOR. A person licensed to practise medicine in Canada. *Canada First Aid Regulations*, C.R.C., c. 1001, s. 2.

QUALIFIED MEDICAL PRACTITIONER. A person duly qualified by provincial law to practise medicine.

QUALIFIED PERSON. 1. A person who, because of knowledge, training and experience, is qualified to perform, safely and properly, a specified job. Canada regulations. 2. (a) In respect of work that is required by law to be performed by the holder of a licence, certificate or other authority; a person who is the holder of such licence, certificate or other authority; and (b) in respect of work that is not required by law to be performed by the holder of a licence, certificate or other authority, a person who, in the opinion of his employer, possesses the knowledge and experience necessary to perform the work safely and competently. *Safe Working Practices Regulations*, C.R.C., c. 1467, s. 2. 3. A person who is growing an insurable crop for sale on one or more acres of land in a province. 4. A person qualified under section 3 to receive benefits of health insurance conferred by this Act. *The Saskatchewan Health Insurance Act*, R.S.S. 1978, c. S-21, s. 2. 5. A person prescribed as being qualified to receive an incentive in the circumstances prescribed or a partner of a partnership who has, pursuant to section 5, been approved by the Minister as being the person qualified to receive an incentive. *Petroleum Incentives Program Act*, R.S.C. 1985, c. P-13, s. 2. 6. A person by provincial law to practise medicine or psychiatry or to carry out psychological examinations or assessments, as the circumstances require, or, where no such law exists a person is, in the opinion of the youth court, so qualified, and includes a person or a person within a class of persons designated by the Lieutenant Governor in Council of a province or his delegate. *Young Offenders Act*, R.S.C. 1985, c. Y-1, s. 13(11).

QUALIFIED PLUMBER. A person who holds a certificate of qualification in the plumbing trade issued under the Industrial Training and Certification Act, and a licence issued pursuant to this Act and regulations or a licence issued pursuant to a by-law made pursuant to section 6. *Plumbing Installation and Inspection Act*, S.N.B. 1976, c. P-9.1, s. 1.

QUALIFIED PRIVILEGE. 1. The legal effect of the defence of qualified privilege is to rebut the inference, which normally arises from the publication of defamatory words, that they were spoken with malice. Where the occasion is shown to be privileged, the bona fides of the defendant is presumed and the defendant is free to publish, with impunity, remarks which may be defamatory and untrue about the plaintiff. However, the privilege is not absolute and can be defeated if the dominant motive for publishing the statement is actual or express malice. *Hill v. Church of Scientology of Toronto*, [1995] 2 S.C.R. 1130. 2. Attaches to the occasion upon which the communication is made, and not to the communication itself. It was explained in this way by Lord Atkinson in *Adam v. Ward*, [1917] A.C. 309 (H.L.), at p. 334: . . . a privileged occasion is . . . an occasion where the person who makes a communication has an interest or a duty, legal, social or moral, to make it to the person to whom it is made, and the person to whom it is so made has a corresponding interest or duty to receive it. This reciprocity is essential. *Botiuk v. Toronto Free Press Publications Ltd.*, [1995] 3 S.C.R. 3.

QUALIFIED PRODUCER. A producer who produces qualifying milk. *Milk Industry Act*, R.S.B.C. 1979, c. 258, s. 1.

QUALIFIED PROPERTY. Limited and special ownership.

QUALIFIED TECHNICIAN. (a) In respect of breath samples, a person designated by the Attorney General as being qualified to operate an approved instrument; and (b) in respect of blood samples, any person or person of a class of persons designated by the Attorney General as being qualified to take samples of blood for the purposes of this section and sections 256 and 258. *Criminal Code*, R.S.C. 1985, c. C-46, s. 254(1) as am. by *Criminal Law Amendment* Act, R.S.C. 1985 (1st Supp.), c. 27, s. 36.

QUALIFIED TITLE. A registered title which is subject to an excepted estate, interest or right arising under a particular instrument or before a particular date, or otherwise specifically described in the register.

QUALIFIED VOTER. A person who (a) is a Canadian citizen; (b) has attained the age of 19 years; and (c) has been ordinarily resident in the settlement, municipality or area in which a plebiscite is to be held for a period of not less than 1 year immediately preceding the date set for voting. *Liquor Act*, S.W.T. 1913 (1st Sess.) c. 26, s. 2.

QUALIFY. *v.* To become legally entitled.

QUALIFYING EXAMINATION. See PARTNERS', DIRECTORS AND SENIOR OFFICERS' ~.

QUALIFYING STUDENT. A person (a) who is a Canadian citizen or a permanent resident within the meaning of the Immigration Act; (b) who is qualified for enrolment or is enrolled at a specified educational institution as a full-time or part-time student for a period of studies at a post-secondary school level; and (c) who intends to attend at a specified educational institution as a full-time or part-time student for a period of studies described in paragraph (b) if it is financially possible for that person to do so. *Canada Student Loan Act*, R.S.C. 1985, c. S-23, s. 2.

QUALITY. *n.* In relation to evidence, weight. See ACCEPTABLE ~; MERCHANTABLE ~.

QUALITY MARK. A mark indicating or purporting to indicate the quality, quantity, fineness, weight, thickness, proportion or kind of precious metal in an article. *Precious Metals Marking Act*, R.S.C. 1985, c. P-19, s. 2.

QUALITY OF ESTATE. The manner in which and the period during which one exercises the right to enjoy an estate or interest.

QUALITY OF GOODS. Includes their state or condition. *Sale of Goods acts*.

QUAMDIU SE BENE GESSERIT. [L. as long as one behaves oneself well] A clause used in connection with appointment to an office such as judge, and contrasted in meaning to durante bene placito (during the pleasure of the appointing body).

QUAM LONGUM DEBET ESSE RATIONABILE TEMPUS, NON DEFINITUR IN LEGE, SED PENDET EX DISCRETIONE JUSTICIARIORUM. [L.] How long a reasonable time should be is not defined in law, but depends on the discretion of judges.

QUANDO ABEST PROVISIO PARTIS, ADEST PROVISIO LEGIS. [L.] When a party's provision is wanting, the provision of the law is there.

QUANDO ALIQUID CONCEDITUR, CONCEDITUR ETIAM ET ID SINE QUO RES IPSA NON ESSE POTUIT. [L.] When anything is granted, that is also granted without which the thing itself could not exist.

QUANDO ALIQUID MANDATUR, MANDATUR ET OMNE PER QUOD PERVENITUR AD ILLUD. [L.] When anything is ordered, everything by which it will be accomplished is ordered too.

QUANDO ALIQUID PROHIBETUR FIERI, PROHIBETUR EX DIRECTO ET PER OBLIQUUM. [L.] When doing anything is prohibited, doing it both directly and indirectly is prohibited.

QUANDO ALIQUID PROHIBETUR, PROHIBETUR ET OMNE PER QUOD DEVENITUR AD ILLUD. [L.] To effectively carry out the object of a statute, one must construe it so that any attempt to do or avoid doing indirectly or circuitously what the statute prohibited or enjoined is not permitted. P. St. J. Langan, ed., *Maxwell on The Interpretation of Statutes*, 12th ed. (Bombay: N.M. Tripathi, 1976) at 137.

QUANDO DUO JURA IN UNA PERSONA CONCURRUNT, AEQUUM EST AD SI ESSENT IN DIVERSIS. [L.] When two titles come together in one person, it is as if they were in different people.

QUANDO JUS DOMINI REGIS ET SUBDITI CONCURRUNT JUS REGIS PRAEFERRI DEBET. [L.] When the titles of the sovereign and a subject concur, the sovereign's should be preferred.

QUANDO LEX ALIQUID ALICUI CONCEDIT, CONCEDERE VIDETUR ID SINE QUO RES IPSA ESSE NON POTEST. [L.] When the law gives something to someone, it is considered to also give that without which the very thing could not exist.

QUANDO LEX EST SPECIALIS, RATIO AUTEM GENERALIS, GENERALITER LEX EST INTELLIGENDA. [L.] Where a law is special, though its reason general, the law should be understood generally.

QUANDO PLUS FIT QUAM FIERI DEBET, VIDETUR ETIAM ILLUD FIERI QUOD FACIENDUM EST. [L.] When more is done than should be done, then it is considered that what should have been done was done.

QUANDO RES NON VALET UT AGO, VALEAT QUANTUM VALERE POTEST. [L.] When a thing does not operate the way I intend, let it operate as much as it can.

QUANDO VERBA STATUTI SUNT SPECIALIA, RATIO AUTEM GENERALIS, GENERALITER STATUTUM EST INTELLIGENDUM. [L.] When the words of a statute are special, though its reason is general, the statute should be understood generally.

QUANTITY. *n.* Amount. Measure. See DOMESTIC QUANTITIES; PAYING ~.

QUANTITY OF ESTATE. The time in which an estate or interest continues.

QUANTITY SURVEY METHOD. A valuation of a building, inclusive of permanent fixtures, using replacement or intrinsic value without allowing for depreciation.

QUANTITY THEORY OF MONEY. Because the level of prices is made a function of money supply, any decrease or increase in the money supply leads to a proportionate decline or increase in the price level. W. Grover & F. Iacobucci, *Materials on Canadian Income Tax*, 4th ed. (Toronto: Richard De Boo Ltd., 1980) at 16.

QUANTUM. *n.* [L.] An amount.

QUANTUM DAMNIFICATUS. [L.] The amount of damage which one suffered.

QUANTUM MERUIT. [L. as much as one earned] "The remedy of quantum meruit exists in two distinct settings. In a contractual setting, remuneration is said to be paid on a quantum meruit basis when, although a valid contract is found to exist in fact and law, there is no clause spelling out in express terms the consideration for the contract. In such circumstances, the Courts award reasonable remuneration to the person who has rendered the services. In an unjust enrichment setting, an action for quantum meruit is based, in general, upon the rendering of services by one person to another who has requested such services be rendered or freely accepted them with the knowledge that they are not rendered gratuitously." *Gill v. Grant* (1988), 30 E.T.R. 255 at 271 (B.C.S.C.) Rowles J.

QUANTUM VALEAT. [L.] As much as it is worth.

QUANTUM VALEBANT. [L. as much as they were worth] A claim for the value of goods sold or disposed of improperly.

QUARANTINE. *n.* (a) In respect of a person or animals, the limitation of freedom of movement and contact with other persons or animals; and (b) in respect of premises, the prohibition against or the limitation on entering or leaving the premises, during the incubation period of the communicable disease in respect of which the quarantine is imposed.

QUARANTINE APPLICATION. The treatment, with methyl bromide, of a commodity, product, facility or means of conveyance where the treatment is intended to prevent the spread of, or to control or eradicate, pests of quarantine significance and is required by the laws of an importing country as a condition of entry or by or under Canadian law. *Ozone-depleting Substances Regulations, 1998*, SOR/99-7, s. 1.

QUARANTINE AREA. An area designated as a quarantine area pursuant to section 3. *Quarantine Act*, R.S.C. 1985, c. Q-1, s. 2.

QUARANTINE PORT. A place where facilities exist to quarantine animals. *Animal Disease and Protection Regulations*, C.R.C., c. 296, s. 2.

QUARE. [L.] Inquire. Used to introduce a statement which is not a settled proposition of law. See QUAERE.

QUARE CLAUSUM FREGIT. [L. why one broke the close] Trespass on the plaintiff's lands.

QUARREL. *n.* A contest; a dispute.

QUARRIABLE SUBSTANCE. Ordinary stone, building or construction stone, sand, gravel, peat moss, clay and soil.

QUARRY. *n.* 1. A pit or excavation in the ground made for the purpose of removing, opening up or proving any mineral other than coal. 2. An open cut from which rock is cut or taken. See PRODUCTS OF THE ~ AND MINE; STONE ~; WAYSIDE ~.

QUARRYING. *n*. Includes excavation for any purpose, drilling, and the removal or transportation of any rock, shale, gravel, sand, earth or other material.

QUARRYING CLAIM. A tract of land containing minerals that have been reserved to the Crown, that gives a person the right to recover sand, gravel, gypsum, peat, clay, marl, granite, limestone, marble, sandstone slate or any stone. *Mines Act*, R.S.M. 1987, c. M160, s. 1.

QUARRY MATERIAL. A substance used in its natural form for construction or agricultural purposes, and includes (a) clay, sand, gravel, stone, topsoil, soil, marl, peat and peat moss; and (b) a mineral rock or stone capable of being cut or polished for use as an ornament, personal adornment or decoration. *Quarry Materials Act*, R.S. Nfld. 1990, c. Q-1, s. 2.

QUARRY MATERIALS. Limestone, granite, slate, marble, gypsum, marl, clay, sand, gravel, building stone, and volcanic ash. *Undeveloped Mineral Areas* Act, R.S. Nfld. 1900, c. U-2, s. 2.

QUART. *n*. 1. 1/4 gallon. *Weights and Measures Act*, S.C. 1970-71-72, c. 36, schedule II. 2. A unit of measurement, containing 40 fluid ounces. *The Liquor Act*, R.S.S. 1978, c. L-18, s. 2.

QUARTER. *n*. 1. The 3-month period ending with the 31st day of March, 30th day of June, 30th day of September or 31st day of December. *Courts of Justice Act*, R.S.O. 1990, c. C.43, s. 127(1). 2. Any period of 3 months commencing on the first day of January, April, July or October in any year. *Air Carrier Regulations*, C.R.C., c. 3, s. 145. See CALENDAR ~; PAYMENT ~.

QUARTER HOUR BLOCK. A period of 15 minutes commencing at one of the following divisions of a clock hour: 00:00, 15:00 30:00 and 45:00. *Radio (F.M.) Broadcasting Regulations*, C.R.C., c. 380, s. 14.

QUARTZ. See GOLD BEARING ~.

QUASH. *v*. 1 . "[In s. 39 of the Supreme Court Act, R.S.C. 1906, s. 139] . . . 'annul' or 'make void.' " *Shawinigan Hydro Electric Co. v. Shawinigan Water Power Co.* (1910), 43 S.C.R. 650 at 653, Fitzpatrick C.J.C. 2. " . . . [A] discharging

or setting aside [of a by-law] and any remedy would be the simple act of quashing in itself. . ." *Gray v. Ottawa (City)*, [1971] O.R. 112 at 115, 19 D.L.R. (3d) 524 (H.C.), Henderson J. 3. Said of the act of setting aside a decision of an administrative tribunal on judicial review.

QUASI. *adv*. [L.] As if; as it were.

QUASI. *pref*. [L.] Similar but not the same as.

QUASI-CONTRACT. *n*. 1. "A contract is in some cases said to be implied by law, which really is an obligation imposed by law independently of any actual agreement between the parties, and may even be imposed notwithstanding an expressed intention by one of the parties to the contrary; it is an obligation of the class known in the civil law as quasi-contracts. *Dominion Distillery Products Co. v. R.*, [1938] 1 D.L.R. 597 at 613, [1937] Ex. C.R. 145, Maclean J. 2. A liability which cannot be attributed to any other legal principle and which requires someone to pay money to another person because non-payment would confer an unjust benefit on the proposed payor. 3. A notional or fictional contract implied in law and not based upon the intention of the parties where no contract exists. *Canada (Attorney General) v. Becker* (1998), 64 Alta. L.R. (3d) 292 (C.A.). See RESTITUTION; UNJUST ENRICHMENT.

QUASI-CRIMINAL OFFENCE. An offence created by provincial law which carries a penalty similar to that for a crime.

QUASI-ESTOPPEL. *n*. Once one party makes a representation about a present or past fact and the other party relies on it detrimentally, the representor cannot repudiate the representation and put forward the true facts. G.H.L. Fridman, *The Law of Contract in Canada*, 2d ed. (Toronto: Carswell, 1986) at 110.

QUASI IN REM. Jurisdiction because the person in question's interest in property exists within that court's territorial jurisdiction.

QUASI-JUDICIAL. *adj*. Describes functions which are judicial in nature but performed by a tribunal. The hearing of a dispute, investigation, inquiry into a matter, determining facts, and the exercising of discretion in a judicial manner are examples of this type of function. See JUDICIAL OR ~ PROCEEDING.

QUASI PARTNERSHIP. " . . . [A]nalogy with partnership . . . is convenient but certainly not legally determinative of the outcome . . . It expresses the reality of situations where shareholders in a company are not mere investors but are participants in its business and rightfully expect that the will continue to play a part in the management of its affairs." *Mason v. Intercity Properties Ltd.* (1987), 37 B.L.R. 6 at 24 the court per Blair J.A.

QUAY. See EX ~.

QUÉ. *abbr.* Québec.

QUEBEC. See PUBLIC LAW OF ~.

QUÉBEC ACT, 1774. "The Québec Act of 1774 (14 Geo. 3, c. 83, s. 8) sealed the fate of the two major legal systems that would govern the law applicable in Quebec: French civil law as it stood before 1760 with its subsequent amendments in Quebec for everything relating to property and civil rights, and the common law as it stood in England at that time, and as subsequently amended, for what related to public law ..." *Laurentide Motels Ltd v. Beauport (City)* (1989), 45 M.P.L.R. 1 at 32, 94 N.R. 1, [1989] 1 S.C.R. 705, 23 Q.A.C. 1, L'HeurueuxDubé J.

QUEBEC NORTH-WEST REGION. That part of the Province of Quebec known as the Quebec North-West Region, comprising the counties of Abitibi-East, Abitibi-West and the parishes of Montbrun and Cléricy of Rouyn-Noranda County. *Quebec North-West Pulpwood Order*, C.R.C., c. 254, s. 2.

QUEBEC PENSION PLAN. The Quebec Pension Plan established pursuant to An Act Respecting the Quebec Pension Plan, chapter R-9 of the Revised Statutes of Quebec, 1977.

QUEBEC-SOUTH REGION. The territory comprising the electoral districts of Beauce and Dorchester and St-Evariste-de-Forsyth, St-Méthode-de-Frontenac, St- Robert-Bellarmin, the parishes of Courcelles and St-Hilaire-de-Dorset, the parishes and villages of St-Gedeon and St-Sebastien, the villages of La Guadeloupe, Lambton and St-Ludger, as well as the townships of Gayhurst, Gayhurst (southeast part) and Lambton, in the electoral district of Frontenac. *Quebec-South Wood Order*, C.R.C., c. 264, s. 2.

[] **QUE. C.A.** *abbr.* Quebec Official Reports (Court of Appeal), 1970-.

QUEEN. *n.* 1. A woman who is the monarch of a kingdom. 2. The Sovereign of the United Kingdom, Canada and Her other Realms and Territories, and Head of the Commonwealth. 3. The Queen is Head of State. She is Queen of Canada. See ROYAL STYLE AND TITLES.

QUEEN CONSORT. The wife of a king who is reigning.

QUEEN DOWAGER. The widow of a king.

QUEEN OF CANADA. The head of state, represented in most capacities within the federal sphere by the Governor General.

QUEEN'S BENCH. 1. In some provinces, the name given to the superior court. 3. In England, a superior court of common law. See COURT OF ~.

QUEEN'S COUNSEL. A barrister appointed counsel to the Crown who wears a silk gown, sits within the bar and in court takes precedence over ordinary barristers.

QUEEN'S ENEMIES. Refers to war and rebellion, not to riots and civil commotions.

QUEEN'S L.J. *abbr.* Queen's Law Journal.

QUEEN'S PEACE. The peace and security of life and property guaranteed by the Crown. All criminal acts defined in the Criminal Code are disturbances of the Queen's Peace.

QUEEN'S PRINTER. Includes government printer or other official printer. *Evidence acts.*

QUEEN'S PRIVY COUNCIL FOR CANADA. The federal cabinet and additional members appointed by the Governor General or ex officio members. See CLERK OF THE QUEEN'S PRIVY COUNCIL; CONFIDENCE OF THE ~; PRIVY COUNCIL.

QUEEN'S PROCTOR. A representative of the Crown who may intervene in a divorce proceeding.

QUEEN'S REGULATIONS AND ORDERS. The Queen's Regulations and Orders for the Canadian Forces. *Military Rules of Evidence*, C.R.C., c. 1049, s. 2.

QUEEN'S WAREHOUSE. (a) A warehouse provided by the Crown; or (b) an area appointed by the collector for the safekeeping of unclaimed abandoned seized or forfeited goods. Canada regulations.

QUE EST LE MESME. [L.] Which is the same.

QUE. K.B. *abbr.* Quebec Official Reports (King's Bench), 1892-1941.

[] **QUE. K.B.** *abbr.* Quebec Official Reports (King's Bench), 1942-1969.

QUE. LAB. CT. *abbr.* Quebec Labour Court (Tribunal du travail)

QUE. L.R.B. *abbr*. Quebec Labour Relations Board (Commission des relations de travail du Québec).

QUE. P.R. *abbr*. Quebec Practice Reports, 1897-1944 (Rapports de Pratique du Québec).

[] QUE. P.R. *abbr*. Quebec Practice Reports, 1945- (Rapports de Pratique du Québec).

QUE. Q.B. *abbr*. 1. Quebec Court of Queen's (King's) Bench Reports. 2. Quebec Official Reports (Queen's Bench), 1892-1941.

[] QUE. Q.B. *abbr*. Quebec Official Reports (Queen's Bench), 1942-1969.

QUERELA. *n*. [L.] A civil proceeding in any court.

QUERELE. *n*. A complaint made to a court.

QUERENS. *n*. [L.] A complainant, inquirer, plaintiff.

QUERENT. *n*. A complainant, inquirer, plaintiff.

QUE. S.C. *abbr*. Quebec Official Reports (Superior Court), 1892-1941 (Rapports Judiciaires du Québec, Cour Superieure).

[] QUE. S.C. *abbr*. Quebec Official Reports (Superior Court), 1942- (Recueils de jurisprudence du Québec, Cour Supérierure).

QUESTION. *n*. 1. An interrogation. 2. " . . . '[I]ssue'." *Blackburn v. Kochs Trucking Inc.* (1988), 25 C.P.C. (2d) 113 at 121, 58 Alta. L.R. (2d) 358, [1988] 34 W.W.R. 272, 86 A.R. 321 (Q.B.), McDonald J. 3. "[In s. 42(1) of the Marital Property Act, 1980, S.N.B. 1980, c. M-1.1] . . . means a point on which the parties are not agreed, that is, it means 'dispute and does not simply mean an interrogatory." *George v. George* (1987), 37 D.L.R. (4th) 466 at 467, 8 R.F.L. (3d) 368, 80 N.B.R. (2d) 357, 202 A.P.R. 357 (Q.B.), Montgomery J. See COLLATERAL ~; INCIDENTAL ~; LEADING ~; MIXED ~; ORAL ~; PRELIMINARY ~; SUBSIDIARY ~; WRITTEN ~.

QUESTION OF FACT. 1. " . . . Where the term is simple and ordinary, and, as it were, can be reduced no further in simplicity or definition, and which to define would require words that themselves need definition, the question is one of fact. The terms 'resident' and 'insulting' are good examples. Where the term gives rise to some complexity, or has acquired a special or technical meaning, the question is likely, but not always, one of law." *Peers v. University Hospi-*

tal (1983), 1 Admin. L.R. 221 at 234, [1983] 5 W.W.R. 193, 4 C.H.R.R. D/1464, 147 D.L.R. (3d) 385, 23 Sask. R. 123 (C.A.), Bayda C.J.S. 2. "The construction of a statutory enactment is a question of law, while the question of whether the particular matter or thing is of such a nature or kind as to fall within the legal definition of its term is a question of fact." *Hollinger Consolidated Gold Mines Ltd. v. Tisdale (Township)*, [1933] 3 D.L.R. 15 at 16, [1933] S.C.R. 321 the court per Cannon J. 3. Questions of law are questions about what the correct legal test is; questions of fact are questions about what actually took place between the parties; and questions of mixed law and fact are questions about whether the facts satisfy the legal tests. A simple example will illustrate these concepts. In the law of tort, the question what "negligence" means is a question of law. The question whether the defendant did this or that is a question of fact. And, once it has been decided that the applicable standard is one of negligence, the question whether the defendant satisfied the appropriate standard of care is a question of mixed law and fact. *Canada (Director of Investigation & Research) v. Southam Inc.*, [1997] 1 S.C.R. 748 (at paragraph 35).

QUESTION OF LAW. 1. " . . . [I]n construing a will, deed, contract, prospectus or other commercial document, the legal effect to be given to the language employed is a question of law . . ." *R. v. Alberta Giftwares Ltd.* (1973), 11 C.P.R. (2d) 233 at 237, [1974] S.C.R. 584, [1973] 5 W.W.R. 458, 11 C.C.C. (2d) 513, 36 D.L.R. (3d) 321, the court per Ritchie J. 2. " . . . [W]ould include (without attempting anything like an exhaustive definition which would be impossible) questions touching the scope, effect or application of a rule of law which the Courts apply in determining the rights of parties; and by long usage, the term 'question of law' has come to be applied to questions which, when arising at a trial by a Judge and jury, would fall exclusively to the Judge for determination; for example, questions touching the construction of documents and a great variety of others including questions whether, in respect of a particular issue of fact there is any evidence upon which a jury could find the issue in favour of the party on whom rests the burden of proof. . ." *Canadian National Railway v. Bell Telephone Co.*, [1939] 3 D.L.R. 8 at 15, [1939] S.C.R. 308, 50 C.R.C. 10, the court per Duff C.J.C. 3. "The construction of a statutory enactment is a question of law, while the question of whether the particular matter or thing is of such a nature or kind as to fall within the legal definition of its term is a question of fact." *Hollinger Consolidated Gold Mines Ltd. v. Tisdale (Township)*, [1933] 3 D.L.R. 15 at 16, [1933] S.C.R. 321 the court per Cannon J. 4. " . . .[W]hether a person's constitutional right has been infringed is a question of law." *R. v. Dunnett* (1990), 26 M.V.R. (2d) 194 at 200, 62 C.C.C. (3d) 14, 111 N.B.R. (2d) 67, 277 A.P.R. 67 (C.A.), Hoyt J.A. (Ayles J.A. concurring). 5. Questions of law are questions about what the correct legal test is; questions of fact are questions about what actually took place between the parties; and questions of mixed law and fact are questions about whether the facts satisfy the legal tests. A simple example will illustrate these concepts. In the law of tort, the question what "negligence" means is a question of law. The question whether the defendant did this or that is a question of fact. And, once it has been decided that the applicable standard is one of negligence, the question whether the defendant satisfied the appropriate standard of care is a question of mixed law and fact. *Canada (Director of Investigation & Research) v. Southam Inc.*, [1997] 1 S.C.R. 748 (at paragraph 35).

QUESTION OF MIXED LAW AND FACT. Questions of law are questions about what the correct legal test is; questions of fact are questions about what actually took place between the parties; and questions of mixed law and fact are questions about whether the facts satisfy the legal tests. A simple example will illustrate these concepts. In the law of tort, the question what "negligence" means is a question of law. The question whether the defendant did this or that is a question of fact. And, once it has been decided that the applicable standard is one of negligence, the question whether the defendant satisfied the appropriate standard of care is a question of mixed law and fact. *Canada (Director of Investigation & Research) v. Southam Inc.*, [1997] 1 S.C.R. 748 (at paragraph 35).

QUESTION OF ORDER. A question about interpreting a rule of procedure which is a matter for the Speaker or, in a committee, for the Chairman to decide. A. Fraser, W.A. Dawson, & J. Holtby, eds., *Beauchesne's Rules and Forms of the House of Commons of Canada*, 6th ed. (Toronto: Carswell, 1989) at 12 and 96.

QUESTION OF PRIVILEGE. A question partly of the law of contempt of Parliament and partly of fact which the House must determine. The question is based on a motion of a member and is put by the Speaker. A. Fraser, W.A. Dawson, & J. Holtby, eds., *Beauchesne's Rules and Forms of the House of Commons of Canada*, 6th ed. (Toronto: Carswell, 1989) at 12.

QUE. TAX R. *abbr*. Quebec Tax Reports.

QUIA EMPTORES. See STATUTE OF ∼.

QUIA FORMA NON OBSERVATA, INFERTUR ADNULLATIO ACTUS. [L.] Because the prescribed procedure was not observed, the proceedings are considered void.

QUI ALIQUID STATUERIT PARTE INAUDITA ALTERA, AEQUUM LICET STATUERIT, HAUD AEQUUS FUERIT. [L.] The one who decides something without hearing one party though they decided rightly, will not be just.

QUI ALTERIUS JURE UTITUR EODEM JURE UTI DEBET. [L.] The one who is clothed in another's right should be clothed in the very same right.

QUIA TIMET. [L.] Because one fears.

QUIA TIMET INJUNCTION. [L. because one fears] 1. " . . . [A]n interim injunction to protect against feared future harm. *Bradley Resources Co. v. Kelvin Energy Ltd.* (1985), 18 D.L.R. (4th) 468 at 471, [1985] 5 W.W.R. 763, 39 Alta. L.R. (2d) 193, 61 A.R. 169 (C.A.), the court per Kerans J.A. 2. It is not necessary to wait for actual damage to occur. Used when there is an apprehension that property will be removed from the jurisdiction. 3. " . . . [A] plaintiff does not have to wait until actual damage occurs. Where such damage is apprehended, an application for a quia timet injunction is an appropriate avenue to obtain a remedy which will prevent the occurrence of the harm. . ." *Palmer v. Forest Stora Kopparbergs Bergslags AB* (1983), (*sub nom. Palmer v. N.S. Forest Industries*) 12 C.E.L.R. 157 at 228, 26 C.C.L.T. 22, 2 D.L.R. (4th) 397, 60 N.S.R. (2d) 271, 128 A.P.R. 271 (T.D.), Nunn J. 4. " . . . [W]ere generally permitted under extreme circumstances which included a real or impending threat to remove contested assets from the jurisdiction." *Aetna Financial Services Ltd. v. Feigelman* (1985), 29 B.L.R. 5 at 16, [1985] 1 S S.C.R. 2, [1985] 2 W.W.R. 97, 55 C.B.R. (N.S.) 1, 56 N.R. 241, 15 D.L.R. (4th) 161, 4 C.P.R. (3d) 145, 32 Man. R. (2d) 241, the court per Estey J. See INJUNCTION ∼.

QUICK ASSET RATIO. The ratio of liquid assets to current liabilities.

QUICK-DONNING MASK. An oxygen mask that can be secured by a person using one hand on the person's face within five seconds, and that provides an immediate supply of oxygen. *Canadian Aviation Regulations*, SOR/96-433, s. 101.01(1).

QUICK FREEZE. Freezing on plates or coils or in cabinets especially designed for quick freezing. *Frozen Food Locker Plant Act*, R.S.M. 1970, c. F170, s. 2.

QUI CONCEDIT ALIQUID, CONCEDERE VIDETUR ET ID SINE QUO CONCESSIO EST IRRITA, SINE QUO RES IPSA ESSE NON POTUIT. [L.] The one who concedes anything is considered to concede that without which the concession is void, without which the very thing would not be able to exist.

QUICQUID DEMONSTRATAE REI ADDITUR SATIS DEMONSTRATAE FRUSTRA EST. [L.] Whatever is added to describe something already described sufficiently has no effect.

QUICQUID NECESSITAS COGIT, DEFENDIT. [L.] When anything is done of necessity, necessity can be used as a defence.

QUICQUID PLANTATUR SOLO, SOLO CEDIT. [L.] Whatever is affixed to the soil goes with the soil. *Canadian Imperial Bank of Commerce v. Alberta (Assessment Appeal Board)* (1990), 73 D.L.R. (4th) 271 at 277, 75 Alta. L.R. (2d) 362, [1990] 6 W.W.R. 425, 109 A.R. 203 (Q.B.), Andrekson J. and *Collis v. Carew Lumber Co.*, [1930] 4 D.L.R. 996 at 999, 65 O.L.R. 520, 38 O.W.N. 237 (C.A.), Middleton J.A.

QUICQUID RECIPITUR, RECIPITUR SECUNDUM MODUM RECIPIENTIS. [L.] Whatever is received is received according to the recipient's intention.

QUICQUID SOLVITUR, SOLVITUR SECUNDUM MODUM SOLVENTIS. [L.] Whatever is paid is paid according to the payer's direction.

QUI CUM ALIO CONTRAHIT, VEL EST, VEL DEBET ESSE, NON IGNARUS CONDITIONIS EJUS. [L.] The one who contracts with another, either is, or should be, familiar with the other's condition.

QUICUNQUE ALIQUID STATUERIT PARTE INAUDITA ALTERA, AEQUUM LICET DIXERIT, HAUD AEQUUM FECERIT. [L.] Anyone who decides without hearing the other side may reach the right result but has not acted justly.

QUI DE UNO DICIT, DE ALTERO NEGAT. [L.] Who speaks of one excludes the other.

QUID PRO QUO. [L. something for something] A consideration.

QUID PRO QUO SEXUAL HARASSMENT. Sexual harassment of this type involves situations in which tangible employment-related benefits are made contingent upon an employee's participation in sexual activity. *Janzen v. Platy Enterprises Ltd.*, [1989] 1 S.C.R. 1252.

QUIET. *v.* To settle; to render unassailable.

QUIET. *adj.* Unmolested, free from interference.

QUIETA NON MOVERE. [L.] A settled situation should not be disturbed.

QUIETARE. *v.* To discharge, quit or relieve of liability.

QUIETE CLAMARE. [L.] To quit claim.

QUIET ENJOYMENT. 1. A covenant that a lessor or anyone claiming through or under the lessor may not enter. 2. ". . . [N]o act of a lessor will constitute an actionable breach of a convenant for quiet enjoyment unless it involves some physical or direct interference with the enjoyment of demised premises." *Owen v. Gadd*, [1956] 2 All E.R. 28 at 32 (U.K. C.A.), Romer L.J. See COVENANT.

QUIETING ORDER. An order establishing the legal existence or corporate status of a municipality, or establishing its proper area and boundaries or any of its boundaries, in order to quiet doubts affecting the same. *Municipal Corporations Quieting Orders Act*, R.S.O. 1990, c. M.51, s. 1.

QUIETUS. *adj.* Acquitted, freed; discharged of any further liability.

QUIETUS REDDITUS. [L.] Quit-rent.

QUI FACIT PER ALIUM FACIT PER SE. [L.] The one who acts through another is considered to act in person. *Courtnay v. Canadian Development Co.* (1901), 8 B.C.R. 53 at 58 (Y.T. Terr. Ct.), Dugas J.

QUI FACIT PER ALIUM PER SE FACERE VIDETUR. [L.] A person who acts through another is considered to act himself.

QUI FRAUDEM AGIT, FRUSTRA AGIT. [L.] The one who commits fraud labours in vain.

QUI HAERET IN LITERA HAERET IN CORTICE. [L. the one who sticks in the letter sticks in the bark] The one who considers only the wording of a document cannot comprehend its meaning.

QUI IN JUS DOMINIUMVE ALTERIUS SUCCEDIT JURE EJUS UTI DEBET. [L.] The one who succeeds to the property rights of another should be clothed with that person's right.

QUI JURE SUO UTITUR NEMINEM LAEDIT. [L.] The one who exercises a legal right injures no one.

QUI JUSSI JUDICIS ALIQUOD FECERIT NON VIDETUR DOLO MALO FECISSE QUIA PARERE NECESSE EST. [L.] The one who does anything by a judge's command is not supposed to have acted with an improper motive because it is necessary to obey.

QUILIBET LICET RENUNTIARE JURI PRO SE INTRODUCTO. [L.] An individual may waive the benefit of a right enacted in his favour.

QUILIBET POTEST RENUNCIARE JURI PRO SE INTRODUCTO. [L.] Anyone may renounce a right introduced in one's own favour. *LeSieur, Re*, [1951] 2 D.L.R. 775 at 778, [1951] O.W.N. 186 (H.C.), Ferguson J. and *Gray Tractor Co. v. Van Troyen* (1924), [1925] 1 D.L.R. 718 at 720-21, [1925] 1 W.W.R. 513, 19 Sask. L.R. 202 (K.B.), Mackenzie J.

QUINELLA. *n.* A type of bet on a race to select, in any order, the first two horses in the official result. *Pari-Mutuel Betting Supervision Regulations*, SOR/91-365, s. 2.

QUI NON IMPROBAT, APPROBAT. [L.] The one who does not disapprove, approves.

QUI NON OBSTAT QUOD OBSTARE POTEST FACERE VIDETUR. [L.] The one who does not prevent what can be prevented is considered to do it.

QUI NON PROHIBET QUOD PROHIBERE POTEST ASSENTIRE VIDETUR. [L.] The one who does not prohibit a thing which can be forbidden is considered to consent.

QUINQUEPARTITE. *adj.* Having five parts or parties.

QUI OMNE DICIT NIHIL EXCLUDIT. [L.] The one who says it all excludes nothing.

QUI PECCAT EBRIUS, LUAT SOBRIUS. [L.] The one who sins while drunk will be punished while sober.

QUI PER ALIUM FACIT, PER SEIPSUM FACERE VIDETUR. [L.] Those who do anything through another are considered to do it themselves.

QUI PRIOR EST TEMPORE POTIOR EST JURE. [L. the one who is first in time is preferred in law] "It is an undoubted principle of law that as between owners of equitable interests the first in time prevails unless he who has acquired it has either done or omitted to do something he is by law required to do and thereby has lost this prior right." *McKillop v. Alexander* (1912), 1 D.L.R. 586 at 588, 45 S.C.R. 551, 1 W.W.R. 857, Idington J.

QUI RATIONEM IN OMNIBUS QUAERUNT RATIONEM SUBVERTUNT. [L.] Those who look for reason in all things subvert reason.

QUI SENTIT COMMODUM SENTIRE DEBET ET ONUS; ET E CONTRA. [L.] The one who enjoys the benefit should also bear the burden; and the opposite. *Canada (Attorney General) v. Ontario (Attorney General)* (1895), [1896] 25 S.C.R. 434 at 533, Sedgewick J.

QUISTCLOSE TRUST. Has been referred to as a purpose trust. The trust that arises is a resulting trust in favour of the supplier of the funds if the funds are not applied for the stated purpose. The name is derived from *Barclays Bank Ltd. v. Quistclose Investments Ltd.*, [1968] 3 All E.R. 651 (H.L.).

QUIT. *v.* 1. With respect to a job, to resign. 2. With respect to leased premises, to surrender possession. See NOTICE TO ~.

QUI TACET CONSENTIRE VIDETUR. [L.] The one who is silent is considered to consent.

QUI TAM. [L. who as well] On a penal statute, an action partly at the Crown's suit and partly at an informer's.

QUIT CLAIM. 1. To relinquish or release any claim to real property. 2. Where a debtor transfers property which is subject to a security interest to a secured party, and the secured party agrees to "settle the claim" it has against the debtor, the resulting agreement must be considered a quitclaim of the debtor's interest in the secured property. *Travel West (1987) Inc. v. Langdon Towers Apartment Ltd.*, 2002 SKCA

51, 217 Sask. R. 233, 265 W.A.C. 233, [2002] 9 W.W.R. 449 (C.A.).

QUIT-CLAIM DEED. The conveyance without promises or warranties only of an interest, if any, which the grantor has in the land. It is often used to release an interest in land, e.g. the purchaser's interest, under an agreement of purchase and sale, which was registered against the title. B.J. Reiter, B.N. McLellan & P.M. Perell, *Real Estate Law*, 4th ed. (Toronto: Emond Montgomery, 1992) at 805.

QUIT RENT. A rent by which a tenant quits and is free of any other service.

QUITTANCE. *n*. An acquittal, a release.

QUI VULT DECIPI DECIPIATUR. [L.] Let the one who wants to be deceived be deceived.

QUOAD. *adv*. [L.] Concerning; as to.

QUOAD HOC. [L.] Concerning that.

QUOAD ULTRA. [L.] Concerning the rest.

QUO ANIMO. [L.] By what mind.

QUOD AB INITIO NON VALET IN TRACTU TEMPORIS NON CONVALESCIT. [L.] What does not go well from the beginning will not improve with the passage of time.

QUOD AB INITIO NULLUM EST, NULLUM EST AD FINEM. [L.] What is void from the beginning, is void in the end.

QUOD AEDIFICATUR IN AREA LEGATA CEDIT LEGATO. [L.] What is built on devised ground passes to the devisee.

QUOD APPROBO NON REPROBO. [L.] What I approve, I do not reject.

QUOD CONSTAT CURIAE OPERE TESTIUM NON INDIGET. [L.] What is well known to a court does not need the help of witnesses.

QUOD CONTRA LEGEM FIT, PRO INFECTO HABETUR. [L.] What is done against the law is held not to have been done at all.

QUOD CONTRA RATIONEM JURIS RECEPTUM, NON EST PRODUCENDUM AD CONSEQUENTIAS. [L.] What is received contrary to the reason of law should not be advanced as precedent.

QUODCUNQUE ALIQUIS OB TUTELAM CORPORIS SUI FECERIT, JURE ID FECISSE VIDETUR. [L.] Whatever one does for the body's safety is considered to have been done legally.

QUOD DUBITAS NE FECERIS. [L.] Do not do what you feel doubtful about.

QUOD EST INCONVENIENS, AUT CONTRA RATIONEM, NON PERMISSUM EST IN LEGE. [L.] What is inconvenient, or contrary to reason, is not permitted in law.

QUOD FIERI DEBET FACILE PRAESUMITUR. [L.] What should be done is easily presumed to have been done.

QUOD FIERI NON DEBET FACTUM VALET. [L.] What should not be done prevails if it was done.

QUOD IN MINORI VALET VALEBIT IN MAJORI; ET QUOD IN MAJORI NON VALET NEC VALEBIT IN MINORI. [L.] What benefits the lesser will benefit in the greater; and what does not benefit the greater will not benefit in the lesser.

QUOD MEUM EST SINE FACTO MEO VEL DEFECTU MEO AMITTI VEL IN ALIUM TRANSFERRI NON POTEST. [L.] What is mine cannot be either lost or transferred to another without either my act or my default.

QUOD NECESSARIE INTELLIGITUR ID NON DEEST. [L.] What is necessarily understood is not omitted.

QUOD NECESSARIUM EST EST LICITUM. [L.] What is necessary is also lawful.

QUOD NON APPARET NON EST. [L.] What does not appear does not exist.

QUOD NON FIERI DEBET, FACTUM VALET. [L.] That which ought not to be done but is valid when done.

QUOD NON HABET PRINCIPIUM NON HABET FINEM. [L.] What does not have a beginning does not have an end.

QUOD NON LEGITUR NON CREDITUR. [L.] What is not read is not trusted.

QUOD NOSTRUM EST, SINE FACTO SIVE DEFECTU NOSTRO, AMITTI SEU IN ALIUM TRANSFERRI NON POTEST. [L.] What is ours cannot be either lost or transferred to another without either our own act or our own fault.

QUOD NULLIUS EST, EST DOMINI REGIS. [L.] What belongs to no one belongs to our lord the sovereign.

QUOD NULLIUS EST ID RATIONE NA-TURALI OCCUPANTI CONCEDITUR. [L.] What belongs to no one is granted to an occupant by natural right.

QUOD NULLUM EST IPSO JURE RES-CINDI NON POTEST. [L.] That which is a nullity cannot be rescinded by the law itself.

QUOD PER ME NON POSSUM, NEC PER ALIUM. [L.] What I cannot do by myself I cannot do through another.

QUOD PER RECORDUM PROBATUM, NON DEBET ESSE NEGATUM. [L.] What is proved by record should not be denied.

QUOD PRIUS EST VERIUS; ET QUOD PRIUS EST TEMPORE POTIUS EST JURE. [L.] What is first is truer, and what is first in time is better legally.

QUOD RECUPERET. [L. that one recovers] In a personal action, the final judgment for the plaintiff.

QUOD REMEDIO DESTITUITUR IPSA RE VALET SI CULPA ABSIT. [L.] What is without remedy prevails by itself if there is no fault in the party who seeks to enforce it.

QUOD SEMEL AUT BIS EXISTIT PRAE-TEREUNT LEGISLATORES. [L.] Legislators pass over what happens only once or twice.

QUOD SEMEL MEUM EST AMPLIUS MEUM ESSE NON POTEST. [L.] What is mine once cannot be more completely mine.

QUOD SEMEL PLACUIT IN ELECTIONE, AMPLIUS DISPLICERE NON POTEST. [L.] What once was pleasing in a choice cannot further displease.

QUOD SUBINTELLIGITUR NON DEEST. [L.] What is understood does not fail.

QUOD VANUM ET INUTILE EST, LEX NON REQUIRIT. [L.] The law does not require what is vain and useless.

QUOD VIDE. [L.] See this.

QUOD VOLUIT NON DIXIT. [L.] "A Judge is to construe, and not to make a will; and if an event has happened for which a testator has not provided, from not having foreseen it, although if he had foreseen it there is a strong probability that he would have provided for it in one particular way, his supposed wishes shall not prevail; quod voluit non dixit: we are to give effect to the expressed, not the conjectural or probable, intention of testators." *Wing v. Angrave* (1860), 8 H.L.C. 183 at 202, 11 E.R. 397 at 404 (U.K.), Lord Campbell, L.C.

QUO LIGATUR, EO DISSOLVITUR. [L.] Whatever binds can also release.

QUO MODO QUID CONSTITUITUR EODEM MODO DISSOLVITUR. [L.] In the way in which the thing is constituted, in the same way it is dissolved.

QUORUM. *n.* [L. of whom] 1. The minimum number of members who must be present for that body to exercise its powers validly. 2. The required number of participants who must participate in the collective decision by assenting to the decision or by dissenting to it.

QUOTA. *n.* 1. The quantity of a product authorized to be produced, marketed or delivered from a particular person or property. 2. The number of a species of game or fish which may be taken during a particular period of time. See GENERAL ACREAGE ~; TARIFF RATE ~; TIMBER ~.

QUOTA ACRES. The acres specified with the approval of the Board in relation to any grain as the basis for the delivery of that grain under a permit book referring to the land described in the permit book. *Prairie Grain Advance Payments Act*, R.S.C. 1985, c. P-18, s. 2.

QUOTA CERTIFICATE. (a) A document issued to a producer certifying the quota assigned to him; or (b) a list containing the names of all producers and certifying the quota assigned to each producer.

QUOTA RULE. Union regulation of a minimum number of workers.

QUOTA SYSTEM. The method by which the quota fixed and allotted to any producer is determined.

QUOT HOMINES TOT SENTENTIAE. [L.] There are as many opinions as there are people.

QUOTIENS DUBIA INTERPRETATIO LIBERTATIS EST SECUNDUM LIBER-TATEM RESPONDENDUM EST. [L.] Whenever a decision for liberty is in doubt it should be decided in favour of liberty.

QUOTIENS IDEM SERMO DUAE SEN-TENTIAS EXPRIMIT; EA POTISSIMUM ACCIPIATUR QUAE REI GERENDAE AP-TIOR EST. [L.] Whenever the same statement offers two meanings, what is better suited to effect the desired end should be adopted.

QUOTIES IN VERBIS NULLA EST AM-BIGUITAS IBI NULLA ESPOSITIO CON-TRA VERBA EXPRESSA FIENDA EST. [L.] When there is no ambiguity in the words then no interpretation contrary to the stated words should be adopted.

QUOUSQUE. *adv.* [L.] How long, how far.

QUO WARRANTO. [L. by what authority] 1. A prerogative writ which challenges the usurpation of a public office. 2. " . . . [C]ivil proceedings. They are instituted by the Attorney-General, or through the intervention of the Attorney-General, . . ." *R. v. Quesnel* (1909), (*sub nom. Tuttle v. Quesnel*) 11 W.L.R. 96 at 98

(Man. C.A.), the court per Howell C.J.A. 3. " . . . [L]ies against persons who claim any office, franchise, or privilege of a public nature, and not merely ministerial and held at the will and pleasure of others . . ." *R. v. Roberts* (1912), 26 O.L.R. 263 at 271, 22 O.W.R. 50, 4 D.L.R. 278 (H.C.), Riddell J.

QUUM PRINCIPALIS CAUSA NON CON-SISTIT, NE EA QUIDEM QUAESEQUUN-TUR LOCUM HABENT. [L.] When the main cause does not stand its ground, then the things which arise out of it have no place either.

Q.V. *abbr.* [L.] Quod vide. See this.

R. *abbr.* 1. [L. regina] Queen. 2. [Fr. reine] Queen. 3. [L. rex] King. 4. [Fr. roi] King. 5. Rule.

RABBIT. *n.* 1. Includes cottontail rabbit, varying hare and European hare. *Game and Fish Act*, R.S.O. 1990, c. G.1, s. 1. 2. A domestic rabbit. *Meat Inspection Regulations*, C.R.C., c. 1032, s. 162.

R.A.C. *abbr.* Ramsay's Appeal Cases (Que.), 1873-1886.

RACE. *n.* 1. " . . . [C]ontest or competition [of speed] . . ." *Mildner v. Saskatchewan Government Insurance Office*, [1962] I.L.R. 1-076 at 368, 40 W.W.R. 86 (Sask. Q.B.), MacPherson J. 2. A test between rivals. *McGill v. Insurance Corp. of British Columbia* (1992), 10 C.C.L.I. (2d) 65 (B.C. S.C.). 3. In a list of prohibited grounds of discrimination, refers to a group of inheritable, physical attributes. 4. A running, trotting or pacing horse-race on which pari-mutuel betting is conducted. *Pari-Mutuel Betting Supervision Regulations*, SOR/91-365, s. 2.

RACE AVERAGE. The average amount bet per race determined by dividing the total monies bet through the pari-mutuel system of a race course during one calendar year by the number of races on which such betting was conducted. *Race Track Supervision Regulations*, C.R.C., c. 441, s. 2.

RACE MEETING. *var.* **RACE-MEETING.** 1. A series of any form of horse races. 2. A series of racing cards that is held by an association at a race-course. *Pari-Mutuel Betting Supervision Regulations*, SOR/91-365, s. 2.

RACE TRACK. *var.* **RACE-TRACK.** 1. A piece of ground specially laid out for horse races, automobile races or other kinds of races. 2. Any place at which harness racing is conducted and pari-mutuel betting is permitted.

RACEWAY. *n.* Any channel for holding wires, cables or bus bars, which is designed expressly for and used solely for this purpose, and unless otherwise qualified in this Code, including rigid, flexible, metallic and non-metallic conduit, electrical metallic tubing, underfloor raceways, lighting fixture raceways, cellular floor raceways, surface raceways, wire-ways, cable-troughs, busways, auxiliary gutters and ventilated cableway. See LIGHTING FIXTURE ~; SURFACE ~; UNDERFLOOR ~.

RACIAL DISCRIMINATION. " . . . [C]learly involves something more than merely burdening a particular individual or group under the law; it involves the imposition of some such burden in a manner which creates or involves some stigma, as where there is 'a denial of the essential worth and dignity of the class against whom the law is directed' or 'a denial based upon unwarranted stereotypes about the capacities and roles of members of that class.'" *R. v. Punch* (1985), [1986] 2 C.N.L.R. 114 at 124, [1985] N.W.T.R. 373, [1986] 1 W.W.R. 592, 48 C.R. (3d) 374, 22 C.C.C. (3d) 289, 18 C.R.R. 74 (S.C.), de Weerdt J. See CONVENTION ON THE ELIMINATION OF ALL FORMS OF ~.

RACIAL PROFILING. There is no dispute about what racial profiling means. . . "Racial profiling involves the targeting of individual members of a particular racial group, on the basis of the supposed criminal propensity of the entire group" . Racial profiling provides its own motivation—a belief by a police officer that a person's colour, combined with other circumstances, makes him or her more likely to be involved in criminal activity. *R. v. Brown* (2003), 173 C.C.C. (3d) 23 (Ont. C.A.).

RACING. *n.* A contest which may be among horses, runners, cars. See HARNESS ~; HORSE ~.

RACING CARD. A number of races that are scheduled to be run consecutively during a specified period on any one day at a race-course. *Pari-Mutuel Betting Supervision Regulations*, SOR/91-365, s. 2.

RACING JUDGE. A person responsible for racing contests.

RACING MEETING. Includes every meeting within the province where horses are raced and where any form of betting or wagering on the speed or ability of horses is permitted, but does not include any meeting were no betting or wagering is permitted even though horses or their owners are awarded certificates, ribbons, premiums or prizes for speed or ability shown.

RACING SECRETARY. A person appointed by an association for the purpose of receiving all entries, scratches and declarations.

RACING STRIP. That portion of a race course on which a race is run.

RACISM. *n.* Intolerance by members of one race characterized by stereotyping, prejudice, and discrimination towards members of another race.

RACK-RENT. *n.* Rent which is not less than two-thirds of the full annual net value of the property out of which the rent arises. *City of St. John's Act*, R.S. Nfld. 1970, c. 40, s. 2.

RAD. *n.* A unit of dose, and is realized when 0.01 joule of energy has been absorbed per kilogram of matter. See MILLI~.

RAD. *abbr.* Radian.

RADAR WARNING DEVICE. Any device or equipment designed or intended for use in a motor vehicle to warn the driver of the presence of radar or other electronic speed measuring equipment in the vicinity.

RADIAL PLY TIRE. A pneumatic tire in which the ply cords that extend to the beads are laid at angles of approximately 90 degrees to the centreline of the tread. Canada regulations.

RADIAN. *n.* The unit for the measurement of a plane angle, being the angle with its vertex at the centre of a circle and subtended by an arc of the circle that is equal in length to its radius. *Weights and Measures Act*, S.C. 1970-71-72, c. 36, schedule I.

RADIATING FRACTURE. A fracture of a flat bone in which fracture lines spread from the centre point of impact. F.A. Jaffe, *A Guide to Pathological Evidence*, 3d ed. (Toronto: Carswell, 1991) at 220.

RADIATION. *n.* 1. Ionizing or non-ionizing energy in the form of atomic particles, electromagnetic or acoustic waves. 2. The emission by a nuclear substance, the production using a nuclear substance, or the production at a nuclear facility of, an atomic or subatomic particle or electromagnetic wave with sufficient energy for ionization. *Nuclear Safety and Control Act*, S.C. 1997, c. 9, s. 2. See IONIZING ~; LASER~; LEAKAGE~; MEDICAL ~ TECHNOLOGY; NON-IONIZING ~.

RADIATION EMITTING DEVICE. 1. (a) Any device that is capable of producing and emitting radiation; and (b) any component of or accessory to a device described in paragraph (a). *Radiation Emitting Device Act*, R.S.C. 1985, c. R-1, s. 2. 2. Any device that is capable of producing and emitting energy in the form of (a) electromagnetic waves having frequencies greater than 10 megacycles per second, and (b) ultrasonic waves having frequencies greater than 10 kilocycles per second. *Canada Dangerous Substances Regulations*, C.R.C., c. 997, s. 2.

RADIATION EQUIPMENT. Equipment or machinery associated with the use or operation of a radiation source, and includes the radiation source itself and any structure used to support or shield the equipment, machinery or radiation source.

RADIATION FACILITY. Any premises or part of premises in which radiation equipment or a radiation source is installed.

RADIATION HEALTH. The science and art of protecting persons from injury by radiation.

RADIATION INSTALLATION. The building or other place, or the part thereof, in which radiation equipment is manufactured, used, handled or tested.

RADIATION SOURCE. A device or substance that emits radiation.

RADIATION THERAPY TECHNOLOGIST. A medical radiation technologist who is registered as a member of the Canadian Association in the discipline of radiation therapy and utilizes radiating emitting devices in the practice of medical radiation technology.

RADIATION WORKER. Any person whose occupation requires that person to be exposed to radiation emitted by radiation equipment.

RADICAL. *adj.* 1. " . . . '[F]undamental' . . ." *Osterkampf v. Osterkampf* (1989), 22 R.F.L. (3d) 153 at 157, 99 A.R. 286 (Q.B.), Sulatycky J. 2. " . . . '[E]xtreme' . . ." *Coskey v. Coskey* (1992), 39 R.F.L. (3d) 449 at 457 (Alta. Q.B.), Cawsey J.

RADIO. *n.* 1. Any transmission, emission or reception of signs, signals, writing, images, sounds or intelligence of any nature by means of electromagnetic waves of frequencies lower than 3 000 GHz propagated in space without artificial guide. 2. Any transmission, emission or reception of signs, signals, writing, images and sounds or intelligence of any nature by means of Hertzian waves. Canada regulations. See CANADIAN ~-TELEVISION AND TELECOMMUNICATIONS COMMISSION.

RADIOACTIVE MATERIAL. *var.* **RADIO-ACTIVE MATERIAL**. (a) Spent nuclear fuel rods that have been exposed to radiation in a nuclear reactor; (b) radioactive waste material; (c) unused enriched nuclear fuel rods; or (d) any other radioactive material of such quantity and quality as to be harmful to persons or property if its containers were destroyed or damaged.

RADIO AND TELEVISION SERVICE TECHNICIAN. A person who: (a) installs, adjusts and repairs radio and television receivers and other domestic electronic equipment; (b) makes adjustments to obtain desired density, linearity, focus, colour and size of television pictures; (c) isolates and detects defects by the use of schematic diagrams, voltage meters, generators, oscilloscopes and other electronic testing instruments; (d) tests and changes tubes and other components; (e) repairs loose connections and repairs or replaces defective parts by the use of hand tools and soldering irons, and understands electronic theory and shop techniques, but does not include a person who is: (f) engaged in the manufacture of radio, television, amplifier or other related electronic equipment; (g) employed in the repair and maintenance of radio, television, amplifier or other related electronic equipment in an industrial plant; or (h) engaged in the wiring of radio, television, amplifier or other related electronic equipment to an external power source.

RADIO APPARATUS. A device or combination of devices intended for, or capable of being used for, radiocommunication.

RADIO-BASED TELEPHONE COMMUNICATION. Any radiocommunication that is made over apparatus that is used primarily for connection to a public switched telephone network.

RADIOCOMMUNICATION. *n.* Any transmission, emission or reception of signs, signals, writing, images, sounds or intelligence of any nature by means of electromagnetic waves of frequencies lower than 3 000 GHz propagated in space without artificial guide.

RADIOCOMMUNICATION CARRIER. A person who operates an interconnected radio-based transmission facility used by that person or another person to provide radiocommunication services for compensation. *Radiocommunication Regulations*, SOR/96-484, s. 2.

RADIOCOMMUNICATION DISTRIBUTION UNDERTAKING. A distribution undertaking, other than a DTH distribution undertaking, that distributes programming services predominantly by means of radio waves. *Broadcasting Distribution Regulations*, SOR/97-555, s. 1.

RADIOCOMMUNICATION SERVICE PROVIDER. A person, including a radiocommunication carrier, who operates radio apparatus used by that person or another person to provide radiocommunication services for compensation. *Radiocommunication Regulations*, SOR/96-484, s. 2.

RADIOCOMMUNICATION USER. A person who operates radio apparatus for personal or government use or for a business other than the business of a radiocommunication service provider; *Radiocommunications Regulations*, SOR 96-484.

RADIODETERMINATION SERVICE. A radiocommunication service that provides for the determination of the position, velocity or other characteristics of an object or physical phenomenon, or for the obtaining of information relating to these parameters, by means of the propagation properties of radio waves; *Radiocommunications Regulations*, SOR 96-484.

RADIO FREQUENCY GENERATOR. See I.S.M. ~.

RADIO FREQUENCY NOISE. Any electrical disturbance produced by any machinery, apparatus or equipment and is capable of being received by a radio receiving apparatus.

RADIOGRAPH. *n.* A Roentgen ray photograph.

RADIOGRAPHER. *n.* A person who practises medical radiological technology.

RADIOGRAPHIC TECHNOLOGIST. A medical radiation technologist who is registered as a member of the Canadian Association in the discipline of radiography and utilizes radiating emitting devices in the practice of medical radiation technology.

RADIOGRAPHY. *n.* The act, process, science or art of making radiographs for use in medical treatment or diagnosis. See INDUSTRIAL ~.

RADIO INSPECTOR. A person authorized by the Minister pursuant to section 345 of the Act to carry out radio inspections. *Crewing Regulations*, SOR/97-390, s. 1(1). (*inspecteur de radio*).

RADIOLOGICAL HEALTH PROTECTION. The science and art of protecting persons from injury by radiation.

RADIOLOGICAL TECHNICIAN. A person who practises the technical aspects of the medical use of ionizing radiation, including Roentgen or X-rays, radium, radioactive isotopes and particles for diagnosis or treatment. See INDUSTRIAL ~; MEDICAL ~.

RADIOLOGICAL TECHNOLOGY. See MEDICAL ~.

RADIOLOGIST. *n.* A legally qualified medical practitioner who holds a specialist certification in diagnostic or therapeutic radiology from the Royal College of Physicians and Surgeons of Canada.

RADIO NOISE. Any electrical disturbance produced by any machinery, apparatus or equipment and is capable of being received by a radio receiving apparatus.

RADIONUCLIDE GENERATOR. A radioactive parent and daughter (a) contained in an ion-exchanging column; or (b) dissolved in a suitable solvent in a liquid-liquid extraction system where the radioactive daughter is separated from its parent by (c) elution from the ion exchange column; or (d) a solvent extraction procedure. *Food and Drug Regulations*, C.R.C., c. 870, c. C.03.001.

RADIOPHARMACEUTICAL. *n.* A drug that exhibits spontaneous disintegration of unstable nuclei with the emission of nuclear particles or photons. *Food and Drug Regulations*, C.R.C., c. 870, c. C.03.201.

RADIO REGULATIONS. The regulations respecting radio made by the Governor in Council and the Minister respectively under sections 342 and 343. *Canada Shipping Act*, R.S.C. 1985, c. S-9, s. 2. See INTERNATIONAL ~.

RADIO-SENSITIVE EQUIPMENT. Any device, machinery or equipment, other than radio apparatus, the use or functioning of which is or can be adversely affected by radio communication emissions.

RADIO STATION. A place in which radio apparatus is located. *Radiocommunication Act*, R.S.C. 1985, R-2, s. 2. See AERONAUTICAL ~; OPTIONAL ~.

RADIO-TELEGRAPH. *var.* **RADIOTELEGRAPH**. *n.* 1. " . . . '[W]ireless system for conveying electric signals or messages'." *R. v. Gignac*, [1934] O.R. 195 at 203, 61 C.C.C. 371, [1934] 2 D.L.R. 113 (H.C.), Armour J. 2. Includes a system of radio communication for the transmission of written matter by the use of a signal code. *Canada Shipping Act*, R.S.C. 1985, c. S-9, s. 2.

RADIOTELEGRAPH ALARM SIGNAL. A signal consisting of a series of 12 dashes transmitted in 1 minute by manual or automatic means, the duration of each dash being 4 seconds and the duration of the interval between consecutive dashes being 1 second. *Ship Station Radio Regulations*, Part II, C.R.C., c. 1474, s. 2.

RADIO-TELEPHONE. *var.* **RADIOTELEPHONE**. *n.* 1. " . . . [W]ireless telephone[s]." *R. v. Gignac*, [1934] 2 D.L.R. 113 at 121, [1934] O.R. 195, 61 C.C.C. 371 (H.C.), Armour J. 2. Includes a system of radio communication for the transmission of speech or, in some cases, other sounds. *Canada Shipping Act*, R.S.C. 1985, c. S-9, s. 2.

RADIOTELEPHONE ALARM SIGNAL. A signal consisting of two substantially sinusoidal audio frequency tones of 2,200 c.p.s. and 1,300, c.p.s. transmitted alternately by manual or automatic means, the duration of each tone being 250 milliseconds. *Ship Station Radio Regulations, Part II*, C.R.C., c. 1474, s. 2.

RADIO WATCH. In respect of a ship, means the period during which a member of the complement is required to be at the ship station and in charge of the radiocommunication equipment. *Crewing Regulations*, SOR/97-390, s. 1(1).

RADIO WAVES. Electromagnetic waves of frequencies lower than 3 000 GHz that are propagated in space without artificial guide. *Broadcasting Act*, S.C. 1991, c. 11, s. 2(1).

RADON PROGENY. The following radioactive decay products of radon 222: bismuth 214, lead 214, polonium 214 and polonium 218. *Radiation Protection Regulations*, SOR/2000-203, s. 1.

RAFT. *n*. Includes any raft, crib, dam or bag boom of logs, timber or lumber of any kind, and logs, timber or lumber in boom or being towed.

RAFTER. *n*. A sloping wood framing member which supports the roof sheathing and encloses an attic space, but does not support a ceiling.

RAFTING. See COMMERCIAL RIVER ~.

RAID. *n*. " . . . [T]he obtaining of search warrants, attendance at the premises of the [respondent] and searching and sometimes seizure of articles or money or both . . ." *Greenback Investments (Hamilton) Ltd. v. O'Connell*, [1972] 3 O.R. 656 at 657 (H.C.), O'Driscoll J.

RAIL. See TRANSPORT BY ~; VIA ~ CANADA INC.

RAILROAD SIGN OR SIGNAL. Any sign, signal or device intended to give notice of the presence of railroad tracks or the approach of a railroad train.

RAIL VEHICLE. A vehicle that is drawn, propelled or driven on rails by means other than by muscular power.

RAILWAY. *n*. 1. " . . . '[A] way on which a train passes by means of rails,' . . ." *Grand Trunk Railway v. James* (1901) 31 S.C.R. 420 at 432, 22 C.L.T. 2, 1 C.R.C. 422, Sedgewick J. 2. " . . . [I]mports locomotion on or over 'rails' furnishing a service within fixed and rigid limits: . . ." *Quebec Railway Light & Power Co. v. Beauport*, [1945] S.C.R. 16 at 40, [1945] 1 D.L.R. 145, 57 C.R.T.C. 245, Rand J. 3. Any railway that the company has authority to construct or operate, and includes all branches, extensions, sidings, stations, depots, wharfs, rolling stock, equipment, stores, property real or personal and works connected therewith, and also any railway bridge, tunnel or other structure that the company is authorized to construct; and, except where the context is inapplicable, includes street railway and tramway. *Railway Act*, R.S.C. 1985, c. R-3, s. 2. See CANADIAN GOVERNMENT ~S; CANADIAN NATIONAL ~ COMPANY; CANADIAN NATIONAL ~S; INDUSTRIAL ~; NATIONAL ~S; PROVIN-

CIAL ~S; TRANSPORT BY RAIL; UNECONOMIC LINE OF ~; VIA RAIL CANADA INC.

RAILWAY CAR. Railway rolling stock.

RAILWAY COMPANY. Any company operating a line of railway in one or more provinces.

RAILWAY CROSSING. Any railway crossing of a highway or highway crossing of a railway and any manner of construction of the railway or highway by the elevation or depression of the one above or below the other, or by the diversion of the one or the other, and any work ordered or authorized by the Agency to be provided as one work or the protection, safety and convenience of the public in respect of one or more railways with as many tracks crossing or crossed as the Agency in its discretion determines. *Railway Relocation and Crossing Act*, R.S.C. 1985, c. R-4, s. 2.

RAILWAY EQUIPMENT. (a) A machine that is constructed for movement exclusively on lines of railway, whether or not the machine is capable of independent motion, or (b) a vehicle that is constructed for movement both on and off lines of railway while the adaptations of that vehicle for movement on lines of railway are in use. *Railway Safety Act*, R.S.C. 1985, c. 32, (4th Supp.) s. 4.

RAILWAY PASSENGER SERVICE. A passenger train service that does not accommodate principally persons who commute between points on the railway.

RAILWAY RIGHT-OF-WAY. Lands that are owned or leased by a railway, are contiguous to that railway's tracks and are required for railway purposes. Canada regulations.

RAILWAY ROADWAY. (a) Outside of a hamlet or an organized hamlet, means a continuous strip of land that is used by a railway company as a right-of-way and includes any railway superstructure on that land; and (b) within a hamlet or an organized hamlet, means a continuous strip of land, not exceeding 31 metres in width, that is owned or occupied by a railway company and includes any railway superstructure on that land. *The Rural Municipality Act, 1989*, S.S. 1989-90, c. R-26.1, s. 2(1).

RAILWAY ROLLING STOCK. Railway passenger, baggage and freight cars. Canada regulations.

RAILWAY STATION. Any location where passenger or freight trains may stop in accordance with the current railway timetable. Canada regulations.

RAILWAY STATION-DWELLING. A railway station, of which a part is used as a dwelling. Canada regulations.

RAILWAY SUPERSTRUCTURE. The grading, ballasts, embankments, ties, rails and fastenings, miscellaneous track accessories and appurtenances, switches, poles, wires, conduits and cables, fences, cable guards, cattle passes, platforms, stockyards, hog shelters, scales, turntables, cinder and service pits, hoists, signals and signal towers, grade crossing protective appliances, water tanks, stand pipes, pump sheds, dams, spillways, reservoirs, wells, pumping machinery, pipelines or bins, sheds or other storage facilities that have a floor space of not more than 9.3 square metres, owned by a railway company or used by it in the operation of a railway. *The Rural Municipality Act, 1989*, S.S. 1989-90, c. R-26.1, s. 2(1).

RAILWAY SYSTEM. Includes a railway owned or operated by a common carrier, together with all buildings, rolling stock, equipment and other properties pertaining thereto.

RAILWAY WORK. A line work or any part thereof, a crossing work or any part thereof, or any combination of the foregoing. *Railway Safety Act*, R.S.C. 1985, c. 32, (4ᵗʰ Supp.) s. 4.

RAIN. *n.* Any water which falls from the atmosphere in the form of solid or liquid precipitation. *Artificial Inducement of Rain Act*, R.S.Q. 1977, c. P-43, s. 1. See ARTIFICIAL INDUCEMENT OF ~.

RAINBOW TROUT. Includes steelhead trout and Kamloops trout.

RAIN WATER LEADER. A conductor inside a building or other structure that conveys storm water from the roof of the building or other structure to a building storm drain or other place of disposal.

RAISE. *v.* To construct, build up.

RAISED CABLE. A cable that is not resting on the river bed.

RAKE. See DRAG ~.

RAM. 1. Some chips store information only as long as the machine is on: they are called "Random Access Memory" chips (RAMs). When the power is turned off, the information stored in the RAMs is lost. *Apple Computer Inc. v. Macintosh Computers Ltd.* (1985), 3 C.I.P.R. 133, 3 C.P.R. (3d) 34 (Fed. T.D.) Cullen J. 2. The computer's memory is typically composed of semiconductor circuits known as chips. There are two types of memory; ROM (Read Only Memory) and RAM (Random Access Memory). Instructions stored in ROM are permanent; they can only be read by the computer not changed or rewritten by it, and do not erase when the machine is turned off. Instructions stored in RAM can be changed or rewritten by the operator at any time and are usually erased when the machine is turned off. *IBM Corp. v. Ordinateurs Spirales Inc./Spirales Computers Inc.* (1984), 27 B.L.R. 190, 80 C.P.R. (2d) 187, 2 C.I.P.R. 56, 12 D.L.R. (4th) 351 (Fed. T.D.), Reed J.

RAM. & MOR. *abbr.* Ramsay & Morin, The Law Reporter (Journal de jurisprudence).

RAMP AREA. The area provided for loading or unloading passengers or cargo, or for refuelling, parking or maintaining the aircraft.

RANCH. See FUR-BEARING ANIMAL ~; FUR ~; MUSKRAT ~.

RANCHER. *n.* A person whose primary occupation is rearing stock from a basic herd and who deals in stock only for that purpose.

RANCHING. See GAME ~; SEA ~.

RAND FORMULA. A plan providing union security and requiring automatic check-off of union dues by employers.

RANDOM ACCESS MEMORY. Some chips store information only as long as the machine is on: they are called "Random Access Memory" chips (RAMs). When the power is turned off, the information stored in the RAM is lost. *Apple Computer Inc. v. Macintosh Computers Ltd.* (1985), 3 C.I.P.R. 133, 3 C.P.R. (3d) 34 (Fed. T.D.) Cullen J. 2. The computer's memory is typically composed of semiconductor circuits known as chips. There are two types of memory; ROM (Read Only Memory) and RAM (Random Access Memory). Instructions stored in ROM are permanent; they can only be read by the computer not changed or rewritten by it, and do not erase when the machine is turned off. Instructions stored in RAM can be changed or rewritten by the operator at any time and are usually erased when the machine is turned off. *IBM Corp. v. Ordinateurs Spirales Inc./Spirales Computers Inc.* (1984), 27 B.L.R. 190, 80 C.P.R. (2d) 187, 2 C.I.P.R. 56, 12 D.L.R. (4th) 351 (Fed. T.D.), Reed J.

RANDOM VIRTUE TESTING. Arises when a police officer presents a person with the opportunity to commit an offence *without* a reasonable suspicion that: (a) the person is already engaged in the particular criminal activity, or (b) the physical location with which the person is associated is a place where the particular criminal activity is likely occurring. *R. v. Barnes*, [1991] 1 S.C.R. 449.

RANGE. *n.* 1. Open land. 2. A spread. 3. A cooking appliance equipped with a cooking surface and one or more ovens. See CROWN ~; NEGOTIATING ~; PAY ~.

RANK. *n.* Includes appointment. *Canadian Forces Superannuation Act*, R.S.C. 1985, c. C-17, s. 2. See BREVET ~.

RANSOM. *n.* The price paid to redeem a prisoner or captive.

RAPE. *n.* " . . . [N]on-consensual sexual intercourse . . ." *R. v. McCraw* (1991), 7 C.R. (4th) 314 at 325, 66 C.C.C. (3d) 517, 128 N.R. 299, 49 O.A.C. 47, [1991] 3 S.C.R. 72, the court per Cory J. See AGGRAVATED SEXUAL ASSAULT; SEXUAL ASSAULT; STATUTORY ~.

RAPID TRANSIT. A public transportation system running on rails or other tracked systems and operating on an exclusive right of way.

RAPINE. *n.* Theft; taking something in defiance of the owner, openly or violently.

RAPTOR. *n.* A bird of the order Falconiformes known as vultures, eagles, falcons and hawks or the order Strigiformes known as owls, and includes its eggs.

RASURE. *n.* Erasing; shaving or scraping.

RATABLE PERSON. A person liable to taxation.

RATABLY. *adv.* " . . . [T]he proportion which the total of the contributions made by a partner bears to the total contributions of all partners to the capital of the partnership." *Emberson v. Fisher*, [1944] 2 D.L.R. 572 at 7, [1944] O.R. 241 (C.A.), the court per Laidlaw J.A.

RATE. *n.* 1. Includes a general, individual or joint rate, fare, toll, charge, rental or other compensation of a public utility, a rule, regulation, practice, measurement, classification or contract of a public utility or corporation relating to a rate and a schedule or tariff respecting a rate. 2. An amount payable under a contract of insurance for an identified risk whether expressed in dollar terms or in some other manner and includes commissions, surcharges, fees, discounts, rebates and dividends. 3. The method of calculating wages. 4. A fixed percentage of value applied equally to all properties within a jurisdiction. See BANK OF CANADA ~; BANK ~; BASE ~; BASIC ~; CANADIAN OWNERSHIP ~; COMMODITY ~; CONTRACT ~; CREDIT~; CRIMINAL ~; DAILY ~; DEBENTURE ~; DISCOUNT~; DOSE-~; DUAL ~ SYSTEM; EFFECTIVE ~; ENTRANCE ~; GOING ~; GUARANTEED ~; INDIVIDUAL ~; JOB ~; NON-CONTRACT ~; ORDINARY PUBLISHED ~; OVERTIME ~; PIECE WORK ~; PREMIUM ~; PRIME ~; ~S; REGULAR ~; SERVICE ~; SEWAGE SERVICE ~; SEWER ~; SINGLE ~; SPECIFIED INTEREST ~; STORAGE ~; TOLL OR ~; VARIABLE ~ AGREEMENT; VARIABLE ~ MORTGAGE; WATER ~; WATER WORKS ~.

RATEABLE. *adj.* 1. Subject to taxation. 2. Proportionate.

RATEABLE LAND. Land liable to taxation.

RATEABLE PORTION. If there are two insurers liable and each has the same policy limits, each of the insurers shall be liable to share equally in any liability, expense, loss or damage; If there are two insurers liable with different policy limits, the insurers shall be liable to share equally up to the limit of the smaller policy limit; and if there are more than two insurers liable, clauses (a) and (b) shall apply mutatis mutandis. *Insurance Act*, R.S.M. 1970, c. I40, s. 272.

RATEABLE PROPERTY. Includes business and other assessments made under the Assessment Act. Ontario statutes.

RATEABLE PROPORTION. (a) If there are two insurers liable and each has the same policy limits, each of the insurers will be liable to share equally in any liability, expense, loss or damage; (b) if there are two insurers liable with different policy limits, the insurers will be liable to share equally up to the limit of the smaller policy limit; and (c) if there are more than two insurers liable, paragraphs (a) and (b) will apply mutatis mutandis.

RATEABLE VALUE. The value of a business interest when less than 100 per cent of the shares are held by the person in question. A. Bissett-Johnson & W.M. Holland, eds., *Matrimonial*

Property Law in Canada (Toronto: Carswell, 1980) at V-9.

RATE BASE. The maximum valuation of assets fixed upon which a public utility may earn a percentage of return.

RATED BED CAPACITY. The number of bassinets, cribs and beds which a hospital is designed to have.

RATED CAPACITY. 1. The maximum load that can be weighed on a weighing machine as set out in the notice of approval. *Weights and Measures Regulations*, C.R.C., c. 1605, s. 57. 2. The amount of chlorine that a plant is designed to produce each day. *Chlor-Alkali Mercury National Emission Standards Regulations*, C.R.C., c. 406, s. 2.

RATED GENERATOR CAPACITY. The aggregate generator capacity obtained by adding together the individually rated capacities of all of the generators on a ship. *Marine Certification Regulations*, SOR/97-391, s. 1(1).

RATED MAXIMUM SOUND PRESSURE. At the frequency of rated maximum sound pressure and with the gain of the hearing aid set to maximum, the lowest value of sound pressure in the coupler at which the total harmonic distortion reaches 10 per cent. *Medical Devices Regulations*, C.R.C., c. 871, s. 1.

RATE MANUAL. The documents of an authorized insurer in which his rules of classification of risks, and the premiums applicable to each, are identified and defined.

RATE OF TAX. See NATIONAL AVERAGE ~.

RATE OF UNEMPLOYMENT. See NATIONAL ~.

RATE OF WAGES. 1. The basis of calculation of wages. 2. (a) The basis of calculation of the wages paid to a person employed whether that basis is remuneration for a period of time worked or for piece work or is any other incentive basis, and (b) where the basis of calculation of the wages paid to a person employed is a combination of such bases of calculation, that combination of bases.

RATE OR TOLL. Any fee or rate charged, levied or collected, either directly or indirectly by any person for the carriage of goods or passengers by a vehicle.

RATEPAYER. *n.* 1. Taxpayer. 2. A person obliged to pay a tax to a municipal corporation.

3. A person who is assessed upon the last revised assessment roll of a municipality. See RESIDENT ~.

RATE PERMITTED. A rate that is a legal and valid rate in respect of the loan and is not in contravention of any Act heretofore or hereafter enacted by the Parliament of Canada. *Money-Lenders Act*, R.S.N.S. 1989, c. 289, s. 2.

RATES. *n.* 1. The charges set or made for the supply of a public utility and includes all conditions of supply pertaining thereto. 2. Rates, surcharges, premiums or any other amount payable by an insured for insurance. See COMPENSATION ~; EASTERN ~; HANDLING ~; IRRIGATION ~; RATE.

RATES OF CONTRIBUTION. The regular net premiums, dues, rates or contributions receivable from the members for the purpose of the payment at maturity of the society's certificates or contracts of insurance. *Insurance acts.*

RATIFICATION. *n.* 1. The act of confirming. 2. "In order to find the parties, in whose name and behalf an unauthorized person has assumed to enter into a contract, by subsequent recognition and adoption it must be shown that either expressly, or impliedly by conduct, the parties whom it is sought to bind have, with a full knowledge of all the terms of the agreement come to by the person who assumed to bind them, assented to the same terms and agreed to abide by and be bound by the contract undertaken on their behalf." *Cameron v. Paxton Tate & Co.* (1888), 15 S.C.R. 622 at 633, Strong J. 3. Agency is created by ratification when an agent does something on behalf of a principal when they are not yet in the relation of principal and agent. Later, however, the principal accepts and adopts the agent's act as if there had been prior authorisation to do what was done. G.H.L. Fridman, *The Law of Agency*, 6th ed. (London: Butterworths, 1990) at 74. 4. Formal approval given to terms negotiated in collective bargaining. 5. " . . . [I]n respect of treaties, the formal adoption by the high contracting party of a previous assent conveyed by the signature of so-called plenipotentiaries." *Canada (Attorney General) v. Ontario (Attorney General)*, [1937] 1 D.L.R. 673 at 677, [1937] A.C. 326, [1937] 1 W.W.R. 299, [1937] W.N. 53 (Can. P.C.), the court per Lord Atkin.

RATIHABITIO MANDATO AEQUIPARATUR. [L.] Ratification is the same as a command.

RATING. *n*. 1. The process by which tax rates are fixed and imposed by local authorities. 2. A person who is a member of a ship's crew other than the master or an officer. Canada regulations. See BOILER ~; CONTINUOUS ~; CREDIT ~; EXPERIENCE ~; FIRE EXTINGUISHER ~; FIRE-PROTECTION ~; FIRE RESISTANCE ~; FLAME-SPREAD ~; GROSS AXLE WEIGHT ~; GROSS VEHICLE WEIGHT ~; LOAD ~; MAXIMUM LOAD ~; POWER ~; PROTEIN EFFICIENCY ~; PROTEIN ~.

RATING BUREAU. Any association or body created or organized for the purpose of filing or promulgating rates of premium payable upon contracts of insurance or which assumes to file or promulgate such rates by agreement, among the members thereof or otherwise.

RATIO. *n*. [L. a reason] 1. The grounds or reason for deciding. 2. A rule for calculating proportions. 3. A calculation of credits and debits. See CLAIMS ~; FREEBOARD ~; FREIGHT TO PRICE ~; FUNDED ~; GAS OIL ~; GROSS DEBT SERVICE ~; ISOPHANE ~; QUICK ASSET ~.

RATIO DECIDENDI. [L.] The grounds or reason for deciding.

RATIO LEGIS EST ANIMA LEGIS. [L.] The reason for the law is the essence of the law.

RATIONABILI ESTOVERIUM. [L.] Alimony.

RATIONABILIS DOS. [L.] A widow's proper share or a reasonable dowery.

RATIONAL CONCLUSION. A conclusion based on and supported by the evidence.

RATIONAL CONNECTION. Between legislative objectives and the means employed to attain them, means showing that the legitimate and important goals of the legislature are logically furthered by the means government chose to adopt. *Lavigne v. O.P.S.E.U.*, [1991] 2 S.C.R. 211.

RATIONALE. See OBJECTIVE ~.

RATIONE MATERIAE. [L.] By reason of the matter.

RATIONES. *n*. [L.] In a suit, pleadings.

RATIONES EXERCERE. [L.] To plead.

RATIONE SOLI. [L.] By reason alone.

RATIONE TENURAE. [L.] In respect or by reason of one's tenure.

RATIONING PROGRAM. A mandatory allocation program extended to include additional measures. Where the Governor in Council considers that the available supplies of a controlled product, energy-related, are or are likely to be in such short supply as to cause the mandatory allocation program to fail unless additional measures are taken, the purchase and sale of the controlled product at any or all levels, including the level of the final consumer or user, be made in such quantities, by such persons and for such uses as may be authorized on documentary evidence. *Energy Supplies Emergency Act*, R.S.C. 1985, c. E-9.

RAW GAS. A mixture containing methane, other paraffinic hydrocarbons, nitrogen, carbon dioxide, hydrogen sulphide, helium and minor impurities, or some of them, that is recovered or is recoverable at a well from an underground reservoir and that is gaseous at the conditions under which its volume is measured or estimated.

RAW HIDE. The skin, with or without the pelage, of big game that is in an unprocessed, whether it be a green, dry or salted condition and includes any part of such skin.

RAW LEAF TOBACCO. Unmanufactured tobacco or the leaves and stems of the tobacco plant.

RAW MILK. Milk that has not been pasteurized.

RAW PELT. The skin, with or without the pelage, of a fur-bearing animal or small game that is in an unprocessed, whether it be a green, dry or salted condition and includes any part of such skin.

RAW WATER. Water that is not potable water. Canada regulations.

RAW WOOL, HAIR OR BRISTLES. Wool, hair or bristles taken from an animal but does not include wool tops, wool waste, wool noils, wool laps, small trade samples of wool, lime pulled wool and hair, scoured wool and hair and carbonized wool and hair.

RAY. *n*. Any transmission of energy in the form of particles or electromagnetic waves with or without production of ions when they pass through matter.

R.C. *abbr*. Roman Catholic.

R.C. DE L'É. *abbr.* Recueils de jurisprudence de la Cour de l'Echiquier.

R.C.L.J. *abbr.* Revue critique de législation et de jurisprudence du Canada.

RCMP. *abbr.* Royal Canadian Mounted Police.

R.C.P.I. *abbr.* Revue canadienne de propriété intellectuelle.

R.C.S. *abbr.* Recueils des arrêts de la Cour Suprême du Canada.

[] R.C.S. *abbr.* Rapports judiciaires du Canada, Cour Suprême du Canada, 1964-.

R. DE J. *abbr.* Revue de jurisprudence.

R. DE L. *abbr.* Revue de Législation (1845-1848).

R.D.F. *abbr.* Recueil de droit de la famille.

R.D.F.Q. *abbr.* Recueil de droit fiscal québécois.

[] R.D.F.Q. *abbr.* Recueil de droit fiscal Québecois, 1977-.

R.D.I. *abbr.* Recueil de droit immobilier.

R.D.J. *abbr.* Revue de droit judiciaire, 1983-.

R.D. MCGILL. *abbr.* Revue de droit de McGill (McGill Law Journal).

R.D.T. *abbr.* Revue de droit de travail.

R. DU B. *abbr.* La Revue du Barreau.

R. DU B. CAN. *abbr.* La Revue du Barreau canadien (The Canadian Bar Review).

R. DU D. *abbr.* Revue du droit (1922-1939).

R. DU N. *abbr.* La Revue du Notariat.

R.D.U.N.-B. *abbr.* Revue de droit de l'Université du Nouveau-Brunswick (University of New Brunswick Law Review).

R.D.U.S. *abbr.* Revue de droit, Université de Sherbrooke.

RE. *prep.* [L.] Concerning, in the matter of.

REACTION. See HYPERSENSITIVITY ~; VITAL ~.

READ. *v.* To vote on a bill in a legislature. A bill must be read three times to become law.

READER. See BRAND ~.

READILY REMOVABLE WINDOW. A window that can be quickly and completely removed from a vehicle without tools and, in the case of a bus having a GVWR of more than 4 535.9 kg (10,000 pounds), shall include a push-out window and a window mounted in an emergency exit that can be manually pushed out of its location in the vehicle without the use of tools, regardless of whether the window remains hinged to one side to the vehicle. *Motor Vehicle Safety Regulations*, C.R.C., c. 1038, s. 2.

READINESS. See CERTIFICATE OF ~; NOTICE OF ~ FOR TRIAL.

READING. *n.* The vote on a bill in a legislature. A bill must undergo three readings to become law. See FIRST ~; SECOND ~; THIRD ~.

READING DOWN. A canon of construction of legislation. Whenever possible a statue is interpreted as having been enacted within the power of the legislature. The doctrine is applied to valid provincial legislation of general application which limits or prohibits some activity which in turn impacts negatively on the functioning of a federal power. General language in a statute which is apt to extend beyond the power of the enacting legislature is construed narrowly to keep it within the permitted scope of power.

READING IN. Where an inconsistency exists in a statute because of something wrongly excluded from it, the result of declaring that provision inoperative is to 'read in' the excluded group or circumstance. The statute is extended by reading in.

READMISSION. *n.* Admission to a hospital of someone who had previously received inpatient care.

READ ONLY MEMORY. Information to be stored permanently can be held in another type of chip called "Read Only Memory" (ROM). Information stored in ROM chips is not lost when the power of the computer is switched off. *Apple Computer Inc. v. Macintosh Computers Ltd.* (1985), 3 C.I.P.R. 133, 3 C.P.R. (3d) 34 (Fed. T.D.) Cullen J. 2. The computer's memory is typically composed of semiconductor circuits known as chips. There are two types of memory; ROM (Read Only Memory) and RAM (Random Access Memory). Instructions stored in ROM are permanent; they can only be read by the computer not changed or rewritten by it, and do not erase when the machine is turned off. Instructions stored in RAM can be changed or rewritten by the operator at any time and are usually erased when the machine is turned off. *IBM Corp. v. Ordinateurs Spirales Inc./Spirales Computers Inc.* (1984), 27 B.L.R. 190, 80 C.P.R.

(2d) 187, 2 C.I.P.R. 56, 12 D.L.R. (4th) 351 (Fed. T.D.), Reed J.

READY FOR JUDGMENT. See CASE ~.

REAL. *adj*. 1. Relating to land as opposed to chattels. 2. Tangible. See CHATTELS ~.

REAL ACTION. The common law proceeding by which a freeholder was able to recover land.

REAL AND SUBSTANTIAL CONNECTION. 1. By tendering his products in the market place directly or through normal distributive channels, a manufacturer ought to assume the burden of defending those products wherever they cause harm as long as the forum into which the manufacturer is taken is one that he reasonably ought to have had in his contemplation when he so tendered his goods. This is particularly true of dangerously defective goods placed in the interprovincial flow of commerce. The approach of permitting suit where there is a real and substantial connection with the action provides a reasonable balance between the rights of the parties. It affords some protection against being pursued in jurisdictions having little or no connection with the transaction or the parties. The above rationale is not limited to torts. *Morguard Investments Ltd. v. De Savoye*, [1990] 3 S.C.R. 1077. 2. The "real and substantial connection" test, which is applied to interprovincial judgments, should apply equally to the recognition of foreign judgments. The "real and substantial connection" test requires that a significant connection exist between the cause of action and the foreign court. Furthermore, a defendant can reasonably be brought within the embrace of a foreign jurisdiction's law where he or she has participated in something of significance or was actively involved in that foreign jurisdiction. A fleeting or relatively unimportant connection will not be enough to give a foreign court jurisdiction. The connection to the foreign jurisdiction must be a substantial one. *Beals v. Saldanha*, 2003 SCC 72, per Major, J.

REAL CRIME. "[One which is] . . . concerned with the reinforcement of society's fundamental values. . ." *Thomson Newspapers Ltd. v. Canada (Director of Investigation & Research, Combines Investigation Branch)* (1990), 54 C.C.C. (3d) 417 at 479, 76 C.R. (3d) 129, 72 O.R. (2d) 415n, 67 D.L.R. (4th) 161, 29 C.P.R. (3d) 97, [1990] 1 S.C.R. 425, 39 O.A.C. 161, 106 N.R. 161, La Forest J.

REAL ESTATE. 1. " . . . [A]ll hereditaments. . ." *Montreal Light, Heat & Power Con-*solidated v. Westmount (Town)*, [1926] S.C.R. 515 at 523, [1926] 3 D.L.R. 466, Anglin C.J.C. (Duff, Mignault, Newcombe and Rinfret JJ. concurring). 2. Includes messuages, lands, tenements and hereditaments, whether freehold or of any other tenure, and whether corporeal or incorporeal, and any undivided share thereof, and any estate, right or interest therein. 3. Includes: (a) real or leasehold property; (b) any business, whether with or without premises, fixtures, stock-in-trade, goods or chattels connected with the operation of the business; and (c) a time-sharing arrangement. 4. An estate in fee simple in land, and does not include any lesser estate or interest therein. *Trust Companies Act*, R.S.A. 1980, c. T-9, s. 1. See IMPROVED ~.

REAL ESTATE BROKER. Any person who carries out a real estate transaction for another and for remuneration.

REAL ESTATE CORPORATION. A corporation incorporated to acquire, hold, maintain, improve, lease or manage real estate or leaseholds or act as agent or broker in the sale or purchase of real estate or leaseholds.

REAL ESTATE INVESTMENT TRUST. 1. A mutual fund the assets of which consist solely or primarily of investments in or loans in relation to real estate, an interest in real estate or a real estate related activity. *Bank Act*, R.S.C. 1985, c. B-1, s. 2. 2. The major kinds of investment are mortgage loans, purchase-leasebacks, construction and development loans, real estate equities and land. D.M.W. Waters, *The Law of Trusts in Canada*, 2d ed. (Toronto: Carswell, 1984) at 446.

REAL ESTATE SALESMAN. An individual, other than an authorized official, who is employed or engaged by a broker (whether registered or not) to take part on behalf of the broker in any of the activities mentioned in the definition of broker.

REAL ESTATE TAX. 1. A tax imposed on an immoveable by a municipal corporation or a school board, regardless of the use made of it. 2. A tax, other than a water tax, levied by a province or provincial agency to finance services that are ordinarily provided throughout Canada by municipalities (a) on all owners of real property and (b) on persons who are lessees or occupiers of real property owned by any person exempt by law, and computed by applying one or more rates to all or a part of assessed value of such real property.

REAL ESTATE TRANSACTION. 1. A transaction for the acquisition, disposal, exchange or renting of real estate, or for the negotiation of a loan secured by a charge on or transfer of real estate, or for the collection of money so secured or money payable as rent for the use of real estate. 2. The purchase, sale, promise of purchase or sale of an immoveable, the purchase or sale of such promise, the exchange or rental of an immoveable, the bulk sale of a stock in trade, a loan secured by the hypothecation or pledging of an immoveable, excluding any act respecting a security within the meaning of the Securities Act. *Real Estate Brokerage Act*, R.S.Q. 1977, c. C-73, s. 1.

REAL EVIDENCE. 1. "Evidence has been found to be 'real' when it referred to tangible items..." *R. v. Wise* (1992), 11 C.R. (4th) 253 at 265, [1992] 1 S.C.R. 527, 70 C.C.C. (3d) 193, 133 N.R. 161, 8 C.R.R. (2d) 53, 51 O.A.C 351, Cory J. (Lamer C.J.C., Gonthier and Stevenson JJ. concurring). 2. "... [E]xists independently of any statement by any witness, ..." *R. v. Schwartz* (1988), 55 D.L.R. (4th) 1 at 26, [1989] 1 W.W.R. 289, 66 C.R. (3d) 251, 88 N.R. 90, [1988] 2 S.C.R. 443, 45 C.C.C. (3d) 97, 56 Man. R. (2d) 92, 39 C.R.R. 260, Dickson C.J.C. (dissenting). 3. All evidence supplied by material objects when they are offered for direct perception by the court. *Military Rules of Evidence*, C.R.C., c. 1049, s. 2(1).

REAL INTEREST METHOD. A method of determining the value of a person's interest in a group pension for the purposes of dividing property in a marriage breakdown. The value of the future income stream is calculated assuming the member will continue to be employed until retirement. Likely future earnings are assumed.

REALIZABLE VALUE. The amount which one would realize through orderly liquidation before considering any costs of the liquidation, e. g. income taxes on the disposal of assets, liquidation commissions or severance pay.

REALIZATION. *n.* The sale of all or virtually all the property, assets and undertaking of a debtor.

REALIZATION PRINCIPLE. In Income Tax, an amount may have the quality of income even though it is not actually received by the taxpayer, but only "realized" in accordance with the accrual method of accounting. The ultimate effect of this principle is clear: amounts received or realized by a taxpayer, free of conditions or restrictions upon their use, are taxable in the year realized, subject to any contrary provision of the Act or other rule of law. *Ikea Ltd. v. R.*, [1998] 1 S.C.R. 196.

REALIZE. *v.* " ... [T]o sell, to convert into money, ..." *Bayne, Re*, [1946] 3 D.L.R. 49 at 50 (N.S. S.C.), Chisholm C.J. (Hall J. concurring).

REAL LIKELIHOOD OF BIAS. See REASONABLE APPREHENSION OF BIAS.

REALM. *n.* A country; a territory subject to a sovereign. See GREAT SEAL OF THE ~; HER MAJESTY'S ~S AND TERRITORIES.

REAL OWNER. (a) A purchaser of the land under an agreement for sale; (b) a person who is entitled to become the owner of land at some future date under a trust; (c) a person on whose behalf the registered owner holds the land as agent; or (d) any person who is entitled to have the land registered in his name.

REAL PROPERTY. 1. " ... [C]orporeal and incorporeal hereditaments ... land [and]... rights in land, ..." *Pegg v. Pegg* (1992), 38 R.F.L. (3d) 179 at 184, 21 R.P.R. (2d) 149, 1 Alta. L.R. (3d) 249, 128 A.R. 132 (Q.B.), Agrios J. 2. Includes messuages, lands, rents and hereditaments whether of freehold or any other tenure whatever and whether corporeal or incorporeal and any undivided share thereof and any estate, right or interest other than a chattel interest therein. 3. The ground or soil and everything annexed to it, and includes land covered by water, all quarries and substances in or under land other than mines or minerals and all buildings, fixtures, machinery, structures and things erected on or under or affixed to land. 4. Includes any estate, interest or right to or in land, but does not include a mortgage secured by real property.

REAL PROPERTY INSURANCE. Insurance against the loss of, or damage to, real or immovable property resulting from any cause not specifically mentioned in other classes of insurance covering real or immovable property. *Classes of Insurance Regulations*, C.R.C., c. 977, s. 33.

REAL PROPERTY TAX. A tax, including a water tax, of general application to real property or any class thereof that is (a) levied by a taxing authority on owners of real property, or where the owner is exempt from the tax, on lessees or occupiers of real property, other than those exempt by law; and (b) computed by applying a rate to all or part of the assessed value of taxable property. *Payments in Lieu of Taxes Act*, R.S.C. 1985, c. M-13, s. 2. See RESIDENTIAL ~.

REAL RIGHT. Jus in re, a full and complete right.

REAL THING. Something immovable and substantial, and any rights and profits which are annexed to or issue out of it.

REAL RISK. A risk which a reasonable person would not ignore as far-fetched or fanciful. The standard of care is based on what a reasonably prudent person would perceive as a real risk of harm to another person.

REALTOR. *n*. A person who belongs to a professional group of real estate dealers who describe themselves as realtors.

REALTY. *n*. Real property; freehold land. See COMMERCIAL ~.

REAL WAGE. The value of a wage in terms of commodities and services which the wage can purchase.

REAR-END DAMAGE. Damage caused to a vehicle by being hit in the rear end.

REARING. *n*. Keeping fish or fish eggs or feeding fish artificially in a fish preserve.

REAR LOT LINE. (a) In the case of a regular shaped lot the boundary line of the lot opposite and furthest in distance from the front lot line; and (b) in the case of an irregular shaped lot, a line 10 feet in length within the lot parallel to and at the maximum distance from the front lot line. Canada regulations.

REAR YARD. 1. A yard extending across the full width of a lot between the rearmost main building or main storage area and the rear lot line. Canada regulations. 2. A yard extended across the full width of a lot upon which a building or structure is situate and from the rear lot line to the part of the building or structure that is nearest to the rear lot line.

REAR YARD DEPTH. The distance measured horizontally from the nearest point of the rear lot line toward the nearest part of the main structure, clear of projections, or the main storage area, as the case may be. Canada regulations.

REASONABLE. *adj*. 1. Refers to a rational inference from evidence or established truths. 2. " . . . [I]mplies a reason related to the purpose of the regulation, a rational connection between purpose and action and, in my view, it also implies a qualification on the nature of the action

taken, that it be reasonable in the circumstances. . ." *Jackson v. Joyceville Penitentiary* (1990), 55 C.C.C. (3d) 50 at 80, 75 C.R. (3d) 174, 32 F.T.R. 96, 1 C.R.R. (2d) 327 (T.D.), Mackay J. 3. "An example of the relatively restrictive approach to reasonableness is found in the decision of Lord Diplock in Secretary of the State for Education & Science v. Tameside Metropolitan Borough Council, [1977] A.C. 1014 . . . (H.L.) at p. 1064, where he stated that a statutory requirement that a public authority exercise a discretion 'reasonably' should be regarded as proscribing 'conduct which no sensible authority acting with due apprehension of its responsibilities would have decided to adopt.' . . . however, a higher standard of proof of reasonableness should be applied in cases where an interest in personal liberty is at stake. In Reg. v. Secretary of State for Home Department, Ex parte Khawaja, [1984] A.C. 74, the House of Lords . . . held that if an immigration officer ordered the detention of any person as an illegal entrant, it would not be sufficient merely to show some reasonable grounds for the action. As a liberty interest was at stake, . . . the immigration officer had to satisfy a civil standard of proof to a high degree of probability that the detained person was an illegal entrant." *Smith v. R.*, [1991] 3 F.C. 3 at 28-9, 42 F.T.R. 81, 14 Imm. L.R. (2d) 57, 4 Admin. L.R. (2d) 97 (T.D.), Cullen J. 4. "A search will be reasonable if it is authorized by law, if the law itself is reasonable and if the manner in which the search was carried out is reasonable." *R. v. Collins*, [1987] 3 W.W.R. 699 at 712, 56 C.R. (3d) 193, 74 N.R. 276, 13 B.C.L.R. (2d) 1, [1987] 1 S.C.R. 265, 33 C.C.C. (3d) 1, 28 D.L.R. (4th) 508, 28 C.R.R. 122, Lamer J. 5. " . . . [T]he term 'reasonable' when used in the context of an interpretation of a provision in a collective agreement means an interpretation that is not absurd, one that is not ridiculous, outrageous, patently unjustifiable, extreme or excessive, but one that is a product of a sensible analysis, which may or may not be flawed, and one that may generally be described as within the bounds of reason. The interpretation does not have to be correct to be reasonable. . ." *University Hospital v. S.E.I.U., Local 333 U.H.* (1986), 26 D.L.R. (4th) 248 at 250, 46 Sask. R. 19, 86 C.L.L.C. 14,064 (C.A.), Bayda C.J.S. (dissenting). 6. " . . . [A]s used in the law of nuisance must be distinguished from its use elsewhere in the law of tort and especially as it is used in negligence actions. . . [In nuisance] 'reasonable' means something more than merely 'taking proper care'. It signifies what is legally right between the parties, taking into account all the circumstances of the case, . . ." *Russell Transport Ltd. v. Ontario Malleable Iron Co.*, [1952] O.R. 621 at 629, [1952] 4 D.L.R. 719 (H.C.), McRuer C.J.H.C. 7. In negligence, to take reasonable care means to take proper care. *Russell Transport Ltd. v. Ontario Malleable Iron Co.*, [1952] O.R. 621 at 629, [1952] 4 D.L.R. 719 (H.C.), McRuer C.J.H.C.

REASONABLE AMOUNT FOR A RE-SERVE. Usually the full amount which a tax-payer received, in either the current or a preceding year, for goods or services which past experience or something else indicates will have to be provided or delivered after the end of the year. One need not estimate the profit on these goods or services since the reserve is not restricted to the estimated costs of any goods still to be delivered or any services still to be rendered. W. Grover & F. Iacobucci, *Materials on Canadian Income Tax*, 4th ed. (Toronto: Richard De Boo Ltd., 1980) at 628.

REASONABLE AND DEMONSTRABLY JUSTIFIED. "To establish that a limit is reasonable and demonstrably justified in a free and democratic society [within s. 1 of the Charter], two central criteria must be satisfied. First, the objective, which the measures responsible for a limit on a Charter right or freedom are designed to serve, must be 'of sufficient importance to warrant overriding a constitutionally protected right or freedom' . . . Secondly, once a sufficiently significant objective is recognized then the party invoking s. 1 must show that the means chosen are reasonable and demonstrably justified. This involves 'a form of proportionality test' . . . There are . . . three important components of a proportionality test. First, the measures adopted must be carefully designed to achieve the objective in question. They must not be arbitrary, unfair or based on irrational considerations . . . they must be rationally connected to the objective. Secondly, the means, even if rationally connected to the objective in this first sense, should impair 'as little as possible' the right or freedom in question . . . Thirdly, there must be a proportionality between the effects of the measures which are responsible for limiting the Charter right or freedom, and the objective which has been identified as of 'sufficient importance' . . ." *R. v. Oakes* (1986), 26 D.L.R. (4th) 200 at 227, [1986] 1 S.C.R. 103, 50 C.R. (3d) 1, 14 O.A.C. 335, 19 C.R.R. 308, 24 C.C.C. (3d) 321, 65 N.R. 87, Dickson C.J.C.

REASONABLE AND PROBABLE CAUSE. "Reasonable and probable cause has been defined as (Hicks v. Faulkner (1878), 8 Q.B.D. 167, at p. 171, per Hawkins J.): ' . . . an honest belief in the guilt of the accused based upon a full conviction, founded on reasonable grounds, of the existence of a state of circumstances which, assuming them to be true, would reasonably lead any ordinary prudent and cautious man, placed in the position of the accuser, to the conclusion that the person charged was probably guilty of the crime imputed.' This test contains both a subjective and objective element. There must be both actual belief on the part of the prosecutor and that belief must be reasonable in the circumstances. The existence of reasonable and probable cause is a matter for the judge to decide as opposed to the jury." *Nelles v. Ontario* (1989), 42 C.R.R. 1 at 20, 49 C.C.L.T. 217, [1989] 2 S.C.R. 170, 37 C.P.C. (2d) 1, 71 C.R. (3d) 358, 60 D.L.R. (4th) 609, 98 N.R. 321, 69 O.R. (2d) 448n, 35 O.A.C. 161, 41 Admin. L.R. 1, Lamer J. (Dickson C.J.C. and Wilson J. concurring).

REASONABLE AND PROBABLE GROUNDS. Requires that the police officer subjectively have an honest belief that the suspect has committed the offence and objectively there must exist reasonable grounds for this belief. Per Sopinka, J. Credibly-based probability. Reasonable probability. Reasonable belief. The context in which the phrase is used and the values underlying it are most important in interpretation of the meaning of the phrase. *R. v. Bernshaw* (1994), [1995] 1 S.C.R. 254, Per L'Heureux-Dube.

REASONABLE APPREHENSION OF BIAS. "The proper test to be applied in a matter of this type was correctly expressed by the Court of Appeal . . . the apprehension of bias must be a reasonable one, held by reasonable and right minded persons, applying themselves to the question and obtaining thereon the required information. In the words of the Court of Appeal, that test is 'what would an informed person, viewing the matter realistically and practically—and having thought the matter through—conclude'. . . . I can see no real difference between the expressions found in the decided cases, be they 'reasonable apprehension of bias', 'reasonable suspicion of bias' or 'real likelihood of bias'. . ." *Committee for Justice & Liberty v. Canada (National Energy Board)*, [1978] 1 S.C.R. 369 at 394-5, 9 N.R. 115, 68 D.L.R. (3d) 716, de Grandpré J. (dissenting).

REASONABLE BAIL. In section 11 of the Charter, refers to the terms of bail. Thus the quantum of bail and the restrictions imposed on the accused's liberty while on bail must be "reasonable". "Just cause" refers to the right to obtain bail. *R. c. Pearson*, [1992] 3 S.C.R. 665, per Lamer, C.J.C.

REASONABLE CARE. A level of care determined by what a reasonable person with the level of knowledge possessed by the person in question would exercise.

REASONABLE CAUSE OF ACTION. " . . . [A] cause of action 'with some chance of success' . . ." *Operation Dismantle Inc. v. R.*, [1985] 1 S.C.R. 441 at 486, 12 Admin L.R. 16, 13 C.R.R. 287, 18 D.L.R. (4th) 481, 59 N.R. 1, Wilson J.

REASONABLE DISCOVERY. [In relation to limitation of actions] the reasonable discovery rule which prevents the injustice of a claim's being statute barred before the plaintiff becomes aware of its existence. *Murphy v. Welsh*, 1993 CarswellOnt 428, 18 C.P.C. (3d) 137, 47 M.V.R. (2d) 1, 156 N.R. 263, 14 O.R. (3d) 799, 65 O.A.C. 103, 157 N.R. 372, [1993] 2 S.C.R. 1069, 106 D.L.R. (4th) 404, 18 C.C.L.T. (2d) 101. Major, J. for the court.

REASONABLE DOUBT. The following explanation for use in a charge to a jury is given: Not an imaginary or frivolous doubt. It must not be based upon sympathy or prejudice. Rather, it is based on reason and common sense. It is logically derived from the evidence or absence of evidence. Even if you believe the accused is probably guilty or likely guilty, that is not sufficient. In those circumstances you must give the benefit of the doubt to the accused and acquit because the Crown has failed to satisfy you of the guilt of the accused beyond a reasonable doubt. On the other hand you must remember that it is virtually impossible to prove anything to an absolute certainty and the Crown is not required to do so. Such a standard of proof is impossibly high. In short if, based upon the evidence or lack of evidence you are sure that the accused committed the offence you should convict since this demonstrates that you are satisfied of his guilt beyond a reasonable doubt. *R.v. Lifchus*, [1997] 3 S.C.R. 320. See BEYOND A ~.

REASONABLE EXPECTATION. 1. " . . . Legitimate, or reasonable, expectation may arise either from an express promise given on behalf of a public authority or from the existence of a regular practice which the claimant can reasonably expect to continue." *Council of Civil Service Unions v. Minister for the Civil Service* (1984), [1985] A.C. 374 at 401(U.K. H.L.), Lord Fraser. 2. Doctrine which applies to resolve ambiguity to achieve a result which might reasonably have been expected by the parties when they entered into the contract. It is up to the insurer to establish that his words clearly and aptly describe the contingency that has arisen and this cannot be done in this case. The court is supposed to avoid an interpretation under the doctrine of "reasonable expectations" which would either give the insurer or the insured a windfall in the form of unanticipated saving or payment. In this case recovery would be for a loss which the plaintiff clearly thought was covered by the insurance policy. The doctrine of reasonable expectations applies to resolve ambiguity to achieve a result which might reasonably be expected by the parties. *Goderich Elevators Ltd. v. Royal Insurance Co.* (1997), 34 O.R. (3d) 768 (Gen. Div.), affirmed on appeal at (1999), 42 O.R. (3d) 577 (C.A.). See LEGITIMATE EXPECTATION.

REASONABLE FORCE. Every one is justified in using as much force as is reasonably necessary (a) to prevent the commission of an offence (i) for which, if it were committed, the person who committed it might be arrested without warrant, and (ii) that would be likely to cause immediate and serious injury to the person or property of anyone, or (b) to prevent anything being done that, on reasonable grounds, he believes would, if it were done, be an offence mentioned in paragraph (a). *Criminal Code*, R.S.C. 1985, c. C-46, s. 27.

REASONABLE GROUNDS. Reasonable probability.

REASONABLE IN THE CIRCUMSTANCES. Although interpretation of the meaning of the phrase "reasonable in the circumstances" [in s. 43 of the Criminal Code, R.S.C. 1985, C-46] is not without difficulty, the phrase clearly provides an intelligible standard for legal debate. The [*R. v. Dupperon* (1984), 16 C.C.C. (3d) 453 (Sask. C.A.)] test requires a court to determine the reasonableness of the force in the circumstances of each case. This approach involves examining the entire context within which the punishment took place, and holds that the test should be objective, applying the standards of the community as a reference point. *Canadian Foundation for Children, Youth & the*

Law v. Canada (Attorney General) (2000), 2000 CarswellOnt 2409, 146 C.C.C. (3d) 362, 188 D.L.R. (4th) 718, 49 O.R. (3d) 662, 36 C.R. (5th) 334, 76 C.R.R. (2d) 251 (S.C.J.)

REASONABLE LIMITS. 1. In section 1 of the Charter, rights are subject to such legal limitation as one can demonstrate is justified in a free and democratic society. 2. " . . . [O]ne which having regard to the principles enunciated in [R. v. Oakes (1986), 26 D.L.R. (4th) 200 (S.C.C.)], it was reasonable for the Legislature to impose . . ." *R. v. Videoflicks Ltd.* (1986), (*sub nom. Edwards Books & Art Ltd. v. R.*) 35 D.L.R. (4th) 1 at 51, 87 C.L.L.C. 14,001, 28 C.R.R. 1, 55 C.R. (3d) 193, 19 O.A.C. 239, 71 N.R. 161, [1986] 2 S.C.R. 713, 30 C.C.C. (3d) 385, 58 O.R. (2d) 442n, Dickson C.J.C. (Chouinard and Le Dain JJ. concurring). 3. A limitation to a constitutional guarantee will be sustained once two conditions are met. First, the objective of the legislation must be pressing and substantial. Second, the means chosen to attain this legislative end must be reasonable and demonstrably justifiable in a free and democratic society. In order to satisfy the second requirement, three criteria must be satisfied: (1) the rights violation must be rationally connected to the aim of the legislation; (2) the impugned provision must minimally impair the *Charter* guarantee; and (3) there must be a proportionality between the effect of the measure and its objective so that the attainment of the legislative goal is not outweighed by the abridgement of the right. In all s. 1 cases the burden of proof is with the government to show on a balance of probabilities that the violation is justifiable. *Egan v. Canada*, [1995] 2 S.C.R. 513, per Iacobucci, J.

REASONABLE MARKET DEMAND. The demand for oil or gas for reasonable current requirements and current consumption or use within and outside the province, together with such amounts as are reasonably necessary for building up or maintaining reasonable storage reserves and working stocks of oil and gas and the products thereof.

REASONABLE NEEDS. Whatever is reasonably suitable for the maintenance of the person in question, having regard to the ability, means, needs and circumstances of that person and of any person obliged to contribute to such reasonable needs.

REASONABLENESS. *n.* [In administrative law] at the reasonableness end of the spectrum, where deference is at its highest, are those cases where a tribunal protected by a true privative clause, is deciding a matter within its jurisdiction and where there is no statutory right of appeal. *Pezim v. British Columbia (Superintendent of Brokers)*, 1994 CarswellBC 232, 92 B.C.L.R. (2d) 145, [1994] 7 W.W.R. 1, 14 B.L.R. (2d) 217, 22 Admin. L.R. (2d) 1, 114 D.L.R. (4th) 385, [1994] 2 S.C.R. 557, (sub nom. *Pezim v. British Columbia (Securities Commission)*) 168 N.R. 321, (sub nom. *Pezim v. British Columbia (Securities Commission)*) 46 B.C.A.C. 1, (sub nom. *Pezim v. British Columbia (Securities Commission)*) 75 W.A.C. 1, 4 C.C.L.S. 117, Iacobucci, J. for the court.

REASONABLE OCCUPATIONAL QUALIFICATION. Equivalent to bona fide occupational requirement and qualification.

REASONABLE PERSON. 1. "[In the context of provocation in criminal law] . . . the ordinary or reasonable person has a normal temperament and level of self-control. It follows that the ordinary person is not exceptionally excitable, pugnacious or in a state of drunkenness. . . particular characteristics that are not peculiar or idiosyncratic can be ascribed to an ordinary person without subverting the logic of the objective test of Provocation." *R. v. Hill* (1985), 51 C.R. (3d) 97 at 114, [1986] 1 S.C.R. 313, 27 D.L.R. (4th) 187, 68 N.R. 161, 25 C.C.C. (3d) 322, 17 O.A.C. 33, Dickson C.J.C. (Beetz, Chouinard and La Forest JJ. concurring). 2. He is not an extraordinary or unusual creature; he is not superhuman; he is not required to display the highest skill of which anyone is capable; he is not a genius who can perform uncommon feats, nor is he possessed of unusual powers of foresight. He is a person of normal intelligence who makes prudence a guide to his conduct. He does nothing that a prudent man would not do and does not omit to do anything a prudent man would do. He acts in accord with general and approved practice. His conduct is guided by considerations which ordinarily regulate the conduct of human affairs. His conduct is the standard "adopted in the community by persons of ordinary intelligence and prudence. Quoted by Major, J. writing for the court in: *Stewart v. Pettie*, [1995] 1 S.C.R. 131. 3. [In the context of a claim for professional negligence] . . . the "reasonable person" who sets the standard for the objective test must be taken to possess the patient's reasonable beliefs, fears, desires and expectations and further that the patient's expectations and concerns will usually be revealed by the questions posed. *De Vos v. Robertson* (2000), 2000 CarswellOnt 44, 48

C.C.L.T. (2d) 172 (S.C.J.). 4. "[In the context of determining the existence of bias] ... it obviously is neither the 'anti-establishment or complaisant' person (Tremblay v. Quebec (Commission des Affaires Sociales) [(1989), 25 Q.A.C. 169 (Que. C.A.)] ... or even someone who is narrow-minded. Nor a functionary in the justice system or a person who knows all the intricacies of the justice system. Rather, it is the average person in society who must serve as the mode." *Lippé c. Charest* (1990), *(sub nom. R v. Lippé)* 60 C.C.C. (3d) 34 at 71, 80 C.R. (3d) 1, [1990] R.J.Q. 2200, 31 Q.A.C. 161, Proulx J.A. 5. [In s. 46(4) of the Personal Property Security Act, S.O. 1989, c. 16] ... one who is a stranger to the transaction but who appropriately determines the correct name (first name, initial of second given name and surname) when conducting an individual specific search." *Haasen, Re* (1992), 13 C.B.R. (3d) 94 at 106, 8 O.R. (3d) 489, 92 D.L.R. (4th) 204, 3 P.P.S.A.C. (2d) 250 (S.C.), Farley J.

REASONABLE SEARCH. 1. "A search will be reasonable if it is authorized by law, if the law itself is reasonable and if the manner in which the search was carried out is reasonable." *R. v. Collins* (1987), 28 C.R.R. 122 at 132, [1987] 3 W.W.R. 699, 56 C.R. (3d) 193, 74 N.R. 276, 13 B.C.L.R. (2d) 1, [1987] 1 S.C.R. 265, 33 C.C.C. (3d) 1, 28 D.L.R. (4th) 508, Lamer J. 2. The criteria which must be met in order that a search be "reasonable" are: (a) a system of prior authorization, by an entirely neutral and impartial arbiter who is capable of acting judicially in balancing the interests of the State against those of the individual; (b) a requirement that the impartial arbiter must satisfy himself that the person seeking the authorization has reasonable grounds, established under oath, to believe that an offence has been committed; (c) a requirement that the impartial arbiter must satisfy himself that the person seeking the authorization has reasonable grounds to believe that something which will afford evidence of the particular offence under investigation will be recovered; and (d) a requirement that the only documents which are authorized to be seized are those which are strictly relevant to the offence under investigation. *Thomson Newspapers Ltd. v. Canada (Director of Investigation & Research)* (1990), 67 D.L.R. (4th) 161 (S.C.C.).

REASONABLE SUSPICION. " ... [A]s a matter of abstract theory, a reasonable suspicion means something more than a mere suspicion and something less than a belief based upon rea-

sonable and probable grounds. . ." *R. v. Cahill* (1992), 13 C.R. (4th) 327 at 339, 12 B.C.A.C. 247, 23 W.A.C. 247 (C.A.), the court per Wood J.A.

REASONABLE SUSPICION OF BIAS. See REASONABLE APPREHENSION OF BIAS.

REASONS. *n.* More than a recital of matters which the decision-maker was required to consider and a statement of conclusions drawn from those matters. Must also enable the person concerned to assess whether he has grounds of appeal. Must be proper, adequate, and intelligible.

REASSESS. *v.* To assess once again.

REASSURANCE. *var.* **RE-ASSURANCE**. *n.* A contract which a first insurer enters into with another insurer to be free wholly or partly from a risk already undertaken.

RE-ATTACHMENT. *n.* A second attachment by one who has attached previously.

REBATE. *n.* A discount; a deduction from a payment.

REBELLION. *n.* Taking up arms against the Crown.

REBUILD. *v.* 1. " ... [A]s applied to an engine, is to renew, to repair, to replace what has become used and inefficient." *Mallory v. Canadian Fairbanks Morse Co.* (1940), [1942] Que S.C. 132 at 134, McDougall J. 2. To make or impose a new tread or new surface or to otherwise alter the surface of a used tire so that it will resemble a new tire, by cutting into or adding rubber to the surface thereof, or by a combination of both. *Highway Traffic Act*, R.S.O. 1990, c. H.8, s. 71.

REBUS SIC STANTIBUS. [L. things standing so] Under these circumstances.

REBUT. *v.* To contradict; to reply.

REBUTTABLE PRESUMPTION OF LAW. 1. " ... [T]hree categories of rebuttable presumptions (s. 241(1)(c) [of the Criminal Code, R.S.C. 1970, c. C-34] ... First, a permissive presumption may tactically require an accused merely to raise a reasonable doubt once the Crown establishes a proved fact giving rise to the presumed fact, failing which the trier of fact may infer the presumed fact. Second, a mandatory presumption legally requires an accused to raise reasonable doubt as to the presumed fact, failing which the trier of fact must infer the presumed fact. Third, a mandatory presumption legally requires an accused to disprove the presumed fact on a balance of probabilities, failing which the trier of fact must infer the presumed fact." *R. v. Hummel* (1987), 36 C.C.C. (3d) 8 at 13, 1 M.V.R. (2d) 4, 60 O.R. (2d) 545, 60 C.R. (3d) 78 (H.C.), Ewaschuk J. 2. A presumption authorized by the National Defence Act, the Criminal Code or other Act of the Parliament of Canada that upon proof of a certain fact or set of facts, another fact exists, unless evidence to the degree required by law renders its existence unlikely. *Military Rules of Evidence*, C.R.C., c. 1049, s. 2.

REBUTTAL EVIDENCE. Evidence which rebuts or contradicts evidence which the defendant or respondent adduced in the case.

REBUTTER. *n*. A pleading.

RECALL. *v*. 1. To call back to work according to seniority standing. A basic and valuable benefit which a person who was actually laid off retains under a collective agreement. 2. In respect of a medical device that has been sold, means any action taken by the manufacturer, importer or distributor of the device to recall or correct the device, or to notify its owners and users of its defectiveness or potential defectiveness, after becoming aware that the device (a) may be hazardous to health; (b) may fail to conform to any claim made by the manufacturer or importer relating to its effectiveness, benefits, performance characteristics or safety; or (c) may not meet the requirements of the Act or these Regulations. 3. For voters to end prematurely the term of an elected official.

RECALL PETITION. A petition issued by the chief electoral officer for the recall of a Member. *Recall And Initiative Act*, R.S.B.C. 1996, c. 398, s. 1(1).

REC. ANN. WINDSOR ACCÈS JUSTICE. *abbr*. Recueil annuel de Windsor d'accès à la justice (Windsor Yearbook of Access to Justice).

RECAPTION. *n*. A remedy to which a party may resort when someone deprives the party of goods or wrongfully detains the party's spouse, child or servant. In such a case, the injured party may lawfully reclaim them, as long as this is not done so that the peace is broken.

RECAPTURE. *v*. If a taxpayer sells an asset at a figure higher than the notional value to which it was reduced by claiming an annual capital cost allowance against previous years' taxable income, an amount equal to that previously claimed allowance now recovered must be

brought into taxable income in the year of sale. D.M.W. Waters, *The Law of Trusts in Canada*, 2d ed. (Toronto: Carswell,1984) at 830.

RECEDITUR A PLACITIS JURIS POTIUS QUAM INJURIAE ET DELICTA MANEANT IMPUNITA. [L.] Abandon the forms of law rather than let crimes and wrongs go unpunished.

RECEIPT. *n*. 1. An acknowledgement in writing that one received money or property. 2. A warehouse receipt. See ACCOUNTABLE ~; DEPOSIT ~; ELEVATOR ~; NEGOTIABLE ~; NON-NEGOTIABLE ~; RENT~; REVENUE ~; WAREHOUSE ~.

RECEIPTS. *n*. All revenue. See ANNUAL ~; CAPITAL ~; FARM PRODUCTS ~.

RECEIVABLE. *n*. Any money owed.

RECEIVABLE. *adj*. " . . . '[T]o be received' . . ." *Wilson & Wilson Ltd. v. Minister of National Revenue*, [1960] C.T.C. 1 at 10, [1960] Ex. C.R. 205, 60 D.T.C. 1018, Cameron J. See ACCOUNT ~; FACTORING OF ~S; LOANS ~.

RECEIVE. *v*. " . . . [T]o 'take into one's hand or possession'. . ." *Manitoba Food & Commercial Workers Union, Local 832 v. Westfair Foods Ltd.* (1980), 7 Man. R. (2d) 260 at 262 (C.A.), the court per Monnin J.A.

RECEIVED. *v*. Actual physical receipt; to be put in possession of a thing. See ACTUALLY ~.

RECEIVER. *n*. 1. A person who was appointed to take possession of property which belongs to a third party. 2. A person appointed by a court to receive the rent and profit of real estate or to collect personal goods. When the appointment is by way of equitable execution, the receiver has the power to sell the personalty and to distribute the rents, proceeds and profits of the real estate to any judgment creditors. C.R.B. Dunlop, *Creditor-Debtor Law in Canada* (Toronto: Carswell, 1981 at 281. 3. " . . . [C]an encompass a receiver-manager. . ." *Cook's Ferry Band v. Cook's Ferry Band Council* (1989), (*sub nom. Minnabarriet v. Cook's Ferry Band Council*) 75 C.B.R. (N.S.) 228 at 232, [1989] 4 C.N.L.R. 105 (Fed. T.D.), Reed J. 4. Any pressure vessel used for the storage or collection of an expansible fluid. See AIR ~; COURT-APPOINTED ~; INTERIM ~; OFFICIAL ~; PRIVATE ~; TELEVISION ~.

RECEIVER AND MANAGER. A person appointed to carry on or superintend a trade, business or undertaking in addition to receiving rents and profits, or to get in outstanding property.

RECEIVERSHIP. *n*. A legal or equitable proceeding in which a receiver is appointed to take over the property of an insolvent company or individual. The receivership operates with respect to all of the assets of the insolvent party. See SOFT ~.

RECEIVING CHARGE. A charge for removing goods from railway flat cars or from the tailgate or bed of motor transport vehicles and moving the goods to an ordinary place of rest when handled by fork lift equipment only.

RECEIVING ORDER. An order which declares a debtor to be bankrupt and which results in the trustee of the bankrupt estate being appointed.

RECEIVING PLANT. A premises to which dead animals are delivered for the purpose of obtaining the hide, skin, fats, meat or other product of the dead animals, or for the purpose of selling or delivering the dead animals or parts thereof to a rendering plant. *Dead Animal Disposal Act*, R.S.O. 1990, c . D.3, s. 1.

RECEIVING STATION. See CREAM ~.

RECENT COMPLAINT. A common law doctrine which allowed the complainant in a rape case to bring evidence of a complaint made shortly after the incident to show that her conduct was consistent with her complaint.

RECENT CONTRIVANCE. Demonstrated by evidence that the witness did not speak of the matter earlier at a time when it would have been natural to speak. The earlier silence is argued as evidence of inconsistency with current statements.

RECENT FABRICATION. An allegation of recent fabrication is no more than an allegation that the complainant has made up a false story to meet the exigencies of the case. The word "recent" means that the complainant's evidence has been invented or fabricated after the events in question and thus is a "recent" invention or fabrication. *R. v. O'Connor* (1995), 25 O.R. (3d) 19 (C.A.).

RECENT POSSESSION. 1. Inferences which can be drawn when it is shown that a person is in possession of property recently stolen. These are determined by the time of theft, the kind of articles stolen, i.e., whether they are the sort of thing which passes rapidly from person to person, or whether the accused would be likely to possess them innocently. P.K. McWilliams, *Canadian Criminal Evidence*, 3d ed. (Aurora: Canada Law Book, 1988) at 5-14. 2. . . . [T]he presumption . . . resulting from the mere circumstances of recent possession of stolen goods, is that the initial possession was gained with the knowledge that the goods were stolen." *R. v. Suchard*, [1956] S.C.R. 425 at 427, 23 C.R. 207,114 C.C.C. 257, 2 D.L.R. (2d) 609, Fauteux J. (Taschereau J. concurring). 3. "Property recently stolen, found in the possession of a person, is always presumptive evidence against that person, unless the possession can be accounted for and explained consistently with innocence." *Reg. v. Exall* (1866), 4 F. & F. 922 at 923, 176 E.R. 850 at 850 (U.K.), Pollock C.B. 4. The unexplained recent possession of stolen goods, standing alone, will permit the inference that the possessor stole the goods. The inference is not mandatory; it may but need not be drawn. Further, where an explanation is offered for such possession which could reasonably be true, no inference of guilt on the basis of recent possession alone may be drawn, even where the trier of fact is not satisfied of the truth of the explanation. The burden of proof of guilt remains upon the Crown. *R. v. Kowlyk*, [1988] 2 S.C.R. 59.

RECEPTACLE. *n*. One or more contact devices, on the same yoke, installed at an outlet for the connection of one or more attachment plugs. See DUPLEX ~; SINGLE ~; SPLIT ~; SUITABLE ~.

RECEPTION CENTRE. 1. Any place established or designated for the purpose of receiving a child for examination, care, treatment, education or rehabilitation. 2. Facilities where inpatient, out-patient, or home-care services are offered for the lodging, maintenance keeping under observation, treatment or social rehabilitation, as the case may be, of persons whose condition, by reason of their age or their physical, personality, psycho-social or family deficiencies, is such that they must be treated, kept in protected residence or, if need be, for close treatment, or treated at home, including nurseries, but excepting day care establishments contemplated in the Act respecting child day care, foster families, vacation camps and other similar facilities and facilities maintained by a religious institution to receive its members or followers.

An Act respecting health services and social services, S.Q. 1979, c. 85, s. 82.

RECEPTIVE BILINGUALS. "... [T]hose who can receive communication in both languages through the written and spoken word but can express themselves in only one language; those who can function in both languages but have a lower level of proficiency in one or in both from unilingual persons; and those who are bilingual only in the particular area of their life's experience." *Assn. of Parents for Fairness in Education, Grand Falls District 50 Branch v. Société des Acadiens du Nouveau-Brunswick Inc.* (1986), 23 C.R.R. 119 at 188, [1986] 1 S.C.R. 549, 66 N.R. 173, 69 N.B.R. (2d) 271, 177 A.P.R. 271, 27 D.L.R. (4th) 406, Wilson J.

RECESS. *n.* 1. The period between Parliament being prorogued and reassembling for a new session. A. Fraser, W.A. Dawson, & J. Holtby, eds., *Beauchesne's Rules and Forms of the House of Commons of Canada*, 6th ed. (Toronto: Carswell, 1989) at 66. 2. A short pause in a sitting of a court.

RECESSION. *n.* A granting again.

RECIDIVIST. *n.* A person who repeatedly commits crimes.

RECIPIENT. *n.* 1. A person to whom any amount is or is about to become payable. 2. A person to whom financial aid is granted. 3. A person to whom an allowance has been granted and includes an applicant for an allowance. 4. A person to whom assistance has been granted. 5. A person to whom a service supplier supplies a taxed service. 6. An economically underprivileged person who receives legal aid. 7. Every person to whom health services or social services are furnished by an establishment or foster family. See FAMILY ALLOWANCE ~.

RECIPROCAL EXCHANGE. 1. A group of subscribers exchanging reciprocal contracts of indemnity or inter-insurance with each other through the same attorney. 2. A group of persons, each of whom agrees to insure each of the others to the extent and in the manner agreed on, in consideration of agreements on their part to insure him. *Insurance Act*, R.S.B.C. 1979, c. 20, s. 1.

RECIPROCAL INSURANCE EXCHANGE. An unincorporated organization which relies on its members or subscribers to underwrite the risks inherent in their activities. An agreement among subscribers sets out a pre-arranged formula used to determine the amounts each subscriber must contribute to a reciprocal insurance fund. Each member pays a base premium and agrees to be assessed for an amount in excess of the premium, a retro-assessment, if liabilities for that year exceed premium income. *Canadian Lawyers Insurance Assn. v. Alberta* (1995), 30 Alta. L.R. (3d) 282 (C.A.).

RECIPROCAL TAXATION AGREEMENT. An agreement referred to in section 32. *Federal-Provincial Fiscal Arrangements Act*, R.S.C. 1985, c. F-8, s. 31.

RECIPROCAL TRANSFER AGREEMENT. An agreement related to two or more pension plans that provides for the transfer of money or credit for employment or both in respect of individual members of the plans. *Pension Benefits acts.*

RECIPROCATING JURISDICTION. A state of the United States of America, the District of Columbia, the Commonwealth of Puerto Rico, a territory or possession of the United States of America, or a province or territory of Canada, which has enacted this Act or provides substantially equivalent access to its courts and administrative agencies. *Transboundary Pollution Reciprocal Access acts.*

RECIPROCATING PROVINCE. A province that has been declared to be a reciprocating province with respect to the deposit of a particular insurer. *Insurance acts.*

RECIPROCATING STATE. 1. A state declared to be a reciprocating state and includes a province or territory of Canada. *Reciprocal Enforcement of Maintenance Orders acts.* 2. A foreign state that is a party to a cultural property agreement. *Cultural Property Export and Import Act*, R.S.C. 1985, c. C-51, s. 37.

RECIPROCITY. *n.* Mutual action.

RECIRCULATION SYSTEM. A system that: (a) maintains circulation of water through a pool by pumps; (b) draws water from a pool for treatment and returns it to the pool as clean water; and (c) provides continuous treatment that includes filtration and chlorination or bromination, and other processes that may be necessary for the treatment of the water.

RECISSION. *n.* Commonly, the ending of a contract because a contract term classified as a condition was breached or a party repudiated or absolutely refused to perform its contractual obligations. B.J. Reiter, B.N. McLellen and P.M.

Perell, *Real Estate Law*, 4th ed. (Toronto: Emond Montgomery, 1992) at 681. 2. Technically, an equitable remedy that restores parties to their position before the contract. B.J. Reiter, B.N. McLellen and P.M. Perell, *Real Estate Law*, 4th ed. (Toronto: Emond Montgomery, 1992) at 681.

RECITAL. *n*. A statement in an agreement, deed or other formal document intended to lead up to or explain the operative part of the document.

RECKLESS. *adj*. 1. Refers to the attitude of a person who is aware that the danger exists that his conduct may cause a result prohibited by criminal law but who persists in the conduct. *R. v. Cooper* (1993), 78 C.C.C. (3d) 289 (S.C.C.). 2. " . . . [H]eedless of consequences, headlong or irresponsible. . ." *R. v. Barron* (1984), 39 C.R. (3d) 379 at 391 (Ont. H.C.), Ewaschuk J. 3. "[In s. 202 of the Criminal Code, R.S.C. 1970, c. C-34] . . . reckless means a person shows carelessness for the consequence of his act so far as the lives or safety of other persons are concerned. . ." *R. v. Canadian Liquid Air Ltd.* (1972), 20 C.R.N.S. 208 at 210 (B.C. S.C.), McKay J.

RECKLESSLY. *adv*. " . . . [I]ntention will be attributed or imputed to an accused where he acts recklessly in the circumstances. In such a situation, 'The term "recklessly" is . . . used to denote the subjective state of mind of a person who foresees that his conduct may cause the prohibited result but, nevertheless, takes a deliberate and unjustifiable risk of bringing it about . . .'": see R. v. Buzzan (1979), 25 O.R. (2d) 705 . . . (C.A.). Depending on the definitional elements of and terms employed in the crime, the accused may be sufficiently reckless to have imputed to him the necessary guilty intention where his foresight indicates to him that the unjustified risk will probably result in the prohibited harm, will be highly probable or, for certain crimes, substantially certain to occur . . ." *R. v. Barron* (1984), 39 C.R. (3d) 379 at 390 (Ont. H.C.), Ewaschuk J.

RECKLESSNESS. *n*. The attitude of a person who is aware that the danger exists that his conduct may cause a result prohibited by criminal law but who persists in the conduct. *R. v. Cooper* (1993), 78 C.C.C. (3d) 289 (S.C.C.).

RECLAIMED. *adj*. In respect of a controlled substance, means recovered, re-processed and upgraded, through processes such as filtering, drying, distillation and chemical treatment, in order to restore the controlled substance to industry-accepted re-use standards. *Ozone-depleting Substances Regulations*, 1998, SOR/99-7, s. 1.

RECLAIMED TEXTILE FIBRE. A textile fibre obtained from a yarn or fabric.

RECLAMATION. *n*. Bringing of land formerly covered by water into a state fit for cultivation.

RECOGNITION. See VOLUNTARY ~.

RECOGNITION AGREEMENT. An agreement in writing, signed by the parties, between an employer or employers' organization, on the one hand, and a trade union or council of trade unions, on the other, under which the trade union or council of trade unions is recognized as the exclusive bargaining agent of the employees in a bargaining unit defined in the recognition agreement.

RECOGNITION CLAUSE. A mandatory provision in any collective agreement which determines the scope of the bargaining unit and the work which falls to that unit.

RECOGNIZANCE. *n*. 1. A person's own promise to appear. 2. "The recognizance contemplated by s. 22 [of the Coroner's Act, R.S.S. 1978, c. C-38] is in the nature of a performance bond: an acknowledgement by the person from whom it is taken that he is indebted to the Crown in the amount fixed therein, provided always, that if he fulfills the condition of the undertaking and appears as required the debt ceases . . ." *McMillan v. Bassett* (1983), [1984] 1 W.W.R. 150 at 154, 29 Sask. R. 272, 9 C.C.C. (3d) 45 (C.A.), the court per Cameron J.A. 3. " . . . [A] bond of record testifying the recognizor to owe a certain sum of money to some other . . ." *R. v. Sandhu* (1984), 38 C.R. (3d) 56 at 63 (Qué. S.C.), Boilard J.

RECOGNIZED CANADIAN SCHEME. Any plan or scheme established to provide pension, superannuation or disability benefits, or any of them, for and in respect of employees (a) of the Government of Canada; or (b) the government of a province of territory of Canada; or (c) of an agency of the Government of Canada or (d) of an agency of the government of a province or territory of Canada; or (e) of a municipality in Canada; or (f) of a school division, school district or school area in Canada; or (g) of an educational institution in Canada; or (h) of a hospital or associated health facility in Canada, or any of them and under which the employees make contributions towards the funding of the plan or scheme. Manitoba statutes.

RECOGNIZED CODE. The code of the American Society of Mechanical Engineers, the British Standards Institution or the code of a similar organization that the Board considers to be of comparable standing. *Steamship Machinery Inspection Regulations*, C.R.C., c. 1492, s. 2.

RECOGNIZED OPPOSITION PARTY. 1. The members of the assembly who belong to a political party that is represented in the assembly four or more members and that is not (a) the political party represented in the assembly by the largest number of members; or (b) the official opposition. *Legislative Assembly Act*, R.S.M. 1970, c. L110, s. 61. 2. A party that (a) holds at least 4 seats in the Legislative Assembly; and (b) received at least 5% of the popular vote in the election immediately preceding the year in which the allowance in subsection (2) is to be paid. *Legislative Assembly Act*, R.S.A. 1980, c. L-10, s. 60.

RECOGNIZED PARTY. 1. The party of a Premier or of a Leader of the Opposition. 2. Any political party that at a general election has or at the general election preceding a by-election had, not less than 10 candidates officially nominated.

RECOGNIZED POLITICAL PARTY. An affiliation of electors comprised in a political organization whose prime purpose is the fielding of candidates for election to the legislature. See LEADER OF A ~.

RECOGNIZED RETAIL STORE. Does not include a dwelling, mail-order office, display room, office, repair or service shop, warehouse, studio or other place of a like nature. *Direct Sellers acts.*

RECOMMEND. *v.* To advise; may encompass a duty to act fairly in making a recommendation.

RECOMMENDATIONS. *n.* " . . . [O]rdinarily means the offering of advice and should not be taken to mean a binding decision. . ." *Thomson v. Canada (Department of Agriculture)* (1992), 3 Admin. L.R. (2d) 242 at 255, 133 N.R. 345, 89 D.L.R. (4th) 218, [1992] 1 S.C.R. 385, 51 F.T.R. 267n, Cory J. (La Forest, Sopinka, Gonthier, McLachlin and Stevenson JJ. concurring).

RECOMMENDATION TO MERCY. Before the death penalty was abolished, a jury who found an accused guilty of murder could accompany their verdict by recommending the prisoner to the Crown's mercy, on certain particular grounds.

RECOMMENDED CONDITIONS OF USE. In respect of a natural health product, (a) its recommended use or purpose; (b) its dosage form; (c) its recommended route of administration; (d) its recommended dose; (e) its recommended duration of use, if any; and (f) its risk information, including any cautions, warnings, contra-indications or known adverse reactions associated with its use. *Natural Health Products Regulations*, SOR/2003-196, s. 1(1).

RECOMMIT. *v.* To send a bill to a Committee of the Whole or any other committee when a member moves an amendment to the third reading motion. A. Fraser, W.A. Dawson., & J. Holtby, eds., *Beauchesne's Rules and Forms of the House of Commons of Canada*, 6th ed. (Toronto: Carswell, 1989) at 214.

RECONCILIATION. *n.* 1. The settlement of differences after an estrangement. 2. " . . . [D]oes not take place unless and until mutual trust and confidence are restored. It is not to be expected that the parties can ever recapture the mutual devotion which existed when they were first married, but their relationship must be restored, by mutual consent, to a settled rhythm in which the past offences, if not forgotten, at least no longer rankle and embitter their daily lives. Then, and not till then, are the offences condoned. Reconciliation being the test of condonation, nothing short of it will suffice." *Mackrell v. Mackrell*, [1948] 2 All E.R. 858 at 860-61 (U.K. C.A.), Denning L.J.

RECONSTITUTED MILK. Milk remade or compounded.

RECONSTRUCTED VEHICLE. A vehicle of a type required to be registered under this Act and materially altered from its original construction by the removal, addition or substitution of essential parts, new or used. *Vehicles acts.*

RECONSTRUCTION. *n.* 1. Renewal, alteration, remodelling of a substantial part of premises. 2. Transferring the assets, or a major part of them, of one company to a new company formed for just that purpose in exchange for shares of the new company to be distributed among the old company's shareholders. H. Sutherland, D.B. Horsley & J.M. Edmiston, eds., *Fraser's Handbook on Canadian Company Law*, 7th ed. (Toronto: Carswell, 1985) at 349.

See AMALGAMATION OR ~; REORGANI-ZATION.

RECONVERSION. *n*. An imaginary process in which an earlier constructive conversion is annulled and the converted property is restored to its original condition in contemplation of law.

RECONVEYANCE. *n*. Conveying mortgaged property again, free from the mortgage debt, to the mortgagor or the mortgagor's representatives after the mortgage debt is paid off.

RECORD. *v*. " . . . [T]o commit to writing or printing . . ." *Excelsior Life Insurance Co. v. Saskatchewan* (1987), 63 Sask. R. 35 at 43 (Q.B.), Hrabinsky J.

RECORD. *n*. 1. Includes any correspondence, memorandum, book, plan, map, drawing, diagram, pictorial or graphic work, photograph, film, microform, sound recording, videotape, machine-readable record and any other documentary material, regardless of physical form or characteristics, and any copy of any of those things. *Personal Information Protection and Electronic Documents Act*, S.C. 2000, c. 5, s. 2(1). 2. In the sense of the record of proceedings before a tribunal, " . . . Must contain at least the document which initiates the proceedings, the pleadings, if any, and the adjudication, but not the evidence, nor the reasons, unless the tribunal chooses to incorporate them." *R. v. Northumberland Comp. App. Trib.; Ex parte Shaw*, [1952] 1 All E.R. 122 at 131 (U.K. C.A.), Denning L.J. 3. "In Farrell v. Workmen's Compensation Bd. . . 26 D.L.R. (2d) 177 . . . the British Columbia Court of Appeal held (. . . at p. 196 and . . . at p. 201) that the record consisted only of the initiating document, the pleadings, if any, and the adjudication (including the reasons if incorporated in the decision) but not the evidence or the supporting documents referred to in the adjudication. . ." *Woodward Stores (Westmount) Ltd. v. Alberta (Assessment Appeal Board Division No. 1)*, [1976] 5 W.W.R. 496 at 511, 69 D.L.R. (3d) 450 (Alta. T.D.), McDonald J. 4. Includes any information that is recorded or stored by means of any device. 5. The history of a person's convictions. 6. Includes the whole or any part of any book, document, paper, card, tape or other thing on or in which information is written, recorded, stored or reproduced, and, except for the purposes of subsections (3) and (4), any copy or transcript admitted in evidence under this section pursuant to subsection (3) or (4). *Canada Evidence Act*, R.S.C. 1985, c. C-5, s. 30(12). 7. "[In ss. 36.3(2)(d) and (e) of the Canada Evidence Act, R.S.C. 1970, c. E-10] . . . used as a generic term to describe various forms of communications or materials which relate or reflect expressions of opinion, information, etc., concerning Cabinet business. In this sense a letter may form part or all of the 'record'." *Smith, Kline & French Laboratories Ltd. v. Canada (Attorney General)* (1983), 38 C.P.C. 182 at 194, [1983] 1 F.C. 917, 76 C.P.R. (2d) 192 (T.D.), Strayer J. 8. A collection of every pleading and proceeding in an action intended for use at the trial. See CARTOGRAPHIC ~ OR DOCUMENT; CERTIFIED ~; COURT OF ~; COURT ~; EMPLOYMENT ~; EXPOSURE ~; IMMUNIZATION ~; INSTRUMENT ~; MANUSCRIPT, ~ OR DOCUMENT; MINISTERIAL ~; PHOTOGRAPHIC ~ OR DOCUMENT; PICTORIAL ~ OR DOCUMENT; PUBLIC ~; PUPIL ~; ~S; SURVEYOR OF ~; TRIAL ~; VIOLATION ~.

RECORDED. *adj*. Entered in the record.

RECORDED ADDRESS. (a) In relation to a person as a shareholder, his latest known postal address according to the central securities register of a bank; and (b) in relation to a person in any other respect, his latest known postal address according to the records of the branch concerned. *Bank Act*, S.C. 1991, c. 46, s. 2.

RECORDED AGENT. A person on record with the Commission on Election Contributions and Expenses as being authorized to accept contributions on behalf of a political party, constituency association or candidate registered under the Election Finances Act. *Corporations Tax Act*, R.S.O. 1990, c. C.40, s. 36.2.

RECORDED SOUND. See DOCUMENT OF ~.

RECORDER. *n*. 1. The mining recorder of the mining division in which is situate the land in respect of which an act, matter or thing is to be done. *Mining Act*, R.S.O. 1990, c. M.14, s. 1. 2. The recorder of the regional assessment appeal court appointed pursuant to subsection (5) of Section 58. *Assessment Act*, R.S.N.S. 1989, c. 23, s. 2. See COCKPIT VOICE ~; VOTING ~.

RECORDING. *n*. Anything on which sounds or images or both are fixed, regardless of form. See AIR TRAFFIC CONTROL ~.

RECORDING AGENT. An agent independent of an insurer but who has the power to bind the insurer by issuing policies, interim receipts and oral coverage.

RECORDING   APPARATUS.   See SOUND ~.

RECORDING EQUIPMENT. Any equipment, device, apparatus, or contrivance, whereby spoken words can be recorded on tape, wire, discs, cylinders, or records, or on any other material or thing, from which those spoken words can be subsequently reproduced. *Manitoba Telephone Act*, R.S.M. 1987, c. T40, s. 1.

RECORD OFFICE. Any land title office and any office of a court in which documents are deposited.

RECORD OF OFFENCES. A conviction for, (a) an offence in respect of which a pardon has been granted under the Criminal Records Act (Canada) and has not been revoked, or (b) an offence in respect of any provincial enactment. *Human Rights Code*, R.S.O. 1990, c. H.19, s. 10(1).

RECORD OF THE PROCEEDING. Includes (a) a document by which the proceeding is commenced; (b) a notice of a hearing in the proceeding; (c) an intermediate order made by the tribunal; (d) a document produced in evidence at a hearing before the tribunal, subject to any limitation expressly imposed by any other enactment on the extent to or the purpose for which a document may be used in evidence in a proceeding; (e) a transcript, if any, of the oral evidence given at a hearing; and (f) the decision of the tribunal and any reasons given by it.

RECORDS. *n*. 1. An all embracing term meaning correspondence, memoranda, completed forms, or other papers, books, maps, plans and drawings, paintings and prints, photographs, films, microforms, motion picture films, sound recordings, tape, video-tapes, computer cards, or other documentary material regardless of physical form or characteristics. 2."[In s. 26 of the Family Law Reform Act, R.S.O. 1980, c. 152] . . . a written record kept by the agency or person in the course of its operations as a trade, business or public agency. . ." *Robertson v. Robertson* (1982), 28 C.P.C. 205 at 210, 127 R.F.L. (2d) 205 (Ont. C.A.), the court per MacKinnon A.C.J.O. See BUSINESS ~; DEPOSIT OF ~; RECORD; TRUST~.

RECORDS MANAGEMENT. A program instituted to provide an economical and efficient system for the creation, maintenance and disposal of public records.

RECORDS SCHEDULE. A prescribed time-table that (a) describes a document's lifespan from the date on which it was created to the date of its final disposition, including the periods of its active and dormant stages either as waste or as a document of legal or historical value to be reserved; and (b) provides instruction permanently as to the manner and time of the disposition of a document. See RETENTION AND DESTRUCTION SCHEDULES.

RECOUNT. *v*. (a) To add again the votes given for each candidate as recorded in the statements of the polls returned by the several deputy returning officers; and (b) to examine and count the used and counted, the unused, the rejected and the spoiled ballot papers.

RECOUP. *v*. 1. To pay back. 2. To hold back something due.

RECOUPMENT. *n*. Complete repayment in that the whole sum of money spent effectively discharges the debt for which, though both parties are liable, the defendant is largely liable. G.H.L. Fridman, *Restitution*, 2d ed. (Toronto: Carswell, 1992) at 242.

RECOURSE. *n*. 1. The right to recover against a party secondarily liable. 2. When a bill is dishonoured by non-payment, an immediate right of recourse against the drawer, acceptor and endorsers accrues to the holder. *Bills of Exchange Act*, R.S.C. 1985, c. B-4, s. 94(2). See WITHOUT ~ TO ME.

RECOVER. *v*. 1. " . . . The usual meaning in the context of the judicial process is that of 'gaining through a judgment or order'. . ." *Centrac Industries Ltd. v. Vollan Enterprises Ltd.* (1989), 70 Alta. L.R. (2d) 396 at 398, 100 A.R. 301, 39 C.P.C. (2d) 136 (C.A.), Lieberman, Stevenson and Irving JJ.A. 2. " . . . [T]he taking of possession of some form of property . . ." *Prism Petroleum Ltd. v. Omega Hydrocarbons Ltd.* (1992), 4 Alta. L.R. (3d) 332 at 348, [1993] 1 W.W.R. 204, 130 A.R. 114 (Q.B.), Egbert J. 3. "[In Mercantile Amendment Act, R.S.O. 1897, c. 145] . . . actually receive. . ." *Bank of Hamilton v. Kramer Irwin Co.* (1911), 3 O.W.N. 73 at 75, 20 O.W.R. 46 (H.C.), Middleton J.

RECOVERABLE GRANT. Any grant, amount in excess of any grant, increment, amount in excess of any increment, monthly benefit, amount in excess of any monthly benefit, tax credit and interest that is required to be paid or repaid by the recipient to Her Majesty under any of the Acts administered by the Minister. *Ministry of Revenue Act*, R.S.O. 1990, c. M.33, s. 12(1).

RECOVERED. *adj*. In respect of a controlled substance, means collected, after the substance has been used, from machinery, equipment or a container during servicing or before disposal of the machinery, equipment or container. *Ozone-depleting Substances Regulations, 1998*, SOR/99-7, s. 1.

RECOVERY. *n*. 1. Obtaining something which was wrongfully taken or withheld from someone, or to which that person is otherwise entitled. 2. That a person who is, or was, a patient is no longer infectious. See CHEMICAL ~ BOILER; DOUBLE ~; ENHANCED ~; HEAT ~ UNIT OR DEVICE; MINERAL ~.

RECOVERY STRATEGY. A recovery strategy included in the public registry, and includes any amendment to it included in the public registry. *Species at Risk Act*, S.C. 2002, c. 29, s. 2(1).

RECOVERY VEHICLE. A motor vehicle that is equipped with a winch and boom device or a wheel life device, or both, and that is designed for towing other motor vehicles by means of that device. *Motor Vehicle Amendment Act (No. 2), 1987*, S.B.C. 1987, c. 61, s. 1.

RECREANT. *adj*. Describes one who yields.

RECREATION. See CROSS-COUNTRY ~.

RECREATIONAL ACTIVITIES. Includes the planned use of all available resources, including finances, leadership, areas and facilities, to meet the needs of residents of the province for recreation during their leisure hours. See OUTDOOR RECREATIONAL ACTIVITY.

RECREATIONAL AGREEMENT. An agreement entered into by a corporation that allows (a) persons, other than the owners, to use recreational facilities located on the common property; or (b) the owners to use recreational facilities not located on the common property.

RECREATIONAL CAMP. Includes a cabin or cottage used for hunting, fishing or leisure and occupied during only part of the year.

RECREATIONAL FACILITY. See PUBLIC ~.

RECREATIONAL FISHING. Fishing for the purpose of exercising the skill of a fisherman or occupying his leisure time.

RECREATIONAL FISHING LICENCE. See ZONE ~.

RECREATIONAL LAND. Land that is not used exclusively as residential land and that is predominantly used for the recreation and enjoyment of its owner or lessee or those, other than persons using the land for agricultural purposes, who are permitted by such owner or lessee to be on the land. *Land Transfer Tax Act*, R.S.O. 1990, c. L.6, s. 1(1).

RECREATIONAL PARK. A park primarily intended to foster the practice of various outdoor recreational activities, while protecting the natural environment.

RECREATIONAL PROPERTY. Land owned by a physical person and used by him principally for recreational or sports purposes.

RECREATIONAL TRAILER. A trailer designed to provide temporary living accommodation for travel, vacation or recreational use.

RECREATIONAL VEHICLE. A vehicular type unit primarily designed as temporary living quarters for recreational, camping, or travel use, which either has its own motive power or is mounted on or drawn by another vehicle.

RECREATION CENTRE. See COMMUNITY ~.

RECREATION FACILITY. Any land, buildings, equipment, or other physical plant, whether publicly or privately owned, used to satisfy the needs and desires of people during their leisure.

RECREATION PROGRAM. A program for the provision of facilities for recreation and for the supervision, encouragement and guidance of recreational activity.

RECREATION SERVICE. Any program for the planned use of recreation facilities to satisfy the needs or desires of people during their leisure.

RECRIMINATION. *n*. A charge which an accused makes against an accuser.

RECTIFICATION. *n*. 1. An equitable remedy which enables the court to make a contract conform with the true intentions of the contracting parties. 2. " . . . [O]perates in a proper case to reform the instruments in order to ensure that they express the agreement actually reached by the parties. . ." *Soni v. Malik* (1985), 1 C.P.C. (2d) 53 at 57, 61 B.C.L.R. 36 (S.C.), McEachern C.J.S.C.

RECTIFIER. *n*. Any pipe, vessel or still into which the spirit is conveyed for the purpose of rectification, re-distillation, filtration or any other process.

RECTIFY. *v*. To make a contract conform to the true intentions of the contracting parties, using the equitable remedy of rectification.

RECTIFYING SPIRITS. The process of refining spirits by re-distillation, filtration or any other process.

RECTITUDO. *n*. [L.] Justice or right; what is legally due; payment or tribute.

RECTOR. *n*. The clergyman acting for the time being as rector of a Roman Catholic parish or the rector of a church or public chapel used for Roman Catholic worship. *Roman Catholic Cemetery Corporations Act*, R.S.Q. 1977, c. C-69, s. 1.

RECTUM. *n*. [L.] 1. Right. 2. The terminal part of the large intestine which opens through the anus. See STARE AD ~.

RECTUM ESSE. [L.] In court, to be right.

RECTUM ROGARE. [L.] To request right.

RECTUS IN CURIA. [L.] Legally right. Rightly before the court.

RECYCLABLE MATERIAL. A product or substance that has been diverted from disposal, and which is organic material from residential, commercial or institutional sources, capable of being composted, or which is a marketable commodity or which is being used in the manufacture of a new product or is being processed as an intermediate stage of an existing manufacturing process.

RECYCLE. *v*. To do anything that results in providing a use for a thing that otherwise would be disposed of or dealt with as waste, including collecting, transporting, handling, storing, sorting, separating and processing the thing, but does not include the application of waste to land or the use of a thermal destruction process

RECYCLED. *adj*. In respect of a controlled substance, means recovered, cleaned by a process such as filtering or drying, and re-used, including re-used to recharge equipment. *Ozone-depleting Substances Regulations, 1998*, SOR/ 99-7, s. 1.

R.E.D. *abbr*. 1. Russell's Equity Decisions (N.S.), 1873-1882. 2. Ritchie's Equity Decisions (Can.) 3. Ritchie's Equity Decisions, by Russell (N.S.). 4. Ritchie's Equity Reports, by Russell (N.S.).

RED CLAUSE. A clause endorsed in coloured ink on a commercial letter of credit which authorizes a bank to accept or pay drafts against the promise that a bill of lading and other documents will be provided when certain goods are shipped. I.F.G. Baxter, *The Law of Banking*, 3d ed. (Toronto: Carswell, 1981) at 156.

REDDENDO SINGULA SINGULIS. [L. by giving each to each] Describes a clause in a document when one of two provisions in the first sentence is appropriated to one of two objects in the second sentence, and the other provision is likewise appropriated to the other object.

REDDENDUM. *n*. [L. that which is to be paid or rendered] The clause in a lease, usually using the words "yielding and paying", which states the amount of the rent and the time at which it should be paid.

REDDIDIT SE. [L.] One gave oneself up.

REDDITARIUM. *n*. The rental of a manor or estate.

REDDITARIUS. *n*. A tenant, one who rents.

REDDITION. *n*. Restoring or surrendering; in the course of legal proceedings formally admitting that lands were the property of the person who sought to recover them, not of the person who made the admission.

REDDITUS. *n*. [L.] Rent.

REDDITUS ASSISUS. [L.] An established or standing rent.

REDDITUS QUIETI. [L.] Quit-rent.

REDDITUS SICCUS. [L.] Rent seck.

REDEEM. *v*. To buy back. See ACTION TO ~.

REDEEMABLE. *adj*. That may be repurchased by the issuer.

REDEEMABLE RIGHTS. Rights which return to the one who conveys or disposes of land once the sum for which such rights are granted is paid.

REDEEMABLE SECURITY. A security which exists for a fixed term and is redeemable at the end of that term at a specified value.

REDEEMABLE SHARE. A share issued by a corporation (a) that the corporation may purchase or redeem on the demand of the corporation; or (b) that the corporation is required by its articles to purchase or redeem at a specified time or on the demand of a shareholder.

REDELIVERY. *n*. Yielding and delivering something back.

REDEMISE. *n*. Re-granting land.

REDEMPTION. *n*. 1. In relation to mutual fund shares of the company, be deemed to be a reference to acceptance by the company of the surrender of those shares. 2. The buying back of securities by the issuer. 3. The right to have property freed from a secured charge. See EQUITY OF ~; PROVISO FOR ~.

REDEMPTION DATE. In the case of a security that is redeemable at more than one specified date, the specified date that gives the lower or the lowest effective rate of interest, as the case may be. *Cooperative Credit Associations Act*, R.S.C. 1985, c. C-41, s. 57(4).

REDEMPTION PERIOD. That period of time within which the owner of a dog or cat that has been impounded in a pound has the right to redeem it.

REDEVELOPMENT. *n*. The planning or replanning, design or redesign, resubdivision, clearance, development, reconstruction and rehabilitation, or any of them, of a redevelopment area, and the provision of such residential, commercial, industrial, public, recreational, institutional, religious, charitable or other uses, buildings, works, improvements or facilities, or spaces therefor, as may be appropriate or necessary.

REDEVELOPMENT TAX. A compulsory levy imposed by a municipality on real property situated within a defined area that is (a) payable by a taxable owner of real property by virtue of his ownership of such property or of specified actions undertaken by him to develop such property; (b) calculated by reference to all or part of the frontage, area or other attribute of land or buildings of the owner; (c) assessed at a uniform rate upon owners of real property liable to pay the tax; and (d) levied for the purpose of financing all or part of the capital cost of the construction or reconstruction of a trunk or arterial road or any other capital service that has been, is being or will be carried out within the defined area.

REDFISH. *n*. A fish of the species Sebastes marinus.

RED HAKE. A fish of the species Urophycis Chuss.

RED-HANDED. *adj*. With the marks of crime fresh on one's person.

RED HERRING. 1. A non-issue. 2. A preliminary prospectus marked in red ink. 3. An issue or fact which seems important but in fact is of no or little importance.

REDIRECTED MAIL. Mail that cannot be delivered as addressed because the addressee has left the place to which the mail was addressed but that can, because the addressee has filed a Request for Redirection of Mail-Holding of Mail card with the postmaster, be redirected for delivery to him at that address. *Undeliverable and Redirected Mail Regulations*, C.R.C., c. 1298, s. 2.

REDISSEISIN. *n*. Recovery of the seisin of a freehold by someone who was disseised and delivery of possession by the sheriff, followed by disseisen again by the same disseisor.

REDITUS. *n*. [L.] Rent.

REDITUS ASSISUS. [L.] An established or standing rent.

REDITUS QUIETI. [L.] Quit-rent.

REDITUS SICCUS. [L.] Rent seck.

REDOCUMENTATION CHARGE. A charge for reissuing or making changes to the billing of inbound cargo arising from changes in original manifests, split delivery or shipments, forwarding instructions or services.

RE-DRAFT. *n*. The second version of a document.

REDRESS. *v*. To give satisfaction or compensation for a wrong or loss sustained.

REDRESS. *n*. Relief in the form of damages or equitable relief.

RED ROT. A condition in which the yolk sac is ruptured permitting mixture of the yolk and white. *Live Stock and Live Stock Products Act*, R.R.O. 1980, Reg. 582, s. 1.

REDUCTIO AD ABSURDUM. [L.] The way to disprove an argument by demonstrating that it leads to an unreasonable conclusion.

REDUCTION INTO POSSESSION. Exercising the right which a chose in action confers so that it is converted into a chose in possession. In this way one may reduce a debt into possession by obtaining payment.

REDUNDANCY. *n*. Unneeded or extraneous material inserted in a pleading.

REDUNDANT ASSET. An asset which is not needed for an on-going operation.

REDUNDANT EMPLOYEE. An employee whose employment is to be terminated pursuant to a notice under section 212. *Canada Labour Code*, R.S.C. 1985, c. L-2, s. 211.

REEL. *n.* 1. (a) A photographic moving picture film; (b) a video, tape; or (c) a cassette; not exceeding 10 minutes in running time. *The Theatres and Cinematographs Act*, R.S.S. 1978, c. T-11, s. 2. 2. 2,000 feet or less in length of standard film or 16-millimetre cinematographic film or 400 feet or less in length of 8-millimetre cinematographic film. *Theatres Act*, R.R.O. 1980, Reg. 931, s. 1.

RE-EMPLOYMENT LIST. A list of persons eligible for appointment to positions in some particular class because they were subject to a lay-off from positions in that same class. *Civil Service acts.*

RE-ENTRANT. See NEW ENTRANT OR ~ TO THE LABOUR FORCE.

RE-ENTRY. *n.* In a lease, a proviso which empowers the lessor to re-enter the leased premises if the rent has not been paid for a certain period.

REEVE. *n.* The principal official of a town.

RE-EXAMINATION. *n.* 1. Examination of a witness by the counsel who first examined that person concerning a new fact which arose out of cross-examination. S. Mitchell, P.J. Richardson & D.A. Thomas, eds., *Archbold Pleading, Evidence and Practice in Criminal Cases*, 43d ed. (London: Sweet & Maxwell, 1988) at 548. 2. Re-examination is used to give a witness an opportunity to explain and clarify testimony which was weakened or obscured during cross-examination. J. Sopinka and S.N. Lederman, *The Law of Evidence in Civil Cases* (Toronto: Butterworths, 1974) at 516.

RE-EXTENT. *n.* Concerning a debt, a second execution by extent.

REF. *abbr.* Reference.

REFER. *v.* 1. With respect to a question, to have it decided by someone nominated for that purpose. 2. To direct a person to someone or something for information or assistance.

REFEREE. *n.* A person to whom a court refers a pending cause so that that person may take testimony, hear the parties, and report back. See BOARD OF ~S; DRAINAGE ~.

REFERENCE. *n.* 1. Sending a whole proceeding or a particular issue to the referring judge, a registrar or other court officer. 2. A question which a government presents to a court for an opinion concerning the constitutionality of an enactment although there is no real dispute. 3. In the context of a reference, the Court, rather than acting in its traditional adjudicative function, is acting in an advisory capacity. The very fact that the Court may be asked hypothetical questions in a reference, such as the constitutionality of proposed legislation, engages the Court in an exercise it would never entertain in the context of litigation. No matter how closely the procedure on a reference may mirror the litigation process, a reference does not engage the Court in a disposition of rights. *Reference re Secession of Quebec*, 1998 CarswellNat 1299, 161 D.L.R. (4th) 385, 228 N.R. 203, 55 C.R.R. (2d) 1, [1998] 2 S.C.R. 217 Per curiam. 4. The lieutenant governor in council may refer a question for opinion to the court of appeal in the province. 5. In order to take accounts or make inquiries, to determine any question or issue of fact, the court may refer any matter to a judge whom the Associate Chief Justice nominates, a prothonotary, or any other person the court deems to be qualified for the purpose so that that person may inquire and report. D. Sgayias *et al.*, *Federal Court Practice 1988* (Toronto: Carswell, 1987) at 499. See ADOPTION BY ~; FEDERAL ~; PATRIATION ~ (1981); PROVINCIAL ~.

REFERENCE CONDITIONS. See STANDARD ~.

REFERENCE PLAN. The plan of survey of a block or part of a lot or on a registered plan of subdivision or part of a registered parcel.

REFERENCE POST. A legal post erected pursuant to subsection (4) to designate the corner of a claim previously designated by a witness post. *Canada Mining Regulations*, C.R.C., c. 1516, s. 15.

REFERENCE STANDARD. A standard that (a) represents or registers a unit of measurement referred to in Schedule I or II or that represents or registers a multiple or fraction of such a unit of measurement; (b) has been calibrated and certified by the National Research Council of Canada; and (c) is or is to be used as a standard for the purpose of determining the accuracy of a local standard. *Weights and Measures Act*, R.S.C. 1985, c. W-6, s. 2.

REFERENDUM. *n.* 1. The direct vote of electors concerning a particular by-law or question.

2. Where the Governor in Council considers that it is in the public interest to obtain by means of a referendum the opinion of electors on any question relating to the Constitution of Canada, the Governor in Council may, by proclamation, direct that the opinion of electors be obtained by putting the question to the electors of Canada or of one or more provinces specified in the proclamation at a referendum called for that purpose. 3. If the Lieutenant Governor in Council considers that an expression of public opinion is desirable on any matter of public interest or concern, the Lieutenant Governor in Council may, by regulation, order that a referendum be conducted in the manner provided for in this Act. *Referendum Act*, R.S.B.C. 1996, c. 400, s. 1(1).

REFERENDUM PERIOD. The period beginning on the day fixed for issuing a writ and ending on the day for its return.

REFERENTIAL BID. A bid which does not stand alone but is understandable only with reference to another bid. *Bank of Nova Scotia v. Yoshikuni Lumber Ltd.* (1992), 74 B.C.L.R. (2d) 19 (C.A.).

REFERRAL. *n*. Includes assignment, designation, dispatching, scheduling and selection. *Canada Labour Code*, R.S.C. 1985, c. L-2, s. 69.

REFERRAL HIRING SYSTEM. A system which permits a union to refer all workers required for a project.

REFERRAL SELLING. Receipt by the purchaser of a product of a commission, rebate or other benefit from the seller, based on sales which other people made to people whom the purchaser named. G.H.L. Fridman, *Sale of Goods in Canada*, 3d ed. (Toronto: Carswell, 1986) at 493. See SCHEME OF ~.

REFERRED BYLAW. A bylaw referred to a vote of either the burgesses or the electors, or both. *The Urban Municipality Act*, R.S.S. 1978, c. U-10, s. 2.

REFILLABLE CONTAINER. 1. A container that is intended to be used more than once for purposes of sale or distribution of a beverage. 2. An approved container for which a cash deposit is made to a retailer or for which a retailer is required to pay a refund.

REFINANCE. *v*. Where used to refer to the refinancing of a foreign debt, means the issue and sale of bonds, debentures and notes or the arranging of loans by the issuer of the foreign debt for the purpose of payment, refunding, refinancing or renewal of the foreign debt.

REFINANCING. *n*. [As used in defining the obligation of a partner under a partnership agreement] contemplates renewing or replacing a mortgage, either because of expiry of the term of the mortgage or because of default and acceleration, not paying the full amount of the debt owing on maturity. The concept of servicing a mortgage debt clearly implies making periodic payments of principal and interest, not retiring the entire debt. *Western Delta Lands Partnership v. 3557537 Canada Inc.*, 2000 CarswellBC 1483, 2000 BCSC 1096 (S.C. [In Chambers]).

REFINED PETROLEUM PRODUCT. A commodity made from oil and, without limiting the generality of the foregoing, includes motor and tractor gasoline, naphtha gasoline, kerosene, diesel fuel, aviation fuel, bunker oil and lubrication products. *The Oil and Gas Conservation, Stabilization and Development Act*, R.S.S. 1978, c. O-3, s. 19.

REFINER. *n*. A person who refines, manufactures, produces, prepares, distils, compounds and blends fuel pet products.

REFINERY. *n*. Any facility where oil or minerals are processed or refined.

REFINING. *n*. Any treatment of smelter product or concentrate to remove impurities, producing a very high grade metal in the metallic state.

REFLECTORIZED. *adj*. As applied to any equipment carried in or on a vehicle or to a traffic control device means treated in such a manner that, under normal atmospheric conditions, and when illuminated by the light from the lamps of any vehicle approaching it will reflect that light so that it is clearly visible from a distance of at least 150 metres. *The Highway Traffic Act*, S.M. 1985-86, c. 3, s. 1.

RE-FLOATING. *n*. The law is uncertain about whether a security instrument which contains a floating charge and crystallizes stays crystallized or re-floats if the security holder changes its mind and discharges the manager and receiver soon after they are appointed. F. Bennett, *Receiverships* (Toronto: Carswell, 1985) at 10.

REFORM. *v*. With respect to an instrument, to rectify it. See LAW ~ COMMISSION OF CANADA.

REFORMATORY. *n*. An institution where offenders are sent to be reformed.

REFRACTORY MATERIALS. Includes fire bricks, plastic refractories, high temperature cement, fire clay and short lived refractories such as melting pots, crucibles and retorts. *Retail Sales Tax Act*, R.R.O. 1980, Reg. 903, s. 1.

REFRACTORY PERIOD. The period during which a triggered pulse generator is unresponsive to an input signal. *Medical Devices Regulations*, C.R.C., c. 871, s. 1.

REFRESH. *v*. With respect to a witness' memory, to refer to a document which may not itself be admissible as evidence.

REFRESHMENT HOUSE. A place conducted by a person, firm or corporation, who sells by retail only all or any of the following: meals and drinks of all kinds for consumption on the premises only, and includes a delicatessen selling cooked meats, cooked vegetables, and cooked fish, not in sealed containers.

REFRIGERANT. *n*. A substance that maybe used to produce refrigeration by its expansion or evaporation. *Operating Engineers Act*, R.S.O. 1990, c. 0.42, s. 1.

REFRIGERANT VESSEL. A pressure vessel that is a component part of a refrigeration system.

REFRIGERATING PLANT. The complete installation of pressure vessels, pressure piping, machinery and appliances of all descriptions by which refrigerants are vapourized, compressed and liquefied in their refrigerating cycle.

REFRIGERATING SYSTEM. A complete installation of pressure vessels, piping, fittings, compressors, machinery and other equipment by which refrigerants are vapourized, compressed and liquefied in their refrigerating cycle.

REFRIGERATION AND AIR-CONDITIONING MECHANIC. A person who: (a) lays out, assembles, installs, maintains in the field any cooling or heating-cooling combination system for residential, commercial or industrial purposes within the limitation of the Energy Act; (b) installs or connects piping for the purposes of conveying refrigerant of all types for either primary or secondary cooling; (c) overhauls or repairs any equipment used in a refrigeration or air-conditioning system; and (d) tests, adjusts, maintains all controls on refrigeration or air-conditioning systems including air-balancing, but does not include a person who is engaged in the repair or installation of single-phase hermetically sealed domestic self-contained units with factory mass produced systems precharged with refrigerant, or a person employed in production commonly known as mass production.

REFRIGERATION PLANT. The complete installation of machinery by which refrigerants are vapourized, compressed and liquefied in their refrigeration cycle.

REFRIGERATOR PLANT. An installation comprised of one or more refrigeration compressors and the equipment used therewith for compressing, liquefying and evaporating a refrigerant.

REFUGE. *n*. 1. An area designated in the regulations as an area in which the hunting of wildlife or exotic animals or of any species, type, class, or group thereof is prohibited. 2. An institution for the care of the young or of adult females to which they may by law be sentenced by a court.

REFUGE AREA. An alcove or extension of a staircase landing for the purpose of accommodating disabled persons in the case of emergency.

REFUGEE. *n*. A person who, by reason of a well-founded fear of persecution for reasons of race, religion, nationality, political opinion or membership in a particular social group, (a) has been lawfully admitted to Canada for permanent residence after leaving the country of his nationality and is unable or, by reason of that fear, is unwilling to avail himself of the protection of that country; or (b) has been lawfully admitted to Canada for permanent residence after leaving the country of his former habitual residence and is unable or, by reason of that fear, is unwilling to return to that country. See CONVENTION ~.

REFUGEE CONVENTION. The United Nations Convention Relating to the Status of Refugees, signed at Geneva on July 28, 1951, and the Protocol to that Convention, signed at New York on January 31, 1967. *Immigration and Refugee Protection Act*, S.C. 2001, c. 27, s. 2(1).

REFUGEE DIVISION. That division of the Immigration and Refugee Board called the Convention Refugee Determination Division. *Immigration Act*, R.S.C. 1985, c. I-2, s. 2.

REFUND. *n*. The restitution or return of a sum received or taken; reimbursement. Generally involves return of money from one party to another. See INCOME TAX ~; PATRONAGE ~.

REFUND OF TAX. The amount of (a) an overpayment of tax paid under the Income Tax Act or collected pursuant to an agreement entered into under section 7 of the Federal-Provincial Fiscal Arrangements and Federal Post-Secondary Education and Health Contributions Act; (b) a payment to an individual by virtue of an agreement referred to in paragraph (a) that is other than a refund of an overpayment of tax paid or collected; (c) an overpayment of unemployment insurance premiums paid under the Unemployment Insurance Act; or (d) an overpayment of contributions paid under the Canada Pension Plan, and any interest paid on any of those overpayments or payments. *Tax Rebate Discounting Act*, R.S.C. 1985, c. T-3, s. 2.

REFUSAL. *n*. "[With knowledge of] . . . the strictures you are under . . . deliberately [flouting] them." *R. v. Docherty* (1989), 101 N.R. 161 at 171,17 M.V.R. (2d) 161, [1989] 2 S.C.R. 941, 51 C.C.C. (3d) 1, 72 C.R. (3d) 1, 78 Nfld. & P.E.I.R. 315, 244 A.P.R. 315, the court per Wilson J. See RIGHT OF FIRST ~.

REFUSE. *v*. 1. For a person who legally has the right and power to have or do something advantageous to decline it. 2. Wilfully failing to comply with an order; imports some guilty knowledge that the actor is not complying with the order.

REFUSE. *n*. Discarded or abandoned materials, substances or objects.

REFUSE TO BARGAIN IN GOOD FAITH. Where one party remains fixed in its bargaining position and refuses to move from the position adopted initially.

REG. *abbr*. 1. [L. regina] Queen. 2. Regulation. 3. Registrar.

REGENCY. *n*. Delegation to another person called the regent of some or all of a sovereign's powers when that sovereign is young, incapacitated or away from the realm.

REGICIDE. *n*. 1. The murder of a monarch. 2. One who murders a monarch.

REGIME. See COMMUNITY PROPERTY~; STANDARD MARITAL ~.

REGION. *n*. 1. A province, a portion of a province, two or more provinces or adjoining portions of two or more provinces. *Department of*

Regional Industrial Expansion Act, R.S.C. 1985, c. R-5, s. 2. 2. A defined geographical area. See ALTIMETER SETTING ~; ATLANTIC ~; FLIGHT INFORMATION ~; GASPESIA ~; GATINEAU VALLEY ~; MATANE ~; NATIONAL CAPITAL ~; NORTHERN ~S; POLAR ~S; PRAIRIE ~; QUEBEC NORTHWEST ~; QUEBEC-SOUTH ~; RIMOUSKI-MATAPÉDIA ~; RIMOUSKI-RIVIÈRE-DULOUP ~; STANDARD PRESSURE ~.

REGIONAL DIFFERENTIAL. See GEOGRAPHIC WAGE DIFFERENTIAL.

REGIONAL INDUSTRIAL EXPANSION. See DEPARTMENT OF ~.

REGIONAL LICENCE. A licence issued by the Commission that authorizes the licensee to carry on distribution undertakings in two or more licensed areas. *Broadcasting Distribution Regulations*, SOR/97-555, s. 1.

REGIONAL MUNICIPALITY. A metropolitan, regional or district municipality as defined in the Act establishing such a municipality and includes the County of Oxford. *Ontario Unconditional Grants Act*, R.S.O. 1980, c. 359, s. 1.

REGIONAL SAFETY OFFICER. 1. A person designated as a regional safety officer pursuant to subsection 140(1). *Canada Labour Code*, R.S.C. 1985 (1st Supp.), c. 9, s. 122. 2. The safety officer designated by the Minister to serve as the regional safety officer in the area in which the federal work, undertaking or business is located. Canada regulations.

REGIONAL SURVEY. A geological, geophysical or geochemical survey for minerals, whether ground or airborne, that is performed (a) in relation to a mineral claim or mining lease but extends beyond the land covered by the mineral claim or mining lease; or (b) on land open for prospecting and staking.

REGIONAL TELEVISION STATION. In relation to a licensed area of a distribution undertaking, a licensed television station, other than a local television station, that has a Grade B official contour that includes any part of the licensed area. *Broadcasting Distribution Regulations*, SOR/97-555, s. 1.

REGIONAL TRAIL. Any footpath, pathway, trail or area of land held in fee simple or as a registered easement or right of way by a regional district and dedicated as a regional trail.

REGIONAL TRANSIT SYSTEM. A transit system that is principally operated within a regional area.

REGISTER. *v.* To file or deposit.

REGISTER. *n.* 1. That part of the records where information respecting registered titles is stored. 2. The register of members and students of a professional body. 3. The record maintained by a registrar for the purpose of recording all registrations, renewals, changes or amendments of registrations, suspensions, cancellations and reinstatements of registrations of brokers or dealers. 4. An entry in an official book kept for that purpose. 5. The register maintained pursuant to the Act of the names of persons and firms entitled to represent applicants in the presentation and prosecution of applications for patents before the Office. *Patent Rules*, C.R.C. , c. 1250, s. 2. 6. The register of Trade-marks. See ANNUAL ~; ASCENDING ~; DESCENDING ~; EDUCATIONAL ~; GENERAL ~; INDIAN ~; SECURITIES ~; TITLE ~; TRAIN ~; VOTING ~.

REGISTERED. *adj.* 1. Filed, listed or holder of a particular status in accordance with an act. 2. Registered as an Indian in the Indian Register. *Indian Act*, R.S.C. 1985, c. I-5, s. 2. 2. Registered in accordance with an act governing a profession. See GROSS ~ TONS.

REGISTERED ANIMAL. An animal for which a certificate of registration has been issued by the registrar of the breed to which the animal belongs or by the registrar of the Canadian National Livestock Records.

REGISTERED CANADIAN AMATEUR ATHLETIC ASSOCIATION. An association that was created under any law in force in Canada, that is resident in Canada, and that (a) is a person described in paragraph 149(1)(l); and (b) has, as its primary purpose and its primary function, the promotion of amateur athletics in Canada on a nation-wide basis, that has applied to the Minister in prescribed form for registration, that has been registered and whose registration has not been revoked under subsection 168(2). *Income Tax Act*, R.S.C. 1985, c. 1 (5th Supp.), s. 248(1).

REGISTERED CANADIAN CHARITABLE ORGANIZATION. See now REGISTERED CHARITY.

REGISTERED CANDIDATE. With respect to an election of a member or members to serve in the Assembly, means a person who has been registered as a candidate for such election by the Commission on Election Finances and whose name has not been deleted from the register of candidates maintained by the Commission with respect to such election. *Corporations Tax Act*, R.S.O. 1990, c. C.40, s. 36(2).

REGISTERED CHARITY. At any time means (a) a charitable organization, private foundation or public foundation, within the meanings assigned by subsection 149.1(1), that is resident in Canada and was either created or established in Canada, or (b) a branch, section, parish, congregation or other division of an organization or foundation described in paragraph 248(1) "registered charity" (a), that is resident in Canada and was either created or established in Canada and that receives donations on its own behalf, that has applied to the Minister in prescribed form for registration and that is at that time registered as a charitable organization, private foundation or public foundation. *Income Tax Act*, R.S.C. 1985, c. 1 (5th Supp.), s. 248.

REGISTERED CLERGYMAN. A clergyman registered to solemnize marriage.

REGISTERED COMPANY. See CANADIAN ~.

REGISTERED CREDITOR. A creditor who is named in a consolidation order. *Bankruptcy Act*, R.S.C. 1985, c. B-3, s. 217.

REGISTERED DOCUMENT. A bill of sale, chattel mortgage, lien note or conditional sale agreement, assignment of book debts and any other document relating to personal chattels registered in the office of a registration clerk for any registration district heretofore or hereafter established for the purpose of registrations of bills of sale, chattel mortgages, lien notes or conditional sale agreements, assignments of book debts and other documents relating to personal chattels. *The Registered Documents Destruction Act*, R.S.S. 1978, c. R-10, s. 2.

REGISTERED EDUCATION SAVINGS PLAN. An education savings plan registered for purposes of the Income Tax Act.

REGISTERED FORM. A security is in registered form if (a) it specifies a person entitled to the security or to the rights it evidences, and its transfer is capable of being recorded in a securities register; or (b) it bears a statement that it is in registered form. *Bank Act*, S.C. 1991, c. 46, s. 83(4).

REGISTERED GROSS TONNAGE. The gross tonnage of a ship as shown on the register of the ship.

REGISTERED HOME OWNERSHIP SAVINGS PLAN. A plan under the Income Tax Act designed to encourage saving for home ownership by which any taxpayer at least 18 years old could contribute an amount completely deductible from income.

REGISTERED INVESTMENT. A trust or a corporation that has applied in prescribed form as of a particular date in the year of application and has been accepted by the Minister as of that date as a registered investment for one or more of the following: (a) registered retirement savings plans, (b) [Repealed.] (c) registered retirement income funds, and (d) deferred profit sharing plans and that has not been notified by the Minister that it is no longer registered under this Part. *Income Tax Act*, R.S.C. 1985, c. 1 (5th Supp.), s. 204.4(1).

REGISTERED LIFE INSURANCE POLICY. A life insurance policy issued or effected (a) as a registered retirement savings plan, or (b) pursuant to a registered retirement savings plan, a deferred profit sharing plan or a registered pension plan. *Income Tax Act*, R.S.C. 1985, c. 1 (5th Supp.), s. 211(1).

REGISTERED MAIL. Includes certified mail.

REGISTERED NURSE. A person who is licensed to practise the profession of nursing and is a registered member, in good standing, of an association.

REGISTERED NURSING ASSISTANT. A person who is the holder of a certificate as a registered nursing assistant.

REGISTERED OFFICE. A head office or chief place of business the address of which is provided to the provincial or federal authority governing the company and where notices and process may be served on the company and certain documents and books must be kept.

REGISTERED ORDER. (a) A final order made in a reciprocating state and filed under this Act or under an enactment repealed by this Act with a court in the Province; (b) a final order deemed to be a registered order; or (c) a confirmation order that is filed. *Maintenance Orders Enforcement acts*.

REGISTERED OWNER. 1. An owner of land whose interest in the land is defined and whose name is specified in an instrument in the registry office. 2. The person registered in a land titles office as owner of the fee simple in land unless it appears from the records of the land titles office that another person has purchased the land under an agreement for sale in which case it means that other person. 3. A person in whose name a vehicle is registered.

REGISTERED OWNER IN FEE SIMPLE. A person registered in the books of the land title office as entitled to an estate in fee simple in real property, and, where used in respect of a lesser estate, includes a person who registers a charge.

REGISTERED PARTY. A political party which has been registered.

REGISTERED PENSION PLAN. 1. A pension plan that is registered and in respect of which a certificate of registration has been issued by the Superintendent under this Act. *Pension Benefits Standards Act*, R.S.C. 1985 (2d Supp.), c. 32, s. 2. 2. A pension plan that is registered with and certified by the Commission as a plan organized and administered in accordance with this Act. *Pension Benefits Act*, R.S.O. 1980, c. 373, s. 1.

REGISTERED REPRESENTATIVE. A person qualified to sell securities.

REGISTERED REPRESENTATIVE EXAMINATION. An examination based on the Manual for Registered Representatives that has been prepared and is conducted by the Canadian Securities Institute and so designated by that Institute.

REGISTERED RETIREMENT INCOME FUND. A retirement income fund accepted by the Minister for registration for the purposes of this Act and registered under the Social Insurance Number of the first annuitant under the fund. *Income Tax Act*, R.S.C. 1985, c. 1 (5th Supp.), s. 146.3(1).

REGISTERED RETIREMENT PLAN. An employees' superannuation plan accepted by the Minister for registration for the purposes of this Part in respect of its constitution and operations for the taxation year under consideration. *Taxation Act*, R.S.Q. 1977, c. I-3, s. 1.

REGISTERED RETIREMENT SAVINGS PLAN. A retirement savings plan accepted by the Minister for registration for the purposes of this Act as complying with the requirements of this section. *Income Tax Act*, R.S.C. 1952, c. 148 (as am. S.C. 1970-71-72, c. 63), s. 146(1)(i).

REGISTERED SUPPLEMENTARY UN-EMPLOYMENT BENEFIT PLAN. A supplementary unemployment benefit plan accepted by the Minister for registration for the purposes of this Act in respect of its constitution and operations for the taxation year under consideration. *Income Tax Act*, R.S.C. 1985, c. 1 (5th Supp.), s. 145(1).

REGISTERED TRADE-MARK. A trade-mark that is on the register. *Trade-Marks Act*, R.S.C. 1985, c. T-13, s. 1.

REGISTERED WEIGHT. The weight in pounds stated upon the permit for a vehicle.

REGISTERING AGENT. The person who is acting as agent for the secured party when submitting a statement for registration but does not include a clerk or other employee of the secured party.

REGISTERING COURT. A court to which an application for the registration of a judgment is made.

REGISTER NUMBER. The number assigned by the board to a motor vehicle, trailer or semi-trailer.

REGISTER OF TITLE AND ABSTRACT INDEX. 1. Includes an instrument received for registration before the closing of the land registry office on the day the tax arrears certificate was registered even if the instrument has not been abstracted or entered in the register or index at that time. *Municipal Tax Sales Act*, R.S.O. 1990, c. M.60, s. 1(3). 2. Include instruments received for registration before 4:30 p.m. on the day immediately prior to the day on which a notice of exercising the power of sale is given. *Mortgages Act*, R.S.O. 1990, c. M.40, s. 31(2).

REGISTER TONNAGE. The register tonnage shown on a ship's certificate of registry. *Canada Shipping Act*, R.S.C. 1985, c. S-9, s. 2.

REGISTRANT. *n.* 1. A securities broker or dealer required to be registered to trade or deal in securities under the laws of any jurisdiction. 2. A person who is registered or required to be registered. See NON-RESIDENT CONTROLLED ~.

REGISTRAR. *n.* 1. The person responsible for the operation and management of a registration system. 2. With respect to a court, the administrative officer who is responsible for filing and issuing particular documents, retaining court files and occasionally for assessing costs. 3. The

officer of the Department who is in charge of the Indian Register. *Indian Act*, R.S.C. 1985, c. I-5, s. 2. See LAND ~; LOCAL ~.

REGISTRAR GENERAL. 1. The provincial officer who registers any birth, death and marriage. 2. The Registrar General as defined in the Vital Statistics Act.

REGISTRARIUS. *n.* [L.] A registrar; a notary.

REGISTRAR OF DEEDS. Includes the registrar of land titles or other officer with whom a title to the land is registered.

REGISTRAR OF LAND TITLES. A registrar of land titles appointed under a Land Titles Act.

REGISTRAR OF MOTOR VEHICLES. The person who from time to time performs the duties of superintending the registration of motor vehicles in a province.

REGISTRARY. *n.* The official whose duty it is to write or keep a register.

REGISTRATION. *n.* 1. (a) Bringing lands under this Act; (b) entering upon the certificate of title a memorandum authorized by this Act, of any document. *Land Titles acts.* 2. A valid and subsisting registration permit. 3. The admission of an individual to membership in a professional association and enrolment of that person's name in a register. 4. The entry of the name of a person in a register. 5. An entry in an official book kept for that purpose. *Yukon Quartz Mining Act*, R.S.C. 1985, c. Y-4, s. 2. 6. Includes both visual indication and printed representation of quantity, unit price or monetary value. *Weights and Measures Regulations*, C.R.C., c. 1605. See CERTIFICATE OF ~; ERROR OF ~; SYSTEM OF ~.

REGISTRATION COURT. The court in the Province (a) in which the registered order is filed under this Act; or (b) that deemed a final order to be a registered order under this Act or under an enactment repealed by this Act. *Maintenance Orders Enforcement acts.*

REGISTRATION JURISDICTION. Employ memorandum and articles of association as incorporating documents. The incorporating officer must ensure that the documents comply with the provisions of the statute, particularly, that there are no illegal objects and that there is no objection to the name. If satisfied that these requirements are met the officer must issue a certificate of incorporation.

REGISTRATION OFFICER. The returning officer shall appoint, for each registration desk, a registration officer to receive, on polling day, the applications for registration of electors whose names are not on the list of electors. *Canada Elections Act, 2000*, S.C. 2000, c. 9, s. 39.

REGISTRUM BREVIUM. [L.) A place where writs are registered.

REGISTRY. *n*. 1. The office of the Registrar. 2. The office of the court. See LAND ~.

REGISTRY ACT SYSTEM. 1. A person acquiring an interest in land registered in this system must examine the title as it is recorded in the Registry Office, and a vendor usually must show that she or he is lawfully entitled to own the land through a chain of title extending back for a period of years. W.B. Rayner & R.H. McLaren, *Falconbridge on Mortgages*, 4th ed. (Toronto: Canada Law Book, 1977) at 127. 2. Under such a system, anyone who acquires interest in land may register a copy of the document which transfers that interest. The registered documents are organized so that any person may, for a small fee, examine those which affect a particular piece of land. In most cases, a claim which is not registered does not affect a later mortgagee or purchaser who acquired an interest for value and without actually being notified of the unregistered claim, but simple registration of a document does not assure its effectiveness. B.J. Reiter, B.N. McLellan & P.M. Perell, *Real Estate Law*, 4th ed. (Toronto: Emond Montgomery, 1992) at 388.

REGISTRY OF DEEDS. Includes the land titles office or other office in which the title to the land is registered. *Railway Act*, R.S.C. 1985, c. R-3, s. 2.

REGISTRY SYSTEM. See REGISTRY ACT SYSTEM.

REGNAL YEAR. A year calculated from a sovereign's accession to the throne, thus 7 Eliz. 2 means the seventh year after the accession of Elizabeth II on February 6, 1952 (February 6, 1958, to February 5, 1959).

REGNANT. *adj*. Reigning.

RE-GRANT. *v*. For a grantor to grant again granted property which came back.

REGRESS. *n*. Entering again.

REGRESSIVE TAX RATE STRUCTURE. A system by which the percentage of income paid in taxes decreases as a taxpayer's income increases.

REGULA EST, JURIS QUIDEM IGNORANTIAM CUIQUE NOCERE FACTI VERO IGNORANTIAM NON NOCERE. [L.] It is a rule that every person is prejudiced by ignorance of law but not by ignorance of fact.

REGULAR. *adj*. Appointed on a permanent basis.

REGULAR ELECTION. An election of members of a council held at regular periodic intervals under which the authority is constituted.

REGULAR EMPLOYEE. An employee who is employed for work which is of continuous full time or continuous part time nature. *Pension (Public Service) Act*, R.S.B.C. 1979, c. 318, s. 1.

REGULAR FORCE. 1. The component of the Canadian Forces, that consists of officers and non-commissioned members who are enrolled for continuing, full-time military service. The maximum numbers of officers and non-commissioned members is authorized by the Governor in Council The regular force includes units and other elements. *National Defence Act*, R.S.C. 1985, c. N-5, ss. 2, 15. 2. The component of the Canadian Forces that is referred to in the National Defence Act as the regular force. *Interpretation Act*, R.S.C. 1985, c. I-21, s. 35. See MEMBER OF THE ~.

REGULAR HOURS. The hours or parts thereof, not exceeding standard hours, during which, from day to day, a person employed is required by the employer to be present for, and engaged upon, the work or services contemplated by the employment.

REGULARITY. The doctrine of regularity derives from the maxim "omnia praesumuntur rite esse act[a]" [all things are presumed to be done properly] and may be stated in essentially the same terms. It was described by Lindley L.J. in *Harris v. Knight* (1890), 15 P.D. 170 (Eng. C.A.) at p. 179 as follows: The maxim, 'Omnia praesumuntur rite esse acta,' is an expression, in a short form, of a reasonable probability, and of the propriety in point of law of acting on such probability. The maxim expresses an inference which may reasonably be drawn when an intention to do some formal act is established; when the evidence is consistent with that intention having been carried into effect in a proper way; but when the actual observance of all due formalities can only be inferred as a matter of probability. The maxim is not wanted where such observance is proved, nor had it any place where such observance is disproved. The maxim only comes into operation where there is no proof one way or the other; but where it is more probable that what was intended to be done was done as it ought to have been done to render it valid; rather than that it was done in some other manner which would defeat the intention proved to exist, and would render what is proved to have been done of no effect. *R. v. Larsen* (1992), 97 Sask. R. 310 (C.A.).

REGULAR LOT. A township lot whose boundaries according to the original plan conform within one degree to the bearings shown for the corresponding boundaries of the majority of the lots in the tier in which the lot occurs. *Surveys Act*, R.S.O. 1990, c. S.30, s. 1.

REGULARLY. *adv.* Opposite of casual or intermittent. Denotes a fixed pattern.

REGULARLY EMPLOYED. A person employed on a continuous basis with allowance for recognized leave periods.

REGULAR MEMBER. A person who is appointed to a rank in the Force. *Royal Canadian Mounted Police Regulations*, C.R.C., c. 1391, s. 2.

REGULAR PAYMENT CONTRACT. A contract in which payments are required at approximately equal intervals and in approximately equal amounts during the term of the contract.

REGULAR RATE. With respect to an employee, means the rate of wages ordinarily paid that employee for work done in regular hours.

REGULAR RUN. The transportation of travellers by an autobus or by a taxi, or of merchandise, by a delivery vehicle, on fixed days and hours, from one point to another or on a round trip.

REGULAR SCHOOL LEAVING AGE. The age at which a person is no longer required by the law of the province in which he resides to attend school.

REGULAR SERVICE. The transportation of travellers by an autobus or by a taxi, or of merchandise, by a delivery vehicle, on fixed days and hours, from one point to another or on a round trip.

REGULAR TRAIN. A train authorized by a time table schedule.

REGULAR UNION DUES. In respect of: (a) an employee who is a member of a trade union, the dues uniformly and regularly paid by a member of the union in accordance with the constitution and by-laws of the union; and (b) an employee who is not a member of a trade union, the dues referred to in paragraph (a), other than any amount that is for payment of pension, superannuation, sickness insurance or any other benefit available only to members of the union. *Labour acts.*

REGULAR WAGE. (a) The hourly wage of an employee; (b) where paid on a flat rate, piece, commission or other incentive basis, the wages of the employee in a pay period divided by the employee's total hours of work during that pay period; (c) where paid on a weekly basis, the weekly wage of the employee divided by the lesser of the employee's normal or average weekly hours of work; or (d) where paid on a monthly basis, the monthly wage of the employee multiplied by 12 and divided by the product of 52 times the lesser of the employee's normal or average weekly hours of work. *Employment Standards Act*, S.B.C. 1980, c. 10, s. 26.

REGULAR WORKING HOURS. As applied to any period means the aggregate for that period of the number of hours in each day of that period that is recognized as the normal working shift for that day in the employment in which an employee is working.

REGULATE. *v.* 1. " . . . [T]he regulation and governance of a trade may involve the imposition of restrictions on its exercise both as to time and to a certain extent as to place where such restrictions are in the opinion of the public authority necessary to prevent a nuisance or for the maintenance of order. But . . . there is a marked distinction to be drawn between the prohibition or prevention of a trade and the regulation or governance of it, indeed a power to regulate [as described in the Municipal Act, . . .] and govern seems to imply the continued existence of that which is to be regulated or governed . . . when the Legislature intended to give power to prevent or prohibit it did so by express words. . . a municipal power of regulation . . . without express words of prohibition, does not authorize the making it unlawful to carry on a lawful trade in a lawful manner." *Toronto (City) v. Virgo*, [1896] A.C. 88 at 93 (Can. P.C.), the board per Lord Davey. 2. Includes govern, control, permit, restrict, prevent, prohibit and exclude and power to prescribe conditions. 3. Includes allow, commence, stop, limit, open, shut and prohibit.

REGULATED FINANCIAL INSTITUTION. (a) A trust company incorporated in Canada; (b) a bank; (c) a treasury branch; (d) an insurance company incorporated in Canada; (e) a credit union incorporated in Canada; or (f) any other corporation approved by the Director.

REGULATED INDUSTRIES DOCTRINE. 1. A person obeying a valid provincial statute may, in certain circumstances, be exempted from the provisions of a valid federal statute. But there can be no exemption unless there is a direction or at least an authorization to perform the prohibited act. *Canada (Attorney General) v. Law Society (British Columbia)*, [1982] 2 S.C.R. 307. 2. " . . . [M]eans that a person obeying a valid provincial statute may, in certain circumstances, be exempted from the provisions of a valid federal statute. But there can be no exemption unless there is a direction or at least an authorization to perform a prohibited act." *R. v. I.O.F.*, [1989] I.L.R. 1-2420 at 9357, 32 O.A.C. 278, 26 C.P.R. (2d) 229 (C.A.), Grange J.A. (Robins and Tarnopolsky JJ.A. concurring).

REGULATED PRODUCT. A natural product of agriculture that is regulated by a commodity board or a marketing agency.

REGULATING. *adj.* Includes authorizing, controlling, inspecting, limiting and restricting.

REGULATION. *n.* 1. A rule of conduct, enacted by a regulation-making authority pursuant to an Act of Parliament, which has the force of law for an undetermined number of persons. *Reference re Language Rights*, [1992] 1 S.C.R. 212. 2. Includes an order, regulation, rule, rule of court, form, tariff of costs or fees, letters patent, commission, warrant, proclamation, by-law, resolution or other instrument issued, made or established (a) in the execution of a power conferred by or under the authority of an Act; or (b) by or under the authority of the Governor in Council. *Interpretation Act*, R.S.C. 1985, c. I-21, s. 2. 3. A regulation, order, rule, form, tariff of costs or fees, proclamation or by-law enacted (a) in the execution of a power conferred by or under the authority of an act; or (b) by or under the authority of the Lieutenant Governor in Council, but does not include an order of a court or an order made by a public officer or administrative tribunal in a dispute between two or more persons. 4. A statutory instrument (a) made in the exercise of a legislative power conferred by or under an Act of Parliament; or (b) for the contravention of which a penalty, fine or imprisonment is prescribed by or under an Act of Parliament, and includes a rule, order or regulation governing the practice or procedure in any proceedings before a judicial or quasi-judicial body established by or under an Act of Parliament, and any instrument described as a regulation in any other Act of Parliament. *Statutory Instruments Act*, R.S.C. 1985, c. S-22, s. 2. 5. A normative instrument of a general and impersonal nature, made under an Act and having force of law when it is in effect. *Regulations Act*, S.Q. 1986, c. 22, s. 1. See CHARTER AND ~S; COLLISION ~S; C.T.C. ~S; DEPARTMENT OF TRANSPORT ~S; FEDERAL ~; INTERNAL ~S; LOAD LINE ~S; PROPOSED ~; QUEEN'S ~S AND ORDERS; RADIO ~S; TONNAGE ~S.

REGULATION-MAKING AUTHORITY. Any authority authorized to make regulations and, with reference to any particular regulation or proposed regulation, means the authority that made or proposes to make the regulation.

REGULATOR. See MARINE TRAFFIC ~.

REGULATORY AGENCY. See PUBLIC ~.

REGULATORY CHARGE. Not a tax if the charge is imposed under a province's regulatory power concerning natural resources (s. 92A(1)), municipal institutions in the province (s. 92(8)), local works and undertakings (s. 92(10)), property and civil rights in the province (s. 92(13)) or matters of a merely local or private nature in the province (s. 92(16)). P.W. Hogg, *Constitutional Law of Canada*, 3d ed. (Toronto: Carswell, 1992) at 749-50.

REGULATORY OFFENCE. "Category of offences created by statutes enacted for the regulation of individual conduct in the interests of health, convenience, safety and general welfare of the public which are not subject to the common law presumption of mens rea as an essential element to be proven by the Crown." *R. v. Wholesale Travel Group Inc.* (1991), 8 C.R. (4th) 145 at 160, 67 C.C.C. (3d) 193, 4 O.R. (3d) 799n, 84 D.L.R. (4th) 161, 130 N.R. 1, 38 C.P.R. (3d) 451, 49 O.A.C. 161, [1991] 3 S.C.R. 154, 7 C.R.R. (2d) 36, Cory J. (L Heureux-Dubé J. concurring).

REHABILITATE. *v.* 1. To treat land from which aggregate has been excavated so that the use or condition of the land, (a) is restored to its former use or condition, or (b) is changed to another use or condition that is or will be compatible with the use of adjacent land. *Aggregate Resources Act*, R.S.O. 1990, c. A.8, s. 1. 2. To restore to former rank, right or privilege. 3. To qualify again. 4. To restore a lost right.

REHABILITATION. *n*. 1. The establishment or the restoration of a disabled person to a state of economic and social sufficiency. 2. One of the principles applied in sentencing individuals convicted of offences. The goal is to rehabilitate the offender. See FINAL ~; PRAIRIE FARM ~ ADMINISTRATION; PROGRESSIVE ~; SENTENCING; VOCATIONAL ~.

REHABILITATION CENTRE. See FUNCTIONAL ~.

REHABILITATION PROGRAM. A program designed to improve the environmental, housing or living conditions of or in a blighted or substandard area. *Alberta Mortgage and Housing Corporation Act*, S.A. 1984, c. A-32.5, s. 1.

REHANDLING. See CONTAINER ~ CHARGE.

RE-HEARING. *n*. 1. Presentation of evidence and argument and the pronunciation of a second judgment in a cause or matter which was already decided. 2. It is perfectly true that an appeal is by way of rehearing; but it must not be forgotten that the Court of Appeal does not rehear the witnesses. It only reads the evidence and rehears the counsel. Neither is it a reseeing court. There are different meanings to be attached to the word 'rehearing'. *Powell v. Streatham Manor Nursing Home*, [1935] A.C. 243 (U.K. H.L.), at p. 249, Viscount Sankey, L.C.

REID VAPOUR PRESSURE. The vapour pressure of gasoline or an associated product at 37.8°C. or 100°F.

REIMBURSEMENT. *n*. 1. Indemnification through repayment to someone of an expense or loss incurred; repayment; refund. Generally involves the intervention of a third person. 2. "In all examples of the word reimbursement there exists a flow of benefits between the respective parties. The person who benefits is under a legal obligation to pay back the amount expended." *Westcoast Energy Inc. v. R., (sub nom. Westcoast Energy Inc. v. Minister of National Revenue)* [1991] F.C. 302 at 319, 91 D.T.C. 5334, [1991] 1 C.T.C. 471, 41 F.T.R. 165, Denault J.

REINDEER. *n*. Deer of the species Rangifer tarandus, native of Northern Europe, or the race Rangifer arcticus asiaticus, native of Northern Asia.

REINFORCED MASONRY. Masonry in which steel reinforcement is embedded in such a manner that the two materials act together in resisting forces.

REINSTATE. *v*. In an insurance policy, to restore buildings or chattels which have been damaged.

REINSTATEMENT. *n*. A remedy available when a labour board proves a claim of unfair dismissal against an employer. It requires that the employer act as though the employee had never been dismissed.

REINSURANCE. *n*. 1. An agreement whereby contracts made by a licensed insurer or any class or group thereof are undertaken or reinsured by another insurer either by novation, transfer, assignment or as a result of amalgamation of the insurers. 2. New insurance under a new policy upon the same risk, which may be in wider or narrower form and which was insured before, that indemnifies the insurer from previous liability. Raoul Colinvaux, *The Law of Insurance*, 5th ed. (London: Sweet & Maxwell, 1984) at 186. See EXCESS OF LOSS ~; FACULTATIVE ~; TREATY ~.

REINSURANCE AGREEMENT. An agreement for reinsurance between the Minister and a province pursuant to subparagraph 3(b)(ii). *Crop Insurance Act*, R.S.C. 1985, c. C-48, s. 2.

REINSURER. *n*. An insurer that, at the request of another insurer, reinsures a risk or part of it that is insured by that other insurer. *Insurance Amendment Act, 1981*, S.A. 1981, c. 49, s. 34.1.

REINTEGRATION LEAVE. Leave granted from a youth custody facility for medical, humanitarian, rehabilitative or reintegrative purposes.

REIT. *abbr*. Real estate investment trust.

REJECT. *v*. To refuse to accept (a statement).

REJECTED BALLOT PAPER. A ballot paper that has been handed by the deputy returning officer to an elector to mark, but, at the close of the poll, has been found in the ballot box unmarked or so improperly marked that it cannot be counted.

REJECTED MATERIAL. Displaced overburden, waste rock, liquid or solid residues and waste matter from mining operations.

REJECTED MATERIALS MANAGEMENT SYSTEM. The aggregate of administrative and technical operations for the removal, haulage, storage, milling and permanent deposit of the tailings of mining, and the moveable and immoveable property allocated to such purposes.

REJOINDER. *n*. The defendant's answer to the plaintiff's reply.

RELATE. *v*. To stand in relation to; to pertain to; to refer to; to concern.

RELATED. *adj*. Having relation to or relationship with something else; concerning, referring, or pertaining to something else.

RELATED COMPANIES. Companies that are members of a group of two or more companies one of which, directly or indirectly, owns or controls a majority of the issued voting stock of the others.

RELATED GROUP. 1. A group of persons each member of which is related to every other member of the group. 2. A group of individuals each member of which is connected to at least one other member of the group by blood relationship, marriage or adoption. *Corporations and Labour Unions Returns Act*, R.S.C. 1985, c. C-43, s. 2.

RELATED INDIVIDUAL. A spouse, parent, child, grandparent, grandchild, greatgrandparent, greatgrandchild, mother-in-law, father-in-law, grandmother-in-law, grandfather-in-law, greatgrandmother-in-law, greatgrandfather-in-law, daughter-in-law, son-in-law, granddaughter-in-law, grandson-in-law, greatgranddaughter-in-law or greatgrandson-in-law.

RELATED MUTUAL FUNDS. Includes more than one mutual fund under common management.

RELATED PERSON. Where used to indicate a relationship with any person, means: (a) any spouse, son or daughter of that person; (b) any relative of the person or of that person's spouse, other than a relative referred to in subparagraph (a) who has the same home as the person; or (c) any body corporate of which the person and any of the persons referred to in subparagraphs (a) or (b) or the partner or employer of the person, either alone or in combination, beneficially owns, directly or indirectly, voting securities carrying more than 50 per cent of the voting rights attached to all voting securities of the body corporate for the time being outstanding.

RELATED PERSON OR COMPANY. In relation to a mutual fund, a person in whom or a company in which, the mutual fund, its management company and its distribution company are prohibited from making any investment.

RELATED PERSONS. Persons are related to each other and are "related persons" if they are (a) individuals connected by blood relationship, marriage or adoption; (b) a corporation and (i) a person who controls the corporation, if it is controlled by one person; (ii) a person who is a member of a related group that controls the corporation; or (iii) any person connected in the manner set out in paragraph (a) to a person described in subparagraph (i) or (ii); or (c) two corporations (i) controlled by the same person or group of persons; (ii) each of which is controlled by one person and the person who controls one of the corporations is related to the person who controls the other corporation; (iii) one of which is controlled by one person and that person is related to any member of a related group that controls the other corporation; (iv) one of which is controlled by one person and that person is related to each member of an unrelated group that controls the other corporation; (v) any member of a related group that controls one of the corporations is related to each member of an unrelated group that controls the other corporation; or (vi) each member of an unrelated group that controls one of the corporations is related to at least one member of an unrelated group that controls the other corporation.

RELATED SALE. With reference to a sales contract, means a sale of goods that is related to the sales contract or is made in connection with or is incidental to the sales contract, whether as an inducement to enter into the sales contract or not and whether made before, at or after the making of the sales contract, and whether it is made with the seller under the sales contract or not.

RELATION. *n*. 1. Next-of-kin of any degree. 2. A doctrine by which an act produces the same effect as it would have if it had happened at an earlier time. See CONFIDENTIAL ~; INDUSTRIAL ~S; LABOUR ~S.

RELATIONAL CONTRACT. "[Governs a] . . . long-term, often multi-party, [arrangement] which [is] realistically, not expected to anticipate all possibilities, but rather, to provide a framework and the terms of reference for the parties' reasonable expectation of their future relationship over an extended period of time. . ." *Miracle Food Mart v. U.F.C.W., Locals 175 &*

633 (1990), 17 L.A.C. (4th) 165 at 182 (Ont.), Marszewski.

RELATIONAL ECONOMIC LOSS. Pure economic loss suffered by a plaintiff as a result of physical injury or property damage to a third party.

RELATIONAL LOSS. A loss which arises from a relationship to the injured party and not directly from injury. *Canadian National Railway v. Norsk Pacific Steamship Co.* (1992), 11 C.C.L.T. (2d) 1 at 43-4, 137 N.R. 241, 91 D.L.R. (4th) 289, [1992] 1 S.C.R. 1021, 53 F.T.R. 79n, Stevenson J.

RELATIONSHIP. See BLOOD ~.

RELATIONSHIP OF INTERDEPENDENCE. A relationship outside marriage in which any 2 persons (i) share one another's lives, (ii) are emotionally committed to one another, and (iii) function as an economic and domestic unit. *Adult Interdependent Relationships Act*, S.A. 2002, c. A-4.5, s. 1(1).

RELATIVE. *n*. 1. " . . . [C]ommonly understood to refer to a relation of consanguinity, close or distant, and to a legally recognized affinity created, for instance, by marriage or adoption." *Leroux v. Co-operators General Insurance Co.* (1990), 44 C.C.L.I. 253 at 259, [1990] I.L.R. 1-2566, 65 D.L.R. (4th) 702, 71 O.R. (2d) 641 (H.C.), Arbour J. 2. A husband, wife, father, mother, grandfather, grandmother, father-in-law or step-father, mother-in-law or step-mother, brother, sister, brother-in-law, sister-in-law, son, daughter, grandson, granddaughter, son-in-law or daughter-in-law or for the members of a community, the superior or his duly authorized delegate. *Election Act*, R.S.Q. 1977, c. E03, s. 2. 3. When used in reference to a child, means the child's grandparent, great-uncle, great-aunt, uncle or aunt, whether by blood, marriage or adoption. *Child and Family Services Act*, R.S.O. 1990, c. C.11, s. 136(1). 4. A person related by blood, marriage or adoption. *Child Welfare Act*, R.S. Nfld. 1990, c. C-12, s. 2. See BIRTH ~; COLLATERAL ~; DEPENDENT ~ REVOCATION; NEAREST ~; NEAR ~.

RELATIVE EXPERTISE. Of an administrative tribunal, recognizes that legislatures will sometimes remit an issue to a decision-making body that has particular topical expertise or is adept in the determination of particular issues. Where this is so, courts will seek to respect this legislative choice when conducting judicial review. *Q. v. College of Physicians & Surgeons (British Columbia)*, [2003] 1 S.C.R. 226.

RELATIVOSUM, COGNITO UNO, COGNISCITUR ET ALTERUM. [L.] Concerning related things, if one is known the other is known too.

RELATOR. *n*. 1. One who rehearses, tells or informs. 2. A person, other than the Attorney General, by whom proceedings are taken under this Act. *Crown Franchise Act*, R.S.B.C. 1979, c. 85, s. 1.

RELATOR ACTION. An action in which a relator seeks an injunction to prevent any interfering with or infringing of a public right, to stop a public nuisance or to force a public duty to be performed or observed. The relator brings this action in the Attorney-General's name after obtaining leave to do so.

RELAY DISTRIBUTION UNDERTAKING. A distribution undertaking that receives the programming services of radio or television programming undertakings and distributes them only to one or more other distribution undertakings. *Broadcasting Distribution Regulations*, SOR/97-555, s. 1.

RE-LAYING. *n*. With respect to shellfish, means the moving of shellfish from a contaminated area to an approved area for the purpose of natural biological cleansing.

RELEASE. *v*. 1. In relation to any information, document, recording or statement, means to communicate, disclose or make available the information, document, recording or statement. 2. Includes spilling, leaking, pumping, spraying, pouring, emitting, emptying, throwing or dumping. 3. In respect of goods, means to authorize the removal of the goods from a customs office, sufferance warehouse, bonded warehouse or duty free shop for use in Canada.

RELEASE. *n*. 1. The termination of the service of an officer or non-commissioned member in any manner. *National Defence Act*, R.S.C. 1985, c. N-5, s. 2(1). 2. A document issued by the Court which releases property arrested by warrant. See CAVEAT ~; LOW-VOLTAGE ~; WORK ~.

RELEASE DATE. See PRESUMPTIVE ~; RIG ~.

RELEASEE. *n*. The person to whom one makes a release.

RELEASOR. *n*. One who makes a release.

RELEVANCE. 1. In its narrow sense, relevance means that the evidence is so related to a fact in issue that it tends to establish it. The evidence proffered here is circumstantial evidence tending to establish identity and is clearly relevant in the narrow sense. The broader meaning given to relevance in [*R. v. Mohan*, 89 C.C.C. (3d) 402, [1994] 2 S.C.R. 9, 114 D.L.R. (4th) 419] requires what the court described as a "cost benefit analysis". Logically relevant evidence may be excluded if its probative value is overborne by its prejudicial effect. The evidence may prove to be misleading, in the sense that its effect on the jury will be out of proportion to its reliability. *R. v. Murrin* (1999), 1999 CarswellBC 3015, 181 D.L.R. (4th) 320, 32 C.R. (5th) 97 (S.C.). 2. In the context of Crown disclosure obligations in a criminal case, information ought not to be withheld if there is a reasonable possibility that the withholding of information will impair the right of the accused to make full answer and defence, unless the non-disclosure is justified by the law of privilege. *R. v. Chaplin* (1994), [1995] 1 S.C.R. 727.

RELEVANCY. *n*. Relationship to that which is the subject of the action.

RELEVANT. *adj*. The basic rule is that all relevant evidence is admissible. Relevance depends directly on the facts in issue in any particular case. The facts in issue are in turn determined by the charge in the indictment and the defence, if any, raised by the accused. To be logically relevant, an item of evidence does not have to firmly establish, on any standard, the truth or falsity of a fact in issue. The evidence must simply tend to "increase or diminish the probability of the existence of a fact in issue". *R. v. Arp*, [1998] 3 S.C.R. 339.

RELEVANT EVIDENCE. Evidence relating to a fact in issue at the trial, and includes evidence that tends to establish the cogency or accuracy of either direct or circumstantial evidence. *Military Rules of Evidence*, C.R.C., c. 1049, s. 2.

RELIABILITY. The requirement of reliability for admissibility of hearsay evidence will be satisfied where the hearsay statement was made in circumstances which provide sufficient guarantees of its trustworthiness. In particular, the circumstances must counteract the traditional evidentiary dangers associated with hearsay. *R. v. Hawkins*, [1996] 3 S.C.R. 1043.

RELICT. *n*. A surviving spouse.

RELICTION. *n*. The sudden receding of sea from the land.

RELIEF. *n*. 1. Remedy. 2. The end result of civil litigation sought by a plaintiff. 3. Alleviation of the consequences of default. 4. Includes every species of relief, whether by way of damages, payment of money, injunction, declaration, restitution of an incorporeal right, return of land or chattels or otherwise. See ANCILLARY ~; COROLLARY ~; CREDITORS' ~ STATUTE; DECLARATORY ~; INTERIM ~; PRAYER FOR ~.

RELIEF AGAINST FORFEITURE. In an appropriate and limited case a court of equity will grant this relief for breach of a condition or covenant when the main object of the deal was to secure a certain result and provision for forfeiture was added to secure that result. F. Bennett, *Receiverships* (Toronto: Carswell, 1985) at 355.

RELIEF EMPLOYEE. An employee engaged to fill a position on a temporary basis as a replacement for the regular incumbent.

RELIEF GRANT. Payment generally made under unusual or anomalous situations and connotes assistance freely given to the destitute.

RELIEF OVER. "[In Ontario Rules of Practice; r. 165-170] . . . In order to claim 'relief over' under those Rules and within the intention thereof, it must appear that the measure of damages in the proceedings as between the defendant and the proposed third party is the measure of damages as between the plaintiff and the defendant." *Drabik v. Harris*, [1955] O. W.N. 590 at 591 (C.A.), the court per Laidlaw J.A.

RELIEF VENT. A vent pipe discharging into a vent stack and connected to a horizontal branch between the first fixture connection and the soil stack or waste stack. *Ontario Water Resources Act*, R.R.O. 1980, Reg. 736, s. 1.

RELIGION. See FREEDOM OF CONSCIENCE AND ~; FREEDOM OF ~.

RELIGIOUS AUXILIARY. A corporation, society, committee, or other organization, that is sponsored, organized, established or set up by a religious denomination and controlled or supervised by, and operated as an instrument or auxiliary of, and in close connection with, that religious denomination. *Cemeteries acts*.

RELIGIOUS BODY. Any church, or any religious denomination, sect, congregation or society.

RELIGIOUS COMMUNICATIONS PRIV-ILEGE. A privilege attached to communications between a confessor and her priest or to other adherents to a religion and their religious adviser.

RELIGIOUS DENOMINATION. An organized society, association, or body, of religious believers or worshippers professing to believe in the same religious doctrines, dogmas, or creed and closely associated or organized for religious worship or discipline, or both.

RELIGIOUS ORDER. Members of a religious community distinct from a secular one.

RELIGIOUS ORGANIZATION. 1. An association of persons, (a) that is charitable according to the law of Ontario, (b) that is organized for the advancement of religion and for the conduct of religious worship, services or rites, and (c) that is permanently established both as to the continuity of its existence and as to its religious beliefs, rituals and practices, and includes an association of persons that is charitable according to the law of Ontario and that is organized for the advancement of and for the conduct of worship, services or rites of the Buddhist, Christian, Hindu, Islamic, Jewish, Baha'i, Longhouse Indian, Sikh, Unitarian or Zoroastrian faith, or a subdivision or denomination thereof. *Religious Organizations' Lands Act*, R.S.O. 1990, c. R.23, s. 1(1). 2. An organization, other than a registered charity, of which a congregation is a constituent part, that adheres to beliefs, evidenced by the religious and philosophical tenets of the organization, that include a belief in the existence of a supreme being. *Tax acts*.

RELIGIOUS SOCIETY. A church, congregation, or other religious society of persons professing or adhering to a religion or religious faith. *Religious Societies' Lands Act*, R.S.M. 1987, c. R70, s. 1.

RELINQUISHMENT. *n*. Giving up, forsaking.

RELIQUA. *n*. [L.] After an account is balanced or liquidated, the remainder or debt which a person still owes.

RELOCATABLE STRUCTURE. A factory built unit which can be used for residential, commercial, industrial or recreational purposes without a permanent foundation.

RELOCATE. *v*. With respect to a worker, means the transfer of the worker, dependants and his or her movable effects to a locality in which he or she has obtained suitable employment.

RELOCATION. See BUILDING ~; HOME ~ LOAN.

RELY. *v*. To be influenced by.

REM. *n*. 1. A dose of ionizing radiation that has the same biological effects as 200-250 kilovolt X-rays whose energy is absorbed by the body or any tissue or organ thereof in an amount of .01 joule per kilogram. 2. [L.] Objective case of "res", meaning thing.

REM. *abbr*. Remanet.

REMAIN. See CREMATED ~S; HUMAN ~S; SKELETAL ~S.

REMAINDER. *n*. That part of a grantor's interest in an estate which is disposed of, but which is postponed to some estate in possession created at the same time. R. Megarry and H.W.R. Wade, *The Law of Real Property*, 5th ed. (London: Stevens, 1984) at 236 and cxxvii. See CONTINGENT ~; VESTED ~.

REMAINDERED BOOK. A book (a) that is sold by the publisher for less than the cost of paper, printing and binding; or (b) that is sold at a reduced price by the publisher and for which the author or copyright owner receives no royalty. *Book Importation Regulations*, SOR/99-324, s. 1.

REMAINDERMAN. *n*. 1. A person who is entitled to the remainder of an estate after some part of that estate has expired or has been extracted. For example, the person who inherits after a life estate is ended. 2. A person with rightful claim to an expectant estate.

REMAIN SILENT. See RIGHT TO ~.

REMAND. *v*. To adjourn a hearing to a future date, ordering the defendant, unless permitted bail, to be kept in the meantime in custody.

REMAND CENTRE. A correctional centre.

REMAND PRISONER. A prisoner (a) remanded in custody by a judge or court; and (b) awaiting trial, or the resumption or conclusion of a trial, for contravention of an Act of the Parliament of Canada or a legislature or of any regulations or order made pursuant to any such act.

REMANENT PRO DEFECTU EMPTO-RUM. [L. they are left on my hands for want of buyers] A return concerning goods taken under a fieri facias which a sheriff makes in certain cases.

REMANET. *n*. [L.] 1. Whatever remains. 2. An action, scheduled for trial in a certain session, which does not come on so that it stands over to the next session.

REMANET IN CUSTODIA. [L.] One remains in custody.

REM. CUSTOD *abbr*. Remanet in custodia.

REMEDIAL CONSTRUCTIVE TRUST. " . . . [T]he acts of the parties are such that a wrong is done by one of them to another so that, while no substantive trust relationship is then and there brought into being by those acts, nonetheless a remedy is required in relation to property and the court grants that remedy in the form of a declaration which, when the order is made, creates a constructive trust by one of the parties in favour of another party. . . A remedial constructive trust is a trust imposed by Court order as a remedy for a wrong . . . the trust itself [is created] by the order of the Court." *Atlas Cabinets & Furniture Ltd. v. National Trust Co*. (1990), 37 E.T.R. 16 at 27, 38 C.L.R. 106, 45 B.C.L.R. (2d) 99, 68 D.L.R. (4th) 161 (C.A.), Lambert J.A. (Hinkson, Toy and Cumming JJ.A. concurring).

REMEDIAL STATUTE. A statute drafted to remedy a defect in the law.

REMEDIATE. *v*. To remove, eliminate, limit, correct, counteract, or mitigate the negative effects on the environment or human health of one or more contaminants.

REMEDIATION. *n*. Action to eliminate, limit, correct, counteract, mitigate or remove any contaminant or the adverse effects on the environment or human health of any contaminant.

REMEDY. *n*. 1. The means by which one prevents, redresses or compensates the violation of a right. 2. Cure for a default. See APPRAISAL ~; APPROPRIATE AND JUST ~; CONSTITUTIONAL ~; CUMULATIVE ~; DISCRETIONARY ~; EQUITY WILL NOT SUFFER A WRONG TO BE WITHOUT A ~; EXTRAORDINARY ~; MUTUALITY OF ~.

REMEDY CLAUSE. Section 24(1) of the Charter, which allows a remedy to be granted to enforce the rights or freedoms the Charter guarantees. P.W. Hogg, *Constitutional Law of Canada*, 3d ed. (Toronto: Carswell, 1992) at 915 .

REMEMBRANCE DAY. November 11, being the day in the year 1918 on which the Great War was triumphantly concluded by an armistice, is a holiday and shall be kept and observed as such throughout Canada. *Holidays Act*, R.S.C. 1985, c. H-5, s. 3.

REMINISCENCE EFFECT. [A forensic psychologist's] testimony included evidence of the reminiscence effect by which recall of a person may increase with time as a person reflects on the memory. *R. v. N. (E.A.)*, 2000 CarswellBC 274, 2000 BCCA 61, 135 B.C.A.C. 154, 221 W.A.C. 154 (C.A.).

REMISE. *v*. To release; to surrender; to return.

REMISSION. *n*. 1. A release; a pardon. 2. A decrease in the length of imprisonment. 3. Every prisoner serving a sentence, other than a sentence on conviction for criminal or civil contempt of court where the sentence includes a requirement that the prisoner return to that court, shall be credited with fifteen days of remission of the sentence in respect of each month and with a number of days calculated on a *pro rata* basis in respect of each incomplete month during which the prisoner has earned that remission by obeying prison rules and conditions governing temporary absence and by actively participating in programs, other than full parole, designed to promote prisoners' rehabilitation and reintegration. *Prisons and Reformatories Act*, R.S.C. 1985, c. P-20, s. 6. See EARNED ~.

REMIT. *v*. To send back.

REMITMENT. *n*. The act of sending back into custody.

REMITTANCE. *n*. Money which one person sends to another. See POSTAL ~.

REMITTEE. *n*. The person to whom one sends a remittance.

REM JUDICATAM. See ESTOPPEL PER ~.

REMORSE. *n*. Feeling of deep regret for wrong done. Can be a justification for leniency in sentencing.

REMOTE AGREEMENT. A consumer agreement entered into when the consumer and supplier are not present together. *Consumer Protection Act, 2002*, S.O. 2002, c. 30, s. 20.

REMOTE CONTROL CIRCUIT. Any electrical circuit which controls any other circuit through a relay or an equivalent device.

REMOTENESS. *n*. 1. Lack of close relation between a wrong and damages. 2. "In Koufos v. C. Czarnikow (The Heron II), [1969] 1 A.C. 350

... [(U.K.H.L.)] ... it was determined that the proper test for remoteness [for recovery of damages for breach of contract] was not the 'reasonable forseeability' of the head of damages claimed as in an action in tort, but whether the probability of the occurrence of the damage in the event of breach should have been within the reasonable contemplation of the contracting parties at the time of the entry into the contract. (Vide Brown & Root Ltd. v. Chimo Shipping Ltd., [1967] S.C.R. 642 per Ritchie J. at p. 648 ..." *Baud Corp., N.V., v. Brook* (1978), (*sub nom. Asamera Oil Corp. v. Sea Oil & General Corp.*) 5 B.L.R. 225 at 237, [1979] 1 S.C.R. 633 [1987-8] 6 W.W.R. 301, 23 N.R. 181, 12 A.R. 271, 89 D.L.R. (3d) 1, the court per Estey J.

REMOTO IMPEDIMENTO EMERGIT ACTIO. [L.] Once the impediment is removed, action emerges.

REMOVAL ORDER. A departure order, an exclusion order or a deportation order. *Immigration Act*, R.S.C. 1985, c. I-2, s. 2.

REMOVE. *v.* To take, move or transport.

REMOVEABLE DEVICES. Detachable dental prostheses to replace natural teeth. *Dental Act*, R.S.Q. 1977, c. D-3, s. 27.

REMOVER. *n.* The transfer of a cause or suit from one court to another.

REMUNERATION. *n.* 1. Payment for services provided. *Sheridan v. Minister of National Revenue* (1985), 57 N.R. 69 at 74, 85 C.L.L.C. 14,048 (Fed. C.A.), the court per Heald J.A. 2. Includes a daily or other allowance for the performance of the duties of a position or office. 3. Includes salary, wages, commissions, tips, earnings for overtime, piece work, and contract work, bonuses and allowances, the cash equivalent of board and lodging, store certificates, credits and any substitute for money. 4. Includes fuel and ships' stores of any kind or any other kind of payment or compensation. *Canada Shipping Act*, R.S.C. 1985, c. S-9, s. 2. 5. Includes a commission or any direct or indirect benefit, any promise of or intention to obtain a remuneration. See FOR ~; ORDINARY ~; PENSIONABLE ~.

RENDER. *v.* To give again; to yield; to return.

RENDERING PLANT. A place (a) where animal by-products are prepared or treated for use in, or converted into, fertilizers, animal food, fats or oils, other than fats or oils used for human consumption, (b) where a substance resulting from a process mentioned in paragraph (a) is stored, packed or marked, or (c) from which a substance resulting from a process mentioned in paragraph (a) is shipped. *Health of Animals Act*, S.C. 1990, c. 21, s. 2(1).

RENDITION. *n.* The surrender of a suspect or convict by international arrangement.

RENEW. *v.* " ... [T]o grant anew ..." *G., Re* (1976), 30 R.F.L. 224 at 227 (N.B. C.A.), the court per Hughes C.J.

RENEWABLE LEASE. A lease containing a covenant by which an option is given to the lessor to renew or extend a term of years as an alternative to payment to the tenant for such improvements as the latter is entitled to be compensated for under the terms of the lease. *Landlord and Tenant Act*, R.S.N.B. 1973, c. L-1, s. 49.

RENEWABLE RESOURCE INDUSTRY. The fishing industry, forestry industry and the agricultural industry in the province. *Health and Post-Secondary Education Tax Act*, R.S. Nfld. 1990, c. H-1, s. 3(9).

RENEWAL. *n.* 1. Refers to the revival of an agreement which has expired, not to extension of an existing agreement. *Manulife Bank of Canada v. Conlin*, [1996] 3 S.C.R. 415. 2 " ... [T]he more 'standard' meaning is the one that assumes the continued existence of the matter 'renewed'. If it is not in existence then the process is really one of recreation rather than renewal. Further, in a general legal context concerned with the renewal of rights, privileges and other interests, conferred under instruments such as leases, contracts and licences, it is, I think, a general understanding that renewal involves the temporal extension of something that is in existence and not the revival of something that has ceased to exist." *R. v. Pleich* (1980), 55 C.C.C. (2d) 13 at 28, 16 C.R. (3d) 194 (Ont. C.A.), the court per Morden J.A. 3. In respect of a lease, includes the extension of the lease and the exercise of any option to continue the lease. *Customs and Excise Offshore Application Act*, R.S.C. 1985, c. C-53, s. 2. 4. Two separate meanings can be ascribed to a "renewal" of an insurance policy. The first meaning results from a continuous policy. Such policies provide for further extensions to the term of an existing contract, subject to the rights of either of the parties to terminate the contract. In a single continuous policy, questions of formation are answered by reference to the original offer and acceptance that initiated the coverage.

By contrast, the other meaning of a "renewal" of an insurance policy involves the situation where a separate and distinct contract comes into existence at each renewal. Automobile insurance renewals fall into the latter category, in that each renewal represents a new contract with its own offer and acceptance. *Patterson v. Gallant*, [1994] 3 S.C.R. 1080. See AUTOMATIC ~; URBAN ~.

RENEWAL AREA. See URBAN ~.

RENEWAL SCHEME. A plan for the renewal of a blighted or substandard area in a municipality See URBAN ~.

RENEWAL STUDY. A study of conditions to identify blighted or substandard areas of a municipality and to recommend required renewal action. See URBAN ~.

RENEWED. *adj*. 1. "[In the context of beneficiary certificates under the Insurance Corporation Act is] . . . applicable to the case of lapsed or forfeited certificates which, perhaps by a new contract inter partes . . . or otherwise, are reinstated." *Long v. Ancient Order of United Workmen* (1891), 25 O.A.R. 147 at 158, Osler J.A. (McLennan and Moss JJ.A. concurring). 2. . . . [M]eant to indicate the keeping alive of the insurance by receipts for premiums." *Cousins v. Moore* (1912), 6 D.L.R. 35 at 44, 42 Que. K.B. 156 (S.C.), Archibald J.

RENOUNCE. *v*. 1. Of a right, to give up. 2. Of probate, for an executor to decline to take probate of a will.

RENOVANT. *adj*. Making new.

RENOVATOR. *n*. Any person who repairs, renovates or alters an upholstered or stuffed article.

RENT. *v*. To let. *Daugherty v. Armaly* (1921), 58 D.L.R. 380 at 382, 49 O.L.R. 310, 19 O.W.N. 573 (C.A.), the court per Meredith C.J.O.

RENT. *n*. 1. " . . . [T]he compensation which a tenant of the land or other corporeal hereditament makes to the owner for the use thereof. It is frequently treated as a profit arising out of the demised land. . ." *Johnson v. British Canadian Insurance Co.*, [1932] S.C.R. 680 at 684, [1932] 4 D.L.R. 281, Lamont J. 2. Includes consideration, whether in money, services or goods, paid, given or agreed to be paid or given by a tenant to a landlord in respect of residential premises including consideration for a privilege, benefit, service, facility or other thing provided, directly or indirectly, by a landlord to a tenant that relates to the use, occupation or enjoyment of residential premises. 3. Rent service, rent charge, and rent seck, and all periodical payments or renderings in lieu or in the nature of rent. *Apportionment acts* 4. Includes any sum payable for the use of a telecommunication service. 5. Includes all annuities and periodical sums of money charged upon or payable out of land. *Limitations Act*, R.S.O. 1990, c. L.15, s. 1. 6. Includes the amount of any consideration paid or given or required to be paid or given by or on behalf of a tenant to a landlord or the landlord's agent for the right to occupy a rental unit and for any services and facilities and any privilege, accommodation or thing that the landlord provides for the tenant in respect of the occupancy of the rental unit, whether or not a separate charge is made for services and facilities or for the privilege, accommodation or thing. *Tenant Protection Act, 1997*, S.O. 1997, c. 24, s. 1, part. See BASIC UNIT ~; CHRONICALLY DEPRESSED ~; DEAD ~; DOUBLE ~; DRY ~; GROUND ~; MAXIMUM ~; OCCUPATION ~; PEPPERCORN ~; QUIT ~; RACK ~.

RENTAL HOUSING PROJECT. A housing project occupied or intended to be occupied primarily by a person other than the owner.

RENTAL OFFICE SPACE. Includes office space that is in a fixed location and office space that is in a structure that may be moved from place to place. *Legislative Assembly Act*, R.S.A. 1980, c. L-10, s. 54.

RENTAL PAYMENT PERIOD. The interval in respect of which rent is payable under a tenancy agreement, but notwithstanding any agreement to the contrary, no rental payment period shall exceed 1 month. *Landlord and Tenant acts*.

RENTAL PERIOD. The interval for which rent is paid. *Residential Tenancies Act*, R.S. Nfld.1990, c. R-14, s. 2.

RENTAL PROPERTY. Property which is rented, is available for rent or was rented when last occupied. *Rental Property Conversion Act*, R.S.N.S. 1989, c. 399, s. 2.

RENTAL RESIDENTIAL PROPERTY. A building or related group of buildings containing one or more rental units but does not include a condominium. *Rental Housing Protection Act*, S.O. 1986, c. 26, s. 1.

RENTALSMAN. *n*. The Rentalsman appointed. *Residential Tenancies acts*.

RENTAL UNIT. Any living accommodations, site for a mobile home or site on which a single family dwelling is a permanent structure used or intended for use as rented residential premises and includes a room in a boarding house or lodging house.

RENTAL VALUE. 1. " . . . [T]he amount of rent which can be obtained for the property, unless there are actual facts connected with same which give it an additional value." *Imperial Oil Ltd. v. Winnipeg (City)*, [1941] 2 W.W.R. 447 at 452 (Man. K.B.), McPherson C.J.K.B. 2. " . . . [S]omething to be assessed for each year; it depends a little, but not much, on long term rental values, and [certainly] is not necessarily determined by the fee simple value of the premises." *W.S. Newton & Co. v. Winnipeg (City)*, [1937] 3 D.L.R. 446 at 447, [1937] 3 W.W.R. 351, 45 Man. R. 258 (K.B.), Dysart J. See NET ~.

RENT CHARGE. A right to receive a periodic sum from land together with the right to use distress to remedy non-payment.

RENT-GEARED-TO-INCOME ASSIS-TANCE. Financial assistance provided in respect of a household under a housing program to reduce the amount the household must otherwise pay to occupy a unit in a housing project.

RENT-GEARED-TO-INCOME UNIT. A unit in a housing project that either is occupied by a household receiving rent-geared-to-income assistance or is available for occupancy by a household eligible for rent-geared-to-income assistance.

RENT PERIOD. The interval at which rent is paid.

RENT RECEIPT. A receipt that is issued to a tenant by a landlord or is endorsed by the landlord, that indicates the amount of rent paid, or the nature and the landlord's evaluation of rent provided by way of services, by the tenant to the landlord in respect of his principal residence for any time period up to one year and that includes: (a) the name of the tenant; (b) the address of the tenant's principal residence; (c) the name and address of the landlord; (d) the amount of rent and the rate at which it is paid or provided; and (e) the time period in respect of which the rent receipt is issued.

RENT REDUCTION FUND. A fund to which contributions, donations, gifts and bequests may be made by the government of a province or by a municipality, social agency, foundation, trust, estate or person for the purpose of reducing the rental of a family housing unit to permit it to be occupied by a family of low income. *National Housing Act*, R.S.C. 1985, c. N-11, s. 2.

RENT SECK. A rent charge with no cause of distress.

RENUNCIATION. " . . . [O]f a contract may be express or implied. A party to a contract may state before the time of performance that he will not, or cannot, perform his obligations. This is tantamount to an express renunciation. On the other hand, a renunciation will be implied if the conduct of a party is such as to lead a reasonable person to the conclusion that he will not perform, or will not be able to perform, when the time for performance arises." *McCallum v. Zivojinovic* (1977), 16 O.R. (2d) 721 at 723, 2 R.P.R. 164, 26 Chitty's L.J. 169, 79 D.L.R. (3d) 133 (C.A.), the court per Howland J.A. See CERTIFICATE OF ~.

RENVOI. *n*. When one determines, by the appropriate choice of law rule, that the questionable issue may be decided according to "the law" of a certain country, the court must decide whether the term "the law" refers to the internal domestic law of that country or to its conflict of laws rules as well. This concept is not firmly entrenched in Canadian law. J.G. McLeod, *The Conflict of Laws* (Calgary: Carswell, 1983) at 198 and 201.

REOPENING CLAUSE. A clause providing for the reopening of negotiations during the term of the collective agreement.

REORGANIZATION. *n*. 1. A court order made under (a) a Corporations Act; (b) the Bankruptcy Act approving a proposal; or (c) any other act that affects the rights among the corporation, its shareholders and creditors. 2. Changes within a company in the way in which different parts of the company relate to one another and changes in the size and objects of the company.

REPAIR. *v*. 1. "[R]estoration to a previously designed or constructed state. . ." *Fry v. Henry* (1985), 64 A.R. 304 at 305 (C.A.), the court per Laycraft C.J.A. 2. " . . . [A]s was pointed out in Foley v. East Flamborough, (1898), 29 O.R. 139 (H.C.), at p. 141 'repair' is a relative term and in Town of Oakville v. Cranston, (1916), 10 O.W.N. 315, at p. 316 (C.A.) . . . Meredith C.J.C.P. said: 'In all cases the question should be—is the road in a reasonable state of repair having regard to the needs of the traffic over it and the means at the disposal of the municipality for the repair of all its roads.'" *Wilson v. Progress (Municipal District)* (1921), 59 D.L.R. 413 at 414, [1921] 2 W.W.R. 1121, 16 Alta. L.R. 265 (C.A.), the court per Harvey C.J. 3. Includes the provision of such facilities and the making of additions or alterations or the taking of such action as may be required so that the property shall conform with the standards established in a by-law.

REPAIR. *n*. An expenditure of money, or the application of labour, skill or materials to, an article for the purpose of altering, improving or restoring its properties or maintaining its condition and includes, (a) the transportation of the article for purpose of making a repair, (b) the towing of an article, (c) the salvage of an article. *Repair and Storage Liens Act*, R.S.O. 1990, c. R.25, s. 1(1). See BUILDING ~S; MAJOR ~S.

REPAIR DESIGN CERTIFICATE. A document issued by the Minister to record the approval of a repair design for an aeronautical product, identified in the document by a serial number or by some other identification unique to the aeronautical product, and that references the documents and data defining the repair design and the limitations and conditions applicable to the aeronautical product as a result of the design change, and includes a repair design approval issued, before the coming into force of these Regulations, pursuant to section 214 of the *Air Regulations*. *Canadian Aviation Regulations*, SOR/96-433, s. 101.01(1).

REPAIRER. *n*. 1. A person who (a) maintains a garage for the purpose of rendering services therein upon motor vehicles, at a charge, price or consideration, in the ordinary course of business; or (b) owns and operates a fleet of five or more motor vehicles, or vehicles, or both, and maintains facilities for the repair of the vehicles. 2. A person who makes a repair on the understanding that the person will be paid for the repair. See AUTO BODY ~; TRUCK TRAILER ~; WATCH ~.

REPAIR GARAGE. A building or part thereof where facilities are provided for the repair or servicing of motor vehicles.

REPAIRMAN'S GARAGE. A place of business primarily designed or used for the purpose of repairing motor vehicles or trailers, but does not include a place of business from which motive fuel, lubricating oil, antifreeze or other similar products, and services incidental to them, are sold or provided except in relation to repairs.

REPAIR SERVICE. The installation, adjustment, repair, restoration, reconditioning, refinishing or maintenance of tangible personal property.

REPARATION. *n*. 1. Restitution. 2. "[In s. 663(2)(e) of the Criminal Code, R.S.C. 1970, c. C-34] . . . would have the additional meaning [to the meaning of restitution which refers to property only] of compensating a victim for loss or damage—both to property and person. . ." *R. v. Groves* (1977), 39 C.R.N.S. 366 at 380, 17 O.R. (2d) 65, 37 C.C.C. (2d) 429, 79 D.L.R. (3d) 561 (H.C.), O'Driscoll J. 3. Reparation for harm done to the victim or to the community is one of the principles applied in sentencing individuals convicted of offences.

REPATRIATION. *n*. 1. Recovering possession of the nationality which a person lost or abandoned. 2. Sometimes used in reference to the patriation of the Canadian constitution. 3. (i) The transfer to a First Nation by the Crown of the Crown's title to a sacred ceremonial object, and (ii) the acceptance by the First Nation of that transfer. *First Nations Sacred Ceremonial Objects Repatriation Act*, R.S.A. 2000, c. F-14, s. 1. See PATRIATION.

REPEAL. *v*. To strike out, revoke, cancel or rescind.

REPEALED. *adj*. Includes revoked or cancelled, expired, lapsed, or otherwise ceased to have effect. *Interpretation Act*, R.S.N.S. 1989, c. 235, s. 7(1).

REPEATEDLY. *adv*. Many times over. More than once or twice.

REPELLANT. *suff*. When used as a suffix (such as moisture-repellant) means constructed, treated or surfaced so that liquid will tend to run off, and cannot readily penetrate the surface.

REPELLITUR A SACRAMENTO INFAMIS. [L.] Someone infamous is not permitted to take an oath.

REPETITUM NAMIUM. [L.] A second, reciprocal distress which takes the place of one which was eloigned.

REPLACE. *v*. 1. To take away and substitute another. 2. In insurance, to restore buildings or chattels which have been destroyed. Raoul Colinvaux, *The Law of Insurance*, 5th ed. (London: Sweet & Maxwell, 1984) at 181.

REPLACEMENT. *n*. In an insurance policy, to put back the insured property in the same position as before the loss.

REPLACEMENT COST. 1. " . . . '[C]ost of reinstatement' . . ." *Shinkaruk Enterprises Ltd. v. Commonwealth Insurance Co.*, [1990] I.L.R. 1-2648 at 10,376, 85 Sask. R. 54, 71 D.L.R. (4th) 681 (C.A.), Bayda C.J.S. (Vancise J.A. and Grotsky J. concurring). 2. " . . . [M]ay mean the cost of repairing the damaged property or the cost of replacing the entire property, depending on the circumstances." *Shinkaruk Enterprises Ltd. v. Commonwealth Insurance Co.*, [1990] I.L.R. 1-2648 at 10,376, 85 Sask. R. 54, 71 D.L.R. (4th) 681 (C.A.), Bayda C.J.S. (Vancise J.A. and Grotsky J. concurring).

REPLACEMENT COST INSURANCE. Any type of coverage under which the insurance company agrees, in effect, to pay the *difference* between actual cash value and full replacement costs." What is insured, simply put, is depreciation. Under replacement coverage, insureds are entitled to receive the amount necessary to rebuild a structure or replace its contents in a new condition, without deducting for depreciation. Recovery is allowed, in the words of many courts, on a new-for-old basis. *Brkich & Brkich Enterprises Ltd. v. American Home Assurance Co.* (1995), 8 B.C.L.R. (3d) 1 (C.A.) appeal to S.C.C. dismissed, reasons of Finch J.A. adopted.

REPLACEMENT PROPERTY. Property bought for a similar or the same use as former property, and, if the former property was used for business purposes, used to gain or produce income from the same business. W. Grover & F. Iacobucci, *Materials on Canadian Income Tax*, 4th ed. (Toronto: Richard De Boo Ltd., 1980) at 517.

REPLACEMENT VALUE. " . . . [W]hat the replacement in stato quo ante the fire of the insured property destroyed or injured would cost, less a reasonable allowance for depreciation. . ." *Colonsay Hotel Co. v. Can. National Fire Ins. Co.*, [1923] S.C.R. 688 at 694, [1923] 2 W.W.R. 1170, [1923] 3 D.L.R. 1001, Anglin J.

REPLACEMENT WORKER. One hired to replace a worker who is on strike. A strikebreaker.

REPLANTING. *n.* The relocating of oysters in ordinary practice to improve their growth, condition or accessibility. *Fishery regulations.*

REPLEADER. *n.* The act or right to plead again.

REPLEGIARE. *n.* [L.] Replevin; redemption of something taken or detained by another by giving a surety.

REPLEVIABLE. *adj.* Able to be replevied or taken back.

REPLEVIN. *n.* " . . . [N]ow called an order for the recovery of possession of personal property, has remained what its new name suggests: a means of getting back the possession which an applicant for the remedy has lost." *Manitoba Agricultural Credit Corp. v. Heaman* (1990), 70 D.L.R. (4th) 518 at 523, [1990] 4 W.W.R. 269, 65 Man. R. (2d) 269 (C.A.), the court per Twaddle J.A. See ACTION FOR ~.

REPLEVISABLE. *adj.* Describes goods for which one may institute replevin proceedings.

REPLEVY. *v.* To redeliver goods which were unlawfully taken or detained to their owner.

REPLIANT. *n.* A party who replies, or delivers or files a replication.

REPLICA FIREARM. Any device that is designed or intended to exactly resemble, or to resemble with near precision, a firearm, and that itself is not a firearm, but does not include any such device that is designed or intended to exactly resemble, or to resemble with near precision, an antique firearm. *Criminal Code*, R.S.C. 1985, c. C-46, s. 84(1).

REPLICANT. *n.* A party who replies, or delivers or files a replication.

REPLICATION. *n.* Formerly in the common law courts of England, a pleading which the plaintiff filed or delivered to answer the defendant's plea or answer or in Chancery, a joinder of issue.

REPLOT. See LAND ~; VALUATION ~.

REPLOTTING SCHEME. See COST OF PREPARING THE ~.

REPLY. *n.* The pleading of a petitioner, plaintiff or party, who institutes a proceeding, in answer to the defendant.

REPLY EVIDENCE. Rebuttal evidence which a plaintiff may present at the end of the defendant's case to contradict or qualify new facts or issues which the defendant raised in the course of presenting her or his case.

REPORT. *n.* 1. " . . . [A]n account of an event. It can be either oral or written. Even an act or gesture that conveys information without words could amount to a report. . ." *Peel (Board of Education) v. B.(W.)* (1987), 36 M.P.L.R. 95 at 103, 24 Admin. L.R. 164, 59 O.R. (2d) 654, 38 D.L.R. (4th) 566 (H.C.), Reid J. 2. A report of a commission, and any newspaper advertisements published under subsection 19(2), and in the Canada Gazette as required pursuant to the provisions of this Act, and the recommendations and reasons therefor set out in the report. *Electoral Boundaries Readjustment Act*, R.S.C. 1985, c. E-3, s. 2. 3. Includes an evaluation of any departmental program of a non-commercial nature, but does not include an appraisal of the performance of any specific officer or employee of a department who is or was involved in administering a program. *The Freedom of Information Act*, S.M. 1985-86, c. 6, s. 39(3). See CONSUMER ~; CREDIT ~; DURHAM ~; ENVIRONMENTAL ASSESSMENT ~; ENVIRONMENTAL PREVIEW ~; LAW ~; OFFICIAL ~; OFFICIAL ~ OF DEBATES; PERSONAL ~; PRE-DISPOSITION ~; PRESENTENCE ~; PROGRESS ~.

REPORTABLE DEATH. A death that must be reported pursuant to subsection 9(1). *Coroners Act*, S.N.W.T. 1985 (3d Sess.), c. 2, s. 2.

REPORTABLE DISEASE. African swine fever, anaplasmosis, anthrax, avian pneumoencephalitis (Newcastle disease), blue-tongue, brucellosis, cysticercosis (bovine), equine infectious anemia, equine prioplasmosis, foot and mouth disease, fowl plague, fowl typhoid, glanders, hog cholera, maladie du coït (dourine), mange, pullorum disease, rabies, rinderpest, scrapie, sheep scab, trichinosis, tuberculosis, vesicular disease of swine, vesicular exanthema of swine, vesicular stomatitis or such other disease as may be designated by the Minister. *Animal Disease and Protection Act*, R.S.C. 1985, c. A-11, s. 2.

REPORTER. *n*. An official court reporter. See COURT ~; PERSONAL ~.

REPORTING AGENCY. A person who furnishes reports for gain or profit or who furnishes reports on a routine, nonprofit basis as an ancillary part of a business carried on for gain or profit. See CONSUMER ~; CREDIT~.

REPORTING ISSUER. An issuer: (a) that has outstanding any securities with respect to which: (A) a prospectus has been filed; (B) a securities exchange take-over bid has been filed; (b) that has filed a prospectus; (c) any of the securities of which have been at any time since the coming into force of this Act listed and posted for trading on any stock exchange; (d) that has issued voting securities with respect to which a prospectus was filed and a receipt for it obtained; (e) that is a company whose securities have been exchanged, by or for the account of that company, with another company or the holders of the securities of that other company pursuant to an amalgamation, merger, reorganization or arrangement where one of the parties to the amalgamation, merger, reorganization or arrangement was a reporting issuer at the time of the amalgamation, merger, reorganization or arrangement.

REPORTING ISSUER EQUIVALENT. A corporation that, under the laws of any Canadian jurisdiction other than British Columbia, is a reporting issuer or an equivalent of a reporting issuer. *Business Corporations Act*, S.B.C. 2002, c. 57, s. 1(1).

REPORTING PAY. A minimum number of hours' pay paid to an employee required to report to work outside the employee's scheduled work time.

REPORTING PERIOD. In relation to a corporation, means a period of time that ends not earlier than 12 months and not later than 53 weeks after its commencement and that ends between October 30 of one calendar year and January 31 of the following calendar year and, in relation to a union, means, with respect to the return required under paragraph 12(1)(a), a calendar year and, with respect to the return required under paragraph 12(1)(b), a fiscal period of the union, and the fiscal period of the union shall be deemed, for the purposes of this Act, to end not later than 12 months after its commencement unless extended with the concurrence of the Minister. *Corporations and Labour Unions Returns Act*, R.S.C. 1985, c. C-43, s. 2.

REPORTING WITNESS. A witness who is permitted to quote an extra-judicial statement. *Military Rules of Evidence*, C.R.C., c. 1049, s. 2.

REPORT STAGE. The stage at which the House, with the Speaker in the Chair, may amend, insert, delete or restore specific clauses in a bill. A. Fraser, W.A. Dawson, & J. Holtby, eds., *Beauchesne's Rules and Forms of the House of Commons of Canada*, 6th ed. (Toronto: Carswell, 1989) at 195.

REPOSSESSION. *n*. Taking back, to which a seller under a sale on credit or a security holder of personal property may be entitled.

REPREHENSIBLE. *adj*. Scandalous, outrageous, deserving of reproof or rebuke.

REPRESENT. *v*. To act for a client as his or her solicitor or attorney. See MIS~.

REPRESENTATION. *n.* 1. A statement of fact, implied or expressed, made by a party to a transaction or tending to facilitate the conclusion of the transaction. 2. Making a statement of facts, reasons or argument on matters that affect the party. 3. A statement concerning a past or existing fact, not a promise concerning a future event or state of affairs. G.H.L. Fridman, *The Law of Contract in Canada*, 2d ed. (Toronto: Carswell, 1986) at 2. 4. Standing in someone else's place for a certain purpose. 5. " . . . The element of representation in s. 163 of the [Criminal Code, R.S.C. 1985, c. C-46] is therefore a suggestion, a depiction to the public. . ." *R. v. Butler* (1992), 11 C.R. (4th) 137 at 184, [1992] 2 W.W.R. 577, [1992] 1 S.C.R. 452, 70 C.C.C. (3d) 129, 134 N.R. 81, 8 C.R.R. (2d) 1, 89 D.L.R. (4th) 449, 78 Man. R. (2d) 1, 16 W.A.C. 1, Gonthier J. (L'Heureux-Dubé J. concurring). 6. Probate, administration, confirmation or other instrument constituting a person the executor, administrator or other representative of a deceased person. *Canada Shipping Act*, R.S.C. 1985, c. S-9, s. 2. 7. A representation, claim, statement, offer, request or proposal that is or purports to be, (a) made respecting or with a view to the supplying of goods or services to consumers, or (b) made for the purpose of receiving payment for goods or services supplied or purporting to be supplied to consumers. *Consumer Protection Act, 2002*, S.O. 2002, c. 30, s. 13(9). See CONSUMER ~; FALSE OR MISLEADING ~; GRAPHIC ~; MIS~.

REPRESENTATION LABEL. A label that contains any representation as to the textile fibre content of the article to which it is applied. *Textile Labelling and Advertising Regulations*, C.R.C., c. 1551, s. 3.

REPRESENTATION VOTE. A vote to determine whether a union should represent a bargaining unit as their bargaining agent.

REPRESENTATIVE. *n.* 1. The person who takes the place of or represents another person. A deceased person's executor or administrator is called a personal representative. 2. Any person who acts on behalf of another. 3. (a) The head of a diplomatic mission or the High Commissioner representing one of Her Majesty's Governments; (b) a counsellor, secretary, attaché or officer of equal rank at an embassy, legation or office of a High Commissioner in Canada; or (c) a consul-general, consul, vice-consul, trade commissioner or assistant trade commissioner, who is a native or citizen of the country he represents and is not engaged in any other business or profession. *Diplomatic (Excise Taxes) Remission Order*, C.R.C., c. 757, s. 2. 4. The owner or charterer of a vessel or an agent of either of them, and includes any person who, in an application for preclearance of a vessel, accepts responsibility for payment of the tolls and charges to be assessed against the vessel in respect of transit and wharfage. *Seaway Regulations*, C.R.C., c. 1397, s. 2. See CHIEF ~; EMPLOYEE ~; EMPLOYEES' ~; FACTORY ~; HEALTH AND SAFETY ~; LEGAL ~; PERSONAL ~; PRISONERS' ~; PUBLIC ~; REGISTERED ~; SAFETY AND HEALTH ~.

REPRESENTATIVE ACTION. 1. " . . . [F]or a proper representative action there must be a 'common interest' of the plaintiff with those he claims to represent, the exertion of a 'common right' or a 'common grievance', normally arising from a 'common origin', but once the alleged rights of the class are denied or ignored it is immaterial that the individuals have been wronged in their individual capacity, provided, of course, that their claims were not for personal damages. It appears to me that the many passages uttered by Judges of high authority over the years really boil down to a simple proposition that a class action is appropriate where if the plaintiff wins the other persons he purports to represent win too, and if he, because of that success, becomes entitled to relief whether or not in a fund or property, the others also become likewise entitled to that relief, having regard, always, for different quantitiative participations." *Shaw v. Vancouver Real Estate Board* (1973), 36 D.L.R. (3d) 250 at 253-4, [1973] 4 W.W.R. 391 (B.C. C.A.), Bull J.A. 2. " . . . [C]an be brought by persons asserting a common right, and even where persons may have been wronged in their individual capacity." *Pasco v. Canadian National Railway* (1989), 34 B.C.L.R. (2d) 344 at 348, [1990] 2 C.N.L.R. 85, 56 D.L.R. (4th) 404 (C.A.), the court per Macfarlane J.A. 3. "An action by members of a corporation challenging allegedly ultra vires acts thus should normally be taken in representative form so that all members or shareholders of the company will be bound by judgment and the company not harassed by a multiplicity of actions. . ." *Gordon v. N.S.T.U.* (1983), 36 C.P.C. 150 at 156, 59 N.S.R. (2d) 124, 125 A.P.R. 124, 1 D.L.R. (4th) 676 (C.A.), the court per MacKeigan C.J.N.S.

REPRESENTATIVE CAPACITY. The capacity of a trustee, executor, administrator, bailee, agent, receiver, liquidator, sequestrator, assignee, custodian, trustee in bankruptcy, guardian of the estate of a minor, committee of the estate of a mentally incompetent person, or any other similar capacity.

REPRESENTATIVE PROCEEDING. When numerous people have the same interest, one or more of them may bring or defend a proceeding for the benefit or on behalf of everyone, or the court may authorize this. See also CLASS ACTION.

REPRESENTATIVE STATUS. See DISCLAIMER OF ~.

REPRIEVE. *n.* The temporary withdrawal of a sentence so that its execution is suspended.

REPRIMAND. *n.* The giving of an official or pointed rebuke. A reproach.

REPRISAL. *n.* Recaption; taking one thing in place of another.

REPRISE. *n.* A deduction, e.g. a rent-charge, from gross annual rent or the value of land.

REPROBATA PECUNIA LIBERAT SOLVENTEM. [L.] Money refused frees the person who offered it.

REPROCESSING PLANT. See GAS ~.

REPRODUCE. *v.* To record any broadcasting material by electrical or mechanical means.

REPRODUCTION. *n.* 1. In relation to copyright infringement, involves the entire work or a substantial part of it and a causal connection between the copyrighted work and the infringing work. The copyrighted work must be the source of the infringing work. Includes making copies of a work. 2. A recording of any broadcast material by electrical, optical or mechanical means. *Television Broadcasting Regulations,* C.R.C., c. 381, s. 2.

REPRODUCTION RIGHTS. Compensation to which copyright holders are entitled when broadcasters make recordings of musical works in another format.

REPTILE. *n.* A vertebrate of the class Reptilia and its eggs.

REPUBLICATION. *n.* Of a codicil or will, execution again by the testator.

REPUDIATION. *n.* 1. " . . . [O]rdinarily means a refusal to carry out all one's obligations under a contract." *Park v. Parsons Brown & Co.* (1989), 27 C.C.E.L. 224 at 242, 39 B.C.L.R. (2d) 107, 62 D.L.R. (4th) 108 (B.C. C.A.), Southin

J.A. 2. To find a repudiation there must be conduct which amounts to total rejection of the obligations of the contract; there must be lack of justification for that conduct; and the repudiation must be accepted by the innocent party who treats the contract as ended. *Norfolk v. Aikens* (1989), [1990] 2 W.W.R. 401 (B.C. C.A.) at 417-418.

REPUGNANCY. *n.* " . . . [W]here one clear clause contradicts another clause equally clear. In a deed where there is a repugnancy the rule is the first shall prevail, but in a will the second: . . ." *Westholme Lumber Co. v. St. James Ltd.* (1915), 21 D.L.R. 549 at 555, 8 W.W.R. 122, 21 B.C.R. 100, 30 W.L.R. 781 (C.A.), Irving J.A. (Macdonald C.J.A. concurring).

REPUGNANT. *adj.* Inconsistent with; contrary to.

REPUTATION. *n.* 1. " . . . [M]erely hearsay, simply what the public says about a person, . . ." *R. v. Sands* (1915), 25 C.C.C. 120 at 123, 28 D.L.R. 375, 9 W.W.R. 496, 25 Man. R. 690 (C.A.), the court per Howell C.J.M. 2. Immediately before a defamatory publication, the long-range composite view which the general public had of the plaintiff's character, credit, honour or good name. R.E. Brown, *The Law of Defamation in Canada* (Toronto: Carswell, 1987) at 1030.

REQUEST. *n.* 1. An active or positive proposal or solicitation. 2. " . . . [T]he requests contemplated in s. 9(1)(e) and the remaining sources of request in s. 9(1)(n) [of the Trade Marks Act, R.S.C. 1970, c. T-10] are made by the Government of Canada, of a Province or by a municipality and by a university or public authority, originate from . . . high authority and, despite polite usage of the word 'request', are . . . mandatory in nature. . ." *Insurance Corp. of British Columbia v. Canada (Registrar of Trade Marks)* (1978), 44 C.P.R. (2d) 1 at 11, [1980] 1 F.C. 669 (T.D.), Cattanach J.

REQUEST FOR PROPOSAL. A call for proposals to meet contractual requirements.

REQUEST MAIL. Mail bearing the return address of the sender and a specific request for the return of the mail. *Undeliverable and Redirected Mail Regulations,* C.R.C., c. 1298, s. 2.

REQUIRE. *v.* 1. To need. *Gourlay v. Canadian Department Stores Ltd.,* [1933] 3 D.L.R. 238 at 240, [1933] S.C.R. 329, the court per Lamont J. 2. " . . . [D]emand as of right, demand with authority." *Canadian Bank of Commerce v. Moth-*

ersill, [1937] O.R. 402 at 404, [1936] 3 D.L.R. 205 (C.A.), Macdonnell J.A. 3. Mandate. 4. Compel.

REQUIRED DEPOSIT BALANCE. A fixed or an ascertainable amount of the money actually advanced or to be advanced under an agreement or arrangement that is required, as a condition of the agreement or arrangement, to be deposited or invested by or on behalf of the person to whom the advance is or is to be made and that may be available, in the event of his defaulting in any payment, to or for the benefit of the person who advances or is to advance the money. *Criminal Code*, R.S.C. 1985, c. C-46, s. 347(2).

REQUIRED INSPECTION. An inspection of an aeronautical product that is required by a maintenance schedule, an airworthiness limitation or an airworthiness directive, except where the airworthiness directive specifies that the inspection may be performed by a flight crew member; *Canadian Aviation Regulations* SOR 96-433, s. 101.01.

REQUIRED TAKE-OFF DISTANCE. The one-engine-inoperative take-off distance or 115 per cent of the all-engines-operating take-off distance, whichever is greater. *Canadian Aviation Regulations*, SOR/96-433, s. 101.01(1).

REQUIRED TAKE-OFF RUN. The one-engine-inoperative take-off run or 115 per cent of the all-engines-operating take-off run, whichever is greater. *Canadian Aviation Regulations*, SOR/96-433, s. 101.01(1).

REQUIRED VISUAL REFERENCE. In respect of an aircraft on an approach to a runway, means that portion of the approach area of the runway or those visual aids that, when viewed by the pilot of the aircraft, enable the pilot to make an assessment of the aircraft position and rate of change of position, in order to continue the approach and complete a landing. *Canadian Aviation Regulations*, SOR/96-433, s. 101.01(1).

REQUIREMENT. *n*. Any demand, direction, order, subpoena or summons. *Business Concerns Records Act*, R.S.Q. 1977, c. D-12, s. 1. See BONA FIDE OCCUPATIONAL ~; BUDGETARY ~S; FIXED CAPITAL ~S; MANPOWER ~; OCCUPATIONAL ~; PERSONAL ~S; SAFETY ~S.

REQUISITION. *v*. To demand necessaries for a military force.

REQUISITION. *n*. 1. A praecipe. 2. A written instruction which requires a court registrar to do something. See CHEQUE ~; OTHER PAYMENT ~; PAYMENT ~.

REQUISITION ON TITLE. A written inquiry to the solicitor for a vendor of real estate requesting that defects and clouds in the title be removed.

RERUM PROGRESSU OSTENDUNT MULTA, QUAE IN INITIO PRAECAVERI SEU PRAEVIDERI NON POSSUNT. [L.] In the course of things many things which could not be averted or foreseen in the beginning arise.

RERUM SUARUM QUILIBET EST MODERATOR ET ARBITER. [L.] Each one is manager and judge of one's own affairs.

RES. *n*. [L.] Any physical thing in which someone may claim a right.

RES ACCESSORIA SEQUITUR REM PRINCIPALEM. [L.] An accessory follows the principal.

RESALE. *n*. 1. A right reserved by the vendor if the purchaser defaults in paying the purchase price. 2. A sale by a producer of a volume of natural gas after that volume has been sold (a) by itself; or (b) as part of another volume of natural gas by the corporation under section 5. *Natural Gas Price Act*, S.B.C. 1985, c. 53, s. 1.

RESCIND. *v*. 1. With respect to a contract, for one or more parties to end it. 2. " ... [D]ischarging [an order] or setting it aside. . ." *Stewart v. Braun*, [1924] 3 D.L.R. 941 at 942, [1924] 2 W.W.R. 1103 (Man. K.B.), Mathers C.J.K.B.

RESCISSION. *n*. 1. " ... [W]ill only occur where the changes go to the very root of the original agreement such that there is patent the intention to completely extinguish the first contract, nor merely to alter it, however extensively, in terms which leave the original subsisting . . ." *Niagara Air Bus Inc. v. Camerman* (1989), 37 C.P.C. (2d) 267 at 285, 69 O.R. (2d) 717 (H.C.), Watt J. 2. Exercise of an option which ends the necessity to perform. B.J. Reiter, B.N. McLellan & P.M. Perell, *Real Estate Law*, 4th ed. (Toronto: Emond Montgomery, 1992) at 681.

RESCISSION CLAUSE. A clause which protects a vendor from action by a purchaser for compensation and specific performance when the vendor cannot convey everything promised and the purchaser claims everything the vendor has with a reduction in the purchase price in compensation. B.J. Reiter, B.N. McLellan &

P.M. Perell, *Real Estate Law*, 4th ed. (Toronto: Emond Montgomery, 1992) at 300.

RES COMMUNES. [L.] Things like light or air which may not be appropriated.

RESCUE. *v.* To knowingly and forcibly free someone from an imprisonment or arrest.

RESCUER. *n.* A person who, having reasonable cause to believe another person to be in danger of his life or of bodily harm, benevolently comes to his assistance.

RESEALING. *n.* Validation of a grant of representation originally issued by a court in a jurisdiction with similar laws and allegiance to the same sovereign, i.e. in the United Kingdom, any territory or province of Canada, the Commonwealth or any British possession. This has the same effect as if the validating court had made the original grant. J.G. McLeod, *The Conflict of Laws* (Calgary: Carswell, 1983) at 404 and 405.

RESEARCH. *n.* 1. Includes any scientific or technical inquiry or experimentation that is instituted or carried out to discover new knowledge or new means of applying existing knowledge to the solution of economic and social problems. *International Development Research Centre Act*, R.S.C. 1985, c. I-19, s. 2. 2. The use of animals in connection with studies, investigation and teaching in any field of knowledge, and, without limiting the generality of the foregoing, includes the use of animals for the performance of tests, and diagnosis of disease and the production and testing of preparations intended for use in the diagnosis, prevention and treatment of any disease or condition. *Animals for Research Act*, R.S.O. 1990, c. A.22, s. 1. See DEMONSTRATION OR ~ PROJECT; ENGINEERING ~ OR FEASIBILITY STUDY; MEDICAL ~ COUNCIL; NATIONAL ~ COUNCIL OF CANADA; NATURAL SCIENCES AND ENGINEERING ~ COUNCIL OF CANADA; SOCIAL SCIENCES AND HUMANITIES ~ COUNCIL OF CANADA.

RESEARCH FACILITIES. Facilities in a teaching hospital provided for research in the health fields associated with the teaching of undergraduate or post-graduate students in the health professions for the purpose of carrying out scientific research, under public support or sponsorship, contributing to the whole body of health knowledge, together with other areas of the hospital to the extent that such other areas service or support the research facilities. *Public Hospitals Act*, R.R.O. 1980, Reg. 862, s. 1.

RESEARCH FACILITY. Premises on which animals are used in research and includes premises used for the collecting, assembling or maintaining of animals in connection with a research facility, but does not include a farm on which pregnant mares are kept for the collection of urine. *Animals for Research Act*, R.S.O. 1990, c. A.22, s. 1.

RESEARCH INSTITUTE. An institution affiliated with a teaching hospital, the sole purpose of which is research in the health fields associated with the teaching of under-graduate or post-graduate students in the health professions for the purpose of carrying out scientific research, under public support or sponsorship, contributing to the whole body of health knowledge, together with auxiliary areas of the institute to the extent that such areas service or support the research facilities.

RESEARCH OR FEASIBILITY STUDY. Includes work undertaken to facilitate the design or analyse the viability of engineering systems, schemes or technology to be used in the exploration for or the development, production or transportation of oil or gas on or from Canada lands. *Oil and Gas Act*, R.S.C. 1985, c. O-6, s. 51(4).

RESEARCH PROGRAM. A program of research and investigation respecting, (a) the more effective use and economic development of lands, (b) the development of income and employment opportunities in rural areas and the improvement of standards of living in those areas, and (c) the development and conservation for agricultural purposes of water supplies and for soil improvement and conservation. *Agricultural Rehabilitation and Development Act (Ontario)*, R.S.O. 1990, c. A.11, s. 1.

RESERVATION. *n.* 1. A clause in a deed by which a donor, grantor or lessor claims or reserves something new out of whatever was granted by the same deed earlier. 2. Power of the Lieutenant-Governor with regard to a bill passed by the Legislature. It is subject " . . . to the restriction that the discretion of the Lieutenant-Governor shall be exercised subject to the Governor General's Instructions." *Reference re Power of Disallowance & Power of Reservation (Canada)*, [1938] S.C.R. 71 at 79, [1938] 2 D.L.R. 81, Duff C.J. (Davis J. concurring). See STREET ~.

RESERVATIO NON DEBET ESSE DE PROFICUIS IPSIS, QUIA EA CONCEDUN-

TUR, SED DE REDITU NOVO EXTRA PROFICUA. [L.] A reservation should not be from the profits themselves, because they were granted, but from new rent beyond the profits.

RESERVE. *v.* For the Governor General to withhold the royal assent from a bill which both Houses of Parliament passed "for the signification of the Queen's Pleasure" or, similarly, for a Lieutenant Governor to withhold assent from a provincial bill for the Governor General's pleasure.

RESERVE. *n.* 1. A tract of land, the legal title to which is vested in Her Majesty, that has been set apart by Her Majesty for the use and benefit of a band. *Indian Act*, R.S.C. 1985, c. I-5, s. 2. 2. A parcel of land reserved for use as a park, recreation area or a school site. 3. " . . . [S]omething set aside that can be relied upon for future use; . . ." *Crane Ltd. v. Minister of National Revenue*, [1960] C.T.C. 371 at 378, [1961] Ex. C.R. 147, 60 D.T.C. 1248, Kearney J. 4. (a) Amounts appropriated from earned surplus at the discretion of management for some purpose other than to meet a liability or contingency known or admitted or a commitment made as at the statement date or a decline in value of an asset that has already occurred; (b) amounts appropriated from earned surplus pursuant to the articles or by-laws of a corporation for some purpose other than to meet a liability or contingency known or admitted or a commitment made as at the statement date or a decline in value of an asset that has already occurred; and (c) amounts appropriated from earned surplus in accordance with the terms of a contract and that can be restored to the earned surplus when the conditions of the contract are fulfilled. See CROWN ~; ECOLOGICAL ~; INDIAN ~; PHEASANT ~; PROBABLE ADDITIONAL ~S; PROVEN DEVELOPED ~S; PROVEN ~S UNDERLYING A PROPERTY; PROVEN UNDEVELOPED ~S; PUBLIC ~; REASONABLE AMOUNT FOR A ~; WHOLLY-PROTECTED ECOLOGICAL ~.

RESERVED LAND. Crown land that has been withdrawn from disposition under this or any other Act. *Land Act*, R.S.B.C. 1979, c. 214, s. 1.

RESERVED ROAD. A parcel of land between or within granted lands reserved by the Crown as the right-of-way for access to and egress from other granted lands or Crown lands, whether or not a road has been constructed thereon. *Crown Lands and Forests Act*, S.N.B. 1980, c. C-38.1, s. 1.

RESERVED TIME. Broadcast time during which, by agreement, facilities of a station are made available for the broadcast of programs or packages of programs supplied by and to be broadcast in a manner determined by a person other than the licensee of the station. *Broadcasting regulations*.

RESERVE FORCE. The component of the Canadian Forces that consists of officers and non-commissioned members who are enrolled for other than continuing, full-time military service when not on active service. The maximum numbers of officers and non-commissioned members in the reserve force is authorized by the Governor in Council, and the reserve force includes units and other elements. *National Defence Act*, R.S.C., 1985, c. N-5, s. 15, as am.

RESERVE FUND. A fund set up by a condominium corporation in a special account for major repair and replacement of common elements and assets of the corporation including where applicable without limiting the generality of the foregoing, roofs, exteriors of buildings, roads, sidewalks, sewers, heating, electrical and plumbing systems, elevators, laundry, recreational and parking facilities. See CONTINGENCY ~.

RESERVE LANDS. Those lands set aside by the Federal government for the exclusive use of Indian people. These lands are regulated under the *Indian Act*, R.S.C. 1985, c. I-5. See CROWN ~.

RESERVE POWER. Power which the Governor General may exercise at personal discretion, i.e. the power to select or dismiss a Prime Minister.

RESERVOIR. *n.* 1. A body of water, whether on private or public lands, created or effected as a result of the construction and maintenance of water control works, and includes a river, stream, creek, watercourse, lake or previously existing body of water that is enlarged, reduced or otherwise affected as a result of the construction and maintenance of water control works. 2. A porous, permeable sedimentary rock formation containing quantities of oil and gas and surrounded by less permeable or impervious rock. See NATURAL ~ IN CANADA; STORAGE ~; UNDERGROUND ~.

RES EXTINCTA. [L.] Something which existed once but no longer does. G.H.L. Fridman, *Sale of Goods in Canada*, 3d ed. (Toronto: Carswell, 1986) at 61.

RES FURTIVAE. [L.] Stolen objects.

RES GENERALEM HABET SIGNIFICA-TIONEM QUIA TAM CORPOREA QUAM INCORPOREA, CUJUSCUNQUE SUNT GENERIS, NATURAE SIVE SPECIEI, COMPREHENDIT. [L.] The word "thing" has a general meaning because it includes both corporeal and incorporeal objects, whatever their type, nature, or species.

RES GESTAE. [L. things done] 1. "One of the earliest definitions of res gestae was given by Cockburn C.J. in his commentary on R. v. Bedingfield (1879), 14 Cox C.C. 341. . . 'Whatever acts or series of acts constitute or in point of time immediately accompany and terminate in the principal act charged as an offence against the accused from its inception to its consummation or final completion, or its prevention or abandonment, whether on the part of the agent or wrongdoer in order to its performance, or on that of the patient or party wronged in order to its prevention, and whatever may be said by either of the parties during the continuance of the transaction with reference to it . . . form part of the principal transaction, and may be given in evidence as part of the res gestae or particulars of it . . ." *R. v. Klippenstein* (1981), 19 C.R. (3d) 56 at 63, [1981] 3 W.W.R. 111, 57 C.C.C. (2d) 393, 26 A.R. 568 (C.A.), the court per Laycraft J.A. 2. A phrase used in the law of evidence to explain the admissibility of words used by a person that shed light upon the quality of the act they accompany. The words are considered to be so interrelated to a fact in issue that they become a part of the fact itself. To qualify, the words must introduce the fact in issue, explain its nature, or form in connection with it one continuous transaction. *R. v. F. (J.E.)* (1993), 16 O.R. (3d) 1 (C.A.).

RESIANCE. *n.* Abode; residence.

RESIANT. *n.* A resident.

RESIDE. *v.* 1. To be physically present someplace. 2. To have a home that is a permanent place of abode to which, whenever a person is absent, that person intends to return. 3. " . . . In some contexts the word 'reside' may clearly denote what is sometimes being called 'being in residence' at a particular house. In other contexts it may mean merely maintaining a house in a fit state for residence. . ." *Sifton v. Sifton, (sub nom. Sifton, Re)*, [1938] 3 D.L.R. 577 at 588, [1938] A.C. 656, [1938] 2 W.W.R. 465, [1938] All E.R. 435, [1938] O.R. 529 (Ont. P.C.), Lord Romer.

4. " . . . [I]n order to show that a corporation resides in Ontario (within the meaning of [Ontario Rules of Practice] Rule 1198), it should appear that the company is incorporated and has its head and controlling office within the jurisdiction where its business is carried on by its members and officers." *Ashland Co. v. Armstrong* (1906), 11 O.L.R. 414 at 415 (H.C.), Boyd C. 5. ["Resident" refers] to having one's home in a particular place "for a considerable length of time", and . . . "residential" [is defined as] "occupied mainly by private houses." No hard and fast line in terms only of length of stay can be drawn as a matter of law. A traveller or tourist may stay in a hotel for a few weeks without being said to "reside" there, just as a person may "reside" in his or her own house for a short period and then find it necessary for some reason to stay elsewhere for an extended period. . . . many factors, in addition to the length of stay, are involved in determining "residence"—whether one lives out of a suitcase or brings all one's possessions to the unit; whether one establishes roots and connections in the local community or remains only a sojourner; whether one is accompanied by family and is employed permanently or semi-permanently in the area; location of bank accounts and other records. *Kamloops (City) v. Northland Properties Ltd.*, 2000 CarswellBC 1172, 2000 BCCA 344, 76 B.C.L.R. (3d) 63, 11 M.P.L.R. (3d) 10, 139 B.C.A.C. 275, 227 W.A.C. 275 (C.A.).

RESIDENCE. *n.* 1. " . . . [C]hiefly a matter of the degree to which a person in mind and fact settles into or maintains or centralizes his ordinary mode of living with its accessories in social relations, interests and conveniences at or in the place in question. It may be limited in time from the outset, or it may be indefinite, or so far as it is thought of, unlimited. . ." *Thomson v. Minister of National Revenue*, [1946] S.C.R. 209 at 225, [1946] C.T.C. 51, [1946] 1 D.L.R. 689, Rand J. 2. The chief or habitual place of abode of a person. 3. Includes any building or part of a building in which the occupant resides either permanently or temporarily and any premises appurtenant thereto. 4. In relation to a person, that person's true, fixed, permanent home or lodging place to which, whenever absent, the person intends ends to return. 5. " . . . [T]he head office or other place designated in the incorporating instrument as being the chief place of business of the corporation." *Canada Life Assurance Co. v. Canadian Imperial Bank of Commerce* (1979), 8 B.L.R. 55 at 63, 27 N.R. 227, [1979] 2 S.C.R. 669, 98

D.L.R. (3d) 670, the court per Estey J. 6. In para. 5(1)(b) of the Citizenship Act, S.C. 1974-75-76, c. 108 is not limited strictly to actual presence in Canada throughout a specified period. " . . . [N]ot strictly limited to actual presence in Canada throughout the period as they were in the former statute but can include, as well, situations in which the person concerned has a place in Canada which is used by him during the period as a place of abode to a sufficient extent to demonstrate the reality of his residing there during the material period even though he is away from it part of the time." *Papadogiorgakis, Re*, [1978] 2 F.C. 208 at 213, 88 D.L.R. (3d) 243 (T.D.), Thurlow A.C.J. 7. "[In s. 335(g) of the Criminal Code, R.S.C. 1927, c. 36] . . . the place where one lives, that is, where ones home is permanently for the time being, . . ." *R. v. Feeny* (1946), 2 C.R. 304 at 308, 63 B.C.R. 131, [1946] 3 W.W.R. 163, 86 C.C.C. 429, [1947] 1 D.L.R. 392 (C.A.), O'Halloran J.A. 8. [In the context of expropriation] . . . occupation of land for the purpose of living on it in a dwelling . . ." *Bank of Nova Scotia v. R.* (1977), 13 L.C.R. 221 at 239, 22 N.S.R. (2d) 568, 31 A.P.R. 568, 80 D.L.R. (3d) (C.A.), the court per Macdonald J.A. 9. A dwelling-place, such as a den, nest or other similar area or place, that is occupied or habitually occupied by one or more individuals during all or part of their life cycles, including breeding, rearing, staging, wintering, feeding or hibernating. *Species at Risk Act*, S.C. 2002, c. 29, s. 2. See ACTUAL ~; CHILDREN'S ~; COOPERATIVE ~; FARM ~; HABITUAL ~; LEGAL ~; ORDINARY PLACE OF ~; ORDINARY ~; PARENT MODEL ~; PERSONAL ~; PRINCIPAL ~; SINGLE FAMILY ~.

RESIDENCE DISTRICT. The territory contiguous to a portion of a highway having a length of 100 m along which there are buildings used for residence purposes only or for residence and business purposes occupying (a) at least 50 m of frontage on one side of that portion; or (b) at least 50 m collectively on both sides of that portion, and includes that portion of the highway.

RESIDENCE OF A CORPORATION. " . . . [T]he head office or other place designated in the incorporating instrument as being the chief place of business of the corporation." *Canada Life Assurance Co. v. Canadian Imperial Bank of Commerce* (1979), 8 B.L.R. 55 at 63, 27 N.R. 227, [1979] 2 S.C.R. 669, 98 D.L.R. (3d) 670, the court per Estey J.

RESIDENCE OF A TRUST. The same residence as that of the trustee. W. Grover & F. Iacobucci, *Materials on Canadian Income Tax*, 4th ed. (Toronto: Richard De Boo Ltd., 1980) at 113.

RESIDENT. *n*. 1. "[In para 5(1)(b) of the Citizenship Act, S.C. 1974-75-76, c. 108] . . . not strictly limited to actual presence in Canada throughout the period as they were in the former statute but can include, as well, situations in which the person concerned has a place in Canada which is used by him during the period as a place of abode to a sufficient extent to demonstrate the reality of his residing there during the material period even though he is away from it part of the time." *Papadogiorgakis, Re*, [1978] 2 F.C. 208 at 213, 88 D.L.R. (3d) 243 (T.D.), Thurlow A.C.J. 2. In relation to a province, a person lawfully entitled to be or to remain in Canada and who makes a home and is ordinarily present in the province, but does not include a tourist, a transient or a visitor to the province. 3. An individual, a corporation or a trust that is not a non-resident. 4. A person admitted to and lodged in a nursing home or other facility. 5. ["Resident" refers] to having one's home in a particular place "for a considerable length of time", *Kamloops (City) v. Northland Properties Ltd.*, 2000 CarswellBC 1172, 2000 BCCA 344, 76 B.C.L.R. (3d) 63, 11 M.P.L.R. (3d) 10, 139 B.C.A.C. 275, 227 W.A.C. 275 (C.A.). See ASSOCIATES OF THE ~; FORMER ~; NON- ~; NURSING HOME ~; ORDINARILY ~; ORDINARILY ~ IN CANADA; PERMANENT ~; SEASONAL ~.

RESIDENT BURGESS. A burgess who resides in a hospital service area and who is a burgess with respect to property or a business situated therein. *The Major Urban Centres Integrated Hospitals Act*, R.S.S. 1978, c. M-2, s. 2.

RESIDENT BUSINESS. A business carried on in or from premises within the municipality. *Municipal Act*, R.S.B.C. 1979, c. 290, s. 497.

RESIDENT CANADIAN. A natural person who is (a) a Canadian citizen ordinarily resident in Canada, (b) a Canadian citizen not ordinarily resident in Canada who is a member of a prescribed class of persons, or (c) a permanent resident within the meaning of subsection 2(1) of the *Immigration and Refugee Protection Act* and ordinarily resident in Canada, except a permanent resident who has been ordinarily resident in Canada for more than one year after the time at which the individual first became eligible to apply for Canadian citizenship.

RESIDENT ELECTOR. As used with respect to a local authority, means an elector whose place of residence is in the authority.

RESIDENTIAL. *adj.* Connected with or related to a residence or residences. See MEDIUM DENSITY MULTI-FAMILY ~; MOBILE UNIT ~; SINGLE FAMILY ~.

RESIDENTIAL AND FARM ASSESS-MENT. See EQUALIZED ~.

RESIDENTIAL BUILDING. 1. A structure that contains one or more dwelling units. 2. A hotel, motel, lodging house, tourist home, apartment house (other than a dwelling), tenement or any building or part thereof which is rented by the day, week, month or year and consists of individually rented rooms or suites (with or without dining facilities) and self-contained apartments. See MULTI-UNIT ~.

RESIDENTIAL CARE. Boarding or lodging, or both, and may include specialized, sheltered or group care in conjunction with the boarding or lodging, or both.

RESIDENTIAL CARE FACILITY. Any building or place, or part of a building or place, where supervisory care or personal care is provided to four or more persons.

RESIDENTIAL COMPLEX. A building , related group of buildings or mobile home park, in which one or more rental units are located, or a site or related group of sites on each of which site is located a single family dwelling which is a permanent structure and includes all common areas, services and facilities available for the use of residents of the building, buildings, park, site or sites.

RESIDENTIAL COMPOSTER. A composter that (a) is located at a residence, (b) is used to decompose manure, food scraps or vegetative matter resulting from gardening, horticulture, landscaping or land clearing, and (c) uses a controlled bio-oxidation process that results in a stable humus- like material. *Activities Designation Regulation*, Alta. Reg. 276/2003, s. 2(1).

RESIDENTIAL DWELLING UNIT. Includes any premises ordinarily occupied or inhabited.

RESIDENTIAL FACILITY. See COMMUNITY-BASED ~.

RESIDENTIAL INSTITUTION. A shelter that provides temporary or continuing care for persons in need and includes (a) homes for the aged, (b) nursing homes, (c) hostels for transients, (d) child care institutions, (e) homes for unmarried mothers, (f) group homes, and (g) any residential institution the primary, purpose of which is to provide residents thereof with supervisory, personal or nursing care or to rehabilitate them socially.

RESIDENTIAL LAND. (a) A parcel on which a single-family detached unit or duplex unit is located; or (b) a residential unit under the Condominium Property Act, that is or was used as a residence. See VACANT ~.

RESIDENTIAL OCCUPANCY. The occupancy or use of a building or part thereof by persons for whom sleeping accommodation is provided but who are not harboured or detained to receive medical care or treatment or are not involuntarily detained.

RESIDENTIAL PARCEL. A parcel of land entered on the assessment roll of a municipality as a separate parcel and on which is situated one or more dwelling units.

RESIDENTIAL PREMISES. (a) Real property used for residential purposes; or (b) real property leased as a site for a mobile home which is used for residential purposes, whether or not the landlord also leases that mobile home to the tenant, but does not include premises occupied for business purposes with living accommodation attached and leased under a single lease. See MUNICIPAL ~; RENTED ~; RURAL ~.

RESIDENTIAL PROPERTY. A building in which, and includes land on which, residential premises are situated. See FARM AND ~; RENTAL~.

RESIDENTIAL REAL PROPERTY TAX. The tax levied by a municipality upon the real property and improvements thereto that are used for a residential purpose.

RESIDENTIAL SERVICE. Boarding, lodging and associated supervisory, sheltered or group care.

RESIDENTIAL STRATA LOT. A strata lot designed or intended to be used primarily as a residence. *Strata Property Act*, S.B.C. 1998, c. 43, s. 1.

RESIDENTIAL TENANCY AGREEMENT. A written, oral or implied agreement to rent residential premises.

RESIDENTIAL UNIT. Any living accommodation used or intended for use as residential premises. *Tenant Protection Act*, 1997, S.O. 1997, c. 24, s. 1, part.

RESIDENT OCCUPANT. A person actually residing on land within a proposed district, or within a district, and who is the owner, tenant or lessee of such land.

RESIDENT OF CANADA. In the case of a natural person, a person who ordinarily resides in Canada and, in the case of a corporation, a corporation that has its head office in Canada or maintains one or more establishments in Canada to which employees of the corporation employed in connection with the business of the corporation ordinarily report for work.

RESIDENT OF THE PROVINCE. A bona fide resident, animus et factum, of the province.

RESIDENT RATEPAYER. As used with respect to a local authority, means a ratepayer whose place of residence is in the authority.

RESIDES IN THE PROVINCE. Is physically present in the province.

RESIDING. *adj*. Staying for an extended time or permanently.

RESIDUAL. *adj*. Relating to the part which remains.

RESIDUAL FAMILY INCOME. The amount remaining when an amount equal to four-thirds of the rounded pension equivalent is deducted from the monthly family income. *Old Age Security Act*, R.S.C. 1985, c. O-9, s. 22.

RESIDUAL INCOME OF THE SURVIVING SPOUSE. The amount remaining when an amount equal to four-thirds of the rounded pension equivalent is deducted from the monthly income of the surviving spouse. *Old Age Security Act*, R.S.C. 1985, c. O-9, s . 22.

RESIDUAL INCOME OF THE WIDOW. The amount remaining when an amount equal to four-thirds of the rounded pension equivalent is deducted from the monthly income of the widow. *Old Age Security Act*, R.S.C. 1985 (1st Supp.), c. 34, s. 5.

RESIDUAL INTEREST. " . . . [T]hat which the owner possesses not only then but also during the currency of the easement." *Chieftain Development Co. Ltd. v. Lachowich* (1982), 129 D.L.R . (3d) 285 at 297, [1982] 1 W.W.R. 37, 23 L.C.R. 298, 17 Alta. L.R. (2d) 106, 32 A.R. 449 (Q.B.), Cormack J.

RESIDUAL LIBERTY. The liberty which remains to a prisoner, the liberty which is permitted to a prison population generally.

RESIDUAL OBLIGATION LEASE. A lease under which the lessor may require the lessee at the end of the lease term to pay the lessor an amount based in whole or in part on the difference, if any, between, (a) the estimated wholesale value of the leased goods at the end of the lease term, and (b) the realizable value of the leased goods at the end of the lease term. *Consumer Protection Act, 2002*, S.O. 2002, c. 30, Sched. A, s. 86.

RESIDUAL UNIT. A bargaining unit the members of which are workers not included in other units approved previously for the plant.

RESIDUAL VALUE. " . . . [T]hat value to the landowner which remains in his hands because of his ability to make some economic use of the land involved in the 'taking' during the term of the 'taking' . . ." *Dome Petroleum Ltd. v. Grekul* (1983), 29 L.C.R. 111 at 118-9, [1984] 1 W.W.R. 447, 28 Alta. L.R. (2d) 260, 5 Admin. L.R. 252, 49 A.R. 256 (Q.B.), Miller J.

RESIDUARY. *adj*. Relating to the part which remains.

RESIDUARY BEQUEST. A gift of any of the testator's personal property which the will did not otherwise give. T. Sheard, R. Hull & M.M.K. Fitzpatrick, *Canadian Forms of Wills*, 4th ed. (Toronto: Carswell, 1982) at 178.

RESIDUARY DEVISEE. The person designated in a will to take the real property which remains after the other devises.

RESIDUARY LEGATEE. The person to whom a testator leaves what remains of a personal estate after all debts and specific legacies are discharged.

RESIDUARY POWER. 1. With respect to the federal parliament; the power conferred by section 91 of the Constitution Act, 1867 to make laws for the "peace, order, and good government of Canada" which is residuary in relation to provincial governments because it is specifically limited to matters not assigned to the provincial legislatures. P.W. Hogg, *Constitutional Law of Canada*, 3d ed. (Toronto: Carswell, 1992) at 435-6. 2. With respect to a provincial parliament, the power conferred by section 92(16) over "all matters of a merely local or private nature in the province." P.W. Hogg, *Constitutional Law of*

Canada, 3d ed. (Toronto: Carswell, 1992) at 540.

RESIDUE. *n*. 1. "[What remained of an estate] . . . after payment of debts, funeral and testamentary expenses." *Prout, Re*, [1943] 2 D.L.R. 125 at 128, [1943] O.W.N. 156 (C.A.), Robertson C.J.O., Fisher and Kellock JJ.A. 2. " . . . [T]he testator meant by the word 'residue' . . . that part of his estate which might remain after the death of his wife. . . the run of this language shows that his mind was directed to what remained of his estate at the death of his wife, and not what remained at his own death." *Wilson v. Wilson*, [1944] 2 D.L.R. 729 at 732, [1944] 2 W.W.R. 412, 60 B.C.R. 287 (C.A.), Smith J.A. (O'Halloran and Roberson JJ.A. concurring). 3. " . . . Not only after the payment of the debts and expenses, but also after the withdrawal of the two specific provisoes or gifts made by the codicil. It seems also clear that the 'residue' means everything that is left after those two deductions and that the annuities are not to be also deducted before the residue is arrived at." *Aldridge Estate, Re* (1916), 28 D.L.R. 531 at 537, 9 Alta. L.R. 512, 10 W.W.R. 701 (C.A.), Stuart J.A. See PESTICIDE ~; WOOD ~.

RESIDUES. *n*. The ingredients of a control product that remain after the control product has been used and includes substances resulting from degradation or metabolism. *Pest Control Products Regulations*, C.R.C., c. 1253, s. 2.

RESIGNATIO EST JURIS PROPRII SPONTANEA REFUTATIO. [L.] Resignation is the spontaneous refutation of one's own right.

RESIGNATION. *n*. 1. Giving up a possession, office or claim. 2. Requires an employee's subjective intention to quit and some objective confirmation by conduct.

RES IMMOBILES. [L.] Immovables.

RES INCORPORALES. [L.] Things which exist only as legal concepts and cannot be touched, such as contractual rights, servitudes, or rights over land like rights of way, easements and profits.

RES INTEGRA. [L.] A point which must be decided on principle because it is not governed by a decision or rule of law.

RES INTER ALIOS ACTA ALTERI NOCERE NON DEBET. [L.] 1. A transaction between some people should not injure another person. 2. . . . The phrase res inter alios acta appears in many of these cases and is used as a

justification, as in Hollington v. Hewthorn, [1984] 1 K.B. 587 (C.A.)], for deciding that what has been decided previously in a criminal Court against one of the parties to a subsequent civil proceeding either may not be admitted against him or may be admitted for a very limited purpose. When the full maxim is examined it becomes obvious that it expressed the principle that a third party should not be injured by things that have been done between others. . . How this principle, designed entirely for the protection of a third can be said to justify a finding that there can be no such thing as issue estoppel arising from a criminal case, is difficult to comprehend. However, until a higher Court shall see fit to re-examine the maxim . . . I must accept the distortion now commonly in use for what it is worth." *Demeter v. British Pacific Life Insurance Co.* (1983), 2 C.C.L.I. 246 at 262-3, 43 O.R. (2d) 33, 37 C.P.C. 277, 150 D.L.R. (3d) 249, [1983] I.L.R. 1-1689 (H.C.), Osler J. 3. . . . [S]omething that has taken place between two parties cannot be used to harm parties who were stranger to a transaction. . ." *Q. v. Minto Management Ltd.* (1984), 44 C.P.C. 6 at 12, 46 O.R. (2d) 756 (H.C.), Steele J.

RES INTER ALIOS JUDICATA ALIIS NEQUE NOCERE NEQUE PRODESSE POTEST. [L.] That which is decided between two parties cannot harm or benefit third parties.

RES IPSA LOQUITUR. [L. the thing speaks for itself] 1. For *res ipsa loquitur* to arise, the circumstances of the occurrence must permit an inference of negligence attributable to the defendant. The strength or weakness of that inference will depend on the factual circumstances of the case. Whatever value *res ipsa loquitur* may have once provided is gone. Various attempts to apply the so-called doctrine have been more confusing than helpful. Its use has been restricted to cases where the facts permitted an inference of negligence and there was no other reasonable explanation for the accident. Given its limited use it is somewhat meaningless to refer to that use as a doctrine of law. It would appear that the law would be better served if the maxim was treated as expired and no longer used as a separate component in negligence actions. After all, it was nothing more than an attempt to deal with circumstantial evidence. That evidence is more sensibly dealt with by the trier of fact, who should weigh the circumstantial evidence with the direct evidence, if any, to determine whether the plaintiff has established on a balance of probabilities a *prima facie* case of negligence against the defendant. *Fontaine v. British Columbia (Official Administrator)* (1997), [1998] 1 S.C.R. 424. 2. . . [U]sed in connection with . . . class of cases where, by force of a specific rule of law, if certain facts are established then the defendant is liable unless he proves that the occurrence out of which the damage has arisen falls within the category of inevitable accident." *Hutson v. United Motor Service Ltd.*, [1937] 1 D.L.R. 737 at 739, [1937] S.C.R. 294, 4 I.L.R. 91, Duff C.J.C. 3. " . . . [D]escribes the situation where the happening of the accident is sufficient in the absence of an explanation to justify the inference that most probably the defendant was negligent and that his negligence caused the injury even though the plaintiff may not be able to establish the precise cause of the accident. . ." *Schanilec Estate v. Harris* (1987), (*sub nom. Rocha v. Harris*) 39 C.C.L.T. 279 at 291, 11 B.C.L.R. (2d) 233, 36 D.L.R. (4th) 410 (C.A.), the court, per Craig J.A. 4. " . . . [W]hen an accident is such as, in the ordinary course of things, does not happen if those who have the management use proper care it is a case of res ipsa loquitur." *Taylor v. Gray*, [1937] 4 D.L.R. 123 at 125, 11 M.P.R. 588 (N.B. C.A.), the court per Baxter C.J.

RESISTANCE. See FIRE ~; INITIAL CRUSH ~; INTERMEDIATE CRUSH ~; PEAK CRUSH ~.

RESISTANT. *suff*. Constructed, protected or treated so that it will not be injured readily when subjected to the specified material or condition. *Power Corporation Act*, R.R.O. 1980, Reg. 794, s. 0.

RESISTING. See FIRE ~.

RES JUDICATA. [L.] 1. A final judicial decision. 2. A plea in defence to an action. 3. "Three requirements for a finding of res judicata are confirmed by the Manitoba Court of Appeal in Solomon v. Smith, [1988] 1 W.W.R. 410 . . . They are: 1. That the same question has previously been decided. 2. That the judicial decision which is said to create the estoppel was final; and 3. That the parties to the judicial decision or their privies were the same persons as the parties to the proceedings in which the estoppel is raised or their privies." *Newman v. Newman* (1990), 26 R.F.L. (3d) 313 at 318, 65 Man. R. (2d) 294 (Q.B.), Davidson J. See COLLATERAL ESTOPPEL; ESTOPPEL PER REM JUDICATAM; ISSUE ESTOPPEL.

RES JUDICATA PRO VERITATE ACCIPITUR. [L.] 1. Until reversed, a judicial decision is conclusive, and its truth may not be contradicted. 2. " . . . [T]he verdict [of acquittal] is binding and conclusive in all subsequent proceedings between the parties to the adjudication. The maxim 'res judicata pro veritate accipitur' is no less applicable to criminal than to civil proceedings." *Sambasivam v. Public Prosecutor, Federation of Malaya* (1950), 11 C.R. 55 at 69, [1950] A.C. 548, [1950] 2 W.W.R. 817 (Malaya P.C.), Lord MacDermott.

RES MAGIS VALEAT QUAM PEREAT. [L.] Let the thing be of effect than have its effect fail.

RES MOBILES. [L.] Movables.

RES NOVA. [L.] A new matter.

RES NULLIUS. [L.] A thing without an owner.

RESOLUTION. *n*. 1. A solemn decision or judgment. 2. A meeting's expression of intention or opinion. 3. The revocation of a contract. 4. Declares the intention of a municipal council regarding a matter of a temporary nature without prescribing a permanent rule. See EXTRAORDINARY ~; ORDINARY ~; PROCESS FOR ~ OF A DISPUTE; SEPARATE ~; SPECIAL ~; UNANIMOUS ~.

RESOLUTIVE CONDITION. Also known as condition subsequent, has the effect of dissolving a contract that had already come into force. G.H.L. Fridman, *The Law of Contract in Canada*, 2d ed. (Toronto: Carswell, 1986) at 413.

RESOLUTO JURE CONCEDENTIS RESOLVITUR JUS CONCESSUM. [L.] The grant of a right ends when the grantor's right ends.

RESOLUTORY CLAUSE. A clause in a deed of sale which provides that on the purchaser's default of payment the vendor may choose to dissolve the sale and retake title to the property clear of any privileges with which the property has been encumbered. D.N. Macklem & D.I. Bristow, *Construction, Builders' and Mechanics' Liens in Canada*, 6th ed. (Toronto: Carswell, 1990-) at 13-40.

RESOLUTORY CONDITION. Something which, when it is accomplished, revokes a prior obligation.

RESOLVED. *v*. Indicates unanimity of sentiment or intention.

RESORT. *n*. A tourist establishment that operates through all or part of the year and that has facilities for serving meals and furnishes equipment, supplies or services to persons in connection with angling, hunting, camping or recreational purposes. See LAST ~; WATER ~.

RESORTED TO. "[Connotes] . . . a frequent or habitual use of the premises for the purposes of prostitution. . ." *Patterson v. R.*, [1968] 2 C.C.C. 247 at 250, [1968] S.C.R. 157, 3 C.R.N.S. 23, 67 D.L.R. (2d) 82, the court per Spence J.

RESORT OF WILDLIFE. Any waters or lands, including highways or roads, that are frequented by wildlife.

RESORT TO CLAUSE. In a wiretap authorization, permits authorities to intercept phone calls in places to which the subjects of the wiretap are believed to resort.

RESOURCE. *n*. Land and in relation to land use, includes water, whether used for agriculture, recreation, wildlife, forest production, or any other beneficial use. See ARCHAEOLOGICAL ~; CHILD CARE ~; ENERGY ~; GEOTHERMAL ~; HERITAGE ~; HISTORIC ~; MINERAL ~; NON-RENEWABLE ~; PALAEONTOLOGICAL ~; RENEWABLE ~; INDUSTRY; ~S.

RESOURCE-BASED INDUSTRY. An industry that uses as a principal material a material (a) the original location of which is not the consequence of human design; and (b) that is in or close to its natural state.

RESOURCE INCOME. Income reasonably attributable to production from oil and gas wells or bituminous sands deposits, oil sands deposits or coal deposits or to any right, licence or privilege to explore for, drill for or recover petroleum or natural gas or to explore for, mine, quarry, remove, treat or process bituminous sands or oil sands or to win or work mines, seams or beds of coal.

RESOURCE MANAGEMENT. See WATER ~.

RESOURCES. *n*. Includes financial support, personnel, equipment, facilities and any other departmental resources which the Minister may make available to a community social service agency or a community placement resource. *Child and Family Services and Family Relations Act* ,S.N.B. 1980, c. C-2.1, s. 1. See ENERGY, MINES AND ~ CANADA; FINANCIAL ~; FISHERY ~; HEALTH ~; NATURAL ~; RESOURCE; WATER ~.

RESOURCES. *abbr*. Newsletter of the Canadian Institute of Resources Law.

RESOURCE TAXES. Taxation of a non-renewable natural resource, electricity facility or forestry resource. These resources may be taxed in place or their primary production may be taxed.

RESOURCE USE PERMIT. A licence, issued under this act, authorizing an activity or course of behaviour or conduct or the occupancy, use, development, exploitation or extraction of a natural resource on or in a recreation area.

RESPECT. *n*. Relation to. See IN ~ OF.

RES PERIT DOMINO. [L.] Risk falls to the owner.

RES PETITA. [L.] Something claimed.

RESPICIENDUM EST JUDICANTI, NE QUID AUT DURIUS AUT REMISSIUS CONSTITUATUR QUAM CAUSA DEPOSCIT; NEC ENIM AUT SEVERITATIS AUT CLEMENTIAE GLORIA AFFECTANDA EST. [L.] The one who judges should be mindful that nothing either more severe or more lenient is done than the case merits; for distinction should not be achieved by either severity or leniency.

RESPIRATORY TECHNOLOGY. The medically supervised and co-ordinated scientific application of techniques and procedures to assist a physician in the safe and effective diagnosis, treatment, and promotion of the well being of patients with respiratory and associated disorders. See PRACTICE OF ~.

RESPIRATORY THERAPY. The practice of respiratory therapy is the providing of oxygen therapy, cardio-respiratory equipment monitoring and the assessment and treatment of cardio-respiratory and associated disorders to maintain or restore ventilation.

RESPITE. *n*. An interruption, reprieve or suspension of sentence.

RESPONDEAT SUPERIOR. [L. let the principal answer] 1. Over the years courts have constricted the once accepted simple proposition captured under the maxim, *respondeat superior*, that an employer who has enabled an employee to cause a person to suffer a loss will be required to compensate the victim. Moreover, the test developed to set limits on an employer's liability for employee wrongdoing has become the test for establishing liability. *B. (P.A.) v. Curry*

(1997), 30 B.C.L.R. (3d) 1 (C.A.). 2. In certain circumstances when a servant acted in the course of employment, the master is liable for the servant's wrongful acts. *Lavere v. Smith's Falls Public Hospital* (1915), 26 D.L.R. 346 at 363, 35 O.L.R. 98 (C.A.), Latchford J. See VICARIOUS LIABILITY.

RESPONDENT. *n.* 1. A person against whom one presents a petition, issues a summons or brings an appeal. 2. A person in the Province or in a reciprocating state who has or is alleged to have an obligation to pay maintenance for the benefit of a claimant, or against whom a proceeding under this Act, or a corresponding enactment of a reciprocating state, is commenced. *Maintenance Orders Enforcement acts.* 3. A person or a department in respect of whom or which or in respect of whose activities any report or information is sought or provided. *Statistics acts.* See CO-~.

RESPONDENTIA. *n.* [L.] The hypothecation of the goods or cargo on a ship to secure repayment of a loan.

RESPONDERE NON DEBET. [L.] One need not answer.

RESPONDING DOCUMENT. In rules 70.03 to 70.14, . . . a statement of defence, defence to counterclaim or affidavit in opposition to an application (Ontario, Rules of Civil Procedure, r. 70.02). G.D. Watson & C. Perkins, eds., *Holmested & Watson: Ontario Civil Procedure* (Toronto: Carswell, 1984-) at 70-3.

RESPONDING PARTY. A person against whom a motion is made. Includes a party or person who will be affected by the order sought. May include a witness.

RESPONSALIS AD LUCRANDUM VEL PETENDUM. [L.] One who appears in court to answer for someone else on the assigned day; an attorney, deputy or proctor.

RESPONSA PRUDENTIUM. [L.] The answers of those who are learned in law.

RESPONSE. *n.* Resulting action; reply. See FREQUENCY ~.

RESPONSIBLE. *adj.* Liable, accountable legally, answerable. See PERSON ~.

RESPONSIBLE GOVERNMENT. The formal head of state (monarch, Governor General or Lieutenant Governor) must always act under the direction of ministers who are members of the majority elected to the legislative branch.

P.W. Hogg, *Constitutional Law of Canada*, 3d ed. (Toronto: Carswell, 1992) at 229.

RESPONSIBLE MEDICAL OFFICER. The physician or one to whom responsibility for the care and treatment of an individual patient has been assigned.

RESPONSIBLE OFFICER OF THE BANK. 1. The manager or assistant manager of the bank or branch thereof. *Business Loans, Guarantees and Indemnities Act*, S.N.W.T. 1983 (1st Sess.), c. 1, s. 3. 2. (a) The manager or assistant manager of the bank or branch thereof; (b) the person for the time being acting as the manager or assistant manager of the bank or branch thereof; (c) the credit committee of the bank or branch thereof; or (d) such other person as may be authorized by the bank or a branch thereof to supervise the making of loans. Canada regulations.

RESPONSIBLE PERSON. A portfolio manager and every individual who is a partner, director or officer of a portfolio manager together with every affiliate of a portfolio manager and every individual who is director, officer or employ of such affiliate or who is an employee of the portfolio manager, if the affiliate or the individual participates in the formulation of, or has access prior to implementation of investment decisions made on behalf of or the advice given to the client of the portfolio manager.

RESPONSIBILITY. *n.* " . . . '[R]esponsibility' within the definition of 'proposal' [in s. 2 of the Department of Environment Act, R.S.C. 1985, c. E-10] should not be read as connoting matters falling generally within federal jurisdiction. Rather, it is meant to signify a legal duty or obligation." *Friends of the Oldman River Society v. Canada (Minister of Transport)* (1992), 3 Admin. L.R. (2d) 1 at 44, [1992] 2 W.W.R. 193, [1992] 1 S.C.R. 3, 84 Alta. L.R. (2d) 129, 7 C.E.L.R. (N.S.) 1, 132 N.R. 321, 88 D.L.R. (4th) 1, 48 F.T.R. 160n; La Forest J. (Lamer C.J.C., L'Heureux-Dubé, Sopinka, Gonthier, Cory, McLachlin and Iacobucci JJ. concurring). See ABSOLUTE ~; SUPERVISORY ~; VICARIOUS ~.

RESSEISER. For the Crown to take control of lands when ouster le main or general livery was misused.

RES SOLI. [L.] Immovables. E.L.G. Tyler & N.E. Palmer, eds., *Crossley Vaines' Personal Property*, 5th ed. (London: Butterworths, 1973) at 14.

RES SUA NEMINI SERVIT. [L.] One's own property cannot be subject to a servitude for one.

REST. See WEEKLY DAY OF ~.

RESTATEMENT OF LAW. A publication of the American Law Institute which deals with a major legal subject by setting out existing law along with desirable or anticipated changes.

RESTAURANT. *n.* A place established and operated as a business which provides, for a consideration, meals and attendant services for the public.

RESTAURATEUR. *n.* Any person who serves or sells meals or refreshments for consumption, for a consideration.

RESTITUTIO IN INTEGRUM. [L.] 1. The fundamental principle is that the plaintiff in an action for negligence is entitled to a sum of damages which will return the plaintiff to the position the plaintiff would have been in had the accident not occurred, insofar as money is capable of doing this. This goal was expressed in the early cases by the maxim restitutio in integrum. *Cooper v. Miller*, [1994] 1 S.C.R. 359, McLachlin, J. 2. In a case in which someone according to strict law lost a right and a court decision restores the original position on equitable principles. 3. Equitable relief given when a contract is rescinded because of fraud or in a similar case in which each party can be restored to its original position.

RESTITUTION. *n.* 1. " . . . [T]he function of the law of restitution 'is to ensure that where a plaintiff has been deprived of wealth that is either in his possession or would have accrued to his benefit, it is restored to him.' Restitution is a distinct body of law governed by its own developing system of rules. Breaches of fiduciary duties and breaches of confidence are both wrongs for which restitutionary relief is often appropriate." *International Corona Resources Ltd. v. Lac Minerals Ltd.* (1989), 44 B.L.R. 1 at 45, [1989] 2 S.C.R. 574, 26 C.P.R. (3d) 97, 69 O.R. (2d) 287, 61 D.L.R. (4th) 14, 6 R.P.R. (2d) 1, 35 E.T.R. 1, 101 N.R. 239, 26 O.A.C. 57, La Forest J. (Wilson and Lamer JJ. concurring in part). 2. The law which relates to any claim, whether quasi-contractual in nature or not, which is based on unjust enrichment. 3. "An examination of the language of these sections [ss. 653 and 654 of the Criminal Code, R.S.C. 1970, c. C-34] indicates that Parliament viewed the term 'restitution' as dealing with the return of identical property obtained as a result of the commission of an offence to its owner; . . . a restoration of property." *R. v. Groves* (1977), 39 C.R.N.S. 366 at 380, 17 O.R. (2d) 65, 37 C.C.C. (2d) 429, 79 D.L.R. (3d) 561 (H.C.), O'Driscoll J.

RESTITUTION ORDER. An order imposed as part of a sentence upon conviction for a criminal offence requiring the offender to restore property to its rightful owner.

RESTORATION. *n.* 1. The restoring of an obliterated monument. *Surveys acts.* 2. The reinstatement of a corporation which has been dissolved or the reinstatement of registration of a foreign company in the province.

RESTORATIVE JUSTICE. The creation of a positive environment for change, healing and reconciliation for offenders, victims and communities. It is a condemnation of criminal actions rather than perpetrators and an integration of offenders into the community rather than a stigmatization or marginalization of them. *R. v. Laliberte*, 2000 SKCA 27, 31 C.R. (5th) 1, [2000] 4 W.W.R. 491, 143 C.C.C. (3d) 503, 189 Sask. R. 190 (C.A.).

RESTORE. *v.* 1. In insurance, to reinstate or replace buildings or chattels which have been damaged or destroyed. Raoul Colinvaux, *The Law of Insurance*, 5th ed. (London: Sweet & Maxwell, 1984) at 181. 2. To reinstate a corporation which was dissolved or to reinstate registration of a foreign company in the province.

RESTORE THE NATURAL ENVIRONMENT. When used with reference to a spill of a pollutant, means restore all forms of life, physical conditions, the natural environment and things existing immediately before the spill of the pollutant that are affected or that may reasonably be expected to be affected by the pollutant. *Environmental Protection Act*, R.S.O. 1990, c. E.19, s. 91(1).

REST PERIOD. The period of time during which workers cease work as they are entitled to under the terms of their employment or a statute.

RESTRAIN. *v.* 1. To place under control when necessary to prevent serious bodily harm to the patient or to another person by the minimal use of such force, mechanical means or chemicals as is reasonable having regard to the physical and mental condition of the patient. *Mental Health Act*, R.S.O. 1990, c. M.7, s. 1. 2. To seize, distrain, confine or hold a stray, prior to impoundment, pursuant to this Act. *The Stray Animals Act*, R.S.S. 1978, c. S-60, s. 2.

RESTRAINING DEVICE. See SAFETY ~.

RESTRAINING ORDER. 1. Refers to an order forbidding a person from being in the presence of another as a term of a recognizance or probation or otherwise. 2. In some provinces, the order of a court to prevent disposal or waste of family property. C.R.B. Dunlop, *Creditor-Debtor Law in Canada*, Second Cumulative Supplement (Toronto: Carswell, 1986) at 211. 3. "... [A] restrictive injunction ..." *Peterson v. MacPherson* (1991), 32 R.F.L. (3d) 333 at 338, [1991] N.W.T.R. 178 (S.C.), de Weerdt J.

RESTRAINT. See HEAD ~; OCCUPANT ~ ASSEMBLY; PELVIC ~; PRODUCT ~ ASSEMBLY; UPPER TORSO ~.

RESTRAINT OF MARRIAGE. In general, any contract designed to prevent someone from marrying is void.

RESTRAINT OF TRADE. Refers to a contract otherwise freely entered into, that restricts a party's future use of skill, time and expertise. G.H.L. Fridman, *The Law of Contract in Canada*, 2d ed. (Toronto: Carswell, 1986) at 368. See CONTRACT IN ~.

RESTRAINT ON ALIENATION. A condition which restrains alienation of absolute interest in either real or personal property is generally considered void because it is repugnant.

RESTRAINTS OF PRINCES. Part of the phrase "arrest or restraints of princes, rulers or peoples" used in marine insurance policies to describe contingencies against which one makes provision. The particular contingency it describes is forcible interference with a voyage by the government of any nation.

RESTRAINT SYSTEM. A removable device designed to be installed in a vehicle for use in the restraint of an infant, a child or a mobility-impaired occupant but does not include booster cushions or vehicle seat belts.

RESTRICTED AREA. 1. An area where explosives, flammable liquids or flammable gases are stored, handled or processed or where the atmosphere contains or is likely to contain explosive concentrations of combustible dust or other combustible suspended material. *Canada Dangerous Substances Regulations*, C.R.C., c. 997, s. 2. 2. An area of an airport designated by a sign as an area whose access by persons or vehicles requires the production of valid identification. *Airport Tariff Regulations*, C.R.C., c. 886, s. 2.

RESTRICTED CHANNEL. In relation to a licensed area of a cable distribution undertaking, a channel of that undertaking that is the same channel on which signals are transmitted by (a) a local television station or a local FM station; or (b) a television station or an FM station that has a transmitter site located outside Canada within 60 km of any part of the licensed area. *Broadcasting Distribution Regulations*, SOR/97-555, s. 1.

RESTRICTED DRUG. Any drug or other substance included in Schedule H. *Food and Drugs Act*, R.S.C. 1985, c. F-27, s. 46.

RESTRICTED FIREARM. (a) A handgun that is not a prohibited firearm, (b) a firearm that (i) is not a prohibited firearm, (ii) has a barrel less than 470 mm in length, and (iii) is capable of discharging centre-fire ammunition in a semi-automatic manner, (c) a firearm that is designed or adapted to be fired when reduced to a length of less than 660 mm by folding, telescoping or otherwise, or (d) a firearm of any other kind that is prescribed to be a restricted firearm. *Criminal Code*, R.S.C. 1985, c. C-46, s. 84(1).

RESTRICTED IMMUNITY. Recognizes that when states enter into commercial or other private transactions with individuals, those individuals must be permitted to bring their disputes before the courts. *Athabasca Chipewyan First Nation v. Canada (Minister of Indian Affairs & Northern Development)*, 2001 ABCA 112, 281 A.R. 38 (C.A.).

RESTRICTED-USE MOTORCYCLE. A vehicle, excluding a power-assisted bicycle, a competition vehicle and a vehicle imported temporarily for special purposes, but including an all-terrain vehicle designed primarily for recreational use, that: (a) has steering handlebars, (b) is designed to travel on not more than four wheels in contact with the ground, (c) does not have as an integral part of the vehicle a structure to enclose the driver and passenger, other than that part of the vehicle forward of the driver's torso and the seat backrest, and (d) bears a label, permanently affixed in a conspicuous location, stating, in both official languages, that the vehicle is a restricted-use motorcycle or an all-terrain vehicle and is not intended for use on public highways.

RESTRICTED VISIBILITY. Any condition in which visibility is restricted by fog, mist, falling snow, heavy rainstorms, sandstorms or any other similar causes. *Collision Regulations*, C.R.C., c. 1416, Rule 3.

RESTRICTED WEAPON. Any weapon, other than a firearm, that is prescribed to be a restricted weapon. *Criminal Code*, R.S.C. 1985, c. C-46, s. 84(1).

RESTRICTION. *n.* Includes a requirement, exception, reservation, covenant, condition, stipulation or proviso. *Crown Grant Restrictions Act*, S.N.B. 1983, c. C-37.1, s. 1. See MARKET~; WORK ~.

RESTRICTIVE COVENANT. " . . . [S]omething in the nature of a negative easement, requiring for its creation and continuance a dominant and a servient tenement . . ." *Hunt v. Bell* (1915), 34 O.L.R. 256 at 262, 24 D.L.R. 590 (C.A.), Garrow J.A. (Meredith C.J.O., MacLaren and Magee JJ.A. concurring).

RESTRICTIVE INDORSEMENT. A notation which prohibits any further negotiation of a promissory note or bill of exchange.

RESTRICTIVE INTERPRETATION. Strict explanation of meaning.

RESTRICTIVE SOVEREIGN IMMUNITY. " . . . [W]hen the Sovereign puts aside his crown, so to speak, and descends to compete in the market place, his special rights, prerogatives and immunities remain with the crown and he becomes an ordinary subject of the law like his competitors . . . distinguishes actions of the state jure imperii from those jure gestionis." *Sparling v. Québec (Caisse de depot & de placement)* (1985), 29 B.L.R. 259 at 274, 22 D.L.R. (4th) 336, [1985] Que. C.A. 164, Tyndale J.A. (Monet and L'Heureux-Dubé JJ.A. concurring).

RESTRICTIVE TRADE PRACTICES COMMISSION. A federal administrative tribunal set up under the Combines Investigation Act.

RESTRUCTURE. *n.* 1. A change that, in the opinion of the Board, is significant in the operations of a manufacturer with respect to his products, methods of production, markets or management procedures and includes, if directly related to such operations, (a) the acquisition, amalgamation or merger of one or more manufacturers described in the definition "manufacturer" or the formation of a corporation or partnership described in paragraph (d) thereof; (b) the acquisition of working capital; or (c) the acquisition, construction or conversion of machinery, equipment, buildings, land or other facilities. Canada regulations. 2. A change that, in the opinion of the Board, is significant in the oper-

ations of a manufacturer or other person eligible for assistance under these Regulations, with respect to its or the person's products, methods of production, markets or management procedures and includes, if directly related to such operations, the acquisition of working capital or the acquisition, construction or conversion of machinery, equipment, buildings, land and other facilities. Canada regulations.

RESTRUCTURING. *n.* Includes the reorganization, refinancing, modernization, rationalization of an enterprise to improve its economic performance. Can include the injection of capital. See INDUSTRIAL ~.

RESUBDIVISION. *n.* The division of a parcel of land involving the modification of a boundary of a lot established by prior subdivision. *Dartmouth City Charter Act*, S.N.S. 1978, c. 43A, s. 2.

RESULT. *v.* With respect to something, to come back to a former owner or that person's representative when the thing was ineffective or only partly disposed of.

RESULT. *n.* 1. " . . . [S]omething which follows as an actual consequence. . ." *Sklar v. Saskatchewan Government Insurance Office* (1965), 52 W.W.R. 264 at 279, [1965] I.L.R. 1-139, 54 D.L.R. (2d) 455 (Sask. Q.B.), Sirois J. 2. " . . . '[T]ally' [of vote] which of course discloses the result . . ." *Alberta Government Telephones v. I.B.E.W., Local 348*, [1986] Alta. L.R.B.R. 112 at 116, Sims (Chair), Thompson and Eifert (Members). See OFFICIAL ~.

RESULT CRIME. One the actus reus of which consists of conduct personal to the defendant, and the causation of substantive harm by this conduct. Penalizes the actual infliction of this harm, and in so doing deters its infliction. *R. v. Hinchey*, [1996] 3 S.C.R. 1128, L'Heureux-Dube, J.

RESULT IN. Leading to; refers to something which is reasonably forseeable; weaker than "to cause".

RESULTING. *adj.* Describes the return of property to the grantor or the remaining in him of property as a result of the implication of law or equity. R. Megarry and H.W.R. Wade, *The Law of Real Property*, 5th ed. (London: Stevens, 1984) at cxxvii.

RESULTING TRUST. 1. " . . . [W]ill be presumed in favour of a person who is proved to have paid the purchase-money for real property in the character of purchaser if the real property is conveyed to another." *Rathwell v. Rathwell* (1978), 1 R.F.L. (2d) 1 at 10, [1978] 2 S.C.R. 436, [1978] 2 W.W.R. 101, 19 N.R. 91, 1 E.T.R. 307, 83 D.L.R. (3d) 289, Dickson J. (Laskin C.J.C. and Spence J. concurring). 2. " . . . [A]rises when a court of equity presumes from the nature of the transaction, the relations of the parties and the requirement of good faith that a trust was intended." *Gerry v. Metz* (1979), 12 R.F.L. (2d) 346 at 351 (Sask. C.A.), the court per Hall J.A. See PRESUMPTION OF ~.

RESULTING USE. A use which is implied.

RESUMMONS. *n.* An additional or repeated summons.

RESUMPTION. *n.* For the monarch to take back land which, through misleading or some other mistake, had been already granted to someone else.

RES UNIVERSITATIS. [L.] Something which belongs to a corporation which all members may use.

RESURVEY. *n.* A survey made for the purpose of placing in correct position monuments lost or incorrectly placed by a previous survey.

RETAIL. *n.* 1. A sale by a retailer directly to a consumer. 2. Any sale of products, excluding meals or refreshments, to a purchaser or to a user for consumption or use but not for resale. See SALE BY ~; SELL AT ~.

RETAIL. *adj.* 1. Refers to sales in small quantities to the end user. *Buchman & Son Lumber Co. v. Ontario Regional Assessment Commissioner, Region 9* (1982), 20 M.P.L.R. 78 at 83, 141 D.L.R. (3d) 95 (Ont. Div. Ct.), Steele J. (O'Leary J. concurring). 2. When used in relation to the distribution and supply of power, refers to the distribution and supply of power at voltages less than 50 kilovolts, but does not refer to works located within a transformer station that transform power from voltages greater than 50 kilovolts to voltages less than 50 kilovolts.

RETAIL BUSINESS. 1. The selling or offering for sale of goods or services by retail. 2. The selling or offering for sale of goods or services for consumption or use and of for resale and includes (a) the selling or offering for sale of goods and services by hawkers and peddlers; and (b) charging the public for admission to a place or facility for educational, recreational, cultural or amusement purposes.

RETAIL BUSINESS ESTABLISHMENT. The premises or place in which or from which a retail business is carried on.

RETAIL DEALER. 1. A person who sells fuel to a purchaser. 2. Any person who sells tobacco to a consumer. 3. Any person who sells or delivers fuel for consumption or use, but not resale.

RETAIL DISTRIBUTION. The sale, lease, rental, exchange or other means of dispersal of film to members of the public, other than retail distributors, wholesale distributors or exhibitors.

RETAIL DISTRIBUTION FACILITIES. Works for the transmission and supply of power at voltages less than 50 kilovolts other than works located within a transformer station that transforms power from voltages greater than 50 kilovolts to voltages less than 50 kilovolts.

RETAIL DISTRIBUTOR. A person who engages in retail distribution on a continual and successive basis.

RETAILER. *n.* 1. Any person who sells or offers to sell an agricultural product directly to the consumer. Canada regulations. 2. A Person who keeps for sale or sells to a consumer gasoline, diesel oil or home heating oil. 3. A person who sells beverages in containers and includes (a) a person, acting or purporting to act on that persons behalf; and (b) a person who controls the normal operation of an automatic vending machine that dispenses beverages in containers. 4. A person who sells books in the course of operating a business, but does not include an exclusive distributor or a book publisher. *Book Importation Regulations*, SOR/99-324, s. 1. See WHOLESALER~.

RETAILER MARGIN. The difference between the price at which a retailer buys from a wholesaler and the price at which the retailer sells to a consumer.

RETAIL ESTABLISHMENT. A building or portion of a building or place in which, as the principal business carried on therein, goods, wares or merchandise are sold or offered or displayed for sale to the general public.

RETAIL HIRE-PURCHASE. Any hiring of goods from a person in the course of his business in which (a) the hirer is given an option to purchase the goods; or (b) it is a agreed that upon compliance with the terms of the contract the hirer will either become the owner of the goods or will be entitled to keep them indefinitely without any further payment; except (c) a hiring in which the hirer is given an option to purchase the goods exercisable at any time during the hiring and which may be determined by the hirer at any time prior to the exercise of the option on not more than two months' notice without any penalty; (d) a hire-purchase of goods by a hirer who himself intends either to sell them or to re-let them for hire by others unless the goods are intended for sale or re-let in a manner to which Part VII of this Act applies; (e) a hire-purchase by a hirer who is a retailer of a vending machine or a bottle cooler to be installed in his retail establishment; (f) a hire-purchase of farm machinery and equipment to which The Farm Machinery and Equipment Act applies; (g) a hire-purchase in which the hirer is a corporation; (h) a hire-purchase of goods the cash price of which exceeds $25,000; and (i) a hire-purchase of goods by a hirer who himself intends to use them or uses them for the primary purpose of carrying on a business, unless the goods are intended for resale or re-let in a manner to which Part VII applies. *Consumer Protection Act*, R.S.M. 1987, c. C200, s. 1.

RETAIL OUTLET. 1. Any station, shop, establishment or other place, whether or not of a kind hereinbefore enumerated, in which any petroleum product is sold or kept for sale by retail. 2. Any premises at which gasoline or an associated product is sold and is put into the fuel tanks of motor vehicles or into portable containers.

RETAIL PURCHASER. 1. Any person who by a sale acquires tangible personal property not for resale but as a consumer and includes also a promotional distributor to the extent that the full fair value of or the purchase price of any goods provided by way of promotional distribution exceeds a payment specifically made by the person to whom the goods are so provided. *Retail Sales Tax Act*, R.S. Nfld. 1990, c. R-15, s. 2. 2. A person who by a sale acquires tobacco not for resale but as a consumer. 3. Any person who purchases fuel oil or gasoline at a sale in the province, where the fuel oil or gasoline is not purchased by that person for resale; but (a) for personal consumption or use, or for the consumption or use of other persons at the purchaser's expense; or (b) on behalf of or as the agent for a principal who desires to acquire the fuel oil or gasoline for consumption or use by that principal or by other persons at the expense of that principal.

RETAIL SALE. 1. A sale, including a sale by auction, of: (a) tangible personal property to a consumer or user for the purposes of consumption or use and not for resale as tangible personal property; (b) taxable services to a user for the purpose of use and not for resale; or (c) tangible personal property to a consumer or user who purchases the tangible personal property for the purpose of providing a taxable service therewith. 2. A sale for purposes other than exclusively for resale, lease or sub-lease.

RETAIL SELLER. A person who sells consumer products to consumers in the ordinary course of business.

RETAIL SPACE. The gross leasable floor area in any building or group of buildings used or intended to be used for the storage, display and sale of goods by retail or the provision of services, excluding areas used or intended to be used (a) for the operation of hotels, motels, theatres and recreation facilities; or (b) as open areas, entrance ways, public washrooms or for the provision of other common facilities.

RETAIL STORE. A building or part of a building which is used or intended to be used for the sale of goods by retail. See RECOGNIZED ~.

RETAIL TRADE. The business of purchasing any goods, wares or merchandise for resale to the public for personal or household use or consumption.

RETAIL VENDOR. Any person who, within a province, sells tobacco to a consumer.

RETAIL WAREHOUSE. " . . . [R]equires a large area and tends to be free standing. It serves both a warehouse and a retail function. It does not have retail in the front of the premises and storage in the back as is the case of the convention retail outlet. Rather than having departments which are individually staffed and where payment is made, there is little staff and the check-out facilities are located at the exit. The level of service is modest at best and there is little or no packaging. One of the chief components of a retail warehouse is its role as a supplier to smaller stores or outlets. . ." *788171 Ontario Ltd., Re* (1992), (*subnom. Barrie (City) Official Plan Amendment 23, Re*) 27 O.M.B.R. 303 at 305, Eisen (Member).

RETAIN. *v*. For a client to engage a solicitor or counsel to defend or take proceedings, to advise or act on one's behalf.

RETAINED EARNINGS. Earnings in excess of declared dividends which are reinvested in the company.

RETAINER. *n.* " . . . [T]he act of employing a solicitor or counsel, or . . . the document by which such employment is evidenced [or] . . . a preliminary fee given to secure the services of the solicitor and induce him to act for the client. . ." *Solicitor, Re* (1910), 22 O.L.R. 30 at 31 (C.A.), the court per Riddell J.A. See SEAT BACK ~.

RETAINING LIEN. A solicitor's right to retain property already in his or her possession until payment of fees due to the solicitor in his or her professional capacity are paid.

RETENTION AND DESTRUCTION SCHEDULES. Define the length of the storage period and eventual disposition of any public document or any class or series of public documents. See RECORDS SCHEDULE.

RETENTION AREA. The area and facilities within the race-course of an association that are provided by the association for the collection and securing of official samples. *Pari-Mutuel Betting Supervision Regulations*, SOR/91-365, s. 2.

RETAINING LIEN. A solicitor's right to retain property already in his or her possession until payment of fees due to the solicitor in his or her professional capacity are paid.

RETINENTIA. *n.* [L.] A group of people who attend on an important person.

RETIRE. *v.* To withdraw from employment.

RETIRED EMPLOYEE. A person who was formerly an employee and to whom or in respect of whom a pension is being paid.

RETIRED JUDGE. A judge who has reached the age where she is eligible to retire and who no longer has judicial duties.

RETIREMENT. *n.* " . . . [A] cessation of or withdrawal from work because of an age stipulation or because of some other condition agreed between employer and employee." *Specht v. R.*, [1975] C.T.C. 126 at 133, [1975] F.C. 150, 75 D.T.C. 5069 (T.D.), Collier J. See AGE OF ~; DELAYED ~; EARLY ~; NORMAL DATE OF ~; ORDINARY ~; REGISTERED ~ SAVINGS PLAN.

RETIREMENT AGE. In relation to an employee, means the earliest age at which a pension benefit, other than a benefit in respect of a disability, is or may become payable to the employee under the terms of a pension plan without adjustment by reason of early retirement. *Pen-*

sion Benefits Standards Act, R.S.C. 1985, c. P-7, s. 2. See COMPULSORY ~; MAXIMUM ~; NORMAL

RETIREMENT DATE. See NORMAL ~.

RETIREMENT INCOME FUND. An arrangement between a carrier and an annuitant under which, in consideration for the transfer to the carrier of property, the carrier undertakes to pay to the annuitant and, where the annuitant so elects, to the annuitant's spouse or common-law partner after the annuitant's death, in each year that begins not later than the first calendar year after the year in which the arrangement was entered into one or more amounts the total of which is not less than the minimum amount under the arrangement for the year, but the amount of any such payment shall not exceed the value of the property held in connection with the arrangement immediately before the time of the payment. *Income Tax Act*, R.S.C. 1985, c. 1 (5th Supp.), s. 146.3(1). See REGISTERED ~.

RETIREMENT METHOD. A method of determining the value of a person's interest in a group pension for the purposes of dividing property in a marriage breakdown. The value of the future income stream is calculated assuming the member will continue to be employed until retirement. Likely future earnings are assumed.

RETIREMENT PENSION. Periodic payments for life intended to replace wages or salary. Intended to guarantee a level of income to a person no longer employed.

RETIREMENT PLAN. See REGISTERED ~.

RETIREMENT SAVINGS PLAN. (a) A contract between an individual and a person licensed or otherwise authorized under the laws of Canada or a province to carry on in Canada an annuities business, under which, in consideration of payment by the individual or the individual's spouse or common-law partner of any periodic or other amount as consideration under the contract, a retirement income commencing at maturity is to be provided for the individual; or (b) an arrangement under which payment is made by an individual or the individual's spouse or common-law partner (i) in trust to a corporation licensed or otherwise authorized under the laws of Canada or a province to carry on in Canada the business of offering to the public its services as trustee, of any periodic or other amount as a contribution under the trust; (ii) to a corporation approved by the Governor in Council for the purposes of this section that is licensed or otherwise authorized under the laws of Canada or a province to issue investment contracts providing for the payment to or to the credit of the holder thereof of a fixed or determinable amount at maturity, of any periodic or other amount as a contribution under any such contract between the individual and that corporation; or (iii) as a deposit with a branch or office, in Canada; of (A) a person who is, or is eligible to become, a member of the Canadian Payments Association; or (B) a credit union that is a shareholder or member of a body corporate referred to as a "central" for the purposes of the Canadian Payments Association Act, (in this section referred to as a "depositary") to be used, invested or otherwise applied by that corporation or that depositary, as the case may be, for the purpose of providing for the individual, commencing at maturity, a retirement income. *Income Tax Act*, R.S.C. 1985, c. 1 (5ᵗʰ Supp.), s. 146(1). See REGISTERED ~.

RETIRING ALLOWANCE. An amount (other than a superannuation or pension benefit, an amount received as a consequence of the death of an employee or a benefit described in subparagraph 6(1)(a)(iv)) received (a) on or after retirement of a taxpayer from an office or employment in recognition of the taxpayer's long service, or (b) in respect of a loss of an office or employment of a taxpayer, whether or not received as, on account or in lieu of payment of, damages or pursuant to an order or judgment of a competent tribunal, by the taxpayer or, after the taxpayer's death, by a dependant or a relation of the taxpayer or by the legal representative of the taxpayer. *Income Tax Act*, R.S.C. 1985, c. 1 (5ᵗʰ Supp.), s. 248.

RETORNA BREVIUM. [L.] Of writs, return.

RETORSION. *n.* Retaliation. Specifically in international law, when one nation is dissatisfied with the treatment of its nationals by another nation, the first nation may declare that it will treat the second nation's nationals similarly.

RETORT. *n.* Any equipment used to recover mercury from mercury contaminated waste. *Chlor-Alkali Mercury National Emission Standards Regulations*, C.R.C., c. 406, s. 2.

RETOUR SANS PROTET. [Fr.] Return with no protest.

RETRACEMENT. *n.* The re-establishment of a line of a previous survey.

RETRACTATION. *n.* In probate practice, withdrawal of renunciation.

RETRACTOR. *n.* A device for storing part or all of the webbing in a seat belt assembly. *Motor Vehicle Safety Regulations*, C.R.C., c. 1038, s. 2. See AUTOMATIC-LOCKING ~; EMERGENCY-LOCKING ~; NON-LOCKING ~.

RETRACTUS AQUAE. [L.] With respect to tides, ebb or return.

RETRAXIT. [L. one withdrew] A proceeding which bars any future action on the same cause, unlike a nolle prosequi which does not bar this, unless it was made after judgment.

RETRIBUTION. *n.* 1. Something given or demanded in payment; punishment based on the notion that every crime demands payment in the form of punishment. 2. Retribution, as an objective of sentencing, represents nothing less than the hallowed principle that criminal punishment, in addition to advancing utilitarian considerations related to deterrence and rehabilitation, should also be imposed to sanction the moral culpability of the offender. Retribution is integrally woven into the existing principles of sentencing in Canadian law through the fundamental requirement that a sentence imposed be "just and appropriate" under the circumstances. Indeed, retribution represents an important unifying principle of our penal law by offering an essential conceptual link between the attribution of criminal liability and the imposition of criminal sanctions. The legitimacy of retribution as a principle of sentencing has often been questioned as a result of its unfortunate association with "vengeance" in common parlance. But it should be clear from my foregoing discussion that retribution bears little relation to vengeance, and I attribute much of the criticism of retribution as a principle to this confusion. As both academic and judicial commentators have noted, vengeance has no role to play in a civilized system of sentencing. *R. v. M. (C.A.)*, 1996 CarswellBC 1000, 46 C.R. (4th) 269, 194 N.R. 321, 105 C.C.C. (3d) 327, 73 B.C.A.C. 81, 120 W.A.C. 81, [1996] 1 S.C.R. 500, Per Lamer, C.J.C.

RETROACTIVE EFFECT. With respect to an act, relation back to a time before that act.

RETROACTIVE ORDER. " . . . [An order] that [changes] past transactions. . ." *Nova v. Amoco Canada Petroleum Co.*, [1980] 3 W.W.R. 1 at 40, 20 A.R. 384 (C.A.), Prowse J.A. (concurring in the result).

RETROACTIVE PAY. The additional portion of wages earned during a period in respect of which a wage increase was awarded which dated back in time.

RETROACTIVE STATUTE. 1. " . . . [O]ne that operates backwards, i.e., that is operative as of a time prior to its enactment, either by being deemed to have come into force at a time prior to its enactment (e.g., budgetary measures) or by being expressed to be operative with respect to past transactions as of a past time (e.g., acts of indemnity). . ." *Royal Canadian Mounted Police Act (Canada), Re*, [1991] 1 F.C. 529 at 548 (C.A.), MacGuigan J.A. 2. " . . . [O]perates forward in time, starting from a point further back in time than the date of its enactment; so it changes the legal consequences of past events as if the law had been different than it really was at the time those events occurred." *Hornby Island Trust Commmittee v. Stormwell* (1988), 53 D.L.R. (4th) 435 at 441, 39 M.P.L.R. 300, 30 B.C.L.R. (2d) 383 (C.A.), Lambert J.A. (Hutcheon J.A. concurring).

RETRO-ASSESSMENT. An assessment required of members of a reciprocal insurance exchange to meet liabilities in excess of those covered by the base premium paid by the members. *Canadian Lawyers Insurance Assn. v. Alberta* (1995), 30 Alta. L.R. (3d) 282 (C.A.).

RETROFIT. *n.* A renovation of the common areas of a building generally undertaken by the landlord. *Martel Building Ltd. v. R.*, 2000 CarswellNat 2678, 2000 SCC 60, 36 R.P.R. (3d) 175, 193 D.L.R. (4th) 1, 262 N.R. 285, 3 C.C.L.T. (3d) 1, 5 C.L.R. (3d) 161, 186 F.T.R. 231 (note), [2000] 2 S.C.R. 860 Per Iacobucci and Major JJ for the court.

RETROGRADE AMNESIA. Blackout or memory loss following a traumatic event. The person affected cannot retrieve stored memories.

RETROSPECTIVE EFFECT. Said of a law which affects acts or facts occurring before it came into force.

RETROSPECTIVE ORDER. " . . . [An order] . . . which [attaches] new consequences to past transactions, such as prospective orders that take into account losses or gains incurred or accrued prior to the effective date of the order. . ." *Nova v. Amoco Canada Petroleum Co.*, [1980] 3 W.W.R. 1 at 41, 20 A.R. 384 (C.A.), Prowse J.A. (concurring in the result).

RETROSPECTIVE STATUTE. 1. " . . . [C]hanges the law only for the future but looks backward by attaching new consequences to completed transactions. It thus opens up closed transactions . . ." *Royal Canadian Mounted Police Act (Canada), Re*, [1991] 1 F.C. 529 at 548 (C.A.), MacGuigan J.A. 2. " . . . [O]perates forward in time, starting only from the date of its enactment, but from that time forward it changes the legal consequences of past events." *Horn Island Trust Commmittee v. Stormwell* (1988), 39 M.P.L.R. 300 at 307-8, 53 D.L.R. (4th) 435, 30 B.C.L.R. (2d) 383 (C.A.), Lambert J.A. (Hutcheon J.A. concurring).

RETROVIRUS. *n.* A virus which uses RNA to pass on genetic information and replicate itself.

RETURN. *v.* To come back to or to go back to a place.

RETURN. *n.* 1. The report of an officer of a court, e.g. a sheriff, which shows how a duty imposed on that officer was performed. 2. The record of any report or information provided by a respondent. *Statistics acts.* 3. A return prescribed pursuant to any revenue act. 4. The returning officer shall declare elected the candidate who obtained the largest number of votes by completing the return of the writ in the prescribed form on the back of the writ. *Canada Elections Act*, S.C. 2000, c. 9, s. 313(1), part. See ANNUAL ~; NET ~ IN ANY YEAR; PATRONAGE ~.

RETURNABLE. *adj.* Used to describe a writ of execution or other kind of writs to which the person to whom they are directed must or may need to make a return.

RETURNABLE CONTAINER. A container belonging to a class of containers with respect to which, at the time of the sale of any such container together with the contents thereof to a purchaser, a specifically identified sum is usually charged and paid upon the express or implied undertaking of the vendor, or of the manufacturer or distributor of the container or its contents, that, upon delivery of that container to such vendor, manufacturer or distributor, or to the agent of any of them, the sum charged to the purchaser with respect to such container will be paid to the purchaser.

RETURN DUCT. A duct for conveying air from a space being heated, ventilated or air-conditioned back to the heating, ventilating or air-conditioning appliance.

RETURNING OFFICER. 1. A person responsible for conducting a municipal or parliamentary election. 2. Appointed for each electoral district and is responsible, under the general direction of the Chief Electoral Officer, for the preparation for and conduct of an election in his or her electoral district. After the issue of the writ, a returning officer appoints the other election officers. *Canada Elections Act, 2000*, c. 9. See ASSISTANT ~; DEPUTY ~; SPECIAL ~.

RETURN OF CONTRIBUTIONS. A return of the amount paid by the contributor into a superannuation account.

REVALORIZE. *v*. Of an amount owing, to revalue it because the debt depreciated between the time it was incurred and the time it was due. J.G. McLeod, *The Conflict of Laws* (Calgary: Carswell, 1983) at 515.

REV. CAN. CRIM. *abbr*. Revue canadienne de criminologie (Canadian Journal of Criminology).

REV. CAN. D.A. *abbr*. Revue canadienne du droit d'auteur.

REV. CAN. D. COMM. *abbr*. Revue canadienne du droit de commerce (Canadian Business Law Journal).

REV. CAN. D. COMMUNAUTAIRE. *abbr*. Revue canadienne du droit communautaire (Canadian Community Law Journal).

REV. CAN. D. & SOCIÉTÉ. *abbr*. Revue canadienne de droit et société (Canadian Journal of Law and Society).

REV. CAN. D. FAM. *abbr*. Revue canadienne de droit familial (Canadian Journal of Family Law).

REV. CRIT. *abbr*. Revue critique (1870-1875).

REV. D. OTTAWA. Revue de droit d'Ottawa (Ottawa Law Review).

REVENDICATE. *v*. To acquire the repossession of. D.N. Macklem & D.I. Bristow, *Construction, Builders' and Mechanics' Liens in Canada*, 6th ed. (Toronto: Carswell, 1990-) at 13-17.

REVENDICATION. *n*. When goods are sold on credit, in some jurisdictions the seller reserves the right to retake them or to hold a lien upon them for the price if it is unpaid. In other jurisdictions, the seller has the right to stop in transitu only when the buyer is insolvent.

REVENUE. *n*. 1. Annual profit; income. 2. All public money collected or due. See CUR-

RENT ~; FEE ~; FLYING ~S; GROSS ~; NET INCOME OR ~; NET ~; NON-RENEWABLE RESOURCE ~; NON-TAX ~; OPERATING ~S; PUBLIC ~; RESOURCE ~; SHAREABLE ~.

REVENUE ACT. A statute imposing a tax or fee.

REVENUE BASE. For a revenue source for a province for a fiscal year relates to the measure of the relative capacity of the province to derive revenue from that revenue source for that fiscal year and has the meaning given to that expression by the regulations. *Federal-Provincial Fiscal Arrangements Act*, R.S.C. 1985, c. F-8, s. 4(2).

REVENUE INSURANCE PROGRAM. A program that is designed to insure a portion of the value of an eligible agricultural product produced or marketed by a producer participating in the program. *Farm Income Protection Act*, S.C. 1991, c. 22, s. 2.

REVENUE LAW. The law concerning noncontractual payments of money to the government or its agencies to maintain programmes for the benefit of everyone within the sovereign's territory.

REVENUE OFFICER. A person who (a) is engaged in or is appointed or employed for the purposes of the collection or management of or accounting for public money; (b) is engaged in the administration of any law under which public money is collected, managed or accounted for; (c) is required by law or contract to collect, manage or account for public money; or (d) receives, holds or is entrusted with public money, whether or not that person was appointed or employed for that purpose.

REVENUE PAPER. Paper that is used to make stamps, licences or permits or for any purpose connected with the public revenue. *Criminal Code*, R.S.C. 1985, c. C-46, s. 321.

REVENUE RECEIPT. Includes all public money except capital receipts.

REVENUE SOURCE. Any of the following sources from which provincial revenues are or may be derived: (a) personal income taxes; (b) corporation income taxes, revenues derived from government business enterprises that are not included in any other paragraph of this definition, and revenues received from the Government of Canada pursuant to the Public Utilities Income Tax Transfer Act; (c) taxes on capital of corporations; (d) general and miscellaneous sales taxes and amusement taxes; (e) tobacco taxes; (f) motive fuel taxes derived from the sale of gasoline; (g) motive fuel taxes derived from the sale of diesel fuel; (h) non-commercial motor vehicle licensing revenues; (i) commercial motor vehicle licensing revenues; (j) alcoholic beverage revenues derived from the sale of spirits; (k) alcoholic beverage revenues derived from the sale of wine; (l) alcoholic beverage revenues derived from the sale of beer; (m) hospital and medical care insurance premiums; (n) succession duties and gift taxes; (o) racetrack taxes; (p) forestry revenues; (q) conventional new oil revenues; (r) conventional old oil revenues; (s) heavy oil revenues; (t) mined oil revenues; (u) domestically sold natural gas revenues; (v) exported natural gas revenues; (w) sales of Crown leases and reservations on oil and natural gas lands; (x) oil and gas revenues other than those described in paragraphs (q) to (w); (y) metallic and non-metallic mineral revenues other than potash revenues; (z) potash revenues; (aa) water power rentals; (bb) insurance premiums taxes; (cc) payroll taxes; (dd) provincial and local government property taxes; (ee) lottery revenues; (ff) miscellaneous provincial taxes and revenues including miscellaneous revenues from natural resources, concessions and franchises, sales of provincial goods and services and local government revenues from sales of goods and services and miscellaneous local government taxes; and (gg) revenues of the Government of Canada from any of the sources referred to in this definition that are shared by Canada with the provinces, other than revenues shared under the Public Utilities Income Tax Transfer Act. *Federal-Provincial Fiscal Arrangements Act,* R.S.C. 1985, c. F-8, s. 4(2).

REVERBERATORY FURNACE. Includes a stationary, rotating or rocking and tilting furnace. *Secondary Lead Smelter National Emission Standards Regulations,* C.R.C., c. 412, s. 2.

REVERSAL. *n.* Making a judgment void because of error.

REVERSE. *v.* To make void, repeal or undo. A judgment is reversed when a court of appeal sets it aside.

REVERSE DISCRIMINATION. 1. When an "affirmative action" program is in place a member of the general population may argue that she is subject to reverse discrimination. Subsection 15(1) of the *Charter* prohibits discrimination on enumerated and analogous grounds, while s. 15(2) permits the adoption of affirmative action programs to ameliorate past discrimination thereby foreclosing the argument of reverse discrimination. 2. " . . . [D]iscriminates against [persons not belonging to one race, for example] because whenever there is a finite number of persons seeking some advantage (in this case employment), to prefer one because of his race is to the disadvantage of another because of the race of the first person." *Athabasca Tribal Council v. Amoco Canada Petroleum Co.,* [1981] 1 C.N.L.R. 35 at 48, [1980] 5 W.W.R. 165, 22 A.R. 541, 112 D.L.R. (3d) 200,1 C.H.R.R. D/174 (C.A.), Laycraft J.A. (McGillivray C.J.A. concurring).

REVERSE ONUS CLAUSE. "In pre-Charter cases the imposition of a reverse onus clause upon an accused was frequently recognized and accepted as an exception to the general rule requiring proof by the Crown of all elements of an offence beyond a reasonable doubt. It was settled, as well, that where the accused was required to discharge an onus relating to an element of a criminal offence, he had to do so according to the civil standard of proof, that is, he had to establish the matter on a balance of probabilities." *R. v. Schwartz* (1988), 55 D.L.R. (4th) 1 at 32, [1989] 1 W.W.R. 289, 66 C.R. (3d) 251, 88 N.R. 90, [1988] 2 S.C.R. 443, 45 C.C.C. (3d) 97, 56 Man. R. (2d) 92, McIntyre J. (Beetz, La Forest and L'Heureux-Dubé JJ. concurring).

REVERSER. *n.* A reversioner.

REVERSE STING. In sting operations, undercover police officers pose as purchasers of narcotics. . . In a reverse sting, undercover police officers offer to sell large quantities of drugs to the target. If the negotiations are successful, the police operatives produce the drugs, give them to the target upon receiving payment and the target is arrested shortly afterwards. *R. v. Jageshur* (2002), 165 O.A.C. 230 (C.A.).

REVERSION. *n.* " . . . [A]n undisposed of estate in property, left in a grantor after he has parted with some particular interest less than the fee simple therein. In the second place, it is an estate which returns to the grantor after the determination of such particular estate . . ." *Ferguson v. MacLean,* [1931] 1 D.L.R. 61 at 67, [1930] S.C.R. 630, Anglin C.J.C. (Rinfret J. concurring). See RUN WITH THE ~.

REVERSIONARY. *adj.* Enjoyable in reversion.

REVERSIONARY INTEREST. " . . . [Future interests in real as well as personal property which are not by operation of law or otherwise interests reserved to the grantor or donor; but are merely interests which take effect at the expiration of a preceding estate or interest, or . . . interests which simply take effect in the future. . ." *Ferguson v. MacLean*, [1931] 1 D.L.R. 61 at 79, [1930] S.C.R. 630, Duff J.

REVERSIONARY LEASE. A lease which takes effect in the future; a second lease which becomes effective after the first lease expires.

REVERSIONARY VALUE. " . . . [S]ome value to the landowner which will accrue to him once the 'taking' has served its use." *Dome Petroleum Ltd. v. Grekul* (1983), 28 Alta. L.R. (2d) 260 at 268, [1988] 1 W.W.R. 447, 29 C.L.R. 111, 5 Admin. L.R. 252, 49 A.R. 256 (Q.B.), Miller J.

REVERSIONER. *n.* A person who has a reversion.

REVERSIO TERRAE EST TANQUAM TERRA REVERTENS IN POSSESSIONE DONATORI, SIVE HAEREDIBUS SUIS POST DONUM FINITUM. [L.] A reversion of land is, so to speak, the return of land to the possession of either the donor or the donor's heirs after the estate granted terminates.

REVERT. *v.* 1. To return; e.g., when the owner of land grants a small estate to another person and when that estate terminates, the land reverts to the grantor. 2. "[T]o . . . 'fall back into' his estate." *Carter v. Goldstein* (1921), 66 D.L.R. 34 at 35, 63 S.C.R. 207, Davies C.J.

REVERTER. *n.* Reversion. See DOMICILE BY ~.

REV. ÉTUDES CAN. *abbr.* Revue d'études canadiennes (Journal of Canadian Studies).

REV. FISCALE CAN. *abbr.* Revue fiscale canadienne (Canadian Tax Journal).

REVIEW. *n.* 1. " . . . [I]s occasionally taken in popular use as meaning more than a first instance 'looking over' or 'examination'. In its legal sense . . . it usually means more than that, as implying a formal, second instance 're-examination' or 'reconsideration' with a view to revision or re-determination if something be found wrong or lacking." *Saskatoon (City) v. Plaxton* (1989), 33 C.P.C. (2d) 238 at 250, [1989] 2 W.W.R. 577, 78 Sask. R. 215 (C.A.), Cameron J.A. (Gerwing J.A. concurring). 2. Except where

the context indicates otherwise, (a) an independent review of records, or (b) the preparation of a report, certificate or comments or the expression of an opinion for the purpose of determining whether financial information appears to be presented fairly. *Chartered Accountants Act*, S.A. 1987, c. C-5.1, s. 1(1). See GENERAL ~; JUDICIAL ~; PAYMENT ~ PERIOD.

REVIEWABLE ERROR. " . . . [A]n arbitrator in construing a statutory provision in the course of an arbitration proceeding commits reviewable error if his or her construction is wrong. . ." *Cape Breton Development Corp. v. U.M.W, District No. 26, Local 4522* (1985), 85 C.L.L.C. 14,041 at 12,222, 68 N.S.R. (2d) 181, 159 A.P.R. 181 (T.D.), MacIntosh J.

REVIEWABLE TRANSACTION. In bankruptcy matters, a transaction which was not at arm's length or was made by people who are "related".

REVIEW BOARD. 1. A board established to review certain orders. *Youth Criminal Justice Act*, S.C. 2002, c. 1, s. 2. 2. A review board established or designated by a province for the purposes of section 30. *Young Offenders Act*, R.S.C. 1985, c. Y-1, s. 2.

REVIEW COMMITTEE. 1. The Security Intelligence Review Committee established by subsection 34(1). *Canadian Security Intelligence Service*, R.S.C. 1985, c. C-23, s. 2. 2. A Review Committee established under section 82. *Canada Pension Plan*, R.S.C. 1985, c. C-8, s. 2.

REVISED ASSESSMENT ROLL. 1. The assessment roll of the municipality as finally passed by the court of revision. *The Urban Municipality Act*, R.S.S. 1978, c. U-10, s. 2. 2. " . . . [T]hat upon which the rates are struck and the financial operations of the municipalities are based . . ." *R. v. McIntosh* (1881), 46 U.C.Q.B. 98 at 105, Cameron J. (Hagarty C.J. and Armour J. concurring).

REVISED STATUTES. 1. A consolidation and declaration of the law as contained in the acts which they supplant; they do not come into force as new or independent statutes. 2. The latest revised and consolidated statutes of a province or the federal government.

REVISED VOTERS' LIST. Where used to refer to the revised voters' list of an electoral division means all the voters' lists prepared for an election in the electoral division as finally revised before polling day at the election.

REVISING AGENT. A returning officer shall appoint revising agents to work in pairs and each pair shall consist, as far as possible, of persons recommended by different registered parties. *Canada Elections Act*, S.C. 2000, c. 9, s. 33(3).

REVISING JUSTICE. A justice of the peace appointed or designated by the Lieutenant-Governor in Council in accordance with this Act to prepare and revise lists of electors for an electoral district or part, when the justice acts in the territory assigned to him or her by the Lieutenant-Governor in Council for the purpose, and includes any such justice sitting as a Court of Revision for a part of the territory so assigned to him or her. *Election Act*, R.S. Nfld. 1990, c. E-3, s. 2.

REVISING OFFICER. A person appointed to revise a list of electors. See ASSISTANT ~.

REVISION. *n*. 1. The arrangement, revision and consolidation of the public general statutes of Canada authorized under the Statute Revision Act. 2. The examination and correction of the meaning and form of a translation and includes the insertion into a translation of changes made in the original text after it has been submitted for translation to the Bureau. *Translation Bureau Regulations*, C.R.C., c. 1561, s. 2.

REVIVAL. *n*. 1. Re-execution of a will by a testator after it was revoked; execution of a will or codicil which shows the intention to revive it. 2. The reinstatement and recreation of a corporation which has been dissolved for failure to file returns or for some other act. 3. "[A corporation through] revival . . . acquires all the rights and privileges and is liable for all the obligations that it would have had if it had not been dissolved . . . ." *Computerized Meetings & Hotel Systems Ltd. v. Moore* (1982), 20 B.L.R. 97 at 106, 40 O.R. (2d) 88, 141 D.L.R. (3d) 306 (Div. Ct.), Callaghan J.

REVIVED COMPANY. A body corporate that is revived for the purpose of enabling it to apply for continuance as a corporation.

REVIVOR. *n*. A motion needed to continue proceedings when the suit abated before final consummation because of death or some other reason.

REV. JUR. FEMME & D. *abbr*. Revue juridique "La Femme et le droit" (Canadian Journal of Women and the Law).

REV. LOIS & POL. SOCIALES. *abbr*. Revue des lois et des politiques sociales (Journal of Law and Social Policy).

REVOCABLE LICENCE. " . . . [E]nables a person to do lawfully what he could not otherwise do: . . ." *National Trust Co. v. Bouckhuyt* (1987), 43 D.L.R. (4th) 543 at 551, 61 O.R. (2d) 640, 23 O.A.C. 40, 46 R.P.R. 221, 21 C.P.C. (2d) 226, 7 P.P.S.A.C. 273, 38 B.L.R. 77, the court per Cory J.A.

REVOCATION. *n*. 1. Undoing something granted; destroying or voiding a deed which existed until revocation made it void; revoking. 2. Cancellation. *Motor Vehicle Act*, R.S.N.B. 1973, c. M-17, s. 2. 3. " . . . [C]ancellation . . ." *R. v. Whynacht*, [1942] 1 D.L.R. 238 at 240, 16 M.P.R. 267, 77 C.C.C. 1 (N.S. C.A.), Chisholm C.J. 4. With respect to a will, for a testator to render it inoperative or annul it by a later act. See DEPENDENT RELATIVE ~.

REVOKE. *v*. To annul, cancel, repeal, rescind.

REVOKED. *adj*. Annulled, cancelled, repealed, rescinded.

REVOKING. *adj*. Annulling, cancelling, repealing, rescinding.

REVOLVING CREDIT. Credit in which amounts drawn on the credit are added back and become re-available as the buyer provides funds to meet acceptances. I.F.G. Baxter, *The Law of Banking*, 3d ed. (Toronto: Carswell, 1981) at 156.

REVOLVING FUND. A fund composed of money, accounts receivable, inventories, liabilities or any combination thereof in which revenues are credited and expenditures charged for a specific purpose.

REVOLVING LOAN AGREEMENT. An agreement under which loans may be made by a lender from time to time with the credit charges being computed from time to time in relation to the total of the balances outstanding on all of the loans.

REVOLVING STORES ACCOUNT. An inventory of goods and materials that are charged against an activity at the time of use rather than purchase.

REWARD. *n*. 1. Something tangible and pecuniary, that is payment or profit. 2. Payment of financial consideration to a person who helped apprehend another charged with an offence. See GAIN OR ~; HIRE OR ~.

REX. *n*. [L. king] Monarch.

REX EST CAPUT ET SALUS REIPUBLI-CAE. [L.] The monarch is the head and guardian of the commonwealth.

REX EST LEGALIS ET POLITICUS. [L.] The monarch is both legal and political.

REX N'EST LIE PER AUSCUN STATUTE SI IL NE SOIT EXPRESSEMENT NOSME. [Fr.] The monarch is not bound by any statute unless expressly named in it.

REX NON DEBET ESSE SUB HOMINE SED SUB DEO ET LEGE QUIA LEX FACIT REGEM. [L.] The monarch should not be subject to any person, but to the deity and the law, for law makes the monarch.

REX NON POTEST FALLERE NEC FALLI. [L.] The monarch can neither deceive nor be deceived.

REX NON POTEST PECCARE. [L.] The monarch cannot do wrong.

REX NUNQUAM MORITUR. [L.] The monarch never dies.

REX QUOD INJUSTUM EST FACERE NON POTEST. [L.] The monarch cannot do what is unjust.

REZONE. *v*. To change the substance of any of the uses permitted in a by-law by zoning at another time. I.M. Rogers, *The Law of Canadian Municipal Corporations*, 2d ed. (Toronto: Carswell, 1971-) at 783.

REZONING. See SPOT ~.

R.F.L. *abbr*. Reports of Family Law, 1971-1977.

R.F.L. REP. *abbr*. Reports of Family Law, Reprint Series.

R.F.L. (2D). *abbr*. Reports of Family Law (Second Series), 1978-1986.

R.F.L. (3D). *abbr*. Reports of Family Law (Third Series), 1986-.

RFP. *abbr*. Request for proposals.

R.G.D. *abbr*. Revue générale de droit (Section de droit civil, Faculté de droit, Université d'Ottawa).

RHETORIC. *n*. The art of speaking with elegance and art.

RHESUS FACTOR. Antigens first found in the rhesus monkey which are carried on red blood cells. Individuals who possess them are called "Rh positive". F.A. Jaffe, *A Guide to Pathological Evidence*, 3d ed. (Toronto: Carswell, 1991) at 225.

RH FACTOR. See RHESUS FACTOR.

RHODODENDRON. *n*. The evergreen shrub, Rhododendron macrophyllum, known as rhododendron. *Dogwood, Rhododendron and Trillium Protection Act*, R.S.B.C. 1979, c. 96, s. 1.

RIB. See TREAD ~.

R.I.B.L. *abbr*. Review of International Business Law.

RICE ORDER. " . . . [A] judicial sale to the plaintiff with a judgment for the deficiency." *Morguard Investments Ltd. v. De Savoye* (1988), 29 C.P.C. (2d) 52 at 55, 27 B.C.L.R. (2d) 155, [1988] 5 W.W.R. 650 (C.A.), the court per Seaton J.A.

RICOCHET EFFECT. See BILLIARD-RIC-OCHET EFFECT.

RIDE. See AMUSEMENT ~.

RIDER. *n*. A clause inserted later. See COAT-TAIL ~; FREE ~.

RIDICULE. *v*. To make fun of someone or something. Making someone or something the object of contemptuous amusement.

RIDING HORSE ESTABLISHMENT. Premises where horses are kept that are let out on hire for riding or used in providing instruction in riding for payment or both. *Riding Horse Establishments Act*, R.S.O. 1990, c. R.32, s. 1.

RIENS ARREAR. [Fr.] Nothing in arrears.

RIENS IN ARRERE. [Fr.] Nothing in arrears.

RIENS PASSE PER FAIT. [Fr.] Nothing passes by deed.

RIENS PER DESCENT. [Fr.] Nothing by descent.

RIENS PER DEVISE. [Fr.] Nothing by devise.

RIFFLARE. To remove something by force.

RIFLE. *n*. A firearm, usually fired from the shoulder, which has a barrel with rifting on the inside surface. F.A. Jaffe, *A Guide to Pathological Evidence*, 3d ed. (Toronto: Carswell, 1991) at 225. See FIREARM; PIECE.

RIFLING. *n.* A sequence of spiral grooves on the inside surface of a firearm barrel which imparts a spin to a projectile. The quantity of grooves and their direction (left or right handed) is one way to classify firearms. F.A. Jaffe, *A Guide to Pathological Evidence*, 3d ed. (Toronto: Carswell, 1991) at 225.

RIG. *v.* To manipulate a bid in an underhanded or fraudulent way.

RIGGING. See BID-~.

RIGHT. *n.* 1. " . . . [I]s defined positively as what one can do." *R. v. Zundel* (1987), 29 C.R.R. 349 at 365, 18 O.A.C. 161, 58 O.R. (2d) 129, 31 C.C.C. (3d) 97, 56 C.R. (3d) 1, 35 D.L.R. (4th) 338 (C.A.), Howland C.J.O., Brooke, Martin, Lacourcière and Houlden JJ.A. 2. " . . . [S]pecific, detailed and imposes a duty; . . ." *R.W.D.S.U., Locals 496, 544, 635, 955 v. Saskatchewan* (1985), 85 C.L.L.C. 14,054 at 12,277, [1985] 5 W.W.R. 97, 39 Sask. R. 193, 21 C.R.R. 286 (C.A.), Bayda C.J.S. 3. Includes power, authority, privilege and licence. *Interpretation acts.* 4. Includes power, authority, benefit, privilege and remedy. *Water Act*, R.S.B.C. 1979, c. 429, s. 1. See ACCESS ~; ACCRUED ~; ACCRUING ~; BARGAINING ~; COLOUR OF ~; CONTINGENT ~; DEPENDENT ~; ENTRANT AS OF ~; FREEDOM; FUTURE ~; IMPRESCRIPTABLE ~; LEGAL ~; LIBERTY; MINERAL ~; MINING ~; OIL AND GAS ~; PERFORMING ~; PETITION OF ~; PETROLEUM ~; PREEMPTIVE ~; PRIVATE ~; PROPERTY ~; PROPRIETARY ~; PUBLIC LENDING ~; REAL ~; ~S; TRAIN OF SUPERIOR ~; VESTED ~ VOTING ~.

RIGHT-HAND. *var.* **RIGHT HAND.** In reference to a highway or the position of traffic thereon means the right when facing or moving in the direction of travel.

RIGHT OF ACCESS. Includes the right to take a child for a limited period of time to a place other than the child's habitual residence.

RIGHT OF ACTION. 1. " . . . [T]he right to institute civil proceedings in court for the determination of a right or claim." *Reference re Sections 32 & 34 of the Workers' Compensation Act, 1983 (Newfoundland)* (1987), 36 C.R.R. 112 at 145, 67 Nfld. & P.E.I.R. 16, 206 A.P.R. 16, 44 D.L.R. (4th) 501 (Nfld. C.A.), Morgan J.A. 2. " . . . A bare 'right of action' is not a right in the ordinary use of the term. It is rather a mere claim to a right, and it only becomes an actual

right when it has ripened into a judgment." *McGregor v. Campbell* (1909), 11 W.L.R. 153 at 161, 19 Man. R. 38 (C.A.), Richards J.A. See CONTRACTUAL ~.

RIGHT OF APPEAL. " . . . [T]he right of appeal is a statutory right, and there is no such right unless it is expressly given." *Dale v. Commercial Union Assurance Co. of Canada* (1981), 22 C.P.C. 29 at 31, 32 O.R. (2d) 238, [1981] I.L.R. 1-1342, 121 D.L.R. (3d) 503 (C.A.), the court per Brooke J.A.

RIGHT OF ASSOCIATION. The right of workers to form unions or other trade associations.

RIGHT OF AUDIENCE. A superior court's inherent right to permit a non-lawyer to appear before it as a representative or advocate for another person.

RIGHT OF CUSTODY. Includes rights relating to the care of the person of the child and, in particular, the right to determine the child's place of residence.

RIGHT OF DISSENT. " . . . [I]n ordinary parlance means just that. But that expression has become a term of art among those involved in this area of the law, and is used by them to describe not just the right to vote against the motion but . . . that 'bundle of rights' that are given to dissentient shareholders in the [Business Corporations Act, S.A. 1981, c. B-15]." *Fitch v. Churchill Corp.* (1990), 47 B.L.R. 97 at 99, 72 Alta. L.R. (2d) 343, 66 D.L.R. (4th) 569, [1990] 4 W.W.R. 256, 105 A.R. 25 (C.A.), Kerans, Lieberman and Irving JJ.A.

RIGHT OF ENTRY. The right to take or resume possession of land by entering it peacefully.

RIGHT OF FIRST REFUSAL. 1. " . . . [T]he party who grants a right of first refusal merely agrees that should he decide to enter a certain type of contract he will first offer to do so with the holder of the right of first refusal: . . . The right of first refusal requires that an offer must first be made as a precondition to the exercise of the right, whereas an option consists of a continuing and irrevocable offer open to the optionee's acceptance. . ." *Brookside Farms Ltd., Re* (1988) 72 C.B.R. (N.S.) 162 at 164 (B.C. S.C.), Campbell L.J.S.C. 2. A right of pre-emption, or right of first refusal, does not give the grantee the unilateral power to compel the grantor to sell the property in question. Instead, the grantor has the sole power to decide whether to make an offer. It is only at that point that the grantee (or lessee) is given the opportunity of purchasing the property. A right of first refusal is a commitment by the grantor to give the grantee the first chance to purchase should the grantor decide to sell. *Mitsui & Co. (Canada) v. Royal Bank*, [1995] 2 S.C.R. 187. See OPTION.

RIGHT OF INTERMENT. A right, acquired by purchase, inheritance or transfer, for the interment of human remains or cremated remains in a lot.

RIGHT OF PRE-EMPTION. A right of pre-emption, or right of first refusal, does not give the grantee the unilateral power to compel the grantor to sell the property in question. Instead, the grantor has the sole power to decide whether to make an offer. It is only at that point that the grantee (or lessee) is given the opportunity of purchasing the property. A right of first refusal is a commitment by the grantor to give the grantee the first chance to purchase should the grantor decide to sell. *Mitsui & Co. (Canada) v. Royal Bank*, [1995] 2 S.C.R. 187.

RIGHT OF PUBLICITY. First coined in *Haelan Laboratories Inc. v. Topps Chewing Gum Inc.*, 202 F.2d 866 (U.S. 2nd Cir. N.Y., 1953), 868, "right of publicity": has since come to signify the right of an individual, especially a public figure or a celebrity, to control the commercial value and exploitation of his name and picture or likeness and to prevent others from unfairly appropriating this value for their commercial benefit. (see *Estate of Presley v. Russen*, 513 F. Supp. 1339 (U.S. D. N.J., 1981)). *Gould Estate v. Stoddart Publishing Co.* (1996), 30 O.R. (3d) 520 (Gen. Div.). See MISAPPROPRIATION OF PERSONALITY.

RIGHT OF SELF-DETERMINATION. ". . . [W]hich underlies the doctrine of informed consent, also obviously encompasses the right to refuse medical treatment. A competent adult is generally entitled to refuse a specific treatment or all treatment, or to select an alternative form of treatment, even if the decision may entail risks as serious as death and may appear mistaken in the eyes of the medical profession or of the community." *Malette v. Shulman* (1990), 2 C.C.L.T. (2d) 1 at 10, 72 O.R. (2d) 417, 67 D.L.R. (4th) 321, 37 O.A.C. 281 (C.A.), the court per Robins J.A.

RIGHT OF SURVIVORSHIP. The right of a surviving joint tenant to take the property of the other, deceased joint tenant.

RIGHT OF USE. The exclusive right to occupy or use property rent-free for the purposes of the undertaking.

RIGHT OF USER. A licence to enter on and use land.

RIGHT OF WAY. *var*. **RIGHT-OF-WAY**. 1. In its traditional sense, a "right of way" is a type of easement, and at common law the acquisition of a right of way does not give the holder a fee simple interest or the right to exclusive possession: E. C. E. Todd, *The Law of Expropriation and Compensation in Canada* (2nd ed. 1992). However . . . in modern usage the term right of way does not always correspond to the common law concept and in some circumstances may refer to a right to the exclusive use and occupation of a corridor of land. *Osoyoos Indian Band v. Oliver (Town)*, [2001] 3 S.C.R. 746, Per Iacobucci J. (McLachlin C.J.C., Binnie, Arbour and LeBel JJ. concurring). 2. " . . . [A] generally understood meaning as the land reserved for placement of a physical improvement such as a railway, transmission line or pipeline. . ." *British Columbia Assessment Commissioner v. Canadian National Railway Co.* (1989), 42 M.P.L.R. 71 at 79 (B.C.S.C.), McLachlin C.J.S.C. 3. The privilege of the immediate use of the highway. 4. Includes land or an interest in land required for the purpose of constructing, maintaining or operating a road, railway, aerial, electric or other tramway, surface or elevated cable, electric or telephone pole line, chute, flume, pipeline, drain or any right or easement of a similar nature. 5. The strip of land between any two railway stations upon which railway tracks run. See EXCLUSIVE ~; RAILWAY ~.

RIGHTS. *n*. 1. Includes estates and interests. *Trustee acts*. 2. Are general and universal and represent the means by which the inherent dignity of each individual in society is respected. See ABORIGINAL ~; AQUATIC ~; BILL OF ~; CIVIL ~; CONJUGAL ~; CUM ~; DOWER ~; EMPLOYER ~; EX ~; INTERMITTENT ~; LEGAL ~; MANAGEMENT ~; MARITAL~; MATRIMONIAL PROPERTY ~; MINERAL ~; MINING ~; MOBILITY ~; NEIGHBOURING ~; OIL SANDS ~; PREROGATIVE ~ OF THE CROWN; REDEEMABLE ~; RIGHT; RIPARIAN ~; SOLE ~; SURFACE ~; SURFACE ~ OPTION; VESTED ~.

RIGHTS ARBITRATION. " . . . [T]he procedure of rights arbitration only comes into play once the negotiations have produced a collective agreement. At that stage any differences arising from the interpretation, application or administration of that collective agreement . . . are required to be resolved by the process of rights arbitration, or grievance arbitration." *Haldimand-Norfolk Health Unit v. O.N.A.* (1981), 81 C.L.L.C. 14,085 at 76, 120 D.L.R. (3d) 101, 31 O.R. (2d) 730 (C.A.), Goodman J.A. (Howland C.J.O., Lacourciére, Houlden and Morden JJ.A. concurring) quoting the O.L.R.B.'s advisory opinion in *Haldimand-Norfolk Regional Health Unit v. Ontario Nurses' Association* (1978), O.L.R.B. Rep. 197 at 198, 78 C.L.L.C. 16,134, [1978] 1 C.L.R.B.R. 475.

RIGHTS HOLDER. See INTERMENT ~.

RIGHT TO A VOTING SECURITY. (a) A security currently convertible into another security that is a voting security; (b) a security carrying a warrant or right to acquire another security that is a voting security; or (c) a currently exerciseable option, warrant or right to acquire another security that is a voting security or a security referred to in subclause (a) or (b). *Securities Act*, S.A. 1981, c. S-6.1, s. 131.

RIGHT TO BEGIN. The right to be first to address a court or jury.

RIGHT TO BE PRESUMED INNOCENT. " . . . [I]s, in popular terms, a way of expressing the fact that the Crown has the ultimate burden of establishing guilt; if there is any reasonable doubt at the conclusion of the case on any element of the offence charged, an accused person must be acquitted. In a more refined sense, the presumption of innocence gives an accused the initial benefit of a right of silence and the ultimate benefit (after the Crown's evidence is in and as well as any evidence tendered on behalf of the accused) of any reasonable doubt: . . ." *R. v. Appleby*, [1972] S.C.R. 303 at 317, 16 C.R.N.S. 35, [1971] 4 W.W.R. 601, 3 C.C.C. (2d) 354, 21 D.L.R. (3d) 325, Laskin J.

RIGHT TO COUNSEL. 1. Everyone has the right on arrest or detention to retain and instruct counsel without delay and to be informed of that right. *Canadian Charter of Rights and Freedoms*, Part I of the *Constitution Act, 1982*, being Schedule B of the *Canada Act 1982* (U.K.),1982, c. 11, s. 10(b). 2. " . . . [T]he right to retain and instruct counsel [in s. 10(b) of the Charter], in modern Canadian society, has come to mean more than the right to retain a lawyer privately. It now also means the right to have access to counsel free of charge where the ac-

cused meets certain financial criteria set up by the provincial legal aid plan, and the right to have access to immediate, although temporary, advice from duty counsel irrespective of financial status. . ." *R. v. Brydges* (1990), 46 C.R.R. 236 at 256, [1990] 2 W.W.R. 220, [1990] 1 S.C.R. 190, 71 Alta. L.R. (2d) 145, 103 N.R. 282, 74 C.R. (3d) 129, 53 C.C.C. (3d) 330, 104 A.R. 124, Lamer J. (Wilson, Gonthier and Cory JJ. concurring). 3. The purpose of the right to counsel guaranteed by s. 10(*b*) of the *Charter* is to provide detainees with an opportunity to be informed of their rights and obligations under the law and, most importantly, to obtain advice on how to exercise those rights and fulfil those obligations. This opportunity is made available because, when an individual is detained by state authorities, he or she is put in a position of disadvantage relative to the state. Not only has this person suffered a deprivation of liberty, but also this person may be at risk of incriminating him- or herself. Accordingly, a person who is "detained" within the meaning of s. 10 of the *Charter* is in *immediate* need of legal advice in order to protect his or her right against self-incrimination and to assist him or her in regaining his or her liberty. Under s. 10(*b*), a detainee is entitled as of right to seek such legal advice "without delay" and upon request. The right to counsel protected by s. 10(*b*) is designed to ensure that persons who are arrested or detained are treated fairly in the criminal process. This court has said on numerous previous occasions that s. 10(*b*) of the *Charter* imposes the following duties on state authorities who arrest or detain a person: (1) to inform the detainee of his or her right to retain and instruct counsel without delay and of the existence and availability of legal aid and duty counsel; (2) if a detainee has indicated a desire to exercise this right, to provide the detainee with a reasonable opportunity to exercise the right (except in urgent and dangerous circumstances); and (3) to refrain from eliciting evidence from the detainee until he or she has had that reasonable opportunity (again, except in cases of urgency or danger). *R. v. Bartle*, 1994 CarswellOnt 100, 33 C.R. (4th) 1, 6 M.V.R. (3d) 1, 19 O.R. (3d) 802 (note), 172 N.R. 1, 92 C.C.C. (3d) 289, 74 O.A.C. 161, 118 D.L.R. (4th) 83, [1994] 3 S.C.R. 173, 23 C.R.R. (2d) 193, per Lamer, C.J.C.

RIGHT TO FLOOD. A right or power to flood or otherwise injuriously affect land for purposes related to the construction, maintenance or operation of a dam, reservoir or other plant used or to be used for or in connection with the generation, manufacture, distribution or supply of power.

RIGHT TO HARVEST. The right to hunt, fish, trap, capture or kill any kind of fish or any kind of wild mammals or birds.

RIGHT TO REMAIN SILENT. " . . . [T]he basis for the non-compellability of the accused as a witness at trial but it extends beyond the witness box. In R. v. Esposito (1985), 20 C.R.R. 102, at p. 108, Martin J.A. outlined its scope: 'The right of a suspect or an accused to remain silent . . . operates both at the investigative stage of the criminal process and at the trial stage.' . . . it is a right not to be compelled to answer questions or otherwise communicate with police officers or others whose function it is to investigate the commission of criminal offences. As with the privilege against self-incrimination, the right to remain silent protects the individual against the affront to dignity and privacy which results if crime enforcement agencies are allowed to conscript the suspect against himself or herself. . ." *Thomson Newspapers Ltd. v. Canada (Director of Investigation & Research)* (1990), 47 C.R.R. 1 at 94, 97, 76 C.R. (3d) 129, 72 O.R. (2d) 415n, 54 C.C.C. (3d) 417, 67 D.L.R. (4th) 161, 29 C.P.R. (3d) 98, [1990] 1 S.C.R. 425, 39 O.A.C. 161, 106 N.R. 161, Sopinka J. (dissenting in part).

RIGHT TO SILENCE. "In R. v. Hebert [1990] 2 S.C.R. 151, this Court found that s. 7 of the Charter includes a right to silence which includes the right to choose whether or not to make a statement to the authorities. In Hebert, Justice McLachlin described the right as follows, at p. 186: 'The essence of the right to silence is that the suspect be given a choice; the right is quite simply the freedom to choose—the freedom to speak to the authorities on the one hand, and the right to refuse to make a statement to them on the other.'" *R. v. Broyles*, [1991] 3 S.C.R. 595 at 605, 9 C.R. (4th) 1, [1992] 1 W.W.R. 289, 68 C.C.C. (3d) 308, 84 Alta. L.R. (2d) 1, 131 N.R. 118, 120 A.R. 189, 8 W.A.C. 189, 8 C.R.R. (2d) 274, the court per Iacobucci J.

RIGHT TO VOTE. "[In s. 3 of the Charter] . . . should be defined as guaranteeing the right to effective representation. The concept of absolute voter parity does not accord with the development of the right to vote in the Canadian context and does not permit of sufficient flexibility to meet the practical difficulties inherent in representative government in a country such as Can-

ada." *Reference re Provincial Electoral Boundaries*, [1991] 2 S.C.R. 158 at 188, [1991] 5 W.W.R. 1, 127 N.R. 1, 81 D.L.R. (4th) 16, McLachlin J. (La Forest, Gonthier, Stevenson and Iacobucci JJ. concurring).

RIGHT TO WORK. 1. The right of an employee to keep a job without being a union member. 2. "[Used to describe] . . . the right not to be regulated. It had little to do with the important personal right of otherwise qualified professional people to have an opportunity to attempt to build a practice in their province and in their chosen communities. One may be deprived of such a right in accordance with the principles of fundamental justice: . . ." *Wilson v. British Columbia (Medical Services Commission)* (1988), 34 Admin. L.R. 235 at 262, 30 B.C.L.R. (2d) 1, [1989] 2 W.W.R. 1, 53 D.L.R. (4th) 17 (C.A.), Nemetz C.J.B.C., Carrothers, Hinkson, Macfarlane and Wallace JJ.A.

RIGHT-TO-WORK LAW. A law which effectively negates union security clauses in agreements. See RIGHT TO WORK.

RIGHT WHALE. Any whale known by the name of Atlantic right whale, Arctic right whale, Biscayan right whale, bowhead, great polar whale, Greenland right whale, Greenland whale, Nordkaper, North Atlantic right whale, North Cape whale, Pacific right whale, pigmy right whale, Southern pigmy right whale, or Southern right whale. *Whaling Convention Act*, R.S.C. 1970, c. W-8, Schedule s. 18.

RIGID FOAM PRODUCT. A product that contains or consists of any of the following types of foam: (a) closed cell rigid polyurethane foam, including one- and two-component froth, pour, spray, injected or bead-applied foam and polyisocyanurate foam; (b) closed cell rigid polystyrene boardstock foam; (c) closed cell rigid phenolic foam; and (d) closed cell rigid polyethylene foam when such foam is suitable in shape, thickness and design to be used as a product that provides thermal insulation around pipes used in heating, plumbing, refrigeration or industrial process systems. *Ozone-depleting Substances Regulations, 1998*, SOR/99-7, s. 1.

RIGOR MORTIS. [L.] The stiffening and contracting of the voluntary and involuntary muscles in the body after death. F.A. Jaffe, *A Guide to Pathological Evidence*, 3d ed. (Toronto: Carswell, 1991) at 225.

RIG RELEASE DATE. The date on which, in the opinion of a district oil and gas conservation engineer, a well drilled for the purpose of discovering or producing oil and gas had been properly terminated. *Territorial Land Use Regulations*, C.R.C., c. 1524, s. 2.

RIM. *n.* 1. A metal support for a tire or a tire and tube assembly, upon which the tire beads are seated. Canada regulations. 2. The unobstructed open edge of a fixture. See DEMOUNTABLE ~; FLOOD LEVEL ~; TEST ~.

RIM-FIRE SHELL OR CARTRIDGE. A firearm cartridge designed to be fired by the action of a firing pin striking the rim area of the cartridge base.

RIOT. *n.* An unlawful assembly that has begun to disturb the peace tumultuously. *Criminal Code*, R.S.C. 1985, c. C-46, s. 64.

RIOT ACT. The name commonly given to the proclamation set out in section 67 of the Criminal Code, R.S.C. 1985, c. C-46 which is read at the time of a riot.

RIPARIA. *n.* [L.] Water which runs between two banks; a bank.

RIPARIAN. *adj.* " . . . [A]pplies to a river and flowing water . . ." *Rickey v. Toronto (City)* (1914), 30 O.L.R. 523 at 524, 19 D.L.R. 146 (H.C.), Boyd C.

RIPARIAN RIGHTS. 1. " . . . [D]o not carry exclusive possession; they exist as incorporeal rights arising from ownership, in the nature of servitudes, among other things, over foreshore." *Canada (Attorney General) v. Higbie, (sub nom. Canada (Attorney General) v. Western Higbie)* [1945] 3 D.L.R. 1 at 44, [1945] S.C.R. 385, Wand J. 2. "The rights enjoyed by a riparian owner are classified as follows in [G.V. La-Forest, Water Law in Canada: The Atlantic Provinces] ([Ottawa: Information Canada,] 1973), at p. 201: '(1) the right of access to water; (2) the right of drainage; (3) rights relating to the flow of water; (4) rights relating to the quality of water (pollution); (5) rights relating to the use of water; and (6) the right of accretion.'" *Welsh v. Marantette* (1983), 27 C.C.L.T. 113 at 125-6, 44 O.R. (2d) 137, 30 R.P.R. 111, 3 D.L.R. (4th) 401 (H.C.), Maloney J.

RISER. *n.* A supply pipe that extends through at least one full storey to convey water. *Ontario Water Resources Act*, R.R.O. 1980, Reg. 736, s. 1.

RISE TIME. The time required for the wave shape to go from 10 per cent to 90 per cent of its amplitude. *Medical Devices Regulations*, C.R.C., c. 871, s. 1.

RISK. *n.* 1. " . . . [I]n insurance contracts refer to the very object of the contract of insurance, the happening of which—the 'loss'—triggers the obligation of the insurer to indemnify the insured or his beneficiary." *Metropolitan Life Insurance Co. v. Frenette*, [1992] I.L.R. 1-2823 at 1784, 89 D.L.R. (4th) 653, [1992] 1 S.C.R. 647, 46 Q.A.C. 161, [1992] R.R.A. 466, L'Heureux-Dubé J. 2. A probability statement about the extent of danger in an ordinary orderly environment. 3. The peril insured against in the policy defines the risk which is the hazard or chance of misfortune or loss at some time in the future. *University of Saskatchewan v. Fireman's Fund Insurance Co. of Canada* (1997), 158 Sask. R. 223 (C.A.). 4. In relation to the emission of an air contaminant as a result of the operation of any work, undertaking or business, a risk that the concentration of that air contaminant in the ambient air in the geographical area in which the work, undertaking or business is situated, either alone or in combination with one or more other air contaminants referred to in the national ambient air quality objectives prescribed in relation to that air contaminant, will exceed the maximum acceptable limit with respect to that air contaminant or combination of air contaminants. *Clean Air Act*, R.S.C. 1985, c. C-32, s. 21(2). See ALL ~S; MATERIAL ~; MORAL ~; SUBSTANTIAL ~; VOLUNTARY ASSUMPTION OF ~; WAR ~S.

RISK ASSESSMENT. " . . . [T]he initial investigation required for the formation of the insurance contract. . ." *Metropolitan Life Insurance Co. v. Frenette*, [1992] I.L.R. 1-2823 at 1784, 89 D.L.R. (4th) 653, [1992] 1 S.C.R. 647, 46 Q.A.C. 161, [1992] R.R.A. 466, L'Heureux-Dubé J.

RISK CLASSIFICATION SYSTEM. In relation to automobile insurance, means the elements used for the purpose of classifying risks in the determination of rates for a coverage or category of automobile insurance, including the variables, criteria, rules and procedures used for that purpose. *Insurance Act*, R.S.O. 1990, c. I.8, s. 1.

RISK FOSTER PARENTS. This designation applies to foster parents who have expressed an interest in adopting a foster child who has been placed with them if that foster child is made a Crown ward. There is an inherent risk in such situations that the duration of foster parenting may be more than just temporary and that strong attachments would be formed. *L. (R.) v. Children's Aid Society of Niagara Region* (2002), 167 O.A.C. 105, 16 O.F.L.R. 127, 34 R.F.L. (5th) 44 (C.A.)

RIVER. *n.* 1. Includes creek, stream or brook. 2. Includes all streams, lakes, creeks and estuaries, and all channels, ravines, gulches and watercourses, natural or artificial, tidal or otherwise, in which water flows constantly, intermittently or at any time, whether salt or fresh. See INTERNATIONAL ~; LAKE AND ~ NAVIGATION; MACKENZIE ~; PRODUCTS OF THE SEA, LAKES AND ~S; SALMON ~.

RIVER BED. The bed and bars of the river to the foot of the natural banks.

RIVER IMPROVEMENT PURPOSE. Clearing and improving the bed, channel and banks of a stream to facilitate the driving and booming of timber.

RIVER RAFTING. See COMMERCIAL ~.

R.J.E.L. *abbr.* Revue juridique des étudiants de l'Université Laval.

R.J.F.D. *abbr.* Revue juridique "La Femme et le droit (Canadian Journal of Women and the Law).

R.J.Q. *abbr.* 1. Rapports judiciaires du Québec, 1875-1891 (Quebec Law Reports). 2. Recueil de jurisprudence du Quéebec.

R.J.R.Q. *abbr.* Rapports judiciaires revisés de la province de Québec (Mathieu), 1726-1891 (Quebec Revised Reports).

R.J.T. *abbr.* La Revue juridique Thémis.

R.L. *abbr.* La Revue Légale (Qué.), 1980-.

[] **R.L.** *abbr.* La Revue Légale (Qué.), 1943-1979.

R.L.N.S. *abbr.* La Revue Légale (N.S.) (Qué.), 1895-1942.

R.L.O.S. *abbr.* La Revue Légale (Qué.), 1869-1891.

ROAD. *n.* 1. Land used or intended for use for the passage of motor vehicles. 2. Includes a street, avenue, parkway, driveway, square, bridge, viaduct, trestle or other passageway designed and intended for, or used by the general public for the passage of vehicles and includes a trail on a frozen lake, river or other body of water or watercourse when such trail is maintained or kept open at public expense. 3. A graded strip of ground, appropriated for travel by motor vehicle, which is not on the right of way of a public highway. See ACCESS ~; CAT ~; COMMON ~; DEPARTMENTAL ~; FEEDER OR SPUR ~; FOREST ACCESS ~; FOREST ~; FORESTRY ~; GRID ~; HAUL ~; HIGHWAY AND ~; HIGHWAY OR ~; IMPROVE A ~; INDUSTRIAL ~; LOCAL ~; LOGGING ~; ON-SITE ~; OPENING A ~; PRIVATE ~; PUBLIC ~; RESERVED ~; RURAL ~; SERVICE ~; TEMPORARY ACCESS ~; TOTE ~.

ROAD ALLOWANCE. 1. Any right-of-way surveyed for the purpose of a road by either the Federal or provincial government survey and includes all rights-of-way provided by virtue of any statute for the purpose of a road, or any right-of-way properly dedicated to the public use as a highway. *Highways and Transportation Department Act*, R.S.M. 1987, c. H40, s. 1. 2. " . . . [S]trips of Crown land reserved from public sale and settlement. They were reserved originally for the sole purpose of making roads when and as roads might be required." *R. v. Alberta Railway & Irrigation* Co., [1912] A.C. 827 at 832, 7 D.L.R. 513 (Can. P.C), Lord MacNaughten.

ROAD AUTHORITY. A body having jurisdiction and control of a common or public highway or road, or any part thereof, including a street, bridge and any other structure incidental thereto and any part thereof.

ROAD BUILDING. The preparation, construction, reconstruction, repair, alteration, remodelling, renovation, demolition, finishing and maintenance of streets, highways or parking lots, including structures such as bridges, tunnels or retaining walls in connection with streets or highways, and all foundations, installation of equipment, appurtenances and work incidental thereto.

ROAD BUILDING MACHINE. *var.* **ROAD-BUILDING MACHINE**. A vehicle (a) that is designed and used primarily for grading of highways, paving of highways, earth moving and other construction work on highways; (b) that is not designed or used primarily for the transportation otherwise of persons or property; and (c) that is only incidentally operated or moved over a highway.

ROAD CROSSING. That part of a road that passes across, over or under a line of railway, and includes any structure supporting or protecting that part of that road or facilitating the crossing. *Railway Safety Act*, R.S.C. 1985, c. 32 (4th Supp.)s. 4(1).

ROAD IMPROVEMENT LINE. The line bordering land required to effect an improvement to the alignment, width or grade of a road, street, lane, sidewalk or other public way. *Local Government Act*, S. Nfld. 1972, c. 32, s. 2.

ROAD LINE. The line between a street reservation and the abutting land.

ROAD LOAD. The power output required to move the vehicle at curb weight plus 400 pounds on level, clean, dry, smooth portland cement concrete pavement or other surface with an equivalent coefficient of surface friction at a specified speed through still air at 68° Fahrenheit and standard barometric pressure of 29.92 inches of mercury, and includes driveline friction, rolling friction and air resistance. *Motor Vehicle Safety Regulations*, C.R.C., c. 1038, s. 103.

ROAD SERVICE VEHICLE. A vehicle operated by or on behalf of a municipality or other authority having jurisdiction and control of a highway while the vehicle is being used for highway maintenance purposes. *Highway Traffic Act*, R.S.O. 1990, c. H.8, s. 133.

ROADSIDE IMPROVEMENT. (a) Any building, structure, fixture or road; (b) any tree, shrub or hedge; or (c) any sign, notice, advertising device or flashing or rotating light.

ROADSIDE PREMISES. Land within 150 m of the centre line of a designated highway.

ROAD RAGE. Misconduct arising when a person reacts in an unreasonable and extreme way in response to the conduct of others using the road or highway.

ROAD TRACTOR. Every motor vehicle designed and used for drawing other vehicles and not so constructed as to carry any load thereon either independently or any part of the weight of a vehicle or load so drawn.

ROAD VEHICLE. A motor vehicle that can be driven on a highway, other than a vehicle that runs only on rails or an electrically propelled wheelchair; a trailer, a semi-trailer or a detachable axle. See COMBINATION OF ~S.

ROADWAY. *n.* 1. That part of a public highway ordinarily used for vehicular traffic. 2. The continuous strip of land owned or occupied by a company as a right of way for its railway leading from place to place within Alberta but does not include (a) land that is outside the limits of the right of way and owned or occupied by the company for station grounds, extra right of way for sidings, spur tracks, wyes or other trackage; or (b) land within the limits of the right of way that is used by the company for purposes other than the operation of the railway. 3. That portion of the surface of land required for access to a well site. 4. With reference to "roadway" as defined in the Motor Vehicle Act, it relates to a portion of a highway that is improved, designed or ordinarily used for vehicular traffic, but does not include the shoulder. For a surface to be a "roadway" it should be currently designed and improved or used for the passage of vehicles. *Busch Estate v. Lewers* 1999 CarswellBC 1730 SC. See LANED ~; ONE-WAY ~; PRIVATE ~; PUBLIC ~; RAILWAY ~; SERVICED ~.

ROB. & JOS. DIG. *abbr*. Robinson & Joseph's Digest.

ROBBERY. *n.* (a) Stealing; and for the purpose of extorting whatever is stolen or to prevent or overcome resistance to the stealing, using violence or threats of violence to a person or property; (b) stealing from any person and, at the time he steals or immediately before or immediately thereafter, wounding, beating, striking or using any personal violence to that person; (c) assaulting any person with intent to steal from him; or (d) stealing from any person while armed with an offensive weapon or imitation thereof. *Criminal Code*, R.S.C. 1985, c. C-46, s. 343.

ROCK. *n.* That portion of the earth's crust which is consolidated, coherent and relatively hard and is a naturally formed, solidly bonded, mass of mineral matter which cannot readily be broken by hand. See BED~.

ROCKET. *n.* A projectile that contains its own propellant and that depends for its flight on a reaction set up by the release of a continuous jet of rapidly expanding gases. *Canadian Aviation Regulations*, SOR/96-433, s. 101.01. See MODEL ~.

ROCK TRENCHING. Any excavation carried out on a mineral claim for the purpose of obtaining geological information.

ROCKWEED. *n.* A brown marine plant of the species Ascophyllum nodosum.

ROD. *n.* 5 1/2 yards. *Weights and Measures Act*, S.C. 1970-71-72, c. 36, schedule II. See GROUND-~; LIGHTNING ~; SQUARE ~.

ROGATORY. See COMMISSION EVIDENCE; COMMISSION ~; LETTERS ~; PERPETUATE TESTIMONY; ~ LETTERS.

ROGATORY LETTERS. A commission in which one judge requests another to examine a witness. See COMMISSION EVIDENCE; COMMISSION ROGATORY; LETTERS ROGATORY; PERPETUATE TESTIMONY; ROGATORY.

ROLL. *n.* 1. The list of the members in good standing of a professional body. 2. A real estate assessment roll. 3. The list of the members in good standing of an order, prepared under this Code. *Professional Code*, R.S.Q., c. C-26, s. 1. See ASSESSMENT AND TAX ~; ASSESSMENT ~; JURORS' ~; STRIKE OFF THE ~.

ROLLED UP PLEA. " . . . [S]tates that the allegations of fact in the libel are true, that they are of public interest, and that the comments upon them contained in the libel were fair. The allegation of truth is confined to the facts averred, and the averment as to the comments is not that they are true but only that they were made in good faith and that they are fair and do not exceed the proper standard of comment upon such matters. *Sutherland v. Stopes*, [1925] A.C. 47 at 62-3 (U.K. C.A.), Viscount Finlay.

ROLLING ANTON PILLER ORDER. The identity of the defendant or defendants is not known at the time the order is granted; the proceeding is commenced against John and Jane Doe. Also, particulars of the alleged infringing activity of the as yet to be identified defendants are not known. A general statement is made in the affidavit filed to support the issuance of the Anton Piller order that the plaintiff is suffering irreparable harm because of the manufacture and sale of counterfeit merchandise, that is, merchandise that infringes the plaintiff's copyright, trademark or other intellectual property rights. Once granted, an Anton Piller order of the rolling type typically lasts for approximately a year, and is executed during that time against numerous individuals and corporate entities identified by the plaintiff's agents. *Nike Canada Ltd. v. Jane Doe* (1999), 174 F.T.R. 131 (T.D.).

ROLLING FORMAT. As applied to any time segment, means a format of presentation of broadcast matter in which one or more musical compositions are broadcast without interruption or accompanying broadcast matter other than (a) matter within content subcategory number 01, 09, 11, 12, 13, 14, 15, 16, 37 or 41, where the interruption for the presentation of such matter occurs on more than one occasion; and (b) matter within content category number 8 or 9. *Radio (F.M.) Broadcasting Regulations*, C.R.C., c. 380, s. 14.

ROLLING STOCK. Includes a locomotive, engine, motor car, tender, snow-plough, flanger and any car or railway equipment that is designed for movement on its wheels on the rails of a railway. *Canada Transportation Act*, S.C. 1996, c. 10, s. 6. See RAILWAY ~.

ROLL-OVER. *n.* " . . . [G]ives a measure of tax relief to surviving members of a family unit by delaying the tax consequences of the deemed realization until the recipient subsequently disposes of the property." *Boger Estate v. Minister of National Revenue* (1991), 43 E.T.R. 27 at 36 (Fed. T.D.), Jerome A.C.J.

ROM. 1. Information to be stored permanently can be held in another type of chip called "Read Only Memory" (ROM). Information stored in ROM chips is not lost when the power of the computer is switched off. *Apple Computer Inc. v. Macintosh Computers Ltd.* (1985), 3 C.I.P.R. 133, 3 C.P.R. (3d) 34 (Fed. T.D.) Cullen J. 2. The computer's memory is typically composed of semiconductor circuits known as chips. There are two types of memory; ROM (Read Only Memory) and RAM (Random Access Memory). Instructions stored in ROM are permanent; they can only be read by the computer not changed or rewritten by it, and do not erase when the machine is turned off. Instructions stored in RAM can be changed or rewritten by the operator at any time and are usually erased when the machine is turned off. *IBM Corp. v. Ordinateurs Spirales Inc./Spirales Computers Inc.* (1984), 27 B.L.R. 190, 80 C.P.R. (2d) 187, 2 C.I.P.R. 56, 12 D.L.R. (4th) 351 (Fed. T.D.), Reed J.

ROMAN CATHOLIC. Includes a Catholic of the Greek or Ukrainian Rite in union with the See of Rome.

ROME STATUTE. The Rome Statute of the International Criminal Court adopted by the United Nations Diplomatic Conference of Plenipotentiaries on the Establishment of an International Criminal Court on July 17, 1998, as corrected by the *procès-verbaux* of November 10, 1998, July 12, 1999, November 30, 1999 and May 8, 2000, portions of which are set out in the schedule. *Crimes Against Humanity and War Crimes Act*, S.C. 2000, c. 24, s. 2(1).

ROOF. *n.* " . . . [T]he cover of a house, a building or a structure . . ." *R. v. Kool Vent Awnings Ltd.*, [1954] C.T.C. 311 at 317, [1954] Ex. C.R. 633, 54 D.T.C. 1158, Fournier J. See FLAT ~; METAL ~ED.

ROOF JOIST. A horizontal or sloping wood framing member that supports the roof sheathing and the ceiling finish, but does not enclose an attic space.

ROOF SPACE. The space between the roof and the ceiling of the top storey or between a dwarf wall and a sloping roof.

ROOM. See AUDIENCE ~; BATH~; BED~; BEVERAGE ~; BILLIARD ~; CELL ~; CHANGE ~; DESIGNATED SMOKING ~; DINING ~; ELECTRICAL ~; ENGINE ~; FIRST AID ~; GAS-PROOF ~; HAZARD-OUS ~; LIVING ~; LUNCH ~; MONEY ~; PERSONAL SERVICE ~; POOL~; PROJEC-TION ~; PUBLIC ~S; SERVICE ~; SHOWER ~; TOILET ~; WASH ~.

ROOMING HOUSE. A place where persons live in separate rooms but share kitchen and bathroom with others.

ROOT CROPS. Parsnips, onion, carrots or rutabagas.

ROOT OF DESCENT. The stock from which one descends.

ROOT OF TITLE. One traces ownership of property from the document which forms the root of title. R. Megarry and H.W.R. Wade, *The Law of Real Property*, 5th ed. (London: Stevens, 1984) at cxxvii.

ROPE. See HOISTING ~; SHAFT ~; TAIL ~.

ROSTER. *n.* The table or list by which one regulates duties.

ROT. See BLACK ~; RED ~; SOUR ~.

ROTA. *n.* [L.] Rotation; succession.

ROTORCRAFT. *n.* A power-driven heavier-than-air aircraft supported in flight by the reactions of the air on one or more rotors. Canada regulations.

ROUGH. *adj.* In relation to softwood lumber, means softwood lumber just as it comes from the saw, whether in the original sawed size or edged, resawn, crosscut or trimmed to a smaller size. *Softwood Lumber Products Export Charge Act*, S.C. 1987, c. 15, Sched., Part 1, s. 1.

ROUGH DIAMOND. A diamond that is unsorted, unworked or simply sawn, cleaved or bruted.

ROUGH PIPING. Gas piping from the meter location to and including all line cocks.

ROUND. *n.* A unit of ammunition composed of projectile, cartridge case, primer and propellant, or, in the case of shotgun ammunition, shell, pellets and wads. F.A. Jaffe, *A Guide to Pathological Evidence*, 3d ed. (Toronto: Carswell, 1991) at 215.

ROUNDNOSE GRENADIER. A fish of the species Coryphaenoides rupestris.

ROUND WEIGHT. The weight of a fish before any part of the fish has been removed. *Fishery regulations*.

ROUNDWOOD. *n.* Any section of the stem of or of the thicker branches of a tree of commercial value that has been felled or cut but has not been processed beyond removing the limbs or bark, or both, or splitting a section of fuel-wood.

ROUTE. *n.* 1. An area within which there are, at any point, one or two directions of traffic flow and that is delineated on two sides by separation lines, separation zones, natural obstacles or dashed tinted lines except that the continuity of such lines or zones may be interrupted where the route merges with, diverges from or crosses another route. *Collision Regulations*, C.R.C., c. 1416, s. 2. 2. In respect of a commercial air service, means the route served by a Class 1 or Class 2 Canadian air carrier between points in any licence when providing a transportation service described in the air carrier's service schedule or service pattern filed with the Committee and in effect. *Air Carrier Regulations*, C.R.C., c. 3, s. 2. 3. The tracks a train or engine may use in passing from one point to another. *Regulations No. O-8, Uniform Code of Operating Rules*, C.R.C., c. 1175, Part III, s. 2.

ROUTE SEGMENT. A part of a route whose ends are identified by (a) a continental or insular geographic location; or (b) a point at which a definite radio fix can be established. Canada regulations.

ROUTING SYSTEM. Any system of one or more routes or routing measures which systems may include traffic separation schemes, two-way routes, recommended tracks, areas to be avoided, inshore traffic zones, roundabouts, precautionary areas and deep water routes. *Collision Regulations*, C.R.C., c. 1416, s. 2.

ROW HOUSE. A detached building divided vertically into three or more dwelling units. Canada regulations.

ROVING RANDOM STOP. A stop which is not motivated on the part of the police officer who orders it by a belief based on reasonable grounds that the driver has committed, or is committing, an offence of any sort, whether it be under the *Criminal Code*, the *Motor Vehicle Act* or the regulations promulgated under the *Motor Vehicle Act*, and which is not ordered as part of any organized program of traffic safety. *R. v. Wilson* (1993), 86 B.C.L.R. (2d) 103 (C.A.).

ROY. *n*. [Fr. king] Monarch.

ROYAL ASSENT. Royal assent to a bill passed by the Houses of Parliament may be signified, during the session in which both Houses pass the bill, (a) in Parliament assembled; or (b) by written declaration. In a province, the Lieutenant Governor gives royal assent to a bill in order to make it a law. Unless the bill contains a clause setting another date, a bill comes into force on the day on which it receives royal assent.

ROYAL CANADIAN MINT. The federal body which produces and supplies circulating, collector and bullion Canadian coins. The Master of the Mint and such other persons as constitute the Board of Directors of the Mint are incorporated as a body corporate under the name of the Royal Canadian Mint. The objects of the Mint are to mint coins in anticipation of profit and to carry out other related activities.

ROYAL CANADIAN MOUNTED POLICE. A federal police force which prevents and detects offences against federal statutes and provides protective and investigative services for federal agencies and departments.

ROYAL COMMISSION. A person or body appointed to inquire into and report on a matter of general public interest.

ROYAL CONSENT. The consent of the Sovereign which a Minister of the Crown gives to a bill or amendment that affects the Crown's prerogative, hereditary revenues, personal interest or property. A. Fraser, W.A. Dawson, & J. Holtby, eds., *Beauchesne's Rules and Forms of the House of Commons of Canada*, 6th ed. (Toronto: Carswell, 1989) at 213.

ROYAL HIGHNESS. A title authorized by British letters patent to apply to the children of any sovereign, the children of the sovereign's sons, and the eldest living son of the eldest son of any Prince of Wales. The Duke of Edinburgh may also be called Royal Highness.

ROYAL INSTRUMENT. An instrument, in respect of Canada, that, under the present practice, is issued by and in the name of the Queen and passed under the Great Seal of the Realm or under one of the signets. *Seals Act*, R.S.C. 1985, c. S-6, s. 2.

ROYAL PREROGATIVE. 1. Generally speaking, in my view, the royal prerogative means "the powers and privileges accorded by the common law to the Crown" (see P. W. Hogg, *Constitutional Law of Canada* (loose-leaf ed.), vol. 1, at p. 1:14). The royal prerogative is confined to executive governmental powers, whether federal or provincial. The extent of its authority can be abolished or limited by statute: "once a statute [has] occupied the ground formerly occupied by the prerogative, the Crown [has to] comply with the terms of the statute". (See P. W. Hogg and P. J. Monahan, *Liability of the Crown* (3rd ed. 2000), at p. 17; also, Hogg, *supra*, at pp. 1:15-1:16; P. Lordon, *Crown Law* (1991), at pp. 66- 67.) In summary, then, as statute law expands and encroaches upon the purview of the royal prerogative, to that extent the royal prerogative contracts. However, this displacement occurs only to the extent that the statute does so explicitly or by necessary implication. *Ross River Dena Council Band v. Canada*, [2002] 2 S.C.R. 816 Per LeBel J. (Arbour, Binnie, Gonthier, Iacobucci, Major JJ. concurring). 2. " . . . [W]hat has been left to the King from the wide discretionary powers he enjoyed at the time he governed as an absolute monarch. . ." *Operation Dismantle Inc. v. R.* (1983), 39 C.P.C. 120 at 156, [1983] 1 F.C. 429 (C.A.), Marceau J.A.

ROYAL PROCLAMATION OF 1763. " . . . In the Supreme Court of Canada in the case of Calder v. Attorney-General of British Columbia (1973), 34 D.L.R. (3d) 145, in a judgment in which Mr. Justice Laskin concurred with Mr. Justice Hall, and said at page 203: 'This Proclamation was an Executive Order having the force and effect of an Act of Parliament and was described by Gwynne J. as the "Indian Bill of Rights". Its force as a statute is analogous to the status of Magna Carta which has always been considered to be law throughout the Empire. It was a law which followed the flag as England assumed jurisdiction over newly-discovered or acquired lands or territories . . . The Proclamation must be regarded as a fundamental document upon which any just determination of original rights rests.' The 1763 Proclamation governed the position of the Indian peoples for the next 100 years at least. It still governs their position throughout Canada, except in those cases when it has been supplemented or superseded by a Treaty with the Indians. . ." *R. v. Secretary of State for Foreign & Commonwealth Affairs*, [1981] 4 .N.L.R. 86 at 92, [1982] Q.B. 892, [1982] 2 All E.R. 118, 1 C.C.R. 254 (U.K. C.A.), Lord Denning M.R.

ROYAL RECOMMENDATION. A communication, attached to a financial initiative of the Crown, which lays down once and for all (unless withdrawn and replaced) the amount of a charge as well as its conditions, objects, purposes and qualifications. A. Fraser, W.A. Dawson, & J. Holtby, eds., *Beauchesne's Rules and Forms of the House of Commons of Canada*, 6th ed. (Toronto: Carswell, 1989) at 183.

ROYAL SEALS. Include the Great Seal of Canada and any other seals or signets that may, with the approval of Her Majesty the Queen, be authorized under this Act. *Seals Act*, R.S.C. 1985, c. S-6, s. 2.

ROYAL STYLE AND TITLES. ELIZABETH THE SECOND, by the Grace of God of the United Kingdom, Canada and Her other Realms and Territories QUEEN, Head of the Commonwealth, Defender of the Faith. *Royal Style and Titles Act*, R.S.C. 1985, c. R-12, s. 2.

ROYALTIES. *n.* 1. "[In s. 3(1)(f) of the Income War Tax Act, R.S.C. 1927, c. 97] . . . does not bear the original meaning ascribed to it as rights belonging to the Crown jure coronae . . . it has a special sense when used in mining grants or licences signifying that part of the reddendum which is variable and depends upon the quantity of minerals gotten. It is a well-known term in connection with patents and copyrights." *Minister of National Revenue v. Wain-Town Gas & Oil Co.*, [1952] 2 S.C.R. 377 at 382, 13 Fox Pat. C. 5, [1952] C.T.C. 147, 16 C.P.R. 73, [1952] 4 D.L.R. 81, 52 D.T.C. 1138, Kerwin J. (Rinfret C.J.C. and Taschereau JJ. concurring). 2. Includes (a) licence fees and all other payments analogous to royalties, whether or not payable under any contract, that are calculated as a percentage of the cost or sale price of defence supplies or as a fixed amount per article produced or that are based on the quantity or number of articles produced or sold or on the volume of business done; and (b) claims for damages for the infringement or use of any patent or regis-

tered industrial design. *Defence Production Act*, R.S.C. 1985, c. D-1, s. 2. 3. ". . . [B]ona vacantia falls within the term 'royalties' . . ." *R. v. British Columbia (Attorney General)* (1922), 68 D.L.R. 106 at 115, 63 S.C.R. 622, [1922] 3 W.W.R. 269, Anglin J. 4. "Assuming then, though without deciding, that the term 'royalties' as used in s. 109 of the Constitution Act, 1867 (30 & 31 Vict.), c. 3 is apt to include fines imposed for infraction of the criminal law, . . ." *Toronto (City) v. R.*, [1932] 1 D.L.R. 161 at 165, 56 C.C.C. 273 (Ont. P.C.), the court per Lord Macmillan. 5. " . . . [T]he English translation or equivalent of 'regalitates', 'jura regalia,' 'jura regia,' . . ." *Ontario (Attorney General) v. Mercer* (1883), 8 App. Cas. 767 at 778, 3 Cart. B.N.A. 1 (Can. P.C.), Selborne L.C. See ROYALTY.

ROYALTY. *n.* 1. A financial consideration paid for the right to use a copyright or patent or to exercise a similar incorporeal right; payment made from the production from a property which the grantor still owns. 2. The amount payable to the Crown for timber harvested on Crown Lands. 3. A payment made for the right or privilege to explore for, bring into production, take or dispose of oil or gas. In its original sense refers to Crown prerogatives or Crown rights . . . The word "royalty" is still used in Canada to describe a payment that is required by a provincial statute to be paid to the province as a share of the production of a resource. Typically, in the case of a resource that the province owns, there is a provincial statute that authorizes the granting of a lease subject to the payment of royalties . . . However, there is no authority that suggests that the word "royalty" must be limited to amounts paid pursuant to such an arrangement. In the context of payments to a province, the word "royalty" may describe any share of resource production that is paid to the province in connection with its interest in the resource. *Mobil Oil Canada Ltd. v. R.* (2001), 2001 FCA 333, 2001 D.T.C. 5668, [2002] 1 C.T.C. 55, 281 N.R. 367, 215 F.T.R. 32 (note) (C.A.) See GROSS ~ TRUST; OIL AND GAS ~ TRUST; PRODUCTION ~; ROYALTIES; TIMBER ~.

ROYALTY INTEREST. Any interest in, or the right to receive a portion of any oil or gas produced and saved from a field or pool or part of a field or pool or the proceeds from the sale thereof, but does not include a working interest or the interest of any person whose sole interest is as a purchaser of oil or gas from the pool or part thereof.

ROYALTY OWNER. 1. A person, including Her Majesty in right of Canada, who owns a royalty interest. 2. A person, other than a working interest owner, who has any interest in a right to receive a portion of the oil and gas produced from any lands or a portion of the proceeds from the sale thereof.

ROYALTY-RELIEF METHOD. Method of valuing intellectual property. Estimation of income stream expected to accrue from the intellectual property asset compared to the cost to rent the asset through a third party licensing arrangement for the economic life of the asset.

ROYALTY YEAR. With respect to an interest, a calendar year or any 12 consecutive months agreed on between a minister and a relevant interest owner.

ROYAL WARRANT. A document, issued by a royal official, by which a tradesperson may act in a certain capacity, e.g. as shoemaker, for a member of the royal family.

R.P. *abbr*. Rapports de Pratique du Québec, 1898-1944 (Quebec Practice Reports).

[] R.P. *abbr*. Rapports de Pratique du Québec, 1945-1982 (Quebec Practice Reports).

R.P.C. *abbr*. Reports of Patent Cases.

R.P.F.S. *abbr*. Revue de planification fiscale et successorale.

R.P. QUÉ. *abbr*. Rapports de Pratique de Québec.

R.P.R. *abbr*. Real Property Reports, 1977-.

R.P.R. (2d). *abbr*. Real Property Reports, Second Series.

R.Q.D.I. *abbr*. Revue québécoise de droit international.

R.R.A. *abbr*. Recueil en responsabilité et assurance.

RRSP. *abbr*. A registered retirement savings plan within the meaning of the Income Tax Act (Canada) that is registered under that Act. *Employment Pension Plan Act*, S.A. 1986, c. E-10.05, s. 1.

R.S. *abbr*. Revised Statutes.

R.S.C. *abbr*. 1. Revised Statutes of Canada. 2. Rules of the Supreme Court.

R.T.P. COMM. *abbr*. Restrictive Trade Practices Commission.

RUBBER. *n*. Includes synthetic rubber, which may be defined by regulations prescribed by the Minister. *Customs Tariff*, R.S.C. 1985, c. C-54, s. 2.

RUBBER TIRE. See SOLID ~.

RUBRIC. *n*. With respect to a statute, its title, which was formerly written in red.

RULE. *n*. 1. A law which an administrative agency or court enacts to regulate its procedure. 2. ". . . [A] set of written directives posted to the attention of employees which must be observed in their day-to-day conduct. Those terms may also encompass unwritten conventions which have, by the usage of a trade or long practice within the work place become so widely accepted by both management and employees that they have gained the force of a rule or a regulation." *Rothmans of Pall Mall Canada Ltd. v. B.C.W., Local 319T* (1983), 12 L.A.C. (3d) 329 at 335 (Ont.), Picher. See ANGLO-CANADIAN ~; BEST EVIDENCE ~; CASPAR'S ~; COLLATERAL ATTACK, ~AGAINST; COLLATERAL FACT ~; DISCOVERABILITY ~; ENGLISH ~; GOLDEN ~; INSTRUMENT FLIGHT ~S; JUDGES' ~S; LOAD LINE ~S; MISCHIEF ~; NEWSPAPER ~; PAROL EVIDENCE ~; PERPETUITY ~; QUOTA ~; REGULATION AND ~; SCATANA ~S; SLIP ~; SURPLUSAGE ~; VISUAL FLIGHT ~S; WORK TO ~.

RULE ABSOLUTE. ". . . [O]ne that is operative forthwith and constitutes an adjudication upon some point at some stage in an action or a proceeding . . ." *R. v. U.F.A.W.* (1967), [1968] 1 C.C.C. 194 at 197, 60 W.W.R. 370, 63 D.L.R. (2d) 356 (B.C. C.A.), Davey C.J.B.C. (Branca J.A. concurring).

RULE AGAINST DOUBLE JEOPARDY. After an accused is tried for an offence and finally convicted or acquitted, that person may not be placed in jeopardy a second time, i.e. be tried again, for the same offence. See AUTREFOIS ACQUIT; AUTREFOIS CONVICT.

RULE AGAINST HEARSAY. Requires that evidence of a witness be restricted to what she or he perceived herself or himself (primary evidence) and excludes anything she or he fathered from other sources.

RULE AGAINST PERPETUAL DURATION. A rule with the same object as the rule against perpetuities, but which is applied to any trust with non-charitable purposes. D.M. Waters, *The Law of Trusts in Canada*, 2d ed. (Toronto: Carswell, 1984) at 282.

RULE AGAINST PERPETUITIES. For an interest in property to be good it must vest no later than 21 years after some life in being when the interest was created. T. Sheard, R. Hull & M.M.K. Fitzpatrick, *Canadian Forms of Wills*, 4th ed. (Toronto: Carswell, 1982) at 231. See PERPETUITY RULE.

RULE IN CLAYTON'S CASE. What is known as the rule in *Clayton's Case* derives from the decision of the English Court of Appeal in *Clayton's Case, Re* (1816), 1 Mer. 572, 35 E.R. 781 (Ch. Div.). The so-called rule—which is really a statement of evidentiary principle—presumes that in the state of accounts as between a bank and its customer the sums first paid in are the sums first drawn out, absent evidence of an agreement or any presumed intent to the contrary: see *Clayton's Case*, per Sir William Grant, at pp. 608—609, Mer. As Morden J.A. remarked in *Greymac* , (p. 677) "the short form statement of the rule . . . is 'first in, first out' '. In the result, where there are competing claims against a shortfall, the shortfall is applied first to the first deposits made, and later contributors to the fund take the benefit of what remains. The role of the rule in *Clayton's Case* in competing beneficiary cases, and its history, were examined thoroughly by this Court in *Greymac*. The application of the rule was rejected as being "unfair and arbitrary" and "based on a fiction" (p. 686). The Court concluded that it was not bound to apply the rule in *Clayton's Case* , and it did not do so. *Law Society of Upper Canada v. Toronto Dominion Bank* (1998), 42 O.R. (3d) 257 (C.A.).

RULE IN HODGES'S CASE. " . . . [I]n a criminal case, where proof of any issue of fact essential to the case of the Crown consists of circumstantial evidence it is the duty of the judge to instruct the jury that before they can find the accused guilty they must be satisfied not only that the circumstances are consistent with an affirmative finding on the issue so sought to be proved but that the circumstances are inconsistent with any other rational conclusion . . . the rule is not one merely of prudent practice but of positive law." *R. v. Mitchell* (1964), 43 C.R. 391 at 401, [1964] S.C.R. 471, 47 W.W.R. 591, 46 D.L.R. (2d) 384, [1965] 1 C.C.C. 155, Cartwright J.

RULE IN PHILLIPS V. EYRE. "As a general rule, in order to found a suit in England for a wrong alleged to have been committed abroad, two conditions must be fulfilled. First, the wrong must be of such a character that it would have been actionable if committed in England . . . Secondly, the act must not have been justifiable by the law of the place where it was done." *Phillips v. Eyre* (1870), L.R. 6 Q.B. 1 at 28-9 (U.K. Ex. Ct.), Willes J.

RULE IN RYLANDS V. FLETCHER. Anyone who, for their own reasons, brings on their land, collects and keeps there anything which may do harm if it escapes, must keep it in at their own peril. If they do not do so, they are prima facie answerable for any damages which result from its escape.

RULE IN SAUNDERS V. VAUTIER. Narrowly it states that a court will not enforce a trust for accumulation, in which no one but the legatee has any interest when an absolute vested gift is made payable at a future event, with direction in the meantime to accumulate any income and pay it with the principal. More broadly it states that, if beneficiaries agree and they are not under a disability, the specific performance of a trust may be arrested, and they may extinguish or modify the trust without referring to the wishes of either the settlor or the trustees. D.M.W. Waters, *The Law of Trusts in Canada*, 2d ed. (Toronto: Carswell, 1984) at 963.

RULE IN SHELLEY'S CASE. If one vests land in trustees in fee simple in trust for some person for life, placing the remainder in trust for that persons heirs or the heirs of that persons body, that person takes an estate tail or equitable fee simple. D.M.W. Waters, *The Law of Trusts in Canada*, 2d ed. (Toronto: Carswell, 1984) at 22.

RULE NISI. " . . . [I]ndicates that the Court is satisfied that a prima facie case has been made out to justify calling upon the other side to make answer at the time and place indicated to the contention upon which the rule was founded." *R. v. U.F.A.W.* (1967), [1968] 1 C.C.C. 194 at 197, 60 W.W.R. 370, 63 D.L.R. (2d) 356 (B.C. C.A.), Davey C.J.B.C. (Branca J.A. concurring).

RULE OF ANTICIPATION. A rule by which discussion of a matter standing on the Order Paper may not be forestalled which depends on the same principle by which the same question may not be raised twice in the same session. The rule states that one must not anticipate a matter if it is contained in a more effective form of proceeding than the proceeding by which one seeks to anticipate it, but one may anticipate it if it is contained in a less effective and equal form. A. Fraser, W.A. Dawson, & J. Holtby, eds., *Beauchesne's Rules and Forms of the House of Commons of Canada*, 6th ed. (Toronto: Carswell, 1989) at 154.

RULE OF CONDUCT. A rule which sets norms or standards of conduct, which determine the manner in which rights are exercised and responsibilities are fulfilled. *Reference re Language Rights*, [1992] 1 S.C.R. 212.

RULE OF LAW. 1. The principles of constitutionalism and the rule of law lie at the root of our system of government. The rule of law, is "a fundamental postulate of our constitutional structure." At its most basic level, the rule of law vouchsafes to the citizens and residents of the country a stable, predictable and ordered society in which to conduct their affairs. It provides a shield for individuals from arbitrary state action. First, the rule of law provides that the law is supreme over the acts of both government and private persons. There is, in short, one law for all. Second "the rule of law requires the creation and maintenance of an actual order of positive laws which preserves and embodies the more general principle of normative order". A third aspect of the rule of law is, "the exercise of all public power must find its ultimate source in a legal rule". Put another way, the relationship between the state and the individual must be regulated by law. Taken together, these three considerations make up a principle of profound constitutional and political significance. *Reference re Secession of Quebec*, 1998 CarswellNat 1299, 161 D.L.R. (4th) 385, 228 N.R. 203, 55 C.R.R. (2d) 1, [1998] 2 S.C.R. 217 Per curiam. 2. " . . . [A] fundamental principle of our Constitution, must mean at least two things. First, that the law is supreme over officials of the government as well as private individuals, and thereby preclusive of the influence of arbitrary power. Second, the rule of law requires the creation and maintenance of an actual order of positive laws which preserves and embodies the more general principle of normative order. Law and order are indispensable elements of civilized life." *Reference re Language Rights Under s. 23 of Manitoba Act, 1870 and s. 133 of Constitution Act, 1867*, [1985] 1 S.C.R. 721 at 748-9, [1985] 4 W.W.R. 385, 35 Man. R. (2d) 83, 59 N.R. 321, 19 D.L.R. (4th) 1, Dickson C.J., Beetz, Estey, McIntyre, Lamer, Wilson and Le Dain JJ. 3.

" . . . [A] highly textured expression, importing many things . . . but conveying, for example, a sense of orderliness, of subjection to known legal rules and of executive accountability to legal authority." *Reference re Questions Concerning Amendment of the Constitution of Canada as set out in O.C. 1020/80* (1981), (*sub nom. Resolution to Amend the Constitution of Canada, Re*) 1 C.R.R. 59 at 99, [1981] 1 S.C.R. 753, [1981] 6 W.W.R. 1, 11 Man. R. (2d) 1, 39 N.R. 1, 34 Nfld. & P.E.I.R. 1, 95 A.P.R. 1, Laskin C.J.C., Dickson, Beetz, Estey, McIntyre, Chouinard and Lamer JJ. 4. Processes which are ultimately predicated on fair and just methods and which theoretically adhere to standards of consistency, predictability of result, and impartiality. S.A. Cohen, *Due Process of Law* (Toronto: Carswell, 1977) at 2.

RULES FOR LIFE-SAVING APPLIANCES. The regulations respecting life-boats, buoyant apparatus and other life-saving equipment made under section 338. *Canada Shipping Act*, R.S.C. 1985, c. S-9, s. 2.

RULES OF CIVIL PROCEDURE. The rules for the Supreme Court and the District Court made under Part V. *Courts of Justice Act*, S.O. 1984, c. 11, s. 1.

RULES OF COURT. Rules made by the authority having for the time being power to make rules or orders regulating the practice and procedure of that court.

RULES OF ENGAGEMENT. The rules governing the use of force in armed combat including issues relating to self defence, proportional use of force, levels of force, definitions of "hostile act" and "hostile intent".

RULES OF NATURAL JUSTICE. The fundamental rules of procedure which must be observed by all who are required to make quasi-judicial decisions. See NATURAL JUSTICE.

RULES OF PLEADING. Rules governing the form that pleadings take which have three basic requirements: (a) to lead the material facts; (b) to deny material facts and (c) to plead an affirmative defence. One might add the right of a party to request, and the court to order, particulars. G.D. Watson & C. Perkins, eds., *Holmested & Watson: Ontario Civil Procedure* (Toronto: Carswell, 1984) at 25-13 and 14.

RULES OF PRACTICE. Unless the context otherwise requires, the Rules of Practice and Procedure of the Supreme Court of Ontario. *Legal Aid Act*, R.R.O. 1980, Reg. 575, s. 1.

RULES OF RACING. (a) In the case of a race held in a province, the rules made by a Commission, and (b) in the case of a foreign race, the rules made by the governing body that regulates the race. *Pari-Mutuel Betting Supervision Regulations*, SOR/91-365, s. 2.

RULING. *n.* 1. Determination obtained by a motion to the court of the propriety of a question in an examination to which one objected without receiving an answer (Ontario, Rules of Civil Procedure, r. 34.12(3)). G.D. Watson & C. Perkins, eds., *Holmested & Watson: Ontario Civil Procedure* (Toronto: Carswell, 1984) at 34-7. 2. " . . . [A] disposition of a motion for non-suit made during the course of a trial is not an order. . . [I]t is instead, in my judgment, what [is] more properly described as a ruling, or a ruling on evidence which is part of the trial process, and it is not appealable until after the trial has been completed." *Rahmatian v. HFH Video Biz, Inc.* (1991), 46 C.P.C. (2d) 312 at 315 (B.C. C.A.), MacEachern C.J.B.C. See SPEAKER'S ~.

RUMMAGE SALE. A place where five or more persons or one or more organizations, or a combination thereof, sell goods for a non-profit purpose.

RUN. *v.* To take effect at a certain place or time. See HIT AND ~; REGULAR ~.

RUN AT LARGE. To be not under control of the owner, either by being securely tethered or in direct and continuous charge of a person, or by confinement in any building or other enclosure or by a fence.

RUNNING AT LARGE. 1. Not being under control of the owner, either by being securely tethered or in direct and continuous charge of a person, or by confinement in any building or other enclosure or by a fence. 2. Off the premises of the owner and not muzzled or under the control of any person. See ANIMAL ~.

RUN-OFF. *n.* A line for carrying electrical power or energy from a rural distribution system to buildings, including the transformer required for transforming the voltage of the said system to the voltage at which the electrical power or energy is to be supplied for the customer's use.

RUN-OFF PARCEL. The parcel of farm land on which a farm subscriber is supplied, or on which a farm applicant is to be supplied, with telephone service by a company, and that parcel continues to be a run-off until the total amount of any construction levy thereon is paid in full

and thereafter until such time as the telephone line located on and serving the run-off parcel is deemed by subsection (1) of section 33 to be abandoned by the company. *The Rural Telephone Act*, R.S.S. 1978, c. R-27, s. 2.

RUNWAY. *n.* An individual landing or take-off surface considered to be heading in one magnetic direction only. See NOISE RESTRICTED ~.

RUNWAY VISUAL RANGE. The range over which the pilot of an aircraft on the centre line of a runway can expect to see the runway surface markings or the lights delineating the runway or identifying that centre line. *Canadian Aviation Regulations*, SOR/96-433, s. 101.01.

RUN WITH THE LAND. Said of a covenant with land conveyed in fee when either the right to take advantage of it or the liability to perform it, passes to the person to whom that land is assigned.

RUN WITH THE REVERSION. Said of a covenant with leased land when either the right to take advantage of it or the liability to perform it, passes to the person to whom that reversion is assigned.

RURAL AREA. Territory not organized as a municipality.

RURAL DISTRIBUTION SYSTEM. A line or lines for the distribution and supply of electrical power or energy to resident occupants outside any city, town or village.

RURAL DISTRICT. 1. A school district situated wholly outside a village, town or city. 2. Any area in the Province except an area within the boundaries of a city or of an incorporated town having a population of more than 1200 according to the last decennial or other census taken under the authority of an Act of the Parliament of Canada. *Rural Electrification Act*, R.S.N.S. 1989, c. 405, s. 2.

RURAL FSA CODE. An FSA code the second character of which is the numeral "0". *Mail Preparation Regulations*, C.R.C ., c. 1281, s. 2.

RURAL GAS UTILITY. A system of pipelines for the distribution and delivery of gas and which provides gas service wholly or primarily to rural consumers.

RURAL LAND. Land in a rural area, other than farm land, forest land, timber land, tree farm land and wild land.

RURAL MAIL BOX. A privately owned mail receiving and dispatching facility designed for outdoor use in a rural area.

RURAL MUNICIPAL AUTHORITY. (a) The corporation of a municipal district or county; or (b) the Minister of Municipal Affairs, in the case of an improvement district or special area. *Rural Gas Act*, R.S.A. 1980, c. R-19, s. 1.

RURAL MUNICIPALITY. A municipality in a county or district.

RURAL RATE DIFFERENTIAL. The amount by which the weighted average rural bill for power exceeds the weighted average municipal bill, expressed as a percentage of the weighted average municipal bill.

RURAL ROAD. A road subject to the direction, control and management of a rural municipality or a road, other than a primary highway, in an improvement district.

RUS. *abbr*. Russell's Election Cases (N.S.), 1874.

RUTABAGA. *n*. That vegetable commonly known as "swede turnip" but does not include the usually smaller species commonly known as "summer turnip".

RVR. Runway visual range. *Canadian Aviation Regulations*, SOR/96-433, s. 101.01.

RYLANDS V. FLETCHER. See RULE IN ~.

S. *abbr.* 1. Section. 2. Second. 3. Length of superstructure.

S.A. *abbr.* Société Anonyme.

SABBATICAL LEAVE. Leave of absence granted to a teacher.

SABOTAGE. *n.* 1. Doing a prohibited act for a purpose prejudicial to (a) the safety, security or defence of Canada; or (b) the safety or security of the naval, army or air forces of any state other than Canada that are lawfully present in Canada. *Criminal Code*, R.S.C. 1985, c. C-46, s. 52. 2. Malicious damaging or destruction of an employer's property by the deliberate conduct of workers.

SACCULAR ANEURYSM. A sac-like aneurysm which arises where a vessel wall is weak. F.A. Jaffe, *A Guide to Pathological Evidence*, 3d ed. (Toronto: Carswell, 1991) at 212.

SACRAMENTUM. *n.* [L.] An oath.

SACRAMENTUM SI FATUUM FUERIT, LICET FALSUM, TAMEN NON COMMITTIT PERJURIUM. [L.] A foolish oath, even if false, does not constitute perjury.

SACRED CEREMONIAL OBJECT. An object, the title to which is vested in the Crown, that (a) was used by a First Nation in the practice of sacred ceremonial traditions, (b) is in the possession and care of the Provincial Museum of Alberta or the Glenbow-Alberta Institute or on loan from one of those institutions to a First Nation, or is otherwise in the possession and care of the Crown, and (c) is vital to the practice of the First Nation's sacred ceremonial traditions. *First Nations Sacred Ceremonial Objects Repatriation Act*, R.S.A. 2000, c. F-14, s. 1.

SADDLE HORSE. Any horse that is ridden, or intended to be ridden, by a person or that person's employees in the daily operation of a farm.

SAE. *abbr.* The Society of Automotive Engineers, Inc. *Motor Vehicle Safety Regulations*, C.R.C., c. 1038, s. 2.

SAFE. See INTRINSICALLY ~.

SAFE-CONDUCT. *n.* 1. Protection through enemy territory. 2. A document which permits travel in hostile territory. See LETTERS OF ~.

SAFETY. *n.* 1. Protection from danger and hazards arising out of, linked with or occurring in the course of employment. 2. In the context of the stalking provisions of the Criminal Code, freedom from physical harm and includes freedom from the apprehension of mental, emotional or psychological harm. 3. Freedom from bodily injury or freedom from damage to health.

SAFETY AND EFFECTIVENESS REQUIREMENTS. The safety and effectiveness requirements set out in sections 10 to 20. *Medical Devices Regulations* SOR/98-282, s. 1.

SAFETY BELT. 1. A combination of: (a) a belt worn around the waist of a worker; (b) all necessary fittings; and (c) a lanyard attached to the belt referred to in subparagraph (a). 2. A personal restraint system consisting of either a lap strap or a lap strap combined with a shoulder harness. *Canadian Aviation Regulations* SOR 96-433, s. 101.01.

SAFETY CARTRIDGE. A cartridge for a gun, rifle, pistol, revolver and other small arms, of which the case can be extracted from the small arm after firing, and which is so closed as to prevent any explosion in one cartridge being communicated to other cartridges.

SAFETY CODE. See ELECTRICAL ~.

SAFETY CONVENTION. The International Convention for the Safety of Life at Sea, 1974, signed at London on November 1, 1974 and the Protocol of 1978 relating thereto, signed at London on February 17, 1978, and any amendments, whenever made, to the Annex to that Convention other than Chapter I of the Annex. *Canada Shipping Act*, R.S.C. 1985, c. S-9, s. 2.

SAFETY CONVENTION SHIP. A steamship, other than a ship of war, a troop ship or a fishing vessel, registered in a country to which the Safety Convention applies, that is on an international voyage and (a) is carrying more than twelve passengers, (b) is of three hundred tons gross tonnage or more, or (c) is a nuclear ship. *Canada Shipping Act*, R.S.C. 1985, c. S-9, s. 2.

SAFETY FILM. Film that does not contain more than thirty-six one-hundredths of one per cent of nitrogen and that, when tested in accordance with the definitions and analytical procedures prescribed by the Canadian Standards Association in its Standard for Safety Film, is shown to be both difficult to ignite and slow burning.

SAFETY FUSE. A fuse for blasting that burns and does not explode, does not contain its own means of ignition, and is of such strength and construction and contains an explosive in such quantity that the burning of such fuse will not communicate laterally with other like fuses. Canada regulations.

SAFETY GLASS. A product composed of glass so manufactured, fabricated, or treated, as substantially to prevent shattering and flying of the glass when struck or broken.

SAFETY GLASS STANDARD. Standard for Glass: Safety, for Building Construction, 12-GP-1b, August, 1971, a standard of the Canadian Government Specifications Board. *Safety Glass Regulations*, C.R.C., c. 933, s. 2.

SAFETY GROUND. A system of conductors, electrodes and clamps, connections or devices that electrically connect an isolated electrical facility to ground for the purpose of protecting employees working on the facility from dangerous electrical shock.

SAFETY GROUNDING. A system of conductors, electrodes and clamps, connections or devices that electrically connect an isolated electrical facility to ground for the purpose of protecting employees working on the facility from dangerous electrical shock.

SAFETY HARNESS. A combination of: (a) a belt worn around the waist of a worker; and (b) straps attached to the belt that pass over the worker's shoulders and around his legs with the necessary fittings and a length of rope, suitable for raising him by the rope without permitting him to bend at the waist.

SAFETY MARK. Includes any design, symbol, device, sign, label, placard, letter, word, number, abbreviation or any combination thereof that is to be displayed on dangerous goods or containers, packaging, means of transport or facilities used in the handling, offering for transport or transporting of dangerous goods in order to show the nature of the danger, or to indicate compliance with the safety standards set for the containers, packaging, means of transport or facilities.

SAFETY MEASURE. A measure designed for the purposes of safety in connection with the design and use of radiation installations, radiation equipment and associated apparatus.

SAFETY NET. A net so placed and supported as to safely arrest any worker who may fall into it.

SAFETY PILOT. A pilot who acts as a lookout for another pilot operating an aircraft in simulated instrument flight; *Canadian Aviation Regulations* SOR 96-433, s. 101.01.

SAFETY REQUIREMENTS. Requirements for the handling, offering for transport or transporting of dangerous goods, for the reporting of those activities, for the training of persons engaged in those activities and for the inspection of those activities. *Transportation of Dangerous Goods acts*.

SAFETY RESTRAINING DEVICE. Any safety belt, safety harness, seat, rope, belt, strap or lifeline designed to be used by an employee to protect that employee from the danger of falling, and includes every fitting or accessory thereto.

SAFETY STANDARDS. Standards regulating the design, construction, equipping, functioning or performance of containers, packaging, means of transport or facilities used the handling, offering for transport or transporting of dangerous goods. *Transportation of Dangerous Goods acts*.

SAFETY STUDDED TIRES. Tires on the periphery of which there have been inserted, either by the manufacturer of the tires or by a person having a permit issued for the purpose by the registrar, studs of any material other than rubber that are of a kind approved in the regulations and that do not protrude beyond the surface of the tires to an extent greater than that specified in the regulations. *The Highway Traffic Act*, C.C.S.M., c. H60, s. 1.

SAFETY ZONE. The area of space officially set apart within a highway for the exclusive use of pedestrians and which is protected or is so marked or indicated by adequate signs as to be plainly visible at all times while set apart as a safety zone.

S.A.G. *abbr*. Sentences arbitrales de griefs (Québec), 1970-.

SAGITTAL. *adj*. In an antero-posterior direction, in the mean plane.

SAID. *adj*. " . . . [G]rammatically applies to the last antecedent . . ." *Toronto General Trusts Co. v. Irwin* (1896), 27 O.R. 491 at 495 (H.C.), Meredith C.J.

SAILING SHIP. 1. Except for the purposes of the Load Line Rules, means (a) a ship that is propelled wholly by sails; and (b) a ship that is principally employed in fishing, not exceeding 200 tons gross tonnage, provided with masts, sails and rigging sufficient to allow it to make voyages under sail alone, and that, in addition, is fitted with mechanical means of propulsion other than a steam engine. *Canada Shipping Act*, R.S.C. 1985, c. S-9, s. 2. 2. Includes every ship provided with sufficient sail area for navigation under sails alone, whether or not fitted with mechanical means of propulsion. *Load Line Rules*, Canada regulations.

SAILING VESSEL. Includes every vessel that is under sail and is not being propelled by machinery. Canada regulations.

SAILING YACHT. A pleasure yacht that is equipped with sails and that is not equipped with a motor.

ST. LAWRENCE RIVER SEASONAL AREA. That part of the St. Lawrence River bounded by the Victoria Bridge in Montreal, a straight line drawn from Cap des Rosiers to West Point, Anticosti Island, and a line drawn along the meridian of longitude 63 degrees west from Anticosti Island to the north shore of the St. Lawrence River. *General Load Line Rules*, C.R.C., c. 1425, s. 2.

ST. LAWRENCE SEAWAY AUTHORITY. A federal body which operates and maintains the seaway and bridges which connect the United States with Canada.

SALARY. *n*. 1. Compensation paid to an employee for labour or services. 2. Remuneration paid for services. See PENSIONABLE ~.

SALARY RATE. See ANNUAL ~.

SALE. *n*. 1. " . . . [T]he primary meaning of sale was the transfer of property to another for a price. . ." *Leading Investments Ltd. v. New Forest Investments Ltd.* (1986), 38 R.P.R. 201 at 213, [1986] 1 S.C.R. 70, 65 N.R. 209, 14 O.A.C. 159, 25 D.L.R. (4th) 161, La Forest J. (Dickson C.J.C. and Lamer J. concurring). 2. " . . . [M]ay be interpreted to mean either a binding agreement for sale or a completed sale. . ." *Leading Investments Ltd. v. New Forest Investments Ltd.* (1986), 38 R.P.R. 201 at 223, [1986] 1 S.C.R. 70, 65 N.R. 209, 14 O.A.C. 159, 25 D.L.R. (4th) 161, Estey J. (McIntyre and Chouinard JJ. concurring). 3. A transaction whereby the retail seller transfers or agrees to transfer the general property in a consumer product to a consumer for a valuable consideration. 4. Includes (a) exchange, barter, sale on credit, conditional sale, sale where the price is payable by installments, transfer of title, conditional or otherwise, and any other contract whereby for a consideration a person delivers goods to another; (b) a transfer of possession, conditional or otherwise, or a lease or a rental determined to be in lieu of a transfer of title, exchange or barter; and (c) the provision of goods by way of promotional distribution. 5. Includes a sale, assignment, transfer, conveyance, declaration of trust without transfer or other assurance not intended to operate as a mortgage, of chattels, or an agreement, whether intended or not to be followed by the execution of any other instrument, by which a right in equity to any chattels is conferred but does not include: (a) an assignment for the general benefit of the creditors of the person making the assignment; (b) a transfer or sale of goods in the ordinary course of any trade or calling; (c) a conditional sale within the meaning of The Conditional Sales Act or an assignment of a conditional sale. *Bills of Sale acts*. 6. Includes a bargain and sale as well as a sale and delivery. *Sale of Goods acts*. 7. In the context of labour relations to accomplish a sale something must be relinquished by the predecessor business on the one hand and obtained by the successor on the other. A sale implies a nexus, an agreement or transaction of some sort between the predecessor and successor employers. There must be a mutual intent to transfer part of the business. *C.A.W., Local 222 v. Charterways Transportation Ltd.*, 2000 CarswellOnt 1253, 2000 SCC 23, (sub nom. *Town of Ajax v. National Automobile, Aerospace & Agricultural Implement Workers Union of Canada, Local 222*) 2000 C.L.L.C. 220-028, 49 C.C.E.L. (2d) 151, (sub nom. *Ajax (Town) v. National Automobile, Aerospace & Agricultural Implement Workers Union of Canada (CAW-Canada), Local 222*) 47 O.R. (3d) 800 (headnote only), (sub nom. *Ajax (Town) v. C.A.W., Local 222*) 185 D.L.R. (4th) 618, [2000] L.V.I. 3109-1, (sub nom. *Ajax (Town) v. C.A.W., Local 222*) [2000] 1 S.C.R. 538, (sub nom. *Ajax (Town) v. National Automobile, Aerospace & Agricultural Implement Workers Union of Canada (CAW-Canada), Local 222*) 253 N.R. 223, 22 Admin. L.R. (3d) 1, (sub nom. *Ajax (Town) v. National Automobile, Aerospace & Agricultural Implement Workers Union of Canada (CAW-Canada), Local 222*) 133 O.A.C. 43 Per Bastarache J. (dissenting). 8. " . . . [I]ndicates to the public that it is a special event different from the regular merchandising technique of the merchant. . . indicates to a potential customer that he is getting a bargain, a price lower than he would ordinarily pay." *R. v. Simpson-Sears Ltd.* (1976), 28 C.P.R. (2d) 249 at 257 (Ont. Co. Ct.), Allen Co. Ct. J. See ACTION FOR ~; AGREEMENT FOR ~; BARGAIN AND ~; BILL OF ~; BULK ~; CLOSING-OUT ~; COMMUNITY ~; CONDITIONAL ~; CONDITION OF ~; CONSUMER ~; CONTRACT FOR ~; CONTRACT OF ~; COUNTRY ~; DIRECT ~; FORCED ~; GENERATION AND ~ FOR DISTRIBUTION TO THE PUBLIC; GROSS ~S; OFF PREMISES ~; ON-PREMISES ~; PARTITION OR ~; PROCEEDS OF ~; PUBLIC ~; RELATED ~; RETAIL ~; RUMMAGE ~; TIME ~; TRUST FOR ~.

SALE AND SELL. Include (a) the exchange, barter and traffic of liquor; and (b) the selling, supplying or distributing, by any means whatsoever, of liquor.

SALE BY DESCRIPTION. " . . . [T]here is a sale by description even though the buyer is buying something displayed before him on the counter: a thing is sold by description, though it is specific, so long as it is sold not merely as the specific thing but as a thing corresponding to a description . . ." *Grant v. Australian Knitting Mills Ltd.*, [1936] S.C. 85 at 100 (Australia P.C.), Lord Wright for their Lordships.

SALE BY RETAIL. Includes sale by auction.

SALE BY SAMPLE. "To constitute a sale by sample, in the legal sense of that term, it must, . . . appear that the parties contracted with reference to a sample, and with a mutual understanding that the sample furnished a description (in this case) of the quality of the oats and that the bulk must conform with the sample." *Wawryk v. McKenzie Co.* (1921), 61 D.L.R. 25 at 26, [1921] 2 W.W.R. 951 (Sask. C.A.), the court per Lamont J.A.

SALE IN BULK. A sale of a stock, or part thereof, out of the usual course of business or trade of the vendor or of substantially the entire stock of the vendor, or of an interest in the business of the vendor.

SALE-LEASEBACK. *n*. A way to raise money on land by which a vendor receives from the purchaser current full market value of both land and the buildings built on the land and becomes a tenant of the purchaser under a long term lease of the property.

SALE OF A CHANCE. The sale of something which the buyer hopes will eventuate.

SALE OF GOODS. 1. A contract by which a seller agrees to transfer or transfers property in goods to a buyer for financial consideration called the price. 2. Includes any transaction in which goods are sold, whether separately or together with services. *Consumer Protection acts.*

SALE OF GOODS ACT. A code which governs a contract of sale of goods.

SALE OF SERVICES. Furnishing or agreeing to furnish services and includes making arrangements to have services furnished by others and any transaction in which services are sold whether separately or together with goods. *Consumer Protection acts.*

SALE ON APPROVAL. The sale of goods with the right of the purchaser to return the goods if the purchaser is not satisfied with them within a specified time.

SALE ON CREDIT. A sale in which payment of the whole price is delayed, or the price is paid in instalments over a period to which the parties agree so that agreed-on interest is paid on the delayed part the purchase price.

SALE PRICE. 1. Actual value of thing exchanged. 2. Amount paid for a thing purchased. 3. The phrase "sale price" is not apt to describe an offered price. In this context, sale price means a price agreed upon between the seller and a buyer who was obtained with the assistance of the co-operating agent. *Rosling Real Estate (Nel-*

son) Ltd. v. Robertson Hilliard Cattell Realty Co. (1999), 1999 CarswellBC 1554 (S.C.).

SALES CONTRACT. (a) An agreement for the sale of goods or services or both for future delivery or performance in whole or in part; (b) an agreement under which the buyer, at some future time, on the happening of an event or the payment of the price or compliance with a condition, will become the owner of goods or entitled to the performance of services or both.

SALES LITERATURE. 1. Includes records, videotapes and similar material, written matter and all other material, except preliminary prospectuses and prospectuses, designed for use in a presentation to a purchaser, whether such material is given or shown to him or her. *Securities acts*. 2. Includes records, videotapes and similar material, written matter and all other material, except terms and conditions of contracts and the written statement required under section 40, designed for use in a presentation to a customer, whether such material is given or shown to the customer. *Commodity Futures Act*, R.S.O. 1990, c. C.20, s. 54(2).

SALESMAN. *n*. 1. An individual employed by a dealer to make trades in securities on the dealer's behalf. 2. A person who goes from house to house selling or offering for sale, or soliciting orders for the future delivery of, goods or services, for or on behalf of a vendor. 3. A person employed, appointed or authorized by a broker to trade in real estate. 4. A person employed, appointed or authorized by an issuer to sell investment contracts. 5. A person who is employed by a licensed insurance agent or broker on a stated salary that is not supplemented by commission, bonus or any other remuneration to solicit insurance or transact, for some other person, an application for a policy of insurance, or to act in the negotiation of such insurance or in negotiating its continuance or renewal, or collects and receives premiums on behalf of an employer only. See COMMODITY CONTRACTS ~; DRIVER ~; INSURANCE ~; ITINERANT ~; MORTGAGE ~; REAL ESTATE ~.

SALESPERSON. *n*. 1. An individual other than an authorized official employed or engaged by a registered mortgage dealer to take part in any of the activities mentioned in the definition of mortgage dealer. *The Mortgage Dealers Act*, C.C.S.M., c. M210, s. 1. 2. A salesperson of a prepaid funeral contract and includes a person who is employed, appointed or authorized by a contract seller to sell prepaid funeral contracts. 3. A person employed, appointed or authorized by a broker to trade in real estate. 4. A person who (a) goes from house to house, (b) contacts occupants of houses by telephone, or (c) through advertising or otherwise carried out by or for the salesperson or by or for the relevant vendor requests occupants of houses to contact him or her by telephone or present themselves to a hotel room or other non-business premises for the purpose of (d) selling or offering for sale goods or services to them, or (e) soliciting orders for the future delivery to them of goods or services for or on behalf of a vendor. 5. An individual who is employed by a dealer for the purpose of making trades in contracts on behalf of such dealer.

SALES STABLE KEEPER. A person who stables, boards or cares for an animal belonging to another person, with the intention of selling or disposing of it, and who receives or is to receive payment for those services whether in the nature of a commission or otherwise.

SALES TAX. The tax imposed under Part IX of the Excise Tax Act and taxes levied under Acts of the legislature of a province in respect of supplies of property or services. See HARMONIZED ~.

SALE TO THE PUBLIC. See DISTRIBUTION AND ~.

SALICYLATE. *n*. A drug used as a fever-reducing agent, analgesic or for local application. F.A. Jaffe, *A Guide to Pathological Evidence*, 3d ed. (Toronto: Carswell, 1991) at 225.

SALINE SOLUTION. An aqueous solution of mineral salts occurring in a natural state and containing more than 1 per cent of mineral salts in solution. *Yukon Quartz Mining Act*, R.S.C. 1985, c. Y-4, s. 2.

SALIVA. *n*. The watery fluid which the salivary glands in the mouth produce.

SALMON. *n*. Includes all kinds and classes of fish usually known and described by the trade names of sockeyes, red and white springs, pinks, chums, cohoes, steelheads and bluebacks. *Fisheries Act*, R.S.B.C. 1996, c. 149, s. 12. See ATLANTIC ~; PACIFIC ~; PINK ~; SLINK ~; SOCKEYE ~; SPENT ~.

SALMON BRINE CURING PLANT. A building, structure, machinery, appurtenances, appliances and apparatus occupied and used in the business of brine curing any species of salmon or of converting any species of salmon into brine cured salmon. *Fisheries Act*, R.S.B.C. 1996, c. 149, s. 12.

SALMON CANNERY. A building, structure, machinery, appurtenances, appliances and apparatus occupied and used in the business of salmon canning, or of converting the natural salmon into canned salmon. *Fisheries Act*, R.S.B.C. 1996, c. 149, s. 12.

SALMON DRY SALTERY. A building, structure, machinery, appurtenances, appliances and apparatus occupied and used in the business of dry salting salmon, or of converting the natural salmon into dry salted salmon, where the salmon are not kept or shipped in a brine solution. *Fisheries Act*, R.S.B.C. 1996, c. 149, s. 12.

SALMONID. *n*. Fish of the order Salmonidae listed in the schedule.

SALMON PLANT. See TIERCED ~.

SALTERY. See SALMON DRY ~.

SALTWATER MARSH. An area, lying between dry land and the ocean or an inlet thereof, which is covered all or part of the time by salt water and which is characterized by aquatic and grass-like vegetation.

SALUS REIPUBLICAE EST SUPREMA LEX. [L.] The well-being of the state is the highest law.

SALUS POPULI EST SUPREMA LEX. [L.] The safety of people is the highest law. *R. v. Carrière*, [1943] 3 B.L.R. 181 at 185, 79 C.C.C. 329 (Que. S.C.), Surveyer J.

SALVAGE. *v*. 1. " . . . [R]escue from threatened loss or injury. . ." *Canadian Pacific Navigation Co. v. "C.F. Sargent" (The)* (1893), 3 B.C.R. 5 at 7 (Ex. Ct.), Begbie L.J.A. 2. " . . . [T]o rescue or save from wreckage, . . ." *R. v. Greenspoon Brothers Ltd.*, [1965] 2 O.R. 528 at 529, [1965] 4 C.C.C. 53 (C.A.), the court per Roach J.A.

SALVAGE. *n*. 1. A reward, not for services attempted without result, but for benefits conferred. A salvor must show that, when the services were rendered, the cargo or ship was in danger of being destroyed. G.H.L. Fridman, *Restitution*, 2d ed. (Toronto: Carswell, 1992) at 281. 2. " . . . [T]hat which is . . . rescued or saved [from wreckage]. . ." *R. v. Greenspoon Brothers Ltd.*, [1965] 2 O.R. 528 at 529, [1965] 4 C.C.C. 53 (C.A.), the court per Roach J.A. 3. Includes second-hand, used discarded or surplus metals, bottles or goods, unserviceable, discarded or

junked motor vehicles, bodies, engines or other component parts of a motor vehicle and articles of every description.

SALVAGE CHARGE. A charge recoverable under maritime law by a salvor independently of contract; it does not include the expense of services in the nature of salvage rendered by the assured or the assured's agents, or any person employed for hire by them, for the purpose of averting a peril insured against. Such an expense, where properly incurred, may be recovered as a particular charge or as a general average loss, according to the circumstances under which it was incurred.

SALVAGE COSTS. 1. A larger share of costs to which the lien claimant who carried an action is entitled. They are calculated on how complex the issues are, the number of claimants and the time it took to resolve their claims. M.M. Orkin, *The Law of Costs*, 2d ed. (Aurora: Canada Law Book, 1987) at 14-5 and 14-6. 2. Because that claimant got the action on for trial, conducted the trial, prepared the formal judgment and distributed the money due under the judgment, she or he may claim a greater share than any other party. D.N. Macklem & D.I. Bristow, *Construction, Builders' and Mechanics' Liens in Canada*, 6th ed. (Toronto: Carswell, 1990) at 12-36.

SALVAGE DEALER. A person who owns or operates a salvage yard.

SALVAGE VALUE. The amount received for plant retired, including insurance proceeds, and includes any amount received for material salvaged from plant retired where the material is sold. See NET ~.

SALVAGE YARD. The premises where used automobile bodies or parts of other vehicles or machinery or used goods, material or equipment of any kind are placed, stored or kept.

SALVATION ARMY OFFICER. Every duly commissioned officer, envoy or auxiliary captain of the religious society known as "The Salvation Army" and duly chosen or commissioned by that society to solemnize marriage and resident in the province. *Solemnization of Marriage Act*, S. Nfld. 1974, c. 81, s. 2. See STAFF OFFICER OR STAFF OFFICER OF THE SALVATION ARMY.

SALVO. [L.] With no prejudice to.

SALVOR. *n*. The person who helps a ship or vessel in distress and thereby earns a reward.

SAME-SEX PARTNER. A person of the same sex with whom the person is living in a conjugal relationship outside marriage.

SAME-SEX PARTNERSHIP STATUS. The status of living with a person of the same sex in a conjugal relationship outside marriage.

SAMPLE. *n*. A small amount of a commodity displayed as a specimen at a private or public sale. See COMMERCIAL ~; COMPOSITE ~; EXPORT STANDARD ~; GRAB ~; OFFICIAL ~; SALE BY ~.

SANATORIUM. *n*. A hospital or part of a hospital set apart as a place for the reception of cases of tuberculosis.

SANCTION. *n*. 1. A punishment or penalty used to enforce obedience to law. 2. A sanction imposed under the Criminal Code must have have one or more of the following objectives: (a) to denounce unlawful conduct; (b) to deter the offender and other persons from committing offences; (c) to separate offenders from society, where necessary; (d) to assist in rehabilitating offenders; (e) to provide reparations for harm done to victims or to the community; and (f) to promote a sense of responsibility in offenders, and acknowledgment of the harm done to victims and to the community. *Criminal Code*, R.S.C. 1985, c. C-46, s. 718.See COMMUNITY ~S; CRIMINAL ~S; ECONOMIC ~; EXTRAJUDICIAL ~.

SANCTUARY. *n*. A place where neither a criminal nor civil process can be executed. See GAME ~; WILDLIFE ~.

SAND. *n*. A soil consisting of particles passing a No. 4 sieve but retained on a No. 200 sieve. *Building Code Act*, R.R.O. 1980, Reg. 87, s. 4.2.1.4. See BITUMINOUS ~S; FINE ~; MEDIUM ~; OIL ~; OIL ~S; TAR ~S.

SAND DUNE. 1. A wind or wave-deposited formation of vegetated or drifting wind-blown sand that lies generally parallel to and landward of the beach and between the upland limit of the beach and the foot of the most inland dune slope. *Environmental Protection Act*, R.S.P.E.I. 1988, c. E-9, s. 1(o). 2. A natural mound of loose sand, which may be covered with grass or other vegetation, found along a lake or ocean shore.

SANDERSON ORDER. 1. A simpler form of a Bullock order by which the unsuccessful defendant must pay the successful defendant's costs directly. The name comes from *Sanderson v. Blyth Theatre Co.*, [1903] 2 K.B. 644. 2. A Bullock order directs an unsuccessful defendant to reimburse the plaintiff for the recovered costs of a successful defendant. A Sanderson order directs that the payment go directly to the successful defendant. The rational behind both orders is the same. Where the allocation of responsibility is uncertain, usually because of interwoven facts, it is often reasonable to proceed through trial against more than one defendant. In these cases, a Bullock or Sanderson order provides a plaintiff with an appropriate form of relief. *Rooney (Litigation Guardian of) v. Graham* (2001), 53 O.R. (3d) 685 (C.A.).

SANITARIUM. *n*. An institution for the care and treatment of mental and nervous illnesses that is licensed under this Act. *Private Sanitaria Act*, R.S.O. 1980, c. 391, s. 1.

SANITARY ACCOMMODATION. Washing accommodation and accommodation containing water closets or urinals.

SANITARY CONDITION. That physical condition of the working environment of an employee that will contribute effectively to the health of that employee by preventing the incidence and spread of disease.

SANITARY DRAINAGE SYSTEM. A drainage system that conducts sewage.

SANITARY FACILITY. A room or rooms containing one or more toilets and one or more washbasins.

SANITARY UNIT. A water closet, urinal, bidet or bedpan washer.

SANITARY WASTE WATER. Waste water from the plumbing system of a building and not mixed with underground or surface water nor with residue from any process.

SANITATION DEVICE. See MARINE ~.

SANITIZE. *v*. 1. To remove bacteria by thermal or chemical means. 2. To clean for the purpose of controlling disease-producing organisms.

SANS CEO QUE. [L.] Without this.

SANS FRAIS. [Fr.] Without cost.

SANS RECOURS. [Fr.] Without recourse.

SARBANES-OXLEY ACT. United States statute enacted in 2002 dealing with securities law and requiring new rules concerning accounting, auditing, disclosure and penalties.

SASK. *abbr*. Saskatchewan.

SASK. BAR REV. *abbr*. Saskatchewan Bar Review.

SASK. L.R. *abbr*. Saskatchewan Law Reports.

SASK. L. REV. *abbr*. Saskatchewan Law Review.

SASK. R. *abbr*. Saskatchewan Reports, 1979-.

SATELLITE TELECOMMUNICATION SYSTEM. A complete telecommunication system consisting of two or more commercial radio stations situated on land, water or aircraft, in this Act referred to as "earth stations", and one or more radio stations situated on a satellite in space, in this Act referred to as "satellite stations", in which at least one earth station is capable of transmitting signs, signals, writing, images or sounds or intelligence of any nature to a satellite station that is in turn capable of receiving and retransmitting those signs, signals, writing, images or sounds or intelligence of any nature for reception by one or more earth stations. *Telesat Canada Act*, R.S.C. 1985, c. T-6, s. 2.

SATELLITE TRACK. A race-course where, by way of inter-track and separate pool betting, bets are taken on races held at a host track. *Pari-Mutuel Betting Supervision Regulations*, SOR/91-365, s. 2.

SATISFACTION. *n*. 1. Compensation under law. 2. Payment for an injury or of money owed. 3. Completion of an obligation by performance or something equivalent to performance. See ACCORD AND ~.

SATISFACTION PIECE. 1. " . . . [A] specialized form of receipt . . ." *Heitman Financial Services Ltd. v. Towncliff Properties Ltd.* (1981), 24 C.P.C. 116 at 120, 35 O.R. (2d)189 (H.C.), Callaghan J. 2. A judgment creditor's formal written acknowledgement, filed in court, that the judgment debtor has fully paid.

SATISFACTORY PROOF OF IDENTITY. In respect of an elector, means such documentary proof of the identity of the elector as is prescribed.

SATISFIED. *adj*. 1. Freed from doubt, anxiety, or uncertainty; having one's mind at rest. 2. Having been paid.

SATISFY. *v*. 1. To free from uncertainty or doubt. 2. To pay completely.

SATIUS EST PETERE FONTES QUAM SECTARI RIVULOS. [L.] It is better to seek the source than to follow rivulets.

SATURATION SOUND PRESSURE. At a specified frequency and under specified operation conditions, means the maximum (r.m.s.) sound pressure obtainable in the coupler from the earphone of the hearing aid at all possible test values of the input sound pressure level.

SAUGER. *n*. Eastern sauger or sand pickerel, Stizostedion canadense.

SAUNA. See PUBLIC ~.

SAUNDERS V. VAUTIER. See RULE IN ~.

SAVING CLAUSE. A provision in a contract stating that if any term is found invalid the rest of the contract will not be affected.

SAVINGS. *n*. Money placed in an account on which no bill of exchange payable on demand may be drawn.

SAVINGS BANK. A Government Savings Bank or a bank or savings bank in Canada.

SAVINGS FUND. See POOLED ~.

SAVINGS INSTITUTION. A bank, credit union, or a trust company.

SAVINGS PLAN. A retirement savings plan or a home ownership savings plan as each is defined in the Income Tax Act (Canada). See EDUCATION ~; HOME OWNERSHIP ~; REGISTERED HOME OWNERSHIP ~; REGISTERED RETIREMENT ~; RETIREMENT ~; STOCK ~.

SAVOUR. *v*. To share the nature of; to seem like.

S.C. *abbr*. 1. Supreme Court. 2. Supreme Court (provincial) [of Judicature]. 3. Superior Court. 4. Same case. 5. Sessions Cases.

SC. *abbr*. [L.] Scilicet. That is to say.

SCAB. *n*. A worker who refuses to join other workers on a picket line.

S.C.A.D. *abbr*. Supreme Court (provincial) [of Judicature] Appellate Division.

SCAFFOLD. *n*. A working platform supported from below.

SCAFFOLDING. *n*. The structure that supports a scaffold.

SCALD. *n*. An injury to the surface which moist heat causes. F.A. Jaffe, *A Guide to Pathological Evidence*, 3d ed. (Toronto: Carswell, 1991) at 225.

SCALE. *v.* To determine the volume and classify the quality of timber.

SCALE. *n.* See BASE RATE ~; SLIDING ~; UNION ~.

SCALE MODEL. A model reduced in size according to a fixed scale or proportion.

SCALE OF PUNISHMENTS. The scale of punishments as set out in subsection 139(1). *National Defence Act*, R.S.C. 1985, c. N-5, s. 2.

SCALER. *n.* A person employed or engaged in the measurement of timber.

SCALING. *n.* 1. The measurement of timber to determine its volume and mass. 2. The determination of the gross and net volumes of round wood in cords, cubic feet, cubic metres, board feet or assumed standards.

SCANDAL. *n.* An action or rumour which affronts one publicly. One may order scandalous matter to be struck from a pleading.

SCANDALIZE THE COURT. " . . . [T]raditionally encompasses two forms of conduct: (a) scurrilous abuse of a court, or of a judge not in his personal capacity but as a judge: . . . and (b) attacks upon the integrity or impartiality of a judge or court: . . . there may be a third form, namely, 'publications that are thought to lower the repute of a judge or court.' " *R. v. Kopyto* (1987), 39 C.C.C. (3d) 1 at 36, 24 O.A.C. 8, 61 C.R. (3d) 209, 62 O.R. (2d) 449, 47 D.L.R. (4th) 213 (C.A.), Houlden J.A. See CONTEMPT.

SCANDALOUS. *adj.* Indecent or offensive and made for the purpose of abusing or prejudicing the opposite party. Unbecoming for the court to hear. Unnecessary allegations bearing cruelly on the moral character of a person.

SCANNED LASER RADIATION. Laser radiation having a time varying direction, origin or pattern of propagation with respect to a stationary frame of reference. *Radiation Emitting Devices Regulations*, C.R.C., c. 1370, s. 1.

SCATTERING GROUNDS. The land within a cemetery that is set aside to be used for the scattering of cremated human remains. *Funeral, Burial and Cremation Services Act, 2002*, S.O. 2002, c. 33.

SCATTERING RIGHTS. Includes the right to require or direct the scattering of cremated human remains on the scattering grounds of a cemetery. *Funeral, Burial and Cremation Services Act, 2002*, S.O. 2002, c. 33.

SCATTERING RIGHTS HOLDER. The person who holds the scattering rights with respect to a scattering ground whether the person be the purchaser of the rights, the person named in the certificate of scattering or such other person to whom the interment rights have been assigned. *Funeral, Burial and Cremation Services Act, 2002*, S.O. 2002, c. 33.

SCAVENGING. *n.* The uncontrolled removal of reusable material from waste at a waste disposal site.

SCC. The English neutral citation for the Supreme Court of Canada.

S.C.C. *abbr.* . . . Supreme Court of Canada. 2. [Fr.] Société commerciale canadienne, one of the words required to be part of a corporate name.

SCHED. *abbr.* Schedule.

SCHEDULE. *n.* 1. An inventory. 2. Additional or appendant writing. 3. Detailed information attached to a statute or regulation. 4. That part of a time table which prescribes class, direction, number and movement for a regular train. See FLEXIBLE ~; INDUSTRIAL STANDARDS ~; RECORDS ~; SERVICE ~.

SCHEDULED FLIGHT. A flight conducted under a published statement of frequency and time of departure and arrival and operated by a commercial air service utilizing commercial aircraft. *Flying Accidents Compensation Regulations*, C.R.C., c. 10, s. 2.

SCHEDULED HARBOUR. Any fishing or recreational harbour or portion thereof included in a schedule prescribed by the regulations. *Fishing and Recreational Harbours Act*, R.S.C. 1985, c. F-24, s. 2.

SCHEDULED TRAVEL TRANSPORTATION. Travel transportation supplied on a regular basis at certain fixed times and for which advance booking is not mandatory.

SCHEDULED WAGE INCREASE. A raise unrelated to work or performance, paid at certain stipulated intervals and based on the length of an employee's service or prior work experience.

SCHEDULE OF HOURS OF LABOR. The schedule of the maximum number of hours in each day or of days in each week, or of both, which any employee shall be permitted to work.

SCHEDULE OF WAGES. The schedule of minimum wages or remuneration payable to any employee.

SCHEME. *n.* 1. A plan for marketing or regulating any natural product. 2. A plan for distributing property among people with conflicting claims. 3. " . . . [I]n the commercial sense of that word, that is a plan, design, formula or programme of action devised in order to attain some end, usually unilaterally described or stated . . ." *Canadian Allied Property Investment Ltd., Re* (1979), (*sub nom. Gregory v. Canadian Allied Property Investment Ltd.*) 98 D.L.R. (3d) 358 at 364, [1979] 3 W.W.R. 609, 11 B.C.L.R. 253 (C.A.), the court per Carrothers J.A. See BUILDING ~; EXPERIMENTAL ~; INSURANCE ~; LOTTERY ~; NEGATIVE OPTION ~; PLANNING ~; PROVINCIAL ~; RECOGNIZED CANADIAN ~; RENEWAL ~; TRAFFIC SEPARATION ~.

SCHEME OF PYRAMID SELLING. A multi-level marketing plan whereby (a) a participant in the plan gives consideration for the right to receive compensation by reason of the recruitment into the plan of another participant in the plan who gives consideration for the same right; (b) a participant in the plan gives consideration, as a condition of participating in the plan, for a specified amount of the product, other than a specified amount of the product that is bought at the seller's cost price for the purpose only of facilitating sales; (c) a person knowingly supplies the product to a participant in the plan in an amount that is commercially unreasonable; or (d) a participant in the plan who is supplied with the product (i) does not have a buy-back guarantee that is exercisable on reasonable commercial terms or a right to return the product in saleable condition on reasonable commercial terms, or (ii) is not informed of the existence of the guarantee or right and the manner in which it can be exercised. *Competition Act*, R.S.C. 1985, c. C-34, s. 55.1(1).

SCHOLARSHIP. *n.* 1. A sum of money awarded with special regard to the quality of the academic work of the person to whom it is awarded. 2. An award of distinction, prize or incentive. 3. Pecuniary assistance granted gratuitously to a student.

SCHOOL. *n.* 1. " . . . [A] place of learning or 'instructional' unit. . ." *Mahe v. Alberta* (1987), 33 C.R.R. 207 at 229, [1987] 6 W.W.R. 331, 54 Alta. L.R. (2d) 212, 80 A.R. 161, 42 D.L.R. (4th) 514 (C.A.), the court per Kerans J.A. 2. The room or building in which instruction is given. 3. A body of pupils that is organized as a unit for educational purposes and that comprises one or more instructional groups or classes, together with the principal and teaching staff and other employees assigned to such body of pupils, and includes the land, buildings or other premises and permanent improvements used by and in connection with that body of pupils. 4. Includes a day school, technical school, high school and residential school. *Indian Act*, R.S.C. 1985, c. I-5, s. 122. See BRANCH ~; COMMERCIAL FLYING ~; CONTINUATION ~; ELEMENTARY ~; FEEDER ~; HIGH ~; HOSPITAL ~; INDEPENDENT ~; INDUSTRIAL ~; JUNIOR HIGH ~; NURSERY ~; PRIVATE ~; PUBLIC ~; SECONDARY ~; SENDING ~; SUBSIDIZED ~; TECHNICAL ~; TRADE ~; URBAN SEPARATE ~; VACATION ~.

SCHOOL AGE. See COMPULSORY ~.

SCHOOL ASSESSMENT. The tax which is levied on the taxable property of a school municipality.

SCHOOL ATTENDANCE. See COMPULSORY ~.

SCHOOL AUTHORITY. 1. A school division, school committee of a county or school district, as the case may be. 2. The board of trustees of school district or school division.

SCHOOL BOARD. 1. A board of education. 2. The board of trustees of a school district. See ROMAN CATHOLIC ~; SEPARATE ~.

SCHOOL BUILDING. A building used for the instruction of school pupils.

SCHOOL BUS. 1. A bus operated for the transportation of children to or from school. 2. A motor vehicle used primarily to transport children to or from school or in connection with school activities.

SCHOOL CORPORATION. Every corporation of school commissioners or trustees and, generally, every commission or board incorporated for the administration of schools. Quebec Statutes.

SCHOOL CROSSING GUARD. A person employed by a municipality, or employed by a person under contract to a municipality, to direct the movement of children across a roadway.

SCHOOL DAY. A day within a school year on which instruction is given or examinations or other educational activities are conducted.

SCHOOL DAY CARE. Day care provided by a school board or a corporation of school trustees to children attending classes and receiving educational services in kindergarten and primary grades in its schools.

SCHOOL DISTRICT. See RURAL AREA OF ~; TOWN ~.

SCHOOL DIVISION. See PUBLIC ~.

SCHOOL HOUSE. *var.* **SCHOOLHOUSE**. Includes the house or building required or used in a district for the imparting of instruction or for offices or other public school purposes; but does not include a building, or a part thereof, constructed, designed, or used solely or chiefly for administrative functions of the school district other than those exercised by principals or teachers. *Public Schools Act*, R.S.M. 1970, c. P250, s. 2. 2. Includes the teacher's dwelling house, the playground, if any, and the offices and premises belonging to or required for a school. *Mortmain and Charitable Uses Act*, R.S.O. 1980, c. 297, s. 8.

SCHOOL LAW. See COMPULSORY ~.

SCHOOL LEAVING. See REGULAR ~ AGE.

SCHOOL LEVY. See PROVINCIAL ~.

SCHOOL LIBRARY. A library intended primarily for students and faculty of a school.

SCHOOL MONEYS. Moneys that are the property of, or are payable to, a school division or a school district.

SCHOOL OF APPLIED SCIENCE. Any Canadian educational institution that conducts science courses leading to degrees in mechanical or electrical engineering.

SCHOOL PERSONNEL. (a) Chief administrative officer and other administrative personnel; (b) building maintenance personnel; (c) secretaries; (d) teachers; (e) persons other than teachers engaged to deliver or to assist in the delivery of special education programs and services, or to assist exceptional pupils; and (f) other persons engaged in the areas of attendance, social services, health services, psychology and guidance.

SCHOOL PROGRAM. All the educational programs and the activities and personnel that a school board is required or permitted to provide.

SCHOOL SECTION. See URBAN ~.

SCHOOL SECURITIES. Bonds, debentures, notes or other evidences of indebtedness of any school corporation in Canada. *Cooperative Credit Associations Act*, R.S.C. 1985, c. C-41, s. 49.

SCHOOL SITE. Land or interest therein or premises required by a board for a school, school playground, school garden, teacher's residence, caretaker's residence, gymnasium, offices, parking areas or for any other school purpose.

SCHOOL TAX. The tax derived by applying the mill rate, as determined by the board of education, to the taxable assessment.

SCHOOLTEACHER. *n.* "[In s. 43 of the Criminal Code, R.S.C. 1970, c. C-34] . . . a person who gives formal instruction in a children's [elementary] school. . ." *R. v. Ogg-Moss* (1984), 6 C.H.R.R. D/2498 at D/2505, [1984] 2 S.C.R. 173, 41 C.R. (3d) 297, 14 C.C.C. (3d) 116, 11 D.L.R. (4th) 549, 5 O.A.C. 81, the court per Dickson J.

SCHOOL TERM. A period commencing July 1 and ending December 31 of the same year or a period commencing January 1 and ending June 30 of the same year.

SCHOOL TRUSTEE. A person elected or appointed as a member of a board.

SCHOOL YEAR. 1. The period commencing on July 1 in one year and ending on June 30 in the next year, both dates inclusive. 2. The period from and including the 1st day of September in one year to and including the 31st day of August in the next year.

SCHOOL ZONE. A zone on a highway identified by a traffic control device as an area where children (a) may be expected to be on the highway; or (b) are permitted to cross the highway at a designated point along the highway. See SEPARATE ~; URBAN SEPARATE ~.

SCIENCE. *n.* Includes the natural and social sciences. *International Development Research Centre Act*, R.S.C. 1985, c. I-19, s. 2. See VETERINARY ~.

SCIENCE COUNCIL OF CANADA. A federal advisory agency on policy concerning science and technology.

SCIENS. *adj.* [L.] " . . . '[K]nowing' . . ." *Waldick v. Malcolm* (1991), 8 C.C.L.T. (2d) 1 at 17, 3 O.R. (3d) 471n, 125 N.R. 372, 47 O.A.C. 241, 83 D.L.R. (4th) 114, [1991] 2 S.C.R. 456, the court per Iacobucci J.

SCIENTER. *adv.* [L.] Knowingly.

SCIENTER ACTION. "At common law the principle of scienter governed the owner's liability for damage caused by his animals. For example, if a dog bit a person liability depended upon proof that the owner of the dog knew or ought to have known of the animal's dangerous character. . . The common law also recognized that certain animals were, by their nature, so dangerous to man that the keeper of them could not be heard to say that he did not know of their character. Scienter, in such a case, was to be conclusively presumed. 'Strict liability' was imposed in such cases, with certain defences permitted. . ." *Brewer v. Saunders* (1986), 37 C.C.L.T. 237 at 242 (N.S. C.A.), the court per Matthews J.A.

SCIENTIA. [L.] Knowledge.

SCIENTIA UTRIMQUE PAR PARES CONTRAHENTES FACIT. [L.] Equal knowledge on both sides makes those who are contracting equal.

SCIENTIFIC APPARATUS. An assembly of objects forming a unit constructed for the purpose of research in any scientific discipline.

SCIENTIFIC INSTRUMENT. An implement, tool or device used for practical or scientific purposes as an instrument for examining or measuring.

SCIENTIFIC METHOD. Scientific method involves the generation of hypotheses and the testing of them to see if they can be falsified or refuted. An hypothesis which is inherently incapable of falsification is also incapable of scientific verification. *R. v. Murrin* (1999), 1999 CarswellBC 3015, 181 D.L.R. (4th) 320, 32 C.R. (5th) 97 (S.C.).

SCIENTIFIC OR EXPLORATORY EXPEDITION. An expedition (a) conducted or sponsored by a scientific or cultural organization, an institution of learning or a foreign government; (b) the participants in which are non-residents of Canada; and (c) the sponsors of which have undertaken to make available to the Government of Canada all information obtained in Canada as a result of the expedition's field studies. *Scientific Expeditions Remission Order*, C.R.C., c. 787, s. 2.

SCIENTI NON FIT INJURIA. [L.] No harm is done to one who knows the risk he runs.

SCI. FA. *abbr*. [L.] Scire facias.

SCILICET. [L.] That is to say.

SCINTILLA JURIS. [L.] A fragment or spark of right.

SCINTILLA JURIS ET TITULI. [L.] A fragment of right and title.

SCIRE FACIAS. [L. that you cause to know] A writ which directs a sheriff to warn or make known to someone to show cause.

SCOPE OF EMPLOYMENT. See ACT WITHIN ~.

SCOPING. *n*. The practice of a tribunal hearing only issues upon which parties disagree so that its hearings are more focussed.

SCORE. See PRELIMINARY ~.

SCOTTISH RING NET. A net that (a) is floated at the top, weighted at the bottom and mounted with rings through which a rope is run; and (b) is set from a vessel so as to enclose an area of water and then closed at the bottom by means of the rope referred to in paragraph (a) so as to form a purse or bag. *Atlantic Coast Herring Regulations*, C.R.C., c. 804, s. 2.

SCOTT v. AVERY CLAUSE. A clause making arbitration a condition precedent to the bringing of an action. Named after *Scott v. Avery* (1856), 25 L.J. Exch. 308, 5 H.L.C. 811 (U.K. H.K.). *Burns & Roe of Canada Ltd. v. Deuterium of Canada Ltd.* (1974), [1975] 2 S.C.R. 124.

S.C.R. *abbr*. Reports of the Supreme Court of Canada, 1876-1922.

[] S.C.R. abbr. 1. Canada Law Reports, Supreme Court of Canada, 1964- (Rapports judiciaires du Canada, Cour Supreme du Canada). 2. Canada Law Reports, Supreme Court of Canada, 1923-1963.

SCRAP. *n*. All waste material including rejected metal, lumber and tree stumps. *Pits and Quarries Control Act*, R.R.O. 1980, Reg. 784, s. 1.

SCRAP AUTOMOBILE. A used automobile that is not in operating condition, is not intended by the owner thereof to be restored to operating condition, and that is kept in the open and primarily for the purpose of salvaging or selling parts therefrom, or for eventual sale as scrap metal, and includes a body or chassis of the used automobile after all or some of the other parts of the automobile have been removed, that is kept for such purposes. *Highways Protection Act*, R.S.M. 1970, c. Z-2, s. 17

SCRAP VEHICLE. Includes any automobile, tractor, truck or trailer that: (a) has no currently valid registration number plates attached thereto; (b) is in a rusted, wrecked, partly wrecked, dismantled, inoperative or abandoned condition; and (c) is located in the open, on private or public property, and does not form part of the stock-in-trade of a business enterprise lawfully being operated by a person. *The Scrap Vehicles Act*, R.S.S. 1978, c. S-40, s. 2.

SCRATCH. See LATE ~.

SCRATCHED. *adj*. In respect of a horse, means a horse that does not start or compete in a race because it is (a) declared a late scratch, (b) determined not to have had a fair start, pursuant to the applicable rules of racing, (c) declared to be a non-contestant, pursuant to the applicable rules of racing, (d) added to the race after betting has begun, in contravention of subsection 52(3), or (e) a horse in relation to which an officer has ordered that betting be closed under subsection 52(4). *Pari-Mutuel Betting Supervision Regulations*, SOR/91-365, s. 2.

SCREEN. See WIRED GLASS ~.

SCREENINGS. *n*. 1. Dockage that has been removed from a parcel of grain. 2. Matter removed in the process of cleaning or grading of cereal, forage or other crop seed.

SCRIBERE EST AGERE. [L.] To write is to do.

SCRIP. *n*. A document entitling the holder to receive something of value.

SCRIP DIVIDEND. A dividend in some form other than cash.

SCRIPT. *n*. 1. Writing. 2. An original or principal document.

SCRIPTAE OBLIGATIONES SCRIPTIS TOLLUNTUR, ET NUDI CONSENSUS OBLIGATIO CONTRARIO CONSENSU DISSOLVITUR. [L.] Written obligations are annulled by writing, and an obligation nakedly assented to is annulled by assent to the contrary.

SCRIVENER. *n*. " . . . [A] person who holds money put into his hands until he has an opportunity of investing. . ." *Fedak v. Monti* (1981), 16 C.C.L.T. 287 at 292 (Ont. H.C.), Steele J.

SCROLL. *n*. A mark which shows the place for a seal.

S.C.R.R. *abbr*. Securities and Corporate Regulation Review.

SCRUBBING PLANT. Any plant for the purifying, scrubbing or otherwise treating, of gas for the extraction or removal from it of hydrogen sulphide or other deleterious substance.

SCRUB BULL. *var*. **SCRUB-BULL**. A bull which is not registered in a herd-book.

SCRUTINEER. *n*. Any person who is appointed by a candidate or that candidate's official agent to represent the candidate in a polling place.

SCRUTINY. *n*. " . . . [I]s an entirely distinct proceeding from a recount; it is an inquiry into the validity of the votes. . ." *West Lorne Scrutiny, Re* (1913), (*sub nom. McPherson v. Mehring*) 47 S.C.R. 451 at 455, Fitzpatrick C.J.

S.C.T.D. *abbr*. Supreme Court (provincial) [of Judicature] Trial Division.

SCUFFING. *n*. A visible erosion of a portion of the outer surface of a brake cup.

SCULPTURE. *n*. 1. An artistic representation or work in three dimensions that is carved, modelled or constructed and includes such a representation that has subsequentially been cast in plaster, metal or other substance that will take on a rigid form. 2. Includes a cast or model. *Copyright Act*, R.S.C. 1985, c. C-42, s. 2. See WORK OF ~.

SCUTTLING. *n*. With respect to a ship, purposeful casting away.

SCUTUM ARMORUM. [L.] A coat of arms, shield.

S.D.A.G. *abbr*. Specially denatured alcohol grade. *Denatured Alcohol Regulations*, C.R.C., c. 568, s. 2.

SEA. *n*. (a) The territorial sea of Canada; (b) the internal waters of Canada other than inland waters; (c) any fishing zones prescribed pursuant to the Territorial Sea and Fishing Zones Act; (d) the arctic waters within the meaning of the Arctic Waters Pollution Prevention Act; (e) such areas of the sea adjacent to the areas referred to in paragraphs (a) to (d) as may be prescribed; (f) any area of the sea, other than internal waters, under the jurisdiction of a foreign state; and (g) any area of the sea, other than the internal waters of a foreign state, not included in the areas of the sea referred to in paragraphs (a) to (f). *Ocean Dumping Control Act*, R.S.C. c. O-2, s. 2. See ARM OF THE ~; BEYOND ~S; BEYOND THE ~S; HIGH ~S; PERILS OF THE ~S; PRODUCTS OF THE ~, LAKES AND RIVERS; TERRITORIAL ~.

SEA CARRIER. The owner or operator of a vessel engaged in the transportation of animals by water.

SEAFARER. *n*. A person who (a) applies for a certificate under the *Marine Certification Regulations*; or (b) is employed or is to be employed in any capacity on a ship. *Crewing Regulations*, SOR/97-390, s. 1.

SEA GOING. Implies something more than travel in salt water and that the term implies the ability to travel upon the open sea and actual travel on the sea outside of protected coastal waters. *Courtenay Assessor Area No. 6 v. Quinsam Coal Corp.*, 2002 BCCA 68, 164 B.C.A.C. 67 (C.A.).

SEA-GOING SHIP. Any ship employed on a voyage any part of which is on the sea. *Canada Shipping Act*, R.S.C. 1985, c. S-9, s. 2.

SEAL. *v*. 1. "[One seals] . . . a contract by placing paper seals opposite the signatures to it . . ." *R. v. Crane* (1985), 55 Nfld. & P.E.I.R. 340 at 342, 162 A.P.R. 340 (Nfld. Dist. Ct.), Barry D.C.J. 2. To take any measures satisfactory to the chief inspector that will effectively prevent the operation or use of a boiler, pressure vessel or plant. *Boilers and Pressure Vessels acts*. 3. To take any measure satisfactory to the chief inspector that will effectively prevent the unauthorized operation or use of an elevating device. *Elevators and Lifts acts*. 4. To perform a formal act by placing a waxed impression, gummed wafer or impression by metal stamp.

SEAL. *n*. 1. A wafer or wax marked with an impression. 2. A gummed wafer or impression made with metal stamp. 3. The portion of a licence that is required to be detached from the licence and cancelled immediately after the wildlife is killed, or a tag that may be supplied with a wildlife licence. *Wildlife Act*, S.S. 1979, c. W-13.1, s. 2. 4. A seal made of some substantial material having a serial number imprinted thereon, and furnished by the returning officer to seal a ballot box. *Municipal Elections Act*, R.S.N.S. 1989, c. 300, s. 2(1). See BROKEN ~; CORPORATE ~; GREAT ~; GREAT ~ OF THE REALM; METAL ~; OFFICIAL ~; PRIVY ~; ROYAL ~S; TRAP ~.

SEALED. See HERMETICALLY ~.

SEALED FIREARM. A firearm sealed or secured in the prescribed manner. *Wildlife Act*, S.N.W.T. 1978 (3d Sess.), c. 8, s. 2.

SEALING. *n*. The hunting for, killing and skinning of seals, the handling and transporting of raw seal pelts from the place where they are killed to the land and the transporting of persons engaged in sealing to and from the killing area and includes searching for seals from helicopters and other aircraft. *Seal Protection Regulations*, C.R.C., c. 833, s. 2. See MECHANICAL ~; PELAGIC ~.

SEALING SHIP. A ship engaged in sealing.

SEAMAN. *n*. 1. Every person, except pilots, apprenticed pilots and fishermen, employed or engaged on (a) a ship registered in Canada; or (b) a ship chartered by demise to a person resident in Canada or having his principal place of business in Canada, when the ship is engaged in trading on a foreign voyage or on a home-trade voyage as those voyages are defined in the Canada Shipping Act, and, if so ordered by the Governor in Council, includes a seaman engaged in Canada and employed on a ship that is registered outside Canada and operated by a person resident in Canada or having his principal place of business in Canada when that ship is so engaged. *Merchant Seaman Compensation Act*, R.S.C. 1985, c. M-6, s. 2. 2. Includes (a) every person, except masters, pilots and apprentices duly indentured and registered, employed or engaged in any capacity on board any ship; and (b) for the purposes of the Seamen's Repatriation Convention, every person employed or engaged in any capacity on board any vessel and entered on the ship's articles, but does not include pilots, cadets and pupils on training ships and naval ratings, or other persons in the permanent service of a government except when used in Part IV where it includes an apprentice to the sea service. *Canada Shipping Act*, R.S.C. 1985, c. S-9, s. 2. See DISTRESSED ~; MERCHANT ~; ORDINARY PRACTICE OF SEAMEN.

SEAMEN'S ARTICLES CONVENTION. The International Convention respecting Seamen's Articles of Agreement adopted by the International Labour Conference at Geneva on June 24, 1926. *Canada Shipping Act*, R.S.C. 1985, c. S-9, s. 2.

SEAMEN'S REPATRIATION CONVENTION. The International Convention concerning the repatriation of seamen adopted by the International Labour Conference at Geneva on June 24, 1926 as modified by the recommendation of the same date respecting masters and apprentices. *Canada Shipping Act*, R.S.C. 1985, c. S-9, s. 2.

SEAPLANE. *n*. 1. Includes a flying boat and any other aircraft able to manoeuvre on water.

Canada regulations. 2. An aircraft capable of landing on or taking off from water. *Life-Saving Equipment Order*, C.R.C., c. 50, s. 2.

SEA PLANT. 1. All benthic and detached marine algae, all marine flowering plants, and includes all brown algae such as fucoids (commonly known as rockweeds) and laminarians (commonly known as kelp), and all red algae including chondrus, gigartina, and furcellaria, and all green algae, or any part or segment of the plants named in this clause. 2. All fucoids (commonly known as rockweeds) and laminarians (commonly known as kelp) but does not include chondrus crispus (commonly known as Irish moss), dulse or eel grass.

SEA RANCHING. That form of aquaculture in which aquatic animals are intentionally released, without restriction, into the natural environment. *Aquaculture Act*, R.S. Nfld. 1990, c. A-13, s. 2.

SEARCH. *v.* 1. Of title, to search in public offices to be sure that the vendor can convey title or interest free of all competing claims. 2. To look for or seek out evidence.

SEARCH. *n.* 1. "In determining whether the beeper monitoring ... constitutes a search [within the meaning of Charter, s. 8], the initial question is whether there is a reasonable expectation of privacy in respect of the monitored activity. If the police activity invades a reasonable expectation of privacy, then the activity is a search." *R. v. Wise* (1992), 8 C.R.R. (2d) 53 at 57, 11 C.R. (4th) 253, [1992] 1 S.C.R. 527, 70 C.C.C. (3d) 193, 133 N.R. 161, 51 O.A.C. 351, Cory J. (Lamer C.J.C., Gonthier and Stevenson JJ. concurring). 2. " ... [I]mplies an effort to find what is concealed, to get past the shield surrounding privacy, to defeat the efforts of an individual to keep hidden certain elements pertaining to his life or personality. . ." *Weatherall v. Canada (Attorney General)* (1990), 78 C.R. (3d) 257 at 265, 58 C.C.C. (3d) 424, 73 D.L.R. (4th) 57, 49 C.R.R. 347, [1991] 1 F.C. 85, 112 N.R. 379, 37 F.T.R. 80n (C.A.), Marceau J.A. (dissenting in art). 3. Examination of original documents, official books and records while investigating a title to land. See BODY CAVITY ~; FRISK ~; PAT DOWN ~; REASONABLE ~; STRIP ~; UNREASONABLE ~.

SEARCH OR SEIZURE. 1. " ... [I]mply an intrusion into the citizen's home or place of business by a third person who looks for and removes documents or things. Searches and seizures are normally effected under a warrant or writ which is addressed to the officer conducting the search or seizure and permits him to enter the premises for those purposes. . ." *Ziegler v. Canada (Director of Investigation & Research, Combines Investigation Branch)* (1983), (*sub nom. Ziegler v. Hunter*) 39 C.P.C. 234 at 259, 8 D.L.R. (4th) 648, [1984] 2 F.C. 608, 51 N.R.1, 8 C.R.R. 47 (C.A.), Hugessen J.A. 2. " ... [E]lectronic surveillance constitutes a 'search or seizure' within the meaning of s. 8 of the [Charter] ..." *R. v. Thompson* (1990), 59 C.C.C. (3d) 225 at 267, [1990] 6 W.W.R. 481, 49 B.C.L.R. (2d) 321, 80 C.R. (3d) 129, 73 D.L.R. (4th) 596, 114 N.R. 1, 50 C.R.R. 1, [1990] 2 S.C.R. 1111, Sopinka J. (Dickson C.J.C., Lamer C.J.C. and L'Heureux-Dubé J. concurring).

SEARCH PERIOD. See TITLE ~.

SEARCH WARRANT. " ... [A]n order issued by a Justice under statutory powers, authorizing a named person to enter a specified place to search for and seize specified property which will afford evidence of the actual or intended commission of a crime." *MacIntyre v. Nova Scotia (Attorney General)* (1982), 132 D.L.R. (3d) 385 at 397, [1982] S.C.R. 175, 26 C.R. (3d) 193, 40 N.R. 181, 49 N.S.R. (2d) 609, 96 A.P.R. 609, 65 C.C.C. (2d) 129, Dickson J. (Laskin C.J.C., McIntyre, Chouinard and Lamer JJ. concurring).

SEA SERVICE. Time spent at sea after the age of 15 years in performing seamanship duties in the deck department of a self-propelled ship regularly engaged in ordinary trading or commercial fishing outside smooth or partially smooth waters. *Master and Mates Examination Regulations*, C.R.C., c. 1444, s. 2.

SEASHORE. *n.* " ... [T]he right of the Crown to the seashore landwards is prima facie limited by the line of the medium high tide between spring and neap, ..." *Turnbull v. Saunders* (1920), 48 N.B.R. 502 at 509, 60 D.L.R. 666 (C.A.), the court per Hazen C.J.

SEASON. See CLOSED ~; CLOSE ~; FIRE ~; GRAZING ~; NAVIGATION ~; OPEN~; SUMMER ~.

SEASONAL AGRICULTURAL WORK. Work of a seasonal nature in agriculture which will provide persons who can legally be engaged at the work site with continuous employment for a period not exceeding 9 months.

SEASONAL CUSTOMER. A customer who requires electricity service for a period of less than 12 consecutive months.

SEASONAL DWELLING. A residence not occupied full time.

SEASONAL EMPLOYEE. An employee whose services are of a seasonal and recurring nature.

SEASONAL EMPLOYMENT. Employment which is not continuous through the year but recurs in successive years. See FULL-TIME ~.

SEASONAL INDUSTRY. An industry that in each year ordinarily suspends production operations completely for one or more periods of at least 3 weeks each, by reason of fluctuations in market demands characteristic of the industry or consequent upon the ripening of crops.

SEASONAL RESIDENT. A person who is not a resident of Canada and who leases for not less than three years or who owns, for seasonal use, a residence in Canada, other than a time-sharing residence or a mobile home. *Seasonal Residents' Remission Order* SI/91-84, s. 2.

SEASONING. *n.* A condiment, spice or herb used for savour but does not include salt.

SEASON OF NAVIGATION. The period from the date of the official opening to the date of the official closing of navigation, both dates inclusive.

SEAT. See ADJACENT ~.

SEAT BACK RETAINER. The portion of a seat belt assembly designed to restrict forward movement of a seat back. *Motor Vehicle Safety Regulations*, C.R.C., c. 1038, s. 2.

SEAT BELT. Any strap, webbing, or similar device designed to secure the driver or a passenger in a motor vehicle.

SEAT BELT ANCHORAGE. Any component, other than the webbing or straps, involved in transferring seat belt load to the vehicle structure, including the attachment hardware, seat frames, seat pedestals, the vehicle structure and any part of the vehicle the failure of which causes separation of the belt from the vehicle structure. *Motor Vehicle Safety Regulations*, C.R.C. 1038, s. 2.

SEAT BELT ASSEMBLY. Any strap, webbing or similar device designed to secure a person in a vehicle in order to mitigate the results of any accident and includes (a) all necessary buckles and other fasteners and all hardware, and (b) a belt assembly that is part of an automatic occupant protection system. *Motor Vehicle Safety Regulations*, C.R.C. 1038, s. 2.

SEAT BELT INJURY. An injury, like a compression fracture of the spine or tear of the bowel and mesentery, caused by bending over a seat belt during sudden deceleration. F.A. Jaffe, *A Guide to Pathological Evidence*, 3d ed. Toronto: Carswell, 1991) at 225.

SEATING CAPACITY. See DESIGNATED ~.

SEATING POSITION. See DESIGNATED ~.

SEA TROUT. An anadromous speckled trout (Salvelinus fontinalis).

SEAWARD BOUNDARY. An imaginary line that is measured seaward from the nearest Canadian land a distance of 100 nautical miles; except that in the area between the islands of the Canadian Arctic and Greenland where the line of equidistance between the islands of the Canadian Arctic and Greenland is less than 100 nautical miles from the nearest Canadian land, there shall be substituted for the line measured seaward 100 nautical miles from the nearest Canadian land such line of equidistance. *Shipping Safety Control Zones Order*, C.R.C., c. 356, s. 2.

SEAWAY. *n.* The deep waterway between the port of Montreal and the Great Lakes that is constructed and maintained pursuant to the Agreement between Canada and the United States providing for the development of navigation and power in the Great Lakes-St. Lawrence Basin, dated March 19, 1941, including the locks, canals and facilities between the port of Montreal and Lake Erie and generally known as the St. Lawrence Seaway. *Canada Marine Act, 1998*, S.C. 1998, c. 10, s. 2.

SECESSION. *n.* Secession is the effort of a group or section of a state to withdraw itself from the political and constitutional authority of that state, with a view to achieving statehood for a new territorial unit on the international plane. In a federal state, secession typically takes the form of a territorial unit seeking to withdraw from the federation. Secession is a legal act as much as a political one. *Reference re Secession of Quebec*, [1998] 2 S.C.R. 217 Per curiam.

SECK. *adj.* Barren; dry. See RENT~.

SECOND. *v.* Refers to an employer transferring an employee to another branch or department. *Belisle Public Service Commission Appeal Board, Re* (1983), 149 D.L.R. (3d) 352 at 358, 49 N.R. 220 (Fed. C.A.), the court per Ryan J.A.

SECOND. *n.* 1. The unit for the measurement of time, being the duration of 9 192 631 770 periods of the radiation corresponding to the transition between the two hyperfine levels of the ground state of the caesium 133 atom. *Weights and Measures Act*, S.C. 1970-1-2, c. 36, schedule 1. 2. Of arc, π/648 000 radian. *Weights and Measures Act*, S.C. 1970-1-2, c. 36, schedule 1.

SECONDARY BOYCOTT. A refusal to deal with a neutral party in a labour dispute in order that that will bring pressure to bear on the employer party with whom there is a dispute.

SECONDARY COURSE. Includes any grade higher than the seventh year of the elementary course.

SECONDARY CREDIT. Credit extended to the supplier of an exporter by the confirming bank. It covers the same goods which are the subject of the confirmed credit to the exporter. I.F.G. Baxter, *The Law of Banking*, 3d ed. (Toronto: Carswell, 1981) at 156.

SECONDARY DIAGNOSIS. 1. A second major diagnosis. 2. An associated mental disorder which manifests an underlying condition or occurs in association with a metabolic or organic disorder or other physical factor.

SECONDARY DROWNING. Acute and even fatal pneumonia hours or days after rescue and apparent recovery from drowning because heavily chlorinated or contaminated water is so irritating to the lungs. F.A. Jaffe, *A Guide to Pathological Evidence*, 3d ed. (Toronto: Carswell, 1991) at 107.

SECONDARY EDUCATION. High school.

SECONDARY EVIDENCE. Proof admitted when primary evidence is lost. For example, a copy, instead of the lost original of a document is secondary evidence.

SECONDARY FOREST PRODUCT. Everything resulting from the processing, treating, manufacturing or breaking down of a primary forest product.

SECONDARY LEAD SMELTER. Any plant or factory in which lead-bearing scrap or lead bearing materials, other than lead-bearing concentrates derived from a mining operation, is processed by metallurgical or chemical process into refined lead, lead alloys or lead oxide. *Secondary Lead Smelter National Emission Standards Regulations*, C.R.C., c. 412, s. 2.

SECONDARY LINE. A pipe for (a) the gathering or transmission of oil or gas in an area; (b) the gathering or transmission of oil, gas, water or any other substance in connection with an order made, or a scheme or operation approved, under the Oil and Gas Conservation Act; (c) the gathering or transmission of water, oil or gas in connection with drilling or production operations in any area; or (d) the gathering and transmission of solids to a solids line, and includes installations in connection with that pipe, but does not include a flow line.

SECONDARY MEANING. 1. In relation to a trade name, means a trade name that has been used in Canada or elsewhere by any applicant or his predecessors so as to have become distinctive in Canada as at the date of filing an application for a corporate name. *Canada Business Corporations Regulations*, C.R.C., c. 426, s. 12. 2. To establish secondary meaning in the appearance of a product the plaintiff must show that, by reason of the appearance, consumers regard products of the same appearance as having one trade source. *Monsanto Canada Inc. v. Novopharm Ltd.* (1996), 123 F.T.R. 224 (T.D.).

SECONDARY PICKETING. 1. " . . . [P]icketing of a third party not concerned in a dispute which underlies the picketing . . ." *Dolphin Delivery Ltd. v. R.W.D.S.U., Local 580, (sub nom. R.S.D.S.U. v. Dolphin Delivery Ltd.)* [1986] 2 S.C.R. 573 at 590, 38 C.C.L.T. 184, 71 N.R. 83, 9 B.C.L.R. (2d) 273, 87 C.L.L.C. 14,002, [1987] 1 W.W.R. 577, 33 D.L.R. (4th) 174, 25 C.R.R. 321, [1987] D.L.Q. 69, McIntyre J. (Dickson C.J., Estey, Chouinard and Le Dain JJ. concurring). 2. " . . . [P]icketing by persons who have no relationship, professional business, or social or otherwise with the persons subjected to the picketing." *683481 Ontario Ltd. v. Beattie* (1990), 44 C.P.C. (2d) 121 at 122, 90 C.L.L.C. 14,041, 73 D.L.R. (4th) 346 (Ont. H.C.), Granger J. 3. " . . . [I]n most cases is a picket line at some place remote from an employer's place of business secondary to the picket line established thereat. . ." *J.S. Ellis & Co. v. Willis* (1973), 73 C.L.L.C. 14,156 at 19 (Ont. H.C.), Cromarty J.

SECONDARY PUBLIC SAFETY ANSWERING POINT. A communication centre to which emergency calls are transferred from a primary public safety answering point that is normally the agency responsible for dispatching emergency personnel. *Emergency "911" Act*, S.N.S. 1992, c. 4, s. 3.

SECONDARY PUPIL. A person enrolled in one of the grades from Grade 8 to Grade 12 in a public school.

SECONDARY SCHOOL. 1. A public school in which accommodation and tuition are provided exclusively or mainly for secondary pupils. 2. An independent school in which tuition or tuition and accommodation are provided primarily for persons who, if they were attending a public school would be enrolled in one of the grades from Grade 8 to Grade 12.

SECONDARY SCHOOL GRADE. Grade 10, 11, or 12, either singly or in combination; and includes grade 9 when that grade is administered and taught by a teaching staff that is also reared to provide instruction in grades 10, 11 and 12 or two of those grades.

SECONDARY SHOCK. A state of shock, caused by sudden reduction in circulating blood volume, which often leads to death. F.A. Jaffe, *A Guide to Pathological Evidence*, 3d ed. (Toronto: Carswell, 1991) at 226.

SECONDARY STRIKE. A strike against one employer with a view to influencing another employer.

SECONDARY TREATMENT WORKS. Water pollution control works that are intended to provide a substantial removal of biodegradable organic material, suspended solids, and bacteria and includes biological treatment works and disinfection works but does not include advanced treatment works.

SECOND BUYER. The person who is the buyer of marketable gas under a resale contract.

SECOND CONVICTION. A conviction, within a certain period after the date of a first conviction.

SECOND DEGREE. See PRINCIPAL IN THE ∼.

SECOND DEGREE MURDER. 1. All murder which is not first degree murder. *Criminal Code*, R.S.C. 1985, c. C-46, s. 231. 2. Murder other than planned or deliberate murder and other than murder of the type specified in s. 231 of the Criminal Code.

SECOND ENGINEER. The engineer next to the chief engineer in the line of authority. Canada regulations.

SECOND-HAND ARTICLE. An upholstered or stuffed article that has been purchased from a retailer but does not include an upholstered or stuffed article returned to the retailer without use and with the original label attached. *Upholstered and Stuffed Articles Act*, R.S.O. 1980, c. 517, s. 1.

SECOND-HAND DEALER. 1. Every person who habitually deals in used articles of any nature whatsoever, and every person who habitually receives, without buying them, used articles and undertakes to sell them. 2. A retail seller whose sales of second-hand consumer products constitute at least 85 per cent of his total number of sales of consumer products, but does not include a retail seller who carries on, in whole or in part, the business of selling motor vehicles. *The Consumer Products Warranties Act*, R.S.S. 1978, c. C-30, s. 2.

SECOND-HAND GOODS. Includes waste paper, rags, bones, bottles, bicycles, automobile tires, old metal and other scrap material and salvage.

SECOND-HAND MATERIAL. Material that has been used other than in a manufacturing process. *Upholstered and Stuffed Articles Act*, R.S.O. 1990, c. U.4, s. 1(1).

SECOND-IN-COMMAND. *n.* A pilot who is designated by an air carrier as second-in-command of an aeroplane or a rotorcraft during flight time. Canada regulations.

SECONDMENT. *n.* The temporary transfer of an employee for a specified period of time to or from one position to another position. *Civil Service Act*, R.S.P.E.I. 1988, c. C-8, s. 1(p).

SECOND MORTGAGE. A charge or mortgage which ranks after a prior charge or mortgage.

SECOND OFFENCE. Refers to a second offence committed after a previous conviction and sentence.

SECOND OR SUBSEQUENT OFFENCE. 1. Ordinarily, the terms 'second offence' and 'subsequent offence' (i.e. subsequent to a second offence) mean successive offences committed against the same section or a predecessor section . . ." *R. v. Negridge* (1980), 6 M.V.R. 255 at 261, 17 C.R. (3d) 14, 54 C.C.C. (2d) 304 (Ont. C.A.), the court per Martin J.A. 2. Refers to a second offence committed after a previous conviction and sentence.

SECOND READING. Parliamentary consideration of the principle of a measure at which time one may consider other methods of reaching its proposed objective. At this stage, the order is made to commit the bill. A. Fraser, W.A. Dawson, & J. Holtby, eds., *Beauchesne's Rules and Forms of the House of Commons of Canada*, 6th ed. (Toronto: Carswell, 1989) at 195.

SECRET. See TRADE ~.

SECRETARY. *n.* 1. The head of a government department. 2. The officer of an association, club or company. 3. The corporate officer who takes minutes of meetings of directors and shareholders, sends out notices of meetings and is in charge of the minute books and other books of the company. H. Sutherland, D.B. Horsley & J.M. Edmiston, eds., *Fraser's Handbook on Canadian Company Law*, 7th ed. (Toronto: Carswell, 1985) at 253. See MUNICIPAL ~; PARLIAMENTARY ~; RACING ~.

SECRETARY OF STATE. 1. A title applied to some members of cabinet or heads of departments. 2. The federal ministry empowered to support multiculturalism and youth and to encourage the use of both official languages.

SECRETARY TREASURER. *var.* **SECRETARY-TREASURER**. A city assessor or tax collector, the secretary-treasurer of a town, new town, village, municipal district, county or school district in a national park and the Deputy Minister of Municipal Affairs in the case of an improvement district or special area.

SECRET BALLOT. See VOTE BY~.

SECRET COMMISSION. A gift or compensation received by an agent without the knowledge of his principal and for which he must account to the principal.

SECRETED. *adj.* Concealed or hidden inside or outside of person's body. *R. v. Monney*, 1999 CarswellOnt 935, 237 N.R. 157, 133 C.C.C. (3d) 129, 171 D.L.R. (4th) 1, 24 C.R. (5th) 97, 119 O.A.C. 272, [1999] 1 S.C.R. 652, 61 C.R.R. (2d) 244.

SECRETOR. *n.* A person who secretes blood group substances in other body fluids like milk, seminal fluid and saliva. About 80 per cent of people are secretors. F.A. Jaffe, *A Guide to Pathological Evidence*, 3d ed. (Toronto: Carswell, 1991) at 225.

SECRET PROFIT. A financial advantage, including a bribe, which an agent receives over and above what the agent is entitled to receive, under the agency agreement, from the principal as remuneration.

SECRET TRUST. " . . . [T]he three necessary requirements to establish a secret trust are an intention on the part of the deceased to create a trust, notwithstanding the apparent benefit to a named legatee; communication of the intention to the intended recipient of the property; and acceptance of the trust by the intended recipient of the property." *Riffel Estate, Re* (1987), 28 E.T.R. 1 at 4, 64 Sask. R. 190 (Q.B.), Matheson J.

SECTA QUAE SCRIPTO NITITUR A SCRIPTO VARIARI NON DEBET. [L.] A suit which is based upon writing should not vary from that writing.

SECTION. *n.* 1. A numbered paragraph in a statute. 2. One of two or more trains running on the same time-table schedule displaying signals or for which signals are displayed. *Regulations No. O-8, Uniform Code of Operating Rules*, C.R.C., c. 1175, Part III, s. 2. 3. A division of land equalling one square mile or 640 acres. See BORDER ~; BOW ~; DEFINITION ~; EDIBLE ~; INTERPRETATION ~; MARINE ~; NOMINAL ~.

SECTIONAL TOWNSHIP WITH DOUBLE FRONTS. A township divided into sections and lots where the usual practice in the original survey was to survey the township boundaries, concession lines and side lines of sections defining section boundaries and to establish the front corners of the lots and section corners. *Surveys Act*, R.S.O. 1990, c. S.30, s. 31(1).

SECTIONAL TOWNSHIP WITH SECTIONS AND QUARTER SECTIONS. (a) A township divided into sections and quarter sections without road allowances between sections where the usual practice in the original survey was to survey the township boundaries and section lines and to establish the section corners and quarter section corners; or (b) a township divided into sections and quarter sections with road allowances between sections where the usual practice in the original survey was to survey the township boundaries and the section lines on the west and south sides of the road allowances and to establish the section corners and the quarter section corners on the surveyed lines. *Surveyors Act*, R.S.O. 1990, c. S.30, s. 42.

SECTIONAL TOWNSHIP WITH SINGLE FRONTS. A township divided into sections and lots where the usual practice in the original survey was to survey the township boundaries, concession lines and side lines of the sections and to establish the front corners of the lots and the section corners. *Surveys Act*, R.S.O. 1990, c. S.30, s. 37(1).

SECTION WIDTH. The linear distance between the exteriors of the sidewalls of an inflated tire, excluding elevations due to labelling, decoration or protective bands. Canada regulations.

SECTOR. *n*. 1. A primary portion or division of the economy. 2. A division of the construction industry as determined by work characteristics and includes the industrial, commercial and institutional sector, the residential sector, the sewers, tunnels and watermains sector, the roads sector, the heavy engineering sector and the pipeline sector. See PRIVATE ~; PUBLIC ~.

SECULAR. *adj*. 1. The dual requirements that education be "secular" and "non-sectarian" refer to keeping the schools free from inculcation or indoctrination in the precepts of any religion and do not prevent persons with religiously based moral positions on matters of public policy from participating in deliberations concerning moral education in public schools. *Chamberlain v. Surrey School District No. 36*, [2002] 4 S.C.R. 710. 2. "Strictly secular" in the School Act can only mean pluralist in the sense that moral positions are to be accorded standing in the public square irrespective of whether the position flows out of a conscience that is religiously informed or not. The meaning of strictly secular is thus pluralist or inclusive in its widest sense. *Chamberlain v. Surrey School District No. 36*, 2000 CarswellBC 2009, 80 B.C.L.R. (3d) 181, [2000] 10 W.W.R. 393, 191 D.L.R. (4th) 128, 143 B.C.A.C. 162, 235 W.A.C. 162, 26 Admin. L.R. (3d) 297 (C.A.), Esson, Mackenzie, Proudfoot JJ.A. 3. Relating to the material world in contrast to spiritual.

SECULARISM. *n*. What secularism does rule out, however, is any attempt to use the religious views of one part of the community to exclude from consideration the values of other members of the community. A requirement of secularism implies that, although the Board is indeed free to address the religious concerns of parents, it must be sure to do so in a manner that gives equal recognition and respect to other members of the community. Religious views that deny equal recognition and respect to the members of a minority group cannot be used to exclude the concerns of the minority group. *Chamberlain v. Surrey School District No. 36*, [2002] 4 S.C.R. 710

SECUNDUM ALLEGATA ET PROBATA. [L.] According to what was alleged and proved.

SECUNDUM NATURAM EST, COMMODO CUJUSQUE REI EUM SEQUI, QUEM SEQUUNTUR INCOMMODA. [L.] It is natural that advantages of anything should follow the person whom the disadvantages follow.

SECUNDUM SUBJECTAM MATERIAM. [L.] Referring to the subject-matter.

SECURE. *v*. To assure. To guarantee.

SECURE CUSTODY. Custody in a place or facility designated by the Lieutenant Governor in Council of a province for the secure containment or restraint of young persons, and includes a place or facility within a class of places or facilities so designated. *Young Offenders Act*, R.S.C. 1985, c. Y-1, s. 24.

SECURED. See OBLIGATION ~.

SECURED CREDITOR. 1. A person holding a mortgage, hypothec, pledge, charge, lien or privilege on or against the property of the debtor or any part thereof as security for a debt due or accruing due to that person from the debtor. 2. A person whose claim is based on, or secured by, a negotiable instrument held as collateral security and on which the debtor is only indirectly or secondarily liable. *Bankruptcy Act*, R.S.C. 1985, c. B-3, s. 2 (part).

SECURED LOAN. A loan in respect of which the collateral security held for the loan is considered adequate to secure repayment of the loan. *The Co-operative Guarantee Act*, R.S.S. 1978, c. C-35, s. 2.

SECURED PARTY. A person who has a security interest.

SECURED TRADE CREDITOR. A creditor of the vendor in respect of (a) stock, money or services furnished for the purpose of enabling the seller to carry on business; or (b) rental of premises in or from which the vendor carries on business, who holds security or is entitled to a preference in respect of a claim. *Bulk Sales acts*.

SECURED TRANSACTION. A transaction with two main elements: that consideration flows from the creditor and creates a debt and that an interest in the debtor's property secures payment of the debt. F. Bennett, *Receiverships* (Toronto: Carswell, 1985) at 27.

SECURE ELECTRONIC SIGNATURE. An electronic signature that results from the application of a technology or process prescribed by regulations. The Governor in Council may prescribe a technology or process only if the Governor in Council is satisfied that it can be proved that (a) the electronic signature resulting from the use by a person of the technology or process is unique to the person; (b) the use of the technology or process by a person to incorporate, attach or associate the person's electronic signature to an electronic document is under the sole control of the person; (c) the technology or process can be used to identify the person using the technology or process; and (d) the electronic signature can be linked with an electronic document in such a way that it can be used to determine whether the electronic document has been changed since the electronic signature was incorporated in, attached to or associated with the electronic document. *Personal Information Protection and Electronic Documents Act 2000*, S.C. 2000, c.5, s. 31 and 48.

SECURE TEMPORARY DETENTION. See PLACE OF ~.

SECURITIES. *n*. 1. (a) Bonds, debentures and obligations of or guaranteed by governments, corporations or unincorporated bodies, whether such corporations and unincorporated bodies are governmental, municipal, school, ecclesiastical, commercial or other, secured on real or personal property or unsecured, and rights in respect of such bonds debentures and obligations; (b) shares of capital stock of corporations and rights in respect of such shares; (c) equipment trust certificates or obligations; (d) all documents, instruments and writings commonly known as securities; and (e) mortgages and hypothecs. 2. Bonds, debentures, promissory notes, and other evidence of debt. 3. (a) Any certificate, instrument or other document constituting evidence: of a right, share or interest in the capital, assets, earnings or profits of an existing or proposed company, or of a person and particularly, but not restrictively, any bond, note, debenture, share, debenture-stock or any title of participation in such capital, assets, earnings or profits; or of a subscription in any proposed company; or of an agreement providing that a sum of money received by a person or company will be repaid or treated as a subscription to shares or interests in the capital or assets of an undertaking at the option of any person or company; or of a share or interest in an association of legatees, heirs or trustees, in a trust estate, in an investment contract or in a bankers' or trustees' security; or of a profit-sharing agreement; or of interest in an oil, natural gas or mining claim or lease or in a voting trust agreement of an oil, natural gas or mining company; or of a lease, right to royalties or other interest respecting an oil or natural gas undertaking; or of a contract of concession under which the concessionary obtains certain special rights respecting the operation of an undertaking; (b) generally a certificate, instrument or document commonly known in the trade as a security or designated as such by the regulations; (c) a certificate, instrument or other document constituting evidence of a right or interest in an option given upon a security within the meaning of the preceding paragraphs. See APPROVED ~; CLASS OF ~; EQUITY ~; GOVERNMENT ~; ISSUED ~; MUNICIPAL ~; OFFEROR'S PRESENTLY-OWNED ~; PROVINCIAL ~; PUBLICLY-TRADED ~; SCHOOL ~; SECURITY; VALUABLE ~.

SECURITIES ADVISER. Any person or company that engages in or claims to engage in the business of advising others, either directly or through publication or writings, as to the advisability of investing in, purchasing or selling specific securities.

SECURITIES COMMISSION. See ONTARIO ~.

SECURITIES DEALER. See CANADIAN ~.

SECURITIES EXCHANGE TAKE-OVER BID. A take-over bid by way of an exchange of securities, whereby the offeror offers to holders of securities of the offeree issuer to exchange them for other securities, is subject to the same regulatory scheme as a take-over bid, mutatis mutandis.

SECURITIES ISSUE. See SPECIFIED ~.

SECURITIES LAW. The law relating to the regulation of the issuance and distribution of shares and debt securities by corporations and governments.

SECURITIES REGISTER. A record of securities which a company issues.

SECURITIES UNDERWRITER. A person who, as principal, agrees to purchase securities with a view to the distribution of the securities or who, as agent for a body corporate or other person, offers for sale or sells securities in connection with a distribution of the securities, and includes a person who participates, directly or indirectly, in a distribution of securities, other than a person whose interest in the distribution of securities is limited to receiving a distributor's or seller's commission payable by a securities underwriter. *Bank Act, 1991*, S.C. 1991, c. 46, s. 2.

SECURITY. *n*. 1. A thing which makes the enforcement or enjoyment of a right more certain or secure. 2. "Security for a debt, in the ordinary meaning of the term, carries with it the idea of something or somebody to which, or to whom, the creditor can resort in order to aid him in realizing or recovering the debt, in case the debtor fails to pay; the word implies something in addition to the mere obligation of the debtor. . ." *Child & Gower Piano Co. v. Gambrel*, [19331 2 W.W.R. 273 at 281 (Sask. C.A.), Martin J.A. (MacKenzie J.A. concurring). 3. A share of any class or series of shares of a corporation or a debt obligation of a corporation and includes a certificate evidencing any share or debt obligation. 4. (a) In relation to a body corporate, a share of any class of shares of the body corporate or a debt obligation of the body corporate, and includes a warrant of the body corporate, but does not include a deposit with a financial institution or any instrument evidencing such a deposit, and (b) in relation to any other entity, any ownership interest in or debt obligation of the entity. *Bank Act*, S.C. 1991, c. 46, s. 2. 5. Sufficient security and one person shall be sufficient therefor unless otherwise expressly required. See AFFECTED ~; CAPITAL ~; COLLATERAL ~; CONVERTIBLE ~; CORPORATE ~; DEBT ~; EQUITY ~; GILT~ EDGED ~; GOVERNMENT INCENTIVE ~; INDEXED ~; MARKETABLE ~; OFFEROR'S ~; PARTICIPATING ~; PERSONAL PROPERTY ~ ACT; PORTFOLIO ~; REDEEMABLE ~; REQUIRED TO GIVE ~; SECURITIES; SHORT TERM ~; THREATS TO THE ~ OF CANADA; UNCERTIFIED ~; UNION ~; VALUABLE ~; VOTING ~.

SECURITY AGREEMENT. An agreement that creates or provides for a security interest.

SECURITY ASSESSMENT. An appraisal of the loyalty to Canada and, so far as it relates thereto, the reliability of an individual. *Canadian Security Intelligence Service Act*, R.S.C. 1985, c. C-23, s. 2.

SECURITY BUSINESS. The business carried on by (a) an alarm service; (b) an armoured car service; (c) a locksmith; (d) a private investiga-

tor; (e) a security consultant; or (f) a security patrol.

SECURITY CERTIFICATE. An instrument in bearer, order or registered form, issued by an issuer evidencing a security. *Business Corporations Act*, R.S.O. 1990, c. B.16, s. 53.

SECURITY CONSULTANT. A person who provides (a) consultation and advice on methods of protecting property from vandalism, intrusion, trespass or theft; or (b) the service of detecting electromagnetic, acoustical or other devices by which private communications or records may be intercepted, transmitted or examined.

SECURITY DEPOSIT. 1. Any money, property or right paid or given by a tenant of residential premises to a landlord or to anyone on the landlord's behalf to be held by or for the landlord as security for the performance of an obligation or the payment of a liability by the tenant or to be returned to the tenant on the happening of a condition. 2. (a) A certified cheque payable to the Receiver General and drawn on payable to which the Bank Act or the Quebec Savings Bank Act applies or on such other financial institutions as may be designated by the Treasury Board for that purpose; (b) a government guaranteed bond; or (c) such other security as may be deemed appropriate by the contracting authority and approved by the Treasury Board. *Government Contracts Regulations*, C.R.C., c. 701, s. 2.

SECURITY DOCUMENT. Any written document including a lease or a mortgage whereby a debtor is required to make payments to a creditor in repayment or partial repayment of an advance of value or while all or any part of the advance is outstanding or unpaid and includes any trading or other covenants that are contained in or are supplemental, incidental or referable to the written document..

SECURITY EMPLOYEE. (a) An individual employed by or engaged in a security business, other than (i) an individual exempted by regulation; or (ii) an individual employed by an armoured car service; and (b) a security patrol salesman.

SECURITY FOR COSTS. Security which a plaintiff may be required to provide in a proceeding to ensure that the plaintiff will be able to pay any costs which may be awarded to the defendant.

SECURITY GUARD. 1. A person who, for hire or reward, guards or patrols for the purpose of protecting persons or property. 2. A person who guards or patrols or provides other security services for the purpose of protecting persons or property and includes a person who (a) supervises and inspects security guards while they are guarding or patrolling; or (b) accompanies a guard dog while the dog is guarding or patrolling. 3. Any peace officer, security policeman, provost, military policeman or member of the Corps of Commissionaires, and includes any officer or man of the Canadian Forces or employee of the Department of National Defence or of the Defence Research Board who has been assigned duties relating to the enforcement of these Regulations. *Defence Establishment Trespass Regulations*, C.R.C., c. 1047, s. 2.

SECURITY GUARD AGENCY. (a) The business of providing the services of a security guard, dog, or both; or (b) the business of guarding, or of guaranteeing the secure transportation and delivery of, the property of others, where a security guard is used to provide security.

SECURITY HOLDER. 1. A person who has an interest in land as security for the payment of money. *Expropriation acts*. 2. A holder of a voting security of a reporting issuer.

SECURITY INSTRUMENT. A contract or instrument that creates a security interest.

SECURITY INTEREST. 1. An interest in collateral that secures payment or performance of an obligation. 2. An interest in or charge upon the property of a body corporate by way of mortgage, hypothec, pledge or otherwise, to secure payment of a debt or performance of any other obligation of the body corporate. 3. A right to or an interest in a deposit in a financial institution that secures payment or performance of an obligation to the financial institution. See AS-SIGNMENT OF ~; PERFECTED ~; PUR-CHASE-MONEY ~.

SECURITY ISSUER. *var.* **SECURITY-IS-SUER.** A person or company that engages in the primary distribution to the public of securities of its own issue.

SECURITY NOTICE. A notice of security interest.

SECURITY OF SUPPLY. In respect of any period, the anticipation of self-sufficiency during each of the five calendar years in that period, taking into account the aggregate of anticipated additions to productive capacity and anticipated adjustments to refining capacity.

SECURITY OF TENURE. 1. A tenant's right to remain in leased premises unless the tenancy is terminated by the landlord for a cause specified in governing legislation. 2. An ingredient of judicial independence. Fixed tenure secure against interference by the executive or appointing authority in a discretionary or arbitrary manner. Removal from office may be for cause only and after an independent review is completed at which the judge has an opportunity to be heard.

SECURITY OF THE PERSON. 1. " . . . [T]he right to 'security of the person' under s. 7 of the Charter protects both the physical and psychological integrity of the individual . . ." *R. v. Morgentaler* (1988), 31 C.R.R. 1 at 87, 82 N.R. 1, [1988] 1 S.C.R. 30, 63 O.R. (2d) 281n, 63 C.R. (3d) 1, 26 O.A.C. 1, 44 D.L.R. (4th) 385, 37 C.C.C. (3d) 449, Wilson J. 2. " . . . The case law leads me to the conclusion that state interference with bodily integrity and serious state-imposed psychological stress at least in the Criminal law context constitute a breach of security of the person." *R. v. Morgentaler* (1988), 31 C.R.R. 1 at 20, 82 N.R. 1, [1988] 1 S.C.R. 30, 63 O.R. (2d) 281n, 63 C.R. (3d) 1, 26 O.A.C. 1, 44 D.L.R. (4th) 385, 37 C.C.C. (3d) 449, Dickson C.J.C. (Lamer J. concurring). 3. " . . . [W]ithin the meaning of s. 7 of the Charter must include a right of access to medical treatment for a condition representing a danger to life or health without fear of criminal sanction. . . must include some protection from state interference when a person's life or health is in danger . . ." *R. v. Morgentaler* (1988), 37 C.C.C. (3d) 449 at 485, 31 C.R.R. 1, 82 N.R. 1, [1988] 1 S.C.R. 30, 63 O.R. (2d) 281n, 63 C.R. (3d) 1, 26 O.A.C. 1, 44 D.L.R. (4th) 385, Beetz J. (Estey J. concurring). 4. " . . . [I]n the context of s. 11(b) [of the Charter], the concept of security of the person should not be restricted to physical integrity. Rather, it should encompass protection against 'overlong subjection to the vexations and vicissitudes of a pending criminal accusation': Anthony Amsterdam, 'Speedy Criminal Trial: Rights and Remedies', 27 Stan. L. Rev. 525 at p. 533 (1975). These vexations and vicissitudes include stigmatization of the accused loss of privacy, stress and anxiety resulting from a multitude of factors, including possible disruption of family, social life and work, legal costs, and uncertainty as to the outcome and sanction. . ." *R. v. Rahey* (1987) 33 C.C.C. (3d) 289 at 300, 75 N.R. 81, [1987] 1 S.C.R. 588, 57 C.R. (3d) 289, 78 N.S.R. (2d) 183, 193 A.P.R. 183, 39 D.L.R. (4th) 481, Lamer J. (Dickson C.J.C. concurring, Estey J. concurring in part). 5. "The common law right to bodily integrity and personal autonomy is so entrenched in the traditions of our law as to be ranked as fundamental and deserving of the highest order of protection. This right forms an essential part of an individual's security of the person and must be included in the liberty interests protected by s. 7 [of the Charter]." *Fleming v. Read* (1991), 82 D.L.R. (4th) 298 at 312, 4 O.R. (3d) 74, 48 O.A.C. 46 (C.A.), the court per Robins J.A.

SECURITY OR SECURITY CERTIFICATE. 1. An instrument issued by a corporation that is (a) in bearer, order or registered form; (b) of a type commonly dealt in on securities exchanges or markets or commonly recognized in any area in which it is issued or dealt in as a medium for investment; (c) one of a class or series or by its terms divisible into a class or series of instruments; and (d) evidence of a share, participation or other interest in or obligation of a corporation. 2. An instrument that is issued by a bank as evidence of a share or other interest in the capital stock of the bank or as a bank debenture of the bank.

SECURITY PACKAGE. A package having a security feature that provides reasonable assurance to consumers that the package has not been opened prior to purchase. *Natural Health Products Regulations*, SOR/2003-196, s. 1.

SECURITY PATROL. A person who, otherwise than as an alarm service, provides, conducts, supervises or inspects a guard patrol or watch of property or a service of responding to a security alarm.

SECURITY TERM. The period during which bonding is required to be maintained whether it be described as a period of time or commences or terminates at the commencement or termination of a licence or privilege.

SECURITY TRANSACTION. The purchase, sale, redemption, exchange, transfer, assignment or other transaction affecting a security. Canada regulations.

SECURITY WITH A CLEARING AGENCY. A security (a) in the form of a security certificate (i) in bearer form, (ii) endorsed in blank by an appropriate person, or (iii) registered in the name of the clearing agency or its nominee or custodian, that is in the custody of the clearing agency, or (b) not in the form of security certificate and that is registered or recorded in the records maintained by or on behalf of the issuer in the name of a clearing agency or its nominee or custodian.

SEDATIVE. *n*. A calming drug.

SE DEFENDENDO. [L.] In self defence.

SEDITION. *n*. Advocating a change of government through the use of force.

SEDITIOUS CONSPIRACY. An agreement between two or more persons to carry out a seditious intention. *Criminal Code*, R.S.C. 1985, c. C-46, s. 59(3).

SEDITIOUS INTENTION. Everyone who teaches, advocates, publishes or circulates any writing that advocates, without authority of law, the use of force as a means of accomplishing a governmental change within Canada is presumed to have a seditious intention. *Criminal Code*, R.S.C. 1985, c. C-46, s. 59(4) in part.

SEDITIOUS LIBEL. A libel that expresses a seditious intention. *Criminal Code*, R.S.C. 1985, c. C-46, s. 59(2).

SEDITIOUS WORDS. Words that express a seditious intention. *Criminal Code*, R.S.C. 1985, c. C-46, s. 59(1).

SEDUCTION. *n*. Inducing a person to have unlawful intercourse.

SEED. *n*. Any plant part of any species belonging to the plant kingdom, represented, sold or used to grow a plant. See COMMERCIAL ~; SPECIALTY ~; UNDESIRABLE ~; WEED ~.

SEED COMPANY OPERATOR. A person who purchases grain from producers for cleaning and processing into seed, for sale.

SEED CORN. Corn grown under contract with a dealer which is intended for sale on a commercial basis for seed purpose.

SEED-CORN. *n*. The seed of hybrid corn, or open-pollinated corn, of every kind or variety for seed purpose.

SEED DEALER. A person who in a province offers by advertisement or otherwise to buy or sell seed directly from or directly to producers or engages in the business of buying or selling seed directly from or directly to producers or accepting seed on a consignment basis directly from producers, but does not include a farmer, rancher or other person buying seed for personal use or selling self-produced seed or a person carrying on business as a merchant in the province and, as an incidental part of the business, selling seed to the public by retail sale only.

SEED GRAIN. Seed of wheat, oats, barley, flax, rye, corn, alfalfa and grass.

SEED STOCK. Includes eggs, alevins, parr, smolt, juvenile and adult fish, crustaceans and shellfish, seeds, spat, seedlings and other forms of aquatic flora and fauna used or intended to be used as the primary source of the aquacultural produce.

SEEPAGE. *n*. 1. Percolation or oozing of water passing through small pores or openings. 2. The escape of water from any irrigation works of a board due to the fact that the works were built with material which, or were constructed in, on or through ground which, because of its porous or pervious nature, allows water to percolate out of the works. *Irrigation Act*, R.S.A. 1980, c. I-11, s. 170.

SEGMENTATION. *n*. Transverse obstructive breaks, many in number, in the blood in vessels in the eye. F.A. Jaffe, *A Guide to Pathological Evidence*, 3d ed. (Toronto: Carswell, 1991) at 225.

SEGREGATED FUND. 1. A specified group of property the fair market value of which causes all or part of the insurer's reserves to vary with respect to any life insurance policy. 2. A fund established by a corporation duly authorized to operate a fund in which contributions to a pension plan are deposited and the assets of the fund are held exclusively for the purposes of that plan alone or that plan and one or more other pension plans.

SEGREGATED FUND POLICY. A life insurance policy under which the amount of benefits payable varies in accordance with the fair market value of the property of the segregated fund relating to the policy.

SEGREGATION. *n*. 1. The act of setting apart, isolating, or secluding a person or body of persons from the general body of persons. 2. [S]egregation, whether administrative or punitive as in this appeal, is a form of incarceration more restrictive than the incarceration experienced by the general prison population. It results in a deprivation of that residual liberty interest possessed by prisoners within our penitentiaries. This deprivation represents a further confinement of the appellant in a prison within a prison. *Winters v. Legal Services Society (British Columbia)*, [1999] 3 S.C.R. 160, Cory, J. dissenting.

SEIGNEUR. *n*. The lord of a seignory or fee manor.

SEIGNIOR. *n*. The lord of a seignory or fee manor.

SEIGNORY. *n*. 1. A manor. 2. A feudal lord's rights. R. Megarry and H.W.R. Wade, *The Law of Real Property*, 5th ed. (London: Stevens 1984) at cxxvii.

SEIGN. QUESTIONS. *abbr*. Lower Canada Reports, Seignorial Questions, vols. A & B (Décisions des Tribunaux du Bas-Canada).

SEIGN. REP. *abbr*. Seignorial Reports (Que.).

SEINE. *n*. A net buoyed at the top and weighted at the bottom that is used to catch fish without enmeshing them. *Quebec Fishery Regulations*, C.R.C., c. 852, s. 2. See BAR ~; BEACH ~; BOAT ~; DRAG ~; SHUT-OFF ~.

SEINE NET. A net with weights at the bottom and floats at the top that is operated to catch fish by dragging the net to a place where the fish may be removed from the water.

SEISED. *adj*. Is applicable to any vested estate for life or of a greater description, and shall extend to estates at law and in equity, in possession or in futurity, in land. *Trustee acts*.

SEISIN. *n*. A freeholder's holding of land. R. Megarry and H.W.R. Wade, *The Law of Real Property*, 5th ed. (London: Stevens, 1984) at cxxvii. See LIVERY OF ~.

SEISINA FACIT STIPITEM. [L.] Seisin forms the basis of descent.

SEISMIC EXPLORATION. Exploration of an area identified as likely to contain oil or gas pools. Bore holes are drilled, loaded with explosives and then detonated. Measurements assist in determining the geologic formations.

SEI WHALE. Any whale known by the name of Balaenoptera borealis, sei whale, Rudolphi's rorqual, pollack whale, or coalfish whale, and shall be taken to include Balaenoptera brydei, Bryde's whale. *Whaling Convention Act*, R.S.C. 1970, c. W-8, Schedule, s. 18.

SEIZED. *adj*. Is applicable to any vested interest for life, or of a greater description, and extends to estates, legal and equitable, in possession, or in futurity, in any land. *Trustee acts*.

SEIZIN. The term "seizin" has its origin in the German expression for "possession" . . . under the custom of Paris, seizin distinguished a legitimate heir from a universal legatee, who was not [translation] "seized as of right" and had to apply to the heir to obtain delivery of his or her legacy in order to be placed in possession . . . seizin does not in any way refer to the transmission of ownership, since that transmission takes place automatically by law and by the will . . . Nor does seizin mean the transmission of possession, since possession is a question of fact. Rather, seizin is [translation] "legal authorization to act *de plano* as the possessor of the inheritance or, better yet, legal empowerment to exercise the rights and actions of the deceased without first having to carry out any formalities" . . . Thus, seizin of legatees refers more to the authority under which they possess property of which they are also the owners. Seizin thus has the effect of avoiding a gap in possession. It confers the rights relating to possession on the legatee, without it being necessary for the legatee to be in actual possession of the bequeathed property . . . Consequently, seizin is [Translation] "the right one has to take effective possession of the patrimony of the *de cujus* and undertake, both passively and actively, the actions available to him or her" *Hall c. Québec (Sous-ministre du Revenu)* (1997), [1998] 1 S.C.R. 220. See SEISIN.

SEIZURE. *n.* 1. " . . . [T]he essence of seizure under s. 8 [of the Charter] is the taking of a thing from a person by a public authority without that person's consent. . . If I were to draw the line between a seizure and a mere finding of evidence, I would draw it logically and purposefully at the point at which can reasonably be said that the individual had ceased to have a privacy interest in the subject-matter allegedly seized." *R. v. Dyment* (1988), 38 C.R.R. 301 at 312, 316, 10 M.V.R. (2d) 1, 66 C.R. (3d) 348, 89 N.R. 249, [1988] 2 S.C.R. 417, 45 C.C.C. (3d) 244, 73 Nfld. & P.E.I.R. 13, 229 A.P.R. 13, 55 D.L.R. (4th) 503, La Forest J. (Dickson C.J.C. concurring). 2. A species of execution in which a sheriff executes a writ of fi. fa. by taking possession of the chattels of the debtor. 3. What takes place when goods are confiscated as a punishment for smuggling. See FREE OF CAPTURE AND ~; LEVY; SEARCH OR ~.

SEIZURE AND SALE. See WRIT OF ~.

SELECT COMMITTEE. A committee of Parliament or a legislature set up to investigate a particular matter.

SELECTION BOARD. A board appointed by the chairman to examine candidates in a competition.

SELECTIVE HERBICIDE. A herbicide commonly used for the control or destruction of weeds in growing crops.

SELF-AGGRANDIZEMENT. *n.* The exaggeration of one's skills or accomplishments.

SELF-CONTAINED DOMESTIC ESTABLISHMENT. A dwelling house, apartment or other similar place of residence in which place a person as a general rule sleeps and eats.

SELF-CONTAINED DWELLING UNIT. A dwelling house, apartment or other similar place of residence that is used or occupied or is intended, arranged or designed to be used or occupied as separate accommodation for sleeping and eating.

SELF-CONTAINED UNIT. A unit of apartment housing accommodation providing living, sleeping, eating, food preparation and sanitary facilities, with or without other essential facilities, but in which no personal service or nursing care is furnished.

SELF-CRIMINATION. See SELF-INCRIMINATION.

SELF-DEFENCE. *n.* 1. Defence of one's person or property directly against another exerting unlawful force. D. Stuart, *Canadian Criminal Law: A Treatise*, 2d ed. (Toronto: Carswell, 1987) at 405. 2. " . . . [A] man who is attacked may defend himself. It is both good law and good sense that he may do, but only do, what is reasonably necessary. . ." *Palmer v. R.*, [1971] 1 All E.R. 1077 at 1088, [1971] A.C. 814, 55 Cr. App. R. 223 (Jamaica P.C.), the board per Lord Morris of Borth-Y-Gest. 3. The basic version of the defence of self-defence is set out in the Criminal Code: every one who is unlawfully assaulted without having provoked the assault is justified in repelling force by force if the force he uses is not intended to cause death or grievous bodily harm and is no more than is necessary to enable him to defend himself. *Criminal Code*, R.S.C. 1985, c. C-46, s. 34(1). Other variations of the defence exist where there is an apprehension of death or grievous bodily harm or where the aggressor is himself attacked.

SELF-DETERMINATION. A right to *external* self-determination (which in this case potentially takes the form of the assertion of a right to unilateral secession) arises in only the most extreme of cases and, even then, under carefully defined circumstances. *External* self-determination can be defined as in the following statement from the *Declaration on Friendly Relations, supra* [*Declaration on Principles of International Law Concerning Friendly Relations and Co-operation Among States in Accordance with the Charter of the United Nations*, GA Res. 2625 (XXV), 24 October 1970], as the establishment of a sovereign and independent State, the free association or integration with an independent State or the emergence into any other political status freely determined by a *people* constitute modes of implementing the right of self-determination by *that people*. The recognized sources of international law establish that the right to self-determination of a people is normally fulfilled through *internal* self-determination—a people's pursuit of its political, economic, social and cultural development within the framework of an existing state. *Reference re Secession of Quebec*, 1998 CarswellNat 1299, 161 D.L.R. (4th) 385, 228 N.R. 203, 55 C.R.R. (2d) 1, [1998] 2 S.C.R. 217 Per curiam. See RIGHT OF ~.

SELF-EMPLOYED PERSON. 1. A person who is engaged in an occupation on his own behalf but does not include a dependent contractor. 2. A person who is engaged in an occupation but is not in the service of an employer.

SELF-EMPLOYMENT. *n.* The work done by an individual on his own behalf.

SELF-GOVERNING. *adj.* Refers to a profession which has been given authority by the legislature to govern itself and to regulate membership in and the conduct of members of the profession.

SELF-GOVERNING PROFESSION. See DISCIPLINARY COMMITTEE.

SELF-GOVERNMENT AGREEMENT. An agreement concluded by a first nation with Her Majesty the Queen in right of Canada and the Yukon Government respecting government by and for the first nation. *Yukon First Nations Self-Government Act, 1994*, S.C. 1994, c. 35, s. 2.

SELF-HELP. *n.* An action in which an injured party seeks redress without resorting to a court.

SELF-IGNITION. *n.* Includes spontaneous combustion where there is no fire.

SELF-IMPROVEMENT EDUCATION. Any education other than vocational education, general education or education for handicapped children within the meaning of this act. *Private Education Act*, R.S.Q. 1977, c. E-9, s. 1.

SELF-INCRIMINATING STATEMENT. A statement by the accused that, if admitted in evidence and believed in whole or in part, would directly or indirectly tend to prove the accused guilty of the charge. *Military Rules of Evidence*, C.R.C., c. 1049, s. 2.

SELF-INCRIMINATION. *n.* 1. Behaviour indicating one's guilt. 2. The principle against self-incrimination was described by Lamer as "a general organizing principle of criminal law". The principle is that an accused is not required to respond to an allegation of wrongdoing made by the state until the state has succeeded in making out a *prima facie* case against him or her. It is a basic tenet of our system of justice that the Crown must establish a "case to meet" before there can be any expectation that the accused should respond. The jurisprudence of this Court is clear that the principle against self-incrimination is an overarching principle within our criminal justice system, from which a number of specific common law and *Charter* rules emanate, such as the confessions rule, and the right to silence, among many others. The principle can also be the source of new rules in appropriate circumstances. *R. v. White*, 1999 CarswellBC 1224, 63 C.R.R. (2d) 1, 240 N.R. 1, 24 C.R. (5th) 201, 135 C.C.C. (3d) 257, 174 D.L.R. (4th) 111, 42 M.V.R. (3d) 161, 123 B.C.A.C. 161, 201 W.A.C. 161, [1999] 2 S.C.R. 417, Iacobucci J. for the majority. See PRINCIPLE AGAINST ~; PRIVILEGE AGAINST ~.

SELF-INDUCED INTOXICATION. It is not a defence to an offence referred to in subsection (3) that the accused, by reason of self-induced intoxication, lacked the general intent or the voluntariness required to commit the offence, where the accused departed markedly from the standard of care as described in subsection (2). *Criminal Code*, R.S.C. 1985, c. C-46, s. 33.1.

SELF-INSURANCE PLAN. A contract, plan or arrangement entered into, established, maintained in force or renewed under which coverage is provided (a) by an employer for all or some of his employees; (b) by a corporation for all or some of its members; or (c) by an unincorporated group of persons for all or some of its members.

SELF INSURER. An individual, partnership or body corporate which retains all or part of a risk for its own account whether or not an excess of loss cover exists to protect itself in the event of a catastrophe.

SELF-LIQUIDATING PROJECT. A project that when completed will, on the basis of conservative estimates, either by reductions in the annual operating and maintenance charges required to be borne by the municipality or by increase of revenues from persons using the services of or otherwise benefiting from the project, result in an increase in the annual net revenue of the municipality sufficient to pay the annual charges for interest on an amortization of the loan.

SELF-LUBRICATING MACHINERY. Machinery that, while in operation, lubricates itself from a supply of lubricant that is sufficient to enable the machinery to operate continuously at full load for a period of not less than 24 hours.

SELF-MAILER. *n*. Any article, other than a postcard, magazine or catalogue, that does not have an outer cover, wrapping or envelope in addition to the paper or material on which is placed the written communication.

SELF-MOBILITY. *n*. Movement of the vehicle by means of a rolling motion of all the weight-bearing wheels. *Motor Vehicle Safety Regulations*, C.R.C., c. 1038, s. 116.

SELF-MURDER. *n*. Suicide.

SELF-NEGLECT. *n*. Any failure of an adult to take care of himself or herself that causes, or is reasonably likely to cause within a short period of time, serious physical or mental harm or substantial damage to or loss of assets, and includes (a) living in grossly unsanitary conditions, (b) suffering from an untreated illness, disease or injury, (c) suffering from malnutrition to such an extent that, without intervention, the adult's physical or mental health is likely to be severely impaired, (d) creating a hazardous situation that will likely cause serious physical harm to the adult or others or cause substantial damage to or loss of assets, and (e) suffering from an illness, disease or injury that results in the adult dealing with his or her assets in a manner that is likely to cause substantial damage to or loss of the assets. *Adult Guardianship Act*, R.S.B.C. 1996, c. 6, s. 1.

SELF-PROPELLED EQUIPMENT. Electrically operated equipment which is capable of moving while it is working or of being moved from place to place under its own power. *Coal Mines Regulation Act*, R.S.N.S. 1989, c. 73, s. 85(1).

SELF-PROPELLED IMPLEMENT OF HUSBANDRY. A self-propelled vehicle manufactured, designed, redesigned, converted or reconstructed for a specific use in farming. *Highway Traffic Act*, R.S.O. 1990, c. H.8, s. 1(1).

SELF-REGULATING BODY. Organization recognized by a government body as one which regulates its own members.

SELF-REGULATORY ORGANIZATION. Association or organization representing registrants that is recognized pursuant to subsection (2). *Securities Act*, S.S. 1984-85-86, c. S-42.1, s. 21.

SELF-SERVING STATEMENT. An exculpatory statement.

SELF-SUFFICIENCY. *n*. A volume of suitable crude oil and equivalent substances available from domestic Canadian hydrocarbon producing capacity that is adequate to supply the total feedstock requirements of Canadian refineries necessary to satisfy the total refined product requirements of Canada, excluding those feedstock requirements necessary to produce specialty refined products.

SELL. *v*. 1. Includes (a) to agree to sell, to offer, keep, expose, transmit, send, convey or deliver for sale; (b) to exchange or agree to exchange; and (c) to dispose of, or agree to dispose of, to any person in any manner for a consideration. 2. Includes offer for sale, expose for sale, have in possession for sale and distribute, whether or not the distribution is made for consideration. 3. Includes lease, transfer or any other manner of disposition. *Employment Standards acts*. See AGREEMENT TO ~; BARGAIN AND ~; SALE AND ~.

SELL AT RETAIL. To sell, transfer or offer to sell or transfer to a purchaser or a transferee for the purpose of use and not for resale or retransfer.

SELL AT WHOLESALE. To sell, transfer or offer to sell or transfer, other than at retail.

SELLER. *n*. 1. A person who sells or agrees to sell goods. 2. Includes a person who is in the position of a seller, as for instance an agent of the seller to whom the bill of lading has been endorsed, or a consignor or agent who has personally paid or is directly responsible for the price. *Sale of Goods acts*. 3. The person who sells or hires out goods by a conditional sale. 4. Includes a person who lets goods on hire by a retail hire-purchase. See BOOK~; CONTRACT ~; DIRECT ~; ITINERANT ~; RETAIL ~; UNPAID ~.

SELLER'S LIEN. See UNPAID ~.

SELLING. See DIRECT ~; REFERRAL ~; TIED ~.

SELLING AGENCY. The person authorized by one or more cooperative associations, one or more, processors or one or more cooperative associations and processors to market an agricultural product under only one cooperative plan. *Agricultural Products Cooperative Marketing Act*, R.S.C. 1985, c. A-5, s. 2.

SELLING GROUP. The persons who, in the course of distribution to the public of securities, are commonly known as the selling group, the members of which acquire securities from an underwriter for the purpose of distribution to the public of those securities or who receive a commission from an underwriter in connection with such a distribution.

SELLING INSTRUMENT. In respect of flow-through shares means a prospectus, registration statement, offering memorandum, term sheet or other similar document that describes the terms of the offer (including the price and number of shares) pursuant to which a corporation offers to issue flow-through shares. *Income Tax Act*, R.S.C. 1985, c. 1 (5ᵗʰ Supp.), s. 66(15).

SELLING OFFICE. Every one who purports to sell or agrees to sell an appointment to or a resignation from an office, or a consent to any such appointment or resignation, or receives or agrees to receive a reward or profit from the purported sale thereof, is guilty of an indictable offence. *Criminal Code*, R.S.C. 1985, c. C-46, s. 124.

SELLING PRICE. See REGULATED ~.

SELLING SHORT. Selling a stock position one does not own, in the expectation that by the time one is required to deliver the shares to the buyer one the share price will have come down.

SEMBLE. *v*. [Fr. appears] A word used to introduce a legal proposition which one does not intend to state definitely.

SEMEN. *n*. The viscous fluid which the penis ejects during orgasm and which consists of spermatozoa from the testis and secretions from the seminal vesicles and prostate gland. F.A. Jaffe, *A Guide to Pathological Evidence*, 3d ed. (Toronto: Carswell, 1991) at 225.

SEMEN BANK. A person who stores semen of domestic animals.

SEMEN PRODUCING BUSINESS. *var*. **SEMEN-PRODUCING BUSINESS**. A business that maintains one or more live stock animals from which it offers semen for sale for the purpose of artificial insemination.

SEMESTER. *n*. A period of studies at an educational institution that is recognized by that educational institution and the appropriate authority for a province as a distinct period within a course of studies at that institution and that is of not less than 13 weeks duration.

SEMI-ACTIVE DOCUMENT. A document in occasional use for administrative or legal purposes.

SEMI-AMBULATORY. *adj*. The ability of a person to move about with the assistance of mechanical aides or devices but not involving assistance from another person.

SEMI-AUTOMATIC. *adj*. 1. In respect of a firearm, means a firearm that is equipped with a mechanism that, following the discharge of a cartridge, automatically operates to complete any part of the reloading cycle necessary to prepare for the discharge of the next cartridge. 2. Refers to machinery requiring the assistance of a human operator to complete part but not all of its functions during each complete cycle of operations. *Export Control List*, C.R.C., c. 601, s. 3358.

SEMI-DETACHED DWELLING. A family housing unit joined by a common or party wall to one other family housing unit.

SEMI-FABRICATING PLANT. A processing plant taking material of mineral origin beyond the refined or primary metal stage and includes a semi-alloys plant, a chemical plant utilizing acid derived from sulphide ores, a zinc die-casting plant, a rolling mill or a small diameter tube mill.

SEMINARY. *n*. " . . . [A] place of education. . ." *Worldwide Evangelization Crusade (Canada) v. Beamsville (City)*, [1960] S.C.R. 49 at 52, 21 D.L.R. (2d) 8, Cartwright J. (Locke and Martland JJ. concurring).

SEMINARY OF LEARNING. A seminary maintained for philanthropic or religious purposes where the participants have dedicated themselves to the purpose and the profits go to the use of the seminary.

SEMINAUFRAGIUM. *n*. 1. Half shipwreck, i.e. in a storm some goods are cast overboard. 2. Such extensive damage to a ship that to repair her would cost more than she is worth.

SEMI-PLENA PROBATIO. [L. semi-proof] The testimony of a solitary person.

SEMI-PRESERVES. *n*. Fish that has been prepared by salting or pickling in brine, vinegar, sugar, spices or any combination thereof and packed so that it may be kept fit for human consumption for a minimum of 6 months by means of refrigeration without freezing. *Fish Inspection Regulations*, C.R.C., c. 802, s. 2.

SEMI-PRESERVING ESTABLISHMENT. An establishment where fish is prepared by salting or pickling in brine, vinegar, sugar, spices or any combination thereof and packed so that it may be kept fit for human consumption for a minimum of 6 months by means of refrigeration without freezing.

SEMI-PRIVATE ACCOMMODATION. A two-bed unit.

SEMI-SKILLED LABOUR. Workers who have some aptitude at a particular job but whose work is not within any of the traditional crafts.

SEMI-TRAILER. *n*. A trailer so constructed that its weight and the weight of its load is carried partly upon an axle of the truck tractor towing it, and partly upon an axle of the trailer.

SEMI-TRAILER TRUCK. Truck tractor and a semi-trailer combined.

SEMPER IN DUBIIS BENIGNIORA PRAEFERENDA. [L.] In doubtful cases always prefer more liberal construction.

SEMPER IN OBSCURIS, QUOD MINIMUM EST SEQUIMUR. [L.] In obscure cases we should always follow what is least obscure.

SEMPER ITA FIAT RELATIO UT VALEAT DISPOSITIO. [L.] A word should always relate back to antecedents so that the disposition of a will has effect.

SEMPER PARATUS. [L.] Always ready.

SEMPER PRAESUMITUR PRO LEGITIMATIONE PUERORUM; ET FILIATIO NON POTEST PROBARI. [L.] The presumption is always in favour of the legitimacy of children; and filiation cannot be proved.

SEMPER PRAESUMITUR PRO MATRIMONIO. [L.] The presumption is always in favour of the validity of a marriage.

SEMPER SPECIALIA GENERALIBUS INSUNT. [L.] Particulars are always included in generalities.

SENATE. *n*. 1. The second federal legislative body whose members are appointed by the Governor General, which means, in fact, by the cabinet. The upper house of the legislature. Appointments are made to represent the regions and the diversity of Canada. Referred to as the chamber of sober second thought. In order to become law a bill must pass through the senate as well as the House of Commons. 2. The governing body of a university or college.

SENATE NOMINEE. A person declared elected under this Act. The Government of Alberta shall submit the names of the Senate nominees to the Queen's Privy Council for Canada as persons who may be summoned to the Senate of Canada for the purpose of filling vacancies relating to Alberta. A person remains as a Senate nominee until (a) the person is appointed to the Senate of Canada, (b) the person resigns as a Senate nominee by submitting a resignation in writing to the Minister determined under section 16 of the Government Organization Act as the Minister responsible for this Act, (c) the person's term as a Senate nominee expires, (d) the person takes an oath or makes a declaration or acknowledgement of allegiance, obedience, or adherence to a foreign power, or does an act whereby the person becomes a subject or citizen, or entitled to the rights or privileges of a subject or citizen, of a foreign power, (e) the person is adjudged bankrupt or insolvent, or applies for the benefit of any law relating to insolvent debtors, or becomes a public defaulter, (f) the person is convicted of treason or convicted of a felony or of any infamous crime, or (g) the person ceases to be eligible to be nominated as a candidate under section 8, whichever occurs first. *Senatorial Selection Act*, R.S.A. 2000, c. S-5, ss. 1, 3..

SENATOR. *n*. A person who is a member of a senate.

SEND. *v*. Includes deliver or mail.

SENIOR CITIZEN. A person 65 years of age or over.

SENIOR CORPORATION. An eligible corporation shares of which are listed on a stock exchange where in its last taxation year ending before the date of the certificate of eligibility the total assets of the corporation are not less than $300,000,000 but not more than $500,000,000. *Stock Savings Tax Credit Act*, R.S. Nfld. 1990, c. S-28, s. 2(1).

SENIOR EXECUTIVE. Any person exercising the functions of a director, or of a president, vice-president, secretary, treasurer, controller or general manager, or similar functions.

SENIORITY. *n*. 1. " . . . [I]s a collective bargaining concept. . . Seniority involves, in the first place, a service relationship among a group of employees . . . or at least more than one—and, as a matter of reciprocal rights inter se and as against the employer, its recognition and enforcement depend on common stipulations governing the group and the employer. This means collective bargaining; and it follows from this that the operation of seniority is, unless otherwise specifically provided, limited to the group covered by the collective agreement." Professor Bora Laskin in *Federal Wire & Cable* Co., as quoted in *Re U.S.W. and Westeel-Rosco Ltd.* (1969), 20 L.A.C. 202 at 205, Weatherill. 2. " . . . [A] term sometimes used in a broad way to refer to length of service—usually length of 'continuous' service—with an employer." *Toronto Star Newspapers Ltd. v. Printing and Graphic Communications Union, Local N-1* (1981), 30 L.A.C. (2d) 267 at 269 (Ont.), Weatherill. See DEPARTMENTAL ~; FROZEN ~.

SENIORITY SYSTEM. Part of a collective agreement which defines who is entitled to some monetary and fringe benefits and who is entitled to a particular job in the case of promotion, transfer or lay-off. Preference is granted to employees based on their length of service with the employer. D.J.M. Brown and D.M. Beatty, *Canadian Labour Arbitration*, 3d ed. (Aurora: Canada Law Book, 1992) at 6-1.

SENIOR JUDGE. Of the Supreme Court of Yukon, of the Supreme Court of the Northwest Territories or of the Nunavut Court of Justice means the judge with the earlier date of appointment to the court in question or, in the case of more than one judge appointed on the same day, means the judge that the Governor in Council may designate as the senior judge. *Judges Act*, R.S.C. 1985, c. J-1, s. 27(9).

SENIOR OFFICER. (a) The chairman or any vice-chairman of the board of directors, the president, any vice-president, the secretary, the treasurer or the general manager of a corporation or any other individual who performs functions for the corporation similar to those normally performed by an individual occupying any such office; and (b) each of the 5 highest paid employees of a corporation, including any individual referred to in subclause (a). See PARTNERS', DIRECTORS' AND ~S' QUALIFYING EXAMINATION.

SENIOR OFFICIAL. With reference to a corporation, (a) the president, vice-president, secretary, comptroller, treasurer or general manager of the corporation; or (b) any other person who performs functions for the corporation similar to those normally performed by persons holding the offices referred to in subclause (a).

SENIOR WATCH KEEPING DECK OFFICER. The watch keeping deck officer next in seniority to the master of a ship.

SENSORY DISABILITY. A disability that relates to sight or hearing. *Access to Information Act*, R.S.C. 1985, c. A-1, s. 3, as am.

SENSU HONESTO. [L.] Describes the interpretation of a statement which does not impute impropriety to anyone concerned.

SENTENCE. *n*. 1. " . . . [U]sed in reference to the determination or pronouncement of punishment or like action following a finding of guilt; . . . utilized to define the fate or punishment of a person who has been adjudged guilty, . . ." *Morris v. R.* (1979), 91 D.L.R. (3d) 161 at 177, [1979] 1 S.C.R. 405, 23 N.R. 109, 6 C.R. (3d) 36, 43 C.C.C. (2d) 129, Pratte J. (Martland, Ritchie, Pigeon and Beetz JJ. concurring). 2. Includes any order or disposition consequent upon a conviction and an order as to costs. *Provincial Offences Act*, R.S.O. 1980, c. 400, s. 92. See ADULT ~; CONCURRENT ~; CONDITIONAL ~; CONSECUTIVE ~S; INDETERMINATE ~; INTERMITTENT ~; PRE-~ REPORT; SUSPENDED ~; TARIFF ~; THRESHOLD ~; YOUTH~

SENTENCING. *n*. 1. The fundamental purpose of sentencing is to contribute, along with crime prevention initiatives, to respect for the law and the maintenance of a just, peaceful and safe society by imposing just sanctions that have one or more of the following objectives: (a) to denounce unlawful conduct; (b) to deter the offender and other persons from committing offences; (c) to separate offenders from society, where necessary; (d) to assist in rehabilitating offenders; (e) to provide reparations for harm done to victims or to the community; and (f) to promote a sense of responsibility in offenders, and acknowledgment of the harm done to victims and to the community. *Criminal Code*, R.S.C. 1985, c. C-46, s. 718. Proportionality is another principle of sentencing which must be applied by the Court. In addition the following principles are applied in sentencing: (a) a sentence should be increased or reduced to account for any relevant aggravating or mitigating circumstances relating to the offence or the offender, and, without limiting the generality of the foregoing, (i) evidence that the offence was motivated by bias, prejudice or hate based on race, national or ethnic origin, language, colour, religion, sex, age, mental or physical disability, sexual orientation, or any other similar factor, (ii) evidence that the offender, in committing the offence, abused the offender's spouse or common-law partner or child, (iii) evidence that the offender, in committing the offence, abused a position of trust or authority in relation to the victim, or (iv) evidence that the offence was committed for the benefit of, at the direction of or in association with a criminal organization shall be deemed to be aggravating circumstances; (b) a sentence should be similar to sentences imposed on similar offenders for similar offences committed in similar circumstances; (c) where consecutive sentences are imposed, the combined sentence should not be unduly long or harsh; (d) an offender should not be deprived of liberty, if less restrictive sanctions may be appropriate in the circumstances; and (e) all available sanctions other than imprisonment that are reasonable in the circumstances should be considered for all offenders, with particular attention to the circumstances of aboriginal offenders. *Criminal Code*, R.S.C. 1985, c. C-46, s. 718. 2. Balancing of these goals is required to fashion a sentence that is just and appropriate and that reflects the culpability of the offender and the circumstances of the offence. See GENERAL DETERRENCE; PROPORTIONALITY; RETRIBUTION; SPECIFIC DETERRENCE; TOTALITY PRINCIPLE.

SENTENCING CIRCLE. An alternative to sentencing by a judge used in aboriginal communities. A sentencing circle is more than a fact-finding exercise with an aboriginal twist. While it assists the judge in fashioning a fit sentence, it is conducted at a quintessentially human level and represents a stock-taking or accountability exercise on the part of the offender and the community that produced the offender. Healing is at the centre of the circle's restorative approach. The validity of the circle here was saved by the attitude, conduct and thinking of the circle participants. *R. v. Taylor* (1997), 1997 Carswell-Sask 720, 122 C.C.C. (3d) 376, 163 Sask. R. 29 (C.A.). The judge, the accused and representatives of the community must participate.

SENTENCING HEARING. Follows a finding of guilt and forms part of the trial procedure.

SENTENTIA CONTRA MATRIMONIAM NUNQUAM TRANSIT IN REM JUDICATAM. [L.] A decision against marriage never becomes res judicata.

SENTENTIA INTERLOCUTORIA REVOCARI POTEST, DEFINITIVA NON POTEST. [L.] An interlocutory judgment may be recalled, but not a final one.

SENTENTIA NON FERTUR DE NO LIQUIDIS. [L.] Judgment does not come about except on clearly defined points.

SEPARALITER. *adv*. [L.] Separately; distributively.

SEPARATE AND APART. These words are interpreted as disjunctive. There must be a withdrawal from the matrimonial obligation with the intent of destroying the matrimonial consortium as well as physical separation.

SEPARATE BUILT-IN COOKING UNIT. A stationary cooking appliance, including its integral supply leads or terminals, and consisting of one or more surface elements or ovens, or a combination of these, constructed so that the unit is permanently built into a counter or wall.

SEPARATE POOL BETTING. Pari-mutuel betting at one or more satellite tracks or in one or more places in one or more foreign countries on a race that is held at a host track, where the money bet on each pool at each satellite track is retained at that satellite track or is combined with the money bet on the corresponding pool at another satellite track or tracks or at a place or places to form one pool from which the pay-out price is calculated and distributed. *Pari-Mutuel Betting Supervision Regulations*, SOR/91-365, s. 2.

SEPARATE RESOLUTION. A resolution that has been submitted to all the members who hold shares of a particular class or series and which is consented to in writing by all those members or passed by the required majority at a class meeting or series meeting.

SEPARATE SCHOOL. Provides a program of education which has a denominational nature by way of formal religious education or by promotion and preservation of Roman Catholic beliefs and values by other means.

SEPARATE STORE OR WAREHOUSE. A store or warehouse that is (a) detached from any dwelling house and situated at a safe distance from any highway, street, public thoroughfare or public place; (b) made and closed so as to prevent unauthorized persons having access thereto and to secure it from danger from without; (c) exclusively used for the keeping of manufactured fireworks and ammunition belonging to Division 1 of Class 6; and (d) well and substantially constructed of suitable material. *Explosives Regulations*, C.R.C., c. 599, s. 127.

SEPARATION. *n*. 1. The decision by a husband and wife to live apart. 2. The termination of employment. 3. With respect to an inpatient in hospital, discharge or death. See CORD ~; FIRE ~; GRADE ~; INNERLINER ~; JUDICIAL ~; PLY ~; SIDEWALL ~; TRAFFIC - SCHEME; TREAD ~.

SEPARATION AGREEMENT. 1. An agreement in writing between spouses who are living or intend to live separate and apart. 2. Includes an agreement by which a person agrees to make payments on a periodic basis for the maintenance of a former spouse or common-law partner, children of the marriage or common-law partnership or both the former spouse or common-law partner and children of the marriage or common-law partnership, after the marriage or common-law partnership has been dissolved, whether the agreement was made before or after the marriage or common-law partnership was dissolved. *Income Tax Act*, R.S.C. 1985, c. 1 (5th Supp.), s.248. 3. Two persons of the opposite sex or the same sex who cohabited and are living separate and apart may enter into an agreement in which they agree on their respective rights and obligations, including, (a) ownership in or division of property; (b) support obligations; (c) the right to direct the education and moral training of their children; (d) the right to custody of and access to their children; and (e) any other matter in the settlement of their affairs. *Family Law Act*, R.S.O. 1990, c. F-3, s. 54, as am. See WRITTEN ~.

SEPARATION OF POWERS. A defining feature of the Canadian Constitution. Refers to the separation of the powers of the executive, legislative and judicial branches of government. The judiciary interprets and applies the law. The legislature decides upon and enunciates policy. The executive administers and implements policy.

SEPARATION ZONE OR LINE. A zone or line separating routes in which ships are proceeding in opposite or nearly opposite directions, or separating a route from the adjacent

inshore traffic zone. *Collision Regulations*, C.R.C., c. 1416, s. 2.

SEPARATOR. *n*. An unfired apparatus specifically designed and used for separating fluids produced from a well into two or more streams.

SEQUENCE LISTING. In respect of an invention, a part of the description describing nucleotide or amino acid sequences and giving other related information. *Patent Rules* SOR/96-423, s. 2.

SEQUESTER. *v*. 1. To place the members of a jury in a private room for their deliberations so that they have no contact with members of the public generally. 2. To prevent the owners from using by setting aside.

SEQUESTRATION. *n*. Property is temporarily placed by some judicial or quasi-judicial process in the hands of persons called sequestrators, who manage it and receive the rents and profits. See WRIT OF ~.

SERGEANT-AT-ARMS. *n*. A Parliamentary official appointed by Letters Patent under the Great Seal who brings people to the Bar to be examined as witnesses, arrests strangers who are improperly in the House or its galleries and who misbehave there and sees to it that people directed to withdraw are removed. A. Fraser, W.A. Dawson, & J. Holtby, eds., *Beauchesne's Rules and Forms of the House of Commons of Canada*, 6th ed. (Toronto: Carswell, 1989) at 61.

SERIAL. *n*. 1. Any book that is first published in separate articles or as a tale or short story complete in one issue in a newspaper or periodical. 2. Any publication issued in successive parts that appear at intervals for an indefinite period.

SERIAL NUMBER. 1. Includes identification number assigned to or placed on a vehicle by its manufacturer as a manufacturer's number and vehicle number. 2. The number or combination of figures and letters of the alphabet assigned to an instrument tendered for filing or registration at the time it is received by the registrar and entered in the instrument register. 3. A combination of letters or figures or both letters and figures by which a device may be traced in manufacture and identified in distribution.

SERIAL TITLE. A run of a serial irrespective of its continuity.

SERIATIM. *adv*. [L.] Separately and in order.

SERIES. *n*. 1. In relation to shares, means a division of a class of shares. 2. A numerical, spatial, or temporal sequence of things which are logically or factually related.

SERIES MEETING. A meeting of members who hold shares of a particular series.

SERIOUS ADVERSE REACTION. A noxious and unintended response to a natural health product that occurs at any dose and that requires in-patient hospitalization or a prolongation of existing hospitalization, that causes congenital malformation, that results in persistent or significant disability or incapacity, that is life threatening or that results in death. *Natural Health Products Regulations*, SOR/2003-196, s. 1.

SERIOUS BODILY HARM. " . . . [F]or the purposes of the section [s. 264.1 of the Criminal Code, R.S.C. 1985, c. C-46] is any hurt or injury, whether physical or psychological, that interferes in a substantial way with the physical or psychological integrity, health or well-being of the complainant." *R. v. McCraw* (1991), 66 C.C.C. (3d) 517 at 523, 7 C.R. (4th) 314, 128 N.R. 299, 49 O.A.C. 47, [1991] 3 S.C.R. 72, the court per Cory J.

SERIOUS DETERIORATION IN THE STATE OF HEALTH. A life-threatening disease, disorder or abnormal physical state, the permanent impairment of a body function or permanent damage to a body structure, or a condition that necessitates an unexpected medical or surgical intervention to prevent such a disease, disorder or abnormal physical state or permanent impairment or damage. *Medical Devices Regulations* SOR/98-282, s. 1.

SERIOUS HARM. Severe physical injury or severe psychological damage. *Corrections and Conditional Release Act*, S.C. 1992, c. 20, s. 99.

SERIOUS INJURY. 1. (a) A fracture of the skull, spine, pelvis, femur, humerus, fibula or tibia, or radius or ulna; (b) an amputation of a major part of a hand or foot; (c) the loss of sight of an eye; (d) a serious internal haemorrhage; (e) a burn that requires medical attention; (f) an injury caused directly or indirectly by explosives; (g) an asphyxiation or poisoning by gas resulting in a partial or total loss of physical control; or (h) another injury likely to endanger life or cause permanent injury, but does not include injuries to a worker of a nature that may be treated through first aid or medical treatment and the worker is able to return to his or her work either immediately after the treatment or at his or her next scheduled shift. *Occupational Health and Safety Act*, R.S. Nfld. 1990, c. O-3, s. 54. 2. An injury that requires admission to hospital.

SERIOUS OR PROLONGED DISABILITY. Does not include a disability of a degree less than 20 per cent estimated in the manner provided by subsection 35(2) of the Pension Act. *Civilian War-related Benefits Act*, R.S.C. 1985, c. C-31, s. 30.

SERIOUS PERSONAL INJURY OFFENCE. (a) An indictable offence, other than high treason, treason, first degree murder or second degree murder, involving (i) the use or attempted use of violence against another person; or (ii) conduct endangering or likely to endanger the life or safety of another person or inflicting or likely to inflict severe psychological damage on another person, and for which the offender may be sentenced to imprisonment for 10 years or more; or (b) an offence or attempt to commit an offence mentioned in section 271 (sexual assault), 272 (sexual assault with a weapon, threats to a third party or causing bodily harm) or 273 (aggravated sexual assault). *Criminal Code*, R.S.C. 1985, c. C-46, s. 752.

SERIOUS QUESTION. In the context of the granting of an interlocutory injunction, Nadon, J. accepted the following definition: 'Serious question' has been considered synonymous with 'chance of success', not 'frivolous or vexatious': 'real prospect of succeeding', and 'probability that plaintiff is entitled to relief'. Without attempting to precisely and conclusively redefine the phrase 'serious question', we can say that it implies a burden of proof of less than the balance of probability, less than fifty-one per cent . . . but more than a 'speculative' risk or a 'mere possibility' from Patricia Carlson, "Granting An Interlocutory Injunction: What is the Test?" (1982) 12 Man. L.J. 109, at 116. *Quebec Trotting & Pacing Assn. v. Canada (Department of Agriculture)* (1993), 1993 CarswellNat 840, 24 Admin. L.R. (2d) 268, 76 F.T.R. 81 (T.D.), Nadon, J.

SERIOUS UNEXPECTED ADVERSE REACTION. A serious adverse reaction that is not identified in nature, severity or frequency in the risk information set out on the label of the natural health product. *Natural Health Products Regulations*, SOR/2003-196, s. 1.

SERIOUS VIOLENT OFFENCE. An offence in the commission of which a young person causes or attempts to cause serious bodily harm. *Youth Criminal Justice Act*, S.C. 2002, c. 1, s. 2.

SERJEANT-AT-ARMS. See SERGEANT-AT-ARMS.

SERMO EST ANIMI INDEX. [L.] Speech is the mind's informer.

SERMONES SEMPER ACCIPIENDI SUNT SECUNDUM SUBJECTUM MATERIAM ET CONDITIONEM PERSONARUM. [L.] Words should always be taken as relating to the subject matter and the occupation of the people mentioned.

SERMO RELATUS AD PERSONAM INTELLIGI DEBET DE CONDITIONE PERSONAE. [L.] A word referring to someone should be interpreted as describing that person's occupation.

SEROLOGY. *n*. The science which concerns antigens and antibodies found in blood and other body fluids. F.A. Jaffe, *A Guide to Pathological Evidence*, 3d ed. (Toronto: Carswell, 1991) at 225-6.

SERUM. See TRUTH ~.

SERVANT. *n*. 1. " . . . [A] person subject to the command of his master as to the manner in which he shall do his work. . ." *Tully v. Genbey*, [1939] 1 D.L.R. 559 at 565, [1939] 1 W.W.R. 161, 46 Man. R. 439 (C.A.), Trueman J.A. 2. " . . . '[E]mployee' . . ." *Atherton v. Boycott* (1989), 36 C.P.C. (2d) 250 at 255 (Ont. H.C.) Cusinato L.J.S.C. 3. A person engaged in employment. 4. Includes agent, but does not include any person appointed or employed by or under the authority of an ordinance of the Northwest Territories or a law of the Legislature of Yukon or of the Legislature for Nunavut. *Crown Liability and Proceedings Act*, R.S.C. 1985, c. C-50, s. 2. 5. When used in relation to the Crown, includes a minister of the Crown. *Proceedings Against the Crown Act*, R.S.O. 1990, c. P.27, s. 1. 6. A person who agrees, freely or for a reward, to give service to another person. 7. A person who is completely subject to the control of a master in relation to what is done and how it is done. See CIVIL ~; DOMESTIC ~; MASTER AND ~; PUBLIC ~.

SERVE. *v*. 1. Of a copy of a legal document, to deliver it to parties interested in a legal proceeding so that they know about the proceeding. 2. To endure; to go through. 3. To be used as.

SERVED. *n*. 1. Served personally. 2. Served personally on a person or on an adult residing at the residence of the person who is at the residence at the time of service, or sent by registered mail to the person at his latest known address.

SERVICE. *n*. 1. Service as a member of the armed forces. 2. With respect to a document, the act of serving it. 3. " . . . [D]oes not necessarily mean 'personal service' . . . means bringing it to the attention of the person to be served." *Canada Trust Co. v. Kakar Properties Ltd.* (1983), 32 C.P.C. 280 at 289, 26 R.P.R. 202 (Ont. Master), Peppiatt (Master). 4. (a) The making of bona fide repairs to a motor vehicle by or under the supervision of an automobile repair mechanic; (b) the painting, stabling, storing or caring for a motor vehicle by a garage keeper. 5. (a) Street lighting; (b) distribution of water; (c) the collection, removal and disposal of ashes or garbage or other refuse; (d) the collection and disposal of sewage and land drainage; (e) fire protection. 6. (a) The conveyance for compensation by a public utility of passengers; (b) the conveyance or transmission for compensation by a public utility of telephone messages; (c) the production, transmission, delivery or furnishing to or for the public by a public utility for compensation of electrical energy for purposes of heat, light and power; (d) the production, transmission, delivery or furnishing to or for the public by a public utility for compensation of gas for purposes of heat, light or power; (e) the production, transmission, delivery or furnishing to or for the public by a public utility for compensation of water; (f) the production, transmission, delivery or furnishing to or for the public by a public utility for compensation of steam heat. 7. Employment. See ACCEPTANCE OF ~; ACTIVE ~; ADMISSION OF ~; AFFIDAVIT OF ~; AIR ~; AIR TRAFFIC CONTROL ~; AIR TRANSPORTATION ~; ALARM ~; AMBULANCE ~; ARMOURED CAR ~; AUGMENTED CHANNEL ~; AUGMENTING ~; BASIC ~; BUS ~; CABLECAST ~; CANADIAN ~; CHILD DEVELOPMENT ~; CHILD TREATMENT ~; CIVIL ~; COMMUNITY ~; COMMUNITY ~ ORDER; COMMUNITY SUPPORT ~; COMPUTER ~; CONSUMER'S ~; CONTINUOUS ~; CONTRACT OF ~; CONTRIBUTORY ~; CORRECTIONAL ~ CANADA; CRANE ~; CREDITED ~; DISCHARGE FROM ~; DOMESTIC ~; EXTRA-JUDICIAL ~; FIRE PREVENTION ~; FOOD ~ PREMISES; FOREIGN ~ OFFICER; IN ~; INTERNATIONAL ~; MEMBER OF A ~; MILITARY ~; MUNICIPAL ~; NEWFOUNDLAND ~; NONWARD ~; OCCUPATIONAL HEALTH ~;

OPHTHALMIC DISPENSING ~; OPTIONAL ~; OVERSEAS ~; PART-TIME ~; PASSENGER-TRAIN ~; PAST ~ CREDIT; PENITENTIARY ~; PENSIONABLE ~; PERIOD OF ~; PERSONAL ~; PILOT~; PLUMBING ~; POST-PAK MAIL ~; POTENTIAL ~; PRIOR ~; PROGRAMMING ~; PROTECTIVE ~; PROVINCIAL ~; PUBLIC ~; PUBLIC ~ COMMISSION; PUBLIC ~ STAFF RELATIONS BOARD; PUBLIC TRANSPORTATION ~; RECREATION ~; REGULAR ~; REGULATED ~; REPAIR ~; REPRESENTATIVE FOR ~; RESIDENTIAL ~; RESOURCE PROTECTION AND DEVELOPMENT ~; SEA ~; ~S; SEWAGE ~; SOFT ~; SPACE ~; SUBSTITUTED ~; SUPPLY ~; TAXABLE~; TEACHING ~; TELECOMMUNICATION ~; TELEGRAPHIC ~; TERMINATING~; TERM OF ~; TERRESTRIAL ~; THROUGH ~; TRANSFER ~; TRANSIT ~ AGREEMENT; TRAVEL~; UNECONOMIC~; UNINTERRUPTED ~; URBAN ~; VESSEL ~; WAR ~; WATER ~; YOUNG OFFENDERS ~.

SERVICEABILITY LIMIT STATES. Those limit states which restrict the intended use and occupancy of the building and include deflection, vibration, permanent deformation and cracking. *Building Code Act*, R.R.O. 1980, Reg. 87, s. 4.1.4.

SERVICEABLE. *adj*. In respect of an aircraft or aircraft part, means fit and safe for flight; *Canadian Aviation Regulations* SOR/96-433, s. 101.01.

SERVICE AREA. The area in which an electric distribution system may distribute electric energy.

SERVICE AT SEA. Service in a ship that normally sailed or operated outside the territorial waters of all countries during World War I, World War II or the United Nations military operations in Korea. *Civilian War-related Benefits Act*, R.S.C. 1985, c. C-31, s. 56.

SERVICE BOX. An approved assembly consisting of a metal box or cabinet constructed so that it may be effectually locked or sealed, containing either service fuses and a service switch or a circuit breaker and of such design that either the switch or circuit breaker may be manually operated when the box is closed.

SERVICE BRAKE. The primary mechanism designed to stop a vehicle.

SERVICE BY MAIL. 1. Service by ordinary mail, registered mail, double registered mail, certified mail and any other form of delivery by a public postal service. 2. With respect to a document, sending a copy along with an acknowledgement of receipt card.

SERVICE CLUB. An association of business and professional people whose objectives are to make contributions of various sorts to the community in which the club exists.

SERVICE CONTRACT. A contract in writing for performance over a fixed period of time, or for a specified duration determined by means other than time, of services relating to the maintenance or repair of a consumer product, whether or not the contract provides for the furnishing of parts or materials to be supplied with or consumed in the performance of such services.

SERVICE CONTROL. A control that is installed on a device by the manufacturer thereof for the purpose of adjustment and that, under normal usage, is not accessible to the user of the device.

SERVICE CONVICT. A person who is under a sentence that includes a punishment of imprisonment for life or for two years or more imposed on that person pursuant to the Code of Service Discipline. *National Defence Act*, R.S.C. 1985, c. N-5, s. 2.

SERVICE CORPORATION. A corporation incorporated to provide, (a) a life company or a foreign life corporation with advisory, management or sales distribution services in respect of life insurance contracts or annuities whose reserves vary in amount depending on the market value of a specified group of assets maintained in a separate and distinct fund; or (b) a mutual fund corporation with advisory, management or sales distribution services.

SERVICE COST. See CURRENT ~.

SERVICE COURT. A court martial and includes the service authorities of a designated state who are empowered by the laws of that state to deal with charges. *Visiting Forces Act*, R.S.C. 1985, c. V-2, s. 2.

SERVICE CREDIT. The credit accruing to an employee because of length of service.

SERVICE CUSTODY. The holding under arrest or in confinement of a person by the Canadian Forces, including confinement in a service prison or detention barrack. *National Defence Act*, R.S.C. 1985, c. N-5, s. 2.

SERVICE DETAINEE. A person under sentence that includes a punishment of detention imposed pursuant to the Code of Service Discipline. *National Defence Act*, R.S.C. 1985, c. N-5, s. 2.

SERVICED HOUSING ACCOMMODA-TION. Housing accommodation for which light, heat, fuel, water, gas or electricity are provided at the expense of the employer.

SERVICE DISCIPLINE. See CODE OF ~.

SERVICED ROADWAY. The part of highway that is improved, designed or ordinarily used for vehicular traffic, and includes the ploughed portion of the shoulder, and, where a highway includes two or more separate serviced roadways, the term "serviced roadway" refers to any one serviced roadway separately and not to all of the serviced roadways collectively. *Motorized Snow Vehicles Act*, R.S.O. 1990, c. M.44, s. 1.

SERVICED VACANT LAND. Land on which there is no building; and which is adjacent to a public street bordering which water and sanitary sewer services are available.

SERVICE ESTATE. The following parts of the estate of a deceased officer or non-commissioned member mentioned in subsection (1): (a) service pay and allowances; (b) all other emoluments emanating from Her Majesty that, at the date of death, are due or otherwise payable; (c) personal equipment that the deceased person is, under regulations, permitted to retain; (d) personal or movable property, including cash, found on the deceased person or on a defence establishment or otherwise in the care or custody of the Canadian Forces; and (e) in the case of an officer or non-commissioned member dying outside Canada, all other personal or movable property belonging to the deceased and situated outside Canada. *National Defence Act*, R.S.C. 1985, c. N-5, s. 42.

SERVICE EX JURIS. Service of process of the court on a person who is outside the territory of the issuing court.

SERVICE FACILITIES. Includes (a) furniture, appliances and furnishings; (b) parking and related facilities; (c) laundry facilities; (d) elevator facilities; (e) common recreational facilities; (f) garbage facilities and related services; (g) cleaning or maintenance services; (h) storage

facilities; (i) intercom systems; (j) cablevision facilities; (k) heating facilities or services; (l) air-conditioning facilities; (m) utilities and related services; (n) security services or facilities. *Residential Tenancies Act*, R.S.O. 1980, c. 452, s. 1.

SERVICE FOR A CONTINUOUS PERIOD. Service for a period of time without regard to periods of temporary suspension of employment.

SERVICE IN A THEATRE OF ACTUAL WAR. (a) Any service as a member of the army or air force of Canada in the period commencing August 14, 1914 and ending November 11, 1918 in the zone of the allied armies on the continent of Europe, Asia or Africa, or in any other place at which the member has sustained injury or contracted disease directly by a hostile act of the enemy; (b) any service as a member of the naval forces of Canada in the period described in paragraph (a) on the high seas or wherever contact has been made with hostile forces of the enemy, or in any other place at which the member has sustained injury or contracted disease directly by a hostile act of the enemy; and (c) any service as a member of the forces in the period commencing September 1, 1939 and ending (i) May 9, 1945, where the service was in any place outside Canada; and (ii) August 15, 1945, where the service was in the Pacific Ocean or Asia, or in any place in Canada at which the member has sustained injury or contracted disease directly by a hostile act of the enemy. *Pension Act*, R.S.C. 1985, c. P-6, s. 2.

SERVICE IN THE FORCE. Includes any period of service as a special constable of the force before April 1, 1960, or any period of service as a member of a provincial or municipal police force, that, in accordance with the regulations, may be counted as service in the Force for the purposes of this Part. *Royal Canadian Mounted Police Act*, R.S.C. 1985, c. R-11, s. 3.

SERVICE IN THE FORCES. See ACTIVE ~.

SERVICE IN THE KOREAN WAR. (a) In the case of a member of the Canadian Forces, any service from the day of the member's departure from Canada or the United States, including Alaska, to participate in the Korean War, until the earliest of (i) the day on which the member next returned to Canada or the United States, including Alaska, (ii) the day on which the member was next posted to a unit that was not participating in the Korean War, (iii) the day on which the unit with which the member was serving, having ceased to participate in the Korean War, arrived at the place to which it had been next assigned, and (iv) October 31, 1953, and (b) in the case of a Canadian merchant mariner of the Korean War as described in subsection 21.1(5), any service during a period described in paragraph 21.1(2)(*b*). *Pension Act*, R.S.C. 1985, c. P-6, s. 3.

SERVICE LIFE. The period of time between the placement of plant in service and its retirement for accounting purposes.

SERVICE LINE. 1. A pipe line used for the transportation or conduct of oil, gas or water to a well-head, drilling rig, surface pit or service tank. 2. A pipe or conduit of pipes, other than a flow line, used for the transportation, gathering or conduct of a mineral or water or other fluid in connection with the producing operations of an operator.

SERVICE MARK. A trade mark used or displayed when a service associated with the mark is performed or advertised.

SERVICE OFFENCE. An offence under this Act, the Criminal Code or any other Act of Parliament, committed by a person while subject to the Code of Service Discipline. *National Defence Act*, R.S.C. 1985, c. N-5, s. 2.

SERVICE OF PROCESS. Bringing the effect or contents of a document to the attention of a person affected.

SERVICE PIPE. 1. A pipe installed by or on behalf of a gas company for the transmission of gas from a distribution main to a meter on the land or premises of the purchaser of the gas. 2. The pipe that conveys water between the main shut-off valve on the public water system and the control shut-off valve in a supply system.

SERVICE PRISON. A place designated as such under the National Defence Act. *Visiting Forces Act*, R.S.C. 1985, c. V-2, s. 2.

SERVICE PRISONER. A person under sentence that includes a punishment of imprisonment for less than 2 years imposed pursuant to the Code of Service Discipline. *National Defence Act*, c. N-5, s. 2.

SERVICE PROVIDER. A contractor providing certain services to the public. The contractor has entered into an agreement with the government to provide these services in place of the government providing them directly itself.

SERVICE RATE. The total amount charged to any person by a public utility for or in connection with (a) the use of a utility system and the connection thereto; or (b) the sending of a communication by a utility system.

SERVICE ROAD. A roadway that is part of a divided highway and that is designed and constructed for use of local traffic as distinct from through traffic.

SERVICE ROOM. A room or space provided in a building to accommodate building service equipment such as air-conditioning or heating appliances, electrical services, pumps, compressors and incinerators.

SERVICES. *n.* 1. " . . . [T]he product of the work supplying it." *Xerox of Canada Ltd. v. Ontario Regional Assessment Commissioner, Region No. 10* (1981), 13 O.M.B.R. 41 at 42, [1981] 2 S.C.R. 137, 127 D.L.R. (3d) 511, Martland, Dickson, Beetz, McIntyre and Chouinard JJ. 2. " . . . '[H]elp' or 'benefit' or 'advantage' conferred. . . *R. v. Laphkas* (1942), 77 C.C.C. 142 at 145, [1942] S.C.R. 84, [1942] 2 D.L.R. 47, Taschereau J. 3. "[In s. 20 of the Charter] . . . means, generally, the administration of public affairs as the same applies to the individual. . ." *Jenkins v. Prince Edward Island (Workers' Compensation Board)* (1986), 15 C.C.E.L. 55 at 65-6, 21 C.C.L.I. 149, 31 D.L.R. (4th) 536, 61 Nfld. & P.E.I.R. 206, 185 A.P.R. 206, 9 C.H.R.R. D/5145 (P.E.I. C.A.), the court per McQuaid J.A. 4. The expression "services provided to land or improvements" by its plain meaning includes electrical services provided to apartments. [The definition of "service" applies] equally to the supply of electricity as to the supply of water or gas. It applies to the apparatus of supply, such as wires and meters, as well as to the supply itself. *B.C. Apartment Owners & Managers Assn. v. New Westminster (City)*, 2001 CarswellBC 1075, 2001 BCSC 684, 19 M.P.L.R. (3d) 249 (S.C.), Shaw J. See ADVISORY ~; ARCHITECTURAL~; CARE~; CEMETERY ~; CHILD CARE ~; COMMUNITY DEVELOPMENT ~; DATA PROCESSING ~; DAY CARE ~; ESSENTIAL ~; FUNERAL ~; HEALTH CARE ~; HEALTH HOME CARE ~; HOMEMAKER ~; HOMEMAKING ~; HOSPITAL ~; IN-HOME ~; INPATIENT~; INSURED ~; LOCAL ~; LOSS OF ~; MANPOWER PROGRAMS AND ~; MEDICAL~; MUNICIPAL ~; NON-PROGRAMMING ~; NON-RESIDENT ~; NURSING ~; OFFICE ~; PER-

SONAL ~; PHYSICIAN ~; PROFES-SIONAL ~; PROTECTION ~; PROTECTIVE ~; RESIDENT ~; SALE OF ~; SERVICE; SOCIAL ~; SUPERVI-SORY ~; SUPPLY AND ~ CANADA; SUP-PLY OF ~; TREATMENT ~; WELFARE ~.

SERVICE SCHEDULE. A written statement of the frequency and time of departure and arrival of flights.

SERVICES DESIGNED TO APPEAL TO EROTIC OR SEXUAL APPETITES OR IN-CLINATIONS. Includes (a) services of which a principal feature or characteristic is the nudity or partial nudity of any person, (b) services in respect of which the word "nude", "naked", "topless", "bottomless", "sexy", or any other word or any picture, symbol or representation having like meaning or implication is used in any advertisement. *Municipal Act*, R.S.O. 1990, c. M.45, s. 225(9).

SERVICE SHAFT. A shaft for the passage of persons or materials to or from a tunnel under construction.

SERVICE SHIP. A registered ship operated by the Government of Canada to obtain scientific data on the high seas and includes weather and research ships. Canada regulations.

SERVICE SHOP. An enclosed building or part of a building in which the repair, sale and servicing of goods is carried on. Canada regulations.

SERVICE SPACE. 1. Space provided in a building to facilitate or conceal the installation of building service facilities such as chutes, ducts, pipes, shafts or wires. 2. Includes galleys, main pantries, laundries, store rooms, paint rooms, baggage rooms, mail rooms, bullion rooms, carpenters' and plumbers' workshops, and trunkways leading to such spaces. *Hull Construction Regulations*, C.R.C., c.1431, s. 2. See VERTICAL ~.

SERVICE STAFF. Domestic service personnel of a diplomatic mission, e.g. cooks, chauffeurs, cleaners.

SERVICE STATION. 1. A place or premises where, for remuneration, motor vehicles are greased, oiled, cleaned and supplied with gasoline, and are given minor repairs. 2. Includes premises used or intended to be used for the retail sale of gasoline. See AUTOMOBILE ~; BAT-TERY ~; GASOLINE ~.

SERVICE STATION ATTENDANT. A person engaged in the servicing and maintenance of motor vehicles who, (a) repairs, changes and balances wheels and tires; (b) changes oil in motor vehicles or lubricates motor vehicles, including lubricating the front wheel bearings and drive shaft; (c) supplies motor vehicles with anti-freezing solutions; (d) replaces cooling-system hoses, engine-driven belts and thermostats; (e) cleans or replaces spark plugs; (f) installs new or rental batteries or battery cables, or recharges batteries; (g) replaces sealed beam units, light bulbs, lenses, fuses and horns; and (h) checks and replenishes fluid levels in hydraulic systems.

SERVICE SUPPLIER. A person who supplies a taxed service to a recipient.

SERVICE TRIBUNAL. A court martial or a person presiding at a summary trial. *National Defence Act*, R.S.C. 1985, c. N-5, s. 2.

SERVICE VALUE. The book cost of plant minus the estimated net salvage value of that plant.

SERVICE VEHICLE. 1. A motor vehicle equipped to refuel, repair or tow road vehicles. 2. (a) A wrecking or tow truck when stopped at the scene of an accident or returning from the scene of an accident with a damaged vehicle in tow; (b) any private or public utility corporation vehicle while engaged at the scene of repair work; (c) snow removal equipment when actually engaged in snow removal operation; or (d) a truck tractor when actually engaged in moving an oversize load for which a permit has been issued. See ROAD ~.

SERVICE WATER HEATER. A device for heating water for plumbing services. See INDI-RECT ~.

SERVIENS AD LEGEM. [L.] Sergeant-at-law.

SERVIENT TENEMENT. The land over which one exercises an easement.

SERVING TRACK. The track serving the storage facility and upon which railway cars are located for loading or unloading purposes. Canada regulations.

SERVITIA PERSONALIA SEQUUNTUR PERSONAM. [L.] Personal services go with the person.

SERVITIUM. *n.* [L.] 1. Service. 2. " . . . [S]ervices in the home. . . the duties of a wife as a worker and manager of his domestic establishment." *Shkwarchuk v. Hansen* (1984), 12 C.R.R. 369 at 373, 30 C.C.L.T. 121, 34 Sask. R. 211 (Q.B.), MacLeod J.

SERVITIUM FEODALE ET PRAEDIALE.
[L.] A personal service due because land was held in fee.

SERVITIUM FORINSECUM. [L.] A service belonging to the monarch.

SERVITIUM, IN LEGE ANGLIAE, RE-GULARITER ACCIPITUR PRO SERVI-TIO QUOD PER TENENTES DOMINIS SUIS DEBETUR RATIONE FEODI SUI.
[L.] Service, in English law, means service which is due from tenants to lords because of their fee.

SERVITIUM INTRINSECUM. [L.] Service due to a lord from tenants on that lord's manor.

SERVITIUM REGALE. [L.] Royal service.

SERVITUDE. See PENAL ~; PRAEDIAL ~.

SESSION. *n*. 1. The period of time between the first meeting of Parliament and a prorogation. One Parliament usually includes several sessions. A. Fraser, W.A. Dawson, & J. Holtby, eds., *Beauchesne's Rules and Forms of the House of Commons of Canada*, 6th ed. (Toronto: Carswell, 1989) at 65. 2. " . . . [T]he period of time during which members of the Legislature are called together for the despatch of public business." *Sessional Allowance under* he Ontario *Legislative Assembly Act, Re,* [1945] 2 D.L.R. 631 at 636, [1945] O.R. 336 (C.A.), McRuer J.A. 3. The sitting of a court. 4. "The word 'term' would be more accurate than 'session' to describe the time prescribed by law for holding court, as a session of the Court is the time of its actual sitting and terminates each day with its rising. The distinction is not always observed, however, and the words are often used interchangeably." *MacDonald v. Dawson* (1955), 20 C.R. 357 at 358, 36 M.P.R. 34, 112 C.C.C. 44 (Nfld. C.A.). the court per Walsh C.J. See FALL ~; SPECIAL ~; SPRING ~; TERM.

SESSIONAL EMPLOYEE. A person who (a) is an employee of either House or of both Houses of Parliament; and (b) is employed for one or more sessions of Parliament.

SESSIONAL INDEMNITY. (a) In relation to a period before October 8, 1970, means the allowances payable to a member pursuant to section 55 and subsection 63(3) of the Parliament of Canada Act; (b) in relation to a period after October 7, 1970 and before July 8, 1974, means (i) in the case of a member of the Senate, five-sixths of the allowances payable to a member

pursuant to section 55 of the Parliament of Canada Act; and (ii) in the case of a member of the House of Commons, the allowances payable to the member pursuant to section 55 of the Parliament of Canada Act; and (c) in relation to a period after July 7, 1974, means the allowances payable to a member pursuant to section 55 of the Parliament of Canada Act. *Members of Parliament Retiring Allowances Act*, R.S.C. 1985, c. M-5, s. 2.

SESSIONAL ORDER. An order which is effective only for the duration of the session in which it was passed. A. Fraser, W.A. Dawson, & J. Holtby, eds., *Beauchesne's Rules and Forms of the House of Commons of Canada*, 6th ed. (Toronto: Carswell, 1989) at 5. See STANDING, SESSIONAL AND SPECIAL ORDERS.

SET. *v*. In respect of fishing gear, to place the fishing gear in the sea so that (a) each end of the gear is anchored in the sea; (b) one end of the gear is anchored in the sea and the other end of the gear is attached to a fishing vessel; (c) the gear is drifting in the sea; or (d) one end of the gear is drifting in the sea while the other end of the gear is attached to a fishing vessel.

SET. *n*. A number of articles of the same general character ordinarily on sale together or intended to be used together, to each of which the same design or variants thereof are applied. *Industrial Design Act*, R.S.C. 1985, c. I-9, s. 2. See CORD ~; LETTER FORM ~.

SET ASIDE. To nullify the order or decision of another decision-maker. A court may set aside the decision or order of an administrative tribunal on judicial review. On appeal, a higher court may set aside the judgment or order of a lower court.

SET DOWN FOR TRIAL. Any step in civil proceedings which indicates that the matter is ready to proceed to trial.

SET-LINE. *n*. 1. A line that is anchored to the sea-bed and has a series of fish hooks attached. Canada regulations. 2. A hook and line that is left in the water unattended.

SET NET. A net that is anchored, staked or otherwise attached to the shore, the bottom or to an anchored boat, buoy or other float to prevent it from drifting freely with the current. Canada regulations.

SET OFF. *var*. **SET-OFF**. 1. "A statutory set-off was available, before the fusion of law and equity, either in equity or at law. It is still available. It requires the fulfilment of two conditions. The first is that both obligations must be debts. The second is that both debts must be mutual cross obligations. Both conditions must be fulfilled at the same time: . . ." *Canadian Imperial Bank of Commerce v. Tucker Industries Inc.* (1988), 48 C.B.R. (N.S.) 1 at 3, [1983] 5 W.W.R. 602, 46 B.C.L.R. 7, 149 D.L.R. (3d) 172 (C.A.), the court per Lambert J.A. 2. "Equitable set-off is available where there is a claim for a money sum whether liquidated or unliquidated: Abacus Cities Ltd. v. Aboussafy [1981] 4 W.W.R. 660 . . . (Alta. C.A.) at p. 666 . . . it is available where there has been an assignment. There is no requirement of mutuality. . . The party relying on a set-off must show some equitable ground for being protected against his adversary's demands: . . . The equitable ground must go to the very root of the plaintiff's claim before a set-off will be allowed: . . . A crossclaim must be so clearly connected with the demand of the Plaintiff that it would be manifestly unjust to allow the plaintiff to enforce payment without taking into consideration the cross-claim: . . . The plaintiff's claim and the cross-claim need not arise out of the same contract: . . . Unliquidated claims are on the same footing as liquidated claims: . . ." *Telford v. Holt* (1987), 21 C.P.C. (2d) 1 at 13, 18, 78 N.R. 321, 54 Alta. L.R. (2d) 193, [1987] 6 W.W.R. 385, [1987] 2 S.C.R. 193, 46 R.P.R. 234, 81 A.R. 385, 41 D.L.R. (4th) 385, 37 B.L.R. 241, the court per Wilson J. 3. " . . . [S]omething in the way of a defence: where claim and cross-claim are merged and the lesser is thereby extinguished. True set-off must be distinguished from procedural set-off, where two unrelated claims are balanced up and a net judgment given: . . ." *Abacus Cities Ltd. v. Aboussafy* (1981), (*sub nom. Aboussafy v. Abacus Cities Ltd.*) 39 C.B.R. (N.S.) 1 at 10, [1981] 4 W.W.R. 660, 124 D.L.R. (3d) 150, 29 A.R. 607 (C.A.), the court per Kerans J.A. 4. In an action to recover money, a cross claim by the defendant for money. 5. Includes counterclaim. *Municipal Courts Act*, R.S.N.S. 1967, c. 197, s. 1. 6. "Where a customer has two accounts with the same bank and one is in credit and the other in debit the bank may set off one against the other and combine the two accounts: . . ." *Bank of Montreal v. R & R Entertainment Ltd.* (1984), 27 B.L.R. 159 at 166, 56 N.B.R. (2d) 154, 146 A.P.R. 154, 13 D.L.R. (4th) 726 (C.A.), the court per Hughes C.J.N.B. 7. Offset is a business or an accounting term. I do not agree with the Royal Bank that offset means the same as the legal term set-off, which normally refers to an amount

claimed by a defendant as a counter-claim or cross claim against a plaintiff arising out of the same subject matter. *Belliveau v. Royal Bank* (2000), 2000 CarswellNB 74, 14 C.B.R. (4th) 17, 23 C.C.P.B. 113, 3 B.L.R. (3d) 43, 224 N.B.R. (2d) 354, 574 A.P.R. 354 (C.A.), Turnbull, J.A. for the court. See EQUITABLE ~; LEGAL ~; STATUTORY ~.

SET OUT. To ignite in the open.

SETTLE. *v*. 1. " . . . [T]o bring a dispute to an end by arrangement of the parties as opposed to by judgment of a court on the merits [and does not necessarily require a compromise]." *Data General (Canada) Ltd. v. Molnar Systems Group Inc.* (1991), 3 C.P.C. (3d) 180 at 187, 85 D.L.R. (4th) 392, 6 O.R. (3d) 409, 52 O.A.C. 212 (C.A.), the court per Morden J.A. 2. With respect to property, to limit it, or the income from it, to several people in succession, so that any person who possesses or enjoys it does not have power to deprive another of the right to enjoy it in future. 3. With respect to a document, to make it right in substance and in form.

SETTLED ESTATE. Land and all estates or interests in land that are the subject of a settlement.

SETTLEMENT. *n*. 1. An agreement by parties in dispute. 2. "[In Human Rights Code, R.S.O. 1980, c. 340] . . . an agreement by the complainant, or perhaps by the Commission, to take no further steps with respect to the complaint in return for some action by the employer, past or promised, to rectify or make compensation for the injury suffered, or believed to have been suffered, by the the complainant employee because of the alleged contravention of the Code. . ." *Ontario (Human Rights Commission) v. Simpsons-Sears Ltd.* (1982), 133 D.L.R. (3d) 611 at 616, 36 O.R. (2d) 59, 3 C.H.R.R. D/796, 82 C.L.L.C. 17,009 (Div. Ct.), Southey J. (Gray J. concurring). 3. An unincorporated community of persons. 4. " . . . [U]nder the former [Bankruptcy] Act [the meaning] was considered by the Supreme Court of Canada in Re Bozanich; A.H. Boulton Co. v. Trusts & Guar. Co., [1942] S.C.R. 130 . . . [Ont.]. In that case Duff C.J.C. at p. 135 cited with approval the statement that the term 'settlement' implies an intention that the property shall be retained or preserved for the benefit of the donee in such a form that it can be traced. In the same case Rinfret J. at p. 139 approved the statement that to qualify as a settlement the end and purpose of the transaction must be a disposition of property to be held for the enjoyment of some other person. . ." *Profile United Industries Ltd. v. Coopers & Lybrand Ltd.* (1987), (*sub nom. Associated Fisheries of Canada Ltd, Re*) 64 C.B.R. (N.S.) 242 at 247, 79 N.B.R. (2d) 62, 201 A.P.R. 62, 38 D.L.R. (4th) 600 (C.A.), Stratton C.J.N.B. 5. " . . . [A] disposition of property to be held, either in original form or in such form that it can be traced, for the enjoyment of some other person . . ." *Geraci, Re,* [1970] 3 O.R. 49 at 51,14 C.B.R. (N.S.) 253, [1970] I.L.R. 1-343, 12 D.L.R. (3d) 314 (C.A.), the court per Jessup J.A. 6. "[The definition in s. 91(2) of the Bankruptcy Act, R.S.C. 1985, c. B-3] . . . has been extended to include an outright gift to a spouse . . . It has within the last decade been extended even further to include a transaction by which the settlor settles property on himself . . . within the last few years the courts on several occasions have characterized as settlements various transactions prior to bankruptcy by which non-exempt property was replaced by the bankrupt with exempt property. . . A settlement within the scheme of the statute occurs when a disposition of property reduces the bankrupt estate available to the trustee for distribution to creditors." *Royal Bank v. Oliver* (1992), 11 C.B.R. (3d) 82 at 89, [1992] 4 W.W.R. 54, 9 C.C.L.I. (2d) 98, 102 Sask. R. 48 (Q.B.), Baynton J. 7. A statute, deed, agreement, will or other instrument, or any number of such instruments, under or by virtue of which land or any estate or interest in land stands limited to or in trust for any persons by way of succession, including any such instruments affecting the estates of any one or more of such persons exclusively. *Settled Estates Act,* R.S.O. 1990, c. S-7, s. 1. 8. A permanent collectivity of habitations continuously inhabited and used. 9. An amount received in respect of a loss or salary or pension benefits arising from the termination of employment of an employee. 10. " .. . [A] permanent indestructible right to take the benefit of the poor laws in a particular parish or place which maintains its own poor. . . A settlement is the right acquired in any one of the modes pointed out by the poor laws to become a recipient of the benefit of those laws, in that parish or place, which provided for its own poor, where the right has been last acquired. . . It may cease, or be destroyed for ever, in the parish or place where it once existed, upon the acquisition of the same right, or any other new right, in any other such parish or place . . ." *Saint John County Hospital v. Peck,* [1924] 2 D.L.R. 163 at 165, 51 N.B.R. 324 (K.B.), Barry J. 11. " . . . [I]s not defined in general terms by any statute. Its meaning must

be derived from the kind of acts and conduct by which a poor person may acquire or change settlement. It is a concept akin to but different from 'residence' (as used in taxing statutes) or 'domicile'. . . A person who had a settlement in district A did not acquire a new settlement in district B if he had been involuntarily moved to an institution in district B, such as an army camp, a naval base, a mental institution, a hospital, jail or penitentiary, a 'senior citizens' complex . . . or, as here, a 'poor house' in district B jointly operated by districts A and B. The settlement from birth or marriage continues until a new settlement is acquired. . . involuntary presence or 'coerced habitation' cannot change settlement . . ." *Yarmouth (District) v. Argyle (District)* (1979), 108 D.L.R. (3d) 321 at 323, 324, 327, 33 N.S.R. (2d) 598, 57 A.P.R. 598 (C.A.), the court per MacKeigan C.J.N.S. 12. Includes a contract, covenant, transfer, gift and designation of beneficiary in an insurance contract, to the extent that the contract, covenant, transfer, gift or designation is gratuitous or made for merely nominal consideration. *Bankruptcy and Insolvency Act,* R.S.C. 1985, c. B-3, s. 2. See INDIAN ~; MARRIAGE ~; METIS ~; MINUTES OF ~; STRUCTURED ~; VIATICAL ~.

SETTLEMENT AGENCY. An organization that provides assistance to refugees to settle in the Province.

SETTLEMENT COUNCIL. A committee of persons resident in a settlement which the Minister recognizes as a representative body of the settlement for the purposes of this Ordinance. *Regional and Tribal Councils Act,* S.N.W.T. 1983 (2d Sess.), c. 7, s. 2.

SETTLEMENT PRICE. Where used in relation to a commodity futures contract, means the price which is used by a commodity futures exchange or its clearing house to determine, daily, the net gains or losses in the value of open commodity futures contracts. *Commodity Futures acts.*

SETTLEMENT PROVISION. See GRIEVANCE ~.

SETTLER. *n.* 1. A person whose application for a settlement lot has been approved but to whom the grant of the lot has not been issued. *Crown Lands Act,* R.S.N.B. 1973, c. C-38, s. 1. 2. A settler occupying colonization land in accordance with Colonization Land Sales Act (chapter T-8). *An Act Respecting the Sales Price* of *Pulpwood Sold by Farmers and Settlers*, R.S.Q. 1977, c. P-25, s. 1. 3. Any bona fide settler occupying lands under the Public Lands Act or engaged in agricultural pursuits involving the clearing and cultivation of land. *Settlers' Pulpwood Protection Act*, R.S.O. 1980, c. 469, s. 1. 4. Any person coming into Canada with the intention of establishing for the first time a residence in Canada for a period exceeding 12 months. Canada regulations. 5. " . . . [O]ne who migrates to a country, different from that previously inhabited, for the purpose of establishing a permanent residence." *H.E. Wakelin v. The Deputy Minister of National Revenue for Custom & Excise* (1990), 3 T.C.T. 2341 at 2346 (C.I.T.T.), Trudeau (Presiding), Hines and Blouin (Members).

SETTLOR. *n.* 1. A person who creates a trust. 2. Any party named or described in a marriage settlement who agrees or is liable to pay any sum or sums of money mentioned therein, or who in any marriage settlement settles, grants, conveys, transfers, mortgages, or charges, or agrees to settle, grant, convey, transfer, mortgage, or charge, any real or personal property upon or to any person. *Marriage Settlement acts.*

SEVER. *v.* To divide.

SEVERABLE. *adj.* Able to be divided.

SEVERAL. *adj.* 1. Individual, separate; the opposite of "joint". 2. A number of things or persons, more than two. See JOINT AND ~.

SEVERAL COVENANT. A covenant made by two or more people which has the same effect as if each person had signed a separate agreement.

SEVERAL INHERITANCE. An inheritance conveyed so that it descends to more than one person separately or by moieties.

SEVERALLY. *adv.* Individually, separately. See JOINTLY AND ~.

SEVERAL TENANCY. A tenancy which is separate and not held jointly with another person.

SEVERAL TORTFEASORS. Those whose acts occur in the same sequence of events causing the damage but who have not acted in common. They are responsible for the same damage, but not for the same tort. John G. Fleming, *The Law of Torts*, 8th ed. (Sydney: The Law Book Co. Limited, 1992) at 255.

SEVERALTY. *n.* Property belongs to people "in severalty" when each person's share can be distinguished in contrast to joint ownership, coparcency or ownership in common in which owners hold undivided shares.

SEVERANCE. *n.* 1. Separation; severing. 2. A court order for the separate trials of two or more people jointly indicted, done in the interests of justice. S.A. Cohen, *Due Process of Law* (Toronto: Carswell, 1977) at 273. 3. Division of one statute into an invalid and a valid part regarding them as two laws concerning two different "matters" because one assumes that the legislature would have enacted the valid part even if it understood that it could not enact the other. P.W. Hogg, *Constitutional Law of Canada*, 3d ed. (Toronto: Carswell, 1992) at 391. 4. A court recognizes that valid and objectionable parts of a contract are separate and gives effect to the former though it refuses to enforce the latter. G.H.L. Fridman, *The Law of Contract in Canada*, 2d ed. (Toronto: Carswell, 1986) at 399. 5. " . . . [T]o put an end to the joint ownership relationship of property." *Laprise (Crow) v. Crow* (1991), 32 R.F.L. (3d) 82 at 93, 101 N.S.R. (2d) 194, 275 A.P.R. 194 (C.A.), the court per Hallett J.A. 6. " . . . [A] complete separation of the employment relationship. . ." *Max Factor Canada v. U.S.W.A., Local 9050* (1988), 33 L.A.C. (3d) 274 at 276 (Ont.), Simmons. 7. " . . . Severance at law of a joint tenancy, therefore, occurs when one or more of the four unities (title, interest, possession and time) is destroyed, either as a result of the actions of one of the joint tenants or as a consequence of the common intention of the joint tenants." *Walker v. Dubord* (1991), 41 E.T.R. 307 at 313-14 (B.C. S.C.), Callaghan J.

SEVERANCE CLAUSE. The section of a statute which provides that, if any part of that statute is judged to be unconstitutional, the rest will continue to be effective. P.W. Hogg, *Constitutional Law of Canada*, 3d ed. (Toronto: Carswell, 1992) at 392.

SEVERANCE PAY. " . . . [T]he nature and purpose of severance pay is similar to the nature and purpose of common law damages for failure to give reasonable notice of termination of employment. The triggering event is the same, namely, termination of employment. Severance pay cushions economic hardship and provides some compensation for loss of employment . . . this payment is made whether or not the employee gets another job . . ." *Mattocks v. Smith & Stone (1982) Inc.* (1990), 34 C.C.E.L. 273 at 279 (Ont. Gen. Div.), Corbett J.

SEWAGE. *n.* 1. The liquid wastes from residences and other buildings, including industrial establishments, and includes ground, surface and storm water. 2. Includes domestic, commercial and industrial wastes, and, unless from natural run-off, drainage and storm water. See HAULED ~.

SEWAGE DISPOSAL SYSTEM. See PRIVATE ~.

SEWAGE FACILITY. Works operated by a municipality that gather, treat, transport, store, utilize or discharge sewage.

SEWAGE SERVICE. The acceptance, collection, transmission, storage, treatment and disposal of sewage, or any one or more of them. *Ontario Water Resources Act*, R.S.O. 1990, c. O.40, s. 74(1).

SEWAGE SERVICE RATE. A charge for the operation, repair and maintenance of sewage works and includes a charge for depreciation, deferred maintenance or a reserve fund for any such purpose. *Municipal Act*, R.S.O. 1990, c. M.45, s. 221(1).

SEWAGE TANK. A sump that is air tight except for a vent and that receives the discharge of sewage from a sub-drain.

SEWAGE TREATMENT FACILITY. Any structure or device or any part or combination thereof used or intended to be used for the purpose of treating, monitoring or holding, sewage, and includes pumps, buildings, piping, controls, other equipment and their appurtenances. *Clean Environment Act*, S.N.B. 1975, c. 12, s. 1.

SEWAGE TREATMENT PROJECT. A project consisting of a trunk sewage collector system, a central treatment plant or both for the collection and treatment of sewage from one or more municipalities.

SEWAGE WORKS. 1. An integral system consisting of a sewer or sewer system and treatment works. 2. Any public works for the collection, transmission, treatment or disposal of sewage, or any part of any such works. See WATER AND ~.

SEWER. *n.* 1. " . . . [I]ncludes channels constructed underground for carrying off waste . . ." *Hall v. Humboldt (Town)*, [1952] 4 D.L.R. 466 at 469, 7 W.W.R. (N.S.) 11 (Sask. C.A.), Martin C.J.S. (Procter, McNiven and Culliton JJ.A. concurring). 2. A pipe or conduit that carries wastewater or land drainage water, or both. 3. A public sewer for common usage for the purpose of carrying away sewage or land drainage, or both. 4. Includes a common sewer, septic tank and a drain, or a combination of them. 5. Includes a drain of any kind except a drain used for the drainage of a house, building or other premises and made merely for the purpose of connecting with a private sewage disposal system or similar receptacle or with a sewer in a public highway. See BUILDING ~; LAND DRAINAGE ~; MAIN ~; SURFACE ~; WASTEWATER ~.

SEWERAGE PROJECT. A sewer or system of sewers or any plants, structures, equipment, pipes, apparatus or other things for or incidental to the collection, treatment or disposal of sewage.

SEWERAGE SYSTEM. A system of sewers designed to carry any waste except water resulting from rain or snow, and includes a system for the treatment of sewage.

SEWERAGE WORKS. All facilities for collecting, pumping, treating and disposing of sewage.

SEWER RATE. A charge for the capital cost of sewage rates.

SEWER SYSTEM. A system of two or more interconnected sewers having one or more common discharge outlets and includes pumping plant, force mains, siphons and other like works. See TRUNK STORM ~.

SEX. *n.* 1. "Gender, . . ." *Janzen v. Platy Enterprises Ltd.* (1986), 8 C.H.R.R. D/3831 at D/3845, [1987] 1 W.W.R. 385, 33 D.L.R. (4th) 32, 87 C.L.L.C. 17,014, 43 Man. R. (2d) 293 (C.A.), Twaddle J.A. 2. Gender, and, unless otherwise provided in this Act, discrimination on the basis of pregnancy or pregnancy-related illnesses is deemed to be discrimination on the basis of sex. *Saskatchewan Human Rights Code*, S.S. 1979, c. S-24.1, s. 2.

SEX CHROMATIN. A cell-nucleus component present only in females which is used to determine the sex of partial human remains. F.A. Jaffe, *A Guide to Pathological Evidence*, 3d ed. (Toronto: Carswell, 1991) at 215.

SEX DIFFERENTIAL. A variation in rates of wage based on the sex of the worker.

SEX DISCRIMINATION. 1. " . . . [P]ractices or attitudes which have the effect of limiting the conditions of employment of, or the employment opportunities available to, employees on the basis of a characteristic related to gender." *Janzen v. Platy Enterprises Ltd.* (1989), 47 C.R.R. 274 at 295, [1989] 1 S.C.R. 1252, 25 C.C.E.L. 1, [1989] 4 W.W.R. 39, 59 D.L.R. (4th) 352, 10 C.H.R.R. D/6205, 58 Man. R. (2d) 1, 89 C.L.L.C. 17,011, 95 N.R. 81, the court per Dickson C.J.C. 2. " . . . Discrimination on the basis of pregnancy is a form of sex discrimination because of the basic biological fact that only women have the capacity to become pregnant. . ." *Brooks v. Canada Safeway Ltd.* (1989), 10 C.H.R.R. D/6183 at D/6193, 26 C.C.E.L. 1, [1989] 4 W.W.R. 193, 89 C.L.L.C. 17,012, 94 N.R. 373, [1989] 1 S.C.R. 1219, 59 D.L.R. (4th) 321, 58 Man. R. (2d) 161, 45 C.R.R. 115, Dickson C.J.C. (Beetz, McIntyre, Wilson, La Forest and L'Heureux-Dubé JJ. concurring).

SEX HORMONE. Any synthetic or natural product represented as having oestrogenic, androgenic, gonadotrophic or progestational properties and any drug consisting in whole, or in part, of sex gland tissue or any extract thereof.

SEX OFFENCE. An offence under section 151 (sexual interference), 152 (invitation to sexual touching), subsection 153 (1) (sexual exploitation), 155 (1) (incest), 160 (1), (2) or (3) (bestiality), 163.1 (2), (3) or (4) (child pornography), section 170 (parent or guardian procuring sexual activity), subsection 173 (2) (exposure), section 271 (sexual assault), subsection 272 (1) (sexual assault with a weapon, threats to a third party or causing bodily harm) or section 273 (aggravated sexual assault) of the Criminal Code (Canada), an offence under a predecessor or successor to a provision set out above or an offence under a provision of the Criminal Code (Canada) that is prescribed. *Christopher's Law (Sex Offender Registry), 2000*, S.O. 2000, c. 1, s. 1.

SEX OFFENDER REGISTRY. The ministry shall establish and maintain a registry containing the names, dates of birth and addresses of offenders, the sex offences for which, on or after the day section 3 comes into force, they are serving or have served a sentence or of which they have been convicted or found not criminally responsible on account of mental disorder and such additional information as may be prescribed. *Christopher's Law (Sex Offender Registry), 2000*, S.O. 2000, c. 1, s. 2.

SEXUAL. See SERVICES DESIGNED TO APPEAL TO EROTIC OR ~ APPETITES OR INCLINATIONS.

SEXUAL ANNOYANCE. One category of sexual harassment. Sexually-related conduct which is hostile, intimidating or offensive but without any direct link to a tangible job benefit or detriment. Creates an offensive work environment for an employee.

SEXUAL ASSAULT. 1. " . . . [A]n assault within any one of the definitions of that concept in s. 244(1) of the Criminal Code . . . which is committed in circumstances of a sexual nature, such that the sexual integrity of the victim is violated. The test to be applied in determining whether the impugned conduct has the requisite sexual nature is an objective one: 'Viewed in the light of all the circumstances, is the sexual or carnal context of the assault visible to a reasonable observer?' (R. v. Taylor (1985), 19 C.C.C. (3d) 156 . . . per Laycraft C.J.A., at p. 162 C.C.C.). The part of the body touched, the nature of the contact, the situation in which it occurred, the words and gestures accompanying the act, and all other circumstances surrounding the conduct, including threats which may or may not be accompanied by force, will be relevant: . . . The intent or purpose of the person committing the act, to the extent that this may appear from the evidence, may also be a factor in considering whether the conduct is sexual. . ." *R. v. Chase* (1987), 37 C.C.C. (3d) 97 at 103, 59 C.R. (3d) 193, [1987] 2 S.C.R. 293, 80 N.R. 247, 82 N.B.R. (2d) 229, 208 A.P.R. 229, 45 D.L.R. (4th) 98, the court per McIntyre J. 2. The true substance of the offence is the violation of the sexual integrity of the victim, and the test to be applied in determining whether there has been such a violation is an objective one. . . Some assaults are so obviously, objectively sexual that nothing more need to be known than that the acts took place. For example, forced intercourse is so obviously a sexual assault that one cannot imagine any circumstances that would deprive them of their sexual character. *R. v. Muchikekwanape*, 2002 MBCA 78, 166 C.C.C. (3d) 144, 166 Man. R. (2d) 81, 278 W.A.C. 81 (C.A.). See AGGRAVATED ~.

SEXUAL COERCION. One category of sexual harassment. Sexually-related conduct which results in some direct consequence, beneficial or detrimental, to the worker's employment status.

SEXUAL HARASSMENT. 1. Any conduct, comment, gesture or contact of a sexual nature (a) that is likely to cause offence or humiliation to any employee; or (b) that might, on reasonable grounds, be perceived by that employee as placing a condition of sexual nature on employment or on any opportunity for training or promotion.

Canada Labour Code, R.S.C. 1985 (1st Supp.), c. 9, s. 247.1. 2. " . . . [I]n the workplace may be broadly defined as unwelcome conduct of a sexual nature that detrimentally affects the work environment or leads to adverse job-related consequences for the victims of the harassment. It is . . . an abuse of power." *Janzen v. Platy Enterprises Ltd.* (1989), 89 C.L.L.C. 17,011 at 16,072, 47 C.R.R. 274, [1989] 1 S.C.R. 1252, 25 C.C.E.L. 1, [1989] 4 W.W.R. 39, 59 D.L.R. (4th) 352, 10 C.H.R.R. D/6205, 58 Man. R. (2d) 1, 95 N.R. 81, the court per Dickson C.J.C. 3. Two basic categories have been identified: sexual annoyance and sexual coercion. See POISONED ENVIRONMENT ~; QUID PRO QUO ~.

SEXUAL INTERCOURSE. For the purposes of the Criminal Code, sexual intercourse is complete on penetration to even the slightest degree, notwithstanding that seed is not emitted. *Criminal Code*, R.S.C. 1985, c. C-46, s. 4(5).

SEXUALLY HARASS. Engage in vexatious comment or conduct of a sexual nature that is known or ought reasonably to be known to be unwelcome. *An Act to Amend the Human Rights Act*, S.N.B. 1987, c. 26, s. 1.

SEXUALLY TRANSMITTED DISEASE. A disease caused by an infectious agent usually transmitted during sexual contact. *Health Protection and Promotion Act*, R.S.O. 1990, c. H.7, s. 1(1).

SEXUALLY TRANSMITTED DISEASES CLINIC. A clinic operated by a minister or a local board for the purposes of prevention and treatment of sexually transmitted diseases.

SEXUAL OFFENDER. See DANGEROUS ~.

SEXUAL ORIENTATION. "[Denotes] . . . an individual's orientation or preference in terms of sexual relationship to others, whether homosexual or heterosexual or perhaps both . . ." *Leshner v. Ontario* (1992), (*sub nom. Leshner v. Ontario (No. 2)*) 16 C.H.R.R. D/184 at D/196, 92 C.L.L.C. 17,035, C.E.B. & P.R.G. 8133 (Ont. Bd. of Inquiry), Cumming, Dawson and Plaut.

SEXUAL PREFERENCE. An individual's preference for sexual relationship with others, either of opposite sex or of the same sex.

SHAFT. *n.* 1. An excavation at an angle of 45 degrees or greater with the plane of the horizon and used or usable for (a) ventilation or drainage; or (b) the ingress or egress of workers or mate-

rials to or from a mine or a part thereof. 2. A long vertical or slanting passage providing access to a mine and includes a winze. 3. Includes sloe, pit and incline. See SERVICE ~; STEERING ~.

SHAFT CONVEYANCE. A conveyance raised or lowered by a mine hoist in a shaft and includes a bucket, a single or multi-deck cage, a skip or a combination of skip and cage.

SHAFT ROPE. A hoisting, tail, balance, guide or rubbing rope.

SHALE. See BITUMINOUS ~; CLAY~; OIL ~.

SHALL. *v.* 1. Is to be construed as imperative. 2. " . . . Parliament when it used the word 'shall' in s. 23 of the Manitoba Act, 1870, and s. 133 of the Constitution Act, 1867 [(30 & 31 Vict.), c. 3] intended that those sections be construed as mandatory or imperative, in the sense that they must be obeyed, unless such an interpretation of the word 'shall' would be utterly inconsistent with the context in which it has been used and would render the sections irrational or meaningless. . ." *Reference re Language Rights Under s. 23 of Manitoba Act, 1879 and s. 133 of Constitution Act, 1867*, [1985] 1 S.C.R. 721 at 737, [1985] 4 W.W.R. 385, 35 Man. R. (2d) 83, 59 N.R. 321, 19 D.L.R. (4th) 1, Dickson C.J., Beetz, Estey, McIntyre, Lamer, Wilson and Le Dain JJ. 3. Is used to indicate mandatory provisions. 4. Must.

SHALL AND MAY. The expression "shall" is to be construed as imperative and the expression "may" as permissive.

SHALL, MUST, MAY. Whenever it is provided that a thing "shall" be done or "must" be done, the obligation is imperative; but if it is provided that a thin "may" be done its accomplishment is permissive.

SHALLOW FOUNDATION. A foundation unit which derives its support from soil or rock located close to the lowest part of the building which it supports.

SHAM. *n.* 1. " . . . [A] transaction purporting to create apparent legal rights and obligations which are at variance with the legal relationships which in fact characterize the arrangement. . . ' *Jodrey v. Nova Scotia* (1980), (*sub nom. Covert v. Nova Scotia (Minister of Finance)*) 8 E.T.R. 69 at 118, [1980] 2 S.C.R. 774, 41 N.S.R. (2d) 181, 76 A.P.R. 181, [1980] C.T.C. 437, 32 N.R. 275, Dickson J. (dissenting) (Ritchie and McIntyre JJ. concurring). 2. "Acts done or documents executed by the parties to the 'sham' which are intended by them to give to third parties or to the court the appearance of creating between the parties legal rights and obligations different from actual legal rights and obligations (if any) which the parties intend to create." *Snook v. London West Riding Investments Ltd.*, [1967] 1 All E.R. 518 at 528 (U.K. C.A.), Diplock L.J.

SHAM TRANSACTION. " . . . [A] transaction conducted with an element of deceit so as to create an illusion calculated to lead the tax collector away from the taxpayer or the true nature of the transaction; or, simple deception whereby the taxpayer creates a facade of reality quite different from the disguised reality." *Stubart Investments Ltd. v. R.*, [1984] 1 S.C.R. 536 at 545, 53 N.R. 241, [1984] C.T.C. 294, 84 D.T.C. 6305, 10 D.L.R. (4th) 1, Estey J. (Beetz and McIntyre JJ. concurring).

SHARE. *n.* 1. An, integral, separate part of a company's authorized capital. H. Sutherland, D.B. Horsley & J.M. Edmiston, eds., *Fraser's Handbook on Canadian Company Law*, 7th ed. (Toronto: Carswell, 1985) at 107. 2. " . . . [I]s not an isolated piece of property. It is rather, in the well-known phrase, a 'bundle' of interrelated rights and liabilities. A share is not an entity independent of the statutory provisions that govern its possession and exchange. Those provisions make up its constituent elements. They define the very rights and liabilities that constitute the share's existence. The Canada Business Corporations Act [S.C. 1974-75-76, c. 33] defines and governs the right to vote at shareholders' meetings, to receive dividends, to inspect the books and records of the company, and to receive a portion of the corporation's capital upon a winding up of the company, among many others. A 'share' and thus a 'shareholder' are concepts inseparable from the comprehensive bundle of rights and liabilities created by the Act." *Sparling v. Quebec (Caisse de dépôt & de placement)* (1988), 41 B.L.R. 1 at 11, 55 D.L.R. (4th) 63, [1988] 2 S.C.R. 1015, 89 N.R. 120, 20 Q.A.C. 174, the court per La Forest J. 3. " . . . [I]ntangible, incorporeal property rights represented or evidenced by share certificates. They are not in themselves capable of individual identification and isolation from all other shares of the corporation of the same class." *Baud Corp., N.V. v. Brook* (1978), (*sub nom. Asamera Oil Corp. v. Sea Oil & General Corp.*) 5 B.L.R. 225 at 235, [1979] 1 S.C.R. 633, [1978] 6 W.W.R. 301, 23 N.R. 181, 12 A.R. 271, 89 D.L.R. (3d)

1, the court per Estey J. 4. A share carrying voting rights under all circumstances or by reason of the occurrence of an event that has occurred and that is continuing, and includes (a) a security currently convertible into such a share; and (b) currently exercisable options and rights to acquire such a share or such a convertible security. 5. Includes a membership interest or ownership interest in a corporation. See APPROVED ~; CLASS A ~; CLASS B ~; COMMON ~; CO-OP ~; CROP ~ AGREEMENT; CROWN ~; DECLARATION OF ~S; EMPLOYEE ~; EQUITY ~; EQUITY ~S; FLOW-THROUGH ~; INVESTMENT ~; ISSUED ~S; JUST AND EQUITABLE ~; MEMBERSHIP ~; MUTUAL FUND ~; NON-EQUITY ~; OFFEROR'S PRESENTLY-OWNED ~S; OWNER'S ~ OF THE COST; PERMANENT ~S; PLAN ~; PREFERENCE ~; PREFERRED ~; PUBLICLY-TRADED ~S; PURCHASER'S COST OF A ~; REDEEMABLE ~; SPECIAL ~; SUBORDINATE VOTING ~; TRANSFERABLE ~; VOTING ~.

SHARE CAPITAL. See NET ~.

SHARE CERTIFICATE. 1. An instrument certifying that the person named in it (the shareholder) is entitled to a certain number of shares of the corporation. 2. " . . . [I]s not in itself a share or shares of the corporation but only evidence thereof, . . ." *Baud Co. N.V. v. Brook* (1978), (*sub nom. Asamera Oil Co. v. Sea Oil & General Co.*) 5 B.L.R. 225 at 235, [1979] 1 S.C.R. 633, [1978] 6 W.W.R. 301, 23 N.R. 181, 12 A.R. 271, 89 D.L.R. (3d) 1, the court per Estey J. 3. " . . . [I]s in no sense a contractual document and even though it is required to be issued under the corporate seal it is not a deed. The holder's legal right depends not on the certificate but upon entry in the share register. A share certificate is not a negotiable instrument whereas a share warrant or a share purchase warrant is." *Henderson v. Minister of National Revenue*, [1973] C.T.C. 636 at 660, 73 D.T.C. 5471 (Fed. T.D.), Cattanach J.

SHARE CLASS. "The concept of share 'classes' is not technical in nature, but rather is simply the accepted means by which differential treatment of shares is recognized in the articles of incorporation of a company. As Professor Welling . . . succinctly explains, 'a class is simply a sub-group of shares with rights and conditions in common which distinguish them from other shares' . . ." *McClung v. Canada (Minister of*

National Revenue) (1990), 50 B.L.R. 161 at 187, [1991] 1 C.T.C. 169, 119 N.R. 101, 91 D.T.C. 5001, [1991] 2 W.W.R. 244, 76 D.L.R. (4th) 217, 49 F.T.R. 80n, [1990] 3 S.C.R. 1020, Dickson C.J.C. (Sopinka, Gonthier and Cory JJ. concurring).

SHARED MEANING RULE. Where two versions of a bilingual statute appear to express different things, the shared meaning rule for the interpretation of bilingual statutes requires that the meaning that is shared by both versions ought to be adopted: The rule is not absolute, however, and can be rejected if the meaning shared between the two statutory versions is contrary to Parliament's intention or the purpose or objects of the enactment. *Canada 3000 Inc., Re* (2004), 2004 CarswellOnt 149 (C.A.).

SHARED-RISK LOAN GUARANTEE. A guarantee under which, after default by the borrower and before Her Majesty's liability is determined, the lender is required to apply any proceeds obtained from realization of the security in satisfaction of the loan. *Regional Development Incentives Regulations*, C.R.C., c. 1386, s. 25.

SHAREHOLDER. *n.* 1. Someone who holds shares in a company. 2. A subscriber to or holder of stock in a company. 3. A shareholder of a corporation and includes a member of a corporation or other person entitled to receive payment of a dividend or to a share in a distribution on the winding-up of the corporation. 4. " . . . [O]ne who has a proportionate interest in its [a corporation's] assets and is entitled to take part in its control and receive its dividends." *Kootenay Valley Fruit Lands Co., Re* (1911), 18 W.L.R. 145 at 147 (Man. K.B.), MacDonald J. See DISSENTING ~; MAJOR ~; SUBSTANTIAL ~ UNANIMOUS ~ AGREEMENT.

SHAREHOLDER AGREEMENT. See UNANIMOUS ~.

SHAREHOLDER LOAN. See SUBORDINATED ~.

SHAREHOLDERS' EQUITY. The value of the interest of the shareholders in a corporation or the amount for which the company is liable to account to the shareholders. The net worth of a corporation.

SHARE ISSUE. See PUBLIC ~.

SHARE MONEY. The money subscribed for shares.

SHARE OFFERING DOCUMENT. A prospectus, offering memorandum or other material, in a form and containing information, that is delivered to eligible investors in connection with obtaining subscriptions for shares. *Share Ownership Plan Act*, S.N.S. 1992, c. 10, s. 2.

SHARE OWNERSHIP PLAN. See EMPLOYEE ~.

SHARE PURCHASE AGREEMENT. See EMPLOYEE ~.

SHARE PURCHASE WARRANT. " . . . [A] certificate which entitles the bearer on surrender of the certificate, on, after or before dates specified, to purchase from the treasury of the company the number of shares stated in the warrant at the price therein provided." *Henderson v. Minister of National Revenue*, [1973] C.T.C. 636 at 656, 73 D.T.C. 5471 (Fed. T.D.), Cattanach J.

SHARES WITHOUT PAR VALUE. " . . . [O]ne of the purposes served by shares without par value is to allow the directors to fix a consideration for the issue of those shares which reflects the current value of the undertaking . . ." *Muljo v. Sunwest Projects Ltd.* (1991), 2 B.L.R. (2d) 221 at 226, 60 B.C.L.R. (2d) 343, 8 B.C.A.C. 53, 17 W.A.C. 53, the court per Goldie J.A.

SHARE WARRANT. A document under a corporate seal which certifies that its bearer is entitled to shares specified in the document.

SHARING SCHEME. See DEFERRED ~.

SHARK. *n.* Any of several species of fish belonging, to the order Pleurotremata (Squaliformes).

SHEARING INJURY. Distortion of the shape of the surface of an organ or tissue caused by a force acting parallel to it. F.A. Jaffe, *A Guide to Pathological Evidence*, 3d ed. (Toronto: Carswell, 1991) at 221.

SHEATHING. *n.* The vertical members of shoring and timbering that are placed up against, and directly resist, pressure from a wall of a trench. *Occupational Health and Safety Act*, R.R.O. 1980, Reg. 691, s. 167.

SHEEP. *n.* A ram, ewe, wether or lamb.

SHEET METAL WORKER. A person who, (a) manufactures, fabricates, assembles, handles, erects, installs, dismantles, reconditions, adjusts, alters, repairs or services all ferrous and nonferrous sheet metal work of No. 10 U.S. Gauge or of any equivalent or lighter gauge and all other materials used in lieu thereof; and (b) reads and understands shop and field sketches used in fabrication and erection, including those taken from original architectural and engineering drawings or sketches, but does not include a person employed in production commonly known as mass production.

SHELF. See CONTINENTAL ~.

SHELF PROSPECTUS. " . . . [H]as come to connote filings with the Securities and Exchange Commission [whereby] an issuer may register any amount of debt or equity securities that it reasonably expects to sell within a two year period and keep such registered securities 'on the shelf' until market conditions are favourable. Issuers are thus enabled from time to time to price and immediately to sell any amount of the shelf-registered securities." *Securities Act, Re* (1984), 7 O.S.C.B. Jan/Feb 583 at 584, Iacobucci, Miles, Kane and Blain (Commissioners).

SHELL. See RIM-FIRE ~ OR CARTRIDGE.

SHELLEY'S CASE. See RULE IN ~.

SHELL FISH. *var.* **SHELLFISH**. 1. All species of mollusks and crustaceans and cuttings, parts and products of all such. 2. Includes clams, mussels, oysters, scallops and other bivalve molluscs. *Fishery regulations*. 3. Oysters, clams, mussels and other bivalve molluscs except scallops.

SHELL FISH CANNERY. A building, structure, machinery, appurtenances, appliances and apparatus occupied and used in the business of shell fish canning, or of converting the natural shell fish into canned shell fish.

SHELTER. *n.* 1. A building or part of a building that is under the supervision of or approved by a director and that may be used for the temporary care of children. 2. The cost of operating a dwelling place. See ICE ~.

SHELTER DECK SPACE. The space contained between the shelter and freeboard decks. Canada regulations.

SHELTERED WORKSHOP. A place of work operated by a charitable organization employing handicapped workers.

SHELTER EQUIPMENT. Any equipment used for the purpose of camping or dining and includes a tent, trailer, tent-trailer, recreational vehicle, camper-back, dining shelter or other similar equipment.

SHELTERING. See DOCTRINE OF ~.

SHERIFF. *n.* 1. Includes bailiff and any officer charged with the execution of a writ or other process. 2. A sheriff enforces any order of a court arising out of a civil proceeding which is enforceable in Ontario, unless an act provides otherwise (Courts of Justice Act, R.S.O. 1990, c. C.43, s. 141(1)). G.D. Watson & C. Perkins, eds., *Holmested & Watson: Ontario Civil Procedure* (Toronto: Carswell, 1984-) at CJA-249.

SHERIFF'S OFFICER. A bailiff.

SHIELD. *n.* A material barrier interposed in the path of a flow of X-rays and having the effect of reducing the dose or dose-rate experienced by any object located beyond the shield. See METAL ~.

SHIELDING. See SHIELD.

SHIFT. *n.* 1. A number of employees whose hours for beginning and terminating work are the same or approximately the same. 2. " . . . [U]sually refers to a predetermined period of time that would ordinarily constitute a day's work . . ." *Dominion Bridge Co. v. U.S.W.A., Local 3390* (1980), 27 L.A.C. (2d) 399 at 401 (Ont.), Adams (Arbitrator). See FIXED-~; LOBSTER ~; SPLIT ~; SWING ~; WORK ~.

SHIFT DIFFERENTIAL. A premium paid to workers who work on shifts other than during the day.

SHIFT ENGINEER. A person who, under the supervision of the chief engineer, is in immediate personal charge of a boiler or steam plant.

SHIFTING USE. An executory or secondary use, which, when executed, derogates from a preceding estate, e.g. land is conveyed to the use of one person provided that when a second person pays a designated sum of money, the estate will go to a third person.

SHIP. *n.* 1. Includes any description of vessel or boat used or designed for use in navigation without regard to method or lack of propulsion. 2. Every description of vessel, boat or craft designed, used or capable of being used solely or partly for marine navigation, whether self-propelled or not and without regard to the method of propulsion, and includes a sea-plane and a raft or boom of logs or lumber. *Canada Marine Act, 1998*, S. C. 1998, c. 10, s. 2. 3. Includes any description of vessel, boat or craft designed, used or capable of being used solely or partly for marine navigation without regard to method or lack of propulsion. *Oceans Act, 1996*, S.C. 1996, c. 31, s. 2. 4. Includes any description of vessel, boat or craft designed, used or capable of being used solely or partly for marine navigation without regard to method or lack of propulsion, but excludes (a) pleasure yachts of less than twenty metres in length; and (b) any vessel, boat or craft, of any length, propelled manually by oars or paddles. *Canada Shipping Act*, R.S.C. 1985, c. S-9, s. 109(1). 5. Includes the hull, materials and outfit, stores and provisions for the officers and crew, and, in the case of vessels engaged in a special trade, the ordinary fittings requisite for the trade, and also, in the case of a steamship, the machinery, boilers, and coals, oils, and engine stores, if owned by the assured. *Marine Insurance Act*, R.S.O. 1990, c. M.2, Sched., s. 31(15). See AIR~; AMID~S; BRITISH ~; CANADIAN ~; CARGO ~; CARTEL-~; CHARTERED ~; CLASSED ~; CONVENTION ~; CROWN ~; DAY ~; DEAD ~; EXISTING ~; EX ~; FACTORY ~; FISHING ~; FREE ALONGSIDE ~; GOVERNMENT ~; GREAT LAKES ~; HAMPERED ~; HOMETRADE ~S; HOTEL ~; INLAND WATERS ~; LOAD LINE CONVENTION ~; LOAD LINE ~; MINOR WATERS ~; MOTOR ~; NEW ~; NON-CANADIAN ~; NUCLEAR ~; OCEAN ~; PASSENGER ~; SAFETY CONVENTION ~; SAILING ~; SEA GOING ~; SEALING ~; SERVICE ~; UNCLASSED ~.

SHIPMENT. *n.* Includes all goods described in an invoice. See DROP ~; DURING THE COURSE OF ~.

SHIP OR SHIPPING. The overt act of any person leading to the movement, by common carrier or other means of public conveyance, of any livestock or livestock product from or to a point outside the province in which that person carries on business.

SHIPOWNER. *n.* The registered owner of a ship or any share in a ship, and includes the lessee or charterer of any vessel having the control of the navigation thereof. *Inland Water Freight Rates Act*, R.S.C. 1985, c. I-10, s. 2.

SHIPPER. *n.* A person sending or desiring to send goods between points in Canada or who receives or desires to receive goods shipped between points in Canada. See DEALER-~.

SHIPPING BILL. A bill accompanying a shipment of fertilizer or supplement. *Fertilizers Regulations*, C.R.C., c. 666, s. 2.

SHIPPING CASUALTY. What occurs when a ship is abandoned, lost, damaged or stranded or when a ship causes damage or loss to another ship.

SHIPPING COMPANY. Any person who carries or offers, advertises or proposes to carry grain between any ports in Canada or between any ports in Canada and the United States. *Inland Water Freight Rates Act*, R.S.C. 1985, c. I-10, s. 2.

SHIPPING CONFERENCE. An association of ocean carriers that has the purpose or effect of regulating rates, charges and conditions for the transportation by those carriers of goods by water.

SHIPPING CONTAINER. A pressure vessel designed and used for the purpose of transporting a gas, vapour, or liquid from one location to another. See RE-USABLE ~.

SHIPPING DOCUMENT. 1. Any document that accompanies dangerous goods being handled, offered for transport or transported and that describes or contains information relating to the goods and, in particular, but without restricting the generality of the foregoing, includes a bill of lading, cargo manifest, shipping order, way-bill and switching order. *Transportation of Dangerous Goods acts*. 2. The insurance policy with terms current in the particular trade; the invoice or written account of the particular goods delivered, their prices and any credit for freight which the buyer must pay the shipowner on delivery; and the bill of lading. Other documents required by the seller, for custom or a contract, i.e. an export licence, may also be included. G.H.L. Fridman, *Sale of Goods in Canada*, 3d ed. (Toronto: Carswell, 1986) at 480.

SHIPPING LAW. The law relating to the shipment of goods and people.

SHIPPING POINT. A depot, station, siding or any other place on a railway at which grain is loaded by or on behalf of a grain buyer.

SHIPPING SAFETY CONTROL ZONE. An area of the arctic waters prescribed as a shipping safety control zone by an order made under section 11. *Arctic Waters Pollution Prevention Act*, R.S.C. 1985, c. A-12, s. 2.

SHIP'S AMMUNITION. Any article or substance on board a vessel and necessary for the safety or defence of a vessel. Canada regulations.

SHIPS BELONGING TO HER MAJESTY. All ships of war and other unregistered vessels held by or on behalf of Her Majesty in right of any Commonwealth country. *Canada Shipping Act*, R.S.C. 1985, c. S-9, s. 2.

SHIP'S COOK. The chief cook or only cook of a ship.

SHIP'S PAPERS. A ship's registry certificate, charter-party, log, bill of lading, bill of health and any other document which describes the ship and her cargo.

SHIPS STORES. The goods listed in the schedules that are taken on board a ship or aircraft for the operation and maintenance thereof or for sale to the officers, crew or passengers during a voyage or flight. Canada regulations.

SHIP STATION. Any radio station established on board a ship that is not permanently moored. *Canada Shipping Act*, R.S.C. 1985, c. S-9, s. 2.

SHIPWRECKED PERSONS. Includes persons belonging to or on board any British or foreign vessel, wrecked, stranded or in distress, at any place within Canada. *Canada Shipping Act*, R.S.C. 1985, c. S-9, s. 2.

SHOCK. *n*. A condition characterized by pallor, low blood pressure, rapid but shallow pulse and clammy perspiration. See NERVOUS ~; PRIMARY ~; SECONDARY ~.

SHOCK-PROOF. *adj*. Equipment that is guarded with grounded metal so that no person can come into contact with any live part.

SHOCK WAVE. A region ahead of an aircraft of abrupt change of pressure and density moving as a wave front at or above the velocity of sound.

SHOOT. *v*. With respect to a drug, to inject intravenously. F.A. Jaffe, *A Guide to Pathological Evidence*, 3d ed. (Toronto: Carswell, 1991) at 219.

SHOOTING PRESERVE. Land that is privately owned and maintained and on which wildlife that has been raised in captivity is kept in captivity, or released, for the purpose of hunting. See PRIVATE ~; PUBLIC ~.

SHOP. *n*. 1. A place where (a) goods are handled or exposed or offered for sale; or (b) services are offered for sale. 2. The part of premises or place in which or from which a wholesale or retail trade or business is carried on. *Shops' Closing Act*, R.S. Nfld. 1990, c. S-15, s. 2(f). 3. "The broad meaning of 'shop' is: (a) a building appropriated to the selling of wares at retail; and (b) a building in which making or repairing of an article is carried on or in which any industry is pursued; e.g. machine-shop, repair-shop, barber's shop . . ." *Hobbs v. Toronto (City)* (1912), 6 D.L.R. 8 at 9, 4 O.W.N. 31, 23 O.W.R. 8 (H.C.), Boyd C. See BAKE ~; BARBER ~; BUCKET ~; CLOSED ~; OPEN ~; PERSONAL SERVICE ~; SERVICE ~; UNION ~; VETCRAFT ~.

SHOP CARD. By the Shop Card Registration Act of 1938, any design, emblem, figure, sign, seal, stamp, ticket, device or other form of advertisement adopted by a labour union. This statute was repealed by the Trade Marks Act of 1953, section 68. H.G Fox, *The Canadian Law of Trade Marks and Unfair Competition*, 3d ed. (Toronto: Carswell, 1972) at 210.

SHOP CHAIRMAN. A union steward chosen by department stewards to chair all the stewards in a plant and to deal with higher management representatives in respect of grievances.

SHOP INSPECTION. An inspection during construction or fabrication.

SHOPLIFTING. *var*. **SHOP-LIFTING**. *n*. Theft of merchandise.

SHOPPING A BID. Soliciting a bid from a contractor with whom one does not intend to deal and then disclosing that bid or using it to reduce the prices bid by other contractors with whom there is an intention to deal.

SHOPPING CENTRE. 1. A development used or intended to be used for the purposes of retail trade and resulting primarily or tended to result in a total of 50,000 square feet or more of (a) new retail floor space or (b) new and existing retail floor space where the new retail floor space exceeds 10,000 square feet, including common areas and related office and warehouse space but excluding parking areas. *Shopping Centre Development Act*, R.S.N.S. 1989, c. 427, s. 2. 2. A building or complex of buildings, which contains or is intended to contain more than one retail store or outlet for the provision of services, or both, but does not include any building or part of a building which is used or intended to be used as a hotel, motel or restaurant. *Shopping Centres (Development) Act*, S.P.E.I. 1979, c. 17, s. 2.

SHOP STEWARD. An officer of a union, a section or branch of a union who is appointed or elected to represent union members. A main function is to hear a worker's complaint or grievance and to assist the worker in processing the complaint or grievance through the procedures provided.

SHORE. *n.* 1. " . . . [P]roperly applies only to the sea or other tidal waters but when used with reference to a lake unaffected by the tide it means prima facie the land adjacent to the water and in the absence of any bank of high land to mark the boundary, extends to the water's edge. . ." *Merriman v. New Brunswick* (1974), 45 D.L.R. (3d) 464 at 468, 7 N.B.R. (2d) 612 (C.A.), the court per Hughes C.J.N.B. 2. " . . . [T]hat space of land on the border of the sea which is covered and left dry by reason of falling of the tide, or in other words, that space of land between high and low water mark." *Mowat v. North Vancouver (District)* (1902), 9 B.C.R. 205 at 205 (S.C.), Irving J. 3. The lands lying between the ordinary high water mark and the ordinary low water mark of a pond, lake, river or body of water. *Quarriable Substances Act*, R.S.N.B. 1973, c. Q-1, s. 1. 4. Includes any shorebound ice that affords a safe landing area. *Life-saving Equipment Order*, C.R.C., c. 50, s. 2. See SEA ∼.

SHORE AREA. See LAKE ∼; OCEAN ∼.

SHORE INSTALLATION. Structures, appliances or machinery affixed to the ground of a prescribed class or kind used in connection with a primary fishing enterprise, but does not include fishing equipment. *Fisheries Improvements Loan Act*, RS.C. 1985, c. F-22, s. 2.

SHORTAGE. *n.* The amount by which the aggregate of the quantity of grain of any grade discharged from an elevator in a period between two consecutive weigh-overs of grain of that grade in the elevator and the quantity of grain of that grade in storage in the elevator at the end of that period is less than the aggregate of the quantity of grain of that grade in storage in the elevator at the beginning of that period and the quantity of grain of that grade received into the elevator during that period. *Canada Grain Act*, R.S.C. 1985, c. G-10, s. 2.

SHORT ENGAGEMENT. A fixed period of service of a member of the regular force as an officer, other than as a subordinate officer, of such duration shorter than an intermediate engagement as is prescribed by regulation. *Canadian Forces Superannuation Act*, R.S.C. 1985, c. C-17, s. 2.

SHORT INTERNATIONAL VOYAGE. An international voyage in the course of which a ship is not more than 200 nautical miles from a port or place in which the passengers and crew could be placed in safety and which does not exceed 600 nautical miles in length between the last port of call in the country in which the voyage begins and the final port of destination. Canada regulations.

SHORT POSITION. Where used in relation to a commodity futures contract, means to be under an obligation to make delivery.

SHORT-RUN FERRY. A ship that operates in partially smooth waters between terminals that are not more than two miles apart and are in line of sight or nearly in line of sight. Canada regulations.

SHORT TERM SECURITY. A bond, debenture or other evidence of indebtedness maturing within 180 days from the date of acquisition thereof.

SHORT TIME DUTY. A requirement of service that demands operation at a substantially constant load for a short and definitely specified time.

SHORT TITLE. The title by which an act is cited.

SHOT. *n.* 1. An explosive charge that has been placed in a bore hole in a mine. 2. The sound of a charge or charges being exploded. See BUCK ∼; CHILLED ∼; HOT ∼.

SHOT FIRER. *var.* **SHOT-FIRER**. 1. A person who is possessed of a certificate of competency as a mine examiner under this or some former Act and who holds a written appointment from the manager of the mine to fire shots in that mine. *Coal Mines Regulation Act*, R.S.N.S. 1989, c. 73, s. 4. 2. A person who has charge of explosives and their use in an underground mine.

SHOT HOLE. *var.* **SHOTHOLE**. *var.* **SHOT-HOLE**. A hole drilled for firing an explosive charge in seismic operations.

SHOT PELLET. In shotgun ammunition, a pellet of lead or lead alloy. F.A. Jaffe, *A Guide to Pathological Evidence*, 3d ed. (Toronto: Carswell, 1991) at 226.

SHOULD. *v.* 1. " . . . In the context of s. 3(1)(d) [of the Young Offenders Act, S.C. 1980-81-82-83, c. 110], I find the word 'should' denotes simply a 'desire or request' . . . and not a legal obligation. *R. v. S. (S.)* (1990), 49 C.R.R. 79 at

94, 57 C.C.C. (3d) 115, 77 C.R. (3d) 273, 110 N.R. 321, [1990] 2 S.C.R. 254, 41 O.A.C. 81, the court per Dickson C.J.C. 2. Used to indicate recommendatory provisions. Canada regulations.

SHOULDER. *n.* Usually it is that portion of the roadbed that extends beyond the improved or asphalt surface of the roadway. There is no limit as to the width of a shoulder. *Busch Estate v. Lewers* (1999), 1999 CarswellBC 1730 (S.C.).

SHOULDER HARNESS. Any device that is used to restrain the upper torso of a person and that consists of a single diagonal upper torso strap or dual upper torso straps; *Canadian Aviation Regulations* SOR/96-433, s. 101.01.

SHOW. *v.* " . . . [T]o demonstrate, prove or establish, . . ." *American Cyanamid Co. v. Ethicon Inc.* (1975), 22 C.P.R. (2d) 75 at 76 (Fed. T.D.), Addy J.

SHOW. *n.* A type of bet on a race to select a horse to finish first, second or third in the official result. *Pari-Mutuel Betting Supervision Regulations*, SOR/91-365, s. 2. See AIR ~.

SHOW CAUSE. 1. The presentation to a court of reasons why a certain order should not take effect. 2. "In s. 457.5(7)(e) of the Criminal Code [R.S.C. 1970, c. C-34] 'To show cause' means not merely to show that the justice made some error, but to show that the detention is wrong." *R. v. English* (1983), 8 C.C.C. (3d) 487 at 491 (Ont. Co. Ct.), Zaler Co. Ct. J.

SHOW CAUSE ORDER. " . . . [I]s simply the document which initiates the hearing under R. 355(4) [of the Federal Court Rules]. The show cause order is analogous to a summons . . . It is at the subsequent hearing, not in the application for the show cause order, that the contempt ultimately must be proved." *Cutter (Canada) Ltd. v. Baxter Travenol Laboratories of Canada Ltd.* (1984), 3 C.I.P.R. 143 at 152, 1 C.P.R. (3d) 289, 56 N.R. 282 (Fed. C.A.), the court per Urie J.A., quoting Dickson C.J.C. for the Court in *Baxter Travenol Laboratories of Canada Ltd. v. Cutter (Canada) Ltd. (sub nom. Baxter Laboratories of Canada Ltd. v. Cutter (Can.) Ltd.)* (1983), 1 C.I.P.R. 46 at 66, [1983] 2 S.C.R. 388, 36 C.P.C. 305, 75 C.P.R. (2d) 1, [1983] R.D.J. 481, 2 D.L.R. (4th) 621, 50 N.R. 1.

SHOW CAUSE SUMMONS. A document which requires a debtor to appear again in court and show why the debtor should not be jailed for contempt of a payment order.

SHOWING. *adj.* " . . . [D]escribing the use being made of the trade mark . . ." *Aerosol Fillers Inc. v. Plough (Can.) Ltd.* (1980), 53 C.P.R. (2d) 62 at 66, [1981] 1 F.C. 679, 34 N.R. 39 (C.A.), Thurlow C.J.A.

SHOW-UP. *n.* Presentation of one suspect for identification. S.A. Cohen, *Due Process of Law* (Toronto: Carswell, 1977) at 83. See LINE-UP.

SHOW-UP PAY. A minimum number of hours pay paid to an employee required to report to work outside the employee's scheduled work time.

SHRIEVALTY. *n.* The jurisdiction or office of a sheriff.

SHRIMP. *n.* A crustacean of the species Pandalus borealis or Pandalus montagui.

SHRIMP COCKTAIL. Shrimp meat packed with sauce, spices, seasonings or flavourings or any combination thereof.

SHRINKAGE. *n.* 1. A reduction in inventory which cannot be accounted for. 2. The loss in weight of grain that occurs in the handling or treating of grain. *Canada Grain Act*, R.S.C. 1985, c. G-10, s. 2.

SHUNTING. *v.* In trucking, the movement of a trailer from one location to another within the employer's yard.

SHURIKEN. *n.* A hard non-flexible plate having three or more radiating points with one or more sharp edges in the shape of a polygon, trefoil, cross, star, diamond or other geometric shape and designed to be thrown as a weapon.

SHUTDOWN. *n.* " . . . [I]nvolves a complete stoppage of production. . . may be complete as is the case when the whole plant is shut down or partial where production takes place in some departments only . . ." *Colonial Cookies v. U.F.C.W., Local 617P* (1990), 13 L.A.C. (4th) 405 at 408 (Ont.), Foisy.

SHUT-OFF SEINE. Netting that is floated at the top, weighted at the bottom and used to impound fish along the shore. Canada regulations.

SHUTTER. *n.* A mechanism that, in its closed position, intercepts the laser beam and prevents the emission of laser radiation from the demonstration laser. *Radiation Emitting Devices Regulations*, C.R.C., c. 1370, s. 1.

S.I. *abbr.* Statutory instrument.

SI AUTEM SACRAMENTUM FATUUM FUERIT, LICET FALSUM, TAMEN NON

COMITTIT PERJURIUM. [L.] If an oath is foolish, the one who takes it does not commit perjury, even if it is false.

SIB. *n*. Someone related by blood.

SIBLING. *n*. A person who has the same biological mother or biological father as another person. See BIRTH ~.

SIBLING SUCCESSOR. Where used with reference to a deceased means a successor to property of the deceased who is a brother, sister, half-brother or half-sister of the deceased. *Statute Amendments (Taxation) Act*, S.M. 1977, c. 58, s. 16.

SIC. *adv*. [L. so, thus] This word is put in brackets in a quoted passage to show that any mistakes or apparent omissions in the quotation appear also in the original source.

SICK AND FUNERAL BENEFITS. Includes insurance against sickness, disability or death. *Insurance acts*.

SICK LEAVE. Time off allowed for illness or disability.

SICKLE CELL CRISIS. Distortion of red blood cells containing an abnormal form of hemoglobin (hemoglobin S) when oxygen tension falls and small blood vessels throughout the body are blocked. F.A. Jaffe, *A Guide to Pathological Evidence*, 3d ed. (Toronto: Carswell, 1991) at 52.

SICKNESS. *n*. Refers to a person in imperfect health which arose from disease or accident. See DECOMPRESSION ~.

SICKNESS INSURANCE. 1. Insurance by which the insurer undertakes to pay insurance money in the event of sickness of the person or persons insured, but does not include disability insurance. 2. Insurance against loss caused by illness or disability of the person or persons insured, other than that arising from accident, old age or death. *Insurance Act*, R.S.B.C. 1979, c. 200, s.1. 3. (a) Insurance against loss resulting from the illness or disability of a person other than loss resulting from death; (b) insurance whereby an insurer undertakes to pay a certain sum or sums of money in the event of the illness or disability of a person; or (c) insurance against expenses incurred for dental care, other than illness or disability or dental care arising out of an accident. *Classes of Insurance Regulations*, C.R.C., c. 977, s. 34. See GROUP ~.

SICK PAY. An earned benefit which compensates employees who otherwise would lose pay by reason of illness.

SICUT ALIAS. [L. as at another time, or heretofore] The name of a second writ dispatched when the first was not executed. See ALIAS WRIT.

SIC UTERE TUO UT ALIENUM NON LAEDAS. [L. use your own property so as not to injure your neighbour's] " . . . [T]he defendant [landowner] can protect himself in any way he pleases as long as in so doing he does not injure his neighbour who is no party to the nuisance." *Canadian Pacific Railway v. McBryan* (1896), 5 B.C.R. 187 at 208 (C.A.), Drake J.A.

SIC UTI SUO UT NON LAEDAT ALIENUM. [L.] Use your own property so as not to injure your neighbour's. *Graham v. Lister* (1908), 14 B.C.R. 211 at 213 (C.A.), Morrison J.A.

SIDE. *n*. 1. The exposed face of the excavation in a strip mine from the surface of the ground to the working level of the pit. *Coal Mines Regulation Act*, R.S.A. 1970, c. 52, s. 2. 2. A limit of a summer resort location that meets a frontage of the location. *Public Lands Act*, R.R.O. 1980, Reg. 879, s. 1.

SIDE EFFECT. An effect on an organ which was not the primary target of a drug, e.g. bleeding in the stomach caused by aspirin. F.A. Jaffe, *A Guide to Pathological Evidence*, 3d ed. (Toronto: Carswell, 1991) at 81.

SIDELIGHTS. *n*. A green light on the starboard side and a red light on the port side each showing an unbroken light over an arc of the horizon of 112.5 degrees and so fixed as to show the light from right ahead to 22.5 degrees abaft the beam on its respective side. In a vessel of less than 20 metres in length the sidelights may be combined in one lantern carried on the fore and aft centreline of the vessel. *Collision Regulations*, C.R.C., c. 1416, Rule 3.

SIDE LINE. See LAST ASCERTAINABLE ~.

SIDE LOT LINE. Any boundary line of a lot that is not a front lot line or a rear lot line. Canada regulations.

SIDE-MEMBER. One of the members of a tribunal who is not the chair of the panel conducting a hearing. Also referred to as winger.

SIDENOTE. *n*. A marginal note.

SIDE TRAWL. An otter trawl designed for or adapted to hauling fish over the side of a vessel. *Fishery regulations.*

SIDEWALK. *n*. 1. That portion of a highway between the curb lines or the lateral lines of a roadway and the adjacent property lines set apart for the use of pedestrians and includes any part of a highway set apart or marked as being for the exclusive use of pedestrians. 2. Includes a footway and a street crossing.

SIDEWALL. *n*. That portion of a tire between the thread and the bead. Canada regulations.

SIDEWALL SEPARATION. The parting of the rubber compound from the cord in the sidewall. *Motor Vehicle Tire Safety Regulations*, C.R.C., c. 1039, s. 2.

SIDE WHARFAGE. 1. A toll charged on a vessel in respect of the period of time that the vessel is loading, unloading or lying in wait in a canal. 2. The charge against a vessel for the use of berthing space at wharf when not engaged in loading or discharging cargo. *Wharf tariffs.*

SIDE WHARFAGE CHARGES. Charges levied on a vessel loading, unloading or lying in wait in a canal.

SIDE YARD. 1. A yard extending from the front yard to the rear yard of a lot upon which a building or structure is situate and from the side lot line to the part of the building or structure that is nearest to the side lot line. 2. A yard between a main building or main storage area and the side lot line extending from the nearest line of the front yard, or the front lot line where no front yard is required by these Regulations, to the rear yard. Canada regulations.

SIDE YARD WIDTH. The distance measured horizontally from the nearest point of the side lot line toward the nearest part of the main structure on the lot, clear of projections, or the main storage area, as the case may be. Canada regulations.

SIDING. *n*. A track auxiliary to the main track for meeting or passing trains.

S.I.D.S. *abbr*. Sudden infant death syndrome.

SIGHT. See AFTER ~; AT ~.

SIGHTSEEING OPERATION. Aerial work in the course of which passengers are disembarked at the point of departure; *Canadian Aviation Regulations* SOR/96-433, s. 101.01.

SIGIL. *n*. [L.] A signature; a seal.

SIGN. *n*. A publicly displayed notice. *National Parks Signs Regulations* C.R.C., c. 1130, s. 2. See COUNTER-~; FISHING BOUNDARY ~; LUMINOUS ~; NAME ~; OFFICIAL ~; PORTABLE ~; RAILROAD ~ OR SIGNAL; TRAFFIC ~; VITAL ~; YIELD ~.

SIGNAL. *n*. Any sign, writing, image, sound or intelligence of any nature transmitted or emitted as a radiocommunication. *Cable Television Regulations*, C.R.C., c. 374, s. 2. See ALARM ~; APPROACH ~; BLOCK ~; CAB ~; DWARF ~; FIRE ALARM ~; FIXED ~; GRADE ~; IDENTICAL ~S; INTERLOCKING ~; PEDESTRIAN CONTROL ~; RAILROAD SIGN OR ~; STANDARD CODE OF ~S; STATION PROTECTION ~; SUPERVISORY ~; TRAFFIC CONTROL~; TRAIN ORDER ~.

SIGNAL CIRCUIT. Any electrical circuit, other than a communication circuit, which supplies energy to a device which gives a recognizable audible or visible signal, such as circuits for doorbells, buzzers, code-calling systems, signal lights and similar devices.

SIGNAL INDICATION. The information conveyed by a fixed signal or cab signal.

SIGNALLING DEVICE. See FIRE ALARM ~.

SIGNALMAN. *n*. A person who, in an industrial establishment or on a construction project, directs vehicle traffic or watches loads.

SIGNATORY. *n*. A person who signs.

SIGNATURE. *n*. 1. " . . . [T]he name or special mark of a person written with his or her own hand as an authentication of some document or writing . . . It is not essential that a signature be in any particular form, as for example, that it include all the given names as well as the surname of the signatory, or that it be legible. Indeed, in some cases, it may amount to no more than a mark." *R. v. Kapoor* (1989), 52 C.C.C. (3d) 41 at 65, 19 M.V.R. (3d) 41 (Ont. H.C.), Watt J. 2. " . . . [S]tamped impressions have been recognized as valid in connection with certain legal documents. Today's business could not be conducted if stamped signatures were not recognized as legally binding. The affixing of a stamp conveys the intention to be bound by the document so executed just as effectively as the manual writing of a signature by hand . . ." *United Canso Oil & Gas Ltd, Re* (1980), 12 B.L.R. 130 at 136, 41 N.S.R. (2d) 282, 76 A.P.R.

282 (T.D.), Hallett J. 3. A mark or sign impressed on something. 4. The name which one writes oneself. 5. A device whereby the "signer" can confirm to the intended recipient that he or she is advising as to the choice selected. That this is accomplished by the use of electronic passwords does not detract from that advice, but rather enhances it. *Newbridge Networks Corp., Re* (2000), 2000 CarswellOnt 1401, 48 O.R. (3d) 47, 186 D.L.R. (4th) 188, 7 B.L.R. (3d) 136 (S.C.J. [Commercial List]), Farley J. See COUNTER~; GUARANTEE OF ~.

SIGNER. See CO~.

SIGNET. *n*. The seal that, under the existing practice in the United Kingdom, is delivered by Her Majesty the Queen to each of her Principal Secretaries of State in the United Kingdom, and includes the lesser signet or second secretarial seal and the cachet. *Seals Act*, R.S.C. 1985, c. S-6, s. 2.

SIGNIFICANT. *adj*. Noticeable; measurably large.

SIGNIFICANT CHANGE. 1. A change that is not within the control of the offeror or of an affiliate of the offeror shall not be considered to be significant unless it is a material change affecting the affairs of the issuer of securities being offered in exchange for securities of the offeree company and, while an offer is outstanding, the exercise of a right contained in a take-over bid or an issuer bid to modify the terms of the offer or to waive a condition of the offer shall be considered to be a variation which changes the terms of the take-over bid or the issuer bid. 2. A change that could reasonably be expected to affect the safety or effectiveness of a medical device. It includes a change to any of the following: (a) the manufacturing process, facility or equipment; (b) the manufacturing quality control procedures, including the methods, tests or procedures used to control the quality, purity and sterility of the device or of the materials used in its manufacture; (c) the design of the device, including its performance characteristics, principles of operation and specifications of materials, energy source, software or accessories; and (d) the intended use of the device, including any new or extended use, any addition or deletion of a contra-indication for the device and any change to the period used to establish its expiry date. *Medical Devices Regulations* SOR/98-282, s. 1.

SIGNIFICANT DISCOVERY. A discovery indicated by the first well on a geological feature that demonstrates by flow testing the existence of hydrocarbons in that feature and, having regard to geological and engineering factors, suggests the existence of an accumulation of hydrocarbons that has potential for production.

SIGNIFICANT INTEREST. A person has a significant interest in a class of shares of a corporation if the aggregate of (a) any shares of that class beneficially owned by the person, and (b) any shares of that class beneficially owned by entities controlled by the person exceeds 10 per cent of all of the outstanding shares of that class of shares of the corporation.

SIGNIFICANTLY MODIFIED. [As found in s. 2(1) of the Controlled Drugs and Substances Act, S.C. 1996, c. 19] denotes changes in or alterations to the physical characteristics of the real property in question that affect its nature in a greatly important manner. The changes must be more than merely transitory and thus imply an element of permanence that affects the physical characteristics of the property in a consequential manner to a noteworthy and readily apparent degree. *R. v. Gisby*, 2000 ABCA 261, 148 C.C.C. (3d) 549, 271 A.R. 303 (C.A.).

SIGN MANUAL. *var*. **SIGN-MANUAL**. The sovereign's signature. See DOCUMENT UNDER THE ~.

SILENCE. See CONE OF ~; RIGHT TO ~.

SILENT. See RIGHT TO REMAIN ~.

SILENT FILM SUBJECT. A subject not adapted for the reproduction of synchronized dialogue, music or any other sound effects.

SILENT PARTNER. A partner who puts money into a partnership without taking an active part in management.

SILICEOUS DUST. Silica dust or other compounds of silicon, including asbestos.

SILICOSIS. *n*. 1. A characteristic fibrotic condition of the lungs caused by the inhalation of silica. 2. A fibrotic condition of the lungs of a worker (a) caused by dust containing silica; and (b) evidenced by specific x-ray appearances or by the results of other scientific tests or examinations, that has resulted in a substantially lessened capacity for work by the worker.

SILK GOWN. The gown worn by Queen's Counsel; thus "to take silk" means to become a Queen's Counsel.

SILT. *n*. A soil, (a) the particles of which are not visible to the naked eye; (b) dry lumps of which are easily powdered by the fingers; (c) that, after shaking a small saturated pat vigorously in the hand, exhibits a wet shiny surface that disappears rapidly when the pat is subsequently squeezed; and (d) that does not shine when moist and stroked with a knife.

SILVER HAKE. A fish of the species Merluccius bilinearis.

SILVICS. *n*. The life history, characteristics and ecology of stands of forest trees. *Forest Management Act*, R.S.P.E.I. 1988, c. F-14, s. 1(t).

SILVICULTURAL TREATMENT. Treatments designed to control the establishment, composition, structure and growth of forests. *Forestry Act*, R.S. Nfld. 1990, c. F-23, s. 2.

SILVICULTURE. *n*. The science and art of cultivating forest crops and, more particularly, the theory and practice of controlling the establishment, composition, constitution and growth of forests.

SIMILAR. *adj*. 1. " . . . [R]anges in definition from 'sameness' to 'partial resemblance' . . ." *R. v. Fraser* (1987), 48 M.V.R. 119 at 122 (Ont. Dist., Ct.), Clements D.C.J. 2. " . . . [B]earing a resemblance to or possessing some of the characteristics of; it is clear that it does not mean 'the same' or 'identical'." *Ruthenian Sisters of Immaculate Conception v. Saskatoon (City)*, [1937] 2 W.W.R. 625 at 628 (Sask. C.A.), Martin J.A. (Mackenzie J.A. concurring). 3. Obviously, "similar" does not mean "identical." Benefits may be similar in kind while differing in quantum. "Similar" does not refer to the system of law in which the benefits originate, the overall regime under which they are administered or the legal process by which they are claimed. To my mind, the legislature's use of the word "similar" in this context was intended to convey the principle that the benefits in question must be of the same *general* nature or character as the benefits described in Part 6 of the British Columbia *Insurance Act* [R.S.B.C. 1996, c. 231]. *Gurniak v. Nordquist*, 2003 SCC 59. 4. "[In interpreting a phrase referring to a tax 'similar to that imposed for the purpose of the provincial revenue'] . . . The choice ranges from the one extreme of saying that it means 'exactly alike' or 'similar' in the sense of being completely the same, to the other extreme of saying that it would apply wherever there is any quality of likeness at all, . . . the proper way to interpret the expression is to treat it as meaning of the same general nature or character. In this way, I think that we avoid both the extremes to which I have referred, and we ought, I also think, to avoid them, for clearly neither would be proper to adopt." *Barnwell Consolidated School District No. 15 v. Canadian Western Natural Gas & Light, Heat & Power Co.* (1922), 69 D.L.R. 401 at 410, [1922] 3 W.W.R. 300, 18 Alta. L.R. 261 (C.A.), Stuart J.A.

SIMILAR FACT EVIDENCE. Evidence which tends to show propensity, which shows past discreditable conduct. In considering the admissibility of similar fact evidence, the basic rule is that the trial judge must first determine whether the probative value of the evidence outweighs its prejudicial effect. In most cases where similar fact evidence is adduced to prove identity it might be helpful for the trial judge to consider the following suggestions in deciding whether to admit the evidence: (1) Generally where similar fact evidence is adduced to prove identity a high degree of similarity between the acts is required in order to ensure that the similar fact evidence has the requisite probative value of outweighing its prejudicial effect to be admissible. The similarity between the acts may consist of a unique trademark or signature on a series of significant similarities. (2) In assessing the similarity of the acts, the trial judge should only consider the manner in which the acts were committed and not the evidence as to the accused's involvement in each act. (3) There may well be exceptions but as a general rule if there is such a degree of similarity between the acts that it is likely that they were committed by the same person then the similar fact evidence will ordinarily have sufficient probative force to outweigh its prejudicial effect and may be admitted. (4) The jury will then be able to consider all the evidence related to the alleged similar acts in determining the accused's guilt for any one act. Once again these are put forward not as rigid rules but simply as suggestions that may assist trial judges in their approach to similar fact evidence. The test for admissibility of similar fact evidence adduced to prove identity is the same whether the alleged similar acts are definitively attributed to the accused, or are the subject of a multi-count indictment against the accused. *R. v. Arp*, [1998] 3 S.C.R. 339.

SIMILAR FACT EVIDENCE RULE. Evidence of discreditable conduct of the accused which the prosecution tries to introduce is inadmissible except when its probative value outweighs its prejudicial effect.

SIMILAR GOODS. In relation to goods being appraised, means imported goods that (a) closely resemble the goods being appraised in respect of their component materials and characteristics; (b) are capable of performing the same functions as, and of being commercially interchangeable with, the goods being appraised; (c) were produced in the same country as the country in which the goods being appraised were produced; and (d) were produced by or on behalf of the person by or on behalf of whom the goods being appraised were produced, but does not include imported goods where engineering, development work, art work, design work, plans or sketches underaken in Canada were supplied, directly or indirectly, by the purchaser of those imported goods free of charge or at a reduced cost for use in connection with the production and sale for export of those imported goods. *Customs Act*, R.S.C. 1985 (2d Supp.), c. 1, s. 45.

SIMILITER. *adv.* [L.] In a like manner.

SIMPLE. *adj.* " . . . '[U]ncomplicated' . . ." *Phoenix Assurance Co. v. Ownix Developments Ltd.* (1976), 11 O.R. (2d) 292 at 294 (H.C.), Weatherston J.

SIMPLE CONTRACT. A contract not under seal.

SIMPLE PROBABILITY. The standard of proof governing most of a damage assessment which involves valuing chances, possibilities and risks according to the degree of likelihood that events will occur or would have occurred. K.D. Cooper-Stephenson & I.B. Saunders, *Personal Injury Damages in Canada* (Toronto: Carswell, 1981) at 84.

SIMPLE TRUST. A trust in which one person holds property in trust for another and, because the trust is not qualified by the settlor, the law determines its parameters. P.V. Baker and P. St. J. Langan, eds., *Snell's Equity*, 29th ed. (London: Sweet & Maxwell, 1990) at 103. See BARE TRUST.

SIMPLEX COMMENDATIO NON OBLI-GAT. [L.] A simple recommendation of goods does not oblige a buyer. *McRae v. Froont* (1870), 17 Gr. 357 at 358 (U.C. Ch.), Mowat V.C.

SIMPLEX JUSTICIARIUS. [L.] A puisne judge, one who is not chief judge of a court.

SIMPLICITAS EST LEGIBUS AMICA. [L.] Simplicity is a friend of the laws.

SIMPLICITER. *adv.* [L.] Without involving any unnamed thing.

SIMPLICITER ET IPSO FACTO. [L.] Simply, directly and from the fact itself.

SIMPLIFIED PENSION PLAN. A defined contribution plan that is administered by a financial institution on behalf of the employees of the employers who have entered into a contract that complies with subsection 11.1(2). *Pension Benefits Standards Regulations, 1985*, SOR/87-19, s. 2, as am.

SIMULATED MEAT PRODUCT. Any food that does not contain any meat product, poultry product or fish product but that has the appearance of a meat product.

SIMULATED POULTRY PRODUCT. Any food that does not contain any poultry product, meat product or fish product but that has the appearance of a poultry product.

SIMULATION. See IMPACT ~.

SIMUL CUM. [L.] Together with.

SIMULTANEOUS INTERPRETATION. It may be useful to keep in mind the distinction between "consecutive" (after the words are spoken) and "simultaneous" (at the same time as words are spoken). Simultaneous interpretation is a complex and demanding task for which court interpreters, unlike conference interpreters, are seldom trained. Moreover, it requires expensive sound equipment with which our trial courtrooms are rarely equipped. In addition, simultaneous interpretation works best when there is a minimum of distraction both for the interpreter and the listener(s), a feature which will not always be present in our busy courtrooms. *R. v. Tran*, [1994] 2 S.C.R. 951.

SINECURE. *n.* A position which has remuneration with no employment.

SINE DIE. [L. without a day being fixed] Indefinitely.

SINE JURI. [L.] Without a right.

SINE PROLE. [L.] Without progeny.

SINE QUA NON. [L. without which not] An indispensible condition or necessity.

SINE SPE RECUPERANDI. [L.] Without hope of recovery.

SINGEING. *n.* An area of skin burned by hot gases which escaped from the muzzle of a firearm all around the wound where the bullet, fired at close range, entered. F.A. Jaffe, *A Guide to Pathological Evidence*, 3d ed. (Toronto: Carswell, 1991) at 226.

SINGLE. *adj.* Unmarried.

SINGLE AXLE. One or more axles whose centres are included between two parallel transverse vertical planes one metre apart.

SINGLE CHARACTER BRAND. A brand consisting of a single character which includes a bar, dot, 1/4 circle or 1/2 diamond.

SINGLE ENTRY. In bookkeeping, an entry made to credit or to charge a thing or person in contrast to double entry of both the debit and credit account of a single transaction.

SINGLE-FAMILY. *var.* **SINGLE FAMILY.** When used to describe a dwelling means a separate building containing only one dwelling unit.

SINGLE-FAMILY DWELLING. A dwelling unit intended for the use of one family only, that consists of a detached house, one unit of row housing, or one unit of a semi-detached, duplex, triplex or quadruplex house.

SINGLE FAMILY RESIDENCE. (a) A unit or proposed unit under the Condominium Act, or (b) a structure or part of a structure, that is designed for occupation as the residence of one family, including dependants or domestic employees of a member of the family.

SINGLE FAMILY RESIDENTIAL. Real property principally used for residential purposes where there is only one dwelling unit and that unit is not a mobile home.

SINGLE FRONT TOWNSHIP. A township where the usual practice in the original survey was to survey the township boundaries, the proof lines and the base lines, if any, and the concession lines for the fronts of the concessions and to establish the lot corners on the front of each concession. *Surveys Act*, R.S.O. 1990, c. S.30, s. 17(1).

SINGLE HOOP NET. A hoop net having one pot.

SINGLE INSURED BOND. A bond under which a company is the only party insured. Canada regulations.

SINGLE PERSON. 1. An adult person who is a widow, widower, unmarried, deserted, separated or divorced and who is not living with another person as husband or wife. 2. An unmarried adult, a widow, a widower or a separated or divorced person but does not include a person, (a) who is a head of a family; (b) who is an employable person under the age of 21 years living with either of his parents or with a person

in loco parentis; or (c) who is living with another person as husband or wife.

SINGLE-PLANT BARGAINING. Collective bargaining between an employer and a union in respect of only one of the employer's plants.

SINGLE RATE. A pay rate which is the same for all employees in a particular job.

SINGLE RECEPTACLE. One contact device, with no other contact device on the same yoke, installed at an outlet for the connection of one attachment plug.

SINGLE-SERVICE ARTICLE. Any container or eating utensil that is to be used only once in the service or sale of food.

SINGLE-SERVICE TOWEL. A towel that is to be used only once before being discarded or laundered for reuse.

SINGLE-TIER MUNICIPALITY. A municipality that is not an upper-tier municipality and that does not form part of an upper-tier municipality for municipal purposes; Ont. Stats.

SINGLE TRACK. A main track upon which trains are operated in both directions.

SINGLE TRANSACTION. A single incident, occurrence, or offence. Can refer to a series of acts which are successive and cumulative.

SINGLE UNIT VEHICLE. A commercial vehicle used for, (a) the transportation and dumping or spreading of sand, gravel, earth, crushed or uncut rock, slag, rubble, salt, calcium chloride, snow, ice or any mixture thereof, asphalt mixes or scrap metal; (b) the transportation of raw forest products.

SINGLE-USE CONTAINER. A non-reclosable container whose contents are to be used in their entirety immediately after the container is opened.

SINGLE WOMAN. 1. A mother or expectant mother who, at the date of conception, was not married to the father of the child. 2. Includes an unmarried woman, a widow, a divorcee, or a woman deserted by or separated from her husband.

SINGULAR. *adj.* Individual, referring to one.

SINGULI IN SOLIDUM. [L.] Joint and several obligors share liability singuli in solidum.

SINK. *n.* 1. (a) a component of the environment that removes or captures specified gases from the atmosphere through natural processes and includes, without limitation, plants and soil, and (b) a geological formation or any constructed facility, place or thing that is used to store specified gases. *Climate Change And Emissions Management Act*, S.A. 2003, c. 16.7, s. 1. 2. A receptacle for general washing or for receiving liquid waste. *Ontario Water Resources Act*, R.R.O. 1980, Reg. 736, s. 1. See BAR ~.

SINKING FUND. 1. An amount which is set aside annually with interest which if capitalized annually will be great enough at maturity to retire the principal with interest. I.M. Rogers, *The Law of Canadian Municipal Corporations*, 2d ed. (Toronto: Carswell, 1971-) at 654. 2. A special account to which is credited annually an actuarially determined amount for the purpose of providing a fund for future payments.

SINK RIGHT. The legal interest, and any commercial or other interest, in a sink. *Climate Change and Emissions Management Act*, S.A. 2003, c. 16.7, s. 1.

SINUOUS BOUNDARY LINE. Those portions of the boundary along the natural line of watershed that are indicated on the map sheets by a series of broken lines.

SI QUIDEM IN NOMINE, COGNOMINE, PRAENOMINE, LEGATARII TESTATOR ERRAVERIT, CUM DE PERSONA CONSTAT, NIHILOMINUS VALET LEGATUM. [L.] Though the testator may have erred concerning the name or names of the legatee, when it is certain what person was meant, the legacy is still valid.

SI QUID UNIVERSITATI DEBETUR SINGULIS NON DEBETUR NEC QUOD DEBET UNIVERSITAS SINGULI DEBENT. [L.] If something is owed to a group it is not owed to the individual members nor do individual members owe what a group owes.

SI QUIS UNUM PERCUSSERIT, CUM ALIUM PERCUTERE VELLET, IN FELONIA TENETUR. [L.] If someone killed one person meaning to kill another, that person is guilty of felony.

SIRE. See IMPROVED~.

SIR JOHN A. MACDONALD DAY. January 11.

SIR WILFRID LAURIER DAY. November 20.

SISTER. *n.* 1. Includes half-sister. *Criminal Code*, R.S.C. 1985, c. C-46, s. 155(4). 2. Includes sister-in-law. See HALF ~.

SITE. *n.* 1. " . . . [M]ight be used to describe a plot of land much larger than that on which a building actually stands, or again might describe the situation or local position of a building. . ." *Victoria (City) v. Bishop of Vancouver Island* (1921), 59 D.L.R. 399 at 406, [1921] 3 W.W.R. 214, [1921] A.C. 384 (P.C.), the board per Lord Atkinson. 2. An area or a place. 3. A parcel of land. 4. A building or structure. See ABANDONED MOTOR VEHICLE ~; AIRCRAFT ACCIDENT ~; AIRPORT ~; ARCHAEOLOGICAL ~; BATTERY ~; BUILDING ~; BURIAL ~; CONSTRUCTION ~; DISCARD ~; HERITAGE ~; HISTORIC ~; IN SITU OPERATION ~; MILL~; MINE ~; MOBILE HOME ~; MUNICIPAL ~; OIL SANDS ~; POWER ~; PROJECT ~; SCHOOL ~; WELL ~; WORK ~.

SITTER. *n.* A person who is responsible for the safekeeping of a person in his charge and who performs no other services.

SITTING. *n.* "Generally speaking, a sitting of a court [as used in the Criminal Code, R.S.C. 1970, c. C-34, s. 645(4)(c)] is said to refer to time during which judicial business is transacted before the court; in that sense, it could mean a day or, again, different days within a given timespan for transacting that court's business." *R. v. Paul* (1982), 27 C.R. (3d) 193 at 203, [1982] 1 S.C.R. 621, 67 C.C.C. (2d) 97, 138 D.L.R. (3d) 455, 41 N.R. 1, the court per Lamer J.

SITTING DAY. A day on which either House of Parliament is sitting.

SITTING DAY OF PARLIAMENT. A day on which either House of Parliament sits.

SITTINGS. *n.* A term or session of court: the part of the year in which one transacts judicial business.

SITTINGS OR SITTING. A sitting of the court for the trial of civil or criminal cases and includes the hearing of a single trial.

SITUATED. ad : 1. " . . . '[L]ocated'." *Brown v. R.* (1979), 105 D.L.R. (3d) 705 at 713, [1980] 3 W.W.R. 360, 20 B.C.L.R. 64 (C.A.), the court per Bull J.A. 2. " . . . [O]rdinarily implies more than mere temporary presence; it implies some element of permanency; it means something more than merely being temporarily in use or temporarily located at a place . . ." *Anderson v. Canadian Mercantile Insurance Co.* (1965), 51 W.W.R. 129 at 139 (Alta. T.D.), Greschuk J.

SITUS. *n.* [L.] A location; a situation.

SIVE TOTA RES EVINCATUR, SIVE PARS, HABET REGRESSUM EMPTOR IN VENITOREM. [L.] Whether evicted from the whole or part of a thing sold, a buyer has the right to be indemnified by the seller.

SIZE FACTOR. The sum of the section width and the outer diameter of a tire determined on the test rim. Canada regulations.

SKCA. The neutral citation for the Saskatchewan Court of Appeal.

SKELETAL REMAINS. Remains of human bodies situated or discovered outside a recognized cemetery or burial ground in respect of which there is some manner of identifying the persons buried therein.

SKELETON BILL. A bill drawn, accepted or indorsed in blank.

SKETCH. *n*. Includes any mode of representing any place or thing. *Official Secrets Act*, R.S.C. 1985, c. O-5, s. 2.

SKETCH PLAN. An adequately dimensioned drawing of the area affected by a lease of all or part of a building situated on land shown on a plan of survey deposited in the land title office. *Land Title Act*, R.S B.C. 1979, c. 219, s. 1.

SKIDDING. *n*. The operation of moving logs or trees by pulling across the terrain. *Occupational Health and Safety Act*, R.R.O. 1980, Reg. 692, s. 107.

SKIDS. *n*. Small portable platforms upon which goods may be consolidated into individual loads for transportation or storage. *Wharfage Charges By-law*, C.R.C., c. 1066, s. 2.

SKILL. *n*. The degree of expertise one has in carrying out the tasks of a job. See MIXED GAME OF CHANCE AND ~.

SKILLED CARE. See OCCASIONAL ~.

SKILLED LABOUR. Anyone who has mastered a job requiring skill; may refer to office workers or craftspeople.

SKILLED TRADESMAN. A natural person who, as a sole operator, carries on a trade or vocation.

SKIN. *n*. 1. In relation to a wildlife or exotic animal, includes its hide or pelt, with or without the pelage, and, in the case of a bird, includes the plumage. 2. The untanned skin of a fur bearing animal stripped from the body. See UNPRIME ~.

SKIN-DIVING FISHING. Fishing under water, with or without self-contained underwater breathing apparatus.

SKQB. The neutral citation for the Saskatchewan Court of Queen's Bench.

SLAMMER. *n*. Slang for jail.

SLANDER. *n*. Making a defamatory statement orally or in a more transitory form. R.E. Brown, *The Law of Defamation in Canada* (Toronto: Carswell, 1987) at 9.

SLANDER OF GOODS. " . . . [A]n action for slander of goods will lie whenever one maliciously publishes a false statement in disparagement of the goods of another and, thereby, causes the other special damage. The false statement may be in writing or by word of mouth. . ." *Rust Check Canada Inc. v. Young* (1988), 22 C.P.R. (3d) 512 at 529, 530 (Ont. H.C.), Watt J.

SLANDER OF TITLE. Writing, speaking or publishing words which impeach a plaintiff's title to any property, real or personal, which that plaintiff owns. I.H. Jacob, ed., *Bullen and Leake and Jacob's Precedents of Pleadings*, 12th ed. (London: Sweet and Maxwell, 1975) at 544.

SLANDER PER SE. In an action for slander, the exceptions to the requirement of special damages are (1) an oral imputation which disparages the reputation of the plaintiff concerning business, work, calling, office, trade or profession; (2) an accusation which imputes the commission of a criminal offence; (3) words which impute a contagious or loathsome disease; (4) words to a woman which impute unchastity. R.E. Brown, *The Law of Defamation in Canada* (Toronto: Carswell, 1987) at 301.

SLASH. *n*. Includes brush and other forest debris. *Forest Act*, R.S.B.C. 1979, c. 140, s. 108.

SLAUGHTER. *n*. Killing for the purpose of processing into food for human consumption.

SLAUGHTER HOG. Any animal of the swine species which is sold to a packer.

SLAUGHTERHOUSE. *n*. An abattoir to which stock is delivered, or in which stock is held for slaughter. *Livestock Brand Act*, R.S.B.C. 1979, c. 241, s. 1.

SLEEPER BERTH. Sleeping accommodation provided in a motor vehicle.

SLEEPING ACCOMMODATION. Includes a campsite where any facility or service is provided for the supply of water or electricity or for the disposal of garbage or sewage.

SLEEPING ACCOMMODATIONS. Includes (a) a hotel or any other building in which lodgings are provided for rent or hire; (b) any building in which lodgings are offered to members of the public on a gratuitous basis; (c) any building in which an educational institution lodges its students; (d) any building, other than a single family residence, in which a religious organization lodges its members; (e) a hospital, sanatorium, infirmary, nursing home or home for the aged; (f) an orphanage or children's home; (g) a jail, reformatory or other penal institution; or (h) an apartment house with three or more self-contained units above the ground floor. *Fire Prevention Act*, R.S.N.B. 1973, c. F-13, s. 1. See BUILDING USED FOR ~.

SLEEPING PARTNER. See SILENT PARTNER.

SLEIGH DOG. A dog used, or capable of being used, from time to time for the purpose of drawing a sleigh, sled, toboggan, or other vehicle, commonly used for carrying goods or persons, and includes the young of any such dog and any dog being trained for that purpose. *Animal Husbandry Act*, R.S.M. 1987, c. A90, s. 28.

SLIDE. *n.* Stationary picture, slide or similar device used in conjunction with a motion picture machine. See PHOTOGRAPHIC ~.

SLIDE-IN-CAMPER. *n.* A device that is constructed and designed to be temporarily placed and carried within a box of a truck or attached to the box of a truck or the chassis thereof, and is a quipped or furnished with beds, stove or other appliances.

SLIDING SCALE. Rates of wages which change automatically in relation to some factor such as the consumer price index.

SLINK SALMON. Salmon that are in poor condition and that are returning to sea after spawning. *Fishery regulations.*

SLIP. *n.* Contains brief particulars of the risk insured and binds the insurer to issue a policy according to its terms. Raoul Colinvaux, *The Law of Insurance*, 5th ed. (London: Sweet & Maxwell, 1984) at 19.

SLIP RULE. " . . . [M]inor corrections to an order can be made. There is no doubt that a court can correct clerical or mathematical errors and other minor slips or omissions in an order so long as the alterations are confined to expounding its manifest intent . . . and it is equally clear that a similar rule applies to orders of administrative bodies, . . ." *Lodger's International Ltd. v. O'Brien* (1983), 4 C.H.R.R. D/1349 at D/1352, 45 N.B.R. (2d) 342, 118 A.P.R. 243, 83 C.L.L.C. 17,014, 145 D.L.R. (3d) 293 (C.A.), the court per La Forest J.A.

SLIVER. *n.* Fibres in a continuous strand, combed or not, not twisted and not exceeding 12 inches in length, and includes tops. *Customs Tariff*, R.S.C. 1985, c. C-54, s. 2.

SLOPE. *n.* An excavation that is driven in the earth or strata of an underground mine at an angle of less than 45 degrees with the plane of the horizon and that is or may be used, (a) for ventilation or drainage; or (b) for the ingress or egress of people, animals or material to or from the mine or part thereof.

SLOT MACHINE. Any automatic machine or slot machine (a) that is used or intended to be used for any purpose other than vending merchandise or services; or (b) that is used or intended to be used for the purpose of vending merchandise or services if (i) the result of one of any number of operations of the machine is a matter of chance or uncertainty to the operator; (ii) as a result of a given number of successive operations by the operator the machine produces different results; or (iii) on any operation of the machine it discharges or emits a slug or token, but does not include an automatic machine or slot machine that dispenses as prizes only one or more free games on that machine. *Criminal Code*, R.S.C. 1985, c. C-46, s. 198(3).

SLOW-BURNING. *adj.* As applied to conductor insulation means the insulation has flame-retarding properties.

SLOWDOWN. *n.* A concerted refusal by employees to maintain the normal production rate.

S.L.R. *abbr.* Statute Law Revision Act of England.

SLUDGE. *n.* The accumulated wet or dry solids that are separated from wastewater during treatment, including the precipitate resulting from the chemical or biological treatment of wastewater.

SLUG. *n.* For a smooth bore gun, a solid projectile made of lead alloy or lead which has rifling engraved to provide spin and ballistic stability. F.A. Jaffe, *A Guide to Pathological Evidence*, 3d ed. (Toronto: Carswell, 1991) at 226.

SMALL AIRCRAFT. An aeroplane having a maximum permissible take-off weight of 5 700 kg (12,566 pounds) or less, or a helicopter having a maximum permissible take-off weight of 2 730 kg (6,018 pounds) or less; *Canadian Aviation Regulations* SOR/96-433, s. 101.01.

SMALL CLAIMS COURT. An inferior court with a limited jurisdiction over civil matters limited as to monetary jurisdiction and as to subject matter.

SMALL FISHING VESSEL. A fishing vessel to which the *Small Fishing Vessel Inspection Regulations* apply. *Crewing Regulations*, SOR/97-390, s. 1.

SMALL-MESH TRAWL NET. A trawl net having a cod end whose mesh size is less than 2 inches extension measure.

SMALL POWER. A load of less than 50 kilowatts.

SMALL PROVINCE. A province (other than Quebec) having a population greater than its population determined according to the results of the penultimate decennial census and less than 1.5 million. *Constitution Act, 1974*, S.C. 1974-75-76, c. 13 reprinted as R.S.C. 1985, App. Document No. 40.

SMALL UNDERTAKING. (a) A person who provides a taxable service exclusively in a place to which admission is granted to persons for the purpose of the presentation to those persons of a programming service by means of telecommunication on payment of a charge or fee through the sale of a ticket or any similar means of admission; or (b) a person who, in any month, provides a taxable service to not more than 200 persons, but does not include a person who, in any month in the year preceding that month, has provided a taxable service to more than 200 persons. *Excise Tax Act*, R.S.C. 1985 (1st Supp.), c. 15, s. 21.1.

SMALL WATER-POWER. A water-power that, in the opinion of the Director, (a) cannot, under average usable flow conditions, produce in excess of 500 horsepower; and (b) is not of primary importance for commercial or primary public utility purposes. *Dominion Water Power Regulations*, C.R.C., c. 1603, s. 69.

SMALL WOOD. Wood casks or barrels of not greater than 150 gallon capacity. Canada regulations.

SM. & S. *abbr.* Smith & Sager's Drainage Cases (Ont.), 1904-1917.

SMELTER. See SECONDARY LEAD ~.

SMELTER RETURNS. See NET ~.

SMELTING, *n.* The chemical reduction of an ore or concentrate to the metallic state, and includes any process of roasting, melting or chemically treating an ore or concentrate to obtain from it a valuable constituent that is in chemical form different from the form of the valuable constituent in the ore or concentrate before it is processed.

SMOKE. *v.* To consume, hold or otherwise have control over an ignited tobacco product.

SMOKE. *n.* Any solid, liquid, gas or combination thereof produced by the combustion of fuel and includes soot, ash and grit.

SMOKE DETECTOR. A device for sensing the presence of visible or invisible particles produced by combustion, and automatically initiating a signal indicating this condition.

SMOKE-FREE ENVIRONMENT. In respect of an enclosed area, an environment where (a) smoking is not permitted, and (b) concentrations of by-products of tobacco combustion are no higher than those prescribed.

SMOKING. *n.* The act of inhaling or exhaling the smoke of a cigarette, cigar or pipe, and includes having control of a lighted cigarette, cigar, pipe or other equipment used for smoking tobacco.

SMOKING AREA. See DESIGNATED ~.

SMOKING ROOM. See DESIGNATED ~.

SMOTHERING. *n.* Suffocation caused by blocking the mouth and nostrils. F.A. Jaffe, *A Guide to Pathological Evidence*, 3d ed. (Toronto: Carswell, 1991) at 226.

SMUDGING. *n.* An area of blackening which powder gases produce around the wound where a bullet fired at close range entered. F.A. Jaffe, *A Guide to Pathological Evidence*, 3d ed. (Toronto: Carswell, 1991) at 226.

SMUGGLING. *n.* The offence of exporting or importing forbidden or restricted goods, or of exporting or importing goods without paying any duties imposed on them.

SNAG. *n.* 1. A dead or dying tree. 2. Any material or object that may interfere with the safe movement of a tree or log or that may endanger a person or any equipment. *Occupational Health and Safety Act*, R.R.O. 1980, Reg. 692, s. 107.

SNAGGER. *n*. An instrument made of a rigid or semi-rigid material with one or more hooks attached in such a manner that each is immovable and inflexible.

SNAGGING. *n*. Fishing for or killing fish by means of a hook or hooks on any instrument manipulated in such a manner as to pierce or hook a fish elsewhere than in the mouth. *Fishery regulations.*

SNARE. *n*. 1. A device for the taking of animals whereby they are caught in a noose. 2. Any instrument used for taking or attempting to take fish, other than a trolling line, hook and line, hook and line and a rod, hook line, dip net, gill net, hoop net, minnow trap, pound net, seine net, spear, trap net or trawl net.

SNARING. *n*. The placing of one or more snares in locations where wildlife are likely to be caught in a noose.

SNEAKWARE. *n*. Software embedded within other software and used by advertisers to monitor an internet user's surfing habits for marketing or demographic research purposes.

SNOW CRAB. A decapod crustacean of the species Chionoeceted opilio.

SNOW CRAB TRAP. A metal or wood framed enclosure covered with netting and with one or more openings.

SNOWMOBILE. *n*. 1. A motor vehicle equipped with either a single or dual-tread and skis. 2. A vehicle that (a) is not equipped with wheels, but in place thereof is equipped with tractor treads alone or with tractor treads and skis, or with skis and a propeller, or is a toboggan equipped with tractor treads or a propeller; and (b) is designed primarily for operating over snow, and is used exclusively for that purpose. See COMPETITION ~.

SNOWMOBILE CONVERSION VEHICLE. A vehicle designed to be capable of conversion to a snowmobile by the repositioning or addition of parts. *Motor Vehicle Safety Regulations*, C.R.C., c. 1038, s. 2.

SNOWMOBILE CUTTER. A sleigh designed to be drawn behind a snowmobile. *Motor Vehicle Safety Regulations*, C.R.C., c. 1038, s. 2.

SNOWMOBILE TRAILER. A trailer primarily designed for the transportation of snowmobiles or snowmobile cutters. *Motor Vehicle Safety Regulations*, C.R.C., c. 1038, s. 2.

SNOW VEHICLE. 1. A motor vehicle desired or intended to be driven exclusively or chiefly upon snow or ice or both, and includes motor vehicles known to the trade as snowmobiles. 2. A vehicle that (a) is not equipped with wheels, but in place thereof is equipped with tractor treads alone or with tractor treads with skis, or with skis and a propeller, or is a toboggan equipped with tractor treads or a propeller; (b) is designed primarily for operating over snow, and is used exclusively for that purpose; and (c) is designed to be self-propelled. See MOTORIZED ~.

SOAR. Society of Ontario Adjudicators and Regulators.

SOC. *abbr*. Society.

SOCAGE. *n*. A kind of tenure with certain temporal services which originally were agricultural. Common free socage is equivalent to freehold tenure.

SOCAN. The society of composers, authors and music publishers of Canada.

SOCIAL ASSISTANCE. 1. Aid in any form to or in respect of a person in need. 2. Any benefit in the form of money, goods or services provided to or on behalf of a person by a province under a program of social assistance, including a program of social assistance designated by a province to provide for basic requirements including food, shelter, clothing, fuel, utilities, household supplies, personal requirements and health care not provided by public health care, including dental care and eye care.

SOCIAL INSURANCE NUMBER. A Social Insurance Number assigned to an individual under the authority of any Act of Parliament. *Canada Pension Plan*, R.S.C. 1985, c. C-8, s. 2.

SOCIAL INSURANCE NUMBER CARD. A Social Insurance Number Card issued to an individual under the authority of any Act of Parliament. *Canada Pension Plan*, R.S.C. 1985, c. C-8, s. 2.

SOCIAL OCCASION. A social gathering at which food, suitable to the occasion and of such quantity and kind as is required by the commission, is served.

SOCIAL PROGRAMS. Includes programs in respect of health, post-secondary education, social assistance and social services, including early childhood development.

SOCIAL SCIENCE BRIEF. A brief in which empirical data is appended to or included in the factum.

SOCIAL SCIENCES AND HUMANITIES RESEARCH COUNCIL OF CANADA. The federal body which promotes and assists scholarship and research in the humanities and social sciences.

SOCIAL SERVICES. Services having as their objects the lessening, removal or prevention of the causes and effects of poverty, child neglect or dependence on social allowance or assistance, and, without limiting the generality of the foregoing, includes (a) rehabilitation services; (b) case work, counselling; assessment and referral services; (c) adoption services; (d) homemaker, day care and similar services; (e) community development services; (f) consulting, research and evaluation services with respect to social service programs; and (g) administrative, secretarial and clerical services, including staff training, relating to the provision of any of the foregoing services or the provision of assistance. See COMMUNITY ~.

SOCIAL WORK. Service that is performed, for remuneration or in a continual way and without immediate supervision, to aid clients to understand and resolve personal, family or social problems, in ways which, in the judgment of the Board as supported by common opinion among social-work educators, authorities and practitioners, require expert and comprehensive knowledge, skills, judgment and ethical conduct of a distinctly professional nature as provided for in education at a university school of social work. *Social Work Act*, R.S.P.E.I. 1988, c. S-5, s. 1.

SOCIÉTÉ COMMERCIALE CANADIENNE. One of the phrases or words which must form part, other than simply in a descriptive or figurative sense, of the name of a corporation.

SOCIETY. *n.* 1. Includes a society or club that is incorporated by an act of a legislature and that has for its object the provision of facilities for the social intercourse and recreation of its members. 2. A religious society, organization or order or a charitable or philanthropic organization. 3. In British Columbia, a society may be incorporated for any lawful purpose or purposes such as national, patriotic, religious, philanthropic, charitable, provident, scientific, fraternal, benevolent, artistic, educational, social, professional, agricultural, sporting or other useful purposes.

Carrying on a business, trade, industry or profession as an incident to the purposes of a society is not prohibited by this section, but a society must not distribute any gain, profit or dividend or otherwise dispose of its assets to a member of the society without receiving full and valuable consideration except during winding up or on dissolution and then only as permitted. See AGRICULTURAL ~; CHILDREN'S AID ~; CLASSIFICATION ~; EXTRAPROVINCIAL ~; FILM ~; FRATERNAL OR SORORAL BENEFIT ~; FRATERNAL ~; FREE AND DEMOCRATIC ~; FREE ~; FRIENDLY ~; HUMANE ~; LOAN ~; MUTUAL BENEFIT ~; NON-PROFIT ~; PERFORMING RIGHTS ~; RELIGIOUS ~.

SOCII MEI SOCIUS MEUS SOCIUS NON EST. [L.] A partner of my partner is not my partner.

SOCKET. *n.* A hole or part of a hole remaining after being loaded with explosives and the charge fired and which is known not to be a misfired hole, and includes so-called "bootlegs" and "old bottoms".

SOCKEYE SALMON. The species of fish known as Oncorhynchus nerka. *Pacific Salmon Fisheries Convention Act*, R.S.C. 1985, c. F-20, s. 2.

SODOMY. *n.* Anal intercourse.

SODRAC. Société du droit de reproduction des auteurs, compositeurs et éditeurs au Canada.

SOFT DRINK. Aerated water to which an essence or syrup is added.

SOFT DRUG. An example is marijuana. *R. v. Randall* (1983), 7 C.C.C. (3d) 363 at 376, 58 N.S.R. (2d) 234, 123 A.P.R. 234, 1 D.L.R. (4th) 722 (C.A.), the court per MacKeigan C.J.N.S.

SOFT RECEIVERSHIP. Reviewing cash flow, assets and accounts payable and reporting so that the security holder may specify particular measures that should be taken to reduce the loan. F. Bennett, *Receiverships* (Toronto: Carswell, 1985) at 4.

SOFT SERVICE. ". . . [P]eople-related ('soft') services [include] libraries and recreation facilities . . ." *Mod-Aire Homes Ltd. v. Bradford (Town) (No. 2)* (1990), 25 O.M.B.R. 12 at 23, 72 O.R. (2d) 683, 49 M.P.L.R. 206 (Div. Ct.), Sutherland J.

SOFT-SHELLED CRAB. A snow crab that has no calcareous growths on the upper surface of the shell and the shell of which is easily bent by thumb pressure on the underside of the claw without breaking.

SOFT TOY. Includes a stuffed toy, a pliable rubber toy and a pliable plastic toy. *Hazardous Products (Toys) Regulations*, C.R.C., c . 931, s. 2.

SOFTWARE. The computer programs which give specific instructions to a computer and permit a user to perform a specific set of tasks or activities. See COMPUTER ~; GEO-IDENTI-FICATION ~; SYSTEMS ~.

SOFTWOOD LUMBER. A product of a sawmill or sawmill and planing mill derived from a log from a tree of coniferous species (order Coniferae) by length-wise sawing that, in its original sawed condition, has at least two approximately parallel flat longitudinal sawed surfaces, and may be rough, dressed or worked. *Softwood Lumber Products Export Charge Act*, S.C. 1987, c. 15, Sched., Part 1, s. 1.

SOIL. *n*. 1. That portion of the earth's crust which is fragmentary, or such that some individual particles of a dried sample may be readily separated by agitation in water; it includes boulders, cobbles, sand, silt, clay and organic matter. 2. Includes the entire mantle of unconsolidated material above bedrock other than minerals. 3. Any land or underground space not submerged in water, excluding an area of land covered by a structure.

SOIL CONDITIONING. See ORGANIC ~.

SOIL MOVEMENT. Subsidence, expansion or lateral movement of the soil not caused by flood, earthquake, act of God or any other cause beyond the reasonable control of the builder.

SOIL STACK. A stack that conveys the discharge of one or more sanitary units with or without the discharge from any other fixture.

SOIL SUPPLEMENT. (a) Any substance or mixture of substances other than a fertilizer, manufactured, sold or represented for use in promoting plant growth or the improvement of the chemical or physical condition of soils to aid growth or crop yields; and (b) includes manipulated manures, sewage sludges, composts or soil conditioners; but (c) does not include unmanipulated animal or vegetable manures, or potting soils or peat soils.

SOIT DROIT FAIT AL PARTIE. [Fr.] Let right be done to a party.

SOJOURN. *v*. 1. "[Applies] . . . to presence in Canada where the nature of the stay is either outside the range of residence or is what is commonly understood as temporary residence or residence for a temporary purpose." *Thomson v. Minister of National Revenue*, [1946] 1 D.L.R. 689 at 704, [1946] S.C.R. 209, [1946] C.T.C. 51, Rand J..2. "One 'sojourns' at a place where he unusually, casually or intermittently visits or stays." *Thomson v. Minister of National Revenue*, [1946] 1 D.L.R. 689 at 707, [1946] S.C.R. 209, [1946] C.T.C. 51, Estey J.

SOLATIUM. *n*. [L. solace] The amount paid to an injured party over and above the actual damage to assuage wounded feelings or for suffering or the loss of pleasure derived from the company of a deceased relative.

SOLATIUM DOLORIS. [L.] A type of moral prejudice that is compensable in Quebec civil law. Compensation for the grief and distress felt when someone close to us dies. *Augustus v. Gosset*, [1996] 3 S.C.R. 268.

SOLDERED. *adj*. A uniting of metallic surfaces by the fusion thereon of a metallic alloy, usually of lead and tin. *Power Corporation Act*, R.R.O. 1980, Reg. 794, s. 0.

SOLDIER. *n*. Any person who served during World War I in (a) the Canadian Expeditionary Force; (b) any of the other military forces of His Majesty; or (c) the military forces of one of the countries allied with His Majesty during World War I if, in the case of a person who served in other than the Canadian Expeditionary Force, that person was born or domiciled in Canada or Newfoundland or was an ordinary resident in Canada or Newfoundland at anytime during the period between August 3, 1904 and the date on which he commenced so to serve. *Memorial Cross Order (World War I)*, C.R.C., c. 1622, s. 2.

SOLE. *adj*. Single; alone; not married. Can be interpreted as principal or real. See CORPO-RATION ~; FEME ~.

SOLE CUSTODY. Custody of a child by one parent only under an agreement or order.

SOLELY. *adv*. One and only; exclusively.

SOLEMN ADMISSION. A plea of guilty when one is arraigned in court. P.K. McWilliams, *Canadian Criminal Evidence*, 3d ed. (Aurora: Canada Law Book, 1988) at 14-7.

SOLEMN DECLARATION. A solemn declaration in the form and manner from time to time provided by the provincial evidence acts or by the Canada Evidence Act. A declaration made knowing that it has the same force and effect as if made under oath or affirmation.

SOLEMNIZATION. *n.* Entering into marriage publicly before witnesses.

SOLEMNIZATION OF MARRIAGE. " . . . Not confined to the ceremony itself. It legitimately includes the various steps or preliminaries leading to it." *Albert (Attorney General) v. Underwood*, [1934] S.C.R. 635 at 639, [1934] 4 D.L.R. 167, the court per Rinfret J.

SOLE PROPRIETORSHIP. An unincorporated business organization having one owner who must and does make all major decisions concerning the business.

SOLE RIGHTS. The right to produce or reproduce a work or a substantial part of it in any way whatever.

SOLE TENANT. One who holds land personally, without any other person.

SOLICIT. *v.* 1. " . . . [T]o endeavour to obtain by asking . . ." *Burns v. Chiropractic Assn. (Alberta)* (1981), 31 A.R. 176 at 177, 16 Alta. L.R. (2d) 128, 125 D.L.R. (3d) 475 (C.A.), the court per Clement J.A. 2. In [s. 195.1 of the Criminal Code, R.S.C. 1970, c. C-34] includes an element of persistence or pressure. It was decided that the mere demonstration by a woman of her willingness and availability for prostitution would not suffice to ground a conviction. In addition, the Crown would be required to prove that her approach to a prospective customer was accompanied by pressure or persistent conduct. . ." *Hutt v. R.* (1978), 38 C.C.C. (2d) 418 at 422-3, [1978] 2 S.C.R. 476, 1 C.R. (3d) 164, [1978] 2 W.W.R. 247, 19 N.R. 330, 82 D.L.R. (3d) 95, Spence J. (Laskin C.J., Dickson, Martland and Estey JJ. concurring). See SOLICITATION.

SOLICITATION. *n.* (a) A request for a proxy whether or not it is accompanied by or included in a form of proxy; (b) a request to execute or not to execute a form of proxy or to revoke a proxy; (c) the sending of a form of proxy or other communication to a security holder under circumstances reasonably calculated to result in the procurement, withholding or revocation of a proxy of that security holder; or (d) the sending, along with a notice of a meeting, of a form of proxy to a security holder by management of a reporting issuer, but does not include (e) the sending of a form of proxy to a security holder

in response to an unsolicited request made by the security holder or on that person's behalf; or (f) the performance by any person of ministerial acts or professional services on behalf of a person soliciting a proxy.

SOLICITATION OF DEPOSITS. An advertisement calculated directly or indirectly to lead to or induce the deposit of money or the investment of money on deposit by members of the public. *Deposits Regulation acts.*

SOLICITING. *n.* Accosting in a persistent manner for purposes of prostitution.

SOLICITING AGENT. An agent of an insurer who submits applications to the insurer for acceptance or rejection but who has no power to bind the company.

SOLICITOR. *n.* 1. In the Province of Quebec, an advocate or a notary and, in any other province, a barrister or solicitor. *Criminal Code*, 1985, c. C-46, s. 183. 2. When used alone, refers to one who does not appear in court regularly but does any of the other work of being a lawyer. 3. "In some jurisdictions there is a distinction between a barrister or counsel and a solicitor. The kind of work which may be undertaken or performed by each is clearly defined. The business of a barrister is advocacy, drafting pleadings and advising on questions of law, while the solicitor interviews clients, takes instructions and prepares the necessary material in the litigation, which is submitted to counsel who will appear at the trial. In those jurisdictions where the distinction exists solicitors do not appear in court." *Griffen v. Spanier*, [1947] 1 W.W.R. 489 at 491 (Sask. C.A.), McNiven J.A. See BARRISTER AND ~; CHANGE OF ~.

SOLICITOR-AND-CLIENT COSTS. 1. These represent all disbursements, charges and fees, taxable by the solicitor against his client as necessary for the proper presentation of the proceeding in respect of which the costs are awarded, but limited to the four corners of that proceeding. *Holloway v. Holloway*, 2001 NFCA 17, 199 Nfld. & P.E.I.R. 1, 600 A.P.R. 1, 6 C.P.C. (5th) 34, [2001] N.J. No. 61, 2001 CarswellNfld 65 (C.A.). 2. "The underlying purpose of an award of costs on the basis of those between solicitor and client is to provide complete indemnification for all costs, including fees and disbursements, reasonably incurred in the course of defending or prosecuting the action but excluding the costs for extra services not reasonably necessary." *Scott Paper Co. v. Min-*

nesota Mining & Manufacturing Co. (1982), 70 C.P.R. (2d) 68 at *79* (Fed. T.D.) Cattanach J.

SOLICITOR AND HIS OWN CLIENT COSTS. "[Allowing the costs which would] . . . provide complete indemnity to her [the client] as to the costs essential to, and . . . 'arising within, the four corners of litigation.'" *Seitz, Re* (1974), 6 O.R. (2d) 460 at 465, 53 D.L.R. (3d) 223 (H.C.), Lerner J.

SOLICITOR AND OWN CLIENT COSTS. These will usually be the same as solicitor and client costs, but where circumstances justify, there will be added any further disbursements, charges or fees that may arise out of the equities as between the solicitor and the client, except such as would result from unreasonableness on the part of the solicitor. *Holloway v. Holloway,* 2001 NFCA 17, 199 Nfld. & P.E.I.R. 1, 600 A.P.R. 1, 6 C.P.C. (5th) 34, [2001] N.J. No. 61, 2001 CarswellNfld 65 (C.A.).

SOLICITOR-CLIENT PRIVILEGE. 1. " . . . [A]n evidentiary rule, invented by Judges in pursuance of public policy, to protect a client against compulsory testimonial disclosure by himself or by his legal advisor in legal proceedings." *Herman v. Canada (Deputy Attorney General)* (1979), 13 C.P.C. 363 at 368, 26 O.R. (2d) 520, 103 D.L.R. (3d) 491, 79 D.T.C. 5372 (C.A.), Lacourcière J.A. (Weatherston J.A. concurring). 2. " . . . [T]he privilege belongs to the client alone. One consequence of this is that confidential communications between solicitor and client can only be divulged in certain circumscribed situations. The client may . . . herself choose to disclose the contents of her communications with her legal representative and thereby waive the privilege. Or, the client may authorize the solicitor to reveal those communications for her. So important is the privilege that the courts have also stipulated that the confidentiality of communications between solicitor and client survives the death of the client and enures to his or her next of kin, heirs or successors in title." *Goodman Estate v. Geffen* (1991), 42 E.T.R. 97 at 125-6, [1991] 5 W.W.R. 389, 80 Alta. L.R. (2d) 293, 125 A.R. 81, 14 W.A.C. 81, 81 D.L.R. (4th) 211, [1991] 2 S.C.R. 353, Wilson J. (Cory J. concurring). 3. Two distinct branches of solicitor and client privilege: the litigation privilege and the legal advice privilege. The litigation privilege protects from disclosure all communications between a solicitor and client, or third parties, which are made in the course of preparation for any existing or contemplated litiga-

tion. The legal advice privilege protects all communications, written or oral, between a solicitor and a client that are directly related to the seeking, formulating or giving of legal advice; it is not necessary that the communication specifically request or offer advice, as long as it can be placed within the continuum of communication in which the solicitor tenders advice; it is not confined to telling the client the law and it includes advice as to what should be done in the relevant legal context. The principles relating to solicitor and client privilege apply in both civil and criminal cases, and they apply regardless of whether the solicitor is in private practice or is a salaried or government solicitor. *Buffalo v. Canada,* (sub nom. *Samson Indian Nation & Band v. Canada*) [1995] 2 F.C. 762 (C.A.). 4. The right, if any, that a person has in a superior court in the province where the matter arises to refuse to disclose an oral or documentary communication on the ground that the communication is one passing between him and his lawyer in professional confidence, except that in certain cases an accounting record of lawyer, including any supporting voucher or cheque, shall be deemed not to be such a communication. *Income Tax acts.* See DOMINANT PURPOSE TEST; LEGAL PROFESSIONAL PRIVILEGE.

SOLICITOR GENERAL CANADA. The federal ministry which controls penitentiaries, paroles and remissions and law enforcement and supervises the National Parole Board, the Correctional Service and the RCMP.

SOLICITOR OF RECORD. The lawyer who is shown on pleadings or other documents filed in a court proceeding as being the lawyer who is acting for a particular party.

SOLICITOR'S J. *abbr.* Solicitor's Journal (Le Bulletin des avocats).

SOLICITOR'S LIEN. A lien which is passive and possessory, the right of a solicitor to continue holding possession of documents or other personal property of the solicitor's client or former client until the solicitor's fees are paid.

SOLID RUBBER TIRE. A tire made of rubber other than a pneumatic tire.

SOLIDS LINE. A pipe for the transmission of a normally solid material whether in suspension or other form and includes installation in connection with that pipe, but does not include a gas line, oil line, fluids line, multiphase line, secondary line, flow line, distribution line or sewer line.

SOLID TIRE. Every tire of rubber or other resilient material that does not depend upon compressed air for the support of the load.

SOLID WASTE. Waste with insufficient liquid content to be free-flowing.

SOLITARY CONFINEMENT. Individual confinement separate from other prisoners, usually an additional punishment or for the protection of the individual or the prison population as a whole.

SOLUM. *n*. The soil or land lying under tidal water and extending seaward from mean high water mark and includes the foreshore.

SOLUM ARBITRIUM ET JUS ET POTESTAS CREANDI. [L.] The sole power, jurisdiction and capacity to create.

SOLUS AGREEMENT. An agreement that one will obtain supplies from one supplier only.

SOLUTIO PRETII EMPTIONIS LOCO HABETUR. [L.] The payment of the price takes the place of purchase.

SOLUTION MINING. Extraction of salt from a geological formation by the injection of water and the recovery of the salt in solution through a well. *Oil, Gas and Salt Resources Act*, R.S.O. 1990, c. P-12, s. 1.

SOLVENCY VALUATION. A valuation of the assets and liabilities of a plan using actuarial assumptions and methods that are in accordance with accepted actuarial practice for the valuation of a plan, determined on the basis that the plan is terminated. *Pension Benefits Standards Regulations, 1985*, SOR/87-19, s. 2, as am.

SOLVENDA IN FUTURO. [L.] To be paid in the future.

SOLVENDO ESSE. [L.] To be solvent.

SOLVENT. *adj*. Having the ability to pay debts as they become due.

SOLVERE POENAS. [L.] To be subject to the punishment specified for an offence.

SOLVIT AD DIEM. [L.] In an action on a bill or bond, a plea that the defendant paid money on the day it was due.

SOLVIT ANTE DIEM. [L.] In an action on a bill or bond, a plea that the defendant paid money before the day it was due.

SOLVIT POST DIEM. [L.] In an action on a bill or bond, a plea that the defendant paid money after the day it was due.

SOLVITUR IN MODUM SOLVENTIS. [L.] Money should be applied the way the payor wishes.

SOMATIC. *adj*. Organic, physical.

SOMATIC DEATH. The first stage of death in which the respiratory, circulatory and nervous systems stop functioning and the body is no longer an integrated organism. F.A. Jaffe, *A Guide to Pathological Evidence*, 3d ed. (Toronto: Carswell, 1991) at 3.

SOMATOFORM DISORDER. A condition in which the patient's physical symptoms suggest a physical disorder but where there are no objective findings of that disorder. The presumption is that the symptoms are linked to non-physical factors, psychological or otherwise.

SON. *n*. A male child.

SONG BIRD. Canary, finch, oriole, cardinal and any other songster.

SONIC FLIGHT. Flight at the speed of a true flight Mach number of one. *Sonic and Supersonic Fright Order*, C.R.C., c. 64, s. 2.

SORORAL BENEFIT SOCIETY. See FRATERNAL OR ~.

SOUND. *v*. To have the basic quality of damages, said of actions brought to recover damages.

SOUND. *n*. See DOCUMENT OF RECORDED ~.

SOUND. *adj*. Free from defects. See ACTUARIALLY ~.

SOUND FILM SUBJECT. A subject adapted for the reproduction of synchronized dialogue, music or any other sound effects.

SOUND IN DAMAGES. See SOUND.

SOUND LEVEL. The intensity of sound expressed in decibels.

SOUND LEVEL METER. A device for measuring sound pressure level that meets the performance requirements for a Type 2 instrument as specified in the International Electrotechnical Commission Standard 651 (1979), *Sound Level Meters*, as amended from time to time. *Canada Occupational Health and Safety Regulations*, SOR/86-304, s. 7.1.

SOUND RECORDING. A recording, fixed in any material form, consisting of sounds, whether or not of a performance of a work, but excludes any soundtrack of a cinematographic work where it accompanies the cinematographic work. *Copyright Act*, R.S.C. 1985, c. C-42, s. 2.

SOUND RECORDING MACHINE. *var.* **SOUND-RECORDING MACHINE**. A device, machine or system that faithfully records speech or other sounds in some permanent form.

SOUP. *n.* A solution of narcotic ready to be injected. F.A. Jaffe, *A Guide to Pathological Evidence*, 3d ed. (Toronto: Carswell, 1991) at 226.

SOURCE. See GAS ~; HEAT ~; INDUS-TRIAL ~; RADIATION ~; REVENUE ~; STATIONARY ~; X-RAY ~.

SOURCE CODE. 1. Both "application" and "operating system" programs can be expressed in what is known as "source code" or in "object code". Most programs are essentially created in "source code" and converted into "object code". "Object code" is more difficult to read or understand by a programmer, because it is a series of 0's and 1's and, to a layman at least, could be described as the language of a computer. *Apple Computer Inc. v. Macintosh Computers Inc.* (1985), 3 C.I.P.R. 133, 3 C.P.R. (3d) 34 (Fed. T.D.) Cullen J. 2. Since the computer only responds to machine language, a computer programme written in another language must be translated. The language in which the programme is written is called the source code and the language into which it is translated is called the object code. Object code in many instances, and in the jurisprudence, I notice, is used as synonymous with machine language and I will adopt that usage. *IBM Corp. v. Ordinateurs Spirales Inc./Spirales Computers Inc.* (1984), 27 B.L.R. 190, 80 C.P.R. (2d) 187, 2 C.I.P.R. 56, 12 D.L.R. (4th) 351 (Fed. T.D.), Reed J. 3. Source code consists of algorithms and looks like lines of text. Source code can be defined as the exact sequence of commands used to instruct a microprocessor on how to execute an algorithm. The source code is in a format that can be read by a computer programmer and consists of names and logical operations represented utilizing the symbols entered on standard, compatible computer keyboard. *Teklogix Inc. v. Zaino* (1997), 79 C.P.R. (3d) 1 (Ont. Gen. Div.).

SOURCE OF CONTAMINANT. Anything that adds to, emits or discharges into the natural environment any contaminant.

SOURCE OF CONTAMINATION. Any activity or condition causing the emission of a contaminant into the environment.

SOURCE OF PROTEIN. Any food that contains protein, but does not include spices, seasonings, flavours, artificial flavours, flavour enhancers, food additives and similar foods that contain only small amounts of protein. *Food and Drug Regulations*, C.R.C., c. 870, c. B.01.101.

SOUR GAS PROCESSING PLANT. A plant that processes raw gas and separates and removes sulphur compounds from the raw gas stream.

SOUVENIR. *n.* A memento of an occasion or place.

SOVEREIGN. *n.* 1. Any supreme or chief person. 2. The Sovereign of the United Kingdom, Canada and Her or His other realms and territories and head of the Commonwealth. See ACCESSION OF THE ~.

SOVEREIGN ACT. A sovereign act is an act done by a sovereign body acting in accordance with its sovereign privileges. *Miller c. R.*, [2001] 1 S.C.R. 407, Bastarache, J. for the court.

SOVEREIGN GOVERNMENT. Includes the Government of Canada, the government of each of the provinces and territories of Canada, and the government of every foreign country or state.

SOVEREIGN IMMUNITY. 1. Canadian courts will not exercise jurisdiction over the property or person of an independent foreign state or sovereign without consent. Any such proceedings may be stayed if the state or sovereign moves to set the proceedings aside or remains passive. A foreign state includes any state which the forum recognizes, de facto or de jure. J.G. McLeod, *The Conflict of Laws* (Calgary: Carswell, 1983) at 68. 2. " . . . [T]he doctrine of absolute sovereign immunity. . . [was] stated by Lord Denning M.R., in Trendtex Trading Corp. v. Central Bank of Nigeria [1977] 1 Q.B. 529 (C.A.) at page 559. Lord Denning said: 'The doctrine grants immunity to a foreign government or its department of state, or any body which can be regarded as an "alter ego or organ" of the government.'" *Ferranti-Packard Ltd. v. Cushman Rentals Ltd.* (1980) 19 C.P.C. 132 at 133, 30 O.R. (2d) 194, 115 D.L.R. (3d) 691 (Div. Ct.), the court per Reid J. See RESTRICTIVE ~.

SOVEREIGN POWER. The power in a state which is supreme.

SOVEREIGNTY-ASSOCIATION. *n.* A compromise proposed in Quebec between outright separation and continuance as a province of Canada. Although it involved the secession of Quebec (sovereignty), it also involved economic association between Quebec and the rest of Canada (association). P.W. Hogg, *Constitutional Law of Canada*, 3d ed. (Toronto: Carswell, 1992) at 125.

S.P. *abbr.* Sessions of the Peace.

SPACE. *n.* A plot of land within a tourist camp, trailer camp or mobile home park designated to accommodate, or accommodating, one camping facility, trailer or mobile home, as the case may be. *Municipalities Act*, R.S.N.B. 1973, c. M-22, s.188. See ACCOMMODATION ~; ANNULAR ~; CONFINED ~; FLOOR ~; HEAD ~; HORIZONTAL SERVICE ~; LOADING ~; MACHINERY ~; MOBILE HOME ~; OCCUPANT ~; PARKING ~; PASSENGER ~; RETAIL ~; ROOF ~; SERVICE ~; SHELTER DECK ~; TOILET ~; TWEEN DECK ~.

SPACE FLIGHT. The period that begins with the launching of a crew member of the Space Station, continues during their stay in orbit and ends with their landing on earth. *Criminal Code*, R.S.C. 1985, c. C-46, s. 7, as am.

SPACE FRAME. A three-dimensional structural system composed of inter-connected members laterally supported so as to function as a complete self-contained unit with or without horizontal diaphragms.

SPACE HEATER. A space-heating appliance for heating the room or space within which it is located, without the use of ducts.

SPACE-HEATING APPLIANCE. An appliance intended for the supplying of heat to a room or space directly, such as a space heater, fireplace or unit heater, or to rooms or spaces of a building through a heating system stem such as a central furnace or boiler.

SPACE STATION. 1. The civil international Space Station that is a multi-use facility in low-earth orbit, with flight elements and dedicated ground elements provided by, or on behalf of, the Partner States. *Criminal Code*, R.S.C. 1985, c. C-46, s. 7, as am. 2. A radio station where radio apparatus that is used for any radiocommunication service is installed in a place located outside the major portion of the earth's atmosphere or is intended to travel beyond the major portion of the earth's atmosphere. *Radiocommunications Regulations*, SOR/96-484.

SPACING AREA. The drainage area required for or allocated to a well for drilling for and

producing petroleum or natural gas, and includes at all depths the subsurface areas bounded by the vertical planes in which the surface boundaries lie.

SPACING UNIT. The area allocated to a well for the purpose of drilling for or producing oil or gas. See POOLED ~; PRODUCTION ~.

SPAM. E-mail messages soliciting purchases of products or services by persons who have not expressed interest in or solicited information concerning the products or services offered.

SPAM FILTER. An electronic automated process that is established by an Internet service provider to analyze incoming messages and that maintains the confidentiality of, and does not reveal to the provider or any person, the content of any message; and rates every incoming message to determine whether it is likely to be spam.

SPANKING. *n.* All social science witnesses accepted a definition of spanking as "the administering of one or two mild to moderate 'smacks' with an open hand, on the buttocks or extremities which does not cause physical harm." Spanking [as defined here] is not child abuse. *Canadian Foundation for Children, Youth & the Law v. Canada (Attorney General)* (2000), 2000 CarswellOnt 2409, 146 C.C.C. (3d) 362, 188 D.L.R. (4th) 718, 49 O.R. (3d) 662, 36 C.R. (5th) 334, 76 C.R.R. (2d) 251 (S.C.J.) for additional discussion *Canadian Foundation for Children, Youth & the Law v. Canada (Attorney General)*, 2004 SCC 4.

SPARKING. See OPEN ~.

SPARSIM. *adv.* [L.] Here and there.

SPEAKER. *n.* 1. With respect to the House of Commons, the representative of the House itself in power, proceedings and dignity; the representative of the House in relation to the Crown, the Senate and other people and authorities outside Parliament; the person who presides over debates and enforces observance of any rule for preserving order. This person is elected by the House itself and, on behalf of the House, controls the accommodation and services in the part of the Parliament Buildings and its precincts which the House of Commons occupies. A. Fraser, W.A. Dawson, & J. Holtby, eds., *Beauchesne's Rules and Forms of the House of Commons of Canada*, 6th ed. (Toronto: Carswell, 1989) at 33 and 47. 2. The speaker of the House of Commons, and, when the office of Speaker is vacant, or when the Speaker is absent from Canada or is unable to act, means the Clerk of the House of Commons or any other officer for the time being performing the duties of the Clerk of the House of Commons. 3. The Speaker of the House of Assembly. 4. The Speaker of the Legislative Assembly. 5. The Speaker of the assembly; and when the office of Speaker is vacant or when the Speaker is absent from the province, or is unable to act, the clerk of the assembly, or any other officer for the time being discharging the duties of the clerk of the assembly. See DEPUTY ~.

SPEAKER'S RULING. Once given, a ruling under standing order 10 must be accepted without appeal or debate. Whether private or public, it becomes a precedent which guides public, officers, members and speakers. A. Fraser, W.A. Dawson, & J. Holtby, eds., *Beauchesne's Rules and Forms of the House of Commons of Canada*, 6th ed. (Toronto: Carswell, 1989) at 50 and 6.

SPEAR. *n.* 1. A lance with barbed or unbarbed prongs that is held or thrown by hand, but does not include a spear gun. 2. An apparatus equipped with one or more points that is capable of catching fish by piercing or impaling them.

SPEAR FISHING. Fishing with a spear propelled by spring, elastic band, compressed air, bow or hand.

SPECIAL. *adj.* 1. Usually means of a peculiar, not general kind. *Wood v. Wood*, 2001 SKCA 2, 13 R.F.L. (5th) 216, 203 Sask. R. 82, 240 W.A.C. 82 (C.A. [In Chambers]). 2. Unusual, uncommon, exceptional.

SPECIAL ACT. A local, personal or private act; an act which applies to a certain kind of person or thing only.

SPECIAL AGENT. One authorized to transact only a particular business for the principal, as opposed to a general agent.

SPECIAL ASSESSMENT. A special frontage assessment or a special local benefit assessment relating to local improvements and includes a special assessment when calculated on a uniform unit rate.

SPECIAL AUTHORIZATION. A special authorization granted for a limited period under this Code to a person who does not hold a permit, to allow him the exclusive practice of the profession mentioned therein and the use of a title reserved to the professionals practising such profession or to allow him only the use of a title reserved to the members of the corporation granting this authorization. *Professional Code*, R.S.Q. 1977, c. C-26, s. 1.

SPECIAL AVIATION EVENT. An air show, a low level air race, an aerobatic competition, a fly-in or a balloon festival. *Canadian Aviation Regulations*, SOR/96-433, s. 101.01.

SPECIAL BINNING. The storing of a parcel or parcels of grain pursuant to a contract, in space in an elevator that is specified in the contract, for the purpose of preserving the identity of the grain. *Canada Grain Act*, R.S.C. 1985, c. G-10, s. 2.

SPECIAL CASE. The statement of a question of law for the opinion of the court by all parties to a proceeding, and which any party applies to have the judge determine.

SPECIAL COMMITTEE. A body the House appoints to inquire into a specified subject. When its final report is presented it ceases to exist. A. Fraser, W.A. Dawson, & J. Holtby, eds., *Beauchesne's Rules and Forms of the House of Commons of Canada*, 6th ed. (Toronto: Carswell, 1989) at 222.

SPECIAL CONSTABLE. A person specially engaged and employed by the Royal Canadian Mounted Police under the authority of the Governor in Council for the particular duty of mounting guard at vulnerable points throughout Canada or for any other similar duty during the War. *Civilian War-related Benefits Act*, R.S.C. 1985, c. C-31, s. 22.

SPECIAL COSTS. 1. " . . . [M]ore or less the old solicitor-and-client costs as described in the 1989 Rules [British Columbia Rules of Court]: . . ." *Bradshaw Construction Ltd. v. Bank of Nova* Scotia (1991), 48 C.P.C. (2d) 74 at 89, 54 B.C.L.R. (2d) 309 (S.C.), Bouck J. 2. The purpose of special costs is to punish a litigant or counsel for misconduct during litigation and deter further misconduct. It is well established that special costs may be ordered for reprehensible conduct falling short of scandal or outrage. Misconduct deserving of reproof or rebuke is "reprehensible". *Chances Housing Cooperative v. Progressive Homes Ltd.*, 2000 CarswellBC 744, 2000 BCSC 596, 46 C.P.C. (4th) 334 (S.C. [In Chambers]).

SPECIAL DAMAGE. 1. Pecuniary loss before the trial. K.D. Cooper-Stephenson & I.B. Saunders, *Personal Injury Damages in Canada* (Toronto: Carswell, 1981) at 29 and 43. 2. Loss of earnings or profits before a trial and pre-trial expenses. K.D. Cooper-Stephenson & I.B. Saunders, *Personal Injury Damages in Canada* (Toronto: Carswell, 1981) at 51. 3. " . . . A private person can bring an action for an alleged or anticipated breach of the law only where that breach would constitute a breach of his private rights or would inflict 'special' or 'peculiar' damage upon him: . . . The common thread which runs through the authorities is that private citizens cannot maintain actions for public nuisance where the suffering and inconvenience complained of is shared by the public or a recognizable class of the public. The ultimate question is simple: is the damage suffered by the plaintiff different from that suffered by other members of the community?" *Stein v. Gonzales* (1984), 31 C.C.L.T. 19 at 22, 58 B.C.L.R. 110, [1984] 6 W.W.R. 428, 14 D.L.R. (4th) 283 (S.C.), McLachlin J.

SPECIAL DAMAGES. " . . . [S]uch as the law will not infer from the nature of the act." *Graham v. Saville*, [1945] 2 D.L.R. 489 at 492, [1945] O.R. 301 (C.A.), Laidlaw J.A. (dissenting in part).

SPECIAL EDUCATION PROGRAM. An education program that is based on the results of continuous assessment and evaluation and which includes a plan containing specific objectives and recommendations for education services that meet the needs of the exceptional pupil.

SPECIAL ENUMERATION. An enumeration of electors within an electoral division other than as part of a general enumeration. *Election Act*, R.S.A. 1980, c. E-2, s. 1.

SPECIAL EXAMINER. An official examiner.

SPECIAL FORCE. Such component of the Canadian Forces as may be established. In an emergency, or if considered desirable in consequence of any action undertaken by Canada under the United Nations Charter, the North Atlantic Treaty or any other similar instrument for collective defence entered into by Canada, the Governor in Council may establish and authorize the maintenance of a component of the Canadian Forces, called the special force, consisting of (a) officers and non-commissioned members of the regular force who are placed in the special force under conditions prescribed in regulations; (b) officers and non-commissioned members of the reserve force who, being on active service or having applied and been accepted for continuing, full-time military service, are placed in the special force under conditions prescribed in regulations; and (c) officers and non-commissioned members not of the regular force or the reserve force who are enrolled in the special force for continuing, full-time military service. The maximum numbers of officers and non-commissioned members in the special force shall be as authorized by the Governor in Council, and the special force shall include such units and other elements as are embodied therein. *National Defence Act*, R.S.C. 1985, c. N-5, s. 2 and 16.

SPECIAL FRANCHISE. Every right, authority or permission, whether exclusive or otherwise, to construct, maintain or operate, within a municipality, in, under, above, on, through, or across any highway, road, street, lane, public place or public water within the jurisdiction of the municipality any poles, wires, pipes, tracks, conduits, buildings, erections, structures or other things for the purpose of bridges, railways, bus lines or other transportation systems or for the purpose of conducting steam, heat, water, natural gas or electricity or any property, substance or product capable of being transported, transmitted or conveyed for the supply of water, heat, light, power, transportation, telegraphic, telephonic or other services.

SPECIAL FUND. A fund set up for a specified purpose and accounted for in a self-balancing financial statement.

SPECIAL HOLIDAY. A day for which an employee is entitled under any act, under any custom or agreement or under a contract of service to be paid wages without being present at work.

SPECIALIA GENERALIBUS DEROGANT. [L.] Special words restrict general ones.

SPECIAL INTEREST. A pecuniary or propriatary interest including physical injury or the risk of injury.

SPECIALIST. *n.* 1. A physician listed by the Royal College of Physicians and Surgeons of Canada as having specialist qualifications. 2. A dentist whose name is entered in the specialists' register. 3. A certified general accountant whose name is entered in the specialists register and who is the holder of a specialists licence. 4. A medical practitioner who is recognized as a specialist by the medical licensing authority of the province in which the practitioner is authorized to practise medicine. *Marihuana Medical Access Regulations* SOR/2001-227, s. 1.

SPECIALIZATION AGREEMENT. An agreement under which each party thereto agrees to discontinue producing an article or service that he is engaged in producing at the time the agreement is entered into on the condition that each other party to the agreement agrees to discontinue producing an article or service that he is engaged in producing at the time the agreement is entered into, and includes any such agreement under which the parties also agree to buy exclusively from each other the articles or services that are the subject of the agreement. *Competition Act*, R.S.C. 1985 (2d Supp.), c. 19, s. 85.

SPECIALLY ASSESSED. Specially charged with part or all of the cost of a work. *Local Improvements acts*.

SPECIALLY CONSTRUCTED VEHICLE. A vehicle which was not originally constructed under a distinctive name, make, model or type by a generally recognized manufacturer of vehicles.

SPECIALLY DENATURED ALCOHOL. Alcohol in suitable admixture with such special denaturants as have been approved by the Minister. *Excise Act*, R.S.C. 1985, c. E-14, s. 243.

SPECIAL MOBILE EQUIPMENT. Every vehicle not designed or used primarily for the transportation of persons or property and incidentally operated or moved over any highway, including road construction or maintenance machinery, ditch digging apparatus, well-boring apparatus, concrete mixers and any other vehicle of the same general class.

SPECIAL MOBILE MACHINE. A vehicle: (a) that is not designed or used for the transportation of passengers or goods and that only uses a highway incidentally to its basic purposes; (b) that is designed and used exclusively for moving earth or construction materials on locations off highways or for general construction or industrial purposes and that only uses a highway incidentally to its basic purposes; or (c) used for the purpose of highway construction and maintenance; but does not include a dumptruck or a truck mounted transit mixer or any other similar mounted machine.

SPECIAL NEED. A need that is related to or caused by a behavioural, developmental, emotional, physical, mental or other handicap. *Child and Family Services Act*, R.S.O. 1990, c. C.11, s. 26.

SPECIAL NEEDS HOUSING. A unit that is occupied by or is made available for occupancy by a household having one or more individuals who require accessibility modifications or provincially-funded support services in order to live independently in the community.

SPECIAL OPERATIONAL INFORMATION. Information that the Government of Canada is taking measures to safeguard that reveals, or from which may be inferred, (a) the identity of a person, agency, group, body or entity that is or is intended to be, has been approached to be, or has offered or agreed to be, a confidential source of information, intelligence or assistance to the Government of Canada; (b) the nature or content of plans of the Government of Canada for military operations in respect of a potential, imminent or present armed conflict; (c) the means that the Government of Canada used, uses or intends to use, or is capable of using, to covertly collect or obtain, or to decipher, assess, analyse, process, handle, report, communicate or otherwise deal with information or intelligence, including any vulnerabilities or limitations of those means; (d) whether a place, person, agency, group, body or entity was, is or is intended to be the object of a covert investigation, or a covert collection of information or intelligence, by the Government of Canada; (e) the identity of any person who is, has been or is intended to be covertly engaged in an information- or intelligence-collection activity or program of the Government of Canada that is covert in nature; (f) the means that the Government of Canada used, uses or intends to use, or is capable of using, to protect or exploit any information or intelligence referred to in any of paragraphs (a) to (e), including, but not limited to, encryption and cryptographic systems, and any vulnerabilities or limitations of those means; or (g) information or intelligence similar in nature to information or intelligence referred to in any of paragraphs (a) to (f) that is in relation to, or received from, a foreign entity or terrorist group. *Security of Information Act*, (was *Official Secrets Act*) R.S.C. 1985, c. O-5, s. 8.

SPECIAL ORDER. An order for a copy of a book that a bookseller or a retailer other than a bookseller does not have in stock and that the bookseller or retailer orders at the request of a customer. *Book Importation Regulations*, SOR/ 99-324, s. 1.

SPECIAL PASSENGER TRADE. A trade in relation to which the Governor in Council has modified the construction regulations or the rules for life-saving appliances in pursuance of this Act. *Canada Shipping Act*, R.S.C. 1985, c. S-9, s. 2.

SPECIAL POWER. The power to appoint from a limited class only, e.g. from among the children of the donee of the power. R. Megarry and H.W.R. Wade, *The Law of Real Property*, 5th ed. (London: Stevens, 1984) at 491.

SPECIAL PROPERTY. Limited or qualified property.

SPECIAL PURCHASER. A person willing to pay more than the fair market value for a given asset because the asset has some special value to that person.

SPECIAL RESOLUTION. A resolution passed by a majority of not less than two-thirds or three-quarters, or other percentage specified by governing legislation, of the votes cast by the shareholders or members who voted in respect of that resolution.

SPECIAL SESSION. A session of the Legislature for which members were paid indemnities less than the annual indemnity for which provision was made at the time of that session. *Legislative Assembly Act*, S.M. 1980, c. 39, s. 9.

SPECIAL SHARE. Any share other than a common share.

SPECIALTY. *n*. A bond, an obligation created by statute, a contract under seal.

SPECIALTY AIR SERVICES. Aerial mapping, aerial surveying, aerial photography, forest fire management, fire fighting, aerial advertising, glider towing, parachute jumping, aerial construction, heli-logging, aerial sightseeing, flight training, aerial inspection and surveillance and aerial spraying services; *Canadian Aviation Regulations* SOR/96-433, s. 101.01.

SPECIALTY AUDIO SERVICE. A programming service provided by a person licensed to carry on a specialty audio programming undertaking. *Broadcasting Distribution Regulations*, SOR/97-555, s. 1.

SPECIALTY CONTRACT. A contract under seal.

SPECIALTY DEBT. 1. A bond, mortgage or debt which one secures by writing under seal. 2. " . . . [S]ometimes used to denote any contract under seal, but it is more often used in the sense of meaning a specialty debt, that is, an obligation under seal securing a debt or a debt due from the Crown or under statute. . ." *Williams v. R.*,

[1942] 3 D.L.R. 1 at 1, [1942] 2 W.W.R. 321, [1942] A.C. 541, [1942] 2 All E.R. 951 (P.C.), the court per Viscount Maugham.

SPECIALTY FOOD. A food that (a) has special religious significance and is used in religious ceremonies; or (b) is an imported food (i) that is not widely used by the population as a whole in Canada; and (ii) for which there is no readily available substitute that is manufactured, processed, produced or packaged in Canada and that is generally accepted as being a comparable substitute. *Food and Drug Regulations*, C.R.C., c. 870, c. B.01.012.

SPECIALTY PRODUCT. A prepackaged product that is (a) a food or beverage that has special religious significance and is used in religious ceremonies; or (b) an imported product (i) that is not widely used by the population as a whole in Canada; and (ii) for which there is no readily available substitute that is manufactured, processed, produced or packaged in Canada and that is accepted as being a comparable substitute. Canada regulations.

SPECIALTY SERVICE. The programming service provided by a person licensed to carry on a specialty programming undertaking. *Broadcasting Distribution Regulations*, SOR/97-555, s. 1.

SPECIAL VFR FLIGHT. A VFR flight authorized by an air traffic control unit that is conducted within a control zone under VMC in accordance with Division VI of Subpart 2 of Part VI; *Canadian Aviation Regulations* SOR/96-433, s. 101.01.

SPECIE. *n*. 1. Metallic money. 2. Something in its own true form, not a substitute, equivalent or compensation.

SPECIES. See ~ AT RISK; ENDANGERED ~; EXTIRPATED ~; ~ OF SPECIAL CONCERN; PROTECTED ~; THREATENED ~; WILDLIFE ~.

SPECIES AT RISK. An extirpated, endangered or threatened species or a species of special concern. *Species at Risk Act*, S.C. 2002, c. 29, s. 2.

SPECIES OF SPECIAL CONCERN. A wildlife species that may become a threatened or an endangered species because of a combination of biological characteristics and identified threats. *Species at Risk Act*, S.C. 2002, c. 29, s. 2.

SPECIFICATION. *n*. 1. "[Details] . . . the kind and type of material to be used to construct a project, . . ." *Bird Construction Co. v. United States Fire Insurance Co.* (1985), 45 Sask. R. 96 at 100, 18 C.L.R. 115, [1986] I.L.R. 1-2047, 24 D.L.R. (4th) 104, 18 C.C.L.I. 92 (C.A.), the court per Vancise J.A. 2. The specification of an invention must (a) correctly and fully describe the invention and its operation or use as contemplated by the inventor; (b) set out clearly the various steps in a process, or the method of constructing, making, compounding or using a machine, manufacture or composition of matter, in such full, clear, concise and exact terms as to enable any person skilled in the art or science to which it pertains, or with which it is most closely connected, to make, construct, compound or use it; (c) in the case of a machine, explain the principle of the machine and the best mode in which the inventor has contemplated the application of that principle; and (d) in the case of a process, explain the necessary sequence, if any, of the various steps, so as to distinguish the invention from other inventions. The specification must end with a claim or claims defining distinctly and in explicit terms the subject-matter of the invention for which an exclusive privilege or property is claimed. *Patent Act*, R.S.C. 1985, c. P-4, s. 27(3), (4). 3. " . . . [A]s applied to pig-iron, refers to the chemical analysis of the iron. . ." *Dominion Radiator Co. v. Steel Co. of Canada* (1918), 43 O.L.R. 356 at 361, 44 D.L.R. 72 (C.A.), Middleton J.A. See PLANS AND ~S.

SPECIFIC BEQUEST. The gift of a certain item of personal estate in a will.

SPECIFIC CHARGE. "One that, without more, fastens on ascertained and definite property, or property capable of being ascertained and defined." *Illingworth v. Houldsworth*, [1904] A.C. 355 at 358, Lord Macnaghten.

SPECIFIC CONTEMPLATION. Of marriage, a direct relationship between the acquisition of a home and a marriage must be shown.

SPECIFIC DETERRENCE. Refers to a sentence intended to discourage the accused from committing the same offence again.

SPECIFIC DEVISE. The gift of a certain item of real property in a will.

SPECIFIC DUTY. A duty imposed as a fixed sum on each article of a class regardless of value of the article.

SPECIFIC GOODS. Goods identified and agreed upon at the time a contract of sale is made. *Sale of Goods acts*.

SPECIFIC INTENT. "[A degree of intent required for some criminal offences. In committing an offence] . . . which involves the performance of the actus reus, coupled with an intention or purpose going beyond the mere performance of the questioned act. Striking a blow or administering poison with intent to kill, or assault with intent to maim or wound, are examples of such offences." *R. v. Bernard* (1988), 38 C.R.R. 82 at 90, 67 C.R. (3d) 113, 90 N.R. 321, 45 C.C.C. (3d) 1, [1988] 2 S.C.R. 833, 32 O.A.C. 161, McIntyre J. (Beetz J. concurring).

SPECIFIC INTENT OFFENCE. An offence requiring a specific intent. See SPECIFIC INTENT.

SPECIFIC LEGACY. " . . . [A] gift of a particular thing. . ." *Rodd, Re* (1981), 10 E.T.R. 117 at 125, 40 Nfld. & P.E.I.R. 239, 115 A.P.R. 239 (P.E.I. S.C.), McQuaid J.

SPECIFIC PERFORMANCE. A court order which compels a person to do something previously promised according to a contractual obligation.

SPECIFIC PREJUDICE. A form of juror prejudice arising from the juror's attitudes and beliefs concerning the particular case and which may render the juror incapable of deciding with an impartial mind.

SPECIFIC TAX. A tax imposed as a fixed sum on each article of a class regardless of the value of the article.

SPECIFIED EDUCATIONAL INSTITUTION. An institution of learning, whether within or outside a province, that offers courses at a postsecondary school level and that is designated by the lieutenant governor in council of that province, either particularly or as a member of a class, as a specified educational institution within the meaning of this Act. *Canada Student Loans Act*, R.S.C. 1985, c. S-23, s. 2.

SPECIFIED INTEREST RATE. The interest rate specified in a mortgage, which a mortgagor is required, under the mortgage, to pay on the outstanding principal of a loan.

SPEC. LECT. L.S.U.C. *abbr.* Special Lectures of the Law Society of Upper Canada.

SPECS. See US DOT ~.

SPECULATION. *n.* This court, in its judgment on appeal in *Willard Miller [Newfoundland (Workers' Compensation Commission) v. Miller* (1998), 167 Nfld. & P.E.I.R. 115 (Nfld. T.D.)]

... has stressed that an inference is different from speculation ... Drawing an inference amounts to a process of reasoning by which a factual conclusion is deduced as a logical consequence from other facts established by the evidence. Speculation on the other hand is merely a guess or conjecture; there is a gap in the reasoning process that is necessary, as a matter of logic, to get from one fact to the conclusion sought to be established. Speculation, unlike an inference, requires a leap of faith. *Osmond v. Newfoundland (Workers' Compensation Commission)*, 2001 NFCA 21, 200 Nfld. & P.E.I.R. 202, 603 A.P.R. 202, 10 C.C.E.L. (3d) 56, [2001] N.J. No. 111, 2001 CarswellNfld 119 (C.A.).

SPECULATIVE RETIREMENT METHOD. A method of determining the value of a person's interest in a group pension for the purposes of dividing property in a marriage breakdown. The value of the future income stream is calculated assuming the member will continue to be employed until retirement. Likely future earnings are assumed.

SPEECH. *n*. " ... [A]udible oral communication." *Tadman v. Seaboard Life Insurance Co.* (1989), 64 Alta. L.R. (2d) 285 at 288, 93 A.R. 83, [1989] I.L.R. 1-2441, 36 C.C.L.I. 215 (C.A.), Belzil, Bracco and Foisy JJ.A. See COMMERCIAL ~; FREEDOM OF ~.

SPEECH FROM THE THRONE. The Governor General's speech which opens a session of Parliament and outlines the legislative programme for that session as planned by cabinet. This speech is written by the Prime Minister. Also refers to the equivalent speech given by a Lieutenant Governor in the legislature of a province setting out the plans of the provincial government.

SPEECH-LANGUAGE PATHOLOGY. The assessment of speech and language functions and the treatment and prevention of speech and language dysfunctions or disorders to develop, maintain, rehabilitate or augment oral motor or communicative functions.

SPEED. *n*. 1. " ... '[R]ate of motion' ... " *R. v. Ley* (1912), 7 D.L.R. 764 at 765, 2 W.W.R. 849, 20 C.C.C. 176 (Alta. T.D.), Walsh J. 2. A colloquial expression for amphetamines. See RESTRICTED ~ AREA.

SPEED BALL. A combination of a depressant such as morphine with a nervous system stimulant such as cocaine. F.A. Jaffe, *A Guide to Path-*ological Evidence*, 3d ed. (Toronto: Carswell, 1991) at 90.

SPEED TEST. " ... [A] test of speed. . . a test of speed without a contest." *Mildner v. Saskatchewan Government Insurance Office*, [1962] I.L.R. 1-076 at 368, 40 W.W.R. 86 (Sask. Q.B.), MacPherson J.

SPEED-UP. *n*. A system intended to increase the productivity of workers.

SPEI EMPTIO. [L.] Purchasing a chance.

SPENDING POWER. A power, though not explicitly mentioned in the Constitution Act, 1867, which is inferred from the powers to legislate in relation to "public property" (section 91(1 A)), to levy taxes (section 91(3)), and to appropriate federal funds (section 106). P.W. Hogg, *Constitutional Law of Canada*, 3d ed. (Toronto: Carswell, 1992) at 150.

SPENT BREACH DOCTRINE. The person seeking to exercise an option to purchase is allowed to exercise it notwithstanding past breaches or deficiently performed conditions precedent provided these breaches have been cured or the conditions remedied, that is, spent, by the time the option is to be exercised.

SPENT SALMON. Salmon that are in poor condition and are returning to the sea after spawning.

SPERMATOZOA. *n*. Male generative cells. F.A. Jaffe, *A Guide to Pathological Evidence*, 3d ed. (Toronto: Carswell, 1991) at 162.

SPERM WHALE. Any whale known by the name of sperm whale, spermacet whale, cachalot, or pot whale. *Whaling Convention Act*, R.S.C. 1970, c. W-8, Schedule s. 18.

SPES RECUPERANDI. [L.] The hope of recovering.

SPES SUCCESSIONIS. [L.] Hope of succession, in contrast to a vested right.

SPIKED WRISTBAND. A leather wristband to which a metal spike or blade is affixed.

SPILL. *n*. 1. A discharge, emission or escape of oil or gas other than one that is authorized pursuant to subsection (4) or any other Act of Parliament or that constitutes a discharge of a pollutant caused by or otherwise attributable to a ship within the meaning of the Canada Shipping Act. *Oil and Gas Production and Conservation Act*, R.S.C. 1985, c. O-7, s. 24. 2. When used with reference to a pollutant, means a discharge,

(a) into the natural environment, (b) from or out of a structure, vehicle or other container, and (c) that is abnormal in quality or quantity in light of all the circumstances of the discharge. *Environmental Protection Act*, R.S.O. 1990, c. E.19, s. 91(1).

SPILLAGE. *n*. Oil or solids escaping, leaking or spilling from a pipeline or any source apparently associated with a pipeline. *Pipeline Act*, R.S.B.C. 1979, c. 328, s. 38. See FUEL ~.

SPINSTER. *n*. An unmarried woman.

SPIRIT. See GRAIN ~; MOLASSES ~; PROOF ~.

SPIRIT OF THE INVENTION. The "spirit of the invention" school in this country relies on *Dominion Manufacturers Ltd. v. Electrolier Manufacturing Co.*, [1934] S.C.R. 436. In that case, which involved a method to pivot handles for coffins, Rinfret J. spoke of "the spirit of the invention" but did so in a direct quote from the patent itself, at p. 443: What the appellant did—and in that his infringement truly consists—was to take the idea which formed the real subject-matter of the invention. It does not matter whether he also adopted the substitution of the two holes for the bar in the pivoting means. The precise form of these means was immaterial. In the language of the patent, they could be changed "without departing from the spirit of the invention". The patent owner, competitors, potential infringers and the public generally are thus entitled to clear and definite rules as to the extent of the monopoly conferred. This in turn requires that the subjective or discretionary element of claims interpretation (e.g., the elusive quest for "the spirit of the invention") be kept to the minimum, consistent with giving "the inventor protection for that which he has actually in good faith invented" (*Western Electric Co. v. Baldwin International Radio of Canada Ltd.*, [1934] S.C.R. 570, at p. 574). Predictability is achieved by tying the patentee to its claims; fairness is achieved by interpreting those claims in an informed and purposive way. *Free World Trust c. Électro Santé Inc.*, 2000 CarswellQue 2728, 2000 SCC 66, 194 D.L.R. (4th) 232, 263 N.R. 150, [2000] 2 S.C.R. 1024, 9 C.P.R. (4th) 168, Binnie, J.

SPIRIT-RECEIVER. See CLOSED ~.

SPIRITS. *n*. 1. Any material or substance containing more than 0.5% absolute ethyl alcohol by volume other than (a) wine; (b) beer; (c) vinegar; (d) denatured alcohol; (e) specially denatured alcohol; (f) an approved formulation; or (g) any product containing or manufactured from a material or substance referred to in paragraphs (b) to (f) that is not consumable as a beverage. *Excise Act, 2001*, S.C. 2002, c. 22. 2. Any beverage that contains alcohol obtained by distillation. 3. Any beverage which contains alcohol mixed with drinking water and other substances in solution, and includes, among other things, brandy, rum, whiskey and gin. See DENATURED ~; RECTIFYING ~.

SPLIT. *v*. With respect to a cause of action, to sue for only a part of a demand or claim, with intent to sue for the rest in another action.

SPLIT. *n*. A longitudinal skin laceration caused when tissue is compressed between bone and a hard surface or hard blunt object. It is distinguished from a cut by its contused edges and possible 'bridging' of the defect. F.A. Jaffe, *A Guide to Pathological Evidence*, 3d ed. (Toronto: Carswell, 1991) at 13 and 226. See DISTRICT OR ~.

SPLIT RECEPTACLE. A duplex receptacle having terminals adapted for connection to a grounded, three-wire supply, such as 120/240 volts.

SPLIT SHIFT. A shift in which there is a break of several hours between the two parts of the shift.

SPLITTER. *n*. An enclosure containing terminal plates or bus bars having main and branch connectors.

SPLIT WORKWEEK. A workweek beginning before and ending after the date of a semimonthly or monthly period.

SPOILED BALLOT. A ballot that on polling day has not been deposited in the ballot box but has been found by the deputy returning officer to be soiled or improperly printed or that has been: (a) handed by the deputy returning officer to an elector to cast the elector's vote; (b) spoiled in marking by the elector; and (c) handed back to the deputy returning officer and exchanged for another ballot paper.

SPOILED BALLOT PAPER. A ballot paper that, on polling day, has not been deposited in the ballot box but has been found by the deputy returning officer to be soiled or improperly printed, or that has been (a) handed by the deputy returning officer to an elector to cast the elector's vote; (b) spoiled in marking by the elector; and

(c) handed back to the deputy returning officer and exchanged for another ballot paper.

SPOKE WHEEL. A rotating member that provides for mounting and support of demountable rims. *Motor Vehicle Safety Regulations*, C.R.C., c. 1038, s. 2.

SPOLIATION. *n*. The loss, destruction or material alteration of an object or document to the prejudice of a party to an action. Raises a rebuttable presumption omnia praesumuntur in odium spoliatoris, against the party who destroyed the documents.

SPOLIATUS DEBET ANTE OMNIA RESTITUI. [L.] The one despoiled should have property restored before all the rest.

SPONSION. *n*. An engagement or agreement made by a public officer such as an admiral or general in wartime either without authority or which exceeds the authority under which it was made.

SPONSOR. *n*. 1. A surety; a person who gives security or makes a promise for someone else. 2. In group insurance the person who enters into the contract with the insurer on behalf of the lives insured, usually an employer. M.G. Baer & J.A. Rendall, eds., *Cases on the Canadian Law of Insurance*, 4th ed. (Toronto: Carswell, 1988) at 48.

SPONTANEOUS. *adj*. Arising from natural impulse without any external prompting or constraint.

SPONTANEOUS EXCLAMATION. The requisite conditions are: (a) an occurrence must produce nervous excitement causing an utterance to be made spontaneously and without reflection; (b) the utterance must have been made before the reflective powers had time to misrepresent or contrive; (c) the utterance must relate to what happened directly before; (d) the declarant must have had the opportunity to observe personally what is described; and (e) in contrast to a declaration admissible as a verbal act, the utterance may be made by a bystander and need not be precisely simultaneous with the act. P.K. McWilliams, *Canadian Criminal Evidence*, 3d ed. (Aurora: Canada Law Book, 1988) at 8-62.

SPONTE OBLATA. [L.] A free present or gift to the Crown.

SPORT. *n*. A physical activity carried on as a contest or involving training and adherence to rules. See AMATEUR ~; FITNESS AND AMATEUR ~ CANADA.

SPORT FISH. 1. Fish that are taken for pleasure and not for sale or barter. Canada regulations. 2. Includes salmon, trout, black bass and tuna.

SPORT FISHING. 1. Fishing for pleasure and not for sale or barter. 2. Fishing carried on as a sport by the use of a line or a rod and line (angling). 3. Fishing for the purpose of exercising the skill of a fisherman or occupying one's leisure time.

SPORT FISHING LICENCE. A licence authorizing a person to engage in sport fishing.

SPORT HUNTING. Hunting with a firearm or a bow and arrow for the sole and specific purpose of killing game.

SPORTING. *n*. Fowling, taking game, or fishing.

SPORTS BODY. A group of natural persons who are individual members of a federation, or a body, association, league or club formed as a legal person to organize or practise a sport.

SPORTS CENTRE. An installation or place equipped and used for sports events.

SPORTS EVENT. A sports event, contest or exhibition in which a contestant may receive a purse or remuneration.

SPORTS STADIUM. 1. An establishment with stepped rows of seats designed and used for presentation of a sporting or athletic event or spectacle, and includes an amphitheatre or arena. 2. A stadium, arena or other facility where members of the public may witness the performance of sports events.

SPOT REZONING. " . . . [A] rezoning of a single parcel of land in the absence of proper planning considerations for the entire area." *Sault Ste. Marie (City) Restricted Area By-Law 77-299, Re* (1978), 9 O.M.B.R. 383 at 384, Smith (Vice-Chair). See SPOT ZONING.

SPOT ZONING. " . . . [T]he creation of districts applicable to single sites in which the form of development was not to be determined by the application of uniform regulations but rather to be approved after a public hearing." *Brown v. Vancouver (City)* (1986), 31 M.P.L.R. 197 at 214, 69 B.C.L.R. 308, 24 D.L.R. (4th) 434 (S.C.), Lander J. See SPOT REZONING.

SPOUSAL AGREEMENT. (a) Any marriage contract or marital agreement, or (b) any separation agreement, or (c) release or quit claim deed, in writing or any other written agreement or other writing between spouses.

SPOUSAL COMMUNICATIONS PRIVILEGE. Communications between spouses are privileged in criminal law and generally in civil proceedings.

SPOUSAL PRIVILEGE. (a) A privilege supplementary to the right of an accused not to be called as a witness against her or himself which depends on the spouse not being compellable or competent as a witness for the prosecution and is subject to the statutory exception in section 4(2) and the common law exception in section 4(5) of the Canada Evidence Act; (b) Section 4(3) of the Canada Evidence Act describes the true privilege in communication made to the spouse who enjoys the privilege. P.K. Mc-Williams, *Canadian Criminal Evidence*, 3d ed. (Aurora: Canada Law Book, 1988) at 352 and 35-3.

SPOUSAL SUPPORT ORDER. A court of competent jurisdiction may, on application by either or both spouses, make an order requiring a spouse to secure or pay, or to secure and pay, such lump sum or periodic sums, or such lump sum and periodic sums, as the court thinks reasonable for the support of the other spouse. *Divorce Act*, R.S.C, 1985, c. 3 (2nd Supp.), s. 15.2.

SPOUSE. *n.* 1. Section 29 [of the *Family Law Act*, R.S.O. 1990, c. F.3] defines "spouse" as "*either* of a man and a woman" who meet the other requirements of the section. It follows that the definition could not have been meant to define a couple. Rather it explicitly refers to the *individual* members of the couple. Same-sex couples are necessarily excluded from this definition, thereby giving rise to the charge that the legislation is underinclusive. *M v. H*, 1999 CarswellOnt 1348, (sub nom. *M. v. H.*) 171 D.L.R. (4th) 577, (sub nom. *M. v. H.*) 238 N.R. 179, (sub nom. *M. v. H.*) 43 O.R. (3d) 254 (headnote only), (sub nom. *M. v. H.*) 62 C.R.R. (2d) 1, (sub nom. *M. v. H.*) 121 O.A.C. 1, 46 R.F.L. (4th) 32, (sub nom. *Attorney General for Ontario v. M. & H.*) C.E.B. & P.G.R. 8354 (headnote only), (sub nom. *M. v. H.*) [1999] 2 S.C.R. 3, Per Cory J. (Lamer C.J.C., L'Heureux-Dubé, McLachlin, Iacobucci and Binnie JJ. concurring). 2. Either of a man or woman who are married to each other. *Divorce Act*, R.S.C, 1985, c. 3 (2nd Supp.), s. 2. 3. A person of the opposite sex to whom the person is married or with whom the person is living in a conjugal relationship outside marriage. *Ont. statutes.* 4. A person who (a) is married to another person, or (b) is living and cohabiting with another person in a marriage-like relationship, including a marriage-like relationship between persons of the same gender. *B.C. statutes.* 5. " . . . [A] man married to a woman, or a woman married to a man. . . A person is a spouse only while married. . ." *British Columbia (Public Trustee) v. Price* (1990), 25 R.F.L. (3d) 113 at 118, 43 B.C.L.R. (2d) 368, [1990] 4 W.W.R. 52, 67 D.L.R. (4th) 481 (C.A.), the court per Lambert J.A. 6. " . . . [A]pplicable to persons living in a common law relationship. . ." *Novick Estate v. Lachuk Estate* (1987), (sub nom. *Novick (Novick Estate) v. Miller (Lachuk Estate)*) 6 R.F.L. (3d) 187 at 199, 55 Sask. R. 216 (Q.B.), Grotsky J. 7. A person of the opposite sex to whom the person is married or with whom the person is living in a conjugal relationship outside marriage. See COMMON LAW ~; DESERTING ~; FORMER ~; HUSBAND; SURVIVING ~; WIFE.

SPP. *abbr.* Species.

SPRAY CONTAINER. A container that permits the dispersal of its contents in the form of a mist and includes a pressurized container and a pump-spray container.

SPREAD. *n.* 1. The difference between rates of interest paid on GICs or other long term investments and the amount charged on money loaned. 2. " . . . [C]onsisting of a put and a call exercisable at different prices." *Posluns v. Toronto Stock Exchange*, [1964] 2 O.R. 547 at 553, 46 D.L.R. (2d) 210 (H.C.), Gale J. 3. In commodities dealing, playing the difference between two contracts with different features, such as maturity date, by buying one contract and selling another one and anticipating a profit from the difference in the prices between the two contracts.

SPREADING FALSE NEWS. A person who wilfully publishes a statement, tale or news that he knows is false and that causes or is likely to cause injury or mischief to a public interest is guilty of an offence. *Criminal Code*, R.S.C. 1985, c. C-46, s. 181.

SPRING. See SUSPENSION ~.

SPRINGBOARD INJUNCTION. One which is issued to prevent the misuse of confidential information. A person who has obtained information in confidence is not allowed to use it as a springboard for activities detrimental to the party who made the confidential communication.

SPRINGING USE. A use like an executory interest which directs property to vest at a future time which need not coincide with the common law termination of a legal estate.

SPRING POLE. A section of tree, or bush which is, by virtue of its arrangement in relation to other materials, under tension.

SPRING SESSION. A session of the Legislature that commences in the first 3 months of any year.

SPRING SWITCH. A switch equipped with a spring mechanism arranged to restore the switch points to normal position after having been trailed through.

SPRINKLER AND FIRE PROTECTION INSTALLER. A person who, (a) plans proposed installations from blueprints, sketches, specifications, standards and codes; (b) lays out, assembles, installs, tests and maintains high and low pressure pipeline systems for supplying water, air, foam, carbon dioxide or other materials to or for fire protection purposes; (c) measures, cuts, reams, threads, solders, bolts, screws, welds or joins all types of piping, fittings or equipment for fire protection of a building or structure; (d) installs clamps, brackets and hangers to support piping, fittings and equipment used in fire protection systems; (e) tests, adjusts and maintains pipe lines and all other equipment used in sprinkler and fire protection systems; (f) operates and utilizes necessary tools and equipment for the installation of sprinkler and fire protection systems, but does not include a person engaged in (i) the manufacture of equipment or the assembly of a unit prior to delivery to a building or site; or (ii) the installation of electrical equipment, devices and wiring not integral or attached to fire protection systems.

SPRINKLERED. *adj*. That the building or part thereof is equipped with a system of automatic sprinklers.

SPRINKLER LEAKAGE INSURANCE. Insurance against loss of or damage to property through the breakage or leakage of sprinkler equipment or other fire protection system, or of pumps, water pipes, or plumbing and its fixtures. *Insurance acts*.

SPRINKLING TRUST. A discretionary trust under the terms of which the trustees are required to distribute the property of the trust among the beneficiaries.

SPUD-IN. *n*. The initial penetration of the ground for the purpose of drilling an oil or gas well.

SPUR ROAD. See FEEDER OR ~.

SPYWARE. *n*. Software embedded within other software and used by advertisers to monitor internet users' surfing habits for marketing or demographic research purposes.

SQUARE FOOT. 1 /9 square yard. *Weights and Measures Act*, S.C. 1970-71-72, c. 36 Schedule II.

SQUARE INCH. 1/144 square foot. *Weights and Measures Act*, S.C. 1970-71-72, c. 36, Schedule II.

SQUARE MILE. 640 acres. *Weights and Measures Act*, S.C. 1970-71-72, c. 36, Schedule II.

SQUARE ROD. 30 1/4 square yards. *Weights and Measures Act*, S.C. 1970-71-72, c. 36, Schedule II.

SQUARE YARD. A superficial area equal to that of a square each side of which measures one yard. *Weights and Measures Act*, S.C. 1970-71-72, c. 36, Schedule II.

SQUATTER. *n*. Someone who occupies land without consent or licence.

SQUATTER'S TITLE. Title acquired by someone who has occupied land without paying rent or in any other way acknowledging superior title for so long that that person acquires indefeasible title.

SQUEEZE-OUT TRANSACTION. A transaction by a corporation that is not a distributing corporation that would require an amendment to its articles and would, directly or indirectly, result in the interest of a holder of shares of a class of the corporation being terminated without the consent of the holder, and without substituting an interest of equivalent value in shares issued by the corporation, which shares have equal or greater rights and privileges than the shares of the affected class.

SQUID. *n*. Cephalopods of the species Illex illecebrasus and Loligo pealei.

SQUIRE. *n*. A contraction of "esquire".

SR. *abbr*. Steradian.

S.R. *abbr*. Saskatchewan Reports, 1979-.

S.R. & O. *abbr*. Statutory rules and orders in England.

S.S. *abbr*. Steamship(s).

SSHRC. *abbr*. Social Sciences and Humanities Research Council of Canada.

STAB. *n.* A penetrating wound with greater depth than width. F.A. Jaffe, *A Guide to Pathological Evidence*, 3d ed. (Toronto: Carswell, 1991) at 13.

STABIT PRAESUMPTIO DONEC PROBETUR IN CONTRATIUM. [L.] A presumption stands until it is proved to the contrary.

STABLE. See HORSE ~.

STABLE KEEPER. A person who, for money or its equivalent, stables, feeds, boards, grazes or cares for animals. See BOARDING ~; SALES ~.

STACK. *n.* A vertical soil, waste or vent pipe which serves more than one fixture. See SOIL ~; VENT ~; WASTE ~.

STACKED. See CUBIC METRE (~).

STACK VENT. The extension of a soil stack or waste stack above the highest connection of a waste pipe to the stack.

STACK VENTING. When used with reference to fixtures means an arrangement such that the connection of the drainage piping from the stack vented fixtures to the stack provides adequate venting to the fixture traps so that no additional vent piping is required. See MODIFIED ~.

STADIUM. See SPORTS ~.

STAFF. See ACADEMIC ~; CLINICAL ~; DENTAL ~; EXAMINING ~; MEDICAL ~; NURSING ~; PERMANENT ~; PROFESSIONAL ~; PUBLIC SERVICE ~ RELATIONS BOARD; SERVICE ~; SUPPORT ~; TEACHING ~.

STAFF-MODEL RESIDENCE. *var.* **STAFF MODEL RESIDENCE**. A residence where program staff are employed for a scheduled period of work or duty.

STAFF OFFICER OR STAFF OFFICER OF THE SALVATION ARMY. Every duly commissioned officer, other than a Probationary Lieutenant, of the religious society known as the Salvation Army and duly chosen or commissioned by the society to solemnize marriage.

STAGE. *n.* 1. A space designed primarily for theatrical performances with provision for quick change scenery and overhead lighting, including environmental control for a wide range of lighting and sound effects and which is traditionally, but not necessarily, separated from the audience by a proscenium wall and curtain opening. 2. A working platform supported from above. See REPORT ~.

STAKE. *v.* In relation to a mineral claim, means to mark the boundaries of a claim area and establish the corner posts of the claim area.

STAKE. *n.* 1. A deposit made in hopes a particular event takes place. 2. A wooden or metal post used to support and prevent the lateral movement of logs.

STAKEHOLDER. *n.* 1. A person who holds money pending the outcome of a wager or bet. 2. A person who holds property or money which rival claimants claim, but who claims no personal interest in that property or money. 3. A person or group having an interest in particular issues facing government. See INTERPLEADER.

STAKEHOLDER GROUP. A group of members of a multi-stakeholder co-operative, (a) with a common interest, or (b) residing within a defined geographical area. *Co-operative Corporations Act*, R.S.O. 1990, c. C-35, s. 1 as am.

STAKER. *n.* A person who stakes a mineral claim.

STAKE TRUCK. A motor vehicle equipped with a platform and normally used for the transportation of packaged goods.

STALE CHEQUE. A cheque which a bank may dishonour after a certain period, without breaching the banker-customer contract simply because it is dated so long in the past.

STALE DEMAND. A claim made so long ago that it is presumed that it was waived.

STALLION. *n.* A cryptorchid.

STAMP. *n.* 1. An impressed or adhesive stamp used for the purpose of revenue by the government of Canada or a Canadian province or by the government of a foreign state. *Criminal Code*, R.S.C. 1985, c. C-46, s. 376(3). 2. Any distinctive mark, label or seal impressed on or affixed to any goods subject to excise, or any distinctive mark, label or seal impressed on or affixed to any package in which any of those goods are contained. *Excise Act*, R.S.C. 1985, c. E-14, s. 2. 3. Includes all stamps or stamped paper, issued, in respect of matters subject to the control of the Legislature, under any law, or under any order-in-council of the Governor of the late Province of Canada or of the Lieutenant-Governor of Québec, founded on or recognized by any of such laws. *Stamp Act*, R.S.Q. 1977,

c. T-10, s. 3. See AGE STRIP ~; CIGAR ~; CUSTOMS DUTY ~S; EXCISE ~; PERFORATED ~S; POSTAGE ~; PRECANCELLED ~; TOBACCO ~; TRADING ~.

STAMP DUTY. A tax raised by placing a stamp on a written instrument like a conveyance or lease pursuant to a Stamp Act.

STAMPED PAPER. Includes all stamps or stamped paper, issued, in respect of matters subject to the control of the Legislature, under any law, or under any order-in-council of the Governor of the late Province of Canada or of the Lieutenant-Governor of Québec, founded on or recognized by any of such laws. *Stamp Act*, R.S.Q. 1977, c. T-10, s. 3.

STAND. *v*. As applied to a vehicle, whether occupied or not, means (a) when required, to cause the vehicle to remain motionless in one place; and (b) when prohibited, to cause the vehicle to remain motionless in one place. See STOP OR ~.

STANDARD. *n*. 1. Something which has authority and tests other things of the same kind. 2. A settled rate. 3. The detailed design specification for a material, product or process, established by a competent body and not automatically mandatory. The standard setting bodies related to health and safety legislation include the Canadian Standards Association, the Canadian Gas Association, the Underwriters Laboratories of Canada, the American Society of Mechanical Engineering, and the National Fire Prevention Association (U.S.). D. Robertson, *Ontario Health and Safety Guide* (Toronto: Richard De Boo Ltd., 1988) at 5-374. 4. " . . . [I]ntended to convey the notion that the goods in connection with which it is used are of high class or superior quality or acknowledged merit." *Standard Ideal Co. v. Standard Sanitary Manufacturing Co.* (1911), [1911] A.C. 78 at 84, 27 R.P.C. 789 (Que. P.C.), the board per Lord MacNaghten. See BUILDING CONSTRUCTION ~; COMMUNITY ~; CSA ~; EMPLOYMENT ~; EXPORT ~ SAMPLE; FUEL CONSUMPTION ~; LOCAL ~; NARROW-NECK GLASS ~; REFERENCE ~; SAFETY GLASS ~; ~S; TRAP ~.

STANDARD CUBIC FOOT. The quantity of gas occupying a volume of 1 cubic foot at 77 degrees Fahrenheit and at a pressure of 29.92 inches of mercury. *Secondary Lead Smelter National Emission Standards Regulations*, C.R.C., c. 412, s. 2.

STANDARD FILM. Cinematographic film of 35 millimetres or more in width.

STANDARD FIRE TEST. A test that develops in a test furnace a series of time-temperature relationships as follows: (a) at the end of the first 5 minutes 1,000°F (538°C); (b) at the end of the first 10 minutes 1,300°F (704°C); (c) at the end of the first 30 minutes 1,550°F (843°C); (d) at the end of the first 60 minutes 1,700°F (927°C). *Hull Construction Regulations*, C.R.C., c. 1431, s. 2.

STANDARD GAUGE. That the space between the rails of a railroad is approximately 1,435 millimetres.

STANDARD MEASURING CUP. A measuring cup that shall, subject to the tolerance permitted under section 7, contain 8 Imperial fluid ounces or 1/5 of an Imperial quart or 227.30 millilitres. *Canada Standard Measuring Cups and Spoons Regulations*, C.R.C., c. 1136, Schedule 1, s. 1.

STANDARD OF AIRWORTHINESS. In respect of the design, manufacture or maintenance of an aeronautical product, means the description, in terms of a minimum standard, of the properties and attributes of the configuration, material and performance or physical characteristics of that aeronautical product, and includes the procedures to ascertain compliance with or to maintain that minimum standard, as specified in Part V. *Canadian Aviation Regulations*, SOR/96-433, s. 101.01.

STANDARD OF PRODUCTION. Means that from every litre or .78924 kg of absolute ethyl alcohol taken for use there shall be produced therefrom not less than one-half kilogram (.5 kg) of acetic acid. *Excise Act*, R.S.C. 1985, c. E-14, s. 190.

STANDARD OF PROOF. A standard which sets the degree of probability which the evidence must establish in order to entitle the party who bears the burden of proof to succeed in proving her or his case or an issue in the case. See also BALANCE OF PROBABILITIES; CIVIL ONUS; CRIMINAL ONUS; BEYOND A REASONABLE DOUBT.

STANDARD OF REVIEW. 1. The leading Supreme Court case on the proper standard of review of a lower court's decision is *Housen v. Nikolaisen*, 2002 SCC 33. Unlike review of decisions by administrative tribunals, the standard of review for reviewing a lower court's decision is determined solely by the nature of the question in issue. Questions of law are reviewed on a standard of correctness (paras. 8-9) while questions of fact and inferences of fact are reviewed on a palpable and overriding error basis (paras. 10-25). Questions of mixed law and fact are also subject to a palpable and overriding error standard unless a pure question of law can be extricated and reviewed on a correctness standard (paras. 26-28). Although *Housen* dealt with appeals from a decision in an action, in *Q. v. College of Physicians & Surgeons (British Columbia)*, 2003 SCC 19 at para. 43, the Supreme Court applied the *Housen* test in reviewing the decision of a judge hearing an application for judicial review. The Supreme Court held that just as much deference should be shown to an application judge's findings as to those of a trial judge who has heard *viva voce* evidence. *Housen* applies to Charter cases in the same way as to other cases (*R. v. Chang*, 2003 ABCA 293 (C.A.) at paras. 7-8; *R. v. Coates* (2003), [2003] O.J. No. 2295, 2003 CarswellOnt 2203 (C.A.) at para. 20 [O.J. No.]). The proper application of section 15 is a question of mixed fact and law. *Misquadis v. Canada (Attorney General)*, 2003 FCA 473 (C.A.). 2. Having regard to the large number of factors relevant in determining the applicable standard of review, the courts have developed a spectrum that ranges from the standard of reasonableness to that of correctness. Courts have also enunciated a principle of deference that applies not just to the facts as found by the tribunal, but also to the legal questions before the tribunal in the light of its role and expertise. At the reasonableness end of the spectrum, where deference is at its highest, are those cases where a tribunal protected by a true privative clause, is deciding a matter within its jurisdiction and where there is no statutory right of appeal. *Pezim v. British Columbia (Superintendent of Brokers)*, 1994 CarswellBC 232, 92 B.C.L.R. (2d) 145, [1994] 7 W.W.R. 1, 14 B.L.R. (2d) 217, 22 Admin. L.R . (2d) 1, 114 D.L.R. (4th) 385, [1994] 2 S.C.R. 557, (sub nom. *Pezim v. British Columbia (Securities Commission)*) 168 N.R. 321, (sub nom. *Pezim v. British Columbia (Securities Commission)*) 46 B.C.A.C. 1, (sub nom. *Pezim v. British Columbia (Securities Commission)*) 75 W.A.C. 1, 4 C.C.L.S. 117, Iacobucci, J. for the court. See CORRECTNESS; CURIAL DEFERENCE; DEFERENCE; JUDICIAL DEFERENCE; PATENTLY UNREASONABLE; UNREASONABLE.

STANDARD PART. In respect of an aircraft, means a part manufactured in conformity with a specification that (a) is established, published and maintained by an organization setting consensus standards or by a government agency, and (b) includes design, manufacturing, test and acceptance criteria and identification requirements; *Canadian Aviation Regulations*, SOR/96-433, s. 101.01.

STANDARD PRESSURE REGION. All of the Canadian Domestic Airspace not within the altimeter setting region. *Canadian Aviation Regulations*, SOR/96-433, s. 101.01.

STANDARDS. *n.* 1. Those rules, tests, measures or specifications by which the quality or grade of a product is determined. 2. The standards for the maintenance and improvement of the physical condition and for the fitness for occupancy. See APPRENTICESHIP ~; CANADIAN ~ ASSOCIATION; SAFETY ~; STANDARD.

STANDARDS COUNCIL OF CANADA. The federal body which encourages voluntary standardization in production, manufacture, construction, performance, quality, the safety of structures and buildings, products and articles.

STANDARD TIME. Except as otherwise provided by any proclamation of the Governor in Council that may be issued for the purposes of this definition in relation to any province or territory or any part thereof, means (a) in relation to the Province of Newfoundland, Newfoundland standard time, being three hours and thirty minutes behind Greenwich time, (b) in relation to the Provinces of Nova Scotia, New Brunswick and Prince Edward Island, that part of the Province of Quebec lying east of the sixty-third meridian of west longitude, and that part of Nunavut lying east of the sixty-eighth meridian of west longitude, Atlantic standard time, being four hours behind Greenwich time, (c) in relation to that part of the Province of Quebec lying west of the sixty-third meridian of west longitude, that part of the Province of Ontario lying between the sixty-eighth and the ninetieth meridians of west longitude, Southampton Island and the islands adjacent to Southampton Island, and that part of Nunavut lying between the sixty-eighth and the eighty-fifth meridians of west longitude, eastern standard time, being five hours behind Greenwich time, (d) in relation to that part of the Province of Ontario lying west of the ninetieth meridian of west longitude, the Province of Manitoba, and that part of Nunavut, except

Southampton Island and the islands adjacent to Southampton Island, lying between the eighty-fifth and the one hundred and second meridians of west longitude, central standard time, being six hours behind Greenwich time, (e) in relation to the Provinces of Saskatchewan and Alberta, the Northwest Territories and that part of Nunavut lying west of the one hundred and second meridian of west longitude, mountain standard time, being seven hours behind Greenwich time, (f) in relation to the Province of British Columbia, Pacific standard time, being eight hours behind Greenwich time, and (g) in relation to Yukon, Yukon standard time, being nine hours behind Greenwich time. *Interpretation Act*, R.S.C. 1985, c. I-21, s. 35.

STANDARD WORKWEEK. The number of working hours in one week beyond which an employee is entitled to be paid at overtime rates.

STAND BY. " . . . Theoretically, the standby is different from a peremptory challenge. Rather than dismissing the potential juror using a peremptory challenge, or challenging for cause, the person is asked to stand by. . . ." *R. v. Bain* (1992), 10 C.R. (4th) 257 at 274, [1992] 1 S.C.R. 91, 69 C.C.C. (3d) 481, 87 D.L.R. (4th) 449, 133 N.R. 1, 51 O.A.C. 161, 7 C.R.R. (2d) 193, Stevenson J.

STANDBY CREDIT. " . . . [D]iffers from the normal letter of credit because it is furnished by way of security, not by way of payment and because payment is made by the issuer only if the principal defaults. . . it is issued by a banker and embodies an undertaking to make a money payment to the beneficiary against a document. . ." *Distribulite Ltd. v. Toronto Board of Education Staff Credit Union Ltd.* (1987), 45 D.L.R. (4th) 161 at 207, 62 O.R. (2d) 225 (H.C.), Campbell J. See LETTER OF CREDIT.

STAND-BY LETTER OF CREDIT. An obligation on the issuing bank to meet any demand for payment by the beneficiary only upon default of the bank's customer to pay or perform its obligations owed to the beneficiary under the underlying contract.

STAND-BY TIME. A period of time that is not a regular working period during which a public servant on written instructions from an official of his ministry keeps himself available for a recall to work. *Public Service Act*, R.R.O. 1980, Reg. 881, s. 10.

STANDING. *n.* 1. " . . . [T]o establish status as a plaintiff in a suit seeking a declaration that legislation is invalid, if there is a serious issue as to its invalidity, a person need only to show that he is affected by it directly or that he has a genuine interest as a citizen in the validity of the legislation and that there is no other reasonable and effective manner in which the issue may be brought before the Court." *Borowski v. Canada (Minister of Justice), (sub nom. Canada (Minister of Justice) v. Borowski)* [1981] 2 S.C.R. 575 at 598, [1982] 1 W.W.R. 97, 24 C.P.C. 62, 24 C.R. (3d) 352, 12 Sask. R. 420, 64 C.C.C. (2d) 97, 130 D.L.R. (3d) 588, 39 N.R. 331, Martland J. (Ritchie, Dickson, Beetz, Estey, McIntyre and Chouinard JJ. concurring). 2. " . . . [I]n order to obtain standing as a person 'interested' in litigation between other parties, the applicant must have an interest in the actual lis between those parties." *Schofield v. Ontario (Minister of Consumer & Commercial Relations)* (1980), 19 C.P.C. 245 at 251, 28 O.R. (2d) 764, 112 D.L.R. (3d) 132 (C.A.), Wilson J.A. 3. When prohibited, means the halting of a vehicle, whether occupied or not, except for the purpose of and while actually engaged in receiving or discharging passengers. See LOCUS STANDI; PUBLIC INTEREST ~.

STANDING ADVANCE. An accountable advance made in a fixed amount to a person required to incur expenditures on a continuing basis and reimbursed to that fixed amount each time an accounting for expenditures is made.

STANDING BODY OF WATER. A lake, pond, reservoir, lagoon, swamp, marsh or any other area containing standing surface water either permanently or intermittently.

STANDING COMMITTEE. 1. A body appointed under a standing order to consider and report on estimates, to examine and report on government agencies and departments and, to conduct any investigation or inquiry which the House requires. Since 1985, they have been given permanent general orders of reference. A. Fraser, W.A. Dawson, & J. Holtby, eds., *Beauchesne's Rules and Forms of the House of Commons of Canada*, 6th ed. (Toronto: Carswell, 1989) at 221-2. 2. The credit committee, supervisory committee, educational committee, membership committee and any other committee elected by the general membership or appointed by the board of directors whose duties shall be continuous during the fiscal year of the credit union. *Credit Union Act*, R.S.P.E.I. 1974, c. C-28, s. 1.

STANDING COMMITTEE ON MANAGE-MENT AND MEMBERS' SERVICES. Advises the Speaker and Board of Internal Economy on matters relating to the administration of the House and Members' services and facilities. It may review and report on operations under the joint administration and control of the House and the Senate. A. Fraser, W.A. Dawson & J. Holtby, eds., *Beauchesne's Rules and Forms of the House of Commons of Canada*, 6th ed. (Toronto: Carswell, 1989) at 58.

STANDING COMMITTEE ON PRIVI-LEGES AND ELECTIONS. The committee which reviews and recommends changes in the Standing Orders of Parliament. A. Fraser, W.A. Dawson, & J. Holtby, eds., *Beauchesne's Rules and Forms of the House of Commons of Canada*, 6th ed. (Toronto: Carswell, 1989) at 5.

STANDING COURT MARTIAL. May try any officer or non-commissioned member who is liable to be charged, dealt with and tried on a charge of having committed a service offence. Every military judge is authorized to preside at a Standing Court Martial, and a military judge who does so constitutes the Standing Court Martial. *National Defence Act*, R.S.C. 1985, c. N-5, s. 173, 174.

STANDING CROPS. Crops standing or growing on the demised premises. *Landlord and Tenant acts.*

STANDING ORDER. 1. A rule or form which regulates procedure in the House of Commons. 2. An order peculiar to a certain institution issued by that institution's head under authority of section 8 of the Penitentiary Regulations.

STANDING PROGRAM. The established programs and the special welfare program. *Federal-Provincial Fiscal Arrangements Act*, R.S.C. 1985, c. F-8, s. 26.

STANDING, SESSIONAL AND SPECIAL ORDERS. The rules and regulations which the House of Commons uses to govern its proceedings. A. Fraser, W.A. Dawson, & J. Holtby, eds., *Beauchesne's Rules and Forms of the House of Commons of Canada*, 6th ed. (Toronto: Carswell, 1989) at 5.

STANDPIPE AND HOSE SYSTEM. A system of pipes and hoses connected to a water supply for the purpose of applying water to a fire.

STANDSTILL AGREEMENT. An agreement between parties to litigation not to take any fur-ther steps in the action pending negotiation of a settlement.

STAND TRIAL. See UNFIT TO ~.

STARBOARD. *n.* In respect of a vessel, means the right side of the vessel looking forward.

STARBOARD HAND BUOY. A buoy that is located on the starboard side (right hand) of the channel when the vessel is proceeding (a) with the flood tide on the sea coast; (b) against the current of a river; or (c) away from the outlet toward the head of a lake.

STARE AD RECTUM. [L.] To stand trial.

STARE DECISIS. [L.] 1. The principle by which a precedent or decision of one court binds courts lower in the judicial hierarchy. P.W. Hogg, *Constitutional Law of Canada*, 3d ed. (Toronto: Carswell, 1992) at 219. 2. " . . . [D]ecided cases which lay down a rule of law are authoritative and must be followed. The general statement is, of course, subject to qualifications, . . . The decisions of our own Supreme Court of Canada until reversed are binding on all Canadian Courts, and the Supreme Court is bound by its own previous decisions . . ." *Reference re Canada Temperance Act*, [1939] 4 D.L.R. 14 at 33, 72 C.C.C. 145, [1939] O.R. 570 (C.A.), McTague J.A. 3. Each panel of an appeal court is bound by the decisions of other panels on questions of law. 4. One trial judge will not, except in extraordinary circumstances, refuse to follow the decision of another judge of the same court.

STARE IN JUDICIO. [L. to litigate in a court] To sue.

STARK HORROR. Stark horror cases usually involve exceptional acts of brutality or cruelty and are considered to be more serious when premeditated and the acts needlessly repeated. An offence of stark horror is often accompanied by indifference or conduct lacking any feeling whatsoever suggesting a sadistic intent that causes terror to the victim, sometimes amounting to outright torture. An offence may be so serious that regardless of the circumstances of the offender, a sentence of life imprisonment is in order. *R. v. Brown*, 2001 NFCA 8, 152 C.C.C. (3d) 26, 591 A.P.R. 346, 197 Nfld. & P.E.I.R. 346 (C.A.).

START. *v.* Of a fire, to kindle, light, place or set out.

STARTER. *n.* 1. An electric controller for accelerating a motor from rest to normal speed, and for stopping the motor, and usually implies inclusion of overload protection. 2. A person designated by an association to start the horses in each race.

STARTING JUDGE. A person responsible for racing starts.

START-UP COSTS. One time costs associated with a new business or a significant change to an existing business.

STASH HOUSE. A place where something is hidden (stashed).

STATE. *n*. 1. A group of people who occupy a certain territory and have an executive and legislative organization under their own, exclusive control. 2. Part of a larger state, i.e. the separate organizations which collectively make up Australia. 3. Includes a political subdivision of a state and an official agency of a state. 4. " . . . [T]he definition of the word 'state' [in s. 2 of the Reciprocal Enforcement of Maintenance Orders Act, R.S.N.B. 1973, c. R-4] is sufficiently broad to include the concept of 'law district' and in Canada it has long been recognized that each province is a separate and distinct law district, . . ." *Brewer (Mousseau) v. Brewer* (1981), 35 N.B.R. (2d) 329 at 340, 88 A.P.R. 329, 22 C.P.C. 143 (C.A.), the court per Richard J.A. 5. Any state or territory of the United States of America and includes the District of Columbia. See ACT OF ~; CONTRACTING ~; DELIVERABLE ~; FEDERAL ~; FLAG ~; FOREIGN ~; LIMIT ~S; MINISTRY OF ~ FOR SCIENCE AND TECHNOLOGY; NATURAL ~; PROVINCE OR ~; RECIPROCATING ~; SECRETARY OF ~; UNITARY ~.

STATE AIRCRAFT. 1. A civil aircraft owned by and exclusively used in the service of Her Majesty in right of Canada or in right of any province. 2. An aircraft, other than a commercial aircraft, owned and operated by the government of any country or the government of a colony, dependency, province, state or territory of any country. Canada regulations.

STATED CAPITAL. The aggregate amount of capital in all stated capital accounts.

STATED CASE. A case tried on the basis of a statement of facts agreed on by the parties.

STATE DOCUMENT. Includes (a) any Act or ordinance enacted or made or purporting to have been enacted or made by a legislature; (b) any order, regulation, notice, appointment, warrant, licence, certificate, letters patent, official record,

rule of Court, or other instrument issued or made or purporting to have been issued or made under the authority of any Act or ordinance so enacted or made; and (c) any official gazette, journal, proclamation, treaty, or other public document or act of state issued or made or purporting to have been issued or made. *Evidence acts*.

STATEMENT. *n*. 1. " . . . [A] written or oral communication. I have no doubt that a nod of the head to indicate yes or a shaking of the head to indicate no would also be considered a 'statement' within the meaning of s. 56 [of the Young Offenders Act, S.C. 1980-81-82-83, c. 110]. . ." *R. v. J. (J.T.)* (1988), 40 C.C.C. (3d) 97 at 123, [1988] 2 W.W.R. 509, 50 Man. R. (2d) 300 (C.A.), Huband J.A. 2. "[In s. 9(1) of the Evidence Act, R.S.C. 1970, c. E-10] . . . there is a mention only of 'a statement'. That 'statement' has been held to include an oral statement: . . ." *R. v. Carpenter* (1982), 1 C.C.C. (3d) 149 at 154, 31 C.R. (3d) 261, 142 D.L.R. (3d) 237 (Ont. C.A.), the court per Grange J.A. 3. An assertion of fact, opinion, belief or knowledge, whether material or not and whether admissible or not. *Criminal Code*, R.S.C. 1985, c. C-46, s. 118 as am. by *Criminal Law Amendment Act*, R.S.C. 1985 (1st Supp.), c. 27, s. 15. 4. The originating process which commences an action (Ontario, Rules of Civil Procedure, r. 14.03(1)). G.D. Watson & C. Perkins, eds., *Holmested & Watson: Ontario Civil Procedure* (Toronto: Carswell, 1984) at 14-3. 5. Any representation of fact whether made in words or otherwise. See ANNUAL ~; BENEFIT COST ~; ENVIRONMENTAL IMPACT ~; EXTRA-JUDICIAL ~; FINANCIAL ~; IMPACT ~; SELF-INCRIMINATING ~; SELF-SERVING ~; ~S; VOLUNTARY ~.

STATEMENT OF ACCOUNT. A written statement of the amount owing by the debtor to the creditor that includes (a) the amount stated on the previous statement of account to be owing; (b) a record of each extension of credit since the previous statement of account; (c) the amount credited to the account since the previous statement of account; and (d) the cost of borrowing accrued since the previous statement of account.

STATEMENT OF ADJUSTMENTS. A detailed statement of all credits and debits resulting in a balance payable by the purchaser to the vendor upon closing a real estate transaction.

STATEMENT OF CLAIM. 1. "[The function of a statement of claim] is not to cast the plaintiff's right of action into formal legal shape but to state the constitutive facts giving rise to the right upon which he relies and to formulate the relief he demands . . ." *Smith v. Upper Canada College* (1920), 57 D.L.R. 648 at 661, 61 S.C.R. 413, [1921] 1 W.W.R. 1154, Duff J. 2. A printed or written statement by the plaintiff in an action which shows the facts relied on to support any claim against the defendant and the remedy or relief sought.

STATEMENT OF DEFENCE. A brief written statement by a defendant to respond to each allegation in a statement of claim: (a) by admission; (b) by denial; (c) by a statement that the defendant does not know; or (d) by a statement of the defendant's own version of the facts.

STATEMENT OF FACTS. See AGREED ~.

STATEMENTS. *n.* Includes: words spoken or written or recorded electronically or electromagnetically or otherwise; gestures, signs or other visible representations. *Criminal Code*, R.S.C. 1985, c. C-46, s. 319(7). See STATEMENT.

STATE OF MIND EXCEPTION. " . . . [E]xception to the hearsay rule has been accepted in the English common law of evidence. The position seems to be that where the intentions or state of mind of the declarant are relevant to a fact in issue, hearsay evidence is admissible, and, indeed, may be the best evidence to prove this. . . The 'present intentions' or 'state of mind' exception to the hearsay rule has been recognized in the Canadian law of evidence . . ." *R. v. Smith* (1992), 15 C.R. (4th) 133 at 141, 139 N.R. 323, 75 C.C.C. (3d) 257, 94 D.L.R. (4th) 590, 55 O.A.C. 321, [1992] 2 S.C.R. 915, the court per Lamer C.J.C.

STATE OF NATURE. " . . . [U]sed in contradistinction to 'residing upon or cultivating' . . ." *Stovel v. Gregory* (1894), 21 O.A.R. 137 at 142 (C.A.), Burton J.A.

STATIC MEASURE. Any measure that measures length, volume or capacity and does not have a moving or movable part that has or can have an effect on the accuracy of the measure. *Weights and Measures Act*, R.S.C. 1985, c. W-6, s. 2.

STATIC WATER LEVEL. The level attained by water in or from a well when no water is being taken from the well. *Water Wells Act*, R.R.O. 1980, Reg. 739, s. 1.

STATION. *n.* 1. A radio or television programming undertaking, or a radiocommunication dis-

tribution undertaking that rebroadcasts the programming service of a radio or television programming undertaking and whose signal is not encrypted and for which no fee is payable to a third party for the undertaking's right to distribute the signal. *Broadcasting Distribution Regulations*, SOR/97-555, s. 1. 2. A facility used for providing aeronautical information or services. *Canadian Aviation Regulations* SOR/96-433, s. 101.01. 3. A location where trains may stop. See AERADIO ~; COAST ~; COMFORT ~; CONTAINER FREIGHT ~; CONTROL ~; CREAM ~; EARTH ~; EGG-GRADING ~; EGG ~; EVISCERATING ~; FARM ~; FILLING ~; FIRSTAID ~; FISH BUYING ~; FISHING ~; GRADING ~; IMMIGRANT ~; INITIAL ~; INTERLOCKING ~; KILLING AND DRESSING ~; LAND ~; MILK RECEIVING ~; MOBILE ~; MOTOR VEHICLE INSPECTION ~; POLLING ~; PROCESSED EGG ~; RADIO ~; RAILWAY ~; REGISTER ~; SERVICE ~; SHIP ~; SKIMMING ~; SPACE ~; TERMINATING ~; TRANSFER ~; VOTING ~.

STATIONARY SOURCE. Any source of emission of one or more air contaminants other than a motor vehicle, ship, train or aircraft.

STATION PROTECTION SIGNAL. A stop and proceed signal equipped with a marker displaying the letters "SPS" used to protect trains or engines occupying the main track in yards or at stations in the block protected by the signal.

STATION WAGON. A dual purpose vehicle designed for transporting not more than 9 persons, with a rear seat accessible from a side door, and designed so that the seats may be removed or folded out of the way to increase the property carrying space in the vehicle.

STATISTICAL INFORMATION. Information relative to the economic, financial, industrial, commercial, social and general activities and condition of persons, whether such information is collected by means of sampling or any other statistical method.

STATISTICAL SURVEY. A survey, the object of which is the collection and arrangement of data or numerical facts concerning one or more subjects.

STATISTICIAN. See CHIEF ~.

STATISTICS. See VITAL ~.

STATISTICS CANADA. The federal body which collects, analyzes, processes and distributes information on the Canadian economy and society and offers statistical users consulting and inquiry services.

STATOCRACY. *n*. Government by the state only, without church interference.

STATU QUO. See IN ~.

STATUS. *n*. 1. The legal capacity or incapacity of an individual in relation to that person's community. 2. "[In s. 9(1)(c)(ii) of the Canadian Human Rights Act, S.C. 1976-77, c. 33] . . . a legal concept which refers to the particular position of a person with respect to his or her rights and limitations as a result of his or her being a member of some legally recognized and regulated group." *Canada (Attorney General) v. Mossop* (1990), 32 C.C.E.L. 276 at 291, 12 C.H.R.R. D/ 355, 114 N.R. 241, [1991] 1 F.C. 18 (C.A.), Marceau J.A. See CONTROL ~; FAMILY ~; FOUNDATION ~; INSURABLE ~; MARITAL~; MARRIAGE~; PEDIGREED ~; REGISTERED ~.

STATUS AND ESSENTIAL POWERS. Attributes of a federally-incorporated company by which, if a province enacts a law which is within its legislative competence, but which would impair those attributes, that law can be held inapplicable to any such federally-incorporated company. P.W. Hogg, *Constitutional Law of Canada*, 3d ed. (Toronto: Carswell, 1992) at 612.

STATUS INDIAN. A person registered as an Indian under the Indian Act or entitled to be registered under that Act.

STATUS OFFENCE. An offence characterized by a "state of being" instead of an "act of doing". D. Stuart, *Canadian Criminal Law: a treatise*, 2d ed. (Toronto: Carswell, 1987) at 69.

STATUS QUO. [L.] The state in which something is or was.

STATUS QUO CLAUSE. A provision in a collective agreement that the conditions which existed prior to an action or circumstance giving rise to a grievance will be maintained until the grievance is settled.

STATUS REPORT. A report, prepared in accordance with the requirements of regulations, that contains a summary of the best available information on the status of a wildlife species, including scientific knowledge, community knowledge and aboriginal traditional knowledge. *Species at Risk Act*, S.C. 2002, c. 29, s. 2.

STATUTABLE. *adj*. Governed or introduced by statute law.

STATUTE. *n*. A law or act which expresses the will of a legislature or Parliament. See ACT OR ~; CODIFYING ~; CONSOLIDATING ~; CREDITORS' RELIEF ~; CURATIVE ~; DECLARATORY ~; ENABLING ~; EQUITY OF A ~; FEDERAL ~; GUEST ~; IMPERIAL ~S; INCOME TAX ~; PENAL ~; REMEDIAL ~; RETROACTIVE ~; RETROSPECTIVE ~; REVISED ~S.

STATUTE BARRED. Said of a cause of action for which proceedings cannot be brought because the limitation period has expired.

STATUTE LABOUR. The inhabitants of a county were required either to do certain work, known as statute labour, annually upon the highways or to pay a levy.

STATUTE OF ELIZABETH. The British statute which first attempted to comprehensively prohibit fraudulent conveyances. C.R.B. Dunlop, *Creditor-Debtor Law in Canada* (Toronto: Carswell, 1981) at 509.

STATUTE OF FRAUDS. The Statute of Frauds requires that certain contracts are in writing or are evidenced by an appropriate memorandum. If one fails to conform to the statutory provisions, the contract is unenforceable. Refers to rules now incorporated in the law in other statutes.

STATUTE OF LIMITATIONS. 1. A statute which prescribes the specified period of time within which criminal charges must be laid or legal actions must be taken. 2. This Court recently described the purpose of limitations legislation in *M. (K.) v. M. (H.)*, (sub nom. *M. c. M.*) [1992] 3 S.C.R. 6. *M. (K.) v. M. (H.)* was a claim for damages for incest brought well after the expiration of the limitation period, even allowing for the plaintiff to reach majority. La Forest J. stated at pp. 29-30: In order to determine the time of accrual of the cause of action in a manner consistent with the purposes of the *Limitations Act*, it is helpful to examine its underlying rationales. There are three, and they may be described as the certainty, evidentiary, and diligence rationales. Statutes of limitations have long been said to be statutes of repose. The reasoning is straightforward enough. There comes a time, it is said, when a potential defendant should be secure in his reasonable expectation that he will not be held to account for ancient obligations. The second rationale is evidentiary and concerns the desire to foreclose claims based on stale evidence. Once the limitation period has lapsed, the potential defendant should no longer be concerned about the preservation of evidence relevant to the claim. Finally, plaintiffs are expected to act diligently and not "sleep on their rights". Statutes of limitation are an incentive for plaintiffs to bring suit in a timely fashion. While these rationales benefit the potential defendant, the Court also recognized that there must be fairness to the plaintiff as well. Hence, the reasonable discovery rule which prevents the injustice of a claim's being statute barred before the plaintiff becomes aware of its existence. A limitations scheme must attempt to balance the interests of both sides. *Murphy v. Welsh*, 1993 CarswellOnt 428, 18 C.P.C. (3d) 137, 47 M.V.R. (2d) 1, 156 N.R. 263, 14 O.R. (3d) 799, 65 O.A.C. 103, 157 N.R. 372, [1993] 2 S.C.R. 1069, 106 D.L.R. (4th) 404, 18 C.C.L.T. (2d) 101. Major, J. for the court.

STATUTE OF QUIA EMPTORES. 1. "The primary purpose of [the Statute of Quia Emptores 1290, 18 Edw. 1, St. 1] was to prevent the practice of the day of subinfeudation which resulted in the feudal landlords losing control of their property. As an incident of the abolition of subinfeudation, the right of unrestricted alienation of fee simple estates was pronounced without loss to the feudal landlords." *Laurin v. Iron Ore Co.* (1977), 7 R.P.R. 137 at 154, 19 Nfld. & P.E.I.R. 111, 50 A.P.R. 111, 82 D.L.R. (3d) 634 (Nfld. T.D.), Goodridge J. 2. "The statutory prohibition against restraints of alienation began with the Statute of Quia Emptores in 1290, 18 Edw. 1, St. 1." *Hongkong Bank of Canada v. Wheeler Holdings Ltd.* (1990), 14 R.P.R. (2d) 1 at 13, 77 Alta. L.R. (2d) 149, 111 A.R. 42, 75 D.L.R. (4th) 307 (C.A.), the court per Lieberman J.A.

STATUTE OF WESTMINSTER. The British statute which repealed the Colonial Laws Validity Act as it applied to the dominions. By section 2(2) it granted each dominion power to amend or repeal imperial statutes which were part of the law of that dominion and it stated that no dominion statute would be void on grounds of repugnancy to an existing or future imperial statute. Section 7(2) clarified that section 2 applied to Canada's provincial Legislatures in addition to Canada's federal Parliament, but that the Parliament and each legislature could only enact laws within their own jurisdiction under the B.N.A. Act. The power to amend or repeal ex-

tended to both future and existing imperial statutes. P.W. Hogg, *Constitutional Law of Canada*, 3d ed. (Toronto: Carswell, 1992) at 50.

STATUTE REVISION. A continuing revision and consolidation of the statutes and regulations of Canada or a province.

STATUTE REVISION COMMISSION. A commission appointed by the Minister of Justice or the Attorney General to carry out a revision and consolidation of statutes and regulations of Canada or of a province.

STATUTORY. *adj*. Governed or introduced by statute law.

STATUTORY AMALGAMATION. Under a prescribed procedure, two or more companies incorporated under one governing act enter into a joint agreement prescribing the terms and conditions of amalgamation and the way to effect it. When the procedure is completed, the amalgamated companies are treated as a single company. H. Sutherland, D.B. Horsley & J.M. Edmiston, eds., *Fraser's Handbook on Canadian Company Law*, 7th ed. (Toronto: Carswell, 1985) at 525.

STATUTORY APPROPRIATION. An amount permitted or directed to be paid from the Revenue Fund.

STATUTORY ARBITRATOR. A person to whom parties are required by statute to resort.

STATUTORY AUTHORITY DEFENCE. " . . . [T]he test applied by the Courts when faced with the decision whether a nuisance may be defended on the ground that it was created pursuant to the exercise of statutory authority takes the form of inquiring whether the statute expressly or impliedly authorizes the damage complained of, and whether the public or other body concerned has established that the damage was inevitable." *Tock v. St John's Metropolitan Area Board* (1989), 1 C.C.L.T. (2d) 113 at 143, 47 M.P.L.R. 113, [1989] 2 S.C.R. 1181, 64 D.L.R. (4th) 620, 104 N.R. 241, 82 Nfld. & P.E.I.R. 181, 257 A.P.R. 181, La Forest J. (Dickson C.J.C. concurring).

STATUTORY CORPORATION. A corporation the business of which is confined to the powers conferred in the statute which created the corporation.

STATUTORY COURT. A court which derives its existence and powers from statute, e.g., The Federal Court of Canada.

STATUTORY DECLARATION. A solemn declaration in the form and manner from time to time provided by the provincial evidence acts or by the Canada Evidence Act. A declaration made knowing that it has the same force and effect as if made under oath or affirmation.

STATUTORY INSTRUMENT. (a) Any rule, order, regulation, ordinance, direction, form, tariff of costs or fees, letters patent, commission, warrant, proclamation, by-law, resolution or other instrument issued, made or established (i) in the execution of a power conferred by or under an Act of Parliament, by or under which that instrument is expressly authorized to be issued, made or established otherwise than by the conferring on any person or body of powers or functions in relation to a matter to which that instrument relates, or (ii) by or under the authority of the Governor in Council, otherwise than in the execution of a power conferred by or under an Act of Parliament, but (b) does not include (i) any instrument referred to in paragraph (a) and issued, made or established by a corporation incorporated by or under an Act of Parliament unless (A) the instrument is a regulation and the corporation by which it is made is one that is ultimately accountable, through a Minister, to Parliament for the conduct of its affairs, or (B) the instrument is one for the contravention of which a penalty, fine or imprisonment is prescribed by or under an Act of Parliament, (ii) any instrument referred to in paragraph (a) and issued, made or established by a judicial or quasi-judicial body, unless the instrument is a rule, order or regulation governing the practice or procedure in proceedings before a judicial or quasi-judicial body established by or under an Act of Parliament, (iii) any instrument referred to in paragraph (a) and in respect of which, or in respect of the production or other disclosure of which, any privilege exists by law or whose contents are limited to advice or information intended only for use or assistance in the making of a decision or the determination of policy, or in the ascertainment of any matter necessarily incidental thereto, or (iv) an ordinance of the Yukon Territory or the Northwest Territories, a law made by the Legislature for Nunavut, a rule made by the Legislative Assembly of Nunavut under section 21 of the *Nunavut Act* or any instrument issued, made or established under any such ordinance, law or rule. *Statutory Instruments Act*, R.S.C. 1985, c. S-22, s. 2.

STATUTORY INTERPRETATION. The process of applying certain principles to determine the meaning of an enactment. See CO-HERENCE, PRESUMPTION OF; CONSECUTIVE INTERPRETATION; CONTEXTUAL APPROACH; GOLDEN RULE; INTERPRETATION; PURPOSIVE INTERPRETATION; STRICTLY.

STATUTORY JURISDICTION. Jurisdiction whose source is a statute which defines the limits within which the jurisdiction must be exercised.

STATUTORY LIEN. A lien on property which arises purely by statute; the lienholder's rights depend on the relevant statutory provisions.

STATUTORY OFFICER. An officer whose duties are set out in statute and are independent in their character. An officer who is not directed by the corporation in the performance of duties. I.M. Rogers, *The Law of Canadian Municipal Corporations*, 2d ed. (Toronto: Carswell, 1971-) at 1423.

STATUTORY OLD AGE. Sixty-five years.

STATUTORY PERSON. A non-living entity which is recognized by law as possessing a legal personality separate and apart from any constituent members. Corporations, societies, the Crown in right of Canada, the Crown in right of a province, foreign sovereigns and foreign states.

STATUTORY POWER. A power or right conferred by or under a statute, (a) to make any regulation, rule, by-law or order, or to give any other direction having force as subordinate legislation; (b) to exercise a statutory power of decision; (c) to require any person or party to do or to refrain from doing any act or thing that, but for such requirement, such person or party would not be required by law to do or to refrain from doing; (d) to do any act or thing that would, but for such power or right, be a breach of the legal rights of any person or party.

STATUTORY POWER OF DECISION. A power or right conferred by or under a statute to make a decision deciding or prescribing, (a) the legal rights, powers, privileges, immunities, duties or liabilities of any person or party; or (b) the eligibility of any person or party to receive, or to the continuation of, a benefit or licence, whether that person or party is legally entitled thereto or not, and includes the powers of an inferior court.

STATUTORY RAPE. "[Refers to] ... sexual intercourse with a person under 16 years of age ..." *R. v. F. (D. W.)* (1987), 36 C.C.C. (3d) 507 at 527, 16 B.C.L.R. (2d) 273, [1987] 6 W.W.R. 481, 35 C.R.R. 36 (C.A.), Anderson J.A. (dissenting).

STATUTORY RELEASE. Release from imprisonment subject to supervision before the expiration of an offender's sentence, to which an offender is entitled under the provision of the Act dealing with remission. *Corrections and Conditional Release Act, 1992*, S.C. 1992, c. 20, s. 99.

STATUTORY SET-OFF. [To net out a debt owed by one person against another owed to that person] " . . . [R]equires the fulfilment of two conditions. The first is that both obligations must be debts. The second is that both debts must be mutual cross obligations." *Telford v. Holt* (1987), 37 B.L.R. 241 at 251, 21 C.P.C. (2d) 1, 78 N.R. 321, 54 Alta. L.R. (2d) 193, [1987] 6 W.W.R. 385, [1987] 2 S.C.R. 193, 46 R.P.R. 234, 81 A.R. 385, 41 D.L.R. (4th) 385, the court per Wilson J.

STATUTORY TAKING. "For there to be statutory taking which gives rise to a claim for compensation, not only must the owner be deprived of the benefit of its property, there must also be a resulting enhancement or improvement conferred upon whatever entity the legislature intended to benefit. Something must not only be taken away, it must be taken over." *Steer Holdings v. Manitoba*, [1992] 2 W.W.R. 558 at 566, 21 R.P.R. (2d) 298, 8 M.P.L.R. (2d) 235, 47 L.C.R. 18, 79 Man. R. (2d) 169 (Q.B.), Kroft J.

STATUTUM AFFIRMATIVUM NON DEROGAT COMMUNI LEGI. [L.] An affirmative statute does not diminish the common law.

STAY. *n.* With respect to proceedings, an action to suspend them. See DAYS ~; LENGTH OF ~.

STAY OF ARBITRATION. An order interrupting an arbitration proceeding until some other action takes place.

STAY OF PROCEEDINGS. 1. A prospective rather than a retroactive remedy. A stay of proceedings does not merely redress a past wrong. It aims to prevent the perpetuation of a wrong that, if left alone, will continue to trouble the parties and the community as a whole, in the future. *R. v. Regan*, [2002] 1 S.C.R. 297, Per LeBel J. (McLachlin C.J.C., L'Heureux-Dubé, Gonthier, Bastarache JJ. concurring). 2. " . . . [A] stopping or arresting of a judicial proceedings by the direction or order of a court. . . A stay may imply that the proceedings are suspended to await some action required to be taken by one of the parties, as, for example, when a nonresident has been ordered to give security for costs. In certain circumstances, however, a stay may mean the total discontinuance or permanent suspension of the proceedings." *R. v. Jewitt* (1985), 47 C.R. (3d) 193 at 203, [1985] 2 S.C.R. 128, [1985] 6 W.W.R. 127, 61 N.R. 159, 21 C.C.C. (3d) 7, 20 D.L.R. (4th) 651, the court per Dickson C.J.C.

STCC. *abbr.* The Standard Transportation Commodity Code as filed with the Canadian Transport Commission.

STCC NUMBER. A number in STCC representing the goods or materials classified under that number.

STCW. The *International Convention on Standards of Training, Certification and Watchkeeping for Seafarers, 1978, as amended in 1995*. *Crewing Regulations*, SOR/97-390, s. 1.

STCW CODE. The *Seafarers' Training, Certification and Watchkeeping Code* of July 7, 1995. *Crewing Regulations*, SOR/97-390, s. 1.

STEAL. *v.* To commit theft. *Criminal Code*, R.S.C. 1985, c. C-46, s. 2.

STEALING. *n.* (a) Stealing is the act of fraudulently and without colour of right taking, or fraudulently and without colour of right converting to the use of any person, any thing capable of being stolen, with intent (i) to deprive the owner, or any person having any special property or interest therein, temporarily or absolutely of such thing or of such property or interest; (ii) to pledge the same or deposit it as security; (iii) to part with it under a condition as to its return which the person parting with it may be unable to perform; or (iv) to deal with it in such a manner that it cannot be restored in the condition in which it was at the time of such taking and conversion; (b) stealing is committed when the offender moves the thing or causes it to move or to be moved, or begins to cause it to become movable, with intent to steal it; (c) the taking or conversion may be fraudulent, although effected without secrecy or attempt at concealment; and (d) it is immaterial whether the thing converted was taken for the purpose of conversion, or whether it was, at the time of the conversion, in the lawful possession of the person converting. *National Defence Act*, R.S.C. 1985, c. N-5, s. 114.

STEAM BOILER. Any boiler, vessel or structure in which steam is generated for power or heating purposes and any boiler, vessel or other appliance in which steam, gas, air or liquid is contained under pressure, and includes all pipes, apparatus and machinery attached to or connected with a steam boiler.

STEAM BOILER INSURANCE. Insurance on steam boilers and pipes, engines and machinery connected therewith or operated thereby, against explosion, rupture and accident and against personal injury or loss of life, and against destruction of or damage to property resulting therefrom.

STEAM DISTILLED WOOD TURPENTINE. A liquid obtained by steam-distillation of the wood of coniferous trees.

STEAM DREDGE. A dredge, the primary power plant of which consists of boilers and steam machinery.

STEAMER. *n.* Except as provided under the Load Line Rules, means any ship propelled by machinery and not coming within the definition of sailing ship. *Canada Shipping Act*, R.S.C. 1985, c. S-9, s. 2.

STEAMFITTER. *n.* A person who, (a) lays out, assembles, installs, maintains or repairs any heating system, cooling system, process system or industrial system; (b) installs or connects piping in any building or structure; (c) installs the piping for any process, including a process that conveys gas, or the tubing for any pneumatic or airhandling system; or (d) reads and understands design drawings, manufacturer's literature and installation diagrams for any system referred to in subclause (a), but does not include a person engaged in the manufacture of equipment or the assembly of a unit, prior to delivery to a building, structure or site.

STEAMFITTER-PIPEFITTER TRADE. Includes (a) the laying out, assembling, fabricating, installing, maintaining or repairing of piping used in connection with heating systems, cooling systems, process systems, industrial systems, pneumatic systems and gas systems but does not include piping used in connection with portable water or sewage systems or piping assembled or installed during the manufacture of equipment prior to delivery to a building, structure or site; and (b) the interpreting of drawings, manufacturer's literature and installation diagrams used in connection with the piping for a heating system, a cooling system, a process system, an industrial system, a pneumatic system or a gas system.

STEAM HOISTING PLANT. A hoist equipped with a drum and a hoisting rope or chain that is driven by a steam-driven prime mover and used for raising, lowering or swinging material.

STEAM PLANT. 1. A plant in which the boilers may be used for generating or utilizing steam and includes any pipe, fitting or other equipment that is attached to the boilers and constitutes one unit with them. 2. A plant in which steam is used for motive power.

STEAMSHIP. *n.* 1. Except as provided under the Load Line Rules, means any ship propelled by machinery and not coming within the definition of sailing ship. *Canada Shipping Act*, R.S.C. 1985, c. S-9, s. 2. 2. Includes (a) every ship that has sufficient mechanical means for propulsion, and does not have sufficient sail area for navigation under sails alone; and (b) every lighter, barge or other ship that is towed and does not have independent means of propulsion. *General Load Line Rules*, C.R.C., c. 1425, s. 2. 3. A ship the propulsive power of which is derived from boilers and steam engines. Canada Regulations. See PASSENGER ~.

STEAM VESSEL. Includes any vessel propelled by machinery, whether under sail or not.

STEEL. *n.* Any metal or combination of metals containing 50 per cent or more, by weight, of iron. *Customs Tariff*, R.S.C. 1985, c. C-54, s. 2. See BLACK ~.

STEERING COLUMN. The structural housing that surrounds a steering shaft. *Motor Vehicle Safety Regulations*, C.R.C., c. 1038, s. 2.

STEERING COMMITTEE. A sub-committee on agenda and procedure which recommends, by report, the way a committee should proceed to study its order of reference and advises on topics like times of sittings, witnesses and subject matters for each sitting. A. Fraser, W.A. Dawson, & J. Holtby, eds., *Beauchesne's Rules and Forms of the House of Commons of Canada*, 6th ed. (Toronto: Carswell, 1989) at 227.

STEERING CONTROL SYSTEM. The basic steering mechanism and its associated trim hardware including any portion of a steering column assembly that provides energy absorption upon impact. *Motor Vehicle Safety Regulations*, C.R.C., c. 1038, s. 2.

STEERING SHAFT. A component that transmits steering torque from the steering wheel to the steering gear. *Motor Vehicle Safety Regulations*, C.R.C., c. 1038, s. 2.

STEERING WHEEL INJURY. An injury, such as rupture of the liver or a "floating chest" caused by the impact of a steering wheel on the upper abdomen and chest of a driver during sudden deceleration. F.A. Jaffe, *A Guide to Pathological Evidence*, 3d ed. (Toronto: Carswell, 1991) at 226.

STENOGRAPHER. *n*. 1. " . . . A Court Reporter is an officer of the court and enjoys an official status. A 'stenographer' on the other hand, is not an officer of the court and enjoys no official status." *R. v. Turner* (1981), 27 C.R. (3d) 73 at 79, [1982] 2 W.W.R. 142, 65 C.C.C. (2d) 335, 14 Sask. R. 321 (C.A.), Bayda C.J.S. (MacDonald J.A. concurring). 2. " . . . [O]ften used to describe persons who transcribe spoken words by simply listening to a voice record of them and without first writing them in shorthand, as well as persons who before transcribing spoken words first write them in shorthand. . ." *Turner v. R.* (1982), 27 C.R. (3d) 73 at 79, [1982] 2 W.W.R. 142, 14 Sask. R. 321 (C.A.), Bayda C.J.C. (MacDonald J.A. concurring).

STEP. *n*. A matter or development in an action which advances the action toward trial.

STEPHENS' DIG. *abbr*. Stephens' Quebec Digest.

STEPPARENT. *var*. **STEP-PARENT**. *n*. In relation to a child, the husband or wife of the child's birth or adoptive parent where the husband or wife is not a birth parent of the child.

STERADIAN. *n*. The unit of measurement of a solid angle, being the angle with its vertex at the centre of a sphere and subtended by an area on the spherical surface equal to that of a square with sides equal in length to the radius. *Weights and Measure Act*, S.C. 1970-71-72, c. 36, Schedule 1.

STEREOTYPE. *n*. A generalization by which a person or group of people is unfairly portrayed as possessing undesirable traits.

STEREOTYPE BLOCK. The printer's block supplied by the Chief Electoral Officer to a returning officer, and of which an impression is printed on the back of each ballot paper by the printer thereof. *Elections acts*.

STERILE TRANSIT AREA. An area in an airport where in-transit passengers, in-transit preclearance passengers or goods that are in transit or precontrolled are physically separated from other passengers and goods.

STERILIZED. *adj*. In respect of canned fish, means fish that has been treated with heat to prevent spoilage and to destroy all pathogenic organisms. *Fish Inspection regulations*.

STERLING. *n*. British money.

STERLING. *adj*. Genuine.

STERNLIGHT. *n*. A white light placed as nearly as practicable at the stern showing an unbroken light over an arc of the horizon of 135 degrees and so fixed as to show the light 67.5 degrees from right aft on each side of the vessel. *Collision Regulations*, C.R.C., c. 1416, Rule 3.

STERN TRAWL. An otter trawl designed for or adapted to hauling fish over an inclined ramp in the stern of a vessel.

STET. [L.] Let it stand.

STEVEDORE. *n*. A person who stows cargo on board a ship.

STEVEDORING. *v*. The loading or unloading of vessels or railway cars.

STEVENS' DIG. *abbr*. Stevens' New Brunswick Digest.

STEWARD. *n*. 1. A person elected to represent union members in a particular part of a plant or department. 2. Has the same meaning as "judge". *Pari-Mutuel Betting Supervision Regulations*, SOR/91-365, s. 2. See ASSOCIATION ~; COMMISSION ~; JOB-SITE ~; PRESIDING ~; SHOP ~; UNION ~.

STEWART. *abbr*. Stewart's Vice-Admiralty Reports (N.S.), 1803-1813.

STICKINESS. *n*. For the purposes of section 118 of Schedule IV, a condition on the surface of a brake cup such that fibres will be pulled from a wad of U.S.P. absorbent cotton when the wad is drawn across the surface of the cup. *Motor Vehicle Safety Regulations*, C.R.C., c. 1038, s. 2.

STILL. *n*. Any distilling apparatus whatever adapted or adaptable to the distillation of spirits. *Excise Act*, R.S.C. 1985, c. E-14, s. 3. See CHEMICAL ~.

STILLBIRTH. *var*. **STILL-BIRTH**. *n*. 1. The complete expulsion or extraction from its mother after at least twenty weeks pregnancy, of a product of conception in which, after such expulsion or extraction, there is no breathing, beating of the heart, pulsation of the umbilical cord, or unmistakable movement of voluntary muscle. *Vital Statistics acts*. 2. If the duration of the pregnancy cannot be determined, the complete expulsion or extraction from its mother of a product of conception, weighing five hundred grams or over, and in which after such expulsion or extraction there is no beating of the heart, pulsation of the umbilical cord or unmistakable movement of voluntary muscle. *Vital Statistics acts*.

STING. *n*. Occurs when a police agent offers to buy controlled drugs or other contraband from a suspected dealer who is arrested when the purchase is made.

STIPEND. *n*. Salary.

STIPENDIARY MAGISTRATE. Includes provincial magistrate, acting provincial magistrate and deputy provincial magistrate. *Stipendiary Magistrate Act*, R.S.N.S. 1967, c. 292, s. 27 (part).

STIPENDIUM. *n*. Pay, wages.

STIPULATED DAMAGE. Liquidated damages.

STIPULATED PRICE CONTRACT. One in which the parties have agreed the contract is to be performed for the amount stated in the tender document.

STIPULATION. *n*. 1. A bargain. 2. In an agreement, a material term.

STIRPES. See PER ~.

STIRRER. *n*. The structure designed to distribute the microwave energy within a cavity. *Radiation Emitting Devices Regulations*, C.R.C., c. 1370, s. 1.

STOCK. *n*. 1. (a) Stock of goods, wares, merchandise and chattels ordinarily the subject of trade and commerce; (b) the goods, wares, merchandise or chattels in which a person trades, or that he produces or that are outputs of, or with which he carries on, any business, trade or occupation. *Bulk Sales acts*. 2. Any horse, cattle, sheep or poultry or any fur-bearing animal. 3. Includes a share, stock, fund, annuity or security transferable in books kept by a company or society established or to be established, or transferable by deed alone or by deed accompanied by other formalities, and a share or interest in it. See DEBENTURE ~; DEFERRED ~; FARM ~; FEED ~; FIRST ISSUE OF ~; ISSUED CAPITAL ~; LISTED ~; LIVE~; NURSERY ~; PENNY ~; PERMANENT ~;

PROCESS ~; PROPERTY IN ~; ROLLING ~; SEED ~.

STOCKBROKER. *n*. . . . [O]ne who buys and sells stock as an agent for others. The relationship between client and broker is that of principal and agent, fiduciary in its nature and one of the governing principles of law demands the fullest disclosure by agent to principal. . ." *R. v. Solloway*, [1930] 2 W.W.R. 516 at 519, 54 C.C.C. 129 (Alta. T.D.), Ives J.

STOCKDEALER. *n*. Includes a person who, whether on his own behalf or as agent for another and whether on a commission basis or otherwise, (a) buys or offers to buy stock; and (b) sells or offers to sell, or has in his possession for sale, or takes out of the Province stock or beef.

STOCK DIVIDEND. 1. " . . . [S]tock distributed to those already holding stock, by way of dividend upon their holdings. It is not a new investment in any sense; it is a mode of distributing accumulated profits in the shape of new stock, which, pro tanto, reduces the value of the stock held." *Fulford, Re* (1913), 14 D.L.R. 844 at 846-7, 5 O.W.N. 125, 29 O.L.R. 375 (H.C.), Middleton J. 2. Includes any dividend paid by a corporation to the extent that it is paid by the issuance of shares of any class of its capital stock.

STOCK ESCROW TRUST. Stock is vested in a trustee who is required to transfer it when a certain event occurs.

STOCK EXCHANGE. "The four essential elements appearing in each definition [of 'stock exchange', Criminal Code, R.S.C. 1970, c. C-34, s. 340(c)] are, namely, a reunion of persons, a particular place, buying and selling, and, finally buying and selling of a particular class of things, namely, securities." *Schecter c. Bluestein* (1981), (*sub nom. Bluestein c. Schecter*) 121 D.L.R. (3d) 345 at 349, 23 C.R. (3d) 39, [1981] C.S. 477, 58 C.C.C. (2d) 208 (Que. S.C.), Malouf J.

STOCK IN BULK. A stock or portion of a stock that is the subject of a sale in bulk. *Bulk Sales acts*.

STOCK IN TRADE. " . . . [G]oods which a merchant has in his possession, for sale or hire. . ." *R. v. North American Van Lines (Alberta) Ltd*. (1986), 2 M.V.R. (2d) 176 at 187, 16 O.A.C. 230 (C.A.), the court per Blair J.A.

STOCK OPTION. "[Takes] . . . the form of negotiable bearer contracts [which] are simply bought and sold like any other commodity for the trading of which there is no exchange. There are six types of stock options: a call; a put; a straddle; a strap; a strip; and a spread. . ." *Posluns v. Toronto Stock Exchange*, [1964] 2 O.R. 547 at 553, 46 D.L.R. (2d) 210 (H.C.), Gale J.

STOCK SAVINGS PLAN. An arrangement, other than a retirement savings plan, between a qualified dealer and an investor under which the dealer holds those eligible securities that the investor: (a) owns; and (b) has designated for the purpose of entitling the investor to a stock savings tax credit for any taxation year.

STOCKTON. *abbr*. Stockton's Vice-Admiralty Reports (N.B.), 1879-1891.

STOCKYARD. *n*. Any area of land in operation as a public market for the purchase and sale of livestock. See PUBLIC ~.

STOLEN. *adj*. "An article is 'stolen' [within the meaning of s. 19 of the Motor Vehicles Act, R.S.O. 1914, s. 207] when some one has committed the act of 'stealing' with reference to it, and not otherwise." *Hirshman v. Beal* (1916), 32 D.L.R. 680 at 688, 38 O.L.R. 40, 28 C.C.C. 319 (C.A.), Riddell J.A. (Lennox J.A. concurring).

STOP. *v*. (a) When required, a complete cessation from vehicular movement; and (b) when prohibited, any halting even momentarily of a vehicle, whether occupied or not, except when necessary to avoid conflict with other traffic or in compliance with the directions of a peace officer or traffic control device.

STOP. *n*. When prohibited, means the halting of a vehicle, even momentarily, whether occupied or not, except when necessary to avoid conflict with other traffic or in compliance with the directions of a police officer or of a traffic control sign or signal. *Highway Traffic Act*, R.S.O. 1990, c. H.8, s. 1(1). See TRANSFER ~.

STOP-CHECK. *n*. Check of vehicle made by police to check for improper registration and deficiencies in vehicles.

STOP ORDER. 1. An order issued on application to the court by someone who claims to be entitled to securities or money held or to be held by the accountant for the benefit of someone else which directs that the securities or money shall not be handled without notifying the applicant or moving party. 2. Order the person to whom it is directed to immediately stop or cause the source of contaminant to stop adding to, emitting

or discharging into the natural environment any contaminant either permanently or for a specific period of time. 3. An order by a client to stop selling a commodity or stock if its price goes down or up to a price set by the client.

STOP OR STAND. When prohibited means any stopping or standing of a vehicle, whether occupied or not, except when necessary to avoid conflict with other traffic or in compliance with the directions of a peace officer or traffic control sign or signal.

STOPPAGE. See WORK ~.

STOPPAGE IN TRANSITU. The right of an unpaid seller to take back the possession of goods sold on credit and to retain them until the buyer, who became insolvent before possessing the goods, tenders the price.

STOPPING. When prohibited, means the halting of a vehicle, even momentarily, whether occupied or not, except when necessary to avoid conflict with other traffic or in compliance with the directions of a police officer or of a traffic control sign or signal. *Highway Traffic Act*, R.S.O. 1990, c. H.8, s. 1(1).

STOPWAY. A rectangular area on the ground at the end of a runway in the direction of take-off and having the same width as the runway, prepared as a suitable area for stopping an aeroplane in the case of a rejected take-off. *Canadian Aviation Regulations*, SOR/96-433, s. 101.01.

STOP WORK ORDER. An order directing that all work cease in a place of employment or on the site of construction.

STORAGE. *n*. Any keeping or retention of tangible personal property for any purpose except (a) for sale in the course of a business, or (b) for the purpose of being processed, fabricated or manufactured into, attached to or incorporated into other tangible personal property. See COLD ~.

STORAGE BATTERY. Includes an electrical storage battery, generator, electrical motor distributor, and the necessary wires, wiring, or parts thereof.

STORAGE CHARGE. 1. The charge made by the licensee of an elevator for maintaining in the elevator a stock of grain available for delivery on presentation of an elevator receipt entitling the holder to the delivery of grain in accordance with the receipt. *Canada Grain Act*, R.S.C.

1985, c. G-10, s. 2. 2. A charge payable on goods remaining on a wharf after the expiration of free time. Canada regulations. 3. A toll charged on goods in respect of the period of time that the goods are stored at a canal. Canada regulations.

STORAGE COMPANY. A person engaged in the business of storing gas.

STORAGE GARAGE. A building or part thereof intended for the storage or parking of motor vehicles and which contains no provision for the repair or servicing of such vehicles.

STORAGE RECEIPT. See GRAIN ~.

STORAGE RESERVOIR. A naturally occurring underground cavity or system of cavities or pores, or an underground space or spaces created by some external means, that may be used for the storage of a hydrocarbon.

STORAGE TANK. A drum, tank, or container of any kind, other than a vehicle fuel tank, in which flammable petroleum products are kept or stored. See BULK ~; HOT WATER ~.

STORAGE-TYPE WATER HEATER. A service water heater with an integral hot water storage tank.

STORE. *v*. 1. To deposit goods while waiting for them to be delivered to another location. 2. When used with reference to water, means collect, impound and conserve.

STORE. *n*. 1. " . . . [A] shop for the sale of goods by wholesale or retail . . ." *Toronto (City) v. Foss* (1912), [1913] 8 D.L.R. 641 at 642, 27 O.L.R. 264, 4 O.W.N. 150 (Div. Ct.), Falconbridge C.J. 2. " . . . [G]oods are stored, sold, and removed from the premises in practically the same condition throughout." *McCormick v. Toronto (City)* (1923), 54 O.L.R. 603 at 605, 25 O.W.N. 155 (H.C.), Wright J. 3. Any building or portion of a building, booth, stall or other place where goods are exposed or offered for sale or auction. See AGENCY ~; CHAIN ~; COLD ~; COMPANY ~; CONSUMABLE ~S; DEPARTMENT ~; DETACHED ~; DRUG ~; GOVERNMENT ~; LIQUOR ~; PUBLIC ~S; RETAIL ~; SEPARATE ~ OR WAREHOUSE; SHIPS ~S; SUPER ~; SURPLUS ~S.

STORED. *adj*. 1. When used with respect to farm produce, means placed in a grain elevator upon terms that the ownership shall remain in the owner of the farm produce until such time as the owner has sold the farm produce and has received due compensation or has removed the farm produce from the elevator. 2. A firearm has been "stored" when it has been put aside and the accused is not making any immediate or present use of it. There is no need to establish that the firearm has been put aside for a "lengthy period". *R. v. Carlos*, 2001 YKCA 6, 155 C.C.C. (3d) 459, 155 B.C.A.C. 95, 254 W.A.C. 95, 48 C.R. (5th) 57 (Y.T. C.A.), Per Ryan J.A. (dissenting).

STOREKEEPER. *n*. A person who sells or exposes for sale goods or produce to consumers from, or at a store or shop of which that person is proprietor or manager.

STORER. *n*. A person who receives goods for storage or reward.

STOREY. *n*. A division of a building between a floor, not below the grade level of the surrounding ground, and the floor or roof next above. See EXIT ~; FIRST ~; HALF ~.

STORM DRAIN. See BUILDING ~.

STORM DRAINAGE PIPING. All the connected piping that conveys storm water to a place of disposal and includes the building storm drain, building storm sewer, rain water leader and area drain installed to collect surface water from the area of a building and the piping that drains water from a swimming pool or from water-cooled air-conditioning equipment but does not include, (a) a main storm sewer; (b) a subsurface drain; or (c) a foundation drain.

STORM SEWER. See BUILDING ~; TRUNK ~ SYSTEM.

STORM WATER. Rain water or water resulting from the melting of snow or ice.

STOVE. *n*. An appliance intended for cooking and space heating. *Building Code Act*, R.R.O. 1980, Reg. 87, s. 1.

STOWAGE. *n*. 1. Money paid for the space where goods are stored. 2. The way a ship is loaded. See BROKEN ~.

STRADDLE. *n*. " . . . [C]onsists of two options, one 'call' and the other 'put', either of which may be exercised independently of the other at any time during the life of the straddle. . ." *Posluns v. Toronto Stock Exchange*, [1964] 2 O.R. 547 at 553, 46 D.L.R. (2d) 210 (H.C.), Gale J.

STRADDLE TREE. Trees whose trunks straddle the common boundary between adjoining properties at ground level. Included therein are three sub-categories: the first includes only those trees planted along a common boundary with the consent of the adjoining owners, or their predecessors in title ("Consensual Trees"). The second encompasses those trees planted on one property but whose trunks have expanded over a common boundary onto the adjoining property ("Straying Trees"). The third includes trees whose origins are unknown ("Voluntary Trees"). *Koenig v. Goebel* (1998), 162 Sask. R. 81 (Q.B.).

STRAIGHT-LINE DEPRECIATION. A uniform annual rate of depreciation of the value of an asset over its useful life.

STRAIGHT TIME. The hours of work defined in a collective agreement as regular straight time hours.

STRAIGHT-TIME PAY. Regular wages excluding bonuses and overtime.

STRAIN. *n*. Aquatic plants or animals that have, or have been bred to have, genetic characteristics that distinguish them from other members of the same species. *Aquaculture Act*, R.S. Nfld. 1990, c. A-13, s. 2.

STRAMINEUS HOMO. [L. man of straw] A person with no means.

STRANDING. *v*. 1. Of a ship, running aground on the shore or a beach. 2. " ' . . . [T]he taking of the ground does not happen solely from those natural causes, which are necessarily incident to the ordinary course of the navigation in which the ship is engaged, either wholly, or in part, but from some accidental or extraneous cause.'" *Rudolf v. British & Foreign Marine Insurance Co.* (1898), 30 N.S.R. 380 at 383 (C.A.), Ritchie J.A. quoting Tindal C.J. in *Kingsford v. Marshall* 8 Bing. 458 at 464, 121 E.R. 470 at 473.

STRANGER. *n*. 1. " . . . [A] person who is not one of my household either as guest or servant and who acts against my will. . ." *Port Coquitlam (City) v. Wilson* (1922), [1923] 1 W.W.R. 1025 at 1032, 1036, [1923] S.C.R. 235, [1923] 2 D.L.R. 194, Duff J. (Anglin, Brodeur and Sir Louis Davies JJ. concurring). 2. ". . . [A]nyone who in lighting a fire or allowing it to escape acts contrary to anything which the occupier could anticipate that he would do: . . . Even if it is a man whom you have allowed or invited into your house, nevertheless, if his conduct in lighting a fire is so alien to your invitation that he should qua the fire be regarded as a trespasser, he is a 'stranger'. . ." *H. & N. Emanuel Greater London County Council*, [1971] 2 All E.R. 835 at 839 (U.K. C.A.), Lord Denning, M.R.

STRANGER TO A TRANSACTION. Someone who takes no part or no part which produces a legal effect in that transaction.

STRANGULATION. *n*. Death caused by compression or constriction of the neck. See LIGATURE ~; MANUAL ~.

STRAP. *n*. 1. A narrow non-woven material used in place of webbing. *Motor Vehicle Safety Regulations*, C.R.C., c. 1038, s. 209. 2. "[A combination of] puts and calls. . . composed of one put and two calls. . ." *Posluns v. Toronto Stock Exchange*, [1964] 2 O.R. 547 at 553, 46 D.L.R. (2d) 210 (H.C.), Gale J.

STRATA CORPORATION. A strata corporation established by the deposit of a strata plan in a land title office. The owners of the strata lots are members of the strata corporation.

STRATA LOT. A lot shown on a strata plan. *Strata Property Act*, S.B.C. 1998, c. 43, s. 1.

STRATA LOT LEASE. A lease of a strata lot arising from the conversion of a ground lease under section 203 (1), and includes an assignment or transmission of a strata lot lease; *Strata Property Act*, S.B.C. 1998, c. 43, s. 199.

STRATA PLAN. The plan which describes the strata lots and which establishes the strata corporation.

STRATOCRACY. *n*. Government by the military.

STRAW CLAIMANT. A corporate shell which has no assets and exists solely for the purpose of commencing or continuing a lawsuit.

STRAY. *n*. 1. An animal that is unlawfully running at large or that has broken into premises enclosed by a lawful fence. 2. A reindeer, found during an annual roundup of a herd held by the owner, that bears the registered mark of another owner. *Northwest Territories Reindeer Regulations*, C.R.C., c. 1238, s. 2. See VALUELESS ~.

STRAY ANIMAL. A domestic animal found on the premises of a person other than its owner.

STRAYING TREE. A tree planted on one property but whose trunks have expanded over a common boundary onto the adjoining property *Koenig v. Goebel* (1998), 162 Sask. R. 81 (Q.B.).

STREAM. A natural watercourse, a small river, including one which flows only in some years.

STREAM OR WATER. 1. Any river, brook, lake, pond, creek or other flowing or standing water. 2. Includes a natural watercourse or source of water supply, whether usually containing water or not, ground water, and a lake, river, creek, spring, ravine, swamp and gulch.

STREET. *n*. A highway, road, square, lane, mews, court, alley and passage, whether a thoroughfare or not. See ONE-WAY ~; PRIVATE ~.

STREET ADDRESS. See MASTER ~ GUIDE.

STREET CAR. 1. Every device propelled by electricity travelling exclusively upon rails when upon or crossing a street. *Motor Vehicle Act*, R.S.N.S. 1989, c. 293, s. 2. 2. Includes a car of an electric or steam railway. *Highway Traffic Act*, R.S.O. 1990, c. H.8, s. 1(1).

STREET CERTIFICATE. 1. " . . . [I]ndorsed in blank . . ." *Stobie Forlong Matthews Ltd., Re*, [1931] 3 D.L.R. 170 at 171, [1931] 1 W.W.R. 817, 39 Man. R. 476, 12 C.B.R. 313 (C.A.), Fullerton J.A. (Dennistoun J.A. concurring). 2. "It is the practice in Ontario and elsewhere for brokers to encourage their customers to permit the registration of the customers' securities in the broker's name in order to facilitate transfer at the time of resale . . . it has become customary for the broker to sign the certificate of transfer, leaving the name of the transferee blank but having the broker's signature guaranteed in such form that the certificate will, in terms of the trade, be 'good delivery'. These certificates then become what is known as 'street certificates', that is transferable without more by delivery. . ." *Canadian Depository for Securities Ltd. v. Toronto Stock Exchange*, [1981] O.S.C.B. 519C at 520C, Knowles (Chair), Bray (Vice-Chair), Morgan, Miles, Webster and Holland (Commissioners).

STREET RESERVATION. The land reserved for a public road, street, lane, sidewalk or other public way.

STREET TRADE. A business carried on in the street, i.e. newspaper vending or peddling.

STRENGTH DECK. The uppermost continuous deck, except in way of an effective superstructure, when the superstructure deck shall be considered the strength deck. *Hull Inspection Regulations*, C.R.C., c. 1432, s. 2.

STRICTI JURIS. [L.] The letter of the law.

STRICTISSIMI JURIS. [L.] Of the strictest law. *Dragun v. Dragun* (1984), 47 C.P.C. 106

at 108, [1984] 6 W.W.R. 171, 30 Man. R. (2d) 126 (Q.B.), Helper J. Calls for the court's most careful attention to ensure adherence to all necessary safeguards of the liberty of the person and the perception that justice is done.

STRICT LEGAL OPERATION. Refers to how legislation as a whole affects rights and liabilities of those subject to its terms. The effect is determined by the legislation itself.

STRICT LIABILITY. 1. Criminal liability based on simple negligence. 2. Imposed in tort law when a lawful activity exposes others to extraordinary risks even though no fault is involved on the part of the "wrongdoer".

STRICT LIABILITY OFFENCE. "Offences in which there is no necessity for the prosecution to prove the existence of mens rea; the doing of the prohibited act prima facie imports the offence, leaving it open to the accused to avoid liability by proving that he took all reasonable care. This involves consideration of what a reasonable man would have done in the circumstances. The defence will be available if the accused reasonably believed in a mistaken set of facts which, if true, would render the act or omission innocent, or if he took all reasonable steps to avoid the particular event. These offences may be properly called offences of strict liability." *R. v. Sault Ste. Marie (City)*, [1978] 2 S.C.R. 1299 at 1326, 3 C.R. (3d) 30, 21 N.R. 295, 7 C.E.L.R. 53, 40 C.C.C. (2d) 353, 85 D.L.R. (3d) 161, the court per Dickson J.

STRICTLY. *adv*. In construing a penal statute, the conduct which gave rise to the charge against the accused or the conduct of anyone for whom the accused may be held answerable must be such as can clearly and unmistakably be demonstrated to fall within the range of conduct which is prohibited by the statute.

STRICTUM JUS. [L.] Law only, in contrast to equity.

STRIKE. *v*. See TO ~.

STRIKE. *n*. 1. Includes a cessation of work or a refusal to work by employees, in combination, in concert or in accordance with a common understanding, and a slowdown of work or other concerted activity on the part of employees in relation to their work that is deigned to restrict or limit output. 2. Includes (a) a cessation of work; (b) a refusal to work; or (c) a refusal to continue to work, by 2 or more employees acting in combination or in concert or in accordance with a common understanding for the purpose of compelling their employer or an employers' organization to agree to terms or conditions of employment or to aid other employees to compel their employer or an employers' organization to accept terms or conditions of employment. 3. [As used in a "force majeure" clause of a contract for the supply of electricity] is not necessarily limited to labour disturbances affecting one's own workforce. [I]f the "officious bystander" were asked about the natural and ordinary meaning of "strike" in subclause 18(d) he or she would say a strike at the pulp mills who accounted for 90 per cent of [the plaintiff's business] was surely caught. [T]here is an answer in this case to the rhetorical questions regarding where to draw the line between strikes besetting customers and those besetting suppliers of customers, suppliers of suppliers of customers, etc. The line surely becomes clear where the plant of one of the contracting parties has had to shut down due to a strike and has virtually no need for electricity. The effect on the customer is exactly the same as if its own workforce had been on strike. *Tenneco Canada Inc. v. British Columbia Hydro & Power Authority* (1999), 1999 CarswellBC 1455, 126 B.C.A.C. 9, 206 W.A.C. 9, 126 B.C.A.C. 9 (C.A.). See ECONOMIC ~; GENERAL ~; ILLEGAL ~; JURISDICTIONAL ~; SECONDARY ~; SYMPATHETIC ~; SYMPATHY ~; TOKEN~; UNAUTHORIZED ~; WILDCAT ~.

STRIKE BENEFIT. An amount paid to a member of a union by the union during a strike.

STRIKEBREAKER. *var.* **STRIKE BREAKER**. A worker hired during a strike to help defeat the strike. See PROFESSIONAL ~.

STRIKE FUND. A reserve accumulated by a union to assist members during a strike.

STRIKE NOTICE. A formal announcement by a union or group of workers that it or they intend(s) to go on strike on a certain date.

STRIKE OFF THE ROLL. To remove the name of a solicitor from the rolls of a court and thereby disentitle that person to practise.

STRIKE OUT. To expunge part or all of a document or pleading, with or without leave to amend.

STRIKER. *n*. An employee who has joined fellow employees in stopping work.

STRIKE-RELATED MISCONDUCT. A course of conduct of incitement, intimidation, coercion, undue influence, provocation, infiltration, surveillance or any other like course of conduct intended to interfere with, obstruct, prevent, restrain or disrupt the exercise of any right under this Act in anticipation of, or during, a lawful strike or lock-out. *Labour Relations Act*, R.S.O. 1990, c. L.2, s. 73(2).

STRIKE VOTE. A vote conducted among members of a bargaining unit to determine whether they should go on strike.

STRIKING COMMITTEE. A parliamentary committee which prepares the membership lists for legislative and standing committees. A. Fraser, W.A. Dawson, & J. Holtby, eds., *Beauchesne's Rules and Forms of the House of Commons of Canada*, 6th ed. (Toronto: Carswell, 1989) at 223.

STRIKING OUT. See STRIKE OUT.

STRIKING PRICE. Where used in relation to a commodity futures option, means the price at which the purchaser of the option has the right to assume a long or short position in relation to the commodity futures contract that is the subject of the option.

STRIKING SURFACE. That part of a book, box or other container of matches that is designed for igniting matches. *Hazardous Products (Matches) Regulations*, C.R.C., c. 929, s. 2.

STRIP. *n*. 1. When applied to iron or steel, means a flat-rolled product of any shape (a) having a width of more than eight inches but not more than twelve inches, and a thickness of 0.2299 inch or less, or (b) having a width of eight inches or less and a thickness of 0.2030 inch or less. *Customs Tariff*, R.S.C. 1985, c. C-54, s. 2. 2. The rectangular portion of the landing area of the airport including the runway prepared for the take-off and landing of aircraft a particular direction. Canada regulations. 3. "[A combination of] puts and calls. . . composed of two puts and one call. . ." *Posluns v. Toronto Stock Exchange*, [1964] 2 O.R. 547 at 553; 46 D.L.R. (2d) 210 (H.C.), Gale J. See MEDIAN RACING ~.

STRIP DEVELOPMENT. " . . . [L]inear development of single depth along a given road as opposed to the subdivision approach of development in depth with more than one layer of lots being developed back from the main access road." *Niagara Escarpment Commission v. Halton (Region) Land Division Committee* (1990), 25 O.M.B.R. 285 at 287, Baines (Vice-Chair).

STRIP MINE. A mine worked by removal of overlying strata and subsequent excavation of exposed coal in flat or substantially flat terrain.

STRIP SEARCH. The removal or rearrangement of some or all of the clothing of a person so as to permit a visual inspection of a person's private areas, namely genitals, buttocks, breasts (in the case of a female), or undergarments. This definition in essence reflects the definition of a strip search that has been adopted in various statutory materials and policy manuals in Canada and other jurisdictions . . . This definition distinguishes strip searches from less intrusive "frisk" or "pat down" searches, which do not involve the removal of clothing, and from more intrusive body cavity searches, which involve a physical inspection of the detainee's genital or anal regions. *R. v. Golden*, 2001 SCC 83.

STROKE. *n*. A popular name for either an intracerebral hemorrhage or brain infarct. F.A. Jaffe, *A Guide to Pathological Evidence*, 2d ed. (Toronto: Carswell, 1983) at 46.

STRONG CIDER. Cider containing more than 7 per cent and not more than 13 per cent of alcohol by volume. *An Act Respecting the Commission de Contrôle des Permis d'Alcool*, R.S.Q. 1977, c. C-33, s. 2.

STRUCK-WORK CLAUSE. A clause in a collective bargaining agreement permitting employees to refuse work on materials coming from a strike-bound plant.

STRUCTURAL ALTERATION. Includes any work or construction which involves any change, modification, replacement, or repair of any supporting member of a building, including the bearing walls, columns, beams or girders thereof.

STRUCTURAL ALTERATIONS OR STRUCTURALLY ALTERED. The application of labour and materials, not including ordinary maintenance to a dwelling unit, where the application of such labour and materials will: (a) effect a change in the dimensions or alter the existing interior plan of the dwelling unit; or (b) extend the lifetime of the dwelling unit.

STRUCTURAL CHANGE. When used to refer to a building, means the alteration, defacement or removal of any normally permanent structural member or surface, whether repaired or not, if the nature of the repair is, or would be, such that other material replaces that which was removed.

STRUCTURAL DEFECT. See MAJOR ~.

STRUCTURAL EXTERMINATION. The destruction, prevention or control of a pest that may adversely affect a building, structure, machine, vehicle or their contents or the use or enjoyment thereof by any person by the use of a pesticide in, on or in the vicinity of the building, structure, machine or vehicle and includes the destruction, prevention or control of termites. *Pesticides Act*, R.S.O. 1990, c. P.11, s. 1(1).

STRUCTURAL PEST CONTROL. The destruction, prevention or control of pests that may adversely affect a building, structure, machine, vehicle or their contents or the use or enjoyment thereof by any person.

STRUCTURAL PLANS. (a) Copies of the architectural and engineering drawings prepared for a condominium project, revised to show all changes made to the date of registration; or (b) plans comparable to architectural drawings containing sufficient information to enable the construction of the building therefrom, where the copies of the original drawings referred to in subclause (a) are unavailable or are inadequate for purposes of construction, mechanically reproduced on such translucent material as the examiner approves. *Condominium Act*, R.R.O. 1980, Reg. 122, s. 1.

STRUCTURE. *n*. 1. "[In s. 26(4)(a) of the Excise Tax Act, R.S.C. 1970, c. E-13] . . . three criteria for determining the existence of a structure: (1) it must be built or constructed; (2) it must rest on or in the ground; (3) it must not be 'a part' of another structure." *Minister of National Revenue v. Plastibeton Inc.* (1986), 86 D.T.C. 6400 at 6402, Can. S.T.R. 80-099, [1986] 2 C.T.C. 211, 11 C.E.R. 369, 68 N.R. 215 (Fed. C.A.), MacGuigan J.A. 2. " . . . [A]nything which is constructed; and it involves the notion of something which is put together, consisting of a number of different things which are so put together or built together, constructed as to make one whole, which then is called a structure." *Hobday v. Nicol*, [1944] 1 All E.R. 302 at 303-4 (U.K. K.B.D.), Humphreys J. (Asquith and Cassels JJ. concurring). 3. "It seems now to be clearly settled that the ejusdem generis rule does not apply to the words 'building or structure' [in the Criminal Code] and that the word 'structure' is not to be confined to something ejusdem generis with 'building': . . . an installation of such a permanent nature as to constitute a structure within s. 389(1)(a) of the Criminal Code [R.S.C. 1970, c. C-34] is one that has been made with the intention that it will continue indefinitely in its present location. It does not have to be a fixture. . . The word 'structure' was intended to go beyond the ambit of the word 'building'. On the other hand, it connotes an installation that is not intended to be temporary and ready for movement . . ." *R. v. Bedard* (1976), 31 C.C.C. (2d) 559 at 562, 566, 20 N.R. 427 (Ont. C.A.), Howland J.A. 4. Any building, plant, machinery, equipment, storage tank, storage place, or fixture of any kind whatsoever erected or placed on, in, over or under any area of land or water. 5. Anything built or made on and affixed to or imbedded in land or affixed to or imbedded in land after being built or made elsewhere, and appurtenances thereto, and, without limiting the generality of the foregoing, includes (a) any building, structure, erection, wharf, pier, bulkhead, bridge, trestlework, vault, sidewalk, road, roadbed, lane, paving, pipeline, fountain, fishpond, drain, sewer, canal, or aqueduct built or made on and affixed to or imbedded in land or affixed to or imbedded in land after being built or made elsewhere, and appurtenances thereto; and (b) any well, mine or excavation drilled, sunk or made in or on land and any appurtenances thereto, and a reference to a structure on land includes a structure in or beneath the surface of the land. See AIR-SUPPORTED ~; FARM ~; NON-RELOCATABLE ~; ON-SITE BUILDING OR ~; PROPORTIONAL TAX RATE ~; RELOCATABLE ~; TEMPORARY WORK ~.

STRUCTURED SETTLEMENT. 1. . . [A]n agreement to pay the plaintiff, as compensation for the damages suffered by him, a sum of money by periodic payments, rather than a lump sum payment." *Fuchs v. Brears* (1986), 44 Sask. R. 112 at 115, [1986] 3 W.W.R. 409 (Q.B.), Vancise J. 2. The periodic payment of damages by means of an annuity; the annuity is purchased by the defendant's casualty insurer from a life insurer. Annuity payments flow to the injured plaintiff as tax-free damages. The annuity contract is owned by the casualty insurer, which guarantees payment to the injured person. The increasing popularity of structured settlements is largely attributable to the cost of gross-up. Because periodic payments flowing to the injured party are non-taxable, gross-up is not an issue. *Wilson v. Martinello* (1995), 23 O.R. (3d) 417 (C.A.).

STRUT. *n.* A transverse member of shoring and timbering that directly resists pressure from a wale or sheathing.

STRYCHNINE. *n.* A vegetable alkaloid extracted from seeds of Strychnos nux vomica; it is a strong convulsant and nervous system stimulant. F.A. Jaffe, *A Guide to Pathological Evidence*, 3d ed. (Toronto: Carswell, 1991) at 226-7.

STUART. *abbr.* Stuart, Vice-Admiralty Reports (Que.), 1836-1874.

STUD. CANON. *abbr.* Studia Canonica.

STUDENT. *n.* 1. A person enrolled or registered in a school. 2. A person enrolled in a course of studies at an educational institution. 3. A person who is pursuing formal education as a full-time or part-time student and is employed by an employer for the purposes of the employer's industry, although not as a learner or an apprentice. *Workers' Compensation Act*, R.S.O. 1990, c. W.11, s. 1(1) . See ARTICLED ~; LAW ~; LICENSED ~; QUALIFYING ~; REGISTERED ~.

STUDENT-AT-LAW. *n.* A person serving articles of clerkship.

STUDENT FINANCIAL ASSISTANCE. Financial assistance provided in the form of a loan, grant, bursary, prize, scholarship, allowance or remission to or in favour of any person who is eligible.

STUDENT HOUSING. A housing project for students and their families.

STUDENT LOAN. A loan made by a bank to a person enrolled as a full-time student at a specified educational institution.

STUDENTS COUNCIL. The executive body of a students' association.

STUDENTS' SUPPLIES. (a) Blank exercise and workbooks whether or not lined but excluding such books as are ruled for bookkeeping or accounting purposes; (b) loose-leaf paper punched for insertion in a loose-leaf binder but excluding such paper as is ruled for bookkeeping or accounting purposes and all loose-leaf paper that is not punched for insertion in a loose-leaf binder; (c) books for drawing upon; (d) music manuscript paper; and (e) schoolbags and satchels.

STUDENT TEACHER. A student engaged in practice teaching while enrolled in teacher education in a recognized teacher education institution.

STUD GUN. A gun which fires a nail, bolt or rivet using an explosive charge. F.A. Jaffe, *A*

Guide to Pathological Evidence, 3d ed. (Toronto: Carswell, 1991) at 227.

STUDY. See ENVIRONMENTAL ~; PERIOD OF STUDIES; RENEWAL ~.

STUDY PERMIT. A written authorization to engage in studies in Canada issued by an officer to a foreign national. *Immigration and Refugee Protection Regulations*, SOR/2001-475, s. 1.

STUFFED ARTICLE. See UPHOLSTERED OR ~.

STUFF GOWN. The court robe worn by lawyers who are not Queen's Counsel.

STUFFING. *n*. Any material used for padding, filling or cushioning, that is meant to be enclosed by a covering.

STU. K.B. *abbr.* Stuart's Reports (Que.), 1810-1835.

STUMPAGE. The amount which is payable to the Crown for timber harvested on Crown lands.

STUMPAGE CHARGES. The amount equal to the total of the amount of the Crown dues and any other amounts added thereto in fixing the price to be paid for Crown timber. *Crown Timber Act*, R.S.O. 1990, c. C.51, s. 1.

STUMP HEIGHT. The vertical distance between the horizontal plane through the top of the stump and the horizontal plane through the highest point of the ground at its base.

STUN GUN. A gun which fires a captive bolt and is used to slaughter cattle. F.A. Jaffe, *A Guide to Pathological Evidence*, 3d ed. (Toronto: Carswell, 1991) at 227.

STURGEON. See DRESSED ~; LAKE ~.

STYLE. *v*. To name, call or entitle someone.

STYLE. *n*. A title; an appellation. See ROYAL ~ AND TITLES.

STYLE OF CAUSE. The name or title of a proceeding which sets out the names of all the parties and their capacity, if other than a personal capacity.

STYRENE. *n*. When used as a base in polyester resin along with a fibrous reinforcing agent, control of exposure to this material is regulated under the Ontario Occupational Health and Safety Act. D. Robertson, *Ontario Health and Safety Guide* (Toronto: Richard De Boo Ltd., 1988) at 5-376.

SUABLE. *adj.* Able to be sued.

SUA SPONTE. [L.] On one's own.

SUBAGENT. *n*. A person employed as an agent by an agent to help transact the affairs of the principal.

SUB-AMENDMENT. *n*. An amendment to an amendment.

SUB-AQUATIC LAND. The bed of a natural body of water including the solum of the sea.

SUBARACHNOID HEMORRHAGE. A hemorrhage into either the brain or the space around it. F.A. Jaffe, *A Guide to Pathological Evidence*, 2d ed. (Toronto: Carswell, 1983) at 46.

SUB-BAILMENT. *n*. When a bailee transfers possession to another with the bailor's consent.

SUB-BROKER DEALER. *var.* **SUB-BROKER-DEALER**. An individual who, being retired from active business or as incidental to his principal occupation and as correspondent of any investment dealer or broker-dealer or both, trades in securities for a part of his time in the capacity of an agent or principal. *Securities acts*.

SUB-CATEGORY. *n*. One of the following classifications within a hazard category in which a chemical product may be classified, in particular: (a) in the case of a Category 1 toxic product, "very toxic", "toxic" and "harmful"; (b) in the case of a Category 2 corrosive product, "very corrosive", "corrosive" and "irritant"; and (c) in the case of a Category 3 flammable product, "spontaneously combustible", "very flammable", "flammable" and "combustible". *Consumer Chemicals and Containers Regulations, 2001*, SOR/2001-269, s. 1.

SUB-CHARGE. *n*. A charge of a charge.

SUB-CHIEF. *n*. An elected member of a band commonly known as sub-chief of the band.

SUB COLORE JURIS. [L.] Under the colour of law.

SUBCOMMITTEE. *n*. A committee which is formed from and acts under a main committee.

SUB-COMMITTEE ON AGENDA AND PROCEDURE. A steering committee which recommends, by report, the way a committee should proceed to study its order of reference and advises on topics like times of sittings, witnesses and subject matters for each sitting. A. Fraser, W.A. Dawson, & J. Holtby, eds., *Beauchesne's Rules and Forms of the House of Com-*

mons of Canada, 6th ed. (Toronto: Carswell, 1989) at 227.

SUB CONDITIONE. [L.] On condition.

SUBCONTRACT. *var.* **SUB-CONTRACT**. *n.* 1. Any agreement between the contractor and a subcontractor, or between two or more subcontractors, relating to the provision of services or materials and includes any amendment to that agreement. *Builders' Lien acts*. 2. A binding agreement between a sub-contractor and a contractor or between a sub-contractor and another sub-contractor (a) for construction, or (b) for improving land, or (c) for the doing of any work or the providing of any services in construction or in improving land, or (d) for the supplying of any materials to be used in construction or in improving land. *Builders' Liens Act*, R.S.M. 1987, c. B91, s. 1. See DEFENCE ~.

SUBCONTRACTOR. *var.* **SUB-CONTRAC-TOR**. *n.* 1. A person who has contracted with a prime contractor or with another subcontractor to perform a contract. 2. A person not contracting with or employed directly by an owner or the owner's agent for the doing of any work, rendering of any services or the furnishing of any material but contracting with or employed by a contractor or under the contractor by another subcontractor, but does not include a labourer. See CONSTRUCTION ~.

SUBCUTANEOUS. *adj.* Beneath the skin.

SUBDIVIDE. *v.* To divide a parcel of land into two or more parcels.

SUBDIVISION. *var.* **SUB-DIVISION**. *n.* 1. " . . . [O]ccurs not only where lots or parcels are divided one from the other, but where interests in such lots or parcels are divided for the purpose of sale. . ." *J.C.D. Holdings Ltd. v. Buie* (1985), 61 B.C.L.R. 119 at 125, 17 D.L.R. (4th) 373 (S.C.), McLachlin J. 2. A division of a parcel by means of a plan of subdivision, plan of survey, agreement or any instrument, including a caveat, transferring or creating an estate or interest in part of the parcel. 3. Improved or unimproved land divided or proposed to be divided into 2 or more lots or other units for the purpose of sale or lease and includes land divided or proposed to be divided into condominium units. 4. That area of an electoral division so designated by the returning officer to enable the efficient conduct of an enumeration. 5. The division of any area of land into two or more parcels, and includes a resubdivision or a consolidation of two or more

parcels. See PLAN OF ~; POLITICAL ~; POLLING ~; RE~.

SUBDIVISION AGREEMENT. An agreement between a council and a developer whereby the developer undertakes to provide basic services in order to develop a plan of subdivision.

SUBDIVISION CONTROL. Legislation to control land division. B.J. Reiter, B.N. McLellan and P.M. Perell, *Real Estate Law*, 4th ed. (Toronto: Emond Montgomery, 1992) at 317.

SUBDIVISION PLAN. See FILED ~.

SUBDIVISION UNIT. (a) A lot shown on the original plan of an original survey and includes a township lot, city lot, town lot or village lot, section, block, gore, reserve, common, mining location or mining claim; or (b) a lot, block, part or other unit of land shown on a plan registered or deposited under the Registry Act or the Land Titles Act. *Registry Act*, R.R.O. 1980, Reg. 898, s. 1.

SUBDRAIN. *n.* A drain that is at a level lower than the building drain and the building sewer.

SUBDURAL HEMORRHAGE. A hemorrhage between the arachnoid mater and the dura mater, usually caused by a trauma. F.A. Jaffe, *A Guide to Pathological Evidence*, 3d ed. (Toronto: Carswell, 1991) at 227.

SUBFEEDER. *n.* Those conductors of a circuit, which being themselves supplied by a feeder and having overload protection, supply, or are intended to supply, one or more branch circuits.

SUBFRANCHISE. *n.* A franchise granted by a subfranchisor to a subfranchisee. *Arthur Wishart Act (Franchise Disclosure), 2000*, S.O. 2000, c. 3, s. 1.

SUBFRANCHISOR. *n.* A person to whom an area franchise is granted.

SUBGALEAL. *adj.* Under the scalp. F.A. Jaffe, *A Guide to Pathological Evidence*, 2d ed. (Toronto: Carswell, 1983) at 117.

SUBINFEUDATION. *n.* Division of land first granted to tenants in chief among their followers. E.L.G. Tyler & N.E. Palmer, eds., *Crossley Vaines' Personal Property*, 5th ed. (London: Butterworths, 1973) at 4.

SUBJECT. *n.* 1. Citizen. 2. The person on whom a personal investigation is carried out or is being carried out. 3. Any matter, theme, incident or description and includes a person, object, place or event. See BRITISH ~; NATURAL-BORN ~.

SUBJECTIVE MENS REA. The accused intended the consequences of his or her acts or knowing of the likely consequences acted recklessly in the face of the risk.

SUBJECT-MATTER. See CERTAINTY OF ~.

SUBJECT MATTER COMPETENCE. The aspects of a court's jurisdiction that depend on factors other than those pertaining to the court's territorial competence.

SUBJECT TO. 1. "In a contract, 'subject to' a stipulated condition, . . . means that the dominant but conditional obligation of the contract, namely, to purchase, is to become operative and effective only on fulfilment of the condition or occurrence of the event stipulated in the condition; unless there is such fulfilment or occurrence the conditional contract never becomes unconditional, operative or binding and the parties are in the same position as if no contract had been entered into. . ." *Kiernicki v.. Jaworski* (1956), 18 W.W.R. 289 at 293 (Man. C.A.), Coyne J.A. 2. "The meaning of the expression 'subject to' in statutes was, in my opinion, correctly stated by the late Professor Elmer A. Driedger in The Composition of Legislation: Legislative Forms and Precedents, 2d ed. (Ottawa: Canadian Government Publishing Centre, Supply & Services Canada, 1976) at pp. 139-40 as follows: 'Subject to—Used to assign a subordinate position to an enactment, or to pave the way for qualifications. Where two sections conflict, and one is not merely an exception to the other, the subordinate one should be preceded by subject to; this reconciles the conflict and serves as a warning that there is more to come.'" *Murphy v. Welsh* (1991), 4 C.P.C. (3d) 301 at 309-10, 30 M.V.R. (2d) 163, 3 O.R. (3d) 182, 81 D.L.R. (4th) 475, 50 O.A.C. 246, the court per Blair J.A.

SUBJECT TO EXCISE. Subject to the provisions of this Act, of any other Act respecting duties of excise or of any proclamation, order in council or departmental regulation published or made under those provisions. *Excise Act*, R.S.C. 1985, c. E-14, s. 2.

SUB JUDICE. [L.] Under consideration by the court.

SUB-JUDICE CONVENTION. The expectation that members of Parliament will not discuss matters that are before tribunals or the courts which are courts of record. A. Fraser, W.A. Dawson, & J. Holtby, eds., *Beauchesne's Rules and Forms of the House of Commons of Canada*, 6th ed. (Toronto: Carswell, 1989) at 153.

SUBLATO FUNDAMENTO CADIT OPUS. [L.] If the foundation is removed, the structure collapses.

SUBLATO PRINCIPALI TOLLITUR ADJUNCTUM. [L.] With the removal of the principal, the adjunct is removed.

SUBLEASE. *var*. **SUB-LEASE**. *n*. 1. A tenant's grant of interest in the leased premises which is less than that tenant's own. 2. Includes an agreement for a sublease where the sublessee has become entitled to have his sublease granted. *Landlord and Tenant acts*.

SUB-LET. *v*. For a tenant to lease the whole or part of the premises during a portion of the unexpired balance of the lease's term.

SUBLICENSE. In patent law, a grant by a licensee of certain licensed rights to a third party, the sublicensee.

SUBLIMINAL DEVICE. A technical device that is used to convey or attempt to convey a message to a person by means of images or sounds of very brief duration or by any other means without that person being aware that such a device is being used or being aware of the substance of the message being conveyed or attempted to be conveyed.

SUBMARINE CABLE. See EXTERNAL ~.

SUBMARINE TRACT. A lot, piece or parcel of land covered or partly covered by the water of the sea or a lake, of which one or more leases have been or may be issued.

SUBMISSION. *n*. 1. Statements and rhetoric urging the trier of fact to make particular findings of fact and apply the law in the manner proposed by the person making the submissions. Made on behalf of a party before a tribunal or court. 2. Acquisition of jurisdiction which it would not otherwise possess by a court because the defendant, by conduct, cannot object to the jurisdiction. This may occur either impliedly or expressly, provided the person submitting is capable of doing so. C.R.B. Dunlop, *Creditor-Debtor Law in Canada* (Toronto: Carswell, 1981) at 470. 3. Definition of an arbitrator's jurisdiction over a particular case, i.e. a written grievance or a separate document. D.J.M. Brown and D.M. Beatty, *Canadian Labour Arbitration*, 3d ed. (Aurora: Canada Law Book, 1988-) at 2-14. 4. A written agreement to submit present or future differences to arbitration whether an arbitrator is named therein or not.

SUBMIT. *v.* 1. To offer, as an advocate, a proposition to a court. 2. To bring under a person's consideration or notice. 3. Deliver.

SUB MODO. [L.] Under restriction or condition.

SUBMORTGAGE. *n.* A mortgage of a mortgage.

SUB NOM. *abbr.* Sub nomine.

SUB NOMINE. [L.] Under a name.

SUBNOTATION. *n.* A written reply to a request for guidance.

SUB-ORDER DELIVERY CHARGE. A charge for the delivery of part of the goods shown on one bill of lading to a person other than the original consignee.

SUBORDINATE. *n.* 1. A person who works under the orders or directions of another and is lower in rank or status. 2. A clause grammatically governed by another clause.

SUBORDINATE BUILDING. A detached building the use of which in relation to another building on the same lot is ordinarily incidental or subordinate to that building. Canada regulations.

SUBORDINATED INDEBTEDNESS. An instrument evidencing an indebtedness of a company that by its terms provides that the indebtedness will, in the event of the insolvency or winding-up of the company, be subordinate in right of payment to all deposit liabilities of the company and all other liabilities of the company except those that, by their terms, rank equally with or are subordinate to such indebtedness.

SUBORDINATED NOTE. An instrument evidencing an indebtedness of a company that by its terms provides that the indebtedness evidenced by it shall, in the event of the insolvency or winding-up of the company, rank equally with the indebtedness evidenced by other subordinated notes of the company but be subordinate in right of payment to all other indebtedness of the company except indebtedness in respect of subordinated shareholder loans.

SUBORDINATED SHAREHOLDER LOAN. A loan made to a company by a share-holder of the company or by a person who controls a shareholder of the company, as the case may be, for a fixed term and under the condition that the indebtedness arising therefrom shall, in the event of the insolvency or winding-up of the company, rank equally with the indebtedness in respect of other subordinated shareholder loans but be subordinate in right of payment to all other indebtedness of the company.

SUBORDINATE LEGISLATION. 1. Legislation of a subordinate body, i.e. one other than a legislature or Parliament, such as a statutory instrument, regulation or by-law. 2. Any regulation, proclamation, rule, order, by-law or instrument that is of a legislative nature and made or approved under the authority of an Act.

SUBORDINATE VOTING SHARE. A common share carrying a right to vote in all circumstances in the issuing corporation that is not a common share with full voting rights.

SUBORNATION. *n.* The crime of getting someone else to do something unlawful.

SUB PEDE SIGILLI. [L.] Under the foot of a seal.

SUBPERIOSTEAL. *adj.* Between the skull and the delicate membrane which covers it. F.A. Jaffe, *A Guide to Pathological Evidence*, 2d ed. (Toronto: Carswell, 1983) at 117.

SUBPOENA. *n.* Document issued by a third party compelling a person to attend proceedings as a witness in order to give testimony. Given under the threat of penalty. See WRIT OF ~.

SUBPOENA AD TESTIFICANDUM. [L.] Under threat of penalty you are required to come to testify.

SUBPOENA DUCES TECUM. [L. subpoena you shall bring with you] 1. A document requiring a witness to give evidence in court or tribunal, or before an examiner and also to bring along documents specified in the subpoena. 2. . . . [A]n order in the nature of a subpoena duces tecum . . . would compel not the production of documents but rather would require the attendance before the inquiry of [a witness] with [her or his] relevant documents." *Canada Deposit Insurance Corp. v. Code* (1988), 49 D.L.R. (4th) 57 at 60 (Alta. C.A.), the court per Kerans J.A.

SUBROGATE. *v.* " . . . [T]o put one in the place of, or to substitute one for, another in respect of a right or a claim." *Big Wheels Transport & Leasing Ltd. v. Richard* (1987), 46 D.L.R. (4th)

108 at 110, 27 C.C.L.I. 243, 70 Nfld. & P.E.I.R. 104, 215 A.P.R. 104 (P.E.I. C.A.), the court per McQuaid J.A.

SUBROGATED. *adj*. Describes the rights acquired by a singly secured creditor in property in which she or he had no rights when a doubly secured creditor realized a claim out of the parcel on which the singly secured creditor had her or his security making it unavailable to the singly secured creditor. W.B. Rayner & R.H. McLaren, *Falconbridge on Mortgages*, 4th ed. (Toronto: Canada Law Book, 1977) at 314.

SUBROGATION. *n*. 1. The principle of subrogation is a device which gives effect to the contract of insurance, protecting the insurer by permitting it to pursue claims against a third party in the name of the insured in respect of losses which have been indemnified. *Pacific Forest Products Ltd. v. AXA Pacific Insurance Co.*, 2003 BCCA 241, 12 B.C.L.R. (4th) 293 (C.A.). 2. " . . . [W]hen one person has been bound to indemnify another against a loss, he is entitled to any benefit in respect of the indemnified loss received by that person over and above the full amount of the loss. From this it follows that the right of subrogation does not arise until there has been recovery in full by the person suffering the loss . . ." *Bigl v. Alberta* (1989), 37 C.C.L.I. 40 at 45, 67 Alta. L.R. (2d) 349, 60 D.L.R. (4th) 438 (C.A.), the court per Laycraft J.A. 3. "The most common [way of avoiding double recovery] is subrogation. Indemnity insurance is subject to the insurer's right to claim back payments to the extent the plaintiff recovers damages. Many statutory benefits, such as worker's compensation, are subject to legislative indemnity provisions." *Ratych v. Bloomer* (1990), 3 C.C.L.T. (2d) 1 at 23, 30 C.C.E.L. 161, 69 D.L.R. (4th) 25, [1990] 1 S.C.R. 940, 107 N.R. 335, 73 O.R. (2d) 448n, 39 O.A.C. 103, [1990] R.R.A. 651n, McLachlin J. (Lamer, La Forest, L'Heureux-ubé and Sopinka JJ. concurring). 4. "To subrogate is to substitute. An insurer to recover a loss by way of subrogation must be able to place itself in the position of the insured. It follows, then, that the insurer is only entitled to make such claims, in the name of the insured, as could have been made by the insured. . ." *Bow Helicopters Ltd. v. Bell Helicopter Textron* (1981), 14 B.L.R. 133 at 142, 16 Alta. L.R. (2d) 149, 31 A.R. 49, 125 D.L.R. (3d) 386, [1981] I.L.R. 1-1415 (C.A.), the court per Haddad J.A. See DOCTRINE OF ~.

SUB SALVO CONDUCTU. [L.] Under safe conduct.

SUBSCRIBE. *v*. 1. To write under. 2. To sign.

SUBSCRIBED AND ISSUED CAPITAL STOCK OF THE COMPANY. As applied to a provincial company having common shares without par value, means the number of the issued common shares of the company.

SUBSCRIBED CAPITAL. The number of shares which subscribers take or agree to take.

SUBSCRIBER. *n*. 1. A person, firm or company supplied with a main line telephone. 2. A household of one or more persons, whether occupying a single-unit dwelling or a unit in a multiple-unit dwelling, to which service is provided directly or indirectly by a licensee; or the owner or operator of a hotel, hospital, nursing home or other commercial or institutional premises to which service is provided by a licensee. *Broadcasting Distribution Regulations*, SOR/97-555, s. 1. 3. Persons exchanging with each other reciprocal contracts of indemnity or inter-insurance. *Insurance acts*. See FARM ~.

SUBSCRIPTION. *n*. 1. An offer from a prospective shareholder to purchase shares of a corporation. 2. Includes fee, due, assessment or other similar sum payable by a member of a society under the bylaws.

SUBSCRIPTION PROGRAMMING SIGNAL. Radiocommunication that is intended for reception either directly or indirectly by the public in Canada or elsewhere on payment of a subscription fee or other charge. *Radiocommunication Act*, R.S.C. 1985, c. R-2, s. 2.

SUBSCRIPTION TELEVISION SYSTEM. An undertaking that distributes encrypted programming services by low-power transmitters using the conventional VHF or UHF television bands. *Broadcasting Distribution Regulations*, SOR/97-555, s. 1.

SUBSEQUENS MATRIMONIUM TOLLIT PECCATUM PRAECEDENS. [L.] A subsequent marriage removes a preceding fault.

SUBSEQUENT. *adj*. " . . . [M]ay have reference to time or to interest. . . the word 'subsequent' [in The Alberta Rules of Court, r. 46] is used in the sense of time . . ." *Corwin v. Avery*, [1925] 2 D.L.R. 599 at 603, [1925] 1 W.W.R. 811, 21 Alta. L.R. 95 (C.A.), the court per Harvey C.J.

SUBSEQUENT CONVICTION. A conviction: (a) within a period of 5 years after the date of a first conviction, either before or after this section comes into force; and (b) that follows a third conviction.

SUBSEQUENT ENCUMBRANCER. A person who has a charge, lien or encumbrance on mortgaged property subsequent to the mortgage in question.

SUBSEQUENT MORTGAGEE. See SUBSEQUENT PURCHASER OR MORTGAGEE.

SUBSEQUENT OFFENCE. 1. "Ordinarily, the terms 'second offence' and 'subsequent offence' (i.e., subsequent to a second offence) mean successive offences committed against the same section or a predecessor section . . ." *R. v. Negridge* (1980), 6 M.V.R. 255 at 261, 17 C.R. (3d) 14, 54 C.C.C. (2d) 304 (Ont. C.A.), the court per Martin J.A. 2. An offence committed within 5 years after the date of a previous conviction. *Excise Act*, R.S.C. 1985, c. E-14, s. 2. See SECOND OR ~.

SUBSEQUENT PURCHASER. 1. Includes a person who, in good faith for valuable consideration and without notice, obtains by assignment an interest in book debts that have already been assigned. *Assignment of Book Debts acts* 2. A person who acquires an interest in goods after the making of a conditional sale thereof. *Conditional Sales acts.*

SUBSEQUENT PURCHASER OR MORTGAGEE. Includes a person who obtains, whether by way of purchase, mortgage, charge or assignment, an interest in chattels or book debts that have already been mortgaged, charged or assigned. *Corporation Securities Registration acts.*

SUBSIDIARY. *n.* 1. A corporation which, in respect of another corporation, is controlled, either directly or indirectly, by that other corporation. 2. A body corporate for which the credit union elects or appoints a majority of the board of directors on the basis of voting rights or shares held in that body corporate by the credit union. 3. A subsidiary, at a given time, of another corporation, hereinafter called "parent corporation", when at least 90 per cent of the issued shares to which are attached full voting rights of its capital stock are owned by such other corporation. See CONTROLLED ~; WHOLLY-OWNED ~.

SUBSIDIARY COIN. A coin other than a gold coin. *Currency Act*, R.S.C. 1985, c. C-52, s. 2.

SUBSIDIARY COMPANY. A company is a subsidiary of another company if, but only if, (a) it is controlled by, (i) that other; or (ii) that other and one or more companies each of which is controlled by that other; or (iii) two or more companies each of which is controlled by that other; or (b) it is a subsidiary of a subsidiary of that other company.

SUBSIDIARY CONTROLLED CORPORATION. A corporation of which more than 50 per cent of the issued share capital, with full voting rights under all circumstances, is owned, directly or indirectly, by another corporation.

SUBSIDIARY CONTROLLED FINANCIAL CORPORATION. A financial corporation of which more than 50 per cent of the issued share capital, with full voting rights under all circumstances, is owned, directly or indirectly, by another corporation. *Financial Corporation Capital Tax acts.*

SUBSIDIARY CONTROLLED OPERATION. A corporation more than 50 per cent of the issued capital stock of which having full voting rights under all circumstances belongs to the corporation to which it is subsidiary.

SUBSIDIARY CORPORATION. A corporation legally transacting business in Canada, under any Act of Parliament, the majority of the shares of which, that have under all the circumstances full voting rights, is owned or controlled directly or indirectly by or for the parent corporation. *Pension Fund Societies Act*, R.S.C. 1985, c. P-8, s. 17(4).

SUBSIDIARY MOTION. A motion, as for reading a bill, to move a question forward through the stages of procedure it must pass before final adoption. A. Fraser, W.A. Dawson, & J. Holtby, eds., *Beauchesne's Rules and Forms of the House of Commons of Canada*, 6th ed. (Toronto: Carswell, 1989) at 174.

SUBSIDIARY QUESTION. An issue which presents itself while the main question before the court is being decided and which must be solved before the main question can be answered. J.G. McLeod, *The Conflict of Laws* (Calgary: Carswell, 1983) at 50-51.

SUBSIDIARY WHOLLY OWNED CORPORATION. *var.* **SUBSIDIARY WHOLLY-OWNED CORPORATION**. A corporation all the issued share capital of which, except directors' qualifying shares, belongs to the corporation to which it is subsidiary.

SUBSIDIES AGREEMENT. The Agreement on Subsidies and Countervailing Measures, being part of Annex 1A to the WTO Agreement. *Special Import Measures Act*, R.S.C. 1985, c. S-15, s. 2.

SUBSIDIZED GOODS. (a) Goods in respect of the production, manufacture, growth, processing, purchase, distribution, transportation, sale, export or import of which a subsidy has been or will be paid, granted, authorized or otherwise provided, directly or indirectly, by the government of a country other than Canada; and (b) goods that are disposed of at a loss by the government of a country other than Canada, and includes any goods in which, or in the production, manufacture, growth, processing or the like of which, goods described in paragraph (a) or (b) are incorporated, consumed, used or otherwise employed. *Special Imports Measures Act*, R.S.C. 1985, c. S-15, s. 2.

SUBSIDIZED PUBLIC HOUSING. A rental unit rented to persons or families of low or modest income who pay an amount geared-to-income for that unit by reason of public funding.

SUBSIDY. *n.* 1. (a) A financial contribution by a government of a country other than Canada in any of the circumstances outlined in subsection (1.6) that confers a benefit to persons engaged in the production, manufacture, growth, processing, purchase, distribution, transportation, sale, export or import of goods, but does not include the amount of any duty or internal tax imposed by the government of the country of origin or country of export on (i) goods that, because of their exportation from the country of export or country of origin, have been exempted or have been or will be relieved by means of remission, refund or drawback, (ii) energy, fuel, oil and catalysts that are used or consumed in the production of exported goods and that have been exempted or have been or will be relieved by means of remission, refund or drawback, or (iii) goods incorporated into exported goods and that have been exempted or have been or will be relieved by means of remission, refund or drawback, or (b) any form of income or price support within the meaning of Article XVI of the General Agreement on Tariffs and Trade, 1994, being part of Annex 1A to the WTO Agreement, that confers a benefit. *Special Imports Measures Act*, R.S.C. 1985, c. S-15, s. 2. 2. The amount by which a premium or other required payment is reduced.

SUB SILENTIO. [L.] Silently.

SUBSISTENCE ALLOWANCE. An amount paid to a worker for the cost of food, travel and lodging while travelling for the employer.

SUBSISTENCE WAGES. Wages adequate only to supply the bare necessities of life.

SUBSISTING EXECUTION. An execution in the hands of a sheriff other than one that by this Act he is directed to disregard. *Execution Creditors acts.*

SUBSTANCE. *n.* 1. Any distinguishable kind of inanimate matter (a) capable of becoming dispersed in the natural environment; or (b) capable of becoming transformed in the natural environment into matter described in subclause (a). 2. In relation to medicine, includes compositions of active and inactive ingredients which are physically mixed together and ingested into the body as a single composition. 3. Of an expert's report, includes the facts upon which the opinion is based as well as the opinion itself. See CLASS OF ~S; DANGEROUS ~; DELETERIOUS ~; DESIGNATED ~; EXPLOSIVE ~; FISSIONABLE ~; FOREIGN ~; LISTED ~; MINERAL ~; OZONE DEPLETING ~; PITH AND ~; PRESCRIBED ~S; QUARRIABLE ~; TOXIC ~.

SUBSTANCE ABUSE. The use of any substance by an individual in quantities that cause a physical or psychological condition that may result in problems for individuals, families or communities.

SUBSTANTIAL. *adj.* "The word 'substantial' has a number of quite different senses, depending on the context in which it is used. . ." *Manning Timber Products Ltd. v. Minister of National Revenue*, [1952] C.T.C. 206 at 207, [1952] 2 S.C.R. 481, [1952] 3 D.L.R. 848, 52 D.T.C. 1148, Taschereau J. (Kerwin, Kellock and Locke JJ. concurring). 2. " . . . '[L]arge quantity', . . ." *Manning Timber Products Ltd. v. Minister of National Revenue*, [1952] C.T.C. 206 at 207, [1952] 2 S.C.R. 481, [1952] 3 D.L.R. 848, 52 D.T.C. 1148, Taschereau J. (Kerwin, Kellock and Locke JJ. concurring). 3. Significant; important; essential.

SUBSTANTIAL BREACH. A breach of a covenant or a series of breaches of a tenancy agreement, the cumulative effect of which is substantial.

SUBSTANTIAL COMPLETION. For a subcontractor the point in time when the sub-contractor is able to sue for his contract price in full, the point when he has performed all he contracted to do.

SUBSTANTIAL COMPLIANCE. "When a statute requires substantial compliance . . . it requires the doing of those things which are of real importance, of substance, having regard to the object and scheme of the Act . . . I would therefore interpret 'substantial' as importing a measure of compliance—has the claimant made a reasonable effort to provide the information that the Act requires for its effective operation. . ." *Ed Miller Sales & Rental Ltd. v. Canadian Imperial Bank of Commerce* (1987), 51 Alta. L.R. (2d) 54 at 57, 37 D.L.R. (4th) 179, 7 P.P.S.A.C. 87, 79 A.R. 161 (C.A.), the court per Stevenson J.A.

SUBSTANTIAL INTEREST. The direct or indirect beneficial ownership of, or the power to exercise control or direction over, equity shares of any corporation that carry more than 10 per cent of the voting rights attached to all outstanding equity shares of the corporation. *Municipal Conflict of Interest Act*, R.S.N.S. 1989, c. 299, s. 2.

SUBSTANTIAL INVESTMENT. A person has a substantial investment in a body corporate where (a) the voting rights attached to the aggregate of any voting shares of the body corporate beneficially owned by the person and by any entities controlled by the person exceed 10 per cent of the voting rights attached to all of the outstanding voting shares of the body corporate; or (b) the aggregate of any shares of the body corporate beneficially owned by the person and by any entities controlled by the person represents ownership of greater than 25 per cent of the shareholders' equity of the body corporate. *Bank Act*, S.C. 1991, c. 46, s. 10.

SUBSTANTIAL ISSUE. "[In s. 37(4) of the Trade Marks Act, R.S.C. 1970, c. T-10] . . . an issue to be tried or, in other words, one where the adverse party might possibly succeed if the allegations raised were established." *Koffler Stores Ltd. v. Canada (Registrar of Trade Marks)* (1976), 28 C.P.R. (2d) 113 at 114, [1976] 2 F.C. 685 (T.D.), Addy J.

SUBSTANTIAL PERFORMANCE. Exists where a contract has been carried out in all its essentials and only technical or unimportant omissions or defects have occurred.

SUBSTANTIAL PURPOSE TEST. "The 'substantial, purpose test' is enunciated by Robertson C.J.O. In Blackstone v. Mutual Life Insurance Co. of New York [[1944] O.R. 328 (C.A.)] at p. 333 [O.R.] where he stated: ' . . . it is not essential to the validity of the claim of privilege that the document for which privilege is claimed should have been written, prepared or obtained solely for the purpose of, or in connection with, litigation then pending or anticipated. It is sufficient if that was the substantial, or one of the substantial, purposes then in *view. . .*'" *Keuhl v. McConnell* (1991), 3 C.P.C. (3d) 22 at 25, 32 M.V.R. (2d) 280 (Ont. Gen. Div.), Chadwick J.

SUBSTANTIAL RISK. A real chance of danger that is apparent on the evidence. *Children and Family Services Act*, S.N.S. 1990, c. 5, s. 22.

SUBSTANTIAL SHAREHOLDER. A person who owns, or who is the beneficial owner of, 10 per cent or more of the voting shares of a body corporate and includes a shareholder who, together with his associates, holds 10 per cent or more of the voting shares of a body corporate.

SUBSTANTIATED. *adj.* " . . . '[P]roven' . . ." *Syndicat des employés de production du Qué. & de l'Acadie v. Canada (Canadian Human Rights Commission)* (1989), 89 C.L.L.C. 17,022 at 16,230, [1989] 2 S.C.R. 879, 62 D.L.R. (4th) 385, 11 C.H.R.R. D/1, 100 N.R. 241, Dickson C.J.C.

SUBSTANTIVE CONSTRUCTIVE TRUST. " . . . In a substantive constructive trust, the acts of the parties in relation to some property are such that those acts are later declared by a court to have given rise to a substantive constructive trust and to have done so at the time when the acts of the parties brought the trust into being. The difference between a substantive constructive trust and a resulting trust may, in cases where the property reverts to the settlor, be no more than a matter of terminological preference. . ." *Atlas Cabinets & Furniture Ltd. v. National Trust Co.* (1990), 37 E.T.R. 16 at 27, 38 C.L.R. 106, 45 B.C.L.R. (2d) 99, 68 D.L.R. (4th) 161 (C.A.), Lambert J.A. (Hinkson, Toy and Cumming JJ.A. concurring).

SUBSTANTIVE LAW. " . . . [C]reates rights and obligations and is concerned with the ends which the administration of justice seeks to attain, . . . substantive law determines [the parties'] conduct and relations in respect of the matters litigated." *Sutt v. Sutt*, [1969] 1 O.R. 169 at 175, 2 D.L.R. (3d) 33 (C.A.), Schroeder J.A. (McGillivray J.A. concurring).

SUBSTANTIVE MOTION. A self-contained proposal, not incidental to any proceeding, which may be drafted or amended so that it expresses a decision of the House of Commons. A. Fraser, W.A. Dawson, & J. Holtby, eds., *Beauchesne's Rules and Forms of the House of Commons of Canada*, 6th ed. (Toronto: Carswell, 1989) at 173.

SUBSTATION. *n*. A part of a transmission line that is not a transmission circuit and includes equipment for transforming, compensating, switching, rectifying or inverting of electric energy flowing to, over or from the transmission line.

SUBSTITUTE DECISION-MAKER. In relation to a person to whom a record, information or an approved agency's decision relates, means, (a) the person who would be authorized under the Health Care Consent Act, 1996 to give or refuse consent to a treatment on behalf of the person to whom the record, information or approved agency's decision relates, if that person were incapable with respect to the treatment under that Act, or (b) any other person who is lawfully authorized to make a decision concerning a community service on behalf of the person to whom the record, information or approved agency's decision relates. *Long-Term Care Act, 1994*, S.O. 1994, c. 26, s. 2.

SUBSTITUTED EXECUTOR. A person appointed to act on behalf of another executor.

SUBSTITUTED SERVICE. Service of a document on a person representing the party to be served, instead of on the party personally or by some means not involving personal service.

SUBSTITUTE TEACHER. A teacher employed on a day-to-day basis as required to replace a teacher who is temporarily absent from his regular duties.

SUB-SURFACE DRAIN. A drain, other than a foundation drain, installed to collect water from subsoil.

SUBSURFACE INVESTIGATION. The appraisal of the general subsurface conditions at a building site by analysis of information gained by such methods as geological surveys, in situ testing, sampling, visual inspection, laboratory testing of samples of the subsurface materials and groundwater observations and measurements.

SUBSURFACE MINERALS. All natural mineral salts of boron, calcium, lithium, magnesium, potassium, sodium, bromine, chlorine, fluorine, iodine, nitrogen, phosphorus and sulphur, and their compounds, occurring more than two hundred feet below the surface of the land.

SUB-SYSTEM. *n*. An identifiable, predesigned, physically integrated, co-ordinated series of parts that function as a unit of the construction of a building.

SUBTENANCY. *n*. A tenancy created by sublease.

SUBTENANT. *var*. **SUB-TENANT**. *n*. 1. A person entering into a lease with a head tenant who reserves at least one day of her or his original term of tenancy. 2. Includes any person deriving title under a sublease.

SUB-UNDERWRITER. *n*. A person who purchases from a principal underwriter the shares or debentures of a company with a view to their sale to the public. *Companies Act*, R.S.N.W.T. 1974, c. C-7, s. 89.

SUBVERSION. *n*. Connotes accomplishing change by illicit means or for improper purposes related to an organisation. *Qu v. Canada (Minister of Citizenship & Immigration)*, 2000 CarswellNat 705, 5 Imm. L.R. (3d) 129, [2000] 4 F.C. 71 (T.D.).

SUBVERSIVE. *adj*. Having a tendency to subvert or overthrow (a government).

SUBVERSIVE OR HOSTILE ACTIVITIES. (a) Espionage against Canada or any state allied or associated with Canada; (b) sabotage; (c) activities directed toward the commission of terrorist acts, including hijacking, in or against Canada or foreign states; (d) activities directed toward accomplishing government change within Canada or foreign states by the use of or the encouragement of the use of force, violence or any criminal means; (e) activities directed toward gathering information used for intelligence purposes that relates to Canada or any state allied or associated with Canada; and (f) activities directed toward threatening the safety of Canadians, employees of the Government of Canada or property of the Government of Canada outside Canada. *Access to Information Act*, R.S.C. 1985, c. A-1, s. 15(2).

SUB VOCE. [L.] Under title.

SUBWAY. *n*. 1. An underground railway. 2. A structure, including the approaches thereto, that carries a highway across and under the railway.

SUCCESSION. *n*. As the case requires, (a) the property of the deceased to which a successor becomes beneficially entitled; or (b) the acquisition by a successor of any property of the deceased by reason of the death of the deceased or a successor's becoming beneficially entitled to property of a deceased by reason of the death of the deceased.

SUCCESSION DUTY. 1. Inheritance tax levied against each beneficiary on an inheritance. 2. Tax on the gratuitous acquisition of property. 3. Tax paid by the person who inherits as a result of an intestacy, a will or an inter vivos gift when the gift arises because of death.

SUCCESSIVE LEGAL INTEREST. (a) The first or particular interest, (b) any following interest, whether the following interest is future, vested or contingent or is an executory interest, or a determinable or defeasible interest, or any interest over thereupon, and (c) a general or special power of appointment, but does not include the interests of landlords and tenants within the meaning of The Landlord and Tenant Act. *Perpetuities and Accumulations Act*, R.S.M. 1987, c. P33, s. 1.

SUCCESSIVE PROSECUTION. When an accused is charged with conspiracy to commit an offence, is tried and convicted or acquitted, and later tried for commission of the separate offence which was the accomplished object of the conspiracy. M.R. Goode, *Criminal Conspiracy in Canada* (Toronto: Carswell, 1975) at 171.

SUCCESSOR. *n.* 1. One who takes another's place. 2. An heir, executor or administrator. *Land Registration Reform Act*, R.S.O. 1990, c. L.4, s. 1. 3. "When used in reference to corporations, . . . generally denotes another corporation which, through merger, amalgamation or some other type of legal succession, assumes the burdens and becomes vested with the rights of the first corporation. . ." *National Trust Co. v. Mead* (1991), 12 R.P.R. (2d) 165 at 177, [1990] 2 S.C.R. 410, [1990] 5 W.W.R. 459, 71 D.L.R. (4th) 488, 112 N.R. 1, Wilson J. (Lamer C.J.C., La Forest, L'Heureux-Dubé, Gonthier and Cory JJ. concurring). 4. In relation to any property of the deceased includes any person who, at any time or on or after the death of the deceased became or becomes beneficially entitled to any property of the deceased (a) by virtue of, or conditionally or contingently on, the death of the deceased; or (b) by virtue of the exercise of any general power of which the deceased was the donee or other holder; or (c) in any case, under any disposition made by the deceased during the deceased's lifetime; or (d) by virtue of the application in respect of the death of the deceased of any law of Canada or a province providing for relief of dependants of deceased persons, and includes (e) any person beneficially entitled to any property of the deceased in default of the exercise of any general power of which the deceased was the donee or other holder; (f) any person as the donee or other holder of any general power created by the deceased in respect of any property of the deceased; and (g) any trustee, guardian, committee, curator or other similar representative of any person mentioned in this clause, in the capacity of trustee, guardian, committee, curator or other representative. See COLLATERAL ~; PREFERRED ~; SIBLING ~.

SUCCESSOR EMPLOYER. A person who acquires the business or assets of an employer.

SUCCESSOR PROVISION. "Section 89 [of The Labour Relations Act, 1977, S.N. 1977, c. 64] is designed to prevent the loss of union protection by employees whose company's business is sold or transferred to another business concern. This provision [is] known colloquially as a 'successor provision' . . ." *W.W. Lester (1978) Ltd. v. U.A., Local 740* (1990), 48 Admin. L.R. 1 at 38, 76 D.L.R. (4th) 389, 91 C.L.L.C. 14,002, 123 N.R. 241, 88 Nfld. & P.E.I.R. 15, 274 A.P.R. 15, [1990] 3 S.C.R. 644, Wilson J. (dissenting) (Dickson C.J.C. and Cory J. concurring).

SUCCESSOR UNION. A union which succeeds another by the process of merger, amalgamation or transfer of jurisdiction.

SUCCURRITUR MINORI: FACILIS EST LAPSUS JUVENTUTIS. [L.] A minor should be assisted: a mistake is easy for youth.

SUCH. *adj.* Associates the word or words it modifies with earlier word or words in a document.

SUCH AS. Has the same meaning as "includes". Words which follow the phrase are examples of or demonstrative of the words or phrases which precede it.

SUDDEN. *adj.* Unexpected; unforeseen.

SUDDEN INFANT DEATH SYNDROME. The sudden death of an apparently well infant, who is usually between three and twelve months old.

SUDDEN PROVOCATION. The wrongful act or insult must strike a mind unprepared for it, that it must make an unexpected impact that takes the understanding by surprise and sets the passions aflame. *R. v. Tripodi*, [1955] S.C.R. 438.

SUE. *v*. To bring a civil action against a person.

SUFFER. *v*. To permit; to allow.

SUFFERANCE WAREHOUSE. A place licensed as a sufferance warehouse by the Minister under section 24. *Customs Act*, R.S.C. 1985 (2d Supp.), c. 1, s. 2.

SUFFERENTIA PACIS. [L. sufferance of peace] A truce.

SUFFERING. See PAIN AND ~;

SUFFICIENT CAUSATION. See MULTIPLE ~.

SUFFICIENT INFORMATION. In respect of the determination of any amount, difference or adjustment, means objective and quantifiable information that establishes the accuracy of the amount, difference or adjustment. *Customs Act*, R.S.C. 1985 (2d Supp.), c. 1, s. 45.

SUFFICIENT OUTLET. The safe discharge of water at a point where it will do no injury to land or roads.

SUFFOCATION. *n*. A fatal oxygen deficiency caused by blockage of the nose and mouth.

SUFFRAGE. *n*. Vote; electoral franchise.

SUFFRAGETTE. *n*. A woman who campaigned for female enfranchisement.

SUFFRAGIST. *n*. A person who campaigned for extended enfranchisement.

SUGAR. See MAPLE ~.

SUGAR BUSH. A stand of trees suitable for the cultivation of maple sugar.

SUGAR BUSH OPERATOR. A person who produces a maple product directly from maple sap.

SUGAR REFINERY. A plant that receives sugar beets or other naturally occurring plants and processes them into marketable sugar products for human consumption and other by-products that can be used for animal consumption.

SUGGESTIO FALSI. [L. suggestion of falsity] Deliberate misrepresentation. *Coffey v. Scane* (1895), 25 O.R. 22 at 34, 15 P.R. 112 (H.C.), Armour J.

SUGGESTION. *n*. A conjecture or representation of something.

SUGGESTIVE. *adj*. Providing evidence of; disclosing.

SUICIDE. *n*. Killing oneself. The intentional act of a party who knows the probable consequences.

SUICIDE PACT. Agreement by more than one person to commit suicide jointly.

SUI GENERIS. [L.] Of one's own class or kind.

SUI JURIS. [L.] Of one's own right, without disability. R. Megarry and H.W.R. Wade, *The Law of Real Property*, 5th ed. (London: Stevens, 1984) at cxxvii.

SUING. *n*. "The ordinary, primary and usual meaning of the word 'suing' [is] the commencement or initiation of an action . . ." *Szeles, Re* (1979), 107 D.L.R. (3d) 393 at 396, [1980] 4 W.W.R. 97, 16 B.C.L.R. 110, 32 C.B.R. (N.S.) 266 (C.A.), the court per Bull J.A.

SUIT. *n*. 1. " . . . [W]as authoritatively defined by the Supreme Court of Canada in Lenoir v. Ritchie (1879), 3 S.C.R. 575. Fournier, J. said, at p. 601, 'The term (suit) is certainly a very comprehensive one, and is understood to apply to any proceeding in a Court of justice, by which an individual pursues that remedy in a Court of justice, which the law affords him. The modes of proceeding may be various, but if a right is litigated between parties in a Court of justice, the proceeding by which the decision of the Court is sought, is a suit.' This definition has been adopted by this court . . ." *Canadian Workers' Union v. Frankel Structural Steel Ltd.*, (1976), 76 C.L.L.C. 14,010 at 51, 12 O.R. (2d) 560 (Div. Ct.), Reid J. 2. A civil legal proceeding brought against one person by another. 3. Includes action. 4. " . . . '[C]ause' or 'action'." *Hampton Lumber Mills v. Joy Logging Ltd.* (1977), 2 C.P.C. 312 at 317, [1977] W.W.R. 289 (B.C. S.C.), Ruttan J. See FRIENDLY~; LAW ~; NON~.

SUITABLE. *adj*. In relation to packing or to containers, means (a) well constructed and in good condition; (b) of such a character and construction that any interior surface with which the contents may come into contact is not dangerously affected by the substance being conveyed; (c) capable of withstanding the ordinary risks of handling and transport by sea; and (d) capable of withstanding any pressure likely to be generated therein. *Dangerous Goods Shipping Regulations*, C.R.C., c. 1419, s. 2.

SUITABLE ALTERNATIVE EMPLOYMENT. Employment which will preserve the existing employment relationship and which is otherwise proper in terms of rate of pay, hours of work and the nature of the work having regard to the circumstances.

SUITABLE EMPLOYMENT. Appropriate employment that allows a worker who has suffered an employment injury to use his remaining ability to work and his vocational qualifications, that he has a reasonable chance of obtaining, and the working conditions of which do not endanger the health, safety or physical well-being of the worker considering his injury. *An Act Respecting Industrial Accidents and Occupational Diseases*, S.Q. 1985, c. 6, s. 2.

SUITE. *n*. A group of connected rooms.

SUITOR. *n*. One who brings a suit or petition.

SULPHATE WOOD TURPENTINE. A terpene liquid obtained as a by-product of the manufacture of chemical wood pulp. *Turpentine Labelling Regulations*, C.R.C., c. 1140, s. 2.

SULPHUR CONTENT. The amount of sulphur in the fuel as determined by standard methods of sampling and testing and in the case of coal shall be determined as organic sulphur. *Environmental Protection Act*, R.R.O. 1980, Reg. 312, s. 1.

SUM. *n*. Quantity or amount of money. See GLOBAL ~; PENAL ~; PRINCIPAL ~.

SUM ASSURED. The principal sum that is payable in event of death where the life insurance money is payable in one sum, or the commuted value of the income or instalments provided on death where the life insurance money is payable otherwise than in one sum, but not including any additional sum payable under the policy on death as a result of accident.

SUM CERTAIN. One of (a) an amount with interest; (b) an amount with specified instalments, with or without an acceleration clause; (c) an amount payable according to the rate of exchange ascertainable from or indicated in a document. I.F.G. Baxter, *The Law of Banking*, 3d ed. (Toronto: Carswell, 1981) at 67.

SUM DEBITUM IN PRAESENTI, SED SOLVENDUM IN FUTURO. [L.] A sum owed now but to be paid in the future.

SUM INSURANCE. The insurer agrees to pay a certain sum of money to the insured if a particular event occurs. John G. Fleming ; *The Law of Torts*, 8th ed. (Sydney: The Law Book Company Limited, 1992) at 395.

SUM INSURED. The named amount to which the insurer's liability is limited by a contract of insurance.

SUMMA EST RATIO QUAE PRO RELIGIONE FACIT. [L.] An argument made for religion carries the greatest weight.

SUMMARY. *n*. An abridgment. See ANNUAL ~.

SUMMARY APPLICATION. A request to a judge or court without a full and formal proceeding.

SUMMARY CONVICTION COURT. A person who has jurisdiction in the territorial division where the subject-matter of the proceedings is alleged to have arisen and who (a) is given jurisdiction over the proceedings by the enactment under which the proceedings are taken; (b) is a justice or provincial court judge, where the enactment under which the proceedings are taken does not expressly give jurisdiction to any person or class of persons; or (c) is a provincial court judge, where the enactment under which the proceedings are taken gives jurisdiction in respect thereof to two or more justices. *Criminal Code*, R.S.C. 1985, c. C-46, s. 785.

SUMMARY CONVICTION OFFENCE. An offence which is tried summarily. This type of offence is less serious. Theft under $5000 is a summary conviction offence. Some offences may be tried by indictment or by summary conviction procedure. See HYBRID OFFENCE; INDICTABLE OFFENCE.

SUMMARY DISMISSAL. " . . . An employer only has cause for summary dismissal if the conduct he complains of is such as to show the servant to have disregarded the essential conditions of the contract of service: . . ." *Valley Rite-Mix Ltd. v. I.B.T., Local 213* (1974), 6 L.A.C. (2d) 339 at 347 (B.C.), Ladner and Wilson.

SUMMARY JUDGMENT. Once the defendant has served a notice of motion or delivered a statement of defence, a plaintiff may apply for summary judgment in respect of part or all of the claim set out in the statement of claim.

SUMMARY JURISDICTION. The ability of a court to make an order or give a judgment on its own initiative at once.

SUMMARY OFFENCE. Offence under any enactment of the Province or any regulation made under any enactment. Nova Scotia statutes.

SUMMARY RETURN. The relatively immediate, as opposed to the eventual, return of the child. *Katsigiannis v. Kottick-Katsigiannis* (2001), 55 O.R. (3d) 456 (C.A.).

SUMMARY TRIAL. A trial conducted by or under the authority of a commanding officer pursuant to section 163 and a trial by superior commander pursuant to section 164. *National Defence Act*, R.S.C. 1985, c. N-5, s. 2.

SUMMARY TRIAL COURT. A court for the summary trial of any person charged with having committed corrupt practices at an election. *Controverted Elections acts*.

SUMMER DRAUGHT. The distance measured from the top of the keel of a ship to the upper edge of the load line that would mark the summer fresh water freeboard calculated in accordance with Part II of this Schedule if that freeboard were assigned to the ship. *Load Lines Regulations (Inland)*, C.R.C., c. 1440, s. 1.

SUMMERFALLOW. *n.* Fallow land that is cultivated or managed in such a way as to conserve soil moisture or to prevent soil from drifting or both.

SUMMER SEASON. The period of time commencing on April 1st in each year and terminating on October 31st next following.

SUMMONITIONES AUT CITATIONES NULLAE LICEANT FIERI INTRA PALATIUM REGIS. [L.] Neither summonses nor citations may be served within the monarch's palace.

SUMMONS. *n.* 1. A citation; a warning to appear in court. 2. Document issued by a court, an agency, board or commission, or another person authorized to issue summonses, requiring a person to attend as a witness at a trial, hearing or examination, to produce documents or other things or to testify before the issuing body or person. 3. A summons or other document issued by a court requiring a person within a province other than the province of the issuing court to attend as a witness at a trial, hearing or examination, to produce documents or other things or to testify before the issuing court. *Interprovincial Summonses Act*, R.S.O. 1990, c. I.12, s. 1. See GARNISHEE ~; JUDGMENT ~; ORIGINATING ~; RE~; SHOW CAUSE ~; WRIT OF ~.

SUMMONS TO WITNESS. Used instead of a subpoena, this document directs a witness to appear in court at a given time and place or to bring certain documents or things along.

SUMMUM JUS, SUMMA INJURIA. SUMMA LEX, SUMMA CRUX. [L.] The most extreme right, the most extreme injury—the strictest law, strictest punishment.

SUMP. *n.* A watertight tank or pit that is open to the atmosphere, (a) which receives storm water or other liquid waste that does not require treatment as sanitary sewage; and (b) from which the storm water or liquid waste it receives is discharged to a sewer or other acceptable point of disposal.

SUMPTUARY LAW. A law to restrain luxury, i.e. excessive apparel.

SUM UP. For a judge to recapitulate evidence or parts of it for a jury, directing what form of verdict they should give. Each counsel has the right to sum up evidence adduced and the judge sums up everything.

SUNDAY. *n.* The first day of the week, also called the Lord's Day.

SUNDAY CLOSING LAW. A law which requires businesses of certain classes to close on Sundays.

SUNDRIES. *n.* Odds and ends; petty things.

SUNK COSTS. The part of an investment required for entry into a particular market which cannot be recovered in the event that the attempt fails.

SUNSET PROVISION. A provision in a statute stating that the act or a portion of it is repealed on a date in the future. May also provide for a review of the statute or provision before the date in the future.

SUP. CT. *abbr.* Superior Court.

SUP. CT. L. REV. *abbr.* The Supreme Court Law Review.

SUPER ALTUM MARE. [L.] On the high sea.

SUPERANNUATION. *n.* The allowance or pension granted to one who is discharged from employment because of age.

SUPERANNUATION FUND. The fund to which a person who is eligible for superannuation contributes.

SUPER FALSO ET CERTO FINGITUR. [L.] Fiction is made from both false and true.

SUPERFLUA NON NOCENT. [L.] Superfluities do no harm.

SUPERINTENDENT. *n.* 1. The person in charge of a place of secure custody and includes a person designated to act on that person's behalf. 2. The person in charge of a hospital or an institution. 3. The person in charge of a correctional institution and includes a person designated to act on that person's behalf. 4. Includes a commissioner, regional supervisor, Indian superintendent, assistant Indian superintendent and any other person declared by the Minister to be a superintendent for the purposes of this Act, and with reference to a band or a reserve, means the superintendent for that band or reserve. *Indian Act*, R.S.C. 1985, c. I-5, s. 2. 5. Includes owner, lessee, manager, operator, director and person in charge. 6. The person who has for the time being the direct and actual superintendence and charge of a hospital. See INDIAN ~;.

SUPERINTENDENT OF INSURANCE. The Superintendent of Insurance of Canada or of a province, according to the person upon whom the law confers the supervision of the insurer concerned.

SUPERIOR COURT. 1. The Supreme Court of a province or territory including the Courts of Appeal in the various provinces. The trial division is known as the Court of Queen's Bench in some provinces. The Federal Court and the Supreme Court of Canada are superior courts. 2. A court not under the control of any other court except by appeal. 3. " . . . [D]escribed in s. 96 [of the Constitution Act, 1867 (30 & 31 Vict.), c. 3] were referred to as 'superior courts' . . ." *Reference re s.6 of the Family Relations Act (British Columbia)* (1982), 26 R.F.L. (2d) 113 at 131, [1982] 1 S.C.R. 62, [1982] 3 W.W.R. 1, 36 B.C.L.R. 1, 131 D.L.R. (3d) 257, 40 N.R. 206, Estey J. 4. A court with jurisdiction throughout a province, not limited to any subject matter. P.W. Hogg, *Constitutional Law of Canada*, 3d ed. (Toronto: Carswell, 1992) at 162. 5. A court of original jurisdiction or of original civil and criminal jurisdiction which has inherent powers. See PROVINCIAL ~.

SUPERIOR COURT OF CRIMINAL JURISDICTION.. (a) In the Province of Ontario, the Court of Appeal or the Superior Court of Justice, (b) in the Province of Quebec, the Superior Court, (c) in the Province of Prince Edward Island, the Supreme Court, (d) in the Provinces of New Brunswick, Manitoba, Saskatchewan and Alberta, the Court of Appeal or the Court of Queen's Bench, (e) in the Provinces of Nova Scotia, British Columbia and Newfoundland, the Supreme Court or the Court of Appeal, (f) in Yukon, the Supreme Court, (g) in the Northwest Territories, the Supreme Court, and (h) in Nunavut, the Nunavut Court of Justice. *Criminal Code*, R.S.C. 1985, c. C-46, s. 2.

SUPERIOR OFFICER. Any officer or non-commissioned member who, in relation to any other officer or non-commissioned member is by this Act, or by regulations or custom of the service, authorized to give a lawful command to that other officer or non-commissioned member. *National Defence Act*, R.S.C. 1985 N-5, s. 2.

SUPERIOR TRAIN. A train having precedence over another train.

SUPERNUMERARY JUDGE. A judge who has elected to give up regular judicial duties and hold office only as a supernumerary judge, thus having a diminished workload. May refer to one who has been appointed for a further term after reaching the mandatory retirement age.

SUPERSEDE. *v.* 1. " . . . [A] meaning that connotes superiority, priority or preference; . . ." *National Trust Co. v. Mass Combines Corp.* (1988), 39 B.L.R. 245 at 249, 69 C.B.R. (N.S.) 171 (Ont. H.C.), Saunders J. 2. " . . . [A] meaning that connotes removal, setting aside, annulment or alteration, followed by a replacement." *National Trust Co. v. Massey Combines Co.* (1988), 39 B.L.R. 245 at 249, 69 C.B.R. (N.S.) 171 (Ont. H.C.), Saunders J. 3. Rescind.

SUPERSEDEAS. *n.* A writ which ordered, when good cause was shown, the stay of an ordinary proceeding which should otherwise proceed.

SUPERSEDING MOTION. A formally independent motion to set aside a question in the course of debate. A. Fraser, W.A. Dawson, & J. Holtby, eds., *Beauchesne's Rules and Forms of the House of Commons of Canada*, 6th ed. (Toronto: Carswell, 1989) at 173.

SUPERSONIC FLIGHT. Flight at speeds in excess of a true flight Mach number of one.

SUPER STORE. " . . . [M]uch larger than an ordinary retail food store and provides the public with a greater range of goods and services. . ." *U.F.C.W., Locals 175 and 633 v. Great Atlantic & Pacific Co. of Canada*, [1981] O.L.R.B. Rep. 285 at 286, [1981] 2 Can. L.R.B.R. 261, MacDowell (Vice Chair), Armstrong and Bourne (Members).

SUPERSTRUCTURE. *n.* 1. (a) Includes grading, ballast, ties, rails, switches and other track appurtenances, bridges, tunnels, culverts, signals and grade crossing protective appliances, telephone and telegraph lines, fencing on the right of way and station platforms; but (b) does not include railway stations, office buildings, water tanks, coal docks, wells, pipe lines, pump houses and equipment, warehouses, dwellings, roundhouses, turntables, shops and tool houses, stock yards, loading platforms or things of a like nature. 2. A decked structure on the freeboard deck extending from side to side of the ship, and includes a raised quarter deck. Canada regulations. 3. The equipment affixed to a hull including masts, rigging and rails, but does not include electronic equipment or the engine of a vessel.

SUPERSTRUCTURE DECK. The deck forming the top of the superstructure. Canada regulations.

SUPERVISE. *v.* To oversee or direct; to monitor.

SUPERVISION. *n.* 1. The provision of counselling services by a probation officer. 2. The caring for, assisting, guiding, protecting, or overseeing of persons. See PERSONAL ~.

SUPERVISOR. *n.* 1. A person who has charge of a workplace or authority over a worker. *Occupational Health and Safety Act*, R.S.O. 1990, c. O.1, s. 1(1). 2. An overseer. 3. A person who is reponsible for the care and management of a child care facility.

SUPERVISORY CARE. The provision of room, board and (a) guidance or supervision in the activities of daily living, or (b) observation or surveillance of the physical well-being, of a person who is ambulatory or semi-ambulatory.

SUPERVISORY RESPONSIBILITY. A duty, whether legal, contractual or otherwise established by mutual understanding, to provide or exercise some form of care, aid, management, guidance or other attention necessary to help a person having diminished capacities with routine requirements of daily living.

SUPERVISORY SERVICES. The regular monitoring of the personal welfare of a resident and the provision of limited or occasional supervision of or assistance to a resident in the performance of activities necessary to his personal welfare.

SUPERVISORY SIGNAL. A signal indicating the need for action in connection with the supervision of sprinkler and other extinguishing systems or equipment, or with the maintenance features of other protection systems.

SUPER VISUM CORPORIS. [L.] Upon viewing the body.

SUPPLEMENT. *n.* 1. Any substance or mixture of substances, other than a fertilizer, that is manufactured, sold or represented for use in the improvement of the physical condition of soils or to aid plant growth or crop yields. *Fertilizers Act*, R.S.C. 1995, c. F-10, s. 2. 2. A monthly guaranteed income supplement authorized to be paid under Part II. *Old Age Security Act*, R.S.C. 1985, c. O-9, s. 2. 3. A mixture of ingredients that supply or are purported to supply nutrients or nutrients and medicating ingredients in sufficient concentration that, when mixed with grain or grain and other carbohydrate materials, in accordance with the directions for use, will produce a complete and balanced feed that is acceptable for registration. *Feeds Regulations*, C.R.C., c. 665, s. 2. See BRIDGING ~; SOIL ~.

SUPPLEMENTAL DEED. A deed expressly in addition to a previous deed.

SUPPLEMENTAL PENSION PLAN. A pension plan organized and administered for the benefit of employees whose membership in another pension plan is a condition precedent to membership in the supplemental pension plan.

SUPPLEMENTAL PLAN. Provisions established for the payment of retirement pensions to employees, including a deferred profit sharing pension plan.

SUPPLEMENTARY ESTIMATES. Estimates presented to obtain moneys in addition to those already appropriated for existing services, for new expenditures in connection with new statutes, to cover unexpected emergency expenditures, or to transfer funds between Votes or to extend a Vote's scope. A. Fraser, W.A. Dawson & J. Holtby, eds., *Beauchesne's Rules and Forms of the House of Commons of Canada*, 6th ed. (Toronto: Carswell, 1989) at 260.

SUPPLEMENTARY LETTERS PATENT. Any letters patent granted to the company subsequent to the letters patent incorporating the company.

SUPPLEMENTARY RETIREMENT BENEFITS ACCOUNT. The Account established in the accounts of Canada pursuant to the Supplementary Retirement Benefits Act.

SUPPLEMENTARY UNEMPLOYMENT BENEFIT PLAN. An arrangement, other than an arrangement in the nature of a superannuation or pension fund or plan or an employees profit sharing plan, under which payments are made by an employer to a trustee in trust exclusively for the payment of periodic amounts to employees or former employees of the employer who are or may be laid off for any temporary or indefinite period. *Income Tax Act*, R.S.C. 1985, c. 1 (5th Supp.), s. 145(1). See REGISTERED ~.

SUPPLIANT. *n.* The one who acts in, or the party who prefers a petition of right.

SUPPLIER. *n.* 1. A person who manufactures, supplies, sells, leases, distributes or installs any article, device or equipment or any biological, physical or chemical agent to be used in a workplace. *Occupational Health and Safety acts.* 2. (a) A person who in the course of his business becomes liable under a consumer transaction to sell, lease or otherwise dispose of goods or to provide services or both, or in the case of an award by chance of goods or services or both, to provide the goods or services awarded; (b) a person who in the course of his business (i) manufactures, assembles or produces goods that are the subject of a consumer transaction; (ii) acts as a wholesaler or distributor of goods that are the subject of a consumer transaction; or (iii) solicits, advertises or otherwise promotes the use, purchase or acquisition in any manner of goods or services that are the subject of a consumer transaction; or (c) a person who receives or is entitled to receive all or part of the consideration paid or payable under a consumer transaction, whether as a party thereto or as an assignee or otherwise, or who is otherwise entitled to be compensated by a consumer for goods or services or both. See BONA FIDE ~; SERVICE ~.

SUPPLIER CREDIT AGREEMENT. A consumer agreement, other than a consumer agreement involving leases to which Part VIII applies, under which a supplier or an associate of the supplier, extends fixed credit to a consumer to assist the consumer in obtaining goods or services, other than credit, from the supplier. *Consumer Protection Act, 2002*, S.O. 2002, c. 30, Sched. A, s. 66.

SUPPLIES. *n.* 1. Materials, equipment and other personal property that is or was required or used by a department for the transaction of its business and affairs, and includes furnishings.

Public Works, Supply and Services acts. 2. " . . . [M]aterials provided for construction work." *Irvine v. Hervey* (1913), 13 D.L.R. 868 at 879, 47 N.S.R. 310 (C.A.), the court per Ritchie J.A. 3. " . . . [G]oods on hand not intended for resale . . ." *Intowner Motel Ltd. v. Hospitality Management Ltd.* (1980), 2 Sask. R. 328 at 331 (Q.B.), Johnson C.J.Q.B. 4. Paper, pens, pencils, note books, scribblers and all other things and materials required by the pupils of any school as an aid to their instruction and education. *The Free Text Book Act*, R.S.S. 1978, c. F-22, s. 2. 5. Petroleum products, feed grain, fodder, repairs to implements and parts, repairs to harness, formaldehyde and other smut control compounds, weed control compounds and gopher poison, and includes such other commodities and such services as the Lieutenant Governor in Council may approve. *The Municipalities Seed Grain and Supply Act*, R.S.S. 1978, c. M-38, s. 2. See CEMETERY ~; DEFENCE ~; FISHING EQUIPMENT AND ~; FUNERAL ~; OFFICE ~; POSTAGE ~; STUDENTS' ~; SUPPLY.

SUPPLY. *v.* 1. " . . . '[F]urnish', 'deliver', . . . the providing what is wanted (in or for the construction of the building)." *W. & B. Construction Ltd. v. Mahaney* (1978), (*sub nom. Mahaney v. W & B. Construction Ltd.*) 4 R.P.R. 5 at 11, 25 N.S.R. (2d) 361, 85 D.L.R. (4th) 425, 36 A.P.R. 361 (C.A.), the court per Coffin J.A. 2. (a) In relation to an article, sell, rent, lease or otherwise dispose of an article or an interest therein or a right thereto, or offer so to dispose of an article or interest therein or a right thereto; and (b) in relation to a service, sell, rent or otherwise provide a service or offer so to provide a service. *Competition Act*, R.S.C. 1985, c. C-34, s. 2.

SUPPLY. *n.* Reservation, transmission, distribution, capacity to provide, dealing in and sale. *Hydro and Power Authority acts.* See BUSINESS OF ~; INTERIM ~; SECURITY OF ~; SUPPLIES.

SUPPLY AND SERVICES CANADA. The ministry which purchases and does accounting for the federal government.

SUPPLY AUTHORITY. Any corporation or person that produces, transmits, delivers or furnishes electrical power or energy to or for a consumer.

SUPPLY DUCT. A duct for conveying air from a heating, ventilating or air-conditioning appliance to a space to be heated, ventilated or air-conditioned.

SUPPLY HOUSE. 1. A manufacturer, jobber or wholesale vendor, making or dealing in gas equipment. 2. A manufacturer, jobber or wholesale vendor or a manufacturers agent dealing in electrical equipment.

SUPPLY LINE. A line used primarily for the transmission of a supply of electrical energy for other than telegraphic, telephonic, signalling or other intelligence purposes.

SUPPLY OF SERVICES. Any work done or service performed upon or in respect of an improvement and includes, (a) the rental of equipment with an operator, and (b) where the making of the planned improvement is not commenced, the supply of a design, plan, drawing specification that in itself enhances the value of the owner's interest in the land. *Construction Lien Act*, R.S.O. 1990, c. C.30, s. 1(1).

SUPPLY SERVICE. Any one set of conductors run by a supply authority from its mains to a consumer's service.

SUPPORT. *n.* 1. "[In Succession Law Reform Act, R.S.O. 1980, c. 488] . . . financial assistance to permit a dependant to provide for the necessities and amenities of life." *Mannion v. R.* (1982), 140 D.L.R. (3d) 189 at 190, 39 O.R. (2d) 609, 13 E.T.R. 49, 31 R.F.L. (2d) 133 (Div. Ct.), the court per Saunders J. 2. Includes maintenance or alimony. *Reciprocal Enforcement of Support Orders Act*, R.S. Nfld. 1990, c. R-5, s. 2. 3. Financial support. See BEARING ~.

SUPPORT ORDER. 1. A child support order or a spousal support order. *Divorce Act*, R.S.C, 1985, c. 3 (2nd Supp.), s. 2. 2. A provision in an order made in or outside Ontario and enforceable in Ontario for the payment of money as support or maintenance, and includes a provision for, (a) the payment of an amount periodically, whether annually or otherwise and whether for an indefinite or limited period, or until the happening of a specified event, (b) a lump sum to be paid or held in trust, (c) payment of support or maintenance in respect of a period before the date of the order, (d) payment to an agency of an amount in reimbursement for a benefit or assistance provided to a party under a statute, including a benefit or assistance provided before the date of the order, (e) payment of expenses in respect of a child's prenatal care and birth, (f) the irrevocable designation, by a spouse or same-sex partner who has a policy of life insurance or an interest in a benefit plan, of the other spouse or same-sex partner or a child as the beneficiary, or (g)

interest or the payment of legal fees or other expenses arising in relation to support or maintenance, and includes such a provision in a domestic contract or paternity agreement that is enforceable. *Family Responsibility and Support Arrears Enforcement Act, 1996*, S.O. 1996, c. 31, s. 1, as am. See FINANCIAL ~.

SUPPORT PROVISION. 1. A provision of an order or agreement for maintenance, alimony or family financial support and includes any order for arrears of payments thereof. 2. A provision in an agreement relating to the payment of maintenance or family financial support that is enforceable by a garnishee summons under provincial garnishment law.

SUPPORT SERVICE. See COMMUNITY ~.

SUPPORT STAFF. Staff other than supervisory officer staff or teaching staff.

SUPPRESSIO VERI. [L.] Suppression of truth.

SUPRA. *prep.* [L.] Above.

SUPRA PROTEST. After protesting.

SUPRAVITAL PROCESSES. Pathological and physiological processes which continue after somatic death, largely at the cellular level. F.A. Jaffe, *A Guide to Pathological Evidence*, 3d ed. (Toronto: Carswell, 1991) at 15.

SUPREMACY. *n.* Sovereignty; pre-eminent authority.

SUPREMACY CLAUSE. Section 52(1) of the Constitution Act, 1982 which gives the Charter power to override other provisions.

SUPREMA POTESTAS SEIPSAM DISSOLVERE POTEST. [L.] Supreme power has the power to dissolve itself.

SUPREME COURT. The Supreme Court of Canada and in some provinces, the name of the province's Superior Court.

SUPREME COURT OF CANADA. The court of law and equity in and for Canada now existing under the name of the Supreme Court of Canada is hereby continued under that name, as a general court of appeal for Canada, and as an additional court for the better administration of the laws of Canada, and shall continue to be a court of record. The Court shall have and exercise an appellate, civil and criminal jurisdiction within and throughout Canada. An appeal lies to the Court from a decision of the Federal Court of Appeal in the case of a controversy between Canada and a province or between two or more provinces. An appeal lies to the Court from an opinion pronounced by the highest court of final resort in a province on any matter referred to it for hearing and consideration by the lieutenant governor in council of that province whenever it has been by the statutes of that province declared that such opinion is to be deemed a judgment of the highest court of final resort and that an appeal lies therefrom as from a judgment in an action.

SUPT. *abbr.* Superintendent.

SURCHARGE. *n.* An additional or extra charge. A charge upon a charge.

SURETY. *n.* 1. ". . . [I]s one who contracts with a creditor that he will be answerable for the debt, default, or miscarriage or another who is the principal debtor and primarily liable." *Schmidt v. Gavriloff*, [1923] 2 W.W.R. 173 at 174, 17 Sask. L.R. 218 (C.A.), Lamont J.A. 2. A person who gives security for another person; a person who assumes a bond for another person. 3. A person who gives a guarantee to the Crown or to a contractor under a bond to pay creditors of the Crown or the contractor. 4. A sufficient surety. 5. A registered company within the meaning of the Canadian and British Insurance Companies Act (Canada) that (a) under the terms of a bid bond, undertakes to pay a sum of money to the obligee in the event that the principal breaches the conditions of the bond; (b) under the terms of a performance bond, undertakes to incur the cost of fulfilling the terms of a contract in the event that the principal breaches the contract; or (c) under the terms of a payment bond, undertakes to make payment to all persons supplying labour and material in the performance of the work provided for in the contract if the principal fails to make payment, and includes any agent, independent agent or underwriter of such registered company, or any person empowered to act on behalf of any such agent, independent agent or underwriter. *Business Loans, Guarantees and Indemnities Act*, S.N.W.T. 1983 (1st Sess.), c. 1, s. 3. See CO ~; PRINCIPAL AND ~.

SURETY BOND. 1. A written promise under seal committing the issuer, the surety, to pay a named beneficiary, the obligee, a sum up to a stipulated amount. Subject to the obligation ceasing if certain specified conditions are met. 2. A guarantee of the performance of an expressed obligation. *Insurance Adjusters Act*, R.S. Nfld. 1990, c. I-8, s. 2.

SURETY COMPANY. A corporation empowered to give bonds by way of indemnity. *Judicature Act*, R.S.O. 1980, c. 223, s. 76.

SURETY INSURANCE. Insurance whereby an insurer undertakes to guarantee (a) the due performance of a contract or undertaking; or (b) the payment of a penalty or indemnity for any default, but does not include insurance coming within the class of credit insurance or mortgage insurance. *Classes of Insurance Regulations*, C.R.C., c. 977, s. 36.

SURFACE. Any ground or water, including the frozen surface thereof. *Canadian Aviation Regulations* SOR/96-433, s. 101.01. See APPROACH ~; BEARING ~; EXTERNAL ~; HORIZONTAL ~; OUTER ~; STRIKING ~.

SURFACE BARGAINING. ". . . [W]hen one pretends to want to reach agreement, but in reality has no intention of signing a collective agreement and hopes to destroy the collective bargaining relationship." *Nova Scotia (Labour Relations Board) v. C.U.P.E.* (1983), 83 C.L.L.C. 14,069 at 12,360, 49 N.R. 107, 60 N.S.R. (2d) 369, 128 A.P.R. 369, 1 D.L.R. (4th) 1, [1983] 2 S.C.R. 311, Laskin C.J.C.

SURFACE DISTURBANCE. (a) The disturbance, exposure, covering or erosion of the surface of land in any manner; or (b) the degradation or deterioration in any manner of the surface of land.

SURFACE FACILITIES. Storage or treatment facilities provided at the disposal site for liquid waste before discharge into the subsurface and includes piping, pumps, valves, tankage, instrumentation and other equipment.

SURFACE HOLDER. The lessee or registered holder of the surface rights to the land on which a mineral claim is or is proposed to be recorded.

SURFACE IMPOUNDMENT. A facility that consists of an excavation or diked area that is formed primarily of earthen materials and is used for the storage of waste.

SURFACE LEASE. 1. A lease or other instrument under which the surface of land is being held for any purpose for which a right of entry order may be made and that provides for payment of compensation. 2. Includes the lease, easement, right of way or other agreement made about a land surface area by an owner.

SURFACE MINE. 1. A mine worked by a strip mining, open pit mining or other surface method, including auger mining. 2. A pit or quarry where metallic or non-metallic rock, mineral bearing substance, earth, clay, sand or gravel is being or has been removed by means of an excavation open to the surface.

SURFACE RACEWAY. A raceway in the form of a channel with a backing and capping for loosely holding conductors and cables in surface wiring.

SURFACE RIGHTS. 1. Includes lands granted, leased or otherwise disposed of for any purpose and in respect of which the mines and minerals thereon or under the surface thereof are by statute or any disposition reserved to the Crown. 2. Every right in land other than the mining rights. *Mining Act*, R.S.O. 1990, c. M.14, s. 1. 3. (a) The land or any portion thereof or any interest therein, except mines and minerals within the meaning of The Land Titles Act, or a right of entry thereon, required by an operation for the purpose of drilling for, producing or recovering a mineral; (b) the right to condition, maintain, reclaim or restore the surface of land where the land has been or is being held incidental to or in connection with either or both of: (i) the drilling for, producing or recovering a mineral; (ii) the laying, constructing, operating, maintaining or servicing a flow line, service line or power line. *The Surface Rights Acquisition and Compensation Act*, R.S.S. 1978, c. S-65, s. 2.

SURFACE RIGHTS OPTION. Any right to acquire the surface rights to land, the mineral rights to which have been acquired by the optionee either prior to the granting of the surface rights option or by the conveyance that itself contains the grant of the surface rights option.

SURFACE SEWER. A sewer that is intended to carry storm and surface water and drainage and includes a surface drain.

SURFACE WATER. 1. " . . . [W]ater flowing through no defined water course. . ." *Wilkinson v. St. Andrews (Rural Municipality)*, [1923] 4 D.L.R. 780 at 793, [1923] 3 W.W.R. 961, 33 Man. R. 381 (C.A.), Trueman J.A. 2. " . . . [T]hose which are produced by rainfall, melting snow, or springs . . ." *Kass v. State Farm Fire & Casualty Co.* (1989), 39 C.C.L.I. 258 at 265, 94 A.R. 152, [1989] I.L.R. 2461, 57 D.L.R. (4th) 290 (Q.B.), Matheson J. 3. Water above the surface of land and being in a river, stream, watercourse, lake, creek, spring, ravine, coulee, canyon, lagoon, swamp, marsh or other body of water. Saskatchewan statutes. 4. Water in a watercourse.

SURGEON. *n.* A member of the medical staff who performs a surgical operation on a patient. See COLLEGE OF PHYSICIANS AND ~S; VETERINARY ~.

SURGERY. See DENTAL ~; VETERINARY ~.

SURGICAL-DENTAL SERVICES. Any medically or dentally required surgical-dental procedures performed by a dentist in a hospital, where a hospital is required for the proper performance of the procedures.

SURGICALLY INVASIVE DEVICE. An invasive device that is intended to enter the body through an artificially created opening that provides access to body structures and fluids. *Medical Devices Regulations* SOR/98-282, s. 1.

SURGICAL OR DENTAL INSTRUMENT. A reusable medical device that is intended for surgical or dental use, including cutting, drilling, sawing, scraping, clamping, hammering, puncturing, dilating, retracting or clipping, without connection to an active device. *Medical Devices Regulations* SOR/98-282, s. 1.

SURMISE. *n.* An allegation; a suggestion.

SURNAME. *n.* Includes a surname, family name or patronymic.

SURPLUS. *n.* 1. The aggregate balances of undivided earnings, statutory reserve and other reserves. *Credit Unions acts.* 2. The amount by which assets exceed liabilities. See COMMON ~; UNALLOCATED ~.

SURPLUSAGE. *n.* The state of having something in excess or over.

SURPLUSAGE RULE. "The 'surplusage rule', which has been developed by the courts over a great many years, is succinctly stated as follows, in Ewaschuk, Criminal Pleadings and Practice in Canada (1983), pp. 222-3: 'If the particular, whether as originally drafted or as subsequently supplied, is not essential to constitute the offence, it will be treated as surplusage, i.e., a non-necessary which need not be proved.' This common law rule is, in effect, the converse of s. 510(3) of the Criminal Code, [R.S.C. 1970, c. C-34] . . ." *R. v. Côté* (1986), 23 C.C.C. (3d) 481 at 498, [1986] 1 S.C.R. 2, 49 C.R. (3d) 351, 64 N.R. 93, 25 D.L.R. (4th) 82, the court per Lamer J.

SURPLUSAGIUM NON NOCET. [L.] Surplusage is not harmful.

SURPLUS ASSETS. Having regard to the prescribed assets and liabilities of a pension plan, the portion of those assets that exceeds those liabilities.

SURPLUS ELECTRICITY. Electricity that is surplus to requirements.

SURPLUS STORES. Any goods, upon which customs duty and excise taxes were paid at the time of the entry of an ocean ship into the coasting trade, that remain on board unused at the time the ship reverts to international service. *Ships Suppliers Drawback Regulations*, C.R.C., c. 493, s. 2.

SURR. CT. *abbr*. Surrogate Court.

SURREBUTTAL. *n*. 1. The calling of evidence by the defence to meet the Crown's rebuttal evidence. P.K. McWilliams, *Canadian Criminal Evidence*, 3d ed. (Aurora: Canada Law Book, 1988) at 31-12. 2. A response to a plaintiff's or appellant's rebuttal of a defendant or respondent's evidence.

SURRENDER. *n*. 1. The giving up by a tenant of premises. 2. An unequivocal, irrevocable and unconditional act to give up a security over property of a debtor. 3. Relinquishment. 4. "The doctrine of surrender is not limited to cases of landlord and tenant . . . As stated by Parke B. in Lyon v. Reed [(1844) 13 M. & W. 285 at 306]: 'This term is applied to cases where the owner of a particular estate has been a party to some act, the validity of which he is by law afterwards estopped from disputing, and which would not be valid if his particular estate had continued to exist. There the law treats the doing of such act as amounting to a surrender.'" *Saskatchewan (Attorney General) v. Whiteshore Salt & Chemical Co.*, [1955] S.C.R. 43 at 46, [1955] 1 D.L.R. 241, Kellock J. (Kerwin C.J.C. and Fauteux J. concurring). 5. " . . . [T]he very act of the tenant in giving up possession and the presence of a new tenant, who was put into possession by the owner, amounted in law to a surrender." *Sandum v. Holmes Estate* (1985), 57 A.R. 300 at 303, 40 R.P.R. 108, 16 D.L.R. (4th) 629 (C.A.), the court per Laycraft J.A. 6. " . . . [F]or the purposes of s. 90 [of the Bankruptcy Act, R.S.C. 1970, c. B-3] is an unequivocal, irrevocable and unconditional act performed prior to voting abandoning for all purposes and for all time as against the debtor the security held by the creditor." *Cadillac Explorations Ltd. v. Kilborn Engineering Ltd.* (1983), 51 C.B.R. (N.S.) 315 at 316, 51 B.C.L.R. 221 (C.A.), Anderson J.A.

SURRENDER BY OPERATION OF LAW. Occurs when the parties to a lease participate in a course of action inconsistent with the continued existence of the lease. Both parties are estopped from denying that a surrender has occurred.

SURRENDERED LANDS. A reserve or part of a reserve or any interest therein, the legal title to which remains vested in Her Majesty, that has been released or surrendered by the band for whose use and benefit it was set apart. *Indian Act*, R.S.C. 1985, c. I-5, s. 2.

SURRENDEREE. *n*. The person to whom one surrenders.

SURRENDEROR. *n*. The person who surrenders.

SURRENDER VALUE. 1. " . . . [T]he amount of money or its equivalent which the company could afford to pay to be rid of the existing policy. . ." *Devitt v. Mutual Life Insurance Co.* (1915), 33 O.L.R. 473 at 477, 22 D.L.R. 183 (C.A.), Riddell J.A. (Falconbridge C.J. concurring). 2. The price in cash which an insurance company will pay when the policy holder surrenders any policy and claims under it to the company. See CASH ~.

SURREPTION. *n*. Getting something by stealth or fraud.

SURREPTITIOUS. *adj*. Stealthy; fraudulent.

SURROGATE. *n*. One who is appointed or substituted for another.

SURROGATE MOTHER. A female person who carries an embryo or foetus derived from the genes of a donor or donors with the intention of surrendering the child at birth to a donor or another person.

SURSUM REDDITIO. [L.] Surrender.

SURTAX. *n*. Tax payable in addition to tax at the standard rate.

SURVEILLANCE. *n*. 1. Location of a person suspected of engaging in criminal activity, following that person, observing their activities and overhearing their conversations with other people. 2. Watching, monitoring of employees by an employer for purposes of the employer. See CONSENT ~.

SURVEY. *v*. To determine the boundaries of a lot with reference to monuments set by previous surveyors; to determine the form and extent and location of a tract of land by linear and angular measurements so that a plan or detailed description can be drawn or given.

SURVEY. *n.* 1. The determination, measurement and establishment of boundaries of land. 2. The establishment, location or definition on the ground of any boundary, limit or angle of any land, size, location, parcel, claim, common, easement, road, street, lane, district, municipality, county or township, or any other location or division of lands or right over lands whether for ownership, title or authority or the origin of any of them. 3. The drydocking of a vessel, the examination and inspection of its hull, boilers, machinery, engines and equipment by an inspector or a surveyor and everything done to such vessel, its hull, boilers, machinery, engines and equipment pursuant to an order, requirement or recommendation given or made by the inspector or surveyor as the result of the examination and inspection so that a safety and inspection certificate might be issued in respect the vessel pursuant to the provisions of the Canada Shipping Act, and the regulations thereunder or, as the case may be, so that the vessel might be entitled to retain the character assigned to it in the registry book of a classification society. *Income Tax Regulations*, C.R.C., c. 945, s. 3600. 4. The accurate determination of the position of mine workings and other parts of a mine by a surveyor using survey instruments suited to the conditions of the survey. *Coal Mines (CBDC) Safety Regulations*, C.R.C., c. 1011, s. 2. See BLOCK OUTLINE ~; BOUNDARY ~; CLASSIFICATION ~; COMPLETE ~; CO-ORDINATE ~; GEOPHYSICAL ~; MARINE ~; ORIGINAL ~; REGIONAL ~; RE~; ~S; WELL SITE SEABED ~.

SURVEY CONTROL. 1. The establishment and maintenance of a series of interrelated survey monuments to which existing and subsequent surveys in accordance with this Act may be related. *The Land Surveys Act*, R.S.S. 1978, c. L-4, s. 60. 2. A network of interrelated survey control markers whose co-ordinate positions form part of the geographical positioning system. *Land Titles Act*, R.S.A. 2000, c. S-26, s. 1.

SURVEYED LOT. An unsubdivided unit of land the boundaries of which are shown on a settlement plan, parcel plan or any plan of subdivision registered.

SURVEYED TERRITORY. That part of a township or seigniory which has been surveyed and divided into lots by the proper authority. *Mining Act*, R.S.Q. 1977, c. M-13, s. 1.

SURVEYING. *n.* The determination of the form of the earth or the position of natural or artificial things, boundaries or points on, above or under the surface of the earth or the collection, storage, management, integration, analysis or representation of spatial and spatially related information pertaining to the earth or the interpreting of or reporting or advising on that information. *Canada Lands Surveyors Act*, 1998, S.C. 1998, c. 14, s. 2. See CADASTRAL ~; LAND ~; PRACTICE OF CADASTRAL ~; PRACTICE OF PROFESSIONAL LAND ~; PRACTICE OF ~.

SURVEY MARKER. See CONTROL ~.

SURVEYOR. *n.* 1. A Canada Lands Surveyor or a person who is entitled to survey lands in a province under the laws of the province. *Canada Lands Surveys Act*, R.S.C. 1985, c. L-6, s. 2. 2. A person who is registered to practise land surveying. 3. A person who practices the profession of land surveying or a person who for gain either direct or indirect makes or does any survey, otherwise than in the employ and under the immediate supervision of a surveyor. 4. A surveyor to a classification society. 5. An inspector, a surveyor of ships employed for that purpose by the government of a country. See CANADA LANDS ~; CHIEF ~; MINE ~.

SURVEYOR GENERAL. A person who is a Canada Lands Surveyor and is appointed as Surveyor General in the manner authorized by law or a person authorized by the Minister to carry out the duties of the Surveyor General. *Canada Lands Surveys Act*, R.S.C. 1985, c. L-6, s. 2.

SURVEYOR OF RECORD. The surveyor who has signed a return of survey.

SURVEY SYSTEM. See CO-ORDINATE ~.

SURVIVING SPOUSE. A person who was another person's spouse at the time of the other persons death. See RESIDUAL INCOME OF THE ~.

SURVIVING SPOUSE WITH DEPENDENT CHILDREN. A surviving spouse of a contributor who maintains wholly or substantially one or more dependent children.

SURVIVOR. *n.* 1. A person who outlives another, who is alive at the death of the other. 2. In relation to a deceased individual, means their surviving spouse or common-law partner.

SURVIVOR PENSION. The pension payable to the surviving spouse or children entitled to a pension.

SURVIVORSHIP. *n.* 1. The living of one of several people after the death of one or all of the group. 2. The right of the joint tenant who outlives the other(s) to the whole of the jointly held estate. See PRESUMPTION OF ~; RIGHT OF ~.

SUSPECT. *n.* " . . . In ordinary parlance, whether someone is a 'suspect' refers to the existence of grounds to believe that the individual has engaged in forbidden activities." *Thomson Newspapers Ltd. v. Canada (Director of Investigation & Research)* (1990), 47 C.R.R. 1 at 67, 76 C.R. (3d) 129, 72 O.R. (2d) 415n, 54 C.C.C. (3d) 417, 67 D.L.R. (4th) 161, 29 C.P.R. (3d) 97, [1990] 1 S.C.R. 425, 39 O.A.C. 161, 106 N.R. 161, L'Heureux-Dubé J.

SUSPEND. *v.* 1. Of a licence, to debar the holder for a period of time from exercising the function or enjoying the privilege authorized or given by the licence. 2. Of an attorney or solicitor, to forbid that person from practising for a certain time.

SUSPENDATUR PER COLLUM. [L.] Let the person be hanged by the neck.

SUSPENDED SENTENCE. 1. Involves the release of the convicted person on certain conditions contained in a probation order. 2. " . . . [S]uspension of the imposition of a sentence . . ." *R. v. Cruickshanks*, [1946] 3 W.W.R. 225 at 226, 63 B.C.R. 102, 2 C.R. 323, 86 C.C.C. 257, [1946] 4 D.L.R. 645 (C.A.), O'Halloran J.A. 3. " . . . [S]uspending the passing of the sentence." *R. v. Switzki*, [1930] 2 W.W.R. 479 at 480, 54 C.C.C. 332, 24 Sask. L.R. 587 (C.A.), the court per Haultain C.J.S.

SUSPENSION. *n.* 1. " . . . [A]n annulment of the rights and obligations accruing during the suspension, and that the parties for the time being are in the same position as if the contract did not exist." *Dominion Sugar Co. v. Northern Pipe Line Co.* (1920), 47 O.L.R. 119 at 129, 51 D.L.R. 548 (C.A.), the court per Hodgins J.A. 2. " . . . [I]n an employment context the term suspension is usually used in the sense of discipline being imposed upon an employee. Section 15(2) [of the Public Service Act, S.B.C. 1985, c. 15], however, is clearly not intended as a matter of discipline because the employer has a disciplinary right completely independently of s. 15(2) by virtue of the collective agreement and the general law. It is more likely that the legislature intended to use the word 'suspension' in the sense of 'the suspension of the contract of employment', meaning that both employer and employee are relieved from any obligation to each other as a result of the contract of employment during the currency of the suspension. . ." *British Columbia (Government Personnel Services Division) v. B.C.G.E.U.* (1990), 22 L.A.C. (4th) 20 at 23 (B.C.), Ladner. 3. A temporary interruption of employment, other than a lay-off at the direction of the employer. 4. Temporary disqualification from the practice of law. 5. Temporary disqualification from the practice of a notary public. See TEMPORARY~.

SUSPENSION SPRING. A leaf, coil, torsion bar, rubber, air bag, and every other type of spring used in vehicular suspensions. *Motor Vehicle Safety Regulations*, C.R.C., c. 1038, s. 2.

SUS. PER COLL. *abbr.* Suspendatur per collum.

SUSPICION. See REASONABLE ~.

SUSPICIOUS CIRCUMSTANCES. In the law of wills, suspicious circumstances may be raised by (1) circumstances surrounding the preparation of the will, (2) circumstances tending to call into question the capacity of the testator, or (3) circumstances tending to show that the free will of the testator was overborne by acts of coercion or fraud. Since the suspicious circumstances may relate to various issues, in order to properly assess what effect the obligation to dispel the suspicion has on the burden of proof, it is appropriate to ask the question "suspicion of what?" Suspicious circumstances in any of the three categories to which I refer above will affect the burden of proof with respect to knowledge and approval. The burden with respect to testamentary capacity will be affected as well if the circumstances reflect on the mental capacity of the testator to make a will. Where suspicious circumstances are present, then the presumption is spent and the propounder of the will reassumes the legal burden of proving knowledge and approval. In addition, if the suspicious circumstances relate to mental capacity, the propounder of the will reassumes the legal burden of establishing testamentary capacity. Both of these issues must be proved in accordance with the civil standard. *Vout v. Hay*, [1995] 2 S.C.R. 876.

SUSTAIN. *v.* ". . . [T]o keep going or to keep up." *Sigurdson v. Reid* (1979), 32 C.B.R. (N.S.) 170 at 172, 17 B.C.L.R. 117 (S.C.), Hutcheon J.

SUSTAINABLE DEVELOPMENT. Development that meets the needs of the present without compromising the ability of future generations to meet their own needs.

SUSTAINABLE DEVELOPMENT STRATEGY. With respect to a department, means the department's objectives, and plans of action, to further sustainable development. *Auditor General Act*, R.S.C. 1985, c. A-17, s. 2, as am.

SUSTAINABILITY. *n.* The integration of environmental, social and economic considerations to ensure that the use, development and protection of the environment enables people to meet current needs, while ensuring that future generations can also meet their needs.

SUSTAINED. *adj.* 1. " . . . '[E]ndured', 'borne' or 'suffered'. . ." *Canadian Imperial Bank of Commerce v. Madill* (1983), 2 C. C.L.I. 75 at 100, 43 O.R. (2d) 1, 150 D.L.R. (3d) 417, [1983] I.L.R. 1-1699 (C.A.), the court per Goodman J.A. 2. Undergone.

SUSTAINED YIELD. The growth of timber that a forest can produce and that can be cut to achieve a continuous approximate balance between growth of timber and timber cut. See PERPETUAL ~.

SUSTAINED YIELD CAPACITY. Capacity when operated under sustained yield management.

SUSTAINED YIELD FOREST MANAGEMENT. A policy, method or plan of management to provide for an optimum continuous supply of timber in a manner consistent with other resource management objectives, sound environmental practice and the principle of sustainable development.

SUSTAINED YIELD MANAGEMENT. The planned use of a forest area whereby the timber produced is periodically removed without reducing the capacity of the area to continue production at an equal or greater rate in perpetuity.

SUTURE. See CRANIAL ~S.

S.V. *abbr.* Sub voce.

SWARMING. *n.* An unprovoked attack on a person in public by a group of persons.

SWEAR. *v.* 1. To put under oath, to administer an oath to. 2. In the case of persons for the time being allowed by law to affirm or declare instead of swearing, includes affirm and declare.

SWEARING. *n.* 1. Declaration under oath. 2. "The essence of swearing [as found is s. 160(a) of the Criminal Code, S.C. 1953-54, c. 51] appears to be a reference to God and in the form of an oath. Often used in legal proceedings and in legal documents as an appeal to the truth by invoking the deity, the word also includes the use of language which is contemptuous or irreverent of God or the deity." *R. v. Enns* (1968), 66 W.W.R. 318 at 320, 5 C.R.N.S. 115 (Sask. Dist. Ct.), Maher D.C.J.

SWEEPSTAKES. *n.* A race declared open to all horses that comply with its conditions, in which the owners of the horses entered contribute to a purse to which is added money contributed by the association.

SWEETBREAD. *n.* The thymus gland of a bovine animal.

SWEETENING INGREDIENT. Sugar, invert sugar, honey, glucose, dextrose or any combination thereof in dry or liquid form. Canada regulations.

SWEET GAS PROCESSING PLANT. A plant that processes raw gas, does not separate any sulphur compounds from the raw gas stream, and releases industrial wastewater to the environment other than by evaporation, by injection into an approved deep well facility, or by directing the industrial wastewater to a wastewater treatment plant.

SWELL. *n.* A can of fish, the top or bottom, or both, of which can have been distorted outward due to spoilage. *Fish Inspection Act*, R.S. Nfld. 1970, c. 132, s. 12. See HARD ~; HYDROGEN ~.

SWIFT. The Society for Worldwide Interbank Financial Telecommunication.

SWIMMING POOL. Any structure, basin, chamber or tank containing or intended to contain an artificial body of water for swimming, diving or recreational bathing and having a water depth of 76.2 centimetres (2 feet 6 inches) or more at any point. See FILL-AND-DRAW ~; FLOW-THROUGH ~; MODIFIED ~; PRIVATE RESIDENTIAL ~; PUBLIC ~.

SWING SHIFT. A shift which overlaps other shifts.

SWITCH. *v.* See BAIT AND ~.

SWITCH. *n.* A device for making, breaking or changing connections in a circuit. See AUTOMATIC ~; DUAL CONTROL ~; ELECTRIC LOCK; GENERAL USE ~; INDICATING ~;

ISOLATING ~; MOTOR-CIRCUIT ~; SPRING ~.

SWITCHBOARD. *n.* A panel or assembly of panels on which is mounted any combination of switching, measuring, controlling and protective devices, buses, and connections, designed with a view to successfully carrying and rupturing the maximum fault current encountered when controlling incoming and outgoing feeders.

SWITCHGEAR. *n.* All devices for controlling, regulating, protecting or measuring the supply of electrical energy, current or voltage to, or in a system, or part of a system.

SWITCHING CHARGE. A charge for each movement over Board railway of a unit of rolling stock. *Harbour Railway Tariff by-laws.*

SYDNEY. See DECLARATION OF ~.

SYLLOGISM. *n.* A form of reasoning in which one draws a conclusion which does not contain the common element of its premises.

SYMBOL. *n.* A shorthand way of visually communicating a message or instruction. See HAZARD ~.

SYMPATHETIC STRIKE. " . . . [T]he idea of workmen in certain industries ceasing work voluntarily and without breach of their contracts to express their sympathy for and moral support of other workmen already on strike. . ." *R. v. Russell,* [1920] 1 W.W.R. 624 at 640, 33 C.C.C. 1, 51 D.L.R. 1 (Man. C.A.), Cameron J.A. (Haggart and Fullerton JJ.A. concurring).

SYMPATHY STRIKE. A strike by workers of one employer to express solidarity with workers of another employer.

SYNALLAGMATIC. *adj.* 1. Involving reciprocal and mutual duties and obligations. 2. Describing a situation in which one party undertakes to another party to do or not to do something, and, if that party fails to perform the undertaking, the law provides a remedy to the other party. G.H.L. Fridman, *The Law of Contract in Canada,* 2d ed. (Toronto: Carswell, 1986) at 10.

SYNCHRONISE. *v.* To agree in time.

SYNCOPARE. *v.* To shorten.

SYNDICATE. *n.* 1. A group of people who join in a venture or undertaking. 2. An underwriting member of the exchange. 3. A syndicate other than a specialized syndicate, constituted under the Professional Syndicates Act, whose mem-

bers are producers and whose object is the study, defence and promotion of the economic, social and moral interests of the producers generally. *Farm Producers Act,* R.S.Q. 1977, c. P-28, s. 1. See FARM ~; PROFESSIONAL ~; SPECIALIZED ~.

SYNDICATE TRUST. Intended to provide protection for the capital contribution of each investor in a group in addition to that provided by any partnership agreement among them, incorporating a company. D.M.W. Waters, *The Law of Trusts in Canada,* 2d ed. (Toronto: Carswell, 1984) at 448.

SYNDROME. *n.* A set of symptoms and signs which happen together. See CRUSH ~; MALLORYWEISS ~; SUDDEN INFANT DEATH ~.

SYNOPSIS. *n.* A brief or condensed statement presenting a combined or general view of something.

SYNTHETIC COLOUR. Any organic colour, other than caramel, that is produced by chemical synthesis and has no counterpart in nature.

SYNTHETIC CRUDE OIL. A mixture, mainly of pentanes and heavier hydrocarbons, that may contain sulphur compounds, that is derived from crude bitumen and that is liquid at the conditions under which its volume is measured or estimated, and includes all other hydrocarbon mixtures so derived.

SYNTHETIC PRODUCTION. The production of petroleum from a mine in a bituminous sands deposit.

SYRUP. See MAPLE ~.

SYSTEM. *n.* 1. " . . . [A] practice. . ." *Creveling v. Canadian Bridge Co.* (1915), 21 D.L.R. 662 at 667, 8 W.W.R. 619, 51 S.C.R. 216, Duff J. (Brodeur J. concurring). 2. " . . . [P]lan . . ." *Mako v. Kelowna (City)* (1988), 40 M.P.L.R. 213 at 215, 53 D.L.R. (4th) 604 (B.C. C.A.), the court per Southin J.A. 3. " . . . [R]efers to the physical aspect of the utility . . . *Charles A. Pender Ltd, Re,* [1940] 3 D.L.R. 39 at 41, 15 M.P.R. 159, 51 C.R.T.C. 230 (N.S. C.A.), the court per Archibald J.A. 4. A telephone, telegraph or radio telecommunication system or a combination of any such systems, or any similar means of communication operated by the use of electrical energy; and also includes all the works, owned, held, or used, for the purpose thereof or in connection therewith or with the operation thereof. 5. A normally interconnected arrangement of insulated electrical conductors for the transmission, distribution and application of electrical energy, and the system may or may not include the generating source. 6. The connection between actions about which one seeks evidence and the act of which the prisoner is accused, i.e. a prisoner has in mind a scheme to obtain money by fraud; the act of which the prisoner is accused is part of a planned fraud; and one seeks evidence that the plan existed, and, therefore, that the prisoner has a guilty mind. P.K. McWilliams, *Canadian Criminal Evidence*, 3d ed. (Aurora: Canada Law Book, 1988) at 11-11. See ADVERSARIAL ~; AIR BRAKE ~; AIR HANDLING ~; ANTILOCK ~; BURGLAR ALARM ~; CABLE ~; CLEARING ~; COMMUNICATION ~; COMPRESSED GAS ~; COMPUTER ~; CONVEYANCE ~; DIFFERENT ~S; DISTRIBUTION ~; ELECTRICAL ~; EMERGENCY LIGHTING ~; EXCHANGE ~; FEUDAL ~; FIRE SUPPRESSION ~; FUEL ~; GAS ~; GEOGRAPHICAL POSITIONING ~; GROUNDING ~; GROUP ~; HORIZONTAL CONTROL ~; HYDRAULIC ~ MINERAL OIL; INDUSTRIAL ~; INFORMATION ~; INFORMATION MANAGEMENT ~; INQUISATORIAL ~; INTERCONNECTED ~S; LAND TITLES ~; LIGHTING ~; LIGHTNING PROTECTION ~; LIGHTNING ROD ~; MAPPING ~; MARKETING PLAN OR ~; METRIC ~; PARIMUTUEL ~; PAYMENTS ~; PIPING ~; PLANT ~; PLUMBING ~; PRESSURE PIPING ~; PRESSURE ~; PUBLIC TRANSIT ~; PURIFICATION ~ ; QUOTA ~ ; RAILWAY ~ ; RECIRCULATION ~; REFERRAL HIRING ~; REFRIGERATING ~; REGISTRATION ~; REGISTRY ACT ~; ROUTING ~; SENIORITY ~; SEWAGE ~; SEWERAGE ~; SEWER ~; STEERING CONTROL ~; SUPPLY ~; TELEPHONE ~; TRANSIT ~; TRANSPORTATION ~; TRANSPORT~; UTILITY VENT ~; WASTE TREATMENT~; WASTE-WATER ~; WATCHKEEPING ~; WATER SUPPLY ~; WATER ~; WATERWORKS ~; WORK ~.

SYSTEMATIC REVIEW. A medical or scientific study which evaluates the strengths and weaknesses of all relevant reported research over a particular period of time. It attempts to allocate a measure of reliability to the strength of the evidence in support of a given proposition.

SYSTEM GOODS. (a) Goods purchased for use directly in a water distribution, sewerage or drainage system; and (b) goods used in the construction of a building, or that part of a building, used exclusively to house machinery and apparatus for use directly in a water distribution, sewerage or drainage system, but does not include chemicals purchased for use or used in the treatment of water or sewage in any such system. *Excise Tax Act*, R.S.C. 1985 (2d Supp.), c. 7, s. 68.23.

SYSTEMIC DELAY. " . . . [T]he delay occasioned by the state's failure to provide for adequate facilities and staff in the timely prosecution of those citizens accused of crime. . ." *R. v. Koruz* (1992), 10 C.R.R. (2d) 113 at 160, 72 C.C.C. (3d) 353, 125 A.R. 161, 14 W.A.C. 161 (C.A.), Harradence J.A. (dissenting).

SYSTEMIC DISCRIMINATION. 1. " . . . [I]n an employment context is discrimination that results from the simple operation of established procedures of recruitment, hiring and promotion, none of which is necessarily designed to promote discrimination. . . is often unintentional. It results from the application of established practices and policies that, in effect, have a negative impact upon the hiring and advancement prospects of a particular group. . ." *Canadian National Railway v. Canada (Canadian Human Rights Commission)* (1987), 27 Admin. L.R. 172 at 195, 87 C.L.L.C. 17,022, 76 N.R. 161, 40 D.L.R. (4th) 193, 8 C.H.R.R. D/4210, [1987] 1 S.C.R. 1114, the court per Dickson C.J.C. 2. Systemic discrimination arises from the existence of a particular policy which creates the discriminatory effect. The effect is usually obvious (e.g. height and weight restrictions). Systemic discrimination arises out of long-standing stereotypes and value assumptions which create the discriminatory effect. Systemic discrimination is quite often the result of unintentional behaviour. There is no desire to exclude certain people or classes of people but, as the result of stereotypes, mind-sets and attitudes which have been acquired over a long period of time, the effect is discriminatory. *Ayangma v. Prince Edward Island*, 2001 CarswellPEI 103, 2001 PESCAD 22 (C.A.).

SYSTEMIC NEGLIGENCE. Negligence not specific to any one victim but rather to the class of victims as a group. *Rumley v. British Columbia*, 2001 CarswellBC 2166, 2001 SCC 69, McLachlin C.J.C., for the court.

SYSTEMIC RISK. The risk that the inability of a participant to meet its obligations in a clearing and settlement system as they become due or a disruption to a clearing and settlement system could, through the transmittal of financial problems through the system, cause (a) other participants in the clearing and settlement system to be unable to meet their obligations as they become due, (b) financial institutions in other parts of the Canadian financial system to be unable to meet their obligations as they become due, or (c) the clearing and settlement system's clearing house or the clearing house of another clearing and settlement system within the Canadian financial system to be unable to meet its obligations as they become due. *Payment Clearing and Settlement Act, 1996*, S.C. 1996, c. 6, Sch., s. 2.

SYSTEMS ACTION. " . . . [O]ne where a person or group with a general public interest as opposed to a strictly personal interest attacks the conduct of a governmental or similar authority on grounds that it has acted unconstitutionally, or that it has violated the principles of natural justice. The environmental actions against mosquito spraying, and the constitutional challenges against censorship laws, or abortion, are typical." *Morgan v. Winnipeg Remand Centre*

(1983), 36 C.P.C. 266 at 279, [1983] 3 W.W.R. 542, 21 Man. R. (2d) 11 (Q.B.), Kroft J.

SYSTEMS SOFTWARE. A combination of computer programs and associated procedures, related technical documentation and data that (a) performs compilation, assembly, mapping, management or processing of other programs; (b) facilitates the functioning of a computer system by other programs; (c) provides service or utility functions such as media conversion, sorting, merging, system accounting, performance measurement, system diagnostics or programming aids; (d) provides general support functions such as data management, report generation or security control; or (e) provides general capability to meet widespread categories of problem solving or processing requirements where the specific attributes of the work to be performed are introduced mainly in the form of parameters, constants or descriptors rather than in program logic. *Income Tax Regulations*, C.R.C., c. 945, s. 1104.

SYSTEM VOLTAGE. The greatest normal effective difference of electrical potential between any two points in a system. *Coal Mines Regulation Act*, R.S.N.S. 1989, c. 73, s. 85(1).

T. *abbr.* 1. Telsa. 2. Tera. 3. Ton (metric).

T.A. *abbr.* Décisions du Tribunal d'arbitrage.

TAB. *n.* A tab that is issued initially with the licence and is issued each year thereafter to indicate that the licence is valid. *Pacific Fishery Registration and Licensing Regulations*, C.R.C., c. 824, s. 2. See REGISTRATION VALIDATION ~; VALIDATION ~.

T.A.B. *abbr.* Tax Appeal Board.

TABLE. *v.* To set aside a matter; to put off; to delay; to postpone.

TABLE. *n.* See BILLIARD ~; TIME ~.

TABLET. *n.* A compressed mixture of active ingredients and various non-medicinal binders.

TABULA. [L.] A writing tablet; a written document.

TABULA IN NAUFRAGIO. [L.—a plank in a shipwreck] A form of tacking of mortgages. R. Megarry and H.W.R. Wade, *The Law of Real Property*, 5th ed. (London: Stevens, 1984) at cxxviii. See DOCTRINE OF THE ~.

TAC. A technical acceptance certificate. *Radiocommunications Regulations*, SOR/96-484

TACIT. *adj.* With respect to a communication of intention, silent. Inferred or understood, but not openly expressed.

TACIT KNOWLEDGE. Knowledge acquired by individuals by experience and not committed to an easily reproducible form as explicit knowledge.

TACK. *n.* Includes all equipment of any kind customarily fitted to or placed on a horse.

TACKING. *n.* 1. Extending a mortgagee's security to cover a subsequent loan. R. Megarry and H.W.R. Wade, *The Law of Real Property*,

5th ed. (London: Stevens, 1984) at cxxviii. 2. A doctrine concerning priorities between competing mortgages on the same property. If a third mortgage is taken without notice of a second and the third mortgagee purchases the first mortgage, the third mortgagee may tack the third mortgage to the first mortgage and so obtain priority. W.B. Rayner & R.H. McLaren, *Falconbridge on Mortgages*, 4th ed. (Toronto: Canada Law Book, 1977) at 195. 3. A doctrine by which a mortgagor's devisees or heirs may not redeem the mortgage without also paying a judgment debt or bond owing by the mortgagor because any equity of redemption in the hands of the devisees or heirs are assets for the payment of that debt. W.B. Rayner & R.H. McLaren , *Falconbridge on Mortgages*, 4th ed. (Toronto: Canada Law Book, 1977) at 196-197. 4. "A first or prior mortgagee may claim priority, up to the face amount of the mortgage, for moneys advanced under the first or prior mortgage subsequent to the registration and advancement of funds under second or subsequent mortgage provided that such first or prior mortgagee did not have 'notice' of the second or subsequent mortgage at the time such subsequent advances were made. The 'notice' previously referred to is actual notice, not constructive notice." *I.W.A. Credit Union v. Johnson* (1978), 6 B.C.L.R. 271 at 280, 4 R.P.R. 181 (S.C.), Hinds L.J.S.C.

TACKLE. *n.* When used in relation to a vessel, means the tackle, machinery, gear, apparatus and appliances used on board the vessel for the loading and unloading thereof.

TAG. *n.* Any type of tag supplied with a licence that is made of cardboard, paper, plastic, metal or any other material. See IDENTIFICATION ~.

TAG-END UNIT. " . . . A tag-end unit, as the name suggests, is ordinarily the last bargaining unit, encompassing all unrepresented employees and fashioned in terms which will ensure no further fragmentation of the bargaining structure. There is only one 'tag-end unit'. There is not a 'tag-end' unit corresponding to each existing bargaining unit . . . a tag-end unit may include a diverse grouping of employees with no strong community of interest with each other." *Teamsters Chemical Energy & Allied Workers Union, Local 424 v. Resco Chemicals & Colours Ltd.*, [1986] O.L.R.B. Rep. 544 at 551, MacDowell (Vice-Chair), Armstrong and Wightman (Members).

TAIL. See FEE ~.

TAILAGE. *n*. Taxes in general.

TAILER. *n*. A device consisting of a manually or spring operated snare attached to the end of a handle that ensnares fish by gripping them around the caudal peduncle.

TAILINGS. *n*. The residue discarded, set aside or impounded during production from a mine.

TAILINGS IMPOUNDMENT AREA. A limited disposal area that is confined by manmade or natural structures or by both.

TAINTED. *adj*. With respect to fish, means fish that is rancid or has an abnormal odour or flavour.

TAKE. *v*. 1. The word "take" in relation to land does not necessarily refer to the acquisition of full title. Rather, *The Dictionary of Canadian Law* (2nd ed. 1995) defines "take lands" as including to "enter upon, take possession of, use and take lands for a limited time or otherwise or for a limited estate or interest". Similarly, several courts including this one have acknowledged that a "taking" of land includes the acquisition of possession and other interests less than full title. *Osoyoos Indian Band v. Oliver (Town)*, [2001] 3 S.C.R. 746 Per Iacobucci J. (McLachlin C.J.C., Binnie, Arbour and LeBel JJ. concurring). 2. To cause a person to come or go with. 3. To physically get something into one's hand or hold. 4. When used in relation to fish or wildlife includes the capturing or the taking into possession of fish or wildlife whether dead or alive.

TAKE-BACK. See VENDOR ~.

TAKE-HOME PAY. Net pay after withholding tax and other deductions.

TAKE-HOME WORK. Work that the employee performs at the place where he resides; but does not include the selling of goods or services.

TAKE LANDS. Includes enter upon, take possession of, use and take lands for a limited time or otherwise or for a limited estate or interest.

TAKE-OFF. (a) In respect of an aircraft other than an airship, the act of leaving a supporting surface, and includes the take-off run and the acts immediately preceding and following the leaving of that surface, and (b) in respect of an airship, the act of freeing the airship from restraint, and includes the acts immediately preceding and following the freeing of that airship from restraint. *Canadian Aviation Regulations*, SOR/96-433, s. 101.01.

TAKE-OFF DISTANCE AVAILABLE. The total of the take-off run available and, where a clearway is provided, the length of clearway declared available by the operator of the aerodrome. *Canadian Aviation Regulations*, SOR/96-433, s. 101.01.

TAKE-OFF RUN AVAILABLE. Means the length of a runway declared available and suitable by the operator of the aerodrome for the ground run of an aeroplane during take-off; *Canadian Aviation Regulations*, SOR/96-433, s. 101.01.

TAKE OVER BID. *var*. **TAKE-OVER BID**. 1. An offer made by an offeror to shareholders of a distributing corporation at approximately the same time to acquire all of the shares of a class of issued shares, and includes an offer made by a distributing corporation to repurchase all of the shares of a class of its shares. 2. An offer to acquire, directly or indirectly, issued and outstanding voting securities of an issuer which is (a) made to an person or company who is in a province; or (b) made to or accepted by any holder in the province of the issuer, where the voting securities subject to the offer to acquire, together with the offeror's voting securities, will carry, in the aggregate, 10 per cent or more of all voting rights attaching to the voting securities of the issuer issued and outstanding at the date of the offer to acquire, and, where two or more persons or companies make an offer or offers to acquire jointly or in concert, the securities subject to such offer or offers to acquire, together with each offeror's voting securities, shall be included in the calculation of the percentage that the voting rights attaching to the voting securities of the issuer to be acquired by the offerors is of all voting rights attaching to the voting securities of the issuer. See SECURITIES EXCHANGE ~.

TAKEN. *adj.* 1. " . . . [L]and is taken under the [Municipal Act, R.S.B.C. 1911, c. 170] when the notice to treat is served. *Hanna v. Victoria (City)* (1915), 22 B.C.R. 555 at 560, 10 W.W.R. 457, 34 W.L.R. 307, 27 D.L.R. 213 (C.A.), Galliher J.A. 2. " . . . [T]he word 'taken' . . . in [Criminal Code, R.S.C. 1970, c. C-34, s. 454(1)] must be held to encompass situations in which the accused surrenders or voluntarily appears." *Alberta (Attorney General) v. Kennedy*, [1983] 1 W.W.R. 406 at 410 (Alta. C.A.), the court per Harradence J.A. 3. " . . . '[A]pprehended' . . ." *R. v. Hughes* (1895), 2 C.C.C. 332 at 334 (Ont. H.C.), Rose J. (Meredith C.J.C.P. concurring).

TAKING. *n.* 1. "For there to be a statutory taking which gives rise to a claim for compensation, not only must the owner be deprived of the benefit of its property, there must be a resulting enhancement or improvement conferred upon whatever entity the legislature intended to benefit. Something must not only be taken away, it must be taken over. . ." *Steer Holdings Ltd. v. Manitoba* (1992), 47 L.C.R. 17 at 23, [1992] 2 W.W.R. 558, 21 R.P.R. (2d) 298, 8 M.P.L.R. (2d) 235, 79 Man. R. (32d) 169 (Q.B.), Kroft J. 2. " . . . [R]efers to the actual seizure and not to the removal of the goods from the premises." *Honens v. International Harvester Co.* (1921), 60 D.L.R. 631 at 635, [1921] 1 W.W.R. 820 (Alta. T.D.), Simmons J. 3. Any capturing, killing or taking into possession any game, whether dead or alive. See STATUTORY ~.

TAKING ACCOUNTS, ACTION FOR. This action was brought against M & L Leasing to indemnify the partners for the payment they made to satisfy the judgment. An action for indemnity or contribution is *not* the appropriate means for partners to seek indemnity; the proper remedy is an action for the taking of accounts. *Lafrentz v. M & L Leasing Ltd. Partnership* (2000), 2000 CarswellAlta 1121, 2000 ABQB 714, 8 B.L.R. (3d) 219, [2001] 1 W.W.R. 629, 85 Alta. L.R. (3d) 233, 275 A.R. 334 (Q.B.), Perras J.

TAKING OFF. In respect of an aircraft, means the act of abandoning a supporting surface and includes the immediately receding and following acts and, in respect of an airship or balloon means the act of freeing the airship or balloon from restraint and includes the immediately preceding and following acts. *Air Regulations*, C.R.C., c. 2, s. 101.

TALCUM EMBOLISM. An embolism caused by talcum powder particles in the circulation.

F.A. Jaffe, *A Guide to Pathological Evidence*, 3d ed. (Toronto: Carswell, 1991) at 218.

TALES. *n.* [L.] Such people.

TALESMAN. *n.* A person called up to be a juror from among the bystanders in a court.

TALION. *n.* The law of retaliation, by which punishments must resemble offences.

TALIS INTERPRETATIO IN AMBIGUIS SEMPER FIENDA EST, UT EVITETUR INCONVENIENS ET ABSURDUM. [L.] Ambiguous words should always be interpreted so that inconvenience and absurdity are avoided.

TALIS NON EST EADEM. [L.] The similar is not the same.

TALLAGE. *n.* Taxes in general.

TALLAGER. *n.* A tax or toll collector.

TALLIAGE. See TAILAGE.

TALLY ADJUSTMENT. See CUMULATIVE ~.

TALLYMAN. See CREE ~.

TAMPONADE. See CARDIAC ~.

TANDEM. *n.* A combination of two axles of a vehicle, exclusive of the front axle of the vehicle, arranged in a fixed position one behind the other.

TANDEM AXLE. Two axles, not more than 72 inches apart when measured at right angles from axle to axle, so arranged that the load carried by each is approximately equal. *Roads Act*, R.S.P.E.I. 1988, c. R-15, s. 1.

TANDEM AXLE WEIGHT. The combined weight which all the wheels on any tandem axle impose on the road.

TANDEM BULLET. 1. A military ammunition in which two projectiles are sequenced in a single round. F.A. Jaffe, *A Guide to Pathological Evidence*, 3d ed. (Toronto: Carswell, 1991) at 227. 2. Two bullets which leave the barrel of a firearm at one firing. F.A. Jaffe, *A Guide to Pathological Evidence*, 3d ed. (Toronto: Carswell, 1991) at 227.

TANGIBLE ASSET BACKING. Adjustment of the book value of liabilities and assets on a balance sheet to fair market value as determined by assuming the concern is viable. A. Bissett-Johnson & W.M. Holland, eds., *Matrimonial Property, Law in Canada* (Toronto: Carswell, 1980) at V-4.

TANGIBLE PERSONAL PROPERTY. (a) Means personal property that can be seen, weighed, measured felt or touched or that is in any way perceptible to the senses, (b) includes electricity, telecommunication and telephone services, (c) includes transient accommodation (d) includes repair services. *Health Services Tax Act*, R.S.N.S. 1989, c. 198, s. 2.

TANGIBLE PROPERTY. Property having a physical existence.

TANK. *n*. 1. A receptacle capable of holding liquids and includes any pipe or conduit through which liquids may pass into the receptacle. 2. A compartment below the deck of a ship suitable for the stowage of cargo. 3. A container for liquids or sludges required in or resulting from the operation of a plant. See CENTRE ~; CUSHION ~; FUEL ~; HOLDING ~; SEWAGE ~; STORAGE ~; VEHICLE ~; WING ~.

TANK CAR. Any vessel described as a tank car in the Regulations for the Transportation of Dangerous Commodities by Rail and is approved by the Commission for chlorine service, but does not include multi-unit tank cars such as the ICC 106A500-X tank car. *Chlorine Tank Car Unloading Facilities Regulations*, C.R.C., c. 1147, s. 2.

TANKER. *n*. Includes a steamship specially constructed for the carriage of liquid cargoes in bulk. Canada regulations.

TANKER FREIGHT COSTS. The costs incurred in the process of transporting petroleum by water.

TANK TRUCK. *var*. **TANK-TRUCK**. A motor vehicle having one or more tanks mounted on the frame or chassis of the vehicle.

TANK TRUCK VEHICLE. A commercial motor vehicle, trailer or semi-trailer used for or capable of being used for transportation of products in bulk and which contains or to which there is attached or upon which there has been placed either permanently or otherwise a closed tank or container having a capacity of 2.3 kilolitres or more.

TANK UNIT. See CARGO ~.

TANK VEHICLE. A vehicle designed for or capable of transporting gasoline or associated products in bulk. *Gasoline Handling Act*, R.R.O. 1980, Reg. 439, s. 1.

TANNER. *n*. A person who is engaged in the business of unhairing, fleshing, tanning, plucking, dressing or dyeing the pelts or skins of wildlife.

TANTUM JUDICATUM QUANTUM LITIGATUM. [L.] The judgment extends to the issues which were tried.

TAP. See FLANGE ~S; INDIVIDUAL ~; PIPE ~S.

TARDIEU SPOT. A small pin-point hemorrhage on the pleural surface of a lung, on a heart or other organ which was at one time considered to indicate asphyxia. F.A. Jaffe, *A Guide to Pathological Evidence*, 3d ed. (Toronto: Carswell, 1991) at 227.

TARE. *n*. 1. An allowance for the weight of the container in which goods are packed. 2. An allowance for the weight of materials and equipment that are weighed with the beef carcass but do not form part thereof.

TARGET AREA. The area within a spacing unit that is allocated for drilling a well.

TARIFF. *n*. 1. "[In the National Energy Board Act, R.S.C. 1970, c. N-6] . . . a list of tolls or rates. . . It has been sometimes defined as 'a schedule of rates together with rules and regulations.' " *Saskatchewan Power Corp. v. TransCanada Pipelines Ltd.* (1981), 130 D.L.R. (3d) 1 at 11, 39 N.R. 595, [1982] 1 W.W.R. 289, 14 Sask. R. 271, [1982] 2 S.C.R. 688, the court per Laskin C.J.C. 2. The schedule of fees to be charged for various legal services. 3. A schedule of fares, rates, charges and terms and conditions of carriage applicable to the provision of a transportation service. See JOINT ~; LOCAL ~.

TARIFF BOARD. The federal body empowered to inquire into and report on anything which relates to goods which are exempt from or subject to customs and excise duty.

TARIFF RATE QUOTA. A limitation on the quantity of goods that are entitled to a specified tariff treatment that may be imported in a specified period. *Customs Tariff*, S.C. 1997, c. 36, s. 2.

TARIFF SENTENCE. " . . . [U]sual range of sentences . . ." *R. v. L. (T.P.)* (1987), (*sub nom. R. v. L.*) 61 C.R. (3d) 1 at 26, 80 N.R. 161, [1987] 2 S.C.R. 309, 82 N.S.R. (2d) 271, 207 A.P.R. 271, 37 C.C.C. (3d) 1, 44 D.L.R. (4th) 193, 32 C.R.R. 41, La Forest J. (Dickson C.J.C., Estey, McIntyre and Le Dain JJ. concurring).

TAR SANDS. A mineral extracted, otherwise than by a well, from a mineral resource which is a deposit of bituminous sands, oil sands or oil shales.

TATTOO. *n.* 1. The introduction of insoluble pigment in the skin either accidentally or for identification or decorative purposes. F.A. Jaffe, *A Guide to Pathological Evidence*, 3d ed. (Toronto: Carswell, 1991) at 227. 2. An area of burned or partly burned powder grains near the wound where a bullet fired at close range entered. F.A. Jaffe, *A Guide to Pathological Evidence*, 3d ed. (Toronto: Carswell, 1991) at 227. 3. Any letter or numeral or combination of the same recorded as allotted.

TAUTOLOGY. *n.* A description of one thing twice in one sentence in equal terms.

TAVERN. *n.* 1. A place arranged for the consumption of beer and weak cider, open only to male persons, subject to section 19. *An Act Respecting the Commission de Contrôle des Permis D'alcool*, R.S.Q. 1977, c. C-33, s. 18. 2. A premises provided with special accommodation facilities and equipment as prescribed in the regulations, where consideration of payment therefor beer and wine are served. *Liquor Control Act*, S. Nfld. 1973, c. 103, s. 2.

TAX. *n.* 1. " . . . [T]he . . . levies . . . are taxes. . . Compulsion is an essential feature of taxation . . . the committee is a public authority, and . . . the imposition of these levies is for the public purposes. . ." *British Columbia (Lower Mainland Dairy Products Sales Adjustment Committee) v. Crystal Dairy Ltd.*, [1933] 1 D.L.R. 82 at 85, [1933] 3 W.W.R. 639 1933 A.C. 168 (P.C.), Lord Thankerton. 2. "Tax is a term of general import, including almost every species of imposition on persons or property for supplying the public treasury, as tolls, tributes, subsidies, excise, imposts, or customs . . ." *Lovitt v. Nova Scotia (Attorney General)* (1903), 33 S.C.R. 350 at 360, Mills J. 3. " . . . [E]very contribution to a public purpose imposed by superior authority is a 'tax' and nothing less." *Monette v. Lefebvre* (1889), 16 S.C.R. 387 at 403, Strong J. (Patterson J. concurring). 4. Any tax, impost, duty or toll imposed or authorized to be imposed by any Act of Parliament or a legislature. See ACCRUED ~; AREA ~; ARREARS OF ~; ASSESSMENT AND ~ ROLL; BUSINESS OCCUPANCY ~; BUSINESS ~; CONSOLIDATED ~ES; CORPORATION ~; CURRENT YEAR ~ES; DEPARTURE ~; DEVELOPMENT ~; DIRECT ~; ESTATE ~; EXCISE ~ES; EXPORT ~; FRONTAGE ~; GENERAL ~; GIFT ~; IN-

COME ~; INCREMENTAL ~; INDIRECT ~; INHERITANCE~; LOCAL IMPROVEMENT ~; LOGGING ~; MUNICIPAL ~; OUTSTANDING ~ES; POLL~; PROPERTY ~; PROVINCIAL ~ OR FEE; REAL ESTATE ~; REAL PROPERTY ~; REDEVELOPMENT ~; REFUND OF ~; RESOURCE ~ES; SCHOOL ~.

TAX ABATEMENT. The percentage that is applied to the "tax otherwise payable under this Part" within the meaning assigned to that expression by subsection 120(4)(c) of the Income Tax Act to determine the amount that is deemed by subsection 120(2) of that Act to have been paid by an individual on account of his tax for a taxation year. *Federal-Provincial Fiscal Arrangements Act*, R.S.C. 1985, c. F-8, s. 26.

TAX A.B.C. *abbr.* Tax Appeal Board Cases, 1949-1971.

TAXABLE. See AMOUNT ~.

TAXABLE CAPITAL GAIN. (a) Subject to paragraphs (a.1) and (a.2), a taxpayer's taxable capital gain for a taxation year from the disposition of any property is 1/2 of the taxpayer's capital gain for the year from the disposition of the property. *Income Tax Act*, R.S.C. 1985, c. 1, (5th Supp.), s. 38, part.

TAXABLE COSTS. 1. "Three distinct categories of taxable costs appear to have been recognized [under the Federal Rules of Court, Tariff B]: (1) disbursements, to which a successful self-represented litigant is ordinarily entitled even at common law; (2) 'costs that would be peculiar to legal counsel', which, evidently, ought to be allowed a successful self-represented lay litigant, and (3) costs, neither disbursements nor 'peculiar to legal counsel', which ought to be allowed that litigant." *Davidson v. Canada (Solicitor General)* (1989), 24 C.P.R. (3d) 129 at 131, 36 Admin. L.R. 251, 47 C.C.C. (3d) 104, [1989] 2 F.C. 341, 98 N.R. 126, 61 D.L.R. (4th) 342 (C.A.), Mahoney J.A. 2. " . . . [T]hose costs which may be taxed by a taxing office under [Saskatchewan Queen's Bench Rules, R. 562(1)]. . ." *Angelstad v. Frederick Estate* (1990), 47 C.C.L.I. 231 at 234 (Sask. C.A.), the court per Sherstobitoff J.A.

TAXABLE FRONTAGE. The actual frontage or, where applicable, the distance which a parcel of land is deemed to abut on the work or highway, and in respect of which parcel the frontage tax is levied for the work or service.

TAXABLE FUEL. Any fuel that may be used for propelling a motor vehicle.

TAXABLE INCOME. With respect to a taxpayer for a taxation year, it is his income for the year plus the additions and minus the deductions permitted. See REVISED ~.

TAXABLE LANDS. See NEWLY ~.

TAXABLE MUNICIPAL PROPERTY. All property owned, operated or managed by a municipality either directly or through the medium of a board or commission for the purpose of producing, transmitting, delivering or furnishing electricity, water or power directly to or for the public. *Assessment Act*, R.S.N.S. 1989, c. 23, s. 2.

TAXABLE PARCEL. Subject to subsection (2), a run-off parcel or other parcel of farm land, any part of which lies within a distance of 100 yards from a telephone line or a proposed telephone line of a company, subject to the exclusions exemptions and conditions provided for by, under or pursuant to sections 3 to 43. *The Rural Telephone Act*, R.S.S. 1978, c. R-27, s. 2.

TAXABLE PROPERTY. 1. Real property and immovables in respect of which a person may be required by a taxing authority to pay a real property tax or a frontage or area tax; *Payments in Lieu of Taxes Act*, R.S.C. 1985, c. M-13, s. 2. 2. Any property or business in a municipality and in respect of which a tax is required to be paid for the raising of revenue for the general purposes of that municipality. *The Hospital Revenue Act* R.S.S. 1978, c H-9, s. 2.

TAXABLE SERVICE. (a) The provision, by means of telecommunication, to the general public or any portion thereof, of any programming service; (b) the commencement or cessation of the provision of a programming service referred to in paragraph (a); (c) the provision of any instrument, device, equipment or apparatus or any part thereof, other than a television receiver, that is (i) used in conjunction with the reception of a programming service referred to in paragraph (a); and (ii) provided by the person providing the programming service or by any person authorized programming or designated by him for the purpose or acting on his behalf or by any person related to him, if the person providing the programming service requires that the instrument, device, equipment, apparatus or part be acquired exclusively from him or any other person referred to in subparagraph (ii); and (d) the installation, disconnection, replacement, re-pair or maintenance of any instrument, device, equipment or apparatus, or any part thereof, other than a television receiver, referred to in paragraph (c), by the person providing the programming service in conjunction with which it is being used or by any other person referred to in subparagraph (c)(ii), but does not include (e) any surveillance or monitoring service, telebanking or teleshopping service or opinion-polling service; (f) any background music service of a nature or kind that is provided in a shopping centre, an office building, a factory or a common area of a condominium or of an apartment building as an accompaniment to shopping, dining, working or other similar activities carried on in such place; or (g) any other service prescribed by regulations made pursuant to section 21.2, that a person providing a programming service referred to in paragraph (a) provides for an additional fee or charge on the request of the person to whom the programming service is provided or that is provided by a person who does not provide a programming service referred to in paragraph (a). *Excise Tax Act*, R.S.C. 1985 (1st Supp.), c. 15, s. 21.1.

TAX ARREARS. The balance unpaid on taxes payable under an act for which payment is past due.

TAXATION. 1. The scheme of imposing charges on persons, income and property for the purpose of raising revenue for the purposes of the legislative authority. 2. Direct taxation refers to taxes imposed on the person intended to pay them. Income and sales tax are direct taxes. Indirect taxation refers to a tax demanded from one person in the expectation that he will indemnify himself at the expense of another person. Customs and excise are indirect taxes when imposed on businesses. 3. The process by which costs awarded to parties at a trial or in relation to work which a solicitor has performed for a client are referred, examined and certified by an officer of the court. 4. " . . . [T]he essence of taxation is that it is imposed by superior authority without the taxpayers consent. . ." *Halifax (City) v. Nova Scotia Car Works Ltd.* (1914), 18 D.L.R. 649 at 652, [1914] A.C. 992 (Can. P.C.), the board per Lord Sumner. 5. " . . . [T]he meaning to be attributed to the phrase 'direct taxation' in s. 92 of the Constitution Act, 1867 [(30 & 31 Vict.), c. 3] is substantially the definition of [of John Stuart Mill]: 'Taxes are either direct or indirect. A direct tax is one which is demanded from the very persons who it is intended or desired should pay it. Indirect taxes are those which are demanded from one person in the expectation and intention that he shall indemnify himself at the expense of another; such as the excise or customs.' "*Cotton v. R.* (1913), [1914] A.C. 176 at 191-3, 5 W.W.R. 662, 13 E.L.R. 371, 15 D.L.R. 283, 26 W.L.R. 207 (P.C.), the board per Lord Moulton. See CERTIFICATE OF ~; LOCAL ~; NET WORTH ~; RECIPROCAL ~ AGREEMENT.

TAXATION AREA. (a) Canada; (b) the United States (except Hawaii); and (c) the Islands of St. Pierre and Miquelon. *Excise Tax Act*, R.S.C. 1985, c. E-15, s. 8.

TAXATION OF COSTS. The review of a lawyer's bill for services or the review of an award of costs in a proceeding by an official of the court. See ASSESSMENT OF COSTS.

TAXATION YEAR. 1. The fiscal year in relation to which the amount of tax is being computed. 2. In the case of a corporation, a fiscal period and in the case of an individual, a calendar year.

TAX AVOIDANCE. Attempts by a taxpayer to minimize or eliminate a tax obligation either by deliberately arranging income earning affairs to benefit from provisions of income tax legislation or by relying on reasonable and different interpretations of that legislation. W. Grover & F. Iacobucci, *Materials on Canadian Income Tax*, 4th ed. (Toronto: Richard De Boo Ltd., 1980) at 993.

TAX BASE. See MUNICIPAL ~;.

TAX BENEFIT. A reduction, avoidance or deferral of tax or other amount payable under this Act or an increase in a refund of tax or other amount under this Act. *Income Tax Act*, R.S.C. 1985, c. 1 (5th Supp.), s. 245(1).

TAX COLLECTION AGREEMENT. 1. An agreement between the Government of Canada and the government of a province pursuant to which the Government of Canada will collect, on behalf of the province, taxes that the province imposes on the incomes of individuals or corporations, or both, and will make payments to the province in respect of the taxes so collected in accordance with the terms and conditions of the agreement. *Federal-Provincial Fiscal Arrangements Act*, R.S.C. 1985, c. F-8, s. 2. 2. Although provinces impose their own income taxes at their own rates, as long as a province uses the same tax base as the federal one, the federal government collects provincial tax on the prov-

inces behalf free of charge. P.W. Hogg, *Constitutional Law of Canada*, 3d ed. (Toronto: Carswell, 1992) at 139.

TAX CONCESSION. Any provision in, or based on the terms of any public or private Act whereby a person is entitled to a benefit or advantage by way of (a) a reduced or fixed assessment or valuation of property, real or personal; (b) a reduced or fixed rate or tax; (c) a variation in the method of paying rates or taxes; or (d) any other benefit or advantage of a like nature. *Assessment Act*, R.S.N.B. 1973, c. A-14, s. 1.

TAX COURT OF CANADA. The Tax Review Board, established by the *Tax Review Board Act*, chapter 11 of the Statutes of Canada, 1970-71-72, was continued under the name of the Tax Court of Canada as a court of record. The Court has exclusive original jurisdiction to hear and determine references and appeals to the Court on matters arising under the *Canada Pension Plan*, the *Cultural Property Export and Import Act*, the *Employment Insurance Act*, Part IX of the *Excise Tax Act*, the *Income Tax Act*, the *Old Age Security Act* and the *Petroleum and Gas Revenue Tax Act*, where references or appeals to the Court are provided for in those Acts. The Court has exclusive original jurisdiction to hear and determine appeals on matters arising under the *War Veterans Allowance Act* and the *Civilian War-related Benefits Act* and referred to in section 33 of the *Veterans Review and Appeal Board Act*. The Court also has exclusive original jurisdiction to hear and determine questions referred to it under section 173 or 174 of the *Income Tax Act* or section 310 or 311 of the *Excise Tax Act*. *Tax Court of Canada Act*, R.S.C. 1985, c. T-2.

TAX CREDIT. A deduction from tax otherwise payable. See EXPLORATION AND DEVELOPMENT EXPENSE ~.

TAX DEBTOR. A person who is liable to make payments under this act. *Income Tax acts*.

TAX DEED. A deed conveying property which has been sold for arrears of taxes to a purchaser.

TAX DRIFT. As a taxpayer's income increases through inflation, the taxpayer drifts upwards into a higher tax bracket. W. Grover & F. Iacobucci, *Materials on Canadian Income Tax*, 4th ed. (Toronto: Richard De Boo Ltd., 1980) at 45.

TAXED COSTS. Costs fixed by the court officer assigned the duty of reviewing and setting the costs to which a party is entitled regarding the costs of litigation.

TAX EQUITY OF A PARTNERSHIP. The fair market value of partnership assets at valuation day, without recognizing the work in progress or inventory of a cash-basis and subject to scaled-down recognition of assets which are intangible. Donald I. Beach, *Explanation of Canadian Tax Reform*, (Toronto: CCH Canadian Ltd., 1972) at 238-239.

TAX EVASION. In a case where the law clearly obliges one to report income and pay tax, a wilful attempt by the taxpayer not to disclose or to suppress income and thus not to pay tax on it. W. Grover & F. Iacobucci, *Materials on Canadian Income Tax*, 4th ed. (Toronto: Richard De Boo Ltd., 1980) at 991.

TAX EXPENDITURE. A feature of the income tax system such as an exemption, exclusion, or deduction which is in fact a method of providing financial assistance and is not required for purposes of administering the income tax itself. W. Grover & F. Iacobucci, *Materials on Canadian Income Tax*, 4th ed. (Toronto: Richard De Boo Ltd., 1980) at 163.

TAX GROSS-UP. *n*. The practice of increasing lump sum awards for future care costs and pecuniary losses in personal injury cases (other than loss of future income) and for pecuniary losses in fatal accident cases to take into account the impact of taxation on the income generated by lump sum awards in respect of those heads of damages. It has been accepted at common law as a proper head of damages to be included in a lump sum award at trial. *McErlean v. Sarel* (1987), 61 O.R. (2d) 396 (C.A.).

TAX HAVEN. See PURE ~.

TAXI. *n*. A motor vehicle other than a bus used to transport passengers for gain or reward.

TAXI CAB. *var*. **TAXICAB**. A motor vehicle other than a bus used to transport passengers for compensation.

TAXI CAB BROKER. Any person who accepts calls in any manner for taxi cabs that are used for hire and that are owned by persons other than that person or that persons family or employer. *Municipal Act*, R.S.O. 1990, c. M.45, s. 232(6).

TAXIDERMIST. *n*. 1. A person engaged in the business of preparing, preserving or mounting heads, skeletons, pelts or skins of wildlife. 2. Any person who engages in the business of the preservation or mounting of migratory birds or their eggs; *Migratory Birds Regulations*, SOR/98-282, s. 2.

TAXI DRIVER. The driver of a motor vehicle having a seating capacity for not more than 9 persons which, with its driver, is operated or plies for hire by members of the public.

TAXING OFFICER. 1. The registrar or other officer appointed for the taxation or fixing of costs or the passing of accounts. 2. An assessment officer.

TAX IN PERSONAM. A tax which is imposed on a person rather than on property.

TAX IN REM. A tax on property rather than on an individual person.

TAX PAYABLE. The tax payable by a corporation for a fiscal year to Her Majesty and includes any amounts fixed by assessment.

TAX PAYABLE UNDER THE FEDERAL ACT. By an individual in respect of the taxation year means the amount determined under subsection (4) of Section 120 of the Federal Act for the year in respect of that individual.

TAX PAYER. *var*. **TAXPAYER**. 1. A person required by a revenue Act to pay a tax. 2. Any person whether or not liable to a tax. *Income Tax acts*. 3. Any person who is entitled to a refund of tax. 4. A person obligated to pay municipal taxes in respect of a residential dwelling. See PRINCIPAL ~.

TAX PURCHASER. A person who purchases land at a tax sale.

TAX RATE. See PROGRESSIVE ~ STRUCTURE; PROPORTIONAL ~ STRUCTURE; PROVINCIAL PERSONAL INCOME ~; REGRESSIVE ~ STRUCTURE; VARIABLE ~ SYSTEM.

TAX RENTAL AGREEMENT. An agreement by which the federal government rents from an agreeing province the right to levy corporate income tax, personal income tax and succession duty. The agreeing province does not levy these taxes, but receives grants ("rent") from the federal government to counterbalance the foregone revenue. P.W. Hogg, *Constitutional Law of Canada*, 3d ed. (Toronto: Carswell, 1992) at 138.

TAYLOR. *abbr*. Taylor's King's Bench Reports (Ont.), 1823-1827.

T.B. *abbr*. Tariff Board.

TBA. *abbr*. To be agreed.

T. BD. *abbr*. Transport Board.

T.B.R. *abbr*. Tariff Board Reports, 1937-1962.

T.C.C. *abbr*. Tax Court of Canada.

T.C.I. *abbr*. Tribunal canadien des importations.

T.C.J. *abbr*. Tax Court Judge.

T.D. *abbr*. Supreme Court, Trial Division.

T.D. BANK. *abbr*. Toronto-Dominion Bank.

TEACHER. *n*. 1. A person who instructs students in a program of instruction. 2. A person holding a valid certificate of qualification to teach in schools. See FULL TIME ~; OCCA-SIONAL ~; PART-TIME ~; PRIVATE SCHOOL ~; PROBATIONARY ~; PUPIL ~; SCHOOL ~; SECONDARY SCHOOL ~; STUDENT ~; SUBSTITUTE ~; TEMPO-RARY ~.

TEACHER AIDE. A person engaged by a board to work in a school under the direction of the principal or other teacher.

TEACHING DAY. A day upon which a school is legally open during the hours prescribed.

TEACHING HOSPITAL. A hospital providing facilities for the instruction of under-graduate and post-graduate students in the health professions in which the treatment of the patient is the function of a team of staff members, including the attending staff physician, a resident physician, an intern physician and a clinical clerk and for which each member of the medical staff and the head of each medical department of the hospital are appointed jointly by the university with which the hospital is affiliated and the board of directors of the hospital. See PARTIAL MEDICAL ~.

TEACHING PERSONNEL. Teachers, classroom assistants and adult educators.

TEACHING SERVICE. 1. The performance of the duties assigned to a teacher by the board of education that employs him. 2. The total period during which a person who holds a valid certificate is employed as a teacher.

TEACHING STAFF. Includes professors, lecturers, instructors, demonstrators, and all others engaged in the work of teaching or giving instruction.

TEACHING YEAR. The 12 calendar months from the first of July. See YEAR OF TEACH-ING.

TEAM. See MINE RESCUE ~.

TEAMING. *n*. Includes all kinds of work done by workers with teams, carts, including hand carts, drays, trucks, cabs, carriages, automobiles and other vehicles. *Workers' Compensation acts*.

TEAMSTER. *n*. The driver of a conveyance who can be hired to carry goods.

TEAM TRACK. A track on railway property which is used for loading or unloading purposes by more than one company or person. Canada regulations.

TEAR BOMBS. Any apparatus or device used to project or emit a gas or any other substance productive of tears.

TEASPOON. *n*. For the purpose of calculation of dosage, a volume of 5 cubic centimetres. *Food and Drug Regulations*, C.R.C., c. 870, c. C.O1.001.

TECH. *abbr*. Technical.

TECHNICAL INSTRUCTION. Instruction pertaining to the mechanical or vocational arts or to any one or more of them.

TECHNICAL LANDING. A landing of an aircraft made solely to obtain ground services required for the aircraft.

TECHNICAL SURVEYS. Geological, geophysical, geochemical, geographical, geodetic, topographical, hydrographic, hydrogeological, geotechnical, oceanographic, meteorological and other similar surveys. *Resources and Technical Surveys Act*, R.S.C. 1985, c. R-7, s. 2.

TECHNICIAN. *n*. 1. A person who engages in the process of artificial insemination or the collection of semen for the purpose of artificial insemination. 2. A person who makes, produces, reproduces, constructs, furnishes, supplies, alters or repairs any prosthetic denture, bridge, appliance or thing to replace, improve or any human tooth or to be used in, upon or in connection with any human tooth, jaw or associated structure for and upon the written prescription of a registered dentist. 3. A person holding a diploma or certificate that shows his qualifications to carry out specific veterinary procedures. See ANIMAL HEALTH ~; DENTAL ~; FILM ~; LABORATORY ~; QUALIFIED ~; RADIO AND TELEVISION SERVICE ~; RADIOLOGICAL ~.

TECHNOLOGICAL CHANGE. (a) The introduction by an employer into the work, undertaking or business of equipment or material of a different nature or kind than that previously utilized by the employer in the operation of the work, undertaking or business; and (b) a change in the manner in which the employer carries on the work, undertaking or business that is directly related to the introduction of that equipment or material.

TECHNOLOGIST. See LABORATORY ~; NUCLEAR MEDICINE ~; RADIATION THERAPY ~; RADIOGRAPHIC ~.

TECHNOLOGY. See BIO ~; DENTAL ~; ENGINEERING ~; MEDICAL RADIATION ~; MINISTRY OF STATE FOR SCIENCE AND ~; RESPIRATORY ~.

TEKTITE. *n.* Any natural form of silicate glass of non-volcanic origin.

TELECOMMUNICATION. *n.* 1. Any transmission of signs, signals, writing, images or sounds or intelligence of any nature by wire, radio, visual, optical or other electromagnetic system. *Copyright Act*, R.S.C. 1985, c. C-42, s. 2. 2. "The term 'telecommunication' as defined in the Criminal Code [R.S.C. 1970, c. C-34], connotes a sender and a receiver. . ." *R. v. McLaughlin* (1980), 18 C.R. (3d) 339 at 349, [1980] 2 S.C.R. 331, [1981] 1 W.W.R. 298, 32 N.R. 350, 23 A.R. 530, 53 C.C.C. (2d) 417, 113 D.L.R. (3d) 386, Estey J. See CANADIAN RADIO-TELEVISION AND ~S COMMISSION.

TELECOMMUNICATION FACILITY. "The combination of the two words connotes, in my view, a physical establishment or combination of physical components employed in the transmission or reception of signals by electromagnetic systems. . ." *R. v. McLaughlin* (1980), 18 C.R. (3d) 339 at 347, [1980] 2 S.C.R. 331, [1981] 1 W.W.R. 298, 32 N.R. 350, 23 A.R. 530, 53 C.C.C. (2d) 417, 113 D.L.R. (3d) 386, Estey J.

TELECOMMUNICATION LINE. A system or arrangement of lines of wire or other conductors by which telephone or other kinds of communications are transmitted and received by electronic means.

TELECOMMUNICATION SERVICE. Any transmission, reception or distribution of signs, signals, words, writing, images, symbols, sounds or intelligence of any nature by means of electromagnetic waves and includes the provision of facilities required for such transmission, reception or distribution. See EXTERNAL ~S.

TELECOMMUNICATIONS COMMON CARRIER. A person who owns or operates a transmission facility used by that person or another person to provide telecommunications services to the public for compensation. *Telecommunications Act*, S.C. 1993, c. 38, s. 2

TELECOMMUNICATIONS FACILITY. Any facility, apparatus or other thing that is used or is capable of being used for telecommunications or for any operation directly connected with telecommunications, and includes a transmission facility. *Telecommunications Act*, S.C. 1993, c. 38, s. 2

TELECOMMUNICATIONS SERVICE. A service provided by means of telecommunications facilities and includes the provision in whole or in part of telecommunications facilities and any related equipment, whether by sale, lease or otherwise. *Telecommunications Act*, S.C. 1993, c. 38, s. 2

TELECOMMUNICATION SYSTEM. See SATELLITE ~.

TELEFERRY. *n.* A device for the conveyance of passengers or chattels above water or land, otherwise than vertically, by means of vehicles supported by cables and more commonly referred to as a gondola lift, aerial cable-car, suspension line or aerial passenger tramway, and includes the land, structures, machinery and approaches necessary to the operation of the device.

TELEFILM CANADA. A federal body empowered to encourage the growth of the private sector Canadian film industry.

TELEGLOBE CANADA. The federal body which provides international telephone, telegraph, telex, facsimile, teleconferencing, data, broadcast and private satellite business services.

TELEGRAM. *n.* Includes cablegram and radiogram.

TELEGRAPH. *n.* 1. Includes telegram, telex and facsimile. 2. Includes wireless telegraph. 3. The expression "telegraph" and its derivatives, in an enactment or in an Act of the legislature of any province enacted before that province became part of Canada on any subject that is within the legislative powers of Parliament, are deemed not to include the word "telephone" or its derivatives. *Interpretation Act*, R.S.C. 1985, c. I-21, s. 36. See RADIO-~.

TELEGRAPH CABLE SHIP. A registered ship used exclusively for the laying or repairing of oceanic telegraph cables. Canada regulations.

TELEGRAPHIC SERVICE. Telegrams, cablegrams and radiograms.

TELEGRAPH TOLL. When used with reference to telegraph, means any toll, rate or charge to be charged by any company to the public or to any person, for the use or lease of a telegraph system or line or any part thereof, for the transmission of a message by telegraph, for installation and use or lease of any instruments, lines or apparatus attached to or connected or interconnected in any manner whatever with, a telegraph system, for any services provided by the company through the facilities of a telegraph system or for any service incidental to a telegraph business. *Railway Act*, R.S.C. 1985, c. R-3, s. 2.

TELEMARKETING. The practice of using interactive telephone communications for the purpose of promoting, directly or indirectly, the supply or use of a product or for the purpose of promoting, directly or indirectly, any business interest. *Competition Act*, R.S.C. 1985, c. C-34, s. 52.1.

TELEPHONE. *n*. Any instrument or device into which messages may be spoken or introduced for transmission over the commission's system by wire, without wires, or by radio transmission or by which such messages may be recorded, heard or seen. See RADIO-~.

TELEPHONE ACCOUNT BETTING. Parimutuel betting conducted by an account holder by means of a telephone. *Pari-Mutuel Betting Supervision Regulations*, SOR/91-365, s. 2.

TELEPHONE ACCOUNT BETTING SYSTEM. The recording devices and related equipment that are used to record and conduct telephone account betting. *Pari-Mutuel Betting Supervision Regulations*, SOR/91-365, s. 2.

TELEPHONE COMPANY. Includes a person or association of persons owning, controlling or operating a telephone system or line.

TELEPHONE LEVY. A levy pursuant to this Act upon land for telephone purposes and includes a construction levy and special levy and a levy required for the repayment of old debentures and loans. *The Rural Telephone Act*, R.S.S. 1978, c. R-27, s. 2.

TELEPHONE LINE. Includes all devices, real estate, franchises, easements, apparatus, fixtures, property, appurtenances and routes used, operated, controlled or owned by any public utility to facilitate the business of affording telephonic communication for hire, and all conduits, ducts, poles, wires, cables, cross-arms, receivers, transmitters, instruments, machines and appliances, connected or used therewith.

TELEPHONE SYSTEM. A system of telephone lines used for the transmission of communications by telephone, and includes all stations, toll offices, exchanges, plant, equipment, wires, cables and works used or connected with it. See MUNICIPAL ~; PRIVATE ~; RURAL ~.

TELEPHONE TOLL. When used with reference to telephone, means any toll, rate or charge to be charged by any company to the public or to any person, for the use or lease of a telephone system, or line or any part thereof, for the transmission of a message by telephone, for installation and use or lease of any instruments, lines or apparatus attached to, or connected or interconnected in any manner whatever with, a telephone system, for any services provided by the company through the facilities of a telephone system or for any service incidental to a telephone business. *Railway Act*, R.S.C. 1985, c. R-3, s. 2.

TELEVISED. See CLOSED CIRCUIT ~.

TELEVISION. See CANADIAN RADIO-~ AND TELECOMMUNICATIONS COMMISSION; RADIO AND ~ SERVICE TECHNICIAN.

TELEVISION PAY-PER-VIEW SERVICE. The pay-per-view service provided by a person licensed to carry on a pay television programming undertaking. *Broadcasting Distribution Regulations*, SOR/97-555, s. 1.

TELLER. *n*. 1. In a bank, a cashier. 2. A person who keeps a tally. 3. A person who issues and cashes tickets for an association. *Pari-Mutuel Betting Supervision Regulations*, SOR/91-365, s. 2. See AUTOMATED ~.

TELSA. *n*. The magnetic induction that is equal to one weber per square metre. *Weights and Measures Act*, S.C. 1970-71-72, c. 36 schedule 1.

TEMPERATURE PLATEAU. A period which may last 1-5 hours after death when the internal body temperature does not fall. F.A. Jaffe, *A Guide to Pathological Evidence*, 3d ed. Toronto: Carswell, 1991) at 227.

TEMPERED GLASS. Glass that has been treated chemically or thermally so that, upon fracture, an entire sheet or pane of the glass disintegrates into many small granular pieces. *Safety Glass Regulations* C.R.C., c. 933, s. 2.

TEMPORARY. *adj.* 1. " . . . [O]pposite in meaning to 'permanent'." *Navin v. Gore Mutual Insurance Co.*, [1980] I.L.R. 1-1170 at 561 (Ont. H.C.), Holland J. 2. Appointed specially for a specified short period of time or until the occurrence of a stated event. 3. In relation to any commission, board or corporation, means established for a specified period of time or until the occurrence of a stated event.

TEMPORARY ABSENCE. Permission for an inmate to leave the institution in which he is imprisoned for a period of time during the time he is serving his sentence. The purpose of a temporary absence program is to contribute to the maintenance of a just, peaceful and safe society by facilitating, through decisions on the timing and conditions of absence, the rehabilitation of prisoners and their reintegration into the community as law-abiding citizens. See UNESCORTED ~.

TEMPORARY ACCESS ROAD. A feeder or spur road that provides access to timber landings within a timber harvesting area and includes bulldozed skid trails, timber landings and other works associated with a timber harvesting operation. *Forestry Act*, R.S. Nfld. 1990, c. F-23, s. 112.

TEMPORARY ADVANCE. Any money paid out of the Consolidated Revenue Fund that is repayable and is chargeable to an activity, but is not evidenced by a promissory note.

TEMPORARY CAVITY. A cavity created momentarily in tissue by a projectile rapidly passing through, its size depends on the projectile's energy and rate of retardation. F.A. Jaffe, *A Guide to Pathological Evidence*, 3d ed. (Toronto: Carswell, 1991) at 227-8.

TEMPORARY DOMICILE. "Temporary" [as used in Town of Canmore Land Use By-law No. 18 of 1986, s. 5] therefore denotes rental on a short-term basis, perhaps for periods of up to 30 days, with no right of renewal. Property that is offered for rent on a daily or weekly basis would qualify as a temporary domicile, even though an occasional occupant might choose to lease the premises for a month or longer. Property that is offered for rent on a longer-term or seasonal basis most likely would not be captured

by the term. *Canmore (Town) v. Fossheim*, 250 A.R. 333, 2000 ABCA 71 (C.A.).

TEMPORARY EMPLOYEE. 1. An employee engaged to perform specific duties because of a temporary increase in the work load. 2. An employee, not being a contractual employee, employed for a specific period or for the purpose of performing certain specified work and whose employment may be terminated at the end of the period or upon completion of the work.

TEMPORARY HOME. A home in which a child may be placed temporarily pending further consideration of his case.

TEMPORARY LAYOFF. *var.* **TEMPORARY LAY-OFF**. A layoff of not more than 13 weeks in any period of 20 consecutive weeks.

TEMPORARY SUSPENSION. Advanced exploration, mining or mine production have been suspended, in accordance with an accepted closure plan, on either planned or unplanned basis, but the site is being monitored on a continuous basis by the proponent and protective measures are in place. *Mining Act*, R.S.O. 1990, c. M.14, s. 139(1).

TEMPORARY WORK STRUCTURE. Any structure or device that is used as an elevated temporary work base for persons or as an elevated temporary platform for materials and includes any scaffold, stage or staging, walkway, decking, bridge, boatswain's chair, tower, crawling board, temporary floor, any portable ladder or temporary means of access to or egress from any of the foregoing, and any safety net, landing or other device used in connection with such a structure.

TEMPUS EST EDAX RERUM. [L.] Time devours things.

TENANCY. *n.* 1. The exclusive right to occupy residential premises granted to a tenant by a landlord, for which the tenant agrees to pay or provide rent for a term that may be terminated by the landlord or tenant. 2. The condition of being a tenant. 3. The relation of a tenant to the property the tenant holds. See ENTIRE JOINT ~; MONTH OF ~; PERIODIC ~; SEVERAL ~; TERM OF ~; WEEK OF ~; YEAR OF THE ~.

TENANCY AGREEMENT. 1. An agreement between a landlord and a tenant for possession or occupation of residential premises, whether written, oral or implied. 2. A written, oral or implied agreement between a tenant and a landlord for occupancy of a rental unit and includes a licence to occupy a rental unit. *Tenant Protection Act, 1997*, S.O. 1997, c. 24, s. 1. See FIXED TERM ~.

TENANCY AT WILL. An interest which permits a grantee to enter into possession of land at the pleasure of the grantor and her or himself.

TENANCY BY ESTOPPEL. Created when a person without title or interest in land or having only an equitable interest in the land, lets a tenant into possession and receives rent from the tenant. The tenant is estopped from disputing the title of the lessor while the tenant remains in possession.

TENANCY BY THE ENTIRETY. A condition like a joint tenancy, which cannot be severed, created through a conveyance to a husband and wife with no words of severance. A. Bissett-Johnson & W.M. Holland, eds., *Matrimonial Property Law in Canada* (Toronto: Carswell, 1980) at 1-11.

TENANCY IN COMMON. A condition in which two or more people have an equal, undivided interest in property. Each of them may occupy all the land in common with the others. Each tenant may dispose of her property by will or deed. There is no right of survivorship as in a joint tenancy.

TENANCY MONTH. The monthly period on which a tenancy is based whether or not it is a calendar month, and unless otherwise specifically agreed on by the landlord and the tenant, the month is deemed to begin on the day on which rent is payable. See MONTH OF TENANCY.

TENANCY YEAR. The yearly period on which the tenancy is based whether or not it is a calendar year and, unless otherwise specifically agreed on by the landlord and the tenant, the year is deemed to begin on the day, or the anniversary of the day, on which the tenant first became entitled to possession. See YEAR OF THE TENANCY.

TENANT. *n*. 1. " . . . [T]he person who, by reason of his possession of occupancy or his rights thereto, whether by privity of contract or estate, for the time being holds the premises under title immediately or mediately from the landlord or his predecessor in title, and by reason of his so holding is the person liable for the time being to pay rent. . ." *Calgary Brewing & Malting Co., Re* (1915), 9 W.W.R. 3 at 565, 25 D.L.R.

859 (Alta. T.D.), Beck J. 2. " . . . [O]ne of a class of persons . . . who have a right to use the premises, not by license or invitation as occasion arises, but by a contract which gives a right to such use continuously during the currency of the contract without licence or invitation." *Watt v. Adams Brothers Harness Manufacturing Co.* (1927), 23 Alta. L.R. 94 at 97, [1927] 3 W.W.R. 580, [1928] 1 D.L.R. 59 (C.A.), Beck J.A. 3. A person who executes a tenancy agreement in possession. 4. Includes an occupant and the person in possession other than the owner. 5. A person who executes a tenancy agreement and to whom an exclusive right to occupy residential premises is granted. 6. Includes a person who pays rent in return for the right to occupy a rental unit and includes the tenant's heirs, assigns and personal representatives. *Tenant Protection Act, 1997*, S.O. 1997, c. 24, s. 1.7. A person who rents land from a landlord for a share of the crop or of the proceeds of the crop produced on such land. See COMMERCIAL ~; HOTEL ~; JOINT ~; LIFE ~; OVERHOLDING ~; PARTICULAR ~; SOLE ~; TERRE ~.

TENANT AT SUFFERANCE. One who overstays the term of his tenancy.

TENANT AT WILL. One who holds possession, without a fixed term, of premises by permission of the owner.

TENANT IN CHIEF. A person immediately beneath the monarch who holds land.

TENANT-OPERATOR. *n*. A person who leases and operates a farm he does not own.

TENANT PUR AUTRE VIE. Tenant for the life of another.

TENANT'S FIXTURES. Fixtures which the tenant installed into the premises for the purposes of his trade. These fixtures do not become part of the structure itself.

TENANTS IN COMMON. Two or more people who have an equal, undivided interest in property; each of them may occupy all the land in common with the others. Each tenant may dispose of their interest by will or deed. There is no right of survivorship as in a joint tenancy.

TENDER. *n*. 1. A payment of the precise amount that is due. To offer a larger amount without asking for change is acceptable, but to offer less is not. If it was agreed that the debt be paid on a certain day, payment after or before that date is not proper, and for the payment to be proper it must be unconditional. C.R.B. Dunlop,

Creditor-Debtor Law in Canada (Toronto: Carswell, 1981) at 21 and 22. 2. " ' . . . [T]o constitute a legal tender the money must be there, and must be produced and seen, but with this exception, that the party to whom a tender is made may by his conduct relieve the debtor from the necessity of producing it, by saying that it need not be produced, for he will not take the money if it be.' " *Matheson v. Kelly* (1875), 24 U.C.C.P. 598 at 601 (Ont.), Hagarty C.J. quoting Knight Bruce, L.J., in *Ex parte Danks; re Farley* 22 L.J.N.S. Bank. 73 at 75. 3. Legal currency. 4. A call for tender by written public advertisement. 5. " . . . [P]art of a system which is designed and intended to take advantage of the competitive factor in the market by inviting, offers to provide a service or product at a price to be stipulated by the individual making the offer and rewarding those who submit the lowest, or lower, offers. . ." *R. v. York-Hanover Hotels Ltd.* (1986), 9 C.P.R. (3d) 440 at 442 (Ont. Prov. Ct.), White Prov. Ct. J. 6. " . . . [A] car used for carrying coal, . . ." *Hollinger v. Canadian Pacific Railway* (1893), 20 O.A.R. 244 at 249, Hagarty C.J.O. 7. A "Tender" is that which a General Contractor submits to an Owner. It is not to a "Bid" which is what a Subcontractor submits to a General Contractor. *Ken Toby Ltd. v. British Columbia Buildings Corp.*, 1997 CarswellBC 1087, 34 B.C.L.R. (3d) 263, [1997] 8 W.W.R. 721, 34 C.L.R. (2d) 81, 31 B.L.R. (2d) 224 (S.C.), Burnyeat, J. 8. An offer to carry out work specified on and subject to the terms and conditions stated at the price quoted. Once a tender is accepted there is a binding contract. See LEGAL ~; LOCK ~; VALID ~.

TENDER OF PAYMENT. The unqualified offer of the specified sum required under a contract.

TENEMENT. *n.* Something which may be held; something which is subject to tenure. See DOMINANT ~; LANDS, ~S AND HEREDITAMENTS; SERVIENT ~.

TENENDUM. *n.* [L. to be held] A clause in a conveyance which describes the tenure by which a grantee holds the grantor's land.

TENOR. *n.* With respect to a document, its effect and meaning in contrast to its exact words. *Maxon v. Irwin* (1907), 15 O.L.R. 81 at 88 (Div. Ct.), Falconbridge C.J.

TENORE PRAESENTIUM. [L.] By the tenor of these presents.

TENOR EST PACTIO CONTRA COMMUNEM FEUDI NATURAM AC RATIONEM IN CONTRACTU INTERPOSITA. [L.] Tenure is an agreement, contrary to the common nature and reason of the fee, which is introduced into a contract.

TENOR EST QUI LEGEM DAT FEUDO. [L.] It is the tenor which regulates the feudal grant.

TENT. *n.* A structure of canvas or similar material supported by a pole or poles.

TENTORIUM CEREBELLI. A fold of dura mater which separates the cerebellum from the cerebrum. F.A. Jaffe, *A Guide to Pathological Evidence*, 3d ed. (Toronto: Carswell, 1991) at 228.

TENT TRAILER. A vehicular portable structure built on its own chassis, having a rigid or canvas top and side walls which may be folded or otherwise condensed for travel.

TENURE. *n.* 1. A way to hold or occupy. 2. The mode in which all land is theoretically owned and occupied. 3. " . . . [I]n the university context means the right to continued [employment] unless there is a sufficient reason for discharge — that is: redundancy, incompetence, seriously unprofessional behaviour, or persistent neglect of duties. The concept of tenure . . . is also applicable to the case of certain other professionals (judges, for example) who are required to exercise an [independent] and critical judgment, and in so doing, may incur the displeasure of powerful individuals and groups. Tenure ensures that an individual's economic security cannot be threatened because he expresses views which might be unpopular, or takes a position of which his employer disapproves, but which does not interfere with his ability to fulfill his professional responsibilities. Tenure has traditionally provided an important safeguard for academic freedom but in recent years it has served the equally important purpose of protecting faculty members against [discharge] for reasons which are wholly unrelated to their intellectual or teaching abilities." *Laurentian University Faculty Assn. v. Laurentian University of Sudbury*, [1979] O.L.R.B. Rep. 767 at 769, MacDowell (Vice-Chair), Archer and Murray (Members). 4. " . . . [T]he granting of tenure to a musician by the Philharmonic Society confers a holding or occupying of a specific position which will be renewed and may not be changed nor become a matter of disengagement without appropriate notice with a right of appeal of these decisions to a committee mainly composed by their peers from the orchestra whose decision is final and binding." *Calgary Philharmonic Society v. Calgary Musicians' Assn., A.F.M. Local 547* (1983), 9 L.A.C. (3d) 324 at 332 (Alta.), Mason. 5. When in reference to the teaching staff, means, subject to such provision as the Board may make an appointment held without term and made or conventionally recognized as made, permanent. *University New Brunswick Act*, S.N.B. 1984, c. 40, s. 1. See PRIVATE ~; SECURITY OF ~.

TENURIAL FORM OF LANDHOLDING. All English land is either in the hands of the monarch or is held by subjects as tenants whose interests in the land one calls estates. E.L.G. Tyler & N.E. Palmer, eds., *Crossley Vaines' Personal Property*, 5th ed. (London: Butterworths, 1973) at 4.

T.E. (QUÉ.). *abbr.* Tribunal de l'expropriation (Québec).

TERA. *pref.* 10^{12}. A prefix for multiples and submultiples of basic, supplementary and derived units of measurement. *Weights and Measures Act*, S.C. 1970-71-72, c. 36, schedule 1.

TERM. *n.* 1. A contract provision which explains an obligation or group of obligations imposed on one or more of the parties. G.H.L. Fridman, *The Law of Contract in Canada*, 2d ed. (Toronto: Carswell, 1986) at 427. 2. "[Used] . . . to designate the length of time for which a person is elected to serve in political office or for which a person is incarcerated as a penalty for the commission of a crime." *R. v. Laycock* (1989), 51 C.C.C. (3d) 65 at 68, 17 M.V.R. (2d) 1 (Ont. C.A.), the court per Goodman J.A. 3. "The word 'term' would be more accurate than 'session' to describe the time prescribed by law for holding court, as a session of the Court is the time of its actual sitting and terminates each day with its rising. The distinction is not always observed, however, and the words are often used interchangeably." *MacDonald v. Dawson* (1955), 20 C.R. 357 at 358, 36 M.P.R. 34, 112 C.C.C. 44 (Nfld. C.A.), the court per Walsh C.J. 4. In relation to any borrowing of money or any loan, means a term stipulated for the repayment thereof and includes a period of extension or renewal of such a term. 5. Of a lease agreement, its limit in time. In the law of real property, the estate granted to a lessor, an estate in years. 6. A period at an approved institution in an approved program of study of not less than 10 weeks du-

ration. See COLLATERAL ~; DISJUNCTIVE ~; EXPRESS~; FUNDAMENTAL ~; IMPLIED ~; PROPORTIONATE ~S; SCHOOL ~; SECURITY ~; SESSION; TRADE ~S; WINTER ~.

TERM CHARTER. A charter of an aircraft for 1 day or for a specified number of consecutive days, months or a combination thereof. Canada regulations.

TERM EMPLOYEE. A person appointed to a position that has been established for a specified period of time ending on a specified date or on the occurrence of a specified event.

TERMINAL. *n.* A storage facility to which petroleum is conveyed from a refinery and which is capable of holding petroleum in storage for resale and receiving petroleum by pipeline or water craft. See AIR-~; HOME ~; TRANSPORTATION ~; ~S.

TERMINAL BALLISTICS. Analysis of the behaviour of projectiles when they strike or penetrate a target. F.A. Jaffe, *A Guide to Pathological Evidence*, 3d ed. (Toronto: Carswell, 1991) at 175 and 213.

TERMINAL CHARGE. A charge at each end of a journey by rail, i.e. for loading or unloading.

TERMINAL CONTROL AREA. An airspace of fixed dimensions that is so specified in the *Designated Airspace Handbook* and within which an air traffic control service for IFR flights is provided. *Canadian Aviation Regulations*, SOR/96-433, s. 101.01.

TERMINAL DECONTAMINATION. The decontamination of (a) the clothing of a person; (b) the physical environment of a person; (c) the contents of the isolation room; and (d) any article or piece of equipment used in the diagnosis or treatment of a person after the person has been removed from isolation or has ceased to be a source of infection or after isolation procedures have been discontinued. *Public Health Act*, S.A. 1984, c. P-27.1, s. 1.

TERMINAL DISINFECTION. Disinfection carried out after recovery, removal or death of a patient. *Public Health Act*, R.R.O. 1980, Reg. 836, s. 1.

TERMINAL ELEVATOR. An elevator the principal uses of which are the receiving of grain on or after the official inspection and official weighing of the grain and the cleaning, storing and treating of the grain before it is moved forward. *Canada Grain Act*, R.S.C. 1985, c. G10, s. 2.

TERMINAL ILLNESS. A medical condition for which the prognosis is death within 12 months. *Marihuana Medical Access Regulations* SOR/2001-227, s. 1.

TERMINALS. *n*. Includes buildings, fixtures, structures, docks, wharves, ramps, landings, approaches, ways, offices and other improvements and facilities, other than land, necessary for or incidental to the operation of ferry, shipping and related services and incidental facilities and improvements. See TERMINAL.

TERMINAL SERVICES UNIT. The personnel who control the use of apron and terminal facilities at an airport.

TERMINATE. *v*. 1. To bring or to come to an end. *Newfoundland v. N.A.P.E.* (1987), 64 Nfld. & P.E.I.R. 280 at 286, 197 A.P.R. 280 (Nfld. C.A.), Gushue J.A. 2. " . . . [I]n the mortgage clause means to end a policy of insurance by some positive act and does not include a termination (expiration) which occurs from the mere passage of time. . ." *Traders Group Ltd. v. Stanley Mutual Fire Insurance Co.*, [1983] I.L.R. 1-1691 at 6515, 47 N.B.R. (2d) 310, 124 A.P.R. 310 (Q.B.), Kelly J. 3. To remove from the employer's payroll and from the employer's workplace.

TERMINATING SERVICE. A telecommunication service by a submarine cable between any place in Canada and any place outside Canada, but does not include any service by a submarine cable wholly under fresh water. *External Submarine Cable Regulations*, C.R.C., c. 1515, s. 2.

TERMINATING STATION. The station at which a schedule is last timed on any subdivision is the terminating station for that schedule, and for an extra train (except work extras) it is the station to which such train is authorized. *Regulations No. O-8, Uniform Code of Operating Rules*, C.R.C., c. 1175, Part III, s. 2.

TERMINATION. *n*. 1. " . . . [W]hen in the context of a breach of contract one speaks of 'termination' what is meant is no more than that the innocent party or, in some cases, both parties are excused from further performance." *Photo Production Ltd. v. Securicor Transport Ltd.*, [1980] 1 All E.R. 556 at 562 (U.K. H; L.), Lord Wilberforce. 2. [Includes] . . . an ending of the contract [of insurance] by time lapse." *Bank of Nova*

Scotia v. Commercial Union Assurance of Canada (1991), 104 N.S.R. (2d) 313 at 319, 283 A.P.R. 313, 6 C.C.L.I. (2d) 178 (T.D.), Tidman J. 3. In relation to a pension plan, means the cessation of crediting of benefits to plan members generally, and includes the situations described in subsections 29(1) and (2). *Pension Benefit Standards Act*, R.S.C. 1985 (2d Supp.), c. 32, s. 2. 4. The severance of a relationship between employer and employee. *Goguen v. Metro Oil Co.* (1989), 1989 CarswellNB 7, 42 B.L.R. 30, 95 N.B.R. (2d) 295, 241 A.P.R. 295 (C.A.), Angers, J.A. for the court. 5. In relation to employment, includes retirement and death. *Pension Benefits Act*, R.S.O. 1990, c. P.8, s. 1. 6. (a) A dismissal, including a constructive dismissal, (b) a lay-off that is effected because of a permanent discontinuance of all of the employer's business at an establishment, or (c) a lay-off including a lay-off effected because of a permanent discontinuance of part of the business of the employer at an establishment, that equals or exceeds thirty-five weeks in any period of fifty-two consecutive weeks. *Employment Standards Act*, R.S.O. 1990, c. E.14, s. 58(1).

TERMINATION DATE. See WELL ~.

TERMINATION OF EMPLOYMENT. Includes a lay-off of a person for a period longer than a temporary lay-off.

TERMINATION METHOD. In marriage breakdown, a method of establishing the value of an accrued pension. The value of the accrued pension is determined assuming that the member terminated employment as at the date of the marriage breakdown. The value of the pension is crystallized as of the date of separation.

TERMINATION OF THE WORK. The date on which the immoveable is ready for the use for which it is intended.

TERMINATION PAYMENT. An amount received by an employee whose office or employment has terminated.

TERM INSURANCE. See INTERIM ~.

TERMINUS AD QUEM. [L.] The end.

TERMINUS ANNORUM CERTUS DEBET ESSE ET DETERMINATUS. [L.] A term of years should be certain and prescribed.

TERMINUS A QUO. [L.] The beginning.

TERMINUS ET FEODUM NON POSSUNT CONSTARE SIMUL IN UNA EADEMQUE

PERSONA. [L.] A term and a fee cannot exist simultaneously in one and the same person.

TERM LIFE INSURANCE POLICY. See GROUP ~.

TERM LOAN. A loan having a fixed date of maturity and includes member and patronage loans having a fixed date of maturity. *Cooperative Corporations Act*, R.S.O. 1990, c. C.35, s. 1(1).

TERM OF APPRENTICESHIP. The interval of time established by regulation that an apprentice is required to serve from entry into to completion of an apprenticeship contract.

TERM OF ART. "Some expressions in common use in documents dealing with legal rights or obligations acquire in a legal context a special meaning different from, or more precise than, their meaning in common speech — they become 'terms of art'." *Prestcold (Central) Ltd. v. Minister of Labour*, [1969] 1 All E.R. 69 at 75, [1969] 1 W.L.R. 89 (U.K. C.A.), Lord Diplock.

TERM OF IMPRISONMENT. Includes the definite term of imprisonment and the indefinite period thereafter to which a person was originally sentenced. *Prisons and Reformatories Act*, R.S.C. 1970, c. P-21, s. 152.

TERM OF TENANCY. The length of time over which a tenancy agreement is to run.

TERMOR. *n*. A person who holds tenements or land for a prescribed number of years.

TERRA. *n*. [L.] Land fit for farming.

TERRA AFFIRMATA. [L.] Land rented out to farm.

TERRA CULTA. [L.] Land which is cultivated.

TERRA DEBILIS. [L.] Barren or exhausted land.

TERRA DOMINICA. [L.] The domain land of a manor.

TERRAE DOMINICALES REGIS. [L.] The domain of the Crown.

TERRAE DOMINIUM FINITUR, UBI FINITUR ARMOURUM VIS. [L.] The right of ownership of land ends where the power of arms ends.

TERRA EXCULTABILIS. [L.] Land which can be ploughed.

TERRA FRISCA. [L.] Land not recently ploughed.

TERRA FRUSCA. [L.] Land not recently ploughed.

TERRA LUCRABILIS. [L.] Land reclaimed from the sea or from wasteland.

TERRA NOVA. [L.] Arable land; land newly converted from woods.

TERRA SABULOSA. [L.] Sandy or gravelly land.

TERRA TESTAMENTALIS. [L.] Allodial land.

TERRA VESTITA. [L.] Land with a crop of corn.

TERRA WAINABILIS. [L.] Land which may be tilled.

TERR. CT. *abbr*. Territorial Court.

TERR. CT. J. *abbr*. Territorial Court Judge.

TERRESTRIAL SERVICE. A radiocommunication service provided by coast, land or mobile stations.

TERRE TENANT. A legal mortgagee because a legal estate was conveyed to her or him; a person who, having a freehold interest in land, possesses the rents and profits, and may at any time, if there is no agreement or reservation to the contrary, convert the legal right of possession into actual possession. W .B. Rayner & R.H. McLaren, *Falconbridge on Mortgages*, 4th ed. (Toronto: Canada Law Book, 1977) at 18.

TERRITORIAL. *adj*. Connected with or limited with reference to a certain territory.

TERRITORIAL COMPETENCE. The aspects of a court's jurisdiction that depend on a connection between the territory or legal system of the state in which the court is established, and a party to a proceeding in the court or the facts on which the proceeding is based.

TERRITORIAL COURT. A court established by Parliament for two federal territories, the Northwest Territories and the Yukon Territory. In Nunavut the court is known as the Nunavut Court of Justice.

TERRITORIAL DIVISION. Includes any province, county, union of counties, township, city, town, parish or other judicial division or place to which the context applies. *Criminal Code*, R.S.C. 1985, c. C-46, s. 2.

TERRITORIALITY. *n*. The state of being connected with or limited to a particular territory.

TERRITORIAL JURISDICTION. The territory where the court is given jurisdiction.

TERRITORIAL LANDS. Lands, or any interest in lands, in the Yukon Territory, the Northwest Territories or Nunavut that are vested in the Crown or of which the Government of Canada has power to dispose. *Territorial Lands Act*, R.S.C. 1985, c. T-7, s. 2.

TERRITORIAL MINISTER. Any minister of the government of a territory.

TERRITORIAL RATIONALE. The rule that any crime is local and that one must commit the offence within a territory for that territory to have jurisdiction to try it. M.R. Goode, *Criminal Conspiracy in Canada* (Toronto: Carswell, 1975) at 160.

TERRITORIAL SEA. 1. " . . . [A]s defined by international law, i.e., the waters and submerged lands to a width of three miles seaward of the coast of the mainland but when the mainland coast is deeply indented or has a fringe of islands in its immediate vicinity, seaward from baselines enclosing these features." *Canada (Attorney General) v. British Columbia (Attorney General)*, [1984] 4 W.W.R. 289 at 299, [1984] 1 S.C.R. 388, 8 D.L.R. (4th) 161, 52 N.R. 335, 54 B.C.L.R. 97, Dickson J. (Beetz, Estey and Chouinard JJ. concurring). 2. In relation to Canada, means the territorial sea of Canada as determined under the Oceans Act and includes the airspace above and the seabed and subsoil below that sea, and in relation to any other state, means the territorial sea of the other state as determined in accordance with international law and the domestic laws of that other state; *Interpretation Act*, R.S.C. 1985, c. I-21, s. 35. 3. The territorial sea of Canada consists of a belt of sea that has as its inner limit the baselines described in the Act and as its outer limit the line every point of which is at a distance of 12 nautical miles from the nearest point of the baselines or where geographical coordinates of points have been prescribed, lines determined from the geographical coordinates of points so prescribed. *Oceans Act*, S.C. 1996, c. 31. 4. "[In s. 2 of Customs and Excise Offshore Application Act, S.C. 1984, c. 17] . . . can be thought of as the area between the shore and a distance 12 miles seaward from thence." *Arctic Offshore Marine Services Ltd. v. R.*, [1986] 2 C.T.C. 179 at 180, 4 F.T.R. 183, 11 C.E.R. 363, Reed J.

TERRITORIES. *n.* 1. The Northwest Territories, which comprise (a) all that part of Canada north of the sixtieth parallel of north latitude, except the portions thereof that are within the Yukon Territory, the Province of Quebec or the Province of Newfoundland; and (b) the islands in Hudson Bay, James Bay and Ungava Bay, except those islands that are within the Province of Manitoba, the Province of Ontario or the Province of Quebec. *Northwest Territories Act*, R.S.C. 1985, c. N-27, s. 2. 2. The Yukon Territory and the Northwest Territories. *Land Titles Act*, R.S.C. 1985, c. L-5, s. 2. 3. The North-West Territories as defined in The North-West Territories Act, 1886, excepting that portion of the said Territories declared by The Yukon Territory Act to constitute the Yukon Territory. *The Interpretation Act*, R.S.S. 1978, c. I-11, s. 21. 4. " . . . [I]nclude waters and submerged lands . . . [An Act for the Union of the Colony of Vancouver Island with the Colony of British Columbia, 1866 (U.K.), 29-30 Vict., c. 67, s. 7]." *Canada (Attorney General) v. British Columbia (Attorney General)*, [1984] 1 S.C.R. 388 at 419, [1984] 4 W.W.R. 289, 8 D.L.R. (4th) 161, 52 N.R. 335, 54 B.C.L.R. 97, Dickson J. (Beetz, Estey and Chouinard JJ. concurring). See HER MAJESTY'S REALMS AND ~; MONEY PAID TO THE ~ FOR A SPECIAL PURPOSE; TERRITORY.

TERRITORIUM NULLIUS. [L.] Territory which is not within the jurisdiction of a party defined by international law.

TERRITORY. *n.* 1. The territories of Canada are the Yukon Territory, the Northwest Territories and Nunavut. 2. A seigniory, a township, a municipality, a territory not organized into a municipality and any part of a seigniory, township, municipality and territory not organized into a municipality. *An Act Respecting Land Titles in Certain Electoral Districts*, R.S.Q. 1977, c. T-11, s. 1. 3. The land areas under the sovereignty, jurisdiction or trusteeship of a country, as well as territorial waters adjacent thereto, and any reference to a country shall be construed, where applicable, as a reference to such territory of that country and any references to a geographical area comprising several countries shall be construed, where applicable, as a reference to the aggregate of respective territories of the countries constituting that geographical area. *Air Carrier Regulations*, C.R.C., c. 3, s. 23. 4. " . . . [O]f the Dominion . . . is all those lands and lands covered with water which form part of or are under the Parliamentary control of the Dominion." *Canadian Pacific Railway v. James Bay Railway* (1905), 36 S.C.R. 42 at 71, Girouard J.

See ACTIVITIES FOR THE DEVELOPMENT OF THE ~; FEDERAL ~; RECIPROCATING PROVINCE OR ~; SELECT ~; SURVEYED ~; TERRITORIES; UNORGANIZED ~; VOTING ~.

TERRITORY OF ORIGIN. The territory for which the original court was exercising jurisdiction. *Canada-United Kingdom Civil and Commercial Judgments Convention Act*, R.S.C. 1985, c. C-30, s. 1.

TERRITORY WITHOUT MUNICIPAL ORGANIZATION. Those parts of Ontario that are without municipal organization, including Indian reservations and provincial parks, but not including property of the Government of Canada used for the purposes of national defence installations, camps or stations. *Private Hospitals Act*, R.S.O. 1990, c. P.24, s. 1.

TERR. L.R. *abbr.* Territories Law Reports (N.W.T.), 1885-1907.

TERRORISM. *n.* 1. [In light of the *International Convention for the Suppression of the Financing of Terrorism, 1999*] "terrorism" in s. 19 of the [*Immigration Act*, R.S.C. 1985, c. I-2] includes any "act intended to cause death or serious bodily injury to a civilian, or to any other person not taking an active part in the hostilities in a situation of armed conflict, when the purpose of such act, by its nature or context, is to intimidate a population, or to compel a government or an international organization to do or to abstain from doing any act." *Suresh v. Canada (Minister of Citizenship & Immigration)*, [2002] 1 S.C.R. 3. 2. [N]ations may be unable to reach a consensus as to an exact definition of terrorism. But this cannot be taken to mean that there is no common ground with respect to certain types of conduct. At the very least, I cannot conceive of anyone seriously challenging the belief that the killing of innocent civilians, that is crimes against humanity, does constitute terrorism. As stated earlier, it is one matter for an organization to pursue political goals such as self-determination and quite another to pursue those goals through the use of violence directed at the civilian population. International human rights codes might not condemn deaths resulting from a civil war, that is to say as between two armed factions. But I know of no authority, international or otherwise, which condones the indiscriminate maiming and killing of innocent civilians. *Suresh v. Canada (Minister of Citizenship & Immigration)*, 2000 CarswellNat 25, 183 D.L.R. (4th) 629, 5 Imm. L.R. (3d) 1, 252 N.R. 1, 18

Admin. L.R. (3d) 159, [2000] 2 F.C. 592, 180 F.T.R. 57 (note) (C.A.), Robertson, J.A. for the court.

TERRORISM OFFENCE. An offence under any of sections 83.02 to 83.04 or 83.18 to 83.23, an indictable offence under this or any other Act of Parliament committed for the benefit of, at the direction of or in association with a terrorist group, an indictable offence under this or any other Act of Parliament where the act or omission constituting the offence also constitutes a terrorist activity, or a conspiracy or an attempt to commit, or being an accessory after the fact in relation to, or any counselling in relation to, an offence referred to in this definition. *Criminal Code*, R.S.C. 1985, c. C-46, s. 2 as am.

TERRORIST ACTIVITY. (a) An act or omission that is committed in or outside Canada and that, if committed in Canada, is one of the following offences: (i) the offences referred to in subsection 7(2) that implement the Convention for the Suppression of Unlawful Seizure of Aircraft, signed at The Hague on December 16, 1970, (ii) the offences referred to in subsection 7(2) that implement the Convention for the Suppression of Unlawful Acts against the Safety of Civil Aviation, signed at Montreal on September 23, 1971, (iii) the offences referred to in subsection 7(3) that implement the Convention on the Prevention and Punishment of Crimes against Internationally Protected Persons, including Diplomatic Agents, adopted by the General Assembly of the United Nations on December 14, 1973, (iv) the offences referred to in subsection 7(3.1) that implement the International Convention against the Taking of Hostages, adopted by the General Assembly of the United Nations on December 17, 1979, (v) the offences referred to in subsection 7(3.4) or (3.6) that implement the Convention on the Physical Protection of Nuclear Material, done at Vienna and New York on March 3, 1980, (vi) the offences referred to in subsection 7(2) that implement the Protocol for the Suppression of Unlawful Acts of Violence at Airports Serving International Civil Aviation, supplementary to the Convention for the Suppression of Unlawful Acts against the Safety of Civil Aviation, signed at Montreal on February 24, 1988, (vii) the offences referred to in subsection 7(2.1) that implement the Convention for the Suppression of Unlawful Acts against the Safety of Maritime Navigation, done at Rome on March 10, 1988, (viii) the offences referred to in subsection 7(2.1) or (2.2) that implement the Protocol for the Suppression of Unlawful Acts against the Safety of Fixed Platforms Located on the Continental Shelf, done at Rome on March 10, 1988, (ix) the offences referred to in subsection 7(3.72) that implement the International Convention for the Suppression of Terrorist Bombings, adopted by the General Assembly of the United Nations on December 15, 1997, and (x) the offences referred to in subsection 7(3.73) that implement the International Convention for the Suppression of the Financing of Terrorism, adopted by the General Assembly of the United Nations on December 9, 1999, or (b) an act or omission, in or outside Canada, (i) that is committed (A) in whole or in part for a political, religious or ideological purpose, objective or cause, and (B) in whole or in part with the intention of intimidating the public, or a segment of the public, with regard to its security, including its economic security, or compelling a person, a government or a domestic or an international organization to do or to refrain from doing any act, whether the public or the person, government or organization is inside or outside Canada, and (ii) that intentionally (A) causes death or serious bodily harm to a person by the use of violence, (B) endangers a person's life, (C) causes a serious risk to the health or safety of the public or any segment of the public, (D) causes substantial property damage, whether to public or private property, if causing such damage is likely to result in the conduct or harm referred to in any of clauses (A) to (C), or (E) causes serious interference with or serious disruption of an essential service, facility or system, whether public or private, other than as a result of advocacy, protest, dissent or stoppage of work that is not intended to result in the conduct or harm referred to in any of clauses (A) to (C), and includes a conspiracy, attempt or threat to commit any such act or omission, or being an accessory after the fact or counselling in relation to any such act or omission, but, for greater certainty, does not include an act or omission that is committed during an armed conflict and that, at the time and in the place of its commission, is in accordance with customary international law or conventional international law applicable to the conflict, or the activities undertaken by military forces of a state in the exercise of their official duties to the extent that those activities are governed by other rules of international law. *Criminal Code*, R.S.C. 1985, c. C-46, s. 83.01

TERRORIST GROUP. An entity that has as one of its purposes or activities facilitating or carrying out any terrorist activity, or a listed entity, and includes an association of such entities. *Criminal Code*, R.S.C. 1985, c. C-46, s. 83.01.

TEST. *v.* 1. Of evidence, to determine veracity. 2. To determine veracity. 3. " . . . [T]o try out, experiment with, check out." *Murray v. Insurance Corp. of British Columbia* (1992), 10 C.C.L.I. (2d) 47 at 56 (B.C. S.C.), Gow J.

TEST. *n.* A standard by which one judges. See ACID ~; APTITUDE ~; BUT FOR ~; DESTRUCTIVE ~; DOMINANT PURPOSE ~; GETTLER-YAMAKAMI ~; HYDROSTATIC ~; LABORATORY ~S; LIE DETECTOR ~; NEIGHBOUR ~; NONDESTRUCTIVE ~; PARAFFIN ~; PARAMOUNT PURPOSE ~; PROPORTIONALITY ~; PULLORUM ~ OR BLOOD ~; SPEED ~; STANDARD FIRE ~ SUBSTANTIAL PURPOSE ~.

TESTABLE. *adj.* With respect to a person, able to make a will.

TESTAMENT. *n.* 1. A bequest of personal property. 2. A will.

TESTAMENTA LATISSIMAM INTERPRETATIONEM HABERE DEBENT. [L.] Wills should have the broadest interpretation.

TESTAMENTARY. *adj.* With respect to a document or gift, made to take effect only after the person making it dies. *Cock v. Cooke* (1866), L.R. 1 P. & P. 241 at 243, Wilde J. See MATTERS AND CAUSES ~.

TESTAMENTARY CAPACITY. Ability to make a valid will. Having a disposing mind and memory, able to comprehend on one's own initiative and volition the essential elements of will-making—property, object, just claims, and revocation of existing dispositions.

TESTAMENTARY INSTRUMENT. Includes any will, codicil or other testamentary writing or appointment, during the life of the testator whose testamentary disposition it purports to be and after his death, whether it relates to real or personal property or to both. *Criminal Code*, R.S.C. 1985, c. C-46, s. 2.

TESTAMENTARY INTENTION. A deliberate fixed and final expression of an intention as to the disposal of property on one's death.

TESTAMENTARY MATTERS AND CAUSES. Includes all matters and causes relating to a grant of or revocation of probate or administration.

TESTAMENTARY TRUST. A trust that arises upon and in consequence of the death of an individual.

TESTAMENTUM. *n.* [L.] A will.

TESTAMENTUM DESTITUTUM. [L.] A forsaken will.

TESTAMENTUM, I.E., TESTATIO MENTIS, FACTA NULLO PROSENTIS METU PERICULI, SED SOLA COGITATIONE MORTALITATIS. [L.] A will, that is, the testimony of the mind, made with no fear of present danger, but in sole contemplation of death.

TESTAMENTUM OMNE MORTE CONSUMMATUM. [L.] Every will is completed by death.

TESTATE. *adj.* Having executed a will.

TESTATION. *n.* Disposition of property by a will.

TESTATOR. *n.* 1. The person making a will, whether the person be male or female. 2. A person who has died leaving a will.

TESTATORIS ULTIMA VOLUNTAS EST PERIMPLENDA SECUNDUM VERAM INTENTIONEM SUAM. [L.] The last will of a testator should be thoroughly fulfilled following that person's true intention.

TESTATRIX. *n.* A woman who has made a will.

TESTATUM. *n.* A part of an indenture, known as the witnessing cause, which begins with the words "now this indenture witnesseth".

TEST CASE. 1. An action whose result determines liability in other actions. 2. "[A case in which there is a] . . . factual or legal relationship between [the case] . . . and . . . other actions depending on its result. . ." *Asbjorn Horgard A/S v. Gibbs/Nortac Industries Ltd.* (1987), 81 N.R. 1 at 2 (Fed. C.A.), Urie J.A. 3. One chosen from a number of cases pending for the purpose of settling issues of law and fact for all. *Rosling Real Estate (Nelson) Ltd. v. Robertson Hilliard Cattell Realty Co.*, 2000 CarswellBC 23, 2000 BCSC 3 (S.C.).

TESTE. *n.* The final part of a writ which gives the date and place it was issued.

TESTES PONDERANTUR, NON NUMERANTUR. [L.] Witnesses should be weighed, not numbered.

TESTES QUI POSTULAT DEBET DARE EIS SUMPTUS COMPETENTES. [L.] The one who calls witnesses must give them appropriate expenses.

TEST GROUP. See CHILD ~.

TEST HOLE. *var.* **TESTHOLE**. 1. A hole drilled for any purpose in connection with geophysical exploration but does not include a shothole, or a well drilled or being drilled for oil, natural gas or water, or a deep testhole. 2. A hole drilled or being drilled (a) with a bore hole diameter of 100 mm or less; or (b) to a depth not exceeding 600 m, to obtain information about a geothermal resource.

TESTIBUS DEPONENTIBUS IN PARI NUMERO DIGNIORIBUS EST CREDENDUM. [L.] When the witnesses are equal in number on both sides, the more worthy should be believed.

TESTIFY. *v.* " . . . [T]he giving of evidence by means of oral communication in a proceeding. . ." *Thomson Newspapers Ltd. v. Canada (Director of Investigation Research, Combines Investigation Branch)* (1990), (*sub nom. Thomson Newspapers v. Canada (Director of Investagation & Research, Restrictive Trade Practices Commission)*) 29 C.P.R. (3d) 97 at 218, 76 C.R. (3d) 129, 72 O.R. (2d) 415n, 54 C.C.C. (3d) 417, 67 D.L.R. (4th) 161, [1990] 1 S.C.R. 425, 39 O.A.C. 161, 106 N.R. 161, L'Heureux-Dubé J.

TESTIMONIAL. *n.* With respect to a food or drug that is represented as containing a vitamin, mineral nutrient or mineral means any dramatized or undramatized pictorial, written or oral representation as to the result that is, has been or may be produced by the addition to a person's diet of that vitamin, mineral nutrient or mineral, as the case may be. *Food and Drug Regulations*, C.R.C., c. 870, c. D.O1.001.

TESTIMONIAL COMPETENCE. The capacity to observe and interpret, to recollect and to communicate. *R. v. Marquard*, [1993] 4 S.C.R. 223.

TESTIMONIAL EVIDENCE. In a broad sense, any evidence about which a competent witness testifies, even to simply identify an object. P.K. McWilliams, *Canadian Criminal Evidence*, 3d ed. (Aurora: Canada Law Book, 1988) at 1-11.

TESTIMONIAL PROOF. Oral testimony by a witness.

TESTIMONIA PONDERANDA SUNT NON NUMERANDA. [L.] Testimony should be weighed not counted.

TESTIMONY. *n.* 1. The evidence which a witness gives viva voce in a court or tribunal. 2. "[In s. 43 of the Canada Evidence Act, R.S.C. 1970, c. E-10] . . . includes both oral evidence and documentary evidence] (Radio Corp. of Amer. v. Rauland Corp., [1956] 1 Q.B. 618 [(U.K.)] and Radio Corp. of Amer. v. Rauland Corp., (Can.) [[1956] O.R. 630 (H.C.)]." *United States District Court, Middle District of Florida v. Royal American Shows Inc.*, [1981] 4 W.W.R. 148 at 152, 58 C.C.C. (2d) 274, 120 D.L.R. (3d) 732, 26 A.R. 136 (C.A.), Lieberman J.A. See PERPETUATE ~.

TESTIS UNUS TESTIS NULLUS. [L.] One witness is no witness.

TEST KIT. An *in vitro* diagnostic device that consists of reagents or articles, or any combination of these, and that is intended to be used to conduct a specific test. *Medical Devices Regulations* SOR/98-282, s. 1.

TEST MARKET FOOD. A food that, prior to the date of the notice of intention respecting that food referred to in subsection (5), was not sold in Canada in that form and that differs substantially from any other food sold in Canada with respect to its composition, function, state or packaging form and includes a food referred to in section B.01.054. *Food and Drug Regulations*, C.R.C., c. 870, c. B.01.012.

TEST MARKET PRODUCT. A prepackaged product that, prior to the date of the notice of intention respecting that product, was not sold in Canada in that form and that differs substantially from any other product sold in Canada with respect to its composition, function, state or packaging form. Canada regulations.

TESTMOIGNES NE POENT TESTIFIE LE NEGATIVE MES L'AFFIRMATIVE. [Fr.] Witnesses cannot prove the negative, but the affirmative.

TEST OF MATERIAL. See CERTIFICATE OF ~.

TEST RUN. See VALID ~.

TEXT BOOK. *var.* **TEXTBOOK**. 1. A treatise which collects decisions or explains principles concerning some branch of the law. 2. A text or other book authorized for use in the schools of the province.

TEXTILE ARTICLE. See CONSUMER ~.

TEXTILE FIBRE. Any natural or manufactured matter that is capable of being made into a yarn or fabric and, without limiting the generality of the foregoing, includes human hair, kapok, feathers and down and animal hair or fur that has been removed from an animal skin. *Textile Labelling Act*, R.S.C. 1985, c. T-10, s. 2. See RECLAIMED ~.

TEXTILE FIBRE PRODUCT. (a) Any consumer textile article; or (b) any textile fibre, yarn or fabric used or to be used in a consumer textile article. *Textile Labelling Act*, R.S.C. 1985, c. T-10, s. 2.

TEXTILE MATERIAL. Textile fibre or fabric or any other textile product of a stage between textile fibre and fabric.

TEXTILES. *n.* Cloth or fabric purchased by the yard or metre but does not include textiles used by a tailor, dressmaker, drapery manufacturer or upholsterer in producing clothing or draperies or in upholstering furniture even where a charge for such textiles is made separately on the invoice to the customer.

TEXTUAL MATERIAL. Manuscripts, records, documents, books, pamphlets and serials or any other material whose primary object is the communication of information through written or printed language.

THC. *abbr*. Tetrahydrocannabinol, an active ingredient of marihuana and hashish. F.A. Jaffe, *A Guide to Pathological Evidence*, 3d ed. (Toronto: Carswell, 1991) at 228.

THE. *Definite article*. Indicates that the noun following it is someone or something previously mentioned or understood from the context.

THEATRE. *n.* 1. Includes any place that is open to the public where entertainments are given, whether or not any charge is made for admission. Criminal Code, R.S.C. 1985, c. C-46, s. 150. 2. A building or hall or any premises, room or place, including an open-air place, to which the public is admitted and that is used for giving vaudeville, dramatic or operatic performances, or for exhibitions of moving pictures. See CHAIN ~; MOTION PICTURE ~; MOVING PICTURE ~.

THEATRE BETTING. Pari-mutuel betting that is conducted in a betting theatre in accordance with these Regulations. *Pari-Mutuel Betting Supervision Regulations*, SOR/91-365, s. 2.

THEATRE FILM EXCHANGE. A film exchange owned or operated by the owner, lessee, or manager of a duly licensed theatre.

THEATRE LICENCE. A licence that is issued by the Executive Director to an association to conduct theatre betting under subsection 85(7). *Pari-Mutuel Betting Supervision Regulations*, SOR/91-365, s. 2.

THEATRE OF ACTUAL WAR. (a) In the case of the South African War, the zone of the military operations in South Africa in which the forces of the United Kingdom of Great Britain and Ireland were engaged prior to June 1, 1902; (b) in the case of World War I, (i) as applied to the army or air forces, the zone of the allied armies of the continents of Europe, Asia or Africa, or wherever the veteran has sustained injury or contracted disease directly by a hostile act of the enemy, and (ii) as applied to the naval forces, the high seas or wherever contact has been made with hostile forces of the enemy, or wherever the veteran has sustained injury or contracted disease directly by a hostile act of the enemy; and (c) in the case of World War II, (i) with respect to a former member of His Majesty's Canadian forces, any place where he has been on service involving duties performed outside the Western Hemisphere, including outside Canada, Newfoundland and the United States and the territorial waters thereof in aircraft or anywhere in a ship or other vessel, which service is classed as "sea time" for the purpose of advancement of naval ratings, or which would be so classed were the ship or other vessel in the service of the naval forces of Canada, and (ii) with respect to a former member of His Majesty's forces other than His Majesty's Canadian forces, or of any of the forces of His Majesty's Allies or powers associated with His Majesty in World War II, such places, zones or areas as the Board may rescribe. *War Veterans Allowance Act*, R.S.C. 1985, c. W-3, s. 37(8). See SERVICE IN A ~.

THEATRE OF OPERATIONS. See SERVICE IN A ~.

THEFT. *n.* Fraudulently and without colour of right taking, or fraudulently and without colour of right converting to his use or to the use of another person, anything whether animate or inanimate, with intent, (a) to deprive, temporarily or absolutely, the owner of it or a person who has a special property or interest in it; (b) to pledge it or deposit it as security; (c) to part with it under a condition with respect to its return that the person who parts with it may be unable to perform; or (d) to deal with it in such a manner that it cannot be restored in the condition in which it was at the time it was taken or converted. *Criminal Code*, R.S.C. 1985, c. C-46, s. 322(1).

THEFT INSURANCE. Insurance against loss or damage through theft, wrongful conversion, burglary, housebreaking, robbery or forgery.

THE KING CAN DO NO WRONG. " . . . It is a general and fundamental rule that the king cannot sanction any act forbidden by law. It is in this sense that the king is under and not above the laws, and is bound by them equally with his subjects. Therefore the laws relating to contracts, as well as other laws, are binding on the sovereign. . . the maxim . . . is further limited by the allowance of the petition of right . . . giving to the subject the right to claim from the sovereign, movables, lands, debts and unliquidated damages . . . This gives the subject the same right he would have by action against another subject." *R. v. McLeod* (1882), 8 S. S.C.R. 1 at 32-3, Fournier J. (dissenting).

THERAPEUTIC ABORTION COMMITTEE. For any hospital, means a committee, comprised of not less than three members each of whom is a qualified medical practitioner, appointed by the board of that hospital for the purpose of considering and determining questions relating to terminations of pregnancy within that hospital. *Criminal Code*, R.S.C. 1985, c. C-46, s. 287(6).

THERAPEUTIC PRIVILEGE. "[An exception to the rule requiring disclosure to form the basis of informed consent which] . . . enables a doctor to withhold from his patient information as to risk if it can be shown that a reasonable medical assessment of the patient would have indicated to the doctor that disclosure would have posed a serious threat of psychological detriment to the patient." *Sidawa v. Bethlem Royal Hospital Governors*, [1985]1 All E.R. 643 at 654 (U.K. H.L.), Lord Scarman (dissenting) adopted in *Haughian v. Paine* (1987), 40 C.C.L.T. 13 at 32, [1987] 4 W.W.R. 97, 55 Sask. R. 99, 37 D.L.R. (4th) 624 (C.A.), the court per Sherstobitoff J.A.

THERAPIST. See DENTAL ~; DENTURE ~; DRUGLESS ~; PHYSICAL ~.

THERAPY. See DENTAL ~; ELECTRO-CONVULSIVE ~; OCCUPATIONAL ~;

PHYSICAL ~; RADIATION TECHNOLO-GIST; RESPIRATORY ~.

THEREUPON. *adv*. Thereafter.

THERMAL CUT OUT. A device affording protection from excessive current but not necessarily short-circuit protection, and containing a heating element in addition to, and affecting, a fusible member which opens the circuit.

THERMAL ELECTRIC POWER PLANT. A facility for the generation of electricity from the combustion of natural gas, oil, petroleum products, coal, wood or plant products or from the use of geothermal energy, and includes all associated structures, machinery, appliances, fixtures and equipment, and storage and handling facilities.

THERMAL INSULATION MATERIALS. Batt, blanket, foam, loose fill, rigid or reflective insulation that is acquired exclusively for the purpose of preventing heat loss and that is, (a) poured, packed, blown, sprayed or otherwise placed in bulk as permanent fill between the confining structural members of a building; (b) material in solid form that is permanently placed between, or attached to, structural members of a building; (c) chemicals to be used to form a permanent thermal insulating foam between the confining structural members of a building, if such chemicals are purchased at the same time, from the same vendor, and in proportions proper for the use of the chemicals as thermal insulating foam; or (d) weather stripping and caulking materials, but does not include, (e) windows and doors of any type and frames therefor; (f) pipe, boiler and duct insulation and wrapping materials; (g) acoustical insulation and acoustical materials; (h) wallboard or drywall; or, (i) any materials incorporated into a building primarily for their structural or decorative value, and materials serving functions other than thermal insulation whether or not such materials have thermal insulating properties.

THERMAL LIQUID BOILER. A pressure vessel the contents of which are heated by a liquid circulated through a tube or tubes that are submerged in water, where the Therm-hour rating of the boiler is more than 17.

THERMAL LIQUID HEATING SYSTEM. One or more thermal liquid heaters in which a thermal liquid that is not pressurized by the application of a heat source is used as the heat transfer medium and includes any connected piping system or vessel.

THERM HOUR. *var*. **THERM-HOUR**. 100,000 British thermal units per hour or 39.3082 brake horsepower.

THERM-HOUR RATING. The rating of a plant determined under an Operating Engineers act.

THESAURIUM. *n*. [L.] A treasure.

THESAURUS. *n*. [L.] A treasure.

THESAURUS COMPETIT DOMINO REGI, ET NON DOMINO LIBERTATIS, NISI SIT PER VERBA SPECIALIA. [L.] Treasure belongs to the monarch, and not to a lord of a liberty, unless this be through special mention.

THESAURUS INVENTUS. [L.] A treasure trove.

THESAURUS INVENTUS EST VETUS DISPOSITIO PECUNIAE, ETC., CUJUS NON EXTAT MODO MEMORIA, ADEO UT JAM DOMINUM NON HABEAT. [L.] A treasure trove is the hiding of money, etc., in a former time of which no memory remains, so that now it has no owner.

THESAURUS NON COMPETIT REGI, NISI QUANDO NEMO SCIT QUI ABSCONDIT THESAURUM. [L.] A treasure does not belong to the monarch, unless no one knows who hid the treasure.

THING. *n*. A subject of dominion or property See REAL ~.

THING IN ACTION. " . . . [A]n anglicization of the more usual and well-known common law expression '[chose] in action'. . ." *Deloitte, Haskins & Sells Ltd. v. Graham* (1983), 47 C.B.R. (N.S.) 172 at 177, [1983] 3 W.W.R. 687, 32 R.F.L. (2d) 356, 25 Alta. L.R. (2d) 84, 144 D.L.R. (3d) 539, 42 A.R. 76 (Q.B.), D.C. MacDonald J. See CHOSE IN ACTION.

THIN SKULL RULE. One who injures another must take his victim as he finds him or her. Makes a tortfeasor liable for a person's injuries even though the injuries are unexpectedly severe because of a pre-existing condition.

THIRD FREEDOM. The privilege of a non-Canadian air carrier, where operating a charter flight, of disembarking in Canada passengers who, or goods that, originated in the territory of the country of the non-Canadian air carrier and includes the privilege of re-embarking such passengers in Canada for the purpose of returning them to that territory. *Air Transportation Regulations*, SOR/88-58, s. 2.

THIRD PARTY. 1. A person who is not a party to an action but from whom a defendant claims relief. The party is not a party at the commencement of the original action but the defendant claims relief from the party and the defendant adds the party to the action. 2. In respect of a request for access to a record under this Act means any person, group of persons or organization other than the person that made the request or a government institution. *Access to Information Act*, R.S.C. 1985, c. A-1, s. 3. 3. A person who is or is about to become indebted to or liable to pay money to a financial corporation liable to pay the tax. *Corporation Capital Tax acts*. 4. A person from whom money is, or will become, due and payable to the defendant. See LEADER OF THE ~.

THIRD PARTY CAUCUS. The group of two or more members who constitute the second largest group sitting in the Assembly in opposition to the Government and who belong to the same political party.

THIRD PARTY CLAIM. A defendant may commence a third party claim against any person who is not a party to the action and who, (a) is or may be liable to the defendant for all or part of the plaintiff's claim; (b) is or may be liable to the defendant for an independent claim for damages or other relief arising out of, (i) a transaction or occurrence or series of transactions or occurrences involved in the main action, or (ii) a related transaction or occurrence or series of transactions or occurrences; or (c) should be bound by the determination of an issue arising between the plaintiff and the defendant. G.D. Watson & C. Perkins, eds., *Holmested & Watson: Ontario Civil Procedure* (Toronto: Carswell, 1984-) at 29-3.

THIRD PARTY DEMAND. A demand by the Receiver General made under the Income Tax Act by which an account debtor who owes money to a debtor-taxpayer must pay to discharge the debtor-taxpayer's debt to the extent of that payment.

THIRD PARTY LIABILITY INSURANCE. Insurance that secures a tortfeasor for personal liability. John G. Fleming, *The Law of Torts*, 8th ed. (Sydney: The Law Book Co., 1992) at 395.

THIRD PARTY PROCEEDING. Serves to enforce duties which a third party owes to the defendant who commences the third party proceeding. See THIRD PARTY CLAIM.

THIRD READING. Parliamentary review of a bill in its final form. A. Fraser, W.A. Dawson, & J. Holtby, eds., *Beauchesne's Rules and Forms of the House of Commons of Canada*, 6th ed. (Toronto: Carswell, 1989) at 195.

THOROUGHFARE. *n*. Any place or structure intended for vehicular or pedestrian traffic, in particular, a road, street, line, sidewalk walkway, bicycle path, snowmobile trail, hiking path, square or public parking area. *An Act Respecting Land Use Planning and Development*, S.Q. 1979, c. 51, s. 1.

THOUGH. *conj*. " . . . [U]sed in the sense of 'but' . . ." *R v. Kimbrough* (1918), 13 Alta. L.R. 412 at 415, [1918] 2 W.W.R. 892, 30 C.C.C. 56, 41 D.L.R. 409 (C.A.), the court per Harvey C.J.

THREAD. See GOLDEN ~.

THREAT. *n*. 1. A denunciation to a person of ill which will befall him. 2. Under the section the threat must be of death or serious bodily harm. It is impossible to think that anyone threatening death or serious bodily harm in a manner that was meant to be taken seriously would not intend to intimidate or cause fear. That is to say, a serious threat to kill or cause serious bodily harm must have been uttered with the intent to intimidate or instill fear. Conversely, a threat uttered with the intent to intimidate or cause fear must have been uttered with the intent that it be taken seriously. Both of these formulations of the mens rea constitute an intention to threaten and comply with the aim of the section. Section 264.1(1)(*a*) is directed at words which cause fear or intimidation. Its purpose is to protect the exercise of freedom of choice by preventing intimidation. The section makes it a crime to issue threats without any further action being taken beyond the threat itself. Thus, it is the meaning conveyed by the words that is important. Yet it cannot be that words spoken in jest were meant to be caught by the section. *R. v. Clemente*, 1994 CarswellMan 152, [1994] 8 W.W.R. 1, 31 C.R. (4th) 28, 168 N.R. 310, 91 C.C.C. (3d) 1, [1994] 2 S.C.R. 758, 95 Man. R. (2d) 161, 70 W.A.C. 161, Cory, J. for the court. 3. The threat [to the safety of the public in s. 672.54(a) of the Criminal Code, R.S.C. 1985, c.C-46] must be more than speculation. It must be supported by the evidence and it must be a real risk of physical or psychological harm to members in the community and the potential harm must be serious. A slight risk of grave harm or a high risk of slight harm will not suffice. The conduct leading to the harm must be criminal in nature. *R. v. Campagna* (1999), 1999 CarswellBC 1961 (S.C.). 4. " . . . [A] 'tool of intimidation which is designed to instil a sense of fear in its recipient': R. v. McCraw . . . [(1991), 66 C.C.C. (3d) 517 (S.C.C.)]. . . may be express or implicit and made by means of words, writings or actions. . ." *R. v. Pelletier* (1992), 71 C.C.C. (3d) 438 at 441(Que. C.A.), the court per Proulx J.A. See UTTERING ~.

THREATENED SPECIES. A wildlife species that is likely to become an endangered species if nothing is done to reverse the factors leading to its extirpation or extinction. *Species at Risk Act*, S.C. 2002, c. 29, s. 2.

THREATS TO THE SECURITY OF CANADA. (a) Espionage or sabotage that is against Canada or is detrimental to the interests of Canada or activities directed toward or in support of such espionage or sabotage; (b) foreign influenced activities within or relating to Canada that are detrimental to the interests of Canada and are clandestine or deceptive or involve a threat to any person; (c) activities within or relating to Canada directed toward or in support of the threat or use of acts of serious violence against persons or property for the purpose of achieving a political objective within Canada or a foreign state and (d) activities directed toward undermining by covert unlawful acts, or directed toward or intended ultimately to lead to the destruction or overthrow by violence of, the constitutionally established system of government in Canada, but does not include lawful advocacy, protest or dissent, unless carried on in conjunction with any of the activities referred to in paragraphs (a) to (d). *Canadian Security Intelligence Service Act*, R.S.C. 1985, c. C-23, s. 2.

THREE AXLE GROUP. Three consecutive axles, not including the front axle of a motor vehicle, (a) that do not form a triple axle within the meaning of clause (p); (b) that are entirely within either a motor vehicle or trailer or semi-trailer, (c) in which the spacings between the consecutive axles do not exceed 2.5 metres; and (d) which are not included in a four axle group within the meaning of clause (h).

THREE-CARD MONTE. The game commonly known as three-card monte and includes any other game that is similar to it, whether or not the game is played with cards and notwithstanding the number of cards or other things that are used for the purpose of playing. *Criminal Code*, R.S.C. 1985, c. C-46, s. 206(2).

THREE CERTAINTIES. The three essential characteristics required to create a trust: (a) certain intention; (b) certain subject-matter; (c) certain objects. D.M.W. Waters, *The Law of Trusts in Canada*, 2d ed. (Toronto: Carswell, 1984) at 107.

THREE CHAIN RESERVE. In Quebec a reserve of at least three chains in depth reserved to the Crown along banks of rivers and lakes. A chain is 66 feet in length. Chain refers to a surveyor's chain.

THRESHER. *n*. A person who threshes or causes to be threshed grain of any kind for another person, or who threshes or cuts and threshes grain, or causes grain to be threshed or cut and threshed for another person, with a harvester thresher, combine, or any other implement that both cuts and threshes grain.

THRESHOLD. See SENSING ~.

THRESHOLD CLAUSE. Requires an employer to appoint the most senior capable applicant even though there are junior applicants who are more capable.

THRESHOLD EFFECT. In respect of a pest control product, means a harmful effect on human health for which the Minister is able to identify a level at which the product will not cause that effect. *Pest Control Products Act*, S.C. 2002, c. 28, s. 2.

THRESHOLD LIMIT VALUE. A Registered Trade Mark of the American Conference of Governmental Industrial Hygienists: the airborne concentration of a substance below which it is ordinarily felt that nearly any worker may be exposed without jeopardizing health. D. Robertson, *Ontario Health and Safety Guide* (Toronto: Richard De Boo Ltd., 1988) at 5-403.

THRESHOLD SENTENCE. A sentence customarily imposed in the same jurisdiction for the same or similar crimes. A guide to judges to help in reducing disparity in sentencing.

THROMBOSIS. *n*. The presence or formation of a thrombus. F.A. Jaffe, *A Guide to Pathological Evidence*, 3d ed. (Toronto: Carswell, 1991) at 228. See CORONARY ~.

THROMBUS. *n*. A brittle, solid clot which forms in circulating blood inside chambers of the heart or blood vessels. F.A. Jaffe, *A Guide* to *Pathological Evidence*, 3d ed. (Toronto: Carswell, 1991) at 228. See MURAL ~.

THROTTLE. *n*. The component of the fuel metering device that (a) connects to the driver-operated accelerator control system and (b) controls the engine speed. *Motor Vehicle Safety Regulations*, C.R.C., c. 1038, s. 2.

THROUGH. *prep*. " ... [M]eans 'in consequence of', 'by reason of'. It does not connote a direct relationship between the cause and its effect, as might the preposition 'by' had it been used." *Petrogas Processing Ltd. v. Westcoast Transmission Co*. (1989), 58 D.L.R. (4th) 156 at 162, 66 Alta. L.R. (2d) 254, [1989] 4 W.W.R. 272, 95 A.R. 112 (C.A.), the court per Belzil J.A.

THROUGH AN ELECTION. The period commencing with the issue of a writ for an election and ending when the candidate or candidates have been returned as elected.

THROUGH HIGHWAY. 1. Any highway or portion thereof at the entrances to which stop signs or yield right-of-way signs are erected at which traffic from intersecting highways is required to stop or to yield right-of-way before entering or crossing the same. 2. A highway or a part of a highway at the entrances to which stop signs are erected.

THROUGH LOT. A lot having frontage on two parallel or approximately parallel streets. Canada regulations.

THROUGHOUT. *prep*. During the whole of.

THROUGHOUT AN ELECTION. Includes the period from the issue of the writ of election until the elected candidate is returned as elected.

THROUGHPUT. See CONTAINER ~.

THROUGHPUT CHARGE. The charge for the inward movement and outward movement of containers but does not include the charge for the crane.

THROUGH TOLL. A combination of separately established tolls.

THUS. *conj*. In accordance with; consequently; therefore.

THYMUS. *n*. A gland in the upper chest which affects immunological functions. F.A. Jaffe, *A Guide to Pathological Evidence*, 2d ed. (Toronto: Carswell, 1983) at 185.

THYROID CARTILAGE. The most important cartilage in the larynx. F.A. Jaffe, *A Guide*

to *Pathological Evidence*, 3d ed. (Toronto: Carswell, 1991) at 228.

TICKET. *n*. 1. A card, pass or other document upon presentation of which the holder is entitled to admission to any theatre, opera house, public hall, show, game, grandstand, race meeting, exhibition or amusement of any kind. *Ticket Speculation Act*, R.S.O. 1980, c. 499, s. 1. 2. A ticket sold under a lottery scheme and includes the contractual rights and obligations between the Corporation and the owner of the ticket. *Ontario Lottery Corporation Act*, R.R.O. 1980, Reg. 719, s. 1. 3. A receipt that is issued by an association for one or more bets on a race; *Pari-Mutuel Betting Supervision Regulations*, SOR/91-365, s. 2. See CASH PURCHASE ~; OUTSTANDING ~; VIOLATION ~; WEIGH ~; WINNING ~.

TICKETING. See DOUBLE ~.

TIDAL WATERS. Waters that are subject to the ebb and flow of tides. Includes the waters of rivers.

TIED SELLING. (a) Any practice whereby a supplier of a product, as a condition of supplying the product (the "tying" product) to a customer, requires that customer to (i) acquire any other product from the supplier or the supplier's nominee; or (ii) refrain from using or distributing, in conjunction with the tying product, another product that is not of a brand or manufacture designated by the supplier or the nominee and (b) any practice whereby a supplier of a product induces a customer to meet a condition set out in subparagraph (a)(i) or (ii) by offering to supply the tying product to the customer on more favourable terms or conditions if the customer agrees to meet the condition set out in either of those subparagraphs. *Competition Act*, R.S.C. 1981 (2nd Supp.), c. 19, s. 77.

TIERCED SALMON PLANT. A building, structure, machinery, appurtenances, appliances and apparatus occupied and used in the business of tiercing or mild curing salmon, or of converting the natural salmon into tierced salmon. *Fisheries Act*, R.S.B.C. 1996, c. 149, s. 12.

TILE. *n*. Tile, pipe or tubing of any material used in the installation of a drainage work.

TILL. *n*. Is of glacial origin, unsorted and heterogeneous and can contain a range of particle sizes including boulders, cobbles, gravel, sands, silts and clays and can exist at any relative density or consistency.

TIMBER. *n.* 1. " . . . [G]enerally treated as connoting growing trees which are a part of the realty and pass with a conveyance of land unless expressly reserved. . ." *Highway Sawmills Ltd. v. Minister of National Revenue*, [1966] C.T.C. 150 at 160 (S.C.C.), Ritchie J. (dissenting). 2. " . . . [I]ncludes spruce, fir and birch deals, planks, boards and scantling. . . the product sawed from logs, irrespective of its dimensions; . . ." *Baxter v. Kennedy* (1900), 35 N.B.R. 179 at 184 (C.A.), Tuck C.J. 3. Trees standing or fallen, logs and bolts, cants, boards and lumber, and any other sawn or shaped product of trees. 4. Standing trees, felled trees, parts of standing or felled trees, shrubs, round logs, wood chips or togs that have been slabbed 1 or more sides. *Forestry Act*, R.S. Nfld. 1990, c. F-23, s. 2. 5. Logs, timbers, boards, deals, scantlings or laths, telegraph poles, railway ties, pitprops, pulpwood, shingle bolts or staves, fence posts and cordwood. 6. Round logs or logs which are slabbed on one or two sides. See CROWN ~; MERCHANTABLE ~; PARTLY PROCESSED ~; STANDING ~.

TIMBER AGREEMENT. Includes any agreement made by the Crown with respect to the cutting and removal of trees and any agreement containing provisions for the cutting and removal of trees and includes any agreement ratified and confirmed by any special Act or general Act.

TIMBER BERTH. Timber licence. See DOMINION ~.

TIMBER DECK CARGO. A cargo of timber carried on an uncovered part of a freeboard deck or superstructurre deck, but does not include a cargo of wood pulp or similar cargo. Canada regulations.

TIMBER DISPOSITION. A forest management agreement, timber licence or timber permit.

TIMBER LAND. *var.* **TIMBERLAND**. 1. Any uncultivated land in the province on which trees or shrubs are growing or standing and any barren, dry marsh or bog, whether such land is owned by the Crown or by private persons. 2. Uncultivated land used or held only or primarily for lumber purposes.

TIMBER LICENCE. 1. Includes pulp and paper licence, Forest Management Licence and any other licence respecting the utilization of timber issued under this Act. 2. Includes any saw mill licence, pulp and paper licence or timber licence

of Crown lands issued by the Minister and any renewal thereof.

TIMBER LIMIT. " . . . [D]escribes a parcel of land with merchantable timber standing upon it. . ." *Highway Sawmills Ltd. v. Minister of National Revenue*, [1966] C.T.C. 150 at 157 (S.C.C.), Cartwright J. (Abbott, Judson and Spence JJ. concurring).

TIMBER LOAD LINE. A special load line to be used only when a ship carrying a timber deck cargo complies with these Regulations and the Load Line Rules.

TIMBER PERMIT. An authorization to cut a quantity of timber specified therein on an area described therein.

TIMBER PROCESSING FACILITY. A facility that processes timber or wood residue or both.

TIMBER PRODUCTS. Logs, piles, poles, bolts, cordwood and other similar products of the forest. See PRIMARY ~.

TIMBER QUOTA. A share of the allowable cut of coniferous timber within a forest management unit and may also include an allocation by area of deciduous timber within a forest management unit. *Forests Act*, R.S.A. 1980, c. F-16, s. 1.

TIMBER ROYALTY. Includes any consideration for a right under or pursuant to which a right to cut or take timber from a timber limit in Canada is obtained or derived, to the extent that such consideration is dependent upon, and computed by reference to, the amount of timber cut or taken. *Corporations Tax Act*, R.S.O. 1990, c. C.40, s. 1(2).

TIME. See AIR ~; ALLOWED ~; BROADCAST ~; CENTRAL STANDARD ~; CLOSE ~; COMMERCIAL ~; DAYLIGHT SAVING ~; DAY ~; DEAD ~; DOUBLE ~; DOWN~; DRIVING ~; FLEX ~; FLIGHT ~; FREE ~; FRINGE ~; GIVE ~; IDLE ~; LIFE~; LOCAL ~; LOST ~; NIGHT ~; ON-CALL ~; PART~; PORTAL ~; POST ~; PRIME ~; PROGRAM ~; RESERVED~; RISE ~; STANDARD ~; STAND-BY ~; STRAIGHT ~; WET ~.

TIME AND A HALF. A wage payment at one and one-half an employees regular rate of pay.

TIME CHARGE. A charge for the period between the time the derrick or crane is ready at the loading location until loading is completed and the period between the time the derrick or crane is ready at the unloading location until unloading is completed. Canada regulations.

TIME CHARTER. A charterparty for a certain time.

TIME IMMEMORIAL. Refers to the year 1189 C.E., the beginning of the reign of Richard I.

TIMELY DISCLOSURE. A requirement of securities regulations for the prompt disclosure by a corporation of information which may materially affect the value of a corporations shares.

TIME OFF. See COMPENSATORY ~.

TIME OF IMPORTATION. In respect of goods, the date on which an officer authorizes, pursuant to this Act, the release of the goods. *Customs Act*, R.S.C. 1985 (2nd Supp.), c. 1, s. 51(6).

TIME OF LAPSING. The time at which the record of alien is removed from the general register. *Real Property Act*, R.S.M. 1970, c. R30, s. 73.

TIME PERIOD. See PRESCRIBED ~.

TIME POLICY. A marine policy is a time policy if the contract insures the subject-matter for a definite period. *Marine Insurance Act*, S.C. 1993, c. 22, s. 29.

TIME SALE. A sale or an agreement to sell under which the purchase price and credit charges in addition to the purchase price, if any, are to be paid by one or more future payments.

TIME SALE AGREEMENT. 1. A document or memorandum in writing evidencing a time sale. 2. (a) An agreement for sale under which the right of property in the goods remains in the seller until the purchase price is paid in full or until some other condition is fulfilled; (b) a sale effected by way of a lien note or by way of any agreement or arrangement made at the time of the sale or subsequent thereto whereby the buyer gives to the seller a chattel mortgage or a bill of sale covering the whole or part of the purchase price of the goods sold; and (c) a sale made pursuant to a contract of bailment under which it is intended that the property in the goods will pass to the bailee on the payment of the purchase price in whole or in part or on the performance of a condition. *Law of Property Act*, R.S.A. 1980, c. L-8, s. 47.

TIME SEGMENT. A quarter hour block.

TIME SHARE AGREEMENT. A consumer agreement by which a consumer, (a) acquires the right to use property as part of a plan that provides for the use of the property to circulate periodically among persons participating in the plan, whether or not the property is located in Ontario, or (b) is provided with access to discounts or benefits for the future provision of transportation, accommodation or other goods or services related to travel. *Consumer Protection Act, 2002*, S.O. 2002, c. 30, Sched. A, s. 20.

TIME SHARE INTEREST. The interest of a person in a time share plan.

TIME SHARE OWNERSHIP PLAN. Any plan by which a person participating in the plan acquires an ownership interest in real property and the right to use or occupy all or part of that property, including accommodation or facilities situated on all or part of that property, for specific or determinable periods of time.

TIME SHARE PLAN. Any time share ownership plan or time share use plan, whether in respect of land situated inside or outside a province, that provides for the use, occupation or possession of real property to circulate in any year among persons participating in the plan.

TIME SHARE USE PLAN. Any plan by which a person participating in the plan acquires a right to use or occupy real property, including accommodations or facilities situated on that property, for specific or determinable periods of time but does not acquire an ownership interest in that property.

TIME-SHARING CONDOMINIUM. Like a freehold or leasehold condominium with the added factor that the purchaser's interest in the common elements and the unit is limited to a certain time period and perhaps also for a certain number of years.

TIME TABLE. The authority for the movement of regular trains subject to the rules. It contains classified schedules, also special instructions relating to the movement of trains and engines.

TIMOCRACY. *n*. Government by those properly qualified to rule.

TIP. *n*. "Section 3(1)(a)(i) [of the Unemployment Insurance (Collection of Premiums) Regulations, C.R.C. 1978, c. 1575], therefore, clarifies or expands the meaning of earnings by telling us that it includes 'any amount paid to him by his employer . . . in satisfaction of . . . a . . . gratuity'. In my view, that is precisely the situation we have in this case. The word 'gratuity' in the English version is the ordinary synonym for tip. The word 'gratification' in the French version [of the Regulations] certainly includes a tip." *Canada (Attorney General) v. Canadian Pacific Ltd.* (1986), 11 C.C.E.L. 1 at 12, [1986] 1 S.C.R. 678, 86 C.L.L.C. 14,032, 66 N.R. 321, 27 D.L.R. (4th) 1, La Forest J. (Dickson C.J., Lamer and Le Dain JJ. concurring).

TIPPED. *adj.* As applied to any fur, means that individual hairs or small groups of hairs have been treated to change their colour. *Fur Garments Labelling Regulations*, C.R.C., c. 1138, s. 2.

TIPPING. In the context of securities legislation, giving insider information or information not generally disclosed to another person.

TIPSTAFF. *n.* A constable attached to a court.

TIRE. *n.* 1. Any tire, made of rubber, chemicals and fabric and steel or other materials, that is designed to contain a gas or liquid. *Motor Vehicles Tire Safety Act*, 1985, c. M-11, s. 2. 2. That part of a wheel, roller or other contrivance for the moving of any object upon a highway, which comes into direct contact with the surface of the highway. *Roads Act*, R.S.P.E.I. 1988, c. R-15, c. 1. See BIAS PLY ~; LIGHT TRUCK ~; METAL ~; PNEUMATIC ~; RADIAL PLY ~; SAFETY STUDDED ~S; SOLID RUBBER ~; SOLID ~; STUDDED ~; TYRE; WIDTH OF ~.

TISSUE. *n.* 1. Includes an organ, but does not include any skin, bone, blood, blood constituent or other tissue that is replaceable by natural processes of repair. *Human Tissue Gift acts.* 2. A part of a living or dead human body and includes an organ but, unless otherwise prescribed by the Lieutenant Governor in Council, does not include bone marrow, spermatozoa, an ovum, an embryo, a foetus, blood or blood constituents. *Trillium Gift of Life Network Act*, R.S.O. 1990, c. H-20, s. 1.

TITLE. *n.* 1. " . . . [A] vested right or title, something to which the right is already acquired, though the enjoyment may be postponed." *O'Dell v. Gregory* (1895), 24 S.C.R. 661 at 663, the court per Strong C.J. 2. " . . . [M]ay simply describe the right (or entitlement) to an interest in property. . ." *Canadian Imperial Bank of Commerce v. 64576 Man. Ltd.* (1990), 1 P.P.S.A.C. (2d) 1 at 7 (Man. Q.B.), Jewers J. 3. The way in which a property owner justly possesses property. 4. A general heading which includes particulars, i.e. of a book. 5. An appellation of dignity or honour. 6. The way in which a landowner justly possesses property. 7. In relation to a loan secured by a mortgage on a long-term lease, means the entire interest of the lessee. See ABORIGINAL ~; ABSTRACT OF ~; BAD ~; CERTIFICATE OF ~; CHAIN OF ~; CLEAR ~; CURE ~; DOCUMENT OF ~; FIRST ~; INDEFEASIBLE ~; INDIAN ~; LONG ~; MINERAL ~; MISTAKE OF ~; POSSESSORY ~; QUALIFIED ~; REGISTER OF ~ AND ABSTRACT INDEX; REQUISITION ON ~; ROOT OF ~; ROYAL STYLE AND ~S; SERIAL ~; SHORT ~; SLANDER OF ~; SQUATTER'S ~.

TITLE INSURANCE. 1. Insurance against loss or liability for loss due to the invalidity of the title to any property or of any instrument, or to any defect in such title or instrument. 2. Insurance against loss or damage caused by defect in the title to real property, or by the existence of liens, encumbrances, or servitudes upon real property, or by other matters affecting the title to real property or the right to the use and enjoyment thereof, or by defect in the execution of mortgages, hypothecs or deeds of trust.

TITLE OF PROCEEDING. Sets out the names of all the parties to a proceeding and their capacity, if other than a personal capacity.

TITLE REGISTER. A book, file, micrographic, electronic or other storage means whereby or wherein are registered the title to land and instruments relating thereto.

TITLE SEARCH PERIOD. The period of 40 years described in subsection 112(1). *Registry Act*, R.S.O. 1990, c. R.20, s. 111(1).

[] **T.J.** *abbr.* Recueils de Jurisprudence, Tribunal de la Jeunesse.

T.J., (QUÉ.). *abbr.* Tribunal de la jeunesse (Québec).

T.L.R. *abbr.* Times Law Reports.

T.M. *abbr.* Trade Marks.

T.O. *abbr.* 1. Taxing Officer. 2. Taxing Office.

TOBACCO. *n.* Tobacco in any form in which it is used or consumed and includes snuff. See CONSUMER OF ~; LOOSE ~; MANUFACTURED ~; RAW LEAF ~; STANDARD LEAF ~.

TOBACCO FARM. One or more parcels of land in respect of which the Commission or the local board determines, (a) the land is suitable for the producing of tobacco, and (b) the producer has provided such buildings or other structures and equipment as are suitable and adequate for the producing of tobacco, and in respect of which the Commission or the local board, as the case may be, allots a tobacco hectarage. *Farm Products Marketing Act*, R.S.O. 1990, c. F.9, s. 20(1).

TOBACCO HECTARAGE. A number of hectares of land fixed and allotted to a person for the producing in any year of tobacco on a tobacco farm. *Farm Products Marketing Act*, R.S.O. 1980, c. 158, s. 21.

TOBACCO MANUFACTORY. Any place or premises where raw leaf tobacco is worked up into manufactured tobacco, and every workshop, office, store-room, warehouse, shed, yard or other place where any of the raw material is or is to be stored, where any process connected with the manufacture or preparation of manufactured tobacco is or is intended to be carried on or where any of the products of the manufacture are or are intended to be stored shall be held to be included in and to form part of the tobacco manufactory to which they are attached or appurtenant. *Excise Act*, R.S.C. 1985, c. E-14, s. 6.

TOBACCO MANUFACTURER. Everyone who manufactures tobacco for himself, or who employs others to manufacture tobacco, other than cigars, whether the manufacture is by casing, packing, cutting, pressing, grinding, rolling, drying, crushing or stemming of any raw leaf tobacco, or otherwise preparing raw leaf or manufactured or partially manufactured tobacco, by the putting up for use or consumption of scraps, waste, clippings, stems or deposits of tobacco, resulting from any process of handling tobacco, or by the working or preparation of raw leaf tobacco, scraps, waste, clippings, stems or deposits of tobacco, by sifting, twisting, screening or any other process. *Excise Act*, R.S.C. 1985, c. E-14, s. 6.

TOBACCONIST. *n.* A person, firm, or corporation, who sells by retail all or any of the following: tobacco, cigars, cigarettes, and tobacconists sundries, including cigarette papers, matches, lighters, cigar and cigarette holders, pipes, pipe cases, pipe cleaners, pouches, humidors, and walking sticks.

TOBACCO PACKER. Any person who, subject to departmental regulations, by himself or his agent, deals in, prepares, packs, stems, re-

constitutes or converts Canadian raw leaf tobacco or employs others to do so. *Excise Act*, R.S.C. 1985, c. E-14, s. 6.

TOBACCO STAMP. Any stamp affixed to any package of manufactured tobacco entered for consumption or to Canadian raw leaf tobacco entered for consumption. *Excise Act*, R.S.C. 1985, c. E-14, s. 6.

TOBACCO STICK. Any roll or tubular construction of tobacco intended for smoking, other than a cigar, that requires further preparation to be consumed. *Excise Act, 2001*, S.C. 2002, c. 22, s. 2.

TODA. Take-Off Distance Available.

TO HAVE AND TO HOLD. In a conveyance, words which show the estate one intends to convey.

TOILET. *n.* 1. A device used for individual disposal of human waste and excrement, and includes a lavatory, water closet and urinal. *Public Toilet Act*, R.S.B.C. 1979, c. 347, s. 1. 2. In relation to a pleasure boat, means equipment designed or used for defecation or urination by humans.

TOILET ROOM. A room that contains a toilet, urinal basin or urinal trough or any combination thereof for the use of employees. *Canada Sanitation Regulations*, C.R.C., c. 1009, s. 2.

TOILET SPACE. Every room containing a bath, shower, water-closet or wash-basin other than a room that is (a) a sleeping room, or (b) used only as a laundry. *Towboat Crew Accommodation Regulations*, C.R.C., c. 1498, s. 2.

TOKEN OF VALUE. See COUNTERFEIT ~.

TOKEN STRIKE. A strike of 1 or 2 days duration to demonstrate the effect of a prolonged strike.

TOLERATE. *v.* To allow; permit.

TOLERATION. *n.* In the context of allegedly obscene materials, the permitting by Canadians of viewing by other Canadians.

TOLL. *n.* 1. Any fee or rate charged, levied or collected by any person for the carriage of passengers and express freight by a public vehicle. 2. Any rate, charge or allowance charged or made for the shipment, transportation, transmission, care, handling or delivery of hydrocarbons or of another commodity that is transmitted through a pipeline, or for storage or demurrage or the like, for the provision of a pipeline when the pipeline is available and ready to provide for the transmission of oil or gas, and in respect of the purchase and sale of gas that is the property of a company and that is transmitted by the company through its pipeline, excluding the cost to the company of the gas at the point where it enters the pipeline. *National Energy Board Act*, R.S.C. 1985, c. N-7, s. 2. See BRIDGE ~; EXPRESS ~; HARBOUR ~; JOINT ~; LOCAL ~; TELEGRAPH ~; TELEPHONE ~; THROUGH ~.

TOLLAGE. *n*. Payment of a toll.

TOLL-BRIDGE. *n*. " . . . [A] bridge for lucre or gain . . ." *Aubert-Gallion v. Roy* (1892), 21 S.C.R. 456 at 469, Taschereau J. (Strong and Patterson JJ. concurring).

TOLL, GAIN OR COMPENSATION. Refers to all forms of compensation for carriage of passengers or property by vehicle.

TOLL-GATHERER. *n*. An official who collects a toll.

TOMALLEY. *n*. An edible by-product of lobster, the ingredients of which have not been ground to a smooth consistency.

TON. *n*. 1. 2,000 pounds. *Weights and Measures Act*, S.C. 1970-71-72, c. 36, schedule II. 2. (a) Where used to calculate weight, 2,000 pounds; and (b) where used to calculate measurement 40 cubic feet. Canada regulations. 3. In respect of cargo, coal or oil means 2,240 pounds. *Esquimalt Graving Dock Regulations*, C.R.C., c. 1362, s. 2. 4. 2,240 pounds. 5. Registered gross tonnage where the reference is to the payment of bounty and underdeck tonnage where the reference is to timber sizes forming the scantlings of vessels. Newfoundland statutes. See GROSS REGISTERED ~S.

TONGUE. See MOTHER ~.

TONIC. *n*. A mineral feed that is represented for the treatment of a specified disease or to aid recovery from a specific disease or debility and is for use only while the disease or debility persists.

TON (METRIC). 1,000 kilograms. *Weights and Measures Act*, S.C. 1970-71-72, c. 36 schedule I.

TONNAGE. *n*. 1. The estimated weight in number of tons which a ship can carry. 2. In relation to a vessel, means (a) the largest gross tonnage of the vessel shown on its certificate of registry or tonnage certificate, as the case may be if that tonnage has been measured in accordance with the rules of a country other than a country listed in the Tonnage of Ships Order; or (b) the gross tonnage of the vessel measured under the Canada Shipping Act, if the largest gross tonnage of the vessel shown on its certificate of registry or tonnage certificate, as the case may be, has been measured in accordance with the rules of a country listed in the Tonnage of Ships Order. Canada regulations. 3. Registered gross tonnage where the reference is to the payment of bounty and underdeck tonnage where the reference is to timber sizes forming the scantlings of vessels. Newfoundland statutes. See GROSS ~; PORT-CALL-~; REGISTERED NET ~; REGISTER ~.

TONNAGE MEASUREMENT CERTIFICATE. A certificate issued by a measurement authority recognized by the Board that sets out the registered gross tonnage of a vessel. Canada regulations.

TONNAGE-RENT. *n*. Rent reserved by a mining lease or something like it consisting of a royalty on every ton of minerals produced by the mine.

TONNE. *n*. 1. 1,000 kilograms. Canada regulations. 2. (a) Where used as a measurement of weight, 1,000 kilograms; and (b) where used as a measurement of volume, 1 cubic metre. *Wharfage Charges By-law*, C.R.C., c. 1066, s. 2.

TON OF REFRIGERATION. The unit for measuring the capacity of a refrigeration plant.

TONS OF REFRIGERATION. Tons of refrigeration computed on the basis of 1 ton of refrigeration per 1.5 motive horsepower.

TOOL. See EXPLOSIVE ACTUATED ~; HAND ~.

TOOL AND DIE MAKER. A person who, (a) sets up and operates to prescribed tolerance engine lathes and milling, grinding, drilling, sawing and boring machines; (b) reads and interprets blueprints, operation and product-related reference charts and tables and selects mechanical measuring, checking and layout tools and devices; (c) performs measuring, checking and layout operations and selects work piece materials and the required cutting tools and abrasives for metal removal operations; (d) performs metal removing operations using hand and power tools and selects work piece clamping and holding devices and product-related components; (e) performs finishing and assembly operations on dies and sets up dies on presses for testing purposes; and (f) manufactures component parts and assembles and tests tools, jigs and fixtures.

TOOLING. *n*. Includes patterns, jigs, fixtures, moulds, models, dies, gauges and punches.

TO PEDDLE. To carry alcohol, spirits, cider, wine or beer on one's person or to transport it with one, or with the aid of another person, with intent to sell it outside any establishment where the sale thereof is allowed.

TOP LEASE. "Top leases" are an accepted business practice in the oil and gas industry. They increase actual drilling and competitiveness because oil companies whose leases have been "topped" have a greater incentive to drill on leased lands. If they do not, they stand to lose the lease and make way for someone else to drill. *Taylor v. Scurry-Rainbow Oil (Sask) Ltd.*, 2001 SKCA 85, 203 D.L.R. (4th) 38, 207 Sask. R. 266, 247 W.A.C. 266, [2001] 11 W.W.R. 25 (C.A.).

TOPOGRAPHY. *n*. The design, however expressed, of the disposition of (a) the interconnections, if any, and the elements for the making of an integrated circuit product, or (b) the elements, if any, and the interconnections for the making of a customization layer or layers to be added to an integrated circuit product in an intermediate form. *Integrated Circuit Topography Act*, S.C. 1990, c. 37, s. 2.

TOPPING UP. The practice, when an employee is off work because of a compensable injury, is paid full salary during the compensation period in exchange for endorsing his benefits over to the employer.

TO PROSPECT AND TO EXPLORE. To carry out work preliminary to mining operations, with the purpose of discovering an ore deposit or an underground reservoir and demonstrating the existence thereof.

TO PROVIDE. When used in relation to services includes to furnish, perform, solicit, or give such services. *Municipal Act*, R.S.O. 1980, c. 302, s. 222.

TOPSOIL. *n*. 1. Soil having the properties that make it suitable for plant growth. 2. That horizon in a soil profile, known as the "A" horizon, containing organic material.

TO PURCHASE. Includes to take as mortgagee or as pledgee. *Warehouse Receipt acts*.

TOP WHARFAGE. A toll charged on goods that are unloaded from or loaded onto a vessel or transhipped between vessels. Canada regulations.

TORA. Take-off run available.

TORRENS REGISTRATION SYSTEM. A land titles system devised by Mr. Robert Torrens of South Australia, first embodied in a statute enacted in South Australia in 1857, then in the Colony of Vancouver Island in 1861 and in the province of British Columbia in 1869. B.J. Reiter, B.N. McLellan & P.M. Perell *Real Estate Law*, 4th ed. (Toronto: Emond Montgomery, 1992) at 502.

TORRENS' SYSTEM. See TORRENS REGISTRATION SYSTEM.

TORT. *n*. 1. Wrong. 2. Provides a means by which compensation, usually in the form of damages, is paid for injuries suffered by a party as a result of wrongful conduct by another. 3. " to restore the injured person [I]ntended person to the position he enjoyed prior to the injury, rather than to punish the tortfeasor whose only wrong may have been a moment of inadvertence. . .' *Ratych v. Bloomer* (1990), 30 C.C.E.L. 161 at 171 39 O.A.C. 103, [1990] 1 S.C.R. 940, 69 D.L.R. (4th) 25, 107 N.R. 335, 3 C.C.L.T. (2d) 1, McLachlin J. (Lamer, La Forest, L'Heureux-Dubé and Sopinka JJ. concurring). 4. "A fundamental proposition underlies the law of tort: that a person who by his or her fault causes damage to another may be held responsible." *Canadian National Railway v. Norsk Pacific Steamship Co.* (1992), 11 C.C.L.T. (2d) 1 at 16, 137 N.R. 241, 91 D.L.R. (4th) 289, [1992] 1 S.C.R. 1021, 53 F.T.R. 79n, McLachlin J. (L'Heureux-Dubé and Cory JJ. concurring). 5. Includes delict and quasi-delict. *Crown Liability Act*, R.S.C. 1985, c. C-50, s. 2. See ACTION FOR ~; ADMINISTRATOR DE SON ~; INTENTIONAL ~; CONTINUING ~; JOINT ~; MARITIME ~; NEGLIGENT ~.

TORTFEASOR. *var*. **TORT-FEASOR**. *n*. 1. A wrongdoer. 2. A party who commits a tort. 3. A person whose wrongful act, neglect, or default has caused the death, or contributed to the cause of death, of the deceased and who, if death had not ensued, would have been liable to him for damages, and includes a person who would have been liable vicariously or otherwise for such damages. *Fatal Accidents acts*. See JOINT ~S SEVERAL ~S.

TORTIOUS. *adj*. Wrongful.

TORTIOUS ACT. A wrongful, injurious or illegal act that results in: (a) loss or damage to the land of an owner or occupant, as the case may be, that is not situated within the surface rights acquired or to be acquired by an operator; and (b) any other loss or damage suffered by the owner or occupant arising out of such act *The Surface Rights Acquisition and Compensation Act*, R.S.S. 1978, c. S-65, s. 60.

TORT LIABILITY. Requires the wrongdoer to pay for damage done to compensate the victim. John G. Flemin *The Law of Torts*, 8 th ed. (Sydney: The Law Book Co., 1992) at 1.

TORTURE. *n.* Any act or omission by which severe pain or suffering, whether physical or mental, is intentionally inflicted on a person (a) for a purpose including (i) obtaining from the person or from a third person information or a statement, (ii) punishing the person for an act which that person or a third person has committed or is suspected of having committed, and (iii) intimidating or coercing the person or a third person, or (b) for any reason based on discrimination of any kind, but does not include an act or omission arising only from, inherent in or incidental to lawful sanctions. *Criminal Code*, S.C. 1987, c. 13, s. 245.4(2). See CONVENTION AGAINST ~.

TO STRIKE. To cease work, or to refuse to work or to continue to work, in combination or in concert or in accordance with a common understanding.

TOTAL. *adj*. Where used in the expression "total and permanent disability" means disability that is severe, in the sense that the employee is incapable of pursuing any substantially gainful occupation.

TOTAL ACTUAL FRONTAGE. The sum of the actual frontage of the parcels of land which actually abuts on the work or highway.

TOTAL AND PERMANENT DISABILITY. Disability to the extent of wholly disabling a person from engaging in any gainful employment.

TOTAL ASSETS. Includes any amount by which (a) the value of any asset of a corporation, as carried on its account books or on its balance sheet, is in excess of the cost of the asset; or (b) the value of an asset of a corporation has been written down and deducted from its income or undivided profits, where that amount (i) is not deductible under the Income Tax Act; or (ii) is deductible under paragraph (n) of subsection (1) of section 20 or subparagraph (iii) of paragraph

(a) of subsection (1) of section 40 of the Income Tax Act but unless required in the regulations to be included, does not include any amount by which the value of an asset of a corporation has been written down and deducted from its income or undivided profits, where that amount is deductible under any provision of the Income Tax Act other than those mentioned in clause (ii) of subparagraph (b). *Corporations Capital Tax acts*.

TOTAL CONTRACT PRICE. The total obligation or consideration, including the cost of borrowing, payable, given, undertaken or assumed by a buyer under a contract for future services.

TOTAL DISABILITY. 1. " . . . [I]n the context of disability insurance does not require the insured person to be completely incapable of any activity-only that his condition is such that ordinary and reasonable prudence will dictate that he should not engage in a given work activity." *Millward v. Maritime Life Assurance* Co. (1988) 90 A.R. 41 at 46 (Q.B.), Lutz J. 2. A disability which prevents an insured from performing a remunerative occupation. Includes the situation where a person must refrain from engaging in his occupation in order to recover from an injury or illness. See PERMANENT ~.

TOTAL FLOOR AREA. The area of all floors of basements, mezzanines, storeys and penthouses in a building, measured from the inside surface of the exterior or boundary walls.

TOTALITY PRINCIPLE. Requires a sentencing judge who orders an offender to serve consecutive sentences for several offences to ensure that the cumulative sentence does not exceed the overall culpability of the offender.

TOTAL LENGTH. In respect of a fish, the distance from the tip of the head with the jaws closed to the tip of the tail with the lobes compressed so as to give the maximum possible measurement.

TOTAL LOADED MASS. 1. The mass of a motor vehicle or combination of motor vehicles, including accessories, equipment and load; such mass may be expressed as the aggregate of the axle loads. 2. The mass of a road vehicle or combination of road vehicles, including accessories, equipment and load.

TOTAL LOADED WEIGHT. 1. The aggregate of the loads on all the axles of one motor vehicle or combination of motor vehicles, including accessories and equipment, plus the weight of the load. 2. The weight of a motor vehicle or combination of vehicles including accessories, equipment and load, expressed as the aggregate of all its axle loads.

TOTAL LOSS. 1. " . . . [I]n the case of a ship the subject of insurance must be either such an entire wreck as to be reduced, as it is said, to a mere 'congeries of planks', or if it still subsists in specie it must, as a result of perils insured against, be placed in such a situation that it is totally out of the power of the owner or the underwriter at any labor, and by means of any expenditure, to get it afloat and cause it to be repaired and used again as a ship." *McGhee v. Phoenix Insurance Co.* (1890), 18 S.C.R. 61 at 70, Strong J. 2. A loss (a) where insured property is destroyed or so damaged as to cease to be a thing of the kind insured; or (b) where the fisherman whose name is on the list in respect of insured property is irretrievably deprived of the property. *Fishing Vessel Insurance Regulations*, C.R.C., c. 325, s. 2. See ACTUAL ~; CONSTRUCTIVE ~.

TOTAL OBLIGATION. The aggregate of the net capital and the credit charges.

TOTAL PAYROLL. The total of all payments and benefits paid or provided to or for the benefit of an employee which are fixed or ascertainable amounts and are calculated at gross value.

TOTAL SUSPENDED MATTER. The non-filterable residue that results from the operation of a plant, that is contained in the effluent from that plant. *Plant Liquid Effluent regulations.*

TOTAL TAXABLE FRONTAGE. The sum of the taxable frontage of the parcels of land which abut or are deemed to abut on the work or highway.

TOTAL WAGE. In respect of any period of employment of an employee, means all remuneration that the employee is paid or is entitled to be paid by his employer, whether or not payment is actually made during that period of employment, in respect of the labour or services that he performs for his employer during that period of employment, and includes: (a) sums deducted from such remuneration for any purpose whatever; (b) remuneration in respect of overtime work that he performs for his employer during that period of employment; (c) remuneration in respect of any annual or special holiday that his employer permits him to take during that period of employment; (d) the cash value of any board or lodging received by the employee as part payment of wages during that period of employment. *The Labour Standards Act*, R.S.S. 1978, c. L-1, s. 2.

TOTE ROAD. An unsurfaced road of a temporary nature over which construction materials and supplies are moved.

TOTIDEM VERBIS. [L.] In just as many words.

TOTIES QUOTIES. [L.] As often as possible.

TOT LOT. An area set aside as a public playground for the use of children of pre-school age. Canada regulations.

TOTO COELO. [L.] All the heavens; the extent of the heavens.

TOUGH GRAIN. Any grain within the meaning of this Act that has a moisture content that classifies it as tough grain in the Canada Grain Regulations made pursuant to the Canada Grain Act. *Prairie Grain Advance Payment Act*, R.S.C. 1985, c. P-18, s. 9(5).

TOUJOURS ET ENCORE PRESZ. [Fr.] Always and still ready.

TOUR. *n.* A round or circle trip performed in whole or in part by air for an inclusive tour price for the period the participants are away from the starting point of the journey. See INCLUSIVE ~.

TOUR FEATURES. All goods, services, facilities and benefits other than accommodation and transportation that are included in an ITC program at the inclusive tour price or made available to tour participants as optional extras at an additional charge.

TOURISM PROMOTION. Mass consumer and trade advertising, including special events support, travel information counselling and other activities designed to improve public relations.

TOURIST. *n.* A person not ordinarily resident who visits a province for a vacation.

TOURIST ACCOMMODATION. (a) Land on which rental units are situate; or (b) land used by the public as a camping ground or trailer park.

TOURIST CAMP. Includes auto camp and any parcel of land or premises equipped with cabins used or maintained for the accommodation of the public, and any parcel of land or premises used or maintained as a camping or parking ground for the public whether or not a fee or charge is paid or made for the rental or use thereof.

TOURIST ESTABLISHMENT. 1. Includes any premises operated to provide sleeping accommodation for the public, the services and facilities in connection with which sleeping accommodation is provided, any premises where lodging, meals, lunches or restroom facilities are offered to the public, and other facilities that are operated as tourist attractions or services. 2. (a) Any premises or boat that provides sleeping accommodation; (b) any campsite equipped for the supplying of water or electricity or the disposal of garbage or sewage; or (c) any picnic area, bathing area or recreation area for the travelling public or persons engaging in outdoor recreational activities, but does not include a private cottage or residence. *Travel and Tourism Act*, S.N.W.T. 1983 (1st Sess.), c. 1, s. 2.

TOURIST HOME. A place where persons reside temporarily on a transient basis while travelling or vacationing.

TOURIST INFORMATION BUREAU. Any establishment whose main activity is the providing of information to the public about lodgings, restaurants, camping and trailer facilities or tourist attractions.

TOURIST INFORMATION CENTRE. A place that is held out to the public as being available for or engaged in furnishing travel information to the public whether for hire or reward or otherwise.

TOURIST OUTFITTER ESTABLISHMENT. A tourist establishment that, (a) throughout all or part of a year furnishes accommodation; (b) may or may not furnish three meals a day; and (c) furnishes equipment, supplies or services to persons in connection with angling, hunting, camping or recreational purposes.

TOUR OPERATOR. A charterer with whom an air carrier has contracted to charter an aircraft in whole or in part for the purpose of operating an inclusive tour.

TOUT TEMPS PRESZ ET ENCORE EST. [Fr.] With respect to a defendant, was always and still is ready.

TOW. *v*. 1. To pull or push any floating object. Canada regulations. 2. To push, pull or otherwise move through the water.

TOW. *n*. Includes every kind of ship, boat, barge, elevator, scow or other floating craft that is not propelled by steam or any other means of propulsion but that is towed by a vessel.

TOWAGE. *n*. 1. The transporting of logs or timber products from one place to another by towing the same through the water by a tugboat, whether towed in booms, rafts or cribs, or on board scows, barges or vessels. 2. A charge for towing service in connection with crane service.

TOW BAR. A towing structure that is connected to the chassis frame of the forward axle of a full trailer and which includes an eye or equivalent device for the purpose of coupling with a trailer hitch.

TOW-BOAT. A ship used exclusively in towing another ship or floating object astern or alongside or in pushing another ship or floating object ahead. *Crewing Regulations*, SOR/97-390, s. 1.

TOW CAR. A motor vehicle used exclusively for towing or rendering assistance to other motor vehicles or to vehicles suffering from a defect or disability in their means of locomotion.

TOWED CONVEYANCE. Includes any sled, cutter, trailer, toboggan or carrier that may be towed by a snowmobile.

TOWING LIGHT. A yellow light having the same characteristics as the "sternlight" defined in paragraph (c) of this Rule. *Collision Regulations*, C.R.C., c. 1416, Rule 3.

TO WIT. Namely.

TOWN. *n*. An area incorporated as a town. See COMPANY ~; SEPARATED ~.

TOWN DISTRICT. A school district situated wholly or in part within a town or city.

TOWN PLAN. See OFFICIAL ~.

TOWN SCHOOL DISTRICT. A school district situated wholly or in part within the limits of a town and includes a school district situated wholly within the boundaries of a local government district.

TOWNSHIP. *n*. Any territory erected into a township. See DOUBLE FRONT ~; EASTERN ~S; FRONT AND REAR ~; SECTIONAL WITH DOUBLE FRONTS; SECTIONAL ~ WITH SECTIONS AND QUARTER SECTIONS; SECTIONAL ~ WITH SINGLE FRONTS; SINGLE FRONT ~.

TOWNSITE. *n.* A subdivision of land into lots intended for residential or business purposes or both, and not adjoining or adjacent to a hamlet, village, town or city. *The Planning and Development Act*, R.S.S. 1978, c. P-13, s. 2.

TOW VEHICLE. A tilt and slide deck truck or a recovery vehicle.

TOXIC. *adj.* 1. Having an immediate or long-term harmful effect on the environment. 2. Acting as or relating to poison.

TOXIC EFFECT. Something caused by an overdose of a drug.

TOXICOLOGY. *n.* The study of poisons, their detection and effects. F.A. Jaffe, *A Guide to Pathological Evidence*, 3d ed. (Toronto: Carswell, 1991) at 228.

TOXICOMANIA. *n.* A pathological condition other than alcoholism, related to the consumption of a toxic substance and disturbing the physical and psychical balance and the social behaviour of persons suffering therefrom.

TOXIC PRODUCT. A chemical product that (a) is capable of causing a lethal effect on a human; (b) is capable of causing a serious and irreversible but non-lethal effect on a human, such as a depressed level of consciousness, muscular weakness or paralysis, acute renal or hepatic failure, arrhythmia, hypotension, dyspnea, respiratory depression, pulmonary edema or optic neuritis; or (c) is identified in Part 1 as a Category 1 toxic product. *Consumer Chemicals and Containers Regulations, 2001*, SOR/2001-269, s. 1.

TOXIC SUBSTANCE. Any chemical, biological or physical agent, or combination of such agents, which may be used in a workplace, to which a worker may be exposed and which may be harmful to that worker. D. Robertson, *Ontario Health and Safety Guide* (Toronto: Richard De Boo Ltd., 1988) at 5-404.

TOXIN. *n.* A poisonous substance which animals, bacteria or plants produce. F.A. Jaffe, *A Guide to Pathological Evidence*, 3d ed. (Toronto: Carswell, 1991) at 228.

TOY. See SOFT ~.

TRACE. See VERTEBRATE ~ FOSSIL.

TRACEABLE. *adj.* Describes property which is commingled with other property so that its individual identity is lost.

TRACE EVIDENCE. Evidence based on examining small amounts of biological material, i.e. blood, soil or textile fibres. F.A. Jaffe, *A Guide to Pathological Evidence*, 3d ed. (Toronto: Carswell, 1991) at 219.

TRACE-MINERAL-SALT FEED. A mineral feed that contains only ingredients incorporated to supply trace mineral elements and salt (NaCl). *Feeds Regulations*, C.R.C., c. 665, s. 2.

TRACHEA. *n.* The windpipe, a tube of cartilage which connects the bronchi with the larynx. F.A. Jaffe, *A Guide to Pathological Evidence*, 3d ed. (Toronto: Carswell, 1991) at 228.

TRACHEOSTOMY. *n.* A surgical operation which opens the trachea to make breathing easier. F.A. Jaffe, *A Guide to Pathological Evidence*, 2d ed. (Toronto: Carswell, 1983) at 186.

TRACHEOTOMY. *n.* A surgical operation which opens the trachea to make breathing easier. F.A. Jaffe, *A Guide to Pathological Evidence*, 2d ed. (Toronto: Carswell, 1983) at 186.

TRACING. *n.* 1. " ... [A] convenient term adopted by many matrimonial property cases to describe the effect of identifying property by a source..." *Harrower v. Harrower* (1989), 21 R.F.L. (3d) 369 at 378, 68 Alta. L.R. (2d) 97, 97 A.R. 141 (C.A.), the court per Stevenson J.A. 2. Tracing at common law and equity is a proprietary remedy. It involves following an item of property either as it is transformed into other forms of property, or as it passes into other hands, so that the rights of a person in the original property may extend to the new property. In establishing that one piece of property may be traced into another, it is necessary to establish a close and substantial connection between the two pieces of property, so that it is appropriate to allow the rights in the original property to flow through to the new property. The question has most often arisen in the context of a trust, when the trustee has improperly disposed of the trust assets. *Agricultural Credit Corp. of Saskatchewan v. Pettyjohn*, [1991] 3 W.W.R. 689, 1 P.P.S.A.C. (2d) 273, 79 D.L.R. (4th) 22, 90 Sask. R. 206 (C.A.) at pp. 702-3 [W.W.R.], per Sherstobitoff, J.A.

TRACK. *n.* 1. The scar caused by repeated injection of drugs directly into a vein. 2. The projection on the earth's surface of the path of an aircraft, the direction of which path at any point is usually expressed in true, magnetic or grid degrees from North; *Canadian Aviation Regulations*, SOR/96-433, s. 101.01. See MAIN ~; PRIVATE ~; RACE ~; SERVING ~; SINGLE ~; TEAM ~.

TRACKING DEVICE. Any device that, when installed in or on any thing, may be used to help ascertain, by electronic or other means, the location of any thing or person. *Criminal Code*, R.S.C. 1985, c. C-46, s. 492.1.

TRACK OPERATOR. A person who owns or operates a race track.

TRACT. *n*. 1. A mining tract. 2. An area within a drilling spacing unit or a pool, as the case may be, within which an owner has the right or an interest in the right to drill for and produce oil or gas. 3. A contiguous area of land which (a) two or more persons jointly have; or (b) two or more persons have an undivided interest in; the right to mine for and remove minerals either because of having joint or common title to those minerals or under a lease or licence from a person or persons having individual, or joint or common, title to those minerals. See MARSHLAND ~; POOLED ~; PRODUCING ~; PRODUCTION ~; SUBMARINE ~; UNIT ~.

TRACTION ENGINE. A mechanically-propelled vehicle running on wheels or caterpillar tracks and designed primarily for traction purposes and not constructed itself to carry a load other than equipment used for the purpose of propulsion, loose tools and equipment, and includes snow ploughs, road conditioning machines and the like.

TRACT OF LAND. An area of land comprising 2 or more parcels, whether contiguous or not.

TRACTOR. *n*. 1. Includes any vehicle designed primarily (a) as a travelling power plant for independent operation or for operating other machines or appliances; or (b) for drawing other vehicles or machines, and not designed for carrying goods or passengers wholly or in part on its structure. 2. A self-propelled vehicle that is designed primarily for traction purposes, and that is not itself constructed to carry any load other than the driver. See FARM ~; MOTOR ~; ROAD ~; TRUCK ~.

TRACTOR-FLOAT COMBINATION. A motor vehicle consisting of a tractor or truck with a float. Canada regulations.

TRACTOR-TRAILER COMBINATION. A motor vehicle consisting of a tractor with a semi-trailer. Canada regulations.

TRACT PARTICIPATION. The share of production from a unitized zone that is allocated to a unit tract under a unit agreement or unitization

order or the share of production from a pooled spacing unit that is allocated to a pooled tract under a pooling agreement or pooling order.

TRADE. *v*. 1. " . . . [E]ngaging in a traffic or in business transactions of bargain and sale for profit or for subsistence. . ." *McCracken v. Sherborne (Township)* (1911), 2 O.W.N. 601 at 603, 23 O.L.R. 81 (Div. Ct.), Britton J. (Falconbridge C.J. concurring). 2. Buying and selling property as a business. 3. Includes, entering into contracts, whether as principal or agent, acting as a floor trader, any receipt by a registrant of an order to effect a transaction in a contract, any assignment or other disposition of rights under a contract except a disposition arising from the death of an individual enjoying rights under a contract, and any act, advertisement, solicitation, conduct or negotiation directly or indirectly in furtherance of the foregoing. *Commodity Futures Act*, R.S.O. 1990, c. C-20, s. 1 as am.

TRADE. *n*. 1. " . . . '[O]ccupation' . . ." *Burns v. Christianson* (1921), 60 D.L.R. 173 at 174, [1921] 2 W.W.R. 366, 16 Alta. L.R. 394 (C.A.) Harvey C.J. 2. The skill and knowledge requisite for or intended for use in any occupation, calling or vocation. 3. Includes industry, craft and business and any branch of any trade, industry, craft or business. 4. The selling, purchasing, exchanging, consigning, leasing or providing of any commodity, right, facility or service on the basis of measure and includes the business of providing facilities for measuring. *Weights and Measures Act*, R.S.C. 1985, c. W-6, s. 2. 5. Includes (a) a disposition of a security for valuable consideration, whether the terms of payment be on margin, instalment or otherwise, but does not include a purchase of a security; (b) participation as a floor trader in a transaction in a security on the floor of a stock exchange; (c) the receipt by a registrant of an order to buy or sell a security; (d) a transfer, pledge, mortgage or other encumbrance of a security of an issuer for the purpose of giving collateral for a debt, or the transfer of beneficial ownership of that security to the transferee, pledgee, mortgagee or other encumbrancer under a realization on that collateral; and (e) any act, advertisement, solicitation, conduct or negotiation directly or indirectly in furtherance of any of the activities specified in paragraphs (a) to (d). *Securities acts*. (i) A disposition or acquisition of or transaction in real estate by sale, purchase, agreement for sale, exchange, option, lease, rental or otherwise; (ii) an offer or attempt to list real estate for a disposition or transaction referred to in subclause (i); or (iii) an act, advertisement, conduct or negotiation directly or indirectly in furtherance of such a disposition, acquisition, transaction, offer or attempt. *Real Estate Agents' Licensing acts.* See ADVENTURE IN THE NATURE OF ~; BALANCE OF ~; BOARD OF ~; BUSINESS OR ~ ASSOCIATION; COASTAL ~; COASTING ~; CONTRACT IN RESTRAINT OF ~; CUSTOM OF THE ~; DAIRY PRODUCTS ~; LIQUIDATING ~; RESTRAINT OF ~; RETAIL ~; SPECIAL PASSENGER ~; STOCK IN ~; STREET ~; WHOLESALE ~.

TRADE AGREEMENT. Any agreement or arrangement relating to international trade to which the Government of Canada is a party. *Customs Tariff Act*, R.S.C. 1985, c. C-54, s. 26.

TRADE AND COMMERCE. 1. A power of the federal Parliament under section 91(2) of the Constitution Act, 1867. P.W. Hogg, *Constitutional Law of Canada*, 3d ed. (Toronto: Carswell, 1992) at 521. 2. " . . . [T]he power to regulate international and interprovincial trade and . . . 'the general regulation of trade affecting the whole of Canada' . . ." *Alex Couture Inc. c. Canada (Procureur general)* (1991), 38 C.P.R. (3d) 293 at 308, 83 D.L.R. (4th) 577, 41 Q.A.C. 1, [1991] R.J.Q. 2534, the court per Rousseau-Houle J.A.

TRADE AREA. The geographic boundaries within which a commercial project can be expected to obtain the vast majority of its sales.

TRADE COMBINATION. Any combination between masters or workmen or other persons for the purpose of regulating or altering the relations between masters or workmen, or the conduct of a master or workman in or in respect of his business, employment or contract of employment. *Criminal Code*, R.S.C. 1985, c. C-46, s. 467(2).

TRADE CREDITOR. See SECURED ~; UNSECURED ~.

TRADE DISPUTE. A dispute between employers and workers or between groups of workers, connected with the employment of a person, the terms or conditions of employment or related matters.

TRADE DIVISION. All unionized employers: (a) in a trade; or (b) in an identifiable class or group of unionized employers in a trade; in a sector or sectors of the construction industry. *Construction Industry Labour Relations Act*, S.S. 1979, c. C-29.1, s. 2.

TRADE FIXTURE. A chattel which is annexed to leased property by a tenant during the term of his tenancy and which may be severed by the tenant at the end of his tenancy when it resumes its character as a chattel rather than a fixture.

TRADE-IN. *n.* Consideration given by a buyer in a form other than money or an obligation to pay money. *Consumer Protection acts.*

TRADE-IN ALLOWANCE. The greater of, (a) the price or value of the consumer's goods or services as set out in a trade-in arrangement, and (b) the market value of the consumer's goods or services when taken in trade under a trade-in arrangement. *Consumer Protection Act, 2002*, S.O. 2002, c. 30, Sched. A, s. 1.

TRADE-IN ARRANGEMENT. An arrangement under which a consumer agrees to sell his or her own goods or services to the supplier and the supplier accepts the goods or services as all or part of the consideration for supplying goods or services. *Consumer Protection Act, 2002*, S.O. 2002, c. 30, Sched. A, s. 1.

TRADE, INDUSTRY OR PROFESSION. Includes any class, division or branch of a trade, industry or profession. *Combines Investigation Act*, R.S.C. 1985, c. C-34, s. 2.

TRADE L. TOPICS. *abbr.* Trade Law Topics.

TRADE MACHINERY. Machinery used at a workshop, except (a) fixed motive power units such as steam engines, steam boilers and things fixed to them; (b) fixed power machinery such as shafts, wheels, drums and things fixed to them, used to transmit motive power to other machinery, fixed or loose; and (c) pipes for steam, gas and water in the workshop. *Chattel Mortgage Act*, R.S.B.C. 1979, c. 48, s. 1.

TRADE-MARK. *var.* **TRADE MARK.** (a) A mark that is used by a person for the purpose of distinguishing or so as to distinguish wares or services manufactured, sold leased, hired or performed by him from those manufactured, sold, leased, hired or performed by others; (b) a certification mark; (c) a distinguishing guise; or (d) a proposed trade-mark. *Trade-Marks Act*, R.S.C. 1985, c. T-13, s. 2. See ASSOCIATED ~S; GENUINE ~; NATIONAL ~; PROPOSED ~; REGISTERED ~.

TRADE MARK AGENT. A person knowledgeable in legal issues relating to trademarks.

TRADE-NAME. *var.* **TRADE NAME.** The name under which any business is carried on, whether or not it is the name of a corporation, a partnership or an individual. *Trade-Marks Act*, R.S.C. 1985, c. T-13, s. 2.

TRADE PRACTICES. See RESTRICTIVE ~ COMMISSION.

TRADER. *n.* Any person who trades in the course of business. See FLOOR ~; FUR ~; TRANSIENT ~.

TRADE SCHOOL. *var.* **TRADE-SCHOOL**. Any school or place in which a trade is taught and includes any course of study whether by correspondence or otherwise offered or operated by any person other than (a) a chartered university in Canada; (b) a department of the Government of Canada or of any province; (c) a board of school trustees; (d) a trade school organized or operated solely for the employees of a corporation, industry or plant; or (e) a school or course exempted by the Lieutenant-Governor in Council. *Trade Schools acts*. See PRIVATE ~.

TRADE SECRET. 1. Must be something, probably of a technical nature, which is guarded very closely and is of such peculiar value to the owner of the trade secret that harm to him would be presumed by its mere disclosure. *Société Gamma Inc. v. Canada (Secretary of State)* (1994), 1994 CarswellNat 1301, 17 B.L.R. (2d) 13, 79 F.T.R. 42, (sub nom. *Société Gamma Inc. v. Canada (Department of the Secretary of State)*) 56 C.P.R. (3d) 58, 27 Admin. L.R. (2d) 102 (T.D.), Strayer J. 2. Any information, including a formula, pattern, compilation, program, method, technique, process, negotiation position or strategy or any information contained or embodied in a product, device or mechanism that (a) is or may be used in a trade or business; (b) is not generally known in that trade or business; (c) has economic value from not being generally known; and (d) is the subject of efforts that are reasonable under the circumstances to maintain its secrecy. *Security of Information Act*, R.S.C.1985, c. O-5, s. 2.

TRADE SIZE. Any size designation traditionally used by the trade, but restricted to products or classes of products manufactured to a standard or specification, so that the designated trade size may be referred to an industry accepted table or chart which then provides the true dimensions of the item in question.

TRADESMAN. *n.* Any person other than an apprentice, who works for remuneration at any designated trade, including an employer who so works. *Apprenticeship and Trades Qualification*

Act, R.S.P.E.I. 1988, c. A-15, s. 1(1)(n). See SKILLED ~.

TRADESPERSON. *n.* A person other than an apprentice, who works for remuneration at any designated trade, including an employer who so works.

TRADE TERMS. Terms in respect of payment, units of purchase and reasonable technical and servicing requirements.

TRADE UNION. *var.* **TRADE-UNION**. 1. Any organization of employees, or any branch or local thereof, the purposes of which include the regulation of relations between employers and employees. 2. A combination, whether temporary or permanent, having among its objects the regulating of relations between employees and employers or between employees and employees or between employers and employers. *Rights of Labour Act*, R.S.O. 1990, c. R-33, s. 1. 3. Such combination, whether temporary or permanent, for regulating the relations between workmen and masters or for imposing restrictive conditions on the conduct of any trade or business, as would, but for this Act, have been deemed to be an unlawful combination by reason of some one or more of its purposes being in restraint of trade. *Trade Unions Act*, R.S.C. 1985, c. T-14, s. 2. See COUNCIL OF ~S.

TRADE UNION BENEFIT SOCIETY. A society, association or corporation, membership in which is restricted exclusively to bona fide members of one trade union and which under the authority of its charter has an assurance or benefit fund for the benefit of its own members exclusively.

TRADING. See INSIDER ~.

TRADING COMPANY. Any company, except a railway or telegraph company, carrying on business similar to that carried on by apothecaries, auctioneers, bankers, brokers, brickmakers, builders, carpenters, carriers, cattle or sheep salesmen, coach proprietors, dyers, fullers, keepers of inns, taverns, hotels, saloons or coffee houses, lime burners, livery stable keepers, market gardeners, millers, miners, packers, printers, quarrymen, sharebrokers, ship-owners, shipwrights, stockbrokers, stock-jobbers, victuallers, warehousemen, wharfingers, persons using the trade of merchandise by way of bargaining, exchange, bartering, commission, consignment or otherwise, in gross or by retail or by persons who, either for themselves, or as agents or factors for others, seek their living by buying and selling or buying and letting for hire goods or commodities, or by the manufacture, workmanship or the conversion of goods or commodities or trees. *Winding-Up Act*, R.S.C. 1985, c. W-11, s. 2.

TRADING STAMP. Any form of cash receipt, receipt, coupon, stamp, premium ticket or other device designed or intended to be given to the purchaser of goods by the vendor thereof or on his behalf, and to represent a discount on the price of goods or a premium to the purchaser thereof, but does not include an offer, endorsed by the manufacturer upon a wrapper or container in which goods are sold, of a premium or reward for the return of that wrapper or container to the manufacturer. *Trading Stamp acts*.

TRADING STAMPS. Includes any form of cash receipt, receipt, coupon, premium ticket or other device, designed or intended to be given to the purchaser of goods by the vendor thereof or on his behalf, and to represent a discount on the price of the goods or a premium to the purchaser thereof (a) that 'May be redeemed (i) by a person other than the vendor, the person from whom the vendor purchased the goods or the manufacturer of the goods; (ii) by the vendor, the person from whom the vendor purchased the goods or the manufacturer of the goods in cash or in goods that are not his property in whole or in part; or (iii) by the vendor elsewhere than in the premises where the goods are purchased; or (b) that does not show on its face the place where it is delivered and the merchantable value thereof; or (c) that may not be redeemed on demand at any time, but an offer, endorsed by the manufacturer on a wrapper or container in which goods are sold, of a premium or reward for the return of that wrapper or container to the manufacturer is not a trading stamp. *Criminal Code*, R.S.C. 1985, c. C-46, s. 379.

TRADITIO INCHOATA. [L.] Incomplete delivery.

TRADITIO LOQUI CHARTAM FACIT. [L.] Delivery gives a deed its voice.

TRADITION. *n*. Handing over; delivering.

TRADITIONAL CHINESE MEDICINE. The promotion, maintenance and restoration of health and prevention of a disorder, imbalance or disease based on traditional Chinese medicine theory by utilization of the primary therapies of (a) Chinese acupuncture (Zhen), moxibustion (Jiu) and suction cup (Ba Guan), (b) Chinese manipulative therapy (Tui Na), (c) Chinese energy control therapy (Qi Gong), (d) Chinese rehabilitation exercises such as Chinese shadow boxing (Tai Ji Quan), and (e) prescribing, compounding or dispensing Chinese herbal formulae (Zhong Yao Chu Fang) and Chinese food cure recipes (Shi Liao).

TRADITIONAL MARRIAGE. " . . . [T]he husband being primarily responsible for the financial support of the family and the wife being primarily responsible for the care of the children and the running of the household. . ." *Overall v. Overall* (1992), 38 R.F.L. (3d) 360 at 367, 79 Man. R. (2d) 125 (Q.B.), Diamond J. See CONVENTIONAL MARRIAGE.

TRADITIONAL OR ARTISTIC CHARACTERISTICS. In respect of any handicraft goods, means (a) any form or decoration used traditionally by the indigenous people; or (b) any form or decoration that represents any national, territorial or religious symbol of the geographical region in which the goods were produced.

TRAFFIC. *v*. 1. To manufacture, sell, export from or import into Canada, transport or deliver, otherwise than under the authority of this Part or the regulations. *Food and Drugs Act*, R.S.C. 1985, c. F-27, s. 38. 2. To sell, buy, barter, solicit or trade or offer to do so. *Wildlife acts*.

TRAFFIC. *n*. 1. Includes pedestrians and ridden, driven, or herded animals and vehicles, and other conveyances, either singly or together, while using a highway for purposes of travel. 2. The traffic of passengers, goods and rolling stock. *Railway acts*. 3. The transmission of and other dealings with telegraphic and telephonic messages. 4. Any persons, goods or mail that are transported by air. *Air Carrier Regulations*, C.R.C., c. 3, s. 2. See AERODROME ~ ZONE; AIRPORT ~; APRON ~; CURRENT OF ~; DIRECTION OF ~ FLOW; EXTRAORDINARY ~; INCIDENTAL ~.

TRAFFIC CONTROL DEVICE. *var*. **TRAFFIC-CONTROL DEVICE**. Any sign, signal, marking or device placed, marked or erected for the purpose of regulating, warning or guiding traffic.

TRAFFIC CONTROLLER. See VESSEL ~.

TRAFFIC CONTROL LIGHT. The light shown by traffic control signal.

TRAFFIC CONTROL SIGNAL. *var*. **TRAFFIC-CONTROL SIGNAL**. 1. A traffic control device, whether manually, electrically, or mechanically operated, by which, when operating, traffic is directed to stop and to proceed. 2. That part of a traffic control signal system that consists of one set of no less than three coloured lenses, red, amber and green, mounted on a frame and commonly referred to as a signal head. *Highway Traffic Act*, R.S.O. 1990, c. H.8, s. 133.

TRAFFIC CONTROL SIGNAL SYSTEM. All of the signal equipment making up the installation at any location. *Highway Traffic Act*, R.S.O. 1990, c. H.8, s. 133.

TRAFFICKING. *n.* Manufacturing, buying, selling, dealing in. See WEAPONS ~.

TRAFFIC LANE. 1. A longitudinal division of a public highway of sufficient width to accommodate the passage of a single line of vehicles. 2. A route within which there is one direction of traffic flow.

TRAFFIC SEPARATION SCHEME. A routing measure that provides for the separation of opposing streams of traffic by appropriate means and by the establishment of traffic lanes.

TRAFFIC SIGN. Includes all traffic-control signals, warning sign-posts, direction-posts, signs, lines, marks or other devices for the guidance of persons using highways. See OFFICIAL ~S.

TRAFFIC SIGNAL. See OFFICIAL ~S.

TRAFFIC ZONE. See INSHORE ~.

TRAIL. *n.* A road which lacks the element of dedication as a highway. See PUBLIC ~; REGIONAL ~.

TRAILER. *n.* 1. " . . . [A] separate vehicle not driven or propelled by its own power but driven by a tractor for the purposes of transporting property. . ." *Humphreys Transfer Ltd. v. Royal Insurance Co. of Canada* (1983), 44 N.B.R. (2d) 528 at 532, 116 A.P.R. 528 (Q.B.), Cormier J. 2. A vehicle so designed that it may be attached to or drawn by a motor vehicle and intended to transport property or persons and includes any trailer that is designed, constructed and equipped as a dwelling place, living abode or sleeping place, either permanently or temporarily, but does not include machinery or equipment used in the construction or maintenance of highways. 3. A vehicle designed for carrying persons or chattels, and for being towed by a motor vehicle and includes a farm trailer but does not include an implement of husbandry that is temporarily towed, propelled or moved upon a highway. 4.

A trailer, a semi-trailer or a mobile home which is used, or intended to be used, as a dwelling, office or commercial or industrial establishment and which has not become an immoveable. *An Act Respecting Municipal Taxation and Providing Amendments to Certain Legislation*, S.Q. 1979, c. 72, s. 1. 5. A film used only for advertising purposes. See BOAT ~; BUS ~; CABIN ~; CABLE REEL ~; FARM ~; FULL ~; HEAVY HAULER ~; HOUSE ~; POLE ~; SNOWMOBILE ~; TENT ~; TRACTOR-~ COMBINATION; TRAVEL ~.

TRAILER CAMP. 1. A parcel of land, not in a Provincial Park or mobile home park, (a) intended as the location for temporary residential purposes of two or more trailers other than mobile homes; or (b) upon which two or more trailers other than mobile homes are located for temporary residential purposes. New Brunswick statutes. 2. Land in or upon which any vehicle, so constructed that it is suitable for being attached to a motor vehicle for the purpose of being drawn or propelled by the motor vehicle, is placed, located, kept or maintained, even if the vehicle is jacked-up or its running gear is removed, but not including any vehicle unless it is used for the living, sleeping or eating accommodation of persons therein. *Municipal Act*, R.S.O. 1990, c. M.45, s. 236(15).

TRAILER COACH. Any vehicle used or constructed in such a way as to enable it to be used as a conveyance upon public streets or highways and includes a self-propelled or non-self-propelled vehicle designed, constructed or reconstructed in such a manner as will permit the occupancy thereof as a dwelling or sleeping place for one or more persons notwithstanding that its running gear is removed or that it is jacked up.

TRAILER CONVERTER DOLLY. A device consisting of one or more axles, a fifth wheel lower-half and a tow bar.

TRAILER COURT. Any tract or parcel of land on which two or more occupied trailer coaches are or are permitted to be harboured whether or not a charge is made or paid for the use thereof and includes any building or structure used or intended for use as a part of the equipment of such trailer court, but does not include an industrial or construction camp.

TRAILER HITCH. A coupling device mounted on the rear of a truck tractor or trailer to which a tow bar may be attached for the purpose of towing a full trailer.

TRAILER PARK. An area that is intended to be used, and is used, primarily as a site for the placing or parking of mobile houses, and includes any buildings or other structures or facilities intended for, or to be used for, cooking, personal cleanliness, washing, health, or sanitation, or any one or more or all of those purposes. *Municipal Act*, S.M. 1970, c. 100, s. 437.

TRAIN. *n.* 1. Includes an engine, locomotive and other rolling stock. 2. An engine or more than one engine coupled, with or without cars, displaying markers. See EXTRA ~; PASSENGER-~ SERVICE; REGULAR ~; SUPERIOR ~.

TRAINING. *n.* 1. Receipt of information and acquisition of practical skills. 2. The process of teaching a dog, (a) hunting skills, or (b) such skills as are necessary for participation in a field trial. *Game and Fish Act*, R.S.O. 1990, c. G.1, s. 811. See LANGUAGE ~; OCCUPATIONAL ~; VOCATIONAL ~.

TRAINING CONTRACT. An agreement between a person engaged in the business of providing a training course and a purchaser under which the person undertakes to provide a training course to the purchaser or to a person designated by the purchaser.

TRAINING COURSE. Any course of study or instruction.

TRAINING FACILITY. See HEALTH ~.

TRAINING PERIOD. A period during which an employee is not expected to be able to do the job for which she was hired but during which she is enabled to do it.

TRAINING PROGRAM. A course or program, other than an apprenticeship program, a work experience program or a student work training program, (a) under which a trainee acquires skill and knowledge in an occupation or a designated occupation, and (b) that is approved, registered or otherwise recognized.

TRAINING SCHOOL. See DRIVER ~.

TRAINING VEHICLE. See DUAL-CONTROL ~.

TRAIN OF SUPERIOR CLASS. A train given precedence by time table.

TRAIN OF SUPERIOR DIRECTION. A train given precedence in the direction specified by time table as between opposing trains of the same class.

TRAIN OF SUPERIOR RIGHT. A train given precedence by train order.

TRAIN ORDER SIGNAL. A fixed signal provided at train order offices used in connection with the delivery of train orders and as prescribed by Rule 91A. *Regulations No. O-8, Uniform Code of Operating Rules*, C.R.C., c. 1175, Part III, s. 2.

TRAIN REGISTER. A book or form used at designated stations for registering signals displayed, the time of arrival and departure of trains, and such other information as may be prescribed. *Regulations No. O-8, Uniform Code of Operating Rules*, C.R.C., c. 1175, Part III, s. 2.

TRAITOR. *n.* A person who betrays a trust; a person guilty of treason.

TRAMMEL NET. A net that (a) is used to catch fish by enmeshing them by means of two different sizes of mesh; and (b) does not enclose an area of water.

TRAMWAY. *n.* Street railroad, railway or tramway for the conveyance of passengers, operated by motive power other than steam, and usually constructed in whole or in part in, under or above public streets, roads, ways and places, and the poles, wires and other appliances and equipment connected therewith. See AERIAL ~; ELECTRIC ~.

TRANQUILIZER. *n.* A drug which induces calmness, used to treat anxiety.

TRANSACTION. *n.* 1. " . . . [A] series of connected acts extending over a period of time. . ." *R. v. Goldstein* (1988), 42 C.C.C. (3d) 548 at 554, 28 O.A.C. 62, 64 C.R. (3d) 360, 32 C.R.R. 320 (C.A.), Houlden J.A. 2. " . . . In its ordinary sense it is understood to mean the doing or performing of some matter of business between two or more persons. 'Transaction' in its broadest sense expresses the concept of driving, doing, or acting as is denoted by the Latin 'transa agere' from which it is derived. . . may and frequently does include a series of occurrences extending over a length of time." *R. v. Canavan* (1970), 12 C.R.N.S. 385 at 388, [1970] 3 O.R. 353, [1970] 5 C.C.C. 15 (C.A.), the court per Schroeder J.A. 3. In relation to securities, includes the purchase, sale or transfer thereof, whether or not the securities had previously been distributed, and includes any act, advertisement, conduct or negotiation directly or indirectly in furtherance of the purchase, sale or transfer thereof. 4. (a) The negotiation for another or others of any trade in real estate wherever situated or, (b) any advertising by a broker, authorized official or salesman, whether of real estate for sale, or lease or for real estate to purchase or take on lease, or (c) the showing of real estate for sale or lease to potential purchasers or tenants, or (d) the collection by a broker, authorized official or salesman of rent, mortgage payments or instalments of purchase money payable under a lease, mortgage or agreement for sale of real estate, except real estate of which he is himself the owner, mortgagee or vendor, as the case may be, or (e) the solicitation or obtaining of a listing, agreement, and includes any conduct, act or negotiation, directly or indirectly, in the furtherance or attempted furtherance of any one or more of the things mentioned in this clause. *Real Estate Brokers Act*, R.S.M. 1987, c. R20, s. 1. 5. Includes purchase or receipt by a salvage dealer and sale or delivery by him. See AVOIDANCE ~; CAPITAL ~; CLOSING A ~; CONSUMER ~; CREDIT ~; EXPORT ~; EXTERNALLY FINANCED ~; GOING PRIVATE ~; INTERNALLY FINANCED ~; MORTGAGE ~; PRIVATE ~; PURCHASE FINANCING ~; REAL ESTATE ~; REVIEWABLE ~; SECURED ~; SECURITY ~; SHAM ~; STRANGER TO A ~; UNCONSCIONABLE ~.

TRANSACTION VALUE. In respect of goods, means the value of the goods determined in accordance with subsection 48(4). *Customs Act*, R.S.C. 1985 (2d Supp.), c. 1, s. 45.

TRANSCRIPT. *n*. 1. Something copied from an original. 2. In a court, an official copy of proceedings. 3. " . . . [A] direct, written copy of words used in a conversation. . ." *R. v. Ouellet* (1976), 33 C.C.C. (2d) 417 at 422, [1977] 2 W.W.R. 295 (B.C. Prov. Ct.), Paradis J.

TRANSFER. *n*. 1. " . . . [T]o give or hand over property from one person to another." *Murphy v. R.* (1980), 8 E.T.R. 120 at 131 (Fed. T.D.), Cattanach J. 2. " . . . [N]ot a term of art and has not a technical meaning . . . All that is required is that [party A] should so deal with the property as to divest himself of it and vest it in [party B], that is to say, pass the property from [A] to [B]. The means by which he accomplishes this result, whether direct or circuitous, may properly be called a transfer." *Fasken v. Canada (Minister of National Revenue)* (1948), [1949] 1 D.L.R. 810 at 822, [1948] C.T.C. 265, [1948] Ex. C.R. 580, Thorson P. 3. The passing of any estate or

interest in land under this Act, whether for valuable consideration or otherwise. *Land Titles acts*. 4. In relation to stock, includes the performance and execution of every deed, power of attorney, act, and thing on the part of the transferor to effect and complete the title in the transferee. *Trustee acts*. 5. Includes transmission by operation of law. *Corporations acts*. 6. A conveyance of freehold or leasehold land and includes a deed and a transfer under a Land Titles act. 7. "[In labour relations context includes] . . . several types of transactions, including exchange, gift, trust, take-overs, mergers, and amalgamations. . ." *W.W. Lester (1978) Ltd. v. U.A. Local 740* (1990), 48 Admin. L.R. 1 at 22, 76 D.L.R. (4th) 389, 91 C.L.L.C. 14,002, 123 N.R. 241, 88 Nfld. & P.E.I.R. 15, 274 A.P.R. 15, [1990] 3 S.C.R. 644, McLachlin J. (Lamer C.J.C., La Forest, Sopinka and Gonthier JJ. concurring). 8. The instrument by which one person conveys to another an estate or interest in land under this Act and includes a grant from the Crown. *The Land Titles Act*, R.S.S. 1978, c. L-5, s. 2. 9. Includes gift, conveyance, assignment, delivery over, or payment of property. *Assignments and Preferences Act*, R.S.N.S. 1989, c. 25, s. 2. 10. . . . [T]o move from one job to another. . ." *Metropolitan Authority of Halifax, Dartmouth & Halifax County v. Correction Officers Assn. (Nova Scotia)* (1983), 10 L.A.C. (3d) 265 at 273 (N.S.), Outhouse and McDougall. 11. In the context of labour relations to accomplish a transfer something must be relinquished by the predecessor business on the one hand and obtained by the successor on the other. A transfer implies a nexus, an agreement or transaction of some sort between the predecessor and successor employers. . . There must be a mutual intent to transfer part of the business. *C.A.W., Local 222 v. Charterways Transportation Ltd.*, 2000 CarswellOnt 1253, 2000 SCC 23, (sub nom. *Ajax (Town) v. CAW, Local 222*) [2000] 1 S.C.R. 538, (sub nom. *Ajax (Town) v. National Automobile, Aerospace & Agricultural Implement Workers Union of Canada (CAW-Canada), Local 222*) 253 N.R. 223, 22 Admin. L.R. (3d) 1, (sub nom. *Ajax (Town) v. National Automobile, Aerospace & Agricultural Implement Workers Union of Canada (CAW-Canada), Local 222*) 133 O.A.C. 43 [Per Bastarache J. (dissenting)]. See AGREEMENT OF ~; EMBRYO ~ BUSINESS; ENERGY ~; INTER-UTILITY ~; LATERAL ~; POWER ~; RECIPROCAL ~ AGREEMENT.

TRANSFERABLE. *adj.* Capable of being transferred.

TRANSFERABLE SHARE. A transferable corporate share that a debtor could freely transfer even if restrictions are placed on its transferability.

TRANSFER AGENT. A person who records the transfer of shares.

TRANSFER CHARGE. See DIRECT ~.

TRANSFEREE. *n.* 1. A person in whose favour a transfer is given. 2. The person to whom any interest or estate in land is transferred whether for value or otherwise. *Land Titles acts.*

TRANSFER HEARING. A hearing to determine whether a young offender will be tried as an adult offender in adult court.

TRANSFER OF OWNERSHIP. Includes any alienation of a motor vehicle.

TRANSFER OPERATION. (a) The loading of oil or an oily mixture on to a ship from a loading facility or from another ship; (b) the unloading of oil or an oily mixture from a ship to an unloading facility or on to another ship; or (c) the transfer of oil or an oily mixture on board a ship. *Oil Pollution Prevention Regulations*, C.R.C., c. 1454, s. 2.

TRANSFEROR. *n.* 1. The person by whom any interest or estate in land is transferred, whether for valuable consideration or otherwise. *Land Titles acts.* 2. A person who gives a transfer.

TRANSFER POINT. See INTER-UTILITY ~.

TRANSFERRED INTENT. "The literature on transferred intent distinguishes between two kinds of situations in which the 'wrong victim' suffers harm at the hands of the accused. The first, sometimes called error in *objecto* involves a mistake by the perpetrator as to the identity of the victim ... It is the second 'wrong victim' situation, sometimes called aberratio ictus or more poetically, 'a mistake of the bullet' that has led to the controversy surrounding the doctrine of transferred intent. In this second situation the perpetrator aims at X but by chance or lack of skill hits Y." *R. v. Droste* (1984), 10 C.C.C. (3d) 404 at 410, [1984] 1 S.C.R. 208, 39 C.R. (3d) 26, 6 D.L.R. (4th) 607, 52 N.R. 176, 3 O.A.C. 179, Dickson J. (Ritchie, Estey, McIntyre, Chouinard and Lamer JJ. concurring). See ABERRATIO ICTUS.

TRANSFER SERVICE. A service to the public with respect to the disposition of dead human bodies, including the transportation of dead human bodies and the filling out of the necessary documentation with respect to the disposition of dead human bodies. *Funeral Directors and Establishments Act*, R.S.O. 1990, c. F.36, s. 1.

TRANSFER STATION. A waste disposal site used for the purpose of transferring waste from a collection vehicle to another carrier for transportation to another waste disposal site. See BULK MILK ~; CREAM ~; MILK ~.

TRANSFER STOP. With respect to a passenger means a stop at an airport by an aircraft from which the passenger deplanes solely for the purpose of emplaning on a connecting flight.

TRANSFER TO USES. A transfer expressed to be given to such uses as the transferee may appoint by transfer, charge or will.

TRANSHIPMENT. *n.* 1. Moving cargo from one vessel to another to forward it to its destination. 2. After goods have been unloaded or in any way removed from the means of transportation by which they came into Canada, their loading, placing on board or within or upon the same or any other means of transportation. *Transhipment Regulations*, C.R.C., c. 606, s. 3.

TRANSHIPMENT TERMINAL. See ENERGY ~.

TRANSIENT ACCOMMODATION. The provision of lodging in hotels, motels, hostels, apartment houses, lodging houses, boarding houses, clubs and other similar accommodation, whether or not a membership is required for the lodging.

TRANSIENT ACCOMMODATION FACILITIES. Facilities where, for consideration, the public may obtain sleeping accommodation and includes motels, hotels, tourist camps, hunting or fishing lodges, out-camps, auto and trailer camp grounds, and similar accommodation facilities.

TRANSIENT TRADER. 1. A person carrying on business in the municipality who: (a) offers to provide services for a price; (b) offers goods or merchandise for sale by retail or by auction; or (c) solicits any person who is not a wholesale or retail dealer for orders: (i) to provide future services for a price; or (ii) for the future delivery of goods or merchandise; and who is not a person: (d) required to be licensed under The Direct Sellers Act; or (e) assessable for the purposes of business taxation in respect of that business. *The Rural Municipalities Act*, R.S.S. 1978, c. R-26, s. 2. 2. Includes any person commencing business who has not resided continuously in the municipality for at least 3 months next preceding the time of his commencing such business there. *Municipal Act*, R.S.O. 1990, c. M.45, s. 236(17).

TRANSIT. *v*. To use the seaway, or a part of it, either upbound or downbound

TRANSIT. *n*. See RAPID ~.

TRANSIT CORPORATION. See MUNICI-PAL ~.

TRANSIT IN REM JUDICATAM. [L.] It becomes res judicata. A judgment against one joint debtor will bar a separate action against another joint debtor, even if the first judgment remains unsatisfied, because the obligation merges in the judgment.

TRANSITIONAL SURFACE. An imaginary inclined plane extending upward and outward from the outer lateral limits of a strip and its approach surface to an intersection with the horizontal surface or other transitional surfaces. *Airport Zoning regulations*.

TRANSIT POLICY. A policy issued to insure against an accident to someone while travelling or to insure goods while they are in transit from place to place. Raoul Colinvaux, *The Law of Insurance*, 5th ed. (London: Sweet & Maxwell, 1984) at 73.

TRANSIT SERVICE AGREEMENT. An agreement for not less than 5 years between the authority and a municipality respecting the provision and maintenance of transit services in a transit service area by means of annual operating agreements. *Urban Transit Authority Act*, R.S.C. 1979, c. 421, s. 1.

TRANSIT SYSTEM. A system for the transportation of passengers and parcel express. See INTERREGIONAL ~; PASSENGER ~; REGIONAL ~.

TRANSIT TERRA CUM ONERE. [L.] Land passes over with its burden.

TRANSIVIT IN REM JUDICATAM. [L.] It has passed into judgment.

TRANSLATION. *n*. The written transposition of words and numbers from one language to another and includes an adaptation that accurately conveys the meaning thereof. *Translation Bureau Regulations*, C.R.C., c. 1561, s. 2.

TRANSMISSION. *n*. 1. " . . . [I]n the ordinary sense of the language, connotes the delivery from an origination point to a reception point. It does not connote a conceptual transfer of something with neither sender nor receiver. . ." *R. v. McLaughlin* (1980), 18 C.R. (3d) 339 at 348, [1980] 2 S.C.R. 331, [1981] 11 W.W.R. 298, 32 N.R. 350, 23 A.R. 530, 53 C.C.C. (2d) 417, 113 D.L.R. (3d) 386, Estey J. (concurring). 2. Applies to change of ownership consequent on death, lunacy, sale under execution, order of court or other act of law, or on a sale for arrears of taxes or on any settlement or any legal succession in case of intestacy. *Land Titles acts*. 3. "[With regard to shares] . . . used to express the legal result which follows on death, but not to express the actual step which is necessary to invest the new holder. That is done by transfer, and that transfer in such a case is effectuated by a change in the register where the shares are registered,. . ." *Brassard v. Smith* (1924), [1925] 1 D.L.R. 528 at 531, [1925] A.C. 371, [1925] 1 W.W.R. 311, 38 Que. K.B. 208 (Que. P.C.), the board per Lord Dunedin. 4. Includes storage. *Gas Utilities acts*. See DOCUMENT OF ~.

TRANSMISSION EQUIPMENT. Any object or objects by which the motion of a prime mover is transmitted to a machine that is capable of utilizing such motion and includes a shaft, pulley, belt, chain, gear, clutch or other device.

TRANSMISSION FACILITY. 1. Any wire, cable, radio, optical or other electromagnetic system, or any similar technical system, for the transmission of intelligence between network termination points, but does not include any exempt transmission apparatus. *Telecommunications Act*, S.C. 1993, c. 38, s. 2. 2. A transmission facility is a facility for the transmission of "intelligence". The phrase "transmission facility" does not, of course, occur in s. 43(5). Yet, the Utilities submit that the term "transmission" in s. 43(5) must be read harmoniously with the definition of "transmission facility" so that in both provisions the thing being transmitted is "intelligence." The Utilities' power poles do not serve to transmit intelligence. They serve to transmit electricity. I agree with the Utilities that a harmonious interpretation of these two provisions is to be preferred. While I do not consider this point to be conclusive, it is another factor suggesting that s. 43(5) does not encompass the Utilities' power poles. *Barrie Public Utilities v. Canadian Cable Television Assn.*, 2003 SCC 28 [Per Gonthier J. (McLachlin C.J.C., Major, Arbour, LeBel, Deschamps JJ. concurring)].

TRANSMISSION LINE. 1. A system or arrangement of lines of wire or other conductors and transformation equipment, whereby electric energy is transmitted in bulk and includes (a) transmission circuits composed of the conductors which form the minimum set required to so transmit electric energy; (b) insulating and supporting structures; (c) substations; (d) operational and control devices. 2. A pipe line, other than a production line, a distribution line, a pipe line within an oil refinery, oil or petroleum storage depot, chemical processing plant or pipe line terminal or station. *Ontario Energy Board Act*, R.S.O. 1980, c. 332, s. 1. See GAS ~; POWER ~; WORKS AND ~S.

TRANSMISSION PIPELINE. A pipe or system of pipes through which natural gas, oil, solids, or a liquid or gas derived from natural gas, oil or solids, whether in suspension or other form is transported and includes compressor or pumping facilities and other equipment related to the operation of the transmission pipeline, associated terminal or storage facilities, but does not include (a) flow lines from wells; (b) secondary lines for gathering that are located within a producing area; or (c) distribution lines that deliver to ultimate consumers. *Utilities Commission Act*, S.B.C. 1980, c. 60, s. 16.

TRANSMISSION SYSTEM. A system for transmitting electricity, and includes any structures, equipment or other things used for that purpose.

TRANSMIT. *v*. 1. " . . . [A]n accurate expression to make use of in relation to every message which is sent from one subscriber to the respondent's telephone exchange system to another. . ." *Electric Despatch Co. v. Bell Telephone Co.* (1891), 20 C.R. 83 at 91, Gwynne J. (Strong J. concurring). 2. To send or convey from one place to another place by physical, electronic, optical or other means. *Canada Post Corporation Act*, R.S.C. 1985, c. C-10, s. 2. 3. "[The Canada Post Corporation Act, S.C. 1980-81-82-83, c. 54] employs 'transmit' as including the whole of the process of sending matter by mail inclusive of both the act of posting and that of delivery. . ." *Canada Post Corp. v. Assn. of Rural Route Mail Couriers* (1987), [1989] 1 F.C. 176 at 192, 88 C.L.L.C. 14,006, 82 N.R. 249, 46 D.L.R. (4th) 716 (C.A.), Hugessen J.A. 4. With respect to electricity, means to convey electricity at voltages of more than 50 kilovolts. *Electricity Act, 1998*, S.O. 1998, c. 15, Sched. A, s. 2.

TRANSMIT BY POST. To transmit through or by means of the Corporation. *Canada Post Corporation Act*, R.S.C. 1985, c. C-10, s. 2.

TRANSMITTER. *n*. 1. A person who supplies a hydrocarbon by pipeline to a distributor. 2. A person who owns or operates a transmission system. *Electricity Act, 1998*, S.O. 1998, c. 15, Sched. A, s. 2.

TRANSMITTING STATION. See RE-BROADCASTING ~.

TRANSPLANT. *n*. The removal of tissue from a human body, whether living or dead, and its implantation in a living human body. *Human Tissue Gift Acts*. See ANIMAL EMBRYO ~ CENTRE.

TRANSPLANTING. *n*. With respect to shellfish, means the moving of shellfish from one shellfish area to another shellfish area for any purpose other than natural biological cleansing.

TRANSPORT. *v*. 1. To convey in or on a vehicle gasoline or an associated product, exclusive of the fuel carried for use in the vehicle. 2. " . . . [I]n the definition of 'traffic' [in s. 2 of the Narcotic Control Act, S.C. 1960-61, c. 35] is not meant in the sense of mere conveying or carrying or moving from one place to another, but in the sense of doing so to promote the distribution of the narcotic to another. . ." *R. v. MacDonald* (1963), (*sub nom. R. v. Harrington*) 41 C.R. 75 at 80, 43 W.W.R. 337, [1964] 1 C.C.C. 189 (B.C. C.A.), the court per Bird J.A.

TRANSPORT. *n*. 1. A method, manner or means of transportation and, without limiting the foregoing, includes aircraft, ships, boats and vessels, elevated, surface or subsurface railways or tramways, elevated cable cars, motor vehicles and trailers, all terrain vehicles, hovercraft, and the hoists, cables, rails, rolling stock, pipelines and conduits used in connection with transport. 2. The transport of goods or passengers, whether by rail or water, for hire or reward, to which this Act applies. See AIR ~; EXTRA-PROVINCIAL ~; LOCAL ~; MEANS OF ~; OFFER FOR ~; PASSENGER ~.

TRANSPORTABLE EQUIPMENT. Electrically operated equipment which requires to be moved to a new position from time to time. *Coal Mines Regulation Act*, R.S.N.S. 1989, c. 73, s. 85(1).

TRANSPORTATION. *n*. 1. With respect to freight, includes the shipment, care, handling, storage and delivery of it. *Motor Carrier acts*. 2.

The operation of a public vehicle and includes the (a) care; (b) handling; (c) assembly or storage in or for transit; or (d) delivery of passengers or goods. See PUBLIC ~; SCHEDULED TRAVEL ~.

TRANSPORTATION FACILITY. Everything necessary for the efficient transportation of persons and goods in a particular manner.

TRANSPORTATION LAW. The law governing the carriage of goods and people.

TRANSPORTATION OF GOODS. The transportation of goods from any place in Canada to any place outside Canada or from any place outside Canada to any place in Canada. *Shipping Conference Exemption Act*, R.S.C. 1985, c. S-10, s. 2.

TRANSPORTATION PLAN. A plan for the control of transportation within a defined area proposing of some specific time the layout of any streets, highways, bridges, railway lines, railway crossings at level or at grade separations, bus routes, rapid transit lines, railway stations, bus terminals, rapid transit stations and wharves and airports within the defined area. *Railway Relocation and Crossing Act*, R.S.C. 1985, c. R-4, s. 2.

TRANSPORTATION PLANT. Plant used for any aspect of pipeline operations or plant held for use under a definite plan for future oil pipeline operations. *Oil Pipeline Uniform Accounting Regulations*, C.R.C., c. 1058, s. 2.

TRANSPORTATION SYSTEM. 1. "[In Assessment Act, R.S.O. 1950, c. 24, s. 37(4) has] . . . a limited meaning and [refers] to a system which is operated to provide transportation as a service to the public, and not one which is operated, almost entirely, for the transportation by a company, on its own premises, of its own goods, as a part of its manufacturing business." *Sault Ste. Marie (City) v. Algoma Steel Corporation Ltd.*, [1961] S.C.R. 739 at 748, 30 D.L.R. (2d) 436, the court per Martland J. 2. A system of transportation facilities including streets highways, paid transit and all types of transportation facilities. See PUBLIC PASSENGER ~.

TRANSPORTATION TERMINAL. An establishment or undertaking operated for the transportation of people or goods by any means, and includes all land, structures and equipment that form part of the establishment or are used in the undertaking.

TRANSPORTATION UNDERTAKING. Any business or undertaking principally engaged in any transportation activity under the legislative authority of Parliament other than any such business or undertaking (a) operated by a person whose principal place of business is outside of Canada, and (b) engaged in transporting goods or passengers, or both, solely between Canada and another country. *National Transportation Act, 1987*, S.C. 1987, c. 34, s. 251(1).

TRANSPORT BOARD. See CANADIAN TRANSPORT COMMISSION; PROVINCIAL ~.

TRANSPORT BY RAIL. The transport of goods or passengers by a company to which the Railway Act applies.

TRANSPORT BY WATER. The transport of goods or passengers, for hire or reward, by means of ships.

TRANSPORT CANADA. The federal ministry in charge of all federally regulated railways, Marine, Air and Surface Transportation Administrations.

TRANSPORT CATEGORY AIRCRAFT. An aeroplane certified pursuant to Chapter 525 of the *Airworthiness Manual* or an equivalent foreign airworthiness standard, or a helicopter certified pursuant to Chapter 529 of the *Airworthiness Manual* or an equivalent foreign airworthiness standard. *Canadian Aviation Regulations*, SOR/96-433, s. 101.01.

TRANSPORTER. *n*. 1. A person regularly engaged in the business of transporting vehicles. 2. A person who supplies a hydrocarbon other than by pipeline to a distributor. See AUTO ~.

TRANSPORT FACILITIES. See BULK ~.

TRANSPORT ORDER. Any order, in a form approved by the Commodity board and issued in the name of the Commodity Board by a duly authorized employee or nominee of the Commodity Board, authorizing the moving or transporting of the regulated product from one place to another. Canada regulations.

TRANSPORT PERMIT. A valid permit in a form approved by and issued under the authority of the Commodity Board authorizing the movement or transportation of vegetable.

TRANSPORT SYSTEM. A system consisting of vehicles or other means of transport.

TRAP. *v*. 1. To conceal and surprise under circumstances which appear safe but mask real danger. 2. To catch or to attempt to catch game or fur bearing animals by means of a spring trap, deadfall, snare or net. See GANG ~PED.

TRAP. *n*. 1. " . . . [A]n intrinsically dangerous situation. The danger should not be apparent but hidden:. . . generally includes some connotation of abnormality and surprise, in view of the circumstances; . . ." *Rubis v. Gray Rocks Inn Ltd.*, [1982] 1 S.C.R. 452 at 466, 41 N.R. 108, 21 C.C.L.T. 64, Beetz J. (Chouinard and Lamer JJ. concurring). 2. A device for catching game. 3. A fitting or device which provides a liquid seal to vent the emission of sewer gases without materially affecting the flow of sewage or waste through it. *Ontario Water Resources Act*, R.R.O. 1980, Reg . 736, s. 1. See BAIT ~; BELL ~; BLACKCOD ~; BODY-GRIPPING ~; BOT-TLE ~; BUILDING ~; COD ~; CRAB ~; DRUM ~; FIXTURE ~; LEG-HOLD ~; MINNOW ~; SALMON ~; SNOW CRAB ~.

TRAPLINE. *var*. **TRAP-LINE**. *n*. An area for which registration is granted to a licensed trapper for the trapping of fur bearing animals.

TRAP NET. 1. A net that is set so as to enclose an area of water into which fish are guided by one or more leaders. Canada regulations. 2. An impounding net supported principally by buoys or floats and held in place by anchors, and in which the top of the crib, pot or car is covered by netting. *Fishery regulations*.

TRAP ORDER. Evidence obtained by a witness concerning the way in which a defendant supplies goods in response to a request which embodies the use of the disputed trade mark. H.G. Fox, *The Canadian Law of Trade Marks and Unfair Competition*, 3d ed. (Toronto: Carswell, 1972) at 450.

TRAPPING. *n*. Taking or attempting to take wildlife by means of a trap or snare.

TRAPPING AREA. 1. The area or location defined and registered under this Act for the taking of fur-bearing animals and fur-bearing carnivores on the area or location by a licensed trapper. 2. An area or location defined and registered under these Regulations for the taking of fur-bearing animals.

TRAP SEAL. The vertical depth of water between the crown weir and the trap dip.

TRAP STANDARD. The trap for a fixture that is integral with the support for the fixture.

TRAUMA. *n*. A wound; an injury.

TRAUMATIC ANEURYSM. An aneurysm which occurs at a point where a blood vessel has

been injured. F.A. Jaffe, *A Guide to Pathological Evidence*, 3d ed. (Toronto: Carswell, 1991) at 212.

TRAUMATIC ASPHYXIA. Suffocation which occurs when the chest is compressed and respiratory movements are prevented. F.A. Jaffe, *A Guide to Pathological Evidence*, 3d ed. (Toronto: Carswell, 1991) at 213.

TRAVEL. *v*. " ' . . . [T]o go from one place to another.' " *Gowan v. Mutual of Omaha Insurance Co.* (1980), 30 N.B.R. (2d) 300 at 302, 70 A.P.R. 300 (Q.B.), Caughey J.

TRAVEL AGENT. 1. A person who issues tickets on behalf of an airline or sells travel services on behalf of a service provider.

TRAVEL ASSOCIATION. A non-profit organization having as its objects the promotion of the tourism industry in its region.

TRAVELLED PORTION. 1. " . . . [T]hat part of the highway over which traffic passes back and forth, or which may be used by traffic." *Beattie v. Owen Sound (Town)*, [1950] O.W.N. 133 at 135 (H.C.), Barlow J. 2. When used in this section as applicable to roads, streets, lanes or highways, means the central portion thereof between the ditches on either side, ordinarily used for vehicular traffic. *Railway Act*, R.S.Q. 1977, c. C-14, s. 121.

TRAVELLER. *n*. A person who, in consideration of a given price per day or fraction of a day, on the American or European plan, or per meal, à table d'hôte, or à la carte, is furnished by another person with food or lodging or both. *An Act Respecting the Commission de Contrôle des Permis D'alcool*, R.S.Q. 1977, c. C-33, s. 2.

TRAVELLING AMUSEMENT. An amusement whose participants travel from place to place, taking part in the amusement.

TRAVELLING EXHIBITION. Any person successively giving exhibitions, concerts or other entertainments in more than one place or locality either for himself or for others.

TRAVELLING EXPENSES. Transportation while on duty and hotel expenses, meals, taxis and gratuities while the employee is away from his employer's place of business. *Martyn v. Minister of National Revenue* (1962), 35 Tax A.B.C. 428, 62 D.T.C. 341 (T.A.B.).

TRAVELLING PICTURE SHOW. A moving picture show which travels about from place to place in a province.

TRAVEL SERVICE. Transportation, accommodation or other service for the use or benefit of a traveller, tourist or sightseer.

TRAVEL TRAILER. Any vehicle designed, built and maintained so that it may be drawn on the highway and primarily built, furnished and used, or intended to be used for overnight or short term shelter.

TRAVEL TRANSPORTATION. See SCHEDULED ~.

TRAVEL WHOLESALER. 1. A person who, in the course of business, supplies his own non-scheduled travel transportation to the public, purchases or acquires from another person rights to travel services for the purpose of resale, or deals with travel agents or other travel wholesalers for the sale of travel services supplied by another. 2. A person who purchases or acquires rights to a travel service for the purposes of resale or who carries on the business of dealing with travel agents or other travel wholesalers for the sale of travel services provided by another.

TRAVERSE. *n.* " . : . [A] denial [by the defendant] of the plaintiffs allegations . . ." *Royal Bank v. Rizkalla* (1984), 50 C.P.C. 292 at 295, 59 B.C.L.R. 324 (S.C.), McLachlin J.

TRAWL. See MIDWATER ~; OTTER ~; SIDE ~; STERN ~.

TRAWLER. *n.* A vessel (a) of an overall length that exceeds 100 feet; and (b) that uses an otter trawl or other trawl of a similar type for catching fish. *Otter Trawl Fishing Regulations*, C.R.C., c. 821, s. 2.

TRAWLING. *n.* Fishing by dragging through the water a dredge net or other fishing apparatus.

TRAWL NET. Any large bag net dragged in the sea by a vessel or vessels for the purpose of taking fish. *Fishery regulations*. See LARGE-MESH ~; SMALL-MESH ~.

T.R.B. *abbr.* Tax Review Board.

TREAD. *n.* The portion of a tire that comes in contact with the road.

TREAD RIB. A tread section running circumferentially around a tire. Canada regulations.

TREAD SEPARATION. The parting of the tread from the tire carcass. Canada regulations.

TREASON. *n.* (a) Using force or violence for the purpose of overthrowing the government of Canada or a province; (b) without lawful authority, communicating or making available to an agent of a state other than Canada, military or scientific information or any sketch, plan, model, article, note or document of a military or scientific character that he knows or ought to know may be used by that state for a purpose prejudicial to the safety or defence of Canada; (c) conspiring with any person to commit high treason or to do anything mentioned in paragraph (a); (d) forming an intention to do anything that is high treason or that is mentioned in paragraph (a) and manifesting that intention by an overt act; or (e) conspiring with any person to do anything mentioned in paragraph (b) or forming an intention to do anything mentioned in paragraph (b) and manifesting that intention by an overt act. *Criminal Code*, R.S.C. 1985, c. C-46, s. 46(2). See HIGH ~; MISPRISON OF ~.

TREASURER. *n.* 1. A person who cares for money or treasure. 2. The person in charge of the securities and funds of a company who deposits these things in the company's bank.

TREASURE TROVE. Any coin, money, gold, silver, bullion or plate buried or hidden in a private place; because its owner is unknown it belongs to the Crown.

TREASURY. *n.* 1. A place where treasure is stored. 2. The fiscal department of a government which controls payment of public money as directed by the legislature or House of Commons.

TREASURY BILL. A bill in certificated form, or a non-certificated security, issued by or on behalf of Her Majesty for the payment of a principal sum specified in the bill to a named recipient or to a bearer at a date not later than twelve months after the date of issue of the bill. *Financial Administration Act*, R.S.C. 1985, c. F-11, s. 2.

TREASURY BOARD. 1. A committee of the Queen's Privy Council for Canada over which the President of the Treasury Board appointed by Commission under the Great Seal presides. The Treasury Board shall, in addition to the President of the Treasury Board, consist of the Minister and four other members of the Queen's Privy Council for Canada to be nominated from time to time by the Governor in Council. The Treasury Board may act for the Queen's Privy Council for Canada on all matters relating to (a) general administrative policy in the public service of Canada; (b) the organization of the public service of Canada or any portion thereof, and the determination and control of establishments therein; (c) financial management, including estimates, expenditures, financial commitments, accounts, fees or charges for the provision of services or the use of facilities, rentals, licences, leases, revenues from the disposition of property, and procedures by which departments manage, record and account for revenues received or receivable from any source whatever, etc. *Financial Administration Act*, R.S.C. 1985, c. F-11. 2. The equivalent body for a provincial government.

TREASURY BOARD OF CANADA. A federal body which advises Cabinet on program selection and promotes judicious use of resources by other federal departments.

TREASURY NOTE. A note in certificated form, or a non-certificated security, issued by or on behalf of Her Majesty for the payment of a principal sum specified in the note to a named recipient or to a bearer at a date not later than twelve months after the date of issue of the note. *Financial Administration Act*, R.S.C. 1985, c. F-11, s. 2.

TREAT. See INVITATION TO ~.

TREATER. *n*. A fired apparatus specifically designed and used for separating gas and water from crude oil.

TREATMENT. *n*. 1. "[In s. 12 of the Charter] . . . Connotes any conduct, action or behaviour towards another person. It is a word of more expansive or comprehensive import than is its disjunctive partner 'punishment', in that it extends, or potentially so, to all forms of disability or disadvantage and not merely to those imposed as a penalty to ensure the application and enforcement of a rule of law . . ." *R. v. Blakeman* (1988), 48 C.R.R. 222 at 239 (Ont. H.C.), Watt J. 2. [Within the meaning of s. 12 of the Canadian Charter of Rights and Freedoms] has a broader scope than punishment. In [*Rodriguez v. British Columbia (Attorney General)*, [1993] 3 S.C.R. 519, 85 C.C.C. (3d) 15], Sopinka J. . . . found that, in the realm of state action, there was a necessary distinction between merely prohibiting certain behaviour and actually subjecting individuals to "treatment". He held that there must be an active state process in operation involving an exercise of state control over the individual, in order for the action, prohibition, or inaction to be considered treatment: p. 611-12. Section 43 [of the Criminal Code, R.S.C. 1985, C-46] does not involve "treatment" of children in the sense contemplated by s. 12 of the Charter.

Canadian Foundation for Children, Youth & the Law v. Canada (Attorney General) (2000), 2000 CarswellOnt 2409, 146 C.C.C. (3d) 362, 188 D.L.R. (4th) 718, 49 O.R. (3d) 662, 36 C.R. (5th) 334, 76 C.R.R. (2d) 251 (S.C.J.). 3. The maintenance, observation, nursing, medical and other care of a patient. 4. With reference to hazardous waste, means any operation for the treatment, recycling or salvaging of the hazardous waste so that it no longer constitutes a danger to the environment, plant or animal life or human health. 5. One, more or all of direction, supervision or treatment of a person for terminating or diminishing his use of or dependency on a narcotic. 6. Concentrating, smelting, refining or any similar process but does not include washing, screening, conveying, loading or other handling methods when they are not combined with treatment. See CHILD ~ SERVICE; DAY'S ~; ELECTRICAL ~; EXPERIMENTAL ~; HEAT ~; MANIPULATIVE ~; MECHANICAL ~; MEDICAL ~; NATIONAL ~; SILVICULTURAL ~; SURGICAL ~; WASTE ~ SYSTEM.

TREATMENT ALLOWANCE. An allowance paid or payable by the Department to or on behalf of a person while under treatment by the Department for a pensionable disability. *Pension Act*, R.S.C. 1985, c. P-6, s. 2.

TREATMENT CENTRE. 1. A nursing home, special care home, sanatorium, psychiatric facility or any other residential facility operated for the purpose of the care and treatment of persons having a physical or mental disability. 2. Any place including a group home, foster home, training centre and reception centre for the reception, detention, custody, examination, care, treatment, education and rehabilitation of a child. 3. A prescribed place where treatment and rehabilitation programmes are available for persons in need of assistance to overcome alcoholism.

TREATMENT FACILITY. See SEWAGE ~; WASTE WATER ~.

TREATMENT POND. A pond, lagoon or other confined area, other than a tailings impoundment area, used to treat an effluent.

TREATMENT PROJECT. See SEWAGE ~.

TREATMENT SERVICES. 1. The broad range of emergency, outpatient and inpatient services provided by a regional community organization and includes (a) detoxification, (b) medical examination and diagnostic assessment, (c) development of a treatment plan for each person participating in a treatment program, (d) short term residential care, (e) rehabilitation measures, (f) counselling, (g) follow-up and support, (h) maintenance of records, (i) evaluation of modes of treatment. *Addiction Services Act*, R.S.P.E.I. 1988, c. A-3, s. 1(k). 2. Services, supplies, appliances and things rendered or furnished for the purpose of or in connection with diagnosis, treatment or care but does not include any basic health services.

TREATMENT WORKS. Buildings, structures, plant, machinery, equipment, devices, intakes and outfalls or outlets and other works designed for the interception, collection, settling, treating, dispersing, disposing or discharging of sewage or land drainage, or both, and includes land drainage, or both, and includes land appropriated for such purposes and uses. See ADVANCED ~; SECONDARY ~.

TREATY. *n.* 1. An agreement between states, political in nature, even though it may contain provisions of a legislative character which may pass into law, produces binding effects between the parties to it. 2. A treaty within the meaning of section 35 of the *Constitution Act, 1982.* 3. In international law, a binding agreement between states. P.W. Hogg, *Constitutional Law of Canada*, 3d ed. (Toronto: Carswell, 1992) at 281. 4. " . . . [A] treaty with the Indians is unique, . . . it is an agreement sui generis which is neither created nor terminated according to the rules of international law. . . it is clear that what characterizes a treaty is the intention to create obligations, the presence of mutually binding obligations and a certain measure of solemnity. . ." *Sioui v. Quebec (Attorney General)* (1990), (*sub nom. R. v. Sioui*) 56 C.C.C. (3d) 225 at 239, [1990] 1 S.C.R. 1025, 109 N.R. 22, 70 D.L.R. (4th) 427, [1990] 3 C.N.L.R. 127, 30 O.A.C. 280, the court per Lamer J. 5. "[In s. 88 of the *Indian Act*, R.S.C. 1970, c. I-6] . . . is not a word of art and . . . it embraces all such engagements made by persons in authority as may be brought within the term 'the word of the white man' the sanctity of which was, at the time of British exploration and settlement, the most important means of obtaining the goodwill and co-operation of the native tribes . . . On such assurance the Indians relied." *R. v. White* (1964), 50 D.L.R. (2d) 613 at 648-9, 52 W.W.R. 193 (B.C. C.A.), Norris J.A. See COMMERCIAL ~; INDIAN ~.

TREATY OF 1908. The treaty between His Majesty Edward VII and the United States respecting the demarcation of the international boundary between the United States and Canada signed at Washington on April 11, 1908. *International Boundary Commission Act*, R.S.C. 1985, c. I-16, s. 2.

TREATY REINSURANCE. " . . . [A] general policy between the original insurer and reinsurer, whereby a certain portion, or all, of the original insurer's risks are insured pursuant to the terms of the treaty by the reinsurer. . ." *Northern Union Insurance Co., Re* (1984), 55 C.B.R. (N.S.) 126 at 130, [1985] 2 W.W.R. 751, 33 Man. R. (2d) 81, [1985] I.L.R. 1-1899, 25 C.C.L.I. 112 (Q.B.), Kroft J.

TREE. *n.* 1. Includes, a growing tree or shrub planted or left growing on either side of a highway for the purpose of shade or ornament. *Municipal Act*, R.S.O. 1980, c. 302, s. 313. 2. A tree that is standing or is down and from which the limbs have not been removed. *Occupational Health and Safety Act*, R.R.O. 1980, Reg. 692, s. 107. See BORDER ~; BOUNDARY ~; CONSENSUAL ~; STRADDLE ~; STRAYING ~; VOLUNTARY ~.

TREE FARM LAND. Land having its best economic use under forest crop and on which (a) there is a stock of young growth in numbers of trees per hectare; (b) an approved working plan provides a reforestation program designed to establish a growing stock in numbers of trees per hectare; (c) there is a stock of mature timber that, according to an approved working plan, will be harvested on a sustained yield basis; or (d) there is any combination of them.

TREE TRESPASS. An action for destruction of a boundary tree. *Koenig v. Goebel* (1998), 162 Sask. R. 81 (Q.B.).

TRENCH. *n.* Any excavation in the ground where the vertical dimension from the highest point of the excavation to the point level with the lowest point of the excavation exceeds the least horizontal dimension of the excavation, such dimensions being taken in a vertical plane at right angles to the longitudinal centre line of the excavation, but does not include a shaft, caisson or cofferdam, or a cutting for the right of way of a public highway or railway. See PREFABRICATED ~ SUPPORT SYSTEM.

TRENCH DEPTH. The vertical dimension from the highest point of the excavation to a point level with the lowest point of the excavation.

TRENCHING. See ROCK ~.

TRESPASS. *n.* 1. " . . . [U]njustified invasion of another's possession. . ." *Harrison v. Carswell* (1975), 75 C.L.L.C. 14,286 at 614, [1976] 2 S.C.R. 200, [1975] 6 W.W.R. 673, 5 N.R. 523, 25 C.C.C. (2d) 186, 62 D.L.R. (3d) 68, the court per Dickson J. 2. All forcible, direct and immediate injury to the plaintiff's person, land or goods. May be committed by propelling a person or object onto the land or by refusing to leave land after a licence to enter has terminated. 3. " . . . [A]n action for the wrong committed in respect of the plaintiff's land by entry on the same without lawful authority." *Point v. Dibblee Construction Co.* [1934] O.R. 142 at 153, [1934] 2 D.L.R. 785 (H.C.), Armour J. 4. Entering or remaining without lawful authority on premises or land owned, occupied or controlled by another. See TREE ~.

TRESPASS AB INITIO. A person who lawfully entered another's land lost immunity from action for trespass if that person abused the privilege by committing a tort against the possessor or the possessor's property. John G. Fleming, *The Law of Torts*, 6th ed. (Sydney: The Law Book Co., 1983) at 95.

TRESPASS BY RELATION. A person who has a right to immediate possession of land may, upon entry, sue for any trespass committed after that right to entry accrued. John G. Fleming, *The Law of Torts*, 8th ed., (Sydney: The Law Book Company Limited, 1992), at 44.

TRESPASS DE BONIS ASPORTATIS. A writ used as a remedy in a case in which something was totally carried away or destroyed. John G. Fleming, *The Law of Torts*, 8th ed. (Sydney: The Law Book Co., 1992) at 52.

TRESPASSER. *n.* Someone who goes on another's land without any lawful authority, right or express or implied licence or invitation, and whose presence is either unknown to the occupier or is objected to if known.

TRESPASS TO CHATTELS. Unlawfully disturbing possession of goods by seizing them or removing them or by damaging them.

TRESPASS TO GOODS. Intentional interference or use of a chattel in such a way as to violate the plaintiff's possessory rights.

TRESPASS TO LAND. The act of entering on land which is in the possession of another person or placing, throwing, or erecting something on that land without any legal right to do so.

TRESPASS TO THE PERSON. Conventionally, the term "cause of action" means the fact or set of facts which give a right to bring an action, which in the case of trespass to the person is complete without resulting harm, meaning such cause of action arises on the commission itself of the wrongful act or, at the instance of a child, when the child reaches adulthood. In the case of negligence, the cause of action is not complete without resulting harm and so the cause of action is traditionally taken to arise on the combination of a wrongful act and resulting harm, subject in the case of an infant to the infant reaching the age of majority. *L. (H.) v. Canada (Attorney General)* (2002), 2002 SKCA 131, 227 Sask. R. 165, [2003] 5 W.W.R. 421, 287 W.A.C. 165 (C.A.).

TRESTLE LADDER. See EXTENSION ~.

TRIACTOR. *n.* A type of bet on a race to select, in the correct order, the first three horses in the official result. *Pari-Mutuel Betting Supervision Regulations*, SOR/91-365, s. 2.

TRIACTOR BET. A bet in which the person placing the bet undertakes to select in the exact order of finish the first three horses to finish in a race. *Race Tracks Tax Act*, R.S.O. 1990, c. R.1, s. 1.

TRIAL. *n.* 1. The hearing of a civil or criminal matter by a court. 2. " . . . In its popular and general sense a trial by jury consists of arraignment and plea, calling and swearing the jury, the opening address of Crown counsel the examination and cross-examination of witnesses for the Crown and for the defence, the closing addresses of counsel, the judge's charge and, last, the jury's verdict. The cases have, by and large, tended to give a rather more restricted meaning to the word 'trial' . . ." *R. v. Basarabas* (1982), 31 C.R. (3d) 193 at 197, [1982] 2 S.C.R. 730, [1983] 4 W.W.R. 289, 144 D.L.R. (3d) 115, 2 C.C.C. (3d) 257, 46 N.R. 69, the court per Dickson J. 3. [In the case of a trial by jury] . . . the trial proper does not start until the accused is given in charge to the jury which stage is, of course, not reached until after the plea has been taken and the adoption of this more restricted meaning of the word 'trial' has been widely accepted in our own courts for many years." *R. v. Dennis* (1960), 30 W.W.R. 545 at 550, [1960] S.C.R. 286, 32 C.R. 210, 125 C.C.C. 321, the court per Ritchie J. 4. " . . . [T]he investigation and determination of a matter in issue between parties before a competent tribunal, advancing through progressive stages from its submission to the court or jury to the pronouncement of judgment." *Catherwood v. Thompson* [1958]

O.R. 326 at 331, 13 D.L.R. (2d) 238 (C.A.), the court per Schroeder J.A. 5. The hearing of a civil or criminal cause. 6. In determining when an accused is required to be present during a trial, three types of actions which courts have found form part of the trial: (1) hearing motions on the admissibility of evidence, (2) communications between the presiding judge, or the Crown, and the jury, and (3) taking the court to view a person, place or thing. *R. v. Tran*, [1994] 2 S.C.R. 951. See FEDERAL COURT— ~ DIVISION; FAIR ~; FIELD ~; JURY ~S; MIS~; NEW ~; NOTICE OF READINESS FOR ~; SET DOWN FOR ~; SUMMARY ~.

TRIAL COURT. 1. The court by which an accused was tried and includes a judge or a provincial court judge. 2. The court which conducts the initial proceedings in civil litigation.

TRIAL DE NOVO. 1. A form of appeal in which the case is retried. 2. The distinction between "an appeal by holding a trial de novo and an appeal to the provincial Court of Appeal is that although the object of both is to determine whether the decision appealed from was right or wrong, in the latter case the question is whether it was right or wrong having regard to the evidence upon which it was based, whereas in the former the issue is to be determined without any reference, except for purposes of cross-examination, to the evidence called in the court appealed from and upon a fresh determination based upon evidence called anew and perhaps accompanied by entirely new evidence. *R. v. Dennis*, [1960] S.C.R. 286, 30 W.W.R. 545, 32 C.R. 210, 125 C.C.C. 321, at 548 [W.W.R.], Mr. Justice Ritchie. 3. A trial de novo envisages a new trial before a different tribunal than the one which originally decided the issue. *McKenzie v. Mason* (1992), 1992 CarswellBC 282, 72 B.C.L.R. (2d) 53, 9 C.P.C. (3d) 1, 96 D.L.R. (4th) 558, 18 B.C.A.C. 286, 31 W.A.C. 286 (C.A.) per Toy, J.A.

TRIAL DIVISION. 1. That division of the Court referred to in section 4 as the Federal Court Trial Division. *Federal Court Act*, R.S.C. 1985, c. F-7, s. 2. 2. The Trial Division of the Supreme Court of Newfoundland referred to in section 3 and Part II of The Judicature Act, 1936. *Judicature Act*, S. Nfld. 1986, c. 42, s. 40.

TRIAL JUDGES. The two judges trying an election petition or performing any duty to which the enactment in which the expression occurs has reference. *Dominion Controverted Elections Act*, R.S.C. 1985, c. C-39, s. 2.

TRIAL PERIOD. A period of time during which an employee is given a chance to demonstrate his or her abilities.

TRIAL PER PAIS. Trial by jury.

TRIAL PREPARATION. The work done at a time reasonably close in time to the trial. May include organization of documents for trial and preparation of exhibit books.

TRIAL WITHIN A TRIAL. An enquiry held by a judge to determine whether a statement or confession is admissible in evidence or to determine other questions of admissibility of evidence or of law which are for the judge alone to determine. The proceeding is held in the absence of the jury. See VOIR DIRE.

TRIB. *abbr*. Tribunal.

TRIB. CONC. *abbr*. Tribunal de la concurrence.

TRIBUNAL. *n*. 1. " . . . [A] generic word which includes courts in its scope. Thus, in this generic sense, all courts are tribunals, but all tribunals are not courts. . .." *Russell v. Radley* (1984), 11 C.C.C. (3d) 289 at 305, [1984] 1 F.C. 543, 5 Admin. L.R. 39 (T.D.), Muldoon J. 2. The first significant difference between courts and tribunals relates to the difference in the manner in which decisions are rendered by each type of adjudicating body. Courts must decide cases according to the law and are bound by stare decisis. By contrast, tribunals are not so constrained. When acting within their jurisdiction, they may solve the conflict before them in the way judged to be most appropriate. . . A second difference lies in the institutional organization and functioning of tribunals, as opposed to that of courts. Tribunals are intended to provide adjudicating bodies with specialized knowledge the courts are unable to offer. They are also designed structurally to provide decisions in a shorter amount of time and with less expense than the courts. *Weber v. Ontario Hydro*, 1995 CarswellOnt 240, 24 C.C.L.T. (2d) 217, 95 C.L.L.C. 210-027, 12 C.C.E.L. (2d) 1, 30 Admin. L.R. (2d) 1, 24 O.R. (3d) 358 (note), 125 D.L.R. (4th) 583, 183 N.R. 241, 30 C.R.R. (2d) 1, 82 O.A.C. 321, [1995] 2 S.C.R. 929, [1995] L.V.I. 2687-1. Iacobucci J. (dissenting in part) (La Forest and Sopinka JJ. concurring). 3. [S]tatutory tribunals created by Parliament or the Legislatures may be courts of competent jurisdiction to grant *Charter* remedies, provided they have jurisdiction over the parties and the subject matter of the dispute and are empowered to make the orders sought. *We-*

ber v. *Ontario Hydro*, 1995 CarswellOnt 240, 24 C.C.L.T. (2d) 217, 95 C.L.L.C. 210-027, 12 C.C.E.L. (2d) 1, 30 Admin. L.R. (2d) 1, 24 O.R. (3d) 358 (note), 125 D.L.R. (4th) 583, 183 N.R. 241, 30 C.R.R. (2d) 1, 82 O.A.C. 321, [1995] 2 S.C.R. 929, [1995] L.V.I. 2687-1. McLachlin J. (L'Heureux-Dubé, Gonthier and Major JJ. concurring). 3. A body or person which exercises a judicial or quasi-judicial function outside the regular court system. 4. One or more persons, whether or not incorporated and however described, on whom a statutory power of decision is conferred. 5. Includes any court, body, authority or person having authority to take or receive information, whether on its or one's behalf or on behalf of any other court, body, authority or person. *Foreign Extraterritorial Measures Act*, R.S.C. 1985, c. F-29, s. 2. 6. Any person or body, from whom an appeal lies to the Court, including any board, commission, committee, municipal authority, Minister, public official, or other public or governmental agency or authority, including the Lieutenant-Governor in Council, but not including a court or judge. *Rules of the Supreme Court*, S. Nfld. 1986, r. 57, s. 57.01. See ADMINISTRATIVE ~; ARBITRAL ~; CANADIAN IMPORT ~; DOMESTIC ~; EXTRA-PROVINCIAL ~; EXTRA TERRITORIAL ~; FEDERAL BOARD, COMMISSION OR OTHER ~; FOREIGN ~; MEMBER OF A ~; REVIEW ~; SERVICE ~.

TRIBUNAL APPEAL. Any appeal authorized by statute to be taken from a tribunal including any matters reserved, case stated or reference referred by a tribunal to the Court. *Rules of the Supreme Court*, S. Nfld. 1986, r. 57, s. 57.01.

TRIBUTE. *n.* A payment made to acknowledge something.

TRIED. *adj.* "[In s. 11 (b) of the Charter] . . . adjudicated and thus clearly encompasses the conduct of a judge in rendering a decision." *R. v. Rahey* (1987), 33 C.C.C. (3d) 289 at 320, 75 N.R. 81, [1987] 1 S.C.R. 588, 57 C.R. (3d) 289, 78 N.S.R. (2d) 183, 193 A.P.R. 183, 39 D.L.R. (4th) 481, La Forest J. (McIntyre J. concurring).

TRIGGER THEORIES. Four approaches have been developed in the U.S. and Canadian jurisprudence for determining the timing of property damage which is latent, or developing over time, and which does not become apparent immediately. The "Exposure Theory", the "Manifestation Theory", the "Injury in Fact Theory" and the "Continuous Trigger or Triple Trig-

ger Theory". *Alie v. Bertrand & Frère Construction Co.* (2002), 62 O.R. (3d) 345 (C.A.).

TRILLIUM. *n.* The plant, Trillium Ovatum, commonly known as western trillium or wake robin.

TRILOGY. *n.* " . . . [A] body of rational and cohesive principles to guide trial Courts in the assessment of damages in personal injury cases. The broad outline of these principles as sketched in three judgments delivered on January 19, 1978, sometimes referred to as the 'trilogy': Andrews v. Grand & Toy Alberta Ltd., [1978] 2 S.C.R. 229 . . . Arnold v. Teno; J.B. Jackson Ltd. v. Teno; Teno v. Arnold, [1978] 2 S.C.R. 287 . . . Thornton v. Prince George Bd. of School Trustees, [1978] 2 S.C.R. 367. . ." *Lindal v. Lindal* (1981), (sub nom. *Lindal v. Lindal (No. 2)*) 19 C.C.L.T. 1 at 23, [1982] 1 W.W.R. 433, 34 B.C.L.R. 273, 129 D.L.R. (3d) 263, 39 N.R. 361, [1981] 2 S.C.R. 629, the court per Dickson J.

TRIMMING. *n.* Any textile fibre product that (a) has been added to a consumer textile article for a decorative purpose; and (b) differs in textile fibre content from the article to which it has been added.

TRIMMINGS. *n.* Trim, ribbon, piping or lace sold by the yard or metre, but does not include trimmings supplied by a tailor, dressmaker, drapery manufacturer or upholsterer in producing clothing or draperies or in upholstering furniture even where a charge for such trimmings is made separately on the invoice to the customer.

TRIP. *n.* See CHARTERED ~; CONTINUOUS ~.

TRIPARTITE. *adj.* 1. Consisting of three parts. 2. Refers to a panel of adjudicators or arbitrators consisting of one member chosen by each party and a third neutral member who is usually the chair.

TRIPARTITE BOARD. A board composed of representatives of labour and management and a neutral or public representative.

TRIPLE AXLE. Any three consecutive axles that, (a) have their consecutive centres equally spaced; and (b) have their consecutive centres more than 1 metre apart; and that, (c) are articulated from an attachment to the vehicle common to the consecutive axles; or (d) are designed to automatically equalize the load between the three axles under all conditions of loading. *Highway Traffic Act*, R.S.O. 1980, c. 198, s. 97.

TRIPLE TRIGGER THEORY. Under this theory, the property damage is effectively deemed to have occurred from the initial exposure to the time when the damage became manifest or ought to have become manifest to the plaintiffs, and if alerted, to the insured. In that case, all policies in effect over that period are called upon to respond to the loss. *Alie v. Bertrand & Frère Construction Co.* (2002), 62 O.R. (3d) 345 (C.A.).

TROLLEY BUS. A bus propelled by electric power obtained from overhead wires.

TROLLEY COACH. A motor vehicle operated with electricity as the motive power through contact with overhead wires.

TROLLING. *n*. Taking or attempting to take fish with rod, hook or line when such rod, hook or line is being drawn through or over water by means of a boat or other water craft being propelled by mechanical or manual means.

TROUT. *n*. Includes char, speckled or brook trout, lake trout or togue, brown or Loch Leven trout, rainbow trout and ouananiche or landlocked salmon. See LAKE ~; RAINBOW ~; SEA ~.

TROVER. *n*. An action on the case, the remedy for a plaintiff who is deprived, by wrongful taking, detention or disposal, of goods.

TROY OUNCE. 480 grains. *Weights and Measures Act*, S.C. 1970-71-72, c. 36, schedule II.

TRU. *abbr*. Trueman's Equity Cases (N.B.), 1876-1903.

TRUANT OFFICER. Includes (a) a member of the Royal Canadian Mounted Police; (b) a special constable appointed for police duty on a reserve; and (c) a school teacher and a chief of the band, when authorized by the superintendent. *Indian Act*, R.S.C. 1985, c. I-5, s. 122.

TRUCE. See COMPULSORY ~.

TRUCK. *n*. 1. Every motor vehicle designed, used or maintained primarily for the transportation of property. 2. A motor vehicle designed for the conveyance of goods, a motor vehicle equipped with lifting device or a motor vehicle on which any machinery is permanently mounted. 3. A motor vehicle or trailer constructed or adapted primarily to carry pods, wares, merchandise freight or commodities but not passengers or luggage. 4. Includes any vehicle, other than a railway car, used in trans-

porting stock. See EXTRA-PROVINCIAL ~ UNDERTAKING; FAMILY FARM ~; FARM ~; FREE ON ~; GOVERNMENT ~; LOADED ~; PUBLIC MOTOR ~; PUBLIC ~; SEMI-TRAILER STAKE ~; TANK ~.

TRUCKER. *n*. A person for hire or reward who transports goods by motor vehicle and who is licensed to do so pursuant to an Act of Parliament or the legislature of a province.

TRUCKING DEPOT. Land where commercial vehicles are stationed and from which they are dispatched. *Commercial Concentration Tax Act*, R.S.O. 1990, c. C.16, s. 1.

TRUCK TRACTOR. *var*. **TRUCK-TRACTOR**. A motor vehicle designed and used primarily for drawing other vehicles and not constructed to carry a load other than a part of the weight of the vehicle drawn and of the load of the other vehicle.

TRUCK-TRAILER. *n*. Any type of trailer vehicle, including a single or multi-axle semi-trailer whereby part of the load is carried on the tractor unit by means of the upper and lower coupler assembly, and a full load bearing trailer, normally hauled by a truck unit, that is registered for use on a highway under the Highway Traffic Act and is used primarily for the transport of equipment or goods but does not include a vehicle, (a) used for transportation solely within an employer's actual place of business; or (b) used for farming operations but not used for carrying a load.

TRUCK-TRAILER REPAIRER. A person engaged in the repair and maintenance of truck-trailers who, (a) disassembles, adjusts, repairs and reassembles suspension systems, including bogies, axles, wheels, and rims, brake systems and electrical systems; (b) inspects, repairs and realigns frames; (c) inspects and repairs appurtenances such as tow-bars, hitches, turntables, landing gear and upper couplers; and (d) inspects, tests, adjusts, overhauls and replaces truck-trailer refrigeration system components, electrical circuits, pressure lines and fittings, and installs and removes truck-trailer refrigeration systems.

TRUE BILL. An indorsement made by a grand jury on a bill of indictment when after hearing the evidence they are satisfied that the accusation is probably true. *R. v. Chabot* (1980), 18 C.R. (3d) 258 at 264, [1980] 2 S.C.R. 985, 34 N.R.

361, 55 C.C.C. (2d) 385, 117 D.L.R. (3d) 527, the court per Dickson J.

TRUE CONDITION PRECEDENT. A future uncertain event upon which the obligations of both parties to the contract are dependent. The happening of the uncertain event is dependent upon the will of a third party.

TRUE COPY. 1. "It has been said (per Kay J., *Sharp v. McHenry*, (1887) 38 Ch. D. 427), that a copy is true if it is true in all essential particulars, so that no one can be misled as to the effect of the instrument, but that if the true effect is mis-stated it is immaterial whether it is mis-stated in favour of one party or of the other." *Commercial Credit Co. v. Fulton Brothers*, [1923] 3 D.L.R. 611 at 618, [1923] A.C. 798 (Can. P.C.), the board per Lord Sumner. 2. A legible copy of the original document produced by manual, photographic, electrical or mechanical means and certified as a true copy by notarial certificate or certificate of the debtor. 3. A copy of a legal document exactly the same as the original with notations, court stamps, signatures of parties and the court registrar, insertions and corrections written in the copy within quotation marks.

TRUE INNUENDO. One in which the defamatory meaning of words depends upon extrinsic circumstances. The words are not per se defamatory in their natural and ordinary meaning.

TRUE MACH NUMBER. The ratio of the true air speed of an aircraft to the local speed of sound at the flight altitude. *Canadian Aviation Regulations*, SOR/96-433, s. 101.01.

TRUE PENAL CONSEQUENCE. " . . . [W]hich would attract the application of s. 11 [of the Charter] is imprisonment or a fine which by its magnitude would appear to be imposed for the purpose of redressing the wrong done to society at large rather than to the maintenance of internal discipline within the limited sphere of activity." *R. v. Wigglesworth* (1987), 32 C.R.R. 219 at 237, [1988] 1 W.W.R. 193, 61 Sask. R 105, 60 C.R. (3d) 193, 81 N.R. 161, 28 Admin. L.R. 294, [1987] 2 S.C.R. 541, 24 O.A.C. 321, 45 D.L.R. (4th) 235, 37 C.C.C. (3d) 385, Wilson J. (Dickson C.J.C., Beetz, McIntyre, Lamer and La Forest JJ. concurring).

TRUNK STORM SEWER SYSTEM. A system for the collection and transmission of storm drainage.

TRUST. *n*. 1. A confidence or reliance which rests expressly or impliedly in a person (the trustee) for the benefit of another (the beneficiary or the cestui que trust). The simplest form of trust requires the trustee to hold property for the beneficiary's benefit. Must possess three essential attributes: certainty of intention, certainty of subject matter, and certainty of objects. 2. " . . . A trust arises . . . whenever a person is compelled in equity to hold property over which he has control for the benefit of others (the beneficiaries) in such a way that the benefit of the property accrues not to the trustee, but to the beneficiaries." *Guerin v. R.* (1984), [1985] 1 C.N.L.R. 120 at 155, [1984] 2 S.C.R. 335, 36 R.P.R. 1, 20 E.T.R. 6, [1984] 6 W.W.R. 481, 59 B.C.L.R. 301, 13 D.L.R. (4th) 321, 55 N.R. 161, Dickson J. (Beetz, Chouinard and Lamer JJ. concurring). See ACCELERATED ~; ACCUMULATION ~; ACTIVE ~; BLIND ~; BONDHOLDER'S ~; BREACH OF ~; CEMETERY OR PERPETUAL CARE ~; CESTUI QUE ~; CHARITABLE ~; CONSTRUCTIVE ~; DECLARATION OF ~; DEEMED ~; DISCRETIONARY ~; EMPLOYEES' CHARITY ~; EQUIPMENT ~; EXECUTED ~; EXECUTORY ~; EXPRESS ~; FOREIGN ~; FROZEN ~; FULLY-SECRET ~; GROSS ROYALTY ~; HALF-SECRET ~; HOLDING ~; IMPERFECT ~; IMPLIED ~; INTER VIVOS ~; INVESTMENT ~; MORTGAGE ~; OIL AND GAS ROYALTY ~; PASSIVE ~; PENSION ~; PERCENTAGE ~; POOLED INVESTMENT ~; PRIVATE ~; PUBLIC ~; RESIDENCE OF A ~; RESULTING ~; SECRET ~; SIMPLE ~; SPRINKLING ~; STOCK ESCROW ~; SUBSTANTIVE CONSTRUCTIVE ~; SYNDICATE ~; TESTAMENTARY ~; UNIT ~; VOTING ~.

TRUST AND LOAN CORPORATION. (a) A corporation that carries on business, or holds itself out, as a trust corporation, (b) a corporation that carries on business, or holds itself out as a loan corporation, or (c) a corporation that carries on business, or holds itself out, as a trust and loan corporation, and is a company licensed under the *Trust and Loan Companies Licensing Act*. *Financial Corporations Capital Tax Act*, R.S. Nfld. 1990, c. F-9, s. 2.

TRUST BUSINESS. The business of providing or offering to provide services to the public as (a) trustee, executor or administrator, (b) guardian of a minor's estate, or (c) committee of the estate of a mentally disordered person.

TRUST CAPACITY. The capacity of a trustee, executor, administrator, bailee, agent, receiver, liquidator, sequestrator, assignee, custodian, trustee in bankruptcy, guardian of the estate of a minor, committee of the estate of a mentally incompetent person, or any other similar capacity.

TRUST COMPANY. A body corporate incorporated or operated for the purpose of offering its services to the public to act as trustee, bailee, agent, executor, administrator, receiver, liquidator, assignee or guardian of a minor's estate or mentally incompetent person's estate and for the purpose of receiving deposits from the public and of lending or investing those deposits. *Trust and Loan Companies Act*, S.N.S. 1991, c. 7, s. 2. See LICENSED ~; PROVINCIAL ~.

TRUST CONDITION. In a contract for purchase and sale of real property, denotes an obligation imposed by one lawyer on the other lawyer concerning the mechanics of closing the transaction.

TRUST CORPORATION. A body corporate incorporated or operated for the purpose of offering its services to the public to act as trustee, bailee, agent, executor, administrator, receiver, liquidator, assignee, guardian of a minor's estate or committee of a mentally incompetent person's estate and for the purpose of receiving deposits from the public and of lending or investing such deposits. *Loan and Trust Corporations Act*, R.S.O. 1990, c. L.25, s. 1. See FOREIGN ~.

TRUST DEED. A separate document in favour of a trust company as trustee for the holders of the instruments which evidences an obligation, the usual way to issue a corporate obligation sold to the public, which may contain a specific charge or mortgage or a floating charge or both. See DEBENTURE ~.

TRUSTEE. *n*. 1. Someone who holds property in trust. 2. Includes a liquidator, receiver, receiver-manager, trustee in bankruptcy, assignee, executor, administrator, sequestrator or any other person performing a function similar to that performed by any such person. 3. An authorized trustee under the Bankruptcy Act (Canada) appointed for the bankruptcy district or division in which the stock of the vendor, or some part of it, is located, or the vendor's business or trade, or some part of it, is carried on, at the time of the sale in bulk; a person who is appointed trustee; and a person named as trustee by the creditors of the vendor in their written consent to a sale in bulk. *Bulk Sales acts*. 4. A person

who is declared by any Act to be a trustee or is, by the law of a province, a trustee, and, without restricting the generality of the foregoing, includes a trustee on an express trust created by deed, will or instrument in writing, or by parol. *Criminal Code*, R.S.C. 1985, c. C-46, s. 2. 5. Any person appointed as trustee under the terms of a trust indenture to which a corporation is a party and includes any successor trustee. 6. A member of a board of trustees. 7. The director of a corporation. See BARE ~; BOARD OF ~S; CUSTODIAN ~; JUDICIAL ~; LICENSED ~; MANAGING ~; OFFICIAL ~; PUBLIC ~; SCHOOL ~.

TRUSTEE DE SON TORT. To be liable as trustees *de son tort*, strangers to the trust must commit a breach of trust while acting as trustees. Such persons are not appointed trustees but "take on themselves to act as such and to possess and administer trust property". *Citadel General Assurance Co. v. Lloyds Bank Canada*, [1997] 3 S.C.R. 805.

TRUSTEE IN BANKRUPTCY. The person in whom a bankrupt's property is vested in trust for creditors.

TRUST FOR SALE. Imposes an obligation on the trustee to sell when the testator or settlor transfers property to the trustee on trust to convert the assets into money, and to distribute or invest these proceeds as directed.

TRUST FUND. 1. Money or property held in trust. 2. Money paid to a contractor by an owner or to a subcontractor by a contractor for the benefit of workers and people who supplied material for a contract. D.N. Macklem & D.I. Bristow, *Construction, Builders' and Mechanics' Liens in Canada*, 6th ed. (Toronto: Carswell, 1990-) at 1-3. See COMMON ~; WORKERS' ~.

TRUST INDENTURE. 1. Any deed, indenture or other instrument, including any supplement or amendment thereto, made by a body corporate under which the body corporate issues or guarantees debt obligations and in which a person is appointed as trustee for the holders of the debt obligations issued or guaranteed thereunder. 2. Any deed, indenture or other instrument, including any supplement or amendment thereto, made by a bank under which the bank issues bank debentures and in which a person is appointed as trustee for the holders of the bank debentures issued thereunder.

TRUST MONEY. All moneys received by a broker other than office money, and, without limiting the generality of the foregoing, includes money that belongs to a client in whole or in part or is to be held on his behalf or to his or another's order or direction. See UNGUARANTEED ~.

TRUST POWER. Imposes an obligation on the donee to exercise the power.

TRUTH SERUM. Sodium amytol or another similar substance.

TSE. *abbr*. Toronto Stock Exchange.

T.T. *abbr*. Tribunal du Travail (Jurisprudence en droit du travail).

T.T.C. *abbr*. Toronto Transit Commission.

T.T. (QUÉ.). *abbr*. Tribunal du travail (Québec).

TUBERCULIN TEST. The introduction into the skin of a person of a substance approved under the Food and Drugs Act (Canada) for the purpose of detecting sensitivity of that person to the tubercle bacillus.

TUBERCULOSIS. See OPEN ~.

TUG. *n*. 1. A steamship used exclusively for towing purposes. *Canada Shipping Act*, R.S.C. 1985, c. S-9, s. 2. 2. A ship used for towing or pushing purposes. *Pacific Pilotage Regulations*, C.R.C., c. 1270, s. 2.

TUGBOAT. *n*. Includes any vessel propelled by steam, combustive, electrical or other similar motive power, whether used exclusively in towage or not.

TUMULTUOUSLY. *adv*. Using actual or threatened force and violence in public disorder, confusion and uproar.

TUNA. *n*. Any fish by the name of tuna and includes fish of the species yellowfin (Thunnus albacares), bluefin (Thunnus thynnus), blackfin (Thunnus atlanticus), albacore (Thunnus alalunga), bigeye (Thunnus obesus), skipjack (Euthynnus elamis), common bonito (Sarda sarda), Pacific bonito (Sarda chiliensis) or false albacore (Euthynnus alletteratus). *Tuna Fishery Regulations*, C.R.C., c. 834, s. 2.

TUNA FISH CANNERY. A building, structure, machinery, appurtenances, appliances and apparatus occupied and used in the business of canning any of the species of tuna fish or of converting the fresh tuna fish into canned tuna fish. *Fisheries Act*, R.S.B.C. 1996, c. 149, s. 12.

TUNNEL. *n*. 1. A subterranean passage made by excavating beneath the overburden, into which a worker enters or is required to enter to work. 2. Includes tunnels, pits, shafts, slopes, airways, way leaves, rights of way, subways, crosscuts between tunnels, logments, sumps, and also all roadways, railways, tramways, haulageways, cableways, passageways, travelling-ways, and all other ways in such tunnels.

TURN AROUND SALES. Refers to persons purchasing gasoline duty-free and then immediately returning to Canada. *1185740 Ontario Ltd. v. Minister of National Revenue*, 2001 FCA 193, 273 N.R. 52, 35 Admin. L.R. (3d) 19, 208 F.T.R. 160 (note) (C.A.).

TURNING-OUT CONDITION. A lifeboat or life raft that is fully equipped but manned only by its launching crew.

TURNKEY. *n*. A gaoler.

TURNKEY PROJECT. " . . . [O]ne that was 100 per cent completed when turned over [to the owner] . . ." *First City Trust Co. v. Woodlawn Properties Ltd.* (1990), 9 R.P.R. (2d) 259 at 272, 80 Sask. R. 299, 66 D.L.R. (4th) 470 (Q.B.), Noble J.

TURPENTINE. *n*. Any of the four products known commercially as gum spirits of turpentine, steam distilled wood turpentine, sulphate wood turpentine and destructively distilled wood turpentine. See GUM SPIRITS OF ~; STEAM DISTILLED WOOD ~; SULPHATE WOOD ~.

TURPENTINE MIXTURE. Any commodity that contains turpentine mixed with any other material.

TURPENTINE SUBSTITUTE. Any commodity that is represented to be a substitute for turpentine or that has applied to it any trade mark, trade name or brand name incorporating the word "turpentine" or any part or simulation of the word "turpentine".

TURPIS CAUSA. [L.] A consideration so vile that no action can be founded on it. See EX TURPI CAUSA NON ORITUR ACTIO.

TURPIS EST PARS QUAE NON CONVENIT CUM SUO TOTO. [L.] A part which does not match the rest is unsightly.

TUTELAGE. *n*. Guardianship; being under a guardian's supervision.

TUTIUS SEMPER EST ERRARE ACQUIETANDO QUAM IN PUNIENDO, EX PARTE MISERICORDIAE QUAM EX PARTE

JUSTITIAE. [L.] It is always safer to err by acquitting instead of by punishing, to act out of mercy instead of justice.

TUTOR. *n*. An instructor; a guardian or protector.

TV. *abbr*. Television.

TWEEN DECK SPACE. A closed space between two consecutive continuous decks and bounded by permanent bulkheads. *Dangerous Goods Shipping Regulations*, C.R.C., c. 1419, s. 16.

TWIN MYTHS. 1. The notions that an "unchaste woman" is likely to have consented to sexual activity and that she is less worthy of belief. 2. Section 276(1) [of the Criminal Code, R.S.C. 1985, c. C-46] addresses the "twin myths". The section provides that evidence of the complainant's sexual activity with the accused or anyone else is not admissible to support an inference that, by reason of the sexual activity, the complainant is more likely to have consented to the sexual activity that forms the subject-matter of the charge; or is less worthy of belief. Section 276(2) operates to exclude evidence of the complainant's sexual activity if its admission would serve only to foster such twin-myth reasoning. Because of the danger twin-myth reasoning poses to the fairness of a trial, evidence of prior sexual conduct of the complainant probative of a relevant issue must be scrutinized under s. 276(2) before it may be admitted to ensure that its probative value is not outweighed by its prejudicial effect. The twin myths relate to "unchaste women". They have nothing to do with pre-pubescent children. *R. v. S. (L.H.)* (1999), 1999 CarswellBC 1018 (C.A.).

TWIST. *n*. In the axis of the bore of a firearm barrel, the inclination of rifling grooves expressed in terms of centimetres or inches of barrel length for one full turn of the grooves. F.A. Jaffe, *A Guide to Pathological Evidence*, 3d ed. (Toronto: Carswell, 1991) at 228. See CANADA ~.

TWISTING. *n*. A practice by which an insurance policy holder is improperly induced by an agent to replace an existing policy with a new policy of less value to the policy holder.

TWO AXLE GROUP. Two consecutive single axles, not including the front axle of a motor vehicle, (a) that are entirely within either a motor vehicle or trailer or semi-trailer; (b) in which the spacing between the consecutive axles is less than 2 metres; and (c) which are not included in a three axle group within the meaning of clause (o) or a four axle group within the meaning of clause (h). *Highway Traffic Act*, R.S.O. 1980, c. 198, s. 97.

TWO-FAMILY DWELLING. A building designed exclusively for occupancy by two families living independently of each other. Canada regulations.

TWO JUSTICES. Two or more justices of the peace, assembled or acting together. *Interpretation Act*, R.S.C. 1985, c. I-21, s. 35.

TWO OR MORE TRACKS. Two or more main tracks upon any of which the current of traffic may be in either specified direction. *Regulations No. O-8, Uniform Code of Operating Rules*, C.R.C., c. 1175, Part III, s. 2.

TWO POST CLAIM. A mineral claim or fractional mineral claim located on or before February 28, 1975 or a two post claim located after January 1, 1978. *Mineral Act*, R.S.B.C. 1985, c. 259, s. 1.

TWO-THIRDS VOTE. The affirmative vote of two-thirds of the members of a council present at a meeting thereof. *Municipal Act*, R.S.O. 1980, c. 302, s. 1.

TWP. *abbr*. Township.

TYPE. *n*. 1. A class of things having common characteristics. 2. (a) When used in reference to personnel licensing, a specific make and model of aircraft, including modifications thereto that do not change its handling or flight characteristics, and (b) when used in reference to the certification of aircraft, a classification of aircraft having similar design characteristics; *Canadian Aviation Regulations*, SOR/96-433, s. 101.01.

TYPE CERTIFICATE. A document issued by (a) the Minister certifying that the type design of an aircraft, aircraft engine, aircraft propeller or aircraft appliance meets the applicable standards for that aeronautical product, as recorded in the type certificate data sheets, and includes a type approval issued before October 10, 1996 under section 214 of the *Air Regulations*, or (b) the foreign airworthiness authority having jurisdiction over the type design of an aeronautical product that is equivalent to a document referred to in paragraph (a) and has been accepted by the Minister for the purpose of issuing a certificate of airworthiness; *Canadian Aviation Regulations*, SOR/96-433, s. 101.01.

TYPE DESIGN. (a) the drawings and specifications, and a listing of those drawings and specifications that are necessary to define the design features of an aeronautical product in compliance with the standards applicable to the aeronautical product, (b) the information on dimensions, materials and manufacturing processes that is necessary to define the structural strength of an aeronautical product, (c) the approved sections of the aircraft flight manual, where required by the applicable standards of airworthiness, (d) the airworthiness limitations section of the instructions for continued airworthiness specified in the applicable chapters of the *Airworthiness Manual*; and (e) any other data necessary to allow, by comparison, the determination of the airworthiness and, where applicable, the environmental characteristics of later aeronautical products of the same type or model; *Canadian Aviation Regulations*, SOR/96-433, s. 101.01.

TYPE FOSSIL SPECIMEN. Any fossil specimen or portion thereof of a biological species used in the original scientific study and published description of that species.

TYPE MINERAL SPECIMEN. Any mineral specimen or portion thereof of a mineral species used in the original scientific study and published description of that species.

TYRE. *n*. That part of a wheel, roller or other contrivance for the moving of any object upon a highway which comes into direct contact with the surface of the highway. *Highway Traffic Act*, R.S. Nfld. 1970, c. 152, s. 2. See TIRE.

U.B.C. L. REV. *abbr*. University of British Columbia Law Review.

UBERRIMAE FIDEL. [L. of the utmost good faith] " . . . [T]here is a limited class of contracts in which one of the parties is presumed to have means of knowledge which are not accessible to the other and is, therefore, bound to tell him everything which may be supposed likely to affect his judgment. They are known as contracts uberrimae fidei, and may be avoided on the ground of non-disclosure of material facts. Contracts of insurance of every kind are in this class. . ." *Gabriel v. Hamilton Tiger-Cat Football Club Ltd.* (1975), 8 O.R. (2d) 285 at 290, 57 D.L.R. (3d) 669 (H.C.), O'Leary J.

UBERRIMA FIDES. [L.] " . . . [A] longstanding tenet of insurance law which holds parties to an insurance contract to a standard of utmost good faith in their dealing. It places a heavy burden on those seeking insurance coverage to make full and complete disclosure of all relevant information when applying for a policy." *Coronation Insurance Co. v. Taku Air Transport Ltd.*, [1991] 3 S.C.R. 622 at 636, [1992] 1 W.W.R. 217, 61 B.C.L.R. (2d) 41, 4 C.C.L.I. (2d) 115, 85 D.L.R. (4th) 609, [1992] I.L.R. 1-2797, 131 N.R. 241, 6 B.C.A.C. 161, 13 W.A.C. 161, Cory J.

UBI ALIQUID CONCEDITUR, CONCEDITUR ET ID SINE QUO RES IPSA ESSE NON POTEST. [L.] Where anything is granted, that without which the thing itself cannot exist is also granted.

UBI CESSAT RATIO, IBI CESSAT LEX. [L.] Where reason ceases, the law ceases.

UBI CESSAT REMEDIUM ORDINARIUM IBI DECURRITUR AD EXTRAORDINARIUM. [L.] When the ordinary remedy fails, recourse is had to the extraordinary.

UBI DAMNA DANTUR, VICTUS VICTORI IN EXPENSIS CONDEMNARI DEBET. [L.] Where damages are given, the losing party should pay the winner's costs.

UBI EADEM RATIO IBI IDEM JUS. [L.] Where there is a like reason, there is like law.

UBI JUS IBI REMEDIUM. [L.] Where a right exists, there is a remedy. When there is no existing line of authority prescribing a just remedy for a wrong, the law must fashion one. *Leacock v. Whalen, Beliveau & Associes Inc.* (1998), 52 B.C.L.R. (3d) 247 (C.A.).

UBI LEX ALIQUEM COGIT OSTENDERE CAUSAM NECESSE EST QUOD CAUSA SIT JUSTA ET LEGITIMA. [L.] Where the law compels anyone to show cause, the cause must be just and lawful.

UBI LEX NON DISTINGUIT, NEC NOS DISTINGUERE DEBEMUS. [L.] Where the law does not distinguish, we should not either.

UBI NON EST PRINCIPALIS NON POTEST ESSE ACCESSORIUS. [L.] Where there is no principal, an accessory cannot be.

UBI QUID GENERALITER CONCEDITUR INEST HAEC EXCEPTIO SI NON ALIQUID SIT CONTRA JUS FASQUE. [L.] Where a grant is interpreted generally, this exception is always implied: that nothing should be contrary to law and right.

UBI SUPRA. [L.] At the place mentioned above.

UBI VERBA CONJUNCTA NON SUNT, SUFFICIT ALTERUTRUM ESSE FACTUM. [L.] Where words do not agree it suffices that one of them is complied with.

U.C. *abbr*. Upper Canada.

U.C. CH. *abbr*. Grant, Upper Canada Chambers Reports, 1846-1852.

U.C. CHAMB. *abbr*. Upper Canada Chambers Reports, 1846-1852.

U.C.C.P. *abbr*. Upper Canada Common Pleas Reports, 1850-1882.

U.C.E. & A. *abbr*. Upper Canada Error & Appeal Reports, 1846-1866.

U.C. JUR. *abbr*. Upper Canada Jurist, 1844.

U.C. JURIST. *abbr*. Upper Canada Jurist (1844-1848).

U.C.K.B. *abbr*. Upper Canada, King's Bench Reports (Old Series), 1831-1844.

U.C.L.J. *abbr*. Upper Canada Law Journal (1855-1864).

U.C.O.S. *abbr*. Upper Canada, King's Bench Reports (Old Series), 1831-1844.

U.C.Q.B. *abbr*. Upper Canada, Queen's Bench Reports, 1844-1882.

UDRP. *abbr*. Uniform Domain Name Dispute Resolution Policy.

U.F.C. *abbr*. Unified Family Court.

UHF. Ultra-high frequency. *Canadian Aviation Regulations*, SOR/96-433, s. 101.01(1).

U.K. *abbr*. United Kingdom.

ULCER. *n*. An open sore of mucous membrane or skin. F.A. Jaffe, *A Guide to Pathological Evidence*, 3d ed. (Toronto: Carswell, 1991) at 228.

ULLAGE. *n*. The percentage indicated in the schedules or the percentage calculated by use of the formula specified, means the percentage of free space to be left in a container in relation to the total capacity of the container. *Dangerous Goods Shipping Regulations*, C.R.C., c. 1419, s. 2.

ULTIMATE HEIR. The person entitled to take by descent or distribution the property of whatsoever nature of an intestate in the event of failure of heirs or next of kin entitled to take that property by the law in force before July 1, 1929. The Crown in right of Alberta is the ultimate heir (a) of any person dying intestate in fact with regard to any property situated in Alberta, and (b) of any person domiciled in Alberta and dying intestate with regard to any movable property or chose in action wherever situated. *Ultimate Heir Act*, R.S.A. 2000, c. U-1, s. 1.

ULTIMATE LIMITATION PERIOD. A limitation period beyond which no extension, postponement or suspension of time for any reason,

such as incapacity or discoverability, can be obtained. The period of 30 years is commonly used.

ULTIMATE LIMIT STATES. Those states concerning safety and include exceeding the load carrying capacity, overturning, sliding, fracture and fatigue.

ULTIMATE NEGLIGENCE. The last clear chance or last opportunity doctrine.

ULTIMATUM. *n*. A final concession, condition or offer.

ULTIMA VOLUNTAS TESTATORIS EST PERIMPLENDA SECUNDUM VERAM INTENTIONEM SUAM. [L.] The testator's last will should be fulfilled according to true intentions.

ULTIMUM SUPPLICIUM. [L. ultimate punishment] Death.

ULTRA. *prep*. [L.] Beyond.

ULTRA-LIGHT AEROPLANE. (a) A single-seat aeroplane that has a launch weight of 165 kg (363.8 pounds) or less, and a wing area, expressed in square metres, of not less than the launch weight minus 15, divided by 10, and in no case less than 10 m², (b) a two-seat instructional aeroplane that has a launch weight of 195 kg (429.9 pounds) or less, and a wing area, expressed in square metres, of not less than 10 m² and a wing loading of not more than 25 kg/m² (5.12 pounds/ft.²), the wing loading being calculated using the launch weight plus the occupant weight of 80 kg (176.4 pounds) per person, or (c) an advanced ultra-light aeroplane. *Canadian Aviation Regulations*, SOR/96-433, s. 101.01.

ULTRA PETITA. [L.] Beyond what is sought.

ULTRASOUND. *n*. Mechanical energy having frequencies above 20 kilohertz.

ULTRA VIRES. [L. beyond the powers] 1. Describes a statute judicially determined to be outside the powers conferred by the Constitution on the legislative body that enacted the statute; it is therefore invalid. 2. That a particular transaction is outside the capacity or power of a corporation. 3. " . . . [I]s not a principle of the English common law and does not rest upon any theory as to the nature of corporations or as to the legal relationship subsisting between a corporation and its governing body . . . It is a rule resting upon the interpretation of the legislative enactments through which the companies to which it applies derive their corporate existence and capacity."

Prevost v. Bedard (1915), 24 D.L.R. 153 at 154, 51 S.C.R. 149, Duff J. 4. Describes an invalid enactment, order or decision made outside the jurisdiction of the body purporting to make it. 5. . . A by-law is ultra vires[:] if it prohibits a condition or activity for which a conviction could be sustained under the criminal law. . . if it is repugnant to the general law. . . if, notwithstanding a general delegated power, it does not conform with a specific power as to the same subject-matter, contained in the same or some other statute. . . if, notwithstanding an apparent general statutory delegation of authority for its enactment, the same subject-matter is dealt with in a comprehensive way in a statute passed in the interest of all the inhabitants of the province, and this is true even in the absence of repugnancy." *Ontario (Attorney General) v. Mississauga (City)* (1981), 15 M.P.L.R. 212 at 222-4, 33 O.R. (2d) 395, 10 C.E.L.R. 91, 124 D.L.R. (3d) 385 (C.A.), Weatherston J.A.

UMBILICAL CORD. The cord containing two arteries and one vein which connects a fetus' navel with the placenta. F.A. Jaffe, *A Guide to Pathological Evidence*, 3d ed. (Toronto: Carswell, 1991) at 228.

UMBILICUS. *n.* [L.] The navel. F.A. Jaffe, *A Guide to Pathological Evidence*, 3d ed. (Toronto: Carswell, 1991) at 21.

UMBRELLA POLICY. [Insurer's] policy expressly and correctly identifies itself as an umbrella policy. An umbrella policy generally provides two types of coverage: standard form excess coverage; and broader coverage than that provided by the underlying insurance including a duty to defend lawsuits not covered by the underlying coverage. An umbrella policy is in effect a hybrid policy that combines aspects of both a primary policy and an excess policy. *Trenton Cold Storage v. St. Paul Fire & Marine Insurance Co.* (2001), 146 O.A.C. 348 (C.A.).

UMPIRAGE. *n.* Performing the duties of an umpire; arbitration.

UMPIRE. *n.* The Governor in Council appoints from among the judges of the Federal Court such number of umpires as the Governor in Council considers necessary for the purposes of this Employment Insurance Act. Umpires hear appeals from board of referees under the Act.

U.N. *abbr.* United Nations.

UNABLE. *adj.* Cannot because of physical inability.

UNA CUM OMNIBUS ALIIS. [L.] Along with everything else.

UNALLOCATED SURPLUS. Includes any net proceeds from the sale of assets on dissolution after the liabilities and the claims of creditors and shareholders have been satisfied.

UNANIMOUS RESOLUTION. A resolution (a) passed unanimously at a properly convened meeting of the corporation by all the persons entitled to exercise the powers of voting by this Act or the by-laws and representing the total unit factors for all the units; or (b) signed by all the persons who, at a properly convened meeting of a corporation, would be entitled to exercise the powers of voting conferred by this Act or the by-laws. *Condominium acts.*

UNANIMOUS SHAREHOLDER AGREEMENT. A written agreement to which all the shareholders of a corporation are or are deemed to be parties, whether or not any other person is also a party, or a written declaration by a person who is the beneficial owner of all the issued shares of a corporation.

UNASCERTAINED GOODS. 1. Goods defined by referring to a genus. G.H.L. Fridman, *Sale of Goods in Canada*, 3d ed. (Toronto: Carswell 1986) at 57. 2. Goods identified only by description. G.H.L. Fridman, *Sale of Goods in Canada*, 3d ed. (Toronto: Carswell, 1986) at 89.

UNAUTHORIZED. *adj.* 1. Done or made without authority, implied, actual or apparent. 2. In relation to a signature or an endorsement, means one made without actual, implied or apparent authority and includes a forgery.

UNAUTHORIZED INVESTMENT OR LOAN. An investment or loan of a company's own funds or its deposits and investment money that is not authorized by, or is expressly prohibited or is made in contravention of any limitations or conditions prescribed.

UNAUTHORIZED LOAN. See UNAUTHORIZED INVESTMENT OR LOAN.

UNAUTHORIZED STRIKE. A strike begun without authority of union officials or by a minority of members of a union.

UNAUTHORIZED USE. The use of a credit card where that use of the credit card (a) is not by the credit card customer; and (b) is not authorized by the credit card customer.

UNAVAILABILITY. *n.* In the context of determining the necessity of admitting hearsay evidence, the unavailability of a witness is determined as follows. Without restricting the precise content of "unavailability", the categories of absence recognized under s. 715 [of the Criminal Code], specifically death, illness, and insanity, offer a helpful guide to the types of circumstances under which it will be sufficiently necessary to consider the admission of the witness's former testimony. *R. v. Hawkins*, [1996] 3 S.C.R. 1043.

UNA VIA ELECTA NON DATUR REGRESSUS AD ALTERAM. [L.] Once one way is chosen, one must not turn back to the alternative way.

UNAVOIDABLE ACCIDENT. A defence to a negligence action. An occurrence which was not intended and which under the circumstances could not be foreseen or prevented by the exercise of reasonable precautions.

UNBECOMING. See CONDUCT ~.

U.N.B.L.J. *abbr.* University of New Brunswick Law Journal.

U.N.B. L. REV. *abbr.* University of New Brunswick Law Journal (Revue de droit de l'Université, du Nouveau-Brunswick).

UNBROKEN LOT. A regular lot whose area is not diminished or increased by a natural or artificial feature shown on the original plan. *Surveys Act*, R.S.O. 1990, c. S.30, s. 1.

UNCALLED CAPITAL. The part of the nominal value of shares a company issued which does not yet need to be paid.

UNCERTAINTY. *n*. In interpreting a will, a general reason to consider some gift or provision void because it is impossible to ascertain what the testator's intention was.

UNCERTIFIED SECURITY. A security, not evidenced by a security certificate, the issue and any transfer of which is registered or recorded in records maintained for that purpose by or on behalf of the issuer. *Business Corporations Act*, R.S.O. 1990, c. B.16, s. 53.

UNCHASTE CHARACTER. " . . . An unchaste character may be indicated where a female person's actions or behaviour have been marked by lewdness, wantonness, or promiscuity, or even by what is sometimes termed looseness, even though there has been no loss of virginity or no indulgence in earlier intercourse. . ." *W. v. Trecartin* (1980), 32 N.B.R. (2d) 621 at

623, 78 A.P.R. 621 (Q.B.), Dickson J. See CHASTE.

UNCLE. *n*. In relation to any person, means a brother of the father or mother of that person.

UNCONSCIONABLE. *adj*. The allegation that a contract is unconscionable is of course a serious one, carrying as it does the implication of unfair use of power amounting to fraud. . . . The term ["unconscionable"] was developed by courts of Equity to refer to bargains that were "contrary to good conscience," against which Equity would grant relief in the form of rescision. *Gindis v. Brisbourne*, 2000 BCCA 73, 72 B.C.L.R. (3d) 19 (C.A.), Per Newbury J.A.

UNCONSCIONABILITY. *n*. 1. " . . . [E]quity will grant relief where there is inequality combined with substantial unfairness, and that in its modern application poverty and ignorance combined with lack of independent advice on the part of the party seeking relief (plus, presumably, some evidence of unfairness) places an onus on the other party to show that the bargain was in fact fair. . ." *Smyth v. Szep* (1992), 8 C.C.L.I. (2d) 81 at 90, 63 B.C.L.R. (2d) 52, [1992] 2 W.W.R. 673, 10 B.C.A.C. 108, 21 W.A.C. 108 (C.A.), Taylor J.A. (Wood J.A. concurring). 2. "The test for setting aside an agreement on grounds of unconscionability was set out by McIntyre J.A. in Harry v. Kreutziger (1978) 9 B.C.L.R. 166 . . . (C.A.) [at p. 173]: 'Where a claim is made that a bargain is unconscionable, it must be shown . . . that there was inequality in the position of the parties due to the ignorance, need or distress of the weaker, which would leave him in the power of the stronger, coupled with proof of substantial unfairness in the bargain.' The essential idea of unconscionability is therefore that of fraud." *Ahone v. Hollowa* (1988), 30 B.C.L.R. (2d) 368 at 374 (C.A.), the court per McLachlin J.A. 3. Refers to a false, misleading or deceptive consumer representation.

UNCONSCIONABLE TRANSACTION. "The Court will exercise its equitable jurisdiction to set aside an unconscionable transaction . . . where undue advantage had been taken of an inequality in bargaining power. . ." *Ronald Elwyn Lister Ltd. v. Dunlop Canada Ltd.* (1979), 9 B.L.R. 290 at 304, 27 O.R. (2d) 168, 32 C.B.R. (N.S.), 4, 50 C.P.R. (2d) 50, 105 D.L.R. (3d) 684 (C.A.), Weatherston J.A. (Lacourcière J.A. concurring).

UNCONSCIOUSNESS. *n*. Is used in the sense that the accused, like the sleepwalker, is shown "not to have known what he was doing"....This excludes the person who is provoked and says, "I couldn't help myself", or who simply professes to be at a loss to explain uncharacteristic conduct. *R. v. Stone*, [1999] 2 S.C.R. 290.

UNCONTESTED DIVORCE. A divorce proceeding in which a respondent does not file a counter-petition or answer.

UNCROPPED. *adj.* Not under cultivation for the purpose of obtaining a crop.

UNCULTIVATED LAND. 1. Land that is in its natural wild state, and includes also land that has been wholly or partially cleared, but is otherwise in its natural state. 2. Land that has not been reclaimed and is not being used for the purpose of tillage, orchard, meadow or pasture, or as land surrounding a dwelling house.

UNDELIVERABLE LETTER. Any letter that for any reason cannot be delivered to the addressee thereof and includes any letter the delivery of which is prohibited by law or is refused by the addressee or on which postage due is not paid by the sender on demand. *Canada Post Corporation Act*, R.S.C. 1985, c. C-10, s. 2.

UNDER. *prep.* 1. Arising out of, i.e. with reference to or arising out of an agreement. 2. With authority from, i.e. a claim is made under a statute when the statute is the source of the right to make the claim. 3. "A claim is made under a statute . . . when that statute is the law which, assuming the claim to be well-founded, would be the source of the plaintiff's right." *Bensol Customs Brokers v. Air Canada* (1979), 99 D.L.R. (3d) 623 at 627, [1979] 2 F.C. 575 (C.A.), Pratte J.A. (Hyde D.J. concurring). 4. " . . . '[W]ith reference to or arising out of an agreement . . ." *Osman v. Callander* (1986), 48 Sask. R. 23 at 24 (Q.B.), MacLeod J.

UNDERBARGAIN. *v.* To enter into a collective agreement which explicitly or by implication does not cover all employees which a plain reading of the certificate authorizing the union as bargaining agent would suggest should be included in the bargaining unit.

UNDER CONTROL. The state of being manoeuvrable in accordance with these Regulations or the regulations under the Canada Shipping Act for preventing collisions at sea. *Air Regulations*, C.R.C., c. 2, s. 101.

UNDER DECK. In a hold, or in a covered space that is enclosed between steel bulkheads and is capable of being effectively closed against the weather. *Dangerous Goods Shipping Regulations*, C.R.C., c. 14, s. 2.

UNDEREMPLOYED WORKER. A person who is able and available to work full-time but is unable to find full-time employment.

UNDERFLOOR-RACEWAY. *n.* A raceway suitable for use in the floor.

UNDERGRADUATE. *n.* A student enrolled at but not graduated from a university or other educational institution.

UNDERGROUND. *adj.* Within the confines of any shaft, tunnel, caisson or cofferdam.

UNDERGROUND MANAGER. Any person who has charge of the underground workings of a mine under the control and supervision of the manager and who possesses a certificate as such issued under this or some former Act. *Coal Mines Regulation Act*, R.S.N.S. 1989, c. 73, s. 4.

UNDERGROUND MINE. A mine that is not a surface mine.

UNDERGROUND MINING CONCESSION. A mining property under private land sold for the purpose of operating mining rights.

UNDERGROUND RESERVOIR. Any mass of rock, consolidated or not, containing natural or artificial cavities, which is suitable to be used for the purpose of storing mineral substances or industrial products or residues or of permanently disposing thereof, or which may become suitable to be so used.

UNDER-INSURANCE. Where an insured is insured for a sum that is less than the insurable value of the subject-matter insured, in the case of an unvalued policy, or less than the value of the subject-matter insured specified by the policy, in the case of a valued policy, the insured is deemed to be self-insured in respect of the uninsured difference. *Marine Insurance Act*, S.C. 1993, c. 22, s. 2.

UNDER LEASE. *var.* **UNDER-LEASE**. 1. A lessee's grant to someone else (the under-lessee, under-tenant, sub-lessee or sub-tenant) of part of the whole interest under the original lease which reserves a reversion to the lessee. 2. Includes an agreement for an under lease where the under lessee has become entitled to have his under lease granted. *Landlord and Tenant acts*.

UNDER LESSEE. *var.* **UNDER-LESSEE**. Includes any person deriving title under or from a lessee or an under lessee. *Landlord and Tenant acts*.

UNDERLYING CONDITION. See PRE-EX-ISTING OR ~.

UNDERPINNING. *n.* Excavation under existing footings, construction of forms flush with the inner edge of the footings and the pouring of concrete to the same width and depth as the existing footings.

UNDERPRIVILEGED PERSON. See ECO-NOMICALLY ~.

UNDER SEAL. Some form mark amounting to a seal has been affixed to the parties' signatures to the contract. See CONTRACT ~.

UNDERSTANDING. *n.* " . . . [A]ppropriate to express a legally binding agreement. Thus, if A. agrees to do something on the understanding (another equally familiar phrase is 'on the footing') that another will do something else that is prima facie party evidence of a legally binding agreement unless the rest of the language used or the surrounding circumstances point to a different conclusion." *Campbell v. Inland Revenue Commissioners*, [1968] 3 All E.R. 588 at 601 (U.K. H.L.), Lord Upjohn.

UNDERTAKE. *v.* To begin, commence; to promise to do something. See OFFER TO ~.

UNDERTAKEN. *adj.* "[In reference to a suit] . . . 'commenced' . . ." *C. v. Director of Children's Aid Society of Winnipeg* (1978), 90 D.L.R. (3d) 94 at 97, 7 R.F.L. (2d) 385 (Q.B.), Hamilton J.

UNDERTAKING. *n.* 1. An assurance. 2. Every kind of business that an association or company is authorized to carry on. 3. An enterprise or activity, or a proposal, plan or program in respect of an enterprise or activity. 4. An undertaking in Form 12 given to a justice or judge. *Criminal Code*, R.S.C. 1985, c. C-46, s. 493. 5. " . . . I adopt the definition of an undertaking proposed by Judge Lesage in . . . Mode Amazone c. Comité conjoint de Montréal de l'Union internationale des ouvriers du vêtement pour dames, [1983] T.T. 227 at 231: '(Translation) The undertaking consists in an organization of resources that together suffice for the pursuit, in whole or in part, of specific activities. These resources may, according to the circumstances, be limited to legal, technical, physical, or abstract elements. Most often, particularly where there is no operation of the undertaking by a subcontractor, undertaking may be said to be constituted when because a sufficient number of those components that permit the specific activities to be conducted or carried out are present, one can conclude that the very foundations of the undertaking exist: in other words when the undertaking may be described as a going concern. In [Barnes Security Service Ltd. c. A.I.M., Local 2235, [1972] T.T. 1], Judge René Beaudry, as he then was, expressed exactly the same idea when he stated that the undertaking consists of "everything used to implement the employer's ideas." ' " *Union des employés de service, local 298 v. Bibeault* (1988), (*sub nom. Syndicat national des employés de la Commission scolaire régionale de l'Outaouais v. U.E.S.*) 35 Admin. L.R. 153 at 209, 95 N.R. 161, [1988] 2 S.C.R. 1048, the court per Beetz J. 6. " . . . [I]s not a physical thing, but is an arrangement under which . . . physical things are used." *Regulation Control of Radio Communication in Canada, Re*, [1932] A.C. 304 at 315, [1932] 1 W.W.R. 563, 39 C.R.C. 49, [1932] 2 D.L.R. 81 (P.C.), Viscount Dunedin for their Lordships. 7. Refers to the whole of the enterprise within which a work or works is or are situated. See BROAD-CASTING RECEIVING ~ BROADCAST-ING ~; COOPERATIVE ~; DISTRIBU-TION ~; ELECTRICITY ~; EXTRA-PROVINCIAL BUS ~; EXTRA-PROVINCIAL TRUCK ~; EXTRA PROVINCIAL ~; FEDERAL WORK, ~ OR BUSI-NESS; GAS ~; INDUSTRIAL ~; LOCAL ~; MOTOR VEHICLE ~; PROGRAMMING ~; PUBLIC UTILITY ~ ; SMALL ~ ; TELE-COMMUNICATIONS ~; TRANSPORTA-TION ~.

UNDERTIME. *n.* Working less time than scheduled or agreed.

UNDER WAY. *var.* **UNDERWAY**. 1. The state of being on the surface of the water but not moored or fastened to any fixed object on the land or in the water. 2. A vessel is under way when it is not at anchor, made fast to the shore or aground.

UNDERWRITER. *n.* A person who, (a) as principal, agrees to purchase a security for the purpose of distribution; (b) as agent, offers for sale or sells a security in connection with a distribution; or (c) participates directly or indirectly in a distribution described in paragraph (a) or (b), but does not include (d) a person whose interest in the transaction is limited to receiving the usual and customary distributor's or seller's commission payable by an underwriter or issuer; (e) a mutual fund that accepts its securities for surrender and resells them; (f) a corporation that pur-

UNDULY

chases shares of its own issue and resells them; or (g) a bank with respect to securities described in this Act and to prescribed banking transactions. *Securities acts.* See LEADING PRINCIPAL ~; SECURITIES ~; SUB-~.

UNDERWRITING. *n.* With respect to a security, means the primary or secondary distribution of the security, in respect of which distribution (a) a prospectus is required to be filed, accepted or otherwise approved pursuant to a law enacted in Canada or in a jurisdiction outside Canada for the supervision or regulation of trade in securities; or (b) a prospectus would be required to be filed, accepted or otherwise approved but for an express exemption contained in or given pursuant to a law mentioned in paragraph (a). *Competition Act,* R.S.C. 1985, c. C-34, s. 5(2).

UNDERWRITING AGREEMENT. Any contract under which a corporation undertakes conditionally or unconditionally to subscribe for shares, bonds or debentures of another corporation with a view to the resale thereof or of a part thereof.

UNDILUTED. *adj.* 1. A condition that does not include air or other gases in excess of the quantity necessary for the processing requirements at a mine or mill. Canada regulations. 2. Not having water added primarily for the purposes of meeting the limits of authorized deposits prescribed by section 5. *Metal Mining Liquid Effluent Regulations,* C.R.C., c. 819, s. 2.

UNDISCLOSED PRINCIPAL. 1. Any person upon whose behalf something is done but whose identity and even the fact of their existence remains unknown to the other party or parties. 2. Any person or company on whose behalf a take-over bid is made whose identity is not disclosed in the take-over bid or in the take-over circular.

UNDISPUTED CORNER. A corner of a parcel of land at which the original post exists, or a corner established under this Act or any predecessor of this Act. *Surveys Act,* R.S.O. 1990, c. S.30, s. 1.

UNDIVIDED INTEREST. A beneficial ownership in common.

UNDOCKING. *n.* The manoeuvring of a ship from a berth.

UNDUE. *adj.* While "undue" is a word of common usage which does not have a precise technical meaning the Supreme Court has variously defined "undue" to mean "improper, inordinate, excessive or oppressive" or to express "a notion

of seriousness or significance." To this list of synonyms, the Concise Oxford Dictionary adds "disproportionate." What is clear from all of these terms is that "undue-ness" is a relative concept. The proper approach to determining if something is "undue", then, is a contextual one. Undue-ness must be defined in light of the aim of the relevant enactment. It can be useful to assess the consequences or effect if the undue thing is allowed to remain in place. *VIA Rail Canada Inc. v. Canada (National Transportation Agency)* (2000), 2000 CarswellNat 2531, 261 N.R. 184, 193 D.L.R. (4th) 357, 26 Admin. L.R. (3d) 1, [2001] 2 F.C. 25 (C.A.).

UNDUE HARDSHIP. The type of hardship contemplated by Section 10 of the *Guidelines* [Federal Child Support Guidelines, SOR/97-175] was "undue", meaning "exceptional", "excessive", or "disproportionate". *Gillespie v. Gormley,* 2003 NBCA 72, 43 R.F.L. (5th) 331 (C.A.).

UNDUE INFLUENCE. 1. " . . . '[U]nconscientious use by one person of power possessed by him over another in order to induce the other to do something." *Berdette v. Berdette* (1991), 33 R.F.L. (3d) 113 at 125, 41 E.T.R. 126, 3 O.R. (3d) 513, 81 D.L.R. (4th) 194, 47 O.A.C. 345 (C.A.), the court per Galligan J.A. 2. " . . . [T]he ability of one person to dominate the will of another, whether through manipulation, coercion, or outright but subtle abuse of power . . . To dominate the will of another simply means to exercise a persuasive influence over him or her. The ability to exercise such influence may arise from a relationship of trust or confidence, but it may arise from other relationships as well. The point is that there is nothing per se reprehensible about persons in a relationship of trust or confidence exerting influence, even undue influence, over their beneficiaries. It depends on their motivation and the objective they seek to achieve thereby." *Goodman Estate v. Geffen* (1991), 42 E.T.R. 97 at 119, [1991] 5 W.W.R. 389, 80 Alta. L.R. (2d) 293, 125 A.R. 81, 14 W.A.C. 81, 81 D.L.R. (4th) 211, [1991] 2 S.C.R. 353, Wilson J. (Cory J. concurring). 3. Influence which overbears the will of the person influenced so that in truth what she does is not his or her own act. *Longmuir v. Holland,* 2000 CarswellBC 1951, 2000 BCCA 538, 81 B.C.L.R. (3d) 99, 192 D.L.R. (4th) 62, 35 E.T.R. (2d) 29 (C.A.) Per Southin J.A. (dissenting in part).

UNDULY. *adv.* "[In the Combines Investigation Act, R.S.C. 1970, c. C-23, s. 32(1)]. . . expresses a notion of seriousness or significance." *Canada v. Pharmaceutical Society (Nova Scotia)* (1992), 10 C.R.R. (2d) 34 at 61, 15 C.R. (4th) 1, 43 C.P.R. (3d) 1, 93 D.L.R. (4th) 36, 74 C.C.C. (3d) 289, [1992] 2 S.C.R. 606, 139 N.R. 241, 114 N.S.R. (2d) 91, 313 A.P.R. 91, the court per Gonthier J.

UNEMPLOYABLE PERSON. A person who is certified by a legally qualified medical practitioner as being unable to engage in remunerative employment by reason of physical or mental disability. See PERMANENTLY ~.

UNEMPLOYED. See ABOUT TO BECOME ~.

UNEMPLOYED PERSON. A person who is able to engage in remunerative employment and who is not so engaged.

UNEMPLOYED WORKER. A worker who is without employment and seeking work.

UNEMPLOYMENT. *n.* " . . . '[T]he state or fact of being unoccupied' . . ." *Martin Service Station Ltd. v. Minister of National Revenue*, [1974] 1 F.C. 398 at 407, 409, 1 N.R. 464, 44 D.L.R. (3d) 99 (C.A.), Pratte and Hyde JJ.A. See AVERAGE NATIONAL RATE OF ~.

UNEMPLOYMENT BENEFIT PLAN. See SUPPLEMENTARY ~.

UNEMPLOYMENT INSURANCE. A contributory, federal social insurance program to provide earnings-related benefits to anyone who is off work or unable to accept or look for work because of injury or other cause. Now known as Employment Insurance.

UNENCRPTYED. *adj.* Refers to an electronic message which has not been processed by a program which encodes it.

UNENCUMBERED INTEREST. The interest that an owner to uses is capable of appointing. *Land Titles acts.*

UNENFORCEABLE. *adj.* Describes a contract which, although it is valid, cannot be sued upon, for example because the Statute of Frauds requires written evidence.

UNEQUAL BARGAINING POWER. Some parties are in no position to negotiate more favourable conditions and they are at times forced to accept unfavourable contractual conditions dictated by their more powerful counterparts, conditions which expose them to unduly harsh penalties in case of default. *Garcia Transport Ltée c. Cie Trust Royal*, [1992] 2 S.C.R. 499.

U.N.E.S.C.O. *abbr.* United Nations Educational, Scientific and Cultural Organisation.

UNESCORTED TEMPORARY ABSENCE. An unescorted temporary absence from penitentiary authorized by the Board taking into account risk of re-offence and other factors. *Corrections and Conditional Release Act*, S.C. 1992, c. 20, s. 99.

UNEXECUTED. *adj.* Of a contract, one of the parties has not completed that party's part of the bargain.

UNEXPENDED CONSUMPTION ALLOWANCE. The portion of a consumption allowance that has not been used during a year. *Ozone-depleting Substances Regulations, 1998*, SOR/99-7, s. 1.

UNFAIR ACTS OR PRACTICES. False, misleading or deceptive consumer representation. See UNFAIR PRACTICES.

UNFAIR BUSINESS PRACTICES. See UNFAIR PRACTICES.

UNFAIRLY DISREGARDS. To unjustly or without cause pay no attention to, ignore or treat as of no importance the interests of security holders. See *Stech v. Davies*, [1987] 5 W.W.R. 563 (Alta. Q.B.).

UNFAIRLY PREJUDICIAL. Acts that are unjustly or inequitably detrimental *Diligenti v. RWMD Operations Kelowna Ltd.* (1976), 1 B.C.L.R. 36 (S.C.)

UNFAIRNESS. See MANIFEST ~.

UNFAIR PRACTICES. (a) A false, misleading or deceptive consumer representation including, but without limiting the generality of the foregoing, (i) a representation that the goods or services have sponsorship, approval, performance characteristics, accessories, uses, ingredients, benefits or quantities they do not have; (ii) a representation that the person who is to supply the goods or services has sponsorship, approval, status, affiliation or connection he does not have; (iii) a representation that the goods are of a particular standard, quality, grade, style or model, if they are not; (iv) a representation that the goods are new, or unused, if they are not or are reconditioned or reclaimed, provided that the reasonable use of goods to enable the seller to service, prepare, test and deliver the goods for the purpose of sale shall not be deemed to make the goods used for the purposes of this subparagraph; (v) a representation that the goods have been used to an extent that is materially different from the fact; (vi) a representation that the goods or services are available for a reason that does not exist; (vii) a representation that the goods or services have been supplied in accordance with a previous representation, if they have not; (viii) a representation that the goods or services or any part thereof are available to the consumer when the person making the representation knows or ought to know they will not be supplied; (ix) a representation that a service, part, replacement or repair is needed, if it is not; (x) a representation that a specific price advantage exists, if it does not; (xi) a representation that misrepresents the authority of a salesperson, representative, employee or agent to negotiate the final terms of the proposed transaction; (xii) a representation that the proposed transaction involves or does not involve rights, remedies or obligations if the representation is false or misleading; (xiii) a representation using exaggeration, innuendo or ambiguity as to a material fact or failing to state a material fact if such use or failure deceives or tends to deceive; (xiv) a representation that misrepresents the purpose or intent of any solicitation of or any communication with a consumer; (b) an unconscionable consumer representation made in respect of a particular transaction and in determining whether or not a consumer representation is unconscionable there may be taken into account that the person making the representation or the person's employer or principal knows or ought to know, (i) that the consumer is not reasonably able to protect his interests because of his physical infirmity, ignorance, illiteracy, inability to understand the language of an agreement or similar factors; (ii) that the price grossly exceeds the price at which similar goods or services are readily available to like consumers; (iii) that the consumer is unable to receive a substantial benefit from the subject-matter of the consumer representation; (iv) that there is no reasonable probability of payment of the obligation in full by the consumer; (v) that the proposed transaction is excessively one-sided in favour of someone other than the consumer; (vi) that the terms or conditions of the proposed transaction are so adverse to the consumer as to be inequitable; (vii) that he or she is making a misleading statement of opinion on which the consumer is likely to rely to his detriment; (viii) that he is subjecting the consumer to undue pressure to enter into the transaction; (c) such other consumer representations under paragraph (a) as are prescribed by the regulations. *Business Prac-*

tices Act, R.S.O. 1990, c. B.18, s. 2. See UNFAIR ACTS OR PRACTICES.

UNFETTERED DISCRETION. The law does not recognize the concept of "unfettered discretion". All discretionary powers must be exercised "according to law" and, therefore, their exercise by administrative officers are subject to certain implied limitations. Those implied limitations are in addition to those which involve procedural deficiencies amounting to breaches of the fairness rules. The expression most often used in the Federal Court is that a discretion must be exercised "judicially". That term is taken to mean that if a decision were made in bad faith, that is for an improper purpose or motive, in a discriminatory manner, or the decision-maker ignored a relevant factor or considered an irrelevant one, then the decision must be set aside. [Whether or not a factor is relevant may be in issue.] The same fate awaits a decision based on a mistaken principle of law or a misapprehension of the facts (as opposed to inferences drawn from accepted facts) or what is commonly referred to as a "palpable and overriding error". More recently, the Supreme Court held that where a tribunal is vested with a "broad discretion" a reviewing court should not disturb the exercise of that discretion unless that tribunal has "made some error in principle in exercising its discretion or has exercised its discretion in a capricious or vexatious manner"; *per* Iacobucci J. in *Pezim v. British Columbia (Superintendent of Brokers)*, [1994] 2 S.C.R. 557, *supra*, at 607]. [Quaere: could this limitation be equated with the "patent unreasonableness" standard of review.] The common law limitations placed on the exercise of an administrative discretion exercised by executive members of government reflect the understanding that all powers granted by Parliament to the executive are fettered only to the extent necessary to ensure that basic tenets of the law are observed. But assuming that the decision-maker has acted "judicially" the question remains whether the discretionary decision may be set aside on other grounds. *Suresh v. Canada (Minister of Citizenship & Immigration)*, 2000 CarswellNat 25, 183 D.L.R. (4th) 629, 5 Imm. L.R. (3d) 1, 252 N.R. 1, 18 Admin. L.R. (3d) 159, [2000] 2 F.C. 592, 180 F.T.R. 57 (note) (C.A.) Robertson JJ.A. for the court. See FETTERING OF DISCRETION

UNFINISHED STONE. Includes crushed stone and what is generally known as blast furnace slag but does not include any stone on which chipping or work other than crushing has been performed in order for the stone to be capable of being mortared to another piece of stone in building a stone structure. *Retail Sales Tax Act*, R.R.O. 1990, Reg. 1013, s. 1.

UNFIT. *adj.* A sentence is "unfit," and will be varied, where: (a) the sentence is clearly unreasonable; (b) the trial judge applied wrong principles; (c) the trial judge ignored or overstressed proper factors; or, (d) the sentence imposed is outside the acceptable range of sentence normally imposed for that type of offence: see *R. v. Shropshire*, [1995] 4 S.C.R. 227, at 249-251. However, it is not enough that there be the application of a wrong principle or a misinterpretation of the facts. Such errors will only lead to a finding of unfitness if they result in the sentence being clearly inadequate or excessive (that is to say, clearly unreasonable). Unfitness, rather than disagreement, is the basis for appellate interference. *Canada v. Domtar Specialty Fine Papers* (2001), 2001 CarswellOnt 1572, 39 C.E.L.R. (N.S.) 56 (S.C.J.), J.W. Quinn, J.

UNFIT FOR FOOD. The product would normally be edible but is inedible by reason of disease, decomposition, injury or other reason.

UNFIT TO STAND TRIAL. Unable on account of mental disorder to conduct a defence at any stage of the proceedings before a verdict is rendered or to instruct counsel to do so, and, in particular, unable on account of mental disorder to (a) understand the nature or object of the proceedings, (b) understand the possible consequences of the proceedings, or (c) communicate with counsel. *Criminal Code*, R.S.C. 1985, c. C-46, s. 2.

UNFORESEEN OPERATIONAL CIRCUMSTANCE. An event, such as unforecast adverse weather, or an equipment malfunction or air traffic control delay, that is beyond the control of an air operator or private operator. *Canadian Aviation Regulations*, SOR/96-433, s. 101.01(1).

UNFUNDED BENEFITS PLAN. A plan which gives protection against risk to an individual that could otherwise be obtained by taking out a contract of insurance, whether the benefits are partly insured or not, and where payments are made by the planholder directly to or on behalf of the member of the plan or to the vendor upon the occurrence of the risk. *Retail Sales Tax Act*, R.S.O. 1990, c. R.31, s. 1(1).

UNFUNDED LIABILITY. Exists when the calculated liabilities of a pension fund exceed the calculated assets of the fund. See INITIAL ~.

UNGUARANTEED TRUST MONEY. Trust money other than guaranteed trust money received by a trust company. *Trust Companies Act*, R.S.C. 1985, c. T-20, s. 2.

UNHAPPY DIFFERENCES. Permission [for counsel of record to withdraw] will almost always be granted in situations where there has been a serious loss of confidence between the lawyer and the client. Such situations are sometimes referred to as a case where the lawyer has "cause to withdraw" or by reason of "unhappy differences" . . . The same is not true of a situation involving the arrangements for the payment of fees. Such a situation would not fall within our understanding of withdrawal for cause or unhappy differences. *R. v. Deschamps*, 2003 MBCA 116, 177 Man. R. (2d) 301, 304 W.A.C. 301, 179 C.C.C. (3d) 174 (C.A.).

UNIDENTIFIED AUTOMOBILE. An automobile with respect to which the identity of either the owner or driver cannot be ascertained.

UNIF. FAM. CT. *abbr*. Unified Family Court.

UNIF. L. CONF. PROC. *abbr*. Uniform Law Conference of Canada, Proceedings.

UNIFORM. *n*. Distinctive clothing worn by an employee, service member, police constable or officer while on duty.

UNIFORM. *adj*. Essentially identical.

UNIFORM CLOSING DAY. (a) Boxing Day, (b) Canada Day, (c) Christmas Day, (d) Good Friday, (e) Labour Day, (f) New Year's Day, (g) Sunday, (h) Thanksgiving Day, (i) any other day the Governor in Council orders and declares by proclamation to be a uniform closing day for the purposes of this Act. *Retail Business Uniform Closing Day Act*, R.S.N.S. 1989, c. 402, s. 2.

UNIFORM CODE. The Uniform Code of Operating Rules set out in the schedule. *Regulations No. O-8, Uniform Code of Operating Rules*, C.R.C., c. 1175, s. 2.

UNIFORM LAW CONFERENCE OF CANADA. Founded in 1918 to harmonize the laws of the provinces and territories of Canada, and where appropriate the federal laws. Makes recommendations for changes to federal criminal legislation based on identified deficiencies, defects or gaps in the existing law, or based on problems created by judicial interpretation of existing law.

UNIGENITURE. *n*. The state of being the only child.

UNILATERAL. *adj*. Having one side.

UNILATERAL CONTRACT. 1. One in which a party makes a promise in return for the performance or forbearance of an act. No counter-promise is made to perform the act or forbearance. Only one party undertakes a promise. 2. In dealing with unilateral contracts, it is clear that the offeree (in this case the plaintiff) can accept the contract so as to make it binding by simply performing and that it is not necessary for the plaintiff to give notice of the acceptance of the contract to the offeror (the defendant). *Ken Toby Ltd. v. British Columbia Buildings Corp.*, 1997 CarswellBC 1087, 34 B.C.L.R. (3d) 263, [1997] 8 W.W.R. 721, 34 C.L.R. (2d) 81, 31 B.L.R. (2d) 224 (S.C.), Burnyeat, J.

UNILATERAL MISTAKE. "To succeed on a plea of unilateral mistake the defendant must establish: (a) that a mistake occurred; (b) that there was fraud or the equivalent of fraud on the plantiff's part in that she knew or must be taken to have known when the agreement was executed that the defendant misunderstood its significance and that she did nothing to enlighten the defendant . . ." *Alampi v. Swartz*, [1964] 1 O.R. 488 at 494, 43 D.L.R. (2d) 11 (C.A.), the court per McGillivray J.A.

UNILINGUAL. *adj*. Knowing and using one language only. Fluent in only one of the two official languages of Canada.

UNIMPROVED LAND. "Unserviced" lands, not just lands without buildings. . . In [*Planet Parking Ltd. v. Metropolitan Toronto Assessment Commissioner*, [1970] 3 O.R. 657 (H.C.)], the court found that the word "unimproved" in the context of the *Assessment Act* [R.S.O. 1970 c. 32] related to the "ordinary and natural" meaning of "improvement" as in "making . . . better" . . . The court rejected "the contention that unimproved land as distinguished from improved land means land without buildings erected thereupon" . . . In the . . . leases, the word "improvement" is used to refer to things other than buildings. Clause 8(a), for example, refers to "any buildings . . . and . . . such other improvements, including construction of roads, water, sewer, electricity and/or gas systems". . . Improvements include services, and conversely "unimproved" means without services. The internal coherence of the rent review clause also supports the view that "unimproved" means un-

serviced. The leases were signed before any buildings were built, so the word "unimproved" would have added nothing to the phrase "unimproved lands in the same state as they were on the date of this agreement" unless it referred to the pre-existing servicing. *Musqueam Indian Band v. Glass* (2000), 2000 CarswellNat 2405, 2000 SCC 52, [2000] 11 W.W.R. 407, 36 R.P.R. (3d) 1, 192 D.L.R. (4th) 385, 82 B.C.L.R. (3d) 199, 261 N.R. 296, 186 F.T.R. 248 (note), [2000] 2 S.C.R. 633, [2001] 1 C.N.L.R. 208 Per Gonthier J. (Major, Binnie and LeBel JJ. concurring).

UNINCORPORATED ASSOCIATION. ". . . [H]as no legal existence, apart from its members, and is not a legal entity capable of suing or being sued." *Tel-Ad Advisors Ontario Ltd. v. Tele-Direct Publications Inc.* (1986), 8 C.P.C. (2d) 217 at 218 (Ont. H.C.), Griffiths J.

UNINCORPORATED MUTUAL FUND. A fund consisting of funds commingled under a collective investment contract managed on behalf of holders by a person who, on request, redeems the units at their net asset value. *Securities Act*, R.S.Q., c. V-1.1, s. 5.

UNINSURED AUTOMOBILE. An automobile with respect to which neither the owner nor driver thereof has applicable and collectible bodily injury liability and property damage liability insurance for its ownership, use or operation.

UNINTERRUPTED SERVICE. The uninterrupted period during which the employee is bound to the employer by a contract of employment, even if the performance of work has been interrupted without cancellation of the contract, and the period during which fixed term contracts succeed one another without an interruption that would, in the circumstances, give cause to conclude that the contract was not renewed. *An Act Respecting Labour Standards*, R.S.Q. c. N-1.1, s. 1.

UNION. *n*. 1. A trade union. 2. " . . . [A]n unincorporated group or association of workmen who have banded together to promote certain objectives for their mutual benefit and advantage . . ." *Astgen v. Smith*, [1970] 1 O.R. 129 at 134, 7 D.L.R. (3d) 657 (C.A.), Evans J.A. 3. Any organization of employees, or any branch or local thereof, the purposes of which include the regulation of relations between employers and employees. 4. The union of the Provinces effected under the British North America Act, 1867, and subsequent acts. *Interpretation Act*, R.S.Q. 1977, c. I-16, s. 61. 5. " . . . [C]orporate or non-corporate action of all kinds and descriptions in the nature of merger or unification of more than one enterprise . . . would embrace proprietorships, partnerships limited and unlimited, corporations established by special Act, or corporations brought into being under general corporate legislation . . . include[s] a union or combination of companies or their respective undertakings by reason of the acquisition by one company of the shares of another company' " *Atco Ltd. v. Calgary Power Ltd.* (1982), 20 B.L.R. 227 at 236 245, [1982] 2 S.C.R. 557, [1983] 1 W.W.R. 385, 23 Alta. L.R. (2d) 1, 41 A.R. 1, 45 N.R. 1, 140 D.L.R. (3d) 193, Estey J. (Beetz, Chouinard and Lamer JJ. concurring). See AFFILIATED ~; CAPTIVE ~; CERTIFIED ~; CLOSED ~; COMMON LAW ~; COMPANY-DOMINATED ~; COMPANY ~; COUNTRY OF THE ~; CRAFT ~; CREDIT ~; CUSTOMS ~; FUND ~; HEALTH CARE ~S; HORIZONTAL~; INDUSTRIAL ~; INTERNATIONAL ~; LABOUR ~; LEGISLATIVE ~; LOCAL ~; MULTICRAFT ~; OPEN ~; POLICEMEN'S ~; SUCCESSOR ~; TRADE ~; VERTICAL ~.

UNION ASSOCIATION. A group of workers constituted as a professional syndicate, union, brotherhood or otherwise or a group of such syndicates, unions, brotherhoods or other groups of workers otherwise constituted, having as its objects the study, safeguarding and development of the economic, social and educational interests of its members and particularly the negotiation and application of collective agreements. *An Act Respecting Occupational Health and Safety*, R.S.Q., c. S-2.1, s. 1.

UNION CONTRACT. See COLLECTIVE BARGAINING AGREEMENT.

UNION DUES. Fees paid by union members to support their union. See REGULAR ~.

UNIONISM. See COMPULSORY ~.

UNIONIZED EMPLOYEE. 1. An employee on behalf of whom a trade union or council of trade unions has been certified as bargaining agent under this Act or voluntarily recognized by an employer, where the certification has not been revoked or the bargaining rights have not been terminated. *Labour Relations Act*, R.S. Nfld. 1990, c. L- 1, s. 54(1). 2. An employee who is employed by a unionized employer and in respect of whom a trade union has established the right to bargain collectively with the unionized employer.

UNIONIZED EMPLOYER. 1. An employer of unionized employees in the geographic area or areas and sector concerned. *Labour Relations acts*. 2. An employer in a trade division in respect of whom a trade union has established the right to bargain collectively on behalf of the unionized employees in that trade division.

UNION GRIEVANCE. A policy grievance. One which affects a number of workers and concerns the same issue with each worker.

UNION LABEL. A label on a product indicating it has been made by unionized workers.

UNION LOCAL. See INDEPENDENT ~.

UNION RIGHTS. Specific provisions which a union frequently attempts to include in the terms of an agreement and which benefit the union itself, its officers or officials. The overriding purpose of such clauses is usually to insure that the union may fully discharge its statutory and contractual function to supervise the terms of the agreement. D.J.M. Brown and D.M. Beatty, *Canadian Labour Arbitration*, 3d ed. (Aurora: Canada Law Book, 1988-) at 9-1.

UNION SCALE. The rate of pay set by a union contract as the minimum rate for a job.

UNION SECURITY. Provisions like voluntary check-off of union dues, union and closed shops which insure that any employees who are the beneficiaries of the agreement share any costs associated with the union's activities. D.J.M. Brown and D.M. Beatty, *Canadian Labour Arbitration*, 3d ed. (Aurora: Canada Law Book, 1988-) at 9-2.

UNION SHOP. A form of union security permitting an employer to hire non-union employees who must become members once employed. See MODIFIED ~.

UNION STEWARD. See SHOP STEWARD.

UNIT. *n*. 1. A group of employees. 2. An individual body of the Canadian Forces that is organized as such, with the personnel and materiel thereof. *National Defence Act*, R.S.C. 1985, c. N-5, s. 2. 3. Includes an identifiable part, portion or instalment of the entire consumer transaction or the consideration for or the subject matter of it. *Trade Practice Act*, R.S.B.C. 1979, c. 406, s. 1. 4. A part of the property designated as a unit by the description and includes the space enclosed by its boundaries and all of the land, structures and fixtures within this space in accordance with the declaration and description.

Condominium Act, 1998, S.O. 1998, c. 19, s. 1(1). 5. That part of the pool or pools to which a unit operation applies that is within the unit area. 6. A square of prescribed dimensions contained in a mineral claim. See ACCOMMODATION ~; AIR TRAFFIC CONTROL ~; APPROPRIATE ~; APRON TRAFFIC CONTROL ~; AXLE ~; BARE LAND ~; BARGAINING ~; BRITISH THERMAL ~; CARETAKER'S ~; COCKTAIL MIXING ~; COMMERCIAL ~; COMPOSITE ~; CONDOMINIUM ~; CONSUMER ~; CONVERSION ~; COOPERATIVE ~; CRAFT ~; DEFECTIVE ~S; DEVELOPED ~; DRAINAGE ~; DRIVE-AWAY ~; DWELLING ~; ECONOMIC FARM ~; EXTENDED CARE ~; FAMILY ~; FIXED COMMERCIAL FISHING ~; FIXTURE ~; FOREST MANAGEMENT ~; FOUNDATION ~; FULLY SERVICED ~; HEAT RECOVERY ~ OR DEVICE; HOSTEL ~; HOUSEKEEPING ~; HOUSING ~; IMPERIAL ~S; INDUSTRIAL ~; INSURANCE~; IRRIGABLE ~; LOCAL GOVERNMENT ~; LONG-TERM ~; MEDICAL SERVICE ~; METRIC ~S; MOBILE ~; MUNICIPAL ~; OBSERVATION ~; PARCEL COMPARTMENT ~; PILOTAGE ~; PLANT ~; POWER ~; PROPOSED ~; PROTOTYPE ~; RENTAL ~; RESIDENTIAL ~; RESIDUAL ~; SANITARY ~; SELF-CONTAINED DWELLING ~; SELF-CONTAINED ~; SPACING ~; SUBDIVISION ~; TAG-END ~; TERMINAL SERVICES ~; TUBER ~; ~S; VOTING ~.

UNIT AGREEMENT. An agreement to unitize the interests of owners in a pool or a part of a pool exceeding in area a spacing unit, or such an agreement as varied by a unitization order. *Canada Oil and Gas Operations Act*, R.S.C. 1985, c. O-7, s. 29.

UNIT AREA. The area that is subject to a unit agreement. *Canada Oil and Gas Operations Act*, R.S.C. 1985, c. O-7, s. 29.

UNITARY STATE. A nation in which supreme authority is in one centre.

UNITAS PERSONARUM. [L.] Unity of people.

UNITED KINGDOM. The United Kingdom of Great Britain and Northern Ireland. *Interpretation acts*. See COURT OF THE ~.

UNITED NATIONS OPERATION. An operation that is established by the competent organ of the United Nations in accordance with the Charter of the United Nations and is conducted under United Nations authority and control, if the operation is for the purpose of maintaining or restoring international peace and security or if the Security Council or the General Assembly of the United Nations has declared, for the purposes of the Convention on the Safety of United Nations and Associated Personnel, that there exists an exceptional risk to the safety of the personnel participating in the operation. It does not include an operation authorized by the Security Council as an enforcement action under Chapter VII of the Charter of the United Nations in which any of the personnel are engaged as combatants against organized armed forces and to which the law of international armed conflict applies. *Criminal Code*, R.S.C. 1985, c. C-46, s. 2 as am.

UNITED NATIONS PERSONNEL. (a) Persons who are engaged or deployed by the Secretary-General of the United Nations as members of the military, police or civilian components of a United Nations operation, or (b) any other officials or experts who are on mission of the United Nations or one of its specialized agencies or the International Atomic Energy Agency and who are present in an official capacity in the area where a United Nations operation is conducted. *Criminal Code*, R.S.C. 1985, c. C-46, s. 2 as am.

UNITED STATES. The United States of America. *Interpretation acts*.

UNIT ENTITLEMENT. Of a strata lot means the number indicated in the Schedule of Unit Entitlement established under section 246, that is used in calculations to determine the strata lot's share of (a) the common property and common assets, and (b) the common expenses and liabilities of the strata corporation. *Strata Property Act*, S.B.C. 1998, c. 43, s. 1.

UNIT HEATER. A suspended space heater with an integral air circulating fan.

UNITIZATION. *n*. (a) The development or production of oil and natural gas; (b) the implementation of a programme for the conservation of oil and natural gas; or (c) the co-ordinated management of interests in the oil and natural gas, within, upon, or under a location, part of a location, or a number of locations that are combined for that purpose pursuant to a unitization agreement entered into under this Act. *Oil and Natural Gas Act*, S.N.B. 1976, c. O-2.1, s. 1.

UNITIZATION ORDER. An order of the Committee made under section 41. *Canada Oil and Gas Operations Act*, R.S.C. 1985, c. O-7, s. 29.

UNITIZED GOODS. Goods in packages that are consolidated, banded or otherwise securely held together to form a single shipping unit in order to facilitate mechanical handling.

UNITIZED OPERATION. 1. The development or production of petroleum and natural gas, or the implementing of a program for the conservation of petroleum and of natural gas or the coordinated management of interests in them in, on or under a location, part of a location or a number of locations combined for that purpose under a unitization agreement under this Act. *Petroleum and Natural Gas acts*. 2. The development or production of geothermal resources or the implementing of a program for the conservation of geothermal resources or the coordinated management of interests in them in, on or under a location, part of a location or a number of locations combined for that purpose under a unitization agreement under this Act. *Geothermal Resources Act*, R.S.B.C. 1996, c. 171, s. 1.

UNITIZED ZONE. A geological formation that is within a unit area and subject to a unit agreement. *Canada Oil and Gas Operations Act*, R.S.C. 1985, c. O-7, s. 29.

UNIT MORTGAGE. Long term financing of a single condominium unit for its potential owner.

UNIT OF ASSESSMENT. Place of business or premises.

UNIT OF TAXATION. An individual; the family member who has the property or legal interest producing income.

UNIT OPERATING AGREEMENT. An agreement, providing for the management and operation of a unit area and a unitized zone, that is entered into by working interest owners who are parties to a unit agreement with respect to that unit area and unitized zone, and includes a unit operating agreement as varied by a unitization order. *Canada Oil and Gas Operations Act*, R.S.C. 1985, c. O-7, s. 29.

UNIT OPERATION. 1. Those operations conducted pursuant to a unit agreement or a unitization order. *Canada Oil and Gas Operations Act*, R.S.C. 1985, c. O-7, s. 29. 2. An operation where, pursuant to an agreement, interests in a mineral are merged, pooled, consolidated or in-tegrated as a single unit, without regard to the boundaries of the separate parcels, for the purposes of (a) the development or production of the mineral within, on or under the parcels, or any specified stratum or strata or portion thereof within the parcels; or (b) the implementing of a program for the conservation of the mineral, or the co-ordinated management of interests in the mineral. *Land Titles Act*, R.S.A. 1980, c. L-5, s. 53.

UNIT OPERATOR. A person designated as a unit operator under a unit operating agreement. *Canada Oil and Gas Operations Act*, R.S.C. 1985, c. O-7, s. 29.

UNIT PRICE CONTRACT. A contract in which it is agreed to measure the work by a convenient unit of measure so that the contractor is paid a fixed price per unit.

UNITRUST. *n*. A guarantee that a would-be "income" beneficiary will regularly receive a fixed percentage on the value of the trust property. D.M.W. Waters, *The Law of Trusts in Canada*, 2d ed. (Toronto: Carswell, 1984) at 867.

UNIT TRACT. The portion of a unit area that is defined as a tract in a unit agreement. *Canada Oil and Gas Operations Act*, R.S.C. 1985, c. O-7, s. 29.

UNIT TRUST. A trust under which the interest of each beneficiary is described by reference to units of the trust.

UNITY OF INTEREST. Said of a joint tenant who has no greater interest in a property than any other joint tenant.

UNITY OF POSSESSION. Said of joint tenants who have undivided possession.

UNITY OF SEISIN. A situation in which someone seised of land which is subject to a profit à prendre, easement or similar right also becomes seised of the land to which that profit or right is annexed.

UNITY OF TIME. Said of joint tenants whose interests must arise at the same time.

UNITY OF TITLE. Said of joint tenants who hold their property by one and the same title.

UNIV. *abbr*. University.

UNIVERSAL COPYRIGHT CONVENTION. A convention drafted under the sponsorship of UNESCO and signed at Geneva in 1952.

UNIVERSAL DECLARATION OF HUMAN RIGHTS. A document adopted by the

United Nations General Assembly on December 10, 1948 which recognizes the 'inherent dignity and . . . the equal and inalienable rights of all members of the human family,' and sets out the fundamental rights to which all persons should be entitled including the right to legal equality.

UNIVERSALITY. *n.* A principle contrasted with territoriality. Permits the exercise of jurisdiction by a state in respect of criminal acts committed by non-nationals against non-nationals wherever they take place. Jurisdiction is based upon the accused's attack upon the international order as a whole and is of common concern to all mankind as a sort of international public policy. Historically, the universality principle has been employed to prosecute piracy and, more recently, hijacking. Under the principle of universality the criminal act is a violation of national law. International law merely gives states a liberty to punish but it does not itself declare the act illegal. By contrast, some acts are crimes under international law. They may be punished by any state which has custody of the accused. *R. v. Finta*, [1994] 1 S.C.R. 701.

UNIVERSAL POSTAL CONVENTION. The Universal Postal Convention drawn by the Universal Postal Union at the 1974 Lausanne Congress.

UNIVERSITARIAN INSTITUTION. A university or an institution affiliated with, incorporated in or annexed to it and providing education leading to the degrees of master, licentiate and doctor. *Teachers Scholarship Act*, R.S.Q. 1977, c. B-7, s. 2.

UNIVERSITY. *n.* "The chief distinguishing characteristic between a university and other institutions of learning is the power and authority possessed by an institution of learning to grant titles or degrees . . ." *London (City) v. Ursuline Religious of the Diocese of London*, [1964] 1 O.R. 587 at 595, 43 D.L.R. (2d) 220 (C.A.), the court per Schroeder J.A.

UNIVERSITY CREDIT. A unit of recognition in respect of the successful completion of a university course.

UNJUST ENRICHMENT. 1. "The determination that the enrichment is 'unjust' does not refer to abstract notions of morality and justice, but flows directly from the finding that there was a breach of a legally recognized duty for which the Courts will grant relief. *International Corona Resources Ltd. v. Lac Minerals Ltd.* (1989), 44 B.L.R. 1 at 45, [1989] 2 S.C.R. 574, 26 C.P.R.

(3d) 97, 69 O.R. (2d) 287, 61 D.L.R. (4th) 14, 6 R.P.R. (2d) 1, 25 E.T.R. 1, 101 N.R. 239, 36 O.A.C. 57, La Forest J. (Wilson and Lamer JJ. concurring). 2. An action for unjust enrichment arises when three elements are satisfied: (1) an enrichment; (2) a corresponding deprivation; and (3) the absence of a juristic reason for the enrichment. These proven, the action is established and the right to claim relief made out. At this point, a second doctrinal concern arises: the nature of the remedy. "Unjust enrichment" in equity permitted a number of remedies, depending on the circumstances. One was a payment for services rendered on the basis of quantum meruit or quantum valebat. Another equitable remedy, available traditionally where one person was possessed of legal title to property in which another had an interest, was the constructive trust. . . . the remedy of constructive trust arises, where monetary damages are inadequate and where there is a link between the contribution that founds the action and the property in which the constructive trust is claimed. . . in order for a constructive trust to be found, in a family case as in other cases, monetary compensation must be inadequate and there must be a link between the services rendered and the property in which the trust is claimed. *Peter v. Beblow*, 1993 CarswellBC 44, 77 B.C.L.R. (2d) 1, [1993] 3 W.W.R. 337, 44 R.F.L. (3d) 329, 48 E.T.R. 1, 150 N.R. 1, 23 B.C.A.C. 81, 39 W.A.C. 81, 101 D.L.R. (4th) 621, [1993] 1 S.C.R. 980, [1993] R.D.F. 369, McLachlin, J. for the majority.

UNKNOWN TROUBLE CALL. A call to police or emergency services where the phone is disconnected before the caller says anything. Treated as a call for help and given priority to all but calls for assistance to an officer in distress.

UNLAWFUL. *adj.* 1. Illegal. 2. ". . . There appears to be three categories of actions or events which are contrary to the law and which sometimes fall into the description 'unlawful' or 'illegal'. These are: (a) offences against statutes prohibiting defined conduct; (b) actions which are without legal consequence in the sense of creating enforceable rights, such as gaming contracts; and (c) actions taken by statutory bodies outside the limits of authority granted or established in the statute. . ." *Nepean Hydroelectric Commission v. Ontario Hydro*, [1982] 1 S.C.R. 347 at 406-7, 18 B.L.R. 215, 132 D.L.R. (3d) 193, 41 N.R. 1, Estey J. (Martland and Lamer JJ. concurring). See ILLEGAL.

UNLAWFUL ACT. " . . . [T]he concept of an unlawful act as it is used in that section [s. 269 of the Criminal Code, R.S.C. 1985, c. C-46] includes only federal and provincial offences. Excluded from this general category of offences are any offences which are based on absolute liability and which have constitutionally insufficient mental elements on their own. Additionally, the term 'unlawfully' . . . requires an act which is at least objectively dangerous." *R. v. DeSousa* (1992),15 C.R. (4th) 66 at 81,142 N.R. 1, 9 O.R. (3d) 544n, 76 C.C.C. (3d) 124, 95 D.L.R. (4th) 595, 56 O.A.C. 109, [1992] 2 S.C.R. 944, 11 C.R.R. (2d) 193, the court per Sopinka J.

UNLAWFUL AND INTENTIONAL INTERFERENCE. To find that there has been unlawful interference, it must be shown that a right protected by the *Charter* was infringed and that the infringement resulted from wrongful conduct. A person's conduct will be characterized as wrongful if, in engaging therein, he or she violated a standard of conduct considered reasonable in the circumstances under the general law or, in the case of certain protected rights, a standard set out in the *Charter* itself. . . There will be unlawful and intentional interference within the meaning of the second paragraph of s. 49 of the [*Charter of Human Rights and Freedoms*, R.S.Q., c. C-12] when the person who commits the unlawful interference has a state of mind that implies a desire or intent to cause the consequences of his or her wrongful conduct, or when that person acts with full knowledge of the immediate and natural or at least extremely probable consequences that his or her conduct will cause. This test is not as strict as specific intent, but it does go beyond simple negligence. Thus, an individual's recklessness, however wild and foolhardy, as to the consequences of his or her wrongful acts will not in itself satisfy this test. *Québec (Curateur public) c. Syndicat national des employés de l'hôpital St-Ferdinand*, 1996 CarswellQue 916, 202 N.R. 321, (sub nom. *Quebec (Public Curator) v. Syndicat national des employés de l'hôpital St-Ferdinand*) 138 D.L.R. (4th) 577, 1 C.P.C. (4th) 183, [1996] 3 S.C.R. 211. L'Heureux-Dubé for the court.

UNLAWFUL ASSEMBLY. An assembly of three or more persons who, with intent to carry out any common purpose, assemble in such a manner or so conduct themselves when they are assembled as to cause persons in the neighbourhood of the assembly to fear, on reasonable grounds that they (a) will disturb the peace tumultuously; or (b) will by that assembly needlessly and without reasonable cause provoke other persons to disturb the peace tumultuously. *Criminal Code*, R.S.C. 1985, c. C-46, s. 63(1).

UNLAWFUL CONDUCT. Includes crime, tort, breach of contract and breach of statute and breach of a fiduciary obligation.

UNLAWFUL INDUSTRIAL ACTION. Industrial action that is prohibited.

UNLAWFUL INTERFERENCE WITH CONTRACTUAL RELATIONS. "The tort of unlawful interference with contractual relations is established where the defendant, with knowledge of a contract and with intent to prevent or hinder its performance, (a) persuades, induces or procures a party to the contract not to perform its obligations, or (b) commits some act, wrongful, in itself, to prevent performance of the contract . . ." *Niedner Ltd. v. Lloyds Bank of Canada* (1990), 72 D.L.R. (4th) 147 at 153, 77 O.R. (2d) 574, 38 E.T.R. 306 (Ont. H.C.), Ewaschuk J.

UNLAWFUL INTERFERENCE WITH ECONOMIC RELATIONS. An emerging tort, refers to someone intentionally employing unlawful means to interfere with a business relationship or expectancy.

UNLAWFUL INTERFERENCE WITH LEGITIMATE BUSINESS EXPECTANCY. The elements of this tort are the existence of a valid business relationship or expectancy, knowledge by the defendant of the relationship or expectancy, intentional interference inducing or causing termination of the relationship or expectancy by unfair or unlawful means, proximate cause and resultant damages.

UNLAWFULLY. *adv.* 1. " . . . [W]ithout legal authority or justification. . ." *R. v. Kapij* (1905), 1 W.L.R. 130 at 136, 15 Man. R. 110, 9 C.C.C. 186 (C.A.), the court per Perdue J.A. 2. As it is used in s. 281 [of the Criminal Code] does not require the commission of an additional unlawful act. Rather, it represents verbal surplusage that enunciates no more than the general defences, justifications, and excuses already available under the Code. It is appropriate to interpret the expression "unlawfully" as meaning "without lawful justification, authority or excuse", as that term is used in s. 281 of the *Criminal Code*; this interpretation is in accord with the purpose of the section which is to prevent and punish strangers intending to deprive a parent (guardian, etc.) of his or her child (the child for whom they act as guardian, etc.). To require that an additional unlawful act occur beyond the physical act of taking the child is at cross-purposes with the mischief Parliament wanted to cure; such an interpretation would not adequately achieve the goal of prevention, and the rights of the parents could not be vindicated. *R. v. Chartrand*, 1994 CarswellOnt 83, 31 C.R. (4th) 1, 91 C.C.C. (3d) 396, [1994] 2 S.C.R. 864, 116 D.L.R. (4th) 207, 170 N.R. 161, 74 O.A.C. 257, L'Heureux-Dubé, J. for the court.

UNLAWFUL OBJECT. " . . . [W]hen used in s. 212(c) [of the Criminal Code, R.S.C. 1970, c. C-34 means] . . . the object of conduct which, if prosecuted fully, would amount to a serious crime, that is, an indictable offence requiring mens rea . . ." *R. v. Vasil* (1981), 20 C. R. (3d) 193 at 224, [1981] 1 S.C.R. 469, 58 C.C.C. (2d) 97, 35 N.R. 451, 121 D.L.R. (3d) 41, Lamer J. (Martland, Dickson, Estey, McIntyre and Chouinard JJ. concurring).

UNLAWFUL PURPOSE. " . . . [I]n Section 423(2)(a) [of the Criminal Code, R.S.C. 1970, c. C-34] unlawful purpose means contrary to law, that is prohibited by Federal or Provincial legislation. . ." *R. v. Gralewicz* (1980), 81 C.L.L.C. 14,070 at 14, [1980] 2 S.C.R. 493, 33 N.R. 242, 54 C.C.C. (2d) 289, 116 D.L.R. (3d) 276, Chouinard J. (Ritchie, Dickson, Beetz and Estey JJ. concurring).

UNLEADED GASOHOL. A mixture of gasoline and ethanol.

UNLEADED GASOLINE. Gasoline to which lead has not been added during the production process.

UNLESS. *conj.* "[In a statutory provision, introduces] . . . an exception or exemption . . ." *Bell v. Grand Trunk Railway* (1913), 48 S.C.R. 561 at 574, 16 C.R.C. 324, 15 D.L.R. 874, Anglin J.

UNLIMITED DIVIDEND RIGHT. The right without limitation as to the amount either to all or to a share of the balance of any dividends after the payment of dividends on any shares entitled to a preference, and includes the right to all or to a share of the balance of any surplus upon winding up after the repayment of capital.

UNLIQUIDATED. *adj.* Not ascertained.

UNLIQUIDATED DAMAGES. Damages whose amount depends on circumstances, and on the parties' conduct or is fixed by an estimate or opinion.

UNLOADED VEHICLE WEIGHT. The weight of a vehicle equipped with the containers for the fluids necessary for the operation of the vehicle filled to their maximum capacity, but without cargo or occupants.

UNLOADING CHARGE. 1. A charge on goods for the unloading thereof from any railway car to the warehouse handling floor. 2. A charge for unloading goods from closed or gondola railway cars or closed motor transport vehicles and moving them to an ordinary place of rest and for all necessary labour and equipment.

UNLOADING FACILITY. Any shore or sea installation that is used for the unloading of oil or an oily mixture from a ship.

UNMARKED PLASTIC EXPLOSIVE. A plastic explosive that (a) does not contain a detection agent, or (b) at the time of manufacture, does not contain the required minimum concentration level of a detection agent as required by the Convention. *Explosives Act*, R.S.C. 1985, c. E-17, s. 2.

UNMARRIED. *adj.* When referring to an individual, means that the individual is not married and has never been married.

UNMARRIED PERSON. Includes a widow, a widower, a divorced person and a married person who, in the opinion of a provincial authority, is living separate and apart from her, or his spouse.

UNNECESSARY. *adj.* Of a pleading, one that alleges immaterial facts.

UNOBSTRUCTED. *adj.* As applied to a roadway or a lane of a laned roadway means not obstructed by a stationary object.

UNOCCUPIED. *adj.* "[In a fire insurance policy applies] . . . to animate occupancy." *Miller v. Portage la Prairie Mutual Insurance Co.*, [1936] 2 D.L.R. 787 at 791, [1936] 2 W.W.R. 104, 3 I.L.R. 377 (Sask. C.A.), the court per Gordon J.A. See VACANT.

UNOCCUPIED PUBLIC LAND. All public land that is not privately owned land.

UNO FLATU. [L. with one breath] With the same intent.

UNORGANIZED DISTRICT. Those parts of the territorial districts that are without municipal organization.

UNORGANIZED TERRITORY. 1. Any part of the province that is not in a municipality, and includes the area of a disorganized municipality. 2. That part of Ontario without county organization. 3. Territory not included in a city, town, village, county or municipal district.

UNPAID SELLER. Within the meaning of this Act (a) when the whole of the price has not been paid or tendered; (b) when a bill of exchange or other negotiable instrument has been received as conditional payment and the condition on which it was received has not been fulfilled by reason of the dishonor of the instrument or otherwise. *Sale of Goods acts*.

UNPAID SELLER'S LIEN. A possessory lien which entitles the creditor to keep the debtor's goods until the debt is paid.

UNPATENTED. *adj*. When referring to land or mining rights, means land or mining rights for which a patent, lease, licence of occupation or any other form of Crown grant is not in effect. *Mining Act*, R.S.O. 1990, c. M.14, s. 1.

UNPRIME. *adj*. Where applied to pelts means that the pelts show natural markings of a dark or bluish colour on the flesh side. *Wildlife Act*, R.S. Nfld. 1990, c. W-8, s. 2.

UNPRIME PELT. A skin or pelt that has been taken other than during the open season and includes a skin or pelt that shows natural markings of a dark or bluish colour on the flesh side.

UNPRIME SKIN. See UNPRIME PELT.

UNPRODUCTIVE LANDS. Rock barrens, muskeg or lands covered by water. *Crown Timber Act*, R.S.O. 1990, c. C.51, s. 1.

UNPROFESSIONAL CONDUCT. Any act or omission by a member of a profession which is an unjustifiable breach of duty to the public, a client, or any other member and includes a breach of the code of ethics.

UNPROTECTED OPENING. A doorway, window or opening other than one equipped with a closure having the required fire-protection rating, or any part of a wall forming part of the exposing building face that has a fire-resistance rating less than required for the exposing building face.

UNQUES. [Fr.] Still, yet.

UNQUES PRIST. [Fr.] Still ready.

UNREASONABLE. 1. The Supreme Court of Canada has introduced a third standard of review in cases where there is a statutory right of appeal. The statutory right of appeal obviates the need to find a jurisdictional error. Because the standard of patent unreasonableness is principally a test for determining whether a tribunal has exceeded its jurisdiction, it will rarely be the appropriate standard of review in statutory appeals. However, because tribunals typically enjoy more expertise and deal with problems of a difficult and complex nature, a standard more differential than correctness was found to be needed. This third standard has been defined as the standard of "unreasonableness". *Canada (Director of Investigation & Research) v. Southam Inc.*, [1997] 1 S.C.R. 748 . 2. In [*R. v. Shropshire*, [1995] 4 S.C.R. 227], the Court concluded . . . that unreasonableness in the sentencing context refers to an order falling outside the "acceptable range" of sentences under similar circumstances. In an adversarial system, it seems logical to assume that if no appeal against sentence is taken, neither of the parties found anything "clearly" unreasonable in it. *R. v. W. (G.)*, 1999 CarswellNfld 253, 138 C.C.C. (3d) 23, 178 D.L.R. (4th) 76, 27 C.R. (5th) 203, 247 N.R. 135, 181 Nfld. & P.E.I.R. 139, 550 A.P.R. 139, [1999] 3 S.C.R. 597, per Lamer, C.J.C. for majority. See PATENTLY ~; REASONABLE.

UNREASONABLE DELAY. Delay which is excessive in the circumstances.

UNREASONABLENESS. *n*. The test of unreasonableness is whether the verdict is one that a properly instructed jury, acting judicially, could reasonably have rendered. *R. v. Mah*, 2002 NSCA 99, (sub nom. *R. v. J.M.*) 207 N.S.R. (2d) 262 (C.A.).

UNREASONABLE SEARCH. Unlawful search, one conducted pursuant to an invalid order.

UNREASONABLE VERDICT. A verdict which a properly instructed trier of fact acting judicially could not reasonably have rendered.

UNREASONABLY. *adv*. "[In s. 455 of the Municipal Act, R.S.B.C. 1960, c. 255] . . . involving action by the council based upon indirect and improper motives or upon irrelevant or alien grounds indicating that in law no discretion was actually exercised at all." *R. v. New Westminster (City)* (1965), 54 W.W.R. 238 at 243, 55 D.L.R. (2d) 613 (B.C. C.A.), McFarlane J.A.

UNRECORDED WATER. Water the right to the use of which is not held under a licence or under a special or private Act. *Water Act*, R.S.B.C. 1996, c. 483, s. 1.

UNRELATED GROUP. A group of persons that is not a related group.

UNSAFE. *adj.* When used in respect of a building means, (a) structurally inadequate or faulty for the purposes for which it is used, or (b) in a condition that could be hazardous to persons in the normal use of the building.

UNSANITARY CONDITIONS. Such conditions or circumstances as might contaminate with dirt or filth, or render injurious to health, a food, drug or cosmetic. *Food and Drugs Act,* R.S.C. 1985, c. F-27, s. 2.

UNSAVOURY. *adj.* A witness is considered unsavoury where it is suspected that his or her evidence is proffered for an ulterior motive—for example, to divert suspicion or blame from himself or herself, or to gain advantage such as immunity from prosecution for the current offence or concessions in relation to another offence, or for monetary reward. *R. v. Campbell,* 2002 NSCA 35, 202 N.S.R. (2d) 170, 632 A.P.R. 170, 163 C.C.C. (3d) 485, 1 C.R. (6th) 343 (C.A.).

UNSECURED CREDITOR. Any creditor of a company who is not a secured creditor.

UNSECURED LOAN. A debt owing that is not secured by a fixed or floating charge, by a hypothecation or pledge, by a guarantee, or otherwise.

UNSECURED TRADE CREDITOR. A person to whom a seller is indebted for stock, money or services furnished for the purpose of enabling the seller to carry on a business, whether or not the debt is due, and who holds no security or who is entitled to no preference in respect of his claim. *Bulk Sales acts.*

UNSEEMLY. *adj.* Competition becomes "unseemly" or unprofessional when it is misleading, contravenes good taste, makes unfavourable reflections on the competence or integrity of another member, or includes subjective claims of superiority that cannot be substantiated. *Assie v. Institute of Chartered Accountants (Saskatchewan),* 2001 CarswellSask 545, 2001 SKQB 396 (Q.B.), Smith J.

UNSERVED COMMUNITY. The licensed area of a distribution undertaking where there is no local radio station and no local television station. *Broadcasting Distribution Regulations,* SOR/97-555, s. 1.

UNSETTLED ACCOUNT. 1. " ... '[U]npaid'." *R. v. Wilkinson,* [1937] 1 W.W.R. 394 at 396 (Alta. C.A.), Lunney J.A. 2. " ... [A]n account the amount of which is not adjusted, determined, or admitted by some act of the parties, such as by the giving of a note, a mutual stating or balancing of the account, or fixing the amount due." *Hall v. Curtain* (1869), 28 U.C.Q.B. 533 at 537 (C.A.), Morrison J.A.

UNSIGHTLY PROPERTY. Any real property or part thereof upon which there is litter, dilapidated buildings, structures or parts thereof, which causes the real property or any part thereof to look unsightly.

UNSKILLED LABOUR. Workers with no identifiable skill or craft.

UNSOLEMN ADMISSION. More than simple speaking; there must be indication that the party is admitting something against interest. P. K. McWilliams, *Canadian Criminal Evidence,* 3d ed. (Aurora: Canada Law Book, 1988) at 147.

UNSOLICITED CREDIT CARD. A credit card that has not been requested in writing by the person to whom the credit card is issued but does not include a credit card that replaces or renews a credit card that was previously issued to that person at that person's request.

UNSOLICITED GOODS. 1. Personal property whose receipt has not been requested by the recipient, but does not include personal property delivered to the recipient that the recipient knew or ought to have known was intended for delivery to another person. 2. Personal property furnished to a person who did not request it and a request shall not be inferred from inaction or the passing of time alone, but does not include (a) personal property that the recipient knows or ought to know is intended for another person, or (b) personal property supplied, under a contract in writing to which the recipient is a party that provides for the periodic supply of personal property to the recipient without further solicitation. *Consumer Protection acts.*

UNSOLICITED GOODS OR SERVICES. (a) Goods that are supplied to a consumer who did not request them but does not include, (i) goods that the recipient knows or ought to know are intended for another person, (ii) a change to periodically supplied goods, if the change in goods is not a material change, or (iii) goods supplied under a written future performance agreement that provides for the periodic supply of goods to the recipient without further solicitation, or (b) services that are supplied to a consumer who did not request them but does not include, (i) services that were intended for another person from the time the recipient knew or ought to have known that they were so intended,

(ii) a change to ongoing or periodic services that are being supplied, if the change in the services is not a material change, or (iii) services supplied under a written future performance agreement that provides for the ongoing or periodic supply of services to the recipient without further solicitation. *Consumer Protection Act, 2002*, S.O. 2002, c. 30, Sched. A, s. 13(a).

UNSOUND MIND. 1. As provided in s. 47 [of the *Limitations Act*, R.S.O. 1990, c. L.15], means in context lack of mental capacity from whatever source to perform the requisite steps called for by the *Limitations Act* or the *Municipal Act*, R.S.O. 1990, c. M.45. *Bannon v. Thunder Bay (City)*, [2002] 1 S.C.R. 716. 2. In the context of the Limitations Act, a person is of unsound mind when he or she, by reason of mental illness, is incapable of managing his or her affairs as a reasonable person would do in relation to the incident, or event, which entitles the person to bring an action. *Bisoukis v. Brampton (City)* (1999), 46 O.R. (3d) 417 (C.A.). See PERSON OF ~.

UNSTANDARDIZED FOOD. Any food for which a standard is not prescribed in this Part. *Food and Drug Regulations*, C.R.C., c. 870, s. B.01.001.

UNSUITABILITY. *n*. A standard applied to probationary employees. Lower standard than "just cause", includes qualities such as having a bad attitude, being unable to get along with colleagues or customers in a reasonable manner.

UNTENABLE PLEA. One that is clearly impossible of success at law.

UNTENANTABLE. *adj*. Refers to the actual physical state of property being unsuitable for occupation by tenants.

UNTIL. *prep*. To.

UNUM EST TACERE, ALIUD CELARE. [L.] It is one thing to be quiet, another to conceal.

UNUMQUODQUE EODEM MODO, QUO COLLIGATUM EST, DISSOLVITUR. [L.] Everything is loosened in the same way that it was bound.

UNUSUAL. *adj*. Not usual; out of the ordinary. See CRUEL AND ~ PUNISHMENT.

UNUSUAL DANGER. In occupier's liability, used in an objective sense, danger which is not usually found in carrying out the task or fulfilling the function which the invitee is expected to carry out or fulfil. What is unusual varies with the purpose for which the invitee enters the premises. *Horton v. London Graving Dock Co.*, [1951] A.C. 737 (U.K. H.L.).

UNVALUED POLICY. A marine policy is an unvalued policy if it does not specify the value of the subject-matter insured and, subject to the limit of the sum insured, leaves the value to be determined in accordance with the Act. Marine Insurance Act, 1993, S.C. 1993, c. 22, s. 30(3).

UNWHOLESOME. *adj*. With respect to fish, means fish that has in or upon it micro-organisms of public health significance or substances toxic or aesthetically offensive to people.

UPC. Universal Product Code.

UPDATING COURSE. A special course of training for certified tradesmen whose skill and knowledge have become inadequate due to innovations and developments in their designated trade.

UPGRADING COURSE. A course of training established for the purpose of supplementing where appropriate the technical knowledge of applicants for certificates of qualification.

UPHOLSTERED FURNITURE. Any furniture that is made or sold with cushions, loose or attached, or is itself stuffed or filled in whole or in part with any stuffing concealed by fabric or other flexible material or any such article that can be used for sitting, resting or reclining purposes.

UPHOLSTERED OR STUFFED ARTICLE. Any object which contains stuffing.

UPLAND GAME BIRD. Includes the following birds and the birds of all species of the following families: tetraonidae, commonly known as grouse, including ruffed grouse, spruce grouse, prairie chickens, sharp-tailed grouse, sage grouse and ptarmigans; phasianidae, commonly known as pheasants and partridges, including ring-necked pheasants, European grey or Hungarian partridges, chukar partridges and quail; meleagrididae, commonly known as wild turkey. *The Game Act*, R.S.S. 1978, c. G-1, s. 2.

UPON. *prep*. Immediately, on the occasion of. Before the act done to which it relates or simultaneously with the act done or after the act is done according to the context.

UPON PROOF. As applied to any matter connected with the licensing of an insurer or other person, means upon proof to the satisfaction of the superintendent. *Insurance acts*.

UPPER TIER MUNICIPALITY. A municipality of which two or more municipalities form part for municipal purposes. Ont. Statutes.

UPPER TORSO RESTRAINT. A portion of a seat belt assembly intended to restrain movement of the chest and shoulder regions. *Motor Vehicle Safety Regulations*, C.R.C., c. 1038, s. 2.

UPSTREAM. *adj*. Closer to a power plant in a power plant/transmission line/electric distribution system sequence.

URANIUM UNDERTAKING. See SPECIFIED ~.

URBAN. *adj*. Relating to a built-up area, a city or town.

URBAN AREA. 1. An area and areas adjacent thereto that are classified by Statistics Canada in its most recent census of Canada as urban. *Railway Relocation and Crossing Act*, R.S.C. 1985, c. R-4, s. 2. 2. A city, town or village.

URBAN CONSTITUENCY. A constituency that is wholly composed of an urban municipality or municipalities.

URBAN DEVELOPMENT PLAN. A plan respecting the development and use of land within or within and adjacent to an urban area whereby it is proposed to control and regulate the use of that land for purposes of industry, commerce, government, recreation, transportation, hospitals, schools, churches, residences, homes for the elderly or for other purposes or classes of users, with or without subdivisions of the various classes. *Railway Relocation and Crossing Act*, R.S.C. 1985, c. R-4, s. 2.

URBAN DISTRICT. A municipality, village or built-up district.

URBAN ELECTORAL DIVISION. An electoral division that comprises the whole or part of an urban municipality.

URBAN FSA CODE. An FSA code the second character of which is any numeral other than "0". *Mail Preparation Regulations*, C.R.C., c. 1281, s. 2.

URBAN MUNICIPAL ADMINISTRATOR. The clerk, secretary treasurer or treasurer of an urban municipality.

URBAN MUNICIPALITY. A city, town or village.

URBAN PLANNING. The guiding and shaping of development, growth, and change in urban centres with the aim of harmonizing as many aspects of the life of the inhabitants and visitors as possible.

URBAN POLLING DIVISION. A polling division that is wholly contained within an incorporated city or town.

URBAN RENEWAL. Action involving redevelopment, rehabilitation and conservation measures taken to renew and repair urban communities and protect them from blight and deterioration.

URBAN RENEWAL AREA. A blighted or substandard area of a municipal area for which a Lieutenant-Governor in Council has approved the implementation of an urban renewal scheme.

URBAN RENEWAL SCHEME. A scheme for the renewal of a blighted or substandard area of a municipal area that includes (a) a plan designating the buildings and works in the area that are to be acquired and cleared in connection with the scheme and for making available to persons dispossessed of housing accommodation by such acquisition or clearance, decent, safe and sanitary housing accommodation at rentals that are fair and reasonable having regard to the incomes of the persons to be dispossessed; (b) a plan describing the proposed street pattern and land use for the area, and the program for the construction or improvement in the area of the municipality services, schools, parks, playgrounds, community buildings and other public facilities; (c) a description of the methods planned for municipal direction and control of the use of land in the area including zoning, building controls and standards of occupancy of buildings in the area; (d) a description of the methods planned for the improvement, rehabilitation or replacement of privately owned facilities, including housing accommodation, that will continue in the area, and the techniques planned for retarding such facilities from becoming substandard; and (e) the estimated costs of the scheme and that will be developed in accordance or in harmony with an official community plan.

URBAN RENEWAL STUDY. A study or survey of conditions aimed at identifying blighted areas, determining housing requirements and providing data upon which an orderly program of housing and urban renewal measures may be based.

URGENT. *adj*. Passage of time will threaten serious irreparable harm.

URGENT NEED OF PROTECTION. In respect of a member of the Convention refugee abroad, the country of asylum or the source country class, that their life, liberty or physical safety is under immediate threat and, if not protected, the person is likely to be (a) killed; (b) subjected to violence, torture, sexual assault or arbitrary imprisonment; or (c) returned to their country of nationality or of their former habitual residence. *Immigration regulation.*

U.S. *abbr.* United States (of America).

U.S.A. *abbr.* United States of America.

USAGE. *n.* 1. " . . . [A] course of conduct which is recognized as being normal in various types of occupations and contractual relationships . . ." *Gainers Ltd. v. United Packinghouse, Food & Allied Workers, Local 319* (1964), 47 W.W.R. 544 at 552, 64 C.L.L.C. 14,030 (Alta. T.D.), Riley J. 2. A practice which a government ordinarily follows, though it is not obligatory. Such a practice may become a convention. P.W. Hogg, *Constitutional Law of Canada*, 3d ed. (Toronto: Carswell, 1992) at 21. See CONVENTION; IMMEMORIAL ~.

USE. *v.* 1. " . . . [U]tilization or employment of, with some aim or purpose. . ." *Andison Estate, Re* (1986), 44 Man. R. (2d) 135 at 137 (Q.B.), Kennedy J. 2. [C]onnotation of the actual carrying into action, operation or effect . . ." *R. v. Chang* (1989), 50 C.C.C. (3d) 413 at 422 (B.C. C.A.), Carrothers J.A. 3. " . . . '[U]se' of property involves control or personal possession of the property by the insured and/or the insured putting the property to his own service. . ." *Kenting Drilling Ltd. v. General Accident Assurance Co. of Canada* (1979), [1980] I.L.R. 1-1168 at 542, [1979] 5 W.W.R. 68, 26 A.R. 90, 102 D.L.R. (3d) 99 (T.D.), Moshansky J. 4. " . . . [T]he working, manipulation, operation, handling or employment of the vehicle, not just merely making use of it by riding in it. . ." *Watts v. Centennial Insurance Co.* (1967), 62 W.W.R. 175 at 177, [1969] I.L.R. 1-220, 65 D.L.R. (2d) 529 (B.C. S.C.), Wilson C.J.S.C. 5. Includes construct, demonstrate, test, operate, handle, repair, service and maintain. *Radiation Health and Safety Act*, S.S. 1984-85-86, c. R-1.1, s. 2. See ENTER AND ~.

USE. *n.* 1. Habitual practice. 2. The employment of a thing to achieve a purpose. 3. The purpose for which land is intended or may be put. 4. Legal interpretation of meaning of the word is context-specific. 5. In relation to a trade-mark, means any use that by section 4 is deemed to be a use in association with wares or services. *Trademarks Act*, R.S.C. 1985, c. T-13, s. 2. 6. The purpose for which land is intended, or to which it may be put. Canada regulations. See ACCESSORY ~; BENEFICIAL ~; CESTUI QUE ~; COMMERCIAL ~; COMMON ~; CONFORMING ~; DEAD ~; DEED TO ~S; DIRECTIONS FOR ~; DOMESTIC ~; ENERGY ~ PROJECT; EXCLUSIVE ~ PORTION; EXISTING ~; FARM ~; ILLICIT DRUG ~; INTERNAL ~; LAND ~ CONTROL LAW; LAND ~ DISTRICT; LAND ~ PLAN; MILEAGE CONTRACT ~; NONCONFORMING ~; ORDINARY ~; OWNER TO ~S; PARENTERAL ~; PASSIVE ~; PERMITTED ~; PRINCIPAL ~; PRIOR ~; RESOURCE ~ PERMIT; RESULTING ~; RIGHT OF ~; SHIFTING ~; SPRINGING ~; TRANSFER TO ~S; UNAUTHORIZED ~.

USE AND OCCUPATION. A person may claim for use and occupation of his land by a person who occupies it without a lease, leasing agreement or a set rent.

USED AUTOMOBILE. An automobile that has been driven for any purpose except delivery to a dealer and servicing.

USED VEHICLE. A motor vehicle which has been sold, bargained, exchanged, given away or title transferred from the person who first acquired it from the manufacturer or importer, dealer or agent of the manufacturer or importer, and so used as to have become what is commonly known as "second hand" within the ordinary meaning thereof.

USEFUL ARTICLE. An article that has a utilitarian function and includes a model of any such article. *Industrial Design Act*, R.S.C. 1985, c. I-9, s. 2.

USEFUL BEAM. The radiation passing through the aperture, cone or collimator of the housing of an X-ray generating tube. Canada regulations.

USEFUL LIFE. The period of time or use, whether full or intermediate, in respect of which an emission standard applies to a vehicle or engine, as set out in the CFR. *On-Road Vehicle and Engine Emission Regulations*, SOR/2003-2, s. 1(1).

USE PERMIT. A permit, issued by the council of a municipality, authorizing the use of a building or other structure for the purpose stated in the permit. *The Planning and Development Act*, R.S.S. 1978, c. P-13, s. 2.

USER. *n.* 1. A person who uses a thing. 2. Enjoyment or use, not the person who uses. 3. A person who within a province utilizes or intends to utilize tangible personal property or a taxable service for personal consumption or for the consumption of any other person at her or his expense, or utilizes or intends to utilize tangible personal property or a taxable service on behalf of or as the agent for a principal who desired or desires to so utilize such property or taxable service for consumption by the principal or by any person at the expense of the principal. 4. A person who prepares a consumer report for her or his own use or causes a consumer reporting agency to prepare a consumer report for her or his use. *Consumer Reporting acts.* See DRUG ~; END ~; METER ~; MIS~; NATURAL ~; NON-NATURAL ~; NON-~; REGISTERED ~; RIGHT OF ~; WATER ~.

USER CHARGE. Any charge for an insured health service that is authorized or permitted by a provincial health care insurance plan that is not payable, directly or indirectly, by a provincial health care insurance plan, but does not include any charge imposed by extra-billing. *Canada Health Act*, R.S.C. 1985, c. C-6, s. 2.

USER CONTROL. A control that is provided on or external to a device by the manufacturer thereof for the purpose of adjustment or operation and that under normal usage, is accessible to the user.

USHER. *n.* A door-keeper; an official who keeps order and silence in a court.

USQUE AD COELUM ET AD INFEROS. [L.] Up to the sky and down to the depths.

USQUE AD MEDIUM FILUM AQUAE. [L.] Just to the middle of the stream.

USQUE AD MEDIUM FILUM VIAE. [L.] Just to the middle of the road.

USQUE AD SOLUM. [L.] As far as the soil.

USSMSG. *abbr.* United States standard metals gauge for sheet iron and steel.

U.S.S.R. *abbr.* Union of Soviet Socialist Republics.

USUAL COVENANT. One of the covenants ordinarily inserted in a deed.

USUAL OR CUSTOMARY AUTHORITY. The authority which an agent in that particular business, trade, profession or place would customarily or normally possess unless the principal expressly said something to contradict it.

USUAL PLACE OF ABODE. The place where one habitually (a) resides; or (b) carries on business; or (c) is employed.

USUFRUCT. *n.* A right of temporary possession, use or enjoyment of the advantages of property belonging to another.

USUFRUCTUARY. *n.* The person who enjoys a usufruct.

USURA EST COMMODUM CERTUM QUOD PROPTER USUM REI (VEL AERIS) MUTUATAE RECIPITUR; SED, SECUNDARIO SPERARE DE ALIQUA RETRIBUTIONE, AD VOLUNTATEM EJUS QUI MUTUATUS EST, HOC NON EST VITIOSUM. [L.] Usury is a certain reward which one receives for the use of a thing (or money) lent; but, secondarily to hope for any return at the will of the party who borrowed is not corrupt.

USURPATION. *n.* Having charge of or retaining something belonging to another by using it.

USURY. *n.* "In ancient times the lending of money at interest was described as the practice of usury. Today, usury is generally thought of as lending money at an excessive rate of interest." *Pioneer Envelopes Ltd. v. British Columbia (Minister of Finance)* (1980), 18 C.P.C. 119 at 121, 21 B.C.L.R. 175 (S.C.), Bouck J.

USUS EST DOMINIUM FIDUCIARIUM. [L.] Use is a fiduciary right of ownership.

USUS NORMA LOQUENDI. [L.] Usage is the rule of speech.

UTC. Coordinated Universal Time.

UTENSIL. *n.* Any article or equipment used in the preparation, processing, packing, service, transport or storage of food, except a single-service article.

UTERO-GESTATION. *n.* Pregnancy.

UTERUS. *n.* The hollow muscular organ in females where embryos develop. F.A. Jaffe, *A Guide to Pathological Evidence*, 3d ed. (Toronto: Carswell, 1991) at 228.

U.T. FAC. L. REV. *abbr.* University of Toronto Faculty of Law Review.

UTILE PER INUTILE NON VITIATUR. [L.] What is useful is not spoiled by what is useless.

UTILITARIAN FUNCTION. In respect of an article, means a function other than merely serving as a substrate or carrier for artistic or literary matter. *Industrial Design Act*, R.S.C. 1985, c. I-9, s. 2.

UTILITIES. *n*. Any one or more of the following: (a) systems for the distribution of gas, whether artificial or natural; (b) facilities for the storage, transmission, treatment, distribution or supply of water; (c) facilities for the collection, treatment, movement or disposal of sanitary sewage; (d) storm sewer drainage facilities. See UTILITY.

UTILITIES OFFICER. A person who assists a municipal authority in the organization, construction, operation and co-ordination, or any of them, of a rural gas utility or a public utility within the boundaries of that rural municipal authority.

UTILITY. *n*. 1. A navigable water, a railway, a highway, an irrigation ditch, an underground telegraph or telephone line, a line for the transmission of hydrocarbons, power or any other substance, or a publicly owned or operated drainage system, dike or sewer. *National Energy Board Act*, R.S.C. 1985, c. N-7, s. 108. 2. Of an invention, depends on whether it will be put into practice by a competent person, do what it assumes to do, and be practical and useful at the time when the patent was granted for the purposes indicated by the patentee. See ELECTRICAL ~; ELECTRIC ~; ENERGY ~; GAS ~; MUNICIPAL ~; MUNICIPAL WATER ~; POWER ~; PUBLIC ~; TELECOMMUNICATIONS ~; UTILITIES; WATER ~.

UTILITY COMPANY. A corporation that carries on business as a distributor or seller to the public of electrical energy, gas or steam or as a generator and seller of electrical energy or steam for distribution to the public.

UTILITY LINE. A pipe line, a telephone, telegraph, electric power or water line, or any other line that supplies a service or commodity to the public.

UTILITY SYSTEM. Equipment or facilities which are available to the public for the purpose of communicating by telephone, teletype or telegraph.

UTILITY VEHICLE. See OFF-ROAD ~.

UTILIZATION. *n*. Use.

UTILIZATION EQUIPMENT. Equipment that utilizes electrical energy for mechanical, chemical, heating, lighting, or a similar useful purpose.

UTI POSSIDETIS. [L.] As you possess.

U.T.L.J. *abbr*. University of Toronto Law Journal.

U. TORONTO FACULTY L. REV. *abbr*. University of Toronto Faculty of Law Review.

U. TORONTO L.J. *abbr*. University of Toronto Law Journal.

UT POENA AD PAUCOS, METUS AD OMNES PERVENIAT. [L.] Though punishment affects few, fear of punishment affects all.

UT RES MAGIS VALEAT QUAM PEREAT. [L. it is better for a thing to go well than to fail] Legislation should be interpreted to give it effect even if a broader interpretation is required. *R. v. C.A.E. Industries Ltd.* (1985), 30 B.L.R. 236 at 245, [1986] 1 F.C. 129, [1985] 5 W.W.R. 481, 61 N.R. 19, 20 D.L.R. (4th) 347 (C.A.), Stone J.A. and *R. v. Victoria Lumber & Manufacturing Co.* (1897), 5 B.C.R. 288 at 300 (C.A.), McCreight J.A. (Walkem and Drake JJ.A. concurring).

UT SUPRA. [L.] As above.

UTTER. *v*. 1. Includes sell, pay, tender and put off. *Criminal Code*, R.S.C. 1985, c. C-46, s. 448. 2. Publish, deliver, put into circulation.

UTTERING COUNTERFEIT MONEY. Every one who, without lawful justification or excuse, the proof of which lies on him, (a) utters or offers to utter counterfeit money or uses counterfeit money as if it were genuine, or (b) exports, sends or takes counterfeit money out of Canada, is guilty of an indictable offence and liable to imprisonment for a term not exceeding fourteen years. *Criminal Code*, R.S.C. 1985, c. C-46, s. 452.

UTTERING FORGED DOCUMENT. Every one who, knowing that a document is forged, (a) uses, deals with or acts upon it, or (b) causes or attempts to cause any person to use, deal with or act upon it, as if the document were genuine, (c) is guilty of an indictable offence and liable to imprisonment for a term not exceeding ten years; or (d) is guilty of an offence punishable on summary conviction. *Criminal Code*, R.S.C. 1985, c. C-46, s. 368.

UTTERING FORGED PASSPORT. While in or out of Canada, (a) forges a passport; or (b) knowing that a passport is forged (i) uses, deals with or acts upon it; or (ii) causes or attempts to cause any person to use, deal with, or act upon it, as if the passport were genuine. *Criminal Code*, R.S.C. 1985, c. C-46, s. 57(1).

UTTERING THREAT. Every one commits an offence who, in any manner, knowingly utters, conveys or causes any person to receive a threat (a) to cause death or bodily harm to any person; (b) to burn, destroy or damage real or personal property; or (c) to kill, poison or injure an animal or bird that is the property of any person. *Criminal Code*, R.S.C. 1985, c. C-46, s. 264.1(1).

U.W.O. L. REV. *abbr.* University of Western Ontario Law Review.

V. *abbr.* 1. Versus. 2. Volume. 3. Volt. 4. Victoria.

VACANCY. *n.* 1. "[In insurance refers] . . . to the absence of inanimate objects, . . ." *Wilson v. INA Insurance Co. of Canada* (1991), 5 C.C.L.I. (2d) 46 at 50, [1992] I.L.R. 1-2808 (B.C. S.C.), Spencer J. 2. " . . . An early but often quoted authority is that of Reville Co. Ct. J. in Re Oil, Chemical & Atomic Workers, Loc. 9-599 and Tidewater Oil Co. (Canada) Ltd. (1963), 14 L.A.C. 233n . . . : ' . . . [A] vacant position for which there is adequate work in the opinion of the company to justify the filling of that position."' *Maplewood Nursing Home Ltd. v. London & District Service Workers Union, Local 220* (1989), 9 L.A.C. (4th) 115 at 121 (Ont.), Hunter. 3. An elected office for which there is no duly elected incumbent. *Local Government Election Amendment Act*, S.S. 1984-85-86, c. 51, s. 3. 4. Includes absence for any reason. *District Courts Act*, R.S. Nfld. 1970, c. 98, s. 2.

VACANT. *adj.* 1. " . . . [A]pplies to the absence of inanimate objects in a premises . . ." *Mohammed v. Canadian Northern Shield Insurance Co.* (1992), 10 C.C.L.I. (2d) 118 at 124, [1992] B.C.W.L.D. 1776 (S.C.), Lamperson J. 2. "[In a fire insurance policy applies to] . . . inanimate objects . . ." *Miller v. Portage la Prairie Mutual Insurance Co.*, [1936] 2 D.L.R. 787 at 791, [1936] 2 W.W.R. 104, 3 I.L.R. 377 (Sask. C.A.), the court per Gordon J.A. See UNOCCUPIED.

VACANT CROWN LAND. The surface of land owned by the Crown and in which no other person has any interest.

VACANTIA BONA. Things found which have no apparent owner. See BONA VACANTIA.

VACANT LAND. A parcel of land separately assessed that has no building thereon, but does not include any improved land. *Municipal Tax Sales Act*, R.S.O. 1990, c. M.60, s. 1(1). See SERVICED ~.

VACANT POSSESSION. 1. " . . . [A] house free of household furniture and effects as well as animate occupancy." *Burke v. Campbell* (1978), 87 D.L.R. (3d) 427 at 432, 20 O.R. (2d) 300, [1979] I.L.R. 1-1148 (H.C.), Craig J. 2. Usual term of an agreement of purchase and sale of residential property. The vendor is required to give vacant possession to the purchaser upon closing.

VACATE. *v.* 1. To cancel; to make ineffective. 2. "[Used in Criminal Code, R.S.C. 1970, c. C-34] . . . to indicate what has occurred is terminated but without impairing what has previously occurred." *Purves v. Canada (Attorney General)* (1990), 54 C.C.C. (3d) 355 at 364 (B.C. C.A.), the court per Legg J.A. 3. To leave, to move out, to empty.

VACATED COMMUNITY. A community the remaining inhabitants of which have moved from the community with financial or other assistance from the province. *Evacuated Communities Act*, R.S. Nfld. 1990, c. E-15, s. 2.

VACATION. *n.* A period of the year during which courts do not conduct ordinary business. See CHRISTMAS ~; LONG ~; SHORT ~.

VACATION CAMP. Any installation, other than an establishment, where children under 18 years of age are sheltered during a period of school vacation and where recreational services and sports, educational or cultural equipment are provided. *Public Health Protection Act*, R.S.Q. 1977, c. P-35, s. 1.

VACATION PAY. Four per cent, or after 6 consecutive years of employment by one employer, 6 per cent of wages of an employee during the year of employment in respect of which the employee is entitled to the vacation. *Canada Labour Code*, R.S.C. 1985, c. L-2, s. 183.

VACATION SCHOOL. A program of instruction offered to students at a time when the school is otherwise closed for vacation.

VACCINATE. *v.* Innoculate with vaccine against brucellosis with vaccine in accordance with the regulations. *Brucellosis acts.*

VACCINATE. *n.* See OFFICIAL ~.

VACUUM BREAKER. A device used in a water supply pipe which, when strategically located, will prevent the reverse flow of water in the pipe by admitting air to the pipe and thereby preclude any back siphonage that might otherwise occur.

VACUUM PACK. A pack in which a minimum amount of packing media is used and the vacuum in the can is created mechanically.

VADE MECUM. [L.] Go with me.

VADIUM. *n.* A pledge or pawn. E.L.G. Tyler & N.E. Palmer, eds., *Cross Vaines' Personal Property*, 5th ed. (London: Butterworth, 1973) at 85.

VAGAL INHIBITION. Cessation of heart beat by stimulating the vagus nerve by immersion in cold water, pressure on the neck or a minor surgical procedure. F.A. Jaffe, *A Guide to Pathological Evidence*, 3d ed. (Toronto: Carswell, 1991) at 228.

VAGINA. *n.* The tubular passage of muscle in females which connects the cervix with the vulva. F.A. Jaffe, *A Guide to Pathological Evidence*, 2d ed. (Toronto: Carswell, 1983) at 186.

VAGRANCY. *n.* Every one commits vagrancy who (a) supports himself in whole or in part by gaming or crime and has no lawful profession or calling by which to maintain himself; or (b) having at any time been convicted of an offence under section 151,152 or 153, subsection 160(3) or 173(2) or section 271, 272 or 273 or of an offence under a provision referred to in paragraph (b) of the definition "serious personal injury offence" in section 687 of the Criminal Code, chapter C-34 of the Revised Statutes of Canada, 1970, as it read before January 4,1983, is found loitering or wandering in or near a school ground, , playground, public park or bathing area. *Criminal Code*, R.S.C. 1985, c. C-46, s. 179(1).

VAGRANT. *n.* " . . . '[I]dle and disorderly person' . . ." *R. v. Knowles* (1929), 65 O.L.R. 6 at 8, 37 O.W.N. 305, 52 C.C.C. 377 (C.A.), Middleton J.A.

VAGUENESS. *n.* " . . . [A] law will be found unconstitutionally vague if it so lacks in precision as not to give sufficient guidance for legal debate. This statement of the doctrine best conforms to the dictates of the rule of law in the modern state, and it reflects the prevailing argumentative, adversarial framework for the administration of justice." *R. v. Pharmaceutical Society (Nova Scotia)* (1992), (*sub nom. R. v. Nova Scotia Pharmaceutical Society*) 43 C.P.R. (3d) 1 at 26, 15 C.R. (4th) 1, 93 D.L.R. (4th) 36, 74 C.C.C. (3d) 289, 10 C.R.R. (2d) 34, [1992] 2 S.C.R. 606, 139 N.R. 241, 114 N.S.R. (2d) 91, 313 A.P.R. 91, the court per Gonthier J.

VAGUS. *n.* A nerve which begins in the brain stem, passes through the neck and the chest and supplies branches to the larynx, carotid bodies, lungs, heart, stomach and abdominal organs. F.A. Jaffe, *A Guide to Pathological Evidence*, 3d ed. (Toronto: Carswell, 1991) at 228.

VALEAT QUANTUM. [L.] Let its weight stand.

VALEAT QUANTUM VALERE POTEST. [L.] It should be taken for what it is worth.

VALID. *adj.* 1. Having force legally. 2. Issued in accordance with the applicable law and the articles of the issuer or validated. *Business Corporations acts.*

VALIDATE. *v.* To render in force for a prescribed period of time.

VALIDITY. *n.* " . . . [T]he quality of being sound and well grounded, . . ." *Ontario (Crime Commission), Re*, (*sub nom. Feeley, Ex parte*) [1962] O.R. 872 at 894,133 C.C.C. 116, 34 D.L.R. (2d) 451 (C.A.), Schroeder J.A. (Aylesworth J.A. concurring).

VALID TENDER. A proposal, bid or offer that is submitted in response to an invitation from a contracting authority and meets all the requirements stipulated in the invitation.

VALLEY. *n.* A hollow or depression of some width bounded by hills or mountains, usually with a stream or river running through it.

VALUABLE CONSIDERATION. 1. Includes: (i) any consideration sufficient to support a simple contract; (ii) an antecedent debt or liability. *Assignment of Book Debts acts.* 2. " . . . [M]ay consist either in some right, interest, profit, or benefit accruing to the one party, or some forbearance, detriment, loss, or responsibility, given, suffered, or undertaken by the other . . ." *Currie v. Misa* (1875), L.R. 10 Ex. 153 at 162 (U.K.), the court per Lusk J. See ADEQUATE ~; FULL AND ~; GOOD CONSIDERATION.

VALUABLE MINERAL IN PLACE. A vein, lode or deposit of mineral in place appearing at the time of discovery to be of such a nature and containing in the part thereof then exposed such kind and quantity of mineral or minerals in place other than limestone, marble, clay, marl, peat or building stone, as to make it probable that the vein, lode or deposit is capable of being developed into a producing mine likely to be workable at a profit. *Mining Act*, R.S.O. 1990, c. M.14, s. 1.

VALUABLE SECURITIES. Includes every document forming the title or evidence of the title to any property of any kind whatever. *Canada Shipping Act*, R.S.C. 1985, c. S-9, s. 2.

VALUABLE SECURITY. Includes (a) an order, exchequer acquittance or other security that entitles or evidences the title of any person (i) to a share or interest in a public stock or fund or in any fund of a body corporate, company or society; or (ii) to a deposit in a financial institution; (b) any debenture, deed, bond, bill, note, warrant, order or other security for money or for payment of money; (c) a document of title to lands or goods wherever situated; (d) a stamp or writing that secures or evidences title to or an interest in a chattel personal, or that evidences delivery of a chattel personal; and (e) a release, receipt, discharge or other instrument evidencing payment of money. *Criminal Code*, R.S.C. 1985, c. C-46, s. 2.

VALUATION. *n.* 1. " . . . [A]n expression of an opinion as to value." *Sanwa Bank California v. Quebec, North Shore & Labrador Railway* (1988), 48 D.L.R. (4th) 360 at 364, 69 Nfld. & P.E.I.R. 220, 211 A.P.R. 220 (Nfld. T.D.), Russell J. 2. " . . . [A] person is appointed to ascertain some matter for the purpose of preventing differences from arising, not of settling them when they have arisen, . . ." *Re Carus-Wilson and Greene* (1886), 18 Q.B.D. 7 at 9 (U.K. C.A.), Lord Esher M.R. 3. " . . . [G]enerally for the purpose of completing the contract engagement between two parties by fixing an amount or arriving at a like result by calculation or by an examination of work done or the inspection of definite articles." *Campbell v. Irwin* (1914), 32 O.L.R. 48 at 61 (C.A.), the court per Hodgins

J.A. 4. The determination of the value of property for taxation purposes. See DUAL ~; GOING CONCERN ~.

VALUATION DATE. The earliest of the following dates: 1. The date the spouses separate and there is no reasonable prospect that they will resume cohabitation. 2. The date a divorce is granted. 3. The date the marriage is declared a nullity.

VALUE. *n.* 1. " . . . [I]n the case of Montreal Island Power Co. v. Laval des Rapides, [1936] 1 D.L.R. 621, [1935] S.C.R. 304. At pp. 621-2 D.L.R., p. 305 S.C.R. [Duff C.J.C.] quotes from a judgment of Lord MacLaren in Lord Advocate v. Earl of Home (1891), 28 Sc. L.R. 289 at p. 293: ' . . . [W]hen it occurs in a contract . . . means exchangeable value—the price which the subject will bring when exposed to the test of competition.'" Continuing, Duff C.J.C. says: 'When used for the purpose of defining the valuation of property for taxation purposes, the Courts have, in this country, and, generally speaking, on this continent, accepted this view of the term "value".' *Withycombe Estate, Re*, [1945] 2 D.L.R. 274 at 286, (*sub nom. A.G. of Alta. v. Royal Trust Co.*) [1945] S.C.R. 267, Hudson J. (Taschereau J. concurring). 2. In real estate law generally means the fair market value of the land, which is based on what a seller and buyer, "each knowledgeable and willing," would pay for it on the open market. . .Market value generally is the *exchange* value of land, rather than its *use* value to the lessee. *Musqueam Indian Band v. Glass* (2000), 2000 CarswellNat 2405, 2000 SCC 52, [2000] 11 W.W.R. 407, 36 R.P.R. (3d) 1, 192 D.L.R. (4th) 385, 82 B.C.L.R. (3d) 199, 261 N.R. 296, 186 F.T.R. 248 (note), [2000] 2 S.C.R. 633, [2001] 1 C.N.L.R. 208, Per Gonthier J. (Major, Binnie and LeBel JJ. concurring). 3. Any consideration sufficient to support a simple contract. *Personal Property Security acts*. 4. Valuable consideration. *Bills of Exchange Act*, R.S.C. 1985, c. B-4, s. 2. 5. " . . . [A] word appropriate to the position of owner. It is the worth of the property to the owner thereof . . ." *MacMillan Bloedel Ltd. v. Port Alberni (City)* (*sub nom. Port Alberni (City) v. MacMillan Bloedel Ltd.*) (1973), 36 D.L.R. (3d) 229 at 236-7, [1974] S.C.R. 83, [1973] 5 W.W.R. 321, Spence J. (Martland, Pigeon and Laskin JJ. concurring). 6. " . . . [I]n assessment statutes refers to current values, not historic values . . ." *Shapiro v. Winnipeg City* Assessor (1987), (*sub nom. Shapiro v. City Assessor for City of Winnipeg*) 43 D.L.R. (4th) 506 at 515,

49 Man. R. (2d) 305 (C.A.), the court per Philp J.A. 7. Fair market value. 8. Assessed value, including improvements. 9. " ... (1) ... the value to the owner as it existed at the date of the taking, not the value to the taker. (2) The value to the owner consisting in all advantages which the land possesses, present or future, but it is the present value alone of such advantages that fails to be determined." *Lake Erie & Northern Railway v. Brantford Golf & Country Club* (1914), (*sub nom. Brantford Golf & Country Club v. Lake Erie & Northern Railway*) 32 O.L.R. 141 at 146, 7 O.W.N. 197 (C.A.), the court per Hodgins J.A. quoting Lord Dunedin in *Cedar Rapids Manufacturing and Power Co. v. Lacoste* [1914] A.C. 569 at 576. 10. "[In the context of appropriation] ... In Diggon-Hibben Ltd. v. The King, [1949] 4 D.L.R. 785 at p. 787 ... the Supreme Court of Canada defined 'value' ... in the following terms: ' ... that the owner at the moment of expropriation is to be deemed as without title, but all else remaining the same, and the question is what would he, as a prudent man, at that moment, pay for the property rather than be ejected from it.'" *Saskatoon (City) v. Shinkaruk* (1987), 38 L.C.R. 193 at 197, 63 Rask. R. 189 (Q.B.), Malone J. 11. " ... [C]ost or saleable value; ..." *Samo v. Gore District Mutual Fire Insurance Co.* (1877), 1 O.A.R. 545 at 568 (C.A.), Patterson J.A. (Burton and Moss JJ.A. concurring). See ACCEPTED ~; ACTUAL ~; AMORTIZED ~; ANNUAL ~; ASSESSED ~; BOOK ~; COMMERCIAL ~; COMMODITY ~ OF GAS; COMMUTED ~; CURRENT ~; ACCOUNTING; DEDUCTIVE ~; DOUBLE ~; DUTY PAID ~; EN BLOC ~; EXCHANGE ~; FACE ~; FAIR ~; FIELD ~; GOING-CONCERN ~; GROSS ~; HERITAGE ~; HOLDER FOR ~; INTRINSIC ~; LENDING ~; LEVIABLE ~; LOAN ~; MARKET ~; NET ~; NOMINAL ~; ORAL LD$_{50}$ ~; PAR~; PRESENT ~; PROBATE ~; PROBATIVE ~; PROPERTY ~; PURCHASER FOR ~; RATEABLE ~; REALIZABLE ~; REPLACEMENT ~; REVERSIONARY ~; SALVAGE ~; SERVICE ~; SURRENDER ~; TAXABLE ~; THRESHOLD LIMIT ~; TRANSACTION ~.

VALUED POLICY. 1. The policy of insurance is based on an agreement as to the value of the item insured. In the event of total loss, the insured can recover the total value and in the event of partial loss, a proportion of the agreed value. 2. A marine policy is a valued policy if it spec-ifies the agreed value of the subject-matter insured. *Marine Insurance Act*, S.C. 1993, c. 22, s. 30(2).

VALUE OF PERSONAL PROPERTY. The assessed value of personal property. See TAXABLE ~.

VALUE OF THE CONTRACT. The contract price or, where there is none established by the contract, the value of the goods to be furnished and the work to be done under the contract.

VALUE OF THE PROPERTY LIABLE. In respect of jurisdiction in matters of salvage, means the value of the property when first brought into safety by the salvors. *Canada Shipping Act*, R.S.C. 1985, c. S-9, s. 2.

VALUER. *n.* 1. A person who appraises or sets value on property. 2. "In determining whether the proceeding ... is a valuation or an arbitration, ... Generally speaking, if the person to whom a reference is made is intended to use his skill and knowledge of the particular subject without taking any evidence or hearing the parties, he is not prima facie an arbitrator, he is a valuer or appraiser." *Pfeil s. Simcoe & Erie General Insurance Co.*, [1986] 2 W.W.R. 710 at 715, 45 Sask. R. 241, 24 D.L.R. (4th) 752, [1986] I.L.R. 1-2055 (C.A.), the court per Vancise J.A.

VALUE RECEIVED. Method of calculating value of constructive trust. The value of the services which the claimant has received. For a monetary award, the "value received" approach is appropriate; the value conferred on the property is irrelevant. *Peter v. Beblow*, 1993 CarswellBC 44, 77 B.C.L.R. (2d) 1, [1993] 3 W.W.R. 337, 44 R.F.L. (3d) 329, 48 E.T.R. 1, 150 N.R. 1, 23 B.C.A.C. 81, 39 W.A.C. 81, 101 D.L.R. (4th) 621, [1993] 1 S.C.R. 980, [1993] R.D.F. 369 McLachlin, J. for the majority

VALUE SURVIVED. Method of calculating value of constructive trust. Where the claim is for an interest in the property one must of necessity, it seems to me, determine what portion of the value of the property claimed is attributable to the claimant's services. The value of that trust is to be determined on the basis of the actual value of the matrimonial property. It reflects the court's best estimate of what is fair having regard to the contribution which the claimant's services have made to the value surviving, bearing in mind the practical difficulty of calculating with mathematical precision the value of particular contributions to the family property. How is the contribution to the property to be determined?

One starts, of necessity, by defining the property. One goes on to determine what portion of that property is attributable to the claimant's efforts. *Peter v. Beblow*, 1993 CarswellBC 44, 77 B.C.L.R. (2d) 1, [1993] 3 W.W.R. 337, 44 R.F.L. (3d) 329, 48 E.T.R. 1, 150 N.R. 1, 23 B.C.A.C. 81, 39 W.A.C. 81, 101 D.L.R. (4th) 621, [1993] 1 S.C.R. 980, [1993] R.D.F. 369 McLachlin, J. for the majority.

VALUE TO OWNER. Used generally in expropriation cases, it is compensatory and may bear no relation to fair market value, market value or fair value. It is the amount the owner would pay for property in lieu of being deprived of the enjoyment and use of it and includes the cost of locating and acquiring a substitute property, opportunity costs and lost income and sometimes quantified emotional factors. A. Bissett-Johnson & W.M. Holland, eds., *Matrimonial Property Law in Canada* (Toronto: Carswell, 1980) at V-9.

VALVE. See BACKWATER ~; FLUSH ~.

VANCOUVER FORMULA. A proposed constitutional amending formula which required agreement of the federal Parliament and two-thirds of the provincial legislatures which represent half of the population of all provinces. P.W. Hogg, *Constitutional Law of Canada*, 3d ed. (Toronto: Carswell, 1992) at 66.

VANDALISM. *n.* " . . . There must be a wrongful intention accompanying the destruction of property to warrant the term 'vandalism'. . ." *Reliable Distributors Ltd. v. Royal Insurance Co. of Canada* (1986), 5 B.C.L.R. (2d) 367 at 370, [1986] 6 W.W.R. 1, 18 C.C.L.I. 267, 30 D.L.R. (4th) 426, [1987] I.L.R. 1-2123 (C.A.), Seaton J.A.

VAPOUR. *n.* The gaseous form of a substance that is found in a solid or liquid state at normal atmospheric pressure. *Consumer Chemicals and Containers Regulations, 2001*, SOR/2001-269, s. 1(1). See INTOXICATING ~.

VAPOUR PRESSURE. The Reid vapour pressure measured in pounds per square inch absolute (psia) that is exerted by a volatile liquid at a given temperature. *Flammable Liquids Bulk Storage Regulations*, C.R.C., c. 1148, s. 2. See REID ~.

VARIABLE CREDIT. Credit made available under an agreement whereby the lender agrees to make credit available to be used from time to time, at the option of the borrower for the pur-

pose of the purchase from time to time of goods, and, without limiting the generality of the foregoing, includes credit arrangements, commonly known as revolving credit accounts, budget accounts, cyclical accounts and other arrangements of a similar nature. *Consumer Protection acts*.

VARIABLE INSURANCE. An annuity or life insurance contract for which the reserves or a part thereof vary in amount with the market value of a specified group of assets held in a separate and distinct fund and includes a provision in a life insurance contract under which policy dividends or policy proceeds may be retained for investment in such a fund. *Insurance Act*, R.S.O. 1990, c. I.8, s. 110(1).

VARIABLE INSURANCE CONTRACT. A contract of life insurance under which the interest of the purchaser is valued for purposes of conversion or surrender by reference to the value of a proportionate interest in a specified portfolio of assets.

VARIABLE RATE AGREEMENT. An agreement that is subject to variations in the true annual percentage rate of the cost of borrowing.

VARIABLE RATE MORTGAGE. A mortgage with a fixed monthly payment whose rate varies with interest rates. If the interest rate goes down, a larger payment is applied to principal, but if the interest rate goes up, any shortfall in interest payment is added to the principal. Can also refer to one where the monthly payments fluctuate with the mortgage rate.

VARIABLE TAX RATE SYSTEM. A system under which individual tax rates are determined and imposed for each property class.

VARIANCE. *n.* 1. Permission to contravene a by-law to permit development of certain land which does not meet criteria prescribed in the by-law. 2. A document without precedential value issued, for an individual circumstance on a single occasion, by a safety officer or safety manager allowing (a) a deviation from the application of an enactment, or (b) a use, other than the standard use, of a regulated product if the proposed use is not specifically prohibited. See MINOR ~.

VARIANTS. *n.* Designs applied to the same article or set and not differing substantially from one another. *Industrial Design Act*, R.S.C. 1985, c. I-9, s. 2.

VARIATION. *n.* An express or implied agreement by which parties agree on a new contract or a new contract term which is mutually convenient and beneficial. See DETRIMENTAL ~ OR ALTERATION.

VARIATION ORDER. An order making changes to a custody or support order made under the Divorce Act.

VARIATION PROCEEDING. A proceeding in a court in which either or both former spouses seek a variation order. *Divorce Act*, R.S.C. 1985 (2d Supp.), c. 3, s. 2.

VARIOUS. *adj*. 1. Different, diverse. 2. Separate, several.

VARY. *v*. To change; to substitute; to alter.

VARYING DUTY. A requirement of service that demands operation at loads and for intervals of time, both of which may be subject to wide variation.

VAULT. *n*. 1. A structure wholly or partially above ground used for the temporary storage of human remains pending burial or other lawful disposition. 2. An isolated enclosure, either above or below ground, with fire-resistant walls, ceilings and floors, for the purpose of housing transformers or other electrical equipment.

V.C. *abbr*. Vice-chancellor.

VECTOR. *n*. An animal that has the potential to transmit a disease, directly or indirectly, from one animal or its excreta to another animal. See ENERGY ~.

VEGETATION. *n*. Any tree, shrub, vine or plant or the fruit or any portion whatsoever of a tree, shrub, vine or plant.

VEHICLE. *n*. 1. " . . . [I]n its original sense conveys the meaning of a structure on wheels for carrying persons or goods. We have generally distinguished carriage from haulage, and mechanical units whose chief function is to haul other units, to do other kinds of work than carrying, are not usually looked upon as vehicles. But that meaning has . . . been weakened by the multiplied forms in which wheeled bodies have appeared with the common features of self-propulsion by motor . . ." *Bennett & White (Calgary) Ltd. v. Sugar City (Municip ality)*, [1950] S.C.R. 450 at 463, [1950] C.T.C. 410, [1950] 3 D.L.R. 81, Rand J. (Taschereau, Estey and Locke JJ. concurring). 2. Any conveyance that may be used for transportation by sea, land or air. 3. Any truck, automobile or other conveyance for use on land but does not include any vehicle running only on rails to which the Rail-

way Act applies. 4. Includes a street car. 5. Any motor vehicle, aircraft or other conveyance designed to be driven or drawn by any means including muscular power, and any part thereof, and includes any equipment necessary for the proper operation of the vehicle and any appurtenances of the vehicle. See ABANDON~; AIR CUSHION ~; ALL TERRAIN ~; AMBULANCE ~; ANTIQUE REPRODUCTION ~; ANTIQUE ~; ARTICULATED ~; CANADIAN ~; CAR POOL ~; COMBINATION OF ~S; COMMERCIAL ~; COURTESY ~; DERELICT ~; DUAL-PURPOSE ~; DUMP ~; EMERGENCY ~; FARM ~; FIRE DEPARTMENT ~; FOREIGN ~; FREIGHT ~; HEAVY DUTY ~; HEAVY ~; HISTORIC ~; JUNKED ~; LIGHT DUTY ~; LIMITED ~; MOBILITY ~; MOTORIZED ~; MOTOR ~; NON-FARM ~; OFF-HIGHWAY ~; OFF-ROAD ~; OPEN-BODY TYPE ~; OUTSIZED ~; OVER-SNOW ~; PASSENGER ~; PLEASURE~; PUBLIC SERVICE ~; PUBLIC ~; RAIL ~; RECONSTRUCTED ~; RECOVERY ~; RECREATIONAL ~; ROAD SERVICE ~; ROAD ~; SCRAP ~; SERVICE ~; SIGHT-SEEING~; SINGLE UNIT ~; SNOWMOBILE CONVERSION ~; SNOW ~; SPECIALLY CONSTRUCTED ~; TANK TRUCK ~; TANK ~; TOW ~; USED ~; WHEELCHAIR ~; WORK ~.

VEHICLE COMPONENT. A seat cushion, seat back, seat belt, headlining, convertible top, arm rest, trim panel including door, front, rear and side panel, compartment shelf, head restraint, floor covering, sun visor, curtain, shade, wheel housing cover, engine compartment cover, mattress cover and the interior of the vehicle including padding and crash-deployed components that are designed to absorb energy on contact by occupants in the event of a crash.

VEHICLE IDENTIFICATION NUMBER. 1. Any number or other mark placed on a motor vehicle for the purpose of distinguishing the motor vehicle from other similar motor vehicles. *Criminal Code*, R.S.C. 1985, c. C-46, s. 354(3). 2. A number consisting of arabic numerals, roman letters, or both that the manufacturer assigns to the vehicle for identification purposes. *Motor Vehicle Safety Regulations*, C.R.C., c. 1038, s. 2.

VEHICLE INSPECTION RECORD. A form required to be completed in accordance with the regulations prior to the issue of a vehicle inspection sticker. *Highway Traffic Act*, R.S.O. 1990, c. H.8, s. 88.

VEHICLE INSPECTION STATION. A site adjacent to a highway designed or used for the purpose of weighing or inspecting vehicles or their contents.

VEHICLE SAFETY ITEM. Any component or equipment forming part of, attached to, or carried on a vehicle, or required to be worn by a passenger in or on a vehicle which may affect the safe operation of the vehicle or contribute to the safety of the driver, passengers or the public.

VEHICLE WEIGHT. See GROSS ~; MAXIMUM LOADED ~; UNLOADED ~.

VEIN. *n*. A blood vessel which carries blood from tissues to the heart. F.A. Jaffe, *A Guide to Pathological Evidence*, 3d ed. (Toronto: Carswell, 1991) at 228.

VEIN OR LODE. Includes rock in place. *Yukon Quartz Mining Act*, R.S.C. 1985, c. Y-4, s. 2.

VELOCITY. See MUZZLE ~.

VENDEE. *n*. The person to whom one sells something.

VENDING. *n*. " . . . [S]elling . . ." *Domco Industries Ltd. v. Mannington Mills Inc.* (1990), 29 C.P.R. (3d) 481 at 490, 107 N.R. 198 (Fed. C.A.), the court per Iacobucci C.J.

VENDING MACHINE. 1. Any self-service device which upon insertion of a coin, coins or tokens, automatically dispenses unit servings of food either in bulk or in package form. 2. A mechanical device that, when coins are deposited therein, dispenses stamps.

VENDITION. *n*. Sale, selling.

VENDITIONI EXPONAS. [L. that you expose for sale] A writ addressed to a sheriff. See WRIT OF ~.

VENDOR. *n*. 1. A person who sells something. 2. Includes a person who barters or exchanges a stock in bulk with any other person for other property, real or personal. *Bulk Sales acts*. See ITINERANT ~; MILK ~; MOBILE HOME ~; REGISTERED ~; RETAIL ~; WHOLESALE ~.

VENDOR'S LIEN. 1. When a vendor sells property on credit, the vendor may be entitled to a lien on it to secure an obligation from the purchaser. B.J. Reiter, B.N. McLellan & P.M. Perell, *Real Estate Law*, 4th ed. (Toronto: Emond Montgomery, 1992) at 781. 2. " . . . [C]an only arise on the sale of land, or of an equitable interest in land, and the lien may exist

in favour of an equitable owner. . ." *Horn v. Sanford*, [1929] 3 D.L.R. 130 at 133, [1929] 2 W.W.R. 33, 23 Sask. L.R. 509 (C.A.), the court per Haultain C.J.S.

VENDOR TAKE-BACK MORTGAGE. A vendor lends the purchaser part of the purchase price in exchange for a mortgage on the property.

VENEREAL DISEASE. 1. Syphilis, gonorrhea or soft chancre. *Criminal Code*, R.S.C. 1985, c. C-46, s. 289(4). 2. Includes syphilis, gonorrhea, chancroid, granuloma inguinale and lympho-granuloma venereum.

VENEREALLY INFECTED PERSON. A person suffering from a venereal disease.

VENGEANCE. *n*. An act of harm, motivated by emotion and anger, as a reprisal for harm inflicted by that person.

VENIAE FACILITAS INCENTIVUM EST DELINQUENDI. [L.] Ease of pardon is an incentive to do wrong.

VENIRE CONTRA FACTUM PROPRIUM. [L.] A later act, incompatible with an earlier act.

VENIRE FACIAS DE NOVO. [L.] You are to cause to come again (for a new trial).

VENT. *n*. 1. A conduit or passageway for conveying the products of combustion from a gas appliance to the outer air. 2. Any mark placed on an animal by the owner or a poundkeeper denoting that the property in the stock bearing it has passed from the owner to some other person. *Brand acts*. See AIR ~; BACK ~; BRANCH ~; CIRCUIT ~; DRY ~; DUAL ~; GAS ~; LOOP ~; RELIEF ~; STACK ~; WET ~; YOKE ~.

VENT CONNECTOR. The part of a venting system that conducts the flue gases or vent gases from the flue collar of a gas appliance to the chimney or gas vent, and may include a draft control device.

VENTILATION. See ADEQUATE ~; FORCED ~.

VENTILATION EQUIPMENT. A fan, blower, induced draft or other ventilation device used to force a supply of fresh, respirable, atmospheric air into an enclosed space or to remove ambient air from such space.

VENTING. See STACK ~.

VENTRAL. See ANTERIOR.

VENTRICLE. *n.* 1. One of two lower chambers in the heart. F.A. Jaffe, *A Guide to Pathological Evidence*, 3d ed. (Toronto: Carswell, 1991) at 229. 2. One of four intercommunicating cavities in the brain which collect cerebrospinal fluid. F.A. Jaffe, *A Guide to Pathological Evidence*, 3d ed. (Toronto: Carswell, 1991) at 229.

VENTRICULAR FIBRILLATION. Ineffective and irregular contractions of the heart ventricles which lead to sudden death. F.A. Jaffe, *A Guide to Pathological Evidence*, 3d ed. (Toronto: Carswell, 1991) at 229.

VENT STACK. A continuous run of vent pipe connected to a soil stack, waste stack or building drain and terminating in the open air.

VENT SYSTEM. A system of piping installed to provide a flow of air to or from drainage piping or storm drainage piping.

VENTURE. *n.* ". . . [C]ommercial speculation attended with some risk . . ." *Cunningham v. Cunningham* (1985), 45 R.F.L. (2d) 395 at 399 (B.C. S.C.), Boyle L.J.S.C. See GROUP MANAGEMENT ~; GROUP ~; JOINT ~.

VENTURE CAPITAL CORPORATION. A Canadian corporation whose objects and activities are confined solely to (a) the provision of financing and loans to Canadian corporations in circumstances that involve the financing or lending corporation in the acquisition, holding or acceptance of hypothecation of equity securities and unsecured debt securities of the corporations being financed; (b) the provision of financial or management consulting services to Canadian corporations whose securities have been acquired by the corporation providing the services in a manner described in paragraph (a) or the provision of such services in contemplation of so acquiring securities; and (c) the provision of financing by participating in a limited partnership as a limited partner. *Bank Act*, R.S.C. 1985, c. B-1, s. 193.

VENUE. *n.* 1. " . . . [T]he place where the charges are laid and the place where the trial takes place: . . ." *R. v. Gagne* (1990), 59 C.C.C. (3d) 282 at 286, [1990] R.J.Q. 2165 (C.A.), Bernier J.A. 2. " . . . [T]he place where the crime is charged to have been committed. . ." *Smitheman, Ex parte* (1904), 35 S.C.R. 490 at 493, 9 C.C.C. 17, the court per Killam J. 3. " . . . [O]riginally indicated the locality of the crime only, has come to indicate with equal propriety, and is more often used to signify, the locality of the trial: as when we speak of the change of venue, which cannot possibly mean a change of the locality of the crime." *R. v. Malott* (1886),1 B.C.R. (Pt. II) 212 at 215 (C.A.), Begbie C.J.A.

VERBA ACCIPIENDA SUNT SECUNDUM SUBJECTAM MATERIAM. [L.] Words should be interpreted according to the subject-matter.

VERBA AEQUIVOCA AC IN DUBIO SENSU POSITA INTELLIGUNTUR DIGNIORI ET POTENTIORI SENSU. [L.] Words which are equivocal and are used in a doubtful sense should be interpreted in the more suitable and stronger way.

VERBA ALIQUID OPERARI DEBENT—DEBENT INTELLIGI UT ALIQUID OPERENTUR. [L.] Words should be effectual—they should be interpreted so that they have some effect.

VERBA CARTARUM FORTIUS ACCIPIUNTUR CONTRA PROFERENTEM. [L.] The words of deeds should be interpreted most strongly against the person using them. *McKenzie v. Kittridge* (1879), 4 S.C.R. 368 at 398, Henry J. and *Barchak Estate v. Anderson*, [1945] 2 D.L.R. 698 at 711, [1945] 1 W.W.R. 657 (Alta. C.A.), Ford J.A. (Harvey C.J.A. concurring).

VERBA CUM EFFECTU ACCIPIENDA SUNT. [L.] Words should be interpreted so that they have some effect.

VERBA DEBENT INTELLIGI UT ALIQUID OPERENTUR. [L.] Words should be interpreted so that they have some effect.

VERBA FORTIUS ACCIPIUNTUR CONTRA PROFERENTEM. [L.] Words are construed against the person proffering.

VERBA GENERALIA RESTRINGUNTUR AD HABILITATEM REI VEL APTITUDINEM PERSONAE. [L.] General words should be limited to the aptness of the subject-matter or the aptitude of the person.

VERBA ILLATA INESSE VIDENTUR. [L.] Words referred to are considered to be included.

VERBA INTENTIONI, NON E CONTRA, DEBENT INSERVIRE. [L.] Words should be subservient to the intent, and not vice versa.

VERBA ITA SUNT INTELLIGENDA UT RES MAGIS VALEAT QUAM PEREAT. [L.] Words should be interpreted so that the thing succeeds more than it fails.

VERBAL. *adj.* Words spoken or written; frequently means spoken rather than written words.

VERBA POSTERIORA, PROPTER CERTITUDINEM ADDITA, AD PRIORA, QUAE CERTITUDINE INDIGENT, SUNT REFERENDA. [L.] Later words, added for certainty, should be referred to earlier words which need clarification.

VERBA RELATA HOC MAXIME OPERANTUR PER REFERENTIAM UT IN EIS INESSE VIDENTUR. [L.] Words referred to in an instrument have the same effect as if they were inserted in that instrument.

VERBATIM ET LITERATIM. [L.] Word by word and letter by letter.

VERBI GRATIA. For example.

VERDICT. *n.* 1. " . . . [T]he finding of a jury . . ." *R. v. Murray* (1912), 8 D.L.R. 208 at 210, 27 O.L.R. 382, 4 O.W.N. 368, 23 O.W.R. 492, 20 C.C.C. 197 (C.A.), Maclaren J.A. (Garrow, Meredith and Magee JJ.A. and Lennox J. concurring). 2. Includes the finding of a jury and the decision of a judge in an action. 3. In the case of an action being tried by a judge without a jury includes judgment. See GENERAL ~; PERVERSE ~.

VERDICT OF ACQUITTAL. Includes a verdict of not criminally responsible on account of mental disorder.

VERDICT OF NOT CRIMINALLY RESPONSIBLE ON ACCOUNT OF MENTAL DISORDER. A verdict that the accused committed the act or made the omission that formed the basis of the offence with which the accused is charged but is not criminally responsible on account of mental disorder. *Criminal Code*, R.S.C. 1985, c. C-46, s. 672.1.

VEREDICTUM, QUASI DICTUM VERITATIS, UT JUDICIUM QUASI JURIS DICTUM. [L.] A verdict is, so to speak, a statement of truth, just as a judgment is a statement of the law.

VERIFY. *v.* "To verify" may well mean something more than "to give notice" i.e., to adduce proof that the fact is true. However, I do not think to verify something to another could mean anything less than giving notice. *Dallas Park Shopping Centre Ltd. v. Buy-Low Foods Ltd.*, 2002 BCCA 585, 6 B.C.L.R. (4th) 302 (C.A.).

VERITAS NIHIL VERETUR NISI ABSCONDI. [L.] Truth fears nothing except concealment.

VERITAS NOMINIS TOLLIT ERROREM DEMONSTRATIONIS. [L.] The truth of the name removes any error in description.

VERMIN. *n.* An animal whose presence may be harmful to the health, comfort or welfare of an animal in a research facility, supply facility or pound.

VERNIX CASEOSA. A greyish-white, greasy substance which covers a fetus' skin. F.A. Jaffe, *A Guide to Pathological Evidence*, 3d ed. (Toronto: Carswell, 1991) at 229.

VERSUS. *prep.* [L.] Against.

VERTEBRATE FOSSIL. The fossilized remains of an animal that possessed a backbone.

VERTEBRATE TRACE FOSSIL. The fossilized trace of a vertebrate.

VERTICAL. *adj.* Not departing from the true vertical plane by more than 45°. *Ontario Water Resources Act*, R.R.O. 1980, Reg. 736, s. 1.

VERTICAL AMALGAMATION. An amalgamation of a holding corporation and one or more of its subsidiary corporations.

VERTICAL SERVICE SPACE. A vertical shaft provided in a building to facilitate the installation of building services including mechanical, electrical and plumbing installations and facilities such as elevators, refuse chutes and linen chutes.

VERTICAL UNION. A union which accepts all workers in an industry as members regardless of their occupations.

VESSEL. *n.* 1. Includes every description of ship, boat or craft used or capable of being used solely or partly for marine navigation without regard to method or lack of propulsion, a dredge, a floating elevator, a floating home, an oil rig, a sea-plane, a raft or boom of logs or lumber and an air cushion vehicle. 2. Where used to indicate a craft for navigation of the water, includes any ship, vessel or boat of any kind whatever, whether propelled by steam or otherwise and whether used as a sea-going vessel or on inland waters only, and also includes any vehicle. *Excise Act*, R.S.C. 1985, c. E-14, s. 2. 3. Includes any ship or boat or any other description of vessel used or designed to be used in navigation. *Canada Shipping Act*, R.S.C. 1985, c. S-9, s. 2. 4. Includes a machine designed to derive support in the atmosphere primarily from reactions against the earth's surface of air expelled from the machine. *Criminal Code*, R.S.C. 1985, c. C-

46, s. 214. 5. Where the context so admits, includes aircraft. See AUXILIARY ~; CANADIAN ~; DANGEROUS OPERATION OF ~S; FERRY ~; FIRED ~; FISHING ~; GIVE-WAY ~; GOVERNMENT ~; MOTOR ~; NON-POWER ~; PLEASURE ~; POWER-DRIVEN ~; POWER ~; PRESSURE~; REFRIGERANT ~; SAILING ~; STEAM ~.

VESSEL BROKER. A person engaged or acting as agent in chartering any vessel or contracting for cargo space for the carriage of grain by water.

VESSEL CONSTRAINED BY HER DRAUGHT. A power-driven vessel which because of her draught in relation to the available depth of water is severely restricted in her ability to deviate from the course she is following. *Collision Regulations*, C.R.C., c. 1416, Rule 3.

VESSEL ENGAGED IN FISHING. Any vessel fishing with nets, lines, trawls or other fishing apparatus which restrict manoeuvrability, but does not include a vessel fishing with trolling lines or other fishing apparatus which do not restrict manoeuvrability. *Collision Regulations*, C.R.C., c. 1416, Rule 3.

VESSEL NOT UNDER COMMAND. A vessel which through some exceptional circumstance is unable to manoeuvre as required by these Rules and is therefore unable to keep out of the way of another vessel. *Collision Regulations*, C.R.C., c. 1416, Rule 3.

VESSEL RESTRICTED IN HER ABILITY TO MANOEUVRE. A vessel which from the nature of her work is restricted in her ability to manoeuvre as required by these Rules and is therefore unable to keep out of the way of another vessel. *Collision Regulations*, C.R.C., c. 1416, Rule 3.

VESSEL SERVICE. Any operation of docking, undocking, turning, shifting or moving a vessel assisted by a tug.

VEST. *v.* 1. With respect to a right or estate, to rest in some person. 2. Of a pension, to obtain or become entitled to an unalterable right to either transfer or withdraw that lump sum to another pension plan or R.R.S.P. or to receive, in the future, a deferred life annuity. A. Bissett-Johnson & W.M. Holland, eds., *Matrimonial Property Law in Canada* (Toronto: Carswell, 1980) at V-91.

VESTED. *adj.* 1. Fixed, accrued, settled, not capable of being defeated by a condition prece-

dent. 2. " . . . [A] future estate or interest is vested when there is a person who has an immediate right to that interest upon the cessation of the present or previous interest . . ." *Re Legh's Resettlement Trusts; Pub. Trustee v. Legh*, [1938] Ch. 39 at 52 (U.K. C.A.), MacKinnon L.J.

VESTED IN INTEREST. With respect to an existing fixed right of future enjoyment.

VESTED IN POSSESSION. With respect to a right of present enjoyment which actually exists.

VESTED PENSION. An individual's pension is vested when the individual has rights to all the benefits purchased by the individual and the employer even if the person is no longer employed by the employer.

VESTED REMAINDER. An expectant interest which is limited or transmitted to the one who is able to receive it.

VESTED RIGHT. 1. " . . . [O]ne which exists and produces effects. That does not include a right which could have been exercised but was not, and which is no longer available under the law. . ." *Quebec (Expropriation Tribunal) v. Quebec (Attorney General)* (1986), 35 L.C.R. 1 at 8, [1986] 1 S.C.R. 732, 66 N.R. 380, the court per Chouinard J. 2. A right which is not contingent or may not be defeated by a condition precedent.

VESTING. *adj.* " . . . [I]n relation to the rule against perpetuities has a special meaning as three conditions must be satisfied before an interest can be said to be vested: (1) the beneficiaries must be ascertained; (2) the interests they take must be determined; and (3) any conditions attached to the interests must be satisfied. . ." *Ogilvy, Re*, [1966] 2 O.R. 755 at 763, 58 D.L.R. (2d) 385 (H.C.), Lieff J.

VESTING ORDER. A court order to give a person an interest in real or personal property which the court has authority to dispose of, encumber or convey.

VETERAN. *n.* Any former member of the North West Field Force and any of the following persons, more particularly described in section 37, namely, (a) a veteran of the South African War; (b) a Canadian veteran of World War I or World War II; (b.1) a merchant navy veteran of World War I or World War II; (c) an allied veteran; (d) a Canadian dual service veteran; (e) an allied dual service veteran; and (f) a Canadian Forces veteran. *War Veterans Allowance Act*, R.S.C. 1985, c. W-3, s. 2(1); and (g) a Canadian merchant navy veteran of the Korean War. See OVERSEAS ~; VOLUNTEER ~; WAR ~S.

VETERANS AFFAIRS. The federal ministry which economically, socially, mentally and physically supports veterans, certain civilians and their dependants.

VETERINARIAN. *n.* A person holding a certificate or licence entitling that person to practise veterinary medicine.

VETERINARY. *n.* A person authorized to practise veterinary science.

VETERINARY AID. A person who is not a qualified veterinarian but who is trained, in a manner prescribed by the by-laws, to carry out certain veterinary procedures. *Veterinary Medical Aid*, R.S.N.S. 1989, c. 490, s. 2.

VETERINARY BIOLOGIC. (a) A helminth, protozoa or micro-organism, (b) a substance or mixture of substances derived from animals, helminths, protozoa or micro-organisms, or (c) a substance of synthetic origin that is manufactured, sold or represented for use in restoring, correcting or modifying organic functions in animals or for use in the diagnosis, treatment, mitigation or prevention of a disease, disorder or abnormal physical state, or the symptoms thereof, in animals. *Health of Animals Act*, S.C. 1990, c. 21, s. 2(1).

VETERINARY DRUG. A substance or combination of substances used or intended or represented to be used as a drug for an animal.

VETERINARY FACILITY. A building, land or vehicle or any combination of them used or intended to be used as a place in or from which to engage in the practice of veterinary medicine. *Veterinarians Act*, R.S.O. 1990, c. V.3, s. 1(1).

VETERINARY LABORATORY. A facility or class of facility, on which or in which diseases are diagnosed.

VETERINARY MEDICINE. 1. That branch of knowledge relating to the prevention, diagnosis and treatment of the diseases of, and injuries to animals. 2. The practice of veterinary medicine includes the practice of dentistry, obstetrics including ova and embryo transfer, and surgery, in relation to an animal other than a human being. *Veterinarians Act*, R.S.O. 1990, c. V-3, s. 1. See PRACTICE OF ~.

VETERINARY SCIENCE. The application of medicine or surgery to an animal, and includes diagnosing, prescribing, treating, manipulating and operating for the prevention, alleviation or correction of a disease, injury, pain, deficiency, deformity, defect, lesion, disorder or physical condition of or in an animal with or without the use of instruments, appliances, medicine, drugs, anaesthetics, or antibiotic or biologic preparations, and also includes the giving of advice in respect of anything, mentioned in this paragraph with a view to obtaining a fee or other remuneration. *Veterinary Medical Act*, R.S. Nfld. 1990, c. V-4, s. 2. See VETERINARY MEDICINE.

VETERINARY SURGEON. A person licensed to practise veterinary medicine, veterinary surgery or veterinary dentistry in a province or territory of Canada.

VETERINARY SURGERY. The surgical, dental or medical treatment of animals, but does not include the castration, spaying, vaccinating or dehorning of animals.

VETO. *n.* 1. A prohibition; the right to forbid. 2. " . . . '[D]isallowance' . . . [refers] to the provisions of secs. 55 and 56 [of the Constitution Act 1867] as applied to a province." *Reference re Initiative & Referendum* Act (*Manitoba*) (1916), 32 D.L.R. 148 at 170, 1 W.W.R. 1012, 27 Man. R. 1, (C.A.), Perdue J.A.

VETROVEC WARNING. What may be appropriate, however, in some circumstances, is a clear and sharp warning to attract the attention of the juror to the risks of adopting, without more, the evidence of the witness. There is no magic in the word corroboration, or indeed in any other comparable expression such as confirmation and support. The idea implied in those words may, however, in an appropriate case, be effectively and efficiently transmitted to the mind of the trier of fact. *R. v. Vetrovec*, [1982] 1 S.C.R. 811, per Dickson, J. A caution to the jury is a matter of the trial judge's discretion and is not required in all cases involving testimony of accomplices or accessories after the fact, there are some cases in which the circumstances may be such that a *Vetrovec* caution must be given. *R. v. Bevan*, [1993] 2 S.C.R. 599.

VEXATA QUAESTIO. [L.] An undecided point.

VEXATIOUS. *adj.* Annoying, distressing; multiplicitous; the bringing of one or more actions to determine an issue which has already been determined; the bringing of actions which cannot succeed or lead to any possible positive outcome.

VEXATIOUS ACTION. 1. "An action may be vexatious if it is obvious that it cannot succeed: . . . or if no reasonable person can possibly expect to obtain relief in it: . . . or if the Court has no power to grant the relief sought: . . . or if the applicant has no status to pursue the remedy, or no proper authority to do so: . . . or if the same relief might be sought in a subsisting action: . . . or if the same purpose might have been effected in a previous action: . . . In some cases the Courts have considered the lack of bona fides in classifying an action as vexatious, as where the plaintiff had no cause of action at all: . . . A legal proceeding may be vexatious even though there were reasonable grounds for its institution if, for instance, the plaintiff is asking for relief in a way which necessarily involves injustice." *Foy v. Foy (No. 2)* (1979), 12 C.P.C. 188 at 197, 26 O.R. (2d) 220, 102 D.L.R. (3d) 342 (C.A.), Howland C.J.O. (Brooke J.A. concurring). 2. Vexatious was said to involve overtones of an irresponsible pursuit of litigation by someone who either knows he has no proper cause of action or is mentally incapable of forming a rational opinion on the topic. *Whitehead v. Taber* (1983), 1983 CarswellAlta 379, 46 A.R. 14 (Q.B.), Crossley, J.

VEXATIOUS PROCEEDING. A proceeding in which the party bringing it wishes only to embarass or annoy the other party.

VFR. *abbr*. The visual flight rules. See DAY ~; NIGHT ~.

VFR AIRCRAFT. An aircraft operating in VFR flight. *Canadian Aviation Regulations*, SOR/96-433, s. 101.01(1).

VFR FLIGHT. A flight conducted in accordance with the visual flight rules. See SPECIAL ~.

VFR OTT. *abbr*. VFR over-the-top; *Canadian Aviation Regulations*, SOR/96-433, s. 101.01(1).

V.G. *abbr*. Verbi gratia.

VHF. *abbr*. Very high frequency. *Canadian Aviation Regulations*, SOR/96-433, s. 101.01(1).

VIA. *abbr*. Via Rail Canada Inc.

VIA. *prep*. By way of.

VIABILITY. *n*. With respect to new-born child, the ability to live after birth.

VIABLE. *adj*. Workable; sustainable.

VIAE SERVITUS. [L. servitude of way] A right of way across another person's land.

VIA RAIL CANADA INC. The federal body which operates trains and manages Canadian passenger rail service, except for commuter trains.

VIA REGIA. [L. royal way] A highway.

VIATICAL SETTLEMENT. The sale of a life insurance policy to a third party. The policy owner receives payment and the purchaser assumes responsibility for premium payment and acquires the right to collect on the policy on maturity.

VIA TRITA. [L.] " . . . [T]he ordinarily travelled portion of the road . . . *Salt v. Cardston (Town)*, [1919] 1 W.W.R. 891 at 898, 46 D.L.R. 179 (Alta. S.C.), Stuart J.

VIA TRITA EST TUTISSIMA. [L.] A well-trodden road is the safest.

VIA TRITA VIA TUTA. [L.] A well-trodden road is a safe road.

VICARIOUS LIABILITY. 1. Liability imposed on one person for the acts of another based on the relationship between the two persons. Liability imposed on an employer for the acts of the employees. 2. In determining whether an employer is vicariously liable for an employee's unauthorized, intentional wrong in cases where precedent is inconclusive, courts should be guided by the following principles: (1) They should openly confront the question of whether liability should lie against the employer, rather than obscuring the decision beneath semantic discussions of "scope of employment" and "mode of conduct." (2) The fundamental question is whether the wrongful act is *sufficiently related* to conduct authorized by the employer to justify the imposition of vicarious liability. Vicarious liability is generally appropriate where there is a significant connection between the *creation or enhancement of a risk* and the wrong that accrues therefrom, even if unrelated to the employer's desires. Where this is so, vicarious liability will serve the policy considerations of provision of an adequate and just remedy and deterrence. Incidental connections to the employment enterprise, like time and place (without more), will not suffice. Once engaged in a particular business, it is fair that an employer be made to pay the generally foreseeable costs of that business. In contrast, to impose liability for costs unrelated to the risk would effectively make the employer an involuntary insurer. (3) In determining the sufficiency of the connection between *the employer's creation or enhancement of the risk* and the wrong complained of, subsidiary factors may be considered. These may vary with the nature of the case. When related to intentional torts, the relevant factors may include, but are not limited to, the following:(a) the opportunity that the enterprise afforded the employee to abuse his or her power; (b) the extent to which the wrongful act may have furthered the employer's aims (and hence be more likely to have been committed by the employee); (c) the extent to which the wrongful act was related to friction, confrontation or intimacy inherent in the employer's enterprise; (d) the extent of power conferred on the employee in relation to the victim; (e) the vulnerability of potential victims to wrongful exercise of the employee's power. *B. (P.A.) v. Curry*, [1999] 2 S.C.R. 534, McLachlin, J. 3. Responsibility in law for the misconduct of another person. John G. Fleming, *The Law of Torts*, 8th ed. (Sydney: The Law Book Co., 1992) at 366. 4. "In the criminal law, a natural person is responsible only for those crimes in which he is the primary actor either actually or by express or implied authorization. There is no vicarious liability in the pure sense in the case of the natural person. That is to say that the doctrine of respondent superior is unknown in the criminal law where the defendant is an individual. . . where the defendant is corporate the common law has become pragmatic, as we have seen, and a modified and limited 'vicarious liability' through the identification doctrine has emerged. . ." *R. v. McNamara (No. 1), (sub nom. R. v. Canadian Dredge & Dock Co.)* [1985] 1 S.C.R. 662 at 692, 45 C.R. (3d) 289, 9 O.A.C. 321, 19 C.C.C. (3d) 1, 19 D.L.R. (4th) 314, 59 N.R. 241, the court per Estey J.

VICARIOUS RESPONSIBILITY. The automatic responsibility of one person for another's wrongdoing through prior relationship only, irrespective of the first person's fault or deed. It is clear common law doctrine in the law of torts that a master can be vicariously liable for a tort committed by a "servant" who acts in the course and scope of employment. D. Stuart, *Canadian Criminal Law: a treatise*, 2d ed. (Toronto: Carswell, 1987) at 522.

VICARIUS NON HABET VICARIUM. [L.] A delegate does not have a delegate.

VICE-CHANCELLOR. *n.* The cleric who holds the office of principal assistant to the chancellor. *An Act Respecting Fabriques*, R.S.Q. 1977, c. F-1, s. 1.

VICE-CONSUL. *n.* An officer in a consulate.

VICE-PRINCIPAL. *n.* A teacher who is appointed to be in charge of a school in the absence of the principal. *Provincial Schools Negotiations Act*, R.S.O. 1990, c. P.35, s. 1.

VICE VERSA. Conversely.

VICINAGE. *n.* Neighbourhood; places next to one another.

VICINI VICINORA PRAESUMUNTUR SCIRE. [L.] Neighbours are expected to know the neighbourhood.

VICTIM. *n.* 1. A person to whom harm was done or who suffered physical or emotional damage as a result of the commission of an offence, and where the person is dead, ill or otherwise incapacitated, the person's spouse, an individual who is cohabiting, or was cohabiting at the time of the person's death, with the person in a conjugal relationship, having so cohabited for a period of at least one year, any relative or dependant of the person, or anyone who has in law or fact custody or is responsible for the care or support of the person. *Federal statutes*. 2. A person who, as a result of the commission of a crime by another, suffers emotional or physical harm, loss of or damage to property or economic harm and, if the commission of the crime results in the death of the person, includes, a child or parent of the person, and a dependant, spouse or same-sex partner of the person, but does not include a child, parent, dependant, spouse or same-sex partner who is charged with or has been convicted of committing the crime. See COMPENSATION OF ~S OF CRIME; CRIME ~.

VICTORIA DAY. The first Monday immediately preceding May 25 is a legal holiday and is kept and observed as such throughout Canada under the name of "Victoria Day" in honour of Queen Victoria.

VICTUALLING HOUSE. A place conducted by a person, firm or corporation, who sells by retail only all or any of the following: meals and drinks of all kinds for consumption on the premises only, and includes a delicatessen selling cooked meats, cooked vegetables, and cooked fish, not in sealed containers. *Shops Regulation Act*, R.S.M. 1987, c. S110, s. 3(1).

VIDE. *v.* [L.] See.

VIDE ANTE. [L.] See an earlier passage in the text.

VIDE INFRA. [L.] See a later passage in the text.

VIDELICET. *adv*. [L.] Namely; that is to say.

VIDEO DEPOSITION. A videorecording made outside of the courtroom in the presence of counsel and the defendant when children are unavailable to give evidence at trial.

VIDEO DISTRIBUTOR. A person who distributes films to a video retailer or to another video distributor.

VIDEO EXCHANGE. Any retail outlet which makes videofilm available to the public.

VIDEOFILM. *n*. Includes videocassette, videodisc and videotape.

VIDEO GAME. An object or device that stores recorded data or instructions, receives data or instructions generated by a person who uses it, and by processing the data or instructions, creates an interactive game capable of being played, viewed or experienced on or through a computer, gaming system, console or other technology.

VIDEO LOTTERY TERMINAL. The video lottery terminal has a video monitor built into the machine. It is operated by touching the video monitor and it can be asked to play a number of different games, one of which is usually a game like the traditional game of the pull-arm slot machine where three spinning wheels come to a stop and a win or a loss depends on the representations on the three wheels and on their alignment. *Great Canadian Casino Co. v. Surrey (City)* (1999), 1999 CarswellBC 2420, 130 B.C.A.C. 189, 211 W.A.C. 189, 7 M.P.L.R. (3d) 33, 71 B.C.L.R. (3d) 199, [2000] 3 W.W.R. 681 (C.A.).

VIDEO MATERIAL. Includes video cassettes, video discs or any medium of the same nature on which a film is recorded.

VIDEO-ON-DEMAND SERVICE. The programming service provided by a person licensed to carry on a video-on-demand programming undertaking. *Broadcasting Distribution Regulations*, SOR/97-555, s. 1.

VIDEO OUTLET. A retail establishment that, for consideration, sells, leases, rents, exchanges or distributes films for use in a video cassette recorder, video disc player or similar device.

VIDEO RETAILER. A person who distributes films to any person.

VIDEO TAPE. See CANADIAN ~.

VIDE POST. [L.] See a later passage in the text.

VIDE SUPRA. [L.] See an earlier passage in the text.

VIDUITY. *n*. The state of being a widow.

VI ET ARMIS. [L.] By force and arms.

VIEW. *n*. 1. A jury's inspection of any controversial thing, place where a crime was committed or person which a judge may order in the interest of justice at any time between when the jury is sworn and when they give their verdict. 2. A visit to a site relevant to the issue at hand by a judge or the hearing panel of an administrative tribunal. See FIELD OF ~.

VIGILANT. See EQUITY AIDS THE ~ AND NOT THE INDOLENT.

VIGILANTIBUS, NON DORMIENTIBUS, JURA SUBVENIUNT. [L.] The laws aid the watchful, not those who sleep.

VIGILANTIBUS ET NON DORMIENTIBUS JURA SUBSERVIUNT. [L.] Equity aids the vigilant not the slothful.

VIGILANTIBUS ET NON DORMIENTIBUS LEX SUCCURRIT. [L.] Law assists the vigilant and not the slothful.

VIGILANTIBUS NON DORMIENTIBUS SCRIPTA EST LEX. [L.] The law assists the vigilant, not the slothful.

VIGILANTIBUS SUBVENIT LEX. [L.] The law helps the vigilant.

VILLAGE. *n*. A small incorporated municipality. Smaller than a town. See RESORT ~.

VILLAGE DISTRICT. A school district situated wholly or in part within a village: but where a village, in which is situated in whole or in part a village district, is incorporated as a town, the district shall for the purposes of this Act become a town district on a date to be determined by the minister. *The School Act*, R.S.S. 1978, c. S-36, s. 2.

VIM VI REPELLERE LICET, MODO FIAT MODERAMINE INCULPATAE TUTELAE; NON AD SUMENDAM VINDICTAM, SED AD PROPULSANDAM INJURIAM. [L.] It is legal to repel force with force, as long as it is governed by a desire to defend; not to take revenge, but to ward off injury.

VIMY RIDGE DAY. April 9, commemorates WWI battle.

VINCULO MATRIMONII. [L.] The bond of matrimony.

VINCULUM JURIS. [L.] The bond of law.

VINDICTIVE DAMAGES. Damages based on punishing the defendant, beyond compensating the plaintiff.

VINTNERS QUALITY ALLIANCE WINE. (VQA wine) wine, (a) that is produced in Ontario from grapes that have been grown in Ontario or from grape juice or grape must produced from such grapes, and (b) that meets the standards of the wine authority. *Vintners Quality Alliance Act, 1999*, S.O. 1999, c. 3, s. 2.

VINYL CHLORIDE. A substance designated under the Ontario Occupational Health and Safety Act. D. Robertson, *Health and Safety Guide* (Toronto: Richard De Boo Ltd., 1988) at 5-416.

VIOLATES. *v.* Includes any disobedience, contravention, infraction, neglect or refusal, and whether or not the act is one of omission or commission.

VIOLATION RECORD. Includes a report, made by any authority acting in an official capacity, that a person has: (i) been found at fault in respect of an automobile accident; or (ii) been convicted of an offence; relating to the use or operation of a motor vehicle. *The Automobile Accident Insurance Act*, R.S.S. 1978, c. A-35, s. 2.

VIOLATION TICKET. Ad document by which a complaint is laid and a summons issued in accordance with Section 32A.

VIOLENCE. *n.* " . . . [C]onnotes actual or threatened physical interference with the activities of others." *R. v. Keegstra* (1990), 1 C.R. (4th) 129 at 236, 77 Alta. L.R. (2d) 193, [1991] 2 W.W.R. 1, 61 C.C.C. (3d) 1, 117 N.R. 1, 114 A.R. 81, 3 C.R.R. (2d) 193, [1990] 3 S.C.R. 697, McLachlin J. (dissenting) (Sopinka J. concurring).

VIOLENTA PRAESUMPTIO ALIQUANDO EST PLENA PROBATIO. [L.] Vehement audacity is sometimes full proof.

VIPERINA EST EXPOSITIO QUAE CORRODIT VISCERA TEXTUS. [L.] An interpretation which eats the bowels out of a text is like a serpent.

VIR ET UXOR CONSENTUR IN LEGE UNA PERSONA. [L.] Husband and wife are held to be one person in law.

VIR ET UXOR SUNT QUASI UNICA PER SONA. [L.] Husband and wife are virtually one person.

VIRTUTE MANDAT. [L.] By virtue of an order.

VIRTUTE OFFICII. [L.] By virtue of office.

VIRULENT DISEASE. (a) Cholera, (b) Diphtheria, (c) Ebola virus disease, (d) Gonorrhoea, (e) Hemorrhagic fever, (f) Lassa fever, (g) Leprosy, (h) Marburg virus disease, (i) Plague; (j) Syphilis, (k) Smallpox, (l) Tuberculosis, or a disease specified as a virulent disease by regulation made by the Minister. *Health Protection and Promotion Act*, R.S.O. 1990, c. H.7, s. 1(1).

VIRUS. *n.* 1. A subcellular parasite dependent on its cellular host to provide material for production of more viruses. 2. A computer program which attacks a host computer.

VIS. *n.* [L.] Any violence, force or disturbance to people or property.

VISA. *n.* A document issued by one country which permits a resident of another to visit the first country. See EMPLOYMENT ~.

VISCERA. *n.* The entrails and inedible internal organs of poultry.

VISIBILITY. *n.* The distance at which prominent unlighted objects may be identified by day and prominent lighted objects may be identified at night. See FLIGHT ~; GROUND ~; RESTRICTED ~.

VISIBLE. *adj.* 1. " . . . [C]apable of being seen, . . . observable, . . . apparent, . . . perceptible to the eye." *Charania v. Travellers Indemnity Co. of Canada*, [1983] I.L.R. 1-1633 at 6276 (Ont. H.C.), Smith J. 2. When applied to lights, means visible on a dark night with a clear atmosphere. Canada regulations. 3. When applied to lights or other signals visible under normal atmospheric conditions.

VISIBLE EMISSION. Any contaminant which can be detected by the naked eye.

VISIBLE MINORITIES. Persons who are non-Caucasian in race or non-white in colour.

VISITATORIAL POWERS. An incident of an eleemosynary corporation. Some educational institutions are eleemosynary corporations. The visitor has general jurisdiction over all matters relating to the statute establishing the corporation and the internal affairs of the corporation.

VISITING FORCE. Any of the armed forces of a designated state present in Canada in connection with official duties and includes civilian personnel designated under section 4 as a civilian component of a visiting force. *Visiting Forces Act*, R.S.C. 1985, c. V-2, s. 2.

VISITOR. *n.* 1. (i) An entrant as of right; (ii) a person who is lawfully present on premises by virtue of an express or implied term of a contract; (iii) any other person whose presence on premises is lawful; or (iv) a person whose presence on premises becomes unlawful after his entry on those premises and who is taking reasonable steps to leave those premises. 2. An inspector for an eleemosynary, ecclesiastical or other corporation or institution such as a university. Has general jurisdiction over all matters relating to the statute establishing the corporation and the internal affairs of an eleemosynary corporation. 3. The officer designated by the competent religious authority. *Religious Corporations Act*, R.S.Q. 1977, c. C-71, s. 1. 4. The bishop of the place or any other person appointed as visitor by such bishop of the place. *Roman Catholic Cemetery Corporations Act*, R.S.Q. 1977, c. C-69, s. 1. 5. "The unique position of a Judge is reflected by s. 7 of the Legal Profession Act [R.S.S. 1987, c. L-10] which designates Judges as visitors of the Society. The title is a hollow and anachronistic one: there is no role or function assigned to a visitor. Nor does a visitor hold an office, or derive any rights from or owe any responsibilities to the Law Society. Whatever it may be, a visitor is not a barrister or solicitor." *Maurice v. Priel* (1989), 36 Admin. L.R. 169 at 178, [1989] 3 W.W.R. 673, 96 N.R. 178, [1989] 1 S.C.R. 1023, 58 D.L.R. (4th) 736, 77 Sask. R. 22, Cory J. (Lamer, Wilson, L'Heureux-Dubé, Sopinka and Gonthier JJ. concurring).

VIS LEGIBUS EST INIMICA. [L.] Violence is inimical to law.

VIS MAJOR. The operation of natural forces and the malicious acts of strangers. John G. Fleming, *The Law of Torts*, 8th ed. (Sydney: The Law Book Co., 1992) at 345. See ACT OF GOD.

VISUAL ARTS. The production of original works of research or expression, which are unique or in limited copies and are conveyed by painting, sculpture, engraving, drawing, illustration, photography, textile arts, installation work, performance, art video or any other form of expression of the same nature. *An Act respecting the professional status of artists in the visual arts, arts and crafts and literature, and their contracts with promoters*, R.S.Q., c. S-32.01, s. 2.

VISUAL FLIGHT RULES. Rules concerning flight under visual control only.

VISUAL METEOROLOGICAL CONDITIONS. Meteorological conditions equal to or greater than the minima specified in Division VI of Subpart 2 of Part VI, expressed in terms of visibility and distance from cloud. *Canadian Aviation Regulations*, SOR/96-433, s. 101.01.

VITAL. *adj.* Essential to or characterizing life. F.A. Jaffe, *A Guide to Pathological Evidence*, 3d ed. (Toronto: Carswell, 1991) at 229.

VITAL REACTION. A tissue reaction like inflammation which occurs during life and can distinguish a pre-mortem from a post-mortem wound. F.A. Jaffe, *A Guide to Pathological Evidence*, 3d ed. (Toronto: Carswell, 1991) at 229.

VITAL SIGN. A physical sign like respiration or pulse which indicates that life is present. F.A. Jaffe, *A Guide to Pathological Evidence*, 3d ed. (Toronto: Carswell, 1991) at 229.

VITAL STATISTICS. The registration of births, deaths and marriages.

VITAMIN. *n.* Any of the following vitamins: (a) vitamin A; (b) thiamine, thiamine hydrochloride or vitamin B_1; (c) riboflavin or vitamin B_2; (d) niacin or nicotinic acid; (e) niacinamide or nicotinamide; (f) pyridoxine, pyridoxine hydrochloride or vitamin B_6; (g) d-pantothenic acid or pantothenic acid; (h) folic acid; (i) biotin; (j) cyanocobalamin or vitamin B_{12}; (k) ascorbic acid or vitamin C; (l) vitamin D or vitamin D_2; (m) vitamin D or vitamin D_3; (n) vitamin E; (o) vitamin K; or (p) any salt or derivative of a vitamin listed in paragraphs (a) to (o). *Food and Drug Regulations*, C.R.C., c. 870, c. D.04.001.

VITIUM CLERICI NOCERE NON DEBET. [L.] A clerical error should do no harm.

VITREOUS HUMOUR. Fluid in an eye ball. F.A. Jaffe, *A Guide to Pathological Evidence*, 3d ed. (Toronto: Carswell, 1991) at 25.

VIVA PECUNIA. [L.] Cattle.

VIVA VOCE. [L.] When describing the examination of witnesses, means orally.

VIVISECTION. *n.* The dissecting of an animal as a scientific experiment.

VIVUM VADIUM. Vif-gage, live gage; pledge.

VIX ULLA LEX FIERI POTEST QUAE OMNIBUS COMMODA SIT, SED SI MAJORI PARTI PROSPICIAT UTILIS EST. [L.] Barely any law can be made which is applicable to everything, but if it regards the majority it is useful.

VIZ. *abbr*. Videlicet.

VLT. *abbr*. Video lottery terminal.

VMC. *abbr*. Visual meteorological conditions. *Canadian Aviation Regulations*, SOR/96-433, s. 101.01.

VOCABULUM ARTIS. [L.] A word of art.

VOCATION. *n*. Any given occupation, whether a trade or a function, by which a person may earn his livelihood.

VOCATIONAL EDUCATION. 1. Education whose immediate object is preparation for the practice of a vocation or trade. 2. Any form of instruction below that of university level, the purpose of which is to fit any person for gainful employment or to increase his skill or efficiency therein and without restricting the generality of the foregoing, includes instruction to fit any person for employment in agriculture, forestry, mining, fishing, construction, manufacturing, commerce, or in any other primary or secondary industry in Canada.

VOCATIONAL REHABILITATION. Any process of restoration, training and employment placement, including services related thereto, whose object is to enable a person to pursue regularly a gainful occupation.

VOCATIONAL SCHOOL. See PRIVATE ~.

VOCATIONAL TRAINING. Training whose purpose is to enable any adult to acquire the competence required to carry on a trade or vocation.

VOCIFERATIO. *n*. [L. outcry] A hue and cry.

VOICEPRINT. *n*. A visual image of a person's voice produced by a spectograph.

VOICE RECORDER. See COCKPIT ~.

VOID. *n*. A space in a grain compartment between the surface of the grain and the crown of the compartment. *Grain Cargo Regulations*, C.R.C., c. 1427, s. 2.

VOID. *adj*. " . . . [L]acking validity and so without legal force." *British Columbia (Minister of Finance) v. Woodward Estate*, [1971] D.T.C. 341 at 348, [1971] 3 W.W.R. 645, 21 D.L.R.

(3d) 681 (B.C. C.A.), Tysoe J.A. See NULL AND ~.

VOIDABLE. *adj*. " . . . [D]oes not necessarily mean 'valid until rescinded.' It is sometimes used to mean 'invalid until validated'; . . ." *American-Abell Engine & Thresher Co. v. Mc-Millan* (1909), 42 S.C.R. 377 at 396, Duff J.

VOIDANCE. *n*. Avoidance.

VOIR DIRE. [Fr.] 1. An initial examination to determine the competency of a juror or witness. 2. " . . . [A] 'trial within a trial'. It is merely a descriptive phrase to describe a procedure which takes place, namely a procedure to determine the admissibility of certain evidence." *R. v. Brydon* (1983), 6 C.C.C. (3d) 68 at 70 (B.C. C.A.), Craig J.A.

VOLENTI NON FIT INJURIA. [L.] 1. Wrong is not done to someone who is willing. 2. " . . . [V]olenti will arise only where the circumstances are such that it is clear that the plaintiff, knowing of the virtually certain risk of harm, in essence bargained away his right to sue for injuries incurred as a result of any negligence on the defendant's part. The acceptance of risk may be express or may arise by necessary implication from the conduct of the parties, but it will arise, in cases such as the present, only where there can truly be said to be an understanding on the part of both parties that the defendant assumed no responsibility to take due care for the safety of the plaintiff, and that the plaintiff did not expect him to." *Dubé v. Labar* (1986), 36 C.C.L.T. 105 at 114-5, 2 B.C.L.R. (2d) 273, 27 D.L.R. (4th) 653, [1986] 3 W.W.R. 750, [1986] 1 S.C.R. 649, Estey J. (McIntyre, Chouinard and Le Dain JJ. concurring). 3. ' . . . [I]nvolves not only knowledge of the risk, but also a consent to the legal risk or, in other words, a waiver of legal rights that may arise from the harm or loss that is being risked. . ." *Waldick v. Malcolm* (1991), C.C.L.T. (2d) 1 at 17, 3 O.R. (3d) 471n, 125 N.R. 372, 47 O.A.C. 241, 83 D.L.R. (4th) 114, [1991] 2 S.C.R. 456, the court per Iacobucci J. See VOLUNTARY ASSUMPTION OF RISK.

VOLT. *n*. The unit of electric potential difference and electromotive force, being the difference of electric potential between two equipotential surfaces of a conductor that is carrying a constant current of one ampere when the power dissipated between these surfaces is equal to one watt. *Weights and Measures Act*, S.C. 1970-71-72, c. 36, Schedule 1.

VOLTAGE. *n*. In respect of an electric circuit, means the greatest root-mean-square voltage between any two conductors of the circuit or between any conductor of the circuit and ground. *Canada Electrical Safety Regulations*, C.R.C., c. 998, s. 2. See EXTRA LOW ~; HIGH ~; LOW ~; MAXIMUM TEST ~; SYSTEM ~.

VOLTAGE OF A CIRCUIT. The greatest root-mean-square (effective) voltage between any two conductors of the circuit concerned.

VOLTAGE TO GROUND. The voltage between any live ungrounded part and any grounded part in the case of grounded circuits, or the greatest voltage existing in the circuit in the case of ungrounded circuits.

VOLUME. See BURSTING ~; NOMINAL ~.

VOLUME OF ABSOLUTE ETHYL ALCOHOL. Such volume measured at 20 degrees Celsius (20°). *Excise Act*, R.S.C. 1985, c. E-14, s. 2.

VOLUME-PRESSURE GAUGE. A device used in conjunction with a meter to compute volume in its relation to pressure where the line pressure fluctuates.

VOLUNTARILY. *adv*. ". . . [O]f one's own free will and without compulsion or constraint. . ." *Ager v. R.* (1983), 7 Admin. L.R. 16 at 23, [1984] 1 F.C. 157 (T.D.), Addy J.

VOLUNTARY. *adj*. 1. In criminal law, made without fear of prejudice or hope of advantage. 2. ". . . '[W]ithout compulsion' . . ." *R. v. British Columbia (Workmens Compensation Board)*, [1942] 2 W.W.R. 129 at 133, 57 B.C.R. 412, [1942] 2 D.L.R. 665 (C.A.), McDonald C.J.B.C. (dissenting) (McQuarrie, Sloan, O'Halloran and Fisher JJ.A. concurring).

VOLUNTARY ADDITIONAL CONTRIBUTION. An optional contribution by an employee to or under a pension plan except a contribution whose payment, under the terms of the plan, imposes on the employer an obligation to make an additional contribution to the plan.

VOLUNTARY AID DETACHMENT. See MEMBER OF ~.

VOLUNTARY APPEARANCE. Appearing before a foreign court on one's own volition.

VOLUNTARY ASSUMPTION OF RISK. [In a negligence claim] "The defence of voluntary assumption of risk is based on the moral supposition that no wrong is done to one who consents. By agreeing to assume the risk the plaintiff absolves the defendant of all responsibility for it . . . Since the volenti defence is a complete bar to recovery and therefore anomalous in an age of apportionment, the Courts have tightly circumscribed its scope. It only applies in situations where the plaintiff has assumed both the physical and the legal risk involved in the activity . . ." *Crocker v. Sundance Northwest Resorts Ltd.* (1988), 44 C.C.L.T. 225 at 239, 86 N.R. 241, 64 O.R. (2d) 64n, [1988] 1 S.C.R. 1186, 29 O.A.C. 1, 51 D.L.R. (4th) 321, [1988] R.R.A. 444, the court per Wilson J. See VOLENTI NON FIT INJURIA.

VOLUNTARY CONTRIBUTION. See VOLUNTARY ADDITIONAL CONTRIBUTION.

VOLUNTARY CONVEYANCE. A conveyance by something like a gift with no valuable consideration.

VOLUNTARY EQUITY ACCOUNT. The sum of the employee additional contribution account together with the vested portion of the employer additional contributions, if any, with accumulated interest.

VOLUNTARY OVERTIME. Overtime work which an employee is not required to perform under a collective agreement and which she may refuse to do if requested.

VOLUNTARY PLEA. Conscious decision of choice by an accused to plead guilty for reasons which she considers appropriate.

VOLUNTARY RECOGNITION. An agreement by the employer to recognize a union as the bargaining agent for the employer's workers.

VOLUNTARY STATEMENT. " . . . [N]o statement by an accused is admissible in evidence against him unless it is shewn by the prosecution to have been a voluntary statement, in the sense that it has not been obtained from him either by fear of prejudice or hope of advantage exercised or held out by a person in authority. " *Ibrahim v. R.*, [1914] A.C. 599 at 609-10 (U.K. P.C.), Lord Sumner for their Lordships.

VOLUNTARY TERMINATION. An act of quitting a job which indicates a subjective intention to quit combined with an objective confirming action.

VOLUNTARY TREE. A tree whose origin is unknown. *Koenig v. Goebel* (1998), 162 Sask. R. 81 (Q.B.).

VOLUNTARY WASTE. ". . . [W]aste is either voluntary or permissive . . . voluntary waste involves an act that is either wilful or negligent. Hence, damage to rented premises caused by a fire started by the negligence of the tenant constitutes voluntary waste and the tenant can be held liable: . . . *Prior v. Hanna* (1987), 55 Alta. L.R. (2d) 276 at 282, 82 A.R. 3, 43 D.L.R. (4th) 612 (Q.B.), Miller A.C.J.Q.B.

VOLUNTAS DONATORIS IN CHARTA DONI SUI MANIFESTE EXPRESSA OBSERVETUR. [L.] The donor's will, clearly expressed in the deed of gift, should be observed.

VOLUNTAS FACIT QUOD IN TESTAMENTO SCRIPTUM VALEAT. [L.] The testator's intention gives a will effect.

VOLUNTAS IN DELICTIS NON EXITUS SPECTATOR. [L.] In crimes, one considers the intention, not the result.

VOLUNTAS REPUTATUR PRO FACTO. [L.] The will is considered to be the deed.

VOLUNTAS TESTATORIS EST AMBULATORIA USQUE AD EXTREMUM VITAE EXITUM. [L.] A testator's will is changeable until the very end of life.

VOLUNTAS TESTATORIS HABET INTERPRETATIONEM LATAM ET BENIGNAM. [L.] A testator's intention always has wide and favourable interpretation.

VOLUNTEER. *n*. Any individual, not in receipt of fees, wages or salary for the services or assistance who renders services or assistance, whether or not that individual has special training to render the service or assistance and whether or not the service or assistance is rendered by the individual alone or in conjunction with others.

VOLUNTEER FIREFIGHTER. A firefighter who provides fire protection services either voluntarily or for a nominal consideration, honorarium, training or activity allowance.

VOLUNTEER LABOUR. Any service provided free of charge by a person outside of that person's working hours, but does not include a service provided by a person who is self-employed if the service is one that is normally sold or otherwise charged for by that person. *Elections acts*.

VOLUNTEER WORK RELATIONSHIP. A relationship between an organization and an individual under which a service is provided for or in relation to or is undertaken in connection with the organization by an individual who is acting as a volunteer or is otherwise unpaid with respect to that service and includes any similar relationship involving an organization and an individual where, in respect of that relationship, the individual is a participant or a student. *Personal Information Protection Act*, S.A. 2003, c. P-6.5, s. 1.

VOTE. *v*. 1. To cast a ballot at an election. 2. To signify agreement or dissent when a question is called at a meeting. See RIGHT TO ~.

VOTE. *n*. 1. A ballot paper which has been detached from the counterfoil, and has been furnished to a voter, and has been marked and deposited as a vote by the voter. 2. Suffrage. 3. A specific segregation of spending authority into a broad category according to intended use such as capital expenditures, operations and maintenance expenditures, and loans. 4. An appropriation under a Supply Act identified in the main or supplementary estimates as a vote. See ADVANCE ~; CASTING ~; FREE ~; LEADERSHIP ~; NO-UNION ~; POPULAR ~; PRE-HEARING ~; REPRESENTATION ~; STRIKE ~; TWO-THIRDS ~.

VOTE BY SECRET BALLOT. A vote by ballots cast in such a manner that a person expressing a choice cannot be identified with the choice expressed.

VOTER. *n*. 1. Any person entitled to vote. 2. Any person who votes at an election. 3. Any person whose name is on any voters' list in force under the Canada Elections Act, or any person entitled to vote at an election of a member of the House of Commons or who has voted at such an election. *Disfranchising Act*, R.S.C. 1985, c. D-3, s. 2. 4. Any person who is or who claims to be registered as an elector in the list of voters for any electoral district; or who is, or claims to be, entitled to vote in any election. See IMPEDITIVE ~; QUALIFIED ~.

VOTER INFORMATION CARD. A card containing information advising a voter where he is qualified to vote.

VOTER POPULATION. The number of electors as determined from the voters' list prepared for use in an immediately preceding provincial general election.

VOTERS LIST. *var*. **VOTERS' LIST**. 1. Includes any list made and revised of persons entitled to vote at an election. 2. A list of electors required to be prepared. See REVISED ~.

VOTES AND PROCEEDINGS. 1. A record of proceedings of the House of Commons. 2. The similar record of the business of a legislative assembly.

VOTING. *n*. Voting at an election or plebiscite. *Election Act*, R.S.A. 1980, c. E-2, s. 1. See CUMULATIVE ~.

VOTING GROUP. Two or more persons who are associated with respect to voting interests in an entity by contract, business arrangement, personal relationship, common control in fact through ownership of voting interests, or otherwise, in such a manner that they would ordinarily be expected to act together on a continuing basis with respect to the exercise of those rights. *Investment Canada Act*, R.S.C. 1985 (1st Supp.), c. 28, s. 3.

VOTING INTEREST. With respect to (a) a corporation with share capital, means a voting share; (b) a corporation without share capital, means an ownership interest in the assets thereof that entitles the owner to rights similar to those enjoyed by the owner of a voting share; and (c) a partnership, trust or joint venture, means an ownership interest in the assets thereof that entitles the owner to receive a share of the profits and to share in the assets on dissolution. *Investment Canada Act*, R.S.C. 1985 (1st Supp.), c. 28, s. 3.

VOTING MEMBER. A member of a council who may vote in the determination of any matter or deliberation put to a vote in such council.

VOTING RECORDER. An apparatus in which ballot cards are used with a punch device for the piercing of ballot cards by the elector to record his or her vote, so that the ballot card may be tabulated by means of automatic tabulating equipment.

VOTING REGISTER. The prescribed form in which to record the names of persons who have received ballots at an election.

VOTING RIGHT. The right to vote for the election of one or more directors excluding a right to vote which is dependent on the happening of an event specified in the instrument of incorporation or this Act.

VOTING SECURITY. Any security other than a debt security of an issuer carrying a voting right either under all circumstances or under some circumstances that have occurred and are continuing. See OFFEROR'S VOTING SECURITIES; RIGHT TO A ~.

VOTING SHARE. Any share that carries voting rights under all circumstances or by reason of an event that has occurred and is continuing. See SUBORDINATE ~.

VOTING STATION. The place where an elector casts his vote.

VOTING SUBDIVISION. That area of a local jurisdiction or ward designated as a voting subdivision by the elected authority or the returning officer.

VOTING TRUST. The rights to vote some or all shares of a corporation are settled upon trustees who under the terms of the trust have authority, with or without restriction, to exercise the voting rights.

VOUCH. *v*. To call on; to rely on; to quote authoritatively.

VOUCHER. *n*. 1. A document which is evidence of a transaction, i.e. a receipt for money paid. 2. An instrument issued under this Act and the regulations that authorizes the supplying of specified goods or the rendering of specified services to the person named therein. *Social Welfare Act*, R.S.N.B. 1973, c. S-11, s. 1.

VOX EMISSA VOLAT, LITERA SCRIPTA MANET. [L.] The spoken word disappears, the written word remains.

VOYAGE. *n*. Includes passage or trip and any movement of a ship from one place to another or from one place and returning to that place. *Canada Shipping Act*, R.S.C. 1985, c. S-9, s. 2. See FOREIGN ~; HOME-TRADE ~; INLAND ~; INTERNATIONAL ~; MINOR WATERS ~; TROPICAL ~.

VOYAGE POLICY. 1. To insure the subject-matter "at and from", from one place to another or others. *Insurance acts*. 2. A marine policy may be a voyage policy or a time policy. A marine policy is a voyage policy if the contract insures the subject-matter "at and from", or "from", one place to another place or other places. *Marine Insurance Act*, S.C. 1993, c. 22, s. 29(1), (2)

VQA WINE. Wine, (a) that is produced in Ontario from grapes that have been grown in Ontario or from grape juice or grape must produced from such grapes, and (b) that meets the standards of the wine authority. *Vintners Quality Alliance Act, 1999*, S.O. 1999, c. 3, s. 2.

VS. *abbr*. Versus.

VULNERABLE. *adj.* 1. " . . . [S]usceptible to harm, or open to injury . . ." *International Corona Resources Ltd. v. LAC Minerals Ltd.* (1989), 35 E.T.R. 1 at 34, 26 C.P.R. (3d) 97, [1989] 2 S.C.R. 574, 69 O.R. (2d) 287, 61 D.L.R. (4th) 14, 6 R.P.R. (2d) 1, 44 B.L.R. 1, 101 N.R. 239, 36 O.A.C. 57, La Forest J. (Lamer J. concurring). 2. In respect of a Convention refugee or a person in similar circumstances, that the person has a greater need of protection than other applicants for protection abroad because of the person's particular circumstances that give rise to a heightened risk to their physical safety. *Immigration regulation.*

VULNERABLE PERSONS. Persons who, because of their age, a disability or other circumstances, whether temporary or permanent, (a) are in a position of dependence on others; or (b) are otherwise at a greater risk than the general population of being harmed by persons in a position of authority or trust relative to them. *Criminal Records Act*, R.S.C. 1985, c. C-47, s. 6.3(1) as am.

VULVA. *n.* The exterior sexual organs of a female: the clitoris, vestibule, labia minora and labia majora. F.A. Jaffe, *A Guide to Pathological Evidence*, 3d ed. (Toronto: Carswell, 1991) at 229.

W. *abbr*. Watt.

WAD. *n*. A cardboard, felt or plastic disc used in shotgun ammunition. F.A. Jaffe, *A Guide to Pathological Evidence*, 3d ed. (Toronto: Carswell, 1991) at 229.

WADCUTTER AMMUNITION. Bullets with flat noses used originally for target shooting. They tend to ricochet and do not penetrate too deeply. F.A. Jaffe, *A Guide to Pathological Evidence*, 3d ed. (Toronto: Carswell, 1991) at 229.

WAFER. *n*. A small circle of red paper used to seal a deed instead of sealing wax.

WAGE. *n*. 1. Any compensation measured by time, piece or otherwise. 2. Salary, pay, commission or remuneration for work. See AVERAGE DAILY ~; BASIC ~; CONSTANT ~ PLAN; DAILY ~; MINIMUM ~; PREVAILING ~; REAL ~; REGULAR ~; TOTAL ~; ~S.

WAGE ADJUSTMENT. See AUTOMATIC ~.

WAGE BRACKETS. The minimum and maximum wage rates for a job.

WAGE DIFFERENTIAL. The different rates of pay for the same type of work. See GEOGRAPHIC ~.

WAGE DISPARITY. A variation of wages paid to workers in similar jobs or in different regions.

WAGE GUARANTEE. A provision in a collective agreement which guarantees an employee the dollar equivalent of a certain number of hours of work every week.

WAGE INCREASE. See PROGRESSIVE ~; SCHEDULED ~.

WAGE PLAN. See CONSTANT ~; INCENTIVE ~.

WAGE PROGRESSION. See AUTOMATIC ~.

WAGER. *n*. "[A contract by which] . . . two persons, professing to hold opposite views touching the issue of a future uncertain event, mutually agree that dependent upon the determination of that event one shall win from the other, and that the other shall pay or hand over to him a sum of money or other stake, neither of the contracting parties having any other interest in that contract than the sum or stake he will win or lose, there being no other real consideration for the making of such a contract by either of the parties. It is essential to a wagering contract that each party may under it either win or lose. . ." *Carlill v. Carbolic Smoke Ball Co.*, [1892] 2 Q.B. 484 at 490-91 (U.K.), Hawkins J.

WAGERING CONTRACT. A mutual promise by which each party gains or loses by the outcome of an uncertain event. Each party's promise is her or his only interest in the transaction. G.H.L. Fridman, *The Law of Contract in Canada*, 2d ed. (Toronto: Carswell, 1986) at 334.

WAGES. *n*. 1. " . . . [A]ny compensation for labour or services." *Davenport Re* (1930), (*sub nom. Davenport v. McNiven*) [1930] 4 D.L.R. 386 at 387, [1930] 2 W.W.R. 263, 42 B.C.R. 468 (C.A.), Macdonald C.J.B.C. 2. Amount paid in respect of employment whether payable by time or by the job or piece or otherwise. 3. " . . . [T]hat tax deductions taken at source by an employer and remitted to Revenue Canada do not lose their character as wages under the Bankruptcy Act, [R.S.C. 1985, c. B-3, s. 68] . . . I do not conclude that all tax refunds are wages. It depends on the nature of the refund. In this case the refund was the result of taxes deducted directly from wages. . ." *Marzetti v. Marzetti* (1992), 14 C.B.R. (3d) 127 at 135, 4 Alta. L.R. (2d) 97, 42 R.F.L. (3d) 76, 94 D.L.R. (4th) 394, 112 A.R.

154, 25 W.A.C. 1543 (C.A.), the court per Major J.A. 4. "Entitlement to damages for wrongful dismissal also falls within the statutory definition of wages [in Labour Standards Act, R.S.S. 1978, c. L-1, s. 2(r)], being a form of compensation for personal services to which an employee is entitled." *Meyers v. Walters Cycle Co.* (1990), 72 D.L.R. (4th) 190 at 192, 32 C.C.E.L. 206, [1990] 5 W.W.R. 455, 85 Sask. R. 222 (C.A.), the court per Sherstobitoff J.A. See ATTACHMENT OF ~; BASIC RATE OF ~; EARNINGS AND ~; FAIR ~; RATE OF ~; SCHEDULE OF ~; SUBSISTENCE ~; WAGE.

WAGON. *n*. Any vehicle used to deliver grain to a country elevator. *Canada Grain Act*, R.S.C. 1970, c. G-16, s. 2. See STATION ~.

WAIF. *n*. Goods found which nobody claimed.

WAIT. See LYING IN ~.

WAITING PERIOD. The interval between the issuance by the Registrar of a receipt for a preliminary prospectus relating to the offering of a security and the issuance of a receipt for the prospectus. *Securities acts*.

WAIVE. *v*. To surrender or renounce a right, privilege or claim.

WAIVER. *n*. 1. Waiver involves the test enunciated in *Western Canada Investment Co. v. McDiarmid* (1922), 15 Sask. L.R. 142 (C.A.), at 146, where Lamont, J.A. said: "To constitute waiver, two essential prerequisites are in general necessary. There must be knowledge of the existence of the right or privilege relinquished and of the possessor's right to enjoy it, and there must be a clear intention of foregoing the exercise of such right." *Ericsson Inc. v. Novatel Inc.*, 2001 ABCA 199, 286 A.R. 190, 253 W.A.C. 190, 12 C.P.C. (5th) 212 (C.A.). 2. "[To forego] . . . reliance upon some known right or defect. It is important that the right or defect, as the case may be, be known, since one should not be able to waive rights of which he was not fully aware or apprised. . . In determining whether waiver applies, the defendant must take steps in the proceedings knowingly and to its prejudice, which amount to foregoing a reliance upon some right or defect. In order to waive a right it must be a known right. . ." *Marchischuk v. Dominion Industrial Supplies Ltd.* (1991), 3 C.C.L.I. (2d) 173 at 176-7, 30 M.V.R. (2d) 102, [1991] 4 W.W.R. 673, [1991] I.L.R. 1-2729, 125 N.R. 306, 80 D.L.R. (4th) 670, 50 C.P.C. (2d) 231, [1991] 2 S.C.R. 61, 73 Man. R. (2d) 271, 3 W.A.C. 271,

the court per Sopinka J. adopting the reasons of the trial judge. 3. " . . . [W]aiver does not confer rights, it repudiates them. If you waive your right to A, it does not mean that you are entitled to B. It means only that you are no longer entitled to A." *R. v. Turpin* (1989), 39 C.R.R. 306 at 329, 69 C.R. (3d) 97, 48 C.C.C. (3d) 8, 96 N.R. 115, [1989] 1 S.C.R. 1296, 34 O.A.C. 115, the court per Wilson J. 4. Surrender of an advantage or right intending not to exercise the advantage or right.

WALE. *n*. A longitudinal member of shoring and timbering that is placed against, and directly resists, pressure from sheathing.

WALK. See CROSS ~.

WALKOUT. *n*. The withdrawal of employees from their place of employment.

WALKWAY. See ENCLOSED ~.

WALL. *n*. The exposed face of an excavation in a surface mine from ground level to the working level. See CAVITY ~; CHINESE ~; DUCTILE FLEXURAL ~; FIRE~; PANEL ~; PARTY ~.

WALLEYE. *n*. Yellow pickerel, Stizostedion vitreum vitreum (Mitchill) and includes dore, perch, pike, walleye pike and yellow pike.

WANDER. *v*. To walk without a specific destination.

WANT OF PROSECUTION. In relation to dismissal of an action, inordinate delay, inexcusable delay, and serious prejudice to the defendants by the delay.

WANTONNESS. *n*. "[In Criminal Code, R.S.C. 1970, c. C-34, s. 202(1)] . . . perhaps a subclass of recklessness. It is a wild, mad or arrogant kind of recklessness and thus closely related to 'wilfulness'." *R. v. Walker* (1974), 26 C.R.N.S. 268 at 273, 18 C.C.C. (2d) 179 (N.S. C.A.), MacKeigan C.J.N.S.

WAR. *n*. Armed conflict. See ARTICLES OF ~; DECLARATION OF ~; ~ CRIME; ~ EMERGENCY; MUNITIONS OF ~; PRISONER OF ~; SERVICE IN A THEATRE OF ACTUAL ~; THEATRE OF ACTUAL ~; WORLD ~ I; WORLD ~ II.

WAR CRIME. 1. An act or omission that is committed during an international conflict, whether or not it constitutes a contravention of the law in force at the time and in the place of its commission, and that, at that time and in that place, constitutes a contravention of the customary international law or conventional international law applicable in international armed conflicts. *Criminal Code*, S.C. 1987, c. 37, s. 1(1). 2. An act or omission committed during an armed conflict that, at the time and in the place of its commission, constitutes a war crime according to customary international law or conventional international law applicable to armed conflicts, whether or not it constitutes a contravention of the law in force at the time and in the place of its commission. *Crimes Against Humanity and War Crimes Act, 2000*, S.C. 2000, c. 24, s. 4.

WARD. *n.* 1. An electoral division. 2. A child committed to the care and custody of the Director or a Society. *Child Welfare acts.* See LOCAL ~.

WARDEN. *n.* 1. The warden of a rural municipality. *Municipal Affairs Act*, S.N.S. 1982, c. 9, s. 2. 2. Includes the Minister, Provincial Forester, district forester, forester, inspector, chief forest ranger, sub-ranger, game warden or other officer appointed under Part II or III. *Lands and Forests Act*, R.S.N.S. 1967, c. 163, s. 84. 3. The chief executive officer of a county council in Ontario. I.M. Rogers, *The Law of Canadian Municipal Corporations*, 2d ed. (Toronto: Carswell, 1971) at 225. See CHURCH~; FIRE ~; PARK ~; PORT ~.

WARD OF THE GOVERNMENT. A child who has been committed to the care and custody of the director or a society. *Child Welfare Act*, R.S.M. 1970, c. C80, s. 2.

WARDSHIP. *n.* Guardianship.

WARDSHIP ORDER. An order of the court making a child a ward of the Crown or of the Court or a society or person. See CROWN ~.

WAREHOUSE. *n.* 1. " . . . [M]ay be for the purpose of receiving goods on bailment where they would be to the order of the bailor, or a repository for storing large quantities of wholesale goods or a building holding large quantities of goods or material and being ancillary to some wholesale or retail business. . ." *Evans v. British Columbia Electric Railway* (1914), 7 W.W.R. 121 at 122 (B.C. S.C.), Schultz J. 2. Any place, whether house, shed, yard, dock, pond or other place in which goods imported may be lodged, kept and secured without payment of duty. 3. Land that is used as a repository, storehouse or shed for the storage of goods and includes any building or structure from which goods are dis-

tributed for sale off the premises, but does not include a building or structure, the primary purpose of which is the sale of goods to the public. *Commercial Concentration Tax Act*, R.S.O. 1990, c. C-16, s. 1 as am. See BONDED ~; BONDING ~; CUSTOMS EXPRESS BRANCH ~; CUSTOMS ~; EXAMINING ~; EX ~; QUEEN'S ~; RETAIL ~; SEPARATE STORE OR ~; SUFFERANCE ~.

WAREHOUSE KEEPER. The owner of a warehouse or, if the warehouse is leased, the lessee of the warehouse. Canada regulations.

WAREHOUSEMAN. *n.* 1. 1. "A person who operates or who has charge of a warehouse . . ." *Canadian Pacific Railway v. Parry Sound (Town)*, [1952] O.W.N. 557 at 558 (H.C.), Schroeder J. 2. A person who receives goods for storage for reward. 3. A person lawfully engaged in the business of storing goods as a bailee for hire.

WAREHOUSER. *n.* A person who receives goods for storing as a bailee for hire. *Warehouse Receipts Act*, R.S. Nfld. 1990, c. W-1, s. 2

WAREHOUSE RECEIPT. 1. A receipt given by any person for any goods in the person's actual, visible and continued possession as bailee thereof in good faith and not as of the person's own property. 2. Includes (a) any receipt given by any person for goods, wares and merchandise in the person's actual, visible and continued possession as bailee thereof in good faith and not as of his own property; (b) receipts given by any person who is the owner or keeper of a harbour, cove, pond, wharf, yard, warehouse, shed, storehouse or other place for the storage of goods, wares and merchandise, for goods, wares and merchandise delivered to him as bailee, and actually in the place or in one or more of the places owned or kept by him, whether such person is engaged in other business or not; (c) receipts given by any person in charge of logs or timber in transit from timber limits or other lands to the place of destination of such logs or timber; (d) Lake Shippers' Clearance Association receipts and transfer certificates, British Columbia Grain Shippers' Clearance Association receipts and transfer certificates, and all documents recognized by the Canada Grain Act as elevator receipts; and (e) receipts given by any person for any hydrocarbons received by him as bailee, whether his obligation to restore requires delivery of the same hydrocarbons or may be satisfied by delivery of a like quantity of hydrocarbons of the same or a similar grade or kind. *Bank Act*, S.C. 1991, c. 46, s. 425.

WAR EMERGENCY. 1. War or other armed conflict, real or imminent, involving Canada or any of its allies that is so serious as to be a national emergency. *Emergencies Act*, S.C. 1988, c. 29, s. 37. 2. (a) A war in which hostilities are being carried on in Canada; or (b) an invasion of Canada by hostile forces; or (c) an insurrection in Canada; or (d) any other emergency due to enemy attack, sabotage or other hostile action.

WARES. *n*. Includes printed publications. *Trademarks Act*, R.S.C. 1985, c. T-13, s. 2. See GOODS, ~ AND MERCHANDISE; PESSURABLE ~.

WAR MEASURES ACT. The now repealed federal statute gave the federal cabinet extraordinary powers when the cabinet declared that a war or insurrection was apprehended or existing. This statute gained notoriety in 1970 when then Prime Minister Trudeau and his Cabinet invoked the Act in peace time for the first time. By doing so they gave authorities extraordinary powers for a period of time. More specific powers are now set out in the *Emergencies Act*, R.S.C. 1985, c. 22 (4th Supp.).

WARNING. *n*. 1. Putting on notice; making aware. 2. No magic combination of words need be resorted to in order to constitute a warning to an employee that their future employment may be at risk due to their conduct. The question in all the circumstances should be whether or not there was such communication to the employee in such a way that the employee should conclude that he stood in danger of being terminated. *Thomas v. Canex Foods Ltd.*, 2000 CarswellBC 1013, 2000 BCSC 748 (S.C.).

WARNING GAS. A gas that immediately identifies its presence by its effect on the senses when a person is exposed to it.

WARRANT. *v*. To justify.

WARRANT. *n*. 1. The order of a judicial authority that a ministerial officer arrest, seize, search or execute some judicial sentence. 2. When used in relation to a warrant for the arrest of a person, means a warrant in Form 7 and, when used in relation to a warrant for the committal of a person, means a warrant in Form 8. *Criminal Code*, R.S.C. 1985, c. C-46, s. 493. 3. A right to subscribe for a share of a corporation. 4. Any record issued by a company as evidence of conversion or exchange privileges or options or rights to acquire shares of the company. *Business Corporations Act*, S.B.C. 2002, c. 57, s. 1(1). 5. In the case of a foreign state, includes any judicial document that authorizes the arrest of a person accused or convicted of crime. *Extradition Act*, R.S.C. 1985, c. E-23, s. 2 See BACK A ~; BENCH ~; CAVEAT ~; DOCK ~; LOCAL ~; ROYAL ~; SEARCH ~; SHARE PURCHASE ~; SHARE ~.

WARRANTEE. *n*. A person to whom one makes a warranty.

WARRANT OF ATTORNEY. An instrument given before an action is commenced by which a debtor names an attorney and empowers the attorney to confess judgment in an action.

WARRANT OF COMMITTAL. An order directing that a person sentenced or committed to prison be taken there and that the keeper of the prison receive the person into custody and imprison the person.

WARRANTOR. *n*. A party who warrants.

WARRANTOR POTEST EXCIPERE QUOD QUERENS NON TENET TERRAM DE QUA PETIT WARRANTIAM, ET QUOD DONUM FUIT INSUFFICIENS. [L.] A warrantor may take exception that a complainant does not hold the land for which the warranty is sought, and that the gift was insufficient.

WARRANTY. *n*. 1. " . . . [A] term in contract which does not go to the root of the agreement between the parties but simply expresses some lesser obligation, the failure to perform which can give rise to an action for damages but never to the right to rescind or repudiate the contract: . . ." *Fraser-Reid v. Droumtsekas* (1980), 103 D.L.R. (3d) 385 at 392, [1980] 1 S.C.R. 720, 29 N.R. 424, 9 R.P.R. 121, Dickson J. (Martland, Estey and McIntyre JJ. concurring). 2. An agreement with reference to goods which are the subject of a contract of sale, but collateral to the main purpose of such contract, the breach of which gives rise to a claim for damages, but not a right to reject the goods and treat the contract as repudiated. *Sale of Goods acts*. See ADDITIONAL WRITTEN ~.

WAR RISKS. The risks of loss or damage arising from hostilities, rebellion, revolution, civil war, piracy, action taken to repel an imagined attack or from civil strife consequent to their happening. *Marine and Aviation War Risks Act*, R.S.C. 1970, c. W-3, s. 2.

WAR SERVICE. 1. Active service during World War II or the Korean War, (a) in His or Her Majesty's naval, army or air forces or in the Canadian or British Merchant Marine, or (b) in any naval, army or air force that was allied with His or Her Majesty's forces and that is designated by the Lieutenant Governor in Council, providing satisfactory proof of such service is produced. Ontario statutes. 2. The total period of service of an employee during World War I, World War II and the Korean War in the Naval, Military or Air Forces of Her Majesty, Her Majesty in right of Canada or Her Majesty in right of the province and includes service in the Merchant Marine, the Auxiliary Forces, the Overseas Forestry Unit and the Rescue Tugs. Newfoundland statutes.

WAR SERVICE INJURY. 1. In the case of an air raid precautions worker other than a duly registered voluntary evacuation worker, any physical injury sustained during the War and arising out of and in the course of his duties as such as a direct result of enemy action, counteraction against the enemy or action in apprehension of enemy attack or during a blackout, test or period of training duly authorized by the senior air raid precautions officer in the designated area in which the injury was sustained, and, in the case of duly registered voluntary evacuation worker means injuries arising out of and in the course of his duties as an evacuation worker. *Civilian War-related Benefits Act*, R.S.C. 1985, c. C-31, s. 30. 2. An injury arising out of and in the course of duties as a member of the Voluntary Aid Detachment. *Civilian War-related Benefits Act*, R.S.C. 1985, c. C-31, s. 43.

WARSHIP. See CANADIAN ~; FOREIGN ~.

WAR VETERANS. Persons who have served in active armed forces, the auxiliary services or the merchant marine of Canada or any of her allies.

WASCHHAUT. *n.* Wrinkling of skin on the feet or hands caused by long exposure to moisture; it can occur before or after death. F.A. Jaffe, *A Guide to Pathological Evidence*, 3d ed. (Toronto: Carswell, 1991) at 229.

WASH. *n.* As applied to distilleries, means all liquor made in whole or in part from grain, malt or other saccharine matter, whether or not the liquor is fermented or unfermented. *Excise Act*, R.S.C. 1985, c. E-14, s. 4. See CAR ~.

WASH BASIN. A receptacle for washing any part of the human body. See BASIN.

WASH ROOM. *var.* **WASHROOM.** A room that contains a wash basin for the use of employees. See PUBLIC ~.

WASTE. *n.* 1. "Waste in law is destruction of a part of the inheritance by a limited owner, such as a tenant for life or years." *"Freiya" (The) v. "R.S" (The)* (1922), 65 D.L.R. 218 at 222, [1922] 1 W.W.R. 409, 21 Ex. C.R. 232, Audette J. 2. ". . . [W]aste is either voluntary or permissive . . . voluntary waste involves an act that is either wilful or negligent. Hence, damage to rented premises caused by a fire started by the negligence of the tenant constitutes voluntary waste and the tenant can be held liable: . . . Permissive waste involves the failure or omission to take some precaution which results in damage to the property." *Prior v. Hanna* (1987), 55 Alta. L.R. (2d) 276 at 282, 82 A.R. 3, 43 D.L.R. (4th) 612 (Q.B.), Miller A.C.J.Q.B. 3. Air contaminants, litter, effluent and refuse. 4. (a) Any substance that, if added to any water, would degrade or alter or form part of a process of degradation or alteration of the quality of that water to an extent that is detrimental to their use by man or by any animal, fish or plant that is useful to man; and (b) any water that contains a substance in such a quantity or concentration, or that has been so treated, processed or changed, by heat or other means, from a natural state that it would, if added to any other water, degrade or alter or form part of a process of degradation or alteration of the quality of that water to the extent described in paragraph (a). *Canada Water Act*, R.S.C. 1985, c. C-11, s. 2. 5. In addition to its ordinary meaning, means "waste" as that term is understood in the oil and natural gas industry, and includes the underground or surface loss of potentially recoverable oil or natural gas and wasteful operations. *Oil and Natural Gas Act*, R.S.P.E.I. 1988, c. O-5, s. 1. 6. Includes ashes, garbage, refuse, domestic waste, industrial waste, or municipal refuse. See AGRICULTURAL ~; AMELIORATING ~; DOMESTIC ~; DOUBLE ~; FARM ~; HAZARDOUS ~; INCINERATOR ~; INDIRECT ~; INDUSTRIAL ~; PERMISSIVE ~; SOLID ~; VOLUNTARY ~.

WASTE AND VENT. See CONTINUOUS ~.

WASTE DISPOSAL SITE. Any land or land covered by water upon, into, in or through which, or building or structure in which, waste is deposited or processed and any machinery or equipment or operation required for the treatment or disposal of waste.

WASTE DISPOSAL SYSTEM. See MARINE CRAFT ~.

WASTEFUL OPERATION. (a) The locating, spacing, drilling, equipping, completing, operating or producing of a well in a manner that results or tends to result in reducing the quantity of oil, gas or crude bitumen ultimately recoverable from a pool or oil sands deposit under sound engineering and economic principles; (b) the locating, drilling, equipping, completing, operating or producing of a well in a manner that causes or tends to cause excessive surface loss or destruction of oil, gas or crude bitumen; (c) the inefficient, excessive or improper use or dissipation of reservoir energy however caused; (d) the failure to use suitable enhanced recovery operations in a pool when it appears probable on the basis of available information that those methods would result in increasing the quantity of oil or gas ultimately recoverable from the pool under sound engineering and economic principles; (e) the escape or the flaring of gas, if it is estimated that, in the public interest and under sound engineering principles and in the light of economics and the risk factor involved, the gas could be gathered, processed if necessary, and it or the products from it marketed, or stored for future marketing, or beneficially injected into an underground reservoir; (f) the inefficient storing of oil, gas or crude bitumen, whether on the surface or underground; or (g) the production of oil, gas or crude bitumen in excess of proper storage facilities or of transportation and marketing facilities or of market demand therefor.

WASTE MANAGEMENT. The collection, handling, transportation, storage, processing and disposal of waste and may include one or more waste disposal sites or techniques. See HAZARDOUS WASTE DISPOSAL FACILITY; HAZARDOUS ~ ENTERPRISE.

WASTE MANAGEMENT PLAN. A plan that contains provisions or requirements for the collection, treatment, handling, storage, utilization and disposal of refuse, sewage and other waste within the whole or a specified part of a municipality.

WASTE MANAGEMENT POWER. Any power conferred by any general or special Act on local municipalities or local boards thereof related to the collection, removal, disposal, treatment, storage, processing, transfer, reduction,

reuse, recovery or recycling of waste. *Municipal Act*, R.S.O. 1990, c. M.45, s. 209(1).

WASTE MANAGEMENT SYSTEM. All facilities, equipment and operations for the management of waste, including the collection, handling, transportation, storage, processing, utilization and disposal of waste, and includes one or more waste disposal sites within such system. See MUNICIPAL ~; PRIVATE ~.

WASTE MATERIAL. (a) Refuse, garbage, rubbish, litter, scrap and discarded material including tailings, offal, machinery, products, vehicles and other articles which are dumped, discarded, abandoned or otherwise disposed of, (b) any material or thing that may be a danger to the health of human beings, animals, wild life or fish, or is of unsightly appearance, and (c) a substance designated as waste material in the regulations. *Waste Material Disposal Act*, R.S. Nfld. 1990, c. W-4, s. 2.

WASTE PIPE. That part of drainage piping that runs from a fixture to a waste stack, soil stack, building drain or sewage tank. See INDIRECT ~.

WASTE STACK. A stack that conducts liquid wastes from one or more plumbing fixtures that are not sanitary units.

WASTE TREATMENT SYSTEM. Any plant or installation used, or intended to be used to treat a contaminant prior to disposal on land, or into air or water and includes a sewerage system. *Environmental Protection Act*, R.S.P.E.I. 1988, c. E-9, s. 1(q).

WASTE WATER. *var.* **WASTEWATER**. Water carrying solid, liquid or gaseous residue from a process, an establishment or a building, mixed or not with underground, cooling, rain or surface water and, unless the context indicates otherwise, underground water, cooling water, rain water and surface water. See DOMESTIC ~; INDUSTRIAL ~; SANITARY ~.

WASTEWATER LAGOON. A wastewater treatment plant that consists of one or more designed and constructed surface impoundments used for biological and physical treatment of wastewater.

WASTEWATER SEWER. A sewer that carries liquid and water-carried wastes from residences, commercial buildings, industrial plants and institutions, together with minor quantities of ground, storm and surface waters that are not admitted intentionally. *City of Winnipeg Act*, S.M. 1971, c. 105, s. 453.

WASTEWATER SYSTEM. Collectively, all of the property involved in the operation of a sewer utility. It includes land, structures, equipment and processes required to collect, carry away and treat wastewater and dispose of the effluent. *City of Winnipeg Act*, S.M. 1971, c. 105, s. 453.

WASTE WATER TREATMENT FACILITY. Any system or method used to treat waste water biologically, chemically, electrically, mechanically or otherwise and includes the water collection system for it.

WASTEWATER TREATMENT PLANT. Any structure, thing or process used for physical, chemical, biological or radiological treatment of wastewater, and includes a structure, thing or process used for wastewater storage, treated wastewater use and disposal, and sludge treatment, storage and disposal.

WASTING ASSET. Property which exists under restriction, such as a natural resource or leasehold.

WATCH. *n.* In respect of a ship, means (a) that part of the complement that is required for the purpose of attending to the navigation or security of the ship; and (b) the period during which a member of the complement is required to be on call or the physical presence of the member is required (i) on the bridge or deck, in the case of a mate or a rating, or (ii) in the machinery space, in the case of a chief engineer, engineer, assistant engineer, engine-room assistant or engine-room rating. Canada Regulations. See DECK ~; ENGINEER ON THE ~; FLIGHT ~ SYSTEM.

WATCHING. *v.* Continuously observing for a purpose.

WATCHING AND BESETTING. Watching is passive and besetting is active. Observing and assailing.

WATCHKEEPING SYSTEM. A system in which the hours of work of watchkeeping persons are such as to ensure regular and systematic surveillance of the ship's operation. *Crewing Regulations*, SOR/97-390, s. 1(1).

WATCH REPAIRER. A person who, (a) makes or fits parts for time-pieces; (b) repairs, alters, takes apart, assembles or reassembles timepieces or any part thereof; (c) determines the condition of time-pieces and estimates the repairs necessary; (d) cleans, polishes or lubricates time-piece movements or any part thereof; or (e) tests, adjusts or regulates time-pieces or any part thereof.

WATER. *n.* 1. Includes flowing or standing water on or below the surface of the earth and ice formed thereon. 2. All water on or under the surface of the ground. 3. A surface or subterranean source of fresh or salt water within the jurisdiction of the province, whether such source usually contains water or not, and includes water above the bed of the sea that is within the jurisdiction of the province, a river, stream, brook, creek, watercourse, lake, pond, spring, lagoon, ravine, gully, canal and other flowing or standing water and the land usually or at any time occupied by any such body of water. *Environmental Assessment Act*, R.S. Nfld. 1990, c. E-14, s. 2. 4. Natural surface and ground water in liquid, gaseous or solid state, but does not include water packaged as a beverage or in tanks. *Trade Agreement Acts*. See BALLAST ~; BODY OF ~; BRACKISH ~; COOLING ~; FIRST OPEN ~; GROUND ~; MAKE-UP ~; MINERAL ~; MUNICIPAL ~ UTILITY; NATURAL ~; NAVIGABLE ~; OPEN BODY OF ~; OPEN ~; PARK ~; POTABLE ~; PROVINCIAL ~; PURE ~ AREAS; RAW ~; SANITARY WASTE ~; STANDING BODY OF ~; STORM ~; STREAM OR ~; SURFACE ~; TRANSPORT BY ~; UNRECORDED ~; WASTE ~; ~S.

WATER AND SEWAGE WORKS. Artificial or natural works used to supply, gather, store, improve, purify, heat, cool or transmit water or to gather, store, process, purify, decompose, transmit or dispose of sewage. *The Family Farm Improvement Act*, R.S.S. 1978, c. F-6, s. 2.

WATER BODY. A lake, pond, river or other body of water that is greater than 2 hectares in extent as determined by the minister. *Forestry Act*, R.S. Nfld. 1990, c. F-23, s. 39.

WATER COLUMN. The aqueous medium superjacent to a defined area of sub-aquatic land. *Aquaculture Act*, R.S.N.S. 1989, c. 18, s. 2.

WATER CONDITIONER. Any water softening chemical, anti-scale chemical, corrosion inhibiter or other substance intended to be used to treat water.

WATER CONTAMINANT. (a) Any solid, liquid or gas, or a combination of any of them, in water; (b) heat in water, resulting in a change in the temperature of surface water or underground fresh water.

WATER CONTROL PROJECT. Any works or undertaking constructed, operated and maintained for the purpose of controlling a lake or stream or stabilizing the water level of a lake or stream.

WATER CONTROL WORKS. 1. Works (a) for the conservation, control, disposal, protection, distribution, drainage, storage, or use of water; or (b) for the protection of land or other property from damage by water; or for all or some of those purposes, and includes any other work necessary or convenient for the use, operation, or maintenance of a work to which subclause (a) or (b) applies or constructed or operated as a complement of such work. 2. Works as defined in The Water Rights Act and includes a facility, plant or contrivance controlling, carrying, measuring, processing or treating water. *The Water Resources Management Act*. R.S.S. 1978, c. W-7, s. 2.

WATER COOLER. A suitable device for storing, cooling and dispensing potable water. *Locomotive and Caboose Sanitation Facilities Regulations*, C.R.C., c. 1155, s. 2.

WATER COURSE. *var.* **WATERCOURSE**. 1. " . . . [A] channel in which water flows, . . ." *Remfy v. Natal (Surveyor-General)*, [1896] A.C. 558 at 560 (Natal P.C.), Lord Davey. 2. " . . . [D]efined channel course or banks where the waters flowed . . . ' . . . a sufficient natural and accustomed flow of water to form and maintain a distinct and defined channel' . . ." *Arthur v. Grand Trunk Railway* (1895), 22 O.A.R. 89 at 90 (C.A.), Hagarty C.J.O. 3. Includes every water course and every source of water supply, whether the same usually contains water or not, and the bed and shore of every stream, river or lake, pond, creek, spring, ravine and gulch. 4. A river, stream, creek, gully, ravine, spring, coulee, valley floor, drainage ditch or any other channel having a bed and sides or banks in which water flows either permanently or intermittently. 5. The full length and width of any river, creek, stream, spring, brook, lake, pond, reservoir, canal, ditch or other natural or artificial channel that is open to the air and includes the bed, banks, sides and shoreline thereof.

WATER-COVERED AREA. Any area covered by flowing or standing water.

WATER DAMAGE INSURANCE. Insurance, other than sprinkler leakage or weather insurance, against loss of or damage to property caused by the escape of water from plumbing or heating equipment of a building or from outside water mains, or by the melting of ice or snow on the roof of a building.

WATER EQUIVALENT. With respect to a given load, means the volume of water at $20 \pm 5°C$ that, when placed in the same plane wave field as the given load, absorbs microwave energy at the same rate as the given load. *Radiation Emitting Devices Regulations*, C.R.C., c. 1370, s. 1.

WATER-EXCURSION CRAFT. A boat or other watercraft, registered under the Canada Shipping Act (Canada), on which members of the public for a fee or other charge are transported for excursion purposes on natural or man-made water bodies.

WATER EXTERMINATION. The destruction, prevention or control in, on or over surface water of a pest by the use of a pesticide. *Pesticides Act*, R.S.O. 1990, c. P.11, s. 1(1).

WATER FREQUENTED BY FISH. Canadian fisheries waters. *Fisheries Act*, R.S.C. 1985, c. F-14, s. 34.

WATER HEATER. See SERVICE ~; STORAGE-TYPE ~.

WATER-INSOLUBLE NITROGEN. Nitrogen insoluble in water when analysed by the method of analysis referred to in section 23. *Fertilizers Regulations*, C.R.C., c. 666, s. 2.

WATER LEVEL. See STATIC ~.

WATER LOT. (a) Any pond or swamp; and (b) any area below the high-water mark of a lake, river, creek or stream.

WATER MANAGEMENT PROJECT. (a) A project to construct a barrier that is of a height exceeding the height prescribed in the regulations to store water or water containing any other substance or to control the level of a body of water or water containing any other substance; (b) a project to construct a new canal capable of conducting an amount exceeding the amount prescribed in the regulations of water or water containing any other substance; (c) a project capable of diverting an amount exceeding the amount prescribed in the regulations of water or water containing any other substance.

WATER PEST CONTROL. The destruction, prevention or control of pests in, on or over a water course that may adversely affect a water course or its use or enjoyment.

WATERPLANE. See MEAN ~.

WATER POLLUTION. (a) The presence in water of any water contaminant in excess of the permissible concentration prescribed by the regulations for that water contaminant; or (b) a change of the temperature of water in contravention of the regulations.

WATER POLLUTION CONTROL WORKS. The works together with the land required for the purpose of treating or holding sewage and for effluent irrigation, and includes: (a) pumps, piping, controls and other equipment required to treat sewage; (b) a system of pipes, pumps, controls and other equipment which convey treated sewage from the point of treatment to the point of disposal; (c) a trunk collector sewer that conveys sewage from the point of the last lateral to the point of treatment; and (d) a pumping station which receives sewage at a point below the last lateral together with the pressure main that delivers sewage from the pumping station to the point of treatment.

WATER POWER. var. **WATER-POWER.** Includes any force or energy of whatever form or nature contained in or capable of being produced or generated from any flowing or falling water in such quantity as to make it of commercial value. See DOMINION ~S; PROVINCIAL ~S; SMALL ~.

WATER PURIFICATION WORKS. Sewer interceptors, sewage treatment plants, diffusers, effluent outlets and subordinate installations.

WATER PURVEYOR. Any person, corporation, municipality or village municipality that offers or supplies, or holds itself out as being available to offer or supply, water for domestic purposes.

WATER QUALITY MANAGEMENT. Any aspect of water resource management that relates to restoring, maintaining or improving the quality of water.

WATER RATE. A tax imposed or levied on the taxable land or other rateable property within a water district.

WATER RESORT. Any beach, shore line, or other place or premises (a) that is on the bank of, contiguous to, adjoining, or in the neighbourhood of, any lake, pond, pool, river, stream, or other body of water, whether naturally existing or artificially created, that is used by persons for swimming, bathing, diving, or wading; and (b) that is available to the public, either without charge, or for the use of which persons are directly or indirectly charged; and includes (c) any place or premises that is or are adjacent to, or in the immediate neighbourhood of, such a place as is hereinbefore described, and (i) that is used for parking motor vehicles or picnicking; or (ii) on which there are facilities for persons to change their clothes; or (iii) that is otherwise used as an adjunct to, or in connection with, any such beach, shore line, place, or premises as is hereinbefore described; and (d) any such beach, shore line, place, or premises that is or are operated or used as part of, or in conjunction with, a motel, hotel, rooming house, boarding house, restaurant, eating place, or place of entertainment, that is available to the public as aforesaid; but does not include the building comprising any motel, hotel, rooming house, boarding house, or restaurant to which clause (d) applies. *Municipal Act*, S.M. 1970, c. 100, s. 440.

WATER RESOURCE MANAGEMENT. The conservation, development and utilization of water resources and includes, with respect thereto, research, data collection and the maintaining of inventories, planning and the implementation of plans, and the control and regulation of water quantity and quality. *Canada Water Act*, R.S.C. 1985, c. C-11, s. 2.

WATER RESOURCES. 1. Includes water storage, drainage and irrigation and any other matters incidental to the management of water resources. 2. All bodies of water in the province.

WATERS. *n.* 1. Any inland water, whether in a liquid or frozen state, on or below the surface of land. *Federal Statutes.* 2. Includes all streams, lakes, ponds, inland waters, salt waters, watercourses and all other surface and ground waters within the jurisdiction of the Province. See ARCTIC ~; BOUNDARY ~; CANADIAN CUSTOMS ~; CANADIAN FISHERIES ~; CANADIAN ~; COASTAL ~; CONVENTION ~; FEDERAL ~; INLAND ~; INTERJURISDICTIONAL ~; INTERNAL ~; INTERNATIONAL ~; MINOR ~ OF CANADA; TIDAL ~; UNDESIGNATED ~; WATER; ~ OF THE PROVINCE.

WATER SERVICE. The taking, collection, production, treatment, storage, supply, transmission, distribution, sale, purchase and use of water, or any one or more of them.

WATERSHED. *n.* An area drained by a river and its tributaries.

WATERSLIDE. *n.* A recreational waterslide flume, including the receiving pool to which it is affixed.

WATERS UNDER CANADIAN JURISDIC-TION. (a) Canadian waters; (b) fishing zones described in section 16 of the *Oceans Act* and prescribed under paragraph 25(*b*) of that Act; and (c) shipping safety control zones prescribed under subsection 11(1) of the *Arctic Waters Pollution Prevention Act. Crewing Regulations*, SOR/97-390, s. 1(1).

WATER SUPPLY. See PUBLIC ~.

WATER SUPPLY CORPORATION. A corporation established by one or more municipalities for the purpose of constructing and operating a water supply project within or for any municipality.

WATER SUPPLY PROJECT. Includes the reservoir facilities, intake systems, pressure systems, treatment facilities and trunk distribution systems that are required to provide a water supply service to one or more municipalities and the inhabitants thereof.

WATER SUPPLY SYSTEM. A water works for the collection, treatment, purification, storage, supply or distribution of water to (a) five or more households, or (b) any business, public building or place of assembly. *Environmental Protection Act*, R.S.P.E.I. 1988, c. E-9, s. 1(t).

WATER SYSTEM. All facilities for storing, pumping, treating and distributing water for domestic, commercial, industrial and fire protective purposes.

WATERTIGHT. *adj.* 1. In relation to a structure, means the structure is capable of preventing the passage of water through it in any direction, under a head of water up to the ship's margin line. *Hull Construction Regulations*, C.R.C., c. 1431, s. 2. 2. Designed to withstand a specific static head of water. *Load Line Regulations (Inland)*, C.R.C., c. 1440, s. 1.

WATERTIGHT COMPARTMENT. In respect of a ship, a space below the main deck that is enclosed by the shell, watertight bulkheads and decks, or by watertight bulkheads and decks and into which direct access from the main deck is gained by means of a hatch or entrance through which downflooding could occur. *Hull Construction Regulations*, C.R.C., c. 1431, s. 100.

WATER USER. (a) The purchaser; or (b) the owner of a parcel of land shown on the assessment roll of a district as containing a number of acres classified as "to be irrigated".

WATER UTILITY. (a) A person who owns or operates in British Columbia equipment or facilities for the diverting, developing, pumping, impounding, distributing or furnishing of water, for compensation, (i) to or for more than the prescribed number of persons or, if no number is prescribed, 5 or more persons, or (ii) to a corporation, and (b) the lessee, trustee, receiver or liquidator of a person referred to in paragraph (a), but does not include (c) a municipality in respect of services furnished by the municipality, (d) a person who furnishes services or commodity only to himself or herself, the person's employees or tenants, if the service or commodity is not resold to or used by others, (e) the Greater Vancouver Water District under the *Greater Vancouver Water District Act*, (f) an improvement district or water users' community under the *Water Act*, (g) a regional district under the *Local Government Act* in respect of the service of the supply of water (i) in bulk to a municipality or electoral area participating in that service, or (ii) to consumers in a municipality participating in that service, (h) a person who supplies water by tanker truck, (i) a person who sells bottled water, or (j) a strata corporation, if the comptroller is satisfied that the owner developers within the meaning of the *Strata Property Act* have ceased to own a majority of the strata lots in the strata plan. *Water Utility Act*, R.S.B.C. 1996, c. 485, s. 1.

WATERWAY. *n.* Stream, river, lake, and includes a dry watercourse. See DEEP ~; ST. LAWRENCE ~.

WATER WORKS. *var.* **WATERWORKS**. Any public, commercial or industrial works for the collection, production, treatment, storage, supply and distribution of water, or any part of any such waterworks.

WATER WORKS RATE. A charge for the capital cost of water works.

WATERWORKS SYSTEM. Any system of plants, wells, structures, equipment, pipes, apparatus or other things for the obtaining, treating, purifying, disinfecting, distributing or supplying of water intended to be used for human consumption or in swimming pools and, without limitation, includes aqueducts, cisterns, culverts, cuts, flumes, mains, pumps, reservoirs, tanks, engines and machinery used in connection with the system.

WATT. *n*. 1. For electric power, the power that will produce energy at the rate of one joule per second, a joule being the energy dissipated when the point of application of a force of 10 million dynes is displaced a distance of one centimetre in the direction of the force. *Electrical and Photometric Units Act*, R.S.C. 1970, c. E-3, s. 2. 2. The power that produces energy at the rate of 1 joule per second. *Weights and Measures Act*, S.C. 1970-71-72, c. 36, schedule 1.

WAVE. See MATERIAL ~; MICRO~; RADIO ~S; SHOCK ~.

WAVELENGTH. *n*. A wavelength in vacuo. *Radiation Emitting Devices Regulations*, C.R.C., c. 1370, s. 1.

WAXED. *adj*. May be used in connection with clean dry rutabagas that have been completely immersed in a wax solution. *Fresh Fruit and Vegetable Regulations*, C.R.C., c. 285, s. 69.

WAY. *n*. Includes any road, street, route, avenue, parkway, driveway, square, place, bridge, culvert, viaduct, trestle and any other way whatsoever. *Highway Traffic Act*, R.S. Nfld. 1970, c. 152, s. 234. See PUBLIC ~; RIGHT OF ~; UNDER ~.

WAY-BILL. *n*. A description of goods which a common carrier transports by land.

WAY OF NECESSITY. 1. A right of way implied in favour of a grantee of land over the land of the grantor when there is no other way by which the grantee can get to the land granted to him. 2. A right of way over land retained by the grantee when the land kept by the grantor is landlocked.

WAYS AND MEANS MOTION. The first step needed before Parliament imposes a new tax, continues an expiring tax, increases the rate of an existing tax or extends a tax to include people not already paying. A. Fraser, W.A. Dawson, & J. Holtby, eds., *Beauchesne's Rules and Forms of the House of Commons of Canada*, 6th ed. (Toronto: Carswell, 1989) at 265.

WAYSIDE PIT. A temporary pit or quarry opened and used by a public road authority solely for the purpose of a particular project or contract of road construction and not located on the road right of way.

WAYSIDE QUARRY. See WAYSIDE PIT.

WB. *abbr*. Weber.

W.C.A.T.R. *abbr*. Workers' Compensation Appeals Tribunal Reporter.

W.C.B. *abbr*. 1. Workers' Compensation Board. 2. Workmen's Compensation Board.

W.D.C.P. *abbr*. Weekly Digest of Civil Procedure.

WEALTH. *n*. The potential or actual resources and possessions of an individual or community which can be expressed in terms of money or measured by some other standard.

WEALTH TAX. See ANNUAL ~.

WEAPON. *n*. 1. (a) Anything used, designed to be used or intended for use in causing death or injury to any person or (b) anything used, designed to be used or intended for use for the purpose of threatening or intimidating any person, and, without restricting the generality of the foregoing, includes any firearm as defined in subsection 84(1). *Criminal Code*, S.C. 1991, c. 40, s. 1. 2. A firearm must come within the definition of a weapon. A firearm is expressly designed to kill or wound. It operates with deadly efficiency in carrying out the object of its design. It followed that such a deadly weapon can, of course, be used for purposes of threatening and intimidating. Indeed, it is hard to imagine anything more intimidating or dangerous than a brandished firearm. A person waving a gun and calling 'hands up' can be reasonably certain that the suggestion will be obeyed. A firearm is quite different from an object such as a carving knife or an ice pick which will normally be used for legitimate purposes. A firearm, however, is always a weapon. No matter what the intention may be of the person carrying a gun, the firearm itself presents the ultimate threat of death to those in its presence. *R. v. Felawka*, 1993 CarswellBC 507, 25 C.R. (4th) 70, 159 N.R. 50, 33 B.C.A.C. 241, 54 W.A.C. 241, 85 C.C.C. (3d) 248, [1993] 4 S.C.R. 199, Cory, J. 3. [In s. 2 of the *Criminal Code* , R.S.C. 1985, c. C-46, for the purposes of interpretation of s. 272(1)(a) of the Code, dealing with sexual assault with a weapon.] [The] French version of the definition of "weapon" ("*arme* ") in s. 2, taken literally, could suggest that for an object to become a weapon, it must be designed, used, or intended to be used for the purpose of causing injury. The English version provides a clarification that is consistent with a sound interpretation of the intent required for an object to become a weapon in all the different sets of circumstances contemplated by the provision. In contrast to the design, the use or the intended use of an object to threaten or intimidate, when an object is actually used in causing death or injury, the English text does not import a requirement that the object be used "for the purpose" of killing or injuring, but merely "in causing" death or injury. *R. c. Lamy*, [2002] 1 S.C.R. 860. See AUTOMATIC ~; HAND CARRIED ~ OR PIECE OF ORDNANCE; LETHAL ~; OFFENSIVE ~; PROHIBITED ~; RESTRICTED ~.

WEAPONS TRAFFICKING. Every person commits an offence who (a) manufactures or transfers, whether or not for consideration, or (b) offers to do anything referred to in paragraph (a) in respect of a firearm, a prohibited weapon, a restricted weapon, a prohibited device, any ammunition or any prohibited ammunition knowing that the person is not authorized to do so under the *Firearms Act* or any other Act of Parliament or any regulations made under any Act of Parliament. *Criminal Code*, R.S.C. 1985, c. C-46, s. 99(1).

WEAR. *n*. A fence or dam set across a river.

WEAR AND TEAR. The waste of any material by ordinary use.

WEATHER CONDITIONS. See VFR ~.

WEATHER INSURANCE. 1 . Insurance against loss or damage through windstorm, cyclone, tornado, rain, hail, flood or frost, but does not include hail insurance. *Insurance acts*. 2. Insurance, other than hail insurance or windstorm insurance, against loss or damage caused by rain, tempest, flood or other climatic conditions.

WEATHER MINIMA. See ITINERANT ~.

WEATHER MODIFICATION ACTIVITY. Includes any action designed or intended to produce, by physical or chemical means, changes in the composition or dynamics of the atmosphere for the purpose of increasing, decreasing or redistributing precipitation, decreasing or suppressing hail or lightning or dissipating fog or cloud.

WEATHER MODIFIER. Any person who engages in an weather modification activity.

WEATHERTIGHT. *adj*. 1. Designed to prevent water from penetrating the ship in any sea conditions. Canada regulations. 2. Capable of preventing the passage of water from exterior space to interior space in any weather condition. Canada regulations.

WEBBING. *n*. A narrow fabric woven with continuous filling yarns and finished selvedges.

WEBCASTING. *n*. Broadcasting an event electronically over the internet.

WEBER. *n*. The magnetic flux that, when linking a circuit of one turn, produces in that circuit an electromotive force of 1 volt as the flux is reduced to 0 at a uniform rate in 1 second. *Weights and Measures Act*, S.C. 1970-71-72, c. 36, schedule 1.

WEDLOCK. See BORN OUT OF ~.

WEED. See NOXIOUS ~; NOXIOUS ~S; WIRE ~.

WEED SEED. The seed of a restricted, noxious or nuisance weed. See SMALL ~S.

WEEK. *n*. 1. Any period of 7 successive days. 2. A period of 7 consecutive days commencing on Sunday. 3. The period between midnight on a Saturday and midnight on the Saturday immediately following. 4. Unless otherwise defined in this act, means the period between zero hours on Sunday night and the same time on the following Saturday night. See CONTRIBUTION ~; FORTY-HOUR ~; PAY ~; WORK ~.

WEEKLY DAY OF REST. Sunday.

WEEK OF LAYOFF. *var*. **WEEK OF LAYOFF**. A week in which one receives less than one-half of the amount one would earn at the regular rate in a normal non-overtime work week, but shall not mean a week in which a person (a) was not able to work or not available for work; (b) was subject to disciplinary suspension; or (c) was not provided with work by the employer by reason of any strike or lock-out occurring at the place of employment or elsewhere.

WEEK OF TENANCY. The weekly period on which the tenancy is based and not necessarily a calendar week and, unless otherwise specifically agreed upon, the week shall be deemed to begin on the day upon which rent is payable. *Landlord and Tenant acts*.

WEIGH. *v*. In relation to evidence, to measure, to ponder, to examine the force of.

WEIGHING. See OFFICIAL ~.

WEIGHING MACHINE. Any machine that measures mass or weight and has a moving or movable part that has or can have an effect on the accuracy of the machine. *Weights and Measures Act*, R.S.C. 1985, c. W-6, s. 2.

WEIGH-OVER. *n*. The weighing and inspection of all grain of any grade in an elevator for the purpose of determining the amount in stock of grain of that grade in the elevator. *Canada Grain Act*, R.S.C. 1685, c. G-10, s. 2.

WEIGHT. *n*. In relation to an aircraft means the maximum permissible take-off weight specified in its certificate of airworthiness or in a document referred to in that certificate. See ACCESSORY ~; AXLE GROUP ~; AXLE UNIT ~; AXLE ~; CATCH-~S; CURB ~; DEAD~; DRAINED ~; DRESSED ~; FRONT AXLE ~; GROSS ~; HEADLESS DRAWN ~; PRODUCTION OPTIONS ~; REGISTERED ~; ROUND ~; TOTAL LOADED ~; VEHICLE CAPACITY ~; WHEEL ~.

WEIGHTED FLY. An artificial fly that is equipped with a weight that causes the fly to sink.

WEIGHT FORFEIT. The amount of money that a boxer, under a written contract to take part in a professional boxing contest or exhibition agrees to pay his opponent upon failure to comply with the weight requirements under the contract.

WEIGH TICKET. *var*. **WEIGH-TICKET**. A receipt that is issued by a grain elevator operator or the operator's employee to the owner of grain or the owner's agent.

WEIGHT OF EVIDENCE. 1. For the evidence of one side to be so far superior to the other's that the verdict should go to the first. 2. The amount of importance attached to any particular piece of evidence.

WEIR. *n*. 1. A trap net constructed of brush and twine or wire netting. *Fishery regulations*. 2. A fence or dam set across a river. See HERRING ~.

WELD. See FORGE ~; FUSION ~.

WELDER. *n*. A person engaged in welding.

WELDING. *n*. The process of welding metals in a molten or molten vaporous state without the application of mechanical pressure or blows.

WELDING EQUIPMENT. Includes plant, machinery, equipment, appliances and devices of every kind and description that are used or intended to be used in the process of fusion welding, brazing and cutting of metals by the application of heat.

WELDING OPERATOR. A person engaged in welding either for self or in the employ of another person on the fabrication or repair of boilers, pressure vessels or pressure piping or any parts of them.

WELDING PROCEDURE. The complete specifications of a process and the technique employed in the welding of various kinds and thicknesses of metals.

WELFARE. *n*. 1. Commonly used to refer to public assistance provided by the province or municipality to persons with minimal financial means. 2. The conditions or facilities, in or near a workplace, provided for the feeding, rest, hygiene or sanitary requirements of a worker. *Workplace Safety and Health Act*, R.S.M. 1987, c. W120, s. 1. See COMMUNITY ~; "GENERAL ~" CLAUSE; HEALTH AND ~ CANADA.

WELFARE CLAUSE. See GENERAL ~.

WELFARE SERVICES. 1. Services, such as case work, homemaker, and day-care, intended to lessen, remove or prevent the causes of poverty, child neglect and dependence on public assistance. 2. Services having as their object the lessening, removal or prevention of the causes and effects of poverty, child neglect or dependence on public assistance, and, without limiting the generality of the foregoing, includes (a) rehabilitation services; (b) casework, counselling, assessment and referral services; (c) adoption services; (d) homemaker, day-care and similar services; (e) community development services; (f) consulting, research and evaluation services with respect to welfare programs; and (g) administrative, secretarial and clerical services, including staff training, relating to the provision of any of the foregoing services or to the provision of assistance.

WELFARE WORKER. See OVERSEAS ~.

WELL. *n*. 1. Any artificial opening in the ground from which water is obtained or one made for the purpose of exploring for or obtaining water. 2. Any opening in the ground, not being a seismic shot hole, that is made, to be made or is in the process of being made, by drilling, boring or other method, (a) for the production of oil or gas; (b) for the purpose of searching for or obtaining oil or gas; (c) for the purpose of obtaining water to inject into an underground formation; (d) for the purpose of injecting gas, air, water or other substance into an underground formation; or (e) for any purpose, if made through sedimentary rocks to a depth of at least 150 metres. *Canada Oil and Gas Operations Act*, R.S.C. 1985, c. O-7, s. 2 as am. 3. A hole made in the ground to locate or to obtain ground water or to test to obtain information in respect of ground water or an aquifer, and includes a spring around or in which works are made or equipment is installed for collection or transmission of water and that is or is likely to be used as a source of water for human consumption. *Ontario Water Resources Act*, R.S.O. 1990, c. 0.40, s. 35(1). 4. A hole or shaft that is or is being drilled, bored or otherwise sunk into the earth (a) through which a geothermal resource is or can be produced; (b) for the purpose of producing a geothermal resource or for the purpose of injecting any substance to assist the production of a geothermal resource; or (c) that (i) extends deeper than 600 m; (ii) has a bore hole diameter of more than 100 mm; and (iii) is intended to obtain information about a geothermal resource. *Geothermal Resources Act*, R.S.B.C. 1996, c. 171, s. 1(1). See ABANDONED ~; BRINE ~; DEEPENED ~; DELINEATION ~; DEVELOPED ~; DEVELOPMENT ~; EVALUATION ~; EXPERIMENTAL ~; EXPLORATORY ~; FLOWING ~; FREEHOLD ~; GAS ~; GEOTHERMAL ~; MULTI ZONE ~; NEW ~; OIL OR GAS ~; OIL ~; PETROLEUM ~; PRODUCING ~; PUMPING ~.

WELL DRILLER. A person who drills or reconditions a well.

WELL-HEAD PRICE. See BASIC ~.

WELL LICENCE. A valid and subsisting licence to drill a well granted pursuant to the regulations.

WELL LICENSEE. The holder of a well licence and subsequent to the drilling of the well, but prior to its abandonment, means the owner of the well.

WELL SITE. 1. The property upon, in or under which an oil well is situate. 2. (a) That portion of the surface of land required for the conduct of drilling or completion operations of a well during the period next following the initial entry upon the land until the well is abandoned or completed; (b) that portion of the surface of land required for the conduct of producing operations

of a well commencing from the completion date of the well.

WELL SITE SEABED SURVEY. A survey pertaining to the nature of the surface or subsurface or the seabed or its subsoil of any frontier lands in the area of a proposed drilling site in respect of a well and to the conditions of the area that may affect the safety or efficiency of drilling operations.

WELL TERMINATION DATE. The date on which a well or test hole has been abandoned, completed or suspended in accordance with any applicable drilling regulations.

WELSH MORTGAGE. A virtually obsolete form of security; to secure a debt, property is conveyed to a creditor without any proviso or condition for reconveyance, usually with no covenant or condition for payment. The essence of the arrangement is that the mortgagee has possession along with receipt of profits and rent. W.B. Rayner & R.H. McLaren, *Falconbridge on Mortgages*, 4th ed. (Toronto: Canada Law Book, 1977) at 6.

WESTERN CANADA. 1. All that part of Canada lying west of Ontario. 2. The Provinces of Manitoba, British Columbia, Saskatchewan and Alberta.

WESTERN HEMISPHERE. The continents of North and South America, the islands adjacent thereto and the territorial waters thereof, including Newfoundland, Bermuda and the West Indies, but excluding Greenland, Iceland and the Aleutian Islands. *Public Service Employment Act*, R.S.C. 1985, c. P-33, s. 48.

WESTERNMOST. *adj*. The half compass circle from but not including true south through west to and including true north.

WEST INDIES. Includes the West Indies and the Bahama and Bermuda Islands. *Canada Shipping Act*, R.S.C. 1985, c. S-9, s. 2.

WEST. L. REV. *abbr*. Western Law Review (1961-1966).

WESTMINSTER. See STATUTE OF ~.

WEST. ONT. L. REV. *abbr*. Western Ontario Law Review (1967-1976).

WET ERBP. The equilibrium reflux boiling point of the brake fluid after it has been humidified under controlled conditions. *Motor Vehicle Safety Regulations*, C.R.C., c. 1038, s. 2.

WETLAND. *n*. 1. Land, (a) that is seasonally or permanently covered by shallow water, or (b) in respect of which the water table is close to or at the surface so that the presence of abundant water has caused the formation of hydric soils and has favoured the dominance of either hydrophytic or water tolerant plants. *Conservation Land Act*, R.S.O. 1990, c. C.28, s. 1. 2. Includes all freshwater and tidal areas that are or may be submerged or periodically submerged under fresh or salt water, including all bodies of water or areas commonly referred to as marshes, salt marshes, swamps, sloughs, bogs, beaches and flats. *Environmental Protection Act*, R.S.P.E.I. 1988, c. E-9, c. 1(v).

WET LEASE. A lease of an aircraft under the terms of which the lessor provides, directly or indirectly, the aircrew to operate the aircraft.

WET LOCATION. A location in which liquids may drip, splash or flow on or against electrical equipment.

WET TIME. Work time lost as a result of bad weather.

WET VENT. A waste pipe functioning also as a vent pipe.

WHALE. See BALEEN ~; BLUE ~; DEAD ~; FIN ~; GRAY ~; HUMPBACK ~; MINKE ~; PILOT ~; RIGHT ~; SEI ~; SPERM ~.

WHALE CATCHER. 1. A ship used for the purpose of hunting, taking, towing, holding onto or scouting for whales. *Whaling Convention Act*, R.S.C. 1970, c. W-8, s. 2. 2. The operator of a boat used for the purpose of hunting whales and towing them to a land station.

WHALE PRODUCTS. Any part of a whale and blubber, meat, bones, whale oil, sperm oil, spermaceti, meal and baleen. *Whaling Convention Act*, R.S.C. 1970, c. W-8, s. 2.

WHALE TREATING. The possession, treatment or processing of whales or of whale products. *Whaling Convention Act*, R.S.C. 1970, c. W-8, s. 2.

WHALING. *n*. 1. Scouting for, hunting, killing, taking, towing or holding onto whales. *Whaling Convention Act*, R.S.C. 1970, c. W-8, s. 2. 2. The scouting for, and the hunting, killing, taking, towing, holding, possessing, eviscerating and processing of whales.

WHARF. *n*. Includes all wharfs, quays, docks and premises in or on which any goods, when landed from ships, may be lawfully placed. *Can-*

ada Shipping Act, R.S.C. 1985, c. S-9, s. 2. See APPROACH ~; EX ~.

WHARFAGE. *n*. 1. A charge levied on goods (a) that are loaded on or unloaded from a vessel at a wharf; or (b) that are placed on, conveyed across, along, over or under a wharf. Canada regulations. 2. A charge imposed in respect of goods, including goods in containers, that are (a) loaded on or unloaded from a vessel; (b) transhipped overside from vessel to vessel; (c) unloaded overside from vessel to water or from water to vessel; (d) landed from or placed in the water; or (e) loaded or unloaded from a vehicle. See SIDE ~; TOP ~.

WHARFINGER. *n*. A person who is appointed to have charge of and to collect the charges in respect of a wharf.

WHEAT BOARD. See CANADIAN ~.

WHEEL. See DISC ~; FISH~; SPOKE ~.

WHEEL BASE. The distance from the centre of the hub of a front wheel to the centre of the hub of the rear wheel on the same side of a motor vehicle, as specified in the lists supplied by the manufacturers.

WHEELCHAIR. *n*. A chair mounted on wheels driven by muscular or other power and used for the carriage of a person who has a physical defect or disability. *Highway Traffic Act*, R.S.O. 1990, c. H.8, s. 1(1).

WHEELCHAIR VEHICLE. A motor vehicle that is used for the transportation, for compensation, of persons in wheelchairs.

WHEEL WEIGHT. The weight indicated when a vehicle is weighed with any wheel or wheels attached to one end of the axle on the scales or weighing device.

WHERE. *adv*. At the same time or at some time after or before.

WHEREAS. *conj*. A word which usually introduces a factual narrative.

WHEREBY. *adv*. By or through which.

WHEY. *n*. The product remaining after the fat and casein have been removed from milk in the process of making cheese.

WHEY BUTTER. Butter made from milk-fat that has been recovered from whey, or from a mixture of such milk-fat and cream, or from a mixture of whey butter and creamery butter.

WHEY POWDER. Dried whey.

WHIP. See CHIEF ~.

WHIPLASH INJURY. An injury to tissues in the neck when the spine is suddenly overextended. F.A. Jaffe, *A Guide to Pathological Evidence*, 3d ed. (Toronto: Carswell, 1991) at 229.

WHIPPING CREAM. Cream that contains 32 per cent or more of milk-fat.

WHIRLPOOL. See PUBLIC ~.

WHISTLE. *n*. 1. Includes a horn of any type approved by the Commission. *Railway Act*, R.S.C. 1985, c. R-3, s. 2. 2. Any sound signaling appliance capable of producing the prescribed blasts.

WHISTLE BLOWER. A person, including an employee, who reports or gives evidence of a violation of a statute or regulation or refuses to work under conditions in violation of legislation.

WHISTLE BLOWER PROTECTION. Protection from, eviction, discharge, discipline, intimidation, coercion, penalty afforded to persons who point out violations by their employer or others of legislation. Protection may be afforded by legislation or by terms of a collective agreement.

WHITE CANE. A cane or walking-stick the major portion of which is white and which is intended for use by a person with impaired vision.

WHITECOAT. *n*. A harp seal that has not begun to moult its white coat. *Marine Mammal Regulations*, SOR/93-56, s. 2(2).

WHITE COLLAR WORKER. A worker employed in office, sales or professional work.

WHITEFISH. *n*. Fish of the species Coregonus clupeaformis, Coregonus nasus or Prosopium cylindraceum.

WHITE HAKE. A fish of the species Urophycis tenuis (Mitch.).

WHITE PAPER. An official government memorandum which sets out a problem and the issues related to it with the policy the government recommends.

WHMIS. *abbr*. Workplace Hazardous Materials Information System.

WHOLE CHEESE. A cheese that is of the original size and shape as manufactured. *Food and Drug Regulations*, C.R.C., c. 870, c. B.08.033.

WHOLE HOUSE. See COMMITTEE OF THE ~.

WHOLESALE. *n*. 1. Any sale of products to a purchaser for resale, standing or after preparation, conditioning or processing. 2. A sale to a person other than a consumer. See SELL AT ~.

WHOLESALE CUSTOMER. Any person who purchases any controlled product in bulk at the wholesale level and includes Her Majesty in right of Canada or any province, any agent thereof and any refiner, distributor, jobber, dealer, public utility, operator of aircraft, railway, ships, trucks and other transportation facilities and such other person as the Governor in Council may by regulation designate as being a large volume user of the controlled product. *Energy Supplies Emergency Act*, R.S.C. 1985, c. E-9, s. 2.

WHOLESALE DEALER.. A person who buys fuel for resale to a person other than a purchaser. 2. Any person who sells tobacco for the purpose of resale.

WHOLESALE DISTRIBUTION. The sale, lease, rental, exchange or other means of dispersal of film to retail distributors exhibitors or other persons who engage in dispersal of films on a continual and successive basis but not to the general public.

WHOLESALE DISTRIBUTOR. A person who engages in wholesale distribution on a continual and successive basis.

WHOLESALE MERCHANT. 1. One who sells merchandise in large quantities to person who are not the ultimate users of the merchandise. 2. "[Deals] . . . with the trade who buy to sell again. . ." *R. v. Pearson* (1894), 1 C.C.C. 337 at 338 (B.C. S.C.), Drake J.

WHOLESALE OUTLET. Any station, shop, establishment or other place in which petroleum products are sold or kept for sale to retailers. *Petroleum Products Act*, R.S.P.E.I. 1974, c. P-4, s. 1.

WHOLESALE PRICE. The consideration for a transfer, sale or delivery _ by a wholesaler to a retailer or to another wholesaler and includes the consideration in a transfer, sale or delivery to a consumer by a wholesaler who is also a retailer. *The Oil and Gas Conservation, Stabilization and Development Act*, R.S.S. 1978, c. O-3, s. 19.

WHOLESALER. *n*. 1. Person who sells to persons other than the end-user or consumer. 2. . " . . . [T]o be one, the sale must not only be in large quantities but it must be to a person other than the end-user. . ." *Buchman & Son Lumber Co. v. Ontario Regional Assessment Commissioner, Region No. 9* (1982) 141 D.L.R. (3d) 95 at 97, 20 M.P.L.R. 78, 14 O.M.B.R. 166 (Div. Ct.), Steele J. (O'Leary J. concurring). 3. Any person, other than an agency, who sells or offers for sale the regulated product to any retailer, peddler, caterer, processor or wholesaler or otherwise than directly to the consumer. Canada regulations. 4. Any person other than a retailer, who sells petroleum products or keeps petroleum products for sale. 5. A person who sells tobacco for the purpose of resale. See LICENSED ~; TRAVEL ~.

WHOLESALER-RETAILER. *n*. A wholesaler who is also a retailer.

WHOLESALE STORE. See CHAIN ~.

WHOLESALE TRADE. The business of purchasing any goods, wares or merchandise for resale otherwise than to the public for personal or household use or consumption.

WHOLLY. *adv*. Exclusively; entirely.

WHOLLY ENCLOSED. A structure having doors or other means capable of impeding the entrance or exit of persons or the escape of fumes.

WHOLLY OWNED. A corporation is wholly owned if all the shares, membership interests or other evidences of interest in the corporation to which are attached votes that may be cast to elect directors of the corporation are held, directly or indirectly, other than by way of security, by, on behalf of, or for the benefit of one of the corporations.

WHOLLY OWNED CORPORATION. See SUBSIDIARY ~.

WHOLLY-OWNED SUBSIDIARY. A corporation that is wholly owned by one or more parent Crown corporations directly or indirectly through any number of subsidiaries each of which is wholly owned directly or indirectly by one or more parent Crown corporations. *Financial Administration Act*, R.S.C. 1985, c. F-11, s. 83.

WHOLLY-PROTECTED ECOLOGICAL RESERVE. An ecological reserve established for the absolute protection of a territory in a natural state.

WIDESPREAD. *adj*. The . . . concept, "widespread", relates to the prevalence or incidence of the bias in question. Generally speaking, the alleged bias must be established as sufficiently pervasive in the community to raise the possibility that it may be harboured by one or more members of a representative jury pool . . . *R. v. Find*, 2001 CarswellOnt 1702, 2001 SCC 32, 42 C.R. (5th) 1, 154 C.C.C. (3d) 97, 199 D.L.R. (4th) 193, 269 N.R. 149, 146 O.A.C. 236, McLachlin C.J.C., for the court.

WIDOW. *n*. A female person whose spouse has died.

WIDOWER. *n*. A male person whose spouse has died.

WIDOW OF A VETERAN. The widow of a person who, being a veteran, died from causes arising during the service by virtue of which he became a veteran. *Public Service Employment Act*, R.S.C. 1985, c. P-33, s. 48.

WIDTH. *n*. 1. Used in reference to a crab, means the maximum distance measured across the widest part of the body shell. *Atlantic Crab Fishery Regulations*, C.R.C., c. 806, s. 2. 2. With respect to a condom, means the linear distance between the longitudinal edges of the condom when the condom is placed flat on a plane. *Medical Devices Regulations*, C.R.C., c. 871, s. 1. See LOT ~; OVERALL ~; SECTION ~; SIDE-YARD ~.

WIDTH OF TIRE. (a) In the case of pneumatic tires, the nominal width of the tire marked thereon by the manufacturer; and (b) in the case of all other tires the actual width of the tire surface in contact with the road.

WIFE. *n*. 1. " . . . [A] legally unambiguous word which describes a status that can only properly be applied to a woman who has voluntarily taken on an obligation, in accordance with the applicable law, to tie herself in a particularly well-understood relationship with one man during their joint lives. A wife is a woman who accepts that her union with her husband is dissoluble during their joint lives only in accordance with the law." *Louis v. Esslinger* (1981), 121 D.L.R. (3d) 17 at 32, [1981] 3 W.W.R. 350, 29 B.C.L.R. 41, 22 C.P.C. 68, 15 C.C.L.T. 137 (S.C.), McEachern C.J.S.C. 2. A woman who has entered into a marriage. See COMMON-LAW ~; DESERTED ~; DESTITUTE ~; HUSBAND; HUSBAND OR ~; SPOUSE.

WILD. *adj*. Wild by nature and in a state of nature.

WILD ANIMAL FARM. An area where wild animals other than fur bearing animals are kept, raised, bred, or propagated, or any combination thereof, in captivity for any purpose.

WILDCAT STRIKE. A strike commenced without the authorization of a union or in violation of a no-strike clause in a collective agreement.

WILD FISH. A fish other than a fish propagated by man in a fish culture facility.

WILD LAND. Land that is not occupied or cultivated.

WILDLIFE. *var.* **WILD LIFE.** *n.* 1. Any non-domestic animal. 2. Any species of vertebrate which is wild by nature and hence not normally dependent on people to directly provide its food, shelter or water. See EXOTIC ~; ILLEGAL ~; RESORT OF ~.

WILDLIFE AREA. See CRITICAL ~.

WILDLIFE FARM. A place in which any wildlife or any exotic wildlife is kept for sale, trade, barter, public exhibition, propagation or for scientific or other purposes.

WILDLIFE HABITAT. The air, soil, water, food and cover components of the environment on which wildlife depend directly or indirectly in order to carry out their life processes.

WILDLIFE MANAGEMENT. The regulation of wildlife populations in their habitats for the purpose of sustaining them for human use or enjoyment in perpetuity.

WILDLIFE MANAGEMENT BOARD. Any board or other body established under a land claims agreement that is authorized by the agreement to perform functions in respect of wildlife species. *Species at Risk Act*, S.C. 2002, c. 29, s. 2(1).

WILDLIFE OFFICER. Any person appointed or authorized by the minister for the purpose of enforcing this act and the regulations. *Wildlife acts.*

WILDLIFE SANCTUARY. Any territory designated by regulation of the Lieutenant-Governor in Council, whose terms and conditions of utilization of the resources are fixed primarily with a view to the conservation of wildlife. *Wildlife Conservation Act*, S.Q. 1978, c. 65, s. 1. 3. An area of land with a particular kind of ecological environment set aside by law or by regulation for the temporary or permanent protection of certain species of animals.

WILDLIFE SPECIES. A species, subspecies, variety or geographically or genetically distinct population of animal, plant or other organism, other than a bacterium or virus, that is wild by nature and (a) is native to Canada; or (b) has extended its range into Canada without human intervention and has been present in Canada for at least 50 years. *Species at Risk Act*, S.C. 2002, c. 29, s. 2(1).

WILFUL BLINDNESS. Occurs when a person who is aware of a need for inquiry declines not to inquire because he does not wish to know the truth.

WILFULLY. *adv.* 1. " . . . [D]eliberately and purposefully. . ." *R. v. Hafey* (1985), (*sub nom. R. v. Stoke-Graaham*) 44 C.R. (3d) 289 at 298, [1985] 1 S.C.R. 106, 67 N.S.R. (2d) 181, 155 A.P.R. 181, 17 C.C.C. (3d) 289, 16 D.L.R. (4th) 321, 57 N.R. 321, Dickson J. 2. " . . . [H]as not been uniformly interpreted and its meaning to some extent depends upon the context in which it is used. Its primary meaning is 'intentionally', but it is also used to mean 'recklessly' . . . The word 'wilfully' has, however, also been held to mean no more than that the accused's act is done intentionally and not accidentally." *R. v. Buzzanga* (1979), 101 D.L.R. (3d) 488 at 498, 500, 25 O.R. (2d) 705, 49 C.C.C. (2d) 369 (C.A.), Martin J.A.

WILFULNESS. *n.* " . . . [M]ust imply both deliberation and knowledge . . . *R. v. Haley* (1985), (*sub nom. R. v. Stoke-Graaham*) 44 C.R. (3d) 289 at 307, [1985] 1 S.C.R. 106, 67 N.S.R. (2d) 181, 155 A.P.R. 181, 17 C.C.C. (3d) 289, 16 D.L.R. (4th) 321, *57* N.R. 321, Wilson J.

WILL. *n.* 1. The written statement by which a person instructs how her or his estate should be distributed after death. 2. Includes a testament, a codicil, an appointment by will or by writing in the nature of a will in exercise of a power and any other testamentary disposition. 3. Includes testament, codicil, and every other testamentary instrument of which probate may be granted. See ADMINISTRATOR WITH ~ ANNEXED; CONDITIONAL ~; DUPLICATE ~; GRANT OF ADMINISTRATION WITH ~; ANNEXED; HOLOGRAPH ~; INTERNATIONAL ~; LETTERS OF ADMINISTRATION WITH ~ ANNEXED; MUTUAL ~S; NUNCUPATIVE ~; TENANCY AT ~.

WILSON APPLICATION. 1. An application, named after the case *Wilson v. The Queen* (1983), 9 C.C.C. (3d) 97 (S.C.C.), to set aside an authorization to wiretap. P.K. McWilliams, *Canadian Criminal Evidence*, 3d ed. (Aurora:

Canada Law Book, 1988) at 13-56 and 13-57. 2. "The current state of the law with respect to testing the admissibility of wiretap evidence is a procedural quagmire. The various procedures that are available have come to be known by the names of the cases that initiated them. [In] the 'Wilson application' . . . [a] hearing takes place before the issuing court, to determine the substantive or subfacial validity of the affidavit. The remedy is the setting aside of the authorization." *R. v. Garafoli* (1990), 60 C.C.C. (3d) 161 at 182, 80 C.R. (3d) 317, 116 N.R. 241, 43 O.A.C. 1, [1990] 2 S.C.R. 1421, 50 C.R.R. 206, 36 Q.A.C. 61, Sopinka J. (Dickson C.J.C., Lamer C.J.C., La Forest and Gonthier JJ. concurring).

WIN. *n*. A type of bet on a race to select a horse to finish first in the official result. *Pari-Mutuel Betting Supervision Regulations*, SOR/91-365, s. 2.

WINDFALL. *n*. Receipt of capital. Refers to timber blown down on a tenant's land was required to be sold and the proceeds invested as capital.

WINDING UP. *var.* **WINDING-UP**. 1. The process of ending the business of a corporation or partnership by settling accounts and liquidating assets. 2. In relation to a pension plan that has been terminated, the process of distributing the assets of the plan.

WINDING-UP ORDER. An order granted by a court under this Act to wind up the business of a company, and includes any order granted by the court to bring under this Act any company in liquidation or in process of being wound up. *Winding-up Act*, R.S.C. 1985, c. W-11, s. 2.

WINDOW. See PUSH-OUT ~; READILY REMOVABLE ~.

WINDSOR Y.B. ACCESS JUST. *abbr*. The Windsor Yearbook of Access to Justice.

WINDSOR Y.B. ACCESS JUSTICE. *abbr*. The Windsor Yearbook of Access to Justice (Recueil annuel de Windsor d'acès à la justice).

WINDSTORM. *n*. A storm with high winds but little or no precipitation. Winds which cause damage.

WINDSTORM INSURANCE. Insurance against loss of or damage to property caused by windstorm, cyclone or tornado.

WIND UP. *var.* **WIND-UP**. The termination of a pension plan and the distribution of the assets of the pension fund.

WINE. *n*. Any beverage containing alcohol obtained by the fermentation of the natural sugar contents of fruits, including grapes, apples and other agricultural products containing sugar, and including honey and milk. See DOMESTIC ~; FORTIFIED ~; MALT-~; MEDICATED ~; NATURAL ~; ONTARIO ~.

WINERY. *n*. A person licensed as a manufacturer of wine for the purpose of sale.

WINGER. *n*. Expression used to refer to two side-members of a tribunal hearing a case; the members of the tribunal, other than the chair.

WING TANK. Any tank adjacent to the side shell plating of a ship.

WINNING TICKET. Includes a ticket that is eligible for refund. *Pari-Mutuel Betting Supervision Regulations*, SOR/91-365, s. 2.

WINTER FISHING. Fishing through the ice during the period between the fall freeze-up and (a) the Thursday preceding the last Sunday in April; or (b) the melting or breaking-up of the ice in the spring, whichever is the earlier.

WINTER FLOUNDER. A fish of the species Pseudopleuronectes americanus (Walb.).

WINTERING. *n*. The occupying, by a vessel, during the non-navigation season of a berth.

WINTERING CHARGE. A rate imposed on a vessel in respect of a period of 30 days or more after December 14 in a year and before April 1 in the following year during which the vessel is (a) moored to a wharf; (b) occupying a berth or any space at or near a wharf; or (c) secured in any manner whatever to a vessel referred to in paragraph (a) or (b).

WINTER MONTHS. The months of January, February, March, April, November, and December, or any of them.

WINTER PERIOD. That period beginning at two o'clock, mountain standard time, in the forenoon of the last Sunday in October in any year and ending at two o'clock, mountain standard time, in the forenoon of the last Sunday in April in the following year. *The Time Act*, R.S.S. 1978, c. T-14, s. 2.

WINTER TERM. The period that commences on December 15 in any year and expires on April 15 in the year next following.

WIPO. *abbr*. World Intellectual Property Organization.

WIRE. *n*. (a) When applied to copper or copper alloys containing 50 per cent or more by weight of copper, means (i) a drawn, non-tubular product of any cross-sectional shape, in coils or cut to length and not over .5 inch in maximum cross-sectional dimension; or (ii) a product of solid rectangular cross-section in coils or cut to length, cold-rolled after drawing and not over 1.25 inches in width or .188 inch in thickness; (b) when applied to aluminum or aluminum alloys, means a non-tubular product of rectangular or square cross-section (whether or not with rounded corners), or, of round, hexagonal or octagonal cross-section, in coils or cut to length and not over .5 inch in maximum cross-sectional dimension; and (c) when applied to metals other than iron, steel, aluminum, aluminum alloys, copper or copper alloys containing 50 per cent or more by weight of copper, means a drawn, non-tubular product of any cross-sectional shape, in coils or cut to length and not over .5 inch in maximum cross-sectional dimension. *Customs Tariff*, R.S.C. 1985, c. C-54, s. 2.

WIRED GLASS. 1. Glass in which a wire mesh has been completely embedded. 2. Glass, not less than one-quarter inch thick, in which a mesh structure of wire is embedded and completely covered.

WIRED GLASS SCREEN. A partition of steel or steel-clad framing containing wired glass panels in which the area of individual panels of wired glass does not exceed 1,296 square inches.

WIRE OF IRON OR STEEL. A drawn, non-tubular product of iron or steel (a) if in coils, with any cross-sectional shape or dimension; (b) if in straight cut lengths, with a maximum cross-sectional dimension of 0.50 inch; or (c) if cold-rolled flat after drawing, with a maximum width of 0.50 inch, in coils or in straight cut lengths. *Customs Tariff*, R.S.C. 1985, c. C-54, s. 2.

WIRE-WAY. *n*. A raceway consisting of a completely enclosed system of metal troughing, and fittings therefor, so formed and constructed that insulated conductors may be readily drawn in and withdrawn, or laid in and removed, after the system has been completely installed without injury either to conductors or their covering.

WIRE WEED. Has the same meaning as horsetail.

WIRING. *n*. Includes any conductor for the conveyance of electric energy, and any conduit, duct, raceway, cable, channel, switch, box, receptacle or other fitting or device associated with any electrical installation.

WIT. See TO ~.

WITCHCRAFT. *n*. 1. Conjuration, sorcery. 2. Fraudulently pretending to use any kind of witchcraft, sorcery, enchantment, or conjuration. *Criminal Code*, R.S.C. 1985, c. C-46, s. 36

WITCH FLOUNDER. A fish of the species Glyptocephalus cynolossus (L.).

WITH COSTS. In the expression "motion dismissed with costs", means that costs will be assessed and paid only when the trial is over.

WITHDRAWAL. *n*. 1. Unlike a stay of proceedings which has statutory basis in Canadian law, withdrawal of charge is based on English common law, in force through section 8(2) of the Criminal Code. 2. " . . . When a charge has been withdrawn, there is no charge on record, and in order to continue the prosecution a new charge would have to be laid. Withdrawing a charge has the effect of ending the proceedings." *R. v. Leonard* (1962), (*sub nom. Crown Practice Rules, Re*) 38 W.W.R. 300 at 303, 37 C.R. 374, 133 C.C.C. 230 (Alta. T.D.), Kirby J. 3. For a defendant to retract a defence by filing and serving written notice. Formerly also meant discontinuance by a plaintiff of part, not the whole, action.

WITHERNAM. *n*. 1. Seizure again; reprisal. 2. " . . . [A]n 'order of withernam' [in the Replevin Act, R.S.B.C. 1960, c. 339] . . . is designed to cover the circumstances where the defendants have taken the property to some other location and allows the sheriff to seize other goods of the defendants to the value of the property removed out of the jurisdiction by the defendants." *Granby Construction & Equipment Ltd. v. Milley*, [1974] C.T.C. 562 at 575, [1974] 5 W.W.R. 292, 47 D.L.R. (3d) 427, 74 D.T.C. 6300 (B.C. S.C.), Bouck J.

WITHIN. *prep*. 1. In relation to time, before the expiration of, at or before, not beyond, not exceeding, not later than. 2. A geographic limitation.

WITHIN CANADA. Includes Canadian waters as defined for the purposes of the Customs Act, chapter C-40 of the Revised Statutes of Canada. *Foreign Enlistments Act*, R.S.C. 1985, c. F-28, s. 2.

WITHIN THE YEAR. Within the 12-month period following the month in which the calculation is made.

WITHOUT DAY. Without being continued on any certain day. See GO ~.

WITHOUT PREJUDICE. 1. "The use of this expression ['without prejudice'] is commonly understood to mean that if there is no settlement, the party making the offer is free to assert all its rights, unaffected by anything stated or done in the negotiations." *Maracle v. Travellers Indemnity Co. of Canada* (1991), 50 C.P.C. (2d) 213 at 222, [1991] I.L.R. 1-2728, 125 N.R. 294, 3 O.R. (3d) 510n, 80 D.L.R. (4th) 652, 3 C.C.L.I. (2d) 186, 47 O.A.C. 333, [1991] 2 S.C.R. 50, the court per Sopinka J. **2.** " . . . [A] party to a correspondence within the 'without prejudice' privilege is, generally speaking, protected from being required to disclose it on discovery or at trial in proceedings by or against a third party." *I. Waxman & Sons Ltd. v. Texaco Canada Ltd.*, [1968] 2 O.R. 452 at 453, 69 D.L.R. (2d) 543 (C.A.), the court per Aylesworth J.A. quoting the trial judge. **3.** " . . . [T]he words 'without prejudice' [endorsing an order] do not operate to freeze time limitations or suspend any other application of the law, but simply prevent the respondent from raising the defence of res judicata and that the endorsement should be given its plain meaning. . ." *Ternoey v. Goulding* (1982), 25 R.F.L. (2d) 113 at 120, 35 O.R. (2d) 29, 132 D.L.R. (3d) 44 (C.A.), Houlden J.A. (Howland C.J.O. concurring).

WITHOUT RECOURSE TO ME. A phrase used to protect the indorser of a note or bill from liability.

WITH PROFITS POLICY. An insurance policy in which any bonus from the profits of the insurance company is allocated to the policy and increases its value.

WITNESS. *n.* 1. " . . . [O]ne who, in the course of judicial processes, attests to matters of fact; . . ." *Bell v. Klein (No. 1)*, [1955] S.C.R. 309 at 317, [1955] 2 D.L.R. 513, Rand J. **2.** A person who gives evidence orally under oath or by affidavit in a judicial proceeding, whether or not he is competent to be a witness, and includes a child of tender years who gives evidence but does not give it under oath, because, in the opinion of the person presiding, the child does not understand the nature of the oath. *Criminal Code*, R.S.C. 1985, c. C-46, s. 118. **2. 3.** Includes a person who, in the course of an action is examined viva voce on discovery or who is cross-examined upon an affidavit, or who answers any interrogatories or makes an affidavit as to documents. **4.** Any person, whether a party or not,

to be examined under this Act. *Supreme Court Act*, R.S.C. 1985, c. S-26, s. 2. **5.** A person who has given or has agreed to give information or evidence, or participates or has agreed to participate in a matter, relating to an inquiry or the investigation or prosecution of an offence and who may require protection because of risk to the security of the person arising in relation to the inquiry, investigation or prosecution, or a person who, because of their relationship to or association with a person referred to above, may also require protection for the reasons referred to in that paragraph. *Witness Protection Program Act, 1996*, S.C. 1996, c. 15, s. 2. See ADVERSE ~; ATTESTING ~; EAR~; EXPERT ~; EYE-~; HOSTILE ~; MATERIAL ~; ORDINARY~; REPORTING ~.

WITNESSING PART. Of a deed or other formal document, the section after the recitals, or after the parties which usually begins by referring to the agreement or intention and then the consideration. The name "witnessing part" refers to the words "This deed witnesseth," which show the document is supposed to record a transaction.

WITNESS POST. A legal post erected pursuant to subsection (2) to designate the corner of a claim. *Canada Mining Regulations*, C.R.C., c. 1516, s. 15.

WITNESS PROTECTION PROGRAM. The purpose of the program is to promote law enforcement by facilitating the protection of persons who are involved directly or indirectly in providing assistance in law enforcement matters in relation to activities conducted by the R.C.M.P. or activities conducted by any law enforcement agency or international criminal court or tribunal in respect of which an agreement or arrangement has been entered into under the Act. The program is administered by the Commissioner of the R.C.M.P. *Witness Protection Program Act*, S.C. 1996, c. 15, s. 3.

WKRS. *abbr.* Workers(').

[] **W.L.A.C**. *abbr.* Western Labour Arbitration Cases, 1966-.

W.L.R. *abbr.* Western Law Reporter, 1905-1916.

[] **W.L.R**. *abbr.* Weekly Law Reports.

W.L.T. *abbr.* Western Law Times, 1890-1895.

WOLF. *n.* 1. The timber wolf, also known as the gray or black wolf and includes the immature young of such animal. *The Wolf and Coyote Bounty Act*, R.S.S. 1978, c. W-15, s. 2. 2. Any of the species Canis lupus L., or Canis latrans Say or any cross breed of either. *Livestock Poultry and Honey Bee Protection Act*, R.S.O. 1990, c. L.24, s. 1.

WOMAN. *n*. A female person of the age of eighteen years or more. See MARRIED ~; SINGLE ~; UNMARRIED ~.

WOMB. See UTERUS.

WOMEN. See CANADIAN ADVISORY COUNCIL ON THE STATUS OF ~; CONVENTION ON THE ELIMINATION OF ALL FORMS OF DISCRIMINATION AGAINST ~; STATUS OF ~ CANADA.

WOMEN'S ROYAL NAVAL SERVICES. See MEMBER OF THE ~.

WOOD. *n*. A group of trees planted or growing on at least 0.5 of a hectare of land with at least 250 trees on each 0.5 hectare of land. *Forestry Act*, R.R.O. 1980, Reg. 397, s. 1. See PROCESSED ~; PULP~; ROUND~; SMALL ~.

WOOD ALCOHOL. Any volatile liquid, whether obtained by the destructive distillation of wood or otherwise, the chief constituent of which is methyl alcohol and which contains not more than 25 per cent by weight of acetone. *Excise Act*, R.S.C. 1985, c. E-14, s. 243.

WOOD FIBRE. The plant tissue contained in trees or wood shrubs.

WOODLANDS. *n*. 1. Lands having at least 1,000 trees per hectare of all sizes or at least 750 trees per hectare measuring over 5 centimetres in diameter or at least 500 trees per hectare measuring over 12 centimetres in diameter or at least 250 trees per hectare measuring over 20 centimetres in diameter (all measurements to be taken at least 1.3 metres from the ground), but does not include a plantation established for the purpose of producing Christmas trees. *Woodlands Improvement Act*, R.S.O. 1990, c. W.10, s. 1. 2. Lands having not less than 400 trees per acre of all sizes, or 300 trees measuring over 2 inches in diameter, or 200 trees measuring over 5 inches in diameter, or 100 trees measuring over 8 inches in diameter (all such measurements to be taken at 4 1/2 feet from the ground) of one or more of the following kinds: white or Norway pine, white or Norway spruce, hemlock, tamarack, oak, ash, elm, hickory, basswood, tulip (white wood), black cherry, walnut, butternut, chestnut, hard maple, soft maple, cedar, sycamore, beech,

black locust, or catalpa, or any other variety that may be designated by order in council, and which lands have been set apart by the owner with object chiefly, but not necessarily solely, of fostering growth of the trees thereon and that are fenced and not used for grazing purposes. *Assessment Act*, R.S.O. 1990, c. A.31, s. 19.

WOODLOT. *n*. 1. An immoveable other than a farm woodlot (a) that is the subject of a forest development plan supervised by the Ministre de l'énergie et des resources or that is, or is intended to be, exploited in a real and continuous manner for domestic, industrial or commercial forest purposes; and (b) that is not used or intended to be used mainly for residential purposes or for purposes of pleasure, recreation or sport. *An Act Respecting Municipal Taxation and Providing Amendments to Certain Legislation*, S.Q. 1979, c. 72, s. 1. 2. An area having not less than, (a) 400 trees per acre of any size, (b) 300 trees per acre measuring more than 2 inches dbh, (c) 200 trees per acre measuring more than 5 inches dbh, or (d) 100 trees per acre measuring more than 8 inches dbh. *Trees Act*, R.S.O. 1990, c. T.20, s. 1. See PRIVATE ~.

WOOD MATCHES. Matches that have splints of wood but does not include such matches if they are attached to a common base. *Hazardous Products (Matches) Regulations*, C.R.C., c. 929, s. 2.

WOOD PROCESSING FACILITY. *var.* **WOOD-PROCESSING FACILITY**. A mill in which timber is manufactured into secondary wood products.

WOOD PRODUCT. Includes pulp, pulpwood, paper, veneer, plywood, lumber, timer poles, posts, chips and any other product accruing from a timber harvesting operation. See PRIMARY ~S.

WOOD RESIDUE. Wood chips, slabs, edgings, sawdust, shavings and hog fuel.

WOODS. *n*. Forest land and rock barren, brushland, dry marsh, bog or muskeg.

WOOD TURPENTINE. See STEAM DISTILLED ~; SULPHATE ~.

WOOL. *n*. Unwashed fleece wool produced in Canada. See RAW ~, HAIR OR BRISTLES.

WORD. See OPERATIVE ~; OVERT ~.

WORDS. *n*. 1. Includes figures, punctuation marks and typographical, monetary and mathematical symbols. 2. Includes pictures, visual images, gestures or other methods of signifying meaning. *Defamation Act*, R.S.N.S. 1989, c. 122, s. 2. See APT DESCRIPTIVE ~; APT ~; GENERAL ~; PRECATORY ~; SEDITIOUS ~.

WORDS OF ART. Words employed in a technical sense.

WORDS OF LIMITATION. Words which effectively restrict the continuation of an estate.

WORK. *n*. 1. " . . . [M]ay mean action or exertion put forth to accomplish some end or it may mean the product of or the result of action or exertion." *Ruthenian Sisters of the Immaculate Conception v. Saskatoon (City)*, [1937] 2 W.W.R. 625 at 628 (Sask. C.A.), Martin J.A. (Mackenzie J.A. concurring). 2. The labour or services an employee is required to perform for an employer and includes time the employee is required to be available for his employment duties at a place designated by the employer but does not include the time spent by an employee in his own living accommodation, whether on or off the employer's premises. 3. The construction, renovation, repair or demolition of property and the alteration or improvement of land. 4. Includes the title thereof when such title is original and distinctive. *Copyright Act*, R.S.C. 1985, c. C-42, s. 2. 5. Includes (a) any bridge, boom, dam, wharf, dock, pier, tunnel or pipe and the approaches or other works necessary or appurtenant thereto; (b) any dumping of fill or excavation of materials from the bed of a navigable water; (c) any telegraph or power cable or wire; or (d) any structure, device or thing, whether similar in character to anything referred to in this definition or not, that may interfere with navigation. *Navigable Waters Protection Act*, R.S.C. 1985, c. N-22, s. 3. 6. The work reasonably required to be performed to explore for, develop or produce minerals. 7. A computer program is a "work" within the meaning of the Copyright Act. Copyright may reside in either a language, or form of language, where it is an original creation of an author: *D.P. Anderson & Co. Ltd. v. Lieber Code Co.*, [1917] 2 K.B. 469 (Eng. K.B.) (telegraph code system); *Pitman v. Hine* (1884), 1 T.L.R. 39 (shorthand system), or, more traditionally, in the particular form of expression of an idea or concept. In my opinion, a program such as this is either a novel language or an expression of thought, albeit in numeric form. In either case it is a work within the meaning of the Copyright Act. *Canavest House Ltd. v. Lett* (1984), 4 C.I.P.R. 103, 2 C.P.R. (3d) 386 (Ont.

H.C.) See ARCHITECTURAL ~; ARTISTIC ~; ASSEMBLY-LINE ~; ASSESSMENT ~; BARGAINING UNIT ~; COLLECTIVE ~; CONSTITUENCY ~; CONSTRUCTION ~; COST OF ~; CUSTOM ~; DAY'S ~; DRAINAGE ~; DRAMATIC ~; EARTH ~; ELECTRICAL ~; ENGINEERING ~; EQUAL PAY FOR EQUAL ~; EXPLORATORY ~; FEDERAL ~ UNDERTAKING OR BUSINESS; FIELD ~; GEOLOGICAL ~; GEOPHYSICAL ~; GEOTECHNICAL ~; HOME ~; HOT ~; HOURS OF ~; INSURED ~; LAWFUL ~; LINE ~; LITERARY ~; MAINTENANCE ~; MINE RESCUE ~; MUSICAL ~; PIPING INSTALLATION ~; PUBLIC ~; RAILWAY ~; RIGHT TO ~; SEASONAL AGRICULTURAL ~; SOCIAL ~; TAKE-HOME ~; ~S.

WORK ACTIVITY PROJECT. A project the purpose of which is to prepare for entry or return to employment persons in need or likely to become persons in need who, because of environmental, personal or family reasons, have unusual difficulty in obtaining or holding employment or in improving, through, participation in technical or vocational training programs or rehabilitation programs, their ability to obtain or hold employment.

WORK-ASSIGNMENT DISPUTE. A dispute with an employer concerning assignment of unorganized employees to work or between unions as to which union's members should do certain work.

WORK CREDIT. Credit given for assessment work performed upon a licence. *Mineral Resources Act*, S.N.S. 1990, c. 18, s. 2.

WORK DAY. 1. The daily period of work. 2. A period of 24 consecutive hours commencing at the time a motor vehicle operator begins his work shift. *Canada Motor Vehicle Operators Hours of Service Regulations*, C.R.C., c. 1005, s. 2.

WORKED. *adj*. In relation to softwood lumber, means matched (provided with a tongued-and-grooved joint at the edges or ends) shiplapped (provided with a rabbeted or lapped joint at the edges) or patterned (shaped at the edges or on the faces to a patterned or molded form) on a matching machine, sticker or molder. *Softwood Lumber Products Export Charge Act*, S.C. 1987, c. 15, Sched., Part 1, s. 1.

WORKER. *n.* 1. An employee. 2. A person who has entered into or works under a contract of service or, apprenticeship, written or oral, express or implied, whether by way of manual labour or otherwise and includes a learner. 3. "The word 'worker' includes: (1) a person who enters into a contract of service, and (2) a person who works under a contract of service. . ." *British Airways Board v. British Columbia (Workers' Compensation Board)* (1985), 61 B.C.L.R. 1 at 16, 13 Admin. L.R. 78, 17 D.L.R. (4th) 36 (C.A.), Macfarlane J.A. (Seaton J.A. concurring). 4. "The definition of 'worker' [in s. 1 of the Occupational Health and Safety Act, R.S.O. 1980, c. 32] applies equally to employment or independent contactor relationships. It does not, for example, restrict the applicability of the statute to contracts of employment as it might have done if the word 'employee' and not the word 'worker' had been used as the correlative to the word 'employer'." *R. v. Wyssen* (1992), 10 O.R. (3d) 193 at 197, 58 O.A.C. 67 (C.A.), Blair J.A. (Dubin C.J.O. concurring). See AIR RAID PRECAUTIONS ~; BLIND ~; BLUE COLLAR ~; CASUAL ~; CHILD CARE ~; DAIRY~; DENTAL HEALTH ~; HOME~; IRON~; MIGRATORY ~; OCCUPATIONAL ~; OUT~; PRODUCTION ~; RADIATION ~; SHEET METAL ~; UNDEREMPLOYED ~; UNEMPLOYED ~; WHITE COLLAR ~; X-RAY ~; YOUTH ~.

WORKER CO-OPERATIVE. A co-operative, the articles of which provide that the co-operative's primary object is to provide employment to its members, and the articles of which provide that it is a condition of membership that, except in circumstances prescribed by the regulations, a member must be employed by the co-operative.

WORKERS' COMPENSATION. 1. A program to provide financial, rehabilitation and medical assistance to any worker who is partially or totally disabled by an accident which arose "out of and in the course of employment" or by an occupational disease. 2. " . . . [I]s paid to partially replace lost wages due to injury on the job. It is not . . . insurance, nor is it damages, nor is it a settlement." *Dixon v. Dixon* (1981), 25 R.F.L. (2d) 266 at 269, 14 Man. R. (2d) 40 (Co. Ct.), Ferg Co. Ct. J. 3. "The primary object of the legislation, broadly speaking, is to provide a mechanism where workmen, who fall within the ambit of the Act and who are injured in the workplace, receive compensation, presumably commensurate with their degree of injury, re-

gardless of fault, and, with respect to any such workman who is killed in the workplace, that their dependants receive such compensation as the Act provides. The latter also applies regardless of where fault may lie. The Legislature has also provided that, in return for such benefits as are guaranteed to the workman, or his dependant, any right of action which might otherwise arise out of the incident which occasioned injury or death is forfeited. This is not a government or funded scheme, but rather it is funded by industrial levy. It is not available to all who find employment in the workplace, but only to those who are employed in industry subject to levy." *Jenkins v. Prince Edward Island (Workers Compensation Board)* (1986), 21 C.C.L.I. 149 at 154, 31 D.L.R. (4th) 536, 61 Nfld. & P.E.I.R. 206, 185 A.P.R. 206, 15 C.C.E.L. 55, 9 C.H.R.R. D/5145 (P.E.I. S.C.), the court per McQuaid J.

WORKERS' COMPENSATION INSURANCE. Insurance of an employer against the cost of compensation prescribed by statute in respect of injury to or disability or death of a worker through accident or disease arising out of or in the course of employment.

WORKERS MOURNING DAY. Throughout Canada, in each and every year, the 28th day of April shall be known under the name of "Day of Mourning for Persons Killed or Injured in the Workplace".

WORKERS' TRUST FUND. Any trust fund maintained in whole or in part on behalf of any worker on an improvement and into which any monetary supplementary benefit is payable as wages for work done by the worker in respect of the improvement. *Construction Lien Act*, R.S.O. 1990, c. C.30, s. 1(1).

WORKING AREA. (a) Any area in which work is being performed on board a ship; (b) with respect to persons employed in the maintenance or repair of a ship, any area immediately adjacent to the ship; and (c) with respect to persons employed in the loading or unloading of a ship, any area on shore that is within the reach of any derrick, crane or other hoisting equipment employed in loading or unloading the ship and the immediate approaches to such an area, but does not include any sheds, warehouses or any part of a wharf forward or aft of the ship's mooring lines. *Safe Working Practices Regulations*, C.R.C., c. 1467, s. 2.

WORKING CAPITAL. 1. Share capital, debenture or bond indebtedness, general reserve fund, deferred dividends or participating reserves and undistributed surplus or deficit accounts. 2. The excess of current assets over current liabilities determined in accordance with generally accepted accounting principles.

WORKING CHAMBER. The part of a project that is used for work in compressed air, but does not include an air lock or a medical lock.

WORKING CIRCLE. See PUBLIC ~.

WORKING CONDITIONS. 1. " . . . [C]onditions under which a worker or workers, individually or collectively, provide their services, in accordance with the rights and obligations included in the contract of employment by the consent of the parties or by operation of law, and under which the employer receives those services. . . a worker's obligation to provide his or her services and the employer's obligation to pay his or her wages. . . the right to refuse to work, the continuation of the right to wages and other benefits, availability, assignment to other duties and the right to return to employment at the end of the assignment or cessation or work . . ." *Québec (Commission de la Santé & de la Sécurité du travail) v. Bell Canada*, [1988] 1 S.C.R. 749 at 798, 801-2, 51 D.L.R. (4th) 161, 21 C.C.E.L. 1, 85 N.R. 295, 15 Q.A.C. 217, the court per Beetz J. 2. " . . . [S]trikes, slow-downs and lock-outs are not 'working conditions' [under the Police Act, R.S.O. 1980, c. 381, s. 29(2)] but rather their very antithesis; they are, in a literal sense, 'non-working conditions'." *Police Assn. (Metropolitan Toronto) v. Metropolitan Commissioners of Police* (1991), 84 D.L.R. (4th) 97 at 102, 5 O.R. (3d) 705, 50 O.A.C. 67 (C.A.), the court per Catzman J.A.

WORKING DAY. 1. A day on which an employee is required to work in his normal working schedule. 2. A day on which the person injured would, but for the injury, be employed in his ordinary work. 3. Any day except a Saturday or a Sunday or other holiday. 4. A day on which teachers are required to give tuition and instruction or the other employees are required to perform their duties. 5. "[May refer] . . . to the community generally . . . to the specific contemplated schedule of the worker." *Prevost v. British Columbia (Workers' Compensation Board)* (1988), 29 B.C.L.R. (2d) 131 at 143, 52 D.L.R. (4th) 513 (S.C.), Southin J.

WORKING EXPENSES. See WORKING EXPENDITURE.

WORKING FACE. Any place in any mine from which coal or another mineral is being cut, sheared, broken or loosened.

WORKING HOURS. 1. The hours during which an employee works or performs some labour or service for the employer. 2. " . . . [R]efer only to the period of time during which an employee is required to undertake his duties and responsibilities . . ." *U.S.W.A. v. Adams Mine*, [1982] O.L.R.B. Rep. 1767 at 1777, 83 C.L.L.C. 16,011, 1 C.L.R.B.R. (N.S.) 384, Adams (Chair). 3. All hours from the time that a motor vehicle operator begins his work shift as required by his employer until the time he is relieved of his job responsibilities but does not include any time (a) during a work shift when he is relieved of his job responsibilities by his employer for authorized meals and rest while en route; (b) spent during stops en route due to illness or fatigue; (c) resting en route as one of two operators or a motor vehicle that is fitted with a sleeper berth; or (d) resting while en route in a motel, hotel or other similar place of rest where sleeping accommodation is provided. *Motor Vehicle Operators Hours of Work Regulations*, C.R.C., c. 990, s. 2. See NORMAL ~; REGULAR ~.

WORKING INTEREST. 1. A right, in whole or in part, to produce and dispose of oil or gas from a pool or part of a pool, whether that right is held as an incident of ownership of an estate in fee simple in the oil or gas or under a lease, agreement or other instrument, if the right is chargeable with and the holder thereof is obligated to pay or bear, either in cash or out of production, all or a portion of the costs in connection with the drilling for, recovery and disposal of oil or gas from the pool or part thereof. 2. Typically, the owner of minerals *in situ* will lease to a potential producer the right to extract such minerals [oil and gas]. This right is known as a working interest. *Bank of Montreal v. Dynex Petroleum Ltd.*, [2002] 1 S.C.R. 146

WORKING INTEREST OWNER. In respect of a parcel of land, a person who has the right to drill for and produce oil and gas from the land.

WORKING PLACE. (a) In relation to a coal mine, means a portion of a coal seam in the underground workings of a coal mine from which coal is being cut, sheared, broken, loosened or removed, and any other part of the underground workings where timbering, rock bolting or drilling operations are in progress; (b) in relation to a mine other than a coal mine, means a portion of the underground workings of a mine in which ore or waste is first broken and removed and includes a place designated by the chief inspector.

WORKING PRESSURE. The pressure at which a boiler or pressure vessel may be used or operated.

WORKING YEAR. One calendar year's continuous service, comprising not less than 225 days of actual work.

WORK INJURY. Any injury, disease or illness incurred by an employee in the performance of or in connection with his work.

WORK IN PROGRESS. An inventory of partly-finished services the value of which is equal to the amount that can be expected to become receivable after the year end.

WORKMAN. *n*. Includes a person who has entered into or works under a contract of service or apprenticeship, written or oral, express or implied, whether by way of manual labour or otherwise. See ORDINARY ~.

WORKMEN'S COMPENSATION. See WORKERS' COMPENSATION.

WORKMEN'S COMPENSATION INSURANCE. See WORKERS' COMPENSATION INSURANCE.

WORK OF ART. 1. A moveable or immoveable property whose conservation is from an aesthetic point of view in the public interest. 2. Includes painting, print, picture, book, sculpture, antique and other similar property. See ARCHITECTURAL ~.

WORK OF ELECTRICAL INSTALLATION. The installation of any electrical equipment, in or upon any land, building or premises, from the point where electrical power or energy is delivered to the point where the power or energy can be used, and includes the maintenance, connection, alteration, extension and repair of electrical installations.

WORK OF JOINT AUTHORSHIP. A work produced by the collaboration of two or more authors in which the contribution of one author is not distinct from the contribution of the other author or authors. *Copyright Act*, R.S.C. 1985, c. C-42, s. 2.

WORK OPTION. The act of participating in community service work as an alternative to incarceration for failure to pay a fine for a summary conviction matter that the person has been ordered to pay by a court of competent jurisdiction.

WORK PERMIT. A written authorization to work in Canada issued by an officer to a foreign national. *Immigration and Refugee Protection Regulations*, SOR/2002-227, s. 2.

WORK PLACE. *var.* **WORKPLACE**. 1. Any place where an employee is engaged in work or the employee's employer. 2. A construction site or any other place where an employee or self-employed person is engaged in work and includes any vehicle or mobile equipment used thereat by an employee. 3. The plant or general work area where an employee normally reports for work and where his current work records are kept. See ENCLOSED ~; ISOLATED ~.

WORKPLACE HAZARDOUS MATERIALS INFORMATION SYSTEM. A Canada-wide system to label any hazardous material intended for workplace use. Suppliers must prepare a Material Safety Data Sheet specifying information required.

WORK RELEASE. The privilege of doing work in the community while serving a sentence in a correctional institution.

WORK RESTRICTION. A limitation on the type or amount of work members of a union will do.

WORKS. *n*. 1. " . . . [P]hysical things, not services'." *Shur Gain Division, Canada Packers Inc., Re* (1991), 85 D.L.R. (4th) 317 at 336, 91 C.L.L.C. 14,046, [1992] 2 F.C. 3, 135 N.R. 6 (C.A.), Desjardins J.A. 2. Includes all property, buildings, erections, plant, machinery, installations, materials, dams, canals, devices, fittings, apparatus, appliances and equipment. 3. Includes all roads, plant, machinery, buildings, erections, constructions, installations, materials, devices, fittings, apparatus, appliances, equipment and other property for the development, generation, transformation, transmission, conveying, distribution, supply or use of power. 4. Retaining walls, dykes, breakwaters, groynes, cribs and other structures designed for the rehabilitation or protection, or both, of property on the shores of lakes, rivers or other bodies of water that have been damaged or eroded by the elements, and includes repairs and improvements to existing works. See APPLIANCES OR ~; CAPITAL ~; DRAINAGE ~; EX ~; FLOOD CONTROL ~; INDEPENDENT ~; IRRIGATION ~; LITERARY AND ARTISTIC ~; ORE REDUCTION ~; PRIVATE ~;

PROTECTION ~; PUBLIC ~ CANADA; PUBLISHED ~; PURIFICATION ~; SECONDARY TREATMENT ~; SEWAGE ~; SEWERAGE ~; TREATMENT ~; WATER PURIFICATION ~; WATER ~; WINTER ~; WORK.

WORKS FOR THE GENERAL ADVANTAGE OF CANADA. By virtue of section 92(10)(c) and section 91(29) of the Constitution Act, the federal Parliament has power to make laws relating to: "(c) Such works as, although wholly situate within the province, are before or after their execution declared by the Parliament of Canada to be for the general advantage of Canada or for the advantage of two or more of the provinces." See DECLARATORY POWER.

WORK SHARING. The distribution of available work to avoid layoffs.

WORK SHIFT. The period in a work day assigned to a motor vehicle operator by the motor carrier by whom he is employed, during which period the motor vehicle operator is continuously on duty except for authorized off duty periods. *Canada Motor Vehicle Operators Hours of Service Regulations*, C.R.C., c. 1005, s. 2.

WORKSHOP. *n*. Premises where manual labour is performed as a trade or for gain, in or incidental to the making, alteration, repair, finishing or adaptation for sale of an article or part of it. See DOMESTIC ~; SHELTERED ~.

WORK SITE. 1. The location or area occupied by an employee, in the course of or in connection with his work. Canada regulations. 2. A location where a worker is, or is likely to be, engaged in any occupation and includes any vehicle or mobile equipment used by a worker in an occupation.

WORK STOPPAGE. 1. A general strike, rotating strike, study session, work slow-down or a refusal or failure to perform the usual duties of employment. 2. " . . . [W]hat essentially characterizes the s. 44 [of the Unemployment Insurance Act, 1971, S.C. 1970-71-72, c. 48] work stoppage and distinguishes it from the claimant's loss of employment is the aspect of 'intent': a work stoppage due to a labour dispute always results from the fact that one or other of the parties to a contract of service does not wish to perform it. If it is the employer who feels this way, the stoppage is called a lockout; if it is the employees who refuse to provide their services,

it is called a strike. . . *Caron v. Canada (Employment & Immigration Commmission)* (1988), 89 C.L.L.C. 14,027 at 12,226, 91 N.R. 1, 55 D.L.R. (4th) 274, [1989] 1 F.C. 628 (C.A.), Hugessen J.A. (Desjardins J.A. concurring).

WORK SYSTEM. A system under which the hours of work of persons associated with the safe operation of a ship are apportioned regularly and systematically among those persons. *Safe Manning Regulations*, C.R.C., c. 1466, s. 2.

WORK TO RULE. 1. A slowdown in production brought about by employees obeying all rules pertaining to their work. 2. Refusing to carry out duties not explicitly included in a job description.

WORK VEHICLE. A vehicle designed primarily for the performance of work in the construction of works of civil engineering and in maintenance, that is not constructed on a truck-chassis or truck-type chassis, but does not include a tractor or any vehicle designed primarily to be drawn behind another vehicle. Canada regulations.

WORK WEEK. *var*. **WORKWEEK**. A week of work established by the practice of the employer or determined by an employment standards officer. *Employment Standards Act*, R.S.O. 1990, c. E.14, s. 1. See COMPRESSED ~; FLUCTUATING ~; SPLIT ~; STANDARD ~.

WORLD INTELLECTUAL PROPERTY ORGANIZATION. Provider of international domain name dispute resolution.

WORLD TRADE ORGANIZATION. The organization established by the World Trade Organization agreement.

WORLD TRADE ORGANIZATION AGREEMENT. The Agreement Establishing the World Trade Organization, including (a) the agreements set out in Annexes 1A, 1B, 1C, 2 and 3 to that Agreement, and (b) the agreements set out in Annex 4 to that Agreement that have been accepted by Canada, all forming an integral part of the Final Act Embodying The Results Of The Uruguay Round Of Multilateral Trade Negotiations, signed at Marrakesh on April 15, 1994. *World Trade Organization Agreement Implementation Act*, S.C. 1994, c. 47, s. 2(1).

WORLD WAR I. The war waged by the German Emperor and His Allies against His Majesty and His Majesty's Allies, and the period denoted by the term "World War I" is the period between August 4, 1914 and August 31, 1921, both dates inclusive.

WORLD WAR II. The war waged by His Majesty and His Majesty's Allies against Germany and Germany's Allies, and the period denoted by the term "World War II" is the period between September 1, 1939 and April 1, 1947, both dates inclusive.

WORM. *n.* Any pipe, condenser or other equipment used or intended to be used for the condensation of spirit vapour. *Excise Act*, R.S.C. 1985, c. E-14, s. 3.

WORSHIP. *n.* The title of a magistrate or mayor.

WORT. *n.* As applied to distilleries, means all liquor made in whole or in part from grain, malt or other saccharine matter, whether or not the liquor is fermented or unfermented. *Excise Act*, R.S.C. 1985, c. E-14, s. 4.

WORTH. See NET ~.

WOUND. *n.* 1. " . . . [A] breaking of the skin, . . ." *R. v. Hostetter* (1902), 7 C.C.C. 221 at 222 (N.W.T. C.A.), the court per Prendergast J.A. 2. The disrupting of tissue caused by violence. F.A. Jaffe, *A Guide to Pathological Evidence*, 3d ed. (Toronto: Carswell, 1991) at 229. 3. " . . . [A]n appropriate description of assault causing bodily harm. . . *R. v. Lucas* (1987), 34 C.C.C. (3d) 28 at 33, 10 Q.A.C. 47, [1987] R.L. 212 (C.A.), the court per L'Heureux-Dubé J.A. See DEFENCE ~; HESITATION ~; PENETRATING ~; PERFORATING ~.

WOUND BALLISTICS. The study of the way projectiles produce wounds. F.A. Jaffe, *A Guide to Pathological Evidence*, 3d ed. (Toronto: Carswell, 1991) at 213.

WRAP-AROUND MORTGAGE. A second mortgage, granted when the first mortgage is small and at a low interest rate, whose principal includes the whole principal of the first mortgage even though the whole amount is not immediately advanced. The second mortgagee must make payments under the first mortgage as long as the second mortgage is valid. If the first mortgage matures, the mortgagee must pay it off and obtain a discharge so the second mortgage becomes a first mortgage. D.J. Donahue & P.D. Quinn, *Real Estate Practice in Ontario*, 4th ed. (Toronto: Butterworths, 1990) at 226.

WRAPPING. *n.* A separate covering or container not part of the item itself.

WRECCUM MARIS SIGNIFICAT ILLA BONA QUAE NAUFRAGIO AD TERRAM PELLUNTUR. [L.] A wreck of the sea means the goods which are brought to shore from the shipwreck.

WRECK. *n.* 1. Jetsam, flotsam, lagan and derelict and any other thing that was part of or was on a vessel wrecked, stranded or in distress; and aircraft wrecked in waters and anything that was part of or was on an aircraft wrecked, stranded or in distress in waters. *Canada Shipping Act, 2001*, S.C. 2001, c. 26, s. 153. 2. Includes the cargo, stores and tackle of a vessel and all parts of a vessel separated from the vessel, and the property of persons who belong to, are on board or have quitted a vessel that is wrecked, stranded or in distress at any place in Canada. *Criminal Code*, R.S.C. 1985, c. C-46, s. 2.

WRECKER. *n.* A person who as a business buys or acquires motor vehicles and dismantles them for the purpose of selling or otherwise disposing of their parts.

WRISTBAND. See SPIKED ~.

WRIT. *n.* 1. The formal order or command of a court which directs or enjoins a person or persons to do or refrain from doing something in particular. 2. A document which originates certain legal proceedings. 3. " . . . [T]he initial process issuing out of the Court." *Fleishman v. T.A. Allan & Sons* (1932) 45 B.C.R. 553 at 560 (C.A.), Macdonald C.J.B.C. 4. The document addressed by the Chief Electoral Officer to a returning officer requiring an election to be held. The Governor in Council or the Lieutenant Governor in Council issues a proclamation directing the Chief Electoral Officer to issue the writ to the returning officer for the electoral district in which the election is to be held. The proclamation fixes the date of the writ and the date of the election. See ALIAS ~; CONCURRENT ~; PLURIES ~; PREROGATIVE ~.

WRITER. See GHOST ~; SHEET ~.

WRITING. *n.* 1. Any term of like import, includes words printed, typewritten, painted, engraved, lithographed, photographed or represented or reproduced by any mode of representing or reproducing words in visible form. *Interpretation Act*, R.S.C. 1985, c. I-21, s. 35(1). 2. " . . . [F]axed proxies . . ." *Beatty v. First Exploration Fund (1987) & Co.* (1988), 40 B.L.R. 90 at 98, 25 B.C.L.R. (2d) 377 (S.C.), Hinds J. 3. "Typewritten documents . . ." *Nesbitt, Re*, [1933] 3 W.W.R. 171 at 173 (K.B.),

Taylor J. 4. " . . . [W]ords already written may be and constantly are 'represented' by a 'do,' or 'ditto,' is familiarly known and a word 'represented' by it is just as effective as if it were written out in full." *Murray v. Haylow* (1927), 60 O.L.R. 629 at 637, [1927] 3 D.L.R. 1036 (C.A.), Riddell J.A. (Latchford C.J. and Masten J.A. concurring). 5. Includes words printed, typewritten, painted, engraved, lithographed, photographed or represented or reproduced by any mode of representing or reproducing words in visible form. *Interpretation Act*, R.S.C. 1985, c. I-21, s. 35. 6. Includes a document of any kind and any mode in which, and any material on which, words or figures, whether at length or abridged, are written, printed or otherwise expressed, or a map or plan is inscribed. *Criminal Code*, R.S.C. 1985, c. C-46, s. 2. 7. Includes a will and any other testamentary instrument whether or not probate has been applied for or granted and whether or not the will or other granted instrument is valid. *Human Tissue Gift acts*. See IN ~.

WRITING, MANUSCRIPT. Includes what is printed, painted, engraved, lithographed or otherwise traced or copied. *Interpretation Act*, R.S.Q. 1977, c. I-16, s. 61.

WRIT OF ASSISTANCE. 1. A writ operated like a search warrant with respect to a crime under the Narcotic Control Act, the Food and Drugs Act, the Customs Act or the Excise Act. It is a general warrant, unlimited in time or place. S.A. Cohen, *Due Process of Law* (Toronto: Carswell, 1977) at 94. 2. " . . . [A] document issued out of the Federal Court which identifies the holder as a person entitled to exercise without a warrant the statutory powers of search and seizure under the relevant statute. It is like an identification card signifying that the holder is entitled to conduct warrantless searches and seizures pursuant to the search and seizure powers conferred by the relevant statute. Consequently, searches under a writ of assistance are warrantless searches by designated persons pursuant to statutory powers." *R. v. Noble* (1984), 16 C.C.C. (3d) 146 at 156, 48 O.R. (2d) 643, 42 C.R. (3d) 209, 6 O.A.C. 11, 14 D.L.R. (4th) 216, 12 C.R.R. 138 (C.A.), the court per Martin J.A.

WRIT OF ATTACHMENT. A writ used to seize property before judgment but only in situations in which a debtor absconds or has absconded from the jurisdiction or hides to avoid service of process. C.R.B. Dunlop, *Creditor-Debtor Law in Canada* (Toronto: Carswell, 1981) at 188.

WRIT OF DELIVERY. A writ of execution directing that goods be delivered by the defendant to the plaintiff.

WRIT OF ELEGIT. A writ under which a sheriff can seize a debtor's chattels and, after their appraisal, deliver enough to a creditor to satisfy the debt. If the debt is still unsatisfied the sheriff can then give the creditor possession of one-half of the debtor's land until its income satisfies the debt. C.R.B. Dunlop, *Creditor-Debtor Law in Canada* (Toronto: Carswell, 1981) at 130.

WRIT OF ERROR. 1. "In the early history of the common law, there was no such thing as a Court of Appeal. Appeals from the decision of a single Judge or Judge and jury were taken by means of a writ of error. When is writ was issued by the Court whose proceedings were questioned, the same Court could set aside the decision it had previously given or grant a new trial." *British Columbia Place Ltd. v. Sweeney Cooperage Ltd.* (1981), 20 C.P.C. 217 at 219, 27 B.C.L.R. 66 (S.C.), Bouck J. 2. A writ in which an appellate court directs a court of record to send the record of an action in which a final judgment was entered so that the appellate court may examine certain alleged errors and may reverse, correct or affirm the judgment, as the case may be.

WRIT OF EXECUTION. 1. The processes available to enforce a judgment; the five main writs are: capias, fi. fa., levari facias, elegit, and extent. 2. The old writ of fi. fa. or its contemporary equivalent. 3. " . . . [C]ommands the sheriff to levy of the goods and lands of the debtor the amount of the judgment debt. Its authority is not limited to property of which the debtor is then presently the owner. It is a warrant to the sheriff to seize and sell any of the debtor which is not exempt from property seizure which he may at any time during its currency be able to find in his bailiwick." *Lee v. Armstrong* (1917), 37 D.L.R. 738 at 749, [1917] 3 W.W.R. 889, 13 A.L.R. 160 (C.A.), Walsh J.A.

WRIT OF EXTENT. A writ by which a sheriff may seize the lands, goods and body of a debtor without having to choose between execution against the person and execution against property. C.R.B. Dunlop, *Creditor-Debtor Law in Canada* (Toronto: Carswell, 1981) at 449.

WRIT OF FIERI FACIAS. An order that someone, out of a party's goods and chattels, collect the sum recovered by the judgment along with any interest on that sum.

WRIT OF Fl. FA. See WRIT OF FIERI FA-CIAS.

WRIT OF HABEAS CORPUS. See HABEAS CORPUS AD SUBJICIENDUM.

WRIT OF POSSESSION. A writ to recover the possession of land.

WRIT OF PROHIBITION. " . . . [L]ies to restrain an inferior Court not only in cases of lack or excess of jurisdiction but in cases in which it is made to appear that there is bias, self-interest or a violation of the principles of natural justice." *R. v. Fodor*, [1938] 2 D.L.R. 290 at 307, [1938] 1 W.W.R. 497, 70 C.C.C. 108 (Alta. C.A.), McGillivray J.A.

WRIT OF SEIZURE AND SALE. The equivalent of a writ of fieri facias.

WRIT OF SEQUESTRATION. 1. An order that four or more people, called commissioners, seize the judgment debtor's personal property and any rents and profits of real property. C.R.B. Dunlop, *Creditor-Debtor Law in Canada* (Toronto: Carswell, 1981) at 279. 2. An order to enforce a writ of delivery which directs a sheriff to seize and hold a person's property and to collect and hold any income from that property until the person obeys the original order. G.D. Watson & C. Perkins, eds., *Holmested & Watson: Ontario Civil Procedure* (Toronto: Carswell, 1984) at 60-2 and 60-10.

WRIT OF SUBPOENA. A writ requiring witnesses to attend to the trial of an action. D. Sgayias *et al., Federal Court Practice 1988* (Toronto: Carswell, 1987) at 307.

WRIT OF SUMMONS. The writ by which an action is commenced.

WRIT OF VENDITIONI EXPONAS. An order that a sheriff sell goods for the best possible price. C.R.B. Dunlop, *Creditor-Debtor Law in Canada* (Toronto: Carswell, 1981) at 400.

WRITTEN. *adj.* 1. Includes words printed, typewritten, painted, engraved, lithographed, photographed or represented or reproduced by any mode of representing or reproducing words in visible form. 2. Printing, lithography and other modes of reprinting or reproducing words in visible form.

WRITTEN HEARING. A hearing held by means of the exchange of documents, whether in written form or by electronic means. *Statutory Powers Procedure Act*, R.S.O. 1990, c. S.22, s. 1(1).

WRITTEN ORDER. An order, in writing, dated and signed by a person to whom a licensed dealer or a pharmacist is authorized to sell a narcotic or controlled drug pursuant to a written order. Canada regulations.

WRITTEN QUESTION. A question designed to gather detailed information from a ministry. A. Fraser, W.A. Dawson, & J. Holtby, eds., *Beauchesne's Rules and Forms of the House of Commons of Canada*, 6th ed. (Toronto: Carswell, 1989) at 119.

WRITTEN SEPARATION AGREEMENT. Includes an agreement by which a person agrees to make payments on a periodic basis for the maintenance of a former spouse, child of the marriage or both, after the marriage has been dissolved whether the agreement was made before or after the marriage was dissolved. *Taxation Act*, R.S.Q. 1977, c. I-3, s. 1.

WRONG. *n.* 1. Deprivation of a right; an injury. 2. The consequence of the violation or infringement of a right. 3. "[In s. 16(2) of the Criminal Code, R.S.C. 1985, c. C-46] . . . '[M]orally wrong' . . ." *R. v. Ratti* (1991), 2 C.R. (4th) 293 at 301, 120 N.R. 91, 62 C.C.C. (3d) 105, 44 O.A.C. 161, [1991] 1 S.C.R. 68, Lamer C.J.C. (La Forest and Cory JJ. concurring). See EQUITY WILL NOT SUFFER A ~ TO BE WITHOUT A REMEDY; NO MAN CAN TAKE ADVANTAGE OF HIS OWN ~; THE KING CAN DO NO ~.

WRONGDOER. *n.* A person who commits a wrongful act and includes any other person liable for such wrongful act and the respective personal representatives, successors or assigns of such persons in this province or elsewhere but does not include an employer or worker in respect of a wrongful act to which subsection 13(1) of the *Workers' Compensation Act*, R.S.P.E.I. 1988, c. W-7, applies or their respective personal representatives, successors or assigns in this province or elsewhere. *Fatal Accidents Act*, R.S.P.E.I. 1988, c. F-5, s. 1(m).

WRONGFUL ACT. A failure to exercise reasonable skill or care toward the deceased which causes or contributes to the death of the deceased.

WRONGFUL BIRTH. An action instituted by parents of a child who was born with birth defects as a result of a planned pregnancy. The tortfeasor has interfered with the mother's right to terminate the pregnancy if an informed option had been available to her.

WRONGFUL CONVERSION. Need not connote a criminal act. Pecuniary loss suffered by reason of dishonest or fraudulent conversion of property.

WRONGFUL DISCRIMINATION. In relation to a bylaw, the bylaw must discriminate in fact and it must do so for an improper motive of favouring or hurting one individual and without regard for the public interest.

WRONGFUL DISMISSAL. The unjustified dismissal of an employee from employment by the employer. 2. In wrongful dismissal cases, the wrong suffered by the employee is the breach by the employer of the implied contractual term to give reasonable notice before terminating the contract of employment. Damages are awarded to place the employee in the same position as he/she would have been had reasonable notice been given." *Piazza v. Airport Taxi Cab (Malton) Assn.* (1989), 26 C.C.E.L. 191 at 194, 69 O.R. (2d) 281, 60 D.L.R. (4th) 759, 234 O.A.C. 349, 10 C.H.R.R. D/6347 (C.A.), Zuber J.A.

WRONGFUL LIFE. 1. An action brought by a person born with disabilities asserting that the person should not have been born at all. 2. " . . . [C]an be defined as an action initiated in the name of the unwanted child who submits that, but for the physician's wrongful conduct, he or she would not have been born at all. These actions arise in situations in which the child is already disabled in utero and the defendant negligently fails to diagnose the condition or inform the mother of the risk so that she can obtain an abortion." *Cherry v. Borsman* (1991), 5 C.C.L.T. (2d) 243 at 255, 75 D.L.R. (4th) 668 (B.C. S.C.), Skipp J.

WRONGFUL PREGNANCY. An action brought by a person who becomes pregnant through some act or omission of the defendant.

WTO AGREEMENT. World Trade Organization Agreement.

WTO MEMBER. A Member of the World Trade Organization established by Article I of the WTO Agreement.

WTO MEMBER RESIDENT. (a) A natural person who is ordinarily resident in a country or territory that is a WTO Member, as defined in subsection 2(1) of the *World Trade Organization Agreement Implementation Act*, other than Canada; (b) a body corporate, association, partnership or other organization that is incorporated, formed or otherwise organized in a country or territory that is a WTO Member, as defined in subsection 2(1) of the *World Trade Organization Agreement Implementation Act*, other than Canada, and that is controlled (i) directly or indirectly, by one or more persons referred to in paragraph (a), or (ii) by a government of a WTO Member, whether federal, state or local, or an agency of one of those governments; (c) a trust established by one or more persons referred to in paragraph (a) or (b) or a trust in which one or more of those persons have more than 50 per cent of the beneficial interest; or (d) a body corporate, association, partnership or other organization that is controlled, directly or indirectly, by a trust referred to in paragraph (c). *Bank Act*, S.C. 1991, c. 46, s. 11.1(1).

W.W.D. *abbr*. Western Weekly Digests, 1975-1976.

W.W.R. *abbr*. Western Weekly Reports, 1912-1916.

[] **W.W.R**. *abbr*. Western Weekly Reports, 1917-1950 and 1971-.

W.W.R. (N.S.). *abbr*. Western Weekly Reports (New Series), 1951-1970.

X-RAY BEAM. See PRIMARY ~.

X-RAY EQUIPMENT. Includes X-ray imaging systems, processing equipment and equipment directly related to the production of images for diagnosis or directly related to irradiation with X-rays for therapy. *Healing Arts Radiation Protection Act*, R.S.O. 1990, c. H.2, s. 1(1). See DIAGNOSTIC ~.

X-RAY FACILITIES. See LABORATORY AND ~.

X-RAY GENERATOR. An assembly of components, including an X-ray tube and its housing and shielding, designed and constructed for the controlled generation of X-rays. *Radiation Emitting Devices Regulations*, C.R.C., c. 1370, s. 1.

X-RAY LOCATION. See PERMANENT ~.

X-RAY MACHINE. An electrically powered device the purpose and function of which is the production of X-rays for the irradiation of a human being for a therapeutic or diagnostic purpose.

X-RAYS. *n*. 1. Artificially produced electromagnetic radiation with peak energy greater than five kilovolts. *Healing Arts Radiation Protection Act*, R.S.O. 1990, c. H.2, s. 1(1). 2. Artificially produced electromagnetic radiation of wave length shorter than 0.25 nonometre.

X-RAY SOURCE. Any device, or that portion of it, that emits X-rays, whether or not the principal purpose and function of the device is the production of X-rays.

X-RAY WORKER. Any person whose occupation, (i) as owner of an X-ray source; (ii) as employee of an owner of an X-ray source; (iii) as a person providing professional or trade services under contract to an owner of an X-ray source; or (iv) as a student undergoing a course of instruction provided by the owner of an X-ray source, requires him to use or operate an X-ray source or to enter regularly a space in which an X-ray source is being operated.

YACHT. See FOREIGN ~; PLEASURE ~; SAILING ~;

Y.A.D. *abbr*. Young's Admiralty Decisions (N.S.), 1865-1880.

YAQUA BLOWGUN. This and any other tube or pipe from which arrows or darts are shot by the breath are hereby declared to be prohibited weapons. *Prohibited Weapons Order, No. 6*, C.R.C., c. 438, s. 2.

YARD. *n*. 1..9144 metre yard. *Weights and Measures Act*, S.C. 1970-71-72, c. 36, Schedule II. 2. The area on a lot unoccupied by a building or structure. 3. The winter quarters of moose, deer or caribou. 4. The winter habitat of big game other than the black bear and the polar bear. 5. A system or tracks provided for the making up of trains, storing of cars and for other purposes, over which movements not authorized by time table or train order may be made subject to prescribed signals, rules and special instructions. *Regulations No. O-8, Uniform Code of Operating Rules*, C.R.C., c. 1175, Part III, s. 2. See ASSEMBLY ~; CONTAINER ~; CUBIC ~; FRONT ~; PACKER'S ~; PUBLIC SALE ~; REAR ~; SALVAGE ~; SIDE ~; SQUARE ~.

YARD ENGINE. An engine assigned to yard service. *Regulations No. O-8, Uniform Code of Operating Rules*, C.R.C., c. 1175, Part III, s. 2.

YARD LIMITS. That portion of the main track or main tracks within limits defined by yard limit signs. *Regulations No. O-8, Uniform Code of Operating Rules*, C.R.C., c. 1175, Part III, s. 2.

YAW. *n*. The angle between the line of flight of a projectile and its longitudinal axis. F.A. Jaffe, *A Guide to Pathological Evidence*, 3d ed. (Toronto: Carswell, 1991) at 229.

YCJA. Youth Criminal Justice Act, S.C. 2002, c. 1.

YEAR. *n*. 1. A calendar year. 2. Any period of 12 consecutive months. 3. Any period of 12 consecutive months, except that a reference (a) to, a "calendar year" means a period of 12 consecutive months commencing on January 1; (b) to a "financial year" or "fiscal year" means, in relation to money provided by Parliament, or the Consolidated Revenue Fund, or the accounts, taxes or finances of Canada, the period beginning on April 1 in one calendar year and ending on March 31 in the next calendar year; and (c) by number to a Dominical year means the period of 12 consecutive months commencing on January 1 of that Dominical year. *Interpretation Act*, R.S.C. 1985, c. I-21, s. 37. 4. Three hundred and sixty-five days. 5. A total of 190 or 195 teaching days. See ACADEMIC ~; CALENDAR ~; CROP ~; CURRENT ~ TAXES; ELECTION ~; ENUMERATION ~; EXECUTOR'S ~; FINANCIAL ~; FISCAL ~; LEAP~; MODEL ~; NET RETURN IN ANY ~; REGNAL ~; REVISAL ~; ROYALTY ~; SCHOOL ~; TAXATION ~; TEACHING ~; TENANCY ~; WITHIN THE ~; WORKING ~.

YEARLY CUSTOMER. A customer who requires electricity service for a period of 12 or more consecutive months.

YEAR OF EMPLOYMENT. 1. Continuous employment of an employee by one employer (a) for a period of 12 consecutive months beginning with the date the employment began or any subsequent anniversary date thereafter; or (b) for a calendar year or other year approved by the Minister under the regulations in relation to an industrial establishment. *Canada Labour Code*, R.S.C. 1985, c. L-2, s. 183. 2. In respect of an employee, means a year in which the employee was paid for at least 1,000 hours of employment. *Labour Adjustment Benefits Act*, R.S.C. 1985, c. L-1, s. 14(4). 3. A period of 12 consecutive months from (a) the date on which the employee's employment actually commenced; or (b) if a common anniversary date is established by an employer for the purpose of determining the vacation and vacation pay of the employees or a group of them, that common anniversary date, and each subsequent period of 12 consecutive months.

YEAR OF TEACHING. Any period of at least 10 months duration, comprised between 1 July of one year and 30 June of the following year, for which an employee has taught, including a similar period for which an employee, after beginning to teach, has pursued further educational studies full time. See TEACHING YEAR.

YEAR OF THE TENANCY. The yearly period on which the tenancy is based and not necessarily a calendar year, and unless otherwise agreed upon, the year shall be deemed to begin on the day, or the anniversary of the day, on which the tenant first became entitled to possession. *Landlord and Tenant acts*. See TENANCY YEAR.

YELLOWTAIL FLOUNDER. A fish of the species Limanda ferruginea (Storer).

YIELD. v. 1. To give way; 2. To earn; to pay. 3.

YIELD. *n.* When used in relation to a redeemable security, means the effective rate of interest that will be returned on the purchase price if the payments of interest specified in the security are made up to and including the redemption date and the security is then redeemed at the specified value. See AREA ~; AVERAGE ~; PER CAPITA ~; PULP ~; SUSTAINED ~; SUSTAINED ~ FOREST MANAGEMENT.

YIELD CAPACITY. See SUSTAINED ~.

YIELDING AND PAYING. In a lease, the first words used in a reddendum clause.

YIELD MANAGEMENT. See SUSTAINED ~.

YIELD SIGN. A sign requiring the driver of a vehicle facing it to yield the right-of-way to traffic of an intersecting or connecting highway. *The Highway Traffic Act*, S.M. 1985-86, c. 3, s. 1.

YKCA. The neutral citation for the Yukon Territory Court of Appeal.

YKSC. The neutral citation for the Yukon Territory Supreme Court.

Y.O.A. Young Offenders Act.

YOKE VENT. A vent pipe connecting a soil stack or a waste stack to a vent stack.

YOU CANNOT DO INDIRECTLY WHAT YOU CANNOT DO DIRECTLY. "The maxim 'you cannot do indirectly what you cannot do directly" is a much abused one. It was used to invalidate legislation . . . It is a pithy way of describing colourable legislation: . . . However, it does not preclude a limited legislature from achieving directly under one head of legislative power what it could not do directly under another head." *Reference re Questions Concerning Amendment to the Constitution of Canada as set out in O.C. 1020/80* (1981), (*sub nom. Resolution to Amend the Constitution of Canada, Re*) 1 C.R.R. 59 at 94, [1981] 1 S.C.R. 753, [1981] 6 W.W.R. 1, 11 Man. R. (2d) 1, 39 N.R. 1, 34 Nfld. & P.E.I.R. 1, 95 A.P.R. 1, Laskin C.J.C., Dickson, Beetz, Estey, McIntyre, Chouinard and Lamer JJ.

YOUNG ADM. *abbr.* Young's Admiralty Decisions (N.S.).

YOUNG OFFENDERS ACT. The Young Offenders Act, chapter 110 of the Statutes of Canada, 1980-81-82-83.

YOUNG OFFENDERS SERVICE. A service provided under Part IV (Young Offenders) or under a program established under that Part. *Child and Family Services Act*, S.O. 1984, c. 55, s. 3.

YOUNG PERSON. 1. A person who is or, in the absence of evidence to the contrary, appears to be twelve years old or older, but less than eighteen years old and, if the context requires, includes any person who is charged under this Act with having committed an offence while he or she was a young person or who is found guilty of an offence under this Act. *Youth Criminal Justice Act*, S.C. 2002, c. 1, s. 2. 2. A person who is or, in the absence of evidence to the contrary, appears to be 12 years of age or more, but under 18 years of age and where the context requires, includes any person who is charged under this Act with having committed an offence while he was a young person or is found guilty of an offence under this Act. *Young Offenders Act*, R.S.C. 1985, c. Y-1, s. 2. 3. A person fourteen years of age or more but under the age of eighteen years. *Criminal Code*, S.C. 1987, c. 24, s. 146(2).

YOUTH. *n.* 1. A male person who has attained the age of 14 years but who has not attained the age of 16 years. *Industrial Safety Act*, R.S.N.S.

1967, c. 141, s. 1. 2. A person whose age is not less than 14 years and not more than 25 years. *Youth Commission Act*, S. Nfld. 1975-76, c. 34, s. 2. See DEPENDENT ~.

YOUTH COURT. A court established or designated by or under an Act of the legislature of a province, or designated by the Governor in Council or the Lieutenant Governor in Council of a province, as a youth court for the purposes of this Act. *Young Offenders Act*, R.S.C. 1985, c. Y-1, s. 2.

YOUTH COURT JUDGE. A person appointed to be a judge of a youth court. *Young Offenders Act*, R.S.C. 1985, c. Y-1, s. 2.

YOUTH CUSTODY FACILITY. A facility designated for the placement of young persons and, if so designated, includes a facility for the secure restraint of young persons, a community residential centre, a group home, a child care institution and a forest or wilderness camp. *Youth Criminal Justice Act*, S.C. 2002, c. 1, s. 2.

YOUTH GROUP. A group composed primarily of persons 18 years of age or under accompanied by their supervisors.

YOUTH JUSTICE COURT. A youth justice court referred to in section 13. A youth justice court is any court that may be established or designated by or under an Act of the legislature of a province, or designated by the Governor in Council or the lieutenant governor in council of a province, as a youth justice court for the purposes of this Act. A youth justice court is a court of record. Certain courts are deemed to be youth justice courts. *Youth Criminal Justice Act*, S.C. 2002, c. 1, s. 2 and 13.

YOUTH JUSTICE COURT JUDGE. A youth justice court judge referred to in section 13. A youth justice court judge is a person who may be appointed or designated as a judge of the youth justice court or a judge sitting in a court established or designated as a youth justice court. Certain judges are deemed to be youth justice court judges. *Youth Criminal Justice Act*, S.C. 2002, c. 1, s. 2 and 13.

YOUTH SENTENCE. A sentence imposed under section 42, 51 or 59 or any of sections 94 to 96 and includes a confirmation or a variation of that sentence. *Youth Criminal Justice Act*, S.C. 2002, c. 1, s. 2.

YOUTH WORKER. 1. Any person appointed or designated, whether by title of youth worker or probation officer or by any other title, by or under an Act of the legislature of a province or by the lieutenant governor in council of a province or his or her delegate to perform in that province, either generally or in a specific case, any of the duties or functions of a youth worker under this Act. *Youth Criminal Justice Act*, S.C. 2002, c. 1, s. 2. 2. The duties and functions of a youth worker in respect of a young person whose case has been assigned to him by the provincial director include supervising the young person in complying with the conditions of a probation order or in carrying out any other disposition made together with it, supervising the young person in complying with the conditions under conditional supervision, giving assistance to a young person found guilty up until the young person is discharged or the disposition of his case terminates, and other duties as required. 3. A probation officer.

Y.R. *abbr*. Yukon Reports.

Y.T. *abbr*. Yukon Territory.

ZONE. *n.* 1. A geological formation, member or zone. 2. A stratum or strata designated by the minister as a zone generally or for a designated area or a specific well. See AERODROME TRAFFIC ~; CONTROL ~; DANGER ~; DISTANT EARLY WARNING IDENTIFI- CATION ~; DOMESTIC CANADIAN AIR DEFENCE IDENTIFICATION ~; EMER- GENCY SERVICE ~; FISHING ~S; LOST CIRCULATION ~; MANAGEMENT AND CONSERVATION ~; NORTH AMERICAN GREAT LAKES ~; NORTHERN ~; PARK- ING ~; PLAYGROUND ~; SAFETY ~; SCHOOL ~; SEPARATION ~ OR LINE; SHIPPING SAFETY CONTROL ~; UNIT- IZED ~; URBAN ~.

ZONE COMMERCIAL LICENCE. A li- cence that authorizes the holder thereof to en- gage in fishing in all waters within a zone.

ZONE FISHERMAN'S LICENCE. A licence that authorizes the holder thereof to engage in fishing in one designated lake within a zone.

ZONE SYSTEM. See COMPREHENSIVE ~.

ZONING. *n.* 1. The control of the use of land. 2. "The objectives of modern zoning legislation are described in [I.M.] Rogers's Canadian Law of Planning and Zoning (Toronto: Carswell, 1973 (looseleaf)) at 115 where the author states: 'Zoning is a form of regulation of property by local governments. It is the division of a munic- ipality into zones or areas and in each area either prohibiting certain uses and allowing all the oth- ers or permitting the uses which may be carried on to the exclusion of all others. . . Zoning is the deprivation for the public good of certain uses by owners of property to which the property might otherwise be put. Underlying planning statutes is the principle that the interest of land- owners in securing the maximum value of their land must be controlled by the community. . . The objective of zoning must be considered from the objective of the public welfare and of all the property within any particular use district.' " *Zive Estate v. Lynch* (1989), 47 M.P.L.R. 310 at 314, 7 R.P.R. (2d) 180, 94 N.S.R. (2d) 401, 247 A.P.R. 401 (C.A.), the court per Macdonald J.A. See DEVELOPMENT CONTROL; SPOT ~.

ZONING BYLAW. " . . . [R]emedial in char- acter in that one of their objectives is to preserve existing property from depreciation. They are designed not only to protect residential neigh- bourhoods against intrusion of buildings to be used for commercial and manufacturing or trade purposes, but to confine commercial and indus- trial purposes to specific parts of the municipal- ity the exclusion of residential construction: . . ." *Zive Estate v. Lynch* (1989), 47 M.P.L.R. 310 at 315, 7 R.P.R. (2d) 180, 94 N.S.R. (2d) 401, 247 A.P.R. 401 (C.A.), the court per Macdonald J.A.